Merry Xmas!
To us!
1989

From BIJBELSE ENCYCLOPEDIE
Revised Edition 1975

W. H. Gispen
B. J. Oosterhoff
H. N. Ridderbos
W. C. van Unnik
P. Visser

Published by J. H. KOK • Kampen

THE EERDMANS BIBLE DICTIONARY

REVISION EDITOR
Allen C. Myers

ASSOCIATE EDITORS
John W. Simpson, Jr.
Philip A. Frank
Timothy P. Jenney
Ralph W. Vunderink

WILLIAM B. EERDMANS PUBLISHING COMPANY
GRAND RAPIDS, MICHIGAN   1987

Copyright © 1987 by Wm. B. Eerdmans Publishing Co.,
255 Jefferson Ave. SE, Grand Rapids, MI 49503

This edition is based on *Bijbelse Encyclopedie*, ed. by W. H. Gispen,
© 1975 by J. H. Kok, Kampen, the Netherlands

Printed in the United States of America

Library of Congress Cataloging-in-Publication Data

The Eerdmans Bible Dictionary

Rev., augm. translation of: Bijbelse encyclopedie.
Rev. ed. 1975.
1. Bible—Dictionaries.   I. Myers, Allen C., 1945-
II. Bible dictionary.
BS440.G7613   1987   220.3   87-13239

ISBN 0-8028-2402-1

PREFACE

This Bible Dictionary is based on a translation of the internationally respected *Bijbelse Encyclopedie,* first published by J. H. Kok of Kampen in 1950 under chief editor F. W. Grosheide, distinguished New Testament scholar and professor at the Free University of Amsterdam for more than forty years, with the assistance of W. H. Gispen (Old Testament, archaeology), F. J. Bruijel (botany and zoology), and A. van Deursen (biblical geography, archaeology, and daily life). In 1975 a thorough revision was published in two volumes, edited by Professor Gispen along with B. J. Oosterhoff, H. N. Ridderbos, W. C. van Unnik, and P. Visser. This edition, upon which the English translation is based, broadened the scope of the original work through the addition of entries on issues of biblical theology; also, the editors incorporated articles from the 1959 second edition of *Christelijke Encyclopedie,* edited by Professor Grosheide and E. P. van Itterzon. A third edition of *Bijbelse Encyclopedie,* with minor corrections, was issued in one volume in 1979.

To further enhance the Dictionary's value as a tool for practical Bible use, this English edition represents another step in the continuing process of revision, reflecting recent archaeological discoveries and the breadth of American biblical scholarship, including insights from critical analysis of literary, historical, and sociological issues. In particular, major articles (including all entries on books of the Bible) have been revised and expanded, and bibliographies reflecting various viewpoints have been added. Although the focus of the Dictionary remains primarily evangelical, the editors have sought to display greater sensitivity to the broad spectrum of interpretation, presenting as objectively as possible divergent perspectives. Accordingly, contributors to the revision represent a variety of denominational stances—including not only Reformed, but also Baptist, Brethren, Disciples, Episcopal, Mennonite, Methodist (and Wesleyan), Pentecostal, Presbyterian, and Independent, as well as Roman Catholic and Jewish.

Underlying the English revision is a sincere desire to preserve not only the ripe scholarship but also the practical sensitivity displayed by the distinguished theologians upon whose efforts this work is based. Following initial review of the *Encyclopedie* by D. E. Holwerda, editing and revision was begun in earnest in August 1980. In addition to the concerns mentioned above, the process of translation in itself has necessitated that particular attention be given to differences in usage between Dutch and English versions of the Bible (where even rendering of name forms may vary), including identification and description of natural phenomena such as plants, animals, precious stones, and the like. To accommodate best the nuances of English Bible translations, this edition is based on the Revised Standard Version, with attention to alternate readings in the King James Version, New International Version, Jerusalem Bible, and others.

Nearly 5000 entries identify all persons and places named in the Bible, as well as animals, plants, and objects. Major entries include each book of the Bible (including the Apocrypha/Deuterocanonical books), literary genres, geographical regions, and pertinent ancient Mediterranean and Near Eastern civilizations. Others explain and interpret important focuses of biblical theology, text and transmission, anthropology, the early Church (including ancient and medieval traditions where appropriate), and extrabiblical writings—matters that the Bible student may encounter in reading or discussion. The editors have introduced pronunciations and, in transliteration, the relevant terms in Hebrew, Greek, and other ancient languages. Illustrations (charts, photos, and line drawings), as well as the twelve-page color map section prepared by Hammond, Inc., are intended to enhance further the reader's understanding.

Entries on subjects not included in the earlier editions are designated by an asterisk (*) following the heading. Articles on previously treated topics in which more than half of the material has been revised (or where an entirely new article replaces the original), or where recent discoveries or interpretations significantly alter the perspective of the original entry, are indicated by a dagger (†). When a name designates more than one person or place, multiple entries are included under the main heading, arranged following the English canonical order of the first citation discussed, rather than purely chronological sequence. Cross references are indicated in the body of the text by the use of capitals and small capitals, and by italicized "see" or "see also" at the end of a paragraph or article. Cross references, including those from KJV readings, generally are omitted when the related entry is within one or two pages of the referent. Gentilic forms often are included in the entry for the person or place from which they are derived.

To restate the desire of the earlier editors, may this Bible Dictionary prove to be a helpful and reliable guide for both reading and study of the Bible.

The Publishers

CONTRIBUTORS

REVISION EDITOR

Allen C. Myers

ASSOCIATE EDITORS

John W. Simpson, Jr.
Philip A. Frank
Timothy P. Jenney
Ralph W. Vunderink

TRANSLATORS

Raymond C. Togtman
Ralph W. Vunderink

CONTRIBUTORS

Neil Bartlett
Belinda J. Bicknell
Steven C. Bouma-Prediger
Gordon P. Brubacher

Gary M. Burge
Kelly L. C. Russell Burton
Benjamin C. Chapman
David A. Dorman
Keith Lynn Eades
R. J. Forbes*
David F. Graf
D. J. de Groot*
Becky Merrill Groothuis
Ron Grove
G. Michael Hagan
William R. Harris
L. Daniel Hawk
Andrew E. Hill
James E. Hoffine
John R. Huddleston
Clayton N. Jefford
Ted J. Jenney
Gregory D. Jordan
Lee E. Klosinski
Gary L. Knapp
J. L. Koole*
Gary A. Lee

Thomas H. McAlpine
Richard E. Menninger
Merrill P. Miller
Larry J. Nyberg
Alan Padgett
James E. Powell
Richard L. Pratt, Jr.
Robert M. Price
Daniel G. Reid
Nicolaus H. Ridderbos*
Barbara J. Saunier
Philip C. Schmitz
Melvin H. Shoemaker
A. Sizoo*
Michael S. Spence
K. Sprey*
Robert E. Stone II
Henry T. C. Sun
Dawn E. Waring
Gerald H. Wilson
Leah Zahler

*Contributor to 1975 edition

ABBREVIATIONS

† Major revision
* New article
Θ Theodotion
a. acre
AASOR Annual of the American Schools of Oriental Research
AB Anchor Bible (Garden City)
AEL M. Lichtheim, *Ancient Egyptian Literature.* 3 vols. (Berkeley: 1973-1980)
Akk. Akkadian
AnBib *Analecta Biblica*
ANEP J. B. Pritchard, *The Ancient Near East in Pictures*, 2nd ed. (Princeton: 1969)
ANET J. B. Pritchard, ed., *Ancient Near Eastern Texts*, 3rd ed. (Princeton: 1969)
AOS American Oriental Series
APOT R. H. Charles, ed., *The Apocrypha and Pseudepigrapha of the Old Testament*, 2 vols. (Oxford: 1913)
Arab. Arabic
Aram. Aramaic
Art. Article (of confession, etc.)
AS Anglo-Saxon
ASOR American Schools of Oriental Research
Assyr. Assyrian
AUM *Andrews University Monographs*
b. Babylonian Talmud
BA *The Biblical Archaeologist*
BAR *Biblical Archaeology Review*
BASOR *Bulletin of the American Schools of Oriental Research*
Bauer F. W. Bauer, *A Greek-English Lexicon of the New Testament and Other Early Christian Literature*, rev. W. F. Arndt and F. W. Danker (Chicago: 1979)
BDB F. Brown-S. R. Driver-C. A. Briggs, *A Hebrew and English Lexicon of the Old Testament* (Oxford: 1907)
BH R. Kittel, ed., *Biblia Hebraica*, 3rd ed. (Stuttgart: 1929)
BHS K. Elliger and W. Rudolph, ed., *Biblia Hebraica Stuttgartensia* (Stuttgart: 1966-1977)
BJS Brown Judaic Studies
BNTC Black's New Testament Commentaries (Naperville)
BSC Bible Student's Commentary (Grand Rapids)
bu. bushel
BZAW *Beihefte zur Zeitschrift für die alttestamentliche Wissenschaft*
ca. *circa*
CBC Cambridge Bible Commentary on the New English Bible (New York)
CBQ *Catholic Biblical Quarterly*
cf. compare, see

CGNTC Cambridge Greek New Testament Commentary (New York)
ch(s). chapter(s)
cm. centimeter(s)
CNT Commentar op het Nieuwe Testament (Kampen)
Comm. Commentary
Copt. Coptic
COT Commentar op het Oude Testament (Kampen)
DNTT C. Brown, ed., *The New International Dictionary of New Testament Theology*, 3 vols. (Grand Rapids: 1975-1978)
EA Tell el-Amarna tablets
EAEHL M. Avi-Yonah, ed., *Encyclopedia of Excavations in the Holy Land*, 4 vols. (Englewood Cliffs: 1975-1978)
EB Early Bronze Age
Eb. Eblaite, Eblaic
ed. edition, editor(s)
Egyp. Egyptian
EJ *Encyclopedia Judaica*, 16 vols. (New York: 1971-1972)
Eng. English
esp. especially
Eth. Ethiopic
fem. feminine
FOTL The Forms of the Old Testament Literature (Grand Rapids)
ft. foot, feet
g. gram(s)
Ger. German
Gesenius W. Gesenius, *Hebrew and Chaldee Lexicon*, trans. S. P. Tregelles (Grand Rapids: 1949)
Gk. Greek
ha. hectare
HBT Horizons in Biblical Theology (Pittsburgh)
Heb. Hebrew
Hitt. Hittite
HNTC Harper's New Testament Commentaries (New York, San Francisco)
HSS Harvard Semitic Series (Cambridge, Mass.)
Hur. Hurrian
IB G. A. Buttrick, ed., *The Interpreter's Bible*, 12 vols. (Nashville: 1952-1957)
ICC International Critical Commentary (Edinburgh)
IDB G. A. Buttrick, ed., *The Interpreter's Dictionary of the Bible*, 4 vols. (Nashville: 1962)
IDBS K. Crim, ed., *IDB, Supplementary Volume* (Nashville: 1976)
IEJ *Israel Exploration Journal*
in. inch(es)
Int *Interpretation*

ISBE	G. W. Bromiley, ed., *The International Standard Bible Encyclopedia,* rev. ed., 4 vols. (Grand Rapids: 1979-1988)
ITC	F. C. Holmgren and G. A. F. Knight, ed., *International Theological Commentary* (Grand Rapids)
j.	Jerusalem Talmud
JAAR	*Journal of the American Academy of Religion*
JAOS	*Journal of the American Oriental Society*
JB	Jerusalem Bible
JBL	*Journal of Biblical Literature*
JPSV	Jewish Publication Society Version (1917)
JQR	*Jewish Quarterly Review*
JSOTS	Journal for the Study of the Old Testament Supplement (Sheffield)
JSS	*Journal of Semitic Studies*
K	Kethib
KAI	H. Donner and W. Röllig, *Kanaanäische und Aramäische Inschriften,* 3 vols., 3rd ed. (Wiesbaden: 1968-1971)
KD	C. F. Keil and F. Delitzsch, *Commentary on the Old Testament* (Grand Rapids)
KJV	King James Version
km.	kilometer
KoB	L. Koehler and W. Baumgartner, *Lexicon in Veteris Testamenti Libros,* 2nd ed. (Leiden and Grand Rapids: 1958)
l.	liter(s)
Lat.	Latin
LB	Late Bronze Age
lit.	literally
LXX	Septuagint
m.	meter(s)
Macmillan	Macmillian New Testament Commentaries (New York)
masc.	masculine
MB	Middle Bronze Age
mg.	margin
mi.	mile(s)
Moab.	Moabite
MSS	Manuscripts
MT	Masoretic Text
n(n).	note(s)
NAB	New American Bible
NASB	New American Standard Bible
NCBC	The New Century Bible Commentary (Grand Rapids)
NCCHS	R. C. Fuller, ed., *New Catholic Commentary on Holy Scripture* (New York: 1969)
NCE	M. R. P. McGuire, et al., ed., *New Catholic Encyclopedia,* 15 vols. (Washington: 1967)
NEB	New English Bible
NICNT	The New International Commentary on the New Testament (Grand Rapids)
NICOT	The New International Commentary on the Old Testament (Grand Rapids)
NIGTC	New International Greek Testament Commentary (Grand Rapids)

NIV	New International Version
NJV	New Jewish Version
NKJV	New King James Version
no(s).	number(s)
NovT Sup	Novum Testamentum, Supplements
NTL	New Testament Library (Philadelphia)
NTSMS	New Testament Studies Monograph Series
OBT	Overtures to Biblical Theology (Philadelphia)
OCD	N. G. Hammond and H. H. Scullard, ed., *Oxford Classical Dictionary,* 2nd ed. (New York: 1970)
O.Eng.	Old English
O.Fr.	Old French
OHG	Old High German
O.Pers.	Old Persian
OSA	Old South Arabic
OTL	Old Testament Library (Philadelphia)
OTS	*Oudtestamentische Studiën*
p(p).	page(s)
℘	papyrus
par.	parallel
PEQ	*Palestine Exploration Quarterly*
Pers.	Persian
Phillips	J. B. Phillips, *The New Testament in Modern English*
Phoen.	Phoenician
PL	J. B. Migne, ed., *Patrologia Latina,* 221 vols. (Paris: 1844-1864)
pl.	plural
pl(s).	plate(s)
ptcp.	participle
Q	Qere
repr.	reprint(ed)
RQ	*Revue de Qumran*
RSV	Revised Standard Version
RV	Revised Version
Sab.	Sabean
Sam.	Samaritan
SAOC	Studies in Ancient Oriental Civilization (Chicago)
SBL	Society of Biblical Literature
SBT	Studies in Biblical Theology (Chicago)
Scot.	Scottish
Sem.	Semitic
ser.	series
sing.	singular
SNTSMS	Society for New Testament Studies Monograph Series (Cambridge)
sq.	square
Sum.	Sumerian
Sup.	Supplement(s)
Syr.	Syriac
Targ.	Targum
TBC	Torch Bible Comentaries (London)
TDNT	G. Kittel and G. Friedrich, ed., *Theological Dictionary of the New Testament,* 10 vols. (Grand Rapids: 1964-1976)
TDOT	G. J. Botterweck, H. Ringgren, and H.-J. Fabry, ed., *Theological Dictionary of the Old Testament* (Grand Rapids: 1974–)
TEV	Today's English Version
trans.	translation, translated by

TS   *Theological Studies*
Tyndale   Tyndale Old Testament Commentaries
(Downers Grove)
Ugar.   Ugaritic
UT   C. H. Gordon, *Ugaritic Textbook.*
Analecta Orientalia 38 (Rome: 1965)
v(v).   verse(s)
VTS   *Supplements to Vetus Testamentum*
Vulg.   Vulgate
WA   Martin Luther, *Werke*, Weimar
Ausgabe (1883–)
WBC   Word Biblical Commentary (Waco)
W.Sem.   West Semitic
yd.   yard(s)
ZAW   *Zeitschrift für die alttestamentliche*
Wissenschaft
ZNW   *Zeitschrift für die neutestamentliche*
Wissenschaft

BIBLICAL AND OTHER
ANCIENT LITERATURE

Old Testament

Gen.   Genesis
Exod.   Exodus
Lev.   Leviticus
Num.   Numbers
Deut.   Deuteronomy
Josh.   Joshua
Judg.   Judges
1-2 Sam.   1-2 Samuel
1-2 Kgs.   1-2 Kings
1-2 Chr.   1-2 Chronicles
Neh.   Nehemiah
Esth.   Esther
Ps(s).   Psalms
Prov.   Proverbs
Eccl.   Ecclesiastes
Cant.   Song of Solomon (Canticles)
Isa.   Isaiah
Jer.   Jeremiah
Lam.   Lamentations
Ezek.   Ezekiel
Dan.   Daniel
Hos.   Hosea
Obad.   Obadiah
Mic.   Micah
Nah.   Nahum
Hab.   Habakkuk
Zeph.   Zephaniah
Hag.   Haggai
Zech.   Zechariah
Mal.   Malachi

Apocrypha/Deuterocanonical Books

1-2 Esdr.   1-2 Esdras
Tob.   Tobit
Jdt.   Judith
Add.Esth.   Additions to Esther
Wis.   Wisdom of Solomon
Sir.   Wisdom of Jesus the Son of Sirach
(Ecclesiasticus)

Bar.   Baruch
Ep.Jer.   Epistle of Jeremiah
Pr.Azar.   Prayer of Azariah
Sg.Three   Song of the Three Young Men
Sus.   Susanna
Bel   Bel and the Dragon
Pr.Man.   Prayer of Manasseh
1-2 Macc.   1-2 Maccabees

New Testament

Matt.   Matthew
Rom.   Romans
1-2 Cor.   1-2 Corinthians
Gal.   Galatians
Eph.   Ephesians
Phil.   Philippians
Col.   Colossians
1-2 Thess.   1-2 Thessalonians
1-2 Tim.   1-2 Timothy
Phlm.   Philemon
Heb.   Hebrews
Jas.   James
1-2 Pet.   1-2 Peter
Rev.   Revelation

Pseudepigrapha

Adam
and Eve   Life of Adam and Eve
Apoc.Abr.   Apocalypse of Abraham
2-3 Apoc.
Bar.   2-3 Apocalypse of Baruch
Apoc.Dan.   Apocalypse of Daniel
Apoc.Mos.   Apocalypse of Moses
Asc.Isa.   Ascension of Isaiah
As.Mos.   Assumption of Moses
1-2-3 En.   1-2-3 Enoch
Ep.Arist.   Epistle of Aristeas
Jub.   Jubilees
Pss.Sol.   Psalms of Solomon
Sib.Or.   Sibylline Oracles
T.Dan.,
T.Jos., etc.   Testament of Dan, Testament of
Joseph, etc. (Testaments of the Twelve
Patriarchs)

Dead Sea Scrolls

1QapGen   Genesis Apocryphon
1QSa   Manual of Discipline, Appendix A
4QFlor   Florilegium
11QPs^a Psalm Scroll A
11QtgJob   Targum of Job

Mishnah and Other Rabbinic Works

ʿAbod. Zar.   *ʿAbodah Zarah*
Ber.   *Berakoth*
Gen. Rab.   *Genesis Rabbah*
Giṭ.   *Giṭṭin*
Maʿas.   *Maʿaseroth*
Mak.   *Makkoth*
Meg.   *Megillah*
Mid.   *Middoth*
Nid.   *Niddah*
Onk.   *Onkelos*
Pesaḥ.   *Pesaḥim*

Qidd.	Qiddušin
Roš Haš.	Roš Haššanah
Šabb.	Šabbath
Sanh.	Sanhedrin
Šebu.	Šebuʿoth
Taʿan.	Taʿanith
Yebam.	Yebamoth

Early Church Writings

Acts Pil.	Acts of Pilate
AP	Acts of Paul
Apost. Const.	Apostolic Constitutions
Augustine	
Civ. Dei	De civitate Dei (City of God)
Conf.	Confessiones
De cons. ev.	De consensu evangelistarum (Harmony of the Gospels)
De doctr. christ.	De doctrina christiana
Ench.	Enchiridion
Quaest.	Quaestiones ad Simplicianum
Barn.	Epistle of Barnabas
Bordeaux Pilgrim	
Itin. Burd.	Itinerarium Burdigalensie
Chrysostom De sac.	De sacerdotio
1-2 Clem.	1-2 Clement
Clement of Alexandria	
Ecl.	Eclogae ex scriptoris propheticis
Misc.	Miscellanies (Stromateis)
Did.	Didache
Epiphanius Haer.	Adversus lxxx haereses (Panarion)
Eusebius	
Chron.	Chronicle
HE	Historia ecclesiastica
Onom.	Onomasticon
Praep. ev.	Praeparatio evangelica
Hippolytus Ref.	Refutatio omnium haeresium (Philosophoumena)
Ignatius of Antioch	
Eph.	Epistle to the Ephesians
Magn.	Epistle to the Magnesians
Philad.	Epistle to the Philadelphians
Polyc.	Epistle to Polycarp
Rom.	Epistle to the Romans
Trall.	Epistle to the Trallians
Irenaeus Adv. haer.	Adversus omnes haereses
Jerome De vir. ill.	De viris illustribus
Justin Martyr	
Apol.	Apologiae
Dial.	Dialogus contra Tryphonem

Mart.Pol.	Martyrdom of Polycarp
Nicephorus Stich.	Stichometry
Origen De prin.	De principiis
Polyc. Phil.	Polycarp of Smyrna, Epistle to the Philippians
Sozomen HE	Historia ecclesiastica
Tertullian	
Adv. Marc.	Adversus Marcionem
Apol.	Apologeticum
De cult. fem.	De cultu feminarum
De orat.	De oratione
De praescr. haer.	De praescriptione haereticorum
De pudic.	De pudicitia

Other Ancient Works

Appian Syr.	Syrian Wars
Cicero De leg.	De legibus
Dio Cassius Hist.	Roman History
Diodorus Siculus Hist.	Library of History
Dionysius of Halicarnassus Rom. Arch.	Roman Archaeology
Gilg.	Gilgamesh Epic
Herodotus Hist.	History
Homer Od.	Odyssey
Josephus	
Ant.	Antiquities of the Jews
Ap.	Contra Apionem
BJ	Bellum Judaicum (The Jewish War)
Livy	
Epit.	Epitomes
Hist.	History of Rome
Philo	
De conf. ling.	De confusione linguarum
De leg.	De legatione ad Gaium
De spec. leg.	De specialibus legibus
De virt.	De virtutibus
Quod omn. prob. lib.	Quod omnis probus liber sit
Pliny (the Elder) Nat. hist.	Naturalis historia
Pliny (the Younger)	
Ep.	Epistulae
Polybius Hist.	Histories
Ptolemy Geog.	Geography
Strabo Geog.	Geography
Suetonius Claud.	Life of Claudius
Tacitus	
Ann.	Annales ab excessu divi Augusti
Hist.	Histories

A. A symbol used to designate the CODEX ALEXANDRINUS.

AARON [âr'ən] (Heb. *'ahᵃrôn*; possibly of Egyptian origin). The brother of Moses and the first high priest of Israel.

I. Biblical Narrative

Aaron was a descendant of Levi and a son of Amram and Jochebed (Exod. 6:20; Num. 26:59; 1 Chr. 6:3). Born eighty-three years before the Exodus, he was three years older than Moses (Exod. 7:7) but younger than their sister Miriam.

When the Lord called Moses to deliver the people of Israel from the Egyptians and Moses protested that he was too slow of speech, the Lord gave him Aaron to speak and prophesy in his stead (Exod. 4:10-16; cf. 7:1-2). At the Lord's command Aaron stretched out his rod to bring plagues to the Egyptians when Pharaoh refused to let the people go (7:1-5; cf. 4:30; 7:8-9; 8:5-6, 16-17). Aaron accompanied Moses in leading the Israelites out of Egypt (12:31) and on the journey through the wilderness (ch. 16). For Israel to win the battle against Amalek, Moses had to keep the staff of God raised over his head; when his arms wearied, Aaron and Hur supported his hands (17:12).

Aaron was permitted to ascend Mt. Sinai with his brother Moses shortly after the Israelites were "introduced" to God there (Exod. 19:24) and again after God gave them the law (24:1). The second time he was among the seventy elders of Israel, all of whom "beheld God, and ate and drank" (24:11). Aaron and Hur were appointed by the people to stand in as leaders when Moses remained on the mountain for "forty days and forty nights" (vv. 12-14, 18). While the Lord prepared the two tables of the law, having informed Moses that he wanted Aaron and his sons Nadab, Abihu, Eleazar, and Ithamar to serve him as priests (Exod. 28:1), Aaron was making a golden calf for the impatient and rebellious people to worship (32:1-6). Called by Moses to account for his action, he could offer only a feeble excuse (32:21-24); yet on account of Moses' intercession the Lord spared him, in spite of his anger (Deut. 9:20). By God's grace, Aaron remained a high priest. (The sons of Levi set a better example as priests, for they carried out the punishment on the Israelites who were guilty of worshipping the golden calf [Exod. 32:25-29].)

Upon the completion of the tabernacle Moses built according to God's specifications (Exod. 35:30–39:43) and after God's instructions to Moses concerning specific cultic regulations (Lev. 1–7), Aaron and his sons were consecrated as God's priests (Lev. 8; cf. Exod. 29). From then on Aaron, who alone was anointed with holy oil (Lev. 8:12), was to be Israel's high priest and mediator and was to enter the holy of holies on the Day of Atonement (16:11-14). The first day of his ministry ended tragically, however. While he performed his first sacrifice to the Lord (9:1-24), his eldest sons Nadab and Abihu "offered unholy fire before the Lord" by making an offering that had not been authorized; they were "devoured" by divine fire for their boldness (10:1-2). Because Aaron possessed the fortitude to obey Moses and suppress his fatherly grief over the death of two of his children (v. 3), God confirmed Aaron and his two remaining sons as his servants. He reminded the sons, through Moses, of their obligation to remain holy (vv. 6-7) and enumerated directly to Aaron his religious duties as high priest (vv. 8-11).

Aaron once again demonstrated his moral weakness after Israel's departure from Mt. Sinai. This time he allowed himself to be manipulated by his sister Miriam into criticizing Moses for his marriage to the Cushite woman and denying that Moses had the exclusive right to the prophetic office (Num. 12:1-2). Though Miriam alone was punished with leprosy (v. 10), Aaron appealed to Moses for mercy on behalf of them both (vv. 9-12).

Sometime later a rebellion by Korah, Dathan, and Abiram (members of the wandering community of Israelites) arose not only against Moses but also against Aaron (Num. 16:3). Korah alleged that since all the Israelites were holy, Moses should not be considered superior in the congregation. When the Israelites again began to murmur against Moses and Aaron after the Lord had the rebels and their families swallowed up by the earth (vv. 31-41), God afflicted them with a plague; he terminated it after Aaron made atonement in behalf of the congregation by standing betwen the living and the dead with a burning censer in his hands (vv. 43-50). Then the Lord once again confirmed

1

Aaron in his priestly office by asking the leaders of each family to bring a rod before him; the rod of Levi, on which Aaron's name was inscribed, was the only one to bud (17:1-12; *see also* AARON'S ROD).

At the end of the wilderness wanderings (in the first month of the fortieth year), Aaron and Moses were refused permission to lead the people into the Promised Land for having failed to "sanctify" the Lord before the faithless and thirsty Israelites (Num. 20:12-13). Shortly thereafter Aaron died at Mt. Hor, having been stripped of his priestly garments by Moses (vv. 22-28).

Aaron's son Eleazar succeeded his father as high priest. According to Num. 20:28 Aaron died on top of the mountain, at the age of one hundred and twenty-three years (32:38; Deut. 10:6 names Moserah as the place of his death, probably in the vicinity of Mt. Hor. The last pentateuchal reference to Aaron is at Deut. 32:50, where the Lord tells Moses that he will die on a mountain just as his older brother had.

II. Religious Significance†

A. *Old Testament*. Aaron's many-sided ministry is mentioned in various parts of the Old Testament, though perhaps the distinction between his role as Israel's co-leader and his office as high priest should not be aggrandized (cf. E. Rivkin, "Aaron, Aaronites," *IDBS*, pp. 1-3). Joshua is aware that Aaron not only inflicted plagues on Egypt but delivered Israel from Egyptian oppression as well (Josh. 24:5-6; cf. 1 Sam. 12:6, 8).

The author of Chronicles portrays Aaron as a priest who made atonement for Israel (1 Chr. 6:49) with his offerings (23:13; cf. v. 32). His descendants are cited as continuing in this capacity.

The Psalms present a rather complete picture of Aaron's duties. It is he who inflicts Egypt with plagues (Ps. 105:26), leads God's people through the wilderness (77:20), and is the focus of a rebellion against his leadership (106:16-17). Three times his office as high priest is designated: at 99:6 (with Moses and Samuel), at 106:16 (distinct from Moses), and at 133:2 (a reference to his consecration as high priest). Ps. 106 is the only Psalm that addresses both his leadership qualities and his cultic obligations.

Surprisingly, the prophets rarely refer to Aaron; they mention neither his moral weakness nor his exemplary behavior. At Mic. 6:4 (cf. Josh. 24; 1 Sam. 12), Aaron is a leader on a par with Moses and Miriam. It is noteworthy that his name is nowhere included in the account of the restored temple (Ezek. 40-47).

B. *New Testament*. When the system for making atonement through sacrifices became obsolete with Christ's death, Aaron's significance for Israel diminished. Here, as in many Old Testament passages, Aaron is less important than Moses. Luke notes that Elizabeth, the wife of Zechariah the priest, is one of his descendants (Luke 1:5) and that Aaron's followers pressured him into making the golden calf (Acts 7:40). The author of Hebrews takes a new look at his importance as high priest. Recognizing the legitimacy of Aaron's divine calling (Heb. 5:4), that author, nevertheless, acknowledges Aaron's priestly office as inferior to that of Christ and argues that even in the Old Testament the Aaronic priesthood was to be

viewed as subordinate to that of Melchizedek, whose order would produce the Messiah (7:11ff.).

AARONIC BLESSING. Another name for the priestly blessing pronounced by Aaron and his sons (Num. 6:22-27). Actually, it is God's own blessing of his people, for he himself commanded Aaron and his sons to "put [the Lord's] name upon the people of Israel" (v. 27). Judging from Lev. 9:22 the high priest pronounced the blessing with his hands lifted up. According to Jewish tradition, after the Exile the blessing was pronounced at the conclusion of the morning and evening sacrifices (W. H. Gispen, *Numeri* 1. COT [Kampen: 1959], p. 118).

The form of this blessing consists of three sentences of two parts each, with the name Yahweh as the second word in each sentence. There is a systematic development from three to seven words:

y^{e}ḇāreḵ^{e}ḵā yhwh   w^{e}yišm^{e}reḵā
("The Lord bless you   and keep you")
yā'ēr yhwh pānāyw 'ēlêḵā   wîḥunnekā
("The Lord make his face   and be gracious
to shine upon you,   to you")
yiśśā' yhwh pānāyw 'ēlêḵā   w^{e}yāśēm l^{e}ḵā šālôm
("The Lord lift up his   and give you
countenance upon you,   peace")

The first sentence presents the blessing in its most general form, the second stresses God's favor and grace, and the third emphasizes God's power over mankind; the climax occurs with the final word "peace." If the three instances of the divine name Yahweh are discounted, the blessing contains twelve words, which may symbolize the twelve tribes of Israel.

While the Church Fathers viewed the blessing in a trinitarian manner — the first part being the work of the Father, the second that of the Son, and the third that of the Spirit — the Old Testament Jewish community, maintaining the unity of God, stressed the fulness of the blessing (so KD at v. 26).

Some of the Psalms echo the individual application of the blessing ("thy servant," "me," Ps. 31:17). Others clearly teach that the blessing was to be regarded as a communal experience ("upon us," 4:6; "we," 80:3, 7, 19). Ps. 67:1, which quotes nearly the entire second sentence of the blessing, relates it to God's people and through them to all the nations (v. 2).

AARONITES [âr'ə nīts]. Another name for the male descendants of Aaron the high priest, who also were called by God to be priests (1 Chr. 12:27; 27:17; KJV, JB "for Aaron" [Heb. l^e'ah^{a}rōn,]; RSV, NIV, following the proposed emendation Heb. liḇnê 'ah^{a}rōn "for the sons of Aaron," read "house/family of Aaron"). In the Psalms they are designated "the house of Aaron" (Heb. bêṭ 'ah^{a}rōn, i.e., "descendants of Aaron," Ps. 115:10; 118:3; at Ps. 115:12; 135:19 the term is parallel with "house of Israel"), while Chronicles calls them "sons of Aaron" (Heb. b^{e}nê 'ah^{a}rōn, 2 Chr. 29:21; 31:19; 35:14 [cf. 1 Chr. 24:31]; NIV "descendants of Aaron").

AARON'S ROD. * The Pentateuch refers to Aaron's "rod" (Heb. maṭṭeh; NIV, JB "staff") on two occasions. At Exod. 7:9-12 Aaron's rod, also considered Moses' property, symbolizes God's victory over Egyptian magic. Here Aaron's rod turned into the serpent which swallowed the serpents which the Egyptians fashioned from their rods. This is the miracle by which God is justified to Pharaoh (cf. v. 19; 8:5-7, 16-17). At Num. 17:6-8 (JB "branch") only this rod blossoms from among the twelve rods brought before God—a reminder that Israel's rebels were challenging leadership bestowed upon Aaron (and Moses) by God. According to the author of the book of Hebrews (Heb. 9:4) the rod (Gk. *rhábdos*; JB "branch") was placed inside the ark, not in front of it as stated at Num. 17:10 (see F. F. Bruce, *The Epistle to the Hebrews.* NICNT [1964], pp. 188-89).

AB [ăb] (Heb. *'ab*). The fifth month of the Hebrew year (July/August); this postexilic name was borrowed by the Jews from the Babylonian Abu. In this month the grapes and figs are harvested and on the seventh day a great fast commemorating the destruction of Jerusalem by Nebuchadnezzar (587/586 B.C.) is held.

ABADDON [ə băd'ən]. In the Old Testament Abaddon (which the RSV renders as a proper name) is the heinous place of the dead (Heb. *'ăbaddôn* "[place of] destruction"; KJV, NIV "destruction"; JB "perdition"); it is linked with Sheol (e.g., Job 26:6), and personifies Death (28:22) and the grave (Ps. 88:11). According to N. J. Tromp (*Primitive Conceptions of Death and the Nether World in the Old Testament.* Biblica et Orientalia 21 [Chicago: 1969], p. 81), it may be one of "many transpositions from the grave to Sheol."

Abaddon is the fiery place of punishment for adulterers (Job 31:12) and the lustful (Prov. 27:20). Never in Abaddon will God's faithfulness or steadfast love be proclaimed (Ps. 88:11) nor the way of wisdom which only he knows (Job 28:20-23). But the Underworld is nonetheless under God's power; it lies constantly exposed to his scrutiny (26:60), like the hearts of human beings (Prov. 15:11).

In the New Testament Abaddon (Gk. *Abaddṓn*), the Hebrew equivalent of Gk. *Apollýon*, is no longer the Underworld but rather the "angel of the bottomless pit," the king of the evil spirits, which in the last days will take on the form of locusts and will torture those human beings who do not bear the seal of God (Rev. 9:11).

ABAGTHA [ə băg'thə] (Heb. *'ăbagetā'*, probably of Middle Iranian origin; perhaps "gift of good fortune"). One of the seven eunuchs of King Ahasuerus (Xerxes I, *ca.* 480 B.C.) who served as his chamberlains (Esth. 1:10).

ABANA [ăb'ə nə] (Heb. *'ăbānâ*; Q *'ămānâ*; cf. RSV mg., KJV mg. "AMANA"). A river in Syria, now called the Barada. From its Anti-lebanon sources the Abana flows south and southeast toward Damascus. Near ancient Abila (a town in Abilene, about 27 km. [17 mi.] west of Damascus) the spring 'Ain Fijeh joins it to double its size. Then the river runs through a gorge to the Ghutah plain, where it divides into seven main branches and a few smaller ones. The city of Damascus arose amid the fields and gardens of this extremely fertile, well-irrigated plain, near the edge of the much-traveled Syrian desert.

When Elisha told the Syrian commander Naaman that seven washings in the Jordan river would cure his leprosy, Naaman exclaimed: "Are not Abana and Pharpar, the rivers of Damascus, better than all the waters of Israel? Could I not wash in them, and be clean?" (2 Kgs. 5:12). Perhaps Naaman was thinking not only of the clearness of the Syrian rivers but also of their sacredness to his fellow countrymen.

ABARIM [ăb'ə rīm] (Heb. *'ăbārîm* "regions beyond"). A mountainous region between the plateau of Moab on the east and the Dead Sea on the west (Num. 27:12; 33:47-48; Deut. 32:49). The mountain range (cf. NIV, JB at Num. 27:12; Deut. 32:49), named Abarim by the people west of the Jordan, is the steep edge of the Moab plateau, extending to the Wâdī Kefrein at Abel-shittim. Its most famous peaks are Nebo (Deut. 32:39), Pisgah (34:1), and Peor (Num. 23:28).

During the wilderness wanderings the Israelites made camp at several places in these mountains before defeating the Amorites (Num. 21:10-20; 33:44). They then moved to the plains of Moab across the Jordan from Jericho (33:47-49). From one of those peaks Moses was able to view the Promised Land before his death (27:12; Deut. 32:49).

In the poetic section of Jeremiah (22:20-23; composed shortly before 597 B.C.) Jerusalem is summoned to announce her own doom from three Transjordanian elevations: Lebanon, Bashan, and Abarim (KJV "passages").

ABBA [ăb'ə, ä'bə] (Gk. *abbá*; Aram. *'abbā'*, emphatic form of *'ab*).† Another name for "father" mentioned three times in the New Testament, always in the context of prayer. Unlike Matthew and Luke, Mark adds the word "Abba" to Jesus' pleading with the Father (14:36), indicating that Jesus prayed in the everyday language of the family, setting a precedent which his Jewish contemporaries would consider disrespectful.

Paul uses the same word to suggest the warmth and confidence with which believers may address God as "Father" (Rom. 8:15; Gal. 4:6).

See also FATHER.

Bibliography. J. Jeremias, *The Prayers of Jesus* (Philadelphia: 1978).

ABDA [ăb'də] (Heb. *'abdâ'*, perhaps abbreviation for "servant of Yahweh").

1. The father of Adoniram, one of Solomon's officials (1 Kgs. 4:6).

2. A Levite, the son of Shammua, who settled after the Exile in Jerusalem (Neh. 11:17); at 1 Chr. 9:16 his name is given as Obadiah the son of Shemaiah.

ABDEEL [ăb'dī əl] (Heb. *'abde'ēl* "servant of God"). The father of Shelemiah, one of Jehoiakim's courtiers (Jer. 36:26).

ABDI [ăb'dī] (Heb. *'abdî*, probably abbreviation for "servant of Yahweh").

1. A Levite of the family of Merari. He was the grandfather of Ethan, a temple singer during the days of David (1 Chr. 6:44).

2. The father of the Levite Kish, a contemporary of King Hezekiah (2 Chr. 29:12).

3. One of those Israelites who had married foreign wives during the ministry of Ezra (Ezra 10:26).

ABDIEL [ăb'dĭ əl] (Heb. *'aḇdî'ēl* "servant of God"). A Gadite who dwelled in Gilead or in Bashan; he was the father of Ahi, the chief of that tribe (1 Chr. 5:15).

ABDON [ăb'dŏn] (Heb. *'aḇdôn,* possibly "service," "servile") (PERSON).

1. The son of Hillel of Pirathon in Ephraim and father of forty sons and thirty grandsons. He was considered a man of wealth and prestige, owning seventy asses (Judg. 12:13-15).

Abdon was one of Israel's last judges, providing leadership for eight years. When he died the Lord gave the Philistines control over the Israelites for many years before the last judge mentioned in Judges — Samson (13:2–16:31) — rose to power.

2. A Benjaminite who dwelled at Jerusalem. He was a son of Shashak (1 Chr. 8:23, 28).

3. The eldest son of the Benjaminite Jeiel and his wife Maacah; he dwelled at Gibeon (1 Chr. 8:30; 9:35-36). Abdon's brother Ner was the grandfather of King Saul (9:35-39).

4. Son of Micah and a court official of King Josiah (2 Chr. 34:20). He is also called Achbor (2 Kgs. 22:12).

ABDON [ăb' dŏn] (Heb. *'aḇdôn*) (PLACE). A levitical city in the tribal territory of Asher (Josh. 21:30; 1 Chr. 6:74) assigned to the family of Gershom. It is probably Khirbet 'Abdeh, today a ruin about 17 km. (10 mi.) north-northeast of Acco. At Josh. 19:28 Ebron should perhaps be rendered Abdon (see M. H. Woudstra, *The Book of Joshua.* NICOT [1981], p. 289).

ABEDNEGO [ə bĕd'nĭ gō] (Heb. and Aram. *ʿaḇēḏ nᵉgô*).† The Babylonian name given to one of Daniel's friends by King Nebuchadnezzar's chief eunuch (Dan. 1:7; 2:49; 3:12-30). If, as many assume, his name is a corruption of the Babylonian deity Nebo (cf. JB note c at 1:7), his new name "Servant of Nebo" would have been the opposite of his original name Azariah, "Yahweh has helped."

Although offered food and drink from the king's table, Daniel, Abednego, and the other two Judahites who had been brought to Nebuchadnezzar's palace to learn Chaldean ways, lived on vegetables and water, which would not violate their dietary laws. For their faithfulness, God blessed them with exceptional learning and wisdom (Dan. 1:8-17). Later, because Daniel pleased the king and was able to interpret dreams, Abednego and the other two men were made officials of the province of Babylon at Daniel's request (2:49). When those three refused to bow down to a golden image erected by Nebuchadnezzar's craftsmen, they were thrown into a fiery furnace. God sent an angel, however, to protect them. Faced with this extraordinary turn of events, the king honored the three men and even showed respect for their religion (3:14-30).

In the parting words of Mattathias (1 Macc. 2:58), Abednego (Azariah) and his two friends were praised

for their fidelity. The only New Testament allusion to them is at Heb. 11:32-34 ("prophets who . . . quenched raging fire"). Here their deliverance may have been used to remind the recipients of this letter that they, too, "could be sure of divine companionship in the midst of [trials] such as the three Hebrews enjoyed" (F. F. Bruce, *The Epistle to the Hebrews.* NICNT [1964], p. 335).

ABEL [ā'bəl]. (Heb. *heḇel, hāḇel*) (PERSON). The second son of Adam and Eve (Gen. 4:1-2); he was a keeper of sheep. While Eve explained the name of her firstborn son, she did not do so with her second. Heb. *heḇel* means "breath," "transitoriness," "vanity," but meaning may have been coincidental to Eve's choosing this name (so G. C. Aalders, *Genesis 1.* BSC [1981], p. 119); others have linked the name with Akk. *aplu* "son."

According to the narrative at Gen. 4:4-5, the Lord approved Abel's offering of the firstlings and their fat, but had no regard for the offering brought by Cain, Abel's older brother. There is no basic difference in the types of offerings and thus no basis for the assumption that animal sacrifices were at that time more acceptable to God than cereal offerings. When Cain sensed God's displeasure with his offering, he was angered and killed his brother in the field, even though the Lord had warned him against such a sin (vv. 6-8). The Lord then protected Cain with a mark (lest someone seek to avenge Abel's death) and expelled him from Eden. In time Adam and Eve had another son, Seth, who took Abel's place.

The name of Abel is not mentioned in the Old Testament outside of the Genesis narrative. In Matthew and Luke he is called the first martyr and a Christ figure (Matt. 23:35 par. Luke 11:50-51). To the author of Hebrews, Abel's death, which cried out for revenge, suggested the blood Christ shed, which brought forgiveness and peace to believers. It was that same author's opinion that Abel's faith is what made his sacrifice more acceptable than his brother's offering (11:4; Gk. *Abel*).

See also CAIN.

ABEL [ā'bəl] (Heb. *'āḇēl*) (PLACE).

1. A place near Beth-shemesh where the Philistines returned the ark of the covenant taken from Israel in a previous battle (so KJV, "the great stone of Abel," 1 Sam. 6:18, following Heb. *wᵉʿaḏ 'āḇēl haggᵉḏôlâ*). Most contemporary versions have "the great stone" (RSV; cf. NIV, JB), following the variant reading *'eḇen* "stone" (see *BH,* KoB, pp. 6-7; see also KD in loc.).

2. For 2 Sam. 20:18, *see* ABEL-BETH-MAACAH.

ABEL-BETH-MAACAH [ā'bəl bĕth mā'ə kə] (Heb. *'āḇēl bêṯ-maʿᵃḵâ* "meadow of the house of Maacah"). A city in northern Palestine, also called Abel (2 Sam. 20:18), Abel of Beth-maacah (vv. 14-15; KJV "Abel, and to Beth-maacah," v. 14, following the MT), and Abel-maim (2 Chr. 16:4). It is first mentioned as a city of refuge for Sheba when he led a revolt in Israel following Absalom's rebellion (2 Sam. 20:14-15). Later it was seized by Ben-hadad, the king of Aram, at the request of King Asa of Judah, who was engaged in a war with Baasha of the northern kingdom (1 Kgs. 15:20). Finally, at the end of the northern kingdom, it was conquered by Tiglath-pileser of Assyria (733 B.C.) (2 Kgs. 15:29; cf. the name "Abilakka" in the records of the Assyrian monarch).

Abel-beth-maacah is usually identified with modern Tell Abil. Situated as it was along the Nahr Bareight, a tributary of the Nahr Hasbani, one of the sources of the Jordan, its alternate name, Abel-maim, would have been an appropriate designation — "meadow of waters." The appellative at 2 Sam. 20:19, "a mother in Israel," would suggest that other villages or cities were under its jurisdiction.

ABEL-KERAMIM [āʹbəl kĕrʹə mĭm] (Heb. *ʾābēl kᵉrāmîm* "meadow of vineyards"). A city in Ammon, to which Jephthah pursued the Ammonites (Judg. 11:33; KJV "plain of the vineyards"). According to some scholars it is now the city of Naʿur, about 14 km. (9 mi.) from Amman.

ABEL-MAIM. Another name for ABEL-BETH-MAACAH.

ABEL-MEHOLAH [āʹbəl mĭ hōʹlə] (Heb. *ʾābēl mᵉḥôlâ* "meadow of dancing"). A city mentioned three times in the Old Testament. In his surprise attack on the Midianites, Gideon sent some of the enemy fleeing as far as the "border of Abel-meholah" (Judg. 7:22), on the western bank of the Jordan. During Solomon's reign it was one of the cities in the district assigned to Baana (1 Kgs. 4:12). Abel-meholah was also the home of Elisha's father (1 Kgs. 19:16) and of Elisha himself (vv. 19-20). Also, according to 1 Sam. 18:19; 2 Sam. 21:8, Adriel, the second husband of Merab, one of Saul's daughters, was a resident of Abel-meholah.

Following Jerome and Eusebius many scholars believe that its location can be identified with either Tell Abû Sifri (approximately midway between the Sea of Gennesaret and the Dead Sea) or Tell el-Maqlûb at the Wâdî el-Yabis, both south of ancient Beth-shan. Others favor a site east of the Jordan.

ABEL-MIZRAIM [āʹbəl mĭzʹrĭ əm] (Heb. *ʾābēl miṣrayim* "meadow of Egypt"). A place along the Jordan where Joseph, accompanied by Egyptian dignitaries, mourned for his deceased father Jacob. According to Gen. 50:11 the name is related to Heb. *ʾābal* ("mourn") and *ʾēbel* ("mourning rites"); its original name was Atad. On the basis of vv. 10-11 ("beyond the Jordan," the "inhabitants of the land") and v. 13 ("carried into the land"), some scholars have judged its location to be in Transjordan, north of the Dead Sea.

See ATAD.

ABEL-SHITTIM [āʹbəl shĭtʹĭm] (Heb. *ʾābēl haššiṭṭîm* "meadow [or brook] of the acacias"). A place of encampment for the Israelites at the end of the wilderness wanderings (Num. 33:49; JB "Abel-hash-shittim"). Usually called Shittim, it is located east of the Jordan, in Moab.

See SHITTIM 1.

ABEZ (Josh. 19:20, KJV). See EBEZ.

ABGAR [ăbʹgər] (Gk. *Abgaros*). A king of Uchama, the son of Uchamo, who reigned over Edessa (*ca.* A.D. 9-46). According to a legend (Eusebius *HE* i.13), Abgar exchanged letters with Jesus concerning the possibility of Jesus' healing his terrible disease. In his reply the Lord promised to send one of his apostles (after his ascension); subsequently Thaddeus, one of the seventy, arrived, healed the king, and promoted the cause of Christianity.

ABI [āʹbī] (Heb. *ʾăbî* "my father"). An abbreviation of the name of Abijah, the mother of Hezekiah (2 Kgs. 18:2).

See ABIJAH 6.

ABIA; ABIAH. See ABIJAH.

ABI-ALBON [āʹbī ălʹbən] (Heb. *ʾăbî-ʿalᵉbôn*). One of David's thirty mighty men (2 Sam. 23:31), called Abiel the Arbathite at 1 Chr. 11:32 (cf. LXX *Abiēl*); he may have been an inhabitant of Beth-arabah (cf. JB). The form Abi-albon is possibly an error for Shaalbon (2 Sam. 23:32).

ABIASAPH [ə bīʹə săf] (Heb. *ʾăbîʾāsāp* "my father has gathered"). A Levite of the family of Korah and contemporary of Phinehas the grandson of Aaron (Exod. 6:24-25). At 1 Chr. 6:23; 9:19 an alternate form Ebiasaph and his son's name are mentioned. The Asaph of 1 Chr. 26:1 (JB "Ebiasaph") may be an abbreviated form (LXX B Abia-Saphar).

ABIATHAR [ə bīʹə thər] (Heb. *ʾebyāṯār* "the father is preeminent"). A descendant of Eli the priest through Phinehas, Ahitub, and Ahimelech. Abiathar was the only son of Ahimelech to escape the sword of Doeg the Edomite, who slaughtered the priests of Nob at Saul's behest because of Ahimelech's aid to David (1 Sam. 22:17-20). Abiathar fled to David who, feeling partly responsible for the tragedy, accepted him among his own people (vv. 20-23).

Abiathar served as David's priest, not only at Keilah (1 Sam. 23:9) but also later when the Amalekites had raided Ziklag (30:7). He advised the future king through the lots of the ephod which he had taken with him from Nob (cf. 23:6). Abiathar continued in this capacity even after the death of Saul and subsequently during David's reign at Hebron and Jerusalem. It may be that Abiathar's son Ahimelech assisted his father in the exercise of his high-priestly office (2 Sam. 8:17).

Throughout the rebellion of Absalom Abiathar remained loyal to King David. He and Zadok intended to carry the ark as they fled Jerusalem (2 Sam. 15:24), but were instructed by David to carry it back into the city (vv. 25, 29). They were also to keep the exiled king informed of new developments (vv. 35-36), which they did (17:15-21).

Surprisingly, near the end of David's long reign Abiathar favored Adonijah rather than David's younger son Solomon for the throne (1 Kgs. 1:7). Perhaps Abiathar, as the descendant of Aaron's youngest son Ithamar, was jealous of Zadok (the descendant of Aaron's elder son Eleazar), the other Davidic high priest (usually mentioned before

Abiathar; e.g., 2 Sam. 15:24-29; so KD *in loc.*). But once the rebel son of David was executed, Abiathar was deposed from his priestly office by Solomon and banished to his estate at Anathoth. He was not given the death penalty because he had carried the ark and had shared in David's afflictions (1 Kgs. 2:26-27). According to the author of Kings, this is how the prophecy concerning Eli's house became fulfilled (cf. 1 Sam. 2:27-36): Eli was one of Abiathar's ancestors and Zadok, who had supported Solomon, replaced Abiathar as high priest (1 Kgs. 2:35). 1 Kgs. 4:4 may indicate that Abiathar, though deprived of his priestly office, had not, however, been deprived of his priestly dignity.

In his account of Jesus' discussion with the Pharisees about David and the meaning of the Sabbath laws, Mark attributes David's eating the Bread of the Presence to the time of Abiathar rather than that of his father Ahimelech, when the incident actually occurred (Mark 2:26; cf. 1 Sam. 21:1-6).

ABIB [ā'bĭb] (Heb. *'āḇîḇ*). The original name of the first Hebrew month, mentioned in connection with the Feast of the Unleavened Bread or the Passover (Mar./Apr.); after the Exile it was called Nisan (Neh. 2:1; Esth. 3:7). Its designation "month of the ears" (Heb. *ḥōḏeš hā'āḇîḇ* "month of young ear of barley [or "other grain"]"; e.g., Exod. 13:4) may point to the new moon nearest to, or preceding, the growth of barley.

According to Josephus, Abib was the first month only of Israel's ecclesiastical year; the so-called civic year ran from autumn to autumn.

See YEAR.

ABIDA [ə bī'də] (Heb. *'aḇîḏā' * "my father knows"). A descendant of Abraham and Keturah through Midian, their fourth son (Gen. 25:4 [KJV "Abidah"]; 1 Chr. 1:33).

ABIDAH (Gen. 25:4, KJV). *See* ABIDA.

ABIDAN [ə bī'dən] (Heb. *'aḇîḏān* "my father judged"). The son of Gideoni; he became the "leader" of the tribe of Benjamin during the wilderness wanderings (Num. 2:22; 10:24). Abidan assisted Moses at the taking of the census (1:11) and made his offering on the ninth day of the dedication of the tabernacle (7:60, 65).

ABIEL [ā'bĭ əl] (Heb. *'aḇî'ēl* "my father is God").
1. A man from the tribe of Benjamin. He was the father of Kish and grandfather of Saul (1 Sam. 9:1-2); also the father of Ner and grandfather of Abner (14:51).
2. One of David's mighty men (1 Chr. 11:32); at 2 Sam. 23:31 he is called Abi-albon the Arbathite.

ABIEZER [ăb'ĭ ē'zər] (Heb. *'aḇî'ezer* "my father is help").
1. A descendant of Manasseh (1 Chr. 7:18). At Num. 26:30 an abbreviated form of his name occurs (Iezer; KJV "Jeezer"). The Abiezrites were given a district in the tribal territory of Manasseh west of the Jordan (Josh. 17:2) which included the city of Ophrah

(to be distinguished from other cities of a similar name). Gideon was an Abiezrite (Judg. 6:11; cf. v. 34).
2. One of David's mighty men, the commander of the ninth division of his army (2 Sam. 23:37; 1 Chr. 11:28; 27:12). He was from Anathoth in Benjamin.

ABIGAIL [ăb'ə gāl] (Heb. *'aḇîgayil, 'aḇiwgayil* [K 1 Sam. 25:18], probably "my father rejoices").†
1. The wife of Nabal, a wealthy shepherd at Maon. When she learned about David's intended revenge against Nabal for insulting David's band of young men, Abigail quietly prepared a large quantity of food to take to David. Upon meeting him, she made obeisance to him, explaining that her husband had acted foolishly and that David should not kill him but, instead, should accept the gift (1 Sam. 25:2-31). Her sensible words and beauty appeased David's anger (vv. 3, 32-34); and he accepted the present (v. 35). When she told her husband the next day what had transpired, he became "as a stone" (v. 37); ten days later he died (v. 38). David subsequently took Abigail as his wife (vv. 40-43), and she dwelled with him at Gath (27:3). When David and his men joined the Philistines in their preparation for battle with Saul, the Amalekites took captive David's wives, Abigail and Ahinoam (30:5). He was, however, able to rescue them (v. 18).

After David had become king at Hebron, Abigail bore him a son named Chileab (2 Sam. 3:3). (At 1 Chr. 3:1 his name is Daniel.)
2. One of the two sisters of David (according to 1 Chr. 2:16) or half sisters (according to 2 Sam. 17:25 where the father of Abigail [Heb. *'aḇîgal*; KJV "Abigal"] is Nahash rather than Jesse, and Zeruiah is Joab's mother rather than Abigail's sister). Most likely Abigail and Zeruiah were daughters of David's mother and Nahash before she married Jesse. If so (but see JB at 2 Sam. 17:25, "Jesse"), then Zeruiah was much older than David and could have borne Joab at about the same time as David's mother bore David.

Abigail married Jether the Ishmaelite (1 Chr. 2:16) or Izri the Ishmaelite (so RSV, JB at 2 Sam. 17:25; probably more accurate than the "Israelite," as KJV, NIV following the MT) and became the mother of Amasa, whom Absalom made captain of David's army. The author of 2 Samuel depicts Izri (NIV "Jether") less favorably than the author of Chronicles, suggesting perhaps that the Ishmaelite seduced Abigail and that therefore Amasa was illegitimate.

ABIHAIL [ăb'ə hāl] (Heb. *'aḇîhayil* "the father is might").
1. A Levite of the family of Merari; he was the father of Zuriel (Num. 3:35).
2. The wife of Abishur of the family of Judah (1 Chr. 2:29).
3. A man from the tribe of Gad; he was the father of seven sons (1 Chr. 5:14).
4. The daughter of David's brother Eliab and wife of David's son Jerimoth. Their daughter Mahalath became the wife of King Rehoboam of Judah (2 Chr. 11:18).
5. The father of Queen Esther and uncle of Mordecai (Esth. 2:15; 9:29).

ABIHU [ə bī'hū] (Heb. *'ăḇîhû'* "he is [my] father"). The second son of Aaron and Elisheba (Exod. 6:23). Nadab and Abihu were permitted to ascend Mt. Sinai and look upon the Lord (24:1, 9-11), and were made his priests (28:1). After they had assisted their father on his first day as high priest (Lev. 9:9), Abihu and Nadab lit their censers and offered "unholy fire" (perhaps meaning "unauthorized") before the Lord (10:1), deviating from the prescribed religious codes. Seeking to impress the Israelites of his holiness, God sent fire from heaven which devoured the two brothers (vv. 2-3). Moses then summoned the sons of Uzziel, Aaron's uncle (rather than Eleazar and Ithamar, Aaron's younger sons, as would have been expected), to bury the bodies (vv. 4-5).

In later history the names of Nadab and Abihu are still associated with this event. Their unacceptable behavior is mentioned in the accounts of the consecration of the Levites (Num. 3:2-4) and the census of the Levites (26:60-61). The description of the brothers in Chronicles is less incriminating; Nadab and Abihu are said to have been succeeded by Eleazar and Ithamar upon their death because they were childless (1 Chr. 24:1-2; cf. 6:3).

ABIHUD [ə bī'hŭd] (Heb. *'ăḇîhûḏ* "my father is majesty"). Listed as the third son of Bela, the son of Benjamin (1 Chr. 8:3). According to *BH* the meaning of Abihud is more correctly "the father of Ehud" (Heb. *'ăḇî 'ēhûḏ*; but cf. LXX *Abioud* "Abiud"). Others have considered it a longer variant of Abiud.

ABIJAH [ə bī'jə] (Heb. *'ăḇîyâ, 'ăḇîyāhû* "my father is Yahweh").

1. One of Aaron's descendants and head of the eighth division of priests under King David (1 Chr. 24:10). According to Luke 1:5 (Gk. *Abia*; KJV "Abia"), Zechariah, the father of John the Baptist, belonged to the division led by Abijah.

2. The seventh son of Becher, a Benjaminite (1 Chr. 7:8; KJV "Abiah").

3. The second son of the prophet Samuel (1 Chr. 6:28). Appointed as judge, he yielded to bribery and injustice with his brother Joel. Because Abijah was not the exemplary leader his father was, the tribal leaders of Israel desired to be ruled instead by a king (1 Sam. 8:1-5).

4. A son of Jeroboam I of Israel (1 Kgs. 14:1). Because of Abijah's sickness, Jeroboam sent his wife (whose name is not given) to the prophet Ahijah to inquire about the child's future (vv. 2-3). Despite her disguise the blind prophet recognized her because God had informed him of her intended visit (vv. 4-5). The aged prophet pronounced doom on the house of Jeroboam but predicted that Israel would mourn his son "because in him there is found something pleasing to the Lord" (v. 13). When his mother returned home and entered the palace, Abijah died as Ahijah had predicted (vv. 12, 17), and he was buried amid widespread mourning (v. 18).

5. The son and successor of King Rehoboam of Judah (2 Chr. 12:16; 13:1); at 1 Kgs. 14:31; 15:1, 7-8 he is called Abijam. His mother was Maacah, daughter of Absalom's daughter Tamar and her husband Uriel (2 Sam. 14:27).

During his short reign (probably two full years, *ca.* 915-913 B.C. [three years according to 1 Kgs. 15:2; 2 Chr. 13:2]), Abijah continued his father's war with Jeroboam I (1 Kgs. 15:6-7). The author of Chronicles describes in some detail Abijah's preparations for battle, Jeroboam's ambush, God's deliverance of Judah, and Abijah's pursuit of his northern enemy (2 Chr. 13:2-20). The Chronicler also adds that Judah's king acquired a large household and had numerous offspring (13:21). Both authors mention Abijah's death and burial at Jerusalem (2 Chr. 14:1; cf. 1 Kgs. 15:8).

While the author of Kings views Abijah as following in the sinful footsteps of his father and thus not wholly committed to the Lord (15:3), the Chronicler portrays him as a religious man who trusted God (13:14, 18); the presentation may be somewhat one-sided in the address to Jeroboam recorded at vv. 5-12. According to 1 Kgs. 15:4-5 it was because of David's faithfulness that the Lord spared Abijah's life and gave him a son.

Abijah is listed in the genealogy of Jesus, between Rehoboam and Asa (Matt. 1:7; KJV "Abia").

6. The mother of King Hezekiah and daughter of Zechariah (2 Chr. 29:1); at 2 Kgs. 18:2 her name is given as Abi.

7. One of the chiefs of the priestly families returning with Zerubbabel from Exile (Neh. 12:4, 7, 17), probably the same as the Abijah mentioned at 10:7 who put his seal to the renewed covenant under Nehemiah. He may have been a descendant of the eighth Aaronic division (**1** above), though his name does not occur with the other returning priests at Ezra 2:36-39.

8. The name of Hezron's wife and grandmother of Tekoa (so NIV, 1 Chr. 2:24; cf. KJV "Abiah" following MT *'ăḇiyyâ*; cf. LXX *Abia*). The RSV and JB consider "Abijah" an epithet of Hezron and render Hezron "his father" (Heb. *'āḇîhu*; cf. *BH*).

ABIJAM [ə bī'jəm] (Heb. *'ăḇiyām* "father of the sea"). A variation of the name of King Abijah of Judah (*see* ABIJAH **5**). Various suggestions have been presented to account for this incongruity.

ABILENE [ăb'ə lē'nī] (Gk. *Abilēnē*). A region in the eastern part of the Anti-lebanon range. Its capital, Abila, was situated along the southwest bank of the upper Barada river (biblical Abana), about 27 km. (17 mi.) from Damascus.

In New Testament times Lysanias was the tetrarch of this district, a historical fact which Luke cites while retelling the beginning of the ministry of John the Baptist (Luke 3:1). After Lysanias' death the tetrarchy was granted to Agrippa I (A.D. 37) and later to Agrippa II (53).

ABIMAEL [ə bīm'ī əl] (Heb. *'ăḇîmā'ēl* "my father is God"). One of the sons of Joktan (Gen. 10:28; 1 Chr. 1:22) and progenitor of a South Arabian tribe.

ABIMELECH [ə bīm'ə lĕk] (Heb. *'ăḇîmelek* "my father is king").

1. A king of the Philistines at Gerar and a contemporary of Abraham. Some scholars have proposed that Abimelech was an official title rather than a personal name (on the basis of the title at Ps. 34 where Abimelech refers to the king of Gath [1 Sam. 21:11]; see **4** below).

Abimelech entered Abraham's life after the destruction of Sodom and Gomorrah, when the patriarch had moved to Gerar (Gen. 20:1). When Abraham told him his wife Sarah was his sister, the king believed him and took Sarah into his house (v. 2). Told by God in a dream that Sarah was really Abraham's wife, Abimelech replied that he had been deceived by Abraham (vv. 3-5). God told him to return Sarah to her lawful husband lest he sin by marrying someone else's wife (vv. 6-7). While scolding Abraham for his deceitful behavior, Abimelech nevertheless dealt generously with him, not only returning his wife to him but giving him gifts and liberty with the land (vv. 9-15). Thereupon the patriarch prayed to God, who removed the barrenness from among the women of Abimelech's house (vv. 17-18).

Sometime later Abraham and Abimelech made a treaty giving Abraham rights to a well Abimelech's men had seized from him; this time the patriarch handsomely paid the king of Gerar in return (21:22-30). The name of the disputed well ("well of the oath") where the pact was signed became the name of the city of Beer-sheba (vv. 31-32).

For the Abimelech of Gen. 26:1-11, 16, 26, see **2** below.

2. Another king of the Philistines at Gerar, most likely the son of **1** above since at least forty years had elapsed between the events mentioned at Gen. 20–21 and those at ch. 26 where this king is mentioned. This time it was Isaac who, forced by a famine, had moved to Gerar (26:1-6), and he, too, called his wife (Rebekah) his sister. Unlike his father, Abimelech did not take Isaac's wife Rebekah for himself, but he did reprove the patriarch after he discovered Isaac's ruse (vv. 8-10). A covenant was concluded between the two men which terminated a dispute over wells, as before (vv. 18-33).

3. A son of Gideon and his Canaanite concubine from Shechem (Judg. 8:31). After his father's death, Abimelech secured the help of his mother's kinsmen at Shechem in a plot to kill his seventy brothers. Receiving a certain number of silver pieces from the temple of Baal-berith to aid his cause, he hired scoundrels to execute his blood relatives "upon one stone"; Jotham, Gideon's youngest son, was the sole survivor (9:1-6). Abimelech was then made "king" by the citizens of Shechem (v. 6).

According to the writer of Judges, God did not let Abimelech's crime go unpunished. After a peaceful reign of three years, the Lord sent an evil spirit to part the inhabitants of Shechem and their "king" (v. 23). Abimelech's subjects became disloyal and permitted Gaal to take over as leader (vv. 26-29). Abimelech, however, upon being informed of Gaal's aspirations by Zebul, the ruler of Shechem in Abimelech's absence, defeated his rival and razed Shechem (vv. 30-45). Even the reputed stronghold, the tower of Shechem, proved to be no defense for the remaining inhabitants; it too was destroyed (vv. 46-49).

Abimelech was less fortunate in attempting to capture nearby Thebez. About to burn the door of the tower of the city, he was mortally wounded by a

millstone dropped on his skull by a woman. Unwilling to die at the hand of a woman, he arrogantly asked his armorbearer to take his life (vv. 50-54). The author ends his account of Abimelech by expressly stating that God requited Abimelech's crime in this manner (v. 56). At 2 Sam. 11:21 Joab refers to Abimelech's death in the context of Uriah's shameful end.

4. Another name for Achish king of Gath, in whose presence David feigned madness (cf. 1 Sam. 21:10-15). If Abimelech is a title of Philistine kings (just as pharaoh is a title for Egyptian rulers), the author of Ps. 34 could have copied it from a source other than 1 Sam. 21:10-15, perhaps from the Annals of King David.

5. (1 Chr. 18:16, KJV). *See* AHIMELECH **2**.

ABINADAB [ə bĭn′ə dăb] (Heb. *ᵃḇînāḏāḇ* "father is noble").

1. A resident of Kiriath-jearim, possibly a Levite, into whose house the ark of the covenant was taken after the horrible slaughter at Beth-shemesh (1 Sam. 6:19–7:2). Abinadab's son Eleazar was consecrated to be in charge of the sacred chest.

Several years later David led a procession in which Abinadab's sons Uzzah and Ahio transported the ark on a new cart pulled by oxen. Before they reached Jerusalem where the king had intended to give the ark a permanent home, the oxen stumbled and the ark was dislodged. Uzzah tried to keep the ark from falling, but was smitten by God for touching it (1 Chr. 13:6ff.).

2. A son of King Saul (1 Chr. 8:33; 9:39) who was slain on Mt. Gilboa by the Philistines along with his father and brothers (1 Sam. 31:2; 1 Chr. 10:2).

3. The second son of Jesse and the elder brother of David (1 Sam. 16:8; 1 Chr. 2:13). He is listed among those who joined King Saul in his encounter with the Philistines (1 Sam. 17:13).

4. The father of a son-in-law of King Solomon and officer of the district of Naphath-dor (1 Kgs. 4:11).

ABINOAM [ə bĭn′ō əm] (Heb. *ᵃḇînōʿam* "father is benevolence"). The father of Barak of the tribe of Naphtali (Judg. 4:6, 12; 5:1, 12).

ABIRAM [ə bī′rəm] (Heb. *ᵃḇîrām* "my father is exalted").†

1. A Reubenite and the son of Eliab. Together with his brother Dathan, he joined the rebellion against Moses and Aaron which was spearheaded by Korah (Num. 16:1). In the end, however, the rebels were "swallowed up" by the earth, and Moses' authority was vindicated (vv. 31ff.). Three times this event is mentioned in the Old Testament: at Num. 26:9 (as a warning), at Deut. 11:6 (as a lesson from the past emphasizing God's power), and at Ps. 106:17 (as an example of Israel's sin during the wilderness wanderings).

2. The eldest son of Hiel of Bethel, who laid the foundations of Jericho "at the cost of" his firstborn (1 Kgs. 16:34). The restoration of Jericho, on which Joshua had pronounced a curse (Josh. 6:26), indicated Israel's progression in ungodliness, but the fulfillment of the curse clearly teaches that God does not allow his will to be disregarded. Some (e.g., W. J. Beecher, "Abiram," *ISBE* 1 [1979]: 10) regard Abiram's death as a foundation sacrifice made by his father at the laying of the foundation of the city.

ABISHAG [ăb'ə shăg] (Heb. *ʾaḇîšag*, possibly "my father is a wanderer"). A beautiful virgin chosen to be David's nurse in his old age. Though she was to lie against him to give him warmth, the king had no sexual relations with her (1 Kgs. 1:1-4).

After David's death his son Adonijah desired Abishag to be his wife and put his request to young King Solomon via Bathsheba, Solomon's mother (2:13-21). Solomon, however, interpreted this as another sign of Adonijah's attempts to become king (vv. 22-24) and had him executed (v. 25). Whatever Adonijah's personal feelings for Abishag may have been, he was clearly thinking about strengthening his claims to the throne (see vv. 15-17).

ABISHAI [ə bī'shī] (Heb. *ʾaḇîšay, ʾaḇšay* "[my] father exists"). The eldest son of Zeruiah, David's sister, and brother of Joab and Asahel (2 Sam. 2:18; 1 Chr. 2:16; 18:2); the name of Abishai's father is not given.

Abishai is first mentioned as a courageous follower of the outlaw David. When David learned that Saul had pursued him into the Wilderness of Ziph, Abishai accompanied him to Saul's camp. Seeing an opportunity to kill Saul while he slept, Abishai was restrained by his commander who instead ordered him to take Saul's spear and water jar (1 Sam. 26:5-12).

Abishai is next mentioned after Saul's death, at the end of a skirmish between the house of Ishbosheth and the house of David (2 Sam. 2:17). Having learned that Abner, Ishbosheth's commander, had killed his younger brother Asahel in self-defense, Abishai and his brother Joab tracked Abner until he offered them a truce; they temporarily abandoned the idea of avenging Asahel's death (vv. 24-30).

In the battle against the Ammonites and Syrians, during which Hanun the king of Ammon insulted David's envoys, Abishai was charged to fight the Ammonites while Joab directed his attention to the Syrians. Each of the two commanders won a victory (2 Sam. 10:9-19; cf. 1 Chr. 19:16-19). According to 1 Chr. 18:12-13, Abishai is given credit for making the Edomites David's subjects. On another occasion Abishai rescued David by killing the Philistine Ishibenob, who was about to run him through with a spear (2 Sam. 21:16-17). Abishai also slew three hundred Philistines (23:18; cf. 1 Chr. 11:20). The record lists him as the most renowned of David's thirty mighty men, if not among the three most valiant (23:19; cf. 1 Chr. 11:21). Though Abishai was a less illustrious warrior than his brother Joab, his thirst for revenge and cruelty against a foe brought him into collaboration with Joab in the unjust death of Abner (2 Sam. 3:30).

He remained loyal to David but twice caused the king to exclaim, "What have I to do with you, you son[s] of Zeruiah?" — once when Abishai wanted to silence the cursing Shimei during the king's exodus from Jerusalem (16:10) and again when Shimei expressed contrition for his earlier behavior (19:21).

ABISHALOM [ə bĭsh'ə ləm] (Heb. *ʾaḇîšālôm*). An alternate rendering of the name Absalom (1 Kgs. 15:2, 10).

ABISHUA [ə bĭsh'ŏŏ ə] (Heb. *ʾaḇîšuaʿ*, possibly "my father is deliverance").

1. A Benjaminite, one of the sons of Bela, and grandson of Benjamin (1 Chr. 8:4).

2. The son of the high priest Phinehas (1 Chr. 6:4) and great-grandson of Aaron (v. 50). According to Ezra 7:5 he was an ancestor of Ezra the scribe.

ABISHUR [ə bī'shər] (Heb. *ʾaḇîšûr* "my father is a wall"). A Judahite of the family of Hezron; a son of Shammai and brother of Nadab. He married Abihail and became the father of two sons (1 Chr. 2:28-29).

ABITAL [ə bī'təl] (Heb. *ʾaḇîṭāl* "my father is dew"). One of David's wives and mother of his fifth son Shephatiah (2 Sam. 3:4; 1 Chr. 3:3).

ABITUB [ə bī'tŭb] (Heb. *ʾaḇîṭûḇ* "my father is goodness"). One of the two sons of Shamaraim and his first wife Hushim (1 Chr. 8:11; KJV "Ahitub").

ABIUD [ə bī'əd] (Gk. *Abioud*, perhaps "my father is majesty"; abbreviation of Abihud). The son of Zerubbabel and an ancestor of Jesus (Matt. 1:13).

ABNER [ăb'nər] (Heb. *ʾaḇnēr, ʾaḇînēr* "my father is a lamp"). The son of Ner and the uncle of King Saul, he became the commander of Saul's army (1 Sam. 14:50-51). While he accompanied the king in battle (1 Sam. 17:55f.), they also shared more peaceful and pleasant circumstances (20:25). At one time his enemy David complimented him for being a very valiant man but reprimanded him as well for not taking better care of the king (26:14-16).

After Saul's death, Abner continued to champion the king's cause. He took Saul's son Ishbosheth to Mahanaim in Transjordan and made him king over the northern tribes (2 Sam. 2:8-10). He then took Ishbosheth's servants and met Joab's force at the pool of Gibeon where, at Abner's proposal, a match was held between twelve young men from each side. Unfortunately, the encounter ended in the deaths of all contestants. In the ensuing skirmish, Abner's men were defeated (vv. 12-17), and Abner himself was pursued by Asahel, the brother of Joab and Abishai. Unwilling to kill the young man, he tried to persuade Asahel to chase others instead. But Asahel continued his pursuit, and Abner killed him in self-defense (vv. 18-23). Faced with attempts at revenge by Joab and Abishai, Abner called for a truce, which Asahel's brothers accepted (vv. 24-28).

Peace, however, was not restored between the houses of Saul and David. While Abner had not wavered in his support of Ishbosheth (2 Sam. 3:6), his master's reproach for having intimate relations with Saul's concubine Rizpah turned his loyalty to David (vv. 6-12). He sent messengers to the king at Hebron with the promise that Abner would bring the northern tribes under his rule (v. 12). Though he accepted Abner's overtures, David insisted that first his wife

Michal, Saul's daughter, should be returned to him. After pressuring Ishbosheth about this matter, David received Michal through Abner's mediation (vv. 13-16). This opened the road toward a treaty, and David invited Abner to Hebron for a feast after Abner had succeeded in winning the northern tribes over as he had promised (vv. 17-20). At the end of the festivities David sent Abner away, everything having been settled (v. 21).

This able commander met his end rather unexpectedly. Abner returned to Hebron at Joab's request. He met the brother of Asahel, whom he had killed, at the gate. Pretending a need to speak to him privately, Joab murdered Abner right there, avenging his brother's death (3:23-27).

Filled with indignation, David not only praised Abner's character, calling him a "prince and a great man," but also offered a eulogy at the warrior's public burial at Hebron (2 Sam. 3:33-34). The people were convinced that their king had had no part in the duplicity or the assassination (vv. 31-39), and David prayed that justice would be served in due time (v. 39; cf. 1 Kgs. 2:5-6, 32).

According to the author of Chronicles, Abner contributed part of the spoil won in battle to the maintenance of the house of the Lord (1 Chr. 26:27-28). His son Jaasiel was the chief officer of the tribe of Benjamin (27:21).

ABRAHAM [āʹbrə hăm] (Heb. *'abrāhām*).† Progenitor of the Israelites and an important figure in salvation history.

I. Name

Originally the name of this patriarch was Abram (Heb. *'abrām*; e.g., Gen. 11:26; 12:1), but God subsequently changed it to Abraham (Heb. *'abrāhām*). According to 17:5 the latter name is composed of Heb. *'ab* "father" and *hmn* "multitude," thus meaning "father of a multitude" (see JB note d at Gen. 17:5). Because several scholars have come to reject such an interpretation on linguistic grounds (e.g., R. E. Clements, "ʿabhrāhām," *TDOT* 1, rev. ed. [1977]: 52), others have suggested relating *rhm* to Arab. *ruham* "multitude" or to an ancient Hebrew root *rhm* (so G. C. Aalders, *Genesis* 1. BSC [1981], p. 306; but see W. H. Gispen, *Genesis* 2. COT [1979], p. 137). As a variant of Abram the name can signify "love of the father" (from Akk. *Abam-rāmā*), "he is of good ancestry" (relating *rhm* to *rm* "exalted"), "the (divine) father is exalted" (a theophorous name), or simply "exalted father" (Clements, pp. 52-53).

Whatever its etymology, the patriarch's name was changed at the renewal of the covenant (Gen. 17:5), when Abraham's only son was the offspring of his maid and Isaac was yet to be born.

II. Chronology

Scholarly opinion has placed the patriarchs as early as Middle Bronze I (*ca*. 2200-1900 B.C.) and as late as the beginning of Late Bronze II (1400-1300 B.C.). Most scholars, however, have proposed a date early in the second millennium based on the following evidence: (1) the scarcity of population in Transjordan between the nineteenth and thirteenth centuries ac-

cords well with the campaign of destruction mentioned in Gen. 14. This would imply that Abraham lived prior to *ca*. 1800; (2) the names of three of the four allied kings in Gen. 14:1 have parallels with names in the period *ca*. 2000-1700. Arioch is equivalent to Arriyuk (or Arriwuk) in the Mari texts (eighteenth century), Tidal is equivalent to Tudkhalia in Hittite texts (nineteenth century and later), and Chedorlaomer is a typical Elamite name from the Old Babylonian period (2000-1700); (3) Mesopotamian power alliances (such as those mentioned in Gen. 14) are common for the period 2000-1750; (4) the patriarchal names have near or exact parallels with Mesopotamian and Egyptian names of the twentieth to eighteenth centuries (e.g., Abram is paralleled by Abarama [from Dilbat], Jacob is paralleled by Yaʿqubil [from Chagar-Bazar]); (5) the southwestern Negeb shows evidence of occupation during Middle Bronze I (specifically the twenty-first to nineteenth centuries), but not for about a millennium before or afterwards. Abraham's and Isaac's pastoral and agricultural activities in this area best coincide with this period; (6) the patriarchal religious concept of the "God of the fathers" is paralleled in cuneiform texts from Cappadocia of the nineteenth century; (7) several customs in the patriarchal narratives, such as the adoption of a servant as heir (Gen. 15:3) and the possession of the household gods as right to inheritance (31:19) are paralleled by customs in the Mari (eighteenth century) and Nuzi (fifteenth century) texts.

More radical critics, such as J. Van Seters and T. L. Thompson, have recently argued on a traditio-historical basis that the patriarchal narratives date from the late first millennium. They allege that there are anachronisms in these narratives (e.g., camels, tents) and that first millennium parallels to patriarchal names exist (Ab[i]ram is like Ahiram); they cite recent studies invalidating several of the parallels between patriarchal customs and those of Mari and Nuzi; and they invoke the difficulty of correlating all the relevant patriarchal stories with a single archaeological period, and the difficulty of reconciling the events of Gen. 14 with archaeology and the known political history of the second millennium.

The chronology supplied by the Bible itself allows a fairly precise dating by means of the following computation. 1 Kgs. 6:1 states that the exodus from Egypt occurred 480 years before the fourth year of Solomon's reign over Israel (967). It therefore would have occurred in 1447, or *ca*. 1445. Accordingly the call of Abram would have taken place *ca*. 2090 (1445 + 30 + 215). Israel dwelt in Egypt for 430 years (Exod. 12:40), suggesting that Jacob went there *ca*. 1875 (1445 + 430). He was 130 years old at that time (Gen. 47:9), and so would have been born *ca*. 2005. Isaac, 60 years old at Jacob's birth (25:26), would have been born *ca*. 2065. Abraham was 100 years old when Isaac was born (21:5), and his birth would thus be dated *ca*. 2165. Since Abram received his call when he was 75 years old (12:4), it would have occurred *ca*. 2090.

Considering the material and textual evidence and the nature of biblical narrative, the birth and calling of Abram must have occurred toward the culmination of Sumerian culture in the Third Dynasty of Ur (*ca*.

2135-2025). The Amorites, West Semitic nomads, and the Elamites, situated in the plain of Khuzistan, exerted pressure upon this kingdom and were eventually responsible for its downfall. It was then replaced by numerous smaller states which were controlled by the Amorites between *ca.* 2100 and 1800.

If this is true Abram came out of a polytheistic environment. For the Sumerians, the universe was controlled by a large pantheon consisting of "superhuman" and immortal gods. The four main gods — An, Ki, Enlil, and Enki — respectively controlled the four main components of the universe — heaven, earth, air, and water. Although nothing of the Sumerian religion is mentioned in the Bible, a reference to "other gods" worshipped by Abraham and his family is recorded in Josh. 24:2.

III. Life

Abraham was the son of Terah, a descendant of Shem. His brothers were Nahor and Haran, who was the father of Lot (Gen. 11:27). Haran died in Ur of the Chaldeans while his father Terah was still alive (v. 28). Abram's wife, who was also his half sister (20:12), was Sarai (11:29). No children had been born to them (v. 30).

As a result of the Amorite incursion, Terah took his family and departed from Ur in southern Mesopotamia for Canaan, but when they arrived in the city of Haran they settled there (v. 31). Haran lay in Paddan-aram (northwest Mesopotamia), some 800 km. (500 mi.) from Ur. Situated at the junction of many caravan routes, it was a flourishing city. The moon-god, Sin, was worshipped in both Haran and Ur, and some scholars have assumed because of this that a close relationship existed between the two cities despite the distance.

Terah died in Haran at the age of 205 (v. 32). Since he was 70 years old when Abram was born, and since Abram was 75 when he departed from Haran (12:4), Terah was 145 years old when Abram left and would have lived many years afterwards in Haran. Note, however, that Stephen says in Acts 7:4 that Abram departed for Canaan shortly *after* the death of his father. Some have thought that Stephen may have been speaking in accordance with a current Jewish tradition also appearing in the Samaritan Pentateuch, which said that Terah died at 145 years of age and that Abram departed from Haran after his death. Others think that Stephen simply erred, or that he meant: "after the Scriptures" mention of his father's death." In Acts 7:2-3, Stephen says that the "God of glory" appeared to Abraham when he was still in Mesopotamia, before he had gone to Haran, and said to him: "Depart from your land . . ." (cf. Gen. 15:7; Neh. 9:7). Does this refer to a calling that occurred in Ur, before the one of Gen. 12:1-3, or does it simply mean that the departure of Abram from Ur took place in accordance with God's providential arrangement? In any case, the significance of Abram's call was that the Lord fulfilled his original promise to Adam (Gen. 3:15) with Abram and his descendants. The latter part of the call (12:3) is best translated: "I will bless those who bless you, and him who curses you I will curse; and in you all the families of the earth shall be blessed" (RSV mg.). The meaning of this line is not

that all the families of the earth would use Abram's name in their blessings (cf. JB note c *in loc.*), but that they would be blessed through the Messiah, the seed of Abram's wife (Aalders, pp. 269-270).

After the call Abram departed in obedience for the land that the Lord would show to him (cf. Heb. 11:8). He took Sarai his wife and Lot his nephew, and all their possessions and dependents, and they arrived in Canaan (Gen. 12:5). The Lord then appeared to him and promised the land to his descendants (v. 7). Next Abram traveled from Shechem to Bethel, and from there he went toward the Negeb region (vv. 6, 8-9). When famine broke out he went to Egypt, where he pretended that Sarai was his sister for their mutual protection. Pharaoh took Sarai into his house and acted charitably toward Abram for her sake. But when the Lord struck Pharaoh with severe plagues, he gave Sarai back to Abram and expelled them from Egypt (vv. 10-20).

Meanwhile, Abram and his nephew Lot had acquired much cattle requiring more pasture land than was available (Gen. 13:5-6). Grumblings among the herdsmen led Abram and Lot to part from each other. Lot chose for himself the entire valley of the Jordan, i.e., the southeastern part of Canaan on both sides of the Jordan river, an exceptionally fertile region inhabited by wicked men (i.e., in Sodom and Gomorrah; 13:2-13). Abram, on the other hand, remained in Canaan, which the Lord once again promised to him and his descendants. He dwelled there by the oak(s) (or terebinth[s]) of Mamre, an Amorite, at Hebron (13:18; cf. 14:13, 24).

According to Gen. 14 Abram defeated the four-king alliance which had made war against Sodom and Gomorrah, and he rescued Lot, who had been taken captive. Melchizedek king of Salem (vv. 18-24), with whom Abram meets, is of great importance as the ideal priest-king in subsequent tradition (cf. Ps. 110:4; Heb. 7).

The Lord then renewed and expanded the covenant with Abram (Gen. 15), promising that Abram's descendants would be as numerous as the stars (v. 5). Abram believed the Lord, who regarded his faith as an act of righteousness (v. 6). Once again, Canaan was promised to him as his inheritance (v. 7). The Lord then confirmed this promise by the customary ancient Near Eastern sign of establishing a covenant; he passed between the pieces of animals that had been slaughtered and divided in two (vv. 8-21).

Since Sarai had borne no children, she gave Hagar, her Egyptian maid, to Abram as a wife, so she might "obtain children by her," i.e., so Hagar might bear children to Abram whom Sarai could later claim as her own (16:1-3). Hagar became pregnant and thereupon despised her mistress. Sarai obtained permission from Abram to do as she pleased with her maid; so she humiliated Hagar until the maid fled (vv. 4-6). The angel of the Lord then appeared to Hagar and sent her back to her mistress with the promise that her own descendants would be very numerous (vv. 7-10). He foretold the birth of a son whom she was to name Ishmael, which means "God hears." Hagar returned and gave birth to a son whom Abram did name Ishmael. Abram was eighty-six years old when Ishmael was born (vv. 11-16).

Gen. 17 tells of the Lord's renewal of the covenant with Abram, who was now ninety-nine years old, and of the institution of the rite of circumcision. At this point Abram's name was changed to Abraham, which is taken to mean "father of a multitude" (see *I*, above). He was then commanded to circumcise all the male members of his household who were eight days old and older (vv. 9-14). Sarai's name was changed to Sarah (both names mean "princess"; v. 15; cf. v. 16). The son she would bear would be called Isaac (meaning "he laughs"; v. 19). Although God blessed Ishmael at Abraham's request, his covenant was to be established with Isaac, who would be born within a year (vv. 20-21; cf. v. 18). Abraham then circumcised Ishmael and all the males of his household according to God's commandment (vv. 23-27).

In Gen. 18, three men appeared to Abraham, two of whom seemed to be angels; the third was the Lord himself. They repeated the promise of a son (vv. 1-15). When they departed in the direction of Sodom, the Lord revealed to Abraham that the outcry against Sodom and Gomorrah had been very great and that he had descended to see if the inhabitants had become more righteous (vv. 16-21). Abraham then interceded with the Lord on behalf of Sodom (vv. 22-23). The following morning Abraham looked toward Sodom and Gomorrah and saw smoke rising from all of the valley (19:27-28). Only Lot was delivered from the destruction, because the Lord remembered Abraham's plea (v. 29).

Abraham then departed from the area of Hebron and journeyed toward the Negeb; he settled between Kadesh and Shur and sojourned in Gerar (20:1). He had Sarah pass for his sister there as he had before. Abimelech, the king of Gerar, had her brought to him (v. 2), but later the Lord appeared to Abimelech and saw to it that Sarah was given back to Abraham. Abimelech also gave to Abraham sheep and oxen, as well as male and female slaves (vv. 3-14). Abraham then interceded with God on behalf of Abimelech, his wife, and his female slaves (vv. 17-18; see B. Vawter, *On Genesis* [Garden City: 1977], pp. 245-46).

When Abraham was one hundred years old, Sarah gave birth to Isaac (21:1-7). Because Ishmael made fun of Isaac on the day that he was weaned, Abraham sent Hagar and Ishmael away (vv. 8-21; cf. Gal. 4:28-31). Gen. 21:22-24 records that Abimelech made a covenant with Abraham regarding a well at Beer-sheba, after which Abraham sojourned for many days in the land of the Philistines (v. 34).

It was in Beer-sheba that the greatest trial of Abraham's already sorely tested faith took place. God commanded him to offer up his son Isaac for sacrifice (22:1-2), and Abraham moved to obey. At the last moment, when Isaac lay bound and Abraham had raised the knife to slaughter him, the angel of the Lord appeared and prevented Abraham from carrying out the sacrifice (vv. 3-12). A ram, whose horns were entangled in the bushes, was then offered in place of Isaac. Abraham appropriately named that place "The Lord will provide" (vv. 13-14; Heb. *yhwh-yir'eh*; KJV "Jehovah-jireh"). The angel of the Lord then renewed the promise that the Lord would bless Abraham and would greatly multiply his descendants.

Afterward Abraham returned to Beer-sheba (vv. 15-19).

Sarah died in Hebron at the age of 127 (Gen. 23:1-2). Since it appears from 17:17 that she was 90 years old when she gave birth to Isaac, he must have been 37 years old when his mother died. Abraham, then, would have been 137 years old. To bury Sarah, Abraham bought the cave of Machpelah from Ephron the Hittite. The detailed record of this transaction (vv. 3-20) nicely illustrates how a purchase was negotiated at that time. The actual price for this grave was four hundred shekels of silver. If a shekel equaled 16.37 gm., then the price was approximately 14.5 lbs. of silver. (Stephen's statement that Abraham purchased a tomb for a sum of silver from the sons of Hamor in Shechem [Acts 7:16] may present a problem, but Stephen was expressing himself very briefly and may have been thinking of Joseph's burial [Josh. 24:32].)

Three years after the death of Sarah, Isaac married Rebekah, the daughter of Bethuel, the son of Nahor (cf. 24:47; 25:20). Abraham had sent his most trustworthy servant back to his own land and family to bring back a wife for Isaac (24:1-9). The Lord guided this servant on his mission in a remarkable way (vv. 10-67). (The city of Nahor [v. 10], located in the vicinity of Haran, appears often in the Mari Letters under the name Naḥur.)

It is possible that the report of Gen. 25:1-6 is meant to be in chronological order and that Abraham married Keturah after the marriage of his son Isaac. However, this would make Abraham at least 140 when he started to beget children by Keturah, and would make the children very young when he sent them away (25:6). It is therefore more likely that he married Keturah while Sarah was yet alive but accorded to her the status of concubine (cf. 1 Chr. 1:32).

Abraham died at the age of 175, and his sons Isaac and Ishmael buried him in the cave of Machpelah with Sarah (vv. 7-10).

IV. Religious Significance

Abram is highly honored among Jews, Christians, and Muslims. To the Jews he is the founder of the Jewish nation, Israel "after the flesh" ("offspring," Ps. 105:6; 2 Chr. 20:7; Isa. 41:8), and God's friend (e.g., Isa. 41:8). The Muslims regard him as founder or reformer of the monotheistic Kaʿba cult, and he is mentioned in greater or less detail in twenty-five suras of the Koran.

In the New Testament Abraham is, next to Moses, the most frequently mentioned Old Testament figure. The Synoptic Gospels list his name three times: Matt. 8:11 par. claims that many from the East will share with Abraham (Gk. *Abraam*) in the kingdom of God; Mark 12:29 par. contains Jesus' utterance that his own Father is the God of the living, of Abraham and the other two patriarchs. For Luke 16:22, *see* ABRAHAM'S BOSOM. John, on the other hand, records only Jesus' remark about Abraham's joy at seeing Christ's "day" (probably the incarnation) and Jesus' claim to be older than this Jewish ancestor (John 8:56-59).

Paul considers Abraham a believer, whose faith is reckoned to him for righteousness (Rom. 4:3; Gal.

3:6, both quotations from Gen. 15:6); he is the father of all believers, Jews and Gentiles alike (Rom. 4:16ff.; cf. Eph. 2:14 for the breaking down of the "dividing wall" between Jew and Gentile). Paul notes that Abraham's circumcision (Gen. 17:22-27) came after his belief (Rom. 4:9-13). In contrast, James looks upon Abraham as one whose faith "was active along with his works" and was "completed by works," specifically by offering his son Isaac on the altar (Jas. 2:21-22, a quotation from Gen. 22:1-14); unlike Paul, James combats "dead faith."

The author of Hebrews summarizes the New Testament perspective on Abraham's significance. The patriarch is the believer par excellence throughout his entire earthly sojourn, because he was looking toward a heavenly home (Heb. 11:8-9). But, as James notes, his faith is shown to be a living faith, tested and triumphant through the required sacrifice of his son Isaac (v. 17; cf. 6:13-14).

Bibliography. J. Jeremias, "Αβρααμ," *TDNT* 1 (1964): 8-9; K. A. Kitchen, *Ancient Orient and Old Testament* (Downers Grove: 1966), pp. 41-56; T. L. Thompson, *The Historicity of the Patriarchal Narratives.* BZAW 133 (1974); J. Van Seters, *Abraham in History and Tradition* (New Haven: 1975); R. de Vaux, *The Early History of Israel* (Philadelphia: 1978), pp. 153-287; D. J. Wiseman, "Abraham Reassessed," pp. 149ff. in A. R. Millard and Wiseman, eds., *Essays on the Patriarchal Narratives* (Leicester: 1980).

ABRAHAM, APOCALYPSE OF. A pseudepigraphal Jewish writing, probably written A.D. 80-100, and extant only in an Old Slavic version (the original language was Hebrew or Aramaic). This work is a midrash on Gen. 15:9-17, relating Abraham's conversion from idolatry to monotheism (chs. 1–8) and his reception of apocalyptic visions concerning the future of his descendants (chs. 9–32). The Christian interpolation in ch. 29 is of special significance, as it reflects a position considerably different from that of the New Testament.

Bibliography. J. H. Charlesworth, *The Pseudepigrapha and Modern Research.* SBL Septuagint and Cognate Studies 7 (Missoula: 1976), pp. 68-69.

ABRAHAM, TESTAMENT OF. A pseudepigraphal Jewish writing, probably from the first century A.D., which is extant in several languages (the original language is not known for certain). In chs. 1–9 Michael the archangel attempts to obtain Abraham's soul, but the patriarch refuses to die unless he can first see the created world. Michael agrees, and chs. 10–14 depict this experience in apocalyptic imagery. Chs. 15–20 relate Abraham's return home and renewed refusal to die, until he is finally deceived by Death posing as an angel.

Bibliography. J. H. Charlesworth, *The Pseudepigrapha and Modern Research.* SBL Septuagint and Cognate Studies (Missoula: 1976), pp. 70-72.

ABRAHAM'S BOSOM [Gk. *kólpos Abraám*]. The place to which the angels carried Lazarus at his death (Luke 16:22; NIV "Abraham's side"). The reference may be to the place next to Abraham at the banquet for the righteous in the world to come (cf. Midrash Exod. 16:4; Matt. 8:11; and the similar phraseology at John 13:23; 21:20; see also JB note h at Luke 16:22), or it may simply refer to a pleasant place of intimate fellowship with him (4 Macc. 13:17; cf. John 1:18, where the image is that of a child reposing on its father's lap). The location of this place is not specified, but a few facts about its relative location can be deduced from the text. It is adjacent to, but not part of, Hades (Luke 16:23, 26); at the same time it is a long way from Hades (cf. "far off," v. 23; "great chasm," v. 26), though within shouting distance (vv. 24-31).

See T. W. Manson, *The Sayings of Jesus* (repr. Grand Rapids: 1979), pp. 296-301.

ABRAM. The original name of Abraham (*see* ABRAHAM *I*).

ABRON [ăb'rən] (Gk. *Abrōna,* Codex Sinaiticus *Chebrōn;* Vulg. *Mambre*). A variant name for the river Khabur, a tributary of the Euphrates (Jdt. 2:24).

ABRONAH [ə brō'nə] (Heb. *'aḇrōnâ* "crossing"[?]). A place where the Israelites encamped during their wilderness wanderings (Num. 33:34-35; KJV "Ebronah"); an oasis, possibly 'Ain Defiyeh, about 12 km. (7.5 mi.) north of Ezion-geber.

ABSALOM [ăb'sə ləm] (Heb. *'abšālôm* "father is [or "of"] peace"). The third son of David and Maacah, the daughter of Talmai, king of Geshur in northern Syria (2 Sam. 3:3 par. 1 Chr. 3:2). He was born at Hebron and grew up to be a very handsome man (2 Sam. 14:25-26). At 1 Kgs. 15:2, 10 he is called Abishalom.

I. Feud and Reconciliation

When Amnon, Absalom's half brother (2 Sam. 3:2), dishonored their beautiful sister Tamar (13:1-14), she took refuge in Absalom's house. When their father heard of this event, he himself was deeply involved with Bathsheba the wife of Uriah (11-12), so he did not justly punish Amnon (13:21). In this way he laid the foundation for future disasters to be visited upon his household, in accordance with Nathan's prophetic word (12:10-12).

Although he managed to conceal his hatred toward Amnon for two full years (2 Sam. 13:22-23), Absalom then had him murdered at a sheepshearing feast and fled to Geshur (vv. 23-28), the home of his maternal grandfather. David must have loved him dearly, for during Absalom's three-year sojourn in Geshur the king mourned for his son "day after day," greatly longing to see him (vv. 37, 39). By means of a clever scheme Joab, Absalom's cousin and his father's commander-in-chief, orchestrated Absalom's return to Jerusalem by having a wise woman of Tekoa speak with the king on behalf of the exiled Absalom. After dwelling in Jerusalem for two more years without being permitted to see the king, Absalom was able at last to persuade Joab to intercede for him and to bring about an official reconciliation between father and son (vv. 28-33).

II. Absalom's Rebellion

Within four years of his reinstatement, Absalom sought to assert his claim of succession and cunningly prepared to revolt against his father's throne, probably during the thirty-second year of David's reign. He was able to win the people's affection (2 Sam. 15:6) on account of the general unrest among the various tribes resulting from the lack of consistent respect for their privileges by the central authority at Jerusalem. Next, he set himself up as king in Hebron with the support of Ahithophel, David's famous counselor and grandfather of Bathsheba (vv. 7-12).

In great haste David fled from Jerusalem (2 Sam. 15:13-16), weeping as he went up the Mount of Olives (v. 30). When the news of Ahithophel's defection reached him, he immediately took measures becoming of a wise king. By sending his faithful Hushai back to Jerusalem to enter into Absalom's service (instead of letting his able counselor accompany him in his flight), David hoped to defeat the counsel of his former advisor (vv. 30-37).

Meanwhile his usurper son had entered the capital with Ahithophel (2 Sam. 15:37; 16:15). He accepted Ahithophel's first advice, to defile the concubines his father had left behind to watch over the king's house (16:21-22); thus any future reconciliation between his father and himself would be impossible. This Absalom did publicly, in a tent pitched on the roof of the palace. (Although it was customary among ancient Near Eastern kingdoms for a ruler to inherit the harem of his predecessor, in terms of Israelite ideology Absalom's action was very loathsome and must be viewed as a fulfillment of Nathan's prophecy to David [12:11-12].) Due to Hushai's influence, however, Absalom did not follow Ahithophel's second counsel (17:1-14). Though he first intended to comply with Ahithophel's plan to pursue and defeat David that very night, Absalom also summoned Hushai for advice. Hushai urged him to take the time to gather all of Israel (from Dan to Beer-sheba) and to lead his force personally to battle (v. 11). This met with Absalom's approval, for the Lord had ordained that Ahithophel's good counsel would be defeated; Absalom's downfall was assured from the very start (v. 14).

III. Death and Burial

Warned by Hushai about Absalom's plans to pursue him in full force, David crossed the Jordan and camped at Mahanaim (17:21, 24). Ahithophel, knowing that his cause was lost, committed suicide (v. 23). In the battle between father and son a short while later, Absalom was defeated in the forest of Ephraim (18:6-8), where David's servants found him alive, "hanging between heaven and earth." His long hair was caught in an oak but his mount had kept on going (v. 9). When Joab was informed of Absalom's condition, he brazenly disregarded David's command just before the battle to "deal gently for my sake with the young man Absalom" (v. 5), and with his own hand thrust three darts into Absalom's heart. His armorbearers completed Absalom's execution (vv. 14-15). Absalom's body was then thrown into a pit over which a mound of stones was raised (v. 17).

When at last David learned about his son's death, he wept bitterly and lamented, "O my son, Absalom, my son, my son Absalom! Would I had died instead of you, O Absalom, my son, my son!" (v. 33). Fearing that the king's behavior would cast a shadow over the victory they had gained, Joab rebuked David and made him speak kindly to his loyal supporters (19:1-8).

IV. Absalom's Monument

During his lifetime Absalom had set up a stone pillar in the King's Valley near Jerusalem (18:18) because he had no sons to perpetuate his name and memory in Israel. (Apparently his three sons mentioned at 14:27 had died before him; his daughter Tamar was to become the mother-in-law of King Abijah.) He may have placed this "monument" on the east slope of the Kidron valley, where a particular Egyptian-Hellenistic style monument dating to the time of the Hasmoneans or Herodians has been called traditionally the "Pillar of Absalom."

Bibliography. C. Conroy, *Absalom, Absalom!*. Analecta biblica 81 (Rome: 1978).

ABSTINENCE. See ASCETICISM.

ABYSS (Gk. *ábyssos*). While the precise term occurs only in the New Testament, the LXX so translates its Old Testament equivalent, Heb. *tᵉhôm* "the deep," "the primeval ocean." According to the ancient Semitic cosmogony, this was a vast body of water below the earth (cf. Exod. 20:4) from which arose springs, brooks, and rivers ("great deep," Gen. 7:11; Isa. 51:10; "recesses of the deep," Job 38:16). Job 41:23 indicates that it harbors a sea monster, the Leviathan.

At Luke 8:31 the abyss is the place of imprisonment of demons, while at Rom. 10:7 it is a synonym of Sheol or the realm of the dead (cf. the contrast with "heaven" at v. 6). Termed "bottomless pit" at Rev. 9:1-2, Gk. *tó phréar tēs abýssos*), 11; 11:7; 20:1, 3 (so RSV, KJV; JB "Abyss," NIV "Abyss," "shaft of the Abyss" [at 9:1, 2]), it is the residence of demons during the current age, before the age to come when they are to be thrown into the lake of fire (19:20; 20:10) — their permanent dwelling place.

ACACIA [ə kā′shə] (Heb. *šiṭṭâ*). A tree or shrub widely distributed in tropical and subtropical regions, especially in Africa, Arabia, and Australia. In southern Palestine and surrounding areas the name designates the native *Acacia seyal* Delile and *Acacia tortilis* Hayne, while in Egypt it indicates *Acacia nilotica* L. (It is not to be confused with the native North American *Robina Pseud-acacia.*) Its wood, heavier and harder than oak, durable and not easily damaged by insects, is an excellent material for cabinetmaking or woodworking.

In the Old Testament it occurs nearly exclusively in the context of the building of the tabernacle, the ark, the altar, and related sacred objects (Exod. 25:5–27:7; 30; 35:7–38:6; Deut. 10:3; KJV "shittim wood"). At Isa. 41:19 it is one of several trees growing in an arid desert.

ACCAD. See AKKAD.

ACCO [ăk'ō] (Heb. *'akkô*). A major port on the Mediterranean north of Mt. Carmel, strategically located on the sea route through the coastal plain known as the plain of Acco. Its natural bay was sheltered by mountains on the east and south (Mt. Carmel), and a branch of the Belus river was nearby. The site is north of modern Haifa.

According to archaeological excavations, the city was apparently founded during the Middle Bronze II period. As a Canaanite city it was a flourishing commercial center. The city fell to the Egyptian pharaoh Seti I (*ca.* 1320 B.C.) and again to the Sea Peoples (twelfth-eleventh centuries), but recovered sufficiently so the Israelite tribe of Asher was unable to "drive out the inhabitants of Acco" and surrounding cities (Judg. 1:31; KJV "Accho"; cf. Josh. 19:29). Later the city fell into the hands of the Assyrian kings, including Sennacherib (701 B.C.) and Assurbanipal (640).

After having lain in ruins for some time, the city was resettled by Athenian colonists in the fourth century B.C. It was subsequently expanded, with a new harbor, by Ptolemy II, who renamed it Ptolemais. Here the Jews fought during the Maccabean wars, and within its walls Jonathan was imprisoned after Trypho had tricked him into sending home a large part of his army (1 Macc. 12:39-49).

In 65 B.C. the city became part of the Roman Empire, and during the reign of Claudius it assumed the status of a Roman colony (coins dating from the imperial period bear the inscription *COL. PTOL* ["Colonia Ptolemais"]). On his return trip from his third missionary journey, the apostle Paul disembarked at this important city in order to visit its church (Acts 21:7).

Acco's subsequent history has been very checkered. During the Crusades it was the last stronghold of the Crusaders until it fell to Saladin in A.D. 1187. Named St. Jean d'Acre by the Crusaders, it still retains the name Acre today. Conquered numerous times in modern history, it has belonged to the state of Israel since 1948. The ancient part of the city (inland a ways and upon a hill) is inhabited almost exclusively by Arabs, while the Jews dwell in the harbor section developed during the Seleucid rule. Neighboring Haifa surpasses it in importance today.

ACCOUNTABILITY.† The circumstances of one's own life which each person (Jew and Gentile alike; 1 Pet. 4:5) will relate before God at the Judgment Day (Rom. 14:12), even acknowledging a "careless" word spoken (Matt. 12:36). In the parable of the talents, a returning landowner takes inventory of the proceeds from the property he has entrusted to his servants. By giving to those who increased their shares while taking from the one who did not, the landowner holds each of his servants accountable for the talents granted to them (Matt. 25:14-30). The point of the parable is that each person is morally responsible for using whatever gifts the Creator bestows upon him.

Luke's account of the parable of the unjust steward is vexing. At the end of the parable the rich man praises his dishonest servant for his "shrewdness" in handling the outstanding account (Gk. *lógos*; Luke 16:8). According to one interpretation (see I. H. Marshall, *Comm. on Luke.* NIGTC [1978], pp. 614-17, for an extensive discussion of various views), the person is complimented for reducing the debt of the rich man's debtors by removing either the interest on it or his own commission. This parable, then, stresses proper use of wealth.

In the parable of the settling of the accounts (Gk. *synárai lógon* "take the account together"), Jesus teaches forgiveness (Matt. 18:23; cf. vv. 21-22).

ACCUSER (Heb. *šāpaṭ*). While usually an accuser is an adversary in a law court (e.g., Job 9:15; KJV, NIV, JB "judge"), in two New Testament passages the term assumes a more special sense. At John 5:45 the Lord states that it is Moses (rather than himself) who accuses (Gk. *katēgoréō*) the Jews before the Father. For if they had listened to Moses' message, they would have been accused by the law and been convicted of sin. In the battle between Michael and the dragon or Satan, John records (Rev. 12:10) that the latter is the accuser (Gk. *katḗgōr*; JB "persecutor") who "day and night" accuses the children of God unsuccessfully before God the Father.

See SATAN; WITNESS.

Bibliography. J. I. Packer, "Accuse(r)," *DNTT* 1:82-84.

ACHAEMENIANS [ä kĭ mĕn ē'ənz] (from Pers. *Hakhāmanish* "friendly in nature"). Another name for the royal house of Persia, from Cyrus II (559-530 B.C.) onward. It was Cyrus who permitted the Jewish exiles to take back to Jerusalem the "vessels of the house of the Lord" (Ezra 1:7). The vast and varied resources of the empire made Achaemenian (or Achaemenid) art possible.

ACHAIA [ə kā'yə] (Gk. *Achaia*). Originally designating only a part of the Peloponnesus, later the name came to designate the entire southern half of Greece. During Greece's independent history, the so-called Achaean League, to which Athens and Corinth belonged, became a significant political force, while afterward (e.g., 251 B.C.) it retained its influence until the Romans destroyed the city of Corinth in 146 B.C. During Roman occupation it became a Roman province south of Macedonia, governed by a proconsul.

On his second and third missionary journeys Paul visited Achaia (cf. Acts 19:21) while Gallio was proconsul of the province (18:12). According to 18:27, Apollos intended to cross over to that region. Stephanas was one of the first converts of the area (1 Cor. 16:15; at Rom. 16:5 KJV "Achaia" should be read "Asia" as in RSV, JB), which (together with Macedonia) sent financial aid to the impoverished church at Jerusalem (Rom. 15:26; 2 Cor. 9:2). The church at Thessalonica, in Macedonia, was held up as an example for the churches of Achaia (1 Thess. 1:7-8).

ACHAICUS [ə kā'ə kəs] (Gk. *Achaikos* "a person from Achaia"). A Christian man from Corinth whom the Corinthian church sent to Paul in Ephesus (1 Cor. 16:17).

ACHAN [ā'kăn] (Heb. *'āḵān*). The son of Carmi of the tribe of Judah (Josh. 7:1), who, after the destruction of Jericho, stole some of the plunder that God had expressly said belonged to him (6:17-19). Consequently, God's anger was aroused, and the Israelites suffered defeat when they attacked the small village of Ai (7:2-5).

When Joshua and the elders of Israel repented before the Lord, God told them that only a proper punishment of the guilty would give them a victory over their enemies (7:6-15). Joshua then drew lots (inferred from Heb. *lākaḏ* "seize, take," i.e., by lot, vv. 15, 18) and Achan was appointed (v. 18). Even though he confessed his sin (vv. 20-21) his possessions were carried away and he and his household were stoned to death in the Valley of Achor (or "trouble"; cf. v. 25; note the alternate form of his name, Achar [meaning "troubler"] at 1 Chr. 2:7).

See ACHOR.

ACHBOR [ăk'bôr] (Heb. *ʿaḵbôr* "mouse").
1. Father of Baal-hanan king of Edom (Gen. 36:38-39 par. 1 Chr. 1:49).
2. The son of Micaiah, he was a court official of King Josiah (2 Kgs. 22:12, 14). At 2 Chr. 34:20 he is called Abdon the son of Micah (*see* ABDON 4). According to Jer. 26:22; 36:12 he may have been the father of Elnathan.

ACHIM [ă'kĭm] (Gk. *Achim*). A postexilic ancestor of Jesus (Matt. 1:14).

ACHIOR [ā'kĭ ôr] (Gk. *Achiōr* possibly from Heb. *ʾaḥîʾôr* "brother of light"). An Ammonite commander under Holofernes, the Assyrian general, who attempted to dissuade his master from attacking the Israelites (Jdt. 5:5ff.). Holofernes' own senior officers disregarded Achior's "religious interpretation of history" (JB note d *in loc.*) and instead threatened him with death (5:22-23). Judith, however, saved his life by decapitating Holofernes. Upon seeing the general's head Achior fainted, but afterward "recognising the mighty works of the God of Israel, believed ardently in him and, accepting circumcision, was incorporated in the House of Israel forever" (14:10); he was one of the few Ammonites to be circumcised (note the command at Deut. 23:3).

ACHISH [ā'kĭsh] (Heb. *ʾāḵîš*, possibly from Hur. *akk sharur* "the king gives"). The son of Maoch and king of the Philistine city of Gath (1 Sam. 21:10).

Twice David sought shelter and protection in Achish's kingdom. After he had fled to Nob, David dwelled in Gath; he pretended to be insane, but rather than assuring protection, his bizarre behavior forced his speedy dismissal from Achish's domain (vv. 13-15). At a later time when pursued by Saul, David returned to Achish, who gave him Ziklag as a dwelling place (27:6) and made him his personal bodyguard (28:2). But when the Philistines were preparing for another battle with Saul, they forced Achish to send David back to Ziklag (29:2-6); perhaps they were not as convinced as Achish of David's loyalty.

If the Achish mentioned at 1 Kgs. 2:39 is the same person (so KD *in loc.*), he must have been a young ruler when David crossed his path. Interestingly, in this passage Achish is said to be the son of Maacah (*see* MAACAH [PERSON] 3).

In the superscription to Ps. 34 Achish is called Abimelech (*see* ABIMELECH 4).

ACHMETHA (Ezra 6:2, KJV). *See* ECBATANA.

ACHOR [ā'kôr] (Heb. *ʿāḵôr* "trouble"). A valley near Jericho where Achan and his family were stoned to death (Josh. 7:24-26). Since the discovery of the Dead Sea Scrolls it has been identified with el-Buqeiʿah, a plain ranging about 6 km. (4 mi.) north-south on the Wâdî Qumran.

In his eschatological prophecies Isaiah refers to the messianic age in which even the arid region of Achor will become "a place for herds to lie" (Isa. 65:10). Beforehand the eighth-century B.C. prophet Hosea had used it as a figure of hope for unfaithful Israel (Hos. 2:15).

ACHSAH [ăk'sə] (Heb. *ʿaḵsâ* "ankle ornament"). Daughter of Caleb (1 Chr. 2:49; KJV "Achsa"), who promised her in marriage to whoever would capture Kiriath-sepher (Debir); Othniel, the son of Caleb's younger brother Kenaz, earned that honor (Josh. 15:16-17 par. Judg. 1:12-14). At Achsah's request, Caleb gave her in addition springs of water in the Negeb (Josh. 15:19 par. Judg. 1:15).

ACHSHAPH [ăk'shăf] (Heb. *ʾaḵšāp̄*, possibly "place of magic"). A city assigned to Asher (Josh. 19:25) after its king — a member of the confederacy initiated by Jabin king of Hazor (11:1) — was killed. It is mentioned in the Egyptian Execration Texts (nineteenth-eighteenth centuries B.C.), the list of towns conquered by Thutmose III (fifteenth century), and the Papyrus Anastasi (thirteenth century). The site is not certain, but many identify it with Tell Kîsân, located in the plain of Acco about 10 km. (6 mi.) southeast of Acco (modern Acre); other possible sites are Tell Berweh and Tell Harbaj.

ACHZIB [ăk'zĭb] (Heb. *ʾaḵzîḇ* "deceit").
1. A city in western Judah between Keilah and Mareshah (Josh. 15:44; cf. Mic. 1:14 where a pun is intended: "the houses of Achzib shall be a deceitful thing [Heb. *ʾaḵzāḇ*]"), identical with Chezib mentioned at Gen. 38:5. Eusebius (*Onom.* 172) points to a hill of ruins near Adullam as the location of ancient Achzib; it is perhaps to be identified with Tell el-Beida, 5 km. (3 mi.) west of Adullam.
2. A town on the Mediterranean coast of Galilee, located within the territory of Asher (albeit not conquered by the Asherites, Josh. 19:29; Judg. 1:31) near the Phoenician border. Excavations at modern ez-Zib, 14 km. (9 mi.) north of Acco, indicate that its Middle Bronze II (nineteenth century B.C.) founders constructed a ditch connecting the Chezib river to the north and a creek to the south, thus making the site a virtual island. The city flourished from the eleventh to sixth centuries, spreading east to the mainland. Among the most important finds at the site are two cemeteries containing numerous rock-cut family tombs dating to the tenth-eighth centuries; they were abandoned when the city's elite fled before the invading Assyrians under Sennacherib, who conquered Achzib in 701.

ACRE (Heb. ṣemeḏ "yoke," i.e., "pair of [oxen]"). A unit of measurement designating the amount of land which a team of oxen can plow in one day, which varied with agricultural methods (1 Sam. 14:14; Isa. 5:10).

ACROSTIC (from Gk. ákros "beginning" and stíchos "row").† A poetic device in which the initial letters of each line or verse (or group of lines) follow a particular sequence, either alphabetical order or that of a particular word or phrase.

Biblical acrostics are frequently found in Wisdom Literature, including wisdom Psalms. In Pss. 111 and 112 each half line begins with a successive Hebrew letter, and in Pss. 25; 34; 145; Prov. 31:10-31 the pattern occurs with each line. Of the five poems which form the book of Lamentations, four are acrostics; chs. 1–2 begin each three-line stanza with the successive letter of the alphabet; in ch. 3 each line (of the three-line stanzas) begins with the appropriate letter; and ch. 4 contains two-line stanzas. Each line in Ps. 119's twenty-two eight-line stanzas begins with the letter assigned (in successive order through the alphabet) to its stanza. The acrostic arrangement of Pss. 9–10 (aleph to lamed, 9:1-19; lamed to tau, 10:1-17) has led many commentators to consider the two a single poem (so LXX). In Ps. 4 the initial letters of the lines (including the superscription or heading) form, in reverse order, Heb. bnr zrwbbl "unto a lamp for Zerubbabel."

The acrostic form, attested also in cuneiform literature, demonstrates the literary skill of the author. While it may at times have been used merely as a stylistic nicety for both reader and listener, it more often served as a mnemonic device for pedagogic purposes in wisdom circles or to express the totality of the ideas addressed in the composition.

ACTS, APOCRYPHAL. See APOCRYPHA, NEW TESTAMENT.

ACTS OF THE APOSTLES. The fifth book of the New Testament.

I. Title

The name "Acts of the Apostles" probably was not the book's original title but was attributed to it by the early Church (as early as the end of the second century A.D.). This is an unfortunate choice, however, for the book does not deal with the activities of all the apostles nor with all activities of the central figures, the apostles Peter and Paul. While it does mention John (3:1-11; 4:13, 19; 8:14), it only lists the other apostles (1:13) or refers to them as a group (e.g., 1:2, 26; 2:14, 37). The book speaks at greater length of Stephen (chs. 6–7), Philip (ch. 8), and Barnabas (4:36-37; 11:22-26; 13–15), none of whom belonged to the original twelve apostles. More importantly, the name does not express the true content and purpose of this New Testament work. (See II below.)

II. Theological Perspective

It is true that Luke describes the words and deeds of the Lord's apostles and servants, but they appear only as his messengers and instruments, agents through whom, and in whom, Christ carried on his work of redemption. In fact, this theological purpose not only constitutes the background of the apostles' ministries, but also their constant motivation and direction.

At the time of his ascension the risen Savior commissioned his apostles to serve as his witnesses (1:8) and was instrumental in the choice of Matthias (Judas' replacement) as the twelfth apostle (1:24-26). At Pentecost he poured out the Holy Spirit from heaven (2:33); he then healed the paralytic (3:6, 12, 16), caused the place where the disciples were praying to shake (4:31), enacted immediate judgment upon Ananias and Sapphira because of their deceit (5:5, 10), and used his angel to free the apostles from prison (5:19-21). In response to the prayer of Peter and John he granted the Holy Spirit to the Samaritans (8:15-17) and sent one of his angels to direct Philip toward the Ethiopian eunuch (8:26). He appeared personally to Saul in order to call him as his apostle (9:3-4; cf. 22:17-21), cured Aeneas (9:34), sent an angel instructing Cornelius to send messengers to Peter (10:3-6), while simultaneously informing Peter in a vision to join them (10:9-20) and afterward pouring out the Holy Spirit on Cornelius' household (10:44-45; cf. 11:15-17). Christ freed Peter from prison (12:7-9), directed the church at Antioch through the Holy Spirit's commissioning of Barnabas and Saul as missionaries (13:2), punished Elymas for his opposition to their ministry on Cyprus (13:11), and healed a cripple at Lystra (14:8-18). Through his Spirit the Lord prevented Paul, Silas, and Timothy from preaching the Word in the Roman provinces of Asia and Bithynia (16:6-7), directing them instead to Troas where by means of a vision he called them to Macedonia (16:8-10). In Philippi he expelled the spirit of divination from the slave girl (16:16-18), sent an earthquake which freed Paul and Silas from prison, and occasioned the conversion of the jailer and his entire family (16:25-32); in Corinth he encouraged Paul by means of a vision (18:9-10); in Troas he gave him the power to raise up Eutychus (20:9-10); and through the Holy Spirit informed him in Ephesus of his coming imprisonment (20:23; cf. 21:10-11). When Paul was a prisoner at Jerusalem, the Lord came to him by night, encouraging him another time, and instructing him about his future witness for his Master at Rome (23:11). Finally, he sent an angel to the apostle when the ship carrying Paul to Rome was involved in a storm (27:23).

Luke states at 1:1 that in his first book (his gospel) he "dealt with all that Jesus began to do and teach, until the day he was taken up." Thus, he is not implying that he will now turn away from the work of Jesus in order to narrate that of his apostles. Rather, he will henceforth relate the Lord's continued acts performed from heaven (7:56) through his apostles and servants on earth.

More specifically, the apostles' role appears in Christ's commission to them at 1:8, but they serve as his witnesses — a recurring theme (1:22; 2:32; 3:15; 4:33; 5:32; 10:39, 41; 13:31), also applicable to the apostle Paul (9:15; 22:15; 23:11; 26:16). Though their witness was one of word and deed, of preaching and performing miracles, their speeches (which follow a standard format with only small divergences, in accordance with the main line of Christian proclamation) occupy a rather large portion of their ministry (e.g., 1:15-22; 2:14-41; 3:12-26; 4:8-12; 7:2-53; 10:34-43). Not only possessing a great deal of similarity, but sometimes even relating events already reported earlier (compare chs. 10 and 11; 22 and 26 with 9), the speeches reveal the nature of the apostles' witness to Jesus and also the manner of its presentation and proclamation in Jerusalem, Judea and Samaria, Syria, Asia Minor, Greece, and finally Rome, the center of the Roman Empire (cf. 1:8); at Rome Paul addresses the Jews living there, testifying about Jesus and proclaiming salvation for all mankind. Acts concludes with the apostle's preaching about the Lord Jesus Christ "quite openly and unhindered" (28:31).

Similarly, the book of Acts describes the effect of this apostolic witness on the conversion of many Gentiles to the Christian faith and on the establishment of the churches, yet Luke does not place the main emphasis here. Though in some passages he could have presented more information about the organization and development of some churches, his accounts are sometimes strikingly brief, and many locations and situations are omitted. Luke's main intent is to record the apostles' testimony concerning the Lord Jesus Christ, a testimony presented in proclamation, sealed by suffering, and confirmed by the Lord himself in the signs and wonders which he performed through them (4:29-32).

On the basis of this clearly implied intention of the book of Acts, one should not hastily conclude that since he does not include Paul's death Luke must have written his second work immediately after the apostle's imprisonment at Rome. Luke was not primarily concerned to give a more or less complete description of the life of this person. Nor should one think that because the book says almost nothing about the apostles other than Peter and Paul, Luke must have been planning to write a third book about their work (so W. R. Ramsay; T. Zahn).

III. Contents

Luke divides the contents of Acts in accordance with the commission given by the Lord to his apostles at 1:8: chs. 2–7 deal with their witness at Jerusalem; 8–12 with their ministry in Judea, Samaria, and Syria; and 13–28 with their work in Asia Minor, Greece, and finally at Rome. The last section can again be subdivided according to the Lord's word to Ananias concerning the apostle Saul (or Paul), the main figure of the preceding section: "he is a chosen instrument of mine to carry my name before the Gentiles and kings and the sons of Israel" (9:15). Thus, in chs. 13–20 Paul is presented as the Lord's witness before the Gentiles, in 22–26 he is portrayed as appearing before rulers, while in the final chapter his testimony before the Jews at Rome is recorded. These do not constitute sharp divisions between the various chapters, but only indications of their general contents.

Acts can also be divided on the basis of people, with chs. 1–12 dealing primarily with Peter's work and 13–28 with Paul's missionary endeavors. In fact, there are remarkable correspondences between the accounts of their respective ministries. The first part presents a number of speeches made by Peter (chs. 2–4; 10–11), the second those of Paul (chs. 13, 17, 20, 22, 26, 28). Each of the two apostles heals a man born lame (3:6-7; 14:8-10). Peter is miraculously freed from prison, as is Paul. The shadow of Peter has healing power (5:15), while handkerchiefs or aprons that had been in contact with Paul's body are also able to cure the sick (19:12). Each of them raises a person from the dead (9:36-40; 20:9-12) and each has to deal with a magician opposing his mission (8:18-24; 13:6-11); both of them are instrumental in imparting the Holy Spirit through the laying on of hands (8:17; 19:6). Some scholars have regarded these passages as a deliberate parallelism which Luke incorporated into his work, but if this were indeed the case, the correspondences would be far greater. Peter is delivered from prison twice (5:19-20; 12:7-11), yet Paul only once (16:25-35); no act of healing by Paul is recorded paralleling Peter's curing of Aeneas (9:34); and unlike Peter, Paul is stoned (14:19) and his name is used in exorcism (19:13-20). Thus, although there is no strict parallelism, the correspondence between the work of the two apostles is to be viewed in the light of the biblical rule that the evidence of two witnesses is to be considered trustworthy (Deut. 19:15; Matt. 18:16).

Beginning Acts with his account of the establishment of the church at Jerusalem (1–2), Luke next describes the rise of the conflict between the apostles and the Jewish authorities (3–4), particularly apparent in the martyrdom of Stephen (6:8–7:60). At the same time, he describes the Church — its constant expansion, internal dangers threatening its well-being, and the development of the special offices. He continues sketching the Church's spread — as a result of the persecution of the believers at Jerusalem — throughout Judea (8:1) and the entire region inhabited by the Jews (8:40; 9:31-43), including Damascus (9:2). Even Samaritans are brought within its fold (8:4-25), as are the Gentiles — first individually, as in the case of the Ethiopian eunuch (8:36-39) and Cornelius and his family (10:1–11:18), later in such great numbers that they begin to form a significant part of the Church (11:19-26). After stating the problem created by Herod Agrippa I for the faithful at Jerusalem and elsewhere in Palestine (12:1-23), as well as the aid offered by the church of Antioch during the famine (11:27-30), at 13:1–21:9 Luke continues his account of the spread of the gospel throughout the Gentile world due to the work of Barnabas and Paul and their helpers. Paul's imprisonments and testimony at Jerusalem (21:33–23:30), Caesarea (23:31–26:32), and Rome (28:16-31) are the conclusion.

IV. Author

Although the name of the author does not appear in Acts, he is clearly the same as the author of the third gospel (1:1; cf. Luke 1:1-4). In his account of Paul's journey from Troas to Philippi (16:10-17) and afterward of his voyages to Jerusalem (20:5–21:18) and to Rome (27:1–28:16), the author repeatedly uses the pronoun "we" (which also appears at 11:28 in a few manuscripts). Thus, the writer indicates that he was a traveling companion of the apostle, a direct witness to Paul's words and works.

Some scholars contend that the "we passages" are taken from the travel records of someone else, which the author partially incorporated into his own writing;

this, however, is unlikely because their language and style fully conform to other passages of Acts and those in the gospel of Luke. Therefore, it is probable that the person using the pronoun "we" is the author of all of Acts. Since both Silas (15:40; 16:19) and Timothy (16:1-3; cf. 20:4-5) had been with the apostle Paul earlier, they can hardly be regarded as the author, for then the pronoun "we" should have appeared sooner in the narrative. The tradition, which began as early as the latter part of the second century, unanimously ascribes the authorship of both Acts and the third gospel to Luke; Luke is not elsewhere described as a person of such importance that a book would be falsely attributed to him in order to gain acceptance. It appears from Paul's letters, moreover, that Luke was with the apostle during both his first (Col. 4:14; Phlm. 24) and second imprisonment (2 Tim. 4:11), as one of Paul's co-workers and "beloved physician" (Col. 4:14).

V. Date

According to his own testimony, Luke wrote Acts after he wrote the gospel bearing his name (1:1); he gives no more precise date. Ch. 28 could have been written as early as A.D. 60/61. A formal comparison of Luke's allusion to Dan. 9:27 with that of Matthew and Mark (Luke 21:20; Matt. 24:18; Mark 14:13) has led some to conclude that his books were written after the fall of Jerusalem. That Luke was dependent on Josephus' *Antiquities* (*ca.* A.D. 93) cannot be conclusively demonstrated, however; the issue here mainly concerns a certain Theudas whose insurrection took place early during the fourth decade according to Acts 5:26, but between 40 and 50 according to Josephus. There is no clear picture of this matter, but there are no compelling grounds either for dating the book after Josephus' work. Acts is possibly cited in a letter of the church of Rome to the church at Corinth (*ca.* 95), and it appears a few years later in other writings of the early Church.

VI. Relation to Pauline Letters

A comparison of Acts with Paul's letters has prompted some to claim that the differences are so great that Acts must be judged inaccurate and could not have been written by a traveling companion and co-worker of the apostle. (Others have raised the unanswerable question whether Luke used some of Paul's letters and, if so, which ones.) There are, to be sure, some undeniable differences where both report the same event. The one occasionally mentions something the other omits, and Luke will at times briefly summarize happenings of some duration (cf. the events after Paul's conversion in Acts 9:10-31; Gal. 2). But differences in reporting do not imply contradictions, as the following examples may show.

(1) There is no disagreement between Paul's refusal to allow Titus to be circumcised in Jerusalem (Gal. 2:3) and Luke's statement (Acts 16:3) that the apostle himself performed circumcision upon Timothy, for the situation was different in either case. Titus was fully a Gentile by descent, and in his case the issue was the necessity of circumcision for salvation. Timothy, by contrast, was a Jew by his maternal line and thus could legitimately receive circumcision

on the basis of nationality. For that reason, Paul cannot be accused of inconsistency, and the example which he presents in Acts 16:3 is not necessarily amiss.

(2) There is no conflict between Paul's words at 1 Cor. 14:5, 27-28 concerning the necessity of an interpreter when someone is speaking in tongues and the absence of such an interpreter at Pentecost (Acts 2:1-13). The importance of Paul's instructions in 1 Corinthians is apparent from a comparison of 1 Cor. 14:23 and Acts 2:13. More basically, in the outpouring of the Holy Spirit described at Acts 2, the listeners were given the ability to understand the words of the apostles, each in his own language (vv. 6-12); by contrast, the "miracle of tongues" at 1 Cor. 14 had lost some of its original power and is more limited in scope, so that a direct understanding of the words spoken was not given to the listeners.

(3) There are many differences between Paul's statements concerning the events after his conversion and the account given by Luke. At Gal. 1:12-16 the apostle does not mention Ananias, whereas Acts 9:10-19 (cf. 22:12-16) reports that the latter was sent to him by the Lord. Paul's narrow escape from the governor of King Aretas (2 Cor. 11:32-33) and his sojourn in Arabia (Gal. 1:17) are passed over by Luke (Acts 9:22-26), who instead mentions Paul's preaching and threatened persecution at Jerusalem (Acts 9:28-30; cf. Gal. 1:18-21). Luke indicates that Paul was introduced to the other apostles by Barnabas and thereafter departed to Tarsus (9:27, 30), whereas Paul himself writes that at that time he "saw none of the other apostles except James" and then traveled to the regions of Syria and Cilicia (Gal. 1:18-19, 21). In each of these cases, however, the two accounts serve to supplement each other and cannot be considered mutually exclusive. A clear agreement between them appears in Luke's description of the apostle's purification (Acts 21:26) and Paul's own statement concerning his rule of conduct (1 Cor. 9:19-22).

(4) A notoriously vexing issue is the relation between the event described at Acts 15 and Gal. 2:1-10. A long tradition of scholars claims that Luke and Paul refer to the same event — the Apostolic Council. To them the arguments against such an identification are in principle answerable, because both authors describe the event from their own distinct point of view (*see* APOSTOLIC COUNCIL).

VII. Text

Two different texts of Acts (the "Neutral" or Alexandrian text and the earlier "Western" text) have been handed down, with some Western manuscripts presenting a much more extensive account than most versions. Among the readings contained in these manuscripts are the following: 11:28, "There was much rejoicing. And as we were gathered together, one of them named Agabus made known through the Holy Spirit that"; 12:10, "and having gone out, they descended the seven steps and went"; 19:9, in the school of a "certain Tyrannus from the fifth until the tenth hour." Readings or interpolations such as these bear a mark of historical accuracy and may well be regarded as authentic. Others, however, obviously could not have belonged to the original text; e.g., 5:38, "and you let them go, not defiling your hands''; 5:39, "neither you, nor kings, nor tyrants.''

In explaining this twofold text tradition, some have suggested that Luke first wrote his more extensive work in the form of a rough draft which he later condensed into a more finished edition and sent to Theophilus. It would then be the latter text which was distributed in the greatest number of manuscripts, finding its way into earlier standard editions of the Greek New Testament (e.g., Westcott-Hort) and the translations based upon them. Some scholars, however, contend that this view is contradicted by the fact that these textual additions vary in character, with many of them clearly betraying that they are later alterations. For example, the variant reading in Acts 15:20, 29 concerning the decision reached at the Apostolic Council at Jerusalem omits the words "and from what is strangled" (cf. RSV mg.) and adds the golden rule in its negative form, i.e., that people must not treat others the way they would not wish to be treated by them. Many would regard this variant reading as authentic, thus understanding the Jerusalem decision to be an ethical rule of conduct rather than a regulation concerning what could be eaten. Those who question this reading contend that (1) it would not have been necessary once again to issue such an explicit ethical rule (see also 21:25); (2) such a decision would have had little relevance to the controversy to be settled, the Gentile believers' obligation to circumcision and Jewish ceremonial law (cf. 11:2-3; Gal. 2:11-14); and (3) those in the early Church who chose, or only had access to, this alternate reading understood the Jerusalem decision as applying to food, and not as setting forth an ethical rule of conduct.

VIII. Value

As an apologist Luke seeks to impress on Theophilus that Christians are not members of another seditious band threatening the legal and moral foundation of the Roman Empire. To that end he records the innocence of Peter and John before the Sanhedrin (Acts 4:23; 5:40), and Paul's clean record before Roman officials — at Philippi where the magistrates apologized for unjustly imprisoning him (16:39), at Corinth where Gallio considered the Jewish charge irrelevant to Roman law (18:14-16), and at Jerusalem where Felix and Festus would have released Paul had he not appealed to Caesar (26:32).

Acts is also valuable in that it is the bridge between the gospels (especially Luke) and most of Paul's letters. The Gospels portray Christ's ministry of reconciliation on earth, while the Epistles address various situations of the churches founded after Christ's resurrection and the outpouring of the Spirit, churches in which Paul labored or wished to labor. Acts presents some interesting details about the initial years of those individual churches.

For the identity of Theophilus, *see* LUKE, GOSPEL OF; THEOPHILUS.

Bibliography. F. F. Bruce, *The Book of Acts.* NICNT (1954); H. J. Cadbury, *The Book of Acts in History* (London: 1955); W. W. Gasque, *A History of the Criticism of the Acts of the Apostles* (Grand Rapids: 1975); E. Haenchen, *The Acts of the Apostles: A Commentary* (Philadelphia: 1971); L. E. Keck and J.

L. Martyn, eds., *Studies in Luke-Acts* (Nashville: 1966); I. H. Marshall, *Luke: Historian and Theologian* (Grand Rapids: 1971); C. H. Talbert, ed., *Perspectives on Luke-Acts* (Danville, Va.: 1978).

ADADAH [ăd'ə dəh] (Heb. *'aḏ'āḏâ*). A city in southern Judah (Josh. 15:22). The name should perhaps be read Ararah (Heb. *'ar'ārâ*) and be identified with Aroer (1 Sam. 30:28), about 19 km. (12 mi.) southeast of Beer-sheba.

ADAD-NIRARI [ā'dăd nĭ rä'rē].†
1. King Adad-nirari I (1307-1275 B.C.) extended Assyrian influence by defeating the Kassite Nasimaruttash and conquering various northern regions; he maintained suzerainty over Mitanni and Hanigalbat.
2. Adad-nirari II (911-891) expanded the economic and military strength of the Assyrian Empire, exerting his influence into Babylonian territory, annexing the strategic city of Arrapḫa, and establishing suzerainty over the Aramean tribes to the west as well as the Temanites and the region along the Habur river to the north. His treaty with the Babylonian king forms a useful base for determining the chronology of this period.
3. Adad-nirari III (810-783) joined his vassals at Hamath in smashing the alliance of Damascus and various northern Syrian tribes. His suzerainty over the Hittites and the peoples of Syria-Palestine was shortlived, and the dynasty's influence was vastly diminished by the growing Urartian power. The usurper Tiglath-pileser III claimed Adad-nirari as his ancestor.

ADAH [ā'də] (Heb. *'āḏâ* "ornament").
1. One of the two wives of Lamech the Cainite. She was the mother of Jabal and Jubal (Gen. 4:19-21, 23).
2. One of the wives of Esau. She was the daughter of Elon the Hittite and the mother of Eliphaz (Gen. 36:2, 4).

ADAIAH [ə dā'yə] (Heb. *'aḏāyâ* "the Lord has adorned").
1. A man from Boskath, and the maternal grandfather of King Josiah (1 Kgs. 22:1).
2. A Levite of the family of Gershom (1 Chr. 6:41).
3. A priest and the son of Jeroham, of the family of Malchijah (1 Chr. 9:12; Neh. 11:12).
4. A Benjaminite, one of the sons of Shimei (1 Chr. 8:21).
5, 6. Descendants of Bani and of Binnui who had to send away their foreign wives (Ezra 10:29, 39).
7. A man of the tribe of Judah; the son of Joiarib (Neh. 11:5).
8. The father of Maaseiah and one of the "commanders of hundreds" upon whom Jehoiada the priest relied in his rebellion against Queen Athaliah (2 Chr. 23:1).

ADALIA [ə dā'lĭ ə] (Heb. *'aḏalyā'*, perhaps from Pers. *āḏārya* "honorable"). One of the ten sons of Haman the Agagite (Esth. 9:8).

ADAM [ăd'əm] (Heb. *'āḏām* "mankind") **(PERSON).** The first human being.

I. Genesis Account

According to the second version of the creation account (Gen. 2:4b–3:24) God formed man (Heb. *hā'āḏām* "ground") from the dust of the ground (Heb. *hā'ᵃḏāmâ* from *'dm* "be red"; cf. "Edom"), breathing life into his nostrils to make him a "living being" (2:7). He then placed him in a garden (v. 8) and charged him with its maintenance (v. 15). In this garden God devised a test of obedience. Giving him the fruit of the garden for his food, God specifically warned Adam that should he eat from one particular tree — the tree of knowledge of good and evil — he would die (v. 17).

Realizing that man was alone (v. 18), God gave him a companion, but not before man himself noted his loneliness as he named the animals (v. 20). Creating woman out of "one of his ribs," God presented her to man, who immediately recognized his counterpart (v. 23). The second account of creation ends with the statement that the man and his wife lived in innocence (v. 25).

In the first version of creation (Gen. 1:1–2:4a) the creation of mankind is described after that of all other creatures. At Gen. 1:26 God is said to propose the idea of man and then create him. In contrast to ch. 2, here man stands for "male and female" (v. 27; cf. v. 28, "them"). Making them both in his (Heb. "our") image and likeness (v. 26), he instructed them to be fruitful and to subdue the earth (v. 28).

Ch. 3 depicts the fall into sin. At the suggestion of the serpent, the woman, who had not personally received the command not to eat from the tree of good and evil, ate some of the forbidden fruit and then gave some to her husband (vv. 1-6). Discovered by God hiding among the trees, the man confessed to the loss of his innocence, but blamed the incident on the woman, who in turn put the blame on the serpent (vv. 8-13). God punished both the woman and the man (vv. 14-20). Because of their awareness of good and evil, God sent them away from the garden, to keep them from eating from the tree of life and thereby reaching immortality (vv. 22-24). And yet God showed them mercy, for his curse included a promise of ultimate victory over the serpent, the real tempter (v. 15).

It is not until ch. 4 that Heb. *'āḏām* (now without the definite article; but see KJV "Adam" already at 2:23; 3:8, 9, 17, 20; NIV 2:20, 21; 3:17, 20, 21) signifies a personal name. Adam loved his wife (named Eve at 3:20), and out of this union were born Cain and Abel (4:1-2; JB "the man"), and later, after Abel's murder by his brother Cain, Seth (v. 25). The last reference to Adam is at 5:1-5, the "generations" of Adam. Here the author reiterates that God created male and female (v. 2), whom he together named "Adam." Noting that Adam's son Seth was created in Adam's own image and likeness, the author concludes the narrative by mentioning Adam's numerous offspring and the length of his life — more than nine hundred years (vv. 4-5).

II. Old Testament Theology

Although its presentation is simple, the account of creation describes complex events. Placed in an idyllic setting, with easy access to nourishment and in harmony with God's other creatures, the man and his wife (later identified as Adam and Eve) lived in a state of concord (cf. 1:31, "good") before falling into sin. To the Jews (cf. 1 Chr. 11:1; Luke 3:38; Jude 14) this was not merely a story or a myth. But the degree of the account's literalness will always remain a subject of discussion among believers (with Aquinas and Calvin, e.g., taking a more literal approach than Augustine). One should not interpret the creation of Eve from Adam's rib too "carnally" (cf. Augustine *Conf.* xii.23) nor assert that the serpent spoke Hebrew. Perhaps the narrative depicts the first (2:4 "of the heavens and earth" and 5:1 "of Adam") of several "generations" or stages of redemption history and thus to some extent shares the factuality of that process.

Interestingly, the author does not develop a theology of sin nor a doctrine of original sin. What he does present, however, are the results of the fall. Adam and Eve's first children killed each other, and subsequently evil assumed such dangerous proportions that God had to send a flood to wipe out every evil (6:5-7). Two other Old Testament passages which refer directly to Adam's sin are ambiguous. At Job 31:33 Job asked rhetorically if he had concealed his transgressions "from men" (so RSV, JB, Heb. *mē'āḏām*; NIV "as men do") or "like Adam" (so KJV, Heb. *ke'āḏām*). At Hos. 6:7 the text may read "at Adam" (so RSV, JB, Heb. *bᵉ'āḏām* par. "there") or "like Adam" (so KJV mg., NIV, Heb. *kᵉ'āḏām*) who violated his covenant with God.

Perhaps as a reaction to Israel's political demise, the figure of Adam attained a greater theological significance during the Hellenistic period. In both the Apocrypha (particularly 2 Esdras and Wisdom) and Pseudepigrapha (e.g., the Books of Adam and pseudo-Clementine writings), as well as rabbinic literature and Philo Judaeus, Adam is depicted prior to the fall as superhuman and almost divine, and the effect of the fall on the entire human race is greatly intensified. *See* ADAM, BOOKS OF.

III. New Testament Interpretation

Of all New Testament writers Paul alone develops a theological perspective on Adam. (The Gospels may imply an analogy between Jesus' temptation and Adam's test, but do not state it explicitly.) The most important and well-known passages are Rom. 5:12 and 1 Cor. 15:29 where the apostle sets forth the parallel between Adam and Christ. The universality of sin (Rom. 2–3), Paul states, is due to "one man" (Gk. *di' henós anthrṓpou*) "in whom" (so KJV mg., Gk. *eph' hṓ*) or "because" (so RSV, KJV, JB, NIV) all human beings "sinned" (5:12). Having concluded that through "one man" sin and death entered the human race (vv. 17-18), he ends ch. 5 with the introduction of another man, Jesus Christ, through whom "righteousness" and "grace" were given (vv. 17-21).

The Corinthians passage by and large agrees with the passage in Romans. After explaining the importance of the resurrection of the dead, possible only on account of Christ's own resurrection (15:1-19), the apostle then links Christ to Adam (vv. 20-22). He notes the same relation between Adam's destructive influence on the human race (without explicitly referring to

Adam's sin) and Christ's life-giving power. At vv. 45-49 he presents an even stronger parallel between them. Adam became a "living being," Christ a "life-giving spirit"; Adam was "from the earth," Christ "from heaven." Paul may echo the Genesis portrayal of Adam's sinless state in Paradise while stressing that his perfection did not match that of Christ.

In addition, Paul writes at 1 Cor. 11:7 that man need not cover his head because he is created in God's image, in contrast to woman whose glory is man. Alluding to Gen. 2:20, he suggests that woman was created for man (v. 9) and is consequently subject to him. In a later passage he repeats the temporal sequence of the creation of Adam and that of Eve. Again he argues Eve's inferior position to Adam, for she was deceived first and not Adam (1 Tim. 2:13-14).

IV. Extrabiblical Parallels

Although no ancient Near Eastern texts have been discovered which directly parallel the biblical account of Adam and Eve in Paradise or the fall, comparisons have been made with various representatives of cuneiform literature. The Akkadian myth of Adapa depicts the failure of "the wise son of Eridu" to attain eternal life for mankind because he heeded the advice of the god Ea not to partake of the food and water of death to be offered by the god Anu (who actually proffered the food and water of life). In the Gilgamesh epic the savage Enkidu is introduced to civilization by the tempting harlot. Gilgamesh obtains possession of the thorny plant which grants him eternal youth (often compared to the biblical tree of life [Gen. 3:22]), but a serpent then snatches it away while he is bathing. Although various elements of these Akkadian narratives are reminiscent of the biblical Adam and the story of Paradise, the overall accounts are vastly different, particularly in their approach to the human condition.

Bibliography. F. Maass, "'ādhām," *TDOT* 1, rev. ed. (1977): 75-87; H. Seebass, "Adam," *DNTT* 1:84-87.

ADAM [ăd'əm] (Heb. *'aḏām*) (**PLACE**). A city at the site of modern Tell ed-Dâmiyeh, about 2 km. (1.2 mi.) south of the mouth of the Jabbok river and about 30 km. (19 mi.) north of the spot where the Israelites crossed the Jordan opposite Jericho (Josh. 3:16).

ADAM, BOOKS OF.† Various pseudepigraphal books concerning the lives of Adam, Eve, Seth, and other Old Testament figures date to the early centuries of the Christian era. Most significant are the so-called Apocalypse of Moses, a Greek text which concerns events following the expulsion of Adam and Eve from the garden of Eden and their subsequent suffering and death, and a Latin text, the Life of Adam and Eve, which includes the disgraced progenitors' attempt at penance and a second temptation by Satan. The two texts are apparently derived from Semitic originals, although no evidence has been found to substantiate a basic book of Adam. Existing versions (e.g., Slavonic, Armenian, Ethiopic) manifest definite Christian insertions.

A gnostic Apocalypse of Adam, preserved in Coptic, embellishes a retelling of the Genesis story with a secret revelation of future events of salvation history which Adam passes on to his son Seth. The work has been attributed to the second century A.D. and demonstrates an important Jewish role in the development of gnosticism.

ADAMAH [ăd'ə mə] (Heb. *'aḏamâ* "earth"). A city in the territory of Naphtali (Josh. 19:36), possibly to be identified with Ḥajar ed-Damm, about 4 km. (2.5 mi.) northwest of where the Jordan river empties into the Sea of Gennesaret (Galilee).

ADAMI (Josh. 19:33, KJV). *See* ADAMI-NEKEB.

ADAMI-NEKEB [ăd'ə mī něk'ĕb] (Heb. *'a ḏāmî hanneqeḇ* "Adami of the pass"). A border city of the tribe of Naphtali (Josh. 19:33; JB "Adami-negeb"; the KJV reads as two names); the name may indicate a contrast to the Adam at the crossing of the Jordan (3:16). It was probably located at Khirbet Dâmiyeh (inhabited already during the Bronze Age), about 10 km. (6 mi.) northwest of Mt. Tabor, by a spring along the caravan route from Hauran to the plain of Acco. Some scholars identify it with Khirbet et-Tell.

ADAR [ā'där] (Heb. *'aḏār* "fulness, glory"; cf. Akk. *adaru*].

1. The twelfth month of the Jewish year (Feb.-March; Ezra 6:15), during which the feast of Purim was celebrated (Esth. 9:17, 19, 21). In the intercalary year, which usually fell every second or third year, a thirteenth month was added which was called "second Adar" (Heb. *we-'aḏār*).

2. (Josh. 15:3, KJV). *See* ADDAR (PLACE).

ADASA [ăd'ə sə] (Gk. *Adasa*). A place near Jerusalem, generally identified with modern Khirbet 'Addâseh, 8 km. (5 mi.) north of Jerusalem. It was here that Judas Maccabeus defeated the Syrian general Nicanor in 161 B.C. (1 Macc. 7:40, 45).

ADBEEL [ăd'bĭ əl] (Heb. *'aḏbe°'ēl*). The third son of Ishmael (Gen. 25:13; 1 Chr. 1:29). The inscriptions of the Assyrian king Tiglath-pileser IV mention a north Arabian tribe, Idiba'il, which dwelt near the border of Egypt.

ADDAN [ăd'ən] (Heb. *'addān, 'addôn*). A city in Babylonia, as yet unidentified. The returning exiles who lived there could not prove their ancestry (Ezra 2:59 par. Neh. 7:61, "Addon").

ADDAR [ăd'är] (Heb. *'addār,* perhaps "abundance") (**PERSON**). A son of Bela the Benjaminite (1 Chr. 8:3), probably the same person as Ard (Gen. 46:21).

ADDAR [ăd'är] (Heb. *'addār,* "abundance" [?]) (**PLACE**). A city along Judah's southern border (Josh. 15:3; KJV "Adar"), west of the Wilderness of Zin; it may have been about 8 km. (5 mi.) northwest of Kadesh-barnea and 66 km. (41 mi.) southwest of Beer-sheba. In the parallel account in Num. 34:4 its name is combined with that of Hezron to read Hazar-addar.

ADDER. *See* SERPENT.

ADDI [ăd′ī] (Gk. *Addi*; cf. LXX *Ióēl* at 1 Chr. 6:21 for MT *'iddô* [MT v. 6]). A preexilic ancestor of Jesus (Luke 3:28).

ADDON. *See* ADDAN.

ADER (1 Chr. 8:15, KJV). *See* EDER (PERSON).

ADIEL [ā′dĭ əl] (Heb. *ʿªḏîʾēl* "God is my ornament").
1. A man from the tribe of Simeon (1 Chr. 4:36).
2. A priest, the son of Jahzerah and father of Maasai (1 Chr. 9:12).
3. The father of Azmaveth, who was put in charge of David's treasuries (1 Chr. 27:25).

ADIN [ā′dən] (Heb. *ʿaḏîn* "voluptuous"). The father and ancestor of a number of Jews returning from exile (454 at Ezra 2:15; 655 at Neh. 7:20). At Neh. 10:6 he is one of the family heads who put their seal on the renewed covenant.

ADINA [ăd′ə nə] (Heb. *ʿªḏînāʾ*). One of David's mighty men, the son of Shiza of the tribe of Reuben (1 Chr. 11:42).

ADINO [ăd′ə nō] (Heb. *ʿªḏînô*). According to the KJV translation of the difficult Hebrew text of 2 Sam. 23:8, the captain of David's mighty men, from Ezno or Ezni (LXX *Adinon ho Asōnaios*); he killed eight hundred people. The RSV and NIV reading is more plausible: "he raised his spear" (JB "wielded his battle-axe"; cf. the parallel at 1 Chr. 11:11).

ADITHAIM [ăd′ə thā′əm] (Heb. *ʿªḏîṯayim*). A city of the tribe of Judah located in the Shephelah (Josh. 15:36). Its precise location is not known, though some have identified it with el-Ḥadîtheh, north of Aijalon.

ADLAI [ăd′lā] (Heb. *ʿaḏlay*). The father of Shaphat, who tended David's herds in the valleys (1 Chr. 27:19).

ADMAH [ăd′mə] (Heb. *ʾaḏmâ*). One of the cities in the valley of Siddim mentioned at the description of the boundaries of the Canaanites (Gen. 10:19). Its king, Shinab, at first a vassal of Chedorlaomer (14:2), joined the kings of Sodom, Gomorrah, and Zeboiim in a revolt against their sovereign (v. 8). Because of its wickedness the city was destroyed along with the other cities of the valley (implied at 19:24-29 and stated specifically at Deut. 29:23). At Hos. 11:8 Hosea cites Admah and Zeboiim as a warning for the recalcitrant Israelites.
See SIDDIM, VALLEY OF.

ADMATHA [ăd mā′thə] (Heb. *ʾaḏmāṯāʾ*, probably from Pers. *admata* "unconquered"). One of the seven princes in the kingdom of the Medes and Persians under King Ahasuerus (Esth. 1:14). These legal advisers (mentioned also at Ezra 7:14) shared the actual power of government (cf. Esth. 1:13-21).

ADMIN [ăd′mĭn] (Gk. *Admin*). An ancestor of Jesus who lived prior to the time of King David (Luke 3:33; KJV, NIV omit).

ADNA [ăd′nə] (Heb. *ʿaḏnāʾ* "pleasure").
1. A son of Pahath-moab and one of those ordered to send away his foreign wife (Ezra 10:30).
2. A priest of the family of Harim who returned with Zerubbabel from exile (Neh. 12:15).

ADNAH [ăd′nə].
1. A man from the tribe of Manasseh who deserted Saul and came to aid David at Ziklag (1 Chr. 12:20; Heb. *ʿaḏnāḥ* "pleasure").
2. A high officer, perhaps commander, under King Jehoshaphat (2 Chr. 17:14; Heb. *ʿaḏnâ*); he was of the tribe of Judah.

ADONAI [ə dō′nī] (Heb. *ʿªḏōnāy* "my lord"). A divine name, generally translated "the Lord" or "my Lord." In the late postexilic period it became a substitute for the unspeakable name of God. The Masoretes wrote the vowels of this name with the consonants of the name Yahweh (*yhwh*), indicating to the reader that it was to be pronounced "Adonay"; later Christian translators read the combination as "Jehovah."

ADONI-BEZEK [ə dō′nī bē′zək] (Heb. *ʾªḏōnîḇezek* "lord of Bezek"). The king of Bezek, a town in southern Palestine. He was defeated by the forces of Judah, who severely mutilated him because of the cruel treatment he himself had inflicted on seventy other kings (Judg. 1:5-7). His own troops returned him to Jerusalem, where he died. He may be identical with Adoni-zedek, king of Jerusalem at the time of the Conquest (so JB; cf. Josh. 10:1-3).

ADONIJAH [ăd′ə nī′jə] (Heb. *ʾªḏōnîyâ*, *ʾªḏōnîyāhû* "Yahweh is my Lord").
1. The fourth son of David, born at Hebron; his mother was Haggith (2 Sam. 3:4 par. 1 Chr. 3:2).
The opening chapter of 1 Kings narrates Adonijah's attempt to secure the throne during the waning years of the reign of his father. Claiming to be David's successor according to the right of primogeniture (1 Kgs. 1:5; cf. 2:15; Amnon, Absalom, and perhaps Chileab had already died, which made him the eldest living son), which his father apparently did not discourage (1:6), Adonijah secured the support of Joab and Abiathar, both powerful influences in the royal court (v. 7). When he invited all but those loyal to Solomon to a feast at En-rogel, he believed that he actually was the successor to the throne of Israel. Meanwhile, however, his aged father, mainly through the intervention of his adviser Nathan, had crowned Solomon (the son of Bathsheba) king (vv. 11-40). Deprived of the security of friends and followers, who fled his festal gathering in fear of attack, Adonijah himself fled to the sanctuary for refuge (v. 50).
At first the young ruler dealt kindly with Adonijah, permitting him to return home in peace (1:50-53). However, when Adonijah asked Bathsheba to intercede for him in obtaining Solomon's permission to marry Abishag the Shunammite, David's former nurse and a member of the royal harem, Solomon correctly interpreted the ploy as a means of usurping his claim to the throne and ordered Adonijah's execution (2:13-25).
2. One of the Levites whom King Jehoshaphat commissioned to instruct the people (2 Chr. 17:8).

3. One of the family leaders who set his seal upon the renewed covenant under Nehemiah (Neh. 10:16). He is perhaps the same as Adonikam mentioned at Ezra 2:13.

ADONIKAM [ăd′ə nī′kəm] (Heb. *'ᵃḏōnîqām* "my Lord has arisen"). The name of a family of returning exiles (Ezra 2:13; Neh. 7:18). He may be the same as the Adonijah mentioned at Neh. 10:16.

ADONIRAM [ăd′ə nī′rəm] (Heb. *'ᵃḏōnîrām* "my Lord is exalted"). The son of Abda; taskmaster over the forced labor under David, Solomon, and Rehoboam (1 Kgs. 4:6; 5:14). He is also called Adoram (2 Sam. 20:24; 1 Kgs. 12:18) and Hadoram (2 Chr. 10:18). Rehoboam sent him to the dissatisfied tribes of Israel, probably to negotiate with them, but to no avail; the people stoned him to death.

ADONIS [ə dō′nĭs] (Gk. *Adōnis*, from Heb. *'āḏôn* "lord"). A Syrian vegetation deity worshipped in Babylonia as Tammuz, believed to die in the heat of summer and to descend to the Underworld in order to arise again in the spring, thereby returning life to nature. Dan. 11:37 may be an allusion to this deity. If Ezek. 8:14 is a reference to the same god, it would seem that the worship of this deity had penetrated even Judah, where it was particularly popular among women.

Gardens in honor of Adonis, symbolizing the deity's death and resurrection, were planted on flat roofs. Proper care of these gardens was supposed to aid nature beyond the point of death and decay while stimulating the growth of vegetation. Isa. 17:10 may be an allusion to such a garden ("pleasant plants"; NIV "finest plants"; JB "plants for Adonis"), in that Heb. *na'ᵃmanim* "pleasant" bears strong resemblance to Ugar. *n'mn* "the desirable one," an epithet of Adonis.

See TAMMUZ.

ADONI-ZEDEK [ə dō′nī zē′dĕk] (Heb. *'ᵃḏōnîṣedeq* "my lord is [the god] Zedek" or "my lord is righteousness"). A king at Jerusalem, like his predecessor Melchizedek. Upon hearing the news that Ai had fallen to Joshua and that Gibeon had made a covenant with him, Adonizedek along with four other Amorite kings encamped against Gibeon (Josh. 10:1-5). When Joshua was notified of this event, he relieved the besieged city and with God's help defeated the combined forces, killed their kings, and had their bodies hung on trees till sunset when they were thrown into a cave (vv. 6-27). It is possible that he is the same as Adonibezek (so LXX vv. 1, 3).

ADOPTION.† In the ancient Near East adoption was an important means of ensuring succession within families and of providing for transmission of property. The practice is suggested in Gen. 15:2ff., which depicts Abraham's adoption of his slave Eliezer of Damascus as his heir. Moses is adopted by the daughter of Pharaoh (Exod. 2:10; cf. Genubath at 1 Kgs. 11:20), and Esther is adopted by Mordecai (Esth. 2:7, 15). Following the establishment of the Israelite covenant at Shechem, land was viewed as the property of Yahweh who consigned it to the various tribal groups; because it could not be sold or transferred other than by means of inheritance, the practice of fictitious adoption may have existed in Israel (note the numerous texts indicating such transactions at Nuzi and elsewhere).

Paul employs the concept as a juridical metaphor with important theological implications. Familiar with the Roman legal custom of adoption, the apostle extended the concept to illustrate that the acceptance of faith brought the believer into the family of God as an adopted child, one who obtained "sonship" in a secondary or derived sense. This sonship contrasts with the direct relationship of Christ to the Father. It is a spiritual adoption which replaces the natural familial relationship with God that had been forfeited through the fall.

At Rom. 8:15 the metaphor ("sonship"; Gk. *huiothesía*, lit. "placing as son") is a reminder of the believer's reponsibility to live in the Christian spirit, a life which might include suffering with Christ (v. 17). V. 23 places adoption in the context of the future "redemption of our bodies," the achievement with all of creation of a consummate filial relationship with God. That this sonship is determined personally (rather than inherited on the basis of blood ties) is evident from 9:4, 6, which indicates that not all Israelites are God's adopted children.

In two other passages Paul provides a larger theological framework for the metaphor of adoption. Christ, he says, came to secure the believers' adoption into the family of God through his act of redemption (Gal. 4:5), thereby terminating their enslavement to sin and permitting them to enjoy the rights of heirs to God's kingdom (v. 7).

Finally, Paul reflects that it is ultimately God who purposes that believers will be as sons through Jesus Christ (Eph. 1:5).

ADORAIM [ăd′ə rā′əm] (Heb. *'ᵃḏôrayim*, possibly "two hills"). A city in Judah which was fortified by Rehoboam (2 Chr. 11:9), later called Adora (1 Macc. 13:20). It has been identified with modern Dûrā, 8 km. (5 mi.) west-southwest of Hebron.

ADRAMMELECH [ə drăm′ə lĕk] (Heb. *'aḏrammeleḵ* "Adar is king") **(DEITY).** A deity of Sepharvaim (possibly near Hamath, in Syria) worshipped together with Anammelech by the Sepharvites whom the Assyrians had moved to Samaria after the fall of the northern kingdom (722/721 B.C.). Because worship included burning their children in sacrifice to this deity (2 Kgs. 17:31), it can be concluded that Adrammelech was a Syrian rather than Assyrian or Babylonian deity, for the Assyrians and the Babylonians did not practice this custom. Adrammelech has been considered identical to the Phoenician god Adar.

ADRAMMELECH [ə drăm′ə lĕk] (Heb. *'aḏrammeleḵ* "Adar is king") **(PERSON).** One of the two sons of Sennacherib of Assyria who, with his brother, murdered his father and escaped to the land of Ararat (2 Kgs. 19:36-37 par. Isa. 37:37-38). Variant forms of the name are found in the works of Abydenus and Polyhistorus.

ADRAMYTTIUM [ăd′rə mĭt′ĭ əm] (Gk. *Adramyttion*). A seaport in Mysia, on the west coast of Asia Minor. On his fourth journey the apostle Paul traveled from Caesarea to Myra in Lycia on a ship from Adramyttium (Acts 27:1-6) before transferring to a ship bound for Rome. After its plunder by Turkish pirates *ca.* A.D. 1100, the port was abandoned; a new settlement (modern Edremit) lies further inland.

ADRIA [ā′drĭ ə] (Gk. *Adrias*). That part of the Mediterranean Sea which is south of Italy and Greece and between Crete and Malta, now called the Ionian Sea. Here the ship carrying Paul and other prisoners was drifting before landing on Malta (Acts 27:27).

ADRIEL [ā′drĭ əl] (Heb. *'aḏrî'ēl* "my help is God"). The son of Barzillai the Meholathite to whom Saul gave his daughter Merab as wife, even though he had already promised her to David (1 Sam. 18:19; 2 Sam. 21:8). Later David gave Adriel's five sons into the hands of the Gibeonites as a payment for the blood-guilt of Saul (2 Sam. 21:8).

ADULLAM [ə dŭl′əm] (Heb. *'aḏullām* "retreat"). A city in the Shephelah region of Judah (at the foot of the central mountain range; cf. Gen. 38:1) believed to be the precursor to modern 'Idelmiyeh, at the foot of Tell esh-Sheikh Madhkûr, about 14 km. (9 mi.) east-northeast of Beit-Jibrîn (Eleutheropolis). At first a royal Canaanite city (Josh. 12:15), Adullam was assigned to Judah after the Israelite conquest (15:35). It was in this area that David sought shelter in a cave during his flight from Saul (1 Sam. 22:1); he even made it his temporary headquarters (2 Sam. 23:13 par. 1 Chr. 11:15). During the divided monarchy King Rehoboam made it a fortified city (2 Chr. 11:7). After the Exile some of the returning Jews settled in Adullam again (Neh. 11:30). In the prophecies of Micah the city may be cited as an allusion to David, who spent years as an outlaw and chief of an army of vagabonds (Mic. 1:15).

ADULTERY (Heb. *n'p*; Gk. *moicheía*). The seventh commandment forbids a married person to have sexual relations with a person who is not his or her spouse (Exod. 20:14; Deut. 5:18; cf. Lev. 18:20). Although Scripture condemns such an act, some Israelites paid no attention to the law; David, for example, broke the marriage bond for the sake of sexual gratification with Bathsheba, the wife of his loyal soldier Uriah (2 Sam. 11:4).

The Mosaic law condemned to death anyone who committed adultery (Lev. 20:10; Deut. 22:22); both parties to the act were subject to punishment. The guilty may have been stoned, as is stipulated in the case of a betrothed virgin (Deut. 22:23-24); according to the Mishnah the punishment was strangulation (*Sanh.* 11:1; cf. 7:4).

The Old Testament applies the term figuratively to Israel's spiritual straying from its covenantal love with Yahweh. Jeremiah notes Israel's apostate behavior in the face of God's fulfilled covenantal obligations (Jer. 5:7).

In the account of the woman caught in adultery and

brought to Jesus, he invites those "without sin" to cast the first stone (John 8:6-8, RSV mg.). The accusers leave the woman unscathed, and Jesus also refuses to condemn her; instead he tells her not to sin again (vv. 9-11, RSV mg.).

ADUMMIM [ə dŭm′ĭm] (Heb. *'aḏummîm* "red rocks"). A mountain pass (so NIV; RSV, JB "ascent"; KJV "going up") on the northern boundary of Judah (Josh. 15:7) and southern boundary of Benjamin (18:17). The modern name, Arab. Tal'at ed-Damm "the ascent of blood," similarly refers to the red limestone rock at the site. The pass is near Han Hatrur, which according to tradition was the site of the Inn of the Good Samaritan on the road from Jerusalem to Jericho (cf. Luke 10:34-35; cf. v. 30).

ADVENT (from Lat. *adventus* "coming"). A term often taken to designate either the incarnation of Christ or the Parousia, his second coming. In the Church, it designates the season immediately preceding Christmas; in the western church it comprises the four Sundays prior to Christmas, whereas in the eastern churches it begins in mid-November.

ADVOCATE (Lat. *advocatus*; Gk. *paráklētos* "one called alongside [of a person]").† A title given to Jesus at 1 John 2:1 (NIV "one who speaks . . . in our defense"). Having stated that believers are still sinners (1:5-10), John further explains that Jesus Christ is their "counsel for the defense" who intercedes in their behalf before the Father on account of his own atoning sacrifice. John may echo Paul's comforting words at Rom. 8:34 about Christ's intercessory work.

The Holy Spirit is called the paraclete, the believer's "Counselor" and advocate (John 14:16). *See* HOLY SPIRIT.

AENEAS [ĭ nē′əs] (Gk. *Aineas*). A man from Lydda who had been bedridden for eight years before Peter healed him of his paralysis (Acts 9:32-35). He may have been a member of a local group of Christians.

AENON [ē′nŏn] (Gk. *Ainōn*, from Heb. *'ēnayim* "double spring"). A place near Salim where John the Baptist was baptizing during the early part of Jesus' ministry (John 3:23). Although this place of abundant water has not yet been identified, Eusebius (*Onom.* xl.1-4) locates it approximately 12 km. (7 mi.) south of Beth-shan, perhaps near modern Umm el-'Amdân.

AEON. *See* AGE.

AFRICA.* Although the continent itself is not named in the Bible, various North African places and peoples figure in the events and imagery of both the Old and New Testaments.

The Table of Nations recorded in Gen. 10 names among the "sons of Ham" Cush, Egypt (Mizraim), and Put (probably Puṭaya near the Nile Delta). In v. 13 Egypt is described as the "father" of Ludim and the Lehabim, generally interpreted as the people of Libya. In linguistic terminology (which bears no ethnic significance) many North African languages have been classified as Hamitic.

Although the Israelites' primary concern in Africa was their powerful adversary, Egypt, the Old Testament does deal with other African peoples, particularly the Cushites or Ethiopians. Cush and Ethiopia may at times be a general designation for areas beyond Egypt (cf. Ps. 72:8-9), but the name usually refers to a particular country south of Egypt (Ezek. 29:10; Esth. 1:1; 8:9). It was a land rich in resources (Job 28:19) and whose wealth was enhanced by commerce (Isa. 45:14). Ethiopia was a strong nation, ruling Egypt during the reign of Tirhakah (689-664 B.C., Twenty-fifth Dynasty; 2 Kgs. 19:9; Isa. 37:9). The physical characteristics of the people were well known (Isa. 18:2; Jer. 13:23). Moses married Miriam, a Cushite woman (Num. 12:1), and Jeremiah was rescued from the cistern into which his countrymen had thrown him by Ebed-melech, an Ethiopian court official (Jer. 38:7-13).

In the New Testament, Jesus and his family took refuge in Egypt (Matt. 2:13ff.). Simon, who bore Jesus' cross (Mark 15:21), may have been a Christian from Cyrene, apparently a vital center in the early Church (cf. Acts 2:10; 11:19-20). Directed by the Holy Spirit, Philip the evangelist instructed and subsequently baptized a eunuch of the Ethiopian (more likely Nubian) court (Acts 8:26-39).

AGABUS [ăg'ə bəs] (Gk. *Agabos*). A New Testament prophet who (like some of his Old Testament predecessors) predicted future events. At Acts 11:27-30 he foretold a great famine during the reign of Claudius which would extend over the entire Roman Empire ("all the world," RSV, KJV; NIV "the entire Roman world"; JB "all the empire"); heeding his words the disciples at Antioch sent a collection to the poor at Jerusalem (v. 30). At the end of Paul's third missionary journey he prophesied at Caesarea concerning Paul's imminent imprisonment at Jerusalem (21:10-11).

AGAG [ā'găg] (Heb. *ʾªgag*, possibly "the raging one"). An Amalekite king whose life, contrary to the express command of the Lord, King Saul spared after having defeated the Amalekites and taken captive their king (1 Sam. 15:1-9). Samuel, however, was more mindful of God's instructions and on the basis of Agag's own infamous cruelties "hewed" him "in pieces" (v. 33).

The Agag at Num. 24:7 may be a title rather than a personal name, symbolizing the enmity of the world against the kingdom of God (cf. LXX *Gōg*).

AGAGITE [ā'gə gīt] (Heb. *ʾªgagî* "descendant of Agag"). A name given to Haman, the enemy of the Jews (Esth. 3:1, 10; 8:3, 5; 9:24; cf. LXX), referring either to King Agag, whom Saul was commanded to kill (1 Sam. 15:1-3), or to the Amalekite nation, Israel's foe since the wilderness wanderings (Deut. 25:17-19).

AGAPE [ä gä′pā] (Gk. *agápē* "love").† In its basic sense the Greek word designates the divine, selfless love which will go to any length to attain the well-

being of its object (*see* LOVE). The term is used in a technical sense in the New Testament to indicate the love feasts (cf. Jude 12) of the early Christians, communal meals which provided religious fellowship and were a means of charity for the poor, widowed, and orphaned of the community.

According to Tertullian, a North African Church Father of the third century A.D., these celebrations observed a particular format:

As it is an act of religious service, it permits no vileness or immodesty. The participants, before reclining, taste first of prayer to God. As much is eaten as satisfies the cravings of hunger; as much is drunk as befits the chaste. . . . After manual ablution . . . each is asked to stand forth and sing, as he can, a hymn to God, either one from the holy Scriptures or one of his own composing — a proof of the measure of our drinking. As the feast commenced with prayer, so with prayer it is closed. (*Apol.* 39)

Apparently the love feast was originally associated with the Eucharist or Lord's Supper (Acts 2:42, 46; 20:11; cf. 1 Cor. 11:20-21), but by the second century the two had become distinct observances. *See* LORD'S SUPPER.

AGATE. A chalcedony (translucent quartz) of various colors (but frequently brown and white concentric bands), greatly prized among peoples of the ancient Near East.

At Exod. 28:19; 39:12 Heb. *šᵉbô* (JB "ruby"; cf. Akk. *šubū*) is the second stone in the third row of precious stones on the high priest's breastpiece. At Isa. 54:12 Heb. *kaḏkōḏ* (LXX, Vulg. "jasper," a red, green, or brown silica) is the material from which the pinnacles of the New Jerusalem will be made; according to Ezek. 27:16 (NIV, JB "rubies") it was an item of trade between Edom (or Aram) and Tyre. Gk. *chalkēdốn* (Rev. 21:19; KJV, NIV "chalcedony"; JB "turquoise") is the third jewel in the foundation of the walls of the New Jerusalem.

AGE (Heb. *ʿôlām*; Gk. *aiốn*).* A period of indefinite duration; the term refers to the past and the future as well as the present. The Hebrew and Greek words occur in various phrases suggesting eternal or "everlasting" conditions (e.g., *mē ʿôlām ʿaḏ ʿôlām* "from everlasting to everlasting," Ps. 90:2; *eis tón aiốna, eis toús aiốnas* "forever" [lit. "to the age(s)"]).

By the late Hellenistic period Jewish thought demonstrates the influence of Zoroastrian eschatology, thus dividing time into distinguishable periods or ages. According to 2 Esdr. 6:7-28, the "first age" ended with Isaac and Esau, and the current age is from Jacob to the final judgment (including the days of the Messiah and the resurrection), with the resurrection age to follow. The New Testament frequently distinguishes between the present age and the age to come (Matt. 12:32; Mark 3:29; cf. Matt. 13:39-40, 49; 24:3; 28:20); the present age is evil (Gal. 1:4), and the age to come is that of the kingdom of God (Heb. 6:5; cf. Luke 11:2). *See* ESCHATOLOGY.

AGEE [ā'gē] (Heb. *ʾāgēʾ*). A Hararite and father of Shammah, one of David's mighty men (2 Sam. 23:11).

AGRAPHA [ăg'rə fə] (Gk. *ágrapha* "unwritten [things]"). Alleged sayings of Jesus not recorded in the canonical gospels. They are found mainly in the apocryphal gospels and the writings of the Church Fathers. Although several hundreds of these sayings are known, few seem to be authentic; among the more reliable are those cited by Tertullian: "No man can obtain the kingdom of heaven who has not gone through temptation" (*De baptismo* 20), and Clement: "Ask for the great things, and God will add to you what is small" (*Strom.* i.24.158). For the most part the agrapha are merely variations or amplifications of canonical sayings; many, particularly in the apocryphal gospels, are markedly inferior in form and content to the canonical material and may well be pious forgeries.

Sayings of Jesus mentioned in the New Testament (e.g., Acts 1:4-5; 11:16; 20:35) are called Logia.

Bibliography. J. Jeremias, *Unknown Sayings of Jesus,* 2nd ed. (Naperville, Ill.: 1964).

AGRICULTURE.† Although only recently have archaeological and comparative studies begun to supplement the biblical record, it is clear that the inhabitants of Palestine were engaged from the earliest times in agricultural pursuits. Excavations at Jericho indicate that as early as *ca.* 7500 B.C. (Prepottery Neolithic A) barley and emmer wheat as well as various legumes were cultivated with the assistance of irrigation. By the time of the Hebrew patriarchs (third millennium) grain farming and horticulture (particularly the growing of grapes, figs, dates, and olives) were well established in the Jordan valley and the foothills (cf. Gen. 13:10), and transhumant pastoralism was introduced into the semi-arid steppe and eventually the uplands (cf. 13:2; 26:14; 37:12; 47:1-12).

Palestinian farmers were heavily dependent on rainfall for the success of their crops. A five-month dry season (mid-May to mid-October) left the land baked hard, and it was not until after the "early rains" (late October-November; Ps. 84:6) that the ground could be prepared; most of the water was provided by the heavy winter rains, but the "latter rains" (March-April; e.g., Jer. 5:24) were necessary to bring the crops to harvest. The best conditions for growing grain were in the hotter and more easily irrigated Jordan valley, which thus has a shorter growing season. Because the Israelites were unable to wrest this region from the Canaanites and Philistines until after the formation of the Monarchy, they were forced to devise terraces in the hill country in order to raise grain; in the process they destroyed vast regions of forest (cf. Josh. 17:18), which impoverished the already rocky soil. Later in the Iron Age the Israelites were able to farm in the desert regions by means of terraces and dams in the beds of seasonally flowing tributaries. In some areas conditions were suitable for a second crop of grain (cf. Amos 7:1).

Bread was the mainstay of the Hebrew diet, and the major grains were wheat (*Triticum sativum*; Heb. *ḥiṭṭâ*) and barley (*Hordeum vulgare* L., spring barley; *Hordeum hexastichon* L., winter barley; Heb. *śeʿōrâ*); a third variety, spelt wheat (*Triticum spelta*; Heb. *kussemeṭ*; KJV "rye," Exod. 9:32), was also used but was considered inferior. Other field crops included beans, lentils, peas, mint, dill, cumin, onions, and leeks. When preparing the soil for these crops it was first necessary, particularly in the hill country, to remove the large stones (Isa. 5:2). Plowing was ac-

Agriculture in Egypt as depicted in wall paintings. Breaking up the ground with hoe and plow, scattering the grain, harvesting, gathering, and threshing (Royal Ontario Museum, Toronto)

complished with a lightweight stick held in the right hand (Luke 9:62) and drawn by harnessed oxen encouraged by means of a long pointed stick or goad (Judg. 3:31; 1 Sam. 13:21; cf. Acts 26:14); at first the plows had copper points, but even the larger and stronger iron point introduced in the tenth century cut no deeper than about 20 cm. (8 in.). Seed was sown by drawing it from a pouch or jar and scattering it with the full hand, or by dropping it through a funnel attached to the plow itself, thereby causing the seed to fall into straight furrows (Isa. 28:25; John 12:24). In order to protect the newly sown seed from being consumed by birds, the farmer immediately covered the seed, perhaps by means of a hoe or harrow (Job 39:10; Isa. 7:25; 28:24; Hos. 10:11; some scholars contend that these references indicate merely breaking up large clumps of soil formed by plowing). Although weeds were a problem for the Israelite farmers, they were occasionally allowed to grow along with the crops lest weeding uproot the growing grain as well (cf. Matt. 13:27-29).

Barley was harvested in April or May, followed approximately a month later by the wheat. The process involved the entire family and on occasion hired reapers. First the grain was gathered by a curved flint or iron sickle; the clumps of grain were held in the left hand and cut near the ground, leaving stubble to be used as provender for the cattle. The cut bunches of grain were put on the ground, to be gathered up by the children and taken to the threshing floor, or put up in sheaves if threshing were to be done in the open field (cf. Judg. 15:5). The threshing floor was an outcropping of rock or a level patch of clay-coated soil where the sheaves of grain might be scattered and the grain loosened from the stalks. This was accomplished by beating the stalks with a stick (e.g., Judg. 6:11) or by driving oxen around the floor to trample the grain (Deut. 25:4) or harnessing them to a cart (Isa. 28:27) or threshing sledge, a heavy drag whose bottom was studded with sharp pieces of basalt or iron (2 Sam. 24:22; Isa. 41:15). Next the grain was winnowed by repeatedly tossing it into the air by means of a wooden fork (Jer. 15:7) or shovel (Isa. 30:24), thus separating the heavier kernels of grain from the chaff, which was driven away by the wind; this was usually done in the late afternoon or evening, when the wind was greater (cf. Ruth 3:2). After the kernels were sifted in a sieve to remove dirt, stones, and other refuse, the grain was stored in jars for home use or kept in barns (Hag. 2:19; Matt. 6:26; Luke 12:18) or granaries (Matt. 3:12).

Various types of grapes were grown, primarily to be used in making wine but also to be dried as raisins. Vineyards, which were ordinarily on a hill (Isa. 5:1; Jer. 31:5) but could also be found near houses (cf. 1 Kgs. 21:1), were protected by a wall or hedge and often a watchtower (Isa. 5:2). Planted in rows approximately 3 m. (10 ft.) apart, the vines required little care during the growing season (July to August or September) other than springtime pruning (Isa. 18:5).

By contrast, olives required considerable attention during the growing stage. Once mature, however, they produced berries for a century or so, and new shoots would sprout from the roots of old trees (cf. Rom. 11:17-24). Olives were ready for harvest by Sep-

tember, but because they ripened slowly the task could be postponed until as late as December. Harvesting was a simple process, often performed simply by shaking the tree or beating the branches with a stick (Deut. 24:20). Although they might be eaten fresh, olives were the most abundant source of cooking oil, obtained by crushing the berries in a press with a millstone or by treading with the feet (Deut. 33:24; Mic. 6:15).

Flocks of sheep and goats were maintained primarily for milk and other dairy products as well as wool. Only rarely was their flesh used for meat, which was generally obtained by hunting. See CATTLE.

The recognition of the land and its products as the gift of God was a central focus of Israelite religion. Indeed, the three major pilgrim festivals are believed to have derived from agricultural observances: the Passover and the Feast of Unleavened Bread, observed in the spring (Exod. 12:1–13:16; 34:18-20; Lev. 23:4-14); Pentecost or the Feast of Weeks, celebrating in June the harvest of the firstfruits of the grain (Exod. 23:16; Lev. 23:15-21); and the Feast of the Ingathering or Booths, commemorating the autumn harvest of grapes (Exod. 23:16; Deut. 16:13-16). The Sabbath may originally have been an agricultural day of rest for farm workers as well as animals, and the sabbatical year may have derived from the practice of allowing fields and vineyards to lie fallow in order to replenish the soil (Exod. 23:10-11; Lev. 25:3-5). Much of the Pentateuchal legislation concerned responsible stewardship of the land and its produce (e.g., Deut. 14:22-29; 22:1-3, 9-10; 24:25), including provision for the less fortunate (24:19-21; 26:12) and the return of a portion as an act of thanksgiving (15:19–16:17).

AGRIPPA [ə grĭp'ə] (Gk. *Agrippas*). See HEROD 3, 4.

AGUR [ā'gər] (Heb. *'agûr*, probably "hireling"). An author or collector of proverbs (Prov. 30:1) and the son of Jakeh of Massa. He was probably a compatriot of Lemuel the king of Massa (31:1).

AHAB [ā'hăb] (Heb. *'aḥ'āḇ* "brother is father").

1. The seventh king of Israel (*ca.* 875-854 B.C.) and the son and successor of Omri (1 Kgs. 16:29).

I. Political Context

While his father was yet alive, Ahab married Jezebel, the daughter of Ethbaal king of Tyre. His alliance with Tyre, through which he strengthened his position against the Syrians, constituted the political background for introducing the worship of the deity Baal. He also allied himself with Judah by having his daughter Athaliah marry the son of Jehoshaphat (2 Kgs. 8:18; cf. 2 Chr. 18:1) and by conducting a military campaign against Ramoth-gilead, which he and Jehoshaphat of Judah initiated (*see III* below). He rebuilt Jericho in order to prevent the recurrence of a Moabite invasion in the east of his kingdom. According to the inscription on the Moabite Stone, Mesha, the king of Moab, had boasted of recapturing Medeba from Israel (*ca.* 865), and Ahab considered his vaunting a sign of future Moabite invasions.

II. Apostasy and Confrontation

Not only did Israel's king Ahab walk in the "sins of Jeroboam the son of Nebat" but he worshipped the Phoenician Baal (Melqart) as well (1 Kgs. 16:31 par.). After ascending to the throne, he built a temple and an altar for this deity in Samaria (v. 32), probably prompted by his ardently religious wife Jezebel, and subsequently promoted Baal worship among the Israelites. Perhaps in his own way he tried to combine the worship of Yahweh with that of Baal. The names of three of his children — Ahaziah, Joram (Jehoram), and Athaliah — contain the theophoric element *yah* or *yahu* "Yahweh," yet Ahab showed little regard for the God of Israel, as is evident from the child sacrifices which accompanied his rebuilding of Jericho (v. 34).

Soon Ahab's apostasy provoked God's anger and he sent Elijah, his devoted and able emissary, with the prophecy of impending drought (17:1). When the drought became severe, Ahab proposed to Obadiah, who had charge of his household, that they divide the land between them and both search for grass in order to feed the livestock (18:5). Upon finally meeting Elijah, for whom he had searched everywhere (v. 10), Ahab greeted the prophet as the "troubler of Israel" (v. 17). Nevertheless, he accepted Elijah's proposal of a duel at Mt. Carmel between himself as representative of the God of Israel and the 850 prophets of Baal and Asherah (vv. 17-45); Ahab was greatly impressed by the Lord's magnificent victory, but Jezebel remained unaffected (19:1-2).

In violation of the covenantal understanding of land as a trust from God and therefore inalienable, Ahab yielded to the temptation of greed and had his wife Jezebel seize the vineyard of his neighbor Naboth, whom she had killed; for this Ahab was severely reprimanded by Elijah (ch. 21).

III. Wars with Syria

Shortly after the contest at Mt. Carmel, King Benhadad I of Syria (853 B.C.) invaded Israel, besieged Samaria (1 Kgs. 20:1), and imposed excessive demands on the people (v. 2). Ahab's reply was defiant (and also prophetic), in the form of a proverb: "Let not him that girds on his armor boast himself as he that puts it off" (v. 11). Encouraged by a prophet of the Lord, he won a brilliant victory over the Syrians then (vv. 13-21), and again the following year (vv. 26-30). Yet, in his misdirected kindheartedness he was foolish enough to spare Ben-hadad's life and make a relatively favorable treaty with him (vv. 30-34). He was reprimanded by a prophet of the Lord (vv. 35-43) and returned to his house in Samaria "resentful and sullen" (v. 43).

After three years of peace (857-854), Ahab returned to battle, seeking to recapture Ramoth-gilead (1 Kgs. 22:1-4). Joined by Jehoshaphat of Judah, who insisted that they learn their fate through God's prophet Micaiah (vv. 9-28), he marched to Ramoth (v. 29) against Micaiah's advice.

Disguised as a common warrior Ahab entered the battle with the Syrians, leaving his ally, Jehoshaphat, in the uncomfortable position of being the only conspicuous royal figure (1 Kgs. 22:31-33). A Syrian archer, however, who drew his bow "at a venture," hit the king of Israel between the "scale armor and the breastplate" (v. 34). Eager, though unable, to leave the scene of the battle, Ahab proved courageous by remaining propped up in his chariot the remainder of the day in spite of his wound. By the time dusk fell he had lost too much blood and died; his body was taken to Samaria and buried there (v. 37).

IV. Appraisal

Ahab's great sin was his introduction and promotion of Baal worship as the official religion of Israel, through which he tempted his subjects to disavow Yahweh. His idolatry was like that of the Amorites, whom the Lord had driven out of the Promised Land in order to make room for his own people (1 Kgs. 21:2-26). His weakness in the murder of Naboth, even though it was instigated and accomplished by his wife, is another instance of his evil character. The Lord's devastating judgment, pronounced through Elijah (v. 19), was executed: after the king's death the dogs licked at his blood which had flowed onto the chariot (22:38), and prostitutes bathed in it — possibly a symbol of Ahab's guilt both in Naboth's death and in introducing the Baal cult. Yet Ahab showed signs of genuine repentance (21:27), which made the Lord delay the destruction of the king's household (vv. 28-29; cf. also the postponement of the anointing of Hazael and Jehu, and his care of the people during drought).

The final verdict of the author of 1 Kings is rather negative, assessing Ahab as a person who, more than anyone else, "sold himself to do what was evil in the sight of God" (21:25), albeit "incited" by his wife. He may have been a competent ruler who won a few political victories, yet these were due to the Lord's help (cf. 20:13, 28). Though he built cities for his subjects, he also constructed an "ivory house" for himself (22:39). Actually, Ahab was a caricature of such theocratic kings as David and Solomon, a person more swayed by his moods and dependent on the action of his assertive wife than one inspired by justice and the love of God. (See Mic. 7:16 for an equally condemnatory judgment.)

The judgment of the writer of Chronicles is less severe than that of the author of Kings. According to 2 Chr. 18, Ahab and Jehoshaphat fought the Syrians, but no reference is made to Ahab's wicked religious and personal deeds, nor a divine judgment on his actions.

V. Archaeological Evidence

Considerable evidence survives at Samaria and elsewhere attesting to Ahab's extensive building activities. The Monolith inscription of Shalmaneser III (858-824) reports that "Ahab the Israelite" battled with two thousand chariots and ten thousand foot soldiers against Shalmaneser at Qarqar (854). The Moabite Stone mentions Ahab's long oppression of Moab (*ANET*, p. 320).

2. The son of Koliah and a false prophet during the time of Jeremiah (Jer. 29:21-23).

AHARAH [ə hârʹə] (Heb. *'aḥraḥ* "brother of Rah" or "a brother's follower"). The third son of Benjamin (1 Chr. 8:1); perhaps the same as Aher (7:12).

AHARHEL [ə här'hĕl] (Heb. *'ʰharḥēl* "brother of Rachel"). The son of Harum of the tribe of Judah (1 Chr. 4:8).

AHASAI (Neh. 11:13, KJV). See AHZAI.

AHASBAI [ə hăz'bī] (Heb. *'ʰhasbay*). The father of Eliphelet, one of David's mighty men (2 Sam. 23:34); possibly an inhabitant of Abel-beth-maacah (20:14; so JB) or of Maacah in Syria (10:6).

AHASUERUS [ə hăzh'ŏ̄o ĕr'əs] (Heb. *'ʰhaswērôš*; Gk. *Assouēros*].†

1. Xerxes I of Persia (Pers. *khshayarsha*; 485-465 B.C.), whose kingdom extended from Ethiopia to India (Esth. 1:1-2) and who married Esther (2:17). A son of Darius the Great, he is the Ahasuerus who reigned between Cyrus and Artaxerxes (Ezra 4:5-7). The LXX calls him Artaxerxes. Tob. 14:15 anachronistically identifies him as Nebuchadnezzar's helper in the conquest of Nineveh; actually, the Mede Cyaxares and Nabopolassar captured the city in 612.

See also XERXES.

2. According to Dan. 9:1, the father of Darius the Mede. Josephus (*Ant.* x.11.4) calls him the son of Astyages I (Cyrus' grandfather; *ca.* 585-550), but this is highly unlikely.

AHAVA [ə hā'və] (Heb. *'ahʰwā'*). A river (Ezra 8:21, 31) on whose banks Ezra assembled those about to return from exile to Jerusalem; there they remained for three days (v. 15), fasting in order that the exiles might humble themselves and ask God for a safe journey (v. 21). Their prayer was answered, and the people marched to Jerusalem without incident (vv. 31-32).

The site may very well have been one of the main canals in Babylonia (possibly near the capital where many Jewish exiles dwelled) used for drainage and irrigation.

AHAZ [ā'hăz] (Heb. *'āḥāz* "he has grasped"; probably a shortened form of Jehoahaz; cf. Akk. *Yauhazi* "Yahweh has grasped").

1. Son and successor of Jotham and Judah's twelfth king at the age of twenty (2 Kgs. 16:2 par. 2 Chr. 28:1). Ahaz began his reign as coregent with his father in 735 B.C.; upon his father's death in 732 he became the sole ruler of Judah and reigned until 716 (cf. 2 Kgs. 16:2 par. 2 Chr. 28:1).

The biblical account portrays Ahaz as a spiritually unfaithful king who, unlike his predecessor David, made molten images, sacrificed his son as a burnt offering, and burned incense to pagan deities first in the valley of Hinnom and finally throughout Judah (2 Kgs. 16:2-4 par. 2 Chr. 28:1-4). As a result, God "brought Judah low" (2 Chr. 28:19; cf. v. 5).

While yet a coregent with his father Ahaz experienced political turmoil. Rezin, the king of Syria, and Pekah, the son of Remaliah of Israel, began attacking Judah, probably in an attempt to win that kingdom to their own anti-Assyrian alliance. Inflicting heavy casualties on Judah (2 Chr. 28:5-15), they marched on to Jerusalem, which they besieged (2 Kgs. 16:5; Isa. 7:1), intent to make the son of Tabeel (probably a

prince of Judah) king of Jerusalem (Isa. 7:6). Meanwhile the king of Edom had recaptured Elath (Eziongeber) and turned this important port into an Edomite city (2 Kgs. 16:5 par. 2 Chr. 28:17). The Philistines, moreover, were raiding the cities in the Shephelah (2 Chr. 28:18).

At this critical juncture Ahaz, overcome with fear, refused to listen to the words of Isaiah the prophet, who had come to encourage Judah (Isa. 7:2-9). Invited by the prophet to ask for a sign, Ahaz again refused. God, however, gave him the sign of the birth of the Immanuel; Judah would be delivered from the Syrian-Israelite invasion (vv. 10-17).

Disregarding God's harbinger of victory, Ahaz instead sent messengers to Tiglath-pileser of Assyria, declaring himself a vassal and seeking Assyrian aid (2 Kgs. 16:7 par. 2 Chr. 28:16). Ahaz even gave as tribute the gold and silver from the temple and palace (2 Kgs. 16:8). (In an Assyrian inscription [*ca.* 734 B.C.] Yauhazi of Judah appears among those paying tribute to Assyria.) Tiglath-pileser responded at once to Judah's plea for help, capturing the Syrian city of Damascus, deporting its people to Kir (see Amos 1:5; 9:7), and killing their king Rezin (2 Kgs. 16:9). Next he marched to Israel, where he captured several cities (2 Kgs. 15:29) and deported the Reubenites, the Gadites, and the half-tribe of Manasseh (2 Chr. 5:26).

According to 2 Kgs. 16:10, Ahaz paid Tiglath-pileser a visit in Damascus, most likely in 732, a year after the Assyrian had captured the city. When he saw "the altar" (probably that of the deity Rimmon), he ordered Uriah the priest to make a replica of it in Jerusalem which would from then on serve as a substitute for the bronze altar on which the sacrifices had been made to Yahweh (vv. 10-16). In payment of the annual tribute to Assyria, Ahaz sent various precious metal objects from the temple; apparently the dismantling of the temple equipment was so extensive that eventually the sanctuary was closed (vv. 17-18; 2 Chr. 28:24).

The writer of Chronicles frequently appears more severe in his judgment of Ahaz than the author of Kings. According to Chronicles, Ahaz' dependence on Assyria became Judah's burden (2 Chr. 28:20-21), and his religious activities intensified his apostasy (v. 22).

Little is known of Ahaz' final years (2 Kgs. 16:19 par. 2 Chr. 28:26; cf. Isa. 14:28). He was buried in Jerusalem (2 Kgs. 16:20), but apparently not in the royal tomb (2 Chr. 28:27), and was succeeded by his son Hezekiah. Ahaz is listed in the royal genealogy at 1 Chr. 3:13 and in that of Jesus (Matt. 1:9).

2. The great-grandson of Jonathan, the son of Saul. He was the son of Micah and the father of Jehoaddah and Jarah (1 Chr. 8:35-36; 9:42).

AHAZIAH [ā hə zī'ə] (Heb. *'ʰhazyâ*, *'ʰhazyāhû* "Yahweh has grasped").

1. A son of Ahab and Jezebel, who succeeded his father as king of the northern kingdom in Samaria. His reign lasted only two years (*ca.* 854-853 B.C.; 1 Kgs. 22:51).

According to the author of 1 Kings Ahaziah did "evil in the sight of God," continuing the religious pattern of his parents and of Jeroboam I (22:52). He, too, worshipped Baal and as a result provoked the Lord to anger (v. 53).

Israel did not fare well in international relations during Ahaziah's reign. Following the death of Ahab Moab revolted, refusing to pay the annual tribute to Israel (2 Kgs. 1:1; 3:4-5); apparently no attempt was made to quell the rebellion until the reign of Jehoram (3:6). Ahaziah sought an alliance with Jehoshaphat of Judah in order to rebuild Ezion-geber and thereby revive trade with Tarshish, but the Judahite king refused (1 Kgs. 22:47-49 par. 2 Chr. 20:35-37).

2 Kings continues the account of Ahaziah's apostasy begun in 1 Kgs. 22:51-53. Injured in a fall at his palace (2 Kgs. 1:2), the king sought recovery — not with the help of the Lord but through the Philistine deity Baal-zebub (v. 2). Through his angel God commanded his servant Elijah to inform the king that his ailments would be terminal because he had failed to pray to the God of Israel (vv. 3-8). In vain Ahaziah twice attempted to arrest the prophet by a contingent of fifty soldiers. Finally, a third party succeeded to bring Elijah to the king, though Elijah did not change the prediction God had given him (vv. 9-16). Ahaziah died "according to the word of the Lord" (v. 17).

Because he lacked an heir, his brother Jehoram ascended the throne (v. 17).

2. The youngest son of Jehoram of Judah and Athaliah the daughter of Ahab and Jezebel (2 Kgs. 8:24-26; 2 Chr. 22:1), who succeeded his father as king after the deaths of his older brothers (according to 2 Chr. 22:1, a band of Arabs had killed them). At 2 Chr. 21:17 he is called "Jehoahaz" (so RSV, KJV; JB, NIV "Ahaziah"), and at 22:6 "Azariah" (KJV). His reign lasted only one year (*ca.* 842), beginning when he was twenty-two years old (2 Kgs. 8:25; the MT of 2 Chr. 22:2 gives his age as forty-two [LXX "twenty"; some MSS "twenty-two"]). He should not be confused with his uncle, King Ahaziah of Israel (**1** above).

Together with his uncle Jehoram, Ahab's successor in the northern kingdom, Ahaziah fought against Hazael the king of Syria at Ramoth-gilead (2 Kgs. 8:28; 2 Chr. 22:5). When his uncle was wounded and returned to Jezreel for recovery, Ahaziah went to pay him a visit (2 Kgs. 8:29), only to witness his execution by Jehu, God's appointed avenger (9:21-26). Ahaziah fled in the direction of Beth-haggan, pursued by Jehu, who shot him with an arrow at the ascent of Gur at Ibleam. He was able to escape to Megiddo, but died there from his wound (vv. 27-29). His body was carried back to Jerusalem and buried in the royal tomb in Jerusalem (2 Kgs. 9:28).

The Chronicler's account of Ahaziah's death is somewhat different. According to 2 Chr. 22:7-9 he did not die from the wounds received in his flight from Jehu, but was killed at Megiddo ("Samaria," v. 9, meaning the territory of Samaria) after the Lord's avenger had reached that stronghold. This account also states that Ahaziah's kinsmen (v. 8; not his own brothers who were already dead, but probably his cousins) were killed before rather than after him (so 2 Kgs. 10:12-14).

While both Kings and Chronicles report Ahaziah's continued observance of Ahab's religious practices (2 Kgs. 8:27; 2 Chr. 22:3), the Chronicler notes that it

was the king's mother Athaliah who encouraged his apostasy. According to Chronicles, Ahaziah's downfall was predetermined by God on account of the Judahite's concern for Joram (vv. 6-7; cf. 2 Kgs. 9:21).

AHBAN [ă′băn] (Heb. *'aḥbān* "brother of a wise person"). The son of Abishur and Abihail and the brother of Molid, of the tribe of Judah (1 Chr. 2:29).

AHER [ā′hər] (Heb. *'aḥēr* "another"). A man from the tribe of Benjamin and the father of Hushim (1 Chr. 7:12). He may be the same person as Ehi (Gen. 46:21), Ahiram (Num. 26:38), or Aharah (1 Chr. 8:1).

AHI [ā′hī] (Heb. *'aḥî* "my brother"; possibly a contraction of Ahijah). The son of Abdiel of the tribe of Gad, who dwelt in Bashan (1 Chr. 5:15). At 7:34 the Hebrew word should probably be taken as an epithet ("my brother," so RSV, JB) rather than as a personal name (KJV, NIV).

AHIAH [ə hī′ə] (Heb. *'aḥîyâ* "brother of Yahweh"). One of those who put their seal to the renewed covenant under Nehemiah (Neh. 10:26; KJV "Ahijah").

AHIAM [ə hī′əm] (Heb. *'aḥî'ām* "mother's brother"). One of David's mighty men. He was the son of the Hararite Sharar (2 Sam. 23:33) or Sachar (2 Chr. 11:35).

AHIAN [ə hī′ən] (Heb. *'aḥyān,* possibly "brotherly"). The son of Shemida of the tribe of Manasseh (1 Chr. 7:19).

AHIEZER [ā′hī ē′zər] (Heb. *'aḥî'ezer* "my brother is help").

1. The son of Ammishaddai. He was a representative from the tribe of Dan during the wilderness wanderings, assisting Moses in the census of the Israelites (Num. 1:12; 2:35) and offering a sacrifice at the dedication of the altar (7:66-72).

2. A kinsman of Saul from Gibeah in Benjamin who defected to David at Ziklag (1 Chr. 12:3).

AHIHUD [ə hī′hŭd] (Heb. *'aḥîhûd, 'aḥîhud* "brother of majesty"[?]).

1. The son of Shelomi. He was a leader of the tribe of Asher appointed to assist Moses in the division of Canaan (Num. 34:27).

2. A son of Ehud of the tribe of Benjamin (1 Chr. 8:7).

AHIJAH [ə hī′jə] (Heb. *'aḥîyâ, 'aḥîyāhû* "brother of Yahweh").

1. The son of Ahitub. According to 1 Sam. 14:3, 8 he was a priest at the time of Saul; he wore the ephod and had charge of the ark of the covenant. He is either the older brother and predecessor of Ahimelech (in which case it must be assumed that he had no sons) or simply Ahimelech himself (cf. 1 Sam. 21–22).

2. A prophet from Shiloh. He tore his garment into twelve pieces and prophesied to Jeroboam the son of Nebat that the Lord would tear ten parts (the northern tribes) from the Solomonic kingdom and give them to Jeroboam (1 Kgs. 11:29-39; 12:15; 2 Chr. 10:15).

Later he foretold the death of Jeroboam's son Abijah and the destruction of the royal house on account of Jeroboam's sins (1 Kgs. 14:1-20; 15:29-30). At 2 Chr. 9:29 he is listed among those who wrote about the acts of Solomon.

3. The father of Baasha king of Israel (1 Kgs. 15:27, 33).

4. One of the sons of Jerahmeel of the tribe of Judah (1 Chr. 2:25).

5. A son of Bela of the tribe of Benjamin (1 Chr. 8:7). At v. 4 he is called Ahoah.

6. One of David's mighty men (1 Chr. 11:36), also called the Pelonite.

7. A Levite during the days of King David; he was put in charge of certain treasuries in the house of God (1 Chr. 26:20).

8. (Neh. 10:26, KJV). *See* AHIAH.

AHIKAM [ə hī′kəm] (Heb. *'ªhîqām* "my brother has arisen"). The son of Shaphan (2 Kgs. 22:12) and father of Gedaliah (25:22). He was one of the officials of King Josiah sent to the prophetess Huldah in order to inquire of the Lord (v. 14; 2 Chr. 34:20). Afterward he protected Jeremiah against King Jehoiakim and his followers (Jer. 26:24).

AHIKAR [ə hī′kär] (Gk. *Achiacharos, Acheicharos*).† The son of Anael and nephew of Tobit (Tob. 1:21). He was grand vizier under the Assyrian king Sennacherib and, after Sennacherib was murdered (2 Kgs. 19:36-37), under his successor Esarhaddon (Tob. 1:22). He was able to use his influence in the court to secure the return of his uncle to Nineveh (v. 22); when Tobit became blind he provided care for him for a time (2:10). Later he participated in the wedding festivities of his relative Tobias (11:18).

The fifth-century B.C. book of Ahikar depicts Ahikar as a legendary figure. Falsely accused by the rebellious Nadan, his adopted son, Ahikar narrowly escapes death for treason through the intervention of a prison guard. When Sennacherib is stumped by the Egyptian pharaoh's puzzle (the resolution of which would determine whether the Assyrian paid or received tribute), Ahikar is brought forward to assist; the crafty sage calls the Egyptians' bluff by sending aloft two boys, carried by eagles, to build the proposed palace midway between heaven and earth. The grateful Sennacherib then restores Ahikar to favor and severely punishes Nadan.

Bibliography. APOT 2:715-784.

AHILUD [ə hī′ləd] (Heb. *'ªhîlûd,* possibly "son's brother"). The father of Jehoshaphat, who was recorder during the reigns of David and Solomon (2 Sam. 8:16; 20:24; 1 Kgs. 4:3). He may also have been the father of Baana, one of the twelve officers of Solomon (1 Kgs. 4:12).

AHIMAAZ [ə hĭm′ĭ äz] (Heb. *'ªhîma'aṣ*).
1. The father of Saul's wife Ahinoam (1 Sam. 14:50).
2. The son of Zadok the priest. Along with Jonathan, the son of Abiathar, he kept David informed of the progress of Absalom's rebellion (2 Sam. 15:27, 36; 17:20). When Absalom died, Ahimaaz in-

sisted on personally relaying the news to the king (18:19-30).
3. One of Solomon's commissary officers, assigned to Naphtali (1 Kgs. 4:15); he was married to Basemath, a daughter of Solomon. Some scholars suggest that the name indicates the father of an officer, whose name has been omitted from the account, and that he may therefore be the same as **2** above.

AHIMAN [ə hī′mən] (Heb. *'ªhîman*).
1. One of the descendants of Anak, the "giants" who inhabited pre-Israelite Palestine (Num. 13:22). Along with his brothers Sheshai and Talmai, he was driven from Hebron by Caleb (Josh. 15:14; Judg. 1:10).
2. A Levite and one of the four gatekeepers of the postexilic temple (1 Chr. 9:17-18).

AHIMELECH [ə hĭm′ə lĕk] (Heb. *'ªhîmelek* "my brother is king").
1. A priest at Nob and the son of Ahitub; he or his brother may also be the Ahijah mentioned at 1 Sam. 14:3, 18. When the fugitive David approached him, Ahimelech supplied his needs (21:1-9). The action, however, was reported to King Saul (22:9-10; cf. superscription to Ps. 52), who condemned the priest and his household to death for assisting the enemy (vv. 11-17). Though the king's own guard refused to execute Saul's command, Doeg the Edomite complied, killing all but Abiathar, one of Ahimelech's sons (vv. 17-20).

On Mark 2:26, *see* ABIATHAR.
2. A son of Abiathar the priest and grandson of Ahimelech **1**. During David's reign he shared an important priestly role with Zadok (2 Sam. 8:17; 1 Chr. 18:16 [KJV "Abimelech," following MT]).
3. A Hittite who defected to David (1 Sam. 26:6).

AHINOAM [ə hĭn′ō əm] (Heb. *'ªhînō'am* "brother is Mot"). A Levite of the family of Kohath, the second son of Levi (1 Chr. 6:25); also an ancestor of Elkanah the father of Samuel.

AHINADAB [ə hĭn′ə dăb] (Heb. *'ªhînāḏab* "brother is noble"). The son of Iddo and one of Solomon's twelve officers; he was in charge of the territory of Mahanaim (1 Kgs. 4:14).

AHINOAM [ə hĭn′ō əm] (Heb. *'ªhîō'am* "brother is friendliness").
1. The daughter of Ahimaaz and wife of King Saul (1 Sam. 14:50).
2. David's second wife (after Saul had given his first wife, Michal, to Paltiel) and mother of his first son, Amnon; she was born in Jezreel (1 Sam. 25:43-44; 2 Sam. 3:2). She accompanied her husband to Gath, where he sought refuge from Saul's pursuits (1 Sam. 27:3). Later, when David dwelled at Ziklag, she was taken captive by the Amalekites but was rescued by David (30:5, 18).

AHIO [ə hī′ō] (Heb. *'ahyô* "little brother").
1. A son of Abinadab, at whose house the ark was temporarily kept. When he and his brother Uzzah drove the ark on a cart en route to Jerusalem (2 Sam.

6:3-4), they came as far as the threshing floor of Nacon (v. 6).

2. A son of Beriah of the tribe of Benjamin (1 Chr. 8:14). On the basis of the LXX some translators prefer to read "his brother" (so JB).

3. A descendant of the Benjaminite Jeiel and Maacah (1 Chr. 8:30-31) and one of the brothers of Kish, the father of Saul (9:35, 37).

AHIRA [ə hī'rə] (Heb. *ʾᵃhîraʿ* "brother is a friend"). The son of Enan of the tribe of Naphtali, assigned to assist Moses in the census (Num. 1:15). At 7:78-82 his offering on behalf of his tribe is described.

AHIRAM [ə hī'rəm] (Heb. *ʾᵃhîrām* "my brother is exalted"). The third son of Benjamin and ancestor of the Ahiramites (Num. 26:38). He is perhaps the same person as Aher (1 Chr. 7:12) or Aharah (8:1).

AHISAMACH [ə hĭs'ə măk] (Heb. *ʾᵃhîsāmāḵ* "my brother has supported"). A man of the tribe of Dan and the father of Oholiab (Exod. 31:6; 35:34; 38:23).

AHISHAHAR [ə hĭsh'ə här] (Heb. *ʾᵃhîšaḥar* "brother is [or of] dawn"). A Benjaminite, one of the sons of Bilhan of the family of Jediael and a mighty warrior (1 Chr. 7:10-11).

AHISHAR [ə hī'shär] (Heb. *ʾᵃhîšār* "my brother has sung"). A high official under King Solomon, put in charge of the palace (1 Kgs. 4:6).

AHITHOPHEL [ə hĭth'ə fĕl] (Heb. *ʾᵃhîṯōpel* "brother of foolishness"[?]). A native of the city of Giloh in Judah (cf. Josh. 15:51) who became David's sagacious counselor (2 Sam. 15:12; 1 Chr. 27:33). He was the father of Eliam and the grandfather of Bathsheba (2 Sam. 11:3), whose husband David had killed so he might marry her himself (vv. 17-27). This may have been the reason for Ahithophel's defection to Absalom when the latter revolted against David (16:15).

Having advised the rebellious son of David concerning his father's concubines and the pursuit of his fleeing father (2 Sam. 16:20–17:4), Ahithophel expected that Absalom would accept his advice, which according to 16:23 was "as if one consulted the oracle of God." When the prince instead agreed with the foolish counsel of David's agent Hushai (17:14), Ahithophel realized that Absalom's cause was lost or that, at any rate, his own position was seriously jeopardized, and so went home and committed suicide (v. 23).

On the theological level, the biblical account contrasts Ahithophel's lack of humility for his betrayal of David with the king's repentance for his shameful behavior with the counselor's granddaughter Bathsheba (2 Sam. 12:13). God heard David's prayer (15:31) and turned Ahithophel's counsel into utter foolishness, although perhaps more as punishment for Absalom than for his accomplice Ahithophel (17:14).

AHITUB [ə hī'tŭb] (Heb. *ʾᵃhîṭûḇ* "my brother is good"; Gk. *Achitōb*).

1. One of the two sons of Phinehas and grandson of Eli; he became the father of Ahijah (1 Sam. 14:3) and Ahimelech (22:9).

2. The son of Amariah and father of Zadok the priest (2 Sam. 8:17; 1 Chr. 6:7-8; cf. 1 Esdr. 8:2; 2 Esdr. 1:1); according to 1 Chr. 9:11; Neh. 11:11 he was Zadok's grandfather.

3. The son of another Amariah and grandfather of another priest named Zadok (1 Chr. 6:11-12). He was an ancestor of Judith (Jdt. 8:1).

AHLAB [ä'lăb] (Heb. *ʾaḥlāḇ* "fat, fruitful"). A town in the territory of Asher from which the Israelites were unable to drive out the Canaanite inhabitants (Judg. 1:31); the Helbah mentioned in the same verse is a duplication of this name (thus omitted in JB). Mahalab (Heb. *mēḥeḇel*; BH *maḥᵃlēḇ*), mentioned in a related account (Josh. 19:29), may be the same town, in which case Ahlab is to be identified with Khirbet el-Maḥālib, about 6 km. (4 mi.) northeast of Tyre. According to the Assyrian annals, Maḥalib was captured by Tiglath-pileser (734 B.C.) and later by Sennacherib.

AHLAI [ä'lī] (Heb. *ʾaḥlay* "Oh, if only!'").

1. The daughter ("sons" at 1 Chr. 2:31 means "descendants") of Sheshan of the tribe of Judah. Because her father had no male heirs, he gave her in marriage to his Egyptian slave Jarha (vv. 34-35); the name of their son is Attai.

2. The father of Zabad, one of David's mighty men (1 Chr. 11:41).

AHOAH [ə hō'ə] (Heb. *ʾᵃhôaḥ* "brotherly"). The sixth son of Bela and grandson of Benjamin (1 Chr. 8:4); the name as represented in the Hebrew text is probably an error (dittography) for Ahijah.

AHOHI [ə hō'hī] (Heb. *ʾᵃhôhî*). The father of Dodo and grandfather of Eleazar, one of David's mighty men (so MT at 2 Sam. 23:9; KJV, NIV, JB "Ahohite").

AHOHITE [ə hō'hīt] (Heb. *ʾᵃhôhî*). A patronymic or gentilic name given to three of David's mighty men: Dodo (1 Chr. 11:12; possibly also at 2 Sam. 23:9, so KJV, JB, NIV), Zalmon (2 Sam. 23:28), and Ilai (1 Chr. 11:29; perhaps the same as Zalmon).

AHOLAH (Ezek. 23:4-5, 36, 44, KJV). See OHOLAH.

AHOLIAB (Exod. 31:6; 35:34; 36:1-2; 38:23, KJV). See OHOLIAB.

AHOLIBAH (Ezek. 23:4, 11, 22, 36, 44, KJV). See OHOLIBAH.

AHOLIBAMAH (Gen. 36:2, 5, 14, 18, 25, KJV). See OHOLIBAMAH.

AHUMAI [ə hū'mī] (Heb. *ʾᵃhûmay*). The son of Jahath of the tribe of Judah (1 Chr. 4:2).

AHUZZAM [ə hŭz'əm] (Heb. *ʾᵃhuzzām* "possessor"). A son of Ashhur and Naarah of the tribe of Judah (1 Chr. 4:6; KJV "Ahuzam").

AHUZZATH [ə hŭz′ăth] (Heb. *'ªḥuzzaṯ* "possession"). A friend (a technical term meaning adviser) of Abimelech the king of the Philistines. He and Phicol accompanied their sovereign, who wished to make a covenant with Isaac (Gen. 26:26).

AHZAI [ă′zī] (Heb. *'aḥzay*, perhaps an abbreviated form of Ahaziah "the Lord has grasped"). A priest at the time of Ezra; the father of Azarel and grandson of Immer (Neh. 11:13; KJV "Ahasai").

AI [ī, ā′ī].
1.† A city in the territory of Ephraim, located near Beth-aven and Bethel (Heb. *hā'ay* "the heap, ruin").

I. History

Settled in the Early Bronze Age (I B, *ca.* 3100 B.C.), Ai is first mentioned at Gen. 12:8 (KJV "Hai"). Upon his arrival in Palestine Abraham received a vision from God after which he pitched his tent between Bethel and Ai. He returned to this spot when the famine that had forced him to move to Egypt had ceased (13:3).

Ai is accorded a prominent role during the Israelite conquest of Canaan. Having conquered the strategic city of Jericho, Joshua sent spies to Ai who brought back the favorable report that the city had only a few inhabitants (Josh. 7:2-3); nevertheless, the first Israelite attack on Ai proved unsuccessful (vv. 4-5). Learning that the defeat was punishment for a violation of the Lord's command to take no spoil at Jericho, the Israelites took vengeance upon the errant Achan and stoned him to death (vv. 10-26); when the attack on Ai was resumed the Israelites succeeded by means of a ruse, in which they feigned a retreat. The city was left a smoldering heap (8:28) and the inhabitants, including the king, were killed (v. 29).

Apparently rebuilt at a later date, the city may be the Aiath mentioned at Isa. 10:28 as one of the cities approached by the Assyrian armies. After the Exile several Israelites of the tribe of Benjamin are said to have returned to Ai (Ezra 2:28; Neh. 7:32; called "Aija" at 11:31).

II. Archaeology

While Ai is located in the biblical account merely as east of Bethel, several sites have been proposed for it, all in the same general region. The most likely identification is the massive mound at modern et-Tell, 3 km. (2 mi.) southeast of Bethel (Tell Beitîn). Excavations at the site have been conducted by J. Garstang (1928), J. Marquet-Krause (1933-35), and J. A. Callaway (1964-72). The postexilic city cited by Ezra and Nehemiah has been identified with Khirbet Haiyân, 1.6 km. (1 mi.) southeast of et-Tell.

Excavations indicate that an unwalled village was established at the site *ca.* 3100, followed by a series of walled cities (3000-2860, 2860-2720, 2720-2400). The latest of these Early Bronze Age cities demonstrates significant Egyptian influence, including public buildings, a large temple in which were found numerous alabaster vessels, and a stone-lined reservoir. The city was violently destroyed *ca.* 2400, most likely at the hands of Amorite invaders, although some attribute its conquest to the Egyptian Fifth Dynasty. Ai was then abandoned and lay in ruins until *ca.* 1200 (Iron Age I), when it was resettled by farmers from the hill country. The village was not fortified and appears to have been abandoned for good following a minor skirmish *ca.* 1050.

The lack of evidence for an occupation of the site during the period assigned to the Conquest (thirteenth century) creates difficulties in understanding the conquest of Ai as recorded in Josh. 7–8. W. F. Albright suggested that the account may refer rather to the conquest of nearby Bethel, proposing that Ai may have served as a fortified outpost for that city (cf. 8:17); note also the similarity in Hebrew terminology and the potential for confusion between Bethel "the city" (Heb. *hā'îr*) and Ai "the ruin" (*hā'ay*). Some scholars suggest that evidence of Late Bronze Age settlement may have been eroded, as at Jericho. Most likely, however, the discrepancy necessitates a reexamination of the nature and date of the Conquest.
Bibliography. J. A. Callaway, "Ai," *EAEHL* 1:36-52.
2. A city in Ammon (Jer. 49:3; so RSV, KJV, NIV following Heb. *'ay*) of unknown location. An alternate reading is "the destroyer is on the march" (so JB, emending *šoḏēḏ 'ālâ*).

AIAH [ā′yə] (Heb. *'ayyâ* "falcon").
1. The son of Zibeon and brother of Anah; one of the chiefs of the Horites (Gen. 36:24, KJV "Ajah"; 1 Chr. 1:40).
2. The father of Rizpah, Saul's concubine (2 Sam. 3:7). His two sons were given to the Gibeonites on account of Saul's evil dealings with them (21:8-11).

AIATH (Isa. 10:28). *See* AI **1.**

AIJA (Neh. 11:31). *See* AI **1.**

AIJALON [ā′jə lŏn] (Heb. *'ayyālôn* "deer-field").
1. A town in the tribal territory of Dan (Josh. 19:42; KJV "Ajalon"); a levitical city (21:24), and for some time a city of refuge (1 Chr. 6:69) in Ephraim. In the Amarna Letters it appears as Aialuna. Aijalon has been located at Yâlô, near Emmaus and 23 km. (14 mi.) northwest of Jerusalem.

Assigned to the Danites, the city remained in Amorite possession, even though its Amorite inhabitants were subject to forced labor (Judg. 1:35). It was here that King Saul later gained a victory over the Philistines (1 Sam. 14:31). During the reign of Rehoboam it belonged to Judah and Benjamin (cf. 1 Chr. 8:13) and became a fortified city (2 Chr. 11:10). According to 28:18 the Philistines raided Aijalon and other Judean cities when Judah's king Ahaz was fighting Pekah, the king of Israel.

The place is especially known for the battle held on its plain between Joshua and the Amorites ("valley," Josh. 10:12). In the pursuit of their enemies the Israelite forces were aided by the moon which stayed "in the valley of Aijalon" (vv. 12-13). At this location Judas Maccabeus defeated Gorgias in 166 B.C. (1 Macc. 3:40; 4:1-15).
2. A city in the tribal territory of Zebulun where Elon the judge was buried (Judg. 12:12). Its site is unknown.

AIJELETH SHAHAR (Ps. 22 superscription, KJV). *See* HIND OF THE DAWN.

AIN [ān] (Heb. *'ayin* "eye" or "spring").
   1. A town located in greater Palestine, west of Riblah (Num. 34:11) and north of the Sea of Chinnereth (Galilee). If the Hebrew represents a place name, its location is uncertain. Proposed locations are near the Yarmuk and the Jordan or Khirbet Dafneh.
   2. A city mentioned before Rimmon at Josh. 15:32; 1 Chr. 4:32; probably the same as En-rimmon (e.g., Josh. 19:7; Neh. 11:29).
   3. A levitical city given to the descendants of Aaron (Josh. 21:16); possibly the same as **2** above.

AIN FESHKA [ān fĕsh′kə]. A saltwater spring approximately 2 km. (1.3 mi.) west of the Dead Sea and 12 km. (7.5 mi.) south of Jericho. It was in nearby caves that the Dead Sea Scrolls were discovered.

AIN KAREM [ān kĕr′əm] (Heb. *'ân kerem* "spring of the vineyard").† Traditional home of Elizabeth and Zechariah and birthplace of John the Baptist, a village in the hill country 8 km. (5 mi.) west of Jerusalem. It is also associated with Mary's visit to her cousin Elizabeth (cf. Luke 1:39-40) during which the birth of Jesus was foretold (vv. 41-56).

AJAH (Gen. 36:29, KJV). *See* AIAH.

AJALON (Josh. 19:42, KJV). *See* AIJALON.

AKAN [ā′kăn] (Heb. *'ăqān* "crooked"). One of the sons of Ezer the Horite, of the family of Esau (Gen. 36:27). At 1 Chr. 1:42 he is called Jaakan (so RSV, JB; KJV "Jakan"; KJV mg., NIV "Akan").

AKELDAMA [ə kĕl′də mə] (Gk. *Akeldamach, Akeldama*, possibly from Aram. *ḥᵃqēl dᵉma'* "field of blood"; another suggestion is "field of sleeping"). The location where Judas committed suicide. At Acts 1:18-19 (KJV "Aceldama") the term is a parenthesis in the explanation of the end of Judas Iscariot, Jesus' disciple and betrayer. After Judas purchased it for thirty pieces of silver and tainted it with his blood, this field was accorded the name "Field of Blood." Luke's account of the origin of this name may be compatible with that at Matt. 27:7-8, which indicates that the chief priests bought it with Judas' betrayal (or blood) money as a place of burial for strangers. Behind the account in Matthew is the idea of a potter's field and the potter's house (Jer. 18:2).
   Tradition (stemming from Eusebius, fourth century A.D.) has located this field on the southern slope of the Wâdī er-Rabâbeh (valley of Hinnom).

AKHENATEN [ä′kə nä′tən] (Egyp. *'kh-n-ìtn* "it is well with Aton").* Amenhotep IV, pharaoh of the Egyptian Eighteenth Dynasty (*ca.* 1363-1347 B.C.) and son of Amenhotep III ("the Magnificent"), with whom he may have ruled for a time as coregent. His queen was Nefertiti. In the sixth year of his reign, he instituted a major religious and cultural revolution, changing his name; abandoning the old imperial religion in favor of the monotheistic worship of a new deity, the sun-god Aton; and moving the capital from Thebes to Akhetaten (Amarna). He had little interest in international politics, and during his reign Egypt lost control of its provinces in Syria and Palestine (*see* AMARNA LETTERS). During this time Egyptian art demonstrated a unique trend toward realism. After Akhenaten's death, during the reign of his son-in-law Tutankhamen, the revolution collapsed, Egypt returned to its traditional religion, and the capital was moved back to Thebes.

AKHETATEN [ä′kə tä′tən] (Egyp. *'kht-ìtn* "place of glory of Aton"). The capital city of the revolutionary Pharaoh Akhenaten (Amenhotep IV, *ca.* 1363-1347 B.C.), modern Tell el-Amarna, 322 km. (200 mi.) south of Cairo on the east bank of the Nile. *See* TELL EL-AMARNA.

AKIBA [ə kē′bə]. A leading Jewish rabbi (*ca.* A.D. 50-136), reckoned among the second "generation" of the Tanaim (lit. "teachers"), expounders of the law. Akiba ben Joseph began the task of collecting and classifying the sayings of the Tannaim and thus, through his disciple Rabbi Meir, who continued the work, exerted considerable influence on the Mishnah; he is regarded as the greatest ethical teacher after Hillel, and his teachings are frequently cited in that work. Akiba actively supported the rebellion of Simon Bar Kokhba against Rome (132-135), recognizing Bar Kokhba's claim to be the Messiah. As punishment for his disobedience of the edict of Hadrian prohibiting study of the Torah, he was taken prisoner and burned alive.

AKKAD [ăk′ăd] (Heb. *'akkaḏ*; Akk. *a-ga-dé*).† A city in northern Babylonia, listed along with Babel and Erech as part of Nimrod's kingdom in the land of Shinar (Gen. 10:10, "Accad"). It was founded as the capital city of Sargon I (*ca.* 2242-2186 B.C.), whose dynasty came to rule Mesopotamia and parts of Syria and Asia Minor. The city and empire flourished politically and culturally during the fifty-six-year reign of Naram-Sin, but Akkad was destroyed (possibly by a coalition of Gutians and Hurrians) during the reign of Šar-kali-šarri (*ca.* 2100) and apparently never rebuilt.
   The name Akkad came to designate the northern part of Babylonia in general, and the term "Sumer and Akkad" was applied as late as the Persian period to all of Babylonia. The linguistic term Akkadian refers to the Semitic language which includes the Assyrian and Babylonian dialects.
   The exact location of Akkad has not been determined, although it is apparently in the vicinity of Sippar or Babylon, possibly modern Tell Der.
   See BABYLONIA.

AKKADIAN [ə kā′dĭ ən] (Akk. *akkadû* "of Akkad").† General designation of various East Semitic dialects, particularly Assyrian and Babylonian. Written on clay or stone in the cuneiform (Lat. "wedge form") script borrowed from the non-Semitic Sumerians, Akkadian is based primarily on triconsonantal roots, inflected both by affixes and internal vowel change; more than a dozen verb stems are attested.
   The earliest known Akkadian dialect is Old Akka-

dian, introduced into Mesopotamia by at least the early third millennium B.C.; it is found in personal names, royal inscriptions and boundary stones, and loanwords in the contemporary Sumerian. Two primary dialects — Assyrian in the north and Babylonian in the south — emerged in the early second millennium, probably as the result of Amorite incursions into Mesopotamia; on the whole, the distinctions between the two were limited to phonology and orthography. Babylonian can be divided into the following subdialects: Old Babylonian (ca. 1950-1530), used also in the administrative correspondence at Mari; Middle Babylonian (ca. 1530-1000), the lingua franca of the ancient Near East (cf. texts from Tell el-Amarna, Ugarit); Standard Babylonian (ca. 1000-600), a written dialect used in administrative documents, Assyrian royal inscriptions, and literary texts; Neo-Babylonian (ca. 1000-612); and Late Babylonian (ca. 625 on). Assyrian subdialects include Old Assyrian (ca. 1950ff.), attested in the Cappadocian mercantile texts and inscriptions from Assur; Middle Assyrian (ca. 1500-1000); and Neo-Assyrian (ca. 1000-612), used in administrative documents, correspondence, royal inscriptions, and literary texts. Various regional dialects, used primarily for diplomatic or administrative purposes, occur in materials from Nuzi, Alalakh, Ugarit, Amarna, and Boghazköy. With the adoption of Aramaic as the official language (ca. 612), Akkadian became highly archaic and eventually fell into disuse.

Akkadian is written from left to right and employs (with corresponding chronological and regional variants) approximately six hundred cuneiform signs (combinations of wedges). These signs, each of which in turn may have several values, are primarily syllabic in value (e.g., *aš*, *ḫal*, *ba*) but may also be word signs (logograms; e.g., *šarru*, Sum. *LUGAL* "king") or determinatives (semantic indicators; e.g., *ilu*, Sum. *DINGIR*, as in *iluAššur* [deity], and *ālu*, Sum. *URU*, as in *iluAššur* [city]; *meš* [plural indicator]). Drawing upon G. G. Grotefend's study of Old Persian texts, the first major breakthrough in the decipherment of Akkadian was accomplished in 1857 by H. C. Rawlinson ("the father of Assyriology"), E. Hincks, J. Oppert, and H. F. Talbot.

Bibliography. J. Friedrich, *Extinct Languages* (New York: 1957); E. Reiner, *Linguistic Analysis of Akkadian* (Hawthorne, N.Y.: 1966).

AKKUB [ăk'ŭb] (Heb. *'aqqûḇ* "pursuer").
1. A son of Elioenai of the royal house of David (1 Chr. 3:24).
2. The head of a levitical family of gatekeepers in the postexilic temple (1 Chr. 9:17; Ezra 2:42; Neh. 7:45; 11:19; 12:25).
3. The chief of a family of postexilic servants (Ezra 2:45).
4. A Levite who expounded the words of the Law which Ezra read before the assembled people (Neh. 8:7).

AKRABATTENE [ăk'rə băt'ə nĭ] (Gk. *Akrabattēnē*). A fortress on the border between Judah and Idumea, near the ascent of Akrabbim, where Judas Maccabeus defeated the Idumeans (1 Macc. 5:3).

AKRABBIM [ə krăb'ĭm] (Heb. *'aqrabbîm* "scorpions"). A mountain pass on the southern border of Canaan (Num. 34:4; Josh. 15:3 [KJV "Maaleh-acrabbim"; NIV "Scorpion Pass"]; Judg. 1:36), to be identified with Naqb eṣ-Ṣafā. In this region Judas Maccabeus defeated the Idumeans (1 Macc. 5:3).

ALABASTER (Heb. *šēš*; cf. Egyp. *šś*; Gk. *alábastron*). A name applied in the biblical text to two types of stone: a calcium carbonate (possibly the white marble of Esth. 1:6), and a gypsum or calcium sulfate, a soft stone, somewhat transparent and sometimes veined. The softer type was frequently used in ancient times in the manufacture of various objects, particularly perfume flasks; many of these were imported into Palestine from Egypt. It was in such a container that the woman who anointed Jesus at Bethany carried the "expensive ointment" (Gk. *alábastron*; "alabaster jar," Matt. 26:7; "alabaster flask," Mark 14:3; Luke 7:37); the statement at Mark 14:3 that "she broke the jar" refers to the seal rather than the jar itself.

ALALAKH [ă lä läh'] (Akk. *a-la-la-aḫ*).* A Syrian city-state of the second millennium B.C., located at modern Tell 'Aṭsānah in the plain of Antioch, modern Turkey. Excavated by C. L. Woolley in 1936-49, the site has yielded an abundance of texts which shed light on the history and social organization of that period. The statue of King Idrimi (ca. 1490) recounts his flight from his native Aleppo, his alliance with Habiru ('Apiru) bands, and his subsequent establishment at Alalakh; included is one of the earliest references to Canaan (Akk. *kina'nim*). Most significant are some 466 cuneiform tablets which record marriage and inheritance customs and indicate much about the social structure. The king ruled autocratically as sole possessor of towns and villages; the hereditary upper class (*maryannu*) were chariot owners; next were the freedmen (*šūzubūtu*), primarily professionals; the masses were the *ṣābē namē*, the semifree rural populace which included the *ḫupšu* and *ḫanû*; at the bottom were the slaves, both prisoners of war and natives who could not pay their debts.

Bibliography. D. J. Wiseman, *The Alalakh Tablets* (London: 1953).

ALAMETH (1 Chr. 7:8, KJV). See ALEMETH 1.

ALAMMELECH (Josh. 19:26, KJV). See ALLAMMELECH.

ALAMOTH [ăl'ə mŏth] (Heb. *'alāmôt*). An uncertain term occurring at 1 Chr. 15:20 and in the superscription to Ps. 46. It may designate the title of a tune ("Maidens," M. Dahood, *Psalms I.* AB [1966], p. 177), a musical instrument (JB "oboe," Ps. 46; "keyed harp," 1 Chr. 15:20; cf. *BH* mg., *'al-'ēlamît* "with Elamite instruments"), or musical instructions indicating that the song was to be sung by young women (taking the term from Heb. *'almâ* "young woman") or in falsetto (BDB, p. 761).

ALCIMUS [ăl'sĭ məs] (Heb. *'elyāqîm* "God sets up"; Gk. *Alkimos* "brave"). A renegade Jew (1 Macc. 7:5, 9), a descendant of Aaron, and a member of the

Hellenistic party during the Maccabean period. Eager to regain the office of high priest (2 Macc. 14:3), he denounced Judas Maccabeus before Demetrius I Soter (162-150 B.C.), who had recently escaped from Rome (vv. 1, 6; 2 Macc. 14:5-10). The king listened to Alcimus, whom he sent with his governor and friend, Bacchides, to the Jews to compel them to accept Alcimus as the next high priest (1 Macc. 7:8). Because they deceived and murdered sixty Hasideans (v. 16) Judas opposed Alcimus, but upon Judas' death (9:18) the Aaronide achieved his goal. His success was brief, however. In the process of renovating the inner court of the temple to conform to Hellenistic standards he died of a stroke (9:54-57).

ALEMETH [ăl′ə mĕth] (Heb. *'ālemeṯ* "concealment") **(PERSON)**.
  1. A son of Becher of the tribe of Benjamin (1 Chr. 7:8; KJV "Alameth").
  2. A descendant of Saul and son of Jehoaddag (1 Chr. 8:36) or Jarah (9:42).

ALEMETH [ăl′ə mĕth] (Heb. *'ālemeṯ*) **(PLACE)**. A city of refuge in the tribal territory of Benjamin (1 Chr. 6:60), also called Almon.

ALEPH [ä′lĭf]. The first letter of the Hebrew alphabet (cf. KJV, NIV, JB at Ps. 119:1), representing the glottal stop (transliterated by '). Its numerical value is one. The Hebrew character (א) is used to designate a fourth-century A.D. Greek manuscript of the Bible, Codex Sinaiticus.

ALEXANDER [ăl ək zăn′dər] (Gk. *Alexandros* "defender of man").
  1. Alexander III of Macedonia, commonly known as Alexander the Great (336-323 B.C.), the son of and successor to Philip the king of Macedonia. His name does not occur in the Old Testament, but the "hegoat" of Dan. 8:5 is considered a veiled reference to him. A summary of his military and political achievements is given at 1 Macc. 1:1-8.
  After Philip's death, the twenty-year-old Alexander fulfilled his father's dream of curbing the Persian influence on Greece. Once secure on the northern frontier, he crossed the Hellespont and terminated Persian rule over the Greek colonies along the west coast of Asia Minor (334). In the famous battle at the narrow plain of Issus (333), Alexander's first real encounter with Darius III of Persia was decided in the Macedonian's favor. He then turned south, conquered Tyre and Palestine, and, without the use of the sword, became the ruler of Egypt. According to Josephus, when he entered Jerusalem the general paid his respects to the high priest, Jaddua, and made an offering in the temple. Whatever the historical reliability of this account, Alexander may have courted the Jews' favor and trust before continuing his march toward Egypt. In Egypt he founded Alexandria on the western part of the Nile Delta, opposite Pharos.
  Having become master of the western part of the Persian Empire, Alexander turned to the east in a final battle with the Persians. He refused Darius' offer to share the Empire (cf. Dan. 8:7), leaving his opponent no choice but to prepare for war. Again Alexander

Alexander the Great depicted as the son of Amon-Re, the Egyptian sun-god (Réunion des Musées Nationaux/ARS, New York)

won (331), and became the undisputed master of the East.
  His expedition to India, however, was less glorious. He went as far as the Jhelum river, where his veterans (weary from eight years of campaigns) refused to continue the journey and Alexander was compelled to return to Babylon.
  While in the process of making the former capital of Babylonia the seat of his new empire, Alexander suddenly died of malaria at the age of thirty-three. His kingdom was soon divided among his generals, the so-called Diadochi ("successors"; cf. the breaking of the horn and the rise of four successor horns at Dan. 8:8); thus his empire came to be divided among Antigonus I and his successors (Macedonia), Seleucus (Asia Minor and Syria), Ptolemy (Egypt), and Eumenes and Lysimachus, founders of the Attalid dynasty (Pergamum).
  Significant though his military feats were and important as the extensive network of roads he con-

structed may have been, Alexander's cultural aims and achievements were even more far-reaching. The Greek language, which he made the official language of the ancient Near East, permitted the translation of the Hebrew Old Testament (at Alexandria) and subsequently the writings of the New Testament. In this way many peoples became familiar with the Jewish and Christian religions, and, through the process of Hellenization initiated by Alexander and implemented by his successors, both the Jews and the Christians were exposed to and challenged by writings of the Greek intellectuals.

Bibliography. R. L. Fox, *Alexander the Great* (London: 1973); J. R. Hamilton, *Alexander the Great* (Pittsburgh: 1974); N. G. L. Hammond, *Alexander the Great: King, Commander, and Statesman* (Park Ridge, N.J.: 1980).

2. * Alexander Balas (Gk. *ho Balas*), ruler of Seleucid Syria (150-145 B.C.). Calling himself Alexander Epiphanes (cf. 1 Macc. 10:1), he solicited the aid of Ptolemy VI Philometer of Egypt (whose daughter Cleopatra he later married), the kings of Pergamum and Cappadocia, and the Roman Senate (which sought to promote civil strife in Syria) and thereby defeated Demetrius I to gain the Syrian throne in 150. To bolster his strength Alexander made Jonathan Maccabeus high priest (Josephus *Ant.* xiii.2.2), which in turn aided the rise of Maccabean influence in Judah (cf. 1 Macc. 10:1–11:19). Alexander proved to be a poor ruler, however, and his father-in-law Ptolemy as well as his own troops switched their loyalties to the invading Demetrius II. Alexander fled and was assassinated soon after.

3.† Alexander Jannaeus (Gk. *Iannaíos*; from Heb. *yônāṯān* "Jonathan"), son of John Hyrcanus and half brother and successor of King Aristobulus I of the house of the Maccabees. As the warlike king and high priest of Judea (103-76 B.C.) he suffered frequent military losses (although actually extending the boundaries of Judea) and became exceedingly unpopular among his subjects because of his pro-Sadducee, Hellenizing tendencies. Wasted by disease during the last three years of his reign, he was succeeded by his wife Salome Alexandra (the widow of Aristobulus I), who reversed his policies by siding with the Pharisees.

4. The son of Simon of Cyrene, the North African who carried Jesus' cross (Mark 15:21); possibly the brother of Rufus mentioned at Rom. 16:13.

5. A relative of the high priest Annas, who, with his kinsmen Caiaphas and John, was present when the apostles Peter and John were examined by the Sanhedrin for healing a lame man at the gate of the temple.

6. A Jew (perhaps himself a smith) who "motioned with his hand" at the assembly in Ephesus, seeking to speak in defense of the Jews concerning the riot against Paul which Demetrius had fomented among the silversmiths. Because the crowd recognized him as a Jew, they prevented him from speaking (Acts 19:33-34).

7. One of two men who had "made shipwreck of their faith" and consequently were "delivered to Satan" by the apostle Paul (1 Tim. 1:19-20). He and Hymenaeus were false teachers who may have abandoned the standard interpretation of the gospel in favor of a form of antinomianism or an early form of Gnosticism.

8. A coppersmith who did "great harm" to Paul and who opposed his message (2 Tim. 4:14-15). He has been variously identified as either **6** or **7** above or as a hostile witness at Paul's trial. The apostle warns that this person might seek to interfere also with Timothy's work at Ephesus.

ALEXANDRA [ăl′ik zăn′drə] (Gk. *Alexandra*). The wife of Aristobulus I (104-103 B.C.), the first Hasmonean to claim the title king, and, upon his death, of his half brother Alexander Jannaeus (103-76), and Alexander's successor as ruler of Judea (76-67). Salome Alexandra conducted foreign policy with finesse and discretion and succeeded in restoring peace among the various Jewish factions; during her reign the Pharisees attained significant power.

ALEXANDRIA [ăl ək zăn′drē ə] (Gk. *Alexandria*). † A city founded by Alexander the Great (331 B.C.), at the conclusion of his conquest of the western part of the Persian Empire, in an effort to unite, culturally and politically, the ancient kingdom of the pharaohs with his envisioned Hellenistic world empire.

I. Location

The city was founded near the island of Pharos, on a narrow strip of land between the Mediterranean Sea and Lake Mareotis, on the western branch of the Nile Delta. This site was an important link with both the East and the Mediterranean world, and its location to the west of the Nile's alluvial fan was a natural breakwater.

II. History

When Alexander's empire was divided after his death, Ptolemy, one of his generals, acquired Egypt (see the allusion at Dan. 11:4) and made Alexandria its capital. Ptolemy and his successors are usually considered the "kings of the south" (see vv. 5-43), who waged battles with the Seleucid kings. V. 16 may refer to the Seleucid victory over Egypt and the acquisition of Palestine, while v. 30 may point to the Roman ultimatum to Antiochus IV Epiphanes that he abandon all hope of conquering Egypt (169 B.C.).

The names of several of the Ptolemaic rulers occur in the Apocrypha (e.g., Ptolemy VI Philometor [e.g., 1 Macc. 1:18]; Ptolemy VII Euergetes [15:16]).

After the battle at Actium (31 B.C.) Cleopatra VII committed suicide because she knew that her dream of uniting Egypt and Rome had been dissipated. During the last years of the intertestamental period and during all of the New Testament era the city was under Roman rule, governed by an imperial prefect.

III. Significance

As a commercial city Alexandria exported wheat (Acts 27:38), books, tapestry, and objects made from precious metals, and imported such articles as wine and olive oil from Greece, horses from Syria, and silk from Africa and the East. Among its architectural highlights was the lighthouse on Pharos, considered one of the seven wonders of the world. Within its boundaries labored such renowned scientists as Claudius Ptolemy, Euclid, and Archimedes. The city provided ample opportunity for a revival of Platonism, directed by Ammonius Saccas and his pupil Plotinus (*ca.* A.D. 230). Finally, its intellectual climate permitted Philo the Jew to attempt a synthesis between the Old Testament and the philosophy of Plato; Clement, and particularly Origen, then achieved a similar synthesis with the New Testament teachings.

IV. Population

As the second most important city of the Roman Empire, Alexandria sheltered a mixed population of Greeks, Egyptians, Romans, and Jews. The primary language was Greek. Jews were brought to Alexandria as slaves or settled there as free men. Many dwelled in the Delta district, east of the royal palace (first century B.C.). They were granted certain privileges by the Romans and enjoyed a measure of political autonomy. They collected the taxes on the river traffic and made an important contribution to the city's trade.

While exposed to the dominant Hellenistic culture, the Jews remained loyal to the monotheistic teachings of the Old Testament. Not all shared Philo's love for allegorization, and many opposed such teachings as apostasy. Upon being forced to place statues of pagan deities in their temple, the Alexandrian Jews sent a delegation to Emperor Caligula in protest. Several Alexandrian Jews were killed during the reign of Nero.

Famed for the libraries of Ptolemy I, Alexandria was an important center for Jewish literature as well. Several apocryphal and pseudepigraphal works were written or translated here. The city's most significant contribution, however, was the Septuagint (LXX), the third-century B.C. Greek translation of the Old Testament which made the biblical writings accessible to the Hellenistic world; probably begun during the reign of Ptolemy II Philadelphus, the LXX was the version of Scripture deemed authoritative in New Testament times and thus the source of many New Testament quotations from the Old Testament.

V. In the New Testament

Alexandria is mentioned frequently in the book of Acts. Alexandrian Jews shared a synagogue (the synagogue of the Freedmen) at Jerusalem with Cyrenians and Libertines; at Acts 6:9 they are recorded as disputing with Stephen, probably concerning the nature of Jesus' messiahship. The eloquent Jew Apollos was from Alexandria (18:24), and his exposition of the Scriptures (v. 25) was probably in the Alexandrian allegorical fashion. The ship carrying Paul to Malta (27:6) and the one which completed the journey to Rome (28:11) were both Alexandrian vessels. According to later tradition, the gospel writer John Mark was the first to bring the gospel to Alexandria and Egypt (Eusebius *HE* ii.16).

Bibliography. J. Marlowe, *The Golden Age of Alexandria* (London: 1971); J. E. L. Oulton and H. Chadwick, *Alexandrian Christianity* (Philadelphia; 1954); E. A. Parsons, *The Alexandrian Library* (New York: 1952).

ALGUM [ăl′gŭm] (Heb. *'algûmmîm*). A type of timber requested of Hiram of Lebanon by King Solomon for the construction of the temple (2 Chr. 2:8) and other projects (9:10). If the Hebrew word is a transposition for "almug" (a very likely possibility), Solomon specified the *Pterocarpus santalinus* L., a scented wood which is extremely suitable for carving. 1 Kgs. 10:12 mentions almug (probably a scribal error), used for supports in the temple and in his own houses, and for musical instruments for the temple choir.

ALIAH. *See* ALVAH.

ALIAN. *See* ALVAN.

ALIEN. *See* SOJOURNER.

ALIYAN BAAL [ăl′ə yăn bāl] (Ugar. *aliyn b'l* "Baal who prevails").† Epithet of the Canaanite god Baal, counterpart (and possibly the son) of Hadad (Akk. *Adad*), the storm and rain god often associated with fertility.

ALLAMMELECH [ə lăm′ə lĕk] (Heb. *'alammelek* "the king's oak"). A town in the territory of Asher (Josh. 19:26; KJV "Alammelech"). Although the site has not been identified, the name is preserved in that of Wadi el-Melek, which drains into the brook Kishon near Mt. Carmel.

ALLEGORY (Gk. *allēgoría*, from *állo* and *agoreúo* "to say something other [than normally intended by the words spoken]").† A figure of speech, often an extended metaphor, frequently employed in Scripture.

I. Biblical Usage

A. *Old Testament.* The RSV renders Heb. *māšāl* as "taunt" (Isa. 14:4; Hab. 2:6), "proverb" (Ps. 49:4), "parable" (Ps. 78:2), and "allegory." The Hebrew word ("[simile, comparison] proverbial saying," KoB, p. 576) can mean parable, which applies spiritually to only a part of the story, and allegory, whereby usually the entire story has a spiritual meaning. Some commentators distinguish parables from allegories.

At Ezek. 17:2 God instructs the prophet to "propound a riddle, and speak an allegory" (so RSV, NIV; KJV, JB "parable") to his fellow countrymen in order to teach them God's faithfulness. The story that follows can indeed be classified as an allegory, for the prophet explains each aspect of his story — the first eagle (Babylon), the young twigs carried to a land of trade (captive Judah taken to Babylon), the second eagle and the bending of the vine (Judah's attempt to secure help from Egypt), and the impossibility of a transplant (the futility of Judah's endeavors). At vv. 22-24 Ezekiel predicts that God will not forsake his people in exile. Sometime afterward God summons his prophet to utter another allegory, this time pointing out Israel's bloodthirstiness and religious unfaithfulness (24:2-14; KJV, NIV, JB "parable"). As a result, Ezekiel appears to his fellow Jews as a "maker of allegories" (20:49; KJV, NIV "parables"; JB "storyteller").

B. *New Testament.* If the distinction between parable (an extended simile) and allegory (a developed metaphor) is a valid one, then Christ's parable of the vine and the branches (John 15:1-10) actually constitutes a genuine allegory. The "figure" (Gk. *paroimía* "dark saying," Bauer, p. 629) of the sheepfold used at John 10:1-5 could be called an allegory, even though Jesus does not clarify all the features of the image. Others of Christ's parables could be labeled allegories as well; certainly the parable of the sower so qualifies (Matt. 13:3-9 par.), because its teachings about the kingdom of God are elucidated point by point (vv. 18-23 par.). (*See also* PARABLE.)

Of a different nature is Paul's "allegory" at Gal. 4:24 (Gk. *allēgoréō* "speak in allegory"; NIV "figuratively"). Here the apostle uses an Old Testament passage to demonstrate that New Testament believers are free of the confines and limitations of the law just as Sarah was blessed beyond the limits of the flesh. This is not a true allegory because Paul does not explain every part (e.g., the meaning of Sarah). Rather, it is an example of typology; the Old Testament historical events have a bearing on the New Testament church and are not merely past Jewish history. At 1 Cor. 10:1-5 Paul selects the Israelites' passage through the Red Sea to suggest baptism. Paul applies this technique only infrequently but may use it also at 1 Cor. 5:6-8; 9:8ff. Eph. 6:13ff. also is an instance of allegory.

II. Early Church

While Paul occasionally takes an Old Testament event and puts it in a New Testament perspective, some of the Church Fathers entirely sacrificed Israel's literal history in the interests of fostering deeper, more spiritual meanings. In other words, they began reading into the text points never implied by the author. Such a method of allegorization is usually associated with the Alexandrian Fathers Clement and Origen (*ca.* A.D. 200). Actually, these thinkers followed the earlier Jewish tradition of Philo and others, which itself may have been borrowed from the Stoics, who applied allegory to the literal meaning of the stories of popular Greek religion.

In his younger years Origen not only elevated the allegorical method of exegesis above the literal and moral methods, but also allied his method with a Platonic framework (esp. in *De principiis*). In his old age, however, he more strongly affirmed the historicity of Scripture's "saving events" (*Contra Celsum*). Unfortunately, he went beyond the limits of typological interpretation established by Paul, thereby depriving the Scriptures of much of their message.

The difficulty with allegorization is, in part, its link with philosophy, particularly Platonism. Classical Christianity may have been enriched by the insights of Plato, but not every Christian adheres to that tradition; even Augustine criticized Origen's excessive use of Platonism. On the other hand, Protestants have not always embraced historical or grammatical exegesis either; many continue to allegorize Canticles and some still read Esther as an allegory.

Bibliography. R. P. C. Hanson, *Allegory and Event* (London: 1959); J. C. McLelland, *God the Anonymous: A Study in Alexandrian Philosophical Theology.*

Patristic Monograph Series 4 (Cambridge, Mass.: 1976).

ALLON [ăl′ən] (Heb. *'allôn* "oak") **(PERSON)**. A man from the tribe of Simeon, the son of Jedaiah and a descendant of Shemaiah (1 Chr. 4:37).

ALLON (PLACE). According to the KJV, a town in Naphtali (Josh. 19:33). It is preferable to read "the oak" (so RSV, JB; NIV "large tree," reading Heb. *'ēlôn* "big tree").

ALLON-BACUTH [ăl′ən băk′əth] (Heb. *'allôn bāḵûṯ* "oak of weeping"). A name given to the burial site of Deborah the nurse of Rebekah (Gen. 35:8; KJV "Allon-bachuth"). Located near Bethel, this tree (JB "Oak of Tears") could be the "palm" under which the later Deborah judged Israel (Judg. 4:5).

ALMIGHTY (Heb. *šadday,* '*ēl šadday*; Gk. *pantokrátōr*).† An epithet of God, derived from the patriarchal deity El Shaddai (Gen. 17:1; 35:11; 49:25; RSV mg.), the "god of the mountains" (cf. Ugar. *ṯdy* "breast"). The name is similar in meaning to epithets of the Amorite Amurru (*bêl šadē*), Canaanite Hadad (*ba'al ṣapōn*), and Hurrian El ('*Il paban-ḫi-wi-ni*) and may have been associated with theophanies of Yahweh in mountain storms (e.g., Exod. 19:16-19). The name occurs in both early and archaizing poetry (e.g., Num. 24:4, 16; Ps. 68:15; 91:1), in passages attributed to the Priestly source (e.g., Exod. 6:2-3), and, much later, in Ezekiel (1:24; 10:5) and the dialogue portions of Job (thirty times). The LXX renders the term Gk. *pantokrátōr* "ruler of all things" (e.g., Job 5:17; 8:5; 11:7), *kýrios* "Lord" (e.g., 6:4, 14; 13:3), and *theós* "God" (Gen. 28:3; 35:11; 48:4).

In the New Testament the term occurs only at 2 Cor. 6:18 and nine times in the book of Revelation.

Bibliography. F. M. Cross, *Canaanite Myth and Hebrew Epic* (Cambridge, Mass.: 1973), pp. 52-60.

ALMODAD [ăl mō′dăd] (Heb. *'almôḏāḏ*) The first of the thirteen sons of Joktan and the grandson of Eber; he was the ancestor of an Arabian tribe (Gen. 10:26; 1 Chr. 1:20).

ALMON [ăl′mən] (Heb. *'almôn*). A city of refuge in Benjamin (Josh. 21:18), identical to Alemeth (1 Chr. 6:60). Located in the vicinity of Anathoth, it is probably to be identified with contemporary Khirbet 'Almît, about 2 km. (1.4 mi.) northeast of Anata.

ALMON-DIBLATHAIM [ăl′mən dĭb′lə thā′əm] (Heb. *'almōn diḇlāṯayim*). A place of encampment during Israel's wilderness wanderings (Num. 33:46), between Dibon-gad and the mountains of Abarim; it is probably identical with the Beth-diblathaim of Jer. 48:22. The name appears on the Moabite Stone in connection with Medeba and Baal-meon. The site may perhaps be identified with Khirbet Deleilât el-Gharbiyeh, 4 km. (2.5 mi.) northeast of Libb.

ALMOND. A tree (*Amygdalus communis* L.) found in Asia Minor, Syria, and Mesopotamia; in Palestine as early as patriarchal times. Jacob used rods of almond in Paddan-aram (Gen. 30:37; Heb. *lûz*; KJV "hazel"; cf. 28:19 for the original name of Luz), and included specimens of the tree in his gift to Egypt (43:11; Heb. *šāqēd*). In the desert Aaron's rod bore ripe almonds (Num. 17:8). The cups of the golden lampstand in the tabernacle were made in the form of almonds (Heb. *mᵉšuqqādîm*; Exod. 25:33-34; 37:19-20).

Blooming at the end of January, before any other tree, the almond tree is a symbol of new life. Jer. 1:11-12 uses it in a play on words: "almond" (Heb. *šāqēd*) and "watching" (*šōqēd*). At Eccl. 12:5 the tree's snow-white flowers represent the white hair of old age.

ALMS (Gk. *eleēmosýnē*). Although no word with the specific meaning of "alms" or "to give alms" occurs in the Old Testament, the practice does seem to have existed. Heb. *ṣedāqâ* "righteous deeds" (Ps. 11:1) came to have the more restricted meaning of gifts to the poor. Concern for the needy, particularly widows and orphans, is evident throughout the Old Testament, and specific legislation concerns provision for the poor (e.g., Lev. 19:10; Deut. 14:28).

The New Testament stresses almsgiving as a mark of righteousness, and Jesus places considerable emphasis on the spirit of such giving; these gifts are to be offered sincerely and should not be used to engender the praise of others (Matt. 6:1-4; cf. Luke 11:4; 12:33). Paul also offers instructions regarding the giving of gifts (e.g., Rom. 12:8; 2 Cor. 9:7), and his own practice is exemplary (Acts 24:17). A good example of heartfelt giving is provided by Cornelius, the centurion at Caesarea, who "gave alms liberally to the people" (Acts 10:2; cf. vv. 4, 31). The apparently heightened concern for almsgiving during this period may indicate a rise in numbers of the poor, particularly in urban areas (cf. Acts 3:2, 10).

See also POOR.

ALMUG. *See* ALGUM.

ALOES [ăl'ōz] (Heb. *ᵃhālîm*; Gk. *alóē*). A general name for the aromatic wood of various plants. Only John 19:39 refers to the true aloe (*Aloe succotrina*

Aloe *(Aquilaria agallocha)*

Lam.), a succulent plant which secretes a bitter fluid used as a purgative and in embalming. Most biblical applications of the term indicate the eaglewood (*Aquilaria agallocha* Roxb.) or sandalwood (*Santalum album* L.), both trees native to India and Malaya but exported to Egypt in ancient times. At Cant. 4:11 the aloe is said to have been growing in the garden at En-gedi. The eaglewood and sandalwood were valued as sources for incense and perfume (Ps. 45:8; Prov. 7:17). "Aloes" at Num. 24:6 probably indicates an oak or terebinth (KJV "trees of lign aloes").

ALOTH (1 Kgs. 4:16, KJV). *See* BEALOTH 2.

ALPHA AND OMEGA [ăl'fə, ō mě'gə]. The first and last letters of the Greek alphabet, signifying "the beginning and the end" (Rev. 21:6), "the first and the last" (22:13; cf. Isa. 44:6; 48:12). The figure may be derived from a rabbinic expression indicating completeness, totality; e.g., at Lev. 26:3-13 God is said to bless Israel "from aleph to tau" (the first and last letters of the Hebrew alphabet; the list of the blessings for obedience to God's statutes begins with aleph [in Heb. *'im-bᵉḥuqqōtay*, v. 3] and ends with tau [in Heb. *qômᵉmîyût*, v. 13]). John applies this title to God (Rev. 1:8; 21:6) as the eternal one, the origin and end of all things; at 22:13 he calls Christ by this name. The letters alpha and omega found frequent use in early Christian art and patristic writings, generally with reference to Christ.

ALPHABET (Lat. *alphabetum*, from Gk. *alpha* and *beta*, the first two letters of the Greek alphabet).† A system of signs representing single sounds of speech. The primary system of writing today is the alphabet which originated among Northwest Semitic peoples in the first half of the second millennium B.C. and which was subsequently modified and transmitted by the Greeks.

Knowledge of the origins and development of alphabetic writing comes primarily from the archaeological discipline of paleography, which studies the inscriptional evidence and classifies the developing sequence of symbols (letter forms). The basic impetus for the formation of the alphabet and for its subsequent modification was a general trend toward simplification among the scribes responsible for records and correspondence. While the alphabet was devised primarily to provide a writing system for a language or dialect which had none (and perhaps secondarily to represent foreign sounds encountered in commerce), it also represented an improvement upon the Egyptian and Mesopotamian systems with their hundreds of symbols indicating specific words or syllabic values. Inspired by the Egyptian hieroglyphic script, the earliest alphabet was comprised of pictographic symbols; these in turn were gradually simplified and refined both for speed and clarity. Many scholars feel that the original symbols were chosen acrophonically, on the basis of words beginning with those sounds (e.g., aleph, representing the glottal stop, from Sem. *'alpu* "ox," symbolized by an ox head; resh from Sem. *rēš* "head," symbolized by a drawing of a human head).

The earliest examples of alphabetic writing are a

number of rock-cut graffiti from Serābiṭ el-Khâdem, a Middle Bronze Age (*ca.* 1500 B.C.) Egyptian mining community in the Sinai peninsula; these so-called Proto-Sinaitic inscriptions appear to represent with pictographic symbols an early Canaanite alphabet used by the Syrian and Palestinian workers. Similar materials dating to the transition from Middle to Late Bronze have been discovered at Canaanite city-states in Palestine, including Lachish, Megiddo, and Hazor. Various inscriptions dating to the Late Bronze Age indicate the increasing abstraction of the symbols and the elimination of vertical and left-to-right writing patterns. With the demise of the Canaanite city-state system at the end of the Late Bronze Age, a number of autonomous nations emerged, accompanied by the diversification of the old Canaanite alphabet into various distinctive "national" scripts. Thus following the rebuilding of Tyre in the twelfth century a distinctively new Phoenician script developed that was to dominate the Tyrian and Sidonian empires and their contacts throughout the Mediterranean. The Hebrew script appears to have diverged from its Canaanite-Phoenician predecessor during the tenth century, shortly after the transition from tribal confederacy to the United Monarchy under David and Solomon. Aramaic inscriptions, including the ninth-century Ben-Hadad stele and the eighth-century Sefire stele, indicate the development of a distinctive script roughly contemporary with the consolidation of Aramean states under Ben-hadad I following the collapse of the Solomonic empire; it was this "square" script which supplanted the Hebrew writing system during the Persian period. Other national scripts which developed from the Canaanite line included Moabite (cf. the Mesha Stone), Edomite, and Ammonite (cf. the Tell Deir ʿAllā inscription).

That the twenty-two character Phoenician alphabet was borrowed by the Greeks is quite clear, both from the order of letters and their names (e.g., Gk. *alpha* from Phoen. *ʾalep; beta* from *bayt*) and from the Greek historians (cf. the use of Gk. *phoinikēía* to indicate the letters). The precise date for the borrowing is much debated; however, while inscriptions indicate that the Greeks experimented with Phoenician letter forms as early as the twelfth century (corresponding to the collapse of Mycenaean civilization), the earliest Greek letters closely resemble the Phoenician characters of the ninth-eighth centuries, the period of extensive Phoenician maritime activity (cf. Phoenician inscriptions from North Africa, Italy, Malta, and Spain). Whereas the Semitic alphabets were primarily consonantal, the Greek alphabet was the first to systematically attempt to indicate vowels, using five of the Semitic consonants (aleph, he, waw, yod, ayin) to represent vowel sounds (alpha, epsilon, upsilon, iota, and omicron); evidence indicates that Old Aramaic, as early as the ninth century, initiated the use of the *matres lectionis* waw, yod, and he for final vowels, but the Greeks were the first to indicate internal vowels. The Greek alphabet was adopted by the Etruscans in the seventh century and subsequently transmitted to the Romans.

Bibliography. F. M. Cross and D. N. Freedman, *Early Hebrew Orthography* (New Haven: 1952); I. J. Gelb, *A Study of Writing* (Chicago: 1963); P. K. McCarter, Jr., *The Antiquity of the Greek Alphabet.* Harvard Semitic Monographs 9 (Missoula: 1975); "The Early Diffusion of the Alphabet," *BA* 37 (1974): 54-68.

ALPHAEUS [ăl fēʹəs] (Gk. *Halphaios*).

1. The father of the apostle James (Matt. 10:3; Mark 3:18; Luke 6:15; Acts 1:13). He is probably the same person as Clopas, the husband of Mary and father of James and Joseph (Matt. 27:56; Mark 15:40; John 19:25), although this identification rests more on tradition than on any actual evidence.

2. The father of Levi the tax collector (Mark 2:14; called Matthew at Matt. 9:9).

ALTAR (Heb. *mizbēaḥ*; Gk. *thysiastḗrion; thymiatḗrion; bōmós*).†

I. Old Testament

A. Purpose. Heb. *mizbēaḥ,* from *zbḥ* "to slaughter" (and subsequently "to sacrifice"), designates a place where various types of sacrifices and offerings (e.g., animal, grain, incense) were presented. (Originally the term may have indicated that animals were placed on the altar and then slaughtered, but in general practice the killing took place in front of the altar [Lev. 1–7; cf. Gen. 22:9].) The altar was the focus of the Israelite sanctuary, hence the phrase "to build an altar" connotes "to establish a sanctuary" (cf. Gen. 12:7-8; 26:25).

The earliest altars mentioned in the Old Testament were erected in commemoration of a divine theophany (e.g., Gen. 8:20; 12:7-8; 13:18; 22:19). Others were set up as a witness to God and frequently were given a commemorative name (e.g., Exod. 17:15, Yahweh-Nissi [RSV "Yahweh is my banner"]; Josh. 22:9-10, 26-27). Such "lay" altars were common even after the centralized cult had been established at Jerusalem under David and Solomon and despite the later reforms of Hezekiah and Josiah (cf. Josh. 8:30-34; Judg. 21:4; 1 Sam. 7:17; 2 Sam. 24:25); monarchic and prophetic opposition to these local altars was not intended to subdue individual piety but rather to lessen the divisive impact of local practices (which had persisted since the days of the tribal confederacy) and prevent further influence by non-Yahwistic elements ("Baalism"). The consecrated altars of the tabernacle and of the Jerusalem temple were symbols of God's eternal presence in their midst.

As the locus of sacrifices and offerings, the altar also functioned as a means of mediation between mankind and God, thereby maintaining or reestablishing the covenant relationship (cf. Exod. 20:24). *See* SACRIFICES AND OFFERINGS.

B. Types of Altars. The patriarchal and family (or lay) altars were primarily of rock or stone. These might be a natural rocky outcropping or large stones used in the exact position in which they were found (e.g., the altar of Manoah, Judg. 13:19-20; cf. 1 Sam. 6:14). More often they were fashioned from unhewn stones heaped together or ordered in a particular fashion (Deut. 27:5-6; Isa. 27:9; cf. 1 Kgs. 18:31-32). No steps were to lead up to the altar (as in many Canaanite altars) lest the person offering the sacrifice profane the altar or expose himself (Exod. 20:26). Also mentioned

Transliteration	Phoenician and paleo-Hebrew	Old Aramaic	Aramaic	Qumran scrolls	Hebrew square characters	Syriac	Nabatean	Old South Arabic	Arabic
ʾ									
b									
g									
d									
h									
w									
z									
ḥ									
ṭ									
y									
k									
l									
m									
n									
s									
ʿ									
p									
ṣ									
q									
r									
ś, š									
t									

Semitic alphabets from their earliest to latest forms

are earthen altars (v. 24), probably heaps of clay fashioned into a bench or table.

The altars of the tabernacle and the temple were the primary responsibility of the priesthood and were considerably more elaborate. According to Exod. 27:1-8; 38:1-7, Moses was given extensive specifications for a square, four-horned altar to be used for burnt offerings. Located in the courtyard of the tabernacle, it was fashioned of acacia or shittim wood covered with bronze. In order that the altar might be transported during the wilderness wanderings, it was hollow (possibly filled with earth when stationary) and equipped with four hooks through which bars might be inserted for carrying. This altar served as a model for that which Solomon constructed in the courtyard of the temple (1 Kgs. 8:64; cf. David's altar at 2 Sam. 24:25); the temple altar was considerably larger and had a bronze gate (2 Chr. 4:1). Apparently neglected by Solomon's successor Rehoboam, it was replaced by a still larger altar (complete with steps or a ramp), which Ahaz patterned after that of Hadad-Rimmon at Damascus (2 Kgs. 16:10-14); the three-tiered altar of holocausts described in Ezekiel's vision (Ezek. 43:13-17) may reflect that constructed by Ahaz. A similar altar of unhewn stone was part of the post-exilic temple (cf. 1 Macc. 4:49).

A smaller horned altar for incense offerings was located within the tabernacle itself, in front of the veil of the ark of the covenant; it was made of acacia wood covered with gold and had gold horns (Exod. 30:1-5; 37:25-28). A similar altar made of cedar covered with gold (called the "golden altar" at 1 Kgs. 7:48; cf. OSA *ḏhb* "gold, perfume") was placed within the inner sanctuary of Solomon's temple (1 Kgs. 6:20-21). Apparently it was sufficiently small so as to be carried off as booty by Nebuchadnezzar (2 Chr. 36:18; cf. 1 Macc. 1:21).

The table for the Bread of the Presence (Exod. 25:23-30; 1 Kgs. 7:48; Ezek. 41:21-22) was a presentation altar for the perpetual offering. *See* BREAD OF THE PRESENCE.

II. New Testament

A. Terminology. The most frequent term for altar in the New Testament is Gk. *thysiastḗrion* (from *thysiázō*, a derivative of *thýō* "to sacrifice"), which has several applications. In both the Old and the New Testament it refers strictly to the altars of the God of Israel. It refers to a number of Old Testament altars, including those of Abraham (Jas. 2:21) and those destroyed because of Ahab's apostasy (Rom. 11:3; cf. 1 Kgs. 19:14). The altar of burnt offering in Solomon's temple is mentioned at Matt. 23:35; Luke 11:51, whereas a similar altar in Herod's temple is indicated at Matt. 5:23-24; 23:18-20; 1 Cor. 9:13; 10:18; Heb. 7:13. (Details of the Herodian altar are uncertain; the Mishnah [*Mid.* 3] describes it as a three-tiered structure based on the Solomonic altar, but Josephus [*BJ* v.5.6] depicts it as a large block with a ramp for access.) The same term is used for the smaller incense altar of Herod's temple; it was there that Zechariah received the vision announcing the birth of John the Baptist (Luke 1:11). Gk. *thymiatḗrion* (from *thymíama* "incense") also indicates the golden altar of incense in the wilderness tabernacle (Heb. 9:4; KJV "censer").

Gk. *bōmós* refers to the Athenian altar of the unknown god (Acts 17:23). The predominant word for altar in classical Greek, the term is restricted to pagan altars in the LXX (note the distinction between *bōmós* and *thysiastḗrion* at 1 Macc. 1:59; cf. v. 54, "desolating sacrilege").

B. Figurative Use. At Rev. 6:9 Gk. *thysiastḗrion* refers to the altar of incense in the heavenly sanctuary; here are offered the prayers of the saints (8:3-4; cf. 16:7). The Jewish Christians to whom the Epistle to the Hebrews was written had no physical altar for burnt offerings; because of the atonement effected by the perfect sacrifice of Christ on the cross, he is called an altar at Heb. 13:10.

III. Archaeology

Excavations in Palestine have uncovered several altars which shed light on the practices of the Israelites and their neighbors. Various Canaanite (Bronze Age) altars have been found, including table or deposit altars at Megiddo (*ca.* 3000 B.C. and another dated to the fifteenth-twelfth centuries); these were probably intended for incense or images. A circular altar of stones and rubble was discovered in an open courtyard at Megiddo (*ca.* 2000-1700); it had four steps and probably was used for ceremonial purposes. Similar structures have been discovered at Lachish and Beth-shean. An altar fashioned from a single limestone block was found at Hazor (fourteenth-thirteenth centuries); part of the top was hewn out for burnt or solid offerings, and a rectangular basin was carved out for blood or liquid offerings.

A stone altar hewn from the natural rock was discovered in the open field at Sarʿa, approximately 22 km. (13.5 mi.) west of Jerusalem; this is thought to be the sacrificial altar which Manoah erected in response to the messenger of the Lord (Judg. 13:19).

Horned altars dating to the period of the Israelite monarchy have been found in sanctuaries at Arad (tenth century, during the reign of Solomon) and Beer-sheba (eighth century). Two small terra-cotta incense altars dating to the Iron Age were discovered at Taanach.

Bibliography. W. F. Albright, *Archaeology and the Religion of Israel,* 5th ed. (Baltimore and Garden City: 1968); R. de Vaux, *Ancient Israel* 2 (New York: 1965).

AL-TASCHITH [ăl tăs′kĭth] (Heb. *ʾal-tašḥēt*). Musical notation in the superscriptions of Pss. 57–59; 75, perhaps the name of a tune (RSV, NIV, JB "Do Not Destroy"; cf. Isa. 65:8).

ALUSH [ā′lŭsh] (Heb. *ʾalûš*). A place where the Israelites encamped between Dophkah and Rephidim (Num. 33:13-14), possibly modern Wâdī el-ʿEshsh.

ALVAH [ăl′və] (Heb. *ʾalwâ*). An Edomite chieftain and a descendant of Esau (Gen. 36:40); at 1 Chr. 1:51 he is called Aliah. He may be the same as Alvan.

ALVAN [ăl′vən] (Heb. *ʾalwān*). The first son of Shobal the Horite and ancestor of a Horite clan (Gen. 36:23); he is also called Alian (1 Chr. 1:40).

AMAD [ā′măd] (Heb. *ʿamāḏ*). A border town of the

An altar with horns from Megiddo (by courtesy of the Oriental Institute, University of Chicago)

territory of Asher near Mt. Carmel (Josh. 19:26). Its precise location is unknown.

AMAL [ā'məl] (Heb. *'āmāl,* possibly "labor, toil"). One of the sons of Helem of the tribe of Asher and head of a family (1 Chr. 7:35).

AMALEK [ăm'ə lĕk] (Heb. *'ᵃmālēq*) (**PERSON**).
1. The son of Eliphaz and his concubine Timna and grandson of Esau (Gen. 36:12). He was the ancestor of the Amalekites.
2. Another name for the Amalekites.

AMALEK [ăm'ə lĕk] (Heb. *'ᵃmālēq*) (**PLACE**). Possibly a region in the territory of Ephraim (Judg. 5:14; so KJV, NIV following MT; see also 12:15; RSV, JB "valley," following proposed emendation *'ēmeq*).

AMALEKITES [ə măl'ə kīts] (Heb. *'ᵃmālēqî*). Descendants of Esau, specifically of his son Eliphaz and concubine Timna (Gen. 36:12). Because Gen. 14:7 attests to the existence of the Amalekites before the birth of Esau, most likely some of the descendants of Esau (the Edomites) later joined the Amalekites; this

passage could also imply that Chedorlaomer and his vassal kings subdued the territory afterward inhabited by the Amalekites.

As nomadic desert people, the Amalekites lived in the vicinity of Kadesh (Gen. 14:7), and later south of Judah's border (the Negeb, Num. 13:29). During Saul's reign they occupied the area from Havilah to Shur "which is east of Egypt" (1 Sam. 15:7; cf. 27:8). At least once they raided the cities north of Kadesh-barnea (Ziklag, 1 Sam. 30:1), and it is possible that they even held an area of Ephraim (Judg. 12:15; RSV, NIV "hill country of the Amalekites" [cf. KJV]; JB "in the land of Shaalim").

The first encounter between Israel and Amalek was at Rephidim during Israel's wilderness wanderings. Israel was "faint and weary," and all who lagged behind were lost to Amalek (Deut. 25:17). The Israelites were able to defeat these enemies, however, because Moses, supported by Aaron and Hur, held up the rod of God (Exod. 17:9-13). After the victory God instructed his servant to record both this event and his prediction of eventual annihilation of the Amalekites (vv. 14-15; cf. Num. 24:20).

The subsequent relations between the two nations were far from friendly. Israel still remembered the cunning manner of Amalek's surprise attack (Deut. 25:17; 1 Sam. 15:2). Moreover, the Amalekites won certain battles over the Israelites, especially during Israel's apostate periods during the judgeships of Ehud and Gideon (first as an ally of Eglon of Moab, Judg. 3:13; and then of the Midianites, 6:3, 33; cf. 10:12). The Amalekites may even have owned part of Ephraim (12:15) at the time.

King Saul received the divine command to destroy Amalek, a command he only partially carried out. After a successful campaign, he destroyed all but Agag the Amalekite king and the best of the cattle (1 Sam. 15:9). God then expelled Saul from the throne and had his prophet Samuel execute Agag (vv. 11, 33). (It is interesting to note that when he was wounded by the Philistines, Saul ordered an Amalekite to kill him [2 Sam. 1:8-10, but cf. 1 Sam. 31:4-5] and was refused.)

During his stay with Achish, king of Gath, David made raids on the Amalekites (1 Sam. 27:8-9), but was unable to exterminate them; upon his return to Ziklag from his rejected enlistment in the Philistine army, he discovered that the Amalekites had burned the city and had taken his wives captive (30:1-2). With the Lord's blessings, however, he pursued the raiders. He located them with the help of an Amalekite slave left behind in the desert, and killed all of them (vv. 7-17) except four hundred young men who escaped on camels. This victory enabled him to regain his lost possessions and his two wives, Ahinoam and Abigail.

With the establishment of the Monarchy Israel was able to curb the Amalekite raids (cf. 2 Sam. 8:11-12). The last biblical reference to these nomads is at 1 Chr. 4:42-43, which indicates that five hundred Simeonites at Mt. Seir destroyed "the remnant of the Amalekites" still living in that region.

AMAM [ā'măm] (Heb. *'ᵃmām*). An unidentified town in the Shephelah, allotted to Judah (Josh. 15:26). It may have been near Beer-sheba.

AMANA [ə mā′nə] (Heb. *'ᵃmānâ*). A mountain peak (Cant. 4:8) in the Anti-lebanon range, near the river Amana (or Abana).

AMARIAH [ăm′ə rī′ə] (Heb. *'ᵃmaryâ, 'ᵃmaryāhû* "the Lord has spoken").

1. The son of Meraioth and descendant of Aaron, of the family of Eleazar (1 Chr. 6:7, 52).

2. A priest, the son of Azariah (1 Chr. 6:11), and an ancestor of Ezra (Ezra 7:3).

3. The second son of Hebron, and a Levite of the division of Kohath during the days of David (1 Chr. 23:19).

4. A chief priest during the reign of Jehoshaphat. He was given jurisdiction over the temple service ("all matters of the Lord," 2 Chr. 19:11). He may be the same as **2** above.

5. A Levite during the time of Hezekiah, assigned to distribute the provisions to the levitical cities (2 Chr. 31:15).

6. A contemporary of Ezra, commanded to send away his foreign wife (Ezra 10:42).

7. A postexilic priest, among those setting their seal upon the renewed covenant of Nehemiah (Neh. 10:3). He may be the same as **9** below.

8. A Judahite of the family of Perez; he volunteered to reside at Jerusalem following the Exile (Neh. 11:4).

9. A priest who returned from Babylon with Zerubbabel (Neh. 12:2); member of a priestly family at the time of the high priest Joiakim (v. 13).

10. The son of Hezekiah and ancestor of the prophet Zephaniah (Zeph. 1:1).

AMARNA. *See* TELL EL-AMARNA.

AMARNA [ə mär′nə] **LETTERS.**† Some 379 cuneiform tablets discovered in 1887 at Tell el-Amarna, site of Akhenaten's capital on the east bank of the Nile river approximately 320 km. (200 mi.) south of Cairo. An additional 200 tablets were destroyed shortly after the discovery.

The texts were written primarily in a dialect of Akkadian (with definite Canaanite influence), the diplomatic language of the period. Approximately 350 represent diplomatic correspondence of Pharaohs Amenhotep III and Amenhotep IV (Akhenaten), who ruled *ca.* 1402-1347 B.C., with the rulers of Babylonia, Assyria, Mitanni, Hatti, and especially with vassal city-states in Syria and Palestine. Thus the Amarna Letters shed important light on the political situation of the period, particularly the shifting balance of power between Egypt, the Hittite kingdom in Asia Minor, Hurrian control of Mitanni in the Upper Habur region, the rising Assyrian kingdom, and Kassite-controlled Babylonia.

The letters portray Palestine in chaos as Akhenaten was distracted from the demands of empire by domestic concerns. Thus the various city-states, each under the rule of a local king or chieftain, often came into conflict with each other, frequently accompanied by internal turmoil and open rebellion. Nearly seventy letters from Rib-addi, ruler over the territory from Gebal (Byblos) north to Simyra, reiterate his constant loyalty to Egypt and plead for military aid against the growing revolt sponsored by Abdu-aširta and his son

Aziru, princes of the neighboring Amurru territory; although the Egyptians did send forces against Abdu-aširta, the rebellion resurfaced under Aziru, who captured Gebal and the Egyptian district capital Ṣumur and then, after having convinced the Egyptians of his loyalty, allied with the Hittites. At the same time, Labayu, ruler of Shechem, rebelled against Egypt and, with the assistance of Habiru ('Apiru) elements, gained control of such major sites as Gezer, Megiddo, and cities in the valleys of Dothan and Jezreel and the plain of Sharon.

Of particular interest to Old Testament studies is the role of the Habiru (Akk. 'Apiru, SA.GAZ). Rather than designating an ethnic group, the term (from Sem. *'br* "to cross [a boundary], to transgress [a covenant]") indicates a political movement whereby individuals, groups, and even entire cities rebel against existing loyalties, cast off both privileges and obligations within their original community, and form a new order based on "illegitimate" military and economic force (cf. Rib-addi's reference to the "curs," the sons of Abdu-aširta who "do what they please"). It is

In an Amarna Letter of *ca.* 1350 B.C., a Kassite ruler complains to Akhenaten about a change in Egyptian policy (by courtesy of the Trustees of the British Museum)

precisely such Habiru (thus the name "Hebrew") activity that scholars have associated with the Israelite conquest of Palestine (cf. Jephthah, Judg. 10:17–11:11; cf. also the activities of the outlaw David, 1 Sam. 21–24). *See* HABIRU, 'APIRU.

Bibliography. *ANET,* pp. 483-490; G. E. Mendenhall, *The Tenth Generation* (Baltimore: 1973), pp. 122-141.

AMASA [ə māʹsə] (Heb. *ᶜᵃmāśāʼ*).

1. A nephew of King David, he was the son of Abigail (David's half-sister) and Ithra (2 Sam. 17:25) or Jether (1 Chr. 2:17) the Ishmaelite. He may be the same as AMASAI 2.

During the initial stages of his rebellion against David's rule, Absalom appointed his cousin Amasa over his army (2 Sam. 17:25). Joab, another of David's nephews and cousin to Absalom, remained loyal to the ousted king. Though David's more able army defeated Absalom's forces in the subsequent confrontation, Joab, against the express command of the king, killed the rebel. The king then invited Amasa to become the commander of his own army, using this gesture of goodwill to reunite the various factions of the house of Judah (19:11-15). This act clearly indicated the king's displeasure with Joab's handling of the rebellion, specifically with the murder of his son Absalom.

Upon returning to Jerusalem following Absalom's unsuccessful revolt, David was notified of another uprising in his kingdom. This time a certain Sheba from Benjamin persuaded most of Israel to desert the king (20:1-2). David first sent Amasa to muster the men of Judah (v. 4). The king then summoned Abishai to pursue the rebel Sheba when Amasa failed to return in the stipulated three-day period (vv. 5-6). When Abishai, with Joab, encountered Amasa at the great stone at Gibeon, Joab treacherously murdered Amasa (vv. 8-10). Apparently, he was jealous of Amasa's appointment as chief of the army and resented the king's disregard for his own loyal service. Although Amasa died in great agony among many onlookers, no one came to his relief. Finally someone carried his body into the field and covered it with a garment (vv. 11-12). The gathered people then continued their pursuit of Sheba.

The aged King David did not forget the incident. Upon his deathbed he reminded Solomon of Amasa's murder (1 Kgs. 2:5). When Adonijah attempted a second revolt, the new king ordered Joab's execution, charging that his father's former general had shed the blood of both Amasa and Abner, two men "more righteous and better than himself" (v. 32).

2. The son of Hadlai from Ephraim. He was among those who opposed their fellow Israelites by showing mercy to the captured men of Judah (2 Chr. 28:12-15).

AMASAI [ə māʹsī] (Heb. *ᶜᵃmāśay*).

1. A Levite, the son of Elkanah, and an ancestor of Samuel (1 Chr. 6:25, 35).

2. Chief of the thirty mighty men of David who came to him in Ziklag along with some of the men of Benjamin and Judah (1 Chr. 12:16-18). He is perhaps the same person as Amasa, the son of Abigail and Ithra.

3. One of the priests who blew the trumpet when the ark was returned to Jerusalem (1 Chr. 15:24).

4. The father of Mahath and contemporary of King Hezekiah (2 Chr. 29:12); although often identified with **1** above, this Amasai lived much later.

AMASHSAI [ə mǎshʹsī] (Heb. *ᶜᵃmaššay*). A priest living in Jerusalem during the time of Nehemiah. He was the son of Azarel (Neh. 11:13; KJV "Amashai"), possibly identical to Maasai (1 Chr. 9:12).

AMASIAH [ǎmʹə sīʹə] (Heb. *ᶜᵃmasyâ* "the Lord has borne"). The son of Zichri of Judah, a volunteer servant of the Lord and a commander over two hundred thousand soldiers (2 Chr. 17:16).

AMAW [āʹmô] (Heb. *ʼammô*).* Homeland of Balaam, west of the Euphrates (Num. 22:5; KJV "the children of his people"). Its capital was Emar, approximately 80 km. (50 mi.) south of Carchemish and southwest of Balaam's city, Pethor (Akk. Pitru). According to the Idrimi inscription, some two centuries earlier (*ca.* 1450 B.C.) Amaw was under the control of Alalakh.

AMAZIAH [ǎm ə zīʹə] (Heb. *ᶜᵃmaṣyâ, ᶜᵃmaṣyāhû* "Yahweh is strong").

1. The eighth king of Judah during the divided monarchy, the son of Joash and Jehoaddan (also Jehoaddin; 2 Kgs. 14:1 par. 2 Chr. 25:1). He ascended to the throne at the age of twenty-five and according to the writers of both 2 Kings (14:2) and 2 Chronicles (25:1) he reigned in Jerusalem twenty-nine years. This would have required that he outlive Joash of Israel by some fifteen years (2 Chr. 25:25), which he probably did not do. It is possible, though, that he reigned twenty-nine years (*ca.* 796-767 B.C.) with his son as coregent for a time.

Having executed his father's assassins (though not their children in accordance with the precepts of Deut. 24:16; 2 Kgs. 14:5-6), Amaziah turned to a plan to recapture Edom, which had been subject to Judah for many years but had been independent since the reign of Jehoram. According to the more extensive account of 2 Chronicles, the king mustered the army of Judah and hired an additional one hundred thousand Israelite soldiers; the Israelites, however, he sent back home in response to a prophet's command (25:5-10). He then led his army to the valley of Salt where he slaughtered ten thousand men of Seir (v. 11; cf. 2 Kgs. 14:7). Next, he marched to Sela (Petra) and won another great victory; here his soldiers even threw many of their captives down to their deaths against the rocky terrain (2 Chr. 25:12; cf. 2 Kgs. 14:7, "took Sela by storm").

Audacious with the successful outcome of his campaign, Amaziah sought a match with Jehoash of Israel (2 Kgs. 14:8). Jehoash declined to fight, or at least attempted to decline by answering Amaziah with a parable about a thistle (vv. 9-10). Judah's king refused to be dissuaded. In the clash with his northern neighbor Amaziah suffered a disastrous defeat at Beth-shemesh in Judah (vv. 11-13). He was powerless against Jehoash, who marched to Jerusalem, broke down part of its wall, and took the temple treasures and those of the royal palace. Freed by his captor, Amaziah then witnessed Jehoash's departure to Samaria with all the booty he had appropriated (vv. 13-14).

2 Chronicles gives Amaziah's defeat a theological perspective. Though at the beginning of his reign he behaved as Yahweh would have him (2 Chr. 25:2), the king returned from his victory over Edom worshipping the Edomite deities, thus provoking the Lord (vv. 14-15). The war with Jehoash and Amaziah's defeat are presented as the result of religious apostasy (v. 20).

Deeply humiliated, the king spent the last years of his reign in misery. The length of that period (fifteen years after the death of Jehoash of Israel, according to 2 Kgs. 14:17 par.) did not outweigh the magnitude of Amaziah's grief and fear. A conspiracy against him assumed ominous dimensions, and he was forced to flee to Lachish (v. 19 par.). Even at Lachish he was not safe, and his pursuers killed him there. His opponents returned his body to Jerusalem in a funeral procession, and he was given a royal burial (v. 20).

While Amaziah is mentioned among the descendants of Solomon (1 Chr. 3:12), his name is absent from the genealogy of Jesus (cf. Matt. 1:8).

2. A man from the tribe of Simeon who was the father of Joshah (1 Chr. 4:34).

3. An ancestor of Ethan, a Levite and temple singer appointed by King David (1 Chr. 6:45).

4. A priest at Bethel, who reported to Jeroboam II of Israel that Amos, the prophet of Judah, had conspired against the king (Amos 7:10-11). When he subsequently tried to oust Amos from Bethel (v. 13), Amos pronounced doom for the northern kingdom and foretold a shameful future for Amaziah himself (vv. 14-17).

AMBER (Heb. *ḥašmal*). A yellowish to brownish translucent fossil resin used for making ornamental objects (Ezek. 1:4, 27; 8:2, KJV; RSV "gleaming bronze"). *See* ELECTRUM.

AMEN [ä′měn′, ā′měn′] (Heb. *'āmēn,* from *'mn* niphal "be firm, reliable"; hiphil "believe, trust in"; Gk. *amḗn*). An exclamation of affirmation or endorsement, frequently used in liturgical contexts.

I. Old Testament

Other than its use as a noun at Isa. 65:16 ("God of truth"; NEB "God of Amen"), Heb. *'āmēn* is an interjection with the meaning "so be it." Uttered in response to another's statement, it indicates agreement or acceptance of the message or command. Thus Benaiah affirms David's promise concerning Solomon's future reign (1 Kgs. 1:36); and, although he may have doubted its actual fulfillment, Jeremiah responds with the wish that Hananiah's prophecy might be fulfilled (Jer. 28:6). "Amen" is frequently used as an endorsement of a covenant (cf. Jer. 11:5), and those who ratify such a relationship accept the appropriate sanctions, whether blessings or curses, upon their obedience or disobedience to the attendant stipulations (e.g., Deut. 27:15-26; Neh. 5:13; cf. Num. 5:22). It may follow a doxology or prayer as a congregational response in worship (e.g., 1 Chr. 16:36; Neh. 8:6) or at the end of a Psalm (Ps. 106:48; note the doxologies

ending four of the five divisions of the book of Psalms; Pss. 41:13; 72:19; 89:52; 106:48).

II. New Testament

In the New Testament "Amen" is spoken in response to the promise of the risen Lord (Rev. 22:20) and a vision of judgment (1:7) as well as to doxologies (v. 6; 5:14). In the Epistles it is written frequently at the conclusion of a doxology (e.g., Rom. 1:25; 9:5; 11:36; 16:27; Gal. 1:5; Phil. 4:20; 1 Tim. 1:17; 1 Pet. 4:11; 5:11) and also as a final blessing concluding the letter (Heb. 13:21; 2 Pet. 3:18; Jude 25). In liturgical use "the Amen" was a standard response (1 Cor. 14:16), uttered in Jesus' name (cf. 2 Cor. 1:20).

As a testimony to their truth and efficacy, Jesus frequently prefaces his remarks with the statement "Truly, truly (Gk. *amḗn*) I say to you" (e.g., Matt. 5:18, 26; John 1:51). He is himself called "the Amen, the faithful and true witness" (Rev. 3:14; cf. Isa. 65:16, NEB).

Bibliography. H. Schlier, "ἀμήν," *TDNT* 1 (1964): 335-38; A. Jepsen, "'āman," *TDOT* 1, rev. ed. (1977): 320-22; H. Bietenhard, "Amen," *DNTT* 1:97-99.

AMENEMOPE [ä′měn ěm′ō pē], **INSTRUCTION OF.**† The collected teachings of Amenemope (also rendered Amen-em-opet) son of Ka-nakht, a minor official and member of Egyptian wisdom circles. Although its anthological nature (typical of much wisdom literature) makes possible a date within the range *ca.* 950-650 B.C., its composition can probably be assigned to the seventh-sixth centuries because of the humbler, less materialistic nature of the writings, in contrast to much of the earlier Egyptian wisdom. The Instruction bears great similarity to the book of Proverbs, particularly Prov. 22:17–23:11, and most scholars accept its (at least indirect) influence on the biblical book. *See* WISDOM LITERATURE.

AMETHYST (Heb. *'aḥlāmâ;* Gk. *amethýstos*). A type of crystalized quartz, deep purple or the color of red wine. It was used in beads in ancient Palestine and in amulets by the Egyptians. In the breastpiece of the high priest it was the third stone in the third row of precious stones (Exod. 28:19; 39:12) and the twelfth jewel in the foundation of the walls of the new Jerusalem (Rev. 21:20).

AMI [ā′mī] (Heb. *'āmî*). An ancestor of a family of "Solomon's servants" (Ezra 2:57), probably the same as AMON 3 (Neh. 7:59).

AMINADAB (Matt. 1:4, KJV). *See* AMMINADAB 1.

AMITTAI [ə mit′ī] (Heb. *'ᵃmittay* "loyal"). The father of the prophet Jonah, from Gath-hepher in the tribe of Zebulun (2 Kgs. 14:25; Jonah 1:1).

AMMAH [ăm′ə] (Heb. *'ammâ*). A hill near Giah, "on the way to the wilderness of Gibeon" (2 Sam. 2:24), where Abner made a truce with Joab his pursuer (vv. 26-28).

AMMI [ăm′ī] (Heb. *'ammî* "my people"). A name given to Israel symbolizing divine acceptance (Hos.

2:1, KJV; RSV, NIV "My people"), in contrast to the name "Not My People" (Heb. *lō' 'ammî*; 1:9), which signified divine rejection of God's people. *See* LO-AMMI

AMMIEL [ăm'ï əl] (Heb. *'ammî'ēl* "my kinsman is God").
1. The son of Gemalli, of the tribe of Dan. He was one of the twelve men sent to spy out Canaan (Num. 13:12).
2. The father of Machir, from Lo-debar in the tribe of Manasseh (2 Sam. 9:4; 17:27).
3. The father of Uriah's wife Bathsheba who later became the wife of David (1 Chr. 3:5). As the result of a transposition of the consonants, the name appears at 2 Sam. 11:3 as Eliam.
4. The sixth son of Obed-edom and a gatekeeper in the temple (1 Chr. 26:5).

AMMIHUD [ə mī'hŭd] (Heb. *'ammîhûd* "my kinsman is exalted").
1. The father of Elishama of Ephraim (Num. 1:10; 2:18; 7:48, 53; 10:22), and an ancestor of Joshua (1 Chr. 7:26).
2. The father of Shemuel, who represented the tribe of Simeon in the division of the land of Canaan (Num. 34:20).
3. The father of Pedahel of the tribe of Naphtali, who assisted in the division of the land (Num. 34:28).
4. The father of King Talmai of Geshur (2 Sam. 13:37; so KJV, RSV; NEB follows MT *'ammîhûr*) and grandfather of Absalom (3:3).
5. One of the returning exiles, a member of the family of Perez the son of Judah; he was the father of Uthai (1 Chr. 9:4).

AMMINADAB [ə mĭn'ə dăb] (Heb. *'ammînādāb* "my kinsman is generous").
1. The father of Nahshon (Num. 1:7) and of Elisheba the wife of Aaron (Exod. 6:23). He was an ancestor of King David (Ruth 4:19) and is mentioned in the genealogies of Jesus (Matt. 1:4; Luke 3:33; KJV follows Gk. *Aminadab*).
2. A Levite, the son of Kohath and father of Korah (1 Chr. 6:22); called Izhar in parallel lists (Exod. 6:21; Num. 16:1; 1 Chr. 6:38).
3. A chief of the levitical family of Uzziel. Along with 112 of his kinsmen he was commissioned by David to carry the ark to Jerusalem (1 Chr. 15:10).
4. The name of several Ammonite kings. *See* AMMON, AMMONITES.

AMMINADIB [ə mĭn'ə dĭb] (Heb. *'ammî-nādîb*). Rendered as a personal name by the KJV (see NIV mg.) at Cant. 6:12, following the LXX and Vulgate. Generally regarded as one of the most difficult texts in the book, it has been rendered in various ways: RSV "in a chariot beside my prince"; JB "on the chariots of my people (Heb. *'ammî*) as their prince (Heb. *nādîb*)."

AMMISHADDAI [ăm'ï shăd'ï] (Heb. *'ammîšadday* "people of the Almighty" or "Shaddai is my kinsman"). The father of Ahiezer of the tribe of Dan (Num. 1:12; 2:25; 7:66, 71; 10:25).

AMMIZABAD [ə mĭz'ə băd] (Heb. *'ammîzābād* "my kinsman has given"). The son of Benaiah, one of David's thirty mighty men. He served as commander of the division for the third month (1 Chr. 27:6, RSV, NIV; KJV "and in his course was Ammizabad his son"; cf. JB).

AMMON [ăm'ən] (Heb. *'ammôn*); **AMMONITES** [ăm'ə nīts] (Heb. *'ammônîm*).† A Semitic people traditionally designated the descendants of Ben-ammi (lit. "son of my people") the son of Lot by his younger daughter (Gen. 19:38); they were considered kinsmen of the Moabites (v. 37) and the Israelites (cf. Deut. 2:19). The territory of Ammon lay to the northeast of the Dead Sea, between the Arnon and Jabbok rivers (Ps. 83:7). Its capital was Rabbath-ammon (modern Amman; *see* RABBAH 2).

I. History

Early in their history (*ca.* 1600 B.C. or even earlier) the Ammonites occupied the territory of the Zamzummim (Deut. 2:20-21). Some scholars contend that at this time the Ammonites were not completely sedentary, and their boundaries seem to have overlapped those of the Amorites. At any rate, Sihon king of the Amorites subsequently captured part of their territory (Num. 21:26-28; Josh. 12:2; 13:10). It was this same king who denied the Israelites passage through his land in the mid-thirteenth century; Israel then defeated him and occupied his territory, but they did not encroach upon the Ammonites (Num. 21:21-25; cf. Deut. 2:19, 37; 3:16; Josh. 13:10, 24-28; cf. Num. 21:24, RSV mg. "the boundary of the Ammonites was strong"). Although Num. 22–24 does not mention their involvement, the Ammonites along with the Moabites were later prohibited from entering the assembly of the Lord because they had hired the diviner Balaam to curse Israel (Deut. 23:3-6; Neh. 13:1-2).

By the time of the Judges the Ammonite state had gained significant strength, and its aggressive military had twice brought it into contact with Israel. The Ammonites joined with the Moabites and Amalekites in regaining for Eglon of Moab some of the Transjordanian territory occupied by Israel; Israel thus came under Moabite control (Judg. 3:12-14). Ammonite religious influence was evident in Palestine at this time (Judg. 10:6), and the Ammonites invaded the territory of Gilead and also waged war with Benjamin and Ephraim before being driven back by Jephthah (10:7–11:33).

In the late eleventh century Nahash king of the Ammonites attempted to capture Israel's Transjordanian territory, advancing as far north as Jabesh-gilead (1 Sam. 11:1-2). Saul established his military authority by decisively defeating him (vv. 5-11; 12:12; cf. 14:47-48). David's relationship with Nahash was cordial (2 Sam. 10:2), but the Ammonite king's son Hanun renewed the hostilities, enlisting military aid from the Syrian states of Beth-rehob, Zobah, Maacah, and Tob (v. 6; 1 Chr. 19:6). David's forces under Abishai and Joab subdued both Aram and Ammon, making them vassals of the Israelite empire; Rabbah was captured and the people subjected to forced labor (2 Sam. 10:9-14; 11:1; 12:26-31).

Throughout the united monarchy the territory remained under an Ammonite governor. When David fled Absalom he was aided by Shobi the son of Nahash (2 Sam. 17:27-29), and Zelek was one of his thirty mighty men (23:37). Solomon included Ammonite women in his harem, including Naamah the mother of his successor Rehoboam (1 Kgs. 11:1; 14:21, 31; 2 Chr. 12:13); these women were instrumental in furthering the worship of the Ammonite god Milcom (Molech) among the Israelites (vv. 5, 7, 33).

During the reign of Jehoshaphat, the Ammonites allied themselves with the Arameans in halting the Assyrian invasion at the battle of Qarqar (853) and then, with the Moabites and Meunim, sought unsuccessfully to impede Judah's military and commercial endeavors (2 Chr. 20:1-30). Later they were forced to pay tribute to Uzziah and Jotham of Judah (26:8; 27:5).

In the eighth century resurgent Assyria became a threat from the northeast. Tiglath-pileser III subdued the Ammonites (733), though he permitted them to retain their own dynasty. Although for the next century they remained faithful tributaries, the Ammonites capitalized upon the feud between Assurbanipal and his brother Šamaš-šum-ukin (ca. 652-648) to assert their independence. In the latter part of the seventh century they were able to taunt Judah (Zeph. 2:8), and turned their energies to the recapture of territory from Gad (Jer. 49:1; cf. Ps. 83:7; Amos 1:13). With the breakup of the Assyrian Empire came widespread attacks by Arab groups, and the Ammonites became Babylonian vassals in return for protection (cf. 2 Kgs. 24:2). Soon, however, they joined neighboring states in conspiring against Babylon (Jer. 27:3). After the fall of Jerusalem in 587/586, the Ammonites provoked further trouble; King Baalis sent Ishmael to Jerusalem to murder the Babylonian governor Gedaliah (Jer. 40:14; cf. 41:11-15). Nebuchadnezzar retaliated (cf. Ezek. 21:19-22), and apparently the Ammonites were sent into exile, thus ending their existence as an independent state.

References to Ammonites following the Exile reflect an entirely different constituency. Nehemiah (ca. 440) was met with considerable opposition by Tobiah (probably the governor of the Persian province of Ammon), who helped to impede the rebuilding of the walls of Jerusalem (Neh. 2:10, 19; 4:3, 7; 6:1). Many of the postexilic Jewish populace had intermarried with Ammonites (13:23-31; cf. Ezra 9:1-2).

During the Hellenistic period Ammon came under Ptolemaic control. The sizable Jewish populace living among the Ammonites was decimated when Judas Maccabeus routed the forces of Timotheus and captured the Ammonite city of Jazer and its environs (ca. 165 B.C.; 1 Macc. 5:6-8, 13). During the first century B.C. Ammon was incorporated into the Nabatean kingdom, and shortly afterward it became part of the Roman Empire.

II. Archaeological Evidence

Excavations at Amman and other sites indicate the presence of a sedentary population as early as 1800 B.C. The extensive contents of a Late Bronze Age (1600-1200) temple discovered at Amman reflect a new, more sophisticated population (cf. Deut. 2:20-21). Indicative of the strength of the Ammonite state in the Iron Age are a series of at least nineteen massive border fortresses (cf. Num. 21:24, RSV mg.). The most extensive finds are from the seventh-sixth centuries — clearly the golden age of Ammonite civilization — and indicate a higher level of culture than in neighboring states including Judah and Israel.

The considerable inscriptional evidence indicates that the Ammonite language was closely related to Hebrew and demonstrates a distinctive Ammonite "national" script after the eighth century. A ninth-century stele discovered at the Amman citadel commemorates the construction of a temple to the chief Ammonite god Milcom (named also on two seals). A fifth-century inscription on a bronze bottle discovered at Tell Sīrān mentions a King Amminadab, and a seventh-century seal names a King Hananel (cf. Hanun, 2 Sam. 10:2-4). Personal names on other seals indicate Arab influence as early as the sixth century, and Greek and Latin inscriptions from Amman point to Arab (Nabatean) dominance by the second century B.C.

AMNON [ăm′nŏn] (Heb. *'amnôn* "trustworthy").

1. The eldest son of David; his mother was Ahinoam of Jezreel (2 Sam. 3:2 par. 1 Chr. 3:1). He raped his half sister Tamar, an atrocity for which he was killed two years later by Absalom, Tamar's full brother (2 Sam. 13).

2. One of the sons of Shimon, and a distant relative of Judah (1 Chr. 4:20).

AMOK [ā′mŏk] (Heb. *'amôq* "deep"). One of the priests and heads of families returning with Zerubbabel from exile (Neh. 12:7); an ancestor of Eber, a priest in the days of the high priest Joiakim (v. 20).

AMON (DEITY). The Egyptian god of the wind (Jer. 46:25); as Amon-Re he was the supreme god of the Egyptian Empire.

AMON [ăm′ən] (Heb. *'āmôn* "trustworthy") **(PERSON).**

1. The son and successor of Manasseh king of Judah (641-639 B.C.); his mother was Meshullemeth. Following his father's idolatrous example, he forsook the worship of Yahweh (2 Kgs. 21:20-22; cf. 2 Chr. 33:22-23). In the second year of his reign, when he was twenty-four years old, his servants conspired and murdered him; they in turn were killed by the "people of the land," who placed on the throne Amon's eight-year-old son Josiah (2 Kgs. 21:23-26; 2 Chr. 33:24-25).

In the New Testament genealogies he is called Amos (Matt. 1:10; Luke 3:25).

2. A governor of Samaria to whom King Ahab committed for imprisonment the prophet Micaiah, who had predicted the king's death in the campaign against Ramoth-gilead (1 Kgs. 22:26 par. 2 Chr. 18:25).

3. A descendant of Solomon's servants who returned to Judah following the Exile (Neh. 7:59); at Ezra 2:57 he is called Ami.

AMORITES [ăm'ə rīts] (Heb. 'ᵉmōrî; from Akk. amurrū "the West, Westerners").† A West Semitic people, named after their tutelary deity (Sum. martu); in Akkadian literature the term also designates the territory of their supposed origins, the desert to the west of Mesopotamia, and in later usage it refers to Syria-Palestine.

As early as the late third millennium B.C. Amorites are mentioned as desert nomads (considered by the Sumerians to be barbarians) living in the region of Palmyra. During the transition from the Early Bronze Age to Middle Bronze I (ca. twenty-third–twenty-first centuries) large groups of Amorites penetrated all parts of the Fertile Crescent. At this time they began to infiltrate Babylonia, where they settled en masse following the collapse of the Third Dynasty of Ur (ca. 1936). Babylon came under Amorite control, the First Dynasty of Babylon, whose most famous ruler was Hammurabi (1792-1750), who headed a coalition of ten Amorite city-states; Amorite control of Babylon ended in 1595 at the hands of the Hittites. More than twenty thousand Akkadian texts document the contemporary Amorite civilization at Mari, modern Tell Hariri on the western bank of the Euphrates; of particular interest for biblical studies are various transhumant tribal federations (basically sedentary pastoralists, segments of whom may have "migrated" seasonally in reaction to climatic and topographical conditions) such as the Bene-Yamina (Benjaminites, lit. "southerners"). Fourteenth-century Egyptian and cuneiform texts refer to an Amorite kingdom in Syria, ranging from Sidon and Damascus north to Arvad. The Amarna Letters mention several Amorite city-states and note their frequent association with Habiru ('Apiru) forces. Although the name Amorite survived as a geographical designation as late as the seventh century, Amorite political power essentially ceased ca. 1000 with the advance of Aramean influence in Syria and Mesopotamia.

The presence of Amorites in Syria and Palestine has been attested in the late third millennium, and the journeys of Abraham have been associated with the extensive Amorite movements ca. 2100-1800. The Old Testament uses the term Amorite as a designation of the pre-Israelite inhabitants of Palestine in general (Gen. 15:16; Josh. 24:15; Judg. 6:10; 1 Kgs. 21:26; cf. Amos 2:9-10). In a narrower sense the term indicates the inhabitants of the hill country of Canaan (Num. 13:29; Deut. 1:7). Biblical use of the name reflects the complex ethnic and sociopolitical nature of Palestine in the Middle Bronze Age (cf. Ezek. 16:3, 45); indeed, by the time of the Israelite conquest the terms Amorite and Canaanite were virtually indistinguishable (cf. Gen. 10:16). Victories over Sihon king of Heshbon and Og king of Bashan, rulers of Amorite city-states east of the Jordan, were a significant factor in the early stages of the Conquest (Num. 21:21-35; Deut. 2:24–3:11; 4:47; Josh. 2:10; 9:10; Ps. 135:11; 136:17-22). Subsequently Joshua confronted Amorites west of the Jordan, defeating the forces of Ai (Josh. 7:7) as well as coalitions such as that headed by the Amorite kings of Jerusalem, Hebron, Jarmuth, La-chish, and Eglon at Gibeon (10:1-27) and the northern Amorites supporting Jabin at Hazor (11:1-14). A remnant of the Amorite population survived in peaceful coexistence with Israel (1 Sam. 7:14; 2 Sam. 21:2; cf. Ezra 9:1), although Solomon subjected them to forced labor (1 Kgs. 9:20-21 par. 2 Chr. 8:7-8).

Because of their association with other deities, Israelite tradition depicts the Amorites as evil (Gen. 15:16; Judg. 6:10; 1 Kgs. 21:26; 2 Kgs. 21:22; cf. Lev. 18:28; 20:22-23; Josh. 24:15).

Bibliography. A. Haldar, Who Were the Amorites? (Leiden: 1971); K. M. Kenyon, Amorites and Canaanites (New York: 1966).

AMOS [ā'məs] (Heb. 'āmôs "burden-bearer").
1. A prophet of the eighth century B.C. whose book is included among the Minor Prophets. He was a native of Tekoa (Amos 1:1), a village some 10 km. (6 mi.) south of Bethlehem overlooking the wilderness of Judah. Amos was not a member of a prophetic guild in training to be a professional prophet (7:14), but was instead a sheep breeder by profession (by no means an undistinguished position; cf. King Mesha of Moab, 2 Kgs. 3:4). As such he probably journeyed with other local sheep breeders to cities such as Jerusalem and Samaria to sell his sheep and wool in the marketplaces. Amos was also a dresser of sycamore trees (Ficus sycomorus L.; Amos 7:14), the fruit of which resembles figs and must be pierced or slit shortly before ripening in order to be edible. It is likely that he owned some property in western Judah (the Shephelah) where such trees were found (1 Kgs. 10:27), since they did not grow near Tekoa. He was thus a landowner who dwelt in the countryside, a background reflected in the rustic images he employs in his prophecy (cf. Amos 3:4, 8, 12; 4:1; 5:8, 19).
2. An ancestor of Jesus (Matt. 1:10; Luke 3:25). See AMON (PERSONS) **1.**

AMOS, BOOK OF.† The third book of the Minor Prophets, chronologically the first of the writing prophets.

I. Date

According to Amos 1:1, the ministry of Amos took place during the reigns of King Uzziah (Azariah) of Judah (783-742 B.C.) and Jeroboam II of Israel (779-747). Because of Uzziah's leprosy, Jotham acted as coregent after ca. 750. Thus, a likely date for Amos' activity was between 760 and 750. His call to be a prophet came "two years before the earthquake" (1:1). Although it is of no help in dating the prophecies more precisely, this must have been a significant event, for it is still alluded to two centuries later, after the Exile, by the prophet Zechariah (Zech. 14:5). According to Josephus, this earthquake resulted when Uzziah himself tried to make an incense offering in the temple but was prevented from doing so by Azariah the priest (Ant. ix.10.4 [223-25]; 2 Chr. 26:16-20).

II. Setting

The period in which Amos prophesied was a time of great prosperity for both Judah and Israel (2 Kgs. 14:23-29; 2 Chr. 26), yet also a time of great excess as well as social and religious decay. In 805 the Assyrians under Adad-nirari III had overwhelmed Damascus, Israel's northern neighbor, and both Uzziah and Jeroboam II capitalized on the absence of the Syrian threat by expanding their borders almost to those of David and Solomon. Israel's control of major trade routes led to the development of a rich merchant class, who shared their wealth with the nobility at the expense of the masses, particularly the small farmers and the peasants. It is to these conditions in the northern kingdom that the Lord called Amos away from following his sheep, saying: "Go, prophesy to my people Israel" (Amos 7:15; cf. 3:8).

III. Contents

At the forefront of Amos' prophecies stand his stinging denunciations of Israel's social sins, particularly the oppression and extortion of the poor by the rich (2:6-12; 3:10, 15; 4:1; 6:4-6). The brutal insensitivity to human concerns which marked the widening gap between social classes is painted in no uncertain terms. The rich "trample upon the poor" (5:11; cf. 2:6, 8), yet "are not grieved over the ruin of Joseph" (6:6). They revel in opulent luxury (3:15; 6:4-6), goaded on by their fat and pampered wives ("cows of Bashan," 4:1). Justice is available only for those who can afford it (2:6; 5:12), and the poor are at the mercy of fraudulent merchants and moneylenders (5:11-12; 8:4-6).

At the heart of Israel's social sickness was their abandonment of the principles of the covenant with the Lord. Amos decries the outward evidence of abuses in ritual and worship (2:8; 4:4-5; 5:21-24), particularly their adoption of pagan practices (8:14) and their contribution to the plight of the poor (2:8; 5:11). He is especially critical of the royal shrine at Bethel (3:15; 7:7-17; 9:1). But even more than reform of cultic practices, Amos stresses the need for a radical cleansing of Israel's whole life, a return to the behavior demanded of the people of God.

Amos conveys oracles of the Lord's judgment, which was to come directly upon Israel. It would come not only upon Damascus, Gaza, Tyre, Edom, Ammon, and Moab (1:3–2:3), nor only to Judah (2:4-5). Indeed, it would come upon the whole family of the Israelites whom the Lord had brought forth out of the land of Egypt (2:6-16; 3:1-2). Amos had to combat the pious self-assurance of those who looked forward to the day of the Lord with the firm conviction that this would be the day of triumph over Israel's enemies, forgetting that they themselves, as the people of God, would be subject to even more severe judgment for their sins (5:18-20; 6:1).

The prophet reports various visions of Israel's coming doom, probably revealed to him even before he departed to preach in the northern kingdom. In the first two, the visions of the locusts and the devouring fire, Amos' pleas on behalf of Israel caused the Lord to repent and withhold action (7:1-6). The vision of the plumb line (vv. 7-9), probably reported to the crowds celebrating the autumn festival as they pressed around the golden calf that had been set up by Jeroboam I (922-901), aroused the wrath of Amaziah the priest, who chased Amos out of Bethel and reported him to Jeroboam II (vv. 10-13).

IV. Theology

Frequently, though somewhat unfairly, Amos is called the prophet of wrath, in contrast to Hosea the prophet of love. The demand that all which interferes with Israel's perfect relationship with God be completely obliterated stems from Amos' understanding of the people's covenant responsibility (3:2) and his concept of God as ever active in nature (4:6-13; 5:8; 9:6, 13) and history (1:3–2:3, 9; 6:14; 9:7).

However, Amos did not prophesy only of calamity. His message held ever open the possibility of Israel's repentance (5:4, 15) and contained the seeds for the doctrine of a faithful remnant (9:8). Indeed, Amos heralded the restoration of Israel's fortunes, the raising up of the fallen "booth of David" (9:11-15), salvation in the promised Messiah. The character of this message of salvation has prompted some to argue that this material was not an original part of the prophecy of Amos, but no justifiable basis exists for this. Throughout the preexilic prophecies of judgment are scattered promises of salvation.

V. Composition

In all likelihood, Amos returned to Judah after having proclaimed judgment upon Amaziah and committed his prophecies to writing in Tekoa. Whether he did the writing himself or a scribe wrote at his dictation cannot be ascertained and is unimportant. Apart from the superscription at 1:1 and the biographical material in 7:10-17, which speak of Amos in the third person, later supplementation of the text has not been proven; such arguments generally are based on matters of content rather than of style.

The book falls naturally into three sections:

A. Chs. 1–2: the proclamation of judgment upon various nations, culminating in the judgment upon Judah and Israel. Each of the eight indictments begins with the formula "For three transgressions of. . . , and for four. . . ."

B. Chs. 3–6: the castigation of the sins of Israel. After an introduction (3:1-8), Israel is reproached especially for cultic and social sins. Three of the discourses are introduced by the formula "Hear this word" (3:1; 4:1; 5:1), and successive oracles in chs. 5–6 begin with "Woe" (5:18; 6:1, 4). Also, the statement, " 'Yet you did not return to me,' says the Lord" occurs five times (4:6, 8-11).

C. Chs. 7–9: five visions of judgment — locusts (7:1-2), devouring fire (vv. 4-6), the plumb line (vv. 7-9), a basket of summer fruit (8:1-14), and destruction of the altar and sanctuary (9:1-10). The story of Amos at Bethel and what took place subsequently is placed in the middle of this (7:10-17). The book ends with a prophecy of salvation, depicting the fallen booth of David and its restoration (9:11-15).

Bibliography. R. S. Cripps, *A Critical and Exegetical Commentary on the Book of Amos,* 2nd ed. (London: 1955); J. L. Mays, *Amos, A Commentary.* OTL (1969); J. D. W. Watts, *Vision and Prophecy in Amos* (Grand Rapids: 1958); H. W. Wolff, *Joel and Amos.* Hermeneia (Philadelphia: 1977).

AMOZ [ā′mŏz] (Heb. *'āmôṣ* "strong"). The father of the prophet Isaiah (2 Kgs. 19:2; Isa. 1:1).

AMPHIPOLIS [ăm fĭp'ə lĭs] (Gk. *Amphipolis* "around the city"). A city in Macedonia located near the mouth of the river Strymon. It was an important station along the Via Egnatia, which ran along Macedonia's southern coast from Thrace. Colonized by the Athenians in 437 B.C., it surrendered to the Spartans in 424. The city was conquered in 357 by Philip of Macedon and in 168 B.C. by the Romans, who made it the capital of the first Macedonian district.

During his second missionary journey, Paul passed through Amphipolis before visiting Thessalonica (Acts 17:1).

AMPLIAS. *See* AMPLIATUS.

AMPLIATUS [ăm'plĭ ā'təs] (Gk. *Ampliatos*). A member of the Christian community at Rome whom Paul calls affectionately "my beloved in the Lord" (Rom. 16:8; KJV "Amplias," following Gk. *Amplias* in some MSS).

AMRAM [ăm'răm] (Heb. *'amrām* "the people are exalted").†
1. The husband of Jochebed and father of Aaron, Moses, and Miriam (Exod. 6:20; cf. Num. 26:59; 1 Chr. 6:3). Though he is named the first son of Kohath (Exod. 6:18; cf. 1 Chr. 6:2), the designation is probably a more general relationship, i.e., a descendant of Kohath. His marriage with his father's sister Jochebed (Exod. 6:20) preceded the restriction against marriage between blood relatives (Lev. 18:18; 20:19; here too the designation may have the more general sense of a female descendant of Levi. Amram lived 137 years (Exod. 6:20).

In the New Testament Amram and Jochebed are praised for their faith in protecting the infant Moses (Heb. 11:23; cf. Exod. 2:1-2).
2. One of the sons of Bani; he was among those whom Ezra commanded to send away their foreign wives (Ezra 10:34).
3. *See* HAMRAN.

AMRAMITES [ăm'rə mīts] (Heb. *'amrāmî*). Descendants of AMRAM 1, a levitical family responsible for the tabernacle (Num. 3:27) and the temple treasures (1 Chr. 26:23).

AMRAPHEL [ăm'rə fĕl] (Heb. *'amrāpel*).† One of the kings mentioned at Gen. 14:1, 9 who fought against the kings of the Cities of the Plain. He was "king of Shinar," possibly the district of Singar in Upper Mesopotamia.

After twelve years as vassals of the Elamite king Chedorlaomer, the kings of Sodom, Gomorrah, Admah, Zeboiim, and Zoar rebelled (Gen. 14:2-4). Before punishing these disobedient subjects, Chedorlaomer secured the support of his allies, Amraphel, Arioch, and Tidal. Together they subdued various peoples both east and west of the Dead Sea (vv. 5-8), thus preventing a general uprising in the area. Chedorlaomer then faced the five rebellious vassal kings in the Valley of Siddim (v. 8) and defeated them. Returning home, the four victorious allies took much spoil, including Lot and his possessions (vv. 11-12).

When he was informed of these events, Abraham took his trained men and pursued the Mesopotamian raiders from Mamre, near Hebron, to Dan. There he divided his forces, routed the enemy, and chased after them as far as Hobah, north of Damascus, before he was able to effect the release of his nephew Lot (vv. 13-16).

The precise identity of Amraphel remains uncertain. Many scholars have identified him with the Babylonian Hammurabi, but both linguistic and chronological considerations make this impossible.

AMZI [ăm'zī] (Heb. *'amṣî* "my strength"; perhaps an abbreviation of Amaziah "the Lord strengthens").
1. A Levite of the family of Merari; he was the son of Bani and an ancestor of Ethan (1 Chr. 6:46).
2. A priest, the son of Zechariah and an ancestor of Adaiah (Neh. 11:12).

ANAB [ā'năb] (Heb. *'ʿanaḇ* "grape"). One of the cities in the hill country of Judah where Joshua defeated the Anakim (Josh. 11:21; 15:50). It has been identified with Khirbet 'Anâb, approximately 24 km. (15 mi.) southwest of Hebron.

ANAH [ā'nə] (Heb. *'ʿanâ*).
1. The son (so RSV, JB; KJV "daughter," following MT; NIV "granddaughter") of Zibeon the Horite and the father of Oholibamah the wife of Esau (Gen. 36:2, 14, 18; 1 Chr. 1:40). According to Gen. 36:24 he discovered the hot springs (KJV "mules") in the wilderness.
2. The fourth son of Seir the Horite (Gen. 36:20, 29; 1 Chr. 1:38, 41). Textual difficulties make the relationship between Anah 1 and 2 highly uncertain; see the commentaries at Gen. 36:24-25; 1 Chr. 1:40.

ANAHARATH [ə nā'ə răth] (Heb. *'ʿanaʿrāṯ*). A city in the valley of Jezreel assigned to the territory of Issachar (Josh. 19:19). Listed among the towns captured by Thutmose III, it has been identified with en-Na'ûrah, 3.2 km. (2 mi.) south of En-dor.

ANAIAH [ə nā'yə] (Heb. *'ʿanāyâ* "the Lord has answered").
1. One of the six men (probably priests) who stood at Ezra's right hand when he read to the people from the book of the law (Neh. 8:4).
2. A chief who, on behalf of his people, set his seal to the renewed covenant under Nehemiah (Neh. 10:22). He may be the same as 1 above.

ANAK [ā'năk] (Heb. *'ʿanāq* "neck"). The son of Arba and ancestor of Ahiman, Sheshai, and Talmai (Num. 13:22; Josh. 15:13-14; 21:11; Judg. 1:20). The name is also taken as a tribal designation equivalent to the Anakim, regarded as the descendants of Anak.

ANAKIM [ăn'ə kĭm] (Heb. *'ʿanāqîm*). A people (KJV "Anakims"; NIV "Anakites") who traced their ancestry to Anak the son of Arba; this same Arba was regarded as the greatest of their number (Josh. 14:15; 15:13). These pre-Israelite inhabitants of Canaan dwelled in the hill country west of the Jordan (11:21), especially in the region of Hebron (14:12-15).

To the Israelites they appeared to be giants ("great and tall," Deut. 9:2), and the report brought back from Canaan by the twelve spies struck the Israelites with terror (Num. 13:28, 31-33; Deut. 1:28). Moses, however, prophesied that once the Israelites crossed the Jordan they would be victorious over these awesome people (Deut. 9:2-3). Subsequently Joshua eradicated them from all of the Promised Land, except for the Philistine cities of Gath and Ashdod where a few remained (Josh. 11:21-23). It was Caleb who expelled Anak's three sons — Ahiman, Shushai, and Talmai — from Hebron (14:12-15; 15:13-14; Judg. 1:10).

Goliath of Gath (1 Sam. 17:4) and giants mentioned at 2 Sam. 21:16-22 par. 1 Chr. 20:4-8 were probably the last Anakim. At Deut. 2:10, 20-21 the Emim and Zanzummim are compared to the Anakim.

ANAMIM [ăn'ə mĭm] (Heb. *ʿănāmîm*). Descendants of Egypt (Gen. 10:13; 1 Chr. 1:11; KJV "Mizraim"), variously considered to be the Kenemites (of the Knmt oasis west of Egypt), Cyrenians, or inhabitants of the Nile Delta.

See also TABLE OF NATIONS.

ANAMMELECH [ə năm'ə lĕk] (Heb. *ʿănammeleḵ*, possibly from Akk. *Anumalku* "Anu is king"). A Sepharvite deity to whom children were sacrificed (2 Kgs. 17:31). Though older commentators identified the Sepharvites with a Mesopotamian people (e.g., KD), more likely they were Syrians worshipping a Syrian deity, possibly the goddess Anath.

ANAN [ā'nən] (Heb. *ʿānān* "cloud"). One of the chiefs setting his seal to the renewed covenant under Nehemiah (Neh. 10:26).

ANANI [ə nā'nî] (Heb. *ʿănānî* "[Yahweh] has revealed himself"[?]). One of the seven sons of Elioenai, a postexilic descendant of David (1 Chr. 3:24).

ANANIAH [ăn'ə nî'ə] (Heb. *ʿănanyâ* "Yahweh has revealed himself"[?]) (**PERSON**). The father of Maaseiah, whose son Azariah assisted in the rebuilding of the walls of Jerusalem (Neh. 3:23).

ANANIAH [ăn'ə nî'ə] (Heb. *ʿănanyâ* "Yahweh has revealed himself" [?]) (**PLACE**). A town which the Benjaminites resettled after the Exile (Neh. 11:32), perhaps el-ʿAzarîyeh (biblical Bethany), about 3 km. (2 mi.) east of Jerusalem.

ANANIAS [ăn'ə nî'əs] (Gk. *Hananias*, from Heb. *ḥănanyâ* "Yahweh has been gracious").

1. A member of the church at Jerusalem, who with his wife Sapphira shortly after Pentecost sold a piece of land and brought some of the proceeds to the apostles as a gift for the poor; they pretended to have donated the entire amount (Acts 5:1-2), for which God's subsequent judgment was death (vv. 5-10).

Ananias' gift-giving, rather than being motivated by the Holy Spirit, was a sin of pretense motivated by self-glory. The incident contrasts sharply with the spontaneous and heartfelt giving of Barnabas mentioned in Acts 4. The account of Ananias has been likened to the narrative of Achan, who was put to death for having stolen part of the spoil from Jericho (Josh. 7).

The sudden deaths of Ananias and Sapphira, perhaps attributable to shock, are presented as divine judgment upon their fraud (cf. W. Neil, *The Acts of the Apostles*. NCBC [1981], pp. 94-95).

2. A disciple in Damascus who was informed in a vision of Saul's conversion and who assisted the blinded apostle in recovering his eyesight and introduced him to the Christian community at Damascus (Acts 9:10-18). Paul himself spoke with appreciation for this devout man (22:12-16). No additional information about him is given in the New Testament, but later tradition indicates that he became bishop of Damascus and died a martyr's death.

3. The son of Nedebaeus, he was a high priest appointed by Herod Agrippa II (*ca.* A.D. 48). According to Acts 23:2 he ordered the Roman tribune Claudius Lysias to bring Paul before him to ascertain the basis of the Jews' charges against the apostle (22:30). When Paul spoke in his own defense, Ananias ordered him struck on the mouth; Paul sharply retorted, but apologized when told he was addressing the high priest (23:2-5). Five days later Ananias went to Caesarea, where Paul had been taken, to accuse him in person before Felix the governor (24:1).

A proud and greedy person, whose cruelty is well attested (cf. 23:2), Ananias was deposed in A.D. 58; six years earlier the emperor Claudius had acquitted him of charges of oppression of the Samaritans. At the outbreak of the Jewish revolt against Rome (66) he was murdered because of his pro-Roman sympathies (Josephus *BJ* ii.17.9 [441-42]).

ANATH [ā'năth] (Ugar. *ʿnt*) (**DEITY**). A West Semitic deity who in Ugaritic literature was goddess of war and love and was sister and consort of Baal. In Israel she may have been worshipped at Beth-anath and Anathoth.

ANATH [ā'năth] (Heb. *ʿănāṯ*) (**PERSON**). The father of Shamgar the judge (Judg. 3:31; 5:6).

ANATHEMA [ə năth'ə mə] (Gk. *anáthema*, from *anatíthēmi* "to place [or set up] something"). Variously translated in the English versions ("anathema" only at 1 Cor. 16:22, KJV), the term originally referred to the votive offering before a deity (cf. LXX translation of Heb. *ḥērem* at Deut. 7:26, "accursed"; Josh. 7:12, "a thing for destruction," i.e., that which is "consecrated [to God]" or "accursed [devoted to destruction]"). In the New Testament it signifies destruction and moral unworthiness. At Rom. 9:3 Paul wishes to be "accursed" (NIV "cursed"; JB "condemned") and cut off from Christ for the sake of fellow Jews, whereas at Gal. 1:8 he hurls this contemptuous ejaculation at those preaching a false gospel (JB, NIV "condemned"; cf. 1 Cor. 16:22). The phrase "Jesus is cursed" (1 Cor. 12:3; JB "Curse Jesus") is an intensive use of the term by Paul to show that nothing unworthy of Christ can ever originate in the Holy Spirit, even while speaking in tongues. At

Acts 23:14 the term indicates the sanctions of an oath (so RSV, NIV; JB "vow"; KJV "curse").

ANATHOTH [ăn'ə thŏth] (Heb. *ʿanāṯôṯ*, perhaps an abbreviation of Beth-anathoth "house of the great Anath"). A levitical city in the territory of Benjamin (Josh. 21:18; 1 Chr. 6:60), northeast of Jerusalem. Abiathar the priest owned property in this city (1 Kgs. 2:26), and David's heroes Abiezer and Jehu called it their home (2 Sam. 23:27; KJV "Anethothite"; 1 Chr. 12:3; KJV "Antothite"; NIV "Anathothite"). The city, which may have been destroyed by the Babylonians as they marched on Jerusalem (cf. Isa. 10:30), was resettled following the Exile by Benjaminites (Neh. 11:32); the census lists of those returning from exile are unclear as to whether the people of Anathoth are a family group or a geographical designation (Ezra 2:23; Neh. 7:27; cf. 10:19).

The city is perhaps best known as the birthplace of the prophet Jeremiah (Jer. 1:1). Although he responded to his fellow citizens' rejection of his prophecy with the prediction of punishment upon them (11:21-23), the prophet willingly purchased his cousin's field in the city as a "possession and redemption" (32:7-9).

The name of the modern city of ʿAnâtâ, approximately 5 km. (3 mi.) northeast of Jerusalem, is reminiscent of the ancient levitical city, but the site of the biblical city is more likely Râs el-Kharrûbeh, 1 km. (.6 mi.) southwest of ʿAnâtâ.

ANATOLIA [ăn'ə tō'lē ə]. *See* ASIA MINOR.

ANCHOR (Gk. *ángkyra*). Whereas earlier anchors consisted merely of a heavy stone or stones, or wood, the anchor mentioned at Acts 27:29-30, 40 was made of iron and had two flukes. In Luke's account of the rescue attempt at sea, the four anchors were lowered from the stern, which kept the ship carrying Paul pointing toward the harbor.

The spiritual anchor of the soul is the believer's hope, which is "moored" to the unchangeable promise of God (Heb. 6:19).

ANCIENT OF DAYS (Aram. *ʿattîq yômîn*).* A title of God in Daniel's vision of the divine judgment (Dan. 7:9, 13, 22), based in part on the biblical view of God's eternal existence (cf. Ps. 9:7; 29:10; 90:2). The imagery depicts God as the divine judge presiding over the heavenly council (cf. Ps. 82:1; 1 Kgs. 22:19).

ANDREW [ăn'drōo] (Gk. *Andreas* "manly"). A fisherman who followed John the Baptist and then became one of the first disciples of Jesus (John 1:35-40; in lists of the apostles he appears among the first four; Matt. 10:2-4; Mark 3:16-19; Luke 6:14-16; Acts 1:13). According to John, it was he who led his brother Simon Peter to Jesus (vv. 41-42). The Synoptic Gospels indicate that Andrew's call came as he and Simon were fishing at the Sea of Galilee near Capernaum with their business partners Zebedee and his sons James and John (Mark 1:16-20; Luke 5:10).

It was Andrew who informed Jesus about the boy with the loaves and fishes prior to the feeding of the five thousand (John 6:8). On another occasion he relayed to Jesus the inquiries of the Greeks concerning the Messiah (12:22). During the discourse at the Mount of Olives he was among those disciples who asked Jesus about the meaning of the destruction of Jerusalem and the end of time (Mark 13:3).

According to the apocryphal Acts of Andrew he died on a cross; various traditions developed regarding the disposition of his body. Andrew has come to be regarded as the patron saint of both Scotland and Russia.

ANDREW, ACTS OF. One of the five apocryphal acts of the apostles traditionally attributed to Leucias Charinus. It was composed in Greek during the third century A.D. (some would date it *ca.* 190) in Greece or Asia Minor. Probably the longest of the apocryphal acts, the book survives only in fragments of various versions and in a Latin epitome by Gregory of Tours (*ca.* 540-594). It was widely accepted by ascetic sects, particularly the Manicheans, who substituted it for the canonical book of Acts.

The book depicts the travels of Andrew, the brother of Peter, through Greece and western Asia Minor and recounts the various miracles and wonders he performs. In Achaia he cures a blind man, revives a dead man, prays for an earthquake to enable him to avoid unjust sentencing, casts out demons, and heals and subsequently converts a woman afflicted with dropsy. In Nicea, he frees the city and its inhabitants of demons who had been stoning to death passers-by. In Nicomedia he again raises a dead man (the account resembles Luke 7:11-17), and in Thrace he and his traveling companions are protected by an angel who turns away the swords of an attacking army. The ascetic ideal is evident in Andrew's prevention of a wedding at Philippi and in his inciting Maximilla to live a life of chastity away from her husband, the proconsul Aegeates. For the latter interference, Andrew is imprisoned and subsequently crucified. During his incarceration and the three days on the X-shaped cross, Andrew issues a series of discourses. Highly Gnostic in character, they concern the true nature of mankind as a pure spiritual being, whose weakness stems from an evil and deceitful enemy who is opposed to peace, and whose deliverance from sin stems from enlightenment.

Prefixed to Gregory's Latin version is an Egyptian tale, the Acts of Andrew and Matthias, which records various miracles by Andrew, including the rescue of Matthias (Matthew in some versions) from cannibals.

ANDRONICUS [ăn drŏn'ə kəs] (Gk. *Andronikos*).
1. A deputy under Antiochus Epiphanes. *See* MENELAUS.
2. A Jewish Christian, perhaps originally from the Jewish community at Tarsus, and fellow prisoner with Paul. Of those to whom the apostle sends his greetings, Andronicus and Junias are called "men of note among the apostles" (Rom. 16:7).

ANEM [ā'nəm] (Heb. *ʿānēm* "two springs"). A levitical city in the tribal territory of Issachar, given to the Gershomites (1 Chr. 6:73); at Josh. 19:21; 21:29 it is called En-gannim, which has been identified with modern Jenîn. For topographical reasons the site is more likely 'Olam, 11 km. (7 mi.) east of Mt. Tabor, or Khirbet 'Anim, 3 km. (2 mi.) northeast of 'Olam.

ANER [ā'nər] (Heb. *'ānēr*) (PERSON). An Amorite who, with his brothers Mamre and Eshkol, aided Abraham in his battle against the four eastern kings (Gen. 14:13, 24). Like the names of the brothers, Aner may be a geographical designation (cf. ANER (PLACE) below; cf. also 1 Chr. 6:70 [MT 55]).

ANER [ā'nər] (Heb. *'ānēr*) (PLACE). A levitical city in the western allotment of Manasseh (1 Chr. 6:70). On the basis of Josh. 21:25 the name should perhaps be read as Taanach, a city on the southern side of the plain of Jezreel.

ANETHOTHITE (2 Sam. 23:27, KJV). An inhabitant of Anathoth.

ANGEL (Heb. *mal'āk* "messenger"; Gk. *ángelos*; Lat. *angelus*). A spiritual being serving God and supporting mankind.

Heb. *mal'āk* can be used not only in reference to an ordinary messenger (e.g., 1 Kgs. 19:2) but also to a divinely sent messenger (e.g., a prophet [Hag. 1:13], or simply the Lord's messenger [Mal. 3:1]); in the latter sense it often refers to spiritual beings or angels. Other Old Testament names are "sons of God" (Heb. *bᵉnê ha'ᵉlōhîm,* clearly implied at Job 38:7 [parallel to "morning stars"]; NIV "angels"; but *see also* SONS OF GOD), and "holy ones" (Heb. *qᵉdōšîm*; e.g., Job 5:1; Ps. 89:5, 7; so RSV, JB, NIV; KJV "saints"). The most common New Testament term is Gk. *ángelos*, "messenger," which is sometimes applied to human beings (Luke 7:24).

According to Scripture, the angels were created before human beings; at Job 38:7 their presence at the creation of the universe is noted. Despite the occurrence of sin (4:18; RSV, NIV "error"; KJV "folly"; JB "fault"), Satan is still permitted access to God (1:6; NIV "angels"). The Scriptures also distinguish between good or faithful angels and fallen angels or demons.

I. Old Testament

The references to angels are more numerous toward the end than at the beginning of the Old Testament. Although the Old Testament supplies little information about the habitation of the good angels, it does indicate that their main task is to serve God (Ps. 103:21), to praise and glorify him (148:2), and to join battle on his behalf (e.g., Gen. 19:1-29 concerning the angels' role in saving Lot and his family during the destruction of Sodom; Ps. 78:49). Together the angels form the army of the Lord (e.g., Gen. 32:2), which appears at significant moments in the history of salvation and is seen by some of the believers (e.g., Elisha and his servant at Dothan [2 Kgs. 6:16-17], Daniel and Zechariah during the night visions); the name "Lord of hosts" (Heb. *yhwh ṣᵉbā'ôṯ*) can best be understood as designating the Lord of the angelic armies (Gen. 32:1; Josh. 5:14-15). Individual angels are mentioned only a few times: Gabriel and Michael in the book of Daniel (8:16; 9:21; 10:13, 21; 12:1).

The Old Testament also speaks of cherubim (e.g., in the description of Ezekiel's vision, Ezek. 10) and seraphim (e.g., in the vision of Isaiah's calling, Isa. 6:1-7).

The "angel of the Lord" (Heb. *mal'ak yhwh*), also called the "angel of God" or the "angel of his presence" (Isa. 63:9), is sometimes distinguished from God, but at other times they are the same. It is actually God who appears to Hagar in the desert (Gen. 16:7-13; 21:17-20), to Abraham when he is about to sacrifice his son (22:11-18), to Jacob as a man wrestling with him (32:24-30; cf. 31:11-13; Hos. 12:4), and to Moses in the burning bush (Exod. 3:2-6). It is God whom Abraham promises will accompany his steward Eliezer (Gen. 24:7, 20) and who may be "the messenger of the covenant" (Mal. 3:1). In these instances the angel of the Lord shares in the nature and power of God and serves as a medium for the divine manifestation (but cf. Zech. 1:11). At other times this angel is a created being with no special relation to God and thus has no part in divine theophany. Such instances include the angel of destruction (2 Sam. 24:16; 2 Kgs. 19:35; *see* DESTROYER) and the angels who support Elijah in the wilderness (1 Kgs. 19:6-7), appear beside the three men in the fiery furnace (Dan. 3:25, 28), and protect Daniel in the lions' den (6:23). In other cases the nature of this angel is ambiguous, as with the angel who appears to Balaam (Num. 22:22) and the "man" who speaks to Joshua (Josh. 5:13-14).

The angelic task on earth is primarily twofold: angels support God's people (e.g., Jacob's vision at Gen. 28:11-12), and they destroy Israel's enemies (e.g., 2 Kgs. 19:35 par. Isa. 37:36; cf. 2 Chr. 32:21). It is God's angel, also, who strikes David when the king is convicted of sin (2 Sam. 24:16-17). Toward the end of the Old Testament history the angels' tasks include interpreting visions given to prophets (e.g., Zech. 1:9) and pleading with God on behalf of Judah's believers (vv. 12-17).

Angelology is greatly expanded in the Apocrypha, where other individual angels are named: Raphael, Uriel, and Jeremiel. Though some scholars attribute this development to Persian influences or interpret the archangels as dethroned pagan deities, these theories have not as yet been proved. Moreover, the accounts clearly teach that these beings are angels — i.e., spiritual servants or messengers of God.

II. New Testament

In the New Testament angels appear first in accounts of the nativity: they announce to Zechariah the birth of his son (Luke 1:11, 18-20) and to Mary the birth of her son (vv. 26-38); they assure Joseph of Mary's faithfulness to him, inform him about her son, and instruct him to take her as his wife (Matt. 1:20-21). After Jesus' birth they proclaim the good news to the shepherds and praise God (Luke 2:9-15). They appear again during Jesus' earthly ministry: after his temptation angels minister to him (Matt. 4:11); an angel appears, strengthening Jesus in the garden as he pleads with the Father (Luke 22:43, RSV mg., KJV, JB, NIV; according to Matt. 26:53 innumerable angels were at Jesus' disposal); and at the resurrection an angel rolls back the stone of the sepulchre (Matt. 28:2-6; Mark indicates only a "young man . . . dressed in a white robe," 16:5; John 20:12, two angels).

Finally, it is said that they will be present at Christ's second coming (e.g., Matt. 16:27; note also the parable of the weeds of the field, 13:39, 41; cf. v. 49).

In other New Testament passages various related angelic duties are outlined. As in the Old Testament, the angels are God's messengers of encouragement to believers. The author of the Epistle to the Hebrews expressly states that angels are "ministering spirits (Gk. *pneúmata*) sent forth to serve, for the sake of those who are to obtain salvation" (Heb. 1:14; cf. the angelic appearance to Peter and Cornelius, Acts 5:19; 10:3).

According to Christ, the angels are spirits (Matt. 22:30 par. Mark 12:25; Luke 20:36) who neither marry nor are given in marriage; they may be endowed with knowledge (cf. 2 Sam. 14:17, 20), but they are not omniscient, for they do not know the time of Christ's second coming (Matt. 24:36). Paul adds that they are subordinate to human beings (1 Cor. 6:3; cf. 1 Pet. 1:12). They form a certain hierarchy, with archangels (Gk. *archángeloi*) above other (regular) angels (1 Thess. 4:16); Gabriel and Michael could possibly be among those archangels (Jude 9; cf. Dan. 10:13, "chief princes"; v. 21, "prince"; 12:1, "great prince"). In addition to angels, thrones, dominions, principalities, and authorities (Col. 1:16) further indicate a distinction of rank among the angelic host.

The seven angels of the churches addressed at Rev. 1:20; 2:1, 8, 12, 18; 3:1, 7, 14 are not real angels as are found in later chapters of the book, but office bearers ("bishops," J. L. McKenzie, *Dictionary of the Bible* [New York: 1967], p. 32; but cf. *TDNT* 1:86).

For the most part the "angel of the Lord" (Gk. *ángelos kyríou*) is portrayed in the New Testament as a created being, a messenger sent by God rather than God himself (e.g., Matt. 1:20, 24; Luke 1:11; 2:9; Acts 5:19; 10:3; 12:17, 23). At Acts 8:26, however, there appears little difference between the angel and the Holy Spirit (cf. v. 29). Only twice is the angel of the Lord identified with God, in both cases in references to Old Testament events (Acts 7:29-34, 37-41). Some scholars would identify the angel of the Lord as Christ's preincarnational manifestations, thus a theophany of the second person of the Trinity (the Son or Logos); others would see the angel as a metaphor for God in human form, the Son of God.

In addition to setting forth the tasks of the good angels, the New Testament teaches the existence of fallen angels whose leader is Satan (*see* SATAN; DEVIL).

III. Theological Reflections

Enlightenment thought, and much of twentieth-century, is skeptical about the existence of angels. The Middle Ages, in contrast, were very much caught up in discussions about the task of these heavenly beings. Even the Church Father Augustine expounded several points on angelology: the creation of the angels (*Civ. Dei* xi.9, 32), the sin of some of them (xi.33) due either to pride (*Ench.* 28) or sexual desire (*Civ. Dei* xv.23); the eternal punishment of the fallen angels; the voids created by those fallen and the redeemed who would fill those voids again (*Ench.* 29), and the manner in which the good angels appear to human beings (59).

A special interest for medieval Christians was the notion of guardian angels. Though the Bible may allude to such angels of protection at Matt. 18:10, it does not actually teach that each believer has a special, personal guardian angel. Guardian angels may perhaps be mentioned at Dan. 4:10, 14, 20; they are certainly discussed during the intertestamental period. Others appeal to such texts as Ps. 91:11 ("guard you in all your ways") or Acts 12:15 for biblical evidence of the existence of guardian angels (see *TDNT* 1:86).

The fall of the angels is a baffling question. Though the Bible clearly holds that some angels fell into sin (2 Pet. 2:4; Jude 6; cf. Rev. 12:7-9 for the fight between the good and evil angels and the victory of the good), it does not explain how this was possible. Human beings were tempted by a serpent (Gen. 3:1-7). But who tempted the angels and why did some — and not all — yield to sin?

The twentieth century by and large prefers a mechanical explanation of human behavior rather than the biblical witness to angelic activity, but it has also stimulated a reevaluation of the speculative attitude of the Middle Ages. The many questions about angels raised by the Bible (such as the nature of the bodily appearance of angels to human beings and Paul's injunction about the women's veil at 1 Cor. 11:10) cannot be convincingly answered because of the absence of the necessary biblical information (see *NCE* 1:513).

Bibliography. W. Grundmann, G. von Rad, G. Kittel, "ἄγγελος," *TDNT* 1 (1964): 74-87.

ANGER. See WRATH.

ANGLE, THE (Heb. *hammiqṣôaʿ*). A tower (2 Chr. 26:9) or a section of the eastern wall of Jerusalem which King Uzziah fortified and which Nehemiah repaired following the Exile (Neh. 3:19-20, 24-25). It may have been located between the Horse Gate and the Water Gate (cf. Neh. 3), perhaps at an angle (Heb. *miqṣôaʿ* "corner post"; 2 Chr. 26:9, KJV "turning of the wall") near the south wall of the temple.

ANIAM [ə nīʹəm] (Heb. *ʾanîʿam* "lamentation of the people"). A son of Shemida of the tribe of Manasseh (1 Chr. 7:19).

ANIM [āʹnĭm] (Heb. *ʿānîm* "springs"). A border city in the hill country of Judah (Josh. 15:50); it is called Ḥawina in the Amarna Letters. According to Eusebius (*Onom.* xxvi.9) it was 9 Roman mi. south of Hebron; it is possibly to be identified with Khirbet Ghuwein et-Taḥtā, 18 km. (11 mi.) south of Hebron.

ANIMALS. Palestine and surrounding regions support a surprisingly abundant animal population and a wide variety of species. Much of this diversity is possible because of the great geographical variation of this area and the attendant climatic conditions. The coastal plain (up to the watershed line) thus has an animal population similar to that of Mediterranean regions; southern Palestine and the Syrian desert support animals common in regions such as the Sahara desert; and other areas are conducive to animals such as those found in the region between the Sahara and Iran and Turkestan.

Positive identification of many of the animals mentioned in the Bible remains difficult, if not impossible, for semantic reasons as well as differences between ancient and modern methods of description and classification. Rather than observing biological characteristics such as are applied by modern Western taxonomy, the Bible views animals in terms of their behavior or habitat; thus, the bat is considered a bird and the whale, a fish. This tendency is especially apparent in the creation story: "sea monsters" (KJV "great whales"; JB "sea-serpents") refers to the large aquatic creatures, and "every living creature . . . with which the waters swarm" suggests the smaller sea animals, including mollusks and crustaceans (Gen. 1:21); "cattle" is a general name for domesticated land animals, while "creeping things" indicates all that move in or upon the ground (v. 24).

For the various species, see the individual entries. *See also* BIRDS.

Bibliography. F. S. Bodenheimer, *Animal and Man in Bible Lands* (Leiden: 1960); G. S. Cansdale, *All the Animals of the Bible Lands* (Grand Rapids: 1970).

ANNA [ăn'ə] (Gk. *Hanna,* from Heb. *ḥannâ* "grace").
1. The wife of Tobit and mother of Tobias (Tob. 1:9, 20). She earned a living for herself and her husband during Tobit's blindness (2:11).
2. The daughter of Phanuel, an aged widow (possibly more than one hundred years old) and a prophetess, whose lineage is traced to the tribe of Asher (Luke 2:36). At the dedication of Jesus she spoke about the child to those who were looking for the "redemption of Jerusalem."
3. The mother of Mary and grandmother of Jesus. She is mentioned in the Protevangelium of James (a New Testament Apocryphon) but not in the New Testament. Long childless, she beseeches the Lord to give her a family, and he comforts her through an angel. At last she conceives a child, rears her till the age of three, and then dedicates her to God by placing her in the temple. In many ways Anna resembles the Old Testament Hannah.

ANNAS [ăn'əs] (Gk. *Hannas,* possibly from Heb. *ḥᵃnanyāhû* "the Lord is gracious"). A Jewish high priest, the son of Seth. He was installed *ca.* A.D. 6 by Quirinius, governor of Syria, and deposed in 15 by Gratus, procurator of Judea. He retained considerable influence afterward, however, partly because of his great wealth. Evidence of his continued power is provided by New Testament accounts of the beginning of John the Baptist's ministry ("in the high priesthood of Annas and Caiaphas," Luke 3:2), the trial of Jesus and his appearance before Caiaphas (John 18:13, 24), and the trial of Peter and John (Acts 4:6). He may have been the high priest mentioned at John 18:19, 22, for according to Jewish law he would still have been the official representative of that office.

All of Annas' five sons became high priests, as did his son-in-law Caiaphas.

ANNO DOMINI [ăn'ō dō'mĭn ĭ] (Lat. "in the year of the Lord"). Reckoning from the birth of Jesus, the dating of years "A.D." and the concept of a "Christian era" resulted from the Easter cycle developed in the sixth century by the Scythian monk Dionysius Exiguus. Rather than the year 753 A.U.C. ("from the founding of the city" of Rome) upon which the system is based, the birth of Jesus is now believed to have occurred somewhat earlier, probably *ca.* 7 or 6 B.C.

ANNUNCIATION. The announcement by the angel Gabriel to Mary concerning the birth of her son Jesus (Luke 1:28-35; cf. a similar announcement to Joseph at Matt. 1:18-25). Greeting and comforting her, the angel tells Mary that she will be "overshadowed" by the Holy Spirit and that her son will rule eternally as king over Israel (Luke 1:32-35).

The words "Blessed are you among women" (v. 28b, KJV, RSV mg.) occur in only a few ancient versions (taken from Elizabeth's greeting at v. 42) and have been omitted in most recent versions (e.g., RSV, JB, NIV).

Zechariah received a similar visit from an angel regarding the birth of his son John the Baptist (vv. 11-20; cf. Judg. 13:2-5).

ANOINT. The custom of smearing or pouring oil on a person or object, in both secular and sacred contexts.

I. Old Testament

In Palestine people anointed themselves in times of gladness (Ruth 3:3, Heb. *sû*ḵ) or after a period of grief such as the death of a child (2 Sam. 12:20; cf. Dan. 10:3). They also poured oil on objects as a symbol of dedication. In such a way Jacob dedicated the stone which served as his pillow at Bethel (Gen. 28:18), and when Moses received the laws of worship he was instructed to anoint the tent of meeting, the ark, and other sacred vessels (Exod. 30:26-30). Dignitaries, especially priests, were anointed before they assumed office (40:13-15); this rite symbolized their consecration (e.g., Lev. 8:12). Some of the prophets were anointed as well (Elisha, 1 Kgs. 19:16). Twice God's people are said to be anointed ones (1 Chr. 16:22; Ps. 105:15).

It was important that Israel's kings be anointed, thus signifying royal competence — e.g., Saul (1 Sam. 10:1), David (16:3, 12-13), Solomon (1 Kgs. 1:39). In the Old Testament they were called the Lord's anointed (Heb. *māšîaḥ*), a title applied specifically to Saul (1 Sam. 24:6; 26:9-11; 2 Sam. 1:14, 16), David (1 Sam. 16:6; 2 Sam. 23:1), and Solomon (2 Chr. 6:42). Isaiah uses it for Cyrus (Isa. 45:1), as does perhaps the author of Daniel (Dan. 9:25). In the Psalms it is a general title for the king (e.g., Ps. 18:50). As such the Old Testament kings may be said to prefigure the great Anointed One, Jesus Christ (*see II* below).

The oil used in the religious ceremony was to contain a proper mixture of spices: 500 shekels of liquid myrrh, 250 shekels of cinnamon, an equal amount of aromatic cane, 500 shekels of cassia, and 1 hin of oil (Exod. 30:22).

II. New Testament

Anointing with oil was common practice in New Testament times. It was a sign of joy and thanksgiving associated with feasts (cf. Ps. 23:5) but was also to be observed when fasting (Matt. 6:17; Gk. *aleíphō*). Oil was used as an emollient in healing (Luke 10:34); such anointing is portrayed as an outward symbol of the miraculous healing power of the divine name (Mark 6:13; James 5:14). Members of the church at Laodicea are instructed to buy salve to anoint their eyes as a symbolic cure for their spiritual blindness (Rev. 3:18; Gk. *enchríō*). When Mary anoints Jesus' feet as an indication of her love, he interprets the act as a symbolic preparation for his burial (John 12:1-8; cf. Mark 14:3-8). At Mark 16:1 the women bring spices to anoint Jesus' body as a token of final respect (cf. Luke 23:56).

The concept of the Lord's anointed is applied to Jesus Christ (Gk. *christós* "anointed one"), who as prophet, priest, and king was viewed as the fulfillment of the promised Messiah (Heb. *māšîaḥ* "anointed"; John 20:31; Acts 5:42; Heb. 1:9, quoting Ps. 45:7). At Luke 4:18 Jesus announces that the Holy Spirit has anointed him (Gk. *chríō,* quoting Isa. 61:1; cf. Acts 10:38). The term Anointed is used by the apostles at Acts 4:26 (quoting Ps. 2:2). *See* CHRIST; MESSIAH.

At 1 John 2:20 all believers are considered to have been anointed by the Holy Spirit.

ANSWER. Gk. *apokrínomai* means "to reply" to a request or a question, and often occurs in conjunction with Gk. *légō* "to speak." At Luke 2:47 Jesus' insightful answers (Gk. *apókrisis*) to the teachers attest not to precocious intelligence but to his understanding of spiritual matters and his relationship to God and the covenantal responsibilities of the Jewish faith (cf. Ps. 119:99-100).

ANT (Heb. *nᵉmālâ*). Several species of ants occur in Palestine and can be found even in the most arid, rocky terrain and in the sandy valleys. Those mentioned in the Bible (Prov. 6:8; 30:25) are most likely harvester ants (*Messor Semirufus*), which live in underground nests; three classes are evident: male, female, and worker (undeveloped female). Feeding primarily on particulate vegetable matter, these ants are most active during the summer, when they collect large quantities of grain from the fields, threshing floors, and barns. Ants do not hibernate, for during the rainy season (winter) they mate, lay their eggs, and care for their young with provisions laid up during the preceding summer (cf. 30:25), replenishing the store, when needed, with the freshly sown grain in the fields or with the young leaves of a variety of plants. It is this industriousness and foresight which earns for the ant its proverbial characterization as small but exceedingly wise (cf. v. 24).

ANTELOPE. A deer-like, hollow-horned ruminant, related to cattle and goats; unlike deer they do not shed their horns. Their normal habitat is Africa, but they have been encountered in large numbers in Palestine.

The Bible distinguishes several species of these graceful animals: the gazelle, most likely the ibex (RSV; Heb. *dîšôn*), and perhaps the oryx (*oryx leucoryx*; cf. LXX *óryx* at Deut. 14:5 for Heb. *tᵉʾô* "wild sheep [?]" [KoB, p. 1016]; KJV "wild ox"), a magnificent animal with striking horns curved back like sabers. The antelope were numbered among the clean animals that could be eaten (Deut. 14:5), and

nets were strung to catch them. At Isa. 51:20 (KJV "wild bull") the condition of Jerusalem's inhabitants after being afflicted by God's anger is likened to that of an antelope trapped in a net.

ANTHOTHIJAH [ăn'thō thī'jə] (Heb. *ʿanᵉṯōṯîyâ*). A son of Shashak of the tribe of Benjamin (1 Chr. 8:24; KJV "Antothijah").

ANTHROPOLOGY. *See* MANKIND.

ANTHROPOMORPHISM. A term signifying God's self-revelation in human form (Gk. *ánthrōpos* "man" and *morphḗ* "form"). The Bible often depicts God in human terms, e.g., attributing to him feet (Exod. 24:10) and arms (6:6). It also describes him as experiencing human emotions such as anger (4:14) and love (20:6).

While God appears quite human to Israel at the beginning of its history and expresses his anger in extremely human terms, he does not let Moses forget his numinous character. Moses is permitted to see his back, but under no circumstances is he permitted to see his face (Exod. 33:21-23). At a later stage of Israel's history Isaiah proclaims the majesty of God (Isa. 40:12-13, 18, 21-26), apparently in an effort to combat a too human, and therefore finite and sinful, concept of Israel's Creator and Redeemer.

In the New Testament God discloses himself in his Son, the Savior. In Jesus God "emptied himself" (Phil. 2:7) and made himself known to human beings (John 14:9).

According to J. Calvin, because God chose to reveal himself to finite — and, after the fall, sinful — people as a holy, eternal being, he had to accommodate himself to human language, emotions, and objects. The Bible leaves no doubt that these anthropomorphic self-disclosures are forms of genuine divine revelation.

Christians continue to have a problem with this phenomenon. Some have taken these corporeal figures literally, thereby presuming God to be a finite being. Others, in reaction, have denied every human element attributed to God and assert that he is unknowable. The Scriptures, however, emphasize both aspects — his divinity and his willingness to participate in the human domain.

Bibliography. W. Eichrodt, *Theology of the Old Testament* 2. OTL (1967).

ANTICHRIST (Gk. *antíchristos*). A demonic adversary of Christ. Although this term occurs only at 1 John 2:18, 22; 4:3; 2 John 7, the concept is present in other biblical passages.

I. Old Testament

Possible roots of this name may be found in the Old Testament. The "sons of Belial" (KJV, Judg. 19:22; 20:13; RSV "base fellows") were extremely wicked individuals who violated all ethical codes of behavior. In one of Daniel's visions the fourth beast with ten horns "made war with the saints" until its kingdom was taken and given to the "son of man" (Dan. 7:7-8, 13, 21-22). This is most likely a metaphor for the Roman Empire, an intensely destructive power. The

Old Testament, however, does not concentrate all evil in one entity serving Satan and called the counter-Messiah.

II. New Testament

John applies the term primarily to those who deny that Jesus is the Christ. At 1 John 2:18 the apostle uses the singular form with reference to a person who will embody all anti-Christian activity, and the plural to indicate that many are already opposing the work of Christ — namely, those who have left the fellowship of believers. At v. 22 he tries to combat the heresy of former believers who now deny the incarnation or the heterodoxy of Cerinthus who taught that Christ descended on the man Jesus only for a time (cf. Irenaeus' reference to a possible meeting between John and Cerinthus; P. Schaff, *History of the Christian Church* 1 [repr. 1978]: 430).

At 1 John 4:1-6 and 2 John 7, the author opposes those who deny that the Word has become flesh. The antichrist is he who would differentiate between the man Jesus and the divine Word. For John the antichrist is not first of all a power opposing God, but one who alters the basic confession of faith in Christ.

Paul believed this person ("man of lawlessness" or "man of sin") would "be revealed" before the return of Christ (2 Thess. 2:3). Writing in apocalyptic language to the Thessalonians, he warns them that this person would display his ominous power just before the Parousia. Thus Paul argued that Christ's second coming was not imminent.

In his description of the man of lawlessness (2 Thess. 2:4), the apostle employs the language of Dan. 11, saying the antichrist would "[exalt] himself against every so-called god" (cf. Dan. 11:36) "or the object of worship, so that he [would take] his seat in the temple of God" (cf. v. 31), and "proclaim himself to be God" (cf. v. 32, the great apostasy; Isa. 14:13-14; Ezek. 28:2ff.). Evidently, Paul found a definite connection between the "man of lawlessness" and historical figures who waged war against God's people; Antiochus IV Epiphanes (alluded to at Dan. 11) may have been such a person. Yet, clearly the emphasis is on the antichrist in the future, not in the past.

The man of lawlessness represents all those who follow him and are committed to his godless philosophy. Just as Christ is united with all believers throughout time, so the antichrist embodies all forms of godlessness — past, present, and future — worked by his disciples. When, after the removal of "what is restraining him now," the man of lawlessness has the opportunity to reveal his concentrated evil power in a caricature of the Righteous One, he will meet Christ, who will destroy once and for all every manifestation of godlessness (2 Thess. 2:7-9).

Many commentators believe that the beast arising from the sea (Rev. 13:1-10) is another description of the apostate nature of the Roman Empire. Certainly some of the Roman emperors of the first century A.D. claimed to be divine. The aged author, John, in language reminiscent of Dan. 7, identifies the antichrist with one "in whom secular authority had assumed the mantle of deity" (R. H. Mounce, *The Book of Revela-*

tion. NICNT [1977], p. 254). At any rate, this creature symbolizes mankind's rebellion against God.

The Bible, however, provides neither a name nor concrete historical details designating a particular person as the antichrist. Attempts have been made at various points in history to identify this evil figure with specific individuals such as Nero, Napoleon III, and Hitler. Most current interpreters are content to view the antichrist as a general embodiment of evil.

ANTIGONUS [ăn tĭ'gō nəs].† The last of the Hasmonean kings, and son of Aristobulus II, with whom he was imprisoned at Rome from 63-57 B.C. After the death of Julius Caesar in 44, he invaded Galilee but was defeated by Herod the Great. Four years later, while Caesar's successor, Mark Antony, was visiting Queen Cleopatra in Alexandria, Antigonus took advantage of Parthian support to become the Jewish king and high priest. He was deposed in 37 B.C. by Herod the Great, who with Roman aid captured Jerusalem, and was executed at Antioch.

ANTI-LEBANON. A mountain range east of the Lebanon mountains, extending from Kadesh (Syria) to Dan. Its highest peak is Mt. Hermon. Other peaks are Amana and Senir (so Cant. 4:4).

ANTIMONY. *See* EYE PAINT.

ANTIOCH [ăn'tĭ ŏk] (Gk. *Antiocheia*). The name of several cities in antiquity.

1. A city in Phrygia near the border of Pisidia (though Acts 13:13 locates it within Pisidia; Gk. *hē Pisidia*), at the foot of Sultan Dăg. The city was settled *ca.* 350 B.C. by people from various lands. In 25 B.C. it became an important Roman colony on the east-west highway from Ephesus to Syria, attracting many merchants including several Jews. According to Josephus (*Ant.* xii.3.4) two thousand Jewish families moved there (*ca.* 200 B.C.).

Paul visited the city on his first missionary journey, after his ministry on Cyprus (13:13-14). Preaching first to the Jews on the Sabbath in their own synagogue, he succeeded in securing an initially favorable reception (v. 43). The next meeting was less friendly, however, because of the jealousy of the Jews over the number of people attending (vv. 44-45). The Jews managed to have Paul and his company evicted from the city, though they were unsuccessful in their attempt to block Gentile conversion (vv. 48-51).

Paul may have revisited the city on his second and third journeys (16:6; 18:23). Though he alluded to the Jewish harassment he had experienced in that city (2 Tim. 3:11), it was here that he first made an impact on Hellenized Jews and Gentiles, from skeptic to sympathizer (v. 48).

Much of the ancient city has been preserved, such as parts of the city wall, a temple of the god Mên, a theatre. The collapsed arches of a Roman aqueduct lie on a barren hill, while on the west are the ruins of the monumental Triple City Gate (*ca.* A.D. 220).

2. A city in Syria (modern Antakya), about 19 km. (12 mi.) east of the Mediterranean Sea, located on the southern bank of the Orontes river and near the green slopes of Mt. Silpius.

Built by Seleucus I Nicator (300 B.C.) as the capital

of the Seleucid kingdom, it became the third most important city of the Roman Empire (after Rome and Alexandria). The layout of the city was a marvel. It was traversed from west to east by a colonnade of four rows of marble pillars between which lay three roads, a central road for the traffic of heavy vehicles and two outer ones for pedestrians, horses, and luxury carriages. A second colonnade began in the north at an island in the Orontes river and ran southward, and the city was thus divided into four districts by a gigantic, glittering, white-marble cross. North of the winding Orontes was the royal Seleucid palace, and on the northeast side of the city was the wall of Tiberius. The enchanting nature paradise of Daphne, where worshippers frequented the temple of Apollo, was to the south; its springs supplied ample water to the city. Archaeological excavations have uncovered mosaic floors of villas, an altar to unknown deities, a temple of Demeter, and numerous sculptures and images of deities. The chalice of Antioch, discovered here, was once heralded as the cup used at the Last Supper; it has been dated to the fourth century A.D.

In New Testament times the city enjoyed an international population of Romans, Greeks, Syrians, Jews, and possibly others. Luke records that some of the persecuted believers moved to Syria (Acts 11:19-20) and started a church. When the Jerusalem church heard this news, it sent Barnabas, who exhorted the believers to remain faithful to the Lord (vv. 22-23). Upon enlisting the help of Saul, the two taught in the city for about one year (vv. 25-26). It was here that the believers were called Christians for the first time (v. 26).

Antioch was the home base of Paul's missionary activities. Three times the local church sent him away to teach (13:1-3; 15:36-40; 18:22-23). When the decision of the Jerusalem Council regarding the salvation of Gentiles was relayed here, it was received with joy (15:30-31). Here also, Paul felt compelled to rebuke Peter for his intolerant behavior toward Gentile believers (Gal. 2:11).

Antioch was very important during the initial spreading of the gospel, located as it was along the road from Jerusalem to Rome. Though the church was exposed to the temptations of wealth and pleasure, not to mention the allure of the cults of Artemis and Apollo, it grew and soon appointed its first bishop. During the early christological controversies the school of Antioch rivalled that of Alexandria, boasting such figures as Theodore of Mopsuestia and Chrysostom. This school held a literal-historical interpretation of biblical exegesis, thereby opposing the allegorical teachings of the Alexandrians.

Bibliography. R. E. Brown and J. P. Meier, *Antioch and Rome* (New York: 1983); G. Downey, *Ancient Antioch* (Princeton: 1963); *A History of Antioch in Syria from Seleucus to the Arab Conquest* (Princeton: 1961); W. A. Meeks and R. L. Wilken, *Jews and Christians in Antioch in the First Four Centuries of the Common Era* (Missoula: 1978).

ANTIOCHUS [ăn tī′ə kəs] (Gk. *Antiochus* "opposer"). The name of at least twelve Seleucid kings reigning over Syria between *ca.* 280 and 65 B.C.

1. Antiochus II Theos (261-246). He is generally identified with the king of the north mentioned at Dan. 11:6 who marries the daughter (Berenice) of the king of the south (Ptolemy II Philadelphus). His former wife, Laodice, subsequently murdered Antiochus and his offspring by Berenice, thereby provoking retaliation from Berenice's brother Ptolemy Euergetes, who invaded Syria.

2. Antiochus III (223-187), grandson of Antiochus II, named the Great on account of his successful expedition against the Parthians. He was first defeated in Palestine by the Egyptian Ptolemy IV Philopator (cf. Dan. 11:11), but eventually wrested control of Palestine from Egypt during the reign of Ptolemy's successor, the infant Ptolemy V Epiphanes (vv. 13-16). In a gesture of peace Antiochus gave his daughter Cleopatra to the young Egyptian king (v. 17).

The last years of his reign were spent in unsuccessful campaigns against Rome. He was twice defeated by the imperial armies (vv. 18-19; 1 Macc. 8:6-8) and was obligated to sign a treaty in which he renounced the area west of the Taurus river (189 B.C.). Two years later he was killed attempting to quell a rebellion among the Armenians.

3. Antiochus IV Epiphanes (175-164), son of Antiochus III; nicknamed Epimanes ("madman," a pun on Gk. *Epiphanēs* "illustrious") because of his cruel tyranny. Early in his reign he supported the Hellenizer Jason in his bid to become the Jewish high priest (2 Macc. 4:7-20), leading to the hellenization of Jerusalem (vv. 10-17). While campaigning in Egypt in 170-169, at which time he captured most of Egypt, Antiochus was compelled to return to Jerusalem to free the city from control by his opponents, at which time he violated the temple and seized its treasures (1 Macc. 1:20-28; 2 Macc. 5:11-26). When in 168 the Romans issued him an ultimatum to let Egypt alone (cf. Dan. 11:30), he concentrated on making Palestine a loyal Seleucid province, which he endeavored to accomplish by imposing Hellenism as a means of unification. It was then that he issued his notorious edict compelling the Jews to "abandon their ancestral customs and live no longer by the laws of God" (2 Macc. 6:1, JB). From then on they were "to profane the Temple in Jerusalem and dedicate it to Olympian Zeus" (v. 2). Particularly offensive to the Jewish population was the erection of a Greek altar (the "abomination that makes desolate," Dan. 11:31; 1 Macc. 1:5) in the temple on the site of the altar of burnt offering. Stringent enforcement of the edict and the merciless punishment of the Jewish offenders backfired, however, when the populace revolted, touching off the Maccabean wars.

By this time Antiochus had turned to the east. Eager to take the riches of the temple of Nanaea, he marched to Elymais but failed in the attempt. Reports of the Maccabean success may have contributed to his insanity and subsequent death (1 Macc. 6:1-16).

4. Antiochus V Eupator ("one with a noble father"; 164-162), who at an early age succeeded his father Antiochus IV. In 162, with the assistance of his kinsman Lysias, the young king sent a large army to Jerusalem, where the Seleucid forces besieged the rebellious Jews (1 Macc. 6:18-54). When Lysias learned that the official regent and guardian, Philip, had returned from Persia, he made a hasty peace with the Jews (vv. 55-60) and then proceeded to defeat Philip at Antioch. The joy of victory was short-lived, for soon both the young ruler (who had swiftly broken the oath with the Jews; v. 62) and his general were murdered by their own army, rallying in support of Demetrius Soter (Antiochus IV's nephew and more direct successor) who had escaped from captivity in Rome (7:1-4; 2 Macc. 14:1-2).

5. Antiochus VI Epiphanes Dionysus (145-142). The son of Alexander Balas of Syria, he was put in power by Trypho, one of his father's chief ministers, and reigned only long enough to stabilize his authority. Trypho then murdered him and assumed the throne himself (1 Macc. 11:39-40, 54; 12:39; 13:31). His reign coincided with the final years of Jonathan Maccabeus, the Jewish leader and high priest (13:40-53).

6. Antiochus VII Sidetes ("one born in Sida" in Pamphylia; 138-129), called Euergetes ("benefactor"); the second son of Demetrius I and brother of Demetrius II. In his retaliatory pursuit of Trypho, who had succeeded Demetrius II upon his capture by the Parthians, Antiochus granted various concessions to the Jewish high priest Simon (Jonathan's successor; 1 Macc. 15:1-14). But having blockaded Trypho in Dor, he revoked these privileges (vv. 25-27). In 135 the high priest, adamant in his refusal to yield to the king, was murdered (while intoxicated) by a son-in-law loyal to the Seleucids (16:11-18).

Antiochus himself invaded Judea in 135 and captured Jerusalem (then headed by the high priest John Hyrcanus); he granted the Jews religious freedom. With Judea again under Seleucid control, Antiochus temporarily gained the upper hand against the Parthians; in 129, however, they released Demetrius II, and Antiochus died in battle against Phraortes II of Parthia.

ANTIPAS [ăn′tə pəs] (Gk. *Antipas,* abbreviation of *Antipatros* "instead of his father").

1. Herod Antipas, son of Herod the Great. He was the tetrarch of Galilee who had John the Baptist imprisoned and beheaded (Matt. 14:1-11 par. Mark 6:14-28) and who mocked Jesus at his trial (Luke 23:7-11). See HEROD 2.

2. A Christian at Pergamum who was martyred on account of his faith (Rev. 2:12).

ANTIPATER [ăn tĭp′ə tər] (Gk. *Antipatros* "instead of his father"). The father of Herod the Great. At first the unofficial ruler of Palestine (63-55 B.C.), in 47 he was appointed procurator of Judea in exchange for his influence in the war between Caesar and Ptolemy. He then secured governorships over Jerusalem and Galilee for his sons Phasael and Herod. Antipater was poisoned by his cupbearer in 43 B.C.

ANTIPATRIS [ăn tĭp′ə trĭs] (Gk. *Antipatris*). A city founded in 9 B.C. upon the ruins of Old Testament Aphek (**1**) by Herod the Great, who named it after his father, Antipater. It was here that Paul spent the night, in the custody of Roman soldiers, en route from Jerusalem to Caesarea where he was to stand trial

(Acts 23:31). The site is located near modern Râs el-'Ain, 16 km. (10 mi.) north of Lod, 65 km. (40 mi.) northwest of Jerusalem, and 40 km. (25 mi.) southwest of Caesarea.

ANTIPHONY. *See* MUSIC.

ANTONIA, TOWER OF [ăn tō′nĭ ə] (Gk. *Antōnia*). A fortress, perhaps that mentioned at Neh 2:8 ("fortress," Heb. *bîrâ* "citadel, castle"; cf. 7:2; KJV "palace"), restored after the Exile by John Hyrcanus (135-105 B.C.) and later enlarged by Herod the Great, who named it Antonia in honor of his patron Mark Antony. It was captured by the Jews when they revolted against Rome and held till A.D. 70 when it was destroyed by Titus' soldiers.

It was in this tower, located at the northwest corner of the temple, that Paul was given safety in the face of an angry mob ("barracks," Gk. *parembolé,* Acts 21:33-37). At its steps Paul tried to address his fellow countrymen (21:40–22:23), but to no avail. When he was brought inside, he was questioned by a Roman centurion, but after mentioning that he was a Roman citizen he was not punished (22:24-29). The tribune realized that Paul's presence in Jerusalem caused division and violence among the Jews and endangered the apostle's own life, so he kept Paul in the tower (23:10, 18-22) just long enough to assemble an escort party to transfer him to Caesarea (vv. 23-33).

Some scholars believe that the judgment seat on the "Pavement" (John 19:13) is the Tower of Antonia. Certain drawings carved into the pavement below the Convent of Our Lady of Zion (probably by Roman soldiers) may depict the same dice game — with money, clothing, and other articles for stakes — as is referred to in v. 24 where the Roman soldiers cast lots for Jesus' robe.

Bibliography. R. M. Mackowski, *Jerusalem, City of Jesus* (Grand Rapids: 1980), pp. 90-101.

ANTONY (Lat. *Marcus Antonius*). A Roman statesman (*ca.* 82-30 B.C.) who served as triumvir along with Octavian and Lepidus. He appointed Herod the Great as vassal king of Palestine, in response to which Herod named the refortified tower at Jerusalem Antonia in his honor. He was defeated by Octavian at Actium in 31; a year later, upon hearing a false report of the death of his consort Cleopatra, he committed suicide.

ANTOTHIJAH. *See* ANTHOTHIJAH.

ANTOTHITE. *See* ANATHOTH.

ANUB [ā′nŭb] (Heb. *'anûḇ* "ripe"). A son of Koz and a descendant of Judah (1 Chr. 4:8).

ANXIETY.† Various degrees of anxiety, ranging from concern to fear and dread, are depicted in both the Old and New Testaments. Anxiety may be the natural concern a parent exhibits for his children (1 Sam. 9:5; 10:2; Heb. *dā'ag*) or that which one feels for the well-being of a fellow (Phil. 2:20; Gk. *merimnáō*; cf. v. 28). It includes personal distress such as that caused by Hannah's barrenness (1 Sam. 1:16; Heb. *śîaḥ*) or

Daniel's dream (Dan. 7:15; Aram. $k^e r\bar{a}$'), as well as the fear and trembling precipitated by war (cf. 1 Chr. 17:9) or natural disaster (Jer. 17:8). The Psalms give frequent expression to such feelings (Ps. 127:2; cf. 102:7; Prov. 12:25).

While loving concern may be constructive (2 Cor. 11:28), Jesus cautions that unnecessary attention to physical needs or the "cares of the world" may hinder the life of faith and the Christian's participation in the kingdom of God (Matt. 6:15-34 par. Luke 12:22-31; cf. Matt. 13:22 par. Mark 4:19; Luke 8:14; see CARE). Rather, one should place his burdens on God, who protects and cares for his people (Phil. 4:6; 1 Pet. 5:7).

APELLES [ə pĕl'ĭz] (Gk. *Apellēs*). A person "approved in Christ," who is greeted by Paul (Rom. 16:10).

APELLES, GOSPEL OF. An apocryphal writing by a certain Apelles, founder of a second-century A.D. Gnostic sect. A modification of the writings of Apelles' teacher, Marcion, the work is known only through references by some of the Church Fathers.

APHARSACHITES [ə fär'sə kīts] (Aram. *$^{'a}pars^e$-$kāyē$', probably from Old Pers. *frasaka*; cf. Akk. *iprasakku*).* According to the KJV (Ezra 5:6; 6:6) a tribe living in Samaria. More recent translations recognize the term as a Persian loanword meaning "officials" or "investigators" (RSV "governors").

APHARSATHCHITES [ə fär'sĭth kīts] (Aram. *$^{'a}par$-$sat^e kayē$', probably from Old Pers. *frēstak* "messenger"). KJV translation indicating a Persian tribe which the Assyrian Assurbanipal resettled in Samaria (Ezra 4:9). This Persian loanword probably means "leading officials" (RSV "governors"; JB "legates").

APHARSITES [ə fär'sīts] (Aram. *$^{'a}pārsayē$'). Generally translated as a gentilic (RSV "Persians"), the term may actually designate an official (Ezra 4:9). The KJV renders the Apharsites as a tribe transplanted to Samaria by Assurbanipal.

APHEK [ā'fĕk] (Heb. $^a p\bar{e}q$ "bed of a stream" or "stronghold").
1. A royal Canaanite city (Josh. 12:18) in the plain of Sharon, northeast of Joppa near modern Râs el-'Ain. During the Conquest Joshua defeated the king of Aphek west of the Jordan. Later, during the judgeship of Eli, the Israelites were twice defeated by the Philistines, who had camped at this site (1 Sam. 4:2, 10); after their second defeat the Israelite ark of the covenant was seized and taken to Philistia. Near the end of Saul's reign another confrontation took place between the Israelites and the Philistines (1 Sam. 29:1), which cost him his life (ch. 31).

In the New Testament the city is called Antipatris (Acts 23:31), so named in honor of the father of Herod the Great, who rebuilt the city *ca.* 35 B.C.

The name of this ancient city appears in texts of several Egyptian pharaohs (Thutmose III, Amenhotep II, Rameses II), and on an inscription of the Assyrian king Esarhaddon. Archaeological research has discovered evidence of the city's continuous occupation from *ca.* 2200 B.C. till *ca.* 1200, when the Philistine city was apparently destroyed. Although much of the excavation was conducted outside the limits of the biblical city, finds include the remains of a Canaanite fortress or palace, a caravansary, and a Roman mausoleum; tombs and rubbish pits have yielded a variety of pottery as well as several cuneiform texts.

2. A city on the border between Canaan and the territory of the Amorites, probably modern Afqā, about 37 km. (23 mi.) northeast of Beirut. It was one of those Canaanite cities not yet conquered at the end of Joshua's life (Josh. 13:14).

3. A city in the tribal territory of Asher (Josh. 19:30), whose inhabitants the Asherites could not expel ("Aphik," Judg. 1:31, so RSV, KJV, JB; NIV "Aphek"). It may be the same as Tell Kurdâneh on the plain of Acco.

4. A city east of the Sea of Chinnereth in biblical Bashan, along the main highway from Damascus to Beth-shan. At this site the Israelites under King Ahab defeated the Syrians (1 Kgs. 20:26-30), and here King Joash of Israel gained a victory over those same enemies, as Elisha had prophesied (2 Kgs. 13:17; cf. v. 25).

APHEKAH [ə fē'kə] (Heb. $^a p\bar{e}q\hat{a}$ "stronghold"). A city in the hill country of Judah, near Beth-tappuah (Josh. 15:53). Its precise location remains unknown; some have proposed el-Ḥadab, on the east side of the Seil ed-Dilbeh.

APHIAH [ə fī'ə] (Heb. $^a p\hat{i}ah$). The father of Becorath of the tribe of Benjamin and an ancestor of King Saul (1 Sam. 9:1).

APHIK. See APHEK **3.**

APHRAH (Mic. 1:10, KJV). See BETH-LE-APHRAH.

APOCALYPSE [ə pŏk'ə lĭps] (Gk. *apokálypsis* "revelation, disclosure"). A genre of writings which concerns visions or prophecies of the end times or the age to come. See APOCALYPTIC; REVELATION, BOOK OF.

APOCALYPTIC [ə pŏk'ə lĭp'tĭk].† A variety of highly symbolic, "revelatory" (from Gk. *apokálypsis* "revelation, disclosure") literature found in both the Old and New Testaments and in extracanonical Jewish and Christian writings from the period 200 B.C.–A.D. 200; also the movement or variety of religious thought which produced this literature.

Both the literature and the system of thought from which it emerged reflect the period of their origins, a time of persecution and oppression during which efforts were made first to Hellenize the Jewish people and then to quell the spread of Christianity. Apocalyptic represents a reaction to this overwhelming social and political force and the ideology which underlies it, while simultaneously expressing total frustration over the failure of the kingdom of God to materialize as anticipated. While scholars attest to the influence of Greek and Near Eastern wisdom literature and some would trace its origins to Persian Zoroastrianism, apocalyptic most likely has its roots in Israelite prophecy, perhaps as early as the sixth century B.C.; it was thus influenced first by the religious and political havoc wreaked by the Babylonian destruction and Exile and subsequently by the economic hardship and religious hostility which followed the Exile.

The apocalypse is the most common literary genre of apocalyptic, found in several variations; but a number of other forms occur with some frequency: the testament, the parable, and the oracle. Dan. 7–12 has long been recognized as apocalyptic, but other Old Testament writings also contain apocalyptic elements, e.g., Isa. 24–27; 56–66; Ezek. 37–48; Zech. 9–14; cf. Jer. 1:11-16; Joel; Amos 7:1-9; 8:1-3. Primary examples of Jewish apocalyptic include 1 (Ethiopic) Enoch, Jubilees, the Testaments of the Twelve Patriarchs, the Sibylline Oracles, the Psalms of Solomon, the Assumption of Moses, 2 (Slavonic) Enoch, the Ascension of Isaiah, 2 Esdras (4 Ezra), the Prayer of Joseph, and the Apocalypses of Abraham, Baruch, Elijah, Lamech, Shadrach, and Zephaniah. The book of Revelation (also called the Apocalypse of John) is the leading example of New Testament apocalyptic, although apocalyptic materials may be found in Matt. 24 par. Mark 13; Luke 21. Christian apocalyptic includes the Apocalypses of Paul and Peter and the Shepherd of Hermas.

Apocalyptic is clearly marked by the traumatic era from which it derives. So entirely hopeless had circumstances become that God was no longer seen as working through historical events to transform the present order; rather, he would come in vengeance to destroy the existing order and to establish for his people a new, heavenly kingdom. This cosmic dualism, contrasting the present evil age and the heavenly age to come, represents a break with the Israelite prophets, who urged God's people to repent and become part of God's righteous remnant; the emphasis now was on the exaltation of believers (who viewed themselves as the remnant) rather than concern for spiritual redemption or atonement for sins. Moreover, the future rested entirely in God's hands, with eschatological events to take place as predetermined (e.g., in the heavenly books; Rev. 5:1; 10:8; 1 Enoch 81:1-3; cf. Matt. 24:36).

Apocalyptic writings thus seek to provide hope for the elect by disclosing through purported visions the predetermined plan of events currently taking place and those about to unfold (Rev. 1:19). Presented as resting upon very ancient and secret traditions, they were often attributed to prominent biblical figures from the earliest stages of Israelite history; frequently this involved the presentation of Israel's history in the form of prophecy by the ascribed author, thereby helping to undergird the promise of future release.

An obvious (and often puzzling) characteristic of apocalyptic is its extensive use of symbolism. At times bearing the influence of ancient Near Eastern and Greek mythologies, the writings portray a colorful variety of strange animals (e.g., Dan. 7–8; Rev. 4:6-9; 5:6ff.; 13; 1 Enoch 85–90; 2 Esdr. 11–12), angels and demons (Dan. 9:21-23; Rev. 5:11; 8–10; 3 Apoc. Bar. 11–17), and the heavenly city (Rev. 21–22; T. Dan. 5:12-13; Apoc. Pet. 15–16), as well as bizarre allegorical representations of past and future events

(e.g., Dan. 9–12; Rev. 17–20; 2 Apoc. Bar. 53–74). Numbers, assigned mystical and often secret meaning, are also employed, perhaps intended to facilitate computation of the date of the end of the current age and the coming redemption (e.g., Dan. 9:1-27; 12:7, 12; Rev. 4:4-10; 11:9-11; 13:18).

Bibliography. J. J. Collins, *The Apocalyptic Imagination* (New York: 1984); P. D. Hanson, *The Dawn of Apocalyptic* (Philadelphia: 1975); E. W. Nicholson, "Apocalyptic," pp. 189-213 in G. W. Anderson, ed., *Tradition and Interpretation* (Oxford: 1979); D. S. Russell, *The Method and Message of Jewish Apocalyptic.* OTL (1964).

APOCRYPHA [ə pŏk′rə fə] (Gk. *apókryphos* "hidden, concealed"). Those writings included in the LXX and Vulgate but not in the Hebrew (MT) or Protestant canon. With minor exceptions, the apocryphal works are 1 Esdras, 2 Esdras (Vulg. 4 Ezra), Tobit, Judith, Additions to the Book of Esther, the Wisdom of Solomon (also called Wisdom), Ecclesiasticus (the Wisdom of Jesus ben Sirach or Sirach), Baruch, the Epistle of Jeremiah, the Additions to the Book of Daniel (or, individually, the Prayer of Azariah, the Song of the Three Young Men, Susanna, and Bel and the Dragon), the Prayer of Manasseh, and 1-2 Maccabees. The LXX omits 2 Esdras (as do Jerome and Luther) but includes 3-4 Maccabees (absent from Jerome, Vulg., and modern versions). For additional information, see entries on the individual books.

Originating in Hellenistic Judaism in the period 200 B.C.–A.D. 100, many of these works were first written in Hebrew or Aramaic and subsequently translated into Greek. Although they were excluded when the Jewish canon was determined at the Council of Jamnia in A.D. 90, they were considered canonical by early Christians until approximately the fourth century. Some early Church Fathers, such as Clement of Alexandria, viewed these "hidden" (i.e., withdrawn from public use) works as having esoteric value, containing secret knowledge accessible only to initiates (cf. 2 Esdr. 12:37-38; 14:4-6, 42-46). But beginning with the end of the second century, many (e.g., Origen, Tertullian) came to regard them as inferior if not heretical, particularly because of their favor among Gnostics and other sects; thus they were restricted from use in public worship and were to be read in private, if at all. By the fourth century they were viewed as spurious and inauthentic (Athanasius); Jerome, who included them in his Latin translation, equated the term Apocrypha with "noncanonical," declaring these books fit for edification but not for the confirmation of dogma. Protestant leaders of the Reformation, following the lead of Jerome, denied the works equal status with the rest of Scripture; Luther, however (followed by the Thirty-nine Articles of the Church of England), accorded them value for personal edification and included them in an appendix to his 1534 translation. At the Council of Trent (1548) the Roman Catholic Church confirmed most of the works as canonical (the Prayer of Manasseh and 1-2 Esdras were not accepted; the Vulgate appends them to the New Testament), although they are sometimes called deuterocanonical ("second canon").

In subsequent years students of the Bible and church history have come to recognize increasingly the value of these books, not only for their insight into the national consciousness of Jews in the Dispersion but also for the light they shed on the history of the "dark age" between the time of Ezra-Nehemiah and the beginnings of the New Testament and for the background of rabbinic and early Christian thought. Although none of these works is quoted in the New Testament (cf. Luke 11:51; 24:44), they discuss such New Testament concepts as eternal life and resurrection and are cited by many of the Church Fathers for apologetic purposes on such issues as the incarnation, sin, and eschatology.

Bibliography. B. M. Metzger, *An Introduction to the Apocrypha* (New York: 1957); G. W. E. Nickelsburg, *Jewish Literature between the Bible and the Mishnah* (Philadelphia: 1981).

APOCRYPHA, NEW TESTAMENT. A vast body of noncanonical religious writings from the first few centuries of the Christian era. Quite popular among the masses of early Christian believers, they range from the relatively orthodox to the bizarre and eccentric. Many were intended to supplement what might be regarded as a paucity of information in the New Testament concerning the lives and activities of Jesus and the apostles; these have by and large been discovered to be based on pious fantasy rather than authentic tradition or historical fact. Other works derive from various heretical sects seeking to attain authority for their views, such as Gnosticism, docetism, and asceticism (*see* NAG HAMMADI). While many of these writings exerted a strong influence on Christian thought from the fourth century through the Middle Ages, none has been accepted as canonical by the Church except among the heretical sects among which individual works derived.

For the most part these apocryphal works can be classified according to types of New Testament writings — gospels, acts, epistles, and apocalypses. Among the apocryphal gospels are those containing legendary accounts of Jesus' infancy and youth as well as the lives of his parents; they include the Protevangelium of James, the Infancy Gospel of Thomas, the gospel of Pseudo-Matthew, Arabic and Armenian infancy gospels, the gospel of the Birth of Mary, the Assumption of the Virgin, and the History of Joseph the Carpenter. Others concern events surrounding (and following) the passion and resurrection: the gospel of Peter, the Acts of Pilate (also called the gospel of Nicodemus), the Apocryphon of John, and the book of the Resurrection of Christ by Bartholomew the Apostle. Some works originated among Jewish-Christian sects (e.g., the gospels of the Ebionites, Hebrews, and Nazarenes), while others derive from heretical sects: the gospels of Bartholomew, Basilides, the Egyptians, Marcion, Philip, and Thomas; the Prayer of Peter; the Wisdom of Jesus; the Diatessaron of Tatian; and the book of the Great Invisible Spirit. Other works are known only by name or from very brief citations by the Church Fathers (e.g., the gospels of Andrew, Apelles, Barnabas, Cerinthus, Eve, Judas Iscariot, the Manichees, Mary Magdalene, Matthias, and the gospel of Truth).

Intended as supplements to or substitutes for the canonical Acts of the Apostles, the apocryphal acts record legends of the travels and heroics of various apostles. These pseudonymous works are generally sectarian in character, both orthodox and antiheretical as well as theologically deviant (Docetic, Gnostic, Manichean). They are popular romances intended to counter the contemporary legends of pagan heroes and foster the ideals of sexual asceticism and martyrdom as well as to reinforce the saintliness of the apostles. Most important are the so-called Leucian Acts, purported to be the product of Leucius Charinus, a disciple of John; these comprise the Acts of Andrew, John, Paul, Peter, and Thomas. Other, later works include the Acts of Andrew and Matthias, Andrew and Paul, Barnabas, James the Great, Paul and Thecla, Peter and Andrew, Peter and Paul, Philip, Thaddaeus, and Timothy; the Apostolic History of Abdias; the Ascents of James; the Martyrdom of Matthew; accounts of the Passion of Paul, of Peter, and of Peter and Paul; and the Preaching of Peter.

A small group of apocryphal writings are pseudonymous epistles and romantic or novelistic works in the form of letters. Among epistles ascribed to Paul (cf. 2 Thess. 2:2; 3:17) are one designated 3 Corinthians, an alleged "lost" Epistle to the Laodiceans (cf. Col. 4:16), an epistle to the Alexandrians, and the purported correspondence of Paul and Seneca. Other works employing epistolary forms include epistles of the Apostles, of Lentulus, and Titus; epistles of Peter to James and to Philip, and of Mary to Ignatius; the correspondence of Christ and Abgarus; and the Clementine Homilies.

Intended to supplement the canonical books with regard to the future course of history and the nature of the afterworld, a number of apocalypses were composed during the apostolic period. These include apocalypses attributed to James, Paul, Peter, Thomas, and the Virgin Mary; the Revelation of Stephen; the Ascension of Isaiah; Sibylline Oracles deriving from Christian sources; and a fifth-century Apocalypse of John.

Other apocryphal works include the Agrapha, collections of sayings attributed to Jesus; and various Gnostic treatises, including the Pistis Sophia, the Wisdom of Jesus, and the books of Jeu. Although contained in early collections, the works of the Apostolic Fathers are now considered to be distinct from the apocryphal writings.

See also entries on the individual works.

Bibliography. E. Hennecke and W. Schneemelcher, eds., *New Testament Apocrypha*, 2 vols. (Philadelphia: 1963-65).

APOLLONIA [ăp'ə lō'nĭ ə] (Gk. *Apollōnia*). A city in Macedonia, located south of Lake Bolbe on the Roman Via Egnatia 56 km. (35 mi.) east of Thessalonica and 44 km. (27 mi.) southwest of Amphipolis. During Paul's second missionary journey, he and Silas passed through the city en route from Philippi to Thessalonica (Acts 17:1). The city has been identified with modern Pollino.

APOLLONIUS [ăp'ə lō'nĭ əs] (Gk. *Apollōnios*).
1. The governor of Coele-Syria and Phoenicia

under Seleucus IV Philopator (187-175 B.C.); he was apparently a native of Tarsus (so RSV, JB; KJV "son of Thraseus"; RSV mg. "son of Tharseas"). He participated in a scheme, carried out by Heliodorus, to rob the temple treasures (2 Macc. 3:5ff.).

2. A governor of Coele-Syria and Phoenicia under Demetrius I and Alexander Balas; according to Josephus (*Ant.* xiii.4.3-4) he was the son of **1** above. Upon his appointment as commander of the rebel Demetrius II's army he challenged Jonathan to battle, only to lose the garrison at Joppa and, following an unsuccessful ambush on the plain, the city of Azotus (Ashdod) and the surrounding towns (1 Macc. 10:69-85).

3. The son of Menestheus, and governor of Coele-Syria and Phoenicia under Antiochus IV Epiphanes (2 Macc. 4:4). He was sent to Egypt to attend the coronation of Ptolemy VI Philometor *ca.* 172 B.C. (v. 21).

4. A military commander of Samaria sent to Jerusalem by Antiochus IV Epiphanes; pretending at first to have come on peaceable terms, he waited until the Sabbath before parading his troops and succeeded in killing an immense number of people (2 Macc. 5:24-27; cf. 1 Macc. 1:29-35). In 166 B.C. he was killed in battle by Judas Maccabeus (1 Macc. 3:10-12). He may be the same person as **3** above.

5. The son of Gennaeus, he was a district governor in Palestine during the reign of Antiochus V Eupator (2 Macc. 12:2).

6. Apollonius of Tyana (d. *ca.* A.D. 100), neopythagorean philosopher and religious reformer. Early anti-Christian writers compiled biographies intended to show him as a rival to Christ, including such legendary features as the announcement of his birth by an angel, travels with his disciples during which he taught and healed, his betrayal at Rome by a disciple, his miraculous disappearance during his trial before Domitian, and his subsequent descent to the netherworld and reappearance to his disciples.

APOLLOS [ə pŏl'əs] (Gk. *Apollōs*, abbreviation of *Apollōnios*; Lat. *Apollonius*). An Alexandrian Jew, who was "well versed in the scriptures" (Acts 18:24). Apparently he had come into contact with John the Baptist or one of his disciples, for he was familiar with John's view of baptism (rather than the one preached by Peter at Pentecost; v. 25). It is not certain when he became a convert to the Christian faith (v. 25).

Soon after Paul had left Ephesus at the end of his second missionary journey, the eloquent Apollos arrived and began his ministry in the Jewish synagogue (v. 26). Upon coming into contact with Priscilla and Aquila, close associates of the apostle, he was invited into their home and instructed "more carefully" in the "way of God."

With a more complete understanding of the nature of the gospel, Apollos set out for Achaia, with the encouragement of fellow believers. There he strengthened the members of the local church and used his newly gained insights into the faith to demonstrate to the Jewish population that Christ was presaged even in the Old Testament (vv. 27-28).

A segment of the Corinthian believers rallied around Apollos, while another segment sided with Paul (1 Cor. 1:12). In his first Corinthian letter, written after his two-year stay at Ephesus and following Apollos' ministry (A.D. 57), Paul criticized the church for its factions. Judging from the tone of Paul's words, the apostle did not lay the blame on his co-worker. Paul not only credited Apollos with following up on his work at Corinth (3:6), but even urged him to revisit the church there (16:12). His censure was directed, instead, toward the Corinthians themselves (3:6-9; 4:6-7).

At Titus 3:13 Paul recommends Apollos to Titus. This time (*ca.* A.D. 63) Apollos was in Crete, southwest of Ephesus and northwest of his native Alexandria. Though his destination was unknown, Paul summoned Titus to send Apollos on his way.

Apollos' awareness of the Scriptures and his skill in preaching (cf. his public confutation, Acts 18:28) may have derived from his Alexandrian background; it was Alexandria that produced the LXX as well as Philo, whose type of allegorical exegesis had profound influence on Alexandrian Jews. Because of these qualities, Luther and later scholars have suggested that Apollos was the unknown author of the Epistle to the Hebrews.

APOLLYON [ə pŏl'yən] (Gk. *Apollyōn*, from *apollýō* "destroy"). An angel, the "prince" of the "scorpions" of the bottomless pit (Rev. 9:11). The Greek name constitutes a "derogatory reference to the Greek god Apollo and those emperors [e.g., Domitian] who claimed a special relationship to him" (R. H. Mounce, *The Book of Revelation.* NICNT [1977], p. 198). This angel may be a divine scourge on those who lack the "seal of God on their foreheads" (v. 4). The Hebrew equivalent, Abaddon, means "destruction" (Job 28:22).

APOSTASY [ə pŏs'tə sĭ] (Gk. *apostasía*).† A term designating the falling away (Gk. *apó* "away from" and *stásis* "rebellion") from the faith. At 2 Thess. 2:3 Paul (himself once accused by the Jews of apostasy from the Old Testament teachings; Acts 21:21) predicts a general apostasy ("rebellion"; KJV "falling away") from the gospel of Christ. Subsequently he writes to Timothy that "in later times" some "will depart from the faith" and heed the "doctrines of demons" (1 Tim. 4:1). In many respects his picture of this future event is remarkably similar to Christ's own prophecy about the spiritual cooling-off of people's love for God and neighbor ("fall away," Gk. *skandalízō*; Matt. 24:10-12).

While the word "apostasy" occurs only occasionally in the Bible, the idea of forsaking fellowship with the living God is found in several passages. Among the Old Testament prophets Isaiah (Isa. 1:2-4), Jeremiah (Jer. 2:17, 19; 5:6 ["apostasy," Heb. *mᵉšûbâ*]), and Ezekiel (Ezek. 14:7) condemn their fellow countrymen in no uncertain terms for such an act. Israel's apostasy before and after the Conquest is mentioned at Ps. 78:56-58, an account of God's great deeds and Israel's faithlessness. In fact, a parallel may be drawn between the spiritual malaise before the Exile in the Old Testament and the religious attitude of indifference prior to the return of Christ in the New Testament. The author of Chronicles interprets the Exile as God's punishment for Israel's attitude of mockery and contempt (2 Chr. 36:16), as does the prophet Jeremiah (Jer. 44:4-6).

A difficult passage is Heb. 6:4-6, which seems to imply that the process of turning from (Gk. *parapíptō* "fall away") God is irreversible. According to J. Calvin (*Commentary on Hebrews and I and II Peter*, ed. D. W. and T. F. Torrance [repr. 1979], pp. 74-77), this is a total apostasy against which the elect have been protected by Christ, and the example is meant as a warning against backsliding within the body of believers.

Bibliography. P. E. Hughes, *A Commentary on the Epistle to the Hebrews* (Grand Rapids: 1977), pp. 206-224.

APOSTLE [ə pŏs'əl] (Gk. *apóstolos*, from *apostéllō* "send"). An official representative charged with a commission. The designation connotes more the form (the authorization of the sender) than the specific content of the commission. Gk. *apóstolos* can be considered the New Testament counterpart to Heb. *šālîaḥ*, which distinguished such Old Testament emissaries as Moses (sent to Pharaoh; Exod. 6:10) and Elijah (sent to Ahab; 1 Kgs. 18:1). Christ is the apostle of God (Mark 9:37) and maintains that "he who receives any one whom I send receives me" (John 13:20; cf. Matt. 10:40).

During his ministry Jesus chose twelve from among his followers to be his apostles — Simon Peter, Andrew, James, John, Philip, Bartholomew, Thomas, Matthew, James the son of Alphaeus, Thaddaeus, Simon the Cananaean (or the Zealot), and Judas Iscariot (Matt. 10:2-4 par.). While he assigned them specific duties prior to his crucifixion, it is really only after his resurrection — when the period of their discipleship had been completed — that their appointment as his apostles could be fully realized (Matt. 28:16-20 par.; Acts 1:8). Among the twelve, three especially played an important role — Peter, James and John, the "inner circle" (cf. Matt. 17:1 par.); of these Peter was frequently the spokesman (e.g., 16:16).

Although he had not been associated with Jesus' ministry, Paul considered himself an apostle and was regarded as such by the early Church. He claims to have seen the resurrected Lord (1 Cor. 9:1; 15:8) and to have received from him his apostolic commission (Gal. 1:15-17). His labors were like those of the twelve apostles, and his ministry, like theirs, was made possible through God's gracious guidance and support. Paul is considered the last of the chosen apostles and the last to witness a post-resurrection appearance of Christ.

The designation apostle is also given to James the brother of Jesus (1 Cor. 15:7; Gal. 1:19) and Barnabas (Acts 14:4, 14; cf. 1 Cor. 9:6). At 2 Cor. 8:23 the "brethren" are called apostles (RSV mg.; RSV, KJV "messengers"; NIV "representatives of the churches"; JB "delegates"), in the general sense of emissaries; the same title is given to Epaphroditus (Phil. 2:25; RSV, KJV, NIV "messenger"; JB "representative").

The twelve apostles were commissioned by Jesus to advance the kingdom of God through the gospel (Matt. 10:1; 28:18-20) and were given the authority to render decisions and maintain discipline (Matt. 18:18;

cf. 16:19) and to forgive sins (John 20:21-23). Moreover, they were to receive the guidance of the Holy Spirit (John 14:26; 15:26-27; 16:13-15; Acts 1:8) and protection against the "powers of death" (Matt. 16:18). (It was this authorization, as well as their exclusive commitment to Christ's cause rather than their own ends, which distinguishes them from the "false apostles" [Gk. *pseudapóstolos*; 2 Cor. 11:13; cf. 12:11].) They were, moreover, representatives and leaders of the New Testament Church, in a sense mirroring the twelve tribes of Israel as God's people. (Thus there may have been a conscious effort to preserve the number twelve by selecting Matthias as Judas' replacement [Acts 1:15-26].) The twelve apostles, then, were the core of the Church from whom the responsibility for preaching the gospel of the risen Savior radiated out to the entire Church population.

With the development of various heresies, the Church in the second century A.D. set doctrinal limits and witnessed the beginnings of a hierarchal succession of ministers. In this way, the Church is an apostolic body, erected on the teaching of Jesus and his apostles.

Bibliography. K. H. Rengstorf, "ἀποστέλλω," *TDNT* 1:398-447.

APOSTLES, EPISTLE OF THE. A second-century A.D. apocryphal letter purportedly composed by eleven of the apostles (including Cephas [not Peter] and Nathanael) and sent to the churches of the east, west, north, and south. Based largely on the four canonical gospels as well as several apocryphal works, it comprises a revelation by the resurrected Jesus providing for his disciples supplementary information about his life and works and his bodily resurrection. The work opens with a denunciation of Simon the sorcerer and Cerinthus.

APOSTOLIC COUNCIL. The meeting in Jerusalem between delegates of the church at Jerusalem and those of the church at Antioch (including Paul and Barnabas), called to resolve a dispute concerning the necessity of circumcision for Gentile converts (Acts 15:1-21). On the basis of Luke's narrative, it appears that the event occurred during the interval between Paul's first and second missionary journeys.

The controversy resulted from the teaching by certain Judeans at Antioch that Gentile converts must submit to circumcision as required by Mosaic law — meaning that they must first become Jews before they could be considered Christians (Acts 15:1). After considerable debate, Peter declared that to God there was no distinction between Jewish and Gentile Christians, and that Gentile converts should not be forced to succumb to a law that even Jews in the past had not been able to bear; he concluded by affirming that salvation is the result of divine grace rather than a human achievement accomplished by an outward rite (vv. 7-11). Peter's words apparently made an impression, for they were received with notable silence (v. 12). The next speakers were Paul and Barnabas, who (as could be expected) also spoke in favor of the Gentiles (vv. 12-13). Finally, James, the brother of Jesus and moderator of the meeting, took the floor. Concurring with Peter that God is also the God of the Gentiles, he concluded by recommending that Gentile converts need only observe the regulations regarding abstention from eating food strangled or sacrificed to idols and to avoid blood and unchastity (vv. 13-22). James' words were effective and his recommendations accepted. The council ended with the appointment of a number of messengers (including the commissioning of Paul and Barnabas) who would relay its decision to the various churches in Paul's missionary territory (vv. 22-30).

The significance of this meeting was enormous. It not only demonstrated that unanimity could be reached among disparate factions within the Church, but it presaged the end — at least in principle — of Judaistic elements in Christianity. Nevertheless, the decisions were not met immediately with general enthusiasm, as some of Paul's letters indicate.

Gal. 2:1-10 may be Paul's account of this council, but several critical difficulties are involved. (1) In the book of Acts Luke mentions that Paul made three visits to Jerusalem after the apostle's conversion: one soon afterward (9:26-28); a second, the so-called famine visit (11:30; 12:25); and a third, when he attended the apostolic council (15:2-4, 12-13). Paul, on the other hand, lists only two visits: the first, three years after his conversion (Gal. 1:18); and the second, fourteen years later (2:1). Most commentators agree that the first visit mentioned by both authors is the same, but they are divided regarding the subsequent visits. (2) Circumcision is of little importance to the Galatians account, which focuses on the content of Paul's preaching and the appropriateness of his endeavors. (3) It is difficult to reconcile the subsequent actions of Paul and Barnabas with the decisions of the apostolic council (Gal. 2:11-21). Moreover, Paul does not report to the Galatians the major decisions of the council regarding the relationship between Gentiles and the Mosaic restrictions.

APOSTOLIC FATHERS. A group of early Christian writers (*ca*. A.D. 100), erroneously held to have been personal students or close associates of the apostles. The name "Apostolic Fathers" originated with J. B. Cotelier, who in 1672 published their writings as *Patres Apostolici aevi* ("Fathers of the Apostolic Age"). Even though the title remains in vogue, it may not do justice to the individual writings. Indeed, the works are quite diverse: pastoral letters (1 Clement, Ignatius), a sermon (2 Clement), a lecture (Epistle of Barnabas), an apocalypse (Shepherd of Hermas), a "manual of discipline" (Didache), and an account of martyrdom (Polycarp). Other works include apologies (Epistle to Diognetus, Apology of Quadratus) and exposition (Papias).

While the Church Fathers considered some of these writings canonical (e.g., 1 Clement and the Shepherd of Hermas) and placed these on a par with the New Testament documents, Athanasius (A.D. 397) and, finally, the Synod of Carthage (397) clearly distinguished between the canonical New Testament and the writings of these first-century authors.

For many centuries the writings of the Apostolic Fathers have been neglected. According to the Protestant Reformers they lacked the lofty theological treatment of Christ and grace which was so ably set forth

by the apostles Paul and John. Commenting on the relationship between the New Testament authors and the writers of these works, R. M. Grant (pp. 7-8) writes:

Historically . . . the writings of the Apostolic Fathers are different from many New Testament books. None of them, as far as we know, wrote a gospel or produced a treatise like Romans or Ephesians. But the extent of the difference can be exaggerated. The Apostolic Fathers were often concerned with practical problems to a degree greater than that reflected in the New Testament books. They were not apostles like Paul, journeying through the Graeco-Roman world in order to proclaim the gospel — though Ignatius provides a partial exception; they were entrusted with the less exciting, but sometimes more burdensome, task of ministering to congregations that the apostles had brought into existence.

The various works are concerned with a variety of common themes, such as God as Creator, Ruler, Redeemer, and Judge; Jesus Christ; the Church, focusing notably on the subjects of unity and ministry; the Christian life; and eschatology, the study and theory of the last things. On the other hand, the works are distinct in emphasis and content. For example, Ignatius is strongly influenced by the teachings of the apostle Paul, while Hermas and Clement exhibit a more Jewish orientation.

Bibliography. R. M. Grant, *The Apostolic Fathers 1: An Introduction* (New York: 1964); J. B. Lightfoot, *The Apostolic Fathers* I/1-II/3 (repr. 1973); P. Schaff, *History of the Christian Church* 2 (repr. 1976): 631-707.

APPAIM [ăp'ī əm] (Heb. *'appayim* "nostrils"). A son of Nadab and father of Ishi, he was a descendant of Jerahmeel of Judah (1 Chr. 2:30f.).

APPHIA [ăf'ī ə] (Gk. *Apphia*). The second of the three persons to whom Paul's Epistle to Philemon was addressed (Phlm. 2). Though designated "sister" (so RSV, JB, NIV; KJV "beloved sister"), she was probably Philemon's wife.

APPIAN WAY [ăp'ī ən] (Lat. *Via Appia*). The second-oldest Roman highway, named after its builder Appius Claudius (312 B.C.). When first constructed it covered the 221 km. (132 mi.) between Rome and Capua; the road was later extended (*ca*. 250) to the port of Brundisium on the Adriatic Sea, at which point ships could be boarded for Epirus, the western terminus of the Egnatian Way. Its 536 km. (333 mi.) bound the two coasts, in essence unifying Italy, and eased trade with Greece and the East.

While traveling this ancient road, Paul was met by delegations from the church at Rome first at Three Taverns (48 km. [30 mi.] south of Rome) and then at the Forum of Appius (64 km. [40 mi.] south of the capital; Acts 28:15).

APPII FORUM (Acts 28:15, KJV). See FORUM OF APPIUS.

APPLE. While Heb. *tappûaḥ* is properly translated "apple" on linguistic grounds, the apple tree known to have existed in ancient Palestine — a tree growing only in isolated areas and producing fruit of poor quality — does not square with the rich biblical imagery, particularly in Canticles. For this reason, scholars have proposed that the fruit was more likely the citron, the orange, or the quince; even more likely is the apricot, a fruit whose trees were imported from China as early as the first century B.C. According to Josh. 15:34, 53; 17:7 this tree was found in such places as Tappuah (in the lowland), Beth-tappuah (in the hill country), and En-tappuah (in the western portion of Manasseh), all of which derived their names from it.

At Prov. 25:11 apples are used figuratively for words aptly spoken. In Canticles the apple is a delightful tree with marvelous fruit (2:3, 5; 7:8). To the "tiller of the soil" it is one of the trees that "wither" at the approaching Day of the Lord (Joel 1:12).

The "forbidden fruit" of Gen. 3:6, usually understood to have been an apple (perhaps on the basis of Cant. 8:5), may have been an apricot.

The expression "the apple of the eye" (Deut. 32:10; Ps. 17:8; Prov. 7:2, Heb. 'îšôn ["little man"] [bat-]'ayin; Zech. 2:8, Heb. bābâ "gate") indicates something precious that is to be protected.

AQUEDUCT [ăk'wĭ dŭkt]. An elevated structure, often supported by series of arches, on which an open channel brought water to cities and dry areas. The three pools of Solomon, about 21 km. (13 mi.) south of Jerusalem, were connected with the capital by means of two aqueducts; built by Herod the Great (30-4 B.C.), they were later repaired by Pontius Pilate (Josephus *Ant.* xviii.3.2[60]).

AQUILA [ăk'wə lə] (Gk. *Akylas* "eagle").
1. A Jew, a native of Pontus, who spent the first years of his married life at Rome before being compelled by an edict of Claudius to leave the capital of the Roman Empire with all other Jews (*ca.* A.D. 49). If this edict was Claudius' reaction to the tumult in the Jewish community caused by the introduction of Christianity, Aquila and his wife Priscilla (or Prisca) may have been Christians while still at Rome.

Having moved to Corinth (Acts 18:2), the couple met the apostle Paul who arrived in that city during his second missionary journey. Because both Aquila and Paul were "tentmakers" (perhaps "leatherworkers"), the apostle stayed at their home (v. 3). Perhaps they accompanied him to Ephesus (v. 19), where they instructed the eloquent Apollos more carefully in the "way of God" (v. 26). According to 1 Cor. 16:19, Aquila and Priscilla had a church in their home.

With the edict against Jews no longer effective after the death of Claudius, Aquila and Priscilla moved back to Rome, starting another household church. They are the first people mentioned in a list of believers to whom Paul sends his greeting at Rom. 16:3. Whatever was the peril they faced on behalf of the apostle (v. 4), Paul and "all the churches of the Gentiles" thanked them for their support.

Paul's last reference to Aquila and Priscilla is at 2 Tim. 4:19. In prison, probably just before his execution, he sent his greetings to them, apparently at Ephesus.

2.* A native of Sinope in Pontus, he was brought to Jerusalem by Hadrian. He was converted to Christianity but was excommunicated and subsequently became a Jewish proselyte and a disciple of Rabbi Akiba. He produced a highly literal Greek translation of the Old Testament which retained official sanction for synagogue use as late as A.D. 533.

AR [är] (Heb. *'ār* "city"). A city (Num. 21:28), a region, or the entire country of Moab (Deut. 2:9). If a city, it was located near the valley of the Arnon (Num. 21:15), along Moab's northern border (Deut. 2:18). In the oracle against Moab (Isa. 15:1), Ar is one of the two principal Moabite towns to be destroyed.

It has been identified with Areopolis and Raabath Moab (cf. Num. 22:36, the "city of Moab," RSV, KJV; NIV "Moabite town"; JB "Ar of Moab"). Because the latter city lies some 22 km. (14 mi.) south of the Arnon, it most likely is not biblical Ar. Another possible identification is modern el-Misna.

ARA [âr'ə] (Heb. *'ªrā'*). A son of Jether, of the tribe of Asher (1 Chr. 7:38).

ARAB [âr'ăb] (Heb. *'ªrāḇ* "ambush"). A city in the hill country of Judah, southwest of Hebron (Josh. 15:52); possibly the birthplace of the Paarai mentioned at 2 Sam. 23:35. The site has been identified as modern er-Râbiyeh, east of Dumah (Deir ed-Dômeh).

ARABAH [ăr'ə bə] (Heb. *hā 'ªrāḇâ*, possibly "the desert").† A region of Palestine distinguished from the coastal plain, the Negeb, the Shephelah, and the mountainous regions. While rendered only occasionally "plain" (Josh. 4:13; Zech. 14:10), it is actually a depression on the eastern side of Palestine.

I. Location

The Old Testament writers describe its location fairly accurately: south of "Chinnereth," "with the Jordan as the boundary," the "sea of the Arabah, the Salt Sea," and the "slopes of Pisgah on the east" (Deut. 3:17; cf. Josh. 12:3, 8; 2 Kgs. 14:25). In related passages they mention Chinneroth (Josh. 11:2), the eastern bank of the Jordan (Deut. 4:49), the Dead Sea or Salt Sea (4:49; Josh. 3:16). At least once its southern part, between the Dead Sea and Ezion-geber, is referred to (Deut. 2:8).

II. History

The Arabah is first mentioned at the end of Israel's wilderness wanderings, after the people had marched from Ezion-geber northward to Moab (Deut. 2:8) and had conquered the territory occupied by Sihon the king of the Amorites, as the location of Moses' rehearsing of God's mighty acts in behalf of his people (1:1). Soon Joshua, his successor, would cross the Jordan just above the Dead Sea (Josh. 3:16), establish Gilgal as his military headquarters (4:19ff.), destroy Jericho (ch. 6), and defeat the inhabitants of Ai (8:14ff.).

The Arabah also figures frequently in the period following the Israelite Conquest. David hid in the wilderness of Maon while pursued by King Saul (1 Sam. 23:24). Abner went through this region in an attempt to escape from the forces of David's commander Joab

(2 Sam. 2:29). The sons of Rimmon took this route — all night — in order to bring Ishbosheth's head to David at Hebron (4:7). During the divided monarchy Jeroboam II considered it part of the eastern boundary of his kingdom (2 Kgs. 14:25). It was here, near the plains of Jericho, that King Zedekiah of Judah, after a successful escape from Jerusalem, was captured by the Chaldeans (2 Kgs. 25:4-5; Jer. 39:4-5; 52:7).

The last reference to the region is symbolic. According to Zech. 14:10, the area from Geba to Rimmon "shall be turned into a plain," thus contrasting with lofty Jerusalem.

ARABAH, BROOK OF THE. *See* WILLOWS, BROOK OF THE.

ARABIA [ə rā′bĭ ə] (Heb. *ʿᵃraḇ* "steppe," "desert-plateau"; Gk. *Arabia*). A large peninsula between the Persian Gulf and the Red Sea.

I. Identification

Classical geographers divided Arabia into three parts: *Arabia Petrea* ("stoney Arabia"), which comprised Moab, Edom, Transjordan, the Arabah, and the city of Petra; *Arabia deserta* ("desert Arabia"), which included the Syrian desert and central Arabia; *Arabia felix* ("fortunate Arabia"), in the south, particularly the coastal regions. The Bible usually refers to *Arabia Petrea* and *Arabia deserta* when this country is indicated (e.g., in the oracle against Arabia at Isa. 21:13 and at Jer. 25:24); at 2 Chr. 9:14; Ezek. 27:21 perhaps both northern and southern Arabia are meant. Paul located Mt. Sinai in Arabia (Gal. 4:25).

The inhabitants of Arabia were known as "people of the wilderness" (Heb. *ʿᵃrāḇî* or *ʿᵃraḇ*) or bedouin; this later became a proper name — Arabs. Living in the desert (Jer. 25:24; cf. 3:2, "wilderness"), these nomadic tribes dwelled as far east as Babylonia (Isa. 13:20) and as far west as Ethiopia ("near the Ethiopians," 2 Chr. 21:16). The Midianites of Gen. 37:28 were from northern Arabia, while the "people of the east" mentioned at Judg. 6:3 lived in *Arabia deserta*.

II. Biblical Times

A. Old Testament. Several Arabian tribes or cities are listed in the Table of Nations: Hazarmaveth, Sheba, Ophir, Havilah, and Jobab (all names of Joktan's sons, descendants of Shem; Gen. 10:26-29). Ishmael was the progenitor of a number of north Arabian tribes (25:12-18).

During the Israelite monarchy, the Israelites and Arabs were mainly trading partners, although the Arabs also could have had some spiritual influence on the Israelites (e.g., Prov. 30:1; 31:1, where Massa may refer to a city in northern Arabia). Gold (1 Kgs. 9:27-28), almug or algum, and precious stones (10:11; 2 Chr. 9:10) were imported from Ophir; frankincense could have been purchased from Sheba (Isa. 60:6; Jer. 6:20). The queen of Sheba, who may have come from northern Arabia, paid Solomon a visit to test his authenticity (1 Kgs. 10:1-13 par. 2 Chr. 9:1-12). The "kings of Arabia" brought gold and silver to King Solomon, likely as an annual tribute (2 Chr. 9:14; cf. 1 Kgs. 10:15). Certainly, during the reign of Jehoshaphat of Judah, the Arabs paid him a large tri-

bute in cattle (2 Chr. 17:11); given the location of Judah and the reference to the Philistines, these Arabs must have dwelled in *Arabia Petrea*.

Soon the tide turned. Jehoshaphat's evil son provoked God, who, as punishment, roused the anger of the Philistines and Arabs against Judah (2 Chr. 21:16-17). Coming from an area close to Ethiopia, these nomads entered Judah in hordes, and were able to penetrate the capital and take the royal possessions as well as nearly all of the king's offspring. That the Arab occupation continued for some time near Judah's eastern border is evident from the battle at Gurbaal (possibly in Edom), which the devout Uzziah of Judah was able to turn to his favor (26:7). In the judgment against the nations Jeremiah includes the kings of Arabia (Jer. 25:24), probably intending Nebuchadnezzar's military victories in 604 B.C. In the oracle against Tyre Ezekiel predicts the end of commercial dealings between the Arabs and that Phoenician city (Ezek. 27:20-22); with the fall of Tyre in 572, Nebuchadnezzar drastically curtailed the extensive trade between the Arabs and their Phoenician neighbor.

After the Exile the Jews again met with opposition from the Arabs. Suspecting a rebellion, a certain Arab named Geshem ridiculed the Jewish attempt to rebuild the walls of Jerusalem (Neh. 2:19). When the Israelites progressed with the work, the Arabs joined other neighboring peoples in plotting the destruction of Jerusalem (4:7).

B. Intertestamental Period. In his fight with "all the Gentiles" surrounding him, Judas Maccabeus had to contend with their Arab mercenaries as well (1 Macc. 5:39). His successor Jonathan, however, enjoyed the friendship of some of the Nabateans (9:35). (To the writer of 1 Maccabees Arabia and Nabatea in northern Arabia were the same.)

C. New Testament. Among the devout Jews worshipping in Jerusalem at Pentecost were Arabians (Acts 2:11), citizens of the Nabatean kingdom governed by King Aretas. At first the relations between Aretas and Herod Antipas, the tetrarch of Galilee, were cordial, but after Herod divorced the Nabatean ruler's daughter, he incurred Aretas' wrath. Incidentally, it was to this Arabian kingdom, which extended over much of the region from the Euphrates to the Red Sea, that Paul fled after his conversion (Gal. 1:17).

III. Significance

The significance of the Arab nation in the Old Testament is twofold. (1) At Gen. 25:12-18 Ishmael is said to be the ancestor of several Arabian tribes. However, according to the southern Arabs, Qahtan (possibly biblical Joktan [10:25-26]) is their original progenitor. (2) Moses' forty-year stay in Midian was in the extreme northwestern area inhabited by Arabian tribes. In the same region the Israelites spent many years of their wilderness wanderings. Some scholars, accordingly, claimed that Yahweh was a northern Arabian desert deity whom the Israelites afterward worshipped as their god — a claim not supported by the Old Testament.

Following the adoption of Islam as their official religion (seventh century A.D.), the Arabs gained a major position in world history. Their South Semitic language, with its many dialects, is now spoken by more than 50 million people; it is the vehicle for a vast body of literature particularly rich in poetry and rhymed prose.

Bibliography. R. A. Nicholson, *A Literary History of the Arabs* (repr. Cambridge: 1956); A. Nutting, *The Arabs* (New York: 1964); G. W. Van Beek, "South Arabian History and Archaeology," pp. 300-326 in G. E. Wright, ed., *The Bible in the Ancient Near East* (repr. 1979).

ARAD [âr´ăd] (Heb. *ʿᵃraḏ*) **(PERSON)**. A son of Beriah and descendant of Benjamin (1 Chr. 8:15).

ARAD [âr´ăd] (Heb. *ʿᵃraḏ*) **(PLACE)**. An important town in the Negeb. After the Israelites had left Kadesh-barnea and were approaching the promised land by way of Atharim, they met with the forces of the Canaanite king of Arad, who defeated them (Num. 21:1). A second confrontation at neighboring Hormah was decided in Israel's favor, however (vv. 2-3; Josh. 12:14 may reflect this second encounter). In this area the descendants of the "Kenite, Moses' father-in-law," settled among the Israelites (Judg. 1:16).

The site has been identified with contemporary Tell ʿArâd, approximately 26 km. (16 mi.) south of Hebron. Recent excavations, however, suggest that the town did not exist at this site during the Middle and Late Bronze Ages; no remains have been found for the period between the destruction of a fortified settlement at Arad (*ca.* 2700 B.C.) and the emergence of a small Israelite village (twelfth-eleventh centuries). Thus, biblical Arad may in fact be a designation for the entire region rather than a specific city. Another possibility is that Tell ʿArâd is the biblical city founded during the United Monarchy, and the Canaanite city is to be identified with Tell el-Milḥ (or Malḥata), 13 km. (8 mi.) to the southwest.

The Israelite village was built on a hill considered to have been a Kenite high place. It may have been King Solomon who built a citadel on this location. A significant discovery is a tenth-century Israelite temple in the northwest corner of the citadel, the main features of which greatly resemble the descriptions of the temple of Solomon and the tabernacle; it had a holy of holies, a courtyard, two altars for burning incense, and an altar for burnt offerings similar to the biblical altar in the tabernacle. Other important finds include some two hundred ostraca, potsherds inscribed in Hebrew and Aramaic, which shed light on the administrative and commercial activities during the time of the Israelite monarchy and the subsequent Persian garrison.

ARAH [âr´ə] (Heb. ʾārah "traveler"[?]).
1. The oldest son of Uldah of the tribe of Asher (1 Chr. 7:39).
2. An Israelite whose descendants (775, according to Ezra 2:5; 652 at Neh. 7:10) returned from the Exile at the time of Zerubbabel; probably the same as the Arah mentioned at Neh. 6:18, whose son Shecaniah was the father-in-law of Tobiah the Ammonite.

ARAM [âr´əm] (Heb. ʾᵃrām) **(PERSON)**.
1. One of the sons of Shem and grandson of Noah; the eponymous ancestor of the Arameans (Gen. 10:22-23; 1 Chr. 1:17).

2. The son of Kemuel and grandson of Nahor, the brother of Abraham (Gen. 22:20-21).
3. A son of Shemer of the tribe of Asher (1 Chr. 7:34).
4. (Matt. 1:3-4; Luke 3:33, KJV). *See* ARNI.

ARAM [âr´əm] (Heb. ʾᵃrām) **(PLACE)**. General designation for the territory and populace of the Arameans (e.g., 2 Sam. 8:5-6; 1 Kgs. 20:20-21; Amos 1:5); *see* ARAMEANS. Aram of Damascus was an important Syro-Aramean city-state at the time of David (2 Sam. 8:6; KJV "Syria of Damascus"; cf. Isa. 7:8, "head of Syria").

ARAMAIC [ăr´ə mā´ĭk] (Heb. ʾᵃramît).† A Semitic language, closely related to Hebrew. Portions of the Old Testament are written in one of its dialects, called Biblical Aramaic.

I. History

The name Aramaic derives from the Arameans, Semitic-speaking people first associated with Northwest Mesopotamia early in the second millennium B.C. The early history of these people (or peoples) is unclear (*see* ARAMEANS), but scholars suggest that in their earliest attempts at writing they used various Canaanite dialects. At any rate, the oldest extant Aramaic inscriptions date from the ninth century (Kilamuwa; cf. Zakir stele, early eighth century).

During the twelfth century groups of Arameans were attested along the Tigris and Euphrates rivers as well as in Palestine and northern Arabia; a century later they had formed several city-states in Syria. Oddly enough, it was as Aramean political independence waned that the language attained its greatest influence. Aramaic became the dominant language of trade and diplomacy, supplanting Akkadian as the lingua franca of the Assyrian Empire (*ca.* 1100-600) as well as in the Neo-Babylonian Empire (*ca.* 600-540). Aramaic reached its zenith as the official language of the Persian Empire (*ca.* 500-300), but declined and was replaced with Greek during the Hellenistic period (following 300). Some dialects continued in use in isolated regions, and a variety of Aramaic survives in the Near East today.

The incident recorded at 2 Kgs. 18:26 par. Isa. 36:11 provides some indication of the spread of Aramaic into Palestine; during Sennacherib's siege of Jerusalem in 701, the Jewish officials request that the Assyrian Rabshakeh negotiate in the diplomatic tongue so the Hebrew-speaking populace might not follow the transactions. After the Exile, however, Aramaic had become so dominant that the reading of the Hebrew scriptures was, of necessity, followed by an Aramaic translation (later standardized in the Targums; cf. Neh. 8:8).

II. Biblical Aramaic

A. *Old Testament.* The language in which certain Old Testament passages are written has been called Biblical Aramaic; at one time labelled Chaldee, it is basically the Official Aramaic dialect prominent throughout the Persian Empire. The earliest biblical example of this dialect is thought to be the name Jegar-sahadutha ("heap of witness," RSV mg.) used by

Laban in his covenant with Jacob (Gen. 31:47). At Jer. 10:11 an Aramaic gloss interrupts the poem, a defense of Yahweh's superiority over idols.

Two portions of the book of Ezra are written in Aramaic. These represent correspondence between local officials and the Persian kings Artaxerxes and Darius concerning the Jews' rebuilding of Jerusalem and the temple (4:8–6:18; cf. 4:7) and a letter from Artaxerxes to Ezra authorizing the latter's mission (7:12-26).

A major portion of the book of Daniel is written in Aramaic (2:4b–7:28), including the accounts of Nebuchadnezzar's dream; his insanity; the story of Shadrach, Meshach, and Abednego; Belshazzar's feast; Daniel in the lions' den; and his first vision. On linguistic grounds this section may have been composed during the fifth-third centuries; the Hebrew portions of Daniel appear to be later, and some scholars suggest that they represent a Hebrew translation of an originally Aramaic work.

B. New Testament. Various Aramaic words or expressions and "Aramaisms" (forms influenced by Aramaic) occur in the New Testament, e.g., "talitha cumi" (Aram. *talyᵉtâ᾽ qûmî* "little girl, stand up"; Mark 5:41); "ephphata" (Aram. *᾽etpᵉtaḥ* "be opened"; 7:34); "Eli, Eli, lama sabachthani" (Aram. *᾽ēlî ᾽ēlî lᵉmâ᾽ šᵉbaqtanî* "My God, my God, why hast thou forsaken me?"; Matt. 27:46; Mark 15:34, "Eloi, Eloi"); "Rabboni" (Aram. *rabbônî* "my Lord"; Mark 10:51; John 20:16); "maran atha" (Aram. *mārana᾽ tâ᾽* "our Lord, come!"; 1 Cor. 16:22). Aramaic influence is apparent in personal names such as Cephas (John 1:42; 1 Cor. 1:12) and Tabitha (Acts 9:36, 40) and in place names, including Akeldama (Aram. *ḥᵃqēl dᵉmâ᾽* "field of blood"; Acts 1:19), Gethsemane (Aram. *gê᾽ šᵉmānê* "oil press"; Matt. 26:36; Mark 14:32), and Golgotha (Aram. *gûlgûltâ᾽* "skull"; Mark 15:22).

It is generally agreed that Aramaic was the common language of Palestine in the first century A.D. Jesus and his disciples spoke the Galilean dialect, which was distinguished from that of Jerusalem (Matt. 26:73). Certain "Hebrew" place names (e.g., John 5:2; 19:13, 17, 20) should more properly be understood as Aramaic (so NIV), as also the "Hebrew language" spoken by Paul (Acts 21:40; 22:2; 26:14; JB, NIV "Aramaic").

III. Divisions

A number of dialects of Aramaic can be distinguished on the basis of locale and period, as well as literary genre. The earliest is Old Aramaic, attested in ninth–eighth-century inscriptions from Syria and Palestine (Zinjirli, Zakir, Sefire) and in inscribed pottery from northern Galilee.

Encouraged in government circles as an administrative lingua franca, Official Aramaic had developed by the late ninth century and came to be the dominant language of the Near East under the Assyrian, Neo-Babylonian, and Persian Empires. It is widely attested in inscriptions, correspondence (including the Elephantine papyri), commercial documents, seals, and graffiti. Following the demise of the Persian Empire, the dialect continued as a literary form (e.g., Daniel, several Qumran texts, Tobit, Enoch, Targum

Onkelos, Targum Jonathan), in legal documents, and in Nabatean and Palmyrene inscriptions and correspondence.

During the period 300 B.C.-A.D. 200, two major divisions became prominent: Western and Eastern Aramaic. The Western (or Levantine) variety is that found in inscriptions from the region of Jerusalem, in certain place names and phrases recorded in the New Testament, and in the Bar Kokhba letters. Three sub-dialects became apparent for the period 200-900: Palestinian Jewish Aramaic, the Galilean dialect of the Palestinian Talmud, Midrashim, and Targums; Christian Palestinian Aramaic, used by Jewish Christians in Palestine and Egypt; and Samaritan, from the region of Shechem.

Eastern Aramaic, first attested in second-century B.C. inscriptions from Uruk, later developed into three primary subdialects, each with its own distinct script: Syriac, known from a vast body of literature including the Peshitta version of the LXX, and adopted by Aramaic-speaking Christians from Persia to China, Asia Minor, Arabia, and Egypt; Jewish Babylonian Aramaic, the language of the Babylonian Talmud; and Mandaic (or Mandean), attested in the religious literature, amulets, and incantation bowls of the Mandeans, a non-Christian Gnostic sect.

In modern times, a variety of Western Aramaic is preserved by a handful of Christian villages in the Anti-lebanon region. Eastern Aramaic, often called Modern Syriac, survives among Christian villagers in northern Syria, the Lake Van region of Turkey, Azerbaijan in the Soviet Union, and northern areas of Iraq and Iran.

IV. Linguistic Character

Phonetically similar to Biblical Hebrew, Aramaic consists of twenty-three consonants. Words are formed primarily on roots of three consonants and are inflected vocally and by the use of prefixes, infixes, and suffixes. Verbs, which are inflected to show person, number, and tense, occur in various stems, including the simple (G or ground; cf. Heb. qₐl), intensive (D or doubling; cf. Heb. piel), and causative (H; cf. Heb. hiphil). Nouns are masculine or feminine in gender and singular, plural, or dual in number; they occur in three states: absolute, construct (genitive relationship), and determinative (an emphatic form indicating the definite article). Direct objects may be indicated by the prefix *lᵉ-* "to."

Tracing its origins to the Phoenician script, a distinctive Aramaic writing system had developed by the ninth century and was used also for Ammonite, Edomite, and other dialects. Its cursive form was the basis of the "square" script adopted by Hebrew *ca.* the second century B.C. Other local variants which derived from the Aramaic script after the fall of the Persian Empire include Nabatean (and, through it, Arabic), Syriac, Mandean, Pahlavi, Parthian, Sogdian, Mongol, and numerous other eastern writing systems.

Bibliography. R. A. Bowman, "Arameans, Aramaic, and the Bible," *JNES* 7 (1948): 65-90; F. Rosenthal, *An Aramaic Handbook*, 4 vols. (Wiesbaden: 1967); *A Grammar of Biblical Aramaic*, rev. ed. (Wiesbaden: 1974).

ARAMEANS [ăr′ə mē′ənz] (Heb. *ʾᵃrām, ʾᵃrammî, ʾᵃrammîm*; Akk. *aramu, arimu, arumu*). A Semitic people, probably named after Arame, a country located somewhere northeast of Syria. The name Aram is used to designate both the people (e.g., 1 Chr. 2:23) and the land from which they came (2 Sam. 15:8; Hos. 12:12; Zech. 9:1). Whereas the KJV consistently refers to these people as "Syrian(s)" (cf. LXX *Syrioi*), the JB and NIV render all Old Testament references "Aramean(s)." The RSV reads "Aramean" in the patriarchal narratives and "Syrians" in passages dealing with Israel's later relations with these nomads. (Actually, the name "Syria" originated in Hellenistic times.)

I. Location

The Arameans settled in Mesopotamia, Syria, and Transjordan. They had strongholds in Aram of Damascus (2 Sam. 8:6; 1 Chr. 18:6, "Syria of Damascus"), in Zobah, in Coele-Syria (between the Lebanon and the Anti-lebanon ranges), and in Beth-rehob near Dan — all in the area that is now called Syria. In Mesopotamia they dwelled in Aram-naharaim, while in Transjordan they occupied the area around Maacah (Aram-maacah) near Bashan.

II. History

Aramean history begins *ca.* 3100 B.C.; at least, nomadic Arameans are known to have been moving through Egypt at that time. During the Amarna Age (*ca.* 1400) their name (Akk. *Aḫlame* "confederates") occured in Akkadian records.

In the Table of Nations Aram, a descendant of Shem, is said to be the ancestor of the Arameans (Gen. 10:22-23). According to Amos 9:7 the Arameans originated in Mesopotamia, in the vicinity of Kir. By *ca.* 2400 B.C. they had crossed the Tigris into Syria. Nahor, the brother of Abraham, became the father of Aram (Gen. 22:20-22). Members of the Aramaean tribe were Bethuel, the father of Rebekah (vv. 22-23), and Laban. Though they settled in Canaan, Abraham had his steward Eliezer return to Haran (biblical Paddan-aram) to ask permission for Rebekah to marry his son Isaac (25:20). Later the aged Isaac sent his son Jacob to the same area to find a wife (28:5), and Jacob served his Aramean kinsman Laban for twenty-one years (31:20, 24). At Deut. 26:5 Jacob is called a "wandering Aramean," perhaps on account of the circumstances of his marriage to Leah and Rachel, Laban's daughters, but more likely as a reference to the Aramean nomadic tradition or to Jacob's relationship to Habiru (ʿApiru) activity.

During the Monarchy Saul fought victoriously against the Arameans at Zobah (1 Sam. 14:47), and later David defeated Hadadezer the king of Zobah (2 Sam. 8:3-4), as well as the Arameans of Damascus (v. 5). Many of the Aramean tribes became subject to Israelite rule and were required to pay an annual tribute. They tried to help the Ammonites — who were also Arameans, traditionally related through Lot (Gen. 11:26-27; 19:30-38) — in their battle with David after the death of Nahash but were defeated (2 Sam. 10:1-19) and no longer dared to offer their support (v. 19).

The Arameans remained subject to Solomon, and to some degree to the first kings of the northern kingdom (but see 1 Kgs. 15:18-20). During Ahab's reign, however, Ben-hadad of Damascus besieged Samaria (1 Kgs. 20:1). Foretold of the Aramean's victory, Ahab not only drove the Arameans away from his capital but also slaughtered them in vast numbers (v. 21). With additional victories over the Arameans behind him, Ahab at last set out to reconquer Ramoth-gilead; this time he was mortally wounded (22:34-37).

Though they were unable to capture Samaria (7:10ff.), the Arameans remained a strong political force during the reigns of Joram and Jehu of Israel (2 Kgs. 8:28-29; 9:32-33). An unnamed king of Israel granted Naaman "the Syrian" passage through his land (5:20; cf. Luke 4:2). But King Joash of Judah was humiliated in war with the Arameans because, as the author of Chronicles puts it, he and his subjects "had forsaken the Lord, the God of their fathers" (2 Chr. 24:24).

Faced with the growing power of the Assyrian kingdom, the Arameans steadily lost cities and territory. In 732 they surrendered Zobah and Damascus (as predicted by Amos [Amos 1:5] as punishment for Aramean cruelty [v. 3]), and shortly thereafter, Hamath (720). With the conquest of Samaria in 732, the Assyrians deported the Israelites to former Aramean areas in Mesopotamia (2 Kgs. 17:6), while the Arameans of Hamath were resettled at Samaria (vv. 24, 30). Though their political and military power was all but gone, isolated Arameans still made warring excursions against Judah and Israel (2 Kgs. 24:2; Jer. 35:11; Isa. 9:12 may refer to Aramean subjects of Assyria). Just before the capture of Damascus, the Aramean king Rezin nearly overpowered Ahaz of Judah (2 Kgs. 16:5), and some of the eastern Aramean tribes joined the Babylonians (Chaldeans) in a mighty victory over Assyria at Nineveh (612). Gradually, however, they became assimilated by the Babylonians.

III. Culture

The cultural contributions of the Arameans, rather than their military might, had a salutary effect on the ancient Near East. They modified the Phoenician alphabet and transmitted it to other peoples, including the Hebrews. Their language — Aramaic — replaced Akkadian and became the lingua franca of the area till it was replaced by Greek when Alexander the Great conquered Persia. Local dialects, however, continued well into the Christian era.

See also SYRIA.

Bibliography. R. T. O'Callaghan, *Aram Naharaim* (Rome: 1948).

ARAMITESS [ăr′ə mīt′əs] (Heb. *ʾᵃrammîyâ* "Aramean woman"). The concubine mother of Machir, the father of Gilead (1 Chr. 7:14). Thus, the inhabitants of Gilead were in part descended from the Arameans.

ARAM-MAACAH [âr′əm mā′ə kə] (Heb. *ʾᵃram maʿᵃḳâ*). An alternate name of Maacah (1 Chr. 19:6; KJV "Syria-maachah"). *See* MAACAH (PLACE).

ARAM-NAHARAIM [âr′əm nā′ə rā′əm] (Heb. *ʾᵃram naḫᵃrayim* "Aram of the rivers"). An area inhabited by the Arameans between the Euphrates and Tigris rivers in northwestern Mesopotamia (the Hebrew term is usually translated "Mesopotamia" in the KJV, RSV, JB). The Hebrew patriarchs are regarded as having come from this region.

Eliezer, Abraham's steward, was sent there to obtain a wife for Isaac (Gen. 24:10). It was the home of Balaam (Deut. 23:4), and it was from this region that Cushan-rishathaim attacked Israel in the time prior to the judgeship of Othniel (Judg. 3:8). The superscription to Ps. 60 may refer to the military engagement between David and a number of Aramean city-states as recorded at 1 Chr. 19:6.

ARAM-ZOBAH [âr'əm zō'bə] (Heb. *ʾᵃram ṣôbâ*). An alternate name of Zobah (superscription to Ps. 60), an Amorite town in the Beqaʿ valley between the Lebanon and Anti-lebanon mountains. *See* ZOBAH.

ARAN [âr'ăn] (Heb. *ʾᵃrān* "wild goat"). The younger son of Dishan the Horite (Gen. 36:28; 1 Chr. 1:42).

ʿARAQ EL-EMIR [âr'ăk ĕl ĕm'ĭr].† Home of the Tobiad dynasty, a family of wealthy Ammonites particularly influential in the Persian period (cf. Neh. 2:19; 6:1, 12, 14, 17; 13:4-8; Zech. 6:9-14). A third-century B.C. inscription on the face of a cliff into which a series of caverns have been dug bears the name "Tobiah." The ruins of a large structure, the Qaṣr el-ʿAbd, are thought to be the mausoleum of the Tobiads, although it may instead be a palace or fortress. The site is located in the Wâdī Sîr approximately 29 km. (18 mi.) east of Jericho and 16 km. (10 mi.) west of Amman.

ARARAT [är'ə răt] (Heb. *ʾᵃrārāṭ*). A country in the region of Lake Van in Armenia, south of the Araxes river. The name is the Hebrew form of Urartu, a people known from Assyrian cuneiform inscriptions.

In the Old Testament the kingdom of Ararat, together with the neighboring kingdoms Minni and Ashkenaz, was summoned to war against Babylon (Jer. 51:27). Actually, the Urartu disappeared as an independent entity and political entity in approximately the early sixth century B.C., when they were destroyed by the Medes coming from the east. Jeremiah may have viewed them as subjects of the Medes who participated in the Median attack against Babylon (cf. v. 11, the "kings of the Medes"). According to 2 Kgs. 19:37 par. Isa. 37:38 (KJV "Armenia"), the sons of Sennacherib fled to this region after having murdered him (681 B.C.).

The "mountains of Ararat" cited as the resting spot of Noah's ark (Gen. 8:4) refer to the mountainous region as a whole, which may have been renowned among the Hebrews as containing the highest mountains in the world. Later Christian tradition focused on one of these peaks, Agri Dag in northeastern Turkey (elevation 5165 m. [16,946 ft.]), as the site of that landing.

ARATUS [är'ə təs] (Gk. *Aretos*). A third-century B.C. Stoic poet from Soli in Cilicia. In his speech on the Areopagus Paul quotes from his poem *Phaenomena* (Acts 17:28).

ARAUNAH [ə rô'nə] (Heb. *ʾᵃrawnâ*). A Jebusite from whom David purchased a threshing floor upon which to build an altar and thereby protect the Israelites from plague (2 Sam. 24:16-25 par. 1 Chr. 21:15-22:1); it was at this site that the angel of destruction had halted the pestilence inflicted on Israel on account of David's census. It was also on this site, traditionally associated with Mt. Moriah, that Solomon built the temple (2 Chr. 3:1).

In the accounts in 1-2 Chronicles, the name is rendered Ornan (Heb. *ʾornān*; cf. 2 Sam. 14:16, *ʾᵃranyâ*; K *ʾôrnâ*), perhaps related to Hur. *iwirne* "chief, ruler."

ARBA [är'bə] (Heb. *ʾarbaʿ* "four"). The father of Anak (Josh. 15:13; 21:11) and regarded as the greatest of the Anakim (14:15). *See* KIRIATH-ARBA.

ARBATHITE [är'bə thīt] (Heb. *hāʿarbāṭi*). A resident of Beth-arabah, a city on the border between Judah and Benjamin. This gentilic is associated with Abialbon, one of David's mighty men (2 Sam. 23:21; "Abiel," 1 Chr. 11:32).

ARBATTA [är băt'ə] (Gk. *Arbatta*). A region to the south of Mt. Carmel whose Jewish inhabitants Simon Maccabeus rescued from the Gentiles in Galilee and brought back to Judea (1 Macc. 5:23). It is probably to be identified with Narbata (Khirbet Beidûs), located between Samaria and Caesarea (cf. Josephus *BJ* ii.14.5, 18.10); other possibilities include Akrabattis, southeast of Shechem (*BJ* iii.3.4-5), or Arubboth, probably in the southern Shephelah of Judah (1 Kgs. 4:10).

ARBELA [är bē'lə] (Gk. *Arbēla*). A place where the Syrian forces of Bacchides besieged and decimated many Jewish inhabitants during his campaign against Judas Maccabeus in 161 B.C. (1 Macc. 9:2). The site is probably to be identified with Khirbet Irbid, 4 km. (2.5 mi.) west of the Sea of Galilee. It was in this same cavernous area (cf. Josephus *Ant.* xii.11.1) that Jewish rebels resisted Herod the Great in 39 B.C. (*Ant.* xiv.15.4-5; *BJ* i.16.204).

ARBITE [är'bīt] (Heb. *hāʿarbî*). An epithet given to Paarai (2 Sam. 23:35), referring either to his father or the city of his residency (cf. Arab, Josh. 15:52).

ARCHAEOLOGY, BIBLICAL.†

I. Definition

The English word "archaeology" ultimately derives from Gk. *archaio-* "ancient" and *logos* "orderly arrangement," and thus means "the orderly arrangement of ancient things." As used in contemporary scholarship, however, it may be defined as "that branch of historical research which draws its evidence from surviving material traces and remains of past human activity" (Blaiklock, p. 259). Biblical archaeology, then, may be defined as that branch of research which draws its evidence from the material remains of Palestine and neighboring countries that bear a relation to the biblical text. Material remains include inscriptions (on stone, clay, metal, parchment, and papyrus), buildings, art, fortifications, weapons, tools, personal implements, and the like.

Recent years have witnessed a growing scholarly objection to the use of the term "biblical archaeology." One reason is the charge that the term implies a particular branch of archaeology whose main function is to confirm the truthfulness of the Bible. A second, related objection is that the term is obsolete, referring to archaeologists' labors from the 1930s to 1960s which supposedly verified much of the Bible's historical accuracy that had been assailed by critical German scholars such as Julius Wellhausen. Indeed, some of these "verifications" have come under scrutiny and have been abandoned. Such objections to the term "biblical archaeology" can be nullified by the prevailing scholarly understanding of the discipline as concerned with the illumination of the biblical text.

II. The Task

A. *Recovery of Materials.* The first step in the archaeologist's task is the selection of a site, a choice which may be motivated by a number of considerations. Literary evidence may have pointed to the historical importance of an ancient site; there may be unsolved chronological problems that one or more sites may solve; or a given site may be more accessible because of availability of supplies or for security reasons.

The next step is the actual recovery of materials. Two methods of accomplishing this may be distinguished — surface exploration and excavation. The first involves the discovery of materials located on the surface of a site. This method has been used since the beginning of serious archaeological endeavor (the nineteenth century), and several significant finds have been made by this method. The most significant are the Rosetta Stone, the key to the decipherment of the Egyptian language, discovered on Napoleon's expedition to Egypt in 1798; and the Behistun Inscription, the key to the decipherment of Assyro-Babylonian cuneiform, first copied 1835-47 by H. Rawlinson.

The second method, which is used more frequently, is excavation. The "target" of excavation is most often the *tell,* which in Arabic means "mound." Tells are formed by the successive establishment of settlements on top of one another during the course of time. That is, after one city was destroyed or became uninhabited, another city would be built upon the ruins.

The first step in excavation is the establishment of a grid for the surface of the mound. This is done by a surveyor, and the grid points are marked by pegs or concrete blocks. The grid usually consists of areas about 5 m. (16 ft.) square, and these constitute the units by which the excavation is organized.

After the grid is established, the archaeologist chooses a starting point and begins excavating. First he removes the plants, rubble, pottery, from the surface of the area and records these as surface finds. He then digs straight downward, leaving earthen balks (ridges of untouched dirt) on all four sides of the area. Caution must be exercised not to dig into the next level of occupation, as the material remains of one

Aerial view of the excavated mound of Megiddo (W. Braun)

occupation must not be mixed or confused with those of another. One safeguard against digging into the next level is to dig a test trench, which involves digging a two- or three-foot trench in the area and smoothing the sides with a trowel. This enables the excavator to see where one level stops and the next begins. The method of excavating one level at a time is known as stratigraphy.

The actual removal of each level is done by the members of the excavation team, usually students, locals, and other interested persons. When the work has progressed close to the floor of each level, however, the experts usually assume the more precise task of debris removal.

Each object found in a given level is placed in a basket identified by site, area, level, and place in the level where the object was found (i.e., street, cistern, room, etc.). Finally, description of the contents of each level is recorded in the archaeologist's notebook, and the entire level is sketched to scale and photographed. Walls and other structures are then dismantled, and the level is cleared to prepare for work on the next level.

Other targets for the archaeologist are tombs and caves. Tombs are frequently difficult to find, since they are usually subterranean and leave little trace of their existence on the earth's surface. They do, however, frequently yield fairly well preserved material remains (e.g., wooden utensils, jewels, seals, furniture) that has been buried with the dead. Caves usually provide information about culture prior to the historical periods covered by the Bible and thus need only be mentioned here.

B. *Dating the Materials.* Part of the archaeologist's task after excavation is dating the level that has been uncovered. Relatively precise dates can be established by pottery sequence-dating, devised in the late nineteenth century by W. M. F. Petrie on his work on Egyptian pottery and refined by subsequent scholars (notably W. F. Albright). This procedure is based on the fact that each period of civilization had its own typical pottery, which differed in shape, color, design, or size. By careful observation of these differences, plus correlation of this evidence with other evidence that produces absolute dates, archaeologists have been able to assign dates to the various types and thus to the levels in which they are found.

Occasionally inscriptions, coins, scarabs containing royal seals, and other materials are found that contain dates which, if found *in situ* (in the level in which they were originally embedded), enable the archaeologist to date a given level precisely. Occasionally chronological references occur in the Bible that also enable precise dating. This is true, for example, in the case of Samaria, which was founded in Omri's seventh year (*ca.* 870 B.C.; 1 Kgs. 16:23-24) and destroyed in 721 (2 Kgs. 17:5-6). For most sites, however, such information is not available.

With the advent of scientific technology, other methods of dating have been devised. Foremost to date is the carbon-14 method, which measures the amount of radioactive carbon present in materials such as bone, wood, shell, and dung. By using a certain formula scientists can assign fairly precise dates to these items, with roughly a 5-percent margin of error.

Thus dated, the articles provide dates for the levels in which they are found.

C. *Interpretation of Data.* Once excavation is completed, the archaeologist must interpret the data retrieved. By examining notes, photographs, and drawings he must determine the major periods of occupation of the site. This can be done by correlating the various levels with datable material remains (pottery, weapons, etc.). The archaeologist must also characterize the material culture of the site from all the available data. Once this is done he will attempt to correlate the data with those of neighboring sites and ultimately of the Near East in general.

Since the process of excavation is destructive, it is incumbent upon the archaeologist to record finds with great care. These records must then be published — usually in preliminary small reports and then in a comprehensive final report — so that the task of interpretation may extend to other competent archaeologists. In this way the inevitable errors or imprecise analyses are frequently corrected and unsolved problems solved.

III. History of Biblical Archaeology

Though the spirit of archaeological endeavor existed as early as the Crusades, the scientific exploration of lands relating to the Bible may be said to have begun with Napoleon's expedition to Egypt in 1798. On this expedition the Rosetta Stone was discovered, and in 1930 it was deciphered by J. Champollion, thus launching the discipline of Egyptology. Mesopotamian archaeology began with P. E. Botta's digging at Nineveh from 1842-43 and A. H. Layard's work on several Babylonian sites in the 1840s. In 1850 H. C. Rawlinson deciphered Assyro-Babylonian cuneiform, and in the late nineteenth and early twentieth centuries R. Koldewey excavated in the city of Babylon. Sumerian culture, the "ancestor" of most Mesopotamian cultures, was brought to light by the work of E. de Sarzec in the late nineteenth century.

Scientific archaeology of Palestine may be said to have begun in 1838, when E. Robinson and E. Smith traveled the country and for the first time identified large numbers of biblical sites through surface exploration. Other significant surface surveys include the work of C. R. Condor and H. H. Kitchener on western Palestine, 1872-78, G. Schumacher's work on Hauran and north Transjordan begun in 1884, and N. Glueck's work on Transjordan begun in 1933 and his work on the Negeb begun in 1952.

Actual excavation in Palestine did not begin, however, until the work of W. M. F. Petrie at Tell el-Ḥesī (once thought to be Lachish, but now believed to be Eglon) in 1890. Following the lead of the classical archaeologist H. Schliemann who began excavating Troy in 1870 by stratigraphic methods, Petrie established the use of stratigraphy and pottery chronology for Palestinian sites.

Other pre-World War I excavations of particular significance include the work of F. J. Bliss and A. C. Dickie at Jerusalem, 1894-97; R. A. S. Macalister at Tell Jezer (Gezer), 1902-09; E. Sellin at Tell Taʿannak (Taanach), 1901-04; G. Schumacher at Tell el-Mutesellim (Megiddo), 1903-05; Sellin and C. Watzinger at Tell es-Sulṭân (Old Testament Jericho),

A view of the Megiddo mound showing several levels of occupation (W. S. LaSor)

1907-09; G. A. Reisner at Sebaṣṭiyeh (Samaria), 1908-10; D. MacKenzie at Tell er-Rumeileh (Beth-shemesh), 1911-12; and Sellin at Tell Balâṭah (Shechem), 1913-14.

However, with few exceptions (notably Petrie and Reisner), pre-World War I excavations were of inferior quality, and erroneous interpretations of the data retrieved were frequent. None of the data of the individual excavations was coordinated, and no general chronological picture of Palestine emerged.

After the war, excavations were resumed. The more significant include the work of J. Garstang and W. J. Phythian-Adams at ʿAsqalân (Ashkelon), 1920-22; C. S. Fisher, A. Rowe, and G. M. FitzGerald at Tell el-Ḥuṣn (Beth-shan), 1921-33; W. F. Albright at Tell el-Fûl (Gibeah), 1922-23; Macalister, J. G. Duncan, and J. W. Crowfoot at the City of David (Ophel) in Jerusalem, 1923-28; Fisher, P. L. O. Guy, and G. Loud at Tell el-Mutesellim (Megiddo), 1925-39; G. Horsfield, Crowfoot, Fisher, and C. C. McCown at Jerash (Gerasa), 1925-34; H. Kjaer and A. Schmidt at Tell Seilûn (Shiloh), 1926; Sellin, H. Welter, and H. Steckeweh at Tell Balâṭah (Shechem), 1926-34; W. F. Badè at Tell en-Naṣbeh (Mizpah), 1926-35; Albright at Tell Beit Mirsim (thought by Albright to be Debir [earlier known as Kiriath-sepher], but recent work suggests that Debir is to be identified with Khirbet Kabûd), 1926-32; Petrie at Tell Jemmeh(?), 1926-27 and at Tell el-Fârʿah (Tirzah), 1928-30; E. Grant and Fisher at Tell er-Rumeileh (Beth-shemesh), 1928-33; Garstang at Tell es-Sulṭân (Jericho), 1929-36; Petrie at Tell el-ʿAjjûl (Beth-eglaim), 1930-34; O. R. Sellers and Albright at eṭ-Ṭubeiqah (Beth-zur), 1931; Crowfoot, K. M. Kenyon, and E. L. Sukenik at Sebasṭiyeh (Samaria), 1931-35; R. W. Hamilton at Tell Abû

Hawâm (Salmonah?), 1932-33; J. L. Starkey at Tell ed-Duweir (Lachish), 1932-38; J. Marquet-Krause at et-Tell (Ai), 1933-34; Albright and J. L. Kelso at Beiṭîn (Bethel), 1934; and C. N. Johns at Jerusalem, 1934-40.

Characteristic of this period were a higher level of organization and better staffing at excavations, careful recording of finds, quicker interpretation of the data retrieved, and correlation of the data of the individual sites. In general, Palestinian archaeology had achieved scientific status.

During World War II and the subsequent Arab-Israeli conflict, archaeological activity all but ceased to exist. Among the more significant excavations after the beginning of the war were B. Mazar (Maisler), M. Stekelis, M. Avi-Yonah, Guy, P. Bar-Adon, and Y. Yadin at Khirbet Kerak (Beth-yerah), begun in 1944; R. de Vaux at Tell el-Fârʿah (Tirzah), 1946-60; de Vaux, G. L. Harding, Y. Saʿad, Sellers, W. L. Reed, and others at the Qumran caves, Khirbet Qumrân, and Wâdî Murabbaʿat, begun in 1948; Mazar at Tell Qasileh, 1948-50; Avi-Yonah at Caesarea, begun in 1950; J. Bowman and B. S. J. Isserlin at Jaffa, begun in 1950; Kelso, A. H. Detweiler, F. V. Winnett, and J. B. Pritchard at Tulul Abû el-ʿAlâyiq (New Testament Jericho), 1950-51; Winnett, Reed, A. D. Tushingham, G. W. Van Beek, and W. H. Morton at Dhîbân (Dibon or Dibon-gad), 1950 and 1956; I. Ben-Dor and M. Dothan at ʿAffuleh (Epher), 1951, and at Khirbet el-Bitar, 1952-54; Kenyon at Tell es-Sulṭân (Jericho), 1952-58; J. Perrot at Tell Abû Matar, 1952; J. P. Free at Tell Dôthâ (Dothan), 1953-64; Ben-Dor, 1947, Dothan, 1954-55, and D. Barag, 1968, at Nahariyeh; Kelso at Beiṭîn (Bethel), 1954, 1957, and 1960; Yadin at Tell el-Qedaḥ (Hazor), 1955-58; Avi-Yonah, N. Av-

igad, Y. Aharoni, I. Dunayevsky, and S. Gutman at
Masada, begun in 1955; G. E. Wright at Balâṭah
(Shechem), 1957-66; Pritchard at ej-Jib (Gibeon),
1956-62; S. Yeivin at Tell Sheikh el-Areini (Gath),
1956-61; Aharoni at Ramat Raḥel, 1959-62; Y. Kap-
lan at Yâfâ (Jaffa), 1955-61; A. Frova, 1959-61, and
Avi-Yonah, 1962, at Qeiṣâriyeh (Herodian part of
Caesarea); Kenyon at Ophel (Jerusalem), 1961-68;
Dothan, Freedman, and J. L. Swauger at Esdûd
(Ashdod), 1962-72; Aharoni at Tell ʿArâd (Arad),
1962-67, and at Tell ed-Duweir (Lachish), 1966; V.
Corbo at Jebel Fureidis (Herodium), 1962-67; Yadin
at Masada, 1963-65; P. W. Lapp at Tell Taʿannak
(Taanach), 1963-68; Wright, W. G. Dever, and others
at Tell Jezer (Gezer), 1964-74; A. Biran at Tell Dan
(Dan), 1966; Mazar at Jerusalem, 1968-77; Aharoni at
Tell es-Sebaʿ (Beersheba), begun in 1969.

Among extra-Palestinian sites excavated, the following deserve at least a brief mention. In Transjordan the
most significant work has been that of Glueck at Ezion-
geber; P. J. Parr and P. Hammond at Petra; H. J. Franken
at Tel Deir ʿallâ (Succoth?); and S. H. Horn, R. S.
Boraas, and L. Geraty at Tell Ḥesbân (Heshbon).

In Syria the most important sites excavated are Car-
chemish, Tell Ḥalâf (Gozan), Râs Shamra (Ugarit),
Tell Hariri (Mari), Tell Atshana (Alalakh), Tell Erfâd
(Arpad), and Tell Mardikh (Ebla).

In Lebanon the most important sites are Baalbek
(Aven?), Byblos, Sidon, Tyre, Kamed el-Loz
(Kumidi), and Zarephath.

In Asia Minor the most significant sites are
Boghazköy (Hattusas), Alaça Hüyük (Euyuk), Kül-
tepe, Karatepe, Alişar, Ephesus, Sardis, Hierapolis,
Smyrna, Pergamum, Thyatira, Philadelphia, and
Laodicea.

IV. Chronological Periods in Palestine

Based primarily on the level of technology, but also
(for the later periods) on political considerations, archaeologists have distinguished certain basic divisions
in the cultural development of Palestine. Although
scholars are far from unanimous regarding the precise
dates of these parameters or the number and limits of
subdivisions in each period, the following main
periods can be identified:

Mesolithic (Natufian)	*ca.* 8000-6000
Prepottery Neolithic	*ca.* 6000-5000
Pottery Neolithic	*ca.* 5000-4000
Chalcolithic (copper tools come into use)	*ca.* 4000-3200
Early Bronze (EB) (copper tools are dominant)	
EB I	*ca.* 3200-2800
EB II	*ca.* 2800-2600
EB III	*ca.* 2600-2300
EB IV (or III B)	*ca.* 2300-2100
Middle Bronze (MB)	
MB I (or EB-MB)	*ca.* 2100-1900
MB II A	*ca.* 1900-1700
MB II B	*ca.* 1700-1600
MB II C	*ca.* 1600-1550
Late Bronze (LB)	
LB I	*ca.* 1550-1400
LB II A	*ca.* 1400-1300
LB II B	*ca.* 1300-1200
Iron I or Early Iron (EI) (iron tools come into use)	
I A	*ca.* 1200-1150
I B	*ca.* 1150-1025
I C	*ca.* 1025- 950
I D	*ca.* 950- 900

Part of the excavation at Megiddo, showing reconstructed walls (by courtesy of the Oriental Institute, University of Chicago.

Iron II or Middle Iron (MI)

II A	*ca.*	900- 800
II B	*ca.*	800- 700
II C	*ca.*	700- 600
Iron III, Late Iron, or Persian	*ca.*	600- 300
Hellenistic	*ca.*	300- 63
Roman	*ca.* 63 B.C.–A.D. 323	
Byzantine	*ca.* A.D. 323-636	
Islamic	*ca.* 636-present	

V. Archaeology and the Bible

A. *Important Correspondences.* Generally speaking, the primary contribution of the archaeology of Palestinian sites (excluding the phenomenal discoveries at Qumran) to the illumination of the Bible is in two areas: intensification in the knowledge of the material culture of Israel in the biblical period, and confirmation of the essential accuracy of many historical statements in the Bible. Knowledge of material culture is intensified by the discovery of buildings, fortifications, art objects, weapons, tools, personal implements, and all material objects that bring ancient life to modern times. Among those finds which confirm historical accuracy are the discoveries of thirteenth-century destruction levels in several Canaanite cities mentioned as conquered by the Israelites in the Conquest (Josh. 5–12) and the confirmation of Babylon's deportation of Judah in 597 B.C. by the Lachish Letters.

The great majority of literary correspondences with the Bible come from extra-Palestinian sites. This is partially because many of Israel's neighbors used clay tablets for writing, which are much more durable than the papyri and other materials used by the Israelites.

An exhaustive listing of all the cases in which archaeology has yielded literary material that sheds light upon the Bible is not practical here, but the following are among the more important.

A Babylonian account of creation was discovered between 1850 and 1854 in the library of Assurbanipal at Nineveh. It became known as Enuma Elish ("when on high") from its opening words, and describes the conflict between the great god Marduk and his female adversary Tiamat which results in the creation of the universe. Its primary similarities with the Genesis account (ch. 1) are that both accounts record a time when the earth was without form and void, the accounts have a similar order of creation events, and both make frequent use of the number seven. The main differences are that the Babylonian account is quite polytheistic while the Israelite is monotheistic, the Babylonian account confuses divine spirit and cosmic matter but the Israelite distinguishes them, and the Babylonian account is part of a ritual hymn recited annually before a statue of Marduk while the Israelite is properly an "account."

In general, scholars believe that the Genesis account is dependent upon the Babylonian. Some scholars, however, are of the opinion that the accounts derive from a common source and that the biblical one was purged of its mythical elements when adapted for the Israelite religion.

The story of a great flood that destroyed mankind is known from a number of Mesopotamian sources, the earliest of which is Sumerian. In the Sumerian account the sole survivor is Ziusudra who survived by riding out the flood in a boat and who subsequently was granted immortality by the gods.

More directly relevant to the biblical account is the Babylonian version of this flood recorded in the eleventh tablet of the Epic of Gilgamesh. In this account Utnapishtim explains to Gilgamesh how he received immortality from the gods after a great deluge. Many details of his story have correspondences with the biblical account. The similarities are as follows: both accounts attribute the deluge to the divine person(s); both relate that the catastrophe was foretold to the hero; both hold that mankind's sin was the reason for the flood (though in different ways); both relate that the hero and his family survived; both state that the hero was commanded by the divine person(s) to build a boat to preserve life; both specify the physical causes and duration of the flood; both relate the name of the mountain where the boat landed; both tell of the sending out of birds to determine the amount of the water's decrease after the flood; both describe the hero's acts of worship after the catastrophe; and both tell of special messages given to the hero after the deluge. The main differences are as follows: the Babylonian account is polytheistic while the Israelite one is monotheistic; the biblical account emphasizes the moral decline of mankind as the reason for the deluge; and the Babylonian account confuses divine spirit and cosmic matter.

As with the creation accounts, conservative scholars generally explain the similarities between these accounts as stemming from a common source, and the differences as the result of the purging of mythical elements from the Israelite account.

The discovery from 1925-41 of thousands of clay tablets written in Babylonian cuneiform at the ancient Hurrian city of Nuzi has thrown light on several customs mentioned in the patriarchal narratives. For example, Abraham's adoption of his servant Eliezer as heir (Gen. 15:2) had long puzzled biblical scholars. The Nuzi tablets, however, show that a childless couple could adopt a servant or freeborn nonrelative as heir. If a son was born at a later time, the adopted son had to yield to him his position as chief heir (as in Abraham's case, 21:1-14).

The Nuzi tablets also shed light on Sarah's giving of her maid to Abraham when she feared she would be childless (Gen. 16:1-16; cf. 30:3, 9). Nuzi laws state that if a man's wife is barren, she must provide him with a slave as wife.

Rachel's theft of her father's teraphim (Gen. 31:34) has been unusually illuminated by the Nuzi texts, which state that possession of the household gods meant leadership in the family. In the case of a daughter's possession of them, her husband was assured rights to her father's property. Rachel's motive is thus clear.

Further information about the patriarchal period comes from the ancient city of Mari on the middle Euphrates. More than twenty thousand clay tablets were found here, containing Akkadian correspondence between Mari's last king Zimri-lim and either his ambassadors or the Babylonian king Hammurabi.

In these texts the (West Semitic) words "kill an ass" occur several times with the meaning "make a covenant" (as the sacrificing of an ass-foal concluded the making of a covenant). This sheds light on the tradition of the Shechemites (Gen. 34), whose god was Baal-berith ("Lord of the Covenant," Judg. 9:4) and who traced their origin back to Hamor ("Ass"). Thus the appellation "sons of the ass" (Gen. 33:19) is probably equivalent to "sons of the covenant," reflecting their origin in an earlier Amorite tribal confederacy.

Other contracts between Mari and the Bible include the frequent discussion of the cities Nahor and Haran in the Mari texts, the mention in the Mari texts of the "binu-iamina" who may possibly have some connection with the Old Testament Benjaminites, the similarities between Mari prophecy and that of the Old Testament, and similarities between Mari adoption customs and those of the Old Testament.

Many parts of the Mosaic law have been paralleled and illuminated by Sumerian, Babylonian, Assyrian, Hittite, and Canaanite law codes. Of particular significance are the Babylonian laws of Lipit-ishtar (ca. 1875 B.C.), the Eshnunna laws (ca. 2000), and the well-known Code of Hammurabi (ca. 1723). In many instances the wording of the Babylonian codes corresponds very closely to that of the Israelites (e.g., compare Hammurabi § 14 with Exod. 21:16), demonstrating that the Israelites shared a common legal tradition with their Near Eastern neighbors (probably acquired upon their entrance into Canaan).

There are, however, basic differences between the codes. The Babylonian codes have no injunctions against lust, do not command that conduct be based upon altruistic motives, and are essentially secular in that they do not command obedience based on respect for the god.

The sensational discoveries at Ras Shamra (ancient Ugarit) since 1928 have all but revolutionized Old Testament studies. The clay tablets found there, written in alphabetic cuneiform, have illuminated the Old Testament in the following ways. The texts provide a much fuller picture of Canaanite religion than was previously possessed. The religious epics give a rather detailed picture of the rainstorm god Baal, who rivaled Yahweh for the loyalties of the Israelites during most of their occupation of Canaan (see 1 Kgs. 16:31; Jer. 7:9). The language of the majority of texts, now known as Ugaritic, has illuminated many words in the Old Testament. For example, "glory" at Ps. 16:9b should instead be read "liver" (i.e., "inner self"), and "high places" in Deut. 33:29 should be read "backs." The Aqhat Epic tells of a just king named Danel who is almost certainly the Dan(i)el referred to at Ezek. 14:14-20, instead of the (later) Daniel mentioned in the biblical book bearing that name.

The discovery of clay tablets in 1887 at Tell el-Amarna (Akhetaton) in Egypt has provided biblical scholars with the earliest examples of the Canaanite language, which was adopted by the Israelites when they entered Canaan (see Isa. 19:18). A number of the texts contain correspondence between the Egyptian pharaohs Amenhotep III and IV and certain kings of city-states in Western Asia; the tablets are written in Akkadian, with Canaanite glosses inserted by the scribes to explain some of the Akkadian words. Besides the occasional light shed on Biblical Hebrew, their most important contribution to biblical studies is the picture they give of the high culture of Canaan in the fourteenth century.

The discovery of the Dead Sea Scrolls since 1947 has had a marked effect on both Old and New Testament studies. The Old Testament manuscripts have revolutionized the study of textual criticism, while the sectarian documents have thrown light on the origins of Christianity and the New Testament. The Qumran biblical manuscripts have provided scholars with copies of all Old Testament books (except Esther) about 1000 years earlier than copies previously possessed. These manuscripts have shown that at least three distinctive text types were in existence in Palestine before the second century A.D. They are the proto-Samarian (a Hebrew text with many readings peculiar to the Samaritan Pentateuch), the proto-Septuagint (a Hebrew text with readings peculiar to the LXX), and the proto-Masoretic (a Hebrew text with readings peculiar to the Hebrew text underlying most modern English translations of the Old Testament). A fourth composite text (one with mixed readings from the other traditions) was also found. The differences between these text types are generally minor, but they do at least show that the Old Testament text was somewhat fluid before the second century A.D.

Many of the beliefs and practices of the Qumran sect have been compared to those recorded in the New Testament. The main points of comparison have been between Qumran and the early Church in Jerusalem (e.g., the relation of baptism to repentance, community property, the number of leaders, a communal meal, antipathy toward the Temple cultus, the Fourth Gospel (e.g., dualism, truth and perversity, brotherly love, the fountain of living waters, apostasy, seasons and feasts, ordinations and baptisms, messianism), and the Pauline corpus (e.g., baptism, the Lord's Supper, the New Covenant, interpretation of the Old Testament ethical imperatives, number of witnesses needed, giving room to God's wrath, singing with understanding), plus other New Testament and early Christian writings. Some (though certainly not all) of these parallels cannot be denied, but it is not necessary to see direct dependence of the New Testament upon the Qumran literature. Given the diverse nature of Judaism in the intertestamental and early Christian eras, the most that can be posited is an ultimate common source for both literatures.

Mention should at least be made of the remarkable discoveries at Tell Mardikh (Ebla) in north Syria since 1975. More than 15,000 tablets have been found, most in a hitherto unknown dialect now identified as paleo-Canaanite. Though it is too early to be certain about many of the proposed correspondences with the Old Testament, these texts may seriously affect the study of Old Testament chronology, language, personal and place names, religion, and many other areas.

Caution must be employed in the application of literary as well as material correspondences to biblical studies. The early twentieth century witnessed frenzied attempts by Assyriologists and biblical scholars to demonstrate the ancient Near East as spiritual ancestor of the Bible. Such leading figures as F. Delitzsch, H. Winckler, A. Jeremias, and P. Jensen contributed to a "pan-Babylonism" which claimed both direct borrow-

Pottery being unearthed at Tell Kittan (by courtesy of the Israel Department of Antiquities and Museums)

ing of Babylonian concepts by the Israelites and an evolutionary pattern of religious development through which the Hebrew religion emerged from the Babylonian. Similar scholarly excesses can be witnessed in connection with the discoveries of Ugaritic material at Ras Shamra, the Dead Sea Scrolls, and the Ebla tablets. More recently scholars have benefitted from the insights of anthropology, linguistics, and related fields with regard to such cultural influence. Although archaeological evidence indicates that the Israelites did indeed borrow or were influenced by both the material and literary forms of their neighbors, the function of these materials was altered to meet the particular ideological perspective of the Hebrew faith.

Archaeology has not illuminated the New Testament to the same degree that it has the Old Testament. Nevertheless, excavation of New Testament sites has provided a "cultural backdrop" against which the biblical story may be read. Excavation of various parts of the Roman Empire has illuminated the structure of its administration and its changing attitude toward the early Church. The discovery of massive quantities of Greek papyri in Egypt has shown that New Testament Greek was the language shared by the rest of the Greek-speaking world and has shed light on the meaning of a number of New Testament words.

B. Does Archaeology "Prove" the Bible? Since the advent of biblical archaeology the claim has often been made that it "proves" the Bible. To this notion two objections may be raised.

First, only a small amount of the biblical text, mostly historical narrative, is open to verification. That is, archaeology can confirm the Bible's assertion that the Israelites invaded Canaan or that Judah was invaded by Babylon, but it cannot confirm, for example, its assertion of God's existence or the deity of

Jesus Christ. Neither can it confirm most psalms or proverbs, or the dialogue between Job and his friends (Job 3–37).

Second, while a number of the Bible's historical statements have been confirmed by excavations, some have not. The destruction of Jericho in Joshua's time (Josh. 6) is a prime example. No level of occupation exists at Tell es-Sulṭân anywhere near the time that the Bible states it was destroyed; perhaps the level was eroded sometime subsequent to the destruction, but the matter remains a problem.

In conclusion, one may ask whether archaeology's confirmation of a few historical statements in the Bible is tantamount to a confirmation of the Christian faith. The answer to this must be an unqualified "no." The nature of the Christian faith is just that — faith, "the assurance of things hoped for, the conviction of things not seen" (Heb. 11:1).

Bibliography. W. F. Albright, *The Archaeology of Palestine,* 4th ed. (Baltimore: 1960); *Archaeology and the Religion of Israel,* 5th ed. (Baltimore: 1968); E. M. Blaiklock, "Archeology," *ZPEB* 1:258-286; J. Gray, *Archaeology and the Old Testament World* (London: 1962); K. A. Kitchen, *The Bible in Its World* (Downers Grove: 1977); P. W. Lapp, *Biblical Archaeology and History* (Cleveland: 1969); W. S. LaSor, "Archeology," *ISBE* 1:235-244; S. M. Paul and W. G. Dever, *Biblical Archaeology* (New York: 1974); K. N. Schoville, *Biblical Archaeology in Focus* (Grand Rapids: 1962); G. W. Van Beek, "Archaeology," *IDB Archeology,* 3rd rev. ed. (Grand Rapids: 1982); M. F. Unger, *Archaeology and the Old Testament* (Grand Rapids: 1962); G. W. van Beek, "Archaeology," *IDB* 1:195-207; G. E. Wright, *Biblical Archaeology* (Philadelphia: 1957); E. M. Yamauchi, "Archeology of Palestine and Syria," *ISBE* 1:270-282.

ARCHANGEL [ärk ān′jəl] (Gk. *archángelos*). Chief of the angels (1 Thess. 4:16) and an epithet of Michael (Jude 9). With the heightened interest in angelology during the Persian and Hellenistic periods, a hierarchy was conceived, headed by various numbers of archangels (e.g., Tob. 12:15; 1 Enoch 87:2-3; 90:31). The seven archangels named by Jewish tradition (Uriel, Raphael, Raguel, Michael, Sariel, Gabriel, and Remiel) may be the angels indicated at Rev. 8:1. *See* ANGEL *I, II.*

ARCHELAUS [är′kə lā′əs] (Gk. *Archelaos*).† The son of Herod the Great by his wife Malthace (Matt. 2:22). Although his succession was challenged by his brother Herod Antipas, he succeeded his father in 4 B.C. as tetrarch of Judea. Archelaus' appointment of Eleazar as high priest and his own marital affairs were an affront to his Jewish subjects. As a result of his brutal oppression of both Jews and Samaritans, Caesar banished him in A.D. 6, naming as his replacement the procurator Coponius.

ARCHER. *See* ARMY; BOW AND ARROW.

ARCHEVITES [är′kə vīts] (Aram. ʾarkāwê; Q ʾarkᵉwāyēʾ). The inhabitants of Erech (Uruk) in Babylonia (Ezra 4:9, KJV; RSV "men of Erech").

ARCHI [är′kī] (Josh. 16:2, KJV). *See* ARCHITE.

ARCHIPPUS [är kĭp'əs] (Gk. *Archippos*). An associate greeted by Paul in his Epistle to Philemon (Phlm. 2) and for whom instructions are provided in the Epistle to the Colossians (Col. 4:17). His "ministry" (v. 17) may have included some of the pastoral duties previously fulfilled by Epaphras (v. 12; cf. Epaphroditus, Phil. 2:25-30), particularly the church at Laodicea (cf. Col. 4:13-16). It is unclear whether Archippus is to be considered the son of Philemon and Apphia or even a member of their house church (Phlm. 2).

ARCHITE [är'kīt] (Heb. *hā'arkî*). A member of a Benjaminite clan near Bethel; the gentilic is applied to Hushai, David's friend and adviser (2 Sam. 15:32; NIV "Arkite"). According to Josh. 16:2 (KJV "Archi"), the clan's territory was at Ataroth (perhaps Ataroth-Adder).

ARCHIVES. A section of the royal treasury in which official documents were stored. Provincial officials requested that the Persian king Darius search the royal archives (Ezra 5:17; Aram. *bêṭ ginzayyā' dî-malkā'*; KJV "king's treasure house"; JB "muniment room"; cf. 7:20 "king's treasury") for Cyrus' decree regarding the rebuilding of the temple at Jerusalem. Subsequently the monarch informed them of the discovery of such a scroll in the "house of the archives" (6:1; Aram. *beṭ siprayyā'* "house of the scrolls") at Ecbatana, his summer residence.

ARD [ärd] (Heb. *'ard* "humpbacked"). A descendant of Benjamin, listed among those ancestral clan leaders who accompanied Jacob to Egypt (Gen. 46:21; Num. 26:40); at 1 Chr. 8:3 he is called Addar. He was the son of Bela.

ARDON [är'dŏn] (Heb. *'ardôn*). The third son of Caleb and Azubah of the tribe of Judah (1 Chr. 2:18).

ARELI [ə rē'lī] (Heb. *'ar'ēlî*). One of the sons of Gad, and grandson of Jacob (Gen. 46:16; Num. 26:17).

AREOPAGITE [är'ĭ ŏp'ə jīt] (Gk. *Areopagitēs*). A member of the prestigious Athenian court which held its sessions at or near the Areopagus. Dionysius, one of Paul's converts, was an Areopagite (Acts 17:34).

AREOPAGUS [är'ĭ ŏp'ə gəs] (Gk. *Areios Pagos*, either "hill of Ares" [cf. KJV "Mars' hill"] or "hill of Arai [or curses]"). A small, barren, limestone hill at Athens, northwest of the Acropolis, to which a stairway hewn out of the rock led from the marketplace. It was on this hill, on a terrace, that the Athenian council (which itself came to be called the Areopagus; cf. JB, NIV) met to pronounce justice. Traces of the benches upon which the justices sat are still visible, and a limestone fragment inscribed "stone" (Gk. *líthos*) discovered near the site may be either the "Stone of Shamelessness" or the "Stone of Pride" upon which accusers and defendants stood.

While the council later met at the Royal Stoa, Paul may have appeared before this illustrious body on the Areopagus itself (Acts 17:19, 22). His famous "Areopagus address" was not so much a formal trial as an opportunity to propound his religious views.

ARETAS [är'ə təs] (Gk. *Haretas*; Nabatean *Ḥâriṭat* "virtuous, pleasing").† The name of several Nabatean rulers.

1. Aretas I, Nabatean despot who imprisoned the fugitive high priest Jason (2 Macc. 5:8; RSV "accused") at the time of Antiochus IV Epiphanes' invasion of Palestine in 169 B.C.

2. Aretas III Obodas. He defeated the Seleucid king Antiochus XII Dionysus to gain control of Coele-Syria and Damascus and then made serious inroads into Judea, forcing Alexander Jannaeus to offer concessions in exchange for his withdrawal. Some ten years later he became embroiled in the struggle for succession to the Hasmonean throne. He gave refuge to Hyrcanus II at Petra and then, with the encouragement of Antipater, marched on Jerusalem where he gained temporary victory over the contender, Aristobulus II. However, the recently appointed Roman legate Scaurus came to the aid of Aristobulus and defeated Aretas at Papyron in 65 B.C.

3. Aretas IV Aeneas (9 B.C.–A.D. 40). When the tetrarch Herod Antipas divorced Aretas' daughter in order to marry his sister-in-law Herodias (Matt. 14:3 par. Mark 6:17; Luke 3:19), Aretas seized the opportunity to send his army against Herod (with whom he had also been embroiled in a boundary dispute). When the Nabateans defeated him, Herod appealed to the Romans, who sent the Syrian proconsul Vitellius to punish Aretas; however, the Roman commander halted his preparations for a campaign against Petra upon learning about the death of the Emperor Tiberius (A.D. 37).

It was shortly thereafter that Paul escaped imprisonment at Damascus (2 Cor. 11:32-33; cf. Acts 9:23-24). His mention of a guard posted by "the governor under King Aretas" (2 Cor. 11:32) suggests that the Nabatean ruler may have been given a measure of local authority under Caligula, Tiberius' successor. Supportive evidence includes a Damascene coin dated 101 of the Pompeian era (A.D. 37) bearing the image of Aretas; in contrast, Damascene coins from the principates of Augustus, Tiberius, and Nero bear the images of those emperors.

ARGOB [är'gŏb] (Heb. *'argōḇ*) (**PERSON**). According to the KJV, a person connected with the slaying of Pekahiah (2 Kgs. 15:25). See ARIEH.

ARGOB [är'gŏb] (Heb. *'argōḇ* "mound") (**PLACE**). A district in Bashan bordering on Geshur and Maacah. It was in the kingdom of Og of Bashan that the Israelites, after their victory over Sihon king of the Amorites, captured sixty cities (Deut. 3:4), which were subsequently assigned to the eastern portion of Manasseh (v. 13).

From Deut. 3:14 it would appear that the region was renamed Havvoth-jair ("the tent villages of Jair"), but 1 Kgs. 4:13 distinguishes between these villages, located in Gilead, and the "sixty great cities with walls and bronze bars" of Argob in Bashan. The Targum places Argob in Trachonitis, south of Damascus; Josephus (*Ant.* viii.2.3) locates it in Gaulanitis (Golan).

ARIDAI [âr'ə dī] (Heb. *'ărîḏay,* possibly from Pers. *haridayas* "delight of Hari"). One of the ten sons of Haman slain by the Jews (Esth. 9:9).

ARIDATHA [ăr'ə dā'thə] (Heb. *'ăriḏāṯā',* possibly from Pers. *haridata* "given by Hari"). One of the ten sons of Haman the Agagite (Esth. 9:8).

ARIEH [ăr'ī ə] (Heb. *hā'aryēh*). Along with Argob, either a victim of or a conspirator in the massacre at the royal palace at Samaria (2 Kgs. 15:25, KJV). The JB and RSV omit the names because of textual difficulties; according to the RSV mg. they should be included with the names of places captured by Tiglath-pileser III (v. 29).

ARIEL [âr'ī əl] (Heb. *'ărî'el* "lion of God"[?]) (PERSON).
1. A member of the delegation sent by Ezra the scribe to obtain ministers for the temple (Ezra 8:16; cf. 1 Esdr. 8:43 "Iduel").
2, 3. Two Moabites ("two ariels of Moab"; KJV "lionlike men"; JB "champions") killed by Benaiah, one of David's mighty men (2 Sam. 23:20 par. 1 Chr. 11:22).

ARIEL [âr'ī əl] (Heb. *'ărî'el* "lion of God" [?]) (PLACE). A cryptic name designating Jerusalem (Isa. 29:1-2, 7) in an oracle concerning both the siege and preservation of the city. The Hebrew term may here designate the hearth of an altar (1QIsaᵃ reads Heb. *'ărû'el* "altar hearth"; cf. Ezek. 43:15-16).

ARIMATHEA [ăr'ə mə thē'ə] (Gk. *Arimathaia*).†
The home of Joseph, a Jewish official in whose tomb the body of Jesus was placed (Matt. 27:57 par. Mark 15:43; Luke 23:50; John 19:38). The town may be the same as Ramathaim-zophim, the home of Samuel (1 Sam. 1:1; 19:19, "Ramah"). It may also be the Rathamin (1 Macc. 11:34) which Demetrius II added to Judea from Samaria. The site is probably modern Rentîs, 14.5 km. (9 mi.) northeast of Lydda. *See* RAMAH 5.

ARIOCH [âr'ī ŏk] (Heb., Aram. *'aryôḵ*).
1. King of Ellasar and an ally of Amraphel, Chedorlaomer, and Tidal (Gen. 14:1); together they mounted a reprisal against the five kings of the valley but were defeated by Abraham's army (vv. 2-17). No positive identification of this monarch has been made, although the name was rather common in second millennium B.C. texts. His district, generally considered to have been in Babylonia, may well have been located between Carchemish and Haran.
2. The captain of Nebuchadnezzar's royal guard (Dan. 2:14-15), empowered to execute the death sentence on Babylon's "wise men." In discharging his duty he met Daniel and introduced him to the king.

ARISAI [âr'ə sī] (Heb. *'ărîsay*). One of the ten sons of Haman the Agagite who were killed by the Jews (Esth. 9:9).

ARISTARCHUS [ăr'ĭs tär'kəs] (Gk. *Aristarchos* "best ruler").† A faithful traveling companion of Paul

from Macedonia. He was dragged into the theater at Ephesus by an angry mob during a riot instigated by Demetrius, a silversmith who was losing business on account of Paul's teaching (Acts 19:29). Because he continued his travels with the apostle, Aristarchus must not have been greatly harmed during the incident, perhaps because he was a Greek. When things had calmed down in the city, he joined a group of men in Greece who went to Troas, where they waited for the apostle (20:4, 6). According to 27:2 Aristarchus even accompanied Paul during his fourth missionary journey, possibly all the way to Rome.
Sometime later Aristarchus is described as a "fellow prisoner" with Paul (Col. 4:10). Whether he stayed with Paul during the resumption of his voyage or went home to Thessalonica, his birthplace, he was among those who shared Paul's first imprisonment at Rome. He is called a "fellow worker" by Paul, with whom he sends greetings to the church at Colossae and to Philemon (Phlm. 24).

ARISTEAS [ăr'ĭs tē'əs] (Gk. *Aristaios*), **LETTER OF.** A pseudepigraphal apologetic book, mistakenly identified as an epistle because of its dedication to the author's brother, Philocrates. It is purportedly a contemporary account of the events related to the Septuagint translation of the Pentateuch. In addition to the translation activities, the book supplies information on such diverse subjects as the release of Jewish slaves through the author's intervention; the gifts given to the high priest Eleazar; descriptions of Palestine, Jerusalem, and the temple cult; and an address of Eleazar concerning the Jewish law.
The author, who claims to be a courtier of Ptolemy II Philadelphus (*ca.* 285-246 B.C.), was apparently an Alexandrian Jew of the first century B.C. Various anachronistic details as well as the recognition of the book's legendary rather than epistolary form have led to the understanding of the work as an attempt to demonstrate the supremacy of Jewish thought and to foster self-confidence among the Alexandrian Jews.
Later Jewish and Christian tradition interpreted Aristeas' account as applying to the translation of the entire LXX, thereby serving to bolster the authenticity and authority of that version. The later version of the legend, which emphasizes the marvelous agreement among the efforts of the seventy (or seventy-two) translators despite the fact that they had worked independently, has no basis in the letter itself; indeed, Aristeas attributes the agreement to the close cooperation of the translators.
Bibliography. R. J. H. Shutt, "Letter of Aristeas," in J. H. Charlesworth, ed., *The Old Testament Pseudepigrapha* 2 (Garden City: 1985).

ARISTION [ăr'ĭs tē'ŏn] (Gk. *Aristiōn*). According to Papias (Eusebius *HE* iii.39.4), "a disciple of the Lord" and, along with the Presbyter John, a primary authority for the gospel traditions. An Armenian manuscript dated A.D. 986 attributes the concluding section of the gospel of Mark (16:9-20) to the Presbyter Aristion, perhaps the same person.

ARISTOBULUS [ăr'ĭs tŏb'yə ləs] (Gk. *Aristoboulos* "best counselor").†

1. The Jewish teacher of Ptolemy VII Physcon (145-116 B.C.) to whom Judas Maccabeus wrote concerning the celebration of the purification of the temple (2 Macc. 1:10).

2. Judas Aristobulus I, the oldest son of John Hyrcanus, and the first of the Hasmoneans to claim the title of king. His reign (104-103 B.C.) was abbreviated by an excruciating ailment which took his life.

3. Aristobulus II, the younger son of Alexander Jannaeus and Salome Alexandra. A contender for the Hasmonean throne, he was temporarily halted by the legitimate successor Hyrcanus II, who marched on Jerusalem with the aid of the Antipater and the Nabatean Aretas III Obodas. With the aid of the Roman general Scaurus, he defeated Hyrcanus and gained the throne. However, in 63 B.C. Pompey captured Jerusalem, and Aristobulus was imprisoned at Rome; he escaped in 56 and attempted to regain power but was again defeated and taken captive to Rome. During the Roman civil war of 49 B.C., Julius Caesar freed Aristobulus and sent him with troops to conquer Judea, but he was poisoned by supporters of Pompey.

4. Grandson of Aristobulus II, and the last of the Hasmoneans. Appointed high priest by his brother-in-law Herod the Great, his popularity enraged the king, who arranged to have him drowned (*ca.* 35 B.C.).

5. The younger son of Herod the Great and Mariamne; father of Herod Agrippa I. He fell victim to his father's jealousy and family intrigue and, with his brother Alexander, was strangled in 7 B.C.

6. A person at Rome, perhaps a Christian, to whose family Paul sent greetings (Rom. 16:10). Some scholars speculate that he is the son of **5** above and brother of Herod Agrippa and was on intimate terms with the Emperor Claudius.

ARK OF NOAH. A vessel made by Noah at God's command to protect him and the animal species during the Deluge. Heb. *tēbâ* (related to Egyp. *db't* "chest," "box," "coffin") is only used to designate Noah's ark and the basket in which the infant Moses was placed (Exod. 2:3, 5).

I. Old Testament

Noah's boat was made of gopher wood (Gen. 6:14) — probably cypress — and consisted of various rooms or compartments (v. 14; Heb. *qinnîm* "nests"), covered with pitch both on the inside and outside. Assuming the Hebrew cubit to equal 44.5 cm. (17.5 in.), the ark's dimensions were approximately 133.5 m. (438 ft.; 300 cubits) long, 22 m. (73 ft.; 50 cubits) wide, and 13.4 m. (44 ft.; 30 cubits) high. It had three decks and a roof (Heb. *sōhar*, KoB, p. 796; so RSV, JB, NIV) or a window (RSV mg., KJV).

Built like an Egyptian transport vessel, the ark was square-cornered, chestlike in shape, with an enormous capacity for cargo. If it is assumed that the animals to be carried in the ark lived in the region where Noah built his vessel, only about thirty-five thousand individual vertebrates had to be accommodated. Moreover, the animals probably hibernated. Thus, the Genesis account of the ark carrying "all" animals — seven pair of clean and two pair of unclean animals — may not be as incredible as it appears at first.

II. New Testament

In the Gospels the second coming of Christ is compared to the Flood. God will allow people to repent of their self-centered life-style until it is too late, as he did when Noah entered the ark (Gk. *kibōtós*) just before the rains came (Matt. 24:37-39 par. Luke 17:26-27). According to the author of Hebrews (Heb. 11:7), Noah constructed the ark in faith; in this way he condemned the world to the Deluge and became an heir to righteousness (cf. 2 Pet. 2:5).

To Peter the ark is a symbol of baptism (1 Pet. 3:20-21).

See also FLOOD.

Bibliography. J. C. Whitcomb and H. M. Morris, *Genesis Flood: The Biblical Record and Its Scientific Implications* (Philadelphia: 1961).

ARK OF THE COVENANT (Heb. *'ārôn habbⁿrît*). A portable chest (cf. "coffin," Gen. 50:26; "chest," 2 Kgs. 12:9-10) to be kept in the tabernacle, and later in the temple of Solomon. The ark contained various cultic articles and served as the meetingplace of the Lord and Israel. Other names for the ark include ark of the Lord (e.g., Josh. 4:11; 6:11), ark of God (e.g., 1 Sam. 4:11, 13, 17, 19, 21), ark of the covenant of the Lord (e.g., Josh. 9:11), ark of the covenant of God (Judg. 20:27), and ark of the testimony (i.e., of the law; e.g., Num. 4:5; 7:89).

I. Construction

Following the Lord's specifications (Exod. 25:10-22), Bezalel made the chest of acacia wood, 2½ cubits long, 1½ cubits wide, and 1½ cubits high. If this cubit refers to the royal Egyptian cubit measuring 52 cm. (20.5 in.), its measurements would have been $130 \times 78 \times 78$ cm. ($51 \times 31 \times 31$ in.). Bezalel then overlaid it inside and out with gold from which all impurities had been carefully removed, and put a golden molding around its upper part; the lid may have rested upon this molding (37:2). It is possible that the golden mercy seat (2½ × 1½ cubits) was also held in place by this molding, preventing it from sliding when the ark was moved; the mercy seat may also have been placed across the top of the ark, resting like a table upon the feet of two decorative cherubim, which were part of the ark itself.

The ark stood upon four feet or pedestals. A ring of gold was fastened to each foot (Exod. 25:3), and two poles made of acacia wood overlaid with gold were drawn through these rings to make a litter (vv. 4-5). They remained in place through the rings even when the chest was not being carried (cf. Exod. 25:15). According to 1 Kgs. 8:8 the ends of the poles were visible from the holy place directly before the open doors leading to the inner sanctuary of the temple.

II. Symbolic Meaning

The cherubim or angelic figures on the ark of the covenant indicated the presence of the Lord. Some scholars have suggested that these cherubim were relief figures. According to Exod. 37:9, "The cherubim spread out their wings above, overshadowing the mercy seat with their wings, with their faces one to another; toward the mercy seat were the faces of the cherubim.'' This could simply mean that the cherubim stood facing one another.

The Lord, who according to Ps. 99:1 ''sits enthroned upon the cherubim,'' is also represented by the mercy seat (Heb. *kappōreṭ*; Gk. *hilastērion*), which symbolically allowed Israel to bring the blood of atonement as close as possible to the throne of the Lord (Lev. 16:14-16; cf. Heb. 9:23-28). The wings of the cherubim covered the mercy seat protectively (cf. Heb. 9:5), which would be possible if their faces looked toward the mercy seat (cf. 1 Pet. 1:12). The position of the cherubim also expressed reverence for the Lord, who met and spoke with Moses from ''above the mercy seat, from between the two cherubim'' (Exod. 25:22). In other words, the mercy seat did not serve merely as a covering for the ark, but had its own significance as well.

III. Contents

Inside the ark a copy of the law was placed as God had instructed Moses (''testimony,'' Exod. 25:16; 40:16; cf. Deut. 10:5, ''tables''). In fact, a copy of the law remained till at least the reign of Solomon (1 Kgs. 8:9). As the expression of God's covenantal concern, the law reminded Israel of its contractual obligations. The jar of manna (Exod. 16:34) and Aaron's rod (Num. 17:4ff.) were probably placed in front of the ark rather than inside with the law (cf. 1 Kgs. 8:9; Heb. 9:4 is somewhat ambiguous).

IV. History

A. Old Testament. Once the ark was placed in the holy of holies of the tabernacle (Exod. 40:21), its care was entrusted to the Levites, specifically the families of the Kohathites (Num. 3:29-31), who carried it whenever the Israelites broke camp (4:11-15). It was the priests, however, who carried the ark during the crossing of the Jordan river (Josh. 3:3), and on other important occasions such as the conquest of Jericho (6:6), the rededication of the people after the destruction of Ai (8:33), and Solomon's dedication of the temple (1 Kgs. 8:3). At the end of the wilderness wanderings, when it had fulfilled its purpose of leading God's people (cf. Num. 10:33-35), the ark was brought to Shiloh (Josh. 18:1), where it may have stayed throughout the period of the judges.

When the Israelites were defeated by the Philistines at Ebenezer, they lost the ark (1 Sam. 4:1-11). Their enemies, afflicted with plagues, were compelled to send it back to them (ch. 5). Arriving in Bethshemesh, it was hastily sent onward to Kiriath-jearim, after the Lord had severely punished the men of Bethshemesh for their disrespectful curiosity (6:19-21). In Kiriath-jearim, the ark was kept at the house of Abinadab, where it was put in the care of his son Eleazar (7:1-2).

It was David who decided to move the ark to Jerusalem. Uzzah and Ahio, the sons of Abinadab, carried it in a new cart that replaced that upon which the ark had been captured (2 Sam. 6:1-5). When the oxen stumbled and Uzzah took hold of the ark to keep it from falling, he was killed for his rashness (vv. 6-7). David then kept it in the house of Obed-edom (vv. 10-11). Three months later the king brought it into Jerusalem amid great rejoicing, and placed it in a tent (vv. 12-19; cf. 1 Chr. 13:14). (Such Psalms as 24, 47, 68 may deal with the bringing of the ark to Mt. Zion.) Solomon later placed the ark in the holy of holies of the temple he had built (1 Kgs. 8:1-9) rather than taking it into battle as his father David had done (2 Sam. 14:11). According to 2 Chr. 35:3, Josiah interpreted this to mean that the ark could now remain at rest in the temple, thereby freeing the Levites to perform other tasks.

The prophet Jeremiah predicted the disappearance of the ark during the restoration, because Jerusalem would then become God's throne (Jer. 3:16-17). After the destruction of Jerusalem and the temple by Nebuchadnezzar (*ca.* 587/586 B.C.), the Bible makes no mention of the ark. In the temples of Zerubbabel and Herod, the holy of holies did not contain an ark. Instead, according to the Jewish tradition, a stone was erected upon which the high priest set the censer on the Day of Atonement (cf. Lev. 16:12ff.).

B. New Testament. Given the changed political situation, the New Testament seldom refers to the ark. Moreover, Israel's religious life had taken a crucial turn. It is mentioned at Heb. 9, where Christ is portrayed as the great high priest who has gone into the holy of holies — once and for all — and finally into heaven itself. At Rev. 11:19 a heavenly counterpart of the ark represents God's faithfulness in fulfilling his covenantal promises in times of crisis.

Bibliography. M. H. Woudstra, *The Ark of the Covenant from Conquest to Kingship* (Philadelphia: 1965).

ARK OF THE TESTIMONY. *See* ARK OF THE COVENANT.

ARKITE [är′kīt] (Heb. *'arqî*). An inhabitant of the town of Arqat, modern Tell ʿArqah, approximately 18 km. (11 mi.) north of Tripoli. At Gen. 10:17; 1 Chr. 1:15 the Arkites are mentioned among the descendants of Canaan. In the Amarna Letters the town is called Irqata; in Roman times it was known as Caesarea Libani. Arkantu, mentioned by Thutmose III, may be the same place.

ARMAGEDDON [är′mə gĕd′ən] (Gk. *Harmagedōn*). A place where, according to Rev. 16:14-16, the kings of the entire world are to assemble for battle on the ''great day of God the Almighty,'' the final overthrow of all evil forces by the might and power of God at the end of time.

This name generally is thought to allude to the historic plain of Megiddo near Carmel (the Greek term is equivalent to Heb. *[har]meʿgiddôn* ''[mountain] of Megiddo''), where Barak and Deborah defeated the Canaanites (Judg. 5:19). This is also the place where Pharaoh Neco mortally wounded King Josiah of Judah (2 Kgs. 23:29-30 par. 2 Chr. 35:22-24). Zech. 12:11 refers to mourning for Hadadrimmon on the plain of Megiddo (perhaps Adad-remmon where Josiah was wounded). The RSV mg. also places Ahaziah's death in the city of Megiddo (2 Kgs. 9:27). However, it is not clear why Armageddon might be called the ''mountain(s) (Heb. *har*) of Megiddo,'' because Megiddo lies southeast of Mt. Carmel (cf. ''plain of Megiddo,'' 2 Chr. 35:22).

ARMENIA (2 Kgs. 19:37 par. Isa. 37:38, KJV). *See*
ARARAT.

ARMLET.† A band worn around the upper arm (cf.
2 Sam. 1:10; KJV "bracelet"; NIV, JB "band/
bracelet on his arm"), to be distinguished from
bracelets which were worn around the wrist (Num.
31:50; according to KoB, p. 81, Heb. '*eṣʿāḏâ* originally meant "ankle chainlet" and later came to mean
"bracelet"). At Isa. 3:20 "armlet" (RSV) actually
refers to a chain between the two ankles which forced
the person to walk with gracious steps ("step-chains
[tickling rings at the ankles]," KoB, p. 809; KJV "ornaments of the legs"; NIV, JB "ankle/foot chains").

While Exod. 35:22 records Israel's willingness to
donate their gold armlets (Heb. *kûmāz,* possibly
"breastplates," KoB, p. 426; KJV "tablets"; JB
"necklaces"; NIV "ornaments") and other possessions to further construction of the tabernacle, Isa.
3:20 depicts the Lord's anger with his people's preoccupation with such worldly decorations.

ARMONI [är mō'nī] (Heb. '*armōnî*). One of the two
sons of Saul and Rizpah whom David handed over to
the Gibeonites, along with five other of Saul's descendants, as payment for the former king's bloodguilt
(2 Sam. 21:8).

ARMY (Heb. *ḥayil*; *ṣāḇāʾ*; Gk. *parembolḗ*;
stráteuma).† Both the form and function of Israel's
military forces varied in accordance with the people's
political and social circumstances. At the time of the
patriarchs, combatants were drawn from the populace
by clan or tribal chieftains in time of impending crisis
(cf. Gen. 14:14-16, where Abram leads a bedouin-
style raid). Similarly, during the wilderness wanderings and the conquest and settlement of Palestine,
small bands were formed for occasional defensive or
aggressive activities (e.g., Exod. 17:8-13); subsequently, charismatic leaders or judges might lead
forces drawn from individual tribes or tribal alignments (Judg. 7:7-23; 12:1-7).

Soon after Saul had assumed his royal duties he
instituted Israel's first professional standing army,
which consisted of three units ("thousands," Heb.

Egyptian armlets

'*alāpîm*) of chosen men (1 Sam. 13:2), personally led
by the king (but cf. 17:55).

David, whose military skill had been evident as
leader of a Habiru ('Apiru) band prior to his kingship,
bolstered the ranks of the army with Israelite and foreign mercenaries. In addition, a civilian militia was
formed with twelve divisions, each of 24,000 conscripted soldiers responsible for one month's service
per year (1 Chr. 27:1-15). David remained commander
of the military, with Joab and Amasa responsible for
the professional and civilian forces, respectively. In
battle, a tripartite division was employed (1 Sam. 13:2;
2 Sam. 18:2). The army was further subdivided into
thousands, hundreds, and fifties (1 Sam. 18:3; 2 Sam.
18:1; 2 Kgs. 1:9). Mercenaries included a select corps
of "mighty men" (2 Sam. 23:8-39; 1 Kgs. 1:8);
others, the Cherethites and Pelethites commanded by
Benaiah, constituted David's bodyguard (2 Sam.
8:17). Under Joab the Israelite army became highly
skilled in siege warfare (2 Sam. 20:15).

During the Monarchy, every Israelite male twenty
years of age or older was subject to military conscription (Num. 1:2-3; 26:2; 2 Chr. 25:5), which was based
on figures drawn from censuses (2 Sam. 24; 1 Chr. 21;
cf. Num. 1). Exemptions were granted to the priests
and Levites (Num. 1:47-48; 2:33) as well as various
others: those who had recently built a house or planted
a vineyard, those engaged to be married, the fearful
and fainthearted (Deut. 20:5-8; 24:5).

David's army consisted primarily of foot soldiers —
lightly armed with bow and arrow, sling and shield
(1 Chr. 8:40; 12:1) or more heavily armed with shield
and spear (vv. 8, 24, 34) — and thus was well-suited
for combat in the Palestinian hill country. Cavalry (at
first using mules rather than horses; 2 Sam. 13:29;
18:9) and chariot units were increased under Solomon,
thereby drastically changing Israel's military character. Solomon had some 1,400 chariots and 12,000
horsemen stationed at Jerusalem and chariot cities
such as Megiddo, Hazor, and Gezer (1 Kgs. 9:15-19;
10:26; 2 Chr. 1:14; 9:25). Later, Ahab sent 2,000
chariots against the Assyrians at Qarqar (cf. his later
alliance with Jehoshaphat of Judah; 2 Chr. 17:28-34).
By the time of Hezekiah, however, the use of mounted
forces apparently had declined (2 Kgs. 18:23).

With the fall of the northern and southern kingdoms, their armies likewise collapsed, and following
the Exile Israel was subject to Persian rule. It was not
until the Maccabean rebellion that Israel again formed
an army. Relying at first on bands of volunteers, Judas
Maccabeus reintroduced conscription and organized
an army of thousands, hundreds, fifties, and tens
(1 Macc. 3:55-56); by the time his brother Simon assumed power, Judea had a standing army of mercenaries (14:32).

When Judea became a Roman province in 63 B.C. a
Roman army was stationed on its soil. Although
Herod the Great contributed his own troops (cf. Luke
3:14; 23:11), New Testament references are primarily
to the Roman legions (e.g., Acts 10:1; 27:1).

Bibliography. Y. Yadin, *The Art of Warfare in Biblical Lands,* 2 vols. (New York: 1963).

ARNAN [är'nən] (Heb. '*arnān*). A descendant of
Zerubbabel, and son of Rephaiah (1 Chr. 3:21).

ARNI [är'nī] (Gk. *Arni*). An ancestor of Jesus (Luke 3:33; KJV, "Aram"; NIV "Ram"). At Matt. 1:3-4 the name is given as Aram (Gk. *Aram*; RSV, JB, NIV "Ram," following the lists of David's descendants at Ruth 4:19 and Judah's descendants at 1 Chr. 2:9-10).

ARNON [är'nən] (Heb. *'arnōn*). A river in Transjordan which flows into the Dead Sea opposite En-gedi; its contemporary name is Wādî Môjib. A number of tributaries and streams unite about 21 km. (13 mi.) east of the Dead Sea, forming the Arnon. The river continues its course through a gorge some 3 km. (2 mi.) wide on top and 37 m. (120 ft.) wide at the bottom, reaching an occasional depth of nearly 700 m. (2300 ft.) (cf. NIV "Arnon Gorge," Deut. 3:8; JB "wadi Arnon" [cf. Heb. *naḥal 'arnōn*], RSV "valley of the Arnon"). Its limestone walls are generally white but at times are laced with darker-colored strata and capped with dark red basalt.

In the Old Testament the river formed the border between the Moabite territory to the south (Num. 21:13) and the Amorite lands (Deut. 2:24) — and later those of the Israelites (Josh. 13:16) — to the north. Except in recounting Israel's early history it is mentioned only three times. At 2 Kgs. 10:33 Hazael of Syria reduced Israel's territory near the Arnon during the reign of Jehu. In the oracle against Moab, Isaiah suggests that the fords of the Arnon may provide a passage to safety for that forsaken tribe (16:2). A subsequent oracle by Jeremiah (Jer. 48:20) predicts Moab's doom — probably Nebuchadnezzar's conquest in 582 B.C. — to be proclaimed along the Arnon.

AROD [âr'ŏd] (Heb. *'arŏd* "humpbacked"). The sixth son of Gad (Num. 26:17).

ARODI [âr'ə dī] (Heb. *'arŏdî*). Descendants of Arod (Gen. 46:16).

AROER [ə rō'ər] (Heb. *'arô'ēr* "juniper"[?]).
1. A city on the northern rim of the Arnon Gorge (Deut. 2:36; 3:12; 4:48), along the southern border of the kingdom of Sihon (Deut. 4:4-5; Josh. 12:2) and subsequently of the tribe of Reuben (Deut. 2:36; Josh. 13:16). It was fortified by Gad, however (Num. 32:34), and later was the first point of David's census (2 Sam. 24:5). The city was in the territory captured by the Syrian king Hazael (2 Kgs. 10:33). According to the Moabite Stone, the Moabite king Mesha fortified it against Israelite attack; Aroer remained in Moabite hands at the time of Jeremiah (Jer. 48:19).

The site has been identified as Khirbet 'Arâ'ir, 5 km. (3 mi.) east of Dhîbân. Situated on the southern edge of the fertile plain surrounding the Kura at a point where that river flows into the canyon of the Môjib (Arnon Gorge), the ancient fortress commanded the great north-south route and its crossing of the Arnon. Remains from the Bronze and Iron Ages, including the main buildings constructed by Mesha, have been discovered. The site was abandoned from the sixth century B.C. until the Nabatean occupation in the second century B.C.
2. A town in Gilead along its boundary with Ammon and located east (Heb. *'al-pᵉnê*, perhaps bet-

ter "opposite, in front of") of the Ammonite city of Rabbah (Josh. 13:25). It has been proposed that the site is south of Rabbah (modern Amman) in the vicinity of es-Sweiwina.
3. A town in the southern Shephelah of Judah (1 Sam. 30:28) with whose inhabitants David divided the Amalekite spoil upon returning to Ziklag. It has been identified with Khirbet 'Ar'arah (cf. Josh. 15:22, "Adadah"), 19 km. (12 mi.) southeast of Beer-sheba.

AROERITE [ə rō'ər īt] (Heb. *hā'ᵃrō'ērî*). A native of Aroer 1 (1 Chr. 11:44). Hothan, the father of two of David's mighty men, was an Aroerite.

ARPACHSHAD [är päk'shäd] (Heb. *'arpaḵšaḏ*). The third son of Shem, the grandfather of Eber (Gen. 10:22, 24; 11:10-13; 1 Chr. 1:17-18; KJV, NIV "Arphaxad"; cf. Luke 3:36, "Arphaxad"; Gk. *Arphaxad*), and an ancestor of the Hebrews (1 Chr. 1:24). Although no etymology has gained general acceptance, many scholars favor an identification of the name with Akk. Arraphu, modern Kirkuk in northeastern Iraq.

ARPAD [är'päd] (Heb. and Old Aram. *'arpāḏ* "support"; Akk. *Arpadda*). A city in northern Syria, identified with Tell Rif' at, about 30 km. (19 mi.) north of Aleppo.

In the Old Testament Arpad is mentioned always in conjunction with Hamath. Once the main city in the region between the Amana mountains and the Euphrates river (*ca.* 1000 B.C.), it was conquered by the Assyrian Tiglath-pileser III after a three-year siege (740). The echoes of this victory were still heard in the Rabshakeh's boasting to the inhabitants of besieged Jerusalem (701 B.C.; 2 Kgs. 18:34 par. Isa. 36:19; cf. Isa. 10:9). Jeremiah's oracle against Damascus also alludes to this event (Jer. 49:23).

ARPHAXAD [är fäk'säd] (Gk. *Arphaxad*).† An unknown king of the Medes who was killed by Nebuchadnezzar (Jdt. 1:1-15). See ARPACHSHAD.

ARROW. See BOW AND ARROW.

ARSACES [är'sə sēz] (Gk. *Arsakēs*).† The throne name of some thirty Parthian kings of a dynasty founded when Arsaces I rebelled against the Seleucid king Antiochus II Soter (*ca.* 250 B.C.).

Arsaces VI (Mithridates I; 171-138) fostered the rise of the Parthian Empire through the conquest of a vast territory, including Media, Persia, Armenia, and Babylonia. When Demetrius II Nicator of Syria invaded Parthian territory, Arsaces' troops captured the Seleucid king and brought him before Arsaces at Hyrcania (1 Macc. 14:1-3). Though imprisoned for some ten years, Demetrius was treated justly by Arsaces and allowed to marry the Parthian king's daughter. At 15:22 Arsaces VI is among those kings whom the Roman consul Lucius orders to refrain from hostility against the Jews.

ARTAXERXES [är'tə zûrk'sēz] (Heb. and Aram. *'artaḥšastā'*).
1. Artaxerxes I Longimanus (464-424 B.C.), the

son and successor of Xerxes I. He subdued revolts in Egypt, which were supported by the Athenians (454), and elsewhere in the Persian Empire.

The king permitted Ezra the scribe to go to Jerusalem in 458 as the head of an official delegation (Ezra 7:7-26; 8:1), but temporarily halted the repairing of Jerusalem (4:7-23). In 445 he authorized Nehemiah to assist in the rebuilding of Jerusalem (Neh. 2:1-7) and sometime after 432 granted him permission to return to that city (13:6).

2. The LXX rendering of Ahasuerus in the book of Esther. Though some scholars have identified him with Artaxerxes II Mnemon, son of Darius II and grandson of Artaxerxes I, more probably he is Xerxes I (486-464).

ARTEMAS [är′tə məs] (Gk. *Artemas*, abbreviation of *Artemí dṓros* "given by Artemis"). One of Paul's companions whom the apostle hoped to send to Crete in order to permit Titus to join Paul at Nicopolis (Titus 3:12).

ARTEMIS [är′tə məs] (Gk. *Artemis*). The Greek goddess of wild animals and the moon, and protectress of the household — the Roman goddess Diana. At Ephesus she was worshiped primarily as an ancient Near Eastern fertility deity, in whose honor the Greek colonists built a temple. This temple, considered one of the seven wonders of the ancient world, was destroyed in 356 B.C. but was rebuilt. Worshippers carried small silver, marble, and terra-cotta images of this temple with them, to be placed inside the actual temple and possibly also in their homes as house shrines.

Paul's work at Ephesus was concluded with an incident described at Acts 19:23-41. Apparently the preaching he did during his third missionary journey made many townspeople turn from the worship of Artemis and cease to purchase these small shrines. After Demetrius, one of the local silversmiths, had presented this charge against Paul, the people rioted, shouting repeatedly, "Great is Artemis of the Ephesians!" (so RSV, NIV; KJV, JB "Diana"). The town clerk settled the crowd by asking rhetorically if anyone there did not know that Ephesus was a "temple keeper" of the great deity and of the "sacred stone [missing in the Greek text] that fell from the sky [lit. "from Zeus"]" (v. 35); this, he pointed out, could not be challenged. (This stone was probably a meteorite which was viewed as resembling multiple-breasted portrayals of the deity.)

ARUBBOTH [ə rŭb′ŏth] (Heb. *ʾărubbôt*). A town in one of Solomon's twelve districts where Ben-hesed was to gather a supply of food for the king one month out of the year (1 Kgs. 4:10; KJV "Aruboth"). Scholars have associated contemporary Arrabeh near Dothan with ancient Arubboth, but the site may have been located toward the southern part of the Shephelah. At 1 Macc. 5:23 it is called Arbatta.

ARUMAH [ə rōō′mə] (Heb. *ʾărumâ* "lofty"). The town in which Abimelech the son of Jerubbaal (Gideon) stayed after having been ousted from Shechem (Judg. 9:41). Arumah was most likely located at what is now Jebel el-ʿOrmeh, 8 km. (5 mi.) southeast of

Ephesian amulet with image of Artemis

Shechem. Pottery sherds at the site dating to the Late Bronze and Early Iron Ages indicate a settlement there during the period of the judges. This steep, isolated hill would have permitted Abimelech a good view of the rebellious city of Shechem.

At v. 31 the RSV and JB emend Heb. *bᵉṭormâ* (KJV "privily"; NIV "under cover," following the LXX) to read *baʾărûmâ* "at Arumah."

ARVAD [är′văd] (Heb. *ʾarwaḏ*; Gk. *Arados*). A city in northern Syria whose inhabitants were employed as rowers on Tyrian ships or as mercenaries near Tyre before its fall (Ezek. 27:8, 11). At 1 Macc. 15:23 Aradus (its Greek name) is listed as one of the cities to which the consul Lucius sent a letter in support of the Jews.

Located on an island now known as Ruad, about 4 km. (2.5 mi.) off the Mediterranean coast and about 48 km. (30 mi.) north of Tripoli, the city (modern Erwâd) was dependent upon the mainland for food and water. Its narrowness (about 730 m. [800 yds.] long and 460 m. [500 yds.] wide) forced the building of multi-story dwellings. After Egyptian influence declined in the area (*ca.* 1164 B.C.), Arvad was able to assume control over some six Phoenician cities. Having survived Assyrian rule, the people of Arvad eventually surrendered to Alexander the Great and permitted him the use of the city's fleet in the conquest of Tyre (333).

ARVADITES [är′və dīts] (Heb. *ʾarwādî*). Inhabitants of Arvad in northern Syria; they are included among the Canaanites (Gen. 10:18; 1 Chr. 1:16).

ARZA [är′zə] (Heb. *ʾarṣāʾ* "gracious"[?]). A steward

of the household of King Elah of Israel in whose home the king, while intoxicated, was murdered by Zimri (1 Kgs. 16:9).

ASA [ā'sə] (Heb. *'āsā'* "healer"; Gk. *Asa*).

1. The son and successor of Abijah (2 Chr. 14:1; 1 Kgs. 15:8, "Abijam") of Judah (912-871 B.C.). Though Maacah is named as Asa's mother (1 Kgs. 15:10), it is more likely that she was Abijah's mother and retained the title of queen mother after his death. The Old Testament generally portrays Asa in a favorable light (1 Kgs. 15:11 par. 2 Chr. 14:2), very unlike his father.

The first ten years of Asa's rule were peaceful (2 Chr. 14:1), in part the result of his father's victory over Jeroboam of Israel. He was able to limit the border conflict with Baasha king of Israel (910-887 B.C.) to a kind of guerilla warfare (cf. 1 Kgs. 15:16, "all their days"). He devoted these years to reforming the cultic practices of his subjects (2 Chr. 14:2-5; cf. 1 Kgs. 15:12) and to fortifying a number of cities (vv. 6-8).

His constructive reign was interrupted (perhaps *ca.* 902 B.C.) by the invasion of Zerah the Ethiopian (probably a commander under the Egyptian Osorkon I). Overwhelmed by the sheer size of Zerah's army (though the number one thousand times a thousand could simply mean the largest possible army; 2 Chr. 14:9; RSV "army of a million"), Asa prayed to the Lord who granted him a great victory over the invaders (vv. 9-15).

Encouraged by the inspiring address of the prophet Azariah, Asa continued his reform program (2 Chr. 15:1-9), and urged the people to renew their covenant with the Lord in a solemn ceremony at Jerusalem (vv. 11-15). He removed his grandmother Maacah from her position as queen mother on account of an image she had raised to Asherah the goddess of fertility — which he subsequently burned (v. 16; cf. 1 Kgs. 15:13). Asa carried out a quite thorough program of reform, except that he did not remove the high places — an omission for which he is not really faulted (2 Chr. 17; cf. 1 Kgs. 15:14).

In the sixteenth year of Asa's reign (not the thirty-sixth as at 2 Chr. 16:1) Baasha invaded Judah and fortified the city of Ramah (which lies between Bethel and Jerusalem), thereby forcing a blockade of the southern kingdom (v. 1; cf. 1 Kgs. 15:17). He probably also recaptured the cities of Bethel, Jeshanal, Ephron and their villages from Asa, which his own father had surrendered to Abijah years earlier (2 Chr. 13:19). Asa did not display the faith in God he had shown when attacked by the enormous Ethiopian host. Rather, this time he appealed to Syria for help. Taking all the silver and gold left in the temple and in his own palace, he offered it as a bribe to Ben-hadad of Syria, who accepted this gesture of political friendship. The Syrian king then broke his league with Baasha, whom he had supported against Judah after the death of his predecessor Tabrimmon (*ca.* 902 B.C.). He then proceeded to capture the cities in the northern part of the northern kingdom, forcing Baasha to abandon his fortification project at Ramah (2 Chr. 16:2-5; cf. 1 Kgs. 15:18-21). This move permitted Asa to remove the stones and timber which Baasha had used at Ramah

and to use them to build Geba and Mizpah in Benjamin (2 Chr. 16:6; cf. 1 Kgs. 15:22). According to 2 Chr. 17:2 Asa must have captured some Ephraimite cities, too.

While the author of Kings does not pass judgment on Asa's decision to seek aid from Syria, the Chronicler records his condemnation by Hanani the seer (2 Chr. 16:7-10). Censuring the king for his lack of faith in the Lord who had rescued him from Zerah, the seer states that because Asa relied on Syria he not only let Ben-hadad escape but also unleashed unremitting warfare between Syria and Judah for the future. Asa might even have set an example for Judah's King Ahaz (his descendant *ca.* 734), who would later appeal to Assyria in order to terminate an invasion by the combined forces of Syria and Israel (2 Kgs. 16:5-9). Enraged by the seer's words, Asa put Hanani in prison and even abused some of his own subjects (2 Chr. 16:10).

Some twenty-three years later (873) Asa contracted a progressive disease in his feet (v. 12; cf. 1 Kgs. 15:23). Though it was at least two years before he died — plenty of time to turn to God for help — instead he sought the healing of physicians (v. 12), perhaps sorcerers. Asa died in 871 and was buried in the royal tomb amid an elaborate funeral (vv. 13-14; cf. 1 Kgs. 15:24).

Jer. 41:9 refers to a cistern made by Asa into which Ishmael threw the bodies of the Israelites he had diverted from their pilgrimage to Jerusalem. In the genealogy of Jesus Asa is mentioned after Abijah and before Jehoshaphat (Matt. 1:7-8).

2. The son of Elkanah, who dwelled in the villages of the Netophathites (1 Chr. 9:16).

ASAHEL [ăs'ə hěl] (Heb. *'ăśâ'ēl* "God has made").

1. The youngest son of Zeruiah, and the brother of Joab and Abishai (2 Sam. 2:18). He was renowned for his swiftness of foot (v. 18), and became one of David's thirty "mighty men" (23:24 par. 1 Chr. 11:26). Asahel is named among those officers in charge of an army division (27:7); he may have been included posthumously, because his son Zebadiah was the actual commander of the fourth division after Asahel's death.

The final moments of Asahel's life are recorded at 2 Sam. 2:18-23. After Ishbosheth's army, led by Abner, was defeated at Gibeon by the forces loyal to David (v. 17), Asahel pursued Abner on foot. Unwilling to kill the young would-be hero out of regard for Joab and their former friendship, Abner told Asahel to chase after one of the other men instead. When Asahel did not heed Abner's warning, the aged warrior at last "smote him in the belly" (v. 23) and killed him. The fate of the young man made a solemn impression on those passing by (v. 23).

At the end of the day the battle was terminated, and Asahel received a burial in his father's tomb at Bethlehem (v. 32). But Joab remembered the incident and later took vengeance by murdering Abner (2 Sam. 3:26-30).

2. One of the Levites who, together with Jehoshaphat's princes, were charged by the king to teach the people from the book of the law (2 Chr. 17:8).

3. One of the overseers assisting in the collection of the contributions for the house of the Lord during the reign of King Hezekiah (2 Chr. 31:13).

4. The father of Jonathan, who opposed (so RSV, NIV, JB; KJV "were employed"; Heb. *ām^e dû 'al* "stood on") Ezra's policy of having the foreign wives of the Jews sent away after the Exile (Ezra 10:15).

ASAHIAH [ăs'ə hī'ə] (2 Kgs. 22:12, 14, KJV). *See* ASAIAH **1**.

ASAIAH [ə zā'yə] (Heb. *'ăsāyâ* "the Lord has made").

1. The "servant" (so RSV, KJV; NIV "attendant"; JB "minister") who, along with other dignitaries, was sent to the prophetess Huldah to inquire of the Lord concerning the book of the law found in the temple (2 Chr. 34:20 par. 2 Kgs. 22:12-14; KJV "Asahiah").

2. A ruler from the tribe of Simeon who participated in the extermination of the Meunim (1 Chr. 4:36).

3. A Levite, a descendant of Merari, and a family head during the days of David (1 Chr. 6:30; 15:6, 11).

4. The firstborn of the Shilonites returning from the exile (1 Chr. 9:5). In a parallel list he is named Maaseiah the son of Baruch (Neh. 11:5).

ASAPH [ā'săf] (Heb. *'āsāp*, possibly "[the Lord] has gathered for himself").

1. One of the Levites who with Heman and Juduthun was put in charge of the "service of song" as the ark was carried to Jerusalem (1 Chr. 6:39; 15:19) and one of those appointed to provide proper praise and thanksgiving to God once the ark was in place (16:4-6). Asaph was primarily a musician (15:19; 16:5) and is credited with having composed Pss. 50, 73-83 (cf. the superscriptions "A Psalm of Asaph"). Asaph the seer of 2 Chr. 29:30 was most likely the same person (cf. Neh. 12:46, "the days of David and Asaph of old").

Asaph's sons "prophesied" through their music during David's reign (1 Chr. 25:1-2), and later descendants appeared as singers under King Josiah (2 Chr. 35:15). A number of them (128 according to Ezra 2:41, or 148 according to Neh. 7:44) returned from Exile and settled in Jerusalem, either as singers or as musicians who performed at the dedication of the temple foundation (Ezra 3:10). They were later assigned to oversee the Levites in the house of the Lord (Neh. 11:22), and to play their trumpets at the dedication of the wall of the city (Neh. 12:35).

Asaph was the son of Berechiah, of the family of Gershom (1 Chr. 6:39).

2. The father of Joah, the recorder of King Hezekiah (2 Kgs. 18:18, 37; Isa. 36:3, 22).

3. The keeper (perhaps "inspector") of the forest owned by Artaxerxes I. He was requested by the king to send supplies to Jerusalem for the construction of the temple and of the city wall (Neh. 2:8).

4. Another name of Abiasaph (a possible alternative to the musician mentioned under **1** above) at 1 Chr. 26:1.

ASAREL [ăs'ə rĕl] (Heb. *'ăśar'ēl*). A son of Jehallelel of the tribe of Judah (1 Chr. 4:16; KJV "Asareel").

ASARELAH (1 Chr. 25:2, KJV). *See* ASHARELAH.

ASCENSION.

1. The departure of Christ to the Father in heaven at the end of his earthly ministry (Gk. *anabaínō,* "go up").

I. The Event

According to Acts 1:9 the Savior "was lifted up, and a cloud took him from [the apostles'] sight." This event is said to have taken place forty days after his resurrection (v. 3; cf. 13:31). In other occurrences the number forty symbolizes a period of preparation; here it may recall the beginning of Christ's exaltation. Whatever the precise length of time might have been, however, it is clear that the ascension took place after the resurrection. Luke describes Christ's appearances at the time of the resurrection (Luke 24:13-49) prior to his final appearance when he ascended into heaven (vv. 50-51).

Luke is the only Evangelist who records the ascension. In fact, this event is the link between the earlier gospel on the life of Christ and the book of Acts, which begins with the initial years of the New Testament church. Luke reports that, having led his disciples to Bethany on the eastern slope of the Mount of Olives, Christ blessed them and parted from them (Luke 24:50-51). While such important manuscripts as ℵ and D omit the addition "and was carried up to heaven [Gk. *kaí anephéreto eis tón ouranón*]" (v. 51), the textual evidence for omission is weak.

Having fittingly recorded the life of Christ in his gospel, Luke elaborates on the ascension at the beginning of Acts ("until the day when he was taken up," cf. Acts 1:2). Here, while he adds the detail about the cloud (v. 9, possibly alluding to the cloud at the transfiguration), he omits the note of joy among the gathered disciples at seeing Christ again. These and other differences are no doubt deliberate, in accordance with Luke's intent; they do not suggest different authors of the two books.

In contrast to Luke's writings, Matthew ends his gospel with Christ's appearance in Galilee when he commissioned his disciples to baptize "all nations" (Matt. 28:16-20). Critical study suggests that Mark's gospel probably concluded at 16:8; in the additional material 16:19 only mentions that Christ "was taken up into heaven." Even John, who often recorded Jesus' statements about going to the Father (John 7:33; 14:12; 16:10) and that Jesus would be "lifted up" (3:14; 8:28), does not include mention of the actual ascension; he only notes that to Mary the resurrected Savior says he is about to ascend to his Father (20:17).

II. Relation to Christ's Humiliation and Exaltation

Christ was crucified, died, was buried, and arose. The ascension constitutes the bridge between his earthly ministry — largely of humiliation — and the exaltation of his heavenly position, sitting at the right hand of the Father and awaiting his second coming. According to Paul the exalted Lord (Phil. 2:9) occupies a position of power and authority (cf. Eph. 1:20). Borrowing the language of the enthronement ritual (Ps. 68:18), the apostle depicts Christ as the one who led a "host of captives" (Eph. 4:8); the terminology is reminiscent of Jesus' own words to Nicodemus (John 3:13) and to his disciples (6:62).

The author of Hebrews speaks of Christ as seated above the angels, at the right hand of God (Heb. 1:3-4), after having "passed through the heavens" (4:14). The Savior entered heaven in order to atone for human sin — a priestly role under the old covenant (9:24-28) — by shedding his own blood (9:12). The author employs the language of power and authority, so prominent in Paul's letters (cf. 1 Pet. 3:22), but uses it to reveal the saving power of Christ's death.

The ascension also anticipates Christ's return. This point is made to the disciples immediately after the ascension (Acts 1:11), and is a part of Peter's address at Pentecost. In the last days the Spirit will be poured out on people, he says, who in turn will "prophesy" about the Day of the Lord (2:17ff.). Then Christ's atoning work will be complete.

III. Significance

The ascension marks the beginning of Christ's dominion over "heaven and earth." He intercedes in behalf of his own (cf. Rom. 8:34), protects his Church against the forces of evil, and one day will have conquered all powers opposing God. Christ's dominion may not always be noticeable; indeed, at times it has been hidden from the world. His Church, however, continues to profess it. *See also* KINGDOM OF GOD.

Bibliography. G. C. Berkouwer, *The Work of Christ* (Grand Rapids: 1965), pp. 202-241; B. M. Metzger, "The Ascension of Jesus Christ," pp. 77-87 in *Historical and Literary Studies* (Leiden: 1968).

2. The title of a number of noncanonical writings such as the Ascension of Moses and the New Testament apocryphal Ascension of Isaiah. Jewish tradition does not ascribe any redemptive significance to these and other ascensions (cf. the ascension of Elijah in a chariot of fire [2 Kgs. 2:1, 11, 16] and the ascension reported in Enoch [71; but see Gen. 5:24]). Nevertheless, these ascensions do highlight the greatness of these Old Testament figures.

ASCENT (Heb. *ma'aleh*). A rising grade, including that of a road or stairway (e.g., 2 Chr. 32:33; Neh. 3:19; 12:37). The term often refers to a mountain pass (so NIV) because it was believed to constitute entrance to a mountain range. Important ascents (so RSV, KJV, JB) in the Old Testament include those of Akrabbim (or the Scorpion pass; Num. 34:4; Josh. 15:3; Judg. 1:36) and Adummim (Josh. 15:7; 18:17).

At 2 Sam. 15:30 the ascent of the Mount of Olives simply means the western slope of the mountain, which David and his entourage climbed as they went east from Jerusalem. Conversely, it was at the "descent" of the same mountain that the Lord was coming down toward the city (Luke 19:37).

ASCENTS, SONG OF (Heb. *šîr hamma'alôt* "song of processions" [KoB, p. 548]). The title (so RSV, JB, NIV; KJV "Song of degrees") of a collection of some fifteen psalms (Pss. 120-134), probably sung by Israelite pilgrims en route to the great feasts at Jerusalem. Since Jerusalem is situated on an elevation, one always ascended when approaching the holy city. While this journey is not exactly divided into fifteen stages, it is appropriate to notice from psalm to psalm the progress made along the way and the arrival at the destination. Thus Ps. 130:1 portrays not only the anguish of a person in distress, but also an outburst from one standing at the foot of the hills on which the city and its temple are built — approaching Jerusalem, the locale of divine forgiveness. Pss. 133 and 134 are farewell songs (the latter is an antiphon).

Other opinions are plausible. These may be songs sung by returning exiles. According to the Mishnah (Mid. ii.5) these songs were sung on the fifteen steps of the stairway leading in the temple from the court of the men to the court of the women (possibly one on each step). Elsewhere they are designated Songs of Degrees (KJV) or Gradual Psalms (KD) on account of their "step-like progressive rhythm of the thoughts."

ASCETICISM (from Gk. *askēsis* "exercise, training").† A term denoting strict self-control as a means of spiritual discipline; it is not found in Scripture. While the Old Testament recognizes the custom of fasting (especially on the Day of Atonement; Lev. 16:29) and upholds the Nazirite vow against intoxicants (Num. 6:2-4), it does not insist upon abstinence from food or from other physical pleasures, provided that indulgence is not abused.

In the New Testament John the Baptist may have led an austere life (Luke 7:33; cf. 1:15), but he did not impose his life-style on others. Jesus himself did not practice asceticism, although he permitted others to fast (Matt. 6:16-18); he was, in fact, once accused of gluttony and drunkenness (Luke 7:34).

At times Paul preferred the single state to married life (1 Cor. 7:7-8), but he never condemned marriage as such (vv. 28, 37-38). His comments must be seen in the context of the nearness of the Parousia (v. 24); the exercise of his body at 9:27 expresses the apostle's aim to preach the gospel and live what he preaches. In fact, he criticized the Colossian heretics for their abstinence from certain foods ("severity to the body") because such an ascetic emphasis is no guard against indulgence (Col. 2:23). In his first Epistle to Timothy Paul warns against those who impose abstinence from foods, because God created food to be received with thanksgiving by believers (1 Tim. 4:3).

At 1 Tim. 4:8 Paul alludes to the value of "bodily training" (Gk. *sōmatikḗ gymnasía*); while he does suggest abstinence, he does, however, note that physical fitness is second to godliness. In other contexts the apostle reiterates the Old Testament commandment against unchaste indulgence (1 Thess. 4:3, Gk. *apéchomai*; cf. 1 Pet. 2:11, "passions of the flesh") and other forms of moral evil (1 Thess. 5:22).

ASENATH [ăs'ə năth] (Heb. *'asenat*; Egyp. *ns-nt* or *'ws-n-n[j]t* "belonging to [or the servant of][the goddess] Neith"). The daughter of Potiphera the priest of On, who became the wife of the Israelite Joseph (Gen. 41:45). Out of this union, which the Old Testament does not condemn, came two children: Manasseh and Ephraim (vv. 50-52; 46:20).

In a second-century A.D. Greek pseudepigraphon (of which translations have also been preserved in Latin, Syriac, and Armenian) Asenath is said to have been a proselyte, not a Gentile wife. Other Jewish legends also attempt to rationalize her Egyptian origins, portraying her as the daughter of Shechem and Dinah, who is later adopted by Potiphera.

ASER [ā′sər] (Luke 2:36; Rev. 7:6, KJV). See ASHER 1.

ASHAN [ā′shən] (Heb. *'āšān* "smoke"). A city originally assigned to Judah (Josh. 15:42), but later, when it was considered too large (19:9), given to Simeon within Judah (v. 7; 1 Chr. 4:32). Ashan was finally inhabited by the Aaronites (1 Chr. 6:59). On the basis of the physical description at 1 Chr. 6:59 some scholars favor reading "Ashan" for "Ain" at Josh. 21:16 (LXX *Asa*). Most likely Borashan (1 Sam. 30:30; Heb. *bôr-'āšān*; KJV "Chorashan"; NIV "Bor Ashan") is the same place. Ashan has been identified with modern Khirbet 'Asan, about 8 km. (5 mi.) west-northwest of Beer-sheba.

ASHARELAH [ăsh′ə rē′lə] (Heb. *'ªśar'ēlâ*). One of the sons of Asaph who with others prophesied with lyres, harps, and cymbals (1 Chr. 25:1-2; KJV "Asarelah"). He is the same as Jesharelah of v. 14.

ASHBEA [ăsh′bĭ ə] (Heb. *'ašbēaʿ*) (1 Chr. 4:21, KJV). See BETH-ASHBEA.

ASHBEL [ăsh′bĕl] (Heb. *'ašbēl*). Either the second (1 Chr. 8:1) or the third (Gen. 46:21) son of Benjamin. At 1 Chr. 7:6 the name is rendered Jediael (Heb. *yᵉdî'ªʾēl* "known to God"), perhaps to avoid alleged pagan connotations in the name Ashbel (cf. Ishbaal "man of Baal").

ASHCHENAZ (Jer. 51:27, KJV). See ASHKENAZ.

ASHDOD [ăsh′dŏd] (Heb. *'ašdôḏ* "fortress"; Gk. *Azōtos*).† One of the five principal cities of the Philistines, about 29 km. (18 mi.) northeast of Gaza and about 5 km. (3 mi.) inland from the Mediterranean coast.

I. History

A. Old Testament. The city is first listed as one of the few cities of the Anakim that the Israelites could not conquer (Josh. 11:22). Though the Lord assigned Ashdod to Judah, that tribe did not occupy it during Joshua's days (13:3 [KJV "Ashdothites"]; 15:46). Subsequently, Ashdod was captured by the Philistines, who ousted the original inhabitants and were able to retain it at least through the judgeship of Samuel, when they defeated Israel at Aphek; after placing Israel's ark in the temple of Dagon as a trophy God punished the captors with a plague (1 Sam. 5:1-7). The Philistines, though often defeated by David, probably did not yield to him this important site. The only time that Ashdod was known to be in Israelite possession was during the reign of Uzziah of Judah (*ca.* 783-750 B.C.), who broke down the city wall and built other cities in the vicinity (2 Chr. 26:6). Though Uzziah was successful in bringing Ashdod under Israelite jurisdiction, this victory was probably only temporary.

In their campaigns of expansion the Assyrians made Ashdod the capital of one of their provinces and imposed the payment of tribute on it. In *ca.* 712 Ashdod rebelled, but the rebellion did not last. Sargon II sent his "commander-in-chief" (Isa. 20:1; Heb. *tārtan*; KJV "Tartan"; JB "cupbearer-in-chief") to quell the opposition and retake the city. (The eighth-century prophet Amos may have been predicting this event as God's punishment of the Philistines for deporting Israelites to Edom [Amos 1:8].) Ashdod then became a strong Assyrian colony (cf. Zech. 9:6; "a mongrel people shall dwell in Ashdod; and I will make an end of the pride of Philistia") till Pharaoh Psamtik I (663-610) incorporated it into his kingdom, after a siege of many years (according to Herodotus, twenty-nine years). Jeremiah's reference to the "remnant of Ashdod" (Jer. 25:20) may have been witness to this eventuality. After the Exile Ashdod provided shelter to some Jews who had married Ashdodite women and who consequently had lost their native tongue (Neh. 13:23-24).

B. Intertestamental Period. During the wars of liberation, Judas Maccabeus successfully captured Ashdod ("Azotus," 1 Macc. 5:68), and his successor, Jonathan, continued Judas' policy of purging the city of Gentile worship (10:84). According to 16:10 John Hyrcanus burned the city down.

C. New Testament. Ashdod is mentioned only once in the New Testament, as the city through which Philip passed en route to Caesarea after his encounter with the Ethiopian eunuch ("Azotus," Acts 8:40). Josephus (*Ant.* xiii.15.4[396]; xiv.4.4[75]) mentions an Azotus on the coast and another about 5 km. (3 mi.) inland.

II. Archaeology

Excavated extensively between 1962 and 1969 by M. Dothan, Ashdod has yielded archaeological discoveries which, together with ancient documents and inscriptions, provide a fairly complete picture of its history.

The history of Ashdod began during the Middle Bronze Period (*ca.* seventeenth century) when it was established as a fortified city covering about 7 hectares (17 acres). In the Late Bronze Period it developed into a commercial center occupied chiefly by Canaanites until about the latter part of the thirteenth century, when it was destroyed.

The Philistines settled in Ashdod a century later, perhaps following its occupation by the Sea Peoples. Judging from the large amount of Philistine pottery the city must have expanded considerably, at a time when Israel and Judah were on the decline. A throne in the form of a female deity may point to an Aegean origin for the Philistines. Four layers of ash may represent successive destructions of the city by Uzziah of Judah, Sargon II of Assyria, Psamtik I of Egypt, and Nebuchadnezzar of Babylon.

Major structural remains and a variety of artifacts suggest that Ashdod was a flourishing city during Greco-Roman times. A coin of Antiochus VIII discovered in the vicinity places the city's conquest by John Hyrcanus after 114 B.C.

The village of Isdud, located on the adjoining hill until abandoned in 1948 in favor of a new city on the coast, preserves the ancient name.

ASHDOTHITES (Josh. 13:3, KJV). Inhabitants of Ashdod.

ASHDOTH-PISGAH (Deut. 3:17; Josh. 12:3; 13:20, KJV). *See* PISGAH.

ASHER [ăsh'ər] (Heb. *ʾāšēr*, from the name of a West Semitic deity).† The eighth son of Jacob and the second son of Zilpah, Leah's maid (Gen. 30:12-13), born in Paddan-aram (35:26). According to 30:13 his name means "happy" (Heb. **ʾōšer* "happiness"; cf. piel of *ʾāšar* "pronounce happy"). It is foretold in the Blessing of Jacob that his descendants would live in a fertile region (49:20), a promise reiterated in the Blessing of Moses (Deut. 33:24).

After the Conquest the Asherites (descendants of the five children of Asher [Gen. 46:17; 1 Chr. 7:30] numbering about 53,400 in the second census [Num. 26:47]) inherited the northwestern part of the promised land, the region from Mt. Carmel to Sidon in the north with the territories of Zebulun and Naphtali in the east (Josh. 19:24-31). According to Judg. 1:31-32 they were unable to conquer such cities as Acco and Sidon, and were thus forced to dwell among the Canaanites, a fate they shared with some of the other tribes of Israel. Some of their cities were occupied by Manasseh (Josh. 17:11).

Settled in such an ideal spot, the Asherites did not participate in Israel's national life as much as other tribes. They did not offer assistance to Deborah and Barak in their battle with the Canaanites, remaining instead "at the coast of the sea" (Judg. 5:17). Their attitude reflected a greater sense of unity with the other tribes some forty years later when they heeded Israel's call for help against the Midianites. Not only did they help defeat the enemy (6:35), but they also pursued them afterward (7:23).

During the Monarchy four of Asher's cities (Josh. 19:30) were given to the Levites (21:30-31; 1 Chr. 6:74-75). Solomon gave a number of its cities in the Cabul region to Hiram of Tyre in exchange for the materials he donated for the construction of the temple (1 Kgs. 9:11-13).

Most of the people of Asher, like those in other northern tribes, were deported to Assyria when Sargon II of Assyria captured Samaria (2 Kgs. 17:6). Of the people who were allowed to stay behind, a few accepted Hezekiah's invitation to come to Jerusalem and participate in the Passover observance (2 Chr. 30:11). The territory of the Asherites may have been included in the reform program of King Josiah of Judah, who *ca.* 622 went as far as Naphtali (2 Chr. 34:6) to rid the northern area of Canaanite worship practices (v. 33). The Asherites are included in the division of land as prophesied by Ezekiel (Ezek. 48:2-3).

In the New Testament Asher is mentioned as the tribe from which the prophetess Anna descended (Luke 2:36; KJV "Aser"). Twelve thousand of its members are among those envisioned as bearing God's protective seal (Rev. 7:6).

ASHERAH [ə shîr'ə] (Heb. *ʾašērâ*). The Hebrew name of an Amorite or Canaanite goddess and the cult object dedicated to her. The KJV consistently renders Heb. *ʾašērâ* "grove," to identify both the goddess and

the pole which belonged to her. The RSV and the NIV distinguish between the two, but not always. The JB most regularly differentiates between the goddess and poles erected in her honor. But a complete distinction is not always possible in the Old Testament (cf. Judg. 3:7, "Asheroth"[pl.]).

Asherah may have been the same as Ashratum, the consort of Amurru, one of the chief deities mentioned in an early Babylonian list of gods; in the Amarna Tablets her name appears in the personal name Abdi-Ashirta ("Servant of Asherah"). The Ras Shamra Texts list her as the spouse of the supreme deity El and the mother of seventy children, including Baal; she is also named "Lady Asherah of the sea." Asherah was the mother goddess, to be distinguished from Astarte, the Canaanite fertility goddess. Centers of worship were located in various countries of the ancient Near East, notably Phoenicia, Israel's northern neighbor.

Heb. *ʾašērâ* refers not only to the goddess but also to the consecrated poles, called either "Asherah" (e.g., Deut. 16:21; Judg. 6:25, 28; NIV "Asherah pole"; JB "sacred pole/post") or "Asherim" (e.g., Exod. 34:13; Deut. 7:5; 12:3; NIV "Asherah poles"; JB "sacred poles"), that represented the deity. At first they may have been living trees (cf. Deut. 16:21), but in later usage were wooden poles, perhaps erected ("set up," 2 Kgs. 17:10) to represent a tree. These poles also may have been carved images of the goddess. Remains of what are believed to be such wooden poles, including those discovered among Bronze Age finds at Shechem, consist merely of postholes in which the rotted timber has left a differently colored soil.

Soon after they had settled in the Promised Land, the Israelites began to worship Asherah, prompting the Lord to punish them for their unfaithfulness toward him (Judg. 3:7-8; NIV, JB "Asherahs"); apparently, God's warnings at Mt. Horeb (Exod. 34:13-14) and afterward (Deut. 7:5) were no longer heeded. When King Ahab married the Phoenician princess Jezebel, worship of Asherah was strongly promoted in the northern kingdom, together with worship of Baal. The prophet Elijah counted some four hundred and fifty of her prophets (and those of Baal), eating at Jezebel's table (no doubt supported by the queen; 1 Kgs. 18:19). Samaria remained a center of worship (2 Kgs. 13:6), and Israel's devotion to Asherah was partly the cause for its deportation to Assyria (17:10, 16).

Worship of this deity was not confined to the northern tribes, however. Some two hundred years later King Josiah of Judah burned the "vessels" and the "hangings" of Asherah (2 Kgs. 23:4, 7; 2 Chr. 34:3, 7) which his predecessor Manasseh had probably had erected in the temple at Jerusalem (2 Kgs. 21:7; cf. 2 Chr. 33:3 ["Asherahs"], 19). Actually, Rehoboam the son of Solomon had already encouraged widespread Asherah worship in this kingdom ("on every high hill and under every green tree," 1 Kgs. 14:23), and Maacah the queen mother had placed an "image" of Asherah in Judah which her grandson Asa destroyed in the brook Kidron (1 Kgs. 15:13; cf. 2 Chr. 15:16; NIV "Asherah pole"). In spite of the efforts of the reform kings (Jehoshaphat, 2 Chr. 19:3; Hezekiah, 2 Kgs. 18:4), the Judahites did not change their cultic patterns and the Exile may have been attributed to this worship (Isa. 27:9; Jer. 17:1ff.; Mic. 5:14). Isaiah contrasts that period with one in which people will exalt their Maker rather than manmade cultic objects (Isa. 17:8).

Bibliography. J. C. de Moor, "'ªshērāh," *TDOT* 1, rev. ed. (1977): 438-444.

ASHEROTH [ə shǐr'ŏth] (Heb. 'ªšērôt). *See* ASHERAH.

ASHES. Often a sign of mourning, sorrow, and repentance. Under such conditions one would put on sackcloth and pour ashes (Heb. 'ēper) on one's head (Isa. 58:5) or "roll" in them (Jer. 6:26). Job sat "among" the ashes (Job 2:8), as did the king of Nineveh when Jonah announced that city would be overthrown (Jonah 3:6). Daniel fasted and used sackcloth and ashes before making his prayer of confession to God (Dan. 9:3). A similar custom occurs in New Testament times to symbolize repentance (Gk. *spodós*; Matt. 11:21 par.).

The ashes (Heb. *dešen*) mentioned at Jer. 31:40 refer to the remains of victims sacrificed to a pagan deity. Though in this way the Israelites perverted this convention, the Lord would eventually make sacred even the ashes of these victims, at the rebuilding of Jerusalem.

The ashes which the prophet used to disguise himself before Ahab (1 Kgs. 20:38, 41, KJV) were probably bandages (so RSV; NIV, JB "headband").

See SACRIFICES AND OFFERINGS.

ASHHUR [ăsh'ər] (Heb. 'ashûr). The son of Caleb and Ephrathah the wife of Hezron (so RSV, JB, following the LXX); according to the KJV and the NIV it was Abiah (or Abijah) who gave birth to Ashhur after the death of her husband Hezron (following the MT). Ashhur became the "father" or founder of Tekoa (1 Chr. 2:24). At 4:5-6 the names of his children are listed.

ASHIMA [ə shī'mə] (Heb. 'ªšîma'). A deity worshipped by the inhabitants of Hamath whom the king of Assyria had deported and resettled in Samaria after the fall of the northern kingdom (2 Kgs. 17:30). Accordingly, some commentators take Amos 8:14 to refer to the same deity ("Ashimah of Samaria"; KoB, p. 94); the MT reads 'ašmaṭ šōmᵉrôn "the guilt of Samaria" (but see LXX Gk. *hilasmós*, "expiation"), the sense of which the KJV ("sin") and the NIV ("shame") have retained.

ASHKELON [ăsh'kə lən] (Heb. 'ašqᵉlôn). A maritime city, about 19 km. (12 mi.) north of Gaza and 16 km. (10 mi.) south of Ashdod.

I. History

Ashkelon is first mentioned in the Egyptian Execration Texts (*ca.* 1850 B.C.) as a rebellious city. According to the Amarna Letters (*ca.* 1350) it had remained a city subject to Egyptian rule, but its citizens revolted during the reign of Pharaoh Rameses II (1280 B.C.); he not only quelled the rebellion but sacked the city at the same time (cf. the stele of Mer-ne-Ptah which mentions this defeat).

At the time of the Conquest, Philistines lived in this and surrounding cities of the plain (Josh. 13:3; KJV "Eshkalonites"). According to Judg. 1:18 the Judahites were able to seize Ashkelon (KJV "Askelon"; cf. 1 Sam. 6:17; 2 Sam. 1:20) only to see it recaptured by the Philistines during the judgeship of Samson (14:19).

The Monarchy produced no change in the city's status. Neither Saul (1 Sam. 6:17) nor David was able to retake it. In his lament over Saul's death David did not wish to broadcast the event to "Gath" or the "streets of Ashkelon" (2 Sam. 1:20), meaning the eastern and western parts of Philistia, or, by extension, its entire territory.

The prophets include the name of the city in their oracles. Amos predicted punishment for Ashkelon's slave trade (Amos 1:8). First subject to Assyria for several years, the people of Ashkelon had to decide whether or not to pay tribute to Nebuchadnezzar of Babylon. When they refused, the Chaldean monarch quickly destroyed the city (604; cf. Jer. 25:20; 47:5-7). Zephaniah, too, foretold doom, but ended his oracle with the prophecy of Israel's occupation of the city (Zeph. 2:4-7).

After the conquests of Alexander the Great, Ashkelon became fertile ground for the spread of Hellenism, developing into an important center of scholarship. The city supported Jonathan, the brother of Judas Maccabeus, in the wars of liberation ("Askalon," 1 Macc. 10:86; 11:61). Herod the Great, who according to tradition was born in Ashkelon, beautified the city with gardens and impressive buildings (Josephus *BJ* i.21.11). In New Testament times Greek learning was much in evidence; even its name had taken the Greek form Ascalon.

Ashkelon remained a city of significance during the first centuries A.D. During the Crusades it was an important port until in 1270 Sultan Baibars ordered it destroyed. Modern Ashqelon, founded in 1953, lies about 1 km. from the ruins of the ancient city.

II. Archaeology

Lady H. Stanhope conducted the first excavation at Ashkelon in 1815. Between 1920 and 1922 the Palestine Exploration Fund sponsored excavations there which enabled scholars to trace the city's history as far back as the Middle Bronze Age (*ca.* 1800). J. Garstang succeeded in uncovering evidence of Philistine occupation and unearthed the Roman "Herod's Cloisters" and a number of statues.

ASHKENAZ [ăsh'kə năz] (Heb. 'aškᵉnaz). The eldest of the three sons of Gomer, the son of Japheth (Gen. 10:3; 1 Chr. 1:6), and the name of a kingdom (Jer. 51:27; KJV "Ashchenaz"). Most likely it was the Scythian kingdom (cf. Assyr. *As-ku-za*). Its connection to the Cimmerian invasions (Herodotus *Hist.* iv.11) accounts for its relation to Gomer.

Allying themselves with the Mannai, the Scythians revolted against Assyria (seventh century B.C.) but were afterward conquered by the Medes and the Persians. In 538 they provided contingents of troops for the Persian attack against Babylon.

ASHNAH [ăsh'nə] (Heb. 'ašnâ).

1. A city in the lowlands of Judah, mentioned in

connection with Eshtaol and Zorah (Josh. 15:33). The nearby village of Aslin is a possible location for this city.

2. Another city in the same region but further south (Josh. 15:43). It is considered the same as modern Idhna near Maresha.

ASHPENAZ [ăsh'pə năz] (Heb. *ʾašpᵉnaz*). The chief of Nebuchadnezzar's eunuchs, charged with recruiting handsome and intelligent Jewish captives of nobility for the king's service (Dan. 1:3-4).

ASHRIEL (1 Chr. 7:14, KJV). *See* ASRIEL.

ASHTAROTH [ăsh'tə rŏth] (Heb. *ʿaštārôt*) (**DEITY**). The plural form of the name Ashtoreth, the Canaanite fertility goddess (NIV "Ashtoreth[s]"). For some time after the Conquest the Israelites worshipped this deity (Judg. 2:13; 10:6). Urged by Samuel to discontinue the practice, they "put away" the Ashtaroth (1 Sam. 7:3-4; cf. 12:10). In calling this goddess "Astarte(s)," the JB links her with Ishtar, the Assyrian goddess of love and fecundity.

ASHTAROTH [ăsh'tə rŏth] (Heb. *ʿaštārôt*) (**PLACE**). A city in Bashan, named after the goddess Ashtoreth in whose honor a sanctuary there was built. According to Josh. 12:4; 13:12, the Rephaim dwelled in this city. Their last king, Og of Bashan, who reigned in Ashtaroth and Edrei (Deut. 1:4; KJV "Astaroth"; Josh. 12:4), was defeated by the Israelites and the city was assigned to the tribe of Manasseh east of the Jordan (Josh. 13:12, 31). Later it became a levitical city of the Gershomites (1 Chr. 6:71).

It has been proposed that modern Tell ʿAshtarah, about 32 km. (20 mi.) east of the Sea of Galilee, occupies the site of ancient Ashtaroth. Scholars remain uncertain about this city's relation to the Ashteroth-karnaim mentioned at Gen. 14:5; perhaps it is best to distinguish them as two neighboring cities. Another proposed identification has been with Beeshterah (cf. Josh. 21:27).

ASHTERATHITE [ăsh'tə răth īt'] (Heb. *hāʿaštᵉrāṯî*). A native of Ashtaroth, used to designate Uzzia, one of David's mighty men (1 Chr. 11:44).

ASHTEROTH-KARNAIM [ăsh'tə rŏth kär nā'əm] (Heb. *ʿaštᵉrôt qarnayim* "Ashteroth of the two horns"). A city in Gilead which Chedorlaomer subdued (Gen. 14:5). The name was later shortened to Karnaim (cf. Amos 6:13, where it is implied that the city was captured by Jeroboam II of Israel), probably the postexilic city Carnaim captured by the Jews during the wars of liberation (1 Macc. 5:26, 43-44). It has been identified with Sheikh Saʿd, about 32 km. (20 mi.) east of the Sea of Galilee; excavations there suggest that it was a great city surrounded by a threefold wall and thus "hard to besiege" (2 Macc. 12:21; KJV "Carnion"). It should not be confused with Ashtaroth, which was situated about 5 km. (3 mi.) to the south.

ASHTORETH [ăsh'tə rĕth] (Heb. *ʿaštōreṯ*). The Canaanite fertility goddess, also called Ashtaroth, Astarte, or Ishtar. Heb. *ʿaštōreṯ* is most likely a deliberate misvocalization of the name Ashtereth or Astarte; the

Ashtoreth, standing on a lion, as goddess of war

Hebrew scribes retained the consonants *ʿštrt* but substituted the vowels of the word *bōšeṯ* ("shame"). The plural form, Heb. *ʿaštārôt*, may signify a more general reference to this deity or may indicate various local cults (cf. Judg. 2:13); it is also rendered "young" (Deut. 7:13; 28:4, 18, 51; KJV "flocks of your sheep"). Ashteroth-karnaim (meaning "the horned Astarte"; Gen. 14:5) may indicate that there was a local sanctuary of the deity in that city. Although both were fertility goddesses, Ashtoreth should not be confused with Asherah (cf. LXX, Vulg. 2 Chr. 15:16; 24:18).

In the Babylonian pantheon this deity, known as Ishtar, was the daughter of the moon-god Sin and later the consort of Anu, the deity of heaven. She is usually regarded as the goddess of love and sensual pleasure or fertility, though the Assyrians also fostered her identification as the goddess of war. Some scholars have conjectured that her double role is related to the evening and morning stars, the former being identified with sexual passion and the latter with war. In Hellenistic times Ishtar became identified with Venus or Aphrodite, the goddess of love; some images which depict her with a beard suggest that she was an androgynous figure. Among the Phoenicians, she was the most important goddess of the Sidonians (1 Kgs. 11:5, 33), probably an astral deity. As the Astarte of the Ugaritic texts she is an ally of Baal, but her functions as giver of life and death were assumed by Baal's sister-consort Anat. The Philistines worshipped her as the goddess of war (1 Sam. 31:10 mentions that they carried Saul's armor to the temple of Astaroth, probably at Beth-shan; cf. 1 Chr. 10:10). She is probably represented among the numerous nude female figurines discovered throughout Syria-Palestine.

By the time of the Israelite confederation many of the populace apparently had become involved at least periodically in cultic observance of the Ashtaroth (cf. Judg. 2:13). It does not appear, however, that they were associated with the Philistine cult at Beth-shan (1 Sam. 31:10). No less a figure than King Solomon engaged in the worship of this deity, particularly after numerous political marriages with foreign women. According to 1 Kgs. 11:5 he introduced the worship of the Sidonian Ashtoreth and the Ammonite Milcom. For that reason God took the kingdom from his son Rehoboam and gave a great portion to Jeroboam (v. 33). Nevertheless, the sanctuaries of Ashtoreth remained until King Josiah of Judah some three hundred years later destroyed them along with other remnants of idol worship (2 Kgs. 23:13). With heightened pressure from the Babylonians and the imminent fall of Jerusalem, Josiah's cultic reforms dissipated and this deity, in its Babylonian manifestation as Ishtar, was worshipped openly ("queen of heaven," Jer. 7:18; 44:17-19).

ASHUR. *See* ASSUR.

ASHURBANIPAL. *See* ASSURBANIPAL.

ASHURITES [ăsh'ə rīts] (Heb. *hā'ăsûrî*). A tribe located between Gilead and Jezreel; Ishbosheth the son of Saul ruled them for a short time (2 Sam. 2:9; NIV "Ashuri"). They are probably Asherites (see KoB, p. 93; cf. NIV mg.), since "Asher" is the collective name for the tribes of Asher, Zebulun, and Naphtali.

ASHVATH [ăsh'văth] (Heb. *'ašwāt*). One of the sons of Japhlet of the tribe of Asher (1 Chr. 7:33).

ASIA (Gk. *Asia*).† A Roman province in New Testament times, located in the western part of Asia Minor and comprising the earlier Attalid provinces of Mysia, Lydia, Caria, and Phrygia; it did not encompass the entire continent of Asia or even a major portion thereof (as did the Seleucid kingdom in the Maccabean period).

Incorporated into the Roman Empire during the second half of the second century B.C., Asia became one of Rome's richest provinces. It retained a great measure of Greek culture, dating back to the fifth and sixth centuries when Greek colonists had settled along its western coast. Some of its important centers of learning were Pergamum, Sardis, Smyrna, and Ephesus.

Jews from Asia were present in Jerusalem at the Feast of Pentecost (Acts 2:9), and some of them later joined other Jews in debating with Stephen in the synagogue (6:9).

Paul intended to visit the province during his second missionary journey, but was "forbidden by the Holy Spirit" to do so (Acts 16:6-7). During his third journey he spent a long time — some two years — at Ephesus, however, and greatly influenced the citizens there (19:10; cf. v. 22; see also Rom. 16:5). Paul's ministry was not as effective among the Asian Jews of Jerusalem, who caused a stir against him for his allegedly bringing Greeks into the temple (Acts 21:27ff.; 24:18ff.). In his letters the apostle indicated his success in establishing churches in Asia (1 Cor. 16:19), but did not hide the less productive side of his ministry there — what he identifies only as "affliction" (2 Cor. 1:8; cf. Acts 20:19).

At the time he wrote Revelation, John addressed some seven churches in this Roman province, of which three (Ephesus, Smyrna, and Pergamum) were significant cities (Rev. 1:4).

The churches in Asia survived anti-Christian opposition during the early part of the second century, and played an influential role in the formation of christological doctrine during the fifth and sixth centuries.

ASIA MINOR. A peninsula between the Black Sea and the Mediterranean Sea, with the Armenian highlands in the East, called in Turkish Anadolu (from Gk. *Anatolia* "the east" or "rising [of the sun]").

The peninsula features a sharp contrast between the coastal area and the interior, a plateau about 1000 m. (3280 ft.) high and surrounded by two mountain ranges: along the Black Sea are the Pontic mountains, a ridge which descends in terraces toward the coast; along the Mediterranean Sea the Taurus and Amanos mountains converge into the Anti-taurus range.

Passage through this rugged region is primarily through two plains, the large central plateau and the southern coastal plain of Cilicia. The latter forms the link between Asia Minor and Syria, and is traversed by an ancient trade route through the Cilician gates — the great highway of Xerxes and Alexander the Great along which Paul and Silas traveled (Acts 15:40-41). The west coast of Asia Minor (with its numerous turns and peninsulas, and protected by a chain of islands) is exceptionally blessed with natural harbors. It was here — on the important west coast — that the ancient Greek colonies as well as several New Testament churches were located (Rev. 2–3).

In Old Testament times Asia Minor was the center of the Hittite empire, the capital of which has been excavated near modern Boghazköy. At the time of Paul's missionary travels the peninsula was divided by the Romans into several provinces: Asia, Bithynia, Pontus, Galatia, Cappadocia, Lycia, and Cilicia. The term "Asia" (e.g., 1 Pet. 1:1) refers to the province of Asia rather than the entire peninsula.

ASIARCH [ā'zhĭ ärk] (Gk. *Asiarchēs*). The title of wealthy and prominent citizens of the Roman province of Asia. They were responsible for managing the games in honor of the emperor, and may have constituted a provincial council of sorts. They were elected for one year only, but reelection was possible. A number of asiarchs may have been the official high priests of the provincial emperor cult.

The Asiarchs appear in Luke's account of the uproar at Ephesus during Paul's third missionary journey. These more educated citizens of Ephesus did not frown on Paul's preaching in the city (Acts 19:31).

ASIEL [ăs'ĭəl] (Heb. *'ăśî' ēl*). The father of Seraiah and great-grandfather of Jehu. He was one of the Simeonite chiefs who sought land in Gedor (1 Chr. 4:35).

ASKELON (1 Sam. 6:17; 2 Sam. 1:20, KJV). *See* ASHKELON.

ASMODEUS [ăz′mō dē′əs] (Gk. *Asmodaios*). An evil spirit (Gk. *daimónion*) mentioned in the apocryphal book of Tobit. In love with Sarah, he killed each of her seven successive husbands. The angel Raphael showed Tobit's son Tobias a way to avoid a similar fate (6:15-18), which the bridegroom (Sarah's eighth) subsequently applied with success (8:3).

In rabbinic literature he is called the "king of the demons," and is sometimes equated with Abaddon (Job 31:12), Apollyon (Rev. 9:11), and Beelzebul (Mark 3:22).

ASNAH [ăs′nə] (Heb. *'asnâ* "thornbush"). One of the temple servants returning from Exile under Zerubbabel (Ezra 2:50).

ASNAPPER (Ezra 4:10, KJV). *See* ASSURBANIPAL.

ASPATHA [ăs pā′thə] (Heb. *'aspāṯā'*, perhaps a Persian loanword). One of the ten sons of Haman the Agagite killed by the Jews (Esth. 9:7).

ASPHALT. *See* BITUMEN.

ASRIEL [ăs′rī əl] (Heb. *'aśrî'ēl* "God has filled with joy"). A descendant of Manasseh (Num. 26:31; Josh. 17:2). According to 1 Chr. 7:14 (KJV "Ashriel") his mother was an Aramean concubine.

ASS. Any of several varieties of hardy, gregarious mammals (*Equus asinus*), smaller than donkeys, either domesticated or wild.

I. Domesticated

A. Old Testament. The Palestinian ass, probably a descendant of the wild Nubian ass (*Equus asinus africanus*), had been domesticated as early as the third millennium B.C. According to Gen. 12:16 Abraham obtained "he-asses" (Heb. *ḥᵃmôr* "red animal" [KoB, p. 310]) and "she-asses" (Heb. *'āṯôn*) from the pharaoh. It is difficult to determine whether all tamed asses — those of Haran (belonging to Jacob; Gen. 30:43), of Uz (belonging to Job; Job 1:3; 42:12), and of the Promised Land — descended from the same stock.

In spite of the fact that the ass was classified as an unclean animal (Lev. 11:1-8; Deut. 14:3-8), its stamina, sprightliness, and speed caused it to be in great demand among the Israelites, even after the Exile (Ezra 2:67 par. Neh. 7:69).They were often kept in herds (Gen. 24:35); but some of them would stray from time to time (1 Sam. 9:3).

The ass, whose color ranged from gray to reddish brown and "tawny" (so RSV at Judg. 5:10; KJV, NIV, JB "white"), was employed as a riding animal by the Hebrews — common and influential alike. Asses were valuable during peacetime (as used by Moses over rugged terrain [Exod. 4:20] and the Shunammite woman en route to Mt. Carmel [2 Kgs. 4:22-25]), and in times of war (as when Samaria was besieged by the Syrians [2 Kgs. 7:7]; or as prophesied in the oracle against the wilderness at Isa. 21:7). In addition, the ass served as a beast of burden, carrying grain (Gen. 42:26) and provisions (Josh. 9:4-5), or plowing the fields (Deut. 22:10), though it was not

yoked like an ox. At Isa. 32:20 the animal is said to "range free," possibly meaning that it was free from danger while human beings used it to cultivate the soil.

Yet indignity attended the ass. Note that the scoundrel King Jehoiakim would suffer the burial of an ass (Jer. 22:19).

B. New Testament. Jesus rode into Jerusalem on a "colt" found tied in the street (so Mark 11:1-10 par. Luke 19:29-40, Gk. *pōlos*; cf. John 12:12-18; Gk. *onárion*). The account echoes Zech. 9:9, which Matthew interprets ambiguously — "the ass (Gk. *ónos*) and the colt" (Matt. 21:7; "and he sat thereon [Gk. *epánō autōn*, "on them"]"). While the animal was still used as a beast of burden, it shared in the Sabbath rest (Luke 13:15; 14:5 [KJV and RSV, NIV, JB mgs.]). The "beast" of the Samaritan could have been a donkey (so NIV; JB "mount") carrying the wounded man (Luke 10:34). 2 Pet. 2:16 recalls the Old Testament story of Balaam's "dumb ass" (Gk. *hypozýgion áphōnon*, "a beast of burden [lit. 'under the yoke']," "incapable of speech" [Bauer, pp. 844, 128]) that restrained the seer from cursing Israel.

II. Wild

Besides the domesticated ass, the Old Testament also mentions the wild ass. Job 39:5 may distinguish between two wild asses: the Syrian wild ass (Heb. *'ārôḏ* [*Equus hemionus hemihippus*]) and the "swift ass" (Heb. *pere'*, the onager [*Equus hemionus onager*]), although the similarities between them should not be ignored. If this is a legitimate distinction, the Hebrews used the onager, which was better known than the other species and dwelled in a larger area, more often than the Syrian species, which was indigenous to the steppes and never successfully domesticated.

At Gen. 16:12 Ishmael is compared to an obstinate and indomitable wild ass (KJV "wild man"; NIV "wild donkey"), while at Jer. 2:24 Israel's apostasy is likened to the lust of a female ass in heat. The swiftness of this animal is made exemplary for the oppressed Moabites (Jer. 48:6; so RSV, JB, following the LXX; KJV "heath"; NIV "bush"); the unnaturalness of a solitary ass is a metaphor for Israel's apostasy at Hos. 8:9.

In a theophany Job is told that God gave the wild ass habitation in the steppes (Job 39:6-8; cf. Jer. 14:6, "bare heights").

ASSASSINS (Gk. *sikárioi*, from Lat. *sicarii* "men with a dagger"). Jewish outlaws who promised political freedom; often they mingled with crowds at festive occasions with daggers hidden under their cloaks to murder those sympathetic to Rome. At Acts 21:38 Paul is mistaken for the Egyptian leader of a band of such men who disappeared into the wilderness after an uprising. *See* ROBBER.

ASSEMBLY. *See* CONGREGATION; MOUNT OF ASSEMBLY.

ASSHUR [ăsh′ər] (Heb. *'aššûr*). (**PERSON**). One of the sons of Shem and the eponymous ancestor of the Assyrians (Gen. 10:22; 1 Chr. 1:17).

ASSHUR [ăsh'ər] (Heb. *'aššûr*) (**PLACE**).

1. A major city in Assyria and at one point its capital (Ezek. 27:23). *See* ASSUR **2.**

2. Another name for Assyria (Num. 24:22, 24; Hos. 14:3 [KJV; RSV, JB, NIV "Assyria"]).

ASSHURIM [ăsh'ə rĭm] (Heb. *'aššûrîm*). A tribe descended from Jokshan and ultimately from Abraham and Keturah, about which little more is known (Gen. 25:3; JB, NIV "Asshurites"). While some commentators suppose them to be related to the Assyrians (perhaps on the basis of v. 18), they are probably an Arabian clan.

ASSIR [ăs'ər] (Heb. *'assîr* "captive").

1. A son of Korah of the tribe of Levi (Exod. 6:24; 1 Chr. 6:22).

2. The son of Ebiasaph (1 Chr. 6:23) and grandson of Korah (v. 37).

3. According to the KJV one of the sons of Jeconiah of Judah (1 Chr. 3:17). The RSV, NIV, and JB refer to him as "the captive."

ASSOS [ăs'ŏs] (Gk. *Assos*). A city built on a volcanic cone on the Gulf of Adramyttium, north of the island of Lesbos off the coast of Asia Minor. Sending his companions ahead by boat around Cape Lectum, Paul took the road from Troas to Assos, a distance of about 32 km. (20 mi.). Because the trip by land was shorter than the voyage by sea, Paul was able to stay longer in Troas before rejoining his friends at Assos (Acts 20:13-14).

The city was founded by the Aeolians of Lesbos (*ca.* 900 B.C.). It was here that the philosopher Aristotle taught for three years (348-345) and that the Stoic philosopher Cleanthes was born. Excavations conducted between 1881 and 1883 unearthed many public buildings and remnants of two city walls. Its contemporary name is Behramköy, a Turkish corruption of the city's Byzantine name.

ASSUMPTION OF MOSES. *See* MOSES, ASSUMPTION OF.

ASSUMPTION OF THE VIRGIN.† A fourth-century A.D. docetic and gnostic gospel included among the works of the New Testament Apocrypha; denounced in the fifth-century Gelasian Decree for its heretical teachings, the work survives in Coptic, Greek, Latin, and Syriac versions dating to the eleventh-fourteenth centuries. Although the versions vary in details and circumstances, the narrative is basically an account of the announcement to Mary (either by the risen Christ or an angel) of her imminent death and transformation, along with accounts of miraculous healings through contact with her body. Also included are Jesus' discourses with his disciples concerning the human soul.

ASSUR [ăsh'ər] (Heb. *'aššûr*; Akk. *Aššur*) (**DEITY**). The main Assyrian deity, after whom the city of Assur, Assyria, and the Assyrians are named; his name occurs in personal names such as Assurbanipal and Esarhaddon. Originally the local god of the city Assur, his name first appears as A-šur in the Cappadocian clay tablets (*ca.* 2000 B.C.) and as A-ušar in the Code of Hammurabi (Old Babylonian; *ca.* 1750). In Babylonian cosmology Assur was identified with An-šar and paired with Ki-šar, thus the universe above and below, respectively. In an Assyrian recension of the Babylonian creation epic (Enuma Elish) he replaces the Babylonian deity Marduk, who himself had replaced the Sumerian chief god Enlil. In Assyrian royal inscriptions he is regarded as the god of war (A-usur).

The deity was most closely connected with the city of Assur, where he lived with his consort Ninlil in the sanctuary Ešarra (Akk. *bît kiššuti* "house of omnipotence"), held to be an earthly copy of a primeval model of the Apsu, the sweet-water ocean; this was the site of the later temple Ehursaggal-kurkurra ("great mountain of the lands"). Assur himself adopted from the Sumerian Enlil the epithet kurgal (Akk. *šadû rabû* "great mountain." He is represented as wearing a tall hat with horns and holding in his left hand a staff and ring, emblems of sovereignty; he stands on two mythical animals, the "red serpent" of Marduk and the horned lion.

ASSUR [ăsh'ər] (Heb. *'aššûr*; Akk. *Aššur*) (**PLACE**).

1. The oldest of the Assyrian cities and at one time the capital; at the height of the Assyrian Empire, however, it was second in importance to Nineveh (cf. Ezek. 27:23, "Asshur"). The city was originally a Babylonian colony. Unlike the other great Assyrian cities (e.g., Dur-Sharrukin, Nineveh, Calah, Arbela) which lay on the east bank of the Tigris river, Assur was situated on the west bank at modern Qal'at Sherqat, about 100 km. (60 mi.) south of Nineveh. The site was excavated *ca.* 1840 by A. H. Layard, who discovered there the annals of Tiglath-pileser I. Between 1903 and 1914 similar excavations were led by W. Andrae, who was able subsequently to outline the history of the city from 3000 B.C.-A.D. 300. Among the finds were a number of temples dedicated to the deities Ishtar and Assur (according to one document there were some thirty-four chapels), fortifications, palaces, and sarcophagi of Assyrian kings, including that of Sennacherib.

2. The country and people of Assyria (Num. 24:22, 24; KJV, RSV "Asshur"; Hos. 14:3; KJV "Asshur").

ASSURBANIPAL [ăsh'ər băn'ə pəl] (Akk. *aššur-bâni-apli* "Assur is creating an heir").† The last great king of Assyria (668-626[?] B.C.); son of Esarhaddon.

Continuing his father's plan of conquering Egypt, Assurbanipal penetrated that country as far south as Thebes, which he destroyed in 663 (cf. Nah. 3:8). He then turned his energies toward quelling the chronic unrest in the outer reaches of the empire — Cimmerian pressure on the Lydians in Asia Minor, the Urartians and Manneans in the north, and the Elamites to the east. In view of these diversions, Assurbanipal's brother Šamaš-šum-ukin (perhaps a twin, and rival in succession of Esarhaddon), viceroy of Babylon, seized the opportunity to rebel in 652, but the Assyrians crushed the revolt after a two-year siege of Babylon (652-650). Subsequently Assurbanipal launched punitive attacks on the Babylonians' Arab and Elamite allies; it is on the basis of these victories and the Assyrian practice of resettling conquered peoples that

Assurbanipal is identified as the biblical Osnappar (Ezra 4:9-10; KJV "Asnapper"). Although the royal annals end at 639, contemporary administrative and literary sources indicate that the remaining years of Assurbanipal's reign were chaotic. The Assyrian Empire crumbled in 612 under his son and successor Sin-šar-iškun.

Despite his constant military activities, Assurbanipal has bequeathed a rich cultural legacy. Reliefs and statues from his palace at Nineveh and temples and public buildings in other cities attest to the quality of Assyrian art. Most significant, however, was his concern for literature; he proclaimed his own ability to read, supported an extensive scribal school which preserved the linguistic and literary heritage of Sumerian and Akkadian, and amassed a vast library at Nineveh of which nearly thirty thousand texts have been excavated.

ASSURNASIRPAL [ăsh'ər năz'ər pəl] (Akk. *aššur-naṣir-apli* "Aššur is guarding the heir"). Assurnasirpal II, king of Assyria *ca.* 883-859 B.C.; son of Tilukti-Ninurta II. After the subjection of Carchemish and the powerful Aramean state of Bit-Adini (868), he was able to force a passage to the Mediterranean Sea. His brutal treatment of defeated peoples earned him a reputation as a cruel leader, but he was nevertheless successful in maintaining a strong regime. He reorganized the provincial government, improved the siege weapons, and built a new capital city (Nimrud) upon the ruins of Calah (Gen. 10:11).

ASSYRIA [ə sĭr'ĭ ə].† An empire and civilization centered in the upper Tigris region of Mesopotamia and, in the first millennium B.C., a major opponent of Judah and Israel. Called Assur in Akkadian sources as well as the Old Testament (Akk. *Aššur*; Heb. *'aššûr*; Num. 24:22, 24; KJV, RSV "Asshur"), it was located north of Babylonia, east of the Syrian desert, south of Anatolia, and west of the Kurdish mountains.

I. History

Material remains indicate that Assyria was inhabited from the earliest prehistoric times. With the transition to a food-producing economy came the beginnings of village life, evident at such sites as Karim Shahir (*ca.* 7000 B.C.) and Jarmo (*ca.* 6000), both east of modern Kirkûk. The period *ca.* 5500-3000 was marked by considerable technological advancement, attested in an array of regional cultural phases emanating from such sites as Hassuna, Samarra, and Tell Halâf; other phases, including the Ubaid, Uruk, and Early Dynastic (or Protoliterate) cultures, were introduced from the south. It was in the Early Dynastic period (*ca.* 2900) that a settlement was established at Assur.

According to the Assyrian King List the earliest Assyrian rulers were nomadic chieftains ("dwellers in tents") of undetermined ethnic origins (probably the non-Semitic "Subarians"), but toward the end of the third millennium Sumerian influence was increasingly felt. The Semitic dynasty of Sargon of Akkad (*ca.* 2300-2230) rebuilt Nineveh, Assur, and Calah, and the region remained under Sumerian control until the Elamites toppled Amar-suen and the Third Dynasty of Ur (*ca.* 2000). The biblical Table of Nations underscores the role of Babylonian peoples in early Assyria (Gen. 10:11-12; cf. v. 22).

As an independent city-state, Assur became a thriving commercial center, linked by caravan trade with colonies in Asia Minor; some three thousand cuneiform tablets document the mercantile activities of Assyrian traders at Kanesh (modern Kultepe) in Cappadocia. Under the Akkadian kings Ilušuma and Sargon I, Assur made inroads into Babylonian territory. In the mid-nineteenth century, however, the movement of the Hittites in Anatolia ended Assyrian trading operations, and Assur itself was dominated briefly by Naram-sin of Eshnunna in the Diyala river region. Shortly thereafter an Amorite chieftain, Šamši-adad I, took the throne at Assur and enabled his son Yašmaḫ-adad to gain control of Mari. With the death of Šamši-adad, the deposed Zimri-lim regained authority at Mari, only to be overthrown by Hammurabi of Babylon. After a brief power struggle Assur became a vassal of the Hurrian empire of Mitanni, and the Old Assyrian period ended (*ca.*

Relief at Calah showing Assurnasirpal hunting lions (by courtesy of the Trustees of the British Museum)

Winged man-headed bull from the palace of King Assurnasirpal II of Assyria (883-859 B.C.) (by courtesy of the Trustees of the British Museum)

1650). Despite its political obscurity during the Dark Age which ensued, the region maintained a degree of agricultural prosperity, as evident from the Nuzi tablets.

Assyria began to regain international prominence with the decline of Mitannian power in the mid-fourteenth century. Assuruballit I (ca. 1365-1330), the first to claim the title "king of the land of Assyria," sent an ambassador to the Egyptian court, gained an alliance with Babylon through the marriage of his daughter to Karaindaš II, and was instrumental in the accession of Assuruballit's descendant Kurigalzu II to the Babylonian throne. Upon Assuruballit's death, Kurigalzu attempted to assume the Assyrian throne, but instead the resultant skirmish seriously weakened Babylon. A normal pattern of succession was established in Assyria, and during the Middle Assyrian period subsequent kings were able to reopen trade routes to the north and west.

Shalmaneser I (1274-1245) halted a rebellion in the western province of Hanigalbat by incorporating the territory and, in what would become characteristic Assyrian practice, deporting the defeated populace; he further defended the northern border against Urartu and established a new capital at Calah (Nimrûd). His

son, Tukulti-ninurta I (1244-1208), focused his attention on Babylon, which he captured and placed under Assyrian dominion for the first time. Seven years later the king was murdered by his son, plunging Assyria into internal disarray and opening the country to Babylonian suzerainty. Assur-reš-išši reasserted Assyrian independence (ca. 1125). His son Tiglath-pileser I (1115-1077) gained the upper hand over the Subarian and Ahlamu (Aramean) tribes; he extended Assyrian control to the Mediterranean, assessing tribute from Byblos, Sidon, and Arvad. However, Aramean pressure persisted and Assyrian resources were overextended, leading to another period of decline. It was these circumstances during the period 1100-900, accompanied by concurrent weakness in Babylon and Elam, that fostered conditions favorable to the rise of the Israelite monarchy under David and Solomon.

A revitalization of Assyrian economic and military fortunes became evident toward the end of the tenth century. The first of the Neo-Assyrian kings, Assur-dan II (934-912) and Adadnirari II (911-891), initiated the pattern of annual military campaigns that would characterize this period (cf. 2 Sam. 11:1, "in the spring of the year, the time when kings go forth to battle"). While the Neo-Assyrian Empire became the dominant power in the ancient Near East, it never attained more than a modicum of stability. Palace intrigues and disputes over succession were commonplace, and each ruler was compelled to suppress rebellion in the provinces and resistance from neighboring peoples. Successive kings would amass enormous strength and increasingly large territories, only to have the empire crumble with the death of the monarch.

Assurnasirpal II (ca. 883-859) halted Aramean incursions in the Euphrates valley, opening the way to the Mediterranean Sea; priding himself on his reputation as a cruel tyrant, he used the tribute extracted from the conquered territories to rebuild the capital at Calah. His son Shalmaneser III (858-824) captured Carchemish and incorporated the territory of the Aramean Bit-Adini before being halted at Qarqar (853) by a coalition headed by Ben-hadad II of Damascus and including Ahab of Israel (cf. 1 Kgs. 20); in 841 he retaliated against the Syrian coalition now headed by the usurper Hazael, plundering the countryside and demanding submission from Syria-Palestine, including Jehu of Israel. Following the regency of Queen Sammuramat (Semiramis), Adadnirari III (810-783) dissolved the coalition of Ben-hadad III at Damascus, thereby providing respite for Israel under Joash (2 Kgs. 13:25; cf. 12:17; 2 Chr. 24:23-24). Shalmaneser IV (782-772) was able to keep Damascus under control despite mounting pressure from the Urartians, thereby enabling Jeroboam II to extend Israel's boundaries to Hamath (2 Kgs. 14:25-28).

Tiglath-pileser III (745-727) usurped the throne and, with his successors, reestablished Assyrian military and economic dominance. Menahem of Israel sought his support by paying tribute (cf. 2 Kgs. 15:19). In response to the plea of Ahaz of Judah for aid against Rezin of Damascus and Pekah of Israel (ca. 734; 16:5-9), Tiglath-pileser mounted another campaign in Syria-Palestine, causing widespread destruction in Israel (15:29); two years later he placed

Hoshea on the Israelite throne (cf. 15:30), then marched on Jerusalem (16:5-6; 2 Chr. 28:17, 19-21). Shortly thereafter he subdued the Chaldeans and established himself king of Babylon under the name Pūlu ("Pul," 2 Kgs. 15:19; 1 Chr. 5:26). Angered by Hoshea's failure to pay tribute, Shalmaneser V (727-722) besieged Samaria, captured the city, and deported its people (722; 2 Kgs. 17:3-6; 18:9-10). Nearly the entire reign of Sargon II (721-705), founder of Assyria's last royal line, was devoted to recapture of the territory held by Tiglath-pileser III; he lost Babylon to the Chaldean Marduk-apla-iddina (Merodach-baladan) for some ten years, but defeated Egyptian-backed coalitions at Qarqar and Ashdod (cf. Isa. 10:5-6, 9; 20:1-6). Under Sennacherib (705-681) the Pax Assyriaca, a period of relative stability and basically free of annual military activity, was marred in 701 by the revolt of Marduk-apla-iddina at Babylon and Hezekiah in Jerusalem, which led to a prolonged siege of Jerusalem (701; 2 Kgs. 18:13–19:37 par. 2 Chr. 32:1-22; Isa. 36–37) and, eventually, the destruction of Babylon (689). One of Sennacherib's wives was Naqî'a or Zakûtu, possibly the daughter of Hoshea of Israel. Her son Esarhaddon Sennacherib

Record of the deeds of King Esarhaddon of Assyria (681-669 B.C.) (by courtesy of the Trustees of the British Museum)

named as his successor, thereby provoking his assassination by his sons Adrammelech and Sharezer (cf. 2 Kgs. 19:37 par. Isa. 37:38). Esarhaddon (681-669), who had been crown prince over Babylon, restored that city; having endured pressure from the Scythians and Cimmerians to the north, he successfully invaded Egypt, defeating Pharaoh Taharqa (Akk. *Tarqū*; "Tirhakah," 2 Kgs. 19:9; Isa. 37:9) at Memphis in 671. Esarhaddon's successor, Assurbanipal (668-626[?]), continued the conquest of Egypt, sacking Thebes and killing Pharaoh Necho in 663 (cf. Nah. 3:8). While Assurbanipal concentrated on attacks from the north and west, his brother Šamaš-šum-ukin, whom Esarhaddon had placed in charge of Babylon, revolted (652). This confrontation, which ended with the rebel's suicide two years later, seriously weakened Assyrian power, and in 612 Nineveh fell to the Chaldean Nabu-apla-usur (Nabopolassar). Josiah's intervention at Megiddo in 609 (2 Kgs. 23:29-30) and a skirmish with the Babylonians at Carchemish in 605 prevented Egyptian aid under Necho II from reaching Assuruballiṭ II at Harran, and Asyrian power was at an end. The region was reduced to a province of later empires.

II. Religion

Largely because of the political vicissitudes of Assyrian history, the religion (as also the culture) of that region closely resembles Babylonian religion, and both derive from the Sumerian. Assur was the national god, the counterpart of the Babylonian Marduk and successor to the Sumerian Enlil; it was he who endowed the kings with power and to whom they dedicated their military forays. Other important deities from the vast pantheon included Sin, the moon-god; Ishtar, goddess of war and love; Ninurta, god of war and the hunt; and Nabu, god of wisdom and writing. More dependent on rain as the source of water and therefore life, Assyrian religion was concerned with atmospheric phenomena, thus the prominence of deities such as the storm-god Adad (West Semitic Hadad). *See* BABYLONIA *II*.

Statues and images of the gods abounded, in which the deities themselves were believed to be embodied and for which were provided detailed instructions for their care and service. Elaborate rituals were performed for the purification and guidance of the king and in honor of the numerous gods. Considerable attention was paid to tutelary spirits and demons, and an extensive corps of specialists was devoted to divination through astrology and the observation of natural phenomena such as the shape and color of animal livers, omens such as animal behavior and freak births, and dreams.

III. Legacy

Excavations as early as those of P. E. Botta at Nineveh (Kuyunjik, opposite Mosul) and Dūr-Šarrukin (Khorsabad, 25 km. [15 mi.] northeast) beginning in 1842 have yielded a wealth of information concerning the literary and material culture of the Assyrians. In particular, the library of Assurbanipal at Nineveh, excavated by A. H. Layard and H. Rassam (1845-1851), contained nearly 26,000 cuneiform tablets including a rich variety of literature. Assyrian kings maintained

King Jehu of Israel bowing before Shalmaneser III of Assyria (858-824 B.C.). A section of the Black Obelisk of Nimrûd (by courtesy of the Trustees of the British Museum)

schools of scribes who, in addition to keeping commercial and administrative records, preserved Sumerian and Babylonian texts as well as Assyrian works which included myths and epics, royal annals and chronologies, correspondence, rituals and omens, wisdom literature, law codes, and reference works such as lexicons and syllabaries for the translation of Sumerian and various Akkadian dialects. Other works attest to Assyrian science and technology in such areas as mathematics, astronomy, medicine, and glassmaking.

Largely influenced by Babylonian culture, the Assyrians also excelled in architecture and art. Successive kings devoted considerable energy to building and embellishing palaces and temples, particularly in the capital cities of Assur, Calah, and Nineveh. Massive statues and ornate reliefs adorned royal and public buildings, and elaborate botanical and zoological parks were maintained in the capitals. Carved ivories, such as those found at Nimrud and Samaria, and stone cylinder seals indicate the skill of Assyrian artists.

Despite their intellectual and artistic advances, the Assyrians cultivated and earned a reputation as cruel barbarians (cf. Isa. 10:12-15). Assyrian kings boasted of their military might and harsh treatment of those they defeated, impaling their victims on spiked poles, burning cities, and carrying off much booty. Many kings, particularly in the Middle and Neo-Assyrian periods, sought to control vast areas by deporting conquered peoples and repopulating their homelands with other displaced captives. Accordingly, the Old Testament (particularly such prophets as Amos, Hosea, Isaiah, Micah, Zephaniah, and Nahum) characterized the Assyrians as barbarous heathens, often used by Yahweh as an instrument of discipline for his own people (cf. Isa. 10:5; Jer. 1:13).

Bibliography. W. W. Hallo and W. K. Simpson, *The Ancient Near East: A History* (New York: 1971); L. L. Orlin, *Assyrian Colonies in Cappadocia* (Hawthorne, N.Y.: 1970); H. W. F. Saggs, *The Greatness That Was Babylon* (New York: 1962).

ASTAROTH (Deut. 1:4, KJV). *See* ASHTAROTH 2.

ASTARTE [ăs tär′tĭ]. The Greek name of the goddess Ashtoreth.

ASTROLOGER (from Gk. *ástron* "star" and *lógos* "study of ").† Unlike the astronomer who studies the magnitudes, movements, and constitutions of the heavenly bodies, the astrologer is interested in the effect of these celestial phenomena on human life. In antiquity astrology was practiced among the Babylonians (as early as 650 B.C.) and the Egyptians (e.g., Ptolemy of Alexandria, second century A.D.).

Magicians, enchanters (KJV "astrologers"), sorcerers, and astrologers (RSV, KJV, JB "Chaldeans" at Dan. 2:2, 4, 5, 10; at 4:7; 5:7 the RSV distinguishes between Chaldeans and astrologers) are summoned to explain Nebuchadnezzar's dreams. Their function does not seem to be limited to interpreting dreams, for King Belshazzar instructs them to explain the writing on the wall (5:7). Daniel is said to have been Nebuchadnezzar's chief astrologer ("chief of the magicians"; 4:9; 5:11), but he confesses that it is God rather than astrology (Aram. *gāzᵉrîn*) that is able to make known the meaning of dreams (2:27-28).

At Isa. 47:13 the astrologers ("those who divide the heavens"; Heb. Q *hōḇᵉrê šāmayim*; KJV, NIV "astrologers") are chided for their inability to predict the fall of Babylon (cf. vv. 10-12).

ASTRONOMY.* Observation of celestial phenomena has been common to most societies since the earliest phases of civilization, but the greatest advances and consequently the earliest influences on modern astronomy can be attributed to the ancient Babylonians. Although much of the Babylonians' interest in stars and planets derived from their religious beliefs, they also looked to the skies for aid in navigation and calendration. Cuneiform tablets from the second millennium B.C. record observations of celestial bodies, their movements, and such phenomena as solar and lunar eclipses; these have been particularly valuable in helping to determine ancient chronologies. By Seleucid times (third-first centuries B.C.) the Babylonians had developed a sophisticated means of observing and predicting lunar phenomena as well as procedures for computing tables of planetary phenomena (ephemerides).

By contrast, Egyptian astronomy was primitive, largely hampered by the limitations of Egyptian mathematics. The Egyptians did, however, devise a calendar dividing the year into twelve months of thirty days each. They also divided the day into twenty-four hours, with the daylight hours varying in length according to the season; by Hellenistic times they had determined hours of equal length, divided into sixty minutes.

The Bible indicates no scientific form of astronomy among the Israelites, although they were certainly aware of astronomical phenomena. The movements of the sun and moon are recorded, particularly eclipses and other occurrences (e.g., Josh. 12:14; 2 Kgs. 20:8-11; Joel 2:31). References to planets may occur at Amos 5:26 (Kaiwan; Heb. *kíyûn*) and Acts 7:43 (Rephan; Gk. *rhaiphán*), both apparently indicating Saturn. For the most part other celestial bodies are called "stars" (Heb. *kôḵāḇîm*; Gk. *astéres*), but constellations are noted: Ursa Major ("the Bear"; KJV "Arcturus"; Job 9:9; 38:32; cf. 37:9), Orion (9:9; 38:31; Amos 5:8), and the Pleiades (Job 9:9; 38:31). Although astronomical phenomena are signs of divine activity (e.g., Isa. 13:10; Dan. 8:10; Matt. 24:29; Rev. 8:10-12), nowhere are they worshipped or is their astrological use encouraged.

Bibliography. O. Neugebauer, *The Exact Sciences in Antiquity*, 2nd ed. (New York: 1969).

ASUPPIM. Heb. *(bêt) hā'ªsuppîm* (1 Chr. 26:15, 17) appears as a proper name in KJV ("[the house of] Asuppim"). It can, however, be translated "the storehouse" as in RSV.

ASYNCRITUS [ə sĭng'krĭ təs] (Gk. *Asynkritos* "incomparable"). A Roman Christian to whom Paul sends his greetings (Rom. 16:14).

ATAD [ā'tăd] (Heb. *'āṭāḏ* "thorny bush"). The original name of a place "beyond" the Jordan where Joseph held a seven-day mourning in behalf of his deceased father Jacob (Gen. 50:10-11). Usually rendered "threshing floor of Atad" (so RSV, KJV, NIV; JB "Goren-ha-atad"), Heb. *gōren hā'āṭāḏ* may better be translated "threshing floor of the thorn bush," indicating a thorny fence which enclosed the threshing floor. The interpretation "a grievous mourning to the Egyptians" may be a popular etymology intended to explain the site's alternate name, Abel-mizraim (v. 11; cf. Heb. *'ēḇel* "to mourn").

Most likely the place was located east of (NIV "near") the Jordan. This would mean that Joseph's party took the longer route around the Dead Sea (the route the Israelites would take many years later) rather than the direct route to Hebron.

ATARAH [ăt'ə rə] (Heb. *'ªṭārâ* "crown"). The second wife of Jerahmeel of the tribe of Judah, and the mother of Onam (1 Chr. 2:26).

ATARGATIS [ə tär'gə tĭs] (Gk. *Atargatis*; abbreviation of Heb. *tr'th*; Gk. *Derketō* "Derceto"). A great Aramean goddess, the consort of Hadad, whose attributes are comparable to those of the Phoenician Astarte or Ashtoreth. She is often depicted as holding a sheaf of grain. Hierapolis (northeast of Aleppo) was the main center of the cult dedicated to this goddess. It was at her temple in Carnaim that Judas Maccabeus slaughtered some twenty-five thousand who had sought refuge therein (2 Macc. 12:26).

ATAROTH [ăt'ə rŏth] (Heb. *'ªṭārôṯ* "crowns," "wreaths").
1. A town in Transjordan, requested as an inheritance from Moses by the Reubenites and Gadites (Num. 32:3), but given to the latter who in turn fortified it (v. 34). Foundations of the ancient place are still visible at modern Khirbet 'Aṭṭārûs, about 13 km. (8 mi.) northwest of Dibon and 16 km. (10 mi.) east of the Dead Sea. The city, which was located on a chain of hills, is mentioned in the Moabite Stone as a conquest by Mesha for the satiation of Chemosh (*ANET*, p. 320).

2. A town on the border between Ephraim and Benjamin (Josh. 16:7). Some would identify it with Tell el-Mazar, whereas others favor Tell Sheikh edh-Dhiab.
3. A town mentioned at Josh. 16:2; probably the same as Ataroth-Addar.
4. Ataroth, "the house of Joab" (1 Chr. 2:54, KJV). See ATROTH-BETH-JOAB.

ATAROTH-ADDAR [ăt'ə rŏth ăd'ər] (Heb. *'āṭrôṯ 'addār* "crowns of Addar"). A town on the boundary between Ephraim and Benjamin (Josh. 16:5; 18:13), possibly identical with the Ataroth mentioned at Josh. 16:2 as the territory of the Archites. Some scholars identify it with Khirbet 'Attara, a town south of Tell en-Nasbeh (Mizpah) along the road from Bethel to Jerusalem, while others suggest Tell en-Nasbeh itself.

ATER [ā'tər] (Heb. *'āṭēr* "crippled," "left-handed").
1. The ancestor of a family that returned from Exile under Zerubbabel (Ezra 2:16; Neh. 7:21).
2. A Levite, the head of a family of gatekeepers returning to Jerusalem with Zerubbabel (Ezra 2:42; Neh. 7:45).
3. One of the Israelite chiefs who set their seal on the renewed covenant under Nehemiah (Neh. 10:17).

ATHACH [ā'thăk] (Heb. *'ªṭāk* "lodging place"). A city in the Shephelah of Judah, to whose elders David gave as a present part of the spoil taken from the Amalekites (1 Sam. 30:30). It is perhaps the same as Ether mentioned at Josh. 15:42; 19:7, this form having resulted from a scribal error.

ATHAIAH [ə thā'ye] (Heb. *'ªṭāyâ* "the Lord helps"). The son of Uzziah of Judah who resided in Jerusalem after the Exile (Neh. 11:4).

ATHALIAH [ăth'ə lī'ə] (Heb. *'ªṭalyâ, 'ªṭalyāhû* "Yahweh is great").†
1. The daughter of Ahab (2 Kgs. 8:18) and granddaughter of Omri (v. 26); her mother was most likely Ahab's wife Jezebel, though the Old Testament does not state this explicitly. Athaliah became the wife of King Jehoram of Judah and the mother of Ahaziah. After eight years of marriage her husband died, and her son succeeded him (v. 26; cf. 2 Chr. 22:2), reigning about one year before he was killed by Jehu of Israel (2 Kgs. 9:27; cf. 2 Chr. 22:7-9).

Upon being informed of the death of this last surviving son (her other sons had been killed beforehand), the queen mother murdered all of her grandchildren except the young Joash, whom Jehosheba, the sister of Ahaziah and wife of the high priest Jehoiada, was able to hide (2 Kgs. 11:1-2; cf. 2 Chr. 22:10-11). Athaliah then proclaimed herself the legitimate sovereign and reigned for six years (842-836 B.C.), the only queen to occupy this position in Judah.

While Athaliah promoted the cult of Baal Melqart, Jehoiada, the faithful priest of Yahweh, bided his time. Having hidden young Joash for six years in the temple (2 Kgs. 11:3), the high priest in the seventh year made a covenant with the captains of the Carites and the guards, which was, in fact, a conspiracy against the queen mother (11:4ff.; cf. 2 Chr. 23:1ff.).

Assured of the young lad's safety, Jehoiada crowned him Judah's next king, with the concurrence of all present (v. 12).

When Athaliah learned about the ceremony and saw her only grandson standing "by the pillar" of the temple, she shouted, "Treason!" (2 Kgs. 11:13-14; cf. 2 Chr. 23:12-13). Since she could no longer depend on her guards, her only recourse was to escape. Not wishing to defile the sacred temple precincts with her blood, the high priest ordered her killed near the royal palace as she made her bid for freedom (vv. 15-16; cf. 2 Chr. 23:14-15). The account closes with Jehoiada terminating Baal worship at Jerusalem (vv. 17-18) and with the installation of Joash as king (vv. 19-20; cf. 2 Chr. 23:20-21).

At 2 Chr. 22:3 Athaliah is portrayed as Ahaziah's counselor for evil, referring to her active support of the Baal cult. At 23:7 she is called a "wicked woman," because she had permitted her sons to break into the temple and take a number of sacred objects for use in the temple of Baal.

2. One of the sons of Jehoram of the tribe of Benjamin, and resident of Jerusalem (1 Chr. 8:26).

3. The father of Jeshaiah, who returned with Ezra from exile. He was of the family of Elam (Ezra 8:7).

ATHARIM [ăth′ər ĭm] (Heb. ᵃṭārîm). Probably a place (so RSV, JB, NIV) of unknown location, where the Israelites were attacked by the king of Arad (Num. 21:1). The KJV, following the LXX and Vulg., renders the term "spies" (emending to haṭṭārîm [see BH]).

ATHBASH [ăth′băsh]. A Hebrew cryptographic scheme in which the first letter of the Hebrew alphabet is exchanged for the last letter, the second for the second to the last (aleph for tau, beth for shin), and so forth. The name is constructed from the first two pairs of substitutes (ʾ ṭbš).

The book of Jeremiah has three occurrences of this scheme (see the mgs. of the versions). At 25:26; 51:41 the king of "Sheshach" (KJV, NIV; JB "Sheshak" in 25:26; Heb. ššk) stands for the king of "Babylon" (so RSV; Heb. bbl). At 51:1 "the midst [lit. "heart"] of them that rise up against me" (KJV; JB, NIV "Leb Kamai," Heb. lb-qmy) points to Chaldea (so RSV;

Heb. kśdym). Some commentators consider the name Elam (49:34-39; Heb. ʿlm) an athbash for Zimki (Heb. zmk).

Bibliography. S. A. Horodezky, "Gematria," EJ 7:170-72.

ATHENIANS [ə thē′nē ənz] (Gk. Athēnaioi). People of Athens (Acts 17:21), whom Luke describes as discussing or learning the latest news or novelty.

ATHENS [ăth′ĭnz] (Gk. Athēnai).† The capital city of the district of Attica in ancient times and the capital of modern Greece. It was probably named after the patron goddess Athena.

I. History

Following partial destruction of their city by the Persians (480 B.C.), the Athenians began rebuilding Athens. During the reign of Pericles (459-429 B.C.) the city entered into its so-called golden age, both culturally and politically. Many temples and civic buildings were constructed, the arts were generously supported, and the consolidation of democracy started by Solon and Pisistratus was realized. The outcome of the Peloponnesian war (431-404) was against Athens, however, as Sparta, better equipped for military maneuvers than its rival, gained the upper hand. Athens cooperated with Philip of Macedonia, but received harsh treatment when its support wavered. After the death of Philip's son Alexander the Great (323 B.C.), Athens regained its cultural prominence. Though the Romans sacked the city in 86 B.C., they named it a free city in recognition of its glorious past.

In New Testament times Athens could still boast of being one of the most famous centers of wisdom, architecture, and art. Though it had been surpassed economically by Corinth and intellectually by Alexandria, the city nevertheless maintained a great reputation.

II. Description

At the center of the ancient city was the ʌcky hill called the Acropolis, which arose some 15ᴜ ʌ. (512 ft.) above sea level, and could be approached from the west via a stately colonnade named the Propylea. Upon this site were erected many temples, of which

The Acropolis of Athens with the large temple to Athena (the Parthenon). Mount Lycabettus is in the distance on the right (Ewing Galloway)

the Parthenon, constructed by Pericles' sculptor, Phidias (*ca.* 438), and the Erechtheion were the principal centers of worship. The Parthenon, dedicated to the virgin goddess Athena, contained a golden image of Pallas Athena.

West-northwest of the Acropolis was the Areopagus, which for many years was the seat of Athens' highest court of justice. Still further northwest was the Agora or the marketplace, a large open space encircled by colonnades, temples, bazaars, and government buildings. It was here that the Athenians spent their time discussing political issues and exchanging goods and services.

III. Biblical References

Brought to Athens ahead of his companions Silas and Timothy, Paul occupied the interim talking to people in the marketplace and the Jews in the synagogue (Acts 17:15-17). If the apostle first entered the city on foot he would have walked along the road where the Greek geographer Pausanias claimed to have observed "altars to gods unknown" (cf. v. 23; *see* UNKNOWN GOD). He accepted an invitation to address the Stoics and Epicureans, though he made only a small impact on them (vv. 32-34). Soon, perhaps three or four weeks later, Paul left the city (18:1), moving on to Corinth without having established a church. Actually, Athens seems to have played no part in Paul's missionary plan.

The New Testament epistles refer only once to Paul's stay in Athens. According to 1 Thess. 3:1, he was left alone in the capital, having sent his faithful companion Timothy to the Thessalonians, recent converts of his. The passage reveals Paul's emotional attachments to these Christians as he tried to proclaim Christ to cynics and mockers of the gospel.

IV. Archaeology

Extensive excavations have been conducted since 1931 by the American School of Classical Studies in the Agora and the northern slopes of the Acropolis. In addition to the numerous public buildings, thousands of art objects and coins have been uncovered. The Stoa of Attalus II has been restored, and in 1970 the Royal Stoa was discovered, the seat of the principal magistrate and site of numerous trials including that of Socrates. In addition, Greek archaeologists have excavated the Acropolis down to bedrock.

Bibliography. C. M. Bowra, *Periclean Athens* (New York: 1971); H. A. Thompson and R. E. Wycherley, *The Agora of Athens* (Princeton: 1972); T. B. L. Webster, *Athenian Culture and Society* (London: 1973).

ATHLAI [ăth'lī] (Heb. *'aṭlay,* abbreviation of *'tlyh* "Yahweh is exalted"). An Israelite of the family of Bebai. He was one of the exiles requested to send away their foreign wives (Ezra 10:28).

ATONE, ATONEMENT. Originally the English word "atonement" meant "the quality of being at one (with)." Later it came to refer to human reunion with God through Christ. The Hebrew and Greek terms designate the manner in which Christ puts the sinner in the right relationship with God.

I. Terminology

A. Old Testament. The word "atonement" occurs nearly one hundred times in the Old Testament, always translated from a form of Heb. *kippurîm* (e.g., Lev. 23:27; 25:9; Num. 5:8) or *kāpar,* usually rendered "make an atonement" (cf. Lev. 16:20, "atone"). Both Heb. *kpr* and *kprym* can be related to Arab. *kpr* "cover" and Akk. *kapāru* "spread over," "wipe off" (KoB, p. 452). Given the context at Gen. 32:20, Heb. *kpr* can most directly be translated "cover" (RSV, KJV "appease"; JB "conciliate"; NIV "pacify"; cf. Prov. 16:6,14) or "to blot out" guilt (cf. Isa. 6:7).

Heb. *kpr* is also rendered "ransom" (Exod. 30:12) or "compensation" (Prov. 6:35, paralleling "gifts"; KJV "ransom"). The KJV also translates the term as "reconcile" (Lev. 6:30; 16:20; Ezek. 45:20; RSV, JB, NIV "atonement"), "purge" (Prov. 16:6; Ezek. 43:20, 26; RSV, JB, NIV "atone/make atonement"), and "put off" (Isa. 47:11; RSV "expiate"; JB "avert"; NIV "ward off with a ransom"); and translates *kprym* as "reconciliation" (e.g., Lev. 8:15; RSV, JB, NIV "atonement").

B. New Testament. The New Testament retains the Old Testament meaning of atone(ment), though it uses the word specifically only once, at Rom. 5:11 (Gk. *katallagḗ*; RSV, JB, NIV "reconciliation"). Gk. *hiláskomai* and cognates are synonyms of Heb. *kpr* and, likewise, designate "cover," "blot out," and "remove guilt." *See also* EXPIATION; RECONCILIATION; REDEMPTION.

II. Biblical Teachings

A. Old Testament. Usually atonement was made through the substitutionary sacrifice of an animal (e.g., Exod. 30:10; Lev. 1:4; 4:20-21). Sometimes it could be accomplished through "loyalty and faithfulness" (Prov. 16:6) or wisdom (v. 14), and sometimes through payment of money (Exod. 30:16; JB "ransom money"). Occasionally human life was required (2 Sam. 21:3ff.). No expiation was possible, however, for a murderer or for one who left his city of refuge before the death of the current high priest (Num. 35:31-33).

In the history of salvation, atonement by the shedding of blood became more and more associated with the shedding of human blood, notably through the prophet Isaiah (Isa. 22:14; 40:2 [of those in exile]; cf. Dan. 9:24). However, when Moses desired to give his own life as a means of reconciliation for the sins of his fellow Hebrews, the Lord refused his "offer" (Exod. 32:32-33). The Old Testament further intimates that one could receive atonement simply by God's grace (2 Chr. 30:18-20; Ps. 78:38; 79:9; Ezek. 16:62-63).

B. New Testament. While retaining the Old Testament cultic concept of "cover," the New Testament links human atonement to Christ. Paul says Christ "died for our sins" (1 Cor. 15:3); Jesus died in order to pay the price for human sins, rather than as a result of them (cf. Isa. 53:5). The apostle confirms this interpretation at 2 Cor. 5:14: "One has died for all," which he explains at v. 21 as "for our sake" (Gk. *hypér hēmṓn*; cf. Gal. 3:13, "a curse for us").

Among several New Testament references to Christ as a sacrifice (e.g., Eph. 5:2) are those made by John ("lamb," John 1:29, 36) and Paul ("paschal lamb," 1 Cor. 5:7). For Paul, however, Christ's blood (e.g., Rom. 5:9) is not merely human blood but, specifically, atoning blood and his death is an atoning sacrifice, recalling the sacrificial arrangement of the old covenant (i.e., Isa. 53:10; see Heb. 7:1-10, 18; cf. 1 Pet. 1:18-20). While Paul stresses the centrality of Christ's vicarious sacrifice, the Synoptic Gospels note that Christ claimed to give his life as a "ransom for many" (Matt. 20:28 par. Mark 10:45; see Exod. 21:30). All three Evangelists record Christ's sincere mention of his eternal sacrifice when at the breaking of the bread he referred to his own body during the Last Supper ("this is my body"; Matt. 26:26-27 par. Mark 14:22-23; Luke 22:19-20).

On the other hand, the New Testament leaves no doubt that atonement is accomplished through the believer's participation with the Lord in his death rather than merely by Christ's death on the cross (Rom. 6:2, 6, 8; cf. Gal. 2:19-20). Thus, Christ not only suffered for the guilt of human sin with his death, but he also freed human beings from the power of sin. Thus, Christ's atonement restores the original relationship between God and man and between human beings, bringing about rejoicing (Rom. 5:11), "life from the dead" (v. 15), and forgiveness (Matt. 6:14-15; cf. 18:21-35; see also Matt. 26:28; Eph. 1:7; Col. 1:14 for the connection between redemption and forgiveness).

III. Theological Reflections†

In view of the colorful tapestry of New Testament teachings concerning the doctrine of the atonement, theologians have attempted to unravel certain of its strands. Some have emphasized Christ's victory over the forces of evil, with Origen (perhaps somewhat crudely) envisioning Christ's humanity as a ransom to Satan (cf. 1 Cor. 15:55-57; Col. 2:15 which proclaim Christ's victory over sin and Satan). Others sought to promote the notion of "satisfaction," the recompense Christ paid to God because God's honor had been violated by sin (Anselm Cur deus homo) or because of his wrath (Calvin Institutes ii.16.1-3, 13; cf. Rom. 5:9 for the reality of God's wrath). Still others chose to emphasize the comfort of the divine love behind the death of Jesus (Abelard, Schleiermacher; cf. John 3:16; Rom. 5:8 for the sacrifice prompted by God's love for humankind).

The scope of Christ's atonement remains a problem for biblical exegetes and theologians. Did Jesus die for all human beings or only for some? Many Calvinists believe that only the elect are the recipients of Christ's benefits (the doctrine of limited atonement). The exegetical difficulty is the meaning of the so-called universalistic texts. Do such passages as 2 Cor. 15:22 ("in Christ all shall be made alive"), 1 Tim. 2:6 ("a ransom for all"), 4:10 ("the Savior of all men") imply that all people without exception will be saved? Or do they teach that people from all nations (i.e., from Jewish and Gentile backgrounds) are included in the divine blessings and that, as a result, these passages do not contradict limited atonement as other New Testament passages profess?

Bibliography. F. W. Dillistone, *The Christian Understanding of Atonement* (Philadelphia: 1968); M. Hengel, *The Atonement: The Origins of the Doctrine in*

the New Testament (Philadelphia: 1981); J. R. Sheets, ed., *The Theology of the Atonement: Readings in Soteriology* (Englewood Cliffs: 1967).

ATONEMENT, DAY OF [*yôm hakkippurîm* "day of the covering over (or propitiation)"]. The most important annual Israelite (and Jewish) fast, held on the tenth day of the seventh month (Tishri; Lev. 23:27; 25:9).

From Lev. 16 it appears that even the high priest could not enter the holy of holies at all times and without special ceremonies; he and his household needed reconciliation, as did the people of Israel and even the sanctuary itself. The Day of Atonement was proclaimed a fast, reminding the Israelites of Yahweh's holiness and their own sinfulness (including the most holy persons). A number of sacrifices were offered, fifteen altogether (sixteen counting the goat of Azazel): twelve burnt offerings and three sin offerings (Lev. 16:5-29; Num. 29:7-11). Including the ram (mentioned separately at Num. 28:8), there were thirteen burnt offerings and four sin offerings. The Israelite sacrifices of reconciliation were similar in function to the purification ceremonies of the ancient Babylonians, Greeks, and Romans.

The Day of Atonement was "a sabbath of solemn rest" (Lev. 16:31), which included a purification ceremony in the tabernacle as well as a general fast. After the high priest had bathed and had put on his linen clothes (rather than his radiant office vestments; v. 4), he chose for himself and his house a young bull for a sin offering and a ram for a burnt offering. From the congregation he took two goats as a sin offering and a ram as a burnt offering. He then had the two goats placed at the entrance of the tent of meeting where he cast a lot, assigning one goat for Yahweh and "one for Azazel." The goat assigned by lot to Yahweh was to be sacrificed as a sin offering, but the other goat was placed before the Lord alive in order to reconcile, i.e., to be dedicated as a scapegoat (vv. 20-22) and subsequently to be driven into the desert, bearing the guilt of Israel's sins.

After lots were cast between the two goats, Aaron killed the bull of the sin offering for himself and his house. Taking next a pan of glowing coals from the altar of burnt offering, he placed ground-up incense on the fire before the face of Yahweh — inside the veil while a cloud of smoke from the incense covered the mercy seat. Then with his finger he sprinkled blood of the bull seven times on the front side of the mercy seat and seven times in front of it, killed the goat of the sin offering, and added the blood of that animal to that of the killed bull, sprinkling the holy place and the horns of the altar of burnt offering.

An indispensable detail of the ceremony was the placing of the live goat before the altar of burnt offering. Leaning with his two hands on the head of the animal, Aaron confessed all the iniquity of the Israelites as well as their transgressions, symbolically placing them on the head of the goat. After this act an appointed person took the animal to the wilderness outside of the camp where he was to free it (cf. Ps. 103:12). (In later years the person customarily threw the goat from the cliffs so that it died.)

Finally, the high priest went to the tent of meeting,

took off his linen clothes, bathed himself, put on his regular vestments, and offered the two rams as a burnt offering in the court, thus reconciling himself and the people. The bull and the goat of the sin offering were placed outside the camp, to be burned totally, including skin, flesh, and dung (Lev. 16:27; see Heb. 13:11). Like the person who had sent the live goat to the wilderness, the one who burned the animal had to wash his clothes and bathe himself. It may have been that the feast offering prescribed at Num. 29:7-11 was given.

The only fast day prescribed in Mosaic law, the Day of Atonement (cf. Exod. 30:10) gained particular importance in postexilic times (cf. Neh. 9:1). Although the fast retained significance in New Testament times (cf. Acts 27:9), the event came to be reinterpreted among Christians in terms of the atoning sacrifice of Jesus Christ as the Great High Priest (Heb. 9:11ff.; cf. 5:5).

ATROTH (Num. 32:35, KJV). *See* ATROTH-SHOPHAN.

ATROTH-BETH-JOAB [ăt′rŏth bĕth jō′ăb] (Heb. *'aṭrôṭ bêṭ yô'āḇ* "crowns of the house of Joab"). A village in the vicinity of Bethlehem, the precise location of which is unknown (1 Chr. 2:54; KJV "Ataroth, the house of Joab"). Rather than a personal name, "Beth-joab" may distinguish this place from others with the name Ataroth.

ATROTH-SHOPHAN [ăt′rŏth shō′făn] (Heb. *'aṭrôṭ šôpān*). A city in Transjordan built by the Gadites (Num. 32:35; KJV "Atroth, Shophan"; but see LXX *Sophar*).

ATTAI [ăt′ī] (Heb. *'attay*, possibly "timely").

1. A son of the Egyptian slave Jarha by Sheshan's daughter. He became the father of Nathan (1 Chr. 2:35-36).

2. One of the Gadites who went over to David at Ziklag (1 Chr. 12:11).

3. A son of Rehoboam and his favorite wife Maacah (2 Chr. 11:20).

ATTALIA [ăt′ə lī′ə] (Gk. *Attaleia*). A harbor city on the southwest coast of Asia Minor, in the Roman province of Pamphylia, about 13 km. (8 mi.) south of Perga. It was built *ca.* 145 B.C. by Attalus II of Pergamum, after whom it was named. Located at the mouth of the Catarrhactes, the city was an important trading center in the region. Its modern name is Antalya.

At the end of his first missionary journey Paul paid the port a brief visit, having come down (Gk. *katabaínō*) from Perga (Acts 14:25). This was Paul's last stop before sailing to Antioch (Syria).

AUDIENCE HALL (Gk. *akroatḗrion* "place of hearing"; so KJV). A room (NEB "audience-chamber") in Herod Agrippa's praetorium at Caesarea where criminal cases were decided. It was here that Paul faced not only Festus the Roman procurator and his five tribunes but also King Agrippa and Bernice, after having appealed to Caesar (Acts 25:23).

AUGUSTAN COHORT [ə gŭs′tən kō′hôrt] (Gk. *speíra Sebastḗ*). A division of the Roman army, a cohort (the tenth of a legion or about 600 soldiers) named after Augustus (rather than the city of Samaria, then named Sebaste). Most likely it was the *Cohors Augusta I*, which, according to inscriptions, was stationed in Syria and at Batanea during the reign of Agrippa II (*ca.* A.D. 55).

This cohort (so RSV, JB; KJV "Augustan band"; NIV "Imperial Regiment") and its centurion Julius were charged to take Paul and other prisoners to Rome (Acts 27:1).

AUGUSTUS [ə gŭs′təs] (Gk. *Augoustos* "the exalted, the venerable"; from Lat. *augur* "divine, consecrate" or *augere* "to increase"). Caesar Augustus; originally named Gaius Octavius, he took on the name Gaius Julius Caesar Octavianus after his adoption by his great-uncle Julius Caesar. Born in 63 B.C., he reigned as the first Roman emperor from 31 B.C. (the battle of Actium) until A.D. 14. The Roman Senate accorded him the name Augustus as a title of honor in 27, in recognition of his efforts to restore order following the Roman civil war. (He had voluntarily resigned the powers of triumvir in 33, relying on annual election as consul by the Senate.) Thereafter he called himself Imperator Caesar Augustus, a title granted as a matter of course to later emperors (cf. Acts 25:21, 25, KJV; RSV "emperor").

Besides the office of the consulate, Augustus also held supreme command over the armies and fleets of the Roman Empire, as well as the government over Egypt (which became his personal domain by his victory in 30 over Antony, his former colleague and rival, who had married Cleopatra, the queen of Egypt, who followed him in death), Syria, Gaul, and the greater part of Spain. In the year 23 he resigned the consulate,

A marble bust of Augustus (by courtesy of the Trustees of the British Museum)

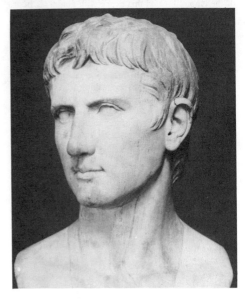

since he felt that this office should not be held by the same person for too long a period of time (despite the yearly election). But in exchange, the Senate gave him for the remainder of his life proconsular authority over the entire empire outside Italy, and determined that the other proconsuls should be answerable to him. He was also named tribune of the people, which gave him the power to oppose any interference from others, even from the Senate.

By his agency, the worship of Apollo was restored in Rome. Upon the Palatine hill he built a glorious temple for Apollo and his sister Diana in order to let it be known that his reign had ushered in a new era. The founding of Troy had been accredited to Apollo, and Augustus followed Vergil in the belief that the Romans were descended from the Trojans. For this reason, the emperor built his palace and the temple of Apollo on the hill where, according to legend, Romulus, the founder of Rome, had dwelt. Thus, Augustus now had supposedly arisen as the founder and leader of Rome's third period of glory. Associating the name Augustus with the ancient popular belief that gods in human form were of greater weight and were usually also larger than ordinary men (cf. Lat. *augere*, hence "he who has been increased"), the emperor thus came to be regarded as "supernatural" or "godly." Although Augustus himself did not propagate or desire such divine worship, he did not oppose its frequent occurrences, especially outside of Italy. In Rome and Italy, this emperor cult mainly took the form of the worship of household gods, among whom the spirit of Augustus also had a place.

In contrast to his predecessors, Augustus was not concerned with the expansion of the Roman Empire over new lands and peoples, but rather with the consolidation of the empire as it then existed and the protection of its borders. A period of peace thus began which was already at that time called the Pax Augusta. Italy — which had been weakened to the point of exhaustion by constant warfare — as well as the rest of the empire greeted this peace with gladness. In an inscription from Halicarnassus in Asia Minor, Augustus is called the "father of the fatherland, Zeus Patroos, and savior of the entire human race, whose leadership has not only fulfilled all prayers, but has given more than was asked for. For land and sea are at peace, the cities prosper through good management, concord, and well-being, everything good increases abundantly and brings forth fruit, and men are full of good hope for the future and good courage for the present." During his reign, the border restrictions between the various countries were removed, so that a one-world empire came into being; and in that unified empire, Greek became the standard spoken and written language.

Augustus died in A.D. 14, succeeded by his stepson and son-in-law Tiberius (A.D. 14-37).

Caesar Augustus is one of the few emperors to be cited by name in the New Testament (Luke 2:1), mentioned in connection with a decree that the entire empire be enumerated in a census for the purpose of taxation.

Bibliography. D. Earl, *The Age of Augustus* (London: 1968); A. H. M. Jones, *Augustus* (London: 1970).

AUTHORITY.† The possession of and right to use power. The concept is frequently extended to include the persons by whom and the sphere within which that power may be exercised.

The Old Testament uses the specific word "authority" only twice, with reference to the ascendance of the righteous to power (Prov. 29:2; Heb. *rābâ* "be great") and Esther and Mordecai's ratification of the letter concerning the Purim festival (Esth. 9:29; Heb. *tōqep* "validity"). Nevertheless, the concept is underscored by the LXX use of Gk. *exousía* ("ability, right") with reference to political power (e.g., Neh. 5:5; RSV "power"; 2 Kgs. 20:13; RSV "realm") as well as the sovereign authority of God (e.g., Dan. 4:34-35; RSV "dominion").

In the New Testament Gk. *exousía* points not to a derived right or a possible claim to authority but to a valid inner authority. Jesus has the authority to teach (Mark 1:22), to forgive sins and cure sickness (Matt. 9:6 par. Mark 2:10; Luke 5:24), and to judge (John 5:27). Just as God was the ultimate source of all power, it was through the full authority of Christ "in heaven and on earth" (Matt. 28:18; cf. John 10:17) that his disciples were able to teach, heal the sick, and cast out evil spirits (Matt. 10:1 par. Mark 6:7; Luke 10:19). Paul also cited his apostolic authority (2 Cor. 10:8; 13:10; cf. 1 Cor. 9:4, 18) and warned others not to abuse their power (cf. 1 Cor. 8:9; RSV "liberty"). Most importantly, it was the power of God acting through the life, death, and resurrection of Jesus Christ that made possible the ultimate authority over all powers, human and superhuman (e.g., 1 Cor. 15:24; Eph. 1:21; Rev. 13:2).

As the Word of God, the Scriptures are regarded as authoritative. *See* BIBLE **V.**

See also POWER.

AUTOGRAPHA [ôt′ə grăf′ə] (Gk. *autográphai* "the writings themselves"). The original manuscripts of the biblical text written or dictated by the biblical authors themselves. All of these, however, have been lost; most were probably written on papyrus, which probably disintegrated early through frequent use. The oldest extant complete manuscript of the Old Testament is the Leningrad Codex (*ca.* A.D. 1009), which is the base for Kittel's *Biblia Hebraica* and the *Biblia Hebraica Stuttgartensia*. The oldest complete manuscript containing the New Testament is the Codex Sinaiticus (*ca.* fourth century).

Many portions of Scripture have been discovered as dating to earlier centuries, thus shortening the length of time between the oldest extant manuscripts and the autographa. 1 Clement (*ca.* A.D. 96) seems to intimate that the church at Corinth still possessed the original letter of Paul near the end of the first century (47:1).

See also BIBLE, TEXT OF THE.

AVA (2 Kgs. 17:24, KJV). *See* AVVA.

AVE MARIA [ä′vä mä rē′ä].* The "Hail Mary" or Angelic Salutation, a prayer to the Virgin Mary based on the greetings of Gabriel and Elizabeth (Luke 1:28, 42). Its liturgical use can be traced to the fifth century; it was introduced into the mass for the feast of the Annunciation in the seventh century, but it did not gain popular use until the end of the twelfth.

AVEN [ā'vən] (Heb. '*āwen* "wickedness").

1. A contemptuous name for the city of Bethel (Hos. 10:8; JB "idolatrous high places"; NIV "high-places of wickedness"), which the prophet Hosea also calls Beth-aven (e.g., 4:15).

2. Another name (Ezek. 30:17, KJV) for the Egyptian city of On (so RSV, JB; Heb. '*ōn*) or Heliopolis (NIV; cf. LXX *Hēliou poleōs*), probably a deliberate pun.

3. A valley in Coele-Syria, where temples were probably located for the worship of Phoenician deities; some scholars view the name as a designation of the temple city Baalbek. At Amos 1:5 it is mentioned in the oracle of doom against Syria.

AVENGER OF BLOOD. Blood relative(s) or fellow tribesmen who avenged the murder of one of their own by killing a member of the family or tribe of the murderer. This practice occurs among modern primitive peoples as it did among the peoples of the ancient Near East. One possible explanation for blood vengeance is the reestablishment of an equilibrium broken by the death; one murder equals another.

In the Old Testament it was the closest relative that avenged the death of the person slain. Patterns of kinship carefully specified the "avenger of blood" (Heb. *gō'ēl haddām*, lit. "redeemer or ransomer of blood," or simply *gō'ēl* [Num. 35:12]), and the responsibilities were clearly defined (35:19-21; Deut. 19:12; etc.).

Mosaic legislation sought to control blood vengeance, however, by distinguishing between accidental manslaughter and intentional murder. In the former case, the killer was permitted to flee to the altar of the Lord (the right of asylum, cf. Exod. 21:14; 1 Kgs. 2:28-31) or to one of the six cities of refuge (Exod. 21:13; Num. 35:9-15; Deut. 19:6-10; cf. Josh. 20:1-9), where he would be safe as long as he remained within its borders until the death of the current high priest. The city of refuge became his place of exile and, in fact, a kind of prison.

The Old Testament records a few instances of blood vengeance: Gideon, who killed those Midianites responsible for the death of his brothers (Judg. 8:18-21), and the Gibeonites who avenged the deaths of their fellows caused by Saul (2 Sam. 21:1-9). However, Joab's execution of his brother, Asahel, in war was not an example of blood vengeance (2 Sam. 3:27, 30; 2 Kgs. 2:5; cf. 2 Sam. 3:31ff.).

Later this custom was abandoned in Israel when various governmental institutions began to administer justice.

AVIM (Josh. 18:23; "Avims," Deut. 2:23; "Avites," Josh. 13:3, KJV). *See* AVVIM.

AVITH [ā'vĭth] (Heb. '*ăwîṭ* "ruin"). A city of Edom and the home of King Hadad, whose father Bedad had defeated the Midianites (Gen. 36:35; 1 Chr. 1:46). Its location has been suggested as Khirbet el-Jiththeh between Ma'ân and el-Basṭa.

AVVA [ăv'ə] (Heb. '*awwā*). A city in Assyria or Syria, possibly the same as Ivvah, from which Shalmaneser V (722 B.C.) took colonists, resettling them in the cities of Samaria whose Israelite inhabitants he had deported to Assyria (2 Kgs. 17:24; KJV "Ava").

AVVIM [ăv'ĭm] (Heb. '*awwîm*) (**PERSON**). The inhabitants of the region later called the Philistine plain, near Gaza, before the Philistines ("Caphtorim") destroyed them and settled in the area (Deut. 2:23; KJV "Avims"; JB, NIV "Avvites"; cf. Josh. 13:3; KJV "Avites").

AVVIM [av'ĭm] (Heb. '*awwîm*) (**PLACE**). A city in the tribal territory of Benjamin (Josh. 18:23; KJV "Avim"), near Bethel and perhaps identical with Ai.

AVVITES [ăv'īts] (Heb. *hā'awwîm*). Inhabitants of Avva (2 Kgs. 17:24) whom Shalmaneser V of Assyria resettled in the cities of Samaria (v. 31; KJV "Avites"). They worshiped Nibhaz and Tartak.

AWL (Heb. *marṣēa'*). A pointed tool used for boring through a slave's ear (Exod. 21:6; Deut. 15:17).

AXE. An instrument for cutting wood; also used as a weapon of war. *See* WEAPONS.

AYYAH [ā'yə] (Heb. '*ayyâ*). A town in the tribal territory of Ephraim (1 Chr. 7:28), to be distinguished from Gaza (KJV "Gaza"; see LXX *Gaza*) in Philistia. Some scholars have suggested a site near Ai or Ai itself.

AZAL [ā'zəl] (Heb. '*āṣāl*). A name mentioned at Zech. 14:5 in connection with the Lord's protection of his people in the day of battle. Whereas the RSV renders it "the side of it" (following the emendation Heb. '*eṣlô*), other versions translate it as a proper name ("Azal," KJV; "Azel," NIV; "Jasol," JB; cf. LXX *Iasod*). It remains unclear whether Azal is the name of a brook ("afflux of Kidron from Olivet," KoB, p. 395) or a place name.

AZALIAH [ăz'ə lī'ə] (Heb. '*ăṣalyāhû* "the Lord has set apart"). The son of Meshullam and father of Shaphan the secretary, mentioned in connection with the discovery of the Book of the Law (2 Kgs. 22:3).

AZANIAH [ăz'ə nī'ə] (Heb. '*ăzanyâ* "the Lord has heard"). The father of Jeshua the Levite, who set his seal to the renewed covenant made under Nehemiah (Neh. 10:9).

AZARAEL [ăz'ə rā'əl] (Neh. 12:36, KJV); **AZAREEL** [ăz'ə rēl] (elsewhere, KJV). *See* AZAREL.

AZAREL [ăz'ə rēl] (Heb. '*ăzar'ēl* "God has helped").

1. A Korahite who went over to David at Ziklag (1 Chr. 12:6; KJV "Azareel").

2. A Levite and a singer during the days of David (1 Chr. 25:18). He was the son of Heman and is the same as the Uzziel of v. 4.

3. The son of Jeroham; he was the leader of the tribe of Dan under David (1 Chr. 27:22).

4. An Israelite descendant of Binnui; he was one of those who had to send away their foreign wives during the administration of Ezra (Ezra 10:41).

5. The son of Ahzai, a descendant of Immer, and the father of Amashsai (Neh. 11:13). He is probably the same as the Azarel of Neh. 12:36 (KJV "Azarael") who along with others played on musical instruments at the dedication of the walls of Jerusalem.

AZARIAH [ăz'ə rī'ə] (Heb. ʿ*azaryâ,* ʿ*azaryāhû* "the Lord has helped").

1. One of Solomon's high officials. He was the son of the high priest Zadok and the brother of Ahimaaz (1 Kgs. 4:2; cf. 2 Sam. 15:27).

2. The son of Nathan who was set over Solomon's officers (1 Kgs. 4:5). He was perhaps one of Solomon's nephews (2 Sam. 5:14).

3. King of Judah (*ca.* 783-742 B.C.); the son and successor of Amaziah (2 Kgs. 14:21; 15:1, 6-8, 17, 23, 27; 1 Chr. 3:12). He is better known by his throne name UZZIAH (**1**).

4. A man of Judah, of the line of Zerah and the family of Ethan (1 Chr. 2:8).

5. A Judahite, the grandson of Obed and son of Jehu, and a descendant of Jerahmeel through the Egyptian slave of Sheshan (1 Chr. 2:38-39). He should be distinguished from **14** below.

6. The grandson of Zadok and son of Ahimaaz (1 Chr. 6:9 [MT 35]).

7. A high priest (1 Chr. 6:10 [MT 5:36]), perhaps the one who opposed King Uzziah when the latter arrogated to himself the prerogatives of the priestly office (2 Chr. 26:17-18).

8. A high priest, the son of Hilkiah and father of Seraiah (1 Chr. 6:13 [MT 39]; 9:11). He was an ancestor of Ezra who lived shortly before the Exile (Ezra 7:1).

9. A Levite, a descendant of the Kohathites and ancestor of Samuel the prophet and Heman the singer (1 Chr. 6:36 [MT 21]).

10. A descendant of Hilkiah and chief officer of the temple at Jerusalem after the Exile (1 Chr. 9:11). He is probably the same as the Seraiah of Neh. 11:11.

11. A prophet, the son of Oded. He encouraged King Asa to proceed with his religious reformation throughout Judah (2 Chr. 15:1-7).

12, 13. Two of the sons of King Jehoshaphat who were killed by their elder brother Jehoram after he had ascended the throne (2 Chr. 21:2-4).

14. A commander who aided in the deposition of Athaliah (2 Chr. 23:1). He was the son of Jeroham.

15. The son of Obed who participated in the revolt against Queen Athaliah (2 Chr. 23:1).

16. The son of Johanan; he was one of the chiefs of the men of Ephraim who compelled Pekah to free the men of Judah whom he had taken captive (2 Chr. 28:12.)

17. The father of Joel, a Kohathite who participated in the cleansing of the temple at the time of Hezekiah (2 Chr. 29:12).

18. A Levite of the line of Merari who, during the reign of Hezekiah, helped in the cleansing of the temple (2 Chr. 29:12).

19. A high priest during the reign of Hezekiah (2 Chr. 31:10).

20. The son of Maaseiah. He repaired the city wall of Jerusalem beside his own house (Neh. 3:23-24).

21. An Israelite who returned from the Exile with Zerubbabel (Neh. 7:7). At Ezra 2:2 he is called Seraiah.

22. One of the Levites who explained (perhaps translated from Hebrew into Aramaic) the words of the law which Ezra read (Neh. 8:7-8).

23. A priest who set his seal to the renewed covenant under Nehemiah (Neh. 10:2).

24. A prince of Judah who took part in the festive dedication of the restored walls of Jerusalem (Neh. 12:33).

25. The son of Hoshaiah; he opposed the prophet Jeremiah (Jer. 43:2; at 42:1 the MT reads Jezaniah; cf. 40:8).

26. The Hebrew name of Abednego, one of Daniel's three friends (Dan. 1:6-7).

AZARIAH, PRAYER OF.† The first of the apocryphal additions to the book of Daniel, inserted in the Greek text (LXX) following Dan. 3:23. Generally it is considered a unit with the Song of the Three Young Men.

The account is an expansion of the story of Daniel's three companions — Shadrach, Meshach, and Abednego — in the fiery furnace, punishment for their refusal to worship the golden image set up by Nebuchadnezzar. Here Azariah (whose Babylonian name was Abednego; Dan. 1:6-7) prays from the midst of the furnace, confessing his sin and seeking God's pardon and deliverance on the basis of Israel's covenant (vv. 1-22; LXX 3:24-45). This is followed by a prose narrative telling how the king's servants continued to stoke the furnace, using naphtha, pitch, tow, and brush to bring the flames to a height of 49 cubits. The Chaldeans themselves were consumed by the fire, but the angel of the Lord joined Azariah and his companions and "made the midst of the furnace like a moist whistling wind" (v. 27; LXX 3:50) so that they remained unharmed.

Attesting to God's previous acts in Israel's behalf, the story offers hope for those at the mercy of Antiochus IV Epiphanes as well as the oppressed of any time.

See also SONG OF THE THREE YOUNG MEN.

AZAZ [ā'zăz] (Heb. ʿ*āzāz* "powerful"). A Reubenite, the son of Shema and father of Bela (1 Chr. 5:8).

AZAZEL [ə zā'zəl] (Heb. ʿ*azāʾzēl*). The name of a goat sent into the desert on the Day of Atonement in order to remove Israel's sins (Lev. 16:8, 10, 26; see NIV mg., "goat of removal"). While the KJV and NIV render the term "scapegoat" (cf. LXX *apopompaíos*), a more generally acceptable translation is the proper name Azazel (so RSV, JB).

Some commentators consider Azazel a kind of desert demon (see JB note at Lev. 16:8; KoB, p. 693), perhaps one of the satyrs (e.g., Isa. 13:21; 34:14). Lev. 16 does not state that this goat is an offering to such a demon; rather, the animal is an insult to it, laden as it is with Israel's sins. Actually, human sin now belongs to the demon.

Later, rabbinic interpretation viewed Azazel as the place in the wilderness to which the goat was sent.

AZAZIAH [ăz'ə zī'ə] (Heb. *ʿazazyāhû* "the Lord is strong").
1. A Levite who played the lyre when the ark of the covenant was brought to Jerusalem (1 Chr. 15:21).
2. The father of Hoshea of the tribe of Ephraim (1 Chr. 27:20).
3. Overseer of the temple during the reign of King Hezekiah (2 Chr. 31:13).

AZBUK [ăz'bŭk] (Heb. *ʾazbûq*). The father of a certain Nehemiah, one of those who worked on the restoration of the walls and gates of Jerusalem (Neh. 3:16).

AZEKAH [ə zē'kə] (Heb. *ʿazēqâ* "hoed ground"[?]). A fortress city south of the valley of Aijalon and opposite Socoh (Josh. 15:35) in the valley of Elah. It has been identified with Tell ez-Zakarîyah, 24 km. (15 mi.) northwest of Hebron.
In the battle with the Canaanite coalition headed by Adonizedek of Jerusalem, Joshua pursued the remnant of the enemy as far as Azekah (Josh. 10:10). In the same area the Philistines later encamped in their engagement with the Israelites (1 Sam. 17:1); again Israel was victorious.
After the revolt of the northern kingdom Rehoboam, the son of Solomon, fortified this city (2 Chr. 11:10), also storing food, oil, and wine in it (v. 11). Azekah was one of the last cities to surrender to Nebuchadnezzar (Jer. 34:7; *ca.* 588 B.C.). In the fourth of the Lachish Letters, the commanding officer of a post north of Lachish informs the commander-in-chief of Lachish that the smoke signals from Azekah can no longer be seen, perhaps implying that the city has already fallen. The city was reoccupied following the Exile (Neh. 11:30).
Ruins at Tell ez-Zakarîyah include fortified towers and a wall, perhaps that of the citadel. A series of underground rooms and passages may have been used for refuge or for storing provisions in time of war. Also discovered were a number of ceramic vessels from the Israelite period bearing the inscription "of (or for) the king."

AZEL [ā'zəl] (Heb. *ʾāṣēl* "noble"). A descendant of Saul and Jonathan, and father of six sons (1 Chr. 8:37-38; 9:43-44).

AZEM (Josh. 15:29; 19:3, KJV). *See* EZEM.

AZGAD [ăz'găd] (Heb. *ʾazgāḏ* "Gad is strong"). An Israelite ancestor of a number of exiles, of whom some returned under Zerubbabel (Ezra 2:12; Neh. 7:17) and some under Nehemiah (Ezra 8:12). He may be the Azgad of Neh. 10:15 who set his seal to the renewed covenant under Nehemiah.

AZIEL [ā'zǐ əl] (Heb. *ʿazîʾēl*). One of the Levites who played the harp as the ark of the covenant was brought to Jerusalem (1 Chr. 15:20). He may be the same as the Jaaziel of v. 18.

AZIZA [ə zī'zə] (Heb. *ʿazîzāʾ* "strong"). An Israelite of the lineage of Zattu; he was compelled to divorce his foreign wife at the command of Ezra (Ezra 10:27).

AZMAVETH [ăz'mə vĕth] (Heb. *ʿazmāweṯ* "Mot [or Death] is strong") (**PERSON**).
1. A Benjaminite whose two sons joined David at Ziklag (1 Chr. 12:3).
2. One of David's mighty men (2 Sam. 23:31 par. 1 Chr. 11:33), from Bahurim.
3. A person in charge of the treasuries in the palace of David (1 Chr. 27:25).
4. A descendant of Saul, and one of the sons of Jehoaddah (1 Chr. 8:36; at 9:42 his father is named Jarah).

AZMAVETH [ăz'mə vĕth] (Heb. *ʿazmāweṯ* "Mot is strong") (**PLACE**). A village near Jerusalem, to which forty-two members of the village clan returned following the Exile (Ezra 2:24); singers from this village participated in the dedication of the wall of Jerusalem (Neh. 12:29). At Neh. 7:28 it is called Beth-azmaveth. The town has been identified with Ḥizmeh, about 3 km. (2 mi.) north of ʿAnâtâ (Anathoth); ruins at the site indicate that the village was built on a rock into which were cut granary cellars and cisterns.

AZMON [ăz'mən] (Heb. *ʿaṣmôn* "strong"). A place on the southern border of Israel (Num. 34:4-5; Josh. 15:4). Its proposed location is near ʿAin el-Qeṣeimeh, 16 km. (10 mi.) northwest of Kadesh-barnea; remains of an Egyptian outpost are still visible.

AZNOTH-TABOR [ăz'nŏth tā'bər] (Heb. *ʾaznôṯ ṯāḇôr* "ears of Tabor"[?]). A site in the territory of Naphtali, perhaps a landmark, where the territories of Naphtali, Issachar, and Zebulun met at Mt. Tabor (Josh. 19:34).

AZOR [ā'zôr] (Gk. *Azōr*). A postexilic ancestor of Joseph and Jesus (Matt. 1:13-14).

AZOTUS. Greek name of ASHDOD.

AZRIEL [ăz'rī əl] (Heb. *ʿazrîʾēl* "God is my help").
1. The head of a family from the tribe of Manasseh living in Transjordan (1 Chr. 5:24).
2. The father of Jeremoth, a chief in the tribe of Naphtali during the days of David (1 Chr. 27:19).
3. The father of Seraiah, the courtier of King Jehoiakim, during the prophetic ministry of Jeremiah (Jer. 36:26).

AZRIKAM [ăz'rə kăm] (Heb. *ʿazrîqām* "my help has arisen").
1. A son of Neariah, a descendant of Zerubbabel and David (1 Chr. 3:23).
2. A son of Azel of the tribe of Benjamin (1 Chr. 8:38; 9:44).
3. A Levite, the son of Hashabiah, and the father of Hasshub (1 Chr. 9:14 par. Neh. 11:15).
4. The commander of the palace at the time of Ahaz; he was murdered along with Maaseiah and Elkanah by the Ephraimite Zichri (2 Chr. 28:7).

AZUBAH [ə zoo'bə] (Heb. *ʿazûḇâ* "deserted one").
1. The daughter of Shilhi and mother of King Jehoshaphat (1 Kgs. 22:42 par. 2 Chr. 20:31).

2. One of the wives of Caleb, the son of Hezron, and mother of three sons (1 Chr. 2:18-19).

AZUR (Jer. 28:1; Ezek. 11:1, KJV). *See* Azzur.

AZZAH (Deut. 2:23; 1 Kgs. 4:24; Jer. 25:20, KJV). *See* Gaza.

AZZAN [ăz'ən] (Heb. *'azzan* "strength"). The father of Paltiel, a chief of the tribe of Issachar (Num. 34:26).

AZZUR [ăz'ər] (Heb. *'azzûr* "the one who received help").

1. An Israelite who, as a representative of the people, put his seal on the new covenant when Nehemiah was governor (Neh. 10:17).

2. The father of the false prophet Hananiah of Gibeon (Jer. 28:1; KJV "Azur").

3. The father of Jaazaniah, a contemporary of Ezekiel (Ezek. 11:1; KJV "Azur").

B. A designation of the biblical MS CODEX VATICANUS.

BAAL [bā'əl] (Heb. *ba'al* "lord," "owner"; Akk. *Bêlu*) (**DEITY**).

I. Name

Heb. *ba'al* can refer to the owner of a house ("[the] man's [house]," Exod. 22:7; NIV "neighbor's"; JB "owner"), of an animal ("owner," 21:28), of a piece of property ("owner," v. 34), of a city ("men [of Jericho]," Josh. 24:11; NIV "citizens"; JB "those who held"), and even of a wife (e.g., Gen. 20:3, "man's [wife]"; NIV, JB "married"). Frequently it is used in compounds (e.g., the "baal of dreams," i.e., "dreamer," at Gen. 37:19). Finally, it is the name of a Canaanite deity.

II. Worship

The Old Testament mentions both Baals (Heb. *beʿālîm*, e.g., Judg. 2:11; 3:7; 8:33; KJV "Baalim") and Baal (e.g., 6:25, 28; 1 Kgs. 16:32; 18:21) as worshipped by the surrounding peoples. Though some believe that each local area had a number of Baals, scholars increasingly favor (on the basis of excavations at Ras Shamra) the view that only one deity specifically named Baal was worshipped in each region. The assumption is that originally Baal, taken as a title of worship and possibly the personification of the sun, was the name of a male deity who subsequently became the principal deity for various regions; the association of his name with that of the location of the cult (e.g., Baal-hazor, 2 Sam. 13:23; Baal-hermon, Judg. 3:3) gives evidence of the varieties of forms in which he was worshipped and may indicate that the various forms came to be viewed as separate deities. Similarly, the veneration of various aspects of the god's character (e.g., his connection with rain or fertility) or other associations (Baal-zebub, "lord of flies," 2 Kgs. 1:2; Baal-berith, "lord of the covenant," Judg. 9:4) may have led to the worship of numerous Baals.

Excavations have shown that the nations surrounding Israel were familiar with Baal. The Babylonians worshipped the deity Bel (see Isa. 46:1; Jer. 50:2; 51:44); in the Amarna Letters he is put on a par with the Babylonian-Assyrian deity Hadad (also Adad or Addu), the god of thunder. Jezebel the daughter of the king of Tyre introduced the Phoenician Baal Melqart ("king of the city") into Israel and promoted his worship at Samaria (1 Kgs. 16:32; cf. 2 Kgs. 10:28 for the destruction of Baal, and vv. 25-27 for the slaughter of the Baal devotees and the demolition of the "house of Baal"). According to some scholars, Jezebel strongly stimulated (rather than introduced) the centuries-old Baal worship in Israel. A temple dedicated to Baal has been excavated at Ras Shamra, near a temple dedicated to Dagon, Baal's father. Several Ugaritic texts mention the name of Baal and his spouse Asherath (Asherah), while others list an Aleyan name (perhaps "strong Baal").

Upon entering Canaan the Israelites came across Baals in various places and soon they also worshipped the fertility deity. In fact, they played spiritual harlotry with Baal-peor already in Transjordan (Num. 25:3-5); according to Num. 25 they were attracted to the sensuous nature of the worship of the Moabite Baal-peor ("owner or lord of Peor"). (At 23:28 Peor is the name of a mountain.) After the death of Gideon the Israelites worshipped Baal-berith (Judg. 8:33; cf. 9:46). At other times they identified their worship of Yahweh with Baal (note the names Bealiah ["Yahweh is Baal" or "Lord," 1 Chr. 12:5] and Beeliada ["Baal knows," 14:7; see also Eliada ("God knows," 2 Sam. 5:16)]).

The book of Judges repeatedly refers to Israel's forsaking the Lord and its worship of Baal without in the least condoning such acts (2:11-14; 3:7; etc.). At 6:25 Gideon receives a commandment from the Lord to break down an altar of Baal which his father had constructed. Other prophetic writings such as Hosea (Heb. *baʿalî*, "my Baal," Hos. 2:16; KJV "Baali"; NIV "my master") equally strongly condemn Baal worship. Thus, it must be assumed that nearly all passages mentioning Baal(s) have been revised in order to defend the claim that Israel gradually developed its proper view of God and ascended from polytheism (the worship of many Baals) to monotheism (the worship of the one God).

III. Character

As the deity of rain and thunder, Baal is also the fertility god. In mythology his reign is curbed, how-

A mid-second millenium figurine of Baal from Tortosa (Tartus, Syria) (Louvre; photo M. Chuzeville)

ever, by the attacks of his enemy Mot, the deity of aridity, sterility, and death. During the spring Mot forces Baal to descend into the underworld, during which period the earth becomes desolate. Mot in turn is killed by the deity Anat who causes the return of Baal to the fields. Then the cycle starts again (note the myth of the dying and rising vegetation-deity Tammuz in Babylonian religion)

Bibliography. W. F. Albright, *Yahweh and the Gods of Canaan* (Garden City: 1968); G. R. Driver, *Canaanite Myths and Legends* (Edinburgh: 1956).

BAAL [bā'əl] (Heb. *baʿal* "lord") (**PERSON**).

1. A personal name, actually a city in the tribal territory of Simeon (1 Chr. 4:33), identical with Baalath-beer.

2. A man from the tribe of Reuben and descendant of Joel who lived before the deportation of the ten northern tribes (1 Chr. 5:5).

3. A Benjaminite and fourth son of Jeiel, a Gibeonite ancestor of Saul (1 Chr. 8:30; 9:36).

BAALAH [bā'ə lə] (Heb. *baʿᵃla* "mistress").

1. Another name for Kiriath-jearim (Josh. 15:9).

2. A mountain on the boundary of the tribal territory of Judah, between Ekron and Jabneel (Josh. 15:11).

3. A city in the southern part of Judah (Josh. 15:29), perhaps the same as Balah (Josh. 19:3) or Bilhah (1 Chr. 4:29). It is presumably Tulul el-Medhbah near Khirbet el-Meshash in the region of el-Mutalla (between Beer-sheba and the Dead Sea).

BAALATH [bā'ə lǎth] (Heb. *baʿᵃlāṯ* "mistress"). A city originally located in the tribal territory of Dan (Josh. 19:44) and afterward fortified by Solomon (1 Kgs. 9:18; 2 Chr. 8:6). It is perhaps identical with Baalah or Kiriath-jearim (Josh. 15:9).

BAALATH-BEER [bā'ə lǎth bē'ər] (Heb. *baʿᵃlaṯ bᵉʾēr* "lady of the well"). A city in the tribal territory of Simeon, the "Ramah of the Negeb" (Josh. 19:8), a place in the Shephelah ("Ramoth of the Negeb," 1 Sam. 30:27), possibly identical with Bealoth (Josh. 15:24) and Baal (1 Chr. 4:33).

See also RAMAH **2.**

BAALBEK [bāl'běk]. A city in the Beqaʿ region of Coele-Syria (modern Lebanon), near the springs of the Orontes, at times identified (though never explicitly in the Old Testament) with the "valley of Aven" (Heb. *biqʿāṯ-ʾāwen,* Amos 1:5). In the Old Testament it was a center of Baal worship; later the Greeks, who identified Baal with Helios (the sun-deity), renamed the city Heliopolis. Impressive ruins representing Egyptian, Phoenician, Grecian, and Roman architectural styles have survived. Particularly well-known are the arresting ruins of a temple complex built by Roman emperors for Jupiter-Heliopolitanus, Venus, and Mercury, the temple of Bacchus, and a Christian basilica.

BAAL-BERITH [bāl bǐr'ǐth] (Heb. *baʿal bᵉrîṯ* "lord of covenant"). A Canaanite deity worshiped by the inhabitants of Shechem during the reign of Abimelech the son of Gideon (Judg. 8:33; 9:4). Abimelech became king over Shechem by means of a covenant, through which he was given seventy pieces of silver from the temple of Baal-berith (9:4). Within three years, however, the relationship had soured and the Shechemites broke the covenant (vv. 22-23; on the "evil spirit" sent by God, see R. G. Boling, *Judges.* AB [1975], pp. 175-76).

The actual name of this deity (also called El-berith in 9:46) may have been Hamor (Heb. *ḥᵃmôr* "ass"), a name with particular significance for a "lord of covenant." At Mari the sacrificial slaying of an ass was such an integral part of treaty making that the expression "to kill an ass" gained the meaning "to conclude a covenant," and the act may well have been part of the transaction between Abimelech and the people of Shechem. Note also the name of Hamor, prince of Shechem, whose descendants are known as the "sons of Hamor" or the "followers of the ass" (Josh. 24:32; Judg. 9:28; cf. Acts 7:16).

BAALE-JUDAH [bā'ə lǐ jōō'də]; **BAALE OF JUDAH** (2 Sam. 6:2). See KIRIATH-JEARIM.

BAAL-GAD [bāl găd'] (Heb. ba'al-gāḏ "lord of good fortune"). A place near Mt. Hermon (Josh. 11:17; 12:7; 13:5), perhaps contemporary Hasbeiyah, but more probably Tell Haus, 20 km. (12.4 mi.) to the north — both at the Wâdī et-Teim.

BAAL-HAMON [bāl hā'mən] (Heb. ba'al hāmôn "lord of wealth"). The name of an unknown place where Solomon had a vineyard (Cant. 8:11). According to some commentators, "vineyard" refers to the royal harem; thus the name could perhaps be a covert allusion to Jerusalem.

BAAL-HANAN [bāl hā'nən] (Heb. ba'al ḥānān "Baal is gracious").
1. A son of Achbor and the seventh king of Edom (Gen. 36:38 par. 1 Chr. 1:49).
2. A native of Gedera and overseer of the olive and sycamore trees in the Shephelah during the reign of David (1 Chr. 27:28); perhaps the same as Hanan, one of David's mighty men (11:43).

BAAL-HAZOR [bāl hā'zôr] (Heb. ba'al ḥāṣôr "lord" or "Baal of Hazor"). A mountain where Absalom invited his brothers during a sheepshearing festival and killed Amnon (2 Sam. 13:23). At the foot of the mountain may have been a settlement with the same name. The most likely identification is Jebel 'Aṣur, a mountain 1032 m. (3386 ft.) high, located 7 km. (4.5 mi.) northeast of Bethel.

BAAL-HERMON [bāl hûr'mən] (Heb. ba'al ḥermôn "lord of Hermon").
1. A mountain east of Mt. Lebanon (Judg. 3:3) where the Hivites dwelled, whom the Israelites could not expel because of the Lord's testing of his people.
2. A city near Mt. Hermon (1 Chr. 5:23), probably identical with Baal-gad. Though some scholars point to Banias at the site of the springs of the Jordan, its identification remains uncertain. F.-M. Abel suggests that it is either a sacred place on Mt. Hermon or on the eastern slope, where a site named Iqlim el-Bellan is located.

BAALI [bā'ə lǐ] (Heb. ba'ᵃlî).† Symbolic name for God, depicting his relationship with his people. Because it connotes the Canaanite Baal, or at least the quality of a pagan human-divine relationship, Hosea substitutes the name Ishmi ("my husband"; so RSV) to call to mind Israel's covenant (Hos. 2:16, KJV; so NJV at v. 18, following MT; RSV "my Baal").
See BAAL (DEITY).

BAALIM [bā'ə lǐm] (e.g., Judg. 2:11, KJV). See BAAL (DEITY).

BAALIS [bā'ə lǐs] (Heb. ba'alîs). King of the Ammonites during the ministry of Jeremiah (Jer. 40:14). He sent Ishmael the son of Nethaniah to murder Gedaliah the governor of Judah in order to bring about the downfall of Judah and to enlarge his own kingdom.

BAAL-MEON [bāl mē'ŏn] (Heb. ba'al mᵉ'ôn "lord of habitation"). An Amorite city at the Moabite border assigned to Reuben and built by the Reubenites (Num. 32:38); also called Beon (v. 3); Beth-baal-meon (Josh. 13:17); or Beth-meon (Jer. 48:23). Its ruins were repopulated by Moabites. The city has been identified with Ma'în, ruins located on the eastern slope of the Shephah mountain ridge, which is the watershed separating the Dead Sea, el-Ghor, and the Arabah from the desert to the east. The valley near the city and the mountain slope are very fertile places, while the western, more stony area provides good pastureland.

BAAL-PEOR [bāl pē'ôr]. See BAAL (DEITY); PEOR.

BAAL-PERAZIM [bāl pǐ rā'zǐm] (Heb. ba'al-pᵉrāṣîm "baal ["lord"] of the breakthroughs"). A place near Jerusalem at the valley of Rephaim where David defeated the Philistines (2 Sam. 5:20 par. 1 Chr. 14:11). The Mt. Perazim mentioned in Isa. 28:21 is an allusion to this event.

BAAL-SHALISHAH [bāl shăl'ə shə] (Heb. ba'al šālišâ). A village in the land of Shalishah in the hill country of Ephraim (1 Sam. 9:4), the home of a man who gave Elisha the "bread of the first fruits" (2 Kgs. 4:42; KJV "Baal-shalisha").

BAAL-TAMAR [bāl tā'mər] (Heb. ba'al tāmār "lord of the palm"). A place (perhaps a landmark rather than a city) in the tribal territory of Benjamin, where the Israelites defeated the Benjaminites (Judg. 20:33-36). According to Eusebius (Onom.) it is Ras et-Tawil, an elevation east of Tell el-Fûl (Gibeah of Benjamin).

BAAL-ZEBUB [bāl zē'bŭb] (Heb. ba'al zᵉbûb "lord of flies"). An idol worshipped at Ekron (2 Kgs. 1:2-18) also named Beel-zebul, to which Ahaziah the king of Israel (ca. 845 B.C.) sent messengers requesting Baal-zebub to cure him. In Phoenicia Baal was also a sun-god, and possibly also a god of flies because flies come to life especially during the heat of the day. Ahaziah could have inquired of this deity not so much on account of the aim to ward off the flies but rather because of the belief that the flies announce changes in the weather. Thus Ahaziah viewed the "Lord of flies" as an oracle deity. Other scholars, however, are of the opinion that the name Baal-zebub is a name of contempt for Baal-zebul. See also BEELZEBUL.

BAAL-ZEPHON [bāl zē'fŏn] (Heb. ba'al ṣᵉpôn "lord of the north," or "Baal of the north wind"). A station along Israel's journey following the Exodus from Egypt, perhaps a designation of a temple or sacred mountain (Exod. 14:2, 9; Num. 33:7). In the annals of

King Sargon is mentioned a deity with the same name, which was worshipped in North Syria and introduced to Egypt (at Memphis) as one of the foreign deities. Baal-zephon was perhaps a sanctuary constructed by the Phoenician merchants who considered their gods to dwell on mountaintops; thus, some scholars are inclined to locate this sanctuary on a mountain not far from the sea, perhaps a small hill near Lake Sirbonis. Others place it on the eastern side of the Nile Delta (where temples of this deity have been discovered), while still others locate it just north of Suez.

BAANA [bā'ə nə] (Heb. *ba'ªnā'* "son of suffering").
1. A son of Ahilud and brother of the chancellor Jehoshaphat (1 Kgs. 4:12), who was Solomon's overseer in the southern part of the valley of Jezreel, from Megiddo to the Jordan.
2. A son of Hushai and overseer of Asher and Bealoth during the reign of Solomon (1 Kgs. 4:16; KJV "Baanah"). His father was probably David's counselor, who gave Absalom the wrong advice (2 Sam. 16:15ff.).
3. The father of Zadok, who helped repair the walls of Jerusalem (Neh. 3:4), perhaps the same as Baanah mentioned at Neh. 10:27.

BAANAH [bā'ə nə] (Heb. *ba'ªnâ* "son of suffering").
1. One of the sons of Rimmon, a Benjaminite from Beeroth. With Rechab his brother he was a general in the army of Ishbosheth, Saul's son and successor. Apparently angered by the lack of punishment for Joab after his murder of Abner, Saul's chief army captain, the two brothers entered Ishbosheth's palace and the king's private chamber, killed him as he napped, decapitated him, and took his head to David at Hebron. David, however, ordered them executed and their hands and feet hung at the pool of Hebron (2 Sam. 4:2-12).
2. A native of Netophah and the father of Heleb (or Heled), one of David's mighty men (2 Sam. 23:29 par. 1 Chr. 11:30).
3. A leader of the Israelites who returned with Zerubbabel from exile (Ezra 2:2 par. Neh. 7:7); he sealed the covenant of Nehemiah (Neh. 10:27).

BAARA [bā'ə rə] (Heb. *ba'ªrā'* "Baal has seen[?]"). A wife of the Benjaminite Shaharaim (1 Chr. 8:8).

BAASEIAH [bā'ə sē'yə] (Heb. *ba'ªśēyâ*). A son of Malchijah and an ancestor of Asaph the musician (1 Chr. 6:40).

BAASHA [bā'ə shə] (Heb. *ba'šā'* "Baal hears" or "the sun is Baal"). The son of Ahijah of the tribe of Issachar (1 Kgs. 15:27), who reigned over the ten northern tribes of Israel from Tirzah, ca. 900-877 B.C. (v. 28). Baasha probably held a high position in Israel's army and was thus able to usurp the throne while King Nadab, son of Jeroboam I, besieged Gibbethon. By killing the king and then all of Jeroboam's descendants, Baasha fulfilled the prophet Ahijah's prophecy (14:7-11) though he did not have the prophet's endorsement of either his conspiracy for the throne or his subsequent cruelty.

Although 1 Kgs. 15:16 would indicate that Baasha was in continuous warfare with King Asa of Judah, it was not until sometime after his reign began that Baasha invaded Judah (2 Chr. 14:1; 15:15, 19). He fortified Ramah (1 Kgs. 15:17), a town a few short miles from Jerusalem, in order to threaten that capital city. No doubt Baasha was angered because many of his own subjects had participated in the celebration and covenant with God connected with Asa's reform (2 Chr. 15:9-15). With the temple moneys, however, Asa bribed the Syrian king, Ben-hadad, and succeeded in having the latter break his alliance with Baasha (vv. 18-20). Ben-hadad's armies then invaded Israel, took some of Baasha's cities, and finally forced Baasha to withdraw from Ramah (v. 21).

Baasha conducted his twenty-four-year reign, as Jeroboam had before him, with sinful disregard of God's commandments (15:34). Although the Lord in turn had Jehu, the son of Hanani, prophesy doom for his house (16:1-4), Baasha himself was one of the few kings of the ten tribes who died a natural death (v. 6). His son, Elah, who succeeded him as king, met a less peaceful end, however; he was murdered two years later (vv. 8-10).

BABBLER. A term (Gk. *spermológos* "one picking up seeds," fig. one who is always "picking up" some information and prating about it without understanding its import) applied to the apostle Paul (Acts 17:18; JB "parrot") by the Athenian philosophers, who considered him "a retailer of second-hand scraps of philosophy" (F. F. Bruce, *The Book of the Acts.* NICNT [1954], p. 351).

BABEL [bā'bəl], **TOWER OF.** The temple tower or ziggurat described in Gen. 11:1-9, a narrative which depicts the consequences of a human attempt to "make a name for ourselves" (v. 4) and offers an explanation for the abundance of human languages (vv. 7-9). The name of the tower and the city, Babel (Babylon; Heb. *bābel*; Akk. *Bāb-ilī* "gate of the gods"), is explained by means of popular etymology from Heb. *bālal* "he confused" (v. 9).

According to the biblical account, the tower was built on a plain "in the land of Shinar" (v. 2), a name which designates that portion of southern Mesopotamia later known as Babylonia. Earlier scholars followed Jewish tradition in assigning the structure to Borsippa (modern Birs Numrud), where a massive temple of Nabû (Nebo) had been located. Recent scholarship, however, has identified it with the smaller but more significant temple tower of Marduk at Babylon. Called in Akkadian Esagila ("house [temple] of the raised-up head"; cf. v. 4; Sum. *É-temen-an-ki* "house of the foundations of heaven and earth"), it was constructed first in Sumerian times and subsequently rebuilt several times (by Nabopolassar, 625-605 B.C.; Nebuchadnezzar, 604-562; and others), suggesting occasion for a Babylonian king who might wish to restore it "with its top in the heavens" (v. 4). Although archaeologists have recovered little more than the foundation of the structure, a height of 90 m. (295 ft.) has been suggested for the tower of unpolished stone covered with baked bricks (cf. v. 3). The tower was destroyed by the Persians during the time of Xerxes I (*ca.* 478) and the rubble removed partially by Alexander the Great and the Arabs, who reused the materials in their own buildings.

On the basis of the third-century B.C. Esagila tablet (a copy of an earlier Akkadian text) and the description of Herodotus (*Hist.* i.181; *ca.* 460), the tower consisted of six square stages constructed upon a platform and topped by a seventh stage, a chapel or sanctuary in which the god Marduk was believed to reside. Steps, which provided access to the various levels, were thought by the Babylonians to allow the deity to descend in order to commune with his human subjects (cf. v. 7). Based on the Esagila tablet, measurements of the various stages have been determined as follows: the first stage, 90 m. (295 ft.) on each side by 33 m. (93 ft.) high; the second, 78 m. (219 ft.) per side by 18 m. (50.5 ft.) high; the third, 60 m. (168.5 ft.) per side by 6 m. (17 ft.) high; the fourth, 51 m. (143 ft.) per side by 6 m. (17 ft.) high; the fifth, 42 m. (118 ft.) per side by 6 m. (17 ft.) high; the sixth (not included on the tablet), 33 m. (93 ft.) per side by 6 m. (17 ft.) high; and the seventh (the sanctuary), 24 m. (67 ft.) per side by 15 m. (42 ft.) high.

Bibliography. A. Parrot, *The Tower of Babel* (London: 1955).

BABYLON [băb'ə lən] (Heb. *bābel* "gate of God"; Gk. *Babylōn*).* Capital of Babylonia, situated on the Euphrates river approximately 80 km. (50 mi.) south of modern Baghdad.

The Hebrew name (translated "Babel" only at Gen. 10:10; 11:9) is based on the Akkadian form *Bāb-ilī* "gate of god," probably a translation of the earlier Sum. *ká-dingir-ki* (written *ká-dingir-ra*); the Greek form, from which the English name is derived, is based on the plural form *Bāb-ilāni* "gate of gods."

The biblical account attributes the city's foundation to Nimrud (Gen. 10:10). A Sumerian text by Šar-kali-šarri of Akkad (*ca.* 2250 B.C.) claims that he restored the temple tower, apparently destroyed during a raid by Sargon of Akkad. Ruled by a governor (Sum. *ensi*) during the Ur III period (*ca.* 2150-2050), the city was captured by the invading Semitic Amorites. Babylon became the capital of the First Dynasty of Babylon, whose best-known king, Hammurabi (*ca.* 1750), restored the city and expanded its influence. The city fell to the Hittites in 1600 and then came under Kassite rule. Following attacks by the Assyrians and Elamites, Babylon was restored by Nebuchadnezzar I in 1124. With the rise of Neo-Assyrian strength in the eighth century, the city was again overcome; the inhabitants' spirited independence brought frequent Assyrian intervention, capped by total destruction under Sennacherib (689). Sennacherib's son, Esarhaddon, restored the city and made it a prosperous vassal city under Šamaš-šum-ukin. After the fall of the Neo-Assyrian Empire in 698, Babylon reached its greatest splendor as capital of the Neo-Babylonian Empire, with extensive building activity under Nabopolassar and Nebuchadnezzar II (605-562); it was in this period that the Jewish exiles were taken captive and transported to Babylon (2 Kgs. 24–25; Matt. 1:11-12, 17). The city passed peacefully to Persian control when Cyrus entered its gates in 539 (cf. Dan. 5:30). It was subsequently destroyed by Xerxes (cf. Ezra 4:6, Ahasuerus) in 478. Although Alexander the Great planned to rebuild the city, Seleucus I Nicator's founding of a new capital at Seleucia led to the demise of Babylon.

Various explorations and excavations of the site were undertaken in the early and mid-nineteenth century, but the most extensive work was carried out by the Deutsche Orientgesellschaft from 1899 to 1917. Surrounded by a massive double-wall fortification system, the city covered approximately 8.4 sq. km. (3.2 sq. mi.). It was entered by eight gates, the most im-

Foundations of the Hanging Gardens at Babylon (J. Finegan)

portant of which was the Ishtar Gate located on the city's north side near Nebuchadnezzar's Summer Palace. The main street, the Processional Way, paralleled the Euphrates river and led 914 m. (1000 yds.) from the Ishtar Gate to Etemenanki, the temple tower or ziggurat, and Esagila, the principal temple, dedicated to Marduk. Excavations have recovered evidence of many other temples (Babylonian texts record more than fifty in the city) as well as the great palace of Nabopolassar and his successors, which may have incorporated the fabled Hanging Gardens.

The city's splendor and the accompanying cosmopolitan atmosphere fostered its reputation, particularly among the Jews (cf. Isa. 13:2-22; Jer. 25:12), as extravagant and morally lax. In the New Testament Babylon is used symbolically for the decadence of Rome (e.g., 1 Pet. 5:13; Rev. 14:8; see ROME).

Bibliography. A. Parrot, *Babylon and the Old Testament* (New York: 1958); O. E. Ravn, *Herodotus' Description of Babylon* (Copenhagen: 1942).

BABYLONIA [băb'ə lō'nĭ ə].† A major civilization in southern Mesopotamia, situated between the Tigris and Euphrates rivers, which flourished from the middle of the third through the late first millennia B.C. The Greeks named the country after the capital Babylon (Gk. *Babylōn*; Akk. *Bāb-ili, Bāb-ilāni* "gate of the god[s]"); in the Bible it is called Shinar (Gen. 11:2; 14:1, 9; Josh. 7:21) and "the land of the Chaldeans" (Jer. 24:5; Ezek. 12:13), but the early inhabitants referred to it as Sumer and Akkad, designating the union of its southern and northern territories.

I. History

Long regarded as the "Cradle of Civilization," southern Mesopotamia witnessed an agricultural revolution and the formation of towns as early as *ca.* 7000 B.C. A "protohistoric" era generally divided into five cultural phases has been attested for the period from *ca.* 6000 to 2500. The earliest was at Eridu (cf. Irad, Gen. 4:18), where discoveries include a series of temples and a variety of ceramic ware. The Ubaid culture, of Semitic Iranian origin, flourished from 4300-3500 and spread into northern Mesopotamia as well. It was succeeded in the south by the Uruk culture of the non-Semitic Sumerians, who introduced pictographic writing and irrigation. Despite their widespread cultural influence, the Sumerians were able to gain political control only in the south, aided there by the appearance of Semites from the west and Subarians or Hurrites from the northeast. In the period *ca.* 3100-2900, characterized by the archaeological discoveries at Jemdet Nasr, an urban revolution took place throughout southern Mesopotamia. This prepared the way for the final protohistoric phase, the Early Dynastic Age or Lagash period, in which, according to the Sumerian King List, "kingship was lowered" from the gods and shared in turn by eleven city-states, with varying degrees of success. Among the rulers of dynasties at Kish, Uruk (Erech), and Ur were the legendary Gilgamesh and Agga, as well as the politically successful Ur-Nanshe and Eannatum. After a period of decline and social abuse, the reformer Urukagina gained control at Lagash; he was succeeded by the powerful Lugalzagesi, who destroyed Lagash and captured

Uruk and Ur, establishing himself as the sole figure in the Third Dynasty of Uruk and extending his control from the Persian Gulf to the Mediterranean.

A Semitic dynasty founded by Sargon of Akkad (*ca.* 2300-2230) overcame Sumerian rule and, centered at the new city of Akkad (Agade) and stabilized by a standing army and strong central government, extended its power into Elam and Anatolia. The northern region of Akkadian control was lost when the Gutians invaded from the northeast and captured Akkad, but Lagash flourished under Gudea, maintaining control of the south until the city-states reasserted their independence *ca.* 2100.

Calling themselves the "kings of Sumer and Akkad," the Neo-Sumerian Third Dynasty of Ur (Ur III; 2113-2006) introduced an era of extensive trade and cultural advances, attested by numerous cuneiform documents. The dynasty was founded by Ur-nammu and included several aggressive kings (e.g., Šulgi, Amar-suen), but Amorite invasions isolated the capital from its empire and Ur fell to the Elamites. This was the end of Sumerian rule in all but local centers (e.g., Isin). It may be that the migration of Abraham belongs to this period of Amorite movement (Gen. 11:31).

Founded by Sumu-Abum (1894), the First (Amorite) Dynasty of Babylon reached its height under Hammurabi (1792-1750), the sixth of that line. As indicated by the Mari Letters, he dominated a coalition of ten city-states; following victories over Rim-sin of Larsa and Zimri-lim of Mari, and aided by treaties with Assyria and Eshnunna, Babylonian rule was stabilized. Hammurabi was instrumental in making Akkadian the dominant language; he instituted Marduk as the most important deity of the Babylonian pantheon, and his law code was based on the earlier reforms of Ur-nammu and Lipit-ishtar. Under Hammurabi's successors the dynasty was weakened by the revolt of the southern Sea-Land tribes, and the city fell to the Hittite Mursilis I in 1595. With the subsequent incursion of the warlike Kassites, Babylonia found itself in a Dark Age which lasted until the rise of Nebuchadnezzar I in 1150.

In the centuries which followed, Babylonia, although always spiritedly independent, suffered repeated humiliation by the dominant Assyrian power. Shalmaneser III (858-824) maintained the upper hand over the Chaldean (Aramean) tribes which had penetrated the south. The Assyrian king Tiglath-pileser III claimed the throne of Babylon in 745 (cf. 2 Kgs. 15:19; 1 Chr. 5:26). Marduk-apla-iddina (Merodach-baladan; 2 Kgs. 20:12; Isa. 39:1), chief of the Chaldean Bīt-Yakin tribe, offered support but later enlisted Elamite aid in wresting Babylon from Tiglath-pileser's son Sargon II; driven out by Sennacherib in 703, Marduk-apla-iddina returned with the aid of a coalition that included Hezekiah of Judah (2 Kgs. 20:12-19; Isa. 39), but was again routed by the Assyrians. Esarhaddon appointed his son Šamaš-šum-ukīn as crown prince over Babylon in 672, but twenty years later the prince committed suicide when his brother Assurbanipal, the Assyrian king, destroyed the rebellious Babylon.

With the death in 627 of Kandalanu, Assurbanipal's appointed successor, Nabû-apla-uṣur (Nabopolassar), the governor of the Sea-Lands region, took the Babylonian throne, thus establishing the Neo-Babylonian or Chaldean dynasty. With the help of Cyaxares and the Medes, Nabopolassar conquered Nineveh in 612. Under Nabû-kudurri-uṣur (Nebuchadnezzar II, 604-562) the Babylonians defeated the Egyptians at Carchemish (605; Jer. 46:2) and then took Syria and Palestine (cf. 2 Kgs. 24:7). Jehoiakim of Judah became Nebuchadnezzar's vassal (v. 1) but later switched his allegiance to Neco II of Egypt, whereupon Nebuchadnezzar retaliated by besieging Jerusalem in 597, sending Jehoiakim into exile and placing Mattaniah (Zedekiah) on the throne. Zedekiah's subsequent revolt led to the Babylonian sack of Jerusalem (587) and the so-called Babylonian Exile of Judah (25:8-26). Nebuchadnezzar, whose military might was matched by his legal and architectural achievements, was succeeded by his son Amel-marduk (Evil-merodach, 562-560; 2 Kgs. 25:27-30 par. Jer. 52:31-34). Nabonidus (556-539) withstood the powers of Media and Lydia, but fled to Tema, whereupon the Persians under Cyrus captured Babylon and killed the coregent Bēl-šar-uṣur (Belshazzar; cf. Dan. 5:30).

Under Cyrus the government of Babylonia was entrusted to the governor Gubaru (Gobryas). The Achaemenids, favorable to the Jews, permitted their return to Jerusalem and encouraged the rebuilding of the temple (Ezra 1:1-11). The death of Cambyses II in 522 led to a brief period of unrest marked by various usurpers to the throne, but order was restored under Darius II (520-485). Darius reorganized the Babylonian government under satraps and local governors, and it was in his reign that construction on the Jerusalem temple was completed (Ezra 4:1-5, 24–6:22).

The Babylonians attempted one final revolt during the reign of Xerxes (486-470; cf. Ezra 4:6, Ahasuerus) but failed. Alexander III (the Great) captured Babylon in 331 and the country came under Hellenistic rule, passing to the Seleucids (312-64). It was later ruled by the Parthians (Arsacids) until captured by the Arabs in A.D. 641.

II. Religion

Because of the complex history of Mesopotamia, it is difficult to distinguish between Sumerian and Assyrian-Babylonian aspects of religion. Many of the deities became interchangeable or fused, partly because Sumerian religious texts were often preserved in Akkadian versions, and many of the allegedly "Semitic" aspects of the later Babylonian religion can be detected at early stages of Sumerian religion.

Nevertheless, many scholars have attempted to characterize Sumerian religion as basically chthonic, that is, having particular interest in the earth and its forces. The Sumerian world view was founded on a desire for order — systematic, consistent, and symmetrical — and their religion aimed to provide "rest" and safety. Nature was viewed as analogous to life, with heaven as the counterpart of earth; what took place above in the heavenly sphere also occurred on earth below. Thus, the earth was represented as a female deity who became pregnant by the male deity who symbolized heaven; at specific times a divine marriage was believed to take place between a deity or

his human representative and a woman, often a temple prostitute, representing the divine bride. Babylonian (and Assyrian) religion, by contrast, has been characterized as concerned with celestial forces such as the sun, moon, and stars as well as the rain, wind, and weather.

The Mesopotamian pantheon consisted of hundreds of deities. More than 2,500 have been discovered through mythological texts, religious records, scribal lists, and personal names; many of these, however, can be understood as merely epithets or characteristics of the major gods, and others may have been "created" by ancient theologians wishing to supply servants and descendants for other gods. Sumerian gods continued to be worshipped under Akkadian names by the Babylonians and Assyrians.

The chief gods included Anu (Sum. An), the god of heaven, king of the gods and the god of kingship; Enlil (or Ellil, also called Bēl), god of the atmosphere and the wind, who possessed the tablets of (human) destiny and wreaked havoc through storm and tempest; and Ea (Sum. Enki), god of the sweet water under the earth and thus of fertility, and god of wisdom and of magic. With these major creative gods the Sumerians also included Ninhursag, the mother goddess. Next in importance were the celestial deities, the moon-god Sin (Sum. Nanna, Su-en) who was viewed at various lunar phases as a young bull or old man, who was god of wisdom, nocturnal judge, and deity of portents and whose main centers of worship were Ur and Haran (cf. Gen. 11:31; Josh. 24:2); the sun-god Šamaš (Sum. Utu), god of justice and preserver of order; and Ishtar (Sum. Inanna; West Semitic Astarte), goddess of the planet Venus (the morning and evening star) and goddess of love and fertility as well as war. Other significant deities were Adad (Sum. Ishkur; West Semitic Hadad), god of thunder; Ninurta, storm god and god of war and hunting; and Nergal, god of the underworld and the plague. The god Tammuz (Sum. Dumuzi; cf. Ezek. 8:14), god of vegetation, is well known in the mythology as a dying and rising god, whose descent into the netherworld and subsequent ascent is credited as the basis of the seasons.

Marduk (perhaps "son of the sun"), offspring of Ea, attained prominence in the Babylonian pantheon as a national deity sometime after the reign of Hammurabi. In the Babylonian Creation Epic (Enuma Elish) he conquers Tiamat, the goddess of chaos, whereupon the other gods establish his temple Esagil ("house with the elevated head") at Babylon and transfer to him the scepter of authority and the tablets of destiny; the final tablet of the epic lists some fifty titles or qualities of Marduk, who subsequently is known also as Bēl ("lord"; cf. the apocryphal book Bel and the Dragon). Marduk's consort is the goddess Sarpanitu ("brilliant as silver"; cf. Zēr-bānītu "creator of seed"), and his son Nabu (Nebo) is the god of writing and science.

According to Babylonian religion, the primary function of mankind was to serve the gods, which included dressing divine images and providing daily gifts of food at the temples. The general populace had no direct access to the deities, so these functions were performed by numerous classes of priests and ritual specialists. The temple personnel included various types of priests and liturgists as well as musicians, singers, prostitutes, prophets, and diviners. Several collections of texts record incantations to be used on particular occasions to ward off evil spirits or demons, and various types of cultic personnel were employed to divine human destinies by dream interpretations, omens as depicted in the entrails of sacrificial animals, and the observations of certain natural phenomena, as well as through ecstatic communications from the deities.

By the time of Hammurabi the king was no longer regarded as divine, although he played an essential role in maintaining the well-being of his people and the fertility of the land. His loyalty to Marduk was reaffirmed each year in the Akitu or New Year festival, in which the king was stripped of royal authority and struck by the priest; after bowing before Marduk for absolution and to pledge himself to maintain his sacred duties, the king's authority was renewed.

III. Legacy

Various aspects of Babylonian civilization (including that of the predecessor Sumerians) were transmitted to other ancient Near Eastern civilizations, among them those of Syria and Palestine. Not the least significant was the development of writing, which evolved from pictographic symbols into an elaborate system of cuneiform symbols (formed on clay by a wedge-shaped stylus), which represented numerous syllabic values as well as entire words and numerals. This script could also be used to write the Eblaic, Hittite, Hurrian, Amorite, Elamite, and Old Persian languages (as well as Sumerian and Akkadian) and was adapted to the alphabetic writing of Ugaritic. Literacy was not widespread, so scribal schools were maintained to record the various commercial and administrative activities, correspondence, legal transactions, treaties, royal edicts, and religious materials (liturgies, omens, and incantations). The schools also produced reference materials, including lexical texts, lists of various entities (stones, stars, plants), and writing exercises as well as a vast body of literature. The latter included not only historical texts such as official chronicles but also rich body of epics, religious poems, proverbs and wisdom literature, prayers, and hymns. Parallels in form as well as content have been attested in the literature of other ancient Near Eastern and Anatolian cultures, and scholars have noted Mesopotamian influence on the biblical writings as well.

The Babylonian concern for justice is evident in the various collections of law. The "codes" (rarely comprehensive compilations of judicial precedents in various categories) reflected existing standards; perhaps best known is that of Hammurabi, containing 282 paragraphs dealing with property, marriage, divorce, theft, commercial and agricultural matters, adoption and inheritance, court procedures, and punishments for crimes. Laws in the modern "legislative" sense occur in royal edicts and decrees issued in a king's first year of reign. Many of these laws exhibit a concern for human welfare and justice and are reflected in modified form in the laws of the Pentateuch.

Cuneiform lists of plants, animals, and minerals indicate the roots of empirical science among the Babylonians. Mathematical texts include procedural tables for multiplication, division, determination of square and cube roots, and exponential functions, and problem texts display significant advances in pre-Hellenistic algebra and geometry. Such skills were combined with accurate observation of astronomical phenomena to chart the calendar and to predict lunar, stellar, and astral phenomena. Omen texts aimed at the diagnosis and prognosis of disease, lists of pharmaceutical preparations and prescriptions, and accounts of treatment for diseases and injuries reveal what is basically a folk medicine closely tied to magic and exorcism.

Bibliography. R. M. Adams, "Developmental Stages in Ancient Mesopotamia," pp. 13-17 in J. H. Steward, ed., *Irrigation Civilizations* (Washington: 1955); W. W. Hallo and W. K. Simpson, *The Ancient Near East: A History* (New York: 1971); O. Neugebauer, *The Exact Sciences in Antiquity,* 2nd ed. (New York: 1969); A. L. Oppenheim, *Ancient Mesopotamia,* 2nd ed. (Chicago: 1977); H. Ringgren, *Religions of the Ancient Near East* (Philadelphia: 1973); H. W. F. Saggs, *The Greatness That Was Babylon* (New York: 1962).

BACA [bā′kə], **VALLEY OF** (Heb. *bākā'* "balsam[?]"). A valley apparently containing trees which exuded resin or gum (the Hebrew term may be related to *bākâ* "weep," hence "weeping trees"). This valley, of unknown identification, apparently was an arid region through which pilgrims passed en route to Jerusalem (Ps. 84:6).

BACCHIDES [băk′ə dēz] (Gk. *Bakchídēs*). Governor of the province Beyond the River, the district between Mesopotamia and Egypt, and faithful friend of the Seleucid king Demetrius I Soter (1 Macc. 7:8), who sent him to Judah to suppress the Maccabean revolt and make Alcimus high priest over the area. He was dispatched a second time after the Syrian general Nicanor was killed in battle and Judas Maccabeus had assumed control of the government (9:1). Following the death of Alcimus, he returned to Judah, where he met with stiff opposition and was forced to meet the proposal of peace as stipulated by Jonathan, the brother of Judas (9:58ff.).

BACCHUS. See DIONYSUS.

BACHRITES [băk′rīts] (Num. 26:35, KJV). See BECHERITES.

BADGER. See LEATHER, ROCK BADGER.

BAG. Various types of bags are mentioned in the Bible. Heb. *ṣᵉrôr* refers to a bag, a pouch, or a bundle (cf. Heb. *ṣûr* "tie or bundle up," 2 Kgs. 12:10 [MT 11]) made from leather or linen drawn together for keeping money (Gen. 42:35; Prov. 7:20; Hag. 1:6, JB "purse") or spices (Cant. 1:13, JB "sachet"). In general, it is a place where valuable things are kept and is used metaphorically in this sense at 1 Sam. 25:29 ("bundle of the living") and Job 14:17 ("my transgression would be sealed up in a bag"). Heb. *kîs* refers to a small bag or purse used by merchants for carrying money (Prov. 1:14), gold (Isa. 46:6), or weights (Deut. 25:13; Prov. 16:11; Mic. 6:11). Heb. *ḥārîṭ* indicates a bag large enough to hold two talents of silver (2 Kgs. 5:23) and is used to designate a woman's handbag (Isa. 3:22, KJV "crisping pins"). Both Heb. *kᵉlî* (1 Sam. 17:40) and Gk. *pḗra* (Matt. 10:10 par. Mark 6:8; Luke 9:3; KJV "scrip"; JB "haversack") refer to a shepherd's bag made of skin and sufficient for one or more days' provisions.

See also MONEY BOX.

BAGOAS [bə gō'əs] (Gk. *Bagoas*). The eunuch in charge of the personal affairs of the Assyrian general Holofernes (Jdt. 12:11). He was instructed to invite Judith to the general's banquet (v. 11) and later discovered her murder of Holofernes (14:14-18).

BAGPIPE. The RSV and JB translation of Aram. *sûmpōnyâ* as "bagpipe" in the list of instruments at Dan. 3:5, 10, 15 is not certain; the KJV renders the term "dulcimer" and the NIV "pipes." The LXX translates *symphōnía*, which suggests a harmony of sounds (cf. Luke 15:25, "music"). The order of the instruments as listed at Dan. 3:5ff. would favor a stringed or possibly percussion instrument.

BAHURIM [bə hyo͝or'ĭm] (Heb. *baḥûrîm* "young men"). A village just east of Mt. Scopus near Jerusalem, possibly Râs eṭ-Ṭmîm near eṭ-Ṭôr on the Mount of Olives. Here Paltiel and Michal parted as she was being returned to David (2 Sam. 3:16). David passed by the town in his flight from Absalom and was cursed by Shimei, a man of the house of Saul (16:5; 19:16ff.; 1 Kgs. 2:8). Shortly thereafter Jonathan and Ahimaaz, spying for David, hid in a well there (2 Sam. 17:18). A variant form of the name is Baharum (1 Chr. 11:33; KJV, NIV "Baharumites"; cf. KJV, NIV 2 Sam. 23:31 "Barhumites").

BAJITH [bā'jĭth] (Heb. *bayiṭ* "house"). A Moabite city east of the Dead Sea near Dibon (Isa. 15:2, KJV). Perhaps Heb. *baṭ-dîḇōn* should be read, rendered "daughter of Dibon" (RSV) and referring to a city (Jer. 48:18). Others read Heb. *bêṭ*, assuming it to be an abbreviation of *bêṭ gāmûl* ("Beth-gamul," v. 23) or a temple (JB "temple of Dibon"; NIV "its temple," i.e., of Dibon).

BAKBAKKAR [băk băk'ər] (Heb. *baqbaqqar*). A Levite who returned from the Captivity and was chosen by lot to dwell at Jerusalem (1 Chr. 9:15).

BAKBUK [băk'bŭk] (Heb. *baqbûq* "flask"). A temple servant whose descendants returned from the Captivity under Zerubbabel (Ezra 2:51; Neh. 7:53).

BAKBUKIAH [băk'bə kī'ə] (Heb. *baqbuqyâ* "the Lord's pitcher"). A Levite (Neh. 11:17) and descendant of Asaph the musician, he was one of those returning exiles who were designated by lot to live at Jerusalem. He was also a gatekeeper and the leader of a group of temple singers (12:9, 25).

BAKERS' STREET (Heb. *ḥûṣ hā᾿ōpîm*). A street in Jerusalem, apparently the place where members of the bakers' guild were concentrated (Jer. 37:21). Because

Heb. *ḥûṣ* has the more general meaning of "the out of doors" or "the ground between the houses" (KoB, p. 283), "bakers' quarter" would be a better translation.

BAKING. *See* BREAD.

BALAAM [bā'ləm] (Heb. *bil῾ām*, perhaps "devourer"). The son of Beor and resident of Pethor on the Euphrates (possibly Pitru on the Sajur river, a tributary of the Euphrates).

I. Narrative

Balaam must have been a noted Mesopotamian diviner. When the Israelites had encamped in the fields of Moab at the end of their long wilderness wanderings, Balak, the king of Moab, feared their strength and numbers. He sent messengers on the twenty-day journey to Mesopotamia in order to have Balaam come to Moab to curse Israel (Num. 22:1-6). When the messengers arrived at Pethor, Balaam refused to go with them, telling them that God had expressly forbidden him to accompany them (vv. 12-13). A second envoy was sent, and this time God granted Balaam permission to go on the condition that he would relay God's message (vv. 15-21). But when Balaam started the journey thinking only of the rewards Balak had promised, God's anger was kindled against him, and he sent an angel with a drawn sword to block his way (v. 22). Balaam's donkey saw the angel and tried to warn him (vv. 23-30), but Balaam himself was unable to see this miracle until a divine act opened his eyes (v. 31). Balaam then acknowledged his sin and offered to return home, but the angel bade him continue his mission (vv. 34-35).

Once Balaam reached Moab, Balak made the proper sacrificial preparations before letting the diviner discharge the duties he had been called on to perform. To Balak's deep indignation, however, Balaam proceeded to bless rather than curse Israel — not once but four times. The account concludes with Balak and Balaam each returning to his own home (24:25).

II. Apparent Problems

Two puzzling details of the narrative should not go unremarked. The first is that Balaam, a Gentile, knew the God of Israel. Some scholars assume that Balaam sought to participate in the power and wisdom of God and that Yahweh obliged him in this respect, but this cannot be demonstrated. However, since Balak summoned Balaam for his divinatory powers, he may have known that Balaam had a special relationship with Israel's God. Furthermore, on the basis of the Mari Letters, Balaam could have been a member of the Mesopotamian *bârû*-priests, priests who were also seers (Akk. *bârû*).

The second is the apparent inconsistency between God's granting Balaam permission to go to Balak and his sudden anger when Balaam actually leaves. While the narrative itself does not specifically mention the cause of God's anger, it appears from 2 Pet. 2:15 (Gk. *Balaam*) that it was Balaam's greed for money that prompted God to punish him. Critical scholars suggest that the difficulties here stem from the conflation of several sources.

III. The Oracles

In four oracles the Lord taught Balak that his plan to weaken Israel would be thwarted. In the first oracle the diviner, Balaam, acknowledges his own inability to curse a people God has blessed (23:7-10), adding in his second oracle that God's own faithfulness prevents him from turning his blessings for Israel into curses (vv. 18-24). Leaving aside all usual pagan omens (24:1), Balaam depicts Israel's future blessings in the third oracle (24:3-9) which will be consummated by Israel's defeat of Moab, as foretold in the last oracle (vv. 15-24). Balaam does not identify the "star of Jacob" or the "scepter"; they could refer to the Messiah. In this way the Spirit of God transformed Balaam's own powers of divination (24:2) and turned him into a prophet for the Lord.

IV. Balaam's Character

Although the narrative itself does not record any negative character traits of Balaam, it indicates that he did not wholeheartedly proclaim God's message. He may even have been vexed by his oracles, and, judging from 24:10, he may have been ousted by Balak without receiving his promised remuneration. Afterward, he is predominantly portrayed in an unfavorable light. Although in ch. 25 the narrative does not attribute Israel's spiritual adultery to Balaam's schemes, he is accused earlier of having counseled the Midianites (possibly Moab's allies [cf. 22:7]) to make the Israelites forsake the Lord and surrender themselves to the Moabite deity Baal-peor (31:16). This may have been the reason the Israelites also killed Balaam when they slaughtered the Midianites (31:8; cf. Josh. 13:22). Elsewhere in the Old Testament (Deut. 23:4, and repeated at Josh. 24:1-10; Neh. 13:2; Mic. 6:5) Balaam is shown in a more moderate light — he is only part of Balak's plot to plague Israel.

In the New Testament, on the other hand, Balaam is viewed either as a mad, wicked person (2 Pet. 2:15; Jude 11) or as one who enticed Israel to sin (Rev. 2:14). Interestingly, his wish to "die the death of the righteous" (Num. 23:10) is not mentioned again anywhere in the Bible.

Bibliography. W. F. Albright, "The Oracles of Balaam," *JBL* 63 (1944): 207-233; K. G. Kuhn, "Βαλαάμ," *TDNT* 1 (1964): 524-25.

BALAC (Rev. 2:14, KJV). *See* BALAK.

BALADAN [băl'ə dən] (Heb. *bal'ªḏān*). The father of Merodach-baladan, king of Babylon and contemporary of Hezekiah king of Judah (2 Kgs. 20:12 par. Isa. 39:1).

BALAH [bā'lə] (Heb. *bālâ*). An unknown city in the southern part of Palestine, assigned to Simeon (Josh. 19:3). It is also called Bilhah (1 Chr. 4:29) or Baalah (Josh. 15:29).

BALAK [bā'lăk] (Heb. *bālāq* "destroyer"). The son of Zippor and king of Moab, who was overcome with fear after the people of Israel had defeated the Amo-

rites and who summoned Balaam in order to curse them (Num. 22–24). After this attempt had failed, he followed Balaam's advice and seduced the people of Israel into idolatry and immorality (Rev. 2:14, Gk. *Balak*; KJV "Balac").

BALD(NESS). Being bald on the forehead (Heb. *gabbaḥaṭ*) or on top of the head (Heb. *qāraḥaṭ*) as such did not constitute for the Israelites a sign of uncleanness (Lev. 13:40-42). However, if baldness were the result of incipient leprosy, then it was considered ceremonial uncleanness (vv. 43-44). Intentional baldness as a mourning custom, particularly as practiced by Gentiles (Isa. 15:2; Jer. 48:37), was forbidden (Lev. 19:27-28; Deut. 14:1); this prohibition was repeated for the priests (Lev. 21:5; Ezek. 44:20). Intentional baldness was considered a sign of shame and contempt (Isa. 7:20; Ezek. 29:18; Amos 8:10) and of slavery (Isa. 3:24); accordingly, the epithet "bald head" implied contempt, hence Elisha's curse of the youths who chided his natural baldness (2 Kgs. 2:23-24). At Isa. 22:12 baldness is demanded as a token of repentance, while at Mic. 1:16 it is encouraged as a sign of mourning because of the deportation of fellow Israelites.

BALM (Heb. *ṣerî, ṣorî*). An aromatic, oily resin produced by the metabolism of various trees and shrubs and exuded when the tree is damaged. Its use for medicinal purposes is alluded to at Jer. 8:22; 46:11; it appears at Gen. 37:25 as an item of trade and at Gen. 43:11 as a gift.

BALM OF GILEAD. A substance with medicinal qualities mentioned at Jer. 8:22; 46:11 (Heb. *ṣorî*), possibly made in Gilead or simply exported from this region to Egypt (see Gen. 37:25) or Phoenicia (Ezek. 27:17). The name of the plant from which this aromatic resin is extracted is not identified (J. A. Thompson, *The Book of Jeremiah*. NICOT [1980], p. 690).

BALSAM. *See* SPICES.

BALSAM TREES. Trees mentioned at 2 Sam. 5:23-24; 1 Chr. 14:14-15 (so RSV, JB, NIV; KJV "mulberry trees"). Heb. *bāḵā'* probably indicates the mastic tree (*Pistacia lentiscus* L.), which is more of a shrub than a tree and secretes a milky sap. A prominent shrub in the Judean hill country, its many branches and hard leaves provide a suitable place of protection or concealment.

BAMOTH-BAAL [bā'mŏth bāl'] (Heb. *bāmôṭ-ba'al* "high places of Baal"). A place north of the Arnon to which Balak took Balaam to view and curse Israel (Num. 22:41). It was assigned to the tribe of Reuben, on whose border it lay, and is listed among the cities under the jurisdiction of Heshbon (Josh. 13:17). It is probably the Beth-bamoth mentioned in the Moabite Stone (line 27; cf. Bamoth, Num. 21:19-20). Although its precise location remains unknown, it was no doubt located on the western edge of the Transjordanian plateau in the region of Mt. Nebo.

The numerous dolmens (boxlike burial structures

consisting of upright stones topped by one horizontal capstone) found on the heights of this area suggest that a temple stood on the peak of this plateau, flanked by dolmens erected in a circle by pilgrims who had come here to fulfill a vow. Sacrifices such as those offered by Balak (Num. 23:2-6) may have been associated with these structures.

BANI [bā´nî] (Heb. *bānî* "founder"; perhaps an abbreviated form of Benaiah).

1. A Gadite, one of David's mighty men (2 Sam. 23:36).

2. A Levite of the line of Merari and a temple singer during the reign of David (1 Chr. 6:46).

3. A man from the tribe of Judah, who was a descendant of Perez (1 Chr. 9:4).

4. Descendants of a Bani appear among those returning from Exile under Zerubbabel (Ezra 2:10; at Neh. 7:15 Bani is called Binnui) and under Ezra (Ezra 8:10).

5. A family, several of whom married foreigners (Ezra 10:29, 34).

6. The father of Rehum, the Levite who worked at the restoration of the walls of Jerusalem (Neh. 3:17).

7. One of the Levites who explained the words of the law which Ezra read to the people (Neh. 8:7). He also took part in the public prayer (9:4-5) and set his seal to the renewed covenant under Nehemiah (10:13).

8. Another Levite who took part in the public prayer in the time of Ezra (Neh. 9:4).

9. One of the "chiefs of the people," who set his seal to the renewed covenant under Nehemiah (Neh. 10:15).

10. The father of Uzzi, the overseer of the Levites at Jerusalem (Neh. 11:22).

BANK. A term occurring in the parable of the pounds (Matt. 25:27, Gk. *trapezítēs*; KJV "exchangers"; Luke 19:23, Gk. *trápeza* "table"). As part of the business of receiving, disbursing, and safeguarding money, some bankers in the ancient Near East loaned funds at interest and exchanged money. In this parable the master scolded his one servant for failure to put his money in the bank, not for safekeeping but for the sake of earning interest. At least in this way the servant would turn the amount entrusted to him into some profit, "high by modern standards, but low in comparison with what the other servants had been able to earn by trading" (I. H. Marshall, *Comm. on Luke*. NIGTC [1978], p. 707).

See also INTEREST; MONEY-CHANGER.

BANNER. The Hebrew terms generally translated "banner" refer either to an identification mark, such as an emblem (usually Heb. *nēs*), or to the colors or standard (Heb. *degel*, e.g., Num. 1:52) around which soldiers rallied in battle. A banner might be a signal (Isa. 5:26; 13:2; 18:3; 30:17; 49:22) or a warning (Num. 26:10).

During the wilderness journey each Israelite tribe had its own banner or standard (Num. 2:2; cf. 1:52). A single standard represented each division of three tribes as the twelve tribes encamped around the tabernacle (2:3, 10, 18, 25, 34) and as they marched (10:14, 18, 22, 25).

Although the precise nature of the Israelite banners is not known, they may have resembled those of other ancient nations, taking the form of an animal image affixed to a pole or spear (as contended by the Targum; cf. Num. 21:8-9 and the symbols in Gen. 49) or names or inscriptions (as indicated in the Qumran War Scroll [1QM]). Moses himself, arms outstretched and holding the rod of God (Exod. 17:9), became a living banner. The altar at Rephidim he called "The Lord is my banner" (v. 15; KJV "Jehovah-nissi"); the Hebrew translated "banner of the Lord" at v. 16 is obscure and may indicate either the altar or the throne of the Lord.

"An army with banners" (Cant. 6:4, 10; Heb. *niḏgālôt*) symbolizes the overpowering love of the lover (cf. 2:4).

BANQUET. *See* MEALS.

BAPTISM. Rite of initiation into the Christian community.

I. Biblical Teachings

A. Origin. The New Testament never mentions the origin of the rite of baptism, but passages such as Acts 2:38, 41 suggest that it was a well known and common rite in the early Church. It most likely arose among Christians from the Jewish practice of baptizing Gentile converts to Judaism when they were circumcised.

B. Mode. At first baptism was accomplished by immersion. Jesus is said to have been coming "up . . . from the water" when John baptized him (Matt. 3:16 par. Mark 1:10; cf. Philip at Acts 8:38-39, going "down into the water" and coming "up out of the water"). It is possible, however, that sprinkling with water became the custom later when large numbers of people were baptized simultaneously (Acts 2:38). Linguistically, Gk. *baptízō* (an intensive form of the vb. *báptō* "dip," "immerse") need not imply baptism by immersion; at Luke 11:38 Jesus "did . . . wash (Gk. *ebaptísthē*, lit. "was washed") before dinner."

C. Initial Practice. 1. John. Baptism (Gk. *báptisma*, less commonly Gk. *baptismós*) is first mentioned in connection with John (who was called the "Baptist" [Gk. *ho baptistḗs*, e.g., Matt. 3:1]), probably because he baptized Jews rather than Gentiles (cf. Mark 1:5). John baptized people during or after their confession of sins (Matt. 3:6). His baptism was called a "baptism of repentance for the forgiveness of sins" (Mark 1:4; cf. Matt. 3:2, 6) signifying that a spiritual change had to take place in recipients which in turn would result in forgiveness of their sins. (That Jesus was also baptized by John does not militate against this interpretation, for the Lord's baptism was a fulfillment of "all righteousness" [Matt. 3:15]).

Contrasting his own baptismal practice with that of Jesus, John states that Christ's baptism would involve the Holy Spirit and fire (Matt. 3:11 par.). This contrast does not imply that John's baptism lacked authenticity, for those baptized by him had no need to be rebaptized. The account at Acts 19:1-7 does not contradict this interpretation because the twelve men rebaptized at the church of Ephesus had been baptized into John's baptism when this rite had ceased to be permissible; see also F. F. Bruce, *The Book of the Acts*. NICNT

(1954), pp. 385-87. But John's baptism was not complete, and would only be complete with the outpouring of the Holy Spirit at Pentecost (Acts 2:3-4).

2. *Jesus*. The Lord himself did not baptize during his earthly ministry. After John's baptism had achieved its purpose (repentance), Jesus' disciples practiced baptism in the Lord's name. (For Paul's charge that Christ did not send him to baptize [1 Cor. 1:17], see F. W. Grosheide, *The First Epistle to the Corinthians*. NICNT [1953], pp. 39-40; G. C. Berkouwer, *The Sacraments* [Grand Rapids: 1969], p. 119.) John's role was a transitional one, with complete baptism after the Spirit's activity within the Church. Interestingly, Christ referred to his own death as a kind of baptism (Luke 12:50).

Upon his ascension into heaven Jesus commanded his apostles to baptize in (Gk. *eis* "into") "the name of the Father and of the Son and of the Holy Spirit" (Matt. 28:19). That people sometimes are baptized only in the name of "Jesus Christ" (Acts 2:38; 10:48) or of "the Lord Jesus" (8:16; 19:5) rather than into the name of the triune God probably is due to Luke's emphasis on baptism as the means of bringing Gentiles and Samaritans into the Church of Christ.

D. Infant Baptism. Infant baptism remains for many a controversial issue, for the New Testament neither presents a clear case for the practice nor commands its observance in any specific words. It cannot be established conclusively when the early Church began to baptize children. However, given the practices of circumcision and the baptism of proselytes, it is likely that the children of converted Christians as well as those born within Christian families were baptized from the earliest times. Many early accounts attest to the baptism of infants as general practice in Asia Minor, France, Italy, North Africa, Egypt, and Palestine (as early as A.D. 200). No accounts have survived indicating debates over the issue as could be expected if the early Church had invented the rite during the second century rather than having received the tradition from the apostles.

The New Testament does indicate that the apostles baptized households (Acts 16:15, 33; 1 Cor. 1:16), a term which in Semitic usage would encompass children; in Old Testament times the Jews baptized not only adult proselytes but their children as well (1 Cor. 7:14 may be understood to include children). Paul relates the Old Testament rite of circumcision performed on children as a symbol of God's covenant with Abraham (Acts 2:39; cf. Gen. 17:7, 12ff.); in Col. 2:11-12 he interprets baptism as replacing circumcision in New Testament practice. Thus infant baptism cannot be rejected without doing violence to the unity between the Old and New Testaments.

E. Meaning. The New Testament does not spell out the meaning of the rite of baptism. For adults, baptism (in connection with profession of faith) signifies and seals the promise of the gospel, that they are visibly incorporated into the Church as a community of believers. At 1 Cor. 12:12-13 Paul, who baptized only a few persons, links baptism with entrance into the one Church. At Tit. 3:5 the apostle speaks of the "washing of regeneration" which urges believers to unburden themselves of sin and renew their lives; at Rom. 6:3-4 he relates baptism to Christ's death; and at Gal. 3:26-

27 he ties it to faith and to unity with others and with God.

A difficult passage is 1 Cor. 15:29, which mentions a baptism "on behalf of the dead." Though some scholars consider this a baptism on the grave of one deceased or a literal baptism of death — a so-called "blood baptism" or martyrdom — thus far a completely satisfactory solution concerning its meaning and significance has not been supplied (see Grosheide, p. 373; F. F. Bruce, *I & II Corinthians*. NCBC [1980], pp. 148-49; *ISBE* 1 [1979]: 426).

II. Theological Reflections

Although nearly all Christians accept the sacrament of baptism, they do not all agree on its interpretation. Baptists, for example, insist on immersion as the proper form and stipulate that only adults may be baptized. Other Protestants have appealed to biblical passages suggesting that sprinkling is adequate and, along with Roman Catholics, accept the administration of the rite to infants. Protestants and Catholics are not agreed upon the issue of baptismal regeneration (rebirth), and charismatics claim the necessity of baptism in the Spirit. Unfortunately, the various viewpoints frequently stem from different biblical texts, and the various denominations interpret key texts in different ways.

See also SACRAMENTS.

Bibliography. G. R. Beasley-Murray, *Baptism in the New Testament* (Grand Rapids: 1962); O. Cullmann, *Baptism in the New Testament* (London: 1950); J. Jeremias, *Infant Baptism in the First Four Centuries* (London: 1960); H. G. Marsh, *The Origin and Significance of the New Testament Baptism* (Manchester: 1941); J. Murray, *Christian Baptism* (Philadelphia: 1952); A. Oepke, "βάπτω," *TDNT* 1 (1964): 529-546.

BAR [bär] (Aram. [*bar*] for Heb. *bēn* "son"). Outside the Aramaic sections of Ezra and Daniel the term occurs at Ps. 2:12 ("Son," KJV, NIV; RSV, JB "his first," following the proposed emendation Heb. *raglāy*) and three times at Prov. 31:2. In the New Testament it is the prefix of such names as Bar-Jesus (Acts 13:6), Bar-Jona (Matt. 16:17), and Barnabas (Acts 4:36).

BAR. Several times the Old Testament speaks of bars being used to lock the gates of cities (Heb. *berîah*, Deut. 3:5; Judg. 16:3; 1 Kgs. 4:13; Neh. 3:3, 13-15; Ps. 147:13; etc.), the doors of houses (2 Sam. 13:17-18), and prisons (Ps. 107:16 par. "doors"); according to Josephus (*BJ* iv.4.6 [298]), the doors of the temple were locked in the same manner (cf. 1 Sam. 3:15; Ezek. 41:23ff.). Such bars, usually wooden beams though sometimes made from iron (Ps. 107:16; Isa. 45:2) or bronze (1 Kgs. 4:13), were inserted into holes in the doorposts on the inner side of the door or gate and were held in place by means of pegs. Another type of bar could be drawn into a locked position from the outside by hand or with a strap; opening such locked doors required a key (Judg. 3:25).

A city with gates and bars was considered safe. Obversely, a city that lost its bars was viewed as fallen (e.g., Amos 1:5; NIV "gate"; JB "gate bars").

Metaphorically bars refer to the domain of the underworld (Heb. *bāḏ*, Job 17:16; NIV "gates"; JB following LXX "with me") or of the sea (38:10; JB "bolted [gate]"). At Lev. 26:13 (Heb. *môṭâ*; KJV "bands"; JB "that bound you") they symbolize oppression.

BARABBAS [bə răb′əs]. A man held in prison at the time of Jesus' trial and chosen by the crowd over Jesus (Matt. 27:16-26 par. Mark 15:6-15; Luke 23:13-25; cf. John 18:39-40). His name may point to a rabbi (Gk. *Barabbas* from Aram. *bar'abbā'* "son of the father") as his father, and thus to a noble birth.

According to John 18:40 he was a robber (perhaps one of the Sicarii); the term (Gk. *lēstēs*) may refer to the zealots' aim to liberate Israel from Roman oppression (see K. H. Rengstorf, *TDNT* 4 [1967]: 261-62). The New Testament does not say that he committed a murder (at Luke 23:19 "for murder" may mean that Barabbas was among those "who had committed murder"; cf. Mark 15:5; Matthew calls Barabbas simply a "notorious prisoner," Matt. 27:16).

According to an ancient tradition Barabbas was named Jesus Barabbas. In that case Pilate would have been asking the crowd to choose between Jesus of Nazareth and Jesus Barabbas.

Bibliography. R. E. Brown, *The Gospel according to John.* AB (1970), pp. 870-72; W. L. Lane, *The Gospel of Mark.* NICNT (1974), pp. 553-54.

BARACHEL [bär′ə kĕl] (Heb. *bārak̄'el* "God blesses"). A Buzite and father of Elihu, Job's fourth friend (Job 32:2, 6; NIV "Barakel").

BARACHIAH [bar′ə kī′ə] (Gk. *Barachias*). The father of Zechariah (Matt. 23:35; KJV "Barachias"; NIV "Berakiah"), possibly the Zechariah who was murdered in the house of the Lord (2 Chr. 24:20-23; so JB note at Matt. 23:35). Some identify him with BERECHIAH 7.

BARAK [bâr′ək] (Heb. *bārāq* "lightning"). The son of Abinoam of Kedesh in Naphtali. Deborah summoned and commissioned him in the name of the Lord to go up to Mt. Tabor with ten thousand men from the tribes of Naphtali and Zebulun to fight against Sisera, the general of King Jabin, who had oppressed Israel for twenty years (Judg. 4:3-7). Barak was willing to fulfill this commission, but only on the condition that Deborah accompany him. Deborah agreed to this, but prophesied that the Lord would "sell Sisera into the hand of a woman" (v. 9). Her words came true after Barak had defeated Sisera. Jael, the wife of Heber the Kenite, killed the general as he was resting in her tent (vv. 12-22).

Barak is included among those judges who delivered Israel at 1 Sam. 12:11 (following the LXX, Syr.; KJV "Bedan," following the MT). In the New Testament he is listed among the heroes of faith (Heb. 11:32), possibly because his refusal to fight may have been Barak's own way of expressing his faith (F. F. Bruce, *The Epistle to the Hebrews.* NICNT [1964], p. 332).

BARBARIAN (Gk. *bárbaros*). To the Greeks everyone who did not speak the Greek language was a barbarian. Thus the word had a linguistic and cultural reference; it was not a contemptuous or coarse expression. In the New Testament all who did not share the Greco-Roman culture were called barbarian ("natives," Acts 28:2, 4 [NIV "islanders"; JB "inhabitants"]; "barbarians," Rom. 1:14 [NIV "non-Greeks"]; Col. 3:11). At 1 Cor. 14:11, Paul uses the word metaphorically in the sense of "one who is not understood, a foreigner" (JB "savage"). When at Luke 17:18 Jesus calls the leper a "foreigner" (KJV "stranger"), he uses Gk. *allogenēs*, a word which appeared in the inscription in the outer court of the temple forbidding Gentiles to enter the temple court.

BARBER. *See* KNIFE.

BAREFOOT. While it was customary in biblical times for people to wear sandals when traveling, at times they went barefooted. Such an act was a sign of reverence (in a religious context; cf. the removal of the sandals by Moses [Exod. 3:5] and Joshua [Josh. 5:15] when addressed by God in a theophany), of mortification (2 Sam. 15:30), and of mourning (2 Sam. 15:30; Ezek. 24:17, 23). Furthermore, it indicated enslavement (during war, e.g., Isa. 20:2-4) and shame (at the refusal of a levirate marriage [Deut. 25:9-10; cf. Ruth 4:7 where it refers to the redemption of a piece of property and of Ruth the widow]).

A difficult point is the contrast between the sending of the disciples (Matt. 10:5ff. par. Mark 6:7ff.; Luke 9:1ff.) and the sending of the seventy(-two) other disciples (Luke 10:1-12). While the former are allowed to wear sandals (Gk. *sandálion*, Mark 6:9, but cf. Matt. 10:10), the latter are instructed not to go on sandals (Gk. *hypódēma*; KJV "shoes"). The "apparent contradiction" (*TDNT* 5 [1967]: 311) may be removed by considering the second (more austere) sending to be original and by interpreting it as an example of unquestioning faith in God's ability to provide for the disciples' needs. Some older commentaries point to the fact that the disciples were to precede the arrival of the Lord himself (10:1) and thus interpret the passage allegorically.

BARIAH [bə rī′ə] (Heb. *bārîaḥ* "fugitive"). A son of Shemaiah, a descendant of David (1 Chr. 3:22).

BARIS [bär′ĭs] (Gk. *báris*). A fortified tower in the northwest corner of Jerusalem, built by the Hasmoneans (who named it the Birah or "capital") on the northeast side of the temple court and rebuilt by the high priest John Hyrcanus (135-105 B.C.) after it had been destroyed by the Seleucids (who called it the Akra). This citadel was a replacement for or restoration of the fortress mentioned at Neh. 2:8; 7:2. The tower was connected to the temple by means of bridges. Herod the Great modified and extended this structure to form the tower of Antonia. Paul was imprisoned here, and he spoke in his own defense while standing upon its steps (Acts 21:35–22:29).

BAR-JESUS [bär jē′zəs] (Gk. *Bariēsous*). *See* ELYMAS.

BAR-JONA [bär jō′nə]. Simon Peter's patronymic (Gk. *Bariōnas*; cf. Heb. *bar yônâ* "son of Jonah").

While at Matt. 16:17 the disciple is called Bar-Jona, the son of Jonah, at John 1:42; 21:15-17 he is named the son of John (KJV "Jona"). It is not certain whether Peter's father had two different names or a single Hebrew name rendered into Greek two different ways.

BAR KOKHBA [bär kŏk'bə] ("son of the star," derived from Num. 24:17, "a star [Heb. *kôkāḇ*] shall come forth out of Jacob"). Surname of Simon (or Simeon), leader of the second rebellion of the Jews against the Romans under Emperor Hadrian. The revolt, which lasted from A.D. 132 to 135, was prepared and supported by Rabbi Akiba. Akiba regarded Bar Kokhba as the Messiah who was to come, and approximately a half million Jews and Samaritans followed him. At first the Romans were repulsed and even forced to abandon Jerusalem. However, Julius Severus, a general summoned from Britain, was able to suppress the rebellion, and in 135 he conquered the city of Bether, Bar Kokhba's headquarters south of Jerusalem. Bar Kokhba was slain while defending Bether. His name has remained a symbol of the Jewish national consciousness, and since 1948 he has been honored in the modern state of Israel as one of the heroes of Jewish freedom.

Various documents discovered in the Judean desert, including Bar Kokhba's personal correspondence in Hebrew, Aramaic, and Greek, have shed light on both the man and the revolt. In these sources he is called by his opponents Bar Koziba, playing on Heb. *kāzāḇ* "a lie," and is accorded the title *nāśî'* (head of the government).

BARKOS [bär'kŏs] (Heb. *barqôs*). A temple servant whose descendants returned from Exile with Zerubbabel (Ezra 2:53; Neh. 7:55).

BARLEY. Barley was the second most important (cf. Deut. 8:8) bread grain in Palestine, being a popular source of food during times of scarcity, especially for the lower classes (e.g., Ruth 2:17), and also serving as provender for horses (1 Kgs. 4:28). It was baked in loaves that were flat and round. Barley sold for half the price of wheat (2 Kgs. 7:1); the value of arable land was assessed in accordance with its yield of barley (Lev. 27:16).

Barley was planted in October, after the "early rains," and it ripened in the spring (March) as the first of the winter grains (Exod. 9:31-32; 2 Sam. 21:9); the harvest took place in March or April. Several kinds of barley, variously having two-, four-, and six-rowed ears of grain, were cultivated, the most common being *Hordeum vulgare* L. and *Hordeum hexastichon*. The plant was clearly distinguished from wheat by the long awns of its chaff (cf. its Hebrew name *śeʿōrâ* "hairy, bristly").

BARN. *See* AGRICULTURE.

BARNABAS [bär'nə bəs] (Gk. *Barnabas*, either "son of consolation" [so KJV] or "son of encouragement" [so RSV, JB, NIV]). The name given to Joseph, a Levite from the island of Cyprus (Acts 4:36).

Barnabas became a Christian early in life, and one of his first acts as a believer was to sell a parcel of land and give the money he received to the apostles for distribution to the poor (v. 37). It was he who brought Paul, after his conversion, to the apostles at Jerusalem (9:27), and it was he who was sent to the newly founded church at Antioch (Syria) (11:22). His successful ministry among the relocated Christians in that city prompted him to secure Paul's assistance, and together they taught many people (vv. 25-26). After a while they brought the money collected in Antioch to the poor at Jerusalem (vv. 29-30).

According to 13:2 both Barnabas and Paul were commissioned by the Spirit to do mission work. During their labors at Cyprus and throughout the first part of their stay in Asia Minor, Barnabas was the chief spokesman. But during the last part of their journey, Paul took over the role of leader. At Lystra Paul was called Hermes (because he was the real speaker) and Barnabas Zeus (14:12). After the first missionary journey both were sent to Jerusalem as delegates to the apostolic Council (15:2), and both were instructed to relay its decisions to the churches (vv. 22ff.).

When Paul invited Barnabas to accompany him on his second missionary journey, they disagreed about whether or not John Mark should join them, and they parted ways; Barnabas took Mark and revisited Cyprus (15:36-39). It appears, though, that their rift was not deep-seated, for Paul continued to speak favorably of his former coworker (1 Cor. 9:6; cf. Gal. 2:1, 9, 13) and paid Mark a compliment (2 Tim. 4:11).

See also BARNABAS, ACTS OF; BARNABAS, EPISTLE OF.

BARNABAS, ACTS OF.† A late (fifth century A.D.) New Testament apocryphal writing, of which only a Greek text has survived; the original, perhaps gnostic, version has been lost. The author of the work, which appears to be dependent on the canonical book of Acts, is unknown. The book is spuriously attributed to Barnabas, a Levite from Cyprus and coworker of Paul.

BARNABAS, EPISTLE OF. One of the writings of the Apostolic Fathers, written *ca.* A.D. 130. Though Clement and Origen ascribed this work to Barnabas, Paul's coworker (most likely because they shared the epistle's allegorical method of explaining Scripture), and considered it canonical, Eusebius and Jerome regarded it noncanonical. The Codex Sinaiticus, however, included the work among the canonical books. Today, scholars commonly consider it a pseudepigraphal work, composed by a Gentile Christian of Alexandria rather than by the Barnabas mentioned in the New Testament.

The epistle consists of four sections: an introduction (ch. 1); a description of the nature of Christian life (chs. 2-17); an exposition of practical rules for living (chs. 18-20); and a conclusion (ch. 21). Its aim is to set forth a correct (i.e., spiritual) view of the Old Testament, in contrast to the literal view defended by the Jews. Furthermore, it claims that Christians are the true covenant people, who are admonished to walk according to the way of light rather than by the way of darkness (ch. 20).

BARSABBAS [bär săb'əs] (Gk. *Barsabbas* "son of Saba" or "son of the Sabbath").

1. Joseph, who was surnamed Justus ("the just one"). Lots were cast to determine whether he or Matthias would replace Judas Iscariot as an apostle (Acts 1:23).

2. Surname of Judas, who was sent with Silas to assist Paul and Barnabas at Antioch (Acts 15:22). Like Silas, he was a prophet (v. 32).

BARTHOLOMEW [bär thŏl'ə mū] (Gk. *Bartholomaios*; Aram. *bar tōlmay* "son of Tolmai"). One of the twelve disciples. Because he is always listed after Philip (Matt. 10:3 par. Mark 3:18; Luke 6:14), sometimes shortly thereafter (Acts 1:13), scholars have identified him with Nathanael, who, according to John (John 1:45-51; cf. 21:2), was led to Jesus by Philip. Other identifications are still possible, however (see L. Morris, *The Gospel According to John*. NICNT [1971], pp. 163ff.).

According to tradition (Eusebius *HE* v.10.3) Bartholomew preached the gospel in India. He died as a martyr by being drowned (cf. the apocryphal Martyrdom of Bartholomew). Jerome (preface to *Comm. Matt.*) mentions a gospel of Bartholomew.

BARTHOLOMEW, GOSPEL OF. One of the New Testament apocryphal gospels (also called Questions of Bartholomew), originally written in Greek, of which Coptic, Latin, and Slavonic recensions have survived. It is dated *ca.* A.D. 400. The work consists of a number of questions which Bartholomew addresses to the risen Lord, Mary, and Satan. It discusses such topics as Christ's descent into hell, the number of souls lost or saved daily, and marriage and virginity.

BARTHOLOMEW THE APOSTLE, BOOK OF. A Coptic writing, probably from the fifth century A.D. or later, consisting of various apocryphal tales purportedly related by Bartholomew to his son Thaddaeus. The work has survived only in fragmentary form.

BARTIMAEUS [bär tə mē'əs] (Gk. *Bartimaios*; possibly Aram. *bar ṭim'ay* "son of Timai"). A blind beggar from Jericho whom the Lord healed as he traveled toward Jerusalem (Mark 10:46-52 par.); that his father had a Greek name need not necessarily imply that Bartimaeus himself was a Hellenist.

Upon hearing that Jesus was passing by, blind Bartimaeus hailed him, calling him "Son of David" (vv. 47-48), convinced no doubt that the Savior would be able to restore his sight. This name may have messianic overtones; at least Jesus did not command him to be silent (as did the people in the crowd who considered his shouting a nuisance). After he was healed Bartimaeus used the respectful title "Rabbi" (Gk. *rhabbouní*, v. 51; *kyrie*, Matt. 20:33 par. Luke 18:41).

BARUCH [bâr'ək] (Heb. *bārûḵ* "blessed").

1. The son of Zabbai. He was involved in the rebuilding of the walls of Jerusalem (Neh. 3:20).

2. A priest who set his seal to the renewed covenant under Nehemiah (Neh. 10:6). He may be the same as **1**.

3. A man from the tribe of Judah. The father of Maaseiah, he was among those who dwelt in Jerusalem (Neh. 11:5).

4. The son of Neriah, and secretary (Jer. 36:4ff., 32) and personal friend (32:12) of the prophet Jeremiah. He may have been of noble birth, given that his brother Seraiah was the quartermaster of King Zedekiah (51:59).

In the fourth year of Jehoiakim (605/4 B.C.) Baruch was asked by Jeremiah to record "all the words of the Lord" spoken to him (36:4). (Though most scholars are unable to reconstruct the content of the scroll on which this request was found, many identify it with the poetic oracles or with the prose discourses found in chs. 1–25 of the book of Jeremiah [see J. A. Thompson, *The Book of Jeremiah*. NICOT (1980), p. 59; see also Keil, *Comm. Jeremiah* (pp. 27ff.) for an older opinion].) Baruch not only complied with Jeremiah's request, but sometime later also read this scroll in the temple (36:10). The royal princes (v. 15), who then summoned Baruch to read to them from the scroll, relayed its horrible message to the king (v. 20). The king in turn read parts of it before burning it. He then ordered that Baruch and Jeremiah be arrested, but the Lord hid them (vv. 22-26). Again Jeremiah asked his amanuensis to record God's oracles against Judah, and once more Baruch wrote down the words of the scroll burned by Jehoiakim, as well as "many similar words" (vv. 27-32). In ch. 45 Baruch is comforted in his state of despondency induced by the recording of these oracles, but he is also warned that his loyalty to Jeremiah would bar him from any future success.

Near the end of Jerusalem's siege by Nebuchadnezzar, Baruch assisted Jeremiah with the purchase of a field (32:12-15) to keep the family from losing property. After the fall of the city and the murder of the governor Gedaliah, both Baruch and Jeremiah were taken to Egypt by fellow Jews (43:6); most likely Baruch was stoned there by his own people (cf. ch. 44). According to Josephus (*Ant.* x.9.1), during the conquest of Jerusalem Nebuzaradan gave Baruch and Jeremiah their freedom at the prophet's request.

The high regard in which Baruch was held is evidenced further by a great number of apocryphal writings attributed to him, such as the book of Baruch and the Apocalypse of Baruch. Other such writings include the Rest of the Words of Baruch, in which Baruch appears in Jerusalem after the deportation of the Jews to Babylon; Ethiopian; Slavonic, and Latin apocalypses of Baruch; and a gnostic book of Baruch, in which Baruch takes the form of an angel and brings a revelation.

BARUCH, APOCALYPSE OF.† A Jewish pseudepigraphal writing. Although both a Greek and a Syriac version have survived, the work was probably originally written in Hebrew or Aramaic shortly after the fall of Jerusalem in A.D. 70. Marked by a legalistic concept of righteousness, it may have been written in imitation of 4 Ezra. The book begins in Jerusalem with the revelation to Baruch, scribe of Jeremiah, of the city's imminent destruction by the Chaldeans. There follow, in the form of a dialogue with God, revelations interpreting the fall of the city as divine judgment (chs. 9–20), as well as the final woes, judgment, the messiah, and the messianic kingdom (chs. 21–34). Also included are a series of allegorical visions concerning the coming of the kingdom, depicted in terms of a forest, a mighty cedar, a fountain, and a vine (chs. 35–46); an account of the resurrection of the righteous and the fate of the wicked (chs. 47–52); and a final vision describing the entire course of history in apocalyptic terms (chs. 53–74).

BARUCH, BOOK OF.† A book of the Old Testament Apocrypha, attributed to Baruch, the secretary of Jeremiah. Scholars agree that it consists of three distinct sections written by different authors and combined by a later editor. Although the book survives in a Greek version (with later translations into Syriac, Latin, Arabic, Ethiopic, Coptic, and Armenian), its poetic parallelism and the book's early liturgical use point to a Hebrew original. The first (prose) section has been dated to the middle of the second century B.C.; the poetic sections may be as late as A.D. 70 but more probably were written in the late Maccabean period, ca. 70 B.C.

In pseudepigraphic fashion, the book depicts Baruch as appearing in Babylon among the exiles. The work constitutes a veritable anthology of quotations from such canonical writings as Jeremiah, Daniel, Job, and Isa. 40–56. The first section (1:1–3:8) includes a historical introduction, a prayer of confession, and a penitential prayer. A poetic section (3:9–4:4) praises Wisdom as God's special gift (the Torah) to Israel. The book concludes with a poetic prayer of lamentation and consolation (4:5–5:9).

Some versions and English translations include as a sixth chapter the so-called Letter of Jeremiah. *See* JEREMIAH, EPISTLE OF.

BARZILLAI [bär zĭl′ī] (Heb. *bārzillay*).

1. A prominent Gileadite of Rogelim who provided various necessities for David and his army during the king's flight from his son Absalom (2 Sam. 17:27-29). After David's victory, Barzillai provided an escort across the Jordan. Because he was eighty years old he declined the king's invitation to join the royal court at Jerusalem, persuading David to substitute his son Chimham (19:31-40). Before his death the king directed his successor Solomon to "deal loyally" with the sons of Barzillai (1 Kgs 2:7).

2. A Meholathite, father of Adriel, the husband of Saul's daughter Merab (1 Sam. 18:19; "Michal" at 2 Sam. 21:8 should be read "Merab").

3. A priest and son-in-law of Barzillai the Gileadite (1), whose name he assumed. According to 1 Esdr. 5:38 his name was originally Jaddus (KJV "Addus"). Because of the name change his descendants were unable after the Exile to prove from the genealogies that they belonged to Israel and accordingly were excluded from the priesthood (Ezra 2:61; Neh. 7:63-64).

BASEMATH [băs′ə măth] (Heb. *bāsᵉmaṯ* "balsam" or "fragrance").

1. One of Esau's wives (KJV "Bashemath") and mother of Reuel (Gen. 36:4, 13, 17). At 26:34 (JB "Basemath") she is called a daughter of Elon the Hittite, whereas at 36:3 she is said to be Ishmael's daughter (at 36:2 Adah is called the daughter of Elon the Hittite). She is probably the same as Mahalath (**1**) at 28:9.

2. The daughter of Solomon and wife of Ahimaaz, Solomon's officer in Naphtali (1 Kgs. 4:15).

BASHAN [bā′shən] (Heb. *habbāšān* "fruitful"). A region in Transjordan, north of Gilead and east of the Sea of Galilee. In general, it extended to Mt. Hermon on the north and the Hauran mountains on the east, with the Yarmuk river as its approximate southern border (Josh. 12:5). Its principal cities were Golan (Deut. 4:43), Ashtaroth, Edrei (1:4), and Salecah (3:10).

Having been victorious over the Amorites, the Israelites continued their march northward to Bashan, the territory of Og (one of the surviving Rephaim [3:11]). After defeating Og at Edrei (Num. 21:33-35; Deut. 3:1-3), they assigned his land mainly to the half-tribe of Manasseh (Deut. 3:13; cf. Num. 32:33). At the beginning of the divided monarchy Bashan belonged to the northern kingdom, but during the reigns of Ahab (1 Kgs. 22:3), Joram (2 Kgs. 8:28), and Jehu (2 Kgs. 10:33) it fell partly or entirely into Syrian hands. Though Jeroboam II was able to reconquer it (2 Kgs. 14–25), Tiglath-pileser III soon incorporated it into his Assyrian Empire (15:29). In the New Testament the area included Gaulanitis, Trachanitis, and Batanea, which were part of Philip's tetrarchy (cf. Luke 3:1, "Trachonitis").

As a fertile plain, Bashan provided luxuriant pastures and prosperity in general (Jer. 50:19; Mic. 7:14). Its famous oak trees were exported to Tyre (Ezek. 27:6), and still grace the plateau. The "mountain of Bashan" (Ps. 68:15) is identified with Jebel Ḥaurân.

Metaphorically, the "bulls of Bashan" (Ps. 22:12) were the unrighteous, and the "cows of Bashan" (Amos 4:1) were the fun-loving women of Samaria who disregarded the needs of the poor. At Isa. 2:13 the "proud and lofty" are compared to the oaks of Bashan.

See also ARGOB; HAURAN.

BASHEMATH. *See* BASEMATH **1.**

BASILIDES [băs′ĭ lĭ′dēz], **GOSPEL OF.** An apocryphal gospel, perhaps a commentary on Luke in which the author attempted to set forth his own contrasting views. The work is attributed to Basilides, a second-century A.D. Gnostic. It is cited by various of the Church Fathers, but of its twenty-four books only a few brief quotations have survived (cf. Clement *Misc.* iv.7).

See GNOSTICISM.

BASIN. The Hebrews used several words to designate an open vessel. Heb. *ᵃgarṭāl* is probably a basket (so KoB, p. 9; RSV "basin," Ezra 1:9; KJV "charger"; NIV "dish"; JB "bowl"), while Heb. *'aggān* is a bowl (so NIV, Exod. 24:6). Heb. *mizrāq* (< Heb. *zāraq* "sprinkle") is a deep bowl into which was poured the blood of the slaughtered animals to be sprinkled on the sides of the altar of burnt offering (Exod. 29:15; cf. 38:3).

The vessel (Gk. *niptér*, from *níptō* "wash off") in which Jesus washed his disciples' feet (John 13:5) may have been a kind of basin, though normally the Jews washed their feet by pouring water over them.

BASKET. In the Old Testament several Hebrew words are rendered "basket." Heb. *dûḏ* may refer to the basket in which the Israelites carried fruit (Jer. 24:1-2) or clay for making bricks in Egypt (Ps. 81:6). Heb. *ṭene'* is a large, deep basket used for carrying the first of the fruit (Deut. 26:2, 4); summer fruit was put into a *kᵉlûḇ* (Amos 8:1). The basket of the baker in prison was a flat basket without a lid, able to contain wares (Gen. 40:16, Heb. *sal*; JB "trays").

Moses' basket was made of bulrushes or papyrus, rendered waterproof with bitumen and mud (Exod. 2:3, 5); according to v. 6 it could be opened. The Hebrew term (*tēḇâ*) means chest (KoB, p. 1017).

In the New Testament Gk. *kóphinos* is a large basket in which bread could be carried (Matt. 14:20 par. Mark 6:43; Luke 9:17 [NIV "basketfuls"]; John 6:13). The basket mentioned at the feeding of the four thousand is Gk. *spyrís* (Matt. 15:37 par. Mark 8:8, 20; NIV "basketfuls"), which was large enough to lower Paul from the wall (Acts 9:25; cf. 2 Cor. 11:33, Gk. *sargánē*, a plaited basket). At Matt. 16:9-10 par. Mark 8:19-20 *kóphinos* and *spyrís* are contrasted.

BASTARD. A name given to those begotten in adultery or incest (Heb. *mamzēr*, Deut. 23:2; NIV "born of a forbidden marriage"). This violation of marriage was such a serious offense that such persons and their descendants were denied admission to the assembly of the Lord, first in the temple and later in the synagogue, to the "tenth generation" (Deut. 23:2) — i.e., forever. (At Zech. 9:6 "a mongrel people" [KJV, JB "bastard"; NIV "foreigners"] refers to a nation of a mixed population.) Since they could not share in the solidarity of the family — its rights and responsibilities — the author of the book of Hebrews calls those not disciplined in the Lord "illegitimate children" (so RSV, NIV; KJV, JB "bastards"; Gk. *nóthos*).

BAT. A very common Palestinian mammal, living in the caves of the Jordan valley and the hill country, sometimes by the hundreds. Usually they are insect-eating animals except for the flying dog of Egypt (*Rousettus egyptiacus*), which feeds on the fruit of the sycamore trees. They have a large wingspan of 90-95 cm. (36-38 in.).

Bats were considered nocturnal birds in antiquity. Scripture mentions the bat as one of the unclean animals (Lev. 11:19; Deut. 14:18, Heb. *ᵃṭallep*). At Isa. 2:20 its dwelling place is in dark caves.

BATANEA [bat ə nē'ə]. Another name for BASHAN and one of the four areas of the kingdom of Herod the Great.

BATH (Heb. *baṭ*). A liquid measure (1 Kgs. 7:26, 38; 2 Chr. 2:10; 4:5; Ezra 7:22; Isa. 5:10). According to Ezek. 45:4, 14, it was one-tenth of a homer and thus the equivalent of the ephah, a dry measure. Excavations at Lachish have uncovered a broken jar, dated to the eighth century B.C., inscribed with the Hebrew letters *bt (lmlk)* "(royal) bath"; the volume of this jar is 22 liters (5.8 gal.).

See WEIGHTS AND MEASURES.

BATHING. In the warm and dusty climate of the ancient Near East frequent washing was essential, though the scarcity of water generally discouraged taking a complete bath. According to Exod. 2:5 members of Pharaoh's court customarily bathed themselves in the Nile, but Pharaoh's own "going out to the water" (7:15; 8:20) could refer to a festival in honor of the Nile deity. Excavations have unearthed Egyptian royal bathing rooms in which the bather sat while water was poured over him. The Babylonians and Assyrians practiced such customs as well. Seven toilets (each containing a large clay water jar and a tray) and five bath chambers have been excavated at Eshnunna in a palace dating to the dynasty of Akkad. The Assyrians, moreover, had bathtubs and footbaths (such as one discovered at Samaria dating *ca.* 900-600 B.C.).

In the Old Testament Heb. *rāḥaṣ* can mean "rinse," "wash" and "bathe" (KoB, p. 887). The Israelites washed their feet after every journey, thus removing the dust from their bodies (e.g., Gen. 18:4; 19:2; 24:32; 43:24); they also washed their hands (Exod. 30:19, 21) and face (Gen. 43:31). Full bathing occurred in the inner court of the homes belonging to the prominent (2 Sam. 11:2; KJV "washing"). While special occasions prompted washing oneself (Ruth 3:3), it was not done during mourning (2 Sam. 12:20; cf. 19:24). The priests were required to wash themselves while serving in the tabernacle and temple (Exod. 40:12; Lev. 8:6; 16:4, 24; Num. 19:7); the bronze laver in the court of the tabernacle (which must have contained faucets) fulfilled that purpose (Exod. 30:17-21). The requirements of ceremonial law stipulated that only the ceremonially clean could approach the Lord; bodily and cultic impurities were symbols of sin-stained imperfection and had to be cleansed (cf. the cleansing of lepers, Lev. 14:8; behavior around those with bodily discharges, 15:5; cleansing of other defilement, 17:15). Even Naaman, a Syrian general, was obliged to wash himself in the Jordan river before being cured of his leprosy (2 Kgs. 5:10). The practice of washing clothes was common and was observed especially for cultic reasons (cf. Heb. piel *kāḇas*, e.g., Exod. 19:10).

The Old Testament customs of washing and bathing recur in the New Testament. Mark records that washing one's hands before a meal had become a tradition (Mark 7:3; Gk. *níptō*), while John is particularly observant of rites of purification (cf. Jesus' summons to a blind man whom he had healed to wash himself in the pool of Siloam, John 9:7). (For John 13:10, *see* FOOTWASHING.)

In metaphorical use, a sword can be "bathed" in heaven (KJV, Isa. 34:5; RSV "drunk its fill"). At Ezek. 23:40 Israel is presented as a woman washing herself in preparation for meeting strangers. Pilate's gesture of washing his hands at the trial of Jesus to convey his innocence is well known (Matt. 27:24; cf. the gesture at Deut. 21:6-7; Ps. 26:6). In a religious context the Israelites are urged to wash themselves of their evil deeds (Isa. 1:16; cf. Heb. 10:22; see also

Acts 22:16), and God is said to be able to wash sinners clean of their sin (Isa. 4:4; cf. Ps. 51:2). Jeremiah contrasts the cleansing of the body with the inward spiritual cleansing necessary for salvation (Jer. 2:22; cf. 4:14).

BATH-RABBIM [băth răb'ĭm] (Heb. *baṭ-rabbîm* "daughter of the multitude"). A gate in the city of Heshbon (Cant. 7:4), facing Rabbah.

BATHSHEBA [băth shē'bə] (Heb. *baṭ-šeḇaʾ* "daughter of abundance"). The daughter of either Eliam (2 Sam. 11:3) or Ammiel (1 Chr. 3:5; here named Bath-shua; cf. NIV mg.) and granddaughter of Ahithophel (2 Sam. 23:34) the counselor of David and Absalom. David fell in love with her, and upon learning that she was carrying his child, had her husband, Uriah the Hittite, murdered (2 Sam. 11:2-21). She then became the king's wife, but the child of their adulterous act died (12:15-23). Later she became the mother of four sons: Shimea, Shobab, Nathan, and Solomon (1 Chr. 3:5; cf. 2 Sam. 3:5).

Upon the advice of Nathan the prophet, Bathsheba persuaded the aged king David to fulfill his oath to make Solomon his successor. In this way she also succeeded in blocking Adonijah's accession to the throne (1 Kgs. 1:11-53). Her attempt to have Adonijah marry Abishag (at Adonijah's own request) failed, however, and resulted in his execution (2:13-25).

In the New Testament, Bathsheba is included in the genealogy of Jesus (Matt. 1:6, the "wife of Uriah").

BATH-SHUA [băth shoo'ə] (Heb. *baṭ-šûaʿ* "daughter of Shua").

1. The Canaanite wife of Judah and the mother of his sons Er, Onan, and Shelah (1 Chr. 2:3). Her designation as the "daughter of Shua" (Gen. 38:2) is not intended to represent a proper name.

2. An alternate form of Bathsheba (1 Chr. 3:5).

BATTERING RAM. An instrument used in war to break through the walls of a besieged city (Ezek. 4:2; 21:22, Heb. *karîm*; 26:9, *mᵉḥî gōḇel*; KJV "engine of war"). It consisted of a movable wooden block (with a metal point) placed on a protected platform. The Israelites became acquainted with such engines of war in Egypt and afterward in Palestine.

BAVVAI [băv'ī] (Heb. *bawway*). The son of Henadad, the "ruler of half the district of Keilah" (Neh. 3:18). He was one of those Levites who aided in the restoration of the walls of Jerusalem under Nehemiah (vv. 17-18). He may be the same as Binnui (v. 24).

BAZLITH [băz'lĭth] (Heb. *baṣlîṭ*). A temple servant whose descendants returned from Exile under Zerubbabel (Neh. 7:54; cf. "Bazluth," Ezra 2:52).

BDELLIUM [dĕl'ĭ əm] (Heb. *bᵉḏōlaḥ*). The identification of this material is uncertain. The appearance of the manna given to Israel in the wilderness is compared to bdellium (Num. 11:7), probably pointing to the transparence of the very fragrant, light yellow gum

secreted by balsam trees (cf. NIV "resin"). However, its association with gold and onyx at Gen. 2:12 may indicate that it is a precious stone.

BEALIAH [bē'ə lī'ə] (Heb. *bᵉʿalyâ* "Yahweh is lord"). A supporter of David whom he joined at Ziklag (1 Chr. 12:5).

BEALOTH [bē'ə lŏth] (Heb. *bᵉʿālôṯ*).

1. A city of the tribe of Judah in the Negeb (Josh. 15:24), probably the same as BAALATH-BEER (19:8).

2. A place in the territory of Asher (1 Kgs. 4:16; so RSV following *BH* and LXX *Baalōth*; KJV, NIV "in Aloth"; JB "in the highlands," following the proposed emendation *maʿᵃlōṯ* "ascents").

BEAN. A leguminous plant (*Vicia faba* L.) of which several varieties (such as the broad or horse bean [*Faba vulgaris* Moench]) were cultivated in ancient times. They were cooked fresh, dried, and ground in a hand mill. They were then prepared with garlic and eaten in the form of groats or grits. At 2 Sam. 17:28 (Heb. *pôl*) they are included in the food gift offered to David at Mahanaim, while at Ezek. 4:9 they are part of the symbol of the siege of Jerusalem. In an emergency they could be used as an ingredient in making bread. According to the Talmud (*Yoma* 18a; cf. Mishnah *Kel.* 17:12), the high priest was forbidden to eat beans on the evening preceding the Day of Atonement.

BEAR. There were originally two subspecies of bears in Syria, namely, the larger yellowish-brown *Ursus arctos isabellinus* dwelling in the shelter of the pine regions of the Anti-lebanon mountains and on the northern slope of Mt. Hermon, and the smaller brown *Ursus arctos syriacus*. The latter (which reached a height of approximately 2 m. [5 ft.]) appeared as far south as Judah (1 Sam. 17:34). Succulent fruits, stems and leaves, new grain, and honey were its favorite foods, though it also ate eggs, young birds, and small animals.

In the Old Testament the dangerous nature of bears, especially of a female robbed of her cubs, is used as a means of illustration. At 2 Sam. 17:7 (Heb. *dōḇ*) the valor of David and his men is likened to the fierceness of a female bear; and at Hos. 13:8 God is said to attack his unfaithful people like a bear. A hungry bear could attack a human being (Amos 5:19), and even devour children (2 Kgs. 2:24). In the eschatological age, however, the cow and the bear will live together harmoniously (Isa. 11:7).

In the vision of the four beasts at Dan. 7:5 the bear is the second animal, symbolizing the Median Empire. It may have been chosen for its strength and fierceness. Its posture ("raised up on one side"), which may be an allusion to its ambling gait, has been variously interpreted (see E. J. Young, *The Prophecy of Daniel* [Grand Rapids: 1949], pp. 144-45). Interestingly, only the feet of the beast at Rev. 13:2 resemble those of a bear (Gk. *árkos*), symbolizing perhaps the trampling of its opponents.

BEARD. The Old Testament distinguishes between the beard (Heb. *zāqān*, Lev. 13:29; JB, NIV "chin") and the moustache (lit. "upper lip," Heb. *śāpām*, Lev.

13:45; NIV "lower part of the face"; 2 Sam. 19:24). As depicted in ancient Near Eastern art, the Israelites and other Semites wore full rounded beards (cf. 2 Sam. 10:4), while the Egyptians (Gen. 41:14), Philistines, and others usually were clean-shaven.

Among the Israelites, to shave the beard was a sign of disgrace or insult (2 Sam. 10:4-5), or a sign of mourning (Isa. 15:2; Jer. 41:5) or sadness (Ezra 9:3). Lepers, who were ritually unclean, were compelled to cover their beards (i.e., moustaches [Lev. 13:45], but possibly their entire lower face, including mouth and upper lip) and thereby appear as mourners (cf. Ezek. 24:17, 22; Mic. 3:7). According to Lev. 19:27; 21:5, the Israelites were not to shave or trim the edges of their beards, which, like the shaving of the hairline and the bald spot, too closely resembled Gentile mourning customs (Deut. 14:1; Jer. 16:6; 47:5; Ezek. 7:18; Amos 8:10; Mic. 1:16) or the Gentile practice of sacrificing hair to their deities.

BEAST. A term used to distinguish any animal from human beings (Heb. *bᵉhēmâ*, e.g., Gen. 6:7; Eccl. 3:18-21). The Old Testament distinguishes between clean and unclean animals (Lev. 11:1-8); the Israelites were permitted to eat only the former. Furthermore, the Israelites divided the animals into two other groups — "wild beasts" (e.g., Exod. 23:11, Heb. *ḥayyâ*; KJV "beasts of the field"; NIV, JB "wild animals"; Mark 1:13, Gk. *thēríon*; NIV "wild animals") and domesticated animals ("cattle," e.g., Gen. 2:20; NIV "livestock"). The latter were subject to the laws of the firstlings (Num. 3:13) and the sabbath observances (Deut. 5:14).

The name "beast" is also used metaphorically (e.g., Ps. 74:19, for Israel's enemies [cf. KJV "multitude of the wicked"]), and is an important symbol in apocalyptic literature. In one of his visions Daniel saw four beasts (7:1-12, Aram. *ḥêwâ*) which represented four earthly kingdoms (v. 17) in opposition to God's kingdom. In a court-like setting (vv. 9-11) God condemns these kingdoms, gives the Son of Man authority over them all (vv. 13-14), and includes the "saints" in his everlasting kingdom (v. 18).

The book of Revelation mentions two animals. The first (a power with anti-Christian tendencies because all authority had already been conferred on Christ; Matt. 28:18) is either the antichrist (arising as it does from the bottomless pit, the domicile of the devils, Rev. 11:7; cf. 2 Thess. 2:3-4) or the godless power of the Roman Empire (the beast coming up from the sea, 13:1, as the dragon or Satan [12:3, 9]; cf. 17:3ff. for the identification of Babylon [Rome] with the beast of blasphemous names). In contrast to the animals seen by Daniel, this is a composite animal, although it incorporates the previous three animals named by Daniel. The second animal (arising out of the earth, 13:11) represents false prophecy (16:13; 19:20; 20:10), which is worshipped by the people (e.g., 13:12, 15); it compels its devotees and others to receive its mark (e.g., 13:16-17; 14:9) and thus to reject the sovereign grace of Christ. In the end, however, Christ triumphs over the beast(s) (19:20; 20:4).

BEATITUDES.† A literary formula, generally beginning with the expression "blessed is" or "happy is" (Heb. *ʾašrê*; Gk. *makários*), which pronounces a blessing upon or declares praise of an exemplary individual. Beatitudes mostly occur in the Psalms (Ps. 1:1; 2:12), wisdom writings (Prov. 8:34; 16:20; Job 5:17), the Gospels (Matt. 13:16; John 20:29), and the book of Revelation (Rev. 14:13; 22:14). Best known is the collection of such sayings in Jesus' Sermon on the Mount (Matt. 5:3-12 par. Sermon on the Plain, Luke 6:20-23).

The two versions of Jesus' beatitudes differ in both form and purpose. The Lucan account contains four beatitudes followed by four contrasting woes (e.g., "Blessed are you poor" [6:20] "but woe to you that are rich" [v. 24]), addressed directly to the audience in the second person. Matthew's blessings are stated more generally, using the third person for the first eight. The first saying in each version is the same, as are Luke's second and Matthew's third, and Luke's fourth and Matthew's ninth. As with the Old Testament beatitudes, Jesus' sayings illuminate God's special favor upon the righteous, here interpreted in terms of participation in the kingdom of heaven. Those contained in Luke's collection stress the great contrast in social and personal relationships between the present situation and that of the kingdom (note the use of the future tense; cf. also "now" in vv. 21, 24). Matthew's beatitudes issue an ethical challenge in light of the kingdom as inaugurated by Jesus' earthly ministry; he encourages steadfast loyalty in the face of affliction, preparing for the lessons on discipleship which follow in the Sermon on the Mount.

See also SERMON ON THE MOUNT.

Bibliography. I. W. Batdorf, *Interpreting the Beatitudes* (Philadelphia: 1966); C. H. Dodd, "The Beatitudes: a form-critical study," pp. 1-10 in *More New Testament Studies* (Grand Rapids: 1968).

BEAUTIFUL GATE. A gate located on the east side of Jerusalem and the temple complex (Acts 3:2, *hē thýra hē hōraía*), named after the beautifully decorated Corinthian bronze doors (according to Josephus *BJ* v.5.3). To those coming from the court of the Gentiles it gave access to the court of the women. It is probably to be identified with the Nicanor Gate rather than the Golden Gate.

BEBAI [bē′bī] (Heb. *bēḇay*).
1. An Israelite whose descendants returned from Exile, some of them under Zerubbabel (Ezra 2:11 par. Neh. 7:16) and some under Ezra (Ezra 8:11).
2. An Israelite, one of the chiefs of the people who set his seal to the renewed covenant under Nehemiah (Neh. 10:15).

BECHER [bē′kər] (Heb. *beker* "young camel"). A son of Benjamin and grandson of Rachel (Gen. 46:21; 1 Chr. 7:6-8; NIV "Beker"); he went to Egypt with Jacob. Although his descendants numbered 20,200 (1 Chr. 7:9), they are not listed in the genealogy of Benjamin (8:1-40) nor do they appear in the census taken in the Transjordan (Num. 26:38-41). A Becher, father of "the family of the Becherites," is mentioned in the latter connection (v. 35), but he belonged to the tribe of Ephraim. Scholars have suggested that after the murder of Becher and other Ephraimites by the men of Gath (1 Chr. 7:20-21), the Benjaminite Becher (MT "Bered") was taken up into the tribe of Ephraim and reckoned among them. At this time his descendants were not numerous enough to be considered a kinship unit and thus they are not mentioned at Num. 26:38-41 and 1 Chr. 8, although they do appear at 1 Chr. 7:6-12.

BECHERITES. Descendants of the Ephraimite Becher (Num. 26:35; KJV "Bachrites"; JB "Bechrite clan"; NIV "Bekerite clan").

BECHORATH (1 Sam. 9:1, KJV). See BECORATH.

BECORATH [bĭ kôr′ăth] (Heb. *b*ᵉ*ḵôraṯ*). A son of Aphiah, of the tribe of Benjamin, and an ancestor of King Saul (1 Sam. 9:1; KJV "Bechorath").

BED.

I. Terminology

A. In the Old Testament. The most common words are Heb. *miṭṭâ* "couch (covers, pieces of cloth, cushions spread out)" (KoB, p. 516), *miškāḇ* "place of lying, couch" (KoB, p. 575), and *'ereś* "couch, divan" (KoB, p. 739).

The poor simply slept on the ground, using their cloaks for covering (Exod. 22:26-27), as did the common traveler (Gen. 28:11). Even Sisera, the general of King Jabin, upon entering the tent of Jael, had only a "rug" for a covering (Judg. 4:18, so RSV, JB; KJV "mantle"). Yet beds were not luxury items, for they were found in the modest homes of the medium at Endor (1 Sam. 28:23; NIV "couch"; JB "divan") and the widow of Zarephath (1 Kgs. 17:19).

The couch on which people could sit during the day could be turned into a bed at night by placing mattresses on it. The homes of the more prominent Israelites contained beds and couches made of ivory (Amos 6:4), and the palace of King Ahasuerus of Persia boasted "couches of gold and silver" (Esth. 1:6). The bed of Og, the king of Bashan, was either a bedstead (so RSV, KJV, JB, NIV) or a sarcophagus (NIV mg.). The "bedchamber" (Heb. *ḥᵃdar hammiṭṭaṯ*, NIV "bedroom"; JB "sleeping quarters") of the palace at Jerusalem (2 Kgs. 11:2 par. 2 Chr. 22:11) was not a children's bedroom, but a special room where "mattresses and counterpanes" (KD *in loc.*) were stored.

Scripture also mentions beds among the Egyptians (Gen. 47:31 [Heb. *miṭṭâ*; JB "pillows"; Heb. *maṭṭeh* "staff," so NIV]; 49:33; Exod. 8:3, "bedchamber"; NIV "bedrooms"), Syrians, and Mesopotamians. From remains excavated at Tell el-Fârʿah (dated to *ca.* 850 B.C.) C. Watzinger reconstructed a bed which reflects Egyptian influence. The ivory beds mentioned at Amos 6:4 (cf. 3:12) are thought to show Assyrian influence.

B. In the New Testament. The usual Greek words are *klínē* "bed, couch" (Bauer, p. 436) and *krábattos* "mattress, pallet" (Bauer, p. 477). In the parable of the lamp Gk. *klínē* could mean a "bench for dining" (W. L. Lane, *The Gospel According to Mark.* NICNT [1974], p. 165, n. 51) used at night as a bedstead or at least a bed with legs under which a lamp could be placed (Mark 4:21 par. Luke 8:16). (In catacombs an-

cient representations of the healing of the lame often depict bedsteads such as these.) Gk. *krábattos* refers to a portable bed or a mattress (e.g., Mark 2:4, JB "stretcher," NIV "mat"; John 5:9-11). At Acts 9:33-34 the "bedridden" (Gk. *katakeímenon epì krabáttou*) Aeneas is urged to "make" his bed; since the verb *strōnnýō* does not have a direct object it could be translated "clothe yourself" (lit. "make yourself ready") or (understanding the object *klínēn*) "set the table for yourself," i.e., get something to eat (F. F. Bruce, *The Book of the Acts.* NICNT [1954], p. 211).

By New Testament times the poor were more likely to have mattresses (Matt. 9:2; Mark 2:4; Luke 5:18).

II. Use of Beds†

While the bed was usually intended as a place for rest or sleep, the sluggard is warned against wasting his time lying on his bed (Prov. 26:14). Love-making could also take place on the bed (e.g., Cant. 3:1), but the author of the book of Hebrews cautions that the marriage bed (*koítē*, 13:4) not be defiled. At Job 17:13; Ps. 139:18 the grave is represented figuratively as a bed.

BEDAD [bē′dăd] (Heb. *b*ᵉ*dad*). The father of Hadad, king of Edom (Gen. 36:35; 1 Chr. 1:46).

BEDAN [bē′dăn] (Heb. *b*ᵉ*dan* "son of Dan" or "son of the judge").

1. A judge whose name appears only in the MT of 1 Sam. 12:11 (so KJV) and of whom nothing further is known. A more likely reading (so RSV, JB, NIV following the LXX, Syriac, and Arabic) is "Barak." Some scholars would read here the name "Abdon" (cf. Judg. 12:13-15).

2. The son of Ulam of the tribe of Manasseh (1 Chr. 7:17).

BEDEIAH [bĭ dē′yə] (Heb. *bēd*ᵉ*yâ* "servant of the Lord(?)"). One of the Israelites who was compelled to send away his foreign wife (Ezra 10:35).

BEE. The wild bee (*Apis mellifica*) of Palestine (Heb. *d*ᵉ*ḇôrâ*), mentioned four times in the Old Testament. In three instances this insect is a symbol of Israel by the Amorites (Deut. 1:44), of the psalmist by his enemies (Ps. 118:12), and of God's people by God himself (Isa. 7:18). While Palestine had an unusually large number of honey-producing plants, only at Judg. 14:8 — a rather peculiar passage — are bees and honey mentioned together.

There is no direct evidence that the Israelites had domesticated the bee (though the phrase "a land flowing with milk and honey [e.g., Exod. 3:8] may suggest so); the Egyptians, however, did breed bees. The modern domestication of bees dates to only 1880. *See also* HONEY.

BEELIADA [bē′ə lī′ə də] (Heb. *b*ᵉ*ʿelyāḏāʿ* "Baal knows"). A son of David born in Jerusalem (1 Chr. 14:7). The name was changed to Eliada ("God knows") at 2 Sam. 5:16; 1 Chr. 3:8 to avoid the pagan element "Baal."

BEELZEBUB [bē ĕl′zĭ bŭb]. See BEELZEBUL.

BEELZEBUL [bē ĕl'zĭ bŭl] (Gk. *Beelzeboul, Beezeboul* "master of the heavenly dwelling"). A name which the scribes derisively applied to Jesus upon his healing of a demon-possessed person (Matt. 12:24 par. Mark 3:22; Luke 11:15; KJV, NIV "Beelzebub"). Although Beelzebul (on the basis of Gk. *Beelzeboub*) has often been identified with the Philistine deity Baal-zebub, the "lord of flies" (2 Kgs. 1:2-3), the name means more likely "Baal the Prince" or the "lord of heaven." Whatever the name's Old Testament associations (in the Old Testament Beelzebul was not identified with the devil or Satan), in the New Testament Beelzebul is believed to be the chief of the demons (Satan). Jesus makes clear that his actions were intended to inaugurate the kingdom of God and were performed in opposition to (and not in subjection to) the kingdom of Satan (Matt. 12:17-28 par.).

BEER [bē'ər] (Heb. *be'ēr* "well").
1. A place where the Israelites encamped during their wilderness wanderings, north of the Arnon (Num. 21:16), perhaps the same as BEER-ELIM (Isa. 15:8).
2. The place to which Jotham, the youngest son of Gideon, fled from his brother Abimelech (Judg. 9:21). It is perhaps to be identified with el-Bîreh, to the east of Mt. Tabor.

BEERA [bē'ə rə] (Heb. *be'ērā'* "well"). A son of Zophah of the tribe of Asher (1 Chr. 7:37).

BEERAH [bē'ə rə] (Heb. *be'ērâ* "well"). The son of Baal, he was a chieftain of the tribe of Reuben and was deported to Assyria by Tiglath-pileser III (1 Chr. 5:6).

BEER-ELIM [bĭr ē'lĭm] (Heb. *be'ēr 'ēlîm* "well of the terebinths"). A place in Moab (Isa. 15:8), probably the same as BEER 1, a place where the Israelites encamped during the wilderness wanderings (Num. 21:16). It has been identified with the Wâdī eth-Themed.

BEERI [bē'ə rī] (Heb. *be'erî* "man of the well").
1. The Hittite father of Esau's wife Judith (Gen. 26:34).
2. The father of the prophet Hosea (Hos. 1:1).

BEER-LAHAI-ROI [bĭr'lə hī'roi] (Heb. *be'ēr laḥay rō'î* "well of the Living One who sees me"). A well on the road to Shur, in the vicinity of Kadesh-barnea and Bered. Here Hagar met the angel of the Lord as she rested during her flight from Sarai (Gen. 16:7-14). Later, Isaac lived near this well (24:62; 25:11; KJV "Lahai-roi").

BEEROTH [bē'ə rŏth] (Heb. *be'ērôt* "wells"). One of the four Hivite cities which, like Gibeon, made a treaty with Israel (Josh. 9:27). It lay on the border between Benjamin and Ephraim (Josh. 18:25) but was assigned to the territory of Benjamin (2 Sam. 4:2) and was the northernmost city of that tribe. Baanah and Rechab, the murderers of Ishbosheth (2 Sam. 4:2-3), were from Beeroth, as was Naharai, one of David's

mighty men and armor-bearer of Joab (23:37 par. 1 Chr. 11:39).

The site of the city has not yet been identified, although some have suggested Nebī Samwil, about 8 km. (5 mi.) northwest of Jerusalem. The city was favored as a resting stop by pilgrims returning home to Galilee, not only because of its water supply but also because it afforded convenient lodging a day's journey from home and outside the territory of the despised Samaritans. According to tradition it was here that Joseph and Mary discovered that Jesus was not among the company with whom they were returning home (Luke 2:44).

BEEROTH BENE-JAAKAN [bĭr'ŏth bĕn'î jā'ə kən] (Heb. *be'ērôt be'nê-ya'aqān*). *See* BENE-JAAKAN.

BEEROTHITE [bē'ə rŏth īt] (Heb. *be'ērôtî*). An inhabitant of Beeroth (2 Sam. 4:3, 5, 9; 23:37, KJV).

BEER-SHEBA [bĭr shē'bə] (Heb. *be'ēr šeba'*; Gk. *Bērsabee*).† A principal city and religious center in the northern Negeb, regarded throughout Israelite history as the southernmost limit of their territory ("from Dan to Beer-sheba," e.g., Judg. 20:1; 1 Sam. 3:20; 1 Kgs. 4:25; cf. 2 Kgs. 23:8; 1 Chr. 21:2; Neh. 11:30). Two possible meanings of the city's name can be traced to the same Hebrew root (*šb'*), "well of the seven" (referring to the seven lambs with which Abraham sealed his covenant with Abimelech, Gen. 21:25-32) or "well of the oath" (commemorating Isaac's covenant with Abimelech, 26:31-33).

Beer-sheba (modern Tell es-Seba') is located in a basin between the Judean mountains to the north and the desert highlands of the Negeb to the south. In ancient times it was the junction of main caravan routes leading both west to Egypt and north to the coast. In patriarchal times both Abraham and Isaac sojourned there with their flocks (Gen. 22:19; cf. 28:10). The city was assigned to the territory of Simeon (Josh. 19:2), although it was considered within the allotment of Judah (15:28). Beer-sheba was an important administrative center at the time of Saul, who stationed two sons there as judges (1 Sam. 8:2), and during the Monarchy (cf. 2 Chr. 19:4). The city was destroyed by Sennacherib in 701 B.C. but was among those cities resettled by the population who returned from the Exile (Neh. 11:27).

At least as early as patriarchal times Beer-sheba was a religious center. Abraham planted a tamarisk tree there in honor of El Olam ("the Everlasting God," Gen. 21:33), a local deity later understood as Yahweh. Before migrating to Egypt Jacob experienced a vision there, perhaps in conjunction with a local oracle (46:1-5). An important shrine was located there in the time of Amos, whose condemnations (5:5; 8:14) allude to the observance of pagan rituals. Archaeological excavations have discovered a large horned altar and the remains of what may have been a temple destroyed during Hezekiah's cultic reforms (2 Kgs. 18:22).

Another Beer-sheba, located in lower Galilee, is mentioned by Josephus (*BJ* iii.3.1 [39]).

BE-ESHTERAH [bē ĕsh'tə rə] (Heb. *be'ešterâ*). A levitical city located in the Transjordanian territory of

Manasseh (Josh. 21:27), perhaps to be identified with Ashtaroth (1 Chr. 6:71). The name is probably a contraction of Beth-astoreth, "house of Astarte."

BEETLE. See CRICKET.

BEGGAR. The Old Testament contains no specific terminology for professional begging, although there are many references to the poor (e.g., Deut. 15:4, 7) and the practice certainly must have existed (cf. Ps. 59:15). Legal provisions for the poor were so strict that begging was indicative of breaking Israel's covenant; thus begging was one of the strongest curses that could be pronounced (Ps. 109:10; cf. 37:25). During the period of the Monarchy owners of small parcels of land lost their possessions to the wealthy landowners, thus widening the class distinction between the permanently rich and the permanently poor. Conditions did not improve after the Exile, and by New Testament times begging was a common practice among the poor and disabled (e.g., Mark 10:46 par., blind Bartimaeus; John 9:8, the blind beggar near the pool of Siloam; Acts 3:2, the lame man at the Beautiful Gate).

See also POOR; POVERTY.

BEGINNING. See CREATION; TIME.

BEHEMOTH [bĭ hē′məth] (Heb. *bᵉhēmôt̪*, intensive pl. of *bᵉhēmâ* "beast"). The name attributed to a large marsh-dwelling mammal, probably the hippopotamus (*Hippopotamus amphibius*), mentioned in the divine discourse at Job 40:15. Here the animal is depicted as an herbivore (vv. 15, 21) living in marshes (v. 21) or the river Jordan (v. 23) and possessing great strength in its loins, muscles, and limbs (vv. 16, 18). The description is intended to impress upon Job the limits of his understanding and ability. Egyptian inscriptions indicate that the hippopotamus lived along the entire length of the Nile river.

Other Old Testament occurrences of the term refer simply to "beasts," either wild or domesticated animals (e.g., Deut. 28:26; 32:24; Isa. 18:6; Hab. 2:17), but in the Apocrypha and Pseudepigrapha it designates a male counterpart to the mythological Leviathan (2 Esdr. 6:49, 52).

BEKA [bē′kə] (Heb. *beqaʿ* "half"). A weight equal to half a shekel or approximately 5.712 g. (.2 oz.), the amount of silver assessed of all male Israelites for the construction of the tabernacle (Exod. 38:26).

See also WEIGHTS AND MEASURES.

BEL [bĕl] (Heb. *bēl*, from Akk. *belu* "master, lord"). The principal Babylonian deity. Like Heb. *baʿal*, the name may simply designate any god or may point to a supreme god. It was first applied as an epithet of the Sumerian Enlil, god of the atmosphere and wind (counterpart to the Canaanite Baal) and one of the original supreme triad of the Sumerian pantheon. He was the son of Ea and father of Nabu (Nebo, Isa. 46:1). Originally he functioned simply as tutelary deity of the city of Babylon, but during the time of Hammurabi he progressively increased in importance. As a Babylonian deity he was identified with Marduk (Merodach; Isa. 46:1; Jer. 50:2; 51:44). He was wor-

shipped in the temple of Esagila and upon E-temen-an-ki, the temple tower of Babylon. During the New Year festival the king of Babylon would bow in submission before Bel, thereby securing the welfare of the land.

BEL AND THE DRAGON.† The last of the additions to Daniel, appended as ch. 14 in the LXX and Vulgate as well as in modern Roman Catholic versions and as ch. 13 in Theodotion's translation.

This addition contains two stories whose primary purpose is to demonstrate the folly of idolatry. In the first tale (vv. 1-22), Daniel challenges Cyrus' contention that the statue of Bel (Canaanite Baal, identified here with Marduk, the chief god of the Babylonian pantheon) is a living god, a claim the king bases on the massive amounts of food and drink which the idol consumes daily. Daniel cleverly spreads ashes over the floor before the temple is sealed and the next day points out the footprints which lead to a secret entrance. The priests, who themselves had been partaking of the offerings, are put to death, and the idol and its temple are given to Daniel, who destroys them.

The second story bears strong resemblance to Dan. 6, upon which it is no doubt based. Daniel refuses to worship a monstrous dragon, which the Babylonians revere as a living god. Believing the creature indestructible, the king grants Daniel permission to slay it "without sword or club" (v. 26). Daniel feeds the beast cakes made from pitch, fat, and hair, and the dragon bursts. Fearing the masses, who charge him with becoming a Jew (v. 28), the king hands over Daniel to be thrown into the lions' den. On the sixth day an angel miraculously transports the prophet Habakkuk from Judea with a meal for Daniel. The king releases him on the seventh day, proclaiming the God of Israel as the one true God and sending into the den Daniel's opponents, whom the starving lions immediately devour.

As with the stories and visions of the book of Daniel and the other additions, these tales point to God's sustaining grace to those who remain faithful to his will.

See also DANIEL, ADDITIONS TO.

BELA [bē′lə] (Heb. *belaʿ* "swallowing up") (**PERSON**).

1. The son of Beor and king of Edom who reigned from the city of Dinhabah (Gen. 36:32-33; 1 Chr. 1:43-44).

2. The eldest son of Benjamin (Gen. 46:21; 1 Chr. 7:6; 8:1). His descendants were the Belaites.

3. The son of Azaz and herdsman ruler of the tribe of Reuben who owned a large amount of territory in the land of Gilead (1 Chr. 5:8-9).

BELA [bē′lə] (Heb. *belaʿ* "swallowing up") (**PLACE**). The original name of Zoar, one of the "cities of the valley" of Siddim (Gen. 14:3), probably located on the southeastern bank of the Dead Sea.

BELAITES [bē′lə īts] (Heb. *balʿî* "belonging to Bela"). Descendants of Bela (Num. 26:38).

BELIAL [bē′lĭ əl] (Heb. *bᵉlîyaʿal* "of no use"; Gk. *Beliar*). Although generally rendered as a proper name in the KJV, the term is translated more precisely as "base fellow" (RSV) or "scoundrel" (NEB). It is used in a variety of senses, ranging from "worthless men" (1 Sam. 2:12; NIV "wicked men") to "perdition" (Ps. 18:4), "villainy" (Nah. 1:11), and "wicked" (v. 15). The specific etymology of the word remains debated, although it may derive from mythological usage (cf. B. Otzen, *TDOT* 2, rev. ed. [1977]: 131-36). T. K. Cheyne has suggested that it may be traced to Belili, a Babylonian goddess of the underworld. A similar form used at Jer. 2:8, 11 (Heb. *lô'-yô'îlû* "does not profit") has been taken as an allusion to the name Baal, the worthless one. In Jewish apocalyptic writings and the pseudepigraphal literature (e.g., Jubilees, Ascension of Isaiah, Testament of Levi, Sibylline Oracles) Belial was another name for Satan, an identification which Paul makes at 2 Cor. 6:15. Noting the rabbinic interpretation of the term (Heb. *b*ᵉ*lî-'ōl* "without a yoke [of the law]"), some commentators explain the expression "man of lawlessness" (e.g., 2 Thess. 2:3, Gk. *ho ánthrōpos tēs anomías*) as a Greek representation of the Hebrew "man of Belial."

BELIEF. *See* FAITH.

BELL. Heb. *pa'ᵃmôn* ("clapper") refers to a gold object fastened to the robes of the high priest, which acted as a warning of his movements in the sanctuary (Exod. 28:33-35; 39:25-26). At Zech. 14:20 it is prophesied that the tinkling ornamental "bells of the horses" (Heb. *m*ᵉ*sillôt*) would bear the same inscription as the turban of the high priest: "Holy to the Lord" (cf. Exod. 28:36; 39:30); in the eschatological age, even the most profane things would be taken up into the service of God.

BELLY. *See* STOMACH.

BELMAIN [bĕl'mān] (Gk. *Belmain*). A village in Palestine where the Jews erected fortifications in their struggle against Holofernes (Jdt. 4:4; KJV 'Belmen'). If Bethulia is another name for Shechem, Belmain may have been located in the vicinity of Dothan, *ca.* 14 km. (9 mi.) north of Samaria (cf. 7:3, where Belmain is called Belbaim).

BELSHAZZAR [bĕl shăz'ər] (Aram. *bēlša'ṣṣar, bēl'šaṣṣar*; Akk. *bēl-šar-uṣur* "may Bel protect the king"). A son of Nabonidus, the last Neo-Babylonian king, and coregent with him *ca.* 553-539 B.C. The impression given by Dan. 5:7-8, that Belshazzar was himself the final king in that line, is not incompatible with the ancient Near Eastern sources. According to cuneiform materials, Nabonidus (Akk. *Nabû-na'id*) was absent from Babylon for political and military reasons for at least ten years of his reign. From the third year of his reign (553) on, he entrusted the kingship to Belshazzar, his eldest son, who became in essence the last acting king of Babylon. Nabonidus returned to defend Babylon shortly before it fell to the Persians in 539, but there is no indication that he relieved Belshazzar of his duties.

Dan. 5 depicts a feast which Belshazzar gave on the last night of his life and reign. During that feast a hand appeared and wrote on the wall the words MENE, MENE, TEKEL, PARSIN, which Daniel interpreted to mean the coming judgment of God. That same night the Persians invaded Babylon and killed Belshazzar. According to Herodotus (*Hist.* i.100-101) Cyrus redirected the waters of the Euphrates and during Belshazzar's feast entered the city by way of the dry riverbed. Xenophon adds that it was Cyrus himself who broke into the palace and killed the king (*Cyropaedia* vii.5.1-36). Akkadian sources mention nothing about Belshazzar's death.

In Dan. 5:2, 11, 18, 22, Belshazzar is called the son of Nebuchadnezzar, but Akkadian sources indicate that he was the son of Nabonidus, the Aramean usurper from Haran who ended Nebuchadnezzar's reign. Some scholars argue that he was descended from the Babylonian king through his mother Nitocris (cf. Herodotus *Hist.* i.188), probably the same queen mentioned at 5:10.

Bibliography. R. P. Dougherty, *Nabonidus and Belshazzar.* Yale Oriental Series 15 (New Haven: 1929).

BELT. *See* CLOTHING.

BELTESHAZZAR [bĕl'tĭ shăz'ər] (Heb. *bēlṭ*ᵉ*ša'ṣṣar*; Akk. *balaṭsu-uṣur* "protect his life"). The Babylonian name given to Daniel during his captivity in Babylon (Dan. 1:7; 2:26; 4:8-9). At 4:8 Nebuchadnezzar interprets the name as derived from the Babylonian deity Bel, but this is probably a popular etymology. The LXX and Vulg. read "Balthasar," which in Roman Catholic tradition became the name of one of the three wise men from the East who visited the infant Jesus.

BEN [bĕn] (Heb. *bēn* "son of"; pl. *b*ᵉ*nê*).† Used as a prefix, a term designating a relationship or condition. Most often it indicates a direct male descendant, but it can also designate a member of a tribe or people ("sons of Israel," Gen. 42:5), national or geographical origin ("son of Jabesh," 2 Kgs. 15:10), or social or professional class ("sons of the prophets," e.g., 1 Kgs. 20:35; 2 Kgs. 2:3). "Sons of God" can refer to believing, godly persons (Gen. 6:2; Hos. 1:10) or angels (Job 1:6; 2:1; 38:7).

See also SON.

BEN-ABINADAB [bĕn'ə bĭn'ə dăb] (Heb. *ben-'ᵃbînādāb* "son of Abinadab"). The son-in-law of Solomon who was made an officer over Naphath-dor (1 Kgs. 4:11; KJV, JB, NIV "son of Abinadab").

BENAIAH [bĭ nā'yə] (Heb. *b*ᵉ*nāyâ, b*ᵉ*nāyāhû* "Yahweh has built").

1. The son of Jehoiada of Kabzeel (a priest, 2 Sam. 23:20; 1 Chr. 27:5). He was a renowned warrior who was in charge of the Cherethites and Pelethites, David's bodyguard (2 Sam. 8:18; 20:23; cf. 23:23), and commander of the third of the twelve divisions of David's army (1 Chr. 27:5). Benaiah smote "two ariels of Moab," killed a lion in a pit, and slew an Egyptian of great stature (2 Sam. 23:20-21 par. 1 Chr. 11:22-23). He remained faithful to David at all times, even during Absalom's rebellion and Adonijah's attempt to seize the crown (1 Kgs. 1:8, 10). At Solomon's command, he executed the death sentence upon Adonijah and Joab (1 Kgs. 2:25, 29-34); the new king then set him over the army in place of Joab (2 Kgs. 2:35).

2. One of David's mighty men. He was from Pirathon in Ephraim (2 Sam. 23:30 par. 1 Chr. 11:31).

3. A prince of the tribe of Simeon (1 Chr. 4:36).

4. A Levite of the second order. He was one of those who played harps and lyres when the ark of the Lord was brought into Jerusalem (1 Chr. 15:18, 20; 16:5).

5. A priest who played upon the trumpet when the ark of the Lord was brought into Jerusalem (1 Chr. 15:24; 16:6).

6. A Levite of the line of Asaph. He was the grandfather of Jahaziel, a contemporary of King Jehoshaphat (2 Chr. 20:14).

7. A Levite during the reign of King Hezekiah. He was one of the overseers of the contributions made to the temple (2 Chr. 31:13).

8-11. Four Israelites whom Ezra compelled to send away their foreign wives. The men were from the families of Parosh (Ezra 10:25), Pahath-moab (v. 30), Bani (v. 35), and Nebo (v. 43).

12. The father of Pelatiah, one of the princes of Israel whom Ezekiel saw in a vision while sitting by the western gate of the temple (Ezek. 11:1, 13).

BEN-AMMI. *See* AMMONITES.

BEN-DEKER [bĕn dē′kər] (Heb. *ben-deqer* "son of Deker"). Officer over Makaz during the reign of Solomon (1 Kgs. 4:9; KJV "son of Deker").

BENE-BERAK [bĕn′ĭ bĭr′ăk] (Heb. *bᵉnê bᵉraq* "sons of lightning"). A city in the inheritance of Dan (Josh. 19:45) located on the coastal plain. The name has been revived in the name of modern Banai Baraq, a suburb of Tel Aviv situated a few miles north of the biblical site.

BENEDICTUS [bĕn′ə dĭk′təs].† Song of thanksgiving by Zechariah in response to the birth of his son John the Baptist (Luke 1:67-79). The first part of the psalm (vv. 68-75), in parallelisms characteristic of Hebrew poetry, expresses thanksgiving for God's fulfillment of messianic promises of salvation. The second division (vv. 76-79) is addressed to the child and describes John's role as the forerunner of Christ.

BENE-JAAKAN [bĕn′ĭ jā′ə kən] (Heb. *bᵉnê yaʿᵃqān* "sons of Jaakan"). A place where the Israelites encamped during their wilderness wanderings (Num. 33:31-32); at Deut. 10:6 it is called Beeroth Bene-jaakan (KJV "Beeroth of the children of Jaakan"). The site is probably to be identified with modern Birein, approximately 11 km. (7 mi.) north of Kadesh.

BEN-GEBER [bĕn gē′bər] (Heb. *ben-geḇer* "son of Geber"). Officer under Solomon over north Gilead and Argob (1 Kgs. 4:13; KJV, JB "son of Geber").

BEN-HADAD [bĕn hā′dăd] (Heb. *ben-haḏaḏ* "son of Hadad"). The name of several Syrian kings who reigned at Damascus.

1. Ben-hadad I, the son of Tabrimmon and grand-

son of Hezion (1 Kgs. 15:18). At the request of King Asa of Judah he broke his alliance with Baasha, king of Israel, and having sent his armies against Israel's cities, he conquered Ijon, Dan, Abel-beth-Maacah, and others (*ca.* 879 B.C.; vv. 18-20). Once in control of the territory of Naphtali, and thus commanding the coastal trade route between Damascus and Egypt, he compelled Baasha to withdraw from Judah (v. 21). According to 2 Kgs. 15:29 the conquered territory again belonged to Israel afterward; perhaps Ben-hadad returned it to Baasha under certain conditions.

2. Ben-hadad II, son or grandson of Ben-hadad I and contemporary of King Ahab (*ca.* 874-853). He besieged Samaria (1 Kgs. 20:1), but his arrogant demands forced the Israelites to make a stiff reply (vv. 7-11). Foretold by a prophet that they would be victorious, the Israelites put the Syrians to flight (vv. 19-21). The following year Ahab defeated him again (at Aphek, vv. 26-30), but in a burst of generosity he spared Ben-hadad's life in exchange for concessions (cities and trade districts at Damascus, vv. 31-34).

If the "king of Syria" mentioned at 1 Kgs. 22:2– 2 Kgs. 6:23 and the Ben-hadad of 2 Kgs. 6:24; 8:7, 9 are the same Ben-hadad II, there must have been a three-year truce between Syria and Israel following the battle at Aphek (1 Kgs. 22:1). If, furthermore, Adad-ʿidri (mentioned in Assyrian inscriptions) is identical with Hadadezer or Ben-hadad, this Syrian king could have fought with Ahab against Shalmaneser III of Assyria and won the battle at Qarqar on the Orontes (853). Soon animosity gained the upper hand again, and the former allies faced each other at Ramoth-gilead, during which battle Ahab lost his life (vv. 29-36). Ten years later Ben-hadad himself died, murdered by his emissary Hazael whom he had sent to Elisha with news of his poor physical condition (2 Kgs. 8:7-15).

On the basis of a ninth-century stele dedicated to the god Melqart, some scholars consider this Ben-hadad to be identical with Ben-hadad I. Such a identification would present certain historical pro ms (cf. 1 Kgs. 20:34) and would require a reign of fifty-seven years for Ben-hadad I. F. M. Cross proposes a new reading for the inscription, on which basis he suggests that another king, whom he designates Ben-hadad III, ruled as a coregent for the last three years of Ben-hadad II's reign (*BASOR* 205 [1972]: 36-42).

3. Ben-hadad III (*ca.* 796-770; Cross calls him Ben-hadad IV), son of Hazael. He continued the successful policy of his aged father, possibly while yet a crown prince, and oppressed Israel (2 Kgs. 13:3) until Jehoash of Israel was able to turn back the Syrians. While Adad-nirari III of Assyria may have weakened Damascus (*ca.* 800) and Joash (son of Jehoahaz) defeated Ben-hadad three times (vv. 24-25), the actual savior of Israel (v. 5) was Jeroboam II, who restored Israel's northern border (14:23-29) either during the reign of this Ben-hadad or that of his successor (cf. Jer. 49:27; Amos 4:14). Ben-hadad III is named on a stele commemorating the victory of Zakir king of Luʿash over Ben-hadad's Syrian coalition (*ca.* 775).

BEN-HAIL [bĕn hāl′] (Heb. *ben-ḥayil* "son of strength"). A prince of the tribe of Judah, whom King

Jehoshaphat sent (with others) through the cities of the southern kingdom in order to instruct the people in the law (2 Chr. 17:7).

BEN-HANAN [bĕn hā'nən] (Heb. *ben-ḥānān* "son of grace"). One of the four sons of Shimon of the tribe of Judah (1 Chr. 4:20).

BEN-HESED [bĕn hē'sĕd] (Heb. *ben-ḥeseḏ* "son of Hesed"). The officer whom King Solomon appointed over Socoh and the entire land of Hepher. He resided at Arubboth (1 Kgs. 4:10; KJV, JB "son of Hesed").

BEN-HINNOM, VALLEY OF. *See* HINNOM, VALLEY OF.

BEN-HUR [bĕn hûr'] (Heb. *ben-ḥûr* "son of Hur").* An officer appointed by Solomon over the "hill country of Ephraim" (1 Kgs. 4:8; KJV, JB "son of Hur").

BENINU [bĭ nī'nōō] (Heb. *bᵉnînû* "our son"). A Levite who set his seal to the renewed covenant under Nehemiah (Neh. 10:13).

BENJAMIN [bĕn'jə mən] (Heb. *binyāmîn* "son of the right hand").

1. The youngest son of Jacob and second son of Rachel, and afterward the name of a tribe. According to Gen. 35:16-20, Rachel gave birth to a son while dying, naming him Ben-oni ("son of my sorrow"). Jacob, however, called him Benjamin (based on a popular etymology, "son of fortune"), because his birth compensated for the loss of his wife.

Benjamin's descendants are listed at Gen. 46:21; 1 Chr. 7:6-12; 8:1-40. In the Blessing of Jacob, Benjamin is characterized as a "ravenous wolf" (Gen. 49:27), while in the Blessing of Moses he is termed the "beloved of the Lord" dwelling by the Lord in safety and enjoying his protection (Deut. 33:12). Often the Benjaminites demonstrated a rude and warlike nature. Although the tribe's condoning of the sexual molestation of a woman by the residents of Gibeah (Judg. 19) may be explained in part by the absence of a king, the heinous act almost led to the extinction of the Benjaminites in a subsequent war (Judg. 20). Ehud the second judge and King Saul were inhabitants of Benjamin (Judg. 3:12-20; 1 Sam. 9:1-2). The Benjaminites were famous for their bowmen and slingers, many of whom were left-handed (Judg. 20:16; 1 Chr. 8:40; etc.).

Josh. 18:11-28 narrates the inheritance that befell Benjamin — between Judah to the south and Ephraim and Manasseh (the inheritance of Joseph, Benjamin's brother) to the north. Thus its borders were the Jordan river and the northern part of the Dead Sea to the east, and the territory of Dan and Judah to the west. Although not a large tribe (smaller in number than most other tribes counted during the wilderness census; Num. 1:37; 26:41), it possessed important cities such as Jericho, Bethel, Gibeon, Ramah, Mizpeh, and Jerusalem.

Judging from the action of Shimei (2 Sam. 16:5-13) and afterward of Sheba (20:1-2), dissatisfaction apparently ruled among the Benjaminites during David's reign. After the monarchies were divided, those Ben-

jaminites living in or near Jerusalem most likely remained faithful to the house of David (1 Kgs. 12:21 par. 2 Chr. 11:1-11). They were the ones who were deported to Babylon along with Judah, but some of their descendants returned with Zerubbabel (Ezra 4:1; 10:9). Others such as Esther and Mordecai remained in the land of their captivity (Esth. 2:5, 7).

Benjamin is mentioned twice in the New Testament. At Rom. 11:1 (in the context of God's dealing with the New Testament Jews) Paul states that he is a Benjaminite, while at Rev. 7:8 Benjamin is one of the New Testament tribes sealed unto salvation.

The Mari Letters (eighteenth century B.C.) mention a tribe named Benjaminites (*binu-yamina* "sons of the right hand," i.e., "sons of the south"), a warlike confederation with extensive pasturelands. While there may be a historical connection between these people and the biblical tribe, the identification remains difficult to prove.

2. The second son of Bilhan, the Benjaminite (1 Chr. 7:10).

3. An Israelite of the family of Harim who had taken a foreign wife (Ezra 10:32). He is probably the same person who worked on the restoration of the walls of Jerusalem and took part in their dedication (Neh. 3:23; 12:34).

BENJAMIN GATE. A gate in the wall of ancient Jerusalem facing the tribe of Benjamin (Jer. 37:13; 38:7). It is perhaps the same as the Sheep Gate (John 5:2), and would thus have been located in the north wall. Others, however, have identified it with the Gate of the Guard or the Muster Gate, which would place it in the east wall (cf. Ezek. 48:32).

BENO [bē'nō] (Heb. *bᵉnô* "his son"). The son of Jaaziah, a Levite (1 Chr. 24:26-27). The Hebrew term may simply be rendered "his son" (so JB; see LXX) rather than a proper name.

BEN-ONI [bĕn ō'nī] (Heb. *ben-'ônî* "son of my sorrow"). A name given by Rachel to her younger son; Jacob, however, changed it to BENJAMIN (Gen. 35:18).

BEN-ZOHETH [bĕn zō'hĕth] (Heb. *ben-zôḥet* "son of Zoheth"). A son of Ishi of the tribe of Judah (1 Chr. 4:20). In view of his name, he is probably the son of Zoheth and the grandson of Ishi.

BEON. *See* BAAL-MEON.

BEOR [bē'ôr] (Heb. *bᵉ'ôr* "torch").

1. The father of Bela, the first king of Edom (Gen. 36:32; 1 Chr. 1:43).

2. The father of the seer Balaam (e.g., Num. 22:5); at 2 Pet. 2:15 he is named Bosor (Gk. *Bosor*, so KJV; RSV, JB, NIV "Beor," following Vaticanus Gk. *Beōr*).

BERA [bĭr'ə] (Heb. *bera'*). King of Sodom defeated when Chedorlaomer invaded the valley of Siddim (Gen. 14:2).

BERACAH [bĕr'ə kə] (Heb. *bᵉrāḵâ* "blessing"). A Benjaminite who defected to David at Ziklag (1 Chr. 12:3; KJV "Berachah").

BERACAH, VALLEY OF (Heb. *ʿēmeq bᵉrāḵâ* "valley of blessing"). A valley near Bethlehem where King Jehoshaphat (*ca.* 850 B.C.) and his soldiers blessed the Lord for delivering them from the invading Moabites and Ammonites (2 Chr. 20:26). Located south of Tekoa, it is perhaps the valley in which Khirbet Bereikut lies.

BERACHAH (1 Chr. 12:3, KJV). See BERACAH.

BERACHIAH (1 Chr. 6:39, KJV). See BERECHIAH.

BERAIAH [bĭ rā'yə] (Heb. *bᵉrāʾyâ* "the Lord has created"). A son of Shimei and descendant of Shaharaim of the tribe of Benjamin (1 Chr. 8:21).

BEREA [bĭ rē'ə] (Gk. *Berea*).*
1. A place in Judah to which Bacchides and Alcimus took their troops after encamping against Jerusalem (1 Macc. 9:4). The site may be identified with el-Bireh, 13 km. (8 mi.) north of Jerusalem.
2. (Acts 17:10, 13; 20:4, KJV). See BEROEA 1.

BERECHIAH [bĕr'ə kī'ə] (Heb. *bereḵyâ, bereḵyahû* "the Lord blesses").
1. A son of Zerubbabel (1 Chr. 3:20; NIV "Berekiah").
2. The father of the singer Asaph and a Levite of the tribe of Gershom (1 Chr. 6:39; KJV "Berachiah").
3. The son of Asa. He was a Levite who dwelt in the villages of the Netophathites after the Exile (1 Chr. 9:16; NIV "Berakiah").
4. One of the four doorkeepers for the ark of the covenant during the reign of David (1 Chr. 15:23; NIV "Berekiah").
5. The son of Meshillemoth. He was one of the chiefs of the Ephraimites who compelled the army of Pekah to release their captives and to send them back to Judah (2 Chr. 28:12-15; NIV "Berakiah").
6. The son of Meshezabel and father of Meshullam, who helped in the restoration of the walls of Jerusalem (Neh. 3:4, 30). His granddaughter married Jehohanan the son of Tobiah the Ammonite (6:18).
7. The father of the prophet Zechariah (Zech. 1:1, 7; NIV "Berekiah"), possibly the same as Barachiah.

BERED [bĭr'ĕd] (Heb. *bereḏ* "hail") (PERSON). The son of Shutelah and grandson of Ephraim (1 Chr. 7:20). See also BECHER.

BERED [bĭr'ĕd] (Heb. *bereḏ* "hail") (PLACE). A place in the Negeb, beyond the well of Beer-lahai-roi (Gen. 16:14). The site has not been determined, although it has been variously identified as ʿAin Muweileh, 20 km. (12.5 mi.) northwest of ʿAin Qedeis, and Khirbet Ḥalaṣeh, 24 km. (15 mi.) southwest of Beer-sheba.

BERI [bĭr'ī] (Heb. *bērî*). A son of Zophah of the tribe of Asher (1 Chr. 7:36).

BERIAH [bĭ rī'ə] (Heb. *bᵉrîʿâ* "excellent").
1. A son of Asher and father of Heber and Malchiel (Gen. 46:17).
2. A son of Ephraim, born after his other sons had been murdered by the men of Gath (1 Chr. 7:23). Heb. *bᵉrāʿâ* ("evil") in this verse resembles Beriah in sound.
3. A son of Elpaal, a Benjaminite, and father of nine sons (1 Chr. 8:14). The inhabitants of Aijalon were descendants of him and his brother Shema (v. 13).
4. A son of the Levite Shimei, of the line of Gershom. Because they were few in number, his sons and those of his brother Jeush were counted as one family (1 Chr. 23:10-11).

BERIITES [bĭ rī'īts] (Heb. *habbᵉrîʿî*). Descendants of BERIAH 1 (Num. 26:44; NIV "Beriite clan").

BERITH (Judg. 9:46, KJV). See EL-BERITH.

BERNICE [bər nēs'] (Gk. *Bernikē* "victorious"). The oldest daughter of King Herod Agrippa I (A.D. 37-44) and sister of Drusilla. After her first husband, Marcus, died, she married his brother and her uncle, Herod of Chalcis. When he too died (48), she remained with her brother Herod Agrippa II, who had succeeded Marcus as king of Chalcis. The incestuous relationship between Agrippa and the twenty-year-old widow proved scandalous, and Bernice persuaded King Polemo of Cilicia to undergo circumcision and marry her. This marriage lasted but a short time, and Bernice returned to the unmarried Agrippa, with whom she appeared as queen on official occasions. Thus they both greeted Festus when he assumed office as procurator, and both heard Paul's speech in his own defense (Acts 25:13, 23; 26:30). She later won the favor of Vespasian's son Titus when he was in Palestine in connection with the Jewish war and became his mistress, but her hopes of marrying him and becoming empress of Rome were unrealized because of the Roman hatred of the Jews (Suetonius *Titus* vii; cf. Dio Cassius *Hist.* lxvi.15).

BERODACH-BALADAN (2 Kgs. 20:12, KJV). See MERODACH-BALADAN.

BEROEA [bĭ rē'ə] (Gk. *Beroia, Berroia*).
1. A city in Macedonia, modern Verria, 65 km. (40 mi.) west of Thessalonica, at the foot of Mt. Bermius. While it lacked the bustle of a commercial town such as neighboring Thessalonica, Boroea was a prosperous center for artisans, farmers, and stonecutters. After being driven out of Thessalonica in A.D. 51, Paul and Silas preached in the synagogue at Beroea (Acts 17:10-11; KJV, NIV "Berea"). Many of the hearers eagerly received the Word and carefully examined the Scriptures. Many Greeks also came to believe, including perhaps Sopater (20:4). However, when the Jews from Thessalonica came and stirred up the people, Paul was compelled to leave the city (17:13-14).
2.† The city of Aleppo in northern Syria, renamed by Seleucus Nicator (312-280 B.C.). Here the high priest Menelaus was executed by Antiochus Eupator for inciting war with the Maccabean forces (2 Macc. 13:3-8).

BEROTHAH [bĭ rō′thə] (Heb. *bērôṯâ*). A city on the northern boundary of Palestine (Ezek. 47:16), probably BEROTHAI.

BEROTHAI [bĭ rō′thī] (Heb. *bērôṯay*). A city of Hadadezer, king of Syria, from which David took much bronze (2 Sam. 8:8). It is probably to be identified with the modern village of Bereitan, 13 km. (8 mi.) south of Baalbek. The parallel passage reads "Cun" (1 Chr. 18:8), possibly the same city (as is Berothah mentioned at Ezek. 47:16).

BERYL [bĕr′əl]. A bluish or bluish-green copper phosphate found on the Sinai peninsula. A precious stone (the first of the fourth row) on the breastpiece of the high priest (Exod. 28:20; 39:13; Heb. *taršîš*). At Dan. 10:6 (NIV "chrysolite") the body of the man whom Daniel saw resembled beryl, symbolizing perhaps "brightness" (KD *in loc.*). Heb. *šōham* may be rendered "beryl" at Ezek. 28:13 (so RSV; KJV, NIV, JB "onyx"; KoB, p. 950 "carnelian"), referring to a stone in the covering of the king of Tyre. In the New Testament Gk. *béryllos* is the eighth jewel adorning the foundation of the wall of the new Jerusalem (Rev. 21:20; JB "malachite").

BESAI [bē′zī] (Heb. *bēsay*). One of the temple servants whose descendants returned from Exile under Zerubbabel (Ezra 2:49 par. Neh. 7:52).

BESODEIAH [bĕz′ə dē′yə] (Heb. *bᵉsoḏyâ* "in the confidence of the Lord"). The father of Meshullam, who assisted in repairing the Old Gate at Jerusalem in the time of Nehemiah (Neh. 3:6).

BESOR [bē′zôr], **THE BROOK** (Heb. *naḥal bᵉsôr*). A brook (NIV "Besor ravine"; JB "Wadi Besor") which probably flowed to the south of Ziklag (1 Sam. 30:9-10, 21). When David pursued the Amalekites after the destruction of Ziklag, a third of his men remained at the Brook Besor, searching for water because of the heat. The stream has been identified with Wâdī Ghazzleh (Israeli "Habesor"), which enters the Mediterranean Sea south of Gaza.

BETAH (2 Sam. 8:8). See TIBHATH.

BETEN [bē′tən] (Heb. *beṭen* "abdomen"). A city in Asher (Josh. 19:25). If Eusebius' identification of Bethseten with Bethbeter (near Ptolemais or Acco) is correct, the site may be identified with modern Abtun, 4 km. (2.5 mi.) east-northeast of Mt. Carmel.

BETH [bĕth] (Heb. *bêṯ*; Gk. *bēth, baith, beth*). Heb. *bêṯ* means "house" and frequently is employed to designate a family or social grouping. The term is commonly the first component of such compound proper names as Bethel ("house of God"), Beth-shean, and Beth-shemesh ("house of the son").

BETHABARA [bĕth äb′ə rə] (Gk. *Bēthabara*). A place where John was baptizing east of the Jordan river, so rendered by the KJV. The oldest and most accurate manuscripts, however, indicate the name as Bethany (so RSV). See BETHANY 2.

BETH-ANATH [bĕth ā′năth] (Heb. *bêṯ ʿᵃnaṯ* "house of [the goddess] Anath"). A Canaanite city that was assigned to Naphtali (Josh. 19:38). The inhabitants were not expelled, but were compelled by the Israelites to do forced labor (Judg. 1:33). The name appears on the lists of several Egyptian pharaohs. Its location is uncertain though some scholars think it is el-Baʿneh, 16 km. (10 mi.) east of Acco.

BETH-ANOTH [bĕth ā′nŏth] (Heb. *bêṯ ʿᵃnôṯ* "house of the goddess Anath"). A city in Judah (Josh. 15:59), probably to be identified with modern Khirbet Beit ʿAinûn, 5 km. (3 mi.) northeast of Hebron.

BETHANY [bĕth′ə nĭ] (Gk. *Bēthania*, possibly "house of misery").

1. A village on the east slope of the Mount of Olives, 15 stadia (approximately 3 km. [2 mi.]) east of Jerusalem (John 11:18). It was here that Jesus lodged during the Passover week (Matt. 21:17; 26:6; cf. Luke 21:37), while staying at the home of Mary and Martha (John 12:12), whose brother Lazarus he had raised from the dead (ch. 11). He was anointed there by Mary at the home of Simon the leper (Matt. 26:6; Mark 14:3). It may be also that on the "outskirts of Bethany" (Luke 24:50, JB) the ascension took place (see I. H. Marshall, *Comm. on Luke*. NIGTC [1978], pp. 907ff.).

Bethany may be identified with the Old Testament village of Ananiah mentioned at Neh. 11:32. Its contemporary name is el-ʿAzarîyeh, a name preserving in part the name of Lazarus. According to Jerome, a church was built on top of Lazarus' grave, and a Muslim-owned grave is still honored as that of Lazarus. A church built in 1953 stands on the alleged site of the house of Mary and Martha.

2. An unknown location "beyond [Gk. *péran*] the Jordan" where John the Baptist preached and baptized (John 1:28; 3:26). Unable to find such a place on the other side of the Jordan (viewed from Jerusalem), Origen proposed to read "Bethabara" (cf. KJV at John 1:28), located about 6 km. (4 mi.) north of the Dead Sea. The better manuscripts read "Bethany," however. Because the apostle distinguishes between this Bethany and the village of Mary and Martha (cf. 11:1; see also R. E. Brown, *The Gospel According to John*. AB [1966], pp. 44-45, n. 28; L. Morris, *The Gospel According to John*. NICNT [1971], p. 142), John may have baptized east of the Jordan near Jericho.

BETH-ARABAH [bĕth är′ə bə] (Heb. *bêṯ hāʿᵃrāḇâ* "house of the Arabah"). A city at the northern border of Judah (Josh. 15:6), in the "wilderness" (v. 61), between Jericho and the Dead Sea. That it was first allocated to Benjamin (18:22) suggests subsequent adjustments in the boundaries. It is probably to be identified with modern ʿAin el-Gharabah, southeast of Jericho and on the north side of Wâdī Qelt.

BETH-ARAM (Josh. 13:27, KJV). See BETH-HARAM.

BETH-ARBEL [bĕth är′bəl] (Heb. *bêṯ ʾarbēʾl*). A place destroyed by Shalman (Hos. 10:14). According to Eusebius (*Onom.* xiv.18) it lay in Transjordan, in the region of Pella, which would be modern Irbid, 32 km. (20 mi.) northwest of Amman. There is, however, also a Khirbet Irbid in Gilead.

BETH-ASHBEA [bĕth ăsh'bĭ ə] (Heb. *bēṯ 'ašbēaʻ*). The residence of the "house of linen workers," probably a guild tracing its origins to (or under the leadership of) Shelah the son of Judah (1 Chr. 4:21; the KJV reads it as a proper name, "house of Ashbea"). Neither the people nor the town is mentioned elsewhere in the Bible.

BETH-AVEN [bĕth ā'vən] (Heb. *bêṯ 'āwen* "house of vanity" or "house of nothing"). According to 1 Sam. 13:5; 14:23, a city west of Michmash near Bethel, and according to Josh. 7:2; 18:12, a city near Ai and Bethel. In their condemnation of Israel's spiritual idolatry, Hosea (Hos. 10:5; cf. 4:15; 5:8) and Amos (Amos 5:5, a pun, "to nought") identify it with Bethel, possibly because the golden calves fashioned by Jeroboam I (1 Kgs. 13:28-29) were worshiped there. In Israel's earlier history, however, Bethel and Beth-aven were two distinct cities. No firm identification of its location has been made, although some scholars suggest el-Bireh, north of Tell en-Naṣbeh.

BETH-AZMAVETH. *See* AZMAVETH (PLACE).

BETH-BAAL-MEON. *See* BAAL-MEON.

BETH-BARAH [bĕth bâr'ə] (Heb. *bêṯ bārâ*). A crossing place or ford on the Jordan, probably south of Beth-shan, taken by Gideon in his pursuit of the fleeing Midianites (Judg. 7:24). Although its location is uncertain, it may be situated in the Wâdī Fârʻah, northeast of Shechem.

BETHBASI [bĕth bā'sī] (Gk. *Baithbasi,* possibly from Heb. *bêṯ-bᵉṣî* "place of marshes"). A place in the wilderness southeast of Jerusalem which Jonathan and Simon Maccabeus defended against Bacchides (1 Macc. 9:62, 64).

BETH-BIREI (1 Chr. 4:31, KJV). *See* BETH-BIRI.

BETH-BIRI [bĕth bĭr'ī] (Heb. *bêṯ-bir'î*). A city belonging to the tribe of Simeon (1 Chr. 4:31; KJV "Beth-birei"). At Josh 19:6 it is called Beth-lebaoth (Heb. *bêṯ lᵉbā'ôṯ* "lair of lionesses"; cf. 15:32, "Lebaoth"). A possible site is Jebel el-Biri, approximately 32 km. (20 mi.) southwest of Beer-sheba.

BETH-CAR [bĕth kär'] (Heb. *bêṯ-kār* "house of a lamb"). An elevated place southwest of Mizpah, beyond which the Israelites pursued the Philistines (1 Sam. 7:11). Its precise location is unknown, although some have proposed its identification with ʻAin Kârim.

BETH-DAGON [bĕth dā'gən] (Heb. *bêṯ-dagôn* "house of Dagon").
1. A town in the territory of Judah (Josh. 15:41). In Assyrian texts (Taylor Prism) it appears as *Bit-Dagannu,* while in Egyptian texts such as the lists of

Rameses III it takes the form *Bet dgn.* The name is preserved in modern Khirbet Dajun, a village 10 km. (6 mi.) southeast of Jaffa.
2. A border city in Asher (Josh. 19:27), probably located at the site of modern Jelamet el-Atiqa, at the foot of Mt. Carmel.

BETH-DIBLATHAIM [bĕth'dĭb lə thā'əm] (Heb. *bêṯ diḇlāṯayim* "house of two fig cakes"[?]). A town in Moab (Jer. 48:22), perhaps the same as Almon-diblathaim (Num. 33:46), which was a resting place during the Exodus. The town is mentioned along with Medeba and Baal-meon in the ninth-century Moabite Stone inscription.

BETH-EDEN [bĕth ē'dən] (Heb. *bêṯ ʻeḏen*). A city mentioned in Amos' oracle of doom directed toward Damascus (Amos 1:5; KJV "house of Eden"). It may be the Bit-adini mentioned in Assyrian texts, an Aramean city-state located between Carchemish and Tiphsah. At 2 Kgs. 19:12 (par. Isa. 37:12) and Ezek. 27:23 this place is called Eden (*see* EDEN 2).

BETH-EKED [bĕth ē'kĭd] (Heb. *bêṯ-ʻeqeḏ* "house of shearing"). A place on the road from Jezreel to Samaria, perhaps to be identified with modern Beit Kâd, approximately 5 km. (3 mi.) east of Jenîn. According to Eusebius it is Bethacath, 24 km. (15 mi.) from Legio in the plain. It was here that Jehu met and killed the kinsmen of King Ahaziah (2 Kgs. 10:12, 14; KJV "shearing house").

BETHEL [bĕth'əl] [Heb. *bêṯ-'ēl* "house of God"] (DEITY). A West Semitic deity, perhaps of Phoenician or Aramean origin, attested in Ugaritic and Phoenician literature and in inscriptions from the time of Esarhaddon (seventh century B.C.) to that of Darius II (fifth century). According to the Elephantine papyri, pagan deities under such names as Eshembethel, Ḥerem-bethel, and ʻAnat-bethel were worshiped along with Yahweh; some of the Jews living in the Elephantine community were named Bethel-nathan, Bethel-nuri, and the like. At one time some scholars held that some of the exiled Jews worshiped Yahweh under the name Bethel.

In the Old Testament Bethel is mentioned as a divine name at Jer. 48:13, probably an epithet for a surrogate worshiped in the northern cult. It occurs also as a personal name at Amos 3:14; as a divine figure regarded as the opposite of Yahweh at 5:5; and at Hos. 10:15 (RSV, JB "house of Israel ").

BETHEL [bĕth'əl] (Heb. *bêṯ-'ēl* "house of God") (PLACE).
1. A prominent center of worship in the Old Testament.

I. History

Bethel is first mentioned with reference to patriarchal times, when Abraham built an altar (Gen. 12:8) and dwelled there following his stay in Egypt (13:3). Here Jacob erected a pillar and consecrated it after seeing angels in a dream ascending and descending a ladder reaching from the earth to heaven, while God reassured him concerning flight from his brother Esau

(28:11-22; cf. 31:13). When upon his return to Palestine Jacob did not keep his vow (33:18–34:31), God directed him to go to Bethel (35:1). Jacob put away the foreign gods (v. 4) and traveled to Bethel, where he built his promised altar to the Lord (v. 7). Again the Lord appeared to him, this time to change his name from Jacob to Israel, and once more Jacob made an offering to the Lord (v. 14).

After the Israelite conquest of the promised land, Bethel was assigned to Benjamin (Josh. 18:22; cf. v. 13), though afterward it became the property of Ephraim (cf. Judg. 4:5; 1 Chr. 7:28). Deborah was a judge near Bethel (Judg. 4:5), and Samuel considered it one of his cities of judgeship (1 Sam. 7:16). During the ministry of Elijah it was the site of a flourishing school of prophets (2 Kgs. 2:3).

While Bethel lost its cultic significance when David made Jerusalem the capital of Israel, it regained a degree of prestige under Jeroboam I, who chose it as a location for his calf worship (1 Kgs. 12:29). Though condemned by a prophet of Judah for this act (1 Kgs. 13:1-3), Jeroboam did not repent but continued in this pattern of worship. The prophets Elijah and Elisha were silent about the pagan religious activities held there, but Amos in the eighth century unequivocally predicted its doom (Amos 5:5; cf. 7:13 where it is considered the "king's [Jeroboam II] sanctuary"). Apparently its idolatrous character was beyond religious reform. Afterward King Josiah of Judah demolished the altar at Bethel, thus terminating whatever cultic role the city still played after the deportation of the inhabitants of the northern kingdom (2 Kgs. 23:15).

II. Identification

The Old Testament supplies several clues to Bethel's general location. It is said to be in the hill country of Ephraim (Judg. 4:5), on the highway toward Shechem and south of Shiloh (21:19), west of Ai (Josh. 7:2; 8:9), and north of Ramah (Judg. 4:5). In the nineteenth century E. Robinson identified the ancient city with modern Beitin. Its alternate name, Luz (cf. Gen. 28:19), may actually have been another site near Bethel (M. H. Woudstra, *The Book of Joshua.* NICOT [1980], p. 258).

III. Excavations†

The site was surveyed in 1927 and first excavated in 1934 by W. F. Albright, with subsequent excavations in 1954, 1957, and 1960 under J. L. Kelso. Evidence indicates a village on the site as early as 3200 B.C., although the city proper was founded not much earlier than 2000. Remains of Canaanite occupation include a city wall, which was frequently rebuilt during the Middle Bronze Age. The site appears to have been leveled by fire *ca.* 1550 and lay in ruins until the fourteenth century, when it was rebuilt to its greatest extent. It attained its architectural height in the thirteenth century, with fine patrician houses and an elaborate sewer and drainage system. Iron Age occupations, following the Israelite conquest, indicate considerably less refined building methods and a relatively primitive culture. By the time of Jeroboam I (tenth century), however, the city was greatly improved and prospered until the early Persian period.

Following the Exile, however, Bethel was but a small village and did not recapture its earlier prominence until its refortification by Bacchides in the Hellenistic period (second century B.C.). Remains indicate that the city flourished in Roman and Byzantine times, but vanished after the Muslim invasion of Palestine.

2. Another name for Bethuel (1 Chr. 4:30) or Bethul (Josh. 19:4), located in the territory of Simeon (1 Sam. 30:27).

BETH-EMEK [bĕth ē'mĭk] (Heb. *bêt hā῾ēmeq* "house of the valley"). A town on the border of the territory assigned to Asher (Josh. 19:27). Mentioned frequently in the Talmud, the name is perhaps preserved in modern Amka, about 10.5 km. (6.5 mi.) northeast of Acco; the probable location of the ancient city is nearby Tell Mîmâs, which bears traces of an Iron Age settlement.

BETHER [bē'thər] (Heb. *beter*). A village southwest of Jerusalem (Josh. 15:59, LXX A *Baither*, B *Thethēr*; cf. LXX *Baiththēr* for Beth-shemesh at 1 Chr. 6:59 [LXX 44]). Some descriptive significance may be derived from Cant. 2:17, where the RSV translates "rugged mountains" (Heb. *hārê bāter*, lit. "mountains of those cut in pieces"). The JB sees here a reference to the ritual cutting of animals in pieces as in the covenant with Abraham (Gen. 15:10), and translates "mountains of the covenant."

Khirbet ej-Jehûdiyeh is identified with the Bether founded by Simon Bar Kokhba as his capital. It was the last Jewish stronghold to fall to the Romans in A.D. 135.

Bibliography. M. H. Pope, *Song of Songs.* AB (1977), pp. 409-411.

BETHESDA [bə thĕz'də] (Gk. *Bēthesda,* probably from Aram. *bêthisdā᾿* "house of mercy"). A pool at the Sheep Gate in the northeastern section of Jerusalem (John 5:2). The pool was renowned for an intermittent spring with curative powers which lasted till the water became mingled with the surrounding water. The sick who sought its cure had to enter the pool immediately after the curative water had been emitted so they might be restored to health (v. 7). Here Jesus healed a paralytic who had been sick for thirty-

The Pool of Bethesda (W. S. LaSor)

eight years (vv. 8-9). Though the better MSS (א L 33) read Gk. *Bēthzatha* ("Beth-zatha," so RSV, NIV mg., JB), the rendering "Bethesda" (so KJV, NIV, JB mg.; based on "Beth Eshdatain" found in the Qumran copper scroll) is "almost certainly correct" (L. Morris, *The Gospel According to John.* NICNT [1971], p. 301).

The pool is very likely the double pool of the St. Anne's Church discovered in 1914. The five "porticoes" (John 5:2) have been related to the colonnades on the four sides and on the partition.

BETH-EZEL [bĕth ēʹzəl] (Heb. *bêṯ hāʾēṣel*). A city in southern Judah, identified with modern Deir el-ʿAṣel, about 16 km. (10 mi.) southwest of Hebron. The prophet Micah cites it in a wordplay on Heb. *ʾāṣal* "to withdraw, withhold" (Mic. 1:11).

BETH-GADER. *See* GEDOR 3.

BETH-GAMUL [bĕth gāʹməl] (Heb. *bêṯ gāmûl* "house of recompense"). A city in Moab against which Jeremiah pronounced judgment (Jer. 48:23). It is probably to be identified with Khirbet ej-Jumeil, about 25 km. (16 mi.) east of Dibon.

BETH-GILGAL [bĕth gĭlʹgăl] (Heb. *bêṯ haggilgāl* "house of Gilgal"). A town in Judah apparently settled by temple singers who participated in the dedication of the rebuilt walls of Jerusalem in the time of Nehemiah (Neh. 12:29). Although it has been identified with both the Gilgal of Benjamin, east of Jericho (Josh. 4:19), and that of Judah (15:7), its location remains uncertain.

BETH-HACCHEREM [bĕthʹhă kĭrʹəm] (Heb. *bêṯ-hakkerem* "house of the vineyard").† Chief city of a district not far from Jerusalem (Neh. 3:14; KJV, NIV "Beth-haccerem") and an elevated area from which smoke or fire signals would be visible (Jer. 6:1; NIV "Beth Hakkerem"). It may be the Karem listed in the LXX of Josh. 15:59. References to the city in the Mishnah and the Qumran literature rule out an earlier identification with ʿAin Kârim, west of Jerusalem. A more likely site is Ramat Raḥel, 3.4 km. (2.1 mi.) south of Jerusalem. Excavations at that site have yielded an Israelite royal fortress and a palace apparently built by Jehoiakim (cf. Jer. 22:13-19). Postexilic seals bearing the names of governors Yehoezer and Ahzai confirm the city's administrative role. A Byzantine church marks the traditional resting place of Mary as she traveled to Bethlehem.

BETH-HAGGAN [bĕth hăgʹən] (Heb. *bêṯ-haggān* "house of the garden"). A town to which King Ahaziah fled from Jehu (2 Kgs. 9:27). It is located approximately 10 km. (6 mi.) south of Jezreel near Ibleam; the modern site is called Jenîn (cf. Engannim, Josh. 19:21; 21:29).

BETH-HARAM [bĕth hârʹəm] (Heb. *bêṯ hārām*). A city of the tribe of Gad, located at the Jordan opposite Jericho (Josh. 13:27; KJV "Beth-aram"); at Num. 32:36 called Beth-haran. Herod the Great changed its name to Livias; Josephus writes that Herod Antipas

called it Julias in honor of Augustus' wife. It is to be identified with modern Tell er-Rameh, north of the Dead Sea and east of the Jordan.

BETH-HOGLAH [bĕth hŏgʹlə] (Heb. *bêṯ ḥoglâ* "house of the partridge"). A village on the boundary between Judah and Benjamin, north of the Dead Sea (Josh. 15:6; 18:19). It was perhaps located at the site of modern ʿAin Hajlah.

BETH-HORON [bĕth hôrʹən] (Heb. *bêṯ-ḥôrôn*, probably "house of [the deity] Hauron"). The name of two cities, namely, Upper and Lower Beth-horon (1 Chr. 7:24), located on the boundary between Ephraim and Benjamin (Josh. 16:3, 5; 18:13-14), about 16 km. (10 mi.) and 12 km. (11 mi.) northwest of Jerusalem. The ancient names are preserved in contemporary Beit ʿUr el-Fōqā (Upper Beth-horon, 533 m. [1750 ft.] above sea level) and Beit ʿUr et-Taḥtā (Lower Beth-horon, 320 m. [1050 ft.] above sea level). At the Conquest Beth-horon became a levitical city (Josh. 21:22), which Sheerah (1 Chr. 7:24) and afterward King Solomon fortified (1 Kgs. 9:17 par. 2 Chr. 8:5).

Commanding a strategic point of the road going to Jerusalem, Beth-horon played an important role in Joshua's battle with the five confederate Amorite kings (Josh. 10:10-11). Retreating from Gibeon, they had to exercise care in descending the ascent of Beth-horon. According to the narrative, God's sending of hailstones and Israel's slaughter of the Amorites (possibly from slopes above the road) all but decimated the Amorite army.

In later Israelite times the city was attacked by Ephraimites displeased with their treatment by King Amaziah of Judah (2 Chr. 25:13). During the Hellenistic period Beth-horon was among those cities fortified by the Jews against the attack of Holofernes (Jdt. 4:4-5). Judas Maccabeus defeated the Syrian general Seron (1 Macc. 3:13-24) and later Nicanor (7:39-43) at Beth-horon; it was later fortified by Bacchides (9:50).

BETH-JESHIMOTH [bĕth jĕshʹə mŏth] (Heb. *bêṯ hayyeʿšimōṯ* "house of loneliness"). A town at the border of the king of Sihon (Josh. 12:3; Num. 33:49; KJV "Beth-jesimoth"; JB "Beth-ha-jeshimoth"), assigned to Reuben after the Conquest (Josh. 13:20), but afterward reconquered by Moab (Ezek. 25:9). It is perhaps to be identified with Khirbet es-Sweimeh, east of the Jordan and north of the Dead Sea.

BETH-JESIMOTH (Num. 33:49, KJV). *See* BETH-JESHIMOTH.

BETH-LE-APHRAH [bĕth lĭ ăfʹrə]. A city mentioned at Mic. 1:10 (KJV "house of Aphrah"; NIV "Beth Ophrah") in a play on words: "in Beth-le-aphrah [Heb. *bêṯ leʿaprâ* "house of dust"] roll yourselves in the dust." It is not unlikely that the Arabs changed the name of this city (which to them sounded like the "house of [the demon] Aphrith") to et-Taiyibeh ("the one of good name"), a site north of Beitîn (L. C. Allen, *The Books of Joel, Obadiah, Jonah and Micah.* NICOT [1976], p. 279, n. 76).

BETH-LEBAOTH. *See* BETH-BIRI.

BETHLEHEM [bĕth'lĭ hĕm] (Heb. *bêṯ leḥem* "house of bread").

1. A village in the territory of Zebulun (Josh. 19:15), about 11 km. (7 mi.) northwest of Nazareth, now called Beit Laḥm. It was the birthplace and burial site of the Israelite judge Izban (Judg. 12:8, 10). Ruins of a synagogue and church indicate that it must have been an important site in antiquity.

2. The northernmost city in Judah (Judg. 19:11-12), 8 km. (5 mi.) south of Jerusalem, called Bit-Laḥmi ("house or temple of Lakhmu," an Assyrian deity) in the Amarna Letters, afterward "house of bread" because of its location in fertile fields within the Judean desert.

I. History

A. In the Old Testament. Bethlehem is first mentioned in the account of Rachel's burial (Gen. 35:19; cf. 48:7). A reference to "Ephrathah (that is, Bethlehem)" is inserted following Josh. 15:59 in the LXX. The Levite serving as a priest in charge of the idol worship in the house of Micah was from this village (Judg. 17:7ff.). So were Elimelech and Naomi (Ruth 1:1). Here Ruth, the Moabite woman, met Boaz (Ruth 3–4), and here, too, David was born (1 Sam. 16:1, 13). As the city of David, it became an important, fortified city under Rehoboam (2 Chr. 11:6). Bethlehem declined in significance, yet the Old Testament records that 123 sons of Bethlehem returned after the Exile to the city of their fathers (Ezra 2:21 par. Neh. 7:26).

B. In the New Testament. Although the last Old Testament reference to Bethlehem is prophetic (Mic. 5:2), it is only in the New Testament that this city gains real prominence as the birthplace of the promised Messiah. As the apostle John states in a rhetorical question: "Has not the scripture said that the Christ is descended from David, and comes from Bethlehem, the village where David was?" (John 7:42). Both Luke (2:4) and Matthew (2:5ff.) record that Christ was born in Bethlehem. Matthew adds that the infamous Herodian massacre of innocent children took place in the same city (2:16-18).

C. In the Early Church. Pilgrims visited Bethlehem as early as the first century A.D. Hadrian (117-138) desecrated the Nativity site, but Constantine was instrumental in the construction of the Basilica of the Nativity above the alleged grotto of Jesus' birth. The grotto, located under the main portion of the transept of this Basilica, differs markedly from the original cave; both the hollow in the limestone and the weak ceiling had to be reinforced in order to withstand the pressure of the superstructure. The present shrine approximates a rectangle, about 14 m. (41 ft.) long by 3 m. (10 ft.) high by an average width of 3 m. (10 ft.). The crypt in which Jesus was born is located at the middle of the east wall; under the altar placed in front of the crypt is a silver star bearing the Latin inscription "Hic de Virgine Maria Jesus Christus natus est" ("Here of the Virgin Mary Jesus Christ was born").

D. Contemporary Bethlehem. Modern Beit Laḥm ("house of meat") is situated 760 m. (2500 ft.) above sea level, near the well of Bethlehem (2 Sam. 23:15-17), which is connected to Rachel's grave by a narrow path. Migdal-eder, resumed to be the field where the

shepherds saw the angels, is probably east of Bethlehem.

II. Traditions

Although the New Testament states only that Christ was born in a manger outside the local inn (Luke 2:7), the ancient tradition of his birth in a cave, mentioned by Justin Martyr (*Dial.* lxxviii.5) and categorically stated by Origen (*Contra Celsum* i.51), may well be correct. An Armenian manuscript dating to 887 attests a cave at Matt. 2:9 ("they [the wisemen] came and stood above the cave where the Christ child was"). However, the reference in the apocryphal Gospel of James is to the cave at Rachel's grave. Caves were used for housing cattle at night, and Mary and Joseph may have sought shelter in just such a cave before the birth of Jesus.

BETHLEHEMITE [bĕth'lĭ hĕm ĭt] (Heb. *bêṯ hallaḥmî*). An inhabitant of Bethlehem of Judah, 8 km. (5 mi.) south of Jerusalem (e.g., 1 Sam. 16:18; 17:58).

BETH-MAACAH. See ABEL-BETH-MAACAH.

BETH-MARCABOTH [bĕth mär'kə bŏth] (Heb. *bêṯ hammar kāḇôṯ* "house of chariots"). A city in the inheritance of Simeon (Josh. 19:5; 1 Chr. 4:31). It was perhaps one of the chariot cities mentioned at 1 Kgs. 9:19; 10:26. A possible identification is Tell Abū Hureirah.

BETH-MEON. See BAAL-MEON.

BETH-MILLO [bĕth mĭl'ō] (Heb. *bêṯ millô'* "house of filling"; Assyr. *mulû* "terrace"). A section of Shechem (Judg. 9:6, 20; KJV "house of Millo"), likely the upper city called "Tower of Shechem" (9:46-47); it was a citadel (cf. Millo of Jerusalem [2 Sam. 5:9; 1 Kgs. 11:27; 2 Chr. 32:5]).

BETH-NIMRAH [bĕth nĭm'rə] (Heb. *bêṯ nimrâ* "house of bitter water"). A city in the inheritance of Gad (Num. 32:36; Josh. 13:27), called Nimrah at Num. 32:3. According to Eusebius (*Onom.* xliv.17), it lay 8 km. (5 mi.) north of Livias (Beth-haram). The name is preserved in Tell Nimrîn (located on the Wâdî Nimrîn in the Transjordan, opposite Jericho), but the oldest settlement of Beth-nimrah (during the Bronze Age) lay in the nearby hills of Tell Bleibil.

BETH-PALET [bĕth pā'lĭt] (Josh. 15:27, KJV). See BETH-PELET.

BETH-PAZZEZ [bĕth păz'ĭz] (Heb. *bêṯ paṣṣēṣ* "house of dispersion"). A town in the tribe of Issachar (Josh. 19:21). The location is not known, although some would locate it at Kerm el-Ḥadîtheh.

BETH-PELET [bĕth pē'lĭt] (Heb. *bêṯ-peleṭ* "house of refuge"). A city in the territory of Judah, located on the southern border toward Edom (Josh. 15:27; KJV "Beth-palet"; Neh. 11:26; KJV "Beth-phelet"). Some scholars would identify it with Tell es-Saqati.

BETH-PEOR [bĕth pē'ôr] (Heb. *bêṯ pᵉʿôr* "house of Peor"). A city in the inheritance of Reuben, located near Mt. Nebo where Moses reminded the Israelites of the covenant stipulations (Deut. 4:46) and was buried (34:6). The city takes its name from Baal-peor, possibly the god of fire, in whose name the Israelites practiced ritual intercourse and human sacrifice (Num. 25:1-5), acts which brought plague upon the entire community (v. 18). According to Eusebius (*Onom.* xlviii.3) the city lay 10 km. (6 mi.) from Livias (Bethharam) on the road to Heshbon; it is perhaps to be identified with Khirbet esh-Sheikh Jâyel.

BETHPHAGE [běth′fə jī] (Gk. *Bēthphagē* "house of [unripe] figs"). A village near the Mount of Olives from which Jesus sent two disciples to fetch an ass and her colt for the triumphal entry into Jerusalem on Palm Sunday (Matt. 21:1); in the parallel passages (Mark 11:1; Luke 19:29) it is mentioned before Bethany, which suggests that Jesus approached from the east. An ancient tradition associates the village with the eastern slope of the Mount of Olives, to the south of Kefr eṭ-Ṭûr.

BETH-RAPHA [běth rā′fə] (Heb. *bêṭ rapaʿ* "house of Rapha" or "house of a giant"). A son of Eshton of the tribe of Judah (1 Chr. 4:12), probably designating a clan or place name.

BETH-REHOB [běth rē′hŏb] (Heb. *bêṭ-rᵉḥôḇ*). A town in the north of Palestine marking the northern limit of the spies' journey (Num. 13:21). According to Judg. 18:28 it was near the city of Laish (later called Dan), perhaps modern Bâniyâs (Caesarea Philippi). 2 Sam. 10:6 mentions Syrian mercenaries from Bethrehob (cf. v. 8, "Rehob") who allied themselves with the Ammonites against Joab. Some scholars would take this as a different town, identifying it with modern Riḥâb, 27 km. (17 mi.) east of Gerash.

BETHSAIDA [běth sā′ə də] (Gk. *Bethsaida* "fisherman's house"). A village on the north side of the Sea of Galilee, the original residence and perhaps the birthplace of three of Jesus' disciples—Andrew, Peter, and Philip (John 1:44; 12:21). Many of Jesus' mighty works took place here (Matt. 11:21; Luke 10:13). The feeding of the five thousand was performed here (Luke 9:10), and here Jesus healed a blind man by spitting on his eyes and laying his hands on him (Mark 8:22-26).

The city (so Luke 9:10; John 1:44; "village" at Mark 8:26) was enlarged or rebuilt by Philip the tetrarch and renamed Bethsaida-Julias in honor of the banished daughter of Emperor Augustus. Josephus (*BJ* ii.9.1[168]) and others locate Bethsaida-Julias in Lower Gaulanitis east of the Jordan. The site has been identified as modern et-Tell, 3 km. (2 mi.) north of the Sea of Galilee; nearby Khirbet el-Araj on the shore of the sea marks the site of the fishing village.

The reference to a Bethsaida "in Galilee" (John 12:21) may be to a suburb west of the river Jordan. The problematic reading at Mark 6:45 "to the other side, to Bethsaida" may be clarified by reading with the Caesarean text Gk. *pròs Bēthsaidan* "to Bethsaida."

BETH-SHAN [běth′shăn, běth shăn′] (Heb. *bêṭ-šan* "house of rest"), **BETH-SHEAN** [běth shē′ən] (Heb. *bêṭ-šeʾan*).† A city strategically located at the juncture of the Jezreel and Jordan valleys. It was located, along with its associated villages, within the territory of the tribe of Issachar (Josh. 17:16), but the city was actually assigned to Manasseh (v. 11; 1 Chr. 7:29); nevertheless, it remained unconquered by the Israelites because the Canaanite inhabitants had "chariots of iron" (Josh. 17:12-16; Judg. 1:27-28). Saul died attempting to wrest the city from the control of the Philistines, who displayed the mutilated bodies of the king and his sons on the city walls (1 Sam. 31:9-12). Apparently Beth-shan was conquered by David, for it appears among the towns in Solomon's fifth administrative district (1 Kgs. 4:12). In Hellenistic times the Greeks called the city Scythopolis (2 Macc. 12:29-30) or Nysa Scythopolis, perhaps based upon a Scythian invasion during the reign of King Josiah, as reported by Herodotus. As Scythopolis it was the chief city of the Decapolis, and the only one west of the Jordan. During the Byzantine era it was the seat of a bishop. After the Arab conquest in A.D. 636, the ancient site, Tell el-Ḥuṣn, was deserted and the name Beisan transferred to the adjacent village.

Excavations at Tell el-Ḥuṣn, conducted from 1921 to 1933 by C. S. Fisher and A. Rowe for the University of Pennsylvania Museum, indicate that the site has been settled almost continuously since Chalcolithic times. In the Late Bronze Age the city apparently functioned as the major Egyptian center in Palestine. It is listed among those cities conquered by Pharaoh Thutmose III (fifteenth century B.C.), and numerous Egyptian remains have been found. Included are a fourteenth-century temple to the local god Mekal, to whom was dedicated a stele inscribed with a prayer; a magnificent relief showing a lion and dog in combat was discovered on a wall of the temple. A victory stele of Seti I (1313-1292) indicates that he reinforced the city's military operations, perhaps with troops from Gath-Carmel; another stele mentions the ʿApiru of Yarmuth, probably the town assigned to Issachar (Josh. 19:21). Two temples, dedicated to Anat (called ʿAntit) and Dagon, were erected in the time of Rameses II and continued in use through the Philistine occupation and into the Israelite period; apparently these were the temples to which the Philistines fastened the armor and head of Saul (1 Sam. 31:10; 1 Chr. 10:10). A large cemetery north of the city has been assigned to this approximate period; it contains several anthropoid coffins (clay coffins bearing human portraits) of dignitaries or mercenaries in Egyptian service. Remains of the Israelite occupation are unimpressive; the relevant strata of the tell bear considerable evidence of destruction by Pharaoh Shishak (*ca.* 920) and the Assyrians or Babylonians. In the postexilic period Beth-shan was little more than a village. A theater, hippodrome, aqueduct, and a great city wall have been discovered, dating to the Roman occupation. Several churches and synagogues as well as a sixth-century monastery survive from Byzantine times.

BETH-SHEMESH [běth shěm′ĭsh] (Heb. *bêṭ šemeš* "house of [the sun-god] Shemesh").

1. A city along the northern border of Judah between Mt. Jearim (Chesalon) and Timnah (Josh. 15:10). Beth-shemesh was a Canaanite city before it

Beth-Shan (Tell el-Ḥuṣn) (W. S. LaSor)

was allocated to the tribe of Dan (called Ir-shemesh at 19:41, probably a reference to a major temple of the sun-god). The Canaanite inhabitants may have resisted Danite occupation, for according to Judg. 1:33 the tribe of Naphthali could impose on them only "forced labor." After the tribe of Dan relocated to the north, the city was designated as belonging to the Levites (Josh. 21:16; 1 Chr. 6:59). It was to Beth-shemesh that the ark of the covenant was returned after the Philistines placed it on a cart drawn by two cows (1 Sam. 6:12-13). During Solomon's reign the city was listed within the second administrative district under the jurisdiction of Ben-deker (1 Kgs. 4:9). It was the scene of the battle between Jehoash of Israel and Amaziah of Judah (2 Kgs. 14:11). The last biblical reference to Beth-shemesh is 2 Chr. 28:18, which records the city's capture by the Philistines during Ahaz' reign. The city was destroyed by Nebuchadnezzar in 588/587.

Beth-shemesh has been identified with Tell er-Rumeileh, 29 km. (18 mi.) west of Jerusalem. It had been associated previously with ʿAin Shems, a site somewhat to the east which preserves the ancient name. Among the remains were a scarab made for the wedding of Amenhotep III and a clay tablet (perhaps an amulet) inscribed in Ugaritic cuneiform script but with the characters formed backward. Evidence of violent destruction suggests that the city was destroyed by the Philistines following their defeat of Shiloh and the removal of the ark to Kiriath-jearim (1 Sam. 6:1–7:2). The tenth-century residence of the district governor appears to have been elevated on an earth-filled platform (millô) such as those at Lachish and Jerusalem. Numerous olive and wine presses indicate that the city was devoted to the dyeing industry and wine-making during the late Israelite period (ca. 950-587). Eighth- and seventh-century jar handles

bear the inscription "for the king" (Heb. lmlk), and one bears the seal of Eliakim, steward of Jehoiachin.

2. A Canaanite city on the border of the tribe of Issachar (Josh. 19:22), most likely contemporary el-ʿAbeidiyeh, 3 km. (2 mi.) south of the Sea of Galilee and east of Khirbet Shamsawi. According to some scholars the Beth-shemesh in Naphtali (19:38) may be the same city.

3. The Egyptian city of On (so JB) or Heliopolis (so RSV) mentioned at Jer. 43:13 (KJV; NIV "temple of the sun"). See ON.

BETH-SHEMITE [bĕth shĕm'īt] (Heb. bêt-haššimši). An inhabitant of Beth-shemesh in Judah (1 Sam. 6:14, 18, KJV).

BETH-SHITTAH [bĕth shĭt'ə] (Heb. bêt haššiṭṭâ "house" or "place of the acacia"). A place mentioned in the account of the battle between the Gideonites and the Midianites (Judg. 7:22), most likely to be identified with modern Shutta on the northern side of the valley of Jezreel, to the east of the fountain of Harod (ʿAin Jalud).

BETH-TAPPUAH [bĕth tăp'yoo ə] (Heb. bêt-tappûah "place of apples"[?]). A city in the hill country of Judah (Josh. 15:53), identified with modern Taffûh, 5.5 km. (3.5 mi.) west-northwest of Hebron. It may be the same as TAPPUAH **3.**

BETH-TOGARMAH [bĕth'tō gär'mə] (Heb. bêt tôgarmâ "house" or "region of Togarmah"). A region north of Palestine where the descendants of Togarmah lived (Ezek. 27:14; 38:6; KJV "house of Togarmah"). Hittite sources mention a Tegarama in Asia Minor, probably the same as modern Gürün (which preserves the name), approximately 200 km. (125 mi.) northwest of Carchemish. It is probably the same as Til-

Garimmu in Cappadocia, mentioned in cuneiform inscriptions and associated with the Cimmerians and Scythians.

BETHUEL [bǐ thōō'əl] (Heb. *bᵉṯûʾēl* "dweller in God").
1. The youngest son of Nahor, Abraham's brother, and Milcah (Gen. 22:22), also called "the Aramean" (25:20; 28:5).
2. A town in the tribe of Simeon near Ziklag (1 Chr. 4:30); at Josh. 19:4 it is called Bethul. The site is probably modern Khirbet el-Qaryatein, northwest of Beer-sheba. Bethel at 1 Sam. 30:27 is probably a misspelling of the same place.

BETHUL. See BETHUEL 2.

BETHULIA [bǐ thōō'lǐ ə] (Gk. *Baituloua, Betuloua, Baitouloua, Baitoulia*). A city in Samaria mentioned only in the book of Judith. The city was strategically located on a hilltop (Jdt. 10:10) opposite Esdraelon near the plain of Dothan (4:6), surrounded by mountains (6:10-12) and with a nearby spring (v. 11). Its fortress was apparently considered a key to the safety of Jerusalem and the temple (8:21, 24). When Holofernes, the Assyrian general of Nebuchadnezzar, besieged the city (7:1ff.), Judith capitalized on an invitation to the general's banquet by beheading him (13:1-10), thus inspiring the Jews to overcome the Assyrians (15:3, 6). The site remains unidentified and the name has been interpreted as a pseudonym for an important city, perhaps Shechem.

BETH-ZAITH [bĕth zā'ĭth] (Gk. *Bēthzaith*, LXX A *Bēzeth*; perhaps from Heb. *bêt zayiṯ* "house of olive"). The place to which Bacchides withdrew and where he slaughtered many of the Jews who had deserted him (1 Macc. 7:19). It has been identified with Khirbet Beit Zeita, about 5 km. (3 mi.) north of Beth-zur; a nearby cistern is said to be the great pit into which the general threw the murdered Jews.

BETHZATHA [bĕth zā'thə] (Gk. *Bethzatha*). A pool in the northeastern section of Jerusalem (John 5:2). This is the form of the name attested in the better manuscripts, and many consider it to be the correct name. See BETHESDA.

BETH-ZECHARIAH [bĕth'zĕk ə rī'ə] (Gk. *Baithzecharia* "house of Zechariah"). The place where Judas Maccabeus defended himself against Antiochus IV Eupator, who had marched against Beth-zur (1 Macc. 6:32-33; cf. Josephus *Ant.* xii.9.4). It is identified with Khirbet Beit Skâriä, 10 km. (6 mi.) northeast of Beth-zur.

BETH-ZUR [bĕth zûr'] (Heb. *bêṯ-ṣûr* "house of rock"). A town in Judah (Josh. 15:58), first occupied by the Calebites (1 Chr. 2:45) and afterward fortified by Rehoboam of Judah (2 Chr. 11:7). After the Exile it was rebuilt and became the capital city of a district (Neh. 3:16).
It played an important role in the Maccabean wars. Fortified by Judas Maccabeus in 164 B.C. (1 Macc. 6:26; KJV "Bethsura"), it surrendered to the Syrians

in 162 (6:31-32, 49). The city was recaptured in 144 B.C. by Judas Maccabeus.
Beth-zur is identified with Khirbet eṭ-Ṭubeiqah, located about 7 km. (4.5 mi.) north of Hebron; at an altitude of 1013 m. (3325 ft.) above sea level, it is one of the highest ancient sites in Palestine. It was also the sole fortress in the western part of Judah, at the upper end of the valley of Elah, and often the site of foreign attacks, as attested by numerous destruction levels at the site. The discovery of numerous coins and jar handles suggests that the city was a thriving commercial center in the late second century B.C. Shortly afterward, however, it was abandoned and never resettled.

BETONIM [bĕt'ə nǐm] (Heb. *bᵉṭonîm* "pistachios"). A city in the territory of Gad (Josh. 13:26), named Botnia or Bothnim by Eusebius (*Onom.* xlviii.11). It is perhaps to be identified with modern Khirbet Baṭneh, approximately 7 km. (5 mi.) southwest of es-Salṭ in Transjordan.

BETROTHAL. See MARRIAGE.

BEULAH [bū'lə] (Heb. *bᵉ'ûlâ* "married").* A symbolic name given to Israel, designating its future prosperity (Isa. 62:4, KJV, NIV). Instead of being forsaken and desolate, Israel will be "married" (so RSV; Heb. *bᵉ'ûlâ* "married"; JB "The Wedded"), lit. "possessed," and its numerous inhabitants will remove the present reproach of its widowhood (E. J. Young, *The Book of Isaiah* [Grand Rapids: 1969], 2:469).

BEVELED WORK. Scrollwork on the bronze stands of the laver in Solomon's temple (1 Kgs. 7:29; KJV "thin work"; NIV "hammered work"; Heb. *ma'ᵃśēh môrāḏ* "work of descent").

BEWITCH.† A term of rebuke used by the apostle Paul at Gal. 3:1 (Gk. *baskaínō*) in regard to the Galatians' yielding to the Judaizing "magicians" who so effectively enticed them that they were unable to see the falsehood underlying the Judaizers' words (see also G. Delling, "βασκαίνω," *TDNT* 1:594-95).

BEYOND THE JORDAN (Heb. *'ēḇer hayyardēn*).† A geographical term designating either the region west (e.g., Gen. 50:10-11, Jacob's burial place [NIV "near the Jordan"; JB "across the Jordan"]; Deut. 3:20, Palestine [NIV "across the Jordan"]) or east (usually, e.g., Judg. 5:17, the inheritance of Gad; Matt. 4:25 [Gk. *péran*; NIV "across the Jordan"; JB "Transjordania"]) of the river Jordan, depending on the writer's viewpoint.

BEYOND THE RIVER. Another name for the area east of the Euphrates from which Hadadezer mustered additional soldiers in his battle with David's general Joab (2 Sam. 10:16 par. 1 Chr. 19:16) and to which Israel was to be deported (1 Kgs. 14:15). Surprisingly, in his farewell address (Josh. 24:3, 14-15) Joshua used a Babylonian viewpoint when he located the homeland of the patriarchs west of the Euphrates. (The RSV usually reads "beyond the Euphrates" when referring to the countries east of that river.) The Persians had their fifth satrapy "beyond," i.e., west of the Euphrates (e.g., Neh. 3:7; KJV "on this side of the river"; NIV "Trans-Euphrates"); it consisted of Syria, Phoenicia, Palestine, and Cyprus. Nehemiah sought the permission of the various governors of this district in order to travel from Susa to Jerusalem (2:7).

BEZAE, CODEX (D). *See* CODEX BEZAE.

BEZAI [bē'zī] (Heb. *bēṣay*). The head of a family that returned from Exile under Zerubbabel (Ezra 2:17 par. Neh. 7:23). One of their representatives set his seal to the renewed covenant (Neh. 10:18).

BEZALEEL (KJV). *See* BEZALEL 1.

BEZALEL [běz'ə lěl] (Heb. *bᵉṣalʾēl* "in the shadow or the protection of God").
1. The son of Uri the son of Hur, of the tribe of Judah. Bezalel and Oholiab were chosen to construct the tabernacle and its furnishings (Exod. 31:1-11; 35:30–36:3; 37:1; 38:22; 1 Chr. 2:20; 2 Chr. 1:5; KJV "Bezaleel").
2. A man of the family of Pahath-moab who was compelled to divorce his foreign wife (Ezra 10:30).

BEZEK [bē'zěk] (Heb. *bezeq*).
1. A city in central Palestine, identical to modern Khirbet Ibziq, which lies between Nablus (Shechem) and Beisan (Beth-shan). Located in the mountains opposite the point where the Wâdī el-Jabis enters the Jordan, it was well suited for Saul's march to Jabesh-gilead (1 Sam. 11:8).
2. A city which later lay within the tribal territory of Judah (Judg. 1:4); perhaps it stood at the site of Khirbet Bezqa, about 5 km. (3 mi.) northeast of Gezer. Here the Israelites defeated the Canaanites and Perizzites, and captured Adoni-bezek.

BEZER [bē'zər] (Heb. *beṣer* "inaccessible") (PERSON). A son of Zophah of the tribe of Asher (1 Chr. 7:37).

BEZER [bē'zər] (Heb. *beṣer* "inaccessible") (PLACE). A city of refuge (Deut. 4:43; Josh. 20:8) and a levitical city (21:36; 1 Chr. 6:78) in Transjordan, perhaps the same city as Bozrah (Jer. 48:24). According to the Moabite Stone, the city was rebuilt and repopulated by the people of Dibon. Bezer is probably to be located at Khirbet Umm el-ʿAmad, 13 km. (8 mi.) northeast of Medeba.

BIBLE.

I. Name

The word "Bible" (Gk. *biblía* "books," from *bíblos* "written document," esp. one written originally on a papyrus) refers to a number of books considered sacred and canonical among Christians. At Dan. 9:2 LXX Gk. *hai bíbloi* (MT Heb. *sᵉparîm* "writings") refers to prophetic Old Testament writings; the earliest Christian usage of this term is found at 2 Clem. 14:2 where it signifies the Old Testament. Other names are "testament" (Gk. *diathḗkē* "covenant") or "covenant" (Heb. *bᵉrîṯ*); at 2 Cor. 3:14 Paul calls the Old Testament "the old covenant." The term "Scripture(s)" designates the Old Testament (Gk. *hai graphaí* "the things written"; e.g., Matt. 21:42). Because the New Testament writings were composed before officially declared canonical, the biblical terms "Scripture(s)" and "old covenant" apply only to the Old Testament. The early Church coined the term "New Testament" in distinction from the Hebrew Scriptures.

II. Division

The Protestant Bible consists of sixty-six books, of which thirty-nine belong to the Old Testament and twenty-seven to the New Testament. In the Roman Catholic versions, which follow the Vulgate, an additional fourteen "deuterocanonical" or apocryphal books are included.

A. Old Testament. Unlike most contemporary English versions of the Old Testament, the Hebrew canon was originally divided into three parts: the Law (Heb. *ṯôrâ* "instruction"), the Prophets (Heb. *nᵉḇîʾîm*), and the Writings (Heb. *kᵉṯûḇîm*). The Law includes the five "books of Moses," also called the Pentateuch: Genesis, Exodus, Leviticus, Numbers, and Deuteronomy. The Prophets in turn are divided into the Former (Joshua, Judges, 1–2 Samuel, 1–2 Kings) and Latter Prophets (Isaiah, Jeremiah, Ezekiel, and the Twelve Minor Prophets, from Hosea to Malachi). The Writings consist of Ruth, Psalms, Job, Proverbs, Ecclesiastes, Song of Solomon (Canticles), Lamentations, Daniel, Esther, Ezra and Nehemiah, and 1–2 Chronicles — the sequence adopted in the Talmud. The MT has subdivided the Writings into three groups: the poetic works (Psalms, Job, and Proverbs), the Scrolls (the Song of Solomon [Canticles], Ruth, Lamentations, Ecclesiastes, and Esther), and the remaining works (Daniel, Ezra and Nehemiah, and 1-2 Chronicles).

The LXX arranges the Old Testament according to the following schema: historic, poetic, and prophetic books. The historic books include Genesis, Exodus, Leviticus, Numbers, Deuteronomy, Joshua, Judges, Ruth, 1–4 Kings (1–2 Samuel, 1–2 Kings), 1–2 Chronicles, Esdras (Ezra), Nehemiah, and Esther. The poetic books comprise Job, Psalms, Proverbs, Ecclesiastes, and the Song of Solomon. The prophetic books are Isaiah, Jeremiah, Lamentations, Ezekiel, Daniel, and the (separate) Twelve Minor Prophets: Hosea, Joel, Amos, Obadiah, Jonah, Micah, Nahum, Habakkuk, Zephaniah, Haggai, Zechariah, and Malachi. (*See also* SEPTUAGINT.)

In the New Testament Christ used this common Old Testament classification. When citing the "law and the prophets" (Matt. 5:17; 7:12; 22:40; Luke 16:16 par. Matt. 11:13), he did not refer merely to the Decalog but rather to the entire Torah. (At Matt. 5:18 par. Luke 16:17; Matt. 12:5; 22:36; 23:23; John 7:49; 12:34 he uses the term "Law" for the Old Testament as a whole.) At Luke 24:44 Christ mentions the "law, the prophets, and the psalms," i.e., the entire Old Testament, while his statement about the blood of Abel (see Gen. 4:8) and that of Zechariah (see 2 Chr. 24:20-21) at Matt. 23:35 par. Luke 11:51 encompasses the entire Old Testament, from Genesis to Chronicles.

Most English versions have adopted the sequence of the LXX, which was retained by the Vulgate.

B. New Testament. The New Testament is divided into the historical books (the four Gospels [Matthew, Mark, Luke, and John] and Acts), the prophetic books (the Epistles), and the Apocalypse (Revelation). The Epistles in turn are subdivided into the major Pauline letters (Romans, 1–2 Corinthians, Galatians, 1–2 Thessalonians), the so-called Prison Letters (Ephesians, Philippians, Colossians, and Philemon), the Pastoral Letters (1–2 Timothy and Titus), Hebrews, and the Catholic Letters (James, 1–2 Peter, 1–2–3 John, and Jude).

See also CANON.

III. Languages and Structure

The Bible reflects the languages of its historical, cultural contexts. Thus, while the Old Testament is written primarily in Hebrew, it also contains Aramaic sections (Ezra 4:8–6:18; 7:12-26; Dan. 2:4b–7:28; Jer. 10:11), as well as some possible Greek words (Dan. 3:5, 7, 10, 15). The language of the New Testament is Koine Greek; in addition, there are several probable Aramaisms (e.g., Matt. 27:46 par.) and terms which show Latin influence (e.g., "centurion," Mark 15:39; "legion," Luke 8:30).

Because the written version of the Old Testament was meant first of all to be read to the Israelites (e.g., Exod. 24:7; Josh. 8:34-35; Neh. 8:4-5, 8), it was divided in the Jewish lectionaries into the Law (Heb. *pārāšôṯ* "explanations") and the Prophets (Heb. *hapṭārôṯ* "conclusions"). While the public readers could recognize larger divisions in these readings, they had to insert additional spaces or breathing pauses (Heb. *pᵉsûqîm*), which may be regarded as the forerunner of the division into verses. The New Testament division into pericopes (large units, intended for daily readings) occurred as early as the second century A.D.; the division of the Epistles into chapters and lections or "reading sections" dates back to Euthalius of Alexandria (*ca.* A.D. 350); the division of Revelation into twenty-two chapters is assigned to the fifth century.

IV. Message

Because the individual books of the Bible were composed over a number of centuries and in various geographical locations, the question of their message and unity is an urgent one. Christians have traditionally believed that each of these (and only these) books was written under the guidance of God, their primary and real author, who brought about one Bible.

The prologue to Sirach (or Ecclesiasticus; *ca.* second century B.C.) states clearly the unity of the Old Testament, and the early Church formally recognized that of the New Testament *ca.* A.D. 200. The Church Fathers confessed the unity of both the Old and New Testaments in their acceptance of the canon. Assisted by various types of biblical criticism, most Christians maintain essentially that assessment.

The core of Scripture's unified message is God's revelation of redemption through his Son Jesus Christ, a revelation unfolded in the Old Testament and fulfilled in the New Testament. Thus, the Bible does not merely comprise a number of individual events reported variously in its many pages. Rather, it contains divine revelation in all its books. Each book, in its own way, renders transparent God's message of redemption, and together they contribute to and form part of the one divine work of redemption. In other words, there is only one Bible, not a series of individual biblical events. (See B. S. Childs, *Introduction to the Old Testament as Scripture* [Philadelphia: 1979].)

This message is enunciated at Gen. 3:15 in the so-called protevangelium. Though God addresses mankind concerning the gospel after the fall into sin, even his prior self-revelation in the Garden as Creator of heaven and earth includes his express right to accomplish redemption in Jesus Christ, for as Creator God has a claim on all living things. Thus, the biblical message is one of redemption or salvation, revealed already in Paradise and afterward through the patriarchs, the prophets, the symbolism of the sacrifices, and finally in God's only-begotten Son.

Gen. 3:15 contains four aspects which are determinative for the entire work of redemption: (1) God will initiate redemption; redemption comes from him; (2) the redeemer is a true human being; redemption comes by the way of the human seed; (3) that seed will bruise the serpent's (or Satan's) head; redemption will entail the destruction of Satan and all his followers; (4) the serpent will bruise the heel of the woman's son; redemption will mean the death of the redeemer. Scripture does not add anything essentially new afterward. Rather, it progressively unfolds this promise in the course of time, permitting the flower and fruit of the New Testament to blossom forth and to ripen on the stem of the Old Testament, while rooting both testaments in the message of salvation. Thus, the secret of the Old Testament is revealed in the New; the message of the New Testament is "concealed" in the Old (so Augustine; see A. D. R. Polman, *The Word of God According to St. Augustine* [Grand Rapids: 1961], p. 115).

The promise of redemption for a world in sin gives rise to the battle between "spirit" (the acceptance of this promise in faith) and "flesh" (the rejection of it in unbelief), which begins in Gen. 4 with the contrast between Cain and Abel. In the continued rejection of this promise, Noah was a "herald of righteousness" (2 Pet. 2:5), a righteousness revealed during the Flood in the judgment of unbelievers and the preservation of believers (Gen. 6:1–9:17). This preliminary judgment and deliverance are prophetic of the complete destruction and perfect blessedness that are to come on the final Day (1 Pet. 3:18ff.).

Placed over against Babel — the power of the antichrist (Gen. 11:1-9) symbolized by the Babel founded by Nimrod (10:8-10) or Babylon (or Rome; Dan. 7) and culminating in present (Rev. 15–17) and future (Rev. 18) Babylon — is the Lord's faithfulness to his calling of Abraham, the father and the firstborn of all believers, who is called out of the darkness of paganism into the light of the gospel (Gen. 12:1-3). The Lord makes a covenant with Abraham promising him that he will be the father of all believers and giving him as a sign the birth of Isaac his own son. In due time Isaac is born, not of Abraham and Hagar or Keturah but of Abraham and Sarah, people "as good as dead" (Heb. 11:11-12; cf. Gen. 21:1-7).

Within this covenantal relationship between God

and Abraham, the promise proceeds by way of the seed of believers: Isaac marries Rebekah (Gen. 24) and together they are blessed with twins. But now the bonds of blood make way for the purposes of God as manifested in election (Rom. 9:11); Jacob and Esau, children of the one covenant, are contrasted as the elected (Jacob the younger) and the rejected (Esau the older). While Esau attaches greater significance to his earthly birthright than to the gracious election of God (Gen. 25:29-34), Jacob, even though he is the elected son, also misuses this grace and seeks his own glory, thus setting a sinful example for the people of God to be named after him (Israel). His descendants are not able to live out of the reality of God's electing grace. Thus, Genesis lays the foundation for the existence of the Israelite nation, which is able to exist only because the "gifts and the call of God are irrevocable" (Rom. 11:29).

According to 1 Cor. 10:6, 11, Israel's rebellion during the wilderness wanderings is a warning to God's people in the Old Testament as well as a means of instruction for New Testament believers. That is, the Old Testament events are first of all actual events in the history of Israel, but they also have meaning for the New Testament Church, the people of God's new covenant. The "typical" significance of these events for the New Testament Church does not mean, however, that every happening in Israel's history will be repeated in the Church, the spiritual Israel. Rather, the Church is to understand the history of Old Testament Israel as its own history.

After Israel, as the bearer of God's promise of redemption, has become a nation in the land of Egypt, it is led out of that "house of bondage (unto sin)," while carrying the Redeemer in its loins (Hos. 11:1; cf. Matt. 2:15). It is for his sake that Israel is called God's son and receives the covenant and the law of the covenant it is to obey in the land of the covenant (Canaan). Paralleling the foundation of the old covenant of Israel "after the flesh," the four New Testament Gospels disclose the foundation for the new and eternal covenant made with spiritual Israel, namely, that of the witness of the "apostles and prophets" (Eph. 2:20). Likewise, Acts parallels the book of Joshua. It is said of Joshua that he was a man filled with the Spirit (Num. 27:18; Deut. 34:9), and that he completed the work of the mediator of the old covenant — Moses — a work that prospered so long as the people of Israel heeded the Word of God. Similarly, the apostles filled with the Spirit of Christ completed the work of the Mediator of the new covenant — Christ — and their work prospered so long as the Church remained true to the Word of its Lord.

The book of Judges portrays the continual departure of God's people from the foundation laid in the covenant of grace and God's continual bringing them back to that covenant through his judges. Kings and Chronicles in turn describe how Israel's theocratic kingship moves further and further away from God instead of leading the people closer to him, thus rendering this theocracy ineffective through the sinful example of Israel's kings. But some of the prophets predict a time when they will finally turn from their sinful ways, in Exile, and learn to look for the real Redeemer, one who is both God and man — the Im-

manuel. Similarly, the New Testament Epistles seek to sustain God's people of the new covenant, while urging them to adhere to the Word. Finally, the exalted Christ, the Lord of the Church, shows in his Revelation to John that the powers of the world are not only unable to bring about deliverance, but continually increase in intensity. Thus, they drive people to commit spiritual apostasy in order that the Church may learn to pray: "Amen. Come, Lord Jesus!" (Rev. 22:20).

From this sketch it is clear that the Old Testament contains, as it were, the seed of the full gospel of Jesus Christ (cf. Gen. 3:15), which will grow in all the parts of the Bible. Thus, all individual books of Holy Scripture are organically related. However, just as the various parts of a plant are not all equally related to the root, not all the parts of Scripture have an equally strong connection to the redemptive work of Jesus Christ. As a result, each individual text must be considered in terms of its immediate and larger contexts, and its place in the whole of the Old and New Testaments, in order to ascertain its precise value within all of Scripture.

V. Authority*

The authority of the Bible stems from its inspiration, in whole and in part, by the Spirit of God in the lives of his people and the work of the authors and transmitters of this Word. Thus the teachings contained therein are held to be authoritative for faith and action. Some branches of the Church have restricted this authority to the Bible itself, while others attribute equal importance to its interpretation by the community of believers (i.e., in the context of Christian tradition) as well as the continuing work of the Holy Spirit through reason and experience. For many conservative believers the acceptance of the full and literal inerrancy or infallibility of the Bible (not a biblical concept) is essential.

Bibliography. J. Barr, *Holy Scripture: Canon, Authority, Criticism* (Philadelphia: 1983); H. von Campenhausen, *The Formation of the Christian Bible* (Philadelphia: 1972); D. K. McKim, ed., *The Authoriative Word* (Grand Rapids: 1983); J. R. Maier and V. L. Tollers, *The Bible in Its Literary Milieu* (Grand Rapids: 1979); J. R. W. Stott, *Understanding the Bible* (Glendale: 1972); G. E. Wright and R. H. Fuller, *The Book of the Acts of God* (Garden City: 1957).

BIBLE, TEXT OF THE.

I. The Old Testament

It is generally held that the Hebrew text of the Old Testament attained its present form through the labor of the Jews *ca.* A.D. 90, after a long process of gradual formation; the length of this process, of course, varied with the different books. Several factors, such as scribal changes and errors, have had some effect on the text.

A. Scribal Changes. The scribes who were responsible for copying the manuscripts introduced three changes.

1. Script. At least by Jeremiah's time the Israelites were using a pointed reed ("pen," Heb. *'ēṭ*, Jer. 8:8) and ink (Jer. 36:18) with which they wrote on animal

skins (or papyrus) joined together to form a scroll (e.g., Jer. 36:13-14; Ezek. 2:9; Zech. 5:1). The characters took the form of the old Hebrew script, which was quite different from that used in modern Hebrew Bibles. Examples of this ancient script are found in the six-line Siloam inscription (*ca.* 700 B.C.), the so-called Gezer Calendar (*ca.* 10th cent.), a number of Israelite seals (8th-7th cents.), the Lachish ostraca (*ca.* 590), and numerous ancient coins dating to various periods of Jewish history. This old Hebrew script, which is very closely related to the old Phoenician and Moabite (found on the Moabite Stone of King Mesha) scripts, was preserved with some modifications in the Samaritan script.

When, after the Exile, Hebrew was gradually superseded by Aramaic, this old script was generally replaced by the Aramaic script. Though originally the Hebrew and Aramaic scripts were closely related to each other, they did develop independently. Jewish tradition (Talmud *Sanh.* 21b) ascribes the change of scripts in Bible texts to one person, Ezra the scribe, but it was really the work of many scribes.

To be sure, even during the first centuries A.D. some biblical manuscripts were still written in the old script, as were fragments of the Dead Sea Scrolls. Gradually the Aramaic script acquired its present form, the so-called square script; this development was completed by the time of Jerome, who wrote the Hebrew characters in their present-day form.

In dealing with problems presented by the Hebrew text, one must take into consideration that much of the text was probably originally written in the old Hebrew script. For example, that the same person is called Heleb at 2 Sam. 23:29 and Heled at 1 Chr. 11:30 is most easily explained on the basis of the old Hebrew consonantal forms of the letters; in old Hebrew the *b* and the *d* were quite similar.

2. Division. On the basis of the Samaria ostraca and the Siloam inscription, by the eighth century Hebrews apparently were using dots or small strokes to separate words. The same method was used in the inscription of the Moabite Stone and in many of the Phoenician inscriptions. This method, however, fell into disuse; in the eighth-century Aramaic inscriptions from Sefire the words were all run together. This method caused mistakes when two distinct groups of consonants were read as one word, or conversely when one group of consonants was split into two words. Thus Amos 6:12 was mistakenly read as "will one plow there with oxen?" (KJV, NIV; Heb. *babbᵉqārîm*), when the correct reading is "does one plow the sea with oxen?" (RSV, JB; Heb. *bᵉbāqar yām*). Similarly, the unintelligible reading *laḥpōr pērôt* "in order to dig ditches" at Isa. 2:20 is to be replaced by *laḥᵃparpārôt* "rats" or "moles" (as in KJV, RSV, JB, NIV). In other instances, word divisions were made in the wrong place, as at Hos. 6:5, where the most probable reading for the conclusion of this verse is "and my judgment goes forth as the light" (Heb. *ûmišpāṭî kāʾôr yēṣēʾ*; RSV, *contra* KJV; cf. JB, NIV). By the fifth century spaces were generally used to divide words, and in the third century special forms were given to certain consonants (*k, m, n, p, ṣ*) appearing at the end of a word; however, some evidence from rabbinic sources (e.g., Palestinian Tal-

mud *Meg.* 1:9) indicates that these forms were not yet totally familiar. (The Dead Sea Scrolls have spaces between the words and also use these final forms of consonants, although not consistently.) The separation of sentences was introduced only later, and then not always made in the correct places. Thus, "my God" at the beginning of Ps. 42:6 (KJV) is to be read with v. 5, so that this verse ends: "my help and my God" (RSV, NIV, JB; cf. Ps. 42:11; 43:5).

3. Vowels and Accents. At first the Hebrew script consisted solely of consonants; the so-called *matres lectionis* (ʾ, *h, y,* and *w*) gradually developed to indicate the presence of long vowels. As long as Hebrew remained the common language this situation presented no serious obstacle to a correct understanding of the text.

Since Aramaic came to replace Hebrew as the vernacular, however, eventually it became necessary to standardize as much as possible the traditional reading of the text and to preserve this for future generations of synagogue worshippers. Thus in the sixth century A.D. vowel points or marks were added to the text to indicate the pronunciation of the words as accurately as possible, and accents clarified the mutual relationships between the words and thereby the meaning traditionally ascribed to larger units within the text. The addition of these vowel and stress marks was part of the contribution of the Masoretes.

B. Textual Corruptions. Meanwhile, the text had been exposed to a long process of historical change. As the number of manuscripts increased greatly, especially those made for private use, the task of transcription was not always entrusted to skilled scribes. In addition, the manuscripts to be transcribed were not always equally legible, either because of frequent use or because of the imperfection of the material used. Another source of textual corruption was the frequent insertion of clarifying comments in the margin for personal use, or substitutions of new words for unclear or obsolete words. Copyists would sometimes think that these insertions belonged in the text and would include them in their transcriptions. A comparison between the Hebrew and Greek texts of the Historical Books provides some idea of the lack of restraint observed with such insertions. Sometimes abbreviations were used, and there was the occasional difficulty in understanding them. This could be the source of a textual corruption at Deut. 32:35, where the Hebrew text has *ly* (lit. "to me"; thus RSV "mine"; cf. KJV, NIV), but the Targum Onkelos, Samaritan Pentateuch, and LXX (followed by NEB, NAB) presuppose a consonantal text *lywm* "for the day," a reading that is also supported by the parallelism of the rest of the verse. Another error was homoioteleuton, which occurs when two identical or similar words are found close to each other and the scribe's eye skips from the first to the second, omitting the words in between. Thus in 1 Sam. 14:41 the Hebrew text (followed by KJV, NIV) omits a sentence included in the LXX and Vulgate (see RSV, JB, NEB) between the first and last occurrences of the name Israel. See further Roberts, pp. 92-100; Würthwein, pp. 105-110.

C. The Text. 1. The MT. It is not surprising that the Jews became more and more concerned about finding a means to check the constant increase in the corruption of the holy text. An attempt was begun in the first century A.D. to arrive at a more accurate fixation of the Hebrew text by means of a rigorous application of a number of rules. Though this endeavor steadily increased in strength, it could be accomplished only after the fall of Jerusalem (A.D. 70) when all of the branches of Judaism submitted to strong rabbinic leadership. Between A.D. 90 and 100 a more or less officially standardized text came into being. The subsequent Greek translations (second century A.D.) show far fewer deviations from the present Hebrew text than the much older LXX translation, and the Hebrew texts used by Origen and Jerome coincide almost completely with those now extant. How the standardization of the text was accomplished can only be guessed. It has been maintained that a standard text came into being during the first century A.D. and that all the later known Masoretic manuscripts are derived from the original authentic manuscript in which the text was fixed. This view was commonly held for some time; at present it is generally accepted that the course of events was much more complicated. It is certain, however, that at the beginning of the first century A.D., and perhaps during the Maccabean period, Jewish scholars (especially under the influence of Rabbi Akiba) worked toward the standardization of the Hebrew text.

Thus, a virtually uniform text, called the "authoritative text," gradually came into being. This uniformity, however, was not complete, for in many places the Masoretes inserted two readings: one indicated by consonants (the so-called Kethib, i.e., "that which is written"), the other by the vowel marks (the Qere, i.e., "that which is to be read"). The former reading is apparently based upon the written traditions, while the latter is perhaps intended to preserve an ancient oral tradition (cf. Gordis). (*See also* KETHIB *and* QERE.) The contribution of the Masoretes extended even further, however. For having arrived at an authoritative text, it was next necessary to guard very carefully against further corruption of this text. To this end they established a number of stringent rules to be followed in the transcription of biblical manuscripts, especially of synagogue scrolls. In addition, they took various measures to insure the regulation and control of manuscripts. They began counting the letters, words, and verses — both for the entire Old Testament and for each individual book — even how frequently a certain word would appear in the Law or in the other two divisions. They also listed all sorts of graphic details to be present in manuscripts recognized as complete: for example, an inverted letter (Heb. *nun*) at Num. 10:34, 36, which indicated that these verses should be transposed; a series of peculiar points placed above and below the Hebrew word, e.g., *lûlē'* at Ps. 27:13, indicated that the word was doubtful; and an open space in the middle of Gen. 4:8 indicated that a clause might be missing.

Considering the amount of labor devoted to the text, one is struck by the degree of respect the Masoretes showed for the text as it had come down to them. The peculiarities of the various biblical books, with all of their archaisms, idiomatic expressions, dialectical nuances, and divergent spellings, were left untouched. Even the disagreements between the various parallel passages were left unchanged. Thus, it is difficult to overestimate the value of the work performed by the Masoretes.

2. *Other Texts.* The most ancient existing manuscripts of part or all of the Hebrew canon include the following: (1) the manuscripts found at Qumrân, the so-called Dead Sea Scrolls; (2) the Nash papyrus; (3) the numerous fragments discovered in the ancient Cairo Genizah, some of which contain parts of the Old Testament text in Hebrew and other languages dating to the sixth to eighth centuries A.D.; (4) the manuscripts of two prominent Masoretic schools, ben Asher and ben Naphtali. The most important of the Asher manuscripts preserved are the Cairo Codex of the Prophets (Codex C; A.D. 895) and the Leningrad Codex (designated by the initial *L*; A.D. 1008), which contains the entire Old Testament. The most significant of the ben Naphtali texts are the so-called Erfurt Codices.

As appears from this brief overview, the extant manuscripts of the Hebrew text are, for the most part, relatively recent. There are three reasons for the lack of older manuscripts: (1) the numerous catastrophes plaguing the Jewish community; (2) the Jewish practice of hiding the manuscripts that had become less valuable and afterward burying them or dropping them into wells; (3) the generally humid climate of Palestine that caused writing materials to deteriorate.

D. Printed Editions. Among the printed editions of the Hebrew text a special place is occupied by the Second Rabbinic Bible. Edited by Jacob ben Chayim and published by Daniel Bomberg at Venice (1524/ 25), this edition enjoyed an almost canonical authority until the twentieth century. It was used as the basis for the first and second Kittel editions. The third (1937) and fourth (1977) editions of *Biblia Hebraica* attempt to reproduce as closely as possible the pure ben Asher text; for this purpose the above-mentioned Leningrad Codex has been used. In a certain sense the form of the present text is much older than that of ben Chayim, for the Leningrad Codex antedates the ben Chayim text by approximately five hundred years, though the differences between the two texts are not extremely significant. The Hebrew University Bible Project is the most ambitious attempt at comprehensiveness; based on the Aleppo Codex (also a ben Asher text, *ca.* A.D. 930), this Bible will provide four critical apparatuses: variants of the early versions, of the Dead Sea Scrolls and rabbinic literature, of the medieval manuscripts, and of peculiarities of scripts, pointing, and accents.

E. Textual Witnesses. Thus far the discussion has focused primarily on the Masoretic Text. In order to come within the reach of establishing the "correct text," insofar as there is such a text, other textual witnesses, especially the ancient translations, must be taken into account. It is the task of the textual critic to compare all of the sources in order to ascertain, where possible, the correct reading of the text. The two best guides to the methodology of text criticism are Roberts and Würthwein; for an excellent survey of the complexities of current text criticism, see Cross and Talmon.

For some time the Septuagint (LXX) enjoyed a position of great authority. Since 1950, however, the

Masoretic Text has gained in significance on account of the discovery of the Dead Sea Scrolls. This development is to be applauded, but a proper evaluation must include two comments. (1) Though the extant Hebrew manuscripts are, generally speaking, rather recent, it must be remembered that after the "authoritative text" was established (perhaps *ca.* A.D. 100), the Jewish scribes took painstaking care to preserve important variants and to prevent further changes from slipping into the text (see C.1 above), and that the scholars responsible for establishing the "authoritative text" used, as much as was in their power, ancient manuscripts. (2) There is no real basis for regarding the Masoretic Text itself as inspired by God and therefore canonical, as happened at times in some Jewish and Christian circles. Nevertheless, the Masoretic Text is the best text available and is for the most part intelligible. There are indeed many obscure passages which naturally have led scholars to assume the presence of textual corruption. While recognizing this fact, may one go further into the past beyond the work of the Masoretes in ascertaining a text's meaning? It must be remembered that the Masoretes had access to better sources than contemporary scholars and made the best possible use of them. There are relatively few instances where their work can be improved upon with a fair degree of certainty.

II. The New Testament

The original copies of the New Testament books (written or dictated [cf. Rom. 16:22] by the authors themselves) have not been preserved. From earliest times countless copies were made that were used among the churches when they read from the Gospels or the Pauline letters during their gatherings. The frequent use of these documents and the fragile nature of the customary writing material of that time (papyrus) necessitated repeated recopying. The original text is separated by at least several copies from the oldest manuscripts handed down; since only a few of these many intermediary manuscripts (papyri) have been discovered, there is an estimated gap of a few centuries. Nevertheless, among Christians there is no real doubt concerning the reliability of the New Testament text, which has been providentially preserved in thousands of manuscripts. With two major exceptions (Mark 16:9-20; John 7:53–8:11) only insignificant details, such as a letter, a word, or a single sentence, are uncertain, and even here the essential content of Scripture is in no way affected. Because of the frequent use of the New Testament Scriptures, far more manuscripts have been preserved than of any other single writing from classical antiquity. And because of the reverence in which the Word of God was held, great care was devoted to the faithful preservation and transmission of the text.

A. *The Written Text.* During the fourth century A.D. papyrus was superseded by parchment, a writing material made by tanning animal skins (mostly from goats and sheep). The use of parchment changed the overall form of the manuscripts. A papyrus manuscript most often took the form of a scroll. In contrast, a parchment manuscript generally was in the form of a codex, i.e., it consisted of a number of pages folded double and placed inside each other. By far the greatest number of extant manuscripts containing all or part of the New Testament are in the latter form.

Originally the Greek text was written in capital letters, without spaces between the words and without punctuation and accent marks; two or three, and later even four, columns appeared on each page. Since the ninth century A.D., manuscripts also contained lower-case letters and a cursive script. From the type of script and the form of the letters the approximate date of a manuscript can be determined; together with the name of the copyist, this date appears on many of the more recent manuscripts.

That approximately two centuries stand between the apostles and the oldest known complete New Testament manuscript is due to the circumstances that prevailed in the early Church. The believers were mainly illiterate people with limited resources, probably lacking for the most part the means of procuring durable, costly copies of the Bible books to be used in their gatherings. In addition, the Church was frequently subject to persecution before the conversion of Constantine the Great (*ca.* 312). One of the means by which the Roman government tried to root out this new religion was through the destruction of its holy books, which the Christians were often compelled to hand over to Roman investigators. And yet, the Church of Christ could not be rooted out, nor could its opponents deprive it of the Word of God, for the New Testament, as well as the Old, was passed down from generation to generation under the guidance of the Spirit.

Because frequent recopying of New Testament manuscripts caused some changes in the text, it is necessary to compare the various extant manuscripts in order to determine the correct scriptural text. Such changes were sometimes made inadvertently by copyists, sometimes deliberately; e.g., in the first three Gospels a word or a report in one Gospel was sometimes altered or supplemented in accordance with a parallel passage in another account.

The task of the textual critic has been greatly simplified by the fact that the numerous manuscripts can be organized into groups according to the location of the church in which they originated, e.g., Palestine or Syria. Much labor was devoted to the accurate transmission of the text at the noted libraries at Caesarea (fourth century) and Alexandria (second and third centuries), as well as later at Constantinople. In the Western part of the Church (Italy, North Africa, and Gaul), a Latin version, in circulation from the second until the end of the fourth century, showed many peculiar deviations from the text used at Alexandria and later at Constantinople. The origin and the significance of the so-called Western text have not as yet been fully fathomed, leaving various questions without satisfactory answers.

Besides the organization of manuscripts into groups, in some cases it is even possible to speak of families of manuscripts, i.e., series of manuscripts which either directly or indirectly go back to one original. Such an arrangement further simplifies the task of assessing the significance of variant readings in the text, for a variant noted in one manuscript will frequently be found in the other manuscripts belonging to the same group or family. Since the middle of the eighteenth century a special method has been followed for designating the New Testament manuscripts in which the letters of the alphabet (A, B, C) refer to manuscripts written in capital letters (uncial manuscripts) and numbers to manuscripts in cursive script (minuscule manuscripts). Some scholars have proposed other systems for designating the manuscripts, but none of these has gained sufficient acceptance.

B. *The Translated Text*. Along with the Greek manuscripts the ancient translations are also of great importance for determining the original Greek New Testament text. Such translations include the Old Latin (third century), the Old Syriac (second century), and the Coptic translations of Upper and Lower Egypt, namely, the Sahidic (third century) and Bohairic (fourth century) versions. Moreover, early writings of the Church Fathers are a tremendous aid, for many of these works repeatedly quoted a New Testament text, thus allowing textual critics a view of the form of the text to which the Fathers had access.

Due to the influence and the labor of the Byzantine Church, the Greek text of the New Testament gradually assumed a more fixed form during the fourth to eighth centuries (the Textus Receptus). While in some sections this text differed slightly from the text of the older manuscripts, once this standard text was adopted, further alteration and corruption were almost entirely eliminated.

C. *The Printed Text*. The invention of printing occasioned a considerable change in the reproduction and transmission of the text. For one thing, the replacement of the pen of the monastery scribes by the printing press greatly diminished the possibility of mistakes and textual alterations.

The first printed edition of the Greek text was completed on January 10, 1514. Directed by Cardinal Ximenes, the Archbishop of Toledo, who initiated this project in 1502 in honor of the birth of Charles V, it soon became known as the Complutensian Polyglot, an edition containing also the Hebrew text of the Old Testament and the Vulgate text of the New Testament (thus *Polyglot* "in many languages"), printed at Acala (Lat. *Complutum*), Spain. It was only in 1520 that Pope Leo X gave permission for its publication, however, and it was put into circulation *ca.* 1522, a few years after the first printed edition of Erasmus.

Erasmus' edition is the first published New Testament text. Requested by Froben, a printer living at Basel, Erasmus' edition was prepared in great haste between September, 1515 and March 1, 1516. Its significance lies more in the timing — the first to appear on the book market — than in its scholarly value. The manuscripts which Erasmus consulted were, according to his own claims, among the oldest and the best, but in reality they were rather recent and of little value. The Greek text of a small portion of the book of Revelation was missing from the manuscripts he consulted, and he had to translate this section back into Greek from the Latin Vulgate, a task in which he was not completely successful.

Erasmus' edition (which was reprinted in 1519, 1522, 1527, and 1535) exerted a great influence on many subsequent editions, e.g., those of the Paris printers Robert and Henri Estienne (Lat. *Stephanus*) which appeared in 1546, 1549, and 1550; the latter

was the first to have marginal notes indicating the readings of some fifteen manuscripts, and its fourth edition (1551) was the first to divide the text into verses (the division into chapters originated with Stephen Langton, *ca.* 1200). T. Beza, the friend of the reformer Calvin, produced no fewer than nine editions of the Greek New Testament between 1565 and 1604, all of which were largely based on Erasmus' editions. Luther used Erasmus' 1519 edition or a reprinting of it, while the Elzevir brothers at Amsterdam published various editions of the Greek New Testament (e.g., in 1624 and 1633) likewise based mainly upon the editions of Erasmus.

Discovery of additional manuscripts, closer study of the writings of the Church Fathers, and other changes brought about a new era in the history of the printed text. Comparison of an ever greater number of manuscripts necessitated the production of editions in which variant readings were noted and the supposedly correct text was printed. In this connection the London Polyglot of B. Walton should be mentioned (1657), an edition in six volumes containing the Greek, Syriac, Latin, Ethiopic, Arabic, and Persian texts, as well as the readings of some fifteen manuscripts. Furthermore, the scholarly English edition of J. Mills deserves mention (1707); it formed the principal source of the 1745 text produced by the noted German theologian J. A. Bengel. Finally, the erudite edition of J. J. Wettstein appeared in 1751/52; it contained the Greek text with the readings of many different manuscripts placed below, as well as explanatory comments including numerous quotations from Jewish, Greek, and Latin writers.

Among modern critical editions K. Lachmann's work (1842-1850) holds a special position, for he attempted to come to grips with the history, the development, and the changes in the written text. C. Tischendorf produced more editions of the text than any other person — no fewer than twenty-four — and his eighth edition (1872) incorporates an immense amount of scholarly material; after his death (1874) the Prolegomena of his work was completed by C. R. Gregory in 1894. An equally valuable work is the English edition of B. F. Westcott and F. J. A. Hort (1881); this edition contains a text which was revised and improved according to principles laid down in its valuable introduction. The popular text of Eberhard Nestle, *Novum Testamentum Graece*, which first appeared in 1898, strikes a balance between the editions of Tischendorf and Westcott-Hort. Subsequent editions include changes made by his son Erwin Nestle, who did not base his editions exclusively upon those of Tischendorf and Westcott-Hort, but used a different reading whenever he thought that a better text could be supplied. Since 1952 (21st ed.) K. Aland has been associated with this text; his involvement with the United Bible Societies' text (see below) as well has led to the wording of the text of the 26th edition (1979) being identical to that of the United Bible Societies' text, though they do differ, especially in the critical apparatus.

New evidence continues to accumulate. Additional manuscripts, discovered in the monasteries of Greece and in the arid sand of Egypt where discarded papyri containing fragments of the Greek New Testament were dug up in great numbers in the vicinity of various ancient cities, necessitated further pursuit of textual criticism. The edition of H. von Soden (1913) was an ambitiously conceived work attempting to determine the New Testament text according to new principles; the resultant text, however, differed only slightly from those of Tischendorf and Westcott-Hort. However, when it became evident that von Soden had worked with a very subjective method, his text, at first applauded, became generally rejected. At the same time not only were still more textual witnesses discovered, but slightly different principles were developed as well, thus necessitating a new general edition of the Greek New Testament. As a result, an edition of the gospel of Mark prepared by S. C. E. Legg appeared at Oxford in 1935, and a similar edition of the first gospel followed in 1940. Yet newer insights were being gained: the Byzantine text, which had long been regarded as inferior, was granted more significance, and other rules for establishing the text came to be accepted. In this connection the names of G. D. Kilpatrick and K. Aland are of particular importance. From 1956 to 1966 an international committee, including K. Aland, M. Black, B. Metzger, and A. Wikgren, worked on a new edition especially for Bible translators and students, *The Greek New Testament* (United Bible Societies; 1st ed. 1966, 3rd ed. 1975).

Bibliography. K. and B. Aland, *The Text of the Greek New Testament* (Grand Rapids: 1987); D. R. Ap-Thomas, *A Primer of Old Testament Text Criticism*, 2nd ed. (London: 1965); F. M. Cross and S. Talmon, eds., *Qumran and the History of the Biblical Text* (Cambridge, Mass: 1975); J. Finegan, *Encountering New Testament Manuscripts* (Grand Rapids: 1974); C. D. Ginsburg, *An Introduction to the Massoretico-Critical Edition of the Hebrew Bible* (1897; repr. New York: 1966); R. Gordis, *The Biblical Text in the Making: A Study of the Kethib-Qere*, 2nd ed. (New York: 1972); P. Kahle, *The Cairo Geniza*, 2nd ed. (London: 1959); B. M. Metzger, *The Text of the New Testament*, 2nd ed. (Oxford: 1968); B. J. Roberts, *The Text and Versions of the Old Testament* (Cardiff: 1951); E. Würthwein, *The Text of the Old Testament* (Grand Rapids: 1979).

BIBLE TRANSLATIONS.†

I. Ancient Versions

In the centuries following the Babylonian Exile, Aramaic-speaking Jews became increasingly less able to understand the Biblical Hebrew of the Old Testament. Thus the synagogue reading of the Hebrew Scriptures was accompanied by an oral paraphrase in Aramaic (cf. Neh. 8:8). These translations or Targums included explanatory material and reinterpretations in light of contemporary conditions and reflect the later Jewish tendency to avoid anthropomorphic representations of God as well as the divine name itself. Many Targums developed in different settings for the various parts of the Old Testament. The most important are the Palestinian Targum (which never had a single authoritative text), which reflects the spoken Aramaic of Jesus' time; the Fragment Targum or Targum Jerusalem II and the Targum Pseudo-Jonathan; and the

official synagogue Targums, Targum Onkelos for the Pentateuch and Targum Jonathan for the Prophets, both of which originated in Palestine but whose wording was fixed in Babylon by the fifth century A.D.

The Jews at Alexandria were likewise unfamiliar with Biblical Hebrew, and in the first half of the third century B.C. the Pentateuch was translated into Greek, with translation of the remaining portions completed during the next two centuries. The Letter of Aristeas contains a legendary account wherein the translation of the Pentateuch was commanded by Ptolemy II Philadelphus (285-247 B.C.) and completed by seventy-two scholars in seventy-two days, hence the name Septuagint (LXX, lit. "seventy"); Philo of Alexandria (*ca.* 25 B.C.–A.D. 40) embellished the account, extending the work to the entire Old Testament and claiming its divine inspiration whereby the individual translators worked independently yet produced seventy-two identical renditions. Examination of the text, however, indicates a combination of numerous versions both literal and free and marked by considerable variance in style, interpretation of the Hebrew, and even order and contents; the latter suggests a variety of underlying Hebrew texts. The Greek-speaking authors of the New Testament quoted from the LXX rather than the Hebrew text, and the LXX became their authoritative scriptures. Its use by Christians for proselytizing and in anti-Jewish polemics, as well as the growing Jewish dissatisfaction with the LXX for being too loose a translation and not based on the current authoritative text (it varied also from the order of the Hebrew canon, led to the more literal translations of Aquila (A.D. 130), Theodotion, and the Ebionite Christian Symmachus. Later revisions of the LXX included one from Origen's Hexapla (A.D. 230-240) and those by Eusebius of Caesarea, Lucian of Samosata, and Hesychius (fourth century). The oldest complete manuscripts of the LXX in existence are the Codex Vaticanus and Codex Sinaiticus (fourth century) and the Codex Alexandrinus (fifth century); significant papyri include those of the Chester Beatty collection (second-fourth centuries), Papyrus Greek 458 of the John Rylands Library (second century), and the Berlin fragments of Genesis (third century). Study of the LXX is useful not only for textual matters (including vocalization of Old Testament proper names) but for insights into Alexandrian and later Jewish theology, including its circumscription of anthropomorphisms (e.g., "power" for "hand," Josh. 4:24) and a tendency toward spiritualization (e.g., the portrayal of the "sluggard" as a "non-religious person" at Prov. 24:30).

Various translations, known as the Old Latin versions, were based on the LXX as early as the second century A.D. in North Africa and Southern Gaul. The multiplicity of such versions necessitated a uniform translation, and in 382 Pope Damasus I commissioned Eusebius Hieronymus, better known as Jerome. Jerome began with a cursory revision of the Psalter on the basis of the LXX, then revised it using Origen's Hexapla and later the Hebrew text. This third translation spurred Jerome's major accomplishment, a translation of the entire Old Testament on the basis of the

Hebrew text, produced 390-405. The Vulgate (so named because it reflects the vernacular of the common people; Lat. *vulgaris*) gained favor over the Old Latin by the eighth century, and in 1546 the Council of Trent designated it the official version for the Roman Catholic Church. The hastily prepared edition issued by Pope Sixtus V (1590) was replaced by that of Clement VIII (1592), which has remained authoritative ever since.

Parts of the New Testament were translated into Syriac, an Aramaic dialect used in various eastern (West Mesopotamian) churches, during the second century A.D. Roughly contemporary was Tatian's Diatessaron, a harmony of the Gospels. Most important of the Syriac versions of both the Old and New Testaments is the Peshitta (lit. "the simple [or plain] version"). The Peshitta translation of the Pentateuch, which follows the Masoretic Text and seems to have been influenced by the Targum Onkelos, may have been initiated in the first century A.D.; other books were completed in the second or third century A.D. and resemble the paraphrases of the Targums, with evidence of revision on the basis of the LXX. The New Testament Peshitta (fourth century) is a revision of the Old Syriac following the Greek text; because the Syrian church did not accept the minor Catholic epistles (2 Peter, 2-3 John, Jude) and Revelation as canonical, they are not included.

Other important ancient translations include the Coptic versions (third-fourth centuries), particularly those in the Sahidic and Bohairic dialects; Gothic (fourth century); Ethiopic (fourth century); Armenian (fifth century); and Arabic (tenth century).

II. Medieval and Reformation Versions

As long as Latin was the official language of the Western Church, there was no need for translation beyond the Vulgate of Jerome. But with the rise of nationalism in the twelfth and thirteenth centuries various efforts were made at translation into the vernacular (e.g., Alfric of Bath [*ca.* 1000], Anglo-Saxon; Peter Waldo [1170] and various scholars at the University of Paris [1226-1250], French). This development was fostered by the use of the printing press (e.g., J. Mentel, 1466) and received its greatest impetus from the Protestant Reformation. The first Bible translated from the original languages into a modern European vernacular was that of M. Luther (1522), a translation characterized by skilled application of Saxon and other German dialects which had profound influence on German language and literature. P. R. Olivétan published the first French Protestant version in 1535 at Serrières in Switzerland; the revision by R. Stephanus (or Estienne) in 1553 is credited as the first to represent chapters and verses. The States-General Bible, published at Leiden in 1637, became the official version for the Dutch Reformed Church.

III. English Versions

The first English translation of the entire Bible was that of J. Wyclif (1380-82). Based on the Latin text, the translation is often stiff and unidiomatic English, but the work represents a concerted effort to render the Bible accessible to the common reader.

A major influence on the history of the English Bible was W. Tyndale, whose work represents the first printed English New Testament (1525, revised 1534) and the first translation from Greek to English. Likewise his Old Testament translation (1530-34) was based on the Hebrew, and the work also relied on Luther's German translation, the Vulgate, and Erasmus' Latin translation. Religious and political opposition forced Tyndale to shift his operation from England to Hamburg, Wittenberg, Cologne, and Worms, and many copies of the early editions were destroyed, largely because of the controversial marginal notes which were critical of liturgical usages. Tyndale was martyred in 1536 at Antwerp, but his translation had great impact on later work (nearly eighty percent of the KJV can be traced to Tyndale) and on the eventual acceptance of the need for translation into the vernacular.

Subsequent works included a conciliatory revision of Tyndale's translation by M. Coverdale in 1535; supplementing Tyndale's work with his own translation from German and Latin, Coverdale produced the first complete English version in print. A compilation of both Tyndale's and Coverdale's work with minor alterations was issued by T. Matthew (probably Tyndale's disciple J. Rogers) in 1537. Building upon the Matthew Bible was a new revision by Coverdale using the Vulgate, Erasmus' translation, and Münster's literal Latin translation of the Hebrew. Variously called Cromwell's Bible, Cranmer's Bible, and the Great Bible, this was primarily Tyndale's version minus the controversial notes; it was widely accepted as the pulpit Bible and strongly influenced the Book of Common Prayer. Forced into exile by the Roman Catholic Mary Stuart, W. Whittingham (assisted by Coverdale) produced a revision of the Great Bible at Geneva in 1560; this Geneva Bible (also called the "Breeches Bible" for its translation of Gen. 3:7) was based upon a high level of scholarship and was widely accepted by the common people.

Seeking to counter the influence of the Protestant translations while rigidly upholding standard Catholicism, Roman Catholics produced an often obscure translation based on the Vulgate ("the authentickk Latin") with attention to the Greek and previous English versions. The work was begun at Douay, France, forced by political pressure to move to Rheims (where the New Testament was translated), then back to Douay (where the Old Testament was finished in 1593); it was published in 1609-10.

Encouraged by the Puritan J. Reynolds, King James I of England commissioned a new translation of the Bible based on the original Hebrew and Greek. Fifty-four scholars (only forty-seven names are recorded) from Westminster, Oxford, and Cambridge, organized into six teams, produced the basic translation, which was then revised by twelve representative translators. Completed in 1611, the work was at first sharply criticized, and numerous revisions were issued from 1613 to 1769, when an official ("Oxford") edition was adopted. Nevertheless, the King James (or Authorized) Version came to be regarded as a major contribution to English literature and still finds widespread use among English-speaking believers. A revision (the Revised Version or ERV) was published in England in 1881-85 (and with modifications in 1901 as the American Standard Version), and enjoyed brief popularity but could not supplant the KJV nor satisfy those who favored its revision.

In the late nineteenth century scholars determined that the New Testament (Koine) Greek was actually a popular rather than literary dialect, a discovery which prompted numerous nonliterary or "modern-speech" translations. Among these were F. Fenton, *The Holy Bible in Modern English* (London: 1895-1905); J. Moffatt, *The Bible: A New Translation* (New York: 1922-24); E. J. Goodspeed, *The New Testament: An American Translation* (Chicago: 1923); A. R. Gordon, T. J. Meek, J. M. P. Smith, and L. Waterman, *The Old Testament: An American Translation* (Chicago: 1927); and J. B. Phillips, *The New Testament in Modern English* (New York: 1958). Although some, such as *The Living Bible* by K. N. Taylor (Wheaton: 1971), are merely paraphrases of earlier English translations, most modern-speech versions are based on the original languages. The New English Bible (1961-1970), sponsored by the Church of Scotland, reflects modern mainstream British scholarship; it relies on various ancient versions including the Dead Sea Scrolls and is often paraphrastic in seeking to avoid overly literal translations of ancient idioms and constructions. Today's English Version (1966-1976; also called the Good News Bible), published by the American Bible Society, applies the insights of modern linguistic study in rendering the text as interpreted by its ancient audience into idiomatic modern English at a level accessible to the average reader.

The most widely accepted English translation of the twentieth century, in terms of both English style and scholarly competence, is the Revised Standard Version (1946-1952). Basing their work on the consonantal Hebrew text and the Westcott-Hort Greek text, the RSV translators also consulted recent manuscript discoveries as well as the most reliable ancient versions; the infrequent conjectural emendations noted in the text were cautiously undertaken.

In 1941 Roman Catholics published the Confraternity of Christian Doctrine Version, a revision of the Douay-Rheims New Testament based on the Vulgate; this translation was itself revised after the 1943 encyclical *Divino Afflante Spiritu* permitted translation from the original languages. Protestant scholars were added to the project after the Second Vatican Council (1962-65), and the entire Bible (including the revised New Testament translation) was published in 1970 as the New American Bible. The Jerusalem Bible (1966) is the English equivalent of *La Bible de Jérusalem*, produced in 1954-55 (and revised in 1961) by French Dominican scholars at the École Biblique in Jerusalem. Notes and introductions were translated from the French, but the biblical translation is based primarily on the Hebrew and Greek. Distinctively Christian in perspective, this version is founded on solid textual, literary, and historical study and is a work of high literary quality.

One hundred conservative scholars contributed to the New International Version (1973-78), which was intended as the twentieth-century equivalent of the King James Version. Based on the MT and the 1550

Greek text of R. Stephanus, the translation represents modern literary rather than spoken English and is cautious though somewhat defensive in interpretation.

Bibliography. F. F. Bruce, *The English Bible* (London: 1970); E. E. Flack, et al., *The Text, Canon, and Principal Versions of the Bible* (Grand Rapids: 1956); J. P. Lewis, *The English Bible from KJV to NIV* (Grand Rapids: 1981); I. M. Price, *The Ancestry of Our English Bible*, rev. ed. (New York: 1956); E. Würthwein, *The Text of the Old Testament* (Grand Rapids: 1979).

BIBLICAL CRITICISM.† A variety of techniques and disciplines have been employed in an effort to determine the exact and original wording of the biblical text and to seek to elucidate its meaning for both its original audience and today by examining matters of authorship, transmission, and application. While a fundamentalist element views this approach as a threat to the authority of the Word, most branches of the Church recognize the importance of such an approach to biblical studies.

I. Textual Criticism

The aim of textual criticism is to establish or restore the original wording of the biblical documents wherever changes have been introduced either by accident or intention during the process of copying and recopying manuscripts. Comparison of manuscripts, translations, and materials contained in quotations is an integral part of this approach. Textual critics seek to determine scribal errors and to explain manuscript differences in terms of social, historical, and theological influences. Establishment of a reliable text is essential to further study and interpretation.

See also BIBLE, TEXT OF THE.

II. Literary and Historical Criticism

Matters of structure, date, and authorship are the primary concern of "higher criticism," a term first applied to biblical studies by J. G. Eichhorn in 1787. Dating may be determined to a degree by historical references within the text (including specific formulas; e.g., Hos. 1:1; Zeph. 1:1), linguistic or stylistic peculiarities which can be compared with other datable writings, or quotation by other works. Structure and authorship are more complex matters and are generally related to questions of sources and editing or redaction. The Bible itself refers to various documents or sources upon which the biblical writers have drawn (cf. Num. 21:14; Josh. 10:13; 1 Kgs. 14:19; *see* BOOK), and in rare instances both a documentary source and the later work which draws upon it are available for comparison (e.g., 1-2 Chronicles and its sources, 1-2 Samuel and 1-2 Kings; note in this regard the value of the Dead Sea Scrolls).

Modern literary criticism received its greatest impetus from the study of the Pentateuch. In 1682 R. Simon noted the duplication of the creation and flood accounts as well as stylistic variations and posited multiple authorship. Building upon H. B. Witter's discovery (1711) of the use of different divine names in these duplicate accounts, J. Astruc (1753) distinguished two pre-Mosaic sources throughout Genesis. This early documentary hypothesis was further developed by J. G. Eichhorn (1780) and K. D. Ilgen

(1798). Subsequent study led to the fragmentary hypothesis of A. Geddes (1792) and J. S. Vater (1802), which claimed a large number of sources. W. M. L. de Wette (1806) developed this conception into the supplementary hypothesis, according to which the Pentateuch was formed from one main writing, the Elohist document, which was supplemented by various Yahwistic fragments; associated with this hypothesis is the work of H. Ewald (1843), F. Bleek, and F. Tuch. In 1857 H. Hupfeld distinguished two sources in Genesis that used the divine name Elohim and subsequently developed the classical documentary hypothesis, which assumes four basic sources: Elohist 1 (E), Elohist 2 (later distinguished as the Priestly source [P]), Yahwist (J), and Deuteronomist (D). Drawing upon the historical-critical research of W. Vatke (1835), K. H. Graf (1866), and A. Kuenen (1869), whose development hypothesis correlated laws and institutions with stages in Israel's religious development, J. Wellhausen related the four-document hypothesis to Israel's religious history; accordingly, the Yahwist source was taken to be the earliest Pentateuchal document. Numerous modifications of this basic theory have been offered, including extensive subdivision of sources (e.g., O. Eissfeldt [1922], R. H. Pfeiffer [1930], G. von Rad [1934]) and redating of the crucial Deuteronomic source (e.g., R. H. Kennett [1920], T. Oestreicher [1923], A. C. Welch [1924], E. Robertson [1950]).

Summarily discredited by those who maintain Mosaic authorship of the Pentateuch, the Wellhausenian position has been supplanted on critical grounds as well. Archaeological studies have disproven much of the Wellhausenian reconstruction of Israelite history and have challenged the wisdom of primarily literary study as well, citing the need for viewing the biblical accounts in the context of their greater Near Eastern social and cultural environment. Of particular influence here have been W. F. Albright and his disciples, J. Bright, G. E. Wright, D. N. Freedman, and F. M. Cross, Jr. More recently the efforts of G. E. Mendenhall and N. K. Gottwald (1979) have stressed sociological analysis, with emphasis on the function and interplay of ideological, material (technological, economic), and social factors. The relationship of social and linguistic structures has been noted in the structural analysis of E. Leach (1969), R. Lack, and R. M. Polzin and in the semasiological studies of P. Ricoeur. Form criticism, which analyzes the social and literary function of basic types of accounts, was applied first to the Psalms and "mythological" accounts by H. Gunkel (1904) and to the law codes by A. Alt (1934); while at first limited to forms thought to have been developed in the oral stage of biblical formation, this approach has more recently been extended to the longer literary compositions as well. Scandinavian scholars, following I. Engnell (1945), have fostered traditio-historical criticism, which advocates the ongoing influence of oral tradition. Canonical criticism, of which B. S. Childs (1979) is a leading exponent, stresses the function of the biblical writings within the community of believers and the context of the entire canon.

New Testament criticism parallels to a large extent the techniques applied to the study of the Old Testa-

ment. A major contribution in the understanding of the Synoptic Gospels (so named by J. J. Griesbach [1774] because so much of their contents can be "harmonized" and examined side by side) was the work of C. Lachmann (1835), who posited Mark as the earliest of the Gospels and the source of much of the material in Matthew and Luke. The material common to Matthew and Luke but not found in Mark was credited to a compilation of Jesus' sayings, called Q by J. A. Robinson (1903). The "Tübingen school" of F. C. Baur (1831) attempted to correlate the Pauline epistles and the early history of the Church, positing a Hegelian opposition of a liberal Paul and the conservative disciples at Jerusalem; later writings, particularly Acts, were viewed as a synthesis or harmonizing of the two positions. Form criticism has played a major role in New Testament studies, applied first by M. Dibelius (1919) and R. Bultmann (1921); primary attention has been paid to the distinction between narratives (pronouncement stories or paradigms, miracle stories and legends or myths) and sayings (wisdom, prophetic and apocalyptic, law pronouncements and rules, parables) and, more recently, to epistle forms (cf. P. Schubert [1939]). Redaction criticism has focused on the ways in which authors or editors (or even "schools"; cf. K. Stendahl [1954]) reworked and presented the various sources or traditions (cf. K. L. Schmidt [1919], C. H. Dodd [1932]). More recent study has turned to the social setting of early Christianity and the diversity of perspectives which produced the New Testament accounts.

Bibliography. B. S. Childs, *Introduction to the Old Testament as Scripture* (Philadelphia: 1979); O. Eissfeldt, *The Old Testament: An Introduction* (New York: 1965); K. Koch, *The Growth of the Biblical Tradition* (New York: 1969); P. Feine, J. Behm, and W. G. Kümmel, *Introduction to the New Testament*, 17th ed. (Nashville: 1975); R. J. Thompson, *Moses and the Law in a Century of Criticism Since Graf.* VTS 19 (1970).

BICHRI [bĭk′rī] (Heb. *bikrî*). The father of Sheba, the Benjaminite who rebelled against David (1 Sam. 20:1ff.). The name probably means a member of the line of Becher (Gen. 46:21; 1 Chr. 7:6, 8).

BICHRITES [bĭk′rīts]. Descendants of Bichri and kinsmen of the rebellious Sheba (2 Sam. 20:14; KJV, NIV "Berites"). The RSV and NEB read Heb. *bikrîm*, thus emending the doubtful MT *bērîm*.

BIDKAR [bĭd′kär] (Heb. *bidqar*, possibly "son of piercing"). Jehu's aide (adjutant[?]) at the murder of King Joram of Israel (2 Kgs. 9:25).

BIGTHA [bĭg′thə] (Heb. *bigethā'*, possibly from Pers. *bagadana, bagadata* "gift of God"). One of the seven eunuchs or chamberlains of the Persian king Ahasuerus (Esth. 1:10).

BIGTHAN [bĭg′thən] (Heb. *bigethān*, Esth. 2:21), **BIGTHANA** [bĭg′thə nə] (Heb. *bigethāna'*, 6:2; both forms possibly from Pers. *bagadana, bagadata* "gift of God"). A eunuch and courtier of King Ahasuerus who with his fellow courtier Teresh conspired against the king (2:21). Upon discovering their plot, Mordecai, the cousin of Queen Esther, had Esther inform the king, who in turn had the men executed (6:2; KJV, NIV "Bigthana").

BIGVAI [bĭg′vī] (Heb. *bigway*). A prominent Israelite who returned from exile with Zerubbabel (Ezra 2:2, LXX Gk. *Bagoui*; Neh. 7:7, LXX *Bago*; 1 Esdr. 5:8, LXX *Enēnios*). Some members of his clan returned at this time (Ezra 2:14; Neh. 7:19; 1 Esdr. 5:14), while the rest returned with Ezra (Ezra 8:14; 1 Esdr. 8:40). A Bigvai, whether this individual or a member of the clan, is listed among those who renewed the covenant (Neh. 10:16).

According to Josephus (*Ant.* xi.7.1 [297-300]), Bigvai (or Bagoses) succeeded Nehemiah as governor of Judah (*ca.* 420-395 B.C.). During his administration the Jews of Elephantine attempted to rebuild their temple, requesting the governor's aid. Also, Jeshua (Jesus or Judas) was murdered in the temple at Jerusalem by his brother, the high priest Johanan (or John). Bigvai, who apparently had some military involvement in the brothers' struggle for the office of high priest, was incensed at the murder of his friend and placed a seven-year limitation on the temple service.

BILDAD [bĭl′dăd] (Heb. *bildaḏ* "son of strife"). One of Job's three friends, from Shuah in northern Arabia (Job 2:11); he may have been a descendant of Shuah the son of Abraham and Keturah (Gen. 25:2).

Drawing upon the wisdom of the ancient sages, Bildad offers three lengthy speeches in defense of what he perceives to be God's case against Job. In the first (Job 8) he argues that Job's misfortune is divine retribution for the misdeeds of Job's children, which case he supports with examples from human tradition and the natural world. In ch. 18 he returns to defend the allegedly "natural order" whereby Job's misfortunes are the inevitable result of his wickedness. His final speech (ch. 25, and possibly 26:5-14) is an attempt to convince Job of his own insignificance in contrast to God's purity and omnipotence. Following God's acquittal of Job, Bildad and the other friends are summoned to present a burnt offering to avert the Lord's anger (42:7-9).

BILEAM [bĭl′ĭ əm] (Heb. *bil'ām*). A levitical city in western Manasseh (1 Chr. 6:70), probably the same as Ibleam.

BILGAH [bĭl′gə] (Heb. *bilgâ* "brightness").
1. The head of a priestly family, the fifteenth of the divisions in service at the time of David (1 Chr. 24:14).
2. A chief of the priests who returned from the Exile with Zerubbabel (Neh. 12:5, 18).

BILGAI [bĭl′gī] (Heb. *bilgay* "brightness"). A priest (or priestly family) among those who set their seals to the renewed covenant under Nehemiah (Neh. 10:8); probably the same as BILGAH 2.

BILHAH [bĭl′hə] (Heb. *bilhâ,* possibly "modesty") (PERSON). A female slave of Rachel, who gave her

to Jacob as a concubine (Gen. 30:3). She became the mother of Dan and Naphtali (30:5-8; cf. 1 Chr. 7:13). After Rachel had given birth to Benjamin on her deathbed, Jacob's oldest son Reuben committed incest with Bilhah (Gen. 35:22; cf. 49:4).

BILHAH [bĭl′hə] (Heb. *bilhâ,* possibly "modesty") (PLACE). A city in the south of Judah (1 Chr. 4:29), also called Balah (Josh. 19:3) and Baalah (15:29). The site has not been identified.

BILHAN [bĭl′hăn] (Heb. *bilhan*).
1. A son of the Horite Ezer, from the mountains of Seir in the land of Edom (Gen. 36:27; 1 Chr. 1:42).
2. A Benjaminite, the son of Jediael and father of seven sons (1 Chr. 7:10).

BILL OF DIVORCE. *See* DIVORCE.

BILSHAN [bĭl′shăn] (Heb. *bilšān* "inquirer"). A prominent Israelite who returned from the Exile with Zerubbabel (Ezra 2:2; Neh. 7:7; 1 Esdr. 5:8, LXX Gk. *Beelsarus*).

BIMHAL [bĭm′hăl] (Heb. *bimhāl,* possibly an abbreviation of *ben-māhal* "son of circumcision"). A son of Japhlet and descendant of Asher (1 Chr. 7:33).

BINDING AND LOOSING. In conferring upon Peter authority as head of the Church (Matt. 16:19), Jesus uses the rabbinic technical terms "to bind" (Gk. *déō*; Aram. *ʾasar*) and "to loose" (Gk. *lýō*; Aram. *šᵉrāʾ*). In rabbinic usage the terms mean "to forbid" and "to permit" with reference to interpretation of the law, and secondarily "to condemn" or "place under the ban" and "to acquit." Thus, Peter is given the authority to determine the rules for doctrine and life (by virtue of revelation and the subsequent leading of the Spirit; John 16:13) and to demand obedience from the Church, reflecting the authority of the royal chamberlain or vizier in the Old Testament (cf. Isa. 22:22; *see* KEYS, POWER OF). This authority is subsequently extended to the other disciples and the entire community of believers (18:18). Their norms (as recorded in Scripture) are in harmony with those to be applied in divine judgment. Accordingly, the community of believers stresses repentance and forgiveness (John 20:23), which many hold to include the authority of the Church to excommunicate and to reconcile.

BINEA [bĭn′ĭ ə] (Heb. *bin'â*). A Benjaminite, the son of Moza and a descendant of Saul (1 Chr. 8:37; 9:43).

BINNUI [bĭn′yŏŏ ī] (Heb. *binnûy* "built").
1. The head of a family whose descendants returned from exile with Zerubbabel (Neh. 7:15); called Bani at Ezra 2:10 (*see* BANI 4).
2. One of the sons of Pahath-moab who was compelled to divorce his foreign wife (Ezra 10:30).
3. The father of thirteen sons who were forced to divorce their foreign wives (Ezra 10:38).
4. A postexilic Levite and contemporary of Zerubbabel (Neh. 12:8), probably the son of Henadad who took part in the rebuilding of the walls of Jerusalem

and set his seal to the renewed covenant under Nehemiah (Neh. 3:24; 10:9). According to Ezra 8:33 he was the father of Noadiah the Levite. This person may have been the same as Bavvai (Neh. 3:18; cf. NIV).

BIRDS.† Palestine has an unusually large and diverse bird population. Although somewhat dated, the research of H. B. Tristram indicates that the ancient Israelites would have been in contact with no fewer than 350 species; more recently, F. S. Bodenheimer has numbered 413 species and subspecies. Three reasons have been suggested for this abundance. (1) Located east of the Mediterranean Sea and west of the Arabian desert, Palestine was part of a great migratory bird route from Africa to Europe and Western Asia (cf. Cant. 2:12; Jer. 8:7; Hos. 11:11). (2) Its semi-tropical climate (dry summers and wet, frost-free winters) is favorable for both migratory and native birds. (3) The land offers a variety of natural habitats conducive to nesting and feeding. While the wilderness areas (especially near the Dead Sea) invite only a few birds (notably the birds of prey), the Jordan valley (with its many bushes and shrubs), Lake Gennesaret (Galilee), and Lake Huleh serve as regions of refuge (cf. Ps. 104:12; Ezek. 31:6). The many cracks in the rocks and the lime soil of the fields as well as the shrubs and trees along the cultivated fields are good places for breeding. Likewise, the numerous thorns and thistles create many shelters, mostly for the smaller songbirds, while other birds feed on the fields and seeds of plants.

In the Old Testament, a number of terms designate birds in general (cf. Heb. *kol ba'al kānāp* "any owner of a wing"; (Prov. 1:17). The most common is *'ôp*, which most often refers to all birds (note its use in such phrases as *kol 'ôp kānāp* "every winged bird," Gen. 1:21), especially as distinguished from fishes and land animals (Gen. 1:26); it can also be used to designate particular species, such as vultures (e.g., Gen. 40:17, 19), game birds (Jer. 5:27), and "winged insects" (Lev. 11:20-21; Deut. 14:19; *see* INSECTS). Another frequent term for birds in general is Heb. *ṣippôr* (Gen. 7:14; Deut. 4:17), although it too can be used for certain species (Ezek. 39:4, 17), particularly game birds (Ps. 124:7; Prov. 6:5) and passerines (Ps. 102:7; cf. 84:3). In the New Testament Gk. *peteínon* is used for birds in general (Matt. 6:26), ranging from birds of prey (Acts 10:12; 11:6) to passerines (Matt. 13:4); its cognate *ptēnós* distinguishes birds from other living creatures (1 Cor. 15:39).

Despite the numerous species of birds in Palestine, the Bible itself names only about fifty. The task of determining the various types on the basis of the biblical materials is made more difficult by the use of some terms for both classes of birds and individual species, and the many terms used only infrequently (some only once) provide little descriptive information. At some points, the biblical account presents a descriptive (rather than scientific) attempt at classification (cf. Lev. 11:13-23; Deut. 14:11-20). (See also entries on individual species and classes of birds.)

Although dietary regulations did permit the eating of some types of birds (Deut. 14:11, 20; cf. Lev. 7:26), they do not seem to have been a major part of the Israelite diet. Game birds ("fowl") are mentioned as food (Neh. 5:18), and various references indicate that hunting or trapping was a common practice (Lev. 17:13; Ps. 124:7; Prov. 1:17; Jer. 5:27). Poultry apparently was not introduced until sometime after the Exile (cf. Matt. 23:37; 26:75; but cf. 1 Kgs. 4:23, "fatted fowl").

Birds were an important part of the theological concept of reality as depicted in the Old Testament. They were created by God on the fifth day (Gen. 1:20) after he had fashioned the firmament (the dome or sky) on the second (vv. 6-8). During the Flood, they were among the creatures which were preserved (7:3, 8), and the raven and dove were sent forth to survey the aftermath (8:7-12). In cultic practice, birds were carefully distinguished as clean and unclean, both as food and as objects of sacrifice (Lev. 11:13-23 par. Deut. 14:11-20; cf. Lev. 5:7).

In both the Old and New Testaments, birds are used for illustrative purposes (e.g., Cant. 1:15). Their care for their young can be compared to God's care for his people (Deut. 32:11; Isa. 31:5; Matt. 23:37). Jesus points to God's concern for the "birds of the air" as reason to quell their anxiety and trust their heavenly Father (Matt. 6:26 par. Luke 12:24). But while God provides shelter for the birds (Ezek. 17:23; 31:6), those who follow his Son are extremely vulnerable (Matt. 8:20). An errant person is likened to a straying bird (Prov. 27:8; cf. Isa. 16:2). God's judgment is depicted as a gathering of eagles or vultures (Matt. 24:48; Rev. 19:17-18, 21; Gk. *órneon*), an image which also portrays the desolation of the fallen Babylon (Rome; 18:2).

See also individual entries.

Bibliography. F. S. Bodenheimer, *Animal and Man in Bible Lands* (Leiden: 1960); A. Parmelee, *All the Birds of the Bible* (New York: 1959); H. B. Tristram, *Flora and Fauna of Palestine* (London: 1884).

BIRDS OF PREY (Heb. *'ayiṭ* "screamer").† Any bird which feeds on carrion or attacks another creature for food. Such birds in themselves were cultically unacceptable, and if eaten they could render a person cultically impure (Lev. 11:13-23; Deut. 14:11-20). Their designation as birds of abomination or unclean birds stems from the covenantal stipulations against eating blood or flesh from which the blood has not been properly removed and against contact with a corpse (Lev. 17); such regulations probably developed as a caution against contagion, although some scholars also associate these birds with foreign cultic practices.

For the most part Heb. *'ayiṭ* is a generic designation for all birds of prey, though at Job 28:7 it appears to single out the vulture (so LXX, KJV) or falcon (RSV; Pope, AB). At Jer. 12:9 *ha'ayiṭ ṣābûa'* may be rendered "a speckled bird of prey" (so RSV, NIV; KJV, JB "speckled bird"), thus depicting Israel as a bird whose "proud plumage" attracts its winged enemies (NEB, following LXX, reads "hyena's lair," over which hover birds of prey). The lists of Lev. 11:13-23 and Deut. 14:11-20 include both land and water birds of various sizes, as well as the bat and winged insects. Many more smaller birds are specified, presumably because they flew lower and with less speed than the eagle and vultures and thus could be identified more easily. Among them are cited various types of falcon (*Falco peregrinus* and *Falco tinnunculus*), harriers, kites (particularly welcome during locust invasions), several varieties of hawks and owls, and the honey buzzard (*Pernis apivorus*), which controls the wasp population.

These birds attempted to prey on the animals which Abraham slaughtered to symbolize his covenant with God (Gen. 15:11; KJV "fowls"). At Job 28:7 (KJV "fowl") the reference suggests desolation and inaccessibility. A similar allusion to utter desolation and helplessness is found at Isa. 18:6. At Ezek. 39:4 God promises to destroy Gog and Magog and to give their flesh to birds of prey (KJV "ravenous birds"; NIV, JB "carrion birds"). The imagery at Isa. 46:11 (KJV "ravenous bird") is to the swiftness and insatiable zeal with which Cyrus carried out God's counsel.

Bibliography. G. R. Driver, "Birds of the Old Testament," *PEQ* 87 (1955): 5-20, 129-140; A. Parmelee, *All the Birds of the Bible* (New York: 1959).

BIRSHA [bûr′shə] (Heb. *biršaʿ*). King of Gomorrah during the time of Abraham (Gen. 14:2). He was defeated after his rebellion against Chedorlaomer (vv. 8, 10-11).

BIRTH. The people of Israel, like the other peoples of the ancient Near East, had only a limited knowledge of the physiological events of conception and gestation. At Job 10:10-11 conception is described as a pouring out of milk and a curdling of cheese, with the fetus then being clothed with skin and flesh and knit together with bones and sinews. If 1 Thess. 4:4 refers to a man's wife, then the wife is the "vessel" (Gk. *skeúos*, KJV; RSV "wife"; but cf. NIV, JB man's own "body") that receives the male sperm. Recognition of the importance of the male contribution to conception may be indicated further by the Israelite custom of determining a child's inheritance only through the father.

The Israelites were acquainted with the correlation between menstruation and birth (Gen. 18:11), but they knew little of the development of the fetus in the mother's womb. To them the process of gestation was a mystery (Eccl. 11:5, Heb. *beṭen*, "womb"; JB "mysteries"), a work of God (Job 31:15; Ps. 139:13; Jer. 1:5), which happened in "secret" (Ps. 139:15) and in a most remarkable manner (v. 14). Luke observes the nine-month duration of pregnancy (Luke 1:36, 56), as well as the movements of the fetus in the womb (vv. 41, 44). Miscarriages are mentioned (Exod. 21:22), as are stillborn children ("untimely birth," Heb. *nēpel* "dropped being," Job 3:16; Ps. 58:8) and children who have died in the womb (Num. 12:12; Jer. 20:17).

When it was her time to deliver, the mother was aided by relatives and neighbors (Ruth 4:14-15; 1 Sam. 4:20) or by a midwife (Gen. 35:17; 38:28; Exod. 1:15-21). The actual delivery occurred on a "birthstool" (RSV, Heb. *ʾobnāyim*, either "stones of delivery" or "genitals"; KJV "stools"; NIV "delivery stool"), two stones (JB; cf. Jer. 18:3, the potter's "wheel") on which the mother sat or knelt. While in labor the mother would place her hands on her "loins" (Heb. *ḥeleṣ*, Jer. 30:6; NIV "stomach"),

possibly to ease the pain or accelerate the birth process (cf. Hos. 13:13, "pangs of childbirth," Heb. *ḥeblê yôlēdâ*; KJV "sorrows of a travailing woman"). Occasionally a woman's endurance failed and she died (Isa. 37:3) (e.g., Rachel [Gen. 35:16, Heb. *beliḏetāh* "in her bringing forth"] and the wife of Phinehas [1 Sam. 4:19-20]). After the umbilical cord was cut, the newborn infant was bathed (Heb. *ruḥaṣt lemišeʿî*), rubbed with salt, and wrapped in swathes of cloth (Ezek. 16:4; cf. Luke 2:7).

Shortly after delivery the parents would give the child a name; at Ruth 4:17 this is done by the women of the neighborhood. In the New Testament, the naming of the child was part of the rite of circumcision, which took place on the eighth day (Luke 1:59, with John the Baptist; 2:21, with Jesus).

When a woman had given birth to a boy, she remained ceremonially unclean for seven days; when the baby was a girl, the mother's uncleanness lasted fourteen days, the same period as for the ritual uncleanness which followed menstruation (Lev. 12:1-5). Afterward the mother was to remain in her house for thirty-three or sixty-six additional days, respectively, and when the time of her impurity had ended she was to make an offering of purification in the sanctuary (vv. 6-8; cf. Luke 2:22-24).

The process of birth and the relationships surrounding it find frequent metaphorical use in the Bible. The Psalmist refers to God's continued care ("from my birth," Ps. 22:10; 71:6), and "from the womb" depicts the lifelong pattern established by the wicked (58:3; cf. Acts 3:2; 14:8). Similarly, one can "give birth" (Gk. *tíktō*) to sin, which in turn "brings forth" (*apokyéō*) death (Jas. 1:15). Reflecting on his misfortunes, Job curses the day of his birth (Job 3:11), wishing he had died an "untimely death" (v. 16); Paul also uses the image of stillbirth (1 Cor. 15:8), wishing he had been born during and not after Christ's earthly ministry. At Eccl. 6:3 the Preacher considers stillbirth to be favorable to a long but miserable life without a burial. Usually the travail of birth is an image of extreme anguish (Isa. 21:3; 26:17; Jer. 49:24; Rom. 8:22; cf. Gal. 4:19 with regard to Paul's relation to the Galatian church); at Isa. 66:7 God's redemptive work is likened to a birth without pain. The woman clothed with the sun (Rev. 12:2) experiences birth pangs symbolizing the torment which precedes the coming of the Messiah (cf. Jer. 13:21; Mic. 4:9-10). In a terrifying threat of judgment, the curses of Deut. 28:56-57 suggest the image of a mother eating her afterbirth because of severe hunger brought on by her disobedience. The act of birth is given a spiritual interpretation in terms of the new birth in water and the Spirit (John 3:3-7).

BIRTH, NEW. See REGENERATION.

BIRTH, VIRGIN. See JESUS CHRIST *III* A; VIRGIN.

BIRTHRIGHT. See INHERITANCE.

BIRTHSTOOL. See BIRTH.

BIRZAITH [bûr zāʾəth] (Heb. *birzāwiṭ* "well of the olive tree"). The son of Malchiel and grandson of

Beriah, a descendant of Asher (1 Chr. 7:31; KJV "Birzavith"). The name may designate a place, probably Birzeit, 21 km. (13 mi.) north of Jerusalem.

BISHLAM [bĭsh'ləm] (Heb. *bišlām*, possibly "peaceful"). One of the Persian officials who sent a letter to King Artaxerxes I objecting to the building activities at Jerusalem (Ezra 4:7). It is more likely that Bishlam is not a personal name, but rather an Aramaic term meaning "son of peace" (cf. LXX *en eirḗnē* "in peace").

BISHOP. A New Testament name for an office bearer or minister of a local church (Gk. *epískopos* "overseer"). Bishops may have been included in the governing body at the church at Ephesus (Acts 20:28, mentioned after elders at v. 17) and at Philippi (Phil. 1:1, along with deacons; NIV "overseers"; JB "elders"); after his first imprisonment Paul recognized the office of bishop (1 Tim. 3:2; Tit. 1:7; NIV "overseer"; JB "president").

According to one acceptable view, both the bishop and the elder (Gk. *presbýteros*) indicated ministers and elders of a church. In the New Testament they were quite similar (cf. Calvin, *Comm.* on 1 Tim. 3:1, ed. Torrance [repr. 1979], p. 223), but during the course of the second century monarchianism arose. The task of the bishop consisted of overseeing the flock ("overseers," Acts 20:28), which included preaching. The requirements of the office are outlined at 1 Tim. 3:1-7; Tit. 1:7-9.

Interestingly, Peter calls Christ the "Guardian" of the Christians in Asia Minor (1 Pet. 2:25; KJV "bishop"; NIV "Overseer"). Elders may be involved in church administration (5:1), but Christ's church is really governed and supported by Christ himself (2:4-8). At Acts 1:20 "office" (Gk. *episkopḗ*; KJV "bishopric"; NIV "place of leadership") refers to the legitimate apostolic succession of the deceased Judas.

See also CHURCH *IV.A.*

BISHOPRIC (Acts 1:20, KJV). See BISHOP.

BITHIAH [bĭ thī'ə] (Heb. *biṯyâ* "daughter of the Lord"). The daughter of the Egyptian pharaoh and wife of Mered of the tribe of Judah (1 Chr. 4:17). Her name shows that she had been converted to the worship of the God of Israel.

BITHRON [bĭth'rŏn] (Heb. *habbiṯrôn*). A gorge in Transjordan (so KJV, NIV, at 2 Sam. 2:29; cf. KoB, p. 160); or a duration of time, parallel "all that night" ("the whole forenoon," RSV; cf. JB "throughout the morning").

BITHYNIA [bĭ thĭn'ĭ ə] (Gk. *Bithynia*). A Roman province in the northwestern part of Asia Minor, on the coast of the Black Sea and adjacent to Paphlagonia in the east and Mysia toward the west and southwest. Its population was a mixture of Thracians, Thyni, and Bithyni.

When on his second missionary journey the apostle Paul attempted to go into Bithynia, "the Spirit of Jesus" prevented him (Acts 16:7), so he proceeded to Troas. Christian churches were soon established in this region, however (1 Pet. 1:1). During the following centuries the province was host to ecumenical councils at Nicea (A.D. 325, 787) and Chalcedon (451), cities in the western part of the province toward the Aegean Sea.

BITTER. In general, something disagreeable to the sense of taste (in the Old Testament, Heb. *mārar* or a derivative; in the New Testament, Gk. *pikrós* or a derivative). The Old Testament mentions bitter herbs (Exod. 12:8), bitter grapes (Deut. 32:32; JB "envenomed"), and bitter water, which comes by its bitterness either naturally ("Marah," Exod. 15:23) or because of a divine curse (Num. 5:17ff.).

Metaphorically, bitterness can express desperation, pain, despondency (Gen. 27:34; Ruth 1:20; 1 Sam. 1:10; Matt. 26:75), and even enmity (Ps. 64:3; Acts 8:23). Bitterness toward fellow Christians is condemned in the New Testament lists of virtues and vices (Rom. 3:14; Eph. 4:31; cf. Col. 3:19; Jas. 3:14). The counsel of God concerning the coming "days" is sweet in the mouth but bitter in the stomach, i.e., because of his harsh judgment (Rev. 10:9-10).

BITTER HERBS (Heb. *mᵉrōrîm*). In order that they might remember the harsh treatment they had suffered in Egypt, the Israelites were instructed to eat the Passover meal with unleavened bread and bitter herbs (Exod. 12:8; Num. 9:11). According to the Mishnah (*Pes.* 2.6) the latter included lettuce (*Lactuca sativa* L.), common chicory (*Cichorium irtybus* L.), watercress (*Nasturtium officinale*), sea holly, and other bitter-tasting herbs. Today Jews celebrating the Seder or Passover meal eat horseradish and lettuce or radishes.

BITTER LAKES. Two connected lakes, the Great and Little Bitter Lakes, which lie to the north of Suez. At one time the lakes were directly connected to the Gulf of Suez and the Red Sea, but the intervening region came to be filled with silt. In modern times the lakes have been again connected to the Red Sea by means of the Suez Canal. Some scholars would locate the place where the Israelites crossed the Red Sea to the south of the Little Bitter Lake; those who favor the southern route for the Exodus would trace the Exodus route along the eastern side of these lakes.

BITTER WATER. See MARAH.

BITTERN. See HEDGEHOG.

BITUMEN. A natural hydrocarbon also called asphalt (cf. LXX Gk. *ásphaltos*; Heb. *ḥēmār* from *ḥāmar* "cover" or "ferment" [KoB, p. 312]), found in clumps on the west bank of the Dead Sea, which the Romans and Greeks named "Sea of Asphalt." When heated it becomes a suitable substance for caulking ships and for cementing the bricks of a house.

At Gen. 11:3 bitumen (KJV "slime"; NIV "tar") is used in the construction of the tower of Babel. Pits containing this substance have been found along the Euphrates. After their defeat some of the kings of

Sodom and Gomorrah fell into such pits near the Dead Sea (Gen. 14:10; KJV "slime pits"; NIV "tar pits"). Moses' basket was caulked with pitch and bitumen (KJV "slime"; NIV "tar"), as were reed boats and rafts in the ancient Near East. Some scholars have suggested that the Egyptians used bitumen for embalming purposes, but this is not widely accepted.

See also PITCH.

BIZIOTHIAH [bĭz'ĭ ō thī'ə] (Heb. *bizyôṯyâ*). Following the MT a town near Beer-sheba ("Hazar-shual," Josh. 15:28; KJV "Biz-jothjah"). The word *beênôṯeyhā* ("her daughters," i.e., surrounding places) should be read, however (cf. LXX and Neh. 11:27).

BIZTHA [bĭz'thə] (Heb. *bizeṯāʾ*). One of the seven eunuchs who served as chamberlains for the Persian king Ahasuerus (Esth. 1:10).

BLACK. *See* COLOR.

BLASPHEMY. The sin of consciously using derogatory language about God. Secondly, it is the "reviling," "mocking," and "slandering" of another human being (cf. Rom. 3:8; 1 Cor. 4:13; 1 Pet. 4:4).

In the Old Testament Nehemiah interpreted Israel's worship of the golden calf in the wilderness as a great blasphemy (Heb. *neʾāṣâ* against God (Neh. 9:18; KJV "provocations"). Isaiah comforted King Hezekiah of Judah by telling him that the Rabshakeh's foul words were an insult against the Lord himself ("reviled," Heb. *gāḏap*, Isa. 37:6; KJV, NIV "blasphemed"; JB "blasphemies uttered"). Especially appalling was the priestly ministry of Eli's sons, which was actually a curse (so JB) to God (Heb. *qālal*; KJV, NIV "made themselves vile/contemptible"). Death by stoning was the punishment for blasphemy (Heb. *nāqab*, Lev. 24:16).

In the New Testament the Jewish Sanhedrin considered that Christ deserved the death penalty on account of his confession at his trial (Gk. *blasphēméō*, Matt. 26:65-66 par. Mark 14:64, Gk. *blasphēmía*; cf. earlier accusations, e.g., Matt. 9:3; John 10:36). Afterward the members of that council lodged the same accusation against Stephen (Acts 6:11). But in Paul's case they themselves used blasphemous language during his preaching of the gospel (Acts 13:45; 18:6, so KJV and partly JB; RSV, NIV have a weaker meaning). Paul in turn attributed the Gentile sin of blasphemy to the Jewish example (Rom. 2:24). Though before his conversion the apostle compelled Christians to blaspheme (Acts 26:11), and was guilty of this sin himself (1 Tim. 1:13), later he warned against dishonoring God's name ("defamed," 1 Tim. 6:1; NIV "slandered"; JB "brought into disrepute") and guarded against creating an occasion for this sin (2 Cor. 6:3; 8:20-21).

Blasphemy at its worst is a sin against the Holy Spirit. When the Jews accused Jesus of being demon-possessed, he stressed the dreadful seriousness of blasphemy against the Holy Spirit; it would not be forgiven, not even in the life to come (Matt. 12:32), and would remain a sin forever (Mark 3:29). *See* SIN.

BLASTUS [blăs'təs] (Gk. *Blastos* "bud"). Chamberlain of King Herod Agrippa I (Acts 12:20). In their dispute with the king, the people of Tyre and Sidon "persuaded" (Gk. *peíthō*; perhaps with a bribe; cf. KJV, NIV, JB) Blastus to use his influence as keeper of the royal bedchamber to secure them an audience with the king.

BLEMISH. Within a religious context, physical imperfection on the part of either the priest or the animal to be sacrificed.

Because the cultic ceremonies in the tabernacle (and later in the temple) were to be performed as perfectly as was humanly possible, a priest suffering from blemishes (Heb. *mûm*, from *muʾûm* "corporeal defect," KoB, p. 489) was forbidden to offer the Bread of the Presence (Lev. 21:17); he was allowed, however, to eat this bread (v. 22). In subsequent prophecies the coming Redeemer is said to be able to deliver his people from these blemishes, especially those of blindness and deafness (Isa. 29:18; 35:5-6; 42:7). In the New Testament the Church (called God's "royal priesthood" at 1 Pet. 2:9) is to appear before the Lord "without blemish" (Eph. 5:27, Gk. *amōmos* "blameless" both physically and morally [see *TDNT* 4 (1967): 830-31]; JB "faultless"; NIV "blameless").

Likewise, animals with physical blemishes were not allowed as sacrificial animals (Lev. 22:20-24) in the tabernacle. In the New Testament Christ is called the "lamb without blemish" (1 Pet. 1:19; JB "without spot") through whose wholeness (Heb. 9:13) cleansing is achieved.

BLESS (Heb. *barak* "bend the knee"; Aram. *berak*; Gk. *eulogéō*), **BLESSED** (Heb. *ʾašrê, barûk*; Aram. *berîk*; Gk. *eulogētós, makários*).† To bless means variously to worship or praise, to bestow goodness and favor, and to invoke such qualities upon another. When applied to God, the terms imply homage or adoration offered in gratitude (Gen. 24:48; Deut. 11:29; Ps. 66:8). God blesses people by granting prosperity or well-being in the form of both physical and spiritual grace (Gen. 39:5; Ps. 24:5). People bless one another by bestowing goods and authority (Gen. 27; 48:9, 15, 20) or by wishing goodwill (Gen. 24:60; Num. 23:11, 20) and by commending a person to God (Ruth 2:20; 1 Sam. 23:21). One might also designate as holy or worthy of honor the Sabbath (Gen. 2:3), work (Deut. 28:8), a sacrifice (1 Sam. 9:13), a place of residence (Prov. 3:33), or food (Mark 8:7).

A standard pattern of blessing or beatitude is often used when invoking a blessing upon another (in the sense "let be praised"; e.g., Ruth 4:14; Matt. 25:34) and in describing the joyful condition of a person "happy" or "fortunate" for having fulfilled certain obligations or lived in an exemplary manner (e.g., Ps. 65:4; Prov. 8:13, 33-34; Matt. 5:11; Luke 11:28). "Blessed" occurs also as an epithet of the Lord (Mark 14:61).

BLESSING (Heb. *berākâ*; Gk. *eulogía*).† The act or means of invoking or granting worship or praise, goodness and favor; also the words used or the gift or quality bestowed. Of particular significance in the ancient Near East was the blessing of a son by his father whereby a man passed on his property and authority to the next generation (Gen. 27; 48:15-16; 49). Blessings were an integral part of the Israelite liturgy and were frequently paired with curses to sanction covenantal stipulations (Deut. 11:29; Josh. 8:34; *see* CURSE). Among the more familiar liturgical blessings is the Aaronic blessing (Num. 6:22-27), through which the Israelites were placed in God's protective care. A person might "be a blessing" through a specific mission or by living an exemplary life (Gen. 12:2; Ps. 37:26; Isa. 19:24). The blessing which Isaac granted to Jacob was held to be irrevocable (Gen. 27:33-35), but failure to live faithfully could bring a curse upon a blessing (Mal. 2:2) just as a curse might be transformed into a blessing (Deut. 23:5; Judg. 17:2; Neh. 13:2).

For the cup of blessing (1 Cor. 10:16), *see* CUP.

BLIGHT (Heb. *šiddāpôn* "scorching"). An injury to the crops caused by the dreaded east wind. With its scorching heat, this wind produced extensive damage to standing crops and vegetation in Palestine and adjacent countries. Its relationship to mildew (1 Kgs. 8:37 par. 2 Chr. 6:28) could indicate a disease brought about by a fungus (*Ustilago carbo*), the spores of which were carried by the wind. At Deut. 28:22; Amos 4:9 (JB "burning"); Hag. 2:17 (RSV, JB "blasting") it comes as a divine punishment.

BLINDNESS. A defect of the eye often caused by the blowing of dust and sand and by the glare of the sun. The Hebrew word is *ʿiwwer* and its cognates, while the Greek noun *typhlós* and verb *typhlóō* occur in the New Testament.

No blind priest was permitted to serve in the tabernacle (Lev. 21:18, 20), and similarly no blind animal could be offered as a sacrifice (22:22; Deut. 15:21; Mal. 1:8). Yet the blind (such as aged Isaac [Gen. 27:1], Eli [1 Sam. 3:2], and the prophet Ahijah [1 Kgs. 14:4]) were to be assisted (Lev. 19:14; Deut. 27:18; cf. Job's exemplary behavior at Job 29:15). Jesus healed many blind persons (cf. the answer to John the Baptist at Matt. 11:5), both individually (e.g., Matt. 12:22) and collectively ("the blind," Matt. 15:30; cf. Luke 7:21). Thus, his healing ministry included the body as well as the spirit. (In the Old Testament also the promised Messiah was to heal the physically blind; cf. Isa. 29:18; 35:5; cf. Luke 4:18 quoting Isa. 61:1-2.)

While gouging of the eyes was practiced by Israel's enemies (by the Philistines on Samson [Judg. 16:21], by Nebuchadnezzar on King Zedekiah [2 Kgs. 25:7]), this custom was considered a disgrace in Israel (1 Sam. 11:2). Nevertheless, God could cause temporary blindness — not only to the men of Sodom (Gen. 19:11) and the Syrians (2 Kgs. 6:18, in sharp contrast to the opening of the eyes of Elisha's servant [v. 17]) but also to the Israelites (cf. Deut. 28:28). Jesus, however, did not always attribute blindness to sin (John 9:2-3), though the magician Elymas was blinded when interfering with Paul's missionary work (Acts 13:11, possibly a case of temporary amaurosis).

Metaphorically, Israel's watchmen are spiritually blind (i.e., without knowledge, Isa. 56:10; cf. 29:9; 42:16ff.). Paul was temporarily blinded physically

(temporary amaurosis; but see Rom. 16:22; Gal. 6:11 for the permanent scars of this event) in order to come to spiritual discernment (Acts 9:9). For that reason he pleaded intensely with his fellow Jews regarding their allegedly spiritual perceptibilities (Rom. 2:19, "a guide to the blind"). Others before him had been struck by Israel's spiritual blindness. Isaiah was called to preach to a nation that would not respond to his message (Isa. 6:9-10, quoted at Matt. 13:14-15 par.). Even here God is sovereign, for it is he who makes people "seeing, or blind" (Exod. 4:11; cf. 2 Cor. 4:4).

Bibliography. F. Graber, "Blind," *DNTT* 1:218-220.

BLOOD (Heb. *dām*; Gk. *haíma*). The essential fluid of human, animal, and even plant life (cf. Gen. 49:11-12; Deut. 32:14).

I. Old Testament

In addition to its literal meaning, blood can be interpreted figuratively as the equivalent of life itself. Thus, the "voice" of Abel's shed blood cries from the ground for vengeance (Gen. 4:10). At Gen. 9:4-6 Noah is forbidden to eat flesh with "its life, that is, its blood," either of animals or of human beings. The prohibition against eating animal flesh from which the blood had not been drained may have been to oppose a cruel, barbaric custom of eating live animals or those whose blood was still warm. Perhaps it implies the future importance of blood for sacrificial purposes. Human bloodshed was forbidden because human beings are created in the image of God (v. 6). When God demanded a reckoning for the blood of a human being, he took human life into his protection and established an intimate connection between blood and life. In this way God hoped to arrest the prevalence of murder spawned when Cain slew his brother Abel.

The Mosaic legislation did not alter this divine prohibition. The blood and the fat of animals were to be brought to the altar, to indicate that they belonged to God rather than to man. The priests could sprinkle the blood on the altar, but, like the other Israelites, could not eat it or the fat (Lev. 3:16-17; 7:22-27). Fat and blood offered upon the altar symbolized atonement and therefore belonged to God alone. During the wilderness period the slaughtering of a sacrificial "ox or a lamb or a goat" could be done only at the door of the tent of meeting (17:3-5). After the Conquest, however, the priests were permitted to sacrifice animals anywhere in Palestine, though they were still not permitted to eat animal blood (Deut. 12:15-16, 21-25; cf. 1 Sam. 14:34).

According to Lev. 17:11, God gave the blood of animals "upon the altar to make atonement for [the souls of his people]; for it is the blood that makes atonement, by reason of the life." The slaughter had to take place on the altar and the sacrifice was to be given to the Lord. The express prohibition against eating animal blood was repeated and observed by the Jews (vv. 10, 12) and the sojourners (v. 13). The cultic significance of the shedding of animal blood reached its highest expression on the Day of Atonement, when the high priest brought it into the holy of holies and sprinkled it on the mercy seat (Lev. 16:14-15). As the essence of life, animal blood atoned for real life; symbolically, it atoned for the sins of the person making the sacrifice.

II. New Testament

In the Old Testament Abraham had to shed some of his own blood when he entered into a covenant with God (Gen. 17:24); later the blood of animals was required as atonement for human sin. In the New Testament, however, it was through Christ's blood that people achieved atonement; according to 1 John 1:7 "the blood of Jesus [God's] Son cleanses us from all sin." On the cross Christ's own innocent blood was shed in place of mankind's sinful blood. (*See also* BLOOD, SHEDDING OF.) The wine at the Lord's Supper became an appropriate symbolic substitute for human blood (cf. Deut. 32:14, the "blood" of grapes).

At the Council of Jerusalem the apostles decided that the Gentile Christians should "abstain . . . from [eating animal] blood . . ." (Acts 15:29), meaning the blood of living animals. In this way, the apostles enforced the Old Testament Jewish rule for churches with a mixed Christian population, while yielding on this point to the Jewish Christians to whom such a practice was immensely offensive.

Bibliography. F. Laubach, "Blood," *DNTT* 1:220-24, 226.

BLOOD, AVENGER OF. *See* AVENGER OF BLOOD.

BLOOD, FIELD OF. *See* AKELDAMA.

BLOOD, FLOW OF (Gk. *rhýsis haímatos*). According to levitical laws, the monthly flow of blood or menstruation made an Israelite woman unclean for seven days (Lev. 15:19ff., RSV "discharge of blood"; KJV "issue"). Everyone who touched her during this period of impurity was rendered unclean until evening.

Jesus' curing of the woman with the "issue of blood" (so KJV; Mark 5:25 par. Luke 8:43; NIV "subject to bleeding" par. Matt. 9:20, Gk. *haimorrhooúsa* "hemorrhage") is of particular interest. Whatever its nature may have been (perhaps menorrhagia or a uterine hemorrhage), the unceasing blood flow rendered her perpetually unclean (and thus completely alone). While her touching of Jesus' garment would have made him ceremonially unclean (cf. Isa. 53:4), the point of the account is that the woman's faith, rather than a magical transference of power, is what brought about her recovery.

BLOOD, SHEDDING OF. According to the author of Hebrews, "there is no forgiveness" without the "shedding of blood" (Gk. *haimatekchysía*, Heb. 9:22). The author refers to the stipulations of the Mosaic legislation regarding the effecting of a covenant and cleansing; sacrifice, whereby the blood of "calves and goats" was shed, was required for purification (vv. 19-21; cf. vv. 25-26). This practice, however, has been superseded by Christ's own blood (v. 14), which was "offered once to bear the sins of

many" (v. 28). The eternal covenant required the death of the mediator in order to become effective.

BLOODGUILT (Heb. *dām, dāmîm* "blood"). The legal guilt incurred basically by the shedding of animal (e.g., Lev. 17:4 regarding a sacrifice outside the tabernacle) or human blood, although the sentence might be extended also to other serious crimes (Lev. 20:18; cf. Josh. 2:19; 1 Kgs. 2:37; Ezek. 18:13). Among those infractions which incur bloodguilt, which could only be expiated with the blood of the one responsible, are the "deliberate murder" of a thief who breaks in during the day (Exod. 22:2-3, in contrast to the "accidental homicide" whereby the owner of the house slays a thief breaking in at night), liability for the accidental death of a person who falls from a roof without a parapet (Deut. 22:8), and blood vengeance against a manslayer within a city of refuge (Deut. 19:10; cf. 2 Chr. 19:10; but cf. Num. 35:27 regarding vengeance outside the city of refuge).

Even royalty were subject to the regulations regarding bloodguilt. At 2 Sam. 21:1 David is commanded to take vengeance upon Saul for having killed the Gibeonites. (Note 1 Sam. 25:26, 33 where Abigail and David praise the Lord for preventing David from usurping divine authority by taking vengeance upon Nabal.) David himself pays with his life for the murder of Uriah (cf. Ps. 51:14). However, in the messianic age even the "bloodstains of Jerusalem" will be cleansed (Isa. 4:4).

Although the term does not occur in the New Testament, Pilate attempts to absolve himself of all responsibility for Jesus' death by shifting the blame for "this man's blood" to the Jews (Gk. *haíma*, Matt. 27:24-25). At Acts 5:28 the council accuses the apostles of making the Jewish leaders responsible for Jesus' death.

BLOODY SWEAT. At Luke 22:44 Jesus' agony is compared to sweat falling to the ground "like great drops of blood (Gk. *hōseí thrómboi haímatos*)." Although the metaphor has been variously understood, the use of Gk. *hōseí* to introduce comparison fits well with the style of this gospel and supports a figurative understanding of the passage.

BLUE. *See* COLORS.

BOANERGES [bō′ə nûr′jēz] (Gk. *Boanērges*, from Aramaic, possibly from Heb. *bᵉnê regeš* "sons of thunder" or *bᵉnê rēgez* "sons of trembling"). A surname given by Jesus to James and John, the sons of Zebedee (Mark 3:17), which would appropriately reflect their rather forceful behavior at a later stage of Jesus' ministry (10:35-39; cf. Luke 9:54).

BOAT. *See* SHIPS AND SAILING.

BOAZ [bō′ăz] (Heb. *bō'az*; Gk. *Boes, Booz*).
1. A kinsman of Naomi from the family of her husband Elimelech. He was a very wealthy man who owned fields outside Bethlehem on which Ruth the Moabitess was allowed to glean (Ruth 2:1, 3ff.). He married Ruth, thereby redeeming the family property,

and preserved the family line by fathering Obed, an ancestor of David (4:17, 22) and Jesus (Matt. 1:5 par. Luke 3:32; KJV "Boos").

2. One of the two bronze pillars in the vestibule of Solomon's temple (1 Kgs. 7:21; 2 Chr. 3:17). *See* JACHIN AND BOAZ.

BOCHERU [bō′kə rōō] (Heb. *bōkֶ°rû* "weepers"). One of Azel's sons and a descendant of Jonathan the son of Saul (1 Chr. 8:38; 9:44).

BOCHIM [bō′kĭm] (Heb. *habbōkîm* "the weepers"). The name given to a place where the Israelites broke into loud weeping on account of the angel's rebuke for their breaking the covenant (Judg. 2:5). Although the actual site is unknown, it must have been located in the hill country west of Jericho. Some scholars have identified it with Bethel; at Gen. 35:8 Bethel is called Allon-bacuth ("Oak of Weeping"), and assemblies were often held there (cf. Judg. 4:5; 20:26-28), often with loud lamenting (20:23, 26; 21:2).

BODY (Heb. *bāśār, gֶ°wiyyâ*; Gk. *sárx, sṓma*).† Semitic thought made no clear distinction between the physical and spiritual or psychological aspects of human existence, hence the Old Testament contains no word which connotes "body" in the modern understanding of the term. Heb. *gֶ°wiyyâ*, which normally indicates a corpse or cadaver, sometimes refers to the living human body, indicating the person as a whole (e.g., Gen. 47:18; Neh. 9:37; Ezek. 1:11, 23). The most common Old Testament term is Heb. *bāśār* "flesh," which designates the whole external being of a person (Lev. 13:3; Ps. 109:24); it is almost interchangeable with *nepeš* "soul" (cf. Ps. 16:9; cf. 84:2) and frequently is mentioned with other parts of the body (Lam. 3:4; Ezek. 37:6, 8). (Semitic perceptions of the roles of various parts of the body differed appreciably from modern Western concepts; e.g., the kidneys [Heb. *kֶ°lāyôṯ*; KJV "reins"] were viewed as the seat of the emotions and the heart [*lēb*] as responsible for thoughts [i.e., the mind]; see the individual articles on parts of the body.) The RSV also translates as "body" terms for specific parts, e.g., Heb. *beṭen* "belly" or "womb" (Deut. 28:4, 11, 18, 53), *gûpâ* "back" (1 Chr. 10:12), *῾eṣem* "bone" (Lam. 4:7).

In the New Testament Gk. *sárx* mirrors the Old Testament term *bāśār*, referring primarily to the external, physical substance (cf. Matt. 24:22; RSV "human being"; Gal. 4:3; RSV "elemental spirits"). Gk. *sṓma* also designates the external aspects of human existence (Matt. 27:59; John 19:31), but a clearer distinction is made between physical and spiritual aspects (Matt. 10:28; 1 Thess. 5:23; Jas. 2:26).

The concept of "body" receives its fullest theological development in the writings of Paul. Here the body is depicted as worldly or fleshly, subject to temptation, weakness, and sin (Rom. 6:12; 7:24; cf. Col. 2:23). It is identified with the inner person, the essential self and locus of the human spirit (Phil. 1:20; Col. 2:9). While the concept of a physical resurrection of the body is clearly expressed (Rom. 8:11, 23; cf. 1 Thess. 4:13-18), Paul stresses also the resurrection of a spiritual body (1 Cor. 15:44, 46). For the metaphor of

the Church as the Body of Christ and the symbolic meanings associated with the Last Supper and love feasts, *see* BODY OF CHRIST.

Bibliography. W. G. Kümmel, *Man in the New Testament,* rev. ed. (Philadelphia: 1963); J. A. T. Robinson, *The Body: A Study in Pauline Theology.* SBT 5 (1952).

BODY OF CHRIST. A Pauline designation of the Church (Gk. *tó sṓma toú Christoú,* 1 Cor. 10:16; 12:27), through which he contends that the many members of the local church (implied at Rom. 12:5) or of the whole Church (e.g., Eph. 2:16; 4:4) are united in Christ (1 Cor. 12:12). According to the apostle, believers are together chosen in Christ ("in him," Eph. 1:4), and participate in his death and resurrection (Rom. 6:6-11), in his exaltation (Eph. 2:6), and in the gift of his Spirit (1 Cor. 12:13), and will witness the glory of his second coming (Col. 3:4). Thus, as "the body of Christ" — a metaphor for the Church's relation to Christ (who also had an earthly body which is [symbolically] present in the partaking of the Lord's Supper) — the Church displays the fullness of him "who fills all in all" (Eph. 1:23). Actually, this designation is a more complete description of God's people. While the term "church" refers to having been called out (Gk. *ek-klēsía*) of the world, "body of Christ" depicts the inner unity of believers in their Savior.

This inner unity cannot be equated, however, with an invisible unity. Rather, it points to a visible bond, just as baptism visibly incorporates the believer(s) into the body of Christ (Rom. 6:3, 5).

In Colossians and Ephesians Paul introduces the headship of Christ over his Church. (In Romans and 1 Corinthians he limits his discussion to the concept of the body of Christ.) The Church grows under Christ's headship (Col. 2:19) and will continue to grow until the end of time (Eph. 4:16).

BODYGUARD. A person or persons rendering physical protection to someone else, usually a high dignitary. David was the captain of Saul's bodyguard (Heb. *mišma῾aṯ,* 1 Sam. 22:14; KJV "bidding") and later the bodyguard of King Achish of Philistia (28:2, Heb. *šōmēr lֶ°rō᾿šî;* KJV "keeper of mine head"). He himself appointed Benaiah as the commander of his own bodyguard (2 Sam. 23:23 par. 1 Chr. 11:25; KJV "guard"). Potiphar was the captain of Pharaoh's guard (Gen. 37:36; 39:1), while Nebuzaradan performed the same function for Nebuchadnezzar of Babylon (2 Kgs. 25:8ff., Heb. *ṭabbāḥîm;* Jer. 39:9ff.), as did Arioch (Dan. 2:14). *See also* GUARD.

BOHAN [bō′hăn] (Heb. *bōhan* "thumb"). A son, grandson, or descendant of Reuben, after whom a monument (perhaps a rock in the form of a thumb) was named. This stone served as a boundary marker between the tribes of Judah and Benjamin (Josh. 15:6; 18:17).

BOIL.† An inflamed swelling of tissue, sometimes of a staphylococcal nature (Heb. *šֶ°ḥin;* Ugar. *šḥn* "burn"). The boils of the sixth Egyptian plague

(Exod. 9:9-11) were related to blains (Heb. *'ăba'bu'ōt* "blisters, vesicles," KoB, p. 8), while Job's "loathsome sores" (Job 2:7; JB "malignant ulcers") may have been smallpox. Hezekiah's boil (2 Kgs. 20:7 par. Isa. 38:21) was more localized and was probably either a furuncle or carbuncle. Its treatment with a fig poultice, prescribed by the prophet Isaiah, provided effective remedy. Discoveries at Ras Shamra revealed similar therapeutic treatments, which are still popular in that part of the world.

BOND.† A means of physical restraint (e.g., Samson's bonds, Judg. 15:14, Heb. *'ăsûrîm*; KJV "bonds"; NIV "bindings") or condition of servitude, as in the frequently occurring expression "bond [Heb. *'āsûr*] and free" (KJV "shut up and left"; JB "fettered and free"; NIV "slave or free"). God will execute all (both the bond and the free) descendants of the wicked kings Jeroboam (1 Kgs. 14:10) and Ahab (21:21; 2 Kgs. 9:8), but will rescue all (NIV; or the few left, so RSV, KJV; JB relates the phrase to the deliverers) his suffering people (2 Kgs. 14:26). To Paul, himself a prisoner (e.g., Acts 26:29, "bonds" [Gk. *desmós*]; JB, NIV "chains"), both the "bond" (KJV, "Gk. *doulós* "slave" [so RSV, NIV, JB]) and the free, thus all Christians, share in Christ's work of redemption (e.g., Gal. 3:28; Col. 3:11).

The bonds of Ps. 116:16 refer to oppression or imprisonment, while those of Isa. 28:22 point to affliction. At Eccl. 7:26 the hands of an evil woman are compared to "fetters" (KJV "bands"; NIV, JB "chains").

An interesting usage occurs at Col. 2:14 where "bond" (Gk. *cheirógraphon* "handwritten"; cf. KJV "handwriting") refers to a document (NIV "written code"), a "signed confession of indebtedness" (F. F. Bruce, *Colossians*. NICNT [1957], p. 238; cf. JB "record of . . . debt") proving human guilt for failure to keep the law. Christ, however, cancelled the power of the law.

BOOK (Heb. *sēper*; Gk. *biblíon*).† In biblical times the book was generally in the form of a scroll (Heb. *megillâ*), a document written on strips of leather or papyrus. These strips were then glued together and rolled up (Ps. 40:8; Isa. 34:4) and sometimes sealed (Rev. 5:1). The text was written in columns (Heb. *delātôt*; cf. Jer. 36:23), and writing was normally confined to one side of the scroll, but both sides might be used when necessary (cf. Ezek. 2:10). Although scrolls might be of various lengths, a standard length was twenty sheets (about 9 m. [30 ft.]); this standard length is the reason for the division of the Pentateuch into five books and, when the unvocalized Hebrew text was translated into Greek, for the division of Samuel, Kings, and Chronicles into two books each.

In Palestine, papyrus, prepared from the inner pith of the papyrus plant (*Cyperus papyrus* L.), replaced leather as a major writing material at the time of the Exodus from Egypt. A letter from Sakkarah attests the use of papyrus in Egypt as early as the Sixth Dynasty (*ca.* 2470-2270 B.C.), and a hieroglyphic sign for the papyrus scroll is present in the earliest Pyramid Texts (*ca.* 3200). By the Persian period (*ca.* 300) books were written on leather and parchment, specially pre-

pared animal skins (cf. 2 Tim. 4:13). It was not until the second century A.D. that the scroll began to be replaced by the codex, a book formed of sheets of papyrus or parchment folded and stitched together and frequently bound within a cover.

In the Old and New Testaments, the term "book" may designate a register, such as a genealogy (Gen. 5:1; Neh. 7:5; Matt. 1:1) or royal chronicles (Esth. 6:1), a document associated with a covenant (Exod. 24:7), or a law book (Deut. 28:61; 29:21, 27; Josh. 1:8; 2 Kgs. 22:8ff.). Frequent references are made to written collections which form the basis of the biblical accounts, including the Book of the Wars of the Lord (Num. 21:14), the Book of Jashar (Josh. 10:13; 2 Sam. 1:18), the Book of the Acts of Solomon (1 Kgs. 11:41), the Book of the Chronicles of the Kings of Israel (1 Kgs. 14:19; 15:31; 2 Kgs. 10:34), the Book of the Chronicles of the Kings of Judah (1 Kgs. 14:29; 15:7; 2 Kgs. 8:23), the Book of the Kings of Israel (1 Chr. 9:1; 2 Chr. 20:34; cf. 2 Chr. 24:27), the Book of the Kings of Israel and Judah (2 Chr. 27:7; 35:27), the Book of the Kings of Judah and Israel (16:11; 25:26), and the Book of the Chronicles (Neh. 12:23). The writings of Moses (2 Chr. 25:4; 35:12; Ezra 6:18; Mark 12:26) and the prophets (Luke 3:4; 4:17-20; cf. Isa. 34:16; Jer. 30:2; Nah. 1:1) are mentioned, and reference is made to individual writings or collections of canonical material (Luke 20:42; Acts 1:1, 20; cf. Mark 12:26; Gal. 3:10); in New Testament usage "the books" (Gk. *tá biblía*) refers to the Old Testament (John 21:25; 2 Tim. 4:13). Mention is also made of various divinely authored books, such as the book of remembrance (Mal. 3:16), the book of truth (Dan. 10:21; cf. 12:1, 4), and the book of life (Phil. 4:3; Rev. 3:5; 13:8; 20:12, 15). *See also* BOOK OF LIFE.

Bibliography. R. P. Dougherty, "Writing upon Parchment and Papyrus Among the Babylonians and Assyrians," *JAOS* 48 (1928): 109-135; J. P. Hyatt, "The Writing of an Old Testament Book," *BA* 6 (1943): 71-80.

BOOK OF LIFE. Just as the Israelites had their genealogical records (e.g., the "book of the generations" [Gen. 5:1], the "book of genealogy" [Neh. 7:5; cf. v. 64; 12:22]), they had a "book of the living [Heb. *sēper ḥayyîm*]" (Ps. 69:28). They believed that in this book God has recorded the names of the living (Ps. 69:28), especially those who desire to be part of his people (Ps. 87:6) and those of his special favor (Ps. 139:16). On the other hand, those who sinned are blotted out of this book, i.e., are accorded an untimely death (cf. Exod. 32:32-33).

Although the Old Testament refers to the future (Isa. 4:3; Ezek. 13:9; Dan. 12:1; Mal. 3:16, "book of remembrance"), it is really in the New Testament that the notion of believers' sharing in eternal life is disclosed. Jesus told his disciples that they should rejoice because their names are "written in heaven" (Luke 10:20), and the apostle Paul remarks at Phil. 4:3 that the names of his colaborers are recorded in the "book of life [Gk. *bíblos zōḗs*]." In fact, this book contains the names of the believers of all times (Heb. 12:23). Those who refuse to yield under persecution and thereby dedicate their lives to the crucified and resurrected Lord (Rev. 3:5) are contrasted with idolaters. The faithful, whose names have been recorded "before the foundation of the world" (Rev. 13:8; 17:8), sahll inherit eternal blessings (21:27); idolaters shall be blotted out.

BOOTH (Heb. *sukkâ*). A temporary place of shelter for people (2 Sam. 11:11; Jonah 4:5) and cattle (Gen. 33:17). These structures were probably made of wattled branches and may have used trees as supports or stilts. At Isa. 1:8 (KJV "cottage"; NIV "shelter"; JB "shanty") the booth is an image of desolation or of something flimsy (Job 27:18). Apparently used by guards who watched over crops about to be harvested, booths were thus associated with the Feast of Ingathering, also called the Feast of Booths.

BOOTHS, FEAST OF (Heb. *hag hassukkôṯ*). One of Israel's three major feasts, also known as the Feast of Ingathering (Exod. 23:16; 34:22) or the Feast of Tabernacles (2 Chr. 8:13). It began on the fifteenth day of the month of Tishri (mid-October, five days after the Day of Atonement or Tishri 10), at the end of the harvest (Exod. 34:22), and lasted one week (Lev. 23:34).

On the first day the Israelites were to cease from their daily work and proclaim a memorial by means of a holy convocation of trumpets (Lev. 23:35). Then for seven days they were to present burnt offerings (v. 36). After the feast proper (i.e., on the eighth day) they were to enjoy another day of rest and to participate in religious activities while making their final offering (vv. 36, 39). All males (slaves as well) were required to participate in this festival.

For the entire length of this feast the Israelites were enjoined to live in booths (Lev. 23:42, Heb. *sukkōṯ*) made from branches of palm trees, "boughs of leafy trees, and willows of the brook" (v. 40), which were woven together. This was to be a reminder of the Lord's care and protection (cf. Ps. 27:5) during their wilderness wanderings (vv. 32-43) and his promise to protect them in the future, especially concerning their harvests (Deut. 16:15). Apparently God's people paid little attention to these precepts; only once does the Old Testament record that an Israelite king fulfilled this obligation (Solomon, at 2 Chr. 8:13). During the reform ministry of Nehemiah, the governor of Judah, the Levites (re)discovered the divine institution of this feast (Neh. 8:13-14), and the Israelites accordingly celebrated it again, following carefully the whole ordinance (vv. 16-18; cf. Ezra 3:4). According to the author of Nehemiah, this was the first time that they had done so since the days of Joshua (8:17). (If this was the case, the feast mentioned at 1 Sam. 1:3-7 most likely was not the Feast of Booths as some have asserted.)

In postexilic Judaism the Feast of Booths became a popular occasion, particularly among Diaspora Jews who undertook lengthy pilgrimages to the temple at Jerusalem. Following the Pharisaic interpretation of Lev. 23:40, the pilgrims carried a lulab (a bundle of myrtle and willow twigs, often held together with a palm frond) in their right hand and a citron in their left as they made their way to Jerusalem; thus these Jews no longer made actual booths of branches. During the evening of the first day the court of women was lit by a golden candlestick, perhaps a symbol of the pillar of fire which accompanied the Israelites on their wilderness wanderings. Often the more prominent men participated in torch dances accompanied by joyful music. During the seven-day observance the priest presented libations after the morning offering, while the choir pronounced the words of Isa. 12:3: "With joy you will draw water from the wells of salvation." No doubt this ceremony commemorated the rock that provided water during Israel's journey in the desert (Num. 20:2-13). Referring to himself as the water of life who can quench thirsty believers, Jesus alludes to this rite (John 7:37-38; see J. Jeremias, "λίθος," *TDNT* 4 [1967]: 277-78), which in New Testament times included a daily procession to the Pool of Siloam for water which was carried back in a golden pitcher for the commemorative libation.

Bibliography. J. C. Rylaarsdam, "Booths, Feast of," *IDB* 1:455-58.

BOOZ. See BOAZ.

BORASHAN [bôr ā'shən] (Heb. *bôr-'ašān* "cistern" or "well of Ashan"). A place in the south of Judah (1 Sam. 30:30), perhaps the same as Ashan. The KJV reads "Chor-ashan," following the Second Rabbinic Bible of Jacob ben Chayyim (1524/25).

BOSCATH (2 Kgs. 22:1, KJV). See BOZKATH.

BOSOM. Heb. *ḥêq* refers to the "under, outer front of [the] human body, where beloved ones, infants [and] animals are pressed" (KoB, p. 296) and to the folds above the belt in the drawn-up upper garment, where money (Prov. 17:23 [NIV "in secret"; JB "under cover of the cloak"]; 21:24 [NIV "concealed in the cloak"]) or other things (e.g., "taunts" at Ps. 79:12 [NIV "laps"; JB "heart"], or "iniquities" at Isa. 65:6 [JB "them"; NIV "laps"]) could be kept. At Job 31:33 Heb. *ḥōḇ* is a pocket "at the inside of the slit of a bedouin's shirt" (KoB, p. 270). Twice bosom is equivalent to a woman's breast (Heb. *daḏ*, Ezek. 23:3, 8; cf. KJV, JB).

In figurative use the bosom indicates intimacy or high regard, probably related to the custom whereby the guest at a feast occupied a place of honor to the right of the principal person, upon whose bosom he reclined. Thus in the parable of the rich man and Lazarus, following his death Lazarus is said to repose in "Abraham's bosom" (Luke 16:22). Likewise, Christ is said to be "in the bosom (Gk. *kólpos*) of the Father" (John 1:18), underscoring his intimate relationship with and place of honor as the son of God the Father. The beloved disciple (13:23; 21:20) is described as lying "close to the breast of Jesus," indicating the Lord's tender regard for him.

The meaning of the gesture of prayer at Ps. 35:13 is difficult to assess. According to the KJV and RSV mg., the psalmist's prayer "returned" into his own bosom, which the NEB and NIV interpret to mean that it was "unanswered" (cf. Matt. 10:13; Isa. 55:11). The RSV reads "I prayed with head bowed on my bosom" (cf. JB, "murmuring prayer to my own heart"), which may suggest humility (see KD *in loc.*). M. Dahood suggests that it simply indicates the prayer's sincerity ("my prayer was like a close friend"; *Psalms* 1. AB [1965], p. 213). Some scholars favor the reading *ḥikkî* "my mouth" as proposed by *BH*.

BOSOR [bō'sôr] (Gk. *Bosor*).

1. A city in Gilead captured by Judas Maccabeus (1 Macc. 5:25, 36). It has been identified with Buṣr el-Ḥarîri, on the southern edge of el-Lejā.

2. (2 Pet. 2:15, KJV). *See* BEOR 2.

BOSORA (1 Macc. 5:26, 28, KJV). *See* BOZRAH 2.

BOTTLE. *See* JAR.

BOUNDARY. The borders or limits of Israel's national territory are described at Num. 34:1-15 (Heb. *gᵉḇûl*, KJV "border"). They depict the extent of the land as stretching from the Brook of Egypt in the south to Hamath in the north, and from the Mediterranean Sea in the west to the Jordan river and the Salt (Dead) Sea in the east; Reuben, Gad, and the half-tribe of Manasseh are outside these boundaries, "beyond the Jordan" to the east. Actually, these boundaries reflect the limits of Israelite occupation in the time of the Davidic empire. Other accounts report Israel as reaching "from Dan to Beer-sheba" (Judg. 20:1; 1 Sam. 3:20; 1 Kgs. 4:25; cf. 1 Chr. 21:2; 2 Kgs. 23:8; Neh. 11:30). Exod. 23:31 cites a list of idealized boundaries from the time of Solomon, from the Red Sea (here meaning the Gulf of Aqaba) to the "Sea of the Philistines" (the Mediterranean), from the wilderness (the Negeb) to the Euphrates; Israel never actually controlled this entire territory, although David did have alliances with most of the nations therein.

Detailed descriptions of the individual territories assigned to the Israelite tribes are provided in Josh. 15–19 (see further the entries on the individual tribes). These boundaries did not remain fixed, particularly during the early years of conquest and settlement, and were subject to various historical and political changes. For instance, Dan lost to Judah its inheritance northwest of Judah (19:41-46) but gained territory in the extreme northern part of Palestine (v. 47). Also, Simeon was originally located in central Palestine, within the allotment of Judah (19:1-9), but was later forced to move farther south.

The boundaries between plots within a tribe were indicated by a double furrow between fields or by means of boundary stones serving as landmarks. Laban and Jacob marked such a boundary by stones after many years of having kept their cattle in a common area (Gen. 31:51-52). Moving these landmarks to the disadvantage of a neighbor was considered a criminal act and was severely punished. The Deuteronomic code expressly warns against such an act (Deut. 19:14; 27:17), as does the book of Proverbs (Prov. 22:28; 23:10; cf. Job 24:2, Heb. *gᵉḇûlâ*). God himself condemns this practice at Isa. 10:13 with reference to the arrogance of Assyria and at Amos 1:13 because of the violations Ammon had committed against the people and territory of Gilead (cf. Hos. 5:10 for a metaphorical use).

God's control over his universe reaches figuratively from the heavenly bodies to earth and to the seasons (Ps. 74:16; 104:9; cf. Job 38:20, "territory"; Jer. 5:22). In his famous Areopagus address (Acts 17:26, Gk. *horothesía*) Paul attributes the boundaries between peoples as "determined" by the Lord of heaven and earth.

BOUNDARY STONES. *See* BOUNDARY.

BOW AND ARROW.† As early as patriarchal times the bow and arrow was the weapon of the nomad (Gen. 21:20) and was used both for hunting (27:3; Isa. 7:24) and warfare (e.g., Josh. 24:12; 1 Kgs. 22:34; Ezek. 39:9). The Israelites themselves, particularly the Benjaminites and the Transjordanian tribes, were experts in the art of shooting arrows (1 Chr. 5:18; 12:2; 2 Chr. 14:8), and many of the neighboring armies (Assyrians, Babylonians, Egyptians, Philistines) had proficient corps of archers.

The bow (Heb. *qešeṭ*; Gk. *tóxon*) was made from hard, resilient wood which could be strengthened by being wrapped with cord or string. Bows were sometimes made of horn or bone, and they could be reinforced with bronze (Job 20:24; Ps. 18:34). The bow usually had either a single or double curve; that used by the Syrians had the shape of an obtuse angle.

The bowstring was a cord of wound thread or was made from ox or camel intestines. The smaller bows may have been simply "drawn" or strung by hand (cf. 2 Kgs. 13:16; Heb. *harkēb yāḏᵉḵā*, lit. "make thine hand to ride [the bow]," KJV mg.). In order to string the larger bows used in battle, however, a person had to "bend" them (Ps. 7:12; Isa. 5:28) by holding one end in place with his feet while pressing the other end down until the bowstring fitted in its notch.

Arrows (Heb. *ḥēṣ, ḥēṣî, rešpeh;* cf. *ben qešeṭ* "son of the bow") were made of reeds or light wood and tipped with metal, flint, or bone (see Job 20:24). The tips were sometimes fashioned in the form of curved hooks, which prevented the victim from removing them from his body. The "fiery shafts" (Ps. 7:13; JB "firebrands"; cf. Eph. 6:16, "flaming darts"; NIV "flaming" or "burning arrows") were arrows wound with hemp, dipped into oil or pitch, and set aflame before being released. Job 6:4 suggests that poison arrows were also used. The archers carried small arrows in a quiver (Heb. *'ašpâ*) on their backs or right sides; they carried the larger ones on their shoulders.

Arrows were used in the practice of divination (belomancy), particularly in Mesopotamia and perhaps also in Israel (cf. Hos. 4:12). Although the details of this practice are unclear, it appears that the diviner might shake the arrows (Ezek. 21:21) or shoot them in the air (2 Kgs. 13:14-19). (On the "miraculous bow" [Ugar. *nḫš*] in the Canaanite Aqhat legend and possibly at Job 20:24; Ps. 18:35, see M. Dahood, *Psalms* 1. AB [1965], p. 115.)

The bow and arrow are used figuratively to represent violence or divine judgment (Ps. 38:2; 64:7; Hab. 3:9). The use of the bow (or "rainbow") as the symbol of the divine covenant (Gen. 9:12-13) may be derived from the common Mesopotamian image (frequently seen in Assyrian reliefs) of the triumphant king returning from battle. The monarch's undrawn bow symbolizes his commitment to the newly won peace; accordingly, the bow represents God's pledge

[124884]

Archers stringing and testing bows; from a relief in Assurbanipal's palace (by courtesy of the Trustees of the British Museum)

never to punish human violence and chaos with divine violence and chaos (see G. E. Mendenhall, *The Tenth Generation* [Baltimore: 1973], pp. 45-48). Others have noted the sexual imagery of the bow and arrow as masculine symbols and the quiver as a feminine symbol (e.g., Gen. 49:24; Ps. 127:4-5; Sir. 26:12; cf. M. H. Pope, "Rainbow," *IDBS*, pp. 725-26).

The lamentation of David over Saul and Jonathan (2 Sam. 1:17-27) has been called the "Song of the Bow" (2 Sam. 1:18; KJV mg. "ode"; NIV "lament"; cf. KJV "the use of the bow"). The RSV deletes this phrase, following the LXX (cf. the rephrasing by the JB).

BOX TREE (Isa. 41:19; 60:13, KJV). *See* PINE.

BOZEZ [bō'zĭz] (Heb. *bôṣēṣ* "shining" or "miry"). One of two rocky crags flanking the mountain pass near Michmash (1 Sam. 14:4), on the north side of the Wâdī eṣ-Ṣuweinît approximately 11 km. (7 mi.) north of Jerusalem. The other crag, to the south of the gorge opposite Geba, was called Seneh.

BOZKATH [bŏz'kăth] (Heb. *boṣqaṭ* "height"). A village between Lachish and Eglon (Josh. 15:39) which was the birthplace of Adaiah the grandmother of King Josiah (2 Kgs. 22:1; KJV "Boscath"). Its location remains unknown.

BOZRAH [bŏz'rə] (Heb. *boṣrâ* "fortified place"; Gk. *Bosorra*).

1. An ancient Edomite fortress city (cf. Jer. 49:22 for its natural defenses), the capital of Edom and that nation's strongest northern city. Its strategic location overlooking the major highways enabled it to develop as a major commercial center, particularly for the textile and dyeing industries. In the prophetic oracles Bozrah is singled out as Edom's target for divine wrath (Isa. 34:6; 63:1; Jer. 49:13; Amos 1:12). (The KJV reads "Bozrah" at Mic. 2:12, but the RSV [cf. also NIV, JB] is probably correct in reading "in a [sheep]fold," following the *BH* emendation *baṣṣirâ*.) The site has been identified as modern Buseirah, approximately 48 km. (30 mi.) south-southeast of the Dead Sea. Excavations have distinguished three major occupations dating to the ninth-eighth centuries B.C.

2. A city in Moab (Jer. 48:24), probably the same as BEZER **2**.

3. A city in Gilead captured by Judas Maccabeus, who killed all of the male inhabitants, then plundered the city and set it on fire (1 Macc. 5:26, 28; KJV "Bosora"). After conquering this Nabatean city in A.D. 105, the Romans made it the capital of their province of Arabia, renaming it Nova Trajana Bostra. According to tradition, the city was evangelized by the mission of the Seventy (cf. Luke 10:1-20), and during the third and fourth centuries it became an important ecclesiastical center. It was visited by Muhammad in the early seventh century, and fell to the Muslims in 634. The site has been located 108 km. (67 mi.) south of Damascus and 35 km. (21 mi.) east of Dera'a, at the southeast border of the Hauran.

BRACELET (Heb. *ṣāmîḏ, šērôṯ*). Ornamental jewelry which a woman wore around her lower arm (Gen. 24:22, 30, 47; Num. 31:50; cf. Jerusalem personified as a woman, Ezek. 16:11; cf. also 23:42). Bracelets might be worn on one or both arms. It is to

Egyptian gold and lapis lazuli bracelet of the tenth century B.C. (by courtesy of the Trustees of the British Museum)

be distinguished from the armlet, worn about the upper arm by both men and women (Heb. *ʾeṣʿāḏâ*, Num. 31:50; 2 Sam. 1:10). At Isa. 3:19 the bracelet is a symbol of pride and haughtiness.

Most bracelets which have been recovered from biblical times are of bronze, although others have been discovered made of silver, iron, glass, and gold. For the most part they took the form of broken rings fitted or pressed together.

BRAIDING. *See* HAIR.

BRAMBLE. *See* THORN.

BRANCH. The translation of several Hebrew and Greek terms designating a shoot or secondary stem of a tree or other plant. In most instances the reference is to a literal bough or branch, but the metaphorical use in certain Old Testament passages is of particular significance.

(1) At Isa. 11:1, a new "branch" (Heb. *neṣer*; JB "scion") will grow out of the roots of the Davidic dynasty. The passage offers hope in the face of the Assyrian might which spelled the interruption of Davidic rule through the Exile (symbolized by the "stump").

(2) The "righteous Branch" (Heb. *ṣemaḥ ṣeḏeq*; Jer. 23:5; 33:15) refers to a member of the Davidic line who would rule with justice and righteousness. In Phoenician the term designates the legitimate heir to the throne, a person divinely chosen even if not the actual son of the predecessor (cf. King Coniah [Jehoiachin], 22:30). Some scholars interpret the reference at 23:5 as a pun on the last king of Judah, Zedekiah (Heb. *ṣiḏqîyāhû* "the Lord is my righteousness"), who was merely a puppet of the Assyrians.

(3) Zechariah (Zech. 3:8; 6:12) mentions "my servant the Branch," who is to rebuild the temple at Jerusalem and thereby inaugurate the messianic age. The reference is clearly to Zerubbabel, the grandson of King Jehoiachin (1 Chr. 3:16, 19). Note the prophet's pun (cf. Akk. *Zêr-bâbili* "scion of Babylon").

BRAZEN SEA (KJV). *See* SEA, MOLTEN.

BRAZEN SERPENT (KJV). *See* BRONZE SERPENT.

BREAD (Heb. *leḥem*; Gk. *ártos*).† In Israel, as throughout most of the ancient Near East, bread was a major factor in the human diet from the earliest times. It was the principal food among the settled population, who were able to tend their own crops, and was also known and valued among the more transient elements (Gen. 14:18; 21:14; 25:34; 27:17; cf. Josh. 9:12). Thus the term (cf. Arab. *laḥm* "meat") came to refer to food in general (e.g., 2 Sam. 9:10; 1 Kgs. 13:8-9, 16-19; 2 Kgs. 25:3; Luke 11:3).

I. Ingredients

Most often bread was made of barley, which ripened relatively early (2 Kgs. 4:42; cf. John 6:9, 13) and was inexpensive (2 Kgs. 7:18) and therefore economical for the masses. Wheat was more highly valued (hence its prominence as an item of trade [1 Kgs. 5:11; Ezek. 27:17] and as a required offering [e.g., Lev. 2]) and thus considered a luxury (Gen. 18:6; Ezek. 16:13, 19; cf. Ps. 81:16; 147:14). Other grains, such as millet and spelt (Exod. 9:32; Isa. 28:25), might have been used in bread, and in times of hardship crushed beans and lentils were mixed in as well (Ezek. 4:9).

II. Preparation

Bread-making appears to have been a daily procedure (cf. Prov. 31:15), performed in the home primarily by the women of the household (Gen. 18:6; Jer. 7:18) or their female servants (Exod. 11:5; Job 31:10; cf. 1 Sam. 8:13). In later times it gained professional status (cf. the evidence of bakers' guilds in Jer. 37:21; cf. also Hos. 7:4). In wealthier households and the palace, the baker held a significant position (cf. Gen. 40:1-2).

After threshing and winnowing, the grain had to be processed into flour or meal. For ordinary use this was accomplished by crushing the grain in a mortar or hand mill (Num. 11:8). Young seed too soft to be milled was placed in a mortar, a large hard stone with a hollow top, and was ground with a pestle. The hand mill consisted of two round stones between which the grain was rubbed or "beat" (Num. 11:8); the bottom stone, generally very hard (Job 41:24), was fastened to the ground, while the upper stone was slid back and forth or rotated to grind the grain. Some grain may have been cooked beforehand and then dried in the sun (cf. 2 Sam. 17:19); at other times it was simply parched (scorched on a fire, then rubbed and separated from its chaff) and eaten (Ruth 2:14; 1 Sam. 15:18; 17:17; 2 Sam. 17:28). The groats or "fine flour" baked for the wealthy or used in offerings (e.g., Lev. 2; 6:20) were first ground and then sifted twice.

The flour was then mixed with water, kneaded in a small wooden trough or bowl (Exod. 8:3; Deut. 28:5, 17), and mixed with a small portion of leavened dough from the previous day's use and allowed to rise (Matt. 13:33; Luke 13:21). In commemoration of the Israelites' hasty exit from Egypt, unleavened bread was required for the Passover observance (Exod. 12:8; Lev. 23:11; Deut. 16:9); because leaven implied fermentation and hence impurity, unleavened bread was required also for cereal offerings (Lev. 2:4; 10:12; cf.

A royal bakery as depicted in Egyptian tomb paintings: mixing dough in a trough, forming the dough into various shapes, baking in a small flat oven set over a fire and in a barrel-shaped oven

7:13; Amos 4:5). The dough was mixed with salt and occasionally oil to enhance its taste (Lev. 2:4; 8:26).

Bread was baked in loaves, usually a thin disk 18 cm. (7 in.) in diameter, although the shape generally was determined largely by the baking process used. The simplest method of baking was to place the bread on large, flat stones upon which a fire had been built; the ashes were removed before the loaf was put in place, then heaped over the top (cf. 1 Kgs. 19:6; Isa. 44:19; John 21:9). These loaves were somewhat thick and had to be turned (Hos. 7:8). Flat, round cakes (or unleavened wafers), which when baked were easily broken (cf. Lev. 2:6), were baked on the outside of a clay or iron griddle (Heb. *maḥᵃbaṯ*; Lev. 2:5; 6:21; 7:9) placed convex side up over a fire built in a pit; softer and thicker cakes could be made by this method with a frying pan (Heb. *marḥešeṯ*, Lev. 2:7; 7:9; *maśrēṯ*, 2 Sam. 13:9), a deeper bowl which had a hole on top into which fitted a lid with a handle. Round, flat loaves (as well as those in special shapes; cf. Heb. *ḥallôṯ*, lit. "ring-shaped loaves," Lev. 2:4; *lᵉḇiḇôṯ*, lit. "heart-shaped cakes," 2 Sam. 13:6, 8, 10), which had to be torn rather than broken, were baked in ovens. These large earthenware jars or cylinders, either built above ground or submerged in the soil, were heated by a fire kindled inside (Hos. 7:6). After the ashes were removed, the loaves were placed on the bottom or sides of the oven; they were not turned and could be removed by hand.

III. Eating Bread

Depending on the type of loaf, bread was either torn or broken. It might be enhanced by spreading or pouring oil over the top (1 Kgs. 17:12). If served with other foods, the bread might be used as a spoon for dipping from the common pot (Matt. 26:23; John 13:26; cf.

Gen. 25:34; 27:17). The normal portion was three loaves per person at each meal (cf. Luke 11:5).

IV. Figurative Use

So essential was bread for human existence that it came to be pictured as a staff upon which one supported himself (Lev. 26:26; Ps. 105:16; Ezek. 4:16; 5:16; 14:13, RSV, KJV; cf. Isa. 3:1). So real might a quality or condition become, so vital a part of one's life, that it was characterized in terms of bread, e.g., "bread of tears" (Ps. 80:5; cf. 42:3), "bread of wickedness" (Prov. 4:17), "bread of idleness" (31:27), "bread of adversity" (Isa. 30:20; cf. Job 3:24).

Bread was considered to be the gift of God (cf. the image of manna in the wilderness, Exod. 16:4; Neh. 9:15; Ps. 105:40; cf. John 6:51). As early as patriarchal times it became a symbol of hospitality, to be shared by strangers and friends alike (Gen. 14:18; Neh. 13:1-2; Matt. 14:15-21).

The act of eating together, commonly called the breaking of bread, created a special relationship and came to be an act symbolizing the formation of a covenant (cf. 1 Kgs. 13:8ff.). In the New Testament, the concept was extended to the love (Gk. *agápē*) feast, a common or cultic meal shared by the entire congregation and including teaching, fellowship, and prayers (Acts 2:42, 46; 20:7), and apparently associated with the observance of the Last Supper (1 Cor. 10:16; 11:21; Jude 12).

Jesus refers to himself as the "bread of life" (John 6:35), the "true bread from heaven" (v. 32) which is the spiritual food (cf. Matt. 4:4 par. Luke 4:4; quoting Deut. 8:3) that provides eternal sustenance (John 6:48-51). This symbolism becomes a vital part of the Last Supper observance (Matt. 26:26 par. Mark 14:22; Luke 22:19; cf. v. 15).

HE PRESENCE (Heb. *leḥem hap-*
f the face"; Gk. *ártoi tễs prosthéseōs*
before [God]"). A continual offering
Lord (Exod. 25:30; Lev. 24:5-9) con-
lve loaves, each made of two-tenths
[4 qts.]) of fine flour, arranged in two
f six loaves each and placed on the holy
gold "outside the veil" on the north side
ace in the tabernacle (Exod. 26:35). The
ater called "Showbread" (Heb. *leḥem*
t "bread of the arrangement [or order-
, 9:32; 2 Chr. 13:11; 29:18; cf. LXX *pros-*
t; cf. Heb. 9:2, RSV mg. "the presenta-
loaves"); other names included "holy
Sam. 21:4) and "bread of God" (Lev.
he bread symbolized Israel's recognition of
provider of daily bread, and the twelve
y have represented the twelve tribes (cf.
4; Lev. 24:5-9).

f frankincense (to which salt had been add-
v. 2:13) was placed on each row of loaves
orial, to be sacrificed when the loaves were
. In order to maintain fresh loaves, the
es (who also baked the bread using special
nd a special oven) brought new loaves each
(1 Chr. 9:32; cf. 23:29; 2 Chr. 13:11). The old
were given to the priests, who ate them in a
ace (Lev. 24:9; cf. 1 Sam. 21:4-7; Matt. 12:4
ark 2:26; Luke 6:4).

table on which the Bread of the Presence was
was made of acacia wood, 2 cubits (approxi-
y .9 m. [3 ft.]) long by 1 cubit (47 cm. [18 in.])
by 1.5 cubits (70 cm. [27.5 in.]) high, overlaid
pure gold and bordered by a golden molding one
breadth wide. At the four corners were golden
s for the acacia-wood poles by which the table was
ied (Exod. 25:23-30 par. 37:10-16). Solomon ap-
ently had ten such tables constructed for his temple
Chr. 4:8), although only one was used at a time (cf.
gs. 7:48; 1 Chr. 28:16; 2 Chr. 4:19).

Regular offerings of bread apparently were
esented in other ancient Near Eastern observances as
ell, particularly among the Babylonians, Egyptians,
nd Hittites. Jeremiah castigates the Judahites for of-
ering cakes for the "queen of heaven" (7:18; 44:15-
19; cf. Isa. 65:11), the Babylonian goddess Ishtar; in
Babylonian practice the deity was often presented with
loaves of sweet bread (Akk. *akâl pâni* "food of the
presence") made of wheat flour, often in multiples of
twelve loaves.

BREAST.† The English term represents a number of
Hebrew and Greek words and uses. Heb. *šaḏ*; *šōḏ*;
Gk. *mastós* refer to the female milk-producing glands
and are used frequently with reference to motherhood
(Gen. 49:25; Ps. 22:9; Luke 11:27; cf. Hos. 9:14;
Luke 23:29 symbolizing divine judgment) and female
beauty (Cant. 4:5-6; Ezek. 16:7). The term can also
refer to the chest or thorax of both males and females
(Aram. *ḥⁿḏî*; Gk. *stēthos*), considered the seat of the
emotions and affections (e.g., Mic. 7:5; John
13:23, 25). Accordingly, beating the breast was a gesture of mourning (Isa. 32:12; cf. Nah. 2:7) and a sign
of anguish or contrition (Luke 18:13; 23:48). Heb.
ḥāzeh indicates the breast portion of animals often

used in sacrifices or wave offerings (Exod. 29:26-27;
Lev. 7:30-31; 8:29; Num. 6:20).

BREASTPIECE (Heb. *ḥōšen*). An article of clothing
worn by the high priest (Exod. 28:15ff.; KJV
"breastplate"; JB "pectoral"), most likely a pouch
(cf. v. 3, "in" it; v. 16 "double," i.e., folded double), about 23 cm. (9 in.) long and wide (thus a
square, v. 16). It was made of the same material as the
ephod or linen apron, to which it was fastened by four
golden rings and golden cords (vv. 22-28). It fitted
over the center of the high priest's chest (his "heart,"
v. 29), and was left exposed by the ephod. On the
breastpiece were four horizontal rows of precious
stones (three in each row), each of which bore the
name of one of the Israelite tribes (vv. 17-21).

This ornamental garment served a twofold purpose.
First, it represented the people to God during the high
priest's presence in the holy place (v. 29). Second, it
conveyed to the people God's judgment (cf.
vv. 15, 30) because on it were mounted two additional
stones, the Urim and Thummim used in the casting of
lots (v. 30).

See also EPHOD; URIM AND THUMMIM.

BREASTPLATE. *See* COAT OF MAIL.

BREATH. Heb. *nⁿšāmâ* refers most commonly to the
physical act of taking in air (from the verb *nāšam* "to
breathe"). Heb. *rûaḥ*, ranging in meaning to include
also "wind," "spirit," and "disposition" (KoB,
pp. 877-79), is often used in a more theological sense
(cf. Gk. *pneúma*, e.g., Acts 17:25; *see* SPIRIT). Heb.
nepeš ("throat," "soul," "living being," "person";
cf. KoB, pp. 626-28) is used at Job 41:21 with reference to Leviathan's breath (parallel to "flame").

In general use, the expression "breath of life"
(Heb. *nepeš ḥayyâ*, e.g., Gen. 1:30; *rûaḥ ḥayyîm*,
6:17; 7:15) simply characterizes "living creatures."
At 2:7 human breath is expressly represented as a gift
of God. Breathing is associated with both the mouth
(Job 41:21; Ps. 135:17) and the nose (e.g., Job 27:3;
Lam. 4:20).

In figurative use, breath refers most commonly to
the "spirit," both human and divine (e.g., Job 27:3;
34:14-15; cf. 15:30). At Job 32:8 it is "the spirit in a
man" (here parallel to "the breath of the Almighty")
which is the source of wisdom and understanding. The
breath of God is capable of inflicting punishment on
mankind (Job 4:9; Isa. 11:4; 30:28; 2 Thess. 2:8; cf.
Dan. 5:23). In Ezekiel's vision the valley of dry bones
is made alive by God's activity ("breath," Ezek.
37:9).

BRICK (Heb. *lⁿḇēnâ*). A common building material
in the ancient Near East. In Mesopotamia baked bricks
were the primary material for foundations and pave-
ments; note their use in the Tower of Babel account
(Gen. 11:3). Sun-dried brick was the chief material in
Egypt and Palestine; baked (or kiln-burned) bricks
were not common until the Roman period. (Stones
were used for foundations in Palestine, but in Egypt
they were reserved for temples and other special
projects.)

A wall painting in the tomb of Rekhmire, vizier of

Pharaoh Thutmose III (1490-1436 B.C.), depicts the fashioning of bricks and may serve to illustrate the contemporary events of Exod. 5, which records the brick-making activities of the Hebrew people while in Egypt. Clay was mixed with water (the Egyptians used the alluvial mud of the Nile) and occasionally straw as a binder when clay was lacking; if the soil contained too much clay, straw could be added to guard against cracking or warping when the bricks were dried (cf. Exod. 5:11). Bricks could either be shaped by hand, as at Neolithic Jericho, or by pouring the mud mixture into molds (Early Bronze Age Palestine). As depicted in the Rekhmire tomb painting, these molds consisted of wooden frames which could be lifted (Nah. 3:14), leaving the bricks to dry in rows. Once dry, the bricks could be stacked until needed.

In Palestine and Egypt the same mud was used for mortar; bitumen was used in Mesopotamia (Gen. 11:3).

BRICKKILN. Because bricks were usually sun-dried in Palestine, Heb. *malle̱bēn* is probably better translated "brickmaking" (so JB, NIV; see KoB, p. 527) at 2 Sam. 12:31, which recounts the task David imposed on the Ammonites captured at Rabbah. At Jer. 43:9 "pavement" (see NIV "brick pavement"; JB "square"), fits the context, while "brick mold" (RSV, JB; NIV "brickwork") adequately portrays the Egyptian art of making bricks at Nah. 3:14.

BRIDE. *See* MARRIAGE.

BRIDE OF CHRIST. An image of the Church and its relationship to Christ. While in the Old Testament the relationship of Judah (Isa. 54:5; cf. Hos. 2:19) or Jerusalem (Ezek. 16:8ff.) to God is described in terms of marital love, it is really in the New Testament that the image finds its fullest development. Paul in particular develops the Church's tie to Christ at 2 Cor. 11:2 ("[pure] bride," Gk. *parthénos* "virgin," so KJV, JB, NIV) and at Eph. 5:25, in the context of human love between husband and wife. According to John, believers are to be wedded to Christ the slain lamb (Rev. 10:7-9; Gk. *gynḗ* "wife"), and in the life to come the new Jerusalem is likened to a bride (21:2; 22:17; Gk. *nýmphē*).

BRIDEGROOM. *See* MARRIAGE.

BRIDEGROOM OF BLOOD (Heb. *ḥa̱tan-dāmîm*). A name which Zipporah gave her husband Moses (Exod. 4:25-26). In order to quell the Lord's anger and spare Moses' life, Zipporah circumcises their firstborn son Gershom (v. 25, "cut off her son's foreskin"). She then touches her husband's genitals (the Hebrew euphemism *raglayim* "feet," v. 25) with the child's foreskin, thereby rendering the rite effective for Moses as well (he apparently had not been circumcised). This account may have been included as an explanation of the transfer of circumcision, previously a rite of puberty or marriage, to a rite performed on infants.

BRIER. *See* THORN.

BRIMSTONE (Heb. *goprît*; Gk. *theíon*). Sulfur, a well-known Palestinian mineral, particularly abundant near the Dead Sea. Accordingly, the terrors of burning sulfur were a vivid image for the peoples of biblical times. Brimstone figured in the divine destruction of Sodom and Gomorrah (Gen. 19:24; cf. Luke 17:29). Partly because of this event this combustible sulfur became the biblical symbol of destruction — not only of the wicked in general (Ps. 11:6; cf. Job 18:15) but also of specific individuals (Isa. 30:33; 38:9). According to John the lake of fire burning with sulfur is a picture of God's punishment of the devil (Rev. 20:10), the beast and false prophets (19:20), and various types of sinners (21:8) at the Day of Judgment.

BRONZE.† An alloy of copper and tin. Heb. *ne̱ḥōšet* (KJV usually "brass") is used to designate bronze and copper as well as alloys of copper and lead, antimony, and other metals. (True brass, an alloy of copper and zinc, was not introduced in Palestine until quite late; cf. Heb. *ḥašmal*, Ezek. 1:4; RSV "gleaming bronze.")

Bronze mirror from Eighteenth-Dynasty Egypt (Royal Ontario Museum, Toronto)

Bronze was in use in Mesopotamia perhaps as early as the late fourth millennium B.C. The Bronze Age in Palestine began *ca.* 3200. This archaeological period, characterized by the use of bronze implements rather than those of stone or iron, has been subdivided into three basic periods: Early Bronze (3200-2100), Middle Bronze (2100-1550), and Late Bronze (1550-1220). The arrival of Abraham and the activities of the patriarchs have been assigned to the Middle Bronze Age, and the Israelite conquest took place in the Late Bronze Age. At the time of the Conquest, the Canaanite inhabitants of Palestine had already become skilled in metalworking with bronze; nevertheless, archaeological remains indicate that bronze had by no means reached common use until the Late Bronze period.

Bronze was used lavishly in the ornamentation of the Solomonic temple (cf. 1 Kgs. 7:13-47; 2 Chr. 4:1-18). Excavations have uncovered various tools and implements, lamps, nails, and jewelry. Copper and bronze were common objects of plunder in war (2 Kgs. 25:13-17 par. Jer. 52:17-23; cf. 2 Sam. 8:8).

BRONZE LAVER (Heb. *kîyôr nᵉḥošeṭ*). A basin (so JB, NIV at Exod. 40:30) located in the court between the tabernacle and the burnt-offering altar, in which the priests and the high priest were to wash their hands and feet before sacrificing on the altar (Exod. 30:17-21; KJV "laver of brass"). This object, made from bronze mirrors donated by "ministering women" (38:8), consisted of a vessel (JB, NIV "stand" at 30:18), perhaps with faucets, and a bronze base. In Solomon's temple the bronze laver was replaced by the molten sea, but it was reinstituted in the temple of Zerubbabel (1 Macc. 4:49).

BRONZE SEA. See SEA, MOLTEN.

BRONZE SERPENT. When at the end of their wilderness wanderings the Israelites became impatient about their daily provisions and complained to Moses and the Lord (Num. 21:5), the Lord punished them by sending fiery serpents by whose poisonous bites many died (v. 6). Listening to their request, and at God's command, Moses made a bronze serpent (Heb. *nᵉḥaš nᵉḥōšeṭ*; KJV "serpent of brass") and erected it on a pole. When members of the tribe became ill, God healed them as they looked upon this statue.

Sometime after the Israelites entered Canaan, they began to worship the bronze serpent and burned incense to it. King Hezekiah, however, terminated their idolatrous activities by destroying the image (2 Kgs. 18:4; KJV "brazen serpent"). See also NEHUSHTAN.

In the New Testament Paul alludes to the punishment in the desert when he warns the Corinthian believers of their responsibilities as adherents of the new covenant (1 Cor. 10:9). According to John, Jesus mentioned to Nicodemus that the Son of Man must be lifted up just as Moses' serpent in the wilderness had been (John 3:14); Jesus was referring to his death on the cross and to his ascension, the culmination of his earthly ministry.

BROOK. A stream of water, generally smaller than a river. The Old Testament usually distinguishes be-

tween a brook (Heb. *naḥal*) and a river (*nāhār*), although *naḥal* sometimes designates a river as well (see, e.g., Deut. 2:37; JB "wadi"; NIV "course"; cf. v. 36). Thus the term "brook" represents what is called in Arabic a *wâdī*, a small stream and its bed; a "brook" might be perennial if supplied by springs, but if dependent upon rainfall it could vacillate between a dry bed or course and a raging river.

In such a shallow brook David picked five smooth stones before his encounter with Goliath (1 Sam. 17:40; JB "river bed"; NIV "stream"). The "deceitful brook" at Jer. 15:18 (KJV "liar") depicts a brook dried up during the hot summer and turned into a bed of grayish-white limestone or gravel. Yet a brook overwhelmed by a large accumulation of water from a sudden downpour can carry away even the soil (Job 14:19; cf. 6:15, "treacherous as a torrent-bed"; KJV "brook"; NIV "intermittent streams"); the Psalmist sees such uncontrollable might as an image of the reality of death (Ps. 18:4). Amos exhorts his countrymen to transform rampant injustice into "righteousness like an ever-flowing stream" (Amos 5:24).

BROOK OF EGYPT. A brook (cf. NIV, JB "wadi") which formed the boundary of Judah's territory (Josh. 15:4, 47, Heb. *naḥal miṣrayim*) and in general that of Palestine (Num. 34:5; implied at 1 Kgs. 8:65 par. 2 Chr. 7:8; cf. Ezek. 47:19). While several scholars favor identification with the Pelusian branch of the river Nile, it is perhaps better to locate it at the Wâdī el-'Arîsh, which flows from the middle of the Sinai peninsula to the Mediterranean Sea south of Gaza.

Other Old Testament accounts make the brook of the Arabah (Amos 6:14) or the Shihor (Josh. 13:3; 1 Chr. 13:5) Israel's southern border. According to *BH*, Gen. 15:18 should read Heb. *naḥal* "brook" (NIV, JB "wadi") rather than *nāhār* "river" (so RSV, KJV) because the river of Egypt commonly designates the Nile.

In Assyrian cuneiform texts the brook of Egypt is called *naḥal [mat] Muṣri* or *naḥal Muṣur*.

BROOM TREE (Heb. *rōṭem*). A shrub or bush found in great numbers in the desert areas of Syria, Palestine, the Sinai, and Egypt, generally identified as the broom tree (*Retama roetam* [Forsk.]; KJV "juniper tree").

Though it hardly has any leaves, its many branches provide some shade for the traveler (cf. 1 Kgs. 19:4; JB "furze bush"). During the spring the bush is full of beautiful white flowers which contain purple stripes and have an almond odor. The tree is one of the area's best charcoal producers (Ps. 120:4; JB "charcoal"; cf. Job 30:4, RSV, based on a change of vowels). The KJV and NIV, following the MT, suggest that in extreme emergencies people might eat the starchy top parts of the plant's roots; but because the roots of the white broom tree are poisonous and nauseating, another plant must be meant here. The "broom of destruction" at Isa. 14:23 (KJV "Besom") is used figuratively, perhaps indicating an implement fashioned from the tree's branches.

BROTHER (Heb. *'aḥ*; Gk. *adelphós*). In its basic sense the term designates male siblings, whether of the same parents (e.g., Abel and Cain, Gen. 4:2, 8), the same father (Joseph and Benjamin, 35:24; 42:15), or the same mother (Shimea, Shobah, Nathan, and Solomon, 1 Chr. 3:5). "Brother" can also designate various other relationships. In the Old Testament, for example, it can mean blood relatives in general (e.g., Abraham and his nephew Lot, Gen. 14:16; NIV "relative"), a friend (e.g., David and Jonathan, 2 Sam. 1:26) or colleague (Ben-hadad and Ahab, 1 Kgs. 20:32), one's companions or fellows (Job 30:29; Prov. 18:9), a member of one's own tribe ("brethren," Num. 8:26), or a member of another nation (e.g., Edom, Deut. 23:7).

In the New Testament Jesus identifies his "brothers," i.e., believers, with those doing the will of the Father (Matt. 12:50 par.), and Paul calls fellow believers "brethren" (Rom. 1:13). According to the author of Hebrews, Jesus was not ashamed to call fellow members of the covenant "brothers" (Heb. 2:11), for they all had "one origin" (here meaning Abraham). At Matt. 7:3-4 he makes "brother" synonymous with "neighbor." Interestingly, although the disciples frequently refer to one another as "brothers" (e.g., Col. 4:7, 9, 15; 2 Pet. 3:15), the term is never applied to Christ.

Bibliography. H. F. von Soden, "ἀδελφός," *TDNT* 1 (1964): 144-46; H. Ringgren, "'āch," *TDOT* 1, rev. ed. (1977): 188-193.

BROTHERLY LOVE (Gk. *philadelphía*). This and related terms ("brotherly affection," Rom. 12:10; "love of the brethren," 1 Thess. 4:9; 1 Pet. 1:22; "brotherly kindness," 2 Pet. 1:7) refer to the mutual love between believers. According to 2 Pet. 1:7, brotherly affection is to be supplemented with the deeper, more perfect love (Gk. *agápē*).

While this specific term does not appear in the Old Testament, the concept is implied in the Mosaic instruction to love one's neighbor as oneself (Lev. 19:17-18; cf. v. 34) and in accounts of intimate friendship (e.g., David and Jonathan, 1 Sam. 18–2 Sam. 1).

BROTHERS OF THE LORD. A New Testament phrase (Gk. *adelphoí toú kyríou,* 1 Cor. 9:5; cf. Gal. 1:19) which has been interpreted to mean Jesus' actual physical brothers and children of both Joseph and Mary, the children of Joseph and a former wife, or Jesus' cousins. In favor of the argument for actual brothers (a view generally identified as Protestant) is the exegetical consideration at Matt. 13:55 par. Mark 6:3 and other passages. The view that they are half-brothers is based mainly on extracanonical information rather than on biblical support. The position that they are cousins (held widely among Catholics) rests on a number of exegetical considerations (*see* JAMES 3) as well as on the dogma of Mary's perpetual virginity (*see* MARY 1). Of the three views the first appears to have the most exegetical justification.

Although at Matt. 12:50 par. Mark 3:35; Luke 8:21 Jesus includes among his brothers all those who do the will of the Father, at Matt. 13:55 par. the primary intention of this phrase is to indicate his own physical brothers. According to the apostle John they accompanied him to the wedding at Cana in Galilee (John 2:12), but did not believe in him (7:5) until Jesus'

resurrection (cf. 1 Cor. 15:7 for Christ's appearance to James). They were among those who "devoted themselves to prayer" in the upper room just before Pentecost (Acts 1:14). Of the four, James became the leader of the Jerusalem church (*see* JAMES 3), and Judas issued the epistle of Jude (*see* JUDE, LETTER OF *I*). The other two, Joseph (or Joses) and Simon, are not further identified in the New Testament.

BUCKLER. A small round shield usually worn on the arm or carried in the hand (Heb. *ṣinnâ,* Ps. 35:2; cf. 1 Kgs. 10:16-17; *soḥērâ,* Ps. 91:4; *magēn,* Cant. 4:4; Jer. 46:3).

BUILD. In addition to literal references to construction, the Bible contains a variety of figurative uses of the concept. In the Old Testament it designates the provision of offspring, both by God (Gen. 16:2; 2 Sam. 7:27) and by man (Deut. 25:9). In the New Testament the term illustrates the formation of the Church and the promotion of its ideals. Paul applies the concept in his discussion of spiritual gifts. Both love (1 Cor. 8:1) and prophecy (14:3) "build up" (Gk. *oikodoméō*) the community of believers, in contrast to the gift of speaking in tongues, which "edifies" only the speaker (14:4; cf. v. 17). Thus the Corinthian Christians are to build one another up (v. 12) as a spiritual house of the Lord (cf. JB "makes the building grow," 8:1).

BUKKI [bŭk′ī] (Heb. *buqqî* "proved of the Lord").
1. A leader of the tribe of Dan; one of those chosen to assist in dividing the Promised Land of Canaan (Num. 34:22).
2. The son of Abishua, a descendant of Aaron (1 Chr. 6:5, 51), and an ancestor of Ezra the scribe (Ezra 7:4).

BUKKIAH [bə kī′ə] (Heb. *buqqîyāhû,* possibly "vessel of the Lord"). A son of Heman and leader of the sixth division of the levitical singers (1 Chr. 25:4, 13).

BUL [bōol] (Heb. *bûl*). The eighth month of the Jewish year (1 Kgs. 6:38), coinciding with the period mid-October to mid-November. It is the month for the sowing of wheat and barley and for the harvesting of olives (in northern Galilee) and winter figs. Also known as the month of rain, its Babylonian name is Marcheshvan.
See also YEAR.

BULL. *See* CATTLE.

BULRUSH. *See* PAPYRUS; REED, RUSH.

BUNAH [bū′nə] (Heb. *bûnâ*). A son of Jerahmeel, a descendant of Judah (1 Chr. 2:25).

BUNNI [bŭn′ī] (Heb. *bunnî, bûnî, bûnnî*).
1. Ancestor of Shemaiah the Levite (Neh. 11:15).
2. A postexilic Levite among those who took the lead in the public confession of guilt (Neh. 9:4).
3. An Israelite who set his seal to the renewed covenant under Nehemiah (Neh. 10:15).

BURDEN. While Heb. *maśśā'* can mean "burden" in the literal sense of a heavy load, in the prophetic writings it is better translated "oracle" (e.g., Isa. 13:1; 14:28; 15:1; 17:1; so RSV, JB, NIV; KJV "burden"; cf. *nāśā' qôl* "lift the voice"). However, at Jer. 23:33-40 the translation "burden" is to be preferred (so RSV, KJV, JB; NIV "oracle") as it reflects a play on words between God's utterance and mankind's understanding of it as a heavy load.

BURIAL.† Respectful treatment of the dead, through appropriate mourning and proper burial, was a significant concern in both the Old and New Testaments. After a person had breathed his last, his eyes were shut (Gen. 46:4) and he was buried, sometimes in his everyday clothing (Ezek. 32:27; cf. 1 Sam. 28:14). Custom dictated that burial (Heb. *qᵉḇûrâ*; the term can mean either the act or the place; Gen. 47:30; Jer. 22:19) should take place on the same day the person had died (cf. Lev. 10:4; Deut. 21:23), probably for sanitary reasons as well as fear of defilement (Num. 19:11-14). To remain unburied was considered shameful or a token of divine punishment (1 Kgs. 14:11; 21:23; Ps. 79:3; cf. 2 Sam. 21:10ff.; Jer. 7:33; cf. also Tob. 1:17-18).

Funeral preparations and practices accompanying burial were basically the same in Old and New Testament times. Members of the family (Zech. 12:12-14) and professional mourners (Eccl.12:5) sang songs of lament accompanied by great weeping and cries of "Alas! alas!" (Amos 5:16). The body was washed (Acts 9:37), wrapped in cloths (Matt. 27:59; John 11:44), and anointed with spices (cf. John 12:7; 19:39). It was then taken to its final resting place, the grave. (*See also* MOURNING.)

Aromatic spices were put into the tomb to combat the smell of putrefaction (2 Chr. 16:14; cf. Jer. 34:5), but this practice was for purification rather than preservation. The embalmings of Jacob and Joseph were rare exceptions among the Hebrews and probably reflect the common Egyptian practice (Gen. 50:2, 26). Sometimes food was left with the dead (Deut. 26:14), but such acts suggest the existence of a cult of the dead and were strictly forbidden (cf. Lev. 19:28). Unlike the Greeks and Romans, the Israelites did not cremate the body, considering that an act of disrespect or vengeance (2 Kgs. 3:27; Amos 2:1; 6:10) and reserved for severe punishment (Lev. 20:14; Josh. 7:25). The burning of the bodies of Saul and his sons by the inhabitants of Jabesh-gilead (1 Sam. 31:12) may have been to prevent further desecration by the Philistines.

Great efforts were made to insure that the individual might be buried in a family tomb, such as the cave at Machpelah which served as the burial site for Abraham, Sarah, and their family (Gen. 49:29-31; cf. 50:13). Archaeological investigation has determined two major types of burial among the Israelites, primary (in which the body is permanently placed in a burial site) and secondary (in which the body is removed from a temporary grave and the skeletal remains relocated in an ossuary or pit, either within the same tomb or at another site; cf. 2 Sam. 21:12-14). Thus, the frequent expression that the deceased had been "gathered to his people" or had gone to "sleep with his fathers" could indicate either primary or secondary burial in a family tomb, as well as the later concept of descent into Sheol (Gen. 25:8; 49:33).

Coffins were rarely used among the Israelites (cf. Gen. 50:26), although they were common among the Egyptians and Philistines. Rather, the body was simply placed in the grave or tomb. Archaeologists have observed several types of tombs; because of the considerable conservatism which accompanies customs concerned with death, however, these types cannot be confined to specific historical or cultural periods. A common type for both individuals and groups in the Early and Middle Bronze Ages was the shaft tomb, consisting of a vertical shaft at one end of a subterranean chamber carved in the limestone rock (cf. Isa. 22:16). In the Late Bronze Age the shaft was often replaced by steps, and the chamber might include a ledge or "bench" on its perimeter, or niches or multiple chambers (often converted caves); such were the family tombs, with recent burials on the benches or niches (cf. 2 Chr. 16:14) and previous remains transferred to a central depression or pit. Sarcophagi and ossuaries (wooden or stone caskets or chests for secondary burials) became common in Hellenistic and Roman times, as did ornate tombs influenced by classical architecture (cf. Matt. 23:27).

See also GRAVE.

Bibliography. J. Callaway, "Burials in Ancient Palestine: From the Stone Age to Abraham," *BA* 26 (1961): 74-91; E. Myers, "Secondary Burials in Palestine," *BA* 33 (1970): 2-29.

BURNT OFFERING.† The commonest form of Israelite sacrifice, performed each morning and evening as well as in special observances for holy days (Num. 28–29). The Hebrew term, *'ōlâ* "ascending," probably refers to that which rises toward God in the smoke (cf. Judg. 13:20). Although the rite was frequently observed in conjunction with other types of offerings and (along with the cereal and drink offerings) was considered part of the "continual offering" (Heb. *tāmîd*; Exod. 29:38-42; Num. 28:1-8; Dan. 8:11-14; cf. 2 Kgs. 16:15), it should be distinguished from acts designated by the terms *zebaḥ* "(communion) sacrifice" (cf. Deut. 12:27) and *minḥâ* "(vegetable) offering" (KJV "meal-" or "meat-offering"). Regulations governing the burnt offering are specified primarily at Exod. 29:38-46; Lev. 1; 6:8-13; Num. 15:1-16; 28–29.

I. Animals

For private or family offerings, various animals were permitted, including cattle, sheep, or goats; turtledoves and pigeons could also be offered, but only by the poor who could not afford domestic animals (Lev. 1:14; 5:7; 12:8; 14:22). Animals from the herd or flock were to be males "without blemish" (cf. Lev. 22:20; Mal. 1:8; Heb. 9:14; 1 Pet. 1:19). On official or solemn occasions (such as the major festivals) when a lamb was to be offered, the animal was to be no more than a year old (Exod. 29:38-39; Lev. 9:3; 12:6; 14:10; 23:12, 18; Num. 6:14; 7:15, 27, 29; Ezek. 46:13). For certain observances, rams or young bulls were preferred (e.g., Exod. 29:15; Lev. 8:18; 22:19; Num. 15:11; 28–29).

II. Accompanying Offerings

Whenever an animal to be sacrificed was of a species from the herd or the flock, the sacrifice was to be accompanied by a cereal offering and a drink offering (Exod. 29:38-46; Num. 15:1-16; 28–29; cf. Ezek. 46:5, 7, 11, 14); these additional offerings were not required with sacrifices of turtledoves or pigeons by the poor.

The quantities of the accompanying offerings were determined in accordance with the animal sacrificed. For example, to the daily morning and evening offerings, each of which required a year-old lamb, were to be added one-tenth ephah (i.e., one omer; 2.183 l. [2 qts.]) of fine flour mixed with "a fourth of a hin" (1.3 l. [1.4 qts.]) of beaten oil and a drink offering of one-fourth hin of wine (Num. 28:5; cf. 15:5). Rams or bulls sacrificed as freewill offerings or in fulfillment of a vow also necessitated additional offerings: for a ram, two-tenths ephah (4.4 l. [4 qts.] of fine flour mixed with one-third hin (1.75 l. [1.8 qts.]) of oil and one-third hin of wine (15:6-7); for a bull, three-tenths ephah (6.5 l. [5.9 qts.]) of fine flour mixed with one-half hin (2.6 l. [2.8 qts.]) of oil and one-half hin of wine (vv. 9-10).

III. Ritual

As with the other major altar sacrifices, the burnt offering followed a prescribed pattern, with specific functions assigned to the worshipper and the priest. The worshipper was required to perform those least tasteful portions of the ritual which might prove ritually defiling to the priest, including presenting, killing, cleaning, and chopping the animal. The priests served as intermediaries with God and performed all functions associated with the altar, including the task of keeping the fire perpetually burning (Lev. 6:9, 12-13).

First the worshipper "brought near" (Heb. *hiqrîb*; Lev. 1:3; RSV "offer") the animal to the door of the tent of meeting, i.e., to the forecourt of the temple or tabernacle, an outer court in which was located the sacrificial altar (Exod. 40:29; cf. ch. 17).

While standing there, the offerer was to "lay his hands" (Heb. *sāmak*, Lev. 1:4) on the head of the sacrificial animal, probably offering an explanation for the sacrifice and perhaps accompanied by a psalm (cf. Ps. 40:6; 51:16, 19; 66:13, 15). It was only after this act that the offering was found acceptable, perhaps acknowledged by priestly words of assurance.

At this point the worshipper was required to kill (Heb. *šāhaṭ*; Lev. 1:5, 11) the animal to the north of the altar; this was the most suitable place for slaughtering the animal, for the ashes were thrown on the east side (v. 16), the laver stood on the west (Exod. 40:30), and the ascent to the altar was on the south. (In offerings made for the whole congregation, the priests themselves slaughtered the animals, assisted by the Levites [Lev. 16:15; 2 Chr. 29:24].) Probably because of the danger that the small quantity of blood might otherwise be lost, the slaughtering of birds was performed upon the altar by the priest himself (Lev. 1:15), who presented the bird and wrung its head from its neck without severing it (cf. 5:8).

After the slaughter, the priests were to "present"

(Heb. *hiqrîb*, Lev. 1:5) the blood, which (if that of an animal from the herd or flock) had been collected in a basin, and throw or splash (*zāraq*, vv. 5, 11) it against the sides of the altar; the blood of birds was to be drained on the side of the altar (v. 15).

The worshipper would then flay the carcass and cut (*nittah*, vv. 6, 12) it in pieces as prescribed in accordance with the natural structure of the body (Exod. 29:17; Ezek. 24:4; cf. v. 6; Judg. 19:29) so the pieces might be laid upon the altar in proper order. Because of a bird's small size, however, the priest would remove the crop with the feathers and deposit it in the ash pit to the east of the altar (Lev. 1:16), then tear the wings without separating them or tearing them asunder and burn the remains on the altar (v. 17). With animals from the flock or herd, the priest would begin burning the head and the fat (vv. 8, 12) while the offerer washed the legs and entrails (vv. 9, 13) in the laver to the west of the altar, to purify them before burning (cf. 2 Chr. 4:6). The priest was to burn the whole animal (vv. 9, 13) except for the skin or hide, which was his compensation for the service (7:8).

IV. Meaning

The primary function of the burnt offering was to appease the Lord by means of "an offering by fire," the smoke of which provided "a pleasing odor to the Lord" (Lev. 1:9; cf. Gen. 8:21), thereby atoning for human sin by propitiating the divine wrath (cf. Eph. 5:2; Phil. 4:18). The numerous stringent requirements associated with the burnt offering, including those which required that the animal be pure ("without blemish") and sufficiently costly (cf. 2 Sam. 24:24), were intended to help incur the Lord's favor. By entering the forecourt of the temple or tabernacle (e.g., Lev. 1:3), wherein the Lord was believed to dwell, the worshipper literally presented himself before the Lord as an expression of surrender or dedication (cf. Gen. 22:3, 6-14; Exod. 18:12; Job 1:5; 42:8). The laying on of hands (Lev. 1:4) is to be understood as the transference of the sinful disposition of the offerer onto the sacrificial animal, thereby making it possible for the animal to take that person's place. This notion of substitution is expressed most fully in the sin offering (cf. Lev. 4; 5:16), and finds particular fulfillment in Christian theology (e.g., John 1:29). Through this transference, a perfect unity was achieved between the offerer and the offering, and it is because of the laying on of hands that the sacrificial animal could serve to cover the sinner before the eyes of the Lord. The significance of the total consumption of the sacrificial animal (e.g., Lev. 1:9, 13) was to destroy totally the sins of the presenter.

BUSH (Heb. *s͏ᵉneh*; Gk. *bátos*). According to tradition the burning bush associated with the theophany through which Moses received his mission from God (Exod. 3:2-4; Deut. 33:16; Mark 12:26 par. Luke 20:37; Acts 7:30, 35) was a thornbush. Some scholars have identified it with the bramble (*rubus discolor*), a shrub which retains its blossom as late as early fall, but the plant is not native to the Sinai region. Other suggestions have included various types of thorny acacia, the blackberry (*rubus collinus*), or a species of gasplant (*Dictamnus albus* L.), as well as the possibility that the flame was actually the glow from a covering of crimson mistletoe (*Loranthus acaciae* Zucc.). Such natural explanations, however, fail to recognize the ancient Semitic mind and its tendency to experience and express occurrences in supernatural terms. The point of the account, therefore, is Moses' awareness of the divine presence.

BUSHEL (Gk. *módios*). A measure for dry wares, nearly equal to 7.4 l. (7.8 qt.). At Matt. 5:15 par. Mark 4:21; Luke 11:33 it designates a vessel (JB "tub"; NIV "bowl") which might be used to cover a light.

BUTTER. *See* DAIRY PRODUCTS.

BUZ [bŭz] (Heb. *bûz* "contempt").
1. One of the sons of Nahor and Milcah (Gen. 22:21). His descendants formed the North Arabian tribe of the same name (Jer. 25:23).

2. The father of Jahdo, of the tribe of Gad (1 Chr. 5:14).

BUZI [bū'zī] (Heb. *bûzî* "my contempt"). A priest, the father of the prophet Ezekiel (Ezek. 1:3).

BUZITE [bū'zīt] (Heb. *bûzî*). A member of the North Arabian tribe of Buz. At Job 32:2, 6 Elihu's father Barachel is said to be of that tribe.

BYBLOS [bĭb'lŏs] (Gk. *Byblos*). Greek name of the ancient city of Gebal, a Phoenician port which was long a center for trade and shipbuilding (cf. 1 Kgs. 5:18; Ezek. 27:9). Among the goods which passed through this port was papyrus imported from Egypt, and it is after these sheets of papyrus (Gk. *biblía*; cf. Eng. "Bible") that the Greeks renamed the city. *See* GEBAL 1.

C. The symbol used to designate the CODEX EPHRAEMI-SYRI.

CAB (2 Kgs. 6:25, KJV). *See* KAB; WEIGHTS AND MEASURES.

CABBON [kăb′ən] (Heb. *kabbôn*). A village in the Shephelah of Judah (Josh. 15:40); perhaps Hebra, a ruin east of Lachish.

CABUL [kā′bəl] (Heb. *kābûl*).
1. A city located in the tribal territory of Asher (Josh. 19:27), now known as Kābûl, about 16 km. (10 mi.) east-northeast of Mt. Carmel and northwest of the Sahl el-Baṭṭof. Situated on a hill between two valleys, the site was settled as early as the Bronze Age.
2. A district in the hill country comprising twenty cities given by King Solomon to Hiram the king of Tyre in gratitude for Hiram's contribution toward the building of the Jerusalem temple (1 Kgs. 9:13). However, to the Tyrian ruler who desired to possess additional cities on the coastal plain rather than in the barren mountain ranges, this was an unacceptable gift (Heb. *keḇal* "as good as nothing"; KoB, p. 422). As yet the area cannot be identified with absolute certainty.

CAESAR [sē′zər] (Gk. *Kaisar*). The surname of the Julian clan, of which Gaius Julius Caesar (*ca.* 101-44 B.C.) was the most famous member. Afterward the name was taken by the adopted Gaius Octavius (Gaius Julius Caesar Octavian), usually known as Augustus, and by subsequent Roman emperors.
Gradually this family name developed into a title. In the eastern part of the Roman Empire "Caesar" referred to the supreme ruler (cf. "Kaiser," "Czar"; cf. also Gk. *basiléus* "king"); in the West the emperor was called Augustus and his sons were each named Caesar, until the second century A.D., when "Caesar" became the title of the specific son designated to succeed to Rome's highest office.
In the New Testament, Caesar is used as the personal name of Augustus (Luke 2:1) and Tiberius (3:1); it also refers to Claudius (Acts 17:7; 18:2). Frequently it is used as a title (e.g., Matt. 22:17-22 par., which deal with paying taxes to Rome), applicable to Tiberius (A.D. 14-37). The Caesar to whom Paul ap-

pealed after the Jews had charged him was Nero (25:12; cf. 21).

CAESAREA [sĕs′ə rē′ə] (Gk. *Kaisareia*). A city on the Palestinian coast, about 37 km. (23 mi.) south of Mt. Carmel, and about 105 km. (65 mi.) northwest of Jerusalem.

I. New Testament

Caesarea was the home of Philip, the deacon-evangelist, and the center of his activity (Acts 8:40). It was there that Peter met with Cornelius, the Roman centurion who accepted the gospel (10:24ff.). The city was the residence of King Herod Agrippa, who died there after having been acclaimed a god by the people of Tyre and Sidon (12:19, 23). Paul visited Caesarea following his first visit to Jerusalem (9:30), and again at the end of his second and third missionary journeys (18:22; 21:8). The apostle later spent two years in prison there before he was given permission to appeal to Caesar at Rome (23:33–26:32).

II. History

Originally Caesarea was a small Sidonian settlement called Strato's Tower. When the Romans (who captured it in 63 B.C.) gave it to King Herod the Great, he embarked upon a building program which lasted some twelve years (*ca.* 22-10), turning the town into a magnificent city in honor of Emperor Augustus, for whom it was renamed.
Eager to have a seaport on Palestinian soil and along the highway from Damascus (Syria) to Egypt, Herod undertook the ambitious project of building a city on sand. He constructed two impressive piers with gigantic breakwaters some 37 m. (120 ft.) deep and two aqueducts to bring water into the city. The city was surrounded by a wall and contained several large buildings including temples, a royal palace, and an amphitheater. In New Testament times, the city — whose population of Greeks, Jews, and Romans numbered between forty and fifty thousand — was the residence of the Roman governor, who like Pontius Pilate stayed temporarily in Jerusalem during the great Jewish feasts. Friction between Jews and Romans here led to riots among the Jews and resulted in the Jewish Revolt of A.D. 66; the Roman legions headquartered

Part of the ruins of Caesarea on the Mediterranean showing typical Herodian masonry (B. Van Elderen)

at Caesarea tortured the Jewish zealots imprisoned there, and the armies of Titus participated in the destruction of Jerusalem in 70.

During the early Christian centuries Caesarea was a seat of bishops and a center of learning boasting such eminent scholars as Origen (*ca.* 200) and the church historian Eusebius (*ca.* 300). Arabs conquered the city *ca.* 640 and in 1265 wrested it from the Crusaders who had held it since *ca.* 1101 amid bitter fighting.

III. Archaeology

Caesarea has been extensively excavated since World War II and a variety of finds uncovered from the Roman, Byzantine, and Crusader periods. Remains of the harbor constructed by Herod Agrippa, including a massive breakwater, can be seen submerged nearly a quarter mile from shore; excavations along the shore have uncovered a series of vaulted buildings — apparently warehouses — and a subterranean sewage system connected to the sea. Ringing the harbor area are various structures including two aqueducts, a hippodrome or stadium, a theater, temple to Augustus, colonnaded street, and amphitheater. During reconstruction of the amphitheater a large stone was discovered bearing an inscription mentioning Pontius Pilate. Other finds include a synagogue of the fourth or fifth century A.D. and a Crusader church.

Bibliography. C. T. Fritsch, ed., *Caesarea Maritima* 1: *Studies in the History of Caesarea Maritima.* BASOR Sup. 19 (1975); L. I. Levine, *Caesarea Under Roman Rule* (Leiden: 1975); A. Negev, "Caesarea," *EAEHL* 1 (1975): 270-285.

CAESAREA PHILIPPI [sĕs'ə rē'ə fĭl'ə pī] (Gk. *Kaisareia hē Philippou*). A city on the southern slope of Mt. Hermon, near the source of the Nahr Bâniyâs,

one of the three springs feeding the Jordan river. The Greeks dedicated the cave from which the water flows to the deity Pan, naming the city Paneas, a name which survives as Bâniyâs, the modern city built on the same location as ancient Caesarea Philippi.

The Romans assigned the district to King Herod the Great (20 B.C.), who erected a white marble temple there in honor of Augustus and placed the image of the emperor near the altar of Pan. After Herod's death in 4 B.C. Philip the tetrarch beautified the city and named it Caesarea; it became known as Caesarea Philippi to distinguish it from the city with the same name on the Palestinian coast to the southwest.

In New Testament times Caesarea Philippi was a place to worship Pan as well as to honor Caesar. It was here, amid the interplay between the forces of nature and the deification of the state in the emperor, that Christ asked his disciples: "Who do men say that the Son of man is?" and Peter replied: "You are the Christ, the Son of the living God" (Matt. 16:13-16 par. Mark 8:27-29).

Herod Agrippa II renamed the city Neronias in honor of Emperor Nero (*ca.* A.D. 50). During the Jewish war both Titus and Vespasian used it as a stopping-place for the Roman armies.

CAESAR'S HOUSEHOLD (Gk. *Kaisaros oikía*). A term designating a sizable number of functionaries, both slave and free, of the emperor's household (rather than the imperial family itself) with whom Paul must have come into contact on several occasions. Those who were Christians sent their greetings to the church at Philippi, with which they were apparently closely associated (Phil. 4:22; JB "imperial household"). The inclusion of their greetings may indicate that this letter was written at Rome, Caesar's home.

CAIAPHAS [kā′ə fəs] (*Kaïaphas*). The surname of Joseph, the son-in-law of Annas the deposed high priest (John 18:13). Valerius Gratus, the Roman procurator preceding Pontius Pilate, had appointed him high priest *ca.* A.D. 18, some eleven years before John the Baptist began his ministry (Luke 3:2). His nineteen-year tenure testified to his ability as a diplomat and an administrator, but he was deposed by Vitellius the Roman governor in Syria in A.D. 36.

It was Caiaphas who proposed that Jesus be sacrificed in place of the entire Jewish nation (11:49-50; cf. Matt. 26:3). Once Jesus was arrested, he was led first to Annas (John 18:12-13) — because he may still have been the legitimate high priest in the eyes of the Sanhedrin or because of the authority he still wielded as former high priest — and then to Caiaphas (v. 24). Matthew records that Caiaphas, the high priest, tore his robes upon Jesus' confession as the Christ, the Son of God (Matt. 26:57, 65; Mark 14:35 and Luke 22:54 do not mention Caiaphas' name). (*See also* JESUS CHRIST *III.E.*).

A few weeks later Caiaphas, accompanied by his father-in-law Annas and other members of the Sanhedrin, investigated Peter and John concerning their authority to preach about the resurrected Jesus (Acts 4:6).

CAIN [kān] (Heb. *qayin*).†
1. The eldest son of Adam and Eve (Gen. 4:1), born after sin had entered into Paradise; he was a tiller of the ground. There is no etymological relationship between Heb. *qayin* ("Cain") and Heb. *qānâ* ("acquire"); it is possible, though, that when Eve named her son she thought of the promise of maternity made to her (3:15) and believed that Cain, begotten with God's help, would reveal a glimpse of the seed that would destroy the serpent (so G. C. Aalders, *Genesis*. BSC [1984] 1:118-19).

According to the Genesis narrative, the Lord paid no attention to Cain's vegetable offerings, but did approve the firstlings which Abel sacrificed from his flock (Gen. 4:4-5). Outwardly, both brothers had made the proper respectful responses, but Cain's motives may have been suspect. He sensed God's displeasure, and became angry and depressed (v. 5).

Noting Cain's anger, the Lord warned him against committing a sin against his brother. If he would do well, he told Cain, he would be "accepted" (4:7; JB he would "lift up" his head, suggesting that Cain would no longer be despondent). Thus, God gave Cain another chance to present an acceptable offering. On the other hand, if he should persist in his anger, sin — portrayed as an animal "couching (so RSV; KJV "lieth"; NIV, JB "crouching") at the door" — would be waiting for him. Yet God urged Cain to master sin (KJV "rule over him," possibly implying that Cain would have power over Abel).

The admonitions were to no avail, for Cain killed his younger brother while they were alone in a field (Gen. 4:8). Called by the Lord to account for his crime, Cain exclaimed "[A]m I my brother's keeper?" (v. 9). Indignant at Cain's rude reply, the Lord cursed him: the soil would no longer yield its potential, and Cain himself would remain a fugitive (vv. 11-12). At this point Cain humbled himself (v. 13), where-

upon the Lord placed a mark on him (not necessarily on his forehead), warning others not to kill the murderer (v. 15).

Having left the "presence of the Lord" (4:16), Cain moved to Nod where he lived with his wife (either his sister [so Aalders, pp. 126, 129] or a woman from another settlement [R. K. Harrison, "Cain," *ISBE* 1 (1979): 571]); out of their union came a son, Enoch. Cain then built a city (which he called Enoch after his son; v. 17), perhaps in an attempt to combine rural and city life or to find security in a "base camp" (Aalders, p. 129; cf. p. 117).

The only other Old Testament reference to Cain occurs in the Song of Lamech, where he is viewed as the prototype of revenge (Gen. 4:24). Some New Testament writers allude to the murder of his brother (Matt. 23:35 par. Luke 11:51) and hold him up as one in whose footsteps the evil ones walk (Jude 11; Gk. *Kain*). Others probe Cain's motives for such a deed. According to 1 John 3:12 he was "of the evil one" (i.e., he drew his inspiration from the Devil) and acted out of envy. The author of Hebrews distinguishes between Abel's sacrifice, which was made in faith and consequently made him righteous, and Cain's offering, which by inference must have lacked such a commitment.

2. (Josh. 15:57, KJV). See KAIN (PLACE).

CAINAN [kā′nən] (Gk. *Kaïnan*).
1. The son of Arphaxad (Luke 3:36; LXX Gen. 10:24; 11:12).
2. Another name for Kenan (Luke 3:37; cf. KJV at Gen. 5:9-14).

CAKE. Because the Israelites were unfamiliar with sugar, their cakes were more like flat, round disks of bread than what is now commonly considered cake or pastry (*see* BREAD). Abraham used fine meal as an ingredient for his cakes (Gen. 18:6), and the manna which fed the Israelites in the wilderness was compared to "wafers," or cakes made from honey (Exod. 16:31; Heb. *ṣappîḥit*).

The Old Testament also mentions cakes made of figs (Heb. *dᵉbēlâ*, e.g., 1 Sam. 25:18; 30:12) and of raisins (Heb. *ʾašîšâ*, e.g., 2 Sam. 6:19; 1 Chr. 16:3). According to Isaiah's oracle against Moab, the Moabites would be deprived of the pleasure of the raisin-cakes made from grapes growing at doomed Kir-hareseth (Isa. 16:7). Although they were legitimately used by worshippers of Yahweh (cf. 2 Sam. 6:19), such "cakes of raisins" (Hos. 3:1; cf. Jer. 7:18) were commonly used as offerings in pagan ceremonies and thus symbolized Israelite apostasy.

CALAH [kā′lə] (Heb. *kālaḥ*; Akk. *Kalḫu*, possibly from Sum. *ka-laḫ* "holy gate").† The capital of Assyria during the Neo-Assyrian period; located at modern Nimrûd near the confluence of the Tigris and the Zab rivers, about 35 km. (22 mi.) south of Nineveh (Tell Kuyunjik).

Excavations indicate that the city was first settled *ca.* 2500 B.C., perhaps by Babylonian immigrants during the Early Dynastic period (cf. Gen. 10:11-12). It is first mentioned in historical accounts during the Middle Assyrian period when it was rebuilt by Shalmaneser I (1274-1245). Assurnasirpal II made the city his capital (*ca.* 833), embellishing it by an extensive building program and increasing its population to nearly seventy thousand. Amid economic distress at home and growing pressure from the Urartians to the north, the city revolted in 746, resulting in the murder of King Assurnirari V and the entire royal family. Although Sargon II (722-705) replaced it as the royal capital with Dur-Sarrukin (Khorsabad), Calah remained a provincial capital until destroyed by the Medes in 614-612.

The ruins of Calah were excavated by A. H. Layard between 1845 and 1851 and by the British School of Archaeology from 1949 to 1963. Among the ruins are the temple and ziggurat (temple tower) constructed by Assurnasirpal in honor of the city's patron deity Ninurta, god of war and hunting (cf. the biblical Nimrod, Gen. 10:9; note the similarity to the site's modern name, Nimrûd). Stone reliefs from Assurnasirpal's palace depict military and hunting scenes, and the arsenal of Shalmaneser III (859-824) has yielded many ivory plaques, figurines, and items of furniture. The Black Obelisk of Shalmaneser discovered at Calah mentions the tribute rendered to the Assyrians by the Israelite king Jehu, son of Omri.

CALAMUS [kăl′ə məs] (Heb. *qāneh*; LXX Gk. *kálamos* at Cant. 4:14). An item of trade produced from an aromatic reed (Ezek. 27:19). *See* SWEET CANE.

CALCOL [kăl′kŏl] (Heb. *kalkōl*). A sage to whom King Solomon is compared (1 Kgs. 4:31; KJV "Chalcol"); he is probably the same as Calcol, the son of Zerah of the tribe of Judah, mentioned at 1 Chr. 2:6. He is included among the "sons of Mahol" (Heb. *bᵉnê māhôl*; 1 Kgs. 4:31), perhaps a personal name (so RSV, KJV, NIV) or an appellative noun meaning "sons of the dance" or "members of the orchestral guild" (JB "cantors").

CALEB [kā′ləb] (Heb. *kālēḇ* "dog"). A common personal name in the Old Testament narrative of the settlement of Canaan and frequently found in genealogical accounts. The meaning of the name may indicate affection and faithfulness or may describe either the fidelity or disobedience of a slave.

1. The son of Jephunneh of the tribe of Judah, and one of the twelve spies whom Moses commanded to observe the land of Canaan (Num. 13:6). Caleb attempted to encourage the Israelites — who had become disheartened because of the report brought by ten of the returning spies (v. 30) — to occupy the land, but he was nearly killed for his boldness (14:6-10). After having received as a reward for his faithfulness the promise that he would successfully enter into Canaan (14:24, 30; 32:12; Deut. 1:36), Caleb, together with Joshua, was spared when a plague took the lives of the other ten spies (Num. 14:37-38). At the second census (near the end of the wilderness wanderings), Caleb was yet alive. Moses appointed him representative from the tribe of Judah for the future assignments of inheritance in Canaan (34:19).

Later when the promised land was divided, the vigorous eighty-five-year-old Caleb asked Joshua if he might have Hebron as his inheritance; his request was granted (Josh. 14:6-15; cf. 1 Chr. 6:56). Caleb then drove the Anakim from Hebron (Josh. 15:13-14; cf. Judg. 1:20) and promised a reward to whoever would capture the city of Debir (Kiriath-sepher): the conqueror was to receive his daughter Achsah for his wife. Othniel, Caleb's youngest brother, took Kiriath-sepher and was rewarded as Caleb had promised (Josh. 15:13-19; Judg. 1:11-15; cf. 1 Sam. 30:14, the "Negeb of Caleb").

Caleb is called the Kenizzite at Num. 32:12; Josh. 14:6, 14. His brother Othniel is named the son of Kenaz at Josh. 15:17; Judg. 1:13; 3:9. According to some scholars, Caleb was a descendant of Kenaz through his father, Jephunneh; Kenaz (of which nothing further is known) in turn was a descendant of Hezron, the son of Peresh, the son of Judah and Tamar.

Difficulties of identification arise from the genealogies in 1 Chronicles. According to 1 Chr. 2:18-20 Caleb, the son of Hezron, was first married to Azubah and then (after her death) to Ephrath, who bore him Hur; Hur in turn became the father of Uri and the grandfather of Bezalel. Because Bezalel was the chief craftsman in the construction of the wilderness tabernacle, Caleb, the son of Hezron, cannot be the same as Caleb, the son of Jephunneh, nor can he be the brother of Jerahmeel as mentioned at 2:42 (but see JB mg. at v. 41). Chelubai (v. 9) may be another name for the Caleb of vv. 18-20, and of vv. 42-49; Caleb the son of Hezron, then, would be an ancestor of Caleb the son of Jephunneh. He, too, may have had a daughter named Achsah (v. 49), as did Caleb the son of Jephunneh. From that perspective, Kenaz would fit in the genealogy between Hezron and Caleb, the son of Hezron. Another possibility is that Jephunneh was a Kenizzite (cf. Gen. 15:19), married to a woman from the house of Caleb, the brother of Jerahmeel; their firstborn son was named Caleb. Jephunneh's second wife would have brought forth Othniel and Seraiah (cf. 1 Chr. 4:13), who were called "sons" of Kenaz, or Kenizzites. As demonstrated by the sociological function of genealogies in various societies, the conflicting relationships and problems of identification may reflect various configurations of kinship groups as well as social and political alignments at various stages in Israelite history.

2. The son of Hezron and brother of Jerahmeel (1 Chr. 2:18-20, 42-50). At v. 9 he is called Chelubai (see above).

CALEB-EPHRATAH [kā′ləb ĕf′rə thə] (Heb. *kālēḇ ʾeprāṯâ*). The place or region where Hezron died before his wife Abiah brought forth his son Asshur (1 Chr. 2:24, KJV; NIV "Caleb Ephrathah"). The RSV and JB render the passage: "Caleb went in to Ephrathah, the wife of Hezron his father, and she bore him Asshur" (following the LXX). According to this version, Ephrathah is the name of Hezron's widow, who gave birth to a son called Asshur by Hezron's son, Caleb. It may be that in joining with his father's wife Caleb claimed his father's possessions.

CALEBITE [kā'lə bīt] (Heb. *kālibî*). Another name of Nabal, a descendant of Caleb the son of Jephunneh (1 Sam. 25:3).

CALENDAR. A system of dividing a year. *See* YEAR.

CALF. *See* CATTLE; GOLDEN CALF.

CALIGULA [kə līg'yə lə].† Gaius Julius Caesar Germanicus, the son of Germanicus and Agrippina Major, and the great-grandson of Augustus, Rome's first emperor. He received this nickname ("little boot") because of his upbringing in a military camp in Germany where his father was commander of the Rhine armies.

Proclaimed emperor at the age of twenty-four, he succeeded Tiberius in A.D. 37 and ruled for approximately four years. Beset by severe personal illness and grief over the death of his favorite sister Drusilla, Caligula ruled despotically and cruelly, instituting treason trials against members of the Roman Senate and executing supporters as well as foes. Convinced of his own divinity, he was a person of great extravagance and enjoyed an immodest number of love affairs; charges by his contemporaries that he was insane are largely unfounded. His relationship with the Senate remained uneasy, and a conspiracy formed against him in 40 led to his assassination in January 41.

Gaius adopted a Hellenistic policy, which in his case meant anti-Jewish. Through his influence Herod I Agrippa succeeded Philip the tetrarch and Lysanias as ruler of Judea (37). Though he did not instigate it, the Jews at Alexandria were actively persecuted in 38, prompting the aged scholar Philo to plead their cause for religious freedom and political rights before Caligula at Rome (40). The emperor enraged the Jews by ordering a statue bearing his image and the name Zeus Epiphanios Neos Gaios to be placed in the temple at Jerusalem (40). Agrippa persuaded him to cancel the edict, but the emperor soon changed his mind again; though work on the statue was begun, the order was never completed.

The New Testament does not mention Gaius' name. Luke cites the names of Augustus (Luke 2:1), Tiberius (3:15), and Claudius (Acts 11:28; 18:2), and alludes to Nero, but fails to include the name of Caligula, at whose ascension to the throne Rome had expected so much.

Bibliography. J. P. V. D. Balsdon, *The Emperor Gaius (Caligula)* (1934: repr. Oxford: 1964).

CALL, CALLING (Heb. *qārāʾ*; Gk. *kaléō* and cognates *klésis*, *klētós*; also *légō*, *phōnéō*, and *chrēmatízō*). A term designating God's summons to a specific task or role and his special relationship to his people.

I. God's Calling of His People

A. Old Testament. Specific individuals were called to certain tasks, as when God called Moses to lead his people out of Egypt (Exod. 3:4, 10) and Samuel to be his servant (1 Sam. 3:1-14). The prophets were called to present God's message (cf. Amos 7:15; Jer. 1:4-19). Likewise, Israel was called to assemble in observance of holy convocations, e.g., during the Sabbath (e.g.,

Lev. 23:2-3), at the end of the Passover (Num. 28:25), and at the Feast of Weeks (Num. 28:26). The book of Isaiah narrates Israel's special position as God's chosen people, the result of God's call. God not only called the Jews from the "farthest corners" (Isa. 41:9), "in righteousness" (42:6), and "by name" (43:1), but also encouraged the religiously undecided to look to Abraham as their own patriarch whom God had called and blessed (51:2; cf. Gen. 12:1-3). Actually, Israel was not founded until it was created by God and he called it by name (43:1; cf. Ezekiel's picture of Israel as an infant girl taken and cared for by God; Ezek. 16:1-7).

B. New Testament. The New Testament echoes the Old Testament's notion of God's call. For instance, Paul states that God "calls into existence the things that do not exist" (meaning that God called Abraham, a heretofore childless man, to be the father of many; Rom. 4:17) and that he is faithful to his covenant (1 Thess. 5:24). Throughout the gospel God's powerful call summons the church (the "called out") to a life of faith.

In the New Testament as in the Old, God's call is always a summons to a special assignment. According to Paul, God calls believers to communion with Christ (1 Cor. 1:9), to peace (7:15), to one hope in Christ (Eph. 4:4), and to eternal life (1 Tim. 6:12). In fact, believers are daily called to their task and must daily respond to it (Phil. 3:13-14). For that reason, they are urged to walk "worthy of the calling to which [they] have been called" (Eph. 4:1).

At 1 Cor. 7:17-23 Paul stresses that believers should remain in the social situation — slavery or otherwise — to which they have been called by God. It is not external circumstances that are important but rather the fact that a person is called and that he walks according to that vocation.

II. Human Response

A. Old Testament. One way in which God's people responded to his call was by calling "upon the name of the Lord" (e.g., Gen. 4:26, with reference to the faithful before the Flood). Often this was done through cultic worship (Ps. 116:17; cf. 1 Kgs. 18:24), sometimes through prayer in times of need (Joel 2:32). While Israel frequently failed to heed God's call, Joel (Joel 2:32) and Zephaniah (Zeph. 3:9) predicted a time when all people turning to God for help will be delivered and serve him.

B. New Testament. Joel's prophecy had been fulfilled, in part, at Pentecost when the Holy Spirit was poured on those who believed in Christ (Acts 2:21). Paul believed that "every one" calling on the Lord would be saved, Jew and Gentile alike (Rom. 10:13; cf. 1 Cor. 1:2). The faithful are further urged to answer their calling with a holy life-style befitting the saints (Rom. 1:7; 1 Cor. 1:2; cf. 2 Tim. 1:9, "called with a holy calling"). Ultimately, Paul contends that both God's call and human response are determined by divine election (e.g., Rom. 8:28-30; 9:11).

See also ELECTION.

CALNEH [kăl'nə] (Heb. *kalnēh*). One of the cities founded by Nimrod, in the land of Shinar (Gen. 10:10,

KJV, NIV). According to the Talmud, Calneh was the important Babylonian city of Nippur, located between Babylon and Erech. Though Gen. 10:10 might very well describe this area, no positive identification between Nippur and Calneh has been made. One proposal, that Calneh is another name for the Akkadian town Kullanî, would require that Calneh be situated much farther north than Gen. 10:10 suggests (cf. 11:2, where Shinar designates Babylonia; cf. Dan. 1:2). The RSV, JB, and NIV mg. render, instead, "all of them (Heb. weḵullānâ)," meaning that the cities mentioned before are all located in the land of Shinar.

At Amos 6:2, Calneh is listed before Hamath (Syria) and Gath (Philistia), perhaps implying a northern location. If the Calneh mentioned in Amos is not the same as the Calneh of Gen. 10, it may be that Amos' reference was to a northern commercial colony named after the more southern mother city.

CALNO [kăl′nō] (Heb. *kalnô*). A city mentioned at Isa. 10:9, which, like Carchemish, was taken by Tiglath-pileser III in 738 B.C. Calno, called Kullanî on Assyrian inscriptions, has been identified with modern Kullanköy, approximately 13 km. (8 mi.) northwest of Aleppo. Should the Calneh of Amos 6:2 — sometimes identified with Kullanî — be the same as Calno, Amos may have known it before its capture by the Assyrians.

CALVARY [kăl′və rĭ]. Latin translation of Golgotha (Vulg. *calvaria* for Gk. *kraníon* "skull," Matt. 27:33 par.; cf. KJV at Luke 23:33).

CAMBYSES [kăm′bĭ′sēz] (Pers. *Kanbujiya, Kambujet*).†
1. Cambyses I, vassal king of Anshan (600-559 B.C.) and father of Cyrus II.
2. Cambyses II, son of Cyrus II and Cassandane the daughter of Pharnaspes, and grandson of Cambyses I. Shortly after Babylon fell to the Persians in 539 B.C., Cambyses was left in charge of that city, representing his father who had departed for Ecbatana. Although he had performed the king's ritual duties at the New Year festival, Cambyses was not permitted the title "king of Babylon" as long as his father remained in control of the empire. He was named regent in 530 prior to Cyrus' last military campaign, against the nomadic tribes beyond the Jaxartes river; when his father died in battle that same year, Cambyses became the sole ruler of Persia.

After lengthy preparations Cambyses in 525 fulfilled his father's plans of invading Egypt, whose Pharaoh Amasis had sought to curb Persian influence in the West. Cambyses defeated the forces of the Egyptian successor Psamtik III (Psammenentis, Psemmetichus) in the eastern Delta; he then tried to gain the Egyptians' acceptance by diplomatically favoring the worship of the Egyptian goddess Neith, whose sanction he sought at Sais. He himself captured northern Ethiopia; his troops took the oasis of Kharga but perished before reaching their goal, the oasis of Amon, and an intended expedition against Carthage was aborted for lack of support. Cambyses died, possibly by suicide, en route to Babylon in 522, shortly after learning that a certain Gaumata had usurped the

throne in Babylon, claiming to be Cambyses' brother Bardiya (Smerdis) — whom Cambyses himself had murdered.

Although the Old Testament does not name Cambyses, he may be one of the three kings alluded to at Dan. 11:2. The Ahasuerus of Esth. 1:1, thought by some earlier scholars to be Cambyses II, is more properly identified with Xerxes I.

CAMEL. Either of two large species of ruminant mammals used for carrying burdens and for transportation.

I. Terminology and Identification

The genus *Camelus* (Lat., from Gk. *kámēlos*; cf. Heb. *gāmāl*) is divided into two species: *Camelus dromedarius*, the dromedary (Isa. 66:20, Heb. *kirkārôṭ*; KJV "swift beasts"; cf. KJV at Isa. 60:6, Heb. **bēḵer*) having one hump, and *Camelus bactrianus*, the two-humped camel.

The dromedary originated in Arabia and appeared in Egypt ca. 3000 B.C. Evidence for its existence in Mari has been supplied by camel bones discovered in the region dating to ca. 2400. It was only much later that this animal appeared in Asia Minor, where it was first mentioned in connection with the battle at Halys (546). References to the camel in Assyria date to ca. 1100, and Mesopotamian drawings of camels have been dated to the tenth century.

The two-humped camel probably originated in central Asia, in the ancient kingdom of Bactria (thus "Bactrian camel") on the Oxus river (Amu Darya). From there some of them spread to Assyria where they are mentioned on monuments dating from 1100 and most notably on the Black Obelisk of Shalmaneser III (ca. 830). Isa. 21:7 may refer to this species.

II. Old Testament

During the patriarchal period Abraham is said to have possessed camels (Gen. 12:16) and given a number of them to his steward on his trip to Paddan-aram (24:10ff.); later Jacob acquired them in Mesopotamia (30:43) and took them with him to Palestine (31:17). While the Egyptians (Exod. 9:3), Ishmaelites (Gen. 37:28), and later the Midianites (Judg. 7:12) and Amalekites (1 Sam. 15:3) owned camels, the biblical record does not indicate their extensive use by the Israelites until David's time (1 Chr. 12:40; cf. 1 Kgs. 10:2 during the reign of Solomon). Camels are also included among the possessions of the exiles returning from Babylon (Ezra 2:67; Neh. 7:69).

Heb. *gāmāl* (cf. Arab. *jamal*) is applied primarily to the one-humped and, later, to the two-humped camel; to the Israelites the difference between these two species must not have been significant, though the Old Testament distinguishes between the heavy beasts of burden (Gen. 37:25) and the more finely built riding animals (1 Sam. 30:17). At 1 Kgs. 4:28 the KJV uses the term "dromedaries," meaning swift-moving camels (Heb. *reḵeš* "team of horses"; cf. RSV "swift steeds"; NIV "other horses"; JB "draught animals").

Camels were used for transportation (e.g., 1 Sam. 30:17) and as beasts of burden (e.g., 2 Kgs. 8:9). Saddles (sometimes a type of canopy) were fastened on the riding camels (Gen. 31:34; KJV "furniture"); the camels of Zebah and Zalmunna had decorative crescents around their necks (Judg. 8:21, 26). Because even the slower-moving pack animals could maintain an average speed of three miles per hour for as much as twelve hours at a stretch, and feed on such desert vegetation as thistles, plant roots, and grasses, camels were of inestimable value to the desert and steppe nomads. Problems did arise, however, when the female camel was in heat (see Jer. 2:23).

Camel hair was sometimes used in making outer garments (see below), and their manure served as fuel. Unlike the Arabs, however, Israelites were forbidden to eat camel meat (Lev. 11:4; Deut. 14:7).

III. New Testament

The outer garment of John the Baptist was made from camel's hair (Matt. 3:4 par. Mark 1:6) and thus was well suited to the austere life in the desert. Such a cloak might have been an emblem of prophetic status.

Speaking figuratively, Jesus commented that wealthy people were less likely to engage in the kingdom of God than a camel to pass through the eye of a needle (Matt. 19:23 par. Mark 10:25; Luke 18:24-25); the literal impossibility of such a feat leads to Jesus' point that "all things are possible with God" (Matt. 19:26 par.). At 23:24 he chides the Pharisees for straining at the gnat and swallowing the camel, playing on the similarity between Aram. *qalmā* "gnat" and *gamlā* "camel" to argue that excessive concern for minute points may result in inattention to important matters.

A relief from the palace of Assurbanipal showing use of camels in warfare (by courtesy of the Trustees of the British Museum)

CAMP. Temporary living arrangements, usually for the military during times of war. In biblical times camp tents may have been set up in a circle or a square which soldiers were to guard continually (e.g., Judg. 7:19, "set the watch"). Often the camp was surrounded by supply wagons that formed a protective wall of defense (Heb. *ma'gāl*, "circle of a camp," KoB, p. 544). The Philistines employed such a camp (1 Sam. 17:20); so did Saul when he was pursuing David (1 Sam. 26:5, 7) — during the battle a contingent of soldiers stayed behind to protect the camp ("remained with the baggage," 1 Sam. 25:13).

Israel's camp in the wilderness was patterned after a military encampment (Num. 2; cf. Heb. *maḥᵃneh*, from *ḥānâ* "decline"). Because God dwelled among his people in the camp, it earned a sacral character: whatever was impure was to be removed and placed outside of the camp. When the Israelites committed the sin of making a golden calf to worship in Moses' absence, he then erected a tent outside the camp in which to meet God (Exod. 33:7-11). Before entering the Promised Land the Israelites were reminded to keep the camp "holy" (Deut. 23:14) because of the Lord's presence within; anything "indecent" might turn him away from his people (vv. 12-14).

The author of Hebrews (Heb. 13:11-12) draws a parallel between the bodies of the animals sacrificed on the Day of Atonement to bear the sins of the people, which were burned "outside of the camp" (Gk. *parembolé*, "camp, barracks, battle line"; Bauer, p. 625) and Jesus' crucifixion "outside of the gate" of Jerusalem. The exhortation that believers go "outside the camp" (i.e., beyond the established fellowship and ordinances of Judaism) and "share [Christ's] degradation" (v. 13, JB) may allude to Moses' actions at Exod. 33:7-11. The "camp of the saints" at Rev. 20:9 may signify the believer's pilgrimage through life (as the Israelites were sojourners in the wilderness) or submission to God's rule.

CANA [kā'nə] (Gk. *Kana,* probably from Heb. *qāneh* "reed"). A village in Galilee, called Cana in Galilee, probably to distinguish it from the Old Testament Kanah, which was in the territory of Asher (Josh. 16:8; 19:28). John mentions Cana three times in his gospel: as the location of Christ's first and second miracles (2:1, 11, the changing of water into wine; 4:46, the healing of the official's son), and as the birthplace of Nathanael, one of Jesus' disciples (21:2).

Ancient and medieval tradition suggests that the site might be identified with Kafr Kennä, about 6 km. (4 mi.) northeast of Nazareth (some even suggest that Nathanael's home was located here). However, contemporary scholars favor Khirbet Qânā, situated on the north side of the el-Battauf, about 14 km. (9 mi.) north of Nazareth.

CANAAN [kā'nən] (Heb. *kᵉna'an*) (**PERSON**). A son of Ham and grandson of Noah (Gen. 9:18, 22); according to 1 Chr. 1:13 Ham's youngest son. He became the ancestor of the people later called the Canaanites (Gen. 10:15ff.).

Canaan was punished for the impropriety of his father's seeing the "nakedness" of Noah (Gen. 9:22-24; *see also* HAM). His grandfather cursed him to be "a slave of slaves . . . to his brothers" (v. 25). This curse, which applies more to his descendants than to Canaan himself, does not imply the slavery of a particular race (as some have held); rather, it suggests the inferior position of the Canaanites before the Conquest relative to the important role played by their neighbors, the Egyptians and the inhabitants of Mesopotamia.

CANAAN [kā'nən] (Heb. $k^e na'an$) (**PLACE**). The territory inhabited by the CANAANITES.

CANAANITES [kā'nə nīts] (Heb. $k^e na'^a n\hat{\imath}$).† The inhabitants of Canaan prior to the Israelite conquest; also an appellation for merchants.

I. Name

Attempts to explain the etymology of the name Canaanites and its geographical referent, Canaan, remain inconclusive. On the basis of a reference to *ma-at ki-in-a-nim* ("land of Canaan") in a fifth-century B.C. inscription of King Idrimi of Alalakh, scholars have identified in the common Akkadian forms *kinaḫni* and *kinaḫḫu* a root *kina* meaning "reed (papyrus)" or "red-purple." Indeed, in the fifteenth-century Nuzi texts the adjective *kinaḫḫu* "Canaanite" occurs in a context which points to the purple dye originally produced in the region. Thus, Canaan and the Canaanites would be related etymologically to red-purple commodities much as Pergamum is identified with parchment and Damascus with damask. Unfortunately, however, linguistic complexities make such a derivation difficult.

More recently scholars have suggested that the name Canaan derived secondarily as a term designating the homeland of a people known as Canaanites. In this view, these people appear to have been neither an ethnic unit nor a nation in the modern sense, but rather a particular social class, notably merchants (cf. Heb. $k^e na'^a n\hat{\imath}$ "merchant," Ezek. 27:3; "trader[s]," Isa. 23:8; Hos. 12:7; Zeph. 1:11; cf. KoB, pp. 444-45). A stele of the Egyptian pharaoh Amenhotep II (1449-1433) lists along with the *maryannu* class of Hurrian chariot nobility and the children of princes some six hundred *kyn'n.w*, most likely a merchant class from a particular Near Eastern locale. Moreover, a Mari letter (eighteenth century) names among various foreigners $^{lu}habbātum$ u $^{lu}Kinaḫnûm$, possibly "thieves and Canaanites" in the sense of "thieves and merchants" or "thieving merchants." It remains unclear whether the gentilic (and thus the geographic) designation derived from the term of the social class or vice versa.

For the most part biblical references to Canaanites indicate the populace of the Late Bronze Age Egyptian province; thus, they are distinguished from the inhabitants of Transjordan and Philistia (Exod. 15:5; Judg. 5:19). The term reflects a cultural group of ethnically diverse people, comprised of various Semitic and non-Semitic elements (cf. Gen. 36:2-3; Ezek. 16:3). At times they are listed among assorted social, political, and cultural classifications (e.g., Gen. 15:19-21; 34:30; Exod. 3:8; Josh. 17:15-18). In later usage the term is used for the Phoenicians, the cultural heirs of the Bronze Age Canaanites (Obad. 20; RSV "Phoenicia"; Matt. 15:22; Gk. *Chananaia*; cf. par. Mark 7:26, *Syrophoinikissa* "Syro-Phoenician").

II. Territory

Egyptian texts from the fourteenth-thirteenth centuries place the southern boundary of Canaan along the military road from Sile to Gaza, along the Wâdī el-'Arish (Brook of Egypt); according to Josh. 15:1-4 this border extended to the southeastern shore of the Dead Sea. The boundary lists of Num. 34:1-12 and Ezek. 47:15-20; 48:1-28 indicate Canaanite territory as bounded on the west by the Mediterranean Sea as far north as the kingdom of Amurru and on the north by the entrance of Hamath, modern Lebweh. On the east the boundary runs south from Hazar-enan to Mt. Bashan and then west to the Sea of Galilee and south again along the Jordan river.

Primary areas of occupation include the coastal plain as far inland as the valley of Jezreel and the Jordan river (Num. 13:29; Josh. 5:1; Judg. 1:1-36).

III. History

Although the area had been inhabited considerably earlier, it is with the influx of peoples from northern Syria and Anatolia and the introduction of urban life at the beginning of the Bronze Age (*ca.* 3200) that Canaanite history is thought to have begun. For all intents, that history is coterminous with the Bronze Age itself, and the course of Canaanite civilization was strongly influenced by the fortunes of the Egyptian Empire to the west and the cultural and political movements within other parts of the ancient Near East and Anatolia.

Indeed, the apparently peaceful existence of the early Canaanite villages and fortified towns was shattered *ca.* 2300 by widespread destruction resulting from raids under the Egyptian Sixth Dynasty and large-scale upheaval accompanied by massive population movements throughout much of the ancient world. During the Middle Bronze Age (specifically MB IIA; *ca.* 2000-1800) the Canaanites were dominated politically and economically by the Egyptian Twelfth Dynasty. It was during this approximate period also that the seeds of classical Canaanite culture were sown, introduced by Amorite movements from the east and north; the migration of Abraham from Haran to Canaan (Gen. 12:4-5) is generally assigned to this period.

With Egypt under Hyksos control in the eighteenth-seventeenth centuries, Canaanite society reached its greatest height. Powerful cities emerged, fortified by massive ramparts of beaten earth. These urban centers and the allied villages and open country which surrounded them formed a network of city-states throughout Palestine, each ruled by a king and the attendant nobility. The economic base for this society was the agricultural produce of the villages, to which the masses of the Canaanite citizenry were aligned.

With the expulsion of the Hyksos in the sixteenth century, Egypt sought to reassert political influence over Canaanite Palestine, accomplished in part by the incursions of Thutmose III (*ca.* 1505-1450). The Late Bronze Age (*ca.* 1550-1200) witnessed further decline of Egyptian power with the advance of the Hittite and Mitannian empires. Increased friction between the Canaanite city-states as well as foreign pressure on them is reflected in the pleas for Egyptian aid recorded in the Amarna Letters. These texts also point to growing dissatisfaction among the Canaanite masses and the appearance of ʿApiru (Habiru) bands which ultimately threatened the existence of that society.

It was during this period of upheaval in Egypt and Canaan that the Hebrews under Moses left Egypt and entered Canaan under Joshua. Various attempts have been made to elucidate the biblical accounts of the Israelite emergence in Palestine, including theories of immigration, military conquest, peasant revolt, and the transformation of frontier areas. It is clear that Israelite control of the region developed gradually and that pockets of Canaanite society remained for some time (cf. Josh. 13:1; 15:63; 16:10; 17:12, 16; Judg. 3:5; 4:2). Nevertheless, the emergence of the Israelite state and the settling of the Philistines along the Mediterranean coast in the thirteenth century constituted the end of Canaanite history.

IV. Legacy

Although portrayed as opponents of the Israelites and a threat to their religious purity (e.g., Exod. 23:32-33; 34:12-16; Deut. 7:2-3, 16, 26), the Canaanites greatly influenced Israelite culture and, indeed, that of civilization in general. Canaanite alphabets, found in middle-second-millennium scripts from Serabit el-Khadem in the Sinai peninsula and the cuneiform texts from Ugarit (Ras Shamra), are the basis for modern Western alphabets. Linguistically, the Canaanite family of Northwest Semitic languages includes Hebrew, Ugaritic, and Phoenician; the language of the texts discovered at Ebla (Tell Mardikh) has been classified tentatively as Paleocanaanite.

Canaanite religion, known largely from the literary and historical texts discovered at Ugarit and the Amarna Letters, acknowledged a great variety of deities, chief of whom was El (Ugar. ʾil "god"; cf. Heb. ʾēl); various local forms of this deity may be reflected in the names El Shadday ("God Almighty"; e.g., Gen. 17:1; 28:3), El Elyon ("Most High"; Gen. 14:18-21), El Olam ("Everlasting God"; Gen. 21:33), and El Bethel ("God of Bethel"; Gen. 31:13). Most prominent in the Ugaritic texts and the Old Testament is the storm and rain god Baal ("lord, master"), also known in numerous local manifestations (e.g., Baal-Peor, Baal-Lebanon; cf. Baal-berith, "lord of the covenant," Judg. 9:4). Other members of the Canaanite pantheon, many of whom have counterparts in Assyrian and Babylonian gods, include Dagon, god of corn; Hadad, the thunder god; and Anat, Astarte, and Athirat (Asherah), variant forms of the goddess of love and the mother goddess. Fertility and procreation were important focuses of Canaanite religion, and ritual prostitution was part of cultic observances. It remains unclear whether human sacrifice was performed (cf. Ps. 106:37-39).

Bibliography. W. F. Albright, *Yahweh and the Gods of Canaan* (repr. 1978); J. Gray, *The Canaanites* (New York: 1964); K. M. Kenyon, *Amorites and Canaanites* (New York: 1966).

CANAANITESS (Heb. *hakkᵉnaʿᵃnîṯ*). A designation for Bath-shua, the wife of Judah (1 Chr. 2:3; NIV, JB "Canaanite woman").

CANANAEAN (Gk. *Kananaios*). An epithet belonging to Simon, one of Christ's disciples, to distinguish him from Simon Peter (Matt. 10:4 par. Mark 3:18; NIV, JB "the Zealot"). Though some claim that he was "zealous for the Lord" (cf. Aram. *qanʾānāʾ* "zealot"; KJV "Canaanite" is a rendering of Gk. *Kananitēs*, attested in less reliable MSS), others consider him to have been a member of the zealot party (cf. "Zealot," Gk. *zēlōtēs*; Luke 6:15; Acts 1:13).

See SIMON (8); ZEAL, ZEALOT.

CANDACE [kănˈdə sī] (Gk. *Kandakē*). The queen of Ethiopia (so KJV, NIV at Acts 8:27; RSV "the Candace"), whose eunuch Philip met on the road between Jerusalem and Gaza. Her realm was probably Nubia with the principal cities of Meroe and Napata, not Ethiopia proper. Candace is not a personal name, but rather a title (similar to "pharaoh"), given to the queens of this territory (cf. JB "the kandake, or queen"). Pyramid graves of a number of Candaces have been discovered near Meroe, dated *ca.* 300 B.C. to A.D. 300. The ancient writers were familiar with the names of several Candaces.

CANDLE (e.g., Job 18:6, KJV). See LAMP.

CANDLESTICK (e.g., Exod. 25:31, KJV). See LAMPSTAND.

CANE. See SWEET CANE.

CANNEH [kănˈə] (Heb. *kannēh*). A Mesopotamian city that maintained trade relations with Tyre (Ezek. 27:23). Some suggest that it is the same as Calneh (Amos 6:2) or Calno (Isa. 10:9).

CANON. The term "canon" (Gk. *kanōn* "law, regulation, rule of conduct," a transliteration of Heb. *qāneh* "reed") refers to the whole of the Scriptures as the authoritative Word of God. Their authority rests on their "God-breathed" (Gk. *theópneustos*; cf. 2 Tim. 3:16) nature and can be accepted only in faith through the testimony of the Holy Spirit in the believer's heart. In addition, it is also used in connection with the traditional sixty-six inspired books, which are first listed in an Easter letter of Athanasius (A.D. 367). The synods of Hippo (393) and Carthage (397) confessed the canonicity of these books, meaning their divine authority. Though Roman Catholics generally believe that the authority of the canonized books is derived from the Church ("proximate and ultimate criterion is the infallible decision of the church," W. G. Most, "Bible, III (Canon)," *NCE* 2:387, but see the text of the article), Protestants for the most part claim that it is the Church's responsibility only to profess and preserve those books that have canonical status. It is more appropriate, in the words of the Belgic Confession (Art. 5): "[to believe] . . . all things contained in them, not so much because the Church receives and approves them as such, but more especially because the Holy Spirit witnesses in our hearts that they are from God" (see also Westminster Confession I.4-5).

I. Scope

The study of the canon is divided into the general and the specific. The latter concerns itself with questions about authorship, place of origin, and date of the individual books of the Bible, as well as about the manner in which they came to be included in the canon; it does not ask whether or not a book belongs within the canon. In this dictionary the question of special canonics is addressed in the separate articles on those books of the Bible whose canonicity has been contested. (See ESTHER; PROVERBS; ECCLESIASTES; SONG OF SOLOMON; HEBREWS; JAMES; JUDE; REVELATION, BOOK OF.)

The study of general canonics, on the other hand, is concerned with the origin, acknowledgment, and extent of the canon as a whole. Though these questions are essentially the same for both the Old and New Testaments, their different answers demand that general canonics be divided into two sections: the Old Testament and the New Testament.

II. Old Testament

A. Origin. Because the Old Testament says little about the process of its own canonization and because scholarly opinion about the historical development of the Old Testament canon has failed to reach consensus, it is best to proceed from the historic moment at which the Old Testament first appears to have been granted recognition — namely, during New Testament times. That the Old Testament was then regarded as a unity appears from the frequent New Testament references to it as the "scriptures" (e.g., Matt. 26:54) and, more cogently, "scripture" (John 10:35); sometimes the term "scripture" refers to more than one Old Testament passage, as, e.g., at John 7:42 which points to at least two different passages (Ps. 89:3-4; Mic. 5:2). Furthermore, some quotations from the Old Testament are introduced with the formula "in the law it is written," even when the passage cited is not from the Pentateuch but from the Psalms or the Prophets (e.g., 1 Cor. 14:21, citing Isa. 28:11-12). These facts do not in themselves prove that the canon of the Old Testament as then accepted contained all thirty-nine books included in most English versions; some books such as Esther and Ecclesiastes are not cited in the New Testament. But Matt. 23:35; Luke 11:51 strongly indicate that this was indeed the case, for in speaking of the blood of Abel and Zechariah, these two passages refer to the first and last books of the Hebrew canon (if the murdered Zechariah is the one mentioned at 2 Chr. 24:20-24), a canon identical to the Old Testament canon of most English versions.

The New Testament refers to the Old Testament as the "old covenant" (Gk. palaía diathḗkē; 2 Cor. 3:14), a name which the Church Fathers also generally accepted. That this Old Testament canon contained the same number of books as contemporary English versions is also apparent from Josephus *Contra Apionem* 1.8, where twenty-two books are listed as trustworthy and as such are to be distinguished from others. These books include the five books of Moses, the thirteen prophetic books (Judges and Ruth are one book, as are Ezra and Nehemiah, Jeremiah and Lamentations, and the twelve minor prophets; the book of Job also belongs to this group), and four books of the Writings. Thus, during the first century A.D. the canon of the Old Testament comprised all thirty-nine books present in English versions.

It appears from the prologue to Sirach ("the law, and the prophets and other books"), however, that the Old Testament canon was completed prior to the first century A.D. as well. Though the dates of Jesus ben Sirach are not known with certainty, most likely he lived *ca.* 180 B.C. This would mean that the Jews were familiar with an Old Testament canon as early as the second century B.C.; such a canon could not have been much older, for the book of Ecclesiastes was not written until the middle of the fourth century.

B. Acknowledgment. It is evident that the New Testament recognizes the canon of the Old Testament as divine in origin and authority. Introduced by the words "as it is written" (in the Law, the Prophets, or the Psalms), the New Testament quotations from the Old Testament serve as proofs to end all disputation. Furthermore, the New Testament speaks of the assured fulfillment of Old Testament predictions, while sometimes ascribing to God an Old Testament quotation in a passage where God did not actually speak (Matt. 19:5, quoting Gen. 2:24). It appears then that the entire Old Testament was recognized as God's own word, probably as early as the time of Jesus ben Sirach.

C. Extent. The process by which the Old Testament became canonical among the Jews remains shrouded in obscurity. Accordingly, the standard nineteenth-century view, which held that the Deuteronomic Code was accepted as canonical *ca.* 621, the Law *ca.* 450, the Prophets *ca.* the third century, and, finally, the Writings during the second century, no longer seems tenable. The lack of consensus among contemporary scholars about the historical formation of the Old Testament may be due in part to the controversy over the theory of unbroken unity between the writing and the collection of an authoritative body of Scripture (see Childs, p. 58 for the degree of distinction between scriptural authority and canonization). Nevertheless, it does seem reasonable that the canonization of the Old Testament went through various stages of development, of which many crucial details are still lacking.

The Hebrew canon had traditionally been divided into the Law (tôrâ), the Prophets (nᵉḇîʾîm), and the Writings (kᵉṯûḇîm). (For an enumeration of the Old Testament books see BIBLE *II.*). The Talmud (*B. Bat.* 14b) speaks of twenty-four books (the Law, or the five books of Moses, Joshua, Judges, Samuel, Kings, Jeremiah, Ezekiel, Isaiah, the Twelve [minor prophets], Ruth, Psalms, Job, Proverbs, Ecclesiastes, Canticles, Lamentations, Daniel, Esther, Ezra [and Nehemiah], and Chronicles), as do 4 Ezra (14:19-48) and Josephus (see above). There was no difference of opinion among the Palestinian Jews concerning the extent of the canon; but differences did exist among the Alexandrian Jews who translated the books of the Hebrew canon into Greek and added to the LXX several other writings which they also considered sources of wisdom and insight. Nevertheless, it was not the intention of the LXX translators to expand the existing Hebrew canon, and the Jewish rabbis have never regarded these additional writings to be equal in status to the books of the Hebrew canon.

The early Church, however, received the Old Testament in the Greek translation and at first ascribed canonical authority to the added books. Several years later the synods of Hippo (A.D. 393) and Carthage

(397) each produced a list of the canonical books. Following Athanasius and Augustine the Church accepted the LXX; even though Jerome argued for a return to the Hebrew canon, he himself included the additional writings of the LXX in his Vulgate translation. The churches of the Reformation, on the other hand, accepted the Hebrew canon but retained the Septuagintal sequence of the books. At the Council of Trent (fourth session, 1546), the Roman Catholic Church declared itself in favor of the broader Old Testament canon. Although 3 Maccabees and 1 Esdras were excluded at first, they were included (along with 3 and 4 Ezra) in the 1592 edition of the Vulgate, placed after the New Testament. Concerning the extent of the Hebrew canon, then, there has been very little contention within the Christian Church; even the Roman Catholic Church came to designate the added books as deuterocanonical. Only the book of Esther was subject to some doubt, mainly in the Eastern Church. Luther did not doubt the canonic character of this book, although he would have preferred that it had not been included in Scripture (it is "less worthy of being held canonical than all the other [books because it] Judaize[s] too much and contain[s] much pagan naughtiness"). *See* APOCRYPHA.

III. New Testament

A. Origin. The question concerning the origin of the New Testament canon is misleading insofar as it can suggest the absence of a canon before the New Testament books were written; in fact, the origin of the New Testament canon is found in the authority of Jesus Christ, not in a more or less fixed collection of writings. Though Christ did accept the writings of the Old Testament as canonical, he also proclaimed his own authority. As the one sent by God for the salvation of mankind (Matt. 11:27; John 5:23-24), he was given authority and power by God and acted accordingly (Matt. 9:6; John 5:27). He demanded obedience of those who followed him and bound them to his word and work — the Word and work of God (John 3:17-18, 34-36). His followers, in turn, recognized Jesus' authority (Matt. 8:8) and gave him the title of "Son of God" (Matt. 14:33; 16:16).

The apostles also recognized the Old Testament books as canonical but acknowledged and preached Jesus Christ as the absolute "canon." Paul made a clear distinction between his own word and that of the Lord (1 Cor. 7:10-12). The early Church recognized as canonical both the Old Testament and Jesus Christ, and in their writings the Apostolic Fathers cited equally quotations from the Old Testament and the words of Jesus.

Jesus made it possible for others to maintain his authority after his departure from earth. He appointed apostles who, guided by his Spirit, would preach his word and carry on his ministry. They were eye-witnesses, able to pass on (Gk. *kērýssein* "preach, witness"; Mark 6:12; Luke 9:2) what they had seen and heard Christ do. The substance of this preaching (Gk. *kérygma* "proclamation, witness") is the affirmation that Jesus Christ is the Son of God come for the redemption of life. This *kérygma* is also called the "gospel" or "evangel" (Gk. *euangélion*, the "glad tidings" or "good news"), for to those who believe, the authoritative word of Jesus Christ is a promise of salvation. The apostles received the Holy Spirit that they might fulfill this task (Acts 1:8). Furthermore, Christ conferred authority upon them by working through them and permitting them to preach about him. As a result, his authority was present not only in their actual speaking (Acts 2:42; 10:44; 15:23-29; 16:4), but also in their letters (Rom. 15:18-20; 1 Cor. 2:1-5; 1 Thess. 5:27; Jude 17). The churches also acknowledged and accepted the apostles' authority. At Eph. 2:20, the apostles are called the "foundation" of the Church which is laid by Jesus Christ, the "cornerstone" (Eph. 2:20; cf. 1 Cor. 3:11; Eph. 4:11).

Next, the Apostolic Fathers (*ca.* A.D. 100) accepted the canonicity of the words preached and written by the apostles (i.e., the Twelve and Paul). They even went so far as to make ascription of words to the apostles a guarantee of canonicity; this concept required an historically complicated explanation for the gospels of Mark and Luke, because these two canonical gospels actually were not composed by any of the original apostles.

Apparently, the Apostolic Fathers had at their disposal written gospels and collected letters of Paul and the other apostles, from which they quoted the words of Jesus and others. The churches of that time also had access to such documents, for the letters addressed to certain congregations were read at their gatherings and passed on to other churches (Col. 4:16; 1 Thess. 5:27; 2 Pet. 3:15-16). From this it appears that the early Church recognized as canonical what is now called the New Testament (then called "the Lord and the apostles"; Gk. *ho kýrios kaí hoi apóstoloi*).

The words of early Christian prophets had no absolute authority (1 Cor. 12:29ff.) and were not recognized as canonical. The Apostolic Fathers, at least, did recognize New Testament prophecy as canonical. This spiritual gift apparently diminished during the second century, and little of the prophetic material has been preserved (cf. Acts 11:27-28).

At the end of the second century, the Church Fathers set up a canon of truth (Gk. *kanón tēs alētheías*) or "rule of faith" (Lat. *regula fidei*) as a criterion of orthodoxy. This rule was derived from the canon but was not regarded as canonical itself; rather it represented a confession of faith, for only "the Lord and the apostles" were considered canonical.

B. Acknowledgment. While it cannot be concluded on the basis of 2 Pet. 3:15-16 that during the second half of the first century Paul's letters were given the same recognition as the Old Testament, it does follow from 3:2 that the New Testament apostles were placed on a par with the Old Testament prophets. (Though in the latter passage the expressions "as it is written" or "the Scriptures say" do not occur, the Apostolic Fathers apparently used these expressions while referring both to the Old Testament and the Gospels and Letters. No doubt because their main intent was to demonstrate to others that Jesus Christ was the long-expected Messiah, these expressions were used more often with quotations from the Old Testament than from the Gospels and Letters.) The early Church also credited the Old Testament with authority equal to that of the Gospels and Letters; leaders read aloud from all of these writings, without discrimination, in their worship services (cf. Justin *Apologia* i.67). At first, however, writings other than those now constituting the New Testament (such as the Shepherd of Hermas and other pseudepigraphal words) were also read publicly during worship services. It was only after the canonical character of a number of writings was unanimously decided that readings during the worship services were limited to the canonical writings.

The authority of the Epistle to the Hebrews, Revelation, and some of the Catholic Letters was long held in doubt, but a qualified consensus finally evolved at the Synod of Hippo (393). The decision to recognize canonicity was adopted by the Synod of Carthage (397). At this assembly a list was compiled of the canonical books of the Old and New Testaments, which alone could be read during public worship. These two synods did not declare outright that these books were canonical. Rather, they acknowledged and officially sanctioned the generally accepted canonicity of those books that now constitute the Old and New Testaments and distinguished between these and other books (e.g., the writings of the Apostolic Fathers and Acts of the Martyrs). The decision of the Church was accompanied by the phrase "we receive," as though God himself caused his Church to confess the canonicity of the New Testament writings. This pronouncement from the North African synods met with general approval in the Western churches, and has been upheld since then (by contrast, the Syrian Church has never accepted as canonical any of the seven Catholic Letters or Revelation). This is perhaps due to the influence of Athanasius (who had already given the same list of canonical books in his Easter letter of 367) and Augustine, for the synodical decisions concurred with their views.

Although the divine "canon" (i.e., Jesus Christ) would ultimately compel the Church to accept the New Testament, three historical factors also prompted the Church to come to such a decision: (1) the self-authentication of the Holy Scriptures (e.g., the Belgic Confession: "[these books] carry the evidence [of authority] in themselves. For the very blind are able to perceive that the things foretold in them are being fulfilled"; cf. Calvin *Inst.* i.8.5); (2) the necessity of having a New Testament to complement the Old Testament; (3) the tradition, namely, that the words of the apostles should be handed down to succeeding generations. The opposition to heretics was also a consideration in this issue, but the concern was more to "close off" the contents of the canon than to acknowledge the status granted to it.

C. Extent. As already observed, the principle of a New Testament canon existed in the authoritative presence of Jesus Christ. The Gospels and Letters were soon accorded authoritative status (*ca.* A.D. 130). Finally, most of the New Testament writings were designated a sacred unity *ca.* 200 (cf. the Muratorian Fragment and Tertullian's writings: all but Hebrews, James, and 2 Peter; the expression "New Testament" appears along with "Old Testament" in the works by Clement of Alexandria (*ca.* 150-215) and Tertullian (*ca.* 160-225).

The confrontation with Marcion (*ca.* 140; he advocated a modified canon containing only passages of divine love [as recorded in Luke's gospel and ten of

Paul's letters] to the exclusion of texts dealing with divine wrath) suggests the existence of an authoritative collection of New Testament writings. Tertullian, Marcion's great opponent, appealed to such a canon in his *Adversus Marcionem*; Marcion's denial of the Church's larger authoritative canon only emphasized the unity of the New Testament documents. The claims of Montanus (a first-century prophet claiming to have ushered in the so-called third stage of new revelations of the Spirit) were further impetus for the Church's confession concerning a definite canon.

Early acknowledgment of the canonical status of the New Testament books corresponds to Christ's ascension and the end of his earthly ministry. Furthermore, God makes himself known in his Word, in which he himself distinguishes between the old and new covenants (Heb. 1:1-2). Just as the Old Testament reveals what was necessary for the old covenant, the New Testament discloses what can be expected for the new: the first and second comings of the Messiah. Once this had been made known, the canon was complete.

The fundamental argument against an open canon is that it would conflict with the nature and purpose of the canon. In an open canon there may arise an authority other than the canon itself which would decide what is or is not to be included.

Bibliography. H. von Campenhausen, *The Formation of the Christian Bible* (Philadelphia: 1972); B. S. Childs, *Introduction to the Old Testament as Scripture* (Philadelphia: 1979); R. M. Grant, *The Formation of the New Testament* (New York: 1965); S. Z. Leiman, *The Canonization of Hebrew Scripture* (Hamden, Conn.: 1976).

CANTICLES. *See* SONG OF SOLOMON.

CAP. The conical hat worn by the Israelite priests (Exod. 28:40; 29:9; Lev. 8:13). *See* TURBAN.

CAPER-BUD. The berry (Heb. *'ăḇîyônâ* "caper-fruit"; JB "caper bush") of a thorny shrub with shiny green leaves and white blossoms, whose reddish-gold seeds stimulate the appetite (thus RSV "desire"; cf. KJV, NIV); ancient people regarded it as an aphrodisiac. At Eccl. 12:5 it characterizes the end of human life (compared to nature which revives with the spring) or is a symbol of old age when the taste buds degenerate and the appetite diminishes.

CAPERNAUM [kə pûr′nĭ əm] (Gk. *Kapharnaoum, Kapernaoum*). A city on the northern shore of the Sea of Galilee (Matt. 4:13), where Jesus based much of his ministry. It was the location of a tax office (Matt. 9:9), and a contingent of soldiers commanded by a centurion was stationed there (Luke 7:2).

I. Identification

According to Matt. 4:13 Capernaum was situated near the Sea of Galilee ("by the sea"), and Matt. 14:34 (par. Mark 6:53) places it not far from the plain of Gennesaret (cf. John 6:16ff.). According to Jewish tradition Rabbi Tankhum was buried at Capernaum, and his name became corrupted to Tell Ḥûm, the name of a hill of ruins about 4 km. (2.5 mi.) northeast of Khan Minyeh. Recent scholarship suggests that this "hill of ruins" may be the site of the ancient city. Earlier scholars favored Khan Minyeh itself, 8 km. (5 mi.) west of the Jordan river. Though the name of the city may have been based on Heb. *kepar nahûm* "the village of Nahum," it was not the home of that Old Testament prophet.

II. Excavations

A large synagogue dating to the third or fourth century A.D. has been unearthed at Tell Ḥûm, perhaps built on the ruins of an older synagogue where Jesus healed the demoniac (Mark 1:23-26 par. Luke 4:31-35) and restored to health a man with a withered hand (Matt. 12:9-13 par. Mark 3:1-6; Luke 6:6-10). This structure, 20 m. (65 ft.) long and two stories high, was made from white limesone and ornately decorated with natural and mythological figures. On one pillar an Aramaic inscription reads: "Alphaeus, son of Zebedee, son of John, made this column; on him be blessing." Other buildings excavated nearby are a fifth-century church (probably a memorial to the apostle Peter), a house church built *ca.* 350 to preserve Peter's original home which had served as a church, and many single-story apartments. Fishhooks found among the artifacts testify that Capernaum was indeed a fishing town. A great number of black basalt stones used in building and for household implements remain throughout the site. From the ruins it appears that the town may have had a population of approximately one thousand residents.

III. New Testament References

Jesus called Capernaum "his own city" (Matt. 9:1). Here, too, presumably close to the synagogue, was the home of Peter's mother-in-law (Matt. 8:14 par. Mark 1:29; Luke 4:38). A paralytic who wished to be healed was lowered through the roof of a house in Capernaum where Jesus was staying (Mark 2:1-3), perhaps the home of Peter and Andrew. In the same city lived the centurion whose servant Jesus healed of paralysis (Matt. 8:5-13 par. Luke 7:1-10), the official whose son he healed (John 4:46-54), and Jairus, the ruler of the synagogue, whose daughter Jesus restored to life (Mark 5:41-42). Another resident was the converted tax collector, Levi (also called Matthew; cf. Matt. 9:9 par. Mark 2:14), who invited business associates and sinners to dine with Jesus. Once, addressing a very large crowd on Capernaum's shoreline, Jesus had to teach from a ship in the harbor (Matt. 13:2 par.).

Although Jesus performed many mighty works in Capernaum — themselves cause for local pride (Matt. 11:23 par. Luke 10:15) — he also warned the city's inhabitants of potential humiliation and perhaps punishment for failure to repent (cf. Matt. 11:23-24).

CAPHARSALAMA [kăf′ər săl′ə mə] (Gk. *Chapharsalama*). According to 1 Macc. 7:31-32 Nicanor, a general of the king of Syria, lost five hundred soldiers in a battle near Capharsalama. Some scholars identify it with Khirbet Selmah near ej-Jîb, about 10 km. (6 mi.) northwest of Jerusalem, or Khirbet Deir Sellām.

CAPHTOR [kăf′tôr] (Heb. *kaptôr*). The Philistines' place of origin according to Jer. 47:4; Amos 9:7 (cf.

Keftiou in Egyptian inscriptions and *Kaptara* in cuneiform texts). Although western Cilicia and the north Syrian coast have been suggested as possible locations, the island of Crete is the most likely identification.

At Gen. 10:14 (cf. 1 Chr. 1:12) the Caphtorim are said to be descendants of the Egyptians, while the Philistines are named descendants of the Casluhim. This seems to conflict with Deut. 2:23, where some of the Philistines are designated Caphtorim. Though some commentators assume that the explanatory phrase "whence came the Philistines" (Gen. 10:14) has been misplaced in the MT and should have appeared after the word "Caphtorim" (cf. *BH*; see also JB), there is little textual evidence for this claim. A possible solution to the discrepancy between Gen. 10:14 and Deut. 2:23 is to assume that some of the Philistines left Crete and settled near the Nile Delta, where the Casluhim lived, before migrating to Philistia in the western part of Palestine.

CAPHTORIM [kăf′tə rĭm] (Heb. *kaptôrîm*). Inhabitants of Caphtor (Gen. 10:14; Deut. 2:23; 1 Chr. 1:11; NIV Caphtorites; JB "Caphtor," at Gen. 10:14 par. 1 Chr. 1:11).

CAPITAL. The decorated top of a pillar or of a pillar-like object. The capitals (Heb. *rō′š* "head") of the tabernacle pillars were overlaid with silver (Exod. 36:38; 38:17-19; KJV "chapiters"; NIV "tops").

On top of the two bronze pillars in Solomon's temple, Hiram, a master craftsman from Tyre, placed a capital (Heb. *kōṭereṭ*) ornamented with a "LILY-WORK," several pomegranates, and a network of worked bronze (1 Kgs. 7:16-20; 2 Chr. 4:12-13; KJV "chapiters"). These were either 5 cubits (2.2 m. [7.3 ft.]; 1 Kgs. 7:16) or 3 cubits (1.3 m. [4.4 ft.]; 2 Kgs. 25:17) high. When Jerusalem was conquered in 587/586 B.C. Nebuchadnezzar had the pillars and their capitals removed to Babylon (2 Kgs. 25:13, 17; Jer. 52:17, 22).

The capitals (Heb. *kaptôr*) of the lampstand in the tabernacle were part of the cups attached to the branches of the lampstand; four other capitals were fashioned from the shaft itself (Exod. 25:31, 33-36; KJV "knops"; NIV "buds"; JB "calix").

The capitals at Amos 9:1 (KJV "lintel"; NIV "tops") may refer to the highest point of the sacred shrine at Bethel or possibly the temple at Jerusalem where there was one altar of burnt offering. At Zeph. 2:14 it is prophesied that vultures and hedgehogs would lodge in the remains of ruined Nineveh; the capitals (KJV "upper lintels"; NIV "columns"; JB "cornices") may have been parts of the local temple or fragments of the palaces.

CAPPADOCIA [kăp′ə dō′shə] (Gk. *Kappadokia*).†
A region in eastern Asia Minor bounded by Galatia and Lycaonia on the west, Pontus on the north, Armenia on the east, and Cilicia and the Taurus mountains on the south. In ancient times major trade routes passed through this barren, mountainous territory, but it was sparsely populated with only a few cities along the Halys river.

As early as 1950 B.C. a colony of Assyrian merchants was established at Kanesh (modern Kültepe) and formed an important link in the extensive donkey caravan trade between Anatolia and Assur. The region was incorporated in the Hittite Empire (*ca.* 1600-1200) and remained under Hittite control until the Assyrians captured Carchemish in 717 (cf. Isa. 10:9). Subsequently it became a Persian satrapy. A native dynasty developed under Seleucid rule, functioning primarily as vassals to that power but enjoying brief independence under Ariarthes III and IV (*ca.* 255-190). Upon the defeat of the Seleucid king Antiochus III in 190, Cappadocia became a client kingdom of the Roman Empire; when the last Cappadocian king, Archelaus, died in A.D. 17, Tiberius annexed the territory as a Roman province.

Judging from the letter to Ariarthes V (163-130 B.C.) cited at 1 Macc. 15:22, a Jewish community must have been located in Cappadocia as early as the second century. Residents of the province are included among the Jewish pilgrims at the Feast of Pentecost in Jerusalem (Acts 2:9). Christianity spread into the region primarily along the route from Tarsus through the Cilician Gates. In his first letter (1 Pet. 1:1) Peter addresses Christian converts from Cappadocia. The capital of the province, Caesarea (Mazaca; modern Kayseri), became a leading center of Christianity, and several important figures in the early Church (e.g., Basil the Great, Gregory of Nyssa, Gregory of Nazianzus) were from Cappadocia.

CAPTAIN.† English rendering of the titles of various types of military leaders, including the "captain of the guard" (Heb. *śar*; Gen. 40:3-4), "captains of chariots" (1 Kgs. 22:31ff.), and leaders of military units including fifties, hundreds, and thousands (e.g., Num. 31:48; 2 Kgs. 1:9ff.). At times the captain appears to be a high-ranking royal aide (cf. 2 Kgs. 7:2, 17, 19; 15:25; Heb. *šālîš*). The title also designates various Assyrian and Babylonian officials (Heb. *rab*; 2 Kgs. 18:24; 25:8-20; cf. Rabsaris, 18:17; Rabshakeh, vv. 17, 19, 26-28, 37).

In the New Testament Gk. *chilíarchos* designates the "leader of a thousand," the head of a cohort of one thousand soldiers (John 18:12; cf. Acts 21:31-36; RSV "tribune of the cohort"). The "captain of the temple" (*stratēgós*; Luke 22:4, 52; Acts 4:1; 5:24, 26) was a high priestly official and head of the temple police.

The KJV uses the term much more frequently, to indicate domestic and civil personnel (e.g., Heb. *ṭipsār*, Jer. 51:27; RSV "marshal"; Nah. 3:17; RSV "scribe"; Gk. *archēgós*, Heb. 2:10; RSV "pioneer") as well as military and political officials (e.g., Heb. *'allûp*, Jer. 13:21; RSV "friend"; *ba'al*, 37:13; RSV "sentry"; *šālîš*, Exod. 14:7; 15:4; RSV "officer"; *śar*, 2 Chr. 8:9; RSV "officer, commander"; *nāśî'*, Num. 2:3ff.; RSV "leader"; *paḥôṭ*, Ezek. 23:23; RSV "governors").

CAPTAIN OF THE TEMPLE [Gk. *ho stratēgós toú hieroú*).† The head of the temple police who was responsible for maintaining order in the Jerusalem temple and thus supervised the cultic personnel. A member of the priestly class, his authority was second only to the high priest. Called "ruler (Heb. *nagíd*) of the house of God" at Neh. 11:11 and "chief officer in

the house of the Lord" at Jer. 20:1, he may have been particularly concerned with the work of the gatekeepers, guards, and other Levites and priests of lesser rank, some of whom were themselves designated "captains of the temple" (cf. Luke 22:4; Acts 5:24, 26). In Mishnaic Hebrew he is called Heb. *sagan hakkōhᵃnîm* "captain of the priests" (cf. the postexilic Jewish "officials" cited at Ezra 9:2; Neh. 2:16; 5:7; 12:40; Heb. *hassᵉgānîm*).

It is this official or one of the subordinate "captains" who arrested Peter and John for preaching about the resurrection (Acts 4:1-3) and who recaptured them after their miraculous escape (5:24, 26). Although Luke uses the plural form in both cases, it was probably the "chief" captain with whom Judas Iscariot conferred concerning Jesus' arrest (Luke 22:4) but the lesser officers who actually apprehended the Master in the garden of Gethsemane (v. 52).

CAPTIVES. In ancient times the inhabitants of cities taken in battle were generally taken captive. Although on rare occasions some might be treated well (1 Kgs. 20:39; 2 Kgs. 6:21-22), many were put to death (2 Sam. 8:7; cf. Judg. 8:7). Women and children might also be brutally slain (2 Kgs. 8:12; 15:16; Amos 1:3; Nah. 3:10), but frequently they were taken as booty along with cattle and other possessions (Deut. 20:10). Those inhabitants of enemy cities who were spared carnage were generally bound in fetters, hand and foot, and marched off to slavery or forced labor. Women, although left unfettered, might be subject to rape by the soldiers who deported them (Nah. 3:5).

The Assyrians, and later the Babylonians, uprooted and resettled captive peoples on a large scale, as Israel and Judah experienced following the fall of Samaria and Jerusalem (cf. 2 Kgs. 17:24; 24:12-16; 25:11-12). Assyrian treatment of captives was particularly harsh and cruel. Captive rulers were sometimes taken to the Assyrian capital and made to pull the chariot of the triumphant king. A ring might be put through the captive king's nose or lips, or, as Hezekiah of Judah (cf. Ezek. 19:9, Jehoiachin), he might be placed in a cage by the city gate as an object of scorn and derision. Captives who rebelled had their hands and feet, noses and ears cut off, their eyes poked out, and their tongues torn from their mouths. Others were sentenced to death, accomplished either by decapitation or impalement; if he was to be impaled, the victim was placed on a pointed stake so that his own weight would cause him to be pierced through the anus, abdomen, or neck. Captives were also sometimes flayed and their skins stretched out on the city wall.

CAPTIVITY. See DISPERSION; EXILE.

CARAVAN (Heb. *'ōrḥâ*; Pers. *carawan*).* In the ancient Near East goods and supplies were transported by merchants and professional carriers who banded together for mutual safety, often with pilgrims and other travelers. Pack animals were primarily asses and, in later times, camels. Such parties passed regularly through ancient Palestine along the major international trade routes connecting Egypt, Mesopotamia, Anatolia, and the Arabian peninsula (Gen. 37:25; Judg. 5:6; Job 6:18-19). Caravans generally lodged or took refuge from desert storms at oases (cf. Isa. 21:13) or caravansaries, permanent hostels which often were walled and had a central open court; often located near a city, the caravansary occasionally became the foundation of a permanent trade center, such as Mari, Petra, Damascus, and Carchemish.

CARBUNCLE. Any of several precious red stones. At Exod. 28:17; 39:10 it is listed as the third stone in the first row of precious stones on the breastpiece worn by the high priest (Heb. *bāreqeṭ* "dark-green beryl"; KoB, p. 156; NIV "beryl"). According to the LXX (Gk. *smarágdos*) it was an emerald (cf. RSV at Ezek. 28:13). Ezekiel included this stone (Heb. *nōpek*, possibly "turquoise, malachite"; so KoB, p. 624; NIV "turquoise") in a description of the covering of the king of Tyre (Ezek. 28:13; RSV "emerald"). At Isa. 54:12 the RSV translates Heb. *'eqdâ* ("beryl," KoB, p. 81; NIV "sparkling jewels"; JB "crystal") as the carbuncle, a dark red stone dug up from the copper mines of the Sinai peninsula; the prophet used this stone to illustrate hope for a future rebuilding of Jerusalem.

CARCAS (Esth. 1:10, KJV). See CARKAS.

CARCASS. The remains of an animal that has died a natural death. Heb. *nᵉḇēlâ* is derived from the stem *nbl* "fall off, wither" (as leaves and flowers). The term is used in reference to the human corpse and to the dead body or carcass of an animal (Lev. 5:2; 11:8, 11, 24-25, 35ff.; Deut. 14:8; cf. Gen. 15:11, Heb. *peleg*). Sometimes carcasses are mentioned together with animals that have been torn by wild beasts (cf. Lev. 17:15; 22:8; Ezek. 4:14; 44:31). The remains of both clean and unclean animals are considered unclean and may not be eaten. In Jewish usage the term designates all flesh that comes from an animal that has not been ritually slaughtered.

The Mosaic legislation gives the impression that contact with the remains of clean cattle or clean wild animals did not render a person unclean, so long as such an animal had been slaughtered or shot (and subsequently slaughtered) and did not die a natural death (cf. Acts 15:20, 29; 21:25, "what is strangled"). The Pentateuch specifies regulations to be followed by an Israelite who had had contact with a carcass (see above citations).

Though the fat from a carcass could in no case be eaten (Lev. 7:24), it could be put to various other uses. It might be used to oil leather, for instance.

Israelites were permitted to give a carcass to a resident alien or sojourner, who though enjoying the privileges of hospitality in Israel was not bound by Mosaic dietary laws; they could also sell carcasses to foreigners, who did not have the status which derived from the bond of hospitality (Deut. 14:21).

CARCHEMISH [kär′kə mĭsh] (Heb. *karkᵉmîš* "city of Chemosh").† An important Syro-Hittite city in northwest Mesopotamia. The site has been identified as a large mound near modern Jerablus, approximately 100 km. (63 mi.) northeast of Aleppo. Strategically situated near the primary ford of the Upper Euphrates river, Carchemish served as a trading post and relay station for merchants from Persia, Babylonia, Asia Minor, Ugarit (Ras Shamra), and Egypt and thus became a wealthy and powerful center throughout much of ancient Near Eastern history.

Excavations at the site indicate that Carchemish was settled as early as Chalcolithic times, and it probably played a vital role in the timber trade between Syria and Mesopotamia during the Ubaid period (4300-3500 B.C.). As depicted in the Mari Letters (eighteenth century) the city flourished as the focus of an independent kingdom until conquered in the fifteenth century by the Egyptian pharaoh Thutmose III. In 1340 the Hittite Šuppiluliumas I captured the city and made it a vassal state under his son Piyassilis. With the fall of the Hittite Empire *ca.* 1200, Carchemish returned to city-state status. In the ninth-eighth centuries it became increasingly vulnerable to the Assyrians, who repeatedly conquered the city and exacted tribute — Assurnasirpal II, 876; Shalmaneser III, 858; Tiglath-pileser III, 740. In response to the general revolt among the provinces which greeted the accession of Sargon II, the Assyrians destroyed and pillaged the city and deported its inhabitants (cf. Isa. 10:9). When the Egyptian pharaoh Neco II marched northward toward Carchemish in 609 seeking to aid the Assyrians against further Neo-Babylonian attacks, he was intercepted in the plain of Megiddo by King Josiah of Judah, who lost his life in the ensuing battle (2 Chr. 35:20-24). The Egyptians continued to Carchemish, where in 605 they and the Assyrians were routed by the forces of Nebuchadnezzar II (Jer. 46:2-12).

Excavations conducted by the British Museum in 1879 and from 1911 to 1920 recovered a number of hieroglyphic inscriptions and statues and reliefs depicting Hittite deities, some in Assyrian dress. Buildings include a palace and temple, a residence with a columned portico (Akk. *bît ḥilani*), and a house with considerable material remains suggesting the bitter struggle of 605.

CAREAH (2 Kgs. 25:23, KJV). See KAREAH.

CARIA [kâr′ĭ ə] (Gk. *Karia*).† A region in southwest Asia Minor, bounded by Lydia on the north, Phrygia on the east, and Lycia on the south. Its main cities were Cnidus and Halicarnassus.

Caria became subject to Croesus of Lydia *ca.* 540 B.C. and subsequently fell under the dominance of the Persian Empire. The western cities were colonized by the Greeks in the fifth century. Following the widespread conquests of Alexander the Great in the late fourth century, the region came under the control of the island of Rhodes until granted independence by the Romans in 168 B.C. According to 1 Macc. 15:23 a copy of a letter from the Roman senate in behalf of the Jews was sent to Caria (*ca.* 139), indicating that, at that time at least, the inland cities had a mixed population. Shortly thereafter (129) the region was incorporated into the Roman province known as Asia.

In New Testament times Caria was still part of that Roman province, so it is not mentioned by its original name. In the book of Acts Luke does refer to two of its chief cities, however. He records that at the end of his third missionary journey Paul stopped at Miletus (Acts 20:15-17) and that the ship carrying the apostle on his voyage to Rome arrived at Cnidus "with difficulty" (27:7).

CARITES [kär'īts] (Heb. *kārî*). Bodyguards (so KoB, p. 454) who helped Jehoiada the high priest protect the Jerusalem temple during the crowning of young Joash (2 Kgs. 11:4, 19; KJV "captains"); they may have performed a function similar to that of the Cherethites. They were from Caria (LXX *Chorri*; JB "Carians"), a region from which came many mercenaries.

CARKAS [kär'kəs] (Heb. *karkas*, possibly "vulture"). One of the seven eunuchs of Ahasuerus, the king of Persia, serving as his chamberlains (Esth. 1:10; KJV, NIV "Carcas").

CARMEL [kär'məl] (Heb. *karmel* "fruit garden").
1. A village in the tribal territory of Judah (Josh. 15:55), identified now with Kermil, about 13 km. (8 mi.) south-southeast of Hebron; the "fertile lands" of 2 Chr. 26:10 may refer to the same place (KJV "Carmel," following Heb. *karmel*; but see KoB, p. 455). The wealthy Nabal had his sheep-shearing business at Carmel (1 Sam. 25:2), and his wife Abigail, the Carmelitess (27:3; 1 Chr. 3:1), might also have had her possessions there.

It was at Carmel that Saul erected a memorial sign after the battle with the Amalekites (1 Sam. 15:12). This was also the birthplace of Hezro, one of David's mighty men (2 Sam. 23:35 par. 1 Chr. 11:37).
2. A mountain range along the border of the tribal territory of Asher (Josh. 19:26), dividing the coastal plain into two parts: the plain of Acco to the north and the plains of Sharon and Philistia to the south. Its highest point has been estimated to be about 530 m. (1742 ft.), at Esfia.

Mt. Carmel was a comprehensive symbol to the Israelites. Jeremiah compares the might of Nebuchadnezzar of Babylon to Mt. Carmel; as the mountain towers loftily over the coastal plain, so the Babylonian ruler appeared powerful and threatening to Egypt (Jer. 46:18; cf. JB "Carmel high above the sea"). Its lush beauty, due to the abundance of rain, is suggested in the imagery at Cant. 7:5 ("Your head crowns you like Carmel"). At Isa. 35:2 the Messiah symbolically receives the majesty attributed to this mountain. On the other hand, Carmel also signifies sadness. God can make the mountain languish (Nah. 1:4) and its top wither (Amos 1:2). A similar picture of destitution is found at Isa. 33:9, pointing to a time shortly after the conquest of the northern kingdom by Assyria in 721 B.C. ("shake off their leaves," Isa. 33:9).

1 Kgs. 18:20-40 describes the contest between Elijah and the Baal priests to determine who worshipped the true God. The sacrifices they made must have taken place at the southeast extremity of the mountain, at what is now el-Mahrakah or Qeren Carmel (the "horn of Carmel"), near the brook Kishon where the Baal prophets were killed (v. 40). The narrative also mentions that the prophet "restored the altar of the Lord" (v. 30), which may have been built during the divided monarchy and destroyed during the reign of Ahab.

Elijah's name is retained in Mt. Carmel's contemporary name, Jebel Mâr Elyâs, "the mountain of the prophet Elias (Elijah)." At the foot of the mountain is the important modern port of Haifa.

CARMELITE [kär'mə līt] (Heb. *karmᵉlî*). An inhabitant of the city of Carmel. Nabal (1 Sam. 30:5; 2 Sam. 2:2; 3:3, KJV; RSV, JB, NIV "of Carmel") and Hezro (2 Sam. 23:35; 1 Chr. 11:37, KJV, NIV; RSV, JB "of Carmel") were from this village.

CARMELITESS [kär'mə lī'tĭs] (Heb. *karmᵉlît*). A female inhabitant of the city of Carmel. Abigail, Nabal's wife, was given this epithet (1 Sam. 27:3; 1 Chr. 3:1; JB, NIV "of Carmel").

CARMI [kär'mī] (Heb. *karmî* "vinedresser"[?]).
1. The youngest son of Reuben, who accompanied the other sons of Jacob to Egypt (Gen. 46:9; cf. Exod. 6:14; Num. 26:6; 1 Chr. 5:3).
2. A Judahite and the father of Achan (Josh. 7:1, 18; called "Achar" at 1 Chr. 2:7).
3. Probably an alternate name for Caleb at 1 Chr. 4:1).

CARMITES [kär'mīts] (Heb. *karmî*). The name of the family (NIV, JB "Carmite clan") whose ancestor was Carmi (**1**) (Num. 26:6).

CARNAIM [kär nā'əm] (Gk. *Karnein, Karnain, Karnion*). An alternate name for Ashteroth-karnaim (1 Macc. 5:26; 2 Macc. 12:21, 26; KJV "Carnion"). *See* ASHTEROTH-KARNAIM.

CARNELIAN. A hard, tough variety of the stone chalcedony having a reddish color. In the Old Testament this precious stone constituted part of the covering of the king of Tyre (Ezek. 28:13, Heb. *'ōḏem* "ruby"; KoB, p. 13; cf. KJV mg., NIV; KJV "sardius"; JB "sard"). In the New Testament the appearance of God is likened to jasper and carnelian (Rev. 4:3; Gk. *sárdion*; cf. KJV "sardine stone"; JB "ruby"), two stones of great significance and worth in antiquity. At 21:20 it is the sixth stone in the foundation of the wall of the New Jerusalem.
See SARDIUS.

CAROB. A leguminous tree (Lat. *Ceratonia siliqua*) native to the eastern Mediterranean, capable of reaching a height of some 16 m. (50 ft.). In Palestine the carob tree flourished particularly in the northwestern part of Galilee between Acco and Tyre as well as in Judea and Transjordan.

Its sweet, pulpy seed pods (8-30 cm. [3-12 in.]) were used as feed for pigs and cattle; it is these on which the prodigal son "would gladly have fed" (Luke 15:16). Some scholars suggest that the "locusts" which John the Baptist ate (Mark 1:6) were actually carob pods.

CARPENTER.† A craftsman (Heb. *ḥārāš ʿēṣ* "engraver of wood"; e.g., 2 Sam. 5:11), who built tools such as plows and threshing boards for agricultural use and constructed houses and other buildings. Some of the tools employed were the axe, hammer and saw, and chisel. At Isa. 44:13 the carpenter is depicted as one who stretched a line, marked it with a pencil, fashioned it with a plane, and marked it with a compass.

David hired Phoenician carpenters to build his palace (1 Chr. 14:1) and the temple in Jerusalem (2 Sam. 5:11). Later King Joash enlisted native carpenters to repair the temple (2 Chr. 24:12; cf. 2 Kgs. 12:11), as did King Josiah (2 Chr. 34:11; cf. 2 Kgs. 22:6). After the Exile Jewish carpenters, who had been deported to Babylon under Nebuchadnezzar (Jer. 24:1; 29:2, KJV, Heb. *ḥārāš*; RSV, NIV "craftsmen"; JB "blacksmiths"), returned to Jerusalem and assisted in the rebuilding of the temple foundation (Ezra 3:7). Isaiah refers to carpenters who produced wooden idols (Isa. 44:13; cf. 41:7).

In the New Testament Jesus himself is called both a carpenter (Mark 6:3) and the son of a carpenter (Matt. 13:55). The Greek term (*téktōn*) used in these references designates a worker shaping wood, metal, or stone; it commonly means "builder."

CARPUS [kär′pəs] (Gk. *Karpos,* possibly from *karpós* "fruit"). A friend of the apostle Paul (perhaps his host) residing at Troas, in whose care Paul had entrusted his books and parchments (2 Tim. 4:13). While in prison awaiting his execution, the apostle asked that these materials be returned to him. The cloak cited here (Gk. *phailónēs*) may have been a case in which books could be placed for protection.

CARRION VULTURE (Heb. *rāḥām, rāḥāmâ*). One of the unclean birds, mentioned along with the pelican, the cormorant, and the stork (Lev. 11:18; Deut. 14:17; KJV "gier eagle"; NIV "osprey"; JB "white vulture"). Called the Egyptian white and black vulture (*Vultur percnopterus*) because of its black flight feathers and white covert feathers, the carrion vulture is the smallest and most common vulture in Palestine. It resembles the raven in size and in its manner of walking and sitting.

CARSHENA [kär shē′nə] (Heb. *karšᵉnāʾ*, possibly from Pers. *keresna* "black"). The first mentioned of the seven princes of the kingdom of the Medes and the Persians called to advise King Ahasuerus (Esth. 1:14). They may have been experts in the law.

CART.† The Old Testament mentions both chariots (especially in accounts of war) and carts, two- or four-wheeled vehicles used for transportation. Because of the hilly terrain they inhabited the Israelites could not use the cart much, unlike the Philistines and the Assyrians, who lived in flatter regions.

Heb. *ʿᵃgālâ* designates a wagon pulled by two oxen (or cows, 1 Sam. 6:7), on which the sacred ark was carried from Philistia back to Israel (1 Sam. 6:7) and later to Jerusalem (2 Sam. 6:3 par. 1 Chr. 13:7). At Amos 2:13 the image of a cart "full of sheaves" suggests a burdensome punishment upon the Israelites for their infidelity. The cart wheel of Isa. 28:27-28 (Heb. *ʾôpan ʿᵃgālâ*) is probably a threshing instrument with teeth like a saw that would crush the grain; such an implement would be too heavy for threshing cummin and would also be unsuitable for grinding bread flour. At Isa. 5:18 the ropes used to pull a cart symbolize man towing sin in his wake.

Joseph had his brothers carried from Egypt to Canaan on four-wheeled Egyptian wagons (Gen. 45:19, 21, NIV; RSV, KJV, JB "wagons"), so they could return again to Egypt with their aged father and his possessions (46:5). The "covered wagons" of Num. 7:3 (Heb. *egᵉlôt ṣāb*) may mean two-wheeled vehicles, but the translation remains uncertain.

See also CHARIOT.

CASIPHIA [kə sïf′ï ə] (Heb. *kāsipyāʾ* "place of silversmiths[?]"; cf. LXX *en argyríō toú tópou* "in silver of the place"). An unidentified place in Babylonia, not far from the river Ahava (Ezra 8:17). It was to this village that Ezra sent a delegation asking Iddo, its leading resident, for "ministers for the house of our God."

CASLUHIM [kăs′lə hïm] (Heb. *kasluḥîm*). Descendants of Egypt the son of Ham (Gen. 10:6, 14; 1 Chr. 1:8, 12; NIV "Casluhites"; JB "Calushluh"), and ancestors of the Philistines. Some scholars believe these people are related to the inhabitants of the region near Mt. Cassius, east of the Nile Delta.

See also CAPHTOR.

CASSIA. *See* CINNAMON.

CASTANETS (Heb. *mᵉnaʿanʿîm* "sistrum"). One of several instruments played as the ark of the covenant was carried to Jerusalem (2 Sam. 6:5; KJV "cornets"). The castanets (so RSV, JB) may resemble the sistrum (so NIV; KoB, p. 539), which consisted of two connected staves between which were loose rods and rings producing a rattling sound.

CASTLE.† A large fortified building mentioned only twice in the RSV. At Neh. 7:2 Hananiah's title "governor of the castle" refers to his position in the citadel north of the temple (Heb. *bîrâ* "castle"; KoB, p. 122; KJV "palace"; NIV, JB "citadel"); on the basis of 1 Chr. 29:1, 19, however, the term could indicate the temple itself (RSV "palace"). The castle of Prov. 18:19 is a "fortified building of small square base and several stories" (Heb. *ʾarmôn*; KoB, p. 88; NIV "citadel"; JB "keep"); here the term symbolizes quarreling, which is as effective a barrier between people as the bar (of the gate) of a castle and as difficult to overcome.

The KJV translates a number of Hebrew words as "castle(s)." The castles of the sons of Ishmael (Gen. 25:16) and of the Midianites (Num. 31:10) were temporary camps (Heb. *ṭîrâ*; so NIV; RSV, JB "encampments") of tents surrounded by piles of stones (cf. KoB, p. 352).

The "castle" (so KJV) where Paul addressed the Jews at Jerusalem (Acts 21:34) and within which he was detained for some time by the Romans (22:24; 23:10, 16) was the tower of Antonia (Gk. *parembolḗ* "barracks"; RSV, NIV; JB "fortress").

CASTOR AND POLLUX (Acts 28:11, KJV). *See* TWIN BROTHERS.

CASTOR-OIL PLANT. A plant (*Ricinus communis* L.) belonging to the spurge family (*Euphorbiaceae*); it can reach a height of 5 m. (16 ft.) in five to six months. Its large hand-shaped leaves (about 1 m. [3 ft.] across) provide abundant shade; its fruit contains three large spotted seeds from which are extracted castor oil and a toxic protein, ricin — extensively used in ancient times as a cathartic.

The plant that God caused to shade Jonah (Jonah 4:6-10) was probably the castor-oil plant (see RSV mg., JB; Heb. *qîqāyôn*; KJV "gourd"; NIV "vine"). This plant grew in one night and sheltered Jonah but withered at the end of the next morning, exposing him to the fierce sun. The point of this incident was to teach the recalcitrant prophet that he should care not only for his own comfort but also for the well-being of the many citizens of Nineveh to whom he was reluctant to preach (vv. 10-11).

CATERPILLAR. The elongated, wormlike larva of a butterfly or moth, mentioned in the Old Testament along with the locust (1 Kgs. 8:37 par. 2 Chr. 6:28; NIV "grasshopper"); at Ps. 78:46 it is probably a synonym for locust (Heb. *ḥāsîl* from *ḥsl* "destroy, consume"). At Isa. 33:4 the gathering caterpillar which voraciously despoils foliage illustrates the savage looting by soldiers after battle.

See also LOCUST.

CATHOLIC LETTERS. A number of New Testament letters which, unlike the Pauline letters addressed to individual churches, were written to a wider and more general (Gk. *katholikós*) readership. The term (Gk. *hai epistolaí katholikaí*) was used as early as the third century A.D. (e.g., by Origen); in the New Testament as in the codices Sinaiticus and Vaticanus, the seven letters are known by individual names: James (written to the "twelve tribes in the Dispersion," Jas. 1:1); 1 and 2 Peter (to the "exiles of the Dispersion," 1 Pet. 1:1; to those "who have obtained a faith of equal standing with ours," 2 Pet. 1:1); 1 and 2 John (to local churches); 3 John (to an individual, Gaius [v. 1], but included among these epistles because of its relationship to 1-2 John); and Jude (to those "who are called," Jude 1). In the English versions of the Bible the Catholic Letters are placed between Hebrews and Revelation. They are sometimes called the General Epistles.

CATTLE.† The extensive Hebrew vocabulary for cattle in the Old Testament represents a variety of domesticated livestock; in collective usage, however, these terms appear imprecise and at variance with the modern Western definition. The generic terms translated in English as "cattle" (e.g., Heb. *behēmâ, miqneh, bāqār*) encompass bovine cattle and oxen as well as sheep and goats (KJV "lesser cattle") and sometimes other animals such as horses, asses (Gen. 47:16-17), and camels (Exod. 9:3-7); at times even wild animals are included (e.g., Deut. 28:36; Jer. 7:33).

Although the particular species of bovine cattle raised by Israelites cannot be identified with certainty, it is probable that they were a breed of the Zebu species, yellowish-brown, brown, black, or mottled animals with bristly hair, curved horns, and a large hump, and native to North Africa and Arabia. Although used primarily for milk and other dairy products (Deut. 32:14; Isa. 7:22), these cattle produced only 400-700 l. (106-185 gal.) of milk per year. Only rarely were cattle used for meat (cf. Gen. 18:7; Luke

15:23), often perhaps only when they had ceased to produce milk and could no longer be used as beasts of burden. Bulls were used as draft animals in the fields, to pull the plow (Deut. 22:10; Judg. 14:18) and drag the threshing sledge (Deut. 25:4; Amos 6:12). They pulled carts and wagons (Num. 7:3; 1 Sam. 6:7; 2 Sam. 6:6) and were used as beasts of burden (1 Chr. 12:40). *See* OX.

Broad-tailed sheep and lop-eared Nubian or Mamber goats, reckoned among the flocks or small cattle, were raised for milk (Prov. 27:27), wool, and hair, as well as for sacrificial purposes. *See* SHEEP; GOAT.

The patriarchs have traditionally been regarded as pastoral nomads, a view supported by evidence of their large herds (e.g., Gen. 32:14-15) and far-flung travels. But other evidence in the patriarchal narratives suggests that they were settled agriculturalists engaged in transhumant herding, seasonal migrations in quest of suitable forage for the livestock (cf. 37:12-17); this is supported by references to their large households (e.g., 20:14; 24:35; 32:5) and involvement with agricultural pursuits and produce (26:12-14; 27:25-29; 43:11; cf. 30:14; 37:5-8). Moreover, in the ancient Near East bovine cattle were raised only in settled regions. This pattern of subsistence would fit also with the Israelite's tending of cattle while in Egypt (45:10; 46:32; 47:1; cf. Exod. 12:32, 38).

Much information regarding the raising of cattle is contained in the legal prescriptions of the Pentateuch. For example, cattle were to be protected under the laws regarding sabbath rest (Exod. 20:10; 23:12) and were to be allowed to consume a portion of the harvest as they labored (Deut. 25:4). Interbreeding was prohibited (Lev. 19:19), and oxen and asses were not to be yoked together for plowing (Deut. 22:10). Other laws apply to theft and damages caused by cattle (cf. Exod. 21:28-22:15), which were regarded as property.

Although all types of cattle were subject to the law requiring sacrifice of firstlings (Exod. 13:12), some were raised specifically for sacrificial purposes, particularly young bulls (29:1, 10-14; Lev. 4:5-12; 16:6; 1 Kgs. 8:63), sheep (Lev. 5:14-19; 16:5), and goats (4:22-5:6; 16:5). Because the bull was regarded as a symbol of fertility in ancient Near Eastern religions (e.g., Canaanite El, Egyptian Apis, Horus), its worship by the Israelites was strongly condemned (cf. Exod. 20:4); nevertheless the practice did occur (Exod. 32; 1 Kgs. 12:28-29; Hos. 8:5-6; 13:2).

In ancient Israel wealth was measured by the extent of one's cattle (Gen. 13:2; 24:35; 26:14; Job 1:3; Isa. 25:2). In figurative use, the bull represented strength and virility (Deut. 33:17; Ps. 22:12; cf. Isa. 10:13). The prophet Amos uses the epithet "cows of Bashan" to reprimand the women of Samaria for wallowing in luxury while ignoring the injustices endured by their fellow Israelites (Amos 4:1).

CAUDA [kô'də] (Gk. *Kauda*). A small island, now called Gaudos, about 37 km. (23 mi.) south of Crete, mentioned in connection with the sudden gale that hit the ship carrying Paul and other prisoners to Rome (Acts 27:16; RSV mg., KJV "Clauda"). By taking shelter to the lee side (south) of the island, the crew was able to survive the tempest (vv. 17-19).

CAULKERS (Heb. *mahⁿzîqê biḏqēḵ* "those who strengthen your breach"). Tradesmen skilled in repairing large leaks in marine vessels (Ezek. 27:9, 27; KJV "calkers"); the task would have involved the use of bitumen or pitch (cf. Gen. 6:14). More precisely, these workers were ships' carpenters, a trade centered at Gebal (Byblos; cf. 1 Kgs. 5:18). Ezek. 27 is a lamentation over "the good ship Tyre," a major Phoenician maritime center.

CAVE.† An opening to the underground caused by water dissolving carbonic acid and lime. In Palestine such openings occurred frequently in the many limestone and sandstone hills.

In biblical times caves (usually Heb. *mᵉʿārâ*) had various uses. They served as dwelling places; Lot and his two daughters lived in a cave (Gen. 19:30), and Elijah stayed in one for some time after his flight from Jezebel (1 Kgs. 19:9). They were also places of refuge in times of persecution. For example, the Israelites had to seek shelter in caves when oppressed by the Midianites (Judg. 6:2), when confronted by the Philistines (1 Sam. 13:6), and when persecuted by Antiochus Epiphanes (Heb. 11:38). The prophet Obadiah hid some one hundred prophets in a cave, probably on Mt. Carmel (1 Kgs. 18:4, 13), when Ahab's wife Jezebel began killing prophets of the Lord. Caves also served as places of burial (e.g., Gen. 23:9, 19-20; John 11:38).

In Ps. 57 David draws a comparison between God, his refuge from enemies, and a cave, a shelter from wild beasts (vv. 1, 4; note the superscription [heading] of the Psalm). In contrast, at the Day of Judgment those who might normally feel secure will seek to escape God's righteous judgment by fleeing into caves (Isa. 2:19; Rev. 6:15; Gk. *spélaia*).

At Jer. 7:11 God's temple is said to have been turned into a "den of robbers," a hideout — usually a cave — where robbers retired to wait until the cries of their victims had died before committing other robberies. Jesus alluded to this text as he drove from the temple all those people who were cheating on the pilgrims (Matt. 21:13; par. Mark 11:17; Luke 19:46).

The more important individual caves named in the Bible were Adullam (1 Sam. 22:1), Machpelah (Gen. 23:9, 19-20), and Makkedah (Josh. 10:16-18).

CEDAR. The cedar of Lebanon (*Cedrus Libani* Loud.) that once graced the Lebanon mountains with magnificent forests is a member of the genus *Coniferae*. The tree can reach a height of about 24-30 m. (80-100 ft.). Its branches start near the ground and grow straight out as the tree grows older, forming horizontal layers. It has short, dark green needles and oval-shaped cones which stand upright.

The cedar (usually Heb. *ʾerez*) is one of the trees mentioned most often in the Old Testament (some seventy times). Ezek. 31:1-18 gives a rather detailed description of its beauty and strength. At Amos 2:9 the might of the Amorites is likened to the cedar's great height.

The cedar of Lebanon figures prominently in the parable which Jotham relates to Abimelech (Judg. 9:15) and in the caution which Jehoash of Israel sends to Amaziah of Judah (2 Kgs. 14:9). Solomon's wisdom included extensive knowledge of trees, "from the cedar that is in Lebanon to the hyssop that grows out of the wall" (1 Kgs. 4:33), meaning the entire "botanical kingdom."

The Psalms present the cedar in a theological context. It is said that God planted the tree (Ps. 104:16) and fixed its boundary (148:9); he can also break it down (29:5). At Ps. 80:10 (MT 11) Heb. *ʾarzê-ʾēl* has been translated the "mighty cedars" (RSV, NIV; cf. KJV "goodly cedars") or the "cedars of God" (KJV mg., JB); thus the tree symbolizes Israel's special relationship to God. In Ps. 92 the reward for righteousness is compared to the growth of a cedar (v. 12).

The durable, brown wood of the cedar has several uses. Burning without smoke and leaving only a few ashes, it provides an excellent fuel. Its fragrant resin, known in ancient times as cedar oil, was used as a preservative for cloth and parchment. Although the symbolism is not clear, cedar wood was used in the purification of a leper (Lev. 14:4, 6, 49-52) and in the ritual of the red heifer, used for purification of a person who had contact with a corpse (Num. 19:6).

Most important, cedar wood served as building material during most of Israel's history. Imported from Phoenicia and exchanged for products from Israel (1 Kgs. 5:10-11), the cedar was used by David in building his house (2 Sam. 5:11 par. 1 Chr. 14:1) and by his son Solomon in the construction of the temple (1 Kgs. 5:10 par. 2 Chr. 2:16; cf. v. 8), particularly the House of the Forest of Lebanon (1 Kgs. 7:1-8). After the Exile cedar wood was again imported for the rebuilding of the temple at Jerusalem (Ezra 3:7) and under Herod near the end of the first century B.C. for yet another rebuilding of Israel's sacred edifice. The Song of Solomon mentions that cedar wood was used for the beams of a house (Cant. 1:17; cf. 1 Kgs. 6:8) and for fashioning a palanquin ("wood of Lebanon," 3:9).

The KJV translation "like a green bay tree" (Ps. 37:35, Heb. *kᵉʾezrāḥ raʿⁿnān*; cf. NIV "like a green tree in its native soil") should probably be emended to read "like the cedar of Lebanon" (so RSV, JB, following the LXX). With regard to the "carpets of colored stuff" (Ezek. 27:24), Heb. *ʾⁿruzîm* is better rendered "made secure" (so RSV; cf. NIV "tightly knotted"); this fits very well with the preceding phrase "bound with cords," rather than the KJV translation "made of cedar."

CEDRON (John 18:1, KJV). See KIDRON.

CELIBACY.* Abstention from marriage in fulfillment of a religious vow. In ancient Israel the practice was rare except among certain sects such as the Essenes at Qumran. In the New Testament celibacy is regarded as a special gift (Gk. *chárisma*), condoned but not commanded by Jesus (Matt. 19:12, "eunuchs for the sake of the kingdom of heaven") and Paul (1 Cor. 7:6-7) as a voluntary form of consecration. In the Eastern branch of Christendom the Council of Nicaea (A.D. 325) affirmed the right of priests and deacons to marry before ordination but not after; bishops must remain celibate. In the Western Church celibacy of the clergy was first instituted by the Council of Elvira (*ca.* 306), but Pope Leo the Great (440-

461) prohibited men from dissolving their marriages upon ordination; the vow of perfect chastity was not required until the eleventh century and even that has been waived at various times in the history of the Church.

CENCHREAE [sĕng'krə ē] (Gk. *Kenchreai*). A seaport about 10 km. (6 mi.) east of Corinth, on the Saronic Gulf. It is mentioned in the writings of Thucydides, Pausanias, and Strabo.

It was at Cenchreae after his ministry at Corinth had come to an end that Paul had his hair cut in fulfillment of a Nazirite vow (Acts 18:18; KJV, NIV "Cenchrea"). According to Rom. 16:1-2 there was a Christian church in Cenchreae where Phoebe, the woman who carried Paul's letter to the Romans, was a deaconess.

CENDEBEUS [sĕn'də bē'əs] (Gk. *Kendebaios*). A general of Antiochus VII, appointed commander-in-chief of the coastal region after Antiochus had defeated Trypho in 138 B.C. (1 Macc. 15:38; JB "Cendebaeus"). Cendebeus strengthened Kedron (southeast of Jamnia), and conducted raids into Judea (vv. 39-41), but soon found himself opposing a large army led by Judas and John, the sons of the aged Simon Maccabeus (16:5). In the ensuing battle, Cendebeus' army was routed, and those soldiers who were not killed took refuge at Kedron (vv. 8-9); others fled to the towers of Azotus (or Ashdod), which John then burned (v. 10).

CENSER.* A small ladle or shovel used for carrying hot coals upon which incense was burned by the Aaronic priests (cf. Num. 16; cf. 2 Chr. 16:18-19) and by the high priest in the purification rite on the Day of Atonement (Lev. 16:12-14).

CENSUS.† The enumeration of a people. In Israel, as throughout the ancient Near East, census figures provided the basis for taxation as well as recruitment for military service and forced labor (corvée).

Shortly after the Exodus the Israelites were enumerated at Mt. Sinai to determine according to tribal unit the males twenty years old and older who would be available for military service (Num. 1:2-46); the total for all Israel was 603,550. A second such census was made at Jericho at the end of the wilderness wanderings (Num. 26:2-50), again to assess military strength and as a basis for the allotment of Canaan (v. 53); the total here was 601,730. Following each of these military enumerations the Levites were counted to determine their assignments over the tabernacle (1:47ff.; 26:57-62; cf. 3:11-37, 40-51; 4:34-49); the total of Levites closely approximated the first-born males of all Israel, for whom they substituted in providing lifelong service to the Lord (3:11-13, 41). Various explanations have been offered regarding the numbers recorded in these accounts. Some scholars suggest that the figures, which even at a high rate of reproduction present a group too large for the period of the wilderness wanderings, were inflated by the authors to portray divine favor upon Israel; others contend that they represent totals retrojected from the period of the Monarchy (cf. Exod. 38:25-26, where the figures for

the silver tax assessment reflect the census of Num. 1). A plausible suggestion is that Heb. *'elep* "thousand" represents a military unit of variable size among the individual social or political units (e.g., tribes, clans), thus significantly reducing the totals reflected; such an interpretation would allow for larger constituencies of the same type of units in the time of the Monarchy.

Toward the end of his reign David commissioned his military leaders to number the people of Israel "from Dan to Beer-sheba," a task which took nearly ten months to complete (2 Sam. 24:1-9 par. 1 Chr. 21:1-5); the total of men available for military service was 800,000 in Israel and 500,000 in Judah according to 2 Sam. 24:9, but 1,100,000 in Israel and 470,000 in Judah according to 1 Chr. 21:5. This enlistment may have been intended to determine the strength of tribal militia to supplement on a rotating monthly basis the standing professional troops (cf. 1 Chr. 27:16-22). The reluctance of Joab to participate in the census and the subsequent plague, a common divine punishment for breach of covenant, suggest that this census was part of a large-scale administrative reorganization and was perhaps evidence of a trend toward royal initiative rather than adherence to the tenets of Israel's covenantal foundations.

Solomon ordered a census of the aliens within Israel in order to provide laborers for the construction of the temple (2 Chr. 2:17-18; cf. 1 Kgs. 5:13; 9:21). The census lists of Ezra 2 par. Neh. 7 represent a compilation of various records, perhaps maintained to demonstrate the legitimacy of the returning exiles as heirs of the true Israel.

Luke's account of Jesus' birth associates the journey of Joseph and Mary to Bethlehem in connection with an enrollment of the entire Roman Empire, or at least of the Roman province of Syria (Luke 2:2-3; cf. J. A. Fitzmyer, *Luke I-IX*. AB [1981], pp. 392-94, 399-405). At Acts 5:37 Luke mentions the revolt of Judas the Galilean "in the days of the census," presumably the census of the governor Quirinius in A.D. 6-7 (cf. Josephus *Ant.* xvii.13). See ENROLLMENT.

Bibliography. G. E. Mendenhall, "The Census Lists of Numbers 1 and 26," *JBL* 77 (1958): 52-66.

CENTER OF THE LAND (Heb. *ṭabbûr hāʾāreṣ* "navel of the earth"). An epithet for a mountain near Shechem, possibly Mt. Gerizim, the highest point in the area and, as it were, the center of the region (Judg. 9:37). At Ezek. 38:12 the "center of the earth" (RSV) may refer to the central region of the land, to the point where numerous highways crossed, or to Jerusalem, the focal point of the world (so JB citing Ezek. 5:5). The JB translation "navel of the earth" (cf. LXX *ómphalos*; Vulg. *umbilicus* "navel") suggests the common ancient conception of a city or shrine (e.g., Delphi, Nippur) as a "navel" binding together the principal realms of the universe — the earth, heavens, and underworld. Although this concept occurs in midrashic Judaism, it does not appear to have developed in Hebrew thought until Hellenistic times (cf. Jub. 8:19; 1 Enoch 26:1).

CENTURION [sĕn tōor'ĭ ən] (Gk. *hekatontárchēs*).† The commander of a "century" — one hundred soldiers — the smallest unit of the Roman army. (In New

Testament times there were ten centuries in a cohort and sixty centuries in a legion, making about six thousand soldiers per legion.) The centurions, often called the backbone of the army, were responsible for keeping discipline, for inspection of arms, for commanding the century in both camp and field, and for the command of the auxiliaries.

Luke mentions two centurions by name: Cornelius, the first Gentile convert (Acts 10:1, 22, 30, 44-47) and Julius, the officer charged to secure Paul's arrival at Rome (27:1, 3, 43).

Though the names of other centurions are not given, they are treated favorably. The centurion stationed at Capernaum was praised by Jesus for his faith, and his servant was healed (Matt. 8:5-13 par. Luke 7:1-10). Another who supervised the crucifixion of Jesus and the other two men confessed, after Christ had died, that he truly was the "Son of God" (Matt. 27:54 par. Luke 23:47; Gk. *hekatóntarchos* "leader of one hundred [men]"; Mark 15:39, 44-55, Gk. *kentyríōn*).

CEPHAS [sē'fəs] (Gk. *Kēphas*, from Aram. *kêpā'* "rock"). *See* PETER.

CEREAL OFFERING (Heb. *minḥâ* "gift, tribute").† An offering of grain (KJV "meal-offering," "meat-offering"; NEB "grain offering"; JB "oblation"), often baked into cakes, offered upon the altar of burnt offerings as part of the daily continual offering. Although it might be observed independently, this "vegetable" offering was most often presented along with other types of offerings and sacrifices. Regulations regarding the cereal offering are outlined primarily in Lev. 2; 6:14-18.

I. Form

In its simplest form the cereal offering might consist of unbaked wheat, finely ground from the inner kernels (Lev. 2:1; 1 Chr. 21:23; Ezek. 43:13), or of barley (Ezek. 13). Coarse grain (possibly including middlings), crushed from the whole ear and parched by fire, was to be presented as an offering of firstfruits (Lev. 2:14, 16; Num. 15:21; Neh. 10:37). In most instances (cf. Lev. 5:11; Num. 5:15) olive oil was to be poured over the flour (and perhaps mixed with it) and frankincense sprinkled on top before a portion of the offering was burned on the altar (Lev. 2:1-2, 15).

Fine flour might also be mixed with oil and baked as loaves or wafers in an oven (Lev. 2:4), fried on a griddle as wafers to be broken and covered with oil (vv. 5-6), or "cooked" (fried) in a pan as cakes (v. 7; *see* BREAD). This bread was to be made with neither leaven nor honey (v. 11), both of which were associated with fermentation and thus, as symbols of decay and corruption, were ritually unclean (cf. Exod. 23:18; 34:25). By contrast, these offerings were to be seasoned with salt, a preservative symbolizing the "salt of the covenant" whereby covenants were sealed throughout the ancient world (cf. Num. 18:19; 2 Chr. 13:5). *See also* BREAD OF THE PRESENCE.

II. Occasions

On certain occasions the cereal offering was to be presented alone rather than in conjunction with other types of sacrifices involving flesh or blood; in these instances neither oil nor incense accompanied the offering. The daily offering of the high priest consisted of wafers fried on a griddle, with half presented in the morning and the remainder in the evening (Lev. 6:20-23; cf. Josephus *Ant.* iii.10.7). Regulations governing the mandatory purification ritual permitted a poor person to offer one-tenth ephah (2.2 l. [2 qts.]) of fine flour as a sin offering (Lev. 5:11-13). Moreover, when a man justly or unjustly suspected his wife of adultery he presented a cereal offering of jealousy, an "offering of remembrance" to assist the priest in determining her guilt or innocence through a trial by ordeal (Num. 5:15-31).

Most often, however, the cereal offering was presented in association with other offerings, perhaps for the purpose of rendering unto the Lord a balanced tribute of animal and vegetable produce (cf. Gen. 4:3-4). As part of the daily continual offering (cf. Neh. 10:33) it normally followed the burnt offering in both the morning and evening sacrifices (e.g., Exod. 29:38-42; Num. 28:1-8; but cf. 1 Kgs. 18:29, 36). Other occasions included the presentation of a guilt (Lev. 7:9-10) or peace offering (vv. 12-14; 8:26), major feasts and festivals (e.g., Ezek. 44:24-25), the ordination of priests and Levites (Lev. 9:4, 17; Num. 8:8), dedication of the tabernacle and the temple (Num. 7; 1 Kgs. 8:64), purification of a leper (Lev. 14:10, 20-21, 31), and the termination of a Nazirite vow (Num. 6:15-19; cf. Judg. 13:19, 23). During the feasts of Firstfruits and Weeks, sheaves of grain and loaves of bread were part of the wave offering; the subsequent offerings of grain and loaves were themselves accompanied by sacrifices of livestock and oblations of wine (Lev. 23:9-21). Detailed regulations specifying the amounts of grain to accompany various types of burnt offerings are provided at Num. 15:1-12; 28–29.

No specific mention of the cereal offering occurs in the New Testament. On the basis of the Old Testament stipulations, however, those instances in which a burnt offering was presented may also have required a cereal offering (cf. Luke 17:11-14).

III. Significance

That portion of the cereal offering which was burned upon the altar constituted a "memorial portion" (e.g., Lev. 2:2, 9, 16; Heb. *'azkārâ*; KJV "the memorial of it"; JB mg. "reminder"), in part commemorating the acts of God in Israel's history but also reminding the participant (and perhaps God as well) of his allegiance to Israel's covenant relationship to the Lord. Particularly in offerings taken from the firstfruits the act constituted a response of thanksgiving for the bounty of the soil (2:14; cf. Exod. 23:16; Deut. 26:10); also, it may have symbolized a liturgical response for the forgiveness of sins accomplished through the preceding burnt offering. The memorial may have had apotropaic significance, serving to appease the Lord and thereby ensure continued good fortune (note Lev. 2:2, 9, 12, "a pleasing odor to the Lord"). The use of incense and particularly the mediation of the priest in presenting the offering symbolized the transformation of that which was common into something holy and therefore suitable to God.

Pragmatically, the cereal offering contributed to the

sustenance of the priesthood. That portion not burned on the altar was to be given to the priests (Lev. 2:3, 10; 7:9-10; Neh. 13:5), to be eaten in a "holy place" beside the altar (Lev. 10:12) or in the courtyard of the tabernacle or temple (6:16). It was inappropriate, however, for the priest to eat any of the cereal offering presented on his own behalf (v. 23; cf. v. 30).

CEREMONIAL LAW. Law regarding primarily the major religious observances and cultic practices. *See* PENTATEUCH; TEN COMMANDMENTS.

CERINTHUS [sə rĭn'thəs] (Gk. *Kērinthos*).† One of the earliest Christian Gnostics, active in Asia Minor *ca.* A.D. 100. According to Irenaeus (*Adv. haer.* iii.11.1), the apostle John wrote his gospel mainly to refute Cerinthus, who credited creation to a less exalted demiurge or angels rather than to God, and who claimed that the special powers of "the Christ" descended upon Jesus at his baptism and departed from him at his death. The Alogi, second-century supporters of Cerinthus, however, maintained that it was Cerinthus himself who had written the gospel of John as well as the book of Revelation. Epiphanius, the fourth-century Church Father, claims (*Haer.* li.7) that Cerinthus had composed a revision of Matthew's gospel, but no evidence of such a work survives; Epiphanius' contention that Cerinthus was a Jewish Christian heretic appears similarly unfounded.

CHAFF. *See* AGRICULTURE.

CHALCEDONY (Rev. 21:19, KJV). *See* AGATE.

CHALCOL (1 Kgs. 4:31, KJV). *See* CALCOL.

CHALDEA [kăl dē'ə] (Heb. *kaśdîm*; Akk. *Kaldu*).† The southern part of Babylonia; according to Assyrian inscriptions of the ninth-seventh centuries B.C., the "land of the Chaldeans" (Akk. *māt Kaldu*) comprised the area between the Euphrates and Tigris rivers near the Persian Gulf. Under the Chaldean dynasty, the last to rule Babylonia (626-539), the name was synonymous with Babylonia (cf. Ezek. 23:15).

I. History

The precise origins of the Chaldeans are not entirely clear, but they appear to have been related to the Amorite groups (Akk. *Amurru* "westerners") active throughout Mesopotamia in the early second millennium B.C. Although some scholars view the designation "Ur of the Chaldees" (Gen. 11:28) as a later clarification of the text, evidence favors the association of Abraham's Terahite ancestors with Amorite elements in southern Babylonia during the Ur III period (2044-1936; cf. Gen. 22:22; Abraham's nephew Chesed is the eponymous ancestor of the Chaldeans; cf. Job 1:17). Later in the second millennium this region was known as the Sea-Lands, comprised of a number of independent chiefdoms. Rebellion among these peoples weakened the hold of the later First (Amorite) Dynasty of Babylon, culminating in the establishment of the First Dynasty of the Sea-Lands, which briefly controlled Babylon itself as the Second Dynasty of Babylon. This domination ceased in 1415 when the Kassites assumed control, but a Second Sea-Land Dynasty (the Fifth Dynasty of Babylon) ruled most of Babylonia *ca.* 1010-980.

The Chaldean chiefdoms, loosely organized into tribal "houses" such as the Bīt-Dakkūri, Bīt-Adini (cf. "Beth-eden," Amos 1:5), Bīt-Amukkani, and Bīt-Yakin, sought socioeconomic independence and political isolation and thus allied themselves accordingly. As a result they were frequently an important factor in the balance of power in Mesopotamia. Strategically situated to control trade on the Persian Gulf, they were a force with which to be reckoned, and the Assyrian kings of the ninth-eighth centuries alternately curried their favor and wrested control of the south through conquest.

With the death of the pro-Assyrian king Nabû-nāṣir of Babylon in 734, the equilibrium was shattered. Ukīn-zēr, chief of the Bīt-Amukkani, revolted against the Babylonian successor and by 732 had seized control of Babylon. The Assyrians under Tiglath-pileser III responded by marching against Babylon. In 729 Ukīn-zēr was routed, but other Chaldean tribes, including the Bīt-Yakin headed by Marduk-apla-iddina (Merodach-baladan), submitted to the invaders and were spared. Shortly thereafter Merodach-baladan enlisted Elamite assistance and captured the throne of Babylon, ruling there until 710 when he was driven out by Sargon II. Upon Sargon's death in 705, the Chaldean returned from Elam where he had fled and regained control of Babylon until again expelled in 703, this time by Sennacherib; it was during this reign that Merodach-baladan dispatched an embassy to Hezekiah of Judah seeking aid against anticipated Assyrian repercussions (2 Kgs. 20:12-19 par. Isa. 39). Another Chaldean, Mušēzib-Marduk (Šūzubu) ruled Babylon from 692-689, and Merodach-baladan's successors continued to foment rebellion among the Sea-Lands peoples. It was their support of the rebellious Šamaš-šum-ukin that led Assurbanipal to destroy Babylon in 648.

Internal strife had weakened Assyria, and upon Assurbanipal's death in 627 the Chaldeans were able to regain the Babylonian throne. Aided by the Medes, Nabopolassar was able to conquer Assur (614) and Nineveh (612), and his Chaldean (or neo-Babylonian) dynasty experienced considerable political and economic success. Under Nebuchadnezzar II (604-562) they defeated the Egyptians at Carchemish (605; Jer. 46:2) and attacked Jerusalem (597), leading to the defeat of Judah in 587 and the Babylonian Exile (2 Kgs. 24-25). Chaldean influence reached its zenith under Nebuchadnezzar II but declined rapidly under his successors Amel-marduk (Evil-merodach, 562-560; 2 Kgs. 25:27-30 par. Jer. 52:31-34), Neriglissar (560-558), and Labāši-marduk (557). Increasing pressure from the Medes and Lydians forced Nabonidus (556-539) to flee to Tema, where he died in exile. With the capture of Babylon by the Persians under Cyrus (539) Chaldean rule ended.

II. Legacy

During their frequent periods in control of the Babylonian throne the Chaldeans apparently maintained the elaborate scribal schools, with their vast literature of religious, historical, and scientific concerns. This was certainly the case under Nebuchadnezzar and others of the last, Chaldean dynasty of Babylon; architecture and building activities flourished under Nebuchadnezzar as well (cf. Dan. 4:30).

The Babylonian expertise in astronomy and astrology was well known, so when in Hellenistic times itinerant magicians, diviners, and astrologers from Babylonia were active throughout the Mediterranean region (including Egypt, Greece, and Rome), the term "Chaldean" was applied, not in its original ethnic or political sense (cf. Ezra 5:12; Dan. 5:30), but as a technical term for these practitioners (2:2-5, 10; 4:7; 5:7, 11; Herodotus *Hist.* i.181-83).

"The language of the Chaldeans" (Dan. 1:4) was most likely an Akkadian dialect similar to that used at Babylon. As did others throughout the ancient Near East, the Chaldeans adopted Aramaic as the lingua franca sometime in the mid-second millennium, but it is incorrect to label that language "Chaldee," as was common until the early twentieth century.

See BABYLONIA.

Bibliography. H. W. F. Saggs, *The Greatness That Was Babylon* (New York: 1964); B. Vawter, *On Genesis* (Garden City: 1977), pp. 167-173.

CHALKSTONES (Heb. *'abnê-gir* "stones of lime"). Soft stones cut from Palestine's limestone rocks and used for building. Isa. 27:9 (KJV "chalk"; JB "lumps of chalk") says the stones of altars would be treated as brittle chalkstones that have been "ground to powder" (JB). The image may suggest that these stones were burned to convert them into lime.

CHAMBERLAIN. An attendant in the bedchamber of a sovereign or lord. See EUNUCH. On Rom. 16:23, see TREASURER, TREASURY.

CHAMELEON. An arboreal lizard (*Chamaeleo chamaeleon*) in the eastern part of the Mediterranean, known for its ability to change the color of its skin. In Palestine, where it is commonly found near trees and water catching its prey with its long, sticky tongue, it was designated one of the unclean animals (Lev. 11:30; Heb. *tinšemet*; KJV "mole"; JB "tinshameth").

CHAMOIS (Deut. 14:5, KJV). See SHEEP.

CHAOS.* A state of emptiness and disorder. At Isa. 24:10 the "city of chaos" (Heb. *tōhû*; KJV "city of confusion"; JB "city of emptiness," mg. "the symbolic city of evil") is one rendered desolate by the ravages of war, no longer habitable for humans, even though a few houses may remain standing. If chaos is the result of mankind's sinfulness, it may be assumed that Edom's forlorn state was God's punishment for their occupation of southern Judah (34:11, "plummet of chaos" par. "line of confusion"; KJV "stones of emptiness"; NIV "plumbline of desolation"; JB "plumb-line of emptiness"; cf. Jer. 49:7-22); from then on Edom would be suitable only for desert birds.

At Isa. 45:18 God is said to have created the earth to be inhabited, not as a purposeless void (KJV "in vain"; NIV "be empty"). This passage is reminiscent of Gen. 1:2, which describes the earth as "without form (Heb. *tōhû*) and void," i.e., utterly empty and inhospitable to both humans and animals (cf. Job 10:22 where Sheol is depicted as a "land of gloom and chaos"). While the biblical account of creation in Gen. 1 does bear similarities to ancient Near Eastern creation myths, this description of the divine purpose in creation omits any reference to a cosmic struggle between God and the forces of Chaos (cf. the Babylonian myth Enuma Elish, according to which Marduk slays the monster Tiamat).

CHARCOAL. See COAL; FUEL.

CHARIOT (Heb. *rekeb, merkābâ*; Gk. *hárma*).† A two-wheeled vehicle, drawn by two or more horses, asses, or oxen, and used primarily for transportation in war.

Use of the chariot is first attested in the Diyala river region of Mesopotamia *ca.* 3000 B.C. It was more than one thousand years later that the solid, disk-shaped wheel was replaced by the spoked wheel. With the introduction of a lighter-weight chariot drawn by horses, the Hyksos gained control of Syria and Egypt in the mid-second millennium. Egyptian adaptation of this vehicle was instrumental in the formation of the New Kingdom (mid-sixteenth century), during which period the Israelites first encountered the chariot. Lavishly ornamented chariots, often preceded by runners, were used by royalty and other dignitaries; during his installation as prime minister, Joseph was permitted to ride in Pharaoh's "second chariot" (Gen. 41:43), and Egyptian chariots escorted the body of his father Jacob to Canaan (50:9). War chariots, manned by a warrior and his shield-bearer, pursued the fleeing Israelites as they crossed the Red Sea (Exod. 14–15). Later, a contingent participated in Shishak's invasion of Israel (*ca.* 920; 2 Chr. 12:3).

The Canaanites also adopted the use of chariots from the Hyksos. Deployment of these vehicles, reinforced with iron plating and studs, prevented the Israelites from conquering the plains and valleys (Josh. 17:16, 18; Judg. 1:19; 4:3); nevertheless, Joshua did succeed in hamstringing the horses and burning the

Tiglath-pileser III in a chariot with driver and attendant (by courtesy of the Trustees of the British Museum)

chariots at Merom (Josh. 11:6, 9), and Naphtali and Zebulun were able to overcome Sisera and his chariot forces (Judg. 4–5). Along the coastal plain, the Philistines used their chariotry to maintain the upper hand over Israel (1 Sam. 13:5).

For the most part, the Israelite chariot had an open frame and carried three people — the warrior or monarch, an aide ("captain," 2 Kgs. 7:2, 17, 19) or shield-bearer (cf. 9:25), and the driver (1 Kgs. 22:34). It may have been David who introduced the martial use of chariots in Israel, applying knowledge gained while a Philistine ally to achieve victory over Philistia and Syria (2 Sam. 8; cf. v. 4 par. 1 Chr. 18:4). Although David's sons Absalom (2 Sam. 15:1) and Adonijah (1 Kgs. 1:5) employed chariots in their efforts to succeed him, it was Solomon who established Israel's chariot forces on a major scale. He acquired substantial numbers of horses from Egypt and elsewhere (10:29) and established chariot cities (9:19) at places such as Megiddo, Hazor, Gezer, and Beth-markeboth ("house of chariots") to protect his borders and maintain these chariot forces. Under the divided monarchy chariots continued to be used by the northern monarchs, particularly Ahab (22:34-35, 38 par. 2 Chr. 18:33-34) and Jehu (2 Kgs. 9:16; 10:15); by the time of Jehoahaz (800), however, military use of the chariot had dwindled appreciably (13:7). Chariots were less commonly used in the hillier terrain of the southern kingdom, although Rehoboam (2 Chr. 10:18) and Josiah (2 Kgs. 23:30 par. 2 Chr. 35:24) had them; Judah apparently relied on Egypt and other nations for chariot troops (cf. Isa. 31:1). The "chariots of the sun" destroyed in Josiah's reforms (2 Kgs. 23:11) apparently were used in the pagan solar cult.

The Assyrians maintained a massive chariot force, such as that which Sennacherib deployed against the Israelites (2 Kgs. 19:23 par. Isa. 37:24) and that of Shalmaneser II which Ahab confronted at Qarqar. Nebuchadnezzar II used chariots when the Babylonians sacked Ashkelon and other Philistine cities (Jer. 47:3). Later, chariots armed with scythes were an important factor in Seleucid warfare, as evidenced in the attacks of Antiochus IV Eupator on Egypt and Judah (Dan. 11:40; 1 Macc. 1:17; 8:6; 2 Macc. 13:2).

The chariot in which the Ethiopian eunuch was seated when Philip joined him was probably a traveling carriage (Acts 8:29-39). The chariots listed as mercantile cargo at Rev. 18:13 (Gk. rhédē) may represent the four-wheeled carriages used by Roman aristocracy, while those to which the locust plague is compared are certainly war chariots (9:9).

In figurative usage, both Elijah (2 Kgs. 2:12) and Elisha (13:14) are called "chariots of Israel and its horsemen," an indication of the might of their prophecy. The two were separated by a chariot of fire (2:11), and Elisha was protected from the Syrians at Dothan by chariots of fire, symbolic of the might of God acting in his behalf. Similarly, the chariot represents the mighty deeds of God in the history of Israel (Ps. 68:17; Hab. 3:8). The heavenly chariots depicted in Zephaniah's visions (Zech. 6:1-8) represent divine messengers, perhaps inaugurating the messianic age.

Bibliography. Y. Yadin, *The Art of Warfare in Biblical Lands* (New York: 1963).

CHARISMATA [kə rĭz′mə tə] (Gk. *charísmata* "free gifts"). Special gifts granted to believers. *See* SPIRITUAL GIFTS.

CHARMER (from Lat. *carmen* "song").† One who chants to achieve a desired effect, either beneficial or harmful, or to ward off evils or evil spirits. *See* EXORCISM.

In the Old Testament the charmer is portrayed as calming a poisonous snake (Ps. 58:5; Heb. *mᵉlaḥᵃšîm* par. "enchanter"; JB "magician"), though as Eccl. 10:11 suggests a charmer is useless if the snake has already bitten someone (Heb. *bāʿal hallāšôn* "master of the tongue"; cf. KJV "babbler"). At Isa. 19:3 it is said that the Egyptian charmers (so KJV; Heb. *ʾiṭṭîm*; RSV "sorcerers"; NIV "spirits of the dead"; JB "wizards"), who used snakes in divinations, would fail because God would confound their plans. Many years earlier the Jews had been forbidden to engage charmers (Heb. *ḥābar ḥeber* "bind with a spell"; cf. JB "uses charms"; NIV "casts spells") because God alone controlled the future.

CHARRAN (Acts 7:2, 4, KJV). *See* HARAN.

CHEBAR [kē′bär] (Heb. *kᵉbār*). A river along which the exiles from Judah dwelled and where Ezekiel received a vision (Ezek. 1:1; 3:15; NIV "Kebar"). Perhaps it is the navigable Euphrates canal (Akk. *nâru kabari*) near Babylon, flowing southeast to a point east of Nippur and rejoining the Euphrates near Uruk (biblical Erech). According to some it may be the modern Shaṭṭ en-Nîl.

CHEDORLAOMER [kĕd′ər lā ō′mər] (Heb. *kᵉdor-lāʿōmer*). A king of Elam, who, together with three kings of small Babylonian kingdoms, invaded the area near the Dead Sea, subdued the kings of Sodom and Gomorrah, and took much spoil and many prisoners, including Lot and his family. Abraham, however, routed the victors and rescued his kinsmen (Gen. 14:1-17).

Though the name Chedorlaomer (*Kutir* [or *kudur*] *Lagamar* "servant of Lagamar") is of Elamite origin, there is no extrabiblical evidence of a specific Elamite king by that name.

See AMRAPHEL.

CHEEK (Heb. *lᵉḥî raqqâ*; Gk. *siagón*).† According to Deut. 18:3, the portion of the burnt offering of an ox or sheep reserved for the priest's sustenance was to include "the two cheeks" as well as the shoulder and stomach. A woman's cheeks, whose softness were a mark of beauty, were often perfumed and bedecked with ornaments, perhaps beads or fringe (Cant. 1:10; 5:13). Perhaps because it was regarded as the seat of modesty (cf. 4:3; 6:7), people in the ancient Near East considered it a particular affront to touch or strike a person on the cheek (1 Kgs. 22:24; Ps. 3:7; cf. Matt. 5:39 par. Luke 6:29).

CHEESE. *See* DAIRY PRODUCTS.

CHELAL [kē′lăl] (Heb. *kᵉlāl* "perfection"). One of the sons of the Israelite Pahath-moab who had to send away his foreign wife when the covenant to abandon mixed marriages was made (Ezra 10:30).

CHELLUH (Ezra 10:35, KJV). *See* CHELUHI.

CHELUB [kē′lŭb] (Heb. *kᵉlûḇ* "basket," "cage").
1. A Judahite, the brother of Shuhah and the father of Mehir (1 Chr. 4:11; NIV "Kelub").
2. The father of Ezri, an overseer of the "field workers" (NIV) of King David (1 Chr. 27:26; NIV "Kelub").

CHELUBAI [kĭ lōō′ bī] (Heb. *kᵉlûḇāy*). A descendant of Hezron of Judah (1 Chr. 2:9), called Caleb at 1 Chr. 2:18, 42.

CHELUHI [kĕl′ə hī] (Heb. *kᵉlûhû,* K *kᵉlûhî*). A son of the Israelite Bani who was compelled to send away his foreign wife (Ezra 10:35; KJV "Chelluh"; NIV "Keluhi").

CHEMARIM [kĕm′ə rĭm] (Heb. *kᵉmārîm* "priests"). A KJV transliteration of the Hebrew word "priests" ("idolatrous priests," RSV, NIV; JB "spurious priests"), referring to the idolatrous priests at Bethel (cf. KJV mg. 2 Kgs. 23:5; Hos. 10:5).

CHEMOSH [kē′mŏsh] (Heb. *kᵉmôš*). The chief deity of the Moabites, mentioned several times on the Moabite Stone and possibly on Sennacherib's hexagonal prism (Akk. *Kam-mu-su-na-ad-bi* "prophet of Kammusu"). The Old Testament calls the Moabites "people of Chemosh" (Num. 21:49; Jer. 48:46).
    According to 2 Kgs. 3:27 Mesha, the king of Moab, offered his eldest son as a sacrifice to appease Chemosh when Israel appeared bound to subdue his people. This brought God's wrath upon the Israelites, who consequently fled Moab and let Mesha escape unharmed. More than a century earlier King Solomon had built a shrine for Chemosh, against God's command (1 Kgs. 11:7, 33). The Judahites worshipped this Moabite deity until Josiah destroyed the shrine which Solomon had built (2 Kgs. 23:13). Jeremiah prophesied that a time would come when a statue of Chemosh would be carried off into exile (Jer. 48:7; perhaps alluding to the termination of Moab as an independent nation, *ca.* 580 B.C.), and the Moabites would be "ashamed" of their deity, who would not be able to deliver them (v. 13).
    At Judg. 11:24 Jephthah mentions Chemosh as the deity of the Ammonites, implying that they, too, worshipped him, perhaps after having subdued the Moabites.

CHENAANAH [kĭ nā′ nə] (Heb. *kᵉnaᶜᵃnâ,* possibly "Canaan").
1. The father of Zedekiah, a false prophet during the reign of Ahab (1 Kgs. 22:11, 24 par. 2 Chr. 18:10, 23).
2. A son of Bilhan of the tribe of Benjamin (1 Chr. 7:10; NIV "Kenaanah").

CHENANI [kĭ nā′nī] (Heb. *kᵉnānî*). A Levite in the days of Nehemiah, who, with the other Levites, set an example concerning the people's confession of guilt (Neh. 9:4; NIV "Kenani").

CHENANIAH [kĕn′ə nī′ə] (Heb. *kᵉnanyāhû, kᵉnanyâ* "the Lord establishes"). A chief of the Levites and temple singers in the days of David; he participated in the ceremony at which the ark was taken from the house of Obed-edom and moved to the city of David (1 Chr. 15:22, 27; NIV "Kenaniah"). Afterward he was appointed with his sons to perform the "outside duties" of officials and judges (26:29; cf. Neh. 11:16).

CEPHAR-AMMONI [kē′fər ăm′ə nī] (Heb. *kᵉpar haᶜammônî* "village of the Ammonites"). A town assigned to the tribe of Benjamin (Josh. 18:24; KJV "Chephar-haammonai; NIV "Kephar Ammoni"). According to some it is probably Khirbet Kefr ᶜAnā, about 5 km. (3 mi.) north of Bethel.

CHEPHIRAH [kĭ fī′rə] (Heb. *kᵉpîrâ*). One of the four cities that had made a covenant of peace with Joshua and the elders of Israel (Josh. 9:17; NIV "Kephirah"). After the Exile the Israelites repopulated Chephirah, along with Kiriath-jearim and Beeroth (Ezra 2:25; Neh. 7:29). The city has been identified with contemporary Tell Kefireh, about 8 km. (5 mi.) southwest of el-Jib (ancient Gibeon).

CHERAN [kĭr′ən] (Heb. *kᵉrān*). The fourth son of the Horite Dishon, who dwelled in the land of Seir (Gen. 36:26; 1 Chr. 1:41).

CHERETHITES [kĕr′ə thīts] (Heb. *kᵉrēṯîm*). A Philistine clan dwelling southeast of Philistia (1 Sam. 30:14, "the Negeb of the Cherethites"; NIV "Kerethites"). Together with the Pelethites they formed the elite of David's army under the capable leadership of Benaiah (2 Sam. 8:18; 20:23; 1 Chr. 18:17). The Cherethites remained loyal to David during Absalom's rebellion (2 Sam. 15:18), aided in the pursuit of Sheba (20:7), and supported the crowning of Solomon (1 Kgs. 1:38).
    According to many contemporary scholars, the Cherethites were originally from Crete (cf. Ezek. 25:16; LXX *Krētes*). This seems to be a more plausible view than other explanations, such as the claim that they received their name from the Phoenician king Chereth, whose kingdom (according to the Shamra texts) was located in the Negeb of Judah, or that Heb. *ngb* "Negeb of the Cherethites" (1 Sam. 30:14) stands for Negba, the region surrounding the city of Beirut which produced some of those who colonized Ugarit during the reign of that city's first Canaanite king.
    See also PELETHITES.

CHERITH, BROOK [kĕr′ĭth] (Heb. *naḥal kᵉrîṯ*). A stream "east of the Jordan" (1 Kgs. 17:3, 5) where, at God's command, the prophet Elijah hid after telling Ahab of imminent drought. Here ravens fed him, and the brook provided him water until it went dry (vv. 6-7).
    The brook is most likely to be identified with one of the wadis in Gilead, but a more precise identification is not currently possible.

CHERUB [kĕr'əb] (Heb. *kᵉrûḇ*). A town (so NIV) in Babylonia; after the Exile a number of people from this town who could not prove their Jewish descent returned to Judah (Ezra 2:59; Neh. 7:61; NIV "Kerub"). The site of Cherub is unknown. According to some commentators "Cherub, Addan, and Immer" can name either one place or three.

CHERUB, CHERUBIM [chĕr'əb, chĕr'ə bĭm] (Heb. *kᵉrûḇ, kᵉrûḇîm*). Winged celestial creatures, introduced into Israelite cosmology from neighboring ancient Near Eastern mythologies. The Hebrew term is probably related to Akk. *kāribu* or *karūbu* "one who prays," "intercessor" (from *karābu* "pray," but also "great, powerful, mighty") or *karibi, kurîbi, karibāti* "gatekeepers," figures of grotesque mythological creatures which guarded the sanctuaries of various deities.

I. Biblical References

According to Gen. 3:24 the Lord drove Adam out of the garden of Eden and placed cherubim with flaming swords at its eastern entrance to guard the tree of life; the author does not describe these beings, assuming that his readers were familiar with them. God is depicted at 2 Sam. 22:11 and Ps. 18:10 as riding on a cherub when he descended to earth; both passages portray the cherub as parallel with "the wings of the wind." Judging from Ezek. 9:3; 10:15-22, the four-winged, four-faced "living creatures" that the prophet Ezekiel saw (e.g., 1:5, 13, 15, 19) were cherubim. Describing them as partly human and partly animal, the prophet may have had in mind the characteristics of two popular mythical species, the serpent-griffons, and lion- or ox-men known from Babylonian and Assyrian mythology. Together the four cherubim carried the "vaulted platform" on which God was enthroned.

Centuries earlier, the Lord had commanded Moses to make two gold-covered wooden cherubim and to place them on the ark of the covenant, actually on top of the mercy seat covering the ark; it was from between these two cherubim that God would speak to Moses and reveal his plans for Israel (Exod. 25:18-22; cf. Heb. 9:5, Gk. *cheroubín*). Exod. 26:1, 31 and 36:8, 35 indicate that pictures of cherubim were skillfully woven into the fabric of the curtains and veil of the tabernacle. Similar images were later carved into the walls of Solomon's temple (1 Kgs. 6:29), and two olivewood cherubim graced the holy of holies (vv. 23-28), above the ark of the covenant (8:6-7). Images of others were woven into the veil of the temple (2 Chr. 3:14) or carved into the panels and stays of the ten stands of the bronze lavers (1 Kgs. 7:29, 36).

The Old Testament mentions several times that the Lord is enthroned "above" or "upon" the cherubim (e.g., 1 Sam. 4:4; 2 Sam. 6:2; 2 Kgs. 19:15 par. Isa. 37:16; Ps. 80:1), who watched his throne on the mercy seat of the ark of the covenant. They are his guardians and special servants symbolizing divine holiness, as is clearly the case at Rev. 4:6 where the four "living creatures" surround God's throne. Cherubim are also part of the adornment of the temple in Ezekiel's vision — on the walls of the inner room and the nave (Ezek. 41:18), on the doors of the nave (v. 25), and throughout the entire temple complex (v. 20).

The description of the king of Tyre as guarded by a cherub at Ezek. 28:14, 16 indicates that the monarch is at the mercy of this celestial servant, who banishes him on account of his transgressions (cf. Gen. 3:24).

II. Material Evidence

Artistic representations of cherubim have been discovered in reliefs and statues at various Near Eastern sites, including Aleppo, Carchemish, Byblos (Gebal), and Taanach. Ivories discovered at Nimrûd and Samaria depict these winged, sphinxlike creatures in considerable detail, with human faces, two wings, and four-legged animal bodies. The griffin, a similar hybrid of lion, eagle, and sphinx, is known from Hittite mythology (cf. Gk. *grýps*). At Nineveh and other Mesopotamian sites immense statues of winged bulls (Akk. *šedu*) have been excavated near the entrances of palaces and other public buildings. It was not until Renaissance times that the cherub was portrayed as a chubby, winged child.

Bibliography. W. F. Albright, "What Were the Cherubim?" *BA* 1 (1938): 1-3.

CHESALON [kĕs'ə lŏn] (Heb. *kᵉsālôn*). A city in northern Judah (Josh. 15:10; NIV "Kesalon"), identified with the contemporary village of Keslâ, about 14 km. (9 mi.) west of Jerusalem.

CHESED [kē'sĕd] (Heb. *keśed*). The fourth son of Nahor and Milcah (Gen. 22:22; NIV "Kesed") and nephew of Abraham. According to some he was the progenitor of the Chaldeans (cf. Heb. *kdśm*).

CHESIL [kē'səl] (Heb. *kᵉsîl*). A city in the Shephelah of Judah, between Eltolad and Hormah (Josh. 15:30; NIV "Kesil"). In some lists of cities it is called Bethul (Josh. 19:4) or Bethuel (1 Chr. 4:30). If these are the same city, Chesil would have been located east of Beer-sheba.

CHESTER BEATTY PAPYRI. One of the oldest and most complete collections of papyrus codices of the Greek Old and New Testaments, acquired in 1931 by A. Chester Beatty of Ireland; other manuscripts from the same codices were acquired by the University of Michigan, Princeton University, and the collections at Cologne and Madrid. The texts represent eleven codices dating to the second-fourth centuries A.D., most likely from a Christian library in the Fayyum (Egypt), and thus are highly significant for the study of textual criticism. The Old Testament manuscripts include parts of nine books, including Genesis, Numbers, Deuteronomy, Isaiah, and Ezekiel; the text of Daniel represents a tradition other than the LXX. Fifteen New Testament books are represented, including the Gospels, Acts, and Revelation; the Pauline Epistles are preserved in a unique order: Romans, Hebrews, 1-2 Corinthians, Ephesians, Galatians, Philippians, Colossians, 1 Thessalonians. Also included are fragments of Ecclesiasticus (Sirach), 1 Enoch, and a treatise on the Passion by Melito, the fourth-century bishop of Sardis.

CHESTNUT TREE (Gen. 30:37; Ezek. 31:8, KJV). *See* PLANE TREE.

The end of Ezekiel 16 in Chester Beatty Papyrus 967 (Chester Beatty Library; photo Pieterse Davison International Ltd.)

CHESULLOTH [kĭ sŭl'ŏth] (Heb. *keṣûlôt*). A city in Issachar (Josh. 19:18; NIV "Kesulloth"), identified with contemporary Iksâl, 5 km. (3 mi.) southeast of Nazareth. Many scholars now identify this town with Chisloth-tabor.

CHEZIB [kĕ'zĭb] (Heb. *kezîḇ*). A place (so MT) where the daughter of Shua gave birth to Shelah (Gen. 38:5; NIV "Kezib"). The NEB, following LXX *chasbí* (which understands the Hebrew term as a derivative of *kāzaḇ* "to stop flowing"; cf. Isa. 58:11; Jer. 15:18), translates here "she ceased to bear children" (cf. Gen. 29:25). See ACHZIB 1.

CHIDON [kī'dən] (Heb. *kîḏōn*). The owner of the threshing floor at the site where Uzzah was killed, having stretched out his hand to prevent the ark of the covenant from falling off the oxcart (1 Chr. 13:9; NIV "Kidon"); the author of Samuel calls him Nacon (2 Sam. 6:6). Though the exact location is unknown, Chidon must have been near the house of Obed-edom in the western part of Jerusalem.

CHIEF PRIEST. See HIGH PRIEST.

CHILD (Heb. *ṭap, yeleḏ*; Gk. *paidíon, téknon*). The Bible, especially the Old Testament, emphasizes that having children is a great blessing (Ps. 127:3; 128:3; cf. Job 5:25). Moreover, childless couples were often ridiculed (Hannah by Peninnah, 1 Sam. 1:6) and despised (Sarah by Hagar, Gen. 16:4); when aged Elizabeth was about to bring forth her firstborn child, she recognized that now her "reproach among men" would be removed (Luke 1:25).

I. Children and the Family

After birth the umbilical cord was cut, and the infant was washed, rubbed with salt, and wrapped in linen cloths ("bands," Ezek. 16:4; "swaddling cloths," Luke 2:7, 12). Often the mother nursed her child (e.g., Sarah, Gen. 21:7) till it was to be weaned at the age of three (Hannah, 1 Sam. 1:22-24). The Old Testament rarely refers to a midwife or a wet-nurse; Rebekah's nurse (Gen. 24:59; 35:8) and the nurse of Jonathan, one of Saul's sons (2 Sam. 4:4), are among the few mentioned by name. Frequently, the mother named the child: Eve named Cain (Gen. 4:1); Leah named her children (Gen. 29:32-35); Rachel named Joseph (30:23; though after her death her husband renamed their son Benoni [35:18]); Manoah's wife named Samson (Judg. 13:24), and Hannah named Samuel (1 Sam. 1:20). There were instances of the father naming the child, as when Abraham named Ishmael and Isaac (Gen. 16:15; 21:3) and Joseph named Manasseh and Ephraim (41:51-52). Some of the names were symbolic, as those of Joseph's sons and Moses (Exod. 2:10). God expressly commanded his prophets Hosea (Hos. 1:4-11) and Isaiah (Isa. 8:3-4) to give their children symbolic names.

The child's first years were entrusted to the mother (Prov. 6:20; cf. 31:1). She continued rearing her daughters till they were married but boys eventually followed their fathers to learn agriculture or a trade. The wealthy had tutors who educated their sons ("guardians," 2 Kgs. 10:1; cf. Isa. 49:23, Heb. *'ōmēn* "foster parents"). The law stipulated that the parents were responsible for the religious instruction of their children (e.g., Deut. 4:9; 6:7, 20-21; 11:19); Timothy was taught by his mother Eunice and his grandmother Lois (2 Tim. 1:5; 3:14-15). According to Exod. 12:25-28; 13:7-8, 14, however, it was the father's responsibility to explain the meaning of the Passover to his sons. (See also EDUCATION.)

Originally, the father's power over his children seemed nearly limitless; he could sell them, at least to fellow Israelites, or have them killed (Gen. 38:24). Later the Mosaic law restricted his power. Should his children refuse to obey him and to pay the respect due him according to the law (e.g., Lev. 19:3; Deut. 5:16), he was required to present his case to the local judges, who were charged with maintenance of law in the community (Deut. 21:18-21). On child sacrifice, see SACRIFICES AND OFFERINGS.

II. Figurative Use*

"Child" is used as a form of address in biblical writings, particularly with reference to a person in a dependent or subordinate relationship, as used by a teacher for a pupil or a leader for followers (e.g., 2 Tim. 1:2; Phlm. 10; cf. Jesus for his disciples; Mark 10:24); Gk. *technía* "little children" indicates particular affection (1 John 2:1; NIV "my dear children").

The term can be used to represent a relationship to a community (Lam. 1:5; Matt. 23:37 par. Luke 13:34), including the covenant community of Israel (*b^enê yiś-ra'ēl* "children of Israel," KJV; JB "sons of Israel"; RSV "Israelites"). It may also indicate possession of a particular quality, such as wisdom (Luke 7:35; Matt. 11:19, KJV) or obedience (1 Pet. 1:14). "Children of light" (Eph. 5:8) designates the followers of Jesus (cf. Matt. 5:14; Luke 16:8); in the Qumran writings the Children of Light are those allied with the Teacher of Righteousness.

In religious usage, the term identifies spiritual allegiance to a particular strain of belief, as "children of Abraham" (John 8:39; Acts 13:26). It may also indicate an underdeveloped faith (1 Cor. 3:1) or sinful behavior (Isa. 30:1; Jer. 4:22).

CHILDBEARING.† In view of the curse God imposed on mankind for the sin in Paradise — that childbearing would be accomplished with great pain (Gen. 3:16; Heb. *hērōn, yālaḏ*) — it is remarkable that the Bible rarely mentions the hardships of delivery. Rather, it emphasizes the prospect of having children, e.g., Eve's conception of both Cain (4:1) and Seth (4:25). Yet the image of the travail of birth does occur in the Old Testament, notably in the writings of the major prophets. Israel pleads with God as a woman writhes in labor (Isa. 26:16-17), and Judah is personified as a woman "gasping for breath" and anxious as her first child is delivered (Jer. 4:31). Twice Jeremiah compares warriors to women who are apprehensive about the outcome of their labor pains (Jer. 48:41, referring to the Moabites; 49:22, to the Edomites), and at least once Micah mockingly asks whether Zion is afraid of future adversity like a woman in travail with no comforter (Mic. 4:9-10). Hos. 13:13 likens the suffering of "refining judgments of God" to the "violent agony" of childbirth.

In the New Testament Paul uses the image of childbirth to describe the torment of all creation (Rom. 8:22) before it is freed from corruption to receive liberty and redemption (see Calvin, *Commentary on Romans*). In an earlier letter the apostle had mentioned that judgment would come like the sudden and inescapable nature of the onset of childbirth (1 Thess. 5:3). His third reference to childbearing, that "woman will be saved through bearing children (Gk. *dia tēs teknogonías*; or "by the birth of the child"), if she continues in faith and love . . ." (1 Tim. 2:15), remains a complex and controversial text. Paul may have been suggesting that childbirth (or "the mediation of life and the bringing up of children"; JB mg.) is instrumental to salvation (though not the ultimate cause; but cf. NIV "will be kept safe"). But he does not limit the woman's role to bringing forth children, for he places this function within the larger context of the virtues of faith and love which all are meant to practice (see Calvin, *Commentary on Timothy*).

CHILEAB [kĭl'ĭ ăb] (Heb. *kil'āḇ*). A son of David and Abigail, the widow of Nabal, born at Hebron (2 Sam. 3:3). Some suggest that his alternate name, Daniel ("God is my judge"; 1 Chr. 3:1), commemorates the divine judgment upon Nabal (1 Sam. 25:39).

CHILION [kĭl'ĭ ən] (Heb. *kilyôn*). The younger son of Elimelech and Naomi, and the husband of Orpah the Moabitess (Ruth 1:2-4; NIV "Kilion"). Chilion, like his brother Mahlon, died early, leaving his wife a widow (v. 5).

CHILMAD [kĭl'măd] (Heb. *kilmaḏ*). A place or a region which traded with Tyre (Ezek. 27:23; NIV "Kilmad"). While some scholars identify Chilmad with the city of Kullimeri in north Mesopotamia (emending *klmd* to *klmr*) and others identify it with the entire country of Media (emending *klmd* to *kl mdy*), in fact, nothing about this place or region is known.

CHIMHAM [kĭm'hăm] (Heb. *kimhām, kimhān*). A son (so 1 Kgs. 2:7; "servant" at 2 Sam. 19:37) of Barzillai the Gileadite, who requested that David favor the lad, rather than himself, for his aid to the king during Absalom's rebellion (vv. 34-37; NIV "Kimham"). David took Kimham with him to Jerusalem (v. 40), where he provided for his physical needs; it is possible that the king gave him a grant of land near Bethlehem, later called Geruth Chimham (Jer. 41:17).

CHIMNEY (Hos. 13:3, KJV). *See* WINDOW.

CHINNERETH [kĭn'ərĕth].
1. A freshwater lake, the Sea of Chinnereth near the city of Chinnereth (Num. 34:11; Josh. 13:27, Heb. *kinneret*; "Chinneroth," Josh. 12:3; so RSV, KJV, JB following Heb. *kin^arôt*), called the Sea of Galilee in the New Testament (e.g., Matt. 15:29). *See* GALILEE, SEA OF.
2. A plain southwest of Chinnereth ("Chinneroth," Josh. 11:2; so RSV, KJV, JB), which the captains of Ben-hadad captured from Baasha of Israel ("Chinneroth," 1 Kgs. 15:20; KJV "Cinneroth"); in the New Testament it is known as the land of Gennesaret (Matt. 14:34).
3. A city in the tribal territory of Naphtali (Josh. 19:35; Heb. *kinnāret* "Chinneroth"; NIV here and other places "Kinnereth"), on the northwest side of the Sea of Chinnereth; it has been identified with modern Tell el-ʿOreimeh.

CHINNEROTH. *See* CHINNERETH.

CHIOS [kī'ŏs] (Gk. *Chios*). An island in the Aegean Sea, about 19 km. (12 mi.) west of Smyrna (contemporary Izmir). At the end of his third missionary journey Paul and his companions sailed from Mitylene past Chios before arriving at Samos the next day (Acts 20:15; NIV "Kios").

CHISLEV [kĭz'lĕv] (Heb. *kislēw*). The ninth month of the Jewish calendar (Nov./Dec.); it was during this month that Nehemiah learned about the fate of the Jews in the Babylonian Captivity (in the twentieth year, Neh. 1:1) and that God's answer to a question about fasting came to Zechariah (Zech. 7:1; KJV "Chisleu"; NIV "Kislev"). On the twenty-fifth day of the month of Chislev the Jews celebrated the Feast of the Renewal of the temple ("feast of the Dedication," John 10:22).

CHISLON [kĭs'lŏn] (Heb. *kislôn* "strength"). The father of Elidad of the tribe of Benjamin (Num. 34:21; NIV "Kislon").

CHISLOTH-TABOR [kĭs'lŏth tā'bər] (Heb. *kislōt tābōr* "slopes of Tabor"). A town in the tribal territory of Zebulun (Josh. 19:12; NIV "Kisloth Tabor"), near modern Iksâl, about 5 km. (3 mi.) southeast of Nazareth. Although many scholars identify the two, the qualifying term "Tabor" (a mountain on the borders of Issachar, Zebulun, and Naphtali) distinguishes this town from Chesulloth in Issachar (Josh. 19:18).

CHITLISH [kĭt'lĭsh] (Heb. *kitlîš* "separation"). A city in the Shephelah of Judah (Josh. 15:40; KJV "Kithlish"; NIV "Kitlish"), perhaps to be identified with Khirbet el-Maghāz, about 8 km. (5 mi.) southwest of Lachish.

CHITTIM. See KITTIM.

CHIUN (Amos 5:26, KJV). See KAIWAN.

CHLOE [klō'ĭ] (Gk. *Chloē* "tender shoot"). Possibly a Christian woman at Corinth (1 Cor. 1:11); members of her household (so NIV, KJV; RSV, JB "Chloe's people") had relayed to Paul at Ephesus that quarrels had arisen among the Corinthian Christians.

CHOIRMASTER. Although the Bible only alludes to a liturgical choir (cf. Neh. 12:31, 38, 40; Heb. *tôdâ* "companies of those who gave thanks"; JB, NIV "choir"), the superscriptions of some fifty-five Psalms include dedications or instructions "to the choirmaster" (also Hab. 3:19; KJV "chief singer"; NIV "director of music"). This rendering (so RSV, JB) is based upon an understanding of Heb. *menaṣṣeah* as a piel (intensive) form of a root *nṣh*, which signifies power and durability (but cf. Targ. "for praise"). See MUSIC.

CHOR-ASHAN (1 Sam. 30:30, KJV). See BORASHAN.

CHORAZIN [kō rā'zĭn] (Gk. *Chorazin*). A city in Galilee whose inhabitants Jesus reproached for disregarding the many works he had performed there (Matt. 11:20-24 par. Luke 10:13-15; NIV "Korazin"). Though it is otherwise unknown (except perhaps for the reference to it in the Talmud (*Menahoth* 85a), it is usually identified with modern Kerâzeh, about 4 km. (2.5 mi.), north of Tell Ḥûm (ancient Capernaum); according to Eusebius it was two Roman miles from Capernaum.

The remains of a synagogue (*ca.* 4th cent. A.D.) have been discovered at the site, as well as a carved seat which may be an example of "Moses' seat" (cf. Matt. 23:2).

CHOSEN. See ELECTION.

CHOZEBA (1 Chr. 4:22, KJV). See COZEBA.

CHRIST (Gk. *Christos*). "Christ" is the New Testament designation of Old Testament "Messiah" (Heb. *māšîaḥ* "anointed"). Frequently the RSV (like the NIV and JB; KJV less often) renders Gk. *ho Christos* of the Gospels as "the Christ," meaning that Jesus is the only true Christ (e.g., John 20:31) or the anointed one specifically prophesied in the Old Testament (e.g., 1 Sam. 2:10; Ps. 2:2). At Acts 4:26, a quotation from Ps. 2:2, the RSV translates Gk. *toú christoú autoú* as "his Anointed," but at Rev. 11:15; 12:10 the same Greek term is translated "his Christ."

The two names of Jesus Christ are not really interchangeable. "Jesus" was the name given to the child at his circumcision (Luke 2:21); when the title, Christ, is used, that passage should be understood as a specific reference to the Savior's office as Mediator, the agent of reconciliation between God and mankind. At times Paul inverts the usual order ("Christ Jesus," e.g., Rom. 3:24; 8:2, 39).

The appellation "anointed one" derives from the ancient Near Eastern custom of consecrating with oil persons who undertake the responsibilities of a high office. Israel was familiar with this practice during Old Testament times, for prophets, priests, and kings were anointed (e.g., 1 Kgs. 19:16; Ps. 133:2) to confirm that they were officially installed in, and declared competent for, their respective offices. Because these Old Testament figures were anointed for only a short time and discharged their offices imperfectly, Israel anticipated the arrival of the Anointed One, who would not be anointed by men and with oil prepared by human hands, but by God, with the Holy Spirit (Matt. 3:16-17 par. Mark 1:10-11; Luke 3:21-22). For that reason Jesus could testify of himself: "The Spirit of the Lord God is upon me, because the Lord has anointed me . . ." (Luke 4:18 quoting Isa. 61:1; cf. Acts 10:38). Thus, the name "Christ" connotes not only his sacred commission as Mediator and Redeemer of his people, but also the authority and power through which he was able to complete this mission.

I. Person

A. *Biblical Teachings.* Unlike the Old Testament dignitaries, Christ was not installed in his office at any specific moment; his actual anointing is held to have occurred before creation. According to 1 Pet. 1:20 Christ was "destined before the foundation of the world" to be the mediator between God and humanity (cf. 2 Tim. 1:9), just as the Father chose his people "before the foundation of the world" (Eph. 1:4). In the words of Paul it was God's purpose "to unite [in Christ] all things . . . in heaven and . . . on earth" before "the fullness of time" (Eph. 1:10).

God made the mystery of Christ's eternal office as Mediator and Redeemer known to his covenant people in the course of time; he promised them that the Anointed One would appear "when the time had fully come" (Gal. 4:4), in order to carry out his divine commission. In the Old Testament God's revelation concerning the Messiah was first given in principle. Then, as the ages passed and the day of his appearance drew near, additional details and clarifications were revealed. He appeared finally as recorded in the New Testament, having been "hidden for [Gk. *apó* "from"; cf. KJV] ages and generations" (Col. 1:26; cf. Rom. 16:25).

Not only is Christ the preexistent Son of God, he

was also a member of the human race. He, like all other men, was born of a woman (cf. Gen. 3:15). His lineage is further specified in God's promise to Abraham that the Messiah would be one of the patriarch's offspring and that all the nations would be blessed by his descendants (22:17-19); Jacob proclaimed from his deathbed that the Messiah would be born of the tribe of Judah (49:10). Later prophecies would disclose further details concerning the Messiah's person and work. According to Isa. 53 the Suffering Servant would be rejected, wounded for the sins of his fellow human beings, and finally die and be buried. Yet at 11:4 he is depicted as the conquering king ready to slay the wicked with the "breath of his lips" and to usher in the eternal kingdom of righteousness. At last, near the end of the Old Testament period, the devout Jews awaited him as the shoot from David's broken royal line (Mic. 5:2).

1. Divinity. The New Testament enlarges the Old Testament understanding of Christ's preexistence. Not only did Christ exist before the foundation of the world, but he existed as the eternal and true God as well (cf. John 1:1). Furthermore, when he came into the world as a man and assumed human "flesh" (John 1:14), he nevertheless remained divine, "God . . . over all [to] be blessed for ever" (Rom. 9:5).

The Church's confession of Christ's divinity is no human fabrication, for it is based upon God's own self-revelation (Matt. 16:17). All of Scripture points to Christ clearly and unambiguously as truly divine (cf. Mic. 5:2; Isa. 9:6). In the New Testament the true divinity of the Savior is proclaimed frequently and is solemnly attested to by Christ himself. Peter confesses that Jesus was "the Christ, the Son of the living God" (Matt. 16:16; cf. Mark 8:29; Luke 9:20); Paul states that Christ, being "in the form of God," did not consider "equality with God a thing to be grasped" (Phil. 2:6); and John praises him as the "true God" possessing "eternal life" (1 John 5:20). When asked by the high priest Caiaphas whether or not he was the "Christ, the Son of God," Jesus answered "You have said so" (Matt. 26:64; cf. Mark 15:2), but on other occasions he declared that the Father and he were one (John 10:30) and that he was (RSV "am") even before Abraham (John 8:58). In his high priestly prayer Christ also refers to the glory he shared with the Father "before the world was made" (17:5). It is in the awareness of his divinity that he forgives sins and heals the sick (Mark 2:5-11 par. Matt. 9:2-7; Luke 5:20-25), and encourages his disciples to believe in him (John 14:1).

In the New Testament Christ is called the Son of God (e.g., Matt. 16:16; 26:63-64), the second member of the trinity. According to the angel who visited Mary, her child would be called "holy, the Son of God" (Luke 1:35). The voice from heaven at the baptism of Jesus testifies that "This is my beloved Son, with whom I am well pleased" (Matt. 3:17 par. Mark 1:10; Luke 4:22). This is not a mere figure of speech or a ceremonious title granted to Jesus, similar to other titles bestowed on earthly kings and judges and occupying divinely sanctioned offices (cf. Ps. 82:1; John 10:34 quoting Ps. 82:6), for the Bible declares that Christ, like the Father, has unique power (John 5:26). The apostle Paul calls him God's "own

Son" (Rom. 8:32), while to John, Christ is the "Word . . . with God" and God himself (John 1:1), the "only Son from the Father" (1:14; cf. 5:18 for Jesus' own claim that God is his Father).

2. Humanity. The New Testament emphasizes no less the humanity of Christ. The eternal Son of God was born "in the likeness of man" and was found "in human form" (Phil. 2:7-8); he is called "the man Christ Jesus" (1 Tim. 2:5); he is the Word that "became flesh and dwelt among us" (John 1:14); and he shared with mankind "flesh and blood" (Heb. 2:14). As a result nothing human was foreign to him. He lived as a man among men, sharing joys and sorrows, partaking food and drink. He was human not only in appearance, but in his very nature. Like all other human beings, he descended from Adam (see his genealogy at Luke 3:38) and was born of a woman (Luke 2:6-7; Matt. 1:18ff.; Gal. 4:4). His ancestors were Abraham (Matt. 1:1) and David (v. 6).

Christ's humanity shared Adam's fallen nature in common with the rest of mankind. Christ came into the world "in the likeness of sinful flesh" (Rom. 8:3), undistinguished from others in spite of his sorrow and grief (Isa. 53:2-3). And yet, though he inherited Adam's sinful nature, he did not succumb to sin. According to the writer of Hebrews, Christ was tempted in "every respect" (cf. the account of his temptations in the Synoptic Gospels) but remained righteous (1 John 2:1; cf. Isa. 53:11), "without sin" (Heb. 4:15; cf. 2 Cor. 5:21). That is, Christ is a "holy, blameless, unstained" high priest "separated from sinners" (Heb. 7:26).

B. Theological Reflection. The Bible teaches that Christ is truly God and truly man. Some New Testament writers may at times stress his humanity while others at times highlight his divinity, yet all agree that the man Jesus was the Son of God. The later Greek-speaking church asked how God could become man, how the two natures could remain distinct, how Christ could be tempted. But because the New Testament writers were not concerned with such questions, they did not provide answers to them.

When the early Church became exposed to the teachings of those who denied Christ's humanity (the Docetists) or his divinity (the Ebionites), it sought to safeguard the biblical view of Christ. In the Nicene Creed, accepted at the Council of Constantinople (381), the Church asserted that Christ was "[b]egotten of His Father before all worlds, God of God, Light of Light, Very God of Very God, Begotten, not made, Being of one substance with the Father, By whom all things were made." Later, in response to the debates over the relation between the human and divine "natures" (Gk. phýsis "nature") the Church further affirmed at the Council of Chalcedon (451) that "This one and the same Jesus Christ, the only-begotten Son [of God] must be confessed to be in two natures, unconfusedly, immutably, indivisibly, inseparately [united], and that without the distinction of natures being taken away by such union, but rather the peculiar property of each nature being preserved and being united in one Person and subsistence, not separated or divided into two persons, but one and the same Son and only-begotten. . . ."

See also CHRISTOLOGY.

II. Offices

As the true Son of God and the true Son of Man, Christ was anointed with the Spirit to be "our chief Prophet and Teacher . . . our only High Priest . . . and our eternal King . . ." (Heidelberg Catechism, XII). Though the Bible does not use the term "offices of Christ" (this terminology was first supplied by Eusebius of Caesarea ca. A.D. 330), the idea of his fulfilling many roles is scriptural. According to Deut. 18:15, God would raise up a prophet (cf. v. 18); at Ps. 110:4 the Lord is called "a priest forever"; and at Zech. 6:12-13 the future "Branch" would have "royal honor, and [would] sit and rule upon his throne." In his threefold office, Christ executes perfectly the office held by Adam before the fall.

A. *Prophet.* Christ, like the Old Testament prophets, was appointed to bring God's message to his people and to reveal God's will. But unlike the messengers of old, Christ was not merely a prophet, but the greatest of the prophets. That is, his message cannot be augmented by future prophets. For in him "are hid all the treasures of wisdom and knowledge" (Col. 2:3), and as God's "only Son" being in the "bosom of the Father" Christ has made the Father known (John 1:18; cf. 15:15 for the special relationship between Christ and the Father). Christ's message pertains to the redemption of sinful people and his forgiveness of those whom he has called, justified, and glorified (Rom. 8:30). Thus, no true knowledge of God and of salvation can be obtained except through Christ, the "light of the world" (John 8:12); those who reject him will remain in spiritual darkness (John 3:18-20), unable ever to discover the way of everlasting life. It is with authority and power that Christ speaks as Prophet, summoning people to believe and to obey his words.

B. *Priest.* According to Ps. 110:4 the Lord said to his anointed: "You are a priest for ever, after the order of Melchizedek," meaning that Christ was a high priest, not as a result of his descent and succession as were the Aaronic priests, but rather on account of a special and unique calling and appointment. The entire priestly service of the Old Testament tabernacle and temple anticipated this great High Priest, who would enter the heavenly sanctuary "not made with hands" (Heb. 9:24).

There were three aspects to Christ's high priestly work. The first was the sacrifice of his life, which both accomplished atonement for sinners and established his own righteousness. Christ's atoning sacrifice had been announced and foreshadowed for many centuries in the entire sacrificial system under the old covenant, especially in the slaying of the Passover lamb. What Aaron and the other Old Testament priests did symbolically and repeatedly, Christ accomplished fully, once and for all time. He appeared at the "end of the age" in order to "put away sin by the sacrifice of himself" (Heb. 9:26); he is the "Lamb of God, who takes away the sin of the world" (John 1:29; cf. v. 36), "our paschal lamb" that has been sacrificed (1 Cor. 5:7). In presenting himself as a sacrifice for human sin, he paid to God the ransom for his own people; in offering himself "once," he bore the "sins of many" (Heb. 9:28). Just as the Old Testament high

priest on the Day of Atonement went into the holy of holies with the blood of the slain animal, so Christ when he ascended into heaven entered into the heavenly sanctuary, not with someone else's blood but his own — the blood of the new covenant which removes sin forever. Thus, he delivers from guilt and condemnation all who believe in him.

Christ, moreover, is capable of doing all things necessary for the salvation of his people. He not only paid for their sin by his "passive obedience," but in his "active obedience" to God he made the sacrifice with a pure heart, with complete dedication to God, and in perfect fulfillment of the law. Thus, he restored for his people what had been corrupted by Adam's fall and performed all that Adam should have done. By imputing his own righteousness to his people he acquired for them an inalienable right to eternal life. *See* ATONE, ATONEMENT.

The second aspect of Christ's priestly work was prayer. He did not merely grant mankind access to God so that they could "draw near to the throne of grace" with "full confidence" (Heb. 4:16; cf. 10:19); he did not merely teach the art of prayer (Luke 11:1-4 par. Matt. 6:9-13), to assure that whoever offered a sincere prayer in his name and pleaded on the basis of his merits would always obtain a hearing from God (John 16:23-24). Christ prayed for his people and pleaded before God on their behalf as the great Intercessor and Advocate, both during his earthly ministry (Luke 22:32; 23:34; John 17) and after entering into the heavenly sanctuary to sit exalted at the right hand of God ("intercedes," Rom. 8:34). Moved to compassion and mercy by the needs of mankind, Christ fully appreciates human struggles and trials; for he is "not a high priest who is unable to sympathize with our weaknesses," since he was tempted in all things like anyone else (Heb. 4:15). His prayers reflect his awareness of human needs and guide his people's own imperfect prayers to heaven where they, purified of any sinful taint, rise as holy incense before the face of God (Rev. 5:8; cf. Ps. 141:2).

The third aspect of Christ's priestly work was to bless his people. One of the duties of the Old Testament priest was to lay his hands on the congregation of Israel and to bless them. By putting the name of the Lord upon them he secured the promise that the Lord would bless them (Num. 6:22-27). Likewise, Christ, who dwelled as a blessing among his people during his earthly ministry and blessed his disciples upon his ascension (Luke 24:50-51), blesses his people from heaven with "every spiritual blessing" (Eph. 1:3). Through his Spirit he pours out his heavenly gifts and sends a never-ending shower of blessings.

Thus, Christ is also the incomparable high priest. For he alone has brought the great sacrifice of atonement, he alone has fulfilled the law on behalf of his people. So, too, he is the only intercessor and bestower of the heavenly blessings, and those rejecting his priestly work in unbelief will be unable to find any other high priest capable of atoning for their sin. They will lack an advocate with God and instead of receiving his blessing will experience eternal judgment.

C. *King.* Christ, too, like the kings of the Old Testament, was anointed for his office. But unlike these predecessors he was not a king among other kings, forced to share power and glory with them. Rather, he was anointed as the eternal King with unlimited power and an eternal rule of righteousness and justice. For centuries the Old Testament foretold of his royal honor (Gen. 49:10; Isa. 9:6; Mic. 5:2; cf. Ps. 110:1-2; Zech. 9:9). In addition, his majestic kingdom was foreshadowed by Israel's theocratic kingship under David and Solomon.

Israel understood little of the unique character of the Messiah's kingship. Just as during Samuel's ministry they had desired a king who would reign over them like the kings of the surrounding nations (1 Sam. 8:5), they had expected that Christ would be an earthly king, who in battle would deliver the Jewish nation from the yoke of the Romans, thus making Israel supreme among the nations (cf. the people's reaction to Jesus' entry into Jerusalem, Matt. 21:9-11 par.; cf. also Satan's temptation, Matt. 4:8-10; cf. Luke 4:5).

In contrast to the Jewish concept of a nationalistic king and their expectation of political freedom, Christ's kingdom is spiritual. As the kingdom of God (or of heaven) it is radically different from any earthly kingdom. It does not rise with outward pomp but is inaugurated within the hearts of Christ's followers (Luke 17:20-21). John notes that Christ's kingdom is "not of this world" (John 18:36), and Paul remarks that it comprises "righteousness and peace and joy in the Holy Spirit" (Rom. 14:17; cf. 1 Cor. 1:10 for the Spirit's role). The author of Hebrews adds that the King rules by his word, which is "living and active, sharper than any two-edged sword . . . discerning the thoughts and intentions of the heart" (Heb. 4:12).

Moreover, Christ's kingship is not limited to the Jewish nation. Christ is the head of the fellowship of believers, the Church (Eph. 4:15), which was bought with his blood and redeemed from the power of the devil; his Church is led by his Spirit and belongs to him in "body and soul" forever. Like a king, Christ protects the Church in times of danger and does not permit any power, not even the power of hell itself, to prevail against it (Matt. 16:18). Like a king, he reigns, graciously and gently but in such a manner that his subjects submit to his authority and obey his voice. Even those unwilling to acknowledge his kingship are incapable of escaping his dominion, for the Father has placed all things under his control and has given him "all authority in heaven and on earth" (Matt. 28:18). According to Paul (Col. 2:15), Christ has disarmed and triumphed over "the principalities and powers," and according to John (Rev. 1:5) he has been made the "ruler of kings on earth."

Christ's kingship may be disregarded on earth and his glory concealed by scorners who "mock the footsteps of [God's] anointed" (Ps. 89:51). But his majesty continues to shine in heaven where he reigns as "King of kings and Lord of lords" (Rev. 19:16). And one day he will return on "the clouds of heaven," exalting believers and humiliating unbelievers (e.g., Matt. 25:31-46). Then the reign of Christ will be ushered in with righteousness, both in heaven and on earth (2 Pet. 3:13; Rev. 21). See KINGDOM OF GOD.

Some theologians believe that Christ occupied these three offices successively. To them Christ was a prophet during his earthly ministry, a priest during his suffering on the cross, and a king after his resurrection and ascension into heaven. However, this view separates the three offices; the New Testament portrays Christ as simultaneously Prophet, Priest, and King. Thus, when he speaks as a prophet his words are clothed with the authority of a monarch (Luke 4:32); when he concedes to Pilate that he is a king, he adds that he came "to bear witness to the truth," like a prophet (John 18:37); and when he performs miracles he reveals his royal power, certifies his prophetic teaching, and is moved by priestly compassion (Matt. 8:17).

See also BODY OF CHRIST.

Bibliography. G. C. Berkouwer, *The Work of Christ* (Grand Rapids: 1965), esp. ch. 4; W. Manson, *Jesus the Messiah* (Philadelphia: 1946).

CHRIST AND ABGAR [ăb'gər] (Gk. *Abgarus*).† New Testament apocryphal epistles, purportedly representing the correspondence between Abgar V (A.D. 9-46), king of Uchama and Edessa, and Christ. The king had heard of Jesus' miraculous abilities and invites the Master to heal him of a serious ailment in exchange for part of his kingdom. According to Eusebius (*Hist.* i.13), who translated the letter purported to have come from the archives at Edessa, Christ declines but promises to send a disciple after the ascension; Eusebius then records the mission of Thaddeus, one of the seventy, who is dispatched by Thomas, heals Abgar, and wins many converts at Edessa. Another version, recorded in the fourth-century Doctrine of Addai, claims that Christ responded orally and sent his portrait, which had been miraculously imprinted on canvas. Although accepted as authentic by the Eastern churches as early as the second century, these pseudonymous writings met with resistance in the West; in 495 the Gelasian Decree placed the work among the apocryphal books.

CHRISTIAN (Gk. *Christianos*; from Lat. *christianus* "belonging to Christ"). An appellation for one who believes in Jesus Christ (Gk. *Christos*), the Son of God and Redeemer of mankind. The term was first applied to the disciples in cosmopolitan Antioch after Paul and Barnabas had taught there for about one year (Acts 11:26).

At Acts 26:28 Luke records Paul as asking Agrippa if he believed the prophet, to which the king retorts: "In a short time you think to make me a Christian!" Peter observes that to suffer (1 Pet. 4:16) and to remember Christ's own suffering on the cross (2:21-25; 4:1) is part of being "Christian."

CHRISTMAS (from Old English *Cristes maesse* "Christ's mass").† Observance commemorating the birth of Jesus. In the Western church, the Feast of the Nativity of Our Lord was first celebrated on December 25 *ca.* A.D. 336, the date apparently chosen to counter the Roman feast Natalis Solis Invicti ("birth of the unconquered sun"), the birthday of Emperor Aurelius. In Alexandria and the Eastern churches the event was originally celebrated on January 6 in connection with the Feast of the Epiphany honoring Jesus' baptism; some branches of the Eastern church still hold to this date. The name, which does not occur in the New Testament, derives from the three masses of the Western rite celebrating the threefold birth of Christ in the Father's bosom, Mary's womb, and the believer's soul.

CHRISTOLOGY. The theological understanding of Jesus Christ, specifically concerning his personhood (as distinguished from the doctrine of the atonement which describes Christ's work of redemption). Though the New Testament portrays Jesus Christ in various ways, and the apostolic preaching may be termed christocentric (e.g., 1 Cor. 2:2), neither Christ's own self-revelation nor his followers' preaching about him should be considered christological, for the Church's reflection on the nature of the person of Jesus Christ did not arise until the first centuries of the early Church.

I. Development

The New Testament — both the Gospels and Paul's letters — clearly states that Jesus Christ is both divine and human (*see* CHRIST *II.A.*). Soon the early Church would be drawn into a fierce and profound debate about the nature of Christ's personhood. Near the end of the first century the Docetists, who (as did the Greeks) identified sin with corporeality, taught that Christ only apparently assumed the human body. They further held that Christ's earthly life, including his suffering and death, was almost an illusion. The Ebionites, on the other hand, denied Christ's divinity, claiming instead that Jesus was merely a human being who was invested with divine power at his baptism (cf. Matt. 3:16-17 par.). Thus, the early Church was faced with two opposing viewpoints which it was responsible to address.

The debate intensified when Arius, a presbyter of Alexandria (*ca.* fourth century A.D.), contended that Jesus Christ was not eternal, did not share in God's divine nature, but was simply the first creature created by God the Father; thus he asserted that salvation was achieved by one who was neither human nor divine. The Church Fathers proclaimed the divinity of Jesus Christ and his equality with the Father at the Council of Nicea (A.D. 325).

A second issue emerged for the Church. If Jesus Christ is divine (the Son of God) and human (the son of Mary), how are the two "natures" related? the Fathers asked. Nestorius caused considerable commotion with his sharp distinction between Christ's divine and human natures. For his views he was condemned at the Council of Ephesus (431), but he may not have advocated dualism to the degree to which he was accused. Nestorius' opponent Eutychus taught that Christ's two natures were so intertwined that, after his incarnation, Christ was one person having one nature. At the Council of Chalcedon (451) the Fathers proclaimed that Christ's two natures were neither wholly separate nor wholly united. *See* CHRIST *II.B.*

II. Theological Reflection

The Christian church has not called together another ecumenical council to further probe the relationship between Christ's divinity and his humanity, nor has the Western branch joined the Eastern branch in its endless debates concerning the one nature and one will of Christ. (Such debates may have contributed to the downfall of Christianity in the East in the face of vigorous Muslim missionary zeal.) Even the Reformers accepted, on the whole, the Chalcedonian formula. The Lutherans have, however, charged the Calvinists with reintroducing a form of Nestorianism, and the Calvinists have launched the countercharge of incipient Eutychianism among Lutherans. Many modern Christians may object to the ancient Church Fathers' infelicitous language, but by and large they accept the Chalcedonian substance because the Chalcedonian Fathers preserved the "essence of Christianity, the absolute character of the Christian religion, and thus also its own independence" (H. Bavinck, *Our Reasonable Faith* [Grand Rapids: 1977], p. 321; cf. pp. 322ff.).

Bibliography. G. C. Berkouwer, *The Person of Christ* (Grand Rapids: 1954), esp. chs. 1–6; O. Cullmann, *Christology of the New Testament,* 2nd ed. (Philadelphia: 1964); I. H. Marshall, *The Origins of New Testament Christology* (Downers Grove: 1976).

CHRONICLES (Heb. *diḇrê hayyāmîm* "words [or events] of the days").† Records of significant events. Often maintained by the palace or temple, these documents might be highly subjective lists of royal donations to shrines or records of military feats, embellishing victories and rationalizing or ignoring defeats. Others, such as the Babylonian date lists or the Assyrian eponym (Akk. *limmu*) lists, labelled each year according to an important political event (or natural occurrence such as an earthquake) or the name of a prominent official, are valuable aids in establishing chronologies. At any rate, these documents represent early attempts at writing history.

Numerous Egyptian and Mesopotamian chronicles have survived in whole or part or are known at least by name from ancient references (cf. Esth. 2:23; 6:1). Such writings existed in ancient Israel also, and they may well have formed the basis for such canonical books as 1-2 Samuel, 1-2 Kings, and 1-2 Chronicles. Indeed, references are made to books of records (Ezra 4:15; "remembrances," Mal. 3:16; cf. Moses' diary, Num. 33:2) and chronicles (Neh. 12:23), including the genealogies by which Israelite descent was proven (Ezra 2:62-63 par. Neh. 7:64-65). Among those annals named are the chronicles of King David (1 Chr. 27:24; cf. 1 Kgs. 11:41, the book of the Acts of King Solomon), the chronicles of the Kings of Israel (1 Kgs. 14:19) and Judah (v. 29), the books of the Kings of Israel and Judah (1 Chr. 9:1; 2 Chr. 16:11; 27:7), and the chronicles of Shemaiah the Prophet and of Iddo the Seer (12:15).

See BOOK.

CHRONICLES, BOOKS OF.†

I. Name

In the Hebrew text the books of Chronicles are called *diḇrê hayyāmîm,* "the events of the days," which the LXX rendered *Paraleipomena* (and the Vulg. in turn adopted as *Paralipomena*), "things passed over or omitted (from other books)." Because the books are a history recording people and events from Adam to the Persian king Cyrus, Jerome suggested the title *Chronicon totius divinae historiae*, "Chronicle of the whole divine history." Luther adopted the name Chronicles, which has become standard in modern translations of the Bible.

Originally the books were a single composition and may even have formed a unit with the books of Ezra and Nehemiah. The division into 1-2 Chronicles was made first in the LXX, based on size rather than contents, and was followed by the Vulgate and later versions. The division was not accepted in Hebrew versions until A.D. 1448.

II. Place in the Canon

In the MT the books are the last of the Kethubhim or Writings, the third and final division of the Hebrew canon, and follow Ezra-Nehemiah. This suggests that Ezra-Nehemiah may have been viewed as a supplement to the historical account in Samuel and Kings and that Chronicles may have been accepted later, perhaps as an appendix to the Writings. The LXX order, followed by Luther, follows the natural sequence of the accounts — Chronicles, apocryphal Esdras, and Ezra-Nehemiah. The English versions follow this order.

III. Contents

Chronicles can be divided naturally into four main units: genealogies from Adam to David and lists of returned exiles (1 Chr. 1–9); the death of Saul and the reign of David (1 Chr. 10–29); the reign of Solomon (2 Chr. 1–9); and the divided kingdom, the kingdom of Judah alone, the deportation to Babylon, and Cyrus' permission for the Jewish exiles to return (2 Chr. 10–36).

IV. Sources

The author of Chronicles relied heavily on a variety of sources, both canonical and noncanonical, for his history of Judah and Israel. The genealogies in 1 Chr. 1–9 rely extensively on the Pentateuch and include official genealogies, lists of tribal allotments, professional guilds, and temple functionaries, and census data. The remainder of the books reflects considerable parallels with the accounts of Samuel and Kings, often seeming to reproduce the MT verbatim yet occasionally diverging in detail or focus. Long held to reflect the author's theologically motivated purposes, these differences now are thought to indicate an older Palestinian text or a midrash or a commentary on Samuel-Kings.

In addition he refers explicitly to official records of kings, including the Book of the Kings of Israel and Judah (2 Chr. 27:7; 36:8), the Book of the Kings of Judah and Israel (2 Chr. 16:11; 25:26; 28:26; 32:32), the Chronicles of King David (1 Chr. 27:24), the Commentary on the Book of the Kings (2 Chr. 24:27), and the Directions of David King of Israel and the Directions of Solomon His Son (2 Chr. 35:4). Also cited are a number of prophetic records, including the chronicles of Samuel, Nathan, and Gad (1 Chr. 29:29), the prophecy of Ahijah and the visions of Iddo (2 Chr. 9:29), and the records of Shemaiah (12:15), Jehu (20:34), and Isaiah (32:32).

V. Author and Date

Scholars in general favor the view that a single author, frequently designated the Chronicler, was responsible for both 1-2 Chronicles and Ezra-Nehemiah. Jewish tradition attributes the books to Ezra (Talmud *B. Bat.* 15a), a position strongly favored by W. F. Albright (*JBL* 40 [1921]: 104-124) yet not universally accepted (see D. N. Freedman, *CBQ* 23 [1961]: 436-442; cf. Matt. 23:35 par. Luke 11:51).

Although the books are clearly postexilic, the issue of date remains hotly contested. If Ezra is accepted as the author, Chronicles would have been written no earlier than 400 B.C.; this is supported by the Davidic genealogy at 1 Chr. 3:10-24 and evidence in the Elephantine papyri. Others have dated the book as early as the ministries of Haggai and Zechariah in 515 (Freedman) or in the Greek period, with dates ranging from 300 or earlier (R. Kittel, R. de Vaux, K. Galling) to 200 or even later than 160 (R. Pfeiffer, C. C. Torrey, M. Noth, H. Cazelles).

VI. Purpose

Considerable doubt has long centered on the accuracy and value of the material in Chronicles, and the author has been charged with bias or careless use of both canonical and noncanonical sources. However, archaeological data and comparison with other ancient Near Eastern records have done much to restore confidence in the historical reliability of these books. Furthermore, increased understanding of the author's chronological perspective on the events recorded and the selectivity employed in interpreting these events for his own postexilic religious, political, and social circumstances have helped to underscore the value of this material.

The overriding concern of the Chronicler's writings is to demonstrate continuity between the returned exiles and the preexilic community in Judah. By concentrating on the glories of David, the ideal ruler, and of his successors, the author seeks to show that the southern kingdom, which had remained faithful throughout the Exile, was the heir of the "true Israel" with whom God had made his perpetual covenant. Predominant interest in the Jerusalem temple and its worship and cultic organization (particularly the Levites) underscores the returned exiles as perpetuating the true Yahwistic faith.

A number of theological concerns underlie the books of Chronicles. Foremost is the direct activity of God in his people's history, demonstrated both by their place at the center of his redemptive plan (1 Chr. 1–9) and by various instances of divine intervention on Israel's behalf in battle (1 Chr. 11:14; 18:6, 13; 2 Chr. 13:15-18; 17:10; 20:22-25). Related to this theme are the issues of divine election — of the saved people who returned from exile, of David and his line for leadership (1 Chr. 28:4, 6), and of Jerusalem (2 Chr. 6:5) and its temple (2 Chr. 7:12, 16) — and covenant (1 Chr. 17; 22:10). Many commentators see here a messianic theology, focused either on the immediate community or on a future David who would combine both royal and priestly functions. A final theological emphasis is divine retribution, portraying the disaster or prosperity of the people as the direct recompense for their adherence to or neglect of God's will (1 Chr. 10:13-14; 2 Chr. 14:5-6; 20:20; 30:8-9).

Bibliography. R. J. Coggins, *The First and Second Books of the Chronicles.*CBC (1976); J. M. Myers, *I Chronicles.* AB (1965); *II Chronicles.* AB (1965); C. C. Torrey, *The Chronicler's History of Israel* (1954; repr. Port Washington, N.Y.: 1973); H. G. M. Williamson, *1 and 2 Chronicles.*NCBC (1982).

CHRONOLOGY, BIBLICAL.† The biblical accounts indicate no absolute, continuous chronology by which all events can be dated, and archaeological findings generally provide only relative correlations. The process of determining dates of persons and events, and occasionally even of historical sequence, is made even more complex by the use of various systems of dating and by the nature of the writings themselves, whose interest is primarily theological rather than precisely historical.

I. Old Testament

A logical starting point in determining chronology is the biblical record itself. Although some persons or events are dated only to a general period (e.g., Gen. 10:1), others are depicted more concretely with reference to a specific event, such as Abraham's arrival in Canaan (16:3), the Exodus (Exod. 16:1; 19:1; Num. 1:1; 9:1; 33:38; 1 Kgs. 6:1), or the Exile (e.g., Ezek. 8:1; 20:1; 24:1), sometimes reckoned from the time of the exile of King Jehoiachin of Judah (2 Kgs. 25:27 par. Jer. 52:31; Ezek. 1:2) or the fall of Jerusalem (Jer. 1:3; Ezek. 40:1).

An important means of determining the precise dates of such biblical events is to extrapolate on the basis of synchronisms, historical events or astronomical phenomena which can be dated by comparison with other ancient sources. For example, the invasion of Palestine by the Egyptian pharaoh Shishak, known from Egyptian annals to have occurred in 926 B.C., is recorded in the Bible as having taken place during the fifth year of Rehoboam (1 Kgs. 14:25). Thus the death of Solomon can be placed at 931, and other events can be postulated accordingly. Unfortunately, however, few synchronisms exist prior to the eighth century; moreover, mention of Israel in the annals of other nations is most rare, particularly for the period preceding the divided monarchy. For the later period, comparison can be made with Mesopotamian records, including the Babylonian and Assyrian king lists, chronicles, and lists of astronomical formations and celestial phenomena. Thus, from Assyrian accounts of Shalmaneser's battle at Qarqar and records listing his tribute from foreign rulers can be dated Ahab's death in 853 and the accession of Jehu in 842; computations based on a solar eclipse which occurred in June 763, the month of Silwan in the ninth year of the Assyrian Assurdan III, provide further aid in dating ancient Near Eastern history and, secondarily, biblical events. Also of value in establishing absolute dates are Egyptian references to the Sothic cycle, a 1460-year period determined by the relationship between the rising of the Nile river and the rising of Sirius (Gk. *Sothis,* the Dog Star) as the morning star, and the second-century

A.D. Canon of Ptolemy, which records astronomical observations and historical events in Mesopotamia and Egypt from 747 B.C. onward.

Among the chronological information provided in the Old Testament are figures for the length of the Israelite sojourn in Israel (400 years, Gen. 15:13; 430 years, Exod. 12:40-41), the wilderness wanderings (40 years, Num. 14:33), the period between the Exodus and the construction of Solomon's temple (480 years, 1 Kgs. 6:1), and the length of the reigns of the kings of Israel and Judah (e.g., 1 Kgs. 15:10; 16:8, 15, 23, 29). Other data include the often extraordinary ages of the antediluvian patriarchs (e.g., Adam, 930 years; Jared, 962 years; Methuselah, 969 years; Gen. 5). Beginning with the determination of Solomon's death at 931 B.C. (see above), one can apply these figures to calculate the dates of Israel's early history. Accordingly, Solomon built the temple in 967, the Exodus occurred *ca.* 1447 (or 1445 on the basis of figures in Judges), Jacob went to Egypt *ca.* 1875, Abraham was born in 2165, the great Flood took place *ca.* 2457, and the world was created *ca.* 4113 (cf. the date 4004 proposed by James Ussher, Anglican archbishop of Armagh, in his 1650-1654 work *Annales Veteris et Novi Testament,* and cited in the margins of the KJV from 1701 onward). *See also* ABRAHAM *II.*

Until the mid-nineteenth century most scholars accepted such numerical calculations, and many conservatives still do. However, critical studies and archaeological evidence have led many to challenge the validity of the numbers recorded. This was prompted in large part by the discrepancies between the figures as recorded in Gen. 5 and 11 in the Hebrew MT and those in the LXX and the Samaritan Pentateuch; moreover, contradictions have been noted between the accounts of the Pentateuch and Judges and, for the later period, between Kings and Chronicles. Apart from claims of textual difficulties, one explanation is that the variant figures represent attempts at various stages of the narrative's transmission to provide more specific details, or at least approximations, for a very ancient account. Some figures may have metaphorical significance (e.g., "forty" meaning "a very long time") or may be a schematic attempt to "balance" the account (e.g., 480 as a "round number" representing twelve generations [another significant number] of forty years ["a long time"]); the precise meaning of most of these figures remains highly conjectural. Moreover, studies of the nature and use of genealogies in other societies, both ancient and modern, suggest that the biblical genealogies are highly schematic as well. Maintained in order to demonstrate the connection between individuals or groups and their very ancient forebears, such lists often are confined to a standard "depth" (e.g., ten generations; cf. Gen. 5, Adam to Noah; 11, Shem to Terah; cf. Matt. 1, three units of fourteen generations, omitting some individuals or "telescoping" history to accommodate the format (*see* GENEALOGY). While some may see such explanations as discrediting the historicity of the biblical accounts, others view them as an effort to better grasp the theological implications of the author's understanding of history.

Comparison with ancient Egyptian and Mesopotamian records has led to significant insights regarding the complexities of chronological reckoning during the period of the Monarchy. Among these have been the use of regnal or throne names and the frequency of coregencies, particularly in Judah (2 Kgs. 15:1-7, 32-33). Moreover, two systems of reckoning kings' reigns were employed: an Egyptian "accession-year" or antedating system, counting the actual year in which a king succeeded to the throne as his first year of reign, and the Mesopotamian "non-accession year" or postdating system, beginning the reckoning from the first full calendar year after accession. By recognizing that Judah applied the antedating system (except for the reigns from Jehoram through Joash) and Israel the postdating system (until Jehoash adopted the antedating system *ca.* 798), discrepancies in figures regarding regnal years can be resolved (cf. 1 Kgs. 12; 2 Kgs. 9:24, 27; 18:10). A related factor is the apparent use of two different means of reckoning the beginning of the regnal year; Judah observed a Tishri calendar, beginning the year in the fall (Sept./Oct.; cf. 1 Kgs. 6:1, 37-38), whereas Israel apparently followed a Nisan calendar, with the New Year in the spring (Mar./Apr.). Recognition of these practices has aided in determining the date of the destruction of Jerusalem as 586 (Ab 7 [Aug. 12], 2 Kgs. 25:8; Ab 10 [Aug. 15], Jer. 52:12). A complicating factor is the presentation of data for both a king of Judah or Israel and the synchronism with his counterpart in the other kingdom in terms of the same system of reckoning. *See also* YEAR.

For further discussion of particular chronological issues, see the individual articles, e.g., EXODUS; EZRA; JUDGES.

II. New Testament

Although the historical period encompassed by the New Testament is considerably more concise than that of the Old, the problems of chronology are no less extensive or complex. Here again the biblical accounts provide little basis for absolute dating through synchronisms with the rest of the ancient world, and much of what is offered is contradictory or vague. Moreover, chronological references are complicated by the existence of several systems of calendrical reckoning.

Although the "Christian era" as determined in the sixth century A.D. (*see* ANNO DOMINI) is calculated from the supposed birth of Jesus in year 753 *ad urbe condita* "from the founding of the city" (of Rome), the actual Nativity is believed to have occurred several years earlier. Matthew places Jesus' birth within the reign of Herod the Great (2:1), who died in 4 B.C.; the account of the Holy Family's flight to Egypt (vv. 13ff.) suggests that Jesus was approximately two years old at the time of Herod's death, thus supporting a date for his birth in 7 or 6 B.C. Luke's reference to the enrollment decree by Caesar Augustus (ruled 43 B.C.-A.D. 14) "when Quirinius was governor of Syria" (Luke 2:1-2), generally dated no earlier than A.D. 6 or 7 (cf. Acts 5:37), suggests that he may simply have been seeking to explain the presence of Mary and Joseph in Bethlehem; more likely is the suggestion that the earlier date represents either

another of a series of censuses or the initial "registration" stage of a census the actual assessment of which took place during the time of Quirinius.

Dates surrounding Jesus' ministry are also problematic. His baptism by John the Baptist is designated as occurring in the fifteenth year of Tiberius and further associated with the rule of Pontius Pilate, the tetrarchs Herod Antipas, Philip, and Lysanias, and the high priests Annas and Caiaphas (Luke 3:1-2). By standard Roman reckoning, which enumerated reigns from the precise day of accession regardless of the civil calendar, the year would be A.D. 28 or 29; by reckoning from Tiberius' appointment as coemperor with Augustus, the date can be brought to A.D. 25 or 26. Although Luke's reference to Jesus' age at the beginning of his ministry as "about thirty" (v. 23) must be recognized as an approximation, it would fit both the earlier dating of Tiberius' fifteenth year and a date for Jesus' birth *ca.* 4 B.C. John's mention of the first Passover of Jesus' ministry in the forty-sixth year of construction on the Herodian temple (A.D. 28 or 29; John 2:13-20) supports the later dating for Tiberius but creates problems for the date of birth. Moreover, the length of Jesus' ministry (and thus also the date of his crucifixion) is subject to considerable debate. Judging from the number and distribution of references to Passover observances during that period, the Synoptic Gospels suggest that the whole of Jesus' earthly work could be confined to one year (cf. Luke 4:19; Clement of Alexandria *Misc.* i.21; Origen *De prin.* iv.5), whereas the gospel of John would support a two- or three-year ministry (John 2:13; 6:4; 11:55; cf. 5:1). Some scholars who equate the Last Supper with the Passover seder contend that Jesus' observance followed an alternate calendar, possibly that of the Essenes (cf. John 13:29; 18:28, suggesting that the disciples celebrated that meal following the crucifixion). April 7, 30 has been proposed as the date of the crucifixion.

The following dates (which have varying degrees of probability) are of relevance to the chronology of the apostolic period. (1) Pilate was procurator of Judea until A.D. 36. (2) Aretas IV, the Nabatean king, probably controlled Damascus from A.D. 37 to his death in 40. (3) Herod Agrippa I (the Herod of Acts 12) died in A.D. 44. (4) Famine conditions probably existed in Palestine from about A.D. 46 to 48. (5) The date of Claudius' expulsion of the Jews from Rome was probably A.D. 49. (6) Gallio was proconsul of Achaia in either 51-52 or 52-53. (7) The date of Festus' replacement of Felix as procurator of Judea is problematic, but was probably in A.D. 59 or 60.

The following general outline, which results from the above dates, is far from absolute, but can be considered probable at most points. (1) The mob stoning of Stephen (Acts 7:58) would probably not have happened during the procuratorship of Pilate, and so can be dated no earlier than A.D. 36. (2) The conversion of Paul was three years (or parts of three calendar years, since time was sometimes reckoned in this fashion) before his escape from the governor of King Aretas in Damascus to Jerusalem (Acts 9:23-26; 2 Cor. 11:32-33; Gal. 1:18) and after the death of Stephen (Acts 7:58; 8:1, 3; 9:1). It occurred, therefore, *ca.* 36-37. (3) Acts does not mean to associate the famine relief visit of Paul and Barnabas (11:27-30; 12:25) and the persecution under Herod (12:1-23) as closely as it may appear (note the vague temporal note at 12:1). The persecution occurred in a Passover season (v. 3) shortly before Herod's death, i.e., in 43 or 44. The famine relief visit may have been some years after Herod's death. (4) The visit of Paul and Barnabas to Jerusalem recounted at Gal. 2:1-10 occurred "after fourteen years," probably meaning parts of fourteen calendar years after Paul's conversion, therefore in *ca.* A.D. 48. This visit is usually considered identical with the apostolic council of Acts 15:1-29, but may be the same as the famine relief visit of 11:29-30; 12:25. (5) Paul arrived in Corinth after the expulsion of the Jews from Rome (18:1-3) and before the accession of Gallio as proconsul of Achaia (v. 12), perhaps eighteen months before (v. 11), unless this figure represents the length of Paul's stay in Corinth as a whole. Paul was in Corinth during his second missionary journey, therefore, from about 49-51 to about 51-53. (6) Festus' accession was two years after some event (24:27; 25:1), probably Paul's arrest in Jerusalem (21:27–22:29) or his being brought to Caesarea (23:16-35), which was in any case shortly thereafter. Paul's departure from Jerusalem was, then, *ca.* A.D. 57-58 and from Caesarea for Rome shortly after Festus's accession, *ca.* 59-60.

The relative dating of Paul's letters can be proposed on the basis of internal evidence, perhaps as follows: 1-2 Thessalonians (although possibly in reverse order), *ca.* 50; 1-2 Corinthians and Galatians (the latter perhaps earlier than one or both of the Corinthian epistles), *ca.* 52-54; Romans, 54; Colossians, Ephesians, and Philemon, *ca.* 58; and Philippians, *ca.* 59 (although some place it *ca.* 54). For further discussion of the setting of the Epistles, see the individual entries.

Bibliography. E. J. Bickerman, *Chronology of the Ancient World*, 2nd ed. (Ithaca, N.Y.: 1980); J. Finegan, *Handbook of Biblical Chronology* (Princeton: 1964); J. J. Gunther, *Paul, Messenger and Exile: A Study in the Chronology of his Life and Letters* (Valley Forge: 1971); R. Jewett, *A Chronology of Paul's Life* (Philadelphia: 1979); G. Ogg, *The Chronology of the Life of Paul* (London: 1968); G. Ogg, *The Chronology of the Public Ministry of Jesus* (1940; repr. New York: 1980); E. R. Thiele, *The Mysterious Numbers of the Hebrew Kings*, rev. ed. (Grand Rapids: 1965).

CHRYSOLITE [krĭs′ə lĭt]. A complex silicate of magnesium and iron, mentioned in the description of the wheels in Ezekiel's vision (Ezek. 1:16; 10:6; Heb. *taršîš*). An olive-green, precious stone, chrysolite was one of the stones covering the king of Tyre (28:13). In the New Testament it is the seventh stone in the foundation of the walls of the New Jerusalem (Rev. 21:20; Gk. *chrysólithos* "gold stone"), thought by some to be yellow topaz.

See also BERYL.

CHRYSOPRASE [krĭs′ə prāz] (Gk. *chrysóprasos*). An apple-green variety of chalcedony, valued as a gem in Egypt, and the tenth precious stone in the foundation of the walls of the New Jerusalem (Rev. 21:20; KJV "chrysoprasus"; JB "emerald").

CHUB (Ezek. 30:5, KJV). See CUB.

CHUN (1 Chr. 18:8, KJV). See CUN.

CHURCH.†

I. Terminology

The English word "church," like Scot. "kirk" (cf. Dutch "kerk"; Ger. "Kirche"), is derived from Gk. *kyriakós* "belonging to the Lord," or more specifically, *kyriakḗ oikía* "belonging to the house of the Lord." In the Old Testament, Heb. *qāhāl* designates an assembly, either religious (e.g., 2 Chr. 30:23; cf. "congregation") or secular (e.g., Jer. 26:17, KJV; RSV "assembled people"). In the New Testament Gk. *ekklēsía* is roughly the equivalent of Heb. *qāhāl* since it connotes the assembly and could be literally translated "meeting called together" (see below). At Acts 19:32, 39, *ekklēsía* refers to a large gathering in the theater at Ephesus, while at 7:38 it refers to the Hebrew community in the wilderness. Usually the Greek term represents God's people as distinguished from others, thus called out (*ek* "out" and *klētos* "called") of the world. Though the New Testament community of believers is intimately bound to its Old Testament counterpart, many Christians hold that the Church is a distinctly Christian concept, based on the teachings of the New Testament and especially those of the apostle Paul.

II. Biblical Teachings

A. Gospels. Of the four Evangelists, only Matthew uses the word *ekklēsía* "church." Following his withdrawal from the crowds to the Phoenician cities of Tyre and Sidon (Matt. 15:21) and his return to Galilee, Jesus asked his twelve disciples about his own identity (16:13). When Peter responded with his confession that Jesus was the "Son of the living God" (v. 16), the Master announced that he would build his Church with this disciple as its foundation (v. 18; *see also* PETER). In one other passage (18:17) the term "church" means a local congregation or a Christian synagogue.

B. Acts. Following the resurrection, the community of believers, which consisted of the twelve apostles and a number of Jewish converts, remained in Jerusalem (Acts 1:12-14; 2:1), eagerly awaiting the coming of the Holy Spirit as promised them by Jesus before his ascension. The church expanded rapidly after Pentecost (2:47, KJV), geographically — into Samaria, Antioch (11:26; 13:1), Caesarea (18:22), and other cities of the Roman Empire (e.g., 15:41; 16:5) — as well as culturally. Gentile Christians were admitted, mainly through Paul's missionary efforts. While Luke focuses on the founding of new churches in various regions and on their local character, he does not fail to mention the collective leadership of various churches (15:22) nor church unity (9:31).

C. Pauline Epistles. Of all the New Testament authors Paul assigns to the Church the greatest variety of roles. Assuming no real distinction between the local churches (e.g., Rom. 16:1, 4, 16; 1 Cor. 1:2) and the Church as a whole (e.g., 1 Cor. 10:32; 12:28; 14:4), the apostle comprehensively terms the Christian community the "body of Christ" (Eph. 4:12, 15) or simply the "body" (4:4), the "commonwealth of Israel" (2:12), the "household of God" (2:19; cf. 1 Tim. 3:15), God's "temple" (Eph. 2:21-22), or Christ's "bride" (5:25).

A unique, though temporary, phenomenon was the establishment of the so-called household churches found in Rome (the "church in their house," Rom. 16:5), Ephesus (1 Cor. 16:19; cf. v. 8), and either Colossae or Laodicea (Col. 4:15; cf. Phlm. 2). Most likely these comprised worship services held in someone's home and attended by the owner and his family, his slaves, and possibly his friends.

Paul's letters contain scattered references to Christian worship. Patterning their services after Jewish worship in the synagogue, the early Christians read Scripture (first the Old Testament and later the letters of the apostles; cf. Col. 4:16; 1 Thess. 5:27), prayed publicly, listened to a sermon, celebrated the Lord's Supper, observed baptism, possibly sang hymns (Eph. 5:19), and at times initiated collections for the poor (1 Cor. 16:1-4).

III. Theological Reflections

Seeking to understand the biblical descriptions of the Church, Christians have formulated four distinct features (commonly called notes) of the Church. They have been less successful in agreeing on the relationships between the Church as people and as organization, and between the Church and the kingdom of God. (Many wish to distinguish further between the militant and triumphant church, between the church on earth and in heaven, and between the visible and invisible church.)

A. *Notes.* Following the affirmation of the Nicene Creed concerning the one, holy, catholic, and apostolic church, theologians have articulated four notes or marks by means of which the Church is to be distinguished from other human groups.

1. Unity. Even though the Christian community is primarily known through its local churches or congregations, there is a unity of faith among Christians of various theological and cultural stripes, a unity that is made possible by the dwelling of the Spirit in the hearts of believers and their union in Christ (cf. Eph. 4:4-6). This spiritual bond, often seemingly absent, provides the basis for a genuinely ecumenical encounter between Christians of diverse denominations.

2. Holiness. While the record of the Church is far from perfect, its members are exhorted to be holy (1 Pet. 1:15) and to cleanse themselves of every defilement (2 Cor. 7:1; 1 Thess. 4:3). Roman Catholics on the whole tend to relegate this note to the organization or hierarchy of the Church (cf. 1 Pet. 2:9), while Protestants generally identify it with the rank and file.

3. Catholicity. Christ's Church is not only one church but is a Church without external qualifications or differentiations. It is meant to include all — Greeks and Jews, slaves and free (Col. 3:11), male and female (Gal. 3:28) — among its members.

4. Apostolicity. The Church's message is based on the teachings of the apostles, the authors of the New Testament. (Paul may be considered an apostle in a broad sense.) Thus, whenever Christians proclaim the gospel as enunciated in the New Testament, they adhere to the apostolic witness as it has been preserved

by the Holy Spirit. Roman Catholics also hold that apostolicity implies unbroken unity between the authority of the apostles and that of the Church's hierarchy.

B. *The Church as People versus the Church as Organization.* The Christian community remains divided about the relationship between the Church as members or individuals and the Church as an organization. Traditionally, the Roman Catholic Church, in adhering to the latter position, has sharply distinguished between the teaching church or the hierarchy, and the listening church or the laity. Post-Vatican II Catholics have placed somewhat greater emphasis on the Church as people.

On the relationship between the Church and the kingdom of God, *see* KINGDOM OF GOD *III.*

IV. Church Government*

The New Testament rarely refers to the manner in which Christ's Church is to be governed; even the apostle Paul mentions the various office bearers — elders, deacons, and bishops — only in his later letters (1 Timothy, Titus; Romans, e.g., is addressed simply to the "saints"; Rom. 1:7). As a result, Christians disagree about the number of special offices and their relationships. The issue of church government is further complicated by the New Testament directive that every believer is to use his or her divinely given talents or gifts (1 Pet. 4:10).

A. *Biblical Teachings.* Just before his ascension, Christ appointed his twelve disciples to be apostles and charged them to preach the good news that he had atoned for sin and had purchased mankind's salvation (Acts 1:8; cf. Matt. 28:16-20). Having been eyewitnesses to Jesus' earthly ministry, they were able to support their message with Christ's own authoritative words. Following the death of Judas, the remaining Eleven chose Matthias as his successor (Acts 1:26) and gradually accepted the divine authority that Paul claimed after his confrontation with the risen Lord near Damascus (cf. Gal. 1:11ff.). The book of Acts records the preaching ministry of Peter (Acts 2–12), Paul (13–28), and, to some extent, John (3:1, 4, 11; 8:14).

When their ministry, which included the care of the poor and the widows, proved too cumbersome and impractical, the apostles chose seven able men to provide financial relief for the Greek widows (Acts 6:1-6). These may have been the precursors of the deacons, though Philip was also an evangelist (8:5, 26ff., 40) and Stephen, an apologist (ch. 7).

Sometime later the early Church instituted the offices of bishop, elder, and deacon (*see also* DEACONESS). Bishops (Gk. *epískopoi* "overseers") were the ministers of local churches, with authority equal to the elders' (their offices may have been the same). According to Acts 20:17 Paul considered the elders to be the ruling body of the Ephesian church; this is one of the few instances that a church where elders had been ordained is identified. The office of elder appeared soon after the selection of the Seven, as elders were appointed at Antioch (Acts 11:30) and in the Galatian churches at the conclusion of Paul's first missionary journey (14:23; cf. Jas. 5:14). Deacons apparently had been appointed at Philippi, for Paul explicitly greets them in the salutation of his Philippian letter (Phil. 1:1). They did not have as much authority as the elders and bishops, however.

Paul certainly recognized these three offices by the time of his first imprisonment, though he did not elaborate on their cooperative relationships. In his specific instructions to the Corinthians about church government, the apostle listed the following offices to utilize spiritual gifts: apostle, prophet, teacher, miracle worker, healer, helper, administrator, and that marked by the gift of speaking in tongues (1 Cor. 12:28). He regards love as the greatest of spiritual gifts (1 Cor. 13) and, so it appears, minimizes the authority of the charismatics in the Corinthian church (cf. also 1:2, where he greets the Corinthian Christians as "saints" without any qualification). In his letter to the Ephesians, he presents a similar catalogue of offices: apostle, prophet, evangelist, pastor, and teacher (Eph. 4:11). Whatever Paul's view of church government may have been, he firmly upheld the leadership of Christ over his people, office bearers and lay people alike (Eph. 1:22; 5:23-24).

B. Theological Reflections. Within a few centuries the early Christians witnessed the growth of a strong and centrally organized hierarchical system, which in the West eventually culminated in the primacy of the Pope, Christ's earthly vicar. Protestants may be divided on the appropriate degree of church government (the Congregationalists, e.g., reject the jurisdiction of a synod or larger ecclesiastical body of office bearers), but they are inclined to repudiate the Roman Catholic claim to papal authority. Protestants may concur with Catholics that Christ builds his Church on a single rock (Gk. *pétra*; playing on Peter's name, *Pétros*; Matt. 16:18), but in their opinion Christ is referring here to Peter's confession (vv. 16-17) and has given this power to all the apostles (18:18) rather than to a particular succession of leaders. Further, Protestants may point out that among the apostles Paul is Peter's equal (cf. Gal. 1:11), and that Peter himself claims only the office of elder (1 Pet. 5:1), reserving the ultimate authority over the church to Christ himself (2:4-10).

See also BISHOP; DEACON; ELDER.

Bibliography. R. Banks, *Paul's Idea of Community* (Grand Rapids: 1980); G. C. Berkouwer, *The Church* (Grand Rapids: 1976); E. A. Judge, *The Social Pattern of the Christian Groups in the First Century* (London: 1960); P. S. Minear, *Images of the Church in the New Testament* (Philadelphia: 1960); E. Schweizer, *The Church as the Body of Christ* (Richmond: 1964).

CHURCH FATHERS.† Bishops and ecclesiastical authorities of the early Christian centuries, renowned for their orthodox doctrine and holy example and whose writings became authoritative in the formative debates of Christian doctrine. Beginning with the Apostolic Fathers, the Ante-Nicene Fathers include second- and third-century A.D. apologists such as Justin Martyr, Athenagoras, Irenaeus, Tertullian, and Clement of Alexandria, as well as the allegorist, mystic, and biblical critic Origen. Among the Post-Nicene Fathers are the dogmatists, expositors, historians, and preachers of the fourth and fifth centuries, including the Greeks Athanasius, Basil, Gregory of Nyssa, Greg-

ory of Nazianus, and John Chrysostom; and Latin writers such as Ambrose, Jerome, and Augustine. Although some scholars would include all ecclesiastical writers prior to the rise of Scholasticism (ninth century), the patristic period generally is viewed as having ended with Gregory the Great (*ca.* 540-604) in the West and John of Damascus (*ca.* 675-749) in the East.

CHUSHAN-RISHATHAIM (Judg. 3:8, 10, KJV). *See* CUSHAN-RISHATHAIM.

CHUZA [kū′zə] (Gk. *Chouzas*).† A steward of Herod Antipas and husband of Joanna, who provided for Jesus and his disciples (Luke 8:3; NIV "Cuza"). Chuza may have been a high functionary at Herod's court, and he and his wife may have been believers among the aristocracy. The name, which occurs on Nabatean and Syrian inscriptions, may be of Aramean derivation.

CILICIA [sĭ lĭsh′ə] (*Kilikia*). A large region in southeastern Asia Minor, bounded to the west and the north by the Taurus mountains and to the east by the Amanus range. In the west, called Tracheia ("rugged"), Cilicia is mountainous, a contrast to the lush plains of eastern Cilicia Pedias ("flat Cilicia"). A main highway through Tracheia went through the famous Cilician Gates, a pass of unmatched grandeur and unrivaled ruggedness, whose cliffs form a narrow defile. Originally, the pass was only a narrow path, but *ca.* 400 B.C. it was widened to allow carriages to pass through; the Romans actually cut a gate into the rocks, which enabled them to control passage through the mountains.

During the second century B.C. Tracheia was the home base of pirates, who were finally outwitted by Pompey in 67 B.C. The Romans left western Cilicia to vassal rulers, and made its eastern part into the province of Cilicia, the capital of which was Antioch of Syria. The two regions were united under Vespasian (A.D. 72).

A Jewish settlement at Cilicia (perhaps Paul's home; Acts 21:39; 22:3) sent supporters to the synagogue at Jerusalem (Acts 6:9). Gentile Christians were in the same district (15:23), and may have learned about Paul's teachings from converts in the adjacent province of Galatia. At any rate, Paul visited Cilicia at the beginning of his second missionary journey (15:41), crossing the Taurus in June (if credence may be lent to a remark by Cicero in a letter to Atticus that snow prevents travel in the Taurus till that month). At an earlier date before his first missionary journey the apostle also had returned to his native Tarsus (Gal. 1:21, which may refer to Acts 9:30).

CINNAMON (Heb. *qinnāmôn*; Gk. *kinnámōmon*). Unlike modern cinnamon (*Cinnamomum zeylanicum* Nees), which originated in Ceylon in the fourteenth century A.D., that mentioned in the Old Testament (*Cinnamomum cassia* Blume) is native to China and was transplanted to Palestine and surrounding countries *ca.* 1650 B.C. Its bark contained a very aromatic oil used as a perfume in the bedroom (Prov. 7:17) and on clothing (Cant. 4:14), and as an ingredient of the holy anointing oil (Exod. 30:23). According to Rev.

18:13 it was a trade product of the city of "Babylon" (Rome).

The dried flowers of the cinnamon were popular among the Israelites as well. Known as cassia, they were an ingredient, along with myrrh and cinnamon bark, in the preparation of holy anointing oil (Heb. *qiddâ*, Exod. 30:24); twice as much cassia had to be used as cinnamon. These dried flowers also served as a perfume, together with myrrh and aloes (Ps. 45:8, Heb. *qᵉṣîʿâ*). Cassia was among the trade wares of Tyre (Ezek. 27:19); the name of Job's second daughter ("Keziah," Job 42:14) may indicate that the fragrance was in high demand in antiquity.

CINNEROTH (1 Kgs. 15:20, KJV). *See* CHIN-NERETH.

CIRCUMCISION.† The removal of the foreskin from the penis.

I. Old Testament

A. The Rite. The earliest reference to circumcision is found at Gen. 17:10-14 where God is said to have commanded Abraham to circumcise (Heb. *mālal*) himself and all other males of his household, including his slaves. According to the account, circumcision is one of the ways God (re)establishes his covenant with Abraham. Though at that time Abraham was ninety-nine years old and his son Ishmael was thirteen (vv. 24-25), God stipulated that from then on all males were to be circumcised on the eighth day following their birth (v. 12; cf. Lev. 12:3), possibly because by that day the mother's impurity was no longer contagious (W. H. Gispen, *Leviticus.* COT [1950], p. 196). The Jews kept the law, performing the rite on the eighth day even when it fell on the Sabbath (cf. John 7:22-23; see also Phil. 3:5). Usually the father performed the act, but if necessary the mother was permitted to do it (Zipporah circumcised Moses' eldest son, Exod. 4:25-26, Heb. *mûlôt*). In later Jewish practice an official, the *mohel*, was charged with this function. In New Testament times the infant also received his name on the day of circumcision (John, Luke 1:59; Jesus, 2:21).

B. Religious Significance. Israel was not the only nation practicing circumcision in the ancient Near East. In fact, the Egyptians, Midianites, Ammonites, Edomites (till *ca.* second century B.C.), Moabites, and Phoenicians considered it a common custom (cf. Jer. 9:26); the Arabs to this day still practice circumcision. Notable exceptions were the Assyrians and the Babylonians in the east, and the Philistines in the west ("uncircumcised," e.g., Judg. 14:3; 15:18).

For the Israelites circumcision was not merely a surgical procedure. It was above all a symbol of God's covenant with Abraham and his descendants. Among other nations circumcision might have been a part of various initiation ceremonies, but to the Hebrew nation it symbolized the physical and spiritual continuity of the Israelite generations. Through circumcision a person became a member of Israel's community and received the right to participate in public worship. The privilege of circumcision was also extended to any strangers among the Israelites; see Exod. 12:48; Num. 9:14. Josh. 5:2-9 expressly states that upon entering

the promised land the Israelites were called again to be circumcised, because while they had been wandering through the wilderness, they had neglected the covenant. Until the rite was accomplished it would be impossible for God to apply his covenant to their children.

Other Old Testament passages also link the physical act of circumcision to its spiritual meaning. When Israel renewed the covenant with God at the end of the wilderness wanderings, Moses summoned his fellow Jews to be circumcised in the "foreskin of [their] heart[s]" (Deut. 10:16), i.e., to love God and to bring their willfulness to an end. Later the major prophets echoed this summons: Jeremiah before Judah's deportation to Babylon (Jer. 4:4) and Ezekiel while criticizing the Israelites for admitting to the temple foreigners "uncircumcised in heart and flesh" (Ezek. 44:7). Clearly, he who was circumcised was expected to respond sincerely to the terms of the covenant.

During the Maccabean period, many Israelite women preferred death to violating the covenant when King Antiochus ordered that their sons should remain uncircumcised (1 Macc. 1:60-64).

II. New Testament

In the New Testament the term "circumcision" (Gk. *peritomḗ*) is used in three senses. (1) When the Jewish Christians insisted that Gentile Christians be circumcised to demonstrate their submissiveness to the law of Moses (Acts 15:2), the matter was referred to the Apostolic Council (v. 5); it was decided that Gentiles did not have to be circumcised (vv. 28-29). Paul permitted the circumcision of Timothy, whose father was not Jewish, out of respect for the Jews Timothy would be teaching among (Acts 16:3), but he remained adamantly opposed to the circumcision of Titus, a converted Gentile (Gal. 2:1ff.). In his letter to the Galatians Paul states that his ministry, unlike Peter's, was to people who were uncircumcised (vv. 7-8). Accordingly his advice to the Galatians was to disregard circumcision (5:2; cf. 6:15).

(2) In another context the apostle reiterated the spiritual dimension of circumcision (Rom. 2:28-29). Physical laceration was valuable, he said, only as long as it was accompanied by obedience to the entire law of Moses; failure to practice all aspects of the law annulled the value of circumcision (v. 25). Paul justified his stance by pointing out that Abraham had faith and obeyed God before he was circumcised; his faith was not dependent on circumcision (4:1-12).

(3) Viewing circumcision as a sign of the old covenant, Paul stressed baptism as a new ritual sign, a "circumcision made without hands, by putting off the body of flesh in the circumcision of Christ" (Col. 2:11-12). This was Paul's final recorded answer to the Jews who emphasized only the physical procedure of circumcision.

CISTERN (Heb. *bôr, bōʾr* [Gen. 37:20-29; Jer. 2:13]). A reservoir for rainwater, commonly cut into a rock. Because streams in Palestine dry up during the summer and are not replenished for several months, it is imperative that the rainwater that falls between late October and the middle of May be stored. Runoff from roofs and other surfaces is also stored. The Is-

Two cisterns at Khirbet Qumrân (B. Van Elderen)

raelites did not always clearly distinguish between cisterns and wells (cf. Prov. 5:15 "cistern" par. "well").

Each Israelite house had its own cistern (2 Kgs. 18:31; Isa. 36:16; at Prov. 5:15ff. the imagery has sexual overtones). Besides private cisterns, of which many have been discovered near ancient sites, there were public cisterns within the city walls. The water cavern under the temple area at Jerusalem with an estimated capacity of over 7 million l. (1.8 million gals.) was such a public cistern.

When a cistern developed cracks, it could no longer hold water. Jeremiah refers to such "broken cisterns" (Jer. 2:13) in describing Israel as having turned from God, the "fountain of living waters," to surrogate deities. However, empty cisterns could serve as temporary prisons (Joseph, Gen. 37:20, 22, 28-29, "pit[s]"; NIV "cistern[s]"; JB "well"; Jeremiah, Jer. 38:6-7; KJV "dungeon"; JB "well") and often trapped the unwary human (e.g., the blind, Matt. 15:14; Luke 6:39, "pit," so RSV, JB, NIV; KJV "ditch") and animal alike (Exod. 21:33-34, "pit"; cf. Matt. 12:11, "pit"; JB "hole"; Luke 14:5, "well"; KJV "pit").

CITADEL (Heb. '*armôn*). The stronghold or fortified area of a city (Ps. 48:13, par. "ramparts"; KJV, JB "palaces") or palace (at Tirzah [1 Kgs. 16:18; KJV "palace"; JB omits] and Samaria [2 Kgs. 15:25; KJV "palace"; JB "keep"]). David took the "stronghold" of Jebus or Jerusalem (2 Sam. 5:7; JB, NIV "fortress"); the psalmist praised God for protecting Jerusalem's citadel against enemies (Ps. 48:3).

During the wars of liberation Simon succeeded in capturing Jerusalem's citadel (*ca.* 142/141 B.C.; 1 Macc. 13:49, Gk. *ákra* "height"). Earlier, Antiochus IV Epiphanes had had a gymnasium built at the foot of the citadel (2 Macc. 14:5). According to Josephus the Hasmonean kings named the Jerusalem citadel the Baris (*Ant.* xviii.91). Rebuilt by Herod the Great and named the Tower of Antonia, it fell to the Romans in A.D. 70.

It was on the acropolis at Athens that Paul looked at the "shrines made by man" (Acts 17:24) — the Parthenon and other Athenian temples. According to some the house of the Philippian jailer was on that city's citadel (cf. 16:34).

CITIES, LEVITICAL. *See* LEVITICAL CITIES.

CITIES OF REFUGE (Heb. '*ārê miqlāt*). A place of asylum granted by Mosaic law (the Book of the Covenant) to those Israelites who had unintentionally killed fellow Israelites, allowing them to escape the law of blood revenge (the so-called *lex talionis*) (Exod. 21:13-14). These were cities that had an altar. The Old Testament records only two incidents in which Israelites made use of this right: Adonijah, David's son, who proclaimed himself king and whose life was spared by Solomon, David's actual successor (1 Kgs. 1:50-53); and Joab, David's general (who was not, in fact, granted asylum by King Solomon on account of the innocent lives he had taken [2:28-34]).

Because not every Israelite who needed to was able to flee to the central sanctuary (the tabernacle or temple), the Lord commanded Moses to urge the Israelites to select from the levitical cities six cities of refuge — three on either side of the Jordan — once they reached the promised land (Num. 35:9-15). Having appointed the three Transjordanian cities of refuge (Deut. 4:41-43), Moses stipulated that after the Conquest the Israelites would be able to appoint the three cities west of the Jordan (Deut. 19:1-3). In this way the cities of refuge would fulfill the function of protection which the national altar had occupied previously. In time Joshua, Moses' successor, set apart these six cities: the three in Transjordan — Gezer in the tribal territory of Reuben, Ramoth in Gilead, and Golan in Manasseh (Josh. 20:8; cf. Deut. 4:41-43) — and the three in Cisjordan — Kedesh in Galilee, Shechem in Ephraim, and Kiriath-arba or Hebron in Judah (Josh. 20:7).

Before asylum could be granted, the "congregation" in one of the cities of refuge (Num. 35:12) would determine whether or not there had been any enmity between the slayer and his victim prior to the crime (Deut. 4:42; 19:4-6; Josh. 20:5). According to Josh. 20:4 it seems that a preliminary hearing before the local authorities preceded the more formal hearing before the assembly (v. 6). (The biblical accounts vary on the location of these inquiries.) If at such a hearing the manslayer was found to have acted unintentionally, he was to remain in the city of refuge to which he had fled (v. 6) "until the death of the high priest" (cf. Num. 35:28), an event which may have effected a general atonement or which may have severed the ties between the manslayer and the city of refuge, of which the Levites and hence the high priest were representative. After the death of the high priest the manslayer could safely return to his own home (Num. 35:28; Josh. 20:6).

CITIES OF THE VALLEY (Heb. '*ārê hakkikkār*).* Five cities — Sodom, Gomorrah, Admah, Zeboiim, and Bela (or Zoar) — in the region of the valley of the Jordan river and the Dead Sea, at Gen. 14:3, 8, 10 called the valley of Siddim. The kings of these cities rebelled against Chedorlaomer of Elam, prompting the battle recorded in Gen. 14. Except for Zoar, the cities were destroyed by the Lord because of their corruption (19:24-29; KJV "cities of the plain").

CITIZENSHIP. The status granted to one who was an inhabitant of or who accorded allegiance to a Greek city-state or the Roman Empire. Roman citizenship could be obtained by birth, by emancipation from servitude, or through naturalization; the tribune of Acts 22:28 had purchased his citizenship (Gk. *politeía*) for a sum of money during the reign of Emperor Claudius. Besides sharing in the usual privileges (such as the right to vote and to own property), Roman citizens could not be scourged (see Acts 22:25) and had the right to appeal their cases to Caesar and to be tried at Rome (25:10-12).

Paul was a Roman citizen by birth (Acts 22:28) and Paul was his Roman name; his Hebrew name was Saul. Apparently his citizenship derived from his father, who may have received the status of Roman citizen near the end of the republic. Though he was also a citizen of Tarsus (21:39), the apostle was numbered among those who had, in addition, obtained Roman citizenship; Tarsus had received the charter of a Roman province in 171 B.C., but few of its citizens actually acquired citizenship in the empire before the end of the first century A.D.

Paul may have been proud of his Roman citizenship and at times, though not always, used it to his own advantage (as when he was about to be whipped at Jerusalem for bringing Greeks into the temple [Acts 22:25; cf. 16:22-23]). His greater interest, of course, was in the spiritual commonwealth. In opposing the Judaizers, the apostle reminded the Philippians and perhaps himself of the common citizenship (so NIV; Gk. *políteuma*; RSV "commonwealth"; KJV "conversation"; JB "homeland") they could anticipate in heaven (Phil. 3:20; cf. Eph. 2:19 for citizenship within the household of God).

CITY (Heb. *'îr*; *qiryâ*; Aram. *qiryâ, qiryāʾ*; Gk. *pólis*). The development of cities was determined by the availability of arable soil, suitable access, the availability of water, and, above all, the possibility of easy defense. Accordingly, many cities were built on a hill — the more isolated, the better. For example, Samaria was built on a hill that offered this natural defense.

The cities of the Bronze Age (both Early Bronze and Late Bronze) featured imposing walls around their entire perimeters. The height of some of these (e.g., of Kiriath-sepher and Jericho) was sufficient to intimidate and deter spies (Deut. 1:28, "fortified up to heaven"). In contrast, the city walls of the Iron Age were neither as high nor as strong; some of these have decayed almost completely, though some that were built on a solid foundation could still be restored. W. F. Albright has suggested that the change in the structure of city walls was due to sociopolitical changes. The heavy circular Bronze Age walls were erected under the order of despotic city kings by people forced into labor.

Among the Israelites it was Solomon whose cities were most impressive. Excavations at Megiddo have revealed walls of hewn stone laid in rows (cf. 1 Kgs. 7:12 for such an elaborate arrangement for Solomon's own palace). Sojourners living in his kingdom were conscripted to build Solomon's cities (9:15, 20-22).

Compared to Mesopotamian cities, the Palestinian cities were small. Megiddo occupied about 5 ha. (12:4 a.), Shechem 4 ha. (10 a.), and Jericho 2.5 ha. (6.2 a.). The wall of Megiddo was only 866 m. (2841 ft.) long, but its height ranged from five to ten m.

(16-33 ft.). Erected on a three-layer foundation of large, unhewn lime stones, the wall was 6 m. (20 ft.) and in places over 8 m. (26 ft.) wide; its plastered gallery was wide enough to permit wagons to be driven on it.

The Gate, often flanked by heavy protruding towers, gave access to the city. A city the size of Jericho had a double wall (cf. Lam. 2:8): an outer wall ("walls," Isa. 26:1) and an inner wall, between which might be living quarters or storage space (2 Sam. 18:24). The citizens could defend their city from parapets and towers. Should the enemy succeed in penetrating the gate, the citizens could enter the citadel or stronghold and from there make their final defense. City streets were narrow, crooked, angular, unpaved, and frequently dirty (Ps. 18:42, "the mire of the streets").

Bibliography. F. S. Frick, *The City in Ancient Israel.* SBL Dissertation 36 (Missoula: 1977).

CITY OF CHAOS (Heb. *qiryaṭ-tōhû*). An epithet for a city of sinners (Isa. 24:10; KJV "city of confusion"; NIV "ruined city"; JB "city of emptiness"), most commonly assumed to be Jerusalem but possibly Babylon, Samaria, Tyre, or a symbolic city of evil.

CITY OF DAVID. *See* DAVID, CITY OF.

CITY OF DESTRUCTION (Isa. 19:18, KJV). *See* CITY OF THE SUN.

CITY OF MOAB (Heb. *'îr môʾāḇ*). A city where King Balak met the seer Balaam; said to have been located on the boundary of Balak's territory, along the Arnon river (Num. 22:36; NIV "Moabite town"); it may be the city mentioned at Josh. 13:9. Most recent scholars identify the City of Moab with Ar, but some suggest that it may be modern el-Medeiyine, bounded by the ravines of the brook Seil Sfi, a branch of the Arnon (cf. Num. 21:14-15).

CITY OF PALM TREES (Heb. *'îr hatteᵉmārîm*). Another name for Jericho or for the surrounding valley, famous for its many palm trees (Deut. 34:3; 2 Chr. 28:15); it was the residence of the Kenites (Judg. 1:16) and, after his conquest, of King Eglon (3:13). According to ancient historians, it took five hours to travel through the palm groves by way of intersecting waterways.

CITY OF SALT (Heb. *'îr hammelaḥ*). A city in Judah (Josh. 15:62), located in the wilderness between Nibshan and En-gedi. Some scholars suggest identification with Khirbet Qumrân on the basis of the remains of buildings from Iron Age II (900-600 B.C.).

CITY OF THE SUN (Heb. *'îr haḥeres*). A city in Egypt mentioned at Isa. 19:18, possibly Heliopolis, renowned as a center of worship of the sun. According to the oracle, this city is to experience salvation for its allegiance to the Lord of Israel, in whose worship it speaks the "language of Canaan," i.e., Hebrew. Another interpretation of this verse proposes that the city will be destroyed (reading Heb. *'îr haheres*; KJV "city of destruction"; JB "Ir Haheres"; cf. NIV), but this view could reflect a scribal resistance to sun worship. A third interpretation links the city with the Messiah, called the "sun of righteousness" at Mal. 4:2. Whatever interpretation, it is certain that there were Jewish settlements in Egypt, even near Heliopolis (first century A.D.).

See also ON.

CITY OF WATERS. Another name for Rabbah (2 Sam. 12:27; NIV "water supply"; JB "water town").

CLAUDA (Acts 27:16, KJV). *See* CAUDA.

CLAUDIA [klô′dĭ ə] (Gk. *Klaudia*, feminine form from Lat. *Claudius*). A Christian woman living at Rome, who, together with other Christians, sent her greetings to Timothy via Paul (2 Tim. 4:21), according to later tradition, the wife of the Pudens and the mother of the Linus mentioned in the same verse, or the wife of Linus.

CLAUDIUS [klô′dĭ əs] (Gk. *Klaudios*).† Claudius I, Rome's fourth emperor (A.D. 41-54), the son of Drusus, and the nephew of Tiberius. Proclaimed emperor by the praetorian guard in the wake of the murder of Gaius (Caligula), Claudius sought to resolve the political problems of his predecessor, revived Rome's religious practices, and led a successful expedition to Britain which resulted in the annexation of a major part of the island to the Roman Empire. Warned by his private secretary Narcissus, he was able to thwart a coup instigated by his third wife. His other secretary, Pallas, prompted Claudius' subsequent marriage with Agrippina, his own niece, and his adoption of her son Nero; it was Agrippina and Nero who ultimately poisoned Claudius.

Recent scholars have emphasized Claudius' devotion to, and competence in, governing the empire. He attempted to rectify Gaius' anti-Jewish policy by permitting the Jews, especially those at Alexandria, to live according to their religious customs as early as A.D. 41. This conciliatory move may have been partly due to his early friendship with Herod Agrippa, the grandson of Herod the Great. Yet, his attitude toward the Jews at Rome remained contrary: he not only forbade them to assemble but also expelled all Jews from the city (*ca.* A.D. 49/50) on account of disturbances. As a result, Aquila and his wife Priscilla were forced to leave Rome and settle at Corinth (Acts 18:2).

According to Acts 11:28 the prophet Agabus predicted that a famine would plague the empire, which Luke assigns to the reign of Claudius. Roman historians in general depict this period as one of worldwide hardship (Dio Cassius *Hist.* lx.11; Suetonius *Claudius* 18).

Bibliography. A. Garzetti, *From Tiberius to the Antonines* (London: 1974), pp. 106-145, 738-741; V. M. Scramuzza, *The Emperor Claudius* (Cambridge, Mass.: 1940).

CLAUDIUS LYSIAS [klô′dĭ əs lĭs′ĭ əs] (Gk. *Klaudios Lysias*). A Roman tribune and commander of the garrison at Jerusalem, which was stationed at the Tower of Antonia near the temple. Probably a Greek (cf. Acts 21:37), he purchased Roman citizenship "for

Coin depicting Emporer Claudius (by courtesy of the Trustees of the British Museum)

a large sum" (22:28) during the reign of Emperor Claudius.

Having rescued Paul from a mob agitated by the apostle's teaching against the law (Acts 21:32-36), Lysias took him inside the tower to beat him (22:23-24). When he learned that Paul was a Roman citizen (vv. 27-29), he untied him and had him appear before the Sanhedrin (22:30); further altercations against Paul made the tribune decide to keep the apostle within the tower (23:10). Having learned that some Jews had sworn to have Paul killed (vv. 20-22), Claudius Lysias had him transferred to Caesarea with a Roman escort (vv. 23-33). Lysias may also have appeared before Felix at Paul's hearing (cf. 24:22).

CLEAN AND UNCLEAN. Israel's cultic and religious life, like that of the surrounding nations, centered around holy places (e.g., the tabernacle), holy persons (the priest), holy times (the Sabbath, the Day of Atonement), and holy acts (sacrifices, offerings, and purifications). Worship of the deity and the ritual purity which that demanded contrast markedly with the violations of acceptable procedure. Furthermore, ritual purity was ultimately bound up with physical and moral purity. To help maintain the purity of the community and thereby to please God, the Israelites took proper precautions with regard to eating certain animals (Lev. 11:1-38, 41; cf. Deut. 14:3-20), childbirth (Lev. 12:1-8), leprosy (13:1–14:57), certain bodily discharges (15:1-33), touching dead bodies and carrion (11:39-40), and captured spoil (Num. 31:23-24).

I. Terminology

The Bible contains an extensive vocabulary with reference to the notions of clean and unclean as well as related concepts such as purity and impurity, holiness and defilement, sacred and profane. Heb. *ṭāhēr* is the word most commonly used in the Old Testament to indicate that someone or something is ritually clean and meets the standards of correct worship; in the piel stem it means "to cleanse." The most frequent term meaning "to be or become unclean" is Heb. *ṭāmē'*; in the piel it signifies "pronounce unclean," and in the hiphil "make unclean."

The terms themselves tell little about the concepts of clean and unclean, receiving their meanings primarily from the contexts in which they are employed. A cursory reading of Lev. 11–15 shows, however, that the Israelites did not contrast physical uncleanliness and spiritual dirtiness. Bodily impurity is of only subordinate importance in the cultic legislation regarding cleanness and uncleanness. Those who were ritually unclean, even though they might have been physically clean, were not permitted to participate in the cultic ceremonies; they were required to spend a certain amount of time purifying themselves before they could be pronounced clean for ceremonial purposes (e.g., those who had touched a carcass were required to wash their clothes but remained cultically unclean until evening; Lev. 11:24-25, 28, 39-40; the leper had to undergo stringent purification measures over a period of many days before being pronounced clean by the priest; ch. 14). Even objects could become unclean (e.g., a garment; 13:47ff.; a house infected by leprosy; 14:43); when possible they were to be rendered clean, but if not possible were to be destroyed.

In the New Testament the terms most often used are Gk. *katharízō* "make clean, cleanse," *katharós* "clean," *akatharsía* and *akáthartos* "unclean." Although the terms are used infrequently, they reflect the Old Testament concepts of ritual, physical, and moral purity and impurity.

II. Laws of Uncleanness

A. *Eating Animals.*† By touching or partaking of certain animals or animal products an Israelite might become instantly impure; thus a variety of dietary laws were observed. Cultic laws specified those animals which were by nature unclean and thus could not be eaten (Lev. 11; Deut. 14:3-20). These included animals which did not both chew the cud and have uncloven feet ("parts the hoof," Lev. 11:3); those which walk on all four feet and flat paws; various "birds of abomination" — flesh-eating scavengers or those which live in swamps or marshes; fish without fins or scales; swarming creatures; those which crawl on their bellies; or those with many feet. Clean animals were to be slaughtered properly; no animal could be eaten which had died of natural causes (Deut. 14:21) or had been torn by beasts (Lev. 17:15) or which still contained blood (Gen. 9:3-4; Lev. 17:11ff.; Deut. 12:23). A kid could not be boiled in its mother's milk (Exod. 23:19; 34:26; Deut. 14:21).

The Old Testament legislation does not specify clearly how a person who had become unclean through contact with or eating of an unclean animal might be purified. Lev. 11:40 instructs him to wash his clothes and remain unclean until evening, suggesting that purification took place on the day in which he had become unclean.

B. *Childbirth.* The law regarding the uncleanness of childbirth (Lev. 12:2ff.) can best be seen against the backdrop of the curse put on women at the time of Eve's sin in the Garden (Gen. 3:16). The Old Testament relates childbirth to God's curse over mankind due to sin; Job implies this (Job 14:4), and David alludes to it (Ps. 51:5).

When the woman delivered a male child, she would be unclean for seven days. During the next thirty-three days she was required to remain "in the blood of her purification" and was forbidden to touch holy objects or enter the holy place until the period of her purification had been completed (Lev. 12:2-4). All in all, she was excluded from participating in the sacrifices for forty days after the birth of her son. (According to Luke 2:22 Mary observed her days of purification before she and Joseph presented her son Jesus to the Lord in Jerusalem.) When the woman delivered a female child, she was to remain unclean for two weeks, and the period of her purification was another sixty-six days. Thus, she was considered unclean twice as long for the delivery of a daughter (v. 5), perhaps because the Jews believed that the birth of a daughter was more difficult than that of a son. Nevertheless, it is difficult to supply a satisfactory explanation for this distinction.

The prescribed offering for purification was a burnt offering consisting of a year-old lamb (11:6) and a sin offering of a dove or a turtledove (v. 6). Should the woman be poverty-stricken, she was permitted to sacrifice two turtledoves, one for a burnt offering and the other for a sin offering (Mary made such a sacrifice after the birth of Jesus; Luke 2:24). Once the sacrifices of purification were tendered, the priest made atonement for her and the woman was declared clean.

C. *Leprosy.* A number of skin diseases which the ancients usually associated with leprosy (LXX Gk. *lépra*) also might render a person unclean. These might include not only leprosy itself but any disease which caused swelling, eruptions, boils, spots, rashes, or abnormal loss of hair (Lev. 13).

This purification procedure was rather complex. First the unclean person, who had been examined by the priest outside of the camp, was to sacrifice two live, clean birds, cedar wood, crimson, and hyssop. One of the two birds was to be killed in an earthen vessel over running water, and its blood was to be sprinkled on the unclean person; the other bird, having been dipped in the blood of the slaughtered bird, was to be released (Lev. 14:2-8). Then the leper had to wash himself, shave his hair, and wash his clothes. Once the ritual was completed, he was permitted to enter the camp, but not yet his tent (14:8). Seven days later the person was to bathe once more, shave himself again, and wash his clothes a second time (14:9). The next day he had to sacrifice two male lambs, one ewe lamb, a cereal offering, and a log (32 l. [.67 pt.]) of oil, as well as a guilt offering of one male lamb. The priest then anointed the diseased person with blood and oil on the right earlobe, thumb, and big toe, and with oil on the head. Finally, the priest made atonement by presenting a sin offering, a burnt offering, and a cereal offering.

In addition to the afflicted person himself, his garments and dwelling might also be considered unclean. While a garment in which the leprous growth was considered deterred might be purified by washing twice, that which was considered still unclean was to be burned (Lev. 13:47-59; 14:33-47). A house in which the disease had been halted could be rendered clean by the atonement ritual, but one in which the disease was considered rampant was to be dismantled and its parts conveyed to an unclean place outside the community (14:45, 48-53).

In New Testament times the leper was taken to the temple of Herod, to the Nicanor Gate between the court of the women and the court of the men. First he took a bath in the hall of the lepers, located in the northwest corner of the court of the women. Then he was to stand at the Nicanor Gate, at the east side of that court, and to bow his head into the court of the men (also called the court of the Israelites) and receive from the priest the blood and oil of the atonement ritual.

D. Bodily Discharges. Various forms of excretions or emissions of blood, semen, and other fluids, particularly those associated with sexual or reproductive functions, were sources of uncleanness. These might include semen produced either intentionally, as in sexual intercourse (Lev. 15:18), or unintentionally, as in nocturnal emission or illness (vv. 2-17). Women were rendered unclean through intercourse as well as during menstruation (vv. 16-19); a man who had sexual contact with a menstruating woman was also unclean for seven days (v. 24). Persons suffering continuous discharge were regarded as perpetually unclean (vv. 2-12, 25-28). Clothing, furnishings, and vessels which a person used while thus unclean were also rendered impure.

The defiling effects of sexual discharges may have originated in primitive taboos or through association with ritual intercourse as practiced among Israel's neighbors. Indeed, the Bible repeatedly defends sexuality as a positive and proper aspect of human existence (e.g., Gen. 2:18-25). It may be that the polluting effects of sexual love are related to the fall of mankind and resultant human sin.

A man who had an ejaculation was considered unclean until evening, as was a woman who participated in intercourse; she was required to bathe in order to become purified (Lev. 15:16, 18). A woman was unclean for seven days during menstruation (v. 19). Persons with a prolonged discharge remained unclean for the duration and for seven days thereafter; whereas a woman need only wait the seven-day period, a man was required also to wash his clothes and bathe in running water (Lev. 15:5-12). Purification also required a sin offering and burnt offering of two turtledoves or pigeons (vv. 13ff.).

E. Dead Bodies. A person who touched a carcass, either of a clean or an unclean animal, was rendered unclean till evening (Lev. 11:39); according to Num. 19:11 touching a dead person yielded a seven-day period of uncleanness. Any such unclean person, like the leper, was to remain outside the camp (Num. 5:2-3) for the duration of his impurity.

The rite of purification for touching an animal carcass required the washing of one's clothes (Lev. 11:40). The cleansing rite for one who had touched a dead person was more complex. The contaminated person was expected to wash himself on the third day of his uncleanness and again on the seventh day (Num. 19:12). A clean person would sprinkle the unclean person with "water of separation," i.e., running

water poured on ashes of a burnt sacrificial heifer (v. 17).

F. Spoil. Partly because of the risk of contamination from corpses and partly because of ritual uncleanness associated with pagan cultic practices, the Israelites were warned of the dangers of spoils gained in battle with Gentiles (Num. 31:21-24). Articles made of skin, animal hair, or wood might absorb uncleanness and so had to be purified through water; other items of various types of metals could not absorb impurity and were to be cleansed with fire and then passed through the water of impurity.

III. Theological Considerations

Because the distinction between clean and unclean is not confined to the Israelites, some scholars (notably R. Smith) have asserted that even the Israelites derived their ritual practices from the concept of taboo, a prohibition against supernatural reprisal. While it cannot be denied that influences from Israel's neighbors penetrated that people's own cultic and religious life, neither could the content of Israel's laws concerning cleanness and uncleanness be attributed to pagan influences without misjudging the divine revelation which directed the establishment of Israel's religious activities.

These laws were not based solely on Israel's own consciousness. On the contrary, the Old Testament explicitly states that these ceremonial laws were given by God to Moses (12:1; 14:1) or to Moses and Aaron (11:1; 13:1; 14:33; 15:1). Israel was to become a holy nation, a nation devoted to God and thus dissociated from sin (Lev. 20:26). In keeping them separate, the Lord aimed to mold the Israelites into a people of pure conduct. Later the prophets would again proclaim the same goal when they called their fellow Israelites to repentance and purity of heart (e.g., Isa. 1:16; cf. Ezek. 36:25). The New Testament, too, would echo the identical message (1 Thess. 4:7; 1 Pet. 1:15-16). Israel was forbidden to ignore its special character, to fall back upon a common or unclean existence (e.g., Lev. 15:31).

Though holiness was the main reason for cultural and religious purity, there are a number of secondary reasons: the cultic motif (the swine in other religions), the motifs of hygiene (some animals are unhealthy and could transmit disease), of nausea (snakes and reptiles were considered loathsome), and of death (predatory birds fed on carrion). Ultimately, the Jews interpreted these regulations simply as royal ordinances to be obeyed and not subject to debate, not unlike God's probationary command to Adam in the Garden (Gen. 2:16ff.).

IV. New Testament

In the New Testament the concepts of clean and unclean concern for the most part an individual's spiritual condition and thus occur primarily in a metaphorical sense. Indeed, the only references to uncleanness in the Gospels concern demon possession and insanity (e.g., Matt. 10:1; Mark 1:23-27; Luke 4:33-36). Although the Old Testament cultic regulations concerning cleanness and uncleanness were still observed, Christ, as the Lamb of God who takes away the sins of the world (John 1:29), is shown to have broken down the partition of law which separated God and mankind (Eph. 2:14-16). Moreover, he speaks to human responsibility, declaring that it is not an external agent that defiles a person but rather that which the person says or does which causes defilement (Matt. 15:11 par. Mark 7:14-23; cf. Acts 15:29; Rom. 15:14-17). While the New Testament does not abrogate the Christian's obligation to flee from every sin (Jude 23), it does demonstrate the mighty works of Christ, who though he opened himself to ritual defilement — for example, by coming into contact with a dead person (Luke 7:11-12; 8:54) and touching a woman who was hemorrhaging (Matt. 9:20-22 par. Mark 5:25-34; Luke 8:44-45) — took upon himself the impurity of sin, thereby redeeming human lives through his reconciliation (cf. 1 Cor. 15:54; Gal. 3:13).

Bibliography. J. Neusner, *The Idea of Purity in Ancient Judaism* (Leiden: 1973).

CLEMENT [klĕm'ənt] (Gk. *Klēmēs* "mild"). One of Paul's fellow workers who probably dwelled at Philippi. According to Phil. 4:3 his name is written "in the book of life." Though some scholars have attempted to identify him with Clement of Rome (one of the Apostolic Fathers), the dates of their lives and different geographical locations make such an identification unlikely.

CLEMENT, EPISTLES OF.* Two writings, a letter and a homily, included among the works of the Apostolic Fathers and traditionally attributed to Clement of Rome, the third bishop of Rome and mistakenly identified by some early writers as a disciple of Peter. Both works were appended to the New Testament in Codex Alexandrinus, and 1 Clement was regarded by some Church Fathers as canonical.

1 Clement, written *ca.* A.D. 96, was sent by the bishop of Rome to the church at Corinth, where a bitter dispute had resulted from the removal of certain presbyters. An important document regarding the development of ecclesiastical hierarchy, the letter exhibits great familiarity with the LXX text of the Old Testament and with various sayings of Jesus as well as the Pauline Epistles and the Letter to the Hebrews.

2 Clement is a sermon intended for Gentile converts and is based on Isa. 54. Concerned with repentance and preparation for the expected judgment, it was composed in the mid-second century, most likely at Corinth or Rome.

CLEOPAS [klē'ə pəs] (Gk. *Kleopas,* probably an abbreviated form of *Kleopatros*). One of the two disciples to whom the risen Lord appeared on the road to Emmaus (Luke 24:18). Some of the Church Fathers identified Cleopas with Clopas, the husband of Mary who stood by Jesus' cross (John 19:25). Whether or not they are one and the same, clearly Cleopas was known to Luke's readers.

CLEOPHAS (John 19:25, KJV). *See* CLOPAS.

CLIMATE OF PALESTINE. *See* PALESTINE.

CLOPAS [klō'pəs] (Gk. *Klōpas*). A person mentioned at John 19:25 (KJV "Cleophas"), whose wife was Mary (so RSV, KJV, JB, NIV; the Greek construction allows for "daughter"). Clopas has been identified with Cleopas, to whom the risen Lord appeared on the road to Emmaus (Luke 24:18) and with Alphaeus, the father of James the Less. *See also* BROTHERS OF THE LORD.

CLOSE OF THE AGE (Gk. *syntéleia toú aiónos*). An expression found only in the gospel of Matthew, designating not only the end of this earthly era (KJV "the end of the world"; cf. JB at 13:39; 24:3), but also the consummation of the entire created universe with the return of Christ (24:3). In the explanation of the parable of the weeds in the field, Jesus made clear that unbelievers would be judged "at the end of time" (13:40, 49, JB), though the gospel ends with Christ's reassurance that he will sustain his disciples till the end (28:20).

See also AGE.

CLOTHING.† Despite the extensive Hebrew and Greek vocabulary for various articles of clothing, dress among the peoples of Palestine and the ancient Near East was basically very simple, and fashions remained somewhat constant over the long period of time concerned.

During the early centuries of Israel's occupation of Palestine, as well as later among shepherds and the poorer elements of society, clothing was fashioned from animal skins (Gen. 3:21; Exod. 25:5). Among the more sedentary segments of Israelite society, particularly with the development of technology, cloth was made of wool spun from fleece (Lev. 13:47) and animal hair woven into coarse cloth (Matt. 3:4). Whereas very coarse sackcloth might be worn for mourning and as a sign of repentance (2 Sam. 3:31), garments might also be fashioned of fine linen or silk (Ezek. 16:13).

The basic unit of clothing for both men and women was a shirtlike tunic (Heb. *keṯōneṯ*; Gk. *chitōn*), an undergarment with long or medium sleeves which reached to the ankles. This undergarment was held together by a girdle or sash of linen (Jer. 13:1) or leather (2 Kgs. 1:8), at times decorated with precious gems (Dan. 10:5); it might also serve to carry a sword (Judg. 3:16; 1 Sam. 25:13) or money (Matt. 10:9) or function as an ink case (Ezek. 9:2). The basic outer garment was the mantle (Heb. *śimlâ*), a square cloth, often decorated with fringes (Luke 8:44) or tassels (Num. 15:38), which was wrapped around the body (Deut. 22:12) and used by shepherds and the poor to cover themselves at night (Deut. 24:13; Jer. 43:12); it might also be used to transport various objects (Exod. 12:34; Hag. 2:12). It was removed while working (Matt. 24:18). A more elegant outer garment was a sleeveless coat or robe (Heb. *me'îl*; also translated "mantle") which designated rank or distinction (e.g., 1 Sam. 18:4; cf. Heb. *'addereṯ*; Jonah 3:6).

The turban (Heb. *pe'ēr*) was the most common form of headdress, a square cloth folded into a triangle and kept in place by a string or wrapped around the head (Job 29:14; Ezek. 24:17). Women also wore veils (Gen. 24:65; 38:14, 19; Isa. 3:18, 20).

Footwear consisted of sandals with leather thongs

(Gen. 14:23) or shoes with hard leather soles and uppers of softer leather (Ezek. 16:10).

See further the individual entries for specific items of clothing.

CNIDUS [nĭ'dəs] (Gk. *Knidos*).† A city in Caria, on the southwestern coast of Asia Minor, opposite the island of Cos. It was "off Cnidus" (Acts 27:7) that the ship carrying Paul and other prisoners to Rome "arrived with difficulty during a storm." The larger, southern harbor with moorings, warehouses, and market places would have provided suitable shelter during the storm, but the captain of the ship chose instead to sail under the lee of Crete.

Colonized by Dorian Greeks, Cnidus has been under excavation since 1967. The sanctuary of Demeter has been discovered, as well as a shrine of Aphrodite, and a number of churches from the Christian era.

COAL. Among the Israelites coal — more likely charcoal than true mineral coal — was used for several purposes. (1) It was used for heating during the cold month of December, for example, in the royal palace (Jer. 36:22, "fire"). Coal provided heat for Peter and others in the court of Jesus' trial during April ("charcoal fire"; Gk. *anthrakía*; John 18:18; KJV "fire of coals"; NIV "fire"). (2) Coal was also used for cooking. With his apostles the risen Lord ate a breakfast heated over a "charcoal fire" (John 21:9). (3) The ironsmith shaped idols (Isa. 44:12; Heb. *peḥām*) or forged weapons (54:16) in the coals of his fire. (4) On the Day of Atonement the high priest used a censer "full of coals of fire" (Lev. 16:12-13; Heb. **gaḥal* "burning charcoals") to produce the incense needed for the ritual offering (Lev. 10:1; Num. 16:46).

At Prov. 26:21 a quarrel is said to feed strife and dissension as charcoal feeds a fire.

COAST, COASTLAND (Heb. *'î*, *gᵉḇûl*).† The shore of either the mainland (e.g., Isa. 23:2, 6) or an island (e.g., Jer. 2:10; 47:4) adjacent to or within the Mediterranean Sea. The KJV frequently translates Heb. *'î* as "island(s)" (e.g., Isa. 11:11; 21:12; 41:1) or "isle(s)" (e.g., Gen. 10:5; Esth. 10:1; Ps. 97:1), and the RSV frequently translates *gᵉḇûl* as "country" or "border" (e.g., Exod. 34:24; Josh. 13:23). "Coastlands" also indicates faraway (Gentile) nations (e.g., Isa. 40–66; Jer. 31:10; Ezek. 26:15).

COAT OF MAIL (Heb. *širyôn*, *širyān*).† A leather jacket reinforced with metal scales (Heb. *qasᵉqassîm*; 1 Sam. 17:5), worn over the torso. The weight of Goliath's coat of mail was five thousand shekels of bronze (about 80 kgs. [176 lbs.]; 1 Sam. 17:5). According to 1 Kgs. 22:34; 2 Chr. 18:33 Ahab was struck between the "scale armor" and the "breastplate," or between the connecting parts near the armpit (KJV "between the joints of the harness"; NIV "between the sections of his armor"; JB "between the corslet and the scale-armor of his breastplate").

Unlike David, who refused to wear a coat of mail on account of its weight (1 Sam. 17:38), most soldiers wore this protective clothing; King Uzziah is credited with supplying coats of mail for his entire army (2 Chr. 26:14). Half of those employed in the rebuilding of the walls of Jerusalem wore such coats while guarding the rest of the work force (Neh. 4:16). A coat of mail was part of the armor worn by both the Egyptians (Jer. 46:4; KJV "brigandines"; NIV "armor"; JB "breastplates") and the Babylonians (51:3).

At Job 41:14 (MT 6) the RSV and JB follow the LXX by emending Heb. *resen* ("bridle"; so KJV, NIV; understood as "double teeth") to *siryôn* "coat of mail" (par. "outer garment"), a reference to the Leviathan's scaly skin. But at 2 Sam. 1:9 Heb. *šāḇāṣ* should probably be rendered "cramp" ("anguish"; so RSV, KJV; NIV "throes of death"; JB "giddiness") rather than "coat of mail" (KJV mg.).

COCKCROW (Gk. *alektorophōnía*).† The third of the four watches of the night assigned by the Romans (evening [6 to 9 p.m.], midnight [9 p.m. to 12 a.m.], cockcrow [12 to 3 a.m.], and morning [3 to 6 a.m.]; Mark 13:35; cf. Matt. 14:25 par. Mark 6:48 for the "fourth watch"); the Jews divided the night into three watches. Cockcrow received its name from the predictable crowing of a rooster near midnight or because of the sound of the bugle that signaled the changing of the guard. Jesus had this period of the night in mind when he warned that Peter would deny him "before the cock crows twice" (Matt. 26:34; Mark 14:30; cf. Luke 22:34; John 13:38).

CODEX. A wooden tablet (or tablets connected with thongs laced through holes bored near the edges). The codex, the earliest form of book — which in Roman times began to replace the more cumbersome scroll — was first used in business and legal transactions. Later Romans experimented with a codex of papyri sheets folded over and sewn together.

The text of the Bible has been handed down in various codices (see below).

CODEX ALEXANDRINUS [ăl'ĭg zăn drē'nəs]. An important Greek manuscript of the Bible dating to the early fifth century A.D., containing the LXX of the Old Testament, nearly the entire New Testament, and the two letters of Clement of Rome; it is usually represented by the symbol **A**. The codex was sent as a gift to James I of England by Cyril Lucar, the patriarch of Constantinople, in 1624, but James died before it could be delivered and the manuscript was officially presented to his successor Charles I in 1627. At present it is stored in the British Museum in London.

CODEX BEZAE [bē'zē]. An important manuscript from the early sixth century A.D., which contains the Gospels (arranged as Matthew, John, Luke, and Mark) and Acts (preceded by the end of 3 John) in both Latin (represented by the symbol *d*) and Greek (**D**) translations, each arranged on opposite pages. In 1562 the French scholar T. de Bèza rescued this manuscript from the burning monastery at Lyons; later, in 1581, he donated it to the University of Cambridge, where it is still stored, hence its frequent designation as Cantabrigiensis.

CODEX CLAROMONTANUS [klăr'ə mŏn tăn'əs]. A sixth-century A.D. manuscript, containing all the letters known to have been written by Paul and those traditionally ascribed to him (e.g., Hebrews). Resembling the Codex Bezae with its Greek (designated by the symbol **D**[P]) and Latin (designated *d*) translations on opposite pages, Codex Claromontanus complements the Western (Greek) text with the inclusion of books not found in Bezae. Claromontanus is a palimpsest; the biblical material has been written over fragments of Euripides *Phaethon*. It was found in a convent at Clermont-en-Beauvais *ca.* 1560 and changed hands several times (portions were stolen and recovered) before it finally found safe lodging at the Bibliothèque Nationale at Paris.

CODEX EPHRAEMI SYRI [ĕf′rī ē′mī sī′rī]. A significant biblical manuscript dating from the early fifth century A.D., originally containing the Scriptures in their entirety; it is designated by the symbol **C**. Of the Old Testament only portions of Job, Prov-

erbs, Ecclesiastes, and Canticles have survived. Nearly all the New Testament books remain, but over them have been written the Greek translations of sermons by a certain Ephraem Syrus from the twelfth century. At present it is housed in the Bibliothèque Nationale at Paris.

CODEX SINAITICUS [sīn′ī ĭt′ə kəs]. An important fourth-century A.D. biblical manuscript that contains a good portion of the Old Testament, the entire New Testament (the only ancient Greek manuscript that does), and two writings of the Apostolic Fathers: the Epistle of Barnabas and the Shepherd of Hermas; it is represented by the symbol ℵ. It is of utmost importance for textual criticism of both the LXX and the Greek New Testament. In 1844 K. Tischendorf discovered part of this vellum manuscript in the monas-

Codex Sinaiticus (a facsimile): part of the Pastoral Epistles (British Library)

tery of St. Catherine at the foot of Mt. Sinai, but it was not until 1859 that he recovered all the leaves, which he purchased for Czar Alexander II of Russia. It remained in St. Petersburg (Leningrad) until 1933, when it was moved to the British Museum in London.

CODEX VATICANUS [văt′ĭ kăn′əs]. A valuable early fourth-century A.D. manuscript that originally contained the entire Greek text of the Bible. The codex in its present state shows evidence of erosion and age, for it now lacks Gen. 1:1–46:28, a number of Psalms, Heb. 9:14–13:25, the Pastorals, and all of Revelation. Most scholars consider it the most valuable extant manuscript. Identified by the symbol **B**, it was probably written in Alexandria. The manuscript has been stored in the Vatican Library at Rome since *ca.* 1470.

CODEX WASHINGTONENSIS [wăsh′ĭng tŏn ĕn′-sĭs]. A fourth- or fifth-century A.D. manuscript of the New Testament, remarkable for its unique script and text type. It contains the four gospels in the Western order: Matthew, John, Luke, and Mark. A particularly striking feature is the insertion at Mark 16:14 of the so-called Freer Logion concerning the present generation of lawlessness and faithlessness as under the dominion of Satan, for which Christ was delivered over to death that people might return to truth and inherit heavenly righteousness. The codex was purchased by C. L. Freer in Cairo in 1906 and is at present part of the Freer Collection in Washington. It is designated by the symbol **W**.

COELE-SYRIA [sē′lĭ sĭr′ĭ ə] (Gk. *Koilē Syria* "hollow Syria"). A valley (Josh. 11:17) between the Lebanon and the Anti-lebanon mountain ranges, now known as the Beqaʿ (cf. biblical Baalbek, "Baal of the *Beqaʿ* ") through which the Leontes river flows southward. According to 1 Macc. 10:69 Demetrius appointed Apollonius governor of this region, a single province which included Phoenicia (but cf. 2 Macc. 3:5-8 where they are considered distinct). Josephus, however, defines Coele-Syria much more broadly — "as far as the river Euphrates and Egypt" (*Ant.* xiv.4.5; cf. *BJ* i.10.8 where it extends even to Damascus).

COINS. *See* MONEY.

COHORT. *See* LEGION.

COL-HOZEH [kŏl hō′zə] (Heb. *kol-ḥōzeh* "all seeing").
   1. The father of Shallum, ruler of the district of Mizpah during the administration of Nehemiah (Neh. 3:15).
   2. Ancestor of Ma-aseiah from Judah, who settled at Jerusalem after the Exile (Neh. 11:5); perhaps identical to **1** above.

COLONY (Gk. *kolōnía*, from Lat. *colonia*). A Roman settlement, founded originally for military purposes; often land given to veterans of the legions. These colonists retained their Roman citizenship and helped establish Roman authority, especially along the main highways of the empire. Emperor Augustus established such colonies as Antioch (Pisidian), Lystra, and Troas — all in Asia Minor.
   Luke mentions explicitly that Philippi was a Roman colony (Acts 16:12); his details regarding the local magistrates' authority to decide criminal cases and impose punishment (cf. v. 22) are very similar to the practice in other Roman colonies of the time. At Phil. 3:20 Paul's instruction to Christians about their "commonwealth in heaven" may be an allusion to Philippi's status as a Roman colony.

COLOR.† The Israelites, unlike their neighbors, apparently were familiar only with a general distinction between colors — esp. between light and dark — and often lacked the words for nuances of color. In fact, they hardly used the word "color" (Heb. *ʿayin*, lit. "eye"). Descriptions of color in the Old Testament are more apt to be circumlocutionary: "speckled and spotted" (describing cattle at Gen. 30:32-33), "striped and spotted" (v. 35), "brightly embroidered garments" (Ezek. 16:18), "plumage of many colors" (17:3; JB "speckled feathers"). Joseph's famous robe (Gen. 37:3, 23, 32) may actually have been just a long-sleeved garment (so RSV, JB, interpreting Heb. **pas* as "extremity") rather than a coat made literally "of many colors" (KJV, understanding **pas* as "variegated"; cf. NIV "richly ornamented"). Some scholars believe that Israel's frequent vague reference to colors can be attributed to the divine prohibition against making graven images.
   The Bible does mention a number of colors, though — notably purple, which was the color worn by the Midianite kings (Judg. 8:26) and by a rich man in a parable of Jesus (Luke 16:19), and scarlet (e.g., material; Exod. 25:4). The Old Testament also refers to white (the color of teeth; Gen. 49:12), black (the color of hair; Cant. 5:11; cf. "very dark," 1:5), green (usually the color of vegetation; e.g., Gen. 1:30), and red (e.g., the color of eyes; Gen. 49:12). Less frequently mentioned are yellow and reddish-white (referring to hair color; Lev. 13:19, 24, 43), and vermillion (the color of a house [Jer. 22:14] and Chaldean paintings [Ezek. 23:14; NIV "red"]).
   The Israelites were also fond of using colors in comparisons. Isaiah chose colors to deliver his words of comfort (Isa. 1:18). The book of Revelation lists several colors with symbolic meaning. The four horses, described in the first four seals, are white (the color of victory; Rev. 6:1; cf. Zech. 6:3), "bright red" (the color of war and bloodshed; v. 4; cf. Zech. 6:2), black (the color of hunger; v. 5; cf. Zech. 6:2), and pale (the color of death; v. 8). White also depicts purity (as of the believers at Sardis and all like them; 3:4-5). Similar meanings are found in other biblical passages: white for purity (Mark 16:5 par.), black for hunger (Lam. 5:10; KJV; RSV, NIV, JB "hot") or mourning (Job 30:28, 30), purple for royal dignity (Esth. 8:15), and grey for wisdom or beauty among the aged (Job 15:10; Prov. 20:29; cf. Isa. 46:4 par., "old age").
   Archaeological discoveries have shed considerable light on the techniques employed by ancient Near Eastern peoples in making dyes and transferring colors. The Babylonians colored stones using several

kinds of clay and then heating them to various temperatures to achieve different colors. The Egyptians prepared colors from a variety of metals (e.g., blue was obtained by heating a copper compound with powdered quartz). In addition to obtaining colors for paintings and pottery, the ancients prepared dyes for clothing by extracting secretions from mollusks and kermes insects (e.g., purple from the *Murex trunculus* and *Helix ianthina* and scarlet from *Coccus ilicia*).

COLOSSAE [kə lŏs′ī] (Gk. *Kolossai*).† A city in the valley of the Lycus river, a branch of the Meander, in the southwest region of ancient Phrygia (Asia Minor). At present it is a ruin near Honaz Dağ (Mt. Cadmus). Originally populated by Phrygians, the city later was given a Hellenistic name.

Of the three major Christian cities in the valley (see Rev. 3:14 for Laodicea), Colossae (about 21 km. [13 mi.] from Hierapolis and about 19 km. [12 mi.] from Laodicea) was the first to have been accorded city status; by New Testament times it was a well-established community. Paul wrote to the local church (Col. 1:2; KJV, NIV "Colosse"), commonly thought to have been founded by Epaphras (inferred from 1:7; 4:12). Among the local church members were Archippus (4:17; cf. Phlm. 2), Onesimus, and his master Philemon (4:8-9; cf. Phlm. 10ff.).

During the seventh and eighth centuries Colossae was occupied by the Saracens. The site has not yet been excavated.

COLOSSIANS, LETTER TO THE. The twelfth book of the New Testament and one of Paul's Prison Letters.

I. Author

Paul did not personally establish the church at Colossae (Col. 2:1), though the effects of his ministry at Ephesus during his third missionary journey could have been felt at Colossae; the two cities were located in the same Roman province of Asia (Acts 19:10, "all the residents of Asia"). It is possible that the church at Colossae was started through the labors of his coworker Epaphras (Col. 1:7). Thus, in a broad sense, the Colossian congregation can be considered to have been Pauline, and Paul could legitimately have written them without violating Epaphras' authority. Although some scholars have argued on the basis of vocabulary and style that the letter represents a second-century attack on Gnosticism, its Pauline authorship is generally accepted.

II. Date and Place of Origin

Paul wrote this letter while a prisoner (4:3, 10, 18) — probably in Rome, though other imprisonments have been suggested (e.g., at Caesarea and Ephesus). If it was written during the Roman imprisonment, the letter would have been composed *ca.* A.D. 61.

III. Purpose

While in prison Paul was visited by Epaphras (1:8), and it was his generally unfavorable report on the Colossian church that prompted the apostle to take up his pen. Epaphras told of influential but false teachers who preached a kind of asceticism, introduced specu-

lation about the origin of the world, and emphasized knowledge (Gk. *gnōsis*). The exact nature of the so-called Colossian heresy is not made clear in Paul's letter, but it must have embraced elements from Judaism and incipient Gnosticism. At any rate, the false teachers were challenging Christ's preeminence and distracting the Colossians from the power of the gospel.

In replying to Epaphras' complaints, Paul first urged the Colossian Christians not to entangle themselves in unnecessary ethical rules (2:16-23), to put off the truly "earthly" lifestyle, and to live a Christian life centered in love (3:5-17). Second, he strongly stressed the centrality of Christ's role in creation and redemption (1:16, 22; 2:13-15), which was loftier than that of the angelic powers worshiped by the Colossians (1:16). Third, the apostle expressed his view that knowledge must not replace faith (1:23; 2:10) or the wisdom found in Christ (1:28).

IV. Contents

After an introductory thanksgiving in behalf of the church and a prayer for the members' continued growth in understanding and love (1:1-14), Paul expands on Christ's power over the principalities of the universe (1:15-23), including his power over sin (1:23–2:7). He continues his letter with an exhortation that the Colossians learn to follow Christ (2:8–3:4) and an outline of various Christian virtues (3:12–4:6). As in his other letters, the apostle concludes with personal greetings (4:7-17).

V. Relation to the Other Prison Letters

Accompanied by Onesimus, a native of Colossae (4:9), Tychicus took Paul's letter to Colossae (4:7-8). On the basis of 4:16 it may be concluded that the Colossian letter was meant to circulate, to be read at least by the neighboring church at Laodicea (cf. 2:1), and possibly by the church at Hierapolis (4:13).

In content the Colossian letter greatly resembles the letter to the Ephesians. Both express the notion of the Church as the body of Christ (1:18) and give nearly identical versions of the household codes (3:18–4:1). There is, however, a slightly different focus on Christ's work — in Ephesians the emphasis is on the Church and the end of all things, while Colossians is directed more toward creation.

Bibliography. F. F. Bruce, *Colossians, Philemon, and Ephesians* NICNT (1984); E. Lohse, *Colossians and Philemon*. Hermeneia (Philadelphia: 1971); R. P. Martin, "Crisis at Colossae," *New Testament Foundations* 2 (Grand Rapids: 1978): 209-222.

COLT. *See* Ass *I.B.*

COMFORTER (John 14:16, 26; 15:26; 16:7, KJV). *See* PARACLETE.

COMMANDER. A title of high rank (most often Heb. *śar*) given to army personnel. During the wilderness wanderings Moses divided Israel's military force into units of thousands and hundreds (Num. 31:14, 52, 54; "captains" at v. 48; so usually KJV). After the Conquest, Saul (1 Sam. 8:12) and David (2 Sam. 18:1) retained this arrangement. Later the Old Testament mentions a commander having control over as few as fifty soldiers ("captain"; 2 Kgs. 1:9ff.; cf. "commanders," 1 Sam. 8:12); this person may have been charged with maintaining internal order within Palestine. Eventually the term no longer implied an officer over a certain number of soldiers, as the number of soldiers per division began to fluctuate.

Joab was David's general ("commander"; 1 Kgs. 1:25), while Abner held a similar position in Saul's army (2:32). A 2 Chr. 23:1 Jehoiada, the high priest, enlisted the protection of five commanders and their soldiers — five hundred men in all — in his attempt to overthrow Athaliah and to crown young Joash king ("captains"; 2 Kgs. 11:4, 9).

COMMANDMENT. *See* LAW.

COMMANDMENT, NEW.†

I. Old Testament

Near Mt. Horeb shortly after their deliverance from Egypt, the Hebrews entered into a covenant with Yahweh through their chief Moses. So that his people might fulfill their covenantal obligations, Yahweh gave them the so-called Ten Commandments (or the Decalog; Exod. 20:1-17), as well as other commandments, contained in the Book of the Covenant (21:1–23:33). The Mosaic law also proclaimed a unifying principle of love, for Lev. 19:18 refers to the human duty to love one's neighbor (i.e., fellow Jews) and Deut. 6:4-5 points to mankind's responsibility to love God: "Hear, O Israel: The Lord your God is one Lord [or "The Lord our God, the Lord is one"]; and you shall love the Lord your God with all your heart, and with all your soul, and with all your might" (see 5:6-21 for a restatement of the Decalog). The commandment to love God with one's entirety — i.e., without any reservation — is linked to the claim that there is only one God, namely, Yahweh.

Scholars have been unable to ascertain when the Hebrews started to connect the two commandments to love both neighbor and God, and to interpret the Decalog in light of that emphasis. It may have been as early as Jesus' ministry (see Luke 10:25-28), in spite of their still strong emphasis on observing the minute details of the law; certainly such an interpretation became common in subsequent centuries.

II. New Testament

The New Testament provides a clearer understanding of the Old Testament connection between law and love.

A. Synoptic Gospels. Retaining the Old Testament summary statements about the Decalog, Jesus replies to the Pharisee (so Matthew) — or to one of the scribes (so Mark) or to one of the lawyers (so Luke) — that the Decalog is based on a twofold commandment of love, first for God and second for one's neighbor (Matt. 22:37-40). Mark quotes the opening sentence of the Shema: "Hear, O Israel: The Lord our God, the Lord is one" (Mark 12:29) before he cites the greatest commandment, and then adds the scribe's concurrence with Jesus' reply and Jesus' commendatory response to his correct answer (vv. 32-34). According to Luke, the lawyer himself gives the answer (Luke

10:27) and raises the further question about the meaning of neighbor (v. 29). Using the parable of the Good Samaritan, Jesus identifies one's neighbor as anyone who crosses one's path, even an undesirable individual (vv. 29-37). While Jesus intends to found the commandment of love primarily on the Decalog, he may have had in mind a wider application to the entire Torah, and possibly to all of the Old Testament teachings (cf. Matthew's addition "all the law and the prophets" [Matt. 22:40]; cf. Talmud *b. Šabb.* 88a: "the threefold Torah").

B. John. Although John does not record Jesus' discourse with the Pharisee, he does, in his own way, reflect on the link between law and love. John records that just before his trial Jesus issued to his disciples a "new commandment" (Gk. *entolē kainē*): they ought to love one another even as their Teacher and Master had loved them before (John 13:34). The new dimension of this commandment is Christians' mutual affection for one another based on Christ's love for them. Actually, this love commandment is an old commandment, as 1 John 2:7; 3:11 clearly teach. At any rate, it became one of the distinguishing features of the early Church (so Tertullian *Apol.* 39).

COMMANDMENTS, TEN. *See* TEN COMMANDMENTS.

COMMEND.† To praise or to present as worthy of confidence. Aware that some Corinthians had challenged his apostolic authority, Paul asks rhetorically whether he is commending himself again (2 Cor. 3:1; Gk. *synístēmi* "stand with"). He answers with an emphatic "no," for the local church is the apostle's letter of recommendation, since the hearts of the membership (so RSV) — as also Paul's (so KJV, JB, NIV, following Gk. *hēmōn*) — had been touched by God for all to see (v. 2). The work he did at Corinth as a servant of Christ, and the results of that work, were his credentials (v. 3). The apostle does not object to praise prudently given (cf. 4:2; 6:4ff.) — in fact he scolds his church for not granting him more respect (12:11). But he refused to follow the unethical practices of the so-called "false apostles," whose credentials were deceptive (10:12) and who commended themselves beyond propriety.

Some commentators believe that Paul did not frown on issuing genuine letters of recommendation, since, e.g., at 1 Cor. 16:10-12 he recommends Timothy to the church at Corinth.

COMMENTARY (from Lat. *commentarius* "annotation").† A work which explains, analyzes, or expounds upon a biblical book or the whole of Scripture. In its original sense it comprised a narrative or historical account, and as such certain works are cited as sources for the Chronicler's history — the Commentary on the Book of Kings (2 Chr. 24:27) and the "story" (Heb. *miḏrāš* "exposition"; NIV "annotations"; JB "Midrash") of the prophet Iddo (13:22).

In Jewish practice, the earliest commentaries on Scripture were those developed for the Jews who returned from the Exile, many of whom could no longer understand the Hebrew language. Originally oral Aramaic paraphrases of the Hebrew text (Neh. 8:8), these explanations were much later written down. Two basic types of midrash developed, the halachic midrash which deals with the legal portions of the canon and the haggadic midrash, a homiletical exposition of the nonlegal portions. The Targum is an Aramaic translation of the Hebrew text dating to the postexilic period; an early form of exegetical work, it is actually a paraphrase. The Talmud represents a collection of rabbinical interpretations of the Law, commenting upon the written law and applying it to Jewish conditions in the period from *ca.* the fourth century B.C. through the sixth century A.D. Extensive rabbinical exegesis in the Middle Ages sought to determine the literal sense of the Scriptures, as well as their allegorical, ethical or homiletical, and mystical meanings.

With the acceptance of the New Testament writings as authoritative, the early Christians developed various means of verse-by-verse exposition on the books of both the Old and New Testaments. Although the earliest known work is that of the Gnostic Heracleon (*ca.* A.D. 180), many of the Church Fathers produced works which are significant not only for their treatment of the biblical text but also for the foundation they provided for Christian doctrine. Among the early commentators two distinct schools of interpretation developed. That of Origen and the Alexandrian commentators was highly allegorical, focusing on the literal, moral, and spiritual aspects of the books. The Antiochian school, represented by Chrysostom, was quite literal and employed a grammatical style of exegesis.

Since the advance of biblical criticism in the nineteenth century, commentaries have sought to elucidate the text in terms of its historical setting (author, date, and, more recently, social, political, and economic matrices), literary character (genre, structure, and function), textual reliability, and philological and grammatical insights. Other works are more popular, stressing exposition of the various passages and their application to contemporary circumstances.

COMMISSION, GREAT. * Jesus' command that his followers "make disciples of all nations" (Matt. 28:18-20), meaning to present the gospel to Gentiles as well as Jews. In view of the reluctance to admit Gentiles even as early as Paul's ministry, as well as the use of the trinitarian formula (v. 19), it has been suggested that this statement was attributed to Jesus by followers of a later time (e.g., second century A.D.), when the universality of the Christian message had been recognized by the early Church.

COMMON (Heb. *ḥōl*; Gk. *koinós*).† In the Old Testament that which is not "holy" or consecrated is considered to be common, such as "common bread" (1 Sam. 21:4) as opposed to the Bread of the Presence. Common people (Lev. 4:27; Heb. *'am hā'āreṣ* "people of the land") are "ordinary" people rather than priests or political rulers.

In the New Testament the concept is primarily that of universality, indicating that which is shared by all, such as common faith (Tit. 1:4) or salvation (Jude 3). In certain occurrences it also indicates that which is ritually unclean (cf. Acts 10:14-15, 28).

COMMUNION. *See* FELLOWSHIP.

COMMUNITY OF GOODS. A form of communal life practiced in the early Church, whereby material goods as well as spiritual qualities were shared. At the end of Peter's stirring address at Pentecost, Luke adds that the recent converts at Jerusalem "had all things in common" (Gk. *eíchon hápanta koiná*). He explained that they had sold all of their property to provide for the poor (Acts 2:44-45). While there are parallels with the Qumran community, the members of the infant Christian church disposed of their possessions voluntarily, unlike those in the Qumran community who were required to share private property. At 4:36-37 Luke mentions a man named Barnabas who, of his own free will, sold a field and gave the proceeds to the apostles. While the account may suggest that all who had possessions or property ("as many as," 4:34) shared their belongings with the poor, this is misleading. For one, Mary, the mother of John, kept her home (12:12).

The apostles who supervised the distribution of money for the poor (Acts 4:35) did not neglect the needy among the Christians. When some of the Greek-speaking widows complained that they had been bypassed, seven men were appointed to manage the distribution of food and goods more equitably (6:1-6).

The ideal of a community of goods was soon abused. At Acts 5:1-11 Luke records the scheme of Ananias and Sapphira, who pretended to have given all of the proceeds from the sale of their property to the apostles, while in reality they had given only a part. Peter rebuked the husband for his deception, but never challenged him for owning property; indeed, it was his to keep or to sell, and the profit was his to disperse as he wished (5:2-4). However, shortly thereafter this communal life was discontinued.

Although Paul is silent about "Christian communism," he does warn against weakening the bond of "common faith" (Tit. 1:4) in relationships with nonbelievers (2 Cor. 6:15); this bond, he says, is strengthened by the Spirit who motivates the faithful to act for the "common good" (1 Cor. 12:7), which would include giving to the needy (Rom. 12:13).

COMPASSION. *See* MERCY.

CONANIAH [kŏn'ə nī'ə] (Heb. *kônanyāhû* "the Lord has established").

1. A Levite entrusted with the supervision of the contributions, the tithes, and the dedicated things during the reign of King Hezekiah (2 Chr. 31:12-13; KJV "Cononiah").

2. A chief among the Levites who contributed to the Passover offering at the time of King Josiah (2 Chr. 35:9).

CONCUBINE (Heb. *pîlegeš*).† A female slave responsible primarily for bearing children to insure continuation of the family name (e.g., Gen. 16:2-4; 30:3). Accordingly, she was regarded as a member of the family (2 Sam. 19:5; 1 Kgs. 11:3; Dan. 5:2-3) and as a legitimate avenue for succession and inheritance (1 Chr. 1:32; cf. Gen. 25:6). Access to the royal concubines was viewed as a legal claim to the throne (2 Sam. 3:7; 16:21-22), hence they were accorded special protection (20:3; Esth. 2:14). Concubines were viewed with affection by their husbands (Judg. 19:1-3), and any assault on their well-being might be cause for vengeance (cf. 19:29). Although frequently their function was to provide sexual gratification ("man's delight," Eccl. 2:8), they might also be given considerable responsibility (2 Sam. 15:16; 20:3).

CONDEMN.† To judge, generally in the negative sense of finding someone guilty. In the Old Testament (most often Heb. *rāša'*) such judgment usually is associated with divine action against the guilty (1 Kgs. 8:32) or unrighteous (Ps. 34:21). The basic meaning of the numerous Greek terms related to this concept (e.g., Gk. *krínō, kríma, krísis*) is to discern or distinguish, but in usage they have derived the negative sense of "determining guilt." Both God (Mark 12:40 par. Luke 20:47; Rom. 8:3) and mankind (Matt. 12:7; Heb. 11:7; cf. Luke 6:37) are depicted as passing judgment.

CONDUIT (Heb. *tᵉ'ālâ* "watercourse"). A water channel or tunnel. According to 2 Kgs. 18:17 par. Isa. 36:2 a contingent of the Assyrian army halted at "the conduit of the upper pool," probably just outside the gate of Jerusalem near the highway leading to the Fuller's Field but within calling distance of the palace. Some commentators identify this conduit, which connected the upper and lower pools (so Isa. 22:9), with a site north of the city, while others suggest a site south of the city. It was at this same location that Ahaz received the divine prophecy concerning the Syro-Ephraimite War (Isa. 7:3). To prevent the enemy from sabotaging this open channel and thus causing a water shortage in the city, Hezekiah built an underground conduit to bring water from the Upper Gihon spring into the city (2 Kgs. 20:20).

CONFESSION.† A declaration associated with worship; it may be either the admission of sin or the profession of faith.

I. Terminology

The Hebrew terms most frequently used to indicate confession also bear the root meaning "to praise," thus underscoring the range of meaning of the English word. The hiphil of Heb. *yāḏâ* means "praise" (e.g., Gen. 49:8) and "confess" (Prov. 28:13). At Josh. 7:19 the RSV renders the term "praise" (JB "pay homage"; KJV "make confession"), in contrast to "acknowledge" at 1 Kgs. 8:33, 35 par. (also at Job 40:14; Ps. 32:5), where the context of repentance (KJV, NIV "confess") would still allow for an element of praise (so JB). Likewise, Heb. *tôḏâ* can be rendered "praise" (e.g., Ps. 26:7, NIV; RSV, KJV, JB "thanksgiving") or "confession" (Ezra 10:11; JB "give thanks").

The principal New Testament word for "confess" (always so rendered by the KJV) is Gk. *homologéō* "say the same thing," perhaps to repeat what God has already said or to declare together (in the congregation; cf. Lat. *confitēri*, from *com* "with" and *fateri* "confess," akin to *fari* "speak"). Usually the RSV renders the term "confess," but at Matt. 10:32 par.; Acts 23:8; Heb. 11:13; 2 John 7 (but see 1 John 4:15) it

is translated "acknowledge" (JB usually "declare"), and at Acts 24:14 (cf. John 1:20) it reads "admit" (see JB, NIV). Cognates are Gk. *homología* ("confession"; 1 Tim. 6:12 [JB "profession"], 13 [JB "spoke the truth"]; 2 Cor. 9:13; Heb. 3:1 [JB "religion"]; 4:14), *exomologéō* ("confess"; Matt. 3:6 par.; Acts 19:18; Phil. 2:11 [JB "acclaim"]; Jas. 5:16; Rev. 3:5 [NIV, JB "acknowledge"]) and "praise" (Rom. 14:11; 15:9) and *anthomologéomai* ("gave thanks," Luke 2:38).

II. Old Testament

Mosaic law stipulated that the Israelites, when guilty of iniquity, should confess their sins (e.g., Lev. 26:40); sometimes they were also required to make an offering to the Lord (Lev. 5:5ff.), while at other times they had to make restitution to whomever had been wronged (Num. 5:7). As a representative of God's people, Aaron, the high priest, was obligated to confess Israel's sin on the Day of Atonement (Lev. 16:21). Outstanding examples of personal confession made on behalf of the Israelites are those by Solomon (1 Kgs. 8:31ff.) and, after the Exile, by Ezra (Ezra 10:1), Nehemiah (Neh. 1:6), and Daniel (Dan. 9:4, 20).

When the Israelites made a confession of sin, they expected that God would forgive them (e.g., Ps. 32:5). It is interesting to note the connection between the confession of sin and the confession of faith, which is an expression of praise to God; for example, Ps. 32, which many consider the prime example of a penitential psalm, is actually a psalm of thanksgiving.

III. New Testament

The New Testament community continued to link the confession of personal or collective sin with confessions of praise. John the Baptist baptized penitent Jews upon confession of their sins (Matt. 3:6; par.), and Jesus included such a confession in his parable of the prodigal son (Luke 15:18).

Although in the New Testament people most commonly confessed their sins to God (1 John 1:9), in two instances people confess to others: Luke 17:4 par., where Jesus urges his disciples to forgive whoever repents of wrongdoing against them; and Jas. 5:16, where James pleads for mutual confession of sins. The Roman Catholic notion of "auricular confession," lit. "confession to the ear" (of a priest), summarized at the Council of Trent (1551) as being of divine origin and necessary for salvation, is ascribed to these texts.

In addition, Jesus Christ can be confessed, as he was by John the Baptist when asked whether this was the promised Messiah (John 1:20, 29-34) and later by Peter at Caesarea Philippi (Matt. 16:13-16 par.). According to Paul (Rom. 10:9-10) a confession of Christ's lordship is necessary to salvation, and according to John (1 John 4:2-3) a sincere declaration of Christ's incarnation is a mark of genuine faith. At Phil. 2:5-10 Paul gives his own confession of faith, adding that Christ's exaltation summons every person to confess him as Lord (v. 11).

There were various reasons for the New Testament community to encourage such confessions of faith. Heresies no doubt influenced the Church (e.g., 1 John 4:2-3), and soon the practice arose of requiring those believers eager to be baptized to recite a public confession. In the face of persecution the faithful were to affirm their loyalty to their Savior; Paul cites the example of Christ giving a "good confession" before Pilate (1 Tim. 3:1). These confessions express the content of the early Church's belief (see 1 Tim. 3:16), as later confessions of faith would continue to do.

The New Testament also records instances of praise as such. Anna "gave thanks to God" at the birth of Jesus (Luke 2:38), and the author of Hebrews urges believers to praise God and acknowledge his name (Heb. 13:15).

Bibliography. O. Cullmann, *The Earliest Christian Confessions* (London: 1949); J. N. D. Kelly, *Early Christian Creeds* (London: 1950); J. T. Sanders, *The New Testament Christological Hymns: Their Historical Religious Background.* SNTSMS 15 (New York: 1971).

CONFIRMATION.* A rite fulfilling the vow or acknowledging and renewing the sacrament of baptism (cf. Gk. *bebaíōsis*). Its beginnings may be traced to the laying on of hands (Acts 8:14-17; Heb. 6:2) and the receiving of the Holy Spirit which accompanied that act (e.g., Eph. 1:13; 4:30; but cf. Acts 2:38). Generally administered, at various ages, to those who have completed a course of instruction in the basic elements of the Christian faith and, in some instances, of a prescribed confessional catechism, the rite has come to represent initiation into full membership in the church. In Roman Catholic practice confirmation traditionally has been administered by the bishop and marked by anointing with oil; since 1971 the rite has been celebrated during the Mass, generally by the priest, who baptizes adults or receives individuals from another branch of the Church.

CONGREGATION (Heb. *ʿēḏâ, qāhāl*; Gk. *ekklēsía*).† Generally a gathering of various types (e.g., Job 15:34; RSV "company"; cf. Ps. 22:16; 82:1), but more specifically the popular assembly or the Israelite religious community. Heb. *ʿēḏâ* (RSV usually "congregation"; from *yʿd* "appoint") refers to the entire community of Israel, particularly that of the wilderness wanderings (Exod. 12:3, 6, 19, 47, "congregation of Israel"; Num. 27:17, "congregation of the Lord"; cf. Lev. 8:4-5), and occurs most frequently in passages attributed to the Priestly source (Exodus-Judges). Heb. *qāhāl* (RSV "assembly"; perhaps from *qwl* "speak") indicates more particularly the gathered community, assembled both for worship and for legislative or judicial purposes, such as the distribution of land and deliberation on internal matters (e.g., Deut. 5:22); the term predominates in the Deuteronomistic history (Deuteronomy-2 Kings) and Psalms. For the most part the LXX translates *ʿēḏâ* as Gk. *synagōgḗ* and *qāhāl* as *ekklēsía*.

Some Jewish exegetes suggest that Heb. *ʿēḏâ* in the Pentateuch indicated the Sanhedrin or supreme court of justice, but this view has met with substantial opposition.

It is sometimes proposed that Gk. *ekklēsía* in the New Testament be rendered "congregation" in order to distinguish between the universal church and local bodies of believers. Although the term sometimes does refer to such local congregations (e.g., Gal. 1:2; 1 Thess. 1:1), it is also used to indicate the Church in general (Eph. 1:22; Col. 1:18). *See* CHURCH.

CONIAH. *See* JEHOIACHIN.

CONONIAH (2 Chr. 31:12-13, KJV). *See* CONANIAH. 1.

CONQUEST.† Standard designation of the Israelite entrance into or occupation of Canaan and the corresponding historical period. Recorded primarily in Num. 13-14, 21-32; Josh. 1-14; and Judg. 1:1-2:5, the process has come to be dated to the late thirteenth century B.C. (those who construct biblical chronology upon a literal interpretation of 1 Kgs. 6:1 place it as early as 1409).

Three major interpretations have been proposed to explain Israel's sudden appearance in the land. The most commonly accepted view, generally thought to represent the literal intent of the biblical accounts, is that the twelve tribes of Israel under Joshua's leadership mounted an all-out conquest of Canaan in order to annihilate completely the previous inhabitants, thereby supplanting Canaanite society with Israelite culture and religion (cf. Josh. 10:40). However, scholars have noted differences in the biblical narratives. The account as presented in Numbers and Joshua depicts all Israel acting under a single leader; based at Gilgal they conquer all or much of the territory west of the Jordan river, which they inhabit following the assembly at Shechem (Josh. 24). In Judges, however, the tribes act individually, with no national leader, and the land west of the Jordan remains to be conquered. While some defend the literal interpretation on the basis of the proleptic or programmatic nature of Hebrew narrative, others see here a conflation of various localized traditions redacted to constitute a common religious tradition or "confession." Archaeological evidence indicates widespread destruction of Canaanite cities in this approximate period followed by the introduction of a new form of culture; at the same time, excavations show that some major sites which figure in the biblical accounts (e.g., Jericho, Ai, Arad) were unoccupied during the entire period concerned.

An alternate interpretation, that of the immigration or settlement of the Israelites, has been advanced since the late nineteenth century. According to this view, numerous waves of "proto-Israelites," of which the Exodus participants were but a small portion, entered Palestine from the time of the patriarchs through that of David. While a certain amount of conflict was involved, the overall process was peaceful, including treaties and intermarriage with the Canaanites.

A more recent position is the model of a peasant revolt, the uprising of native Canaanites against their oppressive city-state aristocracies. The widespread revolution is thought to have been associated with the activities of the ʿApiru (*see* HABIRU), ethnically diverse bands of "outlaws" opposed to the existing social and political orders. Whether precipitated by or simply coinciding with the appearance in Canaan of Israelites fleeing Egypt, the newly independent

Canaanite masses are held to have identified with Yahweh's saving acts in history, which they embraced as their own common tradition.

Each of these theories has merit in view of the literary and traditio-historical aspects of the biblical accounts and can find some support in archaeological evidence, yet each also remains open to debate. Adequate understanding of the emergence of Israel in Canaan may ultimately be gained from a combination of these major theories or from other lesser-known views (e.g., the "frontier" model, whereby Israelite settlements gradually expanded their spheres of influence until the entire land came under Israelite control).

Bibliography. N. K. Gottwald, *The Tribes of Yahweh* (Maryknoll, N.Y.: 1979); M. Weippert, *The Settlement of the Israelite Tribes in Palestine.* SBT 21, 2nd ser. (1971).

CONSCIENCE. The inner voice of a person's spirit which attempts to answer for his deeds and calls him to account before norms that are felt to be binding for himself, his fellow man, and society as a whole. Although no Hebrew term exactly parallels the English word, the corresponding concept is indeed present in the Old Testament. It is said that David's "heart smote him" after he had cut off Saul's skirt (1 Sam. 24:5), that he would have "pangs of conscience" if Nabal and his servants were killed (25:31), and that his "heart smote him" again after he had taken a census of the people (2 Sam. 24:10). At Job 27:6, Job testifies that "my heart does not reproach me for any of my days." In each of these passages, the Hebrew term for "heart" (*lēḇ*) can be interpreted as "conscience." At Job 27:6 the LXX translates the term as *syneídēsis*, the Greek equivalent of Latin *conscientia* "conscience," derived from a verb meaning "to be aware or conscious of something." The Greek term occurs approximately thirty times in the New Testament, some twenty of which are in the letters traditionally attributed to Paul — twelve times in 1-2 Corinthians alone. Its presence in the KJV at John 8:9 (RSV mg. omits the phrase), however, is based upon inferior manuscripts.

The conscience may be unsettled when a person does not subject himself to leadership that has received its authority from God (Rom. 13:5); it can also serve to confirm the law or the Holy Spirit (Rom. 2:15; 9:1). At 1 Cor. 8:7ff.; 10:25ff., the term indicates that mankind has an inner knowledge of the difference between right and wrong, and in this context a weak or strong conscience refers to that of a weak or strong person. The conscience is not invulnerable and cannot serve as an ultimate guide, for it is subject to error and can become corrupt (Titus 1:15). 1 Tim. 4:2 speaks of "liars whose consciences are seared." In contrast to such an evil conscience from which one's heart must be cleansed (Heb. 10:22), the New Testament speaks of a "good" and a "clear" conscience (Acts 23:1; 1 Tim. 1:5, 19; 3:9; 2 Tim. 1:3; Heb. 13:18; 1 Pet. 3:16, 21), i.e., one that is aware of standing in the grace of Christ and under the norm of his gospel. Such a purification of the conscience could not be effected by the sacrifices of the old covenant (Heb. 9:9), for it required the atonement of the blood of Christ (v. 14).

Gk. *syneídēsis* can also refer to a more general awareness, without the moral element of conscience;

the RSV translates it as "consciousness" at Heb. 10:2 and as "mindful" at 1 Pet. 2:19.

CONSECRATE (Heb. *qāḏaš* "set apart," *millē' yaḏ*, lit. "fill the hand," *nāzar* "dedicate"; Gk. *hagiázō* "sanctify").† To dedicate or ordain a person for sacred office (e.g., Exod. 29:33; Lev. 16:32) or an object for sacred purposes (e.g., 2 Chr. 31:6; Ezek. 43:26). See SANCTIFY, CONSECRATE.

CONSTELLATIONS.† The Israelites were familiar with the existence of several stars, including some of the constellations. At 2 Kgs. 23:5 Heb. *mazzālôṯ* (which resembles Akk. *manzaltu* "planet") apparently refers to the zodiac, which the idolatrous Israelites worshiped in addition to the sun and the moon (KJV "planets"). Heb. *mazzārôṯ* refers either to the southern constellation of the zodiac or to the morning star (Job 38:32; see JB, NIV mg.); in this beautifully poetic description of the heavenly host (RSV, KJV "Mazzaroth") God reminds man that the stars are beyond feeble human control. "The chambers of the south" (Heb. *ḥaḏᵉrê têmān*), the constellations of the southern zodiac (NIV "constellations"), are specified as stars created by God (Job 9:9). According to Isa. 13:10, the constellations (Heb. *kᵉsîlîm*) will cease to give light on the Day of Judgment (*see also* ORION).

CONVERSION (Heb. *šûḇ*; Gk. *epistrophḗ*).* A "turning" or "returning" of God to (Num. 25:4; Josh. 7:26) or from mankind (Josh. 24:20), or of mankind to (Deut. 4:30) or from God (1 Sam. 15:11). See also REGENERATION; REPENTANCE.

COPING (Heb. *ṭapᵉḥâ*). Probably a structural detail (JB "wood course"), mentioned in the description of Solomon's royal palace (1 Kgs. 7:9). If this Hebrew term refers to the corbels (cf. Gesenius [p. 324], "projecting stones on the tops of which beams rest") below the roof beams, then the expression "from the foundation to the coping" simply means that the entire wall — from bottom to top (cf. NIV "eaves") — was covered with precious stones.

COPPER. A common reddish metallic element, known in biblical times. Whereas in the Early Bronze Age (3000-2000 B.C.) copper and tin and possibly other metals were melted together to make bronze, in the Middle Bronze Age (*ca.* 2000 B.C.) the use of copper increased considerably. It is possible that the clasps used for holding up the tabernacle curtains were made of copper (Heb. *nᵉḥōšeṯ* "copper or bronze"; Exod. 26:11; but RSV, NIV, JB "bronze"; KJV "brass" [perhaps unknown at that time]), for copper adzes (dating from before the time of the Exodus) have been discovered.

Gk. *chalkós*, rendered "copper" at Matt. 10:9, was a coin worth two "mites"; it was given by a poor widow and exemplified the spirit of generosity (so KJV; Mark 12:42 par. Luke 21:2, Gk. *leptón*); it was one of the smallest copper coins circulated in Palestine.

Copper was mined in the region between the Dead Sea and the Gulf of Aqaba (Deut. 8:9; cf. Job 28:2, "copper smelted from the ore"; Heb. *naḥûš*; KJV "bronze"). At Ezek. 22:18, 20 the RSV renders Heb. *nḥšt* "bronze" (NIV, JB "copper"), but at 24:11 "copper" (JB "bronze").

COPTIC (from Arab. *qubt* "Egyptian"; cf. Gk. *Aigyptios*).† The final phase of the ancient Egyptian language, derived from the spoken form of Late Egyptian, the administrative tongue of the New Kingdom (sixteenth century B.C.); it was used primarily by the native peasant populace. Coptic received its written form from the artificial literary demotic (*ca.* second century A.D.), supplementing the twenty-four characters of the Greek alphabet with seven forms borrowed from demotic. Unlike other forms of Egyptian, it was written from left to right. Although the vocabulary was greatly influenced by Greek, the grammar and syntax derived from Egyptian (e.g., three-consonantal roots, nominal sentences).

At least six dialects of Coptic have been attested, the most important of which were Sahidic and Bohairic. By the fourth century Sahidic was the standard literary language of the Nile Valley (cf. Arab. *al-saʿīd* "Upper Egypt"). Bohairic, which developed in the western Nile Delta, became the official ecclesiastical language in the eleventh century; its use survives in the liturgy of the Egyptian Monophysite church. Long regarded as secondary to the official Greek instituted by Alexander the Great, Coptic was further restricted following the Arab conquest of A.D. 640; by the fourteenth century it was virtually a dead language.

In addition to a number of Gnostic writings among the Nag Hammadi manuscripts, several Coptic versions of the Bible are attested; these contribute significantly to textual criticism, especially with regard to the LXX. Portions of the New Testament were translated into Sahidic by the early third century, and the entire Bible may have been translated as early as 270; the Old Testament portion may be based on Origen's LXX text. The Bohairic version, translated independently of the Sahidic, became the standard Coptic version; it may date from the fourth century, although the only extant manuscripts date to *ca.* the thirteenth century.

COPY. Duplicate of a document. The practice of copying official letters was familiar to the ancients. The book of Ezra refers to at least three such copied letters — one written by unhappy colonists to King Artaxerxes (Aram. **paršegen* "copy"; Ezra 4:11), one by Artaxerxes in response (v. 23), and one to Darius by a provincial governor who feared a revolt by the Jews (5:6). A copy of Haman's decree to annihilate the Jews (Heb. *paṯšegen* [O. Pers. "what is announced for the second time"]; Esth. 3:14) was made for each of the Persian provinces, and Mordecai gave a copy to his cousin Queen Esther (4:8-9). Later, copies of a modified decree, which would permit the Jews to defend themselves, were again sent to the provinces (8:13).

The practice was certainly known also among the Jews. The proverbs of Solomon were copied by the scribes of King Hezekiah (Prov. 25:1; JB "transcribed"). At God's instruction, Jeremiah retained for

safekeeping an "open copy" of the deed to a piece of land he had purchased at Anathoth (Jer. 32:11, 14).

Two interesting instances are related at Deut. 17:18 and Josh. 8:32 (Heb. *mišneh* "double, copy"). According to the first, the "ideal king" would make a copy of the law (possibly the legislation concerning kingship mentioned at Deut. 17:14-17 or a larger section of the law of Deuteronomy) and would read it daily in order to be familiar with the law and behave with respect for God. According to the second reference, Joshua inscribed upon ordinary stones "a copy of the law of Moses" (made either by Moses or by Joshua), perhaps the Decalog (Exod. 20:1-17 or the slightly different version at Deut. 5:6-21).

In the New Testament the author of Hebrews considers the Old Testament sanctuary a "copy" (Heb. 8:5; Gk. *hypodeígma*) of the heavenly sanctuary (KJV "example").

COR [kōr] (Heb. *kōr*). Usually a dry measure a little over 220 l. (58 gal.), as at 1 Kgs. 4:22, where it is said that Solomon's daily provision consisted of thirty cors of fine flour (about 6.5 kl. [185 bu.]; KJV, JB "measures") and sixty cors of meal (about 13 kl. [370 bu.]). *See* WEIGHTS AND MEASURES.

CORAL (Heb. *rāʾmôṯ, penînîm*). The calcareous or horny skeletal deposit produced by the anthozoan polyps, considered a precious commodity. At Ezek. 27:16 coral is listed along with agate as an item of trade between Tyre and Edom. Heb. *rāʾmôṯ* (perhaps "red coral") occurs with crystal as a comparison to the value of wisdom (Job 28:18). At Lam. 4:7 Heb. *penînîm* (RSV "coral"; cf. Job 28:18, "pearls"; KJV "rubies"; NEB "red coral") is used to describe the human body.

CORBAN [kôrʹbăn] (Heb. *qorbān*; Gk. *korban*). An offering dedicated to God, as instituted in postexilic Jewish practice. At Mark 7:11 (par. Matt. 15:5, which omits the term) Jesus decries stringent adherence to ritual to the detriment of human need, citing a person who dedicated to the temple treasury as a "gift to God" (Gk. *dōron*) — thus making inaccessible — funds which would normally have provided support for his parents. It may have been the understanding of such an inviolable dedication that prompted the priests to regard Judas' "blood money" (perhaps taken from the temple treasury; cf. Zech. 11:13) as dedicated to an inappropriate objective and thus unacceptable for religious purposes.

CORE (Jude 11, KJV). *See* KORAH 1.

CORIANDER SEED [kôrʹĭ ănʹdər] (Heb. *gāḏ*; Gk. *kórian*). The fruit of an umbelliferous annual plant (*Coriandrum sativum* L.) which when dried produces a pleasant aroma. Contemporary Arabs still use it on bread and small cakes.

Coriander seed is compared with manna at Exod. 16:31, where manna is said to resemble coriander fruit in shape (but not color) and at Num. 11:7.

CORINTH [kôrʹĭnth] (Gk. *Korinthos*). A city located about 2 km. (1 mi.) south of the narrow isthmus con-

The marketplace of ancient Corinth with the upper part of the city (the Acrocorinth) in the background (Ewing Galloway)

necting mainland Greece with the Peloponnesian peninsula. With the Gulf of Corinth on the west and the Gulf of Aegina (or the Saronic Gulf) on the east. the city was well situated for ocean trade, especially as a transfer port. Merchants from Italy and Spain could go as far as the western harbor of Lechaeum, while those from the east and from Egypt could moor their vessels in the harbor at Cenchreae about 11 km. (7 mi.) east of the city. A specially constructed road (Gk. *díolkos* "haul-across") permitted small ships to be pulled overland across the isthmus rather than attempt the dangerous Cape Malea at the southern point of the Peloponnesus. The Roman emperor Nero planned to cut a canal some 5 km. (3½ mi.) long through the isthmus, but it was not until 1893 that the plan was finally realized.

I. History

Although the site was inhabited as early as the fourth millennium B.C., Corinth first gained significant military and commercial power during the eighth century, when the Greek city-state began establishing colonies in the west. The height of the city's prosperity and fame was reached *ca.* 600.

Corinth sided with Sparta against Athens in the Peloponnesian War (431-404). It became the center of a Hellenic league under Alexander the Great, but was razed by the Roman general Lucius Mummius in 146 B.C. after an anti-Roman uprising.

Rebuilt by Julius Caesar in 44 B.C. and settled with Roman colonists, Corinth became the capital of Achaia and the seat of the Roman government. It surpassed even Athens as a center of science and culture, and as the hub of intercourse between Romans, Greeks, Jews, Syrians, and Egyptians.

Corinth also saw its share of less august attitudes and activities. The city's aristocracy followed only one tradition — the accumulation of wealth — which attracted like-minded sailors. As a result, Corinth was known and identified far and wide as a city of evil, immorality, and frivolousness (cf. Gk. *korinthiázomai* "Corinthianize," i.e., "practice immorality"). The temple dedicated to Aphrodite, built on the highest point of the city, housed some one thousand female priests, who often engaged in religious prostitution with both locals and foreigners (cf. Gk. *Korinthia kórē* "Corinthian girl," i.e., "Corinthian prostitute"). Paul's first letter to the Corinthians particularly reflects the young Christian church's struggle with sexual immorality, which in principle it had abandoned but which, nevertheless, still strongly tempted those believers who did not sever all contact with their fellow Corinthians.

During the second century (*ca.* A.D. 122) Emperor

Hadrian enhanced Corinth by constructing many beautiful public buildings. The city's prosperity continued well into the Middle Ages, when in 1458 the Saracens captured it.

A tremendous earthquake destroyed Corinth in 1858, and once again its inhabitants began to rebuild the ancient city, this time about 5 km. (3 mi.) from the former site.

II. Archaeology

Excavators have been able to determine, to a considerable degree, the location of the important buildings of the ancient Roman city. Corinth was built on two terraces, against the background of an imposing hill called the Acrocorinth (elevation 575 m. [1886 ft.]), which served as a fortress and where the famed temple of Aphrodite was located. The road from Lechaeum was flanked by shops as it neared the agora; a Latin inscription, bearing the word *macellum* ("market"; cf. 1 Cor. 10:25, Gk. *mákellon*; RSV "meat market"), has been discovered near the agora. Between the main shops was the platform (Gk. *béma*) where Paul was brought before the tribunal for teaching contrary to Jewish law (Acts 18:12).

North of the agora was a large basilica, a rectangular hall with two rows of columns, which was used for commercial and judicial functions. The temple of Apollo was west of the basilica, with its Peribolos or paved court to the east across the Lechaeum road. A piece of white marble with an inscription reading "Synagogue of the Hebrews" (Gk. [*Syna*]*gōgē Ebr*[*ai-ōn*]) has been discovered; it appears to have been the lintel over the doorway of a Jewish synagogue, most likely a successor of that in which Paul preached (Acts 18:5).

Of special interest is the Latin inscription *ERASTVS.PRO.AED/S.P.STRAVIT* ("In return for his aedileship [a public office] Erastus has laid the pavement at his own expense"). It may have been laid during the second half of the first century, possibly by Erastus himself, whom Paul calls the city treasurer (Rom. 16:23). Upon assuming the office of curator (*aedilis*) Erastus, a convert and Paul's friend, may have donated the pavement to the city.

Bibliography. American School of Classical Studies at Athens, *Ancient Corinth: A Guide to the Excavations,* 6th ed. (Athens: 1954); J. Murphy-O'Connor, *St. Paul's Corinth* (Wilmington: 1983); G. Theissen, *The Social Setting of Pauline Christianity: Essays on Corinth* (Philadelphia: 1982).

CORINTHIANS, LETTERS TO THE.† The seventh and eighth books of the New Testament, written by Paul.

I. Paul's Ministry at Corinth

Compelled to leave Athens, Paul continued his journey west to Corinth, perhaps slightly discouraged by his apparent lack of success among the Gentiles and Greece's intellectuals (1 Cor. 2:1-5). At Corinth he took his abode with Aquila and Priscilla, who were banned from Rome by a recent edict of Emperor Claudius (Acts 18:1-3). Initially, Paul did not do much mission work, intent as he was on working with the Jews (Acts 18:4); but when Silas and Timothy —

whom he had sent to Thessalonica (1 Thess. 3:1-2) — arrived, Paul vigorously resumed his missionary labors. Because the Jews did not accept his message concerning the Messiah, Paul severed his relationship with them and turned to the Gentiles (Acts 18:5-6).

During the proconsulship of Gallio, the Jews caused an incident, thwarting Paul's work and forcing him to leave sometime later, yet were unable to have him convicted. All in all, Paul stayed some eighteen months in that city (*ca.* A.D. 51; Acts 18:11), encouraged by the Lord's support and announcement that Corinth was a fertile mission field (vv. 9-10). He established a church which was predominantly Gentile, yet included some Jews (cf. Crispus, the ruler of the synagogue; v. 8).

II. The Corinthian Correspondence

According to 1 Cor. 5:9, Paul wrote a letter to the Corinthians in which he warned them against associating with immoral men; he probably wrote this letter from Ephesus, during his third missionary journey. Apparently the Corinthians did not completely understand Paul's instructions and sent a letter back to him, asking him to clarify such issues as marriage, meat offered to idols, the use of spiritual gifts, and the collection for the Jerusalem church (cf. the recurring phrase "Now concerning. . . ," 7:1; 8:1; 12:1; 16:1). He had, moreover, received alarming news about his church at Corinth from Chloe's household (1:11), who personally told him about the divisions within the congregation. Then Stephanas and Fortunatus paid him a similar visit (16:17), while other Corinthians asked him for advice (7:1). As a result, Paul became familiar with the moral abuses reaching incestuous proportions — a man "living with his father's wife" (his stepmother?) (5:1), lawsuits before secular courts (6:1-6), abuses surrounding the Lord's Supper (11:17-34), and the denial of the resurrection of the flesh (15:12). Prompted by these reports, Paul wrote 1 Corinthians (*ca.* 55), actually his second Corinthian letter (1 Cor. 16:8), from Ephesus.

At 1 Cor. 4:17 Paul states that he "sent" (Gk. *epémpsa*; RSV, KJV [cf. JB]; RSV mg., NIV "am sending") Timothy to the Corinthian church. It is not known whether the letter preceded Timothy or whether Timothy ever arrived at the city of Corinth. Because there is not sufficient information about the time between the sending of the two canonical Corinthian letters, only a probable reconstruction can be given.

In 2 Corinthians (written from Macedonia, possibly *ca.* 56) Paul no longer touches on the points at issue in his first letter. Instead he faces other, more dangerous problems: heretics had penetrated his church and attempted to put the Corinthians into a Jewish straight-jacket. Consequently, the Corinthians began to question Paul's apostolicity, particularly one man who had become Paul's great opponent (2 Cor. 2:5-8). The apostle was kept abreast of these developments, however; perhaps he had paid them a short, "painful" visit (implied at 2:1-2), after which he had to leave deeply hurt and seemingly with no positive result. Sometime afterward he sent a "severe letter" (vv. 3-4) to Corinth, his third Corinthian letter, apparently delivered by Titus. When Titus tarried in his return,

Paul traveled to Troas and, unable to find him there, then to Macedonia (vv. 12-13), where he gladly heard that many of the disturbances had cleared up. This was the setting for Paul's fourth letter, 2 Corinthians.

III. Contents and Teachings

A. *1 Corinthians.* After an introductory thanksgiving (1:4-9), Paul lashes out against the dangers to Christian life posed by secular philosophy (1:18–2:16). The main body of the letter deals with Paul's treatment of a number of important issues, ranging from immorality (ch. 5) to lawsuits (6:1-11), marriage (ch. 7), and meat offered to idols (ch. 8). Reminding the believers of the value of Old Testament examples (10:1-13), and urging them properly to observe the Lord's Supper (11:17-34), Paul composes a magnificent song about the virtue of love (ch. 13), extolling it above the other spiritual gifts discussed in ch. 12. He ends his letter with a defense of the reality of the resurrection (ch. 15) and an admonition that the Corinthians take care of the financial needs of fellow Christians at Jerusalem (16:1-18).

From this outline of the contents of 1 Corinthians it is clear that many abuses had penetrated the church established in a city considered notoriously immoral at that time and exposed to the allurements of philosophical and religious visions. Not a small number of this rather large congregation had yielded to these external pressures, thereby rendering Paul's work of no account. Add to this the warring factions of followers of Paul, Apollos, Cephas, and Christ, and Paul must have interpreted the Corinthian scene with sadness. (*See also* CORINTH).

In his response to this situation Paul answers the questions which the Corinthians themselves had raised in their letter to him and expounds on other matters which he deems equally important for them. (1) Concerning the Corinthian question about marriage and bachelorhood, Paul extols the single life (7:7) if self-control can be retained (v. 8), especially under the present trying circumstances (vv. 26-27; perhaps referring to the return of the Lord); nevertheless, he does not condemn marriage. While his linkage of marriage and lust are puzzling (vv. 1-2, 9, 36), he sees no inherent evil in marriage (vv. 9, 28, 36, 39), though the obligation of mutual love may cause the marriage partners "anxiety" not found among bachelors (vv. 32-34). (*See also* MARRIAGE.) (2) Concerning the question about eating meat offered to idols, he attributes no sin to such a practice because the idol does not have any existence (8:4). Paul stresses, though, that the Corinthians abstain from this practice when it jeopardizes the weaker brother with a strained conscience (vv. 8-12). (3) Concerning the question of the nature of the spiritual gifts, Paul reaffirms that there are several such gifts, all given by the one Spirit (12:4) for the maintenance of the unity of the local church, not for personal aggrandizement. Though acknowledging the value of each of these, even that of speaking in tongues when done properly (14:13), Paul compares them to the greatest Christian gift — the virtue of love which outlasts all others. (*See also* SPIRITUAL GIFTS.) (4) Finally, concerning the question about the collection for the poor Christians at Jerusalem, the Corinthian Christians are to set aside a certain sum each week to be taken to Jerusalem upon Paul's arrival at Corinth (16:1-4).

Other equally crucial matters needed Paul's attention. (1) Instead of breaking up the unity of the church by following their favorite preacher — the apostle Paul, eloquent Apollos, impulsive Peter (Cephas), and a certain Christ (1:12; cf. 3:4) — the Corinthians are to look upon their preachers as human beings in the Lord's service (3:5); they plant and water the Corinthian field while God gives the essential increase (v. 6). (2) Instead of outstripping the Gentiles in sexual immorality (incest; 5:1), the Corinthians are to regard their bodies "a temple of the Holy Spirit" (6:19) with which they "glorify" their God (v. 20). (3) In case they are involved in a lawsuit with fellow believers, they should not seek redress in secular courts but arbitration within the church (6:5); and when called upon, they ought to suffer (rather than inflict) injustice (v. 7). (4) When partaking of the Lord's Supper, the wealthy are to wait for the poor and then celebrate this sacrament together without the use of excessive wine (11:20-22, 33) and in remembrance of the true nature of Christ's broken body (vv. 23-26). (5) Lastly, Paul defends the absolute necessity of the doctrine of the resurrection, a conviction he felt called to preach. Instead of denying the resurrection (stated in the powerful sorites: "If there is no resurrection, then Christ has not been raised; if Christ has not been raised, then our preaching is in vain" [15:13-14]), the Corinthians are to affirm it because Christ's resurrection is the foundation of the belief that the dead will be raised (v. 20). (On the "place" of women, *see* WOMAN).

B. *2 Corinthians.* Although this letter lacks clear-cut divisions, the following general outline can be given. Acquainting the Corinthians with his own recent personal troubles (1:1–2:11) and with his happy reunion with Titus (2:12-17), Paul presents his credentials as the legitimate leader of the church (3:1-18). He knows the nature of his calling (5:1-9) and pleads with his fellow Christians to give their hearts to Christ (6:1-18), while praising those who repented (7:1-16). After an interlude about the collection for the poor at Jerusalem, he resumes the subject of his apostolic authority (10:1-18), answering the challenges of the Judaizers (11:1-29) in spite of his own limitations (11:30–12:8).

Unlike 1 Corinthians, 2 Corinthians addresses an altogether different situation — the Corinthian attack on Paul's apostleship. From 2:14-15 and 7:6-7 it appears that some of the issues debated in the first letter had been heeded, though the Corinthians had not as yet given relief to the poor at Jerusalem. While defending himself against attacks from some of the Corinthians, the apostle reminds fellow believers of their obligation to others; they should have the money ready upon his arrival (9:5) and be willing to part with it cheerfully rather than grudgingly (9:6-7). The subject of his own position in the church is treated in ch. 3. Paul does not need letters of recommendation as hucksters do who peddle their own wares (v. 1), for the congregation is Paul's letter of commendation (v. 2). As in 1 Corinthians, the apostles are not to be put in the spotlight because it is God who deserves the applause (ch. 4) as he acts out his works through human beings. Should the Corinthians be interested in some cases of "boasting," Paul lists his credentials as Christ's servant — child of Abraham, floggings, shipwrecks, personal conversion (ch. 11), going so far as to mention his ecstatic experiences (ch. 12).

Ch. 5 includes two interesting doctrinal teachings, with references to life after death and to the doctrine of the atonement — reconciliation (v. 19), but they are only the undercurrent of the letter.

IV. Integrity

Only a few scholars have seriously questioned the Pauline authorship of the Corinthian letters. For 1 Corinthians, both the external evidence (it is frequently quoted in the early Church as being Pauline) and the internal evidence (it presents a credible picture of Corinth where Paul labored for many months) point to Paul as its author. Concerning 2 Corinthians, while the external evidence may not be as strong as that of 1 Corinthians, both the external and internal evidences indicate sufficiently that Paul did compose it. The distinction in temper and tone between 1–7 (gratitude and joy) and 10–13 (harshness) can be explained on the basis of Paul's recent acquaintance with the heretics; it need not necessarily lead to the view that chs. 10–13 contain parts of lost letters, for the early Church did not mention that. On the other hand, the loss of a few Pauline letters prompted some scholars to construct an apocryphal exchange of letters between Paul and the Corinthian church which has been incorporated into the Acts of Paul.

Bibliography. F. F. Bruce, *I and II Corinthians.* NCBC (1971); J. C. Hurd, *The Origin of 1 Corinthians* 2nd ed. (Macon: 1983); H. Conzelmann, *1 Corinthians.* Hermeneia (1975); D. Georgi, *The Opponents of Paul in Second Corinthians* (Philadelphia: 1986); C. K. Barrett, *The First Epistle to the Corinthians.* HNTC (1968); *The Second Epistle to the Corinthians.* HNTC (1973).

CORMORANT [kôr′mə rənt] (Heb. *šālāḵ*). A sea bird (*Phalacrocorax*, of which there are some thirty species. Some species spend the winter in Palestine, along the coast and the banks of the Sea of Galilee, making their nests on the rocks and in the hollows and crevices. They are exceptional swimmers and divers, able to swallow large fish whole because of the elasticity of their gullets. Their extended bodies and long, slender necks are striking.

As a predatory bird, the cormorant is included among unclean birds (Lev. 11:17; Deut. 14:17). Scholars continue to debate, however, the meaning of Heb. *šālāḵ* ("fisher-owl"; see KoB, 978; cf. Gesenius, p. 829, who calls it a species of pelican).

CORNELIUS [kôr nēl′yəs] (Gk. *Kornēlios*). A Roman centurion in charge of the Italian cohort (Acts 10:1) stationed at Caesarea, the administrative center of the Roman government in Palestine. Luke describes him as "a devout man who feared God" (v. 2). Though not a full-fledged proselyte, Cornelius nevertheless gave alms and prayed "constantly" (v. 2). He may have been numbered among the many Gentiles who had adopted some of the Jewish religious practices.

Having learned in a vision that his behavior was acceptable to the Lord, Cornelius followed God's instruction to send for Peter, who was then stationed in Joppa (vv. 3-7). The apostle, who had been prepared by God for an encounter with a Gentile, returned with Cornelius' servants to the centurion's home (vv. 9-24), where he came to understand that God had intended that the Christian community extend to any and all who feared and obeyed him (vv. 34-43). During the address Peter delivered as a result of his new understanding, the Spirit fell on this group of Romans, and Cornelius and his household were baptized (vv. 44-48).

Luke attaches great significance to this first conversion of a Gentile by placing the account shortly after that of Paul's own conversion. Up to this point, the evangelist had described the Church's impact among the Jews and proselytes; now he shifts the focus to the Gentiles, whose conversion would become the special concern of the apostle Paul (chs. 13–20). Luke continues his narrative with Peter facing opposition to his move to accept a Gentile into the Christian fellowship, and then successfully, if only temporarily, silencing his critics (11:18).

CORNER GATE (Heb. *ša'ar happinnâ, ša'ar happōneh* [2 Chr. 25:23]). One of the gates of Jerusalem, near the northwest angle of the wall and the old Ephraim Gate (2 Kgs. 14:13 par. 2 Chr. 25:23). After Joash of Israel had broken down the city wall between the Corner and Ephraim gates, King Uzziah (*ca.* 750 B.C.) fortified Jerusalem and built a tower at the Corner Gate, in an area which lacked natural protection (2 Chr. 26:9).

The Corner Gate, it seems, was not rebuilt after the Exile, when during Nehemiah's administration the city of Jerusalem was restored. Jeremiah speaks of the future restoration of the northern wall as far as the Corner Gate (Jer. 31:38; KJV "gate of the corner"). If the Corner Gate mentioned at Zech. 14:10 is the same as the "former gate" referred to immediately before (cf. JB "that is to say"; KJV, NIV "first gate"), the gate may still have been in ruins at the time of Zechariah (*ca.* 520).

CORNERSTONE. Usually a large stone supporting two walls at right angles to each other. Heb. *'eḇen pinnâ* translates as the foundation stone (Job 38:6 par. "bases") of the earth, so to speak, and the foundation stone of Zion, and is used metaphorically for God's word of assurance to his people (Isa. 28:16). A similar metaphor may be used at Zech. 10:4 (KJV "corner"). Heb. *zāwît* at Ps. 144:12, translated "cornerstones" in the KJV, can best be rendered "corner pillars" (so RSV; similarly NIV, JB; KoB suggests "house").

Ps. 118:22 mentions a capstone (so NIV; Heb. *rō'š pinnâ* "head of the corner"; JB "keystone"), which had been rejected but is now recalled; this verse refers to the Israelites who were being restored to honor by their covenantal God, an appropriate concern in a psalm that was probably composed and sung at the dedication of the temple as reconstructed by Zerubbabel (444 B.C.).

The New Testament provides two commentaries on Ps. 118:22. In the parable of the defiant tenants (Matt.

21:42 par. Mark 12:10; Luke 20:17) Jesus quotes the psalm to emphasize not only that his authority was challenged and rejected by Jewish priests, but also to assert his future glory. Peter also uses this verse to underscore the penalty for unbelief (1 Pet. 2:7; Gk. *kephalḗ gōnías*). When interrogated by the Sanhedrin, the apostles interpreted the psalm as suggesting not only Christ's suffering but also his ascension and reign over the Church. The broadest application of the psalm is found at Eph. 2:20 where the Church is likened to a building whose foundation is the apostles and prophets, and whose cornerstone (Gk. *akrogōniaíos*) is Christ, supporting both the Jews and the Gentiles.

CORRUPTION, MOUNT OF (Heb. *har-hammašḥît*).* A hill to the east of Jerusalem, probably at the southern end of the Mount of Olives (called *harhammîšhâ* "Mount of the Ointment" in rabbinic writings). Here Solomon built high places for the worship of the Sidonian deity Ashtoreth, the Moabite Chemosh, and the Ammonite Milcom (Molech; 1 Kgs. 11:7, 2 Kgs. 23:13).

COS [kôs] (Gk. *Kōs* "summit"). An island near the coast of Caria, northwest of Rhodes. Paul stopped at Cos at the end of his third missionary journey, en route to Jerusalem through Rhodes (Acts 21:1; KJV "Coos").

Settled by the Greeks *ca.* 1500 B.C., Cos became one of the most beautiful harbors of antiquity. As a Greek city-state it played a significant role in the Delian League during the Peloponnesian War (fifth century), and in 354 succeeded in its revolt against Athens. The island was renowned for its medical school, of which Hippocrates was a member, and a sacred shrine dedicated to Asclepius, the god of medicine. The shrine was excavated by R. Herzog between 1898 and 1907.

COSAM [kō'səm] (Gk. *Kōsam*, transliteration of Heb. *qōsēm* "diviner"). A preexilic ancestor of Jesus (Luke 3:28).

COSMOLOGY. See EARTH; WATER; WORLD.

COTTON (Heb. *karpas*; from Sanskrit *karpāsa*, perhaps through Persian). The fruit fibers of the *Gossypium herbaceum* L., probably imported from India. At Esth. 1:6 it is related that some of the curtains of Ahasuerus' palace were made from "white cotton" (KJV "green"; NIV, JB omit). A cuneiform inscription of Sennacherib (705-681 B.C.) mentions that the Assyrian king had planted "trees bearing wool" in the Amanus mountains; thus Ahasuerus well may have been familiar with this exotic plant.

The RSV rendering of Heb. *ḥôrāy* ("white material") as "white cotton" assumes the existence of a cotton industry in Egypt, but this interpretation has been challenged (cf. KJV "network"; JB "white cloth"; NIV "fine linen").

COUNCIL.† An assembly chosen to deliberate various civic, legal, and religious matters. In the Old Testament Heb. *sôḏ* refers to confidential discourse (e.g., Prov. 3:32, "confidence"; so RSV, NIV; KJV "secret") or to a group of intimates (e.g., "company of

merrymakers," Jer. 15:17), including the heavenly council of the Lord, those to whom he confided his deepest thoughts (e.g., Jer. 23:18, 22; cf. Job 15:8).

In the New Testament the Greek word for council, *synédrion*, usually means the Jewish Sanhedrin (e.g., Acts 22:5). At Matt. 10:17 (par. Mark 13:9) it points to local Jewish councils, theoretically in any city with a population larger than 120 Jews (*b. Sanh.* 17b); twenty-three members constituted a tribunal for spiritual matters. In close connection with the local synagogue, these councils possessed the power to expel members from the synagogue and administer corporal punishment, which was normally carried out within the synagogue (see Acts 22:19; 26:11). The Romans permitted these Jewish courts to handle their own judicial system to a degree and even to pass the death sentence. Jesus may have had such a local Jewish council in mind when he gave his own interpretation of the law (Matt. 5:22). A Roman council is mentioned at Acts 25:12.

COUNCIL OF JERUSALEM. See APOSTOLIC COUNCIL.

COUNSELOR.† In Old Testament times the counselor was an employee of the royal court. Ahithophel's counsel (Heb. *ʿēṣâ*; JB, NIV "advice") was revered in the court of King David (2 Sam. 16:23; JB, NIV "advice"); he was succeeded by Jehoiada and Abiathar (1 Chr. 27:34). Jonathan was another of David's counselors (v. 32). The function of a counselor was to advise the king (e.g., 1 Kgs. 12:6-14) on such matters as national defense (Prov. 11:14; JB, NIV "advisers") and plans for war (2 Chr. 22:5; Prov. 24:6; NIV "advisers"), though sometimes this advisory capacity was granted to others (e.g., to the queen mother [2 Chr. 22:3; NIV "encouraged"; JB "gave advice"]).

The Old Testament also mentions counselors in foreign courts. Ezra 7:14-15, 28; 8:25 refer to seven men (Aram. *yeʿaṭ*; NIV "advisers") who constituted a privy "council of advice," advising the Persian monarchs concerning significant events (cf. the seven princes at Esth. 1:14; according to some scholars this royal council was established during the reign of Cyrus I [seventh century B.C.]). In the Aramaic section of Daniel two words are rendered "counselors": *deṭāḇār* (3:2), which points to a royal official ("judge"), one of many in the service of Nebuchadnezzar; and *haddāḇār* (3:24; KoB, p. 1068, suggests "high royal official"; Gesenius, p. 216, "friends or ministers of the king").

Metaphorically, God is said to be a counselor (Ps. 16:7, "gives counsel" par. "instructs"; 32:8; 33:11, "counsel" par. "thoughts"; 73:24), whose testimonies the psalmist considers to be his "counselors" (Ps. 119:24). The rhetorical question at Isa. 40:13 underscores the fact that God is not in need of human advice (cf. Rom. 11:34; Gk. *sýmboulos*). Indeed, the Creator counseled through Christ, the "Wonderful Counselor" (Isa. 9:6; Heb. *peleʾ yôʿēṣ*; KJV "Wonderful, Counselor").

See also HOLY SPIRIT *III.B.2.*

COURTYARD (Heb. *ḥāṣēr*; Gk. *aulḗ*). An architectural enclosure open to the sky, surrounded on all sides by a house or public building. 2 Sam. 17:18 mentions that the courtyard (KJV "court") of a private home contained a well. According to Exod. 8:13 many Egyptians had courtyards with their houses (KJV "villages"). Usually the RSV, KJV, and JB refer to the "court" of the tabernacle (e.g., Exod. 27:9) or temple (e.g., 1 Kgs. 6:36), rather than the "courtyard" (so NIV).

On the basis of Neh. 8:16 it appears that after the Exile the Feast of Booths was celebrated in the courtyards of individual dwellings as well as the temple court and public squares.

The courtyard (Gk. *aulé* "open court"; KJV "hall," "palace") where Peter denied Christ was the lower (cf. Mark 14:66, "below") area of the home of the high priest, separated by a door (John 18:16) from the upper area where the Sanhedrin had questioned Jesus. This open area, like that of any large Hellenistic house, was spacious enough to permit a large fire in the center (Luke 22:55).

Archaeological excavations at various sites have uncovered dwellings in which rooms of widely ranging number were grouped around an inner court. For example, a Middle Bronze Age house at Jericho consisted of five rooms flanking an open court while a Hellenistic dwelling at Gezer contained twelve rooms surrounding the courtyard.

COUSIN.† Though they recognized familial ties with the children of siblings, the Hebrews did not have a word for "cousin." The RSV so renders Heb. *ben-dōḏ* "son of (one's) father's brother" at Jer. 32:8-9, 12, where Jeremiah is said to have purchased a parcel of land from his cousin Hananel, according to his right as cousin (cf. Lev. 25:49; KJV "uncle's son") and at Lev. 25:49 (KJV, JB "uncle's son"), where the law is given regarding redemption of property. But "sons of their father's brothers" is the translation at Num. 36:11 concerning the "cousins" (so NIV) who married the daughters of Zelophehad. The RSV also translates Heb. *baṯ dōḏ* "daughter of (one's) father's brother" as "daughter of his uncle" at Esth. 2:7, where Esther is referred to as the "cousin" (so NIV) of Mordecai.

According to the NIV Mishael and Elzaphan, the sons of Uzziel the uncle of Aaron, were cousins of Nadab and Abihu, Aaron's sons (Lev. 10:4; Heb. *'āḥ*; RSV, KJV "brethren"). At 1 Chr. 23:22 the daughters of Eleazar were married to their "cousins" (so NIV; Heb. *'āḥ*; RSV, JB "kinsmen"; KJV "brethren"), a practice not forbidden by the Mosaic law (cf. Lev. 18:6-18).

The only New Testament reference to a cousin is found at Col. 4:10, where Paul identifies the relationship of Mark to Barnabas (Gk. *ánepsis*; KJV "sister's son" is inaccurate); this helps to explain why Barnabas wanted to take Mark on Paul's second missionary journey (Acts 15:37ff.). At Luke 1:36 Gk. *syngenís* is more accurately rendered "kinswoman" (so RSV, JB) rather than "cousin" (KJV); Luke leaves undecided the degree of kinship between Elizabeth and Mary (see J. A. Fitzmyer, *The Gospel According to Luke I-IX.* AB [1981], p. 352).

COVENANT.† An agreement between two or more parties outlining mutual rights and responsibilities.

I. Near Eastern Covenants

In order to promote greater cohesion among members of a clan, a tribe, or a nation, as well as to encourage greater cooperation between nations, the ancients often formed binding agreements. Among the better known are the so-called Hittite international treaties between the Hittite ruler Hattusilis III and the Egyptian pharaoh Rameses II, and the suzerainty or vassal treaties concluded between the Hittites and states which thus became their vassals. In form these texts usually consisted of (1) the names of the parties involved; (2) a historical survey of past relations between the parties; (3) the stipulations made by the Hittites for their vassals; (4) a list of divine witnesses; and (5) a list of sanctions expressed as the blessings which the divine witnesses would guarantee if both sides should keep the terms of the treaty and the divine curses which would ensue in the event that one of them (mainly the vassals) were to break his obligations. Many of these treaties bound the vassal to the overlord, who would in turn protect the vassal. Similar agreements are known from Mesopotamia (e.g., Assurbanipal's treaty with Qedar; Esarhaddon's vassal treaties; cf. the Mari texts) and Egypt (e.g., the Egyptian version of the treaty between Rameses II and Hittite Hattusilis).

An integral part of a covenant was the ritual slaughtering of an animal and the pronouncement of the formula: "Just as this [beast] is cut up, so may [X] be cut up." Most likely the parties making the covenant thereby declared that whoever might break the agreement would likewise be killed.

II. Terminology

The most common Hebrew word for covenant is Heb. *bᵉrîṯ*, which also means "agreement" or "arrangement." This word may be derived from Heb. *bārâ* "eat bread with," which suggests that the contracting parties symbolized their bond by a common meal at the conclusion of the formal agreement, or from Akk. *birītu* "fetter," which also suggests the bond between them (cf. Akk. *riksu*; Hitt. *išḥiul* "bond"). In the New Testament, as in the LXX, Gk. *diathḗkē* "last will, testament" designates a covenant.

III. Old Testament

The Old Testament lists a number of different covenants: a covenant of friendship between David and Jonathan, Saul's son (1 Sam. 18:3-4; cf. 22:8, "league" [NIV "covenant"]; 23:18), which included "legal" sanctions (20:8); a covenant between King Solomon and one of his subjects, Shemei (1 Kgs. 2:42-46); another between Jehoiada the high priest and the royal guard (2 Kgs. 11:4); a covenant between King David and Abner (2 Sam. 3:12-21; KJV "league"; NIV "agreement"), actually symbolizing a treaty between the ten northern tribes and the two southern tribes governed by David; a covenant between the sovereign and his vassals (implied at 1 Kgs. 4:21 in reference to the tribute paid by the various kings to Solomon); a covenant between the two kings Solomon and Hiram (1 Kgs. 5:12, "treaty" [KJV "league"]); and the covenant between God and his people (see below). Many of these covenants were between two unequal parties, one more powerful than the other.

Ancient covenants were solemnized through certain accompanying rituals, such as the swearing of an oath (e.g., by Abraham's steward Eliezer; Gen. 24:2-3, 9, 41), a shared meal (as between Abimelech and Isaac; 26:28-30), or the exchanging of clothes (as between David and Jonathan; 1 Sam. 18:4). A common ancient Near Eastern custom was the cutting of sacrificial animals into pieces, as mentioned in the account of God's covenant with Abraham (Gen. 15:9-21; cf. Jer. 34:18-20). After the animals were cut lengthwise and the pieces of meat placed opposite one another, the participants walked between the pieces, perhaps symbolizing that whoever would break the covenant would be "cut" like the animals (the standard idiom meaning to make a covenant, Heb. *kāraṯ bᵉrîṯ* "cut a covenant," may derive from this custom).

A central factor in the Judeo-Christian tradition is God's covenant with his people, presented as always initiated by God himself, first with Noah (Gen. 9:8-17), then with Abram (Gen. 15; 17), and later with Abraham's descendants, the Israelites of the Exodus (Exod. 19-24). By contrast, the covenant at Josh. 24 appears to represent an agreement by the various elements of the people Israel to join themselves in a somewhat flexible confederation, vowing their allegiance to the rule of Yahweh rather than to a human sovereign (perhaps to avoid the intolerable circumstances many in their midst had experienced at the hands of the Egyptian pharaoh and the kings of the Canaanite city-states). The Davidic covenant, indicated to have been instituted by God (2 Sam. 7; 1 Kgs. 8:17ff.), formed the foundation for the greatest ruling dynasty in Israelite history.

Many scholars have noted several parallels between Israelite covenants and the ancient Near Eastern treaties. One of the clearest examples is the covenant ceremony at Josh. 24, which contains these basic elements: the preamble, presenting the participants (vv. 1-2); historical prologue describing the previous relations of God and Israel (vv. 2-13); stipulations (v. 14); list of witnesses (v. 22; cf. v. 27); sanctions—curses and blessings (vv. 19-20, 25); provision for deposit of the covenant document and its periodic reading (v. 26); and the oath (vv. 15, 21). It has been suggested that additional stipulations are contained in the legislation represented by the Book of the Covenant (Exod. 20:22-23:33). Numerous examples of curses and blessings can be attested. For example, Yahweh would not protect his chosen people if they violated the sacred ark of the covenant. Accordingly, he permitted the Hebrews to be defeated by the Philistines and the ark of the covenant captured as punishment for the corruption of the priests of Eli (1 Sam. 4:4-11; cf. 2:27-36; 3:11-14). Many years later, after repeated warnings against apostasy, Yahweh is seen to have visited upon his chosen people the most severe of punishments — the Exile.

Following the deportation of the northern tribes to Assyria and the southern tribes to Babylonia, the major prophets envisaged a "new covenant" between Yahweh and his scattered people, called the faithful remnant (see Jer. 31:31-34 for the contrast between the covenant made at Mt. Horeb and the new covenant; cf. Isa. 42:9). Yahweh would forgive the Israelites for their idolatry, would write his will upon their hearts, and would renew the broken bond of fellowship. Furthermore, he would guarantee, according to his "everlasting covenant" or his "covenant of peace" (Ezek. 34:25; 37:26), that one of David's descendants would rule his people (Isa. 55:3 [cf. 61:8]; Jer. 32:37-40; Ezek. 37:25-27; cf. 2 Sam. 7:13) and that one day all nations would share in Israel's covenantal blessings.

Three Old Testament passages employ "covenant" in a metaphorical sense. Jeremiah compares God's covenantal promises to the regular succession of day and night (Jer. 33:20, 25), while Malachi likens a covenant to the marriage bond (Mal. 2:14). Hosea mentions a divine covenant with the animals whereby God intends to protect his unfaithful people (Hos. 2:18).

IV. New Testament

The first-century A.D. Jews continued to draw religious and moral inspiration from God's covenantal faithfulness to their ancestor Abraham (Luke 1:72; Acts 3:25; 7:8; Gal. 3:15, 17) and to their forefathers at Mt. Sinai (2 Cor. 3:14). Though familiar with the Old Testament teachings concerning the covenant, Jesus nevertheless interpreted them in the light of a new (so Luke 22:20; cf. 1 Cor. 11:25) covenant (so Matt. 26:28 par. Mark 14:24) of forgiveness, ratified by his own sacrifice — his own blood shed on the cross and symbolized by the wine of the Last Supper (Matt. 26:28).

Paul makes an even greater distinction between the old and the new covenants. Viewing Jer. 31:31-34 (quoted at Rom. 11:27) as an implied reference to Christ, the apostle focuses not only on Christ's sacrifice (1 Cor. 11:25) but also on his saving work in the transformed hearts of mankind (2 Cor. 3:1-6), even though they might have had no previous religious or social ties with Israel (Eph. 2:12). At 2 Cor. 3:14-18 he supports his distinction between the two covenants by reasoning that the new covenant in Christ issues freedom and grants believers a glimpse of the divine majesty and glory.

The author of Hebrews retains the Pauline contrast between the old covenant made at Mt. Sinai and the new, as well as the Pauline association of Jer. 31:31-34 (quoted at Heb. 8:8; cf. 10:16) with Jesus' sacrificial death. He further concludes, as emphatically as Paul, that Christ's sacrifice on the cross accomplishes genuine mediation between God and sinners (9:1ff., 15, 18ff.; cf. 12:24), but sets forth, in greater detail than Paul, Christ's priestly role as the permanent intercessor to the Father on behalf of his own (7:24-25).

As in the Mosaic covenant, God's covenant in Jesus Christ preserves several parallels with Near Eastern vassal treaties (e.g., the symbolic meal). Again, as in the Old Testament, God initiates this covenant. But the notions of divine forgiveness and the inclusion of people from all nations add unique dimensions.

V. Theological Reflections

Exegetes and theologians have long debated the connection between the old (Old Testament) and new (New Testament) covenants, as well as the nature of the old covenant. Some accept only one covenant between God and man and consider the differences of the several accounts secondary. Others distinguish between the various Old Testament covenants with Noah, Abraham, Moses, and David, as well as the new covenant announced by Jeremiah. Perhaps a balanced view might best be reached by affirming that God's unmerited grace in Jesus Christ is the underlying, unifying principle, and that the particular significance of each covenant, given its social, political, and religious setting, be affirmed.

Bibliography. K. Baltzer, *The Covenant Formulary* (Philadelphia: 1971); G. E. Mendenhall, "Covenant Forms in Israelite Tradition," *BA* 17 (1954): 50-76; repr. E. F. Campbell, Jr., and D. N. Freedman, eds., *The Biblical Archaeologist Reader* 3 (Garden City: 1970): 25-53; M. Weinfeld, "bᵉrîth," *TDOT* 2 (rev. ed., 1977): 253-279.

COVENANT, BOOK OF THE.† Traditional designation of the collection of laws recorded at Exod. 20:23–23:33, also known as the Covenant Code. The title derives from 24:7, which refers to the document read by Moses during the ratification of the covenant at Mt. Sinai; more likely, however, this reference is to "the words of the covenant, the ten commandments" (34:28; 20:1-17). Analysis of the Book of the Covenant shows it to be a collection of various types of laws reflecting an agricultural or transhumant society later in the premonarchic period; some scholars have suggested that the collection represents stipulations such as may have been appended to the covenant of confederation formed at Josh. 24. In form the laws represent both the apodictic ("you shall . . ." or "you shall not . . .") pronouncements common to ancient Near Eastern law codes and the casuistic ("when [or if] a man . . ." or "whoever . . .") laws derived from cases brought before local elders. Although it addresses matters of cultic practice (e.g., 20:23-26; 23:10-12), the Book of the Covenant is concerned primarily with civil and criminal issues regarding slavery (21:2-11), injury to persons and property (21:18–22:17), and the legal process (23:1-9). The highly ethical nature of Israelite law, which derived from the people's religious ideals, is evident in the significance accorded to equity and reciprocity (exemplified by the principle of *lex talionis* "law of retaliation" — "an eye for an eye" — which restricted the right of revenge, thereby preventing the punishment from exceeding the crime; 21:23-25) and the humanitarian concern for all members of society, particularly the disenfranchised — widows, orphans, and aliens (22:21-31).

COVET (Heb. *ḥāmaḏ, 'āwâ*; Gk. *epithymeín*).† To desire material possessions, particularly what belongs to another. One of the basic tenets of the Mosaic law forbids the Israelites to desire (or perhaps "resent") what belonged to their neighbors (Exod. 20:17; Deut. 5:21); as the last commandment of the Decalog, this injunction may stress the self-interest addressed in the preceding commandments regarding relationships with one's neighbors. Certainly covetousness was re-

garded as an issue significant enough to threaten the stability of the Israelite community in its formative stages; but even in the eighth century B.C. the prophet Micah denounced the Israelites for their greed and disregard for their neighbor's rights (Mic. 2:2). In the New Testament it was regarded as a primary sin (Mark 7:22) and a deterrent to true faithfulness (Eph. 5:3). Some scholars have suggested that the very notion of covetousness in one's heart or mind represented the initial stages of concerted action to obtain its goals (cf. Matt. 5:28); indeed, James observes that covetousness promotes war as a means to obtain what is desired (Jas. 4:2).

Paul cites the tenth commandment in elaborating upon the law (Rom. 13:9). At 7:7 he explains that it is the law which exposes the scope of such desire; this does not make the law evil, he says, but indicates that sin is at work even in the law to make mankind more sinful (vv. 7-12).

Whereas the Bible condemns the longing after material goods, it encourages one to strive after spiritual wealth. The psalmist was "consumed with longing (Heb. *ta'ᵃḇâ*) for [God's] ordinances" (Ps. 119:20) and even "faint(s) with longing" for God's salvation (so NIV; v. 81; RSV "languishes"). This attitude prevails in the New Testament as well. Christ asserts that the righteous "longed to see" the truth of his teaching as witnessed by the disciples (Matt. 13:17; KJV "desired"). As an apostle, Paul longed for a heavenly "garment" (2 Cor. 5:2; KJV "earnestly desiring"), i.e., a spiritual body (cf. Phil. 1:23). The author of Hebrews interpreted the desire of the Old Testament heroes for a homeland to be an expression of their faith (Heb. 11:16).

COW. See CATTLE.

COZ (1 Chr. 4:8, KJV). *See* KOZ.

COZBI [kŏz'bĭ] (Heb. *kozbî* "luxuriant"). The daughter of Zur (a chief of Midian), whom the Simeonite Zimri married (Num. 25:6, 14-15). Since Israel's participation in rites associated with Baal-peor (vv. 1-5) had brought a plague as divine retribution, Phinehas killed the couple in order to compensate for Israel's infidelity and thus halt the plague (vv. 7-8; cf. v. 18).

COZEBA [kō zē'bə] (Heb. *kōzēḇâ* "falsehood"). A village in the Shephelah region of Judah (1 Chr. 4:22; KJV "Chozeba"), considered to be the same as Chezib (Gen. 38:5) and Achzib (Josh. 15:44).

CRANE (Heb. *'āgûr*). A tall wading bird of the family *Gruidae*. These migratory birds arrive in Palestine during the spring (March) en route from the south to the northerly beaches. Their diet comprises mostly grains, seeds, sprouts, and wild plants, though on occasion cranes feed on worms, insects, and frogs.

While the identification of any species on the basis of biblical usage is difficult, it may be the crane to which the moanings of the afflicted King Hezekiah are compared (Isa. 38:14; KJV "swallow"; NIV "thrush"). At Jer. 8:7 (NEB "wryneck") the crane is numbered among those birds that instinctively return to Palestine ("keep the time of their coming"), in contrast to the Israelites who at that time were oblivious to the ordinances of their God.

CREATION.† A divine act in which God called into being "heaven and earth" — or all of reality — out of "nothing" or without resorting to any preexisting matter.

I. Terminology

The most common Hebrew word signifying creation is Heb. *bārā'*, which may be related to OSA *br'* "build" and which originally may have meant "separate" or "divide." Less frequently used are Heb. *'āśâ* "make" (e.g., Gen. 1:7, 16, 25, 31), *qānâ* (14:19), and *'āmaḏ* "stand forth" (Ps. 33:9). The New Testament uses Gk. *ktízō* "create" or "produce" (cf. LXX).

II. Biblical Teachings

A. Old Testament. One of the fundamental Hebrew beliefs is that Yahweh is the Creator of the world. This is evident not only from the popular account of Gen. 1–11 but also from other Old and New Testament references. Two distinct accounts of creation have been identified in Gen. 1:1–2:4 and 2:5-25. Basically, Gen. 1 presents a cosmic picture of God's activity, which culminates in the creation of mankind and the Sabbath, while Gen. 2 emphasizes the creation of man and woman and provides the transition to the fall of mankind described in ch. 3.

1. Gen. 1. Israel's history, which commences with Abram's journey to Canaan (Gen. 11:31ff.), is preceded ultimately by the creation of the universe (2:4), then by the "generations" (Heb. *tôlēḏôṯ*, representing divisions of the primeval history) of Adam, the "antediluvian patriarchs," and Noah.

The author of Gen. 1 uses ordinary language to depict the manner in which God created the universe. Introducing his account with a general statement about the creation of the universe "in the beginning" and resulting in an earth without form (v. 2), he next records (some eight times) that God fashioned the various aspects of his creation through speech (vv. 3, 6, 9, 11, 14, 20, 24, 26). Structuring his narrative in terms of six successive days, the author parallels the creation of light and darkness on the first day with the creation of luminaries on the fourth, the creation of the firmament on the second with the creation of fish and birds on the fifth, and the creation of the sea and dry land as well as plants on the third with the creation of land animals and, at last, mankind on the sixth. The author concludes his narrative with a reference to God's rest on the seventh day, thus the origin of the Sabbath (2:2-3).

2. Gen. 2. The author of this account presents a partially detailed view of the creation of mankind, which is portrayed here as occurring first. Man is formed from the dust and given the divine breath of life (2:7). He then is placed in a garden (v. 8) which he is to till and keep (v. 15). When God realizes that man would benefit from a companion, he creates woman from one of man's "ribs" during the man's "deep sleep" (vv. 18, 20-22). This account complements that of Gen. 1 in affirming the creation of male and

female (cf. 1:27) and mankind's dominion over the animal world (2:19-20; cf. 1:26, 28).

3. Other passages. A number of psalms express Israel's faith in Yahweh as the Creator of heaven and earth. Ps. 33:6-9 notes that God created through his word (v. 6; cf. v. 9) and his breath, while Pss. 90:2 and 102:25-27 contrast the eternity of God with the temporalness of his own creation, particularly human beings (Ps. 90:2-3). Job 38–41 presents God's answer to his questioning servant, Job: God created the earth, the sea, the rain, the light, the stars, and the animals — e.g., lions, mountain goats, wild asses, wild oxen, ostriches, horses. The point of these examples is to demonstrate that God's ways are both just and unfathomable (see 42:1-6).

The author of Isa. 40–46 offers another majestic view of God's creative activities (perhaps combatting too anthropomorphic an understanding of Gen. 1). Attempting to comfort the exiles, the author encourages them to trust in the incomparable Yahweh who has revealed himself as the Creator of all things (Isa. 40:26, 28; 42:5). The same exalted Lord, he continues, fashioned the earth as a habitation for people (45:18), specifically his chosen people with whom he made a covenant and whom he redeemed (43:1).

B. New Testament. The New Testament community shares the Hebrew faith in God the Creator (e.g., 2 Pet. 3:5; Rev. 4:11; 10:6). On two occasions Jesus himself refers to the creation of the world. However, instead of explaining how God made the world, he uses the phrase "from the beginning of creation" to indicate the divine order of the universe; thus he seeks to validate the legitimacy of marriage as a creation ordinance (Mark 10:6-9 par.) and predicts an eschatological tribulation the likes of which has never been experienced in the time since the creation of the world (13:19 par.).

Paul, too, touches on the doctrine of creation. In his Letter to the Romans, the apostle observes that even though the created universe displays God's "power and deity" (1:20; KJV "power and Godhead"; NIV "power and divine nature"), people refuse to pay homage to the Creator and serve themselves instead (v. 25). In Colossians he declares that all things, even those which are invisible, have been created by Christ, the image of the invisible God, and that the entire creation coheres in him (Col. 1:16-17). Thus, borrowing from Gen. 1 ("God spoke") and from the Old Testament Wisdom Literature (the creation of Wisdom, Prov. 8:22ff.), Paul hypostatizes Wisdom by identifying it with Christ (cf. Heb. 11:3; 2 Pet. 3:5). In Ephesians he links creation with redemption. God the Creator (3:9) is thus also the Recreator; moreover, Christ grants faith so that the faithful may perform good works (2:10), and fashions a new "nature" through which believers will reflect divine righteousness and holiness (4:23).

III. Relation to Ancient Mythologies

Scholars have pointed out several parallels between the Hebrew view of creation and the Babylonian concept as enunciated in the epic Enuma Elish. Indeed, the Hebrews seem to have borrowed or been influenced by Babylonian expressions and ideas (e.g., the tripartite structure of the universe), perhaps when they

Account of the creation of the world by Marduk and Aruru on a sixth-century B.C. Babylonian tablet from Sippar (by courtesy of the Trustees of the British Museum)

came into contact with those mythologies during the Babylonian captivity, or perhaps even earlier. However, they adapted or "demythologized" the polytheistic Babylonian descriptions to reflect the activities and characteristics of Yahweh. For example, they omitted (at least in Gen. 1) the fierce struggle between Marduk, the deity of order, and Tiamat, the deity of chaos, in which Tiamat was killed and cut into two parts by the victorious Marduk. Some scholars believe that Yahweh's victory over the dragons and Leviathan, celebrated at Ps. 74:13-15, refers to Yahweh's deliverance of his people from Egypt's pharaoh, thus recalling the Exodus; others hold that this passage actually echoes the Babylonian victory of Marduk over Tiamat. Some would also interpret Isa. 27:1 to allude to a fight with a mystical monster (cf. Hab. 3, esp. vv. 8-15).

IV. Faith and Science

The biblical picture of God's act of creation, so the author of Hebrews asserts (Heb. 11:3), is based on divine revelation and is accepted on faith by believers. Thus, in faith the Church has come to affirm that God the Father originated the universe through his Son, the Logos, without depending on preexisting matter (see 2 Macc. 7:28).

With the rise and the phenomenal success of modern science, many have attempted to harmonize the biblical view of creation with the scientific explana-

tion of the origin of the universe. Others have emphasized, however, that the Bible cannot be used as a textbook of information about scientific matters because it deals with matters of faith. Thus the Bible presents the affirmation (the "fact") of creation, whereas science helps to elaborate further the precise manner (the "how") in which this is believed to have taken place. Moreover, scientists acknowledge the hypothetical nature of their explanation, though they consider their hypothesis reasonable, supported as it is by many facts.

Assuming that the Genesis account teaches that the universe was created in six "days," some have seen here a conflict between faith's apprehension and the claims of science. Others have observed that the Bible uses the word "day" in more than one sense. Augustine contends that the first three "days" as presented in Gen. 1 differ from the last three because the sun was created on the fourth day (Conf. xi). The latter interpretation may be compatible with the modern scientific hypothesis of the world's beginnings in the distant past.

Interpreting the Hebrew expression "according to its kind" (Gen. 1:11) to mean "according to its species," some have also seen a conflict between Gen. 1 and the biological classification of species. Others have reasoned that the Hebrews were unfamiliar with modern taxonomy and that v. 11 distinguishes between "vegetation," "plants," and "fruit trees" without any further precision.

The relationship between creation and evolution, between the formation of the world through a free, divine act and a process of the evolution of matter by immanent forces, remains a moot issue. One possible resolution is that Gen. 1 teaches that God created his universe in successive stages without necessarily implying a reduction of higher forms of life to lower forms.

Since the Bible does not pretend to address scientific matters, Christians may never be able to bring the religious view of creation to bear on scientific hypotheses concerning the origin of the world. In faith, however, they affirm that "beyond" the natural causes and seemingly infinite astronomical time there is God who creates, sustains, and redeems his people (cf. Isa. 40:25-26).

Bibliography. L. B. Gilkey, *Maker of Heaven and Earth* (Garden City: 1965); A. Heidel, *The Babylonian Genesis,* 2nd ed. (Chicago: 1963); R. Prenter, *Creation and Redemption* (Philadelphia: 1967); B. Vawter, *On Genesis* (Garden City: 1977), pp. 37-91.

CREEPING THINGS (Heb. *remeś*).† A collective term representing a variety of animals (Gen. 9:3), including on occasion water animals (Ps. 69:34; Hab. 1:14; cf. Gen. 1:20, Heb. *śereṣ,* usually "swarming things"). They are specifically distinguished from birds (e.g., Gen. 6:7), fish (Deut. 4:18), and the larger animals (Gen. 1:24-25; 7:14; 8:17). Although frequently identified as reptiles, the creeping things include all small animals which appear to creep or glide through or upon the ground.

CRESCENS [krĕs′ənz] (Gk. *Krēskēs* "increasing"). A companion of Paul during one of his prison terms

(2 Tim. 4:10). When 2 Timothy was written he had left for Galatia (some texts read Gk. *Gallia* "Gaul"), but the text does not say why.

CRESCENTS (Heb. *śaha̦rōnîm*). Moon-shaped (KoB, p. 916, "little moon [adornment]"; cf. Zakir Inscription, Aram. *šhr,* equivalent of the Babylonian moon-god Sin) ornaments, either of gold or silver, worn by the Midianite kings or their camels (Judg. 8:26, 21; KJV, NIV "ornaments"). At Isa. 3:18 the crescents (KJV "round tires like the moon") constitute part of the tawdry attire of the "daughters of Zion" which the Lord would remove, possibly because of their pagan association.

CRETE [krēt] (Gk. *Krētē*).† A large island (some 250 km. [156 mi.] long) in the Mediterranean Sea, southeast of the Peloponnesus, between Sicily and Cyprus. Its Old Testament name is Caphtor, the original territory of the Philistines (according to Amos 9:7). Crete attained its greatest political and cultural significance as the cradle of Minoan civilization (*ca.* 3000-1500 B.C.).

According to Acts 2:11 some of the Jews residing on Crete attended the Feast of Pentecost at Jerusalem. Later, Christian churches were established there. At Tit. 1:5 Paul instructs Titus to appoint elders in those Christian communities that still lacked effective leadership in Paul's absence. Though the inhabitants of this island were not exemplars of high moral behavior (Tit. 1:12, "liars, evil beasts, lazy gluttons"), there is no reason to believe that the churches did not follow Titus' guidance, as outlined at 2:1–3:11.

Luke mentions that the ship carrying Paul to Rome sailed "under the lee of Crete" (i.e., along its southern coast), past the Cape of Salome, till it reached Fair Havens near Lasea (Acts 27:7-8), the centurion having disregarded the apostle's advice to try for a safer harbor.

Bibliography. S. Hood, *The Minoans* (London: 1971); R. F. Willetts, *The Civilization of Ancient Crete* (Berkeley: 1978).

CRIB (Heb. *'ēḇûs*). Receptacle for fodder. In Palestinian farmhouses the feeding troughs were usually alongside the steps connecting the farmer's living quarters with the lower level where the animals were sheltered. At Prov. 14:4 the crib (so KJV; RSV "grain"; JB "cattle-feed") was where domestic oxen were fed (cf. Job 39:9; JB, NIV "manger"), and, at Isa. 1:3, the ass (cited in contrast to Israel's spiritual ignorance).

The "manger" (Gk. *phátnē*) where Jesus was laid after birth may have been such a feeding trough (Luke 2:7).

CRICKET. One of the clean insects mentioned with locusts and grasshoppers at Lev. 11:22 (KJV "beetle"); probably a species of locust (*Gryllidae*; Heb. *ḥargōl*; so KoB, p. 331; Gesenius, p. 303; JB "hargol").

CRIME.* A violation of community standards, considered so serious as to constitute an offense against the well-being of society. Because in ancient Israel laws (including precedents determined through local

practice) were accorded divine sanction, crimes — whether against persons or property — were regarded also as an offense against God; indeed, the various terms designating the commission of a crime also connote sin (e.g., Heb. *ḥāṭā', 'āwōn, 'āwen*). See LAW.

A considerable range of crimes are delineated in the legal collections of the Pentateuch, but basically they can be classified as crimes against persons, property, or the religious order. Those against persons include murder (e.g., Num. 35:20-21; Deut. 19:11), accidental homicide (vv. 4ff.; cf. Exod. 21:28-32), personal injury (vv. 18-19, 22, 26-27; Deut. 25:11-12), kidnapping (24:7), or sexual infractions such as adultery or unchastity (e.g., Exod. 20:14; Deut. 22:13-30), incest (27:20, 22-23), or bestiality (v. 21; Lev. 18:23). Crimes against property comprise primarily theft (Exod. 22:2-4, 7, 9; Deut. 24:14-15) and damage (Exod. 21:33-36; 22:5-6). Crimes of a specifically religious nature include idolatry and participation in foreign cults (Exod. 20:3-5), blasphemy or false witness (22:28; Lev. 6:3, 5), and sabbath-breaking (Deut. 5:12-15).

In order to preserve the stability of the community it was necessary to compensate the victim and punish the offender. Cases were taken before local elders (or even the king; cf. 1 Kgs. 3:16-28) for mediation to arrive at terms acceptable to both parties. Murder was to be compensated by the death penalty, partially to remove from the community the guilt of compliance in the crime and partially because it was believed that elimination of the offender would restore the security of all citizens (cf. Deut. 19:13). Other crimes were punished humanely and equitably, with care that the penalty not exceed the severity of the crime. Particularly in premeditated or wilfully committed crimes resulting in bodily injury, the punishment was not to exceed the degree of the crime committed (Exod. 21:23-25) and was not to be extended to any person but the actual offender. Monetary penalties for property damage or theft were paid to the victim and might exceed the actual value, perhaps as an exemplary measure (22:1-4, 9). Religious crimes (as well as some sexual offenses) frequently were punished by banishment (31:14; Lev. 18:7-29). See also JUSTICE.

Bibliography. G. E. Mendenhall, *Law and Covenant in Israel and the Ancient Near East* (Pittsburgh: 1955).

CRIMSON. See SCARLET, CRIMSON.

CRISPUS [krĭs'pəs] (Gk. *Krispos,* from Lat. *crispus* "curly"). A former ruler of the synagogue at Corinth who was baptized with several other converts (Acts 18:8); according to 1 Cor. 1:14 he and Gaius were among the very few believers baptized by Paul himself.

CROCODILE. One of the largest reptiles extant, attaining a length of about 6 m. (20 ft.); possibly referred to at Job 41:1 (Heb. *liwyāṯān* "Leviathan"; RSV mg., NIV mg. "crocodile"; so KoB, p. 477; Gesenius, p. 433). The description of this sea monster, especially the arrangement of its scales (vv. 13-17), its immunity to primitive human weapons (vv. 26-29), its agility in the water (v. 32), and, finally, its sheer size (vv. 33-34), may well suggest the Egyptian crocodile (*Crocodilus niloticus*), which probably lived not only in Egypt, but also in Palestine. According to Strabo (*Geog.* xvi.2.27 [C 758]) and Pliny (*Nat. hist.* v.17 [75]) there were a "Crocodile city" (Gk. *Krokodeilōn*; Lat. *Crocodilon*) south of Mt. Carmel and a "Crocodile river." A few crocodiles can still be found in the latter, the river Jabbok, (modern Nahr ez-Zerqā).

The beasts at Ps. 68:30, said to "dwell among the reeds," may be crocodiles or hippopotami.

On Lev. 11:30 ("land crocodile"), *see* LIZARD. *See also* LEVIATHAN.

CROCUS (Heb. *ḥᵃbaṣelet*). Any of a vast genus (*Crocus*) of herbs of the iris family, possibly referred to at Isa. 35:11 (so RSV, NIV; KJV "rose"; JB "jonquil") to symbolize beauty and splendor. The "rose of Sharon" (so the ancient versions) may be a crocus (Cant. 2:1; RSV mg.), but it is more likely the meadow saffron (*Colchicum*; Akk. *ḥabaṣillatu*), which resembles the crocus. The term cannot indicate the rose, which was not found in Palestine until approximately the time of the composition of Ecclesiasticus (early second century B.C.), its first occurrence in biblical literature (Sir. 24:14; Gk. *phytá rhódou*).

CROSS (Gk. *staurós*; Lat. *crux*), **CRUCIFIXION** (cf. *stauróō* "crucify").† Use of an upright stake as an instrument of torture and execution attained particular significance as the culmination of Christ's persecution and thus as a symbol of his atonement for mankind.

Crucifixion is first attested among the Persians (cf. Herodotus *Hist.* i.128.2; iii.132.2, 159.1), perhaps derived from the Assyrian practice of impalement. It was later employed by the Greeks, especially Alexander the Great, and by the Carthaginians, from whom the Romans adapted the practice as a punishment for slaves and non-citizens, and occasionally for citizens guilty of treason. Although in the Old Testament the corpses of blasphemers or idolaters punished by stoning might be hanged "on a tree" as further humiliation (Deut. 21:23), actual crucifixion was not introduced in Palestine until Hellenistic times. The Seleucid Antiochus IV Epiphanes crucified those Jews who would not accept hellenization (Josephus *Ant.* xii.240-41; cf. 1 Macc. 1:44-50), and the Hasmonean Alexander Jannaeus thus executed eight hundred Pharisean rebels of the town of Bethome (Josephus *BJ* i.4.6; *Ant.* xiii.14.2-3). It was the crucifixion of some 3,600 Jews which precipitated the Jewish revolt (A.D. 66; *BJ* ii.14.9). Many Jews and Christians were martyred in this fashion until the practice was abolished by Constantine *ca.* 337 in deference to Christian belief concerning Christ's death.

Originally merely a stake on which the victim was tied or impaled, by Roman times the cross featured a horizontal beam, placed either at the top of the vertical shaft (in the form of the Greek letter *tau*; St. Anthony's cross) or slightly below the top (the traditional Latin cross). The later "Greek" cross comprised vertical and horizontal bars of equal length; the X-shaped St. Andrew's cross also was employed later in Roman times. Judging from first-century A.D. remains from a tomb near Jerusalem, it appears that the victim's feet

were pierced with a single nail which was then driven into a small olivewood board (to keep the feet together) but not into the upright shaft itself. The forearms were nailed to the horizontal bar. A small horizontal board was affixed to the cross at buttocks height to help support the body and prevent collapse, thereby prolonging the suffering. One might agonize on the cross for several days before dying, apparently of suffocation. Thirst was intense and the weight of the body produced inexorable pain; victims were tormented by high fever and convulsions which racked their entire body. Occasionally the executioners prompted death by breaking the victim's bones.

As further humiliation for the victim and as a deterrent to potential offenders, the person condemned to crucifixion was first flogged, then ordered to carry the horizontal crossbeam to the place of execution, where it was hoisted onto the vertical pole. Accordingly, Jesus carried his own crossbeam (John 19:17), though he was later relieved by Simon of Cyrene (Matt. 27:32 par. Mark 15:21; Luke 23:26).

The indignity of the crucifixion, for both the means of punishment (cf. Gal. 3:13) and the crimes with which it was associated, was utter "folly" (1 Cor. 1:17-18), contrasting intensely with the significance of Christ's death as atonement for all mankind (e.g., Eph. 2:16; Col. 2:14). The suffering of the cross is cited to symbolize the self-denial which Jesus' followers must accept — their willingness to renounce their own needs and desires (Matt. 10:38 par. Mark 8:34; Luke 9:23), even one's "old self" (Rom. 6:6; Gal. 2:20).

CROWN.† A headpiece bestowed upon dignitaries and sports champions to signify honor.

According to Exod. 29:6, at the consecration ceremony the high priest was to wear a turban with a "holy crown" (Heb. *nēzer* "diadem") fastened to it by blue lace (28:37). The holy crown on the forehead of the high priest identified him as a holy representative of the people, whose guilt he bore in the sacrifices which they dedicated to the Lord (Exod. 28:38), thereby ensuring that God would forgive the sins which the priest brought to God at the sacrifice.

The crown worn by kings is a symbol of royal power and majesty; at Ps. 21:3 God places a golden crown on the king's head, while at Ps. 132:18 the crown of the anointed is expected to "shed its lustre" over David, in contrast to the shame that would enshroud his enemies. At Prov. 16:31 old age is compared to a "crown of glory," obviously something precious, gained by living a righteous life. The crown (Heb. *ᶜaṭārâ*) worn by King Solomon at his wedding (given by his mother; Cant. 3:11) may be a garland of honor as well as an official diadem (cf. Ezek. 16:32; 23:42). At Zech 6:11 the same term is rendered "crown" (plural in the MT), possibly a single crown fashioned from several intertwined gold and silver bonds to be placed on the high priest Joshua's head to symbolize authority (in the original text Zerubbabel's royal crown may also have been indicated here).

In the New Testament Gk. *stéphanos* means either a wreath given to the winning athlete of a Greek game or a crown. Paul refers to the former at 1 Cor. 9:25, where he states that athletes exercised self-control in order to win the "wreath" (so RSV, JB; KJV, NIV "crown") at the end of the race; the apostle later contrasts this ephemeral reward with the eternal reward believers will obtain in life after death (cf. his own expectation at 2 Tim. 4:8; see also 1 Pet. 5:4 for the "unfading crown of glory" to be handed to faithful elders; cf. the "crown of boasting," 1 Thess. 2:19). A similar meaning is attached to the "crown of life," the recompense of all believers after their intense moral and spiritual testing (Jas. 1:12; Rev. 2:10). In the book of Revelation the latter use is addressed: the church at Philadelphia is warned not to surrender its crown, its symbol of authority, since it will be sustained in the face of persecution (3:11); the elders around God's throne place their "golden crowns" (4:4) before the Lamb (v. 10) who is worthy of all the royal power which their crowns signify.

Also in Revelation Gk. *diádēma* indicates a royal crown (so KJV, NIV; RSV "diadems"; JB "coronet[s]"), worn by the dragon (12:3, unlike the crown worn by the woman with child mentioned at v. 1), the beast (13:1), and the rider of the white horse (19:12) who has many diadems because of his authority over all kings.

CROWN OF THORNS (Gk. *akánthinos stéphanos*).† A wreath, probably fashioned from the leaves and thorns of the akanthos ("thorn") plant, which Roman soldiers placed on Jesus' head following his conviction, in derisive imitation of the victory crown given to Roman emperors (Matt. 27:29 par. Mark 15:17; John 19:2). *See* THORN.

CRUCIBLE (Heb. *maṣrēp*).† A melting pot used for refining silver; most likely it was made of pottery. In Proverbs the term is used metaphorically to depict God's testing or judging of mankind (Prov. 17:3; 27:21).

CRUCIFY. *See* CROSS, CRUCIFIXION.

CRYSTAL (Gk. *krýstallos*).† A nearly transparent quartz, considered by some of the ancients to be frozen water (cf. Heb. *qeraḥ* "ice" at Job 6:16; 37:10; 38:29). At Job 28:18 crystal (Heb. *gāḇîš*; KJV "pearls"; NIV "jasper") is said to be easier to acquire than wisdom. In the vision Ezekiel had of the glory of God, the firmament above the heads of the living creatures was as brilliant as crystal (Ezek. 1:22; KJV "terrible crystal," following MT; NIV "ice").

In the New Testament, crystal is frequently compared to water. The sea of glass in front of God's throne was as clear as crystal (Rev. 4:6). The river of life-giving water was as bright as crystal (22:1), here indicating its sparkling brilliance (cf. the radiance of the New Jerusalem; 21:11).

CUB [kŭb] (Heb. *kûḇ*). An unidentified people mentioned in the prophecy against Egypt (Ezek. 30:5; so RSV mg., JB; KJV "Chub"), possibly the Libyans (LXX *Libyes*; cf. Heb. *lûḇ*; so *BH*; RSV, NIV "Libya"), in Cyrenaica.

CUBIT [kū'bĭt] (Heb. *'ammâ*; Gk. *péchys*).† A unit of measurement, normally the distance from the elbow to the end of the middle finger, about 44.4 cm. (17.5 in.). This figure is based on the Siloam Inscription (*ca.* 701 B.C.), which indicates the length of Hezekiah's tunnel at Jerusalem (about 525 m.) as 1200 cubits.

Since the size of people's bodies varies, the cubit could be only an approximate measure. The Babylonian common cubit measured approximately 49.5 cm. (19.5 in). The Egyptian cubit varied by as much as 2.5 cm. (1 in.); the "common" or standard cubit used in ordinary commerce was 52 cm. (20.5 in.) and the "royal" cubit about 54 cm. (21.7 in.). The "long" cubits mentioned at Ezek. 40:5 could have been these royal cubits, whereas that cited at Deut. 3:11 may be the "common" cubit.

The cubit referred to in the Sermon on the Mount (Matt. 6:27) or at Luke 12:25 represented a measure of time (cf. NIV "a single hour") added to one's life span, not an addition to one's height (KJV "stature"). The 144 cubits measuring either the height or the thickness of the wall of the New Jerusalem (Rev. 21:17) is to be taken symbolically, a multiple of the number twelve, representing the people of God.

CUCKOO (Lev. 11:16; Deut. 14:15; KJV). *See* SEA GULL.

CUCUMBER (Heb. *qiššu'â*).† The fruit of a creeping vine of the family Cucurbitacae. The domesticated cucumbers of Egypt (*Cucumis chate* L.), a staple of their diet for which the Israelites yearned (Num. 11:5), were sweeter than modern European and North American varieties.

Comparison to a temporary guard stand (RSV "booth") in a cucumber field (Heb. *miqšâ*) indicates the exposed position of Jerusalem after the Assyrian forces had destroyed many other cities of Judah (Isa. 1:8). Idols are said to be as lifeless as posts stood up as scarecrows in a cucumber field (Jer. 10:5; KJV "upright").

CULT. *See* WORSHIP.

CULT PROSTITUTE (Heb. *qᵉḏēšâ, qāḏēš*). Personnel associated with pagan temples for the purpose of ritual intercourse, generally to appease the gods and ensure fertility. According to Deut. 23:17 the Israelites were forbidden to engage in cultic prostitution, with either male or female prostitutes (KJV "sodomite"; "whore"), as encouraged in the worship among some of the neighboring nations. That the Israelites could not resist yielding to such temptation is evident from 1 Kings, which mentions male cult prostitutes during the reign of Solomon's son Rehoboam (1 Kgs. 14:24; KJV "sodomites"). It was many years later — even with the vigorous campaigns of King Asa and his son Jehoshaphat (15:12; 22:46), and later, of Josiah, the reform king (2 Kgs. 23:7) — that ritual prostitution was brought under control. 2 Kgs. 23:7 even mentions rooms ("houses") to accommodate cult prostitutes in the temple at Jerusalem.

CUMMIN (Heb. *kammōn*; Gk. *kýminon*). A common annual (*Cuminum cyminum* L.), spelled "cumin" today, included among those seeds sown by the farmer (Isa. 28:25) and threshed with a rod (v. 27). At Matt. 23:23 Jesus chides the scribes and Pharisees for tithing cummin while ignoring that the Mosaic law also requires of them justice, mercy, and faith.

CUN [kŭn] (Heb. *kûn*). One of the two cities belonging to Hadadezer of Syria from which King David pillaged a great amount of the bronze later used by his son Solomon for the construction of the bronze sea and other temple objects (1 Chr. 18:8; KJV "Chun"). Cun, named Conna by the Romans, is the contemporary Râs Ba'albek, a village southwest of Ribleh and about 48 km. (30 mi.) northeast of ancient Berothai.

CUNEIFORM [kū nē'ə fôrm] (from Lat. *cuneus* "wedge").* A writing system employing wedge-shaped signs formed by a stylus on clay tablets and, secondarily, inscribed in stone or metal. Originally pictographic symbols, the signs came to have syllabic (or, in the case of Ugaritic, alphabetic) value. Cuneiform writing is attested in the late third millennium B.C. among the Sumerians and, in the second millennium, became the predominant form of writing in the ancient Near East. Among those languages using cuneiform were Eblaite, Akkadian (Assyrian and Babylonian), Elamite, Hittite, Hurrian, and Old Persian. *See* WRITING.

CUP. A small drinking vessel (2 Sam. 12:3), made of metal (Jer. 51:7), pottery, or leather, and usually used

Detail from the Black Obelisk of Shalmaneser III showing the adaptation of cuneiform writing to stone (by courtesy of the Trustees of the British Museum)

to serve water (Mark 9:41) or wine (e.g., Jer. 25:15). Often it symbolizes the pleasant or bitter experiences of life — the psalmist's cup overflows with God's goodness (Ps. 23:5); the cup of God's wrath must be drunk by Israel (Isa. 51:17), the nations (Jer. 25:15), Edom (Jer. 49:12), or the wicked (Ps. 75:8; cf. Rev. 14:10; 16:19; 18:6).

Matthew (Matt. 20:22) and Mark (Mark 10:39) record that James and John were both willing to drink from Christ's cup of suffering (i.e., indicating their moral participation in his passion), but the Synoptics add that even Jesus himself pleaded with God in Gethsemane to take away his cup (representing testing, or perhaps divine judgment on sin; Matt. 26:39 par. Mark 14:36; Luke 22:42). John, in contrast, relates that Jesus rebuked Peter for defending him with his sword: "Shall I not drink the cup which the Father has given me?" (John 18:11).

The "cup of blessing" (1 Cor. 10:16; cf. 11:25-26) refers to the wine taken at the end of the meal, for which the Jewish family would bless God. Paul likens it to the institution of the Lord's Supper and thus the believer's participation in Christ's death through communion (Matt. 26:27 par. Mark 14:23; Luke 22:17).

The "cup of staggering" points figuratively to God's anger which made his people powerless (Isa. 51:17; "cup [Heb. *kōs*] of his wrath" and "bowl [*qubba'at*] of staggering"; KJV "cup of trembling"). At vv. 22-23 the prophet states that Israel had ceased drinking from this cup and that in the future its enemies would be the ones to experience God's wrath. The "cup of reeling," with which Jerusalem as a fierce adversary would meet its attackers, is represented by Heb. *ṣap*, which means either a basin or a bowl (Zech. 12:2).

CUPBEARER (Heb. *mašqeh* "one who gives drink"). A high official in the ancient Near East who served the king his wine. Because it was common to dispose of monarchs by poisoning, a cupbearer had to be trustworthy to win the confidence of the ruler. It was a mark of honor that Nehemiah, a Jew, was given the office of cupbearer at the Persian court (Neh. 1:11; 2:1).

In Egypt the pharaoh employed a chief cupbearer over several lesser cupbearers (so NIV, JB; RSV, KJV "butler"); the chief cupbearer figures in the account of Joseph's interpretation of dreams (Gen. 40). According to 1 Kgs. 10:5 and 2 Chr. 9:4, Solomon also had such officials in his palace, an indication of the splendor of his court.

The Assyrian Rab-shakeh (Heb. *rab-šāqeh* "chief cupbearer") was an emissary of the Assyrian king (2 Kgs. 18:17ff.; Isa. 36:2), apparently accorded significant administrative duties.

CURSE.† The invocation of harm or injury upon a person (or people), either immediately or contingent upon particular circumstances; a malediction or imprecation. The usual form of the curse follows the pattern "cursed be" or "cursed is (someone)," accompanied by a relative clause declaring the reasons for the imprecation. Both the Old and the New Testaments exhibit an extensive vocabulary regarding cursing; most frequently used are Heb. *'ālâ, 'ārar, qālal*; Gk. *ará* and their derivatives.

To suffer a curse meant to be "cut off," isolated from the matrix of daily life and abandoned to the powers of decomposition and death. Accordingly, the curse was a severe form of punishment and an effective deterrent to antisocial behavior. The curse upon Cain for his brother's murder consigned him to the life of a wanderer and a fugitive, unable to provide agricultural sustenance (Gen. 4:11-12; cf. 3:14). The curse to be accorded a woman guilty of adultery called for her thigh to shrink and her body to swell (Num. 5:21-22). That visited upon the corpse of a prisoner who had been hung was so virulent that, should the corpse remain hanging on the pole during the night, it would render the entire land unclean (Deut. 21:23; cf. the threat of universal judgment for the nation's sins; Isa. 24:1-13, esp. v. 6).

Given the ancient West Semitic identification of word and action, the mere utterance of a curse was considered sufficient to empower its fulfillment. Although an imprecation by a common person might be equally efficacious (cf. Judg. 17:2), that of a king (2 Sam. 3:29; cf. 1 Sam. 14:24-26) or prophet (2 Kgs. 2:24; Num. 22:11ff.; cf. Jer. 11:20) was thought to be particularly potent. Therefore, God prevented Balaam from pronouncing his curses against Israel (Num. 21–22), and David on his deathbed instructed Solomon not to neglect the punishment due Shimei for having cursed him at Mahanaim (1 Kgs. 2:8-9). In particular, to curse either God or the monarch was regarded a crime of utmost significance (Exod. 22:28; 1 Kgs. 21:10). Although Prov. 26:2 notes that an unfounded curse would not come to fruition, the idle utterance of an unjust curse, in anger or in jest, remained extremely dangerous. Because of the potential danger of any curse, people often took great care to render such maledictions harmless. The one who uttered the curse might himself overturn its effect by converting the statement into a blessing (Exod. 12:32; Judg. 17:2), or the curse could be rendered ineffective by killing whoever had pronounced it in the first place (cf. 1 Kgs. 2:8-9). In most instances, a person who had been cursed would invoke God's special protection, proclaiming his innocence (Ps. 26:1-7) or calling for the Lord's wrath to fall on his pursuers (cf. the imprecatory Psalms, e.g., Ps. 10:7-15; 109:17-20).

The curse played an important role in the communal and religious life of ancient Israel, functioning as an effective means of guaranteeing the terms of a covenant or other agreement. Various curses, frequently depicted in highly graphic terms, were appended to the list of covenant stipulations, invoking divine wrath upon the party who might disregard those terms (e.g., Lev. 26:14-33; Deut. 27:15-26; 28:15-68; Josh. 24:20; cf. Judg. 9:15; 1 Cor. 16:22). Similarly, a person might invoke an oath containing a curse to affirm or guarantee the truth of his statements (e.g., Num. 5:19-22; Ps. 7:3-6) or promises (137:5-6). Along with the blessings (the positive sanctions placed on the same stipulations), the curses were pronounced as part of the ritual reenactment of the covenant (e.g., Deut. 27:12-13; Josh. 8:34).

In the New Testament, Jesus himself endured the curse through his passion and death (cf. Gal. 3:10,

13), yet in his great ministry of love commanded his followers to "bless those who curse you" (Luke 6:28; Rom. 12:14). The perplexing narrative of Jesus' cursing the fig tree (Mark 11:12-14, 20-25 par. Matt. 21:18-22), seemingly contradictory to his nature, may have been a symbolic gesture representing his response to the fruitlessness and self-satisfaction of the people.

CUSH [kŏosh] (Heb. *kûš*) (**PERSON**).†
1. The eldest son of Ham and father of Nimrod (Gen. 10:6-8; 1 Chr. 1:8-10).
2. A Benjaminite and an opponent of David (superscription to Ps. 7).

CUSH [kŏosh] (Heb. *kûš*) (**PLACE**).†
1. Territory of the Kassites in northern or central Babylonia (Gen. 2:13; cf. the eponymous ancestor cited at 10:8).
2. A region in Africa, frequently rendered "Ethiopia" (so RSV, e.g., 2 Kgs. 19:9; Esth. 1:1; Isa. 11:11). It should be identified with the Nubian kingdom situated along the Nile river (Isa. 18:1) to the south of Egypt (Ezek. 29:10); it should not be confused with modern Ethiopia (Abyssinia). Often subject to Egyptian control, the region asserted its independence *ca.* the mid-eleventh century B.C.; *ca.* 712-663 Ethiopians ruled Egypt as the Twenty-fifth Dynasty (cf. Tirhakah, 2 Kgs. 19:9 par. Isa. 37:9).
See ETHIOPIA.
3. Possibly a city or district in Midian, northeast of the Gulf of Aqabah (note the parallel at Hab. 3:7; cf. Num. 12:1). Scholars have postulated other districts at Gerar, southeast of Gaza (cf. 2 Chr. 14:9ff.), and in the region of Dedan in South Arabia (cf. Gen. 10:7).

CUSHAN [kŏo'shăn] (Heb. *kûšān*). A people or district cited in parallel with Midian at Hab. 3:7, possibly related to or even identical with Cush.

CUSHAN-RISHATHAIM [kŏo'shăn rĭsh'ə thā'əm] (Heb. *kûšan riš'āṯayim*, possibly "Cushan of the double crime"). A king of Mesopotamia (so RSV, KJV), more likely of a state in northwest Mesopotamia (cf. NIV mg., Heb. *'aram naharāyim* "Aram of the two rivers"; JB emends to Edom, omitting Naharaim), to whom the Lord gave his people as slaves for eight years (Judg. 3:8; KJV "Cushan-rishathaim"). It was Othniel who delivered the Israelites from his rule (vv. 9-10).

CUSHI [kŏosh'ī] (Heb. *kûšî*).
1. (2 Sam. 18:21ff., KJV). *See* CUSHITE.
2. The father of Shelemiah and ancestor of Jehudi who read Baruch's scroll to King Jehoiakim (Jer. 36:14, 21ff.).
3. The father of the prophet Zephaniah (Zeph. 1:1).

CUSHITE [kŏosh'īt] (Heb. *kûšî*). Probably an Ethiopian slave rather than a personal name (note use of the definite article; "Cushi," KJV; 2 Sam. 18:21ff.; NIV "a Cushite"), who was chosen by Joab to relay the news of Absalom's death to King David. Because he was unfamiliar with a shorter route, he arrived after Ahimaaz, who took the "way of the plain" (v. 23);

nevertheless, he succeeded in delivering his message (v. 32).

At Num. 12:1 Moses' wife Zipporah is identified as a Cushite woman, suggesting the identification of Cush as a district in Midian.

CUSTODIAN (Gk. *paidagōgós* "boy guider"). The slave employed by ancient Greek and Roman families as a guardian for boys under the age of sixteen, the conventional age of maturity. These custodians would take the male children to school or to gymnastic exercises, guide their behavior, and thus train them to become responsible adults. They were not educators ("pedagogues") in the contemporary sense of the word.

At Gal. 3:24 Paul compares the law to such a custodian (so RSV; KJV "schoolmaster"; JB "guardian"; NIV "put in charge"), training believers to accept the Lord in faith. Since Paul here is defending the gospel from Judaizing attacks, he emphasizes the negative aspects of the law (at 5:14 he treats the law more tolerantly). At 1 Cor. 4:15 Paul contrasts his role as father of the Corinthian church to the role of other "guides" (so RSV; KJV "instructors"; NIV, JB "guardians"), possibly referring to Apollos and other charismatic leaders highly esteemed by the Corinthians.

CUTHAH [kŏŏth'ə] (Heb. *kûṭâ*; from Akk. *kûtû*). A Mesopotamian city whose inhabitants the Assyrian king Sargon II deported to Samaria in order to repopulate the region formerly inhabited by the exiled northern tribes (2 Kgs. 17:24; called Cuth at v. 30). The site has been identified as Tell Ibrāhîm, northeast of Babylon.

An important Babylonian city, apparently more densely populated after the fall of Babylon than before, Cuthah was the center for the worship of Nergal, the god of the underworld. The displaced populace brought their cult with them to Samaria, where they adopted a syncretistic worship of both Nergal and Yahweh (2 Kgs. 17:30-34).

CUTTINGS IN THE FLESH (Heb. *śereṭ, śāreṭeṭ*).† A form of self-mutilation practiced as a sign of mourning. Because of its association with the pagan cults of Israel's neighbors the Hebrews were forbidden to observe this rite (Lev. 19:28; 21:5; but cf. Jer. 16:6; 41:5). *See* MOURNING.

CYMBAL (Heb. *mᵉṣiltayim, ṣelṣᵉlim*; Gk. *kýmbalon*). A musical instrument, consisting of two metal (perhaps bronze; cf. 1 Chr. 15:19) discs or bowls (cf. Gk. *kýmbē*), held in both hands and struck together. Different sounds (cf. Ps. 150:5) might be obtained from cymbals of different shapes or perhaps by holding the instruments either vertically or horizontally.

Cymbals occur in the account of the festive occasion of the return of the ark to Jerusalem (1 Chr. 15:16, 28; cf. 13:18), and of the dedication of the temple by King Solomon (2 Chr. 5:12-13); Asaph, Heman, and Jeduthun were master cymbalists (1 Chr. 16:5, 42). Later the Levites assumed the functions of cymbalists — during the reign of Hezekiah (2 Chr. 29:25) and, after the Exile, at the dedication of the foundation of

An Assyrian cymbal-player

the temple (Ezra 3:10) and of the walls of Jerusalem (Neh. 12:27).

CYPRESS. Any of a genus of trees (*Cupressus*) that are evergreen conifers often nearly cylindrical in shape. The Italian cypress (*Cupressus sempervirens*), common in many countries bordering the Mediterranean, grows to a height of 30 m. (90 ft.).

The RSV translates Heb. *bᵉrôš* as "fir" (Ps. 104:17; Ezek. 27:5; 31:8), but more often "cypress" (e.g., 1 Kgs. 5:8; Hos. 14:8); the KJV always translates it "fir (tree)." As with other evergreens mentioned in the Old Testament, the identification of this tree is uncertain. *See also* HOLM TREE; PINE.

CYPRUS (Lat. *Cyprium*, from Gk. *kýpros* "copper"). The third largest island in the Mediterranean Sea, 74 km. (46 mi.) south of Cilicia (modern Turkey) and about 96 km. (60 mi.) west of Syria. In the Old Testament it is called Kittim.

I. Geography

Cyprus, reaching a length of 224 km. (140 mi) and a width of 96 km. (60 mi.), has two mountain ranges, the Pentadaktylos along the northern coast, reaching a hieght of 1024 m. (3357 ft.), and the Troodos toward the southwest, reaching a height of 1951 m. (6403 ft.). Between the ranges are the central lowlands, and in the south, the southern uplands. The long slopes and coastal plains in the west and south are conducive to vineyards and orchards of olive and carob trees; the soil, however, is rich enough for other agriculture only in the narrow valleys. Toward the northeast the soil is much more fertile, but yields only one large crop even when properly irrigated.

II. History

Occupied as early as the Neolithic period, Cyprus had become densely populated by the late third millennium B.C., possibly as the result of Anatolian settlement. Trade with the ancient Near East can be traced to this period, reaching extensive proportions by the Late Cypriote period (1600-1050). Achaean colonization was begun in the twelfth century, and the Mycenaean influence on the island was rapid. Situated strategically in the Mediterranean, Cyprus was exposed subsequently to Phoenician and Egyptian influences before it lost its independence in 709 to Sargon II of Assyria. About 560 it became part of the Egyptian kingdom and then the Persian Empire (supplying Xerxes with over one hundred ships in his expedition to Greece in 480); after a brief period of rule by Alexander the Great (333-323), the Roman Empire assumed control (58 B.C.). At first Cyprus was annexed to the province of Cilicia, but after 31 B.C. it became a separate province, governed after 22 B.C. by a Roman legate or a proconsul.

While Cyprus had a Jewish population as early as 320 B.C., the Christian Church made inroads on the island only after many were driven from Palestine by Stephen's death and the ensuing persecution; that the church grew is evident from the missionary activity among the Greeks at Antioch (Syria) by some Cypriote Christians (Acts 11:19-20).

Paul's first missionary journey commenced at Cyprus. Having landed at the eastern port of Salamis (Acts 13:5), Paul, accompanied by Barnabas a native of Cyprus (4:36), preached the gospel to the Jews and, after journeying across the island, to Sergius Paulus, the Roman proconsul stationed at the western harbor of Paphos (vv. 6ff.). Barnabas revisited the island when he and Paul parted company on the eve of the second missionary journey (15:39), but Luke does not comment on the degree of his success. Though Paul passed by Cyprus at the end of his third journey (21:3) and early in the fourth (27:4), Luke does not record that he visited Cyprus again.

CYRENE [sī rē′nī] (Gk. *Kyrēnē*). The capital of the Roman province of Cyrenaica (modern Shakhāt) located east of the Gulf of Sirte, along Libya's northern coast.

Founded *ca.* 632 B.C. by Dorian Greeks from the island of Thera in the Aegean Sea, Cyrene was an important Greek colony, under Greek authority till 440, except for a brief transfer of power to the Persians *ca.* 525. Under Ptolemaic rule (*ca.* 322-96) the city became a well-known center of learning through its medical school and a school of moral philosophy called the Cyrenaic School. In 96 B.C. Cyrene was annexed to Rome, and in 67 it was made a senatorial province together with Crete. Relative prosperity, interrupted only once by a Jewish uprising in A.D. 115, continued till 365, when an earthquake hit the city; its ensuing decline finally ended with conquest by the Arabs (642).

Among the Jewish pilgrims at Jerusalem were visitors from the area of Cyrene (Acts 2:10), distinguished from Egyptian pilgrims. By New Testament times the Jewish population at Cyrene (settled there since 300 B.C.) had become rather sizable, and Cyrenians had a synagogue at Jerusalem (6:9). One of their members, a certain man named Simon, was compelled by guards to carry Jesus' cross along the road to Cal-

vary (Matt. 27:32 par.). It is not known how the gospel infiltrated the Greek city, but a number of these Cyrenian Christians began to preach to the Greeks living at Antioch (Syria) (Acts 11:20); one of them, Lucius, is mentioned among the prophets and teachers of the Antioch church (13:1).

CYRENIANS [sī rē′nī ənz] (Gk. *Kyrēnaioi*). Inhabitants of Cyrene (Acts 6:9).

CYRENIUS (Luke 2:2, KJV). *See* QUIRINIUS.

CYRUS [sī′rəs] (Heb., Aram. *kōreš*; O. Pers. *Kuruš*).† The founder of the Achaemenid dynasty and the Persian Empire; called Cyrus II the Great, to distinguish him from his grandfather Cyrus I (*ca.* 668 B.C.) and Cyrus the Younger (431-401).

I. Life

The son of Cambyses I (Herodotus *Hist.* i.46), Cyrus inherited Persian rule upon ascending to the throne in 559 B.C. Nine years later he conquered the kingdom of the Medes, thereby unifying the two kingdoms (cf. Dan. 5:28, "Medes and Persians"). Shortly thereafter (547), the victor marched westward and defeated Croesus the ruler of Lydia. He then moved eastward to annex Parthia and a region extending as far as India.

While Cyrus' victory over Croesus would profoundly affect not only the fortunes of his son Xerxes (486-465) but also those of the Greek colonists in Asia (and eventually the Greeks on the mainland under Darius [522-486]), it was his successful siege of Babylon that influenced the destiny of the Jews. Though Nabonidus anticipated Cyrus' attack on Babylonia and tried to prepare the capital for a possible siege, the Babylonian forces were defeated by Cyrus along the Tigris in the fall of 539. In the absence of Nabonidus, Babylon was taken on October 12 by a ruse — the course of the river Euphrates had been diverted to permit some of Cyrus' soldiers to cross and enter the city (Herodotus i.191).

Desirous of showing clemency and willing to preserve the Babylonian heritage, Cyrus allowed the Babylonians to continue to worship their own deities. According to the Cyrus Cylinder (*ANET*, p. 315), Marduk, the chief of the Babylonian pantheon, looked favorably upon Cyrus' concessions. At the end of his accession year as ruler over Babylon (539/538), the Persian monarch left the city to assume residence in the old Median city of Ecbatana.

The great conqueror died *ca.* 530, during an expedition against the Massagetae tribes who dwelled on the northeastern frontier (Herodotus i.201-214). Cyrus was buried in a royal tomb outside of Pasargadae, the modern city of Murghab. He was succeeded by his son Cambyses.

II. Biblical References

The author of Chronicles ends his account of the southern kingdom by recalling a prophecy by Jeremiah (Jer. 25:12) and recording Cyrus' role in its fulfillment. In his first year (i.e., during his accession as king of Babylon) Cyrus proclaimed his intent to permit the exiled Jews to return and rebuild the temple at Jerusalem (2 Chr. 36:22-23 par. Ezra 1:1-4). Isaiah,

The Cyrus Cylinder which records the deeds of the king, including the capture of Babylon and the release of the Jewish exiles (by courtesy of the Trustees of the British Museum)

too, in his consolation of Israel (Isa. 40–55) mentions Cyrus' commission to rebuild Jerusalem, with special attention to the temple (44:28). In ch. 45 the prophet calls Cyrus the Lord's "anointed" who would subdue nations and open the gates of Babylon (i.e., permit the exiles to return; 45:1). While the Persian monarch may have been a messianic servant of the Lord, the prophet keeps the focus on God's redemption of his people, of which Cyrus was only the instrument. There is no reason to suggest that Cyrus became a convert. It is more likely that he was interested in having Judah as a buffer nation between hostile Egypt and his own empire.

The book of Ezra depicts the fulfillment of these prophetic passages concerning Cyrus. The author describes the return to Judah of the Jewish exiles during the reign of Cyrus (1:1-2), adding that the monarch returned the vessels which Nebuchadnezzar had taken from the temple almost fifty years earlier (vv. 7-8). Cyrus also offered the returnees a royal grant for the reconstruction of the temple (3:7). When the exiles encountered opposition to this project, they reminded their enemies that Cyrus had given them permission (4:3); so concerned were the opponents over the rebuilding of Jerusalem that they even petitioned the later king, Darius I the Great, to confirm this claim (5:13-17; cf. 6:1-12).

Daniel, who had been taken captive to Babylon by Nebuchadnezzar in 605 B.C., remained in royal service there until at least the first year of Cyrus (Dan. 1:21; cf. 6:28; 10:1). The account of Belshazzar's feast alludes to Cyrus' conquest of Babylon (cf. 5:30-31).

Bibliography. A. T. E. Olmstead, *History of the Persian Empire* (Chicago: 1948), pp. 34-58.

D.

1. A symbol used to designate two biblical manuscripts: Codex Bezae (D) and Codex Claromontanus (D^2).

2. A symbol for the Deuteronomist, a literary document which, according to a number of scholars, was used in the composition of the Pentateuch. It is widely, though not universally, believed that this source approximates the book of Deuteronomy.

DABAREH (Josh. 21:28, KJV). *See* Daberath.

DABBASHETH (Josh. 19:11, KJV). *See* Dabbesheth.

DABBESHETH [dăb'ə shĕth] (Heb. *dabbešeṭ* "hump"). A town in the tribal territory of Zebulun (Josh. 19:11; KJV "Dabbasheth"). Of the possible modern identifications Tell esh-Shammana, near Tell Qeimûn (biblical Jokneam), is the most likely.

DABERATH [dăb'ə răth] (Heb. *dāḇᵉraṭ* "pasture"). A levitical town in the region assigned to Issachar, on the border of Zebulun (Josh. 19:12), identified with contemporary Dabûriyeh at the northwest foot of Mt. Tabor. It was given by God to the Gershonites after the allotment of lands (21:28; KJV "Dabareh"; 1 Chr. 6:72). Rabbith, mentioned at Josh. 19:20, may be the same village.

DAGON [dā'gŏn] (Heb. *dāgôn*).† Ancient Semitic fertility-god, apparently adopted by the Philistines (Sea Peoples) shortly after their invasion of Palestine and regarded as their national god. Upon capturing Samson, the Philistines offered sacrifices to Dagon in his temple at Gaza, perhaps the very structure which the Israelite hero destroyed, killing the Philistines as well as himself (Judg. 16:23-30). Later, when the Philistines had brought the captured ark of the covenant to Ashdod, they placed it in the temple of Dagon beside the statue of their deity, which toppled over twice, severing both its hands and head (1 Sam. 5:2-7); according to 1 Macc. 10:83-85 (cf. 11:4), worship of Dagon continued at Ashdod as late as 160 B.C., when Jonathan destroyed the temple. Archaeological excavations have uncovered an Iron Age temple of Dagon at Beth-shan, probably that where the Philistines displayed the head of Saul (1 Chr. 10:10; cf. 1 Sam. 31:10). Other probable centers of Dagon worship include the cities of Beth-dagon ("house" or "temple of Dagon") in Asher (Josh. 19:27) and Judah (15:41); the name is preserved in the modern sites Beit Dajan, southeast of Jaffa (cf. Akk. Bit-Daganna) and east of Nablus (Shechem).

The deity is attested in third-millennium B.C. inscriptions from southern Mesopotamia and Ebla (Tell Mardikh) in Syria. He was the principal Amorite deity at Mari (eighteenth century), where his cultic personnel included specialists in prophecy and divination. In one of the few mythological references to this god he is cited as the father of the Ugaritic storm-god Baal-Haddu; a temple of Dagon has been discovered at Ras Shamra. Texts or inscriptions from all of the above locales include the name Dagon (more commonly Dagan) as a theophoric element in personal names.

Recent scholarship has identified the name with a Semitic root *dgn,* which concerns clouds and rain. Heb. *dāgān* "grain" is apparently derived from this form, perhaps a secondary development reflecting the transition of the god's authority from weather to cereal (cf. Phoen. *dāgōn* "grain, corn"). The proposed derivation from Heb. *dāg* "fish" (so Jerome, Rashi, Kimchi) has been disproved.

DAINTIES (Heb. *maʿᵃḏān, taʾᵃwâ*; Gk. *liparós*). Tasty foods, especially sweets, consumed at banquets by kings and citizens alike. Scripture does not condemn eating such delicacies (e.g., Gen. 49:20; Job 33:20); in fact, it supports the partaking of special foods on special occasions (Neh. 8:10). But Scripture warns against gluttony (Prov. 23:3; RSV "delicacies"), cautions with regard to the motives of a host (v. 6), and observes the brevity of luxury (Lam. 4:5). The psalmist refuses to compromise himself with the wicked by eating their dainties (Ps. 141:4). The words of the "whisperer" are like "delicious morsels" (Prov. 18:8 par. 26:22), slander which remains in a person's memory.

The dainties (Rev. 18:14) after which Babylon (or Rome) was hankering in John's revelation were the sumptuous foods, the jewelry, and other precious possessions listed at vv. 11-13 — pleasures it no longer would enjoy.

DAIRY PRODUCTS. While the Israelites were familiar with milk, on account of their many herds of small cattle (*see* CATTLE), they often made dairy products rather than drink the milk as it came from the animal. Heb. *ḥālāḇ* ("milk"; KoB, p. 298) is milk curdled by means of churning in contact with pieces of rennet-stomach and made sour through fermentation; it did not spoil for many months. The Hebrews boiled this liquid with groats to make a gruel. *See also* MILK.

Heb. *ḥem'â* has been translated variously as "curds" (RSV, NIV; cf. "curdled milk," Gesenius, p. 285), "cream" (so usually JB), or "butter" (KJV; KoB, p. 308). According to one tradition, it is prepared by beating or simply swinging a goatskin suspended between two branches and filled with milk. Prov. 30:33 suggests that the milk was pressed through a cloth to make butter. The Israelites dipped their bread into fresh butter, which, because of climate and primitive storage facilities, was less solid than that now used in the West. Abraham may have given the divine messenger milk and butter such as this (Gen. 18:8); so might have Jael when she invited Sisera to her tent before killing him (Judg. 5:25). According to Isa. 7:15, 22, "butter and honey" (KJV; RSV "curds") was to be the simple diet of the promised deliverer during his infancy.

Cheese was made by separating the water from the sweet curdled milk. At Job 10:10 this process of curdling cheese (Heb. *geḇînâ*) is used as a metaphor for the creation of human life. The cheeses which David brought to his brothers in the camp (1 Sam. 17:18) were clumps of curds, dried milk (Heb. *ḥᵃriṣê heḥālāḇ* "slices of milk") cut into slices and eaten on bread. The "cheese from the herd" (RSV; Heb. *šᵉpôṭ bāqār*, possibly "curds of the herd"; KoB, p. 1002) given David at Mahanaim (2 Sam. 17:29; NIV "cheese from cow's milk") was similar; this cheese may have been produced at Gilead, which was known for its large herds (cf. Num. 32:26).

DALAIAH (1 Chr. 3:24, KJV). *See* DELAIAH **5.**

DALETH [dä'lĭth] (Heb. *dālet*).† The fourth letter of the Hebrew alphabet, thus used with numerical value in the KJV, NIV, and JB as the heading of the fourth section of the acrostic Ps. 119. The Hebrew character (ד, ד) represents both the dental stop (transliterated *d*) and, with the daghesh, the spirantized interdental (*ḏ*).

DALMANUTHA [dăl'mə noo'thə] (Gk. *Dalmanoutha*). A district to which Jesus withdrew following the feeding of the four thousand (Mark 8:10). The name and location of the district, which is not mentioned in other ancient sources, remains highly problematic. Although the most reliable Greek manuscripts read Dalmanutha at Mark 8:10, other versions cite either Magadan or Magdala (so RSV mg.), and the best texts read Magadan in the parallel account at Matt. 15:39 (KJV "Magdala"). Although some scholars view the name as the incomprehensible vestige of

some Aramaic expression, most likely it designates a location, along with these other sites, on the western shore of the Sea of Galilee (some, however, would place Magadan on the eastern shore, near Gerasa). It may also represent a hypothetical or "ideal" setting for Jesus' ministry in that area, thus pointing up Mark's lack of concern for geographical particulars.

DALMATIA [dăl mā'shə] (Gk. *Dalmatia*). The southern region of the Roman province of Illyricum, located along the northeastern shore of the Adriatic Sea. It was to this district that Titus went after he had completed his work at Crete (2 Tim. 4:10).

DALPHON [dăl'fŏn] (Heb. *dalpôn* "crafty"). One of the ten sons of Haman executed by the Jews for trying to kill all the Jews in Persia (Esth. 9:7).

DAMARIS [dăm'ə rĭs] (Gk. *Damaris*). A woman who, together with a certain Dionysius, was converted to Christianity by Paul's preaching at Athens (Acts 17:34). She may have been a person of social distinction, though she was probably not the wife of Dionysius (as suggested by Chrysostom *De sac.* iv.7).

DAMASCUS [də măs'kəs] (Heb. *dammeśeq*; Aram. *darmeśeq*; Gk. *Damaskos*).† A city in Syria and one of the oldest continuously occupied cities in the world.

I. Geography

Damascus is situated 80 km. (50 mi.) inland from the Mediterranean in the Ghutah, an oasis at the base of Mt. Qasyun; Mt. Hermon is to the southwest. The district received water from the Nahr Baradā (river Abana), which flows from the Anti-lebanon mountains at the west, and the Nahr A'waj (river Pharpar), which lies to the south. Located strategically at the junction of major commercial and military routes, the city was an important center throughout ancient times. The present city, Dimashq ash-Sham, is the capital of modern Syria.

II. History

Although traces of civilization dating to the Chalcolithic period have been found on the periphery of the Ghutah oasis, the city itself seems to have been founded toward the beginning of the second millennium B.C. (*ca.* 2000), perhaps by Arameans. In the patriarchal accounts, Abraham's steward Eliezer is said to have come from Damascus (Gen. 15:2), and it is to this general region that Abraham and his allies pursued the four eastern kings (14:15). The district (Egyp. *Apum*) is mentioned in the eighteenth-century Egyptian Execration Texts.

By the fifteenth century Damascus had come under Egyptian control; it is listed among cities conquered by Pharaoh Thutmose III (*ca.* 1490-1436). In the fourteenth-century Amarna Letters the city ("Damascus in the land of Upe") is named as an Egyptian vassal. Following a brief interlude of domination by the Hittite Empire (*ca.* 1350-1300), Damascus returned to Egyptian control, probably through the treaty of Rameses II and the Hittite Hattusilis.

With the collapse of the Hittite Empire (thirteenth century) the region was invaded by Arameans, who

Houses built into the city wall of Damascus (cf. 2 Cor. 11:32-33) (W. S. LaSor)

established city-states at Damascus and neighboring cities in Syria. It was at the beginning of the first millennium that Damascus came within the purview of the Israelites, when *ca.* 1000 David subdued the Arameans and established garrisons there (2 Sam. 8:5-7 par. 1 Chr. 18:5-7). Israelite authority came to an end in the waning years of Solomon's reign (*ca.* 930), when Rezon of Zobah captured the city, establishing there a powerful Aramean state which defied Israelite authority (1 Kgs. 11:23-25).

Under the divided monarchy, both Judah and Israel sought Damascus as an ally against their Hebrew neighbor (cf. 1 Kgs. 15:18ff. par. 2 Chr. 16:2ff.); having been persuaded by Asa of Judah to break his alliance with the Israelite king Baasha, Ben-hadad I made substantial inroads into Israelite territory. Although twice defeated by Ahab (cf. 1 Kgs. 20:1-34), Ben-hadad II remained a substantial threat to Israel; ironically, Ahab and Ben-hadad were forced to ally themselves against the Assyrian Shalmaneser III, whom they defeated at Qarqar (853). In renewed hostilities, Ahab died in battle with the Syrians at Ramoth-gilead (22:29-36). Hazael usurped the throne at Damascus from Ben-hadad II (or perhaps his coregent and successor Ben-hadad III). Enraged by the Israelite Jehu's submission to Shalmaneser III, Hazael took advantage of a lull in Assyrian pressure to overtake much of the northern kingdom and besiege Samaria (2 Kgs. 10:32-33; 13:1-9). When the Assyrians under Adad-nirari III campaigned against Damascus, Joash of Israel regained control of northern Palestine; although Ben-hadad III (or IV) mounted a campaign against Hamath *ca.* 780, both Damascus and Hamath fell under the sway of Israel's Jeroboam II (14:28). It is unclear whether Jeroboam's onslaught was incomplete or if the Syrians regained control, but in 735 the coalition of Rezin of Damascus and Pekah of Israel encountered Ahaz of Judah in the Syro-Ephraimite War; three

years later, at the instigation of Ahaz, the Assyrians under Tiglath-pileser III invaded Israel and defeated Damascus, killing Rezin and deporting the populace (16:9). Thus the Aramean kingdom of Damascus was destroyed.

While Damascus remained a thriving commercial center, it held little political significance as a province in the Assyrian Empire (Akk. *Dimašqi*) and a garrison city of the fifth satrapy of the Persian Empire. Occupied by Alexander the Great, the city subsequently yielded its prominence to Seleucid Antioch. In the first century B.C. Damascus became the capital of a Nabatean kingdom; although the region came under Roman rule from 64 B.C.–A.D. 37, it remained under a Nabatean governor. Apparently the Nabatean Aretas IV regained control during the rule of Caligula; it was he who ruled the city at the time of Paul's visit (*ca.* 37-40; Acts 9:2ff.; 2 Cor. 11:32). In the early second century A.D. the Roman emperor Trajan incorporated Damascus into the Roman province of Arabia.

Stemming largely from the city's association with Paul's conversion and the apostle's refuge there, Damascus became a thriving center of Christianity. By the early fourth century it had become the seat of a bishop; at approximately this time the Church of St. John the Baptist was constructed on the site of the ancient temple of Hadad. The city came under Islamic influence in 635.

Bibliography. M. F. Unger, *Israel and the Aramaeans of Damascus* (Grand Rapids: 1967).

DAMASCUS DOCUMENT. *See* ZADOKITE FRAGMENTS.

DAMASCUS GATE.† The principal gate in the northern wall of the modern Old City of Jerusalem. Constructed *ca.* A.D. 1538-1539 by Suleiman the Magnificent, it leads to the major north-south street, the Cardo Maximus of the Roman city Aelia Capitolina. The name derives from the early Christian tradition that Paul departed from the city by this gate en route to Damascus (Acts 9). Its Arabic name is Bab el-'Amud ("Gate of the Column"), indicating the column erected there by Hadrian and still standing when the Arabs captured the city in 638.

DAMN, DAMNATION. A term found in the KJV, but changed to "condemn(ation)" in most modern versions. Matthew warns against eternal punishment for the unrighteous (Matt. 25:46; cf. v. 41 "eternal fire"), and Mark cautions that a person blaspheming against the Holy Spirit "is in danger of eternal damnation" (KJV; RSV, NIV, JB "is guilty of eternal sin"). *See* CONDEMN.

DAN [dăn] (Heb. *dān* "he [God] judges") **(PERSON, TRIBE).**† The fifth son of Jacob and first son of Bilhah, the maid of Jacob's wife Rachel (Gen. 30:5-6), and brother of Naphtali (vv. 7-8; 35:25). His mother gave him this name because she interpreted his birth as both a divine judgment and a divine answer to her longing for a son (30:6). Subsequently the name designates a tribe, representing the descendants of Dan.

In the Blessing of Jacob, bestowed upon his sons,

two things are predicted of Dan: that he would judge his own people (NIV "provide justice") and, as a viper, he would bite the horse's heels (49:16-17). By this the aged patriarch may have been alluding to the difficulties Dan would face in adequately administering justice to the Danites who would eventually dwell in the southwestern and extreme northeastern corners of Palestine; he may also have been anticipating Dan's acts of bravery as he resisted the powerful attacks of the Philistines. In the Blessing of Moses, Dan is compared to a powerful lion's whelp leaping from Bashan (Deut. 33:22). According to this prophecy Dan would occupy a region near Bashan in Transjordania; though still timid, the tribe would display its strength in due time.

Dan's search for an inheritance in the Promised Land after the Conquest proved to be more difficult than that of most of the other tribes. Initially Dan was assigned an area between Judah, Ephraim, Benjamin, and the coastal plain; and, according to Josh. 19:40-47, the tribe settled there and stayed for some time. While Dan's boundaries are not precisely given, part of their territory must have been the region later occupied by the Philistines; Ekron, one of the cities assigned to Dan, later became a Philistine city.

The book of Judges describes Dan's struggles to maintain a place of inheritance in Palestine. Pressured by the Amorites, who in turn were coerced by the Philistines, the Danites had to withdraw from the coastal plain to the hill country to the east (Josh. 19:47-48; Judg. 1:34-35), though when this took place is not indicated. (Note that Judg. 5:17 still refers to Dan near the Mediterranean Sea.) But after awhile, perhaps shortly after the death of Joshua, the Danites became overcrowded in the hill country, leading some of them to look for another dwelling place. Judg. 13-16 depicts the Danite victories over the Philistines, and ch. 18 records the move into Laish, a city the Danites from Zorah and Eshtaol captured and renamed Dan (18:27).

On the whole, the Danites did not play a major role in Israel's history. Two of the tribe's more notable representatives were Oholiab, who helped construct the tabernacle (Exod. 31:6), and the judge Samson (Judg. 13-16), both of whom lived before the Monarchy. Ezekiel names Dan in his vision of the apportionments of land (Ezek. 48:1), but the tribe is excluded from John's vision of the 144,000 servants of God (Rev. 7:4-8), perhaps because Dan actively promoted idolatry under King Jeroboam (1 Kgs. 12:29).

DAN [dăn] (Heb. *dān* "he [God] judges") (PLACE).
1. A city along the northern boundary of the tribal territory of Dan (also Israel's northern border), thus generating the expression "from Dan to Beer-sheba" as a designation for all of Israel (e.g., David's census; 2 Sam. 24:2 par.).

Judg. 18 narrates the conquest of Laish (or Leshem at Josh. 19:47) by the Danites. In their search for a new dwelling place, the Danites sent five able men to explore the land. Having noted that the inhabitants of Laish were unsuspecting folk, they reported back to their clan that the city could be easily taken (Judg. 18:2-10). Subsequently, six hundred armed men stole into the city, and enlisting the Levite from the house

of the prophet Micah (or Beth-micah) in Ephraim, took Laish. They rebuilt the city and named it after their ancestor Dan (vv. 14-29). The narrative closes with the new inhabitants of Dan introducing worship of the same idol that had belonged to Micah and had so offended them earlier (vv. 30-31).

The city of Dan is also known for the shrine which King Jeroboam I (*ca.* 925 B.C.) erected in an effort to prevent pilgrims from making their annual journeys to Jerusalem to offer sacrifices; subsequently this shrine, dedicated to calf worship, became a stumbling block to Israel (1 Kgs. 12:25-30; cf. 2 Kgs. 10:29). After Ben-hadad conquered Dan during the reign of Baasha (1 Kgs. 15:16-20), the city was in Syrian hands for some time. While the exact time of its recovery by Israel is not known (possibly by Jeroboam II, *ca.* 760 B.C.; cf. 2 Kgs. 14:25), it fell to the Assyrians in 732 (cf. 2 Kgs. 15:29).

Located in a fertile plain near Beth-rehob (Judg. 18:28), Dan has been identified with Tell el-Qâḍī ("mound of the judge"; Israeli Tel Dan), at the source of the Nahr el-Leddan. A third-century B.C. Greek inscription confirms this identification. Excavations at the site have uncovered the remains of a substantial city as early as the third millennium B.C. During the Middle Bronze Age (mid-second millennium) it was surrounded by massive Hyksos-style earthen ramparts; a large mudbrick gateway formed by two towers joined by an arch has been discovered. Little has been found pertaining to the Danite capture of the city (early twelfth century). In the northern portion of the city, a high place dating to the tenth century has been discovered and, nearby, an Israelite horned altar. A paved royal ceremonial road leads to the eastern gate (ninth century).

2. A city (so KJV, JB), possibly located between Mecca and Medina, or a people (NIV) with whom the Tyrians traded (Ezek. 27:19; Heb. *wᵉdān*). The RSV, following the LXX, omits "and Dan."

DANCE.† The Israelites, like other peoples of the ancient Near East, were accustomed to express their emotions in dance — usually round dances performed by the women (Heb. *mᵉḥōlâ* "round dance"; KoB, p. 512; e.g., Exod. 15:20; Heb. *māḥôl*; Jer. 31:13). The only specific example of male dancing is found at 2 Sam. 6:14 where David dances "with all his might" before the ark; for this his wife Michal accuses him of dancing in the company of "vulgar fellows" (v. 20). On occasion people danced alone, such as Jephthah's daughter upon the victorious return of her father (Judg. 11:34). According to Job 21:11-12 even children engaged in this expression of joy (cf. Matt. 11:17 par. Luke 7:32).

The Israelites danced on a number of festive occasions. The women rejoiced at feasts, during the gathering of the harvest, and at Saul's victory over the Philistines (1 Sam. 18:6-7; cf. 21:11; 29:5). At an earlier time they thanked God in this way for delivering them through the sea of reeds (Exod. 15:20).

Unlike much of contemporary Western dancing, the Israelite men and women never danced together. Frequently the dances were performed within a religious context, as part of many cultic celebrations (Ps. 149:3; 150:4), including those to deities forbidden to Israel

(Exod. 32:19). Like many modern enthusiasts, Israelites "twisted" (Heb. *ḥûl*), "skipped" (Heb. *kārar*), "skipped about" (qal of *rāqaḏ*), and "leaped" (KJV, 1 Kgs. 18:26; Heb. *pāsaḥ*; RSV "limped"; NIV "danced"; JB "performed their hobbling dance") as they expressed themselves in bodily movements.

The Old Testament does not frown on dancing, viewing it as an integral aspect of Jewish life (e.g., Judg. 21:21, 23). Indeed, the author of Ecclesiastes notes that there was an appropriate time for dancing (Eccl. 3:4). It is not surprising that the Hebrews vented their emotions differently in times of mourning, and dancing is seen to contrast with sorrow at Lam. 5:15. But just as the psalmist who was made whole (Ps. 30:11), Israel would find its sadness replaced with dancing once God made their nation whole (Jer. 31:4, NIV).

Unlike the Old Testament, the New Testament records very few instances of dancing. In the parable of the return of the prodigal son, the father's joy is manifested in "music and dancing" (Luke 15:25; Gk. *chorós*). Luke omits mention of merry-making at the marriage feast, though the practice was customary at Israelite weddings (cf. Cant. 6:13); this omission may be explained by the focus of the parable — a lesson in humility (Luke 14:11). The refusal of some children to "dance" (Gk. *orchéomai*) at the bidding of other children (Luke 7:32 par.) most likely refers to the Jews who rejected both the ascetic lifestyle of John the Baptist and the life-affirming attitude of Christ.

DANIEL [dan'yəl] (Heb. *dāniyēl*, *dāniʾēl* "God is my judge").

1. The second son of David, born to him of Abigail (1 Chr. 3:1; LXX A *Dalouia*; LXX B *Damniēl*); at 2 Sam. 3:3 he is called Chileab. No further mention is made of him, which suggests that he died young.

2. A priest of the house of Ithamar who returned from the Exile with Ezra (Ezra 8:2), he was among those who set their seal to the renewed covenant under Nehemiah (Neh. 10:6).

3. A man of exceptional righteousness (so regarded along with Noah and Job in Ezek. 14:14, 20) and wisdom (28:3). The JB follows the Kethib of the Hebrew text, which reads Danel. This person is probably to be identified with the Danel (Ugar. *dníl*) of the Aqht legend from Ras Shamra, who was renowned for his compassion and justice, especially toward widows and orphans. The identification is particularly apt at 28:3, where the king of Tyre is said to be wiser than Daniel (or Danel).

4.† A prophet or visionary of the Exile, the subject of the book of Daniel. One of the noble Israelite youths taken off to Babylon by Nebuchadnezzar during the third year of King Jehoiakim (605 B.C.), he was educated for service in the royal palace and assigned the name Belteshazzar (Dan. 1:1-7). Loyal to the Hebrew religion, he became highly regarded for his skill in interpreting dreams and visions; among those recorded are the dreams of Nebuchadnezzar (chs. 2, 4), the handwriting on the wall of Belshazzar's palace (ch. 5), and Daniel's own dreams concerning the future of the great empires and the coming of the messianic kingdom (chs. 7–12). He attained a high place in the king's service as governor of the province of Babylon and prefect over all the wise men during the reign of Nebuchadnezzar (2:48), third ruler in the kingdom under Belshazzar (5:29), and one of the three presidents over the 120 satraps of Darius I (6:2-3). He continued in royal service until the first year of Cyrus (1:21; 538; cf. 6:28), but is recorded as having received a vision in Cyrus' third year (10:1; 536).

DANIEL, ADDITIONS TO.† Three (or four) apocryphal additions to the book of Daniel. They include the Prayer of Azariah and the Song of the Three Young Men (sometimes considered to be two separate works), inserted after 3:23 in the Greek versions of

Dancers and musicians in an Egyptian tomb painting of the Twelfth Dynasty (by courtesy of the Trustees of the British Museum)

Daniel; the Story of Susanna; and the Story of Bel and the Dragon. The latter two are added to the book of Daniel as chs. 13–14. In English versions, all of these additions are treated as separate compositions.

Probably written toward the end of the second century B.C., these additions do not appear in the Hebrew canon. Whether the additions were composed originally in Hebrew or Aramaic (as seems possible for the Prayer of Azariah and the Song of the Three Young Men) or Greek remains open to debate. Quite possibly these accounts, along with the stories which comprise chs. 1–6 of the canonical book, circulated separately and were rejected by the compiler of the book of Daniel.

See also AZARIAH, PRAYER OF; BEL AND THE DRAGON; SONG OF THE THREE YOUNG MEN; SUSANNA, STORY OF.

DANIEL, BOOK OF.† Account of the activity and apocalyptic visions of Daniel, a noble Israelite taken captive by Nebuchadnezzar and employed in the royal service at Babylon.

I. Place in the Canon

Following the LXX and the Vulgate, English versions place the book of Daniel among the Major Prophets, following Ezekiel (some LXX manuscripts placed it before Ezekiel and Isaiah). The Hebrew canon, however, includes the book among the Writings. Most likely this is because the book was composed too late to be included with the Prophets, which rabbinic tradition considered closed with the death of the prophet Malachi in the fifth century. Less probable is the view that the book is inferior prophecy, failing to address the exiled people in the name of the Lord with words of exhortation toward ethical behavior or of comfort for restoration.

II. Author and Date

Although the book deals primarily with Daniel himself, this does not mean that he was also its author. Indeed, the form of references to "this Daniel" (Dan. 6:3, 28) and the introduction to the accounts of his dreams and visions (7:1) suggest that an unknown author composed the book, perhaps drawing upon first-person reports of the visions as written down or told by Daniel (chs. 7–12) as well as a third-person narrative of Daniel's activity (chs. 1–6). The more thorough detail of the vision accounts as compared to others in the Old Testament suggests that a later editor may have added supplementary material. This later compilation is supported by the Jewish tradition (Talmud b. Bat. 15a) which ascribes responsibility for the book to the "men of the Great Synagogue," a 120-member council which was active in Jerusalem between the time of Ezra (ca. 450) and Simon the Just (270) and allegedly concerned with the canon of the Old Testament.

The notion of a composite work composed by an author-compiler toward the extreme end of the Old Testament period is supported further by the linguistic nature of the book. The language of the section written in Aramaic (2:4b–7:28) generally is held to resemble that of Ezra (more than that of Qumran), though it is somewhat later than the Aramaic of the Elephantine papyri (fifth century). The Hebrew portions, however, are held to resemble Mishnaic Hebrew and, based on the presence of Persian and Greek loanwords as well as historical allusions, are assigned to the Maccabean period (second-first centuries). Final compilation during this late period is supported by the literary nature of the book. The linguistic division between the Hebrew and Aramaic portions does not correspond to divisions of content; indeed, the Aramaic text begins in the midst of the story of Nebuchadnezzar's dream (ch. 2) and concludes between Daniel's first and second visions.

III. Contents

A. Daniel in Babylon. The book can be divided into two main sections on the basis of content and narrative style. Chs. 1–6 consist of six stories, written in the third person, about the trials of Daniel and his three companions in captivity.

Ch. 1 relates the deportation of Daniel to Babylon, where he is educated at the royal court and his name changed to Belteshazzar. He and his companions distinguish themselves by their knowledge and skill. Included is the story of the youths' refusal to abandon the Jewish dietary restrictions and the Lord's rewarding them with superior health.

Ch. 2 records the dream of Nebuchadnezzar in which a colossal statue comprised of various materials is shattered by a rock, which then becomes a great mountain and fills the earth. The Chaldean dream experts are unable to explain the vision, but Daniel interprets the parts of the image as four successive kingdoms — the Babylonian Empire, the Medes and Persians, and the Greek empire of Alexander the Great. (Some would include the Roman Empire as one of the four and would see the feet of the statue as pointing to the period after the fall of Rome when no powerful world empire would be formed.) The stone represents the kingdom of God, which in the end will be victorious over all earthly kingdoms.

Ch. 3 relates the faithfulness of Daniel's three friends, Shadrach, Meshach, and Abednego, in refusing to worship the golden image set up by Nebuchadnezzar. When the king casts them into the fiery furnace, God rewards their loyalty by protecting them from harm.

Written in the form of a proclamation by the king himself, ch. 4 (MT 3:31–4:34) recounts Nebuchadnezzar's dream of a large tree chopped down to its stump. Daniel explains that the tree symbolizes the king, who would be punished for his arrogance by seven years of insanity and then restored upon proof of his repentance. Vv. 34-37 (MT 31-34) are the king's hymn of praise to the God of Daniel.

Ch. 5 tells of the feast of King Belshazzar, the son of the usurper Nabonidus (and perhaps, on his mother's side, related to Nebuchadnezzar; cf. v. 2), at which the party desecrate the vessels from the Jerusalem temple by drinking to their pagan gods. Immediately a hand appears, writing on the wall the cryptic message "MENE, MENE, TEKEL, PARSIN." Summoned at the advice of the queen mother, Daniel explains the words, actually the names of weights, as foreshadowing the demise of Belshazzar and the division of his kingdom among the Medo-Persians. Daniel is richly rewarded, and during that same night the king is murdered, to be succeeded by "Darius the

Mede'' (6:1), more likely Cyrus the Great. (According to extrabiblical sources, the queen mother died eleven days after the entrance of Cyrus into Babylon. Probably Nabonidus had already been taken captive by the time of these events, and his son Belshazzar retained control of only a part of the kingdom. According to the Babylonian Nabonidus Chronicle [*ANET*, pp. 305-7], the crown prince Belshazzar actually ruled as king of Babylon [550-545] while his father stayed at Tema; this would explain the dates given at 7:1; 8:1.)

The story of Daniel in the lions' den at 6:1-28 (MT 2-29) recounts the plot by Daniel's fellow ministers and satraps whereby Darius decrees that for thirty days no one could petition any god or man other than the king. Ever loyal to his faith, Daniel disobeys and is cast into the lions' den as punishment. To Darius' delight, Daniel emerges unharmed, and the king issues an edict favoring the God of the Jews.

B. Daniel's Visions. Chs. 7-12, written in the first person, contain four apocalyptic visions of Daniel and their interpretations. The first (ch. 7), which occurs in the first year of King Belshazzar (*ca.* 550), depicts four beasts that emerge from the sea, one succeeding the other. Just as Daniel had interpreted the visions of others, an angel now explains this vision for Daniel. The beasts represent four kingdoms: the lion with eagle's wings is the Babylonian Empire; the voracious bear is the kingdom of the Medes with its lust for conquest; the leopard with the four wings of a bird stands for the Persians; and the fourth beast, which was "dreadful and exceedingly strong" and which "devoured and broke in pieces, and stamped the residue with its feet" (v. 7), is the kingdom of Alexander the Great. (Here, as in ch. 2, some would include the Roman Empire as one of the four kingdoms.) The ten horns of the fourth beast represent rulers "uprooted" (v. 8) by Antiochus IV Epiphanes, who, according to this vision, is to be the last pagan ruler and is to rule but "a time, two times, and half a time" (perhaps three and a half years; v. 25) before yielding power to the people of God, "the saints of the Most High." Some interpret this eleventh horn as the antichrist, a power directly opposed to God. The "one like a son of man" (v. 13) here indicates a human being, symbolizing the followers of the God of Israel who were to be rewarded for their constant faith despite unbearable circumstances.

The vision in ch. 8, dated to the third year of Belshazzar, describes a mighty ram (the kingdom of the Medes and Persians) which is broken and subdued by a he-goat from the west (Alexander the Great). The great horn of the he-goat is broken and replaced by four others (the successors of Alexander). From one of these horns springs a smaller one, clearly representing Antiochus IV, whose reign is marked by apostasy and persecution (vv. 23-25; cf. 1 Macc. 1:12-15; 2 Thess. 2:3). The imminent end of this wicked ruler "by no human hand" does not fit exactly the situation of Antiochus (cf. 1 Macc. 6:1-16), but may be taken as reassurance of the certain downfall of evil.

Ch. 9 contains the revelation of the "seventy weeks of years" (v. 24), given in the first year of Darius in response to Daniel's fervent prayer and fasting in search of the meaning of Jeremiah's prophecy regarding the desolation of Jerusalem (Jer. 25:11-12). The angel Gabriel explains that despite an extended period of trouble, including wars and sacrilege, the city and temple will be rebuilt and the kingdom of God will be established.

The final vision (chs. 10–12), during the third year of Cyrus, concerns the future of the Jewish people. Following three weeks of fasting and preparation, Daniel stands on the bank of the Tigris and envisions a man clothed in linen and wearing a gold belt. This messenger, perhaps a prominent angel such as Gabriel, reveals events to take place under four Persian kings as well as Alexander the Great and his successors, the struggles between the Seleucids and Ptolemies, and, in great detail, the persecution and apostasy which would occur in the reign of Antiochus IV (11:21-45). Ch. 12 proclaims the ultimate vindication of God's people and the resurrection of the dead (vv. 1-3). Daniel is then instructed to "seal the book" (v. 4) for an indeterminate time; he is assured that soon he would die and go to his rest, ultimately to be rewarded with resurrection "at the end of the days" (v. 13).

IV. Theological Value

The book of Daniel has long given rise to a vast range of conflicting interpretations, largely the result of attempts to determine precise historical identifications for the various points in the prophecies. Interpretation is greatly facilitated and the book's theological perspective greatly enhanced by the recognition of two literary genres employed in its prophecy — midrash (or edifying story) and apocalyptic prophecy. Midrash (chs. 1–6) is based on historical fact, interpreted in terms of God's activity in history, here advanced through the words and deeds of the wise Daniel. Apocalyptic prophecy (2:13-45; chs. 7–12) makes known God's will in timeless terms that have value for every age.

As a whole, the book is sublime in content, and it opens broad perspectives on world history. Each of the stories and visions stresses the understanding of God as active in and responsible for human history, the future of which he makes known to his faithful. In particular, the book is a source of comfort, both for those subject to the atrocities of Antiochus IV and for all the world's oppressed of any age, for it constantly affirms the ultimate rule of God's kingdom through the liberation of those who seek to do his will.

The book's importance is underscored by frequent New Testament references (Matt. 24:15) and allusions (v. 30; Luke 1:19, 26; John 5:29; Heb. 11:33-34; 2 Thess. 2:4) and by the striking similarities of many of the apocalyptic visions in the book of Revelation.

Bibliography. L. F. Hartman and A. A. Di Lella, *The Book of Daniel.* AB (1978); A. Lacocque, *The Book of Daniel* (Richmond: 1979); H. H. Rowley, "The Unity of the Book of Daniel," in *The Servant of the Lord,* 2nd ed. (Oxford: 1965), pp. 249-280; N. H. Porteous, *Daniel.* OTL (1965).

DANITES [dăn'īts] (Heb. *haddānî, bᵉnê-ḍān*). Members of the tribe of Dan (e.g., Josh. 19:47).

DAN-JAAN [dăn jā'ən] (Heb. *dān ya'an*). A city in the northern part of Palestine between Gilead and

Sidon (so KJV, NIV, following MT), possibly in the Transjordan along the road to Damascus; it was included on the circuit Joab followed in taking the census (2 Sam. 24:6b). On the basis of the LXX distinction between *Danidan* and *Oudan*, the RSV emends the MT to "to Dan, and from Dan" (cf. JB, *BH*). Other plausible emendations are Heb. *dān ya'ar* "Dan of the thicket" (so Gesenius, p. 204) and "Dan and Ijon [Heb. *'ywn*]" (NEB), a reading supported by the juxtaposition of these two cities at 1 Kgs. 15:20.

DANNAH [dăn'ə] (Heb. *dannâ* "stronghold"). A city in the hill country of Judah (Josh. 15:49), near Debir (Kiriath-sannah). Though its exact location continues to escape precise identification, proposed sites are Deir esh-Shemsh or Idhna.

DAPHNE [dăf'nĭ] (Gk. *Daphnē* "bay tree"). A suburb of the city of Antioch (Syria), about 8 km. (5 mi.) to the southwest. Located in a magnificent garden some 16 km. (10 mi.) in circumference, Daphne was the site of many sanctuaries, including the exquisite temple of Apollo, at the foot of the ever-flowing springs. Daphne was also a place of asylum, for Onias the high priest fled to Apollo's sanctuary after exposing Menelaus' graft (*ca.* 171 B.C.; 2 Macc. 4:32-33).

DARA. *See* DARDA.

DARDA [där'də] (Heb. *darda'*). One of four famous Israelites whose wisdom was surpassed only by King Solomon (1 Kgs. 4:31). While he is called a "son of Mahol" (so RSV, KJV, NIV), this is probably an epithet designating a member of an orchestral guild (JB "cantor"), since at 1 Chr. 2:6 he is included among the five descendants of Zerah of Judah (so NIV; RSV, KJV, JB "Dara," following MT *dāra'*).

DARIC [dăr'ĭk]. A Persian gold coin weighing about 8.4 g. (.3 oz.), bearing the image of Darius I Hystaspes (*ca.* 500 B.C.) and therefore assumed to have been coined by that ruler; it is possible that the name derived from Akk. *darag mana* (one-sixtieth of a mina). In the Old Testament the term (Heb. *ᵃadarkôn*) occurs at Ezra 8:27 and at 1 Chr. 29:7 (during David's days, likely an anachronism). The coin (Heb. *darkᵉmôn*) included among the exiles' offerings during the reigns of Cyrus (Ezra 2:69) and Artaxerxes (Neh. 7:70-72) may have been a drachma (so NIV, JB; RSV "darics"; KJV "drams").

DARIUS [də rī'əs] (Heb., Aram. *dārᵉyāweš*; O. Pers. *darayava[h]uš* "he who upholds the good").† The name of a number of Persian rulers.

1. Darius the Mede, mentioned only in the book of Daniel. He is depicted as gaining rule over Babylonia in the wake of the capture of Babylon and the death of Belshazzar, who was coregent with his father Nabonidus, the last ruler of the Neo-Babylonian kingdom (Dan. 5:30-31). Said to be the son of a certain Ahashuerus (Xerxes; not Xerxes I cited at Esth. 1:1, the son of Darius I), and by birth a Mede rather than a Persian, this monarch is portrayed as reigning at least one year (Dan. 9:1; 11:1); it is he who ordered Daniel into the den of lions (6:16). While many recent scholars have judged him to be a fictional device of the author of Daniel, various identifications have been proposed. Most likely he is to be equated with Cyrus II the Great, who conquered Babylon in 539; the name Darius may be an alternate title (cf. 6:28 where Aram. *ûḇmalᵉkûṯ* [usually "and the reign"] may begin with the iterative particle waw, meaning "namely...").

2. Darius I Hystaspes (521-486 B.C.), successor to Cambyses II the son of Cyrus II the Great; also called Darius the Great. Although he himself held no direct ancestral claim to succession, he gained kingship by defeating a certain Gaumata who had usurped the throne by posing as Bardiya (Gk. *Smerdis*), who had been murdered by his brother Cambyses II. Much of Darius' reign was consumed in military campaigns both to expand and consolidate Persian territory and to quell revolts within the empire; the more successful of these, as well as an account of his accession, are recorded in the trilingual Behistun inscription carved into the rock at modern Bisitun near Hamadan, Iran. However, not all of his campaigns fared as well as his conquests of Thrace, Macedonia, and the Indus valley. A prolonged bout with the Scythians in the region of the Danube and the Caspian Sea (beginning *ca.* 513) was followed by war with Greece (the Persian Wars) and the defeat of Persian forces at Marathon in 490.

Darius' greatest contributions to the empire were as an administrator. In addition to completing the reorganization of Persian territory into satrapies and determining the annual tribute for each, he fostered commerce by standardizing weights and measures and by establishing both land and sea routes. Persian architecture flourished under his administration, as evidenced by Darius' major building projects at Susa and Persepolis.

Following the policy of Cyrus the Great, Darius was not only tolerant but also supportive of religious freedom among the peoples of the empire. He granted exemptions from taxation and forced labor for priests of the Greek temple of Apollo in Magnesia and built and endowed temples in Egypt; it was during his reign that Zoroastrianism was introduced as an official religion. In the second year of his reign (520) he was informed of the desire of the returned Israelites to resume construction of the Jerusalem temple (Ezra 4:5, 24; 5:1-17); reiterating the decree of Cyrus, he supported their efforts and provided royal revenue for the project, which was completed in 515 (6:1-15). He is probably "Darius the Persian" mentioned at Neh. 12:22.

3. Darius II Ochus (423-404 B.C.), son of Artaxerxes I; also called Nothus ("the bastard") because his mother was a Babylonian concubine. Manipulated during much of his reign by Parysatis, his half-sister and wife, Darius managed to regain Greek cities in Asia Minor by siding with Sparta during the Peloponnesian War (431-404). He is mentioned in the Jewish Aramaic papyri from Elephantine in Egypt.

4. Darius III Codommanus (336-331 B.C.), grandnephew of Artaxerxes II. The last Achaemenid monarch, he suffered repeated defeats at the hands of Alexander the Great and the Macedonian forces (cf. 1 Macc. 1:1-8).

DARKNESS. The absence of light. Often used figuratively in contrast to light in Scripture.

I. Old Testament

According to the larger creation account there was darkness (Heb. *ḥōšeḳ*) upon "the face of the deep" (Gen. 1:2) before God created life and light (vv. 3, 11ff.). Once both the light and the darkness were in existence, they formed a contrast (e.g., v. 4; Job 26:10; 38:19). Created by God (Ps. 104:20; Isa. 45:7), the darkness is subject to its Maker (Ps. 139:12; cf. Job 2:22). Darkness also provides the backdrop of God's revelation at Mt. Horeb (Deut. 5:23-24; cf. 4:11; 2 Sam. 22:12; Ps. 18:11). The prophets depicted the Day of the Lord as being without light (Joel 2:2; Amos 5:18, 20; Zeph. 1:15).

Darkness is used metaphorically for misery (Job 18:18; 23:17 [par. "thick darkness"]; Eccl. 5:17), fright (Job 15:22-23), physical oppression (Ps. 107:10), death (Eccl. 11:8), and spiritual insensitivity (e.g., Isa. 42:7; 60:2). As the antithesis of understanding and righteousness, darkness is the path of fools (Prov. 2:13) and of the wicked (1 Sam. 2:9; Ps. 35:6), both of whom eagerly embrace it (Job 24:14-17; Ezek. 8:12-13).

God has at times caused unscheduled darkness to descend upon the earth. For three days the Egyptians experienced a "plague" of darkness for not letting the Israelites leave Egypt (Exod. 10:21-22); when Israel did escape, darkness foiled Pharaoh's host in their pursuit (14:20). Sometimes God's intervention comes as the darkness of confusion (Job 5:14) and oppression (19:8). But God is able and willing to rescue the faithful (2 Sam. 22:29; Ps. 18:28) and the repentant (Isa. 9:1-2) from eternal darkness. He urges his people to comfort the afflicted and thus to provide light within the darkness of their condition (58:10).

II. New Testament

Gk. *skótos* and its cognate *skotía* (used mainly by John) have the same range of meaning as Heb. *ḥōšeḳ*: from literal darkness (e.g., the three hours of darkness on the day of Jesus' crucifixion [Matt. 27:45 par. Mark 15:33; Luke 23:44]) to moral darkness or evil. John and, to a certain extent, Paul (Rom. 13:12; 2 Cor. 6:14) contrast the realms of light and darkness. The light, as John identified Christ (John 8:12), had come into the world (1:5) in order to lead people out of spiritual darkness (12:46). Though people would reject Jesus' message (3:19), Christ urged his disciples to continue to walk in the light rather than to be misled into spiritual darkness (12:35). 1 John presents an even more pronounced contrast between light — God and the Christian community — and the darkness of the hateful and disobedient (1 John 2:9, 11). But John does not portray the darkness as an independent power alongside God (see R. Bultmann, *Theology of the New Testament* 2 [New York: 1955], p. 18). Indeed, he writes that the darkness "has not overcome" (1:5, Gk. *katélaben* "did grasp" [Bauer, p. 413; cf. JB "could not overpower"]; KJV "comprehended") the light.

The phrase "nether gloom of darkness" (2 Pet. 2:17; Gk. *ho zóphos toú skótous*; KJV "mist of darkness"; JB "dark underworld") refers to the Day of Judgment, which for the false teachers spells complete and timeless darkness (cf. NIV "blackest darkness").

See also LIGHT.

DARKON [där'kŏn] (Heb. *darqôn* "bearer"). One of "Solomon's servants," whose descendants returned from exile under Zerubbabel (Ezra 2:56; Neh. 7:58).

DATES. *See* PALM TREE.

DATHAN [dā'thən] (Heb. *dāṭān*; cf. Akk. *datnu* "strong"). The son of Eliab (Num. 16:1; 26:9), who with his brother supported Korah in challenging Moses' leadership during the wilderness wanderings (16:1ff.). As a result both brothers were "swallowed up" by the earth (vv. 27, 31; cf. Deut. 11:6; Ps. 106:17).

DATHEMA [dăth'ə mə] (Gk. *Dathema*). A fortress in which the Jews took refuge when attacked by the Gentiles (1 Macc. 5:9). From there they sent a cry of distress to Judas Maccabeus, who came to their rescue. Two possible sites have been proposed, Tell er-Ramet and Tell Hamad, east of Carnaim.

DATING. *See* CHRONOLOGY, BIBLICAL.

DAUGHTER.† To the Israelites the word "daughter" (Heb. *baṯ*) has a wide range of meanings. (1) For the most part it refers to one's female offspring; the Old Testament lists the names of daughters as readily as those of sons (e.g., Gen. 11:29, Milcah the daughter of Haran). (2) By extension it signifies a female descendant, perhaps a granddaughter (2 Kgs. 8:26 par. 2 Chr. 22:2, Athaliah the granddaughter [so RSV, NIV; KJV, JB "daughter"] of Omri), or more distant relative. (3) Often it means a female inhabitant of a city (e.g., Judg. 21:21, "the daughters of Shiloh") or a region or country (e.g., Gen. 24:3, "the daughters of the Canaanites"). (4) Frequently it is the personification of a city, such as Jerusalem (e.g., "the daughter of Zion," Isa. 1:8; Jer. 4:31), or of a country (e.g., 46:11, "daughter of Egypt"). (5) In genealogical materials, towns or villages are depicted as daughters, thus indicating their relationship as colonies or dependencies of a state (e.g., Ps. 48:11) or city (1 Chr. 1:50; 2:3, 21, 35, 49; cf. Josh. 15:45; Jer. 49:2-3; RSV "villages"; KJV "daughters").

In the New Testament, Gk. *thygátēr* signifies one's immediate female offspring (e.g., Luke 2:36) as well as a distant descendant (1:5, "daughter of Aaron"; 13:16, "daughter of Abraham"). The term also indicates a city or its inhabitants (Matt. 21:5 par. John 12:15; cf. Luke 23:28). At Matt. 9:22 par., Jesus addresses a woman who had sought his help as "daughter," a term of endearment.

Although the daughter was accorded a social position inferior to that of the son, she was granted certain rights within society, including under certain circumstances the right of inheritance (cf. Num. 27:1-11).

See also FAMILY.

Bibliography. H. Haag, "bath [baṯ]," *TDOT* 2 rev. ed. (1977): 332-38.

DAVID [dā′vĭd]. Israel's second king (*ca.* 1010-970 B.C.).

I. Name

David's Hebrew name *dāwîd* may be derived from the root *dwd* "love," thus meaning beloved — that is, by God (see 2 Chr. 20:37; Heb. *dōḏāwāhû*); it is therefore considered both a personal and a theophoric name. The Mari texts contain the name *dawidum*, which may signify a troop commander; on this basis some scholars suggest that David is a throne name assumed upon his accession, and that his actual name may have been Elhanan (cf. 2 Sam. 21:19).

II. Life

A. *Early Years.* The account of David's life, given at 1 Sam. 16–31; 2 Samuel; 1 Kgs. 1; 2 Chr. 11–29, commences with God's commissioning his aged prophet and judge, Samuel, to replace Saul as king over the twelve tribes because the Lord had rejected him as Israel's legitimate ruler (1 Sam. 16:1). Fearing Saul's displeasure at such a bold act, Samuel pretended to be in Bethlehem to offer a sacrifice to the Lord (vv. 2-4). Here he met Jesse's sons, including his youngest, the ruddy and handsome David, whom he anointed as Israel's next ruler.

According to Ruth 4:18-22 David was the great-grandson of Boaz and the Moabitess Ruth. His father was Jesse, a Judahite living in Bethlehem (1 Sam. 16:3, 10); the name of his mother is not mentioned. David was the youngest of Jesse's seven sons (1 Chr. 2:15; but cf. 1 Sam. 16:10). His oldest brothers were Eliab, Abinadab, and Shammah or Shimea (1 Sam. 16:6, 8-9; 1 Chr. 2:13-15), and his two sisters were Zeruiah and Abigail (2:16). (It is likely that Jesse was actually David's stepfather, that he married David's mother after Nahash, her first husband and David's father, died; this is a generally accepted interpretation of 2 Sam. 17:25.)

David spent much of his youth in the field protecting his father's sheep (1 Sam. 16:11; 17:34-35).

B. *Conflict with Saul.* Almost as soon as David had been anointed as successor, Saul, who would later be his enemy and rival, was tormented by an "evil spirit" of the Lord, and David was summoned into Saul's service to soothe him by playing the harp (1 Sam. 16:14-23). While still a youth David rescued Israel from the dreaded Philistine giant, Goliath, who had blasphemed the living God; with a smooth stone the young lad hit the giant's forehead and killed him (17:1-52). It was after his third feat in defense of Saul and Israel, when David was praised more highly than the monarch himself (18:7), that Saul's jealousy of David became aroused. Thenceforth the king wanted David dead. He tried to spear him with his javelin, but David evaded him by the grace of God (vv. 8-11). Subsequently Saul promised his daughter Michal in marriage to David if David would bring him one hundred Philistine foreskins — a task which the king hoped would be the young man's undoing (vv. 20-25). David, however, killed two hundred Philistines and thus offered the king twice as many foreskins as required; he then married Michal (vv. 26-27).

Seeing that the Lord had protected David and that his subjects favored him highly, Saul then proposed to his son Jonathan that they both kill David (19:1ff.). This idea met with much resistance on Jonathan's part. But once again David was attacked by Saul and escaped, and when yet another attempt was made on his life in his own house, David fled first to Ramah, then to Naioth (vv. 18-19), then back to Ramah. Here he and Jonathan concluded a covenant of friendship (20:41-42) after Jonathan discovered his father's determination to eliminate David (vv. 30-34).

At this point in his life David became an outlaw and vagabond — a prime example of the ʿApiru rebel (*see* HABIRU). His first stop was at Nob where, pretending to be on a secret mission for King Saul, he was able to persuade the priest Ahimelech to permit him and his young companions to eat from the Bread of the Presence, which is forbidden to all but priests (21:1-6). Ahimelech also gave him Goliath's sword which had been put behind the ephod (vv. 8-9). David then stopped at the Philistine city of Gath. Recognizing his potential danger, David feigned madness (v. 13; cf. Ps. 56:1). His bizarre behavior made him despicable to the local king, but also guaranteed his escape (vv. 14-15).

Selecting the cave of Adullam as yet another hiding place, David became the leader of ʿApiru who had become dissatisfied with Saul's rule (22:1-2). While providing shelter for his parents in Moab (vv. 3-5), he was unable to prevent the executions of Ahimelech and the other priests at Nob who had given him aid (vv. 6-19). Acknowledging that he had been responsible for their deaths, he bid Abiathar, Ahimelech's only surviving son, to join the safety of his band (vv. 20-23).

David's band attracted the attention of Saul, who then made a more organized attempt on his life. Proceeding to Keilah where David had defeated the Philistines and freed the Hebrew inhabitants, the king was in an excellent position to take his enemy when David learned from an ephod about Saul's plan and escaped (23:1-14). Saul closed in on David in the wilderness of Maon and seemed eminently successful until, at the last moment, he was called into Canaan on account of a Philistine raid and had to abandon his pursuit of David (vv. 24-29). There is irony in Saul's pursuit of David in Engedi. Hidden in one of the caves in the wilderness there, David had the opportunity to cut a piece from Saul's robe without the king's knowledge (24:1-7). The next day he showed Saul the piece as evidence that he intended him no harm (vv. 8-15). The king, who was obliged to acknowledge David's kindness, conceded that his son-in-law would one day assume the throne of Israel. Accordingly, he made him swear never to kill any of the king's descendants (vv. 16-22). A similar and probably older account is presented in ch. 26, where again the king admitted his pursuit of David was unjustified.

Before returning for protection to Gath, David learned of Nabal and Abigail, a wealthy couple living in Maon in the hill country of Judah. For a time he protected Nabal's property, but he decided to seek revenge when ill-mannered Nabal chided his delegation and denied him and his men a meal on a feast day (25:1-13). Nabal's beautiful and intelligent wife hurried forth with food for the band. David thanked her for averting bloodshed and accepted her generous gift

(vv. 14-35). Though Abigail thus saved her husband from death at David's hand, he died shortly thereafter. With the insult now avenged, David married Nabal's widow (vv. 36-42). At some point during this period David also married Ahinoam, a woman from Jezreel (v. 43), perhaps to replace Michal, whom Saul had given to Paltiel of Laish (v. 44).

David's life remained as vulnerable as before. Reckoning that Saul would one day catch up with him, he elected to place his life in the hands of the Philistine king Achish. The Philistine king not only received his vassal peacefully but also granted him Ziklag as a dwelling place (27:1-7). Slowly David won the king's trust. Making David his personal body-guard (28:2), Achish commanded him and his men to accompany the Philistine army into battle against Israel (29:1ff.). When the other Philistine commanders protested the wisdom of this decision David was angered. However, he returned to Ziklag and was spared the need to choose between fighting and possibly killing his own countrymen and risking Achish's displeasure should he refuse (vv. 2-11).

While the Philistines waged a successful battle against the Hebrews, David arrived at Ziklag to find it had been burned out by the Amalekites. Shocked to see his and his troops' families gone, he barely averted an attack on his life by his own followers, who were bitter over their loss (30:1-6). However, armed with encouragement from the Lord through the ephod, David and his men pursued the Amalekites, surprised them after discovering their location from an exhausted Egyptian, and easily slaughtered nearly all of them. Elated to recover his wives and property, he victoriously entered the ruined city of Ziklag, sharing the captured spoil with all his men and the elders of some Judean cities (vv. 18-31).

At Mt. Gilboa the Israelites were defeated by the Philistines (1 Sam. 31). Upon learning of the deaths of Saul and his son Jonathan, David had the Amalekite informant executed for his alleged part in taking Saul's life (2 Sam. 1:11-16). David grieved over the deaths of Saul and of his dear friend and "brother," Jonathan, whose love was precious to him (vv. 17-27). With his pursuer dead David at last was able to return to Hebron where the inhabitants of Judah subsequently crowned him king (2:1-4).

C. *King.* David can be viewed as having reigned in two phases: over Judah for a period of 7½ years and over all the Hebrew tribes for thirty-three years (2 Sam. 5:4-5; 1 Chr. 3:4; 29:26).

1. Judah. David's first act as king was to thank the inhabitants of Jabesh-gilead for burying the deceased King Saul (2 Sam. 2:4-7). Though he found support for his rule with the tribe of Judah, where he had been born and raised, David soon faced a determined Abner, who, as Saul's commander-in-chief, had Ish-bosheth, one of Saul's surviving sons, crowned king over the other tribes (vv. 8-11). One confrontation between Abner's men and those of Joab, David's general, ended in a temporary truce (vv. 12-29). A disagreement between Abner and Ish-bosheth caused Abner to initiate overtures of friendship to David, who accepted them gladly and at Hebron signed a treaty with him (3:6-21; as part of the agreement, Abner returned David's wife Michal). Unfortunately, David's followers were suspicious of Abner's motives and slew him (vv. 22ff.); so, too, they slew Ish-bosheth, though David condoned neither murder. With no legitimate successor of their own, the northern tribes turned to David to be their king as well (4:1–5:3).

2. All Israel. Having become the sovereign monarch over all twelve of the Israelite tribes at the age of thirty, David used the thirty-three years of his rule to protect his people against enemy attack, to secure a new capital, and to set an example of religious devotion.

a. Military victories. When the Philistines heard that David was no longer a Hebrew outlaw but had, in fact, become king over the twelve Israelite tribes, they sought his life as they had Saul's. David, however, with God's blessings, defeated them at Baal-perazim and in the valley of Rephaim (5:20-25); sometime later he managed to vanquish the Philistines altogether (8:1). With the western border of his kingdom secure, the king sent his army east to conquer the nations of Edom and Moab, and Hadadezer, the king of Zobah (vv. 2-14). Involuntarily David became involved in a confrontation with the Ammonites when their king Hanun insulted a delegation he had sent to pay their respects at the death of Hanun's father. In the ensuing battle, aided by close counsel between David's commanders Joab and Abishai, David's forces defeated the combined Ammonite-Syrian army (10:1-15). Another campaign saw them capture the Ammonite city of Rabbah (11:1; 12:26-31) and begin Ammonite subjection to Israel. Now the kings of the surrounding nations paid tribute to David (8:12), and Israel was able to enjoy a period of peace.

b. Jerusalem. As long as David was king over Judah, Hebron could remain the capital of his kingdom. But when he assumed leadership over the twelve tribes, he had to find another capital, one that would not offend the northern tribes. Selecting Jerusalem (then known as Jebus) as a neutral place, he besieged the city and captured it from the Canaanites (5:6-9). Most likely his men entered the city through the water shaft (v. 8), though the account does not spell out the details of the capture. Once the city was his, David turned it into a strong capital (vv. 9-10).

c. The ark. Remembering that his predecessor Saul had paid little attention to religious matters, David decided to bring the ark of the covenant to his new capital. Thus he not only strengthened Jerusalem by making it a religious center but also relocated the powerful priesthood under his watchful eye. While the participants of a large procession rejoiced in the festive occasion, the ark, which was transported on a new oxcart, began to slide when the oxen stumbled (6:6). When a certain Uzzah touched the ark to keep it from falling, he died instantly, struck down by the Lord (vv. 7-8). Fearful, David left the sacred ark three months in the house of Obed-edom (vv. 10-11). Later, when the Lord's anger had subsided, he organized another procession to carry the ark to its intended destination in the city. At the end of the ceremony the king made burnt offerings and peace offerings and blessed the people who made the procession with him; but his wife Michal, Saul's daughter, mocked her husband for his festive jubilation (vv. 12-23).

Although David had brought the ark to Jerusalem,

he was not satisfied with its location in a tent. Though he was eager to build more suitable accommodations for it, he was informed by the prophet Nathan that it would be David's son who would build the temple (7:1-17). The account is the occasion for the so-called divine charter (v. 13); although David wishes to build a temple (Heb. *bayit*, lit. "house") for the Lord, he is told that his "house" (or dynasty; *bayit*) would be established forever.

Thus far the author of 2 Samuel has painted a picture of David as valiant and righteous. He does not, however, overlook David's weaknesses: sexual temptation and pride.

d. *Adultery*. One day when his army was at war with the Ammonites, David, who already had several wives, was aroused by yet another beautiful woman (2 Sam. 11:1-2). Bathsheba was the wife of Uriah, one of his faithful soldiers, and David had her brought to the royal palace where they engaged in sexual intercourse. Embarrassed by the pregnancy that resulted, David first invited Uriah to return home from battle to spend some time with her. This plan failed because Uriah thought it unseemly to enjoy all the comforts of home while his colleagues fought a war. David then ordered him into battle at the front, and Uriah was killed (vv. 6-21). After the widow had spent the required number of days mourning her husband's death, David married Bathsheba and made her his wife (vv. 26-27). (David's polygamous relations would later pave the way for rivalry among his sons.)

Confident that his conspiracy against Uriah would not be discovered, David did not suspect that the prophet Nathan had come to chastise him with his story about a poor man abused by a wealthy man. When Nathan explained that David was the culprit and that the Lord would use the same "sword" that had murdered Uriah against David's own household, the king repented (12:1-13). Nathan assured David that God had forgiven him for his shameful deed (v. 13), but also informed him that his son, the fruit of his love for Bathsheba, would die (v. 15; cf. 16-23).

Most of the latter part of David's life was marred by dire events apparently precipitated by his adultery. First, Absalom's revenge of his sister's rape and his rebellion against his father are described in great detail (chs. 13–15); next, Shimei's revolt is recorded; Adonijah's attempt to assume the throne precedes David's death.

After Amnon, the son of David and Ahinoam, had dishonored his half-sister Tamar the daughter of David's wife Maacah and sent her away (13:1-19), Tamar found shelter with her brother Absalom, and he wanted to take revenge. Later, when David consented to have Amnon accompany Absalom at the feast of sheepshearers, Absalom arranged for Amnon's death, which elicited a greater reaction from David than Absalom had anticipated and he fled (vv. 30-34). The prophecy of bloodshed in the royal family was being fulfilled.

After three years the king longed for the return of his son, who had taken refuge in Geshur. Joab, David's commander, arranged for his return (13:37–14:24) and again for the reconciliation between father and son another two years later (vv. 25-33). Absalom was not content with the truce, however; instead, he

undermined his father's popularity and plotted a conspiracy, which forced his father to flee to Mahanaim east of the Jordan (15:1–16:14; 17:21-29). In an armed confrontation between Absalom's followers and David's seasoned army headed by Joab, Absalom lost his life (18:1-15). When David was told the news of his son's death, he mourned greatly (vv. 16-33), in spite of his army's victory (19:1-8). With the revolt crushed, the king returned to Judah, where he was welcomed as its legitimate ruler; the other tribes soon followed the southern subjects' example.

Hardly had the king recovered from Absalom's rebellion when he was faced with a second revolt, initiated by a certain "worthless fellow" from Benjamin named Sheba (20:1-2). (Apparently the rivalry between the tribe of Benjamin, Saul's home, and Judah, David's tribe, had not yet ended.) Again his army fought his contest and once more they prevailed (vv. 3-22). While David gave his countrymen rest from battle, he was not able to prevent the final internal uprising, led by his son Adonijah.

e. *Census*. Disregarding the protests of his general, Joab, David commanded him to take a census of all Israelites capable of bearing arms. When Joab reported the result of the census nine months later, David realized that he had sinned (24:10). The Lord, through the prophet Gad, gave the king a choice of punishments: three years of famine, three months of humiliation by his enemies, or three days of a severe plague on the land (vv. 11-14). Casting the sacred lots, David chose the third alternative, and the plague that followed took the lives of some seventy thousand innocent Hebrews (vv. 14-17).

D. *Old Age*. 1 Kings commences with a description of the final years of King David: Adonijah's rebellion, the coronation of Solomon, and David's death.

1. *Adonijah's Rebellion*. Nearing seventy, the aged king had to endure yet another coup within his own household. Adonijah, Absalom's younger brother and David's son by his wife Haggith, made an attempt on the throne, believing that as the oldest surviving royal son, he was the heir. His plans seemed promising, especially when Joab, David's commander, and Abiathar, David's priest, defected in his favor (1 Kgs. 1:1-7). But in the end, all his followers forsook him and he alone had to account for the insurrection (v. 49). Though David did not witness bloodshed this time, Adonijah was killed as an insurgent sometime after his father's death (see 2:19-25).

2. *Coronation of Solomon*. Though Adonijah's plan nearly materialized, David's loyal subjects — Zadok the priest, Benaiah a renowned warrior, Nathan the prophet, and David's mighty men — warned the king of the imminent coup. Securing an audience with the king through Bathsheba and later through Nathan, they reminded David of his promise that Solomon, Bathsheba's son, would succeed him. The king, in full agreement with them, ordered Solomon crowned in the presence of a jubilant crowd (1:8-40).

3. *David's Death*. Sensing that his death was upon him, the weary King David instructed Solomon in his obligations to the Lord, and asked him to revenge Joab for the murders he had committed and Shimei for his curses. He also asked Solomon to deal loyally

with the family of his friend Barzillai (2:1-9). According to 2 Sam. 23:1-7 David's last words were an oracle about a just king, possibly himself, and God's covenant with his descendants. He died at the age of seventy-one (1 Kgs. 2:10).

III. Significance

A. *Old Testament.* The writer of 1-2 Samuel gives a generally favorable impression of David. While not condoning his sins of sexual temptation and pride (cf. 1 Kgs. 15:5) — sins for which David paid dearly — the author reveals him as a person of integrity (cf. 1 Sam. 24:4-7; 26:7-12).

The Chronicler, who used the "Chronicles of Samuel the seer" as one of his sources (1 Chr. 29:29), by and large concurs with the author of Samuel concerning the main events of David's kingship. But he describes David as an even more exemplary king than did his predecessor. The author of Chronicles highlights David's devotion to Yahweh by relating the festive details surrounding the transfer of the ark to Jerusalem (1 Chr. 13:5–16:43) as well as by outlining the duties assigned to the priests and Levites (23:21–26:32). The author deletes the scene of David's adultery along with its bloody consequences, and excuses his sin of pride by attributing the cause of the census to Satan (21:1; cf. 2 Chr. 2:17), not to "the anger of the Lord" (2 Sam. 24:1). The Chronicler also presents David as one chosen by God to replace the unfaithful Saul as king (10:13-14); as a concerned father reminding his son Solomon of the enormous task of building a temple to Yahweh (28:9-21); and as a thoughtful statesman appointing Solomon as his successor (29:1, 19).

As Israel's second king David strove for peace and justice, virtues ascribed to the great King, the promised Messiah. As a man "after [God's] own heart" (1 Sam. 13:14), he lived up to God's expectations for a true king (e.g., 1 Kgs. 11:4, 33-34), unlike Saul, who did not give his heart to Yahweh and did not obey God's statutes and ordinances. As a reward for his loyalty God promised David that his descendants would continue to occupy the throne (e.g., 1 Kgs. 11:12-13, 32, 36; Jer. 33:17). Because some of David's distant descendants became evil rulers (cf. Jer. 36:30-31), the prophets envisaged a righteous king (Isa. 11:1-10; 16:5; cf. Jer. 21:12-14) or a "righteous Branch" (Jer. 23:5; 33:15) to rule in the future, a king who would be the ideal Davidic shepherd, truly ministering to the needs of his subjects (Ezek. 34:23-24; 37:24-25; cf. Hos. 3:5).

David is also portrayed as an excellent musician who composed several psalms, the value and significance of which were recognized by later generations (Neh. 12:24, 45-46). He also invented musical instruments (Amos 6:5; cf. Ezra 3:10). Some of the New Testament writers quote portions from psalms ascribed to David as evidence of their messianic scope or to illustrate other points of religious instruction. (*See also* PSALMS.)

David was courageous, popular, and considerate, displaying sound judgment in choosing Jerusalem as the new capital of the tribes. He was also intensely religious; he prepared a suitable place for the ark and outlined the various cultic and religious duties of priests and Levites. Apt is the psalmist's summary of his character and accomplishments as one who with upright heart shepherded his people and guided them with skilful hand (Ps. 78:70-72).

B. *New Testament.* The Synoptic Gospels record two instances when Jesus refers to David. On one occasion he justifies breaking the Jewish law against working on the Sabbath by appealing to David, who had at one time taken some of the Bread of the Presence, which only priests were allowed to eat (Matt. 12:3 par.). When people called him the Son of David (e.g., 9:27 par.; 15:22 par.), Jesus asked them why he is called Lord as well (22:42-45 par., a quote from Ps. 110:1). Matthew and Luke trace Jesus' genealogy to David (Matt. 1:1, 17; Luke 3:31). Luke also cites the angel's prophecy to Mary that her son would occupy the Davidic throne (1:32).

The author of the book of Hebrews includes David in his list of Old Testament heroes of faith, naming him between the judges and Samuel the prophet (Heb. 11:32).

Bibliography. R. A. Carlson, *David, the Chosen King* (Stockholm: 1964); H. Gaubert, *David and the Foundation of Jerusalem* (New York: 1969); D. M. Gunn, *The Story of King David: Genre and Interpretation.* JSOTS 6 (1978); P. K. McCarter, Jr., *I Samuel.* AB (1980); *II Samuel.* AB (1984).

DAVID, CITY OF (Heb. *'îr dāwîd*).† The fortified city ("stronghold of Zion," 2 Sam. 5:7, 9 par. 1 Chr. 11:5, 7) which David took from the Jebusites after having become king over all twelve tribes. It was later renamed Jerusalem.

Although Joshua had been able to defeat the king of Jerusalem, the city was not included among his conquests (Josh. 10:1-41). The Israelites may later have taken a portion of Jebus or its outskirts (Judg. 1:8), but the Jebusites (a pre-Israelite clan of "Canaanites") remained there until the time of David (Judg. 1:21; cf. Josh. 15:63; Judg. 19:10; 2 Sam. 5:6). Because the city had not been considered among the possessions of any of the twelve tribes, and also because of its central location, it was a politically astute choice for the capital of David's united monarchy.

Excavations have determined the limits of the city as confined to a major portion of the Ophel ridge between the Tyropoeon and Kidron valleys to the south of the present Old City. Approximately 1300 B.C. that portion of the city which extended to the eastern slopes of the ridge was terraced; some of the supporting stone fills (perhaps the "Millo," lit. "filling") and portions of the eastern wall were repaired in the tenth century, probably by David (2 Sam. 5:9 par. 1 Chr. 11:8). Although much of the City of David was obliterated by stone quarrying, particularly at the time of Hadrian (A.D. 135), remains of some buildings survive as well as a necropolis which may have been the burial ground of the kings of Judah (1 Kgs. 2:10; 11:43; 14:31; cf. Neh. 3:16).

The city of David's time encompassed approximately 5 ha. (12 acres) and a population of about 2000. Solomon expanded the city to the north to include the Temple Mount, increasing its size to 13 ha. (32 acres). In the late eighth century Hezekiah further expanded the city to the north and west across the Tyropoeon valley; in postexilic times it was reduced to an area slightly smaller than that of Solomon's city.

Several major underground water channels brought water from the Gihon Spring to the city and its environs; the most notable are the tenth-century Siloam tunnel (probably constructed by Solomon and blocked when the Babylonians destroyed Jerusalem in 586) and Hezekiah's tunnel. The earliest is the so-called Warren's Shaft, which brings the water upward (at one point buckets were used to draw the water up a vertical shaft) and inside the eastern wall, thus providing water in times of both war and peace; openings or "windows" in the channel permitted irrigation of adjacent valleys. This channel, which continued in use until at least the first century A.D., may have been the shaft (Heb. *ṣinnôr*) through which David's men entered the Jebusite city (2 Sam. 5:8).

Bibliography. K. M. Kenyon, *Digging Up Jerusalem* (New York: 1974).

DAY (Heb. *yôm*; Gk. *hēméra*). The Israelites, who divided the year according to a lunar calendar, considered the day to start in the evening and end the following evening. Accordingly, they celebrated the Passover at sunset (Exod. 12:18) and commenced the Sabbath shortly thereafter (Lev. 23:32; Neh. 13:19). To them a twenty-four-hour day consisted of a night followed by a day ("evenings and mornings," Dan. 8:14; "a night and a day," 2 Cor. 11:25). The expression "between the evenings" (JB; cf. RSV mg., KJV mg.) may mean either the brief period between sunset and darkness (so the Samaritans; cf. NIV "twilight") or the longer time span between noon and sunset (so the Pharisees). The Israelite method of reckoning time was similar to that of the Babylonians but differed from that of the Egyptians, for whom the day started at sunrise. The Romans were the first to designate the beginning of the day at midnight.

Some scholars believe that the days of the creation account extended from morning to morning and assume that God created during the daylight hours before the evening. This view is supported by the Jewish understanding of day as the period of daylight (see John 9:4; cf. Gen. 1:5). Others support the opposite viewpoint by citing the recurring phrase "there was evening and there was morning, one day" (Gen. 1:5; cf. 8, 13, 19, 23, 31). (For the length of the days of creation, *see* CREATION.)

Twice the Old Testament reckons a certain day as part of the preceding day; the fifteenth day of the month of Nisan is considered the fourteenth (Exod. 12:18), and the tenth of the month the ninth (Lev. 23:32). The three days of Jesus' burial were actually one full day (Saturday, the Sabbath), and two partial days (Friday and Sunday) (Mark 15:42; 16:1-2).

The Hebrews distinguished between the various days of the week by giving each a different number (e.g., "second day," Gen. 1:8; "the first day of the week," Luke 24:1) rather than a name; the exception was the seventh day, which they called the Sabbath (e.g., Exod. 20:11; Deut. 5:14). Besides many special days, such as the Day of Atonement, the Hebrews also observed "a day of Preparation" each week, the day

preceding the Sabbath (Mark 15:42; cf. John 19:31, 42).

Before the Exile the Hebrews divided the day into morning, noon, and evening (so Ps. 55:17); they also described it in terms of four periods: sunrise (Gen. 19:15, "when morning dawned" [cf. Luke 24:1]; 19:23, when "the sun had risen"; 32:31, "the sun rose" [cf. Mark 16:1]), the heat of the day (Gen. 18:1; 1 Sam. 11:11), the cool of the day (Gen. 3:8), and sunset (Gen. 15:12, 17; Judg. 19:8, "until the day declines"). Other references include daybreak (Gen. 32:26), until "the day breathes" (Cant. 2:17), and the "full day" (Prov. 4:18). By postexilic times the Hebrews used a more precise time division of twelve hours (see, e.g., John 11:9), a method made possible by the recent invention of the sundial (cf. 2 Kgs. 20:9; Isa. 38:8). Under this system the length of the hours varied with the seasons; in summer, when the period of daylight was longer, daytime hours were longer and nighttime hours were shorter than they were in winter when the opposite was true.

Heb. *yôm*, which sometimes meant "then" (e.g., Gen. 4:26, "at the time that" [KJV "then"]) or "when" (2:4; 5:2; Isa. 11:16; KJV "in the day"; cf. RSV Gen. 2:17; Jer. 7:22; Ezek. 20:5; "in the day"), frequently designates the occasion for important events in time: e.g., the day of one's birth (Job 3:1; KJV "his day") and death (e.g., 1 Sam. 26:10; Job 15:32, "time"; cf. the days of one's life [Gen. 26:1; 1 Kgs. 10:21]); the "day of the plague" (Num. 25:18); and the "day of Midian" (Isa. 9:4), i.e., the day of victory over the Midianites (Judg. 7:9ff.). The distant past is described as "days of old" (Isa. 37:26 par.) and the distant future as the "last days" (2 Tim. 3:1; 2 Pet. 3:3; cf. John 6:39-40).

The phrase "to this day" (e.g., Gen. 26:33; Josh. 22:3) signifies that circumstances had continued at least until the time when the author was recording. From a theological perspective, it is God who has created the day (Gen. 1:5, 14; cf. Ps. 74:16) and will uphold the regular sequence of day and night (8:22) until the end of time when he will judge the world. (*See also* DAY OF THE LORD.) For the New Testament believer the time between Christ's first and second coming is the "day of salvation" (2 Cor. 6:2), an era of grace and faith, a period of working "in the day" (John 9:4), i.e., in the light of spiritual and moral discernment (see 11:9; cf. Rom. 13:12-13).

See also EVENING; NIGHT.

Bibliography. S. J. DeVries, *Yesterday, Today and Tomorrow* (Grand Rapids: 1975); G. von Rad, G. Delling, "ἡμέρα," *TDNT* 2:943-953.

DAY OF THE LORD (Heb. *yôm YHWH*; Gk. *hē hēméra toú Kyríou*). The expected consummation of the kingdom of God, often seen as the Lord's anticipated intervention in a particular historical context.

I. Old Testament

The Hebrews believed that Yahweh was both a God of mercy and a God of justice, rendering people their due: salvation to the righteous and damnation to the unrighteous. For centuries they saw God's justice enacted in history; Yahweh not only punished Israel's enemies at the time of the Conquest and during David's reign but also punished his own people's apostasy by deporting the ten northern tribes and later the two southern tribes.

During the time of the later prophets when God's chosen people disregarded his law and contributed to the rampant injustice in Canaan, these prophets warned about a future Day of the Lord, which would bring doom as well as deliverance. Often the prophets stressed the aspects of judgment and condemnation. The ninth-century prophet Joel called it a "great and terrible" day, which none would be able to endure (Joel 2:11), a day of cosmic changes (3:15) and of judgment against the nations surrounding Israel. Similarly, the eighth-century prophet Amos depicted it as a day of darkness and gloom, a day of unexpected disaster (Amos 5:18-20), in a context of judgment against Samaria's wealthy citizens (cf. Joel 2:12-14). After the deportation of the northern kingdom, the eighth-century prophet Isaiah chastised the southern kingdom for its idolatry and envisaged God's righteous recompense for the proud and mighty (Isa. 2:11, 17; cf. 13:6, 9). Finally, Zephaniah (ca. 615 B.C.), sometimes called the prophet of the Day of the Lord, reiterated the stern message of his predecessors, but enlarged its scope to include all people, not just Judah (Zeph. 1:14-18; 2:4-15).

Although the major prophetic emphasis is on judgment, there is a note of comfort. Joel threatens, but he also proclaims Israel's security in their God (Joel 3:16-17); Zechariah very explicitly refers to God's protective care of Israel (Zech. 12–14). Accordingly, the faithful, especially the oppressed, await the Day of the Lord and the vindication of their cause.

II. New Testament

The New Testament, retaining the bipartite message of hope and doom, links the Old Testament Day of the Lord with the coming of the Messiah, a link perhaps anticipated by Malachi (Mal. 3:1ff.). Identifying the promised Messiah with Jesus Christ, the New Testament distinguishes between Christ's first coming — his incarnation — and the second coming, or Christ's return. On the "day of [Jesus] Christ" (Phil. 1:6, 10; 2:16), or on the "day of the Lord Jesus" (2 Cor. 1:14; cf. 1 Cor. 1:8; 5:5), or simply on the "Day" (1 Cor. 3:13), Christ will descend from heaven to judge the living and the dead (Acts 1:11). To the faithful eagerly awaiting his return, he will grant eternal life (Rom. 2:7) and salvation (Acts 2:21).

If the New Testament presents a comforting message of hope to believers, it still issues a clear warning of doom to the impenitent. At Rom. 2:5ff. Paul speaks of God's wrath and fury against the instigators of factions, liars, and the wicked; at 1 Cor. 3:13-15 he asserts that the deeds of individuals will be severely tested on the Day of Judgment. Jude, too, speaks of a day of judgment against malcontents, flatterers, and other evil people (Jude 6), while Peter quotes Joel's apocalyptic version of cosmic change (Acts 2:19-20, quoting Joel 2:30-31).

For the meaning of the "Lord's Day" (Rev. 1:10), see LORD'S DAY.

DAY STAR (Heb. *hêlēl*). Another name for the morn-

ing star (cf. 2 Pet. 1:19; Rev. 2:28) or the planet Venus, which appears in the sky before the sun. At Isa. 14:12 the Babylonian ruler is compared to a "Day Star" (NIV "morning star"), which has fallen from heaven and has been felled like a stately tree. Though the Church Fathers associated this verse with the fall of Satan from heaven (cf. KJV "Lucifer"), it actually speaks of the end of tyranny rather than a prelude to it, as with Satan who after the fall still retained much power. Some commentators link this idea with an ancient myth about the banishment of a divine person from heaven.

The New Testament, which contains Jesus' remark about the fall of Satan (Luke 10:18), does not identify Lucifer with Satan. Instead, the author of 2 Peter suggests that the "morning star" (Gk. *phōsphóros* "light bearer") refers to Christ's second coming, while the aged John possibly alludes to Christ, who will support the church at Thyatira (Rev. 2:28, Gk. *astḗr prōinós*; cf. 22:16).

DAY'S JOURNEY (Heb. *derek yôm*; Gk. *hēméras hodós*). The distance covered by foot during a day's travels (generally limited to an eight-hour period), between 32 and 40 km. (20-25 mi.; Josephus *Vita* 52 [269]), based on a speed of about 4 km. (3 mi.) per hour. Naturally, this will vary with the terrain and the stamina of the traveler.

The Old Testament mentions journeys of one, three, seven, and eleven days' duration (e.g., Exod. 3:1; Num. 11:31; Deut. 1:2; 2 Kgs. 3:9). Jonah's three-day journey through the city of Nineveh points to the amount of time it would take a person to walk leisurely through the city; it does not indicate the size of the Assyrian capital. Jesus' parents traveled one day before retracing their steps to Jerusalem in search of their son, who had chosen to stay and listen to the teachers in the temple (Luke 2:44). The "sabbath day's journey" (Gk. *sabbátou hodós*; Acts 1:12; cf. Exod. 16:29) to which pious Jews were restricted consisted of approximately 1 km. (.6 mi.).

DEACON (Gk. *diákonos*). A New Testament term signifying a servant (e.g., Matt. 23:11) and, by extension, an office bearer — one subservient to God (2 Cor. 6:4) and to the congregation. It is commonly, though not universally, assumed that the office of deacon was instituted shortly after the outpouring of the Spirit on Pentecost (Acts 6:2; Gk. *diakonein* "to serve"). Apparently, the duties of the apostles here had become too extensive, prompting them to suggest that seven be chosen to relieve them of some of their responsibilities (Acts 6:2-6). Two outstanding deacons (or "almoners"; so F. F. Bruce, *The Book of the Acts.* NICNT [1954], p. 130) were Stephen, who would become a great defender of the faith and the first Christian martyr (6:8–8:1), and Philip the evangelist (8:5, 26, 40).

The New Testament never fully explains the various duties accompanying the office of deacon. Acts 6:2 ("serve tables") may well imply responsibility for the common mealtimes or feasts as well as the ministry of distributing to the poor the alms given by fellow believers. Calvin (*Institutes* iv.3.9) distinguishes between two types of deacons: those who distributed alms and those who cared for the sick and the poor.

If Acts 6:1-6 does in fact record the institution of the diaconate, that office apparently existed before the office of elder. Interestingly, the New Testament rarely refers to deacons after Acts 6. Paul mentions them only twice, in letters considered to have been written late in his career — Phil. 1:1, where he refers to the two main offices in the church at Philippi, and 1 Tim. 3:8-13, where he enumerates a deacon's qualities. Though it is not possible to sketch the New Testament development of this office, it is clear that deacons existed near the end of the apostolic age. With the number of believers on the increase, deacons were assigned to local churches, just as were elders and overseers.

According to Paul (1 Tim. 3:8-13), deacons were required to be able to control their tongue and the desire for wealth; while not asked to teach, they did have to believe in the mysteries of the faith. The apostle insisted that a person fulfill these and other requirements before being allowed to discharge the duties of deacon. Indeed, the office was an honorable one and was possibly a stepping-stone to the office of presbyter.

DEACONESS.† Standard translation of Gk. *diákonos* at Rom. 16:1 (KJV, NIV "servant"). In this passage Paul introduces Phoebe, the letter carrier, to the church at Rome as serving the church at Cenchreae near Corinth. Scholarly opinion remains divided concerning the nature of Phoebe's work. Some believe that she functioned in an office similar to that of deacon, while others claim that she was a general "servant" with no official ecclesiastical status.

Modern versions of the Bible, like the commentators, are not consistent in the translation of Gk. *gynaíkas* at 1 Tim. 3:11. The RSV and JB render "the women" and imply deaconesses (cf. RSV mg.; JB note b); the KJV and NIV read "their wives" (but see NIV mg.), suggesting the wives of the deacons. A compromise view is that some women assisted in church ministration, whether or not they were members of a distinct order of deaconesses.

Evidence for the office of deaconess in the early Church is equally scanty. Pliny the Younger (*ca.* A.D. 111) mentioned deaconesses in his report to Emperor Trajan (*Epistle* x.97), but he is one of few Western witnesses to that office in the second and third centuries. By contrast, the Eastern branch of Christianity was much more receptive to women holding official status in the Church.

DEAD. *See* DEATH.

DEAD SEA.† The large salt lake located at the mouth of the Jordan river. The name Dead Sea is first attested in the second-century A.D. writings of Pausanias and Justin, derived apparently from the sea's high saline character which inhibits vegetation. In the earliest Old Testament references it is called the Salt Sea (Heb. *yām hammelaḥ*; e.g., Gen. 14:3; Num. 34:3, 12; Josh. 15:2, 5); subsequently it came to be known as the Sea of the Arabah (Heb. *yām haʿʿrābâ*; e.g., Deut. 3:17; Josh. 3:16; KJV "sea of the plain").

Ezekiel and the postexilic prophets Joel and Zechariah call it the Eastern Sea (Heb. *yām haqqaḍmônî*; Ezek. 47:18; Joel 2:20; Zech. 14:8). Josephus calls it the Sea of Asphalt (or Asphaltitis; *BJ* iv.7.2). It is not mentioned in the New Testament.

The basin of the Dead Sea forms the deepest portion of the Jordan trench, a 565 km. (350 mi.)-long depression in the earth's crust which is an extension of the East African rift valleys. The Dead Sea itself is approximately 80 km. (50 mi.) long. At its greatest width, north of En-gedi, it measures nearly 18 km. (11 mi.) wide, and it has a surface area of about 1036 sq. km. (400 sq. mi.). Its greatest depth is more than 396 m. (1300 ft.); the surface of the Dead Sea lies at an average of 394 m. (1292 ft.) below sea level, making it the lowest point on the surface of the earth. The floor of the Dead Sea is as low as some 792 m. (2600 ft.) below sea level. Moreover, the sea is encircled by mountains and plateaus, making its bottom more than 1585 m. (5200 ft.) lower than the surrounding terrain. By contrast, the southern portion of the Dead Sea located below el-Lisan ("the tongue"; cf. Heb. *lāšôn*; Josh. 15:2, "the bay which faces southward"), a peninsula projecting from the eastern shore and dividing the lake nearly in half some 24 km. (15 mi.) from its southern tip, averages less than 9 m. (30 ft.) in depth. Except for the mouth of the Jordan river in the north and the muddy salt marshes at es-Sebkha in the south, the Dead Sea is bordered by badlands, steep, rocky crags which make access extremely difficult.

The water has an extremely high salt content (magnesium chloride, calcium chloride, potassium chloride, sodium chloride, and other salts), more than 300 g. per liter, or nearly 25 percent solid, approximately six times greater than the salt concentration of the ocean, making it the world's most saline natural body of water. In addition, the region surrounding the Dead Sea is a source of high quality asphalt (cf. Gen. 14:10, which notes the bitumen pits in the valley of Siddim). On the southwestern shore rises Mt. Sedom (Jebel Usdum), the slopes of which are formed by a curious combination of gypsum, salt, limestone, and chalk. The heat of the summer, which makes these minerals dry and brittle, and the erosion caused by the winter rains have brought about the formation of peculiar pillars of salt, often pointed out to tourists as the wife of Lot (Gen. 19:26).

Ancient tradition held that the Dead Sea did not exist prior to the destruction of Sodom and Gomorrah (Gen. 13:19; cf. 14:10; cf. also 2 Esdr. 5:7; Josephus *Ant.* v.1.22, "Sea of Sodom"); such a theory is discounted, however, for topographical studies indicate no such changes within historical times. Archaeological excavations of sites such as Bâb edh-Dhrâʿ on the el-Lisan peninsula and es-Sâfi (perhaps biblical Zoar), south of the Dead Sea, may indicate the remains of the Early Bronze Age cities of the valley (or plain). Such cities, which may have been known or at least remembered in patriarchal times, could well have been destroyed by earthquake (such as that of July 11, 1927), giving rise to phenomena reminiscent of those witnessed by Abraham (Gen. 19:28).

DEAD SEA SCROLLS.† Manuscripts discovered since 1946 in the region of Wâdī Qumrân near the northwest shore of the Dead Sea; they constitute significant early evidence of the biblical text and intertestamental Judaism. Subsequent discoveries at other sites further south are sometimes included in this designation but can be labeled more appropriately Manuscripts from the Judean Desert.

I. Discovery

In late 1946 Muhammed Ahmed el-Hamed (called edh-Dhib "the Wolf"), a bedouin of the Ta'amireh tribe, while allegedly pursuing a lost goat discovered a number of clay jars containing manuscripts in what was later to be called Cave 1 in the cliffs north of Wâdī Qumrân. After a series of encounters involving the bedouins, antiquities dealers, and the Syrian Orthodox monastery of St. Mark, four scrolls and several fragments were purchased by A. Y. Samuel, the Syrian Orthodox metropolitan; three more were obtained by E. L. Sukenik of Hebrew University. (In 1955 the university also purchased the manuscripts of Metropolitan Samuel.)

Scholarly examination of the scrolls and location and further exploration of the site of their discovery were hampered by the war between Arabs and Jews which accompanied the end of the British Mandate and the formation of the state of Israel in 1948. In February-March 1949, when more favorable circumstances prevailed, Cave 1 was located and investigated by G. L. Harding of the Department of Antiquities in Jordan and R. de Vaux of the École Biblique in Jerusalem; thousands of manuscript fragments and pottery remains were discovered, confirming the site as a repository or "library" for scrolls. Additional manuscripts were presented by the bedouins, discovered in caves near the Wâdī Murabba'at, some 18 km. (11 mi.) south of Qumran, and at Khirbet Mird, 8 km. (5 mi.) southwest of the Qumran caves (see V below). In 1952 an expedition examined the hundreds of caves in the area of Qumran, finding pottery in thirty-seven of them; additional manuscripts were discovered in Caves 3-6. The remaining manuscripts were recovered in the 1956 excavations of Caves 7-11.

Articles and photographs of the scrolls as well as

Aerial view of Khirbet Qumrân (by courtesy of the Israel Department of Antiquities and Museums)

partial editions of the texts first appeared in late 1948. It was not until 1950 that the first full edition of the texts from Cave 1 was published, based on photographs of the scrolls from St. Mark's monastery taken in 1947-1948 by J. C. Trever. The first volume contained the Isaiah Scroll and the Habakkuk Commentary; a second volume, published in 1951, contained the Manual of Discipline. A complete edition of the scrolls purchased by the Hebrew University was published in 1954.

II. Origin

A. Site. Excavations conducted from 1951 to 1955 have confirmed the association of the Dead Sea Scrolls with a community which occupied Khirbet Qumrân, north of Wâdī Qumrân. The site occupied a marl terrace beneath the cliffs bordering the el-Buqei'a depression, less than .8 km. (.5 mi.) inland from the northwest shore of the Dead Sea.

The site has been identified as that of the City of Salt (Heb. '*îr-hammelaḥ*) mentioned at Josh. 15:62, a city of substantial size in the eighth-seventh centuries B.C. It was abandoned in the sixth century and rebuilt at the time of the Hasmonean John Hyrcanus (*ca.* 135-104). This later occupation was expanded during the first century B.C. by the community responsible for the scrolls; it seems to have been abandoned briefly following an earthquake in 31 B.C., but was rebuilt and reoccupied by the same group. The inhabitants were routed by fire when the Romans captured the site in A.D. 68 during the First Jewish Revolt; Roman soldiers remained until 73. Jewish rebels used the site temporarily during the Second Jewish Revolt (132-135).

Numbering approximately 200, the community which produced the scrolls apparently slept in caves and tents but conducted a variety of communal activities in the buildings at Khirbet Qumrân. The largest structure was a rectangular hall 22.5 m. (74 ft.) x 14.5 m. (15 ft.) which served as a refectory for common meals as well as an assembly hall. Various workshops included a pottery kiln and storage rooms for ceramic ware (including jars such as those used to store the scrolls), a bakery, laundry, grain mill, and a kitchen with floor ovens. Most important was a scriptorium where the manuscripts were copied; remains include metal and ceramic inkwells, a long, narrow table covered with plaster, and benches. An elaborate water system consisting of an aqueduct, large storage basin, and several cisterns provided water for bathing as well as domestic and industrial use; other cisterns, accessible by stairways, are thought to have been used for ritual washings. The city was fortified by a wall and tower. Outside the complex was a cemetery containing more than 1,100 graves.

Approximately 3 km. (2 mi.) south of Qumran are the remains of 'Ain Feshka, an agricultural outpost of the Qumran community. Here were found stables and other farm buildings as well as facilities for tanning leather.

B. Sect. On the basis of various scrolls devoted to the life and precepts of the community as well as biblical commentaries containing contemporary applications, most scholars have identified the Qumran community as a Jewish sect, most likely a branch of the Essenes and thus a descendant of the orthodox

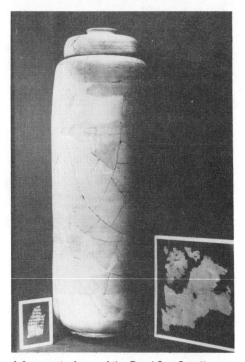

A fragment of one of the Dead Sea Scrolls, one of the jars in which the scrolls were found, and fragments of the linen that the scrolls were wrapped in (by courtesy of the Oriental Institute, University of Chicago)

Hasidim who had opposed the hellenization of Judaism. (Early assessments, which have little current following, placed the sect in the early second century B.C. as opponents of Antiochus IV Epiphanes, as Pharisees or Sadducees, as early Christians or Ebionites, as second-century A.D. Jewish Zealots and rebels against Rome, and even the medieval Karaites.) See ESSENES.

Having rejected as impure the Judaism of the Jerusalem temple community, the Qumran sectarians regarded themselves as the true Israel. Accordingly, they sought to live a life of continuous worship based on strict interpretation of the Jewish law and rigid self-discipline. Admission to the sect required a year of testing, followed by a year of membership with limited privileges; thereafter, members were subject to yearly review. The community was ordered by rank based on spiritual development, and all activities as well as privileges and responsibilities were determined accordingly. Members were distinguished as priests (who had supreme authority), Levites, and laity; they were further divided, at least symbolically, into twelve tribes, with subdivisions of thousands, hundreds, fifties, and tens. The members of the community practiced a form of communism, holding all goods in common and sharing common meals. Once thought to have been a celibate group, the community, although predominantly male, has been found to have included women and children. Following both a lunar and a solar calendar, the sect observed all the Jewish feasts,

with particular emphasis on the Feast of Weeks; cultic acts, including daily prayer at dawn and dusk, were to be observed at the divinely prescribed times. Extreme concern was shown for ritual purity, and ritual ablutions were an integral part of community life.

Having covenanted to become part of the true Israel, the Qumran sectarians felt themselves the potential recipients of the knowledge essential to attain holiness and a life of good works. At the same time, they were conscious of human shortcomings and acknowledged the all-pervading divine grace which enabled their righteousness. All of life was characterized as a struggle between the dual spirits of good and evil, a war between light and darkness. The members believed themselves to be the final generation preceding the great upheaval which would bring about the kingdom of God. Good would prevail through the mediation of a prophet and two messiahs representing Aaron and Israel, or the royal, prophetic, and priestly aspects of Hebrew tradition.

III. Contents

The manuscripts from the eleven Qumran caves comprise most likely a single library of religious writings, or possibly the main community library and some smaller private collections. (One apparent exception is the Copper Scroll from Cave 3, a text inscribed on two copper rolls which details the purported hiding places of a considerable treasure, thought by some to be that of the Jerusalem temple; most likely the scroll is a type of fictional literature belonging to the second-century A.D. Bar Kokhba rebels.) Cave 4, which must have been the main repository, has yielded some 40,000 fragments which have been pieced together to represent nearly 400 manuscripts, about 100 of which are biblical. The scrolls, which on the basis of script and spelling, linguistic usage, and carbon-14 dating of the writing materials can be dated to the period of the Essene community, were relatively well-preserved by the dry air in the caves; however, damage was caused by rats and worms. The texts were written primarily on papyrus or leather, and some of the later manuscripts were on parchment. Some were wrapped in linen and stored in jars similar to those found at Khirbet Qumrân (cf. Jer. 32:14).

Among the texts are portions or fragments of all books of the Hebrew canon with the exception of the book of Esther. The most complete text is that of the Isaiah scroll from Cave 1 acquired in 1947 by St. Mark's monastery; written in the second or first century B.C., it comprises fifty-four columns on seventeen sheets of sheepskin. Among the oldest texts are portions of Leviticus written in paleo-Hebrew script and fragments of 1-2 Samuel dating to the third century. Among the manuscripts discovered, often quite fragmentary, are thirty texts of the book of Psalms, twenty-five of Deuteronomy, nineteen of Isaiah, and fifteen each of Genesis and Exodus. In addition, Hebrew and Aramaic fragments of apocryphal and pseudepigraphal books have been found for works previously known only in translations; among the most important is the Aramaic text of the books of Enoch. Others include portions of Jubilees, the Testaments of Levi and Naphtali, the Prayer of Nabonidus, and the Psalms of Joshua.

Various other texts are related to the Bible, including testimonia (collections of proof texts), florilegia (anthologies of scriptural passages), and phylacteries (biblical quotations to be worn in leather packets affixed to the arm or forehead). Among the more significant related works are the pesharim ("interpretations"), commentaries which expound books of the Bible in terms of the Dead Sea community's historical setting.

The most extensive such work is the Habakkuk Pesher, which presents in thirteen columns the text and exposition of Hab. 1–2. Written in the late first century B.C., the commentary presents the prophet's oracles in terms of contemporary events, which unfortunately remain somewhat vague. The wicked and the righteous (Hab. 1:4) are depicted as the priestly Teacher of Righteousness (perhaps Onias III, Judas Maccabeus, Eleazer, or

A section of the Isaiah scroll (1QIsaᵃ) from Qumran (by courtesy of the Israel Department of Antiquities and Museums)

a future teacher or messiah) and the Wicked Priest (most likely Jonathan Maccabeus, although numerous others have been suggested, including Hyrcanus II and various Hellenizers). Once thought to mean the Seleucids, the Kittim ("Cyprus"), which the scroll inserts for the Chaldeans of Hab. 1:6, represent the Romans who under Pompey subjugated the priestly aristocracy of Jerusalem. Similar pesharim include commentaries on Nahum, Isaiah, and Psalm 37. Other exegetical works include an Aramaic paraphrase, the Targum of Job, and the Melchizedek Document, a midrash on Isa. 61:1. The Genesis Apocryphon is a midrashic collection of first-person stories about the patriarchs, including Lamech, Enoch, Methuselah, Noah, Abraham, and Sarah; based partially on the Genesis accounts, it offers hope for the sectarians as they await the messianic age.

Several scrolls offer insight into the sectarian nature of the Qumran community, in particular its organization and doctrine. Most important is the Manual of Discipline (also called the Rule or Order of the Community; Heb. *serek hayyahad*). The Manual outlines the rules and liturgy of the Dead Sea community, including admission to the sect and penalties for nonconformity, and sets forth the sect's basic doctrines, including the dual spirits of good and evil, the responsibilities of a holy and consecrated life, and the expectations of the end times. The Damascus Document first came to light as one of several documents discovered in 1896 in the genizah (storeroom) of a synagogue in Cairo. Prior to the discovery of additional fragments of the Damascus Document among the Dead Sea Scrolls, this work was known as the Zadokite Fragments. It begins with a veiled description of the historical origins of the Qumran community under the Teacher of Righteousness, which it sets within God's predetermined plan of the ages and the sharp distinction between good and evil persons. This distinction is made the basis of exhortations to erring members of the community. The statutes for the community that comprise the second section of the document are arranged by subject and pertain to vows and oaths, the administration of justice, ritual purification, Sabbath observance, and other matters of life within the community. A Psalms (or Thanksgiving; Heb. *hodayôt*) Scroll consists of original hymns, in language often reminiscent of the biblical Psalms, which extol the might and grace of God; most of the psalms begin with the formulas "I give thanks unto thee, O Lord" or "Blessed are You." Several of the writings are apocalyptic in nature. The War Scroll from Cave 1, also known as The War of the Sons of Light and the Sons of Darkness, depicts the final battle between the forces of good and evil; strongly influenced by accounts of the Maccabean conflicts and marked by details of contemporary Roman warfare, the scroll propounds the biblical concept of holy war, often with apocalyptic detail (cf. the battle of Gog and Magog, Ezek. 38–39). An Aramaic scroll from Cave 5, the so-called New Jerusalem document envisions the age to come (cf. Ezek. 40–48; Rev. 21). The Temple Scroll, consisting of sixty-seven columns and measuring 8.5 m. (28 ft.) in length (the longest of the Qumran manuscripts), describes the ideal sanctuary which the Qumran Essenes hoped to construct in the new age. Written in the late second century B.C., it resembles structurally the book of Jubilees and embodies a harsh polemic against the usurper Jonathan Maccabeus.

IV. Significance

The biblical texts, including the numerous fragments, represent a variety of textual traditions and examples of the principal textual types. Moreover, they are more than 1,000 years older than the Masoretic Text. Thus, they provide important insight into the history of textual transmission as well as help to clarify previously incomprehensible readings. While caution must be exercised in applying the evidence of the Qumran collection with regard to the establishment of the biblical canon, it is possible to note the canonical function of the various biblical and sectarian texts within the Dead Sea community.

A second contribution of the Dead Sea Scrolls concerns the study of intertestamental Judaism, particularly that represented by the Essene faction. The sectarian documents supplement the information supplied by Josephus, Philo, and Pliny, and polemic materials provide insight into other Jewish groups with which the Qumran community had contact or conflict. Doctrinal works and particularly the pesharim are significant for the study of the development of biblical interpretation and of Jewish eschatology and messianism.

The Qumran manuscripts also contribute to an understanding of rabbinic Judaism and Jewish Gnosticism as well as of early Christianity. Because of the sectarian nature of the Dead Sea community, however, it is most likely that any similarities between the ascetic lifestyle of John the Baptist or his teachings and the teaching of Jesus and Paul derive from their common roots in traditional Judaism. There is no reason to conclude that Jesus had any contact with the sect or that he represents the Teacher of Righteousness.

A section of the "Zadokite Document" (CD 11:1-23), discovered in the Cairo Genizah. Fragments of the same sectarian document were found among the Dead Sea Scrolls (Cambridge University Library)

V. Other Manuscripts

In 1952 a variety of biblical and secular texts were discovered in four caves at Wâdī Murabbaʿat. Dating to the period of the Second Jewish Revolt (A.D. 132-135), the biblical writings reflect a unified proto-Masoretic text. Of primary importance is the correspondence of Simeon ben Kosiba (Simon bar Kokhba), leader of the revolt, and his officer Joshua ben Galgula. Texts from this site as well as nearby Naḥal Ḥever, Naḥal Zeʾelim, and Naḥal Mishmar include contemporary letters and Mishnaic Hebrew, Aramaic, Nabatean, and Greek legal documents such as a bill of divorce, a marriage contract, real estate documents, and a census declaration. The texts also provide important information concerning Palestinian toponymy in the Roman and Byzantine periods.

Manuscripts discovered by bedouins in 1953 at Khirbet Mird, a Christian monastery of the fifth-ninth centuries A.D., include Syro-Palestinian biblical fragments and Greek codices, a sixth-century fragment of Euripides' *Andromache* (1,000 years older than previously extant), and a letter from a monk to his superior. The manuscripts are written in Arabic, Greek, and Christian Palestinian Aramaic.

Excavations at the fortress of Masada in 1963-1965 uncovered fragments of Genesis and Leviticus, a Psalms scroll, and Ecclesiasticus. Portions of the Angelic Liturgy from Qumran suggest that members of the Essene sect may have joined the Zealots during their courageous resistance against the Romans; however, the text may have been brought to Masada by Zealots who occupied the Qumran site after the community had been routed. Other documents include Latin papyri from the adjacent Roman garrison.

Bibliography. F. M. Cross, Jr., *The Ancient Library of Qumran and Modern Biblical Studies*, 2nd ed. (1975; repr. Grand Rapids: 1980); J. A. Fitzmyer, *The Dead Sea Scrolls: Major Publications and Tools for Study* (Missoula: 1975); M. Mansoor, *The Dead Sea Scrolls* (Grand Rapids: 1964); J. A. Sanders, "The Dead Sea Scrolls: A Quarter Century of Study," *BA* 36 (1973): 110-148; G. Vermes, *The Dead Sea Scrolls in English*, 2nd ed. (Baltimore: 1975).

DEATH (Heb. *māweṯ, mûṯ*; Gk. *thánatos*).† In its basic sense, the cessation of life on earth. In biblical times death was viewed as a historical event marking the end of a person's existence (e.g., Gen. 25:11; cf. 27:2), the reality of which was final and complete (Eccl. 12:6). At death the body returned to dust (Gen. 3:19) and the spirit to God (Eccl. 12:7); the soul (Heb. *nepeš*) which was the very essence of life departed (Gen. 35:18; 1 Kgs. 12:21).

The inevitability of death was most real to ancient peoples surrounded by pestilence and warfare (Num. 16:29; 2 Sam. 14:14). Indeed, death was virtually certain to one in the throes of disease (Job 18:13) and old age (Rom. 4:19). Nevertheless, one might hope that death would come at the end of a long life (Judg. 8:32; 1 Chr. 19:28) marked by honor and dignity (Num. 23:10; 2 Sam. 3:33). Accordingly, death was rarely welcomed (cf. Job 3:21; Jonah 4:3); in figurative use it came to represent a life without love (1 John 3:14) or a faith without life (Matt. 8:22 par.; Jas. 2:17, 26; cf. Heb. 9:14).

Various images of death are presented in the Bible. It is greedy (Hab. 2:5), seeking to ensnare humans (Ps. 18:4-5; Prov. 13:14), or a city which restricted them within its gates (Job 38:17; Ps. 9:13). Death is personified in terms reminiscent of ancient mythologies (cf. Job 28:22; Jer. 9:21; Rev. 20:13-14), as a royal shepherd (Ps. 49:14), or a grim horseman (Rev. 6:8).

I. The Dead

To the biblical writers death was the contradiction of life (Jer. 21:8; cf. Job 7:21), a separation from earthly existence (Ruth 1:17; Ps. 39:13). It was a state characterized by bitterness (1 Sam. 15:32), pain (Acts 2:24), and fear (Ps. 55:4; Heb. 2:14). Thus, for the ancient Israelites the dead bodies of humans and animals could render a person or object ritually unclean and were to be shunned (Lev. 7:24; 22:8; Num. 19:11, 16, 18); burial was to take place immediately (John 11:17-39; Acts 5:6-10; *see* BURIAL; MOURNING) and no further contact with the spirit of the deceased was to be attempted (Isa. 8:19; *see* MEDIUM).

Viewed as departing to be with their ancestors (e.g., Gen. 15:15; 35:29), the dead were thought to dwell in subterranean oblivion (Prov. 2:18; Jonah 2:6), a dusty (Job 21:26), gloomy void (10:21) of ominous silence (Ps. 94:17) and darkness (Job 10:21-22). The wicked were relegated to a place of fiery torment (Isa. 66:24; Mark 9:44, 46, 48), the "second," spiritual death ("lake of fire"; Rev. 20:6, 13-14).

II. Punishment

As a sanction against behavior which threatened the stability or even the survival of the community, the Israelites imposed the death penalty as punishment for a variety of infractions and as a means of guaranteeing adherence to the stipulations of their covenant with God (e.g., Gen. 3:3; Lev. 10:6-7). Among those crimes which merited capital punishment were murder (Gen. 9:6; Exod. 21:12), blasphemy (Lev. 24:16), incitement to idolatry (Deut. 13:5ff.), fornication (22:20-21), violation of the Sabbath (Exod. 35:2), kidnapping (21:16), striking one's parents (v. 15), and sexual intercourse with animals (22:19; Lev. 20:15-16).

The death penalty was carried out in various ways. Stoning was prescribed for idolatry (Deut. 17:2-7), divination (Lev. 20:27), disobedience toward one's parents (Deut. 21:18-21), Sabbath-breaking (Num. 15:32-36), adultery (Ezek. 16:40; John 8:5), and disrespect toward the king (1 Kgs. 21:13). In order to remove corporate guilt, members of the community participated in the punishment, stoning the offender outside the city limits (Lev. 24:14; Num. 15:36; 1 Kgs. 21:10, 13; Acts 7:58), with witnesses to the crime throwing the first stone (Deut. 17:7; cf. John 8:7). Burning was the punishment for incest (Lev. 20:14), harlotry (Gen. 38:24; Lev. 21:9), and for the taking of consecrated goods (Josh. 7:15, 25). *See* CROSS, CRUCIFIXION.

Sin, as human estrangement from God and thereby the violation or dissolution of the covenant relationship, is presented as the ultimate cause of death (Rom. 6:16, 21, 23). Indeed, it is because of sin that death entered the world to become the common fate of all mankind (Gen. 3:2-7; Rom. 5:12-14; 6:10). Those who persist in sin are already in the clutches of death (Eph. 2:1-2, 5).

III. Victory Over Death

Despite the finality of death, the Israelites maintained the hope that God would enable them to overcome its power (Isa. 25:8; cf. Dan. 12:2). Although numerous instances of resurrection of the dead are recorded (2 Kgs. 4:32-37; Luke 7:11-17; John 11:1-44; Acts 9:36-43), the basic understanding of an afterlife was the establishment of one's name through heirs (Gen. 30:1; Matt. 22:24).

It was through Christ's death and resurrection, however, that the ultimate victory over death was won (Rom. 6:9; 1 Cor. 15:26, 54-55). It is he who has gained possession of the keys of death (Rev. 1:18; cf. Heb. 2:14), depriving it of its power and pain (1 Cor. 15:12-58), and substituting the reality of immortality and life (John 12:24; Phil. 1:21; 2 Tim. 1:10). By taking upon himself human form and thereby grappling with the powers of death (Heb. 2:14-15) he enabled all mankind to pass "from death to life" (John 5:24). Those who believe in him may therefore overcome the weaknesses of the flesh (Rom. 8:13; Col. 3:5), thereby freeing themselves from the power of sin and the restrictions of the law (Rom. 7:4-6).

DEBIR [dē′bər] (Heb. *dᵉḇîr*) (**PERSON**). The king of Eglon who accepted Adonizedek's invitation to join him and other kings of the area in their united pursuit of Israel (whose aim was to conquer the southern part of Palestine; Josh. 10:3).

DEBIR [dē′bər] (Heb. *dᵉḇîr* "back part" or *dᵉḇir* "remote village") (**PLACE**).

1. †An important Canaanite city near Hebron, also called KIRIATH-SEPHER (Josh. 15:15) and KIRIATH-SANNAH (15:49).

When the Israelites entered the promised land, Debir was occupied by the Anakim (11:21). Joshua succeeded, however, not only in capturing the city (after Libnah and Hebron), but also in butchering all of the inhabitants (10:38-39). Later in the narrative the author inserts an account of Debir's retaking by Israel, this time by Othniel, Caleb's brother (15:15-17; cf. Judg. 1:11-13); apparently not all the Anakim of Debir had been killed, and those who survived were able to recapture the town. Debir is last mentioned in the list of cities allotted to the Levites (21:15; cf. 1 Chr. 6:58).

Long identified with Tell Beit Mirsim on the eastern edge of the Shephelah, Debir may more properly be located at modern Khirbet Rabûd, as favored by recent excavations. Situated 12 km. (7.5 mi.) southwest of Hebron, in the hill country of southern Judah, Khirbet Rabûd fits the same watershed pattern as other identifiable sites in the same district (cf. Josh. 15:48-50). Archaeological investigation has shown the site to have been a major fortified city during the Late Bronze and Iron Ages, covering some 5-6 ha. (12-15 acres) at the time of the Israelite Monarchy. It was rebuilt following destruction by Sennacherib in 701 B.C. but was again demolished at the time of Nebuchadnezzar (*ca.* 587) and virtually abandoned. Apart from rock-cut cisterns at the site, Khirbet Rabûd was dependent on water from wells about 3 km. (2 mi.) to the northwest, which would fit the circumstances of the

Achsah-Othniel narrative (Josh. 15:13-19 par. Judg. 1:11-15).

2. A place (Heb. *liḏᵉḇir*; RSV, KJV, NIV "Debir"; Gk. *Daibōn*) in the eastern part of Gilead (Josh. 13:26b), possibly to be identified with LO-DEBAR (cf. JB; see also *BH*), in the vicinity of Mahanaim.

3. A place (so the versions, following MT; LXX has *epí tó tétarton* "to the fourth part") on Judah's northern boundary (Josh. 15:7), possibly Toghret ed-Debr, about 13 km. (8 mi.) east-northeast of Jerusalem.

DEBORAH [deb′ə rə] (Heb. *dᵉḇôrâ* "bee").

1. A nurse who accompanied Rebekah the daughter of Bethuel to her new home in Palestine (Gen. 24:59). The only other reference is to her death at Bethel and to her burial under an oak called "Oak of Tears" (so JB, 35:8; RSV, KJV, NIV "Allon-bacuth").

2. The fourth of Israel's judges, a native of Issachar (implied at Judg. 5:15), and wife of Lappidoth (4:4). As a prophetess (probably a charismatic leader) she ruled that part of Israel between Ramah and Bethel in Ephraim from a site later named the "palm of Deborah" (4:4-5).

The author of Judges focuses on Deborah's capable leadership during Jabin's oppression of the Israelites *ca.* 1200 B.C. Summoning Barak, the son of Abinoam, she commissioned him, in the name of the Lord, to join her in battle with Sisera, most likely the real king; she even acceded to his wish that she accompany him, though she told him at if she went, a woman, not he himself, would receive the honor of killing the enemy (Judg. 4:6-10). When the two armies faced each other, Deborah gave the signal for Barak and his ten thousand men to move down from Mt. Tabor; they then slaughtered the Canaanite charioteers, who had already been routed by God. But it was Jael, the wife of a Kenite, who finally took Sisera's life (vv. 12-22).

The Song of Deborah (Judg. 5:2-31), a twelfth-century B.C. victory hymn, was composed shortly after the Israelite conquest of Sisera at Taanach and was probably first transmitted orally by poets or minstrels. It is regarded as one of the oldest portions of the Old Testament and preserves numerous historical allusions as well as examples of archaic Hebrew usage.

DEBT (Heb. *nᵉšî*; Gk. *opheilé, opheílēma*).* Old Testament restrictions regarding the lending or borrowing of money were intended to prevent undue tension between Israelites, thus serving to maintain the stability of the Hebrew community. The exacting of excessive interest was forbidden (Exod. 22:25; Lev. 25:35-38) so as not to compound an individual's poverty (cf. Deut. 15:4). Creditors were protected by pledges or sureties indicating the debtor's intention of repayment (cf. Exod. 22:26-27; Deut. 24:6, 10-13). Debts were to be cancelled during the seventh year, the year of release (Deut. 15:1ff.; cf. Exod. 23:10-11; Lev. 25). It is apparent, however, that this protective legislation was not always heeded (Amos 2:6-8; 4:1; cf. 1 Sam. 22:2; Neh. 5:1-5; Matt. 23:14). See INTEREST.

Jesus used the terms "debt" and "debtor" figuratively to represent sins and the necessity of forgiveness

(Matt. 6:12; cf. vv. 14-15; 18:23-35; Luke 7:36-50; 11:4).

DECALOG. *See* TEN COMMANDMENTS.

DECAPOLIS [dǐ kăp'ə lĭs] (Gk. *Dekapolis* "ten cities"). A confederation of some ten Hellenistic cities (cf. Josephus *Vita* 65[341], *déka póleis*) settled after the death of Alexander the Great (323 B.C.). For a number of years after Alexander Janneus (103-76 B.C.) had conquered some of them, these cities were subject to Jewish rule. In 63 B.C. the Roman leader Pompey gave them back their independence, and they were placed under the authority of the Roman governor of the province of Syria. By this means the Romans sought to promote Hellenization in the region and to create a barrier against nationalistic Jewish influence from Judea. The Hellenists, for their part, formed the coalition among the ten cities for protection against attack by desert marauders. In New Testament times their common anti-Jewish bond, no doubt, became stronger.

It is not possible to determine the names of all ten cities, since the lists left by Pliny (*Nat. hist.* v.16[74]; A.D. 75) and Ptolemy (second century) differ, at least in part, and the members of the confederation changed from time to time. The original league probably included the following cities: (1) Hippos, on the eastern shore of the Sea of Galilee; (2) Gadara, 13 km. (8 mi.) southeast of the Sea of Galilee; (3) Pella, between the Jabbok river and the Sea of Galilee, near the Jordan; (4) Abila, near the Yarmuk river; (5) Gerasa (modern Jerash), above the Jabbok river in the mountains of Gilead; (6) Philadelphia, at the source of the Jabbok, thus the southernmost city (Old Testament Rabbah); (7) Dion, close to the Yarmuk river and east of the Sea of Galilee; (8) Canatha, the easternmost city, near the Syrian desert; (9) Raphana, northeast of Dion; and (10) Scythopolis (biblical Bethshan), the only city of the ten west of the Jordan. Herod the Great, with the permission of Augustus, incorporated Hippos, Gadara, and Canatha into his kingdom, but after Herod's death these cities were restored to their previous Hellenistic position.

Although the name Decapolis indicates a league of ten cities, there were at least fourteen members, with Damascus an important ally for some time. With the establishment of the Roman province of Arabia, to which Philadelphia and Gerasa were added, the confederation was weakened. Gadara, the original capital of the league, yielded its prominence to Damascus and Scythopolis.

The New Testament mentions Decapolis three times. According to Matthew "great crowds" followed Jesus from Galilee, Jerusalem, and the Decapolis (Matt. 4:25), probably indicating a mixed population with some Jews. Mark records that the healed Gerasene demoniac preached the good news throughout the region of the Decapolis (Mark 5:20), though Luke maintains that the man's activities were restricted to his hometown (Luke 8:39). At 7:31 Mark relates that Jesus passed through the region of the Decapolis (along a route which cannot be retraced) before healing a deaf-mute.

Ancient and modern Gerasa (Jerash, Jordan; cf. GERASA, GERASENES), one of the main cities of the Decapolis (Jordan Information Bureau, Washington, D.C.)

DECEIT, DECEPTION.† Delusion or false dealing with another. A vast array of Hebrew and Greek terms represent various shades of fraudulent behavior. Heb. *rāmâ* (cf. Akk. *ramû* "grow loose") means to forsake (Lam. 1:19; JB "failed"; NIV "betrayed"), trick (Gen. 29:25; so JB), and betray (1 Chr. 12:17). The RSV renders Heb. *šāqar* (piel) "deal falsely" (e.g., Isa. 63:8; KJV "lie") or "lie" (1 Sam. 15:29). The basic sense of Gk. *planáomai* is to wander from the straight path (e.g., Jas. 1:16; KJV "err"; JB "make a mistake"). Gk. *apátē* represents seduction (Rom. 7:11), delight (Matt. 13:22 par. Mark 4:19; JB "lure"), or misleading speech (Rom. 16:18; Col. 2:8). Generated in the human heart (e.g., Prov. 12:20; Jer. 17:9) or in the womb (NIV, Job 15:35; RSV "heart"; KJV "belly"), this vice compounds wickedness (cf. Prov. 15:4).

DECISION, VALLEY OF. *See* JEHOSHAPHAT, VALLEY OF.

DECREE. An official declaration or proclamation, usually in writing. The decree might be posted for public observation, in contrast to the edict, which was written and then read aloud. In the Old Testament the Persian king Darius (the Mede) decreed that he be treated as divine for thirty days (Dan. 6:7; Heb. *'ᵉsār*; RSV "ordinance"); as customary among the Medes and Persians, that stipulation was unchangeable (v. 8; cf. Ezra 6:11; Esth. 8:8-9). The book of Esther records a number of decrees (Heb. *dāṭ* "order, law, regulation") issued by King Ahasuerus (Esth. 3:15; 8:14; 9:14).

In Luke's narrative of the birth of Jesus, Caesar's decree concerning universal enrollment is an important key to dating that event (Luke 2:1; Gk. *dógma* "what seems good"; cf. *TDNT* 2:230-31). The emperor's decrees, which the Christians later were accused of violating (Acts 17:7), were the written laws of the Roman Empire. In other instances the RSV renders the Greek term as "decisions" (16:4; cf. NIV, JB; KJV "decrees"), "ordinances" (Eph. 2:15), and "demands" (Col. 2:14).

Several passages refer to divine decrees (cf. Exod.

15:25, NIV; RSV "statute"). God issues such decrees for mankind because humans cannot penetrate God's mind except as he discloses his intentions (cf. Job 28:10-18). Paul claims that even the degenerate Gentiles knew God's decree, i.e., his moral law, because it was engraved on their consciences when they were born (Rom. 1:32).

DECRETUM GELASIANUM [dĕk'rə təm gĕl ā'sē-ăn'əm].† A Latin document dating in its present form to the sixth century A.D.; traditionally attributed to Pope Gelasius (492-496) but perhaps reflecting the synodical decisions of 382 under Pope Damasus. Of particular significance for the establishment of the Christian canon are its lists of canonical books of both the Old and New Testaments, the writings of the Church Fathers as accepted by the early Church, "apocryphal" biblical and patristic works, and various books rejected as heretical. In addition this compilation includes pronouncements concerning the primacy of Rome and the nature of Christ and the Holy Spirit.

DEDAN [dē'dən] (Heb. *d*ᵉ*dān*). A people in southern Arabia descending from Ham via Cush (Gen. 10:7), or in northern Arabia descending from Abraham and Keturah via Jokshan (25:3). It is quite possible that the Dedanites are a mixture of two different tribes (cf. 1 Chr. 1:9, 32, where the two traditions occur together).

The city of Dedan is connected with Edom and Tema (Jer. 25:23; 49:8; Ezek. 25:13), suggesting possible colonization. It probably was located in the oases of modern el-ʿUlā in the northern Hijaz, south of Tema and northwest of Medina. According to Ezek. 27:20 its inhabitants traded with Tyre, but in the oracle against Arabia the "caravans of Dedanites" (KJV "companies of Dedanim") were warned to be content with lodging in the "thickets" of Arabia, away from the caravan routes, and to aid the fugitives of Kedar (Isa. 21:13). Being merchants themselves, the Dedanites were included among those who recognized the economic value of goods and people seized in war (Ezek. 38:13).

DEDICATION, FEAST OF (Gk. *tá enkaínia* "renewal").† A Jewish festival commemorating the purification and reconstruction of the Jerusalem temple and the dedication of the new altar by Judas Maccabeus in 165/164 B.C., three years to the very day (25 Chislev [Nov.-Dec.]) after Antiochus IV Epiphanes had desecrated it by decreeing pagan sacrifices there (1 Macc. 4:52-59; 2 Macc. 10:5). The modern name of the festival is Hanukkah (Heb. *ḥᵃnukkâ* "dedication").

The eight-day celebration (perhaps patterned after Hezekiah's purification of the temple; 2 Chr. 29:17) was commemorated "with mirth and gladness," by the singing of thanksgiving hymns (notably the Hallel, Pss. 113-118) and processions in which palms and other greenery were carried (2 Macc. 10:7). Many details of the early celebration resembled those associated with the Feast of Booths (Tabernacles), hence its early designation as "the feast of booths in the month of Chislev" (2 Macc. 1:9). After the destruction of the temple in A.D. 70 the feast was observed by the lighting of lamps in private houses (either one lamp each night for each household or person in the household, or increasing or decreasing numbers of lamps marking the successive days), thus its designation "Feast of Lights" (Gk. *tá phôta*; Josephus *Ant.* xii.7.7). Although it may have symbolized the rekindling of the altar fire, the custom is associated traditionally with the legend of Judas' discovery of one day's supply of temple oil which miraculously burned for eight days.

Various other dedicatory observances (Heb. *ḥᵃnukkâ*) are recorded in the Old Testament, including the consecration of the altars in the wilderness tabernacle (Num. 7:10-11, 84, 88) and Solomon's temple (2 Chr. 7:5, 9; cf. 1 Kgs. 8) and the rebuilt walls of Jerusalem (Neh. 12:27).

It was on the occasion of the Feast of Dedication that Jesus described himself as the Messiah, the Son of God (John 10:22-38).

Bibliography. O. S. Rankin, *The Origins of the Festival of Hanukkah, the Jewish New-Age Festival* (Edinburgh: 1930); S. Zeitlin, "Hanukkah: Its Origin and Its Significance," *JQR* 29 (1938/39): 1-36.

DEEP (Heb. *tᵉhôm*).† The primeval ocean, which before creation covered the entire earth. According to Hebrew cosmology which divided the waters of the universe by the dome of the sky (Gen. 1:6-8), it represented the subterranean waters ("water under the earth," Exod. 20:4), the source of both the salt seas (Gen. 1:10) and the fresh waters (cf. Deut. 4:18). An integral part of the divine creation (cf. Gen. 1:2; Ps. 24:1), these waters were the instrument of God in the great Flood (Gen. 7:11; 8:2) and the Exodus from Egypt (Exod. 15:5, 8; Ps. 106:9). An object of fear to the nonseafaring Israelites (cf. Jonah 2:3-5), the deep nevertheless contributed providentially to their survival (e.g., Ps. 78:15; Ezek. 31:4; cf. Gen. 49:25; Deut. 33:13; Ps. 135:6).

Although the Hebrew term is related etymologically to the name of the Akkadian goddess Tiamat, the dragon slain in the creation myth Enuma Elish, its use in the Old Testament appears to have been significantly demythologized. In particular, the Genesis accounts of creation are devoid of any allusion to conflict between a mythological sea monster and God at the time of creation (but cf. Ps. 104:6-7; note also Hab. 3:15 and the Ugaritic myth of the battle between Baal and the Sea). Nevertheless, the Deep is often personified in Hebrew poetry; it is portrayed as speaking (Job 28:14), roaring and lifting its hands (Hab. 3:10), and trembling at the sight of God (Ps. 77:16).

DEER.† A family of cloven-hoofed ruminants, three species of which were known in biblical times: the red deer (*Cervus elaphus*; Heb. *'ayyāl*; RSV, KJV "hart"), the fallow deer (*Cervus dama mesopotamious*; Heb. *yaḥmûr*; RSV "roebuck"), and the roe deer (*Cervus capreolus*; also Heb. *'ayyāl*). As with other terminology regarding animals, Hebrew usage was not consistent, and precise identificaton is difficult if not impossible. Heb. *'ayyāl* may actually have been a generic designation of all deer.

DEGREES, SONGS OF. *See* ASCENTS, SONG OF.

DEHAVITES (dĭ hă′vīts). According to the KJV (following MT *dehāwē′*) one of the nations which the Assyrians deported to Samaria after the Jewish population had been led into exile (Ezra 4:9); some scholars have suggested that they were the people who, according to Herodotus (i.125, Gk. *Daoi*), dwelled southeast of the Caspian Sea. The RSV, NIV, and JB emend the MT to read Heb. *dî hû′* "that is" (cf. LXX B), indicating that the men of Susa were in Elam.

DEKAR (1 Kgs. 4:9, KJV). *See* BEN-DEKER.

DELAIAH [dĭ lā′yə] (Heb. *dᵉlāyâ* "God has raised").
    1. One of the sons of Elioenai, a descendant of David (1 Chr. 3:24; KJV "Dalaiah").
    2. A descendant of Aaron, and the head of the twenty-third priestly division during the days of David (1 Chr. 24:18).
    3. The ancestor of a group of exiles who were unable to prove their Jewish descent and thus secure their Jewish heritage (Ezra 2:60; Neh. 7:62).
    4. The son of Mehetabel and father of Shemaiah. He advised Nehemiah to hide within the temple from those who sought to kill him for rebuilding the temple, but Nehemiah refused (Neh. 6:10-11).
    5. The son of Shemaiah (Jer. 36:12), and one of three princes who urged King Jehoiakim not to burn Jeremiah's prophetic scroll (v. 25).

DELILAH [dĭ lī′lə] (Heb. *dᵉlîlâ*; cf. Arab. *dallatum* "flirt"). A woman living in the valley of Sorek, either a Philistine or an Israelite who sold herself to Israel's oppressors for money. When Samson declared his love for her, she coaxed from him the secret of his strength so she could deliver him to the Philistines. They paid her handsomely for her duplicity (Judg. 16:4-20).
    Although discerning and level-headed, Delilah repaid trust with deception. Perhaps this weakness could more justifiably be excused if she were a Philistine motivated by patriotism rather than if she were a Jew craving power and worldly possessions at the expense of her fellow countrymen. She is not the same person as the prostitute mentioned in v. 1.

DELUGE. *See* FLOOD.

DEMAS [dē′məs] (Gk. *Dēmas*). One of Paul's co-workers who sent his greetings to the Colossian church (Col. 4:14) and to Philemon (Phlm. 24). Later he deserted Paul and headed for Thessalonica because he was "in love with this present world" (2 Tim. 4:10), perhaps in pursuit of some temporal interest or because the apostle's demands had become too rigorous. At any rate, Paul does not call him an apostate, since Demas apparently deserted for personal reasons, not because he no longer believed.

DEMETRIUS [dĭ mē′trĭ əs] (Gk. *Dēmētrios* "follower of [the goddess] Demeter").†
    1. Demetrius I Poliorcetes ("the Besieger"; 336-283 B.C.). The king of Macedonia (294-288) and son of Antigonus I. Seeking to defend the kingdom's southern boundaries against Ptolemy, he was severely defeated at Gaza in 312; other campaigns that same year against the Nabateans and Seleucus also failed.

    2. Demetrius I Soter ("Savior"), king of Syria (162-150 B.C.), and son of Seleucus IV Philopator. In 175 he was sent to Rome to substitute for his uncle Antiochus IV Epiphanes, who was being held hostage as security from the royal family against payment of the indemnity imposed by the treaty of Apamea. When Antiochus IV, who had become king, died in 163, Demetrius petitioned the Roman Senate for release in order to claim the Syrian throne, but he was refused. With the aid of the Greek statesman and historian Polybius, Demetrius escaped the following year and proclaimed himself king, supplanting his young nephew Antiochus V Eupator (1 Macc. 7:1-4; 2 Macc. 14:1-2).
    At first Demetrius took a hard line against the Judean rebels and confirmed the cruel Alcimus as high priest, whom he supported with an army led first by Bacchides and then by Nicanor (1 Macc. 7:5–9:18). When the latter was killed at Adasa, Demetrius sent Bacchides and Alcimus to avenge the general's death; in the ensuing battle at Elasa Judas Maccabeus was killed (160; 1 Macc. 9:1-22).
    Encouraged by the Romans and their allies in Egypt and Asia Minor, and aided by the Syrians' growing discontent with Demetrius' leadership, Alexander Balas sailed from Smyrna and captured Ptolemais (Acco); pretending to be the son of Antiochus IV, Alexander "Epiphanes" (1 Macc. 10:1) sought to challenge Demetrius for the throne. The Syrian enlisted the support of the Hasmonean successor Jonathan Maccabeus, returning Jewish hostages and abandoning fortifications in Palestine. When Alexander named Jonathan high priest, Demetrius offered further concessions (1 Macc. 10:15-44), but he failed to gain the Jews' support. Suspicious of his offers, they allied themselves with Alexander. After two years of conflict, Demetrius was defeated in 150, dying in a deep swamp during the final battle (vv. 48-50; Josephus *Ant.* xiii.2.4).
    3. Demetrius II Nicator ("Victor"), Seleucid king of Syria (145-139, 129-125 B.C.); son of Demetrius I. Returning from protective exile in Asia Minor, the fourteen-year-old Demetrius established himself in Syria with the aid of Cretan mercenaries. He appointed Apollonius as governor in an attempt to subject the resistant Judeans, but Apollonius was routed at Joppa and Ashdod. In 145, however, Ptolemy VI of Egypt became disenchanted with Alexander Balas; in addition to taking his daughter Cleopatra from Alexander and giving her to Demetrius as his wife, he joined forces with the Syrian and together they defeated Alexander near Antioch (1 Macc. 11:1-2). Thus Demetrius gained the kingship.
    Seeking to bolster his monarchy, the inexperienced Demetrius confirmed Jonathan Maccabeus as high priest and provided him territory in Samaria and exemption from tribute. Weakened by these concessions as well as the peacetime release of his troops, Demetrius was forced to enlist Judean help against the claims of Balas' general Trypho and his puppet, the infant Antiochus VI. Angered by Demetrius' failure to fulfill his pledge, Jonathan sided with Trypho, who subsequently murdered the Hasmonean (1 Macc. 11:44–13:24). When Trypho also assassinated Antiochus, the Judean successor Simon Maccabeus endorsed Demetrius in exchange for Judean independence. Seeking to enlist the aid of the Medes against Trypho, Demetrius

expelled the Parthian invaders from Babylonia in 140. The next year he was captured by the Parthian Arsaces VI (Mithradates I); his younger brother Antiochus VII Sidetes succeeded him in Syria. Demetrius was released in 129 to thwart Antiochus' attack on Parthia, but he never regained complete control of Syria; he was assassinated in 125 at Tyre, where he had fled after defeat by the Egyptians.

4. Demetrius III Eukairos ("the timely"), one of three who claimed succession to the throne of his father Antiochus VIII Grypos during the final stages of Seleucid power (95-88 B.C.). Ruling from Damascus, he was enlisted by the Pharisees in 88 against Alexander Janneus, but the latter prevailed.

5. Demetrius of Phalerum, head of the royal library at Alexandria (died 283 B.C.), who according to the Letter of Aristeas suggested to Ptolemy II Philadelphus that the Hebrew Scriptures be translated into Greek (the LXX).

6. A silversmith at Ephesus, a member of a guild which made little silver shrines of the goddess Artemis (Diana) that were used as votive gifts or as souvenirs by pilgrims (Acts 19:23-41). Because Paul's effective preaching significantly threatened the business of the guild, Demetrius instigated a riot and accused Paul and his companions. Peace was restored only when the town clerk had calmed the unruly crowd enough to advise Demetrius of his legal rights in bringing grievances against Paul and his fellows. Because of the frequency of the name Demetrius in Hellenistic times it cannot be proved whether this person is either the Demetrius of 3 John 12 or Demas (a contracted form of the name), Paul's former associate (2 Tim. 4:10).

7. A Christian who received a triple testimony (3 John 12) — from his fellow Christians, from John, and "from the truth itself."

DEMON. A spirit with minor powers. In the Old Testament the RSV renders only Heb. *šēḏ as "demon" (Deut. 31:17; Ps. 106:37 [cf. NIV]; KJV "devil" [LXX Gk. *daimónion*]); this word points to a protective deity (cf. Akk. *šêdu*, a large bull image at the entrance of Assyrian temples or palaces) or to an evil spirit or demon (KoB, p. 949). (Some scholars link *šēḏ with a root śdd "destroy, devastate" and its stem "be Lord" [cf. Arab. *sādda*] or with Arab. *sōḏ* "be black.") The "satyrs" (Heb. *śeʿîrîm* "hairy ones"; KJV "devils"; LXX [*eídōla kaí*] *mátaia*) are either demons represented as he-goats (NIV "goat idols," Lev. 17:7; 2 Chr. 11:15) or actual he-goats (NIV "wild goats," Isa. 13:21; 34:14). The common New Testament word is Gk. *daimónion* (a diminutive of *daímōn*). Less frequent are Gk. *daímōn* (Matt. 8:31) and *diábolos*.

I. Old Testament

The Old Testament often mentions the presence of angels and spirits but rarely refers to demons or evil spirits. The Hebrews worshipped satyrs in the wilderness (Lev. 17:7) and later, at the bidding of Jeroboam I, in Canaan (2 Chr. 11:15). Though their worship at times involved spirits that resembled goats, they did not develop a systematic demonology; God's chosen people were warned against such worship (Deut. 32:17;

cf. Ps. 106:37), just as they were forbidden to worship idols. Two demons are given personal names: Azazel, a spirit of the desert to which the sacrificial goat was sent on the Day of Atonement, and Lilith, the night hag which dwelled in ruins (Isa. 34:14).

II. New Testament

The New Testament, which presupposes the intertestamental development of demonology, depicts demons as evil spirits exercising malevolent influences on people or as foreign deities worshipped through idols (Acts 17:18, "divinities"; cf. Rev. 9:20 where "demons" and idols are distinguished). (The demons to which the Corinthians are said to have offered sacrifices [1 Cor. 8:4; 10:19] were probably impersonal forces.)

Christ's ministry of healing encompassed deliverance from physical and psychological disorders and from demon-possession. Though the Gospels usually distinguish between the two, they occasionally come close to equating one with the other; at Matt. 17:15-18 (cf. Luke 9:39) epilepsy is also called demon-possession, and at Mark 1:26; 9:18, 20, 26 par. a demon is held responsible for a person's seizures.

Jesus, who is credited with healing such demoniacs as the Gerasene (Mark 5:1-20 par.) and Mary Magdalene, who was controlled by seven demons (Luke 8:2; cf. Mark 16:9; KJV "devils"), was generally not moved with compassion for these individuals, but demonstrated with these miracles of exorcism that the kingdom of God (Luke 11:20) is able to conquer Satan's dominion over people (Luke 10:18; John 12:31). To the degree that Satan was in control, Jesus did not hold the demoniacs personally responsible for their actions and utterances as he did Judas Iscariot, who betrayed him. Unlike the Jewish leaders who exorcised demons by means of herbs, Jesus merely commanded the demons "to come out" (e.g., Mark 1:25). His disciples used Jesus' name (Luke 10:17; cf. Acts 16:18), a method which proved so successful that Jewish exorcists adopted it as well (Mark 9:38 par.; cf. Acts 19:13).

While the Gospels describe Jesus' work in curbing the activities of demons in humans, other New Testament writers disclose different demonic activities. Paul warns against the demonic "doctrines" forbidding marriage and encouraging fasting (1 Tim. 4:1-3). But Paul also affirms that not even "principalities" (NIV "demons") can sever the bond of love between Christ and his followers (Rom. 8:38). James makes the provocative comment that even the demons believe that God is one God (Jas. 2:19), but adds that though they tremble before God they do not accept that Christ saved them. Finally, the aged John envisions "demonic spirits," foul spirits originating from the beast who will perform signs and prepare the world's rulers for the final Day of Battle (Rev. 16:14). At 18:2, an allusion to Babylon's previously forlorn state (Isa. 13:20-21), the author compares the proud achievements of mankind with the demonic haunts of foul and hateful creatures.

See also DEVIL; SATAN.

Bibliography. G. B. Caird, *Principalities and Powers: A Study in Pauline Theology* (Oxford: 1956); S. Eitrem, *Some Notes on the Demonology of the New Testament.*

Symbolae Osloenses Sup. 12 (1950); E. Langton, *Essentials of Demonology* (London: 1950).

DEN (Heb. *māʿôn*; Gk. *spélaion*). A hollow or cavern, frequently used as an animals' lair (Job 37:8; Ps. 104:22) or a hiding place for persons (Judg. 15:8ff.; 2 Sam. 17:9; Job 30:6). The terrain in and around Palestine, particularly in the mountains (Judg. 6:2), is marked by caves and hollows created when water containing carbon dioxide dissolved the prevalent limestone deposits.

DENARIUS [dǐ nârʹǐ əs] (Gk. *dēnárion*). A silver Roman coin, weighing 3.8 g. (.13 oz.). In the narrative in which Jesus discusses to whom one should pay taxes he is given a denarius (so JB, NIV; RSV "coin"; KJV "penny") bearing the portrait and inscription of Caesar (Matt. 22:19 par. Mark 12:15; Luke 20:24). Equal in value to the drachma (Luke 15:8, RSV mg.), the denarius was the wage of a day's work (Matt. 20:2, 13; KJV "penny"). Accordingly, the two hundred denarii needed to buy bread for the hungry crowd at the Sea of Galilee would have been the equivalent of eight months' wages (so NIV, Mark 6:37; cf. John 6:7), and the jar of ointment which the poor woman used to anoint Jesus would have cost more than a year's wages (so NIV, Mark 14:5). It has been estimated that the debt of one hundred denarii owed by one servant to another in Jesus' parable on forgiveness was less than fifteen dollars (JB, Matt. 18:28; NIV mg. "a few dollars").

DERBE [dûrʹbǐ] (Gk. *Derbē*).† A city in the district of Lycaonia (Acts 14:6), which in New Testament times still belonged to the Roman province of Galatia, east of Phrygia and west of the territory of Antiochus IV of Commagene. As a frontier city of the province, it was the last stop of Paul's first missionary journey, the city to which he went following his stoning in Lystra at the hands of angry Jews (vv. 19-20). With his helper, Barnabas, he founded a church in Derbe (v. 20) and then returned to Lystra. Paul's second missionary journey commenced at this city. Gaius, who accompanied Paul through Macedonia (Acts 20:4), was from Derbe.

Long identified as located at the mound of Gudelisin, subsequent discovery of two inscriptions — a dedication by the council and citizens of Derbe, and a tombstone of Michael, a bishop of Derbe (fourth century A.D.) — convincingly point to contemporary Kerti Hüyük as the site, about 25 km. (15 mi.) north-northeast of Karaman (ancient Laranda).

DESCENT INTO HELL. The relegation of Jesus (or his soul) to the abode of the dead (Hades) following his death on the cross. This belief is not directly biblical but stems rather from the early Church; although absent in the second-century A.D. Old Roman Creed, it appears to have been known by such second- and third-century Church Fathers as Justin Martyr, Clement of Alexandria, and Origen, and is part of the Apostles' Creed (formulated *ca*. 400). Some exegetes claim biblical support in the Gospel accounts which

indicate that Christ was buried and remained in the grave for three days or parts thereof (cf. Matt. 27:63; note the resurrection "from the dead"; e.g., Matt. 17:9; Acts 4:10). Paul describes Jesus as having descended to the lower parts of the earth before ascending on high (Eph. 4:9). Peter adds that Christ preached to the spirits in prison (1 Pet. 3:19), which may be taken to indicate the dead awaiting judgment (cf. 4:6).

Some theologians interpret the descent into hell to indicate a literal visit to the underworld where Christ liberated the righteous dead from the power of death through the power of his resurrection. Peter, quoting Ps. 16:10, may allude to such a physical presence in and deliverance from Hades (Acts 2:24, 27); however, the passage may also be interpreted as indicating God's victory over death and hell and thus that Christ had been spared from entering that region. Other theologians (e.g., Calvin *Institutes* ii.16.8-13) view Christ's encounter with the grave as the culmination of his earthly suffering, as being completely forsaken by God. The crux of the problem is in the interpretation of the word "grave" — whether it means merely a place of burial, a symbol of God's ultimate judgment over sin, or Jesus' final identification with human sinners.

DESERT.† A barren or partially barren geographical area, usually produced by low rainfall (e.g., the Sinai desert); also a symbol of aridity and desolation.

The most common Hebrew word for "desert" is *miḏbār* (cf. Aram. *dbr* "bring the flock to the pasture"), indicating a barren area resembling a steppe, which would include pasturelands (Ps. 65:12; Jer. 23:10). Less frequent are Heb. *ʿᵃrābâ*, which designates the arid desert (Job 39:6, "steppe" par. "salt land"; KJV "wilderness"; NIV "wasteland") and which indicates the sun's scorching heat during the long summer (*see* ARABAH); Heb. *yᵉšîmôn* applied to a wasteland (Deut. 32:10) with endless stretches of brown and yellow sand, rocks, and valley beds occasionally interrupted by some green growth (*see* JESHIMON); and Heb. *ḥorbâ* "waste places" or "ruins" (e.g., Lev. 26:33, "waste"; NIV "ruins"). Often the Hebrews, through poetic parallelism, treated these words as synonymous. The Greek word for desert is *érēmos*.

Surrounded by the Arabian desert in the east and the Sinai wilderness in the south, the Hebrews were familiar with desert life. Indeed, following the Exodus from Egypt, their ancestors spent forty years in the Sinai wilderness. Their descendants viewed this as Israel's period of discontent with Yahweh (Ps. 78:17-18, 40 [cf. Exod. 16:1ff.]; 106:14), as well as of God's condescension to his people in revelation and grace (Ps. 105:41; Isa. 48:21; cf. Exod. 17:6). Some of the latter prophets describe Israel's wilderness experience as a "desert ideal." Jermiah contrasts Israel's current apostasy to their previous loyalty in the wilderness (Jer. 2:2-3, 6). and Hosea prophesies a recurrence of spiritual fidelity similar to that displayed in the desert (Hos. 2:14-19). God can turn the rivers into a desert (Isa. 50:2); he can, likewise, change the inhospitable wilderness (Job 38:26) into a bed of flowers watered by abundant streams (Isa. 35:1, 6), a group of trees (41:19), and an abode for animals (43:20) —

to demonstrate his power over his creation and to move his people to praise him.

See also WILDERNESS.

DESOLATING SACRILEGE (Gk. *tó bdélygma tês erēmóseōs*).† A phrase derived from Daniel's visions (Dan. 11:31; 12:11; Heb. *[haš]šiqqûṣ [mᵉ]šōmēm* "abomination that makes desolate"; KJV "abomination of desolation"; cf. 9:27), referring to the altar to Zeus Olympios which Antiochus IV Epiphanes erected upon the altar of burnt offering at Jerusalem, thus culminating his persecution of the Jews (1 Macc. 1:54-59; 2 Macc. 6:1-2). Used by Jesus in describing signs of the end of the age, the expression as recorded by Matthew (Matt. 24:15) alludes to Antiochus' desecration, whereas Mark may have had in mind Caligula's near successful attempt *ca.* A.D. 40 to again dishonor the temple (Mark 13:14); Luke's version of the discourse suggests the anticipated final destruction of Jerusalem by the Romans (Luke 21:20). Christ may be referring to the antichrist, whose appearance in the end times is accompanied by a revolt against God (cf. 2 Thess. 2:3-4).

DESTROYER (Heb. *mašḥîṯ*; Gk. *olothreúō*).† The avenging angel of death. During the night of the Israelite Exodus from Egypt this superhuman agent of destruction passed through the land slaying the first-born sons in homes not marked with lamb's blood on the doorposts (Exod. 12:23). In the Old Testament this figure is understood as a divine messenger which the Lord employed to effect his will (cf. 11:4-8). At 2 Sam. 24:16-17 (par. 1 Chr. 21:15, "destroying angel") such an agent punishes Israel for David's census (cf. 2 Kgs. 19:35, where the "angel of the Lord" slaughters the armies of Sennacherib encamped against Jerusalem). In rabbinic thought the Destroyer became a proper name designating a specific angel. It is in this sense that Paul refers to an angel of destruction who punished the Israelites for their rebellion in the wilderness (1 Cor. 10:10; cf. Num. 14:2, 36-37; 16:30-31, 41-50); he may have in mind Satan or his agent (cf. 2 Cor. 12:7; Wis. 18:20-25).

In Joel's account of the locust plague (Joel 2:25) Heb. *ḥāsîl* indicates a type of locust (RSV "destroyer"; KJV "caterpillar"; JB "shearer"; NEB "grub").

DEUEL [dōōʹəl] (Heb. *dᵉʿ û'ēl* "knowledge of God").† A representative of the tribe of Gad in the wilderness (Num. 1:14; 7:42, 47) and the father of Eliasaph. At Num. 2:14 he is called Reuel, probably resulting from a confusion of the Hebrew consonants daleth and resh. *See* REUEL 3.

DEUTEROCANONICAL BOOKS. An alternate name ("second canon") which the Roman Catholic church applies to those books found in the LXX and Vulgate but not in the Hebrew text of the Old Testament. According to the decision of the Council of Trent (1548) and the First Vatican Council (1870) these books, like those of the Hebrew canon, are regarded as possessing divine and canonical authority. *See* APOCRYPHA.

DEUTERO-ISAIAH. *See* ISAIAH, BOOK OF.

DEUTERONOMIC HISTORY.† That portion of the Primary History of Israel consisting of the books Deuteronomy–2 Kings, judged by various critical scholars to have been compiled and edited by one (the Deuteronomist, author of the D source) or more theologians or editorial "schools."

According to this assessment, the history comprises various originally independent materials such as collections of laws, narratives concerning the judges, the "Court History" of 2 Sam. 9–1 Kgs. 2, and the Elijah and Elisha "cycles" — perhaps themselves "complexes" of smaller local traditions. These accounts have been reworked into an editorial framework, largely intended to promote the reforms of the Judahite king Josiah, principally those inspired by the discovery of the law book containing the stipulations of the Mosaic covenant (*ca.* 622 B.C.; 2 Kgs. 22–23 par. 2 Chr. 34–35; *see* DEUTERONOMY, BOOK OF) and, in particular, the centralization of worship at Jerusalem (Deut. 12:5-31). Characteristic of this compilation, with its emphasis on the religious lessons implicit in Israelite history, is the interpretation of events in terms of adherence or disobedience to the Mosaic law; this is most apparent in the assessment of the fall of Samaria and the fortunes or misfortunes of Judah and Israel as the consequence of royal behavior (e.g., 1 Kgs. 15:26, 30; 2 Kgs. 15:3-5) and in the framework superimposed upon the accounts of the judges (Israel sins, God sends an oppressor, the people repent, God sends a deliverer who defeats the oppressor).

Apart from traditional challenges to literary or source criticism, the basic hypothesis of a Deuteronomic history retains widespread acceptance by biblical scholars. However, literary, historical, and theological differences reflected by the various books have led to divergent interpretations of the limits of the history and of the stages of its development. Recent scholarship, although by no means unanimous, suggests three stages of compilation: (1) editing of the book of Deuteronomy in the late eighth-early seventh century B.C. by a northern (perhaps levitical) refugee to Jerusalem following the destruction of Samaria (722); (2) editing of Deuteronomy–2 Kings in light of the Josianic reforms, perhaps by a member of the Judahite court *ca.* 620, before the fall of Jerusalem became apparent; and (3) reediting of the whole for incorporation into the Primary History following the fall of Jerusalem in 587 (cf. 2 Kgs. 23:26), perhaps in Babylon.

See BIBLICAL CRITICISM.

Bibliography. M. Noth, *The Deuteronomistic History.* JSOTS 15 (1981); J. R. Porter, "Old Testament Historiography," pp. 132-152 in G. W. Anderson, ed., *Tradition and Interpretation* (New York: 1979); M. Weinfeld, *Deuteronomy and the Deuteronomic School* (Oxford: 1972).

DEUTERONOMY, BOOK OF.† The fifth book of the Old Testament and the last of the Pentateuch, the "five books of Moses."

I. Name

The English title Deuteronomy derives from the book's designation in the LXX as Gk. *Deuteronomion* "second (or repeated) law," based on the translation of Deut. 17:18 as "this repetition of the law" (from Heb.

mišnēh hattôrâ hazzᵊ'ôṭ "a copy of this law"). The book does not constitute a body of law distinct from that recorded in the preceding books of the Pentateuch; rather, it is an expansion or reinterpretation of the stipulations of the Sinai (Horeb) covenant presented in the context of a renewal of that agreement between Israel and God enacted at the borders of Moab (29:1), hence the repetition or recitation of earlier legislation. Its Hebrew title *'ēlleh haddᵊbārîm* "these are the words," taken from the initial words of the text, reflects the standard opening formula of ancient Near Eastern treaty (covenant) texts.

II. Contents

Interspersed within the narrative of Moses' last days are three discourses which the great leader addresses to the people of Israel in the final stages of their wilderness wanderings. Following a brief introduction, the first oration reviews the history of the people in the wilderness from God's directive at Horeb (Sinai) that they take possession of the promised land through their conquest of Heshbon and Bashan and the allocation of the land east of the Jordan (1:6–3:29; the address concludes with the admonition to faithful obedience to God's laws, particularly those forbidding idolatry (4:1-40). The narrative then recounts Moses' appointment of cities of refuge in Transjordan (vv. 41-43). Moses' second address comprises a review of Israel's laws, including a restatement and exposition of the Ten Commandments as the basis of Israel's covenant (5:1–11:32) and a compilation of specific legislation (12:1–26:15); the discourse concludes with an exhortation or declaration regarding commitment to the covenant (vv. 16-19). Following is a narrative of the covenant renewal ceremony on the plains of Moab (27:1–29:1), depicted in terms of its later observance at Shechem. Moses' third address (29:2–30:20) constitutes a charge to covenant faithfulness. The remaining chapters record the concluding events of Moses' life, including a final charge to the people and the appointment of Joshua as his successor (ch. 31), the "Song of Moses" (32:1-43), the "Blessing of Moses" (ch. 33), and an account of Moses' death and burial (ch. 34).

III. Structure and Origin

Although early literary critics viewed Deuteronomy as primarily the work of the Deuteronomic (D) source, the book has been subjected to numerous critical interpretations and its composition assigned to a variety of authors and editors ranging from Mosaic to postexilic times. Traditionally the book is the work of Moses (although some accept ch. 34 as an appendix perhaps attributed to Joshua), and many critical scholars accept at least the Mosaic roots of its theology and laws. A prominent view is that the core of the book (chs. 12–26) represents the Book of the Law discovered by Josiah in 622/621 B.C. (2 Kgs. 22–23 par. 2 Chr. 34–35) and which formed the basis of his reforms, promoted by editorial elaboration in the form of a "Deuteronomic" or "Deuteronomistic" framework (e.g., chs. 5–11, 30–34); later additions brought the book within the scope of the preexilic "Deuteronomic History" (Deuteronomy–2 Kings) and the exilic "Primary History" (Genesis–2 Kings). An adaptation

of this view dates the compilation of the "Deuteronomic Code" to the reign of Hezekiah (715-687), possibly by northern levitical priests who had fled to Jerusalem following the fall of Samaria in 722. At any rate, the variety of legal, narrative, hortatory, and poetic materials which comprise Deuteronomy suggests a long and complex development prior to the book's canonization by the fourth century B.C. as part of the Pentateuch. *See* BIBLICAL CRITICISM; DEUTERONOMIC HISTORY.

In accordance with its literary and historical setting as well as its primary theme, several scholars have compared the book's structure to the form of ancient Near Eastern vassal treaties. Such treaty components include the preamble (1:1-5), historical prologue (1:6–4:49), declaration of basic principles (chs. 5–11), specific regulations (chs. 12–26), curses and blessings sanctioning the oath (chs. 27–28), invocation of divine witnesses (30:19; 31:19; 32:1-43), and provision for continuity of the covenant (chs. 31–34).

IV. Theology

The core of Deuteronomy's message is the covenant relationship between Israel and God, a concept stressed through both the form and content of the book and summarized in the credal statement of the Shema (Deut. 6:4-5). The Lord is one God, a unique God (4:35, 39), majestic and supreme (3:24; 10:14), who acts in history on behalf of his people (e.g., 1:6–4:49; 29:2-4). Israel is a unique people, chosen by God as a "holy" people (7:6; 10:15; 14:2; 26:19; 28:9) to enjoy a privileged relationship to their Lord (cf. 1:31; 32:6, 9). This covenant relationship, permitted by God as fulfillment of his promises to the patriarchs (7:8; 29:12-13; cf. 4:21), requires obedience to the stipulations set forth at Sinai and elaborated for their contemporary situation (e.g., 4:1; 8:1-6); a central factor of this obedience as presented in Deuteronomy is the centralization of Israelite worship (12:1-31). Israel's adherence to or rejection of these regulations will bring appropriate retribution (chs. 27–28).

Bibliography. R. E. Clements, *God's Chosen People* (London: 1968); P. C. Craigie, *The Book of Deuteronomy.* NICOT (1976); A. D. H. Mayes, *Deuteronomy.* NCBC (1981); G. von Rad, *Deuteronomy.* OTL (1966).

DEUTERO-ZECHARIAH. *See* ZECHARIAH, BOOK OF.

DEVIL (Gk. *diábolos* "slanderer"). Another name for Satan, God's adversary. Whereas the Old Testament contains references to "demons" (so RSV, NIV; KJV "devils") and "satyrs," the New Testament presents a more developed demonology. Here some of the angels are said to have fallen from their state of integrity in heaven and placed themselves under the rule of the devil. As their prince (Matt. 9:34), the devil — called the "father of lies" and the "murderer from the beginning" (John 8:44) — opposed Christ's redemptive work by sending demons into people who then involuntarily became demon-possessed (*see* DEMON).

The devil himself sought to annul Christ's ministry by his temptations in the wilderness, the region where, according to the Old Testament, demons and satyrs existed. Temporarily abandoning the effort after three unsuccessful attempts (Matt. 4:1-11 par. Luke 4:2-13; Mark 1:13 has "Satan"), the devil waited for an opportune moment (Luke 4:13), which came during the passion week when he had Judas Iscariot, one of Jesus' disciples, betray his master (Luke 22:3, "Satan"; John 6:70; 13:2). (Though Luke suggests Jesus' victory over the devil, he also records Christ's awareness of his power [e.g., Luke 8:12; see also Matt. 13:39], especially through his endeavors to block the expansion of the kingdom of God by means of demon possession.) At Acts 13:10 the apostle Paul blinds Elymas on account of his alleged cooperation with the devil.

Through his resurrection Christ broke the power of death and, in principle, the power of the devil (Heb. 2:14; cf. Acts 10:38; 1 John 3:8). God's adversary may still prowl "like a roaring lion" (1 Pet. 5:8), but his reign will end at the great battle of the final tribulation (Rev. 20:10) or at the Day of Judgment (Matt. 25:41). Meanwhile, believers are warned not to play into the hands of the devil (Eph. 4:27) but to resist his wiles (6:11; cf. 1 Pet. 5:9), and office bearers are exhorted to display kindness to unbelievers in the hope that they may escape from the devil's tentacles (2 Tim. 2:25-26).

See also SATAN.

DEVOTED (Heb. *ḥērem*).† Consecrated or set aside for the Lord's purposes; during the formative stages of Israel's existence, particularly the period of the conquest of Canaan, the practice was intensely related to the promotion of the Israelite cause. That which was "placed under the ban" (so NEB) was taboo and inviolable (cf. Lev. 27:28-29) and could not be appropriated for private use (Josh. 6:18; cf. 7:20-21). An integral aspect of the concept of the holy war in ancient Israel was the devotion of various entities for utter destruction, encompassing virtually every living creature — men, women, children, and livestock — as well as material goods (Deut. 20:13, 16; 1 Sam. 15:3). Such destruction often involved burning the conquered city, a preventative measure against epidemic as well as a means of total obliteration. Precious metals were confiscated to bolster the Israelite treasury (later viewed as the priest's portion; Lev. 27:21; Num. 18:14), and bronze and iron might also be used for tools and weapons (Deut. 7:25; Josh. 6:24). Canaanite cities (ostensibly because they might lead the Israelites into sin and apostasy; Deut. 7:1-3; Josh. 2:10; 6:17) were subject to the most extreme execution of the ban (Deut. 20:16-18; cf. 1 Sam. 15:2-3); by contrast, women, children, cattle, and goods from non-Palestinian cities were spared (Deut. 20:10-15). Inconsistencies in the treatment of conquered Palestinian cities (cf. Josh. 8:27; 10:28-39; 11:9, 14; Judg. 21:11-12) suggest that the objects of devotion were determined prior to battle, perhaps through a vow (cf. Num. 21:1-3). Among the Israelites themselves, individuals as well as entire cities who engaged in idolatrous practices or who appropriated devoted goods for themselves — thus undangering the solidarity of the formative nation and its covenant relationship with Yahweh — might be marked for destruction (Exod. 22:20; Deut. 13:12-18; Josh. 7).

The practice of devoting objects in battle became increasingly less common in the time of the judges. Under the Monarchy the distribution of booty was determined by the king, often as a reward for services rendered (1 Sam. 30:21-31; cf. Num. 31:25-54).

In later Hebrew thought the prophets envisioned Israel's enemies as subject to utter destruction (Isa. 34:2, 5; RSV "doomed") and their wealth devoted to the Lord (Mic. 4:13). Although the threat of the "ban of utter destruction" was retained as a sanction against violation of the covenant (Mal. 4:6; RSV mg.), the practice would have no place in the coming reign of God (Zech. 14:11; cf. Rev. 22:3).

DEW (Heb. *ṭal*).† Moisture condensed from warm air by the cool ground. In the understanding of the Old Testament peoples this encompassed both the dew which formed on the ground and the mist that formed almost imperceptibly at night (Num. 11:9; 2 Sam. 17:12). Carried over the land by sea winds, this vapor was condensed as the early morning fog (Exod. 16:13) caused by the sharp drop in temperature during the night; the amount of moisture so produced is suggested by the account of the fleece which signalled Gideon's victory over the Midianites (Judg. 6:36-40). With the rising of the sun, this dew or mist soon disappears (Exod. 16:13-14); thus the transience of Israel's love for God is compared to the dew (Hos. 6:4), and the people are cautioned that their idolatry will lead to their own swift demise (13:3). Essential to Palestinian vegetation, particularly during the dry summer months, dew is viewed as the gift of God (1 Kgs. 17:1; Mic. 5:7), that which promises abundant fertility (Gen. 27:28).

DIAL OF AHAZ [Heb. *maʿᵃlôṯ ʾāḥāz*].† According to the KJV and RSV, a device used to show the passage of time, suggesting a sundial (so KJV, Isa. 38:8) or horologe such as those employed by the Babylonians and Egyptians (cf. Herodotus *Hist.* ii.109). However, the Hebrew term means simply "steps" (so JB) and thus may indicate a stairway (so NIV) upon which a shadow fell, allowing an observer to note the sun's movements; if so, the structure in question may have been erected during Ahaz' renovation of the palace (cf. 2 Kgs. 16:18). The reference occurs in an account marked by obscure Hebrew (2 Kgs. 20:11 par. Isa. 38:8) regarding the ailing King Hezekiah's request that Isaiah provide a sign as confirmation of his recovery, namely that the shadow would regress ten "steps" (again Heb. *maʿᵃlôṯ*) or "degrees" (so KJV).

DIAMOND (Heb. *yahᵃlōm, šāmîr*).† A precious stone, the third in the second row of the high priest's breastplate (Exod. 28:18; 39:11; Ezek. 28:13); the term more likely refers to the green jasper. In the oracle at Jer. 17:1 Judah's sin is etched with a diamond-tipped iron pen; at Ezek. 3:9; Zech. 7:12 Heb. *šāmîr* is rendered "adamant," a stone of impenetrable hardness.

DIANA. The Roman goddess of the forest, often identified with ARTEMIS.

DIASPORA. *See* DISPERSION.

DIATESSARON [dī'ə tĕs'ə rŏn]. A harmony of the Gospels in the form of a continuous narrative, compiled *ca.* A.D. 170 by Tatian. *See* SYNOPTIC GOSPELS; SYRIAC VERSIONS.

DIBLAIM [dĭb'lĭ əm] (Heb. *diḇlayim* "two raisin cakes"). The father of the prostitute Gomer, the wife of Hosea (Hos. 1:3). Unlike symbolic meanings of the names of Hosea's children which follow, no such meaning for Gomer's father's name ("the daughter of pleasure," according to Jerome) seems to be intended here.

DIBLATH (Ezek. 6:14, KJV). *See* RIBLAH.

DIBON [dī'bŏn] (Heb. *dîḇôn*).
1. A city in Transjordan which the Amorites had captured from Moab (Num. 21:30). Though both Reuben and Gad vied for the city as an inheritance (32:3), it was Gad which received the land first (v. 34) and rebuilt the city, naming it Dibon-gad (33:45-46). But when the land was redistributed by Joshua, Dibon was included in Reubenite territory (Josh. 13:9, 17). Although the Moabites apparently reasserted their independence with the division of the Israelite Monarchy, the ninth-century B.C. Moabite Stone, discovered at Dibon, indicates that the territory was under Omride rule for some forty years; according to the inscription, King Mesha of Moab, who calls himself "the Dibonite," recaptured the region *ca.* 840. In the taunting oracle against Moab, Isaiah tells of Moabite defeat during the time of Sennacherib, perhaps at the hands of bedouin raiders (Isa. 15:2, "the daughter of Moab"; v. 9, "the waters of Dibon"; MT "Dimon"). The city is again mentioned in Jeremiah's adaptation of the oracle with regard to Nebuchadnezzar's attack on Moab and Ammon *ca.* 582 (Jer. 48:18, 22; cf. Josephus *Ant.* x.9.7).
Excavations at modern Dhībân, 18 km. (11 mi.) east of the Dead Sea and 5 km. (3 mi.) north of the Arnon river, indicate the presence of a walled city at the time of the Early Bronze Age. The site appears to have been abandoned until the Iron Age (the "Moabite period"), for which extensive building remains have been found. It again flourished in Nabatean and Roman times, as well as the Byzantine and Arabic periods.
2. A town in the Negeb of Judah, toward the eastern border between Hebron and Jekabzeel (Neh. 11:25); perhaps a variant form of, or a textual error for, Dimonah (Josh. 15:22).

DIBON-GAD [dī'bŏn găd'] (Heb. *dîḇôn gāḏ*). An alternate name of DIBON (1) (Num. 33:45-46).

DIBRI [dĭb'rī] (Heb. *diḇrî*, possibly "wordy"). The father of Shelomith of Dan, whose grandson was stoned for cursing and blaspheming God (Lev. 24:11, 14).

DIDACHE [dĭd'ə kī] (Gk. *didachḗ* "teaching"). The oldest known of the so-called church orders, the "Teaching of the Twelve Apostles"; it is reckoned among the books of the New Testament Apocrypha. Originally composed in Greek, the earliest complete text of the Didache is an A.D. 1056 Syrian version

(subtitled "The Teaching of the Lord to the Gentiles by the Twelve Apostles") discovered in 1873 by P. Bryennius in the library of the Jerusalem Patriarchate at Constantinople and published in 1883.
The teachings of the Didache can be grouped into three major sections. The first (chs. 1–6) concerns the doctrine of the "Two Ways," presenting the ethical alternatives of the "way of life" and the "way of death" (cf. Prov. 4:18-19; Jer. 21:8; Matt. 7:13-14). The second part (chs. 7–10) discusses baptism, fasting, prayer, and the Lord's Supper (or perhaps rather the Agape feast). The final section (chs. 11–16) concerns various aspects of church life, including the functions of prophets and traveling teachers, qualifications of bishops and deacons, observance of Sunday worship, and eschatological instructions regarding the return of Christ (cf. Matt. 24).
According to some scholars, the Epistle of Barnabas (chs. 18–20) and the Shepherd of Hermas (both writings of the Apostolic Fathers) quote the Didache, a fact which might indicate that the work was written near the end of the first century A.D. Others assign a later date to the completion of the Didache, citing the existence of an earlier source (first or second century) for the first six chapters and a later source (second-fourth centuries) for the remainder. Rather than indicating textual variants, the various extant versions (e.g., Latin, Coptic, Ethiopic, Georgian) suggest that the work represents a developing tradition encompassing several sources and revisions. The original Greek composition originated at the hands of a convert from Judaism, most likely *ca.* A.D. 100 in Syria, where it was meant to provide a guide to the organization of local churches.

DIDRACHMA [dī drăk'mə] (Gk. *dídrachmon* "double drachma"). A Greek coin equal to the value of two drachmas. Matt. 17:24 records that every male Jew had to pay an annual tax of a half-shekel — or didrachma — for the maintenance of the temple, the law according to Exod. 30:13 (cf. 38:26). Because this coin was no longer issued in Jesus' time (cf. RSV "half-shekel tax"; NIV "two-drachma tax"; KJV, JB "money"), two persons may have joined to pay the combined tax of four drachmas (one tetradrachma or one shekel; Matt. 17:27).

DIDYMUS [dĭd'ə məs] (Gk. *Didymos* "twin"). A surname of the apostle Thomas, the Greek equivalent of Heb. *tᵉʾōm* "twin." Whereas the KJV and the NIV transliterate the Greek term as Didymus at John 11:16; 20:24; 21:2, the RSV and JB translate it as "Twin."
See THOMAS.

DIKLAH [dĭk'lə] (Heb. *diqlâ* "palm grove"). A descendant of Shem through Joktan (Gen. 10:27; 1 Chr. 1:21), and an ancestor of a South Arabian tribe. The site is believed to be an oasis in Saudi Arabia, perhaps the "village" of Daklāh.

DILEAN [dĭl'ĭ ən] (Heb. *dilᵉʿān* "protrusion"[?]). A town in the Shephelah of Judah (Josh. 15:38), possibly to be identified with modern Tell en-Najileh, about 28 km. (17.5 mi.) east of Gaza.

DILL (Heb. *qeṣaḥ*; Gk. *ánēthon*). An umbelliferous herb (*Anethum graveolens* L.) which resembles parsley. The plant was cultivated for its oval-shaped brown seeds, which were used as a condiment in cooking and as a carminative medicine. According to the Mishnah (*Ma'as.* iv.5; Aram. *š^eḇēṭa*) the dill was subject to the tithe (cf. Deut. 14:22), for which Jesus chides the Jewish leaders as paying attention to insignificant matters of the law at the expense of justice, mercy, and faith (Matt. 23:23 par. Luke 11:42, which reads Gk. *pēganon* "rue"; cf. Aram. *šabbārâ*).

The plant cited in Isaiah's parable of the farmer (Isa. 28:25, 27; RSV "dill"; KJV "fitches"; JB "fennel"; NIV "caraway") is probably the nutmeg flower or black cummin (*Nigella sativa* L.), a plant which can reach a height of about 60 cm. (2 ft.) and whose seeds can be easily severed from the husk for use as a condiment. In rabbinic use Heb. *qeṣaḥ* is translated "black cummin" (*Ber.* 40a; so LXX *melánthion*).

DIMNAH [dĭm'nə] (Heb. *dimnâ* "dung"). A levitical city of the Merarites, located in Zebulun (Josh. 21:35). The city may be the same as Rimmon (19:13) or Rimmono (1 Chr. 6:77).
See RIMMON (PLACES) **2**.

DIMON [dī'mən]. A Moabite city (Isa. 15:9; KJV, NIV, following MT *dîmôn*), generally identified with Dibon near the Arnon river (cf. v. 2; so RSV, JB, following Heb. *dîḇôn*; so DSS; LXX *Deimōn*). In this interpretation Dimon is a play on the word "blood" (Heb. *dām*), indicating the amount of blood the Moabites had spilled into the waters of the Arnon. On the basis of the emendation of Heb. *my dymwn* to *mdmn*, Dimon might also be identified with the town MADMEN (Jer. 48:2; Heb. *maḏmēn*), located at Khirbet Dimneh.

DIMONAH [dĭ mō'nə] (Heb. *dîmônâ*).† A town in the Negeb near Edom, mentioned along with Kinah and Adadah (Josh. 15:22), possibly DIBON **1**, which the Jews returning from exile repopulated (Neh. 11:25). Ancient Dimonah is not to be coupled with modern Dimonah, 29 km. (18 mi.) southeast of Beer-sheba, a city founded in 1955.

DINAH [dī'nə] (Heb. *dînâ*, possibly "justice"). The only daughter of Jacob and his wife Leah, born in Paddan-aram (Gen. 30:21; 46:15). The Genesis narrative mentions little about her life beyond the unvarnished account of her dishonoring by Shechem, the son of Hamor, the chief of the region (Gen. 34).

When Dinah, sometime after she had settled with her father at Shechem, went to the nearby city, she caught the eye of the local chief, who "lay with her and humbled her" against her will (34:1-2). Subsequently Shechem fell in love with the Israelite maiden and asked his father to arrange with Jacob for their marriage. Hamor in turn sought to institute extensive intermarriage between the groups and offered Jacob landed property at Shechem — a function which the Israelites regarded as the prerogative of God alone. Jacob's sons pretended to acquiesce to Hamor's proposal on the condition that the Shechemites be circum-

cised (vv. 14-17); but while the males of the city were thus indisposed, Simeon and Levi attacked and massacred them all including Shechem and Hamor, seized their sister, and sacked the city (vv. 25-29). Despite their claim to have vindicated Dinah's honor, Jacob regretted his sons' intemperate response as an invitation to potential reprisal by the local populace (v. 30). At this point God summoned the patriarch to go to Bethel and fulfill the vow he had made previously (35:1-5).

Although Jewish tradition has it that Dinah became either the mother of Asenath, Joseph's future bride, or the second wife of Job, the only additional biblical mention notes simply that she accompanied her father to Egypt (Gen. 46:15).

DINAITES [dī'nə īts] (Aram. *dînāyē'*). According to the KJV, the name of a people deported by Osnapper (Assurbanipal) to Samaria (Ezra 4:9). The RSV, JB, and NIV render the term as an official title, "judges" (cf. LXX *Dinaioi*).

DINHABAH [dĭn'hə bə] (Heb. *dînhāḇâ*). The city from which Bela, an Edomite king, reigned (Gen. 36:32; 1 Chr 1:43). Its location is unknown.

DIONYSIUS [dī'ə nĭsh'əs] (Gk. *Dionysios*). One of a few converts in Athens following Paul's address at the Areopagus (Acts 17:34). Luke indicates that Dionysius was a member of the local government. He may have been Athens' first bishop (cf. Eusebius *HE* iii.4.11; iv.23.3). Others identify him with Denys, the patron saint of France (third century), beheaded on Montmartre (Gregory of Tours *Historia Francorum* i.31). The mystical Neo-Platonic writings of a certain Dionysius the Pseudo-Areopagite were attributed to Dionysus of Athens by their Syrian author (*ca.* A.D. 500).

DIONYSUS [dī'ə nī'səs] (Gk. *Dionysos*).* The Greek god of vegetation, particularly associated with the vine and ivy. Alternately known as Bacchus (so KJV), he was introduced into Greece from Thrace or Phrygia. In Greek mythology he is depicted as dying and rising annually; thus he became associated with the spring fertility rite, the Dionysia or Bacchanalia. As the focus of a mystery cult, he was believed to impart to his followers something of his own power through ecstatic and orgiastic revelry. An alternate version of this celebration involved the participants' tearing to pieces with their teeth a live bull and then consuming its flesh.

Among the excesses of Antiochus IV Epiphanes was his compelling the Jews to wear ivy wreaths in the annual Dionysiac procession (2 Macc. 6:7). His general Nicanor sought to coerce the Jerusalem priests into handing over Judas Maccabeus by threatening to raze the temple and replace it with a temple of Dionysus (14:33).

DIOTREPHES [dī ŏt'rə fēz] (Gk. *Diotrephēs* "nourished by Zeus").† A member of a church in Asia Minor to which Gaius also belonged. In 3 John Diotrephes is accused of excessive self-centeredness and refusal to acknowledge the authority of John the elder. Moreover, he is said to gossip about John, to fail to welcome John's emissaries, and to impede — and even excommunicate — those who sought to be more hospitable (vv. 9-10).

Eager to help fill the vacuum in leadership being created as more and more apostles were approaching old age and dying, Diotrephes objected to John's lingering ecclesiastical authority rather than to a point of doctrine. It appears that he was an ambitious layperson rather than an official or even the local bishop.

DIPHATH [dī′făth] (Heb. *dîpaṯ*). A son of Japheth's son Gomer (1 Chr. 1:6), called Riphath at Gen. 10:3.

DISCIPLE (Gk. *mathētēs* "one who learns").† A student or follower. As used in the New Testament, the English term (from Lat. *discipulus* "pupil") reflects the Greek sense of the disciple as an adherent to the teachings of a particular teacher or school of thought (John 9:28; cf. Matt. 22:16); the followers of John the Baptist are thus identified as disciples (e.g., Mark 2:18; John 1:35, 37). To an extent, the function of the disciple is similar to that of the rabbinical *talmîdîm* (cf. 1 Chr. 25:8; RSV "pupil"), who studied the Law under the guidance of a particular teacher; however, akin to the alternate Greek sense of the disciple as an apprentice, these students themselves sought to gain ordination as teachers.

In the majority of New Testament occurrences, primarily those in the gospels of Luke and John and in Acts, the term has a general application, indicating those who believed in Jesus (e.g., Luke 6:13; John 1:35-50). At times this could indicate a substantial following, such as those who gathered for the Sermon on the Plain (Luke 6:17; cf. KJV) or to witness Jesus' triumphal entry into Jerusalem (19:37). After the resurrection the term gained the standard meaning of a member of the early Church (e.g., Acts 6:1-2, 7; 9:1), hence it was virtually identical with the designation "Christian."

Within the larger body of believers was an inner circle of twelve disciples who were specifically chosen by Jesus to accompany him and assist in his ministry (Matt. 10:1; Mark 3:13-19). In the gospels of Matthew and Mark the term is used in a technical sense to refer to these associates (e.g., Matt. 11:1; cf. Mark 4:10; John 6:66-67). See APOSTLE.

Although in many instances it is difficult to determine whether all adherents or merely the Twelve are indicated (e.g., Matt. 8:21; Mark 6:1), it is apparent that becoming a disciple of Jesus in general meant a transformation of a person's lifestyle. Many of these followers, presumably more than just the inner circle, accepted Jesus' mobile life (cf. Luke 9:57-58). But beyond this, Jesus called all who believed in him to recast their inner lives (cf. 11:1) as well as to minister to others, at the expense of possessions, career, and family (Mark 10:28; Luke 14:26, 33), even to the extent of martyrdom (Mark 8:34-35; Luke 14:27).

Bibliography. R. P. Meye, *Jesus and the Twelve* (Grand Rapids: 1968); K. H. Rengstorf, "μαθητής," *TDNT* 4 (1967): 415-460.

DISEASE.* An impairment of normal physiological or psychological functions associated with infection, imbalance, or deterioration.

The Hebrews considered disease to be sent by God as an expression of divine displeasure or as punishment for wrongdoing (Exod. 4:11; Num. 25:18; Deut. 32:39; John 9:2). With the influence of Persian and Greek thought causation was extended to include Satan (Job 2:7), demonic spirits (Mark 9:17, 25; 1 John 3:8), or human ill will (Job 5:2). The Hebrews considered major body organs to have emotional as well as physiological functions (cf. the heart as the seat of intelligence and will; e.g., 1 Chr. 29:18; Ezek. 18:31; the kidneys as source of passions and desires; cf. Jer. 12:2; RSV "heart"; KJV "reins"; cf. Col. 3:12, KJV "bowels of mercies"), which led to a holistic understanding of the relationship of emotional conditions and physical ailments. Moreover, a basic understanding of the importance of hygiene and the need for physical rest as a preventative of disease underlies much of Old Testament law (e.g., Gen. 2:3; Lev. 11; 15; 18-20).

The New Testament gives no indication that Jesus viewed disease as a form of divine punishment. Rather, he included healing in his ministry as one more means of restoring the divine order of life, to which disease was contrary (cf. Luke 4:18).

On account of semantic difficulties and lack of precise technical description, only the most general identification can be made of most diseases depicted in the Old Testament. Those which Jesus encountered include such common afflictions as blindness, paralysis, leprosy, and mental disorders. See further the individual entries on specific diseases.

DISH.† A vessel for serving and preserving food (Heb. *ṣallaḥaṯ*; Prov. 19:24 par. 26:15; Gk. *trýblion*; Matt. 26:23 par. Mark 14:20) or for presentation of incense or cereal offerings (Heb. *kap* "hand, palm"; Exod. 25:29; 37:16; Num. 4:7; 7:13-14).

In figurative usage the Israelite prophets proclaim that in retribution for Manasseh's apostasy God would destroy Jerusalem, leaving it as a dish wiped and left to drip dry (2 Kgs. 21:13). Jesus chides the Pharisees for their ritual cleansing of only the outside of a dish (Gk. *pínax*; Luke 11:39 par. Matt. 23:25-26, "plate"; cf. Mark 7:14), comparing the practice to the neglect of a person's inner qualities.

DISHAN [dī′shăn] (Heb. *dîšān*). One of the sons of Seir (Gen. 36:21; LXX *Rison*; 1 Chr. 1:38; LXX *Disan*), the father of Uz and Aran (Gen. 36:30; 1 Chr. 1:42); a Horite chief.

DISHON [dī′shŏn] (Heb. *dîšōn*).

1. One of the sons of Seir (LXX *Dēsōn*; Gen. 36:21; 1 Chr. 1:38). He was the ancestor of four Horite tribes (Gen. 36:26; MT *dîšān*; 1 Chr. 1:41; LXX *Daisōn*).

2. The son of Anah and grandson of Seir, a chief of the Horites (Gen. 36:25; 1 Chr. 1:41; LXX *Daisōn*), and the brother of Oholibamah (Gen. 36:25), the wife of Esau (vv. 1-2).

DISPENSATION.* God's dealings with mankind, literally a "giving out." At 2 Cor. 3:7-9 Paul contrasts the splendor of the Old Testament "dispensation of death" (Gk. *diakonía* "service"; KJV "ministration"; NIV "ministry"), mediated through Moses, with the brilliance of the New Testament "dispensation of the Spirit." While the former dispensation brought about death (e.g., blinded the Hebrews as they beheld Moses descending from Mt. Horeb with the tablets of the law), the new dispensation produced righteousness.

In another context the apostle Paul refers to the "commission" entrusted to him, namely the preaching of the gospel (1 Cor. 9:17; Gk. *oikonomía* "household administration"; KJV "dispensation"; NIV "trust"; JB "responsibility"), which may have been a special "administration of God's grace" (Eph. 3:2, NIV; KJV "dispensation"; RSV "stewardship"; cf. Col. 1:25, "divine office"; NIV "commission").

DISPERSION (Gk. *diasporá*).† The scattering of the Jews beyond the borders of Palestine. Unlike the Exile, the Dispersion signified a voluntary departure from Canaan for other countries from the Babylonian Captivity onward.

I. Terminology

The most common Hebrew word for "disperse" is *zārâ* "spread"; both Heb. *zārâ* and *pûṣ* can be rendered "scatter" (e.g., "scatter . . . and disperse"; Ezek. 20:23). Heb. *pāraḏ* (Esth. 3:8) and *napaṣ* (Isa. 11:12) are also translated "dispersed"; *tᵉpôṣâ* is rendered "dispersion" (Jer. 25:34). In the New Testament "Dispersion" is the translation of Gk. *diasporá* (John 7:35; KJV, JB "dispersed"; NIV "scattered"; Jas. 1:1; 1 Pet. 1:1; KJV, NIV "scattered").

II. Causes

No doubt the deportation of the ten northern tribes to Assyria (*ca.* 732 B.C.) and the exile of Judah and Benjamin to Babylonia (587/586) largely contributed to the rise of Jewish settlements outside the Promised Land. Many Hebrews were compelled against their will to make a new life for themselves far from either Samaria, the capital of the northern kingdom, or Jerusalem, the capital of the southern kingdom. Some Israelites had established a Jewish colony at Damascus in Aram earlier (1 Kgs. 20:34; cf. Acts 9:19), but they were a minority, for most preferred to remain in Canaan.

Also contributing to the Dispersion was the search for new trade centers and better business opportunities. Though a great number of the Jews returned to Jerusalem *ca.* 538, many remained in Babylonia and Persia — among them Esther and Mordecai (Esth. 2:5-6; 3:8), Ezra (Ezra 7:1, 8), and Nehemiah (Neh. 1:1; 2:1ff.). Two centuries later many Hebrews moved to Alexandria in Egypt to seek their fortunes there.

III. Spread

Starting *ca.* 581 B.C. when some of the Hebrews who had survived the fall of Jerusalem moved to Upper and Lower Egypt (Jer. 43:5-8; 44:1) and later, after the Exile when the Hebrews founded a Jewish

colony at Elephantine near Aswan (*ca.* fifth century), the Jews gradually spread throughout the entire Hellenistic world, until they were more numerous outside Canaan than inside. According to 1 Macc. 15:22-24, during the second century B.C. they resided in the provinces of Caria, Pamphylia, and Lycia in Asia Minor, on the islands of Delos and Cyprus, in the city of Sparta on the Peloponnesus, and in Cyrene along the shore of Libya. In New Testament times they could be found in Parthia, Elam, Media, and Mesopotamia, in Cappadocia, Pontus, Asia, and Pamphylia in Asia Minor, in Egypt and Libya (Cyrene), and in the capital of the Roman Empire, Rome (Acts 2:7-11). As was his custom, the apostle Paul preached to the Jews before ministering to the Gentiles on the island of Cyprus (Acts 13:5), in Asia Minor at Antioch in Pisidia (13:14-15), at Iconium in Galatia (14:1), at Lystra in Lycaonia (16:1), and at Ephesus in Asia (19:8, 33); in Greece at Thessalonica (17:1-2), Beroea (17:10-11), Athens (17:17), and Corinth (18:1-18); and at Rome (28:17).

IV. Characteristics

On the whole the Hebrews of the Dispersion remained a separate ethnic group from the native population, retaining their own religious customs centered around the local synagogues; in some cities, e.g., Alexandria, they lived in a certain district. By contributing their share to the temple tax and by making the journey to Jerusalem to celebrate the national festivals (see Acts 2:5ff.), they maintained a measure of contact with their home base — Palestine, especially Jerusalem. Some, however, through marrying Gentiles and adopting the Greek language (see John 7:35), lost their separate Jewish identity and became assimilated with the other ethnic groups of the Roman Empire. (This was most likely the fate of the descendants of the deported northern tribes, scattered as they were across the various provinces of the Assyrian Empire.)

While the dispersed Jews enjoyed many political privileges and in some cities were granted a degree of autonomy, many of them were poor. Not all were successful in business or banking as the Jews at Alexandria; many had to be content as farmers and artisans.

V. Significance

For the Old Testament prophets, the Dispersion, with its roots in the Exile, fulfilled God's intention to scatter his unfaithful people (e.g., Ezek. 12:14-15); but it also provided the opportunity for him to gather them one day as well in the messianic age (Isa. 11:12). The Hebrews of the Dispersion were able to acquaint the Gentiles with their religion (cf. 49:6), bequeath to history the Septuagint, and discriminately adopt for their own best features of Hellenistic culture while retaining their Jewish culture. Their contact with alien cultures, however, exposed them to anti-Semitic feelings and reprisals.

In the New Testament James and Peter wrote their epistles to the "twelve tribes of the Dispersion" (Jas. 1:1), the "exiles of the Dispersion" (1 Pet. 1:1). These two authors interpreted their addressees' physical presence outside of Palestine as a physical and spiritual separation from their true home in heaven (1 Pet. 1:4-7; cf. Heb. 11:13-16).

See also EXILE.

Bibliography. V. Tcherikover, *Hellenistic Civilization and the Jews* (1959; repr. New York: 1970).

DISSENSION (Gk. *stásis, dichostasía, schísma*). Disagreement, particularly with regard to factions in the early Church. The primary meaning of Gk. *stásis* is "that which exists (or stands)"; only secondarily does it mean "strife" or "discord" (Acts 15:2). While Gk. *schísma* carries the connotation of severe disagreement, it may also refer to a discussion in which various opinions are aired (John 7:43; RSV "division"; cf. Matt. 9:16 par., "tear").

Paul warns the Corinthian Christians against permitting different viewpoints to produce factions (1 Cor. 1:10ff.). He further cautions them not to permit the various social classes represented in the church to cause fragmentation or discrimination in observance of the Lord's Supper (11:18, 20-21); nevertheless, he does recognize the value of such divisions in theological discussions as serving to distinguish heresies from genuine expressions of the faith (v. 19).

DIVINATION (Heb. *qesem, nāḥaš, mᵉʿônēn*).† The art of determining the future or ascertaining the divine will. Practiced widely throughout the ancient Near East, divination involved the observation and interpretation of natural phenomena or of phenomena deliberately caused by the person or persons interpreting these omens.

Much of the information regarding Near Eastern divination comes from the extensive literature of second- and first-millennia Mesopotamia; performed and recorded as a sophisticated pseudoscience by schools of technical specialists associated with the temples, divination strongly influenced Babylonian and Assyrian monarchs in determining internal operations as well as foreign relations.

The Israelites viewed divination as an inferior form of prophecy (cf. Ezek. 13:4-7; 22:28) and discredited it as a means of divine revelation because it was initiated by humans (cf. Deut. 18:14-15). It was prohibited by law, particularly when associated with heathen magic as a means of influencing the future (Lev. 19:26, 31; Deut. 18:9-14; cf. Lev. 20:27). Nevertheless, various forms of divination were practiced among the Israelites. Among them were the observation of plants (cf. Num. 17:1-11) and animals (1 Sam. 6:7-12). The cup which Joseph ordered hidden in Benjamin's sack (Gen. 44:5, 15) was used in hydromancy or lecanomancy, the observation of water — its surface as moved in the cup or configurations produced by adding drops of oil. Another form was belomancy, the shooting of arrows (2 Kgs. 13:14-19; cf. 1 Sam. 20:18-42; Ezek. 21:21); Hos. 4:2 may indicate rhabdomancy, divination by use of a rod or staff (cf. Exod. 4:4, 17; 17:9). Saul's use of a medium to consult the ghost of Samuel depicts the practice of necromancy (1 Sam. 28:3-25; cf. Isa. 29:4). The Babylonian "chance" oracle (Akk. *egirrû*; cf. Gk. *klēdṓn*), which regarded a predetermined utterance or action as a divine omen, may be reflected in Gideon's interpreta-

One of numerous excavated clay liver models made for use in divination (by courtesy of the Trustees of the British Museum)

tion of the wet fleece (Judg. 6:36-40) and of his troops' drinking patterns (7:4-7) as well as Jonathan's response to the Philistine garrison's remarks (1 Sam. 14:8-12). The teraphim (Judg. 18:14-20), cultic objects of various sizes (cf. Gen. 31:19, 34-35; RSV "household gods"; 1 Sam. 19:13-16; RSV "image"), apparently were related to the Hittite *tarpiš*, which was used in divination (Ezek. 21:21; Zech. 10:2; cf. Hos. 3:4). Discovery of clay liver models at Hazor suggests the practice of hepatoscopy, interpretation of the entrails of sacrificial animals (cf. Ezek. 21:21).

Some forms of divination actually were sanctioned in Israel. Cleromancy, the casting of lots, was performed to attain decisions representing the will of God (Prov. 16:33) in both private and public life: division of the land into tribal allotments or "inheritances" (e.g., Num. 26:55-56; Josh. 17, 19); selection of kings, priests, and other appointees (1 Sam. 10:20-21; 1 Chr. 24:5, 7-19; Acts 1:26); and determination of guilt (Josh. 7:14-15; Jonah 1:7; cf. the ordeal of jealousy, Num. 5:14-30); of particular importance were the Urim and Thummim, attached to the high priest's ephod and consulted in the sanctuary (Num. 27:21; 1 Sam. 23:9-12). Oneiromancy, the interpretation of dreams, is accredited as a means of discerning the mysteries of God (Dan. 2:25-30) and a frequent vehicle for divine revelation; Joseph (Gen. 40:5-8; 41:14ff.) and Daniel (Dan. 1:17; 2:1-11) were acclaimed as skilled interpreters of dreams. On occasion such dreams may have been precipitated by prophets during an induced ecstatic state (cf. 2 Kgs. 3:15; Mic. 3:6; *see* DREAM; PROPHECY).

Bibliography. B. O. Long, "The Effect of Divination upon Israelite Literature," *JBL* 92 (1973): 489-497; A. L. Oppenheim, *Ancient Mesopotamia*, 2nd ed. (Chicago: 1977), pp. 206-227; H. W. F. Saggs, *The Greatness That Was Babylon* (New York: 1969).

DIVINERS' OAK (Heb. *ʾēlôn mᵉʿônᵉnîm*). A tree near Shechem (Judg. 9:37; KJV "plain of Meonenim"; NIV "soothsayers' tree"), probably the same as the oak of Moreh (Gen. 12:6). It is also known as the "oak in the sanctuary of the Lord" (Josh. 24:26) and possibly the "oak of the pillar at Shechem" (Judg. 9:6) or simply the "oak . . . near Shechem" (Gen. 35:4; cf. v. 8). Perhaps part of the sacred grove or temenos at Shechem (cf. Judg. 9:6), the tree may have been named after cultic soothsayers who practiced there.

DIVORCE.† The dissolution of marriage.

I. Old Testament

The Old Testament teachings on divorce can best be understood against the background of the institution of marriage. According to Gen. 2:18ff. God presented the woman to the man as his helper, whom he had created from the man. The author of Genesis then concludes that their love relationship is the basis for monogamous marriage, a complete union between the two partners (v. 24).

Although the Genesis narrative does not include a clause regarding divorce, the Hebrews apparently did divorce, as indicated by a restriction in the law making it permissible only on the grounds of "some indecency" (Heb. ʿerwaṯ dāḇār "shameful matter") that a husband had discovered in his wife (Deut. 24:1). Thus the husband could give his wife a "bill of divorce" (Heb. sēper kᵉrîṯuṯ), send her away, and consider the issue settled. If the divorced woman were to marry another man and again be rejected or be widowed by her second husband, she was not permitted to remarry her former husband (vv. 2-4).

While the Mosaic law permitted, or at least condoned, divorce, the meaning of "some indecency" varied from sect to sect. The rabbinic school of Shammai interpreted it to mean unchastity or adultery; these scholars permitted divorce only when the wife had been sexually unfaithful to her husband. The school of Hillel, on the other hand, understood these words to signify anything unappealing; these teachers allowed the husband to send his wife away even for such a trifle as a burned meal. While Jesus, in Matthew's account, linked divorce with "unchastity" (so RSV at Matt. 19:9), the precise meaning of the ancient phrase "some indecency" is no longer clear. (Commentators suggest that these words do not imply adultery, which was punishable by death [Deut. 22:22], but was not a grounds for divorce.)

Jer. 3:1-8 echoes the intent of the Mosaic law to curb widespread divorce by condemning remarriage between a husband and his divorced wife who had, in turn, been divorced by her second husband. Applying the image of divorce to Israel's spiritual harlotry with Canaanite deities, Jeremiah refers to God's having given his chosen people a spiritual bill of divorce (but see Isa. 50:1, according to which God had not issued a "bill of divorce" to faithless Israel), and Judah's similar unfaithfulness. Unlike literal divorce, however, Israel's spiritual divorce and second marriage to Canaan could be undone by her return to her covenant God in genuine repentance (vv. 11-14).

Mosaic law granted the privilege of divorce only to the husband, but rabbinic interpretation extended this right to the wife as well under certain circumstances, such as when the husband had contracted leprosy. (Still, even in later times, divorce was by and large a husband's prerogative.)

Opposition to divorce seems to have become more intense following the Exile. Malachi records that God hates divorce, specifically between the exiles who had returned to Jerusalem and their first wives — Israelites whom they had exchanged for foreign wives (Mal. 2:13-16). The prophet's condemnation of divorce may also reflect Nehemiah's reform policy regarding marriage between Jews and Gentiles (Neh. 13:23-27) and imply concurrence with Ezra's insistence that the returned exiles divorce their foreign wives (Ezra 9–10).

II. New Testament

A. Gospels. All three Synoptic Gospels contain Jesus' pronouncement on divorce, though each Evangelist presents his own version of Jesus' words.

1. Mark. On the basis of the earliest gospel, it would appear that Jesus maintained a strict view of marriage and divorce. He acknowledged divorce and the issuing of a "certificate of divorce" (Gk. *biblíon apostasíou*) because he recognized that the law had been drafted for Israel's "hardness of heart" (not because the creation ordinance allowed for failed marriages). Nevertheless, he also asserted that divorce could not be encouraged (Mark 10:3-9) on the grounds that divorce and remarriage were tantamount to "adultery," regardless of culpability (v. 12). Thus, he condemned Herod for marrying his brother's wife and indirectly supported John the Baptist for his bold stance opposing Herod (cf. 6:18ff.).

2. Matthew. On the basis of Matthew's gospel, Jesus appears to have been somewhat flexible on the issue of divorce. Matthew records three of Christ's statements: (1) marriage is a creation ordinance which does not allow for dissolution (Matt. 19:4-6); (2) Mosaic law condoned divorce, thereby yielding to the Hebrews' "hardness of heart" (v. 8); (3) unless divorce is generated by "unchastity" (Gk. *porneía*), it is equal to adultery (v. 9). Scholars do not agree on the relationship between these three statements; some claim that Jesus did not permit any divorce (the third statement being invalidated by the first), while others assert that Matthew's account, like the school of Shammai, allows for exceptions — unchastity, sexual unfaithfulness during marriage (not sexual illegitimacy beforehand) and thus justifies divorce (cf. Matt. 5:31-32 for a similar exception).

3. Luke. Luke, who may be in closer harmony with Mark than with Matthew, merely records Jesus' statement about marriage and divorce. Here, Jesus sharpens the Mosaic law, claiming that any divorce implies adultery, even the divorce condoned by the law (Luke 16:18).

B. Paul. At 1 Cor. 7 Paul, though preferring the single state, nevertheless accepts the validity and indissolubility of marriage: neither husband nor wife may divorce (vv. 10-11), even if wives were allowed to do so under Roman law. In the event that the wife does divorce her husband, however, she should remain single if she cannot be reconciled to him (v. 11). (Thus the apostle, too, implies that divorce amounts to adultery; see Mark 10:11-12.)

The marriages concluded between Corinthian believers, mainly women, and unbelievers were a special problem for Paul. Because the Mosaic law did not address this matter, Paul recommended that the believing wife remain married to her unbelieving husband as long as he consented to this arrangement, in hopes of saving him through her own example. Only in the case that the unbelieving partner was no longer satisfied with the marriage would the apostle be willing to grant the believing partner the privilege of a divorce (1 Cor. 7:12-16).

DIZAHAB [dĭz'ə hăb] (Heb. *dî-zāhāḇ* "that which has gold"). An appellation describing the place where Moses delivered his farewell address (Deut. 1:1). Because of the similarity of names, Minet edh-Dhahab, directly east of Mt. Sinai, has been suggested as the site. For geological reasons, edh-Dheibeh, located east of Heshbon and beyond the borders of the Arabah, has also been proposed. However, neither site would have been a suitable campsite.

DO NOT DESTROY (Heb. *'al-tašḥēt*). Most likely the opening words of a tune according to which Pss. 57-59, 75 were to be sung, noted in the superscriptions to those psalms (KJV "Altaschith"). An alternate suggestion is that the words represent a cultic instruction (cf. Isa. 65:8).

DOCETISM [dŏs'ə tĭz'əm]. An early teaching, regarded as heretical, according to which Christ's incarnation (i.e., taking human form) was only a matter of appearance (Gk. *dokéō* "seem"). Thus his suffering, death, and resurrection were aspects of the human Jesus' life in which the divine Christ did not participate (that nature having withdrawn prior to these events).

Docetism is related to a gnostic view of an irreconcilable conflict between two eternal principles — the spiritual (or good) and the material (or evil) — a conflict which precludes the possibility of the Son of God ever assuming human (i.e., material) form. According to the New Testament, those holding this view would utter "Jesus be cursed" (1 Cor. 12:3), would proclaim "another" Jesus (2 Cor. 11:4), or would regard Jesus' suffering and death as foolishness (1 Cor. 1:18).

Among the New Testament writers, John especially challenged the docetic position. In the prologue to the fourth Gospel he wrote: "the Word became flesh and dwelled among us" (John 1:14; cf. v. 1; 1 John 4:2, "Christ has come into the flesh"; 2 John 7, "the coming of Jesus Christ in the flesh").

See also CHRISTOLOGY.

DOCTRINE (Lat. *doctrina*, from *doceo* "teach").* That which has been taught (Gk. *didaché, didaskalía*; RSV also "teaching"). The KJV also uses the term in the archaic sense with regard to the act of instruction (e.g., Mark 4:2; Acts 2:42; 1 Tim. 4:13, 16).

In contrast to the systematic doctrine of the rabbis (KJV, Matt. 16:12; RSV "teaching"), Jesus' teachings as recorded in the Gospels were discursive, relating new interpretations of the law to the contemporary needs of his followers. This instruction, viewed in the light of his death and resurrection and the experiences of his adherents, formed the basis of the doctrine of the early Church, in the modern sense of

fundamental principles accepted by a body of believers. Basically, these beliefs as propounded by the apostles were that Jesus was the Messiah (Acts 3:18), that he had risen from the dead (1:22; 2:24, 32), and that faith in his name was essential to salvation (v. 38; 3:16). By the second century A.D. these beliefs had become sufficiently systematized to be considered orthodox ("sound doctrine"; 1 Tim. 1:10; Titus 1:9; 2:1; cf. 2 Tim. 2:1; RSV "sound words"; 4:3; RSV "sound teaching").

DOCUMENTARY HYPOTHESIS. *See* BIBLICAL CRITICISM.

DODAI [dō'dī] (Heb. *dôḏay* "beloved [of Yahweh]"). An Ahohite and a commander of the second division of David's army (1 Chr. 27:4); he is probably the same as DODO 2 mentioned at 2 Sam. 23:9; 1 Chr. 11:12.

DODANIM [dō'də nĭm] (Heb. *dōḏānîm*). An Ionian people, the descendants of Javan (Gen. 10:4; so RSV, KJV; JB "Dananites"). According to 1 Chr. 1:7 they were also known as Rodanim (so RSV, NIV, following LXX; cf. Gen. 10:4, LXX), the people of Rhodes. G. C. Aalders (*Genesis*. BSC [1981] 1:220) suggests that the name should be "Dardanim," inhabitants along the coast of the Hellespont near ancient Troy, descendants of a certain Dardanus.

DODAVAHU [dō'də vä'hū] (Heb. *dôḏāwāhû* "beloved of Yahweh"). The father of the prophet Eliezer, from Mareshah in Judah (2 Chr. 20:37; KJV "Dodavah").

DODO [dō'dō] (Heb. *dôḏô* "beloved").
1. A descendant of Issachar, the father of Puah, and the grandfather of the minor judge Tola (Judg. 10:1).
2. The son of Ahohi (RSV) or the Ahohite (so KJV, NIV, JB), and the father of Eleazar, one of David's three mighty men (2 Sam. 23:9; cf. 1 Chr. 11:12). He is probably the same as Dodai mentioned at 1 Chr. 27:4.
3. A Bethlehemite, the father of Elhanan who was one of David's thirty mighty men (2 Sam. 23:24; 1 Chr. 11:26).

DOE (Heb. *ya'ălā*).* A metaphor for feminine grace, perhaps used as a term of endearment (Prov. 5:19; KJV "roe"; NIV "deer"; JB "fawn"). Recent philology indicates that it more accurately indicates a female goat or ibex.

DOEG [dō'ĭg] (Heb. *dō'ēg, dō'ēg*). An Edomite who was chief of Saul's herdsmen (1 Sam. 21:7). Detained before the Lord at Nob (so that the priest might pronounce him free of leprosy [see Lev. 13:4], or because he wished to be received into the Israelite community), Doeg witnessed Ahimelech the priest give aid to the fugitive David. The servant then mentioned the incident to Saul (1 Sam. 22:9-11), who charged the priest with conspiracy and condemned him and his family to death (vv. 11-16). When the royal guard refused to obey the king, Doeg killed not only Ahimelech and some eighty other priests, but many women and children as well (vv. 18-19).

According to 1 Sam. 22:22 David had had a premonition that one day Doeg would expose him and Ahimelech to Saul. The superscription to Ps. 52 alludes to these events, but the contents of the psalm do not fit the historical account (cf. vv. 2-4).

DOG (Heb. *keleḇ*; Gk. *kynárion*). A domesticated carnivorous mammal (*Canis familiaris*) considered unclean by Mosaic law; in the Bible most likely the pariah dog and possibly the related greyhound (so KJV at Prov. 30:31; Heb. *zarzîr moṯnayim*; RSV "strutting cock"). The Palestinian dog resembled more closely a wolf than any of the later domesticated breeds. Judging from canine skeletal fragments discovered near Jericho that date to Prepottery Neolithic times, dogs were domesticated long before the beginnings of Israelite history. In the Bible, however, the animal does not appear as a human's companion until Hellenistic and Roman times (Tob. 5:16; Matt. 15:26-27).

The Old Testament describes dogs as wandering in packs through the streets in the evening, often awakening the local residents with their howling (Ps. 59:6, 14-15). Exod. 22:31 admonishes the Israelites to discard improperly butchered meat to such animals. These dogs are depicted as animals with voracious appetites (Isa. 56:11), efficient scavengers (cf. the prophetic accounts of the fates of King Ahab [1 Kgs. 21:19, 23-24; cf. 22:38; 2 Kgs. 9:10, 36] and the household of Baasha [1 Kgs. 16:4]), and powerful enemies of man (Jer. 15:3).

To the Israelites the dog was an object of hatred, not a symbol of affection and loyalty, and the Bible has little good to say about it. The psalmist compares the company of evildoers to a pack of dogs from which he wishes to be rescued (Ps. 22:16, 20; cf. Phil. 3:2). Luke observes that dogs liked Lazarus' sores, treating him as if he were already dead (Luke 16:21). According to Job 30:1 the dog's job was to tend the flock, i.e., to protect it against predators at night — a task it did not always carry out adequately (so Isa. 56:10-11, where blind watchmen are compared to mute dogs).

Given Israel's unfavorable attitude toward dogs, naturally the Israelites looked upon them with scorn. As elsewhere in the ancient Near East (cf. Akk. *kalbu*), calling another person a dog implied contempt (Ishbosheth vis-à-vis Abner [2 Sam. 3:8] or Goliath vis-à-vis David [1 Sam. 17:43]). When David (1 Sam. 24:14) and Mephibosheth (2 Sam. 9:8) later referred to themselves as "dead dog[s]," they were acknowledging their own insignificance (in relating this occurrence 2 Sam. 16:9 records the term as an expression of contempt). The "wages of a dog" (so RSV at Deut. 23:18; cf. KJV) were not low earnings but the acquisitions of a male prostitute (so NIV, JB; RSV mg. "sodomite"). Later the unclean Gentiles were regarded as dogs (cf. Matt. 15:26 par.). It is thus not surprising that, according to Rev. 22:15, dogs are not among those entering heavenly Jerusalem.

The author of Proverbs likens a fool's failure to learn from his mistakes to a dog that returns to its own vomit (Prov. 26:11; cf. 2 Pet. 2:22), and the person involved in others' quarrels to one who provokes a passing dog at the risk of being bitten (v. 17).

Isa. 66:3 contrasts the proper sacrifice of a lamb with the improper sacrifice of a dog, an abomination practiced by the Carthaginians.

DOK [dŏk] (Gk. *Dōk*). A small fortress to which Simon Maccabeus and his two sons were invited for a banquet and where they were murdered, while intoxicated, by Ptolemy, Simon's son-in-law (1 Macc. 16:15-16). Josephus (*Ant.* xiii.8.1[230] ; *BJ* i.2.3[56]) calls this fortress Dagon. The site is probably the fountain known as ʿAin Dûk, about 3 km. (2 mi.) northwest of Jericho.

DOMINION.† Power or authority, indicated in the Bible by several Hebrew and Greek words. Ultimately it is God who has supreme dominion over all creation (e.g., Heb. *māšal*, Job 25:2; *mᵉlûḵâ*, Ps. 22:28; *memšālâ*, 145:13; Aram. *šolṭān*, Dan. 4:3, 34; Gk. *krátos*, 1 Tim. 6:16; Jude 25). Dominion was granted to humans also, as with regard to stewardship of the natural order (Heb. *rāḏâ*, Gen. 1:26, 27; cf. Ps. 8:6) and political power, both that of a monarch or other official (Gen. 37:8; cf. 1 Kgs. 4:24) and that of a conquering nation (Judg. 14:4; cf. Num. 24:19). The control of sin over human lives is depicted as dominion (Heb. *šālaṭ*, Ps. 119:133; cf. 19:13; Gk. *kyrieúō*, Rom. 6:9, 14). In the age to come the messianic king will have universal and everlasting dominion (Dan. 7:14, 27).

Mentioned at Eph. 1:21; Col. 1:16 (cf. KJV, Jude 25; RSV "authority") in conjunction with thrones, principalities, and authorities, dominion (Gk. *kyriótēs*; cf. *kýrios* "lord") appears to designate an order or hierarchy of angels (cf. Eph. 6:12). Paul here insists that Christ alone is the mediator between the Creator and creation, having the full authority of God.

DOMITIAN [də mĭsh'ən].* Titus Flavius Domitian, Roman emperor (A.D. 81-96); the son of Vespasian, he succeeded his brother Titus.

His early reign featured such accomplishments as fortification of the empire in Britain and along the Rhine-Danube frontier, and his building achievements included a new forum and palace at Rome. However, stringent economic measures regulating trade and produce and harsh efforts to legislate public morality led to widespread opposition, particularly among the aristocracy. He became increasingly autocratic, expelling philosophers from Rome and confiscating the property of his opponents. Particularly offensive was his insistence on being addressed as *Dominus et Deus* "Master and God" (cf. Suetonius *Domitian* xiii).

His final years as emperor constituted an infamous reign of terror, characterized by numerous executions and charges of treason against prominent members of the Senate. While this period probably provides the setting for John's apocalypse, it does not appear that Christians in particular were singled out for persecution. Domitian was murdered in 96 as the result of a conspiracy of which his wife Domitia Longina was a part; he was succeeded as emperor by Marcus Cocceius Nerva.

DOOR (Heb. *deleṯ, peṯaḥ*; Gk. *thýra*).† Basically, that opening which serves as an entrance to a dwelling or other structure. In the tents of the Israelite patriarchs and other transhumants the doorway (Heb. *peṭaḥ* "opening"; Gk. *thýra*, Matt. 27:60) was closed off by a flap of coarse cloth (Gen. 18:1; Num. 11:10); in humbler permanent dwellings this might be a curtain or veil or a simple boarded cover which pivoted vertically. Most substantial structures had heavy hardwood doors (Heb. *deleṭ*; cf. the letter *daleṭ*; Gk. *thýra*, Matt. 6:6), generally divided horizontally into two sections and studded with metal or stone.

Beneath the door was a threshold (Heb. *sap, miptān*; KJV usually "door"), a raised stone sill which served to keep out winter floods; sacrificial deposits have been discovered in the foundations of many thresholds, considered sacred throughout much of the ancient Near East. Above the door was a stone or wood lintel (Heb. *mašqôp*), a horizontal beam providing structural support. It was by means of sockets in both the threshold and lintel that the heavy doors pivoted. Vertically the doorway was framed by two wooden posts or jambs (Heb. *mᵉzûzâ*), sometimes overlaid with metal, and fitted into the threshold and lintel. The doors, which opened inward, could be bolted with a wooden bar which crossed the doorposts on the inside and could be slid open by means of a wooden key (cf. 2 Sam. 13:17). The homes of the wealthy often had doorkeepers (Heb. *histôpēp*; Ps. 84:10; cf. 2 Sam. 4:6, LXX Gk. *thyrōrós*) who guarded the entrance and determined who might enter (*see* GATE-KEEPER).

In preparation for the first Passover, the Israelites were instructed to smear blood on the doorposts and lintels of their homes in order to ward off the destroyer (Exod. 12:7, 22-23). Perhaps in commemoration of this event (cf. vv. 24-27) they later inscribed on their doorposts the words of God's commandments (Deut. 6:9; 11:20). In later Judaism a wood or metal case (Heb. *mᵉzûzâ*) containing a parchment (bearing on one side the text of Deut. 6:4-9; 11:13-21 and on the other the divine name Shaddai) was affixed to one of the doorposts, to be touched or kissed when entering or leaving the house. According to Exod. 21:6; Deut. 15:17 if a Hebrew slave who had fulfilled his term of service desired to remain with his master rather than go free, he was to present himself to his master who would mark him by piercing his ear with an awl against the doorpost; "to God" at Exod. 21:6 underscores the sacredness of the doorposts, perhaps because of the household gods placed nearby.

In figurative use, the door is the entrance to the kingdom of heaven (Luke 13:24; Gk. *pýlē*; Acts 14:27, "door of faith") as well as the opening to acceptance or belief (Rev. 3:20). In his allegory of the shepherd and the sheep, Jesus calls himself "the door" (John 10:7, 9) whereby his followers can gain salvation. Paul frequently uses the metaphor of an open door to indicate opportunities for spreading the gospel (e.g., 1 Cor. 16:9; 2 Cor. 2:12; Col. 4:3; cf. Rev. 3:8; 4:1).

DOPHKAH [dŏf′kə] (Heb. *dopqâ*). The first stopping place of the Israelites in their journey after leaving the Wilderness of Sin (Num. 33:12; LXX *Raphaka*; omitted at Exod. 17:1). It has been identified with Serābît el-Khâdim, site of Bronze Age Egyptian mining activity (fourteenth-twelfth centuries B.C.) in the Sinai peninsula.

DOR [dôr] (Heb. *dō̆r, dôr* "habitation").† A Canaanite city assigned to the tribe of Manasseh but not occupied by Israel until the time of David (Judg. 1:27); considered to be the same as Naphath-dor (Josh. 12:13) and Naphoth-dor (11:2). The site is Khirbet el-Burj, slightly north of the small harbor of eṭ-Ṭanṭurâh on the Mediterranean between Caesarea and Mt. Carmel.

Settled as early as the thirteenth century B.C., shortly before the time of Rameses II, Dor fell into the hands of the Sea Peoples (later identified as the Philistines) *ca.* 1190. Visiting the site, the Egyptian emissary Wen-Amon (*ca.* 1100) found it ruled by Beder, a prince of the Tjeker who probably arrived with the Philistines. Dor was part of a coalition (perhaps a pentapolis) headed by King Jabin of Hazor which warred against Joshua (Josh. 11:1-2); its king was defeated by the Israelites (12:23), but apparently the insurgents did not occupy the site (cf. Judg. 1:27). During Solomon's reign the city was sufficiently important to serve as capital of the fourth administrative district under the king's son-in-law, Abinadab (1 Kgs. 4:11). Tiglath-pileser III conquered Dor in 732, making it capital of the Assyrian province of Duru. In the Persian period the city apparently came under Sidonian administration, and a Greek colony was established there. An important Hellenistic fortress, it resisted the attack of the Seleucid Antiochus III the Great in 219. Antiochus VII Sidetes besieged Trypho there *ca.* 139/138, but the usurper escaped (1 Macc. 15:12-13, 25). In 64 B.C. Pompey liberated the city from the Hasmoneans and granted it autonomy.

Archaeological remains at the site indicate its massive destruction in the thirteenth century B.C., probably at the hands of the Sea Peoples. Because only limited excavations have been conducted, little more than ceramic materials have been obtained for the Late Bronze and Iron Age occupations, nevertheless indicating extensive mercantile activity. Considerable architectural evidence has been uncovered for the Hellenistic and Roman periods, including a massive wall and a large building — possibly a temple — with a podium and temenos or sacred enclosure. A Roman theater has been found north of the mound and a basilica to the southeast; both date to the fourth century A.D.

DORCAS [dôr′kəs] (Gk. *Dorkas*; cf. Aram. *ṭᵉbîṭā* "gazelle"; cf. Acts 9:36, 40). A Christian woman living at Joppa, noted and loved for her works of charity, especially for making tunics and other garments for the poor (Acts 9:36, 39). Dorcas died after an illness and was laid in an upper room, following the Jewish custom of purifying the dead (see Mishnah *Šabb.* xxiii.5). Luke records that Peter brought her back to life (vv. 38-41), as the result of which many were converted (v. 42).

DOT (Gk. *keraía*).* A minute detail of the law, cited by Jesus to emphasize the permanence and value of the Old Testament law (Matt. 5:18). Matthew mentions it with the iota, the name for the smallest letter of the Greek alphabet. The Greek term for "dot" ("apex of a letter") refers to small parts of a letter (cf. NIV, "stroke of a pen"; KJV "tittle"), either a mark of distinction between the Hebrew letters or, more probably, a scribal ornament added to various letters.

DOTHAN [dō′thən] (Heb. *dōṯayin, dōṯān*; Gk. *Dōthaim*).† A city located, according to Eusebius *Onom.* lxxvi.13, 12 Roman mi. north of Samaria. The site, confirmed as modern Tell Dôthā, is 22 km. (13.5 mi.) north of Shechem on an important ancient highway through the Jezreel valley.

Occupied as early as the Chalcolithic Age (*ca.* 3000 B.C.), Dothan is mentioned in no written sources except the Bible. It is in the pastureland at Dothan that Joseph discovered his brothers, who cast him into a pit and then sold him to a band of Ishmaelite caravanners (Gen. 37:17ff.). At the time of the divided monarchy the Syrian king Ben-hadad dispatched chariots and troops to besiege the city, seeking to capture the prophet Elisha (2 Kgs. 6:13-14). The city is cited in connection with the attacks of Nebuchadnezzar's general Holofernes against Judea (Jdt. 3:9; 4:6); it was there that his army encamped while surveying Bethulia (7:3).

Excavations at the site have discovered the city wall and evidence of seven levels of occupation during the Early Bronze Age. The city became increasingly prosperous during the Middle Bronze-Iron I periods; significant remains include a citadel inside the city wall and a large family tomb containing numerous artifacts. The most extensive finds are from the Iron II period, that representing the Israelite Monarchy; among them are streets, houses, and a large administrative building. Evidence of destruction by the Assyrians correlates with either the conquest of Tiglath-pileser III (732 B.C.) or the fall of Samaria (721). Occupied briefly by the Assyrians, Dothan was abandoned from the seventh century until the Hellenistic period, when a small settlement with an acropolis was established.

DOUGH. *See* LEAVEN.

DOVE. One of a number of smaller species of pigeons; biblical reference is most often to the rock dove (*Columba livia*), a blue-colored bird with a red breast which lives throughout Palestine and usually makes its nest in caves, wells, and cisterns.

The Old Testament mentions the dove (Heb. *yônâ*; RSV "dove, pigeon") at Gen. 8:8-12 as the bird that finally assured Noah that the waters of the Flood had subsided. The Old Testament offers descriptions of the dove's swift flight (Ps. 55:6) and its nesting habits in rock clefts (Cant. 2:14; Jer. 48:28) and valleys (Ezek. 7:16). Judging from the bird's mournful cooing (Isa. 38:14; 59:11; Nah. 2:7, used metaphorically), the directions to the choirmaster at Ps. 56 ("according to The Dove on Far-off Terebinths," RSV) might indicate that the melody was in a minor key. In Canticles the eyes of the beloved are likened to the bright, clear eyes of the dove (5:12), and a loved one's face recalls a dove's gentleness and beauty (2:14; at 5:2; 6:9 "my dove" is a term of endearment.

In the New Testament Matthew records the saying of Jesus that the disciples were to be as innocent as doves (Gk. *peristeraí*; Matt. 10:16), a common Jewish symbol of sincerity (see Midrash *Cant.* ii.14). All four Gospels use the image of the dove for the

Holy Spirit descending on Jesus at his baptism (Matt. 3:16 par. Mark 1:10; Luke 3:22; John 1:32). The comparison may be to the dove's gentle descent (see further J. A. Fitzmyer, *The Gospel According to Luke I-IX*. AB (1981), pp. 483-84; I. H. Marshall, *Comm. on Luke*. NIGTC (1978), pp. 153-54).

Mosaic law regarded the dove as a clean animal and thus edible (Deut. 14:11, 20); it may have been one of many fowls served to Nehemiah (Neh. 5:18). The "windows" of Isa. 60:8 (RSV, KJV) probably refer to a type of cage or dovecote (JB; NIV "nests") where Israelites kept the domesticated bird. Doves were fed grain and darnel seed. The "dove's dung" (so RSV, KJV, following K *ḥᵃrê yônîm*), sold at an exorbitant price during Ben-hadad's siege of Samaria (2 Kgs. 6:25), was rather a salt substitute (Josephus *Ant.* ix.4.4[62]), cattle dung (Josephus *BJ* v.13.7[571]), or an edible plant (NIV "seed pots"; JB "wild onions").

See also PIGEON; TURTLEDOVE.

DOVE ON FAR-OFF TEREBINTHS (Heb. *yônaṯ 'ēlem rᵉḥōqîm*). Most likely the first words or line of a melody to which Ps. 56 was to be sung (superscription; so RSV; JB "Dove of the distant gods," following LXX *tōn hagíōn* "of the holy ones").

DOWRY.† A gift of money or property usually extended by the bride's family to the groom at marriage. The Old Testament states that the pharaoh gave his daughter a city when she married King Solomon (1 Kgs. 9:16, Heb. *šillûḥîm*; KJV "present"; NIV "wedding gift") and that Laban gave Jacob a handmaid when his daughter Leah became Jacob's bride (Gen. 29:24). The springs of water that Achsah requested for her husband Othniel most likely were to be a wedding present (Josh. 15:19; so RSV; JB, NIV "favor"). After bearing six sons Leah considered that she had brought her husband a "good dowry" (Gen. 30:20; Heb. *zeḇeḏ* "gift, endowment"; KoB, p. 247; NIV, JB "gift"), and she hoped Jacob would accept her love, which thus far he had refused (Gen. 29:21-25, 31; 30:16-17).

The Old Testament also mentions the gift (Heb. *mōhar*) the husband extended to the father of the bride. Shechem was willing to give a "marriage present" (RSV; JB, NIV "price") and a "gift" to Jacob in exchange for his daughter Dinah (Gen. 34:12); David, too poor to give either property or money, was permitted to make a gruesome "settlement" (JB) of slain Philistines for Michal, Saul's younger daughter (1 Sam. 18:25). The compensation to be paid by one who seduced a virgin may have been considered a marriage present (RSV, Exod. 22:17), or money (cf. NIV, JB) to be paid to the girl's father (cf. Deut. 22:29); though treated among the laws concerning property, this does not imply that the bride was to be considered property, for she could own property herself (cf. Josh. 15:18-19 par. Judg. 1:14-15). Although some scholars have considered the *mōhar* a purchase price intended to compensate the bride's family for loss of their daughter and subsequent offspring, the groom's marriage present was merely reciprocation for the dowry, thus completing the exchange as expected in Israel's "gift economy."

DOXOLOGY (from Gk. *doxología, dóxa* "praise" and *lógos* "utterance").† An expression of praise to God. A common Old Testament formula is "Blessed be the Lord" (e.g., Gen. 24:27), in which the speaker mentions God's activities in the lives of his people. Another formula is "Ascribe to the Lord glory" (e.g., Ps. 29:1). Scholars believe that the Old Testament congregation voiced such doxologies at the conclusion of hymns and prayers (1 Chr. 16:36), though 1 Chr. 29:10-13 records similar praise in the opening lines of one of David's prayers (cf. Dan. 2:20-23).

The New Testament has retained both Old Testament formulas for the doxology (e.g., Luke 1:68; Rom. 16:27). In Paul's epistles, doxologies occur in the salutation (Gal. 1:5), as opening thanksgiving (2 Cor. 1:3-5), as a final exhortation (1 Tim. 6:15-16), and in closing comments (Phil. 4:20). Usually the focus of praise is on God the Father, but twice at least the New Testament gives a doxology in behalf of Christ — by the crowd that praised Jesus during his triumphal entry into Jerusalem (Matt. 21:9 par. Mark 11:9; Luke 19:38) and by the four living creatures and twenty-four elders who magnify the name of the Lamb at Rev. 5:12. At Rom. 16:27 the various versions attribute glory to God through Jesus Christ.

The doxology at the close of the Lord's Prayer is omitted by Luke (Luke 11:4) and is not found in the major and more reliable manuscripts of Matthew's gospel (Matt. 6:13; cf. RSV mg., JB mg., NIV mg.; KJV "For thine is the kingdom, and the power, and the glory, for ever"). This ending may be based on 1 Chr. 29:11. It is included in the Didache as well (8:2; cf. 9:2-4; 10:2, 4-5 for the expression of praise in other contexts).

DRACHMA [drăk′mə] (Gk. *drachmé*). A silver Greek coin weighing 4.3 g. (.2 oz.) and valued at one-fourth of a shekel. This may be the meaning of "daric" (Heb. *darkᵉmôn*) at Ezra 2:69; Neh. 7:70-72. In the New Testament the drachma occurs in the parable of the lost coins (Luke 15:8-9, JB; RSV, NIV "silver coins"; KJV "pieces of silver"). It is possible that this coin originated in the east and later circulated in Greece. In New Testament times it was equal to a Roman denarius, or the wage of a day's work (see Matt. 20:2, 9, 13). The fifty thousand "pieces of silver" (Gk. *argyríou*), the value of the magical books burned at Ephesus, were fifty thousand drachmas (so NIV; Acts 19:19).

DRAGNET. See FISHING.

DRAGON (Heb. *tannîn*; Gk. *drákōn* "serpent"). A mythological creature prominent in the creation myths of the ancient Canaanites and Babylonians as a power opposing the gods (e.g., Yam [the sea] vs. Baal and Anat; Tiamat vs. Marduk). See CREATION.

Some passages in the Old Testament have been interpreted as alluding to this primeval creation conflict. Heb. *tannîn* (RSV also "serpent," "sea monster") is the monster whose head God broke upon the waters (Ps. 74:13; NIV, JB "monster[s]") and whom the Lord pierced (Isa. 51:9, where the term parallels Rahab; cf. Hab. 3:8-15). Whatever the influences from mythology, the Old Testament does not personify this crea-

ture as does the Babylonian myth (but cf. JB at Isa. 51:9); rather, it interprets the myth for the purpose of polemics. Isa. 51:9 may refer either to creation or to the Exodus event, since Rahab is often used to personify Egypt. At Job 7:12 Job argues that he is not a sea monster to be guarded against; this, too, may echo Babylonian mythology, although at 38:4-7 it is clearly stated that God created all things.

In the New Testament the dragon (Gk. *drákōn*) figures only in the book of Revelation, where it symbolizes a creature opposing God. Identified as the Devil or Satan (Rev. 12:9), the dragon sought to devour the Christ child but did not succeed (vv. 4ff.). Though still powerful (13:2-4; 16:13), in the end times it will be bound for a thousand years (20:2-3). The author may have purposely used Old Testament imagery for this eschatological conflict (cf. Isa. 27:1 where the term is parallel to Leviathan; JB "sea-dragon").

Bibliography. A. Heidel, *The Babylonian Genesis,* 2nd ed. (Chicago: 1963); M. K. Wakeman, *God's Battle with the Monster* (Leiden: 1973).

DRAGON WELL (Neh. 2:13, KJV). See EN-ROGEL.

DRAUGHT HOUSE (2 Kgs. 10:27, KJV). See LATRINE.

DREAM (Heb. noun *ḥᵃlôm*, verb *ḥālam*; Aram. *ḥēlem*; Gk. *enýpnion, ónar*). A series of perceptions or images experienced during sleep. To the ancient Near Eastern mind, dreams were viewed as somehow connected with the supernatural and thus both feared and sought after because of their potential bearing on persons and events. At the same time, dreams were so commonly experienced by all people that they were often discounted as transient (Job 20:8; Ps. 90:5) and ineffectual (Isa. 29:7-8); one might regard them as unimportant (Ps. 73:20) or accord them more value than they merited (Eccl. 5:3, 7).

Dreams or "night visions" (Heb. *ḥezyôn laylâ, marᵉʾôṯ hallaylâ*) were recognized as an important means of divine communication. Such revelatory dreams might be auditory (cf. Job 33:15-17); in such cases the message was pronounced simply and directly (e.g., Gen. 20:3, 6; 31:10-13, 24; Acts 9:10ff.). At other times dreams might be highly symbolic and thus required skilled interpretation. The Mesopotamian and Egyptian courts employed skilled professionals who sought to interpret such visions as portents of the future (cf. Gen. 41:8; Dan. 2:2); dream books were compiled in which various dream phenomena and their implications were recorded for reference purposes. The Israelites, by contrast, believed that interpretation of dreams could be accomplished only with Yahweh's guidance (Gen. 40:8; Dan. 2:20-23). Two Israelites attained high regard for their skill as oneirocritics: Joseph, who explained not only his own dreams (Gen. 37:6-9) but also those of the pharaoh's butler (Gen. 40:12-13) and baker (vv. 18-19) and of Pharaoh himself (41:25-32); and Daniel, who deciphered Nebuchadnezzar's visions (Dan. 2:27-45; 4:19-27; cf. 7:16 where Daniel requires an angel's interpretation of his vision of the four beasts). Mosaic law prescribed the death penalty for false interpreters who, claiming to know God's will, were eager for a sign or wonder to support their assertions

(Deut. 13:1-5). Twice the prophet Jeremiah warned against such pseudodreamers: against those who introduced Baal worship (Jer. 23:25-32) and those who wished to shorten the length of the Exile (29:8-11). Zechariah criticized those who gave false consolation, causing the Israelites to wander from the truth (Zech. 10:2).

Because of the revelatory value of dreams (cf. Num. 12:6), individuals frequently attempted to induce such visions through incubation, by spending the night in a temple or holy place. The practice was commonly employed by the cultic prophets of Mari, and the kings of Lagash and Ugarit are attested as having sought divine guidance through incubation. Such may be the background for the activities of Saul (1 Sam. 28:6, 15), Solomon (1 Kgs. 3:4-15 par. 2 Chr. 1:3-12; 1 Kgs. 9:2-9 par. 2 Chr. 7:12-22), Ahaz (2 Kgs. 16:15), and Hezekiah (19:1, 14ff.). At times dreams were elicited through incubation even though the individual had not intentionally sought them (e.g., Gen. 28:11-17; 46:1-4; 1 Sam. 3:1-18).

The New Testament accounts surrounding the birth of the Messiah record a number of revelatory dreams. It was by such means that Joseph was instructed to wed Mary (Matt. 1:20), flee to Egypt (2:13), return (v. 19), and go to Galilee (v. 22). The magi also were warned in a dream not to return to their native land along the same route by which they had come (2:12).

Bibliography. J. Obermann, *How Daniel Was Blessed with a Son: An Incubation Scene in Ugaritic.* JAOS Sup. (1946); A. L. Oppenheim, *The Interpretation of Dreams in the Ancient Near East.* Transactions of the American Philosophical Society N.S. 46 (1956): 178-353.

DREGS. A sediment in fermented products. To drink the cup of the Lord's wrath "to the dregs" means to undergo God's punishment to the end. Ps. 75:8 (Heb. *šᵉmārîm*) refers to the wicked who must accept the full share of their punishment. Isa. 51:17 (Heb. *māṣâ*) points to God's people in Exile who had suffered the Lord's chastisement and could now look forward to his comfort (v. 22). *See* LEES.

DRESS. *See* CLOTHING.

DRESSER OF SYCAMORE TREES (Heb. *bôlēs šiqmîm*).* One who prunes sycamore trees to increase their yield or pierces the fruit to allow it to ripen (Amos 7:14; KJV "gatherer of sycamore fruit").

DRINK. The Israelites were familiar with a number of beverages. Besides water (e.g., Exod. 15:23-25) drawn from springs, wells, or cisterns (Jer. 2:13) they drank milk from goats (Prov. 27:27) and sheep (Deut. 32:14; cf. Judg. 5:25), and wine (e.g., Amos 2:8). They also drank vinegar because of its thirst-quenching character (e.g., Num. 6:3).

Recognizing the necessity of drink for human survival, Jesus exhorted his followers to provide drink for the needy (Matt. 25:35, 42). Similarly, the author of Proverbs (Prov. 25:21) and Paul (Rom. 12:20) urge that water be given even to the enemy. Perhaps owing to its life-giving qualities, drink was designated as a form of sacrifice to the Lord (*see* LIBATION). The

water which David's mighty men had obtained from the well at Bethlehem at dire risk to their lives was viewed so dearly by David that he would not drink it but poured it out as an offering to God (2 Sam. 23:13-17). The Israelites were forbidden to drink blood because it was the very essence of life (Lev. 17:14).

The Israelites were familiar with various forms of intoxicating liquor (Heb. *šēkār*, from *škr* "drink oneself drunk"). While the Old Testament does not indicate the precise nature of this "strong drink" (NIV "fermented drink") other than to distinguish it from wine (Heb. *yayin*; e.g., Lev. 10:9; Num. 6:3), the term probably refers to various intoxicants made from apples, dates, and barley. (The Egyptians made a kind of beer from barley, wheat, wild saffron, and salt which could be partially dehydrated to increase its preservability; later the concentrate could be mixed with water [the process may be suggested at Isa. 5:22].) The Bible neither condemns outright nor wholly condones the consumption of strong drink. The psalmist praises God for the wine which would gladden one's heart (Ps. 104:15), and both wine and strong drink were imbibed in Jewish celebrations (Isa. 24:9). Both were employed for medicinal purposes and to alleviate distress (Prov. 31:6). Nevertheless, the perils of strong drink were well known (e.g., Prov. 20:1; Isa. 5:11). Rulers (Prov. 31:4-5; Isa. 56:12), priests (Lev. 10:9-11; cf. 1 Tim. 3:3; Tit. 1:7), and prophets (Isa. 28:7) were to avoid intoxicants so as not to impair their capacity to function; Nazirites and others pledged themselves to abstention (Num. 6:3; Judg. 13:4, 7, 14; Jer. 35:6ff.; Luke 1:15). Drunkenness was viewed as a significant social evil (cf. Gen. 9:20-27; 19:31-38; cf. 1 Sam. 1:15-16; Hos. 4:18; Luke 21:34).

DRINK OFFERING. *See* LIBATION.

DROMEDARY (Heb. *kirkārâ*). A one-humped Arabian riding camel (*Camelus dromedarius*), named among the animals carrying the returned Israelites to Mt. Zion (Isa. 66:20; KJV "swift beast"; NIV "camels"). The Hebrew name (*kirkeret*) may be related etymologically to the verb *krr* "dance," a reference to their undulating motion. *See* CAMEL.

DROPSY (Gk. *hydrōpikós*).* The symptom of a disease in the vital organs, whereby an excess of fluids collects in various parts of the body, indicating an advanced stage of the disease. The Greek term is that employed since the time of Hippocrates (fourth century B.C.). The dropsy condition of the man healed on the Sabbath was advanced (Luke 14:2; so VSS).

DROUGHT. A dryness of the land due to insufficient rain over an extended period of time. The Israelites feared a drought, for it would invariably lead to famine. The drought "caused" by Elijah was so prolonged that Ahab had to travel a great distance to find water and provender (1 Kgs. 17:1ff.).

While not denying natural causes (such as the desiccating effect of the east wind; Hos. 13:15), the Old Testament nearly always interprets droughts to be God's punishment for Israel's sin. Drought is not only numbered among the curses at Deut. 28:22 (emending Heb. *ḥereb* "sword" [KJV] to *ḥōreb* "drought" [RSV,

NIV, JB]) but was also attributed to specific offenses —
the bloodguilt in David's days for the deaths of the
Gibeonites a generation before (2 Sam. 21:1); Ahab's
worship of Baal (1 Kgs. 17:1); Israel's backsliding
during Jeremiah's ministry (Jer. 14:1; Heb. *baṣṣōreṯ*,
possibly referring to Manasseh's purposeful idolatry);
and the postexilic community's negligence in rebuilding
the temple (Hag. 1:7-11).

DRUNKENNESS. *See* DRINK.

DRUSILLA [drōō sĭl′ə] (Gk. *Drousilla*). The third
and youngest daughter (*ca.* A.D. 38-79) of Herod
Agrippa I and the sister of Herod Agrippa II (Josephus *Ant.* xviii.5.4[132]). The marriage to Epiphanes
of Commagene in Asia Minor proposed for her at the
age of six never materialized because the groom refused to be circumcised and embrace Judaism. Her
brother then arranged a marriage for her with Azizus,
king of Émesa in Syria.

Having been married for about one year, the beautiful Drusilla, envied by her elder sister Bernice, accepted the overtures of Antonius Felix the Roman
procurator to divorce her husband and marry him
(a divorcé himself). At the age of forty-two she was
killed in the eruption of Mt. Vesuvius (A.D. 79),
along with Agrippa, her son by Felix.

Luke mentions Drusilla and Felix in his account
of Paul's stay at Caesarea (Acts 24:24-27). Called
a Jewess, she and her husband heard Paul "speak
upon faith in Christ Jesus" (v. 24). According to
the Western text, it was she who prompted her husband to summon Paul.

DUALISM.* A system of thought which views the
world in terms of two irreducible and conflicting elements. Postexilic Judaism, influenced by contact with
Persian Zoroastrianism and its belief in the opposing
forces of good and evil governed by the gods Ormazd
and Ahriman, shows evidence of a developing concept
of a superhuman source of evil (e.g., Satan; cf. Job
1–2; Belial; cf. Nah. 1:15, RSV mg.; 2 Cor. 6:15)
and the eschatological understanding of the present
evil age and a future age to be governed by God
(cf. 2 Esdr. 6:7-9); the distinction is particularly
emphasized in the sectarian writings of the Dead Sea
Scrolls (e.g., Manual of Discipline, War of the Sons
of Light and the Sons of Darkness). Christianity,
like Judaism, rejected the possibility of an evil counterpart to God, but the belief in two ages became an
important part of Christian eschatology (e.g., Matt.
12:32; Gal. 1:4; Heb. 6:5).

Influenced by the metaphysical thought of such Greek
philosophers as Plato and Pythagoras, Hellenistic Judaism as represented by Philo of Alexandria accepted a
distinction between body and soul. The contrast was
maintained and developed by Christianity (cf. Mark
14:38). Paul, in particular, viewed the body of flesh
as evil, the source of sin and therefore death (cf.
Rom. 8; Gal. 5:17); thus the body which he believed
would be resurrected would be a "spiritual body"
(1 Cor. 15:35-58).

DULCIMER (Dan. 3:5, 10, 15, KJV). *See* BAGPIPE.

DUMAH [dōō′mə] (Heb. *dûmâ* "silence") (**PER-
SON**).

1. One of the descendants of Ishmael and ancestor
of a tribe in north Arabia (Gen. 25:14 par. 1 Chr.
1:30). His name is preserved in the name Dûmet
ej-Jendel (modern ej-Jauf), an oasis about midway
between the heads of the Gulf of Aqaba and the
Persian Gulf.

2. The subject of the oracle at Isa. 21:11ff. It may
be a cryptic name (perhaps a scribal error) for Edom
(Heb. *dwmh* for *ʾdwm*; LXX *Idumea* "Edom"; cf.
"Seir," v. 11) or a symbolic reference based on the
meaning of Heb. *dûmâ*, thus indicating the silence
of the night and of death.

DUMAH [dōō′mə] (Heb. *dûmâ* "silence") (**PLACE**).
A city in the hill country of Judah (Josh. 15:52),
identified with contemporary Deir ed-Dômeh, about
10 km. (6.5 mi.) southwest of Hebron.

DUNG (Heb. *gēlel, gālāl, hereʾ, hᵃrî, ṣᵉpîʿê, dōmen,
pereš*; Gk. *skýbalon, kóprion*).† Human dung was
carried out of every city to a heap, also the general
garbage dump (Luke 14:35), which in places long
inhabited became a high "dunghill" (Heb. *ʾašpōṯ,
ʾašpōṯ*; Aram. *nᵉwālî, nᵉwālû*; Gk. *kopría*). There it
was periodically burned. Sitting among the ashes of
the dunghill was a sign of degradation through grief,
of poverty, and of disease (1 Sam. 2:8; Ps. 113:7; Lam.
4:5; RSV "ash heap"; cf. Job 2:8; Isa. 58:5; Jonah
3:6). The transformation of a house's site into a dunghill was a means of degrading the memory of executed persons (Ezra 6:11; perhaps Dan. 2:5; 3:29; cf.
2 Kgs. 10:27); on the day of the Lord Moab will be
humiliated "as straw is trodden down in a dung-pit"
(Heb. *madmēnâ*; Isa. 25:10). The dung of domesticated animals was used for fuel (cf. 1 Kgs. 14:10);
human dung so used made food "unclean" (Ezek.
4:12-13, 15), though in severe siege-induced famine
human feces might even become food (2 Kgs. 18:27
par. Isa. 36:12). Dung was also used for manure (Luke
13:8; cf. Ps. 83:10 [MT 11]).

The dung (*pereš*) of animals sacrificed as sin offerings (i.e., the intestines of the animals and their contents were to be burned "outside the camp" (Exod.
29:14; Lev. 4:11; 8:17; 16:27). To have the dung of
such sacrifices "spread upon your faces" (Mal. 2:3)
was a figure for the severest rebuke.

By contrast to the "surpassing worth" of knowing
Christ, "all things" are regarded by Paul as "dung"
(Phil. 3:8; Gk. *skýbalon*; RSV "refuse").

DUNG GATE (Heb. *šaʿar hā-ʾašpōṯ; šaʿar hā-šᵃpôṯ*).†
A gate of Jerusalem, apparently so named because
of its location near the city's refuse heap (Neh. 2:13;
KJV "dung port"). Following the Exile Malchijah
the son of Rechab assisted in rebuilding this gate
(3:13-14), and festivities took place there at the dedication of the completed wall (12:31). Its site has been
identified in the first (south) wall, thus providing
access to the Tyropoeon valley at the southwestern
corner of David and Solomon's city; it is close to the
present Dung Gate (Arab. *Bab el-Magharibeh*; also
called the Gate of the Westerners or Moroccans [Moors]
Gate), built in the sixteenth century A.D. It is prob-

ably the same as the Potsherd Gate of Jer. 19:2 (Heb. *ḥarsît*).

In New Testament times the Gate of the Essenes, located close to the valley of Hinnom, was sometimes called the Dung Gate (Josephus *BJ* v.4.2).

DUNGEON. *See* Prison.

DURA [do͝or'ə] (Aram. *dûrāʾ*).† A plain in the province of Babylon where Nebuchadnezzar set up a golden image (Dan. 3:1). Among those sites proposed for its location are Dura-Europos, where the Habor and Euphrates rivers meet; a site near Apollonia in the province of Sittakene; and, more probably, Tulul Dura, just south of Babylon. A common element in Mesopotamian place names (cf. Akk. *dûru* "circuit, walled place"), the term may not have been intended as a reference to a specific fortified place (cf. LXX *períbolos* "enclosure").

DURA-EUROPOS (do͝or'ə ûr ō'pəs).* A Hellenistic city at the northern edge of the Syrian desert, located on the western bank of the Euphrates river near its confluence with the Habor river, some 32 km. (20 mi.) northwest of Mari. Founded on the site of the Assyrian fortress Ṣâliḥiyeh by Seleucus I Nicator *ca.* 300 B.C., it became an important trade center and was subsequently occupied by the Parthians, Romans, and Sassanian Persians.

Excavations have uncovered several buildings, the decorations of which are highly significant for the study of religious art history. Several pagan temples have been found containing murals depicting various cultic rituals as well as a large figure of the god Bel. The later of two synagogues (*ca.* A.D. 245) was decorated on all four walls with horizontal bands of tempera *al secco* paintings including fifty-eight interpretations of biblical persons and episodes; an elaborate niche served as a Torah shrine. Nearby is a church, originally a private house (built A.D. 232) which had been enlarged to serve as a chapel accommodating some one hundred people. Profusely decorated with murals of Old and New Testament themes, the church contains a courtyard, pulpit, and baptistry.

DYE.* Although the process of dying materials is not described in the Bible, the Israelites had access to dyed cloth as early as the time of the wilderness tabernacle (Exod. 35:6, 23-26). Dyed goods were prized as the spoil of battle (Judg. 5:30). While there is no indication that the Israelites could not have learned the craft on their own, it is generally suggested that they were influenced by the Egyptians and, especially, the Phoenicians (cf. 2 Chr. 2:7, where Solomon enlists from Hiram of Tyre a man skilled "in purple, crimson, and blue fabrics").

Dyes for various colors were obtained from several sources, including molluscs (red-purple, violet), insects (scarlet), and plants (yellow, orange, red, blue, black). The raw materials for making dyes (Ezek. 27:7, 24) as well as the dyes themselves (cf. Acts 16:14) were important items of trade.

Extensive evidence of the dying industry has been discovered at Tell Beit Mirsim. Dating to the seventh century B.C., the enterprise was conducted out of some thirty homes. The basic arrangement had a room with two round stone vats, on top of which were small openings for dipping the thread to be dyed. Retrieving drains were located around the rims, and basins were placed before or between the vats. Storage jars, presumably to hold the lime or potash used in fixing the dyes, were nearby. Smaller Iron Age operations were also found at Beth-shemesh and Tell en-Nasbeh; materials related to dying, dated to the Hellenistic period, were uncovered at Gezer and Beth-zur.

DYSENTERY (Gk. *dysenteríon*). A disease characterized by severe diarrhea with passage of mucus and blood. According to Acts 28:8 the father of Publius suffered a fever and dysentery (KJV "bloody flux") at Malta; this disease, due to a parasitic microbe (*Bacillus dysenteriae*) and at times fatal, has been proved to be epidemic.

DYSMAS [dĭz'məs] (Gk. *Dysmas*).* The name (also Dismas, Demas, Titus) given by a number of apocryphal Gospels and Acts to the penitent criminal of Luke 23:40-43. Some of these accounts include stories of the kindness of Dysmas to the infant Jesus, the prophecy of the infant concerning the crucifixion of both himself and Dysmas, and the tale of Jesus' last will and testament in which he bequeaths his eternal kingdom to Dysmas, a document signed in blood by both parties. He was later canonized as St. Latro.

E. Designation of the ELOHIST source, considered by source critics to be one of the principal strata of the Pentateuch. *See also* BIBLICAL CRITICISM.

EAGLE (Heb. *nešer*; Aram. *n^ešar*; Gk. *aetós*).† A large diurnal bird of prey belonging to the family *Accipitridae*. As many as eight species have been identified in Palestine, many of which are migratory and spend only a small part of the year there. The biblical references are most likely to the Golden Eagle (*Aquila chrysaëtos*) and the Imperial Eagle (*Aquila heliaca heliaca*); other possibilities include the Steppe Eagle (*Aquila orientalis*) and the smaller Harrier Eagle (*Circaëtus gallicus*). As with other species of birds, the biblical terminology is frequently imprecise and identification remains difficult. Heb. *nešer* is used to indicate both the eagle and the Old World vulture, also a member of the family *Accipitridae* (e.g., Prov. 30:17; cf. Gk. *aetós*, Luke 17:37; RSV mg.); in the lists of unclean birds the two are distinguished (Lev. 11:13; Deut. 14:12; *see* VULTURE).

In the Old Testament the eagle is noted for its swiftness (Deut. 28:49; 2 Sam. 1:23; cf. Jer. 48:40; 49:22) and its ability to swoop from great heights to take its prey by surprise (Job 9:26). From its nest high up the face of a mountain, the eagle uses its sharp vision to spot its prey (Job 39:27-29; cf. Jer. 49:16). In teaching its young to fly, the eagle is said to push its young out of their nest high in the rocks and then hover under them to catch them with its wings as they fall through the air (Deut. 32:11); this exercise is used to symbolize God's fostering of young Israel in the wilderness (cf. Exod. 19:4). The strength (Isa. 40:31) and youthful vigor (Ps. 103:5) of the eagle was proverbial.

The eagle is a popular figure in the prophets as well as in the apocalyptic writings. In Ezekiel's allegory of the eagles (Ezek. 17:1-21) a great eagle represents the Babylonian Nebuchadnezzar, and another eagle stands for the Egyptian pharaoh Psammetichus II. In two of his visions the prophet sees cherubim, one of whose four faces is that of an eagle (1:10; 10:14). One of the four great beasts envisioned by Daniel is a lion with eagles' wings (Dan. 7:4), representing the Babylonian Empire. John's apocalypse mentions a flying eagle with six wings and covered with eyes (Rev. 4:7); at 8:13 an eagle announces impending doom. In a vision concerning Christ and Satan, the woman who had given birth to the male child is given two wings of the great eagle so that she might elude the serpent (12:14).

EAR The physical organ of sound (usually Heb. *'ōzen*) with which human beings and animals receive external stimuli (Job. 12:11). While the Israelites were familiar with the physical ear, they were more concerned with understanding (13:1) and heeding what was heard (e.g., Deut. 6:3; "to give ear" [Heb. *'āzan*] meant "to obey"). Even though the Old Testament community ascribed mankind's ability to hear to God's act of creation (Ps. 94:9; Prov. 20:12), they were also aware of their frequent inability to discern the Maker's message, and the psalmist's more-than-occasional complaint is that God seemed unable to hear his prayers (e.g., Ps. 31:2). Because sin has marred the system of communication between God and mankind (so Isa. 59:2), God must, so to speak, "open" theirs ears (so Elihu to Job; Job 36:10, 15; cf. Ps. 40:6) before they can again hear God's voice and respond (see Isa. 50:5 for the prophets own change in attitude). Then God will hear (see 1 Sam. 8:21; Isa. 59:1 for God's "ears") and answer human prayer.

There is irony in God's commissioning Isaiah to prophesy to Judah and possibly Israel when they were unable to understand (Isa. 6:9-10). Jesus later applied this passage to his own generation because they were not granted insight into the nature of the kingdom of God (Matt. 13:14-15 par.; cf. vv. 16-17). But it should not be forgotten that Isaiah's words came after God had repeatedly warned Israel to repent, and the prophecy may express the end of God's patience with his recalcitrant people (cf. Ahaz' disbelief at Isa. 7), at least for the time being.

In the New Testament Jesus healed the ears of the deaf-mute (Mark 7:35) and the ear of the high priest's slave when it was severed (Luke 22:51). He also repeated the Old Testament charge to hear with one's ears (Matt. 11:15; 13:9); in Revelation John states that in the latter days people should listen to the prophetic voice of the Spirit (Rev. 2:7). To Paul faith results from hearing the preached message of the gospel; unlike the Greeks, the apostle links revelation with the ear, not with the eye (except for 1 Cor. 13:12).

When writing of spiritual gifts to the Corinthian

church, Paul clearly reasons that the human body functions best when all its organs including the ear interact harmoniously (1 Cor. 12:16).

Bibliography. J. Horst, "οὖς," *TDNT* 5 (1967): 543-558.

EAR OF GRAIN. Individual heads of grain (Mark 4:28; Gk. *stáchys*), either of barley (Exod. 9:31; Heb. *'ābîb*) or of wheat (Deut. 23:25; Heb. *melîlâ*), but never of corn. *See* GRAIN.

EARRING.† An ornament worn on the earlobe by Israelite men, women, and even "sons and daughters" (Exod. 32:2-3). Heb. *'āgîl* may be either a ring (so Gesenius, p. 605) or a "circular kind of ornament" (KoB, p. 619), perhaps a disc (cf. Ezek. 16:12, where it is distinguished from the ring on the nose); Heb. *nezem* is any ornamental ring in general (Gen. 35:4; Exod. 32:2), worn either on the ear (Exod. 35:22; Judg. 8:24-26) or in the nose (e.g., Isa. 3:21). At Isa. 3:20 the RSV renders Heb. *lahaš* as "amulets" (cf. JB; NIV "charms"; KJV "earrings"), and the RSV translation of Heb. *tôrîm* (from Heb. *tôr* "turns [of ornament] plaits," KoB, p. 1023 or *tôr* "turtle dove"; cf. LXX) as "ornament" (KJV "rows of jewels"; NIV "earrings") at Cant. 1:10 certainly fits the context. The Israelites were proud of their jewelry and displayed it openly, but they did not object to giving their ornaments to Aaron when he requested them for the construction of the golden calf (Exod. 32:2-3). Later they offered these decorations to meet the expense incurred in building the tabernacle (35:22) and for other offerings as well (Num. 31:50).

EARTH.

I. Terminology

The most common Hebrew words for "earth" are Heb. *'ereṣ* and *'adāmâ*. Heb. *'ereṣ* is used in reference to the earth in contrast to heaven (e.g., Gen. 1:1; 2:1; Deut. 3:24; 30:19; Ps. 68:8), to the sea (Gen. 1:10), and to the Underworld ("land of the living," Isa. 38:11; cf. 26:19, "land of the shades," meaning Sheol); in reference to a certain territory (e.g., "land of Egypt," Gen. 47:13); for the ground as such (e.g., 18:2; 19:1; KJV, NIV "ground"); the life-giving soil (e.g., 1:11-12); and figuratively as a gesture of respect ("bow to the earth," e.g., 37:10) and of mourning (put earth on one's head; 2 Sam. 1:2; 15:32), or as a symbol of endurance (Ps. 72:6-9) or of weakness (Isa. 51:6). Heb. *'adāmâ* (from *'dm* "be red") refers primarily to the soil (e.g., Exod. 20:24) and occurs often in the expression the "face of the earth" (e.g., 32:12), i.e., the surface of the soil. Gk. *gḗ* (e.g., Matt. 5:18) is the New Testament approximation of Heb. *'ereṣ*.

II. Hebrew Cosmology

To the ancient Hebrews the earth was the center of the universe. Above it were the sky and the heavens, and below it were the Underworld, or Sheol, and the waters (e.g., Exod. 20:4; Ps. 24:2; 136:6). (Though at times the Hebrews did cite only heaven and earth as composing the universe [e.g., Ps. 124:8], actually they held to this tripartite concept [e.g., Phil. 2:10]).

The earth, with Canaan at its center (Ps. 74:12), was believed to be one mass of land (cf. the "ends of the earth" [Ps. 65:5] or its "four corners" [Isa. 11:12]) surrounded by an ocean. It rested on pillars (1 Sam. 2:8; Job.9:6; Ps. 75:3) or on firm foundations (Ps. 104:5; but cf. Job 26:7).

III. Theological Meaning

The Old Testament attributes the creation of the earth to God (Gen. 1:1; 2:4; cf. Ps. 124:8), who determined the boundaries of the earth and the sea (Ps. 104:5-9) and arranged the mountains and hills (Isa. 40:12). Though, like man, the earth was created good (Gen. 1:31), it now shares the curse upon human sin (3:17; cf. 6:11-13). But, like man's curse, the curse upon the earth has been tempered by divine grace, and one day, when a new earth is created (Rev. 21:1), it will be removed.

The Bible says that mankind inhabits earth as God inhabits heaven (Ps. 115:16). Though insignificant in relation to heaven ("earth is my footstool," Isa. 66:1), the earth gains in importance as the stage upon which the drama of God's redemption of mankind is enacted. John explicitly states that God loved the world to such an extent that he sent his Son Jesus Christ (John 3:16) to make salvation possible for its inhabitants. Jesus obtained the reconciliation between man and God on earth (on the cross), governs his church, has made it possible for "all the ends of the earth" to worship the Lord (Ps. 22:27-28), to witness salvation (Isa. 52:10), and to participate in the messianic kingdom of peace (Ps. 72:8).

See also WORLD; WATER.

Bibliography. J. Bergman and M. Ottosson, "'ereṣ ['ereṣ]," *TDOT* 1, rev. ed. (1977):388-405; J. G. Plöger, "'adhāmāh ['adāmâ]," *TDOT* 1:88-98; H. Sasse, "γῆ," *TDNT* 1 (1964):677-680; L. I. J. Stadelmann, *The Hebrew Conception of the World.* AnBib 39 (1970):126-154.

EARTHEN VESSELS. Fired pottery utensils used for cooking and storage (cf. Jer. 32:14). According to the ceremonial law, such vessels (Heb. *kelî ḥereś*; NIV "clay pots") were used in the purification of a leper (Lev. 14:5, 50) and in the trial by ordeal (Num. 5:17). When garments on which the sacrificial blood had spilled were cleaned, the absorbent clay pots in which they were boiled were to be destroyed (Lev. 6:28); the same was true for vessels into which an unclean animal had fallen (11:33).

At 2 Cor. 4:7 earthen vessels (Gk. *ostrákinos*) are used figuratively to represent the frailness of the body and, in general, all human limitations (cf. 2 Tim. 2:20; Rev. 2:27; Gk. *keramikós*).

See POTTERY.

EARTHLY (Gk. *epígeios* "belonging to the earth"). That which takes place on earth, in contrast to that which occurs in heaven (e.g., 1 Cor. 15:40, "terrestrial"; so RSV, KJV; NIV, JB "earthly"). The "earthly things" mentioned at John 3:12 probably refer to the discourse between Jesus and Nicodemus concerning spiritual regeneration, while the "earthly tent" at 2 Cor. 5:1 symbolizes the frail human body. In a few instances "earthly" has a negative connotation. At Phil. 3:19 Paul warns against those who do not exchange the Mosaic law for the cross of Christ (cf. the immoral deeds and other vices listed at Col. 3:5; Gk. *epí tês gês* "on the earth"; RSV "what is earthly"). Similarly, James opposes members in the community of believers who espouse a wisdom which is "earthly, unspiritual, devilish" (Jas. 3:15) and which places jealousy and selfish ambition above gentleness and pureness (v. 16).

EARTHQUAKE (Heb. *raʿaš*; Gk. *seismós*). A shaking or trembling of the earth due either to volcanic activity or a slight movement of the earth's crust. Because Palestine is located near a region of active earthquakes, it has experienced numerous earthquakes, which, seismologists assume, are caused by the geologically unstable Jordan (or Rift) valley and the fault lines running east and west through it. The Old Testament mentions an earthquake in the days of King Saul (1 Sam. 14:15) and one during the reign of King Uzziah (*ca.* 760 B.C.), which must have been severe judging from Amos 1:1 and Zech. 14:5. Josephus (*Ant.* xv.5.2) reported an earthquake in 31 B.C. which took the lives of at least ten thousand persons. Since the beginning of the Christian era Palestine has had almost one earthquake per century. That which occurred in 1927 at Nâblus (Shechem) damaged about half of the city and resulted in the loss of some 350 lives.

The Israelites linked such a natural disaster with divine activity; often they viewed earthquakes as punishment from God (e.g., Isa. 29:6), occasionally as a means of revelation — as at Mt. Horeb on which the Lord descended while giving his law (Exod. 19:18). At Ps. 60:2 the psalmist charges God with bringing about quakes and prays for restoration of the cracked soil. Interestingly, the despondent Elijah encountered God in the form of a small voice, not in the preceding earthquake, wind, or fire (1 Kgs. 19:11-12).

Matthew is the only Evangelist who states that an earthquake occurred after Jesus' crucifixion (Matt. 27:51), possibly as a divine judgment (cf. Josephus *BJ* vi.6.3 for a similar happening at the destruction of the temple in A.D. 70). Matthew also notes an earthquake in conjunction with the resurrection (28:2). A great quake freed the prisoners Paul and Silas from their confinement in the Philippian jail (Acts 16:26). According to Christ, earthquakes (even "great" quakes; Luke 21:11) in "various places" (so RSV, NIV at Matt. 24:7 par. Mark 13:8; KJV "divers places"; JB "here and there") will precede the end of the age, a theme John reintroduces at Rev. 6:12.

Bibliography. D. H. K. Amiran, "A Revised Earthquake-Catalogue of Palestine," *IEJ* 1 (1950/51): 223-246; 2 (1952): 48-65.

EAST.† The ancient Hebrews, who recognized four directions of the compass (e.g., Gen. 13:14, Heb. *qēḏem*; Ps. 107:3), identified the east with the rising of the sun (Exod. 27:13, "on the east, toward the sunrise"; Heb. *mizrāḥ* "place of sunrise"; so NIV; [RSV "on the front to the east"; KJV "its east side eastward"]; 38:13; Num. 2:3). The east also signified superstition (Isa. 2:6), righteousness or victory (Isa. 41:2), and deliverance (43:5; cf. Ezek. 43:2; but see Ps. 75:6, Heb. *môṣāʾ*). The psalmist compares the

magnitude of divine forgiveness to the distance between east and west (Ps. 103:12).

In the New Testament Gk. *anatolḗ*, rendered "sunrise" (cf. Gk. *anatéllō* "arise" at Matt. 5:45; 13:6) or "east," represents wisdom (2:1 [cf. 1 Kgs. 4:30]), and war (Rev. 16:12ff.). Jesus likened the certainty and the suddenness of his return with lightning flashing from the east to the west (Matt. 24:27).

EAST, PEOPLE OF THE (Heb. *bᵉnê qeḏem* "children of the east").† A designation for various nomadic or transhumant groups living in the general area east of Palestine, and by extension the territory which they inhabited. "The land of the people of the east" to which Jacob journeyed (Gen. 29:1) included Haran in the region of Paddan-aram, northeast of Palestine between the Euphrates and Tigris rivers; Balaam probably came from the same general area (Num. 23:7, "eastern mountains"; JB "the hills of Kedem"). The people of the east mentioned at Judg. 6:3 were apparently allies of the Midianites and Amalekites who, following their defeat by Gideon's band, fled to Karkor (8:10), southeast of Rabbah (modern Amman); R. G. Boling (*Judges.* AB [1975], p. 125) takes the term "Easterners" at 6:3 as an appositive for the Midianites and Amalekites. The prophets Jeremiah (Jer. 49:28) and Ezekiel (Ezek. 25:4, 10) portray them as Arab tribes from this same area east of Palestine, whereas the eschatological prophecy of Isa. 11:14 suggests that they may encompass the Edomites, Moabites, and Ammonites further to the south.

The people of the east were known for their wisdom; at 1 Kgs. 4:30 their sagacity is favorably compared with Solomon's (cf. Massa, Prov. 30:1; 31:1). It may be in association with this tradition that the wise men who visited the infant Jesus are reputed to have come from the East (cf. Matt. 2:1; Gk. *apó anatolṓn*; cf. Num. 23:7, LXX); suggestions for their origins range from Arabia or the Syrian desert to Parthia or Persia.

EAST COUNTRY (Heb. *ʾereṣ qeḏem*). Most likely the desert region southeast of Palestine, where Abraham sent the sons of his concubines (Gen. 25:6). At Zech. 8:7 the expression *ʾereṣ mizraḥ* ("land of the sunrise") complements *ʾereṣ mᵉḇôʾ* ("land of the sunset"; RSV "west country") to represent the entire world.

EAST GATE (Heb. *šaʿar hammizraḥ*). A gate in Jerusalem mentioned at Neh. 3:29 but not included among the city gates repaired during the governorship of Nehemiah. It may have been a temple gate, the "east gate of the house of the Lord, . . . which faces east" (Ezek. 10:19; 11:1); the "outer gate of the sanctuary," which faced east, was to remain shut (44:1-3) because it was the gate by which the glory of the Lord entered the reconsecrated temple (43:1, 4). At Jer. 19:2 the KJV translates Heb. *šaʿar haḥarsîṭ* (Q, "Potsherd Gate") as "East Gate."

EAST WIND (Heb. *qāḏîm*). Another name for the sirocco, a dry, hot, piercing wind (Job 27:21; Isa. 27:8) from the wilderness (Hos. 13:15; cf. Job 1:19) or the desert (Jer. 4:11; Hab. 1:9; so NIV; cf. KJV, JB). The sirocco blows intermittently between April and June and during the latter part of September. The spring east wind makes the young plants wither quickly (Ezek. 17:10; 19:12), and causes considerable damage to the early crops (Gen. 41:6). On at least two occasions Israel interpreted this wind as an instrument of God: at Exod. 10:13 the east wind brought to Egypt a dense swarm of locusts, and at 14:21 it parted the Reed Sea, allowing the Hebrews to cross.

EASTER.* Festival celebrating the resurrection of Jesus Christ. The name, which has been attested as early as the eighth century A.D., is believed to have derived from annual sacrifices in honor of Eostre, the Anglo-Saxon spring goddess. The Eastern church, following the practice of early Jewish Christians, first observed the celebration on the fourteenth of Nisan, the first day of Passover. The Western church, following the Gospel accounts of Christ's resurrection (Matt. 28:1 par.), set the festival on a Sunday, the first to follow the new moon which occurs on or immediately after the vernal (spring) equinox as determined by the Council of Nicaea (325); thus the dates for Easter may range from March 22 to April 25. Eastern Orthodox churches, which employ a different system of calibration, may observe the festival one, four, or five weeks later.

Following earlier English translations (Tyndale, Coverdale), the KJV at Acts 12:4 reads "Easter" for Gk. *páscha,* the seven-day Passover festival after which Herod Agrippa I intended to sentence and execute Peter.

EASTERN SEA (Heb. *yām haqqaḏmônî*). Another name for the Dead Sea (Ezek. 47:18; Joel 2:20; KJV "east sea"; Zech. 14:8; KJV "former sea").

EBAL [ēʹbəl] (Heb. *ʿēḇāl* "bare").
1. The third son of Shobal and a descendant of the Horite Seir (Gen. 36:23; 1 Chr. 1:40).
2. One of the sons of Joktan whose ancestor was Shem (1 Chr. 1:22; cf. v. 17). In the parallel passage (Gen. 10:28) his name is Obal.
3. A mountain north of Shechem and identified with contemporary Jebel Eslāmîyeh. Rising 940 m. (3080 ft.) above sea level, it is separated by a valley from Mt. Gerizim to the north. It was here that Joshua, following his victory over Ai, built an altar to the Lord (Josh. 8:30), thereby executing the divine command issued to Moses in the wilderness (Deut. 27:4-8). Here, too, he renewed the covenant by inscribing a copy of the Mosaic law on the rock and reading the blessings and curses of the law to the Hebrews who stood on Mts. Ebal and Gerizim; the ark of the covenant he placed in the valley between them (Josh. 8:32-35). In the covenant renewal ceremony half of the congregation pronounced the curses of the law from Mt. Ebal and the other half pronounced the blessings from Mt. Gerizim (Deut. 11:29; cf. 27:13). Because of the negative association of Mt. Ebal which thus derived from this practice, the Samaritan Pentateuch emended Deut. 27:4 to read "Gerizim" as the place where the altar and copy of the law were to be erected.

EBED [ēʹbəd] (Heb. *ʿeḇeḏ* "servant").
1. The father of Gaal the adversary of Abimelech (Judg. 9:26, 35).

2. The son of Jonathan, who, accompanied by "fifty men," returned from exile with Ezra the scribe (Ezra 8:6).

EBED-MELECH [ēʹbĭd mĕlʹĭk] (Heb. *ʿeḇeḏ-meleḵ* "servant [lit. "slave"] of the king"). An Ethiopian "eunuch" (so the MT at Jer. 38:7; LXX omits), probably a court official, who petitioned the Judean king Zedekiah to release the prophet Jeremiah from the cistern into which he had been thrown for preaching surrender to Nebuchadnezzar. The king agreed to his request, and the faithful foreigner, aided by thirty men, succeeded in pulling Jeremiah from the pit (vv. 7-13). In response to this act of kindness, the Lord instructed the prophet, now stationed in the court of the guards, to announce to Ebed-melech that his life would be spared when Jerusalem was destroyed (39:15-18). Though the book of Jeremiah does not specifically mention the Ethiopian among those spared by Nebuchadnezzar (39:10ff.), he may indeed have survived the holocaust.

EBENEZER [ĕbʹə nēʹzər] (Heb. *ʿeḇen hāʿezer* "stone of help").
1. A site at which the Philistines defeated Israel's army (1 Sam. 4:1ff.) and where they captured the ark of the covenant, which the Hebrews had taken to battle (5:1). Located opposite Aphek (modern Râs el-ʿAin), the site may be that of modern ʿIzbet Ṣarṭeh; an ostracon discovered at the site bears an inscription which may be the earliest Hebrew abecedary (elementary alphabet) yet discovered (twelfth-eleventh centuries B.C.).
2. The place where Samuel erected a stone to commemorate a victory over the Philistines (1 Sam. 7:12). The site is described as between Mizpah and "Jeshanah" (so RSV; MT *šēn*), thus north of Mizpah in the vicinity of Burj el-Isanah, about 5 km. (3 mi.) north of Jifneh.

EBER [ēʹbər] (Heb. *ʿēḇer*).
1.† The great-grandson of Shem and the son of Shelah (Gen. 10:21-24; 11:14-17; cf. 1 Chr. 1:17-27) and an ancestor of Jesus (Luke 3:35; KJV "Heber"). He is regarded as the eponymous ancestor of the Hebrews, here understood in an ethnic rather than a social sense (cf. Heb. *ʿiḇrʿ,* which some scholars interpret as "those from beyond [the river Euphrates]," i.e., from Haran; cf. Gen. 11:31; but *see* HABIRU). The name has been associated by some with Ebrum (Eb. *Ibrûm, Ibrium*), under whose kingship the empire of Ebla reached its greatest splendor. At Num. 24:24 Eber should be read as the "region beyond" rather than as a proper name.
2. A descendant of Gad (1 Chr. 5:13).
3. One of the three sons of Elpaal from the tribe of Benjamin (1 Chr. 8:12).
4. The second of a number of sons of Shashak, a Benjaminite (1 Chr. 8:22).
5. A priest and the head of the house of Amok during the postexilic ministry of Jehoiakim (Neh. 12:20).

EBEZ [ēʹbəz] (Heb. *ʿeḇeṣ*). A city within the tribal territory of Issachar (Josh. 19:20; KJV "Abez"); its site is still unknown.

EBIASAPH [ə bīʹə săf] (Heb. *ʿeḇyāsāp* "father has

increased"). A Levite of the lineage of Kohath, said to have been the father of Assir (so 1 Chr. 6:23, 37) or of Kore (9:19). At Exod. 6:24 he is called Abiasaph.

EBIONITES [ē′bĭ ə nīts] (Gk. *Ebiōnaioi*).† An ascetic Jewish-Christian sect which flourished in the second-fourth centuries A.D., subsequently judged heretical (cf. Irenaeus *Adv. haer.* i.26.2).

Some scholars have traced the sect to an eponymous founder, Ebion, but the name probably derives from the members' impoverished state (cf. Heb. *'ebyôn* "poor") as refugees following the destruction of Jerusalem in A.D. 70 during the First Jewish Revolt. Although that designation may have first been applied to all Christians in Palestine (*see* POOR), it appears to have been accorded particular significance by the sect, who identified with Jesus' teachings about the poor and the dangers of material possessions.

Theologically, the Ebionites differed from standard Christianity, earning derision by some Church Fathers for the "poverty" of their christology and their strict emphasis on the Mosaic law (cf. Origen *Contra Celsum* ii.1; Eusebius *HE* iii.27.2). Although some branches of the sect were considered more heretical than others (cf. Origen *Contra Celsum* v.61; Epiphanius *Haer.* XXIX-XXX), for the most part they rejected the Virgin Birth and the incarnation, viewing Jesus as an ordinary man empowered by the Holy Spirit at his baptism, and denied salvation by faith alone. They rejected the Pauline Epistles as well as certain "post-Mosaic" additions to the Pentateuch.

The gospel of the Ebionites, allegedly the only such work accepted by the sect, is known only from fragments cited by Epiphanius (*Haer.* xxx). Identified by some with the gospel according to the Hebrews (cf. Jerome *De vir. ill.* ii), this second-century A.D. apocryphal gospel is actually a Judaistic and Gnostic abridgment of the gospel of Matthew. Beginning with the account of John the Baptist, it includes the call of the disciples, Jesus' baptism, and is said to have included the Last Supper and Christ's passion and resurrection. In addition to various interpretations in keeping with the sect's beliefs, the work records that Jesus abolished the irrelevant portions of Mosaic law, namely the Mosaic sacrifices, but not the law as such. Although some scholars have suggested the Sermons of Peter, a pericope of the Pseudo-Clementine literature, as an Ebionite work, the gospel of the Ebionites remains the only primary source of the group's beliefs.

Despite similarities in the ascetic lifestyles of the Ebionites and the Qumran community which produced the Dead Sea Scrolls, theological differences as well as chronological separation preclude identification of the Jewish Essenes and the Christian Ebionites.

Bibliography. J. A. Fitzmyer, "The Qumrân Scrolls, the Ebionites, and Their Literature," *TS* 16 (1955): 335-372; L. E. Keck, "The Poor among the Saints in Jewish Christianity and Qumran," *ZNW* 57 (1966): 54-78.

EBLA [eb′lə].* Capital of a major Canaanite empire which flourished in the third-second millennia B.C. At the height of its power (*ca.* 2500-2350) Ebla was a city-state of some 260,000 people maintaining political and economic control over lesser vassal cities in an empire stretching as far as Cyprus, Anatolia, the Sinai peninsula, and the Mesopotamian highlands. Despite scattered references to the city in ancient texts and its occurrence on a third millennium map from Nuzi, its location was unknown until 1974, when excavations identified it with Tell Mardikh in northwestern Syria, 67 km. (41 mi.) southwest of Aleppo; the empire itself was unattested prior to the discovery at that site of the palace archive containing some eighteen thousand cuneiform tablets including administrative texts, treaties, and commercial documents.

Preliminary examination of the archive suggests that Ebla had become an advanced civilization by the time Sargon of Akkad formed the first Sumerian empire in 2300. When Sargon recaptured Mari from the Eblaite general Iblul-il and then subjected Ebla, King Ar-ennum was supplanted by Ebrum (Eb. *Ibrûm*; *see* EBER); it was under Ebrum that the empire reached its greatest extent, dominating even Akkad itself. Ebla was destroyed *ca.* 2200 by the resurgent Naram-sin, but the city was rebuilt and survived as a cultural center until *ca.* 1800, the date usually assigned to the Hebrew patriarchs.

Written in cuneiform script, some eighty percent of the texts discovered are composed in Sumerian. The remainder represent a previously unattested language, tentatively identified as Paleocanaanite, a Northwest Semitic dialect related to Phoenician and Biblical Hebrew. Evidence of an efficient scribal class includes scientific lists of animals, geographical atlases, and professional rosters as well as Eblaite grammatical texts, syllabaries for learning Sumerian, and bilingual Sumerian-Eblaite vocabularies. Literary texts include mythological texts, hymns and incantations, rituals, and collections of proverbs.

Some five hundred deities comprise the Eblaite pantheon, chief of whom was Dagon, later to be adopted by the Philistines. Other gods included Rasap (Ugar. *ršp*; Heb. *rešep*), Šamaš, Adad (Hadad), and Astar, a masculine counterpart to Astarte (Ashtoreth). Also attested are Sumerian gods such as Enki and Enlil and the Hurrian Adamma and Astabi. Tentative readings of personal names suggest the presence of the names Il (Canaanite El or the generic term "god") and Ya or Yaw, whose association with Yahu or Yahweh has been hotly disputed.

The impact of Eblaite studies on biblical scholarship cannot yet be ascertained. Because the texts predate biblical events by some six hundred to fifteen hundred years, direct relationship cannot be proven between Eblaite forms of the names Abraham, Ishmael, Esau, and Saul and their biblical namesakes. Eblaite stories of creation and a great flood more closely resemble Mesopotamian versions than biblical accounts, suggesting merely indirect cultural influence. However, the texts provide third millennium documentation of such cities as Salim (forerunner of Jerusalem), Megiddo, Hazor, Gaza, Lachish, and Joppa; of particular interest are references to the cities of the plain recorded in Gen. 14.

Bibliography. P. Matthiae, *Ebla: An Empire Rediscovered* (Garden City: 1981); G. Pettinato, *The Archives of Ebla* (Garden City: 1981).

EBONY (Heb. K *hôḇānîm*, Q *hoḇnîm*). The heavy, black wood of various species of trees belonging to the genus *Diospyros,* notably the species *Diospyros ebenum* König, native to India and possibly to Ethiopia. Ebony, the heartwood of these tropical trees (whose annual growth rings are almost imperceptible), was greatly valued among the ancients who used it for inlaying and for making furniture. Various ebony objects have been discovered in the tomb of Pharaoh Tutankhamen. The Old Testament refers to ebony as an item of trade (Ezek 27:15). According to the KJV and the JB rendering of this passage, the Dedanites, an Arabian tribe, brought this wood to Tyre; in view of the context and on the basis of the LXX reading, the RSV and the NIV attribute this introduction to the inhabitants of Rhodes, who did traffic in an inferior quality of ebony.

EBRON [ē'brən] (Heb. *'eḇrōn*). A town in the tribal territory of Asher (Josh. 19:28; KJV "Hebron"), probably the same as Abdon (so JB, NIV) mentioned at 21:30; 1 Chr. 6:74. The form is generally explained as a copyist's error, reading Heb. resh for daleth.

EBRONAH (Num. 33:34-35, KJV). *See* ABRONAH.

ECBATANA [ĕk băt'ə nə] (Aram. *'aḥmᵉṭā'*; O. Pers. *hagmatāna* "place of gathering"[?]). Originally the capital city of Media, allegedly founded by King Deioces *ca.* 700 B.C. (so Herodotus *Hist.* i.96); after capture by Cyrus the Great in 548, it became the summer residence of the Achaemenid rulers (Xenophon *Anabasis* iii.5.15). According to Ezra 6:2-3 (KJV "Achmetha") a scroll kept in the royal archives there contained a decree of Cyrus concerning the postexilic Jews.

A city of marvelous beauty fortified by seven concentric walls (Herodotus *Hist.* i.98; cf. Jdt. 1:1-5; Polybius *Hist.* x.27), Ecbatana was situated along the primary trade route from Central Asia to northwest Mesopotamia. Ruins of the ancient city are buried beneath contemporary Hamadân, a major trade center of Iran at the foot of Mt. Orontes 290 km. (180 mi.) west-northwest of Tehran. No extensive archaeological excavations have been conducted at the site, but chance discovery of Old Persian inscriptions and gold and silver objects underscores its importance. A tomb traditionally associated with Esther and Mordecai is most likely that of a fifth-century A.D. Sassanian queen.

ECCLESIASTES [ĭ klē'sĭ ăs'tēz], **BOOK OF.**†
Third of the five scrolls (Megilloth) in the Writings, the third division of the Hebrew canon.

I. Name

Ecclesiastes is the English rendering (borrowed from the Latin Vulgate) of Gk. *Ekklēsiastēs,* the title given the book in the LXX. It represents an attempted translation of the book's Hebrew title, taken from the author's pseudonym, Qoheleth (alternately Koheleth; Heb. *qōheleṭ*), which means a person who speaks in the *qāhāl,* the assembly or congregation, and thus one who holds a meeting or gathers around himself a circle of listeners. Customarily rendered "the Preacher," the Hebrew word is a feminine participle, a form used to designate an office or position of dignity as well as

the person who holds the office (cf. Ezra 2:55, 57; Neh. 7:57).

II. Author and Date

Rabbinic tradition, following the author's impersonation in chs. 1–2 and the superscription by a later editor in 1:1, attributes the book to Solomon, the master sage. However, unlike the pseudepigraphic works, the author does not specifically credit the book to Solomon or even use that name; the editor's designation of him as a "son" of David (1:1) could be taken in the sense of a "follower" or disciple. Quite possibly the "Preacher" alluded to Solomonic tradition (and thus helped to earn canonical status for the book) in order to strengthen his evaluation of human wisdom (1:12-18) and pleasure (2:1-11). Indeed, the book contains many statements which do not fit the perspective or lifestyle of a monarch (e.g., 4:1, 13; 5:8 [MT 7]; 7:19; 8:2-4; 9:14-15; 10:4-7). Furthermore, language and sentence structure bear many similarities to Mishnaic Hebrew, and both the highly developed wisdom motifs and the questioning of traditional beliefs and values point to postexilic composition. Accordingly, scholars since the time of Martin Luther have recognized the work as that of an anonymous Jewish wisdom teacher living in Jerusalem sometime in the third century B.C.

III. Contents

Firmly rooted in the wisdom tradition, the book of Ecclesiastes combines empirical observation and reasoned reflection to seek out the very meaning of life and to assess the limits of human satisfaction. The author's highly repetitive style, which is typically Semitic, makes the book difficult to outline. In essence, Ecclesiastes represents an attempt to demonstrate the Preacher's primary conclusion (1:2-3), the basic contrast between God and mankind as evidenced through the limits of human knowledge — particularly concerning the ways of God — a contrast made even more severe by the oversimplifications of traditional wisdom and its smug assessment of human capacity. Throughout the book this conclusion is reiterated, illustrated, and reinforced and interwoven with "words of advice," a second, more positive theme, that people should take pleasure in the simple blessings of life even now as they faithfully adhere to the will of God (2:24-26; 3:12-15, 22; 5:18-20 [MT 17-19]; 8:15; 9:7-10; cf. 11:9–12:1).

The theme of the limitations of human existence is treated in four sections. In 1:4–2:26 the author illustrates the human plight in terms of the very nature of life, the inadequacies of wisdom and pleasure, the common fate of mankind, and the futility of labor. In 3:1–4:16 he points to God's control of human events, the inevitability of death, the prevalence of oppression, the loneliness of wealth, and the ephemerality of prestige. In 5:13 (MT 12)–6:12 he shows the insatiability of the quest for wealth and human inability to know or change the future. Finally, in 8:10–9:12 he demonstrates the inequities of retribution for good and evil, the mysteriousness of God's ways, the certainty of death, and the basic uncertainty of life.

Among the words of advice for the here and now, the Preacher offers admonitions to honor God through pure worship and faithful fulfillment of vows, to anticipate corruption in government, and to maintain a proper perspective on wealth (5:1-12 [MT 4:17–5:11]). In 7:1–8:9 he presents a series of aphorisms in defense of the "good life" — stressing honor, sobriety, caution, compromise, wisdom with wealth, and moderation rather than excessive piety, as well as distrust of women. A final collection of advice (9:13–12:8) contains a parable on the inadequacies of wisdom, various proverbs for practical living, and an allegory on aging.

The book concludes with an epilogue (12:9-14), most likely by an editor, which includes comments on the Preacher's work and intentions, the limitations of all wisdom (including the book of Ecclesiastes), and a final admonition to adhere reverently to God's commandments.

IV. Theology

Both Jewish and early Christian leaders were hesitant to accord the book canonical status, largely because of its rationalistic, overtly negative assessment of traditional beliefs. Nevertheless, Ecclesiastes does indeed make a positive contribution to biblical thought. By contrasting the magnificence of God, his freedom and wisdom, with the limitations of so much of human striving, the book focuses attention on eternal truths and the blessings to be derived from a proper quest for the meaning of existence. The author stresses the unfathomable scope of divine majesty by contrasting God with the all too apparent limits of the human condition. With overstated irony he faults the excesses of standard Hebrew wisdom in comparison with the simple truths to be found in life, the blessings of grace and providence. He urges mankind to live ethically, in the sincere reverence for God which is the sole source of meaning, and in celebration of life itself without concern for personal gain, concentrating rather on gratitude for God's simple gifts of sustenance, purposeful endeavor, and love for all creation.

Bibliography. R. Gordis, *Koheleth — the Man and His World,* 3rd ed. (New York: 1968); D. A. Hubbard, *Beyond Futility: Messages of Hope from the Book of Ecclesiastes* (Grand Rapids: 1976); C. F. Whitely, *Koheleth.* BZAW 148 (1979).

ECCLESIASTICUS. *See* SIRACH, WISDOM OF JESUS THE SON OF.

ECSTASY (Gk. *ékstasis* from Gk. *exístēmi* "stand apart from [the usual]"). A state of heightened emotion in which the normal range of consciousness is exceeded and, especially in religious contexts, a state permitting revelatory experiences.

In the Old Testament, Saul, accompanied by prophets, had such an encounter with the Spirit of God spontaneously (1 Sam. 19:23-24). The prophets' ecstasy, on the other hand, was usually induced by prayer or fasting (Dan. 10:2-9). Though the Old Testament is more concerned with the content of divine revelation than with human experience of God's self-disclosure, Ezekiel (Ezek. 1:1–3:15) and Micaiah (1 Kgs. 22:19-23) may have been describing in part their ecstatic experiences.

In the New Testament Gk. *ékstasis* (rendered "trance") occurs three times in the book of Acts. In one instance Peter receives and recounts the vision of the clean and unclean animals (Acts 10:10; 11:5); Paul alludes to a similar experience while praying in the temple at Jerusalem (22:17). In his second Corinthian letter Paul divulges that fourteen years earlier he had been "caught up to the third heaven" (2 Cor. 12:2), referring most likely to a trance, possibly just prior to his first missionary journey. At 5:13 he remarks that the state of being beside oneself enables communion with God while the normal state of consciousness is conducive to fellowship with believers. This may be a sequel to his warnings in 1 Corinthians against the improper use of spiritual gifts, notably that of speaking in tongues (1 Cor. 14:26-32), which appeared to some as an expression of "madness" (v. 23; cf. Acts 2:13, 15 where the outpouring of the Spirit is interpreted as a state of intoxication).

Bibliography. I. M. Lewis, *Ecstatic Religion* (Baltimore: 1971); A. Oepke, "ἔκστασις," *TDNT* 2 (1964): 449-460.

ED [ĕd] (Heb. *'ēd*). An altar erected at the Jordan river by the Transjordanian tribes (so KJV, Josh. 22:34) symbolizing that they had witnessed (RSV "Witness") God's majesty and faithfulness. Because the name does not occur in the MT, some commenta-

Fragment of an Ecclesiastes scroll from Qumran (by courtesy of the Israel Department of Antiquities and Museums)

tors interpret the qualifying phrase which follows (so NIV "A Witness Between Us that the Lord is God") as its name (cf. Gen. 31:47). The location of the site is unknown.

EDAR (Gen. 35:21, KJV). *See* EDER (PLACE) **2.**

EDEN [ē′dən] (Heb. *ʿēḏen* "delight") **(PERSON).** The son of Joah, and one of the Levites who ministered during the reign of King Hezekiah (2 Chr. 29:12); he may be the same as the person mentioned at 31:15 who assisted in the distribution of the freewill offering.

EDEN [ē′dən] (Heb. *ʿēḏen* "delight") **(PLACE).**
1.† A region in which God planted a garden ("garden in Eden," Gen. 2:8; cf. v. 10; at v. 15 and elsewhere in the Old Testament the garden and the country are identical) as a dwelling place for Adam and Eve.
According to some scholars Heb. *ʿdn* is derived from the Sumerian-Akkadian noun *edinu* "wilderness"; nevertheless, this philological interpretation is not in itself sufficient to link Eden conclusively with a specific location such as the wilderness near the Persian Gulf. Others have connected the name of this garden with Heb. *ʿēḏen* "delight" (cf. Neh. 9:25, "delighted themselves"; Ps. 36:8, "of thy delights") and understand it as "garden of delight" (cf. LXX Gk. *parádeisos tḗs trýphēs* at Gen. 2:15; 3:24). The latter interpretation finds support in the popular understanding of Eden as a lush paradise (cf. Ezek. 36:35; Joel 2:3) fit for God's residence (cf. 28:13; 31:9). *See* PARADISE.
Attempts to ascertain the location of the garden remain largely hypothetical, primarily because of the geographical details provided. In general, it is to be found somewhere "in the east" (cf. Gen. 2:8), which from the standpoint of Palestine would place it in Mesopotamia. More precise identification depends on interpretation of the four rivers said to branch from a common source in Eden (vv. 10-14). Of these only the Tigris (Heb. *ḥiddeqel*; Sum. *idigna*) and the Euphrates (Heb. *pᵉraṭ*) can be identified with certainty; the others, Pishon and Gihon, may be tributaries or rivulets which flow into the Tigris and Euphrates. Moreover, Heb. *yāṣᵉʾā* (RSV "flowed out"; KJV "went out") may more correctly mean here "rises in," suggesting a confluence of the rivers, known as the Shatt el-ʿArab, immediately north of their emptying into the Persian Gulf.
Noting the tendency of the Genesis accounts to provide a historicized setting for common ancient Near Eastern traditions, other scholars view Eden as a symbol of life lived in harmony with God. They take the phrase "in the east" as a reference to the origin of life and light, pointing to the sun's rising in the east.
Eden serves as the setting for what critical scholars regard as a second account of creation and for the narrative of the fall of mankind (Gen. 2:4b–3:24). According to this account God planted the garden for the sake of the man whom he had already created. The garden was described as full of trees, including the tree of life (2:9) and the tree of the knowledge of good and evil (v. 17). Though the man cultivated the garden as he had been charged to do (v. 15), he and the woman ate from the forbidden tree of the knowledge of good and evil and thus disrupted their

harmonious relationship with their Maker. For this they were expelled from the garden, lest they eat from the tree of life and thus gain immortality (3:22-24).
The prophet Isaiah compares Judah's future state with the primordial glory of Eden (Isa. 51:3), suggesting that God's people would be restored to a magnificent Golden Age (cf. Ezek. 36:35). Alluding to the fall of mankind, Ezekiel raises a lamentation over the king of Tyre (28:13). In his allegory of the cedar, the prophet describes Egypt's past splendor as exceeding the glories of Eden (31:9).
2. A city located in Telassar (2 Kgs. 19:12), probably along the upper course of the Euphrates in the vicinity of Carchemish. The "people of Eden" (KJV "children of Eden"; JB "Edenites") are included among those conquered by the Assyrians (2 Kgs. 19:12), and at Ezek. 27:23 Eden is mentioned with other cities that traded with Tyre (cf. Neo-Assyr. *Bit-adini*). The name Beth-eden occurs at Amos 1:5 (*see* BETH-EDEN).

EDEN, HOUSE OF (Amos 1:5, KJV). *See* BETH-EDEN.

EDER [ē′dər] (Heb. *ʿēḏer* "flock") **(PERSON).**
1. A Benjaminite residing at Jerusalem (1 Chr. 8:15; KJV "Ader").
2. A Levite, the second son of Mushi, and a descendant of Merari who lived during the reign of King David (1 Chr. 23:21-23; 24:30).

EDER [ē′dər] (Heb. *ʿēḏer* "flock") **(PLACE).**
1. The name of a tower, possibly a watchtower beyond which Jacob settled following the death of his beloved Rachel (Gen. 35:21; KJV "Edar"; NIV "Migdal Eder"; JB "Migdal-eder"). Located between Bethlehem and Hebron, the site has been proposed as a small village east of Siar el-Ganam or as a place near Keniset er-Rawāt. The same tower occurs at Mic. 4:8 ("tower of the flock"), where it stands for Jerusalem (par. "hill of the daughter of Jerusalem"), which, like a watchtower (so NIV), figuratively overlooks the actions of the people of Eden.
2. A village in the Shephelah of Judah (Josh. 15:21), perhaps Khirbet el-ʿAdar, 8 km. (5 mi.) south of Gaza or a city farther to the east.

EDICT. *See* DECREE.

EDIFICATION. A Pauline metaphor meaning spiritual and moral growth among believers (Gk. *oikodomḗ* "act and result of building"; cf. 2 Cor. 10:8, "building up"; Matt. 7:24, 26 refers to the literal construction of a house). The apostle exhorts mature believers to consider their immature fellows in Christ and to help them "become stronger" (so JB; Rom. 15:2). At 1 Cor. 14 he urges the Corinthian Christians, especially those who had been speaking in tongues (v. 4), to act also for the "benefit" of others and for the "common good" (vv. 17, 26, JB). At 1 Tim. 1:4 the RSV reads "training" (Gk. *oikonomía*; JB "design"; NIV "work") rather than "edifying" (KJV; Gk. *oikodomía*), which is the result of disciplined faith and is nothing like mythic or genealogical "speculations" (so RSV).

EDOM [ē′dəm] (Heb. *'eḏôm*; Akk. *Udumu*; Egyp. *Aduma*).† A country neighboring on Israel, located south of Moab and east of the Arabah; its inhabitants were the Edomites (Heb. *'aḏōmîm*). The name is derived from the common Semitic root *'dm* "red, ruddy," an apt description of the red sandstone and soil in the region, and is an alternate designation for the people's eponymous ancestor Esau (Gen. 25:25, 30; cf. 36:1). In postexilic times many of these people settled in southern Judea, then known as IDUMEA (cf. LXX, Josephus). *See also* SEIR.

I. Territory

Edom's northern boundary ran along the deep ravine of the brook Zered (Wâdī el-Ḥesā), the southern border of Moab. The southern boundary extended, by the tenth century B.C., as far as Ezion-geber (Tell el-Kheleifeh) at the northern tip of the Gulf of Aqabah. Lacking any distinctive geographical features, the western and eastern limits cannot be determined with any degree of precision; such may have been the case in ancient times as well, when the regions were inhabited by nomadic or transhumant peoples perhaps only nominally loyal to Edom. At any rate, Edomite territory extended to both sides of the Arabah, the barren depression which runs north-south between the Dead Sea and the Gulf of Aqabah; to the west it merged with the Sinai wilderness (cf. Num. 20:16), to the east with the Arabian desert.

The core of Edom ranges from an altitude of some 1525-1615 m. (5000-5300 ft.) in the northern portion to 1735 m. (5700 ft.) in the south. The chief strongholds were Bozrah (modern Buṣeirah) in the north and Teman (modern Tawīlân) in the south. The King's Highway, the easternmost road connecting Egypt with Aram (Syria) and Mesopotamia, ran north-south through the middle of this territory; other major routes connected Edom with trade throughout the Fertile Crescent and constituted its primary source of revenue. Much of this region is characterized by miles of red sandstone and limestone (cf. Jer. 49:16; Obad. 3), befitting the biblical description of an area lacking "the fatness of the earth" and deprived of "the dew of heaven" (Gen. 27:39). The slopes of the Seir mountain range (Jebel esh-Shera'), by contrast, receive sufficient copper and iron deposits, an important contributor to Edom's wealth.

II. History

Archaeological evidence attests to the existence of an Edomite civilization between 2300-2000 B.C., which was destroyed *ca.* 1900, possibly by Chedorlaomer (Gen. 14) or some other foreign people. Egyptian texts refer to raids made by Edomite bedouins into Egypt and their subsequent defeat by Pharaoh Rameses III (*ca.* 1170). In the thirteenth-eleventh centuries Egypt controlled the Edomite mines in the Negeb.

The first biblical references to the Edomites are found at Gen. 36, which mentions Edomite chiefs (vv. 15-19, 40-43) and kings (vv. 31-39; cf. 1 Chr. 1:43-51), both descendants of Esau, the brother of Jacob. Though Gen. 36:31 claims that these rulers reigned before King Saul, Hadar (or Hadad), mentioned at v. 39, was actually a contemporary of the Israelite monarch. Most likely their role was that of tribal

chieftain; succession may have been dynastic (cf. 1 Kgs. 11:14) but was probably a nonhereditary position involving, on a rotating basis, leadership of an association of tribes.

The first recorded Israelite contacts with the Edomites occurred after the wilderness wanderings when the Hebrews asked permission to pass through Edom along the King's Highway in order to enter the promised land from the east. The king of Edom, whose name is not given, refused them peaceful passage, however, forcing the Hebrews to go around (Num. 20:14-21; cf. Deut. 2:4-8; Judg. 11:17). Later, after the Conquest, King Saul fought the Edomites (1 Sam. 14:47). This hostility does not seem to have been permanent, though, judging from his friendly relations with a certain Edomite, Doeg, whom he appointed as the chief of his herdsmen (1 Sam. 21:7; cf. 22:9, 18). Saul's successor, David, killed some eighteen thousand Edomites in the valley of Salt, placed garrisons in Edom, and made the Edomites his servants (2 Sam. 8:13-14). (1 Kgs. 11:15-16 attributes David's successful campaign to his general Joab, who during a six-month period killed "every male.")

Hadad III, said to have been Solomon's adversary (1 Kgs. 11:14), was unable to wrest Israelite control from Ezion-geber (9:26); Hadad's descendants may have been deputy governors under Israel rather than local kings (see 22:47), though one of them had the title "king" (2 Kgs. 3:9, 13, 26). The Edomites were unable to regain their independence during the reign of the Judahite king Jehoshaphat (873-839), but they may have made an unsuccessful raid into Judah (cf. 2 Chr. 20:10-12, 22-23) and perhaps were instrumental in the destruction of Jehoshaphat's fleet at Ezion-geber (1 Kgs. 22:48). At any rate, they revolted successfully during the reign of Jehoram, Jehoshaphat's son (2 Kgs. 8:20-22), regaining control of the Arabah and Ezion-geber.

The next centuries saw Edom's fortunes fluctuate. Judah's king Amaziah (800-783), who defeated the Edomites and took their city of Sela (2 Kgs. 14:7 par.), ended Edom's fifty-year period of independence, and Uzziah (Azariah), his son, restored the city of Elath to Judah (v. 22; cf. 2 Chr. 26:2). But Judah's power eventually diminished. Embroiled in a war with the northern tribes and Aram, Ahaz of Judah (735-715) was forced to yield Elath to the Edomites (2 Kgs. 16:6; KJV, NIV "Syria/Aram," following MT Heb. *'arām*). He also suffered an Edomite invasion and victory over his own troops (2 Chr. 28:17).

Meanwhile, the Edomites had to reckon also with a resurging Assyrian Empire, which imposed tribute on them in the reigns of Adadnirari (*ca.* 800 B.C.) and Tiglath-pileser III (*ca.* 732 B.C.). During the next one hundred years, Edom was a vassal of Assyria — under Sennacherib (705-681), Esarhaddon (680-669), and Assurbanipal (669-627) — still paying tribute after an unsuccessful attempt at regaining independence *ca.* 713 (see *ANET*, pp. 287, 291, 294, 298). Edom's kings, though lacking the luster of their predecessors, at least managed to preserve their heritage, till they accepted Babylonian rule under Nebuchadnezzar in 604 (see Jer. 27:3).

Encouraged by the fall of Jerusalem in 587/586 and the subsequent deportation of the people of Judah to

Babylon (see Ps. 137:7; Lam. 4:21-22), the Edomites moved into southern Judah and settled near Hebron. (Nevertheless, several villages remained in Judean hands; cf. Neh. 11:25-28.) During the Persian period more Edomites moved into this region, now called Idumea, pressured by an influx of Nabateans who established their headquarters in the city of Petra; others remained and were assimilated by the Nabateans. Judas Maccabeus attacked the Edomites at Akrabattene, southwest of the Dead Sea, for their continued hostility toward Jews (1 Macc. 5:1-5, 65). During the reign of John Hyrcanus Edom was incorporated into the Jewish nation (135-105 B.C.), submitting even to the Jewish rite of circumcision (Josephus *Ant.* xiii.9.1 [257]; xv.7.9 [253-54]). They regained a measure of power, however, when Antipater, the father of Herod the Great, became the unofficial Jewish ruler of Palestine (63 B.C.), and later when he was appointed procurator of Judea (47 B.C.). During the siege of Jerusalem (*ca.* A.D. 70) the Idumeans sided with the Jewish zealots against the Romans, defending the ancient Jewish city tenaciously rather than mocking its fall as they had done some six hundred years earlier. Soon thereafter they were assimilated by various peoples.

III. Legacy

Archaeological excavations have corroborated the biblical testimony of Edomite idol worship (2 Chr. 25:14, "the gods of the men of Seir"). A pottery figurine of a fertility goddess has been discovered near Buṣeirah, while a pottery plaque representing a mother goddess has been unearthed at Tell el-Kheleifeh. Edom's most popular deity was Qauš (cf. "Koze," Josephus *Ant.* xv.7.9 [253]), the war-god, whose name is attested in several Edomite compound personal names.

The language of the Edomites was a Northwest Semitic dialect related to Biblical Hebrew and Moabite. Although Edomite writing survives only in inscriptions on ostraca, seals, and stamped jar handles, it is thought to have been represented by a sophisticated body of literature. Indeed, the tradition of Edomite wisdom is acknowledged by the Israelites (Jer. 49:7; Obad. 8), and some scholars suggest the origin of the book of Job in Edomite literature (cf. Jobab, Gen. 36:34; Eliphaz the Temanite, Job 2:11).

Despite their cultural if not historical ties (cf. Deut. 23:7; Amos 1:9, 11; Mal. 1:2), the relationship between Israel and Edom, particularly beginning with the Israelite Monarchy, was far from amicable. This constant hostility, probably largely fostered by the Hebrews' intense desire to gain control of the Edomite trade routes, is apparent in the writings of the Judahite prophets. The prophets were particularly offended by the Edomite role in the destruction of Jerusalem (Obad. 10-14), calling for divine retaliation in the form of Edom's total destruction (vv. 1-9; Isa. 34:5-6, 9; Jer. 49:7-22; Ezek. 25:12-14; Mal. 1:3-4). Amos also condemns them for their role in the slave trade (Amos 1:6).

Bibliography. J. R. Bartlett, "The Rise and Fall of the Kingdom of Edom," *PEQ* 104 (1972): 26-37; T. C. Vriezen, "The Edomite Deity Qaus," *OTS* 14 (1965): 330-353.

EDREI [ĕdʹrī ī] (Heb. *'eḏreʻî*).

1. One of the two residence cities of Og, king of Bashan (Deut. 1:4; Josh. 12:4; 13:12). After the Israelites had defeated Og near Edrei (Num. 21:33; Deut. 3:1), the city was assigned to Machir of the tribe of Manasseh (Josh. 13:31).

Located on one of the eastern tributaries of the Yarmuk, Edrei is most likely modern Derʻā, about 48 km. (30 mi.) east of the Sea of Galilee. Ruins of a subterranean city with streets and squares and even individual rooms ventilated by air holes have been discovered.

2. A city in the tribal territory of Naphtali whose location remains unknown (Josh. 19:37).

EDUCATION.† Among the Hebrews, who believed that having children was a divine blessing (e.g., Ps. 127:3; cf. v. 1), education (Heb. *tôrâ* "instruction," "teaching"; from *yārâ* "show" and thus "give direction"; cf. Torah, God's law or rule of conduct) occupied an important place. The Old Testament lists three educational goals: (1) children were to learn about God's mighty acts of deliverance, e.g., his sending plagues upon Egypt (Exod. 10:2), providing for Israel's exodus from Egypt (Deut. 6:20-21; 7:17-19), and institution of the Passover (Exod. 12:26-27; 13:7-8, 14); (2) they were to master such ethical precepts as justice (see Gen. 18:19) in order to mirror God's holiness (Lev. 19:2); and (3) they were to cultivate the faculties of wisdom, prudence, knowledge, and discretion (Prov. 1:2-4), virtues that would help them to get along with others. Clearly the Old Testament views education primarily as an initiation into the "fear of the Lord," which is the "beginning of knowledge" (Prov. 1:7).

I. History

A. Old Testament. The early Hebrews educated their children at home. The father was responsible for his children's religious training and often taught his sons domestic duties, such as tending sheep (1 Sam. 16:11) and working in the fields (2 Kgs. 4:18), as well as a trade; the mother introduced her daughters to household skills — baking (2 Sam. 13:8), spinning, and weaving (Exod. 35:25-26). Though the Hebrews favored sons over daughters, they encouraged their daughters to develop managerial skills (cf. Prov. 31:12-31) and prepared some of them for roles of leadership and influence. Consequently, both parents (cf. 1:8; 6:20) were obliged to instruct their children. Indeed, some mothers are credited as model educators (31:1).

The wealthy employed guardians for the education of their children; according to 2 Kgs. 10:1-2, 5-6, the royal sons were instructed by guardians after the death of their father Ahab. It may be that such guardians taught the children the art of writing. (*See also* WRITING.)

Some scholars believe that the phrases the "band of prophets" (1 Sam. 10:5, 10) and the "company of prophets" (19:20) refer to actual schools or educational institutions for teaching the skill of prophecy. It is certainly true that prophets had disciples (cf. Isa. 8:16), of whom Elisha, Elijah's pupil, was an outstanding example (cf. the use of "master" at 2 Kgs. 2:3; "sons of the prophets," v. 7). The Levites were in charge of instructing their younger members in their religious duties. Often they taught the people God's ordinances (Deut. 33:10) and statutes (Lev. 10:11) as well, sometimes with the encouragement of pious kings such as Jehoshaphat (2 Chr. 17:8-9) and Josiah (35:3).

During and after the Exile the Hebrews established schools, primarily to instill in the children of dispersed Jewish families respect for and familiarity with the Law. (This task was assigned to the scribes, who adopted the method of Ezra, the scribe par excellence.) According to Neh. 8, Ezra, more often called a scribe (Ezra 7:6; Neh. 8:1, 4, 9) than a priest (Neh. 8:2, 9), taught the people the divine law, which he himself had studied diligently (Ezra 7:6, 10). He instructed them from a "wooden pulpit," aided by several Levites who interpreted what he read for the masses (Neh. 8:2-8); it is conceivable that this large-scale program of adult education, which lasted several hours (v. 3, "from early morning to until midday"), was repeated in subsequent years. During the first century B.C. many scribes taught in the synagogues, the official public educational facilities of the day. The Pharisees, who took upon themselves the arduous task of preserving Israel's religious heritage, soon received authority to teach the Law, first in Jerusalem and later in other cities.

B. New Testament. In Jesus' time the synagogues were still the main educational centers for the Jews, though by then the scribes were being replaced by rabbis. The many local synagogues, both within and outside of Palestine, insured intimacy with the Law for those unable to travel to Jerusalem. Jesus, who was taught by the rabbis (Luke 2:46, "teachers") and in turn taught in the various synagogues (e.g., Matt. 4:23), often criticized the scribes according to the standard of the ideal scribe, who should disclose both old and new elements from his store of knowledge (Matt. 13:52). Among the Jewish educators was the famed Gamaliel I, who instructed the apostle Paul (Acts 22:3). The Hebrews of this time did not abandon education in the home, though, for Paul mentions explicitly that Timothy had learned the contents of the Law from his mother, Eunice (2 Tim. 1:5; cf. 2:15).

II. Method and Scope

The book of Proverbs is the Bible's best-known book of instruction. Urging children to listen carefully to their fathers and to heed their advice (1:8-19), the author upholds the value of wisdom (3:13), righteousness (4:18), and work (6:6); he contrasts these with wickedness (4:14; 6:12), sexual promiscuity (6:24-26; 7:6-27), and other vices (6:17-19). By building "precept upon precept" (see Isa. 28:10), a little at a time, and through firm but loving discipline (Prov. 3:11-12) — normally administered by means of a rod (13:24; 23:13-14; 29:15) — the father molded his children into responsible adults.

The Hebrews emphasized God in their education (e.g., Prov. 1:7) and, by and large, excluded secular subjects from their curricula. (This is true more of pious Palestinian Jews, who resented the Greek language and Greek culture, than of the Alexandrian Jews, many of whom could hardly speak Hebrew.) Thus, the Hebrews did not expose their children to the sciences

current in their day — astronomy, physics (the science of nature), biology, and mathematics — subjects highly esteemed among the Greeks and other Near Eastern cultures. Neither did they devote much time to the fine arts, which the Greeks regarded so highly. After all, Moses, who had been instructed "in all the wisdom of the Egyptians" (Acts 7:22), bequeathed to his countrymen the Law, which he learned from God himself rather than from manuals of Egyptian medicine, mathematics, and meteorology.

See also SYNAGOGUE.

Bibliography. G. Bertram, "παιδεύω," *TDNT* 5 (1967): 596-625; M. L. Clarke, *Higher Education in the Ancient World* (London: 1971); W. W. Jaeger, *Early Christianity and Greek Paideia* (Cambridge, Mass.: 1961); I. A. Muirhead, *Education in the New Testament*. Monographs in Christian Education 2 (New York: 1965).

EGLAH [ĕg′lə] (Heb. *'eglâ* "heifer"). One of the wives of King David, and the mother of Ithream (2 Sam. 3:5 par. 1 Chr. 3:3).

EGLAIM [ĕg′lĭ əm] (Heb. *'eglayim*). A town in the country of Moab mentioned in the oracle against Moab (Isa. 15:8). Eusebius (*Onom.* xiii) lists an Agallim, 8 Roman mi. south of Areopolis (biblical Rabbah, modern Amman). Some scholars believe that Eglaim is the same as Rujm el-Jilîmeh and preserves the Byzantine name Aegallim, while others identify the town with Khirbet Jaljul, about 6.5 km. (4 mi.) farther south.

EGLATH-SHELISHIYAH [ĕg′lăth shĭ lĭsh′ə yə] (Heb. *'eglaṭ šᵉlîšîyâ*). A place in Moab mentioned in the prophetic oracles against Moab (Isa. 15:5; Jer. 48:4). Because Eglath-shelishiyah occurs in apposition with Zoar (JB takes it as a gloss at Isa. 15:5) and Horonaim, some commentators regard it as a nickname (KJV "an heifer of three years old") symbolizing the beauty and strength of these two cities. Others, however, view it as a separate place of unknown location (cf. RSV, NIV; JB at Jer. 48:4). Still others interpret the name literally as "the third Eglath," assuming that there were three places with the same name.

EGLON [ĕg′lŏn] (Heb. *'eglôn* "young bull") **(PERSON).**† A Moabite king who together with the Ammonites and the Amalekites defeated Israel, captured Jericho, and oppressed the Hebrews for eighteen years (Judg. 3:12-14). Eglon was murdered by Ehud, Israel's second judge, who had come to deliver Israel's tribute. Pretending to have a private message for Eglon, the Benjaminite plunged his double-edged dagger into the obese king's stomach (vv. 15-25). *See* EHUD.

EGLON [ĕg′lŏn] (Heb. *'eglôn* "young bull") **(PLACE).**† A city in the Shephelah region of Judah near Lachish (Josh. 15:39). Under its king, Debir, Eglon joined the coalition headed by Adonizedek of Jerusalem which sought to punish Gibeon for entering a pact with Joshua (10:3-5). The Israelites prevailed decisively, and the five Amorite kings, who had hidden in the cave at Makkedah, were publicly humiliated and executed (vv. 16-27). Joshua then led the Israelites against Eglon, destroying it and murdering its inhabitants (vv. 34-35). It was subsequently assigned to the tribal territory of Judah (15:39).

Eglon is first attested in the early first-millenium B.C. Egyptian Execration Texts. An additional extrabiblical reference is found in a cuneiform text (*ca.* fourteenth century) from Tell el-Hesī.

Despite extensive explorations in the region, attempts to identify the site of Eglon remain inconclusive. Khirbet ʿAjlân (cf. Eusebius *Onom.* xlviii.18, Gk. *Agla*) was initially proposed, but the site lacks material remains prior to the Byzantine period. W. M. F. Petrie and others later suggested Tell en-Nejîleh. W. F. Albright placed Eglon 5 km. (3 mi.) to the northwest at Tell el-Hesī, which Petrie had identified with Lachish. That site, which many still identify with Eglon, was the first in Palestine to be examined by modern scientific archaeological methods. Eight major periods of occupation were discovered, and the city was shown to have been surrounded by "daughter" villages (cf. Josh. 15:39, 41). Like most other sites in the area, the tell shows massive destruction at the end of the Late Bronze Age (*ca.* 1200). G. E. Wright, however, has suggested that Tell el-Hesī was one of a series of defensive outposts for Lachish (Tell ed-Duweir), 11 km. (7 mi.) north. Following M. Noth, some scholars now favor Tell ʿAiṭûn, located west-southwest of Lachish, as the site, situated more logically from a geographical standpoint on Joshua's route from Lachish to Hebron (Josh. 10:34-37).

EGNATIAN WAY [ĕg nā′shĭ ən] (Lat. *Via Egnatia*). A Roman highway connecting the Adriatic and Aegean Seas, the most important east-west route in the Roman Empire, thus facilitating passage between Rome and Asia Minor. Built after the conquest of Greece in 146 B.C., it stretched from Dyrrhachium (Gk. *Epidamus*; modern Durrës [Durazzo], Albania) through northern Greece to Salonika. Roman merchants and troops could travel along the Appian Way as far as Brundisium (modern Brindisi), the southeasternmost port, and then cross the Adriatic by ship. At Dyrrhachium or Apollonia (modern Vlonë [Valona]), two ports in Epirus on the eastern shore of the Adriatic, they would continue their journey on the Egnatian Way, going as far as Neapolis (modern Kavala), the Aegean seaport of Philippi.

It was along this road that Paul, traveling west, established three churches during his second missionary journey — Philippi, Thessalonica, and Beroea (Acts 16:9–17:14).

EGYPT [ē′jĭpt] (Heb. *miṣrayim*; Gk. *Aigyptos*).† A land in northeastern Africa, sustained by the Nile river, which in ancient times encompassed the territory from the Mediterranean Sea as far south as the Fourth Cataract of the Nile; one of the earliest and greatest civilizations of the ancient world.

I. Name

The name Egypt is derived from Gk. *Aigyptos,* a term first attested in Homer's *Odyssey* (eighth century

B.C.) and is believed to be a transliteration of Egyp. *hwt-k3-pth* "house of the spirit of Ptah" (cf. EA *hikuptah*), an epithet of Memphis, the capital of Lower (northern) Egypt; apparently the term came to be used also for all of Lower Egypt and, by extension, for the entire country (cf. Hos. 9:6; Isa. 19:13). The Egyptians themselves called the country "Black Land" (Egyp. *kmt*; Copt. *kēme*) after the darkness of the soil in the Nile valley, in contrast to the "Red Land" (Egyp. *dašret*), the desert on either side of the valley. They also called their country the "Two Lands" (Egyp. *t3wy*), encompassing both Upper and Lower Egypt, as well as the "Beloved Land" (Egyp. *t3-mr3î*). Heb. *miṣrayim* reflects the common term applied to the country by non-Egyptians from at least the fourteenth century (Ugar. *mṣrm*; EA *miṣri*; Akk. *muṣur, muṣri*; cf. Egyp. *mṣrym,* a derivative meaning "Egyptian"); the suggestion that the term is a dual form incorporating both Upper and Lower Egypt is linguistically unsound. Although in general the Hebrew name designates all of Egypt, at Isa. 11:11 it refers only to Lower Egypt, distinguished there from Pathros (Egyp. *pa-to-resi* "south land") or Upper Egypt (cf. Jer. 44:15).

II. Geography

Ancient Egypt was bounded on the north by the Mediterranean Sea, on the west by the Libyan desert, on the south by the First Cataract of the Nile at Syene (and during the New Kingdom period [after *ca.* 1500] as far as the Fourth Cataract near Meroë), and on the east by the Arabian desert and the Wâdî el-ʿArish, the "Brook of Egypt" (cf. Num. 34:5). The biblical description "from Migdol to Syene" (Ezek. 29:10; 30:6) denotes all of Egypt, from the northeast to the First Cataract (cf. "from Dan to Beer-sheba").

As Hecataeus of Miletus observed in the sixth century (quoted by Herodotus *Hist.* ii.5), "Egypt is the gift of the Nile" and, indeed, not only the country's physical features but its very survival have been determined by that river. Formed by the convergence of the While Nile, Blue Nile, and Atbara rivers and other tributaries (themselves beyond the boundaries of Egypt), the Nile river proper flows northward some 3060 km. (1900 mi.) from Khartoum to the Mediterranean Sea. Seasonal torrential rains in the Ethiopian highlands precipitate the annual inundation of the Nile (July-September), when the volume of the river increases to nearly eight times its lowest capacity in late January. This widespread flooding contributes rich alluvial deposits throughout the Nile valley and helps in the irrigation of fields, without which the virtually rainless land (20 cm. [8 in.] per year at Alexandria, 3 cm. [1.3 in.] at Cairo, scarcely a trace elsewhere) would be nothing more than desert (cf. Isa. 19:5-8).

Just north of modern Cairo the Nile divides (in ancient times it may have had as many as twelve branches) to form an alluvial fan some 250 km. (150 mi.) wide and 160 km. (100 mi.) long. This region, divided into twenty nomes or districts, was known as Lower Egypt and extended as far south as its capital, Memphis. Upper Egypt comprised the 965 km. (600 mi.)-expanse of the Nile valley from south of Memphis to Aswân. This region, a fertile strip ranging from less than 1 km. (.6 mi.) to nearly

The double crown of the two Egypts

20 km. (12 mi.) wide, was divided into twenty-two nomes in predynastic times, which throughout Egyptian history have exerted periodic influence. With the exception of the Amarna period, the capital of Upper Egypt was at Thebes (modern Luxor and Karnak; Egyp. *nw.t imn*; cf. Heb. *nō' 'āmûn*, Nah. 3:8; *nō'*, Jer. 46:25). South of Abydos the Nile branches westward into the Baḥr Yûsûf ("river of Joseph"), which flows northward through the Faiyûm depression and into Lake Karûn (Qarûn; cf. Strabo *Geog.* xvii.1.37, "lake of Moeris").

West of the Nile valley lies the great, arid expanse of the Western or Libyan desert, which comprises nearly three-fourths of modern Egypt (675,000 sq. km. [260,000 sq. mi.]). This limestone plateau, covered with rocks and sand, is marked by a series of oases — natural depressions made habitable by artesian water sources. Parallel belts of sand dunes more than 60 m. (200 ft.) high distinguish the Great Sand Sea, which stretches from the Siwah oases in the northwest to the Jifr el-Kebîr mountain range in the southwest. To the east, between the Nile and the Red Sea, lies the Eastern or Arabian desert, characterized by rugged igneous mountains rich in mineral wealth; drainage from these peaks, several of which are more than 1525 m. (5000 ft.) high (e.g., Jebel Šâyab el-Banât, 2180 m. [7150 ft.]), have led to the formation of a vast number of wadis and larger valleys which impede travel in the region.

III. History

Egyptian history proper is divided conventionally into some thirty-one dynasties, actually distinct historical eras, based upon the writings of the Egyptian priest Manetho (*ca.* 270 B.C.) which record the events between the unification of Egypt by Menes (*ca.* 3200) and the conquest of Alexander the Great (332). Determining precise chronology remains difficult for events prior to the Twenty-sixth (Saite) Dynasty (663), particularly for the third millennium and before.

Human occupation in Egypt has been attested as early as 8000. The development of village life and advances in agriculture, building, and crafts mark the next five millennia of the Prehistoric or Predynastic period, the successive phases of which are identified as Tasian-Badarian, Amratian (or Negadi I), Gerzean (Negada II), and Semainean (Negada III). By the latest phase (late fourth millennium) significant cultural contacts had been made with Sumer, and the numerous local nomes had allied to form the two Egypts, Upper and Lower.

Egyptian history per se begins with the conquest of the delta by southern forces and the unification of the two Egypts under the royal house of Upper Egypt. Perhaps actually a gradual process of alliance and conquest, the formal union traditionally is attributed to Meni (Gk. Menes; probably identical with Narmer), who assumed a dual kingship over the two kingdoms and established a central capital at Memphis. Two southern dynasties from This (Egyp. Tjeni), near Abydos, ruled Egypt during this Archaic or Early Dynastic (also called Protodynastic) period (*ca.* 3200-2700), forging a strong central government and implementing numerous technological advances.

During the reign of the Third Dynasty Egypt entered a new era, known as the Old Kingdom or Pyramid Age (*ca.* 2700-2150), a golden age of culture and prosperity in which Egypt came to rival the Akkad of Sargon. Pharaoh Djoser (or Zoser), through the efforts of his architect Imhotep (also a sage and physician), erected the great Step Pyramid at Saqqârah, history's first large, cut-stone monument. Under the Fourth Dynasty Egypt's architectural achievements reached their zenith, producing the Great Pyramid of Khufu (Cheops) at Gizeh and those of Khafre (Chephren, who also erected the nearby Sphinx and Valley Temple) and Menkaure (Mycerinus). Pyramid building continued throughout the next two dynasties, but these activities seriously strained the economy and governmental administrations; as a result, a trend toward political decentralization began during the Fifth Dynasty, and the mercantile and exploratory ventures of the Sixth (as well as military expeditions against the "sand-dwellers" of southern Palestine *ca.* 2325) also took their toll. By the end of Pepi II's ninety-nine-year reign, the country was in disarray, ripe for civil war.

Almost immediately Egypt entered a dark age known as the First Intermediate Period (*ca.* 2180-2040). The Seventh and Eighth Dynasties (which some scholars would include in the period of the demise of the Old Kingdom) maintained but nominal control over the resurgent local states; some fifteen kings took the throne in little more than two decades. Famine and social upheaval were widespread, and Asiatics (easterners) infiltrated the delta (cf. Instruction for Merikare). In *ca.* 2160 a new dynasty came to the fore under Meribre-kheti I at Heracleopolis (Egyp. Nen-nesset; modern Ahnas el-Medineh) near the Faiyum; the Ninth and Tenth (Heracleopolitan) Dynasties sought to regain control of the delta. Toward the end of the Ninth Dynasty (*ca.* 2133) another dynasty arose at Thebes (Diospolis) which contended with Heracleopolis for control of the north, and in 2040 succeeded in reuniting Upper and Lower Egypt.

On the foundation laid by later kings of the Eleventh Dynasty (who opened quarries at Wâdî Ḥammâmât, initiated trade with Punt, and sought to reconquer Nubia) the Twelfth Dynasty established a new golden age, called the Middle Kingdom (ca. 2000-1786). Its founder, Amenemhet I (Ammenemes), sought systematically to ensure strong and competent leadership: he moved the capital from Thebes to Itj-tawi, 40 km. (25 mi.) south of Memphis, reorganized the nomic structure, and instituted the coregency system to guarantee royal succession. Pharaohs of this dynasty fortified the eastern delta against Asiatic incursions and developed the Faiyûm region, establishing a reservoir at Lake Moeris. Sesostris III (Egyp. Senwosre) completed the subjugation of Nubia to the Second Cataract and invaded Palestine as far as Shechem. Trade was maintained with Crete, and Egyptian influence is attested at Byblos (Gebal), Qatna, and Ugarit. This was also the classical period of Egyptian literature, evident through such writings as the Instructions of Amenemhet, the Tale of Sinuhe, and the Prophecy of Neferti. The dynasty ended with the brief reigns of Amenemhet IV and Queen Sebeknofru (Gk. Scemiophris). It is during this period that most scholars place Abram's visit to Egypt (Gen. 12:10-20).

Once again the central government weakened, and the Thirteenth (Theban) Dynasty found itself rivaled by a line (Fourteenth Dynasty) established at Xois (Khois) in the western delta as well as by rebellious nomes throughout Egypt; the land was plunged into a second dark age, the Second Intermediate Period (ca. 1786-1550). Evidently part of the Middle Bronze II Amorite movements, foreign elements penetrated the eastern delta in two successive waves (ca. 1720 and 1674) and established themselves as the Fifteenth and Sixteenth Dynasties. From their capital at Avaris these foreigners, known as Hyksos (Egyp. ḥq3w ḫ3swt "rulers of foreign lands"), expanded their influence throughout Egypt. In the mid-sixteenth century Kamose, a Theban king of the Seventeenth Dynasty (successors to the weakened Thirteenth), pressed northward, aided by Nubian mercenaries, to attack the Hyksos. The Hyksos were routed by Kamose's brother Ahmose, who extended the campaign as far as Sharuhen in southwestern Palestine (see HYKSOS).

With the "expulsion" (or more likely assimilation) of the Hyksos, Egypt embarked upon a period of expansion and domination, the New Kingdom (or Empire; ca. 1550-1085). Ahmose, considered by many scholars to be the founder of the Eighteenth Dynasty, reunified and stabilized Egypt. His son, Amenhotep I (Amenophis), extended the southern border to the Third Cataract, and his successor Thutmose I (or Thothmes; Gk. Tuthmosis) conquered Cush to just south of the Fourth before advancing to the Euphrates. Thutmose II died after a brief reign, and his wife Hatshepsut seized the kingship from the young Thutmose III, for whom she had been named regent. A powerful leader, she restored numerous temples, completed the building projects of her predecessors, and engaged in peaceful trade. In the twenty-second year of her reign, Thutmose III usurped the throne and immediately began a career of conquest and expansion, which included six campaigns against Kadesh on the Orontes and seventeen in Syria and Palestine; he is considered by some to have been the greatest of the Egyptian pharaohs. His successor Amenhotep II quelled a Syrian revolt at the Orontes,

and Thutmose IV sealed an alliance with the Hittites by marrying a Mitannian princess. Amenhotep III built extensively at Thebes and in Nubia and benignly enjoyed the fruits of empire. In the sixth year of his reign, Amenhotep IV rebelled against the influence of the powerful Amon priesthood in favor of the sun-god Aten, changed his name to Akhenaten, and established a new capital at Akhetaten near modern Tell el-Amarna; but the Amarna correspondence indicates he was preoccupied with the new cult and personal endeavors and ignored the responsibilities of empire (see AMARNA LETTERS). During the brief reigns of Akhenaten's two young sons-in-law, Smenkhkare and Tutankhamen, the Amon priesthood regained control. Dynastic succession was in disarray, passing first to the Aten priest Ay and then to an outsider, the military commander Horemheb, who later quelled a revolt in Syria-Palestine.

Horemheb was succeeded by his vizier, the aged Pera'messu (Rameses I), who inaugurated the Nineteenth Dynasty. Seti I (Gk. Sethos) campaigned in Palestine and Syria, defeating the 'Apiru and concluding a treaty with the Hittite king Muwatallis. During his sixty-seven-year reign Rameses II warred with the Nubians, Libyans, Syrians, and Hittites. At Kadesh on the Orontes he narrowly escaped disaster and defeated the Hittites; after sixteen more years of skirmishes the opponents formed an alliance, reinforced by Rameses' marriage to the Hittite king Ḫattusilis' daughter. Rameses may be remembered best for the construction of numerous monuments and buildings, which included temples at Abu Simbel and Karnak and the royal residence at Pi-Ra'messe (probably biblical Raamses; cf. Exod. 1:11) in the delta. His thirteenth son and successor, Merneptah, raided Palestine and later warded off an invasion by a coalition of Libyans and the Mediterranean Sea Peoples, as recorded in the Israel Stele, which contains the earliest extrabiblical reference to Israel. An early thirteenth-century date for the Exodus would have made Seti I the pharaoh of the oppression and Rameses II the pharaoh of the Exodus (see EXODUS).

A brief period of political chaos, marked by the rapid succession of kings and local rulers in the waning years of the Nineteenth Dynasty, was halted by Sethnakht, who restored order to the delta and established the Twentieth Dynasty. His son Rameses III, last of the imperial pharaohs, repelled an invasion of the Sea Peoples, diverting them to the coast of Palestine. Egyptian rule began a steady decline toward the end of Rameses III's reign, underscored by an assassination plot discovered within the royal harem shortly before the aged king's death. Within a decade the vestiges of Egyptian empire in Asia had crumbled. The remaining decades of the New Kingdom, under Pharaohs Rameses IV-XI, were characterized by official corruption, rampant inflation, labor strikes, and the widespread looting of the royal tombs. Rameses XI was but a nominal ruler, dominated by one Herihor, the high priest of Amon who claimed for himself the royal titulary, and Pinhasy, viceroy of Nubia.

The land — once again fragmented into Upper and Lower Egypt as well as a host of smaller local entities — was ruled by competing dynasties; some scholars view the era of the Twenty-first through Twenty-fifth

Dynasties (*ca.* 1085-664) as a third intermediate period. Nesubanebdet (Smendes) founded the Twenty-first Dynasty, which ruled from Tanis, while at Thebes the descendants of Herihor comprised a line of high priests of Amon who governed Upper Egypt as a theocratic state. Neither state could maintain any substantial foreign policy, and Egyptian prestige suffered abroad, as reflected poignantly in the Misadventures of Wenamun. It was this dynasty which sheltered the fugitive Edomite Hadad from David's advances (1 Kgs. 11:15-22) and with whom Solomon formed a marriage alliance (3:1; 9:16). The Tanite dynasty was succeeded by a powerful line of Libyans from the Faiyûm and delta who ruled from Bubastis in the eastern delta. Sheshonq I (Shoshenq or Shishak), founder of the Twenty-second Dynasty (*ca.* 945-730), stabilized Egypt internally and appointed his son as high priest at Thebes; following the division of the Israelite kingdom, he invaded Palestine and subdued both Judah and Israel (cf. 1 Kgs. 14:25-26 par. 2 Chr. 12:2-9). Sheshonq's successor, Osorkon I, dispatched his Ethiopian general, Zerah, to fight against Judah, but he was only to be routed by Judah's king Asa (14:9-15). Egyptian unity again proved ephemeral, and the land, beset by civil war and ravaged by flood, was once more vulnerable to rival dynasties; another Libyan dynasty, the Twenty-third (*ca.* 817-739), seized control at Thebes (Manetho locates them at Tanis). Two more "official dynasties arose at the end of this period, perhaps overlapping the reigns of their predecessors, while a number of local dynasts (including the sons of reigning kings) vied for power. The Twenty-fourth Dynasty ruled briefly from Sais in the western delta (*ca.* 730-715); its founder, Tafnekht, enlisted the aid of some sixteen local rulers to control much of Middle Egypt, thus provoking the ire of Piankhy, chief of the Nubian kingdom formed at Napata near the Fourth Cataract toward the end of the New Kingdom. Piankhy, who headed the Twenty-fifth Dynasty (*ca.* 730-656), advanced with his army to capture Memphis and rout the northern allies, then installed his daughter as divine votary (or "God's wife") of Amon at Thebes. His brother, Shabaka, again conquered Egypt and eliminated the tenacious Saite Bekenrenef (Bocchoris); although maintaining overtly friendly relations with the Assyrian Sargon II, Shabaka sought to instigate Syrian and Palestinian resistance to the Assyrian invaders. The young pharaoh Shabataka (Shebitku) sent the inexperienced general Taharqa (Tirhakah) to aid Hezekiah of Judah against Sennacherib in 701 (cf. 2 Kgs. 19:9; Isa. 37:9). Later, as pharaoh, Taharqa was defeated by the Assyrian Esarhaddon, who in 671 captured Memphis and established local governors; Taharqa immediately regained the city, only to be driven out by Assurbanipal, who installed Necho I (Niku) as governor at Sais. When the Egyptian pharaoh Tanetamon (Urdamane) sought to recapture Memphis, Assurbanipal retaliated by sacking Thebes, thus ending Ethiopian rule over Egypt (663).

With Assurbanipal preoccupied by revolts in Babylonia, Elam, and Arabia, Pharaoh Psamtik I (Psammetichus) regained control of all Egypt, and his Twenty-sixth (Saite) Dynasty (663-525) ushered in an era of prosperity and artistic nostalgia known as the Egyptian Renaissance or Restoration. In his move to aid his Assyrian allies after the fall of Nineveh,

Necho II was halted briefly at Megiddo, the battle in which King Josiah of Judah was killed (2 Kgs. 23:29); three months later Necho replaced Jehoahaz as king of Judah with his older brother Jehoiakim, who was considered more favorable to the Egyptians (vv. 33-34). Necho's forces were soundly defeated by the Babylonians at Carchemish in 605, and Egypt lost control of Syria-Palestine; nevertheless, the Egyptians were able four years later to prevent Nebuchadrezzar's invasion of their homeland. Hophra (Apries) fostered Zedekiah's rebellion against Babylon in 589 (Jer. 37:5; Ezek. 17:15), provoking Nebuchadrezzar to destroy Jerusalem and to deport its populace three years later. Ahmose II (Amasis) promoted cultural and political relations with Greece (Herodotus calls him "Philhellene"; *Hist.* ii.178). When the Persians conquered Babylon in 539, Cyrus undertook to gain control over Egypt; this Cambyses accomplished (perhaps aided by Pharaoh Ahmose's mercenary Greek generals) by defeating the Egyptian Psamtik III at Pelusium in 525.

The Achaemenids, whom Manetho depicts as the Twenty-seventh Dynasty (525-404), established firm but considerate control over Egypt. Darius I honored the Egyptian religion and promoted commerce by completing or restoring a canal between the Nile and the Red Sea. At his death in 484, however, the Egyptians revolted, encouraged by the Greek victory over Persia at Marathon in 490 — but they were suppressed by Xerxes I, under whom the Egyptian satrapy was ruled more severely. Another revolt in 460 was quelled by Artaxerxes I.

Rebellion against the Achaemenids, inaugurated in 410 by Amyrtaeus of Sais, restored Egyptian independence. Amyrtaeus, the sole pharaoh of the Twenty-eighth Dynasty (404-398), was succeeded by the Twenty-ninth Dynasty (398-378), ruled from Mendes in the delta, who allied with the Spartans and then the Athenians against Persia. The Thirtieth Dynasty (378-341), last of the native Egyptian lines, regained a fragile unity in the land and engaged in substantial building activities, but the economic burden of a Greek mercenary army compounded with rebellion in the Mendesian nomes left Egypt vulnerable to renewed foreign aggression by the Persians. Artaxerxes III Ochus of Persia sacked the delta in 343, and Pharaoh Nakhthorebe II (Nectanebo) spent his last years in retreat in Upper Egypt.

The second Persian domination of Egypt, which Eusebius' version of Manetho labels the Thirty-first Dynasty (341-330), yielded to Macedonian rule after the invasion of Alexander the Great in 332. Alexander, hailed as savior and acclaimed as pharaoh, honored the Egyptian gods at Memphis and consulted the oracle of Amon at Siwah; the city of Alexandria, which he established in the northwestern delta, came to symbolize the union of Egyptian and Hellenistic cultures. Upon Alexander's death Ptolemy I Soter ruled Egypt as satrap under Philip Arrhidaeus and Alexander IV; with the division of Alexander's empire among the Diadochi in 305 Ptolemy became founder of the Ptolemaic Dynasty. The Egyptian provincial organization was preserved, and Alexandria, Naucratis, and Ptolemaïs were accorded self-government as Greek poleis. Ptolemy III Euergetes captured Seleucid land in Syria and Palestine, precipitating prolonged strife with the

Antiochian dynasty. Later Ptolemies, their rule dissipated by internal struggles and incompetent judgment, courted Roman assistance. The last of the dynasty, Cleopatra VII, who ruled as queen with her brothers Ptolemy XIII and XIV and her son Ptolemy XV, sought desperately to preserve Egyptian sovereignty. Despite her diplomatic and personal relationships with Julius Caesar and Mark Antony, though, she failed to divert the advance of imperial Rome; when Octavian (Augustus) occupied Alexandria in 30 B.C. she followed Antony in suicide rather than accept Roman rule. Egypt continued as a Roman province until A.D. 395, when it was incorporated into the Byzantine Empire. Muslim rule was established in 641.

IV. Religion

The complexities of Egyptian religion, characterized by a myriad of deities — sometimes similar yet always distinct, whose functions might coincide or conflict — and disparate, even contradictory mythologies, reflect both the land and its people. Egyptian religion was truly pluralistic as well as syncretistic, as would befit a vast land unified by the river Nile yet easily fragmented into numerous isolated nomes, and whose history saw three millennia of nearly cyclical political fission and fusion.

Although some scholars would trace them to primitive tribal fetishes, most Egyptian deities were first manifested as patrons or protectors of a particular locale, often associated with agriculture (e.g., Ptah and Sekhment at Memphis, Atum at Heliopolis, Sebek at Crocodilopolis). Some developed as part of the great cosmogonies and were accorded cosmic functions (e.g., Nut, goddess of the sky; Geb, god of the earth; Shu, god of the atmosphere). Others gained prominence because of particular responsibilities (e.g., Meshkent, goddess of childbirth; Ma'at, goddess of truth, justice, and reality; Shai, personification of fortune or destiny). Local deities might gain or lose influence in accordance with the political fortunes of their region. Such was the case with Amon of Thebes, who became the patron of the Twelfth Dynasty and under the New Kingdom was acclaimed "king of the gods." When people moved to a new locale, they often continued to worship the gods of their former residence; hence gods might be worshipped in various local manifestations, such as Min at Chemmis in the delta and Koptos, and Neith at Sais and Esna. Deities might acquire new identities or assume a variety of attributes (e.g., Thoth, originally a funerary god from the delta, later moon-god at Hermopolis, god of wisdom, lord of magic, creator of writing, and author of the sacred laws); others were identified or assimilated (e.g., Horus and Re, later Re-Harakhte; Hathor and Isis; Amon and Re; Amon, Min, and Khnum). Deities were also linked mythologically into divine families (e.g., Amon, Mut, and their son, the moon-god Khonsu; Khnum, Satis, and a daughter, Anukis). Frequently the deities were portrayed in animal form, perhaps derived from some aspect of their character (e.g., Horus as a falcon; Mendes and Amon, a ram; Anubis, the jackal); later many were depicted as having a human body but retaining the head of an animal (e.g., Sekhmet, lion; Bast, cat).

Around this multiplicity of gods and goddesses developed an equally complex corpus of mythological interpretations. Such myths, which served as much to reinforce as to explain the existing social order, were the product of various competing priesthoods and often reflected the geographic and dynastic conditions from which they emerged. They were closely related to the daily ritual, which the priests alone performed in the sacred precincts; in rites which reenacted the processes of nature, the priests awoke, bathed, dressed, and fed the divine images. Several versions of creation were prominent. The earliest, from Hermopolis in Upper Egypt, held that the Ogdoad, eight primeval gods who had emanated from the waters of chaos (Nun), created the world and continued to govern the flow of the Nile and the daily rising of the sun. In the theology of Heliopolis (On), the local god Atum first created himself, then by masturbation gave birth to Shu (air) and Tefnut (moisture), who produced Geb (earth) and Nut (sky), and they, in turn, Isis, Osiris, Set, and Nephthys. At Memphis Ptah was viewed as the creator, of whom the Heliopolitan Ennead ("nine") were divine manifestations. Finally, the New Kingdom priests of Thebes, seeking to substantiate Amon's role as chief god, superimposed him upon the earlier cosmogonies.

From the earliest dynastic times the king was regarded as divine, a demigod able to control or at least influence natural phenomena, and thus the embodiment of the sun-god Horus (Behdety). Later he was seen merely as an intermediary between the gods and humans and was called the son of Re, the father of the gods, or in imperial times the son of Atum, creator-god of Heliopolis. Thus, it was only through the king that divine benefits might be extended to the ordinary populace, and his welfare became of prime importance. After death the king was identified with Osiris and thus believed to have been resurrected to live in the afterworld.

The Egyptian belief in an afterlife is underscored by the massive pyramids and other monuments, mummified remains, funerary accouterments, and texts describing elaborate burial rituals. Because many upper-class Egyptians had enjoyed a pleasant earthly life, they believed that the gods would permit them similar pleasures in death; the deceased was provided with food, drink, and personal furnishings (or their magical representations) that would ensure comfort in the future life. The body was embalmed, and the liver, lungs, stomach, and intestines (and after the Middle Kingdom, the brains) were removed and preserved separately in canopic jars. The belief was that if the body were properly preserved, the soul (Egyp. *ba*) would be properly preserved as well. The soul was said to take the form of a bird (often a falcon with the head of the deceased). In the afterlife the person would be protected by his *ka*, a transcendent spirit that had been his double since birth. Elaborate burial rites, which included the "Opening of the Mouth" that made possible the rebirth of the person's soul, would enable the deceased to proceed to the underworld for judgment by Osiris and Thoth and eventually to arise with Osiris in a life of eternal bliss. From the time of the Nineteenth (Ramesside) Dynasty (thirteenth century), increasing concern was given to the rigors of passage to the afterworld with attendant emphasis on rigid conformity to the funerary ritual, perhaps reflecting increased

Relief of Akhenaten and Nefertiti at Tell el-Amarna (fourteenth century B.C.) (Ägyptisches Museum, Staatliche Museen zu Berlin, DDR)

social and political disarray and a decline in the quality of life on earth. At no time does it appear that the lower classes shared the nobles' hope for the afterlife; even if they had been able to afford the mortuary rites, they would have been promised no more than a continuation of their earthly subservience.

Akhenaten's elevation of Aten worship during the Amarna age has been identified by some scholars as a monotheistic revolution. The emphasis was upon the sun disk as the supreme power of life and drew upon existing elements of Egyptian worship (e.g., sun worship, syncretism of Re-Harakhte and Shu) to offer an abstract, universal god perceived as the father of all people, both Egyptian and non-Egyptian, and thus acceptable to all citizens of the empire. Although Aten was deemed the only god worthy of worship, Akhenaten proclaimed himself the god's sole intermediary and his equal. No influence of this religion upon the Yahwism of Moses can be substantiated.

V. Legacy

From the earliest stages of its history, Egyptian culture evidenced significant achievements in technology, art, and intellectual pursuits — aspects of which must have influenced neighboring civilizations, particularly during the periods of Egyptian empire. Much of what the Egyptians accomplished survives today. Perhaps most apparent are those examples of art and architecture represented by monumental structures such as the pyramids at Saqqârah and Gizeh, the Sphinx, and the elaborate temples at Karnak and Luxor, Medinet Habu, and Abu Simbel. Religious art abounds, including statues and figurines of the various deities as well as wall paintings and reliefs depicting mortuary practices and the intricacies of Egyptian beliefs in the afterlife. The tomb furnishings of the young Tutankhamen — furniture, jewelry, personal accessories — suggest the splendor of royal life. Monumental architecture, particularly the statuary of Rameses II, attests to the pride of Egyptian monarchs as well as to the Egyptians' artistic and engineering skill.

A vast and diverse body of literature survives, not only giving testimony to the wit and creativity of the Egyptian people but also providing insights into their history and culture. Victory stelae and other inscriptions provide historical accounts of the Old and Middle Kingdoms, as do royal annals such as those of Thutmose III from the walls of the Karnak temple and official papyri of the New Kingdom and later. Legal texts include various royal decrees and the Egyptian version of Rameses II's treaty with the Hittites under Ḫattusilis. Fictional tales include the stories of Sinuhe, the Shipwrecked Sailor, and the Two Brothers. Among the numerous religious texts are the cosmogonies of Heliopolis, Memphis, and Thebes, mortuary texts (Old Kingdom Pyramid Texts, Middle Kingdom Coffin

Texts and the Book of the Dead), rituals, and incantations, including the seventeenth- or eighteenth-century Execration Texts. Poetry includes hymns and prayers to Amon, Thoth, Osiris, and the Nile as well as to Kings Sesostris III, Thutmose III, Rameses II, and Merneptah, the secular songs of various laborers, and those from memorial banquets. Wisdom literature abounds, comprising proverbs, precepts, and instructions for those charged with the affairs of state, satires, and pessimistic dialogues. Copies of these works and exemplary texts intended as models for correspondence attest to a sophisticated scribal system.

Among the Egyptian advances in the sciences was the observation of astronomical and celestial phenomena, which enabled them to determine a calendar of 365 twenty-four-hour days (twelve months of thirty days plus five intercalary days). By charting the annual inundation of the Nile against this calendar they determined the 1460-year Sothic cycle, which, combined with king lists and other historical accounts, has proven of utmost value to chronological studies. The Egyptian system of mathematics was elementary yet adequate for most practical uses, and with skilled and accurate application proved sufficient for the construction of the Great Pyramids. Simple decimal notations were employed, as well as a rudimentary system of fractions and an unwieldy means of multiplication and division by factoring. Medical texts indicate an awareness of the position and function of the organs and circulatory system and some degree of expertise in the diagnosis and treatment of ailments by medication and surgery as well as by magic.

For the people of Israel Egypt symbolized oppression, the "house of bondage" (Exod. 20:2; Deut. 5:6) from which Moses led God's chosen people; as such it played an integral role in the Exodus theme so central to Hebrew thought (Josh. 24:17; Judg. 6:8-9; Hos. 11:1; cf. Acts 7:9-34; 13:17). Yet throughout their history the people of Palestine turned to Egypt as a haven from famine (Gen. 12:10; 46–47), foreign aggression (1 Kgs. 11:17; 12:2; Isa. 30:2; Jer. 43:7; Ezek. 17:15; cf. Matt. 2:13-15), and religious opposition (Jer. 26:21; cf. Acts 2:10). When Egyptian power waned and Israel could no longer rely upon the political stability that ensued, the Hebrew prophets warned against further dependence upon "that broken reed of a staff" (2 Kgs. 18:21 par. Isa. 36:6; cf. 30:7; 31:1). Moreover, the prophets denounced Egyptian polytheism (Ezek. 30:13, 17; cf. Jer. 44), which they believed had influenced Israel's apostasy from its beginnings in the wilderness (cf. Exod. 32:4; Acts 7:35ff.).

Bibliography. T. Černý, *Ancient Egyptian Religion* (New York: 1952); W. B. Emery, *Archaic Egypt* (Baltimore: 1961); A. Erman, ed., *The Ancient Egyptians: A Sourcebook of Their Writings* (New York: 1966); A. H. Gardiner, *Egypt of the Pharaohs* (New York: 1969); W. C. Hayes, *The Scepter of Egypt*, 2 vols. (New York: 1953-1959); P. Montet, *Eternal Egypt* (New York: 1964); G. Steindorff and K. C. Seele, *When Egypt Ruled the East*, rev. ed. (Chicago: 1957); J. A. Wilson, *The Culture of Egypt* (Chicago: 1956).

EGYPT, BROOK OF. *See* Brook of Egypt.

EGYPTIAN.† The language of the Nile valley; akin to the Semitic and Hamitic language families, it flourished in various stages from the third millennium B.C. through the thirteenth century A.D. It is characterized by triconsonantal roots, causative and reflexive verbal preformatives, occasional doubling of the middle radical, and pronominal forms akin to the Semitic languages, Hamitic reduplication of roots, and etymological similarities to both families as well as a distinctive verbal system lacking preformative pronominal elements.

Five major stages can be distinguished. Old Egyptian was the language of the First-Eighth Dynasties (*ca.* 3100-2160), represented by the Pyramid Texts, biographical texts, and royal decrees. The classical stage of the language is known as Middle Egyptian, which derived from the vernacular of the Ninth Dynasty (twenty-first century) and was adopted for literary and official use through the early Eighteenth Dynasty (*ca.* 1400). This dialect was preserved in religious usage and, with later popular developments, continued in literary and monumental use as late as the Christian era. Late Egyptian (Neo-Egyptian) was instituted among Akhenaten's reforms and reflects numerous morphological and phonological changes characteristic of the current vernacular. Although it never completely replaced Middle Egyptian in written use, Late Egyptian was employed in commercial manuscripts and correspondence through the Twenty-fourth Dynasty (*ca.* 715). Demotic (also called Late or Low Egyptian), which reflects a scribal effort to restore classical Middle Egyptian, takes its name from the script employed in private and official documents from the Saite and Ptolemaic periods (Twenty-fifth Dynasty through Roman conquest, *ca.* seventh century-30 B.C.). The final stage is comprised of the various dialects of Coptic used in the Roman and Byzantine periods, derived from Late Egyptian and influenced by Greek.

Egyptian was written in three major styles of script. Hieroglyphic (Gk. *hierós* "sacred" and *glyptós* "carved") writing was originally pictographic and features ideograms, phonograms, logograms, and phonetic complements but no vowel indicators. Employed primarily in carved inscriptions and wall paintings, it could be written vertically or horizontally (generally right to left, but also left to right) or in a combination of directions or arrangements as required to fit monuments. Hieratic script developed during the Third Dynasty as a cursive form of hieroglyphic more conducive to rapid writing with a sharpened reed and ink on papyrus. It was used largely for religious texts from the Middle Kingdom on and in Greek-Roman times was employed primarily by the priests (cf. Gk. *hieratikós* "priestly"). Demotic is a more simplified form of hieratic which appeared at the time of the Libyan dynasties (*ca.* eighth century); it was the ordinary form of writing (Gk. *dēmotikós* "popular"; earlier called enchorial, from Gk. *enchórios* "in the country, local") used for everyday writing and secular texts.

The language was first deciphered by J.-F. Champollion in 1822 on the basis of the famed Rosetta Stone, a black granite stele discovered by the French officer Bouchard at the ancient fortress of Rašid, 7 km. (4.3 mi.) northwest of Rosetta in the Western Nile delta. Working from the Greek inscription honoring Ptolemeus V Epiphanes (186 B.C.), he was able to decipher the accompanying hieroglyphic and demotic versions.

Bibliography. A. H. Gardiner, *Egyptian Grammar,* 3rd ed. (Oxford: 1957).

EGYPTIAN, THE [ē jĭp′shən] (Gk. *ho Aigyptios*). A noted individual, a false prophet according to Josephus, who claimed he could make the walls of Jerusalem collapse at his command (*Ant.* xx.8.6 [169-171]). He led a band of thirty thousand assassins (*BJ* ii.13.5 [261-63]) or robbers (*Ant.* xx.8.6) to the Mount of Olives intending to capture the capital but Felix the Roman governor anticipated his move and defeated him; only a few of the Egyptian's followers escaped with him.

At Acts 21:38 Claudius Lysias, the Roman tribune, mistook Paul for the Egyptian on account of the mob's violent behavior toward the apostle. When he learned that Paul could speak Greek and was a native of Tarsus, however, he gave him permission to address the people (vv. 37-40). According to the biblical account the Egyptian had a band of four thousand followers, a more plausible figure than that given by Josephus.

EGYPTIANS, GOSPEL ACCORDING TO THE.
1. An apocryphal gospel, written in Greek probably in Egypt during the early second century A.D. Regarded as heretical by Origen (*Hom. in Luc.*), it was used extensively by the Sabellians (Epiphanius *Haer.* lxii.2), the Naassene Gnostics (Hippolytus *Ref.* v.7.9), and the ascetic Encratites (cf. Clement of Alexandria *Misc.* iii.6.45, 9.36-64, 66, 13.92-93). The work, which survives only in quotations by the Church Fathers, is unrelated to the similarly titled work from Nag Hammadi (**2** below).

2.† An esoteric Gnostic tractate, probably written in Greek but surviving in two Sahidic Coptic versions (*ca.* A.D. 150) discovered at Nag Hammadi in Upper Egypt; formally entitled "The Holy Book of the Great Invisible Spirit," the more common designation appears at the beginning of the scribal colophon (Gos. Eg. iii.69.6). Although ascribed to the heavenly Seth, the colophon attributes the work to a certain Eugnostos (or Gongessos). It is typical of mythological Gnosticism and describes the origin of the heavenly world in a series of emanations from the supreme God; it also recounts the origin, preservation, and salvation of the race of Seth. Also included are two sections of hymns praising the divine tetrad of supreme God, Mother Barbelo, Son Jesus, and light-being and an account of the tractate's origin and transmission. The ineffable name is represented by the Greek vowels written twenty-two times each, a magical formula corresponding to the number of letters in the Semitic alphabet.

EHI [ē′hī] (Heb. *'ēhî*). One of the sons of Benjamin mentioned with Rosh at Gen. 46:21; probably to be combined with the following name to read Ahiram (so *BH* Heb. *'hyrm*) listed at Num. 26:38 as a son of Benjamin, or perhaps the same as Aharah at 1 Chr. 8:1.

EHUD [ē′hŭd] (Heb. *'ēhûḏ* "concord").†
1. An Israelite hero, the son of Gera of the tribe of Benjamin (Judg. 3:15). Having made the annual tribute to Eglon the king of Moab, whom Israel was serving at the time, Ehud pretended to have a secret message from God for the king. When the unsuspecting Eglon had dismissed his personnel and rose to hear the divine announcement, the left-handed Ehud stabbed him with a long dagger which the assailant had pulled from his right side (vv. 15-23). Ehud escaped to Seirah, mustered an army, took the fords at the Jordan, and together with other Israelites accomplished a great slaughter of their oppressors (vv. 24-30).

Despite Ehud's role as Israel's deliverer (v. 15), he is not specifically called a judge, possibly because he acted treacherously with Eglon. (He is not mentioned in the list of heroes at Heb. 11.) The account, which some scholars believe to have derived directly from Israelite saga, does not reflect the formulaic Deuteronomistic framework characteristic of the accounts of Israel's judges.

2. The third son of Bilhan and descendant of Jediael, from the tribe of Benjamin (1 Chr. 8:6), probably erroneously inserted in the genealogy of Zebulun at 7:10.

EKER [ē′kər] (Heb. *'eqer* "root"). The third son of Ram, a descendant of Jerahmeel (1 Chr. 2:27).

EKRON [ĕk′rən] (Heb. *'eqrôn* "barren place"; Akk. *Amqarruna*; Gk. *Akkarōn*).† Northernmost of the five principal Philistine cities in Palestine (Josh. 13:3). It was among those cities initially assigned to Dan (19:43) but was later reckoned as Judahite territory (13:3; 15:11).

Although Judah did capture the city for a time (Judg. 1:18), it was soon regained by the Philistines, who reinforced the original Canaanite city-state to maintain control of the Israelite hill country. When the Philistines captured the ark of the covenant they brought it eventually to Ekron (1 Sam. 5:10) before misfortunes associated with its presence prompted them to return it to the Israelites at Beth-shemesh. Israel again reasserted control over the region at the time of Samuel (7:14), but the Philistines were able to retreat to Ekron following David's defeat of Goliath at the valley of Elah (17:52).

Shortly after the division of the Israelite Monarchy (*ca.* 918 B.C.), Ekron was captured by the Egyptian pharaoh Sheshonq I (Shishak; James H. Breasted, *Ancient Records of Egypt* [Chicago: 1906-7] 4: §§ 709-722). Somewhat later the ailing King Ahaziah of Israel (*ca.* 853) sought to consult Baal-zebub, the deity of Ekron (2 Kgs. 1:2), prompting intervention by the prophet Elijah (vv. 3-16).

In the late eighth century Amos denounced Ekron along with the rest of the Philistine pentapolis, warning of their impending doom (Amos 1:8). The city, which may already have felt Assyrian pressure for decades, fell to Sargon II in 712. Although Padi, the city's king, remained loyal to the Assyrians, the aristocracy favored Hezekiah of Judah and sought to revolt; in 701 Sennacherib laid siege to Palestine, isolating Ekron and halting its Egyptian aid, capturing the city and deporting the rebels while reinstating Padi (*ANET*, pp. 287-88).

Although Ekron is known to have provided tribute and laborers to subsequent Assyrian kings (*ANET*, pp. 291, 294) and its doom was foretold by the Hebrew prophets (Zeph. 2:4; Zech. 9:5-9; cf. Jer. 25:20), the city's actual fate during the Babylonian conquest and captivity remains unknown. It is next mentioned as a gift of Alexander Balas to Jonathan Maccabeus for the defeat of Demetrius and the conquest of Ashdod (147 B.C.; 1 Macc. 10:89; Josephus *Ant.* xiii.4.4).

Ekron was first thought to be identified with modern ʿAqir, a village which preserves the ancient name, 16 km. (10 mi.) northeast of Ashdod. The majority of scholars now place it at Khirbet el-Muqennaʿ (Tel Miqne), 31 km. (19 mi.) inland at the eastern edge of the coastal plain; excavations at the site have uncovered a large fortified Iron Age city containing much Philistine ware and, to the northwest, the large Byzantine town noted by Eusebius (*Onom.* xxii.9-10). Others would identify Ekron with modern Qaṭra, 13 km. (8 mi.) northeast of Ashdod, preferring Khirbet el-Muqennaʿ as the site for Eltekeh (Josh. 19:44).

EL [ĕl] (Heb. *ʾēl*; Akk. *ilu*; Ugar. *ʾil*).† The common Semitic designation for a god or deity, used both as a generic term and as a proper name, particularly for the supreme high god. In Biblical Hebrew (translated "God" in most English versions) it is one of the most frequent names for the God of Israel; occurring in both early and late texts, it is found most often in the archaizing poetry of Psalms (seventy-seven times) and Job (fifty-five times) and in those poetic passages of the Pentateuch judged by source critics to be the most ancient. Although the term's etymology is uncertain, it appears to derive from a root meaning "to be strong" or "to be preeminent."

In ancient Canaanite mythology, as supported by the second-millennium B.C. texts from Ugarit, El is the "ancient" or "eternal one," head of the pantheon and primordial father of both gods and mankind. Given the epithet "Bull," he is said to dwell at Mt. Amanus in the north, the cosmic mountain at whose base spring up the waters of creation; there he presides over the assembly of the gods as divine judge (cf. the role of the Old Akkadian and Amorite god Ilu).

The Hebrew term is most often an appellative for the God of Israel (e.g., Exod. 15:2; Deut. 7:9) or one of the pagan gods (Isa. 44:17). However, its occurrences as a proper name bear particular significance for the history of Israelite religion. The appearance of El as a theophoric element in personal names (e.g., Ishmael, Eliezer) suggests that the ancestors of the Israelites worshiped God as El. The various divine names compounded with El (e.g., El Shaddai, El Elyon, El Roi), frequently associated with pre-Israelite shrines (cf. Bethel), represent local manifestations of El, with whom the patriarchs had identified their original clan deities. (See further the individual entries on these compound names of God.) Those scholars who favor a revolt model for the Israelite Conquest of Palestine suggest that the Habiru (ʿApiru) who withdrew from Canaanite city-states in Palestine formed an association (perhaps at Shechem) centered around

the worship of El (cf. El-berith, Judg. 9:46); with the influx of Israelite participants in the Exodus from Egypt, El (God) and Yahweh were recognized as synonymous (cf. El-Elohe-Israel, lit. "El, the God of Israel"; Gen. 33:20; cf. Ps. 68). Hebrew usage suggests that the northern tribes' worship of God as El may have continued in Israel through the divided monarchy (cf. 1 Kgs. 13–14), with Yahweh the name preferred by the southern tribes and subsequently by Judah; with the alliance of the two regions under David and the united monarchy, the identification of El with Yahweh was reinforced. At any rate, after the patriarchal period the two names are used interchangeably, and the various epithets and compounds of El are understood as applying to Yahweh (e.g., "God [El] of glory," Ps. 29:3; "God of vengeance," Ps. 94:1; cf. "God is my salvation," Isa. 12:2).

Bibliography. F. M. Cross, *Canaanite Myth and Hebrew Epic* (Cambridge, Mass.: 1973), pp. 1-75; "*ʾēl*," *TDOT* 1, rev. ed. (1977): 242-261; M. H. Pope, *El in the Ugaritic Texts.* VTS 2 (1955).

ELA [ē'lə] (Heb. *ʾēlāʾ*). The father of Shimei (1 Kgs. 4:18; KJV "Elah").

ELADAH (1 Chr. 7:20, KJV). *See* ELEADAH.

ELAH [ē'lə] (Heb. *ʾēlâ* "oak" or "terebinth").

1. A descendant of Esau, said to have been one of the chiefs of an Edomite tribe (Gen. 36:41; 1 Chr. 1:52). It may, however, be a place name, the Edomite port Elath on the Gulf of Aqabah.

2. (1 Kgs. 4:18, KJV). *See* ELA.

3. The son and successor of Baasha of Israel (1 Kgs. 16:6) and a contemporary of King Asa of Judah (v. 8). The narrative mentions only the end of Elah's reign, a term of less than two full years (*ca.* 877-876 B.C.). While intoxicated in the house of his steward Arza, Elah was murdered by Zimri the cocaptain of the royal chariots (vv. 9-10); Arza may have been an accomplice in the conspiracy. Josephus (*Ant.* viii.12.4 [308]) adds that the murder took place while Elah's army was away attacking Gibbethon. It appears that Elah's reign perpetuated the sins of his father Baasha (1 Kgs. 16:2-4, 10-11).

4. The father of Hoshea, the last king of the northern kingdom (2 Kgs. 15:30; 17:1; 18:1, 9).

5. The second son of Caleb, the grandson of Jephunneh, and the father of Kenaz (1 Chr. 4:15).

6. The son of Uzzi, from Benjamin (1 Chr. 9:8).

ELAH, VALLEY OF (Heb. *ʿēmeq hāʾēlâ* "valley of the terebinth"). A fertile valley in the Shephelah, identified with Wâdî es-Sant ("valley of the acacia"), about 24 km. (15 mi.) west-southwest of Bethlehem; it parallels the Wâdī eṣ-Ṣarâr ("valley of Sorek"), located immediately to the north. Saul and the Israelites encamped in the valley before deploying their forces on a hill on the eastern side of the valley toward Socoh, against the Philistines who were stationed on the western side near Azekah (1 Sam. 17:2-3). It was in this valley, which provided entrance into the Judean hill country, that David slew Goliath and so turned the battle to Israel's favor (vv. 3-54; 21:9).

ELAM [ē'ləm] (Heb. *'ēlām*; Akk. *elamtu* "highland") **(PERSON)**.

1. The first son of Shem (Gen. 10:22; 1 Chr. 1:17) and the eponymous ancestor of the Elamites.

2. One of the sons of Shashak, a Benjaminite dwelling in Jerusalem (1 Chr. 8:24-25).

3. The fifth son of Meshelemiah, a gatekeeper and a Levite during the reign of King David (1 Chr. 26:3).

4. A Hebrew whose descendants returned from exile with Zerubbabel (Ezra 2:7 par. Neh. 7:12; 1,254 in all) and Ezra (Ezra 8:7; seventy-one persons). Among them were Shecaniah, who supported Ezra in reintroducing the Mosaic law (Ezra 10:2-4), and six men who were required to send away their foreign wives (10:26).

5. The head of a family, whose many descendants returned from exile to Jerusalem (Ezra 2:31 par. Neh. 7:34). Even though the number of descendants is the same (1,254), he is called "the other Elam" and is thought to be distinguished from Elam **4.**

6. A chief who set his seal to the renewed covenant (Neh. 10:14).

7. A priest who participated in the ceremony dedicating the walls of Jerusalem (Neh. 12:42).

ELAM (Heb. *'ēlām*; Elam. *ḫaltamti* "land of god"; Akk. *elamtu, NIM* "high land") **(PLACE).†** A country in southwestern Iran, comprising the plain of Khuzistan and the adjacent Zagros mountains; at various points in its history the country also included territory to the northeast and southeast. Although Elam was strengthened commercially by natural trade routes and an abundance of timber and metal resources, the varied terrain hampered political unification; thus it functioned generally as a loose confederation of city-states.

I. History

Urbanization in Elam has been traced to at least the late fourth millennium B.C. Cultural contacts with lower Mesopotamia were high throughout most of the third millennium, and this period saw frequent clashes between the Elamites and their Sumerian neighbors. The Sumerian ruler of Kish is said to have raided Elam *ca.* 2700. Elam invaded Early Dynastic Babylonia *ca.* 2500, Eannatum of Kish subdued Elam and destroyed its capital at Susa *ca.* 2400, and Elam again asserted its independence before falling to Sargon of Akkad (*ca.* 2300). His successor, Naram-sin, effected a treaty with the Elamite dynasty of Awan, but both peoples succumbed to the Gutian invasion *ca.* 2100. Elam remained subject to Lagash and the Third Dynasty of Ur.

With the decline of the Ur dynasty, an Elamite coalition headed by the dynasty of Simash destroyed Ur *ca.* 2030 (*ANET*, pp. 455-463) and deported its king Ibbi-sin to Anshan. Although soon driven from Ur by Išbi-irra of Isin, the governors (Elam. *sukkal-maḫ*) of the Elamite confederation wielded sufficient power to meddle in Babylonian politics, even placing Elamite rulers on the throne of Larsa (Warad-sin, Rim-sin; *ca.* 1800). Elamite emissaries were attested in Syria and Palestine, and their mercenaries were

common in Mesopotamian armies; the activities of Chedorlaomer (Gen. 14:1-17) probably belong to this period. The powerful Hammurabi (1792-1750) checked Elamite expansion, and Elam remained under Babylonian control until both fell to the Kassite invaders in 1595. Little is known of the ensuing dark age, although Elam apparently dissolved into the numerous city-states until subjugated as a Babylonian province when the Kassite Kurigalzu II invaded *ca.* 1330. Under Ḫumban-numena (*ca.* 1285-1266) Elam revived as a unified country; Šutruk-naḫḫunte invaded Babylon, capturing the stele bearing Hammurabi's law code, and Šilhak-inšušinak expanded Elamite control throughout most of Mesopotamia east of the Tigris. Independence ended abruptly when Nebuchadnezzar I sacked Susa *ca.* 1130 and annexed Elam to his Babylonian kingdom. Elam's next three centuries remain shrouded in obscurity.

The remaining centuries of Elamite history are marked by increased pressure from the Medes and Persians as well as various independent tribes. The country gained an appreciable degree of political importance by allying with the Babylonians against Assyria; military aid to Merodach-baladan II, refuge for Babylonian nationalists, and other forms of antagonism were reciprocated by Sargon II, Sennacherib, and finally by Assurbanipal, who destroyed Susa and drove out Elam's last king, Ḫumban-ḫaldaš (*ca.* 640). Many of the leading citizens were deported to Assyria and then resettled in Samaria (cf. Ezra 4:9).

The region around Anshan was taken by the Persians *ca.* 680. Following the fall of Nineveh in 612, the rest of Elam came under Median control (cf. the Median-Elamite attack on Babylon in 596; Isa. 22:2); it was subsequently transferred to the Persians under Cyrus II (*ca.* 550; cf. Jer. 49:35-37), and became the third satrapy of the Persian Empire. Having quelled a revolt early in his reign, Darius I established his residence at Susa (cf. also Esth. 1:1-2). In Hellenistic times the region survived as the semi-autonomous Parthian state of Elymais (cf. 1 Macc. 6:1).

II. Legacy

From the earliest times, Elam was culturally related to the civilizations of lower Mesopotamia, perhaps explaining its inclusion among the descendants of Shem (Gen. 10:22). The native pictographic (Proto-Elamite) script, possibly influenced by the earliest Sumerian writing, was replaced with Akkadian cuneiform following the rule of Sargon of Akkad. Although Elamite royal inscriptions do exist in the linear cuneiform script, Akkadkan remained the official language throughout Elamite history. The agglutinative language appears unrelated to other ancient tongues and has no modern derivatives; trilingual inscriptions of the Persian period have aided in decipherment of that later stage of the language, but classical Elamite remains highly problematic. No native literature is yet known.

Although in prehistoric times Elamite art was quite distinctive, from the third millennium on it bears strong witness to Mesopotamian influence. The greatest artistic accomplishments occur in bronze figures dating to the thirteenth-century period of expansion. Although excavations have been limited, Elamite architecture also appears to have paralleled that of Mesopotamia, particularly the temples and temple towers.

No religious epics or ritual texts survive, but inscriptions and cylinder seals provide basic information concerning Elamite religion. Humban was the chief god, but his consort Kiririsha (called Pinikir at Susa) was head of the pantheon. Other important gods were Nahhunte, the sun-god, and numerous local patrons, most famous of which was In-šušinak ("lord of Susa"). Funerary gifts from royal tombs suggest a belief in an afterlife.

Occupied primarily with the power struggles in Mesopotamia, the Elamites played no great role in Israel's destiny. Portions of the Israelite polulace were exiled in Elam (Isa. 11:11), and Jewish settlements continued there in New Testament times (cf. Acts 2:9). Famed for their skilled archers (Isa. 22:6; Jer. 25:25), the Elamites were scored for their cruel and merciless treatment of other nations (Ezek. 32:24-25). Elam's fortunes are depicted as subject to God's divine plan of punishment and restoration (Jer. 49:38-39).

Bibliography. G. G. Cameron, *History of Early Iran* (Chicago: 1936); E. Porada, *Ancient Iran* (London: 1965).

ELASA [ĕl'ə sə] (Gk. *Elasa*). The place where Judas Maccabeus encamped prior to the battle in which he was slain in 161 B.C. (1 Macc. 9:5). Many of Judas' three thousand troops deserted when confronted by Syrian forces which outnumbered them more than seven to one; nevertheless, Judas was able to defeat the opponents' right wing before he fell in the final skirmish (vv. 8-18). The site is probably modern Khirbet Il'asa between Upper and Lower Beth-horon and 15 km. (9.3 mi.) from el-Bîreh.

ELASAH [ĕl'ə sə] (Heb. *'el'āśâ* "God has made").
1. The last son of Pashhur the priest who promised to send away his foreign wife (Ezra 10:22).
2. The son of Shaphan, and one of the two emissaries whom King Zedekiah sent to Nebuchadnezzar with Jeremiah's letter to the exiles at Babylon (Jer. 29:1-3).

ELATH [ē'lăth] (Heb. *'ēlat* "tall tree"). An Edomite city at the head of the Gulf of Aqabah, in the Old Testament frequently mentioned with EZION-GEBER. It was here that the Israelites turned north and marched toward Edom at the end of their wilderness wanderings (Deut. 2:8). David apparently captured the city following his victory over the Edomites in the valley of Salt (2 Sam. 8:13-14). Solomon later built a fleet at this port (1 Kgs. 9:26-27 par. 2 Chr. 8:17-18). The Edomites recaptured the city from Jehoram during their rebellion against Judah (2 Kgs. 8:20-22), but Uzziah (called Azariah at 2 Kgs. 14:2) "built" (JB, NIV "rebuilt") and restored Elath to Judah *ca.* 670 B.C. (2 Chr. 26:2, "Eloth"; Heb. *'elôt*). The city remained in Judahite control during the reign of Uzziah's son Jotham, but it again became Edomite territory at the time of Ahaz (*ca.* 735; 2 Kgs. 16:6). During Nabatean and Roman times the city was known as Ailah.

Because of the close proximity of the two cities (cf. 1 Kgs. 9:26), many scholars now identify both

Elath and Ezion-geber with modern Tell el-Kheleifeh. The settlement may have been known first as Ezion-geber and subsequently called Elath, a name of later Edomite origin.

EL-BERITH [ĕl bĭr'ĭth] (Heb. *'ēl bᵉrît* "El [or God] of the covenant"). A Canaanite deity worshipped at Shechem (Judg. 9:46; KJV "Berith"). *See* BAAL-BERITH.

EL-BETHEL [ĕl bĕth'əl] (Heb. *'ēl bêt-'ēl*).† A name given by Jacob to an altar he had erected at Bethel (Gen. 35:7), probably meaning "God of Bethel" (so RSV mg., KJV mg., NIV mg.), i.e., Yahweh, who had appeared to him as he fled from his brother Esau (28:10-22). Although less likely, the term may be a divine title, "God Bethel" (cf. LXX *Baithēl*), (*see* BETHEL [DEITY]).

ELDAAH [ĕl dā'ə] (Heb. *'elda'â*). The fifth son of Midian, and one of the grandsons of Abraham and Keturah (Gen. 25:4 par. 1 Chr. 1:33).

ELDAD [ĕl'dăd] (Heb. *'eldāḏ* "God has loved"[?]; cf. Akk. *Dadi-ilu* "Dadi is God"). One of seventy men chosen by Moses and gathered before the tent of meeting. The Lord granted them a measure of the Spirit he had given Moses and permitted them to prophesy for a time (Num. 11:24-25). Though Eldad stayed in the camp with Medad, they too were given the same Spirit and began to prophesy (v. 26). When Joshua became perturbed at the irregularity of Eldad's behavior, Moses replied that he wished that "all God's people were prophets" (vv. 27-30).

ELDER.

I. Old Testament

An older person (usually Heb. *zāqēn* "beard"), and thus a leader in a community. The elders were heads of households, representatives and leaders of tribes, and, at times, the most prominent men of a tribe. On the eve of the Exodus Moses explained to Israel's elders God's plan of deliverance (Exod. 4:29); later he consulted them during the wilderness wanderings (e.g., Lev. 16:25). At Lev. 4:15; 9:1 the elders are said to have assisted in cultic ceremonies (cf. Exod. 24:1, 14). On the advice of his father-in-law, Moses appointed "rulers" over the people who would assist him in administering justice (Exod. 18:24-26), and later, at God's prompting, he selected seventy elders to alleviate his own extensive judicial responsibilities (Num. 11:16, 24).

After the conquest of Palestine, various degrees of elders could be found. Listed in increasing importance within the social hierarchy, they functioned with respect to the household (2 Sam. 12:17; see also Gen. 50:7 for the elders of Pharaoh's house), city (e.g., Succoth [Judg. 8:14, 16], Bethlehem [Ruth 4:2, 4, in a judicial capacity], Jabesh [1 Sam. 11:3], and Samaria [2 Kgs. 10:1]), the various tribes (Gilead [Judg. 11:5, 7-8]), and the northern and southern tribal configurations (1 Sam. 30:26). Distinguished from heads of the tribes (Deut. 29:10; 31:28), "officers" (Heb. *šōṭᵉrîm*; Josh. 23:2; 24:1), and the local judges (Deut. 21:2; Josh.

8:33), elders actually decided many legal cases (Deut. 21:2ff., 19ff.; 22:15-18; 25:7-9 outline a number of their cases) and participated in reading the law (31:9). During the period of the judges, the elders recommended that the ark be brought into battle (1 Sam. 4:3) and were instrumental in establishing the Monarchy (8:4). The elders of Israel accepted David as their king (2 Sam. 5:3) and remained influential during the Monarchy (1 Sam. 15:30; 2 Sam. 17:4, 15) and during the divided monarchy (1 Kgs. 21:16). While they were often the king's counselors (e.g., 1 Kgs. 20:7-8), they also took part in cultic ceremonies (under David [1 Chr. 15:25] and Solomon [1 Kgs. 8:1, 3 par.]), including the reading of the Mosaic law (2 Chr. 34:29 par.).

With the Judahite deportation to Babylon, for which they were partly held responsible (Lam. 4:16; cf. Joel 1:14), the elders thenceforth had to shoulder the burden of leadership alone (Jer. 29:1). They were frequently in the company of Ezekiel, but did not always sincerely wish for divine guidance (Ezek. 20:3; according to Lam. 5:12 they were not respected). After Judah's return to Jerusalem, the elders assisted Ezra in his reform measures (Ezra 10:8, 14). These may be the "elders [Heb. śāḇ "beard"] of the Jews" mentioned at the time of the rebuilding of the temple (5:5, 9; 6:14).

II. New Testament

Among the members of the Sanhedrin, the Jewish supreme governing body, were elders (Gk. *presbýteros* "older"; e.g., Matt. 16:21 par.) who supervised the observance of the law (21:23) and the traditions (15:2 par.). They joined the other ruling authorities in the arrest (26:3) and trial of Jesus (26:57 par.; 27:1), and in the examination of the apostles (Acts 4:5). (*See also* SANHEDRIN.)

The Christian church followed the Jewish custom of granting authority to older persons who had shown laudable wisdom (e.g., 1 Tim. 5:1, "older men" [KJV "elder"]; Heb. 11:2, "men of old" [KJV "elders"; NIV "the ancients"; JB "ancestors"]). Almost from the birth of the Church there were elders who offered leadership (e.g., Acts 11:30; 21:18; cf. Jas. 5:14). The book of Acts cites their influence on the Apostolic Council at Jerusalem (15:6, 22) and afterward (16:4). At what stage of church growth the elders became actual office bearers, alongside of deacons and bishops, remains uncertain. Paul appointed elders in the Galatian churches (14:23) and conferred with the Ephesian elders (20:17). Certainly the office of elder was in existence at least as early as the end of the apostolic age (e.g., 1 Tim. 5:17; Tit. 1:5). (*See also* CHURCH *IV.*) According to 1 Tim. 4:14 the elders (KJV "presbytery") had the authority to bestow "gifts" through the laying on of hands.

Early Christian tradition associates the twenty-four elders of the Apocalypse (Rev. 4:4, 10) with the twelve patriarchs of Israel and the twelve apostles, thus the progenitors of Israel and the Church. More likely, however, they represent an angelic counterpart to the twenty-four priestly and twenty-four levitical orders.

Bibliography. G. Bornkamm, "πρέσβυς," *TDNT* 6 (1968): 651-683.

ELEAD [ĕl'ĭ əd] (Heb. *'elʿāḏ* "God has witnessed").

One of the sons of Ephraim killed by the inhabitants of Gath during a raid (1 Chr. 7:21-22).

ELEADAH [ĕl'ĭ ā'də] (Heb. *'elʿāḏâ* "God has adorned"). A descendant of Ephraim (1 Chr. 7:20; KJV "Eladah").

ELEALEH [ĕl'ĭ ā'lə] (Heb. *'elʿālēh* "God has ascended"). A city in Moab assigned to the Reubenites at the conquest of Transjordan (Num. 32:3, 37); judging from the prophetic oracles of Isaiah (Isa. 15:4; 16:9) and Jeremiah (Jer. 48:34), it later returned to Moabite possession. In the Old Testament it is often linked with Heshbon. Eusebius (*Onom.* lxxxiv.10) viewed it as an important city in the fourth century A.D. The ruins of Elealeh are located at contemporary el-ʿAl, 3 km. (2 mi.) north-northeast of Heshbon, along a main highway.

ELEASAH [ĕl'ĭ ā'sə] (Heb. *'elʿāśâ* "God has made").
1. A son of Helez of the lineage of Jerahmeel of Judah (1 Chr. 2:39-40).
2. The son of Raphah, and a descendant of Saul and Jonathan (1 Chr. 8:37); at 9:43 he is said to be the son of Rephaiah.

ELEAZAR [ĕl'ĭ ā'zər] (Heb. *'elʿāzār* "God has helped"; Gk. *Eleazar*).
1. The third son of Aaron and Elisheba (Exod. 6:23; cf. Num. 3:2; 26:60); he married one of the daughters of Putiel, who bore him a son, Phinehas (Exod. 6:25; 1 Chr. 6:4). Consecrated to the priesthood along with his father and three brothers (Exod. 28:1), his role increased after the sudden deaths of his older brothers Nadab and Abihu (Lev. 10:1-2). As the oldest living son of Aaron he became the chief of the Levites (Num. 3:32) and was Aaron's successor (20:25-28; cf. Deut. 10:6).

As high priest Eleazar participated in the census (Num. 26:1ff., 63). He was asked along with Moses to provide an inheritance for the daughters of Zelophehad (27:2), an act which he and Joshua finally adjudicated after the Conquest (Josh. 17:4). He was instructed to fashion an altar covering from the censers of Korah and his rebellious company (16:37-40). Eleazar also aided Moses in assigning an inheritance to the Reubenites (Num. 32:2, 8) east of the Jordan. Along with Joshua (Num. 27:19, 21), he also provided land for the tribes west of the Jordan (Josh. 14:1; 19:51; cf. Num. 34:17), and cities and pastureland for the Levites (Josh. 21:1). At the end of a distinguished term of service Eleazar died and was buried at Gibeah, a town in the hill country of Ephraim belonging to his son Phinehas (24:33).

Among the descendants of Eleazar were Zadok, a priest serving King David (1 Chr. 6:12; 24:6), and the postexilic scribe Ezra (Ezra 7:5). At the time of David the priests who descended from Eleazar comprised sixteen divisions, double those of the rival branch of priests descended from his younger brother Ithamar (1 Chr. 24:1-4).
2. The son of Abinadab, chosen by the men of Kiriath-jearim to take charge of the ark of the covenant after the Philistines had returned it to the Israelites at Beth-shemesh (1 Sam. 7:1).

3. The son of Dodo, and one of David's three mighty men (2 Sam. 23:9 par. 1 Chr. 11:12). He is credited with having slain many Philistines (1 Chr. 11:13-14).

4. The son of Mahli, and a member of the Merarites (1 Chr. 23:21; 24:28). When he died leaving no male offspring, his daughters were married to their cousins (23:22; RSV "kinsmen"; cf. Num. 36:6-12).

5. The son of Phinehas, and a postexilic priest under Ezra (Ezra 8:33).

6. One of the sons of Parosh who was to divorce his foreign wife (Ezra 10:25).

7. A postexilic priest (Neh. 12:42), perhaps the same as 5 above.

8. The fourth son of Mattathias the priest, surnamed Avaran; he was the brother of Judas Maccabeus (1 Macc. 2:5). He died heroically at Beth-zechariah, having sacrificed his life while attempting to kill an elephant which he supposed to carry King Antiochus IV Eupator (6:43-46).

9. An elderly scribe of high rank, martyred by Antiochus IV Epiphanes (2 Macc. 6:18-31).

10. A postexilic ancestor of Jesus (Matt. 1:15).

ELECT LADY (Gk. *hē eklektē kyría*).† The addressee of 2 John, considered to be either a person (Mary the mother of Jesus, Martha, or a certain Electa) or, more likely, the personification of a local church, whose "children" were its members (2 John 1). Its "elect sister" (v. 13) refers to the church from which John is writing his letter (cf. 1 Pet. 5:13). The reference is not to Peter's wife, who, according to 1 Cor. 9:5, accompanied the apostle on his missions.

ELECTION.† The choice of individuals or groups for a particular relationship or function.

I. Terminology

The most common Hebrew verb referring to election is Heb. *bāḥar* "choose," "examine," "prefer" (KoB, pp. 115-16). Less frequent are Heb. *bāḥîr* "chosen," "elect" (2 Sam. 21:6, KJV, NIV), *bārā'* "create" (Ezek. 21:19; KJV "choose"; RSV, NIV "make"; JB "put up"), *bārar* "choose" (1 Sam. 17:8), and *qābal* "receive" (1 Chr. 21:11; KJV, JB "choose"; RSV "take"). The New Testament usually uses Gk. *eklégomai* "choose out of" and its cognates *eklektós* "chosen," "elect," and *eklogē* "election" (found predominantly in the ancient versions).

II. Biblical Teachings

A. Old Testament. The Old Testament authors use the verb "choose" primarily in three senses. (1) It indicates a human choice. David chose Jonathan as his friend (1 Sam. 20:30) and later chose one of three punishments God offered him for having taken the census (2 Sam. 24:12-15). The craftsman chose wood from which to fashion an idol (Isa. 40:20). (2) It refers to a divine choice of inanimate entities. God chose Jerusalem as his sacred place of worship (1 Kgs. 14:21) and chose the true way for the righteous (Ps. 25:12). (3) It emphasizes a divine choosing of people. Of these three, the last is by far the most important biblically.

According to Deut. 7:6-11 God chose Israel as his people and the object of his love from among all the nations of the ancient Near East. Though the Exodus narrative of the covenant concluded on Mt. Horeb does not contain the verb "choose," it does imply the idea. Israel's history as a separate nation, in a sense, commenced with the events of the Exodus and Israel's wanderings in the wilderness prior to the Conquest of Canaan (Deut. 7:8-9; cf. 4:37). God allowed the Hebrews either to accept his special love and gain his blessing or to reject his kindness and provoke his wrath (vv. 7-10; cf. 30:19). In other words, the divinely initiated covenant recognized and fostered human responsibility: the Hebrews were to be "careful to do the commandment . . . statutes, and . . . ordinances" formulated by Yahweh (v. 11).

At first Yahweh chose a nation and made a covenant with the Hebrew people (Deut. 14:2; Ezek. 20:5). When the Israelites continued to reject that covenant by serving other gods, he permitted them to be deported, either to Assyria, in the case of the northern tribes, or to Babylonia, in the case of the southern tribes. In exile, the Hebrews learned that God would choose individual believers, the so-called remnant, rather than an entire nation as such, and that only these faithful few would realize his covenantal blessings (Isa. 65:22-23).

The earliest examples of divine election occurred with the patriarchs (e.g., Gen. 12:1; 17:9ff.; 25:24ff.). Later, Yahweh chose certain Hebrews — Moses (Ps. 106:23) and Aaron (Num. 16:5; 17:2ff.) — to lead his people through the wilderness and still later he appointed Saul (1 Sam. 10:24) and David (2 Sam. 6:21; Ps. 78:70-71) as their rulers. He also extended his love to his people as a whole (1 Kgs. 3:8) — to David's descendants (Ps. 89:3-4) or to Abraham's offspring (105:6, 43) and, after the fall of Jerusalem, to the faithful remnant, whom he promised a return to Jerusalem (Isa. 14:1-2; 65:8-10; cf. 43:20).

B. New Testament. The New Testament perspective on election demonstrates both continuity with and contrast to the Old Testament teachings. The New Testament writers retain the notion of human choice (e.g., Mary's choice to listen to Jesus rather than to act the hostess to him [Luke 10:42], and Paul's difficult choice between life and death [Phil. 1:22]). But there is no mention of God's preference for the inanimate such as Jerusalem (though the aged John speaks glowingly about the future of Jerusalem, the holy city [Rev. 21:2]). Moreover, the concept of God's chosen people is enlarged. Designating the faithful as "the elect" (perhaps the New Testament equivalent of the Old Testament "remnant"), the Synoptic Gospels record Jesus' promise that they would be sustained during future tribulation (Matt. 24:22, 24 par.), that their cause would be vindicated (Luke 18:7), and that they would gather from all directions at Christ's return (Matt. 24:31 par. Mark 13:27). Paul proclaims that no outside force can prevent the elect from fulfilling their charge to do God's will, secure in Christ's unfailing love (Rom. 8:33). With James he further affirms, as did the Old Testament prophets, that God's choice of the elect is his prerogative (1 Cor. 1:27-28; Jas. 2:5) and is not dependent on human initiative (cf. Rom. 9:11), though it does require a human response (so 2 Pet. 1:10; cf. Col. 3:12).

III. Theological Reflections

Biblical exegetes have called attention to the New Testament link between God's decree of election and his revelation in Christ. According to Eph. 1:4 God "chose us in him [Christ] before the foundation of the world." The Father chose his own people before time began, showing them his love through his eternal Son, who redeemed sinners in time and who as the "Chosen" (Luke 9:35, Gk. *eklelegménos*; p[45] and other important manuscripts; cf. the chosen servant of Isa. 42:1) in turn chose his disciples (Luke 6:13 par.; John 6:70) and, through them, many others.

Whether God's election is universal or restricted continues to be a divisive issue among theologians and the various factions of the community of believers. On the basis of Rom. 9:1ff., the apostle Paul would seem to argue that God did choose one group of people over others, analogous to his choice many centuries ago of one nation, Israel, over countless others. To support this claim he cites Gen. 25:23, which foretells Esau's subjection to Jacob and his hatred for Esau and his descendants (cf. Mal. 1:2-3). (*See also* PREDESTINATION.)

The New Testament writers concentrate on the Christian community as the embodiment of the elect. Within the sphere of the larger community, as also in the communities which make up the Church, individuals respond to the gospel (cf. 1 Pet. 2:9; 1 Thess. 1:4). Thus, to this community belong both Gentiles and Jews (Rom. 11:5, 26ff.), though not all biological descendants of Abraham (9:6–11:12). Christians remain divided over the role of free will in this response as well as the relation of grace to faith and good works.

God chose his elect not that they should be proud and boast of their favored position vis-à-vis those not chosen, but that they should live a life of holiness, that through their lifestyle they should communicate the gospel to others in the hope that they would respond positively to Christ. Out of mercy God bestowed his love on his people, assuring them that their weak and faltering faith was not in vain but would be supported by his unfailing love. God also gave them his love, so that they in turn might love others and praise him for his mercy.

Bibliography. G. C. Berkouwer, *Divine Election* (Grand Rapids: 1960); P. K. Jewett, *Election and Predestination* (Grand Rapids: 1985); G. Nordholt, "Elect," *DNTT* 1:536-543; G. Quell and G. Schrenk, "ἐκλέγομαι, ἐκλεκτός, ἐκλογή," *TDNT* 4 (1967): 144-192; H. H. Rowley, *The Biblical Doctrine of Election* (Chicago: 1952); H. Seebass, "bāchar [bāḥar]," *TDOT* 2, rev. ed. (1977): 73-87.

ELECTRUM. The RV mg. rendering of Heb. *ḥašmal* at Ezek. 1:4, 27; 8:2. Following the LXX (*élektron*) or Vulgate (*electrum*), some scholars consider electrum an alloy containing four parts gold and one part silver; others, on the basis of Akk. *ešmaru* (from Elam. *ilmasu* "inlay" or "bronze") translate it "gleaming bronze" (RSV; NIV "glowing metal"; JB "a sheen like bronze"; KJV "color of amber").

EL-ELOHE-ISRAEL [ĕl ĕl'ō hē īz'rĭ əl] (Heb. *'ēl 'elōhê yiśrā'ēl* "God, the God of Israel" or "mighty is the God of Israel").† The name of an altar erected by Jacob near Shechem, following his safe arrival in Canaan (Gen. 33:20; JB "El, God of Israel"). Jacob associated the altar with his experience at Peniel (vv. 24-32) where he saw God (Heb. *'elōhîm*) "face to face"; it was built to express his faith in the power of God, who had given him a new name: Israel.

Like other divine names compounded with El, this name probably derives from pre-Israelite usage, possibly from the confederation of northern tribes centered around Shechem. With the acceptance of Yahweh as the God of Israel, the name became "Yahweh [or the Lord], the God of Israel" (e.g., Exod. 5:1; Josh. 8:30; Judg. 5:3, 5).

EL ELYON [ĕl' ĕl yōn'] (Heb. *'ēl 'elyôn*).* A name of God, translated "Most High" (cf. Ugar. *'ly*). Generally regarded as having derived from the Canaanite creator god worshipped at pre-Israelite Jerusalem (Salem; cf. Gen. 14:18-20), it was adapted as an epithet of Yahweh (cf. v. 22; Ps. 7:17; 91:9). It is found in the earliest biblical poetry (e.g., Num. 24:16; Deut. 32:8) and later archaizing poetry (e.g., Ps. 78:35; cf. Aram. *'elyônîn*, Dan. 7:18, 22, 25, 27).

ELEMENTAL SPIRITS (Gk. *stoicheía*). A New Testament term usually understood to refer to the stars' powers (NIV "basic principles"; JB "[elemental] principles") over human beings or to angels who, as guardians of the law, seek to control human life (see JB note b at Gal. 4:3). According to H. N. Ridderbos (*The Epistle of Paul to the Churches of Galatia.* NICNT [1953], p. 153 n. 5), however, it is not likely that Paul identified these "spirits" with the astral bodies, for at Gal. 4:3 he used the term to indicate principles by which the Gentiles sought redemption apart from Christ and at Col. 2:20 to link the universe with the world, a human domain ruled by sin. Actually, the apostle considered the Greek term to refer more to primary principles, such as the legal prescriptions which bound the Gentiles and possibly Judaistic ceremonies and ascetic practices. His point is that believers are no longer subject to these human precepts (Gal. 4:3-9; KJV "elements of the world") and should no more be enticed by them (Col. 2:8; KJV "rudiments of the world"). Rather, believers should adhere to the basic features of divine revelation (cf. Heb. 5:12; NEB "the ABC of God's oracles").

ELEPH (Josh. 18:28, KJV). See HA-ELEPH.

ELEPHANT (Gk. *eléphas* "ivory"). Any of the large proboscidean mammals (so called because of their long protruding trunks). Only two species remain: the Indian elephant (*Eliphas indicus*) and the larger African elephant (*Eliphas africanus*). The elephant is prized for the large ivory tusks of the male; in the African species these tusks reach a length of 2.5 m. (8 ft.) and a weight of 90 kg. (198 lbs.) and in the Indian species 1.8 m. (6 ft.) and 20 kg. (44 lbs.).

Native to Southeast Asia, from the foot of the Himalayan mountains to the island of Sumatra, the Indian elephant, it is assumed, must have roamed through many parts of Asia, including northern Syria, where it was hunted by the Assyrians — in the eleventh

Tribute, including an elephant and monkeys, coming from Musri to Assyria (from the Black Obelisk of Shalmaneser III) (by courtesy of the Trustees of the British Museum)

century by Tiglath-pileser I and in the ninth century by Assurbanipal II (*ARAB* 1:247, 519-520). *Ca.* 850 it nearly became extinct due to the expansion of civilization and the growing demand for ivory; this may help to explain why the Old Testament does not mention the elephant. In Hellenistic times elephants were known to the Greeks (Aristotle *Hist. anim.* ix.1 [610a. 15-16]), and in the Jewish wars of liberation they were employed by Antiochus V Eupator (1 Macc. 3:34; 6:30, 45-47).

In Old Testament times the ivory (Heb. *šēn* "tooth") of the Indian elephant was transported from Asia to Palestine and surrounding countries over land or on ships manned by Phoenician sailors. Solomon's Tarshish fleet probably imported African ivory (1 Kgs. 10:22 par.), with which he embellished his palace (v. 18 par.), as did later kings and nobles of the northern kingdom (22:39; Amos 3:15; 6:4). *See* IVORY.

ELEPHANTINE PAPYRI [ĕl′ə făn tī′nĭ pə pī′rĭ]. A number of fifth-century B.C. Aramaic papyri discovered on an island in the Nile river opposite Aswan (biblical Syene), near the First Cataract. The name (Gk. *Elephantinē* "elephant location," possibly because Nubian ivory was traded here) designates the Jewish colony settled during the Persian period (early sixth century B.C.) on the site of Egyptian Iebew, an important trade center which had been the southernmost city of the Old Kingdom. The first group of papyri was purchased from dealers in 1893, but was not published until 1953. A larger collection was purchased after 1900, in stages, and published by A. H. Sayce and A. E. Cowley (1906) and E. Sachau (1911).

The papyri document legal and business transactions, adoption, and other matters. Perhaps some of the Jewish populace migrated to Egypt when social conditions in Judah deteriorated at the end of the sixth century

The island of Elephantine (W. S. LaSor)

Elephantine Papyri: a fifth-century B.C. deed for a house (The Brooklyn Museum, bequest of Miss Theodora Wilbour)

(according to Jer. 43-44 certain Jews moved to Egypt following the fall of Jerusalem in 587/6). At any rate, the refugees led a relatively peaceful existence here until 525, when Cambyses II conquered Egypt and established Persian control; he may have turned the settlement into a garrison to protect the Jews from Egyptian attacks. In *ca.* 410 the Jewish temple was destroyed by the Egyptians; following the wane of Persian influence, the garrison may have been moved in 399, though the Jews continued to live in the area for several centuries.

The papyri also throw light on the Jewish mode of worship. In a temple dedicated to *Yhw* (an abbreviation of Yahweh) the Hebrews also paid homage to 'Anat-bethel, a West-Semitic deity, and Herem-bethel; this suggests a syncretistic attitude on their part. It remains debatable whether or not they celebrated the Passover under the authorization of Darius II (419), as the so-called Passover papyrus implies.

A letter sent to Bagoas, the Persian governor of Judah, in 407 regarding the earlier pillaging of the Jewish temple apparently reiterates a previous letter which petitioned for rebuilding of the sacred shrine. Although no official reply from Jerusalem survives, a memorandum to the Egyptian governor Arsames indicates support for the reconstruction.

The papyri may attest the authenticity of the Aramaic portions of the book of Ezra, notably the letters contained in chapter 4. The letter to Bagoas refers to Sanballat and Johanan the high priest (Neh. 12:22; cf. 13:28).

Bibliography. A. E. Cowley, *Aramaic Papyri of the Fifth Century B.C.* (1923; repr. Osnabrück: 1976); E. G. Kraeling, *The Brooklyn Museum Aramaic Papyri* (1953; repr. Brooklyn: 1969).

ELEVEN, THE (Gk. *hoi héndeka*).† A designation for Jesus' eleven disciples in the brief period succeeding Judas' death and preceding his replacement by Matthias (Acts 1:26). The risen Savior appeared to them on two, possibly three, occasions — at Jerusalem (Luke 24:33), in Galilee (Matt. 28:16), and possibly elsewhere (Mark 16:14). At Acts 2:14 Peter is depicted as the representative of the eleven, an interpretation supported by Codex Bezae (D), which reads the "ten."

See also TWELVE, THE.

ELEVENTH HOUR. See HOUR.

ELHANAN [ĕl hā′nən] (Heb. *'elḥānān* "God is gracious").†
1. The son of Jair (according to 2 Sam. 21:19, Jaareoregim the Bethlehemite), and one of those who conquered a foe of enormous size during David's wars with the Philistines. Most likely his victim was Goliath the Gittite; the parallel account at 1 Chr. 20:5 calls him "Lahmi, the brother of Goliath," perhaps a textual error resulting from confusion with the Hebrew for Bethlehemite or plausibly an editorial attempt to distinguish between this incident and that involving David at 1 Sam. 17:4. Some scholars regard Elhanan as the original name of David, replaced by a throne name (cf. Mari letters, Akk. *dawidum* "commander").
2. The son of Dodo of the tribe of Bethlehem, and one of David's thirty mighty men (2 Sam. 23:24 par. 1 Chr. 11:26). If, as some scholars suggest, he is the same as **1** above, he would be a member of the clan of Jair.

ELI [ē′lī] (Heb. *'ēlî* "exalted"; probably an abbreviation of "God is exalted").† The high priest of the early Israelite shrine at Shiloh and one of the last of the minor judges; in the latter role he is said to have served for forty years (1 Sam. 4:18; ca. 1119-1079 B.C.), which would have made him a contemporary of Samson (but cf. LXX, "twenty years"). Although Eli's ancestors are not mentioned in the Old Testament, he may have been a descendant of Aaron's youngest son Ithamar (so Josephus *Ant.* v.11.5 [361]; cf. 1 Chr. 24:3); another tradition associates him with the rival Eleazar branch (2 Esdr. 1:2-3).

The aged priest first appears, seated beside the doorpost of the temple, as a witness to Hannah's petition for a son (1 Sam. 1:9-18); subsequently the infant Samuel was brought to Eli for dedication to the service of the Lord (vv. 24-28; cf. 2:19-20). Unable to restrain his sons Hophni and Phinehas from their abuse of the priestly office (2:12-17, 22-25; 4:1), Eli received word through an anonymous prophet of the tragic demise of his house (vv. 27-36). The partially blind priest assisted young Samuel in receiving the divine revelation confirming Eli's own fate (3:1-18). In fulfillment of the prophecy, both of Eli's sons died in the Philistine rout of Israel at Ebenezer (4:11, 17); but it was word of the capture of the ark during that same battle which caused the death of the ineffectual though nevertheless devout priest (v. 18; cf. v. 13).

The fate of Eli's descendants, foretold in 2:31-33, was fulfilled by Saul's slaughter of the Elide priests at Nob (22:19). The sole survivor of that massacre, Abiathar (v. 20), subsequently became David's high priest along with Zadok (2 Sam. 20:25), only to be deposed by Solomon for his support of Adonijah's succession (1 Kgs. 2:27; cf. 1:7).

ELI, ELI, LAMA SABACHTHANI [ā′lē ā′lē lä′mə sə bäk′thə nī] (Gk. *ēlí ēlí lamá sabachtháni*, a transliteration of Heb. *'ēlî 'ēlî lāmâ ʿazabtānî*).† A cry uttered by Jesus on the cross, traditionally designated the fourth word on the cross, spoken just before his death (Matt. 27:46); Gk. *elōí* at Mark 15:34 reflects the Aramaic form. Following a three-hour period of darkness, the Savior exclaimed: "My God, my God, why hast thou forsaken me?" echoing the intense suffering of the psalmist (Ps. 22:1 [MT 2]). Some commentators view Jesus' words as an expression of dread at paying the price for human sin to a God who insisted on satisfaction. Others believe his words recall the entire psalm, which ends with a note of praise, to imply that Jesus did not lose faith in the Father.

The similarity between Heb. *'ēlî* "my God" and *'ēlîyāhû* "Elijah" apparently prompted some in the crowd gathered below him to interpret Jesus as calling upon Elijah, the Hebrew prophet who did not die but was taken to heaven and was believed to protect those in danger and affliction.

ELIAB [ĭ lī′əb] (Heb. *'elî'āb* "God is father").
1. A leader of the tribe of Zebulun (Num. 2:7; 10:16) who aided Moses in the census (1:9) and made an offering in behalf of the tribe (7:24); a son of Helon.
2. A Reubenite, the son of Pallu and the father of Dathan and Abiram (Num. 16:1, 12); according to 26:8-9, Numuel was his first son.
3. The firstborn son of Jesse whose height and physical appearance prompted Samuel to consider him Israel's next king; God, however, commanded the prophet to disregard appearance and choose Eliab's youngest brother, David, instead (1 Sam. 16:6-7, 12-13). On one occasion, when stationed in Saul's army, Eliab rebuked David for asking the Israelite troops about the reward to be given to the man who would kill the giant Goliath (17:13, 28-30). Eliab's daughter Abihail married Jerimoth, the son of David, and gave birth to Mahalath, who married Rehoboam (2 Chr. 11:18).
4. A Levite mentioned in the genealogy of Samuel (1 Chr. 6:27); he is also known as Elihu (1 Sam. 1:1) or Eliel (1 Chr. 6:34).
5. A Gadite who joined David at the stronghold in the wilderness, the third of his mighty warriors (1 Chr. 12:8-9), and later an officer in David's band (v. 18).
6. A Levite of the second order appointed as a musician to play harps and lyres (1 Chr. 15:18, 20; 16:5).

ELIADA [ĭ lī′ə də] (Heb. *'elyāḏāʿ* "God knows").
1. One of David's sons born in Jerusalem of an unnamed mother (2 Sam. 5:16; 1 Chr. 3:8); in a parallel list he is named Beeliada (1 Chr. 14:7).
2. The father of Rezon, the adversary of Solomon (1 Kgs. 11:23; KJV "Eliadah").
3. A man from the tribe of Benjamin who assumed a commanding position in the army of King Jehoshaphat (2 Chr. 17:17).

ELIADAH (1 Kgs. 11:23, KJV). *See* ELIADA **2.**

ELIAH (1 Chr. 8:27; Ezra 10:26, KJV). *See* ELIJAH.

ELIAHBA [ĭ lī'ə bə] (Heb. *'elyaḥbā'* "God hides"). A man from Shaalbon, who became one of David's thirty mighty men (2 Sam. 23:32 par. 1 Chr. 11:33).

ELIAKIM [ĭ lī'ə kĭm] (Heb. *'elyāqîm* "God raises up"; Gk. *Eliakeim*).

1. A son of Hilkiah. He was one of three representatives of King Hezekiah who pleaded with the Assyrian Rabshakeh in behalf of the besieged city of Jerusalem (2 Kgs. 18:18 par.); when no agreement was reached Hezekiah sent them to the prophet Isaiah for counsel (19:2). According to Isa. 22:15-25 Eliakim replaced Shebna as "master of the palace" (JB; NIV "palace administrator"; RSV, head of Hezekiah's "household"). Eliakim's authority as described in this prophecy (v. 22) is recalled in describing the role of Christ in determining entrance to the heavenly kingdom (Rev. 1:18; 3:7).

2. The second son of King Josiah whom Pharaoh Neco made vassal ruler over Jerusalem after deposing his elder brother Jehoahaz and deporting him to Egypt (2 Kgs. 23:34 par. 2 Chr. 36:4). By changing Eliakim's name to Jehoiakim ("Yahweh raises up") Neco may have sought to imply Yahweh's approval for this action.

3. A priest who participated in the dedication service of the restored walls of Jerusalem during the administration of Nehemiah (Neh. 12:41).

4. A descendant of Zerubbabel and an ancestor of Jesus (Matt. 1:13).

5. A descendant of King David through his son Nathan and an ancestor of Jesus (Luke 3:30).

ELIAM [ĭ lī'əm] (Heb. *'elî'ām* "God is kinsman").

1. The father of Bathsheba, the wife of Uriah the Hittite (2 Sam. 11:3); at 1 Chr. 3:5 he is named Ammiel ("my kinsman is God").

2. The son of Ahithophel of Gilo, who became one of David's thirty mighty men (2 Sam. 23:34).

ELIAS (KJV). *See* ELIJAH.

ELIASAPH [ĭ lī'ə săf] (Heb. *'elyāsap* "God has added").

1. The son of Lael, and a chief of the Gershonites during the wilderness wanderings (Num. 3:24).

2. The son of Deuel (Num. 10:42) or Reuel (2:14). As representative of the tribe of Gad, he assisted Moses in the census (1:14) and the offering (7:42, 47).

ELIASHIB [ĭ lī'ə shĭb] (*'elyāšîḇ* "God restores").

1. One of the sons of Elioenai, and a descendant of Zerubbabel (1 Chr. 3:24).

2. A priest of the eleventh division during the days of David (1 Chr. 24:12).

3. A Levite and a singer who was forced to divorce his foreign wife (Ezra 10:24).

4, 5. Two Israelites, sons of Zattu and of Bani, who consented to divorce their foreign wives (Ezra 10:27, 36).

6. The son of Joiakim and grandson of Jeshua (Neh. 12:10). As high priest during Nehemiah's first term at Jerusalem, Eliashib joined his fellow priests in rebuilding the Sheep Gate (3:1). But later, in Nehemiah's absence, he prepared a large chamber in the temple at Jerusalem (13:4-6) for Tobiah the Ammonite in defiance of a law barring admission to Ammonites. Eliashib's two sons were Joiada (12:10-11) and Jehohanan (Ezra 10:6); one of his grandsons (via Jehoiada) married a daughter of Sanballat the Horite, reason enough for Nehemiah to expel him from the temple (Neh. 13:28).

ELIATHAH [ĭ lī'ə thə] (Heb. *'elî'āṭâ* "God has come"). One of the sons of Heman who served as a temple musician during the reign of King David (1 Chr. 25:4); by lot he was assigned to direct the twentieth division of musicians (v. 27).

ELIDAD [ĭ lī'dăd] (Heb. *'elîḏāḏ* "God has loved"). The son of Chislon and representative of the tribe of Benjamin chosen to assist in the division of the land (Num. 34:21).

ELIEHOENAI [ĭ lī'ə hō ē'nī] (Heb. *'elyᵉhô'ênay* "my eyes are toward Yahweh").

1. The seventh son of Meshelemiah, a Levite and a gatekeeper of the temple (1 Chr. 26:3; KJV "Elioenai").

2. The son of Zerahiah, and one of the exiles returning with Ezra (Ezra 8:4; KJV "Elihoenai").

ELIEL [ĭ lī'əl] (Heb. *'elî'ēl* "El is God" or "my God is God").

1. The head of a fathers' houses in the eastern half-tribe of Manasseh (1 Chr. 5:24).

2. A son of Toah and father of Jeroham (1 Chr. 6:34); probably the same as ELIAB **4** (6:27) or ELIHU **1** (1 Sam. 1:1).

3. Two Benjaminites, one the son of Shimei and the other the son of Shashak, residing at Jerusalem (1 Chr. 8:20, 22).

4. Two of David's mighty men (1 Chr. 11:46-47).

5. One of the Gadites who joined David at the stronghold in the wilderness (1 Chr. 12:11). He may have been one of David's mighty men.

6. The son of Hebron, and one of the Levites who assisted in bringing the ark to Jerusalem (1 Chr. 15:9, 11).

7. A Levite and one of the overseers appointed by Hezekiah to supervise the temple contributions and tithes (2 Chr. 31:13).

ELIENAI [ĕl'ĭ ē'nī] (Heb. *'elî'ênay*). A descendant of Shimei of the tribe of Benjamin (1 Chr. 8:20).

ELIEZER [ĕl'ĭ ē'zər] (Heb. *'elî'ezer* "my God is my help").

1. Abraham's most trusted servant whom he designates as his heir (Heb. *ben-mešeq,* Gen. 15:2; LXX *ho huiós Masék* "the son of Masek"; KJV "steward"; NIV "inherit my estate"); he is generally said to be from Damascus (Heb. *dammešeq*), although the Hebrew text is unclear. He may have been the "oldest servant" mentioned at 24:2, who, some sixty years later, was charged by Abraham to secure a wife for his grown son Isaac from among Abraham's kinsmen in Mesopotamia.

2. The younger son of Moses and Zipporah (Exod.

18:4), so named because the Lord delivered Moses from Pharaoh. Eliezer's only son was named Rahabiah (1 Chr. 23:17). Some commentators consider that the boy whom Zipporah circumcised was Eliezer (Exod. 4:25; cf. v. 20 "sons"); others believe that his brother Gershom is intended here.

3. One of the sons of Becher, and a grandson of Benjamin (1 Chr. 7:8).

4. A priest and musician who assisted in bringing the ark to Jerusalem (1 Chr. 15:24).

5. The son of Zichri and chief officer of the Reubenites during David's reign (1 Chr. 27:16).

6. The son of Dodavahu of Mareshah. His prophecy against King Jehoshaphat concerning the king's alliance with Ahaziah of Israel terminated the shipbuilding activities at Ezion-geber (2 Chr. 20:35-37).

7. One of the priests commissioned by Ezra to find "ministers" for the temple in Jerusalem from among the inhabitants of Casiphia (Ezra 8:16-17).

8, 9, 10. A priest, a Levite, and a lay Israelite, each required to divorce his foreign wife (Ezra 10:18, 23, 31).

11. An ancestor of Jesus (Luke 3:29).

ELIHOENAI (Ezra 8:4, KJV). See ELIEHOENAI.

ELIHOREPH [ĕlʹə hôrʹĭf] (Heb. *ʾelîḥōrep* "God of autumn"[?]). A high official at the Solomonic court, who with his brother Ahijah fulfilled the office of royal secretary (1 Kgs. 4:3).

ELIHU [ĭ līʹhū] (Heb. *ʾelîhû, ʾelîhû* "He is my God").

1. An Ephraimite, the son of Tohu, and the great-grandfather of Samuel (1 Sam. 1:1); he is called Eliel at 1 Chr. 6:34 and Eliab at 1 Chr. 6:27.

2. A chief of a thousand from Manasseh who defected to David at Ziklag (1 Chr. 12:20).

3. One of the gatekeepers in the temple, of the lineage of Obed-edom (1 Chr. 26:7).

4. One of David's brothers, the chief officer of the tribe of Issachar (1 Chr. 27:18). The name probably should read Eliab (so LXX), thus David's eldest brother mentioned at 1 Sam. 16:6-7.

5. The son of Barachel the Buzite, of the family of Ram (Job 32:2), possibly a descendant of Nahor's son Buz and thus related to Abraham (Gen. 22:20-21). Elihu's speeches (Job 32–37) reiterate and amplify those of Job and his three friends. He chides Job for his human limitations: sinfulness (34:7-8), arrogance (v. 37), and theological superficiality (35:16). In bold contrast, he declares, is the majesty of God (36:27-37:22), whose ways are ultimately just (34:10ff.; 37:23-24) and who in his sovereign wisdom may employ suffering as a test (36:5-15). Although most scholars now concur that Elihu's speeches represent a later insertion into the book of Job, they do serve dramatically as preparation for and transition to the divine disclosure in the whirlwind which resolves the issues at hand. See JOB, BOOK OF.

ELIJAH [ĭ līʹjə] (Heb. *ʾelîyāhû, ʾēlîyâ* "my God is Yahweh"; Gk. *Ēleias*).

1. A ninth-century B.C. Israelite prophet from Tishbe in Gilead, whose ministry had a profound effect not only on his times but also on the intertestamental period and New Testament times. According to some scholars, the accounts of Elijah's activity recorded in 1–2 Kings are taken from an independent source devoted to this powerful prophet.

I. Life and Ministry

A. Defense of Yahweh Worship. Elijah appeared in Israel at a time when Ahab, son of the nefarious Omri, was promoting Baal worship over that of Yahweh, under the influence of his Phoenician wife Jezebel (1 Kgs. 16:29-33). Following a dramatic meeting with Ahab in which the prophet announced the imminence of a severe drought (17:1), which would undermine and attack Israel's faith in the Phoenician deity of fertility, Elijah hid himself at the brook Cherith in Transjordan; there he was sustained by ravens which brought him food and the brook which provided him with water (vv. 2-7). (The length of the drought was about twenty months; the New Testament tradition of three and a half years [so Luke 4:25; Jas. 5:17; cf. 1 Kgs. 18:1 "third year"] may simply refer to a long, indefinite period of time.) When the brook dried up, God summoned Elijah to go to Zarephath, between Tyre and Sidon, where the prophet performed two miracles: he provided food for a widow and her household from a jar of meal and a cruse of oil and restored to life this widow's son (1 Kgs. 17:7-24).

Several months later, when the northern kingdom was still suffering acutely the effects of the drought, Elijah appeared to Obadiah, a royal official who remained faithful to Yahweh (18:3-4). He then confronted Ahab, whom he denounced and challenged to a religious contest (vv. 17-20) on Mt. Carmel between Elijah and 450 prophets of Baal. Elijah permitted his opponents to invoke their deity first, but when their efforts bore no results, he prayed to his God. Yahweh sent fire from heaven that consumed the burnt offering, the wooden altar, and even the water that had been poured over the offering (vv. 20-38). While the bystanders were greatly impressed and confessed their new-found allegiance to Yahweh, Elijah ordered the execution of all of Baal's prophets at the brook Kishon (vv. 39-40). After announcing to the dumb-founded king that rain was about to fall, he prayed seven times to Yahweh on Mt. Carmel's southeastern peak, and the rains commenced (vv. 41-45). In glad celebration, Elijah ran before Ahab the 27 km. (17 mi.) to the royal residence at Jezreel (v. 46).

B. Further Dealings with Ahab. When told about the outcome of the contest, Jezebel was angered at the prospect of having to yield to the worship of Yahweh and threatened to kill Elijah (19:1-2). Fearing the same fate he had imposed on Baal's prophets, Elijah traveled southward, and asked the Lord to take his life (vv. 3-4). However, strengthened by food provided by a divine messenger, he traveled all the way to Mt. Horeb (Sinai), where Moses had received the law many centuries before (vv. 5-8). In a cave he complained bitterly to Yahweh about Israel's indifference to true religion, emphasizing his own faithfulness and the threats on his life (vv. 9-10). Then summoned to the mountain, he endured a strong wind, an earthquake, and a fire before at last the Lord appeared in a "still small voice" (vv. 11-13). But instead of sympathizing with his servant, the Lord charged him with three additional tasks: to anoint Hazael king over

Syria and Jehu king over the northern kingdom, and to anoint Elisha his successor as prophet of the Lord (vv. 15-16). The Lord then indicated how Elijah would be protected against the threats of Jezebel and revealed to his depressed prophet that some seven thousand persons had remained loyal to Yahweh. With his complaint addressed and silenced, the prophet left the mountain (1 Kgs. 19:16-19) to "anoint" Elisha as prophet (vv. 19-21). (It was his successor, however, who would in due time complete the other two tasks; 2 Kgs. 8:7-15; 9:1-10.)

Elijah was sent again to Ahab, who had taken possession of a vineyard belonging to his neighbor Naboth the Jezreelite. After giving Naboth a mock trial, Ahab had had him stoned to death (21:1-17). Obeying the Lord, the prophet appeared, as dauntless as before, to proclaim God's judgment on Ahab's house for the perversion of justice and the shedding of innocent blood (vv. 17-24). Even though the king had committed himself to idolatry, he was visibly shaken; he repented of his wicked deeds, and fasted (vv. 25-27). As a result, the Lord informed Elijah that the prophesied disaster would not befall Ahab's household until after the king's death (vv. 28-29).

C. Encounter with Ahaziah. Eager to recover from an illness, the son and successor of King Ahab, Ahaziah, sent messengers to Ekron to consult the local deity Baal-zebub over whether he might be healed (2 Kgs. 1:1-2). When the messengers returned, they related to the king that a person wearing a garment of haircloth and a leather girdle had instructed them to return to their sovereign and to announce to him that he would not recover (vv. 5-8). Recognizing the prophet by the description of his clothing, Ahaziah disregarded Elijah's message and sent a contingent of soldiers to capture the prophet. When two contingents of fifty men were reported to have been consumed by fire, the captain of the third band begged the prophet to spare his life, asking him to return to the king voluntarily. The prophet consented and repeated his message to the king: Ahaziah would not improve because he had inquired after Baal-zebub rather than after the God of Israel (vv. 9-17).

D. Elijah's Translation. Elijah, like his predecessor Enoch (Gen. 5:25), was translated, i.e., taken to heaven without having died a natural death. When his successor Elisha refused to leave his service at Gilgal, at Bethel, and at Jericho, Elijah finally accepted his company near the river Jordan, which they both crossed when Elijah struck the water with his rolled-up mantle (2 Kgs. 2:1-8). Then Elijah invited Elisha to make a wish, and the younger man asked for a double share of Elijah's spirit (vv. 9-10). As they continued their discourse, Elisha witnessed his teacher's departure in a chariot of fire that separated them and took Elijah to heaven in a whirlwind (v. 11; cf. v. 1). Elisha recognized what had happened, exclaiming, "My father, my father! the chariots of Israel and its horsemen!" (v. 12).

E. Letter to Jehoram. While Elijah's ministry coincided mainly with the reigns of the Israelite kings Ahab (875-854) and his son Ahaziah (854-853), a final prophecy is attributed to him concerning Jehoram (852-841), son of the righteous Jehoshaphat of Judah (873-849). Jehoram, who married the daughter of King Ahab, introduced Baal worship into the southern kingdom (2 Chr. 21:1-6 par. 2 Kgs. 8:16-18). The Chronicler adds that near the end of Jehoram's reign (2 Chr. 21:2) a letter from Elijah found its way to the royal palace in which the prophet accused the king of idolatry and murder and predicted a plague on him and his house (vv. 13-15). Although it is conceivable that Elijah survived until shortly after Jehoram's succession and the subsequent bloodbath, most scholars agree that this document is a later, apocryphal composition; it represents the only reference to either Elijah or Elisha in 1-2 Chronicles and, in distinctive style, is proclaimed in the name of "the Lord, the God of David, your father" (v. 12). More conservative commentators suggest that the prophet composed the letter well before the events for dispatch following his death.

II. Significance

A. Old Testament. As one of the greatest of the Old Testament prophets, Elijah urged the northern kingdom (and to a lesser extent the southern kingdom) to rededicate itself to the worship of Yahweh, the God of the covenant who had appeared to the tribes in the wilderness at Horeb. It is surprising that among the later prophets he is mentioned only by Malachi, who ends his prophetic book with a reference to Elijah's place in the future. Just before the dreaded Day of the Lord Elijah is to return to reconcile fathers and children to true piety and worship and avert divine condemnation (Mal. 4:5-6).

B. Intertestamental Period. Building on the Old Testament tradition of Elijah's mysterious rapture and promised return, Ben Sirach (Sir. 48:10) describes the prophet's future role as one in which he would mitigate God's wrath, restore households, and reunite the twelve tribes. Others view him as the high priest of the eschatological age who will herald the second coming of the Messiah to bring an era of peace and salvation (e.g., 1 En. 89:12).

C. New Testament. The Jews' expectation of Elijah's return and future deeds stayed aflame in New Testament times (KJV "Elias"). According to Matthew (Matt. 27:47, 49) and Mark (Mark 15:35-36) the crowd interpreted Jesus' cry of agony on the cross as a call for Elijah. Some of the Jews identified John the Baptist, the fiery preacher who insisted on being a hermit in the desert, with the Old Testament prophet, perhaps on the basis of the annunciation to Zechariah, John's father (Luke 1:16-17, quoting Mal. 4:5); others associated Jesus and Elijah (Matt. 16:14 par.; Mark 6:15). Though John the Baptist refused such honor (John 1:21, 25), Jesus, as Matthew records, accepted and promoted this identification for him, both when John was in prison (Matt. 11:14) and following his own transfiguration (17:10-13).

All of the Synoptic Gospels include the Transfiguration episode (Matt. 17:3 par.) in which Jesus discourses with Elijah about his "departure" at Jerusalem (Luke 9:31), i.e., about his imminent suffering and death on the cross and possibly his ascension.

In some ways Elijah may be seen as an Old Testament counterpart of Christ, urging people to change their misdirected loyalties. Jesus Christ, however, perfected and completed Elijah's ministry of reconciliation (implied at Mark 9:12; cf. Matt. 17:12-13). Though Elijah ascended to heaven in a chariot of fire, Christ's ascension produced a community of witnesses (rather than a successor) and enabled the risen Lord to pour sanctifying fire on the crowd at Pentecost.

Although the Christian church has preserved the tradition of Elijah's future ministry, it has not lost sight of his historical service. For example, at Luke 4:25-26 Christ relates his work at Nazareth to that of Elijah, who helped the widow of Zarephath rather than Israelite widows at the time of the drought. To Paul the Old Testament account of the preservation of seven thousand believers during Ahab's reign forecast God's continued dealings with the Jews (Rom. 11:2-5). James viewed Elijah's success as the prime example of the power of prayer offered by a righteous person (Jas. 5:16-17).

While the two witnesses at Rev. 11:3 perform miracles similar to those of Moses and Elijah consuming their enemies in fire, and halting the rain (vv. 5-6), they do not necessarily represent those important figures; indeed, they have been variously interpreted as Enoch and Elijah, Zerubbabel and Joshua, Peter and Paul, and God and Christ.

Bibliography. J. Jeremias, "'Ηλ(ε)ίας," *TDNT* 2 (1964): 928-941; H. H. Rowley, *Men of God* (New York: 1963), pp. 37-65; R. S. Wallace, *Elijah and Elisha* (Grand Rapids: 1957); A. Wiener, *The Prophet Elijah in the Development of Judaism* (Boston: 1978).

2. One of the sons of Jehoram, a Benjaminite chief dwelling at Jerusalem (1 Chr. 8:27-28; KJV "Eliah").

3. A postexilic priest of the lineage of Harim who promised to divorce his foreign wife (Ezra 10:21).

4. A son of Elam, likewise the husband of a foreign woman (Ezra 10:26; KJV "Eliah").

ELIJAH, APOCALYPSE OF.†

1. A brief Hebrew apocalypse (Heb. *sēper 'ēlîyāhû* "Book of Elijah") recounting in midrashic style the eschatological secrets revealed to Elijah on Mt. Carmel by Michael. Among the events of the end times are a devastating war which ends the present evil age, the advent of the Messiah and his forty-year reign of plenty, God's righteous new age, a general resurrection of the dead followed by punishment for the wicked and reward for the righteous, and the descent of the heavenly Jerusalem. On the basis of references to wars between Rome and Persia, scholars have proposed the work's origin in A.D. 261 or slightly earlier, although a date in the seventh century is possible. A later Aramaic version (Aram. *Pereq 'Ēlîyāhû* "Fragment of Elijah") also exists.

2. A pseudepigraphal collection of oracles including eschatological motifs and historical accounts presented as predictions. Although it is believed to have been composed in Greek by Alexandrian Jews, the work survives only in a Coptic version dated to the latter third century A.D. and thoroughly Christian in interpretation.

3. An unknown work, perhaps composed in Latin in the second century A.D. (and thus later than Paul), suggested as the source of Paul's quotation (cf. Isa. 64:4) at 1 Cor. 2:9 (Origen *Comm. Matt.* 27:9). It does not appear to be the same as **2** above.

ELIKA [ĭ lī'kə] (Heb. *'elîqā'*). A man from Harod and one of David's thirty mighty men (2 Sam. 23:25).

ELIM [ē'lĭm] (Heb. *'êlim,* possibly from *'ayil* "robust tree"). A place where the Israelites camped during their wilderness wanderings, said to have featured twelve springs and seventy palm trees (Exod. 15:27; Num. 33:9). Generally described as located between Marah and the Wilderness of Zin (Exod. 15:23; 16:1; cf. Num. 33:9-11), Elim was probably located in the Wâdī Gharandel, an oasis about 100 km. (63 mi.) southeast of Suez. It may have been a sacred grove (cf. the possible derivation "gods").

ELIMELECH [ĭ lĭm'ə lĕk] (Heb. *'elîmeleķ* "God is king"). A native of Bethlehem and husband of Naomi. When a severe famine hit the land, Elimelech moved his family to neighboring Moab where he soon died (Ruth 1:1-3), leaving his widow to dispose of his land (4:3, 9). His two sons, Mahlon and Chilion, who had married Moabite women, also died (1:3-5).

ELIOENAI [ĕl'ĭ ō ē'nī] (Heb. *'elyô'ênay* "my eyes are toward my God").

1. The eldest son of Neariah, mentioned among the descendants of Solomon (1 Chr. 3:23-24).

2. A member of the tribe of Benjamin (1 Chr. 4:36).

3. A Benjaminite, one of the sons of Becher (1 Chr. 7:8).

4. (1 Chr. 26:3, KJV). See ELIEHOENAI **1.**

5. A postexilic priest of the family of Pashhur who pledged to divorce his foreign wife (Ezra 10:22).

6. An Israelite, a member of the Zattu clan, who was ordered to send away his foreign wife (Ezra 10:27).

7. A priest who participated in the dedication service for the restored walls of Jerusalem (Neh. 12:41).

ELIPHAL [ĭ lī'fəl] (Heb. *'elîpal* "God has judged"). The son of Ur, and one of David's thirty mighty men (1 Chr. 11:35); in a parallel list (2 Sam. 23:34) he appears as Eliphelet the son of Ahasbai of Maacah.

ELIPHALET (2 Sam. 5:16, KJV). See ELIPHELET **1.**

ELIPHAZ [ĕl'ə făz] (Heb. *'elîpaz,* possibly "God is fine gold" or "God is victorious").

1. The eldest son of Esau and his Hittite wife Adah (Gen. 36:4, 10; 1 Chr. 1:35), and the ancestral father of several Edomite tribes (Gen. 36:11, 15-16; 1 Chr. 1:36).

2. One of Job's three friends, from Teman in Edom (and thus thought to be a descendant of Teman the eldest son of the Eliphaz mentioned as **1** above).

Perhaps because he is the oldest, Eliphaz speaks first in each of the three cycles of speeches intended to console and comfort the stricken Job (Job 2:11). In his first discourse (4:1–5:27) he shows himself to be the most sympathetic of the friends (cf. 4:2-6); nevertheless, he upholds the orthodox view of suffering as divine retribution upon the wicked (5:6-7) and urges Job to repent in total submission (vv. 17-27). The second speech is more harsh, deriding Job for his impiety (15:4) and arrogance (vv. 7-13), and concludes with a vivid description of the fate accorded to the wicked (vv. 20-35). Finally, Eliphaz argues that God is impartial (22:3), hence Job's suffering must be the result of specific sins (cf. vv. 12-20) which the Temanite deduces (vv. 6-11); he concludes with a repeated plea for repentance and reconciliation (vv. 21-30).

ELIPHELEHU [ĭ lĭf′ə lē′hū] (Heb. *'elîpᵉlēhû* "may God distinguish him"). A Levite of the second order, and a musician appointed by David to play during celebrations (1 Chr. 15:18, 21; KJV "Elipheleh").

ELIPHELET [ĭ lĭf′ə lĕt] (Heb. *'elîpeleṭ* "God is deliverance").

1. One of David's sons born at Jerusalem; his mother is unknown (2 Sam. 5:16; KJV "Eliphalet"; 1 Chr. 3:8; 14:7). Although some commentators argue for a second son by the same name, the occurrence of Eliphelet and Nogah at v. 6 may be the result of scribal error or may reflect a conscious editorial expansion of the genealogy in 2 Sam. 5:14-16 (see Elipelet, 1 Chr. 14:5).

2. The son of Ahasbai of Maacah, and one of David's thirty mighty men (2 Sam. 23:34); he is thought to be the same as Eliphal mentioned in a parallel list at 1 Chr. 11:35.

3. The third son of Eshek, a Benjaminite and a descendant of Saul (1 Chr. 8:39).

4. A descendant of Adonikam who returned from exile with his two brothers and a large company of people (Ezra 8:13).

5. A descendant of Hashum who was ordered to divorce his foreign wife (Ezra 10:33).

ELISABETH (e.g., Luke 1:5, KJV). *See* ELIZABETH.

ELISEUS (Luke 4:27, KJV). *See* ELISHA.

ELISHA [ĭ lī′shə] (Heb. *'elîšāʿ* "[my] God is salvation"; Gk. *Elisaios*).† The son of Shaphat, from Abelmeholah (east of the Jordan; 1 Kgs. 19:16), and the successor of Elijah.

I. Call

Summoned by God to appoint Elisha as his successor (1 Kgs. 19:16), Elijah found the apparently wealthy Elisha plowing in a field and anointed him prophet by merely casting his mantle on him (v. 19), to symbolize the assumption of authority. Young Elisha, probably twenty-five years old, committed himself to his new vocation by slaying his yoke of twelve oxen and providing a lavish feast for his neighbors (vv. 20-21).

During the last years of King Ahab and in the reign of his son Ahaziah, Elisha was Elijah's assistant. His own ministry commences shortly after Elijah's ascension. Refusing three times to stay behind — near Gilgal, at Bethel, and at Jericho — Elisha accompanied his aged teacher to the river Jordan, whose waters the elder prophet parted with his rolled-up mantle (2 Kgs. 2:1-8). Knowing (as did his assistant) that the Lord would soon take him to heaven, Elijah granted Elisha his wish of a double share of Elijah's spirit; Elisha was told that if he saw his companion depart, he would indeed receive this request, and when Elijah was taken, Elisha sensed that he had inherited his prophetic powers (vv. 9-12). Taking his teacher's mantle, he returned to the Jordan and used this garment to part the river just as he had seen his master do

(vv. 13-14). With the acknowledgment of his office by the prophetic guilds, Elisha's ministry was started (vv. 15ff.).

II. Ministry

While Elisha's ministry, which covers the span of nearly half a century (*ca.* 849-799 B.C.), is characterized by a great number of miracles, his task was actually three-fold: to heal, prophesy, and complete Elijah's assignments.

A. Miracle Worker. Elisha is primarily known for his many miracles. He purified the polluted waters of Jericho with salt (2 Kgs. 2:19-22); tradition identifies the so-called Elisha's Fountain, the purported site of this incident, with the Sultan's spring ('Ain es-Sulṭân) near ancient Jericho. He increased the amount of oil remaining to a widow so she could sell it to pay her creditors (4:1-8), and he promised the birth of a son to a couple at Shunem and later restored the young lad to life (4:15-17, 32-37). Some of Elisha's miracles were really nothing out of the ordinary; for instance, he administered "meal" as an antidote for the poisonous food at Gilgal (vv. 38-41). That the prophet employed such available techniques should not detract from his activity as a miracle worker.

Elisha helped many people in distress, whether native or foreign, prophets (e.g., 6:1-7) or laypersons. Most familiar is the curing of Naaman, the commander of the Syrian army who suffered the dreaded leprosy (5:1ff.). To Naaman's dismay the prophet ordered him to wash himself seven times in the Jordan; once his servants persuaded him to follow the prophet's prescribed course, he recovered (vv. 9-14).

B. Prophetic Career. Living in times of political unrest, Elisha naturally related his prophecies to Israel's political life. When Jehoshaphat of Judah had joined Jehoram of Israel in a military expedition against rebellious Moab, he summoned Elisha. The prophet predicted a victory for the two kings, a prophecy fulfilled the next day (3:9-20). Of his own accord he saved the life of Israel's king (possibly Jehoram) by warning him about the movements of his enemy, the Syrians (6:8-10). At the height of a famine in Samaria which resulted from a siege by the Syrian king Ben-hadad, the prophet predicted relief would come the next day, which it did (7:12-16).

Even during an illness at the end of his long ministry Elisha remained actively concerned with Israel's political existence. Visited by King Jehoash of Israel, the grandson of Jehu, the prophet ordered the king to shoot an arrow symbolizing his victory over the Syrians (13:14-17). Jehoash was then to strike the ground with the remaining arrows; but the king did so only three times, meaning he would gain only three victories, not enough to destroy Israel's powerful enemy (vv. 18-19).

C. Other Tasks. In conjunction with his political prophecies, Elisha also anointed two kings. In addition to anointing Elisha as prophet, his predecessor Elijah had been directed by God to anoint Jehu and Hazael as legitimate sovereigns (1 Kgs. 19:15-21). This he failed to do, and the task fell to Elisha. Following Samaria's miraculous deliverance from conquest by Syria, Elisha traveled to Damascus, where he met Hazael, the trusted deputy of ill-stricken Syrian king

Ben-hadad. Elisha informed Hazael that the king would recover from his illness but then die (2 Kgs. 8:8-11). Though technically he did not appoint Hazael Syria's next ruler, the prophet did intimate that he would succeed Ben-hadad (vv. 11-15).

Charging one of the prophets to go to Ramoth-gilead to anoint Jehu the son of Jehoshaphat king over Israel, Elisha gave him the proper instructions and a flask of oil (2 Kgs. 9:3). Upon reaching the army headquarters, the man requested a private audience with the captain and officially anointed him as Israel's next ruler (vv. 4-6).

III. Significance

A. *Old Testament.* When Elisha was about to die King Jehoash repeated the words the prophet had spoken at Elijah's departure ("the chariots of Israel and its horsemen," 2 Kgs. 13:14; cf. 2:12). He had considered Elisha Israel's true strength, and the prophet's moral and spiritual influence would not wane with his death. (Note that the author of 2 Kings has inserted an account of a dead person being revived when he touched the buried bones of Elisha [13:20-21].) Elisha had provided strong leadership to a nation constantly threatened by Syrian invasion (Ben-hadad I-II and Hazael) and which frequently displayed only minimal loyalties to Yahweh. In fact, he had served four Hebrew kings: Jehoram, Jehu, Jehoahaz, and Jehoash.

Elisha is often compared with his predecessor, Elijah. Both tended to concern themselves with the needs of the people and both courageously addressed kings and rulers. Yet Elisha was closer to the common Israelite than Elijah, perhaps because of his rural upbringing. While he appeared gentle and genuinely concerned with others (e.g., with his servant at Dothan; 6:15-19), he had his fits of anger and was capable of stern rebuke. He cursed the children from Bethel for mocking his baldness (2:23-24) and meted out leprosy to his servant Gehazi in punishment for his greed (5:25-27). He rendered assistance to Jehoram of Israel only for the sake of Jehoshaphat his ally from Judah (3:14). When one of the northern king's officials failed to believe in a miracle, Elisha arranged for his death (7:2, 18-20).

Although none of the later Old Testament prophets refers to Elisha, the Hebrews did not forget him. Ben Sirach (ca. 200 B.C.) mentions him with Elijah and Hezekiah among the historical ancestors (Sir. 48:12-14). Acknowledging that Elisha was filled with Elijah's spirit, he calls him a firm prophet, one capable of performing incredibly difficult tasks, and a man of miracles.

B. *New Testament.* As Jesus speaks of the rejection he had experienced in his hometown, Nazareth, he draws an analogy between himself and the prophets Elijah and Elisha (Luke 4:25-27; KJV "Eliseus"). The foreigners whom these prophets cured or aided had more faith in the Lord and were more deserving than any Israelites with similar problems (e.g., the four lepers near the gate of Samaria, 2 Kgs. 7:3ff.); Christ implies that he, too, is a prophet who will not be recognized as such among his own people (cf. 2 Kgs. 5:1-19).

Elijah and Elisha can also be likened to John the Baptist and Jesus. John, as it were, commissioned Jesus, who followed John's preaching till the death of the Baptist, at which point he began his own ministry. Jesus, like Elisha, identified with the people and performed several miracles among them. But unlike Elisha's service, Jesus' ministry was superior to John's, since Jesus is the Savior and Reconciler of the world; Elisha's term of service, a continuation of Elijah's, was actually less significant than that of his predecessor. (Elijah's stern prophetic ministry and the contrast of Elisha's service of healing together prefigure the simultaneous presence of judgment and grace in Christ's work of reconciliation.)

Bibliography. L. Bronner, *The Stories of Elijah and Elisha* (Leiden: 1968); R. S. Wallace, *Elijah and Elisha* (Grand Rapids: 1968); J. Gray, *I and II Kings,* 2nd ed. OTL (Philadelphia: 1970).

ELISHAH [ĭ lī'shə] (Heb. *'elîšâ* "God saves"). The firstborn son of Javan the son of Japheth (Gen. 10:4 par. 1 Chr. 1:7). At Ezek. 27:7 Tyre is said to have traded with the "coasts of Elishah," a coastal region between Egypt and Sidon. Though suggested identifications range from Carthage to the Peloponnesus or Sicily, Elishah probably refers in this sense to Alashia, a name found in cuneiform texts (e.g., Amarna Letters), possibly a part of Cyprus.

ELISHAMA [ĭ lĭsh'ə mə] (Heb. *'elîšāmā'* "God has heard").
1. The son of Ammihud, and a leader of the tribe of Ephraim (Num. 2:18; 10:22) who assisted Moses in taking the census (1:10) and who made an offering in behalf of his tribe (7:48, 53). According to 1 Chr. 7:26 he is the grandfather of Joshua.
2. One of David's sons born at Jerusalem of an unknown mother (2 Sam. 5:16; 1 Chr. 3:8; 14:7).
3. A member of the royal family and the grandfather of the notorious Ishmael (2 Kgs. 25:25 par. Jer. 41:1).
4. The son of Jekamiah, and a descendant of Jerahmeel of the tribe of Judah (1 Chr. 2:41).
5. Another of David's sons (so 1 Chr. 3:6); probably a scribal error for Elishua (cf. 2 Sam. 5:15).
6. One of the two priests whom King Jehoshaphat sent among the people of Judah in order to instruct them in the law (2 Chr. 17:8).
7. The secretary of King Jehoiakim (Jer. 36:12, 20).

ELISHAPHAT [ĭ lĭsh'ə făt] (Heb. *'elîšāpāṭ* "God has judged"). One of the five army commanders who assisted Jehoiada in securing kingship for young Joash and indirectly aided in the overthrow of Athaliah (2 Chr. 23:1).

ELISHEBA [ĭ lĭsh'ə bə] (Heb. *'elîšeḇa'* "God is fortune [or] fullness"). The daughter of Amminadab and sister of Nahshon; she married Moses' brother Aaron and bore him four sons: Nadab, Abihu, Eleazar, and Ithamar (Exod. 6:23).

ELISHUA [ĕl'ə shōō'ə] (Heb. *'elîšúa'* "God is salvation"). One of David's sons born at Jerusalem by an unnamed mother (2 Sam. 5:15; 1 Chr. 14:5); because of a scribal error he is incorrectly called Elishama at 1 Chr. 3:6.

ELIUD [ĭ lī'əd] (Gk. *Elioud*). An ancestor of Jesus (Matt. 1:14-15).

ELIZABETH [ĭ lĭz'ə bəth] (Gk. *El[e]isabet*). The wife of Zechariah the priest; according to tradition the couple lived at Ain Karem, a village in the hill country of Judah, about 7 km. (4.5 mi.) west of Jerusalem. While Luke states that she was of priestly descent ("one of the daughters of Aaron," Luke 1:5), he may have meant to imply also that Elizabeth (KJV "Elisabeth") had the same name as Elisheba (Heb. *'elîšeba'* "God is my oath"), the wife of Aaron, the first high priest (cf. LXX Gk. *Elisabeth* at Exod. 6:23). Though portrayed as righteous before God as far as the Mosaic law is concerned, she was unable to bear children (vv. 6-7), which must have prompted social derision. Whatever her own feelings may have been to the angel's message that she would finally bear a son in her late years, she viewed her pregnancy as a sign of God's favor (vv. 24-25).

Luke adds that Elizabeth was the kinswoman (Gk. *syngenís*, v. 36; NIV "relative") of Mary the mother of Jesus, though he is no more specific than that (cf. KJV "cousin"). When visited by Mary, Elizabeth greeted her as one blessed among women, i.e., as the mother of the promised Messiah (vv. 39-45).

Bibliography. J. A. Fitzmyer, *The Gospel According to Luke I-IX.* AB (Garden City: 1981), pp. 322ff.; I. H. Marshall, *Commentary on Luke.* NIGTC (Grand Rapids: 1978), pp. 49ff.

ELIZAPHAN [ĕl'ə zā'făn] (Heb. *'elîṣāpān* "God has hidden [or protected]").

1. The second son of Uzziel, Aaron's uncle (Num. 3:30; called Elzaphan at Exod. 6:22; Lev. 10:4); according to Num. 3:30 he was one of the heads of the Kohathites. Following the sudden death of Aaron's oldest sons Nadab and Abihu, Elizaphan and his brother Mishael were summoned by Moses to remove their dead bodies from the sanctuary (Lev. 10:4). Some of Elizaphan's descendants were among those invited to the festivities observing the return of the ark to Jerusalem (1 Chr. 15:8), while other participated in the cleaning of the temple during the reign of Hezekiah (2 Chr. 29:13).

2. The son of Parnach who represented the tribe of Zebulun in the division of the land (Num. 34:25).

ELIZUR [ĭ lī'zər] (Heb. *'elîṣûr* "God is a rock"). The son of Shedeur (Num. 10:18). As a leader of the tribe of Reuben (2:10), he assisted Moses in taking the census in the wilderness (1:5) and made an offering in behalf of his tribe (7:30, 35).

ELKANAH [ĕl kā'nə] (Heb. *'elqānâ* "God has created" or "possessed").

1. The son of Jeroham, who dwelled at Ramathaim-zophim in the hill country of Ephraim (1 Sam. 1:1); at 1 Chr. 6:27, 34 he is called a Levite, a descendant of Kohath. Elkanah had two wives, Peninnah who bore him children and Hannah who, though barren, was his favorite (1:6). When at last Hannah bore a son, Elkanah accompanied her to Shiloh, where they presented their son Samuel to the Lord (v. 25; 2:11).

2-4. The name of three Levites (1 Chr. 22-23, 25-27, 35-36). While Assir, Elkanah, and Ebiasaph (or Abiasaph) are said to be brothers (and sons of Korah) at Exod. 6:24, at 1 Chr. 6:22-23 they are represented as father, son, and grandson.

5. A Levite of the line of Merari and the grandfather of Berechiah (1 Chr. 9:16).

6. A Benjaminite who joined David at Ziklag and became one of his mighty men (1 Chr. 12:6). He may be the same Elkanah mentioned at 15:23 who was a gatekeeper for the ark.

7. A high official in the royal court at Jerusalem, "next in authority to the king" (2 Chr. 28:7), who was murdered by the Ephraimite Zichri following the defeat of King Ahaz of Judah by Israel and Syria.

ELKOSH [ĕl'kŏsh] (Heb. *hā'elqōšî*). The residence, and possibly the birthplace, of the prophet Nahum (Nah. 1:1; KJV "Elkoshite"); the location remains uncertain. The tradition that identified Elkosh with el-Qôsh, about 50 km. (30 mi.) north of Mosul (near ancient Nineveh), is not borne out by the internal evidence of the book of Nahum; a second tradition, championed by Jerome (*Comm. on Nahum* Prologue), which locates the site at Hilkeseï in Galilee, is also doubtful. There is a degree of plausibility in identifying Elkosh with Begabar, contemporary Beit Jibrîn in Judah (*De vitis prophetarum,* incorrectly attributed to Epiphanius); but because that name does not occur in the Old Testament, others have related Elkosh to Capernaum (Gk. *Kapharnaoum,* transliteration of Heb. *kāpār naḥûm* "village of Nahum").

ELKOSHITE (Nah. 1:1, KJV). See ELKOSH.

ELLASAR [ĕl'ə sär] (Heb. *'ellāsār*). A city in Mesopotamia whose ruler was Arioch, one of the confederates of Chedorlaomer (Gen. 14:1, 9). Most scholars accept H. L. Rawlinson's identification of the site as Larsa (cf. Akk. *[âl] Larsa*), the ancient Babylonian city of the sun-god located between Uruk (biblical Erech) and Ur on the east bank of the Euphrates river. Although the name was relatively common in the mid-second millennium B.C., some have identified the king with Arriwuk (cf. Nuzi *Ariukki*), a vassal of Zimri-lim of Mari, and thus locate the city on the upper Euphrates, between Carchemish and Haran.

ELM. An incorrect translation at Hos. 4:13 (KJV); according to botanists, the elm (*Ulmus campestris* L.) is not a Palestinian tree. See TEREBINTH.

ELMADAM [ĕl mā'dəm] (Gk. *Elmadam*). A preexilic ancestor of Jesus (Luke 3:28; KJV "Elmodam," following Gk. *Elmôdam*).

ELNAAM [ĕl nā'əm] (Heb. *'elna'am* "God is pleasantness"). The father of Jeribai and Joshaviah, two of David's mighty men (1 Chr. 11:46); the LXX lists Elnaam himself as one of the warriors.

ELNATHAN [ĕl nā'thən] (Heb. *'elnāṯān* "God has given").

1. The father of Nehushta, the wife of King Jehoiakim and the mother of Jehoiachin (2 Kgs. 24:8); a resident at Jerusalem. Most likely he is the son of

Achbor mentioned at Jer. 26:22; 36:12, 25 who captured the fugitive prophet Uriah in Egypt and returned him to Jehoiakim. He also joined a number of Judahite princes in reading a scroll dictated by Jeremiah in their attempt to dissuade the king from burning the document. Lachish Ostracon 3 contains the name of an Elnathan, the "commander of the host" of Coniniah who had entered Egypt; this man has not been positively identified.

2. Two (LXX only one) "leading men" (RSV; KJV "chief men") and one "man of insight" (JB omits) who accompanied the returning exiles to Jerusalem (Ezra 8:16).

ELOAH [ĕ lōʹə] (Heb. *ᵉlôah*).* A Hebrew name for God, thought by some to be a later singular derivative of Elohim (Heb. *ᵉlōhîm*; cf. Aram. *ᵉlāh*). The term is used both as a generic designation for a deity (e.g., Job 12:6; cf. Heb. *ʾēl, ᵉlōhîm*) and as a name of the Israelite God (e.g., Isa. 44:8). It occurs in ancient Hebrew poetry dated to the early Monarchy (tenth-ninth centuries B.C.; Deut. 32:15, 17; Ps. 18:31 [par. 2 Sam. 22:32, *ʾēl*]), archaizing poetry of the sixth century (e.g., Hab. 3:3), and nostalgic usage of the exilic and postexilic periods (e.g., 2 Chr. 32:15; Prov. 30:5). Eloah is found most frequently (forty-two times) in the poetic discourses of the book of Job, where the non-Israelite participants would not be expected to use the name Yahweh or other names historically associated with the God of Israel.

ELOHIM [ĕl ō hĭmʹ] (Heb. *ᵉlōhîm*).† A Hebrew term referring to gods in general, and the most frequent Old Testament name for God; it occurs most often in those passages of the Pentateuch which source critics assign to the Elohistic and Priestly sources and in certain "Elohistic Psalms." The etymology of the word is unclear, although it may have derived from a root meaning "strength, power"; the same or a similar root may have been the source of the name El, of which some scholars consider Elohim to be the plural (but *see* ELOAH).

In its earliest uses Elohim appears as a numerical plural with reference to the gods of other nations (e.g., Exod. 12:12; Josh. 24:15; Judg. 5:8; cf. Deut. 32:17). It also occurs with singular meaning for specific ancient Near Eastern deities (1 Kgs. 11:33; 2 Kgs. 1:2-3, 6, 16) and as a generic term for gods (cf. Exod. 22:28, RSV; KJV "gods"; JB mg., NIV mg. "judges").

As a name or designation for the God of Israel, the term is understood as a plural of majesty or an intensive plural, indicating the fullness of the supreme (or only) God (cf. Akk. *ilanu*; EA *ilania* "my gods," designating the deified king). Although some scholars point to a polytheistic background for this form, particularly in instances implying a heavenly council (e.g., Gen. 1:26), the canonical intent is clearly monotheistic, even where the accompanying verbs and adjectives are grammatically plural (e.g., Gen. 20:13; Exod. 22:9 [MT 8]). The name is used interchangeably with and as the equivalent of Yahweh, the covenant God of Israel (e.g., Exod. 5:1; 1 Sam. 5:7-8, 10-11; cf. Exod. 15:2; Judg. 5:3, 5). As such, he is described as holy (Josh. 24:19) and righteous (Ps. 7:9), a God of truth (Isa. 65:16) and justice (30:18; Mal. 2:17)

who is living (Deut. 5:26) and near (4:7; cf. Jer. 23:23) and who acts for human salvation (e.g., Ps. 51:14).

In a few instances the Hebrew term refers to idols (e.g., Exod. 20:33; Isa. 42:17) or to beings with divine attributes (Ps. 82:1; 138:1; cf. 8:5). At 1 Sam. 28:13 it refers to the shade of Samuel (RSV "god"; KJV "gods"; JB "ghost").

Bibliography. H. Ringgren, "'ᵉlōhîm," *TDOT* 1, rev. ed. (1977):267-284.

ELOHIST [ĕlʹō hĭst].† One of the four principal sources or "strands" of the Pentateuch as identified by source critics, and the designation of the author-compiler, school, or tradition which produced it; both are represented by the symbol E. The name derives from the characteristic use in this material of Heb. *ᵉlōhîm* as the name for God, particularly prior to the account of the burning bush (Exod. 3:14-15).

Once thought to be a revision of the YAHWIST (J) source, the E material now is generally viewed by source critics as an independent reworking of various earlier accounts to fit the perspective of the northern kingdom in the ninth century B.C. The prominent interest in the "prophetic" role of Israel's leaders (e.g., Gen. 41:38; Deut. 34:10-12) and the preference for charismatic leadership (e.g., Num. 12:3-8) suggest resistance to institutionalized forms of prophecy and a dynastic monarchy, hence E's probable origin in the prophetic schools akin to those of Elijah and Elisha.

In addition to the use of Elohim for God, the Elohistic writings favor Horeb as the name for the holy mountain (Sinai) where God appeared to Moses (e.g., Exod. 3:1; Deut. 5:2) and Amorites as the designation for the pre-Israelite inhabitants of Canaan (e.g., Gen. 15:16). A northern perspective is reflected in the depiction of Reuben rather than Judah as the principal among Joseph's brothers (37:21, 29) and the focus on such northern sites as Bethel (e.g., 33:18-20) and Shechem (e.g., 37:12-14). A major theme is obedience to the stipulations of the Sinai (Horeb) covenant (Exod. 19–24; cf. Gen. 22:12; Exod. 1:17, 21; 18:21), with appropriate attention to the divine sanctions upon obedience and disobedience (chs. 32–34; cf. 19:5; Num. 14:11-20).

After the fall of Samaria in 721, much of the E material seems to have been revised, perhaps as an attempt to reunite north and south both politically and religiously.

See BIBLICAL CRITICISM; PENTATEUCH.

ELOI, ELOI, LAMA SABACHTHANI (Mark 15:34). *See* ELI, ELI, LAMA SABACHTHANI.

ELON [ēʹlŏn] (Heb. *ʾêlôn, ʾêlōn, ʾēlôn* "oak [or] terebinth").

1. A Hittite whose daughter Basemath (Gen. 26:34) or Adah (36:2) married Esau.

2. The second son of Zebulun (Gen. 46:14), and the ancestral father of the Elonites (Num. 26:26).

3. A minor judge from the tribe of Zebulun who judged Israel for ten years (*ca.* 1076-1066 B.C.; Judg. 12:11). The name may be an etiology based upon his burial place, Aijalon (v. 12; Heb. *ʾayyālôn,* identical to Elon in the consonantal script), suggesting a tree beneath which he issued his oracles (cf. 4:5; 6:11; 9:6).

4. A village in the tribal territory of Dan, between Aijalon and Timnah (Josh. 19:43), possibly Khirbet Wâdī ʿAlin. Some scholars think it is the same as Elon-beth-hanan (1 Kgs. 4:9).

ELON-BETH-HANAN [ēʹlən bĕth hāʹnən] (Heb. *ʾêlôn bêt ḥānān* "Oak of the house of Elon"). A village in the second administrative district of King Solomon, which was required to provide food for the royal palace (1 Kgs. 4:9); perhaps modern ʿAlein, west of Beit Maḥṣir or Tell Qopa, southwest of Yâlō (Aijalon). Some scholars identify the town with Elon mentioned at Josh. 19:43. The suffix "beth-hanan" distinguishes this village from nearby Aijalon, which has the same Hebrew consonants (cf. 21:24 K).

ELONITES [ēʹlə nīts] (Heb. *ʾēlônî*). Descendants of ELON **2** (Num. 26:26).

ELOTH. An alternate form of ELATH.

ELPAAL [ĕl pāʹəl] (Heb. *ʾelpaʿal* "God has wrought"). The head of a family, of the tribe of Benjamin (1 Chr. 8:11-12, 18).

ELPALET (1 Chr. 14:5, KJV). *See* ELPELET.

EL-PARAN [ĕl pârʹən] (Heb. *ʾêl pāʾrān*). A city belonging to the Horites, the southernmost point of Chedorlaomer's military expedition (Gen. 14:6). It must have been located near the head of the Gulf of Aqaba, at the edge of the Wilderness of Paran; some consider it an earlier name for Elath.

ELPELET [ĕl pēlʹĭt] (Heb. *ʾelpāleṭ*). One of David's sons born at Jerusalem, of an unnamed mother (1 Chr. 14:5; KJV "Elpalet"). At 1 Chr. 3:6 the alternate name, Eliphelet, is given; considered by some scholars to be the result of scribal error, its occurrence there may rather be a conscious effort to expand the genealogy recorded at 2 Sam. 5:14-16.

EL SHADDAI [ĕl shădʹī] (Heb. *ʾēl šadday*).† An ancient name for God, generally translated "God Almighty" in English versions (from LXX, NT Gk. *pantokrátōr*); it also occurs in the form Shaddai. Scholars generally interpret the name to mean "God of the (cosmic) mountain" (Ugar. *ṭdy,* originally "breast"; cf. Heb. *šādayim*), possibly adapted from the Amorite storm-god Amurru identified in the Ras Shamra texts with Canaanite El (note the frequent occurrence of the name in the context of divine theophanies; Ezek. 1:24; 10:5; cf. Exod. 19; 1 Kgs. 19). Less plausible derivations include Heb. *śadēh* "field" and *šādad* "destroy" (note the paronomasia at Isa. 23:6; Joel 1:15).

In passages attributed by critical scholars to the Priestly source, the name is that by which the patriarchs knew the "god of the fathers," later identified with Yahweh (Exod. 6:2-3). It is the name by which God revealed himself to Abram when enacting the covenant of circumcision (Gen. 17:1) and to Jacob at Bethel (35:11; 48:3). It is used in blessing formulas by Isaac (28:3) and Jacob (43:14). The name occurs also in early Hebrew poetry (49:25; Num. 24:4, 16; cf. Ps.

68:14) attributed to the eleventh century B.C., the period of the judges (cf. Ruth 1:20-21). It apparently fell into disuse during the Monarchy until revived in archaizing writings of the nostalgic sixth century (e.g., Isa. 13:6; Joel 1:15). It occurs thirty-one times in Job, probably because of its pre-Israelite associations which befit the discourse in that book.

Shaddai appears as a theophorous element in personal names such as Ammishaddai ("Shaddai is my kinsman"; Num. 1:12), Zurishaddai ("Shaddai is a rock"; 1:6), and possibly Shedeur ("Shaddai is light [or fire]"; v. 5).

ELTEKEH [ĕlʹtə kə] (Heb. *ʾelteqēh* "meeting place"). A town within the tribal territory of Dan, between Ekron and Gibbethon (Josh. 19:44), later assigned to the Kohathite Levites (21:23; Heb. *ʾelteqē*ʾ; RSV, JB "Elteke"). According to the Sennacherib prism, the Assyrian king defeated the Egyptian forces there (Akk. *altaqū*) in 701 B.C. and then captured the town and invaded Judah. Scholars remain divided concerning the site of Eltekeh, although it is generally thought to have been north of Ekron and west of Timnah. It was previously identified with modern Khirbet el-Muqennaʿ, but that site is now favored as Ekron; Tell esh-Shalaf is a leading candidate.

ELTEKON [ĕlʹtə kŏn] (Heb. *ʾelteqōn*). A town in the hill country of Judah, named with Beth-zur and Beth-anoth (Josh. 15:59; LXX *Theroum*). The site is thought to be modern Khirbet ed-Deir, about 6.5 km. (4 mi.) west of Bethlehem and 3 km. (2 mi.) south of Ḥauṣan.

ELTOLAD [ĕlʹtōʹlăd] (Heb. *ʾeltôlaḏ* "O El, you beget"). A city listed among the allotments of Judah (Josh. 15:30) and Simeon (19:4), also called Tolad at 1 Chr. 4:29. The proposed location is Khirbet Erqa Saqra, 20 km. (12.5 mi.) southeast of Beer-sheba.

ELUL [ēʹlŭl] (Heb. *ʾelûl*; Akk. *elulu, ululu*; Gk. *Eloul*).† The sixth month of the Hebrew year (mid-August to mid-September). It was on the twenty-fifth day of Elul that the walls of Jerusalem were completed (Neh. 6:15). Later, *ca.* 140 B.C., the Jews recorded the accomplishments of Simon the high priest, dating the inscription the eighteenth day of Elul (1 Macc. 14:27).

See also YEAR.

ELUZAI [ĭ lōōʹzī] (Heb. *ʾelʿûzay* "God is my strength"). One of Saul's "kinsmen" from the tribe of Benjamin, who joined David at Ziklag (1 Chr. 12:5).

ELYMAIS [ĕlʹə māʹəs] (Gk. *Elymais*).* A province in the region between Persia and Babylonia, most likely the equivalent of Elam (cf. Dan. 8:2, VSS) or Susiana, the capital of which was Susa (cf. Ptolemy *Geog.* vi.3; Strabo *Geog.* xv.732, 744). At 1 Macc. 6:1 it is called a city (Gk. *pólis*; cf. Josephus *Ant.* xii.9.1).

ELYMAS [ĕlʹə məs] (Gk. *Elymas*). A Jewish astrologer or wonderworker (Gk. *mágos* "magician") — and thus a "false prophet" — in the employ of the Roman proconsul Sergius Paulus at Paphos on southwestern Cyprus (Acts 13:6-7). When he learned of the proconsul's intention to grant an audience to Paul and Barnabas, Elymas opposed their preaching, fearing that his influence would be diminished by what they would say (vv. 7-8). Exposing his deceit and accusing him of undermining the Lord's work, Paul punished Elymas by striking him temporarily blind (vv. 9-11); the severity of this rebuke, in stark contrast with the apostle's own conversion experience, was sufficient to evoke the proconsul's belief (v. 12).

Some scholars contend that the man's Greek name is etymologically related to his role as magician (v. 8; cf. Arab. *'alim* "wise"); it may also be related to that of the Cypriot magician Atomos (Josephus *Ant.* xx.7.2; cf. the Western text variant Gk. *Hetoimas*). At any rate, it is not a translation of his Hebrew name, Bar-Jesus (v. 6; Gk. *Bariēsous*; cf. Aram. *bar yᵉšûaʿ*).

ELYON. *See* EL ELYON.

ELZABAD [ĕl zāʹbăd] (Heb. *'elzāḇāḏ* "God has given").

1. The ninth of the experienced Gadite warriors who joined David at Ziklag, his stronghold in the wilderness (1 Chr. 12:8, 12).

2. A Korahite gatekeeper during the days of David (1 Chr. 26:7).

ELZAPHAN [ĕl zāʹfăn] (Heb. *'elṣāpān*). A shortened form of Elizaphan, one of the sons of Uzziel (Exod. 6:22; Lev. 10:4). *See* ELIZAPHAN **1.**

EMBALMING (Heb. *ḥᵃnuṭîm*).† The treatment of dead bodies as prevention from decay. Unlike the Egyptians, the Hebrews looked askance at the practice of embalming the dead. The Old Testament mentions only two instances of embalming: Jacob, Joseph's father, whose body the Egyptian "physicians" prepared over a period of forty days (Gen. 50:2-3; cf. Herodotus *Hist.* ii.86), and Joseph himself (v. 26). Both had died important men in Egypt, and the arrangements concerning their burial attest to the honor of their social and political positions. Whether embalming was practiced elsewhere in the ancient Near East is unclear.

Various spices were burned in conjunction with King Asa's burial (1 Kgs. 15:24; 2 Chr. 16:14), probably as a gesture of respect and possibly to signify ceremonial purity as well as to combat the odors of putrefaction; at any rate, his physical preservation was neither the design nor the result. The extraordinary number of spices tucked in the folds of the cloths in which Jesus was wrapped for burial shows that Nicodemus recognized Jesus' authority and possibly that he was willing to demonstrate greater commitment to his Lord upon realization that Christ's earthly life had ended (John 19:39-40). Jewish burial customs required only that sheets be wrapped around the dead person. Incisions in the body, whether to aid in preservation or for any other purpose, were forbidden (cf. Lev. 19:28; 21:5).

Among the Egyptians the desire was to preserve the body from decay, and the belief was that this method would insure the continued identity of the deceased in the afterworld. The Hebrews, on the other hand, admitted no need for physical preservation; they believed that God would extend his presence and care to the grave and would one day resurrect the body. *See* BURIAL; DEATH.

EMBROIDERY. The art of making decorative designs with hand needlework, the ancient forerunner of brocading. Among the items of the tabernacle "embroidered with needlework" (Heb. *maʿᵃšēh rōqēm* "the work of the weaver in colored fabrics"; KJV "wrought with needlework"; NIV, JB "the work of a [skilled] embroiderer") were the screens of the tent door (Exod. 26:36) and of the gate of the court (27:16). The high priest's girdle was also embroidered (28:39; cf. 39:27-29). Bezalel and Oholiab were skilled embroiderers (Heb. *rāqam*), who worked in "blue and purple and scarlet stuff" (35:30-35; 38:23).

Heb. *riqᵉmâ* is used in reference to the dyed woven goods seized following Sisera's defeat (Judg. 5:30); to the fine linen used figuratively to suggest the attention the Lord paid to Jerusalem (Ezek. 16:10, 13); metaphorically to the plumage of the "eagle," Nebuchadnezzar (Ezek. 17:3). Embroidered work was traded between Tyre and Edom (27:16) and cities like Haran (vv. 23-24). Beautiful designs crafted in Egypt were woven into the sails of the Tyrian ships (v. 7). Ps. 45:14 depicts the bride as meeting her groom, the king, dressed in "many-colored robes" (KJV "raiment of needlework"; NIV "embroidered garments"; JB "dressed in brocades").

EMEK-KEZIZ [ēʹmĭk kēʹzĭz] (Heb. *ʿēmeq qᵉṣîṣ* "a valley cut off"). A city in the tribal territory of Benjamin, probably in the Jordan valley near Jericho (Josh. 18:21; KJV "valley of Keziz"). Its exact location remains unknown.

EMENDATIONS OF THE SCRIBES (Tiqqune Sopherim).* A list of eighteen passages in the MT which have been emended to avoid anthropomorphisms or irreverent references to God. The passages include Gen. 18:22; Num. 11:15; 12:12; 1 Sam. 3:13; 2 Sam. 16:12; 20:1; 1 Kgs. 12:16; Jer. 2:11; Ezek. 8:17; Hos. 4:7; Hab. 1:12; Zech. 2:8 (MT 12); Mal. 1:12; Ps. 106:20; Job 7:20; 32:3; Lam. 3:20; 2 Chr. 10:16. Although the list varies in the several rabbinical writings and the Masora to certain Hebrew manuscripts in which it is found and thus is not wholly trustworthy for textual criticism, it remains valuable as an aid to understanding the methodology of early scribal midrashic activity.

EMERALD. A brilliantly green beryl, a rare gem mined at Zabara in Upper Egypt, notably during the reign of Cleopatra. The Hebrew words generally translated emerald more likely refer to the green feldspar: *nōpek* — the first stone in the second row of precious stones on the breastpiece of the high priest (Exod. 28:18; 39:11) and a commodity traded between Tyre and Edom (Ezek. 27:16); and *bārᵉqaṯ* — a precious stone in the covering belonging to the prince of Tyre (Ezek. 28:13, KJV; RSV, JB "carbuncle"; cf. Vulg. *carbunculus*; NIV "turquoise").

Greek *smarágdinos* describes the green of the rainbow surrounding the divine throne at Rev. 4:3. The related term *smáragdos* designates the fourth precious stone adorning the foundation of the wall of the new Jerusalem (21:19).

EMERODS (1 Sam. 5:6-7; 6:4, KJV). See TUMORS.

EMIM [ĕ'mĭm] (Heb. *'ĕmîm* "the terrible ones"). The former inhabitants of Moab dispossessed by the Moabites (Deut. 2:10); a race of giants likened to the Anakim; also known as the Rephaim (vv. 10-11). According to Gen. 14:5 the Emim were defeated by Chedorlaomer at Shaveh-kiriathaim, a plain east of the Dead Sea.

EMMANUEL. See IMMANUEL.

EMMAUS [ĕ mā'əs] (Gk. *Emmaous*). A village where the risen Christ appeared to two of his followers, Cleopas and an unnamed companion; said to be located about "seven miles" (so RSV, NIV, JB; Gk. "sixty stadia"; KJV "sixty furlongs") from Jerusalem (Luke 24:13ff., 28ff.). The location of Emmaus remains unknown. Some scholars favor identification with el-Qubeibeh, the site of a fort called Castellum Emmaus discovered by the Crusaders in 1099, some 11 km. (7 mi.) northwest of Jerusalem. Others would identify it with modern 'Amwâs (ancient Nicopolis), where the Jews gained a victory over Georgias (1 Macc. 3:40, 57; 4:1-26); though it is much further (31 km. [19 mi.]) from Jerusalem, it does preserve the ancient name and was attested by the early Church as the site of Emmaus. A third proposal places Emmaus at Qalôniyeh (Colonia), where, according to Josephus (*BJ* vii.6.6 [217]), Vespasian settled eight hundred Roman veterans; however, this site is too close to Jerusalem (30 stadia or 5.6 km. [3.5 mi.]).

EMMOR (Acts 7:16, KJV). See HAMOR.

EMPEROR.† A title given to the supreme ruler of the Roman Empire; originally a sign of honor bestowed upon a victorious general. Theoretically, the Roman emperors were chiefs of state (Lat. *princeps*) rather than *imperatores*. The emperor to whom Paul appealed for a fair trial (Acts 25:21, 25) was Nero, not Augustus (KJV "Augustus" following Gk. *sebastós*, a transliteration of Lat. *Augustus*; JB "August emperor"). At 1 Pet. 2:13 believers are exhorted to submit to the emperor and other governmental officials.

The Romans granted special honor to the emperor, treating him as if he were a deity, especially after he had died. Among the Greeks there had been no sharp discrimination between human beings and deities, and city founders were often declared divine upon their death. Following the death of Alexander the Great (323 B.C.), the eastern nations viewed all their Hellenistic rulers as divine; even the Hellenistic philosophers ascribed superhuman qualities to the rulers of state.

Julius Caesar (68-44 B.C.) was praised as "a god manifest" and his statue was placed alongside those of the Roman deities. But only after his death was he declared the divine Julius (*divus Julius*). Augustus (30 B.C.–A.D. 14) permitted the erection of temples in the provinces on his behalf, but his official con-

secration did not take place until following his death.

While Tiberius (A.D. 14-37) petitioned divine honor for his predecessor Augustus, he permitted such recognition for himself only in the provinces; after his death the senate did not deify him. Neither was Caligula (37-41) deified by the senate, though while he lived he sought unqualified homage from his subjects and had a temple erected in his own honor. Claudius (41-54) opposed any divine tribute for himself, claiming that such an honor belonged only to the gods; the senate deified him after his death upon the recommendation of Nero (54-68). Because he had been condemned by the senate near the end of his reign, Nero himself failed to receive this extraordinary veneration.

In the provinces more than in Rome, the sovereign was considered more of an absolute monarch, called to his position by providence rather than a magistrate with certain powers granted by law. There the emperor was viewed as a superhuman power, a personification of one of the national deities. Indeed, emperor worship was encouraged by local authorities in the provinces, especially as an instrument of unification in times of unrest.

Tolerant though the Roman Empire was in matters of religious conviction, it was suspicious of conspiracies and collusions against its authority. For this reason it collided with the Christian Church when it became evident that the latter opposed military service and worship of the emperor in favor of worship of the Christian god alone. At various times between A.D. 64 and 314 official magistrates required minimal allegiance to the empire and divine respect for the emperor from all subjects. Refusal of this formality was, in principle, punishable by death. Because the Christians were not a national entity (as were the Jews, who enjoyed freedom of religion), they either had to submit, when asked, to this formality or face the consequences. When many of them, at least at first, refused to submit, they were persecuted in various ways.

The New Testament writers carefully distinguish between worship of God and respect for the government. In his Letter to the Romans, Paul delineates the believer's duties toward the "governing authorities" (Rom. 13:1ff.). He strongly disapproved the actions of people who disregarded Roman rule and failed to pay taxes; he may also have meant to encourage Christian prisoners and servants at the imperial palace to continue to esteem their masters and superiors. Likewise, Peter exhorts believers scattered over Asia Minor to "honor" (Gk. *timáō*) the emperor but to "fear" (Gk. *phobéō* "have reverence, respect for"; so NEB) God (1 Pet. 2:17).

Bibliography. D. Cuss, *Imperial Cult and Honorary Terms in the New Testament.* Parasosis 23 (Fribourg: 1974); L. R. Taylor, *The Divinity of the Roman Emperor* (1931; repr. New York: 1975).

EMPTIED (Gk. *ekénōsen*). A term used in a significant christological passage (Phil. 2:6ff.), actually a hymn (see JB, NIV), in which Paul portrays Christ practicing ultimate self-denial (so RSV, JB; KJV "made himself of no reputation"; NIV "made himself nothing") to take the "form" of a "servant" (RSV, KJV, NIV; Gk. *doúlos* "slave"; so JB). Offering Christ as the example of humility to be emulated by believers, the apostle is not implying that the preexistent Son of God (not the incarnate Savior; cf. A. Oepke, *TDNT* 3 [1965]:661) had deprived himself of all divine attributes and powers and had actually ceased to be divine. Nevertheless, he is suggesting that Jesus did surrender (cf. Isa. 53:12) the glory and majesty he had enjoyed in heaven. Having established in v. 6 that Christ, who though he possessed divine splendor, the "form [Gk. *morphḗ*] of God," did not consider equality with God something to be grasped (RSV, NIV, Gk. *harpagmón* [cf. KJV "robbery"]; JB "cling to") like a war trophy or spoil to be seized, Paul goes on to say that Christ surrendered his majestic life in heaven in order to accept an earthly life of humility and obedience (vv. 7-8).

EN [ĕn] (Heb. *ʿayin* "spring" or "fountain"). The Hebrew word for "spring" (e.g., Gen. 16:7), often a prefix (cf. Arab. *Ain*) in such place names as En-dor, En-eglaim, En-gedi, and En-hazor, all located near springs.

ENAIM [ī nā′əm] (Heb. *ʿênayim* "two fountains" or "double fountain"). An unidentified place "on the road to Timnah" (Gen. 38:14, 21; KJV "open place," "openly"), i.e., in the Shephelah of Judah; perhaps the same as ENAM (Josh. 15:34). Here the widowed Tamar awaited her father-in-law and he, thinking her a temple prostitute, propositioned her.

ENAM [ē′nəm] (Heb. *ʿênām*). A village in the tribal territory of Judah (Josh. 15:34), perhaps the same as ENAIM.

ENAN [ē′nən] (Heb. *ʿênān* "fountains"). The father of Ahira who was a leader of the tribe of Naphtali (Num. 1:15; 2:29; 7:78, 83; 10:27).

END (Gk. *télos*).† A term meaning either "cessation" or "purpose." At Rom. 6:21-22, where the apostle Paul contrasts a life of sin which will result in death with a sanctified life of service which will be rewarded with eternal life, purpose is implied. Both meanings may be applied at 10:4: Christ is both the fulfillment of Mosaic law — having kept all its requirements for man's justification through faith — and the dissolution of the Old Testament law as a means to righteousness.

The phrase "to the end [Gk. *eis télos*, without the definite article]" may refer to the actual termination of persecution (Matt. 10:22; 24:13; cf. Mark 13:13; Rev. 2:26), at the "close [KJV, NIV, JB "end"] of the [present] age" (e.g., Matt. 24:3) when the age of the kingdom of God will be ushered in. (*See also* ESCHATOLOGY; KINGDOM OF GOD). The expression "I am . . . the beginning and the end," attributed to both God and Christ (Rev. 21:6; 22:13), is another designation for God's supreme and unlimited majesty.

EN-DOR [ĕn′dôr] (Heb. *ʿên dōr*, *ʿên dôr*, *ʿên dōʾr* "fountain of Dor" or "fountain of dwelling [or encircling]").† A city assigned to the western portion of Manasseh, near the territory of Issachar (Josh. 17:11; LXX omits), among those cities which the Israelites

had difficulty wresting from Canaanite control (vv. 12-13). The name is preserved in the modern village of Endôr on the northern slope of the Little Hermon mountain (Nebī Daḥī), 6 km. (4 mi.) south of Mt. Tabor; the actual site may be nearby Khirbet eṣ-Ṣafṣafe.

It was here, north of Mt. Gilboa, that Saul consulted the woman "with the familiar spirit" (KJV, 1 Sam. 28:7) concerning the outcome of an impending battle with the Philistines. According to Ps. 83:9-10, Sisera and Jabin were defeated at En-dor; because the account of Judg. 4–5 does not mention such a site, some scholars have proposed the emendation Heb. *ʿên ḥᵃrōd* "En-harod," a site at the foot of Mt. Gilboa (cf. 7:1).

ENDURANCE (Gk. *hypomonḗ*).† One of the virtues of the Christian life cited in the New Testament, produced during suffering and which itself could produce character (Rom. 5:3-4). The Greek term suggests "tolerance," "forbearance," "patience" (KJV, JB), and "perseverance" (NIV). *See also* PATIENCE.

EN-EGLAIM [ĕn ĕg′lī əm] (Heb. *ʿên ʿeglayim* "spring of two calves"). A place on the shores of the Dead Sea where fishermen would spread their nets (Ezek. 47:10). Its exact location remains unknown, although ʿAin Feshkha, about 2 km. (1.5 mi.) from Khirbet Qumrân, is a good possibility; ʿAin Ḥajlah (Beth Hoglah) has also been proposed.

EN-GANNIM [ĕn găn′īm] (Heb. *ʿên gannîm* "spring of gardens").

1. A town in the tribal territory of Judah, in the region near Adullam (Josh. 15:34). Though Khirbet Umm Jina has been suggested as the modern site, a more likely location is ʿAin Fatir, a spring near Beit Jemâl and about 3 km. (2 mi.) south of Beth-shemesh.

2. A levitical city in the territory of Issachar (Josh. 19:21), assigned to the Gershonites (21:29); at 1 Chr. 6:73 it is named ANEM. En-gannim may be identified with modern Jenîn, about 10 km. (6 mi.) from Jezreel (modern Zerʿin), or possibly the nearby Khirbet Beit Jann.

EN-GEDI [ĕn gĕd′ī] (Heb. *ʿên geḏî* "spring of the kid").† A settlement belonging to the tribe of Judah (Josh. 15:62), in the Judean wilderness on the west shore of the Dead Sea, between Wâdī Sudeir and Wâdī ʿAreijeh. Fed by a spring (ʿAin Jidi) from a nearby promontory, En-gedi (modern Tell ej-Jurn) was an oasis known for its vineyards, henna blossoms (Cant. 1:14), and palms (Sir. 24:14). According to Ezek. 47:10 the region between En-gedi and En-eglaim would become an excellent fishing area.

It was in one of the "strongholds" of En-gedi that the outlaw David sought shelter from the continued pursuits of King Saul (1 Sam. 23:29). When the king learned of the outlaw's hideout, he hastened his pursuit and unwittingly chose David's cave in which to relieve himself. Without Saul's knowledge, David cut off a piece from the skirt of the king's robe (24:1-5).

Later, the combined forces of the Moabites, the Ammonites, and the Meunites assembled at En-gedi (actually nearby Hazazon-tamar) after crossing the Dead Sea (2 Chr. 20:2); before they had a chance to face Judah's army at the ascent of Ziz, however, they destroyed one another (v. 23).

Excavations at Tell ej-Jurn indicate that the first permanent settlement was established in the late seventh century B.C., approximately during the reign of Josiah and shortly before the fall of the southern kingdom. Perhaps conquered by the Edomites, the site was not reoccupied until the fifth century (Persian period); this settlement was destroyed by the Nabateans (second century). A Ptolemaic fortress on the site was leveled during the reign of John Hyrcanus (late second century), under whose successors En-gedi was apparently a flourishing administrative center (Josephus *BJ* iii.3.8). During the First Jewish Revolt (*ca.* A.D. 70) the city was leveled, either by raiding Zealots or the Roman forces who quelled them (iv.7.2; Pliny *Nat. hist.* v.15). En-gedi was apparently rebuilt as an administrative center in the early second century A.D., as indicated by commercial enterprises documented in the Naḥal Ḥever manuscripts and military involvements in the Second Jewish Revolt known from the Bar Kokhba letters. But no remains have been discovered at Tell ej-Jurn prior to the third century.

ENGLISH VERSIONS. *See* BIBLE TRANSLATIONS *III*.

EN-HADDAH [ĕn hăd'ə] (Heb. *'ên ḥaddâ*). A village in the tribal territory of Issachar (Josh. 19:21). The site may be modern el-Hadetheh, about 10 km. (6 mi.) east of Mt. Tabor.

EN-HAKKORE [ĕn hăk'ə rī] (Heb. *'ên haqqôrē'* "spring of the partridge" or "spring of the caller"; cf. LXX *pēgē toú epikalouménou*). A spring at Lehi, from which Samson, wearied from battle with the Philistines, drank and regained his strength (Judg. 15:19). The name may derive from Samson's having first called (Heb. *qārā*) upon the Lord for help (v. 18).

EN-HAZOR [ĕn hă'zôr] (Heb. *'ên ḥāṣôr* "spring of Hazor"). A fortified city in the tribal territory of Naphtali (Josh. 19:37). Most scholars propose the site to be Khirbet Haṣīreh, near Ḥazzûr (biblical Hazor) and west or southwest of Kedesh, or a site southwest of Kedesh, on the common border of Naphtali and Asher.

ENLIL [ĕn'lĭl]. The Sumerian god of the atmosphere and the wind, worshipped at Nippur. He was later identified with Marduk. *See* BEL.

EN-MISHPAT [ĕn mĭsh'păt] (Heb. *'ên mišpāṭ* "fountain of judgment"). An oasis, and probably a cult center, in the Negeb where Chedorlaomer and his allied kings defeated the Amalekites (Gen. 14:7). It was later called KADESH or Kadesh-barnea.

ENOCH [ē'nək] (Heb. *ḥªnôk* "founded" or "dedicated" [?]) (**PERSON**).

1. The eldest son of Cain (Gen. 4:17).

2.† One of the sons of Jared (Gen. 5:18) and father of Methuselah (v. 21). A descendant of Adam and Eve through Seth, Enoch is described as one who spent his relatively short life in spiritual communion with

God (vv. 22-23; cf. LXX "was well-pleasing to God"; cf. Jub. 4:17-21). Enoch's ascension to heaven is thought to be indicated at v. 24 ("and he was not [LXX "he was not found"], for God took him [LXX "translated him"]"; cf. 2 Kgs. 2:1, 11). Outside of the Genesis narrative his name occurs only in the royal genealogy at 1 Chr. 1:3 (KJV "Henoch").

In intertestamental writings, Ben Sirach includes his name in the list of Hebrew ancestors (Sir. 44:16), adding that Enoch was an "example for the conversion [JB; Gk. "example of repentance"; so KJV, RSV, Heb. "understanding," i.e., of the mysteries of the universe] of all generations." Similarly, in the Wisdom of Solomon he is portrayed as a righteous man who was "carried off" so that evil might not warp his understanding nor treachery seduce his soul (Wis. 4:11).

The New Testament mentions Enoch's name twice; at Jude 14, where he is said to have been the "seventh generation from Adam," and at Heb. 11:5-6, where he is listed as the second hero of faith. Quoting the LXX nearly verbatim, the author of Hebrews focuses on Enoch's faith as the prerequisite for a life well-pleasing to God.

In the pseudepigraphic 1 Enoch, Enoch appears as one well versed in angelology and astronomy. *See* ENOCH, BOOKS OF **1**.

ENOCH [ē'nək] (Heb. *ḥªnôk*) (**PLACE**). A city built by Cain and named after his eldest son Enoch (Gen. 4:17).

ENOCH, BOOKS OF.†

1. 1 Enoch or Ethiopic Enoch, a collection of pseudepigraphic writings by various authors written during the second-first centuries B.C. and attributed to Enoch (**2**) the son of Jared (Gen. 5:23-24). Originally written in Aramaic or Hebrew and translated into Greek, the work in its entirety survives only in an Ethiopic (Geʿez) translation; fragments of Greek and Latin manuscripts survive as well as Aramaic fragments discovered among the Dead Sea Scrolls.

Frequently described as an apocalypse, the work is a compilation of various types of material including portions of an earlier Apocalypse of Noah, all purportedly the heavenly secrets revealed to the righteous Enoch (cf. Sir. 44:16). Five major sections or "books" can be distinguished. Following a brief introduction concerning the end times (1 En. 1–5), the first section (chs. 6–36) concerns the rebellion of the angels (the "watchers"), Enoch's vision of heaven, and his cosmic travels; these chapters originated before 175 B.C. The Parables (or Similitudes) of Enoch (chs. 37–71) concern the coming judgment (chs. 38–44), the final review by the Son of Man, the preexistent, heavenly Elect One (chs. 45–57), and the aftermath (chs. 58–71); this section appears to have developed from Jewish traditions known around the turn of the era. The book of the heavenly luminaries (chs. 72–82) constitutes an astronomical treatise on cosmic phenomena such as the solar calendar, apparently the focus of theological dispute *ca.* 200 B.C. and later. The fourth section (chs. 83–90) contains two dream visions which foresee the Flood as divine punishment for sin (chs. 83–84) and depict allegorically world history through the messianic kingdom (chs. 85–90); this portion dates to the reign of Antiochus IV Epiphanes (*ca.* 164-160 B.C.). The final book (chs. 92–105) is an epistle to Enoch's children (92:1; actually the author's contemporaries), lamenting the punishment awaiting sinners and exhorting the faithful to have courage and faith, and concluding with a dispute on the existence of retribution; although the date of this section remains uncertain, the early second century B.C. is plausible. The book concludes with an apocryphal account of the birth of Noah (chs. 106–7) and an appendix offering a final note of encouragement to the righteous (ch. 108).

Portions of the work were well known in Christian circles. 1 En. 1:9 is quoted explicitly in the Epistle of Jude (vv. 14-15), and Enoch's appearances to imprisoned spirits associated with the origins of human sin (e.g., 1 En. 1:2; 12–14; 17:1; cf. 65) may lie behind the account at 1 Pet. 3:19. Although the eschatological parables are somewhat compatible with early Christian thought, they lack specifically christological interpretation, particularly in the "Son of Man" references; although they may share a common historical context, nothing suffices to confirm them as either an influence on or the product of Christian theology. The work was accepted as Scripture in various early Christian writings (e.g., Barn. 16:5; cf. 4:3; Clement of Alexandria *Ecl.* ii; Irenaeus *Adv. haer.* iv.16.2), but not universally (cf. Tertullian *De cult. fem.* i.3).

2. 2 Enoch or Slavonic Enoch, also called the book of the Secrets of Enoch (more fully the Secret Book about the Rapture of Enoch the Righteous). Possibly written in Greek at Alexandria during the first century A.D. (although some scholars posit it as a Jewish Christian work of the early third century or even a medieval Bulgarian composition), the book survives only in a Slavonic translation; its interest in sacrificial rites and the Melchizedek priesthood and influence by Zoroastrian cosmogony suggest a possible sectarian origin. Paralleling to a degree the form and content of 1 Enoch, this apocalypse records the ascent of Enoch through the seven heavens (ten according to a longer recension) to the throne of God, where he acquires eschatological and cosmological revelations for his family and spiritual descendants (2 En. 3–37). Stressing God's role as both creator and judge, Enoch's instruction is presented as three books intended for his children (chs. 39–56), Methuselah's brethren and the elders of the people (chs. 57–63), and an assembly of two thousand (chs. 64–65). The work concludes with a final admonition (ch. 66) and Enoch's translation to heaven (ch. 67). Of note are the book's depiction of history as lasting seven thousand years, the last thousand of which will be a "millennium" of rest after which time will come to an end (cf. 32:2).

3. 3 Enoch or Hebrew Enoch, a Jewish work composed in the late third century A.D. or later. This rabbinic interpretation of the Enoch traditions concerns the destiny of Enoch (depicted as the divine servant Metatron), an elaborate angelology, and a description of Sheol. It is marked to an extent by anti-Christian polemic.

Bibliography. J. T. Milik, ed., *The Books of Enoch* (New York: 1976); G. W. E. Nickelsburg, *Jewish Literature Between the Bible and the Mishnah* (Philadelphia: 1981); H. Odeberg, *3 Enoch,* rev. ed. (New York: 1973).

ENOSH [ēʹnōsh] (Heb. *ʹeʹnôš* "man," "mankind"; Gk. *Enōs*). The eldest son of Seth and grandson of Adam (Gen. 4:26; 5:6; 1 Chr. 1:1; KJV "Enos"); the father of Kenan (Gen. 5:9-10). In the New Testament he is called Enos (Luke 3:38). According to Gen. 4:26 the worship of Yahweh was introduced at this early date, well before the time of Moses (cf. Exod. 3:14; 6:3); although the passage remains problematic, it indicates the antiquity of God's revelation to the patriarchs.

EN-RIMMON [ĕn rĭmʹən] (Heb. *ʹen-rimmôn* "spring of the pomegranate"). A city in Judah assigned to the tribe of Simeon (Josh. 19:7); the rendering Ain and Rimmon at 15:32; 1 Chr. 4:32 should be read En-Rimmon (so LXX), but there it is assigned to Judah. Repopulated after the Exile (Neh. 11:29), En-rimmon was a large village in the Christian Era (so Eusebius *Onom.*lxxxviii.17). It is usually identified with Khirbet Umm er-Ramāmîm, 14 km. (9 mi.) northeast of Beersheba, on the road toward Beit Jibrîn (Eleutheropolis).

EN-ROGEL [ĕn rōʹgəl (Heb. *ʹên rōgēl,* possibly "spring of the fuller"). A spring near Jerusalem, which once marked the border between Judah and Benjamin (Josh. 15:7; 18:16). Here David, in exile, received valuable information from a woman concerning the plans of his rebellious son Absalom (2 Sam. 17:17); here, too, a second son, Adonijah, prepared a coup, which nearly succeeded (1 Kgs. 1:9).

Located where the Kidron and Hinnom valleys meet, at a point some 105 m. (345 ft.) below the temple esplanade and well below the nearby Gihon spring, En-rogel provided Jerusalem with a reliable water supply. The spring is approximately 37 m. (123 ft.) deep. Perhaps En-rogel is referred to at Neh. 2:13 under the name of "Jackal's Well" (KJV "dragon well"; cf. JB). Its modern name is Bîr Ayyûb ("spring of Job") because, according to Arab tradition, Job was cured here of his diseases; Jewish tradition calls it the spring of Joab, claiming that Joab, David's general, was among the guests invited here to Adonijah's party.

ENROLLMENT (Gk. *apographḗ*).† A listing or enumeration of people according to family, position, or other social unit. In addition to the census for military conscription (e.g., Num. 1:2-46; 2 Sam. 24:1-9 par.), such records were maintained in early Israel in order to maintain patterns of inheritance (1 Chr. 5:1, 17; cf. v. 7; 4:33) and succession, particularly with regard to the priesthood (2 Chr. 31:16; Ezra 2:62 par. Neh. 7:64). In addition, these genealogical records were essential for establishing the legitimacy of the returned exiles as heirs of the true Israel (1 Chr. 9:1; cf. v. 22). *See* CENSUS; GENEALOGY.

According to Luke 2:1-5, the birth of Jesus in Bethlehem is associated with a decree by Caesar Augustus to enroll the entire Roman Empire ("all the world," v. 1). A number of difficulties posed by Luke's account have raised questions concerning its interpretation and even authenticity. No extrabiblical evidence supports Luke's claim of a universal census during the reign of Augustus, although Augustus did enumerate Roman citizens for statistical purposes and noncitizens in the provinces for taxation and conscription (cf. vv. 1-2,

KJV). Roman practice did not require people to return to their ancestral cities for taxation but rather to be registered where they lived or in the administrative seat of their district; later practice in Roman Egypt (A.D. 104) did require nonresidents to return to their homes for taxation, so it is feasible that such a custom was also observed in Judea where ancestral relationships were traditionally significant. However, why residents of Nazareth in Galilee (under Herod Antipas) would be subject to taxation in Judea remains problematic (cf. Matt. 2:5-6). Moreover, a census known to have been conducted in A.D. 6-7 when Quirinius was governor of Syria (Luke 2:2; Josephus *Ant.* xvii.11.4; cf. Acts 5:37, but note the chronological difficulties there) would not have coincided with the reign of Herod the Great (37-4 B.C.). It has been proposed that Quirinius earlier served as a military commander under the legate S. Sentius Saturninus (9-6 B.C.) or that the "first enrollment" (Luke 2:2, RSV) was the first stage (Gk. *apographḗ* "registration"; coinciding with Jesus' birth during Herod's reign) of a lengthy process, completed some years later (perhaps A.D. 6-7) with the actual tax assessment (Gk. *apotímēsis* "evaluation"; cf. Josephus *Ant.* xviii.1.1) and thus associated with Quirinius (cf. JB, NIV).

Bibliography. R. E. Brown, *The Birth of the Messiah* (Garden City: 1977), pp. 547-556; J. A. Fitzmyer, *The Gospel According to Luke I-IX.* AB (1981), pp. 392-94, 399-405; I. H. Marshall, *Commentary on Luke.* NIGTC (1978), pp. 99-104.

EN-SHEMESH [ĕn shĕm'ĭsh] (Heb. *'ēn šemeš* "spring of the sun").† A landmark spring on the border between the territories of Judah (Josh. 15:7; LXX *pēgē toú hēlíou*) and Benjamin (18:17; LXX "Beth-shemesh"). It is commonly identified with 'Ain el-Hôd, about 4 km. (2 mi.) east of Jerusalem. According to one tradition (*ca.* fifteenth century A.D.) the apostles drank from this spring; since then it has been called "Spring of the Apostles."

EN-TAPPUAH [ĕn tăp'yoŏ ə] (Heb. *'ēn tappûaḥ* "spring of Tappuah" [cf. LXX *pēgē Thaphthōth*). A spring on the southern border of Manasseh (Josh. 17:7) near Tappuah, which belonged to Ephraim (v. 8); apparently the lands watered by the spring were maintained by Manasseh even though the larger town, which protected them, belonged to Ephraim (cf. LXX). The site is probably the spring of Yāsūf, about 13 km. (8 mi.) south of Shechem.

EPAENETUS [ĭ pē'nə təs] (Gk. *Epainetos* "worthy of praise"). One of the Christians to whom Paul sent greetings in his letter to the Romans (Rom. 16:5). Called "beloved," Epaenetus was one of Paul's first converts in the province of Asia (KJV "Achaia," following Gk. *Achaia* in some texts; cf. 1 Cor. 16:15), probably at Ephesus. He was probably a member of Prisca's household, but some scholars believe that he still resided at Ephesus at the time Paul wrote his letter to the Romans.

EPAPHRAS [ĕp'ə frăs] (Gk. *Epaphras*).† A Christian residing at Colossae (Col. 4:12), possibly the founder of the local church (1:7). Having labored intensely

among the Colossian Christians ("on our [Paul's] behalf"), as well as in the neighboring churches of Laodicea and Hierapolis (4:13), Epaphras paid Paul a visit during his first Roman imprisonment. He informed the apostle of the current situation at Colossae, including the believers' faith in Christ and love for one another (1:4-8). According to Phlm. 23 Epaphras was a "fellow prisoner" (Gk. *synaichmálōtos* "fellow prisoner of war"); apparently he was incarcerated with Paul for the sake of the gospel, though no details of his imprisonment are given. His affections for the Colossians did not diminish when he was elsewhere, for on two occasions he sent them his greetings through the apostle (Col. 4:12; Phlm. 23). Deeply grateful for Epaphras's faithful and competent ministry, Paul described him as his "beloved fellow servant" and "a faithful minister of Christ" (Col. 1:7).

Although Epaphras is a shortened form of the name Epaphroditus, there is no sufficient evidence for identifying Epaphras with the Epaphroditus who was active at the church of Philippi (Phil. 2:25; 4:18).

EPAPHRODITUS [ĭ păf'rə dī'təs] (Gk. *Epaphroditos* "handsome"; cf. Lat. *venustus*).† A Christian from Philippi who was sent by the local church to present a gift to Paul during his first imprisonment (Phil. 2:25, "messenger"; Gk. *apóstolos* "one sent"). Epaphroditus also performed evangelistic work ("minister," v. 25) while in Rome. He became dangerously ill, however, either en route to Rome or while in the capital after having presented Paul with the Philippians' gift (4:18). Because of his colleague's distress at being absent from the Philippian Christians and at knowing that they had heard about his recent illness, Paul decided to return Epaphroditus to Philippi (2:25-26). Thanking the church for their gift, a "sacrifice" he called pleasing to God (4:18), the apostle informed them of the seriousness of Epaphroditus' illness, his recovery, and Paul's own joy and relief that Epaphroditus' life had been spared (2:27). Naming him a fellow Christian, a fellow missionary, and a fellow combatant of evil (2:25), Paul seems to have developed a high regard for Epaphroditus and thus affectionately commended him to the Philippian believers (v. 29).

Epaphroditus should not be identified with Epaphras (a shortened form of the name), even though both were present during Paul's prison term at Rome; the former was a member of the church at Philippi, while the latter was attached to the church at Colossae.

EPHAH [ē'fə] (Heb. *'êpâ* "darkness").

1. The eldest son of Midian and grandson of Abraham and Keturah (Gen. 25:4; 1 Chr. 1:33); at Isa. 60:6 the name designates a Midianite tribe bringing gold and frankincense to Jerusalem and proclaiming the praise of the Lord. The Hebrew name may be an·abbriviated form derived from Akk. *Ḫayappa*, an Arab tribe known from inscriptions of Tiglath-pileser III and Sargon.

2. A concubine of Caleb (1 Chr. 2:46).

3. One of Jahdai's sons, of the tribe of Judah (2 Chr. 2:47).

EPHAH [ē'fə] (Heb. *'êpâ*). A unit of dry measure for flour (e.g., Judg. 6:19), barley (Ruth 2:17), and other commodities; equal to one tenth of a homer and equivalent to the bath, a liquid measure (Ezek. 45:11; cf. Isa. 5:10). While Josephus considered the ephah to be a little more than 35 l. (9.25 gal.), it was more likely about 22 l. (5.8 gal.). At Zech. 5:6-10 it designates a container with the capacity of an ephah. *See* WEIGHTS AND MEASURES.

EPHAI [ē'fī] (Heb. K *'ôpay* [cf. LXX *Iōphe, Ōphe*], Q *'êpay* "bird," from *'ûp* "fly"). A Netophathite whose sons were among the "captains of the forces" who came to Gedaliah at Mizpah following the fall of Jerusalem (Jer. 40:8). There the entire assembly was murdered by Ishmael, the son of Nethaniah (41:1-3). In the parallel passage (2 Kgs. 25:23) the words "the sons of Ephai" are omitted.

EPHER [ē'fər] (Heb. *'ēper* "gazelle").
1. The second son of Midian and grandson of Abraham and Keturah (Gen. 25:4; 1 Chr. 1:33); eponymous ancestor of a South Arabian clan.
2. The third son of Ezrah and eponymous ancestor of a Judahite clan (1 Chr. 4:17).
3. The first mentioned in a list of "mighty warriors, famous men," and heads of fathers' houses in the Transjordanian half-tribe of Manasseh (1 Chr. 5:24).

EPHES-DAMMIM [ē'fīz dăm'ĭm] (Heb. *'epes dammîm*). A place between Socoh and Azekah where the Philistines had assembled their armies while preparing for battle with the Hebrews (1 Sam. 17:1). Here David killed the Philistine Goliath (v. 50). Pas-dammim, mentioned at 1 Chr. 11:13, is probably the same place.
The name Ephes-dammim "border of blood" may be derived from the red color of the soil. The modern site is probably Damun, 6.5 km. (4 mi.) northeast of Socoh.

EPHESIANS [ĭ fē'zhənz] (Gk. *Ephesioi*), **LETTER TO THE.†** The tenth book of the New Testament, generally reckoned among Paul's Prison Letters.

I. Addressees

In the older and more reliable manuscripts (B ℵ p[46]), the words "at Ephesus" do not appear at 1:1 (so RSV, JB; cf. NIV). Moreover, although the heading "To the Ephesians" may have been added as early as A.D. 200, it was not originally part of the letter. Indeed, Marcion (*ca.* A.D. 140) viewed the letter as the one sent to the Christians at Laodicea (Col. 4:16). Some scholars have assumed, therefore, that it was not intended solely for the church at Ephesus, but was to circulate between the various churches of the Roman province of Asia until it finally reached the provincial capital Ephesus, from which its name was later derived. The absence of personal greetings as well as references to specific issues or conditions, certainly to be expected in view of Paul's lengthy sojourn at Ephesus, reinforces the claim that this was a circulatory letter. *See also* EPHESUS *I.B.*

II. Authorship

For centuries the Pauline authorship of Ephesians, attested strongly in the early Church, went unchallenged. However, serious questions were raised in the nine-

teenth century. Although conservatives and most British scholars continue to favor Pauline authorship, many American and European scholars maintain serious reservations. Primary objections focus on differences between this letter and the majority of those numbered among the Pauline corpus. Differences of vocabulary (some ninety words not used in other Pauline works but in common use later in the first century A.D.) and style (unusually long chains of phrases and clauses) may be discounted on the basis of artistic temperament or range of subject matter. However, literary parallels to recognized Pauline writings abound, leading some scholars to posit the work as consciously imitative. In particular, the letter closely resembles the style and content of Colossians (Pauline authorship of which scholars also question), although much of the verbal similarity betrays sharply contrasting applications of vocabulary (e.g., Gk. *oikonomía, mystḗrion, plḗrōma*); note the similar attention to Christ as reconciler (2:16; Col. 1:22), the earmarks of the Christian life (Eph. 4; Col. 3:12) in contrast to a life not inspired by Christ (Eph. 2:2-13; 4:18-21, 25-31; Col. 3:5-12), and "household codes" regarding the mutual obligations of husbands and wives (Eph. 5:22-33; Col. 3:18-19), parents and children (Eph. 6:1-4; Col. 3:20-21), and masters and slaves (Eph. 6:5-9; Col. 3:22–4:1) but also the different focuses of Paul's christology (Eph. 1:4; 4:10-13; Col. 1:15; cf. 2:9-10). Most puzzling are statements which suggest a historical and theological setting later than that of Paul (e.g., apparent resolution of the Jewish-Gentile conflict, Eph. 2:15-16; concern for the universal church rather than the local congregation, e.g., 1:22; lack of urgency regarding the second coming and the end times, e.g., 2:7; 3:21; 5:21ff.). Nevertheless, although these arguments in combination make it difficult to prove conclusively Pauline authorship, it does remain possible to maintain that position. An alternate stance favored by some scholars is that the work is the product of a Pauline disciple or an amanuensis.

III. Date and Origin

Assuming that this letter is indeed a Pauline letter, it would have been written during Paul's imprisonment, probably in Rome (3:1; 4:1; 6:20-22; the postscript Gk. *egráphē apó Rōmēs* "written from Rome," however, appears in only a few minor manuscripts), approximately at the same time as the letter to the Colossians, Philippians, and Philemon (*see* PRISON LETTERS). It was brought to the Roman province of Asia by Tychicus (6:21-22) along with the letters to the Philippians and Philemon. These circumstances would date the letter to *ca.* A.D. 62. Those who deny Pauline authorship would date it from 70 to 170.

IV. Contents

On the basis of content, Ephesians can be divided at 3:21. The first three chapters concern spiritual privileges gained through Christ (1:3-14), their implications for believers (ch. 2), and Paul's role in this achievement, motivated and informed by grace (3:1-13). Also included are intercessory prayers for the faithful (1:15-23; 3:14-19) and a concluding doxology (vv. 20-21). In chapters 4–6 the apostle describes the practical consequences of his doctrinal vision. Paul admonishes

Ephesians 1:1-11 from p⁴⁶ (University of Michigan Library)

the Ephesians to live in a manner "worthy of the calling" of the elect (4:1-16), i.e., to abandon their former sinful lifestyles (4:17–5:2) and to practice Christian virtues (5:3-20), specifically love (5:21–6:9); he encourages them also to put on the "armor of God" in their fight against sin and spiritual powers (6:10-20).

V. Theological Significance

In Ephesians Paul seeks to overcome the sharp division between Jews and Gentiles that so plagued the early Church. Echoing his earlier comments on the harmony between the Old Testament people of God and those who follow the New Testament (Gal. 3:28; cf. 1 Cor. 12:12), the apostle proclaims that both can share in Christ's blessings (Eph. 2:11-21). Indeed, sinners — Jews and Gentiles alike — are incorporated into the Church by divine grace (2:5, 8) — specifically, grace through Jesus Christ in whom God elected his people in eternity and through whom he accomplished the reconciliation of the world (1:4-5). The church which he envisions is subject to Christ as its head (1:21-23; 5:23-24) and is securely built upon Christ as the cornerstone (2:20-22). Accordingly, he urges that the entire Christian household should be motivated by a love which transcends all social strata (5:21–6:9) and that all Christians should unite to face their common enemy, "the wiles of the devil," employing spiritual weapons available through faith in God and Christ (6:10-18).

Mindful of the inroads into the church made by incipient Gnosticism, Paul combats the gnostic tendency to minimize Christ's work by reasserting the centrality of the Savior's atoning death on the cross and his subsequent exalted position above the powers of the universe. He responds to the gnostics' emphasis on knowledge with his own emphasis on faith, which is available to all believers. Moreover, the apostle warns against a prevailing immorality that he felt was encouraged by libertine Gnosticism, which lacked ethical principles concerning bodily passions.

Bibliography. T. K. Abbott, *The Epistles to the Ephesians and the Colossians.* ICC (1897); C. H. Dodd, *The Epistle of Paul to the Romans.* MNTC (London: 1932); M. Barth, *Ephesians.* AB, 2 vols. (1974); C. L. Mitton, *Ephesians.* NCBC (1981).

EPHESUS [ĕf'ə səs] (Gk. *Ephesos*).† A seaport in the Roman province of Asia, about 5.5 km. (3.5 mi.) south of the Caÿster river, opposite the island of Samos.

I. History

A. Pre-Christian Period. Conquered from the Carians ca. 1044 B.C. by Androclus of Athens (Strabo *Geog.* xiv.1.3 [632-33], 21 [640]), Ephesus was incorporated into the twelve-city Ionian League. Situated at the intersection of two major overland routes, the city thrived not only as an important port, but as a center of commerce and finance and as a place of worship for pilgrims visiting the sanctuary of the goddess Artemis (still recognized as one of the seven wonders of the ancient world). *Ca.* 555 the Lydian king Croesus captured Ephesus, dedicating it to Artemis (Herodotus *Hist.* i.26). After a subsequent defeat, Croesus was forced to surrender the city to Cyrus the Persian (*ca.* 546). In the Ionian revolt (*ca.* 497), at a time when the noted philosopher Heraclitus made Ephesus his home, it was the only Ionian city-state spared by the Persians.

With his defeat of the Persians in 334, Alexander the Great brought an end to their two centuries of dominion over Ephesus. His successor Lysimachus, one of his generals, forced the populace up the slopes between the steep hills of Coressus (Bülbül Dagh) and Pion (Panajir Dagh) (Strabo *Geog.* xiv.1.21 [640]); Lysimachus also constructed a new harbor and, by concluding a treaty with Ptolemy I, opened the city to Egyptian influence. The latter, however, was thwarted when Seleucus I defeated Lysimachus in 281 (Pausanias, *Description of Greece* 1.16.2) and introduced Hellenism. Seleucid rule lasted until the second century B.C. In 133 B.C. the city was annexed to the Roman Empire as a bequest from Attalus III. Joining Mithradates VI of Pontus, the Ephesians mounted an unsuccessful revolt in 88 B.C. Subsequently Ephesus

The "marble way" in Ephesus (B. Van Elderen)

grew in significance under Roman rule and became the chief seat of Asia early in the Christian Era.

B. New Testament Times. Ephesus began to flourish during the reign of Caesar Augustus, becoming increasingly more cosmopolitan as an international trade center. It was considered one of the most sacred cities of antiquity, largely because of the temple of ARTEMIS and its magnificent statue fashioned from a meteorite. This temple provided a lucrative business for the guild of silversmiths who made miniature silver shrines of the deity (cf. Acts 19:24). The city had its own assembly (vv. 32, 39) over which a town clerk presided (v. 35); Luke records that this clerk successfully quieted the commotion caused when Demetrius, a silversmith, spoke out against Christianity as detrimental to his business.

Paul visited Ephesus on two different occasions. He passed through the city on his second missionary journey in the fall of A.D. 52 following his stay at Corinth (Acts 18:19-21), and returned on his third journey in the spring of 54. While there he taught in the synagogue for three months (19:8) and then for two years in the hall of Tyrannus (vv. 9-10). His ministry was successful: many came to believe in Jesus Christ and demonstrated their new faith with acts of love (v. 18). Luke describes a moving farewell scene between Paul and the Ephesian elders at the end of his third journey, when he stopped at nearby Miletus en route to Jerusalem (20:16-37).

If the Letter to the Ephesians was indeed addressed specifically to the church at Ephesus (*see* EPHESIANS, LETTER TO THE), it reveals certain tensions within that church, among members of families and between slaves and masters who failed to practice genuine love for one another (5:1–6:9). Another letter, written by the aged apostle John (who, according to tradition, spent his last days at Ephesus), compliments the believers for their patience and undying labor in behalf of the risen Christ (Rev. 2:2-3), but also notes the influence of the heretical Nicolaitans, who had diverted many away from their first love (v. 4).

C. Later Years. Damaged by an earthquake during the reign of Emperor Tiberius (A.D. 14-37), Ephesus received yet another setback when its harbor filled with silt, effectively separating the city and the Aegean. (King Attalus of Pergamum [*ca.* 159-138 B.C.] had previously sought to halt the chronic silting by narrowing the channel but actually intensified the problem.) Nevertheless, the Christian church flourished locally, while the Jewish population declined. In A.D. 431 the Council of Ephesus met here to discuss the doctrine of sin and to condemn Nestorius for his sharp distinction between the two natures of Jesus Christ. Today the village of Ayasoluk lies over the site of ancient Ephesus.

II. Archaeology

On the northeast end of the site is the Church of St. John, called Ayasoluk (Gk. *hágios theológos* "holy theologian"), said to be the burial place of John, Jesus' mother Mary, and Timothy, who according to 1 Tim. 1:3 labored at Ephesus in Paul's absence. To the southwest lie the ruins of the Artemision, the famous temple of Artemis, burnt on the birthday of Alexander the Great in 356 B.C. and rebuilt two centuries later; uncovered by J. T. Wood, who began excavations in 1863, the remains measure 128 m. (420 ft.) by 73 m. (240 ft.). Next in a line along the western edge of Panajir Dagh are the ruins of the stadium and the large theater. The theater, which faced the ancient harbor, had a seating capacity of some twenty-four thousand. The main street, 10.5 m. (35 ft.) wide and .8 km. (.5 mi.) long, connected the theater with the harbor and was flanked on either side by a colonnade. Another important feature of the ancient city was the agora, the marketplace located southeast of the harbor; here were located the assembly hall, commercial and administrative offices, and the shrine of the perpetually burning hearth. On the eastern edge of Panajir Dagh is the catacomb of the Seven Sleepers, so-called because, according to tradition, seven young men who had fallen asleep during the Decian persecution (*ca.* A.D. 250) remained dormant until two hundred years later when they awoke and testified to their faith.

Bibliography. J. T. Wood, *Discoveries at Ephesus* (1890; repr. Hildesheim, N.Y.: 1975); O. F. A. Meinardus, *St. Paul in Ephesus and the Cities of Galatia and Cyprus* (New Rochelle: 1978).

EPHLAL [ĕf'lăl] (Heb. *'eplāl*). A Judahite, the son of Zabad, and the father of Obed (1 Chr. 2:37).

EPHOD [ē'fŏd] (Heb. *'ēpōḏ*) (**PERSON**). The father of Hanniel, a leader of the tribe of Manasseh chosen to assist in distributing the Promised Land among the tribes (Num. 34:23).

EPHOD [ē'fŏd] (Heb. *'ēpōḏ*, *'ēpôḏ*, from *'pd* "put [or pull] on") (**OBJECT**).† An article of clothing worn primarily by the Israelite high priest; elsewhere it appears to be an image or some such solid object as well as an object used in divination.

According to Exod. 28:5ff. (cf. 39:2ff.) the ephod worn by the high priest consisted of a sleeveless garment of fine twined lined decorated with gold and blue,

purple, and scarlet material, to which two shoulder pieces were attached and around which fitted a belt. To the shoulder pieces were affixed two onyx stones engraved with the names of the twelve tribes in order of their inception, which served as a permanent memorial before God. At the front of the garment, possibly in an open spot, hung the breastpiece of twelve precious stones symbolizing the twelve tribes.

Although it was usually the high priest and the priests who wore the ephod (e.g., Exod. 28:4; 29:5), young Samuel, while ministering at Shiloh (1 Sam. 2:18), wore a linen ephod (Heb. *'ēpōḏ baḏ*), as did King David during the festive ceremony which accompanied the ark of the covenant to Jerusalem (2 Sam. 6:14; cf. 1 Chr. 15:27). Some scholars discern two types of ephod, with the linen ephod a brief garment such as a loincloth or an apron worn over a longer robe (cf. 1 Chr. 15:27). But, given that the priestly ephod was made of fine linen and that the ephod worn by the priests of Nob was a linen garment (1 Sam. 22:18; see LXX A), they may have been identical.

Three Old Testament passages imply that the ephod was an idol rather than a garment: Judg. 8:27, the ephod made by Gideon at Ophrah to which the Israelites pledged their religious fidelity; 17:5, the ephod fashioned by Micah, alongside the teraphim (cf. 18:14, 17-18 which list four kinds of idols); and Hos. 3:4, where again the ephod is mentioned with the teraphim.

Potential similarities have been noted between the Hebrew ephod (possibly a pullover) and the overgarment (Gk. *ependýtēs*) fashioned on the small statues of various ancient Near Eastern deities (cf. 2 Kgs. 23:7; Isa. 30:22); the Hebrews may have patterned this ephod after such foreign vestments, though making the opening in the front rather than in the back.

The ephod is at times clearly linked with eliciting an oracle from God: by Saul's priest Ahijah at the battle of Michmash pass (1 Sam. 14:3; LXX also vv. 18-19, where the MT reads "ark"), by Saul following that battle (vv. 36-42), by David at Keilah (23:6-12), and again at Ziklag (30:7-8). Most likely the ephod contained a pocket for the Urim and Thummim which were used for divination.

EPHPHATHA [ĕf'ə thə] (Gk. *ephphathá*). An Aramaic expression (transliterated from Aram. *'eṭpᵉtaḥ*), meaning "be opened," used by Jesus in the curing of the deaf-mute (Mark 7:34). As a result, the individual could hear and speak (v. 35). Mark may have intended to preserve Jesus' authentic words. The expression does not imply any magical formula.

EPHRAIM [ē'frī əm] (Heb. *'eprayim*, from *pārâ* "be fruitful"; Gk. *Ephraim*) (**PERSON**). The second son of Joseph and Asenath, and the eponymous ancestor of a tribe by the same name; as with other similar figures, it is frequently difficult to determine whether the individual or the social group is intended. Born in Egypt, probably before the seven-year famine (Gen. 41:50, 52), Ephraim, together with his older brother Manasseh, was adopted by the aged patriarch Jacob after he had arrived in Egypt (48:5). Though the younger of the two, Ephraim received the more significant blessing from Jacob, against Joseph's strong objections (48:12-20). In this blessing, mentioned apart from the blessings upon his sons (49:22-26), Jacob gave Joseph an additional portion (48:22) — in fact, the birthright that really belonged to Reuben as the eldest son (so 1 Chr. 5:1-2). While Ephraim is not given a separate blessing in the Blessing of Moses, again the tribe is promised greater numbers than the tribe of Manasseh (Deut. 33:17).

At the first census taken during the wilderness wanderings, Ephraim's military force appeared a mere 40,500 — well below that of many of the other tribes, and larger only than those of Manasseh and Benjamin (Num. 1:33). At the second census, taken at the end of the journey, Ephraim was even smaller — 32,500; only Benjamin was smaller (26:37). Still Ephraim held an important place among the tribes as the western vanguard of the camp (Num. 2:18-24; Ps. 80:1-2 may be a later allusion).

In the division of Canaan following the Conquest, Ephraim was situated somewhat west of the Jordan, south of Manasseh, northeast of Dan, and north of Benjamin (Josh. 16:5-10); a later description of Ephraim's settlement includes Shechem and Gezer within its boundaries (1 Chr. 7:28-29). At first the Ephraimites were unable to expel the Canaanites from Gezer (Josh. 16:10; Judg. 1:29). According to the Chronicler (1 Chr. 7:28), Shechem was one of the cities reserved for the Ephraimites (cf. Josh. 16:9; see also 17:8), though initially assigned to the tribe of Manasseh (17:2). Apparently Ephraim later acquired a portion of Dan, thus extending its western border to the Mediterranean Sea (16:6, 8).

Located in a fertile, well-irrigated part of Canaan, Ephraim enjoyed protection by the surrounding tribes against foreign attacks. Moreover, the "hill country" constituted a natural defense on the east.

Dissatisfied with the size of their inheritance, the Ephraimites petitioned Joshua, Moses' successor, for an additional allotment. Joshua commanded that they clear a portion of the hill country and expel the Canaanites from the coastal plain (17:14-18). Together Manasseh and Ephraim succeeded in conquering the city of Bethel on Ephraim's southern border (Judg. 1:22-26).

During the period of the judges Ephraim began to assert its power among the tribes. In the Song of Deborah, the tribe is singled out as having fought against Amalek (Judg. 5:14). They chided Gideon the Manassite for not having asked them to join in the battle against the fleeing Midianites when victory was almost certain (8:1-3). They also resented not being called to support Jephthah the Gileadite against the Ammonites (12:1), but Jephthah was less conciliatory than Gideon had been, and his superior forces inflicted heavy casualties upon the Ephraimites (12:2-6). The narrative describing the period of Israel's judges concludes with accounts of the Ephraimite Micah who set up a shrine and appointed priests to serve in it (Judg. 17:1-12), and of the sad fortunes of the Ephraimite Levite and his concubine (19:1ff.).

The period of the Monarchy saw Ephraim allied with Ish-bosheth, Saul's successor, rather than with David (2 Sam. 2:8-10), probably because of the blood ties established by Jacob's wife Rachel between the descendants of Benjamin and Joseph. While the Ephraimites pledged allegiance to David after Ish-bosheth's death (cf. 5:1-3), they quickly joined the other northern tribes in supporting the coup of David's son Absalom (15:13).

The first king of the divided monarchy, Jeroboam I, was an Ephraimite (1 Kgs. 11:26), as was the prophet Ahijah, who promised him the reign over the ten tribes (v. 29). Consolidating Ephraim's powerful position among the northern tribes and mindful of the religious significance of having the ark at Ephraimite Shiloh (Josh. 18:1; 1 Sam. 1:9), the newly crowned king proclaimed Bethel, another Ephraimite town, the seat of religious worship (1 Kgs. 12:28-30).

Slowly Ephraim assumed such a prominent place in the northern kingdom, ahead of Manasseh, that often the name was used to designate the ten tribes as a whole (e.g., 2 Chr. 25:7; Isa. 7:5). This was particularly true with regard to the so-called Syro-Ephraimite War (ca. 734-732 B.C.), whereby Israelite intrigue against Judah and Assyria provoked revenge by the Assyrian Tiglath-pileser III and Israel's reduction to the prior tribal territories of Ephraim and Manasseh (cf. 2 Kgs. 15:29-30, 37; 16:5-9; Isa. 7:1-17; 8:1-15; 10:27-34; 17:1-11; Hos. 5:1-2, 8–6:6; 8:7-10).

Ephraim represented Israel's religious apostasy (Ps. 78:9-10; Hos. 4:17; 5:3; 6:10). Though Yahweh was displeased with Ephraim's (Israel's) unfaithfulness (Hos. 6:4), intending to destroy the land (5:9, 11) and have its inhabitants deported to Assyria (10:6; cf. 9:3), he agonized over this nation, his firstborn (Jer. 31:9, 20; Hos. 11:3, 8). Aware of God's compassion for sinful Ephraim, the prophet Isaiah envisaged an era when the jealousy between Ephraim (Israel) and Judah would disappear (Isa. 11:13). Similarly, Jeremiah presaged that Ephraim would worship again in Jerusalem (Jer. 31:6) instead of committing idolatry at Bethel as under Jeroboam I and II.

The prophet Ezekiel included Ephraim among the tribes that would inhabit the restored Promised Land, between Manasseh and Reuben (Ezek. 48:5-6).

EPHRAIM [ē'frīəm] (Heb. 'eprayim, from pārâ "be fruitful"; Gk. Ephraim) (**PLACE**). A town near Baal-hazor where Absalom intended to kill his half-brother Amnon for dishonoring his sister Tamar (2 Sam. 13:23). It was probably identical to Ephron, mentioned at 2 Chr. 13:19 (RSV mg. "Ephraim"), and Ophrah, listed at Josh. 18:23; 1 Sam. 13:17. It was perhaps to this city that Jesus withdrew following his encounter with the Jewish leaders who were fearful of his influence (John 11:54). The site has generally been identified with eṭ-Ṭaiyibeh, about 21 km. (13 mi.) north-northeast of Jerusalem.

EPHRAIM, FOREST OF. An unknown forest (Heb. ya'ar "woodland"; KJV "wood of Ephraim") east of the Jordan, where David's son Absalom lost his life in his own rebellion against his father, the king (2 Sam. 18:6-15). Because the exiled king of Israel had taken temporary shelter at Mahanaim (17:27) just before the battle, this forest must have been near the Jabbok river.

At the Conquest of Canaan, the tribe of Ephraim was assigned an inheritance west of the Jordan river

(Josh. 16:1-10). Eager to secure additional territory (cf. 17:14-18), some of the Ephraimites may have crossed the river and settled in Gilead where they dwelled as "fugitives of Ephraim" (Judg. 12:4). Another possibility is that Ephraim had been assigned territory east of the Jordan which was subsequently lost to Gilead.

EPHRAIM GATE (Heb. *ša'ar 'eprayim*).† A gate in the northwest wall of Jerusalem where began the road to Shechem and Damascus. During the reign of Amaziah of Judah (*ca.* 800 B.C.) it was located near the Corner Gate, in the older section of the city (2 Kgs. 14:13 par.). After the Exile it may have been reconstructed more to the north of the "Old Gate" (Neh. 12:39) because of the newly constructed Mishneh wall. Here the returning exiles celebrated the Feast of Booths (8:6), and here the second company of Levites marched on the wall toward the Gate of the Guard at the dedication of Jerusalem's restored walls (12:39).

The gate has been variously identified as the Fish Gate, the Gennath or Garden Gate (Josephus *BJ* v.4.2 [142]), and the Middle Gate (Jer. 39:2).

EPHRAIM, HILL COUNTRY OF (Heb. *har 'eprayim*). The western part of the central mountain chain (KJV "mount Ephraim"; JB "highlands of Ephraim") west of the Jordan within the tribal territory of Ephraim (Josh. 17:15), possibly another name for the mountains of Samaria (cf. Jer. 31:5-6); it was a fertile area well suited to vineyards and the cultivation of olives and figs. In this region Deborah judged Israel (Judg. 4:5), and here Elkanah, Samuel's father, made his home (1 Sam. 1:1).

EPHRAIMITE [ē'frī ə mīt] (Heb. *'eprāṯî* [sing.], *'eprayim* [pl.]). A member of the tribe of Ephraim (e.g., Judg. 12:5; RSV, NIV). The KJV renders plural references as "children of Ephraim" (Heb. *bᵉnê-'eprayim*; e.g., Josh. 16:5; cf. JB "sons of Ephraim"); at 1 Sam. 1:1; 1 Kgs. 11:26 the KJV renders Heb. *'eprāṯi* as "Ephrathite."

EPHRAIN (2 Chr. 13:19, KJV). *See* EPHRON (PLACE) **2.**

EPHRATH [ĕf'răth] (Heb. *'eprāṯ*). The second wife of Caleb, and the mother of Hur and Asshur (1 Chr. 2:19); her alternate name is Ephrathah (v. 24; 4:4).

EPHRATHAH [ĕf'rə thə] (Heb. *'eprāṯâ*) (PERSON). Another name for EPHRATH (1 Chr. 2:24; 4:4; KJV "(Caleb-)ephratah").

EPHRATHAH [ef'rə thə] (Heb. *'eprāṯâ*) (PLACE).† A city near which Rachel died giving birth to Benjamin (Gen. 35:16, 19 "Ephrath"). It is traditionally identified with Bethlehem (cf. 48:7; Mic. 5:2; KJV "Ephratah"; cf. Ruth 4:11), 8 km. (5 mi.) south of Jerusalem, although originally it may have been a separate settlement later incorporated into Bethlehem. A nearby Muslim mausoleum preserves the tradition of Rachel's tomb on the road to Bethlehem.

Reference to Rachel's tomb near Zelzah in the territory of Benjamin (1 Sam. 10:2) suggests that Ephrathah

may actually have been located north of Jerusalem near Ramah (cf. Jer. 31:15). Some scholars thus view the identification of Ephrathah with Bethlehem (Gen. 35:19; 48:7) as an interpretive gloss made necessary by a later tradition (cf. Ruth 4:11; Mic. 5:2).

EPHRATHITE [ĕf'rə thīt] (Heb. *'eprāṯî*). A person from the city of Ephrathah (Ruth 1:2; 1 Sam. 17:12). The KJV uses the same gentilic at 1 Sam. 1:1; 1 Kgs. 11:26 to indicate an Ephraimite.

EPHRON [ē'frŏn] (Heb. *'eprôn* "fawnlike") (PERSON). A son of Zohar; a Hittite dwelling at Hebron. After some prodding by Abraham he sold him his field and the cave of Machpelah for four hundred shekels of silver (Gen. 23:8-18; cf. 25:9-10; 49:29-30; 50:13).

EPHRON [ē'frŏn] (Heb. *'eprôn* "fawnlike") (PLACE).
1. A mountain along the northern border of Judah near Kiriath-jearim (Josh. 15:9). Its precise location remains open to question, although el-Qastel, near Mozah (modern Qalôniyeh), is a possibility (R. G. Boling and G. E. Wright, *Joshua*. AB [1982], p. 369).
2. A city in the vicinity of Bethel which King Abijah of Judah captured from Jeroboam of Israel (2 Chr. 13:19; **K** Heb. *'eprôn*; cf. LXX *Ephrōn*; KJV "Ephrain," following **Q** *'eprayin*; cf. RSV mg.); also called Ephraim (2 Sam. 13:23) or Ophrah (Josh. 18:23). The site is modern eṭ-Ṭaiyibeh, about 21 km. (13 mi.) north-northeast of Jerusalem.
3. A large, fortified town attacked and captured by Judas Maccabeus after the residents refused to allow him and his Israelites to pass through to their own land. As the victorious band marched through the streets, they killed all male inhabitants and seized spoil (1 Macc. 5:46-51; cf. 2 Macc. 12:27). This town was located east of the Jordan, opposite Bethshan, perhaps at a site 20 km. (12 mi.) southeast of the Sea of Galilee.

EPICUREANS [ĕp'ə kyŏo rē'ənz] (Gk. *Epikoureioi*).† Members of a philosophical school founded by Epicurus (341-270 B.C.). Epicurus taught that all reality is made up of indestructible and undifferentiated "atoms," whose integration produces life and whose separation produces death. He acknowledged the existence of deities and held that they were composed of atoms like all other beings and were, therefore, corporeal; they did not, however, play a role in human life. This materialistic view of existence was intended, negatively, to free people from anxiety regarding death and the gods; death is the end of everything and, therefore, is nothing to be feared.

Positively, Epicurus' view of existence encouraged people to strive for happiness, wherein pleasure (Gk. *hēdonḗ*) overcomes all trouble, pain, and sorrow. Actually Epicurus developed a hierarchy of pleasures. Most primary were physical enjoyments, of which some were natural and necessary (e.g., food), others natural but not necessary (e.g., sexual union), and others neither natural nor necessary (e.g., fame). Next were the mental pleasures, embracing justice, wisdom, temperance, and peace of mind (*ataraxía* "lack of disturbance"). Despite later opinion, the happiness and pleasure the Epicureans sought was austerely simple to the point of asceticism.

To many Romans of the golden and silver ages (30 B.C.-A.D. 96), Epicureanism meant refinement and finesse. To countless others, however, an Epicurean life represented hedonism, an interpretation buttressed by the flamboyance and excesses of emperors Caligula and Nero. The movement began to wane after *ca.* A.D. 180, paralleling the decline of the Roman Empire; when Rome declared Christianity an acceptable religion *ca.* 323, Epicureanism proved no rival and soon fell into oblivion.

Despite certain similarities between the teachings of Epicurus and the wisdom proclaimed by the Preacher of Ecclesiastes (e.g., Eccl. 2:24; cf. 8:15), significant contrasts between the two (e.g., Qoheleth's affirmation of the law as providing meaning for human existence [12:13-14] and belief in eternal life [v. 7; cf. 3:17; 11:9]) support Ecclesiastes' developing from the stream of biblical and ancient Near Eastern thought rather than Epicurean influence.

Epicureans were in Paul's audience at Athens (Acts 17:18). Although he used the vocabulary of the Epicureans (e.g., *atómos* "atom," 1 Cor. 15:52; RSV "moment"; cf. "pleasure," Titus 3:3), his message of divine judgment and resurrection (Acts 17:31) was contrary to their beliefs.

EPILEPSY (Gk. *seléniázomai*). A disorder of the central nervous system characterized by convulsive attacks and impaired consciousness. Matthew records that Jesus healed many epileptics in Galilee (Matt. 4:24), including a boy whom the disciples had failed to heal (17:14-20). The KJV renders the Greek term as "lunatic," drawing upon its ancient interpretation as the "falling sickness" precipitated by the changed position of the moon. It is not certain whether the illness was still viewed this way in Jesus' day; the record attributes it to demon possession (17:18 par.).

Although Mark and Luke do not mention epilepsy by name, both undoubtedly refer to it. In the passage parallel to Matt. 17:14-20, Mark describes the boy's convulsions accompanied by rigidity and a grinding of teeth (Mark 9:18, 20; cf. Luke 9:39, 42).

EPISTLE (Gk. *epistolé*). See LETTER.

ER [ûr] (Heb. *ʿēr* "watcher" or "watchful"; Gk. *Ēr*).
1. The firstborn son of Judah and the daughter of the Canaanite Shua (Gen. 38:1-3, 12; 46:12; Num. 26:19) or Bath-shua (cf. 1 Chr. 2:3). Er's marriage with Tamar, probably a Canaanitess, ended shortly with his death, attributed to "wickedness in the sight of God" (Gen. 38:7; 1 Chr. 2:3).
2. One of the sons of Shelah; the grandson of Judah and the father of Lecah (1 Chr. 4:21).
3. The father of Elmadam, and an ancestor of Jesus (Luke 3:28).

ERAN [ĭrʹăn] (Heb. *ʿērān*). One of Shuthelah's sons and the grandson of Ephraim (Num. 26:36); called Eden (Gk. *Eden*) in the LXX (v. 40).

ERANITES [ĭrʹə nīts] (Heb. *hāʿērānî*). Descendants of Eran (Num. 26:36).

ERASTUS [ĭ răsʹtəs] (Gk. *Erastos* "beloved"). The city treasurer (so RSV, JB; Gk. *oikonómos*; KJV "chamberlain of the city"; NIV "director of public works") of Corinth, mentioned with others who sent their greetings to the church at Rome (Rom. 16:23); possibly to be identified with Erastus the Corinthian aedile, named in a Latin inscription, who had a section of the city's pavement laid at his own expense. An Erastus is mentioned at Acts 19:22 as an aide of Paul who accompanied Timothy from Ephesus to Macedonia. In his second epistle Timothy greets an Erastus who remained at Corinth (2 Tim. 4:20). Although Erastus appears to have been a common name during this period, it is entirely possible that all of the above references are to the same individual.

ERECH [ĭrʹĕk] (Heb. *ʾereḵ*).† A major Sumerian city (Sum. *Uruk*), located at modern Warka on the eastern bank of the Euphrates river and 65 km. (40 mi.) northwest of Ur. It is named in the Table of Nations as one of the cities founded by Nimrod (Gen. 10:10).

Founded *ca.* 4000 B.C. during the prehistoric Ubaid period, the city was the focus of urban life and a distinctive culture which lent its name to the Uruk period of the early third millennium. It was at this time that residents of the region devised the use of cylinder seals and of pictographic writing, the forerunner of the cuneiform script. Shortly thereafter, the city was governed by a series of legendary kings known from the Sumerian King List, including Gilgamesh, who is credited with construction of the city's first fortifications. Following his destruction of Lagash, Lugalzagesi (*ca.* 2370) captured Uruk, which he ruled in tandem with Ur, and extended his power over all Sumer and Akkad as sole figure in the Third Dynasty of Uruk. Subsequently the city came under the domination of Sargon of Akkad (*ca.* 2300-2230). It was captured by the invading Gutians and liberated *ca.* 2100 by Utuhegal, who reestablished condominion with Ur. Rim-sin of Larsa (*ca.* 1794) annexed Uruk, and with his defeat by Hammurabi the city became part of Babylonia. Although its importance was significantly diminished, the city survived until the fall of the Parthian Empire.

Excavations at the site had uncovered as many as eighteen levels of occupation. Important remains underscore the city's early prosperity and importance, including hundreds of Sumerian economic and administrative texts, royal inscriptions and cuneiform tablets from Babylonian and Persian times, and a distinctive red pottery, polished but unpainted. Several temples and two ziggurats (temple towers) date to the late fourth-early third millennia; the larger ziggurat, some 28 m. (100 ft.) high, is the Eanna ("house of heaven"), dedicated to the sky-god Anu and Inanna (Ishtar).

According to Ezra 4:9-10, the residents of Erech (KJV "Archevites") were deported by Osnapper (probably Assurbanipal of Assyria) to the region of Samaria and other areas within the province Beyond the River.

ERI [ĭrʹī] (Heb. *ʿērî* "watchful"). The fifth son of Gad (Gen. 46:16); his descendants, called the ERITES, are mentioned in the first census taken in the wilderness (Num. 26:16).

ERITES [ĭr′īts] (Heb. *hā′ērî*). Descendants of Eri (Num. 26:16), called Addites in the LXX (v. 25; Gk. *ho Addi*).

ERR. *See* WANDER.

ERUPTION.* A scab (so KJV, JB) or a rash (so NIV). Because the eruptions of incipient leprosy (Heb. *sappahat*; Lev. 13:2; 14:56) were often indistinguishable from rashes caused by something else, all such irregularities underwent ritual examination to determine whether or not they were benign (13:6; Heb. *mispahat*).

ESAIAS [ĭa zā′əs] (Gk. *Ēsaias*) (KJV). *See* ISAIAH.

ESARHADDON [ē′sər hăd′ən] (Heb. *'ēsarhaddōn*; Akk. *Aššur-ah-iddin* "Assur has given a brother").† King of Assyria (681-669 B.C.); the son and successor of Sennacherib and the father of Assurbanipal.

Appointed crown prince over Babylon in 689, Esarhaddon was designated as Sennacherib's successor even though he was not the oldest son. Upon Sennacherib's death at the hands of rival sons (cf. 2 Kgs. 19:37 par. Isa. 37:38), Esarhaddon gained the throne only after defeating the parricides at Hanigalbat and quelling their supporters. His early reign was devoted to suppressing revolts in the provinces, namely the Cimmerians, Manneans, and others to the north, the Sealands to the south, and Syria to the west. Because of Esarhaddon's efficient administration and extensive restoration, Babylon remained securely under Assyrian control.

The pinnacle of Esarhaddon's political accomplishments was his conquest of Egypt. In response to Egyptian instigation of rebellion in Syria and Palestine, Esarhaddon sought to retaliate against Pharaoh Taharqa (biblical Tirhakah) in 675, only to be halted by a sandstorm. He returned with a full-scale campaign in 671, capturing Memphis and forcing Taharqa to flee south into Upper Egypt. Esarhaddon appointed Assyrian advisers to rule the land and proclaimed himself king of Upper and Lower Egypt and Ethiopia, but his success was fleeting. The Egyptians soon revolted and Esarhaddon died in 669 en route to confront the unrest.

Despite his reputation as a cruel and ruthless ruler in the fashion typical of Assyrian monarchs, Esarhaddon demonstrated considerable skill as a leader. His efficient administration is typified by his provisions for succession; in 672 he had named his sons Assurbanipal and Šamaš-šum-ukin (perhaps twins) as successors to the thrones of Assyria and Babylonia respectively and bound the vassal rulers by oath to support them. His extensive building activities are also to his credit, including restoration of the temple tower Esagila and other buildings at Babylon and the construction of a new palace at Kar-Esarhaddon near Nineveh.

ESAU [ē′sô] (Heb. *'ēśāw*; Gk. *Ēsau*).† The firstborn son of Isaac and Rebekah, and the older twin brother of Jacob. He came to be regarded as the eponymous ancestor of the Edomites.

I. Life

A. Birth. Following Isaac's intense pleading in behalf of his barren wife Rebekah, the Lord granted her twins. The firstborn was called Esau, a name said to derive from his reddish (Heb. *'dm*) complexion and his hairy (*śē'ār*) appearance; the younger son, who was born holding tight to Esau's heel, was named Jacob (*ya'ªqōb* "he grasps the heel"; Gen. 25:20-26). The names suggest the later relationship of the Israelites (Jacob's descendants) and the Edomites (cf. Jer. 49:8).

B. Birthright. The young Esau is described as a skillful hunter, who spent his time outdoors, catching game and preparing savory meat for his father, who favored him for that reason (Gen. 25:27-28). Esau was quite different from Jacob, who, like his mother, was a more sedentary person.

Esau revealed a less attractive character, however, when he sold his birthright (vv. 29-34). Returning home from the field, weary and hungry, he noticed the pottage (Heb. *'ādōm*) Jacob was preparing and willingly exchanged his rights of primogeniture for food when his brother suggested the trade. To assure his claim to Esau's birthright, Jacob made him confirm the transfer with an oath. The account ends with the author's indictment of Esau for having "despised" (cared little for) his birthright" (v. 34).

C. Marriage. At age forty Esau married Judith and Basemath, two women from among the people of the land (26:34). Here the narrative indicates only that they made life bitter for Esau's parents (v. 35), probably a reference to their non-Abrahamic descent. Later, when Esau realized Isaac's opposition to his sons' marrying Canaanite women, he defiantly married Mahalath, a daughter of Ishmael, Abraham's son by the Egyptian Hagar (28:6-9; called Basemath at 36:3). According to 36:1-2, he also married Adah, a Hittite, and Oholibamah, a Hivite.

D. Blessing. A pivotal point in Esau's life was the loss of the blessing which would normally have fallen to him as the firstborn of the family — the result of Jacob's cunning (27:1-40). Asked by his aged father to prepare his favorite food, Esau returned from a successful hunt, made the dish according to his father's taste, and presented it to him, fully expecting to receive the patriarchal blessing. Instead, he was informed that his younger brother had already accommodated Isaac's request and had thereby stolen the blessing in his absence. Deeply hurt and realizing Jacob's determination, Esau entreated his father for even a small blessing, which he received: he would spend the remainder of his life away from fertile fields as a man of war, and for a time in subjugation to his brother (vv. 39-40). Esau hoped to kill Jacob after their father died, but Rebekah suggested to Isaac that Jacob be sent to Paddan-aram to secure a wife for himself, and so it was done (vv. 41-46).

E. Reconciliation. Esau and Jacob were reunited some twenty years later following Jacob's return to Canaan. Informed by Jacob's servants that his brother intended reconciliation, Esau, who then dwelled at Seir in Edom, went to meet him accompanied by four hundred of his people (32:3-6; 33:1). Kissing his brother, he inquired after Jacob's possessions and, after much prodding, accepted a gift from him (33:4-11).

When Jacob declined Esau's offer to travel with him or leave some of his men with him, Esau then returned home (vv. 12-17). That Esau no longer nursed a grudge against Jacob is evident from his later willingness to join him in burying their deceased father Isaac (35:29).

II. Interpretation

A. Old Testament. Among the Old Testament prophets, only Malachi offers an interpretation of the Lord's message to Rebekah, namely, that the "two peoples" born of her would be divided and that the elder son would serve the younger (Gen. 25:23); this he sees fulfilled in the subsequent fortunes of Israel and Edom (Mal. 1:2-3). Malachi foresees Edom's continued subjection to God's anger, possibly to be realized as the Nabatean invasion (vv. 3-4).

B. New Testament. In the context of divine election, the apostle Paul cites both God's prediction to Rebekah and Malachi's interpretation (Rom. 9:12-13). Unlike the Old Testament prophet, however, Paul views God's anger against Israel's elder son as originating in heaven prior to Esau's actual deeds, which some would take to mean that God had predestined Esau to eternal damnation.

The author of Hebrews labels Esau an "immoral and irreligious" person, citing as evidence that he had sold his birthright "for a single meal" (12:16), and concludes that Esau failed to receive his father's blessing because he did not find a chance (cf. Midrash *Gen. Rab.* lxv.15 "no Day of Atonement") to repent his earlier folly before the blessing was dispensed (v. 17). In New Testament times his sinfulness was associated with Rome, for which he became a symbol (cf. Jub. 25:1, 8; Philo *De virt.* 208).

ESCAPE, ROCK OF (Heb. *selaʿ hammaḥlᵉqôṯ* "rock of divisions"; so JB).† A place in the wilderness of Maon — perhaps a cliff — where Saul ceased his pursuit of the outlaw David to defend Israel from the aggression of the Philistines (1 Sam. 23:28; KJV, NIV "Sela-hammahlekoth"). The RSV rendering "Rock of Escape" suggests that David was able to "slip away" (Heb. *ḥālaq* hiphil; Gesenius, p. 284; Akk. *ḥalāqu*) while Saul was preoccupied with other problems. Scholars propose identification of the site as Wâdī el-Malâqi, about 13 km. (8 mi.) east-northeast of Maon.

ESCHATOLOGY [ĕs kə tŏl′ə jē] (from Gk. *éschaton* "last thing").* The biblical perspective concerning events to take place in the last days (Gk. *ep' eschátou tôn hēmerôn toútōn*; Heb. 1:2; cf. Heb. *'aḥᵃrîṯ hayyāmîm* "latter days"; Isa. 2:2-4; Hos. 3:5). While the Old Testament highlights the future of the community (Israel), the New Testament pays special attention to the destiny of the individual.

I. Old Testament

The Hebrews worshiped Yahweh as the Lord of history, who not only established his covenant with his chosen people on Mt. Sinai (after delivering Israel from Egypt), but supported the newly founded Hebrew nation as well. While some of the books of the Pentateuch point to God's guidance in the wilderness

wanderings and others, such as 1-2 Samuel and 1-2 Kings, describe God's dealings with the Israelite Monarchy, some of the later prophetic works refer to God's future contact with Israel, usually through the so-called DAY OF THE LORD (or Day of Judgment).

A. Prophets. To the prophets the Day of the Lord represented salvation, hope, and vindication for the righteous as well as judgment and doom for the unrighteous. This is similar to the Mosaic covenant, which promised blessings for those who would keep the covenantal stipulations and curses for those who would disregard their responsibility. Unlike later apocalyptic seers, however, the prophets believed that God would continue to rule history until his Day.

1. Preexilic. Among the preexilic prophets speaking about the Day of the Lord were the eighth-century B.C. prophets Amos and Hosea. The rugged Amos unashamedly told the Samaritan Hebrews that God's Day would mean darkness and gloom, not light as they had hoped (Amos 5:18-20). If Amos tended to downplay God's mercy and compassion for sinful Israel (but cf. 9:11-15), Hosea amply compensated. While not excluding God's judgment, Hosea stressed God's love for Ephraim (Hos. 11:1ff.), God's unwillingness to destroy his "son" (vv. 8-9), and God's eagerness to renew and reinvigorate him (2:15-23).

2. Exilic. Following the fall of Jerusalem in 587/586 and the deportation of the southern kingdom to Babylon, Judah's future looked dismal indeed. Identifying himself with his fellow exiles near Babylon, the prophet Ezekiel spoke not in terms of judgment but prophesied about Judah's new heart and spirit of obedience (Ezek. 36:26-27), its return to the land of its fathers (vv. 28ff.), the unification of the northern and southern kingdoms (37:15-27), their resurrection from the dead (37:1-14), and the new temple and distribution of the land (chs. 40–48). In the same vein, the prophet Isaiah or his successor mentioned Israel's future restoration (Isa. 60–62) and Judah's reign of peace (65:13-25), concluding his message of comfort with the picture of the new heavens and the new earth in which "all flesh shall come to worship" the Lord (66:22-24).

3. Postexilic Prophets. As earlier prophets had linked divine judgment with Israel, Judah, and the surrounding nations, the postexilic prophet Malachi, like Zephaniah (Zeph. 1:14-18; 2:4-15), extended God's judgment to include all the nations, "all the arrogant and all evildoers" (Mal. 4:1). Somber as his message boded for the unrighteous, to believers the prophet's words were inspiring and encouraging: they would experience the healing wings of the sun of righteousness (v. 2).

B. Apocalyptic Seers. Scholars distinguish between the prophetic view of history, in which God remains in control of the historical forces of good and evil, and the apocalyptic perspective. While accepting with the prophets a cataclysmic Day of the Lord, the apocalyptic seers expected a divine intrusion into history through which God would reassert his mastery over human events (*see* APOCALYPTIC). Dan. 7–12 projects a war against the saints, who would receive the kingdom and the ability to judge (7:21-22), the appearance of a king who would exalt himself and honor none but his own name (11:36-43), and a great tribulation and deliverance (12:1-4). In another apocalyptic account, Isa. 24–27, God, it is said, would punish the earthly kingdom (24:21-23), destroy an unknown city, which apparently represents evil (25:1-5), and slay the monster Leviathan (27:1). In addition, he would grant perfect peace to Judah (26:1-5) and restore Jacob's fortunes (27:6). In the intertestamental period the gap perceived between God and the world widened, to be bridged by intermediary eons.

II. New Testament

The New Testament, which reaffirms the Old Testament concept of the Day of the Lord, broadens it as well. The Day of the Lord is taken to mean the first and second coming of Jesus. Here, Israel loses its prominence in the realization of future salvation, and the destiny of the individual is emphasized.

Both Jesus and the apostle Paul incorporated their concern for the future within the general framework of their teaching and preaching. Shortly after his last discourse in the temple, only a few days before his trial and death, Jesus responded to his disciples' inquiry into the nature of the destruction of the temple by explaining that certain signs were to precede the destruction of the temple and the end of the age (Mark 13 par.). In two early letters, written ca. A.D. 51, Paul attempted to correct misunderstandings concerning Christ's return, a subject he evidently discussed with the Thessalonian believers on his second missionary journey. While applauding them for eagerly awaiting Christ's second coming (1 Thess. 1:10), Paul deemed it necessary to point out that both the raised dead and those still alive would together meet the Lord "in the air" (4:17) at an unknown time (5:2, "like a thief in the night"). When the Thessalonian converts interpreted his first letter to suggest that they no longer needed to work on account of Christ's imminent return, Paul replied in a second letter that Christ would not return before certain events had happened (2 Thess. 2:1-4) and that the believers who had fallen idle should resume gainful employment (3:6-13). Though the apostle did not pen such details in his later letters, he repeatedly warned believers concerning the Day of Judgment to come.

A. *Present Eschatology.* Jesus as well as Paul distinguished between the present inauguration of the kingdom — termed "realized eschatology" by C. H. Dodd — and the future completeion of the kingdom. Mark preserves Jesus' pronouncement at the beginning of his Galilean ministry: "The time is fulfilled, and the kingdom of God is at hand; repent, and believe in the gospel" (Mark 1:14; cf. Matt. 4:17). In that God's kingdom has been inaugurated, Jesus is portrayed as victorious over the demons. According to Matthew Jesus has undermined Satan's reign (Matt. 12:28) by performing many miracles (11:4-5) and by bringing about that for which the Old Testament prophets and righteous persons had longed (13:17).

Although Matthew and Mark do not ignore the consummation of the kingdom (e.g., Matt. 19:28; 25:31-46; Mark 13:3-37), Luke seems to have accented the future fulfillment of the kingdom more than the other two Synoptics. If Luke's gospel was composed after A.D. 70, it may reflect an attempt at coping with the delay of Christ's return, as evidenced by his reinterpretation of Mark 1:14 (Luke 4:14-15) and other Markan passages. On the other hand, Luke's shift from the *eschaton* to the *sēmeron* ("today") and Jesus' words about the fall of Satan and about the authority of his disciples (10:18-19) sufficiently indicate that Luke did not seek to interpret Jesus' view of the eschaton with regard to the crisis occasioned in the early Church by the apparent delay of his coming.

At first glance, the apostle John seems to have transposed the Synoptics' horizontal distinction between present and future into a vertical dualism in which believers move from "below" to "above," i.e., from death and earth to life and heaven. Conspicuous are Jesus' assertion that believers possess eternal life already in this life (John 3:36; 5:24), his illustration of the present reality of the resurrection and the continuation of life eternal in raising Lazarus from the dead (11:25-44), and his urgent message that his contemporaries accept him, the light, and thus become children of the light (12:35-36). But John does not reduce horizontal or temporal eschatology to a vertical Platonic or Gnostic dualism. In fact, he explains that the vertical realized destiny of the individual requires the future horizontal consummation of the cosmos as a corrective (e.g., John 12:47-48; cf. 5:28-29).

A similar emphasis on the present is found in Paul's writings. At 2 Cor. 6:2 the apostle interprets Isa. 49:8 to imply that the "acceptable time" and the "day of salvation" have indeed come. In other passages he urges his readers to accept Christ, for he perceives that salvation is very near (Rom. 13:11-14; "at hand," Phil. 4:5).

B. *Future Eschatology.* Other New Testament accounts indicate that Christ, who by bearing the sins of the people made salvation possible (e.g., Heb. 9:26), will return one day to complete his work of redemption (e.g., v. 28; 10:25; Jas. 5:7-9; 1 Pet. 1:5). Because Christ's redemption includes both the individual and the community, it is necessary to consider the destiny of the individual — physical death, the intermediary state of the soul, and the resurrection of the body — as part of the future consummation of the world, which comprises such concepts as the return of Christ, the Day of Judgment, the kingdom of God, and the restoration of heaven and earth.

1. Return of Christ. Christ, who ascended to heaven forty days after his resurrection (Acts 1:3, 11), promised to return with power and glory (Matt. 24:30; cf. 1 Thess. 4:16-17), visible to all (Rev. 1:7). Though Jesus and Paul may have taught the imminence of this event, both cautioned against calculating an exact date for the second coming (Matt. 24:27, 36; 1 Thess. 5:2). (*See* SECOND COMING.)

2. Resurrection. The New Testament explicates Old Testament implications concerning the resurrection of the human body. The Gospels record Jesus' saying that the Lord is a God of the living, not of the dead (Matt. 22:32 par.) and that Jesus believed in the resurrection (on this point he was closer to the Pharisees than to the Sadducees, who denied the possibility of resurrection). Paul also accepted the resurrection of the body. To the Thessalonians he wrote that Jesus, whom he believed to have died and risen again (1 Thess. 4:14), would at his return raise those "asleep," i.e., those who had died, and would gather them along with those still alive (vv. 14-18). To the Corin-

thians the apostle explained that the resurrection of believers is anchored in the resurrection of Jesus himself. Because Christ arose from the dead (1 Cor. 15:4), he will raise to life, when he comes, those who belong to him (v. 23).

Though accepting on faith and on the evidence of Christ's appearance to him the resurrection of the body, Paul wrote very little about the state of the soul between the physical death of the person and the soul's reunion with the resurrected body. The apostle ascribed immortality to God alone (1 Tim. 6:16); he never taught that human beings enjoyed this prerogative. Though careful not to suggest that the person ceases to exist upon dying physically, the apostle did not espouse the Platonic idea of the natural immortality of the soul. In his second Corinthian letter, Paul confessed that he longed for the "clothing" of the resurrected body, whereby mortal life would be immediately supplanted by spiritual existence with the Lord in heaven (2 Cor. 5:1-4). (*See* LIFE; RESURRECTION.)

3. Judgment. The New Testament retains the prophetic distinction between salvation for the righteous and doom for the unrighteous. Jesus, identifying himself with the apocalyptic Son of Man, told his disciples that at the Day of Judgment the nations would be gathered before him to be divided into two groups — those who would receive life eternal and inherit the kingdom of God because they had lived a righteous life, and those who would endure eternal punishment since they had failed to perform good works (Matt. 25:31-46). In John's account, Jesus proclaims a resurrection to either life or judgment, depending on whether one has done good or evil (John 5:28-29; cf. Rev. 20:12-15). Paul teaches a similar type of judgment (Rom. 2:1-11; cf. Gal. 6:7-10). (*See* JUDGMENT *III.*)

4. Future Life. Those persons whom Christ has judged to be righteous will live with him eternally. Though the New Testament authors refer more often to the fact than to the nature of this life eternal, they do indicate that it will be a blessed experience in which sin will reign no longer. Jesus suggests that this "heavenly" existence is devoid of such common activities as eating, drinking, and sexual love (Matt. 22:30 par.); Paul also seems to distinguish between the spiritual, resurrected body and the present, physical, earthly body (1 Cor. 15:42-50).

Although the Bible nowhere specifies that God condemns people to eternal suffering and punishment in hell, the New Testament does indicate that some will lose full fellowship with God. The Bible also warns people against remaining unrighteous, urging them instead to repent, believe, and do good.

According to Paul, all manifestations of earthly power will be overcome at the end of the present age, when Christ has accomplished his mission of redemption and has affirmed to all creation the supremacy of God the Creator; the ultimate victory symbolized here is the subjection of even sin and death to God's authority (1 Cor. 15:24-27).

5. New Earth. Drawing upon Old Testament imagery, notably from Isaiah, the aged apostle John sees the new Jerusalem as a holy city no longer threatened by sin and war, a place where God has direct fellowship with his people (Rev. 21:1ff.). Noticing that heaven and earth are united (cf. v. 2), as they were before the fall, John depicts the restoration of the garden of Eden, watered by the river of life that proceeds from God's throne (22:1-3). John affirms that human beings will enjoy complete redemption in this world.

III. Theological Reflections

During the nineteenth century biblical teachings concerning the last things were often neglected, perhaps because of preoccupation with the improvement of life on this side of the grave. By contrast, in the twentieth century, especially in times of severe social upheavals, certain aspects of eschatology gained attention, most notably among conservative Christians.

A. *Signs of the Times.* Jesus' explanation of the sign to precede the second coming must be viewed against the background of his disciples' question regarding the destruction of the temple in Jerusalem (Mark 13:1-4) and his own comment that the Jewish leaders were unable to interpret God's signs to them (Matt. 16:2-4 par. Luke 12:54-56). Though he has apparently listed the signs sequentially — e.g., antichrists (Matt. 24:4-5 par.), wars and rumors of wars (v. 6 par.), tribulation (vv. 10-12, 24 par.), cosmic changes (v. 29 par.) — Jesus does not necessarily imply that these events would take place chronologically. He apparently resists the temptation of some of his contemporaries to calculate the time of the Parousia (24:27, 36), and seems to suggest that the time between the first and second coming would be filled with tribulation and doom. Indeed, he leaves wide room for God's grace in permitting and making possible the universal proclamation of the gospel (v. 14; cf. Rom. 11:25ff.).

Seeking to calm the Thessalonian Christians, Paul simplifies his description of the period preceding the second coming. He limits the future events to human rebellion and the appearance of the man of lawlessness who would endeavor to gain religious power (2 Thess. 2:3-12). Like Jesus, Paul urges believers to watch and use their time in God's service.

B. *Chiliasm.* Dispensationalists have given primary attention to the opaque content of Rev. 20:1-8 — the thousand-year reign of Christ and the martyred believers before Satan's final assault. Various interpretations of the complex interrelationship of RAPTURE, tribulation, and thousand-year reign continue to divide conservative Christians.

See MILLENNIUM.

Bibliography. W. D. Davies and D. Daube, eds., *The Background of the New Testament and Its Eschatology* (Cambridge: 1956); G. E. Ladd, *The Last Things* (Grand Rapids: 1978); N. Perrin, *The Kingdom of God in the Teaching of Jesus.* NTL (Philadelphia: 1963); H. M. Shires, *The Eschatology of Paul in the Light of Modern Scholarship* (Philadelphia: 1966).

ESDRAELON [ĕz′drĭ ē′lən, ĕz′drĭ lŏn] (Gk. *Esdrēlōn*).* The western portion of the valley of JEZREEL, from which this Greek name is derived (e.g., Jdt. 1:8; 7:3; KJV "Edraelom"); also called the plain of Megiddo (Zech. 12:11) or the Great Plain (1 Macc. 12:49).

ESDRAS, BOOKS OF.† The first two books of the Apocrypha.

I. 1 Esdras

Sometimes known as the "Greek Ezra," this book appears in the LXX as Esdras A and as 3 Esdras in the Vulgate, where it was first regarded as apocryphal. Since the Council of Trent (A.D. 1545-1563) Vulgate editions have relegated the book to an appendix following the New Testament; it is omitted in the Douay-Confraternity edition and the Jerusalem Bible.

The book is a compilation of material paralleling the accounts of 2 Chr. 35-36, Ezra, and Neh. 7:73–8:12, although in slightly different order, covering the period from the reformation under King Josiah (2 Chr. 35) through the public reading of the law by Ezra (Neh. 8:1-12). Also included is a story, apparently based on a Persian tale, concerning a competition among three Jewish pages at the court of Darius I regarding what each thinks to be the most powerful (1 Esdr. 3–4); Zerubbabel wins with his answer that the strength of women is incomparable but that truth prevails over all (4:13-41), earning as his prize the authorization to return to Jerusalem and rebuild the temple.

Although 1 Esdras probably originated during the Maccabean period (most likely ca. 150-100), nothing specific is known about its date, provenance, or authorship. The text represents a freer Greek translation of the original than does the LXX Esdras B (Ezra-Nehemiah), and Josephus chose this version as his primary source for the period covered.

II. 2 Esdras

2 Esdras, also known as the Ezra Apocalypse, is a pseudepigraphal writing which dates from the second century A.D. (which explains its absence from the LXX). Jerome included it in the Vulgate as IV Esdras, appended to the New Testament; it does not hold deuterocanonical authority in Roman Catholic tradition.

Unlike the other apocryphal books, 2 Esdras is an apocalyptic writing. It is a composite work, the main part of which (chs. 3–14) is believed to have been written by a Palestinian Jew in the first century A.D. Although the book is thought to have been composed originally in Hebrew, it was translated subsequently into Greek (of which only fragments survive) and is known primarily from Latin and other translations from the Greek.

Chs. 1–2 (often referred to as 5 Esdras or 2 Esdras and absent from eastern versions) are a later addition depicting Ezra as a prophet called to censure the Jewish people; the section is believed to have been written in the mid-second century by a Jewish Christian leader. The core of the book (chs. 3–14) consists of seven visions of Ezra: (1) Ezra's questions regarding the disproportionate suffering of Zion, and the angel Uriel's answers that God's ways are incomprehensible to humans but that the coming age would bring salvation (3:1–5:19); (2) Ezra's concern regarding divine inequity toward Israel and his questions regarding the end of the age, followed by Uriel's reassurance and signs of the end times (5:21–6:34); (3) discussion of the purposes of creation and the promises of the end times (6:35–9:25); (4) a mourning woman (Jerusalem) transformed into a heavenly city (9:26–10:59); (5) an eagle (Rome) with twelve wings and three heads, interpreted in terms of Daniel's fourth kingdom (Dan. 7),

to be overcome by the Messiah (11:1–12:51); (6) a man rising from the sea (the Messiah; cf. the Son of Man in Dan. 7), who will vanquish a multitude of attackers (ch. 13); (7) Ezra's restoration of the holy Scriptures (ch. 14). In the latter vision Ezra is instructed from a burning bush to restore to writing the holy books, previously destroyed by fire; for forty days and nights he recites the Torah to five scribes, who fill ninety-four books with his dictation (the Vulgate reading "904 books" in 14:44 is corrupt). The Most High directs that the last seventy of these books be reserved for those properly initiated among the wise, but that the twenty-four canonical books (counting as units Samuel, Kings, Chronicles, Ezra-Nehemiah) could be made public. On the basis of this story some of the Church Fathers ascribed the assembling of the Old Testament books to Ezra, a view maintained by Jewish and Christian scholars until the eighteenth century; this view, however, not only lacks credibility but misses the point of the text. The final section, chs. 15–16 (sometimes called 6 Esdras), is a collection of prophetic materials possibly added by a Christian author as late as the end of the third century.

Bibliography. J. M. Myers, *I & II Esdras*. AB (1974).

ESEK [ē'sĕk] (Heb. *'ēśeq* "contention"). A well dug by Isaac's herdsmen, ownership of which the herdsmen of Gerar disputed, thus forcing Isaac to abandon the well (Gen. 26:20). The site, generally believed to have been between Gerar and Beer-sheba, has not been identified.

ESHAN [ē'shən] (Heb. *'eš'ān* "support"). A village assigned to the tribe of Judah and located in the hill country (Josh. 15:52; KJV "Eshean"). Though its exact location is unknown, Eshan may be identified with Khirbet Sama'a (following LXX B *Soma*), about 16 km. (10 mi.) southwest of Hebron.

ESHBAAL [ĕsh'bāl] (Heb. *'ešbā'al* "man of Baal"). The original name of Ishbosheth, one of the sons of King Saul (1 Chr. 8:33; 9:39). See ISHBOSHETH.

ESHBAN [ĕsh'băn] (Heb. *'ešbān*). The second son of Dishon, and a Horite chief (Gen. 36:26; 1 Chr. 1:41).

ESHCOL [ĕsh'kŏl] (Heb. *'eškōl* "[grape-] cluster") **(PERSON).**† An Amorite who dwelled near Hebron, like his two brothers, Aner and Mamre, Eshcol was an ally of the patriarch Abram against Chedorlaomer (Gen. 14:13, 24). The name may be a geographical designation.

ESHCOL [ĕsh'kŏl] (Heb. *'eškōl* "[grape] cluster") **(PLACE).** A valley so named because of a large cluster of grapes that the Hebrew spies brought back following their mission into Canaan (Num. 13:23-24; cf. Deut. 1:24-25, "fruit"). According to Num. 13:22 the valley was located near Hebron; the name is probably to be associated with Eshcol, one of Abram's allies (Gen. 14:13). The name may be preserved in modern Burj Haskeh, about 3 km. (2 mi.) north of Hebron at the head of a wadi abounding in vineyards.

ESHEAN (Josh. 15:52, KJV). See ESHAN.

ESHEK [ē'shĕk] (Heb. *ʿēšeq* "oppressor"). A descendant of Saul's son Jonathan (1 Chr. 8:39).

ESHTAOL [ĕsh'tĭ əl] (Heb. *ʾeštāʾ ôl*). A town in the lowlands of Judah (Josh. 15:33), assigned first to Dan (19:40-41); apparently later, when the Danites were unable to retain their settlements in the area, the town was claimed by Judah (15:33). It was in the vicinity of Zorah and Eshtaol that the Spirit of the Lord began to stir Samson (Judg. 13:25), and in the same region that he was buried (Judg. 16:31). In their search for a place to relocate, the Danites sent five able men from Zorah and Eshtaol to explore Canaan (18:2). Following their favorable report, a contingent of six hundred left Zorah and Eshtaol for Canaan (vv. 8, 11) and captured Laish. Eshtaol can probably be identified with Eshwaʿ, about 2.5 km. (1.5 mi.) east of Zorah and about 21 km. (13 mi.) west of Jerusalem.

ESHTAOLITES [ĕsh'tĭ ə līts] (Heb. *hāʾeštāʾ ulî*). Inhabitants of ESHTAOL, listed among the descendants of Shobal, the son of Caleb (1 Chr. 2:53; KJV "Eshtaulites").

ESHTEMOA [ĕsh'tə mō'ə] (Heb. *ʾešᵗᵉmôaʿ* "listening post") (**PERSON**).
1. The son of Ishbah, and a descendant of Caleb (1 Chr. 4:17).
2. A descendant of Naham's sister, and a Maacathite from the tribe of Judah (1 Chr. 4:19).

ESHTEMOA [ĕsh'tə mō'ə] (Heb. *ʾešᵗᵉmôaʿ* "listening post") (**PLACE**). A levitical city (Josh. 21:14) and a city of refuge (1 Chr. 6:57) in the hill country of Judah; called Eshtemoh at 15:50. Eshtemoa was included among a group of cities that received a share of the Amalekite spoil captured by David at Ziklag (1 Sam. 30:28). According to Eusebius (*Onom.* xxvi.11, lxxxvi.20), a Jewish city of this name still existed as late as the fourth century A.D. Eshtemoa has been identified with modern es-Semûʿ, about 14 km. (9 mi.) south of Hebron.

ESHTEMOH [ĕsh'tə mō] (Heb. *ʾešᵗᵉmōh*). *See* ESHTEMOA (PLACE).

ESHTON [ĕsh'tən] (Heb. *ʾeštôn* "uxorious"[?]). The son of Mehir of Judah, and probably a Calebite; reckoned among the people of Recah (LXX "Rechab") (1 Chr. 4:11-12), perhaps an itinerant metalworking guild.

ESLI [ĕs'lī] (Gk. *Esli*). A postexilic ancestor of Jesus (Luke 3:25).

ESROM (Matt. 1:3; Luke 3:33, KJV). *See* HEZRON.

ESSENES [ĕs'ēnz] (Gk. *Essēnoi, Essaioi*).† An important Jewish sect which flourished in Palestine from the time of the Maccabean revolt (second century B.C.) through the Roman destruction of Jerusalem (A.D. 70). First attested in the writings of Philo of Alexandria, Flavius Josephus, Pliny the Elder, and Hippolytus, the beliefs and practices of the Essenes have been illuminated by the sectarian documents of the community which produced the Dead Sea Scrolls. The etymology of the name, probably never applied by the sect, remains open to debate, although Aram. *ḥasan* "pious" (cf. Heb. *ḥāsîd*) and *ʾᵃsāʾ* "healer" (cf. Gk. *Therapeutai*, a first-century A.D. sect living near Alexandria) are leading possibilities.

I. History

The Essenes are first mentioned as contemporaries of Jonathan Maccabeus (*ca.* 150 B.C.) and are probably to be reckoned among those elements which comprised the Hasideans (Gk. *Hasidaioi*, from Heb. *ḥᵃsîdîm* "pious ones"), a zealous religious party opposed to the growing influence of Hellenism. The Essenes are generally believed to have originated among Palestinian Jews; however, some scholars now suggest that they were an ultraconservative branch among those Jews who remained in Babylonia following the Exile and who ordered their lives according to the tenets of the Damascus Document (*see* ZADOKITE FRAGMENT) so as to prevent recurrence of such a divinely ordained catastrophe. At any rate, following the Maccabean revolt, the Essenes emerged — along with the Pharisees and Sadducees (and possibly the Sicarii; Josephus *Ant.* xviii.18-22) — as a major theocratic party. As such they remained prominent in Jerusalem politics through the reign of Aristobulus I (*ca.* 104 B.C.), but they had become increasingly adverse to the non-Zadokite Hasmonean priesthood and the attendant political compromise.

As a result, they withdrew, first into separatist enclaves in Jerusalem as well as other Palestinian cities and villages, and then into settlements in the desert region northwest of the Dead Sea. At this time the Qumran community was established, which many scholars believe became the headquarters of the Essene movement. When an earthquake destroyed Qumran in 31 B.C., the Essenes may have relocated in the southwest corner of Jerusalem under the auspices of Herod the Great; it is to this occupation that some scholars would date the remains of the Essene Quarter of Jerusalem on Mt. Zion, including latrines and ritual baths as well as the so-called Essene Gate (Josephus *BJ* v.4.2). After the death of Herod, they returned to Qumran, where they remained until the Romans captured the site during the First Jewish Revolt (A.D. 68).

The Essene movement is unattested following the destruction of Jerusalem in A.D. 70, although scattered conclaves may have survived. Others may have been assimilated into other Jewish sects and the Christian church.

II. Beliefs and Practices

Although the Essene adherents were relatively few (numbered at four thousand; Philo *Quod omn. prob. lib.* xii.75; Josephus *Ant.* xviii.1.15), the ancient sources attest divergent and sometimes conflicting beliefs and practices. This has prompted some scholars to view the Qumran community as merely a branch of Essenism, while others question whether it was Essene at all. Such differences may actually reflect variation among Essene settlements, conditions at different historical stages of communal development, or simply the historian's bias.

Basically, the Essenes regarded themselves as the faithful remnant of the true Israel and the core of God's eschatological community, the purity of which they sought to preserve by forming an isolated society devoted to strict observation of the pentateuchal regulations. To strengthen communal bonds and in preparation for God's imminent coming, a communal lifestyle was emphasized, including common meals, study, and bathing. All property was held in common, and resources were provided for individual members on the basis of need. Funds were also maintained to guarantee hospitality toward visitors from other Essene communities (Hippolytus *Ref.* ix.4). Strict adherence to community regulations was required and discipline was severe, intended to guard the holiness of the remnant and also to preserve community solidarity. In addition, some Essenes practiced celibacy (cf. Josephus *BJ* ii.8.13), more likely in accordance with eschatological beliefs rather than ascetic ideals or concern for ritual purity (Philo *Hypothetica* xi.14).

Although they dissociated themselves from the decadence of the Jerusalem temple, the Essenes did — at least for a time — contribute offerings to the temple. To avoid defilement, however, they offered sacrifices within the confines of their own enclave. Utmost attention was devoted to the levitical laws of purity, and regular ablutions were observed, as attested by ruins of ritual pools at Jerusalem and Qumran. Prayers were offered at sunrise and grace recited both before and after meals. Daily study of the scriptures was required, with particular concern for eschatological interpretation. The Sabbath was strictly observed, spent primarily in the reading and discussion of the scriptures in the synagogue. In order to maintain the sanctity of the Sabbath, the Essenes prepared food on the preceding day, and some regulated bodily functions even to the point of denying themselves the opportunity for physical relief of any kind during those twenty-four hours.

Having pledged their loyalty to the Essene cause and vowed to adhere to its strict membership requirements, initiates submitted themselves to a lengthy admission process, intended to test their worthiness and to maintain the purity of the community. According to Josephus (*BJ* ii.8.7), novices spent their first year under spartan conditions beyond the bounds of the community itself. Those who had made progress toward holiness were permitted to observe ritual purification through washing and were admitted to a second, two-year probationary period. Having proven themselves capable of fulfilling all dietary, ritual, and ethical regulations of the community, they were then admitted as full members and allowed to participate in the common meals. Even among full members, however, a hierarchy existed, with priests and elders having superior authority and rights.

III. Relation to Christianity

Although the New Testament contains no mention of the Essenes, scholars have drawn a number of parallels between the teachings of the Essenes and the beliefs of the early Christians. For a short time, some Christians at Jerusalem practiced a form of communism that resembled the lifestyle of the Essenes (cf. Acts 4:32ff.), and many Christians valued the expression of hospitality as highly as did the Essenes (e.g., Matt. 10:11-13; cf. 7:7). And like the Essenes,

Jesus demanded that his followers subordinate family ties to those bonds uniting participants in the kingdom of God (12:46-50 par.).

However, major disparities existed between the Essene and Christian communities. Most of the Christian communities soon abandoned voluntary communism and reintroduced private property. Moreover, both Jesus and Paul considered the cultic codes of the Old Testament as superseded by the coming of Christ; inward purity of heart was more important than ritual conduct, and meticulous observance of rules and regulations detracted from the atonement brought by Christ's death.

Attempts to link Jesus with the Essene movement have largely been abandoned. If any New Testament figure might be associated with them, it would be John the Baptist, the stern preacher of righteousness.

See DEAD SEA SCROLLS.

Bibliography. J. Murphy-O'Connor, ''The Essenes in Palestine,'' *BA* 40 (1977): 100-124; G. Vermès, ''The Etymology of 'Essenes,''' *RQ* 2 (1959/60): 427-443.

ESTHER (Heb. *'estēr*; Pers. ''star'' or ''maiden''). The main character in the book of Esther; her Hebrew name was Hadassah, which means ''myrtle'' (Esth. 2:7). Brought up as an orphan by her cousin Mordecai, Esther lived in Susa, the former capital of Elam, which had been conquered by Persia. She was among the Jews who remained behind in exile during the reign of Ahasuerus (Xerxes I; 485-465 B.C.).

After Queen Vashti was banished from the presence of the king, Esther was chosen from a number of young maidens to be queen in her place. In this position she risked her life to play a decisive role in thwarting Haman's plan to destroy all the Jews in the Persian Empire.

ESTHER, ADDITIONS TO.† Six passages consisting of 107 verses not found in the Hebrew text of Esther, incorporated into the LXX translation to clarify the book's religious motivation. The alleged one-sidedness and the nonreligious character of the canonical book prompted the addition of this material, in which God is mentioned frequently and prayer has a prominent role, and which stresses God's choice of Israel (an emphasis often marred by a strong anti-Gentile bias).

The LXX version interspersed the additions throughout the text. Here the inserted material is identified by alphabetic versification; for example, the seventeen verses added between Esth. 1:1 and 1:2 are designated 1:1a-s. Jerome removed the additions and placed them at the end of the book of Esther, resulting in the traditional numbering 10:4–16:24, unfortunately a somewhat incoherent sequence.

In proper chronological order, the additions are: 11:2–12:6 (LXX 1:a-s), Mordecai's dream foretelling the deliverance of the Jews, and his discovery of a conspiracy against King Ahasuerus; 13:1-7 (LXX 3:13a–g), Ahasuerus' edict ordering the massacre of the Jews; 13:8–14:19 (LXX 4:17a–z), prayers of Mordecai and Esther (the latter lasts for three days); 15:1-16 (LXX 5:1a–f, 2a–b), Esther's appearance before the king; 16:1-24 (LXX 8:12a–x), the king's second edict, denouncing Haman and aiding the Jews; and 10:4–11:1 (LXX 10:3a–11:1), interpretation of Mordecai's dream, and his declaration that the book of Esther is genuine ("These things have come from God"; 10:4).

The additions generally are regarded as of little historical value. Indeed, they contain several contradictions to the canonical book.

ESTHER, BOOK OF.†

The fifth and last of the Megilloth or Scrolls found in the Writings, the third division of the Hebrew canon. It is read in the Jewish synagogue during the Feast of Purim.

I. Contents

This book, in which the name of God is never explicitly mentioned, describes the deliverance of the Jewish people from the total destruction plotted against them during the reign of Ahasuerus, a Persian king generally identified with Xerxes I (485-465 B.C.). The providential arrangement of circumstances thwarts the plan of Haman, the powerful favorite of the king, who sought vengeance upon the Jews because one of them, Mordecai, refused to bow down in obeisance to him (3:1-6).

Angered by the refusal of Queen Vashti to exhibit her beauty at a royal banquet intended to display "the splendor and pomp of his majesty," Ahasuerus orders her deposed (ch. 1). Esther (Hadassah), a Jewish maiden, is among those chosen to fill her place, and she so pleases the king that she is made queen (2:1-18). Mordecai, her cousin and former guardian, overhears a plot to assassinate the king and informs him through Esther, an act recorded in the ancient Book of the Chronicles (2:19-23). Shortly afterward, Haman, who has recently become prime minister, is infuriated by Mordecai's unwillingness to pay homage, and obtains a royal edict decreeing the annihilation of the Jews because their peculiar laws have prevented total allegiance to the king (ch. 3). Mordecai appeals to Esther, who intercedes with the king on behalf of her people (4:1–5:8). Imagining himself at the pinnacle of his power, Haman ironically is commanded to pay homage to Mordecai, for whom he had ordered gallows erected, and to proclaim publicly his greatness in reward for discovering the conspiracy against the king (ch. 6). At another banquet, Esther unveils Haman's plot against the Jews, and he is hanged on the very gallows he had erected for Mordecai (ch. 7). Mordecai is named Haman's replacement as prime minister. A new edict is issued giving the Jews the right to defend themselves against any oppressors, and they begin to take vengeance upon their enemies. The Feast of Purim is instituted to commemorate their marvelous deliverance (chs. 8–10). It is named after the Pur, or lot, which Haman had cast in order to destroy them and to determine an auspicious day to commence the slaughter (3:7; 8:24ff.).

II. Author and Date

The identity of the author of Esther is not known. The Talmud ascribes it to the members of the great synagogue, which had been established by Ezra and Nehemiah in order to lead the Jews who had returned from the Exile into the proper service of God and to deal with religious issues among the Jewish people. Whoever the author may have been, the book must have been written not long after the events it describes. The Feast of Purim had already been instituted at the time of its writing (9:23ff.), and Ahasuerus appears as a king whose reign lies in the past (1:1). However, the description of the Persian Empire, its ceremony and customs, suggests that Persia had not yet fallen to Alexander the Great. Therefore the book must have been written before 330 B.C.

III. Authenticity

Scholars long have been divided over whether the book is a strictly accurate historical account or a romance or short story based upon a historical setting. The basic form of the book as a historical record, references to official documents (2:23; 6:1; 10:2), and the abundance of accurate references to Persian custom support its historicity. Also, Ahasuerus is generally accepted as a Hebrew rendering of the Persian king's name, more commonly known in its Greek form, Xerxes. Archaeological evidence attests a Marduka (Mordecai) as a Persian official at approximately this time. Certain difficulties may be resolved with minimal difficulty. Xerxes' queen was Amestris, which cannot be equated with either Vashti or Esther; however, the king reportedly had a large harem, no doubt with a sequence of favorites. Proper understanding of the pronoun "who" in 2:5-6 reveals a reference to Mordecai's great-grandfather Kish, not an indication that Mordecai himself was taken captive in 597, which would make him 120 years old. Moreover, the charge that the names Esther and Mordecai link the story to the Babylonian deities Ishtar and Marduk may be answered by seeing here a reflection of the standard nomenclature used by the Jews in the Exile. Other details, however, may have been altered for the purposes of the story: Esther's delay in presenting her request to the king, the precise reversal of the fortunes of Haman and Mordecai, and the banquet 180 days long (1:4).

IV. Purpose

Because of serious doubts concerning the book's religious value, both Jews and Christians long were reluctant to admit Esther to their respective canons. Some Jews feared that by instituting a new feast the book implied that Moses was incomplete, but the rabbis came to hold it as equal or even above the Torah, perhaps because of the hope it promised their beleaguered people. It was not admitted to the Christian canon until A.D. 397, and Luther still doubted the book's importance.

The primary message of the book is God's protection of his people, perhaps to be understood through this book as the seed of the woman (Gen. 3:15), through which he preserves and carries on his plan of redemption. The book of Esther prophesies the downfall of the enemies of the Church and of all those who oppose the kingdom of God and his Anointed. This does not mean that all of the actions of Esther and Mordecai are to be commended, for their feelings of hatred and tolerance of violent means of revenge are far from exemplary. Indeed, they probably should not be regarded as the best representatives of the Jewish people at that time because they had not returned to their own land with the other exiles. Nevertheless, the book's powerful message of hope justifies its place in the canon as part of God's special revelation.

Bibliography. B. W. Anderson, *IB* 3 (1954): 821-874; L. H. Brockington, *Ezra, Nehemiah, Esther.* NCBC (1969); C. A. Moore, *Esther.* Anchor Bible (1971); G. F. Knight, *Esther, Song of Songs, Lamentations.* TBC (1955).

ETAM [ē'təm] (Heb. *'êṭām* "place of birds of prey"[?]).
1. A rock to which Samson withdrew following his great victory over the Philistines, and from which the inhabitants of Judah took him in order to bind him and deliver him to their enemies (Judg. 15:8, 11-13). The location may be at ʿAraq Ismaʿin, about 4 km. (2.5 mi.) east-southeast of Zorah.
2. A town assigned to the tribe of Simeon (1 Chr. 4:32); its identification remains unknown.
3. A city in Judah between Bethlehem and Tekoa, one of which King Rehoboam of Judah (*ca.* 920 B.C.) fortified as a defense against Israel (2 Chr. 11:6). Villages related to Etam may be intended in the genealogy of 1 Chr. 4:3. Etam has been identified with Khirbet el-Khôkh, about 3 km. (2 mi.) southwest of Bethlehem, near Artas. In the vicinity is ʿAin ʿAitān, a spring that supplied water to the so-called "pools of Solomon" through aqueducts dating to Hellenistic and Roman times (probably constructed by Herod the Great and repaired by Pontius Pilate; cf. Josephus *Ant.* xviii.3.2 [60]; *BJ* ii.9.4 [175]).

ETERNAL LIFE. *See* LIFE.

ETERNITY. *See* TIME.

ETHAM [ē'thəm] (Heb. *'ēṭām*). The first camp the Israelites made following their departure from Egypt at Succoth, at the "edge of the wilderness" (Exod. 13:20; Num. 33:6-8). At Exod. 15:22 the region is called the wilderness of SHUR. Because of difficulties in determining precisely the route of the Exodus, the site has not yet been determined. A location near the north end of the Bitter Lakes or perhaps north of Lake Timsâḥ is possible.

ETHAN [ē'thən] (Heb. *'êṭān* "enduring").
1. A sage from the east with whom Solomon is compared (1 Kgs. 4:31); possibly the composer of Ps. 89 (superscript; MT v. 1). If the epithet "the Ezrahite" is taken as a scribal error, he may be identified with ETHAN 2 (below).
2. A descendant of Zerah the son of Judah, and the father of Azariah (1 Chr. 2:6, 8). If his brothers Heman and Calcol are the sages named at 1 Kgs. 4:31, he may be identified as ETHAN 1 (above).
3. A Levite, the son of Zimnah and father of Adaiah, and an ancestor of Asaph (1 Chr. 6:42); possibly the same person as JOAH 2.
4. The son of Kishi (1 Chr. 6:44) or Kishaiah (15:17) of the Merarite branch of Levites. With Heman and Asaph, Ethan was appointed to lead singers and musicians in a festive service accompanying the ark to Jerusalem (15:17, 19); perhaps the same as JEDUTHUN 1.

ETHANIM [ēth'ə nĭm] (Heb. *'ēṭānîm* "ever-flowing streams"). The preexilic name of the seventh month

in the Jewish year (Sept./Oct.), of Phoenician derivation; its Babylonian counterpart was Tishri. On the tenth day of this month the Day of Atonement was observed, and the Feast of Tabernacles was celebrated from the fifteenth to the twenty-third. According to 1 Kgs. 8:2-4, the priests took the ark of the covenant to the temple at Jerusalem in the month of Ethanim.
See also YEAR.

ETHBAAL [ĕth'bāl] (Heb. *'eṭbaʿal* "man of Baal"). Ethbaal I, king of Tyre and Sidon for thirty-two years; father of Jezebel, who married King Ahab of Israel (1 Kgs. 16:31). He was a priest of Astarte and usurped the throne by murdering Pheles, the last of Hiram I's descendants (Josephus *Ap.* i.18 [123]). Ethbaal successfully expanded Phoenician commercial activities.

ETHER [ē'thər] (Heb. *'eṭer* "perfume").
1. A village in the Shephelah of Judah (Josh. 15:42), identified with modern Khirbet el-ʿAter, about 3 km. (2 mi.) northwest of Beit Jibrin (Eleutheropolis).
2. A village assigned as part of the inheritance of the tribe of Simeon (Josh. 19:7); probably identical to modern Khirbet ʿAttîr, about 13 km. (8 mi.) north of Beer-sheba.

ETHIOPIA [ē'thĭ ō'pĭ ə] (Heb. *kûš*; Gk. *Aithiopia*).†
In biblical and other ancient usage, the territory of dark-skinned peoples south of Egypt.

I. Name

The modern name stems from the Greek designation for this general area, traditionally explained by popular etymology from Gk. *aíthō* and *óps* "burnt face" (cf. Jer. 13:23); quite possibly the term derives from Egyp. *ḥtk 'pth* "house of Ptah," from which the name "Egypt" is also derived. In the Old Testament period "Ethiopia" appears to have been synonymous with "Cush" (Egyp. *k3s, k3š*), although the MT does not distinguish between the two, rendering Heb. *kûš* throughout. The LXX reads *Aithiopia* with the exception of the genealogical or ethnographic lists (Gen. 10:6-8; 1 Chr. 1:8-10), where Gk. *Chous* is rendered as a personal name (cf. 2 Sam. 18:21-23). For the most part, the English versions follow the LXX readings (KJV except for Isa. 11:11; RSV except for Gen. 2:13).

II. Geography

Throughout much of antiquity Ethiopia was conceived somewhat imprecisely as all territory south of Egypt. The Greeks, in particular, viewed it as the farthest reaches of mankind (Homer *Od.* i.22-24), encompassing even Arabia and India. In Egyptian texts the term designated a smaller region between the Second and Third Cataracts of the Nile river or, more generally, that part of Nubia (modern northern Sudan) between the First and Sixth Cataracts. Biblical references, for the most part, seem to favor this narrower identification; the "rivers of Cush" (Isa. 18:1; Zeph. 3:10) may indicate the Blue and White tributaries of the Nile as well as the Atbara river. At no time in antiquity was Ethiopia identified specifically with the territory of modern Ethiopia (Abyssinia).

III. History

Archaeological evidence indicates that civilization flourished in ancient Ethiopia during the Neolithic and Egyptian Predynastic periods (ca. 8000-3000 B.C.). Abundant mineral resources (cf. Job 28:19) prompted Egyptian raids as early as the Fourth Dynasty (Snefru, ca. 2613), and later trading expeditions were sent by the Sixth-Dynasty pharaohs Merenre and Pepi II (ca. 2200) and by Gudea of Lagash (ca. 2100).

With the establishment of the Middle Kingdom (ca. 2000), Egyptian pharaohs occupied the northern portion of Nubia. Sesostris III (1878-1843) annexed that portion north of the Second Cataract, and for another century Egypt dominated the region, aided by a series of fortresses and trading stations. Apparently little respite was provided by the Second Egyptian Intermediate Period, for the Hyksos rulers continued to occupy Ethiopia. In return for Nubian assistance in overthrowing the Hyksos, the pharaohs of the Eighteenth Dynasty reoccupied Nubia (ca. 1500), extending their control as far south as Napata, near the Fourth Cataract. For the next five hundred years, Ethiopia was administered by a viceroy, the "King's 'Son' in Cush." Under the Eighteenth-Twentieth Dynasties, the land enjoyed peace and prosperity, enhanced by extensive irrigation, the founding of new cities, and the building of numerous temples, including that at Abu Simbel.

With the demise of the Twentieth Dynasty into corruption and ineffective administration, the viceroy Herihor assumed control, forming the Twenty-first Dynasty (ca. 1085-945). During the ensuing Third Intermediate Period, Ethiopian mercenaries aided the Libyan pharaoh Sheshonq I (Shishak; 2 Chr. 12:2-3) in attacking Jerusalem following the death of Solomon. Little is known of subsequent events until ca. 740 when Kashta, who ruled from Napata, conquered Upper Egypt and established the Twenty-fifth (Ethiopian) Dynasty. His son, Piankhy, conquered the remainder of Egypt, and was succeeded by his brother Shabaka, who moved the capital to Thebes and ruled as "King of Cush and Egypt." Taharqa (Tirhakah), who aided Hezekiah of Judah against the Assyrian Sennacherib (cf. 2 Kgs. 19:9; Isa. 37:9), was defeated when Esarhaddon invaded Egypt in 670. His nephew, Tanetamon (Urdamane), attempted to recapture Memphis, but Assurbanipal retaliated, destroying Thebes and ending Ethiopian control of Egypt.

Ethiopian rule continued under Tanetamon's successors from the capital at Napata. The city was sacked ca. 590 by Pharaoh Psamtik II, presumably in order to prevent resurgent Ethiopian control over Egypt. The capital was thus transferred to Meroë, between the Fifth and Sixth Cataracts. Although the Persians apparently invaded the new capital under Cambyses in 522 (cf. Esth. 1:1; 8:9), Meroitic rule continued until the early Byzantine period. Ca. A.D. 350 the city was invaded by ʿEzānā, king of Aksum, and the region came under Abyssinian control.

See EGYPT III.

IV. Biblical Perspective

In the Table of Nations, which depicts geographic and ethnographic distribution genealogically in terms of eponymous ancestors, Ethiopia is represented by Cush, a son of Ham (Gen. 10:6); he is the brother of Egypt, Put, and Canaan, and father of Seba, Havilah, Sabtah, Raamah, and Sabteca (v. 7). Despite the Israelites' generally endogamous preferences, some intermarried with the Hamitic Ethiopians (e.g., Moses; Num. 12:1).

Aware of that country's commercial enterprise (Isa. 45:14) as well as political and military involvements (e.g., Ezek. 30:5-9; Nah. 3:9; cf. Ezek. 38:5), the Israelite prophets held up Ethiopia as the example of a sinful kingdom (Amos 9:7). Not only would Ethiopia fall to the kingdoms of the earth (Isa. 20:3-5), it would also experience the wrath of God (Zeph. 2:12). With Ethiopia, as with Egypt and Seba, he would ransom exiled Israel (Isa. 43:3).

Bibliography. H. Ullendorff, *Ethiopia and the Bible* (New York: 1968).

ETHIOPIAN EUNUCH (Gk. *Aithiops eunoúchos*).† An unnamed minister (*dynástēs*) of the Candace, queen of the ancient Ethiopian kingdom of Meroë, who met Philip the evangelist and accepted the gospel (Acts 8:26-39). Instructed to go south to the desert road leading from Jerusalem to Gaza (v. 26; JB "at noon"), Philip encountered the eunuch seated in his chariot (actually a covered wagon), reading aloud from the book of Isaiah (probably the LXX version). Although as royal treasurer the eunuch would have been acquainted with the Greek language, he could not fully comprehend the text; when the evangelist, who offered to elucidate the troublesome passage, interpreted Isa. 53:7-8 in terms of Jesus as the Suffering Servant, the official embraced Christianity. When the two approached a body of water, the eunuch asked Philip to baptize him (vv. 35-39).

This incident, which some scholars find reminiscent of some of Elisha's activities, sets the stage for Luke's account of the spread of the gospel to the Gentiles (cf. Acts 10:1-48). It shows that even the most remote persons (viewing "Ethiopia" in its broadest ancient usage) and those least acceptable to the stringent tenets of Jewish practice might receive and respond to the gospel.

See EUNUCH.

ETHIOPIC [ē′thĭ ŏp′ĭk] (Eth. *lesāna Geʿez* "the tongue of Geʿez").* The classical language of Ethiopia (Abyssinia); called Geʿez, from Agʿazyan, a tribe from the region of Aksum, the ancient capital. A derivative of Old South Arabic, it was introduced into Abyssinia during the first millennium B.C. and came to supplant the indigenous Cushitic (Hamitic) languages. Bearing many similarities to Old South Arabic and even Biblical Hebrew, it is thought to have developed by the first century A.D. into a distinct dialect, influenced phonologically, morphologically, and syntactically by Cushite; the vocabulary bears traces of Sabean, Greek, and both Jewish and Christian Aramaic influence. The order of the alphabet differs from those of other Semitic languages, and the individual characters of the basically consonantal script may be modified to indicate the accompanying vowel.

Ethiopic flourished as the language of the Aksumite Empire, which in the fourth century A.D. annexed the ancient Meroitic kingdom and embraced Christianity as the national religion; the earliest extant inscriptions are from this period. By the late thirteenth century Geʻez was no longer a spoken language, replaced by Amharic, the dialect of the new imperial capital at Gondar, north of Lake Ṭānā. Its survival as a literary language is evident from writings of the thirteenth-seventeenth centuries, the golden age of Ethiopic literature. Geʻez continues to be the liturgical and theological language of the Ethiopic church. Linguistically, its primary modern derivatives are Amharic (North Ethiopic) and Tigriña and Tigre (South Ethiopic).

Following the conversion of the Aksumite dynasty, an Ethiopic (Geʻez) translation of the Bible was made during the fourth-fifth centuries, apparently based on the LXX and possibly other sources, including the Syriac and MT. The earliest surviving texts date to the thirteenth century. In addition to the books of the LXX canon, the Ethiopic manuscripts include Jubilees, 1 (Ethiopic) Enoch, 4 Esdras, 4 Baruch, and the Eusebian Canons.

ETH-KAZIN [ĕth kāʹzĭn] (Heb. ʻittâ qāṣîn). A town on the border of the tribal territory of Zebulun (Josh. 19:13; KJV, JB "Ittah-kazin"), possibly modern Kefr Kennä, about 7 km. (4.5 mi.) northeast of Nazareth. Roman Catholic tradition identifies it with Cana, where Jesus changed water to wine (John 2:1ff.).

ETHNAN [ĕthʹnən] (Heb. ʻeṯnān "gift"). The youngest son of Ashhur and Helah, and a member of the tribe of Judah (1 Chr. 4:7). Some scholars suggest that the name represents a social unit from Ithnan, located in the Shephelah of Judah (cf. Josh. 15:23).

ETHNARCH [ĕthʹnärk] (Gk. ethnárchēs "ruler of the people," from éthnos "people" and árchōn "ruler"). A title given to an official lesser than an independent king but superior to a TETRARCH; a governor or ruler of a province.

According to 1 Macc. 14:47 Simon Maccabeus was granted the title "commander and ethnarch of the Jews and priests" in recognition of outstanding service to his people. Since Simon's position was acknowledged by Antiochus VII Sidetes, king of the Seleucid Empire (cf. 15:2), Judea apparently had a degree of self-government. Archelaus, the son of Herod, was appointed ethnarch over half of his father's kingdom (Josephus BJ ii.6.3 [93], Ant. xvii.11.4 [317]); cf. Matt. 2:22).

At 2 Cor. 11:32 Paul refers to the "governor" (so RSV, KJV, NIV; JB "ethnarch") of Damascus, said to be responsible to the Nabatean king Aretas IV. This official may have been a Nabatean ethnarch in the service of the Romans or, if the Nabateans then controlled Damascus, a representative of the Nabateans.

ETHNI [ĕthʹnī] (Heb. ʻeṯnî "gift"). A Levite of the Gershomite branch, the son of Zerah, and father of Malchijah (1 Chr. 6:41). At 6:21 he is called Jeatherai.

EUBULUS [ū būʹləs] (Gk. Euboulos "of good counsel"). A Christian at Rome who sent greetings to Timothy (2 Tim. 4:21).

EUCHARIST [ūʹkə rĭst] (Gk. eucharistía "thanksgiving").* The rite of Holy Communion or the Lord's Supper. Among the earliest evidence for this name, which does not occur in the New Testament, are references in the Didache (ix.1), Ignatius of Antioch (Phild. iv), and Justin Martyr (Apol. i.66).

See LORD'S SUPPER.

EUMENES [ūʹmə nēz] (Gk. Eumenēs "well-disposed").† Eumenes II, king of Pergamum (197-159 B.C.); son and successor of Attalus I, whose policy of cooperation with the Roman Empire he continued. Along with Judas Maccabeus (1 Macc. 8:8), he was an ally of the Romans in their war against the Seleucid king Antiochus III (the Great). As a reward for his aid in defeating Antiochus at Magnesium (190) he was granted most of the Seleucid territory in Asia Minor (cf. Livy Hist. Epit. xxxviii.39; Polybius Hist. xxi.45; Appian Syr. xliv). He conducted an extensive building campaign at Pergamum, particularly in the acropolis area.

EUNICE [ūʹnĭs] (Gk. Eunikē "good victory").† A devout woman at Lystra, commended for her "sincere faith" (2 Tim. 1:5); mother of Timothy, whom she instructed in the Christian faith and whom Paul chose as a replacement for his companion Barnabas (Acts 16:1). A Jewish woman who had married a Greek from Lystra, she and her mother Lois had converted to Christianity as a result of Paul's earlier ministry there (cf. 14:6, 21-22).

EUNUCH (Heb. sārîs; Gk. eunoúchos "keeper of the bed").† A castrated male, often accorded a high governmental position such as chamberlain of a sovereign or royal harem. Particularly common in ancient Near Eastern and other oriental courts, the employment of eunuchs in sensitive political roles was introduced through Mesopotamian influence into the Roman and Byzantine Empires. Although no evidence exists for the practice in Egypt, some scholars suggest that Potiphar was a eunuch, hence his harsh reaction to his wife's allegations regarding Joseph (Gen. 37:36; 39:11-20).

The Old Testament mentions eunuchs in the courts of Israel's neighbors (Esth. 1:10, 15; Dan. 1:3, 8-9) and the harem of Queen Jezebel at Jezreel (2 Kgs. 9:32). Other uses of Heb. sārîs may also indicate the role of eunuchs during the Israelite Monarchy (e.g., 2 Kgs. 23:11; 24:12, 15; Jer. 41:16), although at times it appears to designate simply a political or military officer (so RSV; e.g., 1 Sam. 8:15; 1 Kgs. 22:9; 2 Kgs. 8:6; Jer. 52:25; cf. 29:2; 34:19; cf. Akk. ša rēši "one at the head"). Isaiah's prediction that Hezekiah's descendants would be deported as eunuchs at the court of Babylon (Isa. 39:7 par. 2 Kgs. 20:18) may reflect the Assyrian practice of castrating captives. Deuteronomic law prohibited eunuchs from entering the Israelite assembly (Deut. 23:1), but following the restoration of Israel they as well as foreigners would be full members of the community (Isa. 56:3-5; cf. Wisd. 3:14).

In the New Testament, the Ethiopian minister of the Candace, who was instructed and baptized by Philip the evangelist (Acts 8:27-39), was presumably a eunuch; thus Luke indicates that not even this most permanent of ritual defilements could exclude one from acceptance of the gospel and full participation in the body of Christ. Commenting on divorce, Jesus distinguishes between those who are literally eunuchs, either by congenital defect or involuntary castration, and those who figuratively make themselves eunuchs by eschewing marriage and sexual expression in order to devote their energies toward the kingdom of God on earth (Matt. 19:12; cf. Mishnah *Yebam.* viii.4-6). Interpretation of this instruction is often cited as the basis for a celibate clergy; some people in the early Church (e.g., Origen) complied literally.

EUODIA [ū ō′dĭ ə] (Gk. *Euodia* "prosperous journey"). A woman who belonged to the church at Philippi (Phil. 4:2; KJV "Euodias"). She and Syntyche, who both may have held prominent positions in the congregation and had apparently been close associates of Paul (v. 3; on the role of women at Philippi, cf. Acts 16:13ff.), had become embroiled in a dispute of some sort, sufficient enough to prompt the imprisoned apostle to entreat their reconciliation and to enlist one of their colleagues as mediator (*see* YOKEFELLOW).

EUPHRATES [ū frā′tēz] (Heb. *pᵉraṭ*; Akk. *Purattu*; Gk. *Euphratēs*).† The largest river in Western Asia, and one of two important rivers of ancient Mesopotamia.

I. Course

The Euphrates river, also referred to as the "great river" (Heb. *hannāhār haggāḏōl*; Gen. 15:18; Deut. 1:7; Josh. 1:4) or simply the "River" (*hannāhār*; e.g., Num. 22:5; Mic. 7:12; cf. Gen. 31:21; Exod. 23:31, KJV, NIV, JB), is divided into three courses: the Upper, Middle, and Lower Euphrates.

A. Upper Euphrates. Originating in Armenia, the first course of the Euphrates begins as two branches, the western Kara Su ("muddy") and the eastern Murat Su ("clear"), which join north of Malatya in northern Syria. The river then flows southeastward and curves back to the southwest before entering the Syrian plain at Samsat (ancient Samosata), about 80 km. (50 mi.) northwest of the ancient city of Haran.

The river, whose source springs are some 2438 m. (8000 ft.) above sea level, drops the farthest (nearly 305 m. [1000 ft.]) through its first course as it flows through spectacular gorges.

B. Middle Euphrates. Flowing south, the river passes historic Carchemish on its western bank and Aleppo farther inland, and then bends east and southeast. It is joined by the Balikh river, along which Haran is located, and the Habur river. Some 80 km. (50 mi.) farther along its course is the ancient city of Mari and neighboring Dura-Europus. Turning next northeast and then southeast again, the Euphrates reaches the end of its middle section at Hit (ancient Itu). The river drops from 198 to 67 m. (650 to 220 ft.) above sea level along this middle course.

C. Lower Euphrates. Generally flowing in a southeasterly direction, the lower course of the Euphrates in antiquity was much farther to the east than it is today. It passed the ancient cities of Babylon, Kish, Nippur, Erech, and Ur and, at last, after a total journey

of some 3600 km. (2200 mi.) empties into the Persian Gulf. Although a consensus has not been attained, many scholars believe that in ancient times the gulf extended as much as 230 km. (150 mi.) farther to the north so that both the Euphrates and Tigris rivers emptied directly into it; presumably because of silt deposited by these rivers they now merge north of al-Baṣrah to form the Shaṭṭ el-ʿArab, which flows another 190 km. (120 mi.) to the gulf.

Fed by varying rainfall during the winter months, the Euphrates reaches flood stage in April. By September and October it is quite shallow again. The ancients were dependent on the river's water for cultivating their crops and sought to control the water supply by building canals that would prevent the land from flooding in the spring and would provide much needed irrigation in the fall. The Chebar "river" (Ezek. 1:1) may have been one of such canals.

II. Biblical References

The Euphrates served as the lifeblood of the Sumerians and Babylonians, and was a significant trade route between Mesopotamia, Syria, the Mediterranean Sea, and Egypt. But the Euphrates was too far removed from ancient Palestine to have a great affect on the Hebrews. Consequently, the Bible refers to it only sporadically as it influenced Israel's history.

A. Old Testament. According to Gen. 2:14 the Euphrates was the fourth river connected with the garden of Eden, which would suggest that Paradise was located in Mesopotamia. Often the river was cited as the eastern boundary of the region promised to Abraham as his descendants' inheritance (Gen. 15:18; cf. Deut. 1:7; 11:24; Josh. 1:4). Under David and Solomon (cf. 2 Sam. 8:3 par.), and perhaps under Jeroboam II (2 Kgs. 14:25), the Israelites did extend their territory as far northeast as the Euphrates (cf. Isa. 27:12; Zech. 9:10). At Carchemish Nebuchadnezzar's defeat of Pharaoh Neco in 605 B.C. (Jer. 46:2, 6, 10), following Josiah's unsuccessful attempt to block the Egyptians at Megiddo (2 Kgs. 23:29 par.), signaled the end of Egyptian influence in the east (2 Kgs. 24:7) and the beginning of Judah's demise. The Euphrates was also the eastern boundary of the Persian province "Beyond [i.e., west of] the River" (e.g., Ezra 4:11, 17, 20).

The Euphrates occurs twice in symbolic illustrations in the book of Jeremiah. The prophet is commanded

The Euphrates in Anatolia (W. S. LaSor)

by God to bury a "waistcloth" by this river and to retrieve its remains after a time to dramatize how God would curb Judah's pride through the Exile (Jer. 13:1-11). Some commentators interpret Heb. *p^eraṭ* as referring to a spring at Parah, about 6 km. (4 mi.) northeast of Anathoth, Jeremiah's birthplace. Jeremiah later instructs Seraiah to drop a scroll containing an oracle against Babylon into the river, thus alluding to Babylon's future downfall (51:63).

B. *New Testament.* In the book of Revelation the Euphrates is the locale of future divine judgments. Here four angels are kept to be loosed one day and destroy a large number of unbelievers (Rev. 9:14). In another instance an angel pours God's bowl of wrath into the river, causing it to dry up and provide passage for a military force from the east (16:12). Though John may have been alluding to Parthian attacks against the Roman Empire (to be made from beyond the river), his imagery is not confined to historical encounters between these two peoples.

EUROCLYDON (Acts 27:14, KJV). *See* NORTH-EASTER.

EUSEBIUS [ū sē′bĭ əs] (Gk. *Eusebios*).* Eusebius of Caesarea (*ca.* A.D. 260-340), bishop of Caesarea and prolific historian, biblical scholar, and Christian apologist. Educated in the Alexandrian tradition by the presbyter Pamphilus (hence his designation also as Eusebius Pamphilii), his text-critical skills were employed as copyist for the emperor Constantine. His ten-volume *Historia ecclesiastica (Church History)* records the history of the Church from apostolic times until *ca.* 323; the many quotations and paraphrases preserve portions of ancient works which otherwise have not survived. Eusebius' earlier *Chronicle* provides a comparative chronology of ancient Near Eastern, classical, and biblical history. Although he composed extensive commentaries using literal and allegorical modes of exegesis, Eusebius' most important contributions to biblical studies were his *Onomasticon*, a topographical catalogue of biblical sites, and the *Eusebian Canons*, a system of tables indicating parallel passages in the Gospels.

EUTYCHUS [ū′tə kəs] (Gk. *Eutychos* "fortunate"). A young man from Troas who fell two stories from his window seat when he fell asleep during one of Paul's long speeches (Acts 20:9). Luke records that Eutychus died, but that he witnessed Paul revive the youth (vv. 10-12).

EVANGELIST [ĭ văn′jə lĭst] (Gk. *euangelistēs*). Though the Greek noun designates any person who announces the good news about Christ, the usage stresses rather the activity itself. The term is specifically applied to Philip (Acts 21:8), one of the seven original deacons (Acts 6:5), noted for his missionary endeavors at Samaria (8:5).

As church government developed, the evangelist constituted an office, as did apostles, prophets, pastors, and teachers (Eph. 4:11): Timothy fulfilled such a role (2 Tim. 4:5). Though not called to their respective tasks by the Lord himself, evangelists were deemed fully qualified for their missionary activities among the various churches and rendered valuable assistance to the apostles. The office of evangelist disappeared soon after the gospel was put into writing by Matthew, Mark, Luke, and John, commonly known since the third century as the four evangelists.

EVE [ēv] (Heb. *ḥawwâ*).† The first woman, so named by Adam, the first man. Popular etymology links Heb. *ḥawwâ* with *ḥayyâ* "to live"; accordingly, Eve (who bore three sons — Cain, Abel, and Seth; Gen. 4:1-2, 25) is called the "mother of all living" (3:20; cf. LXX Gk. *zōḗ*). Some scholars, following early rabbinic tradition, view the name as consonant with the ancient Semitic word for serpent (i.e., the primeval progenitor of life, thus a mother goddess figure; cf. Aram. *ḥiwyâ*).

I. Genesis Narrative

Sensitive to Adam's loneliness in the Garden, the Lord decided to give him a companion (Gen. 2:18), whom he created from one of Adam's ribs during a deep sleep (v. 21). When the Lord brought her to him, Adam called her "Woman" (Heb. *'iššâ*) because she was taken from "Man" (Heb. *'iš*; v. 23). Even though the woman was created after the man, this does not imply that she is his inferior. As Augustine explained, Eve was created from Adam's "bone" so that she could be his equal, not from his head or the lower parts of his body, lest she be either superior or inferior to him (*Civ. Dei* xii.23; cf. Midrash *Gen. Rab.* xviii.2).

It was the woman who listened to the serpent's enticing words about knowing good and evil and yielded to the temptation to eat from the forbidden fruit (Gen. 3:1-6). When God discovered that she had given her husband part of the fruit, he cursed her: not only would she bring forth children in pain, but she would nevertheless desire her husband and he would rule over her (cf. Heb. *ba'al* "master, husband").

II. New Testament

At 2 Cor. 11:3 Paul introduces Eve in an example of how seduction can lead a believer from devotion to Christ; Eve's experience with the serpent was the most powerful example of Satan's deceptive powers Paul could use to caution the Corinthians against false doctrines and false saviors.

The context of 1 Tim. 2:13-15 is more emotionally charged. Having advised Timothy about the woman's submissive role in public worship, the author justifies her position vis-à-vis the man as follows: Adam was created before Eve, and the woman, not the man, was deceived and transgressed God's commandment (vv. 13-14). In this way he implies that Eve's later creation signified inferiority — a condition aggravated by her vulnerability to Satan's deceit. Thus woman's salvation was held to be through childbearing, if she would persevere "in faith and love and holiness, with modesty" (v. 15).

If these two passages present Eve in an unfavorable light, the scale is balanced somewhat in Paul's letter to the Romans, where it is Adam who is unequivocally charged with introducing sin and death into the human race (Rom. 5:12-19). Some scholars also understand Eph. 5:31, which cites Gen. 2:24, as comparing the relationship of Christ and the Church to that of Adam and Eve prior to the fall (note the portrayal by some early Church Fathers of Mary as a Second Eve).

EVENING (Heb. *'ereḇ*). Sunset, the beginning of the Hebrew day as based on the lunar (cultic) calendar. Heb. *bên hā'arbāyim* (lit. "between the two evenings"; cf. Exod. 12:6, JB, RSV mg.) refers either to the time between sunset and complete darkness (NIV "twilight") or to the time between the sun's zenith at noon (the first evening) and sunset (the second evening). It was at this time that the evening burnt offering and the cereal offering were brought before God (Exod. 29:39-41; Num. 28:4ff.), the incense offering made, and the lamps in the holy places lit (Exod. 30:8). The lambs that were to be prepared for the Passover celebration were also to have been slain in the evening (12:6; Lev. 23:5; Num. 9:3-4), a time which may have coincided with what is now viewed as the afternoon, from 2:30 to 5:00 P.M. (so Josephus *Ant.* xiv.4.3 [65-66]).

See DAY.

EVENING OFFERING. *See* SACRIFICES AND OFFERINGS.

EVERLASTING. *See* TIME.

EVI [ē'vī] (Heb. *'ewî* "desire"). A Midianite king and vassal of the Amorite Sihon. With four other Midianite kings he was defeated and slain by the Hebrews (Num. 31:8; Josh. 13:21) following the Israelite apostasy in the plains of Moab (Num. 25:1-3).

EVIL.† Substantively and descriptively that which is offensive, perverted, or harmful; in the Bible indicative of both natural evil, such as physical disasters, and moral evil, such as deeds against God or one's neighbor.

I. Terminology

The most common word for "evil" in the Old Testament is Heb. *ra'*, which can denote sadness (Gen. 44:34), harm (cf. Lev. 26:6; Deut. 7:15), affliction (Eccl. 6:2; cf. JB "suffering"), or wickedness (1 Sam. 12:17; 1 Kgs. 1:52; JB "malicious"; Ezek. 3:19). Other terms include *dibbâ* "calumny" (e.g., Num. 13:32), *'āwen* (e.g., Job 15:35), *zimmâ* (e.g., Prov. 21:27), and *rāšā'* (Ps. 140:8).

In the New Testament two Greek words in particular are translated as "evil": *kakós* (or *tó kakón*) and *ponērós* (or *hē ponēría*). While the RSV weakens the meaning of *epithymía* at Rom. 6:12; 2 Tim. 2:22; 1 Pet. 1:14 ("passions"; KJV "lusts"; NIV "evil desires"; JB "impulses") and of *tó kakón* at 1 Cor. 13:6 ("wrong"; KJV "iniquity"; NIV "evil"; JB "sins"), it adequately represents the meaning of *ponēría* at Matt. 22:18 ("malice"; KJV "wickedness"; NIV "evil intent") and Gk. *kakopoiéō* at Mark 3:4 ("do harm"; KJV, JB, NIV "do evil").

II. Biblical Teachings

A. *Old Testament.* Though often equating evil with forsaking God (2 Chr. 12:14), transgressing his covenant (Deut. 17:2), or not fearing the Lord (Job 1:1), the biblical authors are also concerned with human evil against one's fellows. Keenly aware of the distinctions between good and evil (e.g., Isa. 5:20; Mic. 3:2; cf.

Mal. 2:17), they define evil as a rejection of God's law, in the sense of both spiritual idolatry (usually expressed as "evil in the sight of the Lord"; e.g., Deut. 4:25; 1 Kgs. 11:6; 2 Kgs. 21:2) and the violation of the rights of others (including the rights of individuals [e.g., 2 Sam. 12:9; Ps. 34:13] and of the community [e.g., Deut. 19:19; 22:21]). Even Israel's desire for a mortal king is seen as an evil (1 Sam. 12:19), because it implies a denial of theocracy.

Human beings are described as evil creatures who devise evil deeds of varying degrees ("much evil," 2 Kgs. 21:6 par.; "more evil . . .," vv. 9, 11; Jer. 7:26; all possible evil, Jer. 3:5; or limitless evil, 5:28), in their hearts (e.g., Job 15:35; Ps. 140:2; Eccl. 9:3) or by their will (Jer. 16:12, NIV "heart"). But they are urged to do good, i.e., to love (or fear) God and their neighbor. The author of Deuteronomy, for instance, repeatedly warns the Hebrews to purge the evil from among them (Deut. 13:5; 17:7, 12; 19:19); later prophets echo the same warning (Isa. 1:16, "cease from evil"; cf. Jer. 18:11; Ezek. 33:11). Their summons is not spoken in vain, for people can do good (Lev. 5:4), as some Old Testament heroes believed they had (Joseph, Gen. 44:4; and David, 1 Sam. 25:21). The authors do not excuse human responsibility because of a poor environment, for the Hebrew kings Menahem (2 Kgs. 15:18), Pekahiah (v. 24), and Pekah (v. 28) are held accountable for their unacceptable behavior in spite of their having been exposed to Jeroboam's evil influence.

The biblical authors struggled with the existential question of the plight of the righteous who strive — seemingly to no avail — to keep the moral law, while the wicked or evildoers apparently prosper. Job, for one, was visited by evil for all his exemplary behavior and integrity (Job 16:11; 30:26). The Old Testament authors respond to this question in three ways. (1) God turns human evil into a good result: when Joseph was unjustly confined to a dungeon in Egypt as a result of his brothers' evil intentions, God used him there to save his family from starvation (Gen. 52:15-22). (2) God uses evil as a test for the righteous: Job suffered trials nearly beyond his ability to endure, but was declared righteous in the end (Job 42:7ff.). (3) Evil does not pay in the long run (Ps. 37:16-17; cf. Prov. 10:29; 11:19; 17:13), for God does judge human deeds — both good and evil (Eccl. 12:14). That God's hand is not always easily discernible in human actions is evident from the psalmist's ambivalence. He triumphantly exclaims that he will see the "recompense of the wicked" (Ps. 91:8), but he also complains bitterly that he feels he has kept his heart clean in vain since the wicked are "always at ease," and "increase in riches" (Ps. 73:12-13).

The biblical authors are very reluctant to implicate God in human evil, for God does not delight in wickedness (Ps. 5:4), and he does support his people (Hos. 7:15; cf. Ps. 97:10, RSV, JB). Nevertheless, they interpret physical evils as sent by God, not only to test the faith of the righteous but also to punish the sin of the unrighteous. God also punishes his people by not permitting their "evil generation" to enter into Canaan (Num. 14:22-24; Deut. 1:34-36); he sends an evil spirit to Abimelech (Judg. 9:23) and later to King Saul (1 Sam. 16:14-16; 18:10). He allows the Babylonians to deport Judah to Babylonia on account of its spiritual idolatry (Ezra 9:13; cf. Jer. 11:17; 18:1-10). But even when God inflicts evil upon his people as a means of punishment for their unfaithfulness toward him, he can be swayed to repentance, as Moses and Jeremiah discovered (Exod. 32:12-14; Jer. 26:3; cf. Jonah 3:10). The exilic prophet Ezekiel comforted the despondent exiles with the claim that the righteous do not suffer for the iniquity of their unrighteous parents and that God wants the wicked to turn from wickedness rather than to receive his punishment (Ezek. 18).

B. New Testament. Jesus was personally acquainted with suffering and temptation, and he encouraged his followers to pray that God would deliver them from "evil" or from the "evil one" (Matt. 6:13; Gk. *apó toú ponēroú*, possibly the "evil one" (RSV mg.), Satan (cf. 13:19; 1 John 2:13-14). Locating the source of moral evil in the human heart (9:4; cf. 15:19) as did the prophets of old, Jesus distinguished between people who do good and those who perpetrate evil (12:34-35). While in Matthew's narrative Jesus concludes that God does not discriminate with such gifts as rain and sunshine — he gives them to the just and the unjust alike (5:45) — in John's gospel he emphatically asserts that only those who do good will receive eternal life, and that those doing evil will reap judgment (John 5:29; cf. 3:19-21 for the distinction between the just and the unjust).

Paul's treatment of the subject of evil is quite extensive. Contrasting those who obey the truth and those who do not, Paul proclaims that the "natural man," the inventor of evil (Rom. 1:30), will suffer tribulation (2:8-9). Those who have accepted Christ, on the other hand, are exhorted to "put to death" their tendencies toward evil (Col. 1:21; 3:5), to hate evil and to do good (Rom. 12:9) rather than continue practicing evil in the hope that it may produce some good (3:8). They are admonished never to repay evil with evil (12:17) but rather with good (v. 21; cf. 16:19; 1 Cor. 14:20). Having personally wrestled with the incongruity of wishing to do good and instead committing evil (Rom. 7:19, 21), Paul drew strength from Old Testament examples (1 Cor. 14:20) as he preached to other believers with similar experiences.

James and Peter make similar observations about mankind's struggle to cope with moral evil. James notes that God is neither tempted by evil nor tempts people (Jas. 1:13) and that people are unable to control their tongues because of a "restless evil" (3:8; cf. v. 6 "a world of evil," so NIV; RSV "an unrighteous world"). Peter warns believers not to use their freedom to commit evil (1 Pet. 2:16), certainly not to repay evil with evil (3:9); rather he encourages them to bless those who wrong them (3:10-12, quoting Ps. 34:12-16).

III. Theological Reflections

Two difficult questions remain. First, how could God, who made the universe and human beings good (Gen. 1:31), have created people with a tendency to do evil? Although logically monotheism does not leave room for the reality of evil (because it excludes dualism and does not accommodate a second deity as creator of evil), the author of Gen. 3 attributes the beginning of moral evil to the disobedience of the first man and woman. Other biblical authors link the serpent who

provided the occasion for sin with Satan, the prince of evil, and place human sin and evil in the larger context of God's duel with Satan.

Second, why does God, who through his son Jesus Christ has conquered death and, in principle, Satan himself, allow evil to be so rampant and Satan to be so powerful? Believers throughout the ages have asked this question. If God is powerful and good, why does he seem to withdraw behind a wall of moral evil? The New Testament, ultimately, points to the second coming (the Parousia) when the righteous will receive their reward and the wicked the punishment they have earned (Matt. 24:36ff.; 25:31-46).

The Bible does not accept the logical propositions that the existence of a good God excludes the reality of evil and that the pervasiveness of evil cancels the presence of a good God. Instead, the Scriptures confess that the Lord created mankind with the possibility of doing evil and that he supports the faithful in their deepest hour of trials and temptations, no matter how incongruous such a confession may seem to be.

On the expression "good and evil," *see* GOOD.
See also SIN.

Bibliography. W. Grundmann, "κακός," *TDNT* 3 (1965): 469-481; G. Harder, "πονηρός, πονηρία," *TDNT* 6 (1968): 546-566; J. H. Hick, *Evil and the God of Love*, rev. ed. (San Francisco: 1977).

EVIL-MERODACH [ē'vəl měr'ə dăk] (Heb. *'ĕwîl mᵉrōdak*; Akk. Amēl-Marduk "man of Marduk"). The son and successor to Nebuchadnezzar II as king of the Neo-Babylonian Empire (562-560 B.C.). In the first year of his reign, Evil-merodach is said to have released from prison Jehoiachin, the deported king of Judah, according him favorable treatment at Babylon (2 Kgs. 25:27-30 par. Jer. 52:31-34). Babylonian tablets confirm the biblical claim that Jehoiachin (*"Ia-ku-ú-ki-nu*, the son of the king of *Ia-ku-du"*; *ANET*, p. 308) received rations as a prisoner of the king of Babylon.

According to the historian Berossus (cf. Josephus *Ap* i.20 [146-47]), Evil-merodach was a very ʳbitrary ruler. His brother-in-law (and successor) Neriglissar (Nergal-šar-uṣur; cf. Nergal-sharezer, Jer. 39:3, 13) led a conspiracy which resulted in Evil-merodach's death.

EWE. *See* SHEEP.

EXACTION.† At Neh. 10:31 Heb. *maśśā'* refers to the amount of money due in the seventh year of a loan; the postexilic Jews were willing to forego this amount ("cancel all debts," so NIV) to foster economic stability within the community. In contrast, the wealthy preexilic inhabitants of Samaria had imposed a stiff tax (JB "extorting levies") on the poor in the form of "exactions [Heb. *maś'ēt*] of wheat," by which they were able to live in luxury (Amos 5:11; KJV "burdens").

At 2 Cor. 9:5 Paul urges the Corinthian Christians to give the gift they had promised the poor at Jerusalem, doing so not grudgingly (Gk. *pleonexía* "avarice"; JB "being extorted"; cf. KJV "covetousness") but with a willing heart.

EXCOMMUNICATION (Lat. *excommunicatio* "outside the realm of communication").† The exclusion of a person or persons from fellowship in a group or community. The preexilic Hebrews temporarily excluded from cultic ceremonies those who committed minor offenses against the ritual regulations and threatened them with permanent exclusion from their society (Heb. *kāraṯ* "cut off"; e.g., Exod. 12:15, 19). The priest Ezra determined that any who failed to appear in Jerusalem to determine the issue of mixed marriages would forfeit all property and would be banished from the postexilic community (Ezra 10:8). Though drastic, this measure was milder punishment than the ban or curse (Heb. *ḥērem*) in which property was destroyed and the offending party put to death (*see* DEVOTED).

In New Testament times Jewish leaders sought to curb the spread of the Christian community by excluding from the synagogue any person who confessed Jesus as the Christ (John 9:22; 12:42). Jesus himself warned his disciples in the hour before he was betrayed and crucified that they would be expelled from the synagogue (16:2). Though at that time the Jews exercised various degrees of excommunication — a temporary exclusion of seven (Heb. *nᵉzîp̄â*) or thirty (*niddûy* or *šammatā*) days and a permanent ban (Heb. *ḥērem*) — it is not certain which form the Jewish leadership had in mind regarding the followers of Jesus. The ostracism implied in the fourth Beatitude (Luke 6:22, "when they exclude you"; Gk. *aphorízō*; cf. Matt. 5:11 "when men . . . persecute you"; *diōkō*) may refer to such exclusion from the Jewish synagogues or simply to social rejection.

Within some branches of the modern church, to be excommunicated means to be denied temporarily or permanently access to the sacraments and participation in congregational worship, loss of ecclesiastical office, and even restriction from public or private contact with fellow believers as a result of serious moral or doctrinal error.

EXEGESIS [ĕk sə jē'səs] (Gk. *exégesis* "bringing out").† The explanation and exposition of a text, with attention to such matters as determination of text, translation and paraphrase, and interpretation of structure, setting, and purpose. Concern for clarification of meaning, prompted in part by cultural and historical separation of author and reader, has necessitated exegesis of the Scriptures since biblical times; methods employed have been literal, allegorical, moral, anagogical or mystical, and, more recently, critical (e.g., literary, historical; *see* BIBLICAL CRITICISM). In the most basic sense, exegesis is concerned with the meaning of a text as regards the author and ancient addressees, but it may also be conducted with a view toward application to the contemporary situation (sometimes called "exposition").

This endeavor requires an understanding of the Bible's historical, sociopolitical, and cultural milieu and a sensitivity to Hebrew and Greek thought. Personal interpretations (eisegesis) must be avoided, a difficult task since the scholar is often influenced by contemporary cultural theories as well as interpretations influenced by Jewish and Christian tradition.

See INTERPRETATION, BIBLICAL.

EXILE. The period when the inhabitants of the southern kingdom of Judah were forced to live in Babylonia (*ca.* 587/586-515 B.C.).

I. Terminology

The usual Hebrew words for "exile" are *gôlâ* and *galûṯ* (rendered predominantly "exile[s]" by the RSV, NIV, and JB), *šᵉḇûṯ* (e.g., in Jeremiah) and *šᵉḇî*. Whereas the KJV nearly always translates these Hebrew words as "captivity," the RSV, JB, and NIV render them either broadly as "captivity" or more explicitly as "exile." The New Testament word is Gk. *metoikesía* "change in home" (Matt. 1:11-12, 17; RSV, JB "deportation"; KJV "carried away"; NIV "exile"; cf. *metoikízō* "send into exile" [Acts 7:43], so NIV; RSV "remove"; KJV "carry away").

II. History

A. Deportation of the Northern Kingdom. Following almost two hundred years of relative peace as a separate kingdom, Israel was faced with a resurgent Assyria, which captured Damascus *ca.* 732 B.C. In the same year the powerful and ruthless Tiglath-pileser III (745-727) invaded the territory of Naphtali, captured its fortified cities, and sent the Hebrew population to Assyria (2 Kgs. 15:29); the Chronicler adds that he also deported the Transjordanian tribes of Reuben, Gad, and Manasseh (1 Chr. 5:6, 26; cf. Isa. 9:1). He then appointed Hoshea, who had murdered Pekah (cf. 2 Kgs. 15:30), as king of Israel. Hoshea was unwilling to accept the role of vassal, however, and revolted after Tiglath-pileser's death in 727. Angered by Hoshea's refusal to pay tribute, Shalmaneser V (727-722), Tiglath-pileser's successor, not only subdued the revolt in 724 but also captured Samaria in 722 (2 Kgs. 17:3-6). As was typical of Assyrian treatment of captive nations, either he or his successor Sargon II (722-705) deported most of the remaining Israelites to Assyria (2 Kgs. 17:6; cf. 2 Chr. 30:1, 10-11). Likewise, he repopulated the area with peoples displaced from the eastern part of the Assyrian Empire (2 Kgs. 17:24-41).

Little is known of the subsequent existence of the deported northern tribes; apparently, as the Assyrians had hoped, they became sufficiently assimilated, losing both their national and their religious identity.

B. Deportation of Judah. Far more significant was the exile of Judah, the southern kingdom (the tribes of Judah and Benjamin). Because they had been able to preserve a margin of autonomy following Sennacherib's siege of Jerusalem in 701 (2 Kgs. 18:13–19:37 par. Isa. 36–37; cf. 2 Chr. 32:1-22), the people of Judah believed that they could regain their freedom from the crumbling Assyrian Empire, in dissolution since the fall of Nineveh in 612. But Judah had to face another powerful foe, the Neo-Babylonian Empire, whose capable leader, Nebuchadnezzar II, quickly defeated Judah's ally and overlord, Egypt, at Carchemish in 605.

According to 2 Kgs. 24, Nebuchadnezzar laid siege to Jerusalem in 598 and, following capture of the city, exiled to Babylon King Jehoiachin, his family, the nobles, a large number of valiant soldiers (a smaller number is given at Jer. 52:28), and craftsmen. Nebuchadnezzar also seized the temple treasures as booty

A Babylonian cuneiform tablet which lists events of the late seventh and early sixth centuries B.C., including the capture of Jerusalem in 598-597 and the deportation of Jehoiachin (by courtesy of the Trustees of the British Museum)

(2 Kgs. 24:11-16; 2 Chr. 36:6; Dan. 1:1-2). The Babylonian monarch made Zedekiah his vassal in Jerusalem, and when Zedekiah refused to pay tribute, Nebuchadnezzar returned to Judah in 587, besieged the city again, and finally leveled it. He took the remaining Jewish rebels, except for the very poorest, to his capital (2 Kgs. 24:20–25:17; 2 Chr. 36:15-21; Jer. 52:3-16). A third deportation took place *ca.* 581 following the murder of Gedaliah, whom Nebuchadnezzar had appointed governor over Judah (2 Kgs. 25:22-26; Jer. 41:2-3). (Meanwhile a sizable number of Hebrews had taken refuge in Egypt [Jer. 43:5-7].)

Unlike their northern counterparts, the people of the southern kingdom returned in 538 when Cyrus the Achaemenid, who had conquered Babylon the preceding year, issued an edict that anyone who wished to assist in building a sanctuary for Yahweh in Jerusalem could go there (2 Chr. 36:22-23). Under Zerubbabel some forty thousand exiles indeed returned to their native country (Ezra 1:1–2:67), where the rebuilding of the temple was completed in 515 (Ezra 6:15) and the walls of Jerusalem nearly a century later.

Not all Hebrews left Babylon and the other cities of their exile (e.g., Susa). During their "seventy years" (cf. Jer. 25:12; 29:10), many had managed to carve a niche for themselves abroad, had married "foreign wives" (cf. Ezra 10:10ff.), and enjoyed a comfortable existence, perhaps enhanced by their willingness to worship the Babylonian deities. As late as the second half of the fifth century leaders such as Ezra the

scribe and Nehemiah the royal cupbearer still resided in Persia.

III. Significance†

The fall of Jerusalem, the center of Judah's worship and the symbol of the Davidic reign, made an indelible impression on the consciousness of the Hebrews, and Judah's deportation to Babylon had a tremendous impact on their religious life. At first the Jerusalem survivors were in a state of shock from the horror of the capture of their ancient city (Lam. 2, 4). They recognized their loss of Jerusalem as God's punishment for their sinful behavior (4:6, 11-14; cf. Lev. 26:33-39; Deut. 4:25-30) and accepted that this event was justified (Lam. 1:18). Indeed, the eighth-century prophets Amos, Hosea, and Micah had denounced the northern kingdom's slackening of commitment to the Israelite covenant and the sanction accorded this "idolatry" by King Jeroboam II (*ca.* 787-747). The major prophets Isaiah and Jeremiah, as well as Zephaniah, had also chastised the southern tribes for their lack of religious and ethical fidelity to Yahweh. Moreover, when the northern tribes had been deported, the author of Kings concluded that their exile was God's punishment for their unfaithfulness (2 Kgs. 17:7-24). Likewise, Judah's captivity was viewed as retribution for their sins (24:3-4; cf. 2 Chr. 32:1-11).

A subsequent generation of exiles bitterly resented Yahweh for making them suffer for the sins of their ancestors (Lam. 5:7); fearful of the future, they even wondered whether their God had forgotten or rejected them (vv. 20-22). The author of Lam. 3, however, urged his fellow exiles to turn to Yahweh (3:40-41) and confess his steadfast love for his people (vv. 22-23).

Jeremiah, who survived the fall of Jerusalem in 587 by several years, recommended that the exiles settle in Babylonia for an extended period, after which Yahweh would permit their return to Jerusalem and would restore their fortunes (Jer. 29:10-14). Even at the beginning of the Exile, the prophet could foretell a time when the spiritually apostate Hebrews would unite to call upon their God once again and receive his new covenant (32:36-44).

Following the first siege of Jerusalem in 597, Ezekiel prophesied in Babylonia till at least 571 (Ezek. 29:17). There he encountered many despondent fellow countrymen who blamed their misery on the sins committed by their fathers (18:2). He could empathize with his people's struggle to worship God in a strange country without the familiar temple; but he could also perceive that God holds each generation (or person) personally responsible for their own deeds, no matter what their ancestors might have done (18:5-24; 33:12-26). Jeremiah continued that, instead of demanding his people's death, God wanted them to live (33:11), to repent, and to have a new spirit (36:26; cf. 24:7). Sensing their sadness over the destruction of the temple and the devastation of the land, Ezekiel encouraged the Hebrews with a vision he had of the new temple (Ezek. 40–44) — a symbol of God's continued faithfulness to his people — and of the division of the land west of the Jordan among the twelve tribes (47:13–48:35), which would be ruled by a Davidic king (34:23-24).

Particular comfort was offered by the words of the author of Isa. 40ff. Yahweh, the only true God (40:18-23), would protect and provide for his wearied people (41:10, 14) and would eventually send his anointed Cyrus (45:1ff.) as their deliverer from foreign servitude. Yahweh was willing to forgive Israel's sins (40:2) and, mindful of his covenant with them (41:8-9), would bless them, and through them all other nations as well (40:5).

The Hebrews, at first haunted by the thought that their uprooted existence was caused by God's punishment for their past unbelief, gradually recognized that, even when deprived of the sanctuary at Jerusalem, they could still turn to God by obeying his ancient law. From a New Testament perspective, God's people were no longer confined to Palestine and were compelled to adapt to a more cosmopolitan lifestyle, which eventually would enable the gospel to be preached worldwide.

See also DISPERSION.

Bibliography. P. R. Ackroyd, *Exile and Restoration*. OTL (Philadelphia: 1968); R. W. Klein, *Israel in Exile*. OBT (Philadephia: 1979); C. F. Whitley, *The Exilic Age* (Philadelphia: 1958).

EXODUS [ĕk′sə dəs] (Gk. *éxodos* "a going out").† Israel's departure from Egyptian captivity, central to Hebrew thought as the primary act of divine deliverance.

I. Biblical Account

For more than four hundred years (Exod. 12:40-41; cf. Gen. 15:13) following Jacob's migration to Egypt his descendants sojourned in that land. Although they had been received hospitably when they had first gone down to Egypt and some (particularly Joseph; 41:1-57; cf. 47:12, 20) had attained high station, they were eventually reduced to state slavery (v. 25; cf. v. 21, LXX, RSV) and forced to engage in corvée labor for various building projects (Exod. 1:11). Their status and living conditions had deteriorated to such a degree that the Israelites entreated their God for deliverance from this "house of bondage" (2:23-25).

In response, the Lord commissioned Moses to petition the pharaoh to release the Israelites. But not only did the Egyptian king refuse, but he increased the severity of the Hebrews' bondage (Exod. 5:6ff.). Pharaoh remained unyielding in this refusal (cf. 7:3), even when the God of Israel, through Moses, inflicted a series of signs and wonders (7:8–10:29) upon the Egyptians. Not until the tenth of these plagues, in which the Lord killed every firstborn male among the Egyptians (11:1-10; 12:29-30), did the pharaoh permit the Israelites to leave (12:31-32). Their own sons spared from God's ravages (11:7; 12:13), the Israelites were hastily dispatched by their captors and provided with abundant supplies and rich spoils (vv. 35-36; cf. v. 32).

But as the people of Israel proceeded under the Lord's direction, Pharaoh and his people realized the consequences of their decision upon the Egyptian labor force and pursued the fleeing Israelites (14:5-9). Trapped between the sea before them and the pharaoh's chariots closing in behind them, the people began to panic (vv. 10-12). But Moses, at God's bidding, divided the waters to provide safe passage for his people. Upon reaching the other shore, they witnessed the waters return, consuming the army of their hated oppressor (vv. 23-28). Thus liberated from centuries of oppression, the Israelites continued their trek through the Sinai peninsula toward their homeland, guided by the divine presence and sustained by his providence.

II. Historical Aspects

Despite the centrality of the Exodus event to Hebrew thought and to the formation and coherence of Israel as both nation and people of God, no direct material or literary evidence of its historical occurrence can be attested apart from the biblical account. However, the silence of the Egyptian record concerning the escape of a host of state slaves and the imperial army's subsequent defeat is not surprising. Moreover, numerous chronological and topographical difficulties impede definitive historical analysis of these events (see below).

The Israelite sojourn in Egypt accords with references in second-millennium Egyptian sources to the presence of Asiatics from Syria-Palestine, particularly in the delta region. The Israelite migration may have been part of Amorite movements during the Second Intermediate Period (*ca.* 1786-1550). However, attempts to link the Joseph stories with the Hyksos period (seventeenth-sixteenth centuries) remain inconclusive; a setting as late as the Eighteenth Dynasty (*ca.* 1558-1303) may also suffice. The use of Semites as corvée laborers in building projects at Thebes and in the delta is attested during the Eighteenth and Nineteenth Dynasties.

Although all of Jacob's descendants are said to have participated in the Exodus (cf. Exod. 1:1-5; 12:50-51), numerical considerations alone pose a problem. Current scholarly consensus suggests that a much smaller group was involved, perhaps represented by the tribe of Levi (note the Egyptian influence on such names as Moses, Hophni, Phinehas, Merari); other proposals include, variously, elements of the Leah (Reuben, Simeon, Judah, Issachar, Zebulun), Rachel (Joseph, Benjamin), or so-called concubine (Dan, Naphtali, Asher, Gad) tribes. Some scholars would address the numerical problem in conjunction with the pharaoh's apparent change of mind (14:5), positing two stages of Israelite escape — one as early as the expulsion of the Hyksos (*ca.* 1550). The "mixed multitude" (12:38; cf. Num. 11:4; NEB "mixed company of strangers"; RSV, JB, NIV "rabble") which ventured forth has prompted identification of the Hebrews with the 'Apiru (Habiru) bands attested throughout the ancient Near East during the second millennium. Many of these same questions of historical interpretation have contributed to the various perspectives regarding the Israelite settlement in or conquest of Canaan (*see* CONQUEST).

The intensity of the divine involvement in history which the Israelites experienced in the Exodus events and the seemingly legendary quality of their portrayal have raised questions concerning the historical reliability of the biblical account. In particular, various attempts have been made to explain the ten plagues and the miraculous crossing of the Red Sea. For example, the plagues may be viewed as severe but reasonable consequences of an unusually high inundation of the

Nile, many providing conditions that would yield further calamity (e.g., reddish-colored microorganisms which kill fish, which in turn decay and infect the frogs, upon which mosquitoes and flies feed and then transmit anthrax to the cattle, in turn causing boils). The miracle at the sea can be explained as a strong east wind draining a marshy "Sea of Reeds" (see *IV,* below). However naturalistic the circumstances surrounding these events, it is important that they be perceived as a means toward a divine end, the workings of God in behalf of his people.

III. Date

On the basis of certain biblical references, the Exodus could be placed in the mid-fifteenth century. According to 1 Kgs. 6:1, the Jerusalem temple was founded some 480 years after the Exodus, in the fourth year of King Solomon (*ca.* 960); thus the Exodus would have occurred *ca.* 1440, near the end of Thutmose III's reign (some chronologies assign this date to Amenhotep II). Judg. 11:26 indicates that at the time of Jephthah (*ca.* 1100) Israel had occupied its Transjordanian territory for some three hundred years; if the Exodus were forty years prior to the Conquest, the date would again be *ca.* 1440. However, these figures may not represent a precise chronology. The 480 years of 1 Kgs. 6:1 may be a symbolic figure, consisting of one generation (standardized at forty years) for each tribal unit; the figure indicated at Judg. 11:26 represents the total reigns of judges as recorded in the book of Judges, with no accounting for overlapping reigns or intermediate periods.

Much of the biblical and extrabiblical evidence favors a date in early thirteenth century. A victory stele of Pharaoh Merneptah, erected *ca.* 1220, records his conquest of Israelite peoples in Palestine, indicating that the Conquest had occurred somewhat earlier. The reference to the enslaved Israelites' building of the store-cities Pithom (probably Tell el-Maskhûṭah; ancient Theku, biblical Succoth) and Raamses (perhaps Tell er-Reṭâbeh, near Qanṭîr) in the eastern delta (Exod. 1:11) accords with the building program of the Nineteenth Dynasty, particularly under Rameses II. Furthermore, archaeological evidence concerning the subsequent wilderness wanderings and Israelite occupation of Canaan supports this date. For example, material remains indicate that Edom and Moab, around which the Israelite band was forced to detour (Num. 20:14-21), did not exist before *ca.* 1300. Moreover, many of the cities mentioned in the biblical accounts of the Conquest (e.g., Lachish, Hazor, Bethel) show evidence of destruction in the late thirteenth century followed by new occupation levels reflecting a different material culture. It would appear, then, that the pharaoh of the oppression was Seti I (1318-1299) and that the Exodus took place under Rameses II (1299-1232).

IV. Route

Numerous difficulties hinder identification of the exact route taken by the Israelites after leaving the delta region. Although archaeological exploration has confirmed the location of some of the sites mentioned, the lack of permanent settlement in the Sinai peninsula has impeded historical continuity of topographical nomenclature. In addition, critical scholars view the narrative of the wilderness wanderings as a composite of accounts representing various historical traditions. Thus, different routes have been proposed.

Scholarly consensus now regards the body of water rendered "Red Sea" in most English versions (Heb. *yam-sûp* "sea of reeds"; so NJV; cf. Papyrus Anastasi III, "Papyrus Lake"; Egyp. *ṭwfi*) to be a fresh-water marsh in the vicinity of Lake Menzaleh. The crossing point may have been in a region where today the lake has extended south because of silting at the Damietta branch of the Nile; other proposals include Lake Timsâḥ, east of Wâdî Ṭumilât, and Lake Sirbonis.

Acknowledging the divine injunction against taking the Way of the Philistines (Exod. 13:17; more accurately the Way of Horus), the normal route between Egypt and Canaan which was fortified by Egyptian troops, the Israelites may have proceeded south on the Way of the Sea along the eastern coast of the Gulf of Suez. Tentative identification of such sites as Marah and Elim in the early stages of the Exodus favors this southern route. The obscurity of later stations suggests the rugged southern terrain where ancient Egyptian copper and turquoise mines were located. Most important to this theory is the traditional identification of Mt. Sinai (Horeb) with Jebel Mûsâ. From here the group headed northeast toward Kadesh-barnea.

A proposed northern route would have the Israelites cross the narrow, sandy spit separating Lake Sirbonis and the Mediterranean Sea, then heading southeast to Kadesh-barnea and a northern Mt. Sinai, perhaps to be located at Jebel Magharah or Jebel Halal. Identification of Baal-zephon with the Egyptian port Tahpanhes (Tell Defneh) would favor this route. A major difficulty is the lack of a natural route crossing the hazardous dunes separating Lake Sirbonis and Kadesh-barnea. An alternate northern route would be the ancient Way to Shur which connects Wâdî Ṭumilât and Kadesh-barnea.

A more central route would have the Israelites traveling east on the ancient Way of the Wilderness (the modern Muslim pilgrim route Darb el-Hajj), which proceeds from Suez to Ezion-geber en route to the Arabian peninsula. Now generally abandoned, this proposal reflected the interpretation of Mt. Sinai as an active volcano, which of necessity placed it in northwest Arabia, also presumed to be the homeland of the Midianites (cf. Exod. 3:1; 18:1). An alternate position would have the Israelites turn northeastward on the Way to the Hill Country of the Amorites; Mt. Sinai might then be located at Ya'allaq.

V. Theological Significance

The Exodus may be considered the central event in Hebrew tradition, the foundation of the understanding of God as acting in human history and the cornerstone of Israel's national identity. In the covenant ceremony at Shechem (Josh. 24), the various tribal configurations which constituted the Israelite confederation acknowledged these events as their common history. (Traditio-historical critics suggest that such circumstances may have prompted the conflation of traditions surrounding the deliverance from Egypt with those of other tribal groups, such as the Sinai theophany and covenant and the wilderness wanderings — and possibly the theme of repeated rebellion or "murmurings.") The

Statues of Rameses II, probably the pharaoh of the time of the Exodus, at Abu Simbel (B. K. Condit)

Passover celebration, perhaps a historical reinterpretation of earlier agricultural festivals, commemorates these events by a liturgical recitation of the story (Exod. 13; cf. Deut. 6:20-25; 26:5-10) and the participants' affirmation of their continued significance.

Historical allusions to the Exodus abound in the Old and New Testaments (e.g., Exod. 20:2; Judg. 6:8, 13; Heb. 11:27-29), often as testimony to the redemptive acts of God (e.g., Ps. 78:12-53; 106:7-46). The prophets repeatedly recall the Exodus as they implore the people to repent from their infidelity (e.g., Isa. 43:16-17; 63:11-13; Ezek. 20:5-26; Hos. 11:1ff.). For the prophets of the Exile the Exodus provided images of hope for God's deliverance from the current bondage (e.g., Isa. 43:19; 48:21; Jer. 16:14-15 par. 23:7-8).

Bibliography. J. J. Bimson, *Redating the Exodus and Conquest.* JSOTS 5 (1978); D. Daube, *The Exodus Pattern in the Bible* (London: 1963); G. Hort, "The Plagues of Egypt," *ZAW* 69 (1957): 84-103; 70 (1958): 48-59; C. de Wit, *The Date and Route of the Exodus* (London: 1960).

EXODUS, BOOK OF.† The second book of the Old Testament, and the second of the Pentateuch or Five Books of Moses. The English title derives from Gk. *éxodos* "departure," the name accorded it by the LXX (cf. Vulg. Lat. *Exodus*) on the basis of its theme of divine deliverance (cf. Exod. 19:1). Its Hebrew name is *we'ēlleh šemôṯ* "these are the names" (also abbreviated as *šemôṯ* "names"), the book's opening words.

I. Contents

The book can be divided into two major sections according to subject matter. Events related to Israel's deliverance from Egyptian bondage are recorded in the first portion (1:1–19:2), from the background of the oppression through the journey to Mt. Sinai (Horeb). The remainder of the book depicts the covenant entered at Sinai and the attendant institution of the Israelite cultus (19:3–40:38).

Following a description of Israelite state slavery under a new pharaoh (1:1-22), the narrative recounts the birth and early career of Moses in the Egyptian court and his flight to Midian (2:1-22), the theophany of the burning bush through which the divine name Yahweh is revealed and Moses is called to deliver his people (3:1–4:17), and his first unsuccessful encounter with Pharaoh (5:1–6:1). The next pericope depicts the contest between Aaron and the Egyptian magicians (7:8-13), followed by the series of ten plagues whereby God demonstrates his supremacy and overcomes the pharaoh's stubborn resistance (7:14–11:10; 12:29-30); it culminates in the release of the Israelite captives and their departure (vv. 31-50). Also recorded are instructions for observance of the Feasts of Passover (vv. 1-13, 21-28) and Unleavened Bread (vv. 14-20) and the consecration of the firstborn (13:1-16). This section of the book concludes with the Israelites' flight toward the Red Sea, their miraculous passage through the sea and the destruction of their Egyptian pursuers (14:10–15:21), and the journey through the Sinai peninsula to the mountain of God.

The second main portion of the book begins with the theophany at Mt. Sinai, the stipulations regarding God's covenant with Israel, and the ceremony ratifying that relationship (19:3–24:18). There follow instructions regarding construction of the tabernacle and its furnishings, priestly vestments and ordination, offerings and sacrifices, and observance of the Sabbath (chs. 25–32).

Following accounts of the golden calf incident, resumption of the journey from Mt. Sinai, and renewal of the covenant (chs. 33–34), the book concludes with the execution of the cultic ordinances and God's continued guidance of his people through the wilderness (chs. 35–40).

II. Composition

Regarded by both Jewish and Christian tradition as the work of Moses, the book of Exodus bears witness to the same complexities of composition as the other Pentateuchal books. Despite its distinctiveness, the book also exhibits a canonical unity with the other parts of the Torah. For example, the opening section (1:1-7) provides a transition from the deaths of Jacob and Joseph (Gen. 50) and the Israelite oppression in Egypt (Exod. 1:8-22). The narrative of the wilderness wanderings (40:34-38) is resumed at Num. 10:11.

The suggestion of critical scholars that the narrative is a conflation of various traditions among the groups comprising the Israelite confederation points to the variety of literary materials employed. The Song of the Sea (15:1-18) is one of the most ancient examples of Hebrew poetry; composed soon after the miraculous events which it celebrates, this victory hymn may be an elaboration of an even earlier poem (cf. v. 21, the Song of Miriam). The book contains three major legal collections. The Decalogue or Ten Commandments (20:2-17; cf. Deut. 5:6-21) represents the stipulations of the Sinai covenant, measures designed to guarantee the stability of the newly constituted people of Yahweh. The laws contained in the Covenant Code or Book of the Covenant (Exod. 20:23–23:33) reflect the agrarian circumstances of the later premonarchic period in Palestine. Critical scholars would assign the cultic instructions (chs. 25–32) to the exilic or postexilic Priestly source. The directions regarding Passover and the Feast of Unleavened Bread (12:1-28) as well as consecration of the firstborn (13:1-16) suggest circumstances following the settlement in Palestine; here they represent the historical reinterpretation of ancient observances in terms of Yahweh's sparing of the firstborn Israelite males and the people's hasty departure.

See PENTATEUCH.

III. Theology

As the primary example of God's redemptive activity in the lives of his people, the Exodus from Egypt constitutes one of the central themes of the Old Testament. This act of divine deliverance came to represent the constitutive identity of the people and nation of Israel, and the truths it spoke about Israel's God formed the basis for pleas of repentance as well as oracles of hope for individual and collective deliverance.

Another major Old Testament theme derives from the Sinai covenant, whereby God chose Israel as his own people and they in turn pledged their allegiance to him (19:5-6; cf. 6:7). Here God's election is reinforced by the people's acceptance of various legal stipulations; in grateful response to the divine grace, they agree to obligations which are to make them a holy nation set aside for God's service.

The detailed specifications for the tabernacle should not obscure another important emphasis of the book of Exodus, the presence of God in the midst of his people (29:45; cf. John 1:14). In addition to this elaborate cultic symbol, the theme is reinforced by the guidance rendered to the Israelites in their wilderness wanderings by the pillar of cloud and the pillar of fire (Exod. 13:21-22; 40:38) and by the various forms of divine providence which sustained them (e.g., 16:1-36; 17:6).

See EXODUS.

Bibliography. B. S. Childs, *The Book of Exodus.* OTL (1974); J. P. Hyatt, *Exodus.* NCBC (1980); M. Noth, *Exodus.* OTL (1962).

EXORCISM (Gk. *exórkōsis,* from *exorkízō* "conjure, bind with an oath").† The practice of expelling demons or evil spirits from a person or place by means of adjurations or rituals.

Despite the widespread practice of divination in the ancient Near East as well as possible evidences among the Israelites, the Old Testament contains no explicit references to exorcism. David's ministry to Saul, who was tormented by an "evil spirit" (1 Sam. 16:14-23; cf. 18:10; 19:9), involved relief of the king's melancholia through music rather than magical formulae. Although some would see the substitutionary function of the scapegoat in carrying off the people's sins as a form of exorcism (Lev. 16:20-22), the earliest reference to the practice is Raphael's instruction for purifying Tobias' marriage chamber (Tob. 6:7, 16-17; cf. 8:3). In the intertestamental period, exorcism is attested at Qumrân (e.g., 1QapGen 20:28-29; 11QPs^a 19:15-16). Numerous Aramaic incantation bowls employing varieties of the ineffable name Yahweh indicate continued use of exorcistic practices among the Babylonian Jews of the sixth-seventh centuries A.D.

In the Synoptic Gospels, Jesus is portrayed as an exorcist in driving out the unclean spirits of demoniacs at Capernaum (Mark 1:21-28 par. Luke 4:31-37) and Gerasa (Mark 5:1-20 par.) and from the Syrophoenician woman (7:24-39 par.) as well as an epileptic boy (9:14-29 par.). This he accomplished by uttering "a word" (Matt. 8:16) or by simply ordering the evil spirit to depart (Mark 9:24). He granted authority to exorcise to his disciples as well (Matt. 10:1; Mark 6:7).

In New Testament times, others among the Jews also practiced exorcism by the Spirit of God (Matt. 12:27 par.). At Ephesus a band of itinerant Jewish exorcists attempted to cast out demons in the name of "Jesus whom Paul preaches," with ineffective results (Acts 19:13-16). Later rabbinic writings condemned such imitative use of Christian incantations (cf. Talmud *j. Šabb.* xiv.4.14d; *ʾAbod. Zar.* ii.2.40d-41a; *b. ʾAbod. Zar.* 27b).

EXPERIENCE.† Several Hebrew and Greek terms generally reserved for concrete processes also are used to depict physical and psychical events. At Eccl. 1:16 Qoheleth concludes that he has "seen" (Heb. *rāʾâ;* KJV, NIV "experienced"; cf. RSV, JB) wisdom and knowledge (cf. NIV, Deut. 11:2; Josh. 24:31; Heb. *yāḏâ;* cf. Heb. 11:5). Repeated exposure and attention to similar circumstances can yield skills or insight, as that for which Moses' assistants were chosen to settle minor disputes during the wilderness wanderings (Deut. 1:13, 15; Heb. *yāḏâ* "know intimately").

In the New Testament, "experience" is always

associated with suffering. For example, at Rom. 5:4 the KJV renders Gk. *dokimē* ("testing, certifying"; RSV "endurance") as "experience," suggesting that believers come to attain hope by patiently enduring trials. As used by Paul, the term implies one's being proved through a test.

EXPIATION.† The restoration of the relationship between God and human beings through some act of atonement. In the Old Testament Heb. *kāpar* (usually in the piel) is a frequently-used term ("cover, appease, atone") sometimes translated "make expiation" in the RSV. Expiation of the sins of the people was the object of the entire system of sacrificial worship (see, e.g., Ezek. 45:17; KJV "reconcile"; RSV "make atonement"; cf. 1 Sam. 3:14; KJV "purged"). The exercise of God's vengeance on the enemies of his people could itself be a way of making expiation for the sins of his people (Deut. 32:43; KJV "be merciful") as could be the death of a murderer (Num. 35:33; KJV "cleansed") or the destructon of idolatrous altars (Isa. 27:9; KJV "purged").

New Testament references to expiation are focused on the atonement accomplished through Christ's crucifixion. Paul refers to Christ as "an expiation (Gk. *hilastērion*) by his blood" (Rom. 3:25; KJV "propitiation"; *hilastērion* is used in LXX and in Heb. 9:5 for the "mercy seat," the covering of the ark of the covenant). Similarly, Christ is called "the expiation (*hilasmós*) for our sins" (1 John 2:2; 4:10; KJV "propitiation") and the one who became a "a merciful and faithful high priest" so that he could "make expiation (*hiláskomai*) for the sins of the people" (Heb. 2:17). In all of these statements, the sacrificial system of the Old Testament is the fundamental framework by which the death of Jesus is interpreted.

See also ATONE, ATONEMENT.

EYE (Heb. *'ayin*; Gk. *ophthalmós*). The organ of sight; also taken to represent the process of apprehending divine revelation.

The Old Testament notes the beautiful eyes of young David (1 Sam. 16:12) and the "weak" eyes of Leah (Gen. 29:17; KJV, NIV mg. "delicate"; cf. JB). To the Hebrews the eye was an indication of well-being (e.g., 1 Sam. 14:27) as well as the showcase of human emotions, such as hatred (Job 16:9) and grief (e.g., Ps. 6:7; 31:9). The expression "in your eyes" (e.g., find favor "in your eyes," do evil "in your eyes") simply meant "in your opinion." (See also APPLE; NEEDLE for other expressions.)

Sensitive as they were to the value of sight and expression, the Hebrews were just as keen to God's spiritual messages. After the fall, which revealed to the man his nakedness (Gen. 3:5, 7), God opened human eyes so that people could understand his law (19:8; cf. 119:18). Assuming interplay between the physical eye and spiritual awareness, the biblical writers point out that God not only sharpened human vision so that Hagar was able to locate water in the desert (Gen. 21:19), and so the two men of Emmaus could identify the risen Christ (Luke 24:31), but he also enhanced mankind's spiritual apprehension. Thus, Balaam was able to see the Lord's angel (Num. 22:31) and to recognize God's blessings for his people (24:4,

16); Elisha's companion at Dothan could perceive God's protective army (2 Kgs. 6:17, 20). On the other hand, though the Hebrews saw "with their own eyes" God's signs and wonders in Egypt and foresaw their own deliverance (Deut. 6:22; 7:19), they did not acknowledge the Lord's care for them, either because they did not receive spiritual illumination (Deut. 29:4, "eyes to see") or because they were made spiritually blind (cf. Isa. 6:10).

Because divine revelation was conceived as being apprehended primarily by the ear, biblical authors seldom speak of actually seeing God. In fact the Hebrews dreaded to "see" God, fearing instant death at having directly confronted his splendor (Exod. 33:20; Isa 6:5). A few Old Testament passages seem to imply, however, that at some time in the future people will see God's beauty (Isa. 33:17) and his majesty and holiness (Ezek. 38:23). This promise the apostle Paul interprets as seeing God "face to face" at the end of time (1 Cor. 13:12) and the apostle John as seeing him "as he is" (1 John 3:2).

The "eyes of the Lord," the Hebrew metaphor indicating divine care (cf. Deut. 11:12), are attentive to his people's plight, in contrast to graven idols that cannot "see" and therefore cannot protect (Ps. 135:16). The Old Testament community prayed that the Lord would continue to guard ("keep his eyes open for") the temple (1 Kgs. 8:29) and heed people's supplications (v. 52), confident that the one who took an interest in their birth (cf. Ps. 139:16) would be able to provide all that might be needed (cf. 2 Kgs. 19:15-16, 20ff.).

See also BLINDNESS.

EYE PAINT. A dark brown or black eye makeup, produced from malachite (a green basic carbonate of copper) or a sulphide of lead (antimony trisulphide in Babylonia), which was applied to the eyelashes and the eyebrows to make the eye more pronounced. A secondary purpose was to protect the eye against the glare of the sun.

In each of the three Old Testament passages where the word occurs, the person using this paint is to be censured. Jezebel sought in this way to impress Jehu (2 Kgs. 9:30; Heb. *pûk* "paint"). Judah, personified as a painted harlot, was seen as wishing to appear beautiful to her lovers (Jer. 4:30, "enlarge" the "eyes with paint"). Jerusalem is represented as an adulteress named Oholibah who painted (Heb. *kāḥal*; cf. Arab. *kuḥl*; JB "kohl," 2 Kgs. 9:30) her eyes before meeting men from distant countries (Ezek. 23:40).

At Rev. 3:18 Gk. *kollýrion* (cf. Lat. *collyrium*) refers to an eyesalve (cf. KJV) produced in Laodicea and called "Phrygian powder," which was applied to the eyes as a paste. Here the Laodiceans are encouraged to use this ointment to heal their vision so that they might know divine salvation.

EZAR (1 Chr. 1:38, KJV). *See* EZER.

EZBAI [ĕz'bī] (Heb. *'ezbāy* "shining"). The father of Naarai, one of David's mighty men (1 Chr. 11:37). The name may be a corrupted reading of "the Arbite" (Heb. *'rby*), an epithet of Paarai (2 Sam. 23:35).

EZBON [ĕz′bŏn].
1. The fourth son of Gad (Gen. 46:16; Heb. *'eṣbōn*; LXX *Thasaban*), called Ozni at Num. 26:16.
2. A son of Bela, of the tribe of Benjamin (1 Chr. 7:7; Heb. *'eṣbôn*; LXX *Asebōn*).

EZEKIEL [ĭ zē′kyəl] (Heb. *yᵉḥezqē'l* "may God strengthen"; Gk. *Iezekiēl*). A prophet of the Exile whose utterances comprise the third of the major prophetic writings. The son of the Zadokite priest Buzi, he was taken into exile under King Jehoiachin's surrender to Nebuchadnezzar in 598 B.C. and lived in his own house at Tel-abib by the canal Chebar between Babylon and Nippur (Ezek. 3:15). He received the prophetic call in 593 (1:2-3) and ministered to his fellow captives for at least twenty-three years; his last dated prophecy is 571 (29:17). The intensity of his prophecy is marked by numerous visions, mute trances, and symbolic actions; the death of his own wife becomes an oracle of the fall of Jerusalem (24:15-27).

EZEKIEL, BOOK OF.† The third book attributed to the Major Prophets, the work of the exilic prophet Ezekiel. In the LXX canon it follows Lamentations.

I. Setting

The prophet's call is placed in Babylon during the fifth year of King Zedekiah's exile (593 B.C.; Ezek. 1:2-3), implying that Ezekiel was among those Jerusalemites deported following the king's surrender to Nebuchadnezzar in 598. A number of scholars have challenged this traditional locale of Ezekiel's ministry, arguing, for example, that the content and allusions of chs. 1–24 necessitate the prophet's presence in Jerusalem; thus they argue that Ezekiel either never left Jerusalem (e.g., V. Herntrich) or that he remained there until the city fell in 587 and was then exiled to Babylon (e.g., A. Bertholet, W. A. Irwin). Others site the prophet's ecstatic transportation in 8:1-4; 11:24-25 as indication that he temporarily returned to Jerusalem. Nevertheless, the majority of scholars support the Babylonian locale, noting, for example, that both prophet and audience were familiar with Jerusalem and remained aware of conditions there, and that they no doubt continued to view themselves as the embodiment of that community.

II. Contents

Ezekiel's prophecies, although not presented in strict chronological order, are grouped thematically, dividing the book into four major sections. Chs. 1–24 comprise oracles of doom, prophecies warning Judah of impending judgment which date prior to the fall of Jerusalem in 587. Following Ezekiel's call and his inaugural vision of the glory of God (1:1-28a), he receives five commissions to prophesy to the "rebellious house" of Israel (1:28b–3:27). Employing various symbolic actions (4:1–5:17), the prophet describes the coming fall of Jerusalem as retaliation for the people's idolatry (ch. 6) and social sins (ch. 7). The temple visions of chs. 8–11, wherein Ezekiel feels himself transported ecstatically to Jerusalem, provide further evidence of cultic abominations and foretell the slaughter of the wicked and the fiery destruction of the city, culminating in Yahweh's departure from his temple. A series of

oracles concerning Jerusalem follows (chs. 12-19), including symbols of the Exile, denunciation of false prophets, mediums, and syncretists, allegories (useless wood of the vine, the unfaithful wife, two eagles [Nebuchadnezzar and Psamtik II]), a discourse on individual responsibility, and laments for Judah. The section concludes with oracles of judgment against the nation (chs. 20–24). First recounting the history of Israel's apostasy in Egypt, the wilderness, and Canaan, the prophet depicts the Exile as a time of purging and offers hope of a new Exodus and restoration of the people to Zion (20:1-44). Four "sword" oracles reiterate the impending judgment (20:45–21:32), followed by a catalogue of Jerusalem's sins (ch. 22). Judah's political alliances are denounced in ch. 23; the allegory of the sisters Oholah (Samaria) and Oholibah (Jerusalem). Another allegory portrays Jerusalem as a badly corroded caldron (24:1-14). Finally, the sudden death of Ezekiel's wife becomes an oracle of Jerusalem's last days (vv. 15-27).

A collection of oracles against foreign nations (chs. 25-32) proclaims doom for their malice demonstrated at the fall of Jerusalem in 587. The oracles are arranged geographically rather than chronologically, proceeding from Judah's immediate neighbors (Ammon, Moab, Edom, Philistia, Tyre, Sidon) to Egypt, symbolic of Israelite bondage prior to the Exodus.

Oracles of restoration and hope, intended to console the exiles following the destruction of Jerusalem, comprise a third major section (chs. 33-39). Having reiterated previous prophecies (ch. 33; cf. 3:16-21; 14:12-23; 18:5-32), the prophet announces Yahweh's judgment upon the wicked shepherds (kings) of Israel (34:1-10) and his desire to distinguish between good and bad sheep (vv. 11-22). An oracle announcing God's victory over Edom (ch. 35) stands in contrast to the promised restoration of Israel, both the land (36:1-15) and the people (vv. 16-38). In the vision of the valley of dry bones (37:1-14) the exiles are brought back to life by the spirit (Heb. *rûaḥ* "wind") of God. The oracle of the two sticks (vv. 15-28) depicts a reunified Israel under a Davidic king. This restored nation will defeat a powerful enemy from the north, Gog king of Magog, with the result that all nations will recognize Yahweh's supremacy (chs. 38–39).

Ezekiel's vision of the restored temple and the city of God (chs. 40–48) pictures a purified cult functioning within a purified community. The dimensions, arrangements, and decoration of the temple, including its gates and courts, are described in chs. 40–42. The purified temple is reconsecrated by the returned presence of God (43:1-12), and the altar of burnt offering is rededicated (vv. 13-26). Ordinances governing cultic personnel and temple services are recorded in chs. 44–46. The sacred river of life will issue forth from the temple, transforming the waters of the Dead Sea and creating a new Paradise for God's people (47:1-12). Israel's future glory is depicted in terms of an ideal land focusing on an ideal city wherein the Lord will live eternally (47:13–18:35).

III. Composition

The arrangement of the book into distinct groupings of prophecy has led scholars to attribute a significant role in its formation to one or more editors. Although

apparent evidences of editorial amplification of some
of the prophecies do not significantly discredit the
traditional view of the book as the product of Ezekiel or
his disciples, some extreme critics (e.g., G. Hölscher,
C. C. Torrey, W. A. Irwin) have discounted the originality of major portions of the work. Accordingly,
some would identify various passages as editorial accretions dating to the time of Nehemiah's reforms
(late fifth century) or later (e.g., some date chs. 38–39
to the time of Alexander the Great). While such extreme
redaction has not been widely accepted, a significant
degree of textual corruption and stylistic infelicities
may be attributed to editors.

The basic unity of the book is upheld by the recurrence of certain characteristics of style. The title "Son
of Man" is applied to Ezekiel by Yahweh some ninety-
three times throughout the book, stressing the humanity
of the agent. Also characteristic is the phrase "I am
Yahweh" which occurs some sixty times, generally
as a recognition formula underscoring the role of the
divine. Oracles are frequently introduced by the dispatch formula "set your face against," directing the
prophet to a particular people or place (e.g., 13:17; 21:2;
25:2). Other formal similarities in Ezekiel's oracles
include introductory formulae such as "the hand of
the Lord came upon me" (e.g., 8:1) or "the word of
the Lord came to me" (e.g., 6:1) or the commands
"hear the word of the Lord" (e.g., 36:1, 4) and
"prophesy and say" (vv. 1, 3, 6).

IV. Evaluation

The intensity of Ezekiel's prophecy is particularly
evident in his ecstatic visions. Taken by a previous
generation of scholars as indication of the prophet's
abnormal psychological health, such instances of total
rapture as well as the contrasting periods of muteness
or aphasia (3:26; 24:27; 33:22) are typical of trance-
like experiences of prophets and mystics attested elsewhere in the ancient world. Particularly characteristic
of Ezekiel is his vivid imagery (e.g., the glory of God,
ch. 1); indeed, several of his visions may be classified
as apocalyptic (cf. the valley of dry bones, 37:1-14;
Gog and Magog, chs. 38–39; the ideal temple and
city, chs. 40–48). The prophet's extensive use of
allegory involves not only literary discourses but also
a number of symbolic actions (e.g., brick mapping
out the siege of Jerusalem, 4:1-3; lying on his side
and eating exiles' rations, vv. 4-17; shaving his head,
5:1-17; digging through the wall of his house, 12:1-16;
cf. response to his wife's death, 24:15-27).

Influence of the prophet's priestly heritage is apparent
throughout the book, including his condemnation of
Israel's acceptance of pagan practices (6:1-7; 8:1-18;
20:27-31) and his vision of the restored temple and
cult (chs. 40–48). Yet because of the book's alleged
divergence from the teachings of the Torah, and because many feared ch. 1 would be misinterpreted by
laity who might hear it read in the synagogue, a
number of the early rabbis found reason to impede its
acceptance as canonical. Nevertheless, Ezekiel came
in time to be regarded as the "father of Judaism."
Indeed, in many ways his prophecy represents a transition from preexilic Hebrew thought to postexilic
Judaism. Like the earlier sixth-century prophets,
Ezekiel interprets the Exile and the destruction of

Jerusalem as divine punishment upon Israel for breach
of covenant (chs. 16, 22). But rather than permit the
people to blame their fate on the sins of their ancestors,
Ezekiel asserts that each individual is accountable
for his own deeds (14:12-23; ch. 18; 33:10-20); this he
demonstrates by the conscientious execution of his
office as "watchman" (3:16-21; 33:1-9). The vibrant
hope which he offers to the exiles focuses on a new
Israel — a people renewed from within, bearing a new
heart and a new spirit (36:26). To this prophet of the
Exile the "shepherd" who would rule over the restored
nation ("my servant David"; 34:23-24; 37:24) indicates
a human figure, whose just and righteous rule would
maintain the divinely sanctioned Davidic line. However,
not only Israel would recognize the authority of God; all
nations would acknowledge his magnificence (38:23).

Ezekiel's eschatological vision is reinterpreted by
the author of the New Testament book of Revelation.
Particularly evident are the apocalyptic images of a
new Jerusalem (Rev. 21:15-27; Ezek. 48:30-35; but
cf. 40:1–48:29) and the sacred river flowing from
the throne of God (Rev. 22:1-2; Ezek. 47:1-12).

Bibliography. W. Eichrodt, *Ezekiel.* OTL (1970);
M. Greenberg, *Ezekiel.* AB 22 (1983); J. W. Wevers,
Ezekiel. NCBC (1982); W. Zimmerli, *Ezekiel.* Her-
meneia (Philadelphia: 1979, 1983).

EZEL [ē'zəl] (Heb. *hā'āzel* "departure"). A stone
where Jonathan and David agreed to meet (1 Sam.
20:19) and where they bade farewell to each other
(vv. 35ff.); its precise location is unknown. The RSV
emends Heb. *'ēṣel hā'eben hā'āzel* "beside the stone
Ezel" to *'ēṣel hā'argāḇ hallā'z* "yonder stone heap"
(cf. JB), following LXX B (Gk. *ergab ekeíno*).

EZEM [ē'zəm] (Heb. *'āṣem*). A city in the territory
of Judah (Josh. 15:29); also assigned to Simeon as
part of that tribe's inheritance (19:3; 1 Chr. 4:29,
'eṣem). At Josh. 15:29; 19:3 the KJV transliterates
the Hebrew name as "Azem." It has been proposed
that the site is modern Umm el-'Azam, about 36 km.
(20 mi.) southeast of Beer-sheba.

EZER [ē'zər] (Heb. *'ēzer* "help").
1. The sixth son of Seir, and one of the Horite
chiefs in Edom (Heb. *'ēzer*; Gen. 36:21, 27, 30; 1 Chr.
1:38 [KJV "Ezar"], 42).
2. A man from the tribe of Judah, and the father
of Hushah (1 Chr. 4:4).
3. One of the sons of Ephraim, whom the inhabitants of Gath killed when he raided their cattle (1 Chr.
7:21).
4. An experienced soldier of the tribe of Gad who
joined David at the stronghold in the wilderness (1 Chr.
12:9).
5. The son of Jeshua and ruler of Mizpah who
aided in rebuilding the walls of Jerusalem at the time
of Nehemiah (Neh. 3:19).
6. A priest who participated in the dedication ceremony of the rebuilt walls of Jerusalem (Neh. 12:42).

EZION-GEBER [ē'zī ən gē'bər] (Heb. *'eṣyôn geber*).
A port at the head of the Gulf of Aqabah, generally
identified as modern Tell el-Kheleifeh, about 3 km.
(2 mi.) west-northwest of Aqabah. The Old Testament

distinguishes between Ezion-geber (or Ezion-gaber at Num. 33:35-36 par. Deut. 2:8; 2 Chr. 20:36, KJV) and Elath (or Eloth) at Deut. 2:8 (but see par. Num. 33:35-36); 1 Kgs. 9:26; and 2 Chr. 8:17. Although the two are traditionally viewed as distinct settlements, many scholars now consider Elath to be a later name for the same site.

Ezion-geber is first mentioned at Num. 33:35 (cf. Deut. 2:8) as a camp from which the wandering Hebrews turned north on their journey to the promised land. It was probably David who captured this village when he subdued Edom (2 Sam. 8:13-14). Solomon built a fleet here which sailed to Africa, Arabia, and India for trade (1 Kgs. 9:26-27 par. 2 Chr. 8:17-18; cf. 10:22). Later King Jehoshaphat rebuilt the Tarshish fleet, but to no avail, for his ships were destroyed in the harbor at Ezion-geber (1 Kgs. 22:48) as divine retribution for his alliance with Ahaziah (2 Chr. 20:37).

A number of strata at Tell el-Kheleifeh were excavated 1938-1940, yielding remains dating from the tenth-fifth centuries B.C. Although no precise dates can be assigned, the first stratum can be identified with the reign of Solomon, while the second and third reflect the periods of Jehoshaphat and Uzziah (or Azariah), who rebuilt the city in the mid-eighth century (2 Kgs. 14:22, "Elath" par. 2 Chr. 26:1-2, "Eloth"). The fourth stratum has yielded evidence of the reign of the Edomite Rezin, who recaptured the city at the time of Ahaz (2 Kgs. 16:1, 6).

The most significant structure at the site is a square, mudbrick building consisting of three small square rooms and three rectangular rooms, dating to the Solomonic period. On the basis of horizontal rows of apertures along the walls, which he judged to be flues and vents, the excavator N. Glueck first assessed the building to be a fortified copper smelter. Later he recognized the apertures as inserts for wooden crossbeams which had been destroyed by fire, and identified the structure as a storehouse and granary. Destruction of this and other buildings may be linked to the invasion of the Egyptians under Shishak ca. 925 (cf. 2 Chr. 12:4).
See ELATH.

EZNITE (2 Sam. 23:8, KJV). See ADINO.

EZRA [ĕz'rə] (Heb. *'ezrā'* "help").
1. A priest who returned from the Exile with Zerubbabel (Neh. 12:1). He was of the house of Meshullam and was priest during the time of the high priest Joiakim (vv. 12-13).
2. A priest of Nehemiah's time (Neh. 12:33), probably the son or grandson of the Ezra cited in v. 1.
3. A priest who was descended from Aaron's son Phinehas by way of Zadok (Ezra 7:1-5) and the author of the book of Ezra and probably also of Nehemiah and 1-2 Chronicles. He was a priest and a scribe skilled in the Torah or law of Moses (v. 6) and apparently held a high position in the service of the Persian king.

According to 7:7 Ezra journeyed from Babylon to Jerusalem in the seventh year of King Artaxerxes I Longimanus (464-424 B.C.), accompanied by a group of Israelites which included priests, Levites, singers, gatekeepers, and temple servants. He was commissioned by the king and his seven counselors to make inquiries concerning Judah and Jerusalem in accordance with the law of God that was in his possession (v. 14). It was of great importance to the Persian king and the stability of his empire that he win the favor of the Jews, for the conquered land of Egypt had proven itself less than trustworthy. For this reason, the king freely gave Ezra silver and gold as an offering to the God of Israel, and he was authorized as well to collect silver and gold throughout the whole province of Babylonia for the same purpose, to be added to the freewill offerings of his own people and priests (vv. 15-16). This money was to be used to buy bulls, rams, and lambs as well as the cereal and drink offerings that were sacrificed with them (v. 17). Ezra also received vessels from the king as gifts dedicated to the service of the temple (vv. 18-19; cf. 8:25), and he was allowed to draw from the royal treasury to provide whatever else was necessary for the temple (7:20). All of the treasurers from the province Beyond the River (the portion of the Persian Empire of which Judah was a part, embracing all of Syria and Palestine up to the land of Egypt as well as the island of Cyprus; "river" here refers to the Euphrates) were commanded to grant promptly all that Ezra requested (up to a prescribed maximum; vv. 21ff.), and all of the Israelite priests, Levites, singers, gatekeepers, temple servants, and other temple functionaries were given exemption from the payment of tribute, custom, or toll (v. 24). In addition, Ezra was authorized to appoint magistrates and judges over all the Jews living in the province Beyond the River, to be understood here as applying primarily to Judah (v. 25).

Upon receiving this commission, Ezra commenced preparations for the journey, gathering up the leading men of Israel (7:28) and assembling at the river Ahava a group of more than fifteen hundred who were to accompany him (8:1-15). When it was discovered that no Levites were present, he added these to the number of his followers (vv. 15ff.). He then proclaimed a time of fasting in order to implore God to grant them a prosperous journey, for he was ashamed to ask the king for the protection of a band of soldiers (vv. 21ff.). The journey was begun on the twelfth day of the first month of Artaxerxes I's seventh year (458), and Ezra's company arrived safely in Jerusalem where those who had returned some eighty years earlier (vv. 24-36).

Approximately four months after his arrival in Jerusalem (compare 7:9 with 10:9) Ezra enacted measures against the widespread practice of Jewish intermarriage with the foreign peoples of the land, successfully persuading the transgressors to send away their foreign wives as well as the children that had been born to them (9:1–10:44). Some thirteen years later (445), in the seventh month of the year of Nehemiah's arrival, Ezra read the law before the people from an elevated wooden pulpit (Neh. 8). According to Jewish tradition, Ezra is responsible for having restored the Mosaic law to writing after it had been burned in the destruction of Jerusalem in 586.
See also EZRA, BOOK OF.

EZRA, BOOK OF.†

1. Origin and Place in Canon

Attributed by Jewish tradition to Ezra the scribe (Talmud *B. Bat.* 15a), the book of Ezra is a continuation of the Chronicler's history of Israel, recounting the return of the exiles to Jerusalem and efforts to re-establish the community. Scholars in general acknowledge that the book, along with Nehemiah, originally formed a unit with 1-2 Chronicles, and both contents and textual tradition indicate that Ezra and Nehemiah originally constituted a single unit in the Hebrew canon and the LXX (Esdras B). Both Origen (third century A.D.) and Jerome (fourth century) acknowledge the two as 1-2 Ezra in contemporary Greek manuscripts; the division was introduced in the Vulgate (1-2 Esdras) and subsequently in a fifteenth-century Hebrew manuscript.

In the English canon, Ezra is placed with the historical writings and follows 2 Chronicles; in the Hebrew canon it is part of the third division, the Writings, and appears out of chronological sequence, before Chronicles.

See also ESDRAS, BOOKS OF.

II. Contents

Chs. 1–6 constitute a brief summary of events between the first return of exiles from Babylon in 538 B.C. in accordance with the decree of Cyrus and the dedication of the temple of Zerubbabel (or the Second Temple) in 515. The book begins with the edict of Cyrus (1:1-4; cf. 2 Chr. 36:22-23), followed by the response to that decree (vv. 5-11). Ch. 2 contains a list of those who returned at this time (cf. Neh. 7). Ch. 3 tells of the rebuilding of the altar and the celebration of the Feast of Booths (vv. 1-6) and the laying of the foundation for the temple (vv. 7-13). Ch. 4 recounts Samaritan opposition to the rebuilding of the temple (vv. 1-6) and of the city walls (vv. 7-24). Renewal of the work and completion of the temple are recorded in 5:1–6:18; the section concludes with an account of the celebration of Passover and the Feast of Unleavened Bread (6:19-22).

Ezra himself first appears in ch. 7, commissioned by Artaxerxes I (465-424) to return to Jerusalem to enforce the law. Ch. 8 depicts Ezra's safe journey and includes a list of exiles who returned with him (vv. 1-20). The book concludes with an account of Ezra's handling of the problem of mixed marriages (chs. 9–10).

III. Literary Aspects

The book of Ezra, like that of Nehemiah, is clearly a compilation of various documents and literary sources. Included are a number of lists, such as the inventory of the temple vessels returned by Cyrus (1:9-11), lists of exiles who returned with Zerubbabel (2:1-70) and Ezra (8:1-14), and lists of Levites (8:15-20) and those who had married foreign wives (10:18-44). Documents include the edict of Cyrus permitting the return (1:2-4, Hebrew; 6:3-5, Aramaic), Artaxerxes' letter authorizing Ezra's return (7:12-26), the letter of Rehum and Shimshai (4:11-16) and Artaxerxes' reply (vv. 17-22), and the letter of Tattenai (5:7-17) and Darius I's reply (6:6-12).

Chs. 7–10, commonly known as the Ezra memoirs, also reflect a variety of sources. This autobiographical material is primarily a third-person narrative, although 7:27–8:34; 9:1-15 is first-person. The Ezra memoirs are concluded, following the first half of the Nehemiah memoirs, in Neh. 7:73b–10:39 (MT 40), where they recount Ezra's reading of the law, the celebration of the Feast of Booths, and the covenant ratifying the law.

Further evidence of the book's complex composition is the inclusion of two sections in Aramaic (4:8–6:18; 7:12-26), the international diplomatic language of the period.

IV. Historicity

Because of the author-compiler's frequent preference for topical rather than strictly chronological arrangement (e.g., note the intermingling of incidents from the reigns of several Persian rulers in ch. 4), biblical scholars have long been suspicious of the book's historical credibility. More recently, however, the historicity of the accounts has gained considerable support from a number of archaeological discoveries as well as study of the Elephantine papyri, fifth-century documents written in Imperial Aramaic which bear strong stylistic resemblance to the Aramaic documents recorded in Ezra.

Of primary concern is the relationship between Ezra and Nehemiah, both of whom the biblical accounts indicate as active during the reign of Artaxerxes. Based on the interweaving of the Ezra and Nehemiah memoirs, the lack of any definite mention of either figure in the other's memoirs, and a conflicting sequence of events as recorded in Josephus and the apocryphal 1 Esdras, many scholars have posited that Ezra followed Nehemiah in the reign of either Artaxerxes II (thus *ca.* 396) or Artaxerxes III (*ca.* 351) or at least during Nehemiah's second governorship (428). However, supported by evidence from the Samaritan papyri from Wâdī Dâliyeh, the Elephantine material, and various seals and inscriptions, the traditional view that Ezra preceded Nehemiah during the reign of Artaxerxes I (thus having returned in 458) has regained favor.

Another conflict is the relationship between Sheshbazzar, designated as having led the first return (1:8) and as governor (5:14) who laid the temple's foundation (v. 16), and Zerubbabel, who heads the list of returnees in ch. 2 and both laid the foundation for (3:10; cf. v. 6) and rebuilt the temple (5:1-2; he is designated as governor throughout the book of Haggai). Although supportive evidence is lacking, Zerubbabel may have led a second group of exiles. Furthermore, it has been suggested that more than one foundation stone was involved, that the work of Zerubbabel represented a "new beginning," or that he played a major role in laying the foundation under Sheshbazzar's authority.

V. Theological Significance

The work of Ezra as recorded in this book (and subsequently in Nehemiah) was of particular value in reforming the postexilic community in terms of its ancient roots in the Mosaic law and thus had great impact on the future life of the Jewish nation, especially with regard to spiritual matters. This is evident in Ezra's efforts to protect the fragile restoration community from unrestrained assimilation by prohibiting intermarriage with the surrounding peoples (chs. 9–10) and especially in the nature of his mission to proclaim and enforce the law (7:12-26).

See also CHRONICLES, BOOKS OF; NEHEMIAH, BOOK OF.

Bibliography. P. R. Ackroyd, *Exile and Restoration.*

OTL (1968); J. M. Myers, *Ezra-Nehemiah*. AB (1965); S. Talmon, "Ezra and Nehemiah (Books and Men)," *IDBS*, pp. 317-328.

EZRAH [ĕz'rə] (Heb. *'ezrâ* "help"). A man of the tribe of Judah (1 Chr. 4:17), listed among the descendants of Caleb.

EZRAHITE [ĕz'rə hīt] (Heb. *'ezrāḥî*). An alternate form of the gentilic Zerahite, designating the descendants of Zerah (1 Chr. 2:6). Ethan and Heman were famous members of this clan (1 Kgs. 4:31; cf. the superscriptions of Pss. 88–89).

EZRI [ĕz'rī] (Heb. *'ezrî* "my help"). The son of Chelub, and supervisor of the work of the crown lands during the days of David (1 Chr. 27:26).

F

FABLE.† An imaginative story composed for didactic or polemical purposes, in which the characters are plants or animals that speak and act like humans. Two Old Testament stories can clearly be classified as fables. In the fable of Jotham (Judg. 9:8-15) the olive tree, fig tree, and vine each reject being made king over all the trees, but the worthless bramble gladly accepts; the bramble represents Abimelech, chosen king by the Shechemites after he had murdered seventy of his kinsmen, the legitimate successors of Jerubbaal (Gideon). In a brief fable (2 Kgs. 14:9 par. 2 Chr. 25:18) Jehoash of Israel checks the arrogance of King Amaziah of Judah by depicting a thistle which is trampled by a wild beast after having sought the daughter of a cedar of Lebanon as wife for its son. Other passages which display similarities to the fable include Nathan's parable of the ewe lamb (2 Sam. 12:1-4), Isaiah's Song of the Vineyard (Isa. 5:1-7), Ezekiel's allegories (e.g., the eagles, Ezek. 17:1-21; the cedar, vv. 22-24; the lioness, 19:1-9), and Paul's account of the parts of the body (1 Cor. 12:14-26).

The KJV translates Gk. *mýthos* as "fable" in the New Testament epistles (e.g., 1 Tim. 1:4; 4:7; 2 Tim. 4:4; 2 Pet. 1:16; cf. Vulg., Lat. *fabula*). The term is more correctly rendered "myth, mythology" (so RSV, JB).

FACE. Literally, the front part of the head of a human being (Heb. *'ap* "nose"; *pānîm,* a plural form; Gk. *prósōpon*), animal, or angel; it is used figuratively in such expressions as the "face of the waters" (Gen. 1:2) and the "face [Heb. *'ayin* "eye"] of the land" (Exod. 10:5).

To the biblical writers, the human face represents the entire person; according to Job 42:9 the Lord accepted "Job's face," i.e., Job himself (so KJV, JB; RSV, NIV "Job's prayer"). Often the face, the most individually identifiable part of the human body, reflects a range of emotions. The psalmist confesses that shame had "covered [his] face" (Ps. 44:15); in describing his grief, Job observes that his "face is red with weeping" (Job 16:16). Elsewhere, joy from a "glad heart" results in "a cheerful countenance" (Prov. 15:13).

The faithful are urged to seek God's face (Ps. 27:8), meaning his favor (see Gen. 33:10), which God might grant (Num. 6:25) or deny by "hiding his face" in anger (Isa. 54:8; cf. Ps. 27:9; see also Lev. 20:3, "set my face against"). In biblical usage the face of God (Heb. *pānîm*) is often idiomatic for the presence of the deity (cf. Gen. 4:16). Thinking anthropomorphically, the peoples of the ancient Near East identified the face of a deity with his "glory," a powerful aura surrounding the deity (cf. Akk. *melammu*). Accordingly, the Israelites were forbidden to look directly upon the divine face lest they be overwhelmed by God's might (cf. the anthropomorphic terms of the instructions preparing Moses for the divine theophany at Exod. 33:20-23). But according to the apostle Paul, in the end time believers will be permitted to see God "face to face" (1 Cor. 13:12), thereby attaining direct and complete knowledge (cf. Gen. 32:30; Exod. 33:11). Meanwhile, they are assured that they can approach God through the face, or person, of Christ (2 Cor. 4:6).

FAIR HAVENS (Gk. *Kaloi Limenes*). A small bay on the southern coast of Crete, east of Cape Littinos and near the city of Lasea (Acts 27:8). The name was probably chosen by the inhabitants in order to attract commerce, but the prevailing southeasterly winds in winter would actually make the harbor unsafe (cf. v. 12).

FAITH.† Human belief in and reliance upon the divine.

I. Terminology

The primary Old Testament words for "believe," "belief," and "faith" are Heb. *'āman* and its cognates *'emûnâ* and *'emet.* The basic meaning of *'āman* is "be steady, firm and trustworthy" (KoB, p. 60); in the hiphil, rendered "to believe," the verb signifies "accept as true" (1 Kgs. 10:7 par. 2 Chr. 9:6; Lam. 4:12; Hab. 1:5), "be sure" (Job 15:22), or "trust" (Jer. 12:6). The meaning of *'emûnâ* is "steadiness," "faithfulness," or "candor" (KoB, p. 60; cf. Isa. 9:7b for the parallel between "believe" and "establish"), while that of *'emet* is "trustworthiness," "faithfulness" (Gen. 32:10), or "truth" (e.g., 42:16; cf. KoB, p. 66).

The New Testament terms are Gk. *pisteúō* "believe" and *pístis* "faith." John uses the verb *pisteúō* to indicate the circumstance of believing; Paul primarily chooses the noun *pístis*, but cf. Rom. 3:22, where he combines the noun and verb to indicate "faith in Jesus Christ for all who believe."

The word "faith" occurs in a variety of expressions: "in good faith" (Heb. *beʾemet*; Judg. 9:15-16, 19), a "breach of faith" (*maʿal*; Lev. 6:2 [MT 5:21]), "full of faith" (Acts 6:5; 11:24), "of little faith," i.e., without confidence that God would provide for the basic human needs (Matt. 6:30; cf. 14:31; 16:8 for the small degree of trust the disciples placed in Jesus' power), a "door of faith" (Acts 14:27), the "word of faith" (Rom. 10:8), the "spirit of faith" (2 Cor. 4:13), the "shield of faith" (Eph. 6:16), and the "breastplate of faith" (1 Thess. 5:8). The Old Testament also portrays faith as undergirding human relationships (e.g., Judg. 9:15). Basically, however, both the Old and the New Testament view faith as mankind's trust in God.

II. Meaning

A. *Old Testament.* It is said of Abraham, the first patriarch, that he believed God (Gen. 15:6), and that God "reckoned it to him as righteousness." Indeed, as an old man, he left all his earthly securities in Haran (12:1), trusting in the Lord's promise of a new country and many descendants. His descendants, likewise, committed themselves to God following their miraculous deliverance from Egypt through the Red Sea (Exod. 14:31) and the ensuing wilderness wanderings. Often, however, the Hebrews' trust in Yahweh, their covenant God, wavered or failed altogether (e.g., Num. 14:11; cf. Ps. 78:22). Such was the case later in the promised land as well (Deut. 32:20, "no faithfulness"; KJV "no faith"; JB "no loyalty"). But even through the peril which destruction and exile would bring to the nation and the land, a core of the people would remain faithful, a remnant who attempted to maintain a life infused by faith (cf. Hab. 2:4).

B. *New Testament.* The New Testament community, like its Old Testament counterpart, identified faith primarily with trust in God. An important emphasis of Jesus' teachings is trust in God, not only for his great power which can accomplish miracles (e.g., Mark 11:20-24 par.; Matt. 9:18-26 par.) but also for his loving concern for the necessities of human existence (Matt. 6:25-33 par. Luke 12:22-31).

In the New Testament, however, the focus is not so much on God's providential care as manifest in various historical events (e.g., the Exodus, the return from exile) as on the coming of his son Jesus Christ, who would establish the kingdom of God. The apostle John, for instance, indicated that those who believed in the Son of Man would have eternal life (John 3:15-16, 36; 6:40, 47; cf. 17:3). Once they had witnessed him perform a miracle (2:11), Jesus' disciples accepted Jesus as sent by God; others did also (v. 23; cf. 4:39; 8:30), most notably upon seeing Jesus raise Lazarus from the dead (11:45; cf. 12:11). At 20:30-31 the apostle writes that he recorded many of the Master's "signs" specifically so that others might believe that Jesus was God's son. John had to acknowledge, though, that the Jewish leaders flatly rejected Jesus' claim of being God's only begotten son (6:36, 64; 7:48; 10:25-26), even after having seen him perform many miracles (12:37).

In addition to frequently linking faith with trust, John elaborates on its content. In Christian faith, people believe that Jesus is "the Christ, the Son of God" (20:31), that he came "in the flesh" (1 John 4:2), that he came from, or was sent by, God the Father (John 16:27 [cf. v. 30; 17:8]; 17:21), that he is "in" the Father (i.e., that they are one) and the Father "in" him (14:10-12), and that he is the resurrection (11:25). Such a belief includes an element of knowledge (4:42; 6:69 par. "know"), but not always empirical knowledge (20:29).

Agreeing with John that human redemption is founded upon faith in Jesus Christ (Rom. 3:22, 25), the apostle Paul cites the gospel as the anchor of faith, God's "power . . . for salvation" (1:16). From this he concludes that God justifies, or restores to wholeness, a person who has faith in Jesus (3:26), or that sinners are justified by faith (5:1; cf. 4:5), which can derive from hearing the gospel of Christ (10:17). Here Paul takes issue with the Judaizers, who held that a person would be justified by obeying the law (cf. Gal. 2:16; Eph. 2:8 for the emphasis on faith; and Rom. 4:3, 9 for Paul's understanding of Abraham's faith; cf. Gen. 15:6). He further concludes that faith is subordinate to love (1 Cor. 13:13–14:1), because believers have received in their hearts the same love that God made manifest in Jesus (Rom. 5:5, 8). As did John, Paul attempts to represent the content of faith: that Jesus is Lord, whom God raised from the dead (Rom. 10:9; 1 Thess. 4:14). (*See* JUSTIFICATION.)

The letter of James contrasts true faith to intellectual knowledge which lacks personal commitment. Comparing some believers with the devils, who also believe that there is only one God (Jas. 2:19), James reasons that good works must be the result of faith, as it was Abraham's faith that made him willing to sacrifice his only son Isaac (vv. 21-23; cf. Gen. 22:1-14).

The letter to the Hebrews summarizes faith as the "assurance [Gk. *hypóstasis*; KJV "substance"] of things hoped for, the conviction [Gk. *élenchos*; KJV "evidence"] of things not seen" (Heb. 11:1). Faith is taking God's promises for certain, even when they have not yet been fulfilled (and thus are not yet seen). Abraham, for instance, obeyed God's call to immigrate to a foreign country, where he and his long-barren wife, Sarah, received a son as God had promised. Yet Abraham was willing to sacrifice Isaac, trusting that God would raise him from the dead (vv. 8-9, 17-19). Abraham, as the other Old Testament heroes of faith, truly accepted God's promise that he would provide them with a better homeland than Canaan here on earth (vv. 13-16). By pointing out that each of the ancient saints trusted God for the promises he made to them and that they acted accordingly, the author of Hebrews hopes to encourage his readers to follow Jesus confidently, expecting that the Master would perfect their faltering faith (12:1-2).

III. Theological Reflections

Faced with growing threats of heresy that would deny the fundamental tenets of the gospel, the early Church formulated summaries of beliefs as definitive of "the Christian faith." Yet Church Fathers like Augustine did not sacrifice subjective faith, which is purely trust in God's promises, to an objective faith, characterized as acceptance of a prescribed set of beliefs (see Augustine *Ench.* v-viii). Later, Luther, who is credited with giving rebirth to the Pauline emphasis on justification by faith, centered his life around obedient surrender to Christ; Calvin, in his own way, attempted to unify trust and experiential knowledge (*Inst.* iii.2.1ff.). The biblical balance between trust and knowledge was, however, nearly lost when scholastic intellectualism — among Catholics and Protestants alike — almost lost sight of personal commitment, and pietism came close to robbing faith of its cognitive dimension.

While some of the New Testament writers provide short statements about the content of the Christian faith, they do not define precisely all its intricate aspects. Yet, true faith essentially must be grounded on belief in Christ's redemptive work. As Paul instructed the Philippian jailer on the requisites of salvation, " 'Believe in the Lord Jesus, and you will be saved' " (Acts 16:31).

IV. Faithfulness

The relationships between God and mankind and between individuals through which trust and belief are enacted can be viewed both qualitatively and duratively. In the Bible this is expressed primarily in terms of loyalty to the covenant relationship, the constitutive factor in Israel's existence as a nation and the focus of their identity as a people. Such faithfulness is frequently attributed to God (e.g., Ps. 33:4; 100:5; 119:90) and is evident through his steadfast love (Heb. *ḥesed*), by which he upholds his gracious covenant (Deut. 7:9; Isa. 61:8; Hos. 2:19-20). Because God has demonstrated such reliability, his people are able to turn to him for deliverance from every need (Ps. 85; Mic. 7:20; 1 Cor. 10:13). Moreover, this divine loyalty is climaxed in the atoning sacrifice of Jesus, the "merciful and faithful high priest" (Heb. 2:17).

In response to God's steadfast love, his people are dutifully compelled to uphold the covenant stipulations (Josh. 24:14; 1 Sam. 12:24; cf. Deut. 7:9). Such faithfulness is a virtue to be employed in all relationships (cf. Luke 16:10-12; Gal. 5:22; 1 Tim. 3:11), but particularly in fulfillment of God's commands (Ps. 111:8; cf. Acts 11:23, Gk. *prosménō*), for which they will be rewarded (1 Sam. 26:23; 1 Kgs. 2:4; Rev. 2:10).

Israel's failure to uphold the covenantal responsibilities is labeled "faithlessness" (Heb. *māʿal, bāgaḏ, mᵉšûḇa*). This designation (e.g., Jer. 3:6, 8, 11-12; cf. Rom. 3:3; 2 Tim. 2:13; Gk. *apisteō*) derives from secular usage regarding breach of marriage (Num. 5:12, 27) or other familial relationship (Jer. 31:22; 49:4; Heb. *šôḇēḇa*). In the New Testament "faithlessness" also denotes lack of belief (cf. John 20:27).

Bibliography. O. Becker and O. Michel, "Faith," *DNTT* 1:593-606; R. Bultmann and A. Weiser, "πιστεύω," *TDNT* 6 (1968):174-228; A. Jepsen, "ʾāman," *TDOT* 1, rev. ed. (1977):292-323.

FALCON (Heb. *ʾayyâ*).† A bird of prey belonging to the family Falconidae; several species of the genus Falco have been attested in Palestine. The bird's keen vision, noted at Job 28:7 (LXX Gk. *gypós* "vulture"; so KJV, JB), would aid it in spotting and striking at its prey, hence its inclusion among the birds of abomi-

nation (Lev. 11:14; JB "buzzard"; KJV, NIV "kite"; cf. Deut. 14:13).

FALL, THE.† The loss of mankind's pristine innocence and tranquility, associated in Jewish and Christian tradition with the temptation and subsequent disobedience of Adam and Eve in the garden (Gen. 3). Although the event itself is not so designated in the Bible, various references do indicate the fall into sin by humans (e.g., 1 Cor. 10:12; 1 Tim. 3:6-7; Jas. 5:12) and angels (cf. 2 Pet. 2:4; Jude 6).

I. Biblical Account

The narrative of the fall is set within the second biblical account of creation (Gen. 2:4–3:24). After depicting the creation of the man (2:7) and the woman (v. 22), the narrative records the circumstances surrounding the disruption of their idyllic primordial state. Eve is approached by a cunning serpent, who arouses her desire for the fruit of the knowledge of good and evil (3:1-3) and instills doubt concerning God's motive in prohibiting that fruit (vv. 4-5; cf. 2:16-17). Realizing that the act would gain them superior skill and insight akin to that of God himself (MT "like gods"; so LXX; cf. v. 22), she eats some of the fruit and shares it with her mate (3:6). The two are immediately aware of what their misdeed represents, and so attempt to hide from God, anthropomorphically portrayed as searching for them in the garden. God, however, obtains a confession of guilt and punishes the perpetrators accordingly. The curses constitute etiological explanations of why serpents crawl (unlike that of vv. 1-5) and of the natural enmity between serpents and humans (vv. 14-15), of the irony between the pain of childbearing and sexual desire (v. 16), and of the paradox which characterizes the tension between mankind and nature and the human necessity of eking out a livelihood (vv. 17-19). Most important, the couple are banished from their earthly Paradise (vv. 23-24).

The complex literary process behind the Genesis narrative has yielded an account rich in symbolism and suggesting a number of mythological motifs (anthropomorphism, etiologies; cf. v. 24). A number of scholars have noted similarities between the biblical account and ancient Near Eastern mythology. For example, the Babylonian Adapa myth depicts the unwise counsel of the jealous god Ea to the sage Adapa, whereby the latter rejects Anu's offer of the bread and water of life and thus loses immortality for himself and mankind. In the Sumerian Gilgamesh Epic, the hero fails in his quest for immortality when a serpent steals from him a plant of eternal youth; earlier, Gilgamesh's companion Enkidu is tempted by a harlot and gains both sexual awareness and wisdom. Yet unlike these myths, the biblical account locates the cause of human failure and misery in rebellion against God's command, not in human weakness, fate, or the trickery of envious gods.

See SERPENT.

II. Interpretation

Since biblical times the fall has been identified as the introduction of sin into the world and, along with it, mankind's subjection to death (Rom. 5:12; cf. Gen. 3:19). In contrast to similar incidents involving the loss of immortality in ancient Near Eastern mythology, the man and the woman are viewed here as responsible for their own action, capable of employing free will rather than subject to a divinely predetermined plan or the wiles of an independent evil force (but cf. Origen *De prin.* ii.8-9; iv.3).

Although the Genesis account does not promulgate a doctrine of original sin, many of the western (Latin) Church Fathers viewed Adam and Eve as the ancestors of all mankind, whose sin was thus transmitted to all successive generations by inheritance (e.g., Augustine *Quaest.*; cf. 2 Esdr. 7:118). By no means as extreme as Pelagius, who denied any evil consequences of the fall, the eastern (Greek) Church Fathers stressed rather the universality of human sin, hence the role of each individual in the fall (e.g., Theodore of Mopsuestia; cf. 2 Apoc. Bar. 54:19). However, whether the circumstances of the fall are interpreted historically or symbolically, that event constitutes the basis for the Christian doctrine of redemption of the world by Christ (cf. Gen. 3:15; Rom. 5:12-19; 1 Cor. 15:22).

Related traditions which derive from the biblical account of the fall include the identification of the serpent as Satan or the devil (Wis. 2:24; cf. Rev. 12:9; 20:2). Another tradition places primary responsibility for sin and the fall upon Eve (Sir. 25:24).

See SIN.

Bibliography. H. Haag, *Is Original Sin in Scripture?* (New York: 1969); B. Vawter, *On Genesis* (Garden City: 1977), pp. 63-91.

FALLOW GROUND (Heb. *nîr*). Ground that has been plowed but intentionally remains uncultivated. Every seventh year the fields in Palestine were to be left unseeded in order to give the land a rest and thus preserve its fertility (Lev. 26:34-35). Whatever grew on that land during the sabbatical year was to be given as sustenance for the poor and livestock (Exod. 23:11; Neh. 10:31; cf. Prov. 13:23; KJV "tillage"; NIV "field"). At Jer. 4:3; Hos. 10:12 the instruction "break up your fallow ground" means "cultivate a new field" or, metaphorically, "come to a renewal of your lives."

FALSE CHRISTS (Gk. *pseudóchristoi*).† Imposters who claim to be messiahs (cf. NEB). In his eschatological discourse on the Mount of Olives just before his crucifixion, Jesus warns his disciples of the many pretenders who would perform "great signs and wonders" (Matt. 24:24 par. Mark 13:22; cf. Luke 21:8). Such figures may have appeared in the traumatic years immediately prior to the destruction of Jerusalem in A.D. 70, proclaiming that they were religious saviors or that the end of time was imminent. The phenomenon, particularly prominent in Judaism from the Hellenistic period through recent modern times, may be attested in the Roman era in such individuals as Theudas and Judas of Galilee (Acts 5:36-37) and Simon Bar Kokhba. These pseudochrists resemble the antichrist in that they imitate Christ's work of redemption and attempt to lead the faithful astray (Matt. 24:24 par.; cf. Rev. 13:11ff.); however, they do not embody the degree of spiritual apostasy and opposition to God's kingdom that is usually associated with the ultimate antichrist (2 Thess. 2:8ff., "the lawless one").

See ANTICHRIST.

FALSE PROPHET (Gk. *pseudoprophḗtēs*).† One who wrongfully claims to be a channel of divine revelation (cf. Jer. 23:16). In the latter stages of the divided Israelite monarchy, the canonical prophets readily denounced the various types of diviners who influenced the royal court (Jer. 27:10; 29:8; Ezek. 13), "prophesying falsely" (Heb. *nibbᵉʾîm laššāqer*; Jer. 27:15) in the Lord's name advice that betrayed the people's best interests (v. 10; 23:32; 29:9). Moreover, many of the professional prophets had lost sight of their calling (cf. 2:8; 23:9-40), instructing the people by "the deceit of their own heart" (v. 26; cf. 14:14) to disregard the word of God and to abandon their covenantal responsibilities (cf. v. 17; Isa. 30:10-11). Ironically, the Israelites failed to discern the lies upon which these oracles were premised (Jer. 23:32; cf. Luke 6:26) and thus brought upon themselves the Exile as divine punishment (Jer. 14:13-16).

The early Church was keenly aware of the perils posed by false prophets who might distract believers from the responsibilities of Christian discipleship (cf. Did. 11:3-12). Jesus warned of such individuals "who come to you in sheep's clothing but inwardly are ravenous wolves" (Matt. 7:15). They claimed supernatural powers (1 John 4:2) and practiced exorcism, using Jesus' name (cf. Matt. 12:27 par.; Acts 19:13-16). The Jewish magician Bar-Jesus (Elymas), who opposed Paul and Barnabas, was a false prophet (13:6). In times of social upheaval the number of false prophets seems to have increased (cf. 2 Pet. 2:4); consequently, they figured prominently in Christian perceptions of the end times (Matt. 24:11, 24 par. Mark 13:22; cf. Rev. 16:13; 19:20; 20:10).

FAMILY (Heb. *bayiṯ* "house," *mišpāḥâ*; Gk. *oíkos*).† The basic social unit, comprised of persons related by kinship and sharing a common residence. The Israelite family was an extended family known as the "father's house" or "household" (Heb. *bêṯ-ʾāb*), consisting of two or more nuclear families (i.e., a married couple and their children) or composite families (an individual with multiple spouses and their offspring). It was both patrilineal and patrilocal, headed by the father or patriarch and consisting of his wife (or wives), married sons and their wives, unmarried children, and grandchildren — all of whom shared the patriarchal residence; other kin (including grandparents), servants, concubines, and sojourners might also be reckoned part of the household (cf. Gen. 46:5-7, 26). The patriarch was the oldest living male, at whose death authority passed to the eldest son and property was divided among all sons. *See also* HOUSEHOLD.

Israelites were encouraged to have large families (cf. Gen. 1:28; 9:1), not only to strengthen the base for production but also to guarantee survival of the people of Israel as a community of faith. The land, which ultimately belonged only to God, was allocated as inalienable to the stewardship of families and could be transferred only through inheritance. Thus, great importance was placed on maintaining the solidarity of families (cf. 1 Tim. 5:4, 8), as evident in the practices of levirate marriage to ensure descendants, blood vengeance, mutual defense (cf. Neh. 4:14), and redemption from debt slavery (Lev. 25:47-49).

Heb. *mišpāḥâ*, generally translated "family" or "clan," represents an association of two or more extended families which occupied the same or adjacent towns. These clusters provided mutual economic and military assistance for the constituent families, particularly prior to the establishment of the Israelite Monarchy. Regular religious festivals were observed within the *mišpāḥâ* (cf. 1 Sam. 20:6, 28-29), perhaps including celebration of local religious traditions.

The concept of family is viewed in a broader sense with regard to the universal fatherhood of God, which encompasses "all the families of the earth" (Gen. 12:3; 28:14; cf. Eph. 3:15). Relationships between God and his people, and similarly between Christ and the Church, are frequently portrayed in terms of human relationships (e.g., Jer. 2:1; 3:14; 2 Cor. 11:2; Rev. 21:2).

See KINSHIP; MARRIAGE.

FAMINE (Heb. *rā'āḇ*, *rᵉ'āḇon*; Gk. *limós*).† An extreme scarcity of food. The Bible records famines during the time of the patriarchs (Gen. 12:10; 41:54), the Judges (Ruth 1:1), the united (2 Sam. 21:1) and divided monarchies (1 Kgs. 17:1ff.), and the Roman period (Acts 11:28). In the ancient Near East, which was particularly dependent upon rainfall, the most frequent cause of famine was drought (Hag. 1:10-11; cf. 1 Kgs. 17:1; 18:1-2). Famine might also result from natural causes such as blight (Amos 4:9) or ravaging insects (e.g., locusts; Joel 1:4-20; Amos 4:9) or from human agentry, particularly warfare (2 Kgs. 6:24–7:20; Isa. 1:7; 3:7); invading armies might deliberately foster famine in order to weaken a city under siege (2 Kgs. 25:3 par. Jer. 52:6; Lam. 4:8-10). The Israelites frequently viewed famine as divine punishment (Deut. 11:17; Isa. 3:1; 51:19; Jer. 29:17-18; Amos 4:6; Mark 13:8) or a form of chastening whereby God would redeem mankind (Job 5:20).

From the onset famine resulted in sharply inflated prices for food (2 Kgs. 6:25; Rev. 6:6). When compounded by threat of military destruction, it produced extreme civil distress and grave damage to the social and moral order, as indicated by reports of cannibalism (2 Kgs. 8:28-29; Lam. 4:10). Frequently families and entire peoples were forced to emigrate in order to find sustenance: Abram (Gen. 12:10), Isaac (26:1), Jacob (46:1–47:12), Elimelech and Naomi (Ruth 1:1-2).

FARTHING (KJV). *See* MONEY.

FASTING (Heb. verb *ṣûm*, noun *ṣôm*; Gk. verb *nēsteúō*).† Deliberate and generally prolonged abstention from eating (and sometimes drinking) as a means of humbling oneself before God (Heb. *kāna'*, niphal; cf. Lev. 16:19, *tᵉ'annû eṯ-napšᵉṯêḵem* "afflict your soul"; RSV "afflict yourselves"). The origins of the practice appear to have been quite ancient, perhaps associated with the rites of mourning (1 Sam. 31:13; 2 Sam. 1:12; cf. 12:20-23). Fasting was observed as a sign of penitence (1 Sam. 7:6; 1 Kgs. 21:27) and an accompaniment to prayer (2 Sam. 12:16-17; Ps. 35:13; Tob. 12:8), and was a means of preparing oneself to receive divine revelation (Exod. 34:28; Deut. 9:9; Dan. 9:3; 10:3; cf. 1 Sam. 28:20; Matt. 4:2 par.).

Mosaic law prescribed fasting only in connection with observance of the Day of Atonement (Lev. 16:29-31; 23:27); otherwise, fast days were voluntary, with the exception of fasts proclaimed in times of national emergency (Judg. 20:26; 2 Chr. 20:3; Joel 2:15; 1 Macc. 3:47). The national trauma which resulted from the destruction of Jerusalem and the Exile which followed prompted regular fasts in observance of these events (Zech. 7:3, 5; 8:19). The length of a fast might be one day (2 Sam. 3:35) or night (Dan. 6:18) or as many as three (Esth. 4:16), seven (1 Sam. 31:13), or forty days (1 Kgs. 19:8).

Jesus echoed the sentiments of the Old Testament prophets in opposing ostentatious fasting as commonly practiced by the Pharisees (Matt. 6:16-18; cf. Isa. 58:3-7; Jer. 14:12; Zech. 7:5). He considered voluntary fasting a legitimate means of attaining humility and for reflecting on God's word (Matt. 9:14-15 par.). In the early Church fasting was observed as a preparation for important decisions (e.g., Acts 13:2-3; 14:23). Weekly fasts became a regular practice (Did. 8:1, Wednesday and Friday).

FAT (Heb. *ḥēleḇ*).† Adipose tissue, particularly that covering the entrails, kidneys, loins, liver, and sometimes the tail of sacrificial animals. Considered the seat of energy and thus one of the most desirable parts of the animal, the fat (or suet) and blood were not eaten but were removed and burned on the altar as the Lord's portion of the sacrifice (Gen. 4:4; Exod. 29:13, 22; Lev. 3–7). In some instances the term refers to the entire sacrifice (e.g., 1 Sam. 15:22; Isa. 43:24). *See* SACRIFICES AND OFFERINGS.

In figurative usage "fat" or "fatness" (Heb. *mišmān*, *dešen*) indicate abundance or fertility (e.g., Deut. 32:15; Judg. 9:9; JB, NIV "oil"; Job 36:16; JB "rich food"; NIV "choice food").

FATHER (Heb. *'āḇ*; Gk. *patér*).† The male parent, either biologically or through adoption (e.g., Gen. 9:23; Num. 3:4; Matt. 4:21-22). In biblical usage the term may also designate a grandfather (e.g., Gen. 28:13) or more remote male ancestor (e.g., 1 Kgs. 15:11, 24), including the eponymous ancestor of a social or political group (e.g., Gen. 10:21ff.; 28:13; 2 Kgs. 19:12; Mark 11:10); the expression "to sleep with one's fathers" thus means to die (e.g., 1 Kgs. 2:10; cf. "gathered to the fathers"; e.g., 2 Kgs. 22:20). The designation "father" is also applied to the founder or representative of an occupation (e.g., Gen. 4:20-21; Jer. 35:6, 8; 1 Macc. 2:54). Elsewhere it is a term of respect for a teacher (e.g., 2 Kgs. 2:12; cf. Prov. 1:8, etc.), prophet (2 Kgs. 13:14), or king (1 Sam. 24:11; 2 Kgs. 5:13); in a similar sense the term has become an appellative of Christian clergy. As with other kinship terminology, "father" is used at times in a jural sense to indicate a political superior in a covenantal relationship (cf. 1 Sam. 24:11) as well as a city or social group from which another settlement or group has developed (cf. 1 Chr. 2:42ff.).

In Israelite society the father was the head of an extended family which resided with him and which reckoned descent through his line. His authority was absolute and included the responsibility of securing wives for his sons (Gen. 24:4) and contracting marriages for his daughters (29:19, 23, 28; Judg. 1:12); he might even sell his daughters as slaves (Exod. 21:7). He was to be honored (Exod. 20:12 par. Deut. 5:16; Mal. 1:6) and obeyed (Prov. 23:22), and serious infractions might incur capital punishment (Exod. 21:15, 17; Deut. 21:18-21). A father was to love and care for his children (1:31; Hos. 11:1-3; Col. 3:21), disciplining them and instructing them in the faith (Deut. 4:9; 6:7; Prov. 1:8; 13:24; 19:18; Eph. 6:4). The father also officiated over religious observances in the family (e.g., Exod. 12:1-14, 21-28). He provided for his children's future by the inheritance accorded sons (e.g., Ezek. 46:18; cf. Num. 27:7-11) and the dowry provided daughters-in-laws (Exod. 22:17). Special provision was made for the care and support of the fatherless (e.g., Exod. 22:22; Deut. 14:29; 24:19-21; cf. Isa. 49:23, "foster fathers"; KJV "nursing fathers").

From early in Israel's history God was regarded as a father (cf. personal names such as Eliab, Joab "God is [my] father"; Abijah, Abiel "my father is God"). Yahweh was recognized as the father of Israel (e.g., Isa. 63:16; Jer. 3:4; Mal. 1:6), both as suzerain in the covenant relationship (e.g., Deut. 7:14) and as creator of the world (e.g., 32:6; Mal. 2:10). Just as the human father, God possesses ultimate authority (Mal. 1:6; Matt. 7:21-23). Similarly, he demonstrates his love and care for his children (Exod. 4:22-23; Deut. 1:31; Jer. 31:9, 20; Matt. 6:26-34; 18:14). The Gospels frequently distinguish between the relationship of God to his son Jesus ("my father") and to the disciples ("your father"; cf. John 20:17). Because of Jesus' particular nature as God's "only begotten son" (1:14, 18) and thus the authority (8:28-38; 14:10) and intimacy (e.g., 1:18; 10:38) they share, mankind has access to the Father only through the Son (14:6). Nevertheless, Jesus urged his followers to approach God intimately, confident of his warmth and grace (cf. Matt. 6:8-9, 32; Rom. 8:15; Gal. 4:6; see ABBA). In later Christian theology God the Father was regarded as the first person of the trinity (cf. Matt. 28:19).

Bibliography. H. Ringgren, "'āḇ ['ābh]," *TDOT* 1, rev. ed. (1977):1-19; G. Schrenk and G. Quell, "πατήρ," *TDNT* 5 (1967): 945-1022.

FATHERLESS. See ORPHAN.

FATHER'S HOUSE (Heb. *bêṯ-'āḇ*).* The basic socioeconomic unit of ancient Israel, an extended family (RSV usually "household"; KJV "house") consisting of the eldest living male of a lineage, his wife or wives, their married sons and grandsons and their wives, and all unmarried children and grandchildren. Other relatives, slaves, concubines, and sojourners were often included. See HOUSEHOLD.

FATHOM (Gk. *orguiá*). A unit of measurement representing the distance between the fingertips of both outstretched arms, equivalent to four cubits or 1.8 m. (6 ft.) (Acts 27:28). See WEIGHTS AND MEASURES.

FEAR (Heb. verbs *yārē'*, *pāḥaḏ*; nouns *yir'â*, *māgôr*, *paḥaḏ*; Gk. verb *phobéō*; nouns *phóbos*, *eulábeia*).† Various degrees of anxious dread or terror, generally

experienced in the face of danger or the suspicion thereof. In the most basic sense, fear arises from threats posed by human agentry (e.g., 1 Kgs. 1:50-51; Job 31:34; Jer. 35:11; Matt. 14:5; cf. Gen. 32:7; 46:3; Matt. 2:22, "be afraid"), the natural world (cf. Amos 3:8), or death (e.g., Job 3:25; cf. 22:10).

However, most frequently the Bible mentions fear as a response to God. At times people fear God because they have sinned and anticipate divine retribution (Gen. 3:10; 20:8; Deut. 9:19); this expectation achieved its fullest expression in the eschatological vision of the Day of the Lord (e.g., Isa. 2:19, 21; 13:6ff.). Fear of God (*mysterium tremendum*) is also precipitated by the overwhelming brilliance and sheer magnificence which surround divine theophanies (e.g., Exod. 3:6; 10:20; Deut. 5:5; Hab. 3:16; Luke 2:9; 7:16; 9:34; cf. the introductory phrase "Fear not," e.g., Gen. 15:1; Isa. 41:10; Luke 2:10; cf. Judg. 6:23); this fear might be accompanied by feelings of awe (*fascinans*; e.g., Gen. 28:17; Matt. 17:6; 27:54; Mark 4:31) and joy (Matt. 18:8; cf. Mark 16:8). Thus representative of these combined emotions, fear connotes a manifestation of great respect or worship (Deut. 28:58; 2 Kgs. 17:7; 1 Pet. 1:17; cf. Judg. 6:10, KJV; RSV "pay reverence to"; NIV "worship"). As it is most commonly expressed, "the fear of the Lord" is equivalent to the Israelite faith in Yahweh (e.g., Exod. 14:31; Josh. 24:14; Ps. 34:11; Jonah 1:9; Luke 1:50; Acts 9:31. In the New Testament, Gentiles drawn to Judaism are called GOD-FEARERS (cf. Acts 10:22; 13:16). Even as new persons in Christ, believers are to remain humble in recognition of their constant dependence upon God (Phil. 2:12, "work out your own salvation with fear and trembling"). Allegiance to the Lord implies a life of service embodied in love and ethical behavior (e.g., Lev. 19:14, 32; Job 4:6; Prov. 14:2; 2 Cor. 7:1; cf. Job 28:28).

The Fear of Isaac (Heb. *paḥaḏ yiṣḥāq*; JB "Kinsman"), whom Jacob acknowledged as his protector (Gen. 31:42) and by whom he swore an oath sealing his covenant with Laban (v. 53), is the ancestral God of the Fathers (cf. Exod. 3:13; Deut. 1:11, 21; Dan. 2:23). This archaic name, the precise etymology of which remains uncertain, reflects the awe and mystery of the divine (cf. B. Vawter, *On Genesis* [Garden City: 1977], pp. 340, 343, "the Awesome One of Isaac").

Bibliography. A. Alt, "The God of the Fathers," pp. 1-100 in *Essays on Old Testament History and Religion* (Garden City: 1968); H. F. Fuhs, "yārē'," *TDOT* 6; R. Otto, *The Idea of the Holy,* 2nd ed. (New York: 1958); R. H. Pfeiffer, "The Fear of God," *IEJ* 5 (1955): 41-48.

FEASTS (Heb. *mô'ēḏ, ḥag*; Gk. *heortḗ*).† Regular celebrations commemorating events of national and religious significance; in ancient Israel, occasions for communal thanksgiving.

I. Old Testament

During the earliest stages of the Israelite nation distinction was made between pilgrim feasts (Heb. *ḥag* "sacred dance, cultic procession") and other festivals (*mô'ēḏ* "appointed time," "season"; RSV, NIV "appointed feasts"; JB "solemn festivals"; NJV "fixed" or "set times"). Although "appointed feast" is a more general term which can encompass all Israelite feasts (e.g., Lev. 23:2, 4, 44; Ezek. 45:17), it also refers specifically to those festivals based upon the lunar calendar, such as the Sabbath and New Moon observances (45:17; cf. 46:11). The designation pilgrim feast came to be limited to three communal celebrations, apparently agricultural in origin and reckoned by the solar calendar: the Feasts of Unleavened Bread, Weeks (Pentecost), and Booths. These festivals involved pilgrimages by the entire family to the temple or other shrine (cf. Exod. 10:9), sacrifices, and common meals (cf. 1 Sam. 1); they were generally accompanied by considerable merriment, including processions, dancing, and revelry (e.g., Ps. 107:27; Isa. 30:29; Hos. 2:11; Amos 5:21-23; cf. syncretistic feasts at Exod. 32:5; 1 Kgs. 12:32).

With the introduction of several new feasts in postexilic times, a new distinction arose, between the "canonical" feasts instituted by the pentateuchal legislation and the "noncanonical" feasts which derived from later custom. Both types of celebrations included specific readings from the Scrolls (Megilloth): e.g., Song of Solomon at Passover, Ruth at Pentecost, Ecclesiastes at the Feast of Booths, and Esther at Purim.

A. *Canonical.* 1. Sabbath. Presumed to be one of the oldest Hebrew festivals, the SABBATH was celebrated every seven days, from sunset Friday to sunset Saturday. It was patterned after the example God set during Creation, of resting one day after six days of work (Gen. 2:2-3); on that day the Hebrews did not perform any work, but spent the time in worship and religious study (Lev. 23:3, "holy convocation"; cf. Exod. 20:8-11).

2. New Moon. At the beginning of each month the Hebrews celebrated the Feast of the NEW MOON (Heb. *ḥdš* "new moon," "month"). On these occasions, like the Sabbath, they abstained from work, made burnt offerings, and sounded the trumpet to symbolize their joy over God's faithfulness toward his chosen ones (Num. 10:10; 28:11-15). At the beginning of Tishri, the seventh month (about mid-September), the Hebrews had a special new moon celebration (Lev. 23:24-25), probably because by then the moon had appeared seven times, a number which symbolized completion or wholeness.

3. Seventh Year. Every seven years the Hebrews were to refrain from cultivating their land to give it, too, a period of rest (Exod. 23:10-11). During that year slaves were freed (Exod. 21:2-6) and the poor could gather whatever grew untended in the fields and vineyards (Exod. 23:10-11; Lev. 25:5-6).

4. Jubilee. The year following the forty-ninth year (the seventh sabbatical year) was to be observed as a year of jubilee, in which slaves received their liberty, people returned acquired property to its rightful owner, and the land enjoyed another period of rest (Lev. 25:8-18).

5. Pilgrim Feasts. a. Passover and the Feast of Unleavened Bread. Originally two separate festivals — a pastoral rite intended to guarantee fertility for the flocks and a pilgrim agricultural feast celebrating the barley harvest — these rites came to be adopted by the Israelites as commemoration of the events surrounding the Exodus from Egypt. This seven-day celebration begins on the fourteenth day of Nisan (March-April),

the first month of the postexilic Hebrew calendar (Lev. 23:4-14; Num. 28:16-25; Deut. 16:1-8). In commemoration of God's sparing the firstborn Israelite males during the tenth plague upon the Egyptians, the ritual includes the slaying of a one-year-old male lamb, the blood of which would be spread on the doorpost of the house. The next seven days the Hebrews were to eat unleavened bread to acknowledge the speed with which God led their forefathers out of Egypt (Exod. 12:1-28).

b. Feast of Weeks. Fifty days after the Passover Sabbath (i.e., at the end of May), the Hebrews celebrated the Feast of Weeks or Pentecost (from Gk. *pentēkostē* "fiftieth"), a one-day feast in which the firstfruits of the wheat harvest were presented to Yahweh (Lev. 23:10-21). This festive day was also known as the Feast of the Firstfruits (Exod. 34:22; cf. Num. 28:26), or the Feast of Harvest (23:16).

c. Feast of Booths. Beginning on the fifteenth day of the seventh month, or Tishri (i.e., early October), the Hebrews observed a seven-day festival in which they dwelled in booths or tabernacles made from branches to symbolize God's protection during the times they had only temporary shelters in which to dwell in the wilderness (Lev. 23:33-36, 39-43). This festival also commemorated the gathering of the harvest (cf. the name "Feast of Ingathering" at Exod. 23:16; 34:22).

B. *Noncanonical Feasts.* 1. Feast of Dedication. To commemorate the dedication or renewal of the temple by Judas Maccabeus in 164 B.C. following its desecration by Antiochus IV Epiphanes three years earlier (1 Macc. 4:52-59), the Hebrews instituted an eight-day celebration starting on the twenty-fifth day of the ninth month or Chislev (i.e., early December) with the lighting of the Hanukkah lamps (Heb. *ḥanukka* "dedication").

2. Purim. On the fourteenth and fifteenth days of the last month, Adar (late February), the Hebrews commemorated their miraculous escape from the plot (Heb. *pûr* "lot") Haman had devised to exterminate those of their ancestors who were living in Persia *ca.* 473 B.C. (Esth. 9:20-25). This two-day feast expressed intense gladness for God's providential care with which he had turned Haman's "lot" against Haman himself.

3. *Simhath Torah.* Immediately following the Feast of Booths, i.e., Tishri 22-23 (early October), the Hebrews celebrated a one- or two-day feast to acknowledge their "joy in the [Mosaic] law" (Heb. *śimḥat tôrâ*), and to signify the completion of their annual reading of the Pentateuch.

III. New Testament

A. *Jewish.* During Jesus' earthly ministry the Jews still observed many of the ancient feasts (Gk. *heortē*), such as the Passover (Luke 2:41) and the Feast of the Unleavened Bread (Matt. 26:17-19 par.), Pentecost (Acts 2:1; 20:16), and the Feast of Tabernacles (or Booths) (John 7:2). They remained very strict about proper observance of the Sabbath and regulated every one of its facets. On the basis of Gal. 4:10, scholars have inferred that the Jews of New Testament times also retained other holy "days," including the New Moon ("months"; cf. Col. 2:16), and the New Year ("years") festivals.

B. *Christian.* Jesus participated in many of the Jewish

feasts: he observed the Sabbath, appeared as many as four times at the Passover feast (John 4:45; 5:1; 6:4; 12:12), and attended part of the Feast of Tabernacles (7:10, 14), and the Feast of Dedication (10:22-23). Just before his death, however, with the institution of the Lord's Supper, he gave new meaning to the Passover by addressing the forgiveness of sins and the granting of everlasting life (Matt. 26:26-29 par.). In the early days of the Church, the Sabbath changed from the last day of the week to the first (cf. Matt. 28:1; Acts 20:7). Paul extended Jesus' abrogation of Old Testament feasts to the New Moon and New Year festivals, as well as other pilgrim feasts (Gal. 4:10; cf. Col. 2:16).

1. Passover. While the KJV renders Gk. *páscha* as "EASTER," a Christian holy day in commemoration of Christ's resurrection from the dead (Acts 12:4), the other versions (RSV, JB, NIV) render it properly as Passover.

2. Pentecost. According to Acts 2:1-4 the Holy Spirit descended on the apostles on the Jewish Feast of Pentecost. Christians reinterpreted this holy day to symbolize the firstfruits of the Spirit.

3. Other. CHRISTMAS, another significant Christian holy day, is not cited in the New Testament; its date, Dec. 25 (in the West), has little scriptural basis. The so-called love (or agape) feast may originally have been associated with the Lord's Supper (*see* AGAPE).

For further details, see the individual entries.

Bibliography. B. Kedar-Kopfstein and G. J. Botterweck, "chagh [ḥag]," *TDOT* 4 (1980): 201-213; H. Schauss, *The Jewish Festivals* (New York: 1973); R. de Vaux, *Ancient Israel* (New York: 1961), pp. 484-517.

FELIX [fē′liks] (Gk. *Phēlix*, from Lat. *felix* "happy"). Antonius Felix, a freedman of emperor Claudius who became procurator of Judea. He probably ruled first over only a portion of Samaria, but in A.D. 48 or 52 was installed as procurator over Judea by Quadratus, the governor of Syria. The relationship of Felix to Cumanus, his predecessor, is not completely clear, and it is possible that they shared the rule for a period of time. Felix was a cruel and tyrannical man. At the same time he sought to suppress the activities of robbers within his realm, he used their services to murder the high priest Jonathan.

After Paul was falsely accused and taken prisoner in Jerusalem, he was sent from the Sanhedrin there to Felix at Caesarea (Acts 23:23-24); when Felix interrogated Paul, the apostle's words about justice, self-control, and future judgment alarmed him and his wife Drusilla (24:24-25). However, he refused to allow Paul to go free, hoping the apostle would bribe him with money (v. 26). When Felix's rule came to an end in A.D. 60, he left Paul in prison in an attempt to please the Jews (v. 27). Later, when his brother Pallas refused to defend him before Nero, Felix was allegedly punished in Rome for poorly managing the procuratorship.

FELLOWSHIP (Gk. *koinōnía*). The communion or common faith, experiences, and expressions shared by the family of believers, as well as the intimate relationship they have with God.

Although the concept is developed most fully in the New Testament, it is inherent in the Israelite covenant. Grounded in the Lord's promise, "I will be with you" (e.g., Exod. 3:12, 16ff.), and governed and maintained by the covenant which was premised on that promise (e.g., Gen. 17:7-8; Josh. 24; Jer. 50:5), Israel enjoyed a unique relationship with Yahweh as the "people of God." Symbolic of God's presence with them were the cloud and the pillar of fire (Exod. 14:24; 40:34-38; Num. 9:15-23), the ark of the covenant (cf. Num. 10:35-36), and the tabernacle and temple (cf. Ps. 11:4; Ezek. 37:27). Although the Israelites were to accord special protection to strangers and foreigners who lived in their midst (Exod. 23:8; Deut. 10:18-19), they came to shun association with such heathen who were not among the chosen people (cf. Exod. 12:43; Neh. 9:2). To such a degree did the fellowship between God and his people determine the lives of the Israelites that the guilt of one who transgressed the covenantal stipulations extended beyond that person to his family and larger social units, and even to the entire nation of Israel (cf. Num. 16:31-32; Josh. 7:1; 2 Sam. 21:1-14; 24:10-17; 1 Chr. 21:12-17).

In the New Testament, the relationship between the Lord and his people is confirmed and strengthened by communion in Christ. Believers are called into fellowship with the Son (1 Cor. 1:9) and thereby also with one another (1 John 1:6-7). For believers this relationship culminates in the celebration of the LORD'S SUPPER, in which each person shares in the body and blood of the Lord in commemoration of his atoning death (1 Cor. 10:16; cf. RSV mg., "communion"). The Church is a token of Christ's fellowship with mankind on earth; Paul calls it the body of Christ, which exists through the fellowship of its members in the Holy Spirit (12:12-31; 2 Cor. 13:14; Eph. 4:4ff.; Phil. 2:1). In the fellowship of believers no distinction is recognized between Jew and Gentile, slave and free, male and female, for belief in Christ has made all one and equal in Christ (Gal. 3:28).

FERTILE CRESCENT.* Designation, coined by orientalist J. H. Breasted, for that semicircular strip of land which arches between Palestine and the Persian Gulf. Contained by the Taurus, Amanus, and Lebanon mountain ranges on the west and the Zagros range to the east, this region consists of plains and foothills relatively conducive to civilization and which contrast sharply with the nearby Arabian and Syrian deserts. Cradle of the Sumerian, Babylonian, Assyrian, and Palestinian civilizations, the Fertile Crescent also served as a landbridge for commerce and military activity between Egypt and the empires of the Tigris and Euphrates valleys.

FESTIVAL. See FEASTS.

FESTUS, PORCIUS [pôr′shəs fĕs′təs] (Gk. *Porkios Phēstos*).† The Roman procurator of Judea who succeeded Antonius Felix. According to Josephus (*Ant.* xx.8.9-11), his administration was more efficient and more sensitive to the Jewish constituents than that of his predecessor, and he succeeded in quelling at least temporarily the insurgent Sicarii (Gk. *sikárioi* "assassins"; from Lat. *sica* "dagger") who were robbing and murdering the populace (cf. Acts 21:38). He died in Palestine *ca.* A.D. 62 and was succeeded as procurator by Albinus.

Immediately upon assuming power at Caesarea, Festus concerned himself with the plight of Paul, who had already been imprisoned for two years under Felix (Acts 24:27). The Jewish authorities sought to have Paul brought before the Sanhedrin in Jerusalem, secretly plotting to have him murdered en route (25:2-3), but Festus shrewdly invited them to present their case upon his return to Caesarea (vv. 4-5, 7). Sensing the personal danger at hand, Paul rejected Festus' conciliatory proposal that he himself try the apostle at Jerusalem and instead requested as a Roman citizen a trial before Caesar (vv. 10-12). King Herod Agrippa II concurred with Festus that Paul was innocent of any capital crime (25:24-27; 26:31), but they were compelled to send him before Claudius (v. 32).

Festus' accession as procurator, regarded as an important key to determining New Testament chronology, nevertheless remains open to debate. Although Eusebius dates this event to A.D. 56 (*Chron.* ii), modern scholarship favors placing it in 60 (or perhaps late 59).

FIELD (Heb. *śāḏeh*; Gk. *agrós*).† That portion of the Israelite landscape not used for human habitation. Generally adjacent to the town or village with which it was allotted (cf. Lev. 25:31, 34; Num. 16:14; Josh. 15:18 par. Judg. 1:14; Josh. 21:12), such land might be distinguished as open (e.g., Lev. 14:53; 2 Sam. 11:11; Ezek. 29:5) or enclosed (e.g., Num. 22:23-24; Prov. 24:30-31). Fields might be cultivated (e.g., Exod. 23:16; Lev. 26:4; Ps. 107:37; John 4:35) or uncultivated (cf. Gen. 25:27; 2 Sam. 11:11; Ezek. 39:10), and might also be used as pastureland (e.g., Num. 22:4; Deut. 11:15; Luke 15:15). Frequent mention is made of the fauna which lived in these areas (e.g., 2 Sam. 17:8; Jer. 14:5; Ezek. 31:6).

In figurative usage, a field represents the entire world (Matt. 13:38), fertile ground for sowing the seeds of the kingdom of heaven (cf. vv. 24, 27, 31). The Corinthian church is depicted as a field which must be nurtured for spiritual growth (1 Cor. 2:9; 2 Cor. 10:15). John describes the present realization of the kingdom of God as "fields . . . already white for harvest" (John 4:35).

FIG TREE. A deciduous member of the mulberry family (*Ficus carica* L.), cultivated for its fruit.

The fig tree is native to the entire Near East and the Mediterranean region and grows exceptionally well along the hills and valleys of Palestine and Syria, particularly in the valley near Tiberias along the Sea of Galilee.

In the wild the fig tree is merely a shrub, but under cultivation it averages 5 m. (15 ft.) in height and sometimes grows to 9-12 m. (30-40 ft.) or more. The fig's branches, covered with a smooth bark, grow haphazardly from a bent trunk. The tree develops a close cover of broad, lobed leaves (cf. Gen. 3:7) which provide ample shade (cf. Mic. 4:4; Zech. 3:10); it can be impossible to see through the foliage, especially when the branches bend toward the ground under the weight of the leaves (cf. John 1:48, 50). Just before

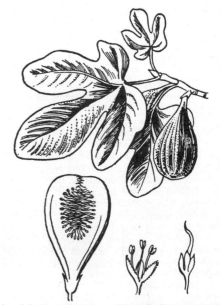

Leaf, fruit, and male and female flowers of the fig

the winter rainy season the fig sheds its leaves; new shoots sprout in March or April, signaling the coming of summer (Matt. 24:32). The petals of the long flower close upon the internal carpels, becoming fleshy and succulent and thus forming the oblong or pear-shaped fruit; technically, the real fruit is the pit rather than the edible pulp of the syconium. The wood of the tree is spongy and thus unsuitable for timber, but once the tree has ceased to be productive the wood might be used as firewood for domestic and sacrificial fires.

In Palestine the cultivation of fig trees was an ancient practice, common already in Canaanite times (cf. Num. 13:23). In that climate the tree produces fruit almost ten months of the year. In March or April the branches put forth new leaf buds. Most of the early green figs (Heb. *pag*; Cant. 2:13), which grow on the stock of the previous year's yield, drop when no more than 5 cm. (2 in.) long (cf. Rev. 6:13, Gk. *ólynthos* "winter fruit"; KJV "untimely figs"; NIV "late figs"); although they do not yet contain juice, they are gathered and eaten for lack of other fruit at that time of year. The remainder of this crop ripens in June for the first actual harvest; because of their juice, these "first-ripe figs" (Heb. *bikkûrâ*; JB, NIV "early figs") are much in demand (cf. Isa. 28:4; Jer. 24:2; Mic. 7:1). A second crop, grown from the new spring shoots, ripens for harvest in August; these "late figs" (Heb. *tᵉʾēnîm*) are the most desirable, full of juice and exceptionally sweet (cf. Judg. 9:11) — approximately 60 percent dextrose. After careful harvesting, lest the figs fall easily to the ground and bruise (cf. Nah. 3:12), the fruit may be collected in baskets (Jer. 24:1-2), ready to be eaten fresh, or dried and pressed into clumps or cakes (Heb. *dᵉḇēlâ*; 1 Sam. 30:12; 1 Chr. 12:40). Because of the fig's medicinal powers, it was applied in antiquity as a poultice for treating boils (2 Kgs. 20:7 par. Isa. 38:21).

As an important form of sustenance the fig tree was greatly honored among the ancient Israelites. Along with the olive tree and gravevine it symbolized the great abundance of the Promised Land (Deut. 8:8). To live under one's vine and fig tree meant, for the Hebrews, to enjoy ideal circumstances (e.g., 1 Kgs. 4:25; 2 Kgs. 18:31 par. Isa. 36:16; Mic. 4:4; Zech. 3:10). In prophecies of divine retribution for Israel's sins the blighted fig tree symbolized national peril (e.g., Jer. 5:17; Hos. 2:12; Joel 1:7, 12; Amos 4:9). In Jotham's parable denouncing Abimelech, the fig tree is too important to serve as king (Judg. 9:10-11). Jeremiah's vision of the baskets of figs (Jer. 24:1-10) distinguished between the exiles (the good figs) and those who remained in Palestine and Egypt (the bad figs). Jesus depicts God as a patient vinedresser in dealing with his people, a barren fig tree (Luke 13:6-9); an alternate interpretation is that Jesus is the vinedresser, interceding for his people against God's judgment. The difficult account of Jesus' cursing the barren fig tree may portray God's judgment on his stubborn people or their legalistic religious practices (Mark 11:13-14, 20-21 par. Matt. 21:18-21).

See also SYCAMORE.

FINGER (Heb. *'eṣbaʿ, qōṭen*; Gk. *dáktylos*).† In the Bible the finger is generally portrayed as an instrument of creativity or productivity (e.g., Isa. 2:8; 17:8; Matt. 23:4; Luke 11:46), often the equivalent of the hand (cf. 59:1, 3). Used anthropomorphically, it represents divine power (e.g., Exod. 8:19; 31:18; Ps. 8:3; cf. Luke 11:20).

In various offerings, the priest was to sprinkle or smear the sacrificial blood on the horns of the altar (e.g., Exod. 29:12; Lev. 4:25), on the front of the mercy seat (16:14), or in front of the tent of meeting (Num. 19:4); in cleansing lepers, the high priest was specifically instructed to use the right finger (Lev. 14:16, 27). The Hebrews were to bind the Pentateuchal laws in phylacteries on their fingers (Prov. 7:3).

As a unit of measure the finger is the twenty-fourth part of a cubit or 1.85 cm. (.73 in.; 1 Kgs. 7:15; RSV; Jer. 52:21). See WEIGHTS AND MEASURES.

FIR TREE. See CYPRESS.

FIRE (Heb. *'ēš*; Gk. *pýr*).*

I. Old Testament

The ancient Hebrews used fire for heat to cook, to make metal malleable (Exod. 32:24), to offer sacrifices (e.g., Gen. 22:6; Lev. 1:17), to dispose of contaminated clothing (Lev. 13:52, 55, 57), and as an effective weapon in war (e.g., Num. 31:10; Josh. 8:8, 19; Judg. 9:49). Frequently fire symbolized a theophany or some other divine activity.

A. Theophany. Fire was one of the means through which Yahweh revealed himself or his will to Israel (cf. Deut. 5:24-26). It was in fire that he concluded a covenant with Abraham (Gen. 15:17), called Moses to be the leader of his people (Exod. 3:2, "burning bush"), showed Israel his protective presence in the wilderness (Exod. 13:21-22; 14:24; 40:38, "pillar of fire"; cf. Num. 14:14), and impressed upon his chosen

people the gravity of his commandments (Exod. 19:18 [cf. 24:17, "devouring fire"]; Deut. 4:33; 5:42). During the reign of King Ahab (*ca.* 860 B.C.), Elijah asked for proof that God was more powerful than Baal, and God answered with fire that consumed the prophet's sacrifice (1 Kgs. 18:24, 38; but cf. 19:11-12, where God does not appear to him in fire but, instead, in a "small voice"). God similarly confirmed human actions at the installation service of Aaron as high priest (Lev. 9:24) and at the dedication of the temple by King Solomon (2 Chr. 7:1).

B. Divine Activity. At times Yahweh used fire to punish people (cf. Lev. 20:14). The inhabitants of Sodom and Gomorrah were burned for their wickedness (Gen. 19:24), the two eldest sons of Aaron for offering "unholy fire" to the Lord (Lev. 10:1-2; cf. Num. 3:4; 26:61), Ahaziah's soldiers for attempting to capture Elijah (2 Kgs. 1:10-12), and the inhabitants of Jerusalem for their idolatry (Jer. 4:4; 17:24). Achan was stoned and burned for taking from among the spoil of Jericho (Josh. 7:15, 20-25). Using the standard ancient Near Eastern image of the deity as surrounded by a fiery aura (Ps. 50:3; *see A* above), the Old Testament writers describe the Lord's wrath as consuming his enemies and punishing his rebellious people (e.g., Pss. 78:21; 97:3; Isa. 30:27; 66:15-16; Jer. 4:4).

While fire quite naturally represents God's anger (Mal. 4:1), it also, at times, manifests his deep love and concern. God uses fire to purify the recalcitrant (3:2; cf. Num. 31:23) and test the faithful (Ps. 66:10-12); to protect his prophet Elisha (2 Kgs. 6:17) and Jerusalem (Zech. 2:5); to carry Elijah to heaven (2 Kgs. 2:11, "chariots of fire"), and to show his perpetual presence with his people (Lev. 6:9, 12-13, in the fire of the burnt offering).

For child sacrifice by fire, *see* SACRIFICES AND OFFERINGS.

II. New Testament

Fire in the New Testament retains the symbolic connotations of theophany (Rev. 1:14; 2:18, "eyes of fire"; cf. 19:12; Heb. 12:29) and judgment. Luke demonstrates familiarity with Moses' call from the "burning bush" (Acts 7:30) and Elijah's request for fire from heaven (Luke 9:54); he observes that during the winter fire provided warmth for Peter (22:55; cf. Mark 14:54) and others (Acts 28:2).

An important emphasis is the eschatological fire as a mode of punishment for the wicked (Matt. 13:40; vv. 42, 50, "furnace of fire"; 18:8-9; 25:41, "eternal fire"; cf. Rev. 20:9-10, 14-15; 21:8), which Luke relates to the burning of Sodom and Gomorrah (Luke 17:29-30). As in the Old Testament, the fire used on the Day of the Lord symbolizes testing, or purifying, as well as punishment. To the Corinthians Paul writes that the believer's spiritual "foundation" would be tested by fire to reveal the endurance of his faith and love (1 Cor. 3:13-15). Luke interprets the outpouring of the Holy Spirit "in the last days" as a sign of God's presence (Acts 2:3, tongues of fire; cf. Matt. 3:11 par. Luke 3:16 for baptism with fire), but also as a sign of judgment (Acts 2:19; cf. Joel 2:30). The author of 2 Peter envisions the Day of the Lord as featuring destruction by fire, rather than water as during the Flood (2 Pet. 3:6-7).

FIRKIN [fûr′kĭn] (Gk. *metrētḗs*). A liquid measure (John 2:6, KJV), approximately equivalent to 38 l. (10 gal.; thus RSV, JB, NIV "twenty or thirty gallons").

FIRMAMENT (Heb. *rāqîaʿ*; Vulg. Lat. *firmamentum*, from LXX Gk. *steréōma* "foundation"). The expanse of sky or heaven (Gen. 1:8) separating the water below (rivers, seas, subterranean waters) from the waters above (precipitation). In ancient Israelite cosmogony the firmament may have been viewed as a dome or curtain (cf. Ps. 104:2) of beaten metal (cf. Heb. *rqʿ* "beat out"; Job 37:18) from which were suspended the stars and planets (Gen. 1:14-17). Rain and other heavenly blessings could pour down upon the earth through windows in the firmament (7:11; 2 Kgs. 7:2; Ps. 78:23-24).

FIRSTBORN (Heb. *beḵôr*; Gk. *prōtótokos*).† The first male offspring of both humans and animals. In English translations the firstborn of animals are often called "firstlings" (e.g., Gen. 4:4; Exod. 13:12-13). See FIRSTFRUITS.

I. Old Testament

With regard to humans, the firstborn usually designates the eldest son of the father. Perhaps stemming from an ancient notion that the firstborn son shared more closely the father's qualities (cf. Gen. 49:3; Deut. 21:17; RSV "first issue of his strength"; NJV "first fruit of his vigor"; Heb. *rēʾšîṯ ʾōnô*), he was specified to succeed the father as male head of the household and larger social units (e.g., Gen. 43:33; Deut. 21:17). The firstborn was accorded greater authority and respect (Gen. 27:19, 37; 37:22) and apparently granted a larger inheritance (Deut. 21:17). Although the rights of the eldest son were protected by law, particularly with regard to polygynous families (vv. 15-17), abundant evidence indicates that fathers could overlook the established patterns (e.g., Gen. 48:17-19; 1 Kgs. 2:15; 1 Chr. 26:10; 28:4). Such flexibility, perhaps engendered by the highly composite nature of ancient Israelite society, may account for instances in which firstborn status is reckoned through the mother (e.g., Deut. 25:6; 1 Chr. 2:50; cf. Heb. *peṭer rāḥam* "the one which opens [the womb]," Exod. 13:2, 12, 15; Ezek. 20:26).

References to the firstborn daughter (Heb. *beḵîrâ*) generally indicate the elder female offspring (e.g., Gen. 19:31, 33, 37; 29:26; 1 Sam. 14:49) and need not imply the eldest child. Although inferior in rank to all male siblings (cf. Gen. 36:22; 1 Sam. 14:49), the elder daughter might receive an inheritance in the absence of brothers (cf. Num. 26:33; 27:1-11).

From the very formative stages of Israel's existence the firstborn of both humans and animals were regarded as the property of God (Exod. 22:29-30; cf. Gen. 4:4). This was later reinterpreted in terms of the Passover events, whereby the firstborn Israelite males were spared during the final plague against Egypt (Exod. 13:2, 12-13; cf. Heb. 11:28).

Firstlings of domestic animals, always reckoned through the mother, were to be offered as sacrifices, perhaps originally in conjunction with the spring fertility rite which was the predecessor of Passover (Exod. 34:19). Bulls and other clean animals were to be sacrificed

when they were eight days old (22:30); their blood was to be sprinkled on the altar, their fat burned, and the flesh given to the priests for food (Num. 18:17-18). In later interpretation the flesh of these firstlings of flock and herd was to be shared by the Israelites themselves in a sacrificial meal at the central sanctuary (Deut. 15:20). (The postexilic temple reconstructed by Zerubbabel included on the south side of the court a "gate of the firstlings" through which these animals were brought to be sacrificed.) Such animals were not to be shorn and were to do no work (v. 19). Blemished animals could not be sacrificed but were to be eaten by the Israelites within their towns; ceremonial cleanness was not required for such occasions, but the blood of the animal was to be poured on the ground (vv. 21-23). A firstling ass or other unclean animal could not be sacrificed; the owner was either to redeem it (Heb. *pāḏâ*) by substituting a clean animal for sacrifice (e.g., a lamb for an ass) or to break its neck (Exod. 13:13; 34:20; Num. 18:15). Later, a monetary fee was substituted for the benefit of the sanctuary. The firstling of an unclean animal was to be redeemed at one-fifth more than the value of the animal as assessed by the priest; if not redeemed, the animal was sold and the money given to the sanctuary (Lev. 27:11-13, 27).

Although the precise manner in which the early Hebrews were to offer their firstborn sons to God is not clear, scholars have not ruled out the possibility of human sacrifice (cf. Gen. 22); indeed, the practice does seem to have been employed during the Monarchy (1 Kgs. 16:34; 2 Kgs. 3:27; cf. Mic. 6:7). Pentateuchal legislation clearly specifies that the firstborn male be redeemed (Exod. 13:11-16; 34:20), either through a substitutionary sacrifice (cf. Gen. 22:13) or five shekels of silver (Num. 18:16), paid when the child was thirty days old (3:46-48; cf. Lev. 27:6). The designation of the Levites as a substitute for the firstborn of Israel (Num. 3:11-13, 40-51) suggests that prior to the establishment of the priesthood firstborn sons from all tribes had been dedicated to such service.

In figurative usage Israel enjoys firstborn status in God's sight (Exod. 4:22; Jer. 31:9). The messianic deliverer, understood as David's successor (Ps. 89:27), is depicted as God's firstborn. The term may also connote superlative quality or status (e.g., "firstborn of death," Job 18:13; Isa. 14:30; NIV "poorest of the poor").

II. New Testament

Jesus is described as the firstborn son of Mary (Luke 2:7; cf. Matt. 1:25, KJV). Roman Catholic and many conservative Protestant scholars interpret Gk. *prōtótokos* here in the sense of "only," contending that Jesus had no younger siblings. Others regard the term as implying status as well as indicating order of birth. It is in this latter, more common sense that Jesus is frequently described as firstborn: exalted and glorified, enjoying a special relationship with God (Heb. 1:6), supreme over all creation (Col. 1:15, 18), founder and head of the Church (v. 18; Rom. 8:29), and, as victor over death, the initiator of new life (Col. 1:18; Rev. 1:5).

At Heb. 12:23 those who have died in the faith are described as "the assembly of the firstborn who are enrolled in heaven"; cf. KJV, JB).

FIRSTFRUITS (Heb. *bikkûrîm, rēʾšît*; Gk. *aparchḗ*).
The first crop which the soil yields in each growing
season.

To acknowledge that all which they received had
come from the Lord, its creator and thus master or
owner (cf. Exod. 13:2; *see* FIRSTBORN), and to guarantee further productivity (cf. Lev. 19:25; Prov. 3:10),
the Israelites were directed to offer the very first
portions (Heb. *rēʾšît bikkûrēʾ*; Exod. 23:19; 34:26; cf.
Lev. 23:10; Num. 18:13) — or perhaps a selection of
the very best (cf. v. 12) — as soon as they were
harvested or processed (Exod. 22:29; cf. 2 Chr. 31:5).
They could partake of nothing until these offerings
had been made (cf. Lev. 23:14). Such offerings might
consist of produce directly from the field, including
cereal, grapes, or fruit, or prepared substances, including grain, wine, oil, and honey. (In some passages
Heb. *bikkûrîm* specifies natural produce and *rēʾšît*
that which has been processed; cf. Num. 18:12-13;
2 Chr. 31:5). Honey and leavening might be added
to make cakes of the coarse meal (Num. 15:20; cf.
Neh. 10:37; Ezek. 44:30; KJV, JB, NJV "dough")
or loaves of the fine flour (Lev. 23:17; cf. 2:11-12).
The cereal offering of firstfruits was made with fresh
kernels of grain, crushed and parched by fire (vv.
14-16). When the Israelites planted fruit trees, they
were forbidden to eat the yield of the first three years.
The harvest of the fourth year was considered holy
and was offered in the sanctuary as praise to the Lord
and then eaten by the priests. Only from the fifth year
could the harvest be eaten by all (19:23-25).

Offerings of firstfruits were made also on behalf
of the entire nation during the annual pilgrim festivals.
On the second day (the day following the Sabbath) of
the Feast of Unleavened Bread, which came to be
incorporated into the Passover celebration, a sheaf of
the firstfruits of the barley harvest was brought to the
priest for a wave offering (Lev. 23:9-14). Pentecost,
also called the Feast of Firstfruits (Exod. 34:22; cf.
Num. 28:26) and the Feast of Harvest (Exod. 23:16)
or Weeks, was celebrated fifty days later at the time
of the wheat harvest. Baskets of produce were to be
placed before the altar (Deut. 26:2, 4; cf. Lev. 23:11ff.)
in commemoration of the deliverance from Egyptian
bondage and the gift of the promised land (Deut.
26:5-10). In addition, other offerings were made at
both of these festivals (Lev. 23:9-21).

Specific portions of the offerings of firstfruits are
not recorded until rabbinic times. The Old Testament
does indicate, however, that in addition to the portion
of the offering which was to be burned as a memorial
(cf. Lev. 2:8-10, 16) this produce was to be given for
support of the priests (Deut. 18:4; Ezek. 44:30); only
those of the priestly households who were ceremonially
clean could eat these portions (Num. 18:11). Chambers
in the second (postexilic) temple were used to store
these gifts (Neh. 10:37, 39; 12:44; 13:5; cf. Mal. 3:10).
Whether the tithe used for the less fortunate among
the populace developed from this practice remains
open to debate.

At Jer. 2:3 Israel is portrayed as set apart for God's
own use, "the firstfruits of his harvest."

In the New Testament the concept of firstfruits
most often appears metaphorically. Paul refers in this
way to the earliest believers in Christ (Rom. 16:5;

1 Cor. 16:15, KJV, JB; RSV, NIV "first converts"),
as do James (Jas. 1:18) and John (Rev. 14:4). In
assuring the Romans that God had not rejected them,
Paul likens them to the dough from which an offering
of firstfruits is made: as the offering is holy, so is
the entire loaf; as the patriarchs had been consecrated,
so are their descendants (Rom. 16:11). At Rom. 8:23,
the term refers to the Holy Spirit which has already
been experienced, the harbinger of the promised redemption. Firstfruits is also applied to Christ himself
as the first to be raised from the dead (1 Cor. 15:20, 23).

FIRSTLING. *See* FIRSTBORN.

FISH (Heb. *dāg, dāgâ*; Gk. *ichthýs*). In biblical usage,
all aquatic animals; no attempt is made to distinguish
species other than the designation of those which have
scales and fins as clean and those without as unclean
(Lev. 11:9-12; Deut. 14:9-10). In the first creation
account fish apparently include, other than the great
sea monsters, "every living thing that moves" in the
water (Gen. 1:21, 28; B. Vawter, *On Genesis* [Garden
City: 1977], pp. 48-49, "swimming creatures"; cf.
Lev. 11:9-10).

Although pools may have been stocked with fish at
Jerusalem and elsewhere in Palestine, the most fertile
habitats for freshwater fish were the Sea of Galilee
and the Jordan river with its tributaries, notably the
Jabbok. Lake Huleh and the swamps to its south were
exceptional breeding grounds; dense papyrus growth
impeded human efforts to catch fish there, and the
abundant mosquitos and other insects provided ample
food for the fish.

Many species common to Palestine are related to
those of the Nile river and northeastern Africa. The
Sea of Galilee contains several species of the family
Cichlidae, with their comblike backfins, such as the
small, brightly colored chromides (e.g., *Chromis
nilotica* Hasselquist) and the Tilapia (e.g., *Tilapia
nilotica* L.) or "St. Peter's fish." The carp family
(*Cyprinidae*) is also amply represented, particularly
with species of barbel (*Barbus*), a delectable fish which
can reach a length of 40-50 cm. (18-20 in.). The
Alburnus sellah of this family — a little fish 12 cm.
(5 in.) long with silver-white scales and resembling
the sardine — is rare here during most of the year,
but appears near the shore in countless swarms from
December to April. Of the catfish family (*Siluridae*),
scavengers characterized by long barbels or feelers
around the mouth, one large species is found in the
Sea of Galilee — the *Clarias macracanthus* Gunth.,
which can reach 1.5 m. (5 ft.) in length and weigh
45 kg. (11 lb.); because of air chambers above the
gills it is able to glide on land in search of food.
One species of eel (*Anguilla vulgaris*) is found near
the shore and in the nearby tributaries. Both the catfish
and the eel were considered unclean animals.

The fish of the lower course of the Jordan and its
tributaries differ little from those of the Sea of Galilee.
The Jordan's strong current carries many fish to the
Dead Sea, where they die and become prey for the
piscivorous birds of the area. No fish can survive in
the Dead Sea itself (cf. Ezek. 47:7-10), but in the
salt springs and brackish brooks which border it are a
variety of small fish.

Fish is mentioned as a part of the Israelite diet as early as the sojourn in Egypt (Num. 11:5, 22), but more commonly in postexilic (cf. Neh. 13:16) and New Testament times (e.g., Matt. 14:17 par.; 15:36; Luke 24:42; John 21:9-13).

In a figurative sense, mankind's fate is that of fish caught in a net (Eccl. 9:12; Hab. 1:14). It is a great fish which swallows Jonah and thus saves from the tempest (Jonah 1:17). In response to questions concerning the temple tax, Jesus instructs Peter that the first fish he shall catch will bear in its mouth a coin to be used as their payment (Matt. 17:27).

In the early Church the fish was a symbol of Christianity. The letters of Gk. *ichthýs* "fish" are an acronym for the confession *Iēsous Christós Theoú Huiós Sōtér* "Jesus Christ, Son of God, Savior."

FISH GATE (Heb. *ša'ar haddāgîm*).† A gate in the northern wall of Jerusalem, presumably named because of its proximity to the fish markets (cf. Neh. 13:16). Manasseh reinforced it early in the seventh century B.C. by an outer wall protecting the city of David west of Gihon and encircling the Ophel ridge (2 Chr. 33:14). Zephaniah, who prophesied early in Josiah's reign (*ca.* 640), mentions it in association with the Second Quarter or Mishneh (Zeph. 1:10). Situated west of the tower of Hananel, it was included in Nehemiah's postexilic reconstruction of the city walls (Neh. 3:3; 12:39).

Some scholars would identify the Fish Gate with the Gate of Ephraim, which led north to the territory of the Ephraimites (cf. Zech. 14:10, "former gate").

Christian tradition long held that Simon of Cyrene entered Jerusalem through the Fish Gate before Roman soldiers enlisted him to carry Jesus' cross (Mark 15:21; Luke 23:26). However, this would have been possible only if Pilate's hall of judgment (Praetorium) had been located within the fortress Antonia.

FISHING. Although fish was apparently part of the Israelite diet at least as early as their Egyptian sojourn (Num. 11:5, 22), references to fishing as either a commercial activity or a means of subsistence are scanty for the Old Testament period. Because for most of this time the Mediterranean coast was controlled by the Philistines and Phoenicians, the Israelites depended on foreign trade for fish (Neh. 13:16; *see* FISH GATE). In New Testament times extensive commercial fishing was conducted on the Sea of Galilee by fishermen organized in guilds (cf. Luke 5:7, 10).

From the earliest times fish were caught using a hook of bone, iron, or simply a thorn attached to a line which was held by hand rather than affixed to a rod (Job 41:1-2; Isa. 19:8; Amos 4:2; Hab. 1:15). Larger fish were caught by means of a spear or harpoon (Job 41:7). The most extensive references, however, are to fishing nets, of which there appear to have been three types. The simplest was a general-purpose net (Heb. *mᵉṣôḏâ*; Gk. *amphíblēstron*) similar to that used in hunting (cf. Heb. *rešeṭ*). Perhaps 4 m. (13 ft.) in diameter and rimmed with stones to make it sink quickly, this throwing net could be used from land or a boat or while standing in the water (Eccl. 9:12; Matt. 4:18; Mark 1:16); hung over the arm until ready, the net was thrown in a wide arc over the fish as

spotted and thus could only be used in the daytime. A long dragnet (Heb. *miḵmereṭ*, *miḵmōreṭ*; Gk. *sagénē*), perhaps 200-250 m. (656-820 ft.) long and 5 m. (16 ft.) wide with heavy weights on one side and floats on the other, could be suspended between two boats and then drawn to shore by ropes (Isa. 19:8; Hab. 1:15-16; RSV "seine"; Matt. 13:47-48); this net was most effective on a slowly sloping sandy shore. Most complex was a series of parallel nets (Heb. *ḥerem*; Gk. *díktyon*) of increasingly narrower mesh (Hab. 1:15-17; Matt. 4:20; Mark 1:18; Luke 5:2, 4-7). Suspended between boats like a seine, it captured fish driven into it by a third craft; used most successfully in deep water near shore (John 21:8, 11), the width of the mesh assured that only large fish would be snared and that smaller ones would escape.

Once the haul was brought to shore, the fish would be sorted as to size and use, and unclean varieties would be discarded (Matt. 13:48). The fish were then dried or salted and transported to market in baskets (Neh. 13:16).

The process of fishing is used figuratively in the prophecy of Ezekiel (Ezek. 26:5, 14; 47:9-10) and in the Gospels (Matt. 13:47-48). A number of Jesus' miracles involved fishing (Luke 5:1-11; John 21:1-8; cf. Matt. 14:13-21 par.). The disciples, many of whom were fishermen by trade, were called to be "fishers of men" (Matt. 4:18-19; Mark 1:16-17; Luke 5:2, 10).

FLAX (Heb. *pešeṭ*, *pištâ*; cf. Akk. *pištu*; Gk. *línon*). An annual herb (*Linum usitatissumum* L.) with lance-shaped leaves spread along a sturdy stem and five-petal blue or white flowers almost 1.5 cm. (.6 in.) long. When dried and combed, the stalks yield linen fibers; the seeds can be crushed to make linseed oil. Many wild species of flax can be found as spring flowers in fallow fields and uncultivated soil.

Flax has been cultivated since ancient times, especially in Egypt along the Nile (Exod. 9:31; Isa. 19:9). From there it was exported to Tyre (Ezek. 27:7), Palestine (Prov. 7:16), and other countries. In Palestine it was cultivated only in those areas with sufficient rainfall or adequate irrigation — near Jericho (Josh. 2:6) or along the coastal plain (1 Chr. 4:21). Flax grown for fiber was sown much closer together than wheat to prevent branching and flowering.

After it was spun into yarn, flax was woven into linen cloth (Prov. 31:13, 24). The priests were usually required to wear linen clothes (Exod. 28:39; Lev. 6:10; cf. Ezek. 44:17). The high priest wore a woolen overgarment, except on the Day of Atonement, when he, too, was dressed entirely in linen (Lev. 16:4, 23). (Linen garments were not to be worn with those of material made from fur or skin [Lev. 19:19; Deut. 22:11].) From the linen taken from Egypt the Jews made curtains for the tabernacle (Exod. 26:1), the veil separating the sanctum sanctorum from the rest of the tabernacle (v. 31), and the curtain over the entrance (v. 36). All parts were made of fine "twined" linen, i.e., several fibers woven into one cord, an art in which the Egyptians had become especially skilled.

Linen clothing was considered a mark of quality and an evidence of wealth (Judg. 14:12; 2 Sam. 6:14; Luke 16:19). The Israelites wrapped it around their dead (Matt. 27:59). It could be made into strong cords (Judg. 15:14); and, because flax was extremely flammable (cf. Judg. 16:9; Isa. 1:31; RSV "tow"), the short, tangled fibers were used as wicks for lamps (42:3; KJV "smoking flax"; Matt. 12:20).

FLEA (Heb. *parʿōš*). A wingless, parasitic insect of the order Siphonaptera whose mouth is particularly adapted for piercing the skin and sucking blood. Their eggs are deposited in the hair or home of the host animal, and the larvae thrive in dry, sandy soil such as that of Palestine. After sparing Saul's life, the rebel David deprecates himself as a minute flea on the carcass of a dead dog (1 Sam. 24:14).

FLESH.†

I. Old Testament

The most common Hebrew word for flesh is *bāśār* (cf. Ugar. *bśr*; OSA *bśr*); less frequent is Heb. *šeʾēr*, which has been linked to *šʾr* "remnant." Flesh refers first of all to the musculature of a human being or animal (Deut. 14:8) or to the skin that covers it (Gen. 2:21; 17:11, 14; Deut. 14:8; 2 Kgs. 5:14). To a lesser degree it signifies the entire person or those with whom one shares the circumstances of life (e.g., Isa. 58:7) and, by extension, people in general (Isa. 40:5; NIV "mankind"). At Gen. 2:23 Adam calls Eve "flesh of my flesh," signifying both kinship and parity.

The Mosaic law stipulated that the Hebrews should sacrifice to God only the flesh, or the meat, of clean animals (*see* SACRIFICES AND OFFERINGS). They were permitted to eat the meat only of clean animals (Lev. 11:1-3; but cf. Deut. 12:15). In a theological context, human beings are described as frail creatures, mere flesh, in comparison to their majestic Creator; Isaiah compares Israel to a sick man wasting away (Isa. 10:18) and contrasts the flesh of the Egyptians to the spirit of God (31:3). Mankind is said to be finite and mortal (40:6-7) and to incline toward sin; thus the psalmist considers them "but flesh," ineffectual and ephemeral (Ps. 78:39). But Ezekiel prophesied that Israel's "heart of stone," its sinful and rebellious nature, would be removed from the "flesh," its personality, and would be replaced by a more malleable heart of flesh that is willing to turn to God's ways (Ezek. 11:19-20; 36:26-27).

II. New Testament

Gk. *sárx,* the word most often rendered "flesh" in the New Testament, has the same range of meaning as the Old Testament Heb. *bāśār* (which it translates in the LXX). Paul also uses Gk. *kréas* in reference to the meat of sacrificial animals (1 Cor. 8:13; cf. Rom. 14:21).

Flesh, the New Testament reiterates, is the physical body (Rev. 17:16), containing such organs as the sexual ones, which some mutilate in the interests of the Old Testament law but in violation of the New Testament spiritual commandments and without respect for what God has created (Phil. 3:2; cf. Gal. 6:13). The "thorn in the flesh" (2 Cor. 12:7) may be a physical ailment with which Paul was afflicted and attributed to his need for humility. According to Acts 2:17, a quotation from Joel 2:28, in the last days God will pour his Spirit on "all flesh" — that is, his spirit will be infused among all individuals. The same notion of human totality and wholeness is expressed at 1 Cor. 6:16, where Paul emphasizes the physical unity between a man and a woman; he is not oblivious, of course, to the wider dimensions of such a relationship (cf. Gen. 2:24; Matt. 19:5 par.).

In the book of Romans, Paul makes two important theological observations on the meaning of flesh. At 7:18, 25 he concludes that his flesh, i.e., he himself (NIV "sinful nature"; JB "unspiritual self"), lacks ethical and spiritual goodness and is subject to sin. He later contrasts the lifestyles of the unregenerate and the believers, explaining that the former, as "flesh," displease God (8:8) and that the latter, as "spirit" (v. 5), are in harmony with God. Having "mortified" the deeds of the flesh (vv. 9, 13), the Roman Christians are urged to exemplify a life "in the Spirit."

John agrees with Paul's interpretation of the distinction between unregenerate and regenerate walks of life; at John 3:6ff. he records Jesus' reminder to Nicodemus that spiritual rebirth must succeed physical birth. Because John seeks to combat an incipient form of Gnosticism that denies Christ's incarnation, the apostle asserts that the eternal Son of God became "flesh" (1:14), i.e., became a human being, and that his sacrifice ("flesh") would nourish all who would acknowledge him (6:51ff.), either through participation in the Lord's Supper or by taking Christ into their innermost being (cf. vv. 56-58).

FLINT (Heb. *ḥallāmîš, ṣōr*). A hard yet impure form of quartz, blackish-gray in color, which is found frequently in Palestine's limestone. Flint breaks naturally into sharp-edged pieces and in antiquity was used for drilling, chiseling, and cutting (Exod. 4:25; Josh. 5:23). Though flint knives belonged to the Chalcolithic period, apparently they were used for circumcision during the Bronze Age — the period of the Exodus from Egypt and the Israelites' entrance into Canaan.

Used figuratively, the hardness of flint serves to describe horses' hooves (Isa. 5:28) as well as the confidence of the Servant of God (50:7). The psalmist alludes to the miracle in the wilderness whereby God turned flint into a pool of water (Ps. 114:8; cf. Deut. 8:15).

FLOCK, TOWER OF THE. *See* EDER 4.

FLOOD.† An Old Testament act of divine judgment wrought against human sin but manifesting God's saving grace in his protection of Noah and his extended family (Gen. 6:5–8:22).

I. Terminology

Heb. *mabbûl,* rendered "flood," may derive from a word meaning a heavenly store of water jars and thus to the heavenly waters; at Ps. 29:10 the term designates the waters above the firmament (Gen. 6:7). The New Testament term is Gk. *kataklysmós* "inundation" (Matt. 24:38-39; Luke 17:27; 2 Pet. 2:5).

II. Genesis Account

Grieved by rampant sin among mankind (Gen. 6:5-7, 11), God decides to destroy his creation. Relating his intentions to Noah, described as the only righteous person alive (vv. 9, 13), God charges him to build an ark, a large sea-going vessel, to provide shelter and a means of escape from the deluge for himself, his family, and the animals (vv. 18-21; 7:2-3). Noah constructs and completes the ark according to divinely given specifications, and at last enters the ark together with his family; God "shut him in" after the animals had entered (6:22–7:16). Next the waters above the firmament ("the windows of the heavens") and below the earth (the "fountains of the great deep") cause a flood that in forty days reaches a depth of 15 cubits (about 7.5 m. [25 ft.]) higher than the "high mountains" (7:20) and destroys all animals and humans (vv. 21-23).

After extinguishing sinful mankind in this way, God causes the rain to stop and the floodwaters to recede. Eventually the ark comes to rest on the mountains of Ararat (vv. 1-5). Forty days later Noah sends out a raven and a dove; when the dove does not return the third time it is sent out, Noah knows that the earth has dried up (v. 13) and that it is safe to exit the ark (vv. 15-19). The narrative concludes with Noah's sacrifice and God's covenant with him (8:20–9:17).

III. Literary Character

Although in its present form the narrative represents a complete unit, a number of scholars have identified it as the compilation of two accounts, representing the Yahwistic (J) and Priestly (P) sources. In addition to such distinctions as use of the divine name ("Lord," Gen. 6:5-8; JB "Yahweh"; "God," vv. 9-13), the terms "flood" and "waters of the flood" (but cf. 9:11 where both occur), figures for the duration of the deluge (forty days and forty nights, e.g., 7:4; more than one year, vv. 11, 24; 8:3-5, 14), number of animals taken (6:19-20; 7:2-3), and causes of the Flood (rainfall, v. 4; water from above and below, v. 11), nearly every aspect of the account is recorded in duplicate. Those who hold a more orthodox view of the narrative's composition accept the differences as a later adaptation of the original narrative intended to underscore the theological significance of the events.

IV. Flood Traditions

Accounts of a universal flood exist in the traditions of nearly every civilization throughout the world, both ancient and modern. While more conservative interpreters take these traditions as proof of a single, historical flood recorded in the Bible, others view them as local traditions, often having developed independently. Anthropologists have noted that in many instances a great flood or other massive destruction serves to explain a discontinuity between documented or otherwise verifiable genealogies and more distant eponymous ancestors.

Of particular interest to biblical studies are three Mesopotamian cuneiform flood stories. The oldest is a Sumerian version (ANET, pp. 42-44), discovered in fragmentary form at Nippur, wherein the pious king Ziusudra responds to the gods' decision to destroy by flood "the seed of mankind"; he constructs a huge boat which bears him afloat for seven days and nights, after which he sacrifices to the gods and is granted eternal life in the land of Dilmun. A well-preserved version survives in Tablet 11 of the Sumerian Gilgamesh Epic (ANET, pp. 93-97). Here, Utnapishtim "the Faraway" aids the hero Gilgamesh in his quest for immortality by relating his own experiences: having been warned by the god Ea of the divine assembly's plan to destroy the world, he constructs a massive ship in which he, his family, and representatives of the living species as well as human craftsmen ride out the deluge, coming to rest on Mt. Niṣir; when the gods learn of the survivors, they dispute the wisdom of the flood as punishment and grant Utnapishtim and his wife immortality while relegating them to a land far distant from other mortals. Fragments of an Old Babylonian story (ANET, pp. 104-6) also survive, partially preserved in an Assyrian version, in which the gods send a series of plagues climaxed by a flood as punishment upon mankind, whose clamor has disturbed the gods' sleep; the protagonist is Atraḥasis ("the exceptionally wise," an epithet of the Sumerian Utnapishtim), who survives the flood much as Noah and the other heroes and provides the bridge to a new, purified creation.

Despite great similarities between these cuneiform versions and the account of the Flood in Genesis, no direct literary continuity can be demonstrated. While many of the details may have been transmitted through cultural contacts in the ancient Near East or as part of the heritage of Hebrews of Mesopotamian origin, differences in motives for and interpretation of the events in the respective accounts preclude any extensive literary dependence.

V. Scientific Issues

When the Flood Narrative is examined in terms of scientific, geological data, a number of problems arise such as the duration, extent, and date of the events recorded. For example, geological evidence for a universal flood would necessitate a date long before historical times, and archaeological remains indicate no significant discontinuity caused by local floods after the fifth millennium B.C. in Mesopotamia and the eighth millennium in Palestine. Ultraconservative "flood geologists" contend that all existing geological formations are the result of the biblical flood. Moreover, numerous explorers and archaeologists have attempted to find the remains of Noah's ark on the Ağri Dağ, the highest mountain of the Ararat range (cf. Gen. 8:4, "mountains of Ararat"). No prospects can be seen for a resolution of these matters as interpreted variously as literal fact or theological application of historical or legendary narrative.

VI. Theological Significance

The Genesis Flood Narrative illustrates divine judgment upon human sin as well as divine mercy toward the righteous. Unlike the gods of Mesopotamian flood stories, the Lord acts neither with irrational anger nor capriciously. Divine providence and grace are also evident in God's preservation of Noah's family and the reestablishment through them of all creation. The covenant with Noah, and thus with purified creation, represents God's promise to mankind never again to disrupt the natural order (Gen. 9:1-17; cf. 8:21-22; cf. also Isa. 54:9); included are stipulations that mankind exercise benevolent stewardship over all creation (Gen. 9:1-7; cf. 1:28-30).

In apocryphal or deuterocanonical literature, the

Flood traditions: a tablet of a Babylonian version of the Sumerian Gilgamesh Epic (by courtesy of the Trustees of the British Museum)

Flood is treated as legend (Wis. 14:6; Sir. 16:7; cf. Gen. 6:1-4). Noah is included among the ancient heroes (Sir. 44:17-18), and is portrayed as a righteous man whose wisdom spared him from destruction (Wis. 10:4).

The New Testament indicates that God's judgment was imposed only after great divine restraint (1 Pet. 3:20). Noah was a great herald of righteousness (2 Pet. 2:5), whose faith brought him through the catastrophe (Heb. 11:7). The return of the Son of Man at the end of the age is compared to the suddenness of the Flood as it swept away Noah's unwary contemporaries (Matt. 24:37-39 par. Luke 17:26-27). Baptism is likened to the Flood: the waters destroy sin and cleanse mankind (1 Pet. 3:20-21).

Bibliography. A. Heidel, *The Gilgamesh Epic and Old Testament Parallels,* 2nd ed. (Chicago: 1963);

J. C. Whitcomb and H. M. Morris, *The Genesis Flood: The Biblical Record and Its Scientific Implications* (Philadelphia: 1961).

FLOUR.† Meal ground from the inner kernels of cereal grains (cf. Deut. 32:14; Ps. 81:16, "the finest of the wheat"; KJV "kidney fat of wheat"). That of ordinary use (Heb. *qemaḥ*) was produced by rubbing grains between stones and sifting off the larger pieces (e.g., 1 Sam. 28:24; 2 Sam. 17:18). Fine flour (Heb. *sōleṭ*; KJV "fine meal") or groats, sifted twice to remove the large pieces as well as the bulkier meal, was served as a luxury (Ezek. 16:13, 19; cf. Gen. 18:6, "fine meal") and was mixed with oil for the cereal offering (Exod. 29:2; Lev. 2:1ff.; 6:20).

See also MEAL.

FLUTE (Heb. *ḥālîl*; Gk. *aulós*).† A wind instrument, actually a shawm or primitive clarinet, made of a hollow reed or wood with fingerholes to produce notes. Held vertically, the flute had a double-reed mouthpiece; a variant form was the double flute (cf. Akk. *ḥalḥallatu*), on which the two pipes could be played individually or simultaneously. The flute could be used as a solo instrument (cf. 1 Kgs. 1:40, "pipes") or played in ensemble (e.g., 1 Sam. 10:5) as accompaniment to joyful songs, religious hymns of praise, or funeral dirges (Isa. 5:12; 30:29; KJV "pipe"; Matt. 9:23; KJV "minstrels").

Heb. *mašrôqîṯā'*, which the KJV and NIV translate "flute" (Dan. 3:5, 7, 10, 15; RSV, JB, NJV "pipe"), was the shepherd's or Pan's pipe, a foreign instrument consisting of a row of pipes of varying length.

Flute player in a relief at Nineveh (Staatliche Museen zu Berlin, DDR)

FLY. Any of various winged insects of the order Diptera. Like all semitropical countries, Palestine has many flies which, along with gnats, make up its most ubiquitous insect population.

Heb. *z°ḇûḇ* (Isa. 7:18; JB "mosquito"), generally interpreted as the common housefly (*Musca domestica*), may actually refer to the larger and more annoying horsefly (*Tabanus arenivagus*). Its filthy habits are evident at Eccl. 10:1, which suggests that infectious matter transported on the leg hairs of the fly flourish when deposited in the perfumer's ointment, causing decay and spreading disease (*see* BAAL-ZEBUB).

Heb. *'ārōḇ* indicates a swarm of insects and thus designates the plague visited upon the Egyptians (Exod. 8:21-22, 24, 29, 31; JB "gadflies"; NJV "swarms of insects"). Among the various species which thrive in the Nile Delta, the stinging fly of the plague may have been the *Stomoxys calcitrans*, a Tabanid whose larvae develop in cow manure and which, when mature, lives off blood obtained by biting the legs of people and animals. An alternate identification would be the Barghaš midge, which infests the eyes, ears, and nose of humans.

FOOD.* The Israelite diet was determined largely by the availability of foodstuffs, a function of modes of subsistence as well as climate and political conditions. Households were responsible for providing their own food, which in the earliest stages and perhaps as a supplement in later periods was obtained by hunting game and gathering plant matter. Nomads and pastoralists depended largely on the produce of the herd and flock, while agriculturalists, who became predominant following the Conquest of Palestine, relied on cereals and vegetables; transhumants (often called "semi-nomads") had access to both animal and vegetable matter dependent upon seasonal and regional variables as well as the limitations of preservation. During the Monarchy and in later periods political conditions permitted Israel to obtain more varied foodstuffs through international trade.

From the time of the Conquest on, cereals were the mainstay of the Israelite diet. Such grains as wheat and barley, and to a lesser degree spelt and millet, were eaten raw, parched, or ground into meal to be cooked or baked into bread. The most important vegetables were beans and lentils, which could be cooked, boiled into pottage, or mixed with flour for bread; others included leeks and onions as well as the condiments mustard, cummin, and dill. Fruits included olives and grapes (generally used for oil and wine), figs, dates, pomegranates, and sycamore figs; nuts such as almonds and pistachios were also common. Meat was never a major part of the diet of ordinary people (but cf. 1 Kgs. 4:23 for its abundance in the royal fare), since domestic animals could better be used for eggs and dairy products; meat was consumed, however, as part of the sacrificial meal and on occasions for the expression of hospitality. Orthodox interpreters hold that meat was not permitted prior to the covenant with Noah (Gen. 9:3), but others cite indications that it was eaten from the earliest times (cf. 1:26, 28-30). Fish was obtained through trade with nations which had access to the Mediterranean Sea and, particularly in New Testament times, by fishing operations on the

Sea of Galilee. Foodstuffs of lesser quality, generally reserved for animal fodder, were eaten by the poor and by all classes in times of shortage. Cultic rules of purity also affected the Israelite diet. In addition to restricting animal matter to that from mammals which part the hoof and chew the cud (Lev. 11:1-8; Deut. 14:6-8) and various "clean" birds, fish, and insects (Lev. 11:9-47; Deut. 14:9-21), the regulations prohibited any food which had been contaminated by contact (through cooking or otherwise) with water defiled by an unclean carcass (Lev. 11:32-38); other legislation governed modes of preparation and combinations of foodstuffs (e.g., Exod. 23:19 par.).

Perhaps because of its universal importance for the preservation of life, the act of eating was considered almost sacred; this is underscored by the common meals associated with sacrifices and which symbolically sealed covenants (e.g., Gen. 31:54) and by the role of food as a token of hospitality (e.g., 18:7). Food was regarded as the gift of God (2:9; Deut. 8:8-10). Accordingly, it was to be among the blessings of the eschatological age (Ezek. 47:6-12; Hos. 2:15, 22; Joel 3:18). Nevertheless, food as the essence of physical sustenance is depicted as of lesser importance than spiritual "food" (Deut. 8:3; Matt. 4:4 par. Luke 4:4; John 6:32-35, 48-58).

On the various types of food as well as modes of subsistence, see the individual entries.

FOOL (Heb. *ʾᵉwîl, kᵉsîl, nābāl, sākāl*; Gk. *áphrōn, mōrós, anóētos*).† In the Bible, foolishness is most often an ethical concept and goes beyond a lack of native intelligence. Although the fool might be one who acts boorishly, naively, or imprudently (e.g., Prov. 10:23; 20:3; cf. 21:20), he is more particularly one who lacks the wisdom which comes with the knowledge of God, someone who in his pride is wise in his own eyes but acts contrary to the will of God and thus does (intentionally or not) what is evil. His foolishness culminates in a denial of the existence of God (Ps. 14:1). The fool reveals his lack of understanding through the wicked deeds which he perpetrates, and his lack of responsibility is evident in the misuse of what has been given to him (1 Sam. 26:21; 2 Sam. 3:33; Matt. 5:22).

In the New Testament, the fool is one who refuses to recognize the truth of God as communicated through the life and resurrection of Jesus Christ (e.g., Luke 24:25; 1 Cor. 15:36; cf. Rom. 1:22). Paul charges the Corinthian Christians to become "fools for Christ's sake" (1 Cor. 4:10; cf. 3:18), pursuing the ways of God which in the eyes of the world appear to be pure folly (1:18-25).

FOOT WASHING. A form of hospitality in the ancient Near East performed upon a guest's entering a house (Gen. 18:4; 19:2; 24:32). Because only sandals were worn (cf. Mark 6:9; Acts 12:8), feet were easily soiled. Priests were thus required to wash their feet as preparation for entering the sanctuary (Exod. 30:19, 21; 40:31). In the home of prominent Jews, a slave was posted at the entrance of the house ready to loosen the sandal straps of those who entered (cf. Mark 1:7; Luke 3:16) and to wash their feet. As a particular sign of hospitality ointment might be used (Luke 7:38,

44-46; John 12:3). Jesus himself washed the feet of his disciples at the Last Supper, symbolizing not only the humble service that would be required of them but also the cleansing of human sin which his death would effect (John 13:3-17). In commemoration of this and as a sign of humility, foot washing was performed in the early Church (cf. 1 Tim. 5:10).

FORCED LABOR (Heb. *mas*).† Compulsory labor for building projects, construction of roads and irrigation systems, and similar undertakings requiring a large work force; also a technical term indicating the corvée, those individuals impressed into such service by the local government or a foreign oppressor. Although the corvée was most common in the dominant ancient Near Eastern empires (cf. Exod. 1:11-14), such a work force was also maintained in Israel during the Monarchy (1 Kgs. 9:21 par. 2 Chr. 8:8; RSV "forced levy") and possibly earlier (however, many critical scholars view references to forced labor following the Conquest as interpretations from the time of the Monarchy; e.g., Judg. 1:28). Israelites and aliens alike might be conscripted for corvée service by means of a census (1 Kgs. 5:13; 2 Chr. 2:17-18), but most often the task was imposed upon conquered peoples (Josh. 16:10; Judg. 1:30, 34-35). The frequent KJV rendering of Heb. *mas* as "tribute" or "tributary" suggests that a subject people might submit to forced labor in lieu of monetary compliance.

FORD (Heb. *maʿᵃbār, maʿbārâ*, from *ʿābar* "pass through" or "over"). A place where a river can be crossed. The Old Testament mentions such points on the Jabbok (Gen. 32:22), Jordan (Josh. 2:7; Judg. 12:5-6; 2 Sam. 15:28; 17:16 [cf. v. 22]), Arnon (Isa. 16:2), and Tigris rivers (Jer. 51:32). In 1 Sam. 13:23; 14:4; Isa. 10:29, the same Hebrew word is used to indicate a mountain pass.

FOREIGNER (Heb. *nēkār, zār*; Gk. *allogenḗs, bárbaros*).* A non-Israelite who comes into temporary contact with the Hebrews as merchant, traveler, or military invader; thus distinguished from the SOJOURNER or resident alien. The term also indicates the gods of foreign nations (e.g., Josh. 24:20; Jer. 5:19; 8:19).

Foreigners could not be kings over Israel (Deut. 17:15) and were restricted in financial transactions (15:3; 23:20). They were prohibited from entering the temple (Ezek. 44:7) and could not participate in cultic observances (e.g., Exod. 12:43; Lev. 22:25). Although the Exile brought some concessions to foreigners (cf. Isa. 56:3, 6), they might still be viewed with suspicion as a potential threat to the Israelite community and religion (cf. Ezra 10:2ff.; Neh. 9:2).

In the early Church, distinctions between Jews and non-Jews were regarded as insignificant because of the universal atonement of Christ (cf. Eph. 2:11-19).

FORERUNNER (Gk. *pródromos*).† One who is sent ahead to prepare the way for others. In nonbiblical sources a technical term indicating a military scout, at Heb. 6:20 it is applied to Jesus as one who has gone to prepare the heavenly sanctuary for his followers (cf. John 14:2). Although the term is not used, the concept occurs at Isa. 40:3-11; Mal. 3:1, and it underlies the ministry of John the Baptist (Matt. 11:10; Mark 1:2-8; Luke 7:27-28).

In an alternate sense, the forerunner might be a herald (cf. 1 Sam. 8:11; 2 Sam. 15:1; 1 Kgs. 1:5; 18:46; Esth. 6:9). Such an interpretation might also fit the role of John the Baptist.

FOREST (Heb. *yaʿar, pardēs, ḥōreš*). In ancient Palestine, the forest region included all of Galilee and the area west of the Jordan river from the coast of the Mediterranean Sea past the watershed line in the central mountains. Modern Golan and Hauran east of the Jordan in the Transjordan were also wooded, and a narrow strip of forest extended south as far as Petra. The forest region was the innermost of the three kinds of terrain which cover the land concentrically: wilderness, steppe, and forest. As late as the third millennium B.C. the entire region was completely covered with trees, but even before the Israelite Conquest large areas — particularly in Bashan — had been brought under cultivation; the newcomers encountered fields of grain, vineyards, olive trees, and orchards (Deut. 6:11; 8:8), and subsequently cleared away much of the forest that remained (Josh. 17:15, 18). As recently as 1860, areas of Palestine were forested much as in biblical times (Isa. 35:2) — e.g., Mt. Carmel, the plain of Sharon, and the western slope of the mountains in Samaria (Josh. 17:15). According to old travel accounts, Judea contained a great deal of forest (cf. 1 Sam. 14:25; 2 Kgs. 2:24), as appears also from the name Kiriath-jearim ("city of forests"). In Transjordan, the oaks of Bashan once formed a thick forest (Zech. 11:2) and were of great value in the shipbuilding industry (Ezek. 27:6). The most important forest region in modern Palestine, made up primarily of oak and Jabbok trees, is in the area between the Yarmuk and Jabbok rivers east of the Jordan; in ancient times it was called the forest of Ephraim (2 Sam. 18:6-8).

Geological conditions and the amount of rainfall affected the density of forests as well as the variety of trees from region to region. Nevertheless, the most common trees throughout all of forested Palestine were the oak, terebinth, and pine, which might occur as isolated trees or in small stands as well as in larger woods or forests. Stands of tamarisk, acacia, and honey locust trees grew in the wilderness area, particularly that near Jericho, in the region of the Dead Sea, along the Wâdī el-ʿArabah, and in the wilderness of Sinai. Such stands might even be large enough to be considered forests. The wooded strip of trees along the banks of the Jordan is called the "jungle of the Jordan" (Jer. 12:5). While these trees often attained strikingly large dimensions both of height and circumference, they never attained the immensity of the cedars of Lebanon. In general, Palestinian forests consisted primarily of comparatively small trees which grew sparsely enough to provide considerable room for undergrowth. Much of the woodland soil was overgrown with brush and shrubs, for the most part evergreen bushes that grew to a height of 1.5-2 m. (5-6.5 ft.). Even more of these regions were overgrown with shrubs growing in thickets along with herbaceous plants. Much of this evergreen brush represented the same species as the larger trees and might be considered dwarf varieties. Such forms may have

developed as a result of the regular use of the forests for firewood, and even more from damage by grazing and browsing livestock (e.g., goats). Some of this undergrowth, however, was naturally low-growing.

In ancient times the forest was not regarded particularly highly (cf. Isa. 29:17). Trees were usually considered valuable only if they bore edible fruit; if this was the case, they were not to be cut down (Deut. 20:19-20). Trees that did not bear fruit were valued only for the shade that they provided (cf. Isa. 10:18, 33-34; 35:1-2; 41:19).

Bibliography. D. Baly, *The Geography of the Bible*, rev. ed. (New York: 1974).

FORK. The Bible contains no references to forks as eating utensils, perhaps meaning that bread and meat were eaten by hand in Palestine and the ancient Near East. A three-pronged fork (Heb. *mazlēg*; KJV "flesh-hook") was used by the priests to remove their portions of sacrifices (1 Sam. 2:13-14); a similar implement (Heb. *mizlāgâ*; KJV "fleshhook"), made of gold or polished bronze (1 Chr. 28:17; 2 Chr. 4:16), was apparently used in sacrifices on the altar in the tabernacle and temple (e.g., Exod. 27:3; 38:3; Num. 4:14).

A six-pronged pitchfork (Heb. *mizreh*; KJV "fan") was used in winnowing to separate chaff from grain (cf. Jer. 15:7; Gk. *ptýon*, Matt. 3:12 par. Luke 3:17; KJV "fan"). The KJV translation of Heb. *šᵉlōš qillᵉšôn* (RSV, NIV, JB "a third of a shekel") at 1 Sam. 13:21 may indicate a similar tool used as a prod or goad (cf. NJV "three-pronged forks").

FORMER PROPHETS.† According to Hebrew tradition, those books attributed ot the "early" prophets Joshua (book of Joshua), Samuel (Judges, 1-2 Samuel), and Jeremiah (1-2 Kings). In later (particularly Christian) tradition they are regarded as historical books.

FORNICATION (Gk. *porneía* "unchastity").* Sexual intercourse performed outside the bonds of marriage, considered an immoral work of the flesh (Matt. 15:19 par. Mark 7:21; cf. Gal. 5:19; Eph. 5:3; Col. 3:5; RSV "unchastity, immorality"). The Old Testament depicts this as "harlotry" or "playing the harlot" (e.g., Gen. 38:24; Deut. 22:21); as such the concept is used figuratively with regard to Israel's abandonment of its covenant ideals (e.g., Isa. 23:17; Ezek. 16:26; cf. Rev. 17:2, 4; 18:3; 19:2).

FORTUNATUS [fôr´chə nā´təs] (Gk. *Phortounatos*, from Lat. *Fortunatus* "favored by fortune"). A Christian from Corinth; a messenger who, with Stephanas and Achaicus, came to Paul in Ephesus bringing news of the Corinthian congregation (1 Cor. 16:17).

FORTUNE (Isa. 65:11). *See* GAD 3.

FORUM OF APPIUS [ăp´ĭ əs] (Gk. *Appiou Phóron*; Lat. *Apii Forum*). A station on the Appian Way, 69 km. (43 mi.) southeast of Rome at modern Faiti. Probably founded during the time of Appius Claudius Caecus, who constructed the highway in 312 B.C., it had become by the first century A.D. an important town (cf. Horace *Satires* i.5.3-6 for a traveler's critique of its accommodations and "stingy tavern keepers").

From this point a canal paralleled the road through the Pontine marshes (a haven for malarial mosquitoes) some 30 km. (19 mi.) to Feronia. A number of Roman Christians traveled to the Forum of Appius to greet Paul following his arrival at Puteoli (Acts 28:15; KJV "Appii Forum").

FOUNDATION (Heb. $y^e s\hat{o}d$, $m\hat{u}s\bar{a}d$; Aram. '$u\check{s}\check{s}ayy\bar{a}$'; Gk. $them\acute{e}lios$, $katabol\acute{e}$).† The base or substructure of a building (1 Kgs. 7:9-10; 2 Chr. 8:16; Ezra 5:16), wall (4:12), or even an entire city (Ps. 137:7; Mic. 1:6). The foundation was accorded definite religious significance in the ancient Near East; Assyrian temples and palaces contained inscribed foundation deposits bearing messages intended solely for the deity, and some scholars believe that human sacrifices may have accompanied the laying of foundations in Palestine and elsewhere (cf. Josh. 6:26; 1 Kgs. 16:34).

In figurative use the term can refer to nations or governments (e.g., Ezek. 30:4; cf. Jer. 50:15, KJV; RSV "bulwarks"), laws (Ps. 11:3), or the moorings of the entire world (e.g., 2 Sam. 22:16 par. Ps. 18:15) and the heavens (2 Sam. 22:8 par. Ps. 18:7). In a temporal sense, "the foundation(s) of the world" refers to the creation (e.g., Ps. 102:25; Isa. 51:13, 16; Rev. 13:8), often underscoring the concept of salvation-history (cf. Matt. 13:35; Luke 11:50; Heb. 4:3; 9:26).

FOUNDATION, GATE OF THE (Heb. $\check{s}a\acute{}ar\,hays\hat{o}d$). A gate in Jerusalem, perhaps providing access to the temple from the royal palace (2 Chr. 23:5; LXX Gk. $t\acute{e}\,p\acute{y}l\bar{e}\,t\acute{e}\,m\acute{e}s\bar{e}$ "middle gate"; cf. Jer. 39:3). The priest Jehoiada positioned guards here in an attempt to capture the usurper Athaliah. In the parallel account it is called the gate Sur (2 Kgs. 11:6; Heb. $\check{s}a\acute{}ar\,s\hat{u}r$).

FOUNTAIN GATE (Heb. $sa\acute{}ar\,h\bar{a}\acute{}ayin$). A gate in the southeastern part of Jerusalem, located near the steps that lead down from the city of David to the Spring Gihon (Neh. 2:14, 15; 12:37). First constructed as part of the Jebusite city which preceded Jerusalem (ca. 1800 B.C.), the gate was rebuilt by Shallum during Nehemiah's postexilic restoration of the city walls; in later times it was known as the Gate of the Spring. Some scholars would identify it with the "gate between the walls" (2 Kgs. 25:4; Jer. 39:4; 52:7).

FOX (Heb. $\check{s}\hat{u}\acute{a}l$; Gk. $al\acute{o}p\bar{e}x$). A carnivorous mammal of the genus Vulpes, family Canidae, of which several species are found in modern Palestine. Most common is the Palestinian fox (Vulpes palaestina), particularly prevalent in the midsection of the country; the largest species is Vulpes flavescens, a brownish-yellow fox found in the region of Galilee. The fox is a solitary, nocturnal animal which burrows its own lair or usurps that of another animal (Matt. 8:20 par. Luke 9:58). Its diet consists of fruit (cf. Cant. 2:15), insects, birds, and mice. Although its slyness is proverbial (Luke 13:32), the fox was considered a worthless animal in biblical times (cf. Neh. 4:3; Ezek. 13:4).

Heb. $\check{s}\hat{u}\acute{a}l$ is also used to designate JACKALS (so RSV, NEB, Ps. 63:10; Lam. 5:18; cf. Judg. 15:4, NEB; R. G. Boling, Judges. AB [1975], pp. 134-135).

FRANKINCENSE (Heb. $l^e\underline{b}\bar{o}n\hat{a}$ "white, shining"; Gk. $l\acute{i}banos$). Olibanum, an aromatic gum resin secreted as a milky-white substance by various species of trees of the genus Boswellia, family Burseraceae, related to the terebinth and shrubs which yield myrrh and balsam. The gum, which exudes as transparent beads from incisions or "resin canals" cut into the bark, slowly congeals and is later pressed into cylindrically shaped yellow pieces which are then ground into powder. When heated or burned it produces a pleasant, penetrating odor similar to that of balsam.

The highest quality frankincense, whiter and more transparent and thus more expensive, was that obtained from the Boswellia carteri, which grows in South Arabia (biblical Sheba; cf. Isa. 60:6; Jer. 6:20) as well as East Africa (e.g., Somalia [biblical Put] and Erythrea [biblical Saba]). Another variety, from the Boswellia thurifera which grows along the eastern coast of India, was imported through Babylon (cf. Rev. 18:13). It is possible that another variety may also have been obtained from the subtropical Jordan valley (cf. Cant. 3:6).

Valued in ancient times for its alleged medicinal qualities (cf. Pliny Nat. hist. xii.14ff.), frankincense was used by the Egyptians as a fumigant and ritual incense. It was one of the major ingredients in the incense (O. Fr. franc encens "pure incense") used in the Israelite sanctuary (Exod. 30:34), offered along with the cereal offering (Lev. 2:1-16) and set forth with the Bread of the Presence (24:7). Its use was forbidden, however, in the sin offering (5:11) and the ordeal by fire (Num. 5:15). Frankincense was among the gifts presented to the infant Jesus (Matt. 2:11).

FREEDMEN, SYNAGOGUE OF THE (Gk. $synag\bar{o}g\acute{e}\,t\acute{o}n\,Libert\acute{i}n\bar{o}n$). A synagogue in Jerusalem attended by "former slaves" (Lat. Libertini; KJV "Libertines"), probably those Jews (or their descendants) taken to Rome as captives by Pompey in 63 B.C. and subsequently liberated (Philo De leg. clv; Tacitus Ann. ii.85). Members of this Greek-speaking congregation disputed with the apostle Stephen (Acts 6:9) and subsequently charged him with blasphemy (vv. 11-12).

Commentators remain divided concerning the precise number of synagogues involved in this dispute. If a single congregation is implied, it was a mixed group of Jews from throughout the Diaspora. At the opposite extreme, five distinct synagogues have been suggested. Some scholars would group the Cyrenians and Alexandrians as one congregation formed by geographical bonds and Jews from Cilicia and Asia Minor as another; the alternate reading Libystinōn "Libyans" might incorporate the so-called "freedmen" into the North African congregation.

FREER LOGION. See CODEX WASHINGTONENSIS.

FRIEND (Heb. $r\bar{e}a\acute{}$, $r\bar{o}\acute{}eh$, '$\bar{o}h\bar{e}\underline{b}$; Gk. $ph\acute{i}los$).† A person with whom one shares affection and commitment; a companion or neighbor. Semantically, the term ranges from a casual acquaintance (e.g., Matt. 5:25; 20:13; cf. Job 2:11) to one who shares an intimate personal bond (e.g., 2 Sam. 15:37; cf. 1 Sam. 18:1).

In technical usage a friend was one who held a position of trust, often involving an intimate association. The "friend of the bridegroom" (Gk. *phílos toú nymphíou*; cf. Heb. *rē'a*, Judg. 14:20; 15:2; RSV "companion"; JB "best man") arranged and presided over the wedding (John 3:29; cf. 2 Cor. 11:2). The "friend of the king" (Heb. *rē'eh hammelek*) was an important official of the royal court, apparently a trusted adviser and intimate companion (1 Kgs. 4:5; 1 Chr. 27:33; cf. Gen. 26:26, RSV "adviser"; 2 Sam. 15:37; 16:16); in the Maccabean period such advisers constituted a distinct privileged class (Gk. *phíloi toú basiléōs*; 1 Macc. 2:18; 3:38; 6:10), of which there were apparently various ranks (10:65).

FRINGE (Gk. *kráspedon*).* The hem or border (so KJV) of a garment. The Hebrews were commanded to wear cords of twisted threads (Heb. *gᵉdilîm*; Deut. 22:12) ending in tassels (*ṣîṣit*; Num. 15:38-39; KJV, NJV "fringes") at the four corners of their garments as a reminder of God's commandments.

When a woman, who had been hemorrhaging for twelve years, touched the fringes of Jesus' garment, she was immediately healed (Matt. 9:20 par. Luke 8:44), as were those sick brought on their pallets to Jesus at Gennesaret (Matt. 14:36 par. Mark 6:56). Although some scholars contend that the garments manifested the Master's own power or that they had magical properties, the gospel accounts stress the individual's faith in reaching out to Jesus as that which effected the healing (Matt. 9:21-22; Luke 8:48). At Matt. 23:5 Jesus condemns the scribes and Pharisees who broaden their fringes as a sign of superior piety.

See TASSEL.

FROG (Heb. *ṣᵉpardēa'*; Gk. *bátrachos*). A tailless amphibian of the order Salientia, and primarily of the family Ranidae, having long hind legs adapted for propulsion through water and leaping on land. The most common frog in North Africa, Syria, and Asia Minor is *Rana ridibunda*, an edible frog about 15 cm. (6 in.) in length, larger and brighter in color than most Western species. In Palestine, where *Rana esculenta* is also found, frogs appear as tadpoles as early as January and flourish during the rainy season. Although the climate in general is too dry a habitat for other amphibians, toads (*Bufo viridis* and *Bufo vittatus*) as well as the tree frog (*Hyla arborea*) are common in the Jordan valley and in the forest regions.

The second plague in Egypt brought droves of frogs out of the rivers and canals into the kitchens and bedchambers of the Egyptians (Exod. 8:2-14); here the term may encompass not only frogs but other types of amphibians. This incident is recalled at Ps. 78:45; 105:30; Wis. 19:10. The frog, which the Hebrews considered unclean (cf. Rev. 16:13) because it lacked fins and scales (Lev. 11:10, 41), had particular significance in this plague because the Egyptians revered it like the Nile itself; moreover, Heket, the Egyptian goddess of childbirth, was portrayed as a frog or a human with the head of a frog.

FRONTLET. *See* PHYLACTERIES.

FRUIT (Heb. *pᵉrî*; Gk. *karpós*).† The edible product of trees and plants, generally the pulp which surrounds the seeds. Fruit was an essential part of the Israelite

diet, consumed fresh, dried, or processed into oil (olives), wine, or cakes (figs, raisins). The most important fruits were olives, grapes, and figs, but others included dates, melons, pomegranates, sycamore figs, mulberries, and nuts, including almonds, pistachios, and walnuts. See further the individual entries.

The period from August to October (Hebrew months Ab-Tishri) were the primary harvest months for orchard crops. The grape harvest began in August, approximately the same time as the late figs. In September pomegranates, almonds, and the first olives were brought in, along with the remainder of the grapes and figs. The most significant portion of the olive harvest was gathered in October. The first portion of each season's crops was to be offered to God as an expression of gratitude (Exod. 23:19; 34:26). Moreover, the produce of all fruit trees was considered unclean the first three years of its yield; that produced during the fourth year was reserved as an offering to God, and only in the fifth year could the fruit be eaten (Lev. 19:23-25).

The vast majority of biblical references to fruit are metaphorical. Children are regarded as the "fruit of the womb" (e.g., Gen. 30:2; Luke 1:42). More frequently, "fruit" depicts the results or consequences of human (e.g., Jer. 17:10; Matt. 7:16-20) or divine (e.g., Ps. 104:13) activity (cf. the "fruit of the Spirit"; Gal. 5:22).

FUEL (Heb. *'oklâ lā'ēš* "food for fire," *ma'ªkōlet*). Combustible material used for heating and cooking. In ancient Israel various forms of wood were used (e.g., Gen. 22:3, 6; Ps. 120:4), ranging from sticks used by the poor (1 Kgs. 17:12) to more massive trees available to the privileged classes (cf. Isa. 44:14-16). Other types of fuel included thorns (Ps. 58:9; Eccl. 7:6) and vines (Ezek. 15:2ff.). The chaff of grain (Matt. 3:12) and hay (6:30) was used for quick heat, whereas dried dung (Ezek. 4:15) burned more slowly. Charcoal, produced from charred wood (cf. Isa. 44:19), was used for heating (John 18:18; in wealthier households contained in a brazier, Jer. 36:22) and cooking (John 21:9) as well as for heating incense (e.g., Lev. 16:12).

At Isa. 9:19 the errant populace of Judah is likened to fuel consumed in the fire of the Lord's wrath. The metaphor is applied to the Ammonites at Ezek. 21:32.

FULFILL (Heb. *mālē'*; Gk. *plēróō*). Temporally and spatially, the coming-to-pass of the days of one's life or of prophecies, promises, and intentions. Nearly all biblical references to fulfillment, both in the Old and New Testament, can be understood on this basis.

Love for God and others ultimately fulfills the covenantal stipulations (Gal. 5:14) as interpreted through the "law of Christ" (6:2), the law of love; indeed, "love does no wrong to a neighbor" (Rom. 13:10), because the law only exists for the good of all.

God's promises of salvation are being fulfilled by Christ's resurrection (cf. Acts 3:18; 13:22, KJV; RSV "do"), for Christ came to fulfill the law and the prophets as recorded in the Old Testament (Matt. 5:17; cf. Luke 24:27, 44), thereby giving them new meaning.

In an eschatological sense fulfillment may be interpreted as events to take place in the end times (cf. Luke 22:16).

FULLER (Heb. *kābas*; Gk. *gnapheús*).† A person who treats woolen and linen fabrics to shrink and thicken them. The process involved beating and treading upon the material as well as scouring it with soap and water (Mal. 3:2) or with fuller's alkali (so JB; NJV "fuller's lye"), a cleanser made from ashes or clay and perhaps mixed with urine and other substances. Finally, the material was stretched in the sun for bleaching.

The fuller's shop was generally located near a water supply and outside the city in an area with sufficient room for drying and bleaching and where the odors yielded in the process would not be so offensive. The Fuller's Field (Heb. *śᵉḏēh ḳôḇēṣ*) which was the meeting place for Isaiah and Ahaz (Isa. 7:3) as well as the officers of Hezekiah and Sennacherib (2 Kgs. 18:17 par. Isa. 36:2) was located near the conduit of the upper pool, perhaps in the vicinity of En-rogel or the Spring Gihon.

The purification of the priesthood in preparation for the day of the Lord is compared to a fuller's cleansing (Mal. 3:2; cf. Jer. 2:22). During the transfiguration Jesus' garments become whiter than any that a fuller could bleach (Mark 9:3).

FULLNESS OF TIME (Gk. *plḗrōma tṓn kairṓn*). The appropriate (or appointed) time for the promised Savior to become incarnate, thus bringing to fruition God's intention (KJV "dispensation") of uniting divine and human purposes (Eph. 1:10; NIV "fulfillment"). The coming of Christ thus completed and brought to an end the previous era of God's activity in human history (cf. JB, "when the times had run their course to the end") and inaugurated his kingdom (Gal. 4:4-5, KJV; cf. Mark 1:15). Others would interpret the fullness of time as coinciding with the second coming of Christ and continuing forever afterward.

FURLONG (KJV; Matt. 14:24, RSV). *See* Stadia; Weights and Measures.

FURNACE.† A brick or stone structure used for heating objects. Heb. *kûr* designates a furnace which smelts metal ore (Ezek. 22:20) or refines gold or other metals (Prov. 17:3 par.), and Heb. *kibšān,* a kiln for firing bricks (e.g., Gen. 19:28). The furnace into which Daniel's three friends were thrown was probably a brickkiln (Aram. *'attûn*), which at Nebuchadnezzar's order was heated to seven times its normal temperature (Dan. 3:19-23); such kilns have been unearthed at Megiddo.

In figurative use the furnace represents the process of human purification. The Egyptian "iron furnace" (Deut. 4:20; 1 Kgs. 8:51) represents the collective experiences during their prolonged captivity in Egypt which molded the Hebrews into a people willing to serve Yahweh. When his people later forsook him in the promised land, God refined them in the "furnace of affliction" (Isa. 48:10), i.e., in Exile, before permitting their return to Jerusalem. In the New Testament, the "furnace of fire" (Gk. *káminos toú pyrós;* Matt. 13:42, 50) refers to divine eschatological judgment.

G

GAAL [gā'əl] (Heb. *ga'al* "loathing"). The son of Ebed. He led the rebellion of the Shechemites against Abimelech **3** but was repelled by Abimelech's deputy Zebul (Judg. 9:26-41).

GAASH [gā'ăsh] (Heb. *gā'aš* "[earth]quaking"). A mountain south of Timnath-serah (Timnath-heres, modern Khirbet Tibneh), *ca.* 32 km. (20 mi.) southwest of Shechem. It is mentioned in reference to Joshua's burial site (Josh. 24:30; cf. Judg. 2:9). The brooks of Gaash (Heb. *naḥ°lê gā'aš*), mentioned as the home of one of David's thirty (2 Sam. 23:30; 1 Chr. 11:32), were located in this region.

GABA (Josh. 18:24; Ezra 2:26 par. Neh. 7:30, KJV). *See* GEBA.

GABAEL [găb'ĭ əl] (Gk. *Gabaēl*).†
1. An ancestor of Tobit (Tob. 1:1).
2. A friend of Tobit and brother (or son) of Gabrias who lived at Rages in Media (Tob. 1:14). Tobit deposited fourteen talents of silver with him and later sent his son Tobias to retrieve the money (4:1, 20; 5:6; 10:2). Gabael returned the sum intact at the wedding feast of Tobias and Sarah (9:2-6).

GABBAI [găb'ī] (Heb. *gabbay*).† A Benjaminite who lived in Jerusalem following the Exile (Neh. 11:8). Some scholars regard the text as corrupt and emend to read "mighty men of valor" (Heb. *gibbōrê ḥayil;* JB "his kinsmen"; cf. v. 14).

GABBATHA [găb'ə thə] (Gk. *Gabbatha,* from Aram. *gabb°ṭā'* "height" or *gabbaḥtā'* "open space").† The Pavement (Gk. *lithóstrōton* "paved area"), a paved courtyard outside of the Praetorium or governor's palace in Jerusalem. Here Pilate judged Jesus and released him to the soldiers to be crucified (John 19:13; cf. v. 16).

According to one established tradition, Gabbatha was located near the Tower of Antonia, Herod's fortress situated north of the temple. This view is supported by Theodosius' (A.D. 530) identification of Pilate's house with the tower as well as the excavation of a paved area measuring 2000 sq. m. (2400 sq. yds.) beneath the convent of the Sisters of Zion and bounded

on the west by the Ecce Homo arch. Others, dating this pavement and the arch to the time of Hadrian (A.D. 135), identify Gabbatha (lit. "back") as a public square in the Upper City, in the vicinity of the Armenian Orthodox seminary east of the modern Jaffa Gate.

GABRIAS [gā'brĭ əs] (Gk. *Gabrias*).* The brother (Tob. 1:14) or son (4:20) of Gabael **2.**

GABRIEL [gā'brĭ əl] (Heb. *gaḇrî'ēl* "man of God" or "God is powerful"; Gk. *Gabriēl*).† A prominent angel; he and Michael are the only two such celestial beings named in the Bible. He appears first as a human messenger, offering an eschatological interpretation of Daniel's vision (Dan. 8:16ff.) and answering Daniel's prayer of repentance with wisdom and understanding (9:22). Luke's gospel identifies Gabriel as the angel who announced the coming birth of John the Baptist (Luke 1:11-20) and Jesus (vv. 26-38). Some scholars would include Gabriel among the seven angels mentioned at Rev. 8:2.

Gabriel attained a prominent position in the pseudepigraphal books of 1-2 Enoch. Here he has become an archangel, one of the four presences that look down from heaven (1 En. 40:3; cf. 9:1). Called one of the Lord's "glorious ones" (2 En. 21:3), he is one of the "holy angels" (1 En. 20:7) seated at God's left hand (2 En. 24:1), exercising supreme power (1 En. 40:9) and interceding on behalf of the martyrs (9:1-11). The Targums attribute to him a central role in events of Israelite history (e.g., Targ. Gen. 37:15; Deut. 34:6; 2 Chr. 32:21).

GAD [găd] (Heb. *gāḏ* "fortune").
1. The seventh son of Jacob, borne by Zilpah, the maid of Jacob's wife Leah; the eponymous ancestor of a tribe. The name derives from Leah's exclamation at Gad's birth (Gen. 30:11; RSV "Good fortune"; Heb. Q *bā' gāḏ* "fortune came"; K *b°gāḏ* "with fortune"). Gad himself had seven sons (46:16; Num. 26:15-18).

The Blessing of Jacob characterizes the tribe of Gad as a raiding band (Gen. 49:19; Heb. *g°ḏûḏ;* cf. RSV mg., NIV); their spirit in battle, which gained for them prime territory in Transjordan, is lauded in the

Song of Moses (Deut. 33:20-21). According to the census taken during the wilderness journey, Gad numbered 45,650 men fit for military duty (Num. 1:24-25); in the second census the total is given as 40,500 (26:15-18). Although Gad did not join Deborah in the battle with Sisera (Judg. 5:17, "Gilead"), they did unite with the other tribes to take vengeance upon Benjamin (20:1). Officers of the Gadites came to David's aid while he hid from Saul at Ziklag (1 Chr. 12:8-15).

The tribal inheritance of Gad lay within the former kingdom of Sihon east of the Jordan, between the territories of Reuben to the south and the half-tribe of Manasseh to the north (Josh. 13:24-28; cf. Num. 32:33ff.). In the prophecy of Ezekiel Gad's portion of the ideal kingdom was to be the furthest south of all the tribes (Ezek. 48:27). This fertile territory served as a place of refuge from the Philistines (1 Sam. 13:7) and sheltered David during Absalom's rebellion (2 Sam. 17:24). Nevertheless, it was subject to attack by the Moabites and Ammonites (cf. 1 Chr. 5:18-22), to whom the territory eventually fell (Jer. 49:1).

2. A prophet (Heb. *nābî'*) and seer (*hōzeh*) during the time of David. When David hid in the cave of Adullam during his flight from Saul, Gad sent him back to Judah (1 Sam. 22:5). When the king incurred the Lord's wrath because he had taken a census of the people, Gad presented him a choice of three punishments (2 Sam. 24:11-14 par. 1 Chr. 21:9-12). Later the prophet commissioned David to erect an altar upon the threshing floor of Araunah, the site where Solomon would later build his temple (2 Sam. 24:18 par. 1 Chr. 21:18). The seer also aided David and the prophet Nathan in the redistribution of tasks among the levitical singers (2 Chr. 29:25). He may have compiled the sources from which 1–2 Chronicles were written (1 Chr. 29:29). Tradition locates Gad's home and his grave at Ḥalhul, about 6 km. (4 mi.) north of Hebron.

3. An Aramaic and old Hebraic god of fortune (cf. Isa. 65:11, JB; RSV "Fortune"; par. *mᵉnî* "destiny"; JB "Meni"). The KJV translates the terms "that troop" and "that number." It is in this sense that Gad appears in place names such as Baal-gad by Mt. Hermon (Josh. 13:5) and Migdal-gad in Judah (Josh. 15:37) and in personal names such as Gaddi, Gaddiel, and Azgad.

GADARA [găd'ə rə] (Gk. *Gadara*), **GADARENES** [găd'ə rēnz] (Gk. *Gadarēnoi*). A major city of the Decapolis and its inhabitants; contemporary Muqeis (or Umm Qeis), about 10 km. (6 mi.) southeast of the Sea of Galilee, near the Yarmuk river. Gadara, with a predominantly Greek population (Josephus *Ant.* xvii.11.4; *BJ* ii.6.3), was an important city of New Testament times. Its territory extended to the Yarmuk river (Pliny *Nat. hist.* v.16.74) and may have included the hot springs of Ematha (or Tell el-Ḥammeh; Eusebius *Onom.* xxii.26). It coins indicate shipping interests, and it is possible the city also owned the stretch of land along the lake between Jordan and Kefar-semaḥ. The slope of the shoreline is quite steep here.

All three Synoptic Gospels relate the story of Jesus healing a demon-possessed man (two men according to Matthew) on the eastern shore of the Sea of Galilee. Jesus ordered the evil spirits out of the man, but permitted them to enter a nearby herd of swine. The demons then entered the pigs, which immediately rushed down the steep slope and drowned in the water (Matt. 8:28-34 par. Mark 5:1-20 par. Luke 8:26-39).

The exact location of this incident is problematic. It may have been among the Gadarenes (Gk. *Gaderēnoi*), Gerasenes (*Gerasēnoi*), or the Gergesenes (*Gergesēnoi*, possibly a variant of *Gerasēnoi*). The similar-sounding towns are within 48 km. (30 mi.) of each other, and each of the three names is represented by at least one of the variant manuscripts for each gospel. The best manuscripts for Mark and Luke (represented by the RSV, JB, NIV) place the event among the Gerasenes, but the city of Gerasa is not located on the shore of the Sea of Galilee, but some 48 km. (30 mi.) to the southeast. The best manuscripts for Matthew, on the other hand, support the city Gadara (represented by RSV, JB, NIV), which does fit the locale. The KJV reads Gergesenes at Matt. 8:28 and Gadarenes at Mark 5:1; Luke 8:26, 37.

Various solutions to the problem have been proposed. Some scholars argue that Mark and Luke were referring to a small town with a similar name located directly on the shore, not the larger Gerasa inland. Two ruins along the shoreline bear the modern names of al-Kursî and Gerga, but there is no direct evidence. Some have suggested that there were two similar deliverances (which might account for the two men in Matthew instead of one) which became confused in the tradition. The best solution seems to be that the original reading of Mark (and therefore Luke) was Gerasa, but Matthew, realizing that this Gerasa was not on the shore, corrected the location to Gadara. It is also possible, since all the variant traditions refer only to the "territory" (Gk. *chōra*) of these cities, that they could all be taken as referring to the same general region.

See GERASA, GERASENES; GERGESENES.

GADDI [găd'ī] (Heb. *gaddî* "my fortune"; Gk. *Gaddi*).
1. The son of Susi of the tribe of Manasseh; one of the spies that Moses sent into Canaan (Num. 13:11).
2. Surname of John, the eldest brother of Judas Maccabeus (1 Macc. 2:2; KJV "Joannan, called Caddis").

GADDIEL [găd'ī əl] (Heb. *gaddî'ēl* "God is my fortune"). The son of Sodi of the tribe of Zebulun; one of the spies sent by Moses into Canaan (Num. 13:10).

GADI [gā'dī] (Heb. *gādî* "my fortune"). The father of King Menahem of Israel (2 Kgs. 15:14).

GAHAM [gā'hăm] (Heb. *gaham* "burning brightly"). A son of Nahor and his concubine Reumah (Gen. 22:24).

GAHAR [gā'här] (Heb. *gahar*). A temple servant whose descendants returned with Zerubbabel from the Exile (Ezra 2:47; Neh. 7:49).

GAIUS [gā'yəs, gī'əs] (Gk. *Gaïos*).
1. A Macedonian Christian who was one of Paul's travel companions. He was dragged into the theater when the silversmiths incited a riot in Ephesus (Acts 19:29).

2. A man from Derbe in Asia Minor who accompanied Paul on his journey from Macedonia to Asia Minor (Acts 20:4). One ancient text, however, gives his home as Doberus in eastern Macedonia, and if this is correct, he could be the same as **1**. Such an identification is also supported by the fact that Acts 19:29; 20:4 cite Gaius with Aristarchus.

3. Paul's host at Corinth when he wrote the Epistle to the Romans (Rom. 16:23).

4. A Christian from Corinth whom Paul had baptized (1 Cor. 1:14). It has been suggested that Gaius's full name was Gaius Titius Justus, and that it is he whom Luke cites as Paul's host in Acts 18:7. He is probably the same as **3**.

5. The person to whom the third Letter of John was sent (3 John 1). He had shown hospitality to fellow Christians, even though they were strangers to him (vv. 5-6). It is possible that it was John who brought Gaius into the faith (cf. v. 4).

GALAL [gā′lăl] (Heb. *gālāl* "tortoise" or "rolling").

1. A postexilic Levite of the lineage of Merari (1 Chr. 9:15).

2. A Levite, son of Jeduthun and father of Shemaiah, of the lineage of Merari (1 Chr. 9:16; Neh. 11:17).

GALATIA [gə lā′shə] (Gk. *Galatia*).† A region in central Asia Minor, named after the Gaulic (Celtic) population which settled there in the third century B.C.; later a Roman province. On the much-debated question of which usage of the term indicates the designation of Paul's epistle (Gal. 1:2), *see* GALATIANS, LETTER TO THE *I*.

In the third century a large number of Gauls migrated from Europe to Asia Minor, where King Nicomedes I of Bithynia enlisted them in a war against his brother. The Gaulic hordes ran rampant in western Asia Minor until confined by the Seleucid king Antiochus I to the high plateaus on either side of the Halys river. This territory was bounded on the north by Bithynia and Paphlagonia, on the south and west by Phrygia, on the east by Pontus, and on the southeast by Cappadocia; its principal cities included Ancyra (modern Ankara), Pessinus, and Tavium. Early Galatia comprised a federation of three Gaulic tribes, governed until 64 B.C. by a council of twelve chieftains, and thereafter was a client state of Rome headed by a series of kings.

Upon the death in 25 B.C. of Amyntas, the last of these Gaulic kings, Galatia became a Roman province. Its territory was expanded to include portions of Isauria, Lycaonia, Paphlagonia, Phrygia, Pisidia, and Pontus. Its capital and chief city was Ancyra. Paul visited several cities here on both his first (Acts 13:14; 14:24) and second (16:1-5) missionary journeys, including Antioch, Iconium, Lystra, and Derbe. The Galatia mentioned at 2 Tim. 4:10; 1 Pet. 1:1 is probably this Roman province.

According to 2 Macc. 8:20 the Seleucids employed Jewish forces against Galatian mercenaries at Babylonia *ca.* 229 B.C. (J. A. Goldstein, *II Maccabees*. AB 41A [1983], pp. 331-34).

GALATIANS [gə lā′shənz] (Gk. *Galatai*), **LETTER**

TO THE.† The ninth book of the New Testament, and one of Paul's major letters.

I. Destination

In the first-century A.D. context of the letter, Paul's use of the term Galatia (Gal. 1:1) remains ambiguous. It may refer to the territory of Galatia, a region in central Asia Minor occupied in the third century B.C. by Gauls (Gk. *Galatai*) and centered around the cities of Ancyra (modern Ankara), Pessinus, and Tavium. This is the "North Galatian" hypothesis. Galatia may also refer to the Roman province, which included both the territory of Galatia and parts of Phrygia, Pisidia, and Lycaonia—a region Paul visited on his first missionary journey (cf. Acts 13:13–14:23). This is the "South Galatian" hypothesis.

Both positions have vigorous defenders. Those preferring the southern hypothesis emphasize Paul's preference for provincial, not geographical names; the suitability of the historical geography of Roman Galatia (see Ramsay); and the silence in Acts of any trip by the apostle into the territory of Galatia. In contrast, defenders of a northern view look to internal evidence in the letter. Certain phrases (Gal. 1:21; 3:1) seem inconsistent with a southern position, as is the nature of the church itself: would a Gentile community so recently wracked by controversy with Judaism (cf. Acts 14:5) now embrace it? Since both theories argue from silence and conjecture, one can only speak guardedly. The southern theory, with its admitted difficulties, still accounts best for the historical and archeological data (see Bruce, pp. 3-18).

II. Date

The date of the letter depends on both the identity of the recipients and the parallels between Galatians and Acts. Paul had visited the churches at least once (Gal. 4:13; some take Gk. *tó próteron* to imply a second visit). If these are the North Galatian churches, then this would have been during his second missionary journey (Acts 16:6), or even on his third, if two visits are meant. In this view Paul would have written the letter either from Corinth (*ca.* A.D. 51-52) or Ephesus (*ca.* 54-55). If Paul wrote the letter to the churches of South Galatia, it could be dated much earlier, immediately after his first missionary journey (cf. Acts 14; *ca.* 48).

Another important consideration is Paul's visit to Jerusalem and the subsequent controversy (Gal. 2:1-10). Is this to be identified with the Apostolic Council (Acts 15), or with the earlier famine relief trip (11:29-30)? Those scholars who favor the earlier visit note that v. 29 is Paul's second visit (as is Gal. 2:1). Again, if the council had already taken place, it would have been possible, even necessary, for Paul to appeal to its decision—but he remains silent. Further, the two conflicts remain significantly different: the Apostolic Council addresses whether Gentile believers should be circumcised (cf. Acts 15:1), while in Galatians Paul defends the sufficiency of his gospel. Finally, Peter's actions (Gal. 2:11-14) seem out of place if they in fact follow the council where he was present. *See also* APOSTOLIC COUNCIL.

It need not be assumed, however, that Paul referred to all of his Jerusalem trips in this letter, especially since the second one was one of duty, the delivery of a collection (cf. 2:10, Gk.). Another reason for identifying the events of Acts 15 with those of Gal. 2 is their common subject. While addressing the issue from different perspectives, both are in fact concerned with those who require Torah and circumcision as part of Christian practice. Paul's apostolic independence likely explains his lack of appeal to the council's decision (cf. Phil. 3:2ff.). Acts 21:21 shows that tensions and misunderstandings remained strong in the Church even after the decision. Finally, identifying Gal. 2 with the visit of Acts 11:29 would make Paul's conversion extremely early, ca. 31.

Thus Paul most likely wrote the Galatian letter some time after the Apostolic Council. His astonishment (Gal. 1:6) and perplexity (4:20) at their hasty desertion points to a conversion in the recent past. A likely date would be 51-52.

III. Occasion

Paul writes to counter the teaching of extremist Jewish-Christian teachers ("Judaizers") who were leading astray members of the Galatian church by a distorted gospel (1:8), and with presumptions of apostolic authority. These troublemakers (v. 7; 5:10) and agitators (v. 12) displayed a persuasive power (cf. 3:1; 5:7-8) in insisting on the necessity of the Hebrew Torah (Gk. *nómos* "law") for Christian belief (3:2; 4:21). With the law came circumcision (6:13; cf. Josephus *Ant.* xx.34ff.), observance of holy days (4:10), and perhaps dietary restrictions (cf. 2:11-14). These Judaizers claimed the authority of the Jerusalem church (cf. 2:12) while denying Paul's apostleship (1:12; the Pseudo-Clementine Homilies preserve this anti-Pauline position; see Betz, pp. 332-33). Some have suggested that there was another kind of Judaizer who taught a libertinism (5:13ff.), but it seems more likely that Paul's intent is to counter the charge of antinomianism (cf. 2:17; Rom. 6:1).

IV. Contents and Message

The book of Galatians follows the form of an apology. In it Paul answers the twin attacks on his status as an apostle and on the gospel of grace in Jesus Christ. Seven sections may be discerned.

The opening lines of Paul's salutation (1:1-5) speak directly to the issues: Paul is an apostle by divine and not human appointment (1:1). His greeting emphasizes deliverance from sin (v. 4), a concern which nagged the Galatians (cf. 2:15-17, 21; 5:16ff.).

An exordium stands in place of the usual thanksgiving (1:6-10; cf. 2 Cor. 1:3-11). It opens with a statement of amazement (Gk. *thaumázō*), a literary convention for responding to bad news. The Galatians have turned away to a different gospel (Gk. *héteros* "different in kind," in contrast to *állos* "other" [Gal. 1:7]). The gospel is at stake; on it hang blessing and curse (vv. 8-9; cf. 6:16).

Next Paul defends his apostleship to the Gentiles (1:11-2:14). He reminds the Galatians that he received his gospel directly from Christ, not secondhand through other apostles (1:11-17), although they did approve it (2:2, 9). He is thoroughly acquainted with Judaism (1:14-15) and has been consistent in rejecting

its circumcision and legalism, even with Peter (2:11-14), thus underscoring his integrity.

The following bridge section (2:15-21) contrasts the law and justification through faith in Jesus Christ (v. 16). Not the law but the grace of God in the crucified Christ is the cure for sin (vv. 19-20).

Paul then begins his main argument: salvation is by grace through faith (3:1-4:31). He starts with an ironic address, appealing to the Galatians' experience of grace apart from law (3:1-5). As Gentiles in Christ, they share by faith the blessing of Abraham (vv. 6-9, 14). In contrast, the Torah leads them not to blessing but to condemnation. Christ fulfills it only by taking its curse (vv. 10-13). As in human covenants, God's promise to Abraham is not annulled by the later giving of Torah (vv. 15-18). The Law still has its place in revealing sinfulness, and in serving as a "custodian until Christ came" (vv. 19-25). In Christ the Galatians enjoyed a new status as children of God (3:26-4:7). To turn to the Law would be to return to the slavery from which Christ freed them (4:8-11; cf. v. 17; 6:13). Paul appeals to them on the basis of their friendship (4:12-20) and then concludes with an allegorical exegesis of Sarah and Hagar (vv. 21-31; *see* ALLEGORY).

A series of ethical exhortations (5:1-6:10) emphasize the Galatians' new freedom in Christ. That freedom is threatened first by the slavery of Torah and circumcision (5:2-12), which obscures "faith working through love" (v. 6). Second, it is threatened by the flesh (Gk. *sárx*) (vv. 13-24). Freedom from the law does not mean indulging the flesh, as might be supposed, but serving one another (v. 14) and bearing the fruit of the Spirit (vv. 22-24). Instead of legalism or indulgence, the Galatians are urged to walk by the Spirit (5:25-6:10).

Paul's closing greeting and benediction summarize his teaching (6:11-18): do not glory in the flesh (v. 12) but rather in the cross of Jesus Christ (v. 14). For in Christ there is not one gospel for Jews and another for Gentiles but a new creation for both (v. 15; cf. 3:28), to become the Israel of God (6:16).

V. Authorship

The Pauline authorship of Galatians is virtually undebated. The early Church accepted the epistle from the beginning (cf. Polycarp *Phil.* iii.3; v.1). The radical criticism of the nineteenth century that denied authorship (e.g., B. Bauer, W. C. van Manen) now finds little support. Likewise, the Tübingen school's sharp antithesis between a Pauline and Petrine (or Jewish) gospel (cf. Gal. 2:7-8, 11-14) remains suggestive but overstated and obscures the more complex and nuanced reality of the New Testament churches.

Bibliography. H. D. Betz, *Galatians.* Hermeneia (1979); R. E. Brown and J. P. Meier, *Antioch and Rome* (New York: 1983), pp. 28-44; F. F. Bruce, *Commentary on Galatians.* NIGTC (1982); W. M. Ramsey, *The Church in the Roman Empire Before A.D. 170,* 7th ed. (London: 1903), pp. 74-111; *St. Paul the Traveller and the Roman Citizen* (London: 1920), pp. 178-193; H. N. Ridderbos, *The Epistle of Paul to the Churches of Galatia.* NICNT (1953).

GALBANUM [găl′bə nəm] (Heb. *ḥelbᵉnâ*; Gk. *chal-*

bánē). A resinous gum derived by drying the milky sap from the roots of a form of fennel or carrot (probably *Ferula galbaniflua* Boise). A herbaceous plant found in Syria, Persia, and Afghanistan, galbanum has a distinct odor which becomes unpleasant when the resin is burned; nevertheless, it was one of the ingredients used to make holy incense, probably added to improve combustion (Exod. 30:34). It was also used in antiquity as a condiment and for medicinal purposes, sometimes taken internally but usually applied as a salve.

At Sir. 24:15 galbanum is used figuratively in describing Wisdom.

GALEED [găl′ī əd] (Heb. *galʿēḏ* "heap of witness"). The name that Jacob gave to the stonepile he and Laban set up to commemorate their covenant and to delineate the boundary between their territories (Gen. 31:47). Laban named the pile Jegar-sahadutha, an Aramaic expression that also means "heap of witness." Etymologically the name may be related to GILEAD.

GALILEE [găl′ə lē] (Heb. *gālîl* "circle" or "district").† The northernmost region of ancient Israel. The name means "district," and is short for "district of the nations." In Isa. 9:1 (MT 8:23) the name is partially translated "Galilee of the nations." Later the area was referred to simply as Galilee.

In the division of the land after the Conquest, this area was originally the territory of Naphtali, Zebulun, and Issachar. After the Captivity, the name Galilee referred to all of Canaan north of Samaria and west of the Jordan river. The area included the Sea of Galilee (formerly called the Sea of Chinnereth), the town of Kedesh (Josh. 20:7; 21:32), and the whole triangular region north of the plain of Esdraelon, with the river Jordan and Lake Huleh on the east, and Mt. Carmel on the west. The famous Highway of the Sea passed through Galilee and contributed to its rich cultural heritage. A precise description of Upper and Lower Galilee in the time of Jesus is given by Josephus in *BJ* iii.3.

According to Judg. 1:30-33, Naphtali, Zebulun, and Issachar did not drive out the Amorites and Hivites whom they had defeated; rather, they settled among these Gentiles. Uprisings were typical (chs. 4-5). Galilee suffered in the Syrian wars (1 Kgs. 15:20), and the whole region seemed to be valued less and less by the monarchy. Twenty of the cities of Galilee were given to Hiram of Phoenicia in exchange for supplies for the construction of the temple at Jerusalem (9:11-13). Galilee was ravaged by Ben-hadad (15:20), and taken again by Tiglath-pileser III for Assyria in 734 B.C. (2 Kgs. 15:29).

In 164 B.C. Simon Maccabeus retaliated against hostile Gentiles throughout Galilee; despite his success much of the Jewish population was forced to flee to Judah (1 Macc. 5:14-23). A series of skirmishes followed involving the forces of Demetrius I, Jonathan Maccabeus, and Tryphon (1 Macc. 9:1-4; 11:63-64; 12:39-40; 13:1-30; Josephus *Ant.* xii.11.1 [420-22]; xiii.5.7 [158-162]; 6.1-6 [187-212]). Aristobulus conquered all but the coastal plain for the Maccabees in 104. When Palestine fell to Pompey and the Romans

in 63 B.C., Galilee became part of Judea. After the death of Herod the Great in 4 B.C. it formed, with Perea, the tetrarchy of Herod Antipas, with its capital (at Sepphoris (xvii.1.4 [317-321]; *BJ* ii.6.3 [93-98])); in A.D. 25 the capital was moved to Tiberias. With the destruction of Jerusalem following the Second Jewish Revolt, Galilee became the new focus of Judaism; important centers of rabbinic study included Jamnia and Tiberias.

The major part of Jesus' ministry, which is described in the Gospels, took place in Galilee. The first miracle occurred in Cana of Galilee. The call of the first disciples (Matt. 4:12-25; Mark 1:16-20), the Sermon on the Mount (Matt. 5-7), and the feeding of the five thousand (John 6:1-15) took place near the Sea of Galilee. Jesus predicted that after his resurrection he would precede his disciples to Galilee (Matt. 26:32), and the Great Commission was given on a mountain in Galilee (28:16-20). Peter's famous confession, "You are the Christ, the Son of the living God" (16:16), was uttered in the region of Caesarea Philippi.

Traditionally Galilee has been regarded as a relatively isolated region within Palestine, particularly subject to hellenization and a hotbed of revolution. The gloom and doom of Galilee, which already in Old Testament times had resulted from political neglect, became proverbial, as reflected in Nathanael's remark about Jesus: "Can anything good come out of Nazareth?" (John 1:46); the coming of Jesus from Nazareth can be seen as a fulfillment of Isa. 9:2 (MT 1): "The people who walked in darkness have seen a great light."

Bibliography. S. Freyne, *Galilee from Alexander the Great to Hadrian, 323 B.C.E. to 135 C.E.* (Notre Dame: 1980); N. Glueck, *The River Jordan* (Philadelphia: 1946), pp. 1-59.

GALILEE [găl′ə lē], **SEA OF** (Gk. *hē thálassa tēs Galilaias* "ring, circle").† The larger of the two lakes in northern Palestine, located in the region in which Jesus conducted the greater part of his public ministry.

The earliest known name for the lake is Chinnereth (Heb. *kinnereṯ;* Num. 34:11; Deut. 3:17; Josh. 13:27), or Chinneroth (Heb. *kinᵃrôṯ;* Josh. 12:3; 1 Kgs. 15:20), a name associated with a town located on its northwest coast (Josh. 11:2; 19:35). This name, which may mean "harp," dates from the fifteenth century B.C. and also identifies the land adjacent to the lake.

A later name, Gennesaret (Gk. *Gennēsaret*), was used in Maccabean times (1 Macc. 11:67) and survives in the Gospels (Luke 5:1). In the second century B.C. the lake was called Tiberias, after a city on its western shore founded by Herod Antipas, King Herod's second son (John 6:1; 21:1).

Galilee is an old name for the territory to the west of the lake, but it seems not to have been associated with the lake itself until the Gospels were written. Gk. *thálassa*, translated "sea" in English versions, is ambiguous in that it can also mean "large lake" (cf. Heb. *yām*), and the Sea of Galilee is actually a large, freshwater inland lake.

The Sea of Galilee lies along the great geological rift which stretches from northern Syria to the southeastern coast of Africa, and which divides Palestine into its western and Transjordanian sections. Located some 212 m. (696 ft.) below sea level, the lake is almost surrounded by mountains of great elevation, relieved only by the plain of Gennesaret on the northwest and a narrow plain before the mountains on the western shore. The lake is 21 m. (13 mi.) long and 13 km. (8 mi.) wide at its widest point. It is fed by Lake Huleh to the north and several other streams, including the "waters of Merom" (Josh. 11:5).

The Sea of Galilee was where Jesus called the first disciples (Matt. 4:18-22 par. Mark 1:16-20), and thousands of people were miraculously fed along its shores (Matt. 15:29-39; Mark 8:1-10; John 6:1-13). Jesus walked upon the waters of the lake (vv. 16-24) and calmed a great storm (Matt. 8:23-27). During the course of his ministry he frequently traversed it by boat (Matt. 15:39; Mark 8:10, 13).

GALL (Heb. *mᵉrōrâ, rō'š;* Gk. *cholé*). Used in two senses, both connoting bitterness.

Heb. *rō'š* (Lam. 3:19; cf. KJV, Deut. 32:32; Heb. *rôš*) refers to a plant with bitter fruit, perhaps hemlock, wormwood, or colocynth. It thus provides apt imagery of the anguish felt by the author of Lamentations. In Matt. 27:34 the evangelist alludes to the LXX of Ps. 69:21 (MT 22), where Gk. *cholé* translates Heb. *rō'š* "poison." Scholars disagree about the purpose of this drink; some hold that the wine-gall mixture was used to ease the pain of the crucified victims, whereas others see it as another cruelty.

Heb. *mᵉrōrâ* can refer to human bile (Job 20:25; NIV "liver"; 16:13, *mᵉrērâ*) or to the venom of snakes (so NIV, JB, 20:14).

GALLERY (Heb. *'attîq*).* A term of uncertain derivation and obscure meaning referring to specific architectural features of the ideal temple envisioned by Ezekiel (Ezek. 40–42).

The term appears most certain at Ezek. 42:3, 5, where it designates a structural feature of the priests' chambers located on the north and south sides of the sanctuary between the temple yard and the inner court. Here the gallery is a terrace or ledge (so NJV; cf. W. Zimmerli, *Ezekiel* 2. Hermeneia [1983], p. 393) in the three-tiered arrangement of the chambers. In the description of the temple hall (41:15-16) the term may designate a corridor (so NEB; RSV "walls"); at v. 16 it may refer to receding steps in the framework of a window (RSV "recessed frames").

At Cant. 7:5 (MT 6) the KJV renders Heb. *rᵉhaṭîm* as "galleries" (cf. LXX Gk. *paradromaís* "spaces for getting through, gaps"), more appropriately a reference to locks of hair (RSV "tresses").

GALLEY (Heb. *'ºnî* "ship"). A large ship or warship propelled by oars. At Isa. 33:21 (NJV "floating vessels"; par. *ṣî 'addîr* "stately ship") Zion is said to no longer need such a ship because its strength now lies in God and not in arms (cf. 2:2-4).

GALLIM [găl'ĭm] (Heb. *gallîm* "heaps").
1. A town in the territory of Benjamin, situated along the route the Assyrians would take as they advanced toward Jerusalem (Isa. 10:30). Although the site has not been confirmed conclusively, it may be

identified with modern Khirbet Ka'kûl, 1 km. (.6 mi.) west of Anathoth. It is probably the same town which was the home of Palti, to whom King Saul had given David's wife Michal (1 Sam. 25:44).
2.* A town in the hill country of Judah, recorded by the LXX between Karem and Bether (JB, Josh. 15:59; cf. NJV mg.). The site may be modern Beit Jalā, located west-northwest of Bethlehem.

GALLIO [găl'ĭ ō] (Gk. *Galliōn*).† Lucius Junius Annaeus Gallio, proconsul of the Roman province of Achaia at the time of Paul's second missionary journey. When the Jews brought the apostle before the tribunal at Corinth, charging that Paul's teachings were contrary to the law, Gallio refused to allow the apostle to defend himself and dismissed the case as an internal Jewish concern (Acts 18:12-16). He further declined to intervene in the assault upon Sosthenes, ruler of the synagogue (v. 17). On the basis of an inscription found at Delphi, these events took place *ca.* A.D. 51-53.

Born Marcus Annaeus Novatus at Cordova, Spain, he was adopted at Rome by the rhetorician Lucius Junius Gallio. Apparently banished for a time to Corsica, he returned to Rome when his brother, the philosopher Seneca, was named tutor to Nero. Following his term in Achaia, Gallio was appointed a substitute consul at Rome. Implicated in a conspiracy against Nero in 65, during which Seneca was killed, he apparently was coerced into committing suicide (Dio Cassius *Hist.* lxii.25).

GAMAD [gā'măd], **MEN OF** (Heb. *gammāḏîm*).† Mercenaries employed in the defense of Tyre (Ezek. 27:11; KJV "Gammadim"; NIV "men of Gammad"; JB "kept watch," following LXX Gk. *phýlakes*). Perhaps they should be identified with the Kumidi from northern Syria, mentioned in the Amarna Letters.

GAMALIEL [gə mā'lĭ əl] (Heb. *gamlî'ēl* "God is my recompense [or reward]"; Gk. *Gamaliēl*).†
1. The son of Pedahzur of the tribe of Manasseh. He was a leader of the tribe during the wilderness wanderings and assisted Moses with the first census of the Israelites (Num. 1:10; 2:20; 7:54, 59; 10:23).
2. Rabban Gamaliel I, called the Elder. According to the Talmud, he was the son of Simon and grandson of Hillel the Elder (other sources call him the son of Hillel), whom he succeeded as a leader of the Sanhedrin. A distinguished teacher of the Law, he was the first to be honored with the title *Rabban* "Our Master" or "Teacher"; the apostle Paul claims to have been one of his students (Acts 22:3; cf. Talmud *b. Šabb.* 30b). Gamaliel was instrumental in establishing liberal Pharisaism and is generally acknowledged for his humane interpretation of the Law (cf. *Giṭ.* iv.1-3); his tolerance is demonstrated by his intervention in the Sanhedrin in behalf of Peter and the apostles (Acts 5:33-39). As a measure of Gamaliel's esteem, the Mishnah notes that when he died (*ca.* A.D. 50) "respect for the Torah ceased, and purity and abstinence died" (*Soṭah* ix.15).
3. Rabban Gamaliel II, grandson of Gamliel I and successor to Johanan ben Zakkai as head of the rabbinic academy at Jabneh (Jamnia) *ca.* A.D. 80-120.

Recognized by the Romans as the head of the Sanhedrin, Gamaliel strengthened Judaism in the post-temple period by reuniting the scribal schools of Hillel and Shammai and by regulating prayer. He was a strict disciplinarian and rigid interpreter of the Law, and basically intolerant of opposition; as the result of a series of excommunications and bitter disagreements, he was removed for a time from his position in the Sanhedrin in favor of Rabbi Eleazar ben Azariah.

4. Rabban Gamaliel III, the son of Rabbi Judah ha-Nasi ("the Prince"), and his successor as head of the Sanhedrin. In the first half of the third century A.D. he completed the redaction of the Mishnah.

GAMES.† The Bible mentions various playful activities, although it provides few details about actual games the people played.

Job 21:11 refers to children's dances, and 41:5 alludes to the amusement children get from keeping pets. At Gen. 21:9 Ishmael's "playing" (Heb. *m^eṣaḥēq* "make sport, play") with his younger brother may have been not so much an innocent pastime as a mockery (so KJV, NIV). 2 Sam. 2:14 suggests a form of wrestling, perhaps a form of belt wrestling, involving twelve young men from Joab's army and another twelve from Abner's band; in this encounter the game degenerated into a bloodbath (v. 16). Jacob may have engaged in a similar wrestling match with the man of God near the Jabbok river (Gen. 32:24); he lost the match when his opponent touched the hollow of Jacob's thigh (v. 25). Another game, foot racing, occurs in a comparison at Ps. 19:5 (MT 6). Though the Hebrews did engage in such physical activities for sport, many resented the Hellenistic athletics introduced by Antiochus IV Epiphanes (1 Macc. 1:10-14) and actively promoted by the high priest Jason, who erected a gymnasium in the vicinity of the temple (2 Macc. 4:7-17).

In one of his discourses Jesus compared his contemporaries to children who chided one another for not joining in their games; imitating their parents, they staged both mock weddings, at which the girls played the flute and the boys performed the round dance, and mock funerals, at which the boys sang dirges and the girls wailed in mourning (Matt. 11:16-17 par. Luke 7:32). At the time of his passion Jesus himself was involuntarily drawn into a guessing game by his captors, who blindfolded him and bid him guess who struck him (Mark 14:65; Luke 22:64; cf. Matt. 26:68).

Perhaps having attended the Isthmian games himself, Paul drew on such competition for spiritual lessons for believers. At 1 Cor. 9:24-25 he compares the Christian life to a race in which, of all those who try, very few would succeed to salvation. He then exhorts the Corinthian Christians, who would have been very familiar with the Isthmian games held biennially near their city, to discipline their bodies like the boxers (vv. 26-27). In other letters the apostle tells of taking precautions against running the race of faith in vain (Gal. 2:2; Phil. 2:16). At 3:13-14 Paul likens the Christian life to a chariot race or a footrace; he writes of his own eagerness to press on toward his goal as a charioteer who must devote full attention to potential dangers ahead and thus could not risk looking back lest he break stride. Similarly, at the end of his life the

author of 2 Tim. 4:7-8 victoriously proclaims to have finished according to the rules of the race, to have maintained his faith in times of trial and distress, and to be ready to receive the victor's crown of righteousness (cf. 2:5; Heb. 12:1-2).

Archaeologists have uncovered various examples of game equipment as well as artistic depictions of games. In Egypt board games similar to checkers have been found, and other board games and dice have been discovered at several sites in Palestine. Some of these board games may have originated in Mesopotamia, where, for example, chess was played in the third millennium B.C. Egyptian wall paintings show ball games and tugs-of-war.

GAMMADIM (Ezek. 27:11, KJV). *See* GAMAD.

GAMUL [gā'məl] (Heb. *gāmûl* "weaned" or "benefited" [?]). A priest and leader of the twenty-second division of the priesthood during the time of David (1 Chr. 24:17).

GANGRENE (Gk. *gángraina*). In ancient Greek usage, a spreading ulcer. At 2 Tim. 2:17 it describes the pernicious spread of heresy (KJV "cankers"). Plutarch employs the term similarly to describe the effect of the calumnies of one Medius, a "flatterer" (i.e., a confidant with evil intent) of Alexander (*Moralia* 65D).

GARDEN (Heb. *gan, karmel;* Gk. *kḗpos*). An enclosed plot of land, generally used for agricultural or recreational purposes. In the ancient Near East gardens often adorned the royal palaces (e.g., the famous hanging gardens of Nebuchadnezzar at Babylon; cf. Esth. 1:5); at Jerusalem the king maintained extensive gardens as a private park (cf. 2 Kgs. 25:4). In Egypt wealthy families also had extensive gardens.

The first garden mentioned in the Bible is in Eden, where olive and fruit trees grew (Gen. 2–3). Flowers, vegetables, spices, and fruit trees were cultivated in gardens (1 Kgs. 21:2; Cant. 5:1; 6:2; Jer. 29:5; Amos 9:14). In Egypt gardens were irrigated with water from the Nile (Deut. 11:10), and archaeological evidence now indicates various forms of irrigation in Palestine (cf. Isa. 58:11; Jer. 31:12). Gardens might also be used as burial plots (2 Kgs. 21:18, 26; John 19:41), and in Israelite times were the locus of pagan sacrifices (Isa. 1:29; 65:3; 66:17).

Gardens are used figuratively as a symbol of prosperity (e.g., Job 8:16; Isa. 51:3; Mic. 7:14) or desolation (Amos 4:9). At Isa. 58:11; Jer. 31:12 the life of the redeemed is likened to a watered garden.

GAREB [gâr'ĕb] (Heb. *gārēḇ* "leprous") (**PERSON**).† An Ithrite and one of David's mighty men (2 Sam. 23:38; 1 Chr. 11:40). The JB, following the LXX and Syriac, lists his home as Jattir.

GAREB [gâr'ĕb] (Heb. *gārēḇ* "leprous") (**PLACE**). A hill that was to become part of the rebuilt, expanded Jerusalem (Jer. 31:38-40). It may have been the hill northwest of the temple and if so would have been the site of the town of Beth-zatha during New Testament times. Another possibility is the hill just southwest of the temple.

GARLIC (Heb. *šûm*). A bulbous herb (*Allium sativum* L.) related to the onion, probably from the Kirghiz steppe, much in demand even in antiquity as a seasoning for food. The laboring Israelites were introduced to garlic and other kinds of spicy foods while in Egypt (Num. 11:5). The small garlic bulbs, wrapped in their own thin skin, were woven together along strings, pressed in a mortar, and rubbed with oil. Sometimes people ate them with bread. The oil contained in the bulb cells gives garlic its sharp odor and strong flavor; in biblical times this oil was considered to stimulate activity and was used against cases of melancholy.

GARMITE [gär′mīt] (Heb. *garmî*).† A gentilic designating the Judahite Keilah (1 Chr. 4:19). Translated literally it means "of Gerem," but no such place is attested; it may be a descriptive term (cf. Heb. *gerem* "bone").

GARRISON. A military post, frequently on the frontier, where a division of soldiers was stationed. Such outposts were used widely in the ancient Near East, and Palestine was often the site of outposts for both Egypt and Mesopotamia as these powers vied for control of the entire Near East.

During the reign of King Saul (*ca.* 1040 B.C.) the Philistines had garrisons near the pass of Michmash, about 11 km. (7 mi.) northeast of Jerusalem (1 Sam. 13:23; 14:1), and at Geba (13:3), Bethlehem in Judah (2 Sam. 23:14 par. 1 Chr. 11:16), and Gibeath-elohim (1 Sam. 10:5), about 5 km. (3 mi.) north of Jerusalem. After defeating the Philistines David succeeded in establishing garrisons at Aram of Damascus (2 Sam. 8:6), and throughout Edom (v. 14 par. 1 Chr. 18:13). The "garrison" placed at Damascus (2 Cor. 11:32, KJV) is actually a "guard" (cf. RSV, JB, NIV) stationed near the city's gates and charged to apprehend Paul.

GASHMU (Neh. 6:6, KJV). *See* GESHEM.

GATAM [gā′təm] (Heb. *ga‘tām*). An Edomite chieftain; a son of Eliphaz and descendant of Esau (Gen. 36:11, 16; 1 Chr. 1:36).

GATE (Heb. *ša‘ar, deleṭ, peṭaḥ;* Gk. *pylón, pýlē, thýra*).† The entrance to a city; specifically, a fortified passageway in the defenses of a walled city. The term also designates the entrance (so NIV) to the Israelite camp in the wilderness (Exod. 32:26), the tabernacle (27:14-16), and the temple (Ezek. 40–47). For specific gates see the individual entries.

Fortified cities such as Jerusalem, Jericho, and Samaria were protected by gates with double doors (cf. Judg. 16:3), usually made of wood (e.g., Neh. 1:3; 2:17) or sometimes plated metal (Ps. 107:16, "door of bronze"; KJV "gates of brass"; cf. JB, NIV), which could be closed and made secure with a wood (Nah. 3:13) or metal (e.g., 1 Kgs. 4:13) bar. The most vulnerable part of a city's defenses, the gate generally was reinforced by towers flanking both sides (cf. 2 Chr. 26:9). Excavations indicate that gates were covered for protection (e.g., Dan; cf. 2 Sam. 18:24) and often featured an upper chamber which functioned as a

lookout or fortress (e.g., Gezer, Shechem; cf. v. 33 [MT 19:1]). Some Middle Bronze cities (e.g., Megiddo) had an indirect access gate, through which entrance was made only after a sharp turn on the access ramp, whereby invading forces would be exposed to defenders within the city. Gates dating to the Solomonic period were characterized by three rectangular rooms on either side (e.g., Hazor, Megiddo), probably guardrooms; those of the divided monarchy generally had only two such chambers on either side. Major cities might have an inner, secondary wall and thus a second gate (2 Sam. 18:24; cf. 2 Kgs. 25:4).

More than simply a passageway, the city gate functioned as a place of assembly and commerce. Here kings held audiences (1 Kgs. 22:10) and prophets proclaimed the Lord's word (e.g., Jer. 17:19), and here Ezra assembled the people for the reading of the law (Neh. 8:1). Merchants traded their wares in or near the gates (e.g., 2 Kgs. 7:1; cf. Neh. 13:15-22); several of Jerusalem's gates are named after the forms of commerce located there (e.g., Fish Gate; 2 Chr. 33:14; Sheep Gate; Neh. 3:1, 32). Most importantly, the gate was where legal matters were adjudicated by the king (e.g., 2 Sam. 18:24ff.) and, most often, the elders of the city (e.g., Deut. 21:18-21; 25:7; Amos 5:10, 15). Here also juridical transactions were performed (e.g., Ruth 4:1).

As the key to a city's defense, the gate symbolizes security (cf. Isa. 28:6); to "possess the gate" means to capture the city (Gen. 22:17; 24:60). Nehemiah permitted the gates of Jerusalem to be open during the heat of the day (Neh. 7:3), but a time was foreseen when God's people would no longer be vulnerable and the gates would remain open forever (Isa. 60:11; Rev. 21:25). The gate represents the limits of a city, hence the injunction that executions be performed and the dead buried "outside the gate" (Heb. 13:12; cf. Luke 7:12); similarly, the gate might signify the entire city (cf. Deut. 12:12ff., Heb. *ša‘ar;* RSV "town") or community (Exod. 20:10). The ideal of hospitality was expressed as kind and generous treatment of the stranger and needy "in the gate" (Gen. 19:1; Amos 5:12).

The gate is a frequent metaphor for power, as in the "gates of death" (Ps. 107:18) or "Sheol" (Isa. 38:10) and the "gates of hell" (Matt. 16:18, KJV; cf. JB, NIV; RSV "powers of death"). Jesus described entrance into the kingdom of God in terms of passage through the narrow pedestrian gate as contrasted with the wider and more frequently used main gate (7:13).

GATEKEEPER (Heb. *šô‘ēr;* Gk. *thyrōrós*). A guard appointed to protect the gates of the city (2 Kgs. 7:10-11; KJV "porter") or the temple (1 Chr. 9:22). King David appointed four thousand gatekeepers to serve in the temple (23:5; 26:1-32). The temple gatekeepers were to be Levites (23:3-5), and their service included caring for the ark (15:23-24), overseeing the freewill offerings (2 Chr. 31:14), and guarding the storehouses located at the gates (Neh. 12:25). The role of the gatekeeper appears more prominent in the postexilic period, when attention to the temple and its personnel increased.

In the Persian court King Ahasuerus (Xerxes I) had

eunuchs who "guarded the threshold" (Esth. 2:21; 6:2), probably serving as royal bodyguards.

In New Testament times gatekeepers were used at the houses of the wealthy (Mark 13:34).

GATH [găth] (Heb. *gaṯ* "winepress"). One of the five major Philistine cities. Its inhabitants were called Gittites.

Situated in the northeastern area of the Philistine plain, Gath effectively controlled the valley west of the Judean hills. It must have been located rather close to Ekron, another Philistine city (1 Sam. 17:52), which provided added defense for the northeastern border of Philistia. Of the proposed sites, Tell eṣ-Ṣâfī, about 19 km. (12 mi.) east of Ashdod, is the most plausible. Although some scholars support Tell Sheikh Ahmed el-ʿAreini (also called Tell el-Menshîyeh), about 11 km. (7 mi.) south of Tell eṣ-Ṣâfī, as the site, excavations there have shown that it was much too small to be Philistine Gath.

When the Israelites conquered Canaan under Joshua, they were unable to expel the Anakim, a race of giants, from Gaza, Ashdod, or Gath (Josh. 11:22). Near the end of his life Joshua acknowledged that still none of the Philistine cities, not even Gath, had been taken (13:3). Later, when the Philistines captured the ark of the covenant, they placed it first in Ashdod, then in Gath (1 Sam. 5:8), before sending it north to Ekron. According to 7:14 the Hebrews succeeded in taking Ekron and Gath near the end of Samuel's ministry.

The Philistines' might returned, however, and they challenged Saul's forces (1 Sam. 13–16). David at last turned the Philistines' (and Gath's) political fortunes. As a young man he defeated Goliath, one of Gath's surviving giants (1 Sam. 17:23, 41-51), and brought about Israel's victory over the Philistines, who returned to Gath and Ekron (vv. 52-54). Soon David himself, envied and pursued by his rival King Saul, was forced to seek shelter in Gath. But Achish's advisors, aware of David's popularity among the Israelites, threatened his life, and David had to feign madness to escape (21:10-15 [MT 11-16]). Later, when Saul's pursuit of David became well known, Achish was willing to receive David and his band of outlaws and even to give him Ziklag, one of the Philistine cities located in western Judah (27:2-6). But when Saul died in battle with the Philistines and David became king, David resumed the conflict with the Philistines. According to the Chronicler he succeeded (1 Chr. 18:1; but see 2 Sam. 8:1); his mighty men killed Goliath's four brothers (2 Sam. 21:21-22). Yet David apparently retained a measure of friendship with Gath's inhabitants, for according to 15:18 some of the Gittites served as his bodyguard.

David's grandson King Rehoboam, who inherited Gath and other Philistine cities from his father Solomon, made Gath a fortified city (2 Chr. 11:8). Gath may have been still in Israelite hands during the reign of King Joash, when Hazael, the king of Syria, attempted to take it before he besieged Jerusalem late in the ninth century (2 Kgs. 12:17). But by the time Uzziah became king of Judah *ca.* 783 B.C., Gath had again become a Philistine city. Uzziah captured Gath and broke down its walls (2 Chr. 26:6).

Toward the end of the eighth century, Sargon II, one of Assyria's most powerful kings, may have sealed Gath's future. His annals relate his conquest of the city (Akk. *Gi-im-tu; ANET,* p. 286), and thereafter Gath does not appear in history. Although the eighth-century prophet Amos alluded to Gath's demise (Amos 6:2) and Micah to its imminent fall (Mic. 1:10), the prophets did not refer to the city in their prophecies of doom, which did include the other major Philistine cities (e.g., Amos 1:6-8; Jer. 25:20; Zeph. 2:4).

Some scholars consider the Gath mentioned at 1 Chr. 7:21 as a site on the Ephraimite border, possibly the Gath-padalla named in the lists of the Egyptian pharaohs Thutmoses III and Sheshonq I (Shishak); the site may be modern Jett on the eastern side of the Sharon plain.

GATH-HEPHER [găth hēʹfər, găth hēʹfər] (Heb. *gaṯ haḥēper* "winepress of the well"). A town on the border of Zebulun (Josh. 19:13; KJV "Gittah-hepher"); the home of the prophet Jonah (2 Kgs. 14:25). According to Jerome it was an insignificant village on the road to Tiberias, about 3 km. (2 mi.) from Sepphoris. This would place Gath-hepher in the vicinity of Tell el-Meshhad, the traditional site of Jonah's tomb, near Khirbet ez-Zurrâ, which the Israelies now call Tell Gath-hepher. The site is about 5 km. (3 mi.) northeast of Nazareth.

GATH-RIMMON [găth rimʹən] (Heb. *gaṯ rimmôn* "winepress by the pomegranate").

1. A levitical city in the territory of Dan that was allotted to the Kohathites (Josh. 19:45; 21:24; 1 Chr. 6:69 [MT 54]). The city may appear in the list of towns that Thutmose III conquered (Egyp. *knt*); if so, it lay in the vicinity of Joppa. On this basis Gath-rimmon has been identified with modern Tell ej-Jerîsheh on the south bank of the river Yarkon, but positive identification remains difficult.

2. A levitical city in the territory of Manasseh allotted to the Kohathites (Josh. 21:25). The text may be corrupt; cf. the LXX and the parallel passage 1 Chr. 6:70 (MT 55), which reads "Bileam" (i.e., IBLEAM).

GAULANITIS [gôlʹə nīʹtĭs] (Gk. *Gaulanitis*). A region in northern Transjordan and a subregion of Bashan. Its borders are roughly Mt. Hermon to the north, the Yarmuk river to the south, the Galilee to the west, and Batanea to the east. Gaulanitis (also Gaulonitis; modern Jôlân or Golan) may be named for the Old Testament levitical city Golan (Deut. 4:43; Josh. 20:8; 21:27). The area formed a part of the tetrarchy of Philip, which also included Batanea and Trachanitis (Trachonitis). Only the latter is mentioned in the New Testament (Luke 3:1); however, Gaulanitis is well known from Josephus (e.g., *Ant.* vii.8.1; viii.4.6; cf. viii.2.3).

Volcanic cones and narrow wadis are dramatic features of this part of the Transjordan plateau. The combination of volcanic soil and good irrigation produced rich farm and pastureland. The area has always been famous for its crops of wheat and cattle, and grain was exported from here during New Testament times. Recently the area has been increasingly surveyed and several important sites excavated (e.g., Tel Anafa, Tel Dan).

See also BASHAN; GOLAN.

GAULS [gôlz] (Gk. *Galatai*).* A Celtic people (Lat. *Galli*) from central and western Europe, specifically the area of modern France and northern Italy. Some segments migrated to Asia Minor in the third century B.C., where they were known subsequently as the Galatians.

Although scholars remain divided, 1 Macc. 8:2 apparently refers to Roman victories over the European Gauls, perhaps in 222 (Polybius *Hist.* ii.18-35) or *ca.* 180 (Livy *Hist.* ix.36.4-15, 43.4, 46.1).

See GALATIA.

GAZA [gā′zə, gä′zə] (Heb. *'azzâ* "the strong"; Gk. *Gaza*). The most important and the southernmost of the Philistine cities, situated 4 km. (2.5 mi.) from the southeastern Mediterranean coast, 80 km. (50 mi.) southwest of Jerusalem, and 66 km. (41 mi.) south of Joppa. It lay on the border to which Joshua forced the pre-Israelite inhabitants to retreat when he conquered southern Palestine (Josh. 10:41). The city was assigned to Judah (15:47), and although the MT of Judg. 1:18 (followed by RSV, KJV) states that Judah conquered Gaza, the LXX states that they did not (followed by JB; cf. NIV mg.). Later the city must have fallen back into the hands of the Philistines, for Samson was held prisoner there (16:21). It represented the southern limits of Solomon's empire (1 Kgs. 4:24). During the reign of Hezekiah, the Philistines were again pushed back as far as Gaza (2 Kgs. 18:8). The city's location on a major caravan route in the coastal plain also long made it attractive to the Egyptians (Jer. 47:1, 5; cf. EA 289, 314-15; *ANET*, pp. 235, 489). The prophets several times pronounced judgment upon Gaza for participation in the international slave trade and for political alignments (Amos 1:6; Zeph. 2:4; Zech. 9:5).

The city was conquered by Cambyses in 529 B.C. and by Alexander the Great in 322. During the Hellenistic period it became prosperous and was thus desired by the Maccabees. The Maccabean commander Jonathan attacked the city, burning and plundering the suburbs, and then made peace on his own terms (1 Macc. 11:61-62). Alexander Janneus captured Gaza and virtually destroyed it in 96 B.C. after a year-long siege (Josephus *Ant.* xiii.13.2-3 [352-364]; *BJ* i.4.2 [86-87]). Pompey later wrested it from the Jews and the city was then rebuilt. Although a Jewish settlement survived there through Byzantine times, the city resisted Christian influence until the fourth century A.D.

According to some scholars the later city of Gaza was built at a new site, closer to the harbor than the ancient site, which lies along the old road to Egypt (Strabo *Geog.* xvi.2.30; cf. Acts 8:26). Others maintain that the original city of Gaza is found in the ruins at Tell el-'Ajjûl, about 7 km. (4 mi.) south of modern Ghazzeh; but this is doubtful, since 'Ajjûl is probably to be identified with Beth-eglaim (cf. Diodorus *Hist.* xix.80). The modern town of Ghazzeh is probably the site of biblical Gaza.

GAZELLE (Heb. *ṣeḇî*). A hoofed ruminant, an antelope of the genus *Gazella*. Gazelles are deerlike animals, swift and shy (2 Sam. 2:18; KJV "roe").

The most common Palestinian gazelle is the *Gazella dorcas* (cf. Acts 9:36, where it is the Greek form of the name Tabitha), a slightly smaller species than the roe and more slender in build, especially in the legs. It is sandy brown, with stripes marking the face and flank, and features ringed horns 30 cm. (1 ft.) long which curve toward the back and then turn upward at the end. In the hills and plains, particularly in the plain of Jezreel, they move about singly or in small groups; in the Negeb, however, herds may number as many as twenty. Another variety, found more on the coastal plain than in the hill country, is the gray *Gazella arabica*, distinguished by its black nose.

The gazelle was numbered among the clean animals the Israelites were permitted to eat (Deut. 14:5; KJV "roebuck"; cf. 1 Kgs. 4:23 [MT 5:3]) but was not sanctioned for sacrifices (cf. Deut. 12:15, 22; 15:22). A popular game animal (cf. Prov. 6:5; Isa. 13:14), the gazelle's speed (1 Chr. 12:8 [MT 9]) and beauty (Cant. 2:9; 4:5; 7:3) were proverbial. The gazelle occurs in an oath formula at Cant. 2:7; 3:5, probably as an euphemistic substitute for a divine name.

GAZEZ [gā′zīz] (Heb. *gāzēz* "shearer").
1. The grandson of Hezron, and son of Caleb by his concubine Ephah (1 Chr. 2:46).
2. The son of Haran and grandson of Caleb (1 Chr. 2:46); nephew of **1** above.

GAZITES [gā′zīts] (Heb. *'azzāṭîm*).* The inhabitants of Gaza (Judg. 16:2; KJV "Gazathites").

GAZZAM [găz′əm] (Heb. *gazzām* "destroyer"). The ancestor or head of a family of temple servants which returned with Zerubbabel from exile (Ezra 2:48 par. Neh. 7:51).

GEBA [gē′bə] (Heb. *geḇa'* "height"). A levitical town (Josh. 21:17; 1 Chr. 6:60), originally assigned to the tribe of Benjamin (Josh. 18:24; KJV "Gaba"), 10 km. (6 mi.) north-northeast of Jerusalem. It represented the northern limits of the kingdom of Judah (2 Kgs. 23:8; Zech. 14:10).

Strategically located opposite the Wâdī eṣ-Ṣuweiniṭ, the deep gorge called the Michmash pass (cf. 1 Sam. 14:5), it was here that Saul encamped against the Philistines (13:16; cf. 14:6ff.). Earlier Jonathan had routed the Philistine garrison here (13:3), and David would later be successful throughout the region (2 Sam. 5:25). King Asa of Judah fortified the city as a border post against the northern kingdom (1 Kgs. 15:22). The prophet Isaiah envisioned it as a lodging point for the Assyrians as they advanced toward Jerusalem (Isa. 10:29). The city was resettled after the Exile, primarily by Benjaminites (Ezra 2:26 par. Neh. 7:30; 11:31) and levitical singers (12:29).

Most scholars now identify Geba as modern Jeba'; some continue to place it at Khirbet et-Tell, although that site has generally been accepted as biblical Ai.

Considerable difficulty lies in distinguishing between Geba and the linguistically similar and geographically neighboring cities Gibeah and Gibeon. For example, most English versions read Gibeah at Judg. 20:10 (MT "Geba"); some scholars would read the same at 1 Sam. 13:3 (so JB, following LXX). At 2 Sam. 5:25 the JB and NIV read Gibeon, following the LXX (cf. 1 Chr. 14:16).

GEBAL [gē'bəl] (Heb. *gᵉḇāl* "border").

1. An ancient Phoenician port, now called Jebeil, strategically located on the Mediterranean coast about 32 km. (20 mi.) north of Beirut. The Greeks renamed it Byblos, perhaps because it was a center for the trading of papyrus (Gk. *biblía*).

Archaeological excavations suggest that Gebal was populated as early as *ca.* 5000 B.C. By *ca.* 3000 the city enjoyed trade with Mesopotamia, Cyprus, and Egypt. During Egypt's Old Kingdom period (*ca.* 2700-2200) Gebal exported to Egypt oil, wine, leather, and great quantities of wood from the eastern slopes of Mt. Lebanon. Peaceful relations with Egypt were interrupted by the Amorite conquest of Phoenician and other western countries *ca.* 2100. The Amorites destroyed the city but then rebuilt it; however, economically and politically Gebal remained subject to Egyptian influence. When the Eighteenth Dynasty expelled the Hyksos from Egypt after 1600 its pharaohs were able to maintain political control over Gebal until the Amarna age (*ca.* 1350) when their grip over Phoenicia loosened; Rib-addi, Egypt's loyal governor in Gebal, sent several pleas for help to Pharaoh Amenhotep IV (cf. EA 137; *ANET*, pp. 483-84). Rameses II restored a measure of Egyptian control over Phoenicia (*ca.* 1285) but *ca.* 1200 Egypt had to grant independent status to Gebal. Wen-amon, charged to buy lumber for Egypt from the ancient maritime city, complained bitterly about the impolite treatment he received from the king there (*ANET*, pp. 25-29).

Gebal enjoyed independence for several centuries. Though the Gebalites thwarted Israel's hopes of conquest (Josh. 13:5; KJV "Giblites"), they later sent skilled craftsmen to Solomon for the construction of the temple at Jerusalem (1 Kgs. 5:18). Later Gebal joined Tyre in a successful battle against the Assyrians (853) but had to share its prestigious position with its southern neighbor. According to Ezek. 27:9, the inhabitants and the "veteran craftsmen" of Gebal were among those who served the Tyrians. The city remained prosperous during the reigns of the Persians, Greeks, Romans, and Muslims.

Excavations at the site, which covers 10 ha. (25 acres), have recovered remains from some twenty-one periods of occupation. Significant discoveries include the late third millennium temple of Hathor, the Amorite temple of Resheph which features standing obelisks, a Roman theatre, and a Crusader castle. The sarcophagus of King Ahiram (tenth century B.C.) contains one of the oldest Canaanite inscriptions in linear alphabetic script, replete with a curse against anyone disturbing the king's remains (*ANET*, p. 661; *ANEP*, nos. 456-59). The fifth-century Phoenician stele of King Yehawmilk delineates his improvements to the temple of Baalat (*ANET*, p. 656; cf. *ANEP*, no. 477).

2. A territory (modern Gibal) southeast of the Dead Sea in the mountains of Seir near Petra, mentioned along with Moab, Ammon, Amalek, and other nations as constituting an alliance against Israel (Ps. 83:7 [MT 8]). According to Josephus (*Ant.* ii.1.2 [6]) Gobolitis was part of Idumea.

GEBER [gē'bər] (Heb. *geḇer* "vigorous one"). The son of Uri; the officer appointed by Solomon over the southern portion of Gilead (1 Kgs. 4:19). Some scholars would identify him as the father of BEN-GEBER (v. 13).

GEBIM [gē'bĭm] (Heb. *gēḇîm* "trenches"). A village north of Jerusalem whose inhabitants fled from the approaching Assyrian army (Isa. 10:31). The site has been suggested as modern Shuʾafat, about 3 km. (2 mi.) north of Jerusalem, but this identification is uncertain.

GECKO [gĕk'ō] (Heb. *ᵃnāqâ* "groaner"). A small, four-legged nocturnal reptile of the family *Gekkonidae*, characterized by its rapid chirping. Of the numerous Palestinian varieties, the *Ptodactylus syriacus* is most common. The gecko is listed among the unclean reptiles which the Israelites were prohibited from eating (Lev. 11:30), probably because it was once considered poisonous.

The KJV renders the term "ferret" (cf. Targ. Aram. *yᵉlaʾ* "hedgehog"), a variety of weasel bred for hunting rats and rabbits.

GEDALIAH [gĕd'ə lī'ə] (Heb. *gᵉḏalyâ*, *gᵉḏalyāhû* "Yahweh is great").

1. (Heb. *gᵉḏalyâ*). The son of Ahikam and grandson of Shaphan, who had been the secretary (scribe) of King Josiah. Nebuchadnezzar appointed Gedaliah governor over those who remained in Judah after the greatest part of the people had been taken into exile (2 Kgs. 25:22). He ruled from Mizpah, where he established some measure of unity among the dispersed people; like his father, he took the prophet Jeremiah under his protection (Jer. 39:14; 40:5-6). The Ammonite king Baal persuaded Ishmael, the son of Nethaniah of the royal family, to murder Gedaliah in Mizpah after he had reigned only two months (or perhaps a little longer). Out of fear of retaliation by Nebuchadnnezzar, the rest of the inhabitants then disregarded the advice of Jeremiah and fled to Egypt under the leadership of Johanan, the son of Kareah (2 Kgs. 25:23-26; Jer. 40:7–41:18).

At Lachish archaeologists have discovered a seal impression of a high court official named Gedaliah, probably to be identified with this governor.

2. (Heb. *gᵉḏalyāhû*). The son of Jeduthun the Levite; leader of the second division of singers during the time of David (1 Chr. 25:3, 9).

3. (Heb. *gᵉḏalyâ*). A priest from the family of the high priest Jeshua who had to send away his foreign wife (Ezra 10:18).

4. (Heb. *gᵉḏalyāhû*). The son of Pashhur; one of the princes who threw the prophet Jeremiah into a cistern for predicting the fall of Jerusalem, then under siege by Nebuchadnezzar (Jer. 38:1-6).

5. (Heb. *gᵉḏalyâ*). The grandson of Hezekiah and grandfather of Zephaniah the prophet (Zeph. 1:1).

GEDER [gē'dər] (Heb. *geḏer* "wall"). A Canaanite royal city conquered by Joshua, presumably located in the Negeb or perhaps the Shephelah (Josh. 12:13). It was the home of Baal-hanan, appointed to supervise David's orchards in the Shephelah (1 Chr. 27:28). According to Eusebius *Onomasticon* it is identified with the tower of Eder (Gen. 35:21), but this site lies too far to the north for this identification to be accurate. Some scholars consider it the same as Beth-gader (1 Chr. 2:51; GEDOR 1), while others emend the text to read Goshen or Gerar.

GEDERAH [gə dîr'ə] (Heb. *geḏērâ* "wall").
1. A town in the Shephelah allotted to Judah (Josh. 15:36; 1 Chr. 4:23; KJV "hedges"). The site may be modern Jedîreh, 6 km. (3.7 mi.) southeast of Gezer, although the identification is uncertain.
2. The home of Jozabad, one of the men who joined David at Ziklag (1 Chr. 12:4). A common topographic name, the town may be located near Gibeon.

GEDEROTH [gə dîr'ôth] (Heb. *geḏērôṯ* "sheepfolds"). A town in the Shephelah that was captured by the Philistines during King Ahaz' reign (Josh. 15:41; 2 Chr. 28:18). Some scholars identify it with modern Qaṭra (Kedron; 1 Macc. 15:39; 16:9), about 7 km. (4 mi.) southeast of Jabneel, although others regard Qaṭra as the site of ancient Ekron.

GEDEROTHAIM [gĕd'ə rō thī'əm] (Heb. *geḏērōṯayim* "sheepfolds"). A town in the lowlands of Judah (Josh. 15:36). Because this name is fifteenth in a list of fourteen towns (so MT), scholars have proposed that it be read literally, "and her sheepfolds" (following LXX; NIV "Gederah [or Gederothaim]").

GEDOR [gē'dôr] (Heb. *geḏôr* "rampart") (**PERSON**). The brother of Kish and uncle of King Saul; eponymous ancestor of a Benjaminite family (1 Chr. 8:31; 9:37).

GEDOR [gē'dôr] (Heb. *geḏôr* "rampart") (**PLACE**).
1. A town in the hill country of Judah situated halfway between Bethlehem and Hebron (Josh. 15:58). The site may be Khirbet Jedur, 12 km. (7.5 mi.) north of Hebron. The mention of Penuel as the father of Gedor (1 Chr. 4:4) probably means that he was the founder of this town. The Beth-gader of 2:51 may be the same town.
2. A Calebite town in the Negeb of Judah, associated with Zanoah and Soco; it was founded by Jered (1 Chr. 4:18).
3. A town in the Negeb indicated as the eastern limits of the territory of Simeon (1 Chr. 4:39-40). Many scholars favor the LXX reading "Gerar."
4. A town in the tribal territory of Benjamin; the home of Joelah and Zebadiah, two of David's mighty men (1 Chr. 12:7). The site may be modern Khirbet el-Gudeirah, 10 km. (6 mi.) west of Gibeon. Some scholars view this as the same city as **2** above.

GE-HARASHIM [gə här'ə shîm] (Heb. *gê' ḥarāšîm* "valley of craftsmen"). A valley in the vicinity of Lod and Ono, probably in the southern part of the plain of Sharon. According to 1 Chr. 4:14 (KJV "valley of

Charashim"), Joab, the son of Seraiah, was the ancestor of the inhabitants of the region; he may have been the founder of a guild of craftsmen who resided here. At Neh. 11:35 most English versions render the Hebrew literally, "valley of craftsmen."

GEHAZI [gə hā'zī] (Heb. *gêḥazî* "valley of vision"). The servant of the prophet Elisha.

Gehazi suggested to his master that the barren Shunammite woman's hospitality to them might be rewarded by the birth of a son, and the woman did indeed conceive (2 Kgs. 4:11-17). Although he later rebuffed the woman when the young man died, Gehazi assisted Elisha in reviving him by means of the prophet's staff (vv. 27-37).

Gehazi greedily tricked Naaman into giving him talents of silver and two festal garments after Elisha had cured the Syrian commander of his leprosy; but because this deceit diminished the honor the prophet had shown toward the God of Israel in refusing to accept any reward himself, Gehazi and his descendants were smitten with the leprosy of Naaman (ch. 5).

It is possible that the conversation between Gehazi and the unnamed king of Judah took place after the servant had contracted leprosy, although the affliction is not mentioned. Because of his relationship with this monarch (possibly Jehoram), Gehazi was able to intercede for the Shunammite woman so that she could regain her possessions.

GEHENNA [gə hĕn'ə] (Gk. *géenna*). Greek form of Heb. *gê hinnōm* "valley of Hinnom" (Josh. 15:8), designating the narrow valley south of Jerusalem. The place was infamous during the monarchic period for the practice of child sacrifice by fire (cf. 2 Kgs. 23:10; Jer. 7:31). In the Hellenistic period the name came to be used metaphorically to denote final punishment by fire, and thus came to be the New Testament name for the place of eternal torment for unbelievers. Both the KJV and RSV translate this word as "hell" (e.g., Matt. 5:29-30; 10:28; 23:15, 33; Mark 9:43-47; Luke 12:5; Jas. 3:6). Matt. 5:22; 18:9 refer to the Gehenna, or hell, of fire (KJV, JB "hell fire").

See HELL *III.*

GELILOTH [gə lĭ'lōth] (Heb. *gelîlôṯ* "circles"). A place on the boundary separating Benjamin and Judah, situated opposite the ascent of Adummim (Josh. 18:17). The site lies along the road from Jericho to Jerusalem, *ca.* 10 km. (6 mi.) from Jerusalem; long identified with Khan el-Aḥmar, the traditional inn of the Good Samaritan, it may rather be ʿArâq ed-Deir, 1.5 km. (.9 mi.) west. It may be the same as the Gilgal mentioned at 15:7; *see* GILGAL **4.**

GEMALLI [gə măl'ī] (Heb. *gemallî* "camel owner" [?]). A man from the tribe of Dan and the father of Ammiel, one of the twelve spies that Moses sent into the promised land (Num. 13:12).

GEMARIAH [gĕm'ə rī'ə] (Heb. *gemaryâ, gemaryāhû* "Yahweh has accomplished").
1. A son of Hilkiah. Sent by King Zedekiah to Nebuchadnezzar at Babylon, he and Elasah carried a

letter from the prophet Jeremiah to the exiles living there (Jer. 29:1-3).

2. A son of the king's secretary Shaphan, and brother of Ahikam. It was in his chamber within the temple that Baruch read Jeremiah's prophecies to the people (Jer. 36:10, 12). Gemariah was one of the princes who opposed King Jehoiakim's burning of the scroll (v. 25).

3. The son of Hissilyahu; mentioned in Lachish Ostracon 1 (*ca.* 590).

GENEALOGY (Heb. *tôlēḏōṯ;* Gk. *genealogía*).† An account of the descent of a person, family, or larger social group.

As demonstrated by anthropological research, the biblical genealogies represent two major types: linear, a vertical form tracing a single line of descent from a living person to a single ancestor, or from an ancestor to a single living person (cf. Luke 3:23-38; Ruth 4:18-22); and segmented, a horizontal or branch form relating many living members by a common ancestor (cf. Exod. 6:14-25). Both types show fluidity among the middle names; names may be omitted or rearranged, or relationships changed. In many societies oral genealogies (especially segmented ones) usually go back four or five generations, occasionally to the tenth; written ones (especially linear types) may be much longer. Whereas Western societies treat them as historical documents, referring to biological kinship, tribal societies use genealogies to express social relationships, to establish personal (or group) status, rights, and obligations. Linear genealogies are used most often to legitimate succession among dynasties.

Of importance to chronology are the ancient Near Eastern king lists. These not only display a fluidity among the middle names but may omit several generations (up to seventy among the Sumerians) between one king and his ancestor. Yet even when separated by numerous generations, the latter may still refer to himself as a "son."

I. Old Testament

Old Testament genealogies are found principally in Genesis and 1 Chronicles and consist of both the linear and the segmented type, often in hybrid arrangement. Genesis lists the "generations" (Heb. *tôlᵉḏōṯ*) of Adam (Gen. 5), Noah (ch. 10), Abraham (through Isaac and Jacob), and Jacob (segmented according to their mothers, the wives Leah and Rachel, the concubines Zilpah and Bilhah; 46:8-27). Exodus traces the levitical line from Levi through Kohath, to Amram the father of Aaron and Moses (Exod. 6:16-20). Numbers continues with the census of Israel (Num. 26:5-50). 1 Chronicles presents the most extensive series of genealogies, from Adam through the Exile (1 Chr. 1–9). Ezra and Nehemiah conclude with the genealogy of the returning remnant (Ezra 2:1-70; Neh. 7:6-63).

The Hebrews, like other ancient Near Eastern peoples, used genealogies to authenticate rights of inheritance (Num. 27:1-11), enhance the social position of outsiders (e.g., Caleb, son of Jephunneh the Kenizzite [Num. 32:12; Josh. 14:6; 15:13], becomes a son of Hezron—part of Judah; 1 Chr. 2:18), establish royal and cultic lineages (e.g., David, 1 Chr. 3; priests, 2 Chr. 31:16-19; Levites, Neh. 7:43-45; temple servants, vv. 46-56), and organize their social geography (Gen. 10;

see also TABLE OF NATIONS). Usually only men are recorded.

Women appear most often as wives and concubines, whose position indicates the relative rank and relationship among the subsequent descendants (e.g., sons of wives are more important than those of concubines; cf. Gen. 35:22-26). On rare occasions women may hold an independent status in a genealogy (Num. 26:33; 1 Chr. 2:16; 3:19). After the Exile genealogies were primarily used to prove biological descent of those claiming to be Hebrews (Neh. 7:61) or of priestly lineage (vv. 63-65). Ezra used these records to purge the people of mixed marriages (Ezra 10), later an important rabbinic function throughout the intertestamental period (*Qidd.* iv.4; Josephus *Ap.* i.7).

1 Chronicles presents the most complete genealogy of the Old Testament. The Chronicler constructs this very complex document from a number of sources: Scripture (e.g., ch. 1 uses Gen. 5, 10–11; 9:2-16 follow Neh. 11:3-22), official genealogies (cf. 4:33; 5:17; 9:1), military census records (e.g., 5:24), official records such as royal chronicles (cf. 27:24), and noncanonical prophetic writings (2 Chr. 12:15). Its highly segmented style expresses both the election of Israel from the nations (ch. 1) and the ideal of the twelve tribes as the people of God (chs. 2–9). The list expresses the conviction that the postexilic remnant (Judah, Levi, and Benjamin) continues the history of Israel, their election, and worship (against Samaritan claims). Here the Chronicler focuses on the breadth (rather than the purity) of Israel, so that as many as possible may be restored to the people of God. These genealogies also demonstrate the postexilic continuity of the Davidic monarchy and the temple. *See* CHRONICLES, BOOKS OF.

II. New Testament

Jesus' genealogy occurs, with different functions, in two gospels. Matthew places it before the description of Jesus' birth (Matt. 1:1-16), as a prologue to both the infancy narrative and the Gospel itself. In Luke it follows Jesus' baptism by John the Baptist, marking the inauguration of his public ministry (Luke 3:23-38).

Matthew structures Jesus' genealogy in terms of three sets of fourteen generations (1:17). The first starts with Abraham and the patriarchs and ends with David (vv. 2-6), largely following the Chronicler's list (cf. 1 Chr. 1:34–3:9). The second traces the royal house of David to Jechoniah and the deportation to Babylon (vv. 6-11); the names follow Chronicles but omit the kings Ahaziah, Joash, and Amaziah (cf. 1 Chr. 3:11-12) as well as Jehoiakim and Jehoiachin (v. 16). The third set begins with Jechoniah, Shealtiel, and Zerubbabel, but then includes nine unknown names before Joseph and Jesus (vv. 12-16). Both the numbering and the division of the lists are significant. The number fourteen carries several messianic connotations. Symbolically, it can indicate completion: the promises to Abraham and David are fulfilled, the time of the Messiah is at hand. Fourteen is also the sum of the numerical value of the Hebrew letters in the name David; thus Jesus is his true heir (cf. Matt. 22:45). According to some scholars, Matthew thus places Jesus firmly within Israel's history as the fulfillment of its promise. To others Matthew dissects history into three equal periods to convey that the new age is about to dawn, that the time is fulfilled.

Luke starts with Jesus' father Joseph and works backward in an ascending line, listing seventy-six names before coming to Adam, "the son of God" (3:38). While the exact number of names remains textually uncertain, seventy-seven are usually accepted (Jesus to Adam; seventy-eight if God is included), thus constituting eleven sets of seven. By ending with Adam, Luke points to Jesus' universal significance, for the Gentiles as well as the children of Abraham. Moreover, by following the line of David's son Nathan, Luke apparently follows another tradition about Davidic lineage, reflecting Jeremiah's prophecy against Jehoiakim (Jer. 22:30; 36:30; cf. Zech. 12:12-13). Others have speculated that Luke intended to picture Jesus as a prophetic figure or as a priestly Messiah, instead of the royal ruler of Pharisaic expectation (as in Matthew).

Comparison of Luke's and Matthew's accounts reveals several differences. Luke's list is considerably longer, listing twenty names from Adam to Abraham and thirty-four more names between Jechoniah and Jesus. After David the two genealogies record different names, agreeing only at Shealtiel and Zerubbabel; both give different fathers to Joseph: Heli in Luke, Jacob in Matthew. By listing Nathan rather than Solomon, Luke implies that Jesus is not of royal descent. Also, Matthew adds explanations, and includes four women: the harlots Tamar (cf. 1 Chr. 2:4) and Rahab, Ruth the Moabitess (Ruth 4:13, 17-21), and Bathsheba, the last wife of David and the mother of Solomon (1 Chr. 3:5).

Accordingly, some scholars suggest that Matthew traces Jesus' biological, and Luke his legal, descent through a levirate marriage. Heli died childless, in this view, which then left his half-brother Jacob to marry Heli's widow, to whom was born Joseph, Jesus' father. Many modern scholars have reversed the order, viewing Matthew as giving Jesus' legal and Luke Jesus' biological descent. Others contend that Matthew reckons Jesus' ancestry through his father Joseph and Luke through Mary, reasoning that Luke 3:23 ("as was supposed") really disregards Jesus' connnection with Joseph.

Scholars have increasingly recognized the popular (as opposed to archival) character of this material. Both Evangelists evidently adopted to their theological purpose genealogical lists of Davidic descendants then circulating in Jewish-Christian circles. In this light, some think that Matthew gives a popular list of royal Davidic lineage, to which Joseph's and Jesus' names have been added. His being a descendant thus refers to the office which Jesus fulfills, as David's son (Matt. 22:45) and one greater than Solomon (12:42). Luke depicts Jesus' biological lineage and his bond with the human race (as shown in the immediately preceding account of his baptism, Luke 3:21-22)—but difficulties and possible duplications in the present list obscure the exact historical details. As in other ancient genealogies, it is the beginning (Jesus) and ending elements (Adam) that are most important.

Bibliography. R. E. Brown, *The Birth of the Messiah* (Garden City: 1979), pp. 57-95; M. D. Johnson, *The Purpose of the Biblical Genealogies* (Cambridge:

1969); R. R. Wilson, *Genealogy and History in the Biblical World.* SNTSMS 8 (New Haven: 1977).

GENERAL EPISTLES. *See* CATHOLIC LETTERS.

GENERATION (Heb. *dôr* "circle"; Aram. *dār* (Dan. 4:3, 34); Gk. *geneá, génnēma*). The "circle" of life, spanning from a man's birth to that of his son; this period was reckoned to be forty years (Num. 32:13; Deut. 2:14). The term was also used to refer collectively to all people living in such a period (Judg. 2:10; Ps. 24:6; 73:15; 112:2; Jer. 2:31; Matt. 11:16; 17:17; Acts 2:40). Time was commonly referred to in increments of generations in the context of blessings (Exod. 17:16; Deut. 7:9) and curses (Exod. 20:5).

A related term is Heb. *tôlēḏôt*, a plural noun derived from the Hebrew verb for "to beget (children)." Translated in most modern English versions as "generations" or "descendants," the term is used almost exclusively in Genesis in listing the family members of such figures as Adam, Noah, and Isaac (e.g., Gen. 5:1; 6:9; 10:1; 25:12, 19). *See* GENEALOGY.

GENESIS, BOOK OF.† First book of the Old Testament and of the Law or Pentateuch.

I. Name

The English name Genesis, which means "origin, generation," was adopted from Gk. *génesis kósmou* "origin of the world," first applied to the book on the basis of its contents by the LXX and later used in the Vulgate. This designation may have been taken from the LXX rendering of 2:4, "this is the book of the generation of heaven and earth." In the Hebrew canon the book bears the title *bᵉrēʾšît* "in the beginning," from its opening words. Some Jewish sources also refer to it as the "book of the creation."

II. Contents

On the basis of subject matter, the book clearly divides into two sections: chs. 1–11, commonly known as the primeval history, and chs. 12–50, the patriarchal history. The two sections constitute an introduction to the history of the people of God as recorded in the books of the Pentateuch.

The primeval history sets forth the origins of the world, mankind, and the human condition. Included are the stories of creation out of chaos (1:1–2:4a); the creation and fall of mankind, the story of the garden of Edem (2:4b–3:24); the conflict between Cain and Abel (ch. 4); the great flood and God's covenant with Noah (6:5–9:17); and the tower of Babel (11:1-9).

The second main section of the book comprises three "cycles" of stories that concentrate on God's call of the patriarchs Abraham, Jacob, and Joseph and his promise of land and posterity. Included in the Abraham cycle (12:1–25:18) are God's call to move from Haran, the stories of Sarah and Pharaoh and Abimelech, Abraham and Lot, the birth of Ishmael by the maid Hagar, Abraham's circumcision, the destruction of Sodom and Gomorrah, the sacrifice of Isaac, and the marriage of Isaac and Rebekah. The Jacob cycle (25:19–36:43) records the rivalry between Jacob and Esau, Isaac's sojourn at Gerar and Beer-sheba, Jacob's dream at Bethel, the stories of Jacob and Laban, Jacob's wrestling with the angel, and the seduction of Dinah. The final portion of the book is the story of Joseph (chs. 37–50), in which he is sold into slavery, attains a high position in the Egyptian court, and is reconciled with his family; also included are the story of Judah and Tamar (ch. 38) and the blessing of Jacob (ch. 49).

III. Literary Aspects

Questions concerning the authorship and date of composition of Genesis are tied closely to those of the origins of the Pentateuch as a whole. Early Jewish and Christian tradition regard Genesis as the first of the books of Moses, although literary and historical factors suggest a long and complex process of composition. (*See* PENTATEUCH; BIBLICAL CRITICISM).

Apart from the sources of narrative strands that a number of scholars have identified, the book as it now stands clearly comprises a variety of literary materials that have been employed to depict the beginnings of the people of Israel. Among them are some of the most ancient Hebrew poetry, such as the song of Lamech (4:23-24) and the blessing or testament of Jacob (49:2-27; cf. 27:27-29, 39-40; 48:15-16). Also included are genealogical records tracing the development of various segments of Israelite society; these vary from simple lists of people and places (the Table of Nations, ch. 10; the descendants of Jacob, 35:22-26; 46:8-27; various Edomite lists, ch. 36) to miniature histories (the descendants of Adam, ch. 5; the generations from Shem to Abraham, 11:10-32; the descendants of Nahor, 22:20-24; the ancestry of Arabic tribes, 25:1-6). Numerous etiological stories, a typical element of much ancient literature, offer explanations for the origins of various social and cultural phenomena as well as the names of peoples and places (cf. 2:23; 3:14-19; 11:1-9; 25:23-26, 30; 32:28; 33:17, 20; 35:10). The stories contained in the primeval history reflect the literary genres of myth or epic, depicting cosmological or anthropological processes for which no historical documentation exists. Some of these accounts, particularly those of Creation and the Flood, bear strong resemblance to other ancient Near Eastern literature; whatever influence this literature may have had on the Bible appears to have been indirect, and the biblical stories clearly establish the events as the activity of the God of Israel. The various parts of the patriarchal cycles have been classified as saga or legend, frequently depicting the patriarchs as folk heroes renowned for their cleverness and mighty deeds; these accounts are rich examples of the storyteller's art.

Structurally, the book can be divided on the basis of the recurrent formula "these are the *tôlᵉdôt*" (5:1, "this is the book of the *tôlᵉdôt*"); the term may be translated "generations" (2:4; 5:1; 6:9; 10:1), "descendants" (11:10, 27; 25:12, 19; 36:1, 9), or "history" (37:2). The sections of the book so designated by this division are 1:1–2:4a, the creation of heaven and earth; 2:4b–4:26, the "generations" or "history of the origin" of heaven and earth; 5:1–6:8, the descendants or "genealogy" of Adam; 6:9–9:29, the history of Noah; 10:1–11:9, the descendants of the sons of Noah; 11:10-26, the descendants of Shem; 11:27–25:11, the history of Terah and his family, which includes Abraham; 25:12-18, the descendants of Ish-

mael; 25:19–35:19, the history of Isaac and his family, which includes Jacob and Esau; 36:1–37:1, the descendants of Esau; and 37:2–50:26, the history of Jacob and his family, which includes Joseph.

IV. Historicity

For those who do not hold to a strictly literal interpretation of the text, the identification of mythological language and folkloristic technique, as well as critical questions concerning composition and literary influence, and alleged incongruities between the biblical accounts and modern science and historiography have given rise to uncertainty regarding the veracity or usefulness of the book of Genesis. Such concerns may be alleviated by a proper understanding of the nature of the biblical account from the perspective of its intended purpose as theological history rather than documentary history in the modern sense. Chs. 1–11 seek to portray theological truths in the framework of a universal human history, portraying in symbolic or pictorial terms the origins of humankind or social phenomena that cannot be substantiated by archaeological or anthropological evidence; rather than addressing scientific issues, the primeval history seeks to show such events as the work in history of the same omnipotent God whose activity has been and continues to be experienced in human lives. The events recorded in the patriarchal narratives represent the unique family histories of those who formed the people of God, accounts preserved and transmitted orally for centuries and accepted by the emergent nation Israel as the remembered past of God's involvement in their collective history; although chs. 12–50 have been shown to reflect the geographical, social, and cultural phenomena of the ancient Near East, they are concerned more with universal theological truths than the particulars of modern chronistic historiography.

V. Theology

The book of Genesis introduces primary theological themes that form the core of both the Old and New Testaments. The opening words of the book establish creation, of which mankind is the highest accomplishment, as the unique prerogative of God, a purposeful process that by its very nature is affirmed as good (1:4, 10, 12, 18, 21, 25, 31). Sin is introduced as willful disobedience (ch. 3), permeating the human condition (4:1-16; 11:1-9) and leading to divine judgment (3:14-24; 6:5–8:22). God's sustaining grace dominates the book as it depicts the beginnings of redemptive history in the call and covenant promise of land and posterity to Abraham, Isaac, Jacob, and their descendants (12:1-3, 7; 13:15-16; 15:7, 18; 17:8; 22:17; 24:7; 26:3-4; 28:13-15; 35:11-12).

Bibliography. G. von Rad, *Genesis*, rev. ed. OTL (1973); E. A. Speiser, *Genesis*, 3rd ed. AB (1979); B. Vawter, *On Genesis* (Garden City: 1977).

GENESIS APOCRYPHON.† A collection of apocryphal stories about the biblical patriarchs, discovered at Qumran in 1947. These Aramaic stories comprise a midrashic exegesis, presented in the first person, of the canonical accounts of such figures as Lamech, Enoch, Methuselah, Sarah, and Abraham, similar to 1 Enoch and Jubilees. The scroll was composed, probably in the late first century B.C. or the first century A.D., as encouragement to the Essene sectarians as they awaited the messianic age. One of the last of the Dead Sea Scrolls to be deciphered, the scroll is poorly preserved, with perhaps as many as one-half of the columns missing. Based on the first portion deciphered it was initially called the Lamech Scroll and thought to be the apocryphal book of Lamech.

See DEAD SEA SCROLLS.

GENIZAH [gə nē′zə] (Heb. *gᵉnîzâ*, from *gānaz* "cover, hide").* The chamber of a synagogue which stores wornout copies of the Torah and other sacred writings no longer fit for use in worship as well as heretical works. Such a chamber, dating to A.D. 886, was discovered at Cairo in 1896; in addition to important biblical and apocryphal manuscripts it contained the Zadokite (or Damascus) Document, which resembles the Qumran Manual of Discipline.

GENNESARET [gə nĕs′ə rĕt] (Gk. *Gennēsaret*). A plain (modern el-Ghuweir) bordering the northwest side of the lake of the same name (also known as the Sea of Galilee). The name may derive from Heb. *gan ha-śar* "garden of the prince" or a similar form (cf. 1 Macc. 11:67, Gk. *Gennēsar;* KJV "Gennesar"; cf. LXX *Chenara;* e.g., Num. 34:11).

According to Josephus (*BJ* iii.10.8 [516-521]) the plain was fertile and well-watered, measuring about 6 km. (4 mi.) long and 4 km. (2.5 mi.) wide. Its subtropical climate, moderated by mountains and lakes, supported a great variety of plant life, among which Josephus mentions palm, fig, olive, and walnut trees as well as grapes.

The fishing industry on the Sea of Galilee contributed as much to the region's prosperity as did agriculture. Josephus claims that Magdala (Tarichea), a city in the south of the plain, had 230 boats holding four sailors each (ii.21.8 [635]).

According to Josephus, Magdala, probably the largest city in Gennesaret, boasted forty thousand inhabitants (ii.21.4). Even if Josephus's figures are inflated, Gennesaret evidently was heavily populated in New Testament times. Another important city, Capernaum, was in the north of the plain.

During at least part of Jesus' Galilean ministry he lived in Capernaum (Matt. 9:1), as did several of the disciples. From there they ranged into the hills and towns of Gennesaret, preaching and healing. Jesus' observation of the agriculture and fishing of Gennesaret must have provided a rich fund of images on which he based many of his parables. *See also* GALILEE, SEA OF.

GENRE. * A classification of literary composition characterized by particular elements of form and content. Initially applied by biblical scholars to assumed elements of oral tradition, attention to such fixed linguistic forms and their characteristic words and formulas has become an important emphasis of form criticism.

Among the first genres identified were various forms of psalms, including the hymn or song of praise (e.g., Pss. 8, 29, 145–150), enthronement psalm (47, 96–99), lament (6, 12-14, 60, 88), and wisdom psalm

(37, 73). Later various genres of narrative were identified, including the chronicle, list, saga, and novelette. Wisdom literature was seen to encompass the proverb, saying, instruction, and disputation. Prophetic books include the oracle and judgment speech. The Gospels contain a variety of genres, including the discourse, parable, miracle story, and narrative. Elsewhere in the New Testament are found the epistle, doxology, and apocalypse.

Once the literary type has been isolated from its canonical context, the form critic examines each genre to determine its setting (the circumstances under which it was written) and intent (e.g., information, narration, proclamation).

Bibliography. K. Koch, *The Growth of the Biblical Tradition* (New York: 1969).

GENTILE. † A non-Hebrew (non-Israelite) person.

I. Terminology

In the Old Testament the concept is expressed most frequently by Heb. *gôy, gôyim* (so KJV; also "heathen, nations"; RSV "nations"; cf. Vulg. Lat. *gentes*). The New Testament term is Gk. *éthnos*, which is the LXX equivalent for both Heb. *gôy, gôyim* and *ʿammim* "nations, peoples"; it generally is translated "Gentiles" with reference to non-Jews (e.g., Luke 21:24; Acts 9:15) and non-Christians (e.g., Matt. 6:7, 32; Eph. 2:11-12) and "nations" with reference to all peoples (e.g., Mark 11:17; Rom. 4:17-18). The KJV also translates Gk. *Hellēnes* as "Gentiles" (RSV "Greeks").

II. Old Testament

The primary distinction between Jews and Gentiles, Israel and the nations, was religious (cf. Ps. 115; Isa. 40:18-20; 44:9-20). Israel itself originated among the nations, a "mixed multitude" ethnically and politically, reflective of the numerous peoples distinguished in the ancient world (Exod. 12:38; cf. Gen. 10; Ezek. 16:3). The patriarchs themselves had been of foreign origin (e.g., Gen. 11:31; 12:1), and, despite the hostilities of the Conquest, the Hebrews maintained a basically peaceful coexistence with the indigenous peoples of Canaan (e.g., Judg. 1:27-36). Concern was shown to demonstrate hospitality to the foreigners sojourning in their midst, even to the point of including them in Israelite worship practices (e.g., Judg. 19:16-21; cf. Lev. 24:22; 1 Kgs. 8:41-43).

Nevertheless, Israel was set apart from the Gentiles as a people chosen by God (Gen. 12:1-3; Deut. 7:6-8) and established as a nation of priestly emissaries to them (Gen. 17:3-8; Exod. 19:3-6). Because of this special relationship with the Lord, it was necessary for Israel to avoid the influences of foreign cults (Deut. 12:30; 18:9, 14). Concern for exclusiveness reached its peak in the fragile community of the restoration, as evident from the dissolution of mixed marriages at the time of Ezra and Nehemiah (Ezra 9–10; Neh. 13:23-30; cf. Exod. 34:15-16).

The nations also were subject to God's authority and were the object of prophetic rebuke when they failed to respond (e.g., Ezek. 25–32; Amos 1–2). At times they were employed as instruments of God's judgment against Israel (e.g., Isa. 45:1-6; Jer. 51;

Hab. 1:5-11). Some postexilic prophets proclaimed the forthcoming destruction of the nations (e.g., Hag. 2:7; Zech. 1:21 [MT 2:4]; 2:8-9 [MT 12-13]). A major postexilic theme, however, was the mission of Israel to the Gentiles (e.g., Isa. 42:1-4, 6), to whom was thus opened membership in the people of God (25:6-8; 56:7; Joel 3:12 [MT 4:12]).

III. New Testament

The loss of political autonomy and the spread of Hellenism caused the Jews to be increasingly wary of Gentiles during the intertestamental period (cf. Wis. 10–19). Many in the early Church, which had emerged among the Jews of Palestine, maintained this opposition to Gentiles, viewing them as morally and religiously inferior (e.g., Matt. 5:47; 6:7; Luke 12:30; Eph. 4:17; cf. 1 Cor. 5:1, "pagans"; 12:2; 1 Thess. 4:5, "heathen"). Indeed, both Gentiles and Jews rigidly opposed the followers of Christ (e.g., Acts 14:1-2; 2 Cor. 11:26).

Although he readily ministered among them (e.g., Matt. 4:15; 8:5-13; Mark 7:31-37), even Jesus excluded the Gentiles from the first apostolic mission, concentrating rather on evangelization of the Jews (Matt. 10:5); in the Great Commission issued following his resurrection, however, he sent the eleven to "make disciples of all nations" (28:19-20). The Christian community remained exclusively Jewish (cf. Acts 2:5ff.) until the stoning of Stephen, after which the church was dispersed, first throughout Judea and Samaria (8:1) and subsequently throughout the Mediterranean world (11:19-21). Peter is credited with converting the first Gentile, the Roman centurion Cornelius (10:1-43). When criticized by conservative Jewish Christians for baptizing Gentiles, Peter declared that the Holy Spirit was open to all without partiality (10:44–11:18; cf. Gal. 2:11-14). Later he defended this position before the Apostolic Council at Jerusalem, as did Paul and Barnabas (Acts 15:1-21); here it was resolved that Gentiles need not observe circumcision in order to participate in the Church. *See* APOSTOLIC COUNCIL.

Paul, the "apostle to the Gentiles" (Rom. 13:11), is particularly responsible for opening the Church to the Gentiles. Beginning with Barnabas a preaching mission at Antioch in Syria (Acts 11:26), he and his associates traveled tirelessly throughout Asia Minor and the Levant (chs. 12–28; cf. 22:21). By opening "a door of faith to the Gentiles" (14:27), Paul aroused the hostility of both Jews and Jewish Christians (Eph. 3:1; cf. Rom. 11:11). In response he proclaimed that God is God of the Gentiles as well as the Jews (Rom. 3:27) and that both have been given the power of salvation (1:16; 9:24). Indeed, he contends that Gentiles "by nature" may comply with God's righteous demands through acts of conscience and faith (2:14-15; cf. Gal. 2:15-21). Nevertheless, he cautions the Gentiles that their justification by faith is not cause for pride (Rom. 11:17-22).

GENUBATH [gə nōō′băth] (Heb. *g^{e}nubaṭ*). The son of the exiled Edomite prince Hadad and his Egyptian wife, the sister of Queen Tahpenes (1 Kgs. 11:20). Born in Egypt, he was raised in the pharaoh's palace.

GERA [gĭr′ə] (Heb. *gērā'* "guest").

1. A son of Benjamin (Gen. 46:21); the eponymous ancestor of a clan. The parallel account (1 Chr. 8:3; cf. v. 5) calls him the son of Bela and thus a grandson (or descendant) of Benjamin; if the reference is to the clan, it may reflect a changed social alignment.

2. A Benjaminite, the father of the judge Ehud (Judg. 3:15).

3. A descendant of Saul, and the father of Shimei, who cursed David upon his flight from Jerusalem (2 Sam. 16:5; 19:16, 18; 1 Kgs. 2:8).

4. A son of Ehud, and the head of a Benjaminite father's house that was exiled to Manahath (1 Chr. 8:6-7). The RSV cites Heglam as his alternate name, whereas other English versions render the Hebrew literally "he removed them" (so KJV) or "led them into exile" (JB; cf. RSV mg.).

GERAH [gĭr′ə] (Heb. *gērâ* "kernel"). A unit of weight equal to one-twentieth of a shekel (Exod. 30:13; Lev. 27:25; Num. 3:47; 18:16; Ezek. 45:12), thus slightly more than .57 g. (.02 oz.).

GERAR [gə rär′] (Heb. *g^{e}rār* "stopping place [?]"). A city near Gaza on the southern boundary of Palestine (Gen. 10:19). Both Abraham and Isaac sojourned there, entering covenants with an Abimelech (perhaps the same individual), called "king of the Philistines" (20:1-2, 15; 26:1, 8). Nevertheless, the city does not appear to have been a major Philistine center (cf. Josh. 13:3). According to the LXX at 1 Chr. 4:39-41, several Simeonite clans raided Gerar and its environs at the time of King Hezekiah, routing the inhabitants and usurping the rich pastureland (so JB and TEV; RSV "Gedor," following MT). The Judahite king Asa pursued the defeated Ethiopians as far as Gerar, plundering the area as well (2 Chr. 14:13-14). The Seleucid Antiochus V Eupator named Hegemonides as governor of the region stretching from Ptolemais to Gerar (2 Macc. 13:24).

On the basis of the name, it has been thought that the city must have been in the vicinity of modern Umm Jerar; thus Tell Jemmeh, 13 km. (8 mi.) south of Gaza, was initially identified as the site. But now most scholars identify Gerar with Tell Abū Hureirah, 18 km. (11 mi.) south of Gaza, on the western bank of the Wâdī esh-Sherî῾ah (the "valley of Gerar," Gen. 26:17). Excavations there have recovered Bronze and Iron Age remains, some of which indicate that the site was prosperous in the Middle Bronze Age (i.e., patriarchal times).

GERASA [gĕr′ə sə] (Gk. *Gerasa*), **GERASENES** [gĕr′ə sēnz] (Gk. *Gerasēnoi*).† A major city of the Decapolis, modern Jerash, located 36 km. (22 mi.) north of Amman. According to Mark 5:1-20 par. Luke 8:26-39, Jesus healed a demoniac in "the country of the Gerasenes" (KJV "Gergasenes"; cf. Matt. 8:28-34, "Gadarenes"); some scholars suggest that this was another site on the shore of the Sea of Galilee. *See* GADARA, GADARENES.

Settled by the Ammonites in the Early Iron Age, Gerasa was reestablished by Alexander IV Epiphanes as Antioch on the Chrysorrhoas. (An alternate tradition attributes the refounding to Alexander the Great.) It was seized by Alexander Jannaeus *ca.* 82 B.C. (Josephus *Ant.* xiii.15.3 [393]; *BJ* i.4.8 [104]), but in 63 B.C. Pompey captured it for Rome, whereupon it became part of the Decapolis. A prosperous commercial center, Gerasa encountered Jewish attacks during the First Jewish Revolt. It became an important Christian center in the fourth century A.D. The Muslims conquered it in 635, and the giant earthquake of *ca.* 746 left the city in ruins.

Excavations begun in 1925 reveal the city to have been a masterpiece of city planning. Encompassed by a 3 m. (10 ft.) wall, the city, which straddled the Chrysorrhoas river, was divided north-south by a colonnaded main street intersected by side streets, also colonnaded. A triumphal arch erected to honor the A.D. 129 visit of the Emperor Hadrian survives, as do the ruins of a circular forum, two theatres, a hippodrome, and several temples.

GERGESENES [gûr′gə sēnz] (Gk. *Gergesēnoi*).† Inhabitants of a town and surrounding territory on the eastern shore of the Sea of Galilee; possibly al-Kursî, opposite Magadalaz. The KJV identifies this as the site of Jesus' healing of the demoniac (Matt. 8:28; RSV "Gadarenes"). *See* GADARA, GADARENES.

GERIZIM [gĕr′ə zĭm], **MOUNT** (Heb. *har g^erizîm*). A mountain in north-central Palestine (modern Jebel eṭ-Ṭôr) with an elevation of 881 m. (2890 ft.), located directly south of Mt. Ebal and forming with it an important pass between Shechem to the east and Samaria to the west. Modern Nablus nestles between the two mountains. Mt. Gerizim was an important sacred site in early Hebrew history. Near it Abram built his first altar after coming into Canaan (Gen. 12:6-7), as did Jacob (33:18-20). On the slope facing Mt. Ebal the tribes of Simeon, Levi, Judah, Issachar, Joseph, and Benjamin, following the command of Moses, gathered after the Conquest to recite the blessings of the Law, while the other tribes, standing opposite them on the slope of Mt. Ebal, responded with the curses (Josh. 8:30-35; cf. Deut. 11:29; 27:11-13). Jotham stood on an outcropping of rock on the slopes of Gerizim as he told his fable of the trees choosing a king (Judg. 9:7ff.).

Later, the mount figured prominently in the rift between Samaria and Judah. According to the Samaritan Pentateuch, which to Samaritans was the only authoritative text, the mountain is the site of Joshua's altar (Deut. 27:4; JB mg.; MT "Mount Ebal"). The Samaritans also held Gerizim to be the mountain on which God commanded Abram to sacrifice his son Isaac, reading Moreh for Moriah (Gen. 22:2; cf. Gen. 12:6). Samaritan tradition also maintains that the "sanctuary of the Lord" of Josh. 24:26 was a temple on Mt. Gerizim. Probably owing to the shift of sacred activity to Jerusalem under King David, and perhaps because of efforts on the part of Judean writers to detract from the importance of northern sites, the mountain is not mentioned again in the Old Testament. Following the Exile, however, the Samaritans maintained the tradition regarding the mountain, establishing a temple there in the fourth century B.C. Although desecrated by Antiochus IV Epiphanes

(2 Macc. 6:2) and later destroyed by the Jewish king John Hyrcanus in 128, the temple site remained the center of Samaritan worship, particularly as a place of Passover observance. Thus the Samaritan woman told Jesus that her ancestors had worshipped on "this mountain" (John 4:20), perhaps as an accusation that the Jews had departed from the tradition of those forefathers common to both Jews and Samaritans. A small community of Samaritans at Nablus still holds annual celebrations of the Passover, Pentecost, and the Feast of Booths on Mt. Gerizim.

Archaeological excavations have uncovered the remains of the temple of Zeus erected by Hadrian in the second century A.D. and possibly the Samaritan temple destroyed by John Hyrcanus. A Middle Bronze Age building on the lower northern slope may be the site of Jotham's proclamation.

GERSHOM [gûr′shəm] (Heb. *gēr^ešōm*).

1. The eldest son of Moses and Zipporah (Exod. 2:22; 18:3). According to popular etymology, the name means "stranger there" (Heb. *gēr šam;* RSV "stranger in a foreign land"). Apparently it was Gershom whom Zipporah circumcised (4:24-26). His descendants were reckoned as Levites (1 Chr. 23:15-16). The KJV, following an errant text, calls him the son of Manasseh at Judg. 18:30.

2. Alternate form of the name Gershon, a son of Levi (1 Chr. 6:16-17, 20, 43 [MT 1-2, 5, 28; 15:7]; his descendants are called Gershomites (6:62, 71 [MT 47, 56]; cf. 15:7).

3. A descendant of Phinehas who returned from the Exile with Ezra (Ezra 8:2).

GERSHON [gûr′shən] (Heb. *gēršôn*). The eldest of Levi's three sons, the father of Libni (Ladan at 1 Chr. 23:7) and Shimei and ancestral father of the Gershonites (Gen. 46:11; Exod. 6:16-17; Num. 3:17-18); elsewhere he is called Gershom (e.g., 1 Chr. 6:16-17 [MT 1-2]) and his descendants Gershomites (e.g., 6:62, 71 [MT 47, 56]). Later his descendants were divided into the families of the Libnites and the Shimeites (Num. 3:21).

During the wilderness wanderings the Gershonites encamped behind the tabernacle on the west side of the Israelite camp (Num. 3:23). They were placed in charge of the covering of the tent of meeting, the screen for its door, the hangings for the surrounding court, and the screen and cords for the door of the court (vv. 25-26), and were responsible for the transportation of these furnishings when the Israelites moved (4:24-28). Ithamar, the son of Aaron, was their overseer in this service (v. 28). To enable them to perform their duties Moses gave the Gershonites two wagons and four oxen (7:7).

Thirteen cities were allotted to the Gershonites from the territories of the northern tribes, including four each from Issachar and Asher, three from Naphtali, and two from the Transjordanian half-tribe of Manasseh (Josh. 21:6, 27-33).

An important Gershonite family at the time of David comprised the descendants (or followers) of Asaph, the guild of temple singers (1 Chr. 6:39-43). Others had charge of the temple treasuries (26:21-22; 29:8). The heads of Gershonite father's houses are recorded at 23:7-11. Gershonites also participated in the cleansing of the temple at the time of King Hezekiah (2 Chr. 29:12-13).

GERUTH CHIMHAM [gĭr′ŏŏth kĭm′hăm] (Heb. *gērûṯ kimhām* "lodging place of Chimham"). The first stopping place of Johanan and Ishmael's captives en route to Egypt (Jer. 41:17; KJV "habitation of Chimham"). The name may designate a caravansary or inn near Bethlehem (cf. Jer. 9:2 [MT 1]; NJV "encampment for wayfarers"; Luke 2:7). The association of this site with Chimham the son of Barzillai (2 Sam. 19:37-38) is unclear.

GESHAN [gĕsh′ən] (Heb. *gêšān* "firm"). The third son of Jahdai; a Calebite of the tribe of Judah (1 Chr. 2:47; KJV "Gesham").

GESHEM [gĕsh′əm] (Heb. *gešem, gašmû* "rain"). An Arab (possibly Edomite) official who joined Sanballat and Tobiah in opposing Nehemiah's reconstruction of the walls of Jerusalem (Neh. 2:19; 6:1-2). At 6:6 the KJV and JB, following the MT, call him Gashmu. Lihyanite Arabic and Aramaic inscriptions contemporary with these events suggest that Geshem was a bedouin chieftain.

GESHUR [gĕsh′ŏŏr] (Heb. *gĕšûr* "bridge").
1. A people situated south of the Philistine pentapolis (Josh. 13:2) against whom David made raids while in exile at Ziklag (1 Sam. 27:8). An alternate interpretation is to read Josh. 13:2 as "Gezerites" (following LXX Gk. *Gesiri;* R. G. Boling and G. E. Wright, *Joshua.* AB [1982], pp. 333, 337), thus placing them to the north of Philistia.
2. A small Aramean principality north of Bashan and separating the kingdom of Israel and Aram (Josh. 13:11; 2 Sam. 15:8; 1 Chr. 2:23). Following the Israelite conquest of Canaan the Geshurites retained their independence within the territory of Manasseh (Josh. 13:13). Later David married Maacah, who was to become the mother of Absalom, to consummate a political alliance with the Geshurite king Talmai (2 Sam. 3:3); after the murder of Amnon Absalom sought refuge with Talmai (13:37; cf. 14:23). During the divided monarchy Geshur was an ally of Aram in raids against Bashan (1 Chr. 2:23).

GESSIUS FLORUS [gĕs′ĭ əs flō′rəs].† The last procurator of Judea (A.D. 64-66). An Asiatic Greek from Clazomenae (western Turkey), his provincial appointment under Nero resulted from the friendship of his wife Cleopatra with the Empress Poppaea Sabina (Josephus *Ant.* xx.11.1). According to Jewish and Roman sources (Tacitus *Hist.* v.10), his harsh policies were primarily responsible for the First Jewish Revolt (66-70) and aimed at obscuring his corrupt administration from imperial authorities (Josephus *BJ* ii.14.3). The culminating act was his extraction of seventeen talents from the temple treasury in 66, prompting protests in which Roman soldiers plundered the upper markets of Jerusalem and crucified 3,600 Jews, including a number of women, children, and equestrians. After a futile attempt to quell the rebellion, C. Cestius Gallus, the Roman governor of Syria, allegedly sent an official report to Nero placing the blame for the initial outbreak on Florus (ii.20.1). The emperor's verdict and Florus' fate remain unknown, although it is generally assumed that he was banished. Josephus' account, however, is filled with exaggerated rhetoric and overstatements, creating some suspicion of his interpretation of the events. Florus' seizure of the temple funds probably was dictated by imperial pressure to collect the Judean tribute in arrears and was inspired by Nero's general exactions from Rome and the provinces (Tacitus *Ann.* xv.45; Suetonius *Nero* 32, 38). These measures were taken after the great fire of Rome in 64. Although a dozen provincial officials were prosecuted for maladministration before 62, no such corruption is known to have taken place thereafter during Nero's reign.

GESTAS [gĕs′təs] (Gk. *Gestas*).* The name ascribed in apocryphal writings to the unrepentent thief crucified with Jesus (cf. Luke 23:39). Other forms of the name are Gistas, Gesmas, Stegmas, and Dumachus. *See* DYSMAS.

GETHER [gē′thər] (Heb. *geṯer*). A son of Aram and grandson of Shem (Gen. 10:23; 1 Chr. 1:17); the eponymous ancestor of an Aramean principality.

GETHSEMANE [gĕth sĕm′ə nĭ] (Gk. *Gethsēmani,* from Aram. *gaṯ š^emānê* "oil press"). The place where Jesus went to pray during the night on which he was betrayed (Gk. *chōríon* "field"; Matt. 26:36; Mark 14:32) and where he often met with his disciples (Luke 22:39; John 18:2). It was named for a press that was located there, perhaps in a cave since the cool underground temperatures would have been preferable for pressing olives. According to John 18:1 a garden was situated at the foot of the Mount of Olives.

Tradition identifies a grotto near the so-called Tomb of the virgin as Gethsemane. This grotto is now under the care of the Franciscans, and across the road from it lies a garden with some ancient olive trees. Between 1919 and 1924 the Church of All Nations was built here, within which is the traditional Rock of the Agony. The actual garden of Gethsemane was probably somewhere near these shrines, but the tradition offers no certainty and is subject to objection. For example, although it is possible for olive trees to live for more than two thousand years, Josephus reports that in the siege of Jerusalem under Titus (A.D. 70) all the trees within the circumference of 20 km. (12 mi.) were cut down *BJ* v.12.4 [523]).

GEUEL [gū′əl] (Heb. *g^e′û′ēl* "majesty of God"). The son of Machi from the tribe of Gad; one of the twelve spies sent into the land of Canaan (Num. 13:15).

GEZER [gē′zər, gĕz′ər] (Heb. *gezer* "portion"; Akk. *Gazru*). A royal Canaanite city, about 11 km. (7 mi.) southeast of Lydda (Josh. 12:12).

Gezer was an Egyptian outpost in the time of Thutmose III and is mentioned frequently in the Amarna Letters. Joshua defeated Horam, the king of Gezer (10:33), but the Israelites were unable to drive out the other Canaanites (16:3, 10; Judg. 1:29). Gezer became a levitical city in the tribal territory of Ephraim

(Josh. 21:21). According to 2 Sam. 5:25 David defeated the Philistines "from Geba to Gezer"; thus the city must have been in Philistine hands during his reign. Solomon later acquired the city as dowry for his wife, an Egyptian princess (1 Kgs. 9:16). In the eighth century B.C. the fortress of Gezer fell into the hands of Tiglath-pileser III, who memorialized his victory here in a relief at Nimrud (*ANEP*, no. 369). In the war of liberation under the Maccabees Judas had to secure the city, and it was later retaken by his successor Simon, who strengthened the fortifications and built there a residence for himself (2 Macc. 10:32; 1 Macc. 13:34ff.; RSV "Gazara"). Gezer still had a fortress at the time of the Crusades, and the crusaders also built there a western citadel called Mont Gisart.

After this time, however, the city's influence waned and it was buried under what came to be known as Tell Jezer. This mound was established as the site of ancient Gezer by the discovery of a series of rocks that bear the inscription "boundary of Gezer." Partial excavation of the site between 1902 and 1909 revealed that the city had been inhabited since the Early Bronze Age. The most important finds include an Early Bronze watercourse hewn out of the rocks, measuring about 13 m. (43 ft.) in length with a slope of 5.5 m. (18 ft.); a number of large monoliths set upright in a row; and an agricultural calendar from the time of the Israelite monarchy (*ca.* 950). This calendar (*ANET*, p. 320) is one of the oldest Hebrew inscriptions, and thus is valuable for the history and development of the Hebrew script and language. Since it lists agricultural events for a twelve-month year it is also important sociologically and as an indicator of early Hebrew calendrical reckoning, especially since it begins with the fall rather than the spring, contrary to Old Testament practice. In 1964 new excavations were undertaken which have made possible a fuller and more precise evaluation of the results of the earlier work. The fortifications and gateways that Solomon added to the city walls (1 Kgs. 9:17) have been identified and have proven very similar to discoveries of contemporary fortifications at Hazor and Megiddo (v. 15). Later investigations also uncovered ten monoliths, each measuring about 3m. (9 ft.) in height.

GEZRITES (1 Sam. 27:8, KJV). *See* GIRZITES.

GHOST, HOLY. *See* HOLY SPIRIT.

GIAH [gī'ə] (Heb. *gîaḥ* "spring").† An unidentified site along the route taken by Abner as he fled from Gibeon to the Arabah (2 Sam. 2:24). The Hebrew text may be corrupt, and recent scholarship favors a reading based on the LXX Gk. *Gai* (cf. Heb. *gay'* "valley").

GIANTS. Several Old Testament texts seem to refer to people of unusually large stature. At Num. 13:32-33 the Israelite spies who ventured into Canaan returned with fearful reports about the huge size of the inhabitants. Og king of Bashan is often considered a giant because he had an iron bed roughly 4 m. (13 ft.) long and 2 m. (6 ft.) wide (Deut. 3:11). The most famous giant, of course, was Goliath, who was about 3 m. (9 ft.) tall, with armor and weapons of corresponding size (1 Sam. 17:4-7). Such size may have been the result of genetic abnormality, as suggested by 2 Sam. 21:20, which describes one giant as having six fingers on each hand and six toes on each foot.

See also ANAKIM; NEPHILIM; REPHAIM.

GIBBAR [gĭb'är] (Heb. *gibbār* "hero"). The ancestral home of persons who returned with Zerubbabel from exile (Ezra 2:20). The name may be a corruption of Gibeon, which appears in the parallel list (Neh. 7:25).

GIBBETHON [gĭb'ə thŏn] (Heb. *gibbᵉtôn* "height"). A town near Baalath in the initial territory occupied by Dan (Josh. 19:44). Although it had been assigned to the Levites (21:23), the city long remained in the hands of the Philistines. The Israelite king Baasha killed his predecessor Nadab as the latter was besieging Gibbethon (1 Kgs. 15:27). Later Omri also tried to capture Gibbethon but was forced to cut his siege short when he heard that Zimri had killed Baasha's son and successor Elah at Tirzah; the army promptly proclaimed Omri king and marched to Tirzah, which they captured (1 Kgs. 16:15-18).

Eusebius and Jerome claim that Gibbethon was 26 km. (16 mi.) from Caesarea, but this is too far north; Josh. 19:44-45 mentions Gibbethon in close connection with Jehud, which was only a few miles north of Lydda. It is most likely that Gibbethon was a border city near Gezer, on the eastern edge of the coastal plain; thus many scholars identify it with modern Tell el-Melât, about 5 km. (3 mi.) east of Gezer.

GIBEA [gĭb'ĭ ə] (Heb. *gibᵉā'* "hill").* A Judahite, the son of Sheva and Caleb's concubine Maacah (1 Chr. 2:48-49). The name may designate a site in the hill country near Hebron, perhaps founded by Sheva.

GIBEAH [gĭb'ĭ ə] (Heb. *gibᵉâ* "hill").†
1. A city of Judah that lay in the hill country southwest of Jerusalem (Josh. 15:57). Some scholars identify it with el-Jeba', 19 km. (12 mi.) southwest of Jerusalem, although a site further south may be more appropriate.
2. A town in the hill country of Ephraim (Josh. 24:33; KJV "in a hill"; cf. NJV). It had been assigned to Aaron's son Eleazar, who was buried there, and became the inheritance of Phinehas.
3. A city in the tribal territory of Benjamin, one of the unwalled villages founded at the close of the Late Bronze Age along the watershed ridge north of Jerusalem. Because of the frequency of the name Gibeah, the city is often designated "Gibeah of Benjamin" (e.g., Judg. 20:10; 1 Sam. 13:2, 15; cf. Judg. 19:14; 1 Chr. 11:31) or "Gibeah of Saul" (e.g., 1 Sam. 11:4; Isa. 10:29). At Josh. 18:28 the KJV and NJV read "Gibeath," following an older feminine form of the name preserved in the MT. The town may be the same as Gibeath-elohim at 1 Sam. 10:5 (KJV, RSV mg. "hill of God").

Gibeah first appears as the setting of the rape murder of the Ephraimite Levite's concubine, which flagrantly violated the ideal of hospitality and led to civil war against Benjamin; as a result, the city was destroyed and the Benjaminites vanquished (Josh. 19–20; cf. Hos. 9:9; 10:9). Some form of settlement survived, for Saul was born at Gibeah and later joined a prophetic guild there, receiving confirmation of his atonement as king (1 Sam. 10:5, 10, 26). Saul rebuilt the city as his capital (cf. 15:34; 22:6), and from there he marshalled Israelite forces against the Ammonites (11:1-11) and Philistines (e.g., 14:2, 16) as well as the fugitive David (23:19; 26:1). According to 13:2 the Philistines maintained a garrison there, apparently intending to seize Benjaminite territory. Three of David's mighty men came from Gibeah (2 Sam. 23:29; 1 Chr. 12:3). According to the KJV and NIV, following the MT at 2 Sam. 21:6, the bodies of Saul's murdered sons were displayed at Gibeah (RSV, JB "Gibeon"; cf. NJV mg.). Josephus reports that Titus encamped at "Gabath Saul" to reconnoiter Jerusalem during the First Jewish Revolt (*BJ* v.2.1 [51-52]).

Isa. 10:29 places the city slightly north of Jerusalem along the advance of the Assyrian army (cf. Hos. 5:8; Josephus *BJ* v.2.1 [51], 30 stadia). Excavations have established that Gibeah is to be identified with modern Tell el-Fûl, a site about 5.5 km. (3.4 mi.) north of Jerusalem. The lowest stratum contains the ruins of an Iron Age village that was destroyed by fire, perhaps as a result of the events described in Judg. 19–20. The next occupation features the remains of Saul's fortress-palace; a tower and part of the wall survive. Other strata represent occupations of varying prosperity during the divided monarchy (seventh-sixth centuries) as well as the Hellenistic and Roman periods.

4. (2 Sam. 6:3-4, KJV). *See* KIRIATH-JEARIM.

GIBBEATH (Josh. 18:28, KJV). *See* GIBEAH 3.

GIBEATH-ELOHIM [gĭb′ĭ ăth ĕl′ō hĭm] (Heb. *gib*ʿ*aṯ hā*ʾ*elōhîm* "hill of God").* A hill where Saul, as predicted by Samuel, joined a band of prophets in ecstatic prophecy as a sign of his election to the Israelite kingship (1 Sam. 10:5-6). It is generally thought to be the same as the Gibeah (3) of Saul (so v. 10), an identification supported by Saul's recognition by the inhabitants (v. 11). Other proposed sites include the nearby Nebī Samwil and Bethel.

GIBEATH-HAARALOTH [gĭb′ĭ ăth hā ăr′ə lŏth] (Heb. *gib*ʿ*aṯ hā*ʿ*ᵃrālôṯ* "hill of foreskins").† A place near Gilgal, between Jericho and the Jordan river, where before their entry into Canaan Joshua circumcised the Israelites who had been born on the journey from Egypt (Josh. 5:3; KJV "the hill of the foreskins"). The site is unidentified.

GIBEON [gĭb′ĭ ən] (Heb. *gib*ʿ*ôn*, from *gb*ʿ "hill").† A city about 8 km. (5 mi.) northwest of Jerusalem, identified with modern el-Jîb. Called "a great city" in Joshua's time (Josh. 10:2), Gibeon was one of four Canaanite (or Hivite) cities (with Chephirah, Beeroth, and Kiriath-jearim; sometimes referred to as the Tetrapolis) which were spared from destruction during the Israelite conquest. The Gibeonites, masquerading as foreigners, concluded a covenant with Israel (Josh. 9:1-15). When the ruse was discovered three days later, Joshua honored the covenant and spared the Gibeonites (vv. 16-19), but made them hewers of wood and drawers of water (v. 21), evidently one of the lowest forms of servitude (cf. Deut. 29:10-11), and

in these capacities they served the congregation of Israel and the altar (Josh. 9:27). When a coalition of five Amorite kings besieged Gibeon, Joshua came to Gibeon's rescue, destroying the Amorites and liberating the city (10:1-27). This was the famous battle during which it is said the sun stood still (vv. 12-14; cf. R. G. Boling and G. E. Wright, *Joshua*. AB [1982], pp. 282-84, 286-88). Subsequently Gibeon was assigned to the tribe of Benjamin (18:25) and designated a levitical city.

A century and a half later, the armies of David and Ishbosheth fought at the pool of Gibeon after twelve young men from each side, at the instigation of Abner and Joab, felled each other in a mock battle (2 Sam. 2:12-17). During the rebellion of Sheba, Joab treacherously killed Amasa near the "great stone" in Gibeon (20:8-10). King Saul evidently attempted to destroy the Gibeonites in violation of Joshua's covenant between the Israelites and the Gibeonites. Because of Saul's bloodguilt, Israel suffered three years of famine under David's rule. In expiation David allowed the Gibeonites to hang seven of Saul's sons and grandsons on "the mountain of the Lord" (21:1-9; KJV, NIV "Gibeah of Saul"; cf. Gibeath-elohim). The same site may be the "great high place" or pagan shrine where the Lord appeared to Solomon as he was offering a sacrifice and granted his request for wisdom to govern his people (1 Kgs. 3:4-5). In David and Solomon's days the high place was the site of the tabernacle or tent of meeting (1 Chr. 16:39; 21:29; 2 Chr. 1:3, 13). The great pool of Gibeon figured once again as the place where Johanan gained leadership of the remnant of Judah spared from Babylonian exile (Jer. 41:12). At the pool he overtook Ishmael, a rebel who had killed the Babylonian-appointed governor of Judah, Gedaliah, and rescued the captives Ishmael had taken; Ishmael himself escaped to the Ammonites (vv. 11-18). The prophet Jeremiah also mentions Gibeon as the birthplace of the false prophet Hananiah (28:1). Gibeonites are included among those who returned from the Exile and helped rebuild the temple (Neh. 3:7; 7:25). It is safe to assume that the Gibeonites had been absorbed into the people of Israel by the time of the Exile.

The modern site of el-Jîb is now accepted as biblical Gibeon. First proposed by E. Robinson in 1838, this identification was confirmed by J. B. Pritchard's excavations at el-Jîb in 1956-62. Evidence for the identification existed before excavations began, including the linguistic similarity of "Gibeon" and "el-Jîb," a large rock to the northeast (perhaps that of 2 Sam. 20:8), and the Nebī Samwil, a 900 m. (3000 ft.) hill which rises 2 km. (1.3 mi.) from el-Jîb and dominates the surrounding area (the "high place" mentioned above). Excavations uncovered near-conclusive evidence, including two extensive water systems: a tunnel leading to a cistern fed by a spring dating from the tenth century B.C., and a large pool (cf. 2 Sam. 2:13) consisting of a 10.7 m. (35 ft.)-deep cylinder in which a staircase spirals down to an underground passage which in turn leads to a reservoir 24 m. (80 ft.) below surface level. Debris discovered in the pool included a number of jar handles inscribed with the legend *gbʿn gdr* in seventh-century script. The word *gbʿn* is a clear reference to Gibeon, and the entire phrase may mean "from the vineyards of Gibeon," an interpretation supported by the discovery of sixty-three storage cellars for wine jars, evidence of a flourishing wine-making industry. Nearby tombs have also provided evidence of occupation during the Middle and Late Bronze periods, just prior to Joshua's time.

Bibliography. J. B. Pritchard, *Gibeon, Where the Sun Stood Still* (Princeton: 1962).

GIBLITES (Josh. 13:5, KJV). *See* GEBAL 1.

GIDDALTI [gĭ dăl´tī] (Heb. *giddaltî* "I have magnified"). A son of Heman and leader of the twenty-second division of musicians in the service of the sanctuary (1 Chr. 25:4, 29).

GIDDEL [gĭd´əl] (Heb. *giddēl* "he [God] has caused to grow").
1. A temple servant whose descendants returned with Zerubbabel from the Exile (Ezra 2:47 par. Neh. 7:49).
2. A servant of Solomon whose descendants returned with Zerubbabel from the Exile (Ezra 2:56 par. Neh. 7:58).

GIDEON [gĭd´ĭ ən] (Heb. *giḏʿôn* "one who fells, hewer"). The youngest son of Joash, from the Abiezrite line of Manasseh. His home was in Ophrah (Judg. 6:11), a city of uncertain location. Though it is difficult to determine precisely when Gideon most likely lived, the events recorded took place *ca.* 1200 B.C. Gideon was called to be a judge during the seven years that Israel came under the dominion of Midian as divine punishment for their evil deeds (6:1). Together with the Amalekites and the "people of the East," the Midianites would attack Israel and destroy their crops and flocks as far as Gaza, leaving them with nothing. Out of fear the Israelites made their homes in dens, caves, and strongholds in the mountains (vv. 2-6), and begged the Lord for deliverance. He sent a prophet to rebuke them for their apostasy (vv. 7-10), but at the same time also sent an angel to commission Gideon to deliver Israel from the power of the Midianites (vv. 11-17). After the Lord had reassured him, Gideon built an altar, which he called "The Lord is peace" (vv. 21-24; NJV "Adonaishalom"). That night the Lord commanded Gideon to destroy the altar of Baal and the sacred pillar of Asherah that stood beside it. When the inhabitants of the city discovered what Gideon had done and demanded that he be handed over to them to be killed, his father Joash said to them that if Baal were a god, he could "contend for himself" (vv. 25-31); thus Gideon was given the name Jerubbaal, meaning "Baal shall contend" or "contender against Baal" (v. 32); at 2 Sam. 11:21 the name appears as Jerubbesheth, an alternate spelling of Jerubbosheth, in which "Baal" is replaced by Heb. *bōšeṭ* "shame".

Later Gideon summoned the tribes of Manasseh, Zebulun, and Naphtali to battle against the Midianites, Amalekites, and the people of the East, who were encamped in the valley of Jezreel (6:33-35). At Gideon's request Yahweh gave him a sign of victory with the dew and the fleece (vv. 36-40). After selecting three hundred men from the original thirty-two thousand by various tests (e.g., whether they would lap water "like a dog" [Calebite?]; 7:4-6), Gideon and his small army defeated the Midianites and put them to flight (vv. 19-23). The Israelites then offered him the kingship in honor of his victory, but Gideon refused because he desired to preserve the theocracy. Instead he asked that each of the troops give him the earrings they had taken as spoil, and with these, which amounted to 1700 shekels (about 30 kg. [60 lbs.]) of gold, he made an ephod (8:24-27).

Gideon manifested many praiseworthy characteristics as judge of Israel, and the people encountered no war for forty years after his defeat of Midian. But in spite of the decisive victory that God had given him, Gideon succumbed to sin in making the ephod, thus provoking the continued apostasy of Israel and the destruction of Gideon's house after his death at the hands of Abimelech (8:33–9:6). Nevertheless, his great victory lived on in the memory of Israel (Ps. 83:9, 11 [MT 10, 12]; Isa. 9:4; 10:26), and at Heb. 11:32 he is listed as one of the heroes of faith.

GIDEONI [gĭd´ĭ ō´nī] (Heb. *giḏʿōnî* "one who fells, hewer"). The father of Abidan, who led the tribe of Benjamin during the wilderness journey (Num. 1:11; 2:22; 7:60, 65; 10:24).

GIDOM [gī´dəm] (Heb. *giḏʿōm* "a cutting off, desolation"). A place in the vicinity of Rimmon 1, *ca.* 5 km. (3 mi.) east of Bethel, to which the Israelites pursued the Benjaminites after defeating them in civil war (Judg. 20:45; JB "Geba").

GIHON [gī´hŏn] (Heb. *gîḥôn*, from *gîaḥ* "gush, burst forth").†
1. The second of the four rivers flowing out of Eden, described as winding through (so NIV) or encircling (so JB) the entire land of Cush (Gen. 2:13). Although some scholars suggest either the Diyala or Kerkha rivers, most likely Gihon represents a tributary or rivulet of the Euphrates river.
2. A spring in the Kidron valley on the eastern slopes of the Ophel ridge; a vital source of water for biblical Jerusalem. Located south of the temple area, it is today called ʿAin Sittī Maryam (or "Fountain of the Virgin") or ʿAin Umm ed-Daraj ("Spring of the Mother of Steps"; cf. Neh. 12:37). The Hebrew name derives from the periodic (two to five times daily) gushing of the spring from its origin in a natural cave.

An underground conduit constructed by the Jebusites allowed David to capture the city for his capital (2 Sam. 5:8). The spring was regarded as a sacred site and thus was the locus for the anointing of Solomon (1 Kgs. 1:33, 38, 45).

During the Monarchy the waters of Gihon were collected in a nearby reservoir and conveyed by aqueduct south to another pool, the modern Birket el-Ḥamra, and used for irrigation of the adjacent valley. At the onset of the Assyrian invasion of Jerusalem, King Hezekiah diverted the waters through an elaborate underground system, the 536 m. (1758 ft.) Siloam tunnel, which brought the water supply to the pool of Siloam in the Tyropoeon valley, safely within the fortified city (2 Kgs. 20:20; 2 Chr. 32:30; *ANET,*

p. 321). Later Manasseh expanded the city walls to a point west of Gihon (2 Chr. 33:14).

GILALAI [gĭ lā´lī] (Heb. *gilᵃlay*). A levitical musician who participated in the procession at the dedication of the rebuilt walls of Jerusalem (Neh. 12:36).

GILBOA [gĭl bō´ə], **MOUNT** (Heb. *har haggilbōaʿ* "mount of the bubbling fountain"). A mountain 529 m. (1737 ft.) high, the peak of a chain of hills at the eastern edge of the valley of Jezreel. Situated south of the hill of Moreh in the tribal territory of Issachar, it is identified with modern Jebel Fuqûʿah, 11 km. (7 mi.) west of Beth-shan; the name is preserved in the modern village of Jelbôn on the southern slope.

It was here that Saul and the Israelites encamped against the Philistines at Shunem on the hill of Moreh (1 Sam. 28:4) and where, in the ensuing battle, he took his own life after three of his sons were slain (31:1, 8 par. 1 Chr. 10:1, 8; 2 Sam. 1:6, 21). Apparently it was here also that Gideon's forces encamped against the Midianites near the hill of Moreh (Judg. 7:1; cf. 6:33).

GILEAD [gĭl´ĭ əd] (Heb. *gilʿāḏ* "monument of stones [?]") **(PERSON)**.†

1. The son of Machir and grandson of Manasseh, and the eponym of the tribe and territory of Gilead (Num. 26:19-30; 27:1; 36:1; 1 Chr. 2:21, 23; 7:14, 17). Little is known of Gilead himself or of the characteristics of the tribe. According to Judg. 5:17, however, Gilead remained in Transjordan rather than join Deborah and Barak against Sisera; some scholars suggest that this reflects political instability within the tribe at that time and that the tribe of Gilead was supplanted by Gad. *See* GILEAD (PLACE).

2. The father of the illegitimate warrior Jephthah, who judged Gilead at the time of the Ammonite invasion (Judg. 11:1-2, 8, 11). The name may be a patronymic.

3. A descendant of Gad, and the eponymous ancestor of a clan within that tribe (1 Chr. 5:14).

GILEAD [gĭl´ĭ əd] (Heb. *gilʿāḏ* "monument of stones" [?]) **(PLACE)**.† A region in Transjordan (Deut. 3:8, 10). Sometimes the name refers to all of Israelite Transjordan (e.g., Josh. 22:9), but often it is restricted only to the areas between the Jabbok and Arnon rivers to the south (i.e., Reuben and Gad; cf. Num. 32:29) or between the Jabbok and Yarmuk to the north (i.e., Manasseh; cf. Josh. 17:5). Gilead is a rugged highland area (cf. Gen. 31:21, 23, 25) cut by river valleys and bordered by Bashan to the north, Moab to the south, Ammon to the east, and the Jordan river to the west. Important settlements in the southern portion were Jogbehah and Gerasa, and along the Jabbok river, Mahanaim, Succoth, and Peniel. The area north of the Jabbok was heavily forested, and so was a place of refuge. It was here that David first fled (cf. 2 Sam. 17:21-22) and then fought against Absalom in the "forest of Ephraim" (18:6). The northern, wooded region was a source of plants from which incense was made, as well as medicine such as the proverbial balm of Gilead (Jer. 8:22; 46:11). Gilead also offered ex-

cellent pastureland (Num. 32:1), and flocks of goats are depicted descending from its slopes in Cant. 4:1.

During the period of the Israelite conquest the area was held by the Amorite king Sihon. The Israelites under Moses defeated him to possess the land (Num. 21). This first battle for the possession of Gilead was followed by several others, and at times Moab and Ammon extended into Gilead and Gilead encroached into Bashan (cf. Josh. 17:5; 2 Kgs. 10:33; Mic. 7:14). The city Ramoth-gilead was fought for repeatedly. Gilead is named in David's conquests (Ps. 60:7 [MT 9] par. 108:8 [MT 9]). During the ninth and eighth centuries B.C. Syria was a threat, and Gilead traded hands between Israel and Damascus; Amos condemned the Syrians of Damascus who had "threshed Gilead with threshing sledges of iron" (Amos 1:3) and "ripped up women with child in Gilead" (v. 13). In 733 Tiglath-pileser III exiled the residents of Gilead (2 Kgs. 15:29). Zechariah had predicted their exile and return (Zech. 10:10). During the postexilic period the Jews in Gilead were attacked by the Gentiles of the area and had to call on Judas Maccabeus to rescue them (1 Macc. 5:9-51).

At Judg. 7:3 the KJV and NIV follow the MT in reading "and depart from Mount Gilead" at the end of Yahweh's command that Gideon put the Midianites to flight (RSV "and Gideon tested them," following LXX). The NEB follows the consonantal Hebrew text in reading "Mount Galud," thus placing the action at modern ʿAin Jālûd, west of the Jordan (cf. R. G. Boling, *Judges.* AB [1975], pp. 142, 145, "Mount Fearful"; Akk. *galadu* "be afraid").

Bibliography. N. Glueck, *The Other Side of the Jordan* (1940; repr. Cambridge, Mass.: 1970); M. Ottosson, *Gilead: Tradition and History* (Lund: 1969).

GILGAL [gĭl´găl] (Heb. *gilgāl* "circle [of stones]".)†

1. A place near Jericho (Josh. 4:19), prominent during the Conquest and the early years of the Monarchy. The site remains uncertain, although many scholars would place it in the neighborhood of Khirbet el-Mefjer.

Before the assault on Ai and Jericho the Israelites set up a camp at which they deposited the twelve stones gathered from the Jordan riverbed (vv. 19-20). Joshua was charged with circumcising there the generation born to the slaves who had escaped from Egypt. The Lord declared that this act "rolled away" the reproach of Egypt, so the place was called Gilgal (cf. Heb. *gālal* "roll").

Several important events in early Israelite history took place at or near Gilgal. The Gibeonites deceived Joshua there to make a treaty after the destruction of Ai (9:6), and there they requested aid from him when Adonizedek of Jerusalem attacked them (10:6-7, 9, 15, 43). Joshua divided the land west of the Jordan among the tribes at Gilgal (14:6). An angel journeyed from there to rebuke the Israelites for violating covenant obligations (Judg. 2:1), and Ehud the Benjaminite delivered Israel by assassinating King Eglon of Moab near Gilgal (3:12-30).

Some two centuries later the judge Samuel's circuit was bounded by Bethel, Gilgal, and Mizpah (1 Sam. 7:16). After anointing Saul as Israel's first king, Samuel directed him to Gilgal, now a prominent cultic center where his kingship would be publicly affirmed (10:8; 11:14-15).

Israel's bid for freedom from Philistine oppression began when Jonathan attacked a Philistine post at Geba; Saul assembled the Israelites at Gilgal to prepare for battle (13:2-4). When it appeared Samuel would not arrive to offer sacrifice before the army disbanded due to low morale, Saul gave the burnt offering; subsequently Samuel rebuked Saul and declared that God had rejected him as king (ch. 15).

In later monarchic history Gilgal is named as the place where the people of Judah met David as he returned to Jerusalem after the collapse of Absalom's rebellion (2 Sam. 19:15). In the eighth century the site is reviled as a place of pagan or apostasized worship by Hosea (Hos. 4:15; 9:15; 12:11), Amos (Amos 4:4; 5:5), and Micah (Mic. 6:5).

2. A site north of Bethel mentioned in the Elijah-Elisha story cycle. Elijah and Elisha traveled from Gilgal to the Jordan river, where Elijah was taken up in a whirlwind (2 Kgs. 2:1). Elisha later returned to Gilgal after raising the Shunammite woman's son from the dead, and rendered harmless a spoiled stew a company of prophets was eating (4:38-41).

A possible identification is modern Jiljilieh, in the hill country 13 km. (8 mi.) north of Bethel.

3. Possibly a Canaanite city in Galilee (Josh. 12:23; KJV, following MT; RSV "Goiim in Galilee," following LXX).

4. A site on the border of Judah between Jerusalem and Jericho, opposite the ascent of Adummim (Josh. 15:7). At 18:17 it is called Geliloth. Some scholars identify this Gilgal with the postexilic Beth-gilgal (Neh. 12:29). The site is generally considered to be modern Khan el-Aḥmar (the traditional Inn of the Good Samaritan), but archaeological evidence suggests a location near ʿAraq ed-Deir, 1.5 km. (.9 mi.) to the west (R. G. Boling and G. E. Wright, *Joshua*. AB [1982], p. 367).

5. A site which Demetrius passed en route to his siege of Jerusalem (1 Macc. 9:2). The text (LXX Gk. *Galgala*) should probably be rendered "Galilee" (so JB; cf. Josephus *Ant.* xii.11.1 [421]; LXX, Josh. 22:10).

GILGAMESH [gĭl′gə mĕsh] **EPIC.**† An Akkadian poem recounting the exploits of the legendary King Gilgamesh, here called two-thirds god and one-third human. It is apparently based upon Sumerian stories associated with Gilgamesh, a Semitic king of the Second Early Dynastic period who fortified Uruk (biblical Erech, modern Warka) and defeated King Agga of Kish (cf. *ANET*, pp. 44-52). Discovered among Assurbanipal's archives at Nineveh, the epic consists of eleven tablets composed *ca.* 2000 B.C. and a twelfth which was added somewhat later (pp. 72-99); other copies were discovered at Megiddo (dating to the fourteenth century) and Ugarit as well as fragments of Hittite and Hurrian versions from Boghazköy (pp. 503-7). Its Akkadian title is *Ša nagbu imuru* "He who saw everything."

Disturbed by Gilgamesh's violent and lustful rule, the people of Uruk petition the gods, who direct the goddess Aruru to fashion Enkidu as a rival to the king. Gilgamesh, however, sends a temple prostitute to se-

duce the wild man, and thereafter becomes a close friend of the newly civilized man. Together they slay the monster Huwawa, as well as the bull of heaven sent by the goddess Ishtar. The gods decree that Enkidu must die, and the mourning Gilgamesh, suddenly aware of his own finitude, sets out to learn the secret of immortality from Utnapishtim, the sole survivor of the Flood and the only human to attain eternal life. But the king fails to accomplish the three tests for immortality as related by Utnapishtim and resigns himself to earthly existence.

Scholars have observed various similarities, if not parallels, to biblical accounts, particularly in the account of the Deluge and the great ship and in Enkidu's attainment of mortality as the result of his sexual awareness. Most agree, however, that any literary relationship can only be secondary. *See* FLOOD.

Bibliography. A. Heidel, *The Gilgamesh Epic and Old Testament Parallels*, 2nd ed. (Chicago: 1949).

GILOH [gī′lō] (Heb. *gilōh*). A town in the hill country of Judah (Josh. 15:51); the home of Ahithophel ("the Gilonite"; 2 Sam. 15:12; 23:34). Though widely accepted, the identification of Giloh with Khirbet Jala, about 8 km. (5 mi.) north-northwest of Hebron, encounters a difficulty at Josh. 15:48-51, which seems to locate Giloh southwest of Hebron. At 2 Sam. 23:34 the RSV and JB render the name Gilo (KJV, NIV "Gilonite").

GIMZO [gĭm′zō] (Heb. *gimzô* "place of sycamores" [?]). A Judahite city located in the lowland region near the Philistine plain. It was captured by the Philistines at the time of Ahaz (2 Chr. 28:18). The site is modern Jimzū, about 5 km. (3 mi.) southeast of Lod (biblical Lydda).

GINATH [gī′năth] (Heb. *gînaṯ*). The father of Tibni, who unsuccessfully rivaled Omri for the Israelite throne (1 Kgs. 16:20-21).

GINNETHOI [gĭn′ə thoi] (Heb. *ginnᵉṯôy*). A priest who returned from the Exile with Zerubbabel (Neh. 12:4; KJV "Ginnetho"). He may be the same as Ginnethon 2 (cf. NIV).

GINNETHON [gĭn′ə thŏn] (Heb. *ginnᵉṯôn*).

1. A priest who set his seal to the renewed covenant at the time of Nehemiah (Neh. 10:6 [MT 7]).

2. The head of a priestly father's house at the time of the high priest Joiakim (Neh. 12:16). If the name is an eponym for the entire family, it may encompass **1** above. Some would also identify him with Ginnethoi.

GIRGASHITE [gûr′gə shīt] (Heb. *girgāšî*). A people mentioned only in the lists of the original inhabitants of Canaan dispossessed by Israel (e.g., Gen. 15:21; 1 Chr. 1:14; Neh. 9:8). They may have lived near the Sea of Galilee in the area of Transjordan that later was inhabited by the Gadarenes, Gerasenes, or Gergesenes.

GIRZITES [gûr′zīts] (Heb. K *girzî*; Q *gizrî*). Mentioned along with the Geshurites and the Amalekites in 1 Sam. 27:8 (KJV "Gezrites"; NJV "Gizrites") as nations that since ancient times had inhabited the area "as far as Shur to the land of Egypt, meaning between

Philistia and Egypt." Except that they were defeated by David when he resided at Ziklag, nothing about these people is known.

GISHPA [gĭsh′pə] (Heb. *gišpā'*). An overseer of the temple servants at the time of Nehemiah (Neh. 11:21; KJV "Gispa"). Some scholars consider the name to be a corruption of Hashupa in the list at Ezra 2:43.

GITTAH-HEPHER (Josh. 19:13, KJV). *See* GATH-HEPHER.

GITTAIM [gĭt′ī əm] (Heb. *gittayim* "two winepresses"). A place of unknown location to which the Beerothites fled to avoid Saul's persecution (2 Sam. 4:3). Following the Exile Benjaminites resettled there (Neh. 11:33). According to Eusebius *Onomasticon* the town lay between Antipatris and Jamnia, but the Madeba Map places it between Beth-dagon and Lod. The name may appear in the Amarna Letters as Akk. *Gamteti.*

GITTITE [gĭt′īt] (Heb. *gittîm*). A gentilic designating inhabitants of the Philistine city of Gath (e.g., 2 Sam. 6:10-11; 15:18).

GITTITH [gĭt′īth] (Heb. *gittît*). A term of unclear meaning which occurs in the superscriptions to Pss. 8, 81, 84. The instruction that the psalms be performed "according to The Gittith" (so RSV) may refer to a tune or musical style associated with Gath, the accompaniment of a musical instrument from that city (cf. JB "on the ... of Gath"; NJV "on the Gittith"), or in honor of a person from Gath. Revocalization of the Hebrew consonants permits the meaning "to be sung while treading the winepress," suggesting a psalm associated with celebrations of the wine harvest (cf. LXX; KJV "upon Gittith").

GIZONITE [gī′zə nīt] (Heb. *gizônî*). A gentilic applied to Hashem, one of David's mighty men (1 Chr. 11:34). No person or place named Gizon, from which the term could be derived, is known; thus scholars suggest emending the text to "Gunite" (cf. LXX) or "Gimzonite" (cf. *BHS*).

GLASS [Heb. *z^ek̂ôk̂ît;* Gk. *hýalos*. An amorphous, inorganic, usually transparent or translucent substance consisting of a mixture of silicates formed by fusing silica with a flux and stabilizer into a mass that, when cooled, becomes rigid.

Discovered *ca.* 2500 B.C. in the East, glass was shaped into various objects by the Phoenicians *ca.* 1400 and by the Egyptians, following military campaigns led by Thutmose III (*ca.* 1490-1436). For the next thirteen centuries or so the Egyptians, like the Phoenicians, produced opaque glass decorations by casting their glass in a mold or by heating and shaping the molten glass into several small rods that would be fastened together in a larger composition; the latter method flourished especially during the Hellenistic age, notably in Alexandria. *Ca.* 50 B.C. the technique of glass blowing was invented, which permitted craftsmen to fashion a vase, bottle, beads, or other decoration by blowing air through a hollow metal tube into

the measure of molten glass suspended from the end of it. According to Josephus the Phoenicians were excellent glass blowers (*BJ* ii.20.2 [189-191]).

At Job 28:17 glass (so RSV, JB) or crystal (so KJV, NIV) is mentioned along with precious metals and jewels as being unequal to the value of wisdom. Not always available in large quantities, glass was much treasured among the ancients.

In his apocalyptic work the aged John twice uses the expression "sea of glass," though his meaning is vague. At Rev. 4:6 John envisions a sea of clear glass before the throne of God, perhaps suggesting majesty and purity (cf. 21:18), or calmness as a contrast to the stormy seas with which the Hebrews were familiar. Whatever its meaning the background for "sea of glass" in this context is found at Exod. 24:10 and other Old Testament passages mentioning a transparent object near God's throne. At Rev. 15:2 the phrase may signify an ordeal that the faithful must endure before they are able to enter God's presence, just as the Old Testament saints had to cross the Red Sea before entering the Promised Land (cf. vv. 3-4 where the victorious martyrs sing the Song of Moses to commemorate Israel's passing through the sea); it might also indicate God's fierce judgment upon the "peoples and multitudes and nations and tongues" (17:15), which like the beast (13:1) are associated with the sea (see 15:2 for the element of fire present in the sea).

On the KJV reading at 1 Cor. 13:12; Jas. 1:23, *see* MIRROR.

GLEANING (Heb. *leqeṭ,* from *lāqaṭ*). The practice of gathering leftover ears of grain, fallen grapes, or other fruit after the harvest. Mosaic law forbade the owner of a field to collect this food, for it was to be

Glass vase in the form of a pomegranate; Cyprus, fourteenth century B.C. (Corning Museum of Glass)

left for the poor, the sojourner, the fatherless, and the widow (Lev. 19:9-10; 23:22; Deut. 24:21). Thus Ruth the Moabite widow went to glean in one of Boaz's fields upon her arrival at Bethlehem (Ruth 2:2ff.); Boaz, pleased with her concern for her aged and grieving mother-in-law, ordered his workers to assist her beyond the letter of the law (vv. 15-16).

The prophets used the imagery of gleaning to suggest utter desolation and destruction. Israel had been thoroughly stripped; all its possessions had been taken as carefully and completely as the grapes are picked from the vine (Jer. 6:9). The imagery of Micah conveys that the world is like a gleaned orchard, with no godly people left (Mic. 7:1-2). According to Jeremiah God would clean the Edomites out of Judah more thoroughly than a grape gatherer cleaned a vineyard— the gatherer at least would leave gleanings (Jer. 49:9; cf. Obad. 5). In contrast, Damascus's future was somewhat brighter, for there gleanings would be left (Isa. 17:6).

GLORY. That aspect in a person or God worthy of praise, honor, or respect; often associated with brightness or splendor in theophanies.

I. Terminology

Several Hebrew words are translated "glory." The most common and important is *kābôḏ* (from *kābēḏ* "be heavy, weighty, burdensome"; cf. Isa. 22:24). Two related words are *hāḏār,* which carries an aesthetic dimension (e.g., the splendor of God's work, Ps. 90:16), and *hôḏ,* God's sovereignty over all things (Ps. 148:13; NIV "splendor"; Hab. 3:3), more often translated "honor."

The LXX translates *kābôḏ* and related words with Gk. *dóxa.* This translation unifies glory with its manifestations, and gives the word clear theological prominence by covering the greatness and majesty of God. In the intertestamental period Greek-speaking Jews used *dóxa* for both Aram. *yiqārāʾ* "glory" and *šᵉkînâ,* God's tabernacling presence, a concept prominent in later Judaism.

The New Testament inherited this complex of meanings, using *dóxa* in the classical Greek sense of "reputation" (cf. Luke 14:10), in the Hebrew sense of weighty (2 Cor. 4:17), and for the Shekinah (Jas. 2:1; 1 Pet. 4:14). Most often, though, the New Testament follows the LXX's broad understanding of *dóxa* as glory with all its attendant manifestations.

II. Usage

A. Secular. Used of people or creation, glory is that importance which people typically honor: wisdom (Prov. 25:2); might (2 Kgs. 14:10); wealth (Ps. 49:16-17 [MT 17-18]; Esth. 1:4; Matt. 6:29). Glory can refer to the quality of a land (Isa. 35:2); or of people: age (Prov. 16:31); strength (20:29); or outward appearance (Job 19:9; cf. "comeliness," Isa. 53:2; Heb. *hāḏār*).

B. Old Testament. The Pentateuch associates God's glory (i.e., his aura, the sheer magnificence of his presence) with theophanies, acts of salvation, and acts of judgment. This glory is a devouring fire, shrouded with clouds on Mt. Sinai (Exod. 24:16-17). In clouds and fire, God's glory accompanied Israel through the wilderness (cf. 13:21), filled the tabernacle (40:34-38) and the temple at their completion (cf. 1 Kgs. 8:10-11; 2 Chr. 7:1-3), and sanctified the beginning of the cultic service (Lev. 9:23). While God shrouded his glory from Israel, he did give Moses a glimpse of its brilliance (Exod. 33:18ff.). God displays his glory in salvation: in victory over Pharaoh at the Red Sea (14:4) and in providing Israel with manna (16:7). When the people of Israel rebel (e.g., by following Korah's false priesthood or longing for Egypt at Meribah) glory also accompanies the Lord's subsequent judgment (Num. 16:42ff.; 20:2ff.).

According to the prophets Isaiah and Ezekiel, God's glory is again encountered in theophany (Isa. 6:6), and is declared in judgment on idolatrous Israel (2:10; Ezek. 10:18) and the nations (Isa. 10:16). In contrast to human glory, God maintains an unshakable covenant with his faithful remnant (42:8). Everyone shall see the glory of salvation he gives Israel (40:5; 46:13). This glory is protection for the obedient (58:5-8) and is fulfilled when Israel becomes a kingdom of priests (61:6), declaring God's glory to the nations (66:18-19). Ezekiel consoles the people with the promise of the return of God's glory to fill a new temple of an obedient people (44:2-8).

In the Psalms God's glory rests in his mighty works, manifest in creation (e.g., Pss. 19, 29, 104). Israel worships Yahweh for his mighty works of salvation in history (66; 145:4-12; cf. 29:2; 105; Isa. 42:12). He is the victorious king of glory (Ps. 24:7-10), whose presence now rests on Zion (26:8; 63:2 [MT 3]). He shows his glory in working salvation (85:9 [MT 10]). God's glory is the promised blessing for the faithful (73:24).

The Old Testament also proclaims the eschatological hope that the whole earth "shall be filled with the glory of the Lord" (Num. 14:21; cf. Isa. 6:3), when all the nations shall bless him (Ps. 66:2-4; 138:4-5). The messianic kingdom will dawn fully when the nations will know the Messiah's glory and peace (Isa. 60:1-3; cf. 11:6-9; Hab. 2:14).

C. New Testament. The New Testament modifies the Old Testament understanding of glory to include that of Christ as well. Just as in the Old Testament glory referred to salvation, so in the New Testament it is revealed in the Messiah's work of deliverance.

Glory is an essential attribute of God, "the Father of glory" (Eph. 1:17), who is praised for redemption in Christ (Gal. 1:5). God's glory is displayed in brightness and splendor at Christ's birth (Luke 2:9), and is part of eschatological hope (Rom. 5:2; cf. Rev. 21:11, 23).

In the Synoptic Gospels Christ shares in glory at the Parousia, when he comes with vindication and judgment, "in the glory of his Father" (Matt. 16:27; Mark 8:38; cf. 1 Pet. 4:13). Christ possesses his own glory through his death and resurrection (Luke 24:26; cf. 9:26, 32), which is already acclaimed in his works (cf. 5:25).

According to John Jesus' glory preexisted with the Father (17:24; cf. 1:1). It is revealed through Jesus' works (17:4) as full of grace and truth (1:14), signs (Gk. *sēmeía*) inviting belief (2:11; 11:4, 40). The cross is the culminating sign, the hour of Christ's glorification (12:23). God glorifies Jesus in his resurrection (13:31-32; cf. 1 Pet. 1:21), and continues to do so through the work of the Spirit (John 16:14).

Paul reports that Christ, raised by God's glory (Rom. 6:4), now shares in glory, which is his by perfect obedience (3:23ff.). Indeed, he is "the Lord of glory" (1 Cor. 2:8). With God, Christ now dispenses the riches of his glory (Phil. 4:19; cf. Eph. 3:16). Through him and his gospel God's glory is seen (2 Cor. 4:6); and through him glory is returned to God (Rom. 16:27).

Elsewhere in the New Testament Christ is accorded glory for his suffering and death (Rev. 5:12-13). Jesus is the "man" of Ps. 8:4-6 (MT 5-7) whom God has crowned with glory and honor because of his vicarious suffering (Heb. 2:6-9).

God is glorified through Jesus (1 Pet. 4:11; Jude 24-25). He is glory's "lamp" (Rev. 21:23), the reflection of glory, showing the true character of God (Heb. 1:3; cf. 2 Cor. 4:4). Therefore, people glorify God for Jesus' miraculous works (Luke 18:43), and especially for his work of atonement (Rev. 7:9-12; cf. 1:5-6). The Church's doxologies return glory to God for his wisdom (Rom. 11:33-36), strengthening power (16:25-27), and deliverance from sins (Gal. 1:4-5; 2 Tim. 4:18).

Glory is the work of the Spirit (John 16:14), which equips the Church with gifts (1 Pet. 4:11) to let it bear fruit to the Father's glory (John 15:8). Through the Spirit, the Church lets the glory of God in Christ shine throughout its life (cf. 2 Cor. 3:18; 4:6). Believers are the image and glory of God (1 Cor. 11:7) through their obedience (2 Cor. 9:13; Phil. 2:11), holiness (1 Cor. 6:18-20), purity (Phil. 1:11), good deeds (1 Pet. 2:11-12), and willingness to suffer for Christ (Rom. 8:17-18; 1 Pet. 4:13-16). The Church glorifies Christ by praying (John 14:13), giving generously (2 Cor. 9:13), and living in unity and love (John 17:27), filled with confidence in God's promises (Rom. 4:20; 2 Cor. 1:20). The people of God are to give glory in everything, leading lives worthy of the gospel (1 Cor. 10:31; 1 Thess. 2:12). Glory climaxes God's electing salvation (Rom. 8:30). Believers will share his glory, living in his presence in new bodies, on a new heaven and new earth (1 Cor. 15:43; Rev. 19:7; 21:22-26).

Bibliography: I. Abrahams, *The Glory of God* (1925; repr. New York: 1973); G. von Rad and G. Kittel, "δοκέω, δόξα," *TDNT* 2 (1964): 232-255; A. M. Ramsey, *The Glory of God and the Transfiguration of Christ* (New York: 1949).

GLOSS.* A scribal note, originally written in the margin or above a line, which in the process of transcription became incorporated into the text. As ascertained by textual critics, such annotations may have been intended to explain or elaborate upon a passage (e.g., Josh. 1:15, "and shall possess it"), indicate a variant reading (cf. 1 Sam. 12:13, "for whom you have asked"; lacking in LXX), or add a pious restatement or theological corrective (e.g., Ps. 51:14 [MT 16], "thou God of my salvation").

GNAT (Heb. *kēn, pl. *kinnîm*). A general term referring to small, winged, biting or stinging insects, perhaps the midge (*Chironomidae*; Arab. *barghaš*),

associated with the third plague which Yahweh visited upon Egypt (Exod. 8:16-18; Ps. 105:31; KJV "lice"; JB "mosquitoes"; NJV "swarms of insects"). The image of Aaron's staff striking the dust of the earth to bring forth the plague of gnats aptly conveys their minute size, which permits them to enter the eyes, ears, and noses of their human victims.

Gnats are used symbolically in Matt. 23:24, where Jesus, criticizing the Pharisees and teachers of the law, describes them as straining out a gnat (focusing on ceremonial manners) while swallowing a camel (neglecting justice, mercy, and faith).

The RSV rendering of "gnats" (JB "vermin"; NIV "flies") for Heb. *kēn* at Isa. 51:6 is problematic, since the singular form does not occur elsewhere. Here the KJV "in like manner," following the LXX, seems more appropriate (cf. NJV).

GNOSTICISM [nŏs′tə sĭz əm].† A diverse religious and theosophical movement of the first three centuries A.D. The name derives from the means of salvation: the Gnostic is saved through possessing a special knowledge (Gk. *gnōsis*). Gnosticism best refers to the organized expressions of the second and third centuries. Although scholars sometimes apply the term to Gnostic tendencies of the first century, evidence for a pre-Christian Gnostic movement is inconclusive.

I. Sources

Knowledge of this movement derives largely from the patristic works against it, and from original texts. Major patristic works include Irenaeus *Adversus omnes haereses*, Hippolytus *Refutatio omnium haeresium*, Tertullian *Adversus Marcionem*, Clement of Alexandria *Miscellanies*, and Origen *Commentary on John*.

Before the twentieth century only a few Gnostic texts were known, but in 1946 a large library of thirteen Coptic codices was discovered near Nag Hammadi, Egypt. These works reveal a more complex, and less specifically Christian movement. See NAG HAMMADI.

II. Beliefs

The central Gnostic doctrine is the ontological dualism between the supreme, ineffable God of love and the material world, considered evil or, at best, indifferent. Between God and matter lie a host of spiritual powers, collectively termed the fullness (*plērōma*) of God. From its lowest rank comes the creator, a demiurge identified with the Old Testament Yahweh. Fallen spiritual powers, often linked with astral referents, now rule the world.

Some human beings (i.e., the Gnostics) possess a divine spark (*pneúma*), an inner self different from the soul (*psychē*). Although imprisoned in the body, the pleroma is their true home. Made aware of their unfortunate plight through revelation (most often mediated by some divine savior), they may now ascend to their home by means of this gnosis. This is not an intellectual, but a mystical knowledge, a true seeing and hearing.

The focus of Gnostic redemption is not on God, but ultimately upon the individual's self-understanding and the resulting freedom it provides.

III. Roots

Gnosticism borrowed from many traditions in the Hellenistic world. While the exact relationship between these sources remains cloudy, four areas are discernible.

A. *Platonic Philosophy.* Gnosticism owed much to classical Greek philosophy, particularly Middle Platonism. Prominent ideas included the soul as a divine spark, imprisoned in the body; creation by a flawed demiurge; dualism between spirit and matter; knowledge of the One (*tó hén,* i.e., God) given intuitively through revelation, often in secret. Similar teachings are found in the so-called hermetic literature, a collection of Greek and Latin mystic writings attributed to Hermes Trismegistus. The high value of Plato among the Gnostics is seen in the inclusion of his *Republic* among the Nag Hammadi codices.

B. *Oriental Religion.* Gnosticism's cosmology derived principally from Persian and Mesopotamian religion. The ontological dualism of Zoroastrianism became the touchstone for Gnostic thought. Accordingly, two cosmic powers wage war in the material world: Ahura Mazda, the power of goodness and light, with his angels; and Ahriman, the wicked spirit or the power of darkness, with his demons. These powers (particularly those of Ahriman) were set in an astrological context that was originally Babylonian. Some scholars have noted the parallels with the Persian Mithraic mysteries, which taught the soul's ascent through the planetary spheres to reunion with God.

C. *Judaism.* First-century Judaism shows several points of likely influence upon the emerging Gnostic movement. Apocalyptic literature and the Dead Sea Scrolls both show clear affinities with subsequent Gnostic themes. Both are marked by strong dualisms (e.g., light/dark, the world to come/the present evil age). Both emphasize knowledge. At Qumran it is esoteric, the "hearing of deep things" (1QM 10:11). In apocalyptic, revelation discourses (a protognostic term) and visions unfold God's salvation. Although marked by pessimism toward the world, theirs remains an ethical or eschatological dualism rather than an ontological one.

At Alexandria Philo Judaeus put a Hellenistic face on Judaism. In a series of works for Gentiles he reconciled the Old Testament with philosophy by an allegorical exegesis that found mystical and philosophical truth beneath the literal narrative. This method was widely adopted by Christians and Gnostics. Philo's most important contribution was his identifying the Logos of philosophy with the biblical Wisdom (*sophía;* cf. Prov. 8), as the intermediary between the transcendent God and a universe flawed with evil.

Gnosticism also liberally borrowed motifs and names from the book of Genesis. By Gnostic allegorization these were twisted so that, e.g., the Fall no longer referred to a human event but to the fall of Sophia ("Eve") from the godhead.

D. *Christianity.* Increasingly, scholars recognize that Christianity's proclamation of a divine savior provided the catalyst for the Gnostic movement. Many Gnostics traced their teaching back to him and the secret teaching he purportedly revealed after the resurrection. Gnostic christologies offer a savior without the incarnation (a Christ-spirit) who gives knowledge instead of calling for faith (cf. Mark 12:14; Gal. 2:16).

IV. New Testament

As the Gnostic movement coalesced in the last half of the first century the New Testament Church increasingly found itself confronting false teachings with Gnostic colorings.

Paul dealt with a culture already familiar with some elements of the Gnostic synthesis. He addresses opponents at Corinth "puffed up" with knowledge (1 Cor. 8:1), who emphasize an esoteric wisdom, imagining themselves mature (Gk. *téleios*), and thus an elite group (2:6). But Paul argues that it is not knowledge but love that builds up (8:1; 13:8); not secret wisdom, but the foolishness of the cross (1:18; 2:7-8); not spiritual elitism, but the mind of Christ (2:16; Phil. 2:5ff.).

Writing to the Colossians, Paul challenges a teaching that had fused Hellenistic thinking and syncretistic Judaism into an incipient Gnosticism. This position evidently held that Christ was only part of the pleroma of God. Rather, Paul insists, he is the image of God, the ruler of all spiritual powers (Col. 1:15). Where the heresy taught asceticism (2:21, "Do not handle . . . touch . . . taste") as a means to escape the rule of the "elemental spirits" (*stoichéa;* 2:8), Paul proclaims the liberating power of Christ (vv. 11-15; 3:10).

The Pastoral Epistles present one of the clearest pictures of the developing Gnosticism. In 1 Timothy, the author censures self-proclaimed teachers of the Law (1 Tim. 6:4) who teach a false gnosis (v. 20), marked by fervid speculation into Jewish myths and genealogies (1:4; 4:7; cf. Tit. 1:14). They proclaim a spiritual resurrection already realized (2 Tim. 2:18). This is all accompanied by an asceticism regarding food (1 Tim. 4:3) and marriage (2:15; 5:14; Tit. 2:4)— a position echoed by later Gnostics (cf. Irenaeus *Adv. haer.* i.24.2).

In 1 John the apostle strongly resists similar trends. False teachers have taken his ethical dualism (light/dark, 1 John 1:5-6; God/evil one, 5:19) to be ontological. As a consequence they replaced the incarnation with a purely spiritual Christ (4:2; *see also* DOCETISM), substituted knowledge for belief (3:23; cf. 5:20), and pretended to an exalted spiritual status ("in the light," "sinless"; 1:7-8) disconnected from the atonement (2:2; 5:6-10). As at Corinth, theirs is a supposed spirituality apart from the ethical (2:3, 10-11). Denying the God of love revealed in Jesus Christ (4:8), they are instead "the spirit of antichrist" (v. 3) and deceivers (2 John 7).

Some scholars believe that the Nicolaitans were early Gnostics, noting their seeming boast to know "deep things"—a Gnostic term (Rev. 2:6, 15, 24). Before this temptation to spiritual adultery and immorality (v. 20), believers are to stand fast (vv. 3, 25).

V. Postapostolic Gnosticism

Gnosticism began taking formal shape in the late first century. One of the earliest systems is that of Simon Magus (cf. Acts 8:9-24), a religious leader among the Samaritans. Subsequent developments identified Simon himself as the heavenly revealer. He is traditionally accompanied by his consort Helen, an embodiment of Sophia. The Church Fathers labeled Simon as the father of all heresies.

Cerinthus was another of the early Gnostics. By tradition a contemporary of the apostle John, he believed the Christ (the spirit) descended on the man Jesus at his baptism and departed from him before the crucifixion.

In the second century Gnosticism reached full form and produced several major schools. The most prominent school was that of Valentinus. Educated in Alexandria, he came to Rome (ca. A.D. 136), and there accepted Christianity. His Gospel of Truth lies close to both the gospel of John and second-century Christian thought. However, later works diverged from these norms, and Valentinians developed a complex mythological system. The Valentinian school mirrored Christianity's claim to apostolic continuity, asserting that Valentinus' teacher, Theudas, was a disciple of Paul. Their apologetics showed the same allegorical method of exegesis (e.g., Ptolemaeus *Letter to Flora*), demonstrated in their commentary on John, allegedly the first such work.

Basilides was an older contemporary of Valentinus who taught at Alexandria and Rome. He produced a highly philosophical system that stressed God's ineffability. As with the Valentinians, his original vision evolved into a more mythological one, featuring five powers and numerous angels.

Some scholars consider Marcion a Gnostic. A native of Pontus, he was active at Rome as a teacher and moral reformer. Like the Gnostics, he distinguishes between the unknown, loving Father (the God of Jesus) and the creator Demiurge, a deity of cold justice identified with Yahweh. To support his reading, Marcion "de-Judaized" the New Testament (having already rejected the Old Testament), leaving a canon consisting of Luke and the ten letters ascribed to Paul. Like the Gnostics he also taught a rigorous asceticism, but he differed from their emphasis on the innate divinity of the inner self and their speculative mythology.

Gnosticism declined rapidly in the third century as Christianity countered with apologetic attacks as well as systematic biblical and theological work. In the fourth century Gnostic teachings experienced a revival in Manicheism, a radically dualistic sect which caught the imagination of many, including young Augustine; yet while it borrowed Gnostic elements (e.g., an emphasis on esoteric wisdom) Manicheism incorporated them into a discrete religious system. Gnosticism, as a movement, was dead.

VI. Evaluation

Gnosticism threatened to swamp Christian belief with speculative mythologies and a radical subjectivity. Out of the crisis the early Church developed structures of authority (the episcopacy and canon) and began the task of biblical exegesis and systematic theology. In rejecting Gnosticism, the Church affirmed the unity of Old and New Testaments, of Creator and Redeemer, as well as the priority of love. Although some Church Fathers adopted Gnostic elements, their apologies demonstrated the sufficiency of Christian answers for the Gnostic (and human) questions: "who we were and what we have become . . . wither we are hastening (and whence we are being redeemed)" (Irenaeus *Adv. haer.* i.24.4).

Bibliography. R. M. Grant, *Gnosticism and Early Christianity,* 2nd ed. (New York: 1966); H. Jonas, *The Gnostic Religion,* 2nd ed. (Boston: 1963); R. M. Wilson, *The Gnostic Problem* (Chicago: 1958); E. M. Yamauchi, *Pre-Christian Gnosticism* (Grand Rapids: 1973); K. Rudolph, *Gnosis* (San Francisco: 1983).

GOAD (Heb. *dor^eḇan;* Gk. *kéntron*). A long stick with a pin or a pointed spike attached. The farmer used the goad to make his cattle, especially his oxen, move; in some cases an oxgoad (Heb. *malmāḏ,* from *lāmaḏ* "learn") served as a powerfully effective weapon, as Shamgar demonstrated in his fight with the Philistines (Judg. 3:31). During the reign of King Saul the Israelites lacked metalsmiths and had to rely on the Philistines to repair their goads (1 Sam. 13:21; cf. LXX). At Eccl. 12:11 the "sayings of the wise" are compared to goads, in that they prod the student to acquire wisdom.

The second account of Paul's conversion near Damascus relates the Lord's comment: "It hurts you to kick against the goads [i.e., against the Lord]" (Acts 26:14; KJV "pricks"; cf. 9:5, KJV). Perhaps borrowing a common Greco-Latin saying meaning that it was useless to resist the will of the gods, Luke portrays Paul as pricked by his conscience with doubt over his compliance in Stephen's death and persecution of other believers.

GOAH [gō′ə] (Heb. *gō'â* "lowing").† An extension of the hills encompassed within the rebuilt city of Jerusalem as envisioned by Jeremiah (Jer. 31:39; KJV "Goath"). Identification remains uncertain, partly because of uncertainty regarding the precise location of Gareb. Recent scholarship favors a setting west of the ancient city near the juncture of the Tyropoeon and the Transversal valleys; an alternate interpretation places Goah to the southeast, where the Tyropoeon, Hinnom, and Kidron valleys meet. The JB includes Goah in Zechariah's account of the eschatological battle (Zech. 14:5).

GOAT.† A hollow-horned ruminant belonging to the same subfamily as sheep. The Bible employs a large number of words for goats, an indication of the goat's importance in ancient life. In Hebrew the generic word for goat is *'ēz* (pl. *'izzîm;* cf. Gk. *aíx*), also used for she-goats and elliptically for goats' hair (Exod. 26:7). Heb. *śā'îr* (lit. "hairy") usually means he-goat and is used of goats offered as sacrifices; it is sometimes used in combination with *'ēz.* The most common word for he-goat is *'attûḏ,* although *ṣāpîr* (2 Chr. 29:21; Dan. 8:5, 8, 21) and *tayiš* (e.g., Gen. 30:35; Prov. 30:31) also occur. Heb. *g^eḏî* refers to the kid (young goat); it appears also in the place name En-gedi (1 Sam. 23:29). Hebrew has several words for wild goats: *yē'ēl* (Ugar. *y'l;* cf. Heb. *ya'ªlâ,* Prov. 5:19; RSV "doe," but probably a female mountain goat); *'aqqô* (so RSV) and *zemer* (Deut. 14:5; RSV "mountain sheep"; KJV "chamois"; NEB "rock-goat"). In Greek the common word for goat is *trágos* (Heb. 9:12-13, 19; 10:4); cf. *ériphos* (Matt. 25:32) and the diminutive *eríphion* "kid" (v. 33).

The wild antecedent of modern domestic goats was probably the bezoar goat (*Capra hircus aegagrus*), which had long scimitar-like horns up to 130 cm. (50 in.) long. It was usually reddish-brown with black and white markings. Paleolithic remains of it, as well as of another wild species, *Capra primigenia,* have been found in the Antelios cave in the mountains of Lebanon, and, some archaeologists claim, at Palestinian sites. *Capra primigenia* may be related to the Nubian ibex (*Capra ibex nubiana*) whose territory extended as far north as Lebanon. Most scholars believe that the wild goat of the Old Testament was the Nubian ibex or its antecedents. Wild goats usually lived at high elevations (Ps. 104:18; cf. Job 39:1, "mountain goat"), on the rocks near En-gedi close to the western shore of the Dead Sea (1 Sam. 24:1-2), in the southern Negeb (attested by drawings), occasionally in the vicinity of Jerusalem, and possibly in the Sinai peninsula. Wild goat meat was lawful for the Hebrews to eat (Deut. 14:5). On "wild goats" at Isa. 13:21; 34:14 (NIV), see SATYR.

The earliest evidence for the domestication of the bezoar goat comes from Jericho about 7000 B.C. By the Bronze Age varieties with twisted horns had been bred. The early biblical domestic goats may have been of the scimitar-horned or a twisted-horn variety, or a breed closer to the modern Syrian or Mamber goat (*Capra hircus mambrica*). The latter, unlike the bezoar, has a convex nose, drooping ears as long as 35 cm. (14 in.), and long hair usually blackish-brown in color (cf. Cant. 4:1). The speckled and spotted goats at Gen. 30:32 were quite rare throughout Syria. The horns of both the male and female are fairly long—up to 71 cm. (28 in.) on the male—but there are marked differences between the sexes in length, shape, and posture.

In ancient economy goats were very useful and thus were a measure of wealth (cf. 1 Sam. 25:2; 2 Chr. 17:11). They probably preceded and outnumbered cows in providing milk for human consumption (Deut. 32:14; Prov. 27:27), and their meat was lawful (Lev. 7:23; Deut. 14:4). Goat's hair was woven into tent cloth, one variety of which was used in the tabernacle (Exod. 26:7), as well as tough fabric for clothing (25:4; 36:14; 1 Sam. 19:13, 16). Goatskin, when tanned, provided leather (e.g., Num. 4:6; cf. Josh. 9:4; 1 Sam. 1:24). Unlike sheep, goats can subsist on scant vegetation, but their grazing habits can be ruinous to trees and shrubs, the leaves of which they can reach by standing nearly erect on their hind legs. Such habits may account for much of the denuding of biblical lands.

Goats figured prominently in the sacrificial rites of Israel (Ps. 50:9, 13; 66:15; Isa. 1:11). Firstling goats were to be offered to the Lord (Num. 18:17). Most goat sacrifices specified a he-goat (e.g., Lev. 1:10; 4:23; 22:19; Num. 7:16-17; 2 Chr. 29:21; Ezek. 43:22, 25), although some required a she-goat (Lev. 4:28; 5:6; cf. Gen. 15:9). The Passover called for a year-old male goat or lamb (Exod. 12:5). Two he-goats were required as a sin-offering on the annual Day of Atonement, one of which was chosen by lot as the "scapegoat" released into the wilderness (Lev. 16:5, 7-10; *see* AZAZEL). According to the New Testament the blood of Jesus Christ has replaced the blood of goats as the atoning sacrifice, now offered once for all (Heb. 9:12-13, 19; 10:4).

In figurative usage the he-goat, because of its role as leader of the flock (Jer. 50:8), served as an image of human leadership (cf. Dan. 8:5-8), and the stately strides of he-goats and kings are compared (Prov. 30:31). These exalted images of goats in the Old Tes-

tament gave way in the Christian era to the negative image of the goat in Matt. 25:31-46, where the goats, separated from the good sheep, represent the wicked at the day of judgment (cf. Ezek. 34:17ff., where both sheep and goats are divided into good and wicked groups).

GOATSKINS (Heb. *taḥaš;* Gk. *aígeion dérma*).† Part of the material used in the covering of the tabernacle (Exod. 26:14; 36:19; 39:34; Num. 4:25), donated by the people (Exod. 22:5; 35:7, 23). It was also used to cover the ark and the vessels and utensils of the altar (Num. 4:6, 8, 10-12, 14).

The meaning of Heb. *taḥaš* is debated. The KJV "badgers' skins," like the RSV "goatskins," has no philological basis (cf. JB "fine leather"). The NEB "porpoise-hide" (cf. B. S. Childs' (*The Book of Exodus.* OTL [1974], p. 514, "dolphin skins") reflects the possible Arabic cognate *tuḥas* "dolphin" (so NJV) or "dugong" (NIV "sea cow"), the latter of which is found in the Red Sea. The only other occurrence of the Hebrew term is at Ezek. 16:10, where it refers to footwear and thus to leather (cf. Egyp. *ṯḥś* "leather"; so RSV), which would seem to support the view that *taḥaš* was from a commonly available animal like the goat and not a relatively rare creature such as other options suggest. Moreover, the people of Israel would hardly have had access to large numbers of dolphin skins. But the matter must remain uncertain.

The New Testament mentions goatskins only at Heb. 11:37, where they are said to have been the clothing of prophets and other holy persons (cf. the "hairy mantle" of Zech. 13:4). Such ascetic dress was later common for Near Eastern monks.

GOB [gŏb] (Heb. *gōḇ, gôḇ* "pit"). The setting for two battles between the Israelites, led by David, and the Philistines (2 Sam. 21:18-19). The parallel account at 1 Chr. 20:4 gives the site as Gezer.

GOD. That gracious Person revealed in and through the Bible as the Sovereign Creator of the universe, and the merciful redeemer and faithful preserver of mankind.

1. Knowledge of God

A. Metaphysics. Both Christians and non-Christians have approached God through philosophical reasoning. This approach develops a definition of God, often abstract and vague, which is focused on his transcendence ("an inscrutable power"), perfection ("the highest of all beings"), or absoluteness (cf. Anselm). In extreme instances these descriptions of the divine may stand in hostility against revelation, or only tolerate the biblical God with the greatest difficulty. In Christian theology, such a method becomes a means of systematizing, developing, or completing the biblical data. In all these approaches the biblical view is one, or the sole, instance of some general definition. By resorting to such inherently abstract categories, this approach continually runs the danger of becoming only the reflection of what people think or sense the divine to be, rather than a true description of how he was revealed himself.

B. Natural Theology. Closely related to a metaphysical approach, natural theology seeks to know God through creation (cf. Ps. 19) and human experience (cf. Rom. 1:20). Like the metaphysical approach, this creates a general doctrine of God into which the biblical evidence must then accommodate itself. As with all human knowledge, its conclusions mix truth with hope, self-delusion, and error. In its extreme forms, natural theology asserts the continuity of God with creation and may result in either a pantheism or in the depersonalizing of God. Most theologians, though, treat natural theology as a jumping-off point to knowledge gained through Scripture. However, the lack of consensus within natural theology and the necessary tentativeness of its method may make it an unreliable partner for gaining a true knowledge of God. Although employed by many traditions, natural theology dangerously undercuts the uniqueness and necessity of scriptural revelation by substituting human conceptions about the divine for divine self-disclosure.

C. Biblical Theology. The Bible knows little of knowledge gained by philosophical speculation or reasoning from nature. Even less does it entertain the possibility of atheism (cf. Ps. 14:1). God is. Unlike the anthropocentric ways of attempting to know God, this knowledge is theocentric: God discloses himself; it is a divine gift, not a human achievement.

The Fall makes this revelation necessary. Sinful people cannot rightly know the holy God. Although God has revealed himself in creation and in human conscience, people reject that revelation for idolatry and self-deification. Sin has blinded their understanding, leaving them unable to properly perceive God (Eph. 4:18). In the face of willful ignorance, God restores what mankind itself can no longer find.

As the One who initiates this knowledge, God is properly the subject of knowledge. By giving himself concretely in acts of salvation, the interpreting words and records of his people, and his incarnation, God is also the object of this knowledge.

The biblical knowledge of God rests foremost with his self-disclosure through acts of salvation in the midst of history, from Abraham to the apostles. Accompanying this action, God gives his word as record, testimony, and interpretation of these deeds. God speaks, and in speaking shows his character and expectation for people. Salvation and word come together in the revelation of Jesus Christ. As the fullness of deity present bodily (Col. 2:9) Jesus reveals God through the reconciling act of salvation on the cross, his teaching, and in his presence. This knowledge is by the Spirit, who inspires Scripture, witnesses to its truth, testifies to salvation, and guides God's people. The Spirit brings this knowledge of God into concrete embodiment in the repentance and faith of believers. Thus human knowledge is not only about God, but genuine knowledge of God. This threefold work of God in revelation, acts of salvation in teaching, and his inspiring presence testifies to his character, confessed in the Church as being triune: Father, Son, and Holy Spirit.

See REVELATION.

II. Old Testament

A. Name. God's self-revelation in history is under-

scored by the giving of his name, in Semitic thought tantamount to disclosure of his true character. This name gives authority (Exod. 3:13), is called upon in worship (Gen. 12:8), is feared (Deut. 28:58), praised (Ps. 7:17 [MT 18]), and glorified (86:9). To treat the Lord's name as empty or vain is to blaspheme God (Exod. 20:7; Lev. 24:16; cf. Jer. 32:34). To trust God's name is to trust God (Ps. 33:21); to proclaim it is to proclaim his deeds (Exod. 9:16; Isa. 12:4). *See* NAME.

God is known by various names in the Old Testament, among the most frequent of which is El (Heb. *'ēl* "power, might"). Also the generic Semitic designation for a deity and the title of the head of the pantheon, as a personal name for the God of Israel El is particularly common in the patriarchal accounts; it occurs also in various compound forms, very ancient appelatives that may express divine attributes or local manifestations (e.g., El Elyon, El Shaddai; cf. El-Elohe-Israel). Another general name is Elohim, a plural form representing the godhead, the very fullness of deity; it may be related grammatically to Eloah, which occurs primarily in poetry. Probably, only Yahweh, the name revealed to Moses, is the personal name of God (*YHWH*; Exod. 3:14); later regarded as too sacred for utterance, it is generally represented in English texts as "the Lord." By giving Israel this name God implicitly promises continuing presence and help (10:2; Isa. 49:23). The name occurs also in the compound "Yahweh (Lord) of hosts." Other names ascribed to God include Rock (Deut. 32:18), Judge (Gen. 18:25), Father (Isa. 63:16), and the Holy One of Israel (49:7; Jer. 50:29).

For further information on specific names see the individual entries. *See also* I AM WHO I AM; YAHWEH.

B. Revelation. Theology uses a variety of categories derived from philosophy to understand who God is. Traditionally it describes God in terms of attributes such as eternity, self-existence, immutability, omniscience, and omnipotence. The Old Testament, however, declines this formal path, and instead knows God through three distinctive relationships.

1. *Personal Relationship.* Yahweh is Israel's God, the God of Abraham, Isaac, and Jacob (Exod. 6:3), and they are his people (e.g., Lev. 26:12; Jer. 31:33). By giving his name he thus can be called upon (Ps. 99:6), and in turn he responds (Isa. 58:9). This is a personal, not a magical name, publicly known, guarded against vain misuse (Exod. 3:14; 20:7). This relationship is expressed formally by a covenant, the motive of which lies in God's gracious self-commitment and love (34:6; Deut. 7:7-8). It takes active shape in redeeming Noah (Gen. 9:8-17), calling Abraham (chs. 12, 15, 17), and in rescuing and making covenant with Israel (Exod. 19–20). In creating relationship, Yahweh gives Israel his law (Heb. *tôrâ*), which is his personal will, refusing cultic manipulation, and demanding personal faithfulness in return (Isa. 1:12-17; Amos 2:4; 5:21ff.). In the face of Israel's rejection and rebellion Yahweh shows himself as the preserver of this relationship by raising judges (Judg. 2:11-18), renewing the covenant (2 Kgs. 23:1-3), and promising blessing to a repentant remnant (Ezek. 37:24-28; Hos. 2:21-23; Joel 2:18-27).

Through this relationship Yahweh reveals himself as the living God (Deut. 5:26; Jer. 10:10), who maintains a living relationship with his people. God expresses this through personalistic traits of love, anger, anguish, patience, hatred, jealousy, and joy, and with personalistic titles: he is Israel's next-of-kin, their Redeemer (Isa. 41:14), a father (Mal. 1:6), Israel's husband (Hos. 1–3), one who cares tenderly (Jer. 14:17; Hos. 11:8). In turn, Israel's approach to God echoes and reinforces this personalistic language. Israel can question God, utter laments (e.g., Ps. 74:1-11), and cry out (Jer. 14:19; Hab. 1:2), because they are in a living relationship with the Living God.

2. Unique Sovereign. Yahweh is one God, and God alone (Deut. 6:4), with no other gods before him (Exod. 20:3; Isa. 45:5). He is sovereign in graciously electing Israel (Deut. 7:7-10), making covenant with them as suzerain (Exod. 19–20), and claiming unconditional loyalty (24:7). His sovereignty and election rest in the freedom expressed in his name (Exod. 3:14). Grace and mercy cannot be demanded, but are God's to bestow in freedom (33:19).

Yahweh is Lord over all the earth (Josh. 3:11; Ps. 97:5), the judge of the nations (e.g., Amos 1–2) who promises them salvation through Israel (Isa. 2:2-4; 66:18). He is transcendent over time (Ps. 90:2), human knowledge (139:6), and, indeed, everything in heaven and earth (1 Kgs. 8:27). As Lord, God is the high and lofty one (Isa. 57:15) whose aura none can see and still live (Exod. 33:20).

3. Creator. As the Lord of his people and the nations, and as the establisher of relationship, Yahweh is also the Creator. Creation expresses God's might and sovereignty: formed by his word (Ps. 33:6), established by his wisdom and power (Prov. 3:19-20; Jer. 10:12), formed as by a potter (Isa. 29:15-16). As Creator, God holds in control the forces of chaos and destruction (Ps. 46; 74:13-14). He is the source of fertility (Deut. 7:13-14; 11:13-17), and his law and wisdom express his intention for creation (Pss. 19, 104). Yahweh created the earth for habitation (Isa. 45:18), and will climax salvation with the creation of a new heaven and earth (e.g., 66:22).

C. Revealed Character. In revealing himself God also reveals his character, termed in traditional theology his "communicable" attributes. These are as varied and numerous as his action. Yahweh is righteous (e.g., Neh. 9:8; Jer. 9:24), and his righteousness is displayed preeminently in the covenant relationship maintained with Israel through acts of deliverance and salvation (e.g., 1 Sam. 12:7; Ps. 103:6; cf. Judg. 5:11). God acts to preserve this relationship by judging the nations (Isa. 10–13), Israel (Amos 5:1-24), and individuals (Jer. 31:30) and by vindicating the cause of the poor and oppressed (Ps. 14:5; 35:10; Amos 2:6ff.). This righteousness which is promised to the repentant (Isa. 45:20-25), is the basis for a confident appeal for God's help in times of need (e.g., Ps. 4:1 [MT 2]; 26:1).

God is holy, as expressed through his radical separation from creation (Hos. 11:9) and characterized by his presence and action. Holiness can be virtually synonymous with God's deity, emphasizing his absolute might which works awesome deeds (Exod. 15:11), judges nations (Ps. 99), and inspires dread (Isa. 8:13). Moreover, it indicates the gulf between God's moral perfection and human sinfulness (cf. 6:1-5). God is

the Holy One (e.g., Ps. 89:18 [MT 19]; Isa. 1:4) who separates Israel for himself (Exod. 19:6; Lev. 19:2). Accordingly, he demands righteousness (e.g., Jer. 7), obedience (Gen. 22:1-19), and exclusive worship (Josh. 24:19). The holiness of his presence also invests various symbols of the covenant (e.g., the Sabbath, Exod. 20:8). For those who violate it, God's holiness is a consuming fire (Lev. 10:1-3; Isa. 10:17). Yet to the contrite God shows holiness in redemption (43:3), even to the nations (Ezek. 28:25).

God shows mercy in forgiveness (2 Sam. 24:14; Ps. 51; Dan. 9:9), deliverance (Ps. 69:16-18 [MT 17-19]), in fulfilling his promise (Deut. 13:17; cf. Jer. 33:26), and in gathering an exiled Israel (Isa. 14:1; Jer. 12:15). His mercy and love are born of passionate caring for Israel as a parent (Isa. 49:15; Jer. 31:20) and even as a spurned husband (Hos. 1–3). In love, Yahweh wills this fellowship by graciously electing Israel (Deut. 7:7) and giving them his Law. The relationship demands exclusivity, which if rejected brings judgment (Jer. 13:14). Yet God's wrath is not a permanent attribute, but a "footnote" to his love (Eichrodt 1:262; cf. Isa. 54:7). That love lets Israel see past the experience of punishment to God's intended salvation (Lam. 3:22-33).

God abounds in faithfulness (Exod. 34:6). His works (Ps. 111:7) and his word (119:138) both give confidence. He is reliable in keeping his promise (Isa. 25:1), in protection (Ps. 91:2), and in bringing salvation (Isa. 49:7). God can be counted on (Deut. 32:4), for he is true (Jer. 10:10). He is constant in steadfast loving care for Israel (Heb. ḥesed; Ps. 25:10). He is faithful in recompense (Isa. 61:8), in promised forgiveness (1:18; cf. Neh. 9:32-33), and in gracious love, even for an apostate Israel (Jer. 31:3; Hos. 2:20-23). In redemption God is not so much faithful to the covenant as to himself and his will (cf. Isa. 43:21–44:6). In steadfast love and faithfulness God shows his goodness (Ps. 100:5), in creation (Gen. 1), the Law (Ps. 119:39), deliverance (145:7), and salvation (Isa. 52:7). God's constant faithfulness is the biblical meaning underlying the formal attribute of immutability.

D. Anthropomorphisms. Where most moderns think of God in spiritual terms (cf. John 4:24), the Old Testament freely uses concrete human imagery. God speaks, acts, walks, forms, fights, and repents. He has hands, feet, eyes, a face, a back. He feels anger, anguish, pain, joy, expresses regret. Usually thought of in male terminology, the Bible also uses female imagery. Yahweh is the God of mercy and compassion (Heb. raḥamîm; cf. reḥem, "womb"; i.e., the one who shows maternal compassion). Yahweh gave birth to Israel (Deut. 32:18), comforts them like a mother (Isa. 49:15), and pants and cries out as a woman in labor to bring Israel to salvation (42:14). Yet amidst this imagery the Old Testament does not forget Yahweh's essential distinctness. He is God, not man (Hos. 11:9; cf. Isa. 40:25), the Holy One whose ways surpass human understanding (55:8-9). It is not until the LXX and the Targums that anthropomorphic language was systematically tempered (e.g., substituting an angel for God at Exod. 24:10).

More than a metaphor, anthropomorphic language underscores the truth of God's person: Yahweh is the

God who acts and maintains relationship. He is intimately involved with the world and near to his people (Deut. 4:7). He is the incomparable One who nonetheless invites reverence and trust (Isa. 46:3ff.). Such imagery reflects God's condescension and accommodation. God descends beneath his loftiness to speak with people according to their capacity for knowledge, a capacity bestowed in virtue of their creation as his image bearers. This self-giving finds its fulfillment and climax in the incarnation; in Jesus Christ, God takes human form to accomplish his revealing and reconciling purposes (cf. John 14:9).

III. New Testament

A. *Name*. The LXX equivalent of Heb. *'el* and *'elōhîm*, Gk. *theós* represents the generic term for deity as well as the most common name of God (cf. 2 Cor. 4:4, "god of this world'). Often used with other ascriptions such as Lord or savior, it denotes the God of Israel (Acts 2:30; Rom. 11:1), the living God (Matt. 26:63). Usually the title of the exalted Jesus (e.g., Rom. 10:9; Phil. 2:11), Gk. *kýrios* occurs as the equivalent of the Old Testament name Yahweh (e.g., Matt. 11:25), most often in citations of the Old Testament (e.g., Mark 1:3; Luke 1–2). Other names ascribed to God reflect Old Testament usage as well, including Holy One (Acts 2:27; 1 John 2:20), Almighty (Gk. *pantokrátòr*, the LXX translation of Heb. *ṣᵉbā'ôt* "hosts"; 2 Cor. 6:18; Rev. 16:14), the Most High (Mark 5:7 Acts 7:48), Savior (Luke 1:47; 1 Tim. 1:1), and King (v. 17; Rev. 17:14, "King of kings").

B. *Relation to the Old Testament*. The New Testament knows no other God than the same self-revealing God of the Old Testament. It demonstrates its essential continuity with the Hebrew scriptures through numerous quotations, which it claims are now fulfilled in Christ (Luke 24:27). Yet the New Testament reflects in its language and theology (cf. Gk. *logos* in John) the thought world of the first century A.D. More importantly, it boldly claims that God has decisively spoken in Jesus Christ (Heb. 1:1-2); indeed, he can only be understood in terms of Christ, "the image of the invisible God" (Col. 1:15).

Still, the fundamental relationships and attributes are everywhere assumed. God is the Creator (Acts 17:28; cf. Col. 1:15-16). He is the exalted king of time and nations (Rev. 15:3-4; cf. 2 Pet. 1:16-18), electing, blessing, and saving his people (Eph. 1:3-8; cf. Rom. 8:28ff.). Above all, he is the living God (Heb. 10:31) who fulfills his covenant promise of old (Acts 2:14-36; 1 Pet. 2:10-12) and summons a new people (v. 9) to a new covenant (Heb. 8:8-12; cf. Rom. 9:22-31). He is the Father who sends his Son in love (1 John 4:9), from whom every family is named (Eph. 3:15). In fulfilling his promise, God extends his faithfulness in a direction previously only hoped for: his family includes not only Israel, but Greeks, barbarians, slaves, and freedmen (Gal. 3:28; Col. 3:11).

God's character or attributes as set forth in the Old Testament are generally assumed. He is holy (Matt. 6:9; Rev. 4:8), as his people also are to be (1 Pet. 1:16). He is righteous (Matt. 6:33), revealed through faith (Rom. 1:17) and seen in Christ's atoning death (3:26). He is a God of justice displaying righteous wrath (Rom. 1:18ff.; cf. Matt. 13:24-30, 47-50). Yet

this wrath is penultimate, for through Jesus, God shows mercy and love (Rom. 5:8; Eph. 2:4-6) to deliver mankind from the wrath to come (1 Thess. 5:9). He is the God of mercy (Jas. 5:11). God is faithful in all his dealings (1 Cor. 1:9; 1 Thess. 5:24), even in the face of human failings (2 Tim. 2:13). God is true (John 3:33; 7:28), as is his word (17:17; cf. 2 Tim. 3:14-16); he keeps his covenant through Jesus (Rom. 15:8; cf. Eph. 4:21). It is impossible for him to be false (Heb. 6:18).

The New Testament also significantly expands upon Old Testament thought on God. Jesus announces that God's kingdom is at hand (Mark 1:15). Prophesied and longed for by the Hebrews (cf. Ps. 145:13; Dan. 2:44), this kingly rule has now begun in the works and teaching of Jesus the Messiah (Luke 4:21; cf. Matt. 12:28). Although not a worldly kingdom (John 18:36), nevertheless it is in the midst of the world (Luke 17:21; KJV, NIV "within you"; JB "among you"), already taking root (cf. Matt. 13:1-9, 31-32). Membership is by regeneration (Matt. 18:3; John 3:3) and is characterized by obedience to God's will (Matt. 7:21), putting aside all (Mark 10:23-25), walking by the Spirit (cf. Gal. 5:22-23), and by love and forgiveness (Matt. 5:38-48; Luke 19:11:27). This kingdom is a gift found in the presence of Jesus (Matt. 16:19; Luke 12:32), especially for the poor in spirit (Matt. 5:3) and the persecuted (v. 10). It is a kingdom that inspires the worship of the Church (Heb. 12:28). Yet it is also a coming kingdom for which believers pray (Matt. 6:10) and which Jesus the Messiah brings to fulfillment with glory as its king and judge (25:31-46). Then God will invite all to fellowship with him at the messianic banquet (Luke 14:15-24; 22:30; Rev. 19:9), and Christ, in turn, will deliver up the kingdom to his Father, who will be all in all (1 Cor. 15:24-28).

Another distinctive mark of the New Testament understanding of God concerns his love. Not only is God himself love (1 John 4:8) but love characterizes his kingdom. Where the Old Testament speaks of God's love for Israel in collective terms, here it becomes personalized in Christ, who is the means of God's love for a sinful humanity (John 3:16). This perfect love is an expression of the Father's love for the Son from eternity (5:20; 17:24). Standing in Christ, believers discover that they too share in the Father's electing love (Eph. 1:4-6; cf. John 13:1), which is theirs by his Spirit (Rom. 5:5). Mankind is to imitate God's love (Eph. 5:2; cf. Mark 12:29-31; 1 John 4:20-21): in forgiveness (cf. Luke 11:4; Acts 7:60), sacrifice (1 John 3:16), love for enemies (Matt. 5:43-48), and service even to the least (25:40). Love is the living testimony of following God in Christ (John 13:35).

C. *Self-Revelation*. 1. Father. In the Bible, God as Father refers to a social, not generative metaphor. It speaks of a relationship of authority, and love, rather than one of origin with its sexual overtones (i.e., God as male), as found in Greek and Mesopotamian cultures.

God's fatherhood preeminently denotes that relationship seen and shared in Jesus, who has now made God known (John 1:18), the Father from whom come grace and peace (e.g., Rom. 1:7). God's fatherhood receives its clearest expression in the relationship between Father and Son (e.g., 15:6; 2 Cor. 1:3). Father and Son share a unity of will (John 10:30) and mutual knowledge (Matt. 11:26-27). Jesus enacts the words and works of his Father (John 5:19; 7:17), such that the Father is directly revealed (14:9-11). The Father sends his Son in love (17:18), and is with him in his passion (16:32). In turn, the Son obeys, even to death on a cross (Luke 23:46) and the accompanying estrangement (Mark 15:34). Their relationship is characterized by Jesus' address, "Abba, Father" (Mark 14:36), a term of intimate familiarity not used earlier of God.

In Christ believers also are sons (Rom. 8:14), or children (1 John 3:1-2), who themselves may address God as "Abba, Father" (Rom. 8:15; Gal. 4:6). This relationship is a gift of his Spirit, known through adoption (v. 5). It is thus eschatological: as children of the Father (cf. Acts 17:29), Christians are heirs of his kingdom (Rom. 8:17), anticipating the sharing of his fullness and nature (Eph. 3:19; 2 Pet. 1:4). In the present they live knowing his fatherly care and goodness (Matt. 6:25-33), doing his will (12:50), giving thanks (Eph. 5:20), and accepting his discipline (Heb. 12:7-8), that in all things he may be glorified (Matt. 5:16).

2. Son. In the New Testament God's self-revelation becomes radically personal in Jesus Christ, the Son of God, who is both the means of this revelation and its incarnation.

Christ's words and acts reveal God. He speaks with authority (Matt. 7:29), proclaims imminent salvation (Luke 19:9), and offers the presence of divine forgiveness (Mark 2:10). God is powerfully present in Jesus' exercising work (Mark 3:11) and particularly in his death (15:39). By him the goal of knowing and being known by God comes near (Gal. 4:9). God reveals the varied aspects of this salvation through Christ: as grace and truth (John 1:17), judgment (Rom. 2:16), righteousness and justification (3:22, 24), salvation (cf. 7:25), resurrection (1 Thess. 4:14), confidence (2 Cor. 3:4), eternal predestination (Eph. 1:5), and glory (1 Pet. 4:11). Such is God's revelation that believers utter the "Amen" to the glory of God (2 Cor. 1:20) through Christ, the unique avenue to God (John 14:6).

3. Holy Spirit. Again God's Spirit communicates his presence, activity, and power. The Spirit is a Person who directs, speaks, forbids, appoints, bears witness, is tempted, resisted, and grieved. It is the Advocate who proceeds from the Father (John 15:26; so JB; RSV, NIV "Counselor") and is sent by the Son (16:7); it is Christ's "alter ego" who continues his work (14:16). Salvation by Christ's grace and the Father's love is always with the fellowship of the Holy Spirit (2 Cor. 13:14).

The Spirit continues Christ's ministry among God's people, convicting them of truth (John 15:26; 1 John 5:7-8), bringing good news of God's love (Rom. 5:5), sanctifying (2 Thess. 2:13), sealing (Eph. 1:13), and leading them to utter with their Lord, "Abba Father" (Gal. 4:6). The Spirit of God is the distinguishing mark of the Christian, a necessity for confession (Rom. 8:9; 1 Cor. 12:3; cf. John 3:5). It brings the new life in Christ once impossible for sinners (Rom. 7:6; 8:2ff.), strengthening believers that they may be filled with the very fullness of God (Eph. 3:16-19).

Although the New Testament does not explicitly delineate a doctrine of the trinity, it does provide the foundation for its subsequent development. It implicitly poses the trinitarian problem of God's unity and the differentiation of his self-revelation. Throughout, the New Testament writers confess that God is one, in unity with his self-revelation in the Old Testament (Mark 12:29; Rom. 3:30), effecting one work of salvation (Eph. 4:6). Yet his salvation is proclaimed in the name of the Father, Son, and Holy Spirit, e.g., at baptism (Matt. 28:19; cf. Did. 7:1) and in benediction (2 Cor. 13:14). Similar triadic formulae occur in descriptions of salvation and its effects (Rom. 15:30; Gal. 3:11-14; Eph. 4:4-6; 1 Pet. 1:2). The same pattern also structures the presentation of the gospel itself (e.g., Rom. 1–8: the judgment of God, 1:18–3:20; justification through faith in Jesus Christ, 3:21–8:1; life in the Spirit, 8:2-30). In all ages this tension between God's unity and his self-revelation remains inescapable for those who confess Jesus Christ as Lord. Never completely resolved, this mystery teaches the depth of the riches, wisdom, knowledge of God as Father, Son, and Holy Spirit.

Bibliography. H. Bavinck, *The Doctrine of God* (Grand Rapids: 1951); W. Eichrodt, *Theology of the Old Testament.* OTL (1961) 1:206-288; H. Thielicke, *The Evangelical Faith* 2: *The Doctrine of God and of Christ* (Grand Rapids: 1977); G. E. Wright, *God Who Acts: Biblical Theology as Recital.* SBT 8 (1952).

GOD-FEARERS (Gk. *sebómenoi, eusebés* "devout ones").* Gentiles who out of respect for Judaism attended the synagogue services and observed some of the Jewish law but were not full converts to Judaism; not having undergone circumcision (Acts 10:2; cf. 13:50; 16:14; 17:4, 17; 18:7).

See FEAR; PROSELYTE.

GODLESS.† Alienated from God, both in state and in activity; over against God, thus actively in opposition to him. The godless (Heb. *ḥānēp*; KJV "hypocrite") have no standing before God (Job 13:16); their joys are momentary (20:5), and their hopes will perish (8:13; 27:8; Prov. 11:7; Heb. *'ônîm;* KJV "unjust"); they cherish anger (Job 36:13), oppress the good (Ps. 119; Heb. *zēd;* KJV "proud"), do evil, and speak folly (Isa. 9:17). Usually implicit is an allegiance to something other than God (2 Sam. 23:6; Heb. *beliyaʿal;* KJV "sons of Belial"; perhaps a common noun meaning "worthless person"; cf. Judg. 19:22, "base fellows"), such as idolatry (cf. Jer. 2:11; Hos. 4:12) or worldliness (cf. Jer. 23:15). Related terms include the "wicked" (Heb. *ʿawîl;* e.g., Job 16:11), "impious" (Ps. 74:18, 22), or "fool" (14:1; Heb. *nābāl*).

In the New Testament "godless" (Gk. *bébēlos;* KJV "profane") refers to "silly myths" (1 Tim. 4:7) and false knowledge (6:20; 2 Tim. 2:16), in all likelihood a reference to Gnostic myths and teachings. The "ungodly" (Gk. *asebés*) may encompass the Old Testament sense of "godless" (e.g., Jude 14-19), but the term is also extended to depict all humanity in its sinfulness. Thus the law was given for the ungodly (1 Tim. 1:9), and Christ died for and justifies the ungodly (Rom. 4:5; 5:6).

GODLY (Heb. *ḥāsîḏ*; Gk. *eusebeía*).† A term designating one who exercises loving-kindness (cf. Heb. *ḥeseḏ*) toward others (Mic. 7:2; KJV "good man") and demonstrates faithfulness to God (Ps. 12:1 [MT 2]; 86:2; KJV "holy"; cf. 52:9 [MT 11]; KJV "saints"). It occurs primarily in the Pastoral Epistles and 2 Peter, the translation of several related Greek words (*eusebeía, eusebôs, eusebés; cf. eulabeía,* Heb. 5:7) connoting piety (e.g., 1 Tim. 2:2, "a quiet and peaceable life, godly and respectful in every way"). Such a devout life is contrasted specifically with the heretical views of the Gnostics (4:7-8; 6:3; cf. Tit. 1:1, "godliness"). The author of 2 Peter employs the term to contrast the moral life of Christians with the behavior of the libertines (2 Pet. 1:6-7; 3:11; cf. 2:9).

GOG [gŏg] (Heb. *gôg*; Gk. *Gōg*).
1. The son of Shemaiah and father of Shimei, of the tribe of Reuben (1 Chr. 5:4).
2. The ruler of the land of Magog. At Ezek. 38:2; 39:2 Gog is called the "chief prince of Meshech and Tubal," although this phrase could also be translated "the prince of Rosh, Meshech, and Tubal" (so NEB, JB). According to the prophecy, the Lord would command Gog and a great army to march from the far north against Israel. But Gog would be defeated in the mountains of Israel by means of frightful judgments sent by the Lord.
The identity of Gog is a subject of much dispute. At Ezek. 38:17 Yahweh refers to former contact with Gog through the prophets of Israel, yet he is mentioned only in the oracles in chs. 38–39 and at Rev. 20:8. It may be that Gog is being used as a symbol for the neighboring heathen nations that threatened Israel (cf. the numerous prophecies against the nations). The LXX and Samaritan Pentateuch have Gog in place of Agag at Num. 24:7, and at Amos 7:1 the LXX reads "Behold, King Gog is a locust"; however, neither reference sheds any light on this problem.
Some scholars call Gog the Old Testament antichrist, citing the appearance of Antiochus IV Epiphanes and the defeat of the Syrians at the hands of the Maccabees as the fulfillment of Ezekiel's prophecy. Moreover, according to some scholars Antiochus serves as a type of antichrist in the book of Daniel. The appearance of Gog and Magog at Rev. 20:8 would then describe the antichrist's last attack against the Church and the people of God and his ultimate defeat. It should be noted, however, that the names of the nations that Gog commands indicate his location to be in Asia Minor, far to the north of Israel; the antichrist who is to come in the latter days is to arise from the midst of Christendom. Gog might better be regarded as a personification of the enmity that the heathen nations felt for the people of Israel.
Several historical figures and events may have furnished the material for Ezekiel's imaginative description: e.g., Gyges, king of Lydia (Akk. *Gugu;* Magog thus could be Akk. *māt Gûgu* "land of Gog") or Alexander the Great. Some connect Gog with Sum. *gug* "darkness," and thus make the reference to a personification of evil. Another possibility is that the name Gog was merely taken from Magog, and that Magog itself meant *māt Gaga,* the land of Gaga, mentioned

in the Amarna Letters and probably located north of Syria. It is also possible that Gog and Magog are not historical names at all, but were coined by Ezekiel as a cryptic reference to a future ruler who would oppose the people of Gog and would lead a large group of heathen nations as a united force against Israel and the Church.
See MAGOG.

GOIIM [goy'ĭm] (Heb. *gôyim* "nations"). Probably a small tribe of people that lived in Galilee (Josh. 12:23; KJV "Gilgal," following MT; RSV, NEB "Galilee," following LXX). The same group may also be part of the place name Harosheth-ha-goiim, "Harosheth of the Goiim," Sisera's base from which he fought Barak (Judg. 4:2, 16). Tidal (whom some identify as the Hittite king Tudḫaliyas) is called king of Goiim at Gen. 14:1, 9 (KJV "nations"). The tribe mentioned in Josh. 12:23 may have been descended from this earlier people, although some scholars identify them as a branch of the Philistines.

GOLAN [gō'lăn] (Heb. *gôlān*). A city of refuge located east of the Jordan in the district of Bashan, in the territory allotted to the tribe of Manasseh (Deut. 4:43; Josh. 20:8; 21:27). According to 1 Chr. 6:71 (MT 56) it was also designated a levitical city, assigned to the Gershonites. Some scholars propose an identification with modern Saḥem el-Jōlân, about 28 km. (17 mi.) east of the Sea of Galilee; however, this would place the city outside the district of Golan, an area that in the Old Testament comprised the territories of the Geshurites and the Maacathites and later called Gaulanitis.

GOLD. The most frequently mentioned metal in the Bible. The land of Arabia was an important source of gold in the ancient world, and the Old Testament mentions two regions famous for their gold production, Havilah (Gen. 2:11-12) and Ophir (1 Kgs. 10:11), which may be located there.
Gold has been highly valued since earliest times, especially for the making of ornaments (Gen. 24:22). It was smelted in a crucible or furnace (Prov. 17:3), and goldsmiths worked the metal into figures, including idols (Isa. 40:19). It could be beaten flat with a ham-

Gold pectoral from Byblos in Phoenicia, nineteenth century B.C. (Louvre; photo M. Chuzeville)

mer (41:7) or drawn into threads to be woven into garments (Ps. 45:13 [MT 14]). "Pure gold" (Heb. zāhāḫ sāgûr, lit. "closed gold") refers to the highest quality gold, which was finely wrought and pressed into very fine sheets or gold leaf. This gold was required for the construction of the tabernacle furniture (e.g., Exod. 25:11, 17, 31; 30:3) and for the temple (1 Kgs. 6:20-35; 1 Chr. 28:14-18; 2 Chr. 3:4-10). Solomon, who imported a large amount of gold, even used it on his ivory throne (1 Kgs. 10:18).

The golden calves that Aaron and the Israelites set up in the wilderness (Exod. 32:4) and those erected at Bethel and Dan by King Jeroboam (1 Kgs. 12:28) may have been made of stone or wood and overlaid with gold. Idols were also often made of wood or stone and then gilded (e.g., Deut. 7:25; Isa. 30:22; Hab. 2:19).

Gold was one of the gifts brought by the Wise Men to the infant Jesus (Matt. 2:11). The golden denarius was the most valuable Roman coin and was worth twenty-five silver denarii. (cf. 10:9).

GOLDEN CALF (Heb. 'ēgel massēḵâ, 'egel zāhāḫ).† An image cast in the form of a calf or bull; a common element of ancient Near Eastern religion (see CATTLE) and a byword for apostasy in the Old Testament.

The Israelites, weary of waiting for Moses to descend from the mountain (possibly Sinai), urged Aaron to make an idol that could "go before them" in their journey (Exod. 32:1-35). The text does not state whether the intent was to make an image of Yahweh, but in any event Aaron does not protest or hesitate to act. He collected gold earrings from the people and melted them down to be fashioned into an idol. The people proclaimed it to be the god who brought Israel out of Egypt (cf. Neh. 9:18; Ps. 106:19-23). Aaron built an altar before the idol and declared a festival to Yahweh; the following day's sacrifices soon turned into wild revelry. When Moses and Joshua descended to the camp the sight caused Moses to shatter the stone tablets of the Ten Commandments; he then burned the idol, ground it into powder, and forced the people to drink it in water (cf. Deut. 9:15-21). The nation was cleansed from this transgression after Moses ordered faithful Levites to restore order in the camp with the sword, and Yahweh struck the people with an unidentified plague.

During the divided monarchy Jeroboam I of Israel (ca. 922-901 B.C.) placed a calf in each of the traditional sanctuaries of Dan and Bethel (1 Kgs. 12:26-33) as part of the plan to legitimize his rule. While he may actually have intended to foster worship of Yahweh, Jeroboam's actions were denounced as pagan (v. 30; 2 Kgs. 10:29; 17:16; 2 Chr. 13:8). Rehoboam, Judah's first king (ca. 922-915), also placed calf idols in sanctuaries (11:15). The calf worship mentioned in the mid-eighth-century oracles of the prophet Hosea (Hos. 8:5-6; 10:5-6; 13:2) may allude to these or similar abuses or may refer more generally to increased syncretism in Israelite religion.

GOLDEN GATE.† A gate in the eastern wall of the temple esplanade in the Old City of Jerusalem. The name (Arab. Bab ed-Daheriyeh) derives from Lat.

aurea, a misreading of "Beautiful Gate" (Gk. Hōraía) in Acts 3:2; although most scholars discredit its association with the biblical gate, it may mark the site of the Susa Gate through which the high priest proceeded for the sacrifice of the red heifer on the Mount of Olives (Mishnah Mid. i.3; cf. Ezek. 10:19; 11:1; 43:1).

The Golden Gate is a double gate, consisting of two arches called Bab eṭ-Ṭubē "Gate of Penance") and Bab er-Raudhonē ("Gate of Mercy"); according to tradition, the columns which separate the passageways were given to King Solomon by the Queen of Sheba. The Ottoman Turks, who constructed the gate, walled it up soon thereafter, presumably because both Christian and Jewish tradition held that the Messiah would use it to enter the city (cf. Ezek. 44:1-3).

GOLDEN RULE.† Jesus' command that his followers treat others as they themselves would be treated. The positive form of the statement occurs at Matt. 7:12, where it concludes a portion of the Sermon on the Mount concerning prayer; Jesus underscores its teaching as the summation of the Law and the Prophets. Luke presents the rule as Jesus' instruction concerning the Christian reaction to one's enemies (Luke 6:31).

This principle, worded negatively, occurs some years earlier in the teachings of Hillel the Elder (Talmud b. Šabb. 31a), who calls it "the whole Law." It is found in Hellenistic Jewish literature (Ep. Arist. 207; Tob. 4:15; cf. 2 En. 61:2) and as an ethical precept in earlier Greek writings (e.g., Isocrates Nicocles 61; Herodotus Hist. iii.142; vii.136) and elsewhere (e.g., Confucius Analects xv.23).

GOLGOTHA [gŏl'gə thə, gŏl gŏth'ə] (Gk. Golgotha).† The site of Christ's crucifixion. The name, defined by the Gospel writers as "the place of a skull" (Matt. 27:33; Mark 15:22; John 19:17; cf. Luke 23:33; KJV "Calvary"), is the Greek transliteration of Aram. gûlgaltā' "skull" (cf. Vulg. Lat. Calvaria, whence Eng. "Calvary"). According to Origen, Golgotha was named after the skull of Adam, who was allegedly buried there. It is more likely that the name derived from a rocky protuberance located there that had the shape of a skull, but other explanations have also been given.

The New Testament reports that Jesus' crucifixion took place outside the city (Heb. 13:12), in keeping with both Roman custom and Jewish law. The site was near the city (John 19:20), and since it is said that there were many passersby (Matt. 27:39; Mark 15:29), it was probably beside a road.

In 336 Constantine the Great (284-337) built the Church of the Holy Sepulchre on what is said to have been the traditional site of Golgotha. The church stands in what is now the western part of the Old City; inside is a pile of rock about 3 m. (15 ft.) high, and 40 m. (130 ft.) away is a site that has been identified as the tomb of Jesus. The church was destroyed by the Arabs and then rebuilt by the Crusaders in 1130; after its destruction by fire in 1808, it was restored again but very imperfectly. The church has long been a focal point of political agitation among Arabs, Jews, and Christians, and it is now controlled by the Muslims.

The main question about this traditional site of the tomb of Jesus has been whether it lay outside the city walls during the New Testament period. A further difficulty is presented by the possibility that the hill changed a great deal under Emperor Hadrian (117-138), who rebuilt Jerusalem into the thoroughly pagan city of Aelia Capitolina and declared it off limits to Jews. Discussions have long been more emotional than factual, but most scholars now favor this traditional location as the correct one.

In 1885 the British general Charles Gordon suggested that Golgotha lay farther to the north, proposing a site on a hill north of the Turkish city wall, near the modern Damascus Gate. The area contains a number of simple graves from the Byzantine period, one of which is designated the "Garden Tomb." This rock formation, roughly resembling a human skull and called "Gordon's Calvary," lacks the support of both archaeology and early Church tradition.

Bibliography J. Finegan, *The Archaeology of the New Testament* (Princeton: 1970).

GOLIATH [gə lī'əth] (Heb. *golyāṯ*).† The Philistine giant slain by David in single combat at the valley of Elah (1 Sam. 17). Goliath may have been from among foreign mercenaries hired by the Philistines and quartered at Gath (2 Sam. 21:22; 1 Chr. 20:8).

Physically imposing and heavily armed and armored (1 Sam. 17:4-7), Goliath challenged Saul's army to bring out a champion to fight him. The outcome of their combat would decide the war's outcome. Young David, bringing provisions to his brothers in the battle lines, took up the challenge. Disdaining Saul's heavy armor, the shepherd felled the giant with a single stone from his sling and routed the Philistines (vv. 38-51). Goliath's arms and armor may have been dedicated to Yahweh (21:9); thus Ahimelech the priest later returned his sword to David at Nob, as he fled from Saul (vv. 1-9; 22:10).

A certain Elhanan (Heb. *'elḥānān* "God is gracious") is described as having killed Goliath the Gittite (2 Sam. 21:19); the giant is called Lahmi at 1 Chr. 20:5. Some scholars regard Elhanan as David's original, preregnal name (*see* ELHANAN 1).

GOMER [gō'mər] (Heb. *gōmer*).

1. The eldest son of Japheth, listed in the Table of Nations as the eponymous ancestor of a people (Gen. 10:2-3 par. 1 Chr. 1:5-6). The name is probably equivalent to Akk. *Gi-mir-ra-a*, who are the same as the Cimmerians appearing in Greek sources as early as Homer. The Cimmerians were a nomadic people who lived north of the Black Sea and later moved southward and settled in Cappadocia. They put an end to the kingdom of Lydia, and Gyges, one of the Lydian kings, died in battle against them. At Ezek. 38:6 Gomer is again linked with other sons of Japheth (Magog, Meshech, Tubal) as well as sons of Ham (Cush and Put), all of whom form part of Gog's army.

2. A prostitute, possibly associated with a fertility cult; the daughter of Diblaim. God commanded the prophet Hosea to marry her as a symbol of Israel's unfaithfulness and God's grace (Hos. 1:2-3).

GOMORRAH [gə mōr'ə] (Heb. *'ămōrâ*). One of the five cities in the valley of Siddim defeated by Abraham (Gen. 14:2-3, 8). God destroyed the city along with Sodom because of the wickedness of its inhabitants; only Lot and his family survived (19:24-29). Sodom and Gomorrah thus became proverbial for wickedness and divine punishment (e.g., Deut. 29:23 [MT 22]; 32:32; Matt. 10:15); while many take this account to be a condemnation of homosexuality (cf. Jude 7), the focus of divine displeasure is rather the citizens' disregard for the Near Eastern practice of hospitality (cf. Gen. 19:8).

It is not certain whether the cities of the valley lay in the northern or southern part of the Dead Sea basin. Some proponents of the northern hypothesis suggest that Sodom and Gomorrah formed twin cities, which they see substantiated in the excavations at Teleilât el-Ghassûl, north of Moab in the Jordan valley. More recent evidence, however, favors a southern location. It is thought that the area of these cities remained a wasteland for centuries (cf. Zeph. 2:9) and that later it was submerged when the water level of the Dead Sea rose. According to Josephus (*BJ* iv.8.4 [483-85]) traces of the cities could still be seen beneath the surface of the water during his time. Therefore some have sought Gomorrah on the southeast coast of the Dead Sea at Seil en-Numeiriah, in the delta region formed by streams entering the Dead Sea from Moab and the valley of Siddim. Most likely the site is situated slightly to the north, at the mouth of the stream Seil 'Esal south of the el-Lisan peninsula.

GOOD (Heb. *ṭôḇ*; Gk. *agathós, kalós*).† While philosophy often sees "the good" simply as an abstract ideal or moral norm, the Bible overwhelmingly presents goodness as a practical experienced reality.

Goodness is part of human experience. Although English versions use a variety of words, the Old Testament prefers Heb. *ṭôḇ* to indicate both practical and aesthetic dimensions, such as the values of fruit and grain (Gen. 2:9; 41:5), hospitality (26:29), prosperity (Hos. 10:1; JB "richer"), old age (Gen. 15:15), reputation (Isa. 56:5; RSV "better than"), loyalty (1 Sam. 29:9; RSV "blameless"), unity (Ps. 133:1), and patience (Prov. 16:32). It is the delight in beauty (Gen. 24:16; RSV "fair"; Deut. 6:10), sweetness (Jer. 6:20), fragrance (Cant. 1:3), and musical ability (1 Sam. 16:17). These many aspects coalesce in the "good land" as God's blessing (Exod. 3:8; Deut. 8:7-10). Material and spiritual goods alike are God's gift (1 Tim. 4:4-5).

Supremely, God is good. This goodness is not simply that reflected in or extended from creation. Rather, it is the goodness of grace, the object of praise and thanksgiving (Ps. 106:1; 107:1; Jer. 33:11). While God shows his goodness in creation (Gen. 1), most often it is that faithfulness shown in the covenant: redemption from Egypt and care in the wilderness (Exod. 18:9); the gift of the land (cf. Josh. 24:20); teaching and law (Jer. 6:16); the temple (cf. Ezra 3:11); forgiveness (Hos. 3:5); care for the needy (Ps. 68:10 [MT 11]); strength in time of trouble (Hab. 1:7); and the promise of restoration and a new covenant (Zech. 8:15; cf. Jer. 32:40), now fulfilled gloriously in Jesus Christ (Tit. 3:4), in the saving word of the gospel (Heb. 6:5), and the new life it brings (Phil. 1:6). God's name is good (Ps. 54:6 [MT 8]), as are the Spirit and its fruit (Ps. 143:10; Gal. 5:22). This goodness is for the true Israel, the pure in heart (Ps. 73:1; cf. mg.; Mic. 2:7), for those who wait in hope (Lam. 3:25). Apart from God's fellowship there is no good (Ps. 16:2); only he is good (Matt. 19:17). While no person can lay claim to God's goodness (Ps. 14:3; Rom. 7:18), this fellowship is now possible through Christ's ministry (Heb. 9:11; 10:1).

God expects people to do good to one another (Luke 6:35). Although unable to keep or attain that moral good which justifies (Gk. *tó agathón*, Rom. 7:13), people do show practical goodness constantly (Luke 11:13). Perverting this goodness brings judgment (Isa. 5:20). The Bible everywhere summons people to discern good and evil (Deut. 30:15; Heb. 5:14) and so choose the good (e.g., Ps. 34:15 [MT 16]; 5:14; Rom. 12:9; 1 Thess. 5:15). This choice is not blind, for God shows the way (1 Kgs. 8:36; cf. Ps. 25:8) through good commandments (119:39, 68; Prov. 4:2; cf. Rom. 7:12): do justice (Amos 5:14-15), refuse to lie (Ps. 52:3 [MT 5]), seek peace (34:14 [MT 15]), be impartial (Prov. 18:5), defend the weak (Isa. 1:17). What is good? To do justice, love kindness, and walk humbly with God (Mic. 6:8).

Good works are the expected result of this way, the good fruit of the Christian's life (Matt. 7:17; cf. Jas. 3:17). They are the purpose of God's election and salvation (Eph. 2:10; Col. 1:10; Tit. 2:14), the harvest of the good soil that hears and believes the gospel (Matt. 13:8, 23), the fruit that cannot be hid (1 Tim. 5:25; cf. Matt. 5:16). These works are the Christian's duty (1 Tim. 6:12); the Christian's true wealth and adornment (2:10; 6:18; cf. 5:10; 2 Tim. 2:21).

Bibliography. W. Grundmann, "ἀγαθός," *TDNT* 1 (1964): 10-18; Grundmann and G. Bertram "καλός," *TDNT* 3 (1965): 536-556; I. Höver-Johag, "ṭôḇ," *TDOT* 5 (1986): 296-317.

GOOD FRIDAY.* The Friday preceding Easter, observed in commemoration of the crucifixion (Mark 15:42; Luke 23:54; John 19:31; cf. Matt. 27:62); called Great Friday in the Eastern Church. In the Church year it is traditionally a day of fasting and penance. Post-reformation practice observed by both Roman Catholics and Protestants includes a service from noon to 3 p.m. marking Jesus' agony on the cross (Matt. 27:45; Mark 15:33; Luke 23:44).

GOOD NEWS. *See* GOSPEL.

GO OUT AND COME IN (Heb. *yāṣāʾ ûḇāʾ*).† A Hebrew idiom depicting the conduct of everyday affairs (e.g., Josh. 14:11), used primarily as a technical term for the functions of officials. It is applied to national leaders such as Moses (Deut. 31:32) and his successor, Joshua (Num. 27:17, 21), to David as both military commander and king (1 Sam. 18:13, 16; 29:6; 2 Sam. 5:2), and to the Assyrian king Sennacherib (2 Kgs. 19:27). In this sense it may derive from the picture of a military leader "going forth" (cf. 1 Chr. 20:1) before his people (e.g., Deut. 20:1; 1 Sam. 8:20). The expression occurs in a wisdom context in Solomon's plea for the technical skills necessary as monarch (1 Kgs. 3:7; 2 Chr. 1:10; cf. 2 Kgs. 11:8).

The idiom also represents the function of the high priest as he serves in the holy place (Exod. 28:35; 34:34; Lev. 16:17) and consults the oracles (Num. 27:21). Elsewhere it suggests cultic duties performed by the king (2 Chr. 23:7; Ezek. 44:3; 46:2, 8, 10, 12; cf. 42:14). This priestly sense occurs in the New Testament with regard to the ministries of Jesus (Acts 1:21; cf. the implication of Jesus as the Door, John 10:9) and Paul (Acts 9:28).

Bibliography. H. D. Preuss, "yāṣāʾ," *TDOT* 6.

GOPHER WOOD (Heb. *ʿaṣê-gōper*).† The material from which Noah was instructed to build the ark. The term appears only at Gen. 6:14, and no cognates have been found in other ancient Near Eastern languages. Some scholars associate it with the construction of the Mesopotamian *kufa* boat, which was made of branches or reeds and palm leaves and sealed with bitumen (cf. *Gilg.* xi.20-69). Most likely this resinous wood comes from some variety of conifer, probably a cypress (cf. G. Westermann, *Genesis 1-11* [Minneapolis: 1984], pp. 388, 391, 420, "teak-wood").

GORGIAS [gôrʹjəs] (Gk. *Gorgias*).† A general of Antiochus IV Epiphanes. With Nicanor and Ptolemy, he was appointed by the regent Lysias to lead Seleucid forces against the Jews (1 Macc. 3:38; cf. 2 Macc. 8:9). In 166 B.C. he attempted an unsuccessful raid of Judas Maccabeus' camp near Emmaus, failing when the numerically inferior Jews trapped the Syrians within the temporarily vacated encampment (1 Macc. 4:1-24). As military governor of Idumea and other regions in Judea (Josephus *Ant.* xii.8.6 [250], "Jamnia"; cf. 2 Macc. 10:14, "the region") he successfully repelled the unsanctioned attack of Joseph and Azariah on the garrison at Jamnia (1 Macc. 5:55-62). Some time later Judas defeated Gorgias at Jamnia, cutting off his arm and causing him to flee to Marisa (2 Macc. 12:32-37).

GOSHEN [gōʹshən] (Heb. *gōšen*).

1. A region in the eastern Nile delta where Jacob's family settled (Gen. 45:10; 46:28–47:6). Goshen lay west of the Wâdī Ṭumilât and east of the Nile, but the precise limits are uncertain. Goshen was given as grazing land to the descendants of Jacob (Gen. 46:28-34; 47:1); as the habitation of the Israelites, it was exempted from the last seven of the plagues that struck the rest of Egypt (Exod. 8:22; 9:4, 26; 10:23).

2. A part of Canaan that was conquered by Joshua (Josh. 10:41; 11:16); perhaps the region of low hills in southwest Palestine. It may have been named after 3 below.

3. A city of the hill country of Judah (Josh. 15:51); a possible identification is modern Ẓâharîyeh about 19 km. (12 mi.) southwest of Hebron.

GOSPEL (Gk. *euangélion* "good news"; cf. Lat. *evangelium*; AS *god-spell* "good tidings").† Good news, specifically the good news of salvation through Jesus Christ (Matt. 11:5 par. Luke 4:18; Heb. 4:2, 6; 1 Pet. 1:12). In classical Greek the term originally designated the reward given to a messenger of good tidings and later came to mean the good news itself. The LXX has retained the first meaning at 2 Sam. 4:10; 18:22 (RSV "reward") and the second at Isa. 40:9; 52:7; 61:1.

Attempting to encourage the Jews in their exile, Isaiah predicted that a "herald of good tidings" (Isa. 40:9; JB "joyful messenger"), possibly Zion itself (so RSV, KJV), would announce that Yahweh would protect his despondent people (vv. 9-11) and that, as sovereign, he would usher in a new age for his chosen people (52:7). At 61:1-4 the herald, this time the prophet empowered and anointed by the Spirit of the Lord, proclaimed to the exiles that their harsh captivity had finally ended. God's wish for them was that they return to Judah to rebuild the ruined city and restore their languishing fields. Though his message contained a note of warning—the day of divine vengeance had also arrived (v. 2)—on the whole his words were a welcome comfort to the mourning Jews.

Among the New Testament authors, Paul most thoroughly treats the nature of the gospel; he uses Gk. *euangelízesthai* twenty-one times. For Paul, the "good news" was that God had bought salvation through the death of Jesus Christ independent of the rules and regulations that characterized Judaism. Other writers, with the exception of Luke (who uses the verb twenty-five times), seldom use the term; the apostle John omits it altogether.

Matthew and Mark preserve the saying of Jesus that the gospel would be preached in all the world before the end would come (Matt. 24:14; Mark 13:10). Both also record Jesus' promise to the woman who anointed him that her deed would be remembered as the gospel was proclaimed (Matt. 26:13 par. Mark 14:9). Mark further implies that those who spread the gospel risked the loss of their possessions or their lives "for my sake and the gospel's" (8:35; 10:29). Luke, on the other hand, records that Jesus sent his twelve disciples to preach the gospel ("the kingdom of God") to the Jewish villages (Luke 9:2, 6) and that Jesus himself preached "the gospel" in the temple (20:1). *See* GOSPELS.

The book of Acts mentions that the apostles preached the good news in many Samaritan villages following their persecution at Jerusalem (Acts 8:25). Philip, one of the seven deacons, proclaimed the same message from Azotus to Caesarea (v. 40). At the Apostolic Council, Peter declared that God had sent him to preach "the word of the gospel" to the Gentiles (15:7); later, Paul received in a vision God's summons to preach the good news to Macedonia (16:10; cf. 2 Cor. 2:12).

The apostle Paul, who confessed that he was called to "testify to the gospel of the grace of God" (Acts 20:24; cf. Rom. 1:1; 1 Cor. 1:17), proclaimed the incarnate, crucified, and resurrected Christ (Rom. 1:3; 1 Cor. 1:17) who appeared to his followers after his resurrection (15:1-8). Preaching Christ in various cities of the Roman Empire (Rom. 15:19), Paul stressed that the gospel is God's power unto salvation for all believers, manifesting the righteousness of God, but veiled to all those who do not believe (1:16-17; cf. 2 Cor. 4:3-4).

Paul insisted that he preached an untainted gospel "without cost" to the Corinthians (1 Cor. 9:11-23; 2 Cor. 11:7). His opponents, who apparently depended on the local congregations for support, challenged his preaching with a "different (Gk. *héteros*) gospel" (Gal. 1:6). Paul responded vehemently, accusing them of distorting the gospel for their own profit and defending his own apostleship (2 Cor. 10:1–12:13) and his message ("my gospel," Rom. 2:16; 16:25; "our gospel," 2 Thess. 2:14). Paul's message was based on the Old Testament in which the gospel was "promised beforehand ... in the holy Scriptures" (Rom. 1:2; 10:15, quoting Isa. 52:7, LXX; Eph. 6:15; cf. Luke 4:18, where Christ applies Isa. 61:1 to himself).

At Gal. 1:7 the apostle Paul contrasts the gospel of the Judaizers with another (KJV "different") gospel. Paul felt the Judaized gospel denied salvation as a free gift ("by grace") and was thus "contrary" to the gospel of Jesus Christ (vv. 8-9; cf. 1 Tim. 1:3; 6:3). This "other gospel," perhaps represented by Peter's message to the uncircumcised, was unlike Paul's own in that it preached circumcision for the Jewish Christians (Gal. 2:7) and obedience to the Jewish law. The readings of the RSV ("not that there is another gospel") and the NIV ("which is really no gospel at all") best represent Paul's position: a salvation that was not completely by grace was no salvation at all.

The aged Peter makes a rather cryptic statement that the gospel was preached to the "dead" that they might live "in spirit" and not be judged like those who continue to disobey God's gospel of sound moral living (1 Pet. 4:6, 17). Similarly, the elderly John relates his positive message of love to an impending judgment when he records the angel's "eternal gospel," of the fear, or reverence, of God (Rev. 14:6).

GOSPELS.† A genre of literature, peculiar to Christianity, about the life of Jesus Christ. The term is specifically used to refer to the four canonical gospels of Matthew, Mark, Luke, and John.

"Gospel" is derived from AS *god-spell* "good news," which accurately translates Gk. *euangélion*. Mark used the term to introduce his account of Jesus' earthly ministry (Mark 1:1). The term was eventually expanded to include any work which dealt with the same subject—the birth, ministry, suffering, death, and resurrection of the Messiah. The earliest reference to this term as a type of literature was *ca.* A.D. 150 by Justin Martyr (*Apol.* i.66), "the memoirs ... which are called Gospels."

The Gospels cannot be understood as simple records of events. The four canonical Gospels are complex literary works of a high order. None of them are "objective" biographies in the nineteenth-century sense, nor do they follow the tenants of modern historiography. Each of the authors carefully selected and shaped his material with an eye toward both his own understanding of Jesus Christ and the needs of the community to which he was writing.

Mark, for instance, designed his gospel to answer the question "Who was Jesus Christ?" (cf. Mark 1:27; 2:7). The structure of his gospel is easily analyzed by relating each character or event to this central question. The teachers of the law (14:61-65), the people of the land (6:3, 14-16; 10:48; 11:9-10; cf. 12:35-37), nor Pilate knew (15:2), and even the disciples were ignorant until after the fact (e.g., 8:29; cf. Matt. 16:16); but God (Mark 1:11; 9:7), and even the demons (1:24; 3:11; 5:7), knew from the outset. The ultimate proof of the divinity of Christ (for Mark) was not his miracles or his teaching. It was only at the cross that Jesus Christ was revealed for who he truly was—the Son of

God. So the confession of the centurion is the climax of the book and restates Mark's premise (15:39).

Matthew writes to Jewish Christians. His concerns are Jesus the Messiah as king of the Jews and teacher of the law. One of his primary concerns is Jesus' relationship to the law—both to its keeping (Matt. 5:17-20) and to its prophecies of the Messiah (e.g., 1:1-17, 21-23; 2:5-6). Accordingly, Matthew's gospel uses a high number of Old Testament quotations. Jesus (for Matthew) is the new lawgiver who is greater than Moses (5:21-48). Thus, only Matthew places the giving of the Beatitudes on a mountainside (cf. Luke 6:17, "a level place") like that of Sinai, where the law was given to Moses (Exod. 19).

Luke's concern is not with the future coming of the risen Christ, but the mission of the Church in the meantime (cf. the angel's rebuke at Acts 1:9-11). So his gospel focuses on Jesus' relationships with those that were oppressed—the women (Luke 1:5-56; 4:38; 7:11-17, 36-50; 8:1-3, 43-48), the Samaritans (9:51-56; cf. 10:25-37), and the poor (6:20).

These three gospels together are called the Synoptic Gospels because of their interrelationship. While each has a different emphasis, their writings share common incidents and events, even to the point of using identical language in some places. Scholars, observing these many similarities, have concluded that either several of the gospels were largely dependent on the first one written (usually considered to be Mark) or that all had access to the same material in an even earlier collection of material (usually assigned the designation "Q," from Ger. *Quelle* "source"). To this common material each author then added his own distinct contribution. This riddle of order, priority, and dependence among the three gospels is called the Synoptic Problem. *See* SYNOPTIC GOSPELS.

John's gospel stands alone in the canon. It may well be the most complex gospel of all. In simple Greek John manages to handle extraordinarily difficult theological questions, such as the preexistence of Christ (John 1:1-18; 8:48-58). John's gospel also takes the most freedom with chronological order. Jesus' meal with the disciples before his betrayal, for example, is never called the Passover (13:2; RSV "supper"). The Passover could not occur until after the paschal lamb had been slain and, for John, Jesus was that paschal lamb; so John places Jesus on the cross at the time when the lambs were being slaughtered ("not a bone of him shall be broken" [19:36, quoting Exod. 12:46]). John is conscious of other liturgical settings in both early Christianity and Judaism; it has even been argued that his gospel may have been organized around the annual cycle of synagogue readings. Finally, John uses the characters in his narrative as types. Each is "larger than life," particularly "the Jews," who as a group are depicted as hostile to the Messiah and his message.

Despite their differences of emphasis, each of these authors shared a single premise. They believed that the life of Jesus—his actions and his words—set the standard for those that would follow. He was the living Torah for them, replacing (or at least modifying) the Mosaic Torah. Authority for Christian living was rooted in these memories of Jesus' actions. A gospel, then, could not be simply biographical; it had to be polemical.

Other gospels have survived which were not included in the canon for one reason or another. These writings are called apocryphal gospels. They include the gospel of Thomas, the gospel of the Hebrews, and the gospel of the Egyptians, among many others. These works can be divided loosely into three groups: those that share a largely common tradition with the Synoptics, those that are primarily gnostic, and those that are mostly legendary. All of these are valuable sources for understanding the diversity of Christian thought in the first several centuries. *See* APOCRYPHA, NEW TESTAMENT.

For additional information on specific canonical and apocryphal gospels see the individual entries.

Bibliography. F. C. Grant, *The Gospels: Their Origin and Growth* (New York: 1957); C. H. Talbert, *What Is a Gospel? The Genre of the Canonical Gospels* (Philadelphia: 1977).

GOTHIC VERSION.† A translation of the Greek Bible into Gothic, begun *ca.* A.D. 341 by Bishop Ulfilas, apostle to the Danube region (Sozomen *HE* vi.37). The oldest extant Teutonic writing, it is an extremely literal rendering of the early Byzantine text, although similarities to the Old Latin suggest its completion after Ulfilas and the Gothic Christians were driven into Moesia *ca.* 348. For this translation Ulfilas devised a twenty-seven character alphabet based on the Greek and Latin alphabets and Old German runes.

The version survives only in six fragmentary manuscripts dating to the fifth-sixth centuries, including five palimpsests and Codex Argenteus, which is written in silver and gold letters on purple vellum. Only a few verses of Gen. 5, Ps. 52, and Neh. 5-7 survive, as do fragments of the Catholic Epistles and the Gospels, arranged in the Western order (Matthew, John, Luke, Mark).

GOURD.† The "gourds" (Heb. *paqquʿōt*) gathered from a wild vine by one of the "sons of the prophets" (2 Kgs. 4:39) were colocynths (*Citrullus colocynthus*, also called bitter apples), bitter yellow or pale green fruits the size of an orange with strong purgative qualities, which can be poisonous on that account. The colocynth was the model for relief work on the wall paneling and the molten sea of Solomon's temple (1 Kgs. 6:18; 7:24; Heb. *peqāʿîm* "gourd-shaped"; KJV "knops"). At 2 Chr. 4:3, the relief on the molten sea is said to be of oxen (Heb. *beqārîm*); RSV supplies "gourds" from the parallel, 1 Kgs. 7:24. The plant under which Jonah found shade (Jonah 4:6-10; Heb. *qîqāyôn*) was probably not a gourd (so KJV), but a castor oil plant (*Ricinus communis*).

GOVERNMENT.† Although the Bible presents a variety of political institutions, detailed information is often fragmentary and inferential. Nonetheless, government is consistently understood in the context of God's covenant and of his sovereignty over the world.

Theocracy (Gk. *theokrátia* "God rules"), normally understood as government by God or mediated through his revelation and/or priesthood, is the underlying tenet of biblical thinking about government.

Israel was a community constituted by a covenant with their suzerain, Yahweh (Exod. 19:4-6). He is their lawgiver, judge, and ruler. This covenant provides the context for and the measure of every political organization. Although the forms of governing may vary, Yahweh remains Israel's true king and lord (Judg. 8:23; 1 Sam. 12:14-15; Pss. 93–100).

During the tribal period specially called leaders mediated God's rule, rallying the people to the Lord's cause. In their absence the people went their own way (Judg. 2:17). Under the Monarchy, theocratic rule centered on the king, but only as he lived in obedience to God's law and will (Deut. 17:14-20). Refusal led ultimately to the political destruction of the kingdom. After the Exile, Israel's government was explicitly theocratic, under the leadership of the high priest, priests, and scribes.

In New Testament times believers awaited the day when God will reign directly (Rev. 21:3). In the meantime, their practical relationship with earthly rulers continued to be informed by the Old Testament understanding of theocracy, yet modified by the confession that Jesus Christ is Lord (Phil. 2:11). Christians live in society as citizens of another kingdom, established by God and not by politics (John 18:36). Even though the state and its institutions owe their existence to God (Rom. 13:1; cf. John 19:11), the government's powers are subordinate to God's sovereignty (Luke 20:25). The rebellious denial of this concept, embodied through despotism, is an abomination (Rev. 13; cf. Dan. 6:6-18; 11:31-32). God charges the state with certain responsibilities: to do justice, approve the good, condemn evil (Rom. 13:4), and promote the general welfare so that all may live in peace (1 Tim. 2:2; cf. Ps. 72:1-4). Christian citizenship before such responsible authority includes submission, payment of taxes, and affirmation through prayer (Rom. 13:1-6; 1 Tim. 2:1-2; 1 Pet. 2:13-16). Yet Christian loyalty can never be unconditional, for allegiance belongs first to God (Acts 5:29).

I. Old Testament

A. Tribal Israel. From the patriarchs to Saul's reign, Israel held a tribal form of government similar to that of other peoples of the region (cf. Gen. 25:13-16). This form is portrayed in terms of kinship patterns, with relationships expressed by blood, marriage (cf. Judg. 1:16), covenant (cf. Josh. 14:14), and service (Gen. 17:27). See GENEALOGY.

Four groupings are distinguished among tribal Israel (cf. Josh. 7:16-18). The household or "father's house" (Heb. *bêt-'āb*) consists of parents, children, grandchildren, unmarried kin, slaves, and strangers, all living together. The clan (*mišpāḥâ*) represents several related households living in close proximity, later identified with the district or village. The clan is the center for feasts (1 Sam. 20:6, 29), settling disputes, and providing the basic military unit, the thousand (*'elep*; e.g., Judg. 6:15). The tribe (*šēbeṭ, maṭṭeh*) is an association of clans claiming a common ancestor, who recognize a common leader (*nāśî'*) and rally to his aid (*šēbeṭ* "staff"). In Canaan tribes became increasingly identified with regions, rather than as ethnic divisions. Together the tribes (usually numbered at twelve, if with varying membership; cf. Gen. 35:23-26; Num. 1:20-47) constitute the people of Israel, whose primary identity is established by covenant (Exod. 19–23; Josh. 24), focusing on one God,

sharing the same feasts, law, and aversion to non-Israelite practices (Judg. 19:30). Although ideally distinct, in practice the jural boundaries between the various political levels were often obscured (cf. 17:7; 18:1).

Under the covenant, all adult males fit for military service composed the assembly or congregation (*'ēdâ, qāhāl*). This group ratified the covenant (Exod. 24:1-8), witnessed cultic practices (Lev. 8:3; Num. 8:9-10), heard reports (13:26ff.), and divided booty (31:26-27).

Routine governance of clan and tribe rested with the elders (*zeqēnîm*, from *zāqān* "beard"). These were the princes and judges (Exod. 2:14; cf. 4:29), the nobles (Job 29:10), the chiefs and leaders (Josh. 22:14), the heads of households, and men of economic or military eminence (e.g., Judg. 6:12; Ruth 2:1)—a practical aristocracy who ruled on behalf of the community (cf. Judg. 11:5). As their titles indicate, they led the military (as *śārîm* "captains"), judged disputes and interpreted the law, and gave wisdom in administering the community's affairs. From their ranks Moses appointed his commanders and judges (Exod. 18:13-26; Deut. 1:15).

Alongside the councils of elders, tribal Israel recognized several types of offices, some the result of a divine call, others by the people's appointment. Both cases presume recognized prowess and wisdom. The leader (*nāśî'*) is the chief political authority of the clan or tribe (Num. 7:2), who represents them in cultic matters (11:16ff.) and leads in war (1:1-16): a chief. As Yahweh's appointed leader (Exod. 3:10), Moses assumed many of the chiefs' responsibilities as judge (18:13), mediator of religious life, and leader in battle (17:8-11). This same pattern of leadership continued with Joshua (cf. Deut. 34:9). Israel also appointed "heads" (*rôš*), who were both military leaders and judges (Exod. 18:25-26; Deut. 1:13; Judg. 11:11). These offices were perpetuated in each town throughout the Monarchy (16:18; cf. 1 Chr. 23:4). As recorded in the book of Judges God raised up charismatic leaders for some (if not all) of the tribes (Judg. 2:16), to serve as military deliverers (*môšî[a]'* "messiahs") as well as adjudicators (*šōpeṭîm*). These singular offices were not hereditary, for only Yahweh was the king of Israel (cf. 8:23). See JUDGE.

B. Monarchy. In the face of internal anarchy (Judg. 21:25) and external threats (cf. 1 Sam. 4:1-10; 11:1-2), Israel looked for a king. Moses had anticipated this and gave theocratic guidelines for kingship (Deut. 17:14-20). Yet Israel rejected this limited notion of monarchy and sought a king "like the other nations," opening the door to absolutism, false glory, and inevitable idolatry (1 Sam. 8:5-18). Only rarely would the divine ideal be realized (2 Kgs. 12:2; 18:3; e.g., 13:14).

The Monarchy institutionalized many aspects of the earlier office of judge. The king was God's anointed (1 Sam. 9:16; 1 Kgs. 1:39) and, as such, inviolable (1 Sam. 24:6). With his anointing, the king was invested not only with the diadem but with the covenant stipulations as vassal king of Yahweh (2 Kgs. 11:12; cf. Deut. 17:18-20). Although coups occurred, in Judah the office remained dynastic, restricted to David's descendants (2 Sam. 7:8-16), while in Israel it remained largely charismatic, with strong leaders called by God and anointed by the hierarchy (1 Kgs. 11:31; 14:7; 19:6; cf. Hos. 8:4).

Under the king, local government continued as before, with most affairs in the hands of the elders (cf. 1 Kgs. 21:8). In larger cities and towns the king appointed a royal deputy to oversee his interests and collect taxes (22:26). Judges and other officials also became subject to royal appointment (1 Chr. 23:4; 26:29).

For administrative and tax purposes Solomon divided the kingdom into districts, twelve for the northern regions, with a separate one presumably for Judah, each with its own head (1 Kgs. 4:7-28).

A variety of court functionaries, generally termed servants or officials (*śārîm*), carried out the royal administration. 1 Kgs. 4 lists the major offices under Solomon. These include the manager of the king's estate, later vizier or prime minister, second only to the king (2 Kgs. 19:2; Isa. 22:15, 20-22; cf. Gen. 41:40); the recorder who brought the king news, served as his spokesman, and supervised royal protocol; the royal secretary, second in rank to the master of the palace (2 Kgs. 18:18), whose scribes became a sizeable official body, handling all official records, tabulations, and correspondence (cf. Jer. 36:10-12); the supervisor of the corvée (1 Kgs. 12:18); and the chief revenue officer ("over the officers," 4:5), charged with collecting taxes and provisions for royal use. The Bible also notes an informal office variously termed counselor (2 Sam. 16:23), the king's priest (20:26), or king's friend (1 Kgs. 4:5).

C. Postexilic Period. Under Persian rule the Jews enjoyed cultural and religious autonomy, while military and political control rested with imperial governors and their administrations. Judah was a province in the larger satrap Beyond the River (Ezra 5:6), and was divided into districts for taxation purposes, each with its own ruler (Neh. 3:9-18). This basic structure remained, with varying boundaries, into the Roman period.

Matters affecting the religious and cultural life of the people rested in the hands of the chief priest (Ezra 3:2), the priests and Levites, and the elders. These interpreted and taught the Law (7:6, 10), judged and punished under official oversight (10:8), and rebuilt the temple (6:7). During Roman rule the Sanhedrin, a body of seventy-one elders, priests, and scribes, represented Jewish interests in Palestine.

Locally, elders continued to gather in council to supervise the life of the villages, much as they had before (Ezra 10:14; cf. Jdt. 7:23).

II. New Testament

The first-century A.D. government of Palestine was a patchwork of surrogate kings and direct Roman rule. The century began with Herod the Great savagely ruling Palestine (cf. Matt. 2:16). Three sons succeeded him. Archelaus was the ethnarch (lit. "governor of the people") of Idumea, Judea, and Samaria, but his bloodthirstiness was as bad as his father's (cf. v. 22), so the Romans exiled him in A.D. 6. Philip was tetrarch (minor prince) of northern Transjordan (Luke 3:1). Herod Antipas was tetrarch of Galilee and Perea; he beheaded John the Baptist, monitored Jesus' ac-

tions, and humiliated him during his trial (9:7-9; 23:6-12). Herod Agrippa succeeded these three; he ruled a united Palestine, but died suddenly at Caesarea (Acts 12). After the exile of Archelaus, Tiberius appointed Pontius Pilate procurator of Judea; procurators were military governors, appointed to rebellious or newly conquered territories. Later procurators of Judea were Antonius Felix (Acts 23:24) and Porcius Festus (24:27).

Lesser administrative officers included tax collectors (usually Romans, but cf. Luke 19:2-10), centurions (Luke 7:1-10; Acts 10:1; 27:1), and lictors (Gk. *rhabdýchoi* "police"; Acts 16:35).

Bibliography. N. K. Gottwald, *The Tribes of Yahweh* (Maryknoll, N.Y.: 1979); S. Mowinckel, *He That Cometh* (Nashville: 1956), pp. 21-95; A. N. Sherwin-White, *Roman Society and Roman Law in the New Testament* (Oxford: 1963); R. de Vaux, *Ancient Israel* (New York: 1961).

GOVERNOR.† A ruler of a territory, province, or city, appointed by a king.

Old Testament references to a governor most commonly designate the imperial administrators of Babylon and Persia. The usual term (Heb. *peḥâ*, from Akk. *bēl pāḥati* "lord of a district") designates an administrative level below that of satrap (cf. Dan. 3:2). Tattenai, then, serves as governor (Aram. *peḥâ*) under the satrap of Babylon and Trans-euphrates (RSV "Beyond the River") and as superior to other local governors (Aram. *'aparsaṭ kāyê*, from O. Pers. *frastāka*) under him (Ezra 5:6). Zerubbabel (Hag. 1:1) and Nehemiah (Neh. 5:14) were appointed by the king to this lesser governorship over Judah. Nehemiah is also called a *tiršāṭā*, a Persian title of respect (from *taršta* "feared, reverenced," thus "his excellency"; Neh. 7:65; 10:1 [MT 2]).

In preexilic settings the title is relatively rare and less distinct. The governor of a district (Heb. *śārê mᵉdînâ*) combines civil and military functions (1 Kgs. 20:14ff.). The ruler of a city (*śar*) may be called governor (e.g., 22:26), although the Hebrew term refers to a much broader range of positions than does *peḥâ*. At 2 Chr. 23:20, "governors" (*môšēl*, ptcp. *māšal* "to rule"; cf. Gen. 45:26) refers to high officials, who with captains (*śārê*) and nobles overthrow Athaliah. Joseph is also called a governor (*šallîṭ*), a high official or vizier in Pharaoh's court (42:6).

In the New Testament, governor (Gk. *hēgemenón*) generally denotes the ruler of a Roman province (Matt. 10:18; 1 Pet. 2:14). Luke uses the term to designate three Roman offices: the proconsul, who governs a senatorial province (Sergius Paulus of Cyprus, Acts 13:7; Gallio of Achaia, 18:12-13); a legate, a military official governing an imperial province (Quirinius of Syria, Luke 2:2); and the procurator or prefect, who rules a country in the name of the emperor with the help of a resident army (e.g., Pontius Pilate, 3:1; Felix, Acts 23:24; and Festus, 24:27).

The governor (*ethnárchēs*) of King Aretas (2 Cor. 11:32) is likely his deputy, or perhaps a local chieftain. *See* ETHNARCH.

GOZAN [gō′zăn] (Heb. *gôzān;* Akk. *Guzana*). A city and district in northwest Mesopotamia, situated on the river Habor (called in the Old Testament the "river of Gozan"; cf. RSV, NJV, 1 Chr. 5:26; "river Gozan," following MT). The Assyrian king Tiglath-pileser III deported the Reubenites, Gadites, and the Transjordanian portion of Manasseh to this region (2 Chr. 5:26). With the fall of Samaria, Shalmaneser V or Sargon exiled some of the northern populace here as well (2 Kgs. 17:6; 18:11). Later Sennacherib boasted to King Hezekiah of the Assyrians' earlier conquests in Gozan (19:12 par. Isa. 37:12).

Modern Tell Halâf, east of Haran, has been posited as the site, perhaps the same as the Gauzanitis cited by Ptolemy (*Georg.* v.18).

GRACE.† God's unmerited favor toward humanity and especially his people, realized through the covenant and fulfilled through Jesus Christ.

I. Old Testament

Three Hebrew words are used to express this concept. Heb. *ḥēn* often designates the favor (so RSV) the strong bestow on the weak (e.g., KJV, Gen. 33:8ff.), especially by kings (1 Sam. 27:5; Esth. 5:8). The term can emphasize the freedom of God's grace (Gen. 6:8; Exod. 33:12ff.; Jer. 31:2) or personal qualities that bring his blessing: faithfulness (Prov. 3:4), humility (3:34; cf. Jas. 4:6), understanding (Prov. 13:15).

The related verb *ḥānan* "be gracious" designates the action of unmerited favor toward another in the context of need. It presupposes love (cf. Deut. 7:7-8) but cannot be presumed (Exod. 33:19). The psalmist cries for graciousness in the stress of loneliness (Ps. 25:16), hunger (111:4-5), and sin (51:1 [MT 3]). God denies grace in judgment (Deut. 7:2; Isa. 27:11), yet offers grace for the repentant (Amos 5:15). Isaiah proclaims that the Lord "exalts himself to show mercy (*ḥānan*)" to those who wait for him (Isa. 30:18). God's graciousness is the object of hope (Gen. 43:29; Num. 6:25) and of praise (Ps. 67).

Heb. *ḥeseḏ* (KJV "mercy," following RSV, LXX; "steadfast love") further enlarges the Old Testament understanding of grace. God not only grants periodic favor but continues in gracious relationship with his people. Between people, *ḥeseḏ* denotes a committed loyalty (e.g., Gen. 47:29) created by acts of kindness (cf. Josh. 2:12; Ruth 3:10) or by covenant (1 Sam. 20:8), one implying the other (Gen. 21:23; 1 Kgs. 20:31ff.). God's *ḥeseḏ*, however, flows from his love, not from obligation. He created the world in steadfast love (Ps. 136:4-9), and fills it accordingly (33:5; 119:64). Out of love he calls to covenant a people who were nothing (Deut. 7:6-9), delivers them, and gives his law (Exod. 20:2-6). This grace calls people to covenant loyalty (Num. 14:18-19) and graciousness toward one another (Mic. 6:8; cf. Ps. 109:16). Yet even when Israel fails as his people (Hos. 6:4, 6), he remains their gracious God, welcoming the repentant (10:12; Ps. 51).

Grace fills the Psalms, which confess that God's *ḥeseḏ* endures forever (Ps. 136). Often paired with "faithfulness" (Heb. *'emeṯ*; LXX Gk. *alḗtheia* "truth"), this is the grace of salvation experienced in history, which continues despite Israel's sins (106:1, 7) and gives hope (107:39-43). It gives confidence for times of need (31:7), even in the face of death (86:13).

Grace accompanies (23:6) and crowns a believer's life (103:4).

These words come together in Exod. 34. God proclaims his name as the one who has saved Israel (v. 14), who now makes a covenant (v. 1). He shows graciousness (*ḥēn*) to his people's distress and abounds in love (*ḥeseḏ*) and faithfulness (*'emeṯ*) (v. 6). He is loyal (*ḥeseḏ*) to the covenant, forgiving the people's iniquity, rebellion, and sin, even to the thousandth generation. Israel uses these same words to express praise (e.g., Ps. 86:15; 103:8), repentance (Joel 2:13; Mic. 7:18; cf. Jonah 4:2), and covenant renewal (2 Chr. 30:9; Neh. 9:17). It is this grace so richly displayed that Christ fulfills (John 1:16).

II. New Testament

The New Testament word for grace, Gk. *cháris,* is related to the verb *chaírō* "rejoice." In secular usage the term indicates that which brings joy and pleasure or wins favor. This broad meaning is reflected in the use of "favor" in Luke-Acts (e.g., Luke 1:30; 2:40; Acts 7:10).

The Gospels rarely use the word "grace," although its substance permeates them in the life and teaching of Jesus. He reflects God's self-giving, sent in love (John 3:17), with divine purpose (Luke 4:4), becoming a servant (Mark 10:45). Jesus' life manifests grace in seeking the lost sheep of Israel (Matt. 9:36; 10:6; Luke 15:4ff.; John 10): the poor (Matt. 19:21), social outcasts (Luke 5:30-32), women (8:2), and children (Mark 10:14-15). He preaches grace: a seeking God (Luke 15); salvation made possible (Mark 10:17-31); a new covenant (Luke 22:19-22); and love for enemies (Matt. 5:43-44; Luke 10:27ff.). God demonstrates grace by sending Jesus to the cross for human sin and then by the resurrection. Now reigning as Lord, Jesus Christ inaugurates a new age of grace.

A. Paul. This new grace holds a key position in Paul's letters. Nearly two-thirds of all uses of *cháris* are found there.

According to Paul, God's grace is inseparable from his love expressed in Jesus Christ (Rom. 1:7; 1 Cor. 1:3). Christ mediates salvation. Rich, he became poor (2 Cor. 8:9); in glory, he took the form of a servant (Phil. 2:7); through him, God reconciled mankind to himself (2 Cor. 5:18-21), "while we were yet sinners" (Rom. 5:8).

The grace of Jesus Christ is through the cross (Gal. 2:20; Eph. 1:20; cf. Rom. 5:9). God freely justifies all who believe, by faith and grace (3:24-25; cf. 5:1). Grace is the antithesis of law (Gal. 5:4), human wisdom (2 Cor. 1:12), and sin (Rom. 6:1). God, rich in mercy (cf. Heb. *ḥeseḏ*) and love, brings children of wrath alive (Eph. 2:4-5).

This grace is received by faith (v. 8). In faith, one experiences grace's abundance (Rom. 5:17; Eph. 1:7; 2:7). Yet faithlessness, by legalism (Gal. 2:21; 5:4) or negligence (1 Cor. 15:2; 2 Cor. 6:1), can render this grace in vain. While grace cannot be presumed, in its abundance it can be wholly trusted as adequate for every sinner (cf. 1 Tim. 1:15-16).

God's graciousness in Christ is multiplied throughout the world through his people (2 Cor. 4:15). God gives Paul grace to preach in his mission to the Gentiles (Rom. 15:15; Eph. 3:8; cf. Acts 20:24). The

Church receives this same grace for its offices and ministries (Rom. 12:3-8; Eph. 4:7, 11-12). Believers show God's graciousness in the ministry of relief (2 Cor. 8:7), in godly living (cf. Tit. 2:11ff.), and in gracious speech (Eph. 4:29ff.; Col. 4:6).

In Paul's greetings and benedictions grace (*cháris*) echoes the standard Hellenistic greeting *chaírein* (cf. Luke 1:28; Jas. 1:1; RSV "Greeting"). Combined with peace (from Heb. *šālôm* "wholeness, well-being, salvation"; cf. Num. 6:25), these words focus on the God of peace (Rom. 15:33) who brings people into relationship with himself in Christ and into peace with one another (Eph. 2:14ff.). The closing, "grace . . . be with you" (Rom. 16:20; Gal. 6:18, "your spirit"), prays for their continuance in the salvation of Christ and for the presence of God which he mediates. This rich language was adopted by the early Church in epistles (e.g., Revelation, 1 Clement) and liturgies (e.g., 2 Cor. 13:14).

B. Other Uses. In Acts *cháris* most often refers to the salvation being worked out in believers' lives (e.g., Acts 11:23; 13:43). Occasionally, Luke here also follows Paul's identification of grace and the gospel (15:40; 20:24).

In Hebrews the term follows the LXX usage (for Heb. *ḥēn*). God gives kingly favor through Christ to those who come to him in time of need (Heb. 4:16). This grace calls for faith (cf. 11:6). Believers are not to scorn grace (10:29) nor ignore it in sloth (12:15), but are to be strengthened by grace in their hearts (13:9).

1 Peter makes frequent reference to putting grace into practice in holiness (1 Pet. 1:13ff.), humility (5:5), and the employment of spiritual gifts (4:10). Even suffering may be a means of grace (5:10).

From creation to consummation, the Bible tells of God's grace. Jesus Christ does not replace the splendor of the Old Testament (cf. Exod. 34:6), but now brings it to fullness in grace and truth (John 1:16-17; cf. Heb. 1:1-2), freely bestowed on mankind, to return to him in praise (Eph. 1:6).

Bibliography. H. Conzelmann and W. Zimmerli, "χάρις," *TDNT* 9 (1974): 359-415; N. Glueck, *Ḥesed in the Bible* (1967; repr. New York: 1975); J. Moffatt, *Grace in the New Testament* (New York: 1931).

GRAIN. The cultivation of grain began early in Palestine's history, both in the steppe regions, which were the first to be settled, and in the wooded areas. Fields were planted mainly with barley and wheat, but the cultivation of millet and spelt is also mentioned (Isa. 28:25; Ezek. 4:9). Grain was grown in Palestine even before the time of the patriarchs, but they themselves are not known to have been farmers; only Isaac is specifically mentioned as a sower of grain (Gen. 26:12). When the Israelites arrived in Palestine, they took over the cultivation of the land from the previous inhabitants (Deut. 8:8). At Gen. 27:28; Deut. 7:13 "grain and wine" are used figuratively to represent the entire yield of the land.

The several grains that were grown in the area were used for a variety of purposes and could be prepared in a number of ways. Wheat might be eaten raw, as it was picked (23:25; Matt. 12:1). It might also be parched with fire when the kernels were either half or fully ripe (Lev. 2:14; 23:14; 1 Sam. 17:17). Most of the wheat harvest, however, was milled into flour for making bread, which was not only a dietary staple but important among the sacrifices that were brought to the sanctuary. Barley was often harvested while still green for use as animal fodder, and the ripened kernels also were fed to horses (1 Kgs. 4:28). Barley was less important than wheat as a flour for bread, but the Bible has several references to its use in loaves (cf. Ruth 3:15; 2 Sam. 17:28; John 6:9).

The precise meaning of Heb. *hārîpôt*, which appears at 2 Sam. 17:19 (RSV "grain"; KJV "ground corn"; NJV "groats"); Prov. 27:22 (RSV "crushed grain"; KJV "wheat"), is unclear. It may designate grain which was moistened so that it could be finely crushed in a mortar and then spread out to dry. The term may also refer to sand which was added to the grain to aid in milling.

GRAPES (Heb. *ʿēnāḇ* "ripened grapes"; *bōser* "early grapes"; Gk. *staphylé*).† A primary agricultural product of the ancient Near East, grapes frequently are used symbolically or figuratively in the Bible, primarily in the context of judgment. Eliphaz the Temanite tells Job that the wicked man will be like a vine stripped of its immature grapes (Job 15:33; Heb. *bēser*), a judgment echoed in prophecies against Edom by Jeremiah (Jer. 49:9) and Obadiah (Obad. 5). At Joel 3:13 (MT 4:13); Rev. 14:18-19 the wicked are described as grapes which are harvested and thrown into the winepress of God's wrath.

A vine can produce good or bad grapes. The Song of the Vineyard (Isa. 5:1-7) illustrates how Israel, God's tenderly cultivated vine, is condemned for yielding the bad grapes (Heb. *bᵉʾušîm* "wild grapes") of wickedness instead of righteousness. Similarly, Jesus employs grapes when he teaches that a plant is recognized by its fruit (Matt. 7:15-20; Luke 6:43-45). The apostle Paul cites by analogy the fruit of the vineyard in defending his right to material support from those he had evangelized (1 Cor. 9:7).

Perhaps the best-known biblical quotation in which grapes are employed is "The fathers have eaten sour grapes, and the children's teeth are set on edge." This proverb implies that one generation's sins would affect the lives of those in succeeding generations (cf. Exod. 20:5; Deut. 24:16). Jeremiah (Jer. 31:29-30) and Ezekiel (Ezek. 18:1-32) countered this belief by stating that each person was responsible for his sins alone.

For agricultural aspects of grapes, *see* VINE, VINEYARD.

GRASS. In biblical usage a number of terms designate, with little apparent distinction, grass and related forms of herbage.

Heb. *ʿēśeḇ* is a general term for grass (e.g., Deut. 29:23 [MT 22]; Ps. 72:16; JB "common grass"; 92:7 [MT 8]; JB "weeds"; Amos 7:2; JB "greenstuff"; Mic. 5:7 [MT 8]). Elsewhere the RSV translates the term as "herb" (e.g., Deut. 32:2), "plants" (e.g., 2 Kgs. 19:26 par. Isa. 37:27), and "vegetation" (Zech. 10:1). The KJV frequently renders it "herb" (e.g., Gen. 1:11-12, 29-30; Exod. 9:22, 25) or "herbs" (e.g., Prov. 27:25; Jer. 12:4). The Hebrew term refers to food eaten by animals (Deut. 11:15; Ps. 106:20) as well as humans (Gen. 1:29; 3:18; NJV "grains"). The Aramaic form *ᵃśaḇ* occurs at Dan. 4:15, 25, 32-33 (MT 12, 22, 29-30); 5:21.

Another general term for grass is *ḥāṣîr* (also "herbage"). It refers to food for animals (1 Kgs. 18:5; Job 40:15; Ps. 104:14) and is used symbolically of mankind's temporal, mortal existence (90:5; 103:15; 129:6; Isa. 40:6-8). At Prov. 27:25 the term means "hay" (so KJV, NIV; RSV "grass"; cf. JB).

Heb. *dešeʾ* (KJV often "herb") may refer to forage (Job 6:5; 38:27; Jer. 14:5), newly-sprouted vegetation (2 Sam. 23:4; cf. Gen. 1:11-12; RSV "vegetation"), and human transitoriness (2 Kgs. 19:26 par. Isa. 37:27; Ps. 37:2; RSV "tender grass"). The Aramaic form *deteʾ* "tender grass" occurs at Dan. 4:15, 23 (MT 12, 20).

Heb. *yereq* means literally "green, greenness," but by metonymy refers to grass (e.g., Num. 22:4). Elsewhere the term is translated "green thing" (Exod. 10:15) or "verdure" (Isa. 15:6; NJV "vegetation").

The New Testament term for grass is Gk. *chórtos*, which is used in the LXX chiefly for Heb. *ʿēśeḇ*. It refers to grass which is found in a field or meadow (Matt. 14:19; Mark 6:39; John 6:10; Rev. 8:7; 9:4) and to wild grass, in contrast to cultivated plants (Matt. 6:30 par. Luke 12:28; Jas. 1:10-11; 1 Pet. 1:24). The RSV also translates it as "plants" (Matt. 13:26; JB "new wheat"; cf. NIV), "blade" (Mark 4:28; NIV "stalk"; JB "shoot"), and "hay" (1 Cor. 3:12).

GRASSHOPPER (Heb. *ʾarbeh, ḥāgāḇ*).† An insect whose numbers and voracious appetite were a threat to agriculture in the ancient Near East.

In ancient times, as today, the words grasshopper (family *Tettigoniidae*) and locust (or short-horned grasshopper; family *Acrididae*) were used interchangeably. While both insect families belong to the order *Orthoptera*, grasshoppers do not swarm or migrate in the manner of locusts.

In the Bible grasshoppers are listed among the clean insects that the Israelites could eat (Lev. 11:22); only the thorax was eaten, after being broiled or dried. Their jumping ability may be referred to indirectly at Eccl. 12:5, where mankind is admonished to remember God before troubled days or advanced age comes, when the grasshopper will be forced to drag itself along the ground.

Grasshoppers also occur metaphorically in the Bible. At Num. 12:33 the spies sent into the promised land estimate that they were no bigger than these insects in comparison to the giant Nephilim inhabiting the land. The people of the earth are as numerous as grasshoppers before God's throne (Isa. 40:22). The onslaught of Israel's enemies is likened to the advance of a swarm of grasshoppers (Nah. 3:15-17; cf. Joel 1:4; 2:25).

See LOCUST.

GRAVE (Heb. *qeḇer, qᵉḇûrâ*).† An excavated place for burial of the dead. In general terms graves were located outside cities or villages in biblical times, although exceptions were made for rulers. Occasionally a person was buried beneath his house (1 Sam. 25:1; 2 Chr. 33:20), a custom attested by excavated Canaan-

ite dwellings. The usual practice was to bury a person in an individual grave within a family burial complex, hence the expressions "to sleep with one's fathers" (e.g., 2 Kgs. 14:16; 20:21) and "be buried with one's fathers" (e.g., 14:20; 15:7).

Archaeological excavations in Palestine have uncovered a large number of ancient graves. Graves varied widely in their form, and no specialized vocabulary for their classification or description is encountered in the Bible. In its simplest form the grave was merely a shallow trench, perhaps covered with a heap of stones to protect the remains (cf. Josh. 7:26; 2 Sam. 18:17) and appropriately marked (e.g., Gen. 35:8, 20). Caves frequently were used for interment because of their convenience (cf. 25:9), with bodies lowered into them from above. Large burial chambers were built into them, including horizontal compartments into which bodies were deposited. Sometimes a semicircular niche was hewn into the rock, creating a ledge onto which the body was placed. Also, a kind of stone coffin could be made by digging a trough in the niche floor (cf. Matt. 27:59-60). Although no evidence of cremation has been found, secondary burials are attested at 2 Sam. 21:12-14 and by the numerous ossuaries discovered dating to the Hellenistic and Roman periods.

The grave often has a figurative meaning in the Bible. The Hebrews believed that after earthly life the dead continued to exist, separated from God, in a twilight world called Sheol (Heb. *šᵉʾôl*, often translated "the grave" in English versions). For example, the biblical writers compared jealousy (Cant. 8:6) to the grave and the words of adulteresses (Prov. 5:5; 7:27) to Sheol. A frequently expressed hope is that God will rescue the dead from the grave (Ps. 49:14-15; cf. KJV, Hos. 13:14; 1 Cor. 15:55).

See BURIAL; SHEOL.

GREAT SEA [Heb. *hayyām haggādôl*].† The common name used in the Old Testament for the Mediterranean Sea (e.g., Num. 34:6-7; Josh. 1:4; Ezek. 47:10; cf. Ps. 104:25; 107:23), because it was larger than the other seas known to the Israelites (i.e., the Dead Sea, the Sea of Galilee, and the Red Sea). The Akkadian name "Western Sea" was also used (Deut. 11:24; 34:2; Joel 2:20; Zech. 14:8), distinguishing it from the Dead Sea, which was the eastern sea (e.g., Ezek. 47:18). At Exod. 23:31 it is called "the sea of the Philistines." The Assyrians and Babylonians also used the name "Upper Sea," and the Romans Lat. *Mare Internum* "Interior Sea" or *Mare Nostrum* "Our Sea." Most frequently the Mediterranean is simply referred to as "the sea" (Heb. *hayyām*; Gk. *hē thálassa*) (e.g., Gen. 49:13; Num. 13:29; Josh. 15:46; 1 Kgs. 18:43; Jer. 25:22; Ezek. 26:16; Jonah 1:4; Acts 27:5). It served as the western boundary of the territory of Judah (Josh. 15:12) as well as of Israel itself (23:4; Ezek. 47:15, 19-20; 48:28).

The Mediterranean Sea is situated in an intercontinental basin with Europe to the north, Africa on the south, and Asia to the east. Its maximum length from the western limit Strait of Gibraltar to the eastern coast of Lebanon is more than 3700 km. (2300 mi.). The maximum longitudinal distance between the coasts of modern Yugoslavia and Libya is nearly 1370 km. (850 mi.). If one includes the Sea of Marmara (be-

tween the Aegean and Black Seas), it covers nearly
2,512,300 sq. km. (970,000 sq. mi.). The Western
Mediterranean is deeper on the average, but the deepest soundings have been obtained in the eastern basin
south of Greece with a depth of 4850 m. (15,900 ft.)
below sea level. The surface water temperature varies
from a February low of 10-12°C. (50-54°F.) to an
August high of 25-29°C. (77-84°F.). The salinity is
considerably higher than the Atlantic or the Black Sea
because of the heavy losses of water by evaporation,
with the saltiness increasing from west to east.

Historically the Mediterranean basin has been a
melting pot for the peoples and civilizations intermin-
gled through migration, military conquest, political
consolidation, and commerce. The Mediterranean
world was first united by Alexander the Great in the
Hellenistic Empire in 331 B.C. Then, after years of
disintegration, the region was again united under the
Roman Empire in 31 B.C., with Palestine submitting
to the invading army of Pompey in 63 B.C.

The Phoenicians were early leaders in seafaring
commerce on the Mediterranean. Hiram, king of Tyre,
sent experienced seamen to serve as consultants to the
infant fleet of Solomon (1 Kgs. 9:26-28 par. 2 Chr.
8:17-18). Solomon's merchant fleet of ocean-going
vessels utilized the harbor at Ezion-geber in the Red
Sea; and, although called ships of Tarshish (1 Kgs.
10:22 par. 2 Chr. 9:21), there is no evidence for an
Israelite shipping fleet sailing the Mediterranean. The
timber used for building the temple was formed into
rafts and thus transported by sea from Lebanon (1 Kgs.
5:9). The Greeks and the Romans used the sea extensively, thus the Roman designation "Our Sea." The
development of international traffic on the Mediterranean in New Testament times certainly contributed
to the missionary travels of Paul, Barnabas, Silas, and
others (e.g., Acts 17:14), and played a significant role
in the rapid growth of Christianity.

GREAVES (Heb. *miṣḥaṭ*). Pieces of armor that protect the soldier's shins. Goliath wore bronze greaves
(1 Sam. 17:6). Greaves were also a standard part of
Greek and Roman armor.

GREECE (Heb. *yāwān*; Gk. *Hellas*).† A major ancient civilization rooted primarily in a confederation
of city-states in the southern Balkan peninsula. During
the biblical period the Greeks influenced the peoples
of the ancient Near East culturally and, at times,
politically.

I. Name

The modern name Greece (Lat. *Graecia*) is apparently
quite late, applied to the people and their civilization
by the Romans following the invasion of Italy by the
Greek general Pyrrhus in the late third century B.C.
Prior to that time Gk. *Hellas* was used to designate
the locus of Greek civilization, although not in a strictly
geographical sense (derived from the collective *Hellēnes*, an appellative for those who fostered that culture). Even as late as Homeric times (*ca.* eighth
century) various local appellatives (e.g., *Achaioi, Ar-
geioi, Danaoi*) were extended to all Greeks.

In the biblical Table of Nations Javan (Heb. *yāwān*;
Gen. 10:4 par. 1 Chr. 1:7) apparently designates the

Ionians, the earliest Greek-speaking inhabitants of
Attica (cf. Dan. 8:21; 10:20; 11:2; Zech. 9:13,
"Greece"). At 1 Macc. 1:1 Gk. *Hellas* represents Heb.
kittim "Kittim" (so RSV), since by this time *yāwān*
had come to mean the Seleucid kingdom; at Acts 20:2
Hellas refers to the Roman province of Achaia. In
New Testament usage Gk. *Hellēn* may designate an
inhabitant of Greece, in the broader sense (e.g., Acts
16:1; Rom. 1:14). More often it denotes a Gentile or
non-Jew (e.g., 10:12; Gal. 3:28). It may also refer to
a Greek-speaking Jew of the Diaspora (e.g., Mark
7:26; cf. Acts 6:1, "Hellenists"; Gk. *Hellēnistai;* KJV
"Grecians").

II. Geography

Greece proper generally is limited to that portion of
the lower Balkan peninsula situated between the fortieth and thirty-sixth parallels. The mountainous terrain and irregular coastline that divide the land into
a number of distinct regions long served as a deterrent
to political unification. Northern Greece is separated
from the plains of Macedonia by a string of minor
ranges, including the Acroceraunian to the west and
the Cambunian to the east, the latter crowned by Mt.
Olympus (2920 m. [9570 ft.]); the southern limits of
the region are formed by the Gulfs of Ambracia and
Maliac and the Othrys mountains. The north-south
Pindus mountain range, often called the backbone of
Greece, separates Epirus to the west and Thessaly to
the east in northern Greece; Thessaly is further divided from Magnesia and the Aegean coast by the
Ossa and Pelion mountains and by Lake Boebeis and
the Gulf of Pagasae. Spurs of the Pindus divide central
Greece into Acarnania and Aetolia to the west and
Attica, Phocis, and Boetia to the east; interspersed
here are the smaller states of Aenis, Doris, Locris,
and Malis. To the south the Peloponnesus (called Morea
in medieval times) is nearly severed from central Greece
by the Gulf of Corinth and the Saronic Gulf save for
the 6.5 m. (4 mi.)-wide Isthmus of Corinth. Achaia
occupies the northern coast of the peninsula, with Elis
to the west. Inland is Arcadia, a limestone plateau
with several lofty mountains to the north; it is the only
major Greek district inaccessible by sea. Messenia and
Laconica to the south are relatively fertile regions,
while Argolis to the east features lowlands that vary
by the season from malarial swamp to barren plain;
these districts are characterized by a jagged coastline
with numerous small harbors and three major gulfs,
the Messeniac, Laconic, and Argolic.

The several islands of the Ionian and Aegean Seas
as well as Crete in the Mediterranean to the south
played important roles in the history and civilization
of ancient Greece. Off the western coast lie the Ionian
islands, which include Corfu (modern Corcyra), Leu-
kas, Cephalonia, Ithaca, Zante (modern Zakinthos),
and, opposite the Laconic Gulf, Cythera. Even more
numerous are the various groups of islands in the Aegean Sea. The submerged continuation of the mountains stretching southeast from Mt. Olympus form the
Northern Sporades (lit. "scattered islands") east of
the Magnesian peninsula, including Skiathos, Sko-
pelos, and Skiros. Euboea, the largest of the Aegean
islands, extends the mainland Othris and Oeta mountain ranges and parallels nearly the entire coast of

central Greece from Epicnemedian Locris to the eastern tip of Attica. The Cyclades comprise two submerged mountain ranges and include Andros, Tinos, Naxos, Delos, Paros, Kea, Milos, and Thira. Salamis and Aegina are located in the Saronic Gulf. Modern reckonings of the Greek isles include not only Thasos, Samothrace, and Lemnos off the coast of Thrace, but also the numerous islands along the western coast of Asia Minor, such as Lesbos, Chios, Samos, and Ikaria as well as the Dodecanese ("twelve"), of which Patmos, Leros, Cos, Rhodes, and Karpathos are the most important.

III. History

The earliest traces of Greek settlement are found at Knossos on Crete and at various sites in the Aegean islands and along the coast of the mainland dating to the Early Neolithic I period (6100-5100 B.C.). This relatively complex society was reinforced during the course of the third millennium by immigrants from Asia Minor who fostered the use of bronze and copper. Local chieftains amassed power, and trade flourished among the islands and with Anatolia, setting the stage for the Early Helladic era on the mainland and the parallel Early Minoan period on Crete.

During the Middle Helladic era (2000-1600) the mainland experienced alternate periods of conflict between the new, Greek-speaking, indigenous populations and periods of peaceful coexistence. Central and eastern Crete, however, flourished both politically and culturally under the strong rule of the Knossos dynasty. The achievements of Minoan civilization, which reached its height *ca.* 2000-1570, are evident in architecture (multistoried residences, elaborate palaces decorated with colored frescoes), arts and crafts (metalwork, jewelry), and the development of pictorial and linear writing. Equally noteworthy are the absence of both fortifications and a warrior class.

The fusion of indigenous "Pelasgians" and newcomers on the mainland produced in the Late Helladic period (*ca.* 1650-1150) the great Mycenaean civilization, named from Mycenae in Argolis, the focus of a confederation of city-states and the first such site discovered. The Mycenaeans traded extensively with the kingdoms of the Levant and proved themselves aggressive militarists, dispatching forces (including charioteers) against such powers as Cyprus and Egypt; although scholars remain divided concerning the demise of the Minoans, their displacement *ca.* 1400 may have come at the hands of the Mycenaeans. Much of the Mycenaean success was forged at the expense of the peasantry and slaves captured in war. In general Mycenaean culture was derivative, imitating that of the Minoans and the Near East; distinctive features include massive burial circles for military heroes and the domed tombs of kings as well as gold work, including inlaid weapons and foil death masks.

Events in Greece during the twelfth century accord with the wide-scale disruption and dislocation characteristic of the end of the Bronze Age throughout the ancient world. The mainland and islands were invaded, spelling not only the end of Mycenaean civilization but also the beginning of a cultural dark age. New hordes of immigrants appeared, displacing the existing populations. Among them were the Dorians,

Greek-speaking barbarians, elements of which are traced variously to the Danube valley and to Epirus in northwestern Greece. They ravaged Macedonia, Mycenae, and Crete before settling in the southern Peloponnesus. In the process they forced native Aeolian peoples from Thessaly and central Greece to seek refuge in Thrace, the Aegean islands, and Asia Minor. Likewise, the Ionians fled Achaia for Attica, eventually driving the inhabitants to the Cyclades and western Asia Minor.

In the ninth and eighth centuries Greek civilization revived, perhaps most evident through the reappearance of writing (now in alphabetic form) and the literature which evolved (e.g., Homer, Hesiod). Trade was resumed, providing contact with the outside world, and regional ties were established at home, often through leagues formed around the worship of common deities. Of particular importance was the rise of a new political order. The Ionians clustered around the old Mycenaean citadels on the mainland, and those whom they had displaced established similar alignments in the islands and Asia Minor; these city-states (Gk. *pólis*), actually loose "tribal" confederations, were administered first by local kings or chieftains and later by magistrates. More than one hundred such states emerged in Dorian Crete, established by constitution and generally headed by annually elected village magistrates and a permanent council of elders. Occasionally, as at Corinth and Sicyon, tension between the traditional aristocracy and the emergent oligarchy over political succession provided opportunity for a dictator or tyrant (Gk. *týrannos*) to usurp control. At Athens the reformer Draco sought unsuccessfully to shift power away from the clans; in 594 the archon Solon succeeded in creating a new social and political order representative of the entire citizenry. Elsewhere, new political alignments between city-states led to increased strength and prosperity. Sparta, formed at the beginning of the seventh century by the union of five Dorian villages in Laconica, asserted itself against villages and by 720 controlled the neighboring district of Messenia; similar unions were formed at Megara, Corinth, and Thebes. Moreover, city-states began to establish colonies for agricultural purposes as well as trade; by the middle of the sixth century hundreds of such settlements had been founded in the islands and Asia Minor as well as in Mediterranean Europe and North Africa. The resultant commercial and territorial competition between city-states often led to strife. Megara yielded its southern territory to Corinth and later lost the island of Salamis to the Athenians. Sparta was defeated by Argos in 669 and then lost several colonies through revolt before settling the score with Argos in 546. Having prospered under tyranny for some thirty-six years, Athens, with the aid of Spartan forces, revolted in 510 against the descendants of Pisistratus; the ensuing civil unrest was quelled through the democratic reforms of Cleisthenes, and Athens was able to withstand the subsequent aggression of Sparta and allied Peloponnesian states.

Greek expansion came to an abrupt halt with the rise of the Persian Empire. Cyrus the Great defeated Croesus of Lydia in Asia Minor, an ally of Sparta, which was at the time the dominant Greek state. Cyrus continued to overrun Greek territory in Asia Minor, and his successor Darius I employed captured Greek forces to gain control by 500 of all Greek territory outside the mainland. Chafing under Persian-appointed tyrants, the Ionians revolted in 499 with the aid of Athens and Eretria. Despite initial successes at Sardis, the Hellespont, and Bosporus, the Ionians inexplicably yielded the offensive, and the Athenians withdrew. The Persians, apparently supported by certain Greek factions, reconquered Cyprus and Caria and in 495 scored a decisive naval victory at Lade; by 493 they had regained control in Asia Minor. As punishment the Persians destroyed Miletus, home of the Ionian leader Aristagoras, and in 490 they sailed against Athens and Eretria. Having reduced Euboea, they landed at Marathon, but the Athenians prevailed there and in the later Persian ambush at Phalerum. Persian forces massed in Asia Minor, but the death of Darius I and rebellion in Egypt delayed action until 480, when Xerxes led Persian troops from Sardis against the Hellenic Symmachy, a defensive alliance of thirty Greek states headed by Sparta. While the fleets fought three indecisive battles at Artemesium in northern Euboea, the armies battled at the pass of Thermopylae; despite heavy losses, the Persians won and proceeded to rampage through Boetia and Attica, putting the Athenians to flight. The Greeks then lured the Persian fleet to Salamis and prevailed although heavily outnumbered. The Persians burned Athens the following spring, but the Greeks were victorious at Plataea and routed the Persian navy at Mycale on the Aegean coast. The increased Athenian might compelled Sparta to acquiesce leadership of the alliance; Athens and several Ionian states then formed the Delian League, which warred almost continuously with Persia until 449.

With the Persian threat curbed after the assassination of Xerxes the ephemeral unity of the Greek states dissipated, largely because of the propensity toward democracy in Athens. In 461 the Athenians broke with Sparta and initiated a treaty with Argos, the Spartans' archenemy, and Megara; Sparta in turn allied with Corinth and Thebes, a hegemony acknowledged by the Thirty Years Peace accepted in 445. Athens entered the Age of Pericles (443-429), a golden age of democracy, economic prosperity, and the flourishing of philosophy and the arts. But the attendant expansion of the Athenian Empire to encompass some 425 city-states angered the Spartan alliance, and in 431 hostilities erupted in the great Peloponnesian War. Despite disproportionate losses of population and resources, a decade later the two sides declared this first stage of the war (called the Archidamian War) a stalemate and found themselves, under the terms of the Peace of Nicias, allied against their own supporters in the Peloponnesus and Argos. This fifty-year pact lasted but five years. The ostracized Alcibiades, a would-be successor to Pericles, incited the Spartans to attack Athens from Decelea in 413. Two years later the impoverished Athenians adopted an oligarchy, but in 410 the masses revolted and instituted a broadened democracy. That same year Alcibiades returned, leading Athens to victory at Cyzicus and gaining election as strategos; he was deposed in 407 when the Greek fleet was defeated near Notium. With Persian aid the

Peloponnesian forces besieged Athens by land and sea throughout the winter of 404; the starving Athenians surrendered in the spring, their city, empire, and institutions in total collapse. The victorious Spartans themselves experienced internal dissension over repressive policies and external resistance by allies and subject states. From 399 to 394 Sparta battled Persia for control of Asia Minor; the Persians retaliated, assisted by Argos, Athens, Corinth, and Thebes, in the Corinthian War (395-387).

By the mid-fourth century most Greek city-states were in dire straits, and Hellenic unity was recognized as the only hope for survival. To the rescue came Philip II of Macedonia, a crafty diplomat and ruthless militarist who first unified Macedonia and then commenced a systematic assault on the Greek city-states and leagues. The Athenians, some of whom viewed Philip as a valuable ally against the resurgent Persians, joined with Thebes but were routed by Philip and his son Alexander at Chaeronea in 338. Now master of all Greece, Philip united all but Sparta into the Corinthian League, granting the states autonomy and charting the course for war with Persia. Upon Philip's assassination in 336 the young Alexander rose to power. Having quelled two rebellions in Thebes (336-335), he embarked on the Persian campaign. He defeated the Persian satraps of Asia Minor in 334 and a year later overcame Darius III Codommanus at Issus. Proceeding along the coast he subjugated Tyre and Syria (332) and "liberated" Egypt, where he founded Alexandria (331). He then crossed the Tigris and Euphrates, putting Darius' troops to flight at Arbela. In 330 Alexander burned Persepolis in retaliation for the 480 destruction of the Acropolis. Calling himself successor to the Achaemenids, he conquered western Iran and Sogdiana, then set forth to master India as far as the river Hydaspes (modern Jhelum), where his troops balked and he was compelled to return to Babylon (326). There he reorganized the Persian Empire, taking upon himself the threefold crowns of king of Persia, hegemon of the Corinthian League, and king of Macedonia. While planning to extend his rule into Arabia Alexander contracted swamp fever and died in 323 at age thirty-three. *See* ALEXANDER 1.

Upon Alexander's death Greece attempted to reassert independence but was suppressed by Antigonus. Alexander's direct descendants were cast aside, and prolonged conflict ensued for control of the vast empire (the Wars of the Diadochi ["Successors"], 323-280). Three major dynasties shared the legacy: those of Antigonus I Gonatas in Macedonia and Greece, Seleucus over Syria and Asia Minor, and Ptolemy in Egypt and the southern Levant. Peace was short-lived on the mainland, and Macedonia could manage not even token control of the cities, aligned in the Aetolian and Achaean leagues that warred throughout much of the third century. Philip V earned the disfavor of the emergent Roman state by siding with Carthage in the Second Punic War (215). Rhodes and Pergamum invited Roman intervention in the Second Macedonian War (200-196), and the Romans began to forge steady inroads into Greek affairs. When Perseus of Macedonia refused to disband his coalition army, the Romans invaded, setting off the Third Macedonian War (171-167) that resulted in the division of Macedonia into four kingdoms. At the first sign of renewed resistance in 148 the Romans seized the region and established it as the province of Macedonia. Two years later they crushed a revolt by the Achaean League, dissolved all the Greek leagues, destroyed Corinth and enslaved its citizens, and replaced democracy with oligarchy. In 145 the defeated city-states were incorporated in the province of Macedonia; Athens and Sparta were permitted to remain autonomous.

IV. Legacy

Although the Greeks borrowed much from the ancient Near East (e.g., the Phoenician alphabet, Babylonian astronomy and mathematics, aspects of Near Eastern mythology), they developed a unique worldview and a largely rational perspective that can clearly be distinguished as Greek. Despite their geographical and political fractiousness, the Greeks shared a basically unified culture, which they recognized as distinct from all others (hence the differentiation between matters Greek or Hellenic [Gk. *Hellēnes*] and those which were not [*bárbaros* "foreign," i.e., "non-Greek"]). Many of their artistic, scientific, and political accomplishments constitute the foundations of Western civilization.

A vast corpus of Greek literature is attested, although much has been lost or survives only through brief quotations in the works of others. The roots of that literature may be found in oral "epic cycles" formed during the Mycenaean era. The development of alphabetic writing in the centuries after the Greek migrations, fostered by the relative stability of the city-states, gave impetus to the creation of such poetic classics as the Homeric epics (the *Iliad* and *Odyssey*) and the didactic *Works and Days, Catalogues,* and *Theogony* of the Boetian farmer Hesiod. Various types of poetry, primarily religious and intended for recitation to musical accompaniment, emerged during the eighth-seventh centuries, including the elegy, individual and choral lyrics, and iambic poetry. Ironically, Greek literature attained its highest form at the time of the Persian conflicts (mid-sixth to mid-fifth centuries). In addition to the choral lyrics of Pindar of Thebes, Greek drama flourished at this time, an outgrowth of religious festivities; noteworthy are the tragedies of Aeschylus (e.g., *Oresteia*), Sophocles (*Antigone, Oedipus Rex*), and Euripedes (*Medea, The Trojan Women*) and the comedies of Aristophanes (*The Clouds, The Birds*). Prose writing, which developed after the sixth century, included the writings of the philosophers, historical works (Herodotus, Thucydides, Xenophon), rhetoric, and oratory (Antiphon, Andocides, Demosthenes).

Distinctively Greek art is first evident in the tenth century, represented by the angular, rectilinear designs on pottery of the geometric period. The eighth-seventh centuries constitute a period of orientalization stemming from trade with the Phoenicians and Asia Minor; mythical animals, curvilinear patterns, and silhouettes with incised outlines are characteristic. During the Archaic Period (*ca.* 650–480) the Greeks began to produce freestanding sculpture, most notably of nude youths (Gk. *Koúros*) and gowned women (*Kórē*), as well as elaborate temple friezework; red-figured vase painting appeared after 530. The classical period of Greek art (*ca.* 480–330) coincides with the height of Greek power; it featured the statues of Myron and Phidias in the fifth century and of Praxiteles and Scopas in the fourth and the Parthenon sculptures of Polyclitus. Greek art, represented by schools of realism as well as idealism, was diffused throughout the ancient world following the conquests of Alexander; well-known works of this period include the Nike ("Victory") of Samothrace, busts of Alexander, and the Aphrodite of Antioch on the Meander (the "Venus de Milo," from its discovery on Melos).

Greek religion was this-worldly, dominated by superhuman deities. It developed from Minoan religion, which focused on the Great (or Earth) Mother (later known as Hellotis or Demeter), and featured an extensive pantheon introduced during the second-millennium immigrations. Among the most important deities were the father and creator Zeus, god of weather; his wife Hera, goddess of the hearth; the sea-god Poseidon; Ares, god of war; the sun-god Apollo; Hermes, god of thieves and merchants; Artemis, goddess of the hunt; Athena, patron of the arts, crafts, and sciences; and Aphrodite, goddess of love. The major deities served as patrons of the city-states and, with numerous minor deities, were worshipped in various local manifestations. Over time, often the result of changed political circumstances, some deities experienced transformation, and new cults arose. For example, the law-giver Apollo gained prominence through the popularity of his oracle at Delphi. The cult of Dionysus, god of wine, became an important focus of orgiastic worship and drama. Of later significance were the cult of Asclepius, god of medicine, the syncretistic cult of Sarapis (from the Egyptian Osiris and Apis), and the mystery cults of Demeter at Eleusis and of Orphism. On a popular level Greek religion also featured family (ancestral) cults and theurgy, a form of sorcery.

In the sixth century Greek thinkers began to seek rational explanations for the world order. Ionian natural philosophy, traced first to Thales of Miletus, sought a "beginning" (Gk. *archē* "prime matter or cause"). Pythagoras of Samos saw harmony in the universe while distinguishing soul and body, thought and the senses. In the fifth century Heraclitus of Ephesus sought truth in rational thought, identifying change as the first principle of the world. The Sophists ("teachers of wisdom") viewed knowledge itself as a "good" and established a form of education stressing rhetoric, dialectics. and civics. Socrates, known for his method of cross-examination, sought by the inductive method to determine the nature of values and thus to arrive at universal truths which might be taught for ethical living. Foremost among Socrates' pupils was Plato (427–347), whose theory of ideas contrasted the realm of existence with that of forms or ideas (e.g., truth, beauty, the Good); his political works stressed wisdom, courage, and justice. Plato's greatest student was Aristotle of Stagira (384–322), founder of the Lyceum at Athens, whose vast knowledge and insights encompass the fields of ethics, politics, literary criticism, and metaphysics; he contributed significantly to the scientific method in terms of analytical thinking, empirical methodology, and speculative construction. Developments in the Hellenistic period included Stoicism, which viewed the world as divinely ordered on rational principles to which mankind must, by freedom of will, conform; and Epicureanism, a largely hedonistic philosophy concerned with the attainment of pleasure and the avoidance of pain.

Closely related to the philosophical quests was the development of Greek science. In the sixth century Pythagoras expanded philosophy by seeking to explain the world order through mathematics, physics, and astronomy. Democritus advanced solid geometry, but the greatest strides were made by Euclid (*ca.* 300) in his systematic textbook *The Elements* and by Archimedes of Syracuse (*ca.* 287–212). During the Hellenistic era the Greeks expanded upon Babylonian astronomy; Heraclides of Ponticus and Aristarchus of Samos concluded that the earth rotated on its own axis as well as around the sun, but Hipparchus of Nicaea, in addition to cataloging the stars and astral phenomena, arrived at the more popular notion of celestial movement around the earth. Perhaps the greatest achievements were in the field of medicine. Hippocrates of Cos (469–399), who stressed rational treatment of illness as a natural phenomenon rather than divine punishment, advanced the theory of the four vital forces or humors. Herophilus of Chalcedon and Alexandria discovered the function of the brain and nervous system, and Erasistratus of Ceos studied the circulatory system.

See HELLENISM.

V. Biblical Contacts

Advanced through the conquests of Alexander the Great, Greek culture permeated the ancient world, including not only conquered territories but even the very conqueror of Greece, Rome. Influence on the biblical world is evident from the Hellenistic period on. Scholars have argued the Hellenistic character of such Old Testament books as Daniel and Ecclesiastes. Specific references include the he-goat of Daniel 8:5-8, generally identified as Alexander (cf. 11:3). The imposition of Hellenistic civilization on Palestine was particularly offensive to the Jews, and the excesses of Antioches IV Epiphanes provoked the Maccabean Revolt. The apostle Paul confronted Greek civilization directly in his preaching missions (Acts 16–18, 20); many scholars contend that he introduced into Christianity a Greek perspective.

Greek influence on the New Testament is evident not only in the language in which it is recorded but also in certain discernible literary genres (e.g., epistolary formulas and possibly apocalyptic). Moreover, a number of quotations from Greek literature occur. Acts 17:28b is taken from the *Phaenomena* of Aratus, a Stoic poet from Soli in Cilicia (315–239). The first part of the verse is often attributed to Epimenides, a sixth-century Cretan poet named as one of the seven sages of Greece and regarded by his people as a prophet (cf. Diogenes Laertius *Vitae* ii.112). The quotation at Titus 1:12 is ascribed to Epimenides *De Oraculis,* a collection of oracular proverbs and noteworthy sayings; some attribute it instead to Callimachus (305–240). The proverb cited by Paul at 1 Corinthians 15:33 may be traced to Thais, written by the Attic comic poet Menander (342–290).

Bibliography. W. K. C. Guthrie, *A History of Greek Philosophy,* 5 vols. (Cambridge: 1962–1975); N. G. L.

Hammond, *A History of Greece to 322 B.C.,* 2nd ed. (New York: 1967); H. D. F. Kitto, *The Greeks* (Baltimore: 1951); M. I. Rostovtzeff, *Social and Economic History of the Hellenistic World,* rev. ed., 2 vols. (New York: 1957).

GREEK. † The language of Greece and its colonies; following the conquests of Alexander the Great the lingua franca of the Hellenistic world. The second oldest branch of the Indoeuropean family, Greek is attested as early as the mid-second millennium B.C. It attained its classical form in the period from Homer (eighth century) to Alexander, during which the Attic dialect became primary. Greek was used by both the Roman and Byzantine empires; the Roman emperors and senate issued decrees in Greek translation, and the Roman church held services in Greek until the third century A.D. In addition to the literary form of Modern Greek, Greek influence is seen in the form of the Russian and Serbian alphabets. As the language of the New Testament, classical philosophy, and early science, Greek has exercised an important role in the formation of Western culture.

The Greek of the Hellenistic through Byzantine eras, and thus of the Septuagint and the New Testament, is called Koine (Gk. *Koinē* "common"), not only because it represents a commingling of the various dialects but primarily because it served as the vernacular of commerce and politics. Its commonness throughout the eastern Mediterranean world proved of inestimable value for the spread of the gospel.

Basically, Koine Greek represents a simplification of the Attic or classical Athenian dialect, with some elements of Ionic (eastern Aegean). Distinctions in vowel usage were less clear (e.g., omicron and omega were pronounced the same, as were epsilon and the alpha-iota diphthong), pronunciation of consonantal clusters varied, and the rough breathing was no longer pronounced. The use of noun case forms declined (particularly the dative), and the dual number disappeared; the perfect and aorist tenses moved toward assimilation, and the optative was abandoned; the conjunctive *hína* plus the subjunctive came to replace the infinitive and, at times, the imperative. At the same time, the Koine tended toward emphatic (and thus redundant) expression, most obvious in abundant use of pronouns and the compounding of verbal affixes.

Koine Greek includes a conservative literary strain intended as a means of preserving the language of classical Attic prose. The Koine of the Bible, however, represents the "living" language attested in thousands of extrabiblical papyri, inscriptions, and ostraca discovered in the past century. Although scholars remain divided as to whether Jesus knew or used Greek, it certainly was employed by at least those apostles of Hellenistic origin (e.g., Paul, Mark). Differences in Greek style, although less apparent in translation, range from the literary excellence of Luke to the educated but less refined writings of Paul and the elementary language of Revelation. Because of its particular interests and context, New Testament Koine demonstrates occasional semiticisms (e.g., Matt. 19:5; Luke 1:34) and latinisms.

Bibliography. J. H. Moulton, W. F. Howard, N. Turner, *A Grammar of New Testament Greek,* 4 vols.

(Edinburgh: 1908-1976); A. T. Robinson, *A Grammar of the Greek New Testament in the Light of Historical Research* (1914; repr. Nashville: 1934).

GREEK VERSIONS.* To accommodate Jews dispersed throughout the Hellenistic world, and to a lesser extent interested non-Jews, it became necessary to translate the Hebrew scriptures into Greek, the common language. The most influential, and probably the earliest, such translation was the Septuagint (LXX), ascribed by the Letter of Aristeas to seventy-two scholars commissioned by Ptolemy II Philadelphus (285–247) for the Jewish community at Alexandria. It is the version quoted by the New Testament writers and constituted the scriptures of the early Church. *See* SEPTUAGINT.

Recent manuscript discoveries at Naḥal Ḥever and in Egypt suggest that independent translations of the MT and other Hebrew texts had appeared as early as the first century B.C. (e.g., Proto-Lucianic, *Kaige*). Christian acceptance of the LXX and their use of it in anti-Jewish polemics caused the Jews to repudiate the accuracy of that version and to seek suitable replacements. The earliest clear example of such an effort is the work of Aquila (**2**) of Sinope in Pontus, Jewish proselyte and student of Rabbi Akiba; now considered a revision of the *Kaige* text, this version (*ca.* A.D. 130) is literal to the point of distorting meaning (intentionally so in messianic passages). Also literal but more faithful to Greek idiom is the translation of the Ebionite Symmachus (*ca.* 170); seeking to avoid anthropomorphisms, it tends at times toward paraphrase rather than translation. Toward the end of the second century Theodotion, a Jewish proselyte at Ephesus (or perhaps an Ebionite Christian), revised the *Kaige* text on the basis of the MT or another Hebrew text. His work bears distinct similarity to New Testament quotations of the Old Testament which vary from the LXX. Theodotion's rendering of Daniel was viewed by the early Church as superior to that of the LXX.

In the early third century the Alexandrian theologian Origen compiled his HEXAPLA, a parallel record of the MT and important Greek versions including Aquila, Symmachus, and Theodotion as well as fragmentary representation of others (now called Quinta, Sexta, and Septima). The LXX as recorded by Origen notes Greek words not represented in the MT and incorporates Theodotion's rendering of Hebrew material lacking from the LXX. At approximately the same time Lucian of Antioch issued a revision of the late first-century B.C. "Proto-Lucianic" text; characterized by conflate readings of several versions, it is regarded by many scholars as a revision of the LXX. Two revisions of Origen's modified LXX text came to prominence in the third century, that of Eusebius of Caesarea and Pamphilus, which gained favor in Palestine, and that of the Alexandrian Hesychius.

See BIBLE, TEXT OF THE.

Bibliography. E. Würthwein, *The Text of the Old Testament* (Grand Rapids: 1979).

GREETING.† A salutation. In words and gestures, the greetings of the Bible are often more expansive than those of Western culture and can include the obligation of hospitality (Gen. 18:2ff.). Greetings are set aside only in matters of urgency (cf. 2 Kgs. 4:29).

A greeting extends a wish for the happiness or blessing of the other, e.g., by God's presence (Ruth 2:4; cf. Judg. 6:12) and graciousness (Gen. 43:29). Subjects greet their king with a wish for a long or eternal life (1 Kgs. 1:31; Dan. 2:4; cf. 1 Sam. 10:24).

The most characteristic greeting is "well-being, prosperity"; e.g., 1 Sam. 25:6). Commonly, this greeting was an inquiry after the other's well-being (Heb. *šāʾal lᵉšālôm;* 10:4; 17:22; cf. Eng. "How are you?"). The New Testament infuses this standard greeting with new depth. It is the peace (Gk. *eirḗnē*) of the gospel, given by the disciples on their mission (Matt. 10:12-13; Luke 10:5), by the risen Christ (John 20:19, 21), and in apostolic salutation (e.g., Rom. 1:7; 1 Cor. 1:3). It is a peace extended to all, irrespective of their status (Matt. 5:47; cf. Mark 12:38). Peace is also the customary word of departure and benediction (e.g., 1 Sam. 1:17; Acts 16:36; 1 Pet. 5:14; cf. Num. 6:26).

The standard Greek greeting *chaíre, chaírete* "rejoice" is used in joy (Luke 1:28; RSV "Hail"; Jas. 1:1-2; cf. Phil. 4:4) as well as mocking (Mark 15:18); it is withheld from false teachers (2 John 10).

Gestures also form an important part of greeting. These include clasping the beard (2 Sam. 20:9), embracing (Gen. 29:13; Acts 20:37), and kissing (Gen. 33:4; Luke 7:45; 15:20). Kneeling marks the usual greeting given to one's superior (Gen. 42:6; 1 Sam. 24:8; 1 Kgs. 1:16) or to God's representative (1 Sam. 28:14; cf. Matt. 8:2; 9:18). The ancient Near Eastern custom of kissing the feet or ground in obeisance was considered disgraceful by the Israelites and was reserved for the nations (Ps. 2:12; cf. Esth. 8:3). The greeting of a holy kiss extends the peace and unity that echoes God's reconciliation (2 Cor. 13:11-13; cf. Luke 15:20).

Letters in the ancient world open with greeting formulas. In the Bible the formula is: sender, addressee, salutation ("peace"; Ezra 5:7; Dan. 6:25; Jude 2; or "greeting"; Acts 15:23; Jas. 1:1). Letters normally closed with a greeting as well (v. 29; Rom. 16:3-23). The New Testament greeting of "grace and peace" (Gk. *cháris kaí eirḗnē*; 1:7; 1 Pet. 1:2; Rev. 1:4) proclaims the salvation of God and Christ as both gift and eschatological reality (cf. Rom. 5:1).

GRIDDLE (Heb. *maḥᵃḇat*). A flat plate made of clay or iron (cf. Ezek. 4:3) upon which cakes or bread was baked (Lev. 2:5; 6:21 [MT 14]; 7:9). The griddle usually was placed on stones over a fire. Small depressions or holes in the cooking surface inhibited food from sticking. The advantages to a griddle were portability, cooking control, and cleanliness (in keeping bread out of the fire).

See BREAD.

GRINDING (Heb. *ṭāḥan*). The processing of grain into flour, generally by rubbing or pulverizing between two stones turned by hand or with the aid of animals. In the ancient Near East the task generally was relegated to women, to servants or slaves (Exod. 11:5), or to prisoners (Judg. 16:21) or the conquered as a form of humiliation (Isa. 42:7; Lam. 5:13).

This domestic task is the setting for Christ's words

on watchfulness for his coming in glory (Matt. 24:41). Cessation of this activity marks God's judgment (Jer. 25:10).

At Eccl. 12:3-4 the "grinders" (Heb. *ṭōḥᵃnôṯ*) refers to the molars, in an allegory about aging (vv. 1-7); worn down and few in number, they are now only suitable for chewing soft food.

GUARANTEE [Gk. *arrabṓn*]. A commercial term for the deposit or down payment that secures a legal claim or makes a contract binding. It is used figuratively in the New Testament for God's gift of his Spirit to believers as a guarantee of their full inheritance in Christ (Eph. 1:14; KJV "earnest") and their share of immortality (2 Cor. 5:5).

GUARD (Heb. *šāmar, nāṣar;* Gk. *tēréō, phylássō*). As a verb the term means to watch over and protect, to have charge of, or to keep. The ordinary use speaks of guarding prisoners (Josh. 10:18; Acts 12:4), a palace (2 Kgs. 11:5), or a gate (Neh. 13:22). It may indicate guarding against something: intruders in the Garden (Gen. 3:24), invaders (2 Kgs. 9:14), or enemies (Ps. 12:7 [MT 8]; 25:20). A person may guard or protect another from danger: Nabal, by David (1 Sam. 25:21); believers, by angels (Ps. 91:11) and by God (Isa. 27:3).

These same words are used in a theological sense with regard to keeping the covenant (cf. Ezek. 17:14) and for pursuing wisdom. Believers must guard their ways (Ps. 39:1 [MT 2]), wisdom (Prov. 5:2), instruction (4:13), and the truth entrusted them (1 Tim. 6:20; 2 Tim. 1:14).

The noun form designates a person or troop responsible for protecting a person or place, as well as a member of the royal retinue. In Israel the king's escort (*rāṣîm* "runners") acted as couriers (2 Chr. 30:6) or executioners (1 Sam. 22:17) in addition to guarding the palace (2 Kgs. 11:4-6) and treasury (1 Kgs. 14:27). Absalom assembled fifty as part of his pretension to the throne (cf. 2 Sam. 15:1ff.). Following ancient Near Eastern practice, these were often foreigners. David's "mighty men" (*gibbōrîm*) include Uriah the Hittite (23:39), along with Pelethites, Chelethites, and Gittites (15:18). David himself served in a similar capacity with the Philistines (1 Sam. 28:2).

In foreign courts one finds "officers of the *ṭabbā-ḥîm*" ("butchers," from *ṭābaḥ*, "to cook, slaughter"); the title's origin remains obscure. In biblical usage the term designates not a function, but high court officials: Potiphar, in charge of the royal prison (Gen. 39:1); Nebuzaradan, one of Nebuchadnezzar's chief officers responsible for the temple's destruction and the exile of Jerusalem's inhabitants (2 Kgs. 25:8ff.); and Arioch, the king's "provost marshall" who executed the king's decrees (Dan. 2:14; Aram. *ṭabbaḥayyā'*).

Other words for "bodyguard" describe the function more directly. David guards (*šōmēr*) the head of Achish the Philistine (1 Sam. 28:2). The participle *mišmaʿaṯ* (from *šāmaʿ* "to hear") characterizes the bodyguard's personal obedience and responsiveness to the king (22:14; 2 Sam. 23:23 par. 1 Chr. 11:25).

Elsewhere guards watch over (*mišmār*) prisons (Neh. 4:22-23; cf. Acts 12:10), gates (1 Chr. 9:23), and Jesus'

grave (Gk. *koustōdía*; Matt. 27:65). The guards in the courtyard (*hypērétēs*; 26:58; Mark 14:54) are servants of the court (cf. Matt. 5:25). John the Baptist's executioner (Mark 6:27) is a *spekoulátōr*, one of Herod Antipas' bodyguards. See PRAETORIAN GUARD.

The guardroom (Heb. *tāʾ hārāṣîm*, lit. "room of the runners") was a chamber in the Jerusalem temple for storage of various treasures (1 Kgs. 14:28 par. 2 Chr. 12:11; KJV "guard chamber"; cf. Ezek. 40:7, 36).

GUARD, COURT OF THE (Heb. *ḥᵃṣar hammaṭ-ṭārâ*).* A room or open area in the palace compound where prisoners (such as Jeremiah) were detained during the Babylonian siege of Jerusalem (e.g., Jer. 32:8, 12; 38:6, 13, 28; KJV "court of the prison").

GUARD, GATE OF THE (Heb. *šaʿar hammaṭṭārâ*). A gate of postexilic Jerusalem at which a company was stationed during Nehemiah's rededication of the walls (Neh. 12:39; KJV "prison gate"). The context favors locating it in the city wall near the temple complex, either identical to the Muster Gate (3:31; RSV mg. "Hammiphkad Gate") or farther south near the tower which projected from the royal palace in the vicinity of the court of the guard (v. 25).

GUDGODAH [gŭd gōʹdə] (Heb. *gudgōḏâ*).† A place where the Israelites encamped during the wilderness wanderings (Deut. 10:7; LXX Gk. *Gadgad*), the first site mentioned after Moserah (Moseroth) where Aaron died. At Num. 33:32-33 it is called Hor-haggidgad.

GUEST. See SOJOURNER.

GUM. See SPICES.

GUNI [gooʹnī] (Heb. *gûnî* "painted" [?]).
1. A son of Naphtali (Gen. 46:24; 1 Chr. 7:13); eponymous ancestor of the Gunites (Num. 26:48).
2. The father of Abdiel of the tribe of Gad (1 Chr. 5:15).

GUR [gûr] (Heb. *gûr* "dwelling"). An ascent near Ibleam, where Jehu's archers fatally wounded King Ahaziah of Judah (2 Kgs. 9:27). Derived from the verb *gûr* "sojourn, stay, dwell," the name apparently indicates a resting place on some elevated point between Ibleam and Megiddo; it may have originated with an isolated caravanserai there. The exact site remains unknown, although recent scholarship favors Gurra, near Taanach; an alternate proposal is Khirbet Kara.

GURBAAL [gûrʹbāl] (Heb. *gûr-bāʿal* "dwelling of Baal"). A town occupied by Arabs (i.e., bedouin), captured by King Uzziah in his campaign to secure Judah's western and southern boundaries (2 Chr. 26:6-8). Probably located in the vicinity of Edom, it may be identified with Jagur (Josh. 15:21).

GYMNASIUM (Gk. *gymnásion*).* A Greek center for physical education and recreation as well as moral and literary training. The pinnacle of Hellenistic education, it constituted a preparatory school for aristocratic males who had attained puberty (cf. 2 Macc. 4:9; Gk. *ephēbeíon;* RSV "body of youth"; JB "youth center''). More importantly, the gymnasium served as a means of establishing Hellenic solidarity and maintaining Hellenistic values, particularly in outlying cities of the empire.

When the high priest Jason obtained permission from Antiochus IV Epiphanes to establish a gymnasium in the vicinity of the Jerusalem temple (1 Macc. 1:14; 2 Macc. 4:9-12), it offended the pious Jews. Not only were Jews enticed to embrace Hellenistic culture (v. 10), but many youths felt compelled to disguise surgically the evidence of their circumcision (1 Macc. 1:15; cf. Josephus *Ant.* xii.v.1 [241]). The gymnasium was one of many abuses that precipitated the Maccabean Revolt.

H

H.* Symbol for the Holiness Code, a body of legal material (Lev. 17–26) within that portion of the Pentateuch attributed to the Priestly source. *See also* Biblical Criticism.

HAAHASHTARI [hā′ə hăsh′ tə rī] (Heb. *hā′ᵃḥaštārî*).* Offspring of Ashhur and Naarah (1 Chr. 4:6). This otherwise unknown family is listed among geographic and ethnic components of Judah.

HABAIAH [ha bā′yə] (Heb. *ḥᵒbayyâ* "the Lord has hidden"). A priest whose descendants returned from the Exile with Zerubbabel. Because they were unable to prove their priestly descent, they were excluded from the priesthood (Ezra 2:61-63). At Neh. 7:63 he is called Hobaiah (KJV "Habaiah").

HABAKKUK [hə băk′ək] (Heb. *ḥᵃbaqqûq*). A preexilic prophet of Judah whose prophecy is recorded in the book of Habakkuk. The name may derive from Heb. *ḥābaq* "embrace" (2 Kgs. 4:16; Eccl. 3:5); the Vulgate form (Lat. *Habacuc*) presupposes Heb. *'ābaq* "wrestle." An alternate derivation is from Akk. *ḥambaqûqu*, a garden plant (cf. LXX Gk. *Ambakoum*; Θ *Ambakouk*).

Very little can be ascertained concerning the identification or provenience of this prophet. Historical allusions and linguistic characteristics of his prophecy suggest that he ministered in Judah *ca.* 600 B.C. Thus the rabbinic tradition that he was the son of the Shunammite woman (cf. 2 Kgs. 4:16ff.) is anachronistic. The LXX superscription to Bel and the Dragon attributes that book to Habakkuk son of Jeshua of the tribe of Levi (cf. 1 Esdr. 5:58), apparently inferred from liturgical use of the psalm in Hab. 3 (*see* Habakkuk, Book of *III*), but again chronological factors prohibit making him a contemporary of Daniel. Another tradition, long discredited, assigns him to the Zerahites of the tribe of Simeon.

According to Bel 33–39 a prophet named Habakkuk was taken by an angel of the Lord from Judea to Babylon in order to deliver pottage to Daniel, who had been cast into the lions' den a second time. Although Theodotion's translation clearly identifies this Habakkuk as the canonical prophet, the LXX does not even identify him as a prophet. Most scholars regard this passage as a later addition, perhaps from another writing about Habakkuk.

HABAKKUK, BOOK OF.† The eighth of the twelve Minor Prophets.

I. Origin

The book itself contains no reference to the prophet's lineage or place of residence, nor are any of his utterances sufficiently dated. The superscription attributing Hab. 3 to "Habakkuk the prophet" (Heb. *nābî'*) and notations implying the psalm's liturgical use (vv. 3, 9, 13, 19) suggest to some scholars that he was a cultic prophet associated with the Jerusalem temple. *See* Habakkuk.

As the result of divergent interpretations of historical allusions, the book has been dated as early as *ca.* 700 B.C. (following the invasion of Sennacherib) and as late as 170 (in the Seleucid period). Of primary importance for dating are references to the imminent threat posed by the Chaldeans (1:6; cf. vv. 5, 7-11). Although some scholars would view vv. 2-5 in terms of the Assyrian threat prior to the fall of Nineveh in 612, the prophecies, taken as a whole, best suit the circumstances of the resurgent Neo-Babylonian Empire following their defeat of the Egyptians at Carchemish in 605 and immediately prior to the fall of Jerusalem to Nebuchadnezzar in 587. The disarray pictured in vv. 2-5 conveys the internal conditions of Judah in the face of certain destruction (cf. v. 4 as a reference to the short-lived reforms of Josiah). Thus the prophecies of Habakkuk best fit the period *ca.* 612-587, most likely during the reign of Jehoiakim (*ca.* 609-598). Habakkuk would then be an approximate contemporary of the prophets Jeremiah, Zephaniah, and Nahum.

II. Contents

In the opening passage (1:2-4) the prophet laments the violence and lawlessness which pervade Judean society and implores the Lord to intervene. The divine oracle which follows (vv. 5-11) proclaims God's intent to dispatch the savage Chaldeans ("that bitter and hasty nation," v. 6) to administer justice upon his errant people. The prophet then complains that the proposed cure exceeds the ills at hand (vv. 12-17). He is unable to comprehend how a righteous God could choose as his instrument such as evil people: "why dost thou look upon faithless men, and art silent when the wicked swallows up the man more righteous than he?" (v. 13). Waiting eagerly upon his watchtower (2:1), the prophet receives another oracle (vv. 2-5): the arrogant shall fall but the righteous will prevail. The Chaldeans, in their oppression of the righteous, are wicked and arrogant, but those who live by the righteousness of God will be preserved by their unswerving faith and trust in the Lord.

Habakkuk then delivers a taunt song against the Chaldeans (2:6-20), comprised of five oracles of woe. Here he castigates them for their oppression of Judah and surrounding nations, for plundering and self-gratification, and for idolatry. He concludes with a call to submission before the Lord (v. 20).

The book concludes with a prayer of Habakkuk (Heb. *tepillâ*), actually a psalm depicting Yahweh's theophany. Following a vivid description of the Lord's mighty acts in history, no doubt anticipating the destruction to be wreaked by the Chaldeans, the prophet declares his unyielding faith in the triumph of God over adversity (vv. 16-19).

III. Literary Aspects

The diversity of materials within the book, compounded by problems of interpretation, has led a number of critical scholars to challenge the book's unity and even its authorship — in whole or in part — by the prophet Habakkuk. Of particular issue is whether the concluding psalm (ch. 3), which represents a unique genre among the biblical prophets, was part of the original composition. Some view the liturgical notations as evidence that it was added later from a cultic collection, but such instructions are generally secondary; if not authored by the prophet himself, the work may have been part of a collection formed or used by Habakkuk. Significant support for the psalm's later inclusion stems from its absence in a second-century B.C. commentary (pesher) from Qumran (1QpHab); but rather than prove that the poem was not at this time part of the canonical book (at least in the textual tradition represented), its omission may simply indicate that its content (particularly the prophet's concluding affirmation) did not accommodate the commentator's purpose or historical circumstances. Indeed, the mythological motifs and linguistic archaizing of Hab. 3 are fully in keeping with the nostalgic poetry prompted by the burgeoning paranoia of Habakkuk's era. Moreover, similarities of vocabulary and theme demonstrate the unity of the canonical book, including God's activity in Israelite history past, present, and future (1:6; 3:3-15), the motif of the prophet's "seeing" and "hearing" (2:2-3; 3:7, 16; cf. v. 2, NEB), and characterization of the enemy as wicked (1:4, 13; 3:13).

The book of Habakkuk uniquely draws upon a variety of literary genres. In the opening portion, the alternating laments or complaints of the prophet and the divine oracles which follow comprise a dialogue between Habakkuk and God. The five woes, which some scholars contend derive from various historical circumstances, form a unified diatribe against the oppressive Chaldeans. Even the psalm may represent a compilation of materials, including a theophany of the Lord's approach (vv. 2-7; cf. Deut. 33:2; Judg. 5:4), a mythological account of God's battle with the forces of nature (vv. 8-15), and an affirmation or hymn (vv. 16-19); all are artistically bound by various stylistic devices, including an envelope construction (vv. 2, 16-19) and metrical balance.

IV. Theology

The collected utterances which comprise the book's opening dialogue show Habakkuk to be an individual deeply perplexed by the discrepancy between the tenets of his religion and his perception of God's dealings with Judah. He questions why God has not dealt authoritatively with Judah for abandoning their covenant ideals. When told that God will punish them at the hands of the Chaldeans, he challenges God's motives in employing a wicked and heathen people to chasten his own chosen people. But like Job he resolves that the Lord, although by inscrutable means, has always acted in his people's behalf and will continue to do so. His response therefore must be to remain faithful and trust in God (cf. Rom. 1:17; Gal. 3:11; Heb. 10:38).

Bibliography. W. F. Albright, "The Psalm of Habakkuk," pp. 1-18 in H. H. Rowley, ed., *Studies in Old Testament Prophecy Presented to T. H. Robinson* (Edinburgh: 1950); W. H. Brownlee, *The Midrash Pesher of Habakkuk*. SBL Monograph 24 (Missoula: 1979); D. E. Gowan, *The Triumph of Faith in Habakkuk* (Atlanta: 1976).

HABAZZINIAH [hăb'ə zĭ nī'ə] (Heb. *ḥabaṣṣinyâ*). The grandfather of Jaazaniah the Rechabite whom Jeremiah tested (Jer. 35:3-10; KJV "Habuziniah").

HABIRU [hä'bĭ rōō] ('APIRU) [ä'pĭ rōō] (Akk. *ḥabiru, ḥapiru, apiru*; Egyp. *'pr.w*; Ugar. *'prm*; Sum. sa-gaz).† Anomalous groups of people attested throughout the ancient Near East from the late third millennium through the twelfth century B.C. More precise definition of these people, their origins, and status is hampered by lack of consensus regarding the etymology of the name. Sum. sa-gaz appears to represent either Akk. *šaggāšu* "murderer, aggressor" or *ḥabbātu* "robber" or "migrant." Many scholars trace the word to W. Sem. *'br* "to cross [a boundary], to transgress [a covenant]." Others, citing Egyptian and Ugaritic forms, derive it from W. Sem. *'pr* as meaning "one who receives food rations" (cf. Akk. *epēru* "provide with food").

Habiru are first mentioned during the Ur III period (2044-1936 B.C.) as wreaking destruction throughout the Syrian steppeland, defiant of Sumerian authority. In the Mari texts (eighteenth century) they comprise various bands which pillage the Mesopotamian countryside, either independently or in alliance with local city-states or peasant groups. During the same period, King Irkabtum of Alalakh concluded a treaty with Habiru forces, as did several Hittite kings in subsequent centuries. References to the Habiru are most frequent in the fourteenth-century Amarna correspondence, recording the encounters of Egyptian vassals with Habiru activity throughout Syria and Palestine. They represent small bands or entire cities which had cut themselves off from the established social and political order in order to become self-sufficient, forming alliances or engaging in periodic raids for economic support; a sizable number were in the service of the insurgent Abdu-aširta and his successors, founders of the Amurru kingdom. Habiru are last mentioned as political prisoners in Egypt during the twelfth century.

Originally considered by scholars as an ethnic designation, the name Habiru is now known to have identified peoples of diverse origins, including West Semitic and Akkadian as well as Hurrian and other non-Semitic backgrounds. Thus the majority of scholars have come to regard the Habiru as a sociopolitical category comprised of individuals and groups detached by choice from the predominant order. These uprooted peoples are not to be confused with foreign immigrants or prisoners of war, and the frequent reports of their dependency (e.g., receiving rations or subsidies, contracting as mercenaries or clients, serving in various professional, military, or menial capacities) may simply indicate a willingness to derive sustenance from the established society, particularly in times of relative stability maintained by a strong political power. Descriptive evidence of Habiru "outlaw" or refugee activity is provided most amply in the Mari and Amarna texts, but the pattern fits the circumstances of other periods and locales as well; for example, in the mid-fifteenth century the fugitive King Idrimi of Alalakh found refuge among kindred spirits in a Habiru settlement on the Phoenician coast. This standard interpretation of Habiru activity in the ancient Near East is an important element of the revolt model proposed for the Israelite conquest of Palestine.

An alternate interpretation views the Habiru as nomadic groups united by blood kinship which existed on the fringes of Near Eastern society, but having penetrated cultivated territories rather than restricted to the desert regions. This pattern would support the settlement model of gradual Israelite occupation of the land. However, textual evidence implies that Habiru origins were overwhelmingly urban, and many groups continued to maintain settled bases for their operations.

A number of factors suggest a connection between the Habiru and the biblical Hebrews (Heb. 'ibrî). On etymological grounds, adherents of such an identification favor the derivation of both names from 'br "cross [a boundary], transgress." Many scholars contend that the name "Hebrew" did not become a gentilic until the time of the Monarchy, suggesting its possible origin as a class designation. Moreover, the diverse ethnic composition of the Habiru accords with Bronze and Iron Age Palestine, including Israelite "tribes" apparently unified by fictive kinship. The extramural operations of the Amarna Age Habiru, although preceding the Israelite Conquest by nearly one hundred years, seem to mirror the circumstances of formative Israel, whether self-disenfranchised elements of Canaanite-dominated Palestine or escaped Habiru captives from Egypt. Habiru roots might even be traced to the patriarchal period (cf. Jacob's role as a "fugitive Aramean"; Deut. 26:5; RSV "wandering Aramean"). Under the Confederation, the mercenaries employed by Abimelech to take Shechem

(Judg. 9:4) and the disenfranchisement of the illegitimate Jephthah and his subsequent leadership of a robber band (11:2-3) fit the pattern of Habiru activity. Even in the early stages of the Monarchy, Habiru were found in the service of both the Philistines (e.g., 1 Sam. 13:3; 17:8; RSV "Hebrews"; cf. 13:7, KJV, NIV, NJV) and Israel (14:21). A prime example was David (29:3), who with a contingent of malcontents, debtors, and other misfits (22:2) sustained himself as a client of Achish of Gath (27:1–28:2; 29:8) and by raiding Israel's enemies (27:8-12; cf. 29:27-31). Thus it would appear that the biblical Hebrews constituted one segment of the larger Habiru movement. *See* HEBREW (PEOPLE).

Bibliography. M. Greenberg, *The Ḥab/piru*. AOS 39 (1955); G. E. Mendenhall, *The Tenth Generation* (Baltimore: 1973), pp. 122-141.

HABOR [hā′bôr] (Heb. *ḥābôr*; Akk. *Ḥabûr*). The modern Nahr el-Khābur, a tributary of the Euphrates river. Originating in the vicinity of Haran (perhaps near the city or region of Gozan; 2 Kgs. 17:6; "the river of Gozan"; cf. 1 Chr. 5:26; RSV "the river Gozan"), it flows southwesterly and enters the Euphrates at Circesium, north of Mari. It was along the shores of this river, now flanked by the ruins of numerous ancient settlements, that "the king of Assyria" (probably Shalmaneser V [727-722]) settled the inhabitants of vanquished Samaria (2 Kgs. 17:6; 18:11; cf. 1 Chr. 5:26). The name should not be confused with that of the river Chebar (Heb. *kᵉbār*; Ezek. 1:1).

HACALIAH [hăk′ə lī′ə] (Heb. *ḥªkalyâ* "the Lord afflicts"). The father of Nehemiah (Neh. 1:1; 10:1; KJV "Hachaliah").

HACHILAH [hə kī′lə] (Heb. *ḥªkîlâ*). A hill along the border of the Wilderness of Ziph where David hid from Saul (1 Sam. 23:19; 26:3). Said to be south of Jeshimon, its precise location is not known.

HACHMONI [hăk′mō nī] (Heb. *ḥakmônî* "the wise"). The father of Jehiel who attended the sons of King David (1 Chr. 27:32). The Hebrew form is the same as that of the gentilic Hachmonite and may simply indicate his membership in that family (so NEB).

HACHMONITE [hăk′mō nīt] (Heb. *ben-ḥakmônî*). The family of Jashobeam, a chief among David's mighty men (1 Chr. 11:11). The reading Tahchemonite at 2 Sam. 23:8 is a textual error (KJV "Tachmonite"; JB "Hachmonite").

HADAD [hā′dăd] (Heb. *ḥªdad*).

1. The eighth son of Ishmael and grandson of Abraham (Gen. 25:15; KJV "Hadar"; 1 Chr. 1:30).

2. An Edomite king. The son of Bedad (Gen. 36:35-36; 1 Chr. 1:46-47); he ruled from Avith.

3. An Edomite king who reigned from Pau (1 Chr. 1:50-51). Because of a textual error, his name appears as Hadar at Gen. 36:39.

4. An Edomite ruler who fled Joab's massacre but later returned as an adversary of Solomon (1 Kgs. 11:14-22, 25; at v. 17 the MT has Heb. *ªdad*).

5.† The West Semitic storm-god. As Baal ("the

lord'') he was head of the Ugaritic pantheon (Ugar. *Hd*); Mt. Saphon, north of Ugarit, was not only his home but also the assembly of the gods. Known to the Assyrians as Adad (Akk. *Addu, Haddu*; cf. Sum. Ishkur), he wielded lightning as a weapon of destruction, yet as "controller of the floodgates of heaven and earth" he governed the beneficial rains which foster life. He was later regarded as a giver of oracles. The Arameans regarded Hadad as their national god, who established the monarchy and from whom each new king received authority; accordingly, in the biblical period several Aramean kings are named Ben-hadad ("son of Hadad"). He was given the epithet Ramman "thunder" (cf. 2 Kgs. 5:18, "Rimmon"; Akk. *ramānu* "roar, thunder"). Hadad may also be identified with the Hittite god Teshub and the Amorite Ammuru.

HADADEZER [hăd′ə dē′zər] (Heb. *hᵃḏaḏʿezer*; Akk. *Adad-idri* "Hadad is help").

1. The king of Zobah (2 Sam. 8:3-12; 10:16, 19; 1 Kgs. 11:23; 1 Chr. 18:3-11; 19:16, 19), a powerful Aramean ruler who controlled not only the city-state of Zobah in the Biqaʿ but also portions of Ammon and the region west of the Upper Euphrates river. Enlisted to aid the Ammonites against David's retaliation, Hadadezer and his Syrian allies were among the forces defeated by Joab at Rabbah (2 Sam. 10:6-14). He gathered new troops for a second battle at Helam, but the Israelites again prevailed (vv. 15-18; cf. 8:3-6); as a result, David exacted heavy tribute from the Arameans and extended his control in Transjordan (8:7-8; 10:19). At 2 Sam. 10:16, 19 and the passages in 1 Chronicles the KJV renders the name as Hadarezer (cf. NJV mg.).

2. *See* BEN-HADAD 2.

HADADRIMMON [hā′dăd rĭm′ən] (Heb. *hᵃḏaḏrimmôn*). A composite name of the West Semitic storm-god (Akk. *Addu* and *ramānu*, both meaning "thund[er]"), probably a local manifestation of the Canaanite Baal worshipped in the region of Megiddo. At Zech. 12:11 Judah's despair over the Davidic ruler they have martyred apparently is compared to seasonal mourning associated with this Baal cult, commemorating one aspect of his periodic dying and rising as a god of vegetation (cf. *ANET*, pp. 139-141). Some scholars would associate this passage with lamentation over King Josiah, who had been slain in the ill-advised battle with Pharaoh Neco at Megiddo in 609 (cf. 2 Chr. 35:24-25).

Hadadrimmon may also be a place name, probably derived from the local cult, and thus the location for the rites mentioned at Zech. 12:11. Identified by some as Rummaneh, a village near biblical Taanach, the site is more likely the Roman city Legio (modern el-Lejjun), slightly more to the east in the plain of Megiddo. This site, which the fourth-century A.D. Bordeaux Pilgrim calls Maximianopolis, is 27 km. (17 mi.) east of Caesarea and 16 km. (10 mi.) west of Jezreel (*Itin. Burd.* xix.20). According to Jerome, Maximianopolis was formerly called Adadremmon.

HADASHAH [hə dăsh′ə] (Heb. *hᵃḏšâ* "new city"). A city in the tribal territory of Judah, located in the

Shephelah region near Lachish (Josh. 15:37). Its site was once thought to be modern Hatta between Dikrin and Ashkelon, but a more accurate conjecture is Khirbet el-Judeide, between ʿArâq el-Menshîyeh (also called Tell Sheikh Aḥmed el-ʿAreini) and Khirbet ʿAjlân.

HADASSAH [hə dăs′ə] (Aram. *hᵃḏāssâ* "myrtle"). The original Hebrew name for Esther (Esth. 2:7) or a title given her (from an epithet of the goddess Ishtar; Akk. *ḥadaššatu* "bride").

HADATTAH (Josh. 15:25, KJV). *See* HAZOR-HADATTAH.

HADES [hā′dēz] (Gk. *hádēs*).* The realm of the dead, derived from the name of the Greek god of the underworld. In the LXX the term translates Heb. *šᵉʾôl*, the gloomy underworld abode of the departed (Eccl. 9:10; Isa. 7:11; *see* SHEOL). During the intertestamental period Hades came to be regarded as a place where the deceased awaited judgment (1 En. 22:3-4, 9-13). At some point it gained the interpretation as a place of reward for the righteous (cf. v. 9; but note Ps. Sol. 14:6-7; 15:11-15).

See HELL.

HADID [hā′dĭd] (Heb. *ḥāḏîḏ* "sharp"). A city of Benjamin located in the vicinity of Lod and Ono (Ezra 2:33; Neh. 7:37). According to Eusebius, Hadid (called Aditha) lay about 6.5 km. (4 mi.) northeast of Lydda (Lod) on a steep hill, the site of the modern village of el-Ḥadîtheh. This ancient city existed at least as early as the time of Pharaoh Thutmose III (early fifteenth century B.C.), whose inscription in the temple of Amon at Karnak lists it among the 165 towns he captured in Palestine. It was rebuilt and fortified by Simon Maccabeus (1 Macc. 12:38) and again by the Roman emperor Vespasian (Josephus *BJ* iv.9.1).

HADLAI [hăd′lī] (Heb. *ḥaḏlāy* "patient"). The father of the Ephraimite Amasa who would not accept Judahite captives following Ahaz' defeat by Damascus and Pekah of Israel (2 Chr. 28:12).

HADORAM [hə dôr′əm] (Heb. *hᵃḏôrām* "Haddu [Hadad] is exalted").

1. The son of King Tou of Hamath, who was sent by his father to congratulate King David on his victory over Hadadezer (1 Chr. 18:10). At 2 Sam. 8:10 he and his father are called Joram and Toi.

2. A descendant of Joktan, and the ancestor of an Arabian tribe (Gen. 10:27; 1 Chr. 1:21).

3. An official of King Rehoboam who was taskmaster over the forced labor (2 Chr. 10:18). At 1 Kgs. 4:6 he is called Adoniram and at 12:18, Adoram, a shortened form of that name.

HADRACH [hăd′răk] (Heb. *ḥaḏrāḵ*; O. Aram. *ḥzrk*; Akk. *Ḥatarikka*). A Aramean city-state, named with Damascus and Hamath as enemies of Israel (Zech. 9:1). The site has been identified as Tell Āfis, 45 km. (28 mi.) southwest of Aleppo. Here was discovered in 1908 the stele of Zakir, king of Hamath and Luʿash (ca. 800 B.C.), who withstood a siege of the city by an Aramean coalition headed by Ben-hadad III. Named among the Syrian cities allied with King Azariah (Uzziah) of Judah (742), Hadrach was made an Assyrian province by Tiglath-pileser III. Zech. 9:1-6 may record its subsequent unsuccessful revolt against Sargon II (720).

HADRIAN [hā'drĭ ən]. Publius Aelius Hadrianus (A.D. 76-138), Roman emperor 117-138. A second cousin and ward of his predecessor Trajan, his succession to office was difficult and he spent much of his reign solidifying his authority by streamlining the Roman bureaucracy and by extensive travels throughout the empire (he spent twelve years away from Rome).

He rebuilt Jerusalem, which had been destroyed in A.D. 70, as the Roman city Aelia Capitolina, populated by Gentiles and featuring a temple to Jupiter constructed on the site of the Jewish temple. This act, compounded by his legislation against circumcision, provoked Jewish rebellion under Simon Bar Kokhba. Hadrian himself spent much of 134 in Jerusalem attempting to suppress this revolt, which was finally quashed by Julius Serverus in 135. By contrast, Hadrian was generally lenient toward Christians, despite having erected a temple to Venus on the site of Jesus' tomb. Quadratus wrote an apology for the Christian faith addressed to this emperor (Eusebius *HE* iv.3.1-2), and Justin Martyr (*Apol.* i.68) relates the contents of a letter sent by Hadrian to a proconsul in Asia forbidding the use of anonymous complaints and questionable processes against Christians.

HA-ELEPH [hā ē'lĭf] (Heb. *hā'elep* "the ox"). A Benjaminite town in the vicinity of Jerusalem (Josh. 18:28; KJV "Eleph"). On the basis of LXX A (Gk. *Sēlaleph*), the name is probably to be read Zela-eleph.

HAGAB [hā'găb] (Heb. *ḥāgāb* "locust"). A temple servant whose descendants returned from exile with Zerubbabel (Ezra 2:46).

HAGABAH [hăg'ə bə] (Heb. *ḥᵃgābâ* "locust"). Head of a family of servants who returned from the Exile under Zerubbabel (Ezra 2:45). At Neh. 7:48 he is called Hagaba.

HAGAR [hā'gär] (Heb. *hāgār* "wandering" or "fleeing"). The Egyptian maid of Sarai (Gen. 16:1), perhaps one of the maidservants given to Abram by the pharaoh (12:16; note that the name is Semitic). In accordance with custom, the barren Sarai gave her servant to Abram to fulfill the Lord's promise that her husband would have a son of his own (15:3-4; 16:1-4); legally the child would be considered Sarai's own. But when Hagar conceived, she scorned her mistress, and Sarai—with Abram's tacit approval—responded by mistreating her and causing her to flee toward Egypt (vv. 4-6). The angel of the Lord appeared to Hagar in the wilderness, however, and sent her back to Sarai with the promise that the maid's offspring would be greatly multiplied (vv. 7-10). Following her return she bore a son, whom the eighty-six-year-old Abram named Ishmael (vv. 15-16).

A second account (21:8-21) records events following the birth of Isaac, Abraham's son by Sarah. Distressed to see Ishmael playing with (KJV, NIV "mocking") Isaac at a family feast celebrating the latter's weaning, Sarah asked Abraham to expel the slave and her son lest Ishmael share his father's inheritance (vv. 8-10). Assured by God that, though Isaac was his true heir, Ishmael would not be overlooked (vv. 12-13), Abraham conceded, and Hagar fled with her son to the Wilderness of Beer-sheba. Their provisions depleted and the boy dying of thirst, an angel of the Lord renewed God's promise for Ishmael and directed the two to a well (vv. 15-19). Hagar later obtained for her son an Egyptian wife (v. 21).

Paul refers to these incidents allegorically, portraying Hagar as "the present Jerusalem," bearing children to slavery in the old covenant (Gal. 4:21-31). By contrast, Isaac is the son of a free woman, a child of promise representing grace and freedom from the law.

HAGGADAH [hə gä'də] (Heb. *haggaḏâ* "narration, instruction"). In postbiblical Judaism, any nonprescriptive scriptural interpretation. Thus the Haggadah deals mainly with the historical portions of the Old Testament and reflects upon their doctrinal and ethical content and ramifications. For the most part, the Haggadah embellishes the stories of the Bible by means of folklore, sagas, and legends, as well as by proverbs and parables.

HAGGAI [hăg'ī, hăg'ĭ ī] (Heb. *ḥaggay* "festal," perhaps "born on a feast day").† A postexilic prophet whose utterances are recorded in the book of Haggai. Although his four prophecies can be dated to the year 520 B.C., little else is known about his life or background. Because no prophecy of his survives concerning the rededication of the temple in 515, many scholars consider him to have been an old man in 520, perhaps one who had seen the former temple (Hag. 2:3). Alternate tradition holds that he was a young man who returned from exile with Sheshbazzar in 538.

Although he and his contemporary Zechariah were largely responsible for promoting reconstruction of the temple, no evidence exists that they conducted a joint ministry (cf. Ezra 5:1-2; 6:14). Nevertheless, the two are linked in rabbinic tradition, and some Versions ascribe to them certain of the Psalms (LXX, Pss. 146-149; Vulg., 112, 146-147). The latter association may be the basis for the Christian tradition that Haggai was of priestly descent (but cf. Hag. 2:11-13, where he defers to the priests).

HAGGAI, BOOK OF.† The tenth of the Minor Prophets.

I. Origin

Haggai's four pronouncements are dated to a four-month period during the second year of the Persian Darius I Hystaspes (520 B.C.), under whom indigenous religious activities were supported throughout the empire. These prophecies appear to have been recorded sometime after the fact, as evident by reports of their effect upon Zerubbabel, the high priest Joshua, and the populace of postexilic Jerusalem

(Hag. 1:12, 14-15). While the prophet himself may have been responsible for the finished book, various factors suggest that it was compiled by a disciple—indeed a likelihood if the prophet were advanced in years at the time of his ministry (*see* HAGGAI). Haggai, identified as "the prophet" (e.g., 1:1, 4, 12), is depicted throughout in the third person. Moreover, although prophetic utterances were generally poetic in form, Haggai's are recorded as prose, suggesting that they have been paraphrased.

II. Contents

The book opens with an oracle (1:1-11) addressed to Zerubbabel, governor of Judah, and Joshua the high priest, dated the first day of the sixth month (mid-August). Calling for resumption of work on the temple, the prophet reproves the people for having concerned themselves rather with furnishing their own dwellings; indeed, the present drought and attendant agricultural failure and economic woes are signs of the Lord's displeasure. The impact of these words is plain, for three weeks later construction had begun (vv. 12-15).

A second prophecy, dated to the twenty-first day of the seventh month (mid-October), encourages Zerubbabel, Joshua, and the people to continue with the restoration despite concern that this new structure might not attain the grandeur of its predecessor (2:1-9). The Lord promises protection and support for their endeavors and pledges that the new temple will prosper (vv. 4-9; cf. Heb. 12:26-29).

In an oracle dated to the twenty-fourth day of the ninth month (mid-December), the prophet is given a series of questions for the priests regarding ritual cleanness (Hag. 2:10-14). The interpretation is unclear, but apparently the people's previous reluctance to rebuild the temple had rendered their current efforts unclean, thus the continuing misfortunes of the land (v. 17). Nevertheless, the Lord will yet reward their repentance with prosperity (v. 19). An alternate interpretation is that the offer of the Samaritans ("this people," v. 14) to assist with reconstruction be refused lest the temple itself be made unclean (cf. Ezra 4:1-3). Some scholars regard Hag. 2:15-19 as a separate prophecy which more correctly follows 1:15.

The final oracle (2:20-23), addressed to Zerubbabel on the same day as the third utterance, proclaims that God is about to disrupt the existing order and that Zerubbabel, his "chosen," would be exalted "like a signet ring" (v. 23), symbolizing restoration of the Davidic line and the advent of the messianic kingdom.

III. Significance

The book of Haggai provides valuable information regarding the events and religious circumstances of the early postexilic period, thus supplementing and offering a perspective different from the Chronicler's accounts. It becomes apparent that any zeal for rebuilding the Jerusalem temple had flagged shortly after the initial return under Sheshbazzar (538), perhaps partially because the land had suffered measurably since its destruction forty-eight years earlier and partially because many capable and successful Jews who could have assisted had chosen to remain in Babylon.

Some interpreters regard Haggai's concern for rebuilding the temple as having a trivializing effect upon the Hebrew faith, focusing on outward, physical aspects rather than the spiritual and ethical as stressed by earlier prophets. But in view of the historical circumstances, such a project was essential to the very survival of the physical community as well as its religion. Thus Haggai and his contemporary, Zechariah, actually were responsible for guaranteeing the continuation of the Hebrew people.

Moreover, Haggai played a significant role in directing postexilic Israel toward the messianic hope of God's promised redemption. Perhaps viewing the revolts which accompanied Darius' accession as evidence of the shifting world order (cf. 2:6-7, 21-22), he reveled in the restoration of the Davidic line as accomplished by the governorship of Zerubbabel (cf. 1 Chr. 3:19), the "servant" whom God had chosen (Hag. 2:23; cf. Isa. 42:1). Furthermore, the "splendor" and "treasures" which were to characterize the restored temple (Hag. 2:7-9) are comparable to the magnificence envisioned for the messianic age.

Bibliography. J. G. Baldwin, *Haggai, Zechariah, Malachi.* Tyndale (Downers Grove: 1972); G. A. Smith, *The Book of the Twelve Prophets.* Expositor's Bible (repr. Grand Rapids: 1956), 4:613-620.

HAGGEDOLIM [hăg′ə dō′lĭm] (Heb. *haggᵉḏôlîm* "the great men"). The father of Zabdiel the overseer who lived in Jerusalem after the Exile (Neh. 11:14; JB "Haggadol"). Perhaps the passage should be translated "Zabdiel, the son of the great men," as in the KJV.

HAGGI [hăg′ī] (Heb. *ḥaggî* "born on a feast day"). Son of Gad and grandson of Jacob and Zilpah (Gen. 46:16).

HAGGIAH [hă gī′ə] (Heb. *ḥaggîyâ* "festal" [i.e., "born on a festal day"]). A Levite and descendant of Merari (1 Chr. 6:30).

HAGGITES [hăg′īts] (Heb. *haḥaggî*). Descendants of Haggi (Num. 26:15).

HAGGITH [hăg′ĭth] (Heb. *ḥaggîṯ* "festive"). One of the wives of David; the mother of Adonijah (2 Sam. 3:4; 1 Kgs. 1:5, 11; 2:13; 1 Chr. 3:2).

HAGIOGRAPHA [hăg′ĭ ŏg′rə fə] (Gk. *hagiographa* "sacred writings").† The third division of the Hebrew canon of the Old Testament, also called the Kethubim (Heb. *kᵉṯûḇîm*) or Writings. The last to be accepted into the cannon, these books vary greatly in form and content, including poetry (Psalms, Lamentations), wisdom (Job, Proverbs, Song of Solomon, Ecclesiastes), apocalyptic (Daniel), folklore (Ruth, Esther), and history (1-2 Chronicles, Ezra-Nehemiah).

HAGRI [hăg′rī] (Heb. *hagrî* "my beauty" [?]). The father of Mibhar one of David's mighty men (1 Chr. 11:38). The KJV renders his name as Haggeri. The parallel account (2 Sam. 23:36) reads "Bani the Gadite" (NIV "son of Hagri"; either Heb. *bny hgdy* here or *bny hgry* in 1 Chr. 11:38 is a textual corruption).

HAGRITES [hăg'rīts] (Heb. *hagri'îm, hagrî'îm, hagrîm*). A pastoral tribe or confideration which lived east of Gilead in Transjordan (1 Chr. 5:10, 19-20; Ps. 83:6), apparently regarded as the descendants of Hagar (so NIV, Ps. 83:6). Associated with such other enemies of Israel as the Edomites, Moabites, and Ishmaelites, they were defeated by the Reubenites and Gadites during the time of Saul. Jaziz, the steward of David's flocks, was a Hagrite (1 Chr. 27:30; Heb. *hagrî*). The KJV renders the term variously as Hagarenes, Hagarites, Hagerites, and Hagrites.

HAHIROTH [hə hī'rŏth] (Heb. *hahîrōt*). A place in the eastern Nile Delta, an early point in the exodus from Egypt (Num. 33:8; JB, NIV "Pi-hahiroth"; NJV "Pene-hahiroth"). *See* PI-HAHIROTH.

HAI (Gen. 12:8; 13:3, KJV). *See* AI.

HAIL, HAILSTONES (Heb. *bārād, 'eben 'ēlgāḇîš*; Gk. *chálaza*). Precipitation that falls as bits of ice or hard snow, frequently accompanying severe thunderstorms during the rainy season in Palestine and capable of inflicting severe damage (e.g., Josh. 10:11; Hag. 2:17). Yahweh, whose storehouses are an arsenal for snow and hail (Job 38:22), deploys hail against the enemies of Israel (e.g., Exod. 9:23-24; Ps. 18:13-14; Ezek. 38:22) and wields it as a means of punishing the wicked (e.g., Isa. 28:2, 17; Ezek. 13:11, 13; Rev. 8:7; 16:21).

HAIR (Heb. *śē'ār, śa'ªrâ*; Gk. *thrix, kómē*).† Judging from literary references as well as Egyptian and Mesopotamian art, a variety of hair styles were worn in Palestine and the ancient Near East. To an extent hair style was a matter of fashion, at least among the upper classes who were particularly open to foreign influence. Nevertheless, long hair appears to have been the rule among the Hebrews (cf. Ezek. 8:3), both men and women (cf. Cant. 4:1; 7:5).

The Israelites observed various, sometimes contradictory restrictions concerning the hair, perhaps because they accorded it religious significance as a symbol of human vitality and certainly because they sought to avoid pagan practices. Although occasional trimming with a razor or knife was apparently accepted as good grooming (cf. 2 Sam. 14:26), the Israelites were directed not to "round off the hair on your temples or mar the edges of your beard" (Lev. 19:27) as the pagans did in mourning (but cf. Ezra 9:3; Jer. 7:29). Disheveled hair, hanging loose, was a common token of grief (e.g., Josh. 7:6; Job 2:12) but was forbidden to the priests (Lev. 21:10; cf. 10:6). Religious vows sometimes proscribed cutting the hair (Num. 6:5; Judg. 13:5; 16:17), but the consecration of Levites involved shaving the body (Num. 8:5-7; cf. Isa. 7:20). Tonsure, which the Old Testament notes as peculiar to certain Arab peoples (Jer. 9:26; 25:23; 49:32), may also have been adopted by some prophetic guilds as a badge of office (cf. 1 Kgs. 20:35-43; 2 Kgs. 2:23). Lepers were required to wear their hair loose (Lev. 13:45) but were to shave their heads in the ritual of cleansing and restoration (14:8-9). Apparent reference is made also to the pagan rite of cutting the hair and weighing it as a sacrifice to the gods (Ezek. 5:1; cf. 2 Sam. 14:26).

Excessive attention to grooming and ornamentation is derided by the prophets (Isa. 3:24) and in the Epistles (1 Tim. 2:9; 1 Pet. 3:3). Although hair generally seems to have been combed straight, it might also be wavy (Cant. 5:11; KJV "bushy"; JB "palm fronds"; NJV "curled") or plaited (7:6, JB; RSV "like purple"; NIV "like royal tapestry"; 1 Pet. 3:3). Isa. 3:18, 23 mention headbands and turbans as adornments (NIV "tiaras"; cf. Jdt. 10:3), and the privileged even sprinkled gold dust on their hair (Josephus *Ant.* viii.7.3). Anointing with oil or perfumed water was a token of hospitality and a sign of prosperity (e.g., Ps. 23:5; 92:10).

In New Testament times Palestinian men adopted the Roman style of closely cropped hair (cf. 1 Cor. 11:14), whereas long hair was deemed appropriate for women (vv. 5-6, 15).

Although infinitesimal in size (cf. Judg. 20:16), God has numbered the seemingly innumerable hairs of our heads (Matt. 10:30 par. Luke 12:7; cf. Ps. 40:12; 69:4); in his loving care not a single hair will perish (1 Sam. 14:45; 2 Sam. 14:11; 1 Kgs. 1:52; Luke 21:18).

HAKKATAN [hăk'ə tăn] (Heb. *haqqāṭān* "the small one"). A descendant of Azgad, and the father of Johanan who returned from Babylon with Ezra (Ezra 8:12; 1 Esdr. 8:38).

HAKKOZ [hăk'ŏz] (Heb. *haqqôṣ* "the thorn-[bush]"). The head of the seventh division of priests during the time of David (1 Chr. 24:10). Descendants of Hakkoz were among those who had returned with Zerubbabel from the Exile. Most members of his family were excluded from the priesthood because they could not prove their priestly descent (Ezra 2:61-62; Neh. 7:63-64); however, it appears from Neh. 3:4, 21 that priestly descent was proven for some. *See* KOZ.

HAKUPHA [hə kū'fə] (Heb. *hªqûpā'* "crooked"). A temple servant whose family returned from the Exile with Zerubbabel (Ezra 2:51; Neh. 7:53).

HALAH [hā'lə] (Heb. *hªlah*). A region in the Assyrian Empire, possibly near Haran or the river Habor. It was one of the areas where Tiglath-pileser III relocated captives from the Transjordanian tribes (1 Chr. 5:26); Shalmaneser V also exiled Israelites there following the fall of the northern kingdom (2 Kgs. 17:6; 18:11).

HALAK [hā'lăk], **MOUNT** (Heb. *hāhār hehālāq* "bald (or smooth) mountain," i.e., one without vegetation). A mountain in the Negeb, located east of the Arabah toward Edom, which marked the southern boundary of Joshua's conquests (Josh. 11:17; 12:7). The probable site, which also preserves the name, is modern Jebel Halâq, 42 km. (26 mi.) southeast of Beer-sheba.

HALAKHAH [hä'lä kä'] (Heb. *hªlākâ* "the way," from *hālak* "walk, go"). In its basic sense, a teaching or precept that serves as a practical guide for living; also spelled Halachah, Halakah. In postbiblical Judaism, Halakhah came to mean the legal body of rules and regulations established and passed down by the scribes and rabbis as they interpreted and applied the law of Moses. In contrast to the Haggadah, which deals with the narrative portions of the Old Testament, the Halakhah is a juridical and casuistic interpretation of those sections of the Old Testament that are concerned with the law. Since Mosaic legislation is generally quite broad, it became the task of the rabbis to apply these broad ordinances to specific cases; if a particular incident arose that was not covered by one of these general regulations, they sought a solution through inference from the law and through the combination of various elements present in the law. Such casuistic interpretation proceeded mainly from debates among small groups of rabbis; as a majority vote established new legal requirements, the additions became unalterable and irrevocable. In New Testament times the Sadducean scribes regarded only the Mosaic legislation as authoritative, but the Pharisees asserted that the Halakhah was as binding as the pentateuchal laws themselves. Until A.D. 70 Jerusalem was the center for this method of interpretation; later centers included Jamnia, Tiberias, and Babylon.

The Halakhah were at first passed down orally, but as the amount of material increased the oral tradition gradually became too difficult to maintain. Toward the end of the second century A.D., the Halakhah were written down, forming the Mishnah; this in turn became the subject of the large body of interpretive literature known as the Gemara. Thus the Halakhah comprises the greatest portion of the Talmud.

HALF-TRIBE (Heb. *ḥᵃṣî šēḇeṭ*). *See* MANASSEH.

HALHUL [hăl'hŭl] (Heb. *ḥalḥûl*). A city in the tribal territory of Judah, located in the hill country near Beth-Zur (Josh. 15:58). It has been identified as modern Ḥalḥûl, 6 km. (4 mi.) north of Hebron. According to tradition, a mosque in this city contains the grave of Jonah.

HALI [hā'lī] (Heb. *ḥᵃlî* "collar"). A place on the border of the territory allotted to Asher (Josh. 19:25; LXX A Gk. *Tholi;* B *Aleph*). Although the site remains uncertain, it may be Khirbet Râs Alî, south of Tell el-Harbaj.

HALICARNASSUS [hăl'ə kär năs'əs] (Gk. *Halikarnassos*).* The largest and strongest city of Caria, situated on an excellent harbor on the Ceramic Gulf 90 km. (55 mi.) south of Ephesus. Colonized by the Dorians, the city remained under Carian rule even after its capture by the Persians. In retaliation for its support of the Persians, Alexander the Great destroyed the city in 334 B.C., after which it never regained its previous glory. One of the seven wonders of the ancient world, the tomb of King Mausolus (377-353), was located here, and the city was acclaimed as the birthplace of the historians Herodotus and Dionysius. The site is partially occupied by the modern village of Bodrum.

A cosmopolitan Hellenistic city, Halicarnassus apparently had a sizable Jewish population. According to 1 Macc. 15:23, the Roman senate dispatched a letter in 139 B.C. urging tolerance toward the Jewish

inhabitants. Nearly a century later the city granted them religious liberty (Josephus *Ant.* xiv.10.23).

HALLEL [hăl'əl] (Heb. *hallēl* "praise thou").† A song of praise. The title is specifically applied to certain psalms prescribed by Jewish tradition for the major festivals and for the daily morning services.

The "Egyptian Hallel" (Pss. 113-118), so called because it recounts God's activity in the history of Israel beginning with the Exodus, was sung at the principal annual feasts and in celebration of the New Moon. During the Passover Seder, Pss. 113-114 (or in some traditions only Ps. 113) were sung before the second cup and the meal itself and 115-118 following the meal but before the fourth cup; according to the Mishnah, the Levites chanted these psalms as the paschal lamb was being slaughtered (*Pesaḥ.* v.7). It was probably part of this Hallel which Jesus and his disciples sang at the conclusion of the Last Supper (Matt. 26:30 par. Mark 14:26).

The Talmud (*Ber.* 4b; *Pesaḥ.* 118a) and Mishnah (*Taʿan.* iii.9) identify Ps. 136 as the "Great Hallel"; other traditions apply the title to Pss. 135-136 or 120-136. Sung at the daily morning prayers, this Hallel praises God for his mighty deeds. Ps. 136 is arranged antiphonically for congregational singing.

Another Hallel collection, Pss. 146-150, was also used in the morning services.

HALLELUJAH [hăl'ə lōō'yə] (Heb. *halᵉlû-yāh* "praise ye Yah [Yahweh, the Lord]"; Gk. *Allēlouia;* Lat. *Alleluia*).† An exclamation of praise. Most English versions translate the Old Testament occurrences as "praise (ye) the Lord" (JB "Alleluia"); at Rev. 19:1ff. it is transliterated as "Hallelujah (so RSV, NIV) or "Alleluia" (KJV, JB). Although the term forms a compound in the LXX and Vulgate, it does not appear to have been hyphenated in the Hebrew text, suggesting an imperative with a shortened form of the divine name as its object; a Jewish tradition, perhaps seeking to disavow any such use of the sacred name, contends that it was a very ancient cultic acclamation of unknown etymology.

The term occurs twenty-four times in the book of Psalms (Pss. 104-106, 111-113, 115-117, 135, 146-150), generally either introducing or concluding the Psalm (or both). Indeed, with the exception of 135:3; 147:1 where it is essential to the content, it appears to have been a liturgical formula. Such "Hallelujah Psalms" may have been derived from collections of hymns used in the temple services (cf. 106:48 where the term concludes Book IV of the Psalter), perhaps chanted antiphonally (cf. 1 Chr. 16:4, 36). In later passages (Tob. 13:18; Rev. 19:1, 3-4, 6; cf. 3 Macc. 7:13) "Hallelujah" is sung by the heavenly chorus. Adopted by the early Church, it remains in liturgical use in many forms, particularly in the Eastern churches.

HALLOHESH [hă lō'hĕsh] (Heb. *hallôḥēš* "the whisperer, charmer"). The father of Shallum (Neh. 3:12); one of those who set the seals to the renewed covenant under Nehemiah (10:24).

HAM [hăm] (Heb. *ḥām* "hot"; cf. W. Sem. *Ḥammu,* a deity) (**PERSON**). One of Noah's three sons, usually mentioned after his older brother Shem and before Japheth (e.g., Gen. 5:32; 1 Chr. 1:4); however, according to Gen. 9:24 he was the youngest of the family (so RSV; KJV "younger"). Born many years before the Flood (cf. 5:32; 7:11), Ham witnessed the moral decline of his contemporaries, but he and his wife were allowed to accompany his parents and brothers in the ark (7:13) and thus were saved from the Deluge (8:18) and subsequently included in the divine blessing bestowed upon Noah's family (9:1, 9).

Ham's only recorded act is an unfortunate one. Apparently rather than making amends upon finding Noah drunk and naked in his tent, Ham reported his discovery to his brothers, who promptly covered their father's indiscretion (9:21-23). When Noah realized what had transpired, he angrily cursed his youngest son by condemning his own youngest son, Canaan (10:6), to servitude under Shem and Japheth (9:24-27). Some critical scholars contend that the story represents an originally separate tradition in which Noah's sons were Shem, Japheth, and Canaan.

Ham's sons are mentioned after those of Japheth, not only in the so-called TABLE OF NATIONS (Gen. 10:6-20), but also in the genealogies of 1 Chr. 1-9 (1:8-16). The "tents of Ham" (Ps. 78:51) and the "land of Ham" (Ps. 105:23, 27; 106:22) refer to Egypt (cf. Egyp. *Kem* "land of Egypt"), the home of one of Ham's descendants (also called Egypt). However, at 1 Chr. 4:40 those who "belonged to Ham" are apparently the Canaanites.

HAM [hăm] (Heb. *hām*) (PLACE). A city in Transjordan where the Zuzim were defeated by the armies of Chedorlaomer and his allies (Gen. 14:5; but see LXX Gk. *éthnē ischyrá háma autoís* "strong nations with them"), possibly at Tell Hâm, north of the Jabbok and about 7 km. (4.5 mi.) southwest of Irbid.

HAMAN [hā'mən] (Heb. *hāmān*). The grand vizier or highest official in the Persian Empire under King Ahasuerus (Xerxes); son of Hammedatha (Esth. 3:1). In the book of Esther he appears as Mordecai's adversary and is labelled "the enemy of the Jews" (v. 10). He is called "the Agagite" (e.g., 3:1, 10), which would suggest that he was a descendant of Agag, the Amalekite king. Many, however, think that Haman was a true Persian and suggest that "Agagite" means only that he was a spiritual descendant of the nation of Amalek, one of Israel's bitter enemies. Most likely, the term refers to a region near Media (cf. Akk. *Agazi*). In any case, Haman was infuriated by Mordecai's refusal to do obeisance to him and determined to destroy all of the Jews in the kingdom (v. 6). However, this plan was foiled by the efforts of Esther and Mordecai, and Haman was hanged on the very gallows he had erected for Mordecai (7:10); in the purge which followed his ten sons were also killed (9:6-10).

HAMATH [hā'măth] (Heb. *ḥ*ᵃ*māṯ* "citadel"; Akk *Amātu*).† An important city in Syria (cf. Amos 6:2, "the great"), strategically located at modern Ḥama, 120 km. (75 mi.) south-southwest of Aleppo on the Orontes river, where it dominated the main trade route between Asia Minor and the south. Settled during the Neolithic period, it was an important Hittite royal city

and, after 1200 B.C., a strong and prosperous independent kingdom. David, who had extended Israel's northern boundaries as far as the limits of the region controlled by Hamath (cf. 2 Sam. 8:6; 10:16), maintained an alliance with Toi, king of Hamath (8:9-12). Solomon infringed upon that territory, establishing store-cities there (2 Chr. 8:4). Although Hamath was able to recoup some of this area, the city-state's power gradually began to wane with the ascendancy of the Assyrian Empire. In the ninth century Shalmaneser II captured some of the towns under Hamath's control. A century later, during a period of Assyrian weakness, Jeroboam II again extended Israel's borders as far north as the Hamath frontier (2 Kgs. 14:25, 28). Soon thereafter Tiglath-pileser III deported some of the city's inhabitants, but the Hamathites resisted. *Ca.* 720 Sargon II (and possibly later Sennacherib; 18:34; 19:13; Isa. 10:9) quelled Hamath's opposition, deporting the city's populace to Samaria (2 Kgs. 24; cf. v. 30, worshippers of the Assyrian Ashima); in turn, some of the Israelites were resettled around Hamath (Isa. 11:11). During the Maccabean conflict, Jonathan confronted the troops of Demetrius stationed in the region of Hamath (1 Macc. 12:24-25), renamed Epiphania after the Seleucid Antiochus IV Epiphanes.

The "entrance to Hamath" (Heb. *l*ᵉ*ḇô ḥ*ᵃ*māṯ*), depicted as the ideal northern boundary of Israel (e.g., Num. 13:21; Josh. 13:5; Judg. 3:3; Ezek. 47:15; 48:1), probably represents the southern limits of territory controlled by Hamath. Thus it would be located in the upper Beqaʿ valley, most likely in the vicinity of Riblah. Some scholars prefer to read the term as a place name following the transliteration Lebo-hamath (cf. ancient Lebo [modern Lebweh], 22 km. [14 mi.] north-northeast of Baalbek).

HAMATHITES [hā'mə thīts] (Heb. *haḥ*ᵃ*māṯî*). The inhabitants of Hamath, reckoned among the descendants of Canaan (Gen. 10:18; 1 Chr. 1:16).

HAMATH-ZOBAH [hā'măth zō'bə] (Heb. *ḥ*ᵃ*māṯ ṣôḇâ*).† A town or region conquered by Solomon (2 Chr. 8:3). Some scholars consider the name an alternative designation for ZOBAH, possibly reflecting the circumstances of the Persian period (when 1-2 Chronicles was composed), at which time Zobah was part of the province of Hamath. The town and incident are absent from the parallel account at 1 Kgs. 9:17-19, prompting some to derive the term from a textual corruption based on Heb. *ḥômāṯ* "wall" at v. 15 (cf. Ezek. 47:17; *g*ᵉ*ḇul ḥ*ᵃ*māṯ* "border of Hamath"). At 2 Chr. 8:3 LXX B reads Gk. *bai Zóba*, suggesting the reading "Beth-zobah" or "house of Zobah."

HAMITES [hăm'īts].† The descendants of Ham, the youngest son of Noah. According to the Table of Nations (Gen. 10) they comprised four branches, each traced to one of Ham's sons: Cush, Egypt, Put, and Canaan (vv. 6-20).

Linguistically and, by extension, culturally, the term refers to those peoples who speak Hamitic languages. Closely related to the Semitic languages (and thus classified as Hamito-Semitic [or sometimes Afro-Asiatic] languages), this family includes the

Berber languages of North Africa and the Canary Islands, Ancient Egyptian, the Cushitic (or Eastern Hamitic) languages of Ethiopia and Somalia, and the Chad languages of northern Nigeria (primarily Hausa). Some scholars would also include the Nilo-Hamitic languages of East Africa.

HAMMATH [hăm´ăth] (Heb. *ḥammaṭ* "hot springs").
1. A fortified town in the tribal territory of Naphtali (Josh. 19:35). It was located at Ḥammâm Ṭabarîyeh, 3 km. (2 mi.) south of Tiberias on the western shore of the Sea of Galilee. Frequently mentioned in the Talmud, the city has been renowned since ancient times for its medicinal springs (cf. Josephus *Ant*. xviii.2.3 [36]). It is probably the same as Hammoth-dor (Josh. 21:32) and Hammon (1 Chr. 6:76).
2. The home of the Kenites of the family of Rechab (1 Chr. 2:55); its location is not known. Some regard this reference as a personal name, but Heb. *bā´îm* in this verse means "who come from" and not "who are descended from."

HAMMEDATHA [hăm´ə dā´thə] (Heb. *hammᵉḏāṯā´*; Pers. *mâhdāta* "given by the moon"). The father of Haman (Esth. 3:1, 10; 8:5; 9:10, 24).

HAMMELECH [hăm´ə lĕk] (Heb. *hammelek* "the king").* Translated by the KJV as a personal name at Jer. 36:26; 38:6. "The king's son" (so RSV, NIV; JB "Prince") may actually designate any male of the royal household.

HAMMER (Heb. *maqqeḇeṯ, paṭṭîš*). A tool used for pounding as well as fashioning from crude material by smiths and masons; generally a smooth or shaped stone held directly in the hand or by a handle affixed to a hole bored in the stone. Various samples have been discovered at sites throughout the Near East. The Bible mentions the use of the hammer to hew stone (1 Kgs. 6:7; Jer. 23:29), work iron (Isa. 44:12) and other metals (Jer. 10:4), and pound tent pegs into the ground (Judg. 4:21). At Jer. 51:20 Heb. *mappēṣ* (RSV "hammer") is more correctly a weapon of war (KJV "battle-axe"; NIV "war club"; JB "mace").
The hammer is used figuratively in the book of Jeremiah as an image for the power of God's word (Jer. 23:29) and his destructive might (51:20, RSV). It also appears as a symbol for worldly power (50:23).

HAMMOLECHETH [hă mŏl´ə kĕth] (Heb. *hammōleḵeṯ* "the queen"). The sister of Gilead (1 Chr. 7:18; KJV "Hammoleketh"), progenitor of several tribes.

HAMMON [hăm´ən] (Heb. *ḥammôn* "hot spring [?]").
1. A city on the border of the tribal territory of Asher (Josh. 19:28). It is probably to be identified with modern Umm el-'Awāmîd, located on the Mediterranean coast at Wâdī el-Hamûl, approximately 8 km. (5 mi.) northeast of Râs en-Naqûrah; a stele dedicated to the deity Milk-Astarte has been discovered at the site.
2. A city in Naphtali allotted to the Gershomite Levites (1 Chr. 6:76). It is probably the same as HAMMATH 1 (Josh. 19:35) and Hammath-dor (21:32).

HAMMOTH-DOR [hăm´əth dôr´] (Heb. *ḥammōṯ dō´r* "warm springs of Dor"). A levitical city in the tribal territory of Naphtali (Josh. 21:32). Hammon (1 Chr. 6:76) and Hammath (Josh. 19:35) are probably alternate names for this city.

HAMMUEL [hăm´yoo̅ əl] (Heb. *ḥammû´ēl*). Son of Mishma and father of Zaccur, of the tribe of Simeon (1 Chr. 4:26; KJV "Hanuel").

HAMMURABI [hăm´ə rä´bī].† The sixth and most important king of the First (Amorite) Dynasty of Babylon; son of Sin-muballit. In addition to his famous law code, Hammurabi's reign is well documented by correspondence, royal inscriptions, and administrative texts, which underscore his proficiency as a diplomat, military strategist, and a strong, humanitarian administrator. Sometimes dated as early as 2123-2081 B.C. and as late as 1704-1662, he is now generally accepted as having reigned 1792-1750, placing him toward the end of the period widely ascribed to the patriarchs. His name, which is of Amorite (West Semitic) origin, is probably better transliterated 'Ammurapi; some scholars associate it with a West Semitic god Ḥammu or 'Ammu, but the form may also mean "people" (W. Sem. *ḥamm*), and the second element may mean "restorer" or "healer" (**rp*') or "great" (cf. Heb. *rab*). The earlier identification of Hammurabi with Amraphel of Gen. 14 has been discredited on both linguistic and historical grounds.
Building upon the modest territorial expansion begun by his father, Hammurabi managed, as head of a coalition of some ten city-states, to conquer the cities of Uruk and Isin and by his twelfth year of rule had extended Babylon's rule as far as Rāpiḫu. Nearly two decades of peace ensued, during which he engaged in numerous building projects, including several temples and canals. In his twenty-ninth year Hammurabi turned on his ally Rim-sin of Larsa, annexing all lands previously captured by Larsa. He then defeated Išme-dagan of Assyria as well as the kingdoms of Mari and Eshnunna. By the end of his reign he had created an empire of "Sumer and Akkad" which stretched from the Persian Gulf as far as Hit and Mari on the Euphrates river and Nineveh on the Tigris as well as Gutium and Subartu to the east. Nevertheless, without Hammurabi's powerful and creative personal leadership the empire crumbled under his son and successor Samsu-iluna.
The reign of Hammurabi is regarded as a golden age in Mesopotamian history. Babylon became a center of learning; an efficient scribal class produced and preserved much Sumerian and Babylonian literature, and Akkadian came to the fore as the language of business and administration. Marduk, who would later head the Babylonian pantheon, attained prominence as god of the empire's capital. Perhaps most noteworthy is Hammurabi's concern for justice as demonstrated in his code of laws (*ANET*, pp. 163-180), compiled toward the end of his reign. Inscribed on a massive stele, of which several copies apparently were distributed among major cities of the land, this collection of some 282 case laws summarizes the current application of justice, to a large extent an interpretation and

modification of reforms previously brought about under Ur-nammu and Lipit-ishtar. Included are precedents regarding judicial procedure, theft, property damage, treatment of slaves, commerce, agriculture, debts and deposits, marriage and family relations (including inheritance and sexual infractions), and liability for physical injury. Although punishments would seem harsh today and distinctions are made on the basis of social rank, the code represents an attempt to maintain the Babylonian social order fairly and with restraint. The prologue to the code hails Hammurabi's piety and his establishment of peace and prosperity, while the epilogue proclaims the justice of his reign, particularly evident in his concern for the less fortunate.

HAMONAH [hə mō'nə] (Heb. *hᵃmônâ* "multitude"). A city near the valley of Hamon-gog ("multitude of Gog," Ezek. 39:15-16) the name of which served as a reminder of the multitudes of Gog's army that were buried nearby. Most likely the location is near Baal-hamon in the valley region between Abarim and the mouth of the Jordan. An alternate identification would be el-Lejjun (Legio, possibly Hadadrimmon), in the valley of Megiddo. It is also possible that Hamonah was not a city at all. A minor emendation in the text (v. 16) would allow the translation "and an end has come to his commotion," which would fit perfectly in the context (cf. NEB, "so no more shall be heard of that great horde").

HAMON-GOG [hā'mən gŏg'] (Heb. *hᵃmôn gôg* "multitude of Gog").† A valley where the forces of Gog are to be buried (Ezek. 39:11, 15). Also called the Valley of the Travelers (v. 11; Heb. *'ōḇᵉrîm*; NIV "those who travel east toward the Sea"), it may be associated with the Abarim (*"ᵃḇārîm* "region beyond") mountains in northern Moab between the Dead Sea and the plain of Moab (so JB, following Vulg.).

HAMOR [hā'môr] (Heb. *hᵃmôr* "he-ass"). The Hivite ruler of Shechem whose son, also named Shechem, defiled Jacob's daughter Dinah. In retribution her brothers Simeon and Levi killed both Shechem and his father (Gen. 34). Hamor is identified as the progenitor of the inhabitants of Shechem at Josh. 24:32; Jgs. 9:28 (cf. Acts 7:16, where the name is confused with Machpelah; KJV "Emmor"); these descendants ("sons," Gen. 33:19) sold Jacob the land upon which he erected an altar (v. 20) and where later Joseph was buried (Josh. 24:32).

HAMRAN [hăm'răn] (Heb. *hamrān*).* The eldest son of Dishon (1 Chr. 1:41; KJV "Amram"; NIV "Hemdan"). At Gen. 36:26 he is called Hemdan.

HAMUL [hā'məl] (Heb. *hāmûl* "spared"). A son of Perez and grandson of Judah (Gen. 46:12; 1 Chr. 2:5).

HAMULITES [hā'mə līts] (Heb. *hehāmûlî*). Descendants of Hamul, a clan or subdivision of Judah (Num. 26:21).

HAMUTAL [hə mū'təl] (Heb. Q *hᵃmûṭal*; K *hᵃmîṭal*; LXX Gk. *Amital* "father-in-law is dew"). Wife of King Josiah of Judah, daughter of Jeremiah of Libnah, and the mother of Kings Jehoahaz and Zedekiah (2 Kgs. 23:31; 24:18; Jer. 52:1). At 2 Kgs. 24:18; Jer. 52:1 the MT reads Hamital (so JB). Some think that the lioness of Ezek. 19:2 is a reference to Queen Hamutal.

HANAMEL [hăn'ə měl] (Heb. *hᵃnam'ēl* "God is gracious"). The son of Shallum and cousin of Jeremiah, from whom the imprisoned prophet purchased a field at Anathoth during the Chaldean siege of Jerusalem (Jer. 32:7-15; KJV "Hanameel").

HANAN [hā'năn] (Heb. *hānān* "gracious," possibly from *hānanyâ* "Yahweh has been gracious").
1. A Benjaminite leader and son of Shashak (1 Chr. 8:23).
2. A Benjaminite, one of the descendants of Saul and Jonathan (1 Chr. 8:38; 9:44).
3. Son of Maacah, and one of David's mighty men (1 Chr. 11:43).
4. A son of Igdaliah. During the time of Jeremiah his "sons" (perhaps members of a prophetic guild) had a chamber in the temple (Jer. 35:4).
5. The ancestor of a family of temple servants who returned from the Exile with Zerubbabel (Ezra 2:46; Neh. 7:49).
6. A Levite who aided Ezra in interpreting the law (Neh. 8:7) and who sealed the covenant (10:10). He may be the Hanan, a son of Zaccur, mentioned at Neh. 13:13 as an assistant to the treasurers appointed over the storehouses.
7, 8. Two family heads who set their seals to the renewed covenant under Nehemiah (Neh. 10:22, 26).

HANANEL [hăn'ə něl], **TOWER OF** (Heb. *migdal hᵃnan'ēl* "tower of 'God is gracious'").† A tower or fortress along the northern wall of Jerusalem, located on the northwestern corner of the Ophel-Moriah spur overlooking the temple. First mentioned by the prophet Jeremiah (Jer. 31:38) and, after the Exile, by Zechariah (Zech. 14:10) as the northeastern corner of the restored Jerusalem, it was located between the Fish Gate and the Sheep Gate (Neh. 3:1; 12:39). Called the "fortress (Heb. *bîrâ*) of the temple" (2:8), it was the site of the Maccabean citadel (e.g., 1 Macc. 4:41), rebuilt by Antiochus IV Epiphanes as the Seleucid Akra (Josephus *Ant.* xxi.362-64, 369, 405-6) and again by John Hyrcanus I as the Hasmonean Baris (xviii.91). Here Herod the Great built the Fortress Antonia (xviii.92; *BJ* i.75, 118), a massive tower with four smaller towers at each corner, the tallest of which guarded the temple precincts to the southeast.

HANANI [hə nā'nī] (Heb. *hᵃnānî* "gracious").
1. The father of the prophet Jehu (1 Kgs. 16:1; 7; 2 Chr. 19:2; 20:34). Hanani was himself a seer, and King Asa, who had an alliance with the Syrian king Ben-hadad, imprisoned him because he criticized this alliance (2 Chr. 16:7-10).
2. A Levite, leader of the eighteenth division of temple musicians during the time of David (1 Chr. 25:4, 25).

3. A priest from the family of Immer. He was one of those who had taken foreign wives (Ezra 10:20).

4. A brother (more likely a kinsman) who reported that the Jews in the devastated city of Jerusalem were in distress (Neh. 1:2-3). He and HANANIAH **3**, the governor of the castle, were later given charge of the city (7:2).

5. A levitical musician who participated in the dedication of the city walls during the time of Nehemiah (Neh. 12:36).

HANANIAH [hăn′ə nī′ə] (Heb. *ḥᵃnanyāhû, ḥᵃnanyâ* "Yahweh has been gracious").

1. A Levite, the leader of the sixteenth division of the temple singers during the time of David (1 Chr. 25:4, 23).

2. One of the commanders in the army of King Uzziah (2 Chr. 26:11).

3. The father of Zedekiah, who was one of the high officials under King Jehoiakim (Jer. 36:12).

4. A false prophet from Gibeon; the son of Azzur. He broke the yoke that Jeremiah wore to symbolize Judah's oppression by Babylon as a divinely authorized burden and announced, in direct opposition to Jeremiah's prophecy, that the people would be delivered from the yoke of Nebuchadnezzar within two years (Jer. 28:1-11). In accordance with the subsequent word of the Lord, Hananiah died two months later (vv. 12-17).

5. Grandfather of the sentry Irijah who seized Jeremiah (Jer. 37:13ff.).

6. One of Daniel's three friends. The chief of Nebuchadnezzar's eunuchs changed his Hebrew name to Shadrach ("Command of Aku"; Dan. 1:6-7).

7. The son of Zerubbabel and father of Pelatiah and Jeshaiah (1 Chr. 3:19-21).

8. A Benjaminite, son of Shashak (1 Chr. 8:24).

9. An Israelite of the family of Bebai who had to send away his foreign wife (Ezra 10:28).

10. A perfumer who worked at restoring the walls of Jerusalem (Neh. 3:8). He may be the same Hananiah who repaired the wall above the Horse Gate (v. 30).

11. The governor of the castle (Heb. *bîrâ* "fortress"), a "faithful and God-fearing man" whom Nehemiah placed in charge of Jerusalem along with his own brother, Hanani **2** (Neh. 7:2).

12. An Israelite leader who, on behalf of his family, set his seal to the renewed covenant under Nehemiah (Neh. 10:23).

13. A priest and head of the house of Jeremiah during the time of the high priest Joiakim who returned with Zerubbabel from Babylon and participated in the dedication of the walls (Neh. 12:12, 41).

HAND (Heb. *yāḏ*; Gk. *cheír*).† In addition to numerous literal references to the hand as a part of the body, it occurs some thirteen hundred times in a figurative sense, drawing upon its function as an instrument of creativity and production and as a vehicle for strength and action. The hand connotes power and authority (cf. Jer. 38:4; Ezek. 8:9), principally that of God (e.g., Exod. 13:9; Deut. 7:8; cf. Ps. 78:42, KJV; RSV "power"). Similarly, it means control or custody (e.g., Gen. 9:2; Josh. 9:25-26; Luke 24:7). To lay

one's hand upon someone may mean to exercise dominion over that person (e.g., 1 Sam. 5:6-7; Ezek. 39:21) or to harm him (e.g., Gen. 22:12; 2 Chr. 23:15). That which is in one's hands is the person's responsibility (Ps. 7:3; cf. 1 Sam. 19:5; 28:21). "By the hand of" implies agency (e.g., Exod. 16:3; Ps. 77:20). Prophetic inspiration is described as the hand of the Lord being upon the prophet (e.g., Ezek. 1:3; 3:14, 22; cf. 2 Kgs. 3:15; RSV "power"), implying both agency and transference.

In the Bible various gestures employ the hands. Lifting the hands is a sign of praise or invocation (e.g., 1 Kgs. 8:22; Ps. 44:20; cf. Exod. 8:5-6, 17; 2 Kgs. 5:11). Clapping the hands is a sign of acclamation of a king (2 Kgs. 11:12) or God (e.g., Ps. 47:1; 98:8; Isa. 55:12; cf. Lam. 2:15). Placing one's hands upon another implies the granting of blessing (e.g., Gen. 48:14-15; Mark 10:16; for this gesture as a means of transferring authority or guilt, *see* LAYING ON OF HANDS). Pledges and even alliances were sealed by "giving" or "striking" (i.e., shaking) hands (e.g., 2 Kgs. 10:15; KJV, Prov. 6:1; 17:18; RSV "give a pledge"; cf. Exod. 23:1, "join hands"; 1 Sam. 22:11). Washing the hands implies disavowal of guilt or complicity (Deut. 21:6; Ps. 26:6; Matt. 27:24). In biblical times folding the hands implied laziness (Prov. 6:10; 24:33); not until much later was it adopted as a posture of prayer.

Euphemistically, the hand designates the male genitals (Isa. 57:8; RSV, NIV "nakedness"; JB "sacred symbol"; NJV "lust"; cf. Ugar. *yd* "love").

HANDBREADTH (Heb. *ṭepaḥ, ṭōpaḥ*). A linear measure corresponding to the width of the hand, approximately one-sixth of a cubit or 7.4 cm. (2.92 in.) (e.g., 1 Kgs. 7:26; 2 Chr. 4:5). *See* WEIGHTS AND MEASURES.

HANDKERCHIEF (Gk. *soudárion*; Lat. *sudarium*, from *sudor* "perspiration"). A small cloth used for wiping the mouth, nose, brow, etc. (Acts 19:12), possibly a form of headdress (cf. Luke 19:20) used as a burial cloth (John 20:7; RSV "napkin"; 11:44; RSV "cloth").

HANES [hā′nĭz] (Heb. *ḥānēs*).† A place where Egyptian and Israelite envoys met to consider an alliance (Isa. 30:4), generally identified as Anusis or Heracleopolis Magna (modern Ihnâsiyeh el-Medina), capital of the twentieth Upper Egyptian nome some 129 km. (80 mi.) southwest of Cairo. The Hebrew name is probably a transliteration of Egyp. *Ḥwt-nnì-nsw* "mansion of the king." Some scholars would favor a site in the eastern Delta, thus more accessible to the Israelites.

HANNAH [hăn′ə] (Heb. *ḥannâ* "grace, favor").† A wife of Elkanah the Ephraimite, and mother of Samuel. For a long time Hannah was childless, for which she was harassed by Elkanah's other wife, Peninnah (1 Sam. 1:6; cf. v. 2). During the family's annual pilgrimage to the sanctuary at Shiloh she vowed that if the Lord would grant her a son she would dedicate the child to his service (v. 11), a petition which the priest Eli assured would be fulfilled

(v. 17). Accordingly, when she had given birth to Samuel, she brought the young boy to the sanctuary to fulfill her vow (vv. 22, 24-28); during subsequent pilgrimages she provided her son with a priestly robe (2:19-20). Hannah later gave birth to three more sons and two daughters (v. 21).

The Song of Hannah (2:1-10), a psalm traditionally attributed to Hannah, extols God's benevolence by describing his mighty acts. Stylistic features such as the use of divine names (e.g., Heb. ṣûr "rock," v. 2) and royal allusions ("anointed," v. 10) suggest to some that the poem was composed somewhat later than Hannah, probably in the early tenth century B.C. and perhaps in response to the birth of a royal heir. If so, it may have been associated with Hannah because of the reference to a barren wife giving birth to a large family (v. 5).

HANNATHON [hăn'ə thŏn] (Heb. ḥannāṯôn). A city in the tribal territory of Zebulun (Josh. 19:14). In the Amarna Letters this city is called Ḥinatuna. Various sites have been proposed, including Kefr ῾Anā (biblical Ono) and Deir Hanna, which suggest the biblical name, as well as Tell el-Harbaj. A leading possibility is Tell el-Bedeiwîyeh on the western side of the el-Battof plain (the plain of Zebulun), 9.6 km. (6 mi.) north of Nazareth. Bronze Age remains in this region indicate the presence of an ancient settlement. In addition, this location coincides with details at Josh. 19, for Hannathon lay north of both Rimmon (modern Rummâneh, on the south side of the plain) and the valley of Iphtahel, which is probably the valley of the Wâdī el-Melek, a brook that runs through the western portion of the plain.

HANNIEL [hăn'ĭ əl] (Heb. ḥannî'ēl) "God has been gracious").
1. The son of Ephod, and a leader of the tribe of Manasseh. He represented his tribe in the division of the land of Canaan (Num. 34:23).
2. A son of Ulla, and a leader of the tribe of Asher (1 Chr. 7:39; KJV "Haniel").

HANOCH [hā'nŏk] (Heb. ḥanôḵ "dedicated").
1. A son of Midian and grandson of Abraham and Keturah (Gen. 25:4; 1 Chr. 1:33; KJV "Henoch").
2. The oldest son of Jacob's oldest son, Reuben (Gen. 46:9; Exod. 6:14; 1 Chr. 5:3). His descendants became the family of the Hanochites (Num. 26:5; Heb. haḥănôḵî).

HANUKKAH [hä'nə kə] (ḥănukkâ "dedication"). See DEDICATION, FEAST OF.

HANUN [hā'nən] (Heb. ḥānûn "favored").
1. The son of Nahash, and his successor as king of the Ammonites. David sent envoys to Hanun with condolences on the death of Nahash, but the leaders of the Ammonites aroused him against David; he seized the messengers, shaved off half their beards, and cut off one side of their garments. In the war that ensued, Hanun was defeated and his people forced into slavery (2 Sam. 10:1-11:1; 12:26-31; 1 Chr. 19:1-20:3).
2. An Israelite who aided in the restoration of the walls of Jerusalem at the time of Nehemiah (Neh. 3:13).

3. The sixth son of Zalaph who aided in the restoration of Jerusalem's walls (Neh. 3:30); possibly the same as 2.

HAPAX LEGOMENON [hä'pŏx lə gŏ'mə nən] (Gk. hápax legómenon "once read").* A term that is found only one time in a certain body of literature (e.g., a Hebrew term found only once in the Old Testament).

HAPHARAIM [hăf'ə rā'əm] (Heb. ḥăpārayim). A city in the tribal territory of Issachar (Josh. 19:19; KJV "Haphraim"). Mentioned in the list of Palestinian towns conquered by the Egyptian Shishak (Egyp. ḥprm), it is generally thought to have been located at modern eṭ-Ṭaiyibeh, about 14 km. (9 mi.) northwest of Beth-shan. Some scholars, following Eusebius (Onom.), identify the site as Alphraia (modern Khirbet el-Farriyeh), 9.6 km. (6 mi.) northwest of Roman Legio (probably biblical Hadadrimmon, modern el-Lejjun).

HAPPIZZEZ [hăp'ə zēz] (Heb. happiṣṣēṣ). The leader of the eighteenth division of priests during the time of David (1 Chr. 24:15; KJV "Aphses").

HARA [hâr'ə] (Heb. hārā' "hill country"). The city or district to which the Assyrians deported some of the Israelite captives (1 Chr. 5:26). The absence of the term in the LXX and at 2 Kgs. 17:6; 18:10 (MT "the cities [LXX "mountains"] of Media") casts doubt upon the credibility of this reading. But if the text is correct, Hara might be identified with the town of Ara, which with its villages constituted one of the nineteen districts of Hamath mentioned by Tiglath-pileser III (ANET, pp. 282-83).

HARADAH [hə rā'də] (Heb. ḥărādâ "terror"). A place where the Israelites stopped during the wilderness journey (Num. 33:24-25). The location is not known.

HARAN [hâr'ən] (Heb. hārān "mountainous") **(PERSON)**.
1. The son of Terah and brother of Abraham and Nahor; he fathered a son, Lot, and two daughters, Milcah and Iscah (Gen. 11:27-29). Haran died in the Chaldean city of Ur while his father was still alive.
2. A descendant of Judah; the son of Caleb by his concubine Ephah (1 Chr. 2:46).
3. A son of Shimei; a Levite of the line of Gershom who was a head of the family of Ladan during the time of David (1 Chr. 23:9).

HARAN (Heb. ḥārān; Akk. Ḥarrânu; Gk. Charran) **(PLACE)**.† A city on the Balikh river, a northern tributary of the Euphrates, 39 km. (24 mi.) southsoutheast of Urfa (ancient Edessa). It was to this city that Terah moved from Ur of the Chaldees (Gen. 11:31; Acts 7:2, 4; KJV "Charran"), and there he died (Gen. 11:32). His son Abram and daughter-in-law Sarai and Lot, his grandson by the deceased Haran, departed from this city en route to Canaan (12:4-5), but Terah's other son, Nahor, remained (cf. 24:10). Seeking to escape Esau's wrath, Jacob settled there with his uncle Laban (27:43; 28:10); Jacob prospered at Haran, marrying there Laban's daughters Leah and Rachel (29:4ff.).

Probably founded in the mid-third millennium B.C., by the eighteenth century Haran had become an important commercial center, and it remained such through the Hellenistic period (cf. Ezek. 27:23); it lay on important caravan routes linking Nineveh in Mesopotamia with cities in northern Syria and Egypt with Asia Minor. A cosmopolitan city of mixed population, Haran was coveted by various Anatolian and Mesopotamian powers and fell to the Assyrian Shalmaneser I in the early thirteenth century (cf. 2 Kgs. 19:12 par. Isa. 37:12). It is listed among the cities conquered by Sennacherib (Akk. *ir Harrani*), and served as an important provincial capital; following the fall of Nineveh in 612 it served as the Assyrian capital until sacked by the Babylonians in 609. During the Greek and Roman periods the city was known as Carrhae; it was here that the Roman triumvir Crassus was annihilated by the Parthians in 53 B.C., and here the emperor Caracalla was murdered in A.D. 217 prior to a battle with the Parthians.

Associated with the Babylonian moon-god Sin since the Ur III period (*ca.* 2000 B.C.), Haran remained a focus of lunar cults well into the Christian period, as attested by excavations at the site and supported by subsidiary temples discovered at nearby Sultantepe and Aşagi Yarimcâ.

HARARITE [hârʾə rīt] (Heb. *hahᵃrārî, hāʾrārî* "mountain dweller" [?]). A gentilic, possibly indicating the inhabitants of a place or region in the hill country of Judah or Ephraim. The name might also be taken from Araru, a place mentioned in the Amarna Letters in connection with Dumah, Anab, and Adoraim, in which case it would have been located near Hebron. Three of the mighty men of David are called "the Hararite": Agee (2 Sam. 23:11), Shammah (v. 33) or Shagee (1 Chr. 11:34), and Sharar (2 Sam. 23:33) or Sachar (1 Chr. 11:35).

HARBONA [här bō′nə] (Heb. *harᵉbônāʾ, harᵉbônâ;* cf. Pers. "donkey driver"). A eunuch of Ahasuerus, king of Persia (Esth. 1:10). He suggested that Haman be hanged on the very gallows he had made for Mordecai (7:9).

HARE (Heb. *ʾarnebet*). A herbivorous rodent of the family Leporidae, a mammal closely related to the rabbit. Various species have been attested in Palestine, including the *Lepus syriacus*, an animal slightly smaller than its European counterpart (*Lepus europaeus*); it is common in wooded and cultivated areas throughout the northern part of Palestine, particularly in the valley of Esdraelon. A smaller variety, with a light, sand-colored back, is the *Lepus aegypticus*, found in the Negeb and the Jordan valley.

"Because it chews the cud but does not part the hoof," the hare is classified as an unclean animal (Lev. 11:6; Deut. 14:7). Actually, it is not a ruminant but may have appeared as such to ancient observers because of its constant chewing movements.

HAREPH [hârʾĕf] (Heb. *ḥārēp* "early born" or "insolent"). A son of Hur and grandson of Caleb, of the tribe of Judah. He was the father (or founder) of Beth-gader (1 Chr. 2:51; *see* GEDER).

HARHAIAH [här hā′yə] (Heb. *ḥarhᵃyâ* "the Lord rages"). The father of the goldsmith Uzziel, who aided in the restoration of the walls of Jerusalem under Nehemiah (Neh. 3:8).

HARHAS [här′hăs] (Heb. *ḥarḥas*). The grandfather of Shallum, husband of the prophetess Huldah (2 Kgs. 22:14). At 2 Chr. 34:22 he is called Hasrah.

HAR-HERES [här hĭr′ĭz] (Heb. *har-ḥeres* "mountain of the sun"). A place in the tribal territory of Dan, but which the Danites were unable to take from the Amorites (Judg. 1:35; KJV, NIV "mount Heres"). It is thought to be the same as Ir-shemesh ("city of the sun," probably Beth-shemesh [Tell er-Rumeileh]), a city assigned to Dan (Josh. 19:41). The name may be preserved in modern Hirsa, which lies up the slope of the mountains southeast of Yâlō (biblical Aijalon).

HARHUR [här′hûr] (Heb. *ḥarḥûr* "fever"). A temple servant whose descendants returned from the Exile with Zerubbabel (Ezra 2:51; Neh. 7:53).

HARIM [hâr′ĭm] (Heb. *ḥārim* "dedicated").
1. The leader of the third division of the priesthood at the time of David (1 Chr. 24:8). It was probably his descendants who were led back from exile by Zerubbabel (Ezra 2:39; Neh. 7:42; 12:15). Several members of this priestly family had taken foreign wives (Ezra 10:21); and a representative of this family set his seal to the renewed covenant under Nehemiah (Neh. 10:5).
2. An Israelite (not a priest) whose descendants returned from the Exile with Zerubbabel (Ezra 2:32; Neh. 7:35). Several members of this family took foreign wives (Ezra 10:31). Malchijah, apparently from this family, worked on the restoration of the walls of Jerusalem (Neh. 3:11).

HARIPH [hâr′ĭf] (Heb. *ḥārîp*, possibly "autumn" or "insolent"). An Israelite whose descendants returned from the Exile under Zerubbabel (Neh. 7:24); he may be the same person as Jorah in the parallel account (Ezra 2:18). Either he or a representative of his family set his seal to the renewed covenant under Nehemiah (Neh. 10:19).

HARLOT (Heb. *zānâ, zōnâ*; Gk. *pórnē*).† A female prostitute; in the general sense, one who engages in extramarital sexual relations for commercial purposes (cf. Gen. 38:17; Prov. 6:26; Luke 15:30). Common throughout Palestine and the ancient Near East (e.g., Judg. 16:1), they would dress enticingly and frequent public places (Gen. 38:14-15; JB, NIV "prostitute"; Ezek. 16:16ff.), seeking to lure their customers (cf. Prov. 7:6-27) back to the houses of their enterprise (cf. Josh. 2:1; 1 Kgs. 3:16; Jer. 5:7). Harlotry was condemned by the Israelites (Deut. 22:21; Prov. 23:27; KJV "whore"; Amos 2:7); its practitioners were held in low esteem (Gen. 34:31; Matt. 21:31-32; cf. Amos 7:17), regarded as religiously unclean (cf. Lev. 21:7, 9; cf. 19:29).

Of far greater concern to the Israelites was the practice of cultic prostitution common among the non-Israelite religious (e.g., Num. 25:1), particularly that of the Canaanite fertility goddess Astarte. Both men

(Deut. 23:18; Heb. *keleḇ* "dog"; RSV mg. "sodomite"; NIV "male prostitute") and women (*qᵉḏēšâ* "consecrated woman") dedicated their lives to the deity, performing sexual acts with worshippers so as to encourage the deified forces of nature to imitate them and thus guarantee continued productivity and prosperity. Cultic prostitution was specifically prohibited in the Hebrew faith (Deut. 23:17) and the wages earned by the practice rejected as a temple offering (v. 18). Nevertheless, many gave in to non-Israelite influence, participating in the foreign rites (1 Kgs. 14:24) and even introducing prostitution into the Israelite cult (e.g., 1 Kgs. 22:38; 2 Kgs. 23:7; Jer. 2:20; Hos. 4:13-14).

Israel's unfaithfulness to the covenant with Yahweh is depicted, perhaps at times literally (cf. 1 Chr. 5:25), as "playing the harlot" after foreign gods (e.g., Isa. 1:21; Jer. 3:1). Jerusalem's religious infidelity is described at length in Ezekiel's allegory of the unfaithful wife (Ezek. 16:1-63, esp. vv. 15-43). Foreign cities, regarded as apostate not only because of their fertility cults but also for their greed for wealth and power, are depicted as harlots (e.g., Isa. 23:16-18; Nah. 3:4ff.; cf. Rev. 17:1ff.).

HARMON [här′mən] (Heb. *haharmônâ*). An unspecified place of banishment (Amos 4:3; KJV "the palace"; JB "Hermon"). Otherwise unattested, it is the place to which the guilty women of Samaria would be cast forth. If they were to be punished while yet alive, it might have been a place of exile for captives, located perhaps beyond Damascus (cf. 5:27; Targ. "beyond the mountains of Armenia"; LXX "mountain of Romman"; NIV mg. "O mountain of oppression"). If they were to be killed as punishment, it could have been a reference to a place near Samaria where corpses were thrown (NJV "on the refuse heap").

HARNEPHER [här′nə fər] (Heb. *ḥarneper*). A son of Zophah of the tribe of Asher (1 Chr. 7:36).

HAROD [hâr′ŏd] (Heb. *ḥᵃrōḏ* "trembling").
   1. The spring where Gideon and his army camped before routing the Midianites (Judg. 7:4; KJV "well"). It is probably to be identified with modern 'Ain Jālûd on the eastern border of the valley of Jezreel north of Mt. Gilboa. The water flows out of a hollow in the rocks here and forms a small lake, the headwaters of Nahr Jālûd. This may also be the fountain near which Saul encamped prior to his defeat by the Philistines at Gilboa (1 Sam. 29:1).
   2. The home of Shammah and Elika, two of David's mighty men (2 Sam. 23:25). The site may be Beth-hadutu (variously rendered Haduru, Haduri, Harudra, Haruri, Haruru, Haron), 6 km. (3.8 mi.) from Jerusalem, which according to Jewish tradition was considered the beginning of the wilderness. This would favor identification with Khirbet Khareidan, a site on the road between Jerusalem and Mar Sāba on the brook Kidron.
   At 1 Chr. 11:27 the KJV calls Shammah "the Harorite" (MT Heb. *ḥᵃrôrî*), following a textual error confusing the Hebrew letter resh with daleth (2 Sam. 23:25, *ḥᵃrōḏî*).

HAROEH [hə rō′ə] (Heb. *hārō'eh* "the seer"). A son of Shobal and descendant of Judah (1 Chr. 2:52). At 4:2 he is called Reaiah.

HAROSHETH-HAGOIIM [hə rō′shĕth hə goi′ĭm] (Heb. *ḥᵃrōšeṯ haggôyim* "forest of the Gentiles"). The home of Sisera, the commander of the Canaanite king Jabin's army (Judg. 4:2, 13, 16). Some scholars propose Tell el-Harbaj as the site because it fits the topographical details of the biblical account, but a more likely possibility would be Tell 'Amr, near modern el-Ḥarithiyeh, which may preserve the ancient name; unfortunately, the latter site has yielded no remains prior to the tenth century B.C. It may be the same as Muḥrašti mentioned in the Amarna Letters, a site in the plain of Sharon.

HARP (Heb. *nēḇel, kinnôr;* Gk. *kithára*). A stringed musical instrument, plucked or strummed with both hands and used primarily for worship (cf. Ps. 33:2; 57:8; 81:2; 92:3; 108:2; 1 Macc. 4:54). Although the instruments to which these terms refer cannot be identified with certainty, the harp represented by Heb. *nēḇel* (KJV "psaltery") most likely consisted of strings stretched on an open frame, perpendicular to the sound board. Whether large and stationary or small and portable, a variety of these harps are depicted in drawings from ancient Babylonia, Assyria, and Egypt. Ps. 33:2; 144:9 refer specifically to the ten-stringed harp (NIV "lyre"). The strings of the instrument represented by Heb. *kinnôr* (RSV "lyre") were probably strung across the top of a broad, flat sound board. Aram. *pᵉsantērîn* at Dan. 3:5, 7 (KJV "psaltery") is derived from Gk. *psaltḗrion*.

The harp is seldom mentioned in connection with secular functions (Isa. 5:12; 14:11; NJV "lutes").

HARSHA [här′shə] (Heb. *haršā'* "mute"). A temple servant whose descendants returned from the Exile with Zerubbabel (Ezra 2:52; Neh. 7:54).

HART (Heb. *'ayyāl*). The adult male deer (the female is called the hind, Heb. *'ayyalâ, 'ayyaleṯ*), generally associated with the European red deer *(Cervus*

Harp found at Ur

elaphus), a species now limited to areas north of Palestine but possibly prevalent in that region in biblical times (cf. 1 Kgs. 4:23). In biblical usage, its power and agility (Isa. 35:6; cf. Cant. 2:9, 17; 8:14; RSV "stag") are proverbial.

HARUM [hâr'əm] (Heb. *hārûm* "exalted"). A Judahite, father of Aharhel (1 Chr. 4:8).

HARUMAPH [hə rōō'măf] (Heb. *ḥªrûmap*, probably "cleft nose"). The father of Jedaiah, who worked on the restoration of the walls of Jerusalem (Neh. 3:10).

HARUPHITE [hə rōō'fît] (Heb. K *ḥªrîpî*, Q *ḥªrûpî*). A gentilic applied to Shephatiah, a Benjaminite who came to David's aid at Ziklag (1 Chr. 12:5). It appears to be based on an unknown place name, perhaps derived from Hareph or Hariph.

HARUZ [hâr'ŭz] (Heb. *ḥārûṣ* "gold" or "industrious"). The father of Meshullemeth, King Manasseh's wife; she was the mother of King Amon (2 Kgs. 21:19).

HARVEST (Heb. *qāṣîr, tªḇû'â;* Gk. *therismós*).† The gathering of agricultural crops. In ancient Israel, a primarily agrarian society, the harvests of major crops became the occasions for the three principal pilgrim feasts: Passover (actually the earlier Feast of Unleavened Bread with which it was combined) marking the barley harvest in April or May (Exod. 34:18-20), Pentecost (the Feast of Weeks) observing the wheat harvest in June (Lev. 23:15-21; Exod. 23:16, "feast of harvest"), and the Feast of Booths or Tabernacles in October celebrating the grape harvest (Deut. 16:13-16; Exod. 23:16, "feast of ingathering"). Other harvests included flax in March and April (Josh. 2:6), the summer fruits (grapes and late figs) in August and September, and olives from mid-September to mid-November. For further information on specific crops see the individual entries; *see also* AGRICULTURE.

Harvesting generally involved the entire family as well as hired workers; indeed, participation was expected of all Israelites (cf. Prov. 10:5; 20:4). Grain and other produce might be gathered by hand, but most often the sickle was used (Joel 3:13; Mark 4:29); implements were employed to harvest other crops as well (e.g., sticks for beating olive trees; Isa. 17:6). Because all produce was regarded as the gift of God, portions of the firstfruits (in the case of fruit trees, entire harvests; Lev. 19:23-25) were presented as offerings (23:10; Exod. 22:29). Moreover, out of concern for the underprivileged and the sojourner, portions of the yield were left unharvested to permit gleaning (Lev. 19:9; 23:22; Deut. 24:19-20).

In figurative usage, Jesus depicts the task of enlisting followers for the kingdom of God in terms of harvesting (Matt. 9:37; 13:30; John 4:35); elsewhere the harvest represents the end of the age (e.g., Matt. 13:39; Rev. 14:15). The frightful implications of a ruined harvest underlie such a portrayal of divine affliction (e.g., Isa. 16:9; 17:11; Jer. 5:17) and the dreaded day of the Lord (51:33; Joel 3:13).

HASADIAH [hăs'ə dī'ə] (Heb. *ḥªsaḏyâ* "Yahweh is kind").

1. A son of Zerubbabel (1 Chr. 3:20).

2.* An ancestor of Baruch and son of Hilkiah (Bar. 1:1).

HASHABIAH [hăsh'ə bī'ə] (Heb. *ḥªšaḇyâ, ḥªšaḇyāhû* "the Lord has taken account").

1. A Levite of the line of Merari; an ancestor of Ethan (1 Chr. 6:45).

2. A Levite of the line of Merari; the father of Azrikam and an ancestor of Shemaiah (1 Chr. 9:14; Neh. 11:15).

3. A son of Jeduthun; leader of the twelfth division of the levitical singers (1 Chr. 25:3, 19).

4. A Hebronite. He and his kinsmen were appointed officers over Israel west of the Jordan during the time of David (1 Chr. 26:30).

5. Son of Kemuel; chief officer of the tribe of Levi at the time of David (1 Chr. 27:17).

6. A chief of the Levites during the time of King Josiah (2 Chr. 35:9; 1 Esdr. 1:9; KJV "Assabias").

7. One of the Levites who accompanied Ezra on his return to Jerusalem (Ezra 8:19; 1 Esdr. 8:48; KJV "Asebia"), responsible for the temple treasures (Ezra 8:24; 1 Esdr. 8:49; KJV "Assanias"). He may be the same Hashabiah who set his seal to the renewed covenant under Nehemiah (Neh. 10:11) and who was chief over the temple singers (12:24).

8. An Israelite layman who pledged to divorce his foreign wife (Ezra 10:25, RSV; KJV, JB, NIV "Malchijah"; 1 Esdr. 9:26, "Asibias").

9. A Levite; ruler of half the district of Keilah. He aided in the restoration of the walls of Jerusalem at the time of Nehemiah (Neh. 3:17).

10. A Levite descended from Asaph (Neh. 11:22).

11. The head of the priestly family of Hilkiah during the time of the high priest Joiakim (Neh. 12:21).

HASHABNAH [hə shăb'nə] (Heb. *ḥªšaḇnâ*, abbreviated form of Hashabneiah). An Israelite who set his seal to the renewed covenant under Nehemiah (Neh. 10:25).

HASHABNEIAH [hăsh'əb nē'yə] (Heb. *ḥªšaḇnªyâ* "the Lord has considered me").

1. The father of HATTUSH **2**, who worked at rebuilding the walls of Jerusalem (Neh. 3:10).

2. A Levite who participated in the ceremony preceding ratification of the covenant (Neh. 9:5); perhaps the same as HASHABIAH **7**, **8**, or **10**.

HASHBADDANAH [hăsh băd'ə nə] (Heb. *ḥašbaddānâ*). An Israelite, probably a Levite, who stood at Ezra's left side and interpreted the law as it was read (Neh. 8:4; KJV "Hashbadana"; 1 Esdr. "Nabariah"; KJV "Habarias"). He may have been the same as HASHABNEIAH **2**.

HASHEM [hā'shĕm] (Heb. *hāšēm*). A Gizonite, one of David's mighty men (1 Chr. 11:34). The parallel passage at 2 Sam. 23:32 reads "the sons of Jashen."

HASHMONAH [hăsh mō'nə] (Heb. *ḥašmōnâ* "fruitfulness"). A place where the Israelites stopped during the wilderness journey (Num. 33:29-30). Eusebius identifies Hashmonah with Asemona (biblical Azmon), in the vicinity of Kadesh-barnea ('Ain Qedeis). Some scholars assign the ruins near 'Ain el-Qeṣeimeh, about 16 km. (10 mi.) northwest of Kadesh-barnea, to Hashmonah.

HASHUBAH [hə shōō′bə] (Heb. *ḥªšuḇâ* "consideration[?]"). A son of Zerubbabel (1 Chr. 3:20).

HASHUM [hā′shəm] (Heb. *hāšum*). An Israelite whose descendants returned from the Exile under Zerubbabel (Ezra 2:19; Neh. 7:22). It was probably a representative of this family who stood at Ezra's left during the reading of the law (8:4; 1 Esdr. 9:44 "Lothasubus") and who set his seal to the renewed covenant (Neh. 10:18). Members of this family were required to give up their foreign wives (Ezra 10:33; 1 Esdr. 9:33; KJV "Asom").

HASIDEANS [hăs′ə dē′ənz] (Gk. *hasidaíoi*).† A pietistic Jewish movement which came to prominence in Palestine during the Hellenistic period. The name represents the Greek transliteration of Heb. *ḥªsîḏîm* "pious, devout," a designation derived from *ḥeseḏ* "steadfast love, loving kindness" and marked by devotion toward God and faithfulness to one's obligations (cf. 2 Chr. 6:41; Ps. 85:8; RSV "saints"; 50:5; RSV "faithful ones"). No direct connection exists between these Jews and the German mystics of the twelfth-thirteenth centuries A.D. or the modern Hasidic movement, founded in eighteenth-century Poland by Israel ben Eliezer (Baal Shem Tob "Master of the Holy Name"). *See* SAINTS.

In the face of increased pagan influence, the Hasideans were committed to strict observance of the law and a revival of Jewish ritual; thus their roots may be sought as early as the late fourth century B.C. when the first inroads of Hellenism were felt in Palestine. They are first mentioned as militant protectors of the law against the desecrations of the Seleucid Antiochus IV Epiphanes (1 Macc. 2:42; KJV "Assideans"; RV mg. "Chasidim"; *ca.* 167); although they preferred to suffer torture and martyrdom rather than defile the Sabbath—even in self-defense (1:62-63; 2:29-38; cf. Talmud *Nid.* 17a), many heeded Mattathias' zealous reinterpretation of the law (1 Macc. 2:39-41) and joined in the Maccabean revolt (cf. 1 En. 90:10). Some years later, following the Seleucid siege of Jerusalem, internal disarray led the Syrians to restore religious freedom to the Jews (1 Macc. 6:55-63); accepting the overtures of the Aaronic priest Alcimus, who sought to become high priest, many of the Hasideans abandoned the Maccabean cause and agreed to peace (7:12-16). However, Alcimus' accomplice, the general Bacchides, slaughtered sixty of the pietists (v. 16; cf. v. 19). Although some scholars interpret 2 Macc. 14:6 as Alcimus' attempt to garner Demetrius I's support, the passage may indicate renewed Hasidean participation in the revolt (cf. 1 Macc. 7:18; Josephus *Ant.* xii.10.2). *See* MACCABEES.

Two later Jewish sects, the Pharisees and the Essenes, are thought to have originated as rival factions of the postrevolutionary Hasideans.

HASIDIM. *See* HASIDEANS.

HASMONEANS [hăz′mə nē′ənz] (Gk. *Asamomaios*, from Heb. *ḥašmān* "fruitfulness [?]").† The dynasty of Jewish high priests and kings which ruled Judea from the Maccabean revolt until the Roman conquest under Pompey in 63 B.C. The name is derived from Asamonaeus (Hashman; Josephus *Ant.* xii.6.1 [265]), a priest descended from Joarib (1 Macc. 2:1; 1 Chr. 24:7, "Jehoiarib") and ancestor of Mattathias, the founder of the dynasty. Some would trace the name further to the place names Hashmonah or Heshmon.

The designation "Hasmonean," which does not occur in 1-2 Maccabees, is not generally applied to the early leaders of the dynasty (but note *Ant.* xiv.16.4 [490-91]; xx.10.3 [238], 5 [247, 249]; Mishnah *Mid.* 1.6); rather, they are called Maccabees, from the epithet of Judas (Heb. *mqby* "hammerlike"; 1 Macc. 2:4). In 167 the aged Mattathias resisted Seleucid attempts to introduce pagan practices into Palestine and fled with his five sons, thus initiating the revolt (1 Macc. 2:15-28). A year later he was succeeded by his son Judas, who soon proved himself a skilled warrior, driving back the Syrians to restore temple worship in 165 (*see* DEDICATION, FEAST OF). Judas was able to withstand renewed attack in 163 by the Syrian regent Lysias, who was compelled to grant the Jews religious freedom (6:28-63). Judas, however, continued to seek political independence and perished two years later at Elasa (7:4–9:22). His brother Jonathan persisted in the fight, compelling the Syrian general Bacchides to accept terms of peace (9:55-73); skillfully taking advantage of the struggle for succession between the Seleucids Alexander Balas and Demetrius I, he was appointed general and high priest (10:22-66).

When Jonathan was assassinated in 143 by the Syrian usurper Trypho, he was succeeded by his brother Simon, who agreed to support Demetrius II against Trypho and thus obtained total Judean independence in 142 (13:33-42; *Ant.* xiii.6.7 [213-24]). Subsequently he was acclaimed high priest, with succession guaranteed to his successors; many regard this as the true beginning of the Hasmonean dynasty. Judea prospered under Simon, but he and two of his sons were murdered in 135 by his ambitious son-in-law Ptolemy. Simon's son, John Hyrcanus (135-104), withstood the siege of Jerusalem by the Seleucid Antiochus VII Sidetes and extended Judean rule into Transjordan and Edom as well as Samaria. His reign was marred by internal religious conflict, which cost him the support of the Pharisees (xiii.10.5-6 [288-296]). Judas Aristobulus I imprisoned his mother, whom Hyrcanus had designated his political successor, as well as his brothers and claimed the title of king. Mortally ill, he reigned but one year, during which he captured Galilee and compelled its inhabitants to be circumcised (xii.11.3 [319]). Salome Alexandra, Aristobulus' widow, released her imprisoned brothers-in-law and appointed as king and high priest Alexander Jannaeus (103-76), whom she later married. The militant Alexander restored Judea's borders almost to the historic limits of David's glorious empire, despite numerous setbacks and the costly retaliations of his foes as well as the revolt of his own people. His brutality and hellenizing tendencies earned the enmity of the Pharisees. By contrast his widow and successor, Alexandra (76-67), favored the Pharisees. She appointed her son Hyrcanus II as high priest while seeking to minimize the role of her other son, Aristobulus II, who had seized the Sadducean strongholds. The rival brothers both sought Roman aid to succeed their mother, but Aristobulus won out over Hyrcanus and his allies, the Idumean Antipater and the Nabatean Aretas III; nevertheless, Aristobulus had so antagonized Pompey that the Roman forces turned on Jerusalem, capturing the city in 63 B.C. and thus ending both Judean independence and Hasmonean rule.

With Aristobulus imprisoned in Rome, Hyrcanus II was installed as high priest and ethnarch, actually the puppet of Antipater. Through a series of escapes, Aristobulus and his sons continued to foment rebellion and fan Jewish hopes, but he was assassinated in 49 B.C., shortly after his release by Julius Caesar. With the aid of the Parthians, Aristobulus' sole surviving son, Antigonus II, declared himself king and high priest in 40 B.C., but the Roman favorite, Herod the Great, captured Jerusalem in 37 and beheaded Antigonus. Alexandra, Herod's mother-in-law and daughter of Hyrcanus II, coerced Herod through Antony and Cleopatra to set aside his own appointment of Ananel as high priest and install her son, Aristobulus III; soon afterward Herod arranged the drowning of the popular seventeen-year-old. In addition to murdering Hyrcanus II (30 B.C.), Alexandra (28), and his wife Mariamne (29), Herod sought to avoid further Hasmonean influence by convicting and executing in 7 B.C. Alexander and Aristobulus, his remaining sons by Mariamne.

See further the individual entries; *see also* MACCABEES, BOOKS OF.

HASRAH [hăz'rə] (Heb. *hasrâ*).†
1. The grandfather of Shallum (2 Chr. 34:22; 2 Kgs. 22:14; "Harhas").
2. The head of a family who returned to Jerusalem with Zerubbabel following the Exile (1 Esdr. 5:31; KJV "Azara"). The name is omitted in the parallel accounts (Ezra 2:49; Neh. 7:51).

HASSENAAH [hăs'ə nā'ə] (Heb. *hassᵉnā'â*). The head of a family whose members assisted in repairing the walls of Jerusalem (Neh. 3:3). See SENAAH.

HASSENUAH [hăs'ə nōō'ə] (Heb. *hassᵉnu'â*, *hassᵉnû'â* "wrathful").
1. The father of Hodaviah; a man of the tribe of Benjamin whose descendants lived in Jerusalem after the Exile (1 Chr. 9:7; KJV "Hasenuah").
2. The father of Judah, who was second in command of Jerusalem during the time of Nehemiah (Neh. 11:9; KJV "Senuah").

HASSHUB [hăsh'əb] (Heb. *haššûb* "considerate").
1. A Levite of the line of Merari; the father of Shemaiah (1 Chr. 9:14; Neh. 11:15).
2. A son of Pahath-moab who aided in the rebuild of the walls of Jerusalem (Neh. 3:11).
3. An Israelite who helped to rebuild the walls of Jerusalem (Neh. 3:23). Either he or **2** above set his seal to the renewed covenant under Nehemiah (Neh. 10:23).

HASSOPHERETH [hă sŏf'ə rĕth] (Heb. *hassōperet* "the scribe"; Gk. *Assaphiōth*). The head of a family or guild of "Solomon's servants" who returned from the Exile with Zerubbabel (Ezra 2:55; KJV "Sophereth"; 1 Esdr. 5:33; KJV "Azaphion"). See SOPHERETH.

HASUPHA [hə sōō'fə] (Heb. *hᵃśûpā'*, *hᵃśupā'*). A temple servant whose descendants returned from the Exile with Zerubbabel (Ezra 2:43; Neh. 7:46; KJV "Hashupha; 1 Esdr. 5:29; KJV "Asipha").

HATE (Heb. *śānē'*; Gk. *miséō*). Aversion or hostility. Biblical usage represents a broad range of nuances from intense malice to simple disregard as expressed between individuals and groups and between God and mankind.

According to the Old Testament, hatred may stem from wickedness (Ps. 26:5), ill will (25:19), apostasy (101:3), or political differences (Dan. 4:19 [MT 16]). The wicked hate those who are righteous (Prov. 29:10), just as the righteous hate those who sin (e.g., Ps. 119:113, 163). In its most intense expression, hatred connotes deliberation and intent (Num. 35:20; cf. Deut. 4:42; 19:4ff.; RSV "enmity"). Elsewhere it may indicate the existence of a grudge (Gen. 27:41) or merely rejection or repulsion (Judg. 11:7; 2 Sam. 13:22). With regard to husbands and wives, hate indicates the dissolution (or perhaps a diminution or restriction; cf. Gen. 29:31; Deut. 21:15) of the marriage bond (KJV, 22:13, 16; RSV "spurns"; 24:3; RSV "dislikes"). It is with regard to such a covenantal relationship that hatred is proscribed as a threat to the stability of the community of believers (Lev. 19:17). Hatred between God and mankind, in particular, focuses on the covenant. To "hate" God means to reject or break the covenant relationship with God (e.g., Exod. 20:5; Deut. 5:9; Ps. 68:2 [MT 2]). Accordingly, God hates behavior which is not conducive to the covenant (e.g., Deut. 16:22; Prov. 6:16-19; Isa. 1:14; Amos 5:21).

The New Testament also exhibits a variety of interpretations of hatred. Covenantal ties are implicit in Jesus' instructions that a disciple must "hate" his family and even his own life (Luke 14:26), thereby subordinating all to Christ. Likewise, one cannot serve two masters, for he will naturally subordinate one to the other (Matt. 6:24; cf. Rom. 7:15). Because Christ was the corporeal and apprehensible manifestation of the "light" of God's love, one must consciously and without compromise eschew the "darkness" of sin and the resultant disruption of relationship to both God and one's fellows (e.g., John 3:20-21).

HATHACH [hā'thăk] (Heb. *hᵃtāk*). A eunuch belonging to the Persian king Ahasuerus, appointed to attend Queen Esther; it was through him that she learned from Mordecai about Haman's plot against the Jews (Esth. 4:5-6, 9-10; KJV "Hatach").

HATHATH [hā'thăth] (Heb. *hᵃtat*). A son of Othniel (1 Chr. 4:13).

HATIPHA [hə tī'fə] (Heb. *hᵃtîpā'* "captive"). A temple servant whose descendants returned from the Exile with Zerubbabel (Ezra 2:54; Neh. 7:56; 1 Esdr. 5:32; KJV "Atipha").

HATITA [hə tī'tə] (Heb. *ḥ°ṭîṭā'*). A levitical gatekeeper whose descendants returned with Zerubbabel from the Exile (Ezra 2:42; Neh. 7:45; 1 Esdr. 5:28; KJV "Teta").

HATTIL [hăt'əl] (Heb. *ḥaṭṭîl*). A family of "servants of Solomon" whose descendants returned from the Exile with Zerubbabel (Ezra 2:57; Neh. 7:59; 1 Esdr. 5:34; KJV "Hagia").

HATTUSH [hăt'ŭsh] (Heb. *ḥaṭṭûš*).
1. A son of Shemaiah and grandson of Shecaniah (1 Chr. 3:22); a postexilic descendant of David who returned from the Exile with Ezra (Ezra 8:2; 1 Esdr. 8:20; KJV "Lettus"; here called a "son" of Shecaniah).
2. The son of Hashabneiah who repaired a portion of the walls of Jerusalem (Neh. 3:10).
3. A priest who returned from exile with Zerubbabel (Neh. 12:2). He may be the same Hattush as the priest who set his seal to the renewed covenant under Nehemiah (10:4).

HAURAN [hôr'ən] (Heb. *ḥawrān* "hollow [or crater] district").† A district in Transjordan east of the Sea of Galilee and north of the Yarmuk river. In Ezekiel's vision of the restored land it marks the ideal northern and eastern limits of Israel (Ezek. 47:16, 18). Roughly coterminous with the region of Bashan, Hauran was bordered on the east by the slopes of Jebel ed-Druze (Akk. *šadê* *ᵐᵃᵗHa-ú-ra-ni;* Lat. *mons Alsadomus;* P. C. Craigie, *Deuteronomy,* NICOT [1976], p. 119, "Mount Hauran"; cf. Ps. 68:14-15), which reaches a height of some 1830 m. (6000 ft.). The district is characterized by fertile lava soil, which in Hellenistic and Roman times made it the breadbasket of Palestine.

Attested as early as the Egyptian Nineteenth Dynasty (thirteenth century B.C.; Egyp. *Ḥuruna*), Hauran came under control of Aramean Damascus at the time of the Israelite divided monarchy. The Assyrian Shalmaneser III records a victory there in 842 (*ANET*, p. 280), and Assurbanipal (668-*ca.* 626) suppressed a revolt in the district during his ninth campaign (p. 298). During the fourth century the area was populated by Jews, Greeks, and Nabateans, among whom control shifted frequently. It was conquered by the Maccabeans in the second century, but Alexander Janneus lost it to the Nabateans in 90 B.C. Pompey incorporated the province, then known as Auranitis, into the Decapolis. Augustus entrusted it to Herod the Great (*ca.* 23 B.C.); and after the death of the tetrarch Herod Philip, Caligula gave it to Herod Agrippa I (A.D. 37). Following the war against Rome (85), Hauran came again under Nabatean rule, but in 106 Trajan made it part of the Roman province of Syria.

HAVILAH [hăv'ə lə] (Heb. *ḥ°wîlâ* "a stretch of sand," from *ḥôl* "sand").†
1. A son of Cush and grandson of Ham (Gen. 10:7; 1 Chr. 1:9).
2. A son of Joktan and descendant of Shem (Gen. 10:29; 1 Chr. 1:29).

3. A land through which the PISHON river flows, abundant in fine gold, bdellium, and onyx (Gen. 2:11-12). Although the river has been variously located, its identification with the Wâdī el-Dhawasir would favor placing Havilah on the western coast of Arabia, north of Yemen (cf. Sab. *Haulan*); in the Table of Nations (Gen. 10), if the genealogies are read as geographical designations, Havilah is associated with Arabian place names (vv. 7, 29 par. 1 Chr. 1:9, 29; see 1 and 2 above). It was apparently the eastern limit of the Ishmaelite territory (Gen. 25:18; NJV "Havilah, by Shur, which is close to Egypt"; B. Vawter, *On Genesis* [Garden City: 1977], p. 281, "Havilah-by-Shur"); according to some scholars, this reference denotes a different locality, perhaps farther north on the Arabian peninsula or along the Persian Gulf (cf. Strabo *Geog.* xvi.4.2). 1 Sam. 15:7 records, in similar language, Saul's pursuit of the Amalekites; some would favor reading here "Hachilah" (1 Sam. 23:19; 26:1, 3; cf. P. K. McCarter, Jr., *I Samuel.* AB (1980), pp. 258, 261 "from the Wadi," Heb. *mnḥl*).

HAVVOTH-JAIR [hăv'ŏth jā'ər] (Heb. *ḥawwŏt yā'îr* "the tent-villages of Jair").† A group of villages in Argob, a district of Bashan (Deut. 3:4, 14; KJV "Bashan-havoth-jair"), and Gilead (Num. 32:40-41; Judg. 10:4; KJV "Havoth-jair"; cf. 1 Kgs. 4:13), captured by Jair and thus renamed (Num. 32:41; Deut. 3:14; Judg. 10:4; cf. Josh. 13:30, "towns of Jair"; P. C. Craigie, *Deuteronomy.* NICOT (1976), p. 122 n.5, "house" or "realm" of Jair, Ugar. *ḥwt*). The number of villages varies (sixty, Deut. 3:4; Josh. 13:30; cf. 1 Kgs. 4:13; thirty, Judg. 10:4; LXX "thirty-two"; twenty-three, 1 Chr. 2:22), perhaps reflecting different phases of political alliances (cf. R. G. Boling, *Judges.* AB [1975], pp. 186-88; a similar understanding may explain the seemingly incongruous affiliations of Jair (*see* JAIR 1). At the time of the divided monarchy those villages in Gilead were captured by Geshur and Aram (1 Chr. 2:22-23).

HAWK (Heb. *nēṣ*).† Any of various species of diurnal birds of prey belonging to the families Accipitridae and Falconidae. Several species have been attested in Palestine, most commonly the sparrow hawk *(Accipiter nisus)*, marsh harrier *(Circus aeruginosus)*, and hen harrier *(Circus cyaneus)*, nesting and breeding in the northern Palestinian hills around Galilee and Mt. Carmel and wintering in the Jordan valley near the Dead Sea and in the region of Beer-sheba. They build crude nests of twigs in large trees or on mountain crags, and feed on smaller birds and poultry, reptiles, insects, and small mammals; accordingly, the Israelites regarded them as unclean (Lev. 11:16; Deut. 14:15; given the uncertainty of Hebrew terminology and classification, several species of hawk may be included in the lists of Lev. 11:13-19; Deut. 14:11-18). The soaring flight of these birds is noted at Job 39:26).

After Yahweh's day of vengeance, Edom is to become the haunt of various creatures, including hawks (Isa. 34:11, RSV; Heb. *qā'aṭ*; KJV "cormorant"; JB "pelican"; NIV "desert owl"; NJV "jackdaws").

HAZAEL [hā'zǐ əl] (Heb. *ḥ°zâ'ēl, ḥ°zā'ēl;* Akk. *Haza'ilu* "God sees"). King of Damascus (*ca.* 843-

ca. 798 B.C.). A commoner in the service of the royal court, Hazael usurped the throne of Damascus and became a powerful ruler, withstanding Assyrian aggression and antagonizing both Israel and Judah (cf. 2 Kgs. 13:3; Amos 1:3-5).

Sent by Ben-hadad II (or a coregent Ben-hadad III) to inquire of Elisha concerning the king's infirmities (2 Kgs. 8:7-9), the prophet informed Hazael that the messenger would himself succeed the ailing ruler and come to inflict evil on the Israelites (vv. 10-13); feeling himself commissioned by Elisha (cf. 1 Kgs. 19:15-16), Hazael returned home, murdered the king, and seized power (2 Kgs. 8:15). Shortly thereafter he engaged the coalition of Jehoram of Israel and Ahaziah of Judah at Ramoth-gilead, forcing the wounded Jehoram's flight to Jezreel, where he was slain by his general Jehu (vv. 28-29; 9:14-26).

Unaided by any ally, Hazael retained Damascus against the assault of the Assyrian Shalmaneser III in 841 despite heavy losses of surrounding territory. Shalmaneser inflicted further damage in central Syria *ca*. 837, but again Hazael held firm, causing the Assyrian to forsake further efforts against Damascus. Hazael was thus able to focus attention on Palestine, where he captured all of Jehu's territory in Transjordan (20:32-33); subsequently he decimated Jehoahaz's forces and so barraged Israel that the Syrians were able to move at will through the land (cf. 13:4-7, 22). He gained control of Gath and the important trade routes in Philistia (12:17) but was dissuaded from taking Jerusalem by the Judahite king Joash, who offered treasures from the temple and the royal palace (v. 18; cf. 2 Chr. 24:23-24).

Hazael died *ca*. 798, and was succeeded by his son, Ben-hadad III (or IV; *see* BEN-HADAD 3; 2 Kgs. 13:24). More than eight centuries later Hazael's role in building Damascus was noted by Josephus (*Ant.* ix.4.6 [93]). An ivory couch inscribed as belonging to "our lord Hazael" was discovered at modern Arslan Tash, site of the Assyrian provincial capital Ḥadâtu, and may have been among loot seized in the raids of Adadnirari III (cf. *ANET*, pp. 281-82).

HAZAIAH [hə zā′yə] (Heb. *ḥᵃzāyâ* "Yahweh has seen"). An ancestor of the Judahite leader Maaseiah, who lived in postexilic Jerusalem (Neh. 11:5).

HAZAR-ADDAR [hā′zər ăd′ər] (Heb. *ḥᵃṣar-'addār* "strong village [or enclosure]").† A place on the southern border of Canaan (Num. 34:4), toward Edom. Listed between Kadesh-barnea and Azmon, it is apparently the same as Hezron in the account of Judah's southern boundary (Josh. 15:3; the parenthetical reference to Addar here [KJV "Adar"] suggests either that the name was no longer recognized as a compound or that two sites were combined in the Numbers passage). Location of this settlement remains uncertain; Khirbet el-Qudeirât, 11 km. [7 mi.] northwest of Kadesh-barnea and the site of an important stronghold during the Monarchy, has been suggested.

HAZAR-ENAN [hā′zər ē′nən] (Heb. *ḥᵃṣar ʿēnān* "village of the spring"). The northeastern point of the ideal boundaries of Palestine (Num. 34:9-10); called

Hazar-enon (Heb. *ḥᵃṣar ʿēnôn*) at Ezek. 47:17-18; 48:1). Ezek. 48:1 places it on the northern boundary of Damascus "over against Hamath" (NJV "with Hamath to the north"). The probable site is modern Qaryatein, a large village with a deep spring about 112 km. (70 mi.) northeast of Damascus toward Palmyra.

HAZAR-GADDAH [hā′zər găd′ə] (Heb. *ḥᵃṣar gaddâ* "village of Gad [or fortune]"). A city in the Negeb region of Judah (Josh. 15:27), near Beer-sheba. Its precise location has not been determined, although Khirbet Ghazza, southwest of Râs Zuweira, has been suggested.

HAZARMAVETH [hā′zər mā′vĭth] (Heb. *ḥᵃṣar-māwet* "village of death [or Mot]").† A son of Joktan and descendant of Shem (Gen. 10:26; 1 Chr. 1:20). Included in a series of place names in the Table of Nations, it has been identified with Hadramaut, a district in the southern Arabian peninsula corresponding to the eastern portion of the modern Aden protectorate; this ancient state, with its capital at Shabwah (Sabteca), became rich and powerful through control of the frankincense trade.

HAZAR-SHUAL [hā′zər shoo′əl] (Heb. *ḥᵃṣar šûʿāl* "village of the fox"). A town in the Negeb assigned to Simeon (Josh. 19:3; 1 Chr. 4:28), always mentioned in association with Beer-sheba; at Josh. 15:28 it is listed among the allotment of Judah (cf. 19:9). It was resettled following the Exile (Neh. 11:27). Although various sites have been proposed, the location remains uncertain.

HAZAR-SUSAH [hā′zər soo′sə] (Heb. *ḥᵃṣar sûsâ* "horse enclosure"). A city in the Negeb assigned to Simeon (Josh. 19:5; 1 Chr. 4:31, "Hazar-susim"; Heb. *ḥaṣar sûsîm*), possibly a commercial or military installation (e.g., 1 Kgs. 4:26; 9:19; 2 Chr. 8:6; cf. Beth-marcaboth "house of chariots"). It may have been Sbalat Abū Susein, 32 km. (20 mi.) west of Beer-sheba.

HAZAZON-TAMAR [hăz′ə zŏn tā′mər] (Heb. *ḥaṣᵉṣōn tāmār*, possibly "sandy stretch with palms"). An Amorite city conquered by Chedorlaomer and his coalition (Gen. 14:7). At 2 Chr. 20:2 it is identified with En-gedi on the western shore of the Dead Sea; the name may be preserved in modern Wadī el-Ḥaṣāṣa, an oasis slightly northwest of ʿAin Jidi. It may also be the same as Tamar, a city in southeastern Judah rebuilt by Solomon (1 Kgs. 9:18; cf. Ezek. 47:19; 48:28).

HAZER-HATTICON [hā′zər hăt′ə kŏn] (Heb. *ḥᵃṣēr hattîḵôn* "middle village [or enclosure]"). A place at the northern limits of the ideal Israel, on the border of Hauran (Ezek. 47:16; KJV "Hazar-hatticon"). It may be the same as Hazar-enon in v. 17.

HAZERIM [hə zĭr′ĭm] (Heb. *ḥᵃṣērîm* "villages").* Unwalled settlements (cf. Lev. 25:31) in southwestern Palestine, inhabited by the Avvim (Deut. 2:23, RSV, NIV; JB "encampments"; cf. Neh. 11:25). The KJV translates the Hebrew term as a place name.

HAZEROTH [hə zĭr'ŏth] (Heb. *ḥᵃṣērôṯ* "settlements"). A place where the Israelites stopped during the wilderness journey. While here, Miriam and Aaron turned against Moses, for which Miriam was punished with leprosy (Num. 11:35; 12:1-10, 15-16; 33:17-18). Hazeroth may have been located at modern 'Ain Ḥaḍrā, an area of springs in the northeastern part of the Sinai peninsula, 48 km. (30 mi.) northeast of the traditional site of Mt. Sinai (Jebel Mûsā).

HAZIEL [hā'zĭ əl] (Heb. *ḥᵃzî'ēl* "vision of God"). A Levite; a descendant of Gershom and son of Shimei (1 Chr. 23:9).

HAZO [hā'zō] (Heb. *ḥᵃzô* "vision"). A son of Nahor and Milcah (Gen. 22:22). The term may represent a clan or other subgroup associated with Hazu, a region in the vicinity of Hauran mentioned in inscriptions of the Assyrian king Esarhaddon.

HAZOR [hā'zôr, hŏt'zôr] (Heb. *ḥāṣôr* "enclosure"). †
1. A major city in Upper Galilee, identified as modern Tell el-Qedaḥ (also called Tell el-Waqqâṣ), 14 km. (8.7 mi.) north of the Sea of Galilee and 8 km. (5 mi.) south of Lake Huleh. Strategically situated on the plain of Huleh where it controlled the Way of the Sea (the major trade route connecting Egypt with Syria and Anatolia to the north and Mesopotamia to the east), Hazor became the largest Canaanite city in the second millennium B.C.

First mentioned in the nineteenth-century Egyptian Execration Texts (Egyp. *ḥḏw3i*), Hazor appears as an important commercial center in the Mari correspondence (eighteenth century). It is named among those cities conquered by the pharaohs Thutmose III (1490-1436), Amenhotep II (1438-1412), and Seti I (*ca.* 1301-1287). In the Amarna Letters the king of Hazor affirms his loyalty to Egypt despite charges of aggression against cities in Bashan and Tyre and the claim that he had joined the 'Apiru (EA 148). Having become a dominant political force in the Middle Bronze Age (cf. Josh. 11:10), Hazor, headed by its King Jabin, during the early stages of the Israelite conquest of Canaan formed a coalition to ward off the Hebrew onslaught (11:1-5); Joshua decisively defeated the Canaanite allies by the waters of Merom and, singling out the city for having led the opposition, burned Hazor (vv. 6-14). The Israelite success was not enduring, however, and under the Confederation the judge Deborah suppressed a revolt by another king of that city, also called Jabin, and his general Sisera (Judg. 4:2-24; 5:19-20). Subsequently Hazor was allotted to the tribe of Naphtali (Josh. 19:36). Solomon rebuilt and fortified the city as a garrison for the plain of Huleh (1 Kgs. 9:15). Its prominence ended with the conquest by the Assyrian Tiglath-pileser III in 732 (2 Kgs. 15:29). During the Maccabean conflict Jonathan was ambushed on the plain of Hazor by Demetrius I Soter but gained a substantial victory (1 Macc. 11:67-74; Josephus *Ant.* xiii.5.7; Gk. *Asōr*).

Excavations at Tell el-Qedaḥ, a large mound 40 m. (131 ft.) high and covering some 12 ha. (30 acres), have discovered twenty-one distinct levels of occupation, the earliest dating to the twenty-seventh century (Early Bronze Age). Periodically abandoned, this unfortified settlement contained no substantial permanent structures until the eighteenth century (MB II), at which time a sudden increase in population necessitated the addition of a rectangular "enclosure" measuring some 72 ha. (178 acres) to the north of the mound. Identified in J. Garstang's preliminary explorations of 1928 as a military encampment, this area was fortified by ramparts of beaten earth, a deep fosse, and a Hyksos-style glacis; subsequent excavations by

Solomonic gate and casement walls at Hazor (L. T. Geraty)

Y. Yadin (1955-1958, 1968) identified this area as a "lower city," characterized by various dwellings and public buildings. Of particular interest is a temple, rebuilt in four phases, the latest of which (thirteenth century) strongly resembles Solomon's temple with entrance hall, main hall, and holy of holies, replete with numerous cultic vessels. During this period Hazor reached the apex of its prosperity and was the largest of the Canaanite cities, some ten times the size of Megiddo. Both the upper and lower cities were leveled in the late thirteenth century in conjunction with the Israelite conquest. Although the lower city never was rebuilt, the Israelites established a limited settlement in the upper city; among the remains, however, is an eleventh-century shrine ("high place") of a deity other than Yahweh. Extensive rebuilding, including massive walls and gates similar to those of Gezer and Megiddo, marks the tenth-century Solomonic city. Evidence of conflagration in the early ninth century points to the activity of the Syrian Benhadad II (cf. 1 Kgs. 15:20; 2 Chr. 16:4). Reconstruction of the city under the Omride dynasty, most likely by Ahab, included a citadel and a large pillared building; originally identified as one of Solomon's stables, it is now recognized as a storehouse. An underground water system, composed of an entrance building, a vertical shaft some 30 m. (98 ft.) deep, and a sloping tunnel, was constructed at the southern edge of Tell el-Qedaḥ. Buildings from the reign of Jeroboam II (786-746) are primarily commercial in nature; this level was apparently destroyed by earthquake (cf. Amos 1:1). Subsequently the city's fortifications were enhanced to meet the growing Assyrian threat. As evident from a layer of debris 1 m. (3.3 ft.) thick, Hazor was violently destroyed by the forces of Tiglath-pileser III. The city was never resettled as such, save for citadels at the western edge of the site during the Assyrian (seventh century), Persian (fourth century), and Hellenistic (second century B.C.) periods.

Bibliography. Y. Yadin, *Hazor* (London: 1972); *Hazor: The Rediscovery of a Great Citadel of the Bible* (New York: 1975).

2. A city in the Negeb assigned to Judah (Josh. 15:23). Following LXX B, some scholars read this as a compound with the name which follows, "Hazorithnan," which they identify with el-Jebarîyeh, a site on the Wâdī Umm Ethnān some 60 km. (37 mi.) southwest of Beer-sheba.

3. (Josh. 15:25, KJV). *See* HAZOR-HADATTAH.

4. A city in southern Judah, apparently earlier known as KERIOTH-HEZRON (Josh. 15:25) and identified with modern Khirbet el-Qaryatein, 7 km. (4.5 mi.) south of Maon. The KJV reads two separate names here.

5. A town resettled by the Benjaminites following the Exile (Neh. 11:33). It has been identified with modern Khirbet Hazzûr, 5 km. (3 mi.) northwest of Jerusalem.

6. An unidentified kingdom in the Arabian peninsula east of Palestine, defeated by Nebuchadnezzar in 598 B.C. (Jer. 49:28-33). It may have comprised a cluster of unwalled villages (Heb. *ḥāṣēr*).

HAZOR-HADATTAH [hā'zôr hə dăt'ə] (Heb. *ḥᵃṣôr*

ḥᵃdattâ "new enclosure [or Hasor]"). A town in the Negeb region of Judah, toward Edom (Josh. 15:25; KJV "Hadattah"). The site may have been modern el-Hudeira, 9.6 km. (6 mi.) southeast of Maon.

HAZZELELPONI [hăz'ə lĕl pō'nī] (Heb. *haṣṣᵉlelpônî*). A woman of Judah from the town of Etam, designated as the sister of the "sons of Etam" (1 Chr. 4:3).

HEAD (Heb. *rō'š*; Gk. *kephalé*).† In literal usage, the uppermost division of the body, both of humans (e.g., Gen. 49:16; Matt. 5:36) and of animals (e.g., Lev. 3:8; 2 Kgs. 6:25). By extension, the term also designates the top portion of inanimate objects (e.g., 1 Sam. 5:4; Ps. 24:7, 9).

To the ancient Hebrews, the heart rather than the head was the seat of the intellect and imagination (but cf. Dan. 2:28; 4:5, 10, 13). Yet in many ways the head is portrayed as the focus or symbol of human identity, as demonstrated by such gestures as bowing one's head in submission (John 19:30) or lifting it in pride (e.g., Judg. 8:28; Ps. 140:9 [MT 10]); guilt for one's misdeeds returns upon his head (e.g., Josh. 2:19; Esth. 9:25; Acts 18:6). Paul upheld the contemporary convention whereby men were to pray or prophesy with their heads covered and women with theirs uncovered (1 Cor. 11:2-16).

Applied metaphorically, the term refers to a prominent person, one of honor or authority who ranks above (i.e., "at the head of") a family or community (e.g., Exod. 6:14, 25; Deut. 3:28; Isa. 7:8-9). Elsewhere it indicates a source or point of origin (e.g., Ezek. 16:25; cf. Exod. 12:2; Judg. 7:19; RSV "beginning"), a meaning particularly frequent in Hellenistic and gnostic sources. Paul presents Christ as the head of the Church, which is his body (Eph. 1:22-23; Col. 1:18). According to Col. 2:19, Christ is the source from which the Church is nourished and "grows with a growth that is from God." Interpreters differ, however, as to whether Paul implies a hierarchy of authority in the order God-Christ-man-woman (1 Cor. 11:3) or simply portrays the order of creation (i.e., "head" as source); according to the latter view, man and woman are interdependent, with man the initial cause of woman and woman the instrumental cause of woman.

Bibliography. M. Barth, *Ephesians 4-6.* AB (1974).

HEADDRESS (Heb. *pᵉ'ēr*). A type of head covering, perhaps practical as well as ornamental (Isa. 3:20; KJV "bonnet"). The Hebrew term designates also the turban (Ezek. 24:17, 23), the garland worn by the bridegroom (Isa. 61:3), and the linen cap worn by the priests (Exod. 39:28; Ezek. 44:18).

HEALING (Heb. *marpē*, from *rāpā'* "heal"; Gk. *therapeía*).* The restoration to a sound physical or psychological state or to the greatest degree of health (Heb. *šālōm* "completeness, welfare") possible given such limits as age and dismemberment. The process might involve regeneration as well as restoration, which included rectification of a sinful condition for which disease was often considered divine punishment (Ps. 38:3; cf. Isa. 38:10-20).

Ultimately, God is the source of healing (e.g., Gen. 20:17; Exod. 15:16). Healing might be effected through prophets who acted as God's agents (e.g., 2 Kgs. 5:3-14; 2 Kgs. 20:1-7 par. Isa. 38) as well as purification rituals performed by priests (cf. Lev. 15). By the Hellenistic period professional physicians had gained a prominent role, relying on magic and superstition as much as actual medical treatment (cf. Sir. 38:1-15).

As part of his ministry of restoring humanity to wholeness, Jesus healed a variety of physical and psychological ailments (e.g., Luke 7:21-22; cf. 4:18). Although in some instances a demonstration of faith was a necessary condition for healing (e.g., Matt. 9:21-22, 28-29; Luke 17:19), it does not always appear to have been a prerequisite (cf. Mark 1:31; Luke 22:51). The apostles also were entrusted with the ministry of healing (Matt. 10:1; cf. Acts 3:6-7, 16; 8:7; 9:12), and many in the early Church exhibited gifts of healing (e.g., 1 Cor. 12:10, 28).

See DISEASE; see also the individual entries on specific diseases.

HEART (Heb. *lēḇ, lēḇāḇ;* Gk. *kardía*). In general usage, the core of the person. The term has a wide range of applications which include physical being, personality, emotions, intellect, will, and relationship with God.

The Old Testament refers to the heart no fewer than 854 times by the Hebrew terms *lēḇ* and *lēḇāḇ*, and once by *libbâ* (Ezek. 16:30). Usually there is no appreciable difference in meaning between the first two words, the choice between them often being determined, evidently, for stylistic or emotional reasons. The linguistic roots of the terms are obscure. Heb. *lēḇ* may be related to a verb which means "to press flat." If so, the approximate meaning of heart could be "fixed point" or "core."

In the great majority of cases the Hebrew words refer to the human heart. Only three texts refer to the heart of an animal (2 Sam. 17:10; Job 41:24; Dan. 5:21; KJV "heart"; RSV "mind"), where heart does not refer to the bodily organ but rather to what typifies or characterizes the animal. This is especially clear in Job 41:24 where the skin of the Leviathan, and not its literal heart, is as hard as stone. Heart is also used twenty-six times in reference to Yahweh, and again that which is typical or representative of him is the primary meaning.

The word heart occurs only a few times in the Old Testament in reference to the physical organ or to a particular region of the body such as the breast (Exod. 28:29-30; 1 Sam. 25:37; 2 Sam. 18:14; 2 Kgs. 9:24; Ps. 37:15; 38:10; 45:5; Cant. 8:6; Hos. 13:8; KJV "heart"; RSV "breast"; Nah. 2:7; KJV, RSV "breasts," following MT), and even in some of these verses it indicates more than the bodily organ alone. The explanation of this apparent ambiguity lies in the fact that Hebrew thought forms were concrete rather than abstract; the Hebrew mind naturally expressed inward psychological or religious states by speaking of the condition of the heart. Such biblical uses of heart include references to emotions, intellectual activity, volition and morality, and spiritual condition. In the realm of emotions, the heart may be hateful

(Lev. 19:17) or loving (Deut. 13:3), courageous or fearful (2 Sam. 17:10; Isa. 35:4), sad (Neh. 2:2) or glad (Prov. 27:11), envious (23:17) or trustful (31:11). Many passages employ heart with reference to thought or intellectual activity (Judg. 5:16; 1 Chr. 29:18; Ps. 4:4; 10:6; Mark 2:6; Luke 1:66; 2:19; KJV, Gen. 27:41). The heart's connection with thinking in Hebrew thought is so close that modern translations such as the RSV frequently translate *lēḇ* or *lēḇāḇ* by "mind" or "understanding" (Job 12:3; Prov. 16:9; Jer. 7:31). Similarly, the heart is the seat of the will and thus the source of good or evil qualities or behavior (Deut. 8:14; Prov. 6:18; 11:20, KJV; RSV "mind"). Generally the Bible characterizes the human heart as full of evil (Gen. 8:21), deceitful and corrupt (Jer. 17:9), and in need of transformation through God's grace (Ps. 51:10; Ezek. 36:26).

In more than three hundred cases where the word refers to the human heart it has a spiritual significance and refers to a person's relationship with God. This does not mean that in its religious sense the heart has no relationship to a person's thoughts, intentions, and feelings, but rather that these are motivated and driven by the heart, which is the religious point of departure for all of human life. The religious use of heart in the Old Testament, however, expresses not only directedness toward God, but often also appears in the context of turning away from him (e.g., Deut. 8:14, 17; 9:4; 2 Chr. 26:16, KJV; Isa. 9:9; 10:12, KJV; 47:8; Ezek. 31:10; Hos. 13:6; Obad. 3). As the source of virtually every manifestation of human religion and as that point in the person to which the revelation of God is ultimately directed, the human heart forms the focal point of God's dealings with the person.

This Old Testament meaning of heart is continued in the New Testament, particularly the Gospels (Matt. 6:21; 15:18-19; 22:37; Luke 6:45; John 14:1, 27) and the letters of Paul. As in the Old Testament, the New Testament word for heart (Gk. *kardía*) can indicate a person's mind, will, and feelings, but Paul's use of the term in reference to the spiritual or religious quality of human life expresses the idea that all of these facets of personhood are spiritually determined (cf. 2 Cor. 3:14ff., KJV; RSV "mind"; Phil. 4:7). Paul explicitly declares the connection between the heart and God, saying that God's revelation bears witness to or within the human heart as the true center of human existence (cf. Rom. 2:14ff.). Just as the heart or core of a person's being is the recipient of divine revelation, so it is the subject of the response, positive or negative, one makes to God. With the heart one believes (Rom. 10:10), desires (1:24), obeys (6:17), and performs the will of God (Eph. 6:6). The redeemed heart is the dwelling place of Christ (3:17) and of his peace (Col. 3:15) and love (Rom. 5:5).

The use of the word heart in all of these contexts suggests that on the deepest level human beings are guided and determined from one central point which represents their true humanity, the heart. This is true both of their response to the revelation of God and of their responsibility for their own thinking, willing, and acting.

HEARTH (Heb. *môqᵉḏâ, harʾēl, ʾᵃriʾēl*).* In its basic sense, a depression in the ground in which was built a fire for cooking or heating. In cultic usage the hearth was the upper portion of the altar of burnt offering upon which the sacrifice was burned (Lev. 6:9; Ezek. 43:15-16). At Ezek. 46:23-24 the hearths in Ezekiel's ideal temple are used for boiling sacrifices.

HEAVEN (Heb. *šāmayim;* Gk. *ouranós*).

According to the threefold Semitic worldview, heaven was the firmament, a tentlike vault (cf. Isa. 40:22; Ps. 104:2) supported by pillars (Job 26:11) and separating the subterranean waters from those above (Gen. 1:6-8). From this canopy were suspended the planets and stars (vv. 14-17), and through its windows were dispensed various forms of precipitation (e.g., Gen. 7:11; Josh. 10:11; cf. Job 38:22, 29). At times the term simply denotes the sky (e.g., Ps. 147:8). As in Akkadian, the expression "heaven and earth" refers to everything that exists, the universe in its totality (e.g., Gen. 1:1; Matt. 5:18; Acts 7:24). Although later Judaism envisioned as many as seven strata of heaven (e.g., Test. Levi 2:7-3:9; Asc. Isa. 6:13; 7:13ff.; cf. 2 Cor. 12:2), the plural form of the Hebrew term as well as the occasional use of the Greek plural (e.g., Matt. 3:16; 24:29; 2 Cor. 5:1; Eph. 4:10) and the Hebrew expression "heaven of heavens" (e.g., Deut. 10:14; Neh. 9:6; cf. 1 Kgs. 8:27 par. 2 Chr. 6:18; Ps. 148:4; RSV "highest heaven") represent merely a superlative or intensified application of the name.

Heaven is the dwelling place of God (e.g., Jonah 1:9; Matt. 5:16, 45; 6:1, 9), the site of his throne (Ps. 11:4; Isa. 66:1) from which he looks down upon human affairs (Ps. 14:2; 33:13) and issues his ordinances (Deut. 4:36; Neh. 9:13; cf. Ps. 2:4). The Israelite tabernacle and temple were held to be patterned after this divine abode (Heb. 8:5; 9:24). God is accompanied in heaven by his angels, who execute his commands (Gen. 21:17; 22:11; Matt. 18:10), and here the heavenly tribunal holds forth (1 Kgs. 22:19-22; Job 1:6ff.; 2:1ff.; Zech. 3:1-2).

At the incarnation Jesus descended from heaven to earth (John 3:13; cf. 1:2), and after completing his ministry of redemption he returned there (Acts 1:11), to return at the end of time (Matt. 24:30; 1 Thess. 1:10).

The concept of heaven as a place of reward for the faithful is rare in the Old Testament (Elijah, 2 Kgs. 2:11; cf. Gen. 5:24; Ps. 72:24). In Christian interpretation it becomes the believer's inheritance (1 Pet. 1:4), an abode provided by God (2 Cor. 5:1-5; cf. John 14:2; Phil. 3:20) as a reward for faithful service (Matt. 5:12; 6:20; cf. Col. 1:5).

Heaven itself is to experience the turmoil of the final days (e.g., Hag. 2:6; Mark 13:31; Rev. 12:7-12), giving way to the creation of a new order, a "new heaven and a new earth" (Isa. 65:17; 66:22; 2 Pet. 3:13; Rev. 21:1).

As Jewish reverence for the divine name increased, "heaven" was employed occasionally as a substitute (Dan. 4:23 [MT 20]; Mark 11:30; Luke 15:18, 21; John 3:27). This may account for Matthew's use of the expression "kingdom of heaven" (e.g., Matt. 3:2) as the equivalent of the "kingdom of God" in Mark and Luke.

Bibliography. W. M. Smith, *The Biblical Doctrine of Heaven* (Chicago: 1968).

HEBER [hē'bər] (Heb. *ḥeḇer* "companion, associate").

1. A son of Beriah and descendant of Asher (Gen. 46:17; 1 Chr. 7:31-32). He is the eponymous ancestor of the Heberites. (Heb. *ḥeḇrî;* Num. 26:45) and thus, according to some scholars, also of the Habiru 'Apiru) or the Hebrews.

2. A Kenite, descended from Hobab. He had separated from the main body of Kenites, settling near Kedesh (Judg. 4:11); it was there that his wife, Jael, murdered Sisera by driving a tent peg through his temple as he slept (vv. 12-24).

3. A descendant of the Judahite Ezrah and his Jewish wife (1 Chr. 4:18); the ancestor or founder of Soco.

4. A Benjaminite, the son of Elpaal (1 Chr. 8:17).

5. (Luke 3:35, KJV). *See* EBER 1.

HEBREW (LANGUAGE).† The language of the Hebrew people, and the primary language of the Old Testament. A Northwest Semitic language and a dialect of Canaanite, it is called in the Old Testament the "language (lit. lip) of Canaan" (Heb. *śᵉp̄aṯ kᵉnaʿan;* Isa. 19:18) or "Judahite" (*yᵉhûḏît;* RSV "the language of Judah"; 2 Kgs. 18:26, 28; Neh. 13:24; Isa. 36:11, 13). The designation "Hebrew" is first attested in the prologue to Sirach (cf. Josephus *Ant.* x.8). In the New Testament, Gk. *Hebraís* (thus Lat. *Hebraeus*) refers to that dialect of Palestinian Aramaic spoken in the first-second centuries A.D. (e.g., John 5:2; 19:13, 17, 20; Acts 21:40; Rev. 9:11).

Biblical Hebrew developed from Canaanite as a separate dialect during the early centuries of the second millennium B.C. On the basis of biblical tradition, which identifies the core of the Hebrew people as of Aramean origin (cf. Deut. 26:5), these newcomers apparently at that time borrowed the language from their Canaanite predecessors in Palestine. Although preserved primarily in the Old Testament writings, Biblical Hebrew is known also from various inscriptions (e.g., the eleventh-century ʿIzbet Ṣarṭah inscription, the late tenth-century Gezer calendar, and the Siloam inscription [*ca.* 705]), the Samaria Ostraca (*ca.* 770), the Lachish Letters (*ca.* 587), seals, and coins. In its present form the Old Testament is believed to represent a stage of the language as standardized during the Israelite Monarchy. Nevertheless, it contains material dating from the twelfth through second centuries B.C., including both ancient and archaizing poetry as well as later contributions whose style and vocabulary suggest Aramaic, Persian, and Greek influence; dialectal differences (cf. Judg. 12:6) and the possible use of explanatory glosses further point to the geographical and chronological diversity of Biblical Hebrew as a living language. During the postexilic period Hebrew was replaced by Aramaic as the spoken language (cf. Neh. 8:8; 13:24) but it continued as the literary and liturgical language, as evident from manuscripts such as Sirach and, especially, the Dead Sea Scrolls. Biblical Hebrew apparently fell into disuse following the successful revolts against Rome in the first-second centuries A.D.

Hebrew is an alphabetic language consisting of twenty-two consonants, some of which (called *begad-kepat:* beth, gimel, daleth, kaph, pe, taw) occur as both stops and spirants. Written from right to left, in its earliest stages it adopted the predominantly round, closed Phoenician script; this Paleohebrew writing was replaced during the Persian period by the square, open Aramaic alphabet familiar from modern printed texts. Although some fourteen vowel sounds have been distinguished, none were written in the earliest texts; rather, pronounciation was transmitted orally (thus a word written *qtl* might be pronounced *qatal, qatūl, qotēl, qᵉtōl, qittal,* or *quttal*). Beginning in the ninth century B.C. certain consonants were employed as *matres lectionis* ("mothers of reading") to indicate final vowels (he for ā or ō, waw for û, yodh for ī); by postexilic times waw (û or ô) and yodh (ê or î) were used also to indicate medial vowels and diphthongs. In the ninth-tenth centuries A.D. the Masoretes, rabbis of the school of Tiberias, developed a system of lines and points to "vocalize" the text, thus fixing the ancient vowel system as accurately as possible. Other symbols were devised to indicate stress and pause. Moreover, the letters of the Hebrew alphabet were assigned numerical values according to their sequence, prompting at various stages of Hebrew scholarship symbolic interpretations of names and expressions.

Numerous similarities occur between Biblical Hebrew and other Semitic languages, most notably the triconsonantal root for both verbs and nouns which may be modified by affixes or vowel inflection to indicate such factors as gender, number, tense, or relationship. Syllables begin with consonants and may be open (ending with a vowel) or closed (ending with a consonant); they may end but not begin with a cluster of two consonants. Hebrew verbs, nouns, and adjectives indicate gender (masculine and feminine) and number (singular, plural, and dual, which denotes paired entities); verbs also indicate person (speaker, one spoken to, and one spoken of). Seven verb stems express various aspects of action: qal, the simple or basic form; niphal, simple passive or reflexive; piel, intensive; pual, passive intensive; hiphil, causative; hophal, passive causative; and hithpael, reciprocal or intensive reflexive. Each stem occurs in the perfect (suffixing) and imperfect (prefixing) states, expressing complete or incomplete action respectively, as well as infinitives, participles, and the imperative state. Nouns may originate as such or as derivatives from verbal roots; the basic (or unmarked) form is generally the masculine singular, from which arise the feminine, plural, and dual forms. Case endings (e.g., nominative, genitive, and accusative) are absent from Biblical Hebrew, except perhaps in the most vestigial form in some archaic material. Possession is indicated by the construct (or bound) state of a noun (unstressed or inflected) in conjunction with pronominal suffixes or a modifying or restrictive (absolute) noun. Adjectives, either predicative or attributive, agree with the noun modified in gender and number. Prepositions may be independent words or particles prefixed to other words

as are conjunctions and interrogative pronouns. Normal syntax generally follows the order verb, subject, object, adverb or prepositional phrase; deviations, apart from the more flexible poetic style, are usually intended for emphasis. Obscure constructions as well as vocabulary may be enlightened by comparison with other Semitic languages, particularly Ugaritic and Phoenician.

Later forms of Hebrew include Mishnaic (or Rabbinic) Hebrew, a derivative of the colloquial Palestinian Hebrew of the Hellenistic and Roman periods refined as a scholastic language; it was the literary medium of the rabbinical academies and is preserved primarily in the Mishnah and other Tannaitic writings. During the Middle Ages attempts were made to imitate classical Hebrew as a literary language, with various degrees of success. In the tenth-fifteenth centuries A.D., particularly among Jews in the Iberian peninsula, Medieval Hebrew became the vehicle for exquisite poetry as well as philosophical and scientific literature; this language exhibits strong Arabic influence in vocabulary and syntax. Modern (Israeli) Hebrew developed as a conscious revival by nineteenth-twentieth century Zionists. Originally based upon Biblical as well as later stages of Hebrew, it has become a living language strongly influenced by Western technological society and thus often differs vastly from the classical Hebrew of the Bible.

Bibliography. W. Gesenius, E. Kautzsch, and A. E. Cowley, *Hebrew Grammar* (Oxford: 1910); A. Sperber, *A Historical Grammar of Biblical Hebrew* (Leiden: 1966).

HEBREW (Heb. *ʿiḇrî;* Gk. *Hebraios*) (**PEOPLE**).† A gentilic term referring to the Israelite people and their ancestors. It occurs primarily as an ethnic or political designation (e.g., Gen. 43:32; Exod. 2:11, 13) applied to the Israelites by foreigners (e.g., by Egyptians, Gen. 39:14, 17; Exod. 1:16-19; by Philistines, 1 Sam. 4:6, 9) or by Israelites themselves when addressing non-Israelites (e.g., Gen. 40:15; Jonah 1:9). By the monarchic period it had been superseded largely by the expression "people of Israel" (Heb. *bᵉnê yiśrāʾēl* "sons of Israel"; KJV "children of Israel"). In the New Testament "Hebrew" refers to Jewish people in both Palestine and the Diaspora (Acts 6:1; Phil. 3:5).

According to the Table of Nations, the Hebrews are descended from an eponymous ancestor, EBER 1 (Heb. *ʿēḇer;* cf. Eb. *Ibrûm, Ibrium*), a descendant of Shem and ancestor of several peoples (Gen. 10:21-31; 11:14-26; 1 Chr. 1:17-27); thus the term might be seen to include not only the descendants of Abraham but also those of Nahor (the Arameans) and Lot (Moabites and Ammonites). Standard interpretation favors restricting the term to Abraham and his family, perhaps as a derivative of Heb. *ʿēḇer* "opposite side, region beyond" applied by the indigenous population of Canaan to those who had come from beyond the Euphrates. This same root (*ʿbr*) may also indicate one who had "crossed a boundary," which would favor an identification of the Hebrews with the HABIRU [ʿApIRU]), an ethnically diverse social class comprised of dissident and disenfranchised peoples who lived on the fringes of Bronze Age society. Abraham and his family may have been considered part of this movement (Gen. 14:13; LXX Gk. *perátēs* "outlander"). The freebooter status of the Habiru may explain the distinction between Hebrews and Israelites at 1 Sam. 14:21.

HEBREWS, GOSPEL ACCORDING TO THE.†

An apocryphal Greek gospel which originated among Jewish Christians in Egypt during the late first-early second centuries A.D. Although it may have approximated in length the gospel of Matthew (cf. Nicephorus *Stich.*), the work now survives only in fragments quoted by Clement of Alexandria, Origen, and Cyril; it is attested also by Hegesippus, Eusebius, and possibly Papias. Jerome claims to have translated the book into Greek and Latin from an Aramaic original, but his citations from the work were probably borrowed from Origen; moreover, he appears to have confused this gospel with both the gospel of the Ebionites and the gospel of the Nazarenes.

Once regarded by scholars as a forerunner of the gospel of Matthew, it is now recognized as a later work, but any dependence on the canonical gospels remains subject to debate. In addition to sayings of Jesus not included in canonical collections, this gospel includes syncretistic mythological accounts of Jesus' preexistence and life. A fragmentary reference to the temptation depicts Jesus' "mother, the Holy Spirit" carrying him away by one of the hairs of his head (cf. Ezek. 8:3; Bel 36). Another passage describes a postresurrection appearance of Jesus to his brother, James the Just (cf. 1 Cor. 15:7); James, a leader of the Jewish Christians at Jerusalem, is presented here as foremost among the apostles.

HEBREWS, LETTER TO THE.

The nineteenth book of the New Testament, written by an unknown author. In most translations it is placed between the Pauline letters and the so-called Catholic Letters.

I. Contents

Unlike other New Testament letters, which open with a salutation and introduction of the author and addressees, the Letter to the Hebrews abruptly starts with a theological discourse concerning the superiority of God's message as proclaimed by his Son "in these last days" to the divine revelation previously communicated by the Old Testament prophets (Heb. 1:1-2). According to this new revelation, Christ (v. 3), having completed his earthly ministry, is seated at the right hand of the Father, thereby holding a position infinitely superior to the angels (vv. 4-14), through whose mediation the divine law had been given (2:1-2). As a result, anyone who rejects salvation as it is offered through Christ must be more severely† punished than the one who has been disobedient only to the (Old Testament) law (vv. 2-4). Indeed, the "world to come" has been made subject to Christ, who through his suffering became a human being and thus was able to help others overcome their weaknesses (vv. 5-18). Further, Christ can be regarded as "worthy of . . . much more glory than Moses" (who delivered the law to Israel), just as in a household the son has much more honor than a servant (3:1-6). The author then warns of the dangers of unbelief and compares the Old Testament promise of rest in Canaan with the New Testament promise of salvation in Christ (3:7-4:13).

Depicting Christ as the sinless great High Priest (4:14-16), the author next discusses the distinctions of this high priesthood—"after the order of MELCHIZEDEK" (5:1-6:8). Christ's priesthood is greater than that of Aaron and his descendants because it is perfect and eternal (7:1-28). The new covenant which he mediated is more lofty than the old which merely prefigured the new (8:1-13). Moreover, Christ's sacrifice—made "once for all [Gk. *ephápax*])"—terminates the value of the Old Testament cultic sacrifices (9:11-10:18), which likewise pointed to Christ's supreme sacrifice on the cross (9:1-10). The author stresses that those who persist in denying the sacrifice and salvation offered by Christ will receive divine judgment more horrible than any punishment with which those who violated the old covenant were inflicted (10:28-31).

In order to provide strength for those who must endure sufferings and hardships (10:32-39), the author supplies a list, drawn from the old covenant, of devout persons who, in faith, awaited the promised salvation (11:1-40). Such a "cloud of witnesses" (12:1) can be a source of encouragement for the weary to persevere in faith and to regard their trials as divine discipline (vv. 1-29). The book concludes with general exhortations, warnings and advice, personal information, a greeting, and a benediction (ch. 13).

II. Theological Significance

The Letter to the Hebrews occupies a unique place among the New Testament writings. It is significant, not so much for its view of history as divided into two periods but much more for its connecting these two historical periods with the two divine testaments and covenants. The "present age" (9:9), a concept found also in Paul's letters and implied by the prophets of old, is a span of time that lasts until Christ's (first) coming and even longer for those who remain unaffected by his message of hope. The new age or the "age to come" (6:5), however, commences with Christ's incarnation (cf. 1:2, "these last days") and moves toward its eschatological fulfilment (e.g., 9:26). The author anchors this eschatological dualism in his view of the two covenants. In the former covenant (or testament) Aaron and his descendants were to mediate between Yahweh and his people. Because every testament contains its goal within itself as well as the means toward it, the Aaronic testament in a certain sense accomplished its goal, namely the restoration of the broken relationship between God and man (4:16). But the former covenant really pointed to the new and eternal covenant of Christ (cf. Ps. 110:4; Heb. 5:6, 10), initiated by God in grace (13:20), for Christ the great High Priest brought sinful mankind and holy God together.

Although the present age precedes in time the age to come, just as the Aaronic covenant came historically before the new covenant in Christ, the two ages also run concurrently: the present age continues for those who refuse to accept Christ's message of salvation, and the age of salvation, which dawned with Christ's first coming, will radiate its magnificent beauty at his second coming. In order to highlight the distinction between Christ and Aaron and the superiority of Christ over his Old Testament counterpart, the author exchanges his temporal metaphor for a spatial image: the Aaronic covenant points upward to the heavenly covenant of Christ ("copy and shadow of the heavenly sanctuary," 8:5; 9:23), who as the heavenly Son, seated on his throne (8:1), fulfilled the requirements necessary to bring believers into communion with God, as the heavenly Christ identifies with earthly sinners (4:14-15), and, finally, as the heavenly High Priest brings the eternally valuable sacrifice (10:4-22). From this point of view the author circumscribes faith as a "conviction of things not seen" (11:1); the patriarchs, who were pilgrims during their earthly life (vv. 13-14), looked for a better (i.e., "heavenly") country (v. 16).

But the focus on the heavenly reality of the earthly copies does not "look away from an eschatological future to a present world of invisible reality" (G. E. Ladd, *A Theology of the New Testament* [Grand Rapids: 1974], p. 573). The fulfilment of the age to come is to happen in time, and the heavenly Christ is also a thoroughly human Christ, who "in every respect has been tempted as we are" (4:15). Faith, moreover, is sketched as the "assurance of things hoped for" (11:1)—the realization of events in history such as the keeping of the Passover (v. 28), the crossing of the Red Sea (v. 29), and the conquest of Jericho (v. 30). Like the apostle Paul, the author of this text tempered his "enthusiasm" for Platonism with a loyalty to the Hebrew heritage that upholds God's acting in history and in time.

III. Style

Because several "exhortations" (e.g., 12:5, Gk. *paraklēsis* "comfort, exhortation"; cf. 13:22) tend to interrupt the didactic sections of the book at various points, and in view of the author's rhetorical style, which fits more a personal address than a written letter, Hebrews has been considered a homily, or a collection of sermons. It may also be a public document with literary overtones.

IV. Purpose

From various indications (e.g., 10:28-29) it appears that the addressees were in grave danger of falling into apostasy. They may have neglected their faith because of the threat of persecution, although none had as yet been martyred (12:4). Thus, the writer clarifies the glory of the Christian faith and warns against an apostasy that no further repentance would absolve (6:4-6).

V. Addressees

From the earliest manuscripts, the letter has borne the superscription "[t]o the Hebrews" (Gk. *pros Hebraious*), suggesting that it was directed to Christians of Jewish background. This suggestion, though not made by the author himself, may have arisen in the early Church. Some scholars (e.g., B. F. Westcott, W. M. Ramsay) contend that its recipients were Palestinian Jews while others cite Hellenistic influences and place them in Alexandria; still others (e.g., T. W. Manson) claim that these were Jewish Christians living in

Rome. Indeed, the Letter to the Hebrews was known in Rome probably before the end of the first century A.D. (cf. the correspondence of Clement of Rome with the church at Corinth, A.D. 96). Moreover, 13:24 can be understood to refer to Christians who, having emigrated from Italy, sent their greetings to those yet remaining in the capital of the Roman Empire.

VI. Date

If Hebrews was known to Clement of Rome *ca.* A.D. 96, this work could not have been written much after A.D. 90. The fact that Timothy, Paul's helper and companion *ca.* A.D. 50 (Acts 16:1), was still alive (Heb. 13:23), together with the consideration that the author as a second-generation believer received the message of salvation from those who personally heard Christ himself preach it (cf. 2:3), favors an approximate date of *ca.* A.D. 80 or 85. Some, however, would date it *ca.* 60, prior to the fall of the Jerusalem temple and well before any persecutions under Nero.

VII. Authorship

No definite teachings concerning authorship of this anonymous book emerged in the early Church prior to the end of the second century A.D. Clement of Alexandria contended that it was the work of Paul (who as "apostle to the Gentiles" sought anonymity) translated into Greek by Luke (Eusebius *HE* vi.14.4). Origen, who viewed the teachings as basically Pauline and attributed the work to a disciple of the apostle, nevertheless held reservations: "the diction and phraseology are those of someone who remembered the apostolic teachings . . . but who wrote the epistle, in truth, God alone knows" (vi.25.13-14). The work remained anonymous in the Western church until the fourth century, perhaps in part because the church at Rome refused to accept the possibility of a second repentance (e.g., 12:17). Among the Reformers, Luther ascribed authorship to Apollos, an Alexandrian Jew familiar with Philo's allegorization. The KJV, however, identifies the book as "the epistle of Paul the Apostle." Nevertheless, if the later date proposed is at all near the mark, Paul could not have been the author. Most scholars now support this denial of Pauline authorship on the basis of style and content.

The author of this letter, whoever he may have been, was well versed in the teachings of the Old Testament, especially in the Psalms, which he frequently quotes. Through interpreting the meaning of Old Testament events typically (i.e., as types pointing to Christ) rather than allegorically (as did Philo) his notion of the heavenly sanctuary most assuredly is influenced by Platonic idealism mediated through Philo and others. Some scholars believe that the author may have been acquainted with the lifestyle of the Essenes and the Qumran community.

The author's portrayal of Christ's priestly ministry adds a valuable dimension to Paul's perspective of Christ's work of reconciliation and his insistence that salvation is made possible through faith, not by means of following the precepts of the Mosaic law. Yet both writers balance judiciously between Christ's humanity and his divinity.

VIII. Canonicity

Although the Western church for some time refused to accord Hebrews canonical status, the Latin Fathers at last, following the example of the Eastern church, included this remarkable work in the list of canonical books compiled at the synods of Hippo (A.D. 393) and Carthage (397).

Bibliography. F. F. Bruce, *The Epistle to the Hebrews*. NICNT (Grand Rapids: 1964); P. E. Hughes, *A Commentary on the Epistle to the Hebrews* (Grand Rapids: 1977); T. W. Manson, *The Epistle to the Hebrews* (London: 1951); J. Moffatt, *A Critical and Exegetical Commentary on the Epistle to the Hebrews*. ICC (Edinburgh: 1924).

HEBRON [hē′brən] (Heb. *ḥeḇrôn* "association, confederacy") **(PERSON).**†
  1. A Levite, the third son of Kohath (Exod. 6:18; Num. 3:19; 1 Chr. 6:2, 18; 23:12) and father of four sons (v. 19; 24:23). His descendants were called Hebronites (Heb. *ḥeḇrônî*; Num. 3:27; 26:58; 1 Chr. 26:30-31) or "the sons of Hebron" (15:9).
  2. A Calebite and son of Mareshah; he was the father of four sons (1 Chr. 2:42-43). This name and the others in the genealogy (as well as those of **1** above) may actually be place names.

HEBRON (PLACE).† A city in the hill country of Judah, identified with modern er-Rumeideh, approximately 30 km. (19 mi.) south-southwest of Jerusalem. Situated some 927 m. (3040 ft.) above sea level and thus the highest city in the region west of the Jordan river, ruins at the site (Deir el-Arba‘in) overlook a fertile district of vineyards and orchards. Initially called Kiriath-arba ("city of four"; e.g., Gen. 23:2; 35:7; the name suggests an ancient confederation [Heb. *ḥeḇrôn*] of neighboring cities; cf. 14:13, 24), the city was founded *ca.* 1700 B.C. ("seven years" before Zoan was rebuilt as the Hyksos capital; Num. 13:22).

It was at Mamre (modern Râmet el-Khalîl, 3 km. (1.8 mi.) to the north (perhaps the focus of the ancient confederation), that Abraham had pitched his tent (Gen. 13:18) and where the Lord appeared to him prior to the destruction of Sodom and Gomorrah (18:1). When his wife Sarah died, Abraham purchased from Ephron the Hittite a cave in the field of Machpelah "to the east of Mamre" as her burial site (23:17-19); Abraham (25:9-10), Isaac, Rebekah, Leah, and Jacob were buried there as well (49:29-32; 50:12-13). Established slightly to the east of er-Rumeideh at the time of the Crusades, modern Hebron is believed to preserve the site of this cave; the mosque Haram el-Ibrahimi el-Khalîl marks the site of a sixth-century A.D. basilica and an earlier Herodian enclosure commemorating the tombs of the patriarchs. The modern city is called el-Khalîl, from the traditional Muslim epithet of Abraham as "the friend (of God)" (cf. 2 Chr. 20:7; Isa. 41:8; Jas. 2:23).

As a Canaanite royal city (Josh. 12:10), Hebron exhibited the ethnic diversity of pre-Israelite Palestine; its inhabitants included the legendary Anakim (Num. 13:22; Josh. 11:21; cf. 14:15; 15:13), Amorites (Gen. 14:13), Hittites (23:3ff.), and Canaanites (Judg.

1:10). Hebron was among the strongly fortified cities scouted by the Israelite spies (Num. 13:22). When Joshua attacked the confederated Amorite cities, he captured and hanged Hoham the king of Hebron (Josh. 10:1-27); subsequently he besieged the city itself and utterly destroyed it (vv. 36-37). The city was allotted to Caleb for his role in its capture (14:12-13; Judg. 1:20; cf. v. 10). Later it became a city of refuge (20:7) and a levitical city (21:11). Hebron was among the cities upon which David bestowed the spoil of Ziklag (1 Sam. 30:31). It was here that he was anointed king of Judah (2 Sam. 2:4), ruling from Hebron over the southern coalition for seven and a half years (v. 11; 5:5); after the elders of Israel came to Hebron to anoint him king over the northern tribes as well (v. 3; cf. 1 Chr. 12:23), he moved the capital to the more neutral Jerusalem. During David's reign at Hebron he negotiated a covenant with Abner to strengthen his claim to the northern throne (1 Sam. 3:12-21); later, his general Joab murdered Abner in the city gate (vv. 27, 30). The head of the assassinated Ishbosheth, Saul's son, was buried in Abner's tomb, and his murderers were hanged beside the pool of Hebron, probably modern Birket es-Sultan (4:12). Several of David's sons were born at Hebron (3:2-5), including Absalom, who proclaimed his rebellion there (15:7ff.). Shortly after the division of the monarchy, King Rehoboam fortified the city (2 Chr. 11:10). It was among the towns resettled by the people of Judah following the Exile (Neh. 11:25, "Kiriath-arba"). But the Edomites (Idumeans) had extended their control in this region, and Hebron remained in their control until destroyed by Judas Maccabeus (1 Macc. 5:65). The city was again rebuilt, but was destroyed by the Romans during the First Jewish Revolt (A.D. 68; Josephus *BJ* iv.9.9).

The KJV reading "Hebron" at Josh. 19:28 (RSV "Ebron") is better rendered Abdon (so JB, NIV; cf. 21:30).

HEDGEHOG (Heb. *qippōḏ*). A small mammal of the genus Erinaceus, characterized by a protective coat of dense, erect spines; when startled or attacked it rolls itself into a ball. Various species have been found in Palestine, including the *Erinaceus sacer* in the central mountainous regions and the long-eared *Erinaceus auritus* in the coastal plain and the Negeb. The hedgehog feeds primarily on insects, but will also eat mice, frogs, and plants. It is basically nocturnal and lives in hollow stumps or rocky crevices, thus fitting its biblical description as an inhabitant of devastated cities (Isa. 14:23; KJV "bittern"; NEB "bustard"; Zech. 2:14; JB "heron"; NIV "screech owl"). At Isa. 34:11 the RSV translates the term as "porcupine" (JB "hedgehog"), a rodent of the family Hystricidae which ancient observers may have considered a larger variety of the same species.

HEGAI [hĕg′ī] (Heb. *hēgay, hēgē′*). A eunuch of the Persian king Ahasuerus who was in charge of the royal harem. He won the trust of Esther when she was preparing for her meeting with Ahasuerus (Esth. 2:3, 8, 15). At v. 3 the KJV reads "Hege."

HEGEMONIDES [hĕj′ə mō′nə dēz] (Gk. *Hēge-*

monidēs "leader" [?]).* A Syrian official whom Antiochus named governor of the district from Ptolemais to Gerar at the time of Philip's attack on Antioch (2 Macc. 13:24; KJV "principal [governor]," referring to Judas Maccabeus).

HEGLAM [hĕg′ləm] (Heb. *heglām*).* A son of Ehud, and the father of Uzza and Ahihud; an alternate name for Gera (1 Chr. 8:7; KJV "he removed them"; RSV mg. "he carried them into exile").

HEIFER (Heb. *'eglâ, pārâ*).* A young cow which has not produced a calf. Although employed in agricultural pursuits such as threshing (Hos. 10:11), the heifer is mentioned most frequently in association with religious rites, including the ratification of a covenant (Gen. 15:9) and the expiation of murder (Deut. 21:1-9). *See* Ox.

Of particular significance is the rite for purifying a person defiled by contact with a corpse (Num. 19:1-22). A red (or reddish-brown) heifer (Heb. *pārâ 'ᵃdummâ*, lit. "red cow"), unblemished and never yoked for work, was brought to the priest to be slaughtered outside the camp (vv. 2-3). Some of the blood was sprinkled toward the front of the tent of meeting (v. 4), but the remainder of the carcass, including the blood and dung, was burned, along with cedar wood, hyssop, and scarlet thread. The ashes were then gathered and stored, to be mixed with spring water as the "water for impurity" sprinkled in the actual purification ritual (vv. 9, 13, 18-19). Although the person or object sprinkled was cleansed, the priest as well as those who burned the heifer, gathered the ashes, and sprinkled the water were rendered unclean (vv. 7-8, 10, 19). The rite, which may have been adapted from pre-Israelite practice, was also performed for some articles taken as booty (31:23).

HELAH [hē′lə] (Heb. *hel'â* "necklace"). One of the two wives of Ashur, the ancestor of Tekoa (1 Chr. 4:5, 7).

HELAM [hē′ləm] (Heb. *hêlām*).† A place in the Transjordan near the northern border of Gilead where David defeated the Syrians (Arameans) under Hadadezer (2 Sam. 10:16-17). The name appears in the LXX of Ezek. 47:16, situated between Damascus and Hamath. Although the location of the site is disputed, it may be the same as the Alema of 1 Macc. 5:26, 35.

HELBAH [hĕl′bə] (Heb. *helbâ*).† A town in the territorial allotment of Asher, the Canaanite inhabitants of which the Israelites were unable to expel (Judg. 1:31). The name is thought to be a duplication of Ahlab in the same verse (thus JB omits) and may be identified with Mahalab (modern Khirbet el-Maḥâlib; cf. Josh. 19:29).

HELBON [hĕl′bŏn] (Heb. *helbôn*). A city famed for its wine and honey (Ezek. 27:18), which are mentioned in inscriptions of Nebuchadnezzar and also by the Greek geographer Strabo. It is identified with modern Halbûn, a village 29 km. (18 mi.) north of

Damascus in a region of the Anti-lebanon valley that is still a center for the cultivation of grapes.

HELDAI [hĕl′dī] (Heb. *helday*).

1. A Netophathite and descendant of Othniel; commander of the twelfth division of David's army (1 Chr. 27:15). In the parallel list of David's mighty men he is called Heled (11:30). He is probably the same as the Heleb of 2 Sam. 23:29.

2. A Jew still living in Babylon at the time of Zechariah; he was among those who brought gold and silver for the crown of Joshua the high priest (Zech. 6:10, 14). At v. 14 the KJV and NJV, following the MT, read "Helem" (Heb. *helem*; LXX *hypoménō* "wait for").

HELEB [hē′lĕb] (Heb. *heleb*). One of the "thirty," David's mighty men; the son of Baanah of Netophah (2 Sam. 23:29; JB, NIV "Heeled"). *See* HELDAI 1.

HELECH [hē′lĕk] (Heb. *hêlēk*).* A source of the mercenary forces of Tyre (Ezek. 27:11; KJV "your army"; JB "their army"). The name may designate Cilicia in southeastern Asia Minor (cf. Akk. *Ḥilakku*).

HELED [hē′lĕd] (Heb. *heled*). One of David's mighty men; the son of Baanah of Netophah (1 Chr. 11:30). *See* HELDAI 1.

HELEK [hē′lĕk] (Heb. *helek*). A son of Gilead and descendant of Manasseh (Num. 26:30; Josh. 17:2); eponymous ancestor of the Helekites.

HELEM [hē′lĕm] (Heb. *hēlem*).

1. A descendant of Asher (1 Chr. 7:35; LXX B Gk. *Balaam*; LXX A *huiós Elam*). At v. 32 he is called Hotham.

2. *See* HELDAI 2.

HELEPH [hē′lĕf] (Heb. *hēlep*).† A town on the border of the territory assigned to Naphtali (Josh. 19:33). Identification of the site remains uncertain; possible locations are modern Khirbet 'Arbathah, slightly northeast of Mt. Tabor, and Beitliph, in the hill country of Galilee some 18 km. (11 mi.) west of Tell Qades.

HELEZ [hē′lĕz] (Heb. *heles* "strength, vigor").

1. A Pelonite of the tribe of Ephraim; commander of the seventh division of David's army (1 Chr. 11:27; 27:10). At 2 Sam. 23:26 he is called "the Paltite."

2. A Judahite and descendant of Jerahmeel; the son of Azariah and father of Eleasah (1 Chr. 2:39).

HELI [hē′lī] (Gk. *Hēlei*, from Heb. *'ēlî*).* The father of Joseph, according to Luke's version of Jesus' genealogy (Luke 3:23).

HELIODORUS [hē′lĭ ə dôr′əs] (Gk. *Hēliodōros* "gift of Helios [or the sun]").† A high official of the Syrian king Seleucus IV Philopator (187-175 B.C.) dispatched to confiscate the temple treasury at Jerusalem, a depository for the funds of widows and orphans (2 Macc. 3:7-14). In response to the prayers of the people and the high priest Onias, the plan was thwarted by divine intervention in the form of a horseman in gold armor and two strong young men (vv. 22-26). He was restored from his wounds by Onias' intercessory prayers and subsequently testified to the deeds of the supreme God (vv. 31-39). A variant account occurs in 4 Macc. 3:19–4:14, in which Apollonius, governor of Coelesyria and Phoenicia, plunders the temple (cf. 2 Macc. 3:5-7).

Heliodorus is mentioned also by Appian (*Syr.* 45) and an inscription found in the temple of Apollo at Delos. He was implicated in the assassination of Seleucus IV, who had been his childhood friend, and was expelled by supporters of the successor, Antiochus IV Epiphanes.

HELIOPOLIS [hḗ′lĭ ŏp′ə lĭs] (Heb. *bêṯ šemeš*; Gk. *hēlíou pólis* "house of the sun [god]"). †

1. The Egyptian city ON, capital of the thirteenth nome of Lower Egypt and center for worship of the sun-gods Atum and Re (cf. Jer. 43:13; KJV "Bethshemesh"; NIV, NJV "temple of the sun" [JB adds "at On"]).

2. Greek name for BAALBEK.

HELKAI [hĕl′kī] (Heb. *ḥelqāy*, perhaps a shortened form of Hilkiah). A priest during the time of the high priest Joiakim (Neh. 12:15).

HELKATH [hĕl′kăth] (Heb. *ḥelqaṯ* "portion"). A town on the border of the territory assigned to Asher (Josh. 19:25). It was later a levitical town set aside for the Gershonites (21:31). At 1 Chr. 6:75 it is called Hukok. Located near the Kishon river in the vicinity of Mt. Carmel, the site may be either modern Tell el-Harbaj or Tell el-Qassis.

HELKATH-HAZZURIM [hĕl′kăth hăzh′ŏŏ rĭm] (Heb. *ḥelqaṯ haṣṣurîm* "field of flints [or knives] or "field of opponents"). A place near the pool of Gibeon where twelve combatants of Joab's forces and twelve of Abner's slaughtered each other in a tournament of champions (2 Sam. 2:16; KJV mg. "field of strong men"; JB "Field of Sides"; NIV mg. "field of hostilities").

HELL.† The English word "hell," as employed in the KJV, translates four words in the original biblical languages: Heb. *še′ôl*, and Gk. *hádēs, géenna* (Gehenna) and *tartaróō* (a reference to Tartarus). The RSV transliterates as Sheol and Hades; these names generally signify the abode of all the dead, whether blessed or damned. On the other hand, the RSV associates both *géenna* and *tartaróō* with hell, signifying, as used in the New Testament, a special place of punishment for the wicked. The progressive biblical use of these terms provides a history of the development of the doctrine of hell as the eternal destiny of the damned. Although seeds of the later doctrine of hell exist in the Old Testament, particularly in the prophets, the doctrine did not approach its developed form until intertestamental and New Testament times.

I. Sheol

The KJV translates Heb. *še′ôl* thirty-one times as "hell," thirty-one times as "the grave," and three times as "the pit." Both the literal meaning of the word and its derivation are unknown; none of the theories proposed is universally accepted. Attempts to derive it from Akkadian have failed to convince most scholars. Some scholars relate the term to Heb. *šā′â* "to lie waste"; Sheol then would refer to a desolate, inhuman region where no life can exist and which is a horror to all who behold it. Since such a region was thought to be located under the earth, some have suggested "underworld" as the best translation. Others believe that *še′ôl* means "cavern, hollow, deep (place)," from the Hebrew root *š′l*. Another widely accepted view is that *še′ôl* derives from a root meaning "ask, inquire." This theory connects Sheol with the practice of necromancy, the consultation of the dead through mediums. Sheol would be the abode of the spirits thus consulted.

Whatever the precise meaning of Sheol, the Old Testament speaks of it as the abode of the shades (Job 26:5-6; Ps. 88:10 [MT 11]; Prov. 2:18; 9:18 [RSV mg.]; Isa. 14:9; 26:14, 19). The Hebrew word for shades (*rᵉpā′im*) means lit. "the limp, powerless ones." Other texts characterize Sheol as dark, gloomy, chaotic, and silent (Job 10:21-22; Ps. 94:17), a "land of forgetfulness" whose inhabitants are weak, cut off from the experience of God's presence, and no longer praise him (Pss. 88:4-6, 10-12 [MT 5-7, 11-13]; 115:17; Isa. 14:9-10; 38:18). Yet there the weary find rest (Job 3:17), and Sheol is not beyond the reach of God's presence and power (Ps. 139:8; Amos 9:2). Old Testament writers employ various images of Sheol including a gated city (Job 38:17; Isa. 38:10) or a voracious mouth which swallows up the dead (Isa. 5:14). Except for an oblique reference to Sheol as a place of thirst (v. 13), the Old Testament nowhere suggests that it is a place of torment for the wicked. Rather, it is the general abode of all the dead.

See also SHEOL.

II. Hades

The LXX consistently uses Gk. *hádēs* to translate *še′ôl*. The Greek term had a long history of usage in the classics, where it designates the underworld in general, the abode of all the dead. Hades is translated as "hell" in the KJV but is transliterated in the RSV. Acts 2:27 quotes Ps. 16:10 with reference to the resurrection of Christ. It is literally the "gates of Hades" (Matt. 16:18, RSV mg.) that shall not prevail against the Church; the RSV suggests that the image of the gates represents the power of Hades, the "powers of death." In the story of the rich man and Lazarus, however, the rich man in Hades is said to be in torment and suffering from thirst (Luke 16:23-24; cf. Isa. 5:13). The reference to flame as the source of the torment suggests that, in this parable at least, Hades is virtually synonymous with Gehenna. Rev. 20:14 maintains the distinction between Hades and the place of torment by fire (usually Gehenna in the New Testament) but depicts their ultimate union when Death and its realm, Hades, are thrown into the lake of fire.

III. Gehenna

The word Gehenna represents the nearest biblical approach to the developed doctrine of hell as the place of the damned. Thus the RSV employs the English word "hell" almost exclusively for Gehenna (Gk. *géenna*). The name comes from the Hebrew expressions *gê hinnōm*, *gê ben-hinnōm*, and *gê bᵉnê-hinnōm*, which mean respectively "valley of Hinnom," "valley of the son of Hinnom," and "valley of the sons of Hinnom." All refer to a valley south of Jerusalem which became infamous for its sacrificial site called Topheth where children were offered to the god Molech during the reigns of such wicked kings of Judah as Ahaz and Manasseh (2 Chr. 28:3; 33:6). King Josiah defiled the site during his reforms so that children no longer would be sacrificed there (2 Kgs. 23:10), but the valley may have been used again for such practices after his time (Jer. 7:31-32; 19:2-6; 32:35). As punishment for this, Jeremiah proclaimed that in the future the valley of the son of Hinnom would be called the valley of slaughter since many would be slain there and, for lack of room elsewhere, the dead would be buried in Topheth (7:32; 19:6).

In later Jewish thought the name of this place of infamy and horror became associated with the growing belief in the existence of a place where the wicked would be punished for eternity (cf. Isa. 66:24). Likewise the conviction was growing that a final resurrection and judgment would come, separating those destined for "everlasting life" from those destined for "everlasting contempt" (Dan. 12:2). The site of this judgment was variously placed in the valley of Jehoshaphat (Joel 3:12ff. [MT 4:12ff.]; according to tradition this is the Kidron valley) and on the Mount of Olives (Zech. 14:3ff.). The image of Gehenna as the place of punishment for the wicked is also used in later Jewish writings (As.Mos. 10:19; 2 Esdr. 7:36; 2 Apoc. Bar. 59:10; 1 En. 27:2-3; 48:9; 54:1; 90:26-27; 103:8), where it often has strong associations with darkness and burning fire.

The New Testament use of Gehenna continues the development of the concept of a place of eternal punishment. Except for Jas. 3:6, it is used only in the Synoptic Gospels. Drawing heavily on Jewish apocalyptic literature, the Gospels characterize Gehenna as a place of "unquenchable fire" (Matt. 5:22; 18:9; Mark 9:43; Jas. 3:6; cf. Matt. 3:10, 12; 7:19; 18:8; 25:41; Luke 3:9, 17 where fire is mentioned without naming Gehenna) and as a valley or pit into which one's body may be cast (Matt. 5:29-30; Mark 9:45, 47; Luke 12:5). It is probably safe to assume that the lake of fire of Rev. 20:14 is identical with Gehenna, into which Death and Hades are thrown. The limited use of the Gehenna-fire imagery in the New Testament should be noted. Although it cannot be ignored, particularly since it appears primarily in the teachings of Jesus, its limited use and the nearly total lack of concrete imagery for hell in Paul's writings suggest that this is not the only way to speak of the destiny of those who reject God.

IV. Tartarus

The only other appearance of English "hell" in the RSV is in 2 Pet. 2:4 where the Greek text uses a verb form of the classical name Tartarus meaning "consigning to Tartarus." In classical thought Tartarus was the lowest part of the underworld and a place of punishment over against Elysium, the place of the blessed. Thus it was distinct from Hades, the general abode of the dead, although in popular usage the two terms may have been interchangeable. In 2 Peter the name is used of the infernal region to which the rebellious angels were consigned, and hence here signifies a place of punishment of the wicked.

HELLENISM [hĕl'ə nĭz əm].† Greek civilization, including culture, thought, and institutions, particularly as diffused throughout the Mediterranean world and the ancient Near East by the conquests of Alexander the Great (336-323 B.C.).

Apart from military colonies, the primary means of transmitting this civilization was the Greek polis or city-state. These carefully planned cities typically featured a marketplace (Gk. *agorá*), long, colonnaded boulevards, temples, theaters, baths, and a gymnasium. The city-states were semiautonomous, governed by elected magistrates, a senate of the aristocracy, and an assembly of all free citizens.

The cosmopolitan Hellenistic cities were conducive to the Greek ideals of free inquiry and the development of the intellect, particularly in terms of philosophy and science, literature and the arts. Education became a central concern, and libraries flourished. Advances were made in medicine, astronomy, and mathematics. Poets, playwrights, and sculptors attained new horizons of human expression and creativity, and philosophers explored aspects of metaphysics, ethics, and logic.

Hellenism encountered Judaism with varying degrees of success. Alexandria in Egypt became the intellectual center of the Diaspora. Here the Septuagint was produced in the second century B.C., and here Philo Judaeus (*ca*. 30 B.C.–A.D. 40) developed an allegorical interpretation of the Old Testament, envisioning the Jewish law as a philosophical system and attributing to the Logos an important creative and intermediary role. Elsewhere the Jews were thoroughly hellenized, often maintaining their unique identity solely through observance of the law and synagogue worship. With the support of the priestly aristocracy, Antiochus IV Epiphanes established Jerusalem as the Greek polis Antioch in Judea, ruled by a council (Gk. *boulē*) comprised of temple officials and featuring a gymnasium and other typically Hellenistic attributes (cf. 1 Macc. 1:11-15; 2 Macc. 4:9-16). However, resistance among the Jewish masses heightened when Antiochus attempted to supplant Judaism with worship of Olympian Zeus (1 Macc. 1:41-64), culminating in the Maccabean war.

The formative Christianity of Jesus and the disciples exhibited little Hellenistic influence, yet Pauline theology bears traces of Greek thought. Moreover, the same qualities of Hellenistic civilization which fostered the spread of Christianity throughout the Mediterranean world also introduced new interpretations of the faith and created tensions within the body of Christ (cf. Acts 15).

Bibliography. E. Hatch, *Influence of Greek Ideas on Christianity* (1800; repr. New York: 1957); M. Hengel, *Judaism and Hellenism*, 2 vols. (Philadelphia: 1974); W. W. Tarn, *Hellenistic Civilisation*, rev. ed. (Cleveland: 1961).

HELLENISTS [hĕl'ə nĭsts] (Gk. *Hellēnistai*).†

Greek-speaking Jews, usually contrasted with the Aramaic-speaking "Hebrews" (Acts 6:1; 9:29; KJV "Grecians"; NIV "Grecian Jews"). At 6:1 they constitute a minority in the church at Jerusalem, where they complain of unfair treatment in the support of their widows. Those cited at 9:29 were vocal opponents of Christianity, bent on murdering Paul.

HELON [hē'lŏn] (Heb. *ḥēlōn* "strength"). The father of Eliab of the tribe of Zebulun (Num. 1:9; 2:7; 7:24, 29; 10:16).

HELPER (Heb. *ʿāzar*; Gk. *antílēmpsis*).† In the Old Testament a helper is one who provides aid or relief, most notably the Lord (e.g., Ps. 30:10; 54:4). Eve (RSV "a woman") is created as a helper or partner for the man (Gen. 2:18, 20; KJV "a help meet for him"; JB "helpmate"; E. A. Speiser [*Genesis*, 3rd ed. (1979), p. 17] reads "an aid fit for him," meaning one "alongside" or "corresponding to him").

At 1 Cor. 12:28 Paul numbers helpers (KJV "helps") among the functions performed by members of the body of Christ. Although some interpret this as a reference to the office of deacon, the term means rather aid given to weaker members by the stronger (NIV "those able to help others"; W. F. Orr and J. A. Walther, *I Corinthians*. AB [1976], p. 287, "ministries of aid"; cf. Acts 20:35; 27:17, RSV mg., KJV).

HEM (Matt. 9:20; 14:36, KJV). *See* FRINGE.

HEMAN [hē'mən] (Heb. *hêmān* "faithful").

1. A wise man, one of those whom Solomon was said to have surpassed in wisdom (1 Kgs. 4:31). Like Carcol and Darda he was a son (probably a member of the guild) of Mahol. At 1 Chr. 2:6 these three are named as descendants of Zerah of the tribe of Judah; cf. the superscription of Ps. 88, where Heman is called an Ezrahite.

2. The son of Joel and grandson of Samuel. A Levite of the Kohathite line who was a temple singer and played the cymbals during the time of David (1 Chr. 6:33; 15:19). He was a leader of the temple singers (2 Chr. 35:15), and his division was among those that served the tabernacle and altar at Gibeon (1 Chr. 16:39, 41-42); all fourteen of his sons played and sang under his direction in the temple service (25:4-6). Heman also appears among those who participated in the dedication of Solomon's temple (2 Chr. 5:12). At 1 Chr. 25:5 he is called the king's seer (cf. 2 Chr. 35:15).

3. A Horite descended from Esau (Gen. 36:22; so RSV, following LXX; MT Heb. *hêmām*; so KJV); at 1 Chr. 1:39 he is called Homam.

HEMDAN [hĕm'dăn] (Heb. *hemdān* "pleasing"). A Horite, son of Dishon and descendant of Seir (Gen. 36:26). At 1 Chr. 1:41 he is called Hamran (KJV "Amram").

HEMORRHAGE. *See* BLOOD, FLOW OF.

HEN [hĕn] (Heb. *hēn* "favor"). The son of Zephaniah, according to the MT (Zech. 6:14; so KJV,

NIV). The RSV and JB read "Josiah," following the Syriac and v. 10.

See JOSIAH **2**.

HENA [hĕn'ə] (Heb. *hēnaʿ*). A Syrian city conquered by Sennacherib in 838 B.C. and incorporated along with the surrounding territory into the Assyrian Empire, thus held up as a warning of the imminent doom of Jerusalem (2 Kgs. 18:34; 19:13; Isa. 37:13). In the LXX it is called Gk. *Ana* or *Anag*, and in the annals of Assurnasirpal it appears as Akk. *Anat*. Various proposals have been offered for its identification, including modern Anah on the Euphrates as well as a location in the general area of the Persian Gulf. The suggestion that the name designates a deity rather than a city has generally been rejected.

HENADAD [hĕn'ə dăd] (Heb. *hēnādād* "favor of Hadad").† Eponymous ancestor of a levitical family or guild that returned from exile with Zerubbabel (Ezra 3:9). Members of this group assisted in rebuilding the walls of Jerusalem (Neh. 3:18, 24) and sealed the renewed covenant (10:9).

HENNA (Heb. *kōper*). A shrub (*Lawsonia inermis* L.) with dark-green bark, light green leaves that are slender and oblong, and long clusters of white flowers having a strong fragrance. In the ancient Near East henna was the "bride's flower," and because of its fragrance (cf. Cant. 4:13; KJV "camphire"; M. H. Pope, *Song of Songs*. AB [1977] translates "cypress" following LXX Gk. *kýpros*) it was often kept in houses or worn by women. During Solomon's time henna grew in the vineyards of Engedi (1:14). Since very early times in Egypt and Mesopotamia the dried leaves have been pulverized to make a yellowish-red pigment for coloring the hair, nails, and extremities.

At 7:11 the NJV reads "henna shrubs" (Heb. *kepārîm*; NIV mg. "henna bushes"; RSV, KJV "villages").

HEPHER [hē'fər] (Heb. *hēper*) (**PERSON**).

1. A son of Gilead and descendant of Manasseh (Num. 26:32; 27:1; Josh. 17:2; LXX Gk. *Hopher*); eponymous ancestor of a clan or other social group known as the Hepherites (Heb. *heprî*; Num. 26:32).

2. A descendant of Judah; son of Ashhur and Naarah (1 Chr. 4:6; LXX Gk. *Hēphal*).

3. A Mecherathite; one of David's mighty men (1 Chr. 11:36; LXX Gk. *Hopher*).

HEPHER [hē'fər] (Heb. *hēper*) (**PLACE**). A Canaanite city whose king Joshua defeated (Josh. 12:17). "All the land of Hepher," along with Arubboth and Socoh, comprised Solomon's third administrative district (1 Kgs. 4:10); R. G. Boling and G. E. Wright identify Hepher as a clan occupying a district in the Sharon valley north of Shechem (*Joshua*. AB [1982]). The precise location of Hepher has not yet been determined; possible sites include modern Hafireh and Tell Ibshar.

HEPHZIBAH [hĕf'zĭ bə] (Heb. *hepsî-bāh* "my delight is in her").

1. The wife of King Hezekiah and mother of Manasseh (2 Kgs. 21:1).

2. A new name for Jerusalem, symbolizing its restored status (Isa. 62:4, KJV, NIV); the RSV renders the name literally, "My delight is in her" (JB "My delight").

HERBS. A general term designating all forms of green plants suitable for human consumption. As with much biblical terminology for natural phenomena, usage is frequently imprecise by modern standards. Herbs included vegetables (Heb. *yaraq*; Prov. 15:17) and condiments such as cummin, mint, and dill (Gk. *láchanon;* Luke 11:42). Generally herbs were gathered from the fields where they grew wild (Heb. *ʿēśeḇ*; Gen. 2:5; Prov. 27:25; *ʾōrâ*; 2 Kgs. 4:39).

For specific information see the individual entries. *See also* BITTER HERBS.

HERES [hĕr'ĭz], **ASCENT OF** (Heb. *maʿᵃlēh heḥāres*).* The immediate route by which Gideon returned upon halting his pursuit of the Midianites (Judg. 8:13, RSV, JB, NIV; NIV "Pass of Heres"). The NJV seems to place the preceding battle at this site (cf. R. G. Boling, *Judges.* AB [1975], pp. 154, 156). The site, which remains unknown, is distinct from that of Har-heres.

HERES, MOUNT (Judg. 1:35, KJV, NIV). *See* HAR-HERES.

HERESH [hĭr'ĕsh] (Heb. *ḥereš*).† A Levite who returned from the Exile (1 Chr. 9:15; LXX B Gk. *Rharaiēl*). The name is lacking from the parallel account at Neh. 11:15-16.

HERESY (Gk. *haíresis*, from *hairéō* "take, choose").* In New Testament usage, a sect or party. Derived from the Hellenistic concept of philosophical schools (cf. Eusebius *Praep. ev.* xiii.12.10), the term was applied to various branches of Judaism, such as the Sadducees (Acts 5:17; RSV "party") and Pharisees (15:5). Christianity was viewed by many as such a sect of Judaism (24:5, 14; 28:22). Eventually the term came to designate factions representing divergent opinions within the early Church (1 Cor. 11:19); such divisions Paul denounced as a work of the flesh (Gal. 5:20; RSV "party spirit"). Not until the second century A.D. did "heresy" come to indicate false doctrine (Ignatius Eph. 6:2; Trall. 6:1; cf. 2 Pet. 2:1).

HERETH [hĭr'ĕth] (Heb. *ḥeret*). A forest in the tribal territory of Judah where David took refuge from Saul (1 Sam. 22:5; KJV "Hareth"). The name may be preserved in modern Kharas, a site 11 km. (7 mi.) northwest of Hebron east of Khirbet Qîlâ (biblical Keilah). The territory may have been under Philistine control at the time (cf. 23:3).

HERMAS [hûr'məs] (Gk. *Hermas*). A Christian in Rome to whom Paul sent his greetings (Rom. 16:14).

HERMAS [hûr'məs], **SHEPHERD OF.**† An early Christian apocalyptic work traditionally reckoned among the writings of the Apostolic Fathers.

The book comprises three principal divisions, the Visions, Mandates, and Similitudes. In the first four visions experienced by the author—although these may actually be literary devices—he is guided by the woman Rhoda, who symbolizes the Church and whom Hermas identifies as his former mistress and owner. Beginning with the fifth vision, which serves as an introduction to the remainder of the book, the revealer is a shepherd, the mysterious angel of repentance. The shepherd delivers twelve mandates regarding matters of faith and practice, intended to enable the new Christian to distinguish between the way of righteousness and that of evil. The visions and mandates are then further illuminated by ten similitudes (parables or allegories). Best known is the ninth similitude, which develops and reinterprets the third vision, the parable of the tower; the tower, which represents the Church, is constructed of various stones—types of believers, some of whom must repent or be removed.

This work, with its emphasis on the reality of sin among baptized Christians and the possibility of repentance (albeit only once without fear of judgment), is an important source concerning life and beliefs in the early Church. Used in the instruction of catechumens, it was regarded as canonical by several ante-Nicene Fathers (e.g., Irenaeus, Clement of Alexandria); in the Codex Sinaiticus it followed the New Testament books, along with the Epistle of Barnabas.

Composed originally in Greek, the complete text survives only in two Latin versions; it has also been found in an Ethiopic version as well as Coptic and Middle Persian fragments. Written at Rome, the book may have been written as early as the late first century A.D., but the Muratorian Canon attributes it to the brother of Pope Pius I (*ca.* 150). Despite early tradition (Origen *Comm. on Romans*), the author is probably not to be identified with the Hermas of Rom. 16:14.

HERMENEUTICS. *See* INTERPRETATION, BIBLICAL.

HERMES [hûr'mēz] (Gk. *Hermēs*) **(DEITY).** A Greek deity, son of Zeus; messenger and attendant of the gods, patron of orators, and god of merchants and thieves. He was the protector of sheep and cattle and functioned as a fertility god.

Drawing upon a myth known in Asia Minor in which Zeus and Hermes appeared in human form to the Phrygians Baucis and Philemon (Ovid *Metamorphoses*), the people of Lystra likened Paul, as chief speaker, to the messenger Hermes (Acts 14:12). The KJV reads "Mercurius," the Latin name for this god.

HERMES [hûr'mēz] (Gk. *Hermēs*) **(PERSON).** A person at Rome to whom Paul sent his greetings (Rom. 16:14).

HERMOGENES [hər mŏj'ə nēz] (Gk. *Hermogenēs* "born of Hermes"). A Christian who, with Phygelus and others in the Roman province of Asia, turned away from Paul (2 Tim. 1:15). It is unclear whether the defection was over theological differences or to avoid Roman persecution.

HERMON [hûr′mən], **MOUNT** (Heb. *har ḥermôn* "consecrated mountain"). The highest of the Antilebanon mountains, forming the southern spur of that range. Snow-capped much of the year, it bears the modern Arabic names Jebel el-Thalj ("mountain of the snow") and Jebel el-Sheikh ("gray-haired mountain"). In ancient times the Amorites called the mountain Senir and the Sidonians Sirion (Deut. 3:9). It is actually comprised of three peaks, the highest of which is *ca.* 2804 m. (9200 ft.) above sea level; this feature may be intended by the plural form in the MT of Ps. 42:6 (KJV "Hermonites").

Long regarded as a sacred mountain (cf. Judg. 3:3; 1 Chr. 5:23; "Baal-hermon"), Mt. Hermon marked the northern limits of Joshua's conquests (Josh. 11:17; 12:1). The sources of the Jordan river are located on its slopes, and currents of cool air passing over the mountain carry moisture to the surrounding lower areas (Ps. 133:3). Cant. 4:8 refers to lions and leopards which inhabited the wilds of this range.

HEROD [hěr′əd] (Gk. *Hērōdēs*). The Idumean family which governed Palestine for the Roman Empire 37 B.C.–A.D. 70. The dynasty was founded in the early first century B.C. by Antipater I, who was appointed governor (Gk. *stratēgós* "general") of Idumea by Alexander Janneus. Antipater (or Antipas) II gradually accumulated power by manipulating the Hasmonean Hyrcanus II and earned the favor of the Roman hierarchy; in 47 B.C. Julius Caesar named him procurator of Judea.

The family was nominally Jewish, compelled with all Idumean peoples to accept circumcision and embrace Judaism following their conquest by John Hyrcanus in 125 B.C.

1. Herod the Great (73-4 B.C.), second son of Antipater II, who named him governor of Galilee at age twenty-five in 47. For his immediate capture and execution of troublesome bandits, Herod gained the early admiration of the Romans and Galilean Jews, although this action incurred the wrath of the Sanhedrin. He then repelled the Hasmonean Antigonus' invasion of Galilee. Following the assassination of Antipater, the Roman triumvir Mark Antony installed Herod and his elder brother Phasael as tetrarchs of Judea. In 40 Jerusalem was besieged by Parthian forces, who installed Antigonus as king; Phasael committed suicide in Parthian custody, and Herod fled to Rome, where he was named king of Judea. The Roman army drove out the Parthians in 38, and Herod gained the throne a year later by defeating Antigonus.

Herod's reign was basically peaceful, and he demonstrated both military skill and political prowess, particularly in consolidating support among his Jewish subjects and in maintaining good relations with the Roman leaders. After the death of his benefactor Antony, he managed to win the favor of Augustus (Octavius). With the aid of both Antony and Augustus, Herod enlarged the boundaries of Judea to the north and south. Moreover, his reign was one of great splendor, marked by the spread of Hellenistic culture

and a building program unrivaled in the country's history. Herod constructed a series of massive fortresses, and he rebuilt and adorned on a magnificent scale cities such as Samaria, Jerusalem, and Jericho; Strato's tower, which he renamed Caesarea in honor of Augustus, became the Roman capital of Palestine. In true Hellenistic fashion, he built theaters and stadia and sponsored plays and athletic contests—all offensive to the Jews; nevertheless, his greatest building project was the reconstruction of the temple at Jerusalem, begun in 20 B.C.

In stark contrast, Herod's domestic life was filled with turmoil, fostering his natural tendency toward cruelty and instability. He married ten wives, many for political reasons, including Mariamne, the granddaughter of the Hasmonean Hyrcanus II, and another Mariamne, daughter of the high priest Simon. Palace intrigue was rampant, spurred largely by Herod's sister Salome and Alexandra, mother of the Hasmonean Mariamne, and scores of assassinations and executions ensued, including those of Hyrcanus II, Mariamne, her brother the high priest Aristobulus, and three of Herod's own sons. Herod's shifting favor, complicated by the assassinations, necessitated numerous revisions of his choice as successor; the sixth version of Herod's final will, although disputed, named Archelaus as king of Judea and Samaria and Philip and Antipas as tetrarchs of the remaining territory. Herod died of arteriosclerosis in 4 B.C., shortly after executing his son Antipater and (unsuccessfully) ordering his sister Salome and her husband Alexas to murder several leading Jews in the hippodrome at Jericho, ostensibly to guarantee a period of national mourning at the time of Herod's death.

It was toward the end of Herod's reign that Jesus was born (Matt. 2:1). Matthew reports that Herod viewed the birth as a threat to his own power (v. 3). Not only did he seek to destroy Jesus (v. 13), he also ordered the massacre of all male children at Bethlehem under the age of two (v. 16), a deed which, although otherwise unattested, was typical of Herod's cruelty.

2. Herod Antipas (*ca.* 21 B.C.–A.D. 39), son of Herod the Great and his Samaritan wife Malthace, tetrarch of Galilee and Perea during the life of Jesus. He founded Tiberias as his capital city, in honor of the emperor who had bestowed on him the dynastic title Herod, by which he is designated in the New Testament. He became enamored of his niece Herodias, wife of his half-brother Herod II (called "Philip" in the New Testament), and married her, renouncing his first wife, daughter of the Nabatean king Aretas IV. This offended the Jews, and John the Baptist publicly renounced Antipas, who ordered his imprisonment (Matt. 14:3-5 par.); subsequently Antipas was manipulated into presenting the head of John as a favor to Herodias' daughter Salome (vv. 6-11 par.).

Antipas, who viewed Jesus as a successor to the troublesome Baptist (Matt. 14:1-2 par.), may have considered a plot against him (Luke 13:31-33). Later, Pontius Pilate sent Jesus as a Galilean to Antipas for judgment, but the tetrarch returned him to Pilate for condemnation (23:7-12).

In A.D. 36 Aretas retaliated for the earlier humiliation of his daughter, defeating Antipas' forces in a border skirmish. Tiberius dispatched Roman troops, but upon the emperor's death the mission was abandoned. The successor, Caligula, installed Herodias' brother Agrippa I as king over the territory of Philip, another son of Herod the Great (cf. Luke 3:1). The jealous Herodias convinced Antipas to seek similar treatment at Rome, but Agrippa accused him of being in league with the Parthians. For this Antipas, accompanied by Herodias, was exiled to Lyons in Gaul.

3. Herod Agrippa I (10 B.C.–A.D. 44), son of Aristobulus and grandson of Herod the Great and the Hasmonean Mariamne; brother of Herodias and nephew of Herod Antipas. Sent to Rome after the assassination of his father, he was raised in the imperial court and became the friend of Tiberius' son Drusus. As a young man he lived extravagantly, and, after fleeing in poverty to Palestine, he incurred the enmity of his benefactor Antipas. Returning to Rome in A.D. 36, he gained the friendship of Gaius Caligula but was imprisoned for an indiscreet remark concerning the emperor. Upon Tiberius' death six months later, the successor Caligula named Agrippa king over Herod Philip's territory, and through his complicity in Antipas' banishment Agrippa gained control of the Galilean tetrarchy. Seeking to persuade Caligula to forego erecting an imperial statue in the Jerusalem temple, Agrippa was in Rome when the emperor was assassinated. He interceded with the senate to enable Claudius' succession. For this the new emperor granted him Judea and Samaria. Agrippa's territory, which he ruled as king A.D. 41-44, now equaled that of Herod the Great.

Agrippa I earned the good will of his Jewish subjects by at least superficially respecting the Jewish law and by persecuting the Christian church. He executed James the son of Zebedee (Acts 12:2; "Herod") and imprisoned Peter (vv. 3-5). He died suddenly in A.D. 44, shortly after his subjects had hailed him as a god (cf. vv. 20-23).

4. Agrippa II (A.D. 27-ca. 100), son of Agrippa I. Raised in the Roman court, he was only seventeen at his father's death and considered too young to govern his territories, which were thus placed under procurators. In A.D. 50 he succeeded his uncle Herod as king of Chalcis (in modern Lebanon), which the emperor Claudius exchanged in 53 for the larger territory of Herod Philip (Batanea, Trachonitis, Gaulanitis) and the region of Abilene that had been ruled by Lysanias. Shortly after his succession in 54 Nero added several cities, including Tiberias, Tarichea, Julias, and Abila.

Partly because of an incestuous relationship with his sister Bernice, Agrippa held little favor among the Jews. He exercised control over the priesthood, and perhaps because of this religious authority Festus asked him to hear Paul's defense (Acts 25:13–26:32; "Agrippa"). Agrippa enlarged the palace of the Hasmoneans at Jerusalem and also undertook construction projects at Caesarea. When the First Jewish Revolt broke out in 66 he sided with Vespasian, and after the conquest of Jerusalem in 70 he accompanied Titus to Rome, where he was appointed praetor. He died ca. 100, the last of the ruling Herods.

See ARCHELAUS; PHILIP 6, 7.

Bibliography. S. H. Perowne, *The Life and Times of Herod the Great* (London: 1956); *The Later Herods: The Political Background of the New Testament* (London: 1958); S. Sandmel, *Herod: Profile of a Tyrant* (Philadelphia: 1967).

HERODIANS [hĭ rō'dĭ ənz] (Gk. *Hērōdianoi*). Partisans of the house of Herod. Although primarily a political party, they were religiously oriented and joined the Pharisees in opposing Jesus' teachings (Mark 3:16; 12:13 par. Matt. 22:16).

HERODIAS [hĭ rō'dĭ əs] (Gk. *Hērōdias*). The daughter of Aristobulus and Bernice, and half-sister of Herod Agrippa I. She first married Herod Philip (Herod II), the son of Herod the Great and Mariamne, daughter of the high priest Simon. She abandoned her husband to marry her half-brother Herod Antipas, her own uncle, who likewise divorced his current wife, the daughter of the Nabatean king Aretas IV. John the Baptist condemned this exchange, for which he was imprisoned, and Herodias, seeking to advance the fortunes of her daughter Salome, instigated her request for the head of John (Matt. 14:3-11 par. Mark 6:17-28; Luke 3:19-20). When Agrippa was named king over Herod Philip's territory, the ambitious Herodias urged her husband to seek similar honors; but Antipas was convicted of treason, and Herodias acquiesced to accompany him into exile in Gaul.

HERODION [hĭ rō'dĭ ən] (Gk. *Hērōdiōn* "heroic"). A Christian in Rome whom Paul greeted as his "kinsman," i.e., fellow countryman (Rom. 16:11).

HERODIUM [hĭ rō'dĭ əm] (Gk. *Hērōdeion*).† A fortress-palace built by Herod the Great at modern Jebel el-Fureidis, 6.5 km. (4 mi.) southeast of Bethlehem. Constructed from 24-15 B.C., the complex features seven stories of buildings some 762 m. (2500 ft.) atop a conical-shaped mountain; it is fortified by massive concentric walls and a steeply sloping glacis. Herod requested that he be buried at this luxurious desert retreat (cf. Josephus *BJ* i.33.9 [670-73]), but excavations have yet to locate his tomb.

It was at this site in 40 B.C. that Herod was ambushed by Antigonus, but he was able to counter and decisively defeat his Hasmonean attackers. After Herod's death the Romans selected Herodium as capital of a Palestinian toparchy. Along with Machaerus and Masada, the city was one of the last Jewish strongholds during the First Jewish Revolt, falling to the Romans in A.D. 72. It was reoccupied briefly during the Second Jewish Revolt (ca. 132).

An earlier fortress erected by Herod to defend the Idumean frontier was also called Herodium. Possibly near the foot of Mt. Nebo in Perea, its location remains unknown.

HERODOTUS [hĭ rŏd'ə təs].* A fifth-century B.C. Greek historian (ca. 484-ca. 424), whose nine-part *History* earned him the appellation "father of history" (Cicero *De leg.* i.1). Based on eyewitness accounts, oral and written traditions, and archaeological observations accumulated during his own travels, this work records the relationships between Greece and ancient Near Eastern peoples from the rise of Croesus as king of Lydia (560) through the end of the Persian War (478).

HERON (Heb. *'ᵃnāpâ* "short-tempered"). Any of several long-necked, long-legged birds of the family Ardeidae; biblical usage also so designates birds of similar species. According to Lev. 11:19 and Deut. 14:18, the several species of heron found even today in Palestine and surrounding regions were considered unclean. Some (e.g., the purple, slender, and the small silver herons) live there year round, while others (e.g., the blue, the cattle egret, and night heron) are winter guests.

The purple heron (*Ardea purpurea*), named after the dark purple color of its breast and sides, is found along the Jordan, the Kishon, and at the seacoast.

The blue heron (*Ardea cinerea*) has been attested in nearly all countries of the ancient Near East as far north as sixty degrees latitude. They fly slowly across Palestinian lakes in groups of fifteen to twenty, or quietly search for their prey on the shores.

The slender heron (*Ardeola ralloides*) is a smaller species having a strong, black beak, a long, flat crest of yellowish-red feathers with dark points, and reddish-yellow feathers on the sides of its head. Its shoulders and back are reddish and the rest of its body is white. This species breeds in overgrown swamps.

The cattle egret or buff-backed heron (*Ardeola ibis*), a white bird with red markings, little resembles the common heron; its body and legs are both quite short. It can be found in the countries along the southern coast of the Mediterranean Sea, throughout all of Africa, and in West Asia; in Egypt it is a very common bird, flocking by the hundreds to the steppes when the locusts swarm. In Palestine, too, this species is very common, breeding in large groups in the Huleh region. Often they sit on or near grazing cattle to pick insects off these animals.

The little egret (*Egretta garzetta*) is smaller than the standard silver heron, but is just as beautiful a silver-white. This species feeds mainly on small fish and is seen frequently in the Nile region.

The night heron (*Nycticorax nycticorax*) is easily identified by its squat posture, its short, thick beak, relatively short legs, and broader bill. Its head and chest are greenish-black; its neck and throat, an ashy gray; its breast and belly are straw yellow; and its legs are the color of flesh. Behind its head are three long, white, threadlike ornamental feathers. Though the night heron may occasionally spend the entire year in Palestine, it usually migrates from place to place and spends only part of its cycle in Palestine. A gregarious bird, it might winter anywhere in Africa where there is sufficient water and forest cover. It feeds on fish in the evening.

HESED (1 Kgs. 4:10, KJV). *See* BEN-HESED.

HESHBON [hĕsh'bŏn] (Heb. *ḥešbôn*).† A Moabite city located east of the Dead Sea, whose territory was contested by Israelites, Amorites, and Moabites from the time of the Israelite penetration of Transjordan to the end of Ahab's reign (mid-ninth century B.C.).

Heshbon was first taken by the Israelites when Sihon, king of the Amorites, refused their request for passage through his territory (Num. 21:21-31). The Reubenites and later the Gadites settled in the area of Heshbon after Sihon's defeat (Num. 32; Josh. 13:15-

28; 21:38-39; 1 Chr. 6:81). During the period of the Judges, Heshbon was again in Moabite hands, until Ehud's assassination of King Eglon signaled Moab's overthrow (Judg. 3:12-30). Heshbon remained an Israelite possession until the Moabite king Mesha seized it after Ahab's death. The city was Moabite from that time until its capture by the Ammonites (seventh century), and is featured in the oracles of Isaiah and Jeremiah (Isa. 15–16; Jer. 48).

Heshbon (then called Esbus) was incorporated into the Nabatean kingdom in Hellenistic times. It was captured by Alexander Janneus in the first century B.C. during the Maccabean Revolt, became an autonomous city, and gained the right to mint its own coinage (Josephus *Ant.* xiii.15.4 [397]). Heshbon was annexed to Roman Syria as Palestine became a province of that empire. It was the seat of a Christian bishop in the Byzantine period and later served as a district capital under the Mamelukes.

The site has been confirmed as modern Tell Ḥesbân, 56 km. (35 mi.) east of Jerusalem and 19 km. (12 mi.) southwest of Amman. Excavations at the site have determined nineteen phases of occupation from 1200 B.C. to A.D. 1500.

The absence of remains prior to 1200 B.C. may point to the transhumant character of the community in that period; some scholars interpret this lack of evidence to mean that Sihon's city was located at another site, perhaps nearby Jalul. Ammonite ostraca discovered at Tel Ḥesbân indicate a prosperous period of occupation in the seventh-sixth centuries. The most extensive remains are from the Hellenistic and Roman periods.

HESHMON [hĕsh'mŏn] (Heb. *ḥešmôn* "fruitfulness"). A place in the tribal territory of Judah between Hazar-gaddah and Beth-pelet, in the vicinity of Beersheba (Josh. 15:27). Its precise location is not known.

HETH [hĕth] (Heb. *ḥet*).† The second son of Canaan (Gen. 10:15 par. 1 Chr. 1:13), and eponymous ancestor of the Hittites (Gen. 23:10). Biblical references to the Hittites denote the populace of Neo-Hittite city-states in Syria and related elements among the pre-Israelite population of Canaan. Abraham purchased his burial cave at Machpelah from Hittites (ch. 23; 25:10; 49:32), and Rebekah and Isaac discouraged Jacob from marrying Hittite women (27:46), whom they also referred to as "Canaanite women" (28:1, 8).

HETHLON [hĕth'lŏn] (Heb. *ḥetlôn*). A place on the ideal northern boundary of Israel. It is mentioned at Ezek. 47:15 and 48:1 in connection with Damascus, Hamath, and Berothah. Its precise location is not known, but a possible identification is modern Heitela, northeast of Tripoli.

HEXAPLA [hĕx'ə plə] (Gk. *hexaplá* "sixfold").† An elaborate critical edition of Old Testament versions compiled A.D. 230-*ca.* 245 by the Alexandrian biblical critic and theologian Origen (Origenes Adamantius, *ca.* 185-*ca.* 254). Presented in six parallel columns are the Hebrew text in both Hebrew characters and Greek transliteration and the Greek versions of

Aquila, Symmachus, the Septuagint (with sigla denoting variance from the original Hebrew), and Theodotion. Three additional Greek versions are included for the Psalms. Origen's express purpose for this work was to equip Christians for discussion with the Jews, who relied on the Hebrew text.

The original text, comprising some six thousand folios in fifty volumes, was kept in the library at Caesarea and apparently was destroyed by fire in the Islamic conquest of 653. Fragments of the text were discovered at Milan in 1895. Although no portions of the Hebrew column survive, the LXX text was widely copied. A translation of that Greek text into Syriac, known as the Syro-Hexapla, was made by the Jacobite bishop Paul of Tella in A.D. 616-17 and preserves Origen's critical symbols.

Origen also produced an edition of the four Greek versions, the Tetrapla, which was either an earlier draft or a later abridgement of the Hexapla.

HEXATEUCH [hĕx'ə tŏok]. † The first six (Gk. *héx*) books of the Old Testament (Genesis-Joshua), viewed by some critical scholars as a major component of the primary history of Israel (Genesis–2 Kings). This proposal, which has largely been abandoned, is based on identification in these books of the major documentary sources (particularly the Priestly source, which was not attested in the books Judges–2 Kings) and on matters of content.

See BIBLICAL CRITICISM; PENTATEUCH.

HEZEKIAH [hĕz'ə kī'ə] (Heb. *ḥizqîyâ, ḥizqîyāhû, yeḥizqîyâ, yeḥizqîyāhû* "Yahweh [is] my strength").

1. The fourteenth king of Judah (*ca.* 715-687 B.C.), son of Ahaz and Abijah (**6**). Hezekiah came to the throne at age twenty-five (2 Kgs. 18:2; 2 Chr. 29:1); his accession date is synchronized with the Assyrian king Sennacherib's invasion of Palestine in 701, Hezekiah's fourteenth regnal year (2 Kgs. 18:13 par. Isa. 36:1). The events of Hezekiah's reign are recorded at 2 Kgs. 18–20; 2 Chr. 29–32; Isa. 36–39. He is described as an able and pious ruler (2 Kgs. 18:3-8; cf. Sir. 49:4) who led Judah in the dangerous years of Assyrian dominance and who fought deep-seated apostasy from Yahwism in Judah. He is named among Jesus' ancestors at Matt. 1:9-10; KJV "Ezekias."

The groundwork for the challenges Hezekiah would face was laid during the reign of his father, Ahaz (*ca.* 735-715). When Pekah of Israel and Rezin of Damascus formed an anti-Assyrian alliance which Judah refused to join, they attacked just as Ahaz took the throne (2 Kgs. 15:37). As Edomites and Philistines joined the attack Ahaz appealed to Assyria's Tiglath-pileser III for help, against the prophet Isaiah's admonition to trust in Yahweh (Isa. 7). The Assyrians struck swiftly, and in little more than a decade Judah's enemies had ceased to exist. Nevertheless, Judah was left an Assyrian vassal. Political subservience to Assyria meant recognition of their gods, and Ahaz placed a copy of an Assyrian altar in the Jerusalem temple. Contemporary prophetic passages (2:6-8, 20; 8:19-20; Mic. 5:12-14) and 2 Kgs. 16:2-4 illustrate the upwelling of both native and imported pagan practices during Ahaz' reign.

After Ahaz' death Hezekiah carefully worked at freeing Judah from Assyrian political and religious domination. He not only eliminated idols, divination practices, and human sacrifice, but he also did away with cult objects long associated with Yahwism. The latter included a bronze snake which was reputed to have been made by Moses himself (18:4). Hezekiah also attempted to close local shrines of Yahweh, which were often centers of pagan practices.

During Sargon's reign Hezekiah resisted Egyptian overtures to participate in an ill-fated coalition against Assyria, but upon Sennacherib's accession he formally witheld tribute (2 Kgs. 18:7) as uprisings spread from Mesopotamia to Palestine. Ignoring Isaiah's warnings, Hezekiah became a ringleader in the revolt and negotiated a treaty with Egypt (Isa. 30:1-7; 31:1-3). He began to prepare Jerusalem to withstand a siege, and dug the Siloam tunnel to assure the city's water supply (2 Kgs. 20:20; 2 Chr. 32:30). In 701 Sennacherib crushed resistance in Palestine and defeated an Egyptian relief army. Judah's fortified cities were reduced, one by one, until Hezekiah was shut up in Jerusalem "like a bird in a cage," according to Sennacherib's annals (*ANET*, p. 288). Seeing no way out, Hezekiah sued for terms. Tribute to Assyria was vastly increased, and some of Hezekiah's daughters became Assyrian concubines.

It is possible that 2 Kgs. 18:17–19:37 records a second revolt against Assyria, with the result that Hezekiah was besieged in Jerusalem once more, but with Isaiah's assurances that the city would not fall (Isa. 14:24-27; 17:12-14; 31:4-9; cf. 2 Kgs. 19:29-34). The Assyrians were subsequently turned back, either because of an epidemic in their army (2 Kgs. 19:35) or because Sennacherib was suddenly required at home (v. 7).

It was during this period that Hezekiah fell ill, but was granted fifteen years more life as an answer to prayer. His song of praise to Yahweh is recorded at Isa. 38:10-20. Upon Hezekiah's death in 687 the long revolt of Judah against Assyria ended, as his son Manasseh made peace.

2. (1 Chr. 3:23, KJV). *See* HIZKIAH **1**.

3. The head of a family whose descendants returned to Palestine with Nehemiah after the Babylonian exile (Ezra 2:16; Neh. 7:21). His Babylonian name was Ater, and both names are among those who set their seal to the renewed covenant (Neh. 10-17; KJV "Hizkijah").

4. One of the ancestors of the prophet Zephaniah (Zeph. 1:1; KJV "Hizkiah").

HEZION [hē'zĭ ən] (*ḥezyôn* "vision"). King of Syria; father of Tabrimmon and grandfather of Benhadad I (1 Kgs. 15:18). Many scholars identify him with REZON (cf. 11:25).

HEZIR [hē'zər] (Heb. *ḥēzîr* "swine, boar").

1. Leader of the seventeenth division of priests during the time of David (1 Chr. 24:15).

2. A Levite who sent his seal to the renewed covenant under Nehemiah (Neh. 10:20).

HEZRO [hĕz'rō] (Heb. K *ḥesrô*, Q *ḥesray* "entrenched"). A man from Carmel (**2**); one of David's mighty men (2 Sam. 23:35; KJV "Hezrai"; 1 Chr. 11:37).

HEZRON [hĕz'rən] (Heb. *ḥeṣrôn, ḥeṣrōn* "enclosed") (**PERSON**).
  1. The third son of Reuben (Gen. 46:9; Exod. 6:14; 1 Chr. 5:3). His descendants are called Hezronites (Num. 26:6).
  2. A son of Perez and grandson of Judah (Gen. 46:12; 1 Chr. 2:5; 4:1). His descendants constituted the Hezronite family of the tribe of Judah (Num. 26:21; cf. 1 Chr. 2:9ff.). He is listed among the direct ancestors of David and the royal house of Judah (Ruth 4:18-19) and occurs in both versions of Jesus' genealogy (Gk. *Esrōm*; Matt. 1:3; Luke 3:33; KJV "Esrom").

HEZRON [hĕz'rən] (Heb. *ḥeṣrôn* "enclosure") (**PLACE**).† A city on the southern border of Judah, west of Kadesh-barnea (Josh. 15:3). At Num. 34:4 the name is combined with ADDAR; scholars are uncertain whether the compound name or the listing as separate sites is correct. The precise location of the town has not yet been determined. *See* HAZAR-ADDAR.

HIDDAI [hĭd'ī] (Heb. *hidday* "cheerful"). An Israelite from Gaash who was one of David's thirty mighty men (2 Sam. 23:30). At 1 Chr. 11:32 he is called Hurai.

HIDDEKEL [hĭd'ə kĕl] (Heb. *hiddeqel;* Akk. *Idiglat;* Sum. Idigna). KJV name for the Tigris river (so RSV), following the MT (Gen. 2:14; Dan. 10:4).

HIEL [hī'əl] (Heb. *hî'ēl* "God lives").† A man of Bethel who rebuilt the city of Jericho during the time of King Ahab (1 Kgs. 16:34). He is said to have sacrificed two of his sons, Abiram and Segub, and buried them under the foundation in fulfillment of the word of the Lord as spoken centuries earlier by Joshua (Josh. 6:26). Although such sacrifices are attested in Israel and the ancient Near East for this period by archaeological and literary evidence, it is uncertain whether Hiel intentionally slaughtered his offspring or if their death—either by natural or accidental causes—occurred coincidentally during the forbidden reconstruction and was thus interpreted as divine punishment in accordance with Joshua's curse.

HIERAPOLIS [hī'ə răp'ə lĭs] (Gk. *Hierapolis* "holy city"). A city in southwestern Asia Minor overlooking the Lycus river; it survives as modern Pamukkale, 10 km. (6 mi.) north of Laodicea and 19 km. (12 mi.) northwest of Colossae. In ancient times it was a cult center for various Anatolian deities and prospered in the textile trade. Remarkable limestone formations were created on the terraces by water cascading from the hot mineral springs above. Epaphras, who was imprisoned with Paul, had ministered to this city, into which Christianity was introduced during the first century A.D. (Col. 4:12-13).

HIERONYMUS [hī'ə rŏn'ə məs] (Gk., Lat. *Hierōnymos*).*

  1. A district governor at the time of Antiochus V who antagonized the Jews (2 Macc. 12:2).
  2. Latin form of JEROME.

HIGGAION [hĭ gā'yŏn] (Heb. *higgāyôn*).† A musical notation of uncertain meaning, possibly indicating either a flourish or a quiet passage (Ps. 9:16; cf. JB "muted music"). Elsewhere the Hebrew term is translated as a musical sound (Ps. 92:3; RSV, NIV "melody'; KJV "solemn sound"; JB "rippling [of the harp]"; NJV "ten-stringed [harp]"). It can also connote "meditation" or "thought" as at 19:14 (JB "whispering"; NJV "prayer") and Lam. 3:62 (NIV "mutter"; NJV "pratings").

HIGH PLACE (Heb. *bāmâ*).† A place of worship, located on hilltops or man-made platforms. Old Testament accounts usually associate high places with pagan religious practices.
  High places were a common fixture of Canaanite religion when the Israelites entered Palestine. The common ancient Near Eastern cosmology held that the earth was flat, and that the gods dwelt in the heavens above. Consequently, a worship center located on an elevation had a better chance of gaining their attention.
  The layout and activities associated with high places varied. Some were open-air affairs with altars, sacred pillars (asherim), and idols, often located in groves of trees. Other high places had buildings erected upon them. The most elaborate was the famed ziggurat of the Marduk temple in Babylon: it is thought by many scholars to be the model for the tower of Babel (Gen. 11:1-9).
  On the eve of the conquest of Canaan Yahweh included the destruction of high places in his instructions to Moses (Num. 33:52), and they are identified elsewhere with such despicable activities as human sacrifice (2 Kgs. 16:4; 2 Chr. 33:6; Jer. 19:4-5), cultic prostitution (1 Kgs. 14:23-24), and divination (2 Kgs. 17:17). Balak the Moabite brought the diviner Balaam to a high place to survey the Israelites before attempting to curse them (Num. 22:41).
  Despite Yahweh's injunction, high places continued to exist throughout Israel's history, particularly after the establishment of the Monarchy. When Saul sought out Samuel to enlist his aid in recovering his father's lost donkeys, he was told that the seer had come to sacrifice on the high place (1 Sam. 9:11-19). After he was anointed king, Saul was met by a band of prophet-musicians who descended from a high place (10:5, 10).
  During David's reign the high place at Gibeon achieved some prominence (1 Chr. 16:39; 21:29), which extended into Solomon's reign (2 Chr. 1:3, 13).
  While 1 Kgs. 3:3 explains that people continued to sacrifice on high places "because there was no house (temple) built for the name of Yahweh until those days," the reigns of Solomon and those who followed in the divided monarchy are marked with references to thoroughly pagan religious practices on high places.
  When Israelite and Judean kings married foreign princesses, a common aspect of ancient international

relations, they were obliged to provide them with high places or shrines where they could worship their native gods. By this means polytheism was spread and reinforced in Israelite society (1 Kgs. 11:6-8).

Some kings, notably Hezekiah (2 Kgs. 18:4) and Josiah of Judah (23:4-20; 2 Chr. 34:3-7), mounted campaigns to eradicate the high places. More often, however, references are made to kings who "walked in the way of the Lord" without removing these installations (1 Kgs. 22:43; 2 Kgs. 12:3; 14:4; 15:4, 35; 2 Chr. 15:17; 20:33).

HIGH PRIEST (Heb. *hakkōhēn haggādōl* "the great priest," *hakkōhēn hammāšiaḥ* "the anointed priest").† The Old Testament mediator between Yahweh and the people of Israel who, in addition to performing sacrifices and rituals like other priests, acted to expiate the sins of the nation on the annual Day of Atonement. He is alternately called the chief priest (Heb. *kōhēn hār'ōš;* e.g., 2 Kgs. 25:18 par. Jer. 52:24; 2 Chr. 19:11).

The high priest descended from Eleazar, the son of Aaron. The office was normally hereditary and was conferred upon an individual for life (Num. 25:10-13). The candidate was consecrated in a seven-day ceremony which included investiture with the special clothing of his office as well as anointments and sacrifices (Exod. 29:1-37; Lev. 8:5-35).

The high priest was bound to a higher degree of ritual purity than ordinary levitical priests. He could have no contact with dead bodies, including those of his parents. Nor could he rend his clothing or allow his hair to grow out as signs of mourning. He could not marry a widow, divorced woman, or harlot, but only an Israelite virgin (Lev. 21:10-15). Any sin committed by the high priest brought guilt upon the entire nation and had to be countered by special sacrifice (4:1-12). Upon a high priest's death manslayers were released from the cities of refuge (Num. 35:25, 28, 32).

The book of Exodus (28:2-39) extensively details the special garments worn by the high priest. These consisted of a robe or outer garment, an ephod, breastplate, coat or undergarment, turban, and a girdle. It seems that the ephod and breastplate were permanently fastened together (v. 28). The robe was a sleeveless blue garment worn under the ephod, reaching perhaps to the feet and decorated along the skirt with embroidered pomegranates (cf. Num. 15:38-41) alternated with golden bells. The coat, worn beneath the robe, had sleeves and also reached the feet (Exod. 28:39). A golden plate engraved with the words "Holy to the Lord" was fastened to the front of the turban with blue lace (v. 36). Known as the "holy crown" (Heb. *nēzer haqqōdeš,* 29:6), this plate was intended to remove the iniquity of the "holy things which the sons of Israel consecrate" (28:38). Josephus (*Ant.* iii.7.6) indicates that the holy crown also had a three-tiered diadem worn over the turban and decorated with a floral design.

The Day of Atonement, celebrated on the tenth day of the month of Tishri, was Israel's great annual feast. It is the only day of fasting prescribed in Mosaic law, and the high priest was central to its celebration. The high priest left his home seven days before the feast began to live in an apartment in the temple. When the Day of Atonement came he bathed (Lev. 16:4) and made an offering. He then changed into linen garb to officiate at the atonement ceremonies. First, a young bull was brought before the high priest. Placing his hand upon its head, the high priest recited his sins and those of his household. After he sacrificed the bull, the high priest took its blood into the holy of holies, which he censed with incense. He then sprinkled the blood once on the mercy seat and seven times on the front of the ark. The second sacrifice, for the sins of the people, involved a goat chosen by lot from an identical pair. After slaughtering the goat, the high priest entered the sanctuary a third time, sprinkling the ark seven times with the goat's blood. Then he sprinkled the ark's veil seven times with the bull's blood, and another seven with goat's blood. He mixed together the remaining blood and smeared it on the horns of the golden altar of incense (Exod. 30:1-10). The first two sacrifices served to rid items associated with worship of pollution. The third sacrifice removed the people's guilt. After the high priest placed his hand upon the second goat and confessed the sins of the people, the scapegoat was led through the people to a site in the wilderness where it was killed. Once more the Israelites could stand blameless before God.

When the sacrifices were complete the high priest laid aside his linen garb and put on his rich clothing. Then he made burnt offerings which included the fat of the bull and goat that had been sacrificed on the temple grounds (Lev. 16:24). After another ritual bath the high priest changed again to linen and entered the holy of holies for the final time, recovering the censer which had stood therein throughout the sacrifices.

The office of high priest took on different dimensions after the Exile. It gained the qualities of prestige and dignity which had formerly been held by the king. In 520 B.C. the high priest Joshua and the Davidic governor Zerubbabel were identified as equals (Hag. 1:1, 12, 14; 2:2, 4), the "two anointed" of Yahweh (Zech. 4:14).

This political involvement became more pronounced. By the second century the high priest presided over a group of priests, scribes, and heads of families which formed the early Sanhedrin. During the Greek period the office of high priest was the target of ambitious and unscrupulous people, but the years of the Maccabean Revolt saw the restoration of some of its former glory.

For Christians, Jesus of Nazareth is understood to be the perfect high priest (cf. Heb. 5:5-10; 6:20). He took upon himself the sins of the entire world, and is the mediator of the new covenant between God and humankind. *See* MELCHIZEDEK.

The prayer which forms John 17, and the final portion of the Upper Room discourses (John 13–17) prior to Jesus' arrest in the Garden of Gethsemane, is often designated the High Priestly Prayer. The longest of the recorded prayers of Jesus, it is characterized by tenderness toward the disciples and those who would believe through them, and the triumphant expectation of Christ's victory. In 17:1-5 Jesus prays about his forthcoming passion and asks that God's will be done in him. In vv. 6-19 Jesus prays for the disciples; Jesus' self-consecration (v. 19) sets him apart to do God's will through his death. Finally, Jesus prays for those who will believe as a result of the disciples' ministry (vv. 20-26); he requests that God glorify them with a sense of unity analogous to the relationship between the Father and the Son.

HIGHWAY (Heb. *m^esillâ*).† As a land bridge between Asia and Africa situated between the Mediterranean Sea and the Syrian desert, Palestine supported a network of highways and lesser roads which peoples from the Hittites to the Romans utilized for trade and military purposes. Paved highways only came to Palestine with the Romans, but even the earlier highways clearly made travel easier and more direct.

Geography dictated the location of highways throughout the ancient Near East. The major international route was the Way of the Sea. This highway had its origin in the Lower Nile. It followed the coast, then cut through the Jezreel valley to Hazor and Damascus. From thence the highway branched north to Aleppo and south through Tadmor, to meet again at Mari. The highway proceeded southward along the Euphrates river, finally meeting what is now called the Persian Gulf. A major corollary of the Way of the Sea was known as the King's Highway. This route passed through the Transjordanian hill country, very near the desert. Although a secondary route, it anchored many east-west routes to the Way of the Sea. The King's Highway is mentioned in the Old Testament in conjunction with the Israelites' request for permission to traverse Edomite (Num. 20:17, 19; Judg. 11:14-20) and Amorite (Num. 21:22; Deut. 2:27) lands in their drive to Transjordan.

Most occurrences of the term figure in historical narratives (Judg. 20:31, 32, 45; 21:19; 1 Sam. 6:12; 2 Kgs. 18:17 par. Isa. 36:2; 7:3). The term is also used figuratively in poetry and prophecy (Isa. 11:16; 33:8; 49:11; 59:7; cf. Judg. 5:20; RSV "courses"; Joel 2:8; RSV "path").

HILEN [hī'lən] (Heb. *ḥîlēn*).† A village in the hill country of Judah, allotted to the Kohathite family of the Levites (1 Chr. 6:58). At Josh. 15:51; 21:15 it is called Holon.

HILKIAH [hĭl kī'ə] (Heb. *ḥilqîyâ* "Yahweh is my portion").†
1. The father of Eliakim, who was steward during the reign of King Hezekiah (2 Kgs. 18:18, 26; Isa. 22:20; 36:3).
2. The son of Shallum; high priest during the reign of King Josiah (1 Chr. 6:13; Ezra 7:1-2). It was he who discovered the law book while repairing the temple (2 Kgs. 22:4-14 par. 2 Chr. 34:9-22) and who subsequently became a leader in Josiah's reforms (2 Kgs. 23:4 par. 2 Chr. 35:8). One tradition calls him the brother of Jeremiah.
3. The son of Amzi; a Levite of the line of Merari (1 Chr. 6:45).
4. The son of Hosah; a Merarite Levite who lived in David's time (1 Chr. 26:11).
5. One of those who stood by Ezra when he read the law (Neh. 8:4); perhaps a layperson.
6. A chief priest and head of a priestly house who

returned from exile with Zerubbabel (Neh. 12:7, 21). Some scholars identify him with **5** above.
7. A priest from Anathoth; father of the prophet Jeremiah (Jer. 1:1).
8. The father of Gemariah, whom King Zedekiah sent to Nebuchadnezzar (Jer. 29:3).
9. An ancestor of Baruch, the servant of Jeremiah (Bar. 1:1, 7; KJV "Chelcias").
10. The father of Susanna (Sus. 2, 29, 33; KJV "Chelcias"). Some identify him with **2** above.

HILL COUNTRY (Heb. *har*).† The gradually ascending but rugged central ridge of Palestine, lying between the coastal plain and the Jordan river valley. It is bordered on the south by the wilderness of the Negeb and on the north by the varied terrain of Galilee.

The hill country played a role in Israelite plans for invading Canaan. Missions under both Moses (Num. 13) and Joshua (Josh. 2) to spy out the land proceeded along the central ridge. A reckless attempt to attack northward along it, against Moses' counsel, led to a defeat at the hands of the Canaanites and Amalekites at Hormah (Num. 14:44-45).

The hill country is mentioned in various phases of the invasion of Canaan. Joshua and the Israelites descended from the hill country and crossed the Jordan (after its waters were miraculously held back; Josh. 3:14-17) prior to the battles of Ai and Jericho. Later the Israelites rallied behind Joshua to protect the Gibeonite cities against the five Canaanite kings, led by Adonizedek of Jerusalem (10:1-27). This victory permitted the Israelites to attack southward through the hill country, capturing the major cities of Bezek, Schechem, Bethel, and Jerusalem.

HILLEL [Heb. *hillēl* "he greatly praised").†
1. The father of the judge Abdon, from the town of Pirath in Ephraim (Judg. 12:13, 15).
2. Hillel the Elder (*ca.* 60 B.C.–A.D. 20), rabbinic sage and a determinant force in the development of the oral law. A Babylonian native of Davidic descent, Hillel went to Jerusalem at age forty to study with the expositors Shemaiah and Abtalion. He so distinguished himself that he was named *nāśî* ("prince") of the Sanhedrin, a title inherited by his successors.

Tradition describes Hillel as a skilled teacher characterized by patience, humility, and piety, who was tolerant and conciliatory toward his opponents. His seven rules for interpretation of Scripture were highly influential in Pharisaic and Talmudic hermeneutics. Hillel and his disciples interpreted the Law more leniently than his contemporary Shammai. A number of his sayings and maxims have been preserved, many of which resemble the teachings of Jesus; perhaps best known is Hillel's version of the Golden Rule: "What is hateful to you, do not do to your neighbor; this is the whole Torah, all else is but commentary." A major enactment of Hillel is the *prozbul* (from Gk. *prós Boulé* "before the assembly"), which cancelled the Deuteronomic legislation requiring remission of all debts in the Sabbatical Year (cf. Deut. 15:2).

Hillel is generally regarded as the grandfather of

Gamaliel I, Paul's teacher, although some sources would make him his father.

Bibliography. N. N. Glatzer, *Hillel the Elder: The Emergence of Classical Judaism*, rev. ed. (New York: 1956).

HIN [hĭn] (Heb. *hîn*; Egyp. *hn*). A liquid measure equal to one-sixth of a bath, approximately 3.6 l. (1 U.S. gal.) *See* WEIGHTS AND MEASURES.

HIND (Heb. *'ayyalâ, 'ayyaleṭ*).† The adult female deer. Although the exact species cannot be identified with certainty, biblical references are probably to a variety of the European red deer *(Cervus elaphus)*. The Old Testament notes the hind's beauty (Prov. 5:19), surefootedness (2 Sam. 22:34 par. Ps. 18:33 [MT 34]; Hab. 3:19), and fertility (Job 39:1-4; Jer. 14:5; cf. Gen. 49:21, JB; Ps. 29:9, NJV; cf. RSV mg.). Adjuration by the "hinds of the field" at Cant. 2:7; 3:5 may represent a substitute for a divine name or simply a reference to procreative capacity.

See HART.

HIND OF THE DAWN (Heb. *'ayyeleṭ haššaḥar*).† Perhaps the name of a tune or a similar musical instruction, mentioned in the superscription to Ps. 22 (KJV "Aijeleth Shahar"). The phrase suggests a common theme of the Psalms, God's help to the needy (cf. 46:5).

HINNOM [hĭn'əm], **VALLEY OF** (Heb. *gê hinnōm*).† A deep valley south of Jerusalem, delineating the boundary between Judah and Benjamin (Josh. 15:8; 18:16). Some early traditions identified it with the Kidron valley east of the city and at the foot of the Mount of Olives, and some scholars have suggested that before the Monarchy the name was applied to the Tyropoeon valley, a north-south valley within Jerusalem separating the Ophel hill from the Upper (western) City on Mt. Zion. Most scholars now identify Hinnom with the Wâdī er-Rabâbi, a broad and deep gorge which begins west of the city near the modern Jaffa Gate and curves south of the city to meet with the Kidron valley at En-rogel. It is also called the valley of the son of Hinnom (Heb. *gê ḇen-hinnōm*; e.g., Josh. 15:8; 2 Chr. 28:3; Jer. 32:35; NJV "Valley of Ben-hinnom"; JB also "wadi Hinnom") and the valley of the sons of Hinnom (Heb. *gê ḇᵉnê-hinnōm*; 2 Kgs. 23:10, K; KJV "valley of the children of Hinnom").

At least as early as the Monarchy the valley (cf. Jer. 2:23) was associated with pagan cults which practiced human sacrifice to Molech and Baal (2 Kgs. 23:10; Jer. 19:5; 32:35); even the kings of Judah participated in such abominations (2 Chr. 28:3; 33:6). Accordingly, Jeremiah prophesied that in the Day of Vengeance Hinnom would be known as the valley of Slaughter (Jer. 7:32; 19:6). The infamy of these rites gave rise to the concept of Gehenna (a Greek transliteration of the Hebrew name) as a fiery place of punishment (cf. 2 Esdr. 7:36, RSV, KJV mg.; Matt. 5:22, RSV mg.).

HIRAH [hī'rə] (Heb. *ḥîrâ*). An Adullamite friend (MT Heb. *rēʿēhû*; LXX, Vulg. "shepherd," from

rōʿēhû) of Jacob's son Judah (Gen. 38:1, 12, 20-23). It was when Judah was visiting Hirah that he met the daughter of the Canaanite Shua whom he married (v. 2).

HIRAM [hī'rəm] (Heb. *ḥîrām, ḥîrôm*; abbreviation of *ᵃḥîrām* "[my] brother is exalted").†

1. Hiram I, king of Tyre (986-935 B.C.), a contemporary and friendly ally of David and Solomon. During Hiram's reign Tyre became the dominant city on the Phoenician coast and a prosperous commercial center. Hiram is credited with extensive building activity and with the colonization of such Mediterranean islands as Cyprus, Sicily, and Sardinia. He also erected new shrines to the gods Melqart and Astarte and inaugurated a new pilgrim feast in honor of Melqart.

According to the Old Testament, Hiram's first contact with Israel was shortly after the capture of Jerusalem, when he supplied craftsmen and raw materials for the construction of David's palace (2 Sam. 5:11 par. 1 Chr. 14:1). External evidence suggests that this arrangement actually may have been with Hiram's father Abibaal, who dispatched Hiram as his messenger (Josephus *Ant.* viii.5.3), or that it occurred toward the end of David's reign (cf. *Ap.* i.17-18, which would place Hiram's accession at 969). Hiram's long affection for David is attested at 1 Kgs. 5:1.

This cordial relationship continued upon the succession of David's son Solomon. Hiram provided timber for the construction of the temple, in exchange for which Solomon supplied wheat, beaten olive oil, and wine (1 Kgs. 5:11 par. 2 Chr. 2:10). This commercial alliance was complemented by a treaty of peace (1 Kgs. 5:12), perhaps symbolized by Solomon's marriage to a Phoenician princess (cf. 11:1; Eusebius *Praep. ev.* x.11). Twenty years later Solomon gave Hiram twenty cities in Galilee, apparently as repayment for Hiram's financial support of the temple project; Hiram, however, was dissatisfied with the inland sites, derisively labelling then CABUL ("worthless"; 1 Kgs. 9:10-14). The cities may have been collateral pending payment of the debt, for at 2 Chr. 8:2 Solomon is said to have rebuilt and resettled these cities "which Hiram had given him." Hiram also joined Solomon in lucrative maritime ventures based at the Israelite port of Ezion-geber, offering the guidance of experienced Phoenician sailors and probably also aiding in shipbuilding (vv. 26-28; 10:11, 22; 2 Chr. 8:17-18; 9:10, 21).

Upon his death Hiram was succeeded by his son Baal-eser I.

In 2 Chronicles his name occurs as Huram (**1**) (e.g., 2 Chr. 2:3, 11-12; 8:2, 18; 9:10).

2. A Tyrian metalsmith enlisted by Solomon for the ornamentation of the temple (1 Kgs. 7:13-14, 40, 45). *See* HURAM **2.**

3. Hiram II, king of Tyre (739–ca. 730 B.C.), called "king of the Sidonians." He greatly expanded the territory controlled by Tyre despite the aggression of the Assyrian Empire. Texts dating to 738 and 734-32 list him among territories paying tribute to Tiglath-pileser III (*ANET*, p. 283). In 733-32 he entered a coalition with Rezin of Damascus and the king of Ashkelon against Assyria; when the rebellion was quashed Hiram alone was pardoned.

4. Hiram III, king of Tyre (551-532 B.C.). Apparently a loyal vassal of King Nabonidus, he was summoned from Babylon to succeed his brother Maharbaal (Merbal; Josephus *Ap.* i.158-59). With the accession of Cyrus in 539 Tyre became part of the Persian Empire.

5. Hiram IV, king of Tyre and a contemporary of the Persian king Darius I Hystaspes (521-486 B.C.). Herodotus (*Hist.* vii.98) refers to him as Siromos.

Bibliography. H. J. Katzenstein, *The History of Tyre* (Jerusalem: 1973).

HIRELING (Heb. *śāḳîr*; Gk. *misthōtós*). A day laborer or paid worker. Unlike the slave, he was not considered a member of the master's household because he was hired only for a specific period of time, perhaps as short as a day. Accordingly, the transitory nature of the hireling's status became proverbial (cf. John 10:12-13).

One of the regulations concerning the hireling states that his wages were to be paid to him daily (Lev. 19:13); having to wait for his wages could create great hardship for such a person, and this ordinance was intended to guard against oppression of the hireling on the part of the employer (Deut. 24:14-15; Job 7:2; Jer. 22:13; Jas. 5:4). It appears from Deut. 15:18 that a hireling was paid twice as much as it cost to sustain a slave. Since he was not a member of the household, a hireling who was in service to a priest was not allowed to eat of the holy things (Lev. 22:10). The expression "according to the years of a hireling" (Isa. 16:14; 21:16) indicates a period which was measured to the day.

HISTORY.* From the ancient perspective, the events and circumstances of the past as remembered and transmitted, in both oral and written form.

The Bible contains a substantial amount of historical material, including the universal events of the "Primary History" contained in Gen. 1–11, the more particular record of Israel's development from the patriarchs through the fall of Samaria and Jerusalem in Gen. 12–2 Kings, the Chronicler's account of the Monarchy and the postexilic period in the books of 1-2 Chronicles and Ezra-Nehemiah, the life and teachings of Jesus in the four Gospels, and the history of the early Church in the book of Acts. Other bits of historical information can be found in the prophetic books and the Writings, including Ruth, Esther, and Daniel. Historical writings among the apocryphal books include 1 Esdras, 1-2 Maccabees, and perhaps Tobit and Judith.

Various types of historical data occur, including genealogies, census figures and tribal allotments, annals and chronicles, and the cherished deeds of Israel's leaders and people, often preserved in almost legendary form. All of these materials have been woven together in a distinctively religious, didactic fashion to comprise what theologians call "salvation history" (Ger. *Heilsgeschichte*) or redemptive history, a confessional account of the acts of God in human (and specifically Israelite) history.

The RSV translates as "history" Heb. *tôlēdōt*

"generations" (Gen. 37:2), indicating the genealogy or family history of Jacob, and *dibrê* "words" (2 Chr. 9:29), with reference to the chronicles of the prophet Nathan (cf. 1 Chr. 29:29).

See CHRONICLES, BOOKS OF; DEUTERONOMIST.

Bibliography. J. R. Porter, "Old Testament Historiography," pp. 125-162 in G. W. Anderson, ed., *Tradition and Interpretation* (Oxford: 1979); G. E. Wright, *God Who Acts: Biblical Theology as Recital.* SBT 8 (1952).

HITTITES [hĭt'īts] (Heb. *bᵉnê ḥēt*, *ḥittîm*; Akk. *Ḫatti*).† An Indoeuropean people who formed a powerful Anatolian empire in the second millennium B.C.; later an ethnic component of city-states in northern Syria and the Tauros mountain region of southeastern Anatolia.

I. History

Adopting the name Ḫatti from the non-Indoeuropeans who had inhabited south-central Anatolia in the third millennium, the Hittites appear as immigrants from the northeast *ca.* 2000. Hittite names are found in the archives of the Old Assyrian trading colony at Kanesh (modern Kultepe) *ca.* 1800. Later tradition notes a King Pithanas who conquered Nesas (perhaps Kanesh), which his son Anittas (who called himself "Great King") established as the Hittite capital. Labarnas gained control of several independent Anatolian city-states and is thus regarded as the founder of the Hittite Old Kingdom. Hittite interest turned toward northern Syria under Labarnas' son Ḫattusilis I, whose son and successor Mursilis I moved the capital to Ḫattusas (modern Boghazköy) and later captured Aleppo and defeated Babylon (*ca.* 1595, or 1531 following the low chronology), thus ending the First (Amorite) Dynasty of Babylon. Nevertheless, the rise of the Hurrians coupled with internal dissension curbed Hittite power for more than a century.

Codification of Hittite law in the early fifteenth century by Telepinus, generally regarded as the last king of the Old Kingdom, signalled a renewed vitality. A new, more stable dynasty established by Tudḫaliyas II was able to resist encroachment by the Egyptian Thutmose III (*ca.* 1468) and to expand Hittite influence. Šuppiluliumas I (*ca.* 1386-1356/1380-1350) consolidated Hittite power in Anatolia and spread the Hittite Empire by conquering city-states in northern Syria and subjugating Mitanni. Despite winning the allegiance of Egyptian vassal cities in Syria, Šuppiluliumas sought to maintain peace with Egypt; however, a failed marriage alliance with Tutankhamen's widow and the concomitant murder of the Hittite envoy precipitated a state of war. Rebellion among the provinces as well as Egyptian aggression occupied Šuppiluliumas' successor, Mursilis II; Mursilis' Plague Prayer (*ANET*, pp. 394-96) interprets the outburst of plague as divine punishment for breach of covenant with Egypt. Territorial ambitions of the Egyptian Nineteenth Dynasty culminated in the Hittite king Muwatallis' indecisive victory at Kadesh on the Orontes (*ca.* 1297/1286); sixteen years later Ḫattusilis III and Rameses II concluded the Silver Peace (*ANET*, pp. 199-203), a parity treaty sealed by the marriage of a Hittite princess to Rameses. Despite aid from this

The King's Gate at the Hittite capital of Ḫattusas (Boghazköy) (B. K. Condit)

new ally, Hittite power waned as the result of increased rebellion among subject peoples and famine caused by drought. The empire collapsed with the destruction of Ḫattusas by the invading Sea Peoples (*ca.* 1200).

From the twelfth to the eighth centuries Hittite civilization survived in a number of city-states in northern Syria and the Taurus mountain range, called in Akkadian records the "land of Ḫatti." Among these Neo-Hittite (or, less correctly, Syro-Hittite) states were Aleppo, Arpad, Carchemish, Hamath on the Orontes, and Sam'al. Already kept in check by the more extensive Aramean kingdoms, these states were conquered by the Assyrians *ca.* 720.

II. Biblical References

Hittites, traced to the eponymous ancestor Heth, are reckoned among the descendants of Canaan (Gen. 10:15 par. 1 Chr. 1:13). They are recorded among the pre-Israelite population of Canaan, particularly in the region of Hebron (Gen. 23:3-20) and the central hill country (Num. 13:29), and their territory is among that promised to the Israelites for conquest (e.g., Gen. 15:20; Deut. 7:1; Josh. 1:4). Abraham purchased from the Hittites the field of Machpelah as a family burial plot (Gen. 23), and his descendants married their daughters (26:34; 27:46). Scholars identify these people with the Neo-Hittites of northern Syria; thus Jerusalem's ancestry is said to be Hittite and Amorite, reminiscent of the Assyrian designation of the region as "Ḫatti and Amurru."

Tidal king of Goiim, an ally of Chedorlaomer (Gen. 14:1), may be identified with Tudḫaliyas I. David, whose officers included the Hittites Ahimelech (1 Sam. 26:6) and Uriah (2 Sam. 11:3ff.), maintained diplomatic relations with King Toi of Hamath (8:9-12). Solomon entered marriage alliances with the Hittites (1 Kgs. 11:1) and traded with the Hittite city-states (10:29). Later kings apparently formed military alliances with them as well (cf. 2 Kgs. 7:6).

III. Culture

Excavations at Boghazköy and other Anatolian sites have uncovered extensive remains of art, architecture, and literature which illuminate the development of Hittite civilization. Some ten thousand clay tablets were discovered in the royal archive, representing literary, administrative, and legal texts. From these texts scholars have determined that the predominant language of the Old Kingdom and the empire was a western Indoeuropean tongue, called by the Hittites Nesian (or Nesite) after their first capital; the cuneiform script was adopted *ca.* 1600. Two other Indoeuropean languages are also in evidence, Luwian (the language of Arzawa; cf. EA 31-32) and Palaic. With the fall of the empire hieroglyphic Hittite, closely related to Luwian, became the language of the Neo-Hittite states.

Hittite law, once generally accepted as the forerunner of Old Testament law, is in general more humane than other Mesopotamian law, particularly with regard to compensation and retaliation as well as women's rights. In international relations the inclination was toward diplomacy and clemency; study of Hittite treaty texts has been a valuable aid to interpretation of the biblical concept of covenant.

The Hittites worshipped a myriad of deities, many associated with isolated local shrines. The head of the pantheon was the weather-god Teshub, apparently adopted from the Hurrians; his consort Ḥepa and their son Sharruma also figure prominently. The official state religion focused on the sun-goddess Arinna, patron of Ḥatti and advisor to the monarchy. Hittite theology viewed these various deities as primary forces behind natural phenomena and historical processes, and divination and magic were important aspects of religious practice.

Bibliography. O. R. Gurney, *The Hittites*, 2nd ed. (Baltimore: 1961); H. A. Hoffner, "The Hittites and Hurrians," pp. 197-228 in D. J. Wiseman, ed., *Peoples of Old Testament Times* (New York:1973).

HIVITES [hĭv'īts, hī'vīts] (Heb. *ḥiwwî*). A people dispossessed during the Israelite invasion of Palestine (Exod. 3:8, 17; 13:5, 23:23, 28; Deut. 7:1; Josh. 3:10). Little is actually known about the Hivites, and they are mentioned in no extrabiblical sources.

The Hivites are described as the descendents of Canaan, the son of Ham (Gen. 10:15; 1 Chr. 1:15). At Gen. 34 Shechem, son of Hamor the Hivite, violates Jacob's daughter Dinah. Hamor, Shechem, and all the males in their city submit to circumcision so Shechem can marry Dinah, but her brothers Simeon and Levi kill them all soon afterwards. Gibeon's Hivite inhabitants employ a ruse to escape destruction at the hands of the Israelites, at the price of becoming their servants (Josh. 9). Other Hivites joined the northern Canaanite coalition which Joshua defeated at the Waters of Merom (Josh. 11:3, 19). Hivite cities were included in David's enumeration of the fighting men of Israel, an act punished by a three-year famine in Israel (2 Sam. 24).

The Hivites cannot be identified with any certainty. Some scholars suggest that the name is interchangeable with that of the Horites (cf. Gen. 34:2; Josh. 9:7, where the MT reads "Hivites" and the LXX "Horites"); indeed, only the middle consonant of the gentilics Hivite, Hittite, and Horite differs in the Hebrew spelling. Moreover, extrabiblical sources suggest that the areas of Hivite occupation coincide with the region of city-states ruled by a Hurrian aristocracy.

HIZKI [hĭz'kī] (Heb. *ḥizkî*, an abbreviated form of Hezekiah). A Benjaminite; son of Elpaal (1 Chr. 8:17; KJV "Hezeki").

HIZKIAH [hĭz kī'ə] (Heb. *ḥizqîyâ* "strength of Yahweh," a form of Hezekiah).

1. A son of Neariah and descendant of Zerubbabel, thus a member of the royal house of Judah (1 Chr. 3:23; KJV "Hezekiah").

2. (Zeph. 1:1, KJV). *See* HEZEKIAH **4.**

HOBAB [hō'băb] (Heb. *ḥōḇāḇ* "beloved").† The son of Reuel (Num. 10:29; KJV "Raguel"). He was either the father-in-law (so RSV, JB; Heb. *ḥōṯēn*), brother-in-law (NIV; cf. KJV), or son-in-law (R. G.

Boling, *Judges*. AB [1975], p. 57; so LXX from Heb. *ḥāṯān*) of Moses. He and his descendants were Kenites, travelling metalsmiths apparently related to the Midianites (Judg. 1:16; 4:11). No doubt because of the geographical expertise gained through his trade he was invited by Moses to accompany the Israelites in their wilderness wanderings (Num. 10:29-32).

HOBAH [hō'bə] (Heb. *ḥōḇâ* "the hidden").† A place north of Damascus to which Abraham pursued Chedorlaomer and the kings allied with him (Gen. 14:15). The name is preserved in Ḥoba, the ruins of which are located 96 km. (60 mi.) northwest of Damascus. However, some scholars associate it with the territory of Ube mentioned in the Amarna Letters, a region whose capital was Tell el-Salihiye, 16 km. (10 mi.) east of Damascus.

HOBAIAH [hō bā'yə] (Heb. *ḥªḇayyâ*).† A family of returning exiles unable to prove their priestly descent (Neh. 7:63; KJV "Habaiah"). *See* HABAIAH.

HOD [hŏd] (Heb. *hôḏ* "majesty"). A son of Zophah of the tribe of Asher (1 Chr. 7:37).

HODAVIAH [hŏd'ə vī'ə] (Heb. *hôḏawyâ, hôḏawyāhû* "praise the Lord").

1. A son of Elioenai and descendant of Zerubbabel (1 Chr. 3:24).

2. The head of a family in the half-tribe of Manasseh (1 Chr. 5:24).

3.† The son of Hassenuah of the tribe of Benjamin (1 Chr. 9:7). Some scholars consider the name here to be a corruption of Heb. *wîhûḏâ*, in which case he would be the same as the Judah of Neh. 11:9.

4. A Levite whose descendants returned from the Exile under Zerubbabel (Ezra 2:40). At Neh. 7:43 he is called Hodevah. It is likely that Judah, at Ezra 3:9, refers to the same person; the Hebrew reading "sons of Judah" (so RSV, KJV) should probably be changed to "sons of Hodaviah," since the reference is to Levites.

HODESH [hō'dĕsh] (Heb. *ḥōḏeš* "new moon"). A wife of Shaharaim, the Benjaminite (1 Chr. 8:9).

HODEVAH [hō dē'və] (Heb. K *hôḏ^ewâ*, Q *hôḏ^eyâ*). A Levite whose family returned from exile with Zerubbabel (Neh. 7:43). *See* HODAVIAH **4.**

HODIAH [hō dī'ə] (Heb. *hôḏîyâ* "Yahu is my splendor").

1. The husband of a Judahite woman; brother-in-law of Naham (1 Chr. 4:19).

2. One of the Levites who interpreted the law to the people of Jerusalem when Ezra read it publicly at the Water Gate (Neh. 8:7-8; 1 Esdr. 9:48; KJV "Hodijah"). He also helped lead the worship on the day of penitence (Neh. 9:5). He may be the same as **3** or **4.**

3. A Levite who signed Ezra's covenant (Neh. 10:10).

4. Another Levite who endorsed Ezra's covenant (Neh. 10:13).

5. A leader of the people and signer of Ezra's covenant (Neh. 10:18).

HOE (Heb. *ma'ḏēr*, *'āḏar*). A tool consisting of an iron blade set at the end of a slightly bent shaft, used to prepare the ground for planting (Isa. 5:6; KJV "dig"; 7:25; KJV "mattock"). *See* MATTOCK.

HOGLAH [hŏg'lə] (Heb. *ḥoglâ* "partridge"). One of the five daughters of Zelophehad the Gileadite (Num. 26:33; 27:1). She and her sisters received an inheritance in Manasseh, since they had no brothers (Josh. 17:3); they married cousins, so that their inheritance would remain in the tribe of Manasseh (Num. 36:11). The name, which also occurs in Samaria Ostracon 47, may also be a place name (cf. Beth-hoglah).

HOHAM [hōhăm] (Heb. *hôhām*). An Amorite king of Hebron who, along with four other kings, sought to take vengeance upon the Gibeonites for making peace with Israel. He and his allies were defeated by Joshua at Beth-horon and hanged (Josh. 10:3-4, 23-27).

HOLINESS CODE.† Name ascribed by critical scholars to Lev. 17–26, originally derived from the recurring statement "You shall be holy; for I the Lord your God am holy" (e.g., 19:2; cf. 20:26); represented by the symbol H. Regarded by some scholars as an independent code inserted into the Priestly narrative, these chapters constitute more properly a loose collection of legal material concerning such matters as sexual conduct and civil damages and, in particular, cultic prescriptions regarding the priesthood, sacrifices, festivals, and the Sabbatical Year. These "laws of holiness" reflect the Israelite concern for ethical and cultic purity befitting their unique relationship with God (cf. chs. 18–20).

See LEVITICUS, BOOK OF; BIBLICAL CRITICISM.

HOLINESS, HOLY.†

I. Terminology

The wide range of English words that express holiness are Teutonic (holy, holiness, hallow) or Latin (sacred, sacerdotal, consecrate; sanctify, sanctuary, saint) in derivation. In Scripture they usually translate two basic words: Heb. *qāḏôš* and Gk. *hágios*. The Hebrew root *qdš* (noun *qōḏeš*; adj. *qāḏôš*; verb *qāḏēš*) suggests cutting off or separation: in cultic usage, separation from mundane existence and for the service and worship of God. In later usage it came to mean primarily the separation, the "wholly otherness," of God himself in relation to everything creaturely. Several other Hebrew terms are used in connection with *qāḏôš*: *ḥerem*, which refers to things "devoted" or set apart to God, particularly as an offering (e.g., Lev. 27:28); *nāzar* "to consecrate, separate" (15:31; Ezek. 14:7) from which the name Nazirite derives (Num. 6:8; cf. RSV mg.); *ṭōhar* "purity" and the piel of *ṭāhar* "to purify," the ritual correlate of *qōḏeš*; and *ḥasîḏ* "holy one" (RSV "faithful," "godly one"), which is related to *ḥeseḏ*, God's love, faithfulness, and mercy. The LXX and New Testament employ Gk. *hágios* and its derivatives as the nearest equivalent to *qāḏôš*; as a rule it is preferred to the more common *hierós*, a word the LXX and New Testament avoid because of its wide usage in relation to pagan religions

(but cf. forms of *hierós* in 2 Tim. 3:15 and in reference to the temple and the Jewish priesthood). Other Greek words related in meaning to *hágios* include *hosiós*, sometimes used as an equivalent of *hasîḏ* (Acts 2:27; 13:35 quoting Ps. 16:10; Acts 13:34 quoting Isa. 55:3; 1 Tim. 2:8; Tit. 1:8; Heb. 7:26); *semnós* "pure" (e.g., Phil. 4:8); and *hagnós*, which suggests moral purity (2 Cor. 7:11; 1 Tim. 5:22).

II. Biblical Teachings

Holiness lies at the heart of biblical teaching; it ties together and in a sense contains all of the other great themes of Scripture. It is first and foremost the root or core of God's being, encompassing all other divine attributes, and therefore is central to the life of God's people. The whole of the Jewish and Christian understandings of God and his relationship to his people is summed up in the command, "You shall be holy; for I the Lord your God am holy" (Lev. 19:2; cf. 1 Pet. 1:15).

A. Old Testament. The Jewish concept of holiness grew from cultic roots. Manifest concretely in the sanctuary (Ps. 28:2) and all that was associated with it, holiness characterized the temple site (1 Chr. 29:3; Isa. 11:9; 56:7; 64:10) as well as its chambers (Ezek. 42:13; 46:19) and courts (Isa. 62:9), and the city of Jerusalem (Neh. 11:1, 18; Isa. 48:2; 52:1). Other places theophanic vision and divine presence likewise were holy, including the holy ground of Sinai (Exod. 3:5) and the place near Jericho (Josh. 5:15). God's presence in the camp of the Israelites rendered it holy (Deut. 23:14). All objects related to cultic service were holy—all offerings and sacrifices (e.g., Lev. 7:1), tithes (Deut. 26:13), and priestly vestments (Lev. 16:4). Such cultic holiness was a physical and communicable property (Exod. 29:37; 30:29; but cf. Hag. 2:12). Furthermore the times set apart by God for worship were holy, (Gen. 2:3; Exod. 20:8; Neh. 9:14; 10:31 [MT 32]; Isa. 58:13), as was the jubilee (Lev. 25:12).

The cultus, however, was meaningless without the covenant in which it was established. Through God's covenant with the people of Israel he created a holy people, communicating to them his holiness by dwelling in their midst (Deut. 7:6; 26:19; Jer. 2:3). The people were holy as set apart from other nations who were profane. Within the people, some were accorded a special degree of holiness, owing to their special functions: the priests and Levites (Exod. 29:1ff.; Lev. 8:12, 30; 21:8), Nazirites (Num. 6:5ff.), warriors involved in holy war (1 Sam. 21:5-6; cf. Isa. 13:3), and the prophets (2 Kgs. 4:9; Jer. 1:5).

In every instance, whether with things or people, it was the presence of God that imparted holiness. The Israelites expressed this with particular power in their reverence for God's "holy name," which constituted the actual presence of God with them (Lev. 20:3; 22:2; 1 Chr. 16:10, 35; Ps. 33:21; 103:1). The name of God was opposed to everything profane, but God's holiness transcends even this earthly duality of sacred and profane. His holiness stands over against everything creaturely (Isa. 40:25); thus holiness, even in people, is never natural but always bestowed since it is properly God's alone. The Old Testament usually specifies rites of consecration by which people and things were made holy. When something was made holy, it then partook of God's own holiness, transcending itself in order to become literally representative of God's holiness. Hence angels, because of their proximity to God, are called "holy ones" (Job 5:1; Ps. 89:6-7 [MT 7-8]; cf. Mark 8:38; Acts 10:22; Rev. 14:10).

By the time of the prophets the notion that God's holiness belonged to his person became so strong that holiness was virtually synonymous with God's deity (e.g., Isa. 6:3; cf. 5:16; Hos. 11:9). Thus only God is said to sanctify himself; Heb. *niqdaš* "show oneself holy" is used only with God as the subject (e.g., Lev. 10:3; Num. 20:13; Isa. 5:16; Ezek. 20:41). To one standing under the transcendent mystery of God's holiness, it appears as a "terrible good" (cf. Ps. 99:3; 111:9), evoking awe sometimes to the point of terror (cf. "the fear of the Lord") and at the same time an all but irresistible fascination (cf. R. Otto).

Among people, then, holiness was a condition bestowed by God through consecration, but in turn it brought demands, particularly that of purity (Deut. 7:6). The scope of that demand is spelled out in the Holiness Code (Lev. 17–26); all of its rules, both cultic and personal, follow from the basic command, "You shall be holy; for I the Lord your God am holy" (19:2). Here holiness is linked to the language of ritual purity (*ṭōhar*), and the supernatural categories of holy and profane coincide in some measure with the natural distinction between clean and unclean. The prophets, however, stress not merely ceremonial purity, but inward holiness; this development paralleled the development of the concept of holiness as God's personal essence. The personal character of God's holiness is seen in two aspects of holiness which the prophets greatly enriched: God's moral perfection (Hab. 1:13), and holiness not simply as the nature of God's being but as that being expressed through the will and action of God in judgment and redemption (e.g., Isaiah). Isaiah's characteristic name for God, "the Holy One of Israel" (e.g., Isa. 12:6; 17:7), expresses the dual orientation of holiness: to God as the Holy One and to the people of Israel placed under the awesome fact of God's holiness and thus for whom holiness ought to be a defining characteristic. Because of Israel's chronic unholy behavior, however, God becomes to the unclean a fire of judgment (10:16-17; cf. Hos. 6:10; 9:4). Yet to the remnant of the faithful he is truth and life (Isa. 10:20-21) and the fire of holiness becomes a purifying fire (cf. 6:6-7). The remnant is to be holy, living under the protection and light of God's holiness and awaiting the time when holiness will triumph (4:3-6). Thus the prophets' final word is that God's holiness, because it also includes his love, mercy, and faithfulness (*ḥeseḏ*), is ultimately redemptive and not destructive, and that redemption to the end of holiness is wholly divine and not human (Hos. 11:9).

B. *New Testament.* The New Testament writers were firmly grounded in the Old Testament concept of holiness. Thus allusions to and imagery derived from the Jewish cultus are full of references to cultic holiness (e.g., the sanctuary, Matt. 24:15; Jerusalem, 27:53; Rev. 11:2; the scriptures, Rom. 1:2; the law, 7:12; prophets, Acts 3:21). The continuity between the testaments, then, is great, but the New Testament transposes all of this into the context of the new people of God and new covenant, and in the process further develops the prophetic emphasis on spiritual and ethical holiness and its foundation in the person and character of God. Although relatively few explicit references to God's holiness appear in the New Testament, that foundation remains the center of the Christian conception of holiness.

1. God the Father. The Lord's Prayer is the best known reference to the Father's holiness. "Hallowed be thy name" (Matt. 6:9 par. Luke 11:2) is clearly within the Hebrew tradition of the holy name of God; this does not suggest that the one praying hallows God's name, but rather that he assents that God alone sanctifies his name. Jesus reinforces that connection between the Father's holiness and his name in the high-priestly prayer (John 17:11). The Father is also clearly in view in 1 Pet. 1:15-17 where he calls people to holiness because he himself is holy. The book of Revelation is saturated with the sense of God's holiness, repeating Isaiah's trisagion (Rev. 4:8) and conjoining praise for God's holiness with praise for his glory, honor, and power issuing in creation (cf. v. 11).

2. Jesus Christ. Though few, the references to Jesus' holiness are weighty with significance. For Luke, Jesus' holiness is grounded in his miraculous birth, receives an external sign in his baptism (by which Jesus is seen to be the bearer of the Holy Spirit), and is manifest in his triumphs over unclean spirits. The demons themselves acknowledge Jesus as "the Holy One of God" (Luke 4:34), as does Peter in his confession (John 6:69; cf. 1 John 2:20). The peculiarly unceremonial character of Jesus' holiness is most striking in view of his constant contact with things and people considered "unclean" (e.g., lepers, prostitutes, unlawful food). Jesus' holiness has strong associations with his love and his power, but it also contains an element of judgment which is seen, for instance, in the temple cleansing. His holiness, therefore, is not merely like that of the God of the prophets; it is God's own holiness, and it reveals the deity of Christ. Having been consecrated by the Father before being sent into the world (John 10:36), Jesus also consecrates himself (17:19; Gk. *hagiázō* with the reflexive pronoun), an act of which only God is capable. Similarly Jesus is called "the holy one, the true one" (Rev. 3:7), attributes which he shares with the Father (6:10). Moreover, just as the prophets saw God's holiness issuing in the redemption of unholy Israel, so Jesus' holiness issues in the sanctification of believers through his atoning self-sacrifice (Heb. 2:11, 14; 10:10, 14) and the blood of his new covenant (10:29; 13:12). Christ is both the holy priest entering the heavenly sanctuary and the holy and spotless victim, the paschal lamb (1 Cor. 5:7; Heb. 9:25-26). By his own divine holiness he is able to sanctify others, again as only God can do (Eph. 5:26; Heb. 9:13).

3. Holy Spirit. The increasing use of the name Holy Spirit in the New Testament indicates not only that God's Spirit is to be identified with God himself in some sense, but also that the Spirit communicates God's essential being by communicating his holiness. Like Christ, the Spirit is shown to be divine in its sanctifying work (Rom. 15:16). In this Christ and the

Spirit (sometimes called the Spirit of Christ; e.g., 8:9) are linked in holiness and its outworking, and because of that link the Spirit can impart holiness to the Church (2 Thess. 2:13). See HOLY SPIRIT.

4. The Church. The redemptive work of Christ and its application through the Holy Spirit creates a new people of God (1 Pet. 2:9) which like Israel is called to be holy (1:16; cf. Lev. 11:44). Sanctified by Christ and in the Spirit 1 Cor. 1:2; 6:11; Eph. 5:26), its members are united in fellowship with the saints and are made a "holy temple in the Lord" in which the Holy Spirit dwells (2:12-22), both individually and corporately. Thus the Church's holiness is not its own, but it is the holy and sanctifying presence of God within it. Although the word "saints" sometimes suggests the heroes of the faith, its characteristic reference is to all Christians, who are "called to be saints" (Rom. 1:7; 1 Cor. 1:2) "in Christ Jesus" (Phil. 1:1), and are "God's chosen ones, holy and beloved" (Col. 3:12). In this is often an eschatological thrust which, like the book of Revelation, links holiness with a participation in the glory of God, "the inheritance of the saints in light" (1:12; cf. Acts 20:32; Eph. 1:18).

Although the complete revelation of the glory of holiness may lie in the future, holiness itself *(hagiasmós)* is a state which is already in existence and at the same time a process toward that eventual fulfillment (Rom. 6:19, 22; 1 Thess. 4:3-4, 7). The holy people of God are called to holy living precisely because they have been made holy in Christ, not as a means to that holiness. Holiness issues in holy action and holy bearing (cf. "holy and blameless"; Eph. 1:4; Col. 1:22), and the New Testament is often at pains to specify the spiritual and ethical characteristics of that holy life— from the Sermon on the Mount to the letters to the churches in Revelation. In its ethical dimension holiness is characterized by purity of heart (Matt. 5:8; cf. 1 Tim. 1:5; 2 Tim. 2:22; Jas. 1:27) and the mutual service of love among the saints which builds up the body of Christ (Eph. 4:12-16). At root it is a sacrificial life which participates in the sacrificial life of Christ (Rom. 12:1; cf. Phil. 2:17; 3:10). As such it is wholly opposed to the life of uncleanness, that which conforms to the world (Rom. 12:2). The apostle Paul suggests that the communion in holiness is so strong that it may be communicated, as among members of a family, so that children of a believer and an unbeliever are not unclean but are holy (1 Cor. 7:14). The holy temple of God, the Church, is thus aptly called "the communion of the saints" who are bound together in the fellowship of the Holy Spirit (2 Cor. 13:14), in the supplying of each other's needs (e.g., Rom. 12:13), in the sign and seal of the holy kiss (1 Cor. 16:20; 2 Cor. 13:12; 1 Thess. 5:26), and in participation in the sanctifying fellowship of baptism (1 Cor. 6:11) and the Lord's Supper (cf. 1 Cor. 10:16-17), having in common one "most holy faith" (Jude 20).

Bibliography: R. Otto, *The Idea of the Holy*, 2nd ed. (London: 1950); S. Neill, *Christian Holiness* (New York: 1960).

HOLM TREE (Heb. *tirzâ*).† In biblical usage probably the holm oak (*Quercus ilex* L.), a small evergreen resembling the holly (Isa. 44:14, RSV; cf. Sus. 58; Gk. *prínon*). The true holm tree (*Ilex aquifolium*

L.) is a holly and is not found in this setting. Other possible identifications include the cypress (*Cupressus sempervirens* L.; so KJV, JB, NIV) and the plane tree (*Platanus orientalis* L.; so NJV).

HOLOFERNES [hŏl′ə fûr′nēz] (Gk. *Olophernēs*).† Chief general of the Assyrian army, commissioned by King Nebuchadnezzar to punish the territories of western Asia for failing to aid in the king's war on Media (Jdt. 2:4-13). With his enormous army Holofernes pillaged the eastern Mediterranean, seeking also to destroy all worship but that of the Assyrian king. Despite Jewish resistance and the warning that their god made the Jews invincible, Holofernes laid siege to Bethulia. There he was deceived and beheaded by the widow Judith (13:1-10), who thereby liberated the city.

No such general is known from Assyrian records. However, Diodorus Siculus notes a Persian general Holofernes who invaded Asia Minor at the command of Artaxerxes III in 350 B.C. (*Hist.* xxxi.19.2-3).

HOLON [hō′lŏn] (Heb. *ḥōlōn, ḥōlôn*).

1. A city in the hill country of Judah (Josh. 15:51) later assigned to the Levites (21:15). At 1 Chr. 6:58 it is called Hilen. Most scholars identify the site as modern Khirbet ʿAlîn, 16 km. (10 mi.) northwest of Hebron in the region of Beth-zur.

2. A city in the tableland of Moab (Jer. 48:21). The site remains unknown.

HOLY OF HOLIES (Gk. *hágia hagíōn*).* The innermost and most sacred precinct of the Israelite sanctuary (Heb. 9:3, RSV; KJV "holiest of all"). See MOST HOLY PLACE.

HOLY ONE OF ISRAEL (Heb. *qᵉḏôš yiśrāʾēl*). A name of God which represents not only his separateness and uniqueness but also his special relationship to the people Israel (cf. Exod. 19:6; Lev. 19:2). It occurs primarily in the book of Isaiah (twenty-five times; e.g., Isa. 1:4; 43:3; 60:9) and in other contemporary sources (e.g., 2 Kgs. 19:22; Ps. 71:22; 78:41; Jer. 50:29).

HOLY PLACE (Heb. *haqqōḏeš, māqôm qāḏôš;* Gk. *tópos hagíos, hágia*).* The outer compartment of the Israelite sanctuaries, the main chamber in which priests performed routine duties such as tending the lampstands, the table of the Bread of the Presence, and the altar of incense.

In the tabernacle, this chamber was separated from the most holy place by a tapestried veil (Exod. 26:33); the holy place measured 8.9 m. (29 ft.; 20 cubits) long and 4.5 m. (14.5 ft.; 10 cubits) wide and high. In Solomon's temple it was separated from the most holy place by a wall with olivewood doors carved and overlaid with gold (1 Kgs. 6:2, 31-32); its dimensions were double those of the tabernacle. The height of the chamber in the Herodian temple was slightly greater (Josephus *BJ* v.5.5).

HOLY SEPULCHRE.* The tomb in which Jesus' body was interred, a rock-hewn cave intended as the burial place for Joseph of Arimathea (Matt. 27:57-60;

Gk. *mnēmeíon;* cf. v. 61, *táphos*). Located outside the walls of Jerusalem in a garden near the place of crucifixion (John 19:20, 41), the precise location remains open to debate.

Long-standing tradition, strengthened by recent archaeological excavations, favors a site within the Church of the Holy Sepulchre, a twelfth-century A.D. Crusader basilica in the Christian quarter of the modern Old City. This structure replaces earlier churches marking the site of Constantine the Great's fourth-century Church of the Anastasis. Earlier the Roman emperor Hadrian had leveled Jerusalem following the Second Jewish Revolt and built in its place the Roman Aelia Capitolina; on the traditional site of Jesus' tomb, at Hadrian's time in the midst of a city square, he had constructed a temple to Venus.

HOLY SPIRIT (Heb. *rûaḥ qāḏôš;* Gk. *pneúma hágion*).† The third person of the trinity.

I. Terminology

Heb. *rûaḥ* may be rendered as "breath," "wind," or "spirit." English translations inevitably divide what to the Hebrew mind was a single, complex meaning in which natural, psychic, and supernatural aspects were comprehended (cf. Ezekiel's vision of the dry bones; Ezek. 37:9-10 and mg). Nevertheless, distinctions may be drawn which justify the choice of meanings. "Breath" is usually that of the mouth or nostrils, and sometimes signifies "spirited" behavior (Job 4:9; 9:18; 15:30; cf. 2 Sam. 22:16 par. Ps. 18:15 [MT 16]). It is the "breath of life" (Gen. 6:17; 7:15, 22; Ezek. 37:5-6, 8-10; cf. v. 14; RSV "Spirit"; also Ps. 146:4; Jer. 10:14), which is from God alone and is the equivalent of the animating spirit (Gen. 2:7; Heb. *nišmaṯ ḥayyîm*). The "breath" of God is thus creative (cf. Ps. 33:6, par. the "word of the Lord" suggesting breath as speech). Likewise the Old Testament often regards wind as a divine phenomenon, sent from God or heaven (Gen. 8:1; Exod. 14:21; Num. 11:31; Job 26:13; KJV "spirit"; Hos. 13:15); it also sometimes signifies elemental chaos (Prov. 25:14) or emptiness (Job 6:26; 7:7; Ps. 78:39; Eccl. 1:14; Isa. 41:29). The combination of these two meanings makes wind a fitting image of divine judgment, as in the image of winnowing grain and scattering the chaff to the winds. In its third aspect, *rûaḥ* may refer to the human spirit: the animating center of life, human qualities or dispositions such as courage (Josh. 5:1; Ps. 76:12 [MT 13]), the prophetic spirit (Num. 27:18), or the new spirit (Ezek. 11:19; 18:31; 36:26), all the direct work of God in human life. The term also is used of angelic or demonic beings (Judg. 9:23; 1 Sam. 16:14-16, 23). For its use in reference to the Spirit of God, see below, *II.*

Gk. *pneúma*, similarly, means "breath," "wind," and "spirit" and suggests an underlying unity as in *rûaḥ*. Life-breath is again equivalent to spirit (e.g., Matt. 27:50; Luke 8:55; John 19:30); it is explicitly connected with the Holy Spirit in 20:22 and is an image of divine judgment (2 Thess. 2:8). Wind is frequently used in the ordinary sense; but just as in the Old Testament the wind is God's instrument, so in the Gospels it is subject to Jesus' command (Luke 8:24). "Wind" and "spirit" are often bound together: wind

and the Holy Spirit are alike independent of human control (John 3:8), a mighty wind accompanies the Pentecostal outpouring of the Holy Spirit (Acts 2:2, 4), Philip is caught up by the Spirit as by a wind (8:39), and angels are equated with winds (Heb. 1:7; cf. Ps. 104:4). The term also very often refers to the human spirit. In particular the New Testament, recalling the Old Testament prophecies, speaks of the new life as the life of or in the Spirit and as the creation of the Holy Spirit. Paul contrasts flesh and spirit (e.g., Gal. 5:19-22), where the latter signifies the whole of human life as indwelt by and subject to the Spirit of God. Thus in both Testaments, the term "spirit" in whatever context points, directly or indirectly, to the agency of the Spirit of God.

In older English usage, particularly in liturgical contexts, the name Holy Ghost occurs, often interchangeably with Holy Spirit. It derives from O. Eng. *hālza* (or *hāliz*) *gāst* (cf. M. Eng. *haligast;* OHG *geist* "spirit").

II. The Spirit of God

The title "Holy Spirit" occurs in the Old Testament only three times: at Ps. 51:11 (MT 13) in the context of spiritual cleansing and in Isa. 63:10-11 in the context of the Spirit's presence with the Israelites in the wilderness wanderings. It also occurs in the Apocrypha and Pseudepigrapha (e.g., 2 Esdr. 14:22; Sir. 48:12; Mart. Is. 5:14; Ps. Sol. 17:37 [42]) and in numerous rabbinic writings. In the New Testament the title "Holy Spirit" appears nearly one hundred times, more than half in Luke and Acts, less frequently in the other gospels, Romans, and Hebrews, and three or fewer times in 1-2 Corinthians, Ephesians, 1 Thessalonians, 2 Timothy, Titus, 1-2 Peter, and Jude. Of the remaining New Testament books all but Philemon, James, and 2-3 John refer to the Spirit by other titles. The frequent KJV designation "Holy Ghost" has been superseded in ordinary usage and modern translations by "Holy Spirit." Other titles in the Old Testament include "the Spirit of God" (e.g., Exod. 31:3; also Matt. 3:16; Rom. 8:9, 14; cf. 1 Pet. 4:14), "the Spirit of the Lord" (e.g., 1 Sam. 16:13; also Acts 5:9), and "the Spirit of the Lord God" (Isa. 61:1). To these the New Testament adds "the Spirit of [the] Father" (Matt. 10:20); "the Spirit of Jesus" (Acts 16:7); "the Spirit of Jesus Christ" (Phil. 1:19); "the Spirit of Christ" (Rom. 8:9; 1 Pet. 1:11); "the Spirit of [the] Son" (Gal. 4:6); and "the Counselor" (only in John 14–16; so RSV, NIV; KJV "Comforter"; JB "Advocate"; Gk. *paráklētos*).

Besides breath and wind, the chief images include the dove (Matt. 3:16; Luke 3:22; John 1:32), God's arm (Isa. 63:12), hand (31:3), or finger (Luke 11:20; cf. Matt. 12:28), and fire (3:11; Luke 3:16; Acts 2:3; cf. Old Testament fire imagery as representative of God's presence, communication, or judgment).

The Old Testament usually does not suggest a personal conception of the Holy Spirit; on the other hand the Spirit is not always regarded as merely an impersonal force. This might be explained by the Hebrew delight in personification, exercised with particular zest in the rabbinic writings, but the root may go deeper, ultimately to the personal character of Israel's God and thence to his divine agency and presence through the Spirit. In a few Old Testament passages a more personal view of the Holy Spirit is evident. It is capable of grief (Isa. 63:10) and patience (Mic. 2:7), and cannot be directed or instructed by people (Isa. 40:13). When the Spirit is said to direct or lead individuals (Ps. 143:10) or to instruct God's people (Neh. 9:20), it acts as a personal agent, and the breath/spirit of Ezek. 37:9-10 is addressed as a person. By any reckoning the Old Testament evidence points to the objective reality of the Holy Spirit who, as the power and presence of God, is itself divine. The full development of the personal conception of the Holy Spirit, however, came only after the expansion of the Spirit's work in the New Testament era.

III. Work

A. *Old Testament.* 1. In creation. From the beginning God acted in the creation through his Spirit, who "was moving over" (lit. "brooding over") the waters as a bird brooding over its eggs (Gen. 1:2). Not only active in the original creation, however, the Spirit is also at each instant the giver and sustainer of all life, the ongoing creator of all creatures (Ps. 104:30), and especially the animator of human beings (Gen. 6:3; Job 27:3; 33:4; 34:14). In this regard the human spirit, i.e., the life in a person, is given by God (Zech. 12:1; cf. Isa. 42:5) and to God it returns at death (Eccl. 12:7). In parallel with the word of God, the Spirit (breath) of God created the heavens (Ps. 33:6).

2. Empowering individuals for service. The special work of the Spirit focuses on equipping and energizing various individuals for special service or tasks. It empowers artisans like Bezalel for the building of the tabernacle (Exod. 31:3; 35:31). Most often the Spirit is said to prepare and endow individuals for leadership: filling Joshua with "the spirit of wisdom" (Deut. 34:9; cf. Num. 27:18); preparing judges for Israel (e.g., Judg. 3:10; 6:34; 11:29; 13:25); giving Samson extraordinary physical powers (14:6, 19; 15:14); and guiding kings (1 Sam. 11:6; 16:13; cf. 10:6, 10).

A special aspect of the Spirit's empowering of individuals is the inspiring of prophets for the communication of God's word. Generally, the Spirit is said to instruct Israel (Neh. 9:20) and give warnings through the prophets (v. 30). The Spirit indwells Joseph (Gen. 41:38); the Spirit possessed by Moses is apportioned among the elders (Num. 11:17, 25-26, 29); and Balaam (24:2), Saul and his messengers (1 Sam. 10:6, 10; 19:20, 23), David (2 Sam. 23:2), and others (1 Chr. 12:18; 2 Chr. 20:14; 24:20) are its instruments for prophecy. The Spirit addresses and transports Ezekiel in vision (e.g., Ezek. 2:2; 3:12; 11:1, 5). Through Joel God promises a universal outpouring of this same Spirit (Joel 2:28 [MT 3:1]).

3. In the renewal of creation. The end of the Spirit's work in the fallen, estranged world is not only preservation but renewal of creation. Usually this work is corporate and eschatological. It is the content of the prophets' messages, where judgment of sin and promise of renewal are often intimately bound together. Israel is to be cleansed "by a spirit of judgment and by a spirit of burning" (Isa. 4:4; cf. 30:28). A foretaste of this work of the Spirit was given in the Exodus (63:11; cf. vv. 12, 14). At the restoration of Israel the Spirit is to come "from on high" (32:15ff.).

Then he will make of the wilderness a "fruitful field" and will bring justice, righteousness, peace, trust, security, and rest. The Spirit is promised to Israel's descendants (44:3) and its enduring presence to the covenant people (59:21; cf. Ezek. 39:29). Renewal in the Spirit, however, is not merely external, but internal as well, giving people a "new spirit" and "a heart of flesh" (11:19; 18:31; 36:26; cf. Ps. 51:10-12 [MT 12-14]); indeed, the Spirit itself is to be within them (Ezek. 36:27; 37:14). Such work can proceed only by the Spirit of God, "not by might, nor by power, but by my Spirit" (Zech. 4:6).

4. In the Messiah. The Spirit's work in developing leaders and prophets and in renewing creation comes to a focus in the messianic promises. The Spirit anoints and rests upon the Messiah (Isa. 61:1; cf. 42:1), imparts to him wisdom and understanding, counsel and might, knowledge and the fear of the Lord (11:2), and fills him with the Spirit's own power (Mic. 3:8).

In the Old Testament, then, the Spirit is first and foremost the power of God, the agent or agency by which God gets things done. It is true power, unlike earthly powers (Isa. 31:3; Zech. 4:6), and is in fact the only power; even demonic power is ultimately referred to the Spirit (1 Kgs. 22:21-23 par. 2 Chr. 18:20-22; cf. the figure of Satan in Job). The Spirit is omnipresent (Ps. 139:7) and above all others in wisdom and power (Isa. 40:13-14). As the creator and sustainer of creation (Job 34:14-15) it is able to direct nature itself in judgment upon the nations (Isa. 34:16). Its power is not neutral but morally good (Ps. 143:10). Finally, it is not created but is of God, being God's very presence and power.

B. *New Testament.* 1. Jesus. The Gospels contain relatively few references to the Holy Spirit, principally because the Spirit properly belongs to the postresurrection age of the Church and because Jesus rarely offered theological explanations of his acts. The exceptions to this reticence relate either to Jesus' birth and the validation of his ministry or to the extension of that ministry to the disciples and through them to the Church; two special passages in John treat the Holy Spirit in more detail (John 3; 14–16).

For Matthew and Luke, the work of the Spirit in Jesus' life originates from Jesus' conception by the Holy Spirit (Matt. 1:18; Luke 1:35). Its theological importance includes the creative "overshadowing" of Mary by the Spirit, recalling the creative "brooding" of Gen. 1 and thereby maintaining the unity of the Godhead's acts in the Word becoming flesh. John, too, was filled with the Holy Spirit (Luke 1:15-17), but by virtue of his conception Jesus was one with God in a unique way. The Spirit's special work in Jesus continued in Jesus' baptism, when the Spirit descended on him in the form of a dove and the heavenly voice declared Jesus' divine sonship (Mark 1:10-11), which Luke sees as his "anointing" with the Holy Spirit (Acts 10:38). This was a permanent act (cf. John 1:33), unlike the temporary inspiration of prophets, and it was concrete and personal, bringing authority and power that are God's alone (cf. Matt. 7:29 par. Mark 1:22; Luke 4:32, 36). A further contrast with John appears here, for Jesus was to baptize with "the Holy Spirit and with fire" (Matt. 3:11), echoing the prophetic note of salvation in judgment. Following the baptism, the Spirit impelled Jesus into a confrontation with evil in the wilderness temptation. Jesus, "full of the Holy Spirit" and "led by the Spirit for forty days in the wilderness" (Luke 4:1-2; Matt. 4:1; Mark 1:12), returned to Galilee "in the power of the Spirit" (Luke 4:14). He exhibited his victory over evil by casting out demons "by the Spirit of God" (Matt. 12:28; cf. Luke 11:20). He identifies sin against the Holy Spirit as the deliberate refusal to recognize the work of the Spirit in his miracles or, worse, regarding that power as unclean or of Beelzebub (Mark 3:28-30; cf. Matt. 12:31-32; Luke 12:10). Thus Jesus, by the power of the Holy Spirit, performed works which were present signs of the kingdom of God or announcements of its dawning, and proclaimed the gospel of the kingdom by the same power. By that proclamation he was revealed as the "Servant of the Lord" (Luke 4:18, citing Isa. 61:1-2; cf. Matthew's similar use of 42:1-2 in Matt. 12:18). This relationship between the Holy Spirit and the kingdom of God in Jesus' ministry is attested also in a rare but significant variant reading of the Lord's Prayer (Luke 11:2), where some manuscripts read "may the Holy Spirit come upon us and cleanse us"; the identification of the two phrases has become a keynote of Eastern Orthodox theology.

2. The disciples. The gospel narratives suggest that the Spirit's work in and through Jesus was not only foundational but also the firstfruits of further work. Jesus promised to the disciples the same effects of the Spirit's power as he had experienced. The Spirit would be active in and on them both in proclamation and in signs and wonders. It would "teach" the disciples what to say when they were challenged (Luke 12:12; cf. Mark 13:11), presumably much as the prophets were inspired. Jesus also imparted to the disciples authority and power over demons and sickness, and ultimately the power to forgive sins (John 20:22-23); such power, as Jesus himself suggested, could only be the work of the Spirit (Matt. 12:28). Jesus repeated the promise of the Holy Spirit near the end of his ministry. John stresses the aspect of knowledge and truth in his references to the "Counselor" (Paraclete) who is "the Spirit of truth" (John 14:16-17). Sent from the Father, the Spirit would bear witness to Christ through the disciples' witness (15:26-27) and enable them to understand Christ's person and work (14:26). Similarly, Luke emphasizes the "power from on high" which is "the promise of my Father" (Luke 24:49; Acts 1:5, 8). John explains that the Spirit was not granted earlier because "Jesus was not yet glorified" (John 7:39). After the resurrection, Jesus imparted the Spirit to the disciples, breathing on them and saying, "Receive the Holy Spirit," to the end that they were empowered to forgive or condemn (20:22-23).

The culmination of this transfer of the Spirit and its divine powers to the disciples came at Pentecost, when those gathered together received the baptism of the Holy Spirit (Acts 1:5). The experience itself was an illustration of the Spirit's nature and activity as understood even in the Old Testament, for it was accompanied by "the rush of a mighty wind [Gk. *pneúma*]," "tongues as of fire," and the gift of proc-lamation "in other tongues" (Acts 2:1-4); it was the beginning of the outpouring of the Spirit on "all flesh" promised by Joel (Acts 2:16-21, quoting Joel 2:28-32). The immediate result was the baptism of new converts. Although in Acts the correlation of water baptism and receiving the Holy Spirit is inconsistent, as a rule the two are united (Acts 2:38; cf. v. 41; 8:38; 16:15, 33; 18:8; 22:16; cf. also John 3:5), although exceptions occur in extraordinary circumstances (Acts 8:14-17; 10:44-48; 19:2-6).

3. The Church and the New Creation. In the New Testament, the Old Testament doctrine of creation is presupposed throughout and therefore needs no expansion. The Epistles turn to the Spirit's work in the renewal of creation, particularly as begun in the community of believers. The descent of the dove at Jesus' baptism was the beginning of the new creation. There is a cosmic dimension to renewal in the Spirit which Paul articulates in Rom. 8:18-23, where the renewal of the suffering creation is promised in the "firstfruits" of the believers' renewal (cf. 2 Cor. 1:22; 5:5; Eph. 1:13-14). The latter, personal aspect is dominant in Paul's doctrine of the Spirit's work. In the first instance the Spirit indwells the hearts of believers as the presence of Christ within them, initiating a radical transformation from death to life. Thus the Spirit of God can be called the "Spirit of Christ" (Rom. 8:9-11; cf. 1 Pet. 1:11). The Spirit's work, however, is not merely individual; rather the individual believer, being now "in Christ," is brought into a new whole which is the new creation of the Spirit, exhibited in the body of Christ, the Church (1 Cor. 12:13; cf. Eph. 2:19-22; 4:4). Baptism concretely signifies the "washing of regeneration and renewal in the Holy Spirit" (Tit. 3:5) and the new unity with and in Christ (Eph. 4:4-5), the new birth (John 3:3-8), and the "living water" of the Spirit (7:38-39).

In the Epistles the specific activities of the Spirit all serve the end of creating this new community in Christ, sanctifying its members and endowing them with gifts in order to build up and extend by mission the community of faith. Life in the Spirit is the life of sanctification (Rom. 15:16; 1 Cor. 1:2); because of the finished work of Christ it is already accomplished (6:11), yet it is also an ongoing process oriented towards an eschatological fulfillment (Gal. 3:14; 5:5; Eph. 1:13-14). In this process the Spirit is a "guarantee" of faith (2 Cor. 5:5-7; cf. 4:13), enabling belief in the foolishness of the gospel. The sanctifying Spirit brings freedom—freedom from the slavery and corruption of the old life and freedom to be children of God (3:17; Rom. 8:15-16, 21; Gal. 4:6-7; 5:1-5; cf. the Johannine "Spirit of truth" which brings freedom; John 14:17; 16:13; cf. 1 John 2:20-21). Paul analyzes the old slavery and the new freedom in terms of flesh and spirit. The life of the flesh, in one aspect, is life under the law (Gal. 3:2-5); the Spirit is contrasted to the "letter" (KJV, 2 Cor. 3:6; RSV "written code"; cf. Rom. 2:29; 7:5-6). In fact the "flesh" is not only evil desires and acts, but all human capacity, efforts, or guarantees, including morality and the law, whereas the Spirit is God's holy action which is not subject to human control. Paul therefore counsels the Galatians to abandon the "works of the flesh" and to walk by the "fruit of the Spirit," where the plural "works" indicates futility and dissipation but the singular "fruit" suggests the integrity and wholeness that comes only as a gift of the Spirit and not through human effort (Gal. 5:16-24). When the Spirit indwells the believer, even the body becomes holy, "a temple of the Holy Spirit" that must be kept pure (1 Cor. 6:18-20). For the individual the Spirit also teaches and interprets prayer (Rom. 8:26-27).

The center of all of the Spirit's gifts and actions in believers is love, which is "of the Spirit" (Rom. 15:30) and is the first of the fruit of the Spirit (Gal. 5:22). The gifts of the Spirit, centering in love, are given not for the individual alone but for the common good of the Church (1 Cor. 12:7; cf. Eph. 4:4-7). Thus a chief evidence of the Spirit's work is the edification of the whole Church, which by the power of the Holy Spirit is united "into one body" (1 Cor. 12:13). A further criterion of genuine spiritual gifts is the confession "Jesus is Lord" (v. 3). Among the gifts of the Spirit there is no fixed hierarchy (cf. 1 Cor. 12:13, 28), but now one, now another is exercised for the benefit of the Church, just as the body of Christ itself is characterized by equality (vv. 14-25). Likewise the establishment of church order under the Spirit reflects a varying balance between freedom and order as the Spirit leads and the situation demands (Acts 20:28; 1 Cor. 14; cf. 1 Tim. 1:18; 4:14; 2 Tim. 1:6). Finally, as the Spirit was promised to the disciples for their mission of proclaiming the kingdom, so also it continues to lead and aid those called to the offices of proclamation. Indeed, the Spirit always leads (Rom. 8:14) and enlightens (1 Cor. 2:9-11) all believers, but it also renews and raises up individuals in special ways, enabling them to preach the gospel in power (e.g., Acts 4:8, 31; 6:3; 13:9; 1 Cor. 2:4) and sending them out (e.g., Acts 8:29; 10:19; 13:2, 4).

Thus in the New Testament the role of the Holy Spirit achieves a greater prominence and a more personal character than in the Old Testament. The new age that dawned in the ministry of Jesus and began in power at Pentecost is called the "dispensation of the Spirit," the splendor of which exceeds that of the Law (2 Cor. 3:8). The Old Testament theme of the Spirit as the power of God is assumed and developed in the New, but a new emphasis on the Spirit as a unifying power emerges. It is united to the work of Christ, making the members of the body of Christ partakers of his death and resurrection and in so doing uniting those members to one another. As "the spirit of glory" (1 Pet. 4:14) it does all this to the glory of God, and brings believers into the sphere of that glory so that they now taste "the powers of the age to come" (Heb. 6:5). The character of the new creation of the Spirit, promised in the Old Testament, is revealed in the New as a new life lived "in Christ" and "in the Spirit" which yields spiritual fruit and which is to culminate in resurrection for all who believe. Finally, the New Testament applies the Old Testament understanding of the Spirit as the Spirit of prophecy to the whole of Scripture, which is the Spirit's own word (Acts 1:16; 4:25; 28:25; Heb. 10:15; 2 Pet. 1:21).

See SPIRITUAL GIFTS.

Bibliography: C. K. Barrett, *The Holy Spirit and the Gospel Tradition* (London: 1947); F. D. Bruner, *A Theology of the Holy Spirit* (Grand Rapids: 1970);

G. W. H. Lampe, *God As Spirit* (New York: 1977); C. F. D. Moule, *The Holy Spirit* (Grand Rapids: 1978); E. Schweizer, *The Holy Spirit* (Philadelphia: 1980).

HOMAM [hō′măm] (Heb. *ḥômām* "destruction"). A son of Lotan and grandson of Seir the Horite (1 Chr. 1:39). At Gen. 36:22 his name appears as Heman (3) (KJV "Hemam").

HOMER [hō′mər] (Heb. *ḥōmer*). A dry measure equal to ten ephahs or baths (Ezek. 45:11) as well as the cor (v. 10). It was the equivalent of approximately 228 l. (58 gal.). See WEIGHTS AND MEASURES.

HOMILY (Gk. *homilía*). A simple address, consisting of a paraphrase of a substantial portion of Scripture, having more the character of a Bible reading than a sermon. Directed toward practical matters, it was frequently used as a method of preaching in the early Christian church. The letter to the Hebrews could be regarded as one or more homilies (e.g., ch. 11), and although the epistles of Paul appear to be genuine letters written to address specific topics, his letter to the Ephesians may constitute a homiletic reworking of the letter to the Philippians.

The Greek term appears only at 1 Cor. 15:33, where it would be best translated as "talk, conversation": "bad conversation (KJV "communications"; RSV "company") ruins good morals."

HONEY (Heb. *dᵉbaš*; Gk. *méli*).† A sweet, viscid, and nutritional fluid produced by bees from flower nectar; also a similar sweet fluid derived from fruits or juices. Most Old Testament references to honey concern the wild variety (e.g., Judg. 14:8-9; 1 Sam. 14:25-26, 29, 43; cf. Matt. 3:4 par. Mark 1:6). Even though apiculture is not definitely attested until Hellenistic times, it does appear that domesticated honey was produced somewhat earlier (cf. 2 Chr. 31:5, where honey is included among the offerings of firstfruits).

Although honey might be sufficient to sustain life in the absence of other produce (2 Sam. 17:29; Isa. 7:22; cf. v. 15), it is generally viewed as a luxury (e.g., Gen. 43:11; 1 Kgs. 14:3) and was an item of international trade (Ezek. 27:17). Because it was subject to fermentation honey was prohibited in the cereal offering (Lev. 2:11).

Honey occurs often in figurative usage, primarily as an expression of abundance (e.g., a land "flowing with milk and honey"; Exod. 3:8, 17; Josh. 5:6; Jer. 11:5; cf. Deut. 8:8; Job 20:17). Of course, honey typifies sweetness (Cant. 4:11; Ezek. 3:3; Rev. 10:9-10), including the palatability of God's commandments (Ps. 19:10) and his nourishment of Jerusalem (Ezek. 16:13).

HOOK.† Heb. *wāw* designates a hook or peg from which curtains and other hangings were suspended in the Israelite tabernacle (e.g., Exod. 26:32; 27:10-11); these curtains were fastened together by hooks or pins (*qeres;* 35:11; 39:33; KJV "taches").

Heb. *ḥakkâ* refers to the simple fishhook (Isa. 19:8; Hab. 1:15; cf. Matt. 17:27; Gk. *ánkistron*); at Job

41:1 it is viewed insufficient for catching the monster Leviathan. A similar device may be intended by Heb. *ḥaḥ* (e.g., 2 Chr. 33:11; Job 41:2; Ezek. 29:4) and *ṣinnôt* (Amos 4:2), terms generally translated "thorn" (cf. Job 5:5; Prov. 22:5).

HOOPOE [hoo'pō] (Heb. *dûḵîpat*). A beautiful yet peculiar bird (*Upupa epops*), the only species of the family Upupidae. The hoopoe is characterized by a cinnamon or buff-colored body and a high, gold crest, tipped with black; its back and wings are marked with black and white bands. Some 30 cm. (12 in.) long, the hoopoe is also identified by its long, curving beak, its erratic flight, and hawing call. Common throughout Africa and Europe, the hoopoe migrates to Palestine during March and broods there. It eats various types of insects and worms, for which it forages in manure piles, hence its inclusion among the birds declared ceremonially unclean (Lev. 11:19; Deut. 14:18).

HOPE.† Confident expectation, ranging in degree from an ordinary desire felt with eager anticipation to a defining characteristic of those who seek God and experience his grace. In the latter (theological) sense hope is a virtue constitutive of God's people, both Israel in the Old Testament and the Church in the New Testament.

I. Terminology

No single Hebrew word corresponds directly to the English word "hope." More than a dozen Hebrew words may be so translated but each has its own nuances. Noun forms include several words that mean hope, expectation: *miqweh* (e.g., Jer. 14:8), *tiqwâ* (Job 4:6, where it parallels *kislâ* "confidence"; Ps. 71:5; Jer. 31:17; Zech. 9:12), *tôḥelet* (Ps. 39:7 [MT 8]; Prov. 10:28), and *mabbāt* (Isa. 20:5-6). Other nouns carry the general sense of confidence or trust: *beṭaḥ* (cf. Ezek. 28:26; RSV "securely"), *kesel* (Ps. 78:7; cf. Prov. 3:26, RSV "confidence"), and *mibṭāḥ* (Jer. 17:7; so KJV; RSV "trust"). Another noun, *śēber*, means hope in the sense of waiting with hope (Ps. 119:116; 146:5). Likewise Hebrew employs several verbs meaning "to hope": *yāḥal* "to wait with hope, endure" (e.g., Pss. 31:24 [MT 25]; RSV "wait for"); 33:18, 22), *qāwâ* "to wait, expect, look for, hope in" (e.g., Jer. 14:22; cf. RSV "wait for," Gen. 49:18; Isa. 40:31), *śābar* "to wait, look for, hope for" (Isa. 38:18), and *ḥasâ* "to have hope, take refuge in" (Prov. 14:32). The LXX translated many of these words, though none exclusively so, by Gk. *elpís, elpízō*; KJV frequently "to trust."

It is helpful to distinguish among the basis of hope, the object of hope, and the activity of hoping. In both Hebrew and Greek the noun forms tend to express the ground or basis of hope, that by reason of which one hopes. This is not the same as the immediate object of hope. These objects are sometimes specified, especially in passages where eschatological concerns are the focus, but the frequent omission of an apparent object suggests that the ground or guarantee of hope is the decisive factor. The verb forms, on the other hand, emphasize the human response, activity, or attitude to that foundation.

II. Biblical Teachings

In both testaments hope appears frequently in mundane contexts. Ruth speaks of her hope for a husband (Ruth 1:12); Job speaks generally of his hopelessness (Job 7:6; 17:15; 19:10); a man is hopeless in the face of the strength of Leviathan (41:9 [MT 41:1]); a father hopes for his son to turn out right (Prov. 19:8). There is also hope for a tree to survive and grow after it has been cut down (Job 14:7). Paul frequently expresses his hope to visit the churches and people to whom his epistles are addressed. But another class of hopes more closely addresses the focus of biblical hope. The biblical writers distinguish between hopes that are ill-founded and vain, and hopes that have a sure foundation. The range of ill-founded hopes is as wide as the human capacity for self-deception. It is vain to place one's hope in military might (Isa. 31:1-3), in one's own wisdom (Prov. 26:12) or righteousness (Ezek. 33:13), in riches (Prov. 11:28), or even in the temple (Jer. 7:9-10) or the law of Moses (John 5:45). All of these are inadequate bases of hope, and indeed, for the unrighteous person who trusts in such things, there is no hope (Job 8:13; 11:20; 27:8; Prov. 10:28; 11:7). Thus the majority of scriptural references to hope elucidate the only true foundation of hope, God. In this there is a remarkable continuity between the Old and New Testaments.

In the Old Testament, true hope is always directed to God (e.g., Ps. 39:7 [MT 8]; 71:5; Isa. 8:17). In his despair the Psalmist exhorts himself to "hope in God" (Ps. 42:5, 11 [MT 6, 12]; 43:5) because God is himself the "hope of Israel" (Jer. 14:8; cf. 50:7), and indeed the hope of all the earth (Ps. 65:5 [MT 6]). At times the writers specify acts or attributes of God as reasons for hope: hope is based on God's steadfast love and mercy (Ps. 33:18, 22; Lam. 3:24), his power in nature (Jer. 14:22), his sutaining power (God's "arm"; Isa. 51:5). The object of hope is often omitted in the Old Testament, but it is clear that a general desire for God's salvation is implied, both personal salvation (Ps. 119:166) and corporate salvation for Israel (Jer. 29:11; 31:17). The means whereby hope is inspired in the people's hearts is God's word, the center of which is the covenant (Ps. 119:43; 130:5). Because of his love, God has established himself as the hope of Israel through covenants with his people. God's pledge of himself and of his blessing is at the center of Old Testament hope. Israel, especially in the Monarchy, had shaped its hopes in accordance with what it conceived as the concrete fulfillment of God's promises. These expectations were shattered in the Exile (Ezek. 37:11), and while the hope of restoration to the land of promise continued, the prophets began to emphasize the expectation of a Messiah who would redeem his people. Israel's true situation, as the prophets realized, is summed up in the curious phrase "prisoners of hope" (Zech. 9:12), for even in the midst of captivity—to their own folly and to foreign conquerors—God's people endure in the hope of salvation "because of the blood of my covenant with you" (v. 11).

The same concept of hope informs the whole of the New Testament. Although the word itself rarely occurs in the Gospels, its spirit is clearly discernible in the messianic office of Jesus and his salvific work. The extension of hope to the Gentiles, who were otherwise without hope, being "strangers to the covenants of promise" (Eph. 2:12), is declared in Matt. 12:21, which quotes the LXX version of Isa. 42:4: "in his name will the Gentiles hope" (cf. Rom. 15:12 with its similar use of Isa. 11:1, LXX). Luke-Acts tends to employ hope in continuity with the messianic tradition: the disciples' hope that Jesus was the Messiah (Luke 24:21), apparently frustrated at the cross, was revived and fulfilled in the resurrection of Christ (Acts 23:6; 24:15; cf. 2:26, which quotes the psalmist's hope of resurrection [Ps. 16:9]).

In the Epistles the theology of hope is fully developed and becomes an explicit and prominent theme. As in the Old Testament, God himself is the Christian's hope; he is "the God of hope" (Rom. 15:13; cf. 1 Tim. 4:10; 1 Pet. 1:21). But Paul also identifies Jesus Christ as the ground of hope ("Christ Jesus our hope," 1 Tim. 1:1; cf. Eph. 1:12; 1 Thess. 1:3), the evidence of which is the resurrection (1 Cor. 15; 1 Pet. 1:3). The work of hope comes "by the power of the Holy Spirit" (Rom. 15:13; Gal. 5:5). Hope is produced through the witness of the written scriptures (Rom. 15:4), but the new covenant provides "a better hope" (Heb. 7:19) because of the promises inherent in the priesthood of Christ (6:18-19).

The New Testament provides a rich complex of associations regarding the object of hope. That object is personal salvation (1 Thess. 5:8), but it is also corporate, "the one hope" that binds the Church together (Eph. 4:4). It is "the hope of righteousness" (Gal. 5:5), of resurrection (1 Thess. 4:13), eternal life (Tit. 1:2; 3:7), and the "glorious inheritance in the saints" (Eph. 1:18) which is the "splendor" of Christ (2 Cor. 3:12ff.) and "the glory of God" (Rom. 5:2). This hope is heavenly (Col. 1:5), but the whole of creation is caught up in it as well (Rom. 8:20ff.). The echo of Zechariah's paradoxical "prisoners of hope" in Paul's assertion that "the creation was subjected to futility . . . in hope" (v. 20) suggests that hope is most truly itself when it occurs in the context of darkness, suffering, or persecution. Thus Christian hope is a "living hope" (1 Pet. 1:3) which provides power and protection for the Christian life ("for a helmet the hope of salvation," 1 Thess. 5:8). So pervasive is it that even Paul's hope to send Timothy is hope in Christ (Phil. 2:19). It is a reasonable hope to be verbally confessed (Heb. 10:23) and accounted for (1 Pet. 3:15). Hope also finds expression in rejoicing (Rom. 12:12), in certainty (Heb. 11:1), in perseverance (Rom. 8:25), and in holy living (1 John 3:3).

In Scripture hope often is substantive as well as active. One may "have" hope, since to do so is to possess God who is hope. Thus hope came to be regarded as one of the "theological" virtues in the triad of faith, hope, and love (e.g., Rom. 5:1-5; Eph. 4:1-6; 1 Thess. 1:3; Heb. 6:10-12). The three belong together and always function as one; none is possible without the other. As an act, hope may be thought of as the prospective totality of the response of faith to love, i.e., to God who is love. Love is the "greatest of these" virtues in that it is primary, being the very nature of God who is the source and goal of hope, but

all three virtues—faith, hope, and love—abide (1 Cor. 13:13).

HOPHNI [hŏf'nī] (Heb. *ḥopnî*; Egyp. *ḥfn(r)* "tadpole"). One of the sons of Eli, and a priest at Shiloh (1 Sam. 1:3). Like his brother Phinehas, he acted very wickedly as priest (2:12-17), bringing the judgment of the Lord down upon himself (cf. vv. 27-36; 3:11-18). He was killed in the battle of Aphek in which the Philistines captured the ark of the covenant (4:1-18).

HOPHRA [hŏf'rə] (Heb. *ḥopra*ʿ; Egyp. *w3ḥ-ib-r*ʿ "the heart of Ra endures"; Gk. *Apries*).† An Egyptian pharaoh of the Twenty-sixth Dynasty, who ruled 589-570 B.C. Responding to King Zedekiah's plea for assistance in his rebellion against Nebuchadnezzar II of Babylon (cf. Ezek. 17:11-21), Hophra invaded Judah in 589; although the Babylonian forces were diverted temporarily, the Egyptians apparently withdrew before Jerusalem had been delivered, and Nebuchadnezzar returned to capture the city as the prophet Jeremiah had warned (Jer. 37:5-11; cf. Ezek. 29:1-16).

Egypt flourished during the reign of Hophra, but he fell victim to domestic unrest instigated by his successor Ahmose II (Amasis). When Egyptian troops were roundly defeated aiding the Libyans against the Greeks at Cyrene, the pharaoh was deposed and probably murdered. Jeremiah, who had fled with other Jews to Tahpanhes in the delta, had predicted Hophra's downfall (Jer. 44:30).

HOR [hôr] (Heb. *hōr hāhār* "Hor the mountain").

1. A mountain or ridge on the border of Edom on which Aaron died and was buried (Num. 20:22; Deut. 32:50; cf. 10:6, which places these events at Moserah). Long-standing tradition (cf. Josephus *Ant.* iv.4.7) identifies Mt. Hor with Jebel Nebī Harun ("mountain of Aaron") near Nabatean Petra; however, this twin-topped sandstone mountain, which stands some 1460 m. (4800 ft.) high, is located in the middle of Edomite territory rather than on the border. A more likely identification would be Jebel Madurah, 24 km. (15 mi.) northeast of Kadesh.

2. A mountain marking the northern boundary of Israelite territory (Num. 34:7-8). Suggested identifications include Mt. Hermon and Jebel Akkar, a spur of the Lebanon range west of Tripolis.

HORAM [hôr'ăm] (Heb. *hōrām* "haughtiness"). A king of Gezer who tried to aid the city of Lachish in its defense against Israel, but who was himself defeated by Joshua (Josh. 10:32-33).

HOREB [hôr'ĭb] (Heb. *hōrēḇ, ḥōrēḇ* "wilderness, desolate region"), **MOUNT.**† The mountain of God, also called Sinai; critical scholars assign those passages using the name Horeb to the Elohist and Deuteronomist strata of the Pentateuch.

It was here that Moses experienced the theophany of the burning bush (Exod. 3:1), and here God presented to him the terms of his covenant with Israel (e.g., Deut. 4:10, 15; 5:2; cf. Exod. 19-20). It was from this point that the Israelites set forth for

Kadesh-barnea (Deut. 1:2, 6, 19). Later, the prophet Elijah received a vision at Mt. Horeb instructing him to anoint Hazael as king of Syria and Jehu over Israel and to name Elisha as his own successor (1 Kgs. 19:8, 11).

Some scholars consider Horeb to be distinct from Mt. Sinai, perhaps a peak or rocky site in an otherwise low region through which the Israelites wandered. Others view the name as a general designation for the entire chain of mountains in the Sinai peninsula, thus derived from that of a specific mountain; in the same sense, the Hebrews often used the term "mountain" (Heb. *hār*) to indicate a mountainous region.

See SINAI, MOUNT.

HOREM [hôr'ĕm] (Heb. *ḥōrēm* "consecrated"). A fortified city in the tribal territory of Naphtali (Josh. 19:38), presumably in northern Galilee. Its precise location is unknown.

HORESH [hôr'ĕsh] (Heb. *ḥōreš* "wood"). A place in the Wilderness of Ziph where David hid from Saul and where he made a covenant with Jonathan (1 Sam. 23:15-19). The KJV translates "in a wood" rather than a place name, but it appears unlikely that the area was ever wooded. The site is usually identified as Khirbet Khoreisa, which preserves the name, 9.6 km. (6 mi.) southeast of Hebron.

HOR-HAGGIDGAD [hôr'hə gĭd'găd] (Heb. *ḥōr haggiḏgāḏ* "hole of Gidgad").† A place where the Israelites encamped during the wilderness wanderings (Num. 33:32-33). At Deut. 10:7 it is called Gudgodah; the LXX reads Gk. *Gadgad* in both passages. The location of the site remains uncertain; attempts to identify it with Wâdī Ghadhaghedh, a branch of the Wâdī Jerafeh in the eastern Sinai peninsula, have been discounted for linguistic reasons.

HORI [hôr'ī] (Heb. *ḥōrî*, *ḥōrî* "cave-dweller").
1. A son of Lotan and a descendant of Esau (Heb. *ḥōrî*; Gen. 36:22; 1 Chr. 1:39).
2. The father of Shaphat who was one of the twelve spies Moses sent into Canaan; of the tribe of Simeon (Heb. *ḥōrî*; Num. 13:5).

HORITES [hôr'īts] (Heb. *ḥōrî*, *ḥōrîm* "cave-dweller[s]" [?]).† The original population of Seir, prior to its occupation by the Edomites (Gen. 14:6; 36:20; Deut. 2:12, 22).

Textual differences make it difficult to identify the Horites with confidence. The LXX refers to Horites at Gen. 34:2; Josh. 9:7, where the MT reads "Hivites"; moreover, both passages refer to inhabitants of central Palestine. Some scholars have distinguished between these two groups, often identifying the central-Palestinian Horites with the Hurrians. The name may actually reflect an Egyptian administrative term for southern Transjordan (cf. Akk. *Ḥurru*). *See* HUR-RIANS.

Bibliography. E. A. Speiser, "Ethnic Movements in the Near East in the Second Millennium B.C.," *AASOR* 13 (1933): 26-31.

HORMAH [hôr'mə] (Heb. *ḥormâ* "devotion").† A city in Judah, located south of Jerusalem. Hormah

became a possession of the tribe of Simeon when Joshua cast lots for the land at Shiloh (Josh. 15:30; 19:4; 1 Chr. 4:30). The meaning of its name is obscure, but it may relate to sanctifying a burnt offering to a deity.

At Num. 14:45; Deut. 1:44 Hormah is described as the place to which the Amalekites, Amorites, and Canaanites repulsed Israelite forces which were attempting an invasion of the northern hill country. Another account indicates that Hormah got its name when the Israelites made good on a vow to defeat the king of Arad (Num. 21:3). A third version tells how the tribes of Judah and Simeon allied to destroy the city of Zephath, and then renamed it Hormah (Judg. 1:17).

Hormah is included in the list of kings conquered by Joshua (Josh. 12:14). It was one of the cities to which David sent booty from the defeat of the Amalekites, perhaps in gratitude for their hospitality toward him in his brigand days (1 Sam. 30:30).

Various attempts to identify the site include Tell esh-Sheri'ah, 19 km. (12 mi.) northwest of Beersheba; Tell el-Milḥ, 13 km. (8 mi.) southwest of Tell 'Arâd; and Tell Meshash (Tel Masos), 6 km. (3.7 mi.) west of Tell el-Milḥ.

HORN (Heb. *qeren*, *šôpār*; Aram. *qeren*; Gk. *kéras*). A musical instrument; also a container for liquids or the oil poured on those anointed to a specific task. It is uncertain whether they were ever made from metal; most likely they were made from animals' horns.

The horn is often a symbol of power, help, victory, and glory (Deut. 33:17). "To exalt one's horn" (1 Sam. 2:1, 10, KJV) means to grant victory, while "to cut off one's horn" (Jer. 48:25) refers to defeat. The prophets predicted the future rise of the horn, a power opposing God (Zech. 1:18-21; Dan. 7:8; Rev. 13:1). At 5:6, however, the Lamb, or Jesus Christ, has seven horns to symbolize his power.

HORNET (Heb. *ṣir'â*). A large insect of the order Hymenoptera, a wasp which lives with thousands of others in a multicelled cellulose nest the hornets make by chewing the bark of trees. Though they prove useful to humans by masticating large numbers of insects to feed their larvae, they cause great damage to ripe fruit and the bark of trees.

Most common in Palestine is the *Vespa orientalis*, a large yellow or reddish-brown species considered to be more malicious and aggressive than Western varieties. Its sting is particularly painful, and the aftereffects last several days, often paralyzing smaller victims so the hornet can suck out vital fluids; multiple stings may prove fatal to humans. Thus the hornet occurs as a figure for divine intervention in driving out the pre-Israelite inhabitants of Palestine (Exod. 23:28; Deut. 7:20; Josh. 24:12; NJV "plague").

HORNS OF THE ALTAR (Heb. *qarnôṯ hammizbēaḥ*).† Horn-shaped projections at the four corners of the altar of burnt offering (Exod. 27:2; 38:2; Ezek. 42:15) and the altar of incense (Exod. 30:2; 37:25). Overlaid with gold or bronze, they formed one piece with the altar. On special occasions such as the consecration of priests (29:12) or the Day of Atonement (Lev. 16:18) and in conjunction with the sin offering (ch. 4) the blood of sacrificial animals was spread on the horns.

Although their precise symbolism remains unclear, the horns are thought to have represented divine strength and holiness. Fugitives, other than those guilty of wilful murder (cf. Exod. 21:14; 1 Kgs. 2:28ff.), might gain asylum by grasping these projections (1:50-53). Amos prophesies that God will cut off the horns of the altar as punishment for Israel's transgressions (Amos 3:14).

Horned altars of various sizes, apparently incense altars as well as those used in sacrifices, have been discovered at various biblical sites (e.g., Beer-sheba, Dan, Gezer, and Megiddo).

See ALTAR.

HORONAIM [hôr'ə nā'əm] (Heb. *hôrōnayim* "two caves").† A place in southern Moab, apparently located at the foot of the Moabite plateau (Jer. 48:5). It is named in oracles against Moab (Isa. 15:5; Jer. 48:3, 34), and is mentioned in the Moabite Stone as a place defeated by King Mesha (Moab. *Ḥwrnn*). According to Josephus, it was captured from the Arabs by Alexander Jannaeus (*Ant.* xiii.15.4 [395-97]) but returned by Hyrcanus (xiv.1.4 [14-18]). It is probably to be identified with modern el ʿAraq.

At 2 Sam. 13:34 the name may be a dual form for Upper and Lower Beth-horon (cf. MT Heb. *midderek* *'aḥ^arāyw* "from the road behind him").

HORONITE [hôr'ə nīt] (Heb. *ḥōrōnî*). An appellation given to Sanballat, one of those who opposed Nehemiah in the rebuilding of the walls of Jerusalem (Neh. 2:10, 19; 13:28). The name could mean that Sanballat was from Horonaim, in which case he would have been a Moabite. Josephus, however, calls him a Samaritan, which suggests that he was from Beth-horon.

HORSE (Heb. *sûs, pārāš, 'abbîr, rekeš;* Gk. *híppos*). In the ancient Near East the horse was used for military, transportation, and hunting purposes (for the wealthy), and only rarely for pulling burdens or in agriculture. The horse appears in the Bible in the contexts of war and ceremony, and it is used in symbolic language.

Horses are not included among the animals possessed by the patriarchs in the second millennium B.C. They first appear in the Cappadocian Tablets (nineteenth century), but not as frequently as do asses. A century later the Mitanni, an Aryan people, introduced the two-wheeled war chariot to northern Mesopotamia, as the Kassites gained control of Babylonia with similar vehicles. The Hyksos (eighteenth-sixteenth centuries) brought the horse chariot to Egypt, and the Amarna Letters (fourteenth century) tell of their use in Palestine.

In early Israel horses were associated with pagan wealth and luxury (Deut. 17:16; 1 Sam. 8:11). The Israelite armies were not equipped with chariots until King David's reign (2 Sam. 8:4). During Solomon's reign the great numbers of horses Israel possessed were indicative of the nation's wealth and military

power. Solomon purchased horses and chariots from Egypt for his own use, and sold them to other nations as well (1 Kgs. 10:28-29). He built extensive stables for his horses and established a quota system to supply their fodder (4:26-28). Horses became so commonplace in Jerusalem that both the city wall and the royal palace had a Horse Gate (2 Chr. 23:15; Neh. 3:28; Jer. 31:40).

That horses continued to be important down to the end of the kingdoms of Israel and Judah is attested by both extrabiblical and biblical sources. Assyrian king Shalmaneser III's annals (ninth century) tell of the two thousand chariots King Ahab of Israel contributed to an unsuccessful anti-Assyrian coalition, and Sennacherib (eighth century) lists horses among the booty he took from Judah. The prophet Isaiah scorned Judah's reliance upon Egypt's horses and chariots as a sign of apostasy (Isa. 2:7; 31:1). Later, Zechariah prophesied that they would be abandoned in the messianic age (Zech. 9:10). In the last days of the southern kingdom Jeremiah stated that Judah's kings would ride in triumph through Jerusalem's gates on chariots and horses if they would obey Yahweh (Jer. 17:24-25; 22:4).

The strength, swiftness, and other physical characteristics of the horse lent themselves to comparisons and figurative references in the poetical and prophetic books of the Old Testament (e.g., Ps. 32:9; Isa. 63:13; Jer. 12:5; Ezek. 23:20). Job 39:19-25 gives the most complete description of the horse in the Bible.

Horses also figure in the apocalyptic imagery of the New Testament book of Revelation. In Rev. 6:2, 4-5, 8 four horses are symbolic of the judgments inflicted upon the earth by their riders (cf. Zech. 6:1-7). Judgment is also executed by cavalry whose supernatural horses have lions' teeth and serpentine tails (Rev. 9:17, 19). In the victorious scene at the end of time Christ and his hosts ride on white horses (19:11, 14, 19, 21).

HORSE GATE (Heb. *šaʿar hassûsîm*). A gate of Jerusalem located at the southeast corner of the temple complex, north of the Water Gate and the Ophel wall and near the palace (Jer. 31:40). It was restored at the time of Nehemiah (Neh. 3:28). This may be the same gate associated with the murder of Queen Athaliah (2 Kgs. 11:16; 2 Chr. 23:15).

HOSAH [hō'zə] (Heb. *ḥōsâ* "refuge") **(PERSON).** A Levite from the line of Merari. He was a gatekeeper of the tent which David pitched for the ark when he brought it to Jerusalem (1 Chr. 17:38). Later Hosah, his sons, and their kin were responsible for guarding the west gate of Shallecheth (26:10-11, 16).

HOSAH [hō'zə] (Heb. *ḥōsâ* "refuge") **(PLACE).** A city on the northern boundary of Asher, in the vicinity of Tyre (Josh. 19:29). Most likely the Usu of Egyptian and Assyrian inscriptions, Hosah may be identified with modern Tell Rashīdīyeh, 4 km. (2.5 mi.) south of Tyre.

HOSANNA [hō zǎ'nə] (Gk. *hōsanná*).† An exclamation shouted at Jesus by the crowds who greeted his triumphal entry into Jerusalem (Matt. 21:9 par. Mark

11:9-10; John 12:13) and by children in the temple (Matt. 21:15). Derived from Ps. 118:25 (Heb. *hôšî'a-nā'* "save us, we pray"), which apparently became a liturgical cry for divine mercy through the reading of the Hallel Psalms, the expression later became associated with Jewish eschatological hopes (cf. v. 26, quoted at Mark 11:9).

HOSEA [hō zā'ə] (Heb. *hôšēa'* "may Yahweh save").† An eighth-century B.C. prophet of the northern kingdom whose message is preserved in the book of Hosea. The Hebrew form of his name is identical to that of HOSHEA. At Rom. 9:25 the KJV renders the name as Osee.

Apart from the name of his father, Beeri, few specifics are recorded regarding Hosea's life. His ministry to Israel began shortly after that of Amos and may have spanned some forty years, from the latter days of King Jeroboam II of Israel (779-747) to the rise of King Hezekiah of Judah (*ca*. 715; Hos. 1:1); some scholars find no indication that he prophesied after the fall of Samaria in 721. No consensus has been reached concerning the prophet's background, in particular whether he was associated with the priesthood or the official prophets, and some even question whether he was a native of the northern kingdom. His troublesome marriage to Gomer, generally accepted as factual, is analogous to the relationship between God and Israel.

HOSEA, BOOK OF.† The first book of the Minor Prophets, one of the earliest and longest of the Book of the Twelve.

I. Background

Hosea's ministry began in the latter years of King Jeroboam II of Israel (779-747 B.C.), a period of peace and prosperity. But, as Hosea had prophesied (Hos. 1:4), the stability of the northern kingdom was shattered following Jeroboam's death by a series of royal assassinations that brought to the throne in a fifteen-year period six kings—Zechariah, Shallum, Menahem, Pekahiah, Pekah, and Hoshea. Israel's internal decay was accompanied by increasing pressure from the east, the empire-minded Tiglath-pileser III of Assyria (745-727). Israel alternately submitted to Assyrian pressure and rebelled against it in alliance with Syria and Egypt; the attempt of King Pekah and the Syrian king Rezin to coerce Judah's support led to the Syro-Ephraimite War (735-732; cf. 5:8-15). Hosea's prophecies herald the Assyrian siege of Samaria in 721 (13:16 [MT 14:1]), but it is unclear whether any later utterances are recorded; according to 1:1 his ministry continued until the reign of Hezekiah of Judah (*ca*. 715-687).

Although some scholars question whether Hosea was a native of the northern kingdom, he was acutely aware of Israel's religious and political situation. Most likely he prophesied at such major Israelite centers as Samaria (e.g., 7:1; 8:5-6), Bethel (e.g., 10:5, "Beth-aven"), and Gilgal (e.g., 12:11 [MT 12]). Moreover, he demonstrates familiarity with such northern sites as the valley of Achor (2:15 [MT 17]), Adam (6:7), Gibeah, and Ramah (5:8).

Hosea's proclamations suggest that he was affiliated with the official prophets (Heb. *n*e*bî'îm*; cf. 6:5; 12:10, 13 [MT 11, 14]). Some scholars, however, assert that he arose from the priestly class (cf. 4:4-9).

II. Contents

The book opens with a biographical account of Hosea's ministry (1:1) and, in particular, his tumultuous marriage (1:2-3:5). Following God's command, Hosea marries the prostitute Gomer, who bears him three children symbolically named Jezreel, Not pitied, and Not my people (1:2-2:1 [MT 2:3]); this marriage is likened to Yahweh's relationship to the faithless Israel (2:2-23 [MT 4-25]). In ch. 3 Hosea is instructed to redeem his wife from harlotry.

Chs. 4-14 comprise utterances from throughout Hosea's ministry. In ch. 4 he states the Lord's case against Israel, citing the corruption of the religious leaders (vv. 4-10) as well as the idolatrous practices of the masses (vv. 11-19); these themes are reiterated in 5:1-7. The prophet denounces both Israel and Judah for their roles in the disgraceful Syro-Ephraimite War (5:8-6:6) and threatens divine judgment upon them (5:12-15; 6:4-6). Through Hosea the Lord rebukes his people for breach of the covenant as evident through religious syncretism (6:7-11; 8:4-6, 11-13; 9:1-9), civil strife (6:22-7:7; 8:4, 14), and the quest for national security by means of alignment with foreign nations (7:8-16). Hosea traces Israel's spiritual history, including the apostasy at Baal-peor (9:10-14; cf. Num. 25) and the Benjaminite assault upon the Levite's concubine at Gibeah (Hos. 10:9-15; cf. Judg. 19). He proclaims the Lord's compassionate chastisement in Hos. 11:1-11, then reiterates the divine outrage at Israel's faithlessness (11:11 [MT 12:1]-13:11), culminating in the prophecy of Samaria's destruction (13:12-16 [MT 14:1]). The book concludes with a call to repentance and the promise of divine forgiveness (ch. 14).

III. Literary Aspects

On the basis of style and content, the book divides into two distinct sections. The narrative depicting Hosea's marriage (chs. 1-3) is generally considered to be factual, although some posit elements of allegorization (particularly in the names of Hosea's children) in ch. 2. Some scholars have questioned whether the woman in ch. 3 is Gomer or a second wife, but the chapter does appear to parallel ch. 1. The third-person account in chs. 1-2 may have been compiled by a disciple, with ch. 3 an autobiographical version by the prophet himself (so Andersen and Freedman, p. 58).

The second, larger portion of the book consists of prophetic oracles, apparently grouped somewhat chronologically according to subject matter or linked by catchwords. The usual forms of prophetic speech are often not distinguishable, and the style displays a blending of poetic and prosaic diction. This suggests the conscious literary compilation of originally oral material by the prophet or a disciple; further evidence includes the recurrent theme of the prophetic lawsuit (Heb. *rîb* "contend, accuse"; cf. 4:1, 4; 12:2 [MT 3]), akin to standard legal practice at the city gate.

Some scholars suggest that the book was composed in Judah, where Hosea or his followers had fled upon the fall of Samaria. Textual corruption, perhaps introduced by Judahite scribes, has long been blamed for difficulties in translating these chapters; more recent scholarship, however, defends the authenticity of the material, suggesting that it reflects a distinctive northern dialect of Hebrew influenced by Aramaic.

IV. Theology

Hosea's ministry was dominated by one major concern, Israel's breach of covenant with God. This he sees most clearly in the assimilation of Canaanite religious practices by the Israelite cult—condoned and even fostered by the priestly and prophetic leadership—and the accompanying decline in ethical, social values. Moreover, he views Israel's maneuvering for political alliances and power as a rejection of God as the people's sole source of security and sustenance. The intended intimacy of this covenant Hosea depicts in terms of personal experience (chs. 1–3) as well as the covenant history of Israel (cf. 2:15 [MT 17]; 9:10; 11:1), underscored by his reference to God by the name Yahweh, which had been revealed to Moses (e.g., 1:9; 12:9 [MT 10]; cf. Exod. 3:14; 6:7).

Hosea has been characterized as a prophet of love. Indeed, the inevitable destruction of Israel as punishment for this breach is presented as an act of divine compassion (Hos. 9:15; 11:5-7; 13:9). This constant love provides the hope for Israel's restoration and salvation (2:21-23 [MT 23-25]; 11:8-11; 14:4-7).

Bibliography. F. I. Andersen and D. N. Freedman, *Hosea.* AB (1980); W. Brueggemann, *Tradition for Crisis: A Study in Hosea* (Richmond: 1968); H. W. Wolff, *Hosea.* Hermeneia (Philadelphia: 1974).

HOSHAIAH [hō shā'yə] (Heb. *hôšaʿyâ* "Yahweh has saved").

1. The father of Azariah (**16**), the antagonist of Jeremiah (Jer. 42:1; 43:2).

2. A prince of Judah who led the second contingent of Judahites in the procession at the dedication of the repaired walls of Jerusalem (Neh. 12:32).

HOSHAMA [hōsh'ə mə] (Heb. *hôšāmāʿ* "Yahweh has heard"). A son of King Jeconiah (Jehoiachin), born while his father was in captivity (1 Chr. 3:18).

HOSHEA [hō shē'ə] (Heb. *hôšēaʿ* "may Yahweh save").

1. The original name of Joshua the son of Nun (Num. 13:8; KJV "Oshea"). Moses changed the form and meaning of the name (v. 16), thereby affirming the saving acts of Yahweh (Heb. *yᵉhôšuaʿ* "Yahweh saves").

2. The son of Azaziah; chief officer of the Ephraimites at the time of David (1 Chr. 27:20).

3. The Hebrew form of the name HOSEA; the eighth-century prophet of Israel whose utterances constitute the book of Hosea.

4. The last king of the northern kingdom (*ca.* 732-722 B.C.). The son of Elah, he gained the throne by conspiring and killing King Pekah (2 Kgs. 15:30); the Assyrian Tiglath-pileser III boasts complicity in Hoshea's accession (*ANET*, pp. 283-84; Akk. *A-ú-si-ʾ*). The evil character of his reign is characteristically condemned, although the biblical account notes he was not as bad as his predecessors (17:2).

By Hoshea's time much of the Israelite territory had been incorporated into the Assyrian Empire, and Hoshea was subjected to heavy tribute. Upon the death of Tiglath-pileser in 727, Hoshea revolted, seeking the aid of the Egyptian pharaoh So (v. 4; Heb. *sw*'; Akk. *Sibe*; possibly Osorkon IV of the Twenty-third [Libyan] Dynasty). The Assyrian successor Shalmaneser V retaliated by invading Israel in 724, forcing Hoshea to submit. But because the Assyrian was unconvinced of Israel's loyalty he imprisoned Hoshea and laid to Samaria for three years (vv. 4-5). The city fell in Hoshea's ninth year, and the Assyrians deported its citizens to various locations in Mesopotamia (v. 6; 18:9-12).

5. One who set his seal to the renewed covenant under Nehemiah (Neh. 10:23).

HOSPITALITY. See SOJOURNER.

HOST OF HEAVEN (Heb. *ṣᵉḇāʾ haššāmayim*).† Old Testament name for the celestial bodies. Derived from military usage (cf. Gen. 21:22, 32; Judg. 4:2, KJV; RSV "army"), the term connotes the vastness of creation, over which the Lord exercises command (Isa. 34:4; 45:12; Jer. 33:22; cf. Isa. 40:26). Elsewhere it designates the angels who attend the heavenly throne (1 Kgs. 22:19 par. 2 Chr. 18:18).

The worship of cosmic phenomena was an important aspect of Mesopotamian religion and became increasingly prevalent in Israel during the divided monarchy (e.g., 2 Kgs. 17:16; 23:4-5; 21:3, 5 par. 2 Chr. 33:3, 5; Amos 5:26; cf. Deut. 4:19; 17:3).

See LORD OF HOSTS.

HOTHAM [hō'thəm] (Heb. *ḥôṭām* "signet ring").

1. A man of the tribe of Asher; a son of Heber and grandson of Beriah (1 Chr. 7:31-32).

2. A man from Aroer (1 Chr. 11:44; KJV "Hothan"). His sons, Shama and Jeiel, were among the mighty men of David.

HOTHIR [hō'thər] (Heb. *hôṭîr* "abundance"). A son of the singer Heman (**2**), appointed by David to head the twenty-first division of levitical musicians (1 Chr. 25:4, 28).

HOUR (Heb. *môʿēḏ*; Gk. *hóra*).† A division of the daylight period from sunrise to sunset, roughly analogous to the division of the night into watches. With the invention of the sundial in the postexilic period, the Hebrews divided the day into twelve equal segments (John 11:9). Rather than standardized units, these hours varied in length proportionate to the seasonal fluctuations in amount of daylight. Thus, references to specific hours must be considered approximations (e.g., third hour, the beginning of the third twelfth of daylight [*ca.* 9:00 A.M.; Matt. 20:3; Mark 15:25; Acts 2:15]; the sixth hour [*ca.* noon; Matt. 20:5; 27:45; Mark 15:33]; the ninth hour [*ca.* 3:00 P.M.; Matt. 20:5; 27:45-46; Mark 15:33-34; Acts 3:1; 10:30]). The eleventh hour designates the final period of daylight and often symbolizes waning opportunity (e.g., Matt. 20:6, 9; cf. 1 John 2:18, "the last hour").

An hour may also indicate an important moment or an appointed time (KJV, Dan. 3:6, 15; Aram. *šāʿâ*; RSV "immediately"; NJV "at once"; Matt. 8:13;

RSV "moment"; cf. Jer. 46:17; Luke 22:53; John 5:28; Rom. 13:11; Rev. 3:10). In the Gospels this usage applies most frequently to the events of Jesus' death and resurrection (e.g., Matt. 25:13; Mark 14:35, 41; John 2:4; 7:30; 17:1).

See DAY.

HOUSE (Heb., Aram. *bayiṯ;* Gk. *oíkos*).† A dwelling or place of residence. In this basic sense, the term encompasses the simplest peasant dwellings (perhaps even caves or tents; cf. Gen. 33:17) as well as the palaces of the nobility.

From the Early Bronze Age (*ca.* 3200-2100 B.C.) on, most Palestinian houses were located in fortified cities and their dependent villages, which offered both security and such urban services as water. To date scant evidence of village life has been recovered to shed light on the housing of the rural masses; presumably these dwellings were merely shacks to win agriculturalists returned for meals and shelter for the night. In the cities houses were clustered together with adjoining walls. Those in the interior formed irregular blocks encircled by streets, while others were adjacent to or part of the city walls (Josh. 2:15).

Founded on bedrock or rocky terraces (cf. Matt. 7:24-27), houses were constructed of loose or quarried stone, when available, and mud-dried brick, covered with clay plaster. Walls might be reinforced with stone pilasters. Floors were generally of beaten clay, and roofs were formed from wooden beams (Cant. 1:17) covered with branches and clay (cf. Ps. 129:6; Isa. 37:27). Doorways consisted of a wooden lintel upon two upright posts, and the few windows were often merely small openings in the wall (cf. Josh. 2:15).

The basic plan of the Israelite house was rectangular. Presumably the homes of the poor were one-room affairs. Ample evidence exists of multi-roomed houses constructed around a courtyard. In addition to housing for the extended family, rooms were provided for livestock, cooking, storage, and commercial enterprises such as carpentry and dyeing and weaving. The flat roofs, accessible by a ladder or stairway and protected by a parapet (Deut. 22:8), provided additional sleeping space (1 Sam. 9:25; 2 Sam. 11:2; 2 Kgs. 4:10) and served as a place for drying crops and performing acts of worship (Acts 10:9; cf. 2 Kgs. 23:12).

The homes and palaces of the nobility were more elaborate, featuring hinged doors and latticed windows and decorated with wood carvings, paintings, mosaics, and inlaid ivory (cf. Amos 3:15; 6:4). Such structures have been discovered at Tirzah, capital of the northern kingdom, and among remains of the Persian period at Lachish. In the New Testament period Hellenistic and Roman influence is particularly apparent in the adoption of a large outer court or atrium, surrounded by rooms accessible to the public, and a private, inner court or peristyle with the family quarters. Rooms, halls, or even component buildings which comprised the royal palace or other magnificent structures might also be designated as "houses"; for example, the House of the Forest of Lebanon was a part of Solomon's palace, decorated with cedar and furnished with many treasures (1 Kgs. 7:2-5; 10:17,

21; cf. Isa. 22:8). The winter house of the king may have been originally such a unit of the palace (cf. Jer. 36:22); elsewhere it appears to have been a separate residence akin to the luxurious structures at Herodian Jericho (Tulûl Abū el-ʿAlâyiq; cf. Amos 3:15).

In the Old Testament the designation house of God (Heb. *bêṯ ʾelōhîm*) or house of the Lord *(bêṯ yhwh)* refers to the Israelite tabernacle or temple as the residence of God (e.g., Exod. 23:19; 1 Kgs. 8:11; Neh. 6:10; Dan. 1:2; Heb. 10:21; cf. Judg. 17:5, MT; so NJV; RSV "shrine"). Foreign temples are named in similar fashion (e.g., "house of Dagan," 1 Sam. 5:2, 5; cf. 31:10; RSV "temple of Astarte").

The term "house" is also applied to the spider's web (Job 8:14; cf. 27:18, MT), the human body (4:19), or a container (Deut. 6:11; cf. Isa. 3:20, MT). Used figuratively it designates an abode, such as Sheol (Job 17:13; cf. 30:23; Eccl. 12:5), or a condition, such as slavery ("house of bondage"; e.g., Exod. 13:3; Deut. 5:6).

For "house" as a designation for a dynasty or a social unit such as a family or tribe, *see* FAMILY; FATHER'S HOUSE; HOUSEHOLD.

HOUSEHOLD (Heb. *bayiṯ;* Gk. *oíkos, oikía*).* The extended family or father's house, the basic social unit of ancient Israel (so RSV, JB; KJV "house"; NIV "family"). A patrilocal residential unit, it was headed by the eldest male of the lineage and might comprise as many as five generations of the family. In addition to the family head and his spouse, it included unmarried children, sons and their wives and children. Moreover, it encompassed dependent persons such as adopted sons (cf. Gen. 15:2), servants or enlisted personnel (14:14), and resident aliens. Despite its size (cf. 26:1-27), the household was subordinate to the clan (Heb. *mišpāḥâ;* cf. Josh. 7:14).

The household was self-sufficient with regard to subsistence, education, and social control. This autonomy is underscored by the group solidarity evident in the accountability of the entire unit for one member's transgressions (e.g., Josh. 7:1-15; cf. 2:12; Gen. 7:1) and particularly in religious observance (e.g., Gen. 18:19; 35:2; Deut. 15:20; Josh. 24:15). Such corporate identity may underlie the application of the designation "house" or "household" for larger units such as lineages or dynasties (e.g., 2 Sam. 7:11, 13, 16 par. 1 Chr. 17:10, 12, 14; 2 Kgs. 8:18, 27; Ps. 115:10, 12), tribes (e.g., Exod. 2:1; Judg. 10:9), or even the state (e.g., 1 Sam. 7:2-3; 1 Kgs. 12:21, 23; cf. Ruth 4:11).

The New Testament frequently records the conversion and baptism of a person and his entire household (e.g., John 4:53; Acts 11:14; 16:15, 33; cf. Luke 19:9). Such families may have formed the basis of the house churches (1 Cor. 16:19). By extension, the entire Church is called the household of God (Eph. 2:19; 1 Tim. 3:15; 1 Pet. 4:17; cf. Heb. 3:2-6) or the household of faith (Gal. 6:10).

The so-called "household lists" of the Epistles (e.g., Eph. 5:21–6:9; Col. 3:18–4:1; 1 Pet. 2:13–3:9) are compilations of obligations conducive to the stability of the family.

See FAMILY.

HOZAI [hō'zī] (Heb. *ḥōzāy* "the seers"). According to the MT the author of chronicles concerning King Manasseh of Judah, a source used by the author of 2 Chronicles (so JB, NJV; KJV mg. "Hosai"). The RSV, KJV, and NIV read "the seers," following the LXX (Gk. *tōn horóntōn;* cf. v. 18, Heb. *haḥōzîm* "the seers") and one Hebrew version.

HUKKOK [hŭk'ŏk] (Heb. *ḥûqōq* "chasm"). A town in the tribal territory of Naphtali (Josh. 19:34), generally identified with modern Yāqûq, near Jebel Habaqbuq about 5 km. (3 mi.) west of Chinnereth.

HUKOK [hōō'kŏk] (Heb. *ḥûqōq*). A city within the tribal territory of Asher assigned to the Gershonite Levites (1 Chr. 6:75). Elsewhere it is called Helkath.

HUL [hŭl] (Heb. *ḥûl*). According to the Table of Nations, a son of Aram and grandson of Shem (Gen. 10:23; 1 Chr. 1:17). The territory inhabited by his descendants cannot be identified with certainty; suggestions include the Arabian peninsula, the region of Lake Huleh, and the Armenian border (cf. Hulia, a site mentioned in Assurnasirpal's annals).

HULDAH [hŭl'də] (Heb. *ḥuldâ* "weasel"). A prophetess living in Jerusalem during the time of King Josiah. She was the wife of Shallum, the keeper of the wardrobe (perhaps that of the king or temple). After the Book of the Law had been found in the temple and read to Josiah, the king sent a delegation to Huldah asking her to inquire of the Lord on his behalf. She proclaimed that judgment would come upon Jerusalem, but not until Josiah had died, so that he would be spared the sight of the evil that was to come (2 Kgs. 22:14-20 par. 2 Chr. 34:22-28). The prophecy was fulfilled with the death of Josiah at Megiddo in 609 B.C.

HULEH [hōō'lə], **LAKE.**† The northernmost and smallest of the three lakes along the course of the Jordan river, situated some 16 km. (10 mi.) north of the Sea of Galilee. Known in Arabic as Baḥret el-Ḥûleh or Baḥret el-Kheit, it is merely 2 m. (6.5 ft.) above sea level and measures 6 km. (4 mi.) long, with its greatest width toward the north (3 km. [2 mi.]).

Immediately to the south is Jisr Benāt Ya'qûb ("Bridge of Jacob's Daughters"), a thirteenth-century A.D. Arab route which links the mountains of Galilee and the Jôlān region of the Transjordan. The area to the north, which occupies the Jordan rift at the southwestern foot of Mt. Hermon, is called the Huleh basin. In 1958 this impenetrable marshy area as well as Lake Huleh itself was drained by the Israeli government.

Lake Huleh is not named in the biblical accounts. Scholars have abandoned the earlier identification of this lake with the waters of Merom (Josh. 11:5, 7).

HUMTAH [hŭm'tə] (Heb. *ḥumtâ* "fortress"). A city in the tribal territory of Judah, mentioned between Aphekah and Kiriath-arba or Hebron (Josh. 15:54). Its precise location is unknown.

HUNDRED, TOWER OF THE (Heb. *migdal hammē'â*). A tower in or along the northern wall of Jerusalem, located between the Fish Gate and the Sheep Gate (Neh. 3:1; 12:39; KJV "tower of Meah"). It is mentioned as part of the wall reconstructed by Nehemiah. Listed preceding the Tower of Hananel, it apparently overlooked the temple from the northwestern portion of the Ophel-Moriah spur, on the site where Herod the Great later constructed the Fortress Antonia. The name may derive from the designation of a military unit, suggesting that the tower functioned as a garrison.

HUNDREDWEIGHT (Rev. 16:12, RSV). *See* TALENT.

HUNTING (Heb. *ṣayiḏ,* from *ṣûḏ; ṣayyad* "hunter").† Hunting was a highly developed art in the ancient Near East. While the spread of agriculture and the rise of cities relegated hunting to secondary importance as a source of food, the Bible and other literature provide insights into the equipment and tactics used in the hunt. Hunting imagery is used throughout the Bible.

Nimrod (Gen. 10:9) and Esau (25:27) are the only hunters named in the Old Testament. Generally, hunting was practiced only occasionally and by the anonymous people whose livelihood was agriculture or animal husbandry. Hunting for pleasure (with hounds, hawks, or falcons), as depicted in Egyptian, Phoenician, and Assyrian monuments, is not found in the Bible.

Hunting implements included the bow and arrow (Gen. 27:3), the sling (1 Sam. 17:40, 49-50), lasso, spears, traps, nets, and deadfalls. Swords, spears, slings, and clubs were also used defensively, to protect human beings and livestock against predators. Hunting fowl was more common than hunting four-footed game; often such creatures could simply be chased until they tired, whereupon the hunter would dispatch them with a stone.

The patience and deadly intent of the hunter are the basis for metaphorical comments in both the Old and the New Testament. Prominent themes include man hunting down man (Mic. 7:2; cf. 1 Sam. 24:11, KJV), Yahweh's relentless judgment (Job 10:16; Jer. 16:16; cf. Isa. 24:17-18; Jer. 48:43-44), and attempts to snare Jesus or believers in their words (cf. Mark 12:13; Luke 11:54; 1 Tim. 3:7; 2 Tim. 2:26).

HUPHAM [hū'fəm] (Heb. *ḥûpām*). A son or descendant of Benjamin; eponymous ancestor of the Huphamites (Num. 26:39). He is probably the same as Huppim (Gen. 46:21), although at 1 Chr. 7:12, 15 the latter is said to be the son of Ir.

HUPPAH [hŭp'ə] (Heb. *ḥuppâ* "canopy, protection"). The head of the thirteenth division of priests at the time of King David (1 Chr. 24:13). The Hebrew name suggests the wedding baldachin in the modern synagogue.

HUPPIM [hŭp'ĭm] (Heb. *ḥuppîm* "coast people").† A descendant of Benjamin (Gen. 46:21; 1 Chr. 7:12).

At 1 Chr. 7:15 he appears to be a descendant of Manasseh. The name, which has apparently become the eponym of an Israelite subgroup, is probably a variant form of Hupham.

HUR [hûr] (Heb. *ḥûr*).

1. An Israelite who, with Aaron, supported Moses' arms during the battle against the Amalekites at Rephidim in order that the rod of God might remain upraised and the Israelites prevail (Exod. 17:10-12). Later he and Aaron served as chief judges while Moses and Joshua ascended Mt. Sinai to receive the tablets of the law (24:14). Interestingly, he is not mentioned in the account of the golden calf (ch. 32). According to later Jewish tradition, Hur was the husband of Moses' sister Miriam (cf. Josephus *Ant.* iii.2.4 [54]).

2. A Judahite; the father of Uri and grandfather of Bezalel (Exod. 31:2; 35:30; 38:22; 1 Chr. 2:19-20; 2 Chr. 1:5). Among his descendants are reckoned the people of Kiriath-jearim, Bethlehem, and the Manahathites (1 Chr. 2:50-54; 4:4). Josephus identifies him with **1** above, the husband of Miriam (*Ant.* iii.6.1 [105]).

3. A king of Midian and vassal of the Amorite king Sihon (Josh. 13:21). He was one of five Midianite kings slain along with Balaam in Moses' retaliation for the incident at Peor (Num. 31:8).

4. The father of the officer over the hill country of Ephraim, who was responsible for providing Solomon's palace with food (1 Kgs. 4:8, KJV, JB; RSV "Ben-hur").

5. The father of Rephaiah, who helped repair the walls of Jerusalem (Neh. 3:9).

HURAI [hŏŏr'ī] (Heb. *ḥûray*).† One of David's mighty men (1 Chr. 11:32). At 2 Sam. 23:30 he is called Hiddai.

HURAM [hŏŏr'əm] (Heb. *ḥûrām*, from *'aḥîrām* "brother of the exalted").†

1. Alternate form of the name Hiram, used in 2 Chronicles particularly for Hiram I, king of Tyre.

2. A Tyrian metalworker employed by Solomon for technical assistance in the ornamentation of the temple (1 Kgs. 7:13-14, 40, 45 par. 2 Chr. 2:13-14; 4:11-16). His father was Tyrian and his mother an Israelite from Naphtali (1 Kgs. 7:14; 2 Chr. 2:14 identifies her as from the adjacent territory of Dan). In 1 Kings he is called Hiram (**2**), and at 2 Chr. 2:13; 4:16 his name occurs as Huram-abi.

3. A Benjaminite; the son of Bela (1 Chr. 8:5).

HURAM-ABI [hŏŏr'əm ā'bē] (Heb. *ḥûrām 'aḇî* "Huram is my father").† The Tyrian craftsman employed by Solomon for the metalwork of the temple (2 Chr. 2:13; KJV "Huram my father"; NJV "my master Hurdam"; 4:16; KJV "Huram his father"). *See* HURAM **2.**

HURI [hŏŏr'ī] (Heb. *ḥûrî* "cotton weaver"). A man of the tribe of Gad; the son of Jaroah and father of Abihail (1 Chr. 5:14).

HURRIANS [hŏŏr'ī ənz].† A non-Semitic people

who formed the powerful empire of Mitanni and were instrumental in the diffusion of Sumero-Akkadian culture.

I. History

The Hurrians are first attested by a Late Akkadian text *ca.* 2400 B.C. to the area of Urkish, located in the Taurus mountain range north of Carchemish, which was to remain the center of their civilization throughout their history. Other texts indicate that prior to *ca.* 2000 they were situated in the region east of the Tigris and north of the Upper Zab rivers. After the fall of the Third (Neo-Sumerian) Dynasty of Ur (1936), the Hurrians gradually penetrated Upper Mesopotamia and northern Syria; their presence was particularly important at Alalakh.

Buoyed by the weakening of the Hittite Old Kingdom, the Hurrians formed a number of city-states which subsequently contributed to the fall of the Hittite kingdom *ca.* 1500. Most powerful of these states was Mitanni (Akk. Ḫanigalbat). Ruled from its capital at Washukkanni, near biblical Haran, by an Indoeuropean aristocracy, Mitanni formed an empire of Hurrian and Amorite city-states stretching from Alalakh to Nuzi; even Assyria was reduced to a vassal.

Hurrian dominance was ended scarcely a century later with the rise of the Hittite Empire under Šuppiluliumas I (*ca.* 1386). Nevertheless, Hurrian influence continued, culturally as well as politically. Hurrians formed the ruling aristocracy of several city-states, as evident in the Amarna Letters. Accordingly, Nineteenth Dynasty Egyptian texts (late fourteenth century) refer to Syria-Palestine as "Ḫuru-land." With the influx of new peoples, particularly the Sea Peoples in the twelfth century, Hurrian influence diminished. Apparently assimilated with other peoples, the Hurrians are last attested in the region of Lake Van during the early first millennium.

II. Legacy

Far more important than their brief political success through the Mitanni Empire was the Hurrians' cultural and social influence on the ancient Near East. Already in the third millennium the Hurrians had adopted the cuneiform syllabary to their own language, a still largely undeciphered tongue apparently akin to Urartian. By the end of their history Hurrian forms were evident in the nomenclature of Mari, Alalakh, Ugarit, and the Hittite dynasty of Suppiluliuma, and Hurrian loanwords are abundant in the Hittite language. Hurrian literary, lexical, and religious texts have been discovered in the archives of Mari, Boghazköy, and Ugarit, and a Hurrian letter is included among the Amarna Letters.

Having assimilated much of Sumero-Akkadian culture early in their history, the Hurrians transmited it, with adaptations, westward to Syria and especially the Hittites. This was particularly the case with religion; in addition to several syncretistic Hurrian deities, the Hittites adopted the Hurrian weather-god Teshub, his consort Ḫepa, and their son Sharruma.

Hurrian social and legal practices are well described in several thousand cuneiform tablets discovered in Nuzi (modern Yorghan Tepe), Arrapḫa (modern Kirkuk), and other sites. However, their influence on the

Old Testament patriarchs, once an important aspect of the exegesis of Gen. 12–50, is now largely discredited. Nevertheless, the Hurrian aristocracy which ruled so many feudal states in Mesopotamia and Syria-Palestine introduced new forms of military technology, such as the composite bow, scaled armor, and the war chariot. These influenced not only the mode of warfare but social organization as well; several ancient Near Eastern societies now featured an aristocracy of chariot warriors (Hur. *maryannu*).

III. Biblical References

Although they comprised a ruling class in fourteenth-century Palestine, as attested by the Amarna Letters for such cities as Shechem, Taanach, and Megiddo, the Hurrians do not appear to have constituted a substantial element in the region's population then or at any other time in the biblical period. Attempts to identify the Hurrians with the biblical Horites or even the Hivites remain difficult on historical, onomastic, and linguistic grounds.

Bibliography. I. J. Gelb, *Hurrians and Subarians* (Chicago: 1944); E. A. Speiser, "The Hurrian Participation in the Civilization of Mesopotamia, Syria and Palestine," pp. 244-269 in J. J. Finkelstein and M. Greenberg, eds., *Oriental and Biblical Studies* (Philadelphia: 1967).

HUSHAH [hŏosh'ə] (Heb. *ḥûšâ* "haste"). A place in the hill country of Judah, founded by Ezer (1 Chr. 4:4). It was the home of Sibbecai ("the Hushathite"), one of David's mighty men (2 Sam. 21:18; 1 Chr. 11:29; 20:4; 27:11; called Mebunnai at 2 Sam. 23:27). The site is generally identified with modern Husan, southwest of Bethlehem.

HUSHAI [hŏosh'ī] (Heb. *ḥûšay*). A friend and confidant of King David (2 Sam. 15:37; 1 Chr. 27:33). An Archite, he was the father of Baana, an officer of King Solomon (1 Kgs. 4:16). He played an important role during the rebellion of Absalom by posing as an adviser and dissuading Absalom from following Ahithophel's counsel (2 Sam. 15:32-33; 16:16–17:14); moreover, he kept David apprised through the sons of the priests Zadok and Abiathar (15:34-36).

HUSHAM [hŏosh'əm] (Heb. *ḥušām*, *ḥûšām*). A Temanite who became king over Edom after the death of Jobab (Gen. 36:34-35; 1 Chr. 1:45-46).

HUSHATHITE [hŏosh'ə thīt] (Heb. *ḥûšāṭî*). A gentilic designating an inhabitant of Hushah (2 Sam. 21:18; 23:27; 1 Chr. 11:29; 17:11; 20:4).

HUSHIM [hŏosh'īm] (Heb. *ḥûšîm*, *ḥušîm*, *ḥušim*).
1. A son of (or a social group descended from) Dan (Gen. 46:23). The form Shuham occurs at Num. 26:42.
2. The sons of the Benjaminite Aher (1 Chr. 7:12). The Hebrew text of this verse is difficult to interpret.
3. A wife of the Benjaminite Shaharaim and mother of Abitub and Elpaal (1 Chr. 8:8, 11).

HUZ (Gen. 22:21, KJV). *See* Uz.

HUZZAB [hŭz'əb] (Heb. *huṣṣab*).† According to the KJV and NJV, a personal name. This obscure Hebrew word, found only at Nah. 2:7 (MT 8), has been translated variously by the English versions. The RSV renders it "mistress," a reference to the palace of Nineveh (cf. TEV, "the queen"). Others view it as a verbal form derived either from *yāṣab* "to set or station oneself" (cf. NASB, "it is fixed") or *nāṣab* "to take one's stand" (cf. NIV, "it is decreed").

HYENA (Heb. *'îyîm*).† A carnivorous, nocturnal animal of the genus *Hyaena*; a carrion-eater noted for its cowardliness. The Palestinian hyena is the striped hyena (*Hyaena striata*), found from North Africa to India. In the Bible the hyena is associated with desolation and abandoned human habitations (Isa. 13:22; 34:14; Jer. 50:39; KJV "wild beasts of the islands"; NJV "dragons"; cf. Sir. 13:18; Gk. *hýaina*).

The place name Zeboim (Heb. *ṣᵉbōʿîm*) also means "hyenas" (Neh. 11:34); at 1 Sam. 13:18 it designates the Wâdī Abū Dabāʿ.

HYKSOS [hĭk'sōs] (Egyp. *ḥq3w ḫ3swt*).* Foreign rulers of the Fifteenth and Sixteenth Dynasties of Egypt (*ca.* 1700-1500 B.C.). Interpreted as "shepherd kings" by the Egyptian priest Manetho (*ca.* 280; Josephus *Ap.* i.14 [75-82]), the Egyptian term means more precisely "rulers of foreign lands."

This largely Semitic (Egyp. "Asiatic") aristocracy apparently entered Egypt in two waves (*ca.* 1720 and 1674) as part of the larger Middle Bronze II Amorite movements which coincided with the beginning of the Second Intermediate Period in Egypt. Their rise to power was a gradual process of infiltration facilitated by the decentralization of Egyptian authority at the end of the Thirteenth Dynasty. Ruling from Avaris (perhaps Tell ed-Dabʿa) in the Nile Delta, they extended their rule south toward Thebes and gained influence commercially and culturally as well as politically in Syria-Palestine and the Mediterranean. Long thought to have been expelled by the resurgent Theban dynasty and driven into Palestine, the Hyksos may actually have fallen in a civil war, after which they were simply assimilated.

Characteristically Hyksos innovations as evidenced by archaeological excavations in Egypt and Palestine include fortifications of beaten earth featuring a sloping, plastered revetment (cf. Hazor, Tell Beit Mirsim); and a distinctive style of scarab.

Attempts as early as Josephus to link the Hyksos period with the Israelite sojourn in Egypt or the expulsion of the Hyksos with the Israelite Exodus are replete with chronological difficulties and have been largely dismissed.

HYMENAEUS [hĭ'mə nē'əs] (Gk. *Hymenaios*). An opponent of Paul, named after the Greek god of marriage. Hymenaeus is mentioned with the false teachers Alexander (7) (1 Tim. 1:19-20) and Philetus (2 Tim. 2:17-18). He is said to have abandoned the faith by teaching that the final resurrection had already taken place. Paul "delivered him to Satan" (i.e., excluded him from the church) so that Hymenaeus might learn not to blaspheme (1 Tim. 1:20).

HYMN. A sacred song; a song of praise or thanksgiving to God. The oldest collection of such songs in the Bible is the book of Psalms, but other religious songs are included as well: The Song of the Sea (Exod. 15:1-18), the Song of Moses (Deut. 32:1-43), The Song of Deborah (Judg. 5), the Song of Hannah (1 Sam. 2:1-10), the Magnificat of Mary (Luke 1:46-55), the Benedictus of Zechariah (1:68-79), and the Nunc Dimittis of Simeon (2:29-32). From 2 Chr. 29:27-28 it appears that often the Hebrew Psalms were sung with accompaniment.

The New Testament uses three words for Christian songs: "psalms (Gk. *psalmós*) and hymns *(hýmnos)* and spiritual songs *(hōdḗ pneumatikḗ)*" (Eph. 5:19; Col. 3:16). During the Passover night the Lord and his disciples sang the psalms (Pss. 113–118).

At Eph. 5:14 and 1 Tim. 3:16 fragments are retained of old Christian hymns; these are recognizable from the meter of the Greek text. On the basis of Acts 16:25; 1 Cor. 14:26; Eph. 5:19; and Col. 3:16 it can be surmised that the singing of hymns was customary among even the first Christians, as confirmed in A.D. 112 by Pliny the Younger (*Ep.* x.97).

HYRCANUS [hûr kā′nəs] (Gk. *Hyrkanos*).†

1. A Tobiad (RSV "son of Tobias"), the eighth son of Joseph and grandson of Tobias. Born *ca.* 226 B.C., he became estranged from his family by ingratiating himself with the Ptolemaic rulers. After murdering two of his brothers, he fled to the Transjordanian fortress at ʿArāq el-Emīr, where he established himself as an independent ruler loyal to the Ptolemies even after the conquest of Syria-Palestine by the Seleucid Antiochus III the Great (Josephus *Ant.* xii.4.6-11 [186-236]). He apparently deposited in the temple treasury a substantial amount of the riches he had amassed by preying on the surrounding populace (2 Macc. 3:11; KJV "Hircanus"). Shortly after the succession of the powerful Antiochus IV Epiphanes in 175 Hyrcanus committed suicide.

2. John Hyrcanus I, Hasmonean high priest and king of Judea (135-104 B.C.). The youngest son of Simon Maccabeus, he turned back the Seleucid invasion of Judea in 137 and gained the throne two years later upon the assassination of his father and two brothers. Antiochus VII Sidetes immediately renewed his campaign against Judea and, after besieging Hyrcanus at Jerusalem for an entire year, forced him to concede to heavy tribute, the taking of hostages, and disarmament of Jewish forces (Josephus *Ant.* xiii.7.4–8.3 [228-248]; *BJ* i.2.5 [61]). Capitalizing on the death of Antiochus at the hands of the Parthians in 129 and the internal disarray faced by his successor Demetrius II, Hyrcanus renewed his father's alliance with Rome and thus regained his independence. He expanded Jewish control by conquering Medeba in Transjordan, Shechem to the north, and Idumea in the south; some years later his sons captured Samaria and the valley of Esdraelon.

Hyrcanus established himself as a fearsome ruler by destroying the Samaritan temple at Mt. Gerizim and forcing the Idumeans to accept circumcision and the Jewish law (*Ant.* xiii.8.4–9.1 [249-258]; *BJ* i.2.6-7 [62-66]). Moreover, he broke with the dominant,

pietistic Pharisees and sided with Sadducees, who favored his Hellenistic, monarchic tendencies. Thus, while Hyrcanus reestablished Judea's independence and enhanced its political fortunes, he transformed the Hasmonean dynasty into a largely secular power. He was succeeded by Judas Aristobulus I, the eldest of his five sons.

3. John Hyrcanus II, eldest son of Alexander Jannaeus and Salome Alexandra and grandson of John Hyrcanus I. He succeeded his father as high priest in 76 B.C. and upon his mother's death in 67 became ethnarch, an office he was forced to relinquish three months later to his aggressive younger brother Aristobulus II. When Pompey captured Jerusalem in 63 he reinstated Hyrcanus as high priest, but the real power was held by the Idumean Antipater (Josephus *Ant.* xiv.2.3–4.5 [29-79]; *BJ* i.6.3–7.7 [128-158]; Dio Cassius *Hist.* xxxvii.15-17). Following rebellions by Aristobulus and his son Alexander, Gabinius, the Roman proconsul of Syria, reorganized the Palestinian administration and deposed Hyrcanus. After Julius Caesar had defeated Pompey, Hyrcanus demonstrated his loyalty, for which Caesar renamed him high priest and nominal ethnarch; again he was but the puppet of Antipater, now procurator of Judea. In 47 Antipater appointed his sons Herod (the Great) and Phasael as governors of Galilee and Jerusalem, respectively; they also overran Hyrcanus, and in 42 Mark Antony made them tetrarchs of Judea. Two years later Aristobulus' son Antigonus enlisted Parthian assistance to depose Hyrcanus and Phasael and thus become king. He mutilated Hyrcanus by chopping off his ears, thereby rendering him unsuitable to regain the high priesthood. Hyrcanus was taken captive to Parthia, but was permitted to return in 36. He was executed in 30 by Herod the Great, thus ending the Hasmonean claim to the throne.

HYSSOP [hĭs′əp] (Heb. *ʾēzôḇ*; Gk. *hýssōpos*). A fragrant, aromatic plant of the Labiatae family. True hyssop (*Hyssopus officinalis* L.) does not grow in Palestine. Thus, in the Bible hyssop may refer to several species, most likely majoram of the Syrian and Egyptian varieties (*Origanum maru* L.). These shrubs are capable of growing in desert regions or along mountain slopes and in the cracks and clefts of the soil or even in walls (1 Kgs. 4:33).

The hyssop, or marjoram, plant grows to a height of 1 m. (3.3 ft.) and features stalks of many branches with small, fragrant, green leaves. The numerous hairy branches favor its use as a brush or aspergillum for ritual purposes (Exod. 12:22; Num. 19:6, 18; Ps. 51:7; cf. Heb. 9:19) or for the cleansing of lepers (Lev. 14:4, 6, 49-52). Moreover, like other labiates such as mint and thyme, marjoram contains a volatile oil making it attractive as a purifying agent. The use of hyssop as an aspergillum may explain the "sponge" full of vinegar that the Roman guards raised to Jesus' lips as he hung upon the cross (John 19:29; cf. also the use of hyssop in flavoring wine), or perhaps John alludes to the sacrificial nature of Jesus' death; although the stalks of the plant become woody as new shoots form each growing season, this would not have been sufficient to support a sponge (cf. par. Matt. 27:48; Mark 15:36; Gk. *kálamos* "reed").

I

I AM WHO I AM (Heb. *'ehyeh 'ªšer 'ehyeh*).† An expression used to explain Yahweh, the covenant name of the God of Israel, given to Moses when he encountered the burning bush (Exod. 3:14). It is also rendered "I will be what I will be" or, perhaps more correctly, "I create what(ever) I create." *See* YAHWEH.

IBEX [ī′bəks] (Heb. *dîšōn*). An animal listed among those which the Israelites were permitted to eat (Deut. 14:5; KJV "pygarg"). The Palestinian ibex may have been a wild goat of the genus *Capra ibex nubiana*, characterized by backward-curving horns.

IBHAR [īb′här] (Heb. *yiḇḥār* "He [God] chooses"). A son of David, born in Jerusalem (2 Sam. 5:15 par. 1 Chr. 14:5).

IBLEAM [īb′lĭ əm] (Heb. *yiḇlᵉʿām* "confusion of the people"). A city in the tribal territory of Issachar, between Jezreel and Megiddo (2 Kgs. 9:27), assigned to Manasseh (Josh. 17:11) though not immediately conquered (Judg. 1:27). R. G. Boling and G. E. Wright (*Joshua*. AB 6 [1982]: 413) read "near" at Josh. 17:11, placing the city in proximity to Manasseh's border with Issachar.

According to LXX Josh. 21:25 Ibleam (Gk. *Ieblaam*) was a levitical city (cf. 1 Chr. 6:70 [MT 55], Bileam). The name *Y-b-ra-ʿa-mu* occurs in a temple inscription at Karnak listing the conquests of Thutmose III in Palestine. King Ahaziah of Judah was mortally wounded by Jehu's forces at the ascent of Gur nearby (2 Kgs. 9:27), and, following the LXX, Shallum assassinated King Zechariah of Judah there (15:10).

The site has been identified as Tell Belʿameh, 16 km. (10 mi.) southeast of Megiddo and 2 km. (1.3 mi.) south of Jenin.

IBNEIAH [īb nē′yə] (Heb. *yiḇnᵉyâ* "Yahweh builds up"). A Benjaminite who dwelled in postexilic Jerusalem; the son of Jeroham (1 Chr. 9:8).

IBNIJAH [īb nī′jə] (Heb. *yiḇnîyâ* "may Yahweh build up"). A Benjaminite who dwelled in Jerusalem; the father of Reuel (1 Chr. 9:8).

IBRI [īb′rī] (Heb. *ʿiḇrî* "Hebrew"). A Levite, son of Jaaziah and descendant (or follower) of Merari (1 Chr. 24:27).

IBSAM [īb′săm] (Heb. *yiḇśām* "fragrance of balsam"). A descendant of Tolah, from the tribe of Issachar (1 Chr. 7:2; KJV "Jibsam").

IBZAN [īb′zăn] (Heb. *'iḇṣān* "swift"). A minor judge who governed Israel for seven years after the time of Jephthah (Judg. 12:8-9). His home was Bethlehem in Zebulun, northeast of Nazareth on its border with Asher (cf. Josh. 19:15). No more is known of Ibzan other than that he had thirty sons and thirty daughters.

ICHABOD [īk′ə bŏd] (Heb. *'î-ḵāḇôḏ* "where is glory?"). The son of Phinehas and grandson of Eli. His mother, who died at his birth, named him in response to the Philistine capture of the ark of the covenant (1 Sam. 4:22; the name may refer to the "glory" or presence of Yahweh).

ICONIUM [ī kō′nĭ əm] (Gk. *Ikonion, Eikonion*). The capital city of Lycaonia in south-central Asia Minor, north of Lystra near the Phrygian border; modern Konya.

According to ancient tradition, Iconium existed even before the Flood, after which it was rebuilt. Prometheus, so it was believed, had made new people out of mud, giving life to those drowned; for this reason the Iconians believed that the name of their city was derived from Gk. *eikṓn* "image." A prosperous agricultural and commercial center on the major trade route linking Ephesus and Syria, Iconium was apparently originally a Phrygian city. Following Seleucid and Pontic rule, the city was incorporated into the Roman Empire as part of the province of Galatia. *Ca.* A.D. 41 the emperor Claudius gave this city, which he renamed Claudiconium, to military veterans as a place to retire.

Paul and Barnabas visited Iconium during the first and second missionary journeys (Acts 13:51–14:6, 21-23). The population at that time consisted of Hellenized Galatians, Roman officials and veterans, and Jews. Iconium was then a center of the wool and textile industry, so Paul could easily have found work and shelter. Despite their early success, Paul and Barnabas fled for Lystra and Derbe when Jews and Gentiles alike threatened to stone them to death (cf. 2 Tim. 3:11). They later returned to strengthen the young church and to appoint officials. Timothy was a native of Iconium (Acts 16:2), as was the convert Thecla (*see* PAUL AND THECLA, ACTS OF).

ICHTHUS [ĭk'thəs] (Gk. *ichthýs* "fish"). The sign of the fish, used by the early Church as a secret Christian insignia as well as a symbol representing Christ and the Eucharist in art and literature. This symbol may derive from an appellation for the disciples, "fishers of men" (Luke 5:10), or from Jesus' miraculous feeding of the five thousand (Matt. 14:13-21 par.). The word is an acronym whose letters represent *I(ēsous) Ch(ristos) Th(eou) Y(ios) S(ōtēr)*, meaning Jesus Christ, Son of God, Savior.

IDALAH [ĭd'ə lə] (Heb. *yid'°lâ*). A city in the tribal territory of Zebulun (Josh. 19:15). In the Talmud it is called Ḥuryēh (*j. Meg.* i.1). The site is modern Khirbet el-Ḥawârah, 1 km. (.6 mi.) south of Bethlehem in Galilee.

IDBASH [ĭd'băsh] (Heb. *yidbāš* "as sweet as honey"). A son of Etam, from the tribe of Judah (1 Chr. 4:3).

IDDO [ĭd'ō].†

1. (Heb. *'iddô*). The father of Ahinadab, an administrative officer in Mahanaim, on the Jabbok river, during Solomon's reign (1 Kgs. 4:14).

2. (*yiddô*). A Levite of the clan of Gershom (1 Chr. 6:20 [MT 6]). At v. 41 (MT 16) he is called Adaiah.

3. The son of Zechariah, and the one whom King David appointed as an officer over the half-tribe of Manasseh in Gilead (1 Chr. 27:21).

4. (*'iddô*). A seer and prophet who prophesied against kings Rehoboam and Abijah of Judah and Jeroboam of Israel in the tenth century B.C. (2 Chr. 9:29 [K *ye'dî*, Q *ye'dô*]; 12:15; 13:22). His collected prophecies were a source used in the Chronicler's history.

5. (*'iddô, 'iddô'*). The grandfather of the prophet Zechariah (Zech. 1:1, 7; Ezra 5:1; 6:14).

6. (*'iddô*). Head of a family of Levites in Casiphia, a village of Jewish exiles on the Chebar river in Babylon. He responded to Ezra's request for temple servants to accompany him to Jerusalem (Ezra 8:16-17; 1 Esdr. 8:45-46; KJV "Saddeus, Daddeus").

7. (*'iddô'*) The head of a priestly house that returned to Jerusalem following the Exile (Neh. 12:4, 16); possibly the same as 5.

8. (Gk. *Ēdais*). One of the Jews whom Ezra forced to give up their foreign wives and children (1 Esdr. 9:35; KJV "Edes"). He is called Jaddai at Ezra 10:43 (Heb. Q *yidday*).

IDOLATRY (Gk. *eidōlolatría*). In the Old Testament, the worship of gods other than Yahweh, especially through images representing them. The New Testament extends the concept to include any ultimate confidence in something other than God, e.g., covetousness, surrender to appetites (Eph. 5:5; Phil. 3:19; Col. 3:5; cf. 1 Sam. 15:23; Matt. 6:24).

In the ancient Near East the Sumerians may have been the first to develop an extensive pantheon and mythology. Their gods included An, the god of heaven, and his consort Ninḫursag, who was believed to be the creator of humans; the earth-god Ki; Enlil, god of air; Enki, lord of the waters or the abyss; and Nanna, the moon-goddess whose daughter was Inanna, wife of Dumuzi. The Babylonians adapted Sumerian deities, Inanna and Dumuzi becoming Ishtar, goddess of love and fertility, and Tammuz, and Enki becoming Ea. Ea's son Marduk gradually emerged as chief in the Babylonian pantheon. The Assyrians in turn accepted the Babylonian deities. In the Assyrian system Ishtar was equal in power to Ashur, the chief local deity. Egyptian religion grew out of a variety of local systems which were rather fluid over time and elements of which eventually merged. Most of these mythologies featured the emergence of the gods from chaos (sometimes itself regarded as a deity). Eventually the sun-god Re was regarded as the chief god, creator of other gods, the world, and mankind. The pharaoh was sometimes regarded as identical with or the son of Re. Egypt's chief deities were usually represented in human form; others appeared as human bodies with animal heads or were associated with totem animals. Thus Sebek was represented by the crocodile, Anubis by the jackal's head, others by vulture, cat, or cow. An important "family" group was that of Osiris, the dying and rising god of agriculture, and his consort Isis, their son the falcon-headed Horus, and his son Thoth, the bringer of culture. The Canaanites' chief gods were El, the creator, and his son Ba'al, a storm and/or vegetation god (also called Haddu or Hadad) who, having been challenged and killed by Mot, god of death, was resurrected. Both El and Ba'al were represented by the bull (virility) or as riding on a bull. Asherah, variously identified as El's or Ba'al's consort (Anath, Astarte, Ashtaroth) was a fertility goddess portrayed as particularly savage and bloodthirsty. The cult of Ba'al and Asherah played on carnality, fornication, and drunkenness, and thus was regarded as particularly dangerous for the Israelites. Similarities between the deities of these cultures allowed identification of deities with each other, so that Ishtar, for example, could be recognized and worshipped under other names such as Inanna, Isis, Astarte, Ashtaroth, Anath, and Shaushka (Hittite).

The idols mentioned in the Bible (Heb. *semel, selem, heḇel, ṣîr*; Gk. *eídōlon*) were man-made images representing the gods. They were carved from wood, clay, or stone ("graven images"; Heb. *pesel* [Lev. 26:1; Deut. 4:23; cf. 2 Chr. 33:22; Isa. 40:19; 44:17]), or were cast metal ("molten images"; Heb. *massēḵâ* [Hos. 13:2; Nah. 1:14], *neseḵ* [Isa. 41:29; 48:5; cf. Jer. 10:14; 51:17], *nāsîḵ* [Dan. 11:8]). Others were wood carvings overlaid with precious metal (Isa. 30:22; Jer. 10:3-5). The smallest idols were figures worn as amulets (Gen. 35:4; Isa. 3:18-20). Somewhat larger figures called teraphim ("household gods"; Gen. 31:19, 34-35; 2 Kgs. 23:24) probably had both religious and legal significance in families; passed down from father to heir, they betokened the rightful succession. Major centers of cultic activity housed large statues and monuments. Canaanite cultic furnishings also included "pillars" (Heb. *maṣṣēḇâ*; Exod. 23:24; 1 Kgs.

14:23), "incense altars" (Heb. *hammānîm;* Lev. 26:30; Isa. 17:8), and "Asherim" (KJV "groves"), which were probably wooden columns, perhaps carved, devoted to the goddess Asherah (Heb. *'ašērîm;* Exod. 34:13; Deut. 12:3; 2 Kgs. 17:10). Certain sites were deemed inherently holy and thus most suitable for shrines and worship, especially mountains and "high places" (Deut. 12:2; Isa. 57:7; Jer. 3:6; Hos. 4:13) and stands of green trees (1 Kgs. 14:23; Hos. 4:13).

Idols evidently were distinguished from the gods themselves. At least at more sophisticated levels of pagan religion, the gods were conceived as essentially invisible and immortal beings, often associated with various natural forces. Yet the images were also in some sense identified with the deities and were regarded as localizations of or points of access to the god's purported power. Thus various rites grew up around the idols which accorded worship to the gods but which were also designed to entreat and even coerce the gods to exercise their power on behalf of the worshipper. Pagan sacrificial rites bore a superficial resemblance to the sacrificial system of Israel; they included burnt offerings (2 Kgs. 17:32; 2 Chr. 28:4; Hos. 12:11 [MT 12]), food and drink offerings (Isa. 57:6; Ezek. 16:19), and incense offerings (2 Kgs. 16:4; 17:11; 23:5; Ezek. 6:13). Such cultic similarities may have been influential in the Israelites' frequent lapses into pagan worship, even leading at times to human sacrifice (Deut. 12:31; 2 Kgs. 3:27; 17:17; 2 Chr. 28:3).

Throughout its history Israel was in constant contact with the idolatrous religions of its neighbors, and was constantly tempted to emulate them. The patriarchs had derived from Mesopotamian roots. Abraham's father Terah, and perhaps Abraham himself before his call, "served other gods" (Josh. 24:2). Laban's teraphim played a part in the life of Jacob's family, though perhaps more as a legal than a religious factor; in any case Jacob eventually did away with them (Gen. 35:2; cf. 31:19, 30-35). The Israelites in Egypt worshipped idols (Josh. 24:14; Ezek. 20:7-8; 23:2-8). During the wilderness wanderings prohibitions of idolatry were repeated (Exod. 34:14-17), but Israel continued to yield to the temptation, sacrificing to satyrs (Lev. 17:7), worshipping Baal of Peor at Shittim (Num. 25:1-5), and demanding the creation of the golden calf (Exod. 32:1-6). The latter probably was intended to represent Yahweh, or to be a "seat" for him, much in the manner of the bulls of Apis (Egypt) or of Ba'al (Canaan). The motif was revived by Jeroboam I, who placed golden bulls at Bethel and Dan in an attempt to establish new centers of worship for the northern kingdom of Israel (1 Kgs. 12:28-30). The prophetic warnings that mixed marriages would lead to religious syncretism in Canaan (Exod. 34:12-16) were borne out by several episodes during the Monarchy. Solomon succumbed to the religious practices of his foreign wives (1 Kgs. 11:4-8), Ahab established Baal worship as a national religion (16:30-33), Ahaz (2 Kgs. 16:3 par. 2 Chr. 28:3) and Manasseh (2 Kgs. 21:1-7; 2 Chr. 33:6) practiced human sacrifice (cf. 2 Kgs. 23:10; Ps. 106:37-38; Jer. 32:34-35). By Jeremiah's time idolatry was rampant (Jer. 2:28), and residents of Judah burned incense to the "queen of heaven" in the belief that it would secure their prosperity (44:15-19).

All this was of course contrary to the true character of both Israel and its God. The demand to reject idolatry and to worship Yahweh alone was enunciated clearly in the Mosaic law (Exod. 20:3-5). Israel belonged to the Lord, its legitimate "husband" (Isa. 54:5), and was not to "play the harlot after other gods" (e.g., Exod. 34:15-16; Lev. 17:7; 20:5; Judg. 2:17). Israel devised a vocabulary of idolatry rich in derogatory and contemptuous names for idols: *'elîlîm,* literally "gods of no respect," "things of nought," or "nonentities" (e.g., Lev. 19:4; Isa. 2:8; Hab. 2:18, RSV "dumb idols"); similarly *heḇel* "vanity," "empty thing" (2 Kgs. 17:15); *'êmîm* "terrors" or "frightful visions" (Jer. 50:38); *gillûlîm,* a word deriving either from a verb meaning "to roll," suggesting transportable idols, or "dung pellets" (e.g., Deut. 29:17 [MT 16]); *šiqqûṣîm* "detestable" or "abominable idols" (2 Chr. 15:8); *'āwen* "sorrow" (Isa. 66:3); *mipleṣet* "horror" or "object of trembling" (1 Kgs. 15:13 par. 2 Chr. 15:16); *'āṣāḇ,* something fashioned, but also a pun on "grieve," hence a thing of grief (1 Chr. 10:9; Ps. 106:36; Isa. 10:11; Hos. 10:6). This tone of mockery characterizes the prophets' denunciation of idolatry. They point out the contradiction of worshipping objects made by hand (Isa. 2:8; 44:12-20; Hab. 2:18). Above all, they contrast the power of Yahweh to the impotence of idols (Isa. 41:5-7; 42:17; 44:9; 45:20; Jer. 10:14-15; 51:17-18), Yahweh's powerful word of knowledge to the "empty wind" of idols (Isa. 41:26, 29; 44:7), his incomparable and unrepresentable being to these paltry images (40:18-20; cf. Deut. 4:15), the true marriage of Israel and Yahweh to the spiritual fornication of idolatry (Mic. 1:7). In short, there is no comparison to the true God; beside him "there is no god" (Isa. 44:6; cf. 40:25). The question of the object of idolatrous worship, whether a statue or a natural force or a demonic being, becomes insignificant; the very existence of idols meant that the object of worship, however conceived, was by nature unworthy of worship and therefore false.

If the Exile dealt a blow to Judah's tendency toward idolatry, the abominations of the idolatrous Antiochus IV Epiphanes, with his descration of the temple, and the resistance to him by the Hasmoneans, signalled the doom of idolatry as a real choice for Israel (cf. 1 Macc. 2). The scant references to idolatry in the Gospels suggest that it may have been virtually nonexistent at the time. As the Christian mission expanded, however, the near-universal idolatry of Greco-Roman culture became a matter of intense practical concern. Athens, for instance, was a city "full of idols" (*kateídōlos;* Acts 17:16), one of which was devoted to "the unknown god"; and in Ephesus the apostolic preaching occasioned a riot of the silversmiths who traded on the cult of Artemis there (Acts 19:23ff.). Paul's teachings on idolatry echo many Old Testament themes. Idols have "no real existence" (1 Cor. 8:4; cf. Acts 19:26). Idolatry is earthly (Col. 3:5; cf. Phil. 3:19) and immoral (1 Cor. 5:10-11); sexual and social disorder follow from it, and it brings judgment and death (Rom. 1:18-32). Because of this "pollution," Paul counsels Christians to keep away from idols (Acts 15:20; cf. 1 John 5:21). In the matter of eating meat that had been offered to idols, Paul asserts that, although sacrifices to idols are really made to demons, the meat itself is not thereby impure and its consumption is lawful; but since the context of its source might offend some Christians, and since such a practice would not build up the body of Christ, Christians would be wise to abstain (Acts 15:29; 1 Cor. 8; 10:14-30; cf. Rev. 2:14, 20; Exod. 34:15). For Paul, however, idolatry is only symptomatic of the deeper disease of human alienation from God, and so he speaks figuratively of idolatry as any allegiance to something other than God. In most cases that allegiance is ultimately to oneself; it is making an idol of oneself and one's desires (Rom. 1:18-32; Gal. 5:19-21).

IDUMEA [ĭd′o͞o mē′yə] (Gk. *Idoumaia, Idoumea* "[land] of the Edomites").† The Hellenistic Greek name for the territory south of Judea then inhabited by the Edomites, who had been displaced from their territory by the Nabateans; in the LXX and Josephus the term designates EDOM proper. Located west of the Dead Sea, Idumea stretched from Beer-sheba to Beth-zur, thus reaching to within 24 km. (15 mi.) of Jerusalem.

The origins of Idumea as a country began with the migration of Edomites after most of the Jews had been deported to Babylon, leaving Judah unoccupied. The Nabateans established a strong kingdom in Edomite territory, and some of the Edomites moved north and west, mingling with the Jews who remained. Although the Seleucids at times controlled parts of Idumea, the territory was independent at the outset of the Maccabean Revolt (cf. 1 Macc. 4:61). Judas Maccabeus attacked the Idumeans at Akrabattene and Hebron (5:3, 65). John Hyrcanus I annexed the territory to the Hasmonean state and forcibly converted the Idumeans to Judaism. Alexander Janneus placed the region under an Idumean governor, and in 63 B.C. Pompey granted Idumea local rule. In 37 B.C. Herod the Great reannexed the territory to Judea. (The Herodian dynasty, stemming from the procurator Antipater the Younger, was Idumean and thus nominally Jewish.) After Herod's death Idumea became part of Archelaus' ethnarchy and, following the First Jewish Revolt, was incorporated into the province of Syria.

Idumea is mentioned only once in the New Testament, where it is simply stated that part of the great crowd that came to Jesus during his ministry of healing originated in Idumea (Mark 3:8). The KJV erroneously identifies Edom as "Idumea" in Isa. 34:5-6; Ezek. 35:15; 36:5.

IEZER [ĭ ē′zər] (Heb. ′î′ezer).† Abbreviated form of the name Abiezer (**1**). A descendant of Manasseh, he was the eponymous ancestor of the Iezrites (Num. 26:30; KJV "Jeezer," "Jeezerites").

IGAL [ī′găl] (Heb. *yig′āl* "he [God] redeems").
1. A spy from the tribe of Issachar sent by Moses to scout the land of Canaan (Num. 13:7).
2. The son of Nathan of Zobah, one of David's mighty men (2 Sam. 23:36). 1 Chr. 11:38 lists instead Joel the brother of Nathan.
3. A son of Shemaiah, and a descendant of Zerubbabel (1 Chr. 3:22; KJV "Igeal").

IGDALIAH [ĭg′də lī′ə] (Heb. *yigdalyāhû* "great is Yahweh"). A Rechabite, the father of Hanan, whose

descendants or followers had a chamber in the temple (Jer. 35:4).

IGNATIUS [ĭg nā′shəs], **EPISTLES OF.**† A collection of seven early Christian letters written by Ignatius, bishop of Antioch in Syria.

Ignatius was arrested and taken to Rome to be killed by wild animals in the amphitheater. As he was being transported to Rome he wrote four letters from Smyrna (to the churches of Ephesus, Magnesia, Tralles, and Rome) and three from Troas (to the churches of Philadelphia and Smyrna, and to Polycarp).

The seven letters of Ignatius are a very well-known part of the literature of the Apostolic Fathers. They were written during the time of Trajan (A.D. 98-117). The so-called long recension contains six other letters purporting to be from Ignatius but from a much later period.

These epistles are similar in many ways to those of the New Testament, including general similarities in vocabulary, style, themes, idioms, and allusions that show familiarity with the writings of Paul and John and with Hebrews.

The most remarkable feature of these epistles is Ignatius' eagerness to die as a martyr. His attitude toward his impending doom is far different from that of Paul, who was at least ambivalent about his departure from this world. Paul put himself in the hands of God. Ignatius hoped that he would be lucky enough to reach Rome and have the privilege of proving his Christianity and his manhood by fighting the beasts. In writing to the people at Rome, he expresses his fear that out of their love for him they will attempt to save him from death and thus keep him from meeting God.

These epistles are important theologically because of their strong support of the authority of the office of bishop. None of the institutions of worship was considered valid to Ignatius without the presence of the bishop. All members of the congregation were to submit to the bishop as to Christ. The letters also show the historical presence of such heresies as Judaizing tendencies and Docetism, which held that Jesus only appeared to suffer and die on the cross; Ignatius condemns such heresies.

Bibliography. W. R. Schoedel, *Ignatius of Antioch.* Hermeneia (Philadelphia: 1985).

IIM [ī′ĭm] (Heb. ′*îyîm* "ruins").†
1. A city in the southern part of Judah near the Edomite border, between Baalah and Ezem (Josh. 15:29). A possible site is modern Deir el-Gami north of Beer-sheba and south of Anab.
2. (Num. 33:45, KJV). *See* IYIM.

IJE-ABARIM (KJV). *See* IYE-ABARIM.

IJON [ī′jŏn] (Heb. ′*iyôn* "ruin"). A store-city of Israel, conquered by Ben-hadad king of Syria (at the instigation of King Asa of Judah; 1 Kgs. 15:20 par. 1 Chr. 16:4) and later by the Assyrian Tiglath-pileser III (2 Kgs. 15:29). At 1 Kgs. 15:20 the cities are mentioned in sequence from north to south, while the Syrians came from Damascus. Thus Ijon must have been located in the plain north of Abel-beth-maacah, between the rivers Līṭānī and Ḥesbānī. Modern ed-Dibbîn, on the road from Sidon to Damascus, has been suggested as the site, but without archaeological support. The district and town Merj-ʿAyyûn preserve the name.

IKKESH [ĭkʹĭsh] (Heb. *'iqqēš* "crooked"). A man from Tekoa; the father of Ira, one of David's mighty men (2 Sam. 23:26; 1 Chr. 11:28; 27:9).

ILAI [ĭʹlī] (Heb. *'îlay*). An Ahohite and one of David's mighty men (1 Chr. 11:29). At 2 Sam. 23:28 he is called Zalmon.

ILLYRICUM [ĭ lĭrʹə kəm] (Gk. *Illyrikon*). A Roman province in the northwestern Balkan peninsula, stretching along the eastern coasts of the Adriatic Sea from the borders of Italy to Macedonia and inland as far as the Danube (corresponding approximately to modern Yugoslavia and Albania).

Greek penetration of the region was restricted to the coastal areas and adjacent islands. The first colony was established at Corcyra in the eighth century B.C., perhaps to exploit the silver deposits of northern Albania, but the Dalmatian coasts further north had little to attract traders or settlers. Gold deposits in the interior were not worked until after the Roman conquest. The most noteworthy of the coastal peoples were the Ardiaei, whose skill with small pointed-prow galleys made them effective raiders of merchant ships in the Adriatic. The first Roman actions in the region were precipitated by these Illyrican pirates (229-219). By 167 B.C., the area was under Roman control. The campaigns of Octavian (35-33 B.C.) and Tiberius (12-9 B.C.) extended the region of the Illyrican province to the Danube. After the native revolt of A.D. 6-9, this territory was divided into two provinces, Pannonia in the north (formerly Illyricum Inferius) and Dalmatia in the south (formerly Illyricum Superius). Legionary fortresses at Burnum and Tilurium defended the coastal settlements and commanded the major routes leading to the interior. The provincial capital of Dalmatia was Salone (modern Solin), where there was a Jewish community and, by the third century, a thriving Christian community as well.

Paul's claim to have preached the gospel from Jerusalem "as far round as Illyricum" (Rom. 15:19) is ambiguous and difficult to interpret. Some scholars contend his activities in Macedonia and Achaia along the Egnatian road (Acts 20:1-2; cf. 2 Cor. 2:13) may have embraced parts of Illyricum (cf. Strabo *Geog.* vii.7.4). Others suggest the phrase implies only that the borders of Illyricum were reached, since the only allusion to mission activity in the region is Titus' later commission to Dalmatia at the close of Paul's career (2 Tim. 4:10). Under Tiberius, the major cities of the Adriatic coast were connected by a number of strategic roads to the military bases and settlements in the Save valley. In plaques commemorating these constructions, the phrase "the boundaries of Illyricum" (Lat. *ad fines provinciae Illyrici*) seems to refer to the Italian frontier, not the Pannonian-Dalmatian border. In the early Roman Empire, all the Danubian provinces were grouped into a single customs area (the *portoricum publicum Illyrici*), further suggesting that the term maintained its general sense.

Bibliography. J. J. Wilkes, *Dalmatia* (Cambridge, Mass.: 1969); A. Mócsy, *Pannonia and Upper Moesia* (Boston: 1974).

IMAGE. *See* IDOLATRY.

IMAGE OF GOD.† A designation of the distinguishing nature of humanity as originally created; in the New Testament Jesus Christ restores to fulness the image of God, both in himself and in the redeemed.

The central passage for the image of God is Gen. 1:26, where Adam is said to have been created "in" God's image (Heb. *ṣelem*; cf. v. 27; 5:3; 9:6) and "after" his likeness (Heb. *dᵉmûṯ*; cf. 5:1, 3). The precise meaning of the phrase has been the subject of much scholarly explanation and speculation. The uses of "image" in other biblical contexts carry the meaning of concrete representation, as in statues, pictures, and the like. The bearing of this on interpretation of the image of God should not be too lightly dismissed. The history of interpretation, however, has largely rejected a concrete or physical interpretation—since God is spirit and has no physical form to be represented—in favor of various spiritualizing interpretations such as personality, self-consciousness, immortality, rationality, freedom of will, moral agency, or creativity. A purely spiritual interpretation, however, tends to ignore the basic unitary character of Hebrew anthropology in which human nature is always viewed as a psychosomatic unity. Thus, for example, to regard the image of God as rationality alone reflects a Greek rather than Hebrew emphasis; in the latter, reason, the heart, volition, and moral sensibility are a single fact. This suggests that a proper understanding of the image of God should not be sought in particular faculties or capacities alone, but rather in the one nature that they all inform, i.e., in the wholeness of human nature which includes but is not limited to embodiment. Within this view, various human characteristics may be subsumed, some of which are suggested or implied in other biblical uses of "image" and "likeness." Of these, two seem to have in view the wholeness, including physicality, of human nature. Seth is "in" the likeness and "after" the image of his father Adam (5:3, reversing the construction of 1:26). Here Seth's humanity, which is to say his resemblance to Adam, can hardly omit the physical resemblance. Moreover, murder is prohibited because it violates the image of God as embodied in the victim (9:6). This too must include at least the aspect of physical violation, although it also suggests the more abstract concept of the sacredness of human life and thus of human dignity and standing before God. Two more abstract implications may be involved in the verses immediately following Gen. 1:26. "Image" is repeated in v. 27 and followed by the distinction of male and female. Some theologians see this as a suggestion that the image of God includes the notion of relation in unity. Whether this is taken to be a prototrinitarian implication or not, it is still thought to indicate that the image of God has a corporate dimension (cf. K. Barth, *Church Dogmatics* III.1-2). The next verse (v. 28) speaks of Adam and Eve's dominion over creation; hence lordship is sometimes seen as a further element in the image of God (cf. Ps. 8:5-8 [MT 6-9]). Beyond this evidence, the supposition that reason, will, freedom, and the like constitute the image of God must be derived from general systematic or philosophical reflection rather than directly from textual evidence.

A second interpretive question is whether image and likeness are to be distinguished. Biblical usage is not consistent, yet the history of theology exhibits various theories which, for instance, identify image with natural reason and likeness with supernatural grace or original righteousness. The point of these theories is to answer the question of the effect of the fall on the image of God in mankind. Neither the Old nor the New Testament countenance the idea of the complete loss of the image of God after the fall (Gen. 9:6; 1 Cor. 11:7; Jas. 3:9 all assume its persistence). Nevertheless, most interpreters agree that the image of God has been radically distorted by sin—faculties dimmed, relations broken, dominion become tyranny—yet not wholly lost.

In the New Testament the image (Gk. *eikṓn*) and likeness (Gk. *homoíōma, homoíōsis*) of God are redefined in terms of Jesus Christ, who is the "image of the invisible God" (Col. 1:15), the "express image" of God's nature (Heb. 1:3, KJV; Gk. *charaktḗr* "engraved (or stamped) image"), and the "likeness of God" (2 Cor. 4:4). In each instance the reference of the image must be to deity; an exact image would be identical with the original. Thus in Christ dwells "the fulness of God" (Col. 1:19; 2:9), and he preexisted in the "form of God" (Phil. 2:6). On the other hand, the image of the invisible God became visible in the incarnation. The prologue to John's gospel suggests that the Logos assumed the humanity which was created in his own image (John 1:4, 9, 13-14). If mankind is in the image of God, then Jesus the man is supremely and perfectly so (v. 14; 14:9). Some theologians infer from such considerations that the incarnate Word was in fact the prototype of all humanity. Hence even the body is a part of the image of God and must be taken into consideration, and even more so in the light of the New Testament doctrine of the eschatological restoration of the image in Christ and the ultimate refashioning of the body in glorification (Phil. 3:21). The image of God as revealed in Jesus Christ, moreover, relates to his offices which sum up the Old Testament themes discussed above: as prophet he reveals the image of God in knowledge (cf. Col. 3:10), as priest in holiness, and as king in righteousness and lordship.

The end of the recapitulation of the image of God in Christ is soteriological; it aims at the redemption and restoration of fallen humanity. Thus believers are to be refashioned into the likeness of Christ (2 Cor. 3:18) who is the last Adam. The redeemed then constitute a new humanity; they are new creatures (5:17), conformed to the image of Christ (Rom. 8:29). The new person is thus conformed to the true image of God; but this involves participation in the ground of Christ's own nature as image of God, participation in the divine nature (2 Pet. 1:4; cf. 1 Pet. 5:1). Paul occasionally stresses the rational and ethical element in this renewal, wherein believers are to have the mind of Christ (Phil. 2:5; cf. 2 Cor. 10:5), are renewed unto knowledge after the image (Col. 3:10), and are created in righteousness and holiness (Eph. 4:22-24; Col. 3:9-11). The corporate dimension to the image of God in humanity is also suggested in the Pauline doctrine of the Church as the body of Christ. Although renewal has begun already, in the present age the contradiction between the renewed image and the old, distorted "Adamic" image persists. Even in Christ the contradiction was apparent, though not actual, in that he came in the "likeness of sinful flesh" (Rom. 8:3; cf. "the form of the servant," Phil. 2:7; cf. Heb. 2:17). The New Testament, however, asserts the eschatological perfection of all promises regarding the renewed image. At last Christians will bear the image of the "man of heaven" (1 Cor. 15:49). The context of this promise, again, is the promise of resurrection wherein even the body will participate in the renewed image. "Our lowly body" will be made "like his glorious body" (Phil. 3:21). This likeness is based on the ultimate vision of Christ "as he is" (1 John 3:2).

Bibliography. G. Berkouwer, *Man: The Image of God*. Studies in Dogmatics (Grand Rapids: 1962); F. Horst, "Face to Face: The Biblical Doctrine of the Image of God," *Int* 4 (1950):259-270; G. Kittel, G. von Rad, H. Kleinknecht, "εἰκών," *TDNT* 2 (1964): 381-397.

IMAGERY.† The Bible has a wealth of pictorial language and graphic literary forms, largely because it deals with supernatural matters that cannot be expressed adequately in direct terms.

The concrete figures employed in much of this imagery were most suitable for the mindset and worldview of the ancient audience for and among whom these writings were produced. Not only in poetry—which forms a substantial part of the Old Testament—but also in prose, figurative usage abounds in the form of anthropomorphisms (specifically God's activity in human history; e.g., Gen. 3:8ff.; Deut. 5:4) and in concrete images taken from agriculture (e.g., Jer. 8:13; Matt. 13:24-30), commerce (e.g., Luke 19:11-27; 2 Pet. 2:1), and domestic life (e.g., Jer. 18:1-12; Matt. 13:33).

Specific genres employed include the allegory, an extended metaphor, generally in the form of a story in which each detail imparts spiritual meaning (e.g., Eccl. 12:3-7; John 10:1-5); fable, a didactic story employing animals or plants which act as humans (e.g., Judg. 9:8-15); proverb, a wisdom saying derived from common human experience or observation (e.g., Ezek. 16:44); and parable, a brief narrative similar to the allegory but devised to impart a single idea (e.g., Matt. 21:33-44; Luke 15:11-32). See further the individual articles.

Ideally, the various symbols employed are to point beyond themselves to a truth which is unseen, and to illuminate and explain that truth in such a way as to make it accessible and useful for the formation of the hearer's or reader's faith. In some instances the image employed may actually pass over into the reality of what it itself represents.

IMITATION (Gk. *miméomai*). A self-sacrificial following after Christ, to be adopted in emulation of the apostles (e.g., 1 Thess. 1:6; 2 Thess. 3:7, 9; Heb. 13:7).

While he confesses that he himself is not perfect, Paul challenges Christians in the young churches to follow his example (1 Cor. 11:1; cf. Phil. 3:12). One should imitate the model of Christ (cf. Eph. 4:32), the ideal set forth by God (5:13), and emulate good rather than evil (John 11).

The concept is more fully expressed by Gk. *akoloutheō,* with the sense "follow (as a disciple)" or "obey," as used primarily in the Gospels. The term implies more than merely copying Jesus' lifestyle (Matt. 16:24; John 8:12), stressing particularly a readiness to face one's own possible destruction (Matt. 16:24; Mark 8:34; Luke 9:23). It occurs in those passages where Christ calls his disciples (Mark 1:18) and where the disciples respond (Matt. 4:20; Mark 2:14; Luke 5:11). Such a "coming after" suggests a relationship between master and pupil that also removes the parties from other social ties (Matt. 8:22; Luke 9:61). Even the crowds that followed Jesus demonstrated a form of imitation that showed recognition and relatedness. Such imitation is focused on Christ's messiahship (Mark 10:21; John 8:12). At Rev. 14:4 those who have remained morally pure are the redeemed who follow the Lamb "wherever he goes."

IMLAH [ĭm'lə] (Heb. *yimlâ* "fulness"). The father of the prophet Micaiah (1 Kgs. 22:8-9 par. 2 Chr. 18:7-8; KJV "Imla").

IMMANUEL [ĭ măn'yŏŏ əl] (Heb. *'immānû 'ēl*; Gk. *Emmanouēl* "with us [is] God").† The symbolic name of a child whose birth, foretold by the prophet Isaiah, would be a sign to King Ahaz that the Lord would deliver Judah from its enemies (Isa. 7:14; 8:8; cf. v. 10). The New Testament identifies the name with Jesus (Matt. 1:23, "Emmanuel").

The prophecy of Immanuel came *ca.* 735 B.C. during a crisis in Ahaz' reign. Judah had been threatened by kings Rezin of Syria and Pekah of Israel, who wished to make Ahaz an ally against the Assyrians. But Ahaz preferred to side with Assyria, and subsequently did so (cf. 2 Kgs. 16:5-9; 2 Chr. 28:16-21). Isaiah assured Ahaz that he need neither fear the exhausted strength of Rezin and Pekah, nor align himself with Assyria. He offered a sign from God of Ahaz' own choosing to authenticate this. Ahaz, perhaps feigning piety to mask his unbelief, refused to ask God for the sign. Therefore Isaiah announced that God would give a sign in spite of Ahaz: the birth of a child, during whose early years (Isa. 7:16) the northern allies would be destroyed. Tiglath-pileser III of Assyria did indeed deliver Judah from the threat of the allies, destroying Damascus in 732 (2 Kgs. 16:9) and Samaria in 722, but at the cost of making Judah his vassal.

The identity of the child Immanuel and his mother has been the subject of continuing controversy among biblical scholars, owing in part to exegetical difficulties in the Isaiah passage and in part to the lack of corroborating historical evidence. The exegetical difficulties revolve around several ambiguities in the Hebrew text. (1) Most scholars now agree that Heb. *'almâ* (KJV, NIV "virgin," following LXX; RSV, NJV "young woman," following MT; JB "maiden") means a young woman of marriageable age. Heb. *bᵉṯûlâ,*

often cited as the ordinary word for virgin, has been shown to be ambiguous, sometimes also designating a married woman (Joel 1:8), and therefore unsuitable here if "virgin" is the intended meaning. The presumption of virginity is therefore valid, but not strictly necessary. Further, the article used here with *'almâ* may be definite ("the young woman"), indefinite ("a young woman") or generic ("young women"). If the sign was to have any meaning to Ahaz, it must have had a specific reference. (2) The verb *hārâ* "shall conceive" may also be rendered "is pregnant" (cf. RSV mg., JB, NJV). Conservative scholars generally prefer the future tense as more appropriate to the context. (3) Textual variants exist that support translating *wqr't* as either "[she] shall call," "you [singular] shall call," or "he shall be called" (passive). The majority of scholars prefer the first construction, following the MT. (4) The "sign" may be seen as a promise, or a threat, or both. Here the interpretation depends on the relationship between Isa. 7:14 and the broader context of the so-called "book of Immanuel" (7:1–12:6), and the weight attached to the New Testament use of v. 14. Isaiah's original intent, to assure Ahaz that he had nothing to fear from the allies, indicates that the sign was first to be a promise of deliverance. Subsequent verses, however, include elements of both promise and threat (especially 7:15–8:15), which is characteristic of many prophetic pronouncements: God's actions and the instruments of his will constitute both a threat to the unrighteous and a promise to the righteous. The New Testament identification of Immanuel with Jesus, linked with such other messianic sections of the book of Immanuel as 11:1ff., suggests that the ultimate nature of the sign is promise.

Such considerations do not solve the problem of the identity of Immanuel and his mother. The solutions offered to this riddle fall into four basic options.

(1) A collective immediate reference. This solution, characteristic of some nineteenth- and twentieth-century critical scholars, interprets the article with *'almâ* as generic and thus suggests that "Immanuel" is to be a general indication that deliverance could be expected during the early years of the new generation. This approach ignores the New Testament evidence, divorces the prophecy from the messianic content of other related passages, and fails to see the need for a specific fulfillment.

(2) A single immediate reference. Two figures have been proposed most often as immediate fulfillments of the prophecy: a son of Isaiah or a son of Ahaz. On the former hypothesis Immanuel is identified with Isaiah's second son Maher-shalal-hash-baz, and the name Immanuel is linked to the aspects of promise in the sign whereas the name Maher-shalal-hash-baz ("the plunder hastens, the prey speeds") represents the aspects of threat. In this case Immanuel's mother could not have been Isaiah's first wife, the mother of Shear-jashub, but may have been a posited second wife (called "the prophetess" in 8:3) to whom Isaiah was about to be married at the time of the prophecy and who thus qualifies as a virgin. Further support for this position is found in the New Testament's typological use of Isaiah's children (Heb. 2:13; cf. Isa. 8:18). Other scholars propose that the young woman was a wife of Ahaz; thus the son would most likely have been Hez-

ekiah. This interpretation is supported by the broader context of the messianic character of the royal line of David. Also, like the rival theory, it makes sense of the dual nature of the sign as promise and threat, where Hezekiah represents the ultimate survival of the royal line. This theory, however, runs into serious difficulties with regard to chronology. On the evidence of 2 Kgs. 16:2; 18:2, Hezekiah would already have been nine years old when the prophecy was uttered, and a judgment on the validity of this solution then becomes a question of the reliability of the 2 Kings chronology.

(3) A single future reference. This possibility is based on the New Testament identification of the young woman with the Virgin Mary and of Immanuel with Jesus (Matt. 1:22-23). Some scholars maintain that Heb. 'almâ necessitates a supernatural birth, since the subject of the sign could hardly have been the child of an immoral unmarried woman. This solution takes seriously the authority of the New Testament interpretation of Old Testament prophecies, but ignores the consideration that Isaiah's words to Ahaz must have had some recognizable contemporary meaning for the king.

(4) A double (typological) reference. A serious regard both for the contemporary situation of Ahaz and for the Matthean interpretation of Isa. 7:14 seems to demand a double fulfillment, wherein Immanuel and his mother are viewed typologically; i.e., the young woman is proximally Ahaz' or Isaiah's wife and the Virgin Mary prospectively, and Immanuel is proximally Hezekiah or Maher-shalal-hash-baz and prospectively Jesus.

The lack of other historical evidence for the contemporary identity of Immanuel does not prejudice the need for such an identification; lacking such evidence, any solution to Immanuel's immediate identity must be tentative. This solution, however, does full justice to the messianic and Davidic context of the Immanuel prophecy. The birth of Jesus is thus seen as the ultimate fulfillment of the meaning of Immanuel—"God with us," the culmination of this theme which is a constant in the covenantal history of God's dealings with his people—and as the sign of humanity's deliverance from sin and death.

See also VIRGIN.

IMMER [ĭm'ər] (Heb. *'immēr* "lamb") **(PERSON).** The leader of a priestly division at the time of David (1 Chr. 24:14). Pashhur, Jeremiah's opponent, was a member of this priestly family (Jer. 20:1). Descendants of this line returned with Zerubbabel from captivity (1 Chr. 9:12; Ezra 2:37; cf. Neh. 7:40; 11:13) and participated in the rebuilding of the city wall (Neh. 3:29). Two men of this line had taken "foreign women" as wives (Ezra 10:20).

IMMER [ĭm'ər] (Heb. *'immēr*) **(PLACE).** A city in Babylonia from which the Jewish exiles returned (Ezra 2:59; Neh. 7:61). The site is unknown.

IMMORALITY (Gk. *porneía*).† Sexual activity contrary to biblical principles. The RSV also translates the Greek term as "fornication" (so KJV throughout), "unchastity," and "impurity."

Paul is particularly concerned with such behavior, listing it among the works of the flesh (Gal. 5:19). He views it as a deterrent to participation in the kingdom of God (1 Cor. 6:9-10; Gal. 5:19-21) and suggests marriage as a proper preventative to immoral sexuality (1 Cor. 7:2). Specific concerns include incest (5:1) and prostitution (6:12-20; cf. 2 Cor. 12:21).

In the book of Revelation, immorality is used figuratively with regard to pagan practices, including idolatry and sacred prostitution (Rev. 2:14, 20-21).

IMMORTALITY (Heb. *'al-māweṭ*; Gk. *athanasía, aphtharsía, áphthartos*).†

I. God

In the Old Testament, the God of Israel is the "Everlasting God" (Heb. *'ēl 'ôlām*, Gen. 21:33; cf. Ps. 90:2), enthroned as Lord forever (9:7 [MT 8]; cf. Jer. 10:10); his love and righteousness are everlasting (Ps. 103:17; 111:3; Isa. 54:8; Jer. 31:3). The idea of God's eternity is closely linked with the idea of God as the source of all life, the living God who is God of the living (Deut. 5:26; Josh. 3:10; Ps. 42:2 [MT 3]; 84:2 [MT 3]; Jer. 10:10; cf. Isa. 38:11). Similarly, the New Testament affirms that God alone has immortality (Gk. *athanasía* "deathlessness," 1 Tim. 6:16; cf. Rom. 1:23; 1 Tim. 1:17)—i.e., he alone is immortal by nature. 1 Timothy also suggests that God's immortality is of a piece with his creativity as the giver of all life (6:13) and his transcendent holiness and glory (he "dwells in unapproachable light," v. 16).

II. Mankind

A. Greek and Biblical Views. The question of human immortality inevitably involves a comparison of biblical and Greek views of the subject. The Greek view, expounded classically in Plato's *Phaedo*, is based on an anthropological dualism of body and soul. The body is gross, corruptible, subject to illusion. The soul, on the other hand, is immortal, eternal, essentially divine, and in a sense infallible, belonging properly to the realm of the ideal. In this life the soul is imprisoned in the body, which easily tyrannizes over the soul. Hence life ought to be a process of liberation, the weaning of the soul away from alien matter through engagement with the eternal ideas that lie behind material things. Death is the culmination of the process, the final liberation of the soul from the body, and thus is a friend and not an enemy; through death the soul is released from the prison of the body to its true home. This view is noble, full of apparent light, answers to an important dimension of human experience (the sense of alienation), and is attractive. It has influenced both Hellenistic Judaism and the history of Christian thought. Indeed, the salvation of the "immortal soul" has sometimes been a commonplace in preaching, but it is fundamentally unbiblical. Biblical anthropology is not dualistic but monistic: human being consists in the integrated wholeness of body and soul, and the Bible never contemplates the disembodied existence of the soul in bliss. Death is the enemy of this integrity and not the friend of the soul. Immortality, in Greek thought, is of the nature of the soul, which is essentially unaffected by death except insofar as it is liberated. This involves no conflict, but rather is a peaceful escape from creation. Biblical immortality, on the contrary, is an end which is achieved through a dramatic conflict with death and involves a new creation in which the integrity of body and soul is restored and perfected.

B. *Old Testament.* The only Hebrew word approaching "immortality," *'al-māwet* "not-death" (Prov. 12:28; so NIV, NASB), is controversial; the RSV, JB, and NEB follow the LXX reading derived from Heb. *'el-māwet* "to death." Thus any conclusion based on the word is tenuous. But the Old Testament exhibits a developing hope for eternal life—the positive correlate of immortality. Human life—"spirit," "the breath of life"—is a gift of God, the source of life, and remains God's possession and prerogative. Hence in the Old Testament there is no question of native human immortality. God is the Lord of the living, and has no concourse with the dead (Isa. 38:18; cf. Ps. 88:10-12 [MT 11-13]). The imagery regarding the inhabitants of Sheol, however, suggests some shadowy and incomplete continuing existence of the dead (e.g., Job 3:16-19), though the "shades" in Sheol (not souls) cannot be said to be living. Several passages refer to everlasting punishment (e.g., Ps. 9:6 [MT 7]; 78:66; Isa. 33:14; Jer. 23:40), although many of these may refer to endless infamy of reputation rather than to personal survival. More positive expressions of hope of continuing life appear in the Psalms. If God is the God of life, there is hope that life and communion with him will continue (cf. Ps. 17:15; 73:24); the Psalmist hopes for ransom from the power of Sheol (16:10; 49:15 [MT 16]). Even more explicitly, the "pleasures for evermore" at Zion, the eternal mount (133:3; cf. 125:1-2), suggest hope for eternal life.

Since Hebrew thought has no concept of the independent existence of the soul, it is natural that the hope for eternal life should eventually be recognized as a hope for resurrection. Seeds of this hope appear most clearly in Isa. 26:19, where revivification of the dead, the raising of bodies and the light of glory falling on the land of shades follows the assertion of God's ultimate victory over death (25:8). Less explicitly, resurrection as a reward for the suffering servant (53:9-12), Job's hope of bodily vindication (Job 19:25-26), the resurrection of Ezekiel's "dry bones" (Ezek. 37), and the stories of bodily assumptions (Enoch, Gen. 5:24; Elijah, 2 Kgs. 2:10-11) all contribute to the development of resurrection hope. The idea becomes fully explicit in Daniel, where eternal life is seen to entail a double bodily resurrection of "some to everlasting life, some to shame and everlasting contempt" (Dan. 12:2). Daniel's doctrine of eternal life is hardly, as some have maintained, influenced by the Greek view of the immortality of the soul; it is the reawakening of those "who sleep in the dust of the earth" and therefore, in keeping with Hebrew anthropology, embodied—a prospect the Greeks found repugnant and ludicrous (cf. the derision which greeted Paul's proclamation of the resurrection at Acts 17:31-32). To be sure, Greek influence did enter into Hellenistic Judaism (cf. Wis. 1:15; 2:23-24; 3:4-8). In Palestinian Judaism the doctrine of the resurrection, allied with the doctrine of the two ages or worlds—this age and the age to come (cf. Mishnah *Sanh.* x.1-3)—was widely accepted, although it remained controversial into New Testament times and was particularly opposed by the Sadducees. The decisive development of the doctrine came in the New Testament.

C. *New Testament.* The New Testament doctrine of immortality builds on the Old Testament views of God as "life-in-himself" and as life-giver, and of mankind as a unity which ultimately entails the hope of resurrection. The two themes come together in decisive focus and fulfillment in the person of Jesus Christ and his resurrection. Thus the New Testament view is always christocentric and is concerned with not merely the negative concept of deathlessness but rather with the positive and richer concept of eternal life through resurrection/re-creation.

Eternal life is made manifest in Christ (1 John 1:2), whom the Father has granted "to have life in himself" (John 5:26). As bearer of the essential divine life Jesus confronted and endured death, the "last enemy" (1 Cor. 15:26), in body and soul and yet emerged victorious in the resurrection. Therefore he has conquered death and as the "last Adam" has reversed the legacy of sin bequeathed by the first Adam (Rom. 6:23; 1 Cor. 15:22, 45-49), thereby becoming the "first fruits of those who have fallen asleep" (v. 20) and a "life-giving spirit" (v. 45). Thus eternal life for mankind is also from Christ (1 John 5:11, 20). God has invited people to share in the life that is in Christ, "who abolished death and brought life and immortality to light through the gospel" (2 Tim. 1:10). Eternal life is a gift, through Jesus Christ, to those whom God has ordained (John 17:2; Acts 13:48; cf. 1 Cor. 15:23). The evangelist John expresses this in images of food and drink—the living water and food (John 4:14; 6:27)—and by reference to the "words" of Jesus (6:68; 10:28) as well as Old Testament scripture which points to Christ (5:39).

To be in Christ is to be a new creation (2 Cor. 5:17). Immortality is thus not inherent in the old creation. But as Christ is the firstfruit of the resurrection, so Christians are born anew of imperishable seed (1 Pet. 1:23), the spiritual seed of the last Adam. The life of the new creation is the life that proceeds from Christ. It is a sharing of the divine nature (2 Pet. 1:4; cf. 1 Cor. 15), a participation with Christ as joint heirs of the imperishable inheritance (1 Pet. 1:4; cf. 1 Cor. 9:25; Heb. 9:15), an exchange of the image of the earthly Adam for the image of the "man of heaven" (1 Cor. 15:49), and it results in the assumption of the "eternal weight of glory" (2 Cor. 4:17). The new life, however, as it was achieved by Christ only through his death on the cross, can come only by the death of the old life. Believers must be buried with Christ in baptism in order to be raised with him "by the glory of the Father" to "newness of life" (Rom. 6:4; cf. Col. 2:12). The Holy Spirit, the agent of the new life, implants the spiritual life in the inner person first; the new creation grows from within and is "renewed every day" (2 Cor. 4:16; Eph. 3:16). Because of this, death, though it still rules over the body, cannot separate mankind from the love of God in Jesus Christ (Rom. 8:39).

Eternal life is not simply a quality of life now, nor merely a future goal that has no reference to this life. Rather, an eschatological tension of "now" and "not yet" characterizes all New Testament pronouncements on the subject, though the emphasis on one aspect or the other may vary. For Paul the redeemed are alive in Spirit now—the new life; in the life to come they will be alive in body—the resurrection (Rom. 8:9-11). The aspect of eternal life now begins in being "buried" with Christ (6:4), in the renunciation of the flesh (Matt. 19:29; John 12:25). But to be dead to the flesh means to be alive to the will of God. Therefore the New Testament echoes the Old Testament view that to keep the commandments is to live (Lev. 18:5; Deut. 5:33; cf. Matt. 19:16 par.; 25:46; John 12:50; 1 Tim. 6:12). Such work is done in Christ, or as Paul says, it is "sowing to the Spirit" in order to reap the fruit of eternal life (Gal. 6:8; cf. John 4:36). Thus John repeatedly connects belief in Christ with eternal life (3:15-16; 5:24; 17:3; 1 John 5:13; cf. 1 Tim. 1:16). Eternal life is the end of sanctification, which is already begun by the Holy Spirit (Rom. 6:22).

The classic statement of the dual aspects of eternal life held together inextricably in communion with Christ is recorded by John: "he who eats my flesh and drinks my blood has eternal life [now], and I will raise him up at the last day [to come]" (John 6:54). Eternal life comes now by the mutual indwelling of the believer and Christ (vv. 56-57). Paul makes the same eucharistic point in speaking of the bread and wine as participation or communion in the body and blood of Christ (1 Cor. 10:16). The Lord's table is thus the place where the "now"of eternal life comes to a spiritual and physical focus.

If such spiritual life is the center of Christian immortality, it is incomplete—even impossible (cf. Mark 12:27)—without resurrection. The healing ministry of Jesus may be viewed as a foretaste of the ultimate integrity of salvation, the renewal of both body and soul. The very physicality of the Lord's Supper suggests the same integrity. That is why Paul speaks of immortality only in connection with the resurrection of the body. The presence of the Spirit within the believer now, in fact, is the guarantee of the ultimate reclothing of the resurrection body (2 Cor. 5:5), which Paul likens to Christ's "glorious body" (Phil. 3:21; cf. 2 Cor. 3:18)–a "spiritual" body (1 Cor. 15:44) now animated by the power of the Holy Spirit rather than subject to the power of sin and death. What is sown perishable, dishonored, weak, physical, and mortal is to be raised imperishable, glorious, powerful, spiritual, and immortal (vv. 42-44, 53). Mortality is not so much left behind as "swallowed up by life" (2 Cor. 5:4).

Thus, true immortality is nothing like a stripping of the soul of the grossness of the body that hinders it. Rather, the spiritual/physical nature of mankind now, as fallen creatures, is comparatively naked and shameful. It is as if humans are not embodied enough yet; mankind must be further clothed before being fully sanctified (2 Cor. 5:4). The promise of immortality is the promise of the renewed integrity of soul and body in a participation in the glory of Christ.

Bibliography. J. Baillie, *And the Life Everlasting* (New York: 1933); P. Benoit and R. Murphy, eds., *Immortality and Resurrection* (New York: 1970); H. Küng, *Eternal Life?* (Garden City: 1984); G. W. E. Nickelsburg, Jr., *Resurrection, Immortality and Eternal Life in Intertestamental Judaism* (Cambridge,

Mass.: 1972); E. Rohde, *Psyche: The Cult of Souls and Belief in Immortality among the Greeks*, 8th ed. (Freeport, N.Y.: 1925); K. Stendahl, ed., *Immortality and Resurrection* (New York: 1965).

IMNA [ĭm'nə] (Heb. *yimnā'* "may [God] defend"). A son of Helem from the tribe of Asher (1 Chr. 7:35).

IMNAH [ĭm'nə] (Heb. *yimnâ* "good fortune").
1. A son of Asher, whose descendants are called Imnites (Gen. 46:17; KJV "Jimnah"; Num. 26:44; KJV "Jimna," "Jimnites"; 1 Chr. 7:30).
2. A Levite and father of Kore (2 Chr. 31:14).

IMRAH [ĭm'rə] (Heb. *yimrâ* "stubborn"[?]). A son of Zophah, from the tribe of Asher (1 Chr. 7:36).

IMRI [ĭm'rī] (Heb. *'imrî* "of eloquent speech").
1. An ancestor of Uthai, a Judahite who returned from exile (1 Chr. 9:4). He may be the same as AMA-RIAH (7) (of which the name Imri may be a shortened form) in the parallel account at Neh. 11:4.
2. The father of Zaccur (Neh. 3:2).

INCARNATION (Lat. *incarnatio* "taking on flesh"). A theological term referring to the embodiment of God in Jesus of Nazareth.

I. Biblical Teachings

Of the four Evangelists only Mark omits the birth of Jesus from his gospel. Instead, he begins his record of Jesus' ministry with John's preaching of the kingdom and Jesus' baptism (Mark 1:1-11). Matthew and Luke both give accounts of Jesus' birth before they narrate his public ministry. Both indicate that Jesus was born the son of Mary and therefore was a human being (Matt. 1:16; 2:1; Luke 2:6-7). However, they also assert that he was an unusual person, for he lacked a human father (Matt. 1:18; Luke 1:34) and his birth is linked with the presence of the spirit of God (Matt. 1:20-23; Luke 1:35). According to these two Evangelists, Jesus was both divine and human at his birth and continued thus through his life (cf. Matt. 11:25-27 par. Luke 10:21-22 for Jesus' unique relationship to God the Father).

It is John who best presents the concept of the incarnation. In contradistinction from Matthew and Luke who mention Jesus' humanity before his divinity, John begins his gospel with Christ's preexistence in heaven (the Word with God; John 1:1) and shortly thereafter affirms that the Word became "flesh" (v. 14); "flesh" in this context refers to the corporeal person. Though he has not used the term "incarnation," he is explicit about the reality of Christ's humanity. Nevertheless, although John's approach is more metaphysical, it does not contradict Matthew and Mark.

Some scholars have hypothesized that notions of divine incarnations held by Hellenistic mystery religions or Gnosticism prompted John to respond with the concept of the Word (Gk. *Lógos*) assuming human flesh. It may be safer to conclude that as John began to fathom the meaning and significance of Jesus' death he came to understand the significance of Jesus' birth. Although John does not probe the mystery of the incarnation, he does support both Christ's humanity (cf.

19:34) and his divinity. Note that Christ's "becoming" human does not cancel his divinity (cf. 14:10 for the unity between the Father and the Son and 20:31 for the purpose of John's gospel). *See* WORD.

II. Theological Reflections

Analogies of the incarnation may be sought in other religions. The Hindus believe in the incarnation of Vishnu, of whom some Buddhists consider Buddha to be the human form. The Egyptians viewed the pharaoh as an incarnation of the god Re, and several other ancient peoples believed that their kings were divine. The apostle John, however, proclaims that Jesus is God's permanent and only incarnation (John 1:14).

John's views of the incarnation may have been rejected by his Jewish contemporaries (cf. John 6:41-42; 10:31). Even today some Christians debate the circumstances and interpretation of the divine being appearing in human form. But as Athanasius (*ca.* A.D. 330) sensed, a proper view of the incarnation is indispensable to a proper view of the atonement. *See* CHRIST.

Bibliography. D. M. Baillie, *God Was in Christ* (New York: 1948); M. D. Goulder, ed., *Incarnation and Myth* (Grand Rapids: 1979).

INCENSE (Heb. $q^e \underline{t}\bar{o}re\underline{t}$ "smoke, odor of (burning) sacrifice, perfume").† A compound of gums and spices which produces smoke and a strong perfume when burned. Incense burning was a common practice in ancient Near Eastern religions. Archaeologists have unearthed incense altars from numerous cultures throughout the Fertile Crescent, and the Old Testament often speaks of the use of incense in pagan religious rites.

The incense used in Israelite worship consisted of frankincense and other elements as specified in Exod. 30:34-38. It was initially prepared by Bezalel of the tribe of Judah (31:11), who, along with Oholiab of the tribe of Dan, received wisdom from God to design and build the tabernacle and all its equipment. Equal parts of fragrant spices, onycha (a musky substance derived from the shells of sea animals), galbanum (a bitter gum resin), and pure frankincense were formed into lumps, which were then preserved with salt. Prior to being burned some of the hardened incense would be finely ground (Lev. 16:12). This incense could be used only in cultic activities, and its production for private use was expressly forbidden (Exod. 30:37-38). It was unlawful to offer any other incense before Yahweh (Lev. 10).

Fragrant incense was one contribution God required of the Israelites for his sanctuary (Exod. 25:6). Exod. 30:1-6 details the construction and ornamentation of the tabernacle's portable incense altar (Heb. *mizbaḥ haqq^e ṭōreṭ*). The altar was made of acacia wood, with horns on the four corners, all overlaid with gold. Four gold rings, placed on opposite sides of the altar, permitted it to be hand-carried on poles. When the tabernacle was erected this altar was to be placed before the veil of the ark of testimony, in front of the mercy seat which rested upon the ark (v. 6; 40:5, 26-27). Upon completion of the tabernacle representatives from each of the twelve tribes presented offerings, including ten-shekel-weight (115 g. [4 oz.]) gold incense

bowls (Heb. *ḳap* "palm [of the hand]," indicating the size) filled with incense (Num. 7). Only the high priest could burn the daily incense offering before God (Exod. 30:7-8; cf. Num. 16). In blessing the tribe of Levi before his death Moses listed incense burning as one of their duties (Deut. 33:10).

The incense altar and the practice of burning incense played a part in the complex rituals for sin atonement in ancient Israel. Atonement for the sins of an Israelite or the high priest included smearing a portion of the blood from a sacrificed bull upon the horns of the incense altar (Lev. 4:7). On the national day of atonement the high priest burned two handfuls of fragrant incense in a censer before the mercy seat. The smoke thus produced protected the priest from a fatal glimpse of the presence of God (16:12-13).

With the advent of the monarchy incense burning became an element of the worship conducted in the Jerusalem temple. The furnishings of Solomon's temple included an incense altar of gold (2 Chr. 26:16) and golden firepans for transporting the coals used to kindle the incense (1 Kgs. 7:50). The latter were replaced during the temple repairs under King Joash (2 Chr. 24:14); these and the other temple furnishings were plundered when Jerusalem fell to the Babylonians in 587 B.C. (2 Kgs. 25:14 par. Jer. 52:18-19). It was also apparently customary to burn incense at the burial of kings (2 Chr. 16:14; Jer. 34:5).

Most references to incense burning during Solomon's reign and those of the subsequent kings of Israel and Judah are in connection with its use in pagan worship. Solomon's wealthy and powerful kingdom produced a cosmopolitan society in which foreign princesses whom the king married were permitted to continue worshipping their own gods (1 Kgs. 11:8). Long-dormant native paganisms also regained their popularity (Jer. 7:9; Ezek. 8:11), and Yahwism was seriously challenged (Jer. 11:13; 44). The prophetic condemnation of these practices was unconditional. Some monarchs attempted to remove the "high places" with their incense altars (2 Kgs. 23:5; 2 Chr. 14:5 [MT 4]; 34:4, 7). But Isaiah, Jeremiah, and Ezekiel warned that all the nations would face judgment for burning incense to other gods (Isa. 17:8; Jer. 1:16; 19:13; 48:35; Ezek. 6:4, 6). Isaiah prophesied that Israel would be delivered when no incense altars or other idolatrous practices remained (Isa. 27:9).

The offering of incense continued in New Testament times (e.g., Luke 1:10; Rev. 5:8). In figurative usage, prayer was likened to the fragrant smoke of the incense, wafting its way to God (Rev. 8:3-4; cf. Ps. 141:2).

INCEST (Heb. *teḇel, zimmâ*). Sexual relations between close blood relatives. This practice is forbidden at Lev. 18:6-18, and the penalty of death prescribed at 20:11-12, 14, 17 (KJV "confusion"). If a man had sexual relations with his aunt or a sister-in-law, both parties were to be made "childless," although the means is not specified (Lev. 20:19-21).

From 1 Cor. 5:1ff., it appears that a man had had sexual relations with his father's wife (perhaps the man's stepmother) and that this behavior was permitted by the congregation at Corinth; Paul, however, severely condemned it (v. 5). The fact that Jews at this time permitted a proselyte to marry his stepmother may explain this situation in Corinth. The punishment which Paul recommended was also directed toward the congregation, for in their spiritual arrogance they had become blind to this sin.

INDIA (Heb. *hōddû*; O.Pers. *hinduš*).† In biblical usage the country which formed the eastern boundary of Ahasuerus' (Xerxes I) territory (Esth. 1:1; 8:9), specifically the northwestern region of the subcontinent through which the Indus (*Hondu*) river flows (including modern Pakistan and the Indian provinces of Gandhara and Sind). The region "from India to Ethiopia" (also 1 Esdr. 3:2; Add.Esth. 13:1; 16:1) had been conquered and incorporated into the Persian Empire by Darius I Hystaspes (Herodotus *Hist.* iii.94-106).

Although the Israelites may have had trade contact, however limited and indirect, with India (cf. 1 Kgs. 10:11; Ezek. 27:15-36), the region was not truly opened to the West until after the conquests of Alexander the Great (mid-fourth century B.C.). Indeed, the Seleucids employed elephants and "Indian drivers" (mahouts) in warfare (1 Macc. 6:37). The reference to Antiochus III the Great's control of provinces in India (8:8), however, is generally disputed; Seleucus I Nicator had ceded much of the territory conquered by Alexander to the Indian ruler Chandragupta Maurya in 305. In the second century Demetrius II Nicator, the Greek king of Bactria, did invade and subjugate territory in northern and central India as far as Pataliputra. Subsequently the Indian Pushyamitra was able to confine Greek rule to the region of Punjab until the Greeks were driven out by the Scythians (Sakas), perhaps with Parthian assistance, *ca.* 80 B.C.

INGATHERING, FEAST OF (Heb. *ḥag hā'āsîp*). *See* BOOTHS, FEAST OF.

INHERITANCE (Heb. *naḥᵃlâ*).† The transference of property from one generation to another (to be distinguished from transference of familial or other social authority, which constitutes descent).

Throughout the ancient Near East, the standard inheritance pattern was from father to son (cf. Prov. 19:14). In Israel, each son was to receive a portion of the father's estate, and the firstborn son was accorded a double portion (Deut. 21:15-17). Ample evidence does exist for other patterns of inheritance. Job divided his property among his three daughters as well as his sons (Job 42:15). According to Exod. 21:4, the offspring of a slave (but not the slave himself) could be granted a portion of the estate. Specific provision is made for instances where a father died without having produced sons, as in the case of Zelophehad's daughters (Num. 27:1-11); the preferred ranking of heirs was sons, daughters, brothers of the deceased, father's brothers, nearest remaining kinsmen. The institution of levirate marriage (Deut. 25:5-10) was concerned with continuation of the family line (descent) rather than inheritance.

Following the Conquest inheritance was particularly associated with the promised land, which was understood as Israel's inheritance from Yahweh (cf. Exod. 6:8; 32:13; Deut. 12:10). Indeed, the Hebrew

noun *naḥᵃlâ* came to designate specifically land within Canaan, the various apportionments assigned to the tribal units (e.g., Josh. 13:23; 19:9). The verb *nāḥal* came to mean in its various stems "give (or assign) as an inheritance" (hiphil; e.g., 1 Chr. 28:8), "divide up as a share" (piel; e.g., Josh. 13:32; qal; Num. 34:17-18). The assignment of the tribal territories by lot (Josh. 19:51) implies the active role of Yahweh in distributing these "inheritances" (cf. the LXX term for *naḥᵃlâ*, Gk. *klēros* "that which is assigned by lot"). Through the Sinai covenant the Israelites came to be stewards of the land, of which Yahweh remained ultimately the owner. Accordingly they were forbidden from transferring their "inheritance" beyond the jural-familial group to which it was assigned; Naboth's refusal to grant King Ahab his family vineyard clearly illustrates the Israelites' tenacity to this principle (1 Kgs. 21; cf. Ezek. 46:16-18). Social legislation restricting marriage of daughters within their own tribe is intended to prevent alienation of property by means of the dowry (Num. 36; cf. Boaz' redemption of the Moabite Ruth; Ruth 4). For similar reasons Gilead's sons resist the potential inheritance by Jephthah, son of a harlot and therefore of questionable paternity (and whose loyalty to the tribe thus could not be assured; Judg. 11:2). Abraham's adoption of the Damascene Eliezer (Gen. 15:3-4) suggests the practice attested at Nuzi and Mari through which "inviolable" property was transferred by means of adoption.

Jerusalem and the temple are called God's inheritance (Ps. 79:1; Jer. 12:7, "heritage"), as are his chosen people (v. 8; Exod. 34:9; Deut. 9:26, 29). Elsewhere the object of inheritance may include lies (Jer. 16:19), God's testimonies (Ps. 119:111), and a variety of intangibles: e.g., honor (Prov. 3:35; KJV "glory"), wind (11:29), folly (14:18, KJV).

In addition to the legal sense of the transmission of property (e.g., Luke 12:13), inheritance in the New Testament has a profound theological meaning. The "inheritance of the saints" (Eph. 1:18; Col. 1:12) is eternal life (Matt. 19:29; Luke 10:25; 18:18) and partnership in the kingdom of God (cf. Matt. 5:5), transmitted to all (Eph. 3:6) through Jesus Christ as God's heir (21:43; Heb. 1:2). It is often depicted as the reward for faithful obedience (Rom. 4:13ff.; Col. 3:24; Heb. 6:12) and as requiring moral behavior (Gal. 5:21; Eph. 5:5).

INK (Heb. *dᵉyô*; Gk. *mélan*).† In antiquity, black ink was produced by mixing the soot of burned resin, pitch, fir wood, or oil (lampblack) with gum and water, oil, or other liquids. Generally the ink was dried into solid cakes which had to be moistened with liquid before using. Red ink, in which red ocher or iron oxide replaced the soot, was used in Egypt and later, on the evidence of the Dead Sea scrolls, in Palestine. The Old Testament mentions ink explicitly only at Jer. 36:18, but elsewhere implies that ink could be blotted out (Exod. 32:33; Ps. 69:28 [MT 29]) or washed off (Num. 5:23). The rabbinic writings emphasize the difference between ink, which could be blotted out, and other writing substances (caustic or vitriol, red dye, gum preparations, copperas [sulfate of iron]) which left an indelible impression (e.g., Mishnah *Soṭah* 2:4). In the New Testament Gk. *mélan* (lit. "black") suggests the general use of black ink (2 John 12; 3 John 13); Paul uses the term to contrast a message written in perishable ink with messages of the Holy Spirit written indelibly on human hearts (2 Cor. 3:3).

Hebrew scribes kept ink and brushes in wood, horn, ivory, or metal cases that could be worn on or in a girdle (Ezek. 9:2; KJV "inkhorn"; RSV "writing case"). *See* WRITING.

INN. A place of lodging while traveling. The KJV generally renders Heb. *mālôn* as "inn," but the RSV translation, "lodging place" (Gen. 42:47; 43:21; Exod. 4:24; Jer. 9:2 [MT 1]; cf. Josh. 4:3, 8; Isa. 10:29) is more correct. The term implies nothing more than a level stretch of ground on which to sleep (cf. NJV "encampment," Gen. 21:27).

Gk. *katályma*, which both the KJV and RSV translate as "inn" at Luke 2:7, is derived from a verb which means "to loosen, unharness." Thus the word refers to a place where one stables animals for a night or for a somewhat longer period. The same Greek term is used at Mark 14:14; Luke 22:11 for the setting of the Last Supper, with the meaning "guest room" (KJV "guest chamber"). "Inn" also appears at Luke 10:34 as the translation of Gk. *pandocheíon*, a place where any traveler would be received and given a night's lodging; this place had an innkeeper (v. 35) who provided food and care to the wounded man left there by the Samaritan. The Near Eastern ideal of hospitality implicit in these terms underlies the use of Gk. *xenía* at Acts 28:23 (RSV "lodging"); Phlm. 22 (RSV "guest room"; cf. JB); the reference here is primarily to the hospitality shown a guest, and only secondarily to the place where the guest is lodged.

INNER MAN (Gk. *ho ésō ánthrōpos*). An expression used by Paul at Eph. 3:16 (cf. "inmost self" [Gk. *noús*; Rom. 7:22] and "inner nature" [2 Cor. 4:16]) to distinguish the spiritual self, which only God can see, from the "outer man," whom others see and who is subject to the law of sin. The difference between the inner and outer person is not one of soul and body or spirit and flesh, nor of grace and sin, believer and unbeliever.

INNOCENTS, MASSACRE OF THE.† The slaughter of all male infants two years of age or under in the vicinity of Bethlehem, ordered by Herod the Great (Matt. 2:16-18). Through this atrocity Herod sought to destroy the infant King of the Jews of whom he had learned from the wisemen (vv. 2-6). From the biblical account the incident appears to be, at least in part, the reason for the Flight to Egypt (vv. 13-15).

The early Church numbers the victims in the tens to hundreds of thousands, but population figures based on archaeological data suggest that the figure may actually have been twenty or less. Although the incident is not recorded in Josephus' detailed documentation of Herod's final years, it accords completely with other evidence of Herod's paranoia and cruelty (Josephus *Ant.* xvi.11.7; xvii.2.4; 6.5-6). No mention is made of these events in Luke's gospel, and purported later references (e.g., Rev. 12:1-4; As.Mos. 6:2-6) have been disproven.

Scholars have noted the similarity between the Mas-

sacre of the Innocents and Pharaoh's slaughter of the Hebrew male infants at the time of Moses' birth (Exod. 1:15ff.).

INSCRIPTION (Heb. *miktāb*; Gk. *epigraphé*).† A legend or epigraph engraved or written on a hard surface, generally intended for public notice. Such an inscription was affixed to the turban of the high priest, identifying him as "Holy to the Lord" (Exod. 39:30; KJV "writing"; cf. 28:36). In the New Testament the term also refers to the legends on coins (Matt. 22:20 par.; KJV "superscription").

Most notable is the plaque mounted on Jesus' cross specifying the charges against him (Mark 15:26 par. Luke 23:38; cf. Matt. 27:37). According to John 19:19-20 (Gk. *títlon* "title") it read, in Hebrew, Greek, and Latin, "Jesus of Nazareth, the King of the Jews" (frequently portrayed artistically as the Latin acronym "I[esus] N[azarenus] R[ex] I[udaeorum]").

INSECTS (Heb. *šereṣ hā'ôp* "winged insects").† The biblical accounts designate as insects only small, winged invertebrates which hop or swarm, either on land or in the air (cf. KJV "fowls that creep," "flying creeping things").

According to Deut. 14:19, all winged insects were proscribed as unclean for eating. Lev. 11:20-23, however, distinguishes between those insects which "go upon all fours" (probably a reference to their swarming movement, regardless of the number of legs) and those "which have legs above their feet" (i.e., large, bending rear legs for hopping). Only the latter, which include certain species of locust, were regarded as clean.

Because the Hebrew terminology varies in its application, precise identification of species remains problematic. See further the individual entries.

INSPIRATION.† A theological concept encompassing phenomena in which human action, skill, or utterance is immediately and extraordinarily supplied by the Spirit of God. Although various terms are employed in the Bible, the basic meaning is best served by Gk. *theópneustos* "God-breathed" (2 Tim. 3:16), meaning "breathed forth by God" rather than "breathed into by God" (Warfield).

I. Biblical Period

In the biblical period a wide variety of effects is attributed to the Holy Spirit, including artistic skill (Exod. 35:30-35), military prowess and feats of superhuman strength (e.g., Judg. 3:10; 11:29; 14:6, 19; 15:14), ecstatic or spiritual music (1 Chr. 25:1-5; 1 Cor. 14:26; Col. 3:16), speaking in tongues (Acts 2:4; 1 Cor. 12:10), prophetic ecstasy (e.g., 1 Sam. 10:10-13), and the inspired confession of martyrs (Matt. 10:19-20). Preeminently, the Spirit inspired the prophets of Israel, Judah, and the early Church. The inspiration of the Old Testament prophets forms the most important precedent for scriptural inspiration. The various collections of the prophets' inspired utterances naturally came to be venerated as Scripture. So the Prophets eventually took their place in the canon alongside the Law (as did the Writings later still). Though it is common in reconstructing "the biblical doctrine of inspiration" to cite various texts from the Old Testament prophets, this practice may be misleading as it risks confusing one type of inspiration (that of the written Scripture) with another (that of the inspired speakers who did not write down what they said). It is a safer procedure to examine New Testament statements about Scripture, i.e., about the Scripture of the early Christians, the Old Testament.

II. The New Testament Doctrine

Contemporary extrabiblical sources attest to a conception of inspiration wholly miraculous in nature and reducing the human writers to passive instruments. Scripture, therefore, was seen as being without error and as legitimately to be read on several levels as well as harmonized when it seemed to contradict itself. This is found in explicit statements such as Philo's characterization of a prophet as "an interpreter for God, uttering words formed within his being; and to God we can attribute no error" (De praem. et poen. 55). The exegetical practices of both Palestinian and Alexandrian Judaism imply that the very words of the text have been carefully chosen and intricately combined with more than human wisdom. And the stories of the translation of the Septuagint, wherein all seventy translators working in isolation arrive at exactly the same rendering (Philo Vita Mosis 7), and of Ezra's restoration of the lost Scriptures by divine dictation (2 Esdr. 14:22-26, 37-48), seem to presuppose that the original composition of Scripture was of the same kind.

It seems hard to deny that Jesus and the New Testament writers held much the same conception of Scripture. In their usage the categories "law" and "prophecy" had so interpenetrated that all of Scripture might be considered as either "the Law" (e.g., John 10:34, where Jesus quotes Ps. 82:6 but calls it "your law") or "the oracles [i.e., prophecies] of God" (Rom. 3:2). All portions of Scripture are considered binding ("scripture cannot be broken" [John 10:35], i.e., as a rule or law is "broken"), and the production of all Scripture is conceived on analogy with the spoken words of the prophets.

This view is as clearly implied in exegetical practice as stated in explicit teaching. In Jesus' rebuttal to the Sadducees (Mark 12:26-27) he attempts to prove that the doctrine of resurrection may be found in the Pentateuch, seeing it implied in the present tense "I am." That Jesus believes in the wholly divine nature of Scripture is evident not only in that he sees the tense of a single verb as irrefutable scriptural proof, but also in that he seeks out such subtle meanings beneath the surface sense of the text (cf. Paul's exegesis of Gen. 12:7 in Gal. 3:16). The same conviction is expressed in Luke 16:17, "But it is easier for heaven and earth to pass away, than for one dot of the law to become void."

Equally important are the many ascriptions of cited Old Testament texts simply to God, even when the words of a narrator or some human character are quoted (e.g., Acts 13:34; Heb. 1:5); God is regarded as the author of the Scriptures quoted, regardless of who may have held the pen (cf. Matt. 19:4; 1 Cor. 6:16).

The writer of 2 Pet. 1:20-21 pictured the human writers of Scripture as mere instruments, not as collaborators with God; the passage speaks in the first instance of the Old Testament prophets, but clearly from the context they are being practically identified with the writers and compilers of the books bearing their names. 2 Tim. 3:16 provides the classical statement for the New Testament doctrine of biblical inspiration: "All scripture is inspired by God and profitable for teaching, for reproof, for correction, and for training in righteousness." A striking parallel to this passage is found in the Brihadaranyaka Upanishad ii.4.10: "As clouds of smoke proceed by themselves out of a lighted fire kindled with damp fuel, thus, verily, O Maitreyi, has been breathed forth from this great Being what we have as Rig-Veda, Yajur-veda, Sama-veda, . . . [and] Upanishads. . . . From him alone all these were breathed forth." The ideas match perfectly, illustrating that to ascribe "God-breathedness" or inspiration to a text has traditionally meant to lift it out of the realm of human literature.

III. Early and Medieval Church

After the period of the apostles, the conception of inspiration may be said to have remained the same, if it did not tend toward an even more mechanical view. The view is occasionally found (also shared by Philo) that the writers of Scripture wrote in a mantic trance state. Augustine describes the biblical writer as "an amanuensis for God, who must provide him with a graceful style as well as with the content of his writings" (Conf. xii.36). Origen says "that the sacred books are not the works of men, but that they were composed and have come down to us as a result of the inspiration of the Holy Spirit" (De prin. iv.9). Certainly his famous schema of three levels of interpretation (reduced from the fivefold system of his mentor Clement of Alexandria) presupposes Origen's belief in the thoroughly superhuman character of Scripture.

Recent attempts have been made to show that many early Christian theologians did not hold to a strict conception of inspiration and inerrancy. Appeal is made to statements such as that of Augustine to the effect that the four evangelists wrote "as each remembered, in accordance with his native powers, either briefly or at greater length" (De cons. ev. ii.12.27), or the admission of Origen that the literal sense of the Scriptures sometimes makes no sense or is false. But it is misleading to attribute to them any systematic "doctrine" of a "divine-human confluence" since these occasional statements stand side by side and unreconciled with other statements by the same writers upholding the traditional view, as cited above. This line of reasoning also ignores the fact that such statements are more likely intended as apologetics for inerrancy than denials of it. Origen retreats to an allegorical interpretation or to the explanation that God was "accommodating" himself to human language or perception precisely in order to clear Scripture from the charge of error. Admittedly, such a procedure may seem counterproductive in its effects since it does imply that the literal sense of the text is in error. But this is embarrassing only to moderns who, unlike Origen, reject any but a literal interpretation of Scripture.

In the medieval period, the greatest single advance in the conception of inspiration was Thomas Aquinas' distinction between prophecy or revelation as a grace affecting the intellect (i.e., imparting new knowledge) and inspiration as a grace affecting the judgment (i.e., guiding and directing the biblical writer to select, correct, and set forth in a particular way prior knowledge, derived from divine or mundane sources). This interpretation enabled subsequent thinkers to deal more plausibly with the many elements in Scripture which need not have been immediately revealed by God (e.g., historical records and personal observations).

IV. Modern Views

At the time of the Reformation, Martin Luther held that particular scriptural writings are authoritative and canonical only if they "preach and bear Christ." In the light of this "canon within the canon," Luther could relegate James, Jude, Hebrews, and Revelation to deuterocanonical status. But perhaps surprisingly, Luther did not integrate such observations with his doctrine of inspiration and infallibility, which remained at least formally within traditional bounds.

John Calvin, adhering to tradition, maintained that God had "dictated" the Scriptures, and (as had Augustine) Calvin attributed the diverse literary styles of the writers to the Holy Spirit. Like Origen, he occasionally appealed to divine "accommodation" to explain unseemly passages, usually anthropomorphisms. Generally, he sought to harmonize factual and theological discrepancies.

During the seventeenth century Roman Catholic, specifically Jesuit, thinkers sought to understand the phenomena of the text (e.g., factual difficulties and diverse literary styles) and to reconceive the doctrine of inspiration. Leonhard Lessius (Leys) proposed three new models for understanding inspiration: 1) "content inspiration," whereby God provided the thoughts but left their expression in words to the biblical writers' discretion; 2) "concomitant inspiration," the notion that inspiration consisted simply in a divine superintendence resulting in freedom from error; 3) "consequent inspiration," the idea that a writing might be composed solely by human initiative and under human power but later be approved by the Spirit, henceforth to be received as inerrant and canonical. The second and third theories were soon to be abandoned or condemned, but the first became predominant in Jesuit circles from the 1840s to the 1890s.

The rise of biblical higher criticism has probably been the greatest influence on the formation of new doctrines of inspiration. Basically three positions have resulted. Upholders of verbal inspiration continue to believe that every verse of Scripture was God-breathed, but now a greater role is assigned to the human writers. Their individual backgrounds, personal traits, and literary styles were authentically theirs, but had been providentially prepared by God for use as his instrument in producing Scripture. The Scriptures had not been dictated, but the result was as if they had been (A. A. Hodge, B. B. Warfield). Some verbal inspirationists, both Protestant and Catholic, claim that either inspiration or its effect of inerrancy was restricted only to matters of faith and morals (John Cardinal Newman, Baron Friedrich von Hügel, Llewellyn J. Evans, Henry Preserved Smith, Charles Augustus Briggs, Daniel P. Fuller). Others contend that Scrip-

ture makes use of ancient genres of pseudonymity or legend which make the rubric inerrancy inapplicable.

Far more radical a reaction to higher criticism has been the modernist or liberal view of inspiration, that only the religious experiences recorded in the Bible are inspired and function as mirrors of God's progressive revelation (Harry Emerson Fosdick), or that the inspiration of the Bible is the quality of "religious genius" imparted to it by the spiritual depth of the writers (C. H. Dodd), or that Scripture is inspired by the "Spirit of the Christian community" (Friedrich Schleiermacher). The neo-orthodox view returned to Luther's dynamic view of the gospel as the locus of biblical authority. The Bible is held by neo-orthodox thinkers to *contain* the Word of God, i.e., the saving message of Christ, and to *become* the Word of God to the hearer or reader as he or she is existentially addressed by it.

The three basic views which developed in response to higher criticism are far from incompatible, at least in principle. The first may be said to imply the other two. According to it, God's providence prepared the "religious geniuses" needed to write the Scripture (cf. Warfield: "If God wished to give his people a series of letters like Paul's, he prepared a Paul to write them"). And verbal inspirationists certainly believe that "the Word of God is quick and powerful" (Heb. 4:12, KJV) and liable to come alive to the reader as the neo-orthodox hold. The difference is that adherents of the liberal and neo-orthodox views see the critical difficulties with the text as being too great to make verbal inspiration plausible any longer, though not so great as to obscure the religious greatness of the Bible as human literature (liberalism) or to impede the power of the gospel message contained in the text (neo-orthodoxy).

Bibliography. J. T. Burtchaell, *Catholic Theories of Biblical Inspiration since 1810* (Cambridge: 1969); C. H. Dodd, *The Authority of the Bible*, rev. ed. (New York: 1962); H. J. Forstman, *Word and Spirit: Calvin's Doctrine of Biblical Authority* (Stanford: 1962); B. Vawter, *Biblical Inspiration* (Philadelphia: 1972); B. B. Warfield, *Limited Inspiration* (Grand Rapids: 1962).

INTEREST (Heb. *nešeḵ* "a bite"; Gk. *tókós* "interest").†

I. Ancient Near East

Loaning both money and produce on interest was a widespread practice in all parts of the ancient Near East, as attested by an enormous body of literature. Rates varied both with the locale and with the type of loan. In Lower Mesopotamia interest rates were fixed at 20-25 percent for loans of silver or grain, while in Upper Mesopotamia rates on money were higher at 33-50 percent. Interest rates in Egypt at Elephantine during the Ptolemaic period were 12 percent. Rome permitted only a maximum rate of 12 percent interest at the time of Christ.

Rates of interest, exchange rates, and trade were normally fixed and regulated by the state. The laws of Eshnunna (§18A) and the Code of Hammurabi (§§88-96) both establish interest rates. The latter, in particular, carefully defines the respective rights of both borrower and lender. Moneylenders were penalized the full amount of the loan for loaning at higher than the established rates (§90). Lenders were required to bear some of the risk of the loan. Traders who were robbed were not required to repay either the loan or the interest (§103). If a free man borrowed money against the future produce of a field and the crop was destroyed either by flood or drought, all interest was forfeited for the year (§48). The presence of such detailed laws demonstrates the probability of widespread abuse of these practices.

II. Old Testament

The Mosaic law attempted to regulate many of these abuses. Yahweh, as sovereign of Israel, exercised royal prerogative by establishing acceptable economic practices. Israelites were forbidden to loan on interest to fellow Israelites (which is probably why exact interest rates for Israel are unavailable), but were permitted to do so to foreigners (Exod. 22:25 [MT 24]; Lev. 25:35-38; Deut. 23:19-20). Heb. *nešek* (RSV "usury") stands alone in Exodus and Deuteronomy, but later laws also use *tarbît* (RSV "increase"; KJV "usury"); the Septuagint regularly uses Gk. *tokós* to translate *nešek* and various forms of *pleonázō* to translate *tarbît*. Unfortunately, the distinction between these two types of interest remains unclear.

Security was sometimes given in earnest of payment. Judah gave Tamar his signet, cord, and staff (Gen. 38:17-18). The security could also be a garment, which had to be returned by sundown (Exod. 22:26-27 [MT 25-26]; Deut. 24:10-13), or an animal (Job 24:3). A lender was forbidden to take anything that the borrower needed as a means of livelihood, such as a millstone (Deut. 24:6).

There is no evidence that any of these regulations was followed. Rather, Ezekiel, Nehemiah, and Job decry the practices of the moneylenders (Neh. 5:1-13; Job 24:3; Ezek. 18:13; 22:12).

Israelites who could not pay their debts often sold themselves or their children into (temporary) slavery (Lev. 25:39ff.; 2 Kgs. 4:1-7; Neh. 5:5). These bondservants were to be freed every seventh year, and their debts forgiven, unless they preferred to remain slaves (Exod. 21:2ff.; Deut. 15:12-18).

A biblical proverb notes that wealth gained by usury is fleeting and will eventually revert to the poor (Prov. 28:8).

III. New Testament

Gk. *tokós* occurs only twice, in the parable of the talents (Matt. 25:27; Luke 19:23). Here Jesus uses the example, but fails to comment on the practice itself. The various forms of *pleonázō* "increase," while appearing more frequently, do not yield any additional insights into the economic practices of the times. John the Baptist exhorts the soldiers and tax collectors not to increase the amounts they collect from the people (3:12-14). Paul claims to have overcharged no man (2 Cor. 7:2; 12:17-18). Unfortunately, the term lacks its specialized use in the Septuagint, and not all occurrences of this word mean interest; both *pleonéktēs* and *pleonexía*, for instance, simply connote covetousness without any specific reference to charging unlawful interest.

INTERPRETATION, BIBLICAL.†

I. The Task of Interpretation

The interpreter of the Bible is concerned first to discover the meaning of the text in its original context (which process is called "exegesis"), then to show the meaning of the text for his or her own era (the process of "hermeneutics," from Hermes the divine messenger). The latter will be the main concern here.

II. The Age of Allegory

Given a Scripture held to be divinely inspired, devout minds in all religions and throughout history have inferred that such a text must conceal several levels of meaning beneath the plain surface sense. Sometimes this belief stems from dissatisfaction with the text: as it stands, it seems unworthy of divine inspiration, so profundities are discovered behind this genealogy or beneath that love canticle. Other times the belief in divine inspiration stems from great appreciation for the plain sense of the text: more and deeper riches are sought from the same treasure chest.

In the era of Jesus and the early Church several methods of plumbing the depths of the text had already been devised by both Jews and Gentiles. The apocalyptic sectarians of the Dead Sea (Qumran) Scrolls employed the *pesher* ("interpretation," in the sense of "solution") technique, whereby individual Scripture texts were now seen as fulfilled by events in the sect's own history and thus rightly interpreted for the first time. That is, the true meaning was not to be found by contextual exegesis, but from a kind of apocalyptic hindsight. Much the same notion is to be found in Acts 2:16-21; 1 Pet. 1:10-12.

The scribes and rabbis developed various sets of midrashic, or hermeneutical, rules such as the seven attributed to Hillel, designed to extrapolate from biblical texts to matters where Scripture was silent. One such technique was *Qal wa-homer:* what is true in a less important case (mentioned in Scripture) applies no less to a more important one (not mentioned there), and vice versa. Jesus argues in precisely this way in John 10:34-36.

More philosophically inclined Jews, paramountly Philo of Alexandria, employed allegory, a technique first developed by rationalistic Stoics who sought to salvage abstract truths from the myths of the Homeric epics. The Stoic Pseudo-Heraclitus defined allegory as "saying one thing and signifying something other than what is said" (*Quaestiones homericae* 6). Paul uses allegory in Gal. 4:21-31, as do many of Jesus' parables (e.g., Matt. 13:24-30, 36-43; Mark 4:2-20), though some scholars attribute the allegorizing element to the early Church.

Allegory was the favorite method of interpretation among most ancient Christian writers, and found particular acceptance at Alexandria, the home of Philo, Clement, and Origen. Several of the Church Fathers (e.g., Tertullian, Clement of Alexandria, Origen, Augustine, and Jerome) set forth two-, three-, four-, or fivefold systems of interpretation which culminated in the widespread medieval belief that every verse of Scripture had four senses: literal, allegorical (= theological), tropological (=morally exhorting), and anagogical (=eschatological). Hand in hand with the multiplicity of interpretations went the claim that biblical interpretation must be controlled by the tradition of the Church. Heretical meanings might be pressed from the text as readily as orthodox ones unless some controls were set up. Tertullian, in fact, advised orthodox apologists not to wage a losing battle against the Gnostics by citing Scripture; it would be safer to appeal to orthodox tradition.

III. The Dawn of Literalism

Although the allegorical method dominated most of Christian history, it did not go totally unopposed. The heresiarch Marcion championed literalism, seeking to rule out orthodox attempts to christianize the Old Testament by allegorical interpretation. In the third century, the Egyptian bishop Nepos wrote his *Refutation of the Allegorists*. But literalism only gained a solid foothold in the Church with the school of Antioch, which under Diodorus of Tarsus and Theodore of Mopsuestia in the fourth and fifth centuries grew to challenge the Alexandrian school. Theodore's extant writings show him going so far in his rejection of allegorizing as to claim, e.g., that only four of the Psalms (2, 8, 45, and 110) were genuinely messianic, since they alone seemed to have a literal messianic reference—unlike Ps. 22 which could be read messianically only by allegory. The voice of the Antiochenes was silenced in the sixth century in the wake of the Nestorian crisis, because the christological heretic Nestorius had been Theodore's disciple and brought his teachings under suspicion.

The cause of literalism was revived in the Middle Ages by Hugh of St. Victor and his disciples Richard and Andrew, teachers of a canonical lay order in Paris, who adopted many of the exegetical insights of the near-contemporary literalist rabbi Solomon ben Isaac ("Rashi"). On this basis, Andrew of St. Victor declined even to interpret Isa. 7:14 messianically.

In the fourteenth century, Franciscan professor Nicholas of Lyra wrote a lengthy biblical commentary in which he maintained the primacy of the literal meaning. Mystical senses there might be, but they must proceed from and not violate the plain sense of the text. Martin Luther was later to acknowledge his debt to Lyra for his literal exegesis, though he rejected the Franciscan's toleration for any other sense: "I consider the ascription of several senses to Scripture to be not merely dangerous and useless for teaching but even to cancel the authority of Scripture whose meaning ought to be always one and the same." Luther wanted simply "the naked text" (*WA* xl, 567; xxv, 142). He sought to put an end to allegory, advocating instead the grammatico-historical method: the only meaning which one may ascribe to the text is that which its human author intended, as one is able to reconstruct it in the historical context and with ordinary rules of grammar. Hand in hand with the grammatico-historical method of interpretation went Luther's motto, *Sola Scriptura* ("Scripture alone"). For if interpretation is no longer a matter of esoteric oracle-mongering, interpreters no longer need the infallible oracle of tradition to tell them what Scripture says. Indeed, if the meaning of Scripture is plain to the ordinary Christian, then the tables may be turned: tradition may be judged at the bar of Scripture.

With Luther, the hermeneutical tide seems to have turned. Thenceforth all Protestants, and eventually many other Christians as well, began to concentrate on the literal sense, almost to the exclusion of any other. Luther himself, however, was not a completely consistent literalist, since he continued in a heavily allegorical christological reading of many Old Testament prophecies and stories. Subsequent Protestants have been, unwittingly, even less consistent. Most continue to accept "double fulfillments" of prophecies (such as Isa. 7:14) which, though traditionally taken as predicting Jesus Christ, do not seem messianic in any literal sense. Many Protestants (e.g., Calvinist "covenant" theologians) also accept Roman Catholic spiritualizations of Old Testament promises to Israel as applying instead to the Church. And the common apologetical strategy of harmonizing "apparent contradictions" results in rejecting the "plain" or "apparent" sense of a theologically disturbing text in favor of a more pleasing but less natural interpretation.

A new chapter in biblical interpretation was opened when the grammatico-historical method was supplemented by the historical-critical method. The latter may be said to be implicit in the former, since it insists that for Scripture to be understood rightly, it cannot be exempt from the ordinary canons of historical and literary study, even when such study indicates the presence of such factors as legends, pseudonymity, and theological diversity.

IV. Contemporary Approaches

In the wake of historical criticism, many questions of interpretation have been reopened and debated with new passion. Some interpreters hold that the Bible's teaching is so permeated with prescientific cosmogony and myth that its truth can only be maintained via a hermeneutic of "demythologizing" (Rudolf Bultmann) or "deliteralizing" (Paul Tillich), interpreting the myths to reveal the self-understanding of faith that is presupposed by and communicated in the prescientific framework.

To other interpreters the paramount challenge is the theological and ethical diversity among biblical writers. Some advocate the use of a "canon-within-the-canon" (Ernst Käsemann) to discriminate between superior and inferior or central and peripheral elements (cf. also Bultmann). Others (Helmut Koester, James D. G. Dunn) see the wide range of biblical viewpoints as a charter legitimating an equally broad range of canonically Christian viewpoints today.

The diversity of modern cultures to which Scripture must be applied is seen by many as a challenge equal to that of the Bible's own diversity. Feminist interpreters (e.g., Virginia Ramey Mollenkott and Paul K. Jewett) apply "content criticism" to accentuate what they see as the central biblical or Pauline thrust toward egalitarianism at the expense of other female-subordinationist texts which are deemed aberrant or peripheral. Third World theologians (e.g., Kwesi A. Dickson) and Western missiologists (like Charles H. Kraft) point to the diversity of the canon and allow that, e.g., Old Testament texts which presuppose thought-patterns and cultures similar to those of the Third World might be better models for Third World Christians than the New Testament.

Liberation theologians (including Gustavo Gutiérrez and Juan Luis Segundo) have adopted a Marxian hermeneutic whereby the Sitz im Leben ("setting in life") of the interpreter is just as important as that of the text: the interpreter must radically scrutinize his or her own agenda to make sure the resultant biblical interpretation will facilitate the liberation of the oppressed rather than rationalize their oppression.

Many conservative Protestants have shown some sympathy with various of these concerns, but others have attempted to construct hermeneutical controls which would disallow most of these approaches. Some fundamentalist organizations and schools have attached hermeneutical codes to their doctrinal statements. The often bewildering diversity of interpretations has even moved some Protestants to look again in a Catholic direction, seeking to replace a seemingly eroded biblical authority with one or another variety of ecclesiastical or traditional authority.

See BIBLICAL CRITICISM.

Bibliography. J. D. G. Dunn, *Unity and Diversity in the New Testament* (Philadelphia: 1977); R. M. Grant, *A Short History of the Interpretation of the Bible*, rev. ed. (New York: 1963); B. Jowett, "The Interpretation of Scripture," pp. 312-323 in *Religious Thought in the Nineteenth Century*, ed. B. M. G. Reardon (Cambridge: 1966); D. H. Kelsey, *The Uses of Scripture in Recent Theology* (Philadelphia: 1975); R. N. Longenecker, *Biblical Exegesis in the Apostolic Period* (Grand Rapids: 1975).

IOB [yōb] (Heb. *yôḇ*).* A son of Issachar (Gen. 46:13; KJV "Job"). The JB and NIV read "Jashub," following the form of the name in the parallel accounts (Num. 26:24; 1 Chr. 7:1).

IOTA [ī ō'tə] (Gk. *ióta*). The ninth letter of the Greek alphabet, corresponding to Eng. *i* and Heb. *yodh*. Its numerical value is ten. At Matt. 5:18 it is noted as the smallest letter in the contemporary Hebrew and Aramaic script (KJV "jot"; JB "dot").

IPHDEIAH [ĭf dē'yə] (Heb. *yipdᵉyâ* "may the Lord deliver"). The head of a household from the tribe of Benjamin; a son of Shashak (1 Chr. 8:25; KJV "Iphedeiah").

IPHTAH [ĭf'tə] (Heb. *yiptaḥ* "may God open [the womb?]"). A city in the Shephelah of Judah (Josh. 15:43; KJV "Jiphtah"). Although the site has not been identified positively, it is frequently identified as modern Tarqūmīya, 10 km. (6 mi.) northwest of Hebron, between Wâdī Tarqūmīya and Wâdī Afrandš in the vicinity of Ashan.

IPHTAHEL [ĭf'tə ĕl] (Heb. *yiptaḥ-'ēl* "God opens" or "may God open"). A valley along the border between the tribal territories of Zebulun and Asher (Josh. 19:14, 27; KJV "Jiphthahel"). It is most likely the valley now known as Wâdī el-Melek, northwest of Nazareth.

IR [ĭr] (Heb. *'îr*). A son of Bela from the tribe of Judah (1 Chr. 7:12).

IRA [ī'rə] (Heb. *'îrā'*).

1. A man of the lineage of Jair from the tribe of Manasseh, called a priest (Heb. *kōhēn*) of David (2 Sam. 20:26; KJV "chief officer"). The Hebrew term may designate here a special role of confidence in David's court, apparently as private priest to the king (cf. 8:18).

2. The son of Ikkesh from Tekoa; one of David's mighty men (2 Sam. 23:26; 1 Chr. 11:28) and captain of the division guarding the temple in the sixth month (27:9).

3. An Ithrite who was one of David's mighty men (2 Sam. 23:38; 1 Chr. 11:40). On the basis of some ancient versions, which call him a Jattirite, he is sometimes identified with **1**.

IRAD [ī'răd] (Heb. *'îrāḏ*).† The son of Enoch and grandson of Cain (Gen. 4:18). He is thought to be the same as Jared in the genealogy at 5:15-20.

IRAM [ī'răm] (Heb. *'îrām* "vigilant"). The eponymous ancestor of an Edomite clan (Gen. 36:43 par. 1 Chr. 1:54).

IRI [ī'rī] (Heb. *'îrî*). A Benjaminite (1 Chr. 7:7); probably the same as IR.

IRIJAH [ī rī'jə] (Heb. *yir'îyāyh* "Yahweh sees"). A sentry at the Benjamin Gate who apprehended the prophet Jeremiah as he sought to leave Jerusalem to claim his inheritance at Anathoth, charging him with deserting to the Chaldeans (Jer. 37:13-14).

IR-NAHASH [ĭr nā'hăsh] (Heb. *'îr nāḥāš* "city of a serpent").† It is unclear whether this term refers to a city or is a personal name. At 1 Chr. 4:12 the Judahite Teninnah is described as the father (perhaps as "founder") of Ir-nahash. The argument for place-name identification comes from 1 Chr. 4:14, where Joab is named as the father of Ge-harashim ("valley of the craftsmen"; KJV "valley of Charashim"). At Neh. 11:35 Ge-harashim is translated as a place name, "valley of craftsmen."

IRON (Heb. *barzel;* Aram. *parzel;* cf. Akk. *parzillu;* Ugar. *brḏl;* from Sum. *bar-gal*).† A malleable, strong metal whose name is associated with an important period of material culture, the Iron Age (in Palestine, *ca.* 1200-300 B.C.).

During the Bronze Age in the ancient Near East (*ca.* 3200-1200 B.C.), the art of casting bronze had been so refined that that metal was commonly used for most domestic, commercial, and military requirements. Even though copper and tin, the constituent elements in bronze, were scarce and difficult to mine, the easy availability of bronze had hindered the development of iron technology. Iron ore was plentiful (cf. Deut. 8:9), but iron had only been available in the form of wrought iron, which was softer and less durable than bronze; thus it was regarded as a semiprecious metal.

Technological and social factors combined to bring the Iron Age to Palestine. An unknown craftsman in Asia Minor discovered that quenched and reheated iron emerged as a strong and durable metal; Hebrew tradition points to Tubal-cain, "the forger of all instruments of bronze and iron" (Gen. 4:22). Although the scientific basis for this—that the furnace charcoal added carbon to the iron and reheating removed a material which made the iron brittle—was unknown until modern times, a manufacturing method had been found which paved the way for the widespread use of iron.

The thirteenth century saw the irruption of the Sea Peoples from Asia Minor into the eastern Mediterranean. A variety of ethnic groups, vigorous and militarily adept, pushed into Palestine by land and sea. One result was the disruption of traditional trade routes in the region, including sources of supply for bronze; another was the introduction of iron to the area by the Philistines. Palestine had been a part of the Egyptian Empire, and while the Egyptians were able to repulse the Sea Peoples from Egypt itself, Palestine fell into the hands of such peoples as the Israelites and Philistines. The Philistines dominated the seacoast and occupied strategic points on the plain of Esdraelon and the Jordan valley, and friction between them and the Israelites was inevitable (1 Sam. 13:19-22). Iron weapons, war chariots, and a centralized organization made the Philistines and their allies (cf. Judg. 4:3, JB) a constant threat to the Israelites which was not eliminated until David became king.

Iron soon became popular for use in sword blades, spearpoints (17:7), and arrowheads, but it also came to be used for tools and farm implements (2 Sam. 12:31; Job 19:24; Jer. 17:1; Amos 1:3). King Og of Bashan had a bed (perhaps a sarcophagus?) made of iron (Deut. 3:11). Vast quantities of iron were used in the construction of the Jerusalem temple (1 Chr. 22:3, 14, 16; 29:2), and various members of the royal court contributed 100,000 talents of iron (about 3,450 metric tons) to the service of the temple (1 Chr. 29:7).

Various implements and ornaments have been discovered in Palestine dating to as early as the late twelfth century. An ancient iron mine has been discovered at Mugharet el-Wardeh, near biblical Penuel, and various installations identified with smelting and ironworking have been suggested at Megiddo and Tell Jemmeh, dating approximately to the time of Solomon.

The strength of iron was also referred to figuratively in the Old Testament. Yahweh brought Israel out of Egypt, the iron-smelting furnace (Deut. 4:20; 1 Kgs. 8:51; Jer. 11:4). The mighty Behemoth has limbs like bars of iron (Job 40:18), and the Leviathan crushes iron like straw (41:27 [MT 19]). Stubborn Israel's neck is likened to an iron sinew (Isa. 48:4).

IRON (PLACE) (Josh. 19:38, KJV). *See* YIRON.

IRPEEL [ĭr′pĭ əl] (Heb. *yirpeʾēl* "God heals"). A city in the tribal territory of Benjamin (Josh. 18:27), probably located in the hill country north of Jerusalem. Some scholars place it at modern Rafat, north of Gibeon, which is some 10.5 km. (6.5 mi.) northwest of Jerusalem.

IRRIGATION.† An artificial means of watering crops, used throughout the ancient Near East, primarily for cereal crops. The practice of irrigation demanded a high degree of cooperation from the people of the societies in which it was practiced. The precise origins

of irrigation are unknown, but the practice could have begun when pastoralists planted seeds in the rich silt left by the retreating waters of a flooded river.

While irrigation was utilized across the Fertile Crescent in ancient times, differences in climate, terrain, and the availability of water made for a variety of irrigation techniques. In Egypt the Nile river was the source of irrigation water. Dependably flooding from July to September of each year, the Nile's retreat deposited a thick layer of fertile mud on Egyptian farmland. The regularity of the Nile floods permitted the development of canal systems (also used for transportation) and catch basins to retain the maximum amount of water for use in the drier months. The *shadûf*, a balanced pole with a bucket on one end and a weight on the other, was used to lift water from the river or a catch basin to the level of a tilled field; this device is still in use today.

The combination of largely mountainous terrain, heavy rainfall (especially in winter, October through April), and a shortage of arable flatland required a different kind of irrigation in Palestine. Indeed, great variations in terrain elevation made for vastly different climatic characteristics within short distances, and water from rivers was less abundant. (Palestine's topography consists of a coastal plain, highlands, the Rift valley, the Transjordanian plateau, and desert areas, with the coastal plain, highlands, and western plateau receiving most of the rainfall.) Farmers overcame the shortage of farmland and countered the threat of erosion by building hillside rock terraces whose low walls retained the soil and permitted irrigation with water stored in catch basins and cisterns. Terraces dating from approximately 1500 B.C. have been found in Galilee, and many have been located in the vicinity of Jerusalem.

Evidence of a sophisticated irrigation system dating to the third millennium has been discovered at Jâwa, situated along Wâdî Rajîl some 130 km. (80 mi.) east of the Jordan river near the Jordan-Syria border.

Mesopotamian farmers, situated between the great Euphrates and Tigris rivers, also faced unique natural conditions. Unlike the Nile, these rivers flooded unpredictably, threatening to wash out farmland. Furthermore, 2.4-2.7 m. (8-9 ft.) spring tides in the Persian gulf increased soil salinity. Accordingly, irrigation was a major concern in Mesopotamian societies. In the third millennium B.C. the Sumerians maintained a complex system of canals, dikes, and reservoirs. At Sumer gods were depicted carrying pickaxes and baskets for repairing canals, and *patesi* (agricultural rulers) were appointed to build and repair canals. A cuneiform text now called the "Farmer's Almanac" cautions a young farmer to avoid opening his dikes too wide when preparing his field for planting. The Babylonians also devoted energy and resources to the canals; their maintenance was considered to be a sign of the king's faithfulness to the gods.

IR-SHEMESH [ĭr shĕm′ĭsh] (Heb. *ʿîr-šemeš* "city of the sun").† A Canaanite city allocated to the tribe of Dan (Josh. 19:41); probably the same as Har-heres, which the Danites were unable to conquer (1:35). Called elsewhere Beth-shemesh (1), the site has been identified as Tell er-Rumeileh.

IRU [ī′rōō] (Heb. *'îrû*). A son of the Judahite Caleb, from the lineage of Jephunneh (1 Chr. 4:15).

ISAAC [ī′zĭk] (Heb. *yiṣḥāq, yiśḥāq* "he laughed").† The child of promise for Abraham and Sarah, the living sign of God's faithful dealings with them. As the link between the cycles of Abraham and Jacob stories, Isaac's position is of less prominence than either of the other patriarchs, yet his life provides examples of faith in and obedience to Yahweh.

Abraham's advancing age and Sarah's continued barrenness threatened the perpetuation of that patriarchal line. Abraham (Abram) attempted to alter the situation, first perhaps through his relationship with his nephew Lot (Gen. 13), next by adopting Eliezer of Damascus as a member of his household (15:2-3), and then by impregnating Sarah's maidservant (ch. 16). The last of these efforts gained him a son, Ishmael. But on more than one occasion God had promised Abraham a more direct heir of his own flesh (15:4; 17:15-19), and during a visit with Abraham and Sarah at Mamre the Lord gave notice that a son would be born to them within a year (18:9-15). Thus it came about that Isaac was born in Abraham's one-hundredth year (21:5); his circumcision when he was eight days old was the first such act among the Hebrews (v. 7; cf. 17:11-12; Acts 7:8). The name Isaac is traced to the incongruity of the child's birth to a couple of such advanced age (Gen. 17:17; 18:12-15; cf. 21:6).

The expulsion of Ishmael (21:8-14) and Abraham's treatment of sons subsequently born to other wives (25:1-6) were intended to assure transmission of his material property and spiritual promise solely through Isaac (21:12).

The single recorded episode of Isaac's youth is found in ch. 22, where God commands Abraham to offer his precious son as a burnt offering on a mountain in Moriah. The poignancy builds as father and son ascend to the sacrifice site, and Isaac innocently asks, "Where is the lamb for the burnt offering?" Abraham replies that God will provide the lamb, and then prepares to sacrifice his son. Only the angel's call stays the father's hand, and God promises to reward Abraham's faithfulness by blessing him and multiplying his descendants (cf. Heb. 11:17-19).

Some years later the aged Abraham solemnly charges his most trusted servant to journey to Mesopotamia to obtain a wife for Isaac from among the women of his family (Gen. 24). The apparent dual purpose of this mission is to keep Isaac in Canaan while preventing him from marrying a pagan Canaanite woman. The servant's mission meets with success, as the beautiful Rebekah agrees to marry forty-year-old Isaac, sight unseen (25:20).

Isaac's wife is barren, as Sarah was (25:23). But unlike his father, Isaac responds to the situation by praying to Yahweh and waiting upon him in faith. The birth of Esau and Jacob, when Isaac is sixty, answers his prayers, but a prophecy (v. 23) foretells the brothers' rivalry (cf. the relationship between Isaac and Ishmael). As the boys grow, Isaac comes to favor Esau, while Rebekah prefers Jacob; this division of parental loyalties is to have tragic consequences. Other parallels between the lives of Abraham and Isaac are apparent in ch. 26. God's promise to Abraham is reiterated to Isaac in vv. 3-5. When a famine drives Isaac to Gerar, he claims Rebekah is his sister, for he is fearful that men who covet her beauty will kill him to obtain her (vv. 6-11). Isaac's abundant flocks and material riches (vv. 12-16) are reminiscent of his father's fortune. During his transhumance in the valley of Gerar he clears a number of wells which Abraham had dug, only to be pursued by herdsmen who argue that the water is theirs (vv. 17-22). Finally Isaac returns to Beer-sheba, where Abraham and Abimelech had made a covenant; Yahweh appears to him at night and identifies himself as the God of Abraham, pledging to bless Isaac and to increase the number of his descendants. In response Isaac builds an altar and settles in the area (vv. 23-25; cf. 21:27ff.).

As Isaac nears death, he asks his son Esau, a skillful hunter, to prepare a game stew for him before receiving the paternal blessing (power-laden words intended to strengthen and grant prosperity to the one who received them). Overhearing her husband, Rebekah acts quickly to secure the blessing for Jacob instead. She sends her favored son to get choice kids from the flock so she may prepare a stew, in the hope that, by presenting it to Isaac, the younger son would receive his father's blessing (27:5-10). Jacob protests that Isaac might recognize him because of his smooth skin, although Isaac's eyesight is failing; Rebekah clothes him in Esau's finest garments, and places pieces of goatskin on his hands and neck to simulate Esau's hairiness. Isaac is initially skeptical that the one who brings him the stew is Esau, but he finally eats it and unwittingly pronounces his blessing on Jacob (vv. 27-29). Isaac and Esau alike are scandalized when the ruse is uncovered, but nothing can be done: once a blessing is pronounced it cannot be recalled. The story of Isaac closes with the patriarch knowing that his blessing is with a deceitful son, with Esau hating his brother and plotting to kill him, and with Jacob fleeing the land of his inheritance, never to see his mother again.

Isaac died at the age of 180 years, and Esau and Jacob buried him in the cave at Machpelah where Sarah, Abraham, and Rebekah had been buried (35:27-29; 49:31).

The importance of Isaac to Israelite tradition is implied by the frequent references to "the God of Abraham, the God of Isaac, and the God of Jacob/Israel" (e.g., Exod. 3:6, 15-16) and "the Fear of Isaac" (Gen. 31:42). At Amos 7:9 Isaac occurs in poetic parallel with Israel as a designation for the northern kingdom. In the allegory at Gal. 4:21-31 Paul likens Christians to Isaac as "children of promise," heirs to the spiritual inheritance.

ISAAC, TESTAMENT OF. An Old Testament pseudepigraphical writing, probably composed in the first century B.C. and preserved only in Arabic and Coptic versions. It was subject to Christian adaptation in the second or third century A.D. yet retained its original character, which resembles concerns of the Qumran community: the emphasis on fasting and on ritual and moral purity.

ISAIAH [ī zā′ə] (Heb. *yᵉša'yāhû, yᵉša'yâ* "Yahweh is salvation").† A major Old Testament prophet, whose ministry in and utterances against Jerusalem and Judah are recorded in the book of Isaiah.

Little is known of the prophet's background other than that he was the son of Amoz (Isa. 1:1). His wife is identified only as "the prophetess" (8:3), and their sons are named symbolically Shear-jashub ("A remnant shall return"; 7:3) and Maher-shalal-hash-baz ("The spoil speeds, the prey hastes"; 8:3, 18).

Because of his ready access to the court and his seeming lack of inhibition in confronting monarchs (cf. chs. 7, 36–39), scholars have often suggested that Isaiah was of noble, if not royal, descent; others contend that he was a cultic priest (cf. 6:1-8).

Isaiah's call came *ca.* 740 B.C., "the year that King Uzziah died" (6:1), and his ministry extended to the reign of Hezekiah (1:1), sometime after Sennacherib's seige of Jerusalem in 701 (36:1–39:8 par. 2 Kgs. 18:13–20:19). According to tradition the prophet was martyred at the time of King Manasseh (*see* ISAIAH, ASCENSION OF).

Because the book of Isaiah includes prophecies concerning events during and after the Exile, critical scholars generally attribute portions of the book to one, two, or more prophets in addition to Isaiah (esp. Deutero-Isaiah, chs. 40–55; Trito-Isaiah, chs. 55–66). For the issues involved, see ISAIAH, BOOK OF.

The Hebrew form of the name Isaiah designates various other Old Testament persons (so NEB), which most English versions render as JESHAIAH. In the New Testament the KJV uses the form Esaias, following Gk. *Ēsaias.*

ISAIAH, ASCENSION OF.† An apocryphal account of a visionary experience of Isaiah the son of Amoz and his subsequent martyrdom.

This New Testament apocryphal book was composed in Greek during the second century A.D.; it is preserved only in an Ethiopic translation. A major part of the book (Asc.Isa. 1–5) preserves an earlier Jewish midrash on 2 Kgs. 21:16, the Martyrdom of Isaiah. Recorded here are the prophets' alleged predictions concerning the evil King Manasseh of Judah, which culminate with his having the prophet sawn in two (cf. Heb. 11:37). Inserted into this section is a Christian apocalypse, the Testament of Hezekiah, Asc.Isa. 3:13b–5:1), which predicts the descent of Christ from the seventh heaven, the persecution and rule of the world by the satanic Beliar, and the Lord's final victory.

In Isaiah's visionary trip to the seventh heaven (chs. 6–11), he sees the glory of the Lord praised in each successive heaven. The details of the birth, death, and resurrection of Jesus Christ are given to Isaiah in the vision, and he relates them to Hezekiah. It is because of Isaiah's determination to maintain his testimony that he has seen the Lord (cf. Isa. 6:1).

The book bears traces of both Gnostic and Docetic thought.

ISAIAH, BOOK OF.† The first book of the Latter Prophets, which contains the utterances of the prophet Isaiah.

I. Critical Issues

As is true of other Old Testament prophetic books, Isaiah is a compilation, an anthology of prophetic speeches as well as accounts of symbolic actions and historical and biographical narrative. The complex arrangement does not appear to be systematically chronological.

The form and unity of the canonical book were established at least by the second century B.C., as demonstrated by the Dead Sea Scrolls manuscripts (esp. 1QIs^a) and implied by Ben Sira (Sir. 48:17-25). From a literary standpoint, the book can be divided into two major sections, Isa. 1–39 and 40–66, on the basis of content and, concomitantly, theological concerns. Indeed, the majority of critical scholars accept the view suggested as early as Abraham ibn Ezra (twelfth century A.D.) that only the first portion can be ascribed to the eighth-century B.C. prophet Isaiah, a contemporary of Amos, Hosea, and Micah. The second section is attributed to an unknown prophet, commonly designated Second or Deutero-Isaiah, living among the Jews in Babylon toward the end of the Exile (*ca.* 550-538). Many scholars further identify chs. 56–66 as the work of Third or Trito-Isaiah, addressed to the restoration community perhaps in the period immediately preceding Ezra and Nehemiah. More extreme critics posit even more "Isaiahs."

Stylistic considerations are no longer a major factor in arguments concerning the book's authorship; liberal as well as conservative critics recognize that usage may depend on subject matter, setting, or purpose, as well as the prophet's personal development. A compromise position allows for the compilation of the book by Isaiah's disciples (cf. 8:16; Talmud *b. B. Bat.* 15a), with the inclusion of later material influenced by and expanding upon the concerns of the eighth-century prophet. The primary issue dividing critical scholars and conservative or traditional interpreters (the latter many of whom view the theory of multiple authorship as challenging biblical inerrancy) remains the nature of biblical prophecy. If prophecy is essentially predictive (foretelling rather than "forthtelling"; *see* PROPHECY), the historical allusions (e.g., Isa. 44:28; 45:1) and theological concerns of the second portion of the book would not be unseemly for a prophet living some 150 years before the events addressed.

II. Contents

The book opens with a collection of prophecies concerning Jerusalem and Judah (Isa. 1–12). The initial chapter serves as a general indictment and preface to Isaiah's ministry. Chs. 2–4 announce the elevation of Zion (2:2-5) and the coming day of the Lord (vv. 6-22), with the resultant chaos (ch. 3); the preservation of the faithful is intimated in 4:2-6. The Song of the Vineyard (5:1-7) is an allegory of judgment against the people of God; a series of reproaches or "woes" follows. Ch. 6 is an autobiographical account of Isaiah's commission and his inaugural vision, set in the Jerusalem temple. A series of prophecies related to the Syro-Ephraimite war (*ca.* 734) includes the signs of Shear-jashub, Immanuel, and Maher-shalal-hash-baz (chs. 7–8). The messianic king is heralded in 9:2-7 (MT 1-6). Yahweh's wrathful judgment is to be expressed through his instrument, Assyria (9:8 [MT 7]–10:34). Ch. 11 offers the hope of a messianic king ("the root of Jesse") and a new age. The collection ends with a song of thanksgiving (ch. 12).

Chs. 13–23 are comprised of oracles against foreign nations and cities: Babylon (13:1–14:23; 21:1-10), Assyria (14:24-27), Philistia (vv. 28-32), Moab (chs. 15–16), the Syro-Ephraimite alliance (Damascus and Israel; 17:1-6), Egypt (chs. 18–20), Edom (21:11-12), Arabia (vv. 13-17), and Sidon (ch. 23). Also, Jerusalem is warned of impending doom (22:1-14); vv. 15-25 castigate Shebna, one of Hezekiah's leading officials.

The "Isaiah Apocalypse" (chs. 24–27) includes eschatological prophecies of universal judgment and destruction interspersed with songs of victory and thanksgiving. Isa. 26:7-19 is a psalm proclaiming trust in God's help.

A second major collection of prophecies concerning Jerusalem and Judah is contained in chs. 28–35. The "Assyrian cycle" (chs. 28–31) consists of denunciations of religious and civil leaders (28:1-22), the parable of the farmer (vv. 23-29), and warnings to Hezekiah not to ally with Egypt in rebellion against Assyria (chs. 30–32). Ch. 33 is a prophetic liturgy of oracles and lamentations. The "Little Apocalypse" (chs. 34–35) contrasts Yahweh's day of vengeance against the nations with the restoration of Zion.

Regarded variously as an appendix to chs. 1–35 or an interlude between the major sections of the book, chs. 36–39 recount Sennacherib's attempt(s) to seize Jerusalem (chs. 36–37), Hezekiah's illness and recovery (ch. 38), and the embassy sent by Merodach-baladan (ch. 39). The narrative parallels the account in 2 Kgs. 18:23–20:19.

Commonly known as the Book of Consolation, chs. 40–55 offer comfort to the exiles, promising God's imminent salvation and the restoration of Israel. Chs. 40–48 specifically address the situation in Babylon, proclaiming deliverance to Jacob (Israel). Following a series of proclamations that the people take comfort and "prepare the way of the Lord" (40:1-11), the prophet exalts God as creator of the universe (vv. 12-31). In ch. 41 he employs the form of a prophetic lawsuit to detail Yahweh's working in history through the Persian king Cyrus. The first "Servant Song" presents the mission of God's chosen servant, Israel, to "bring forth justice to the nations" (42:1-4; some scholars include the hymn to God's glorious victory in vv. 5-9). Israel is further depicted as God's deaf and blind servant (42:18–43:7), a witness to the nations (vv. 8-13). Oracles of deliverance and restoration follow (43:14–44:8). Vv. 9-20 is a masterpiece of satire on the futility of idolatry. In 44:23–45:25 the prophet details Yahweh's commissioning of Cyrus as his "shepherd" and the subsequent conversion of the nations. He then contrasts the might of the Lord with the impotence of the Babylonian deities (ch. 46). Ch. 47 is a lamentation over the fall of Babylon. This group of oracles concludes with a summary of Yahweh's activity in history (ch. 48). Chs. 49–55 expand upon the preceding prophecy in the Book of Comfort. In the second Servant Song (49:1-6) the Servant elaborates upon his call and mission as "a light to the nations." Vv. 7-26 are an oracle of restoration. The third Servant Song (50:4-11; some consider v. 9 the end of the song) expresses the Servant's firm confidence in God's vindication despite suffering and rejection. The depiction of Yahweh's promise for the offspring of Abraham (51:1-16) and his majesty in the redemption of his people (51:17–52:10) culminate in the command to return to Jerusalem (vv. 11-12). The fourth Servant Song (52:13–53:12) proclaims the suffering and death of God's chosen people as an act of atonement. The collection ends with a song of assurance for Israel and a triumphal hymn celebrating Israel's restoration.

The remainder of Isaiah is a collection of oracles regarding matters of concern to the restoration community. Chs. 56–57 contrast righteousness (observance of the Sabbath; 56:1-8) and wickedness (corrupt leadership, idolatry), followed by words of consolation (57:14-21). The requirements of true religion are set forth in ch. 58 (cf. Mic. 6:6-8). Isa. 59 is a summons to national confession and repentance. Poems celebrating the glory of the restored Jerusalem, the mission of the Servant people, and the vindication of Zion are preserved in chs. 60–62. Isa. 63:1-6 describes the vengeance of God. A lamentation and prayer for mercy (63:7–64:12) are answered by God's promise of punishment for the wicked and "new heavens and a new earth" for the righteous (chs. 65–66).

III. Theology

The book of Isaiah presents a well-developed doctrine of God. Throughout the book Yahweh is depicted as the Holy One of Israel (e.g., 1:4; 37:23; 45:11; 60:9, 14; cf. 5:16; 40:25), separated from mankind (Heb. *qāḏôš* "holy," lit. "set apart") by his very transcendence (cf. 8:13); Isaiah especially defines holiness in terms of physical and moral purity (cf. 6:3ff.), which helps to explain God's wrath against human sin, particularly among his covenant people (e.g., 1:2-4; 5:8-25). Yahweh is supreme, Lord of the whole earth (6:3), in stark contrast to the deities worshiped by Israel's neighbors (2:8, 18-21; 37:19); many scholars have interpreted this Isaianic emphasis as the first real evidence of monotheism in Israel. It is he who created the universe (45:11-12) and who orders it according to his plan (44:24-28), including direct divine involvement in historical events (e.g., 7:18-20; 10:5ff.; 45:1ff.). In particular, God is the savior of his people, delivering them from human foes (e.g., 11:11-16; 49:25; 63:1ff.) and, in an eschatological sense, vindicating or justifying them by faith (45:21-23; 49:1-26; cf. 7:9). Closely related is the image of God as Redeemer of his people, who as their "next of kin" (cf. Lev. 25:25) ransoms them from captivity (Isa. 35:9-10; 43:14–44:8; 52:3-9).

Unlike the book of Jeremiah, which anticipates the total annihilation of Israel, Isaiah's prophecy guarantees the preservation of at least a core of God's people, symbolized in the name of his son Shear-jashub ("A remnant shall return"; 7:1-9; 11:10-16; 37:32). Only those who are faithful to the covenant stipulations will be included in this number (cf. 10:19-22; 30:15), a prerequisite which implies repentance (4:2-6; cf. 7:9).

The figure of the Messiah, God's anointed, is identified specifically at 45:1 as Cyrus, king of Persia. For the most part, however, God's chosen instrument appears to be a scion of the house of David (7:10-17), an ideal king (9:2-7 [MT 1-6]; cf. 32:1-8) who will inaugurate a kingdom of peace and righteousness (11:1-9), an age of paradise regained (vv. 10-16). The writers of the New Testament, for whom the book of Isaiah held special appeal, understood these messianic passages as heralding Jesus Christ. The Servant of the Lord, whether identified as a specific historical individual (e.g., Cyrus, Zerubbabel) or the people Israel, was commissioned to bring forth justice; as thus depicted in Isaiah this Suffering Servant does not truly conform to the Old Testament understanding of the Messiah as an ideal king but was rather so interpreted later in terms of Jesus (e.g., Matt. 12:17-21; Luke 2:32; Phil. 2:7-11). *See* SERVANT OF THE LORD.

The postexilic focus of much of Isaiah includes a universalizing trend in Hebrew thought. Indeed, the exiles are instructed that God's salvation is to reach "the end of the earth" (49:6; 52:10) and that his glory will be shown to "all flesh" (40:5; 66:18-19). The mission of the Servant is to "bring forth justice to the nations" (42:1-4) and to be "a light to the nations" (42:6), so that all will turn to the Lord (45:6, 22-23; 55:5; cf. 56:3-8).

Bibliography. B. S. Childs, *Isaiah and the Assyrian Crisis.* SBT, 2nd ser. 3 (1967); R. E. Clements, *Isaiah 1–39.* NCBC (1980); W. L. Holladay, *Isaiah: Scroll of a Prophetic Heritage* (Grand Rapids: 1978); J. D. Smart, *History and Theology in Second Isaiah* (Philadelphia: 1965); C. Westermann, *Isaiah 40–66.* OTL (1969); E. J. Young, *The Book of Isaiah,* 3 vols. (Grand Rapids: 1965-1972).

ISCAH [ĭz'kə] (Heb. *yiskâ*). A daughter of Haran and the sister of Milcah (Gen. 11:29) and Lot (v. 31).

ISHBAAL [ĭsh'bäl] (Heb. *'îš-ba'al* "man of Baal").† Probable original form of the name of King Saul's son ISHBOSHETH (1 Chr. 8:33; 9:39). Most English versions render the name as Eshbaal.

ISHBAH [ĭsh'bə] (Heb. *yišbaḥ*). A Judahite, son of Mered and the Egyptian princess Bithiah (1 Chr. 4:17). He is called the father of Eshtemoa, which may mean the founder of that city.

ISHBAK [ĭsh'băk] (Heb. *yišbāq* "may he be victorious"[?]). A son of Abraham and his concubine, Keturah (Gen. 25:2; 1 Chr. 1:32); eponymous ancestor of an Arabian nation.

ISHBI-BENOB [ĭsh'bī bē'nŏb] (Heb. *yišbî ḇᵉnōḇ* "citizen of Nob").† A Philistine, a descendant (or devotee) of the legendary giants (Rephaim). Ishbi-benob sought to kill David, but Abishai came to David's rescue and killed the Philistine instead (2 Sam. 21:16-17). The text appears to be corrupt (cf. Gob at v. 18), and various alternatives have been proposed.

ISHBOSHETH [ĭsh bō'shĕth] (Heb. *'îš-bōšeṭ* "man of shame"). One of Saul's sons, whose name was changed from Ishbaal (RSV "Eshbaal"), which means "man of Baal" (1 Chr. 8:33; 9:39). Although the "Baal" element of the name, which may be translated literally "lord" or "master," could have been an epithet of Yahweh, it has come to be interpreted as a reference to the Canaanite deity. Whether the name change occurred during Ishbosheth's time or later in the history of biblical transmission is unclear.

After the death of Saul and three of his sons, Saul's cousin Abner took Ishbosheth to Mahanaim in Transjordan and made him king over all the tribes except Judah, whose king, David, was in Hebron (2 Sam. 2:8-11). Ishbosheth's reign lasted only two years (v. 10). Because David ruled at Hebron seven and one half years (v. 11), Ishbosheth's time at Mahanaim may have taken place after Abner's successful conquest of the Philistines in behalf of Ishbosheth or after Ishbosheth had managed to subject the other eleven tribes to his rule. As long as David and Ishbosheth remained their vassals, the Philistines tolerated this development—perhaps because it benefited their policies to have two kings ruling Israel. An alternate view is that Ishbosheth's reign occurred immediately after Saul's death, leaving David yet to rule in Hebron for another five and one half years (cf. vv. 10-11). Indeed, Ishbosheth proved unable to resist David's increasing strength (cf. 2:13–3:1). Some scholars, however, contend that Ishbosheth's reign was fully concurrent with that of David at Hebron.

Ishbosheth came increasingly into conflict with his ambitious general Abner. When Abner consorted with Saul's concubine Rizpah, quite possibly an attempt to usurp royal authority, Ishbosheth objected. The angry Abner sought to ally himself with David (3:6-21), but he was murdered by Joab. Without his powerful commander, Ishbosheth's effectiveness as a monarch dissipated (4:1). He was murdered in his sleep by two of his captains, and David buried him in Abner's grave at Hebron (vv. 5-12).

ISH-HAI [ĭsh-hī] (Heb. *'îš-ḥay* [K], *'îš-ḥaḥ* [Q]).* According to 2 Sam. 23:20, RSV mg., the father of Benaiah (1). Most English versions render the Hebrew "a valiant man" or a similar phrase (Heb. "son of a valiant man").

ISHHOD [ĭsh'hŏd] (Heb. *'îšᵉhôḏ* "man of vigor"). A son of Gilead's sister Hammolecheth of the tribe of Manasseh (1 Chr. 7:18; KJV "Ishod").

ISHI [ĭsh'ī] (Heb. *'îšî*) (NAME OF GOD).* Symbolic name to be used for God, representing his covenant with Israel (Hos. 2:16; RSV "my husband"). *See* BAALI.

ISHI [ĭsh'ī] (Heb. *yiš'î* "salutary") (PERSON).
1. The son of Appaim, a Jerahmeelite of the tribe of Judah (1 Chr. 2:31).
2. A Judahite, the father of Zoheth and Ben-zoheth (1 Chr. 4:20).
3. A man from the tribe of Simeon whose sons (or followers) defeated the Amalekites at Mt. Seir and then occupied the area (1 Chr. 4:42-43).
4. The head of a father's house in the half-tribe of Manasseh which occupied territory in Transjordan (1 Chr. 5:24).

ISHIAH (1 Chr. 7:3, KJV). *See* ISSHIAH 1.

ISHIJAH (Ezra 10:31, KJV). *See* ISSHIJAH.

ISHMA [ĭsh'mə] (Heb. *yišmā'* "may God listen"). A son of Etam, from the tribe of Judah (1 Chr. 4:3).

ISHMAEL [ĭsh'mĭ əl] (Heb. *yišmā'ē'l* "may God hear").

1. The son of Abraham by his Egyptian slave Hagar; the older half brother of Isaac (Gen. 25:12; 1 Chr. 1:28).

The story of Ishmael is bound up with one of the strongest themes of the Abraham stories, the search for an heir for the patriarch. Because Sarah was barren (Gen. 11:30), Abraham initially considers making his orphaned nephew Lot, the nearest male relative, his heir (ch. 13), and then adopts Eliezer of Damascus, a member of his household (15:2-3). Despite the Lord's assurances to Abraham (vv. 4-5), Sarah's concern leads her to offer her maid Hagar to Abraham in yet another attempt to obtain an heir (16:1-6; cf. the similar arrangement recorded in a Nuzi text whereby the first wife has authority over children produced by slave women). Hagar's successful conception prompts her to deride Sarah, whose harsh treatment drives Hagar away.

Two accounts in Genesis advance the story of Ishmael from this point. In 16:7-14 the angel of God comes upon Hagar and advises her to return to Sarah's service. Then the angel declares that her descendants, like Abraham's, will be too numerous to count, and that her son Ishmael would be a wild man whose life would be marked by conflict. In ch. 17 God repeats the promises of a son to Abraham and blessings to Ishmael, whereupon all males in the household are circumcised as a sign of the covenant.

The sequence of events is arranged differently in ch. 21. Here Isaac has been born, and Sarah casts out Hagar and Ishmael when she sees the latter playing with her newly weaned son. Abraham gives Hagar food and water, and she and Ishmael wander in the wilderness of Beer-sheba. When the water runs out Hagar waits for death, but God hears the boy's cries and his angel delivers the promise that Ishmael would be a great nation.

Few details are known about the balance of Ishmael's life. He married an Egyptian woman (21:21), participated in Abraham's burial at Machpelah (25:9), and lived to be 137 years old (v. 17). Vv. 16-18 give a brief account of Ishmael's sons and the regions they inhabited (cf. 1 Chr. 1:29-31).

In Jewish and Moslem tradition Ishmael came to be regarded as the ancestor of desert-dwelling tribes. Arabs venerate Ishmael as their forefather, and according to Moslem tradition he and Hagar are buried in the sacred Ka'aba in Mecca.

2. The son of Nethaniah and descendant of Elishama, a member "of the royal family" of Judah; leader of the insurgents who assassinated Gedaliah, the caretaker governor of Judah (2 Kgs. 25:23-25; Jer. 40:8–41:18). Ishmael and other "captains of the open field" had come before the Babylonian-appointed official at Mizpah, where the governor urged cooperation with the Babylonians. Two months later Ishmael and his followers killed Gedaliah and many others before being forced to flee to his Ammonite supporters across the Jordan river.

3. The third son of Azel of Benjamin, a descendant of Saul (1 Chr. 8:38; 9:44).

4. The father of Zebadiah, governor of Judah during Jehoshaphat's reign in the ninth century (2 Chr. 19:11).

5. The son of Jehohanan; one of the five "commanders of hundreds" of Judah to obey the orders of the high priest Jehoiada by making the child Joash king and executing the usurper, Queen Athaliah (2 Chr. 23:1ff.).

6. A son of Pashhur named among those sons of priests ordered to put away their foreign-born wives during Ezra's reforms (Ezra 10:22).

ISHMAELITES [ĭsh'mĭ ə līts] (Heb. *yišmᵉ'ē'lîm*).† Peoples who traced their ancestry through Abraham's first son, Ishmael (cf. Gen. 25:12-18). These desert-dwelling peoples inhabited regions of North Arabia, ranging from Lower Egypt to the Euphrates river, from the early second millennium until the eighth/seventh centuries B.C. They appear infrequently in the Old Testament, but the name "Ishmael" has been found in texts at Mari and in Assyrian annals. Little is known of them, save for their prowess as archers (cf. 21:20).

Joseph's brothers sold him to camel-riding Ishmaelite traders on their way from Gilead to Egypt (37:25-28; 39:1; KJV "Ishmeelites"), with assistance of Midianites (37:25-28); at v. 36 the Ishmaelites are apparently identified with the Midianites. (Some scholars believe the appearance of Ishmaelites and camels is anachronistic here; according to patriarchal genealogies Ishmael himself would have been a contemporary of Joseph, and evidence of domesticated camels is first found in twelfth-century Egyptian records.)

During the period of the judges the Ishmaelites are again closely linked with the Midianites. Upon defeating the latter Gideon obtained some of their gold earrings from the Israelite spoils; Judg. 8:24 suggests that these were a distinguishing mark of the Ishmaelites.

Individual Ishmaelites are mentioned in Chronicles. These include Jether, who with David's sister Abigail was parent to Amasa (1 Chr. 2:17); and Obil, who was responsible for King David's camels (27:30). At Ps. 83:6 [MT 7], the Ishmaelites are counted among the peoples who conspired against Israel.

ISHMAIAH [ĭsh mā'yə] (Heb. *yišma'yâ* "Yahweh hears").

1. A Gibeonite, a leader of the Benjaminite thirty and one of the mighty men who came to David's aid at Ziklag (1 Chr. 12:4; KJV "Ismaiah").

2. The son of Obadiah, chief officer of Zebulun at the time of David (1 Chr. 27:19).

ISHMERAI [ĭsh'mə rī] (Heb. *yišmᵉray* "the Lord protects"). A son of Epaal; head of a Benjaminite father's house (1 Chr. 8:18).

ISHPAH [ĭsh'pə] (Heb. *yišpâ*). A son of Beriah, from the tribe of Benjamin (1 Chr. 8:16; KJV "Ispah").

ISHPAN [ĭsh'păn] (Heb. *yišpān*). A Benjaminite, son of Shashak (1 Chr. 8:22).

ISHTAR [ĭsh'tär].* The Assyrian goddess of the Morning and Evening Star (the planet Venus) and of love and fertility; the equivalent of the Sumerian Inanna (Innin). The offspring of the moon-god Sin and consort of Anu, the god of heaven, Ishtar may originally have been a male deity (cf. OSA, Canaanite Athtar). During the early second millennium B.C. Ishtar also became known as goddess of war; it was in this capacity that she was instrumental in the election of kings and their protector in battle. In time Ishtar came to be the predominant Assyrian goddess, assimilating the characteristics of several inferior goddesses. Represented by the eight-pointed star, she is occasionally called Belit ("Mistress" or "Lady").

Ishtar is associated with the vegetation deity Tammuz (Sum. Dumuzi). In the myth of her descent to the netherworld Ishtar is imprisoned and afflicted by the goddess Ereškigal, escaping only through the assistance of Ea, goddess of wisdom. During her captivity all fertility and production cease.

Ishtar was worshipped in various manifestations at Uruk, Nineveh, and Arbela, as well as by the Hurrians and Hittites. Her cult often included ritual prostitution and ecstatic prophecy. At Babylon Nebuchadnezzar II erected an elaborate gate in her honor, marking the end of the sacred processional route.

The Queen of Heaven worshipped in the latter years of Judah (Jer. 7:18; 44:17-19, 25) may be a manifestation of Ishtar, perhaps introduced by Manasseh (2 Kgs. 21).

ISH-TOB [ĭsh′tŏb].* KJV translation of Heb. *ʾĭš-ṭôb* "men of Tob" (so RSV) at 2 Sam. 10:6, 8. *See* TOB.

ISHVAH [ĭsh′və] (Heb. *yišwâ*). The second son of Asher (Gen. 46:17; KJV "Ishuah"; 1 Chr. 7:30; KJV "Isuah"). He is not mentioned among the families of Asher's sons at Num. 26:44.

ISHVI [ĭsh′vī] (Heb. *yišwî*).

1. The third son of Asher (Gen. 46:17; KJV "Isui"; Num. 26:44; KJV "Jesui"; 1 Chr. 7:30; KJV "Ishuai"), whose descendants are called the Ishvites (Num. 26:44; KJV "Jesuites").

2. A son of Saul (1 Sam. 14:49; KJV "Ishui"). Some scholars would identify him with Ishbosheth.

ISIS [ī′sĭs].* An Egyptian goddess, the "giver of life"; sister and wife of the grain-god Osiris, in whose absence she served as regent, and mother of Horus, considered the ancestor of all pharaohs. Isis had great magical powers and was the protector of children. She assimilated the characteristics of Hathor, Septet/Sothis, and several other goddesses.

According to mythology Isis sought the corpse of the murdered Osiris, hovering above it in the form of a swallow. Her tears of mourning were said to be the origin of the annual Nile flood. She later gathered the dismembered parts of Osiris' body, mutilated by his brother and rival Seth, and with the aid of other gods brought him back to life. In another myth she poisons the sun-god Re until he divulges the name of the supreme god.

From meager origins in the delta province of Sebennytus, Isis was elevated with her family to the pantheon of Re. Her cult flourished throughout the Greco-Roman world until the sixth century A.D.

ISLAND, ISLE (Heb. *ʾîy*; Gk. *nēsíon, nésos*).† The islands cited in the Bible are those of the Mediterra-

nean Sea; among those specifically mentioned are Caphtor (probably Crete), Cauda, Cyprus, Malta, and Patmos. The KJV frequently translates the Hebrew term as "isle" or "island" in passages where the context shows its meaning to be "coast" or "coastland" (so RSV), i.e., the eastern Mediterranean coastland including areas from Egypt to Phoenicia (e.g., Gen. 10:5; Ps. 97:1); thus the essential meaning of the Hebrew is probably "land adjacent to the sea," whether on island or mainland.

ISMACHIAH [ĭz′mə kī′ə] (Heb. *yišmakyāhû* "Yahweh supports"). A Levite at the time of King Hezekiah. He was an overseer of the temple tax (2 Chr. 31:13).

ISMAIAH (1 Chr. 12:4, KJV). *See* ISHMAIAH **1.**

ISPAH (1 Chr. 8:16, KJV). *See* ISHPAH.

ISRAEL [ĭz′rē əl, ĭs′rə əl] (Heb. *yisrāʾēl*).†

1. The alternate name of the patriarch JACOB, given to him after he wrestled with God at Peniel (Gen. 32:28 [MT 29]). At 35:10 God bestows the name on the occasion of his promise to Jacob at Bethel.

Gen. 32:28 explains the name by the popular etymology "He who strives with God" (NJV "beings divine and human"; cf. JB mg. "May God show his strength"), from Heb. *šārâ* "contend." Other interpretations suggest that the root means "persevere" or that the name derives from *šrr* "rule," *yšr* "be upright," or *ʾšr* "happy, blessed."

2. The name ascribed to the descendants of Jacob as well as to the socio-political organization (ideally the twelve tribes who traced their origins to Jacob's sons) which in Old Testament times constituted the "people of God." It occurs, in parallel with Jacob, in what scholars consider the earliest poetic components of the Bible (e.g., Gen. 49:2, 7; Num. 23:7, 10, 23; Deut. 33:10). A frequent designation for this entity is "sons [KJV "children"] of Israel" (Heb. *bᵉnê yisrāʾēl*); similar usages include "house of Israel" (*bêt yisrāʾēl*) and "kingdom of Israel" (*mamleket yisrāʾēl*). In poetic usage the name Jeshurun also occurs (Deut. 32:15; 33:5, 26; Isa. 44:2). The gentilic "Israelite" occurs only rarely (Lev. 24:10; 2 Sam. 17:25; 1 Chr. 2:17).

Israel is first attested outside the Bible in the Egyptian Merneptah stele (*ca.* 1225 B.C.; *ANET,* p. 378), which commemorates the pharaoh's conquests in Palestine. The Moabite Stone (*ca.* 380; *ANET,* p. 320) mentions Omri, "king of Israel" (the northern kingdom). In the annals of the Assyrian king Shalmaneser III (858-824; *ANET,* p. 279) King Ahab is called "the Israelite" (*ᵐᵃᵗSir-ʾi-la-a-a*); in general Akkadian texts refer to the northern kingdom as the "land" (*mat*) or "house of Omri" (*bît Ḫu-um-ri-a*).

I. Formative Period

The precise circumstances of Israel's origins as a people are difficult to ascertain and subject to interpretation of the biblical accounts and supplementary historical data. Gen. 11:31ff. points to God's call of Abram to migrate with his family from Ur of the Chaldees to Canaan, with the promise that they would become a great nation. Diverse origins are suggested by the historical "credo" at Deut. 26:5-9, which traces Israel's descent from "a wandering (NJV "fugitive") Aramean"; cf. Ezek. 16:3: "Your origin and your birth are of the land of the Canaanites; your father was an Amorite, and your mother a Hittite." The emergence of Israel may be reckoned, in an anthropological sense, to evidence of the people's conception of themselves as distinct from neighboring peoples (e.g., Moabites, Ammonites, Gen. 13:9; Edomites, 25:19-34; Arabian tribes, 21:13, 20) or, politically and militarily, to Joshua's wars of conquest or the conflict of Samson, Saul, and David with the Philistines.

The Exodus from Egypt and the subsequent wilderness wanderings are important biblical themes, and the events associated with them may be reckoned justifiably as the beginnings of the people Israel (cf. Deut. 32:9-10). Linked to Jacob's migration to Egypt in patriarchal times (Gen. 46-47), the Exodus tradition encompasses the subjection of Jacob's descendants to slave labor (Exod. 1), the efforts of Moses to gain their release (plague narratives; chs. 7:8-11:10), the Passover (ch. 12), and the deliverance at the Red Sea (chs. 14-15). The revelation of the name Yahweh (3:14) and the Sinai covenant (chs. 19-24) each may also be regarded specifically as the origin of Israel.

Following M. Noth, many scholars have focused on the Confederation of the twelve tribes as the formative point in Israel's history. Whatever the circumstances of Israel's establishment in Canaan (conquest, settlement or infiltration, revolution), the result of the Shechem covenant (Josh. 24) was a religious and ethical union centered on allegiance to Yahweh as sovereign. Some scholars have suggested that it was at this point that the whole of Israel adopted Yahweh worship and, concomitantly, the Exodus tradition as a common heritage. (Thus the *-el* component of the name designating this Yahwistic people may derive from an earlier, pre-Yahwistic association of clans or tribes within the Confederation.)

II. Monarchy

The "charismatic" leadership of the period of the judges, characterized by shifting configurations of tribal alliances and relative anarchy (Judg. 21:25), proved politically ineffective in the face of resurgent ancient Near Eastern powers, most immediately the Philistines. Accordingly, the people demanded a traditional monarchy (1 Sam. 8). In many ways a charismatic leader typical of the judges (cf. 11:1ff.), Saul was chosen king at Gibeon, apparently only over a coalition of the northern tribes; the remaining tribes were to constitute Judah, which came under the aegis of David.

David's kingdom, traditionally identified as the beginning of the "United Monarchy" because it constituted the later "divided" kingdoms of north and south, is increasingly recognized as a dual monarchy which united under a powerful and crafty ruler two separate coalitions of tribes (cf. the separate accounts of David's accession; 2 Sam. 2:1-11; 5:1-5; also 19:44), solidified by the selection of Jerusalem (formerly Jebus) as capital. The permanent militia, organized to ward off the Philistine threat, along with David's economic and military administrative system provided the basis for the subsequent expansion of Israel's territory "from

Dan to Beersheba" (24:2). Yet although firmly established as a political state, Israel under David lost sight of the covenant ideals and became increasingly paganized.

Solomon faced the challenge not only of broadening his own political base but of prolonging Israel's "Golden Age" and, indeed, preserving the tenuous unity of the empire. He took decisive measures to bolster the central government by realigning administrative districts across traditional tribal lines (1 Kgs. 4:7-19) and assumed an active role in matters related to the newly constructed temple (e.g., 2:27, 35; 8:14-66). Furthermore, he sought to strengthen Israel economically through international trade (9:26-28; 10:11; 2 Chr. 9:14), diplomatically by means of numerous alliances (cf. 1 Kgs. 11:1-3), and militarily by establishing a chariot force (10:28-29) and through construction of border fortresses and other installations (9:19). But the taxation and forced labor necessary to provide these measures (5:13; 9:15ff.) overburdened the populace, and Solomon's accommodation of non-Israelite religion (cf. 11:1-13, 33) significantly modified the nation's character.

III. Northern Kingdom

Following the death of Solomon *ca.* 922 B.C. the northern tribes (with the exception of Benjamin) refused to sanction the Davidic successor Rehoboam, ostensibly because he would not pledge to alleviate their economic constraints (1 Kgs. 12:1-15), and thus dissolved the dual monarchy (v. 16). Jeroboam of Ephraim was acclaimed king of the northern kingdom (12:20; cf. 11:29-40), which retained the name Israel. Ruling from Shechem (or perhaps a number of "capitals"), he established at Bethel and Dan royal shrines to rival Jerusalem (12:26-29).

Continual warfare with Judah (vv. 21-24; 14:30; 15:16), primarily over boundaries, and the threat imposed by the resurgence of other ancient Near Eastern states contributed to (or compounded) the instability of the newly formed state. In the second year of his reign Nadab, the son of Jeroboam I, was assassinated by Baasha of Issachar, who usurped the throne and executed all remaining rivals of Jeroboam's line (vv. 27-29). Baasha's own son and successor Elah met a similar fate at the hand of his officer Zimri (16:8-12), who ruled but seven days before committing suicide under siege by the general Omri (vv. 15-18), whom the army proclaimed king.

Having overcome a rival faction headed by Tibni (16:21-22), Omri established himself as king (v. 23). According to extrabiblical sources he demonstrated considerable ability, subduing Moab and forming alliances with the Phoenicians. Following the precedent of David at Jerusalem, he founded as his capital Samaria, which he had purchased as his personal property (v. 24). Material and political prosperity continued under Omri's son Ahab, who fortified cities (22:39), allied with Judah (ch. 22; 2 Kgs. 8:26), and was able for a time to withstand the Arameans of Damascus (1 Kgs. 20, 22) and to resist the Assyrians at Qarqar (cf. *ANET,* pp. 278-79). Yet despite their political expertise the Omrides exhibited little concern for the ideals of Israel's covenant with Yahweh. This is particularly exemplified by Ahab's accommodation of the Melqart cult fostered by his Tyrian wife Jezebel (1 Kgs. 16:32-33; 18:19) and his disregard for the inviolability of the land as a trust from the Lord (ch. 22).

With the support of the prophet Elisha, the army officer Jehu raised a bloody coup against the ineffectual Jehoram and the vestiges of Omride rule (2 Kgs. 9–10). Jehu's religious purge, however, lost him and his successors, Jehoahaz and Joash, the support of their Phoenician and Judean allies and thus weakened Israel against the resurgence of Damascus and Moab (10:32-33; 13:20). The power vacuum created by the decline of Damascus and Assyria allowed Israel under Jeroboam II to regain territory and to enjoy peace and, for the privileged class, prosperity (cf. Amos 2:6-8; 5:10-12).

Following the death of Jeroboam II in 753, the northern kingdom experienced almost continual internal turmoil. In a twenty-year span, five kings occupied the throne: Zechariah, Shallum, Menahem, Pekahiah, Pekah; palace intrigue and civil war were the norm, and the people looked to Egypt and Assyria for aid. Although he endured as monarch for ten years, Menahem was forced to tax the nobility (2 Kgs. 15:19-20) to raise tribute for Tiglath-pileser III of Assyria, who later apparently seized territory along Israel's northern coast. Pekah allied with Damascus and other neighboring states against Assyria, but Judah refused to cooperate; the Syro-Ephraimite allies attacked Jerusalem, and Ahaz of Judah appealed to Tiglath-pileser to intervene. In 733 the Assyrians obliged, dividing Galilee and Transjordan into three provinces, deporting the urban nobility, and installing their own leaders (v. 29). Hoshea, leader of the pro-Assyrian faction, bought time for Israel, usurping the throne and submitting to Assyria (v. 30; *ANET*, p. 284)

But early in the reign of Shalmaneser V, Hoshea rebelled, refusing tribute and foolishly soliciting assistance from an Egyptian state then in disarray (2 K. 17:4). Assyrian forces immediately captured the Israelite king and all of his kingdom save the capital. Two years later (722/721) Samaria fell to Shalmaneser. His successor, Sargon II, deported the populace to Mesopotamia and Media (v. 6) and resettled other captive peoples—the forebears of the Samaritans—in their place as the basis of the new Assyrian province Samerīna (vv. 24ff.; *ANET*, pp. 284-85). As a political state Israel ceased to exist.

For parallel events in the history of the southern kingdom, see JUDAH.

IV. Concept

Whatever the earliest (pre-Yahwistic) associations of the name Israel, in the biblical accounts the concept is first and foremost the people of God (Heb. *'am-YHWH;* cf. Judg. 5:11, 13; 1 Sam. 2:24), no matter what their historical, political configuration. Thus the name is used on occasion to designate the southern kingdom, Judah, following the fall of Samaria (e.g., Isa. 5:7; Jer. 10:1) or the postexilic restoration community (Ezra 2:2). Implicit in the national consciousness was the notion of this people as a cultic community bound by covenant with "Yahweh, the God of Israel" (e.g., Josh. 24:2, 23; Judg. 11:23) who chose them as his own for faithful service (cf. Isa. 49:3). This religious ideal underlies the prophetic promises of res-

toration for a faithful remnant (e.g., 43:14–44:5) and the creation of a "New Israel" (Jer. 30–31). This vision was eventually expanded to include "non-Israelites" (cf. Isa. 2:3 par.; 45:14, 22-23; Zech. 8:20-23).

In the New Testament also Israel is understood primarily as the people of God, genealogical descendants of the nation Israel as well as those who have covenanted with Yahweh (e.g., Matt. 8:10 par.; 19:28; cf. Jdt. 4:1; 2 Macc. 1:25-26). Thus Jesus as the "King of Israel" (John 1:49; 12:13) is sovereign over the people of God. In some passages the concept of Israel has been extended to encompass the followers of Christ (e.g., Acts 13:23; cf. Rom. 11); in others—particularly the Pauline epistles—a clear distinction is made between those who are Israelites "according to the flesh" (cf. Rom. 9:2; 1 Cor. 10:18) and the true "Israel of God" (Gal. 6:16). Indeed, the emerging view is that Christians have supplanted "the Jews" as the elect people of God (1 Pet. 2:9-10; cf. Rom. 9:6-13; Gal. 4:21-31; Heb. 1:1-2).

See further the individual articles on specific individuals and events.

Bibliography. W. F. Albright, *From the Stone Age to Christianity,* 2nd ed. (Garden City: 1957); J. Bright, *A History of Israel,* 3rd ed. (Philadelphia: 1981); J. H. Hayes and J. M. Miller, eds., *Israelite and Judaean History.* OTL (1977); R. de Vaux, *The Early History of Israel,* 2 vols. (Philadelphia: 1978); H.-J. Zobel, "yiśrā'ēl," *TDOT* 6.

ISSACHAR [ĭs'ə kər] (Heb. K *yiśśāḵār*; Q *yiśśāḵār* "hired worker" or "let there be recompense").†

1. The ninth son of Jacob, the fifth born by Leah; his birth and the etymology of the name are associated with Reuben's discovery of mandrakes in the field (Gen. 30:14-18). He was the eponymous ancestor of an Israelite tribe (cf. the lists of descendants at 46:13; Num. 26:23-25; 1 Chr. 7:1-5).

The tribal territory of Issachar was bounded by Manasseh on the south and west, Zebulun and Naphtali on the north, and the river Jordan on the east. The region included Mt. Tabor (where they shared a sanctuary with Zebulun; Deut. 33:18-19), part of the valley of Jezreel, and such cities as Jezreel and Shunem (Josh. 19:17-23). While the heart of Issachar's settlement was on the plateau between Mt. Tabor and the river Jalud, the tribal allotment apparently extended south of the Jalud and included Mt. Gilboa; perhaps isolated from the main Issachar occupation by unconquered Canaanite territory, this southern portion was annexed by Manasseh (cf. 17:10-11; cf. R. G. Boling and G. E. Wright, *Joshua.* AB 6 [1982]: 413).

Issachar was a large tribe (cf. Num. 1:28-29; 26:25), characterized in the Blessing of Moses as a "strong ass," situated in a good and beautiful land (Gen. 49:14-15), sitting astride major trade routes to the sea (cf. Deut. 33:18-19). In love with the riches of trade and the land, the tribe submitted itself to forced labor (or perhaps simply a vassal relationship) for the Canaanites like an obliging pack animal that lets itself be overburdened (Gen. 49:14-15).

Issachar regained its independence when Deborah led it to victory against Jabin and Sisera (Judg. 5:15). Prominent leaders from the tribe include Tola the judge

(10:1-2), and the Israelite kings Baasha who established his capital and the royal residence within its borders (1 Kgs. 15:27–16:4), and Elah (vv. 5-10). During the monarchy Issachar was known for its knowledge (1 Chr. 12:32), its wealth (v. 40), and its continuing faithfulness (2 Chr. 30:18).

2. The seventh son of Obed-edom; a Korahite gatekeeper at the time of David (1 Chr. 26:5).

ISSIAH [ĭ shī'ə] (Heb. *yiššîyâ, yiššîyāhû* "may Yahweh forget [my sin]'").

1. A son of Izrahiah, descendant of Uzzi from the tribe of Issachar (1 Chr. 7:3; KJV "Ishiah").

2. One of the warriors who joined David's forces at Ziklag (1 Chr. 12:6 [MT 7]; Heb. *yiššîyāhû*; KJV "Jeshiah").

3. A Levite, the second son of Uzziel (1 Chr. 23:20; KJV "Jesiah"; 24:25).

4. A Levite of the family of Rehabiah (1 Chr. 24:21).

ISSHIJAH [ĭ shī'jə] (Heb. *yiššîyâ* "may Yahweh forget"). A Levite forced by Ezra's reforms to relinquish his foreign-born wife (Ezra 10:31; KJV "Ishijah").

ISUAH (1 Chr. 7:20, KJV). *See* ISHVAH.

ISUI (Gen. 46:17, KJV). *See* ISHVI **1.**

ITALA [ĭ tăl'ə].† One of the earliest Latin versions of the Bible (Augustine *De Doctr. Christ.* ii.15.22), generally presumed to have been completed prior to or independent of the Vulgate (although some scholars identify it with that work). Itala is sometimes used as a collective designation for the Vetus Latina (OLD LATIN Versions) and is also taken as specifying the Italian branch of that text. It is sometimes called Italia, which may derive from a version popular in northern Italy.

ITALIAN COHORT (Gk. *speíra Italikḗ*).† A Roman military unit stationed at Caesarea (Acts 10:1; KJV "Italian band"). The centurion Cornelius, a Gentile "God-fearer," was an officer in this unit. Since Caesarea was the capital of Palestine under the Roman procurators, the name of this cohort probably means that it was made up of all native Romans, "regular" troops and not auxiliaries. Inscriptions support the presence of this unit in Caesarea from A.D. 69 to 157.

In the Roman military structure, a cohort represented one tenth of a legion. Ideally, a cohort consisted of 600 legionaries, but auxiliary cohorts such as those stationed in Palestine had 760 foot soldiers and 240 cavalry. The biblical use of the term, however, is less precise (cf. 2 Macc. 8:21, where the term describes one quarter of an army numbering 6,000 soldiers, thus 1,500 men); indeed, a unit of such size would not have been needed to arrest Jesus in Gethsemane (John 18:3, 12). It seems better, therefore, to understand a cohort as simply a military subunit of indeterminate size.

ITALY (Gk. *Italia*).† Originally the southern "toe" portion of the Mediterranean peninsula separating the Tyrrhenian and Adriatic seas. By the mid-third century B.C. the name came to designate the entire region

south of Liguria and Cisalpine Gaul; in popular usage it referred to all territory south of the Alps (Polybius *Hist.* v.29). The Romans designated as Italian all non-Roman inhabitants of the peninsula. Traditionally the name is held as deriving from a thirteenth-century king known as Italus (Dionysius of Halicarnassus *Rom. Arch.* i.12.35); some scholars trace it to *Vitelia* "Calf Land," an early designation for the southwestern toe region.

Geographically, Italy can be divided into two distinct parts. Continental Italy, comprised of the Po valley in the north, was a rustic, backward district in ancient times, isolated from the forefront of Mediterranean culture. Peninsular Italy stretches some 1050 km. (650 mi.) from north to south along its rocky backbone, the Apennine mountains; its greatest width is 240 km. (150 mi.). Lesser ranges further divide the region into numerous compartments, producing distinct cultural groups and long hampering political unification. The only navigable river is the Tiber, which flows through Rome.

Italy was inhabited as early as Paleolithic times. The earliest cultural groups included the Liguorians and the lake-dwelling Palafitte. These were supplanted in the Bronze Age by the Indoeuropean Terramara in the north and the Apennine culture in central Italy. Villanovan culture was an important Iron Age (first millennium) influence, as was the influx of peoples from Anatolia and the Near East. Greek colonies were established on the southern coast and Sicily, and Phoenician culture was introduced by Carthaginian merchants. The Etruscans, who formed a twelve-city league in Etruria on the western side of the peninsula, extended their control north into the Po valley and south into Latium and Campania; at the height of their power they joined with Carthage to drive the Greeks from Corsica (535). The expansion of Rome under the Republic (after 509) brought conquest of and alliance with the various Italian states (by 264); in 90 B.C. Roman citizenship was extended to all Italy. After the fall of the Roman Empire in A.D. 476 Italy remained divided until 1870.

Paul met Aquila and Priscilla at Corinth after they were driven from Italy by Claudius' expulsion of the Jews from Rome (Acts 18:2). After Paul was set free by Agrippa, he and his companions set sail on an Alexandrian ship bound for Rome (Acts 27:1, 6). The letter to the Hebrews concludes with an ambiguous expression of greetings from "those who come from Italy" (Heb. 13:24).

See ROME.

ITHAI [ĭth'ī] (Heb. *'îtay*).* A Benjaminite, the son of Ribai of Gibeah; a mighty man of David's army (1 Chr. 11:31). In the parallel account (2 Sam. 23:29) he is called Ittai (**2**).

ITHAMAR [ĭth'ə mär] (Heb. *'îtāmār* "place of palms"). The youngest son of Aaron (Exod. 6:23; 1 Chr. 6:3 [MT 5:32]; 24:1).

Together with his father and brothers, Ithamar was consecrated to serve as a priest (Exod. 28:1; 1 Chr. 24:2; cf. Lev. 8–9); he and Eleazar gained prominence when Nadab and Abihu were destroyed (Lev. 10; Num. 3:4). Ithamar was responsible for calculating the gold, silver, and copper used for the tabernacle, i.e., for tallying the costs (Exod. 38:21). As head of the Gershonites and the Merarites, he directed their responsibilities in service to the tabernacle (Num. 4:21-33). The organization of his priestly line is denoted at 1 Chr. 24:4-6. The priestly line of Eli at Shiloh was apparently descended from Ithamar, and one of his descendants, Daniel (2), returned from exile with Ezra (Ezra 8:2).

ITHIEL [ĭth'ĭ əl] (Heb. *'îṯî'ēl* "God is with me").
1. A Benjaminite in postexilic Jerusalem; ancestor of Sallu (Neh. 11:7).
2. A person addressed, with Ucal, in the wisdom discourse of Agur the son of Jakeh (Prov. 30:1). The terms are not rendered as proper names in the LXX or Vulgate, and various translations have been proposed. For example, Heb. *le'îṯî'ēl* can also be read as *lā'îṯî'ēl*, meaning "I am weary, O God," and *wᵉ'uḵāl* as *wā'ēḵel* "I faint" or "pine away."

ITHLAH [ĭth'lə] (Heb. *yiṯlâ* "height"). A city in the tribal territory of Dan (Josh. 19:42; KJV "Jethlah"). The location is unknown, although some have suggested modern Siltah, 7 km. (4.3 mi.) northwest of Beth-horon.

ITHMAH [ĭth'mə] (Heb. *yiṯmâ*). A Moabite, and one of David's mighty men (1 Chr. 11:46).

ITHNAN [ĭth'năn] (Heb. *yiṯnān*). A city in the Negeb, on the southern border of the tribal territory of Judah (Josh. 15:23). Located near Kedesh and Ziph, the site, though not decisively identified, may be modern Khirbet el-Jebarîyeh on the Wâdî Umm Ethnān, 60 km. (37 mi.) southwest of Beer-sheba. Some scholars read the name with the preceding town, thus Hazor-ithnan.

ITHRA [ĭth'rə] (Heb. *yiṯrā'*).* The father of Amasa and husband of David's sister Abigail. At 2 Sam. 17:25 the MT calls him an Israelite (so RSV mg.; NIV "Jether, an Israelite"), but the LXX reading "Ishmaelite" is considered correct (so 1 Chr. 2:17, "Jether the Ishmaelite"; see JETHER 2).

ITHRAN [ĭth'răn] (Heb. *yiṯrān*).
1. A son of Dishon and grandson of Seir the Horite (Gen. 36:26; 1 Chr. 1:41).
2. A son of Zophah of the tribe of Asher (1 Chr. 7:37); probably the same as JETHER 4.

ITHREAM [ĭth'rĭ əm] (Heb. *yiṯrᵉ'ām* "abundance of people"). The sixth son of David, born at Hebron to his wife Eglah (2 Sam. 3:5 par. 1 Chr. 3:3).

ITHRITES [ĭth'rīts] (Heb. *yiṯrî*). A clan or similar unit from the tribe of Judah located at Kiriath-jearim (1 Chr. 2:53). Ira and Gareb, two of David's mighty men, came from this group (2 Sam. 23:38; 1 Chr. 11:40). Some interpreters believe the Ithrites were derived from a person named Jether or a city by the name of Jattir or Jether.

ITTAH-KAZIN (Josh. 19:13, KJV, JB). *See* ETH-KAZIN.

ITTAI [ĭt'ĭ] (Heb. *'ittay, 'iṯay* "father" or "[God] is with him").
1. A man from Gath, commander of six hundred Philistines who remained loyal to David during Absalom's rebellion (2 Sam. 15:19-22). David named him, along with Joab and Abishai, to lead his forces in battle at the forest of Ephraim (18:2, 5).
2. The son of Ribai from Gibea of Benjamin; one of David's mighty men (2 Sam. 23:29). He is called Ithai at 1 Chr. 11:31.

ITURAEA [ĭt'ōˌōr ē'ə] (Gk. *Itouraia* "land of the Ituraeans"). A region to the northeast of Galilee, part of the tetrarchy of Philip (Luke 3:1). The name comes from the Ituraeans, a people of Ishmaelite stock (the Jetur of Gen. 25:15; 1 Chr. 1:31; 5:19).

The Ituraeans were driven from their original Transjordanian home by the people of Israel, possibly as early as the initial Israelite settlement in Palestine (5:19) or David's reign (so Eupolemos in Eusebius *Praep. ev.* ix.30). They settled in the region of Mt. Hermon and the Anti-lebanon and became notorious for their barbarity and banditry (Strabo *Geog.* xvi.2.20; Cicero *Philippicae* ii.112). When Josephus speaks of Aristobulus (104-103 B.C.) forcing the Ituraeans to convert to Judaism (*Ant.* xiii.3 [318]), he is referring to inhabitants of Galilee, which had been within the Ituraean sphere of influence but was thenceforth associated with Judea. The Ituraeans' short-lived political independence (*ca.* 85-37 B.C.), with a capital at Chalcis in the Beqaʿ valley, ended before the Roman rise to power. Repeated Roman redistribution of the region into various political units has obscured boundaries; nevertheless, Ituraean territory apparently was for the most part added to the kingdom of Herod the Great and the province of Syria.

Philip's tetrarchy, described by Luke as consisting of Iturea and Trachonitis, included with the regions east and northeast of the Sea of Galilee (Gaulanitis, Batanea, Trachonitis, and Auranitis) probably only the southern part of the region that had been ruled by the Ituraeans, namely, the area around Philip's capital of Caesarea Philippi on the southern slopes of Mt. Hermon. It is possible that the phrase "and Trachonitis" employs Gk. *kaí* "and, even" in an explanatory sense; thus the tetrarchy would be referred to as "the region of the Ituraeans, that is, Trachonitis." In any case, Philip's domain is to be distinguished from the parts of the former kingdom of the Ituraeans ruled by Lysanias under the name of Abilene and later under the direct rule of Rome as part of the province of Syria.

IVORY (Heb. *šēn* "tooth," *šenhabbîm*, perhaps "tooth (i.e., tusk) of elephant"; Gk. *elephántinos*).†
In the Bible as throughout the ancient world, raw ivory and ivory carvings were a token of wealth and luxury (cf. Amos 6:4), to be traded (Ezek. 27:15; Rev. 18:12), treasured, and demanded in tribute (*ANET*, pp. 237, 282).

Although tusks or teeth of several large mammals could be used, the preferred source of ivory was elephant tusk, acquired from herds in northern Syria, or by trade with Africa and India (cf. 1 Kgs. 10:22). Prized for its color, with a texture and hardness similar to wood, ivory was used in intricate inlays (e.g., Ezek.

Important discoveries of ivory carvings in Palestine include a large Canaanite cache at Megiddo (stratum VII, *ca.* twelfth century B.C.) and more than five hundred pieces at Samaria (*ca.* eighth century). Other important finds in Syria-Palestine include an inlaid bedframe from Arslan Tash, several exquisite pieces from Ugarit, as well as numerous pieces from Nimrûd. The close similarity of the Nimrûd ivories to finds in Samaria leads many to think they are booty and tribute from Assyrian campaigns against Syria and Israel (cf. *ANET,* p. 288).

The author of the Song of Solomon uses ivory in two metaphors: the lover's body (KJV "belly") is like an ivory statue, smooth, shining, adorned with jewels (Cant. 5:14); while the beloved's neck is an "ivory tower" (7:4), stately like the towers of Jerusalem (cf. 4:4).

Bibliography. *ANEP,* nos. 125-132; W. G. Dever and S. M. Paul, eds., *Biblical Archaeology* (New York: 1973), pp. 204-207; N. Avigad, "Samaria," *EAEHL* 4: 1039, 1044-46.

IVVAH [ĭv'ə] (Heb. *'iwwâ*).† A Syrian city-state among those captured by the Assyrians in the eighth century B.C. (2 Kgs. 18:34; 19:13; Isa. 37:13; KJV "Ivah"). It may be the same as Avva (2 Kgs. 17:24; KJV "Ava"), residents of which the Assyrians uprooted and settled in Samaria after the defeat of the northern kingdom.

IYE-ABARIM [ī'yə āb'ə rĭm] (Heb. *'îyê hā'ăbārîm* "ruins of Abarim"). A place in the desert, east of Moab (Num. 21:11; 33:44; KJV "Ije-abarim"), where the Israelites camped during the wilderness wanderings. At 33:45 it is called Iyim. It is probably in the vicinity of Mahaiy, southeast of the Dead Sea near the brook Zered.

IYIM [ī'yĭm] (Heb. *'îyîm* "mounds").* A contracted form of Iye-abarim (Num. 33:45; KJV "Iim").

IYYAR [ē'yär] (Heb. *'îyār*). The second month of the Hebrew calendar (April/May); this name, derived from Akkadian usage, superseded the Canaanite name Ziv.

IZHAR [ĭz'här] (Heb. *yiṣhār* "may [God] be radiant").†
1. A Levite, a descendant of Kohath and father of Korah (Exod. 6:18, 21; Num. 16:1; 1 Chr. 6:18, 38 [MT 2, 22]). He is the eponymous ancestor of the Izharites (Num. 3:19, 27; KJV "Izehar"; 1 Chr. 26:23). At 6:22 (MT 6) he is called Amminadab (**2**).
2. A Judahite whose mother was Helah (1 Chr. 4:7; K *yiṣhār*; KJV "Jezoar"). Some scholars view this name as a variant of Zohar (cf. Q *wᵉṣōhar* "and Zohar").

IZLIAH [ĭz lī'ə] (Heb. *yizlî'â* "eternal"). A son of Elpaal and descendant of Shaharaim from the tribe of Benjamin (1 Chr. 8:18; KJV "Jezliah").

IZRAHIAH [ĭz'rə hī'ə] (Heb. *yizraḥyā* "Yahweh appears" or "shines forth").† The son of Uzzi and descendant of Tola, from the tribe of Issachar (1 Chr.

Eighth-century B.C. ivory plaque found at Nimrûd (British Museum; photo by W. S. LaSor)

27:6), joined together in plaques, or used ornamentally in such artifacts as game boards and cosmetic boxes. Techniques included figures in the round, high and low relief, open work, insets of glass and jewels, and overlays of gold.

In Israel, ivory is especially associated with the king and aristocracy. Solomon's great ivory throne was ornamented with lions and a calf, and overlaid with gold (1 Kgs. 10:18-20 par.); similar pieces for a throne with lions in the round have been found at both Samaria and Nimrûd. The palace that Ahab built, the "ivory house" (22:39; cf. Ps. 45:8 [MT 9]; Amos 3:15), suggests the splendor of his reign as typified by lavish use of ivory inlays in furniture and doors. Artifacts discovered at Samaria employ Egyptian and Syrophoenician themes: e.g., sacred trees, the woman at the window, stags drinking—appropriate ornaments for the son-in-law of the Sidonian king (1 Kgs. 16:31). For Amos, ivory was a symbol of the indolent luxury that ignored God and the needs of the poor (Amos 6:4; cf. 2:6-8).

7:3). At Neh. 12:42 he is called Jezrahiah, leader of the levitical singers at the time of Nehemiah.

IZRAHITE [ĭz′rə hīt] (Heb. *yizrāḥ* "rising, shining"). A gentilic applied to Shamhuth, commander of the fifth division of David's army (1 Chr. 27:8). Although some scholars interpret the name as a derivative of Izrahiah, it is probably related to the Zerahites at v. 11.

IZRI [ĭz′rī] (Heb. *yiṣrî* "[Yahweh] has fashioned" [?]). A leader of the fourth division of temple musicians at the time of David (1 Chr. 25:11), perhaps a "son" (guild member) of Jeduthun. He may be identified with Zeri at v. 3.

IZZIAH [ĭ zī′ə] (Heb. *yizzîyâ* "may Yahweh purify"). An Israelite who had to send away his foreign wife; a son of Parosh (Ezra 10:25; KJV "Jeziah").

J

J. Symbol of the Yahwist (Ger. *Jahvist,* from Heb. *YHWH* "Yahweh" or "the Lord"), the earliest of the primary sources which critics ascribe to the Pentateuch. *See* Biblical Criticism.

JAAKAN [jā′ə kən] (Heb. *yaʿᵃqān*). A Horite, son of Ezer and descendant of Seir (1 Chr. 1:42; KJV "Jakan"; NIV "and Akan"); called Akan at Gen. 36:27. The name occurs also in Bene-Jaakan (Num. 33:31-32) and Beeroth Bene-jaakan (Deut. 10:6), where the Israelites encamped during the wilderness wanderings.

JAAKOBAH [jā′ə kō′bə] (Heb. *yaʿᵃqōḇâ* "may [God] protect"). A prince of the tribe of Simeon (1 Chr. 4:36).

JAALA [jā′ə lə] (Heb. *yaʿᵉlā* "female mountain goat"). One of Solomon's servants, whose descendants (or guild) returned with Zerubbabel from captivity (Neh. 7:58). At Ezra 2:56 he is called Jaalah (Heb. *yaʿᵉlâ*).

JAALAM. *See* Jalam.

JAANAI (1 Chr. 5:12, KJV). *See* Janai.

JAAR [jā′ər] (Heb. *yaʿar* "forest").† Place where the ark of the covenant is said to have been discovered (Ps. 132:6; KJV "the wood"). The name may be a form of Kiriath-jearim, at which the ark had been lodged for twenty years (1 Sam. 7:1-2; 2 Chr. 1:4).

JAARE-OREGIM [jā′ə rī ôr′ə jĭm] (Heb. *yaʿᵃrê ʾōrᵉgîm*).† The father of Elhanan (2 Sam. 21:19), called Jair in the parallel account (1 Chr. 20:5). This form apparently is the result of a scribal error inserting Heb. *ʾōrᵉgîm* ("weavers") from the end of the verse (NIV "Jair the weaver"). *See* Jair 3.

JAARESHIAH [jâr′ə shī′ə] (Heb. *yaʿᵃrešyâ* "may Yahweh plant"). Head of a Benjaminite father's house in Jerusalem (1 Chr. 8:27; KJV "Jaresiah").

JAASIEL [jā ā′zĭ əl] (Heb. *yaʿᵃśîʾēl* "God acts").†
  1. A Mezobaite, one of David's mighty men (1 Chr. 11:47; KJV "Jasiel").

2. The son of Abner; chief of the tribe of Benjamin at the time of David (1 Chr. 27:21). He may be the same as **1.**

JAASU [jā′ə sōō] (Heb. K *yaʿᵃśô,* Q *yaʿᵃśay* "may Yahweh act"). An Israelite who was required to send away his foreign wife (Ezra 10:37; KJV "Jaasau"; NJV "Jaasai"; cf. LXX "and they did").

JAAZANIAH [jā āz′ə nī′ə] (Heb. *yaʿᵃzanyāhû, yaʿᵃzanyâ* "Yahweh hears"). On the basis of inscriptional evidence (including Lachish Ostracon 1), a common name in preexilic Palestine.
  1.† A military captain who remained in Judah following the fall of Jerusalem and aided Gedaliah, the governor appointed by the Babylonians (2 Kgs. 25:23). Called the son of the Maacathite, he may be the same as Jezaniah mentioned at Jer. 42:1 (RSV "Azariah" [25]; cf. 43:2). An engraved seal "belonging to Jaazaniah, servant of the king" was discovered at Tell en-Naṣbeh (Mizpah?) and may have been associated with this individual.
  2. The son of the Rechabite Jeremiah (Jer. 35:3).
  3. The son of Shaphan; in Ezekiel's temple visions one of the elders of Judah who committed idolatry in the Jerusalem temple (Ezek. 8:11).
  4. The son of Azzur; one of twenty-five individuals who gave "wicked counsel" in Jerusalem (Ezek. 11:1).

JAAZER [jā ā′zər] (Num. 21:32; 32:35, KJV). *See* Jazer.

JAAZIAH [jā′ə zī′ə] (Heb. *yaʿᵃzîyāhû* "may Yahweh strengthen"). A son (of follower) of the Levite Merari; father of Beno, Shoham, Zaccur, and Ibri (1 Chr. 24:26-27). He and his descendants are not named among the sons of Merari at Exod. 6:19; 1 Chr. 23:21.

JAAZIEL [jā ā′zĭ əl] (Heb. *yaʿᵃzîʾēl* "may God strengthen"). A Levite of the second order, a gatekeeper and singer at the time of David (1 Chr. 15:18). This name should be read for Aziel at 15:20 and Jeiel at 16:5.

JABAL [jā′bəl] (Heb. *yāḇāl*). The first son of Lamech and Adah; the ancestor of nomadic and transhumant shepherds (Gen. 4:20; cf. v. 2).

JABBOK [jăb′ək] (Heb. *yabbōq*). A major eastern tributary of the Jordan river, now called the Nahr ez-Zerqā ("the blue river") after the color of the water. The Jabbok originates at a spring north of Amman (biblical Rabbah) and flows first north and then northwest through a progressively deeper gorge until it enters the Jordan just north of Tell ed-Dâmiyeh (biblical Adam).

In biblical times the river formed a boundary separating the territory of Sihon, the Amorite king of Heshbon, from that of Ammon and Bashan (Num. 21:24; Deut. 2:37; Josh. 12:2; Judg. 11:13, 22). Jacob crossed the Jabbok when he and his family returned from Paddam-aram (Gen. 32:22).

JABESH [jā′bĭsh] (Heb. *yāḇēš* "arid") (PERSON).* The father of King Shallum of Israel (2 Kgs. 15:10, 13-14). Some scholars suggest that the term is a place name indicating Shallum's provenience.

JABESH [jā′bĭsh] (Heb. *yāḇēš* "arid") (PLACE).* A principal city of Gilead ("Jabesh of Gilead"). *See* JABESH-GILEAD.

JABESH-GILEAD [jā′bĭsh gĭl′ĭ əd] (Heb. *yāḇēš gilʿāḏ* "Jabesh of Gilead").† A city located east of the Jordan river and south of the Sea of Galilee. Many scholars have identified the site as modern Tell el-Maqlûb on the northern side of Wâdī Yâbis, a site first inhabited late in the fourth millennium B.C. and marked by numerous potsherds from Israelite times; Eusebius' identification of this site some 9.7 km. (6 mi.) from Pella on the road to Gerasa (*Onom.* cx.12-13) supports this identification. Recent scholarship favors Tell Abū Kharaz, 32 km. (20 mi.) south of the Sea of Galilee where the wadi joins the Jordan valley.

Jabesh-gilead is first mentioned in Judg. 21, when the Israelites put to the sword nearly all of its inhabitants as punishment for refusing to join in the punitive war against the Benjaminites and Gibeah (vv. 8-12); the four hundred virgins who survived the slaughter were subsequently given as wives to the remaining Benjaminite men so that tribe would not cease to exist (v. 4).

Shortly after Saul was anointed as Israel's first king the nation's sovereignty was challenged when Nahash the Ammonite attacked Jabesh-gilead. The dual intent of this attack was to exact tribute and gain honor for Nahash by mutilating the men of the city (1 Sam. 11:1-2; "Jabesh"). Apparently the Ammonites were so confident of Israel's military impotence that they permitted Jabesh-gilead's inhabitants a week to find rescuers (11:3). Saul forcefully rallied Israel (11:6-7) and thereby gathered a large force, the news of which elated Jabesh-gilead (vv. 9-10). Saul's victory over the Ammonites by means of a dawn attack after a forced march (v. 11) authenticated his kingship in the eyes of many (vv. 12-15).

Jabesh-gilead also figured in events that followed Saul's death. In their triumph over Saul at Mt. Gilboa, the Philistines beheaded him and hung his body and those of his sons on the city wall of Beth-shan (1 Sam. 31:8-10). Upon hearing of this disgrace the valiant men of Jabesh-gilead travelled nearly 63 km. (39 mi.) by night to retrieve the bodies for cremation and burial

at Jabesh (vv. 11-13). Upon being anointed king over Judah, David sent greetings to the people of Jabesh-gilead lauding their act of loyalty to Saul (2 Sam. 2:4b-7); some scholars regard this as an attempt to gain their support for his kingship.

JABEZ [jā′bĭz] (Heb. *yaʿbēṣ*) (PERSON). The eponymous ancestor of a Judahite family (1 Chr. 4:9). The popular etymology that his name derives from a difficult childbirth (Heb. *ʿōṣeb* "pain") is implicit in his prayer for protection from harm (*ʿāṣab*, v. 10).

JABEZ [jā′bĭz] (Heb. *yaʿbēṣ*) (PLACE). A town in Judah, probably near Bethlehem. It was the home of several families of scribes (1 Chr. 2:55).

JABIN [jā′bĭn] (Heb. *yāḇîn* "He [God] builds" or "discerns").

1. A Canaanite king of Hazor who led a coalition against Joshua at the waters of Merom. He was defeated and slain, and Hazor was burned (Josh. 11:1-15).

2. "King of Canaan," the ruler of Hazor who severely oppressed the Israelites during the time of the judges. The Israelites under Deborah and Barak defeated Jabin's forces, commanded by Sisera (regarded by many scholars as king of Harosheth-ha-goiim), thus advancing their control in Canaan (Judg. 4:2-24; 5). Some identify this ruler with (1), but the name appears to be a dynastic title or throne name dating from at least the Mari period.

JABNEEL [jăb′nĭ əl] (Heb. *yabnᵉʾēl* "Yahweh causes to build").

1. A town on the northern boundary of Judah (Josh. 15:11), called Jabneh at 2 Chr. 26:6 and Jamnia in Hellenistic times (cf. 1 Macc. 4:15). For a time the Philistines occupied the town, but King Uzziah recaptured it for Judah (2 Chr. 26:6). According to Eusebius, Jabneel was located between Diospolis (Lydda) and Ashdod. The site is modern Yebnā, a large village on the Nahr Rubin 6.5 km. (4 mi.) from the Mediterranean at a point 14.5 km. (9 mi.) north-northeast of Ashdod.

2. A town on the border of Naphtali (Josh. 19:33), perhaps located at modern Khirbet Yemmā, 11 km. (7 mi.) southwest of Tiberias. Settled in the Bronze Age, this site remained occupied into the Roman-Byzantine and Arabic periods.

JABNEH [jăb′nə] (Heb. *yabneh* "he causes to build"). An alternate name for JABNEEL (1) (2 Chr.26:6).

JACAN [jā′kən] (Heb. *yaʿkān* "saddening"). A man from the tribe of Gad, living in Bashan during the reigns of King Jothan of Judah and King Jeroboam II of Israel (1 Chr. 5:13; KJV "Jachan").

JACHIN [jā′kən] (Heb. *yāḵîn* "he establishes" or "will establish").

1. A son of Simeon and grandson of Jacob (Gen. 46:10; Exod. 6:15), whose descendants constituted the family of the Jachinites (Num. 26:12). At 1 Chr. 4:24 he is called Jarib (KJV mg. "Jachin").

2. The leader of the twenty-first priestly division at the time of David (1 Chr. 24:17). His family was among

those enlisted to repopulate postexilic Jerusalem (1 Chr. 9:10; Neh. 11:10).

JACHIN [jā′kən] (Heb. *yāḵîn* "he will establish") **AND BOAZ** [bō′ăz] (*bō˓az* "in it is strength").† The twin pillars of bronze created for Solomon by Hiram of Tyre, situated to the right and left of the entrance porch of the Jerusalem temple (1 Kgs. 7:15-22, 40-42; 2 Chr. 3:15-17; Jer. 52:20-23). The pillars' names may derive from a dynastic formula inscribed upon them.

Although detailed information is available regarding the pillars' decoration, accounts of their dimensions differ. Their height is recorded as 18 cubits (6.6 m. [22 ft.]) in the MT of Kings and Jeremiah, and as 35 cubits (15.8 m. [52 ft.]) in the LXX of Chronicles and Jeremiah. The MT of Kings and Jeremiah describes their circumference as 12 cubits (5.3 m. [17.5 ft.]) while at 1 Kgs. 7:15 the LXX reads 14 cubits (6.3 m. [21 ft.]).

Jachim and Boaz were hollow and "four fingers" (one-sixth cubit [7.5 cm. (3 in.)]) thick (Jer. 52:21). Each pillar was surmounted by a bowl-shaped capital, decorated by bronze grillwork, lily leaves, and pomegranates The height of the capitals is said to have been 3, 4, or 5 cubits (2 Kgs 25:17; 1 Kgs 7:19; Jer. 52:22, respectively).

Scholars disagree over whether Jachin and Boaz were free-standing or were connected to the temple entrance. The former argument is based on 2 Chr. 3:17, and free-standing temple columns have been excavated in Tyre. The latter position may be supported by 1 Kgs. 6:4 (cf. Akk. *bît ḫilâni*) and temple porticoes with columns found at northern Assyrian sites.

After Jerusalem fell to the Babylonians in 587 B.C. Jachin and Boaz—like many temple furnishings—were broken up, and their metal taken to Babylon (2 Kgs. 25:13-17; Jer. 52:17ff.).

JACINTH [jā′sinth] (Heb. *lešem;* Gk. *hyákinthos*).† In the Old Testament, a reddish-orange precious stone, probably a variety of zircon which varies from translucent to transparent. It was the first stone in the third row of the high priest's breastplate (Exod. 28:19; 39:12; JB "hyacinth"). The KJV renders the term "figure" from LXX Gk. *ligýrion*. Also called electron by the Greeks, this stone was imported by the Phoenicians from the Far West as well as from the mouth of the Po (Ligurian) river in northern Italy.

At Rev. 21:20 the jacinth is the eleventh stone in the foundation of the New Jerusalem. Judging from 9:17, where the adjectival form describes the riders' breastplates, the stone is the dark blue sapphire (so RSV, JB; RSV mg. "hyacinth"). According to ancient sources it was known also in a yellow variety.

JACKAL (Heb. *tannîm* [masc.], *tannôt* [fem.], *tannîn, šû˓āl*).† A doglike, nocturnal, carnivorous mammal (*Canis aureus*) found throughout the eastern Mediterranean. In size and features, the jackal bears similarities to both the wolf and the fox. It is a strongly built animal with a moderately long tail and short ears, and its fur is a mixture of reddish-brown and gray shades. The snout is more pointed than that of a wolf but broader than that of a fox. In lifestyle it resembles the fox, with which it may be confused.

Jackals are social creatures forming packs of up to two hundred individuals; they communicate in long high-pitched howls or wails (Mic. 1:8; cf. Isa. 13:21-22; Jer. 50:39). Jackals wander near cities and villages, attracted by the smell of carrion and refuse, which they prefer above other foods, although they will eat almost anything edible. Although useful in disposing of carrion, jackals cause much damage to poultry, grapes, and vegetable crops, particularly during the dry season.

In biblical usage the jackal occurs most frequently as an image of desolation and desertlike conditions (e.g., Job 30:29; Ps. 44:19 [MT 20]; Isa. 35:7, MT; Jer. 9:11 [MT 10]; 10:22; 14:6; 49:33; 51:37). At Lam. 4:3 the image of a creature suckling its young favors "jackals" rather than KJV "sea monsters."

Some controversy surrounds the translation of Heb. *šû˓āl,* variously rendered in the RSV as "fox" or "jackal." The creature in Ps. 63:10 (MT 11) must be the jackal (so RSV), since foxes do not eat carrion. Lam. 5:18 (RSV) and Ezek. 13:4 (JB, NIV) may also intend jackals rather than foxes in an environment of desolation and ruins.

JACKAL'S WELL (Heb. *˓ên hattannîn*).* A well or spring (so NJV) in the Hinnom valley, situated between the Valley Gate and the Dung Gate (Neh. 2:13; KJV "dragon well"). Some scholars identify the site as En-rogel.

JACOB [jā′kəb] (Heb. *ya˓ăqōḇ;* Gk. *Iakōb*).†

1. The younger son of Isaac and Rebekah, and the twin brother of Esau; patriarch and father of the twelve tribal ancestors of Israel.

The name is linked to Heb. *˓qb,* from which are derived the noun *˓āqēḇ* "heel" and the verb *˓āqaḇ* "to seize at the heel," hence "to beguile" or "to overreach, supplant." The name thus can mean "he takes the heel" or "supplants." These etymologies may well allude to incidents in the patriarch Jacob's life: his grasping of his twin brother Esau's heel at their birth (Gen. 25:26; cf. Hos. 12:3 [MT 4]), and his appropriation of Esau's birthright as firstborn (27:36; cf. Jer. 9:4 [MT 3]). The name may well be a shortened form of *ya˓ăqōḇ-˒ēl* "may God [or El] protect" or "God protects"; this form occurs as the name of places in Palestine conquered by the Egyptian pharaoh Thutmose III (fifteenth century B.C.) and on artifacts dating from the Hyksos period. A similar name appears on Mesopotamian clay tablets dating from the eighteenth century.

Jacob's story occupies a central position in the book of Genesis (Gen. 25–50). The Lord had told Rebekah before their birth that the older son would serve the younger (25:23; cf. Rom. 9:12). Jacob was born grasping Esau's heel (Gen. 25:26). When he grew up he was evidently a quiet pastoralist (v. 27); Esau, a hunter, on the other hand, was rough and impetuous. Once, when Esau was in extreme hunger, Jacob coerced him into selling his birthright in exchange for a pot of lentils (vv. 29-34). Moreover, Jacob, with his mother's urging, received the blessing of the firstborn from his father through imposture (27:1-45). It was Esau's intention to kill Jacob after the death of Isaac, which he supposed was imminent; but Rebekah instructed her favorite son to flee to his uncle Laban in Haran (27:41–28:5).

On his journey from Beer-sheba to Haran, Jacob rested at Bethel, apparently the site of an ancient sanctuary. There he saw in a dream a ladder reaching to heaven on which angels ascended and descended (28:10-17); this structure probably resembled the massive outdoor staircases leading to upper stories in Palestinian houses. At the top of the ladder stood the Lord, who promised Jacob that during his sojourn outside of Canaan, in spite of his sin, he would be protected by God's presence and that, when God so determined, he would return safely to the land of his kindred and occupy the place of the firstborn. Still the bargainer, Jacob promised to serve the Lord if he would indeed protect Jacob and provide him with food, clothing, and a safe return (vv. 20-22).

Jacob's stay with Laban was characterized by trickery on the uncle's part, much in Jacob's own style. Desiring to marry Laban's daughter Rachel, for which right he labored seven years, he was tricked by his host into marrying her unattractive older sister Leah, who was substituted for Rachel on their wedding night (30:15-26); the deceit was possible because the bride was veiled, even in the nuptial bed. Laban then promised that Jacob could indeed marry his beloved Rachel after an additional seven-year period of service (vv. 27-30). In Mesopotamia Jacob fathered eleven sons and one daughter: by the fertile Leah, Reuben, Simeon, Levi, Judah, Issachar, Zebulun, and the daughter Dinah; by Leah's maid Zilpah, Gad and Asher; by the barren Rachel's maid Bilhah, Dan and Naphtali; and finally by Rachel herself, Joseph (29:31–30:24). Laban required that Jacob serve him, not only for his wives, but also for his flocks; again through a cunning bit of scheme and counterscheme, Jacob became prosperous at Laban's expense (vv. 25-43). Finally, when he sensed that Laban and his sons envied him on account of his good fortune, he secretly fled from Haran with his entire household (31:17-21). Laban, further angered at Rachel's theft of the household gods, pursued them, but in a dream God warned him not to harm Jacob (vv. 22-24). Laban and Jacob made a covenant in the hills of Gilead that neither would harm the other, after which Jacob returned home (vv. 44-55 [MT 32:1]).

Despite reassurance of God's continued protection (32:1-2), Jacob feared meeting Esau upon his return through Seir; Jacob's anxiety was heightened by his messengers' report that his brother was already en route with four hundred men. Overcome by fear, he divided his household and flocks in two, so that if Esau could slay one part the other would escape (vv. 3-8). He sought further to ease the meeting by sending lavish gifts to Esau (vv. 14-21). His prayer for divine protection (vv. 9-13) led to the decisive event of his life. At Peniel ("the face of God," v. 32), Jacob met a man with whom he wrestled. Though lamed by a dislocated hip, Jacob would not release his opponent until the man blessed him. From the blessing it became clear that the "man" was God himself, who gave Jacob the new name Israel ("he who strives with God and with men"; v. 28; cf. Hos. 12:4-5). In the end Jacob's encounter with Esau was peaceful and full of brotherly tenderness, but he did not follow Esau to Seir as he had promised, settling instead first at Succoth and then near Shechem (Gen. 33). There Shechem, the son of Hamor, assaulted and dishonored Jacob's daughter Dinah (ch. 35). Her brothers pretended to accept a plan of appeasement whereby the men of Shechem were circumcised, but while the latter were recuperating, Simeon and Levi attacked the city, killing all the males.

Having first buried his family's foreign gods (idols) and amulets under the oak near Shechem, Jacob and his family next journeyed to Bethel in response to God's command (35:1-7). There God appeared again to Jacob, blessed him, confirmed his new name Israel, and promised that "a nation and a company of nations" would come from him and that the land promised to Abraham and Isaac would be given to Israel's descendants (vv. 9-12). Shortly thereafter, as they travelled to Ephrath (Bethlehem), Rachel died after giving birth to Jacob's last son, Benjamin (v. 19).

In the subsequent chapters of Genesis Jacob's story becomes secondary to the story of his favorite son Joseph. In a fit of jealousy reminiscent of Jacob's own jealousy of Esau, Joseph's brothers sold the lad into slavery (37:1-28). Jacob, believing that Joseph had been killed by a beast, swore that he would mourn his son until his own death (vv. 29-35). A last Jacob received the news that his son was in fact alive and ruled over all of Egypt (45:26). Determined to see his son again before he died, Jacob left Canaan for Egypt, receiving along the way at Beer-sheba another promise from God that his offspring would be a great nation in Egypt (46:1-4). When he arrived in Egypt and met Pharaoh (47:1-12), Jacob was 130 years old. Shortly before his death ten years later, he blessed the sons of Joseph, Ephraim and Manasseh (48:8-20), and foretold the future of his twelve sons (ch. 49). He made Judah the heir of the promise (v. 10). According to his own desire, Jacob was buried in Abraham's burial site, the cave at Machpelah (vv. 29-32; 50:13). The Egyptians mourned his death for seventy days, and after his burial his sons returned to Egypt (50:3, 14). The events of Jacob's life cannot be dated with any precision, but can be more generally placed in the early to middle centuries of the Middle Bronze Age (ca. 2000-1700 B.C.).

The Scriptures give an honest portrait of Jacob as a deceiver who thought he could succeed through trickery and human calculation. In the context of the social structures of his time his aim was high: to receive the blessing of the firstborn, which was not a mere expression of good will and hope but a substantive gift which, once given, could not be taken back. For Jacob it involved not only the inheritance of Canaan but also the promise of salvation for his people given to Abraham and Isaac. The paradox of Jacob's life was that his schemes and efforts appeared to be effective; he did receive the blessing of the firstborn, his hard work and scheming in Laban's household did win him prosperity, and most decisively his apparent victory over God at Peniel resulted in God's blessing and the symbolic change of his name to Israel. Yet by his death Jacob had learned that all blessings came from the Lord alone (cf. 49:18). Indeed, he had learned the truth of his earlier confession, "surely the Lord is in this place; and I did not know it" (28:16). Jacob could be regarded as a hero of the faith (Heb. 11:21) attesting to God's faithfulness and grace. His importance in the development of Israelite religion is indicated by the references to Yahweh as "the God of Jacob" (e.g., Ps. 20:1 [MT 2]; 46:7 [MT 8]; Isa. 2:3; Mic. 4:2; cf. Exod. 3:6, 15-16; Matt. 22:32 par.; Acts 3:13) or the "King of Jacob" (Isa. 41:21).

As the ancestor of the nation of Israel, Jacob became the prototype of his descendants—indeed of the entire nation of Israel—who frequently displayed the same mixture of faults and faith. His names, Israel and Jacob, both became identified with and representative of the nation itself. At times the two names are used in parallel (e.g., Num. 23:23; 24:5; Isa. 44:21); in other passages the name Jacob alone stands for the nation (Deut. 32:9; 33:28; Ps. 44:4 [MT 5]; 87:2; 147:19; Isa. 27:9; Jer. 31:7, 11; Obad. 10; Mic. 5:7 [MT 6]; cf. "house of Jacob," Isa. 2:5-6; Obad. 17-18; Luke 1:33), the "servant" of the Lord (e.g., Isa. 41:8; 48:20; Jer. 46:27).

2. The father of Joseph, according to Matthew's genealogy of Jesus (Matt. 1:15-16; cf. Luke 3:23).

JACOB'S WELL (Gk. *pēgē toú Iakōb*). A well on the northeastern foot of Mt. Gerizim, 76 m. (250 ft.) southeast of Shechem (modern Tell Balâṭah). The only biblical reference to the well is at John 4:6, 12, which records Jesus' meeting with the Samaritan woman; the well is situated "near the field that Jacob gave to his son Joseph" (cf. Gen. 33:18-19; Josh. 24:32) at Sychar, "a city of Samaria" (John 4:5). The traditional well, Bîr Yaʿqûb, is both a spring and a cistern situated at the intersection of important trade routes; the shaft is 41 m. (135 ft.) deep. A Byzantine church was built on the site and rebuilt during the Crusades; a modern Greek Orthodox church remains uncompleted.

JADA [jāʹdə] (Heb. *yāḏāʿ* "he [God] cared"). A Judahite, son of Onam and brother of Shammai; father of Jether and Jonathan (1 Chr. 2:28, 32).

JADDAI [jădʹī] (Heb. *yaddô* K, *yadday* Q). An Israelite who was required to send away his foreign wife (Ezra 10:43; KJV "Jadau"). At 1 Esdr. 9:35 he is called Iddo (**8**).

JADDUA [jădʹŏo ə] (Heb. *yaddûaʿ* "known").
1. One of the "chiefs of the people" who set his seal to the new covenant under Nehemiah (Neh. 10:21 [MT 22]).
2.† The son of Jonathan (or Johanan), the last mentioned of the high priests (Neh. 12:11). According to v. 22 he was a priest about the time of the Persian king Darius III Codomannus (336-331 B.C.), who fell to Alexander the Great (cf. Josephus *Ant.* xi.8.4-5 [326-339]).

JADDUS [jădʹəs] (Gk. *Iaddous, Ioddous*).* A priest whose descendants, because he had adopted the name of his father-in-law Barzillai the Gileadite, were unable to prove their levitical descent upon their return from exile (1 Esdr. 5:38; KJV "Addus"). *See* BARZILLAI **3**.

JADON [jāʹdŏn] (Heb. *yāḏôn* "he rules"). A Meronothite who helped repair the walls of Jerusalem (Neh. 3:7).

JAEL [jāʹəl] (Heb. *yāʿēl* "mountain goat").† The Kenite woman who killed the Canaanite army commander Sisera after his defeat by the Israelites under Barak and Deborah. The name is also found as an Amorite village in the Mari period.

Jael's actions are recorded both in a prose account (Judg. 4:17-22) and the Song of Deborah (5:24-27), one of the oldest examples of Hebrew literature and probably the more authoritative of these versions. These accounts differ in major details, and neither reveals Jael's motive. While the Kenites had long been associates of the tribe of Judah (cf. 1:16), they are not listed among those fighting the Canaanites; indeed, 4:17 indicates that Heber and Jabin were allies, so it is difficult to suggest that Jael killed Sisera out of a sense of obligation to Judah.

According to the Song of Deborah, Jael lulled Sisera into complacency by hospitably offering him milk and curds, only to drive a tent peg into his skull as he ate. The prose account provides more of a context for what took place. Jael invited the exhausted and pursued Sisera into her tent. When Sisera asked for water Jael gave him milk and then covered him with a blanket. Before collapsing into sleep Sisera charged Jael to keep watch near the tent entrance and to deny that anyone was in the tent. Then, as he slept, Jael hammered a tent peg into his skull and greeted the pursuing Barak with the news that his enemy was dead.

JAGUR [jāʹgər] (Heb. *yāḡûr* "may [God] sojourn [with him/them]"). A city in the southern part of Judah near Edom (Josh. 15:21), most likely Tell Gur, about 16 km. (10 mi.) east of Beer-sheba.

JAHATH [jāʹhăth] (Heb. *yaḥaṭ* "He [God] will snatch away").
1. A Judahite, the son of Reaiah; ancestor of the Zorahite families Ahumai and Lahad (1 Chr. 4:2).
2. A Levite, son of Libni and descendant of Gershom (1 Chr. 6:20, 43).
3. A descendant of Gershom; chief of the sons of Shimei (1 Chr. 23:10-11).
4. A Levite, son of Shelomoth and descendant of Izhar (1 Chr. 24:22).
5. A Levite, descendant of Merari and overseer of the work force repairing the temple at the time of King Josiah (1 Chr. 34:12).

JAHAZ [jāʹhăz] (Heb. *yāhaṣ, yahᵉṣâ, yāhᵉṣâ* "a trodden (or) open place" [?]). A city in Transjordan where the Israelites defeated the Amorite king Sihon after he had refused them permission to pass through his territory (Num. 21:23-24; Deut. 2:32-34; Judg. 11:19-22). After the conquest of Canaan Jahaz was among the cities assigned to the tribe of Reuben (Josh. 13:18; KJV "Jahazah"); it was later given (with its pasturelands) to the Merarite Levites (21:36; 1 Chr. 6:78 [MT 63]; KJV "Jahzah").

Jahaz remained an Israelite possession until the mid-ninth century B.C., when King Mesha of Moab seized it during his revolt against Israel. According to the

Moabite Stone, the Israelite king Omri had stayed there before Mesha's armies captured the city and annexed it to the district of Dibon (*ANET*, p. 320). Jahaz is mentioned also in prophetic oracles against Moab (Isa. 15:4; Jer. 48:21 [RSV "Jahzah"; KJV "Jahazah"], 34).

The site of Jahaz has not been positively identified. Suggestions include Khirbet el-Medeiniyeh, on the edge of the desert 19 km. (12 mi.) southeast of Medeba; Jālûl, 56 km. (35 mi.) east of Medeba; Khirbet et-Teim, 1.6 km. (1 mi.) southwest of Medeba; and Umm el-Walid, 12 km. (7.5 mi.) southeast of Medeba.

JAHAZIAH (Ezra 10:15, KJV). *See* JAHZEIAH.

JAHAZIEL [jə hā′zĭ əl] (Heb. *yaḥᵃzî'ēl* "may God see").
1. A Benjaminite who came to David in Ziklag (1 Chr. 12:44 [MT 5]).
2. A priest at the time of David, appointed to sound the trumpet before the ark (1 Chr. 16:6).
3. A Kohathite Levite, third of the "sons" of Hebron (**1**) (1 Chr. 23:19; 24:23).
4. The son of Zechariah, "a Levite of the sons of Asaph" (1 Chr. 20:14) who prophesied to Jehoshaphat that Judah would be victorious over the Moabites and Ammonites (vv. 14-17, 20-30).
5. The father of Shecaniah, who returned with Ezra from captivity in Babylon (Ezra 8:5).

JAHDAI [jä′dī] (Heb. *yāhdāy* "may Yahweh lead"). A Calebite, perhaps a wife or concubine of Caleb, from whom are descended six offspring (1 Chr. 2:47).

JAHDIEL [jä′dĭ əl] (Heb. *yaḥdî'ēl* "may God rejoice"). The head of a father's house in the half-tribe of Manasseh (1 Chr. 5:24).

JAHDO [jä′dō] (Heb. *yaḥdô* "may [God] rejoice"). The son of Buz from the tribe of Gad (1 Chr. 5:14).

JAHLEEL [jä′lĭ əl] (Heb. *yaḥlᵉ'ēl* "wait for God"). A son of Zebulun (Gen. 46:14), and eponymous ancestor of the Jahleelites (Heb. *hayyaḥlᵉ'ēlî;* Num. 26:26).

JAHMAI [jä′mī] (Heb. *yaḥmay* "may Yahweh protect"). The head of a father's house among the descendants of Tola from the tribe of Issachar (1 Chr. 7:2).

JAHZAH [jä′zə] (Heb. *yahᵉṣâ*).† Alternate name of JAHAZ, a city in the tableland of Moab (Jer. 48:21; KJV "Jahazah").

JAHZEEL [jä′zĭ əl] (Heb. *yaḥṣᵉ'ēl* "God apportions"). A son of Naphtali (Gen. 46:24); at 1 Chr. 7:13 his name is given as Jahziel. His descendants are called Jahzeelites (Heb. *hayyaḥ ṣᵉ'ēlî;* Num. 26:48).

JAHZEIAH [jä zē′ə] (Heb. *yaḥzᵉyâ* "may Yahweh see"). The son of Tikvah; an Israelite who opposed Ezra's order to divorce foreign wives (Ezra 10:15; KJV "Jahaziah").

JAHZERAH [jä′zə rə] (Heb. *yaḥzērâ*). A priest and the son of Meshullam (1 Chr. 9:12). He may be the same as Ahzai at Neh. 11:13.

JAHZIEL [jä′zĭ əl] (Heb. *yaḥᵃṣî'ēl*). Alternate form of JAHZEEL, a descendant of Naphtali (1 Chr. 7:13).

JAIR [jā′ər] (Heb. *yā'îr,* "may he [God] shine" or "enlighten").
1. A descendant of Manasseh (Num. 32:41; Deut. 3:14; Josh. 13:30; 1 Kgs. 4:13); 1 Chr. 2:21-23 traces his descent through Judah as son of Segub and grandson of Hezron. Jair, possibly a place name, is associated with HAVVOTH-JAIR, the tent-cities or villages of Argob (Bashan) and/or Gilead.
2. A Gileadite who judged Israel twenty-two years (Judg. 10:3-5); possibly the same as or a descendant of **1**. His thirty sons were said to possess "thirty cities, called Havvoth-jair." He was buried in Kamon.
3. (Q *yā'îr* "may he awaken"; K *yā'ûr*). The father of Elhanan, who killed the Gittite Lahmi (1 Chr. 20:5). At 2 Sam. 21:19 his name is given as JAARE-OREGIM.
4. The father of Mordecai (Esth. 2:5).

JAIRITE [jā′ə rīt] (Heb. *yā'irî*).† A gentilic attributed to Ira, David's priest (2 Sam. 20:26). Ira was a descendant of Jair the Manassite of Gilead (*see* JAIR **1**). Following the LXX and other versions, some scholars prefer to read "Jattirite" (Heb. *yattirî*), i.e., a native of Jattir (e.g., 1 Sam. 30:27; cf. 2 Sam. 23:38, "Ira the Ithrite").

JAIRUS [jā′rəs, jī′rəs] (Gk. *Iaïros*).†
1. A ruler of the synagogue in Capernaum whose twelve-year-old daughter Jesus raised from the dead (Matt. 9:18-26 par. Mark 5:22-43; Luke 8:41-56). Matthew and some manuscripts of Mark do not name Jairus; thus some scholars see Luke's use of the name as an attempt to supply an appropriate name based on the Hebrew equivalent *yā'îr* "may he awaken." Differences in detail in the three accounts do not alter the substance of the event. Jesus' comment to the professional mourners gathered at Jairus' house that the girl was not dead but sleeping (Mark 5:39; but cf. 1 Thess. 5:10) may have meant that the girl was in a comalike state, but Luke speaks of her spirit returning to her, clearly indicating resuscitation. All of the accounts are interrupted by the healing of the woman with a hemorrhage.
2. (Add.Esth. 11:2, KJV). *See* JAIR **4**.

JAKAN (2 Chr. 1:42, KJV). *See* JAAKAN.

JAKEH [jā′kə] (Heb. *yāqeh* "discerning").† The father of Agur the sage (Prov. 30:1). The verse has been variously interpreted. Some scholars see Jakeh as an acronym for Heb. *YHWH qāḏôš hû'* "Yahweh, blessed is he." *See* MASSA.

JAKIM [jā′kĭm] (Heb. *yāqîm* "may [God] establish").
1. A son of Shimei from the tribe of Benjamin (1 Chr. 8:19).
2. The leader of the twelfth division of priests at the time of David (1 Chr. 24:12).

JALAM [jā'ləm] (Heb. *ya'lām*). An Edomite chief, the son of Esau and Oholibamah (Gen. 36:5, 14, 18; 1 Chr. 1:35; KJV "Jaalam").

JALON [jā'lŏn] (Heb. *yālôn*). A son of Ezrah from the tribe of Judah (1 Chr. 4:17).

JAMBRES [jăm'brĭz] (Gk. *Iambrēs*). According to 2 Tim. 3:8, one of two Egyptian sorcerers who opposed Moses (cf. Exod. 7:11, 22). The name may be a Grecized form of "John" (but cf. Heb. *mamrê* "opponent" or "apostate"). *See* JANNES.

JAMBRI [jăm'brī] (Gk. *hoi huioí Iambri* "the sons of Iambri"). A band of robbers from Medeba in Transjordan, who took captive and murdered John, a brother of Judas Maccabeus (1 Macc. 9:36). John's brother Jonathan avenged his death during a wedding feast (vv. 37ff.). The Jambri were probably Amorites (Josephus *Ant.* xiii.1.2 [11] "sons of Amaraius"; cf. Num. 21:30-31).

JAMES [jāmz] (Gk. *Iakōbos*, from Heb. *ya'ªqōḇ*).†
1. An apostle of Jesus; the son of Zebedee and the elder brother of John. He was one of those first called to be a disciple (Matt. 4:21 par.) and (with Peter and John) belonged to the inner circle among the disciples (17:1; 26:37; Luke 8:51). Remarkably, the Bible mentions him very little.

His father was a fisherman, and James and John helped in the business. Peter and Andrew were their partners (Matt. 4:21; Luke 5:10). His mother was most likely Salome, a sister of Mary the mother of Jesus. This would make James the cousin of Jesus (Matt. 27:56; cf. Mark 15:40; 16:1; John 19:25). Whenever James and John are mentioned the name of James is almost always mentioned first (but cf. Luke 9:28; Acts 1:13), which suggests that James was the elder. For this reason he is generally known as James the Great.

Jesus referred to James and John as Boanerges ("sons of thunder"; Mark 3:17), probably an indication of their disposition. He also found it necessary to rebuke them for their attitude toward the Samaritan village which refused them entry (Luke 9:51-56) and for their desire for personal glory (Mark 10:35-45; cf. Matt. 20:20-28). After the resurrection of Christ, James went with the other apostles to Jerusalem (Acts 1:13) only to be executed by Herod shortly thereafter (12:2).

Only a few legends about James are recorded outside the Bible. Eusebius quotes Clement of Alexandria when he writes that James forgave Herod (*HE* ii.9.2-3). The apocryphal Apostolic History of Abdias details some of the miracles James performed. A very late tradition tells how James preached in Spain and was ultimately buried there.

Traditionally, James the son of Zebedee is called "James the Great," while James the son of Alphaeus is referred to as "James the Less."

2. James the son of Alphaeus, an apostle of Jesus (Matt. 10:3; Mark 3:18; Luke 6:15; Acts 1:13); commonly called James the Less (or James the Younger [RSV]).

This James is mentioned only in the lists of the disciples, where he always heads the third group of four names. Little more than his name is known. It has been speculated that he was related to Levi (who is also called the son of Alphaeus; Mark 2:14), but this is unlikely since the two are never linked together in the Gospels. He may possibly be the same as James the son of Mary (**4** below).

3. James the Just, the brother (or half-brother) of Jesus (Matt. 13:55 par. Mark 6:3; Gal. 1:19).

The New Testament and early Christian writers all refer to this James as the brother of Jesus. Most of the ancient Church, however, rejected this evidence because of the belief in the perpetual viginity of Mary. Several different options were proposed in order to reconcile these beliefs. The first was that James was actually the cousin of Jesus. The second was that Joseph already had several children before he married Mary. Thus Joseph's older sons came to be known as the brothers of Jesus.

It was this James who assumed leadership of the church in Jerusalem while the other apostles were gone on missionary journeys. James the son of Zebedee had already been killed, and the James mentioned in this context is never called the son of Alphaeus. Indeed, one who was the brother of Jesus, even though not one of the Twelve, would have had the stature necessary for such leadership.

James dominates the accounts of official actions of the council at Jerusalem; he cast the deciding vote when the question of Gentile circumcision was discussed (Acts 15:13). Paul visited him at Jerusalem after his third missionary journey (21:18), as he had done earlier shortly after his conversion on the Damascus road (Gal. 1:19; cf. 2:9, 12). It was James and the elders of the church who advised Paul to join in sacrifices at the temple (Acts 21:17-26). It was emissaries from James who supported Peter against Paul (Gal. 2:12). When Peter was freed from prison, he requested that James be informed (Acts 12:17).

Apparently James the brother of Jesus did not at first believe in the messianic claims of Jesus (cf. John 7:5), yet he remained in contact with the apostles after the crucifixion (Acts 1:14). So it seems likely that the appearance of the risen Lord to James (1 Cor. 15:7) was probably to this brother of Jesus.

This James is also the most likely author of the epistle of James. James was one of those strongly tied to Jewish law (Acts 21:17-26; Gal. 2:12)—and the content of the epistle suggests at least a vigorous ethic toward works. On the basis of this evidence and v. 9, James could even be considered the head of the party of the Judaizers.

According to Church tradition, James was the first bishop of Jerusalem. Jewish Christianity placed James above Peter and Paul. According to several sources, James was martyred; Eusebius quotes Hegesippus to this effect (*HE* ii.23.4-18) and Josephus, although differing in details, collaborates the story (*Ant.* xx.9).

4. A son of Mary (Matt. 27:56; Mark 15:40; 16:1; Luke 24:10), probably either the mother of Jesus (cf. **3** above) or her sister (cf. **1** above).

5. James the father (KJV "brother") of Judas, one of the Twelve (Luke 6:16; Acts 1:13). Nothing else about this individual is known.

JAMES, APOCRYPHON OF.* A Coptic writing found in the Nag Hammadi library; also called the Apocalypse of James.

Three such revelations in the name of James have been found in the Nag Hammadi writings discovered in Upper Egypt in 1946. Very little is known about the two found in Codex VII; the first appears to be a dialogue between Jesus and James, the second the sayings of James the Just. The third document, found in Codex II, calls itself an apocryphon (an esoteric revelation of truth) and purports to have been written in Hebrew by James (perhaps **3**, the brother of Jesus) and delivered in epistolary form upon Christ's ascension. It was probably written in the second century.

The author claims that he and Peter received this revelation directly from the Lord during the 550 days (in contrast to the 40 days of Acts 1:3) between the resurrection and the ascension of Jesus. This knowledge was not given to the other apostles. James and Peter then witnessed the ascension, heard the prayers and hymns of the angels, and promised to deliver this secret truth to the children of God. The apocryphon is considered to be of Valentinian Gnostic origin.

Bibliography. E. Hennecke and W. Schneemelcher, *New Testament Apocrypha* 1 (Philadelphia: 1963): 333-38.

JAMES, ASCENTS OF.* A Jewish-Christian (Ebionite) book referred to by Epiphanius (*Haer.* xxx.16). According to the passage cited, James the brother of Jesus is the hero and defender of circumcision, yet the opponent of the temple and the sacrificial system. He slanders Paul of Tarsus, a Greek who submitted to circumcision because he wanted to marry a daughter of the high priest; when he was denied, Paul became bitter and began to write against circumcision.

Presumably, the book was called "Ascents," or "Steps," because James spoke to the crowds from the steps of the temple (cf. Clement *Recognitions* i.66-71).

JAMES, EPISTLE OF.† The first of the so-called Catholic Letters.

I. Authorship

The author introduces himself as "James, a servant of God and of the Lord Jesus Christ" (Jas. 1:1). Of the New Testament persons named James who might have written this epistle, the (half) brother of Jesus seems most likely. He does not claim to be an apostle, but he could be considered one in the broad sense (cf. Acts 15:13; Gal. 1:19). The apostle James, the son of Zebedee, had already been killed by the time this letter was written, and James, the son of Alphaeus, does not seem to have played a significant role in the early Church. A number of scholars hold that the work is pseudonymous—perhaps even a Christian reworking of an earlier Jewish writing—or the product of yet another James.

II. Addressees and Date

James addresses his letter to the "twelve tribes in the Dispersion" (Jas. 1:1). According to one view, this is a name for the Jewish Christians. Not all of the literal twelve tribes of Israel were in exile, for some of the deported Jews had returned from Babylon already in Cyrus' day. Furthermore, a book that was addressed only to Jews would not have been included in the Christian canon. It is also possible that the author refers to the Christian community as a whole by this figurative name (cf. Matt. 19:28). The word "dispersion" seems to imply that the readers lived at some distance from Jerusalem (cf. 1 Pet. 1:1). It is possible that James wrote to Jewish Christians who had fled to Syrian Antioch after Herod's persecution (see Acts 11:19).

If the author is identified as the Lord's brother, then the epistle must be dated before A.D. 62, when James was martyred. It is possible that James wrote the epistle near the end of his life, but some considerations would point to a slightly earlier date, about A.D. 50, which would make James the earliest of the New Testament writings. For example, there is no mention of the promise having been extended to the Gentiles or of the Jewish-Gentile controversy, which would imply a date before Paul. The simplicity of life and church order and the use of the word "assembly" (Gk. *synagōgḗ*) also favor an early date. Those who argue the book's later (70-130) composition cite its idiomatic Greek and possible awareness of certain Pauline writings.

III. Contents and Teachings

Following a brief salutation (Jas. 1:1), the author immediately addresses the question of the significance of trials in the Christian life (vv. 2-18). He then outlines the ethical implications of the gospel (vv. 19-26), the impartiality of faith (2:1-13), and the necessity of works (vv. 14-26). The second major section of the epistle is comprised of several moral injunctions (3:1-5:12). The conclusion discusses prayer and confession (vv. 13-18), followed by concluding words of encouragement (vv. 19-20).

James gives practical advice about the distinctive character of the Christian lifestyle. Christians should be slow to anger (1:19) and should control their tongues (3:6; cf. 1:26) and their passions (4:1-3). They should be humble (v. 6) and avoid jealousy (4:5) and slander (vv. 11-12). They are to embrace "pure and undefiled" religion, keeping themselves unstained by the world and visiting orphans and widows in their affliction (1:26). James further addresses the economic plight of the poor, urging the rich not to be preoccupied with or hoard wealth (5:1-6). Christian relationships should be open and without prejudice (2:1-9).

Concerned as he is to prod the recipients of his letter to be "doers of the word, and not hearers only" (1:22), James also reminds them to live their daily lives in the light of the will of God (4:14-15), in whose image they are created (3:9). While he is not as doctrinally profound as Paul, James does have a theological framework. God is said to be the Father (1:27) who gives perfect gifts (v. 17), even the gift of trials through which he transforms faith into steadfastness (v. 3) and incorporates believers into his kingdom (2:5); God does not, however, "tempt" (i.e., lead) believers into sin (1:13). Jesus Christ is called Lord (v. 1; cf. 2:1 "Lord of glory"), who will return quickly to judge the world (5:7-9). The wisdom "from above," in sharp contrast to the "earthly" wisdom of mankind, is the source for producing "good fruits" (3:13-17) through which believers experience fellowship with God (4:8).

Concerning important doctrinal affirmations, the classical theologians quoted the expression, "the Father of lights with whom there is no variation or shadow due to change" (1:17, RSV) in support of the doctrine of divine changelessness. Others have extensively debated James' connection between faith and works as they pertain to mankind's justification before God (2:14-26); some (e.g., Luther and Barth) reason that James contradicted Paul because he affirmed that believers are justified by faith and works, not only by faith as Paul confessed, while others assert that James complemented Paul's view (see JUSTIFICATION). Historically, Roman Catholics and Protestants have interpreted differently James' comments on the anointing of the sick by the elders of the Church (5:14).

IV. Canonicity

James' letter, like all Jewish-Christian writings except the gospel of Matthew, has not always and everywhere been accepted as canonical. For various reasons (e.g., skepticism about its authorship, its Semitic background, nondoctrinal character, supposed anti-Pauline stance), the book was not cited as Scripture until Origen in the third century. Even Luther called it an "epistle of straw" in the first edition of his German Bible, though he did not repeat this negative phrase in later editions. Calvin, on the other hand, was "fully content to accept this epistle," because he could find "no fair and adequate cause for rejecting it" (*Comm. James*, ed. D. W. Torrance and T. F. Torrance [Grand Rapids: 1972], p. 259).

Bibliography. J. B. Adamson, *The Epistle of James.* NICNT (1976); P. H. Davids, *The Epistle of James.* NIGTC (1982); M. Dibelius-H. Greeven, *James.* Hermeneia (1976); J. H. Ropes, *The Epistle of St. James.* ICC (1916; repr. 1978).

JAMES, PROTEVANGELIUM OF.† A New Testament apocryphal book that relates a pious and fanciful account of Mary and the nativity of Jesus.

It is generally accepted that this book was composed in Greek in the mid-second century, perhaps in Egypt. The oldest manuscript dates from the third century. The title "Protevangelium" ("First Gospel") was first used in the sixteenth century, derived from the notion that the book's contents were earlier than those of the canonical accounts. Origen called it simply the book of James, and the Gelasian Decree refers to it as the gospel of James the Less.

The pseudonymous author, ostensibly James the brother of Jesus, describes the miraculous birth of Mary. He records that Joachim, her father, fasted forty days in the wilderness and Anna, Mary's mother, was visited by the angel of the Lord. In her joy at the promise of a child, the aged Anna vowed that the child would be dedicated to the service of the temple. At the age of twelve, Mary was given to Joseph through a miraculous sign in the temple; but, despite her pregnancy at age sixteen and the subsequent birth of Jesus, she remained a virgin all her life.

The book presupposes the canonical infancy stories, and obviously draws heavily upon the narratives of Matthew and Luke (e.g., the decree of Augustus, Jesus'

birth in a cave, the star, the Wise Men). However, it also records the cessation of nature at Jesus' birth, the restoration of Salome's hand by contact with the infant, John the Baptist's miraculous escape from Herod, and Herod's murder of Zacharias.

The primary purpose of the book appears to be the glorification of Mary. Indeed, many of the attributes accorded to Jesus in the canonical gospels are here attested for Mary. Although the immaculate conception of Mary is not noted, all the other elements of mariology are supported. The author is careful to harmonize the perpetual viginity of Mary with all the biblical data; Joseph was a widower and had children before Mary was given into his care.

The book was an important factor in the development of devotion to Mary. It influenced other apocryphal writings and provided the basis for numerous artistic masterpieces.

Bibliography. E. Hennecke and W. Schneemelcher, eds., *New Testament Apocrypha* 1 (Philadelphia: 1963): 370-388.

JAMES THE GREAT, ACTS OF.† An apocryphal account of the later ministry and martyrdom of James the son of Zebedee.

This fanciful book was probably written in Greek but is now extant only in Latin as Book IV of the Apostolic History of Abdias. It describes the preaching of James, the conversion of the magician Philetus (cf. 2 Tim. 2:17), and the opposition of Philetus' mentor, Hermogenes (cf. 1:15). Hermogenes was powerless to harm James and eventually began to burn his magical books; James told him to throw the books into the sea so that the smoke would not harm the unwary. The Jews finally had James arrested, and after preaching to them from the prophets, James was dragged before Herod and beheaded (cf. Acts 12:2). En route to his execution, James was able to convert and baptize the scribe who had delivered him to Herod; this man, Josias, was also beheaded with James.

JAMIN [jā'mĭn] (Heb. *yāmîn* "right hand" or "good fortune").

1. A son of Simeon (Gen. 46:10; Exod. 6:15; 1 Chr. 4:24), eponymous ancestor of the Jaminites (Heb. *hayyāmînî,* Num. 26:12).

2. A Judahite, son of Ram and descendant of Jerahmeel (1 Chr. 2:27).

3. A Levite who translated into Aramaic the portions of the Law read by Ezra so the people could understand (Neh. 8:7-8).

JAMLECH [jăm'lək] (Heb. *yamlēḵ* "may [God] let rule"). A prince of the tribe of Simeon (1 Chr. 4:34).

JAMNIA [jăm'nĭ ə] (Gk. *Iamneia*). A town on the coastal plain of Judah, 6 km. (4 mi.) inland from the Mediterranean Sea and 48 km. (30 mi.) from Jerusalem; modern Yebnā. Jamnia served as the base of operation of the Seleucid generals Gorgias (1 Macc. 4:15; 5:58), Apollonius (10:69), and Cendebeus (15:40) in their war against the Hasmoneans. When Judas Maccabeus heard that the Jamnians were planning to exterminate their Jewish fellow citizens, he burned the harbor and fleet (164 B.C.; 2 Macc. 12:8-9; KJV

"Jamnites"). The city was conquered by Judas' brother Simon *ca.* 142 (Josephus *Ant.* xiii.6.7 [215]), and it remained in Jewish hands until 63 B.C. when Pompey freed it, annexed it to Syria, and restored it to its earlier inhabitants (*Ant.* xiv.5.3 [75]; *BJ* i.7.7 [156]; i.8.4 [166]). From the Romans its rule (and revenue) passed to Herod, who gave it to his sister Salome (*Ant.* xvii.8.1 [189]; she in turn bequeathed it to the empress Julia (xviii.2.2 [31]). Nevertheless, throughout this period it remained a predominantly Jewish city. According to Philo (*De leg.* cxcix-cciii) it was the the erection of a clay brick altar in Jamnia and its destruction by the Jews that inspired Gaius' plan to erect a gold statue of himself in the Jerusalem temple (A.D. 40; *BJ* ii.16.1-2 [184ff.]).

According to talmudic tradition, during the Jewish War (A.D. 66-70) Johanan ben Zakkai, a prominent Pharisaic leader in Jerusalem, escaped to Vespasian's camp and requested permission to found a school (Yeshiva) in Jamnia (*b. Git.* 56b). After the fall of Jerusalem in 70 the power of the Jerusalem Sanhedrin was assumed by the Beth-din ("law court") of Jamnia, and there Judaism under Johanan's leadership sought to reconstitute itself in the face of the national tragedy (Mishnah *Roš Haš.* iv.1-3). Thus from 70-132 the city was the spiritual and intellectual center of Judaism, during the period in which the foundations of rabbinic Judaism were laid.

Scholarship has long held that the council of Jamnia of A.D. 90 was the occasion of the final fixing of the Jewish canon. More recent studies have shown that the evidence is not so clear, either for the convening of such a council or for such specific results. With the outbreak of the Bar Kokhba revolt in 132, Jamnia's prominence as a Jewish center ceased (*b. Roš Haš.* 31a-b). By the fifth century the city was predominantly Christian.

For the earlier history of the city, *see* JABNEEL 1.

JANAI [jǎ'nī] (Heb. *ya*ʿ*nay* "may the Lord answer"). A descendant of Gad living in Bashan (1 Chr. 5:12; KJV "Jaanai").

JANIM [jǎn'ĭm] (Heb. *yānîm* "slumbering"). A place in the mountains of Judah, in the vicinity of Eshan and Beth-tappuah (Josh. 15:53; KJV "Janum"). The site has not been identified; one possibility is modern Beni Naʿim, 6 km. (4 mi.) east of Hebron.

JANNAEUS, ALEXANDER. *See* ALEXANDER 3.

JANNAI [jǎn'ī] (Gk. *Iannai*), The son of Melchi, an ancestor of Jesus dating from after the Exile (Luke 3:24; KJV "Janna"). The name does not occur in the Old Testament.

JANNES [jǎn'ĭz] (Gk. *Iannēs* probably from Aram. *yôḥānāʾ*).† An Egyptian court magician who, with JAMBRES, opposed Moses according to 2 Tim. 3:8, the Targum (Aram. *yannîs, yamb*ᵉ*rîs,* from the Greek), and other writings from the first century A.D. onward. In the original account of their activities (Exod. 7:11-12, 22; 8:7; 9:11) these magicians are not named. An otherwise unattested apocryphal book of Jannes and Jambres is mentioned in the Decretum Gelasianum (sixth century A.D.).

JANOAH [jə nō'ə] (Heb. *yānôaḥ* "resting place").

1. A city on Ephraim's northern tribal border (Josh. 16:6-7). It has been identified with modern Khirbet Yānûn, 11 km. (7 mi.) southeast of Shechem.

2. A city of upper Galilee, in the territory of Naphtali. Janoah was captured and its population deported as a result of the 734 B.C. campaign of the Assyrian Tiglath-pileser III in Palestine (2 Kgs. 15:29). Once thought to be located at modern Janûḥ, east of Tyre (cf. Yanoam in the annals of Thutmose III; *ANET*, p. 237), the site is now suggested as Tell en-Nâʿimeh, 8 km. (5 mi.) northeast of Kedesh.

JAPHETH [jā'fĭth] (Heb. *yepeṯ, yāpeṯ* "may [God] enlarge''; Gk. *Iapheth*).†

1. A son of Noah. He is presented as either the second (e.g., Gen. 9:23-27) or the third (7:13; 9:18; 10:1-2) of Noah's three sons. Like the other members of the family, Japheth and his wife were spared from the Flood by Noah's ark (7:13; 9:18). Later Japheth and his brother Shem were compelled to cover their father's nakedness without so much as looking at him (9:20-23).

Noah's blessing, that God "enlarge (Heb. *yapt*) Japheth," letting him "dwell in the tents of Shem" with Canaan as his slave (9:27), has generally been understood as a prophecy of the respective fortunes of the descendants of Shem, Japheth, and Canaan. Since the expression "dwell in the tents of" is subject to various interpretations (e.g., geographic, with or without violence; religious), numerous identifications of Japheth have been proposed, from the Amurru to Alexander the Great. Most likely the account in ch. 9 portrays Japheth as the eponymous ancestor of the Philistines; according to the Table of Nations (10:3-5 par. 1 Chr. 1:5-7), however, he is the ancestor of peoples to the north of Israel, including the Medes, Etruscans, and numerous Anatolian peoples. The rabbis, followed by some Christians, understood the prophecy to refer to the translation of the Torah into Greek.

Attempts to identify Japheth with the Greek titan Iapetos, father of Prometheus, have proved inconclusive.

2. A region north of Arabia, perhaps in Asia Minor (Jdt. 2:25). Here Holofernes surrounded and routed the Midianites.

JAPHIA [jə fī'ə] (Heb. *yāpîaʿ* "may [God] be radiant") (PERSON).

1. An Amorite king of Lachish, who with other leaders of the coalition headed by Adonizedek was routed by Joshua at Beth-horon (Josh. 10:3) and subsequently slain (vv. 22-27).

2. A son of David, born in Jerusalem (2 Sam. 5:15). His mother, perhaps a concubine, is not indicated.

JAPHIA [jə fī'ə] (Heb. *yāpîaʿ* "may [God] be radiant") (PLACE). A town on the southern border of Zebulun (Josh. 19:12), identified with modern Yâfâ, 2.5 km. (1.5 mi.) southwest of Nazareth. Josephus fortified the town with a double wall (*Vita* 45 [230]; 52 [270]). Under severe Roman attack the Jewish warriors did not have time to close the outer gates, and those forces embroiled in savage battle between the walls perished; the Romans then entered the city, killing every male and taking women and children captive.

JAPHLET [jăf'lĭt] (Heb. *yaplēṭ* "may [God] deliver").† A son of Heber from the tribe of Asher (1 Chr. 7:32-33). He may have been the ancestor of the Japhletites (Heb. *yaplēṭî*), a group whose territory marked the southern boundary of the Joseph tribes (Josh. 16:3; KJV "Japhleti").

JAPHO (Josh. 19:46, KJV). *See* JOPPA.

JAR.† Clay vessels of several varieties, used in biblical times for liquid and dry storage.

Heb. *kaḏ* refers to a vessel used for carrying water (Gen. 24:14; KJV "pitcher"; cf. Gk. *kerámion;* Mark 14:13 par.) and for storing flour (1 Kgs. 17:12, 14, 16; KJV "barrel"); it was sealed with a stopper. The *gāḇîʿa* was a type of pitcher for serving water or wine (RSV, Jer. 35:5; KJV "pot"). The *baqbuq* was another pitcher, whose narrow neck aerated water passing through it; the resulting sound gave it its name (cf. 1 Kgs. 14:3, where it is used for storing honey; KJV "cruse"). The *nēḇel* was a large, round-bottomed wine storage jar that was set upon rings for stability (Jer. 13:12; KJV "bottle"; JB "jug"; cf. Gk. *hydría*; John 2:6-7; KJV "waterpot").

Heb. *paḵ* designates a small flask used for carrying anointing oil (1 Sam. 10:1; RSV "vial"; 2 Kgs. 9:1, 3; RSV "flask"; KJV "box"), as was the oval-shaped *ʾāsûḵ* (from *sûḵ* "pour for anointing"; 2 Kgs. 4:2; KJV "pot"). Gk. *alábastros* is used for a small alabaster juglet used for perfume (Matt. 26:7 par.; KJV "box").

Glazed ceramic jar from Iran, *ca.* 800 B.C. (Royal Ontario Museum, Toronto)

JARAH [jâr'ə] (Heb. *yaʿrâ* "honeycomb"). The son of Ahaz and father of Alemeth, Azmaveth, and Zimri; a descendant of Saul (1 Chr. 9:42). At 8:36 he is called Jehoaddah.

JAREB [jâr'ĭb] (Heb. *yārēḇ*).† At Hos. 5:13; 10:6 the KJV reads Heb. *mlk yrb* as a personal name. More likely, the text should be divided *mlky rb* (*malkî rāḇ "great king"; so RSV, JB, NIV), a Hebrew form of the Akkadian honorific title *šarru rabû* (cf. Sefire I.B.7). The NJV retains the MT form, rendering *yrb* (on the basis of the root *ryb* "strive, contend") as "patron king" (cf. Isa. 1:17; 3:13; 19:20; 51:22; JB mg. "to an avenging king").

JARED [jâr'ĭd] (Heb. *yereḏ, yāreḏ* "descent"; Gk. *Iared*). A son of Mahalalel and father of Enoch, from the lineage of Seth (Gen. 5:15-20; 1 Chr. 1:2; Luke 3:37; KJV "Jered"). According to Gen. 5:20, Jared lived 962 years.

JARESIAH (1 Chr. 8:27, KJV). *See* JAARESHIAH.

JARHA [jär'hə] (Heb. *yarḥāʿ*). An Egyptian slave belonging to Sheshan the Jerahmeelite (1 Chr. 2:34). Because Sheshan had no sons, he gave his daughter as a wife to Jarha in order to produce an heir (v. 35; cf. Exod. 21:4).

JARIB [jâr'ĭb] (Heb. *yārîḇ* "may he contend").†

1. A son of Simeon (1 Chr. 4:24). Because he is called Jachin (1) at Gen. 46:10; Exod. 6:15; Num. 26:12, many scholars consider the reading here to be a scribal error.

2. One of the leaders whom Ezra dispatched to Casiphia to obtain ministers for the temple (Ezra 8:16; cf. 1 Esdr. 8:44; KJV "Joribas").

3. A priest whom Ezra ordered to give up his foreign wife (Ezra 10:18; cf. 1 Esdr. 9:19; KJV "Joribus").

JARMUTH [jär'mŭth] (Heb. *yarmûṯ* "height").

1. A city located in the Shephelah region of Judah (Josh. 15:35). The Canaanite king Piram of Jarmuth (10:5) was part of a five-city league which opposed Joshua's invasion (vv. 3-27; 12:11). Returning from exile in Babylon, the Judahites repopulated the city (Neh. 11:29).

The site is generally identified as modern Khirbet Yarmûk, 24 km. (15 mi.) west of Bethlehem in the Elah valley near Zâharîyeh. This well-protected site bears traces of walls and pottery from the Bronze and Iron ages as well as from the Hellenistic through the Byzantine periods. It is probably the site 13 km. (8 mi.) north-northeast of Eleutheropolis (modern Beit Jibrîn) noted by Eusebius.

2. A city in Issachar given to the Gershonite Levites (Josh. 21:29). It is probably the same as Ramoth listed at 1 Chr. 6:73 and Remeth at Josh. 19:21. The site may be modern Kôkab el-Hawā, 11 km. (7 mi.) north of Beth-shan; an alternate suggestion is er-Râmeh, 17 km. (10.5 mi.) south of Jenîn (biblical En-gannim).

JAROAH [jə rō'ə] (Heb. *yārôaḥ*). A man of the tribe of Gad who lived in Basham; son of Gilead and father of Huri (1 Chr. 5:14).

JASHAR [jā'shər], **BOOK OF** (Heb. *sēper hay-yāšār*).† A Hebrew document, most likely a collection of ancient epic songs (Josh. 10:13; 2 Sam. 1:18; KJV "Jasher"; perhaps LXX 1 Kgs. 8:12-13, 53). Heb. *yāšār* commonly designates "one who is honest, righteous, upright"; in the title of this work it may be an allusion to the poetic personal name of Israel, Jeshurun. Through the heroes of Israel's past this ancient work may set forth the ideal of a righteous Israel.

The passages attributed to the book of Jashar include a poetic version of Joshua's command that the son and moon stand still (Josh. 10:12-13) and David's lament over the death of Saul and Jonathan (2 Sam. 1:19-27). At the end of Solomon's prayer at the dedication of the temple (1 Kgs. 8:53, LXX) the LXX places a lengthier version of the poetic fragment found at 8:12-13, MT, attributing it to the "book of Song" (cf. Heb. *šyr*); this reference may involve an accidental transposition of the consonants in the name Jashar.

The book of Jashar appears to have been an anthology of songs, epic in nature, recounting the upright acts of heroic leaders in Israel's history. Some scholars have suggested that it also included the Song of Miriam (Exod. 15:21) and the Song of Deborah (Judg. 5). Containing material perhaps as old as the Amarna period, the book may have been put into final form during the creative period of Solomon's reign. Along with such works as the book of the Wars of the Lord (Num. 21:14) it provides evidence for the use of sources in the writing of the historical records of ancient Israel.

JASHEN [jā'shən] (Heb. *yāšēn*).† One of David's thirty mighty men (2 Sam. 23:32). The MT reading "sons of Jashen" (Heb. *bᵉnê yāšēn*) derives from a dittography with the preceding name Shaalbon (perhaps a gentilic, Shaalbonite). At 1 Chr. 11:34 he is called HASHEM the Gizonite.

JASHOBEAM [jə shō'bǐ əm] (Heb. *yāšob'ām* "let the people return [to God] [?]").
1. A Hachmonite and chief of the mighty men of David (1 Chr. 11:11). At 2 Sam. 23:8 the name appears as "Josheb-basshebeth a Tah-chemonite" (KJV "the Tachmonite that sat in the seat"), a copyist's error; the more plausible LXX rendering, Ishbosheth, is taken by some as evidence for an original form Ishbaal ("man of Baal"; so JB; cf. NIV mg.).
2. The son of Zabdiel and a descendant of Perez; one of David's commissioners (1 Chr. 27:2-3). According to many scholars he is the same as 1 above. If so, the epithet Hachmonite (11:11) would refer to an ancestor of this household (cf. 27:32, "son of Hachmoni").
3. A Korahite from the tribe of Benjamin who joined David at Ziklag (1 Chr. 12:6 [MT 7]). It is possible that this reference is also to the same person.

JASHUB [jā'shəb] (Heb. *yāšûb* "may he return").
1. The third son of Issachar (Num. 26:24; 1 Chr. 7:1 K *yāšîb*); eponymous ancestor of the Jashubites (Num. 26:24). The name appears as Iob (*yōb*) at Gen. 46:13, but the LXX reading (*Iasoub*) suggests that the letter *š* was omitted from the Hebrew through scribal error.

2. One of the exiles who divorced their foreign wives (Ezra 10:29).

JASHUBI-LEHEM [jə shoo'bī lē'hĕm] (Heb. *yāšubî-lehem*).† According to the KJV, a descendant of Shelah the Judahite (1 Chr. 4:22). The NIV and NJV read Jashubi Lehem as a place name; the RSV does similarly, translating "and returned to Lehem" (cf. JB, "Bethlehem"). The NJV links this place with Moab as territories from which the Judahites had obtained wives (cf. JB; Ruth 1).

JASIEL (1 Chr. 11:47, KJV). *See* JAASIEL.

JASON [jā'sən] (Gk. *Iasōn* "healing").† A name common among Hellenistic Jews, chosen as a substitute for both Joshua and Jesus.
1. A son of a certain Eleazar (not the brother of Judas Maccabeus) whom Judas sent with Eupolemus in 161 B.C. to seek a treaty with Rome (1 Macc. 8:17).
2. The father of Antipater, sent by Jonathan as an ambassador to Rome in 144 B.C. (1 Macc. 12:16). He may be the same as 1.
3. A high priest before the time of the Maccabees (174-171 B.C.); son of Simon II and brother of Onias III. Jason was hated by the people because he obtained the high priesthood by corrupt means (bribery of Antiochus IV Ephiphanes) and because he forced the Jews to conform to Greek customs (2 Macc. 4:7-22). Jason built a sports stadium within sight of the Jerusalem temple, with the result that the priests lost enthusiasm for the sacrifices and were drawn away from their religion. In 171 Menelaus outbid Jason for the office of high priest, and Jason went into hiding in Ammonite territory (vv. 23-29). Thinking that Antiochus was dead, Jason was able to regain the high priesthood by attacking Jerusalem with a small army and mercilessly slaughtering many of his fellow Jews; he was soon forced to flee again, however. After being imprisoned by the Nabatean ruler Aretas (1) and escaping to Egypt, Jason died at sea en route to Sparta (5:5-10).
4. A Cyrenian historian who composed a five-volume work on the history of the Maccabean revolt which forms the basis for 2 Maccabees. Included are depictions of the battles against Antiochus IV Epiphanes and his son Antiochus V Eupator, and the divine interventions that enabled the faithful Jews to overcome all odds (2 Macc. 2:19-23). Jason's history — apparently technical, dull, and highly statistical — was completed sometime after 160 B.C.
5. A Jewish Christian who entertained and aided Paul and Silas at Thessalonica (Acts 17:5-9). He was among those arrested because of their association with the missionaries and later released.
6. A companion and "kinsman" of Paul who sent greetings to the church at Rome (Rom. 16:21). He may be the same as 5.

JASPER (Heb. *yāšpēh*; Gk. *iaspis*).† A greenish, translucent variety of quartz of the type called chalcedony. The stone is the third (and last) on the fourth row of the high priest's breastplate (the LXX places it third and last on the second row) (Exod. 28:20;

39:13). Jasper is also one of the precious stones that cover the anointed cherub in Ezek. 28:13 (Heb. *yāhªlōm*; RSV elsewhere "diamond"; Heb. *yāšpēh*, RSV "onyx").

In the New Testament the gem is mentioned only in the book of Revelation. Here, God appears on the throne as a light of jasper and carnelian (Rev. 4:3); the radiance of the Heavenly Jerusalem is like jasper (21:11); and the walls of the city and its first foundation course are made of jasper (21:18-19).

JATHNIEL [jăth'nĭ əl] (Heb. *yaṯnîʾēl* "God grants"). A Korahite gatekeeper of the sanctuary; the fourth son of Meshelemiah (1 Chr. 26:2).

JATTIR [jăt'ər] Heb. *yattîr* "surpassing [?]"). A levitical city in the hill country of Judah (Josh. 15:48; 21:14; 1 Chr. 6:57 [MT 42]), to which David sent a portion of the booty he had seized from the Amalekites (1 Sam. 30:27). According to Eusebius, Jattir was an important Byzantine Christian settlement. The site is thought to be modern Khirbet ʿAttîr, 21 km. (13 mi.) south-southwest of Hebron.

JAVAN [jā'vən] (Heb. *yāwān*; Gk. *Ióvan, Iaōn, Hellas, hoi Hellēnes*). The fourth son of Japheth and grandson (or a descendant) of Noah; father of Elishah, Tarshish, Kittim, and Dodanim (Gen. 10:2, 4; 1 Chr. 1:5, 7).

As in Greek, Assyrian, and Egyptian sources, the name refers in the Old Testament to the Greeks and their lands. Isaiah mentions Javan as one of the distant coastal nations who will yet see God's glory (Isa. 66:19; NIV "Greece"). Ezekiel describes Javan as a nation of slave and bronze traders (Ezek. 27:13); according to Joel 3:6 (MT 4:6), Judah and Jerusalem were sold as slaves to these people (RSV "the Greeks"). The Hebrew form is also found at Dan. 8:21; 10:20; 11:2 with reference to the kingdom of Alexander the Great of Macedon (RSV "Greece"); Seleucid Greeks may be the reference of the term at Zech. 9:13. Ezek. 27:19 (MT) mentions Javan (so JB) as trading with Tyre, but this verse presents textual difficulties (RSV "and wine," following LXX).

JAW, JAWBONE (Heb. *lᵉḥî*).† The bony structure which forms the framework of the mouth. Samson used such a bone from an ass as a weapon against the Philistines (Judg. 15:15-17; cf. v. 17, Ramath-lehi "hill of the jawbone").

The jaw occurs frequently in a figurative sense, particularly with regard to the bridling of an enemy (e.g., Isa. 30:28). At Hos. 11:4 God liberates his people by easing the yoke on their jaws (NIV "neck"; cf. F. I. Andersen and D. N. Freedman, *Hosea*. AB [1980], pp. 574, 581-82).

The Hebrew term can be translated also as "cheek." Possible overlapping of these meanings can be noted at Job 41:2; Ezek. 29:4; 38:4 (cf. Hos. 11:4, JB).

JAZER [jā'zər] (Heb. *yaʿzēr, yaʿªzêr* "he [God] helps"). An Amorite city conquered by the Israelites at the time of Moses (Num. 21:32; KJV "Jaazer") and assigned to Gad (32:1, 34-35; Josh. 13:25) and subsequently to the Merarite Levites (21:39; 1 Chr. 6:81

[MT 66]). Joab began the census for King David at Aroer and continued along the Israelite border toward Jazer (2 Sam. 24:5; cf. Num. 21:24; KJV "strong," following MT). Late in David's reign skilled warriors were enlisted from among Hebronites living there (1 Chr. 26:31). After the death of the Israelite king Ahab in 852 B.C., the region was conquered by Mesha of Moab (cf. Isa. 16:8-9; Jer. 48:32, where it is cited in oracles against Moab). In the Hellenistic period Judas Maccabeus captured the city from the Ammonites (1 Macc. 5:8; Josephus *Ant.* xii.8.1 [329]).

Khirbet es-Sar, 15.5 km. (9.6 mi.) west of Philadelphia (modern Ammân, Rabbah of the Ammonites), accords with the Azer or Iazer noted by Eusebius and Jerome, but the site has yielded no remains earlier than Iron II. Khirbet es-Sireh, 2.4 km. (1.5 mi.) to the northeast, is another possibility but also lacks archaeological support. A more likely location is Khirbet Jazzir, situated on the Wâdī Šaʿib, 4 km. (2.5 mi.) south of es-Salt.

JAZIZ [jā'zĭz] (Heb. *yāzîz*). A Hagrite overseer of the cattle belonging to David (1 Chr. 27:30 [MT 31]).

JEALOUSY (Heb. *qinʾâ*; Gk. *zélos*).† In biblical usage, one of two possible aspects of a single active emotion. In the positive sense it is "jealousy for" someone and as such is righteous "zeal," a concept used of both humans and God; in the negative sense it is "jealousy of" someone and thus is sinful and related to envy. The same Hebrew and Greek terms designate both aspects and thus the appropriate nuance must be determined from the context.

I. Divine Jealousy

The Old Testament frequently affirms that God is a "jealous God" (e.g., Exod. 20:5), and intensive nominal forms are used exclusively of God (Heb. *qannāʾ*; e.g., Exod. 34:14; Deut. 4:24; *qannôʾ*; e.g., Josh. 24:19; Nah. 1:2). The substantive "jealousy" (*qinʾâ*; e.g., Num. 25:11; Job 5:2; KJV "envy"; Ps. 79:5) and the verb "be jealous" (*qānāʾ*; e.g., Gen. 37:11; KJV "envied"; Num. 11:29) are used in reference to both divine and human, righteous and sinful, jealousy. At times God is said to exercise his "jealous wrath" (Ps. 79:5), and he is capable of being provoked to jealousy (78:58; par. "anger"). Divine jealousy in every instance is the just response to a challenge to God's sovereignty and particularly to the breaking of his covenantal relationship with Israel (i.e., unfaithfulness). In the latter sense the prophets sometimes employ the metaphor of marriage, where God is represented as the jealous husband and Israel the adulterous wife (Ezek. 16:42), in reference to Israel's repeated lapses into idolatry. If this jealousy is God's "negative" response to Israel's sin, it is based on two positive facts: (1) God's faithfulness and ultimately his mercy in relation to his people, and thus his "zeal" as Israel's champion and defender; and (2) God's uniqueness and holiness which is violated by Israel's idolatry (e.g., Josh. 24:19; Ezek. 39:25). The New Testament also suggests that idolatry provokes God to jealousy (e.g., 1 Cor. 10:22). Theologians often interpret the application of such language to God as mere anthropomorphism and thus too easily dismiss it. Yet all language about God is necessarily anthropomorphic, and the question of the meaning of such language has been distorted by an uncritical acceptance of the Greek notion of divine impassibility. Thus the meaning of God's jealousy must be sought in God's character as the holy One, and it is perhaps a measure of the love and esteem in which he holds creation that the rebellion of a creature infinitely lower than himself could be said to occasion jealousy in him.

II. Human Jealousy

As with all human qualities, jealousy can be either a positive emotion or a sinful perversion. In its positive expression, jealousy or zeal is, like God's jealousy, a concern for another's good. It is "jealousy for"— sometimes for God, as in the case of Elijah who was "jealous for the Lord" in his confrontation with the priests of Baal (1 Kgs. 19:10, 14); and sometimes for another person, as in the case of a husband's legal right to his wife's faithfulness (Num. 5:14). The necessary selfless character of positive jealousy is harder to maintain here, but since it is based on a genuine legal right, it is legitimate; thus the Mosaic law specifies a procedure for testing those suspected of adultery (vv. 11-31). The apostle Paul speaks of his "divine jealousy" (Gk. *theoú zélō*) for the Corinthians (2 Cor. 11:2).

On the other hand, human jealousy is almost inevitably sinful. In contrast to righteous jealousy, the sinful perversion is based on the belief that one is entitled to something to which one has no natural right. Examples of this type of jealousy abound in the Bible: e.g., the jealousy of Jacob's other sons over the special favor accorded to Joseph (Gen. 37:11; cf. Acts 7:9); jealousy of those in positions of power, as Dathan and Abiram's jealousy of Moses (Ps. 106:16-18; cf. Num. 16:1-40). The Wisdom Literature warns of the dangers of jealousy and its almost inevitable connection with sinful self-indulgence (e.g., Job 5:2; Prov. 6:34; Cant. 8:6). In the New Testament jealousy appears in lists of vices; Paul classifies it among "works of the flesh" (Gal. 5:20; cf. Rom. 13:8-14). Such jealousy is destructive and divisive (1 Cor. 3:3; 2 Cor. 12:20; cf. Jas. 3:14-16). Characteristically, however, Paul also suggests that jealousy itself, like other sins, can serve an ultimately redemptive purpose; it can be used by God to achieve his providential plan. Thus Paul explains that redemption has been extended to the Gentiles in order to provoke the jealousy of Israel, to the end of inspiring the Jews to faith in Christ (Rom. 10:19; 11:11, 14; cf. Acts 5:17ff.; 17:1-15, where the jealousy of Jewish leaders is aroused by the success of the Christian mission).

JEARIM [jē′ə rĭm, jē′ə rīm], **MOUNT** (Heb. *har yeʿārîm* "mountain of forests").† A mountain on the northern border of Judah (Josh. 15:10). On this ridge is located Chesalon (Heb. *kesālôn* "loins, back"), modern Keslā situated 14.5 km. (9 mi.) west of Jerusalem. Some scholars have identified it with Mt. Seir to the north across Wâdī Chesalon.

JEATHERAI [jē ăth′ə rī] (Heb. *yeʿaṭray*). A Levite of the Gershonite line (1 Chr. 6:21; KJV "Jeaterai"). At v. 41 he is called Ethni; one of these forms may

have resulted from scribal confusion of the Hebrew consonants nun and resh.

JEBERECHIAH [jə bĕr′ə kī′ə] (Heb. *yeberekyāhû* "Yahweh blesses"). The father of Zechariah **17**, who witnessed Isaiah's symbolic prophecy to King Ahaz (Isa. 8:2). Jeberechiah may have been the father-in-law of Ahaz and the grandfather of Hezekiah (cf. 2 Chr. 29:1).

JEBUS [jē′ bŏŏs, jē′bəs] (Heb. *yebûs*).† A Canaanite town, seized by David as the site for his capital and renamed Jerusalem (Josh. 18:28; Judg. 19:10; 1 Chr. 11:4; cf. 2 Sam. 5:6). The name may derive from a clan which constituted the city's pre-Israelite inhabitants, reckoned among the descendants of Canaan (Gen. 10:16; Heb. *yebûsî*; cf. Ezek. 16:3, 45, which suggests a Syro-Hittite background for the city). Jebus does not occur in extrabiblical sources, but the name Jerusalem is attested in sources dating to the third and second millennia B.C. (cf. EA Akk. *Urusalim*); although the specific limits of the site are not certain, archaeological remains indicate occupation as early as the third millennium.

The Jebusites were among several non-Semitic peoples living in the hill country of Canaan in the vicinity of Jerusalem at the time of the Conquest (Num. 13:29; Josh. 3:10; 11:3; cf. Gen. 15:21). Their king, Adonizedek, led an Amorite coalition formed to oppose Joshua (Josh. 10:1-5), and they are numbered among the peoples who were "not driven out" (15:63; Judg. 1:21; cf. 1:8, where Joshua's forces destroyed the city; cf. also 19:1-12). The city is listed among the border towns of both Benjamin (Josh. 18:16, 28) and Judah (15:8).

When David sought a royal city from which to rule he chose one that belonged to neither Israel nor Judah—Jebus/Jerusalem, which remained in Jebusite hands. In spite of the city's impressive defenses, David succeeded in conquering the Jebusites, thus making Jerusalem his own (2 Sam. 5:6-9; cf. 1 Chr. 11:4-8; Zech. 9:7). Nevertheless, 2 Sam. 24:16-25, which recounts David's purchase of the threshing floor of Araunah the Jebusite (later the site of the temple), indicates that the Jebusite presence continued even after David's conquest. Later, during the reign of Solomon, the remaining Jebusites were conscripted for the royal corvée (1 Kgs. 9:20-21).

JECAMIAH (1 Chr. 3:18, KJV). *See* JEKAMIAH **2**.

JECHONIAH. *See* JECONIAH **1**.

JECOLIAH [jĕk′ə lī′ə] (Heb. *yekolyāhû*, *yekolyâ* "Yahweh is able"). The wife of King Amaziah of Judah and mother of Azariah **3** (Uzziah; 2 Kgs. 15:2; KJV "Jecholiah"; 2 Chr. 26:3).

JECONIAH [jĕk′ə nī′ə] (Heb. *yekonyâ*, *yekonyāhû* "Yahweh will establish").

1. Alternate name of King JEHOIACHIN of Judah. In the genealogy of Jesus at Matt. 1:11-12 he is called Jechoniah (Gk. *Iechonias;* KJV "Jechonias").

2. A levitical chief during King Josiah's reign (1 Esdr. 1:9; KJV "Jeconias"). At 2 Chr. 35:9 he is called CONONIAH (**2**).

3. Alternate name of King Jehoahaz of Judah (1 Esdr. 1:34; KJV "Joachaz"). *See* JEHOAHAZ **3.**

JEDAIAH [jə dā′ yə, jə dī′ yə].†
　1. (Heb. *yᵉdāyâ* "Yahweh has favored"). The son of Shimri, and a clan leader in the tribe of Simeon (1 Chr. 4:37).
　2. (Heb. *yᵉdaʿyâ* "Yahweh knows"). A priest who settled in postexilic Jerusalem (1 Chr. 9:10).
　3. The eponymous ancestor of the second division of priests (1 Chr. 24:7).
　4. The "sons of Jedaiah," a priestly family descended from Jeshua; the census of the first return numbers 973 members of this division (Ezra 2:36; Neh. 7:39; cf. 12:19, 21).
　5. (Heb. *yᵉdāyâ*). The son of Harumaph who helped repair the walls of Jerusalem under Nehemiah (Neh. 3:10).
　6. (Heb. *yᵉdaʿâ*). The son of Joiarib; a postexilic priest residing in Jerusalem (Neh. 11:10). He may be the same as **2**, who is represented as a colleague of Joiarib.
　7. A "chief" among the priests and Levites who returned to Jerusalem with Zerubbabel (Neh. 12:6).
　8. Another levitical "chief" who returned with Zerubbabel (Neh. 12:7).
　9. An exile from whom the prophet Zechariah was commanded to extract silver and gold for the crown (LXX "crowns") of the high priest Joshua as a memorial (Zech. 6:10, 14).

JEDIAEL [jə dī′əl] (Heb. *yᵉdîʿaʾēl* "known by God").
　1. A Benjaminite, ancestor of mighty warriors (1 Chr. 7:6, 10-11). The genealogy in which he is named may actually be that of Zebulun, which is not listed here among the northern tribes.
　2. A son of Shimri, and one of David's mighty men (1 Chr. 11:45).
　3. A military chief from the tribe of Manasseh, who deserted to David at Ziklag (1 Chr. 12:20 [MT 21]).
　4. The second son of Meshelemiah; a Korahite gatekeeper for the ark at the time of David (1 Chr. 26:2).

JEDIDAH [jə dī′də] (Heb. *yᵉdîdâ* "beloved"). The mother of King Josiah of Judah; daughter of Adaiah of Bozkath (2 Kgs. 22:1).

JEDIDIAH [jĕd′ə dī′ə] (Heb. *yᵉdîdyâ* "beloved of Yahweh"). A name which Yahweh bestowed upon the infant Solomon through the prophet Nathan (2 Sam. 12:25). Some scholars suggest that this was the king's throne name.

JEDUTHUN [jə dōo′thən] (Heb. *yᵉdûtûn, yᵉdutûn, yᵉdîtûn*).
　1. A chief musician listed with Asaph and Heman as serving in David's tabernacle (1 Chr. 16:41-42; 25:6) and Solomon's temple (2 Chr. 5:12). In addition to providing music (1 Chr. 16:41), Jeduthun and his "sons" (perhaps members of his levitical guild) served as prophets (25:1, 3; cf. 2 Chr. 35:15, where Jeduthun is called the "king's seer"). Parallel listings suggest that Jeduthun may be identified the same as Ethan, a descendant of Merari (1 Chr. 15:17, 19). The name Jeduthun appears in the superscriptions of Pss. 39,

62, and 77, perhaps indicating a musical form or liturgical tradition associated with this individual or his guild (cf. 89, Ethan).
　2. A Korahite Levite; the father of Obed-edom, who with his descendants served as gatekeeper for the ark (1 Chr. 16:38, 42; cf. 1 Chr. 26:1, 4, 8).

JEEZER (Num. 26:30, KJV). *See* AHIEZER **1**.

JEGAR-SAHADUTHA [jē′gər sā′ə dōo′thə] (Aram. *yᵉgar śāhᵃdûṯāʾ* "heap of witness").† The name given by the Aramean Laban to the mound of stones erected to commemorate his covenant with Jacob (Gen. 31:47). Jacob named it, in Hebrew, Galeed.

JEHALLELEL [jə hăl′ə lĕl] (Heb. *yᵉhallelʾēl* "may God shine forth").
　1. A descendant of Judah (1 Chr. 4:16; KJV "Jehaleleel").
　2. A Merarite Levite; the father of Azariah **18** (2 Chr. 29:12; KJV "Jehalelel").

JEHDEIAH [jĕ dē′yə] (Heb. *yehdᵉyāhû* "may Yahweh rejoice").
　1. A descendant of Shubael; a Levite at the time of David (1 Chr. 24:20).
　2. A Meronothite; overseer of the she-asses of David (1 Chr. 27:30).

JEHEZKEL [jə hĕz′kĕl] (Heb. *yᵉhezqēʾl* "may God give strength"). The leader of the twentieth division of priests at the time of David (1 Chr. 24:16; KJV "Jehezekel").

JEHIAH [jə hī′ə] (Heb. *yᵉhîyâ* "the Lord lives"). A gatekeeper for the ark at the time of David (1 Chr. 15:24).

JEHIEL [jə hī′əl] (Heb. *yᵉhîʾēl* "may God give life").†
　1. (1 Chr. 9:35, KJV). *See* JEIEL **2**.
　2. (1 Chr. 11:44, KJV). *See* JEIEL **1**.
　3. A Levite of the second order among those who played the harp at the installation of the ark in Jerusalem (1 Chr. 15:18, 20) and throughout David's reign (1 Chr. 16:5).
　4. A son of Hachmoni who advised or tutored David's sons (1 Chr. 27:32).
　5. A Gershonite Levite who supervised the temple treasury at the time of David (1 Chr. 29:8). Other members of his family or guild also served in this capacity (1 Chr. 26:21-22).
　6. A son of King Jehoshaphat of Judah (2 Chr. 21:2).
　7. A descendant of David's chief musician Heman who assisted in Hezekiah's reform (2 Chr. 29:14, Q; so JB, KJV, NIV; RSV "Jehuel").
　8. An overseer in the temple at the time of Hezekiah's reform (2 Chr. 31:13). He may be the same as **7**.
　9. A chief officer among the priests during Josiah's reforms who assisted in the Passover celebration (2 Chr. 35:8; cf. 1 Esdr. 1:8; RSV mg. "Esyelus"; KJV "Syelus").
　10. The father of Obadiah **10**, who returned with Ezra from the Babylonian captivity (Ezra 8:9; cf. 1 Esdr. 8:35; KJV "Jezelus").

11. A descendant of Elam, and the father of Shecaniah, who took a leading role in Ezra's marriage reforms (Ezra 10:2; cf. 1 Esdr. 8:92).

12. A descendant of the priest Harim who pledged to divorce his foreign wife (Ezra 10:21; cf. 1 Esdr. 9:21; KJV "Hiereel").

13. One who sent away his foreign wife (Ezra 10:26; cf. 1 Esdr. 9:27; KJV "Hierielus"). He may be the same as **11**.

JEHIELI [jə hī'ə lī] (Heb. *yᵉhî'ēlî*). A gentilic form designating the descendants of JEHIEL 5 (1 Chr. 26:21-22).

JEHIZKIAH [jē'hĭz kī'ə] (Heb. *yᵉhizqîyāhû* "may Yahweh give strength").† A son of Shallum; one of the chiefs from the tribe of Ephraim at the time of King Pekah (2 Chr. 28:12).

JEHOADDAH [jə hō'ə də] (Heb. *yᵉhô'addâ*). A Benjaminite; the son of Ahaz and father of Alemeth, Azmaveth, and Zimri (1 Chr. 8:36; KJV "Jehoadah"). At 9:42 he is called Jarah.

JEHOADDAN [jə hō'ə dən] (Heb. *yᵉhô'addān* "Yahweh is delight"[?]). The mother of King Amaziah of Judah (2 Chr. 25:1); called Jehoaddin in the Kethib of 2 Kgs. 14:2 (so RSV).

JEHOAHAZ [jə hō'ə hăz] (Heb. *yᵉhô'āḥāz* "Yahweh has grasped").

1. The eleventh king of Israel, son and successor of Jehu (2 Kgs. 10:35). According to the date formulas in 13:1, 10 he reigned from 814 to 800 B.C., suggesting that the first three of his "seventeen years" (v. 1) constituted a coregency with his father.

Characterized as continuing the covenantal abuses of his predecessors (vv. 2, 6), Jehoahaz incurred the Lord's wrath in the form of repeated attack by the Syrian king Hazael and his son Ben-hadad (vv. 3, 22; cf. 10:32-33). His forces drastically reduced (13:7), Jehoahaz repented for a time and was granted respite through an unnamed "savior" (vv. 4-5), perhaps Jeroboam II or Adad-nirari III of Assyria. Upon his death, Jehoahaz was buried in Samaria and succeeded by his son Joash (**4**; v. 9).

2. The seventeenth king of Judah, fourth son of Josiah and Hamutal the daughter of Jeremiah of Libnah (2 Kgs. 23:30-31 par. 2 Chr. 36:1; 1 Chr. 3:15). He, rather than his elder brother Eliakim (cf. 3:15), was acclaimed king when his father died in battle at Megiddo.

The twenty-three-year-old Jehoahaz ruled in Jerusalem but three months (609 B.C.) before the Egyptian pharaoh Neco II imprisoned him in Riblah and installed in his place Eliakim (Jehoiakim **1**); subsequently, Neco deported Jehoahaz to Egypt, where he died (2 Kgs. 23:31-34 par. 2 Chr. 36:1-4; cf. Jer. 22:10-12; Ezek. 19:2-4).

He is called Shallum at 1 Chr. 3:15; Jer. 22:11 and Jeconiah at 1 Esdr. 1:34 (KJV "Joachaz").

3. An alternate form of AHAZIAH 2, king of Judah *ca.* 842 B.C. (2 Chr. 21:17; cf. 22:1).

JEHOASH. *See* JOASH 3, 4.

JEHOHANAN [jē'hō hă'nən] (Heb. *yᵉhôḥānān* "Yahweh is gracious").†

1. A Korahite Levite; the sixth son of Meshelemiah who served as a gatekeeper in the temple (1 Chr. 26:3).

2. A Judahite commander of a thousand in King Jehoshaphat's army (2 Chr. 17:15).

3. The father of Ishmael, commander of a hundred who joined Jehoiada's palace coup against Queen Athaliah (2 Chr. 23:1). He may be the same as **2**.

4. The son of the high priest Eliashib, in whose room Ezra fasted when preparing for the covenant renewal (Ezra 10:6; KJV "Johanan"; 1 Esdr. 9:1; KJV "Joanan"). Jehohanan's connection with Ezra is an important element in the chronology of the period, particularly if, as some scholars contend, he is the same as the high priest Johanan (**11**; Neh. 12:22-23) or Jonathan (**11**; v. 11). It is unclear when he became high priest.

5. One of the Israelites who had married foreign wives; a son of Bebai (Ezra 10:28; 1 Esdr. 9:29; KJV "Johannes").

6. The son of Tobiah the Ammonite, Nehemiah's opponent (Neh. 6:18; KJV "Johanan"). He married the daughter of Meshullam, who helped repair Jerusalem's walls (cf. 3:4, 30).

7. The head of the priestly house of Amariah at the time of the high priest Joiakim (Neh. 12:13).

8. A priest who officiated at the dedication of the walls of Jerusalem (Neh. 12:42).

JEHOIACHIN [jə hoi'ə kĭn] (Heb. *yᵉhôyāḵîn* "Yahweh establishes"). Nineteenth king of Judah (598/597 B.C.); son and successor of Jehoiakim and Nehushta, the daughter of Elnathan. He is also called Jeconiah (1 Chr. 3:16-17; Esth. 2:6; Jer. 24:1; 27:20; 28:4; 29:2; cf. Matt. 1:11-12, "Jechoniah") and Coniah (Jer. 22:24, 28; 37:1).

Jehoiachin was eighteen years old in 597 B.C. when he assumed the throne in Jerusalem (2 Kgs. 24:8), where he reigned but three months (2 Kgs. 24:8; according to 2 Chr. 36:9, he was eight years old and reigned three months and ten days). When Nebuchadnezzar II of Babylon marched against Jerusalem, Jehoiachin surrendered; the Babylonians then took the king captive, looted the temple and palace, and exiled to Babylon the entire royal court, the nobility, military classes, and skilled workers (2 Kgs. 24:10-16). Nebuchadnezzar then installed Jehoiachin's uncle, Mattaniah (Zedekiah) as king (v. 17).

Tablets discovered in the Babylonian archives (dated between the tenth and thirty-fifth year of Nebuchadnezzar's reign, i.e., between 595/4 and 570/569) bear the name of Jehoiachin (Akk. *Ia-'-kin, Ia-ku-ú-ki-nu*; *ANET*, p. 308). Called "the king of the country of *Ia-ḫu-da*," he is recorded as having received deliveries of sesame oil. Five of his sons, who are not named (cf. 1 Chr. 3:17-18; perhaps born in Babylon while their father was a prisoner), are also listed, along with "eight men from the land of *Ia-ḫu-da*." After thirty-seven years of captivity, Jehoiachin was freed shortly after the ascension of Evil-merodach (Amel-marduk) to the throne (2 Kgs. 25:27-30 par. Jer. 52:31-34).

In later Jewish tradition Jehoiachin is viewed favorably, but the biblical account does not support such a view (2 Kgs. 24:9; cf. Jer. 22:20-30).

JEHOIADA [jə hoi'ə də] (Heb. *yᵉhôyāḏāʿ*) ("Yahweh knows").†

1. The father of Benaiah, who served as a military official for David (2 Sam. 8:18 par. 1 Chr. 18:17; 2 Sam. 23:20, 22 par. 1 Chr. 11:22, 24 [KJV "the son of a valiant man of Kabzeel"]; 1 Kgs. 1:8) and Solomon (1 Kgs. 4:4). Jehoiada is further identified as a priest (1 Chr. 27:5; KJV "chief priest"), a "prince" of the house of Aaron who came to David's aid at Hebron (12:27).

2. A high priest in Jerusalem who rose to prominence during the reign of Athaliah (*ca.* 842-837 B.C.). When Athaliah attempted to exterminate the royal family, Jehoiada and his wife Jehosheba rescued and secretly harbored the infant Joash (Jehoash) for six years (2 Kgs. 11:1-3; 2 Chr. 22:10-12). In the seventh year Jehoiada was instrumental in leading a coup against Athaliah and establishing Joash as king (2 Kgs. 1:4-21 par. 2 Chr. 23:1-21).

While Jehoiada lived, he influenced Joash toward reform, but after the priest's death Joash reversed many of his previous actions (2 Kgs. 12:1-18 par. 2 Chr. 24:1-22); his subsequent murder of Jehoiada's son Zechariah led to the king's demise (vv. 20ff.). Jehoiada died at the age of 130 years and was buried in a royal tomb as reward for his good service to Judah and to Yahweh (vv. 15-16).

3. A son of Benaiah and grandson of Jehoiada **2**; successor to Ahithophel as the king's counselor (1 Chr. 27:34). Some scholars identify him with **1**.

4. (Neh. 3:6, KJV). *See* JOIADA **1**.

5. Alternate form of JOIADA **2** (Neh. 13:28).

6. A priest in Jerusalem during the ministry of Jeremiah (Jer. 29:26).

JEHOIAKIM [jə hoi'ə kĭm] (Heb. *yᵉhôyāqîm* "Yahweh will lift up" or "establish").†

1. King of Judah 609-598 B.C. The second son of Josiah (1 Chr. 3:15) and Zebidah, Jehoiakim (originally named Eliakim) was passed over when his father was killed at Megiddo and his younger brother Jehoahaz was made king. Three months later Pharaoh Neco deposed Jehoahaz and made the apparently pro-Egyptian Eliakim king, changing his name to Jehoiakim (2 Kgs. 23:29-36 par. 2 Chr. 36:1-5).

After the battle of Carchemish (605), in which Nebuchadnezzar defeated Neco, Jehoiakim became a Babylonian vassal (Jer. 46:2). After three years Jehoiakim rebelled in hope of forming an alliance with Egypt (2 Kgs. 24:1; Dan. 1:1), perhaps buoyed by a military standoff at the Egyptian border in 601. Nebuchadnezzar retaliated by instigating harassment by bands of Chaldeans, Syrians, Moabites, and Ammonites, and in 598 Nebuchadnezzar himself laid siege to Jerusalem (Dan. 1:1). It is unclear whether Jehoiakim died sometime during this siege (cf. Jer. 22:19) or was carried off to Babylon (2 Chr. 36:6-7; Dan. 1:2). His son Jehoiachin succeeded him to the throne (2 Kgs. 24:6). The Babylonian Chronicle independently corroborates many of these events.

Scripture harshly condemns Jehoiakim (cf. Jer. 22:13-19; 36:29-31). To him are attributed countless "abominations" (2 Chr. 36:8) and all the "sins of Manasseh" (2 Kgs. 24:3-5). He persecuted and murdered the prophet Uriah, who opposed his religious abuses

and pro-Egyptian policies (Jer. 26:20-23), and refused to heed the prophecies of Jeremiah, even burning the scroll upon which they were written (36:1-32).

2. A high priest, son of Hilkiah and descendant of Shallum, to whom the exiles sent an offering (Bar. 1:7).

JEHOIARIB [jə hoi'ə rĭb] (Heb. *yᵉhôyārîḇ* "may Yahweh contend").† A priest during the reign of King David (1 Chr. 24:7); eponymous ancestor of a priestly house among the returned exiles (9:10). At Neh. 11:10 he is called Joiarib.

JEHONADAB [jə hŏ'nə dăb] (Heb. *yᵉhônāḏāḇ* "Yahweh is generous").† Alternate form of JONADAB.

JEHONATHAN [jə hŏn'ə thən] (Heb. *yᵉhônāṯān* "Yahweh has given").†

1. A Levite who traveled among the cities of Judah teaching the Torah during the reign of Jehoshaphat (2 Chr. 17:8).

2. KJV form of JONATHAN (**8**) at 1 Chr. 27:25, following the MT.

3. A postexilic priest, head of the father's house of Shemaiah (Neh. 12:18).

JEHORAM [jə hôr'əm] (Heb. *yᵉhôrām* "Yahweh is exalted").† The name also occurs in a contracted form, Joram (*yôrām*).

1. King of Israel (*ca.* 852-841 B.C.); the son of Ahab and Jezebel, and brother and successor of Ahaziah. Difficulties in correlating the regnal formulas associated with Jehoram's accession have led to the suggestion that his counterpart, Jehoram of Judah (**2**), began as a coregent with his father Jehoshaphat (cf. 2 Kgs. 1:17; 3:1). Thus the twelve-year reign accorded to Jehoram of Israel (v. 1) generally is accepted as accurate.

Although he is recognized for having abandoned the pagan images worshipped by his parents (v. 2), the biblical judgment on Jehoram is far from favorable ("he did what was evil in the eyes of the Lord"). His lack of faith is evident in his interpretation of God's activity in the events of his day (cf. v. 13; 6:33).

Following Ahab's death Moab revolted against its suzerain Israel (1:1; 3:4-5), an event corroborated by the inscription of King Mesha of Moab (*ca.* 850; *ANET*, pp. 320-21). Jehoram marched against Mesha, aided by Jehoram of Judah and the Edomite king (2 Kgs. 3:4-8). Miraculously rescued from thirst in the wilderness (vv. 9-12), the allies devastated Moab. However, as they lay siege to Kir-hareseth, the last remaining city, the desperate Mesha offered his eldest son as a burnt offering in full view of the revulsed attackers, who withdrew.

Jehoram's reign was marked by intermittent warfare with the Syrians of Aram, who raided Israelite territory (5:2) and laid siege to its cities (6:8-7:20). Jehoram himself was wounded at Ramoth-gilead, where he had sought to repel the Syrians under Hazael (8:28-29).

While Jehoram was recovering at Jezreel, the general Jehu was anointed king over Israel and fomented rebellion throughout the northern kingdom. Jehoram went forth to confront the usurper, but he was slain by Jehu's arrow and his body dumped in Naboth's vineyard, thus fulfilling Elijah's prophecy (1 Kgs. 21:17-19). Jehu then killed Jehoram's mother Jezebel and his brother-in-law Ahaziah, son and successor of Jehoram of Judah, bringing to an end the Omride dynasty (2 Kgs. 9:27, 30-37; cf. 1 Kgs. 21:28-29).

2. King of Judah (849-841 B.C.); son of Jehoshaphat and husband of Athaliah, daughter of Ahab and Jezebel. According to 2 Kgs. 8:17 par., he became king at age thirty-two and reigned eight years; v. 16 places his accession in the fifth year of Jehoram of Israel (849), but 1:17 indicates that he had already ruled one year when his northern counterpart took the throne (852). Scholars suggest that he began as coregent with his father in 853 and became sole ruler in 849.

Immediately upon gaining power Jehoram executed his brothers and some of the nobility (2 Chr. 21:2-4), perhaps because they opposed his paganizing practices (cf. v. 13). An important influence on his reign, typically characterized as evil, was his marriage to the Omride Athaliah (v. 6; cf. vv. 11, 13; 2 Kgs. 8:18). The Chronicler reports that the prophet Elijah rebuked Jehoram, forecasting divine punishment in the form of a Philistine and Arab invasion and the king's fatal illness (2 Chr. 21:11-15; cf. vv. 16-19).

Jehoram's reign was marred by rebellion, by the Edomites to the east and by Libnah, a city on the Philistine border, to the west (2 Kgs. 8:20-22 par. 2 Chr. 21:8-10). Jehoram died "with no one's regret" and was accorded no ceremony, buried apart from the royal cemetery (vv. 19-20; but cf. 2 Kgs. 8:24). He was succeeded by his son Ahaziah (also called Jehoahaz), who was apparently dominated by the widowed Athaliah (2 Kgs. 8:26-27; 2 Chr. 22).

3. A priest at the time of King Jehoshaphat (2 Chr. 17:8).

JEHOSHABEATH [jə hō shăb′ĭ əth] (Heb. *yᵉhô-šaḇ′aṯ* "Yahweh is fullness").† The daughter of King Jehoram of Judah; she spared Ahaziah's son Jehoiada from the queen mother Athaliah (2 Chr. 22:11). At 2 Kgs. 11:2 she is called Jehosheba.

JEHOSHAPHAT [jə hŏsh′ə făt] (Heb. *yᵉhôšāpāṭ* "Yahweh judges").†

1. The son of Ahilud; a recorder in the courts of David and Solomon (2 Sam. 8:16; 20:24 par. 1 Chr. 18:15; 1 Kgs. 4:3).

2. The son of Paruah, and an officer of Solomon responsible for Issachar's portion of the royal provisions (1 Kgs. 4:17).

3. The fourth king of Judah (873-849 B.C.); son of Asa and Azubah the daughter of Shilhi (1 Kgs. 22:42).

Upon gaining the throne Jehoshaphat fortified Judah against Israel (2 Chr. 17:2; cf. vv. 12-19), but overall his reign was marked by a constant quest for peace and friendship with the northern kingdom (1 Kgs. 22:44). This concord is typified by the marriage of his son Jehoram to Athaliah, the daughter of Ahab and Jezebel (2 Chr. 18:1), although the pagan influences thus introduced would later cause Judah much distress (2 Kgs. 8:18, 27). Jehoshaphat lent support to Ahab's expedition to Ramoth-gilead, where Ahab

was killed and Jehoshaphat's own life endangered (1 Kgs. 22:2-40; 2 Chr. 18:3-34). Upon his safe return home, Jehoshaphat was met by the seer Jehu, who reprimanded him for helping "the wicked" who "hate the Lord" (19:2). Jehoshaphat apparently allied with Ahaziah, the son of Ahab, in an unsuccessful maritime expedition (2 Chr. 20:35-36; cf. 1 Kgs. 22:48-49). Subsequently he joined with another of Ahab's sons, Jehoram, and the king of Edom against Mesha of Moab (2 Kgs. 3:4ff.).

Evidence of Jehoshaphat's success in international affairs includes the respect accorded him by neighboring peoples (2 Chr. 17:11), his apparent suzerainty over Edom (1 Kgs. 22:47), and the account of a great victory over the allied Moabites, Ammonites, and Meunites at En-gedi (2 Chr. 20:1-30).

Jehoshaphat's reign is viewed favorably. He followed the righteous example of David (2 Chr. 17:3-4, MT), forsaking the Baals and faithfully serving the God of Israel. Though he did not remove the alternate sanctuaries (high places) used for the worship of Yahweh, he did remove those dedicated to the Baals as well as the Asherah and other accoutrements of cultic prostitution (1 Kgs. 22:43, 46; 2 Chr. 17:6; 19:3). Frequent notice is made of his concern for the word of the Lord (1 Kgs. 22:5ff. par. 2 Chr. 18:4ff.; 20:3-19, 20). Moreover, Jehoshaphat sent "princes," Levites, and priests into the cities of Judah to teach the people the law of the Lord (17:7-9). He also reorganized the judicial system, urging fairness and impartiality in accordance with the covenantal ideal (19:5-11).

Jehoshaphat reigned for twenty-five years and was buried in the city of David. His son Jehoram succeeded him as king (21:1-3). At Matt. 1:8 he is listed among the ancestors of Jesus (KJV "Josaphat").

4. The son of Nimshi and father of King Jehu of Israel, who supplanted the Omride dynasty (2 Kgs. 9:2, 14).

JEHOSHAPHAT [jə hŏsh′ə făt], **VALLEY OF** (Heb. *ʿēmeq yᵉhôšāpāṭ*).† A valley, mentioned by the prophet Joel (Joel 3:2, 12 [MT 4:2, 12]), to which during the days of the messianic restoration of Judah and Jerusalem God will summon the pagan nations to be judged for their treatment of Israel. At v. 14 the same locale is twice called the valley of decision (Heb. *ʿēmeq heḥārûṣ*).

Scholars disagree over whether the valley of Jehoshaphat was a real or symbolic place. Those who favor a real place have identified it with the valleys of Hinnom or Kidron.

JEHOSHEBA [jə hŏsh′ə bə] (Heb. *yᵉhôšeḇaʿ* "Yahweh is fullness"). The daughter of King Jehoram of Judah, sister of King Ahaziah, and wife of the high priest Jehoiada. When the queen mother, Athaliah, had the entire royal family killed, Jehosheba saved Joash, the youngest of Ahaziah's sons, by hiding him in a bedchamber (2 Kgs. 11:2). At 2 Chr. 22:11 her name is given as Jehoshabeath.

JEHOSHUA (Num. 13:16, KJV), **JEHOSHUAH** (1 Chr. 7:27, KJV). *See* JOSHUA.

JEHOVAH [jə hō'və].† A name of God, devised during the Renaissance by artificially combining the consonants of the name Yahweh (held by the Jews to be unutterable) and the vowels of the substitute name Adonai ("the Lord"). See YAHWEH.

JEHOVAH-JIREH [jə hō'və jī'rə] (Heb. *YHWH yir'eh*).* The name given by Abraham to the place where God provided him a ram to be offered in place of Isaac (Gen. 22:14, KJV; NJV "Adonai-yireh"; RSV, NIV "the Lord will provide"; cf. JB). The location remains uncertain, although tradition favors the site of the Solomonic temple; an alternate suggestion is the sanctuary of the oak of Moreh at Shechem.

JEHOVAH-NISSI [jə hō'və nĭs'ī] (Heb. *YHWH nissî*).* Moses's name for the altar commemorating the Israelite victory over the Amalekites at Rephidim (Exod. 17:15, KJV; NJV "Adonai-nissi"). The RSV and NIV translate literally, "The Lord is my banner."

JEHOVAH-SHALOM [jə hō'və shā'ləm] (Heb. *YHWH šālôm*).* The name which Gideon gave to the altar he constructed at Ophrah (Judg. 6:23, KJV; NJV "Adonai-shalom"; mg. "My Lord, 'All-is-well'"). The RSV and NIV render the Hebrew literally, "The Lord is peace" (JB "Yahweh-Peace").

JEHOZABAD [jə hō'zə băd] (Heb. *yᵉhôzābāḏ*, "Yahweh has given").†
1. A servant of Joash of Judah who participated in the king's assassination. According to 2 Kgs. 12:21 (MT 22) (Heb. *yôzābāḏ*) he was the son of Shomer, but 2 Chr. 24:26 (MT *zābāḏ*) calls him the son of Shimrith (a variant of Shomer?), a Moabite woman. He in turn was assassinated by Joash's son and successor, Amaziah **1** (2 Kgs. 14:5).
2. The second son of Obed-edom; a Korahite Levite and gatekeeper for the temple (1 Chr. 26:4).
3. A Benjaminite commander of thousands during the reign of Jehoshaphat (2 Chr. 17:18).

JEHOZADAK [jə hō'zə dăk] (Heb. *yᵉhôṣāḏāq* "Yahweh is righteous").† The son of the chief priest Seraiah who was exiled to Babylon by Nebuchadnezzar (1 Chr. 6:14-15 [MT 5:40-41]); father of the postexilic high priest Joshua, who helped to rebuild the temple (Hag. 1:1, 12, 14; Zech. 2:2, 4; KJV "Josedech"). In Ezra and Nehemiah the name appears as JOZADAK.

JEHU [jē'hū] (Heb. *yēhû'* "he is Yahweh").
1. A prophet and son of Hanani who announced the Lord's judgment against King Baasha of Israel (*ca.* 900-877 B.C.) (1 Kgs. 16:1, 7, 12). He is generally identified as the same prophet who warned King Jehoshaphat of Judah in 853 of the Lord's anger against him for having joined the wicked King Ahab of Israel in battle against the Syrians (2 Chr. 19:2); as a result Jehoshaphat led Judah in renewal of devotion to the Lord. According to 20:34 the acts of Jehoshaphat were written by Jehu in his chronicles and recorded in the Book of the Kings of Israel.
2. A revolutionary general who led a bloody coup d'état, purging the Omride dynasty and the house of

Ahab from Israel, and who then reigned as the tenth king of the northern kingdom (841-814 B.C.). Jehu was the son of Jehoshaphat, the grandson of Nimshi (2 Kgs. 9:2, 14), but is referred to also as Jehu the son (or descendant) of Nimshi (1 Kgs. 19:16; 2 Kgs. 9:20; 2 Chr. 22:7).

Jehu first appears as a member of the personal body guard of King Ahab (2 Kgs. 9:25), and was a witness to the murders of Naboth the Jezreelite and his sons. He accompanied Ahab from Samaria to Jezreel to inspect and take possession of Naboth's vineyard, which Ahab now claimed for himself. There in the vineyard Jehu observed the dramatic encounter between the king and the prophet Elijah, hearing the Lord's judgment against the house of Ahab for this and many other evil deeds (v. 26; cf. 1 Kgs. 21:17-19, 28-29); with an almost missionary zeal Ahab and his Sidonian wife Jezebel had introduced the Tyrian Baal and Asherah in Israel and promoted their worship. In response to Elijah's announcement of divine judgment (v. 21), Ahab repented, thus postponing judgment to the next generation (vv. 27-29). Jehu was without doubt reminded of Elijah's words when Ahab was slain at Ramoth-gilead and the dogs licked up his blood (22:38; cf. 21:24).

After more than fourteen years, the time was ripe for judgment to fall upon the house of Ahab, with Jehu as the Lord's chosen sword of execution. The announcement first came to Elijah at Mt. Horeb (19:16-17), but the anointing was not carried out until the time of the prophet Elisha. While Jehoram, the son of Ahab and king of Israel, was recuperating from battle wounds inflicted by the Syrians, Ahaziah king of Judah went to Jezreel to visit him. This left the army of Israel, encamped at Ramoth-gilead, under the command of Jehu. Elisha dispatched one of the sons of the prophets with a flask of oil to Ramoth-gilead, where he privately anointed Jehu king over Israel (2 Kgs. 9:1-10).

When Jehu came out of the house after his anointing, he hesitated to tell his fellow commanders the prophet's purpose in coming. But the secret could not be kept. The officers hastily created a throne on the steps and blew the trumpet to proclaim Jehu king (v. 13). Immediately Jehu mounted his chariot and headed for Jezreel, for he knew that King Jehoram (Joram) was there. As they came within sight of the city, a watchman on the tower spied the approaching group of riders. Horsemen were sent out to meet them and ascertain their purpose, only to be told to fall in behind them. Finally, the watchman announced to King Jehoram what has become proverbial: "The driving is like the driving of Jehu . . . for he drives furiously" (v. 20). Realizing it was Jehu approaching, Jehoram and Ahaziah of Judah set out in their chariots, meeting him at the property of Naboth the Jezreelite. When Jehoram saw that Jehu intended to act treacherously, he attempted to flee. But Jehu drew his bow and the arrow pierced the king's heart (v. 24). Likewise Ahaziah fled, only to have Jehu's soldiers pursue and shoot him as well (v. 27; cf. 2 Chr. 22:9).

When Jehu entered Jezreel, Jezebel met him at the gate and mockingly called him "Zimri, murderer of your master" (v. 31; cf. 1 Kgs. 16:9, 20). Jehu called out to the eunuchs in her chamber to throw Jezebel down, and her blood splattered on the wall and on the horses which trampled her (2 Kgs. 9:33); when her attendants came to bury her, they found only the skull, feet, and palms of her hands; the dogs had eaten her flesh, and thus fulfilled the prophecy of Elijah (vv. 36-37).

Jehu then took bold steps to destroy every male of the royal line of Ahab, and thus to consolidate his own power over Israel. He sent word to the guardians of Jehoram's seventy sons and the elders of Samaria to select the best of their master's sons (descendants) to take Ahab's throne (10:1-3). Jehu challenged them to support this new king, but they pragmatically responded with submission to Jehu himself. Jehu then commanded them to prove their loyalty by bringing the heads of Jehoram's sons to him at Jezreel by the next day, which they did (vv. 6-7). Likewise, Jehu slaughtered the "great men," friends, and priests associated with the house of Ahab (v. 11).

Jehu's craftiness and bloody violence were exercised further in his "zeal for the Lord" (v. 16). Pretending to serve Baal, he called together all the prophets and worshippers of Baal to offer a great sacrifice to Baal (v. 19). He appointed eighty men to surround the sanctuary, and they massacred all who were inside and then demolished the sacred pillar and the temple of Baal, converting the place into a latrine. Thus Jehu destroyed Baal worship in Israel (v. 8).

The historical record of 2 Kings primarily narrates Jehu's revolution. His reign proper is summarized in only a few brief verses (10:28-36). Although he was not always faithful to the covenantal law, he did execute divine judgment upon the house of Ahab. His dynasty ruled Israel for four generations (841-752), longer than any other house over the northern ten tribes. However, Jehu did witness the decline of both Israel and Judah through the constant aggression of King Hazael of Syria. In 842 the Assyrian king Shalmaneser III asserted authority over Israel, and the famous Black Obelisk pictures Jehu together with a group of Israelites bearing tribute before the king (*ANEP*, nos. 351, 355); the stele's inscription records the "tribute of Jehu, son of Omri (Akk. *Ia-u-a mār Ḫu-um-ri-i)" (ANET*, p. 280; cf. p. 281). The Chronicler gives only a brief summary of Jehu, for he was interested not in Israel but in Judah (cf. 2 Chr. 22:7-9).

3. A Judahite of the family of Jerahmeel; the son of Obed and father of AZARIAH 5 (1 Chr. 2:38).

4. The son of Joshibiah, and a descendant of Simeon. He was a clan leader at the time of King Hezekiah of Judah (1 Chr. 4:35).

5. A mighty Benjaminite warrior from Anathoth and a kinsman of Saul who joined David's army at Ziklag (1 Chr. 12:3).

JEHUBBAH [jə hŭb'ə] (Heb. *yᵉḥubbâ* "hidden"). A son of Shemer and descendant of Beriah from the tribe of Asher (1 Chr. 7:34; **K** *yaḥbâ*). The Qere reads "and Hubbah" (cf. LXX B).

JEHUCAL [jə hōō'kəl] (Heb. *yᵉḥûkal* "Yahweh is powerful"). The son of Shelemiah, sent by King Zedekiah to solicit the prayers of the prophet Jeremiah (Jer. 37:3). At 38:1 he is called Jucal.

JEHUD [jē'hŭd] (Heb. *yᵉḥûḏ* "praise").† A city in the tribal territory of Dan (Josh. 19:45), probably located at modern Yehudīeh, 13 km. (8 mi.) southeast of Joppa. LXX B reads Gk. *Azōr* (cf. Akk. *Azuru*; *ANET*, p. 287), which has been identified with modern Yazur, 6 km. (3.7 mi.) southeast of Joppa.

JEHUDI [jə hōō'dī] (Heb. *yᵉhûḏî* "Jew, Judean").† A court official sent by the princes to summon Baruch to bring Jeremiah's prophecies before King Jehoiakim (Jer. 36:14); later Jehudi himself read the scroll to the king, who cut off portions and burned them (vv. 21, 23). The gentilic form of the name suggests that Jehudi was of foreign origin.

JEHUDIJAH [jē'hə dī'jə] (Heb. *hayᵉḥuḏiya* "Jewish [woman]").* The Jewish wife of Mered (1 Chr. 4:18, KJV). The RSV translates literally, "his Jewish wife" (NIV "Judean"); the JB reading makes her the spouse of Eshtemoa in v. 17.

JEHUEL [jə hōō'əl] (Heb. **K** *yᵉḥû'ēl*; **Q** *yᵉḥî'ēl*).* A levite who assisted with Hezekiah's reforms (2 Chr. 29:14, RSV); probably the same as JEHIEL 5 (so KJV, JB, NIV).

JEHUSH (1 Chr. 8:39, KJV). *See* JEUSH 3.

JEIEL [jə ī'əl] (Heb. *yᵉ'î'ēl* "God has healed" or "preserved").†
1. A chief of the tribe of Reuben (1 Chr. 5:7).
2. An ancestor of the Gibeonites and King Saul (1 Chr. 9:35, Q; K "Jeuel"; KJV "Jehiel"). The RSV inserts the name at 8:29, following LXX.
3. A son of Hotham the Aroerite; one of David's mighty men (1 Chr. 11:44, Q; K "Jeuel"; KJV "Jehiel").
4. A levitical gatekeeper and musician who played the lyre when the ark was brought to Jerusalem (1 Chr. 15:18, 21; 16:5b); at 1 Chr. 15:24 he is called Jehiah. At 16:5b the name may better be read as Jaaziel (cf. 15:18; v. 20, "Aziel").
5. A Levite of the line of Asaph; an ancestor of Jahaziel, who prophesied victory for King Jehoshaphat (2 Chr. 20:14). He may be the same as **4**.
6. A secretary who prepared a military roster for King Uzziah (2 Chr. 26:11).
7. (2 Chr. 29:13, KJV). *See* JEUEL **2**. Perhaps the same as **4**.
8. A chief of the Levites who contributed to the Passover offering at the time of Josiah (2 Chr. 35:9; cf. 1 Esdr. 1:9, "Ochiel").
9. (Ezra 8:13, KJV). *See* JEUEL **3**.
10. A son of Nebo who was compelled to divorce his non-Israelite wife (Ezra 10:43).

JEKABZEEL [jə kăb'zĭ əl] (Heb. *yᵉqabṣᵉ'ēl* "God gathers").† A city of Judah near the Edomite border (Neh. 11:25). *See* KABZEEL.

JEKAMEAM [jĕk'ə mē'əm] (Heb. *yᵉqam'ām* "may the kinsman establish"). The fourth son of Hebron (1 Chr. 23:19); head of a levitical father's house (24:23).

JEKAMIAH [jĕk'ə mī'ə] (Heb. *y^eqamyâ* "may Yahweh lift up").

1. A Judahite, son of Shallum and descendant of Jerahmeel (1 Chr. 2:41).

2. A son or descendant of King Jeconiah (Jehoiachin) of Judah (1 Chr. 3:18; KJV "Jecamiah").

JEKUTHIEL [jə kōō' thǐ əl] (Heb. *y^eqûṭî'ēl* "may God sustain"). A man from the tribe of Judah, descendant of Mered and father of Zanoah (1 Chr. 4:18).

JEMIMAH [jə mī'mə] (Heb. *y^emîmâ* "little dove" [?]). The first of Job's three daughters, born to him after he had surmounted his trials (Job 42:14; KJV "Jemima").

JEMUEL [jĕm'yŏŏ əl, jə mōō'əl] (Heb. *y^emû'ēl*). A son of Simeon (Gen. 46:10; Exod 6:15). At Num. 26:12; 1 Chr. 4:24 he is called Nemuel.

JEPHTHAH [jĕf'thə] (Heb. *yiptāḥ,* "he [God] shall open [the womb]").† A military leader who defeated the Ammonites and Philistines in Transjordan and subsequently became a judge in Israel (Judg. 10:6–12:7).

Jephthah was the illegitimate son of Gilead, born in the town of the same name. When his half-brothers grew up, they drove him away so he would have no claim to their inheritance. Jephthah fled northeast to the land of Tob where he became the leader of a band of outlaws (11:1-3).

In the meantime, the Philistines and Ammonites had overpowered the Israelites as divine punishment for their idolatry (10:6-8). The Israelites endured eighteen years of oppression, but matters came to a head when the Ammonites crossed the Jordan and camped at Gilead (v. 9). Then the Israelites repented of their idolatry and prayed for deliverance (vv. 10-16).

The elders of Gilead, lacking an effective leader, appealed to Jephthah to command the Israelite forces. Reminded of the past injustice, the Gileadites promised that Jephthah would rule after the battle (11:4-11). Jephthah returned to Gilead and immediately opened diplomatic relations with the king of the Ammonites, who accused the Israelites of wrongfully seizing the land when they came up from Egypt. Jephthah responded that Israel had intended to pass through the land peacefully until Sihon, the former Ammonite king, launched an unprovoked attack. God had then given Israel the victory and the Ammonite territory, where they had now lived for many years. The Ammonite king refused this interpretation and prepared for battle (vv. 12-28).

The Spirit of the Lord came upon Jephthah, and he advanced against the Ammonite forces, vowing that if he were victorious whoever met him upon his return he would offer for a burnt offering (v. 31, RSV). When he did indeed return home victorious, the first one to meet him was his only child, a virgin daughter with no husband or son to redeem her from his vow; yet she told him to keep his pledge after a two-month postponement during which she might mourn her virginity. Jephthah consented and at the end of the allotted time kept his vow. In commemoration of these

events it became customary for Israelite maidens to lament the daughter of Jephthah four days each year (vv. 34-40).

After the successful conclusion to the battle, some men from the tribe of Ephraim challenged Jephthah, claiming that they had been intentionally left out of the conflict—for which they intended to punish Jephthah by burning both him and his house. Jephthah responded that he had called them to battle, but the Ephraimites had not come. War broke out between the two parties, but the Gileadites soon had the Ephraimites on the run. Taking the fords of the Jordan, they identified the fugitive Ephraimites by a difference in dialect (the Ephraimites said "Sibboleth" ["stream"] instead of "Shibboleth"). According to 12:1-6, the Gileadites killed forty-two thousand Ephraimites during the conflict.

Jephthah continued to judge Israel until his death six years later, whereupon he was buried at Gilead (v. 7; so RSV, following LXX).

The Jephthah narrative raises a number of questions, but none is more important than that of human sacrifice (cf. Gen. 22; 2 Kgs. 16:3; 21:6, as well as abundant archaeological evidence supporting this practice). There is no way to determine whether Jephthah intended his vow to mean a human sacrifice (the Hebrew indefinite relative pronoun *'^ašer* can mean either "whoever" or "whatever [so KJV, NIV]"), but certainly he did not intend to promise the life of his only child. Nevertheless, the narrative clearly reports that he kept his vow.

JEPHUNNEH [jə fŭn'ə] (Heb. *y^epunneh* "may he [God] turn").

1. The father of Caleb, from the tribe of Judah (e.g., Num. 13:6; Josh. 14:13); also called a Kenizzite (vv. 6, 14; Num. 32:12; cf. 1 Chr. 4:15).

2. A son of Jether, from the tribe of Asher (1 Chr. 7:38).

JERAH [jĕr'ə] (Heb. *yeraḥ* "moon"). A son of Joktan and descendant of Shem (Gen. 10:26 par. 1 Chr. 1:20). He was probably the eponymous ancestor of a place in South Arabia.

JERAHMEEL [jə rä'mē əl] (Heb. *y^eraḥm^e'ēl,* "may God have mercy").

1. The firstborn son of Hezron and descendant of Judah through Tamar (1 Chr. 2:9, 25-27); brother of Caleb (v. 42). He was the ancestral head of the Jerahmeelites, a clan living on Judah's southern frontier, whose territory David raided while in the service of Achish (1 Sam. 27:10); later David distributed a portion of the spoils to the Judahite elders living there (30:29). Some scholars think that 1 Chr. 2:9 refers to an adoptive rather than lineal relationship and that this material may reflect the social history of the Jerahmeelites.

2. A Merarite Levite, the son of Kish 3 (1 Chr. 24:29).

3. A member of the royal court sent by King Jehoiakim of Judah to seize Jeremiah and Baruch (Jer. 36:26). His title, "the king's son," may designate one of royal birth but not an heir (NEB "a royal prince";

cf. JB), or perhaps one of the king's officers (NEB mg. "deputy"; cf. 1 Kgs. 22:26). The KJV renders the Hebrew literally, "son of Hammelech."

JERED [jĕr'əd] (Heb. *yereḏ*).†
1. A son of Mered by his Jewish wife; the father of Gedor (1 Chr. 4:18).
2. (1 Chr. 1:2, KJV). See JARED.

JEREMAI [jĕr'ə mī] (Heb. *yᵉrēmay*). A son of Hashum; an Israelite who had to divorce his foreign wife (Ezra 10:33).

JEREMIAH [jĕr'ə mī'ə] (Heb. *yirmᵉyāhû, yirmᵉyâ* "Yahweh lifts up" or "establishes").
1. The father of Hamutal, wife of King Josiah (2 Kgs. 23:31; 24:18 par. Jer. 52:1). A resident of Libnah, he was the grandfather of King Jehoahaz and King Zedekiah.
2. The head of a father's house in the half-tribe of Manasseh (1 Chr. 5:24).
3. A Benjaminite who came to David's aid at Ziklag (1 Chr. 12:4 [MT 5]).
4. The name of two Gadite officers who joined David at Ziklag (1 Chr. 12:10, 13 [MT 11, 14]).
5. A priest who sealed the new covenant of Nehemiah (Neh. 10:2 [MT 3]).
6. A priest, also the head of a father's house, who returned with Zerubbabel from the Exile (Neh. 12:1, 12).
7. A priest who participated in the dedication of the walls of Jerusalem at the time of Nehemiah (Neh. 12:34). He may be the same as 5 above.
8. A prophet from Anathoth whose ministry is recorded in the book of Jeremiah; son of the priest Hilkiah (Jer. 1:1). His prophetic call came in the thirteenth year of King Josiah (*ca.* 627 B.C.), suggesting that he was born early in Josiah's reign or during that of his predecessor Manasseh. Jeremiah's ministry spans some forty years during the reigns of the final five kings of Judah. After Jerusalem fell to the Babylonians in 587 he was allowed to remain in Judah with the poorer elements of the populace; but after the assassination of the Babylonian governor Gedaliah the prophet was forced to flee to Egypt. See JEREMIAH, BOOK OF.
9. The son of Habazziniah and father of Jaazaniah, a Rechabite contemporary with the prophet Jeremiah (Jer. 35:3).

JEREMIAH, BOOK OF.† The recorded utterances and activities of the prophet Jeremiah; the second of the Major Prophets in the Old Testament canon.

I. Origins

The book of Jeremiah has been recognized as "an anthology of anthologies," a compilation of various collections of Jeremiah's oracles and pronouncements as well as biographical and autobiographical accounts of his life and ministry. Jer. 36 suggests that significant portions of the book may have been dictated by the prophet to his friend and secretary Baruch; other portions, particularly the biographical material in the second half of the book, are often attributed to the memoirs of this close associate.

II. Setting

Jeremiah's ministry extended more than forty years, encompassing much of the reigns of the last five kings of Judah. Thus he was a contemporary of the prophets Zephaniah, Nahum, Habakkuk, and Ezekiel. His call came in 627 B.C., before the discovery of the lawbook gave impetus to Josiah's reforms. The death of Assurbanipal *ca.* 626 led to the demise of Assyrian power, and Josiah was able to assert Judah's independence. Most of Jeremiah's recorded activities refer to events and circumstances following the death of Josiah at Megiddo in 609. Josiah's son and successor Jehoahaz (Shallum) ruled only three months before he was deposed by the Egyptian pharaoh Neco and deported to Egypt. In his place Neco installed Jehoiakim, who soon abandoned his father Josiah's reforms. The resurgent Babylonians under Nebuchadnezzar II routed Neco's forces at Carchemish in 605 and thus gained control of Syria and Palestine. Buoyed by the Neo-Babylonians' failure to subjugate Egypt in 601, Jehoiakim sought to regain independence for Judah. But Nebuchadnezzar retaliated, laying siege to Jerusalem; in 598 he captured the city, looted the temple, and exiled the king, Jehoiakim's successor Jehoiachin (Jeconiah or Coniah), and many of the nobility. Zedekiah, whom the Babylonians then named king, bowed to his advisors' pressure to join an Egyptian coalition against Babylon. Nebuchadnezzar again invaded Judah, destroying Jerusalem and the temple in 586 and deporting the king and most of the population. When the Babylonian governor Gedaliah was assassinated, many of the Jews who had remained (including Jeremiah) fled to Egypt.

III. Contents

Following a superscription identifying the prophet and the extent of his ministry (Jer. 1:1-3), ch. 1 recounts Jeremiah's call (vv. 4-10) and initial visions (vv. 11-19).

The first half of the book (chs. 2–25) is comprised primarily of oracles against Judah and Jerusalem. Chs. 2–6, which date from the time of Josiah, include an indictment of Israel's apostasy (ch. 2), a plea for repentance (3:1–4:4), and announcement of the coming judgment (4:5–6:30).

The next collection (chs. 7–20) dates mostly from the reign of Jehoiakim. It begins with the temple sermon (7:1-15), in which Jeremiah decries the false sense of security derived from the mere presence of Solomon's temple, and the denunciation of pagan and syncretistic worship (7:16–8:3). Various oracles are preserved in 8:4–10:25: Judah's backsliding and indifference, a barren vine, a lament over Judah, uncircumcision of the heart, and a satire on idolatry. Jeremiah's discourse on the broken covenant (11:1-17) provokes an attack on his life (11:18–12:6). Ch. 13 records the prophet's symbolic burial of the linen waistcloth (vv. 1-11) and the allegory of the wine jar (vv. 12-14). A series of laments follows: drought, famine, and the fall of Jerusalem (14:1–15:9), and a personal lament over the prophet's inner struggles (vv. 10-21). Jeremiah's life is depicted as a symbol of the coming judgment (16:1-13), followed by various sayings: judgment, conversion of the nations, trust in God, keeping the Sabbath (16:14–17:27). The allegory of the potter (18:1-12) and the symbolic actions of the broken flask (19:1-13) are presented in the context of the prophet's public persecution (18:18-23; 19:14–20:6). The section concludes with Jeremiah's further struggle about his calling and an expression of deep personal despair (vv. 7-18).

Chs. 21–25 focus primarily on the reign of Zedekiah. The section opens with Zedekiah's inquiry of Jeremiah concerning the invasion by Nebuchadnezzar, and the prophet's counsel to surrender (21:1-10). Oracles concerning the royal house follow, including the duties of the king, utterances regarding Jehoahaz, Jehoiakim, and Jehoiachin, and the promise of a messianic ruler (21:11–23:8). Vv. 9-40 contain oracles against the prophets of Judah. The vision of the basket of figs (ch. 24) concerns the exiles and those who remained in Palestine after the fall of Jerusalem. The collection concludes with Yahweh's judgment upon the nations (ch. 25).

The second major section of the book (chs. 26–45) consists of biographical material, generally identified as "Baruch's memoirs." Ch. 26 recounts Jeremiah's temple sermon, the resultant trial, and his narrow escape from death. Employing a symbolic yoke, Jeremiah warns against Judah's entering the Egyptian coalition against Babylon (ch. 27); his confrontation with the prophet Hananiah follows (ch. 28). Jeremiah's correspondence with the exiles in Babylon is preserved in ch. 29. Chs. 30–33, the "Book of Consolation," include oracles of the restoration of Israel and Judah (chs. 30–31), an account of Jeremiah's purchase of land in Anathoth (ch. 32), and prophecy of the restoration of Judah and Jerusalem ("the righteous Branch"; ch. 33). Jeremiah warns Zedekiah of the impending siege of Jerusalem (34:1-7), addresses the broken pledge of the slave owners (vv. 8-22), and extols the fidelity of the Rechabites (ch. 35). Ch. 36 relates Jeremiah's dictation of the scroll to Baruch and its burning by Jehoiakim. After twice consulting with Zedekiah and being imprisoned for his prophecies, Jeremiah instructs the king to surrender to Babylon (chs. 37–38). The fall of Jerusalem and Jeremiah's release from prison are recorded in 39:1–40:6. The memoirs continue with accounts of further Judean revolt and the assassination of Gedaliah, the Jews' flight to Egypt, and Jeremiah's prophecy there (40:7–44:30). The compilation concludes with an earlier oracle of deliverance addressed to Baruch (ch. 45).

Chs. 46–51 are a collection of various oracles against foreign nations: Egypt (ch. 46), the Philistines (ch. 47), Moab (ch. 48), Ammon (49:1-6), Edom (vv. 7-22), Damascus (vv. 23-27), neighboring Arab peoples (vv. 28-33), Elam (vv. 34-39), and Babylon (chs. 50–51).

The book concludes with a historical account of the fall of Jerusalem (ch. 52; par. 2 Kgs. 24:18–25:30).

IV. Literary Aspects

The anthological nature of the book of Jeremiah is perhaps most evident when attempting to determine precisely the chronology of the prophet's ministry and at times the setting or intent of the prophecies. The book's complex literary development is further suggested by comparison of the Hebrew and Greek (LXX) versions. Several passages (approximately 12 percent

of the canonical book, which some scholars thus interpret as expansions in the Hebrew text) are lacking in the LXX (e.g., 33:14-26; 39:3-14). Moreover, in the LXX the oracles against foreign nations (chs. 46–51) are grouped, in a different order, between 25:13 and 15 of the Hebrew text. Jer. 10:11 is in Aramaic.

Prose and poetic forms are juxtaposed throughout the book. Most characteristic of Old Testament prophetic writings are the poetic oracles, which include judgment speeches (e.g., 2:2-3, 5-37; 46:2-12), sayings (e.g., 10:2-10, 12-16), and laments (e.g., 14:2-10, 17-22). Of particular importance in understanding Jeremiah as a person are the poetic confessions or personal laments (e.g., 15:10-21; 17:14-21; 20:7-18). In addition to biography (e.g., chs. 26–29, 36–45) and historical narrative (ch. 52), the prose materials include oracles (e.g., ch. 24), sermons (e.g., 7:1-15), allegory (18:1-12), symbolic actions (e.g., 13:1-11; 19:1-2, 10-11), and epistles (ch. 29). Among the various literary devices which the prophet employs are rhetorical questions (e.g., 2:32; 18:14-15), paronomasia (e.g., 1:11-12; 14:8; 17:13), and wisdom formulas (e.g., 13:12).

V. Theology

At the core of Jeremiah's thought is his concern for the relationship between God and mankind. The book focuses primarily on the relationship between God and his covenant people as embodied in the surviving kingdom of Judah, but it is concerned also with the relationship between God and the prophet Jeremiah himself and that between God and all humanity (specifically "the nations"). God has loved his people "with an everlasting love" and has remained faithful to them (31:3), delivering them from oppressors and otherwise directing the events of history (e.g., 2:6ff.). Indeed, he is the lord of creation (e.g., 5:22, 24; 27:5). But Judah has rebelled against God and violated the terms of the covenant (2:29), turning toward the gods of neighboring peoples (e.g., vv. 23-28) and concerning themselves with cultic observances (7:1-15) rather than ethical behavior (5:26-28). Unless the people repent and "return" (Heb. *šûḇ*; e.g., 3:1–4:4) to the covenantal ideals (e.g., 7:5-6; 18:11; cf. the language of the covenantal lawsuit, 11:20; 20:12; 25:31), punishment is inevitable (e.g., 26:4-6; 38:17-23). Indeed, God was to employ Judah's very enemies as the instrument of punishment, bringing destruction upon his chosen people (4:11ff.; 27:6-9).

Yet despite the fall of Jerusalem and the exile of its people, the "sorrowful" Jeremiah is able to look with hope beyond the political and religious catastrophe. Even as the city was within the clutches of the invading Babylonians, Jeremiah purchased the estate of his cousin Hanamel at Anathoth, thus demonstrating his faith that Yahweh would one day restore his people (ch. 32). The prophet's correspondence with the exiles in Babylon envisions a day when the people would be returned to their land and their fortunes regained (ch. 29; cf. 30:18-22). A day would come when the people again sought the Lord, and he would enact with them a "new covenant" of obedience and fellowship, "written upon their hearts" (31:31-34). Moreover, God was to restore the line of David, raising "a righteous Branch," a Messiah, who would "execute justice and righteousness in the land" (23:5-6; 3:14-16).

V. Evaluation

Because his ministry is one of the most thoroughly documented in the Old Testament, Jeremiah is perhaps the best known of the prophets. His personal struggles with the prophetic calling (e.g., 1:7, 9; 20:14-18) and his straightforward proclamation which resulted in both isolation and personal danger (e.g., 15:10-21; cf. 11:18ff.; 20:7) show him to be sensitive, honest, and courageous. Jeremiah's devotion to the word of God set him in stark contrast with many of his contemporaries among the prophets (cf. 28:1-17). The intensity of his faith and his uncompromising commitment indeed make Jeremiah a "a prophet like Moses" (cf. Deut. 18:18).

Bibliography. J. Bright, *Jeremiah,* 2nd ed. AB 21 (1978); W. L. Holladay, *Jeremiah: Spokesman Out of Time* (Philadelphia: 1974); J. A. Thompson, *The Book of Jeremiah.* NICOT (1980); J. G. S. S. Thomson, *The Word of the Lord in Jeremiah* (London: 1959).

JEREMIAH, LAMENTATIONS OF. *See* LAMENTATIONS, BOOK OF.

JEREMIAH, LETTER OF.† A book of the Apocrypha, supposedly a letter written by the prophet Jeremiah in 597 B.C. to those citizens of Judah about to be exiled to Babylon (cf. Jer. 29). Regarded as canonical by Origen and others of the Greek Church Fathers, the letter occurs as an independent book following Lamentations in most LXX manuscripts. In the Vulgate and some Greek and Syriac manuscripts it constitutes the sixth chapter of the deuterocanonical Baruch (so KJV, which entitles it the "Epistle of Jeremy").

Actually the work is a homily based on an Aramaic passage in the canonical book (10:11), imploring the exiles to eschew the idolatry of their neighbors in Bablyon. It is reminiscent of Isa. 44:9-20; Jer. 10:1-16; and similar passages which mock the inefficacy of human-crafted pagan idols. Following the superscription (Ep.Jer. 1) and an introduction setting forth the reason for and nature of the exile (vv. 2-7), the book consists of nine stanzas decrying the folly of pagan worship, all but the last ending with a refrain drawn from Jer. 10:11.

Based on linguistic considerations and historical factors, most scholars now date the work to the Hellenistic period, specifically the end of the fourth century. Others, however, would place it in the time of John Hyrcanus I (end of the second century) or the first century B.C. (cf. 2 Macc. 2:2). Scholarly consensus has long set its composition in Alexandria (cf. Ep.Jer. 19, which may suggest Hellenistic Egyptian rites), but some recent scholars posit Mesopotamian (cf. vv. 31-32, 40-43) or Palestinian (cf. v. 1) origins.

Recent scholarship, citing apparent Hebraisms and other usuages which may reflect translation, contends that the book was composed in Hebrew; some scholars favor a Greek or Aramaic original. The earliest extant versions are Greek, including a fragment containing vv. 43-44 discovered in Qumran Cave 7.

Bibliography. C. A. Moore, *Daniel, Esther, and Jeremiah: The Additions.* AB 44 (1977), pp. 317-358.

JEREMIEL [jə rĕm'ĭ əl, jĕr ə mī'əl] (Lat. *Hieremihel,* from Heb. *yᵉraḥmᵉʾēl* [?]).* The archangel who responded to the questions of the righteous dead concerning resurrection (2 Esdr. 4:36; KJV "Uriel"). He is presumed to be the same as Ramiel or Ramael (so Syr.; cf. 2 Bar. 55:3) or Remiel (1 En. 20:8, mg.).

JEREMOTH [jĕr'ə mōth, jĕr'ə mŏth] (Heb. *yᵉrēmôṯ* "swollen").

1. A Benjaminite, son of Becher (1 Chr. 7:8; KJV "Jerimoth"). Some scholars regard this genealogy as that of Zebulun.

2. A son of Elpaal; head of a Benjaminite father's house (1 Chr. 8:14). He may be the same as JEROHAM 2 at v. 27.

3. A Merarite Levite; a son of Mushi (1 Chr. 23:23); called Jerimoth (4) at 1 Chr. 24:30.

4. Leader of the fifteenth division of levitical singers at the time of David (1 Chr. 25:22). He is probably the same as JERIMOTH 5 (so NIV).

5. A chief officer of Naphtali; the son of AZRIEL 2 (1 Chr. 27:19; Heb. *yᵉrîmôṯ*; so KJV).

6. A son of Elam, listed among those who divorced their foreign wives under Ezra (Ezra 10:26; 1 Esdr. 9:27; KJV "Hieremoth").

7. A son of Zattu who divorced his foreign wife during Ezra's reform (Ezra 10:27; 1 Esdr. 9:28; KJV "Jarimoth").

8. A son of Bani, listed among those who put away their foreign wives under Ezra's reform (Ezra 10:29 K; KJV "Ramoth," following Q; 1 Esdr. 9:30; KJV "Hieremoth").

JERIAH [jə rī'ə] (Heb. *yᵉrîyāhû* "may Yahweh see").† The head of a levitical house; son of Hebron and descendant of Kohath (1 Chr. 23:19; 24:23). He was chief of the Hebronites at the time of King David. At 26:31 he is called Jerijah (Heb. *yᵉrîyâ*).

JERIBAI [jĕr'ə bī] (Heb. *yᵉrîbay*). A son of Elnaam; one of David's mighty men (1 Chr. 11:46).

JERICHO [jĕr'ə kō] (Heb. *yᵉrēḥô, yᵉrîḥô, yᵉriḥô, yᵉrîḥōh*).† An important city situated about 16 km. (10 mi.) northwest of the Dead Sea in the Jordan valley. Also called "the city of palms/palm trees" (Deut. 34:3; Judg. 1:16; 3:13; 2 Chr. 28:15), biblical Jericho has had a moving and significant history that can be divided into two parts—the Canaanite/Israelite period and the period of the Hasmonean/Herodian city.

Jericho is situated in a fertile plain referred to as the "plains of Jericho" (Josh. 4:13; 2 Kgs. 25:5; cf. Deut. 34:3) near the Jordan river, directly west of Moab (e.g., Num. 22:1; Josh. 13:32), close to the hills of eastern Benjamin (Josh. 2:16, 22), and at the border separating the territories of Ephraim and Benjamin (16:1-2). It is 28 km. (17 mi.) east-northeast of Jerusalem and 11 km. (7 mi.) west of the Jordan. The surroundings were pleasant, and ancient writers praised its palm and balsam trees (cf. the adjacent oasis, ʿAin es-Sulṭân); accordingly, some would interpret the name to mean "a scented place," but others pursue the meaning "city of the moon," suggesting ancient worship of the West Semitic moon-goddess there (cf. Heb. *yārēaḥ* "moon").

I. Biblical References

Its location along a major east-west trade route made Jericho a key city for commerce, and its strategic setting would have made it an important conquest for the Israelites after crossing the Jordan. It was here that the Israelite scouts encountered the harlot Rahab (Josh. 2), after which the people crossed the miraculously halted waters of the Jordan "opposite Jericho" (3:14-17). According to 6:20, the walls of the city fell down flat when the Israelites, bearing the ark of God, sounded their trumpets. Joshua's company destroyed the city (v. 21; cf. Heb. 11:30), and the entire region was assigned to Benjamin (Josh. 18:12, 21). During the period of the judges, Jericho was conquered by the Moabite Eglon in his suppression of Israel (Judg. 3:13).

When Jericho later came under Ammonite rule, David sent messengers to console the new king Hanun on the death of his father, who had been on friendly terms with Israel. Hanun, however, shamed the messengers by shaving off half of their beards so that they were compelled to remain in Jericho until their beards grew out (2 Sam. 10:1-5 par. 1 Chr. 19:1-5).

At the time of Ahab (ninth century B.C.) the city was rebuilt by Hiel of Bethel, who sacrificed his first-born son in laying its foundation and his youngest son in setting up its gates (1 Kgs. 16:34), thus fulfilling Joshua's curse (Josh. 6:26). Shortly thereafter Elisha encountered a local prophetic guild at Jericho and learned that his master Elijah would soon depart (2 Kgs. 2:4-5); it was here that he was acknowledged as Elijah's successor (vv. 15-18) and performed an inaugural miracle (vv. 19-22). During the Syro-Ephraimite conflict (*ca.* 734), Ephraimite chiefs gave respite to Judean captives at Jericho (2 Chr. 28:15). It was here also that the Babylonians captured Zedekiah, the last king of Judah, as he fled Nebuchadnezzar (2 Kgs. 25:5-6 par. Jer. 39:5-6; 52:8-9). After the Babylonian captivity, Jericho was once again occupied (Ezra 2:34), and its inhabitants helped to rebuild Jerusalem (Neh. 3:2).

The Synoptic Gospels include three accounts of Jesus' restoring the sight of blind men just outside Jericho (Matt. 20:29-34; Mark 10:46-52; Luke 18:35-43). Jesus encountered the tax collector Zacchaeus at Jericho (19:1-10), and the parable of the Good Samaritan is set on the Jerusalem-Jericho road (10:30).

II. Archaeology

Extensive excavations have been conducted at Tell es-Sulṭân (C. Warren, 1867; E. Sellin and C. Watzinger, 1907-1909; J. Garstang, 1930-1936; K. M. Kenyon, 1952-1958), with much attention devoted to the city walls and evidence of the site's occupation at the time of Joshua's invasion. Jericho was first occupied in the Mesolithic period (*ca.* 9000), and a stone wall var-

iously dated from 8000-6000 underscores the tradition of Jericho as the oldest walled city in the world. Other periods of occupation have been dated to the Chalcolithic period (fourth millennium), Early Bronze I (*ca.* 3200-2800), and Middle Bronze I (*ca.* 2100-1900) and II (*ca.* 1900-1500).

According to Garstang, a double wall consisting of a thin outer wall and a brick inner defense wall was the wall that fell before the Israelites *ca.* 1400. But Kenyon vigorously disagreed, claiming that these remains were actually two walls much earlier than Joshua. The lack of conclusive evidence for a city of any substance destroyed in the fourteenth-thirteenth centuries or a subsequent Late Bronze (Israelite) occupation thus supporting Joshua's conquest continues to perplex scholars. Possible explanations include erosion or other forces having obliterated the remains or the less likely possibility that the site then occupied was actually another tell in the area.

Jericho apparently remained unoccupied until the eighth century. Substantial remains of an unwalled settlement have been dated to the seventh century. The site was abandoned after the Babylonian invasion in the early sixth century.

In the second century B.C. settlement was resumed at Tulûl Abū el-ʿAlâyiq, situated along both banks of the Wâdī Qelt approximately 1.5 km. (1 mi.) south of the Old Testament city. The Hasmonean kings selected this site for their winter residence, and Herod the Great lavishly renovated "New Testament Jericho" and its royal palace, adding sunken gardens, guest houses, a Roman bath, and public buildings. The city survived capture by Vespasian *ca.* A.D. 68. Evidence of its continued occupation dates to the time of Bar Kokhba (132-135) and the Bordeaux Pilgrim (333).

Shortly thereafter this site also was abandoned and replaced by a Byzantine city 1.5 km. (1 mi.) to the east. Modern Jericho (Arab. *Erikha*) is located on this site.

Bibliography. K. M. Kenyon, *Digging Up Jericho* (New York: 1957); Kenyon *et al.*, "Jericho," *EAEHL* 2:550-575.

JERIEL [jĕrʹī əl] (Heb. *yᵉrîʾēl* "may God see"). A son (or descendant) of Tola; head of a father's house in the tribe of Issachar (1 Chr. 7:2).

JERIJAH [jə rīʹjə] (Heb. *yᵉrîyâ* "may Yahweh see"). A chief of the Hebronites (1 Chr. 26:31). Elsewhere he is called JERIAH.

JERIMOTH [jĕrʹī mŏth] (Heb. *yᵉrîmôṯ* "swollen").
1. A son of Bela; a "mighty warrior" listed among the heads of Benjaminite fathers' houses (1 Chr. 7:7).
2. (1 Chr. 7:8, KJV). See JEREMOTH 1.
3. A Benjaminite mercenary (one of the "mighty men") who joined David at Ziklag (1 Chr. 12:5 [MT 6]).
4. A Merarite Levite; son of Mushi (1 Chr. 24:30). He is the same as JEREMOTH 3 (23:23).
5. A Levite musician in David's time; one of the "sons of Heman" (1 Chr. 25:4). See JEREMOTH 4.
6. (1 Chr. 27:19, KJV). See JEREMOTH 5.

7. A son of David, and father of Mahalath, Rehoboam's wife (2 Chr. 11:18).

8. One of the levitical overseers of the temple treasury under Hezekiah (2 Chr. 31:13).

JERIOTH [jĕr′ī ŏth] (Heb. *yᵉrî·ôṯ* "tents").† Apparently a wife of Caleb the son of Hezron (1 Chr. 2:18); the MT reading is unclear. Other possibilities are that Jerioth may be an alternate name for Azubah or that Azubah was previously married to a man named Jerioth. The JB makes Caleb the father of Azubah, Ishshah, and Jerioth.

JEROBOAM [jĕr′ə bō′əm] (Heb. *yārob̠ᵉʿām* "may the people multiply").

1. Jeroboam I, the first king of the northern kingdom (*ca.* 922-901 B.C.); an Ephraimite of Zeredah, the son of Nebat and Zeruah (1 Kgs. 11:26).

As a young man, Jeroboam led an abortive revolt against Solomon (cf. 12:24, LXX). An officer on the king's building projects, he was made head of the corvée of the house of Joseph because of his demonstrated ability (11:27-28). Such forced labor had long irritated Israel (cf. Deut. 26:6-7), and Ahijah the prophet fanned their discontent into open revolt (1 Kgs. 11:29-39), promising kingship to Jeroboam (cf. 1 Sam. 10:1; 16:1; 2 Kgs. 8:13). Thereupon Jeroboam fled for his life to Pharaoh Shishak of Egypt, thus escaping Solomon's wrath (1 Kgs. 11:40).

Having learned that Solomon's son Rehoboam had gone to Shechem to be confirmed as successor to the throne, Jeroboam returned from Egypt (12:1-2). When the young king foolishly rejected the northern tribes' request to lighten their burdens (v. 3), they rejected his rule, thus ending the dual monarchy (vv. 4-16, 19). Instead, they acclaimed Jeroboam as king over the ten tribes (v. 20).

Jeroboam made Shechem his first capital, fortifying it as well as Transjordanian Penuel (v. 25). Later he moved his residence to the more defensible Tirzah (14:17). His reign was marked by continual warfare with Judah (vv. 19, 30; 15:6-7; 2 Chr. 12:15), including at least one major defeat at the hands of Rehoboam's son Abijah/Abijam (ch. 13). Inscriptions at Karnak confirm that Israel was also devastated by Shishak (*ANET,* pp. 242-43; 1 Kgs. 14:25-26).

Afraid that the temple worship in Jerusalem would erode his support, Jeroboam erected golden calves at Bethel and Dan for Israel's worship (12:26-30); although not meant as idols but as pedestals for Yahweh, the calves were soon enmeshed in a syncretistic blend with Baalism, the symbol of which was the bull (cf. Hos. 8:5-6; 13:2; *see* GOLDEN CALF). Jeroboam appointed new priests representing all strata of society except the Levites (1 Kgs. 12:31; cf. 2 Chr. 11:14-15); on occasion he himself officiated at the sacrifices (1 Kgs. 12:32-33). He also reorganized the cultic calendar, moving the Feast of Booths from the fifteenth day of Tishri to the following month of Bul. These religious innovations drew the ire of the religious orthodoxy, and came to typify "the sins of Jeroboam" in which the kings of Israel would walk (e.g., 15:30, 34; 16:26, 31) and which eventually led to Israel's apostasy and fall (2 Kgs. 17:21-23). Indeed, Jeroboam persisted in this apostasy despite repeated warnings;

neither the oracle of doom spoken by an unknown Judean prophet (1 Kgs. 13:1-10), nor the word of the old prophet Ahijah, nor even the death of his own son (14:1-18) made Jeroboam repent (13:33). This obstinacy became the sin of his house and ended with its extermination (v. 34; 15:29).

2. Jeroboam II, the tenth king of Israel (786-746 B.C.), the son and successor of Joash, and the fourth king of Jehu's dynasty. During his reign the ten northern tribes reached their zenith of wealth and power. Taking advantage of a Damascus weakened by Assyrian raids (*ca.* 802) and Assyria's temporary preoccupation with internal conflicts, Jeroboam was able to restore Israel's boundaries from "the entrance of Hamath as far as the Sea of the Arabah" (i.e., to the southern end of the Dead Sea), as Jonah the son of Amittai had prophesied (2 Kgs. 14:25; cf. Amos 6:13-14). He extended Israel's power over the kingdoms of Damascus and Hamath, reconquering the territory which had belonged to Judah at the time of David (2 Kgs. 14:28). He thus became the deliverer of the nation from the hand of the Syrians (13:5), the savior whom God raised up to preserve his people (14:27).

Yet Israel's prosperity under Jeroboam, benefitting primarily the burgeoning aristocracy, gave rise to injustice, immorality (Amos 2:6-7), religious syncretism (5:26), and opulent self-indulgence (6:4-6). Despite God's mercy, the disease proved terminal (cf. 2 Kgs. 14:27); soon after Jeroboam died the ten tribes perished in their apostasy (*ca.* 722; 17:6-23).

JEROHAM [jə rō′hăm] (Heb. *yᵉrōḥām* "may he have compassion").†

1. An Ephraimite; the father of Elkanah and grandfather of the prophet Samuel (1 Sam. 1:1). According to 1 Chr. 6:27, 34, he was a Levite.

2. A Benjaminite (1 Chr. 8:27); possibly the same as the Jeremoth of v. 14. Some scholars would identify him with **3.**

3. The father of the Benjaminite Ibneiah, who was a postexilic resident of Jerusalem (1 Chr. 9:8).

4. A postexilic priest living in Jerusalem (1 Chr. 9:12) and the father of Adaiah (Neh. 11:12).

5. A Benjaminite of Gedor whose two sons joined David at Ziklag (1 Chr. 12:7). Some scholars would identify him with **3.**

6. The father of AZAREL **3**, tribal chief of Dan at the time of David (1 Chr. 27:22).

7. The father of AZARIAH **13**, a commander of a hundred who incited the revolt against Athaliah (2 Chr. 23:1).

JEROME [jə rōm′].† Eusebius Hieronymus (A.D. 342-420), a scholar and monk known most for the Latin Vulgate translation of the Bible. Yet although the Vulgate is normally associated with Jerome's name, he was not its only translator/reviser. Pope Damasus commissioned Jerome in 382 to produce a standard Latin Bible to replace the numerous Old Latin versions. Jerome completed a revision of the Gospels on the basis of a Greek manuscript; three versions of the Psalms, one of which, the "Gallican Psalter," based on the LXX text in Origen's Hexapla, came to be accepted as the Psalter of the Vulgate; Latin revisions of the rest of the Hebrew canon, for which he had recourse to the Hebrew; and translations of Tobit and Judith. Some at least of the rest of the Vulgate Bible (which includes all of the Apocrypha) is not from Jerome but from Old Latin versions and other revisers.

JERUBBAAL [jĕr′ə bāl] (Heb. *yᵉrubba'al* "let Baal [or "the master"] contend" or "multiply").† The name given to Gideon to commemorate his destruction of his father's altar to Baal at Ophrah (Judg. 6:32). At times this name is identified as an alternate appellative (7:1; 8:35), but at others it is clearly a substitute for Gideon (e.g., ch. 9; 1 Sam. 2:11); some scholars view this as evidence of different sources. The euphemistic form Jerubbesheth occurs at 2 Sam. 11:21.

JERUBBESHETH [jə rŭb′ə shĕth] (Heb. *yᵉrubbāšeṯ* "let shame contend" or "multiply").† A substitute form of the name Jerubbaal (2 Sam. 11:21), devised to avoid pronunciation of the Baal element.

JERUEL [jə rōō′əl] (Heb. *yᵉrû'ēl* "founded by El"). An area of the Judean wilderness between En-gedi and Tekoa, situated at the ascent of Ziz (2 Chr. 20:16). Here King Jehoshaphat defeated a coalition of Ammonites and Moabites.

JERUSALEM [jə rōō′sə ləm] (Heb. *yᵉrûšālayim, yᵉrûšālēm* "city of peace, wholeness [or "Salem"]").† The city of David, capital of Judah and the united monarchy; holy city of Judaism, Christianity, and Islam.

I. Geography

Jerusalem is located along the central mountain ridge

of Palestine, 58 km. (36 mi.) east of the Mediterranean and 26 km. (16 mi.) west of the northern tip of the Dead Sea. It is just east of the ancient north-south road from Shechem to Hebron and 13 km. (8 mi.) south of the convergence of the east-west road from Jericho and those leading west to various points on the Mediterranean. The city is situated *ca.* 640-770 m. (2100-1500 ft.) above sea level in a relatively level plateau of the Benjaminite highlands.

The ancient city is bounded on the east by the Kidron valley, which separates it from the Mount of Olives, and on the west and south by the Hinnom valley. No distinctive physical features define the northern limits of the city as it merges with the central mountain chain, thus leaving that side vulnerable to attack. The city is divided into two main ridges by a central north-south valley, the Tyropoeon, which joins the Hinnom and Kidron valleys at the southeastern corner of the city and forms Wâdī en-Nâr. The eastern ridge between the Tyropoeon and Kidron valleys consists of Mt. Moriah or the Temple Mount to the north and the narrow, steeply sloping Ophel to the south. The larger western ridge between the Hinnom and Tyropoeon valleys can further be divided by the east-west Transversal valley, a branch of the Tyropoeon; Mt. Ghareb in the north, corresponding to the modern Christian Quarter, was the highest part of the ancient city; to the south was the so-called Upper City, the lower portion of which is now erroneously called Mt. Zion.

The main water supply for the city was the Spring Gihon, also known as the Virgin's Fountain (modern 'Ain Sittī Maryam) or 'Ain Umm ed-Darāj, located in the Kidron valley outside the northern end of David's original city. At various stages of the city's history shafts or tunnels were employed to make the spring

Jerusalem from the south with the Mount of Olives on the right (Matson Photo Service)

accessible to the city, and its intermittent flow necessitated the construction of aqueducts and storage pools. En-rogel (probably modern Bîr Ayyûb), some 210 m. (690 ft.) south of where the Hinnom and Kidron valleys join, was less accessible to the walled city and probably did not constitute a major source of water.

II. History

The earliest evidence of settlement, dated to the Paleolithic and Mesolithic periods, was discovered on the ridge west of the Hinnom valley overlooking the Rephaim valley. Jerusalem proper was first settled on the Ophel ridge during the Chalcolithic period (end of the fourth millennium B.C.), followed by an unwalled village in the third millennium; this may be the Salim listed in preliminary publications of the Ebla tablets (ca. 2400).

Remains of a walled city encompassing the western ridge and eastern slopes of Ophel have been dated to the Middle Bronze period (2100-1550). Called Aushamem or Rushalimum in the nineteenth-century Egyptian Execration Texts, this may be the Salem of which Melchizedek was king (Gen. 14:18).

In the Late Bronze Age (1550-1200) the city came under Canaanite (Jebusite) control (cf. 10:16). In the fourteenth-century Amarna Letters Abdu-ḥepa, the Amorite king of Jerusalem (Akk. *Urusalim*), complains of Habiru (ʿApiru) activity and is himself accused of raiding other Palestinian cities. The apparently mixed ethnic character of the populace is reminiscent of Ezek. 16:3, 45. Although included in the territory allotted to Benjamin (Josh. 18:16, 28), the city (called Jebus) resisted the advancing Israelites (10:1ff.) and remained in Jebusite hands throughout the period of the Confederacy (15:63; Judg. 1:21; 3:5; cf. 1:8). Ca. 1300 the eastern slopes were terraced with stone (cf. Heb. *millô'* "filling"; perhaps the Millo of 2 Sam. 5:9 par. 1 Chr. 11:9).

Having been named king over Israel as well as Judah in the eighth year of his reign at Hebron, David sought Jerusalem as a neutral site from which to maintain his dual kingship. This he accomplished, not by sending his commander Joab through the vertical water shaft from the Spring Gihon into the walled city (so RSV), but by cutting off the tunnel which led from the shaft to the water supply (2 Sam. 5:6-8; 1 Chr. 11:4-6; cf. JB, NJV). The "stronghold of Zion," scarcely a prime location from either a commercial or military standpoint, represented a wise political choice for David's capital. Centrally located in previously unconquered territory between Judah and Benjamin, the "city of David" became the religious center of the kingdoms as well with David's relocation of the tabernacle and the ark of the covenant at the sacred threshing floor of Araunah (Ornan), presumably on Mt. Moriah north of the city (2 Sam. 6:1-15; 24:18-25; 1 Chr. 22:1; 2 Chr. 3:1). David apparently repaired the Millo and the city wall (2 Sam. 5:9) and constructed a palace within the fortified city (v. 11). It remains uncertain where with relation to Ophel his royal tomb was located (cf. 1 Kgs. 2:10; Neh. 3:16).

Solomon's massive building campaign included extensive renovations within Jerusalem. Most important was the construction of the temple of Yahweh on Mt. Moriah, an elaborate, multichambered structure bearing district Phoenician influence (1 Kgs. 6–8 par. 2 Chr. 2–4). The palace and administrative complex included the House of the Forest of Lebanon (1 Kgs. 7:2-5), the Hall of Pillars (v. 6), Hall of the Throne (v. 7), residential quarters (v. 8), and other structures (vv. 9-12). Solomon rebuilt and extended the city walls (3:1), thus increasing the city's size from 4.5 to 13 ha. (from 11 to 32 a.); its population likewise had grown from two to six thousand. It is unclear whether settlement had yet expanded to the southwestern hill (Upper City). Evidence of increased paganization within the now cosmopolitan city included shrines to non-Israelite deities, apparently located south of the Mount of Olives (11:7).

Shortly after the northern tribes withdrew from the dual monarchy, Pharaoh Shishak of Egypt raided Jerusalem (14:25). Nevertheless, the city continued to flourish as the cultic center of Judah (cf. the evidence of the great wealth amassed by the temple; 15:18). Apart from King Joash's repair of the temple (2 Kgs. 12:4-16 [MT 5-17]), building activity in the ninth and eighth centuries was restricted primarily to reconstruction and reinforcement of the city walls and other defenses (e.g., 15:35; 2 Chr. 26:9, 15; 27:3) in response to constant attack or threatened attack by Judah's neighbors (e.g., 2 Kgs. 12:17 [MT 18]; 16:5). In addition to repairing and cleaning the temple (2 Chr. 29:3-19), Hezekiah (ca. 715-687) responded to the Assyrian defeat of the northern kingdom by strengthening the city walls and fortifying it with gates and towers (32:5; cf. Isa. 22:10); most notably, he sought to safeguard the vital water supply by enclosing the Gihon Spring and channeling its waters through the Siloam tunnel (2 Kgs. 20:20; 2 Chr. 32:2-4; Isa. 22:9; Sir. 48:17). Although Hezekiah himself was taken captive, the city did survive siege by Sennacherib (2 Kgs. 18:13ff.; 19:35-36 par. Isa. 37:36-37; *ANET*, pp. 287-88). Archaeological evidence indicates that by this time the city had spread to the western hill (cf. 2 Kgs. 22:14 par. 2 Chr. 34:22, "Second Quarter"), although the walls apparently only extended to the Tyropoeon valley; it encompassed some 60 ha. (150 a.) and had a population of twenty-four thousand. In the seventh century Manasseh built an outer wall to the original city on Ophel (2 Chr. 33:14), and Josiah's religious reforms included destruction of the pagan shrines (34:3-4) and repair of the temple (2 Kgs. 22:3ff. par. 2 Chr. 34:8ff.). Soon thereafter Jerusalem felt the might of the Neo-Babylonian Empire. In 597 Jehoiachin and all but the poorer classes were taken captive by the Babylonians (2 Kgs. 24:10-16; 2 Chr. 36:10; Ezek. 40:1). Nebuchadnezzar I besieged the city in 588 (2 Kgs. 25:1-2; Jer. 39:1; 52:4-5; Ezek. 24:1-2); in less than two years Jerusalem was torn by famine and internal disorder (2 Kgs. 25:3-4 par. Jer. 52:6) and fell to the Babylonians, who destroyed the temple and burned the city (2 Kgs. 25:9-10, 13-17; Jer. 52:13-14, 17ff.) and deported the remaining populace (2 Kgs. 25:11-12, 21; Jer. 52:28-30).

Following the Exile Jerusalem was vastly reduced in size and grandeur. Only a small number of the exiled Jews returned, and combined with the few who had been allowed to remain behind and the "people of the land" the population was barely two thousand. Nevertheless, efforts were made immediately to re-

Jerusalem in the time of Jesus portrayed in the Jerusalem Temple model. Herod's palace is in the foreground, the temple and its courts are in the background, and the Antonia and two of the three palace towers are on the left (W. S. LaSor)

store the temple; despite local opposition work was completed by ca. 516 (Ezra 3:1–4:6; 4:24–6:22). Yet not until the mid-fifth century did Nehemiah repair the fortifications of the city, now apparently little more than a mound of rubble confined to the eastern portion of the Ophel ridge (Neh. 2:11-17; 3:1-32; 12:31-43).

Under Ptolemaic and Seleucid rule (third-early second centuries) Jerusalem became largely hellenized. Greek influence was felt particularly under Antiochus IV Epiphanes (175-164), who ravaged the temple (1 Macc. 1:21-23; 2 Macc. 5:15-21) and erected therein an altar to Zeus (1 Macc. 1:54; 2 Macc. 6:2); he further fostered Hellenism by constructing a gymnasium (1 Macc. 1:14; 2 Macc. 4:9-12) and promoting athletic competition (v. 17). His supporters among the Jews built a citadel within "the city of David," or perhaps to its north (1 Macc. 1:33; 14:36). The Maccabean revolt ended such abuses, and Judas Maccabeus restored the temple in 164 (4:36-59; 2 Macc. 10:1-8). Remains of buildings and fortifications encompassing the entire western ridge, perhaps those of Simon (14:37), have been discovered and dated to this period.

In 63 B.C. Pompey conquered Jerusalem for Rome, breaching the walls of the temple. Antigonus, aided by the Parthians, captured the city in 40, but Herod the Great regained it in 37. As king of Judea (37-4) he conducted an extensive building program, strengthening the Hasmonean walls and reinforcing the city's defenses with a second and third wall, the precise locations of which remain open to debate. He constructed an elaborate palace with three towers on the western ridge (later the headquarters of the procura-

tor) and rebuilt the Hasmonean fortress (Gk. Bāris) northwest of the temple as the Fortress Antonia. His most important project was rebuilding the temple and enlarging its precincts. Other innovations included a theater, marketplace or public square, aqueducts and reservoirs, and a porticoed walkway or bridge (Gk. Xystos) connecting the temple area and the Upper City. Many of the events of Jesus' life (e.g., presentation in the temple, Luke 2:22-39; annual pilgrimages, vv. 41-50; temptation by Satan, Matt. 4:5 par. Luke 4:9; passion and resurrection, Matt. 21–28 par.) and ministry (e.g., John 2:13-25; 5:1-18; 7:1ff.) took place in Herodian Jerusalem, as did Paul's arrest and appearance before the Sanhedrin (Acts 21:27–23:10) and the council concerning the role of Gentiles in the Church (15:1ff.; cf. Gal. 2:1-10). Many traditional sites have been preserved commemorating events of this period. Jerusalem's population at this time has been estimated to have been between twenty and fifty thousand.

Discontented with harsh and insensitive Roman rulership, the Jews of Jerusalem revolted in A.D. 66, and the Christian inhabitants fled. Vespasian laid siege in 68 but withdrew when acclaimed emperor. Four legions commanded by his son Titus surrounded and captured the city in 70, burning the temple, slaughtering or enslaving the populace, and razing all but the towers of the palace. In 135 Hadrian responded to the Bar Kokhba revolt by plowing under the rubble of Jerusalem and erecting on the western hill a thoroughly Roman city, Aelia Capitolina, from which all Jews were banned. In the fourth century the em-

A sixth-century A.D. mosaic map of Jerusalem in a Byzantine church (the Madeba Map) (Jordan Information Bureau, Washington, D.C.)

peror Constantine restored the city as a Christian center; his mother Helena established shrines at many of the traditional sites.

For further information (e.g., gates, buildings) see the individual entries.

III. Ideal City

As the focal point of Israel's religion. the seat of Yahweh's anointed (Davidic) king, and, through the presence of the tabernacle and the temple, the earthly dwelling place of God (e.g., Ps. 48:1-3; Isa. 2:3), the real Jerusalem came in time to symbolize the people and kingdom of God (cf. Isa. 2:2-3; 40:4; Luke 21:24). See ZION.

In their despair the exiles envisioned a rebuilt Jerusalem (cf. Ezek. 36:28). That vision came to denote a transformed city, an ideal capital for God's kingdom (chs. 40–48; to be named "The Lord is there," 48:35; cf. Mal. 4:1) and the foundation of his new creation to be realized at the end of time (Rev. 21:1–22:5).

Bibliography. K. M. Kenyon, *Jerusalem: Excavating 3000 Years of History* (New York: 1967); W. S. LaSor, "Jerusalem," *ISBE* 2 (1982): 998-1032; R. M. Mackowski, *Jerusalem, City of Jesus* (Grand Rapids: 1980); Y. Yadin, ed., *Jerusalem Revealed* (New Haven 1976).

JERUSHA [jə rōō'shə] (Heb. *yᵉrûšāʾ* "possession"). The daughter of Zadok and mother of King Jotham of Judah (2 Kgs. 15:33). At 2 Chr. 27:1 the form Jerushah occurs.

JESHAIAH [jə shā'yə] (Heb. *yᵉšaʿyāhû, yᵉšaʿyâ* "deliverance" or "salvation of Yahweh" [= Isaiah]).
1. A son of Hananiah and grandson of Zerubbabel, listed among the descendants of Solomon (1 Chr. 3:21; KJV "Jesaiah").
2. A son of Jeduthun, and leader of the eighth division of levitical singers at the time of David (1 Chr. 25:3, 15).
3. The son of Rehabiel; a Levite who served in David's treasury under Shebuel (1 Chr. 26:25).
4. An Elamite; son of Athaliah who returned to Jerusalem with Ezra's party (Ezra 8:7).
5. A Merarite Levite who returned with Ezra to

serve in the temple (Ezra 8:19; 1 Esdr. 8:48; KJV "Osias").
6. A Benjaminite, father of Ithiel 1 and ancestor of Sallu (Neh. 11:7; KJV "Jesaiah").

JESHANAH [jĕsh'ə nə] (Heb. *yᵉšānā* "old [city]").†
A city on the border of Israel and Judah taken by Abijah during his war with Jeroboam I (2 Chr. 13:19). It is probably also mentioned at 1 Sam. 7:12 (so RSV, JB; KJV, NIV "Shen," following MT Heb. *šēn*). Later the headquarters of Antigonus' general Pappus, the city was captured by Herod the Great (Roman Isanas; Josephus *Ant.* xiv.15.12 [458]). The site has been identified as modern Burj el-Isâneh, 5 km. (3 mi.) north of Jefneh and 10.5 km. (17 mi.) north of Jerusalem.

JESHARELAH [jĕsh'ə rē'lə] (Heb. *yᵉšarʾēlâ*). A son of Asaph; leader of the seventh division of levitical singers at the time of David (1 Chr. 25:14; NIV "Jesarelah"). He is called Asharelah at v. 2 (KJV, NIV "Asarelah").

JESHEBEAB [jə shĕb'ĭ ăb] (Heb. *yešebʾāb*). The leader of the fourteenth division of priests at the time of David (1 Chr. 24:13).

JESHER [jē'shər] (Heb. *yēšer, yešer* "righteous"). A son of Caleb and Azubah and grandson of Hezron (1 Chr. 2:18).

JESHIMON [jə shē'mən, jə shī'mən] (Heb. *hayyᵉšîmôn*).* A general Hebrew term for the desert or wilderness (e.g., Deut. 32:10; Ps. 106:14), much less frequent than the parallel Heb. *miḏbār* (cf. Isa. 43:19-20). It is rendered as a proper name in the English versions with reference to two locations.
1. The eastern limits of the mountains of Judea, situated south and east of Hebron and reaching to the northwest shore of the Dead Sea (1 Sam. 23:19, 24; 26:1, 3; JB "the wastelands"). The region was a popular haunt for fugitives and ascetics.
2. The salty desert region northeast of the Dead Sea and east of the Jordan river, below Mt. Pisgah (Num. 21:20; 23:28, KJV; RSV "desert"; NIV "the wasteland").

JESHISHAI [jə shīsh'ī] (Heb. *yᵉšîšay* "old, worthy of honor"). A Gadite; son of Jahdo and father of Michael (1 Chr. 5:14).

JESHOHAIAH [jĕsh'ə hī'yə] (Heb. *yᵉšôḥāyâ* "Yahweh bows [?]"). A prince of a Simeonite father's house (1 Chr. 4:36).

JESHUA [jĕsh'ōō ə, jə shōō'ə] (Heb. *yēšûaʿ* "Yahweh is salvation" [= Joshua]) (PERSON).†
1. The leader of the ninth division of priests at the time of David (1 Chr. 24:11; KJV "Jeshuah"). His descendants may have been among those who returned from captivity in Babylon (cf. Ezra 2:36; Neh. 7:39).
2. A Levite of Hezekiah's time, who aided in the distribution of the priests' portion of the offerings (2 Chr. 31:15).

3. The eponymous ancestor of a levitical family or guild that returned with Zerubbabel from Babylon (Ezra 2:2 par. Neh.7:7; 1 Esdr. 5:8; KJV "Jesus"), numbered among the "sons of Pahath-moab" (Ezra 2:6 par. Neh. 7:11; 1 Esdr. 5:11).

4. The head of a levitical guild that returned with Zerubbabel from exile (Ezra 2:40 par. Neh. 7:43; 1 Esdr. 5:26; KJV "Jessue"), numbered among those who assisted in rebuilding the temple (Ezra 3:9). He was among those who helped explain the law (Neh. 8:7) and led in worship (9:4-5; 12:8). At 12:24 he is called the son of Kadmiel, but their precise relationship is not clear (cf. Ezra 2:40; Neh. 7:43; 10:9).

5. A priest, the son of Jozadak (Jehozadak) who with Zerubbabel restored regular worship (Ezra 3:2-9) and rebuilt the temple (5:2; Sir. 49:12; KJV "Jesus"). He was the first high priest after the Exile according to Haggai and Zechariah ("Joshua"; Hag. 1:1, 12-14; Zech. 3:1-8; cf. 6:11), both of whom encouraged him with promises of the Lord's help. Some of his sons were among the priests who divorced their foreign wives (Ezra 10:18). His son Joiakim was a contemporary of Nehemiah (Neh. 12:26).

6. The father of the Levite Jozabad, who accompanied Ezra to Jerusalem (Ezra 8:33; 1 Esdr. 8:63; KJV "Jesu"). He may be the same as **4**.

7. The father of Ezer, who repaired a section of the walls of Jerusalem (Neh. 3:19).

8. Alternate form of Joshua, son of Nun (Neh. 8:17).

9. The son of Anaziah; a postexilic Levite who sealed the renewed covenant (Neh. 10:9 [MT 10]). He is probably the same as **4**.

JESHUA [jĕsh'ōo ə, jə shōo'ə] (Heb. *yēšûaʿ* "Yahweh is salvation") (**PLACE**). A town in southern Judah reoccupied after the return from captivity (Neh. 11:26). It is thought to be the same as Shema (Josh. 15:26), modern Tell es-Saʿwī, 19 km. (12 mi.) east-northeast of Beer-sheba.

JESHURUN [jĕsh'ōo rən] (Heb. *yᵉšurûn*).† Another name for Israel, which occurs only in poetry. Jeshurun is considered to be a hypocoristicon (diminutive, or term of endearment) that may emphasize its root meaning of "upright." The term occurs in two ancient poems: the song of Moses (Deut. 32:15; tenth century B.C.) and the Blessing of Moses (33:5, 26; eleventh century). It is found also in Isa. 44:2 (KJV "Jesurun"), concerning the redemption and restoration of Israel.

JESIAH (1 Chr. 12:6; 23:20, KJV). *See* ISSHIAH **2, 3**.

JESIMIEL [jə sĭm'ĭ əl] (Heb. *yᵉśîmiʾēl* "may God establish"). A chief from the tribe of Simeon contemporary with King Hezekiah (1 Chr. 4:36).

JESSE [jĕs'ē] (Heb. *yišay*, *ʾîšay*; Gk. *Iessai*). The son of Obed and grandson of Boaz and Ruth, a descendant of Perez and the father of King David (Ruth 4:21-22; Matt. 1:5-6; Luke 3:31-32).

Jesse was a modest landholder of the tribe of Judah, and one of the elders of Bethlehem (1 Sam. 16:4-5).

Jesse fathered eight sons, the youngest of whom was David (17:12-14; 1 Chr. 2:13-15 lists only seven), and two daughters (v. 16; 2 Sam. 17:25 calls them daughters of Nahash). When David was summoned to Saul's court Jesse sent gifts to the king (1 Sam. 16:20). Later, when David was a fugitive from Saul, Jesse and his household joined their son at the cave of Adullam; from there David sent his parents to Moab for safekeeping (1 Sam. 22:1-4).

Although "son of Jesse" was used derisively of David (cf. vv. 7-9; 1 Kgs. 12:16), it came to be a revered title (1 Chr. 29:26; Acts 13:22). Likewise, "the root of Jesse" became a symbol of God's promises fulfilled in the Messiah (Isa. 11:1, 10; Rom. 15:12).

JESUI (Num. 26:44, KJV). *See* ISHVI.

JESUS [jē'səs] (Gk. Iēsous; from Heb. *yᵉhôšuaʿ* "Yahweh will save").

1. The father of Sirach and grandfather of the author of Ecclesiasticus (Sir., Prologue).

2. Joshua ben Sira (Jesus son of Sirach), author of Ecclesiasticus.

3. *See* JESUS CHRIST.

4. An ancestor of Jesus Christ (Luke 3:29; RSV "Joshua," KJV "Jose").

5. Jesus Barabbas. *See* BARABBAS.

6. (Acts 7:45; Heb. 4:8, KJV). *See* JOSHUA **1**.

7. A Jewish Christian also called Justus (**3**) (Col. 4:11).

JESUS CHRIST.† The Savior, the Son of God, the Son of Man.

I. Name

The given name Jesus means "savior"; it is the Greek equivalent of Jeshua (Heb. *yēšûaʿ*, from *yᵉhôšuaʿ* "Yahweh saves" [= Joshua]). Christ is a title, indicating that he is the "anointed one," the Messiah (from Heb. *māšiaḥ*).

Although the name Jesus was common in Hellenistic-Roman Palestine, only Jesus Christ embodied the full sense of the name, by saving his people from their sins. The name was not arbitrarily given by Joseph and Mary, but was divinely chosen and revealed to them (Matt. 1:21; Luke 1:31) as most appropriate for the Savior of the world.

In the biblical accounts Jesus is usually called "Jesus of Nazareth" (e.g., 24:19), "Jesus, Son of David" (Mark 10:47), "the Nazarene" (14:67), or "the son of Joseph" (John 1:45). By far the most common designation used by biblical writers was simply "Jesus." The compound Jesus Christ occurs only five times in the Gospels but is more common in Acts and the Epistles.

II. Chronology

It is not the purpose or intention of the New Testament writers to give precise dates for the birth and death of Jesus. Nevertheless, scholars have been able through comparative research to determine these dates with general accuracy. The birth of Jesus occurred before the death of Herod the Great (Matt. 2:1), which is known to have taken place in 4 B.C., and during the reign of Caesar Augustus (27 B.C.–A.D. 14; Luke 2:1). The birth of Jesus is further limited by its connection with the census of Quirinius (vv. 1-5), but dating for that event is problematic (generally placed in A.D. 7). Most scholars date the birth of Jesus early in 6 B.C. or late in 5 B.C.

The public ministry of Jesus began when he was "about thirty years of age" (3:23). His baptism by John the Baptist is set in the "fifteenth year of the reign of Tiberius Caesar" (v. 1), which may be assumed to be A.D. 29. The duration of the public ministry of Jesus was apparently about three years (John mentions three Passover feasts). The New Testament does not give a detailed chronology for other events in Jesus' ministry; it is often necessary to research, hypothesize, and make general approximations in order to date a particular event.

There is still some disagreement among scholars about the day and date of the crucifixion of Jesus. Traditionally it has been held to have occurred on Friday, Nisan 15, A.D. 33, but reckoning from a birth date of 7/6 B.C. the date of crucifixion may be rather A.D. 26/27. Jesus predicted his death and his resurrection on the third day (Matt. 16:21; Mark 8:31; Luke 9:22). He was crucified and his body was placed in the tomb on the preparation day (Friday), the day before the Sabbath (John 19:31). Jesus' disciples discovered the empty tomb and talked with him on the first day of the week (Matt. 28:1; Mark 16:1-2; Luke 24:13).

III. Life

The various events associated with the life of Christ witness to the identity of Jesus as the Messiah. The main sources of information about his life are the four Gospels. Because these offer four different accounts of the facts, and because the four Evangelists wrote independently and selectively according to their own unique purposes, a complete, chronological biography cannot be reconstructed. There has been much debate and critical study concerning the relationship of the Gospels to each other and to historical fact, especially since the rise of eighteenth-century rationalism. Traditional theologians have attempted to overstress the need for harmony among the accounts. Liberal and rationalistic theologians have often denied the supernatural and resorted to reconstruction in their quest for the real, human, "historical Jesus." Others have stressed the importance of the Word, the interpretation of the Word, or the "Christ of faith" in distinction to the "Jesus of history." Still others have focused on the inner life of Jesus and how he conceived of himself irrespective of the truth of his claims. Mythology, or theological meaning, evolution of religions, and the study of literary sources have been the consuming passions of others.

Only a brief summary of the main events of Jesus' life can be presented here.

A. Birth. The birth of Jesus Christ may be foreseen in Old Testament messianic prophecies (e.g., Isa. 7:14; 11:1; Mic. 5:2) and is proclaimed in the New Testament as the fulfillment of such prophecies (e.g., Matt. 1:22-23). Jesus was "conceived . . . of the Holy Spirit" and born of the virgin Mary (v. 20; cf. Luke 1:31-35). Accordingly, he is called the Son of God. Joseph is

The traditional location of Jesus' birth, the Grotto of the Nativity in Bethlehem (W. S. LaSor)

regarded not as his biological father but as the husband of Mary and the protector of the infant. Yet both Joseph and Mary may have been of the lineage of David (assuming that the genealogy of Matt. 1 is that of Joseph and the genealogy of Luke 3 is that of Mary).

The exceptional nature of Jesus' work was to be implied from the association of his birth with Bethlehem, the city of David. Moreover, Luke reports that the birth of Jesus was announced by angels singing praise to God (2:8-14). The aged Simeon underscored the significance of this birth in the temple at the presentation of Jesus when he said, "mine eyes have seen thy salvation (Gk. *sōtḗrion*; cf. Heb. *yĕšûʿâ*)" (vv. 29-35). According to Matthew's record magi from the East paid homage to the child (Matt. 2:1-11). Clearly, Jesus' birth was no ordinary birth (John 1:14; cf. Rom. 8:3).

Jesus himself never appeals to his unique birth. Even his apostles refer to it rarely. Mark entirely omits the birth from his Gospel, and John treats it in a metaphysical context. Paul's references are to the risen Lord and his state of exaltation. Matthew and Luke provide most of the information about the birth and its theological implications.

B. Childhood. Unlike apocryphal works, which narrate many unusual details of Jesus' childhood, the New Testament records only one incident that occurred in the childhood of Jesus. When he was twelve years old, he participated in the celebration of the Passover in Jerusalem (Luke 2:41-51). Luke's statement that Jesus "increased in wisdom and stature," evidently indicating normal human development, suggests in general terms that Jesus was prepared for his divinely commissioned task (v. 52).

C. Baptism and Temptation. Jesus' baptism in the Jordan river by John the Baptist and his temptation in the Judean desert were his inauguration to ministry. He was baptized to "fulfil all righteousness" (Matt. 3:15), meaning that it was necessary for him to experience what mankind experiences in all respects. As he was being baptized the Holy Spirit descended on him in the form of a dove (v. 16 par. Mark 1:10; Luke 3:22), and a voice from heaven was heard identifying and commissioning him to his mediatorial task.

The significance of the baptism is perhaps highlighted by the ordeal of the temptation that followed it. By comparison, Adam had been tempted under more felicitous circumstances, yet quickly fell into sin. Jesus, however, resisted an intense, threefold attack by Satan (Matt. 4:1-11 par.), who offered him the glory and supremacy of victory without the suffering and death of the cross. Despite the very reality of the temptation, Jesus could not and did not sin (cf. Heb. 4:15). He was determined to fulfill his commission and experience the suffering and death of the cross in order to save his people from their sins.

D. Public Ministry. Since all four of the Gospel writers perceive of the cross and the resurrection as the climactic acts of God in redemptive history, their emphasis is on these events and the circumstances that led up to them. The public ministry of Jesus from the baptism to the passion week is represented by selected incidents and characteristic discourses. Although the exact chronology of Jesus' public ministry is far from certain, it may be categorized into two periods: an apparently brief ministry in Judea and a longer, more systematic itinerant ministry in Galilee.

1. *Judea.* The Judean ministry is reported in the gospel of John. The preaching of John the Baptist prepared the way for the introduction of Jesus as "the Lamb of God, who takes away the sin of the world" (John 1:29). The Pharisees and leaders at Jerusalem rejected John's testimony, but the disciples accepted Jesus and became his followers. Andrew, Peter, Philip, and Nathanael believed that Jesus is the Son of God (v. 49).

In this early Judean ministry Jesus performed miracles and signs that revealed his power and drew people to him (4:48), establishing his claim of messianic authority. The first "sign," or miracle, was performed at Cana in Galilee, when Jesus visited a wedding and turned the water into wine for the guests (2:1-11). In John's account the most spectacular public act of this aspect of Jesus' ministry was his cleansing of the temple by routing the money changers with a whip (vv. 13-25), an act which supported Jesus' messianic claims (cf. Ps. 69:9 [MT 10]). On this occasion Jesus also made a cryptic reference to his death and resurrection (v. 19). The Synoptic Gospels record the cleansing of the temple in a different chronological order, at the end of Jesus' public ministry (Matt. 21:12-13; Mark 11:15-19; Luke 19:45-46).

Another well-known incident from this early ministry is Jesus' conversation with Nicodemus, a Jewish official, concerning the new birth (John 3:1-21). This basic dialogue on the principle of regeneration assumes the truth of Jesus' claim to be the Messiah, and shows that "whoever believes in him" (v. 15) will experience eternal life.

En route to Galilee Jesus had a remarkable discussion with a woman at the well in Samaria; here, Jesus revealed himself as Messiah and encouraged the woman's efforts to make him known (4:1ff.).

2. *Galilee.* The Galilean ministry of Jesus Christ began with the healing of an official's son at Cana, which evoked the faith of the man himself and his entire household (vv. 46-54). Later he performed many more such miracles: healing a paralyzed man (Matt. 9:1-8 par.), Jairus' daughter, who was at the point of death (Mark 5:21-43 par. Luke 8:40-42, 49-56; cf. Matt. 9:18-26), and a hemorrhaging woman (Luke 8:43-48), driving out demons (Matt. 8:28-34 par.), and calming a storm on the Sea of Galilee (Mark 4:35-41).

Much of Jesus' ministry focused on the common people (e.g., Matt. 4:13-21 par.; 8:2-4 par.), many of whom were outside the mainstream of acceptable Jewish society (e.g., 8:5-13 par.; 15:21-28 par.). Somewhat representative of his dealings with people was the selection of apostles such as Matthew, a tax collector who responded to Jesus' call immediately (9:9 par.). Such dealings drew the ire of the Pharisees, who criticized Jesus for eating with sinners; his response was that "those who are well have no need of a physician" (vv. 10-13 par.).

Jesus spoke of the nature of his ministry in the Sermon on the Mount; he had not come to destroy the law but to fulfill it (5:17). Such utterances led to frequent controversies with the Pharisees, who were threatened by Jesus' authority and tried, at any cost, to maintain their hold on the people (cf. Mark 2:7ff.); e.g., the Pharisees accused Jesus of breaking the Sabbath (2:23–3:6).

During the last winter of his ministry, Jesus continued his teaching and miracles in Judea and Perea, on his way to Jerusalem. On at least three occasions Jesus predicted that he would go to Jerusalem, suffer many things at the hands of the chief priests and scribes, and die. Yet he seemed determined to go there (Luke 9:51-62). Most of the information about the ministry on the way to Jerusalem comes from the gospel of Luke: the sending out of the seventy disciples in ministry (10:1-24), the woes against the Pharisees (11:37-54), and the conversion of Zacchaeus (19:1-10).

E. The Passion. After Jesus had prepared his disciples for their future ministry and informed them of his own imminent death (Mark 8:31–9:1), he continued his determined journey toward his appointed "hour" (John 17:1) in Jerusalem. Upon reaching Bethany, near Jerusalem, he raised Lazarus from the dead (11:38-44); this is the incident that would prompt the high priest Caiaphas to persuade the leaders to seek Jesus' life (vv. 49-53). When he entered the city riding on a donkey, the crowd was jubilant because they expected that Jesus would now assume the role of their long-expected Messiah (cf. Zech. 9:9)—he would lead them to victory over their oppressors (Mark 11:1-10 par.).

The Pharisees, seeing Jesus' popularity with the common people as a threat to their own power, became more and more determined in their plot to kill Jesus, and when Judas offered to betray him, they gladly accepted his offer. Judas took some soldiers and some officers of the Pharisees and chief priests (John 18:3) and led them to Jesus, betraying him with a kiss. Jesus was then taken to the house of Annas, where he was questioned about his disciples and his teaching. From there he was then sent to Caiaphas, where he was blindfolded, struck, and reviled (Luke 22:63-65). Two witnesses were secured to establish a false charge against him, but when that failed, they accused him of blasphemy on the basis of his claim to be the Messiah and condemned him to death (Mark 14:53-65).

Although the sentence of death was determined by the leaders of the Jews, it was carried out by the Romans, who simply approved of the prior trial at the demand of the chief priests (Mark 15:1-15). Pilate perceived that it was an unjust sentence and attempted to release Jesus by means of a customary pardon at the feast (vv. 6-10); the chief priests, however, stirred the crowd to have Barabbas released instead. Jesus was then delivered to the Roman soldiers, mocked, beaten, and crucified. Plotted by the calumny of his own people and carried out by the cruelty of wicked individuals, Jesus' death was nevertheless the accomplishment of God's plan (Acts 2:23).

F. Resurrection and Ascension. On the third day Christ arose from the dead, according to the Scriptures (1 Cor. 15:3-4) and his own prediction (Mark 10:32-34 par.). For forty days after his passion Jesus presented himself alive by many incontrovertible proofs (Acts 1:3). During this time he also taught his disciples of the kingdom of God in more detail, reaffirmed his commission to them, and promised the pouring out of the Holy Spirit (vv. 3-5). Then, as the disciples watched, Jesus was taken up through the clouds into heaven (vv. 9-11). *See* RESURRECTION; ASCENSION.

IV. Teachings

The teachings of Jesus Christ comprise the whole system of Christian doctrine in seminal form. During his ministry on earth Jesus explained and interpreted the Old Testament message; he was the embodiment of its principles and the fulfillment of its prophecies. He was the Word of God incarnate (John 1:1, 14). By both his teachings and his life, he made God known to mankind (v. 18).

Jesus taught people to believe in him as the Messiah, the Son of God, sent by the Father to die on the cross and draw all people to him. The way of salvation and eternal life is believing in Jesus Christ (3:14-16). The public and private ministry were aimed at the

A tomb at Heshbon which closes with a rolling stone, as did the tomb of Jesus (cf. Mark 15:46) (B. Van Elderen)

conversion and teaching of the disciples (followers) of Jesus. He taught about the kingdom of God on earth, prayer, the Holy Spirit, and eschatology; he taught in sermons (discourses), private conversations, debates, parables, and by his own example.

The Sermon on the Mount is representative of the teaching of Jesus (Matt. 5–7; cf. Luke 6:17-49). True happiness, Jesus taught in the beatitudes, belongs to those who live according to the principles of the kingdom. Believers are the salt of the earth. Righteousness is not legalistic and external like that of the Pharisees, but consists in fulfilling the true spirit of the Old Testament laws and commandments. Prayer is not empty and repetitious words, but true inner communication with the Father in the manner that Jesus prescribes. There is no security in materialism, but true riches are to be stored up in heaven, safe from thieves and decay. Life for Jesus' followers in the kingdom of God is serene, peaceful, and trusting, with no need for anxiety and care. People should not be critical and judgmental toward others, but should be accepting and forgiving; they should follow the golden rule—"do for others what you would have them do for you." People responded positively to such teachings of Jesus, "for he taught them as one who had authority, and not as their scribes" (Matt. 7:29).

In several parables, Jesus taught the nature of the kingdom of God by means of comparisons to things in everyday life (13:1-52). God's Word is like seed sown on different kinds of soil—different kinds of people respond in different ways to the Word. The good grain and the weeds are allowed to grow together in the field until the harvest, just as good people and bad people coexist in the kingdom until the end of the age. The growth of the kingdom of God is like that of the mustard seed, rapid and strong. The response to Jesus' teaching in parables, even when it was not understood, was characterized by wonder: "Where did this man get this wisdom?" (v. 54).

Jesus taught the most profound and central truths of Christianity with powerful impact. He said to Martha, "I am the resurrection and the life; he who believes in me, though he die, yet shall he live, and whoever lives and believes in me shall never die" (John 11:25-26). His illustration was the resurrection of Lazarus.

Much of the teaching of Jesus centered on his claims of being sent into the world by the Father to accomplish redemption. He knew and predicted that he would be rejected by the leaders of the people and suffer and die in Jerusalem. He knew that he would not continue to teach, help, and encourage his followers, but he taught them that he would send them another counselor and helper from the Father, the Holy Spirit, who would continue the teaching of Jesus (John 14:15-26).

See CHRIST; CHRISTOLOGY.

Bibliography. G. C. Berkouwer, *The Person of Christ* (Grand Rapids: 1954); G. Bornkamm, *Jesus of Nazareth* (New York: 1960); H. Conzelmann, *Jesus* (Philadelphia: 1973); A. Edersheim, *The Life and Times of Jesus the Messiah* (1886; repr. Grand Rapids: 1971); H. C. Kee, *Jesus in History,* 2nd ed. (New York: 1977).

JESUS, WISDOM OF.† A Gnostic writing dating from the first three centuries A.D.; also known as the

Sophia of Jesus Christ. The work was originally written in Greek but is now extant only in two Coptic manuscripts, one of which was part of the Nag Hammadi library discovered near the ancient Christian monastery at Chenoboskion in Egypt.

The work appears to be a recasting and christianizing of a non-Christian Gnostic philosophical treatise, the Epistle of Eugnostos, into a dialogue between the resurrected and exalted Christ and his twelve disciples, together with seven holy women. The Savior responds to their questions by imparting numerous cosmic revelations (drawn largely from Eugnostos) concerning the existence of an invisible, supercelestial realm beyond human reckoning and the divine beings who inhabit that world.

JETHER [jē'thər] (Heb. *yeṭer* "abundance").

1. The oldest son of Gideon (Judg. 8:20). His father ordered him to kill the Midianites Zebah and Zalmunna as vengeance, but the youthful Jether was afraid to comply.

2. The father of Absalom's commander Amasa (1 Kgs. 2:5, 32), an Ishmaelite (1 Chr. 2:17). At 2 Sam. 17:25 he is called Ithra ("the Ishmaelite," RSV mg.; MT Heb. *hayyiśrᵉʾēlî* "Israelite").

3. A son of Jada and descendant of Jerahmeel; he died childless (1 Chr. 2:32).

4. A son of Ezrah, from the tribe of Judah (1 Chr. 4:17).

5. A man from the tribe of Asher (1 Chr. 7:38), apparently identical to Ithran the son of Zophah in v. 37.

JETHETH [jē'thĕth] (Heb. *yᵉṭēṭ*). A descendant of Esau; a chief and eponymous ancestor of an Edomite clan (Gen. 36:40; 1 Chr. 1:51).

JETHLAH (Josh. 19:42, KJV). *See* ITHLAH.

JETHRO [jĕth'rō] (Heb. *yiṭrô* "highness" or "eminence" [?]).† A priest of Midian, the father-in-law of Moses (Exod. 3:1; 4:18). At 2:18 he is called Reuel, which some scholars interpret as a clan name. In two passages Moses' father-in-law is called Hobab (Num. 10:29 [perhaps referring to Reuel]; Judg. 4:11, RSV); while some scholars identify Jethro with Hobab, others interpret Heb. *ḥōṭēn* variously as "brother-in-law" (Judg. 4:11, NIV) or "son-in-law." Some view the variant names as reflecting different traditions.

When Moses fled Egypt he took refuge with Jethro in Midian. Having protected Jethro's daughters, Moses was welcomed into the priest's household, marrying his daughter Zipporah, and tending the flocks (Exod. 2:16–3:1). Later, when Jethro came to Moses at Mt. Sinai, he rejoiced at Israel's deliverance and Yahweh's revelation, offered thanksgiving sacrifices, and gave Moses counsel concerning the administration of justice (ch. 18). Jethro and his party did not go with Moses (v. 27).

Jethro was a Kenite, an itinerant smith related to the Midianites (Judg. 1:16). Some scholars think that Moses learned about Yahweh from Jethro and the Kenites, but the evidence remains highly inferential and, some think, contrary to other texts (Exod. 18:11; cf. 6:3). Some scholars contend Jethro was likely a

priest of El, the God of the patriarchs (cf. Reuel, "friend of El").

JETUR [jē'tər] (Heb. *yᵉṭûr*). A son of Ishmael (Gen. 25:15 par. 1 Chr. 1:31); eponymous ancestor of the Ituraeans. His descendants were among the peoples against whom the Transjordanian tribes of Israel made war (5:19).

JEUEL [jə ū'əl, jōō'əl] (Heb. *yᵉʿûʾēl* "God has saved" [?]).

1. The head of a father's house of Zerah of the tribe of Judah; a clan listed among the returning exiles who settled in Jerusalem (1 Chr. 9:6).

2. A Levite of the sons of Elizaphan; one of fourteen who cleansed the temple during Hezekiah's renewal (2 Chr. 29:13; KJV, NIV "Jeiel"). He may be the same as JEIEL **4**.

3. A son of Adonikam, named among those accompanying Ezra to Jerusalem (Ezra 8:13; KJV "Jeiel"; 1 Esdr. 8:39).

JEUSH [jē'ŭsh] (Heb. *yᵉʿûš; *"may [God] come to rescue").

1. A son of Esau and Oholibamah; an Edomite chief (Gen. 36:5, 14 [K *yᵉʿîš*], 18; 1 Chr. 1:35).

2. A son of Bilhan, a mighty warrior from the tribe of Benjamin (1 Chr. 7:10; K *yᵉʿîš*).

3. The second son of Eshek, and a descendant of Saul; a Benjaminite (1 Chr. 8:39; KJV "Jehush").

4. A Gershonite Levite, the son of Shimei (1 Chr. 23:10). Because he had only a few sons, his family was reckoned with that of Beriah as one father's house (v. 11).

5. A son of Rehoboam and Mahalath (2 Chr. 11:19).

JEUZ [jē'ŭz] (Heb. *yᵉʿûṣ*). A son of Shaharaim, and head of a Benjaminite father's house (1 Chr. 8:10).

JEW (Heb. *yᵉhûḏî*; Aram. *yᵉhûḏay, yᵉhûḏāyēʾ*; Gk. *Ioudaios*), **JUDAISM** (Gk. *Ioudaïsmos*).* Originally a gentilic noun derived from Judah (Heb. *yᵉhûḏâ*), the name of a son of Jacob and Leah, the tribe named for him, and the kingdom of Judah. The Hebrew term for Judahite(s) was used before and after the destruction of the southern kingdom for persons of that country (2 Kgs. 25:25; Neh. 1:2; Jer. 34:9), whose language was "the language of Judah" (Heb. *yᵉhûḏît*; 2 Kgs. 18:26 par.; Neh. 13:24), that is, Hebrew. The term came into greatest use after the Exile, however. Those who returned from captivity in Mesopotamia were known as Jews (Ezra 6:14; Neh. 13:23), as were the descendants of those who remained in Mesopotamia (Esth. 3:6) and of those who had not gone into exile. Gk. *Ioudaios* and Lat. *Judaeus* became the usual terms in those languages for the people of the province of Judea and their coreligionists dispersed in Mesopotamia and the Roman Empire. The English word "Jew" is derived from the Hebrew by way of Greek, Latin, and Old French.

Judaism apparently represented at first particular zealousness with regard to the religion of the Jews (2 Macc. 2:21; 14:38; Gal. 1:13-14), but has come to be the standard abstract term for that religion. Judaism is, then, the religion of the Old Testament worshippers of Yahweh as modified by exile, return, dispersion, the double destruction of the temple (587 B.C. and A.D. 70), the development of the synagogue as a local place of worship, the growth of eschatological ideas, the development of the detailed interpretation and living-out of the law of Moses as the center of religious and cultural life, and numerous other factors, influences, and events down to the present day.

To call Judaism "the religion of the Jews" is less exclusive and therefore preferable to defining Jews as "those who practice Judaism." Jews regard Jews as Jewish even if they do not practice Judaism. But neither is ancestry the sole determinant of Jewishness. Proselytes, or converts to Judaism, have always been at least theoretically acceptable to Jews, and often welcomed. The most obvious distinction between Jews and Gentiles during the Hellenistic period was circumcision (cf. Gal. 2:7).

In the New Testament "the Jews" are portrayed as the consistent adversaries of Jesus and the Church's preaching of the gospel. At the heart of this portrayal are the narratives of Jesus' trial and execution, in which the role of the Jewish leaders (Mark 14:1-2, 10-11, 43, 53-65; 15:1, 10 par.) and the crowds in Jerusalem for the Passover (Matt. 27:25; Mark 15:11-15) are emphasized. Here the Jews of Judea are held responsible for the death of Jesus (Acts 2:23; 7:52; 1 Thess. 2:14-15), but it is not until after the New Testament that the account is altered to eliminate the Roman role altogether and to have Jews actually nail Jesus to the cross (as in the second-century gospel of Peter). The Jews are also portrayed as the opponents of Jesus and Christianity by the Synoptics' treatment of the Pharisees and other Jewish groups (e.g., Matt. 23; Mark 2:23–3:6) and the repeated reference in the gospel of John to "the Jews" as the opposition to Jesus (e.g., John 5:10-18; 6:41; 7:1, 13), and in Acts as those who reject and oppose the gospel as preached by Paul (Acts 9:22-23; 13:45-50; 18:12-15; 20:19; 21:11; 26:7; cf. 1 Thess. 2:14-16).

The fundamental failure of the gospel mission "to the circumcised" (Gal. 2:7) is regarded as a tragedy (Rom. 9:1-5, 30-33; 10:1-3; 11:7-10), but the existence of Christian Jews is, nonetheless, recognized (Acts 13:43; 14:1; Rom. 11:1-5; cf. John 8:31), and they are regarded as "Jews," not as persons who have departed from Judaism for another religion (Acts 21:39; Gal. 2:13). Paul argues that the Jews who have not believed still have a place in God's plan which will come to fruition in their salvation (Rom. 11:11-31). There is no doubt in the New Testament that those who believe in Jesus are the spiritual heirs of Old Testament religion (e.g., 2:26-29; ch. 4; cf. Rev. 2:9; 3:9), but not until after the New Testament is this broadened to mean that the Old Testament prophets preached Christianity to adherents of the false Jewish religion (as in Ignatius *Magn.* 8–9) or that the name "Israel" could be applied straightforwardly to the Church (as it is for the first time by Justin Martyr *Dial.* cxxx).

JEWELS.† Biblical usage prefers to refer to jewels by name (e.g., Cant. 5:14; cf. Rev. 21:19-20), as "something fashioned" (Heb. *kᵉlî;* e.g., Ezek. 16:17),

or as "precious" (1 Kgs. 7:9) or "costly stones" (10:2) rather than by an abstract noun "jewel."

Their beauty, durability, size, and rarity made jewels a natural form of wealth to be gained by trade (Ezek. 27:22) or seized as booty (Num. 31:50). Whether loose or in settings, jewels were given as gifts (1 Kgs. 10:10) and inheritances (2 Chr. 21:3), adorned crowns (2 Sam. 12:30), decorated the sanctuary (2 Chr. 3:6) and the priest's ephod (Exod. 28:15-21), and were stored in the royal treasury (2 Chr. 32:27). Stones were set in various articles of jewelry, including signets, bracelets, and necklaces (cf. Isa. 3:18-23). *See* ORNAMENTS.

Archaeological finds include evidence of various forms of semiprecious stones, including amber, coral, and pearl. Nevertheless, precise identification of jewels cited in the biblical accounts remains difficult owing to differing means of classification and variations in terminology. For specific jewels see the individual entries.

Jewels were dressed, given rounded, convex forms, and polished to heighten their color and brillance. The modern technique of faceting was not used. Frequently they were engraved, especially horizontally stratified stones (e.g., black and white onyx) where the engraving would then appear in a contrasting color to the polished surface (cf. Exod. 28:12).

Jewels set the standard of splendor for God's wisdom (Prov. 3:15) and kingdom (Matt. 13:45-46), and describe the magnificence of his appearance (Rev. 4:3) and of the new Jerusalem (Isa. 54:11-12). The twelve stones of the priest's ephod (Exod. 28:15-21) represent the twelve tribes, and were taken symbolically to refer to the cosmos (Wis. 18:24). The New Jerusalem's foundation of twelve jewels signifies the twelve apostles (Rev. 21:14, 19-20) and, with the twelve gates of pearl (vv. 12, 21), underscores the glorious salvation promised the twelve tribes as now fulfilled in the Lamb.

JEWISH CHRISTIANS. The earliest Christians were all Jews. As such they continued their participation in the temple worship while the forms of Christian worship were developing (Acts 2:46; 3:1). After the conversion of Gentiles at Joppa, distinctions were first made between Christian Jews, "the believers from among the circumcised" (10:45), and Gentile believers in Jesus (cf. Gal. 2:12-13). It was in Antioch, first center of Gentile Christianity, that a new term, "Christians," had to be coined (Acts 11:26).

A dispute arose in the Jerusalem church after the conversion of the Gentiles at Joppa (v. 2). But its basis was a lack of information—apparently some did not know that the particular Gentiles Peter had been associating with were now Christians. The dispute was easily resolved (v. 18), but that this was not to be the end of the matter is shown already by the difficulty with which Peter was persuaded to receive Cornelius (10:9-16) and by the evangelistic energy of the leaders of the "Hellenists" (8:5-13, 26-40; 11:19; cf. 6:1-6). The latter led to the founding of the church at Antioch (11:20-21), which was itself the basis of the mission into Cyprus and Asia Minor of Paul and Barnabas (chs. 13–14).

A group within the Jerusalem church which apparently accepted the Gentile Christians as only incomplete Christians needing circumcision was formed in opposition to the developments at Antioch. It may have been only when they went to Antioch to teach their position to the Gentile Christians that this group learned of Paul and Barnabas' work (15:1-2). The complaints of this group, who were "false brethren" in Paul's view (Gal. 2:4), led to the APOSTOLIC COUNCIL at Jerusalem, which rejected their position (Acts 15:5-29). But their position did not go away so simply but continued and developed in a number of directions, as can be seen from what happened again at Antioch (Gal. 2:11-13), at Galatia (1:6-9; 3:1; 4:17-20; 5:2-12), and possibly at Philippi (Phil. 3:2, 18-19), Corinth (2 Cor. 11:4-5, 12-15), Colossae (Col. 2:8, 11, 16-23), and Crete (Titus 1:10-16; 3:9).

This position, which was basically that the true followers of Jesus should be and remain Jews faithful to the law of Moses, became the basis of the EBIONITES and other second-century Jewish-Christian groups deemed heretical by the broader stream of (predominantly Gentile) Christianity and of the views represented in the anti-Pauline Kerygmata Petrou and related writings. Gentile Christianity itself became more extreme in the opposite direction (cf. Rom. 11:17-22), the results ranging from the rejection of Old Testament Israel as always heedless and sinful (Barnabas; Ignatius *Magn.* 8-9) to the Marcionite rejection of the Old Testament and anti-Jewish Gnosticism. The moderate Jewish Christianity of the early period, which included a broad range of view and persons, such as Paul, Peter, and James, and which was clearly open to letting Gentile Christians remain Gentiles, was lost in this bifurcation.

JEWISH REVOLTS.* Armed revolts by Jews against the Roman Empire in Palestine in A.D. 66-74 and 132-135 and in Mesopotamia, Cyrenaica, Egypt, and Cyprus in 115-117.

I. Background

The Maccabean revolt against Antiochus IV Epiphanes became a model both for the possibility of successful revolution and for the ideal of independent self-government in Palestine. Judean independence under the Hasmoneans persisted until the Roman takeover by Pompey in 63 B.C.

Roman rule through Herod the Great, his offspring, and Roman governors was intolerable to those who held dear the ideal of independence. Numerous Jewish revolts occurred in Herod's territory after his death, some with messianic overtones. The memory of their suppression dissuaded many Jews in the following decades from revolt against Rome. When Archelaus was deposed in A.D. 6, Judea became for the first time a province under direct Roman rule. Unrest characterized the province, but until the death in A.D. 44 of Herod Agrippa I, whose reign beginning in A.D. 41 was the only brief interruption of direct Roman rule before 66, this took the form of generally nonviolent responses to Roman outrages, which often involved the threat of desecration of the temple in Jerusalem. From 48, however, violence increased.

This period, from Antiochus IV on, saw the growth of the activist Jewish piety characterized by "zeal" (cf. Num. 25:6-13), which sought the purification of the land and the people of Israel from violations of the law of Moses. The Gentile occupation of the land was, of course, offensive to this piety. Jewish apocalyptic literature, while it began earlier, came to its greatest importance at this time. At the heart of apocalyptic literature was the hope of Israel's eschatological salvation from foreign rule. Throughout this period it was questioned whether Roman rule should be considered tolerable for those obedient to the law of Moses (cf. Matt. 22:17 par.). When Judea came under direct Roman rule and a census was taken in A.D. 6, Judas the Galilean put forth his radical interpretation of Exod. 20:3, according to which the Jews could have "no lord but God," i.e., no non-Jewish ruler (cf. Pss. Sol. 17:15). This became the ideological orientation for the continuing agitation for revolt against Rome.

II. The War of A.D. 66-74

War had long been on the horizon when in A.D. 66 a number of events led to revolt. In conflicts between the Jews and the Greeks of Caesarea, the Roman government sided with the Greeks. While hostilities were breaking out in Caesarea, Gessius Florus, the procurator of Judea — accustomed to enriching himself at the expense of Jews—took seventeen talents from the temple treasury. When two men mocked Florus' "poverty," he opened a part of Jerusalem to a rampage by Roman soldiers in which scores of Jews were killed. The next day the people were to show their acceptance of Florus' authority by giving their customary salutation to two Roman cohorts coming in from Caesarea; but Florus arranged that the soldiers not return the salutation. As a result, revolutionary elements among the people gained the upper hand over those who wished to avoid confrontation with Rome, and war was under way.

Within a few months all Roman soldiers and those Jewish forces opposing the revolt—including the soldiers of Herod Agrippa II—were driven from Jerusalem or killed. In every Palestinian town containing both Jews and Gentiles war broke out. The effects were felt in some places in the Diaspora as well. The army of Cestius, the legate of Syria, attacked Jerusalem but was forced to withdraw and was attacked near Beth-horon while returning to Syria. In 67 Roman armies under Vespasian and Titus captured all of Galilee and Gaulanitis from the rebel forces. The more radical leaders of the revolt gained control in Jerusalem and instituted a reign of terror during the winter of 67-68. The Roman armies continued to subjugate significant parts of Palestine. But with Nero's death in June 68 and the three ensuing short imperial reigns, Vespasian was forced to halt military operations for a year. Yet by the time of Vespasian's acclamation as emperor in July 69 the Jewish rebel forces held only Jerusalem and the fortresses of Machaerus, Herodium, and Masada. Those in control of Jerusalem were fighting among themselves.

Jerusalem fell to the siege of Vespasian's son Titus in Spring-Summer 70. The temple was destroyed by fire, as was most of the rest of the city. Herodium and Machaerus fell in 72, and Masada in 74. Those of the population of Palestine who remained were severely impoverished. The tax which had gone from every Jew to the support of temple was replaced by a Roman tax for the support of the temple of Jupiter Capitolinus in Rome. The books of 4 Ezra (= 2 Esdr. 3–14) and 2 Baruch are apocalyptic reflections on the disaster which had befallen the Jews.

Not only was the temple—the central focus of Jewish worship—gone, but the Sanhedrin, the central authority among the Jews, was destroyed. The rabbis in the pharisaic tradition who concentrated on scholarly study and exposition of the law became the leaders in the reconstitution of Judaism. Jamnia, near the Mediterranean coast, was the first center of this rabbinic activity, under the leadership initially of Johanan ben Zakkai.

According to a tradition preserved by Eusebius, the Christians of Jerusalem left the city early in the war and went to the Gentile city of Pella in Perea. Although this tradition has been questioned, it is likely that few Judean Christians participated in the First Jewish Revolt, since links had existed between the church in Jerusalem and Gentile Christianity (Acts 15:22-29; Gal. 2:1-10). But in this the Judean Christians were not united (Acts 15:1, 5; Gal. 2:4, 12). A significant issue in the study of the New Testament is the degree to which, if at all, the documents in the New Testament reflect a date subsequent to the war by speaking obliquely of Jerusalem's destruction (e.g., Luke 21:20-24; cf. par.; Eph. 2:14), by reflecting a new polemical relationship between Christianity and Judaism now in its post-A.D. 70 form, or by portraying Christianity in its best light before the Roman government, thereby dissociating it from rebellion.

III. The Second-Century Revolts

In Alexandria, Egypt, the first century A.D. witnessed conflicts, sometimes quite bloody, between the large Jewish population and the Gentile majority. These conflicts increased during the time of the revolt in Palestine and after the revolt when refugees came in from Palestine. While the emperor Trajan was involved in the conquest of Mesopotamia (115), Jewish revolts broke out in Alexandria and Cyrene that spread to all of Cyrenaica, Egypt, and Cyprus. The Jews in the newly conquered lands of Mesopotamia revolted as well, forcing Trajan's retreat and the eventual abandonment of Roman conquest of the Parthian Empire by Trajan's successor, Hadrian. The revolts ended under Hadrian after Trajan's death in 117, but left considerable destruction in Egypt, Libya, and Cyrenaica. Cyrenaica was depopulated enough to require colonization after the war. Jews were barred entry to Cyprus, but the war also helped to insure that Jewish culture and learning would have a home free from Roman control in Mesopotamia.

The revolt of 132-135 was caused by two unrelated decisons of Emperor Hadrian. He banned circumcision as a barbaric practice in general, not specifically as a Jewish custom, and took steps to build a Roman (thus Gentile) city and temple at Jerusalem. It is possible that these decisions, disastrous from a Jewish standpoint, were preceded by a period in which Hadrian took a conciliatory approach to the Jews and possibly even planned for a rebuilding of the Jewish temple

at Jerusalem. At any rate, because of the decisions involving circumcision and Jerusalem, the Jews of Palestine begin in secret to gather arms. When Hadrian left the East in 132 they revolted. At first, messianic claims were associated with a number of local heroes, but soon Simon bar Kosiba (Bar Kokhba) emerged as the dominant figure with the support of Rabbi Akiba, one of the most significant persons in the development of early rabbinic learning. Christian Jews, unable to agree with Bar Kokhba's messianic claims, were persecuted for their nonparticipation in the revolt. The insurrection was put down at great cost to Roman forces. The land of Palestine was, on the whole, devastated by the war. Jerusalem was rebuilt as Aelia Capitolina, a Roman city from which Jews were barred. Systematic persecutions of Jews by the Roman government began after suppression of the revolt.

Bibliography. H. H. Ben-Sasson, ed., *A History of the Jewish People* (Cambridge, Mass.: 1976), pp. 330-35, 368-373; D. M. Rhoads, *Israel in Revolution 6-74 C.E.* (Philadelphia: 1976); E. Schürer, *The History of the Jewish People in the Age of Jesus Christ,* 1 (Edinburgh: 1973): 484-513, 529-557.

JEWRY (Dan. 5:13, KJV). See JUDAH. (Luke 23:5; John 7:1, KJV). See JUDEA.

JEZANIAH [jĕz′ə nī′ə] (Heb. $y^ezanyāhû$ "Yahweh hears").† A captain of Judah's army who joined the Babylonian governor Gedaliah at Mizpah following the fall of Jerusalem (Jer. 40:8; so KJV, NIV at 42:1, following MT; RSV "Azariah"). At 2 Kgs. 25:23 his name occurs as Jaazaniah (1). He is probably the same as AZARIAH 16 (Jer. 43:2).

JEZEBEL [jĕz′ə bĕl, jĕz′ə bəl] (Heb. ′îzeḇel; Gk. Iezabel).

1. The daughter of King Ethbaal of Sidon, and wife of King Ahab of Israel; a woman of strong character, whose wickedness and cruelty—an evil influence upon Ahab (1 Kgs. 21:25)—have become proverbial.

Jezebel promoted Baal worship in Israel, aided in that effort by a temple which Ahab built for that deity in Samaria—perhaps in fulfillment of the alliance with Sidon that constituted the basis for their marriage (1 Kgs. 16:31-32). She was responsible for the murder of many of the prophets of Yahweh in Israel (18:4, 13). At her urging and with her financial support, some 450 prophets of Baal and 400 prophets of Asherah had entered the land (v. 19). When informed that Elijah had killed all these prophets following the contest on Mt. Carmel, Jezebel promised vengeance (19:1) but did not succeed. She later had Nabath stoned to death so she could obtain his coveted vineyard for her husband—blatantly disregarding the Israelite view of the land as an inalienable trust from God (21:1-16).

The scene at Jezreel was one of accursed beauty (2 Kgs. 9). After her son Joram (Jehoram) had been slain, Jezebel knew that she herself had not long to live. She "painted her eyes, and adorned her head" (v. 30), and greeted the victorious Jehu mockingly and despisingly (v. 31). In response the general had his henchmen throw her out of the window so that her blood spattered against the wall; then they trampled on her. After he had eaten and drunk, Jehu gave the order to bury the "cursed woman," but "no more of her than the skull and the feet and the palms of her hands" could be found (vv. 34-35). Jehu interpreted this consequence as the fulfillment of Elijah's words against the house of Ahab following the death of Naboth (v. 37; 1 Kgs. 21:23; cf. 2 Kgs. 9:6-7).

2. A woman at Thyatira "who calls herself a prophetess" and was tempting Christians there to practice idolatry (Rev. 2:20-23). She was a woman of some influence in the congregation there, whom some scholars contend on the basis of a few manuscripts was the wife of the congregation's leader. The name is probably symbolic rather than the woman's given name (cf. v. 14).

JEZER [jē′zər] (Heb. *yeṣer*).* The third son of Naphtali (Gen. 46:24; 1 Chr. 7:13); eponymous ancestor of the Jeezerites (Heb. *hayyiṣrî*; Num. 26:49).

JEZIAH (Ezra 10:25, KJV). *See* IZZIAH.

JEZIEL [jēz′ĭ əl] (Heb. **K** *yᵉzû′ēl* **Q** *yᵉzî′ēl* "God gathers" [?]). A Benjaminite and son of Azmaveth who came to David at Ziklag (1 Chr. 12:3).

JEZLIAH (1 Chr. 8:18, KJV). *See* IZLIAH.

JEZOAR (1 Chr. 4:7, KJV). *See* IZHAR **2.**

JEZRAHIAH [jěz′rə hī′ə] (Heb. *yizraḥyâ* "Yahweh appears" or "shines forth").† The leader of the levitical singers in Nehemiah's temple (Neh. 12:42). At 1 Chr. 7:3 he is called Izrahiah.

JEZREEL [jěz′rĭ əl] (Heb. *yizrᵉᵉ′eʾl* "God sows") (PERSON).

1. A son of Etam and descendant of Judah (1 Chr. 4:3); probably the eponymous ancestor of a town in Judah (cf. Josh. 15:56).

2. The firstborn son of Hosea and Gomer (Hos. 1:4). The name was chosen to symbolize God's judgment against Israel for Jehu's bloody accession to power at the valley of Jezreel (vv. 4-5, 11 [MT 2:2]; cf. 2 Kgs. 9-10) as well as the future restoration of Israel (Hos. 2:22 [MT 24]).

JEZREEL [jěz′rĭ əl] (Heb. *yizrᵉᵉ′eʾl* "God sows") (PLACE).

1. A city in the tribal territory of Judah (Josh. 15:56), presumably in the hills south of Hebron. It was the birthplace of Ahinoam, one of David's wives (1 Sam. 25:43; 2 Sam. 2:2). Some scholars suggest that the site may be modern Khirbet Ṭarrâmā, 9 km. (6 mi.) southwest of Hebron, but the identification is not without problems.

2. A valley that separates Galilee from Samaria. The valley is a geological fault basin whose abundant water supply made it one of the most fertile regions in Palestine (as implied by its name). It also served as a major communications artery through the hills from Acco on the Mediterranean Sea to the Jordan valley, and from Egypt north through Galilee and Syria to Phoenicia. Accordingly, the valley of Jezreel figures prominently in important military actions in the

early days of Israel. Some scholars distinguish the western portion as the valley of Esdraelon or the plain (or valley) of Megiddo.

At the time of the Israelite conquest of Palestine the Jezreel valley was occupied by Canaanites whose iron chariotry prevented the tribes of Ephraim and Manasseh (Joseph) from displacing them (Josh. 17:16). During the period of the judges Gideon and the northern tribes routed a coalition of Amalekites, Midianites, and "people of the East" encamped there (Judg. 6:33–7:23). David's forces encamped "by the fountain which is in Jezreel" against the Philistines at Aphek (1 Sam. 29:1). Later Saul and his sons fell in battle against the Philistines on Mt. Gilboa, located in the eastern section of the valley (1 Sam. 31).

The valley of Jezreel is mentioned also in the prophecies of Hosea, who declared that Israel's strength would be broken there (Hos. 1:4-5, 11 [MT 2:2]) as punishment for the murders committed there during Jehu's purge *ca.* 842 B.C. (2 Kgs. 9–10).

3. A border city in Issachar (Josh. 19:18), identified with modern Zerʿîn, 11 km. (7 mi.) north of Jenin. Strategically located along major trade routes in the valley of Jezreel, it sits at the head of the Beth-shean corridor and commands a view of the plain of Esdraelon.

Because it is not mentioned in extrabiblical sources of the second millennium B.C., the city is believed to have been settled first by the Israelites. Jezreel grew in importance during the monarchy, first as a city of Solomon's fifth administrative district (1 Kgs. 4:12) and later as a royal city (18:45-46), perhaps the location of the winter palace (cf. Amos 3:15). There Ahab seized the vineyard of Naboth (1 Kgs. 21) and Jehu executed his bloody coup (2 Kgs. 9:14-37).

JEZREELITE [jěz′rĭ ə līt] (Heb. *hayyizrᵉʿēʾlî*).* A gentilic designating Naboth, a resident of Jezreel (**3**) in Issachar (1 Kgs. 21; 2 Kgs. 9:21, 25).

JEZREELITESS [jěz′rĭ ə lī′tĭs] (Heb. *yizrᵉʿēʾlît*).* A gentilic applied to David's wife Ahinoam, who came from Jezreel (**1**) in Judah (1 Chr. 3:1; KJV 27:3; 30:5; 2 Sam. 2:2; 3:2).

JIBSAM (1 Chr. 7:2, KJV). *See* IBSAM.

JIDLAPH [jĭd′lăf] (Heb. *yiḏlap* "he weeps"). A son of Nahor and Milcah (Gen. 22:22).

JIMNA, JIMNAH. *See* IMNAH **1.**

JIPHTAH (Josh. 15:43, KJV). *See* IPHTAH.

JIPHTHAHEL. *See* IPHTAHEL.

JOAB [jō′ăb] (Heb. *yôʾāḇ* "Yahweh is father").

1. The second son of Zeruiah, David's sister, and brother of Abishai and Asahel (1 Chr. 2:16); commander of David's army (2 Sam. 8:16).

Joab probably joined David, as had his brothers, when David was still fleeing from Saul. Apparently he already held a position of leadership when he prevailed over Abner in the contest at Gibeon (2 Sam. 2:12-32). Subsequently he killed Abner, ostensibly because the latter had killed Joab's brother Asahel in the skirmish at Gibeon but also because he appeared to be a rival as commander of the army (3:22-29). This prompted David to pronounce a terrible curse over Joab and his house, though he himself was too weak to punish Joab and Abishai (vv. 28-29, 31-39).

According to 1 Chr. 11:6 (cf. 2 Sam. 5:8), Joab was the first to capture the water supply of Jebus (Jerusalem) and thus earn the reward that David had promised: the chief command of his forces. He then restored a part of the city of David (1 Chr. 11:8). Later he defeated the Ammonites and their Aramean allies at Jericho in retaliation for their humiliation of David's envoys (2 Sam. 10:1-14 par. 1 Chr. 19:1-19). In a second campaign he besieged the Ammonites at Rabbah, enabling David to take that city (2 Sam. 11:1; 12:26-31; 1 Chr. 20:1-3). It was at this time that Joab assisted his king in the murder of Uriah the Hittite (2 Sam. 11:14-25). After David's victory over Edom Joab remained there for six months to slay all the males (1 Kgs. 11:15-16).

Joab persuaded David to return his son Absalom to Jerusalem from Geshur where he had fled after the murder of Amnon (14:1-24); two years later Absalom burned Joab's field in order to prevail upon the general to request an audience with David in Absalom's behalf (vv. 28-33). Joab was opposed to Absalom's insurgence against the throne and ended the rebellion by killing the rebellious son (18:9-18); when David's grief eclipsed any joy at the victory Joab accused the king bluntly of ill-advised devotion to an enemy (19:5-8). Joab also was able to quell the later rebellion by Sheba against David (20:1-22), and regained his position as commander of the forces by murdering Amasa, whom David had appointed (19:13; 20:8-10).

Though Joab warned David to refrain from taking a census, the king refused to pay heed and thus incurred the ravages of a three-day plague as punishment for his pride (2 Sam. 24:1-9; 1 Chr. 21:1ff.). The loyal commander carried out David's command, but because the king's order was abhorrent to him he did not enumerate Levi and Benjamin.

Joab may have based his support of Adonijah, the son of David and Haggith, on the consideration that the kingdom would be more secure with David's eldest surviving son on the throne than the young Solomon (1 Kgs. 1:7, 19). Of those invited to Adonijah's feast, Joab was the first to sense danger (v. 41). On his deathbed David had instructed Solomon not to let Joab's "gray head go down to Sheol in peace" (2:6), recalling that even in times of peace Joab had shed the blood of war (vv. 5-6). When Solomon had Adonijah killed because of his request to marry Abishag (vv. 13-25), Joab fled to the tabernacle and took hold of the horns of the altar. Because he refused to come out Solomon ordered Benaiah to kill him there (vv. 28-34; cf. Exod. 21:14). Joab was buried in his house in the wilderness (1 Kgs. 2:34), and Benaiah succeeded him as commander (v. 35).

Joab was loyal to David and served him as a competent and successful general without compromising his honor. He was audacious, yet energetic and of inestimable value to the dynasty. But he was also vengeful and ambitious and felt no compunction for murder. Nevertheless, his intention was to serve his country, even when he supported Adonijah's rebellion. Yet he deserved the death penalty which Solomon imposed upon him. He had lacked the devotion to the fear of God and faithfulness to the covenantal ideal so indispensable to an Israelite of such social and political distinction.

2. A Judahite, the son of Seraiah and descendant of Kenaz, and "father" (or settler) of Ge-harashim ("valley of Craftsmen") (1 Chr. 4:14).

3. Father (or ancestor) of the "sons of Pahath-moab" who were among the first to return from exile (Ezra 2:6; 8:9; Neh. 7:11).

JOAH [jō'ə] (Heb. *yôʾāḥ* "Yahweh is brother").

1. The son of Asaph, and a recorder in the court of King Hezekiah. He was one of the three officials sent by the king to the Assyrian representatives at the siege of Jerusalem *ca.* 701 B.C. (2 Kgs. 18:18, 26, 37 par. Isa. 36:3, 11, 22).

2. A Levite and son of Zimmah from the family of Gershom (1 Chr. 6:21 [MT 6]). He may be identical with the Joah who, with his son Eden, participated in the temple reforms begun under King Hezekiah (2 Chr. 29:12).

3. The son of Obed-edom; a Levite appointed to be a gatekeeper in the temple (1 Chr. 26:4).

4. The son of Joahaz; an official of King Josiah commissioned to repair the temple (2 Chr. 34:8).

JOAHAZ [jō'ə hăz] (Heb. *yôʾāḥāz*, contraction of *yᵉhôʾāḥāz* "Yahweh has grasped" [= Jehoahaz]). The father of Joah 4 (2 Chr. 34:8).

JOANAN [jō ă'nən] (Gk. *Iōanan*, from Heb. *yôḥānān* "Yahweh has been gracious"). The grandson of Zerubbabel, and an ancestor of Jesus (Luke 3:27; KJV "Joanna"), perhaps to be identified with Hananiah (1 Chr. 3:19).

JOANNA [jō ăn'ə] (Gk. *Iōana, Iōanna* "Yahweh is gracious"). The wife of Chuza, Herod's steward (Luke 8:3). One of the women whom Jesus had healed, she followed him and his disciples, providing for them as they traveled in Galilee (v. 4). She was one of the women who discovered the empty tomb on Easter morning (24:10; cf. 23:55).

JOARIB [jō'ə rĭb] (Gk. *Iōarib*).* Head of the priestly family from which was descended Mattathias, who with his sons initiated the Maccabean revolt (1 Macc. 2:1; 14:29; KJV "Jarib"). At 1 Chr. 24:7 he is called Jehoiarib.

JOASH [jō'ăsh] (Heb. *yᵉhôʾāš, yôʾāš* "Yahweh has given"; *yôʿāš* "Yahweh has aided").

1. (Heb. *yᵉhôʾāš, yôʾāš*). An Abiezerite of the tribe of Manasseh, and father of Gideon the judge (Judg. 6:11). Evidently the owner (or caretaker) of the Asherah and the altar to Baal which Gideon destroyed, Joash nonetheless stood by his son against the townspeople of Ophrah (vv. 25-31). It was from his rejoinder that Gideon's new name, Jerubbaal, was derived (v. 32).

2. A son of King Ahab of Israel, and an associate of Amon, the governor of Samaria. He imprisoned

Micaiah after the prophet had prophesied defeat for Ahab (1 Kgs. 22:26-27 par. 2 Chr. 18:25-26). Some scholars suggest that "king's son" is a title.

3. The ninth king of Judah (*ca.* 837-800 B.C.); the son of Ahaziah and Zibiah of Beer-sheba. He is also called Jehoash (2 Kgs. 11–12; 2 Chr. 22:10–24:24). Although he did "what was right in the eyes of the Lord all his days" (2 Kgs. 12:2), the biblical account remains cool in its portrait, doubtlessly colored by the closing years of his reign.

As an infant Joash narrowly escaped the massacre of the royal heirs by the queen mother Athaliah, when he was hid by his aunt Jehosheba, wife of Jehoiada the high priest (11:1-3). At seven Joash was anointed king by Jehoiada in the presence of the royal guard, the Levites, and representatives of the people (v. 4; 2 Chr. 23:1-2). Athaliah's cry of "Treason" was useless; the usurping queen was summarily executed. In the wake of the coup, Jehoiada renewed the covenant "between the Lord and the king and people" and another between the people and the Davidic king. Afterward they went out and destroyed the temple and priest of the Tyrian Baal, which the former queen had established (2 Kgs. 11:17-18).

The people of Judah rejoiced at Joash's ascension to the throne. So long as Jehoiada lived and instructed him, the young king did well in the sight of the Lord, although local worship did continue upon the high places. The major work of Joash's reign was the restoration of the temple, ignored and desecrated by the former queen (2 Chr. 24:7). The first such attempts were entrusted to the priests, who were to use money from the collections at their discretion (2 Kgs. 12:5), and to the Levites, who went to the cities of Judah to gather the temple tax (2 Chr.' 24:5; cf. Exod. 30:11-16). Yet by the twenty-third year of his reign the priests had not yet made repairs, nor had the Levites pressed them to do so (2 Kgs. 12:6; 2 Chr. 24:5). In response, Joash took the building program away from the priests and instituted stricter accounting measures (2 Kgs. 12:8, 15). The collection was now gathered in a chest at the gate of the temple, under the joint supervision of the king's scribe and the high priest; the masons and carpenters were paid directly. The people welcomed the new procedure, and soon the temple was fully restored, with the extra gold and silver used for new dishes and utensils (2 Chr. 24:8-12).

After the death of Jehoiada, the princes of Judah influenced Joash to let them again openly serve their Asherim and idols. Both king and princes ignored the prophets of Yahweh (2 Chr. 24:17-19). When Zechariah the son of Jehoiada, Joash's benefactor, spoke against their idolatry, prophesying God's coming judgment, the king had him stoned in the court of the temple (vv. 20-22; cf. Luke 11:51).

Judgment came swiftly. Before the year's end King Hazael of Syria marched against Jerusalem. Although the Syrians came with relatively few troops, they were still able to defeat the much larger Judean army. Joash was able to stop them only with gold, gained by emptying the palace and stripping the temple of its votive offerings (2 Kgs. 12:17-18; 2 Chr. 24:23-24).

Shortly afterward Joash came to a violent end, when two of his officers murdered him as he slept in the fortress of the Millo. He was buried in the city of David, but not in the royal sepulchre (2 Kgs. 12:19-21; 2 Chr. 24:25). His son Amaziah succeeded him as king (2 Kgs. 12:21; 2 Chr. 24:27).

4. The twelfth king of Israel (801-786 B.C.); the son of Jehoahaz. He is also called Jehoash (2 Kgs. 13:10-25; 14:8-17). Although he is characterized as continuing in the sins of Jeroboam (13:11), Joash's reign did enjoy divine favor (v. 23; cf. Josephus *Ant.* ix.8.6 [177]) and military success.

On the basis of the biblical account, the key event of his reign was his visit with the dying Elisha (13:14-19). His greeting was filled with respect (v. 14; cf. 2:12; in contrast, 6:31, 33). By means of the symbolic action of shooting arrows, the prophet predicted Joash's three victories over the Syrians, while underscoring the king's limited faith (vv. 18-19).

Militarily, Joash proved himself as the savior of Israel (v. 5), defeating the Syrians and recovering the cities lost by Jehoahaz (v. 25). When King Amaziah of Judah foolishly provoked him to war, Joash crushed him in battle at Beth-shemesh, then captured Jerusalem, and reduced Judah to the status of a vassal state (14:8-14). Joash was buried in Samaria with the kings of Israel. His son, Jeroboam II, succeeded him (v. 16).

An inscription of Assyrian king Adad-nirari III lists "Joash (Akk. *Ia-'a-su*) of Samaria" among those paying tribute *ca.* 796.

5. A Judahite, the son of Shelah (1 Chr. 4:22).

6. (Heb. *yōʿāš*). A Benjaminite from the clan of Becher (1 Chr. 7:8).

7. (Heb. *yâʾāš*). A son of Shemaah of Gibeah who joined David at Ziklag. He was second in command of the "mighty men," Benjaminite warriors who could use both bow and sling (1 Chr. 12:1-3).

8. (Heb. *yōʿāš*). The overseer of David's stores of oil (1 Chr. 27:28).

JOATHAM (Matt. 1:9, KJV). *See* JOTHAM **2**.

JOB (Gen. 46:13, KJV). *See* IOB; JASHUB.

JOB [jōb] (Heb. *ʾiyôb*), **BOOK OF.**† In the English versions, the eighteenth book of the Old Testament and the first of the poetical books; in the Hebrew canon, the second of the Writings. The book recounts the trials and resultant crisis of faith experienced by Job of Uz.

I. Origins

Scholars remain divided, only in part by their understanding of the nature of Scripture, as to whether the book derives from the experiences of an actual person named Job or represents a folkloristic treatment of the common plight of mankind. The name Job is attested for Palestinian chieftains cited in the Egyptian Execration Texts (Egyp. *ʾybm*; *ca.* 2000 B.C.) and the Amarna Letters (Akk. *Ayyâb*; *ca.* 1350), perhaps meaning "where is (my) Father." Other suggested etymologies include "opponent" (of Yahweh, or treated by God as such), from Heb. *ʾyb* "enemy," or "the penitent one" (cf. Arab. *ʾwb* "return").

The author of the book is not named; rabbinic tradition (cf. *B. Bat.* 14b) and some early Christian authors attributed the work to Moses. The apparent antiquity of the prose introduction (Job 1:1–2:13) and epilogue (42:7-17) is supported by details suggestive of the patriarchal period (early second millennium), e.g., Job's personal offering of sacrifices in the absence of a priesthood or central shrine (1:5; 42:8), the reckoning of wealth similar to that of Abraham and Jacob (1:3; 42:12; cf. Gen. 12:16; 32:5 [MT 6]), and Job's longevity (Job 42:16-17). Moreover, at Ezek. 14:14, 20 Job is mentioned along with the ancient heroes Noah and Daniel (Ugar. *Dan'el*). Some conservative scholars date the book of Job as early as Solomon (tenth century), while others favor the seventh century. Pointing to the poetic style, critical scholars generally place the final editing in exilic or postexilic times, primarily the fourth century.

Similarities between the book of Job and other ancient Near Eastern writings have frequently been noted. In particular, the Egyptian Protests of the Eloquent Peasant (*ANET*, pp. 407-410) and Admonitions of Ipuwer (*ANET*, pp. 441-44) and Akkadian Ludlul Bēl Nēmeqi (*ANET*, pp. 434-37, 596-600), Dialogue about Human Misery (*ANET*, pp. 438-440), and the Babylonian Theodicy (*ANET*, pp. 601-4) are comparable in content and/or form. Other works suggested include the Egyptian Dispute over Suicide (*ANET*, pp. 405-7), Akkadian Pessimistic Dialogue between Master and Servant (*ANET*, pp. 437-38), Hittite Tale of Appu, and the Indian legend of Hariscandra. Yet despite any similarities to or parallels with other ancient literature, the book of Job remains unique in its approach to the matter of human (particularly righteous) suffering.

II. Contents

The book opens with a prose prologue (chs. 1–2) depicting the pious character and attendant prosperity of Job, and his devastation as a result of the testing prompted by Satan's challenge to Yahweh.

Job 3:1–42:6 constitute the core of the book, a collection of poetic dialogues and individual discourses addressing the issue of Job's (and mankind's) suffering. The section opens with Job's soliloquy lamenting his circumstances and cursing his very existence (ch. 3). Chs. 4–27 comprise a poetic dialogue, three cycles of speeches (chs. 4–14, 15–21, 22–27) by Job and three friends—Eliphaz, Bildad, and Zophar—who seek variously to comfort him and to ascertain the cause of his calamity. Ch. 28 is the first of the monologues, a hymn on the value and inaccessibility of wisdom, variously attributed to Job, Zophar, or the poet. In the monologue which follows (chs. 29–31) Job offers his final defense to the friends, a poetic complaint protesting his innocence. A new character now appears, Elihu, who utters four discourses (chs. 32–33, 34, 35, 36–37) admonishing Job and defending God's justice. The section concludes with a poetic discourse between God, who speaks from the whirlwind (38:1–40:2, 40:6–41:34 [MT 26]), and Job, who expresses contrition and allegiance (40:3-5, 42:1-6).

In the prose epilogue (42:7-17) God assails the "comforters," vindicates Job, and restores his fortunes.

III. Literary Aspects

Despite the variety of its component parts and the complexity of its composition, the book of Job is on the whole a unified presentation of the fortunes of the man from Uz and the attempt to place them in theological perspective. This is not to dismiss the probability that various elements of the canonical book originated from different hands in different historical periods. Most scholars agree that the prose framework derives from an ancient account of human suffering and that the poetic discourses represent the later theological reflections of the author. Some scholars point to various passages as later accretions (e.g., the wisdom psalm, ch. 28; the Elihu speeches; Yahweh's second speech, 40:15–41:34 [MT 26]) or indicative of editing or difficulties in transmission (particularly the third cycle of the dialogue, which lacks a speech by Zophar).

The book as a whole does not fit the standard classifications of literary genre. It has been likened, in whole or part, to the Greek drama, the parable or allegory (*B. Bat.* 15a), covenantal lawsuit (Heb. *rîb*), complaint or lament, and philosophical debate. It is comprised of various form-critical elements, including prose narrative, poetic lament (ch. 3), complaint (e.g., chs. 6–7; 13:23–14:22), hymn (e.g., 12:13-25; 36:24–37:13), and prophetic judgment speech (22:5-11). Wisdom forms abound, including proverbs (e.g., 6:14; 12:5-6; 32:7), rhetorical questions (e.g, 4:7; 15:2-3; 34:13, 17-19, 31-33), wisdom sayings (e.g., 4:10-11; 5:17-18), and appeal to ancient tradition (15:17-19).

The language of the book is perhaps the most problematic of any Old Testament work, largely because of the numerous rare words and unusual morphology and syntax. This is more often the cause of rather than the result of difficulties in transmission, as reflected in frequent variants among the versions. The difficulties stem in part from archaic or archaizing usages. Many scholars, noting the frequent apparent aramaisms, suggest that the work was composed in a nonstandard dialect of Hebrew or that the present book is a translation from an Aramaic or perhaps Edomite original.

IV. Theology

The book of Job is universally recognized as an attempt to explain the ways of God to mankind, and is particularly understood as wrestling with the causes of human suffering, especially undeserved suffering. As such it has become the subject of countless artistic and literary interpretations. Indeed, Job's lamentations and his dialogue with the supposed comforters do seek to comprehend Job's pitiful condition in terms of the classical doctrine of retribution, which views loss of fortune, health, and the like as divinely ordained punishment for sin (cf. Lev. 26; Deut. 28). Yet although the book argues against that interpretation, its overall purpose actually is not to "solve" the problem of suffering. Rather, the book underscores above all the sovereignty of God—the freedom to act at will, to test Job and to restore his fortunes, to form and maintain all creation (e.g., 38:26).

The man Job emerges as a model of faith. Racked by misfortune despite his demonstrated righteousness and piety, Job reexamines and defends his actions and his loyalty to God, challenging not only the friends but even God himself. Yet even in the face of perplexity and the seeming hopelessness of his condition, Job maintains his trust in God, confident that his

"Redeemer lives" (19:25-27) and that somehow he would be sustained (42:2). His example reveals the possibility—and necessity—of steadfast loyalty to God, who is purposeful yet compassionate and merciful (cf. Jas. 5:11).

Bibliography. F. I. Andersen, *Job.* Tyndale (1976); R. Gordis, *The Book of God and Man* (Chicago: 1965); H. H. Rowley, *The Book of Job.* NCBC (1980); P. Sanders, ed., *Twentieth Century Interpretations of the Book of Job* (Englewood Cliffs: 1968).

JOB, TESTAMENT OF.† One of a number of Jewish works from the two centuries surrounding the turn of the Christian era written in the form of a testament, i.e., where an aged father (after the fashion of Jacob at Gen. 47–50) calls his heirs to him at his deathbed, dispenses both property and moral exhortations, then dies and is mourned.

The Testament of Job was originally written in Greek, probably in Egypt, possibly by members of the Jewish sect known as the Theraputae (described in Philo's *Vita Contemplativa*). Some editing by Christians may have occurred. It follows the narrative framework of Job (LXX) and adds a good deal of haggadic legend, often expanding incidents mentioned only briefly in the biblical text. The bulk of the material focuses on Job's confrontation with Satan and his discussion with the three kings.

The work delivers its primary message of endurance in the midst of trial by presenting Job as the chief example of this virtue. A secondary feature is its unusually great interest in women. The passing of the higher and more spiritual inheritance to Job's daughters rather than to his sons is remarkable in that age, and the daughters' speaking in angelic languages is one of very few extrabiblical references to glossalalia, although it is questionable whether this section was written earlier than Pauline epistles such as 1 Corinthians.

JOBAB [jō'băb] (Heb. *yôḇāḇ*; Gk. *Iōbab* "jubilation").
1. A son of Joktan (Gen. 10:29; 1 Chr. 1:23).
2. The son of Zerah from Bozrah and king of Edom (Gen. 36:33; 1 Chr. 1:44-45).
3. The king of Madon and one of the kings defeated by Joshua (Josh. 11:1; 12:19).
4. A Benjaminite and son of Shaharaim (1 Chr. 8:9).
5. A Benjaminite and son of Elpaal (1 Chr. 8:18).

JOCHEBED [jŏk'ə bĕd] (Heb. *yôḵeḇeḏ* "the Lord is majesty"). The wife of Amram and mother of Aaron, Moses, and Miriam (Num. 26:59). She was also her husband's aunt (Exod. 6:20).

JODA [jō'də] (Gk. *Iōda*). The son of Joanan and ancestor of Jesus (Luke 3:26; KJV "Juda").

JOED [jō'ĕd] (Heb. *yôʿēḏ* "the Lord is a witness"). The grandfather of Sallu of the tribe of Benjamin (Neh. 11:7).

JOEL [jō'əl] (Heb. *yôʾēl* "Yahweh is God").
1. The elder son of the prophet Samuel. He and his brother Abijah were appointed by their father to be judges in Beer-sheba, but they perverted justice and accepted bribes (1 Sam. 8:1-3). According to 1 Chr. 6:33 (MT 18); 15:17 he was a Korathite Levite and the father of the singer Heman. The RSV and NIV, following the LXX and Syriac, read his name at 6:28 (KJV "Vashni," following MT Heb. *wᵉhaššēnî* "and the second"; cf. JB).
2. A prince of the tribe of Simeon at the time of Hezekiah (1 Chr. 4:35).
3. A Reubenite, the father of Shemaiah (Shema; 1 Chr. 5:4, 8).
4. A chief of the tribe of Gad who dwelled in Bashan (1 Chr. 5:12).
5. A Kohathite Levite and an ancestor of Samuel (1 Chr. 6:36 [MT 21]; cf. 1 Sam. 1:1). Some scholars would identify him with Shaul (1 Chr. 6:24 [MT 9]).
6. A son of Izrahiah of the tribe of Issachar; an officer contemporary with King David (1 Chr. 7:3).
7. One of David's mighty men and the brother of Nathan (1 Chr. 11:38). At 2 Sam. 23:36 he is called Igal the son of Nathan.
8. A chief of the Gershomite Levites who assisted David in bringing the ark to Jerusalem (1 Chr. 15:7, 11).
9. The son of Ladan (23:8) who, with his brother Zetham, had charge of the temple treasuries (1 Chr. 26:21-22). He is probably the same as **8**.
10. The son of Pedaiah; chief officer of the half-tribe of Manasseh at the time of David (1 Chr. 27:20).
11. A Kohathite Levite, the son of AZARIAH **16**. He assisted in cleansing the temple at the time of Hezekiah (2 Chr. 29:12).
12. A postexilic Israelite who was required to divorce his foreign wife (Ezra 10:43).
13. The son of Zichri; overseer of the Benjaminites in postexilic Jerusalem (Neh. 11:9).
14. The prophet Joel, the son of Pethuel (Joel 1:1; LXX "Bethuel"). His utterances comprise the book of Joel. *See* JOEL, BOOK OF.
15. The archangel Joel; also called Jaoel, Jahoel, or Jehoel (e.g., Apoc. Mos. 29:4; 43:5; Apoc. Abr. 10:3; 17:13).

JOEL, BOOK OF.† The second of the minor prophets.

I. Origins

Other than his identification as the "son of Pethuel" (Joel 1:1), the book provides no direct information concerning the prophet Joel. From his knowledge of and concern for cultic (temple) matters (e.g., 1:13-14; 2:12-17; scholars also note the possible liturgical associations of some of the prophecies) and allusions to Jerusalem (e.g., 2:7, 9; cf. 3:1, 6, 20 [MT 4:1, 6, 20]), he appears to have lived in the vicinity of Jerusalem. He may well have been a cultic prophet associated with the Jerusalem temple; he does not appear to have been a priest (1:13; 2:17).

The date of Joel and thus the historical locus of his prophecies remain uncertain because the book offers no clear chronological references. Much of the prophecy appears to be a reaction to a significant national tragedy (3:2 [MT 4:2]; cf. 2:27), but scholars have been unable to identify even that with certainty. The book has been dated as early as the coregency of King

Joash of Judah and the priest Jehoiada (late ninth century B.C.), the eighth century (on the basis of its placement in the canon between Hosea and Amos [LXX following Micah]), the years immediately preceding the fall of Jerusalem (597-587), after the rebuilding of the temple (*ca.* 515-500; thus contemporary with Haggai and Zechariah), the end of the fifth century, or as late as the third century (particularly by critical scholars who see later accretions to the work, i.e., reference to Ptolemy I Soter's capture of Jerusalem in 312). On linguistic and historical grounds, a date *ca.* 400 presents the fewest difficulties.

II. Contents

On the basis of content the book may be divided into two parts, in keeping with the division of the Hebrew text into chs. 1–2 and 2–4 (Eng. 1:1–2:17 and 2:18–3:21, following LXX and Vulgate). From a form-critical perspective some scholars prefer the division 1:1–2:17 and 2:18–3:21. Regardless of the precise point of division, the book does exhibit a basic unity of both form and content.

The first portion concerns a devastating plague of locusts, understood variously as a literal infestation of insects; an allegorical portrayal of waves of foreign invasion; or, most likely, an apocalyptic account of divine judgment experienced—presumably in the recent past—by Judah. Following the opening superscription (1:1), this section begins with an announcement of the crisis (vv. 2-7), followed by a summons for various components of the community (Judah) to lament their circumstances and to repent (vv. 8-14). Vv. 15-20 contain various expression of lamentation. Joel 2:1-11 is a cry of alarm, warning that the present disaster is but a harbinger of the impending Day of the Lord. A call to repentance follows (vv. 12-17), imploring the nation as a whole to "return" and instructing the priests to prepare a ceremony of communal lamentation. To this God responds (vv. 18-27), promising deliverance from plague and famine and renewal of the covenant; many scholars consider these verses to be the turning point of the book and the introduction to the concluding portion.

The remainder of the book focuses on the day of the Lord, a future time of judgment upon the nations and blessing for Judah and Jerusalem. An outpouring of God's spirit and various divine portents will herald this final great "day" (2:28-32 [MT 3:1-5]). Yahweh summons to the valley of decision (Jehoshaphat) the enemies of Judah and Jerusalem, "all the nations" (3:1-3 [MT 4:1-3])—specifically addressed in vv. 4-8—whereupon commences a holy war between the nations and the warriors of God (vv. 9-12). The book concludes with a series of strophes contrasting the desolation of the nations and the prosperity of Zion (vv. 13-21).

III. Theology

Of primary concern to Joel is the coming day of the Lord. Although stressed here more than in any other Old Testament prophetic book, this theme is not unique to Joel: according to Isa. 2:4, 6-22, Yahweh would judge his own people as well as the nations (cf. Mal. 4:3, 5 [MT 3:21, 23]); the prophet Amos warned Israel not to expect vindication but wrath (Amos

5:18-20); Zephaniah threatened universal destruction yet offered hope for the humble righteous (Zeph. 1–2). Joel begins with a very real crisis that he and his fellows had experienced at the hands of the nations (locusts), treating it as a warning of the even greater disaster that the future day of the Lord could bring upon the people of God if they did not return to the covenant ideals. In stark contrast, Joel proclaims that through such national repentance the day of the Lord could become, rather, an eschatological time of salvation and vindication for Judah/Israel; Yahweh's wrath would be directed instead against the nations. Accordingly, scholars see in Joel's prophecies the beginnings of apocalyptic eschatology, expressed in universal terms to include Israel as well as the nations.

Joel depicts God as sovereign over creation and history. The imagery of theophany portrays the quaking of the earth and the blackening of the sky (Joel 2:2, 11) and the acting of God in his people's history brings devastation to the land (1:7, 10-12, 17-20; cf. 3:19 [MT 4:19]) as well as the promise of restored bounty (2:24-26; 3:13, 18 [MT 4:13, 18]). The Lord himself commands (2:11) and expels (v. 20) the forces of destruction.

The spirit of God empowers the entire nation to experience renewed life through the covenant, strengthening them to endure the coming judgment and opening them to a direct relationship with God (expressed in terms of prophetic revelation; 2:28-29 [MT 3:1-2]). This promise to "all flesh" applies here to all of Judah/Israel; in his Pentecost sermon Peter reinterprets the passage for all of humanity (Acts 2:17-21; cf. 10:45).

Bibliography. G. W. Ahlstrom, *Joel and the Temple Cult of Jerusalem.* VTS 21 (1971); L. C. Allen, *The Books of Joel, Obadiah, Jonah and Micah.* NICOT (1976); H. W. Wolff, *Joel and Amos.* Hermeneia (1977).

JOELAH [jō ē'lə] (Heb. *yôʿēʾlâ* "Yahweh lifts up"). A son of Jeroham of Gedor who came to David's assistance at Ziklag (1 Chr. 12:7 [MT 8]).

JOEZER [jō ē'zər] (Heb. *yôʿezer* "Yahweh is a helper"). A Benjaminite who came to David at Ziklag (1 Chr. 12:6 [MT 7]). He is further identified as a Korahite.

JOGBEHAH [jŏg'bə hə] (Heb. *yogbᵉhâ* "situated on high"). A Transjordanian city, part of the territory of the Amorite king Sihon allotted to Gad (Num. 32:35). It was situated on the caravan route by which Gideon pursued the Midianites (Judg. 8:11). The site has been identified as modern Khirbet el-Ajbeihât, about 10 km. (7 mi.) northwest of ʿAmmân (Rabbah).

JOGLI [jŏg'lī] (Heb. *yoglî* "may God reveal"). The father of the Danite leader Bukki (Num. 34:22).

JOHA [jō'ə] (Heb. *yôḥāʾ*).
1. A Benjaminite, son of Beriah (1 Chr. 8:16).
2. A son of Shimri; one of David's mighty men (1 Chr. 11:45). He is given the gentilic "Tizite."

JOHANAN [jō hā'nən] (Heb. *yôḥānān* "Yahweh has been gracious").†

1. The son of Kareah; a captain of the "forces in the open country," likely freebooters that remained after Jerusalem's fall (568 B.C.). Loyal to Gedaliah, the Babylonian-appointed governor of Judah (2 Kgs. 25:23-24; Jer. 40:7-12), Johanan warned him of Ishmael's assassination plot and later avenged the murder, pursuing and defeating Ishmael (40:13–41:18). Afraid of Babylonian reprisal, Johanan and his company ignored the Lord's word to stay, and fled to Egypt, taking the prophet Jeremiah with them (42:1–43:7).

2. The eldest son of King Josiah of Judah (1 Chr. 3:15). He did not succeed his father, but is thought to have died at an early age. Some scholars would identify him with JEHOAHAZ **3.**

3. A son of Elioenai, and a descendant of David (1 Chr. 3:24).

4. The father of the priest Azariah (**7**), who served in Solomon's temple (1 Chr. 6:9-10 [MT 5:35-36]).

5. A Benjaminite who joined David at Ziklag (1 Chr. 12:4 [MT 5]).

6. One of the renowned Gadite warriors who came to David at his desert stronghold (1 Chr. 12:12 [MT 13]).

7. The father of Azariah (**16**), an Ephraimite chief (2 Chr. 28:12; JB, NIV "Jehohanan," following MT).

8. A member of the clan of Azgad who returned from the Exile with Ezra; the son of Hakkatan (Ezra 8:12; 1 Esdr. 8:38; KJV "Johannes").

9. (Ezra 10:6, KJV). *See* JEHOHANAN **4.**

10. (Neh. 6:18, KJV). *See* JEHOHANAN **6.**

11. The successor to Joiada as high priest, and "son" (perhaps "grandson" or "descendant"; cf. Neh. 12:11, where "Jonathan" may be a scribal error) of Eliashib (vv. 22-23). The Elephantine papyri date Johanan as high priest in the reign of Darius II (*ca.* 410 B.C.; cf. Neh. 12:22). Josephus also mentions a high priest Johanan (Gk. *Iōannēs*) who murdered his brother Jeshua in the temple, but his confused chronology casts doubt whether this is the biblical Johanan. Identification of this Johanan with JEHOHANAN **4** at Ezra 10:6 (so KJV); 1 Esdr. 9:1 would necessitate dating Ezra after Nehemiah.

JOHN (Gk. *Iōannēs;* from Heb. *yôḥānān* "Yahweh is gracious").†

1. The father of Mattathias (**1**) and grandfather of Judas Maccabeus; son of the priest Simeon **2** (1 Macc. 2:1).

2. The oldest son of Mattathias (**1**), surnamed Gaddi (1 Macc. 2:2; some MSS read "Caddi"). Sent to the Nabateans by his brother Jonathan to store the Maccabees' belongings, he was ambushed and killed by the "sons of Jambri" from Medeba (9:35-36; cf. vv. 37-42).

3. The father of Eupolemus and son of Accos (1 Macc. 8:17), accorded royal concessions by Antiochus III (2 Macc. 4:11).

4. John Hyrcanus I; son of Simon and nephew of Judas Maccabeus; commander of Simon's forces (1 Macc. 13:53; 16:1) and subsequently high priest. *See* HYRCANUS **2.**

5. John Hyrcanus II. *See* HYRCANUS **3.**

6. An envoy of the Jews to Lysias (2 Macc. 11:17).

7. John the Baptist. The son of the priest Zechariah and Elizabeth. Because Elizabeth is called a "kins-woman" (Luke 1:36) of Mary, John is traditionally regarded as a cousin of Jesus Christ; the precise application of the kinship term is not clear. John the Baptist is perhaps the most enigmatic figure in the New Testament.

Luke relates the story of his birth in terms reminiscent of that of Isaac (vv. 5-25; cf. Gen. 18:9-15). Like Abraham and Sarah, Elizabeth and Zechariah were advanced in years, but still childless. Both births were announced by angels, and in both cases one of the future parents disbelieved the prophecy. While on duty at the temple, the priest Zechariah was visited by the angel Gabriel, who predicted that his wife would bear a son whom they would call John. This son was not to drink wine or any fermented drink, but would be "filled with the Holy Spirit" from birth. He would minister in the spirit and power of the prophet Elijah, and he would herald the coming of the Lord. When Zechariah doubted, the angel told him that he would be unable to speak until after the baby was born. Elizabeth soon became pregnant as foretold and gave birth to a son. When a dispute arose with the neighbors and kinfolk over the naming of the child, Zechariah wrote that the boy would be called John. Immediately Zechariah regained his ability to speak. The birth occurred approximately six months prior to that of Jesus (v. 36).

Nothing else is known of John's youth except that he remained in the wilderness until the beginning of his public ministry (vv. 57-80).

The beginning of John's ministry is dated to the fifteenth year of the reign of Tiberius Caesar, when

Herod's fortress of Machaerus where John the Baptist was imprisoned and killed. The hills of Judea, across the Dead Sea from the fortress, are in the background (A. D. Baly)

Pontius Pilate had begun to serve as governor of Judea (*ca.* A.D. 28-29; 3:1-2). As a person, John was certainly unique: his outward appearance reminded many of the prophet Elijah, for he wore a garment made of camels' hair and a leather belt, and he ate the food of the poor—locusts and wild honey (Mark 1:6; cf. 2 Kgs. 1:8). His ministry was primarily conducted in southern Judea near the Jordan river. John's audience included not only those receptive to his message, but also Pharisees and Sadducees; John publicly castigated them as a "brood of vipers" (Matt. 3:7)—a sentiment no doubt shared by many of his followers among the common people.

John's message was twofold. First, he preached the coming of the Messiah and his kingdom (John 1:6-8, 19-22). Second, he stressed a baptism of repentance, intensified by his apocalyptic anticipation of God's wrath (Luke 3:3-14 par.). Yet John made clear that the one he preceded would baptize not with water but with the Spirit (Mark 1:7-8 par.). It was he who baptized Jesus in the Jordan river (Matt. 3:13-17 par.)

As the forerunner of Jesus, John's life and ministry frequently paralleled yet never equaled that of Jesus (cf. the annunciation of and the events surrounding his birth [Luke 1-2] through various aspects of his ministry and death). What set John apart from his contemporaries and made him of particular value to the Christian community was his testimony supporting Jesus as the Messiah (John 1:19-36). Many of John's disciples would later become disciples of Jesus: Andrew and John among the first (vv. 35-42), followed by Apollos (Acts 18:24-26) and the twelve "disciples" at Ephesus (19:1-7).

John himself created such a stir that Herod imprisoned him out of fear that he might start a political revolution (Mark 6:14-29 par.). According to Josephus, Herod imprisoned John and executed him in the Maccabean-Herodian fortress Machaerus near the Dead Sea (*Ant.* xviii.5.2).

Some scholars have suggested that John the Baptist was associated (perhaps through his father Zechariah) with the Qumran community. Although such a connection cannot be demonstrated with any certainty, John did share many similarities with that sect. His rejection of Pharisaic Judaism (Matt. 3:7), his withdrawal from society into a simpler lifestyle (vv. 1-5), his emphasis on baptism and purity (v. 11; John 3:25-27), his stress on the Holy Spirit and judgment (Matt. 3:11-12), and the nature of the Messiah he expected (John 1:32; but cf. Matt. 11:1-15; Luke 7:18-35) are all points that he shared with the Qumran community.

Bibliography. C. H. Kraeling, *John the Baptist* (New York: 1951); W. Wink, *John the Baptist in the Gospel Tradition.* NTSMS 7 (1968).

8. John the Apostle. The son of Zebedee and the younger brother of James; an apostle of Jesus and perhaps also his cousin (John's mother, Salome, may have been a sister of Mary the mother of Jesus; cf. Matt. 27:56; Mark 15:40; John 19:25). He and his brother James shared with their father in an apparently thriving (cf. Mark 1:20) fishing business. Simon Peter was also a partner in this enterprise (Luke 5:10).

Initially a disciple of John the Baptist, John and

Andrew were the first to become Jesus' apostles (John 1:35-40; cf. Matt. 4:21-22 par.). John was one of the "inner circle" that included his brother James and Peter. Together these three witnessed Jesus' raising Jairus' daughter from the dead (Mark 5:37), the transfiguration on the mountain (Matt. 17:1), and Jesus' prayer in the garden of Gethsemane (Mark 14:33).

John seems to have had a fiery disposition, for he and his brother were called Boanerges, meaning "sons of thunder" (Mark 3:17). John rebuked a man for casting out demons in Jesus' name because he was not actually one of his followers (Luke 9:49). He and James asked Jesus to call down fire from heaven to consume a Samaritan village that would not receive them (v. 54). Moreover, both boldly asserted that they were willing to become martyrs in order to receive the highest positions in the coming kingdom (Mark 10:35ff.).

Few of the above events are mentioned in the gospel of John, and John is never even mentioned there by name. The gospel may, however, contain information about his actions during the last days of Jesus' ministry on earth. If he is to be identified as the unnamed disciple "whom Jesus loved," he sat beside Jesus at the Last Supper and asked him who the betrayer would be (John 13:23). He gained entrance to the house of Caiaphas for himself and Peter (18:15). He stood next to Mary the mother of Jesus at the crucifixion and afterwards cared for her (19:26-27). Outrunning Peter, he became the first disciple to see the empty tomb (20:1-10). If John was the author of the gospel, the last scene in that book was intended to correct an apparently widespread belief among early Christians that he would live until the return of Christ; the writer carefully points out that this was not what Jesus had said (21:20-24).

The balance of the New Testament offers scant biographical information on the apostle John. He is mentioned in Acts three times, each in the company of Peter: at the healing of the lame man (Acts 3:1-10), at their subsequent interrogation before the Sanhedrin (4:1-22; cf. 5:17-42), and as an emissary from the Jerusalem council to Samaria (8:14-25). Paul mentions John in his letter to the Galatians as one of those in Jerusalem "reputed to be pillars" (Gal. 2:9).

Church tradition concerning John is contradictory. Some speculate that John may have been a priest; he may have been personally acquainted with the high priest (cf. John 18:15), and tradition mentions his wearing the sacerdotal plate (Eusebius *HE* v.24.3). The strongest tradition is that John moved to Ephesus (e.g., Justin Martyr *Dial.* lxxxi.4), became the bishop of the churches in Asia Minor (cf. Apost. Const. vii.46), and there died a natural death of old age—a late tradition even lists John as one of those martyred for his faith. Yet others contend that John died young (cf. Philip of Side, fifth century A.D.). Tertullian's account of John's being plunged into boiling oil and then exiled on the isle of Patmos is based on the understanding of the apostle as the author of Revelation.

Church tradition also ascribes to John the authorship of five New Testament books: the gospel of John, the three epistles attributed to John, and Revelation. Current scholarship is divided on this question. Polycarp and his student Irenaeus (second century) are among the earliest Church Fathers to associate the gospel with John the apostle, but the anonymity of the author and the book's divergence from the Synoptic Gospels make the identification uncertain. Despite some difficulties, most critical scholars view the epistles as the product of the same author as the gospel. Few modern scholars, however, would identify the John of Revelation with John the son of Zebedee (cf. Dionysius of Alexandria, third century). See further the individual entries on those books.

9. John Mark. *See* MARK, JOHN.

10. According to the gospel of John, the father of Simon Peter (John 1:42; KJV "Jona"; 21:15-17; KJV "Jonas"). In Matthew the name occurs in the form Simon Bar-jona (Matt. 16:17).

11. A relative and perhaps a successor of Annas the high priest; one of those who interrogated Peter and John before the Sanhedrin (Acts 4:6).

JOHN, ACTS OF.* A third-century apocryphal book that purports to supplement the canonical book of Acts by giving a history of all the acts of the apostle John. The work is attributed as early as the fourth century to Leucius Charinus, purportedly an eyewitness of the events recorded and author of several other apocryphal acts.

Composed toward the end of the second century, this book is the earliest of several apocryphal acts collected by the Manichaeans. Like other apocryphal works of this type, the Acts of John records in rather loose order a series of exaggerated miraculous events that extol the central figure. The book includes several narratives: John's journey to Rome; his exile on Patmos and return to Ephesus (a later addition); a journey from Miletus to Ephesus; the preaching of the gospel; ministry in Ephesus; a partridge playing in the dust; a journey from Laodicea to Ephesus; and a lengthy account of John's death. Largely because of its Docetic character, particularly evident in John's lengthy discourse on the life, death, and nature of Christ, the work was condemned by the Second Nicene Council of 787 as worthy only of destruction.

Of the original Greek work, which equaled approximately the length of the gospel of Matthew, perhaps only two-thirds survives. A Latin translation was known by the end of the fourth century. The book was combined with other ascetic and Gnostic writings in various collections in Syriac, Armenian, Georgian, Coptic, Arabic, and Ethiopic. Reworked versions of much of the contents are contained in some versions of the fifth-century account of John's activities on Patmos attributed to (pseudo-)Prochorus.

JOHN, APOCRYPHON OF.† An early Gnostic apocryphal book detailing a vision of the apostle John. Although attested by the Church Fathers (cf. Irenaeus *Adv. haer.* i.29-31), little was known about this book until the discovery of the Nag Hammadi library in Egypt in 1946. A fifth-century papyrus (Berolinensis 8502) had been purchased for the Berlin Museum in 1896, but it was often confused with the gospel of Mary, with which it was filed. The work is now pre-

served in Codices I, III, and VIII of the Gnostic library of Nag Hammadi.

The book was called an apocryphon, meaning "secret," because it revealed the esoteric Gnostic gospel. It is believed to be identical to another apocryphal book known as the Apocalypse to John. The very early date of this work is attested by the fact that Irenaeus quotes from it in writing against heresies *ca.* A.D. 180. The Apocryphon enjoyed remarkable prestige between the second and eighth centuries; it is now one of the primary sources for the beliefs of the original Gnostics.

Like other Gnostic gospels, the Apocryphon of John begins with the narrative of a vision in which secret information is given to the "author" (here John) by a divine revealer (the resurrected Christ), and develops into a dialogue with interspersed comments. Among the issues raised are the origin of evil, creation of the spiritual and material realms, and the human struggle for release from mortal constraints.

JOHN, GOSPEL OF.† The last of the four Gospels and the fourth book of the New Testament.

I. Relationship to Synoptics

The gospel of John is more philosophical than the Synoptic Gospels; it refers to Jesus as the Word, the Light, the Truth, and the Way, and uses more abstract, philosophical language. The Synoptics focus on a more concrete description of the early Galilean ministry. Ninety percent of the content of John is not discussed in the other three Gospels. The fourth gospel discusses only seven miracles (yet includes the raising of Lazarus, which the Synoptics do not; 11:1-44; 12:9-11), does not refer to exorcism, and lacks parables. Unlike the Synoptics, John depicts the early period of Jesus' ministry as taking place in Judea (2:22); *see* JESUS Christ III. *D*. Moreover, John records several discourses not found in the Synoptics, including Jesus' conversations with Nicodemus (3:1-15) and the Samaritan woman (4:7-30).

Scholars have discussed at length this relationship between John and the Synoptics and have concluded, in general, that John's material comes from an independent tradition that is similar but not identical to the sources of the Synoptics. John had his own unique viewpoint (cf. John 20:30-31), selected and shaped his material according to his own purposes (21:25), and thus complemented the Synoptics.

II. Author

According to early Church tradition, the fourth gospel was written by the apostle John, the son of Zebedee. Although the work does not mention John by name (perhaps out of modesty), several internal evidences do support or at least suggest his authorship. According to 21:20-24, the author is a disciple of Jesus and associate of Peter. The phrase "the disciple whom Jesus loved" may refer to John. This individual had intimate fellowship with Jesus (13:23-25) and witnessed the piercing of Jesus' side during the crucifixion (19:35) and other events in the life of Jesus. John's reference to Jesus as the "Word" (Gk. *lógos*) should be taken as alluding to God's word in creation (Gen.

John 6:59-70 in the papyrus codex Bodmer II ($\mathfrak{p}^{66}$; second-third century) (Bodmer Library, Geneva)

1; cf. Ps. 33:6, 9) rather than as the basis for objection to John's authorship on the grounds of alleged Hellenistic (or Gnostic) influence. *See* Logos.

III. Place and Date

Tradition traced as early as the second century (e.g., Polycarp, Irenaeus) testifies that John composed his gospel at Ephesus in his old age. Yet apostolic authorship has often been challenged; indeed, Clement of Alexandria (late second century) identifies John as the latest of the four Gospels, which would place it too late for even an elderly contemporary of Jesus. However, a fragment of Rylands papyrus 457 ($\mathfrak{p}^{52}$), dated *ca.* A.D. 125, contains John 18:31-33, 37-38, which would preclude a later date.

IV. Purpose

Scholars are divided as to whether John wrote to supplement or to correct the Synoptic accounts, or to combat current heresies. At 20:31 John himself clearly states his purpose for writing: "...that you may believe that Jesus is the Christ, the Son of God, and that believing you may have life in his name." Succinctly expressed here are three themes that recur throughout John's gospel: Jesus is the Christ, the Son of God; God calls people to true commitment and belief in Jesus as the Christ; and believers in Christ possess a distinctive quality of eternal life that others cannot share.

V. Historical Reliability

Some scholars have alleged that because John goes beyond merely recording the facts of the life of Christ and seeks to interpret those facts, his gospel has little historical reliability. It must be stated that although John does give penetrating insights into the new birth (3:1-21), eternal life (4:7-30), and resurrection after death (11:23-44), he does so within a historical con-

text that has been validated and confirmed. The account of Jesus' conversation with the woman at the well (ch. 4) supplies valuable information about the Samaritan way of life, for example. John also gives information about the historical and physical contexts of the gospel that is not found in the Synoptics (e.g., the wedding at Cana, 2:1-12; the discourse with Nicodemus, 3:1-21). Cana (2:1), the pool of Siloam (9:7), and the brook Kidron have been readily identified. The Bethzatha pool (5:2; KJV, NIV "Bethesda") has been excavated, and John's description of its five porches has been confirmed. No doubt remains as to the historical reliability of the gospel.

VI. Content and Theology

The content of the gospel reflects John's primary interest in theology rather than biography, and the Gospel is structured to achieve his stated purpose (20:31). Of particular importance is John's emphasis on the incarnation. In the prologue (1:1-14) Jesus is introduced as the Word, and his deity is clearly stated: "In the beginning was the Word, and the Word was with God, and the Word was God" (v. 1). John also stresses the relationship between Jesus and God, the Son and the Father. The fact that Jesus is the Christ, the Son of God, is established on the testimony of John himself and the disciples (vv. 15-51). Jesus' ministry is to reveal God. John records a series of miracles as "signs" of Jesus' deity, presenting them in his own unique way along with the statements and teachings of Jesus. The miracles selected are: turning water into wine (2:2-11); healing the noble's son (4:46-54); healing the paralyzed man (5:1-15); feeding the five thousand (6:1-14); walking on the water (vv. 15-21); healing the blind man (9:1-41); raising Lazarus; and the miraculous catch of fish (21:6-11). The "I am" statements of Jesus recorded by John also testify to Jesus' deity. Jesus claimed to be the bread of life (6:35), the light of the world (8:12), the door (10:7), the good shepherd (v. 11), the resurrection and the life (v. 25), the way, the truth, and the life (14:6), and the true vine (15:1).

Also of primary importance is John's emphasis on the necessity of faith for the eternal life (e.g., 3:15-20; 7:38-39). Throughout the gospel John portrays the Jewish leaders as rejecting Jesus' claims: "His own people received him not. But to all who received him, who believed in his name, he gave power to become children of God" (1:11-12).

Bibliography. C. K. Barrett, *The Gospel According to St. John,* 2nd ed. (Philadelphia: 1978); R. E. Brown, *The Gospel According to John,* 2 vols. AB 29-29A (1966-1970); F. F. Bruce, *The Gospel of John* (Grand Rapids: 1983).

JOHN, LETTERS OF.† Three brief New Testament books attributed to the apostle John.

I. Form

2-3 John clearly resemble the standard format of an ancient epistle, and the length of each would conform with the limits of a single papyrus sheet. The longer 1 John, by contrast, although it has always been classified as such, does not display the usual features of a letter. Like Hebrews, it lacks an epistolary conclusion; moreover, it has no formal salutation or greeting, and no specific person is named. Yet even though the contents of this writing may be viewed as a tractate or a sermon, most scholars classify it as a letter addressed to a specific situation in one of the young churches.

II. Author

Although the author does not identify himself directly in any of the three epistles (in the salutations to 2-3 John he refers to himself as "the elder"), the consensus of scholars is that the apostle John, the son of Zebedee, wrote these letters. Tradition and internal evidence, notably similarities of style and content, support the view that both the gospel and the Epistles are the work of the same person. Some scholars caution, however, that the works did not achieve canonicity as a unit and thus may have originated with different authors.

III. Origins

From the fatherly tone of these writings, scholars surmise that John was of venerable age at the time of their writing. The apostle is believed to have spent his later years at Ephesus in a supervisory role, and it is assumed that he would have written the letters at this time, after the writing of the gospel. Since church order seems to be more fully developed in these letters, a date near the end of the first century would seem appropriate. The Epistles as well as the gospel of John are mentioned in the Muratorian Canon (*ca.* A.D. 200), and there are references and allusions to at least some of the Epistles in the Church Fathers dating to the first half of the second century.

IV. Contents and Theology

John's purpose in writing the Epistles was not purely evangelistic, but rather to encourage maturity in the Christian life—joy and assurance (1 John 1:4; 5:13).

John also wrote to correct certain doctrinal errors brought in by false teachers.

A. 1 John. Here John encourages believers to continue to walk in light and fellowship with God, who is light (1:1–2:8), to love one another (2:9–4:21), and find assurance in faith, the "victory that overcomes the world" (5:1-21). In this longest of the three Epistles, the apostle balances positive encouragement with warning as he counsels believers in various issues of the faith: fellowship with God, sin, Jesus as the Advocate, keeping the commandments, love, recognizing false teachers, assurance of victory and eternal life, answers to prayer, and the Christian walk in general.

B. 2 John. This shorter letter is addressed to "the elect lady and her children," presumably a symbolic reference to a specific church and its congregation, and concludes with greetings from "the children of your elect sister," another congregation. As in 1 John, the author encourages the recipients to continue to seek the truth and to love one another (vv. 4-6). A specific concern, however, is adherence to sound doctrine (vv. 7-11), warning the believers not to show hospitality to false teachers; strangers (traveling evangelists) should hold genuinely to the doctrine of Christ and be proven before they are helped by Christians.

C. 3 John. This letter is of similar size and content to 2 John, but is written to an individual by the common name of Gaius rather than to a church. The apostle contrasts the steadfastness and warmth of Gaius (vv. 3, 5-8) with the self-centered, obnoxious behavior of Diotrephes, who resists John's authority (vv. 9-10). The letter also also offers encouragement for Demetrius (v. 12).

Bibliography. R. E. Brown, *The Epistles of John.* AB 30 (1983); I. H. Marshall, *The Epistles of John.* NICNT (1978).

JOHN MARK. *See* MARK, JOHN.

JOHN THE DIVINE, DISCOURSE OF ST.† The standard Greek version of the apocryphal ASSUMPTION OF THE VIRGIN.

The legend of the Assumption existed in Latin, Syriac, Coptic, Arabic, and Greek versions. It probably originated in Egypt sometime after the beginning of the fifth century. This Greek form is extant in manuscripts of the eleventh-fourteenth centuries, and was edited by the New Testament textual critic Constantin von Tischendorf.

The narrative begins after the Ascension of Jesus and depicts Mary's life in association with the apostles, her death in the presence of Jesus (who had returned to earth in bodily form), the miraculous disappearance of her body, the reappearance of Jesus with Mary in the heavenly chariot, and her final assumption into heaven with Jesus.

JOIADA [joi′ə də] (Heb. *yôyāḏāʿ* "Yahweh knows").
1. The son of Paseah who restored the Old Gate in Jerusalem under Nehemiah (Neh. 3:6; KJV "Jehoiada").
2. A priest during the reign of Darius and the son of the high priest Eliashib (**5**) (Neh. 12:10-11, 22; 13:28; RSV "Jehoiada").

JOIAKIM [joi'ə kĭm] (Heb. *yôyāqîm* "Yahweh raises up"). A postexilic high priest; the son of Jeshua (**4**) and the father of Eliashib (**5**) (Neh. 12:10, 12, 26).

JOIARIB [joi'ə rĭb] (Heb. *yôyārîḇ* "Yahweh contends").

1. A "man of insight" sent by Ezra to Iddo in Casiphia, requesting levitical priests for the temple (Ezra 8:16).

2. A Judahite; son of Zechariah (**28**) and father of Adaiah, and ancestor of Maaseiah (Neh. 11:5).

3. A priest who returned with Zerubbabel from captivity in Babylon (Neh. 11:10; 12:6), head of a priestly house (v. 19). At 1 Chr. 9:10 he is called Jehoiarib.

JOKDEAM [jŏk'dĭ əm] (Heb. *yoqḏeʿām*). A city in the tribal territory of Judah (Josh. 15:56). The LXX reads Jorkeam (cf. 1 Chr. 2:44). The site may be modern Khirbet Raqaʿ between Juttah and Ziph, south of Hebron.

JOKIM [jō'kĭm] (Heb. *yôqîm* "Yahweh lifts up"). A son of Shelah, from the tribe of Judah (1 Chr. 4:22).

JOKMEAM [jŏk'mĭ əm] (Heb. *yoqmeʿām*).† A levitical city in the tribal territory of Ephraim (1 Chr. 6:68). Solomon included it in the district administered by Baana (1 Kgs. 4:12; KJV "Jokneam"). It may be the same as Kibzaim at Josh. 21:22 (cf. R. G. Boling and G. E. Wright, *Joshua*. AB 6 [1982], pp. 489-490). The site has been suggested as modern Tell esh-Sheikh Dhiab, 22 km. (13.6 mi.) north of Jericho.

JOKNEAM [jŏk'nĭ əm] (Heb. *yoqneʿām*). A Canaanite royal city in Carmel defeated by Joshua (Josh. 12:22), situated on a brook near the border of Zebulun with Manasseh (19:11). It was subsequently assigned to the Merarite families of the Levites (21:34).

Jokneam is mentioned in a list of cities captured by Thutmose III. The site is identified as modern Tell Qeimûn near the Kishon brook, 20 km. (12.5 mi.) southeast of Haifa and 11 km. (7 mi.) northwest of Megiddo. Thus the city was strategically situated near a pass leading to the Jezreel valley.

Variant forms of the name in the LXX have frequently led to confusion of this site with JOKMEAM (cf. 1 Kgs. 4:12, KJV).

JOKSHAN [jŏk'shăn] (Heb. *yoqšān*). A son of Abraham and Keturah, and eponymous ancestor of various Arabian peoples (Gen. 25:2-3; 1 Chr. 1:32).

JOKTAN [jŏk'tăn] (Heb. *yoqṭān* "younger [son]" [?]). A son of Eber and descendant of Shem, and eponymous ancestor of several Arabian peoples (Gen. 10:25-29 par. 1 Chr. 1:19-23).

JOKTHEEL [jŏk'thĭ əl] (Heb. *yoqṯeʾēl*).

1. A city in the Shephelah of Judah. Although presumably in the vicinity of Lachish, its precise location is unknown (Josh. 15:38).

2. A name given by King Amaziah of Judah to the conquered city of Sela, the capital of Edom (2 Kgs. 14:7).

JONA [jō'nə] (Gk. *Iōannēs*).† John, the father of Simon Peter (John 1:42, KJV). *See* JOHN **10**; BAR-JONA.

JONADAB [jō'nə dăb] (Heb. *yônāḏāḇ*, *yᵉhônāḏāḇ* "Yahweh is generous" or "noble" or "Yahweh has impelled").† The forms Jonadab and Jehonadab alternate.

1. The son of Shimea, David's brother, and friend of David's son Amnon, for whom he devised a plan to dishonor Amnon's half-sister, Tamar, and thereby establish a claim to royal succession (2 Sam. 13:3, 5, 32). Later, when Absalom avenged his sister's rape, Jonadab assured David that only Amnon among his sons had been killed (v. 35). Some would identify him with David's nephew Jonathan the son of Shimei who killed the Gittite giant (21:21 par. 1 Chr. 20:7; cf. LXX).

2. The son of Rechab the Kenite (Jer. 35:6; cf. 1 Chr. 2:55) who established the strict ordinances of the Rechabite order (Jer. 35:6-19). He was an associate of Jehu, whom he aided in exterminating the house of Ahab and the priests of Baal at Samaria (2 Kgs. 10:15, 23).

JONAH [jō'nə] (Heb. *yônâ* "dove"; Gk. *Iōnas*).† The son of Amittai from Gath-hepher; the central figure of the book of Jonah. The prophet Jonah predicted that King Jeroboam II would reconquer Israel's border "from the entrance of Hamath as far as the Sea of the Arabah [the Dead Sea]" (2 Kgs. 14:25). He apparently later undertook a mission to Nineveh, which is the focus of the prophetic book. In the New Testament the KJV calls him Jonas (Matt. 12:39-41; 16:4; Luke 11:29-32).

JONAH, BOOK OF.† The fifth of the minor prophets.

I. Content

Unlike the other prophetic books, Jonah is not a collection of the prophet's utterances (his only pronouncement is recorded in 3:4). Rather, it is primarily a narrative of events surrounding one Jonah the son of Amittai, in many ways reminiscent of the accounts of Elijah and Elisha.

The book opens with God's commissioning of Jonah to preach to Nineveh and the prophet's flight to Tarshish to avoid that task (Jonah 1:1-3). God responds by stirring up a storm at sea. The pagan seamen pray to their respective deities, then determine by lot that responsibility for the maelstrom falls to Jonah. They cast him into the sea, whereupon the Lord quells the storm (vv. 4-16). God rescues Jonah by appointing "a great fish" to swallow him up (1:17 [MT 2:1]). Sheltered in the belly of the fish for three days and nights, Jonah offers a psalm of thanksgiving for divine deliverance (2:1-9 [MT 2-10]). Then Yahweh directs the fish to vomit out Jonah upon dry land (v. 10 [MT 11]).

The Lord calls Jonah a second time to preach repentance to Nineveh (3:1-2). This time Jonah complies, and the Ninevites turn from their evil ways and embrace Yahweh (vv. 3-9). Thereupon God "repents of the evil which he had said he would do to them" and shows mercy toward them (v. 10). To this Jonah reacts angrily, either dismayed that his oracle of doom has been rendered sterile or resentful that God's grace has been extended seemingly without qualification to this non-Israelite people (4:1-4). He withdraws to a booth outside the city (v. 5), where God first provides a plant to shelter him (v. 6) and then sends a worm to destroy the plant and sun and wind to torment the recalcitrant prophet (vv. 7-8). The account concludes with a final word of God to Jonah explaining the depth of God's love for all creation and thus the basis of his grace (vv. 9-11).

II. Author and Date

The central figure of the book is generally identified as the late eighth-century prophet from Gath-hepher associated with the court of King Jeroboam II of Israel (2 Kgs. 14:25). Yet on the basis of language and viewpoint many scholars date the work significantly later, in both the preexilic and postexilic periods. No consensus exists that the book does record actual events involving the historical prophet or that it is instead a pseudonymous composition.

Numerous factors have been cited as evidence of postexilic composition, but much of the evidence remains inconclusive: aramaisms and late Hebrew usage (e.g., 1:5-7, 12); use of the perfect in referring to Nineveh (which fell in 612 B.C.) and royal titulature (3:3, 6); similarities to the thought of Isa. 40-55, Jeremiah, Ezekiel, and Joel; and the argument that Jonah's universalism was intended to counter the alleged exclusiveness of Ezra and Nehemiah. Nevertheless, most scholars focus on a sixth-century date for the book.

III. Interpretation

Of particular importance to understanding the meaning and purpose of the book, as well as matters of background, is its literary form.

Conservative scholars and others who view Jonah literally take it to be a historical narrative similar to those concerning Elijah and Elisha in 2 Kings and biographical passages in other prophetic books. A key factor is acceptance of the miraculous aspects of the great fish and the plant and worm. Other important issues are Nineveh's repentance, for which no extrabiblical evidence exists, and the manner (specifically the language) in which Jonah addressed the Assyrians.

Most recent interpreters consider the book to be a parable or allegory, akin to the wisdom genre of mashal. It has been labeled a "prophetic narrative," more specifically a short story or novella, with didactic intent. The literal meaning of the Hebrew name Jonah is "dove," used elsewhere as a symbol for Israel (cf. Ps. 74:19; Hos. 11:11); this suggests that the book may be a symbolic portrayal of Israel's mission as the people of God: preexilic disobedience (flight to Tarshish), Exile (storm at sea), a reluctant "light to the nations" (proclamation at Nineveh). As a parable, the entire story would have a single main point: Jonah (an individual, Israel, or other group) is unable to understand and unwilling to fulfill God's purpose. Jesus interprets Jonah's being swallowed and vomited by the "whale" as a simile or prefiguring of his own death

and resurrection (Matt. 12:39-40; Luke 11:29-30), which is to bring about the repentance of many (Matt. 12:41; 16:4; Luke 11:32).

Some scholars see in Jonah a midrashic exegesis of passages dealing with God's grace and mercy (e.g., Exod. 34:6; Ps. 84:16 [MT 17]; etc.).

IV. Theology

The book of Jonah portrays God as sovereign, who directs both the elements of nature (1:4, 9, 17 [MT 2:1]; 2:10 [MT 11]; 4:6-8) and historical events (3:5) to accomplish his purpose, which is the redemption of mankind (2:10; 3:10). Jonah comes painfully to realize that Yahweh is God not only of Israel but of all nations (4:11), and that his grace is universal (3:10).

Related to this understanding of God is the picture provided of the role of the prophet and of prophecy itself in attaining God's purpose. By proclaiming God's word Jonah is able to bring about their change of heart and thereby to nullify the threatened consequences of the prophecy.

Bibliography. G. C. Aalders, *The Problem of the Book of Jonah* (London: 1948); L. C. Allen, *The Books of Joel, Obadiah, Jonah and Micah.* NICOT (1976), pp. 173-235.

JONAM [jō′nəm] (Gk. *Iōnam*). An ancestor of Jesus; the son of Eliakim and father of Joseph 9 (Luke 3:30; KJV "Jonan").

JONAS [jō′nəs] (Gk. *Iōnas,* from Heb. *yônâ*).
1. Name given to the prophet Jonah in the New Testament and Apocrypha of the KJV.
2. (John 21:15-16, KJV). *See* JOHN 3.

JONATHAN [jŏn′ə thən] (Heb. *yᵉhônāṯān, yônāṯan,* "Yahweh has given"; Gk. *Iōnathan*).
1. The son (or descendant) of Gershom, the son of Moses (Judg. 18:30; KJV "son of Manasseh," following MT, which inserts a suspended letter nun [*n*] into the original reading "Moses"; the rabbis so altered the text to show that Jonathan was unworthy to be Moses' son, but rather was spiritual kin to the wicked King Manasseh [cf. 2 Kgs. 21:1-18]).

Jonathan was the young Levite from Bethlehem whom Micah the Ephraimite hired to be priest at his shrine (Judg. 17:7-13). When the Danites stole Micah's graven images, Jonathan gladly left Micah to be their priest instead. The Danites erected the stolen idols at Dan (formerly Laish), where Jonathan and his descendants served as priests of the tribe of Dan until the Exile (18:14-20, 30-31).

2. The eldest son of King Saul and Ahinoam, and one of the noblest figures of the Old Testament: brave, inspiring (cf. 1 Sam. 14:7), loyal, self-sacrificing, and a devoted friend.

Jonathan served as the chief lieutenant of Saul's army (1 Sam. 13:2). Although he likely also fought against the Ammonites (ch. 11), his first recorded battle was the attack on the Philistine outpost at Geba (13:3). When the Philistines seized Michmash, Israel's army wilted before the powerful foe (vv. 5-22)—until Jonathan showed his prowess and courage. Aided only by his armor-bearer he attacked the enemy camp, sending it into panic (14:6-15); then Saul struck with the army, and the confusion turned to a rout. This great victory was clouded by the king's rash vow that all should abstain from food on the day of battle. Although Jonathan had unwittingly broken the ban, he was ready to pay its penalty in loyalty to God and his father; but the people ransomed him, noting that his victory was a sign of God's pleasure, not his anger (vv. 24-30, 43-45).

More than a warrior, Jonathan showed himself the devoted friend of David. As the young David told the court of his defeat of Goliath, Jonathan "loved him as his own soul" (18:1). The two made a covenant of friendship between them (cf. 20:23), with Jonathan giving his robe, armor, sword, and bow as tokens (18:3-4). Later, when the jealous Saul plotted to kill David, Jonathan not only brought warning but worked for peace between the two (19:1-7). As Saul's hatred increased, Jonathan again attempted reconciliation, even taking himself the brunt of his father's anger; but when all efforts failed, Jonathan helped David escape (ch. 20). Later at Ziph, the two friends renewed their covenant; Jonathan renounced his claims to the throne, agreeing that David should be the next king and Jonathan his first minister (23:16-18).

Yet neither his unswerving friendship with David nor Saul's rage separated Jonathan from his father. He fell with Saul in battle on Mt. Gilboa (31:1-2). The inhabitants of Jabesh-gilead (cf. 11:5ff.) took their bodies from the wall of Beth-shan where the Philistines had descrated them, and buried them beneath the tamarisk tree in Jabesh (31:11-13). David later moved their bones to the ancestral tomb of Kish in Zela (2 Sam. 21:13-14). In his lament over Saul and Jonathan, also known as the Song of the Bow, David mourned the death of father and son, and particularly his love for Jonathan (1:19-27). David also remembered their friendship by bestowing all of Saul's holdings on Jonathan's sole surviving son Mephibosheth (ch. 9).

3. The son of the priest Abiathar (2 Sam.15:27). During Absalom's revolt, he passed on Hushai's reports to King David at Mahanaim (v. 36; 17:15-22). Later he sided with Adonijah, bringing news that Solomon had been anointed king (1 Kgs. 1:42-43); for this he presumably shared his father's banishment (2:26-27).

4. The son of Shimei, David's brother, who killed an abnormal Philistine giant who had taunted Israel at Gath (2 Sam. 21:21 par. 1 Chr. 20:7 "son of Shimea"). *See* JONADAB 1.

5. One of David's mighty men; son of Shammah the Hararite (so NIV, 2 Sam. 23:32-33, following LXX; according to 1 Chr. 11:34 the son of Shagee).

6. A son of Jada, and descendant of Jerahmeel, listed in the genealogy of the Judahites (1 Chr. 2:32-33).

7. The son of Uzziah who served as overseer of the royal treasuries outside the capital (1 Chr. 27:25; KJV "Jehonathan").

8. The uncle (Heb. *dôd*) of King David. Known for his keen perception, he served as David's counselor and scribe (1 Chr. 27:32). The meaning of the Hebrew kinship term is not certain, and some thus identify him with **4.**

9. The father of Ebed, who returned with Ezra from Babylon (Ezra 8:6).

10. The son of Asahel; one who opposed Ezra's measures concerning foreign wives (Ezra 10:15; cf. 1 Esdr. 9:14).

11. A high priest; the son of Joiada and father of Jaddua (Neh. 12:11). He is probably the same as Johanan **11** (v. 22).

12. The head of the priestly house of Malluchi when Joiakim was high priest (Neh. 12:14).

13. The father of Zechariah **28**, who led the levitical musicians at the rededication of Jerusalem's walls (Neh. 12:35).

14. The state secretary at whose house Jeremiah was imprisoned for treason (Jer. 37:15, 20; 38:26).

15. A son of Kareah, one of the commanders who joined Gedaliah after Jerusalem's fall (KJV, NIV, Jer. 40:8; RSV omits, following LXX; cf. 2 Kgs. 25:23). The MT reading may be a case of dittography.

16. The fifth son of Mattathias, surnamed Apphus (1 Macc. 2:5). He succeeded Judas Maccabeus as leader of the Jewish revolt (9:28-31). Devastated by the death of Judas and the resurgence of the Hellenists, the rebels under Jonathan were at first able to wage only guerrilla warfare (cf. vv. 23-24). Yet when the high priest Alcimus died in 159 B.C. no successor was named, and two years later the Syrian general Bacchides returned to Antioch. Urged by the Hellenists to return to Judah, he was defeated by Jonathan at Beth-basi and forced to accept terms of peace. Headquartered at Michmash, Jonathan's forces gained strength, aided in part by a power struggle between Demetrius I and Alexander Balas. Alexander emerged victorious in 150 and, admiring Jonathan, appointed him general, governor, and high priest (10:22-66). In 146 Demetrius II Nicator forced Alexander to flee, allowing Jonathan to attempt an unsuccessful siege of the citadel (Akra) at Jerusalem, then held by Hellenistic Jews (11:20-37). Demetrius confirmed Jonathan's offices, granted religious privileges to the Jews, and gave Jonathan control of the three southern districts of Samaria. Demetrius' army rebelled in 143, and Diodotus Trypho, a general of Alexander Balas, usurped the throne as regent of Alexander's son Antiochus VI Epiphanes. Trypho gave Jonathan civil and religious authority over the Jews and named his brother Simon military commander; but threatened by Jonathan's military (11:60-74) and political success (cf. his alliances with the Romans and Spartans; 12:1-23), Trypho imprisoned Jonathan and in 143 murdered him at Baskama in Transjordan (12:24–13:24). Trypho then assumed control of Syria, while Simon Maccabeus ruled Judea.

17. The son of Absalom; sent by Simon Maccabeus to Joppa, which he captured (1 Macc. 13:11).

18. A postexilic priest who led in prayer at the sacrifice offered by Nehemiah (2 Macc. 1:23).

JOPPA [jŏp'ə] (Heb. *yāpô, yāpô'* "beautiful"; Gk. *Ioppē*).† A coastal city on the border of the original territory of Dan (Josh. 19:46; KJV "Japho"), 56 km. (35 mi.) northwest of Jerusalem; modern Jaffa or Yafo. The name is attested in the list of Egyptian pharaoh Thutmose III (Egyp. *ypw*; *ANET*, p. 242), the Amarna

Letters (Akk. *Ia-pu, Ia-a-pu*), and the annals of Sennacherib (*Ia-ap-puu, Ia-u-u*; *ANET*, p. 287).

Joppa was not a city of major significance in the Old Testament. Its primary importance was as a seaport, hence Deborah's reproachful question, "Dan, why did he abide with the ships?" (Judg. 5:17). King Hiram of Tyre cut timber needed for Solomon's building projects and floated it in rafts by sea to Joppa (2 Chr. 2:16; cf. 1 Kgs. 5:9). After the return of the exiles the Sidonians and Tyrians also shipped cedar by sea to Joppa for the rebuilding of the temple at Jerusalem (Ezra 3:7). When the prophet Jonah balked at preaching the Lord's message in Nineveh, he fled to Joppa and found a ship going to Tarshish (Jonah 1:3).

In the Hellenistic period Joppa suffered much in war, experiencing frequent conquest by such figures as Alexander the Great and Ptolemy I of Egypt. Judas Maccabeus was unable to conquer the city, although he did destroy the harbor (2 Macc. 12:3-9). His brother Jonathan succeeded in capturing Joppa but lost it again (1 Macc. 10:69-85; Josephus *Ant.* xiii.4.4 [88-101]). Finally their brother Simon established a Jewish garrison there (12:33-34), and the city remained in Jewish control for two hundred years (cf. 13:11; 14:5, 34), although later as an autonomous city of Roman Syria. The last of Joppa's frequent destructions came at the hand of the Roman general (and later emperor) Vespasian, who crushed it in A.D. 68 during the First Jewish Revolt (Josephus *BJ* iii.9.2 [414]).

In the New Testament Joppa was the city where Peter restored to life the disciple Tabitha (Dorcas) (Acts 9:36-42). It was there in the house of Simon the tanner that Peter had the rooftop vision which led to the first preaching of the gospel of Christ to the Gentiles (10:9-48).

Excavations have determined seven major strata of occupation from the Middle Bronze through the Hellenistic periods. Important discoveries include the ornamented city gate of Rameses II and a Bronze Age temple.

JORAH [jôr′ə] (Heb. *yôrâ* "early rain"). An Israelite whose descendants returned with Zerubbabel from captivity (Ezra 2:18). At Neh. 7:24 his name is given as Hariph.

JORAI [jôr′ī] (Heb. *yôray* "Yahweh instructs"). The head of a Gadite father's house in Bashan; a son of Abihail (1 Chr. 5:13).

JORAM [jôr′əm] (Heb. *yôrām*, contracted form of *yᵉhôrām* "Yahweh is exalted").
1. The son of King Toi of Hamath, sent by his father to congratulate David on his victory over Hadadezer (2 Sam. 8:10). In the parallel account he is called Hadorezer (**1**), son of Tou (1 Chr. 18:10).
2. Alternate form of JEHORAM **1** and **2**.
3. A Levite descended from Eliezer the son of Moses (1 Chr. 26:25).

JORDAN [jôr′dən] (Heb. *yardēn*; Gk. *Iordanēs*). The largest and most important river in Palestine, extending from its sources near Mt. Hermon in the north to its outlet in the Dead Sea. The etymology of the name Jordan is a point of controversy among linguists: cf. Indo-European *yor* "year" plus *don* "river," thus "perennial river"; Sem. "rapidly descending stream," from the root *yrd* "to descend." It is also known by the Arabic name esh-Sherî'ah ("the drinking place").

The Jordan river is located in a valley which is the northern extension of the Rift valley. This geological fault stretches from southeastern Africa through Palestine, to Syria. The fault determined the basic course of the Jordan and of its Transjordanian branches: the Yarmuk, Jabbok, Arnon, and Zared. Occasional earthquakes and landslides, along with hot springs, are lingering signs of the area's volcanic past.

Tracing its winding course over 320 km. (200 mi.), through a bed of basalt, the Jordan is 30.5 m. (100 ft.) wide (wider during spring floods) and 1 to 3 m. (3 to 10 ft.) deep. Numerous fords are found throughout its length.

The sources for the river include, from east to west, the Nahr Bâniyâs, Nahr el-Leddan, Nahr Ḥasbânî, and Nahr Bareighith. As the Jordan flows southward it passes through the Huleh valley, in ancient times Lake Huleh. In biblical times the region was a tropical swamp, characterized by an abundance of papyrus.

The Sea of Galilee is next, as the river descends rapidly over a 11-km. (7-mi.) stretch. The favorable climate and abundance of water here have made Galilee important for agriculture throughout history.

The Jordan then descends nearly 180 m. (590 ft.) from the Sea of Galilee to the Dead Sea. Rapids, whirlpools, and constantly changing banks are characteristic of this area. Thick jungles are found in the lowlands of the valley, while its highlands are suitable for farming and grazing. With eight tributaries below Galilee, the lower Jordan valley was a natural site for the foundation of settlements such as Jabesh-gilead, Jericho, and Beth-shan.

The Jordan figures prominently in events recorded in the Bible. It is first mentioned in the Old Testament in the account of Abram and Lot (Gen. 13:10-11): when the two decided to separate, Lot chose to take his herds to the rich plain of the Jordan. Later, Jacob crossed the river on his journey to Aram (32:10).

The Jordan was the final obstacle facing the Israelites before they could enter into the promised land. Moses' dying wish was to cross the river (Deut. 3:23-25), and to do so was Joshua's first command from the Lord (Josh. 1:2). The miraculous dry crossing of the Jordan (chs. 3–4; cf. Exod. 14–15) opened the way for the destruction of Jericho and the subjugation of the Canaanites.

The Jordan remained a military obstacle through the period of the judges into the early Monarchy. Control of the river's fords was critical in a number of battles (Judg. 3:28-29; 7:24-25; 12:5-6; cf. 1 Sam. 22:3-4; 2 Sam. 17:22; 19:1ff.).

Some of the stories of Elijah and Elisha are set in the Jordan valley. There they and their disciples gathered, and in that vicinity the two prophets performed a number of miracles (2 Kgs. 2; 5:1-14; 6:1-7).

The Jordan is also the backdrop for events recorded in the Gospels. John the Baptist came out of the wilderness to baptize in the Jordan (Matt. 3:1-12 par.), and it was there that Jesus was baptized (vv. 13-17 par.). During part of his public ministry Jesus traveled along the eastern bank of the river (Luke 12–18), and he crossed it at Jericho as he began his final journey to Jerusalem.

Bibliography. N. Glueck, *The River Jordan*, rev. ed. (New York: 1968).

JORIM [jôr'ĭm] (Gk. *Iōreim*, from Heb. *yᵉhôrām* "Yahweh is exalted"). An ancestor of Jesus; father of Eliezer and son of Matthat (Luke 3:29).

JORKEAM [jôr'kĭ əm] (Heb. *yorqᵉ'ām*).† The son of Raham, and a descendant of Caleb (1 Chr. 2:44). Most scholars interpret these names as settlements in the territory of Judah. The LXX B reads this name for the city Jokdeam at Josh. 15:56, suggesting that one of the forms is a scribal variant. The site may be modern Khirbet Raqa' near Ziph, in the hill country south of Hebron.

JOSABAD (1 Chr. 12:4, KJV). See JOZABAD 1.

JOSAPHAT (Matt. 1:8, KJV). See JEHOSHAPHAT 3.

JOSE (Luke 3:29, KJV). See JOSHUA 5.

JOSECH [jō'zĭk] (Gk. *Iōsech*). An ancestor of Jesus listed in Luke's genealogy (Luke 3:26; KJV "Joseph").

JOSEDECH. See JEHOZADAK.

JOSEPH [jō'səf] (Heb. *yôsēp, yahôsēp* "may [God] add [posterity]'").
1. The eleventh son of Jacob and the oldest of Rachel, his favored wife. Like Isaac and Jacob before him, Joseph was born to a formerly barren woman to whom God had shown compassion (Gen. 30:22-24). Joseph's ability to interpret dreams and his administrative gifts were to have dramatic consequences for his life in Egypt, earning him the confidence of the pharaoh and as a result high position. He was the eponymous ancestor of an Israelite tribe.

After Joseph's birth his family returned from Paddan-aram (northwest Mesopotamia) to Canaan and eventually settled at Hebron. There the family lived as transhumants, camping in different places as they followed their flocks and herds.

Jacob doted on Joseph, the son of his old age, and gave him a *kᵉtōnet passîm* (lit. "long robe with sleeves"), the fabled "coat of many colors." The exact nature of this garment is uncertain (cf. 2 Sam. 13:18-19, where Tamar wears one), but when Joseph received it his brothers' jealousy was kindled (Gen. 37:3-4). Their anger only increased when Joseph had dreams which suggested that they would one day be subservient to him (vv. 5-11). When Jacob sent Joseph to check on his brothers as they cared for the herds, they plotted to kill him (vv. 12-20). Only Reuben's pleas persuaded the others to spare Joseph's life. They stripped him of his coat, threw him into a dry cistern, then sold him to passing traders (Ishmaelites or Midianites?) bound for Egypt (vv. 21-28). The brothers covered up Joseph's disappearance by dipping his coat

in goat's blood, and the news broke Jacob's heart (vv. 29-35).

Like countless other Canaanites taken into Egypt, Joseph was sold into the service of an Egyptian household (cf. Papyrus Brooklyn 35.1446), in his case that of Potiphar, the captain of Pharaoh's guard. With the help of God Joseph prospered, and he was soon in charge of all aspects of the house and fields. Unfortunately, the lust of Potiphar's wife for the handsome slave led to Joseph's being falsely accused of seducing her and imprisoned (Gen. 39:6b-20; cf. the Egyptian Tale of Two Brothers; *ANET*, pp. 23-25). Despite this reversal, the prison warden soon entrusted Joseph with charge of the prison.

During his imprisonment Joseph correctly interpreted the dreams of the royal cupbearer and baker, and asked the former to remember him to Pharaoh upon his release (Gen. 40). The cupbearer forgot Joseph, however, and he languished in prison for two more years. Then Pharaoh dreamed first of seven gaunt cows devouring seven healthy ones, followed by seven thin heads of grain consuming seven full heads (this parallelism in dreams is found in ancient Egyptian literature). The inability of Pharaoh's wisemen to unravel the meaning of these dreams reminded the cupbearer of Joseph, whom he recommended to the ruler. Joseph was quickly summoned, and God enabled him to explain Pharaoh's dreams, which foretold the coming of seven years of plenty in Egypt to be followed by seven years of famine (ch. 41). After suggesting that the pharaoh appoint an able administrator to oversee the collection and storage of the harvest in the years of abundance, the thirty-year-old Joseph found himself selected for the post (perhaps that of vizier). The royal signet ring, fine linen clothing, gold chain, and chariot Pharaoh bestowed upon the Hebrew were signs of royal favor and of great power (vv. 41-43). In addition, Pharaoh gave Joseph a new name, Zaphenath-paneah (Hebrew transliteration of Egyp. "the god speaks and he [who bears the name] lives"), and Asenath the daughter of Potiphera priest of On for his wife.

Joseph's planning paid off, for the severity of the famine made "all the earth" suffer (Gen. 41:57). Like many other inhabitants of Canaan, Joseph's brothers travelled to Egypt to buy food. Recognizing them, Joseph slyly accused his brothers of being spies, held Simeon hostage, and commanded the others to bring to Egypt their youngest brother Benjamin (42:6-27). When Jacob heard of the demand made by the unnamed Egyptian official he refused to let Benjamin go to Egypt. But soon the food ran out again, and he was forced to send his sons back to Egypt with presents—and his youngest son (42:36–43:15). Joseph's dinner invitation upon their return to Egypt did nothing to lessen his brothers' apprehension, but their presence deeply affected him (v. 30). Curiously, Joseph played a final ruse on his brothers: he had his silver drinking and divination cup hidden in Benjamin's bag of grain, then declared that whoever was found with it would become his slave (44:1-9). The discovery of the cup devastated Joseph's brothers, for they knew what effect their leaving Benjamin in Egypt would have upon Jacob. Judah made a passionate plea for the lad's freedom and offered to substitute as Joseph's slave (vv. 18-34). Joseph could restrain himself no longer and revealed his true identity to his incredulous brothers. He invited them all to bring their households and herds to Egypt, an invitation reiterated by Pharaoh (45:16-20).

Joseph's family was established in Egypt with God's promise of future greatness (46:2-4; ch. 47). At the end of his life Jacob blessed Joseph and his other sons (ch. 48; 49:22-26). Upon his father's death, Joseph had Jacob's body embalmed in a manner which only wealthy Egyptians could afford (50:2-3) and returned him to Canaan with a large burial party (vv. 7-11).

Joseph died when he was 110, an age the Egyptians associated with great wisdom (v. 26).

Perhaps four hundred years after the time of Joseph, the Hebrews had become slaves in Egypt and were led out of bondage in the great Exodus. The tribes of Ephraim and Manasseh, Joseph's descendants, became part of a new people, Israel. After the conquest of Palestine the "Joseph tribes" settled in the region between the Sea of Chinnereth (Galilee) and the Salt (Dead) Sea. *See* EPHRAIM; MANASSEH.

Bibliography. D. B. Redford, *A Study of the Biblical Story of Joseph (Genesis 37–50)*. VTS 20 (1970).

2. The father of Igal of the tribe of Issachar, one of those chosen by Moses to spy out Canaan (Num. 13:7).

3. A son of David's musician Asaph (or member of his levitical guild) who participated in the ministry of prophecy accompanied by music (1 Chr. 25:2, 9).

4. A descendant of Binnui; a postexilic Jew who had married a foreign woman (Ezra 10:42).

5. A head of the priestly father's house of Shebaniah during the days when Joiakim was high priest (Neh. 12:14).

6. An ancestor of Judith (Jdt. 8:1).

7. A military commander under Judas Maccabeus who sought personal glory by instigating an attack upon Jamnia but was routed (1 Macc. 5:18, 55-62).

8. According to 2 Macc. 8:22; 10:19, a brother of Judas Maccabeus; he is not named among the sons of Mattathias at 1 Macc. 2:1-5.

9. The husband of Mary and putative father of Jesus. According to Matthew he was a Bethlehemite carpenter who later settled in Nazareth, but Luke's account has him journey from Nazareth to Bethlehem to comply with the census edict. Joseph appears rarely other than in the birth and childhood narratives in Matthew and Luke; he is not mentioned in Mark, and is named only twice in John in references to Jesus as the "son of Joseph" (John 1:45; 6:42). Accordingly, it is generally assumed that Joseph died before Jesus' public ministry began (cf. apocryphal writings which depict Joseph as a widower at the time of his marriage to Mary, thus rationalizing the existence of Jesus' siblings).

Little is known of Joseph. The genealogies of Jesus (Matt. 1:2-16; Luke 3:23-38) trace descent through David to show that Jesus (through his legal father Joseph) belonged to that royal line (some scholars trace Davidic ancestry also through Mary). Luke states that Joseph was already living in Nazareth when he became betrothed to Mary (Luke 1:26-27), meaning that the couple had announced publicly their intention to

marry but had not yet begun to live together. Matthew (Matt. 1:18-21) records Joseph's consternation upon discovering that Mary was pregnant and his offer to divorce her as permitted by Jewish law in cases of alleged adultery.

Reassured of Mary's purity and informed by an angel in a dream of the nature of the child she carried, Joseph proceeded with the marriage. After the birth of Jesus, Joseph received further angelic instruction, first to escape Herod's wrath by fleeing to Egypt and subsequently to return to Palestine (Matt. 2:13-15, 19-25). Luke's account depicts Joseph as a pious Jew, participating annually in the Passover festival (Luke 2:41).

Bibliography. R. E. Brown, *The Birth of the Messiah* (Garden City: 1979).

10. A brother of Jesus (Matt. 13:55; KJV "Joses").

11. A wealthy and respected member of the Jewish Sanhedrin from Arimathea in the central hill country of Judea who provided his tomb for Jesus' burial (Matt. 27:57; Mark 15:43). Joseph was a devout Jew (Luke 23:50-51) and a secret follower of Jesus (Matt. 27:57; John 19:38). He boldly approached the Roman governor Pilate and asked to be given Jesus' corpse (Matt. 27:58; Mark 15:43-45; John 19:38; cf. Deut. 21:22:23). With the aid of Nicodemus Joseph anointed and wrapped Jesus' body for burial, and placed it in his hewn-rock tomb (Matt. 27:59-60; Mark 15:46; Luke 23:53; John 19:39-42).

12. A brother of James the younger (Matt. 27:56; KJV "Joses"; cf. Mark 15:40).

13. An ancestor of Jesus; father of Jannai and son of Mattathias (Luke 3:24).

14. (Luke 3:26, KJV). *See* JOSECH.

15. An ancestor of Jesus who lived between the time of David and Zerubbabel; father of Judah and son of Jonam (Luke 3:30).

16. A candidate for the apostle's seat vacated by Judas. He was called Barsabbas and surnamed Justus (1) (Acts 1:23). *See* BARSABBAS 1.

17. The given name of BARNABAS (Acts 4:36; KJV "Joses").

JOSEPH, PRAYER OF.* A Jewish (or perhaps Jewish-Christian or Gnostic) pseudepigraphal writing, probably dating to the first century A.D. Of an original eleven hundred lines only three fragments amounting to nine Greek sentences have survived, preserved in the writings of Origen; Joseph (the son of Jacob) himself is not mentioned in the surviving portions. The Prayer of Joseph presents an exalted Jacob as the earthly incarnation of the angel Israel, claiming superior heavenly rank over the angel Uriel. The work seems related to early Jewish Merkabah mystical traditions.

JOSEPH AND ASENATH [ăs′ə năth].* An example of the Hellenistic romantic novel. This intriguing Jewish work is a fictional attempt to explain why it was not improper for the Hebrew patriarch Joseph to marry Asenath, the daughter of an Egyptian priest (Gen. 41:45, 50; 46:20).

The first part of the story describes in some detail and from Asenath's viewpoint her idolatrous life, her introduction to Joseph, her subsequent repentance and conversion, and their marriage. The second part records events whereby her life is endangered by Pharaoh's firstborn son (aided by various of Joseph's brothers), but she is rescued, thus showing how God protects his new convert. The key point of the story is the spiritual progression of Asenath from one who worships idols to one who takes refuge in the Lord, the God of Joseph. By this progression she becomes the prototype for all who would take refuge in the God of Israel, and the second part of the story serves to reinforce her decision.

Joseph and Asenath was written in Greek at the turn of the Christian era, probably in Egypt. Its widespread popularity is suggested by the large number of manuscripts which survive.

JOSEPH THE CARPENTER, HISTORY OF.† A short apocryphal book on the life and death of Joseph the husband of Mary.

The book originated in Egypt ca. the beginning of the fifth century. First written in Greek, it is extant in two dialects of Coptic, Bohairic and Sahidic (chs. 14–24).

The book is intended to glorify Joseph and thus his feast day. Chs. 1–11 relate the circumstances of Joseph's life before the birth of Jesus (he was an aged widower at the time of his marriage to Mary), the miraculous birth of the Messiah, and narratives of Jesus' early childhood; these chapters depend heavily on the Protevangelium of James and the gospel of Thomas. Chs. 12–32 portray Joseph in his sickness and death at age 111 as a model for the saints; included is Jesus' eulogy over his earthly father. The work shows obvious influence from Egyptian religion and Gnosticism.

JOSEPHUS, FLAVIUS [flā'vĭ əs jō sē'fəs]. A Jewish general and historian who was born A.D. 37-38 to an aristocratic family of priests in Jerusalem and who died after 100 in Rome. His Hebrew name was Joseph ben Mattathias.

Josephus became a Pharisee after examining at first hand the different varieties of Judaism which existed in Judea. In A.D. 63 he went to Rome to obtain the liberation of a group of Jewish priests. He was impressed with Rome's power and, as Judea moved toward revolt, attempted to persuade Jews that war against Rome was foolish. When war did break out in 66, Josephus took on an important generalship of Jewish forces in Galilee. In July 67 he was captured after the Roman siege of Jotapata, but gained the favor of the Roman general Vespasian by predicting that the latter would become emperor. Two years later Vespasian did become emperor and his son Titus assumed leadership of the Roman forces in Judea. Josephus served as an interpreter and performed other duties for Titus. After the fall of Jerusalem (70), Josephus lived in Rome under the patronage (mainly) of the Flavian emperors.

The extant writings of Josephus are the *Jewish War* (*BJ*), the major source for the history of the revolt and war, written in the A.D. 70s; the *Jewish Antiquities*, a history of the Jews from the creation of the world to the time of the revolt, written in A.D. 93-94; and two later and smaller writings, *Contra Apionem*

(*Against Apion*; *Ap.*), a defense of the Jews and Judaism against the attacks of Apion and other anti-Jewish writers; and the autobiographical *Life* (*Vita*), primarily a defense of Josephus' position in the early part of the war against Justus of Tiberias, another writer who accused Josephus of much of the responsibility for the revolt. Josephus' writings are important not only for the history of the war and the events leading up to it, but also for the nature of the parties within first-century Judaism, which he interprets for his Gentile audience as different philosophical schools. Furthermore, through the *Antiquities* and *Contra Apionem*, he provides insight for the nature of Jewish apologetics and the opposition it had to face, the latter of which is heavily represented by quotations in *Contra Apionem*.

A Slavonic translation of the *Jewish War* (possibly from the Aramaic original rather than from Josephus' Greek revision, though this is unlikely) has passages not contained in the Greek, some of which describe John the Baptist, Jesus, their work, and the persecution of Christians in Palestine after the death of Agrippa I. Whether these passages are authentic is disputed; it is certain that they contain at least a few Christian interpolations.

Bibliography. H. St. J. Thackeray, R. Marcus, A. Wikgren, and L. H. Feldman, eds., *Josephus*, 9 vols. Loeb Classical Library (Cambridge, Mass.: 1926-1965); D. M. Rhoads, *Israel in Revolution 6-74 C.E.: A Political History Based on the Writings of Josephus* (Philadelphia: 1976).

JOSES [jō'zĭz] (Gk. *Iōsēs*).
1. One of the brothers of Jesus (Mark 6:3). At Matt. 13:55 he is called Joseph (KJV "Joses").
2. A brother of James the younger (Mark 15:40, 47). At Matt. 27:56 he is called Joseph (KJV "Joses").
3. (Acts 4:36, KJV). See JOSEPH 17; BARNABAS.

JOSHAH [jōsh'ə] (Heb. *yôšâ*). The son of Amaziah (2), and a prince of the tribe of Simeon at the time of Hezekiah (1 Chr. 4:34).

JOSHAPHAT [jōsh'ə făt] (Heb. *yôšāpāṭ* "Yahweh judges").†
1. A Mithnite and one of David's mighty men (1 Chr. 11:43).
2. A priest at the time of David, responsible for blowing the trumpet before the ark of the covenant as it was brought to Jerusalem (1 Chr. 15:24; KJV "Jehoshaphat").

JOSHAVIAH [jōsh'ə vī'ə] (Heb. *yôšawyâ*). A son of Elnaam, and one of David's mighty men (1 Chr. 11:46).

JOSHBEKASHAH [jōsh'bĭ kā'shə] (Heb. *yošbᵉqāšâ*). The leader of the seventeenth division of singers at the time of David; a son of Heman (1 Chr. 25:4, 24).

JOSHEB-BASSHEBETH. See JASHOBEAM 1.

JOSHIBIAH [jōsh'ə bī'ə] (Heb. *yôšibyâ* "Yahweh causes to dwell safely"). The father of Jehu and son of Seraiah; prince of the tribe of Simeon at the time of Hezekiah (1 Chr. 4:35; KJV "Josibiah").

JOSHUA [jŏsh'ōō ə] (Heb. *yᵉhôšuaʿ* "Yahweh saves"; Gk. *Iēsous*).

1. The son of Nun, a member of the tribe of Ephraim (1 Chr. 7:20-27), and Moses' lieutenant and successor. Originally he was named Hoshea (Num. 13:8; KJV "Oshea").

Throughout the wilderness wanderings Joshua was Moses' trusted "minister" (Heb. *mᵉšārēṯ*; e.g., 11:28; RSV elsewhere "servant"), a witness to his most sacred tasks (cf. Exod. 17:14). As a young man (Num. 33:11) he proved himself as commander of Israel's forces in battle against the Amalekites (17:8-13).

Joshua was not only Moses' military lieutenant, but his disciple: accompanying his master up Mt. Sinai and remaining there for forty days while Moses met with God (24:13-18; 32:15-17); remaining as custodian in the tent of meeting, where he assisted Moses (33:11); and zealously guarding his patron's prophetic office (Num. 11:26-29).

Joshua was one of the twelve spies Moses sent into Canaan (13:8, 16; KJV "Jehoshua"). With Caleb he distinguished himself for his steadfast trust in the Lord's promises; in the face of the negative report of the other spies, Joshua and Caleb encouraged the people to trust God, but Israel rejected their pleas and sought to stone them (14:4-10). For their faith and courage, the Lord permitted only Joshua and Caleb to enter the Promised Land (v. 30; 26:65; cf. 1 Macc. 2:55; Heb. 3:17-18).

At the Lord's direction, Moses consecrated Joshua as his successor to complete his work (Num. 27:12-23; Deut. 3:28; 31:14). Joshua was filled with the same spirit of wisdom as his mentor (34:9; cf. Sir. 46:1). The book of Joshua clearly parallels his career to that of Moses (Josh. 1:15, 17; 3:7; 4:23; 8:32; cf. 3:5; 5:15).

Under Joshua's leadership Israel firmly established themselves in the land, breaking the back of the more powerful Canaanite resistance (chs. 6–12; esp. 11:23). After these initial victories Joshua allotted territory to each tribe as their inheritance (chs. 13–21). At the end of his life Joshua again summoned all Israel to exhort them to steadfastness, and to renew the covenant (23:1–24:28). Joshua died at the full age of 110 and was buried in his own inheritance at Timnath-serah (24:29).

2. A man of Beth-shemesh, in whose field the ark of the covenant stopped after the Philistines had sent it away (1 Sam. 6:14).

3. A governor of Jerusalem at the time of King Josiah (2 Kgs. 23:8).

4. Alternate form of JESHUA **5**, the first postexilic high priest, as used in Haggai and Zechariah.

5. An ancestor of Jesus (Luke 3:29; KJV "Jose").

JOSHUA, BOOK OF.† The first book of the Former Prophets and the sixth of the Old Testament canon, named after its principal figure, Joshua the son of Nun.

I. Contents

The book of Joshua continues the historical account of the Israelites' entrance into Canaan, recording events following the death of Moses (Deut. 34). It depicts the conquest of the promised land (Josh. 1–12) and the division of the territory among the twelve tribes (chs. 13–21).

The book begins with Yahweh's commissioning of Joshua to lead Israel in conquest of Canaan (1:1-9) and Joshua's instructions (specifically to the officers and the Transjordanian tribes) to prepare for the invasion (vv. 10-18). Anticipating the first arena of conquest, Joshua sends spies to reconnoiter the territory around Jericho; here they are given refuge by the harlot Rahab (ch. 2). Reminiscent of events at the Red Sea (Exod. 14–15), the waters of the swollen Jordan river part, allowing the people to cross over on dry ground (Josh. 3); the Israelites commemorate this event with stone memorials and renewal of the covenant in their camp at Gilgal (4:1–5:12).

After the appearance to Joshua of the angelic commander of Yahweh's army (vv. 13-15), the Israelites lay siege to Jericho; as they march around it for the seventh day, the walls collapse and the Israelites utterly destroy all but their protector Rahab and her family (ch. 6). Following this initial success, the Israelites fail at first to conquer Ai, hampered by Achan's disobedience to the covenant; after he is stoned to death for his offense, the invaders succeed in capturing that city (8:1-29). Fulfilling Moses' command (Deut. 27:4-5), Joshua builds an altar on Mt. Ebal and the people observe a covenant ceremony (Josh. 8:30-35). The Gibeonites, pretending to have traveled a long distance, trick Joshua into entering an alliance, thereby sparing from conquest their cities in the central highlands (ch. 9). The pact is tested as Joshua defends Gibeon against a coalition of five Amorite cities (10:1-27); success is aided by the miraculous halting of the sun and moon. The account of this initial stage of conquest ends with a summary of Joshua's campaigns in the south (vv. 28-43). Ch. 11 recounts the Israelite victory over Jabin king of Hazor and his allies (vv. 1-15) and outlines Joshua's conquests in the north (vv. 16-23). The section concludes with a summary of Israel's victories both east and west of the Jordan (ch. 12).

With the assurance that he himself will direct the conquest of the remaining non-Israelite enclaves, the Lord instructs the aged Joshua to divide among the tribes the entire land (13:1-7). There follow lists of the tribal allotments: territories assigned by Moses to the Transjordanian tribes (13:8-33); land assigned by Joshua at Gilgal to Judah and the Joseph tribes, Ephraim and Manasseh (chs. 14–17); and his allotment to the remaining seven tribes at Shiloh (chs. 18–19). The section concludes with the appointment of cities of refuge (ch. 20) and levitical cities (21:1-42).

Having assisted in the conquest of the land, the Transjordanian tribes return to their territories, erecting as a sign of unity an altar at the Jordan (21:43–22:34). Significantly later, when hostilities have subsided, Joshua in his final days of life assembles "all Israel" for his farewell address, charging them to remain faithful to the covenant (ch. 23). He then gathers the tribes at Shechem for a ceremony of covenant renewal (24:1-28). The book concludes with the death and burial of Joshua (vv. 29-31), Joseph (v. 32), and Eleazar (v. 33).

II. Origin and Composition

The origin and formation of the book of Joshua remain the object of continued controversy among scholars. Although the Talmud (*B. Bat.* 14b, 15a) attributes the book to its central figure, the book itself gives no conclusive indication of authorship, at least for its final form (cf. Josh. 24:26). Its canonical position as first among the Former Prophets is generally taken as one factor distinguishing it from the composition of the Pentateuch. Nevertheless, earlier critical scholars noted resemblances between the contents of Joshua and the various sources identified in the five books of the Torah; accordingly, the book was regarded as a continuation of the account in Deuteronomy, hence constituting the final book of the Hexateuch. Others note similarity to the editorial hand of the Deuteronomic historian, thus viewing it as part of a larger Deuteronomic history that concludes with 1–2 Kings.

Various types of materials have been used in the composition of the book, including possible eyewitness accounts (e.g., Josh. 5–7; 14:6-12), border and town lists, archival material (e.g., "the book of Jashar," 10:13; cf. 18:9), and cultic materials (e.g., ch. 24). Critical scholars, in particular, have noted inconsistencies (e.g., between border and town lists, which perhaps reflect different historical periods) and duplications (cf. 4:5-7, 9; ch. 7; 22:9-34). Some scholars suggest that various collectons of tribal traditions are represented (e.g., Benjaminite material in chs. 2–11), with a final editing intended to depict "all Israel" as participating in conquest of the entire land; to further complicate matters, archaeological evidence suggests a longer, more diversified process (cf. Judg. 1:1–2:5; *see* CONQUEST; JERICHO). Such expressions as "to this day" (e.g., 4:9; 5:9; 7:26) are taken as evidence that the work was compiled at some distance from the actual events. A conservative approach to these complexities, which favors the essential unity of the book, notes its thematic arrangement and episodic or proleptic treatment of events, offering provisional summaries of events to be presented later in considerable detail.

III. Theology

A major focus of the book is Yahweh's giving of the land to his people Israel, accomplished through the Conquest and presented as fulfillment of his promise to Moses (Josh. 1:2-6; 11:23; 21:43-45), originally made to Abraham (Gen. 12:1, 7) and repeated to Isaac (26:3), Jacob (28:4, 13; 35:12), Joseph (48:4), the remaining sons of Jacob (50:24), and to their descendants as they wandered through the wilderness (e.g., Deut. 5:31; 9:6; 11:17). To assure fulfillment of his promise, Yahweh himself directs the events of the Conquest. As the divine warrior it is he, rather than the human historian led by Joshua, who accomplishes victory (e.g., Josh. 3:10; 6:16; 10:14; 11:6-8; cf. 5:13-15); those areas which remain in non-Israelite hands will yet be conquered under Yahweh's direction (13:2-6; 23:5). Finally, it is the Lord who directs the allotment of territories to the individual tribes (v. 7; 17:4; 18:6; 19:51; 23:4).

The covenant relationship between God and Israel is of primary concern throughout the book. Upon crossing the Jordan river those who had been born during the wilderness wanderings are circumcised in a covenant ceremony at Gilgal (5:2-9). The bond is reaffirmed on Mt. Ebal following the Israelite victory at Ai (8:30-35), and at the conclusion of the Conquest all Israel gathers at Shechem to renew the covenant (24:1-28). Particular emphasis is placed on obedience to the covenant stipulations, underscored by the sanctions of blessings and curses (1:16-18; 23:6-8, 14-16; 24:19-20); the vengeance taken upon Achan (ch. 7) is to be understood in terms of his violation of the taboo regarding booty and the danger his actions thus posed for the covenantal community.

Having entered the promised land (1:13, 15) and having essentially completed the conquest of Canaan (11:23; 22:4), Israel attained "rest" (NEB "security") from hardship and conflict (14:15; 21:44; AB "cessation of hostilities"; 23:1). The concept entails not only respite from life's turmoil—a time of peace earned through covenantal faithfulness—but also the hope for future blessing; as such it forms the basis for the eschatological understanding of heaven as mankind's ultimate place of rest (cf. Heb. 3:7–4:10).

Bibliography. R. G. Boling and G. E. Wright, *Joshua.* AB 6 (1982); J. Gray, *Joshua, Judges and Ruth.* NCBC (1986); J. A. Soggin, *Joshua.* OTL (1972); M. H. Woudstra, *The Book of Joshua.* NICOT (1981).

JOSIAH [jō sī'ə] (Heb. *yō'šîyāhû* "Yahweh sustains").

1. The son of King Amon of Judah and Jedidah the daughter of Adaiah of Bozkath. He ruled from 640 to 609 B.C. (2 Kgs. 22:1).

Josiah was eight years old when he began to reign following the assassination of his father, coming to power at a time when Assyrian power was in decline (Assur fell in 614 and Nineveh in 612). As a result he had more political leeway than had his predecessors Manasseh and Amon, although that was not the sole reason for his campaign against the worship of Baal. In the twelfth year of his rule he purged Judah and Jerusalem of the pagan high places, the Asherim, and the graven and molten images (2 Chr. 34:3). He even pressed his religious reformation into the territory of the former northern kingdom, pulling down the altar in Bethel (1 Kgs. 13:2) and slaying the priests of the high places in the cities of Samaria and burning their bones on their own altars (2 Kgs. 23:20; 2 Chr. 34:6-7). The accounts of 2 Kgs. 23:1-25; 2 Chr. 34:1-7 present a detailed picture of these far-reaching reforms.

According to the biblical account, Josiah was prompted in his zeal by the book of the law found in the temple during the eighteenth year of his reign by the high priest Hilkiah (2 Kgs. 22:8-20; cf. 2 Chr. 34:8-28, where the discovery follows the reforms detailed in vv. 3-7), hidden there perhaps in time of Assyrian oppression. Some scholars contend that this book was the entire Pentateuch, while most recent scholars identify it as only Deuteronomy or a portion of that book (esp. chs. 12–26); some have suggested that it was composed by a prophetic or priestly party. At any rate, this law book apparently made such a deep impression on Josiah (some scholars contend that

Josiah's reforms stem rather from a desire to centralize the cult) that he sent a delegation to the prophetess Huldah, who predicted that the catastrophe mentioned therein would not be delayed though the king would die in peace. After having called together the elders of Judah and Jerusalem, Josiah read them the words of this "book of the covenant" and pledged to follow its stipulations (2 Kgs. 23:1-3 par.). He celebrated the Passover in Jerusalem, an occasion which had not been celebrated in Israel since earlier in the Monarchy (v. 22 par.). Nevertheless, the Lord remained adamant in his anger against Judah on account of the provocations rendered by Manasseh (v. 26) and because Israel had repented only half-heartedly (cf. Jer. 1–20).

It is not certain what led Josiah to march against Pharaoh Neco when the Egyptians came to the aid of Assyria; perhaps he wanted to reclaim the former territories of the northern kingdom in order to restore the unity of the Davidic and Solomonic empire. Perhaps he wanted to impress Nabopolassar of Babylon. Whatever his motives, they were never realized; Josiah was killed in the battle against Neco at Megiddo (2 Kgs. 23:29; 2 Chr. 35:20-24). His servants carried his body in a chariot to Jerusalem where Jerusalem and all Judah mourned him (2 Kgs. 23:30; 2 Chr. 35:24-25). The people of Judah acclaimed his son Jehoahaz as Josiah's successor, but the Egyptians replaced him with a younger son, Jehoiakim, whom they found more amicable to their cause.

Matthew lists Josiah among the ancestors of Jesus (Matt. 1:10-11; KJV "Josias").

2. The son of Zephaniah (Zech. 6:10; KJV "Hen"), in whose house the prophet Zechariah crowned the high priest JOSHUA 4/JESHUA 5.

JOSIBIAH (1 Chr. 4:35, KJV). See JOSHIBIAH.

JOSIPHIAH [jŏs′ə fī′ə] (Heb. *yôsipyâ* "Yahweh adds"). An Israelite whose son Shelomith returned with Ezra from captivity in Babylon (Ezra 8:10).

JOT. See IOTA.

JOTBAH [jŏt′bə] (Heb. *yoṭbâ* "pleasantness"). The home of Haruz, father of Meshullemeth and grandfather of King Amon of Judah (2 Kgs. 21:19). According to Jerome Jotbah was located in Judah, but this has not been confirmed. If so, the site may be ʿAin aṭ-Ṭaba, 30 km. (20 mi.) north of Aqabah. Some scholars would identify the location as Jotapata (Khirbet Jefât), in the valley of Zebulun west of Lake Gennesaret.

JOTBATHAH [jŏt′bə thə] (Heb. *yoṭbāṭâ* "pleasantness" [?]). A region with many flowing brooks (Deut. 10:7; KJV "Jotbath") where the Israelites sojourned in their wilderness wanderings (Num. 33:33-34). This area was probably located in the Arabah north of Eziongeber; some scholars identify it with ʿAin aṭ-Ṭaba and thus with Jotbah.

JOTHAM [jō′thəm] (Heb. *yôṯām* "Yahweh is perfect"; Gk. *Iōatham*).

1. The youngest son of Gideon (Jerubbaal), and sole survivor of the slaughter of his seventy brothers

by Abimelech, the son of Gideon's concubine (Judg. 9:5). In the fable of the trees and the bramble, Jotham denounced the Shechemites for making Abimelech king (vv. 7-20); the prophetic closing curse was fulfilled three years later (v. 57). In the intervening years Jotham took refuge at Beer (v. 21).

2. King of Judah, son of Uzziah and Jerusha the daughter of Zadok (2 Kgs. 15:32-38; 2 Chr. 27:1-9). Jotham was twenty-five years old when he began his sixteen-year reign: first as coregent for his father (750-741/740), who was stricken with leprosy (v. 5; 2 Chr. 26:16–27:1); then as sole ruler to 735, when Ahaz became coregent and ended Jotham's rule. He died in 732. The relationship of this chronology with certain statements about Hoshea remains unclear (cf. 2 Kgs. 15:30; 17:1).

Throughout his reign Jotham continued Uzziah's policies. He followed his father's example and "did what was right in the eyes of the Lord" (15:34; 2 Chr. 27:2), but without Uzziah's arrogance. While under his rule Judah enjoyed great prosperity, yet the people continued in idolatry (2 Kgs. 15:35), greed, and the contempt born of wealth (2 Chr. 27:2; cf. Isa. 2:8; 5:8-23).

Jotham built the upper (northern) gate of the temple (2 Kgs. 15:35) and extended the wall on Mt. Ophel (2 Chr. 27:3). Moreover, he established strategic cities in the hill country, and forts and towers throughout Judah (v. 4). When the Ammonites rebelled following Uzziah's death (*ca.* 739), Jotham suppressed them and exacted heavy tribute (v. 5). Along with traditional holdings, Jotham's Judah controlled southern Transjordan (cf. 1 Chr. 5:17), Moab, and Edom, reaching from Ammon to the port of Ezion-geber.

Like his father, Jotham maintained a common anti-Assyrian policy with Israel and Syria. Faced with the renewed activity of Tiglath-pileser III, the pro-Assyrian party in Jerusalem elevated Ahaz as coregent; this effectively retired Jotham and curbed his foreign policy, thus precipitating the Syro-Ephraimite War (cf. 2 Kgs. 15:37; Isa. 7:1ff.).

Matthew lists Jotham in the genealogy of Jesus (Matt. 1:9; KJV "Joatham").

3. A Judahite; son of Jahdai, and descendant of Caleb (2 Chr. 2:47).

JOZABAD [jō′zə băd] (Heb. *yôzāḇāḏ* "Yahweh has bestowed"; shortened form of *yᵉhôzāḇāḏ*).†

1. A Benjaminite from Gederah who joined David's forces at Ziklag (1 Chr. 12:4 [MT 5]; KJV "Josabad").

2. A man from the tribe of Manasseh who deserted Saul to join David at Ziklag as a commander of his army (1 Chr. 12:20).

3. Another Manassite commander of a thousand who deserted to David at Ziklag (1 Chr. 12:20).

4. A Levite appointed by Hezekiah as an overseer at the temple (2 Chr. 31:13).

5. A chief of the Levites who contributed to the Passover offering at the time of Josiah (2 Chr. 35:9; 1 Esdr. 1:9, "Joram").

6. A Levite, a son of Jeshua who helped count the temple vessels which Ezra returned from Babylon (Ezra 8:33; 1 Esdr. 8:63; KJV "Josabad").

7. A Levite among those who had married foreign women (Ezra 10:23). He may be the same as **6**.

8. A priest and descendant of Pashhur who married, then divorced a foreign woman (Ezra 10:22; 1 Esdr. 9:22, "Gedaliah"; KJV "Ocidelus").

9. A Levite who helped to interpret the Law as Ezra read it (Neh. 8:7; 1 Esdr. 9:48; KJV "Joazabdus"). He may be the same as **6** or **7**.

10. A chief of the Levites in charge of external repairs on the temple (Neh. 11:16). He may be the same as **6**, **7**, or **9**.

JOZACAR [jō′zə kär] (Heb. *yôzākār* "Yahweh has remembered").† A servant of King Joash of Judah who, with Jehozabad, murdered the king (2 Kgs. 12:21; KJV "Jozachar"; some MSS read "Jozabad"; so NIV). In the parallel account he is called Zabad (2 Chr. 24:26).

JOZADAK [jō′zə dăk] (Heb. *yôṣāḏāq* "Yahweh is righteous," shortened form of *yᵉhôṣāḏāq*). Alternate form of JEHOZADAK, the father of the high priest Jeshua/Joshua (Ezra 3:2, 8; 5:2; 10:18; Neh. 12:26).

JUBAL [jōō′bəl] (Heb. *yûḇāl* "horn player"). A son of Lamech and Adah, and the younger brother of Jabal. He was the "father" (or "inventor") of musical instruments (Gen. 4:21).

JUBILEE, YEAR OF (Heb. *šᵉnaṯ hayyôḇēl* "the year of the ram's horn").† The fiftieth year in a cycle of Sabbatical Years observed in ancient Israel, when land that had been leased by families to avert poverty reverted to its original owners, and indentured Israelite servants were set free. The sounding of the ram's horn throughout the land inaugurated the Year of Jubilee, which began on the Day of Atonement, the tenth day of the seventh month, Ethanim (Sept.-Oct.).

The Year of Jubilee brought to a close a cycle of seven Sabbatical Years (Lev. 25; cf. Exod. 23:10-11). God decreed that after every six years of planting the land the seventh year should be a "Sabbath" in which the land and all people and animals who worked it rested. Humans and animals then lived off the abundance of the sixth year's harvest (Lev. 25:20-21).

The proclamation of Jubilee had implications for Israelite society in the areas of land tenure and human servitude. While each of the twelve tribes had been assigned a portion of land upon entering Canaan, Yahweh had made it clear that the land belonged to him alone, and that the people sojourned there at his pleasure (Exod. 19:5; Lev. 25:23). Yet God's ownership did not preclude the Israelites from selling or leasing landholdings among themselves, particularly to avoid poverty.

During the years preceding the Jubilee the next-of-kin of those who had sold their land had the duty of buying back or "redeeming" it (v. 25), as did the original owners if they returned to prosperity (v. 26). This redemption price was to be calculated relative to the number of years during which the buyer had use of the property (vv. 15-17, 27). Special rules applied for redemption of houses and the fields of the Levites (vv. 28-34). The onset of the Year of Jubilee required that all land sold during the preceding forty-nine years be returned to the original owners or their descendants. The Jubilee is also mentioned in connection with

the dedication of a field to the sanctuary of the Lord (27:16-25). To redeem it the owner had to pay an additional fifth of the field's value, proportional to the number of years remaining between its redemption and the next Jubilee. If the field went unredeemed or was sold to someone else, it became the possession of the sanctuary priest upon the next Jubilee.

The phenomenon of indentured slavery in Israel was also addressed by the Jubilee legislation. When poverty forced an Israelite to sell himself into the service of a countryman, he was to be treated as a hired hand, not as a slave (25:40, 42). Then when the Year of Jubilee came, the indentured one and his sons were to be released so they could return to their own land.

Although scholars disagree over whether the Year of Jubilee was ever actually practiced in Israel because of its radical social implications, the institution stands as an example of God's concern for equality among his people and the maintenance of the ancient tribal lands.

JUBILEES (Gk. *tá Iōbēlaia, hoi Iōbēlaioi*), **BOOK OF**.† An important postbiblical Jewish writing, classified as an apocalypse, intended as a call to obedience to Torah, the law of God. Reckoned among the pseudepigraphal writings, this "Little Genesis" is a rewriting of Gen. 1–Exod. 12, presented as an angelic revelation to Moses on Mt. Sinai.

The author's many revisions stress that because the law, written and oral, goes back to Moses it is all the more to be obeyed. Accordingly, the book depicts the patriarchs as observing statutes and customs unknown in their day. The author places his own exhortations in their mouths and presents Abraham as a model of many virtues. The frequent quotation and paraphrase of Scripture is often followed by Halakhah (legal commentary) on some element in the narrative. The author is convinced that wholesale obedience to Torah and avoidance of Gentile practices will usher in a new age in which the Jewish people will once again enjoy God's favor.

A notable feature of this work is the emphasis on a special 364-day calendar and the theological importance attached to this, particularly as opposed to the lunar calendar. Certain days were to be sacred, others profane, and it was a crucial part of Torah to observe sabbaths and sacred festivals on the appropriate days. Related to this is the book's temporal understanding of world history, in which the period from creation to the Exodus is divided into forty-nine "Jubilees" of forty-nine years each.

The discovery of the Dead Sea Scrolls has yielded numerous theological and legal similarities between those Essene texts and the book of Jubilees. Indeed, two of the Qumran writings treat Jubilees as authoritative. Although Jubilees does not reflect the break with the Jewish religious establishment so prominent in the scrolls, it is quite likely that it stems from a group of Hasidim or Essenes who stood in the same line of tradition as the Qumran community.

Jubilees is to be dated toward the mid-second century B.C., and may have been written *ca.* 168-167, shortly before the pollution of the temple by Antiochus IV Epiphanes. The author of Jubilees was a Palestinian Jew who wrote in Hebrew. The work was translated into Greek and Syriac, and from Greek into Latin and Ethiopic. Only in Ethiopic is the whole work extant; fragments of Greek and Latin texts survive, and portions of Hebrew manuscripts were discovered at Qumran. The work was well known into the twelfth century A.D., then forgotten until the mid-nineteenth century.

JUCAL [jōō'kəl] (Heb. *yûḵāl* "Yahweh is powerful"). The son of Shelemiah; an opponent of Jeremiah who sought to kill the prophet by casting him into a cistern (Jer. 38:1-6). At 37:3 he is called Jehucal.

JUDA (Luke 3:26, KJV). *See* JODA.

JUDAH [jōō'də] (Heb. *y^ehûḏâ*; Gk. *Ioudas*).†

1. The fourth son of Jacob and Leah (Gen. 35:23; 46:12; Exod. 1:2; 1 Chr. 2:1). The etiological account at Gen. 29:35 derives the name from the hiphil form of Heb. *yāḏâ* "to throw or cast," "to praise" (cf. 49:8).

Virtually all the information available about Judah the man is found in Genesis. He plotted with his brothers to be rid of Joseph, but convinced them to sell the lad into slavery instead of killing him (Gen. 37:26-27). He married the Canaanite Shua and established a family (38:1-5), and his widowed daughter-in-law Tamar tricked him into impregnating her after his son Onan had failed to do so (vv. 8-30).

When famine struck Canaan after Joseph had gained renown in Egypt, Judah accompanied his brothers to buy food from Pharaoh's storehouses. Judah convinced Jacob (Israel) to allow his youngest brother Benjamin to go on a second journey to Egypt, as Joseph had demanded (43:3-5, 8-10). When Joseph employed a ruse to keep Benjamin with him (ch. 44), Judah asked that he be enslaved instead of the youth (vv. 18-33).

Like all of Jacob's sons, Judah (here probably the eponymous representative of the later social group [2]) accepted Joseph's invitation to settle in Egypt (46:12, 28). Jacob's blessing of Judah characterized him (or the tribe, according to critical scholars as reflecting here the time of David) as a ferocious lion, destined to be a ruler (49:8-12).

At Matt. 1:2 (KJV "Judas"); Luke 3:33 he is listed among the ancestors of Jesus.

2. The putative descendants of Judah; a tribe of Israel which became established in southern Palestine (cf. Heb. *yhd*, Arab. *whd* "lowland") after the Exodus, and subsequently a coalition of tribes which constituted the southern counterpart of the kingdom of Israel. The name occurs in Assyrian inscriptions as Akk. *Ia-ú-du* and the gentilic *Ia-ú-da-ai* "Jew."

I. Early History

During the wilderness wanderings Judah camped to the east of the tent of meeting, led by Nahshon the son of Amminadab (Num. 2:3); with Issachar and Zebulun the tribe formed a "division" of Israel which led the people on the march (v. 9; 10:14). The census figures given in Numbers place the population of the tribe at approximately seventy-five thousand (1:26-27; 2:4; 26:22); if not purely idealistic, these figures may indicate simply the equivalence of seventy-five basic

military units (Heb. *'elep*). Judah was among the tribes Moses commanded to stand upon Mt. Gerizim across the Jordan to pronounce blessings on Israel (Deut. 27:12). Moses' final blessing suggests that Judah was relatively insignificant at the time, requiring military aid from the other tribes (33:7).

During the conquest Judah, as one of the "Leah tribes," was in the thick of the battle which displaced the Canaanites from much of the hill country and the Negeb (Judg. 1:1-20; cf. Josh. 11:21-23), but with all Israel in general Judah was unable to drive out all of the indigenous population (Judg. 1:19).

Judah's territory (Josh. 15) encompassed primarily the central hill country (the region between Jerusalem and Hebron) and the largely uninhabitable Negeb (the desolate "wilderness of Judah"; Judg. 1:16). It was bounded by a combination of Benjaminite, Gibeonite, and Philistine cities to the north; by the Dead Sea to the east; by Edom to the south; and by unconquered Canaanite cities and Philistine territory to the west. In addition to the territory allotted to Simeon ("because the portion of the tribe of Judah was too large for them"; Josh. 19:1-9), other subgroups were assigned land within Judah: e.g., Caleb (14:13-15; 15:13-19), Jerahmeel (cf. 1 Sam. 27:10), Othniel (Josh. 15:19), and the Kenites (Judg. 1:16); some scholars contend that these lists reflect circumstances during David's kingship. Hebron, the largest town in Judah, was designated as one of the cities of refuge (Josh. 20:7), and the Levites received nine towns in Judah as part of their inheritance (21:4, 9-16).

The Israelites' inability to occupy all of Palestine resulted in the need to repulse a steady stream of attackers during the period of the judges (twelfth century B.C.). Othniel, the first of the judges, came from Judah (Judg. 3:9-11). Eventually the growing power of the Philistines and Ammonites led to the establishment of the monarchy in the eleventh century.

II. Monarchy

The Benjaminite Saul, Israel's ill-fated first king, enjoyed considerable support in Judah. Thirty thousands (contingents) of Judah responded to his demand for volunteers to repulse the Ammonite attack on Jabesh-gilead (1 Sam. 11:8), and ten thousands joined in the war against the Amalekites (15:4).

The Philistine attack at Socoh on Judah's western border provided the setting for one of David's first exploits, and led to a great victory over Israel's enemy (ch. 17). David's growing popularity aroused Saul's jealousy, forcing the young hero to flee, first to the Philistine city of Gath and then to Judah's desert of Ziph (22:5); Saul pursued David through the wilderness with no success, but David was finally forced to seek Philistine protection. David's ties with Judah remained strong; after rescuing the inhabitants of Ziklag from the Amalekites (ch. 30) he sent a portion of the spoils to the elders of Judah.

After Saul died in battle David was anointed king over Judah in Hebron (2 Sam. 2:1-4) and reigned there seven and a half years (vv. 10-11). Israel, however, was ruled by Saul's son Ishbosheth, whose two-year reign was marked by warfare between the two states (vv. 12-32). Upon the assassination of Ishbosheth, the northern tribes also acclaimed David as king, thus establishing a dual monarchy (5:1-5; cf. 1 Sam. 18:16). David moved quickly to consolidate his position. He captured Jerusalem from the Jebusites and made it the royal capital; he then journeyed from Kiriath-jearim in Judah to accompany the ark of the covenant to Jerusalem, which became the cultic center of Judah and Israel (2 Sam. 6:1-15).

When Absalom rebelled against David he too had himself anointed at Hebron (15:10-12). Judah's elders, fearful that the king would exact revenge for this act, refrained from welcoming David on his return to Jerusalem. But in an adroit political move David allayed their fears and succeeded in reuniting Judah and Israel (19:11-15; cf. vv. 8b-10). Israel, however, soon felt that David was showing undue favor to Judah, leading to a rebellion headed by the Benjaminite Sheba (19:41–20:2); using Judahite troops David suppressed this rebellion as well (20:4-22).

Solomon's reign (ca. 961-922) consisted in large measure of maintaining the territory acquired in his father's lifetime and exploiting the economic potential of perhaps the strongest and richest Near Eastern state of its time (1 Kgs. 4:24-25). The organization of "all Israel" into twelve districts to supply the royal household's needs (v. 7) may have exempted the southern component of the dual kingdom from Solomon's levies (cf. v. 19). Solomon's ambitious building program included fortification of several Judahite cities, all located on or near trade routes: Beth-shemesh, Ashan, Arad, Beer-sheba, Baalath-beer, and Hazar-addar. Judah was also the gateway to Israel for copper ore from the mines in the Timna valley and for goods imported through the Red Sea port of Ezion-geber. Perhaps of greatest impact on Judah's future was Solomon's construction of the temple at Jerusalem (ch. 6).

III. Southern Kingdom

Despite Solomon's success in maintaining the fragile coalition of north and south, his son Rehoboam's truculence toward the northern tribes led them to reject continued rule by the Davidic dynasty (1 Kgs. 12:1-17; 2 Chr. 10:1-17), thus producing two small, weak kingdoms from the remnants of what had been, briefly, a mighty nation. Yet from the outset, the kingdom of Judah enjoyed certain advantages over the northern kingdom: the Davidic dynasty remained intact in Judah, promoting a sense of continuity; and Jerusalem, the center of national political and religious life for nearly a century, remained in Judah. Although Judah's territory diminished, particularly in the south and west, Benjamin's loyalty to David's house secured Jerusalem for the southern kingdom. Henceforth, Judah's political life was marked internally by alternating episodes of brief glory and political intrigue, and externally by the need to fight or placate a host of enemies, both large and small.

Rehoboam (ca. 922-915) made no attempt to force the northern tribes back into political union, and he fortified against them some fifteen cities in northern Judah (11:5-12). Thus when the Egyptians under Pharaoh Shishak attacked numerous cities, including Jerusalem, they were unable to penetrate the central hill country (1 Kgs. 14:25-26; 2 Chr. 12:2ff.).

During the reigns of Abijah (915-913) and Asa (ca.

913-873) Judah faced border incidents with Israel (ch. 13) and Ethiopian attack (14:9-14). Baasha of Israel invaded Benjamin, threatening Jerusalem, but Asa bribed Ben-hadad I of Damascus to break his treaty with the northern kingdom and send an army into Galilee to draw off Baasha's troops (1 Kgs. 15:16-22).

Asa's son Jehoshaphat (ca. 873-849) enjoyed a fruitful reign. Like his father a loyal Yahwist, he fortified his kingdom both morally and militarily (2 Chr. 17; 19:4-11). Although convinced by Ahab of Israel to join an ill-fated attack on Ramoth-gilead (ch. 18), Jehoshaphat later successfully waged war against Moab and Ammon (20:1-30). An attempt to revive the Red Sea trade came to naught when the newly constructed ships were wrecked (1 Kgs. 22:48-49; 2 Chr. 20:35-37).

Jehoshaphat strengthened peaceful relations with Israel through a marriage alliance involving his son Jehoram and Athaliah, the daughter (or sister) of the Omride Ahab. But Judah's fortunes were reversed during Jehoram's reign (ca. 849-842). Edom revolted, as did Libnah on the Philistine border (2 Kgs. 8:20-22). Moreover, upon taking the throne Jehoram slaughtered all his brothers, and his queen fostered pagan worship in Jerusalem (2 Chr. 21:4, 11). Castigated by the Israelite prophet Elijah, Jehoram came to endure God's punishment in the form of sickness and strife (vv. 12-20).

Ahaziah, an inexperienced young man, ruled briefly (842) under the sway of his mother and her advisors. Following an abortive attack on the Arameans in concert with Israel, Ahaziah became a victim of Jehu's coup in the northern kingdom (2 Kgs. 9:1-28; 2 Chr. 22:1-9). Athaliah then seized power in Judah (842-837) and systematically liquidated the royal family; only the infant Joash escaped death (2 Kgs. 11:1-3; 2 Chr. 22:10-12). Intrigue followed intrigue. The chief priest Jehoiada sheltered Joash (Jehoash) for six years while he himself formed alliances with the commanders of loyalist military units and the Levites. At age seven Joash was crowned king, whereupon Athaliah was executed and the Baal temple destroyed (2 Kgs. 11:4-21; 2 Chr. 23). Jehoiada apparently acted as Joash's regent, and under his tutelage the king repaired the temple (2 Kgs. 12:1-16; 2 Chr. 24:1-14). Upon the chief priest's death, however, Joash abruptly took up pagan ways (2 Chr. 24:17-19; cf. 2 Kgs. 12:3 [MT 4]). Not long afterward the Arameans invaded Judah, either plundering (2 Chr. 24:23) or exacting tribute from Jerusalem (2 Kgs. 12:17-18). Joash, wounded in battle, was subsequently killed in his bed by a faction avenging his murder of the prophet Zechariah (2 Chr. 24:25-26; cf. 2 Kgs. 12:20-21).

The growth of Assyrian power in the early eighth century cowed the Arameans, allowing Israel and Judah some measure of peace. Yet Amaziah of Judah (ca. 800-783) waged war against Edom (2 Kgs. 14:7) and enticed Jehoash of Israel to a confrontation at Beth-shemesh; Amaziah was captured and Israel invaded Jerusalem (2 Kgs. 14:8-14; 2 Chr. 25:5-24).

Both Israel and Judah experienced a renaissance under kings Jeroboam II (ca. 793-753) and Uzziah (or Azariah; ca. 783-742). Uzziah restored Judah's military and commercial fortunes, repairing Jerusalem's defenses and reequipping the army, regaining control of Edom, fortifying caravan routes in the Negeb, and reopening the Red Sea port of Ezion-geber (2 Kgs. 14:22; 2 Chr. 26:9-15).

But soon this prosperity ended as the campaigns of Tiglath-pileser III of Assyria (745-727) cast a shadow over the small states of Syria-Palestine. King Menahem of Israel offered tribute to Assyria, but his son Pekah formed an anti-Assyrian coalition with Damascus and the Philistine cities; when Jotham of Judah (742-735) refused to join the coalition, its members made ready to attack Judah (2 Kgs. 15:37). Ahaz (735-715) had barely succeeded Jotham when the kingdom was simultaneously invaded from the north, west, and south (16:5-6; 2 Chr. 28:5-8, 17-18). In desperation Ahaz appealed to Tiglath-pileser for aid (2 Kgs. 16:7-8; 2 Chr. 28:16; cf. Isa. 7:1–8:15). Assyrian forces swiftly lanced southward through Syria, Palestine, and Philistia, halting only at the Egyptian border. As a vassal of Assyria, Ahaz succumbed to foreign religious influence (2 Kgs. 16:10-18; 2 Chr. 28:24-25).

After Israel fell to the Assyrians in 722/721, Ahaz' son and successor Hezekiah (715-687) determined to renew his nation's loyalty to Yahweh and to regain unobtrusively its political independence. He destroyed age-old pagan worship sites (2 Kgs. 18:4; 2 Chr. 31:1), purified the temple, and reestablished regular Yahwistic observances there in an attempt to centralize worship (chs. 29–31). Although long encouraged to join widespread revolt throughout the Assyrian Empire, Hezekiah waited until after the death of Sargon in 705; he then withheld tribute (2 Kgs. 18:7) and moved swiftly to fortify Jerusalem and other Judean cities (20:20; 2 Chr. 32:1-5, 30), joined yet another anti-Assyrian coalition, and allied with Egypt (cf. Isa. 30:1-7; 31:1-3). Assyrian retribution was swift; Sennacherib smashed all resistance in Syria and Palestine in 701 (2 Kgs. 18:13-16). Forty-six fortified cities in Judah fell, and though Jerusalem withstood a siege (chs. 18–19; 2 Chr. 32; Isa. 36–37), Hezekiah was forced to sue for terms.

Hezekiah's young son Manasseh (ca. 687-642) quickly submitted as a vassal of Assyria, then at the peak of its power. Manasseh, and his son Amon (742-740), reverted to the injustice and pagan practices common in Ahaz' day, paying homage to Assyria's gods and permitting the worship of Canaanite deities to displace that of Yahweh in the temple (2 Kgs. 21:3-7; 2 Chr. 33:2-9; cf. 2 Kgs. 21:10-11, 16; 24:3-4).

Assyria's vast empire proved to be indefensible, with frequent revolts and the constant threat of powerful enemies including Egypt in the west, Indoeuropeans such as the Medes in the north, and Babylonia in the east. Smaller states thus were given breathing space, and Judah finally regained independence under Josiah (ca. 640-609). Established on the throne through a pro-Yahwistic coup, Josiah purified the temple and initiated widespread religious reform, which gained impetus through discovery of the "book of the law" (2 Kgs. 22–23; 2 Chr. 34). In a desperate bid to turn back invading Babylonians from the heartland of the crumbling empire (the capital Nineveh had fallen in 612), Assyria allied with its old enemy Egypt. When an Egyptian army under Pharaoh Neco II advanced

toward Carchemish on the Euphrates river to reinforce the Assyrians, Josiah inexplicably sallied forth to attack the surprised Neco, only to die in battle in 609 (2 Kgs. 23:29-30; 2 Chr. 35:20-25). Josiah's son Jehoahaz (Shallum) reigned only three months before Neco deposed and deported him, placing his pro-Egyptian brother Eliakim (Jehoiakim; 609-598) on Judah's throne and extracting heavy tribute (2 Kgs. 23:31-35; 2 Chr. 36:2-4; cf. Jer. 22:10-12).

Initially the resurgent Babylonians lacked the strength to attack Egypt, which had taken control of Syria and Palestine. But in 605 Nebuchadnezzar routed the Egyptians at Carchemish. The Babylonian advance was temporarily checked when Nebuchadnezzar returned home to be crowned king, but by late 604 his armies had returned, taking Ashdod and deporting its leading citizens. Faced with the prospect of fighting the Babylonian army, Jehoiakim pledged his allegiance to Nebuchadnezzar instead (2 Kgs. 24:1a), but when a pitched battle on the Egyptian border caused the Babylonians to withdraw temporarily, Jehoiakim foolishly rebelled (v. 1b). Nebuchadnezzar sent various contingents against Judah (v. 2; Jer. 35:11) until his army could march against it in 598. Jehoiakim's revolt was predictably short-lived. Nebuchadnezzar entered Jerusalem, deported Jehoiakim in chains, and looted the temple (2 Chr. 36:6-7). The Babylonians placed Jehoiakim's son Jehoiachin (Coniah) on the throne, but after three months he was taken to Babylon, along with the cream of Judah's nobility, military leaders, intellectuals, and artisans, and an immense treasure (2 Kgs. 24:8-16; 2 Chr. 36:9-10; Jer. 22:24-30). Then Jehoiachin's uncle Mattaniah (Zedekiah) was placed on the throne.

Judah was a confused and agitated nation after the deportation of 597. Signs of Judah's impending death abound in the prophetic writings (e.g., Jer. 27–29; Ezek. 21:25-27). No longer able to await the ideal moment, Zedekiah rebelled against Babylon with no outside support (2 Chr. 36:11-16). The Babylonians reacted swiftly and decisively, blockading Jerusalem in early 588 (2 Kgs 25:1; Jer. 21:3-7; 52:4) and reducing Judah's outlying fortified cities one by one. The Babylonians withdrew briefly when an Egyptian army advanced on Jerusalem, but soon resumed the siege (37:5-10). Jerusalem held out for an entire year. Zedekiah wished to surrender (38:14-23), but the Babylonians breached the city walls in July 587, just as the defenders' food supply ran out. The king sought to escape but was captured and deported to Babylon (2 Kgs. 25:4-7; Jer. 52:6-11). Nebuzaradan, the commander of Nebuchadnezzar's guard, looted the temple, put Jerusalem to the torch, and leveled the city walls. Certain of the leaders of Judah were hauled before Nebuchadnezzar and executed, and another group was deported, leaving only the poorest citizens behind (2 Kgs. 25:8-21; 2 Chr. 36:17-20; Jer. 39:8-10).

Judah was subsequently organized into a Babylonian province. Gedaliah was appointed governor but ruled only briefly before assassinated (2 Kgs. 25:22-25; Jer. 40:7–41:18).

IV. Exile and After

After the Babylonian conquest Judah was an impoverished, virtually depopulated land, a half-century of whose history is silent. Nebuchadnezzar continued to campaign elsewhere in Palestine and Egypt, but returned to Judah to conduct a third deportation in 582 (Jer. 52:30). Some fifty years later internal dissension, combined with Persian invasions, led to the end of the Babylonian Empire when Cyrus entered Babylon in October 539. In 538 Cyrus issued a decree ordering the reestablishment of the Jews in Palestine, including provisions for rebuilding the temple in Jerusalem (2 Chr. 36:22-23; Ezra 1:1-4; 6:3-5).

Sheshbazzar, a prince of Judah, was placed in charge of the restoration, and set out with a band of former exiles of unknown size. The early years, characterized by the prophet Zechariah as days of "small things" (Zech. 4:10), were filled with hardship and unfulfilled dreams of recapturing past glories. As other groups of exiles filtered into Judah, friction developed between them and the inhabitants of the land, aggravated by poor crop yields (Hag. 1:9-11; 2:15-17) and slow progress on the temple's reconstruction (v. 3; Ezra 3:12).

Sheshbazzar's nephew Zerubbabel succeeded him as governor (perhaps in 538), and a series of high priests, beginning with Jeshua (5) assumed responsibility for spiritual affairs in Judah. Despite opposition by Tattenai, the Persian governor of Transeuphrates, which included Palestine, and others, the temple was completed in 515 (6:13-18).

Although it is difficult to determine the chronology precisely, in the mid-fifth century Nehemiah was appointed governor of the Persian province of Judah and given permission to rebuild the walls of Jerusalem (Neh. 2:1-8). In what may have been a second term as governor, Nehemiah instituted various social and religious reforms intended to ensure the stability of the postexilic community (ch. 13). Perhaps during this phase of Nehemiah's tenure as governor the scribe Ezra also arrived from Babylon (Ezra 7:1-26), restoring to prominence the law of Moses (Neh. 8).

Included in the 333 B.C. conquest of Palestine by Alexander the Great, Judah came under Seleucid rule during the Hellenistic period and subsequently formed the core of the Hasmonean state. By the time of the Roman occupation of Palestine, the name Judah, or more properly Judea, designated a region rather than a self-governing political unit (cf. Luke 1:39).

In the New Testament Jesus is presented as a descendant of the tribe of Judah (Heb. 7:14; cf. Rev. 5:5). At Rev. 7:14 Judah heads the roster of "the sealed."

See further the individual articles on specific persons and events.

Bibliography. J. Bright, *A History of Israel,* 3rd ed. (Philadelphia: 1981); J. M. Miller and J. H. Hayes, *A History of Ancient Israel and Judah* (Philadelphia: 1986); H.-J. Zobel, "yᵉhûḍâ," *TDOT* 5 (1986): 482-499.

3. A Levite, ancestor of a family that supervised work on the postexilic temple (Ezra 3:9). He may be the same as HODAVIAH **4.**

4. A Levite who had married foreign women (Ezra 10:23).

5. The son of Hassenuah; a leader who settled in Jerusalem after the Exile (Neh. 11:9).

6. A Levite who returned from exile with Zerubbabel (Neh. 12:8).

7. A leader of Judah who participated in the dedication of Jerusalem's rebuilt city wall (Neh. 12:34).

8. A priest and musician present at the dedication of the wall (Neh. 12:36).

9. An ancestor of Jesus (Luke 3:30; KJV "Juda").

JUDAISM. *See* JEWS, JUDAISM.

JUDAIZERS.* While the word "Judaizers" does not appear in the New Testament, it has come to represent the situation addressed by Paul's letter to the Galatians. It derives from Gk. *Ioudaïzō* at Gal. 2:14 (RSV "to live like Jews"; KJV "to live as do the Jews"; cf. Esth. 8:17, LXX, for Heb. *yāhaḍ,* hithpael; KJV "became Jews," RSV "declared themselves Jews"), where it refers to the adoption of Jewish practices by Gentiles. The "Judaizers" were those who sought to compel the Galatian Christians to be circumcised.

The fundamental problem facing the Galatians was that certain persons from outside their own congregations, who are only briefly mentioned, were making distinctions among Christians—that is, between themselves as better and the Galatians as lesser Christians. Gal. 4:17 can be translated "They exercise zeal [cf. 1:14] toward you not rightly. Rather they desire to exclude you so that you will be jealous of them." In Paul's view, any making of distinctions among Christians creates a situation of compulsion, inasmuch as a way is offered to the "lesser" Christians to rise to the higher level by conforming to certain behaviors. The compulsion was for the Galatians to be circumcised (6:12) and, apparently, to observe Jewish feast days, new moons, Sabbaths, and perhaps Sabbatical Years (4:10). In Paul's view this amounted to the substitution of "a different gospel" for the true gospel (1:6), which would make the preaching and hearing of the gospel vain (3:4; 4:11), and a retreat from the Spirit to the flesh (3:2-3). The Galatians were about to receive circumcision (perhaps some already had) without fully understanding it as an institution into a life in which all of the Torah was observed (5:2-3).

Part of Paul's counterargument is that the making of distinctions among Christians and the compulsion that goes with it were rejected not only by the apostle himself but also by the leaders of the Jerusalem church (2:1-10; cf. Acts 15:1-29; *see* APOSTOLIC COUNCIL). The making of distinctions (Gal. 2:12-13) and the compulsion that goes with it (v. 14) did, however, arise later at Antioch, affecting even some of those who were leaders in the solution that had been reached at Jerusalem. Perhaps Paul tells of his agreement with the Jerusalem apostles and his confrontation with Peter at Antioch because the "Judaizers" who were troubling the Galatians (cf. 5:10, 12) claimed some association with the authoritative leaders of the Jerusalem church. They were at least probably related in some way to the "false brethren" of 2:4 (cf. Acts 15:1, 5) and those who came to Antioch as representatives of James (Gal. 2:12). But for Paul there could be no appeal to human authority where "the truth of the gospel" (v. 14) that he had received from Christ and had passed on to the Galatians (1:8-12) was at stake. The same disdain for human opinion (v. 10) was in Paul's view not held by the "Judaizers," whose actions were carried out partly to avoid persecution—apparently Jewish persecution directed only against Christians whose understanding of faith in Christ threatened adherence to the law (6:12).

Judaizing tendencies continued to be a problem confronted by Paul. At Corinth one of the many emphases of a troublesome group of opponents was the authority of the Jerusalem apostles (2 Cor. 11:4-5; cf. 1 Cor. 1:12; 3:21-23). Paul's letter to the Christians at Rome presents in a modified and developed form much of the teaching on the law and the gospel found in Galatians; perhaps a similar problem is being confronted. At Philippi, as at Galatia, a campaign to circumcise Gentile Christians may have developed (Phil. 3:2-3). At Colossae circumcision, observance of food laws, and observance of feast days, new moons, and Sabbaths were aspects of a heresy being urged on the Colossian Christians (Col. 2:8, 11, 16-23). In the Pastoral Epistles a heresy is spoken of which is concerned with the law, circumcision, and other aspects of Judaism (1 Tim. 1:7; Titus 1:10, 14; 3:9).

JUDAS [jōō′dəs] (Gk. *Ioudas*, from Heb. *yᵉhûdâ*).†
   1. Judas Maccabeus; the third son of Mattathias and leader of the revolt against Antiochus IV Epiphanes (1 Macc. 2:4). Having already fled Jerusalem when Antiochus desecrated the temple in 167 B.C. (vv. 1-14), Mattathias and his sons precipitated the revolt against Seleucid paganization by refusing to offer the required pagan sacrifice (vv. 15-48).

Judas succeeded his father a year later and led the rebels to defeat first the combined Gentile and Samaritan forces of the Syrian governor Apollonius (3:10-12) and then the large army of Seron at Bethhoron (vv. 13-26). He routed the Syrians under Gorgias and Lysias, enabling the Jews to recapture Mt. Zion and purify the temple on 25 Chislev 164, the event commemorated by the Feast of Hanukkah (4:36-61). Judas then attacked Idumea to the south, Ammon and Gilead to the east, across the Jordan river, Galilee to the north, and the coastal plain to the west, thus securing Judean political freedom (ch. 5). Lysias declared himself regent with the young Antiochus V Eupator and marched to defeat Judas at Beth-zechariah (6:32-47). The Syrian then laid siege to Jerusalem, but pressured by the advance of the legitimate regent Philip, granted the Jews religious freedom in exchange for Judas' pledge to destroy the walls of Jerusalem (vv. 55-63).

Judas then sought political freedom from the Seleucids. Demetrius I Soter, however, usurped the throne, assassinating Antiochus V and Lysias and confirming the appointment of the Hellenistic sympathizer Alcimus as high priest (7:1-25). Demetrius then dispatched troops under Bacchides to march on Judea and, when the Hasidim soon abandoned support of Alcimus and returned to Judas' aid, reinforcements under Nicanor. Judas defeated Nicanor at Adasa (vv. 26-50) and formed a treaty with Rome (ch. 8). Demetrius then sent Bacchides and Alcimus back to Ju-

dah; many of the Judean soldiers fled and, before Roman assistance could arrive, Judas was slain in battle at Elasa (9:1-22). He was succeeded by his brother Jonathan.

See HASMONEANS.

2. Judas the son of Chalphi. A commander in the army of Jonathan (1 Macc. 11:70) who with Mattathias **2** remained with Jonathan when all the others fled in the ambush at Hazor.

3. A son of Simon Maccabeus and brother of John Hyrcanus. Judas and John were commissioned as leaders of the fight for the Jewish nation when their father, Simon, had grown old; together they defeated Cendebeus (1 Macc. 16:2-10).

4. One of those who wrote to Aristobulus and the Jews in Egypt; apparently a person of high standing in Jerusalem (2 Macc. 1:10). Some have identified him with Judas Maccabeus.

5. (Matt. 1:2-3, KJV). *See* JUDAH **1**.

6. A brother of Jesus, one of four mentioned at Matt. 13:55; Mark 6:3. He is generally held to be "Jude, the brother of James," author of the Letter of Jude (Jude 1).

7. Judas Iscariot [ĭs kâr′ē ət]; one of the twelve apostles and the betrayer of Jesus. The meaning of the appellative Iscariot (cf. Luke 22:3; John 14:22) remains uncertain, although various etymologies have been suggested, including "liar" (cf. Aram. *'yš šqr'* "man of the lie"), "dyer," "dagger bearer" (from Lat. *sicarius*), and "man of Issachar." A commonly accepted meaning is "man from Kerioth," supported by its reading as a gentilic by several MSS; the location of Kerioth is uncertain, but it is believed to be in Judea. The same name is associated with Judas' father Simon at John 6:71; 13:26.

Judas Iscariot is infamous for his betrayal of Jesus, attested by all four Gospels (Matt. 26:47-56 par.) and foretold by Jesus himself (John 6:70-71). He accomplished this heinous act by leading the soldiers and officers of the chief priests and Pharisees to the garden, where he betrayed Jesus by a prearranged signal—a kiss of greeting.

Although Judas is mentioned in all the lists of the apostles, his selection and calling are not described. It may be assumed that his call was not different from that of the other apostles. His general behavior was probably not different either; he evidently heard the words of the Savior, saw the miracles, and performed the various responsibilities of the disciples. According to John 12:5-6; 13:29, his penury as treasurer of the group was tempered by greed and theft. Indeed, greed prompted Judas to go to the chief priests and bargain with them for the betrayal of Jesus (Matt. 26:14-16 par.).

Judas plotted and waited for an opportunity to betray Jesus. During the Passover meal, Jesus predicted that one of the disciples would betray him; Judas left the room and continued to follow his plan. Familiar with Jesus' habits, Judas found an opportunity and led the soldiers to the garden of Gethsemane where, as prearranged, he betrayed the Master with a kiss. After Jesus had been condemned to death, Judas was overwhelmed with remorse. He went to the chief priests and elders and, throwing down the thirty pieces of silver he had received from them, went and hanged himself (27:3-5; Acts 1:18-20).

Speculation abounds concerning the phenomena of the betrayal of Jesus by Judas, from the point of view both of theology and the accomplishment of the atonement through the Cross as presented in the biblical account, and of the dynamics of the personality of Judas. Why did Jesus choose Judas and entrust him with the moneybox? Why did Judas first join the disciples and then turn traitor? Was he attempting to force Jesus to exercise temporal—or suprahuman—power? There are, however, no certain answers.

8. The son (or brother) of James; one of the twelve apostles—not to be confused with Judas Iscariot—mentioned only at Luke 6:16; John 14:22. He is thought to be the same as Thaddaeus (or Lebbaeus) named at Matt. 10:3 (so KJV; cf. RSV mg.); Mark 3:18. Some scholars identify him with **6.**

9. Judas the Galilean; a Zealot and the leader of an insurrection during the census of A.D. 6-7, which represented the imposition of Roman rule and taxation on Judea (Acts 5:37).

10. An otherwise unknown person in whose house on Straight Street Paul stayed in Damascus (Acts 9:11). Paul was evidently baptized and commissioned in this man's house.

11. Judas Barsabbas; a prominent member (and "prophet") in the church at Jerusalem, chosen by the apostles and elders to accompany Paul and Barnabas in encouraging the Gentiles in Antioch, Syria, and Cilicia (Acts 15:22-35). Judas and Barnabas were to explain in person the decision of the church in Jerusalem concerning the responsibility of the Gentile Christians with regard to the Mosaic law. According to the KJV of v. 34 (omitted by RSV, NIV; cf. JB mg.), Judas returned to Jerusalem without his companion Silas. He may be the brother of Joseph Barsabbas (**16**).

JUDAS, GOSPEL OF. * An apocryphal gospel described by Irenaeus (*Adv. haer.* i.28.9) and mentioned in Epiphanius' writings against heresies (*Haer.* xxxviii.1.5). Ascribed to the Cainite Gnostic sect, it was probably written in the mid-second century A.D. No portion of the work survives. According to Irenaeus, it represents Judas Iscariot in a favorable light as an enlightened Gnostic who betrayed Jesus for the noble purpose of bringing about the redemption of mankind.

JUDE, LETTER OF. † The last of the Catholic (or General) Epistles of the New Testament.

I. Author

Although he refers to aspects of the apostolic period as somewhat in the past, the author presents himself as "Jude, a servant of Jesus Christ and brother of James" (Jude 1). He is traditionally identified as one of Jesus' brothers (Matt. 13:55; Mark 6:3; JUDAS **6**), rather than Judas (**8**) the son (or brother) of James listed among Jesus' disciples at Luke 6:16; John 14:22. Some scholars regard the book as pseudonymous.

II. Contents

Following the opening salutation (vv. 1-2), Jude explains the reason for writing: despite his eagerness to write of "common salvation" (v. 3), he finds himself compelled to address a negative theme, a caution against "ungodly persons who pervert the grace of our God into licentiousness" and deny the messiahship of Christ (v. 4). These false teachers, furthermore, had interrupted the Christian love feasts with their carousing (v. 12). Thus prompted by an unforeseen development, Jude decided to defend against heresy the faith "once for all delivered to the saints" (v. 3).

In vv. 5-16 Jude reminds the faithful that the heretics, whom he compares to "waterless clouds," "wild waves of the sea," and "wandering stars," would not escape divine punishment (vv. 12-13), just as earlier rebels—the fallen angels and the inhabitants of the wicked cities of Sodom and Gomorrah (vv. 6-7)—did not escape. In fact, he concludes, their doom had been announced long ago by Enoch, who prophesied about a future judgment for "all the ungodly" (vv. 14-15).

Toward the end of this short work, Jude exhorts the recipients to increase their "most holy faith," to pray in the Holy Spirit, and to support one another in love—thereby resisting the immorality practiced by their intruders (vv. 20-22). In the closing doxology, Jude points to God, in whose glorious presence they will one day rejoice (v. 24), and to "the only God, our Savior through Jesus Christ" (vv. 24-25).

III. Addressees and Date

Jude addresses the letter to the "beloved in God the Father" (v. 1), but neither identifies these readers nor their place of residence. Some scholars have suggested that the heretics attacked in the work represented an early branch of Gnosticism, the charges are sufficiently broad as to apply to most any faction. The recipients of the epistle may well be Jewish-Christians somewhere in Asia Minor.

Scholars frequently have noted many similarities between Jude and 2 Peter, especially 2 Pet. 2 (cf. verbal similarities; e.g., Jude 13 and 2 Pet. 2:17). Yet similarities to 1 Enoch (e.g., Jude 6-15) and the Assumption of Moses (e.g., Jude 12-14, 16) are absent in 2 Peter. Arguments have been adduced that both Jude and 2 Peter were the earlier, as well as that both relied on an independent source, a homiletic work used to support those in danger of being tempted by a heresy of a Gnostic nature. Most recent scholars, however, favor the dependence of 2 Peter on Jude (*see* PETER, SECOND LETTER OF). Thus the date of Jude should be sought *ca.* A.D. 90.

IV. Canonicity

Despite its reliance on the pseudepigraphic works noted above, Jude's little tract gained considerable respect among Church Fathers of the second century, including Clement of Alexandria and Tertullian, and it was accepted in the Muratorian canon. Yet Eusebius (*ca.* 324) called the work "spurious" and "disputed" (*HE* ii.23.25; 25.3; vi.13.6; 14.1). By the time of Athanasius (367) it had been accepted as the last of the Catholic Letters.

Bibliography. Richard J. Bauckham, *Jude, 2 Peter.* WBC (1983); B. Reicke, *The Epistles of James, Peter, and Jude.* AB 37 (1964).

JUDEA [jo͞o dē'ə] (Gk. *Ioudaia*).† The Greek and Latin form of Judah. In biblical usage it occurs first in accounts dating from the Persian period (Ezra; Nehemiah; cf. Tob. 1:18) as the designation for the postexilic Jewish state.

Although in preexilic times Judah comprised essentially the southern half of Palestine (approximately 5180 sq. km. [2000 sq. mi.]), in the Persian period it was reduced to primarily the small region around Jerusalem. In the broadest sense, the independent Maccabean state encompassed nearly all of Palestine, but in reality this larger "empire" was governed by a smaller Judea, along with Samaria and Galilee a "district" of Palestine (cf. 1 Macc. 11:28, 34; Strabo *Geog.* xvi.2.21); Herod the Great was king over much the same territory. The Judea of Herod's son, the ethnarch Archelaus, included Idumea and Samaria, but not Galilee and Perea (cf. Matt. 19:1; Luke 23:5; Acts 10:37). Subsequently Judea was incorporated into the Roman province of Syria, ruled from Caesarea by Roman-appointed procurators (cf. Luke 3:1; RSV "governor").

The wilderness of Judea, where John the Baptist first preached (Matt. 3:1), was the barren region between the central hill country and the Dead Sea and between Jerusalem and Hebron.

JUDGE (Heb. *šōpēṭ*).† In a special, technical sense, one of the charismatic leaders who "delivered" Israel or a portion of that entity during the premonarchic period of the Israelite confederation.

The term derives from common Semitic *špṭ*, which means basically "to exercise authority" and thus "to govern" (e.g., MT, 1 Kgs. 3:9; 2 Kgs. 15:5). The twelve persons recorded in the book of Judges as having "judged" Israel (the noun *šōpēṭ* is not used) are depicted as "saviors" (*mōšīᵃ*) empowered by Yahweh to lead one or more tribes in resolving a particular crisis (e.g., Othniel delivered Judah from the hands of Cushan-rishathaim [3:1-11]; Gideon of Manasseh led a coalition of northern tribes against the Midianites [chs. 6–8]); the office was temporary, and no dynastic succession was established. The scant information provided about the six "minor" judges (Shamgar, Tola, Jair, Ibzan, Elon, Abdon) may indicate that their administrations were relatively peaceful. The complex chronology of the book suggests that several of the judgeships overlapped. Moreover, many scholars contend that during the so-called period of the judges Israel was a loosely knit confederation of relatively autonomous tribes (identified by earlier scholars as an amphictyony), bound primarily by their common allegiance to Yahweh as acknowledged through the Shechem covenant (Josh. 24; *see* ISRAEL *I*).

Although Heb. *šōpēṭ* and related forms do occur with reference to the administration of justice in the more common legal sense, that function was performed typically by the elders or family heads with regard to civil matters (e.g., Exod. 18:13-26; Deut. 1:13-17; cf. Ruth 4:1-12); only during the Monarchy was justice administered by royally appointed officials (cf. 2 Chr. 19:5-7), and even then generally by the king (cf. 1 Kgs. 7:7; 1 Chr. 23:4). Matters of religious interpretation were adjudicated by the priests (e.g., Deut. 17:12).

With regard to God as judge *see* JUDGMENT. *See also* JUST, JUSTICE.

Bibliography. J. L. McKenzie, *The World of the Judges* (Englewood Cliffs: 1966); A. D. H. Mayes, *Israel in the Period of the Judges.* SBT, 2nd ser. 29 (1974).

JUDGES, BOOK OF.† The second book of the Former Prophets and the seventh of the Old Testament, recounting aspects of Israel's history between the death of Joshua and the birth of Samuel.

I. Contents

The book opens with a summary of the Israelite conquest of Canaan (Judg. 1:1–2:5). Recorded are the invasion of the south by Judah and Simeon (1:1-21), the incomplete conquest by the Joseph tribes, Ephraim and Manasseh (vv. 22-29), and the fortunes of the northern tribes (including Dan, here still located west of Benjamin along the Philistine plain; vv. 30-36). The introduction concludes with a religious assessment of the Conquest: having disobeyed Yahweh's command to make no covenant with the indigenous population, Israel would now face them as adversaries (2:1-5).

The core of the book focuses on the activities of the various judges (Heb. *šōpᵉṭîm*, from which it derives its name) who "saved" and "judged" (or "ruled"; *see* JUDGE) Israel at the time of the Confederation (2:6–16:31). A theological introduction (2:6–3:6) distinguishes the Israelites of Joshua's time from the present generation (2:6-10) and sets forth the cyclic pattern of Israel's disobedience, a divinely appointed punishment, repentance and the sending of a "savior," and a period of "rest" under the judge's administration (vv. 11-19); 2:20–3:6 views the events to follow as Yahweh's "testing of Israel." Summaries of the careers of two "major" judges follow—Othniel of Judah, who delivered Israel from oppression by Cushan-rishathaim (3:7-11), and the Benjaminite Ehud, who foiled King Eglon of Moab (vv. 12-30)—followed by a brief mention of Shamgar, who slaughtered six hundred Philistines (v. 31). Chs. 4–5 recount the defeat of Sisera and the Canaanites in the plain of Esdraelon by Deborah of Issachar, aided by Barak of Naphtali; ch. 4 is a prose account and ch. 5 the twelfth-century B.C. Song of Deborah. The narrative concerning Gideon (Jerubbaal) of Manasseh (6:1–8:32) includes a detailed account of his call and the expulsion of the invading Midianites (chs. 6–7), the displeasure of the Ephraimites at not being summoned sooner (8:1-3), Gideon's continued pursuit of the Midianites (vv. 4-17), and his refusal to accept kingship (vv. 22-23). By contrast, his son Abimelech openly seeks kingship, slaughters all but Jotham of his seventy brothers, suppresses rebellion at Shechem, and is mortally wounded by a woman at Thebez (ch. 9). Brief notice is made of the judges Tola of Issachar and Jair of Gilead (10:1-5), followed by an introduction to the remaining five judges: the apostasy of Israel and the resultant oppression (vv. 6-16). The next pericope relates the summons of Jephthah, illegitimate son of Gilead and head of an outlaw band in Hauran, and his defeat of the Ammonites (10:17–11:33); Jephthah's unfortunate vow (vv. 30-31, 34-40); and his punishment of the recalcitrant Ephraimites (the "Shibboleth" incident; 12:1-6). The judges Ibzan of Bethlehem (in Judah), Elon of Zebulun, and Abdon from Ephraim are mentioned in vv. 8-15. The career of Samson of Dan is preserved in chs. 13–16: his birth and Nazirite vow (ch. 13), his marriage to a Philistine woman and various mighty feats against the Philistines (chs. 14–15), his relationship with and betrayal by Delilah (16:4-22), and his destruction of the Philistine temple of Dagon—and himself (vv. 23-31).

The concluding chapters record other events of the period. To atone for stealing silver from his mother, Micah the Ephraimite builds a shrine and enlists a Levite as priest (ch. 17); the Danites migrate to new territory in the north, kidnapping en route Micah's Levite and installing him as priest of their shrine at Laish (ch. 18). Chs. 19–20 recount the rape murder of a Levite's concubine by the Benjaminites of Gilead and the punitive wars of the other tribes against Benjamin; ch. 21 depicts measures to obtain wives for the Benjaminites and thus preserve the tribe.

II. Setting

The events recorded in the book of Judges provide insight into the formative period of Israel in Canaan (twelfth-eleventh centuries). The various accounts accord with the understanding of early Israel as a loose confederation of basically autonomous tribes (e.g., 17:6; 21:25, "every man did what was right in his own eyes"; cf. also the varieties of religious practice; e.g., chs. 17–18). Although the judges are portrayed as delivering or ruling "the people of Israel," the narratives suggest that their spheres of influence actually were limited to a particular tribe (cf. 3:27-29; 12:8-15) or an impromptu coalition (e.g., 5:13-18; 6:34-35). Instances of bitter conflict between tribes (12:1-6; ch. 20) are tempered by concern for the survival of the covenant community (ch. 21).

Chronological references in the book of Judges, which total 410 years, are difficult to correlate with a span of little more than two centuries between the Exodus and the reign of Saul as delimited by literary and archaeological sources. Some of the figures given may be rounded or figurative numbers (e.g., forty, eighty, and twenty years, probably multiples of a standard generation); yet even if a generation were reckoned more realistically at twenty-five years, the total could not reasonably be reduced to less than 280 years. This suggests that the individual judgeships were not only geographically restricted but also often contemporaneous.

III. Literary Aspects

A great variety of material is preserved in the book of Judges, including what may well be eyewitness accounts. Based on its archaic style and historical allusions, the Song of Deborah (5:2-31) has been dated ca. 1125, making it one of the oldest portions of the Old Testament. Other accounts may have been preserved as oral tradition by the various tribes and clans. Indeed, Jotham's fable (9:7-15) and Samson's riddles (14:14, 18; 15:16) suggest traditions preserved in tribal lore.

The various narratives have been preserved within a theological framework characterized by a classic pattern: the people of Israel "did what was evil" by serving other gods, an angry Yahweh sends an alien nation to punish them, the people cry to the Lord for help, he raises up a deliverer who defeats or drives out the oppressor, the land has rest. Scholars have sought in the summaries of the twelve judges a schematic attempt to represent all "Israel," but this is problematic; the Gileadites Jair and Jephthah may represent eastern Gilead and Gad, the vaguely identified Shamgar may align with either Reuben or Simeon, and Deborah of Issachar may be associated with Naphtali through her general Barak. This intent may also account for the inclusion of the "minor" judges—perhaps more an indication of the compiler's access to traditions than to the actual significance of these individuals. Other literary patterns have been proposed as well, such as the alternation of exemplary and unexemplary judges (e.g., Othniel and Ehud, Jephthah and Samson).

Although the Hebrew text of Judges has long been regarded as well preserved, the major LXX manuscripts (Alexandrinus and Vaticanus) are widely divergent and thus are both printed in modern editions. Alexandrinus is generally regarded as more reliable.

IV. Origins

Rabbinic tradition ascribes Judges to the prophet Samuel, but the book itself contains no reference to authorship. Earlier critical scholars saw in its various components similarities to Pentateuchal sources and thus regarded it, with Joshua, as part of a larger work, continuing (if not concluding) the narrative begun in Genesis. Recent scholars place the book within the "Deuteronomic history," Joshua–2 Kings.

References to the events recorded as prior to the establishment of kingship in Israel (18:1; 19:1) suggest that the book was composed at the time of the United Monarchy. Critical scholars, identifying the theological framework of the book with the work of the Deuteronomic historian(s), point to further stages of editing in the eighth-seventh and sixth centuries.

V. Theology

The book of Judges is to be regarded as religious history, as readily apparent from the framework given the careers of the judges. This theological orientation may also explain the divergence between the description of the Israelite conquest in 1:1–2:5 and that of Josh. 14–15.

Throughout God is portrayed as sovereign over history, employing non-Israelite peoples as his instruments in testing and punishing his covenant people. Central to his direction of historical events is the faithfulness of Israel to the covenant relationship: when Israel disobeys, God punishes; when the people repent and obey, he sends a deliverer, thus demonstrating his own constant faithfulness (2:1-5, 11-19; 2:20–3:6).

Bibliography. R. G. Boling, *Judges*. AB 6A (1975); J. Gray, *Joshua, Judges and Ruth*. NCBC (1986).

JUDGMENT (Heb. *mišpāṭ, pᵉlîlîyâ*; Gk. *dikaiokrisía, kríma, krísis*).† In the civil, legal sense judgment is given by the elders, king, or another authority. In a technical sense it refers to military action or conquest (Ps. 149:9; Ezek. 23:24). Most often, judgment is the product of a "controversy" or lawsuit (Heb. *rîb*). See JUDGE; LAWSUIT.

I. Old Testament

God's judgment is also cast in this royal-legal mold. God is the heavenly ruler who vindicates Israel with acts of deliverance (Exod. 6:6), who judges against Edom and Moab (Isa. 34:5; Jer. 48:21), whose judgments uphold his covenant and include his law (Ps. 105:7; 119:137), to whom Israel appeals to arise and give his judgment against their present enemies (7:6 [MT 7]; 76:9 [MT 10]). By his prophets the Lord summons Israel to judgment in the language of a lawsuit, and he stands to pronounce judgment (e.g., Isa. 3:13-14). This judgment was partially fulfilled with Jerusalem's destruction, yet also anticipates the final Day of the Lord (Joel 3:2 [MT 4:2]).

See DAY OF THE LORD.

II. New Testament

In the New Testament judgment may refer to the "sentence of condemnation" (cf. Luke 23:40) issued by the state or God (Rom. 5:16; 13:2), to "lawsuits" (cf. 1 Cor. 6:7), or to decisions ("unsearchable judgments") by which God governs (Rom. 11:33; Rev. 15:3-4).

Closely related is the eschatological "day of judgment" (Matt. 10:15; 2 Pet. 3:7; 1 John 4:17), a day of divine wrath (Rom. 2:5, "righteous judgment"), woe (cf. Matt. 23:13-36), and fiery punishment and separation from God (5:22; 2 Thess. 1:5-10). On that day God will pronounce judgment against all who violated his law (Matt. 5:21ff.), spurned mercy (Jas. 2:13; but "mercy triumphs over judgment"), and his new covenant (Heb. 10:26-30; "a fearful prospect of judgment"), as well as against the ungodly (2 Pet. 2:9; Jude 15-16), the fallen angels (2 Pet. 2:4ff.; cf. 1 Cor. 6:3), and the antichrist (cf. 2 Thess. 2:1-12).

Believers also will receive judgment. God will judge their works (2 Cor. 5:10; cf. 1 Cor. 3:12-13), and bring to light the truth of their lives and faith (1 Cor. 4:5; cf. 1 Pet. 1:7). He will also pronounce a verdict of acquittal or righteousness, based not on works but on Christ, who bore their judgment already in the flesh by his life and blood (Rom. 5:16; cf. 8:31-34). By his Spirit God gives believers confidence in his love for them in Christ, and of his righteous verdict (1 John 4:17).

God's final judgment is already experienced in the world's rejection of Christ (John 3:19; 12:31); and in the Church, in its discipline (1 Cor. 5:3; 11:29), in the growth of love (1 John 4:16ff.), and in the joyful steadfastness in the face of persecution (2 Thess. 1:5-10; cf. 1 Pet. 1:7-8).

III. Last Judgment

Although the term itself does not occur, the biblical accounts point to a final judgment at the end of history whereby God or Christ will assign both the "living and the dead" to eternity in heaven or hell, as each deserves (1 Tim. 4:1; cf. Acts 10:42; Rev. 22:12). On that final, unspecified day, all who have passed away will be raised from the dead and will be judged with those who are still living. Those who have lived righteous lives will receive eternal life, while those who

have spent their days in unrighteousness will suffer eternally (John 5:28-29, "resurrection of judgment"; cf. Rev. 20:11-15; 22:12). Believers are urged to prepare themselves for this event (cf. Matt. 24:42, 44 par.; 25:13) and to await Christ's return and their deliverance from God's wrath (cf. 1 Thess. 1:10); others are exhorted to repent and to believe (cf. Matt. 3:8-10; Acts 17:30-31).

Although the general features of the doctrine concerning God's final judgment are clear, several questions arise. First, are there two divine judgments— one during or at the end of a person's life (John 3:18, 36) and another general judgment at the end of time— or only one? Some scholars believe that such a second judgment confirms the first. Second, is judgment according to works (Matt. 16:27; 25:31-46; Rom. 2:6-8; 2 Cor. 5:10) compatible with salvation by grace through faith (Eph. 2:8)? Some theologians maintain that God's sovereignty and human responsibility are ultimately compatible rather than contradictory emphases. Third, is God's judgment, especially on unbelievers, fair? Some exegetes point out that God will judge each person on the basis of his or her response to the measure of revelation God has given that individual (e.g., the Phoenician cities of Tyre and Sidon were not judged as though they had been exposed to God's nature as fully as had the Hebrew cities of Bethsaida and Capernaum [Matt. 11:20-24 par. Luke 10:13-15], and the Gentiles, likewise, were not to be judged according to the standards of Israel's law [Rom. 2:12-16]). Fourth, what does Paul mean concerning the saints' part in the judgment of the world and mankind's judgment of angels (1 Cor. 6:2-3); or Matthew, regarding the angelic role in the separation between the righteous and the unrighteous (Matt. 13:49-50) and in gathering the elect from diverse places (24:31)? Paul, alluding to Dan. 7:22 ("saints of the Most High"), may have identified the saints with "the associates of the Son of Man" (F. F. Bruce, *I & II Corinthians*. NCBC [1980], p. 60).

See also ESCHATOLOGY.

JUDGMENT SEAT (Gk. *bḗma*). A seat on a raised platform from which officials could hear legal cases and address the population. Pontius Pilate sat upon such a judgment seat in an area known as "The Pavement" when the crowd decided whether to free Jesus or Barabbas (Matt. 27:19; John 19:13), and Herod Agrippa I occupied one while delivering the address during which he was struck with a fatal illness (Acts 12:21; RSV "throne"; JB "dais"). The apostle Paul was brought before the judgment seats of the proconsul Gallio at Corinth (18:12; so KJV; RSV "tribunal") and the procurator Festus at Caesarea (25:6; RSV "seat"). Lysias, the regent of Antiochus IV Epiphanes, also was seated on a *bḗma* when he negotiated with the residents of Ptolemais (2 Macc. 13:26).

A large, ornate platform overlooking the agora at Corinth bears the Latin term *rostrum*, the equivalent of Gk. *bḗma*, and is generally held to be the "tribunal" before which Paul was brought.

JUDITH [jōō'dĭth] (Heb. *yᵉhûḏîṯ* "Jewish woman"; Gk. *Ioudith*).

1. A wife of Esau and daughter of the Hittite Beeri

(Gen. 26:34). According to some, she was the same as Oholibamah.

2. The principal character of the book of Judith; a descendant of Merari and widow of Manasseh. Characterized as beautiful, wealthy, and pious, she demonstrated great courage in delivering Jerusalem from Nebuchadnezzar's army and killing the general Holofernes. *See* JUDITH, BOOK OF.

JUDITH, BOOK OF.† A book of the Old Testament Apocrypha relating the heroic deeds of Judith of Bethulia.

I. Contents

On the basis of content the book divides into two distinct parts. Jdt. 1–7 provide the setting for the drama. Nebuchadnezzar, "king of the Assyrians," declares war on the Medes under King Arphaxad (1:1-6); although the Persians and western nations (including the Jews) refuse to aid the cause (vv. 7-11), he succeeds in defeating the Medes (vv. 12-16). "Very angry with the whole region" (v. 12), Nebuchadnezzar commissions his general Holofernes to carry out his revenge against the West (2:1-13). Holofernes marches against Damascus, and his enormous army quickly reduces the city (vv. 14-27); fear and terror spread throughout the West, and the various nations voluntarily capitulate (2:28–3:9). Yet when the Assyrians encamp against Judea, the "people of Israel" cry out to God for help in resisting attack (ch. 4). Achior, leader of Holofernes' Ammonite allies, advises the Assyrian that the Jews will be invincible so long as they heed the law of God; to suceed he must catch them in sin against God (ch. 5). Holofernes rejects the advice and delivers the bound Achior over to the Jews, to share their fate (ch. 6). The stage is set as Holofernes advances to Bethulia and cuts off the city's water supply (7:1-18); the citizens urge their leaders to surrender, but Uzziah, the chief elder, urges them to delay five days (vv. 19-32).

Chs. 8–16 comprise the story of Judith. Epitomized as extremely pious, rich, and beautiful (8:1-8), Judith summons the elders to hear her plan to rescue the city and thus ultimately to preserve the temple at Jerusalem and the very survival of the Jews (vv. 9-36). Praying that God will sanction her efforts (ch. 9), she beautifies herself (10:1-5), departs the city with her maid, and arrives at the enemy camp, where she is ushered before Holofernes (vv. 11-23). She informs the general that the desperate Jews of Bethulia are about to sin by consuming consecrated food, and thus will be ripe for defeat (ch. 11). As Holofernes' house guest, Judith remains pious in prayer and ablution (12:1-9). The Assyrian general, enamored by her charms, invites her to a private banquet (vv. 10-20). As the inebriated Holofernes slumbers, Judith beheads him with his own sword (13:1-10a); then, concealing his head, she departs the camp, purportedly to bathe, and returns to Bethulia (vv. 10b-20). Upon seeing Holofernes' head, Achior converts to Judaism (14:1-10); the Assyrians, by contrast, panic and flee, and are easily decimated by the Jews (14:11–15:7). Judith is led triumphantly to Jerusalem (15:8-13; 16:18-20) and utters a hymn of thanksgiving (vv. 1-17). The land

has rest, and Judith lives in honor to a great age (vv. 21-25).

II. Literary Aspects

Although on general appearance the book is a historical account, numerous anachronisms and factual inaccuracies preclude identifying it as such. For example, the Babylonian Nebuchadnezzar (605-562 B.C.) is depicted as ruling the Assyrians (1:1, 7) from Nineveh, which had fallen in 612. Moreover, the Jews are said to have just returned from the Exile and have rebuilt the temple—which Nebuchadnezzar had not yet destroyed (5:18-19). Other passages are geographically confusing (e.g., 2:21, 24-25).

As a literary work, many have judged Judith to be, on the basis of both the story itself and its presentation, superior to the somewhat comparable canonical book of Esther. Although some scholars have sought to classify it as an apocalypse (cf. 16:15, 17), the book is more properly a Jewish adaptation of the Hellenistic novel (cf. the alternation of extended speeches and narrative) or a story told in folkloristic style with a didactic, theological purpose. Indeed, it is characterized throughout by the use of irony—e.g., the character and role of Judith; the fortunes of Holofernes; the contrasting motives for and responses to the advice given the general by Achior and Judith; and the perhaps intentional historical inaccuracies.

The original Hebrew form of the book is reflected both idiomatically and syntactically in the LXX Greek translation. Nevertheless, Old Testament quotations follow the LXX readings.

III. Origins

Attempts to date with precision the composition of Judith on the basis of historical allusions (e.g., attempts to identify Nebuchadnezzar with Antiochus IV Epiphanes or Hadrian) have proven generally fruitless. References to Hellenistic practices (e.g., 3:7; 12:15; 15:13) and the role of the high priest and Sanhedrin (e.g., 4:6, 8; 11:14) as well as resemblances of the story to aspects of Judas Maccabeus' defeat of Nicanor (1 Macc. 7:43-50) suggest a date in the Maccabean period, *ca.* 150-125 B.C. Accordingly, and pointing to certain of the pietistic values stressed, some scholars ascribe the book to a Palestinian Jew of the mid-second century B.C., perhaps an early adherent of Pharisaism.

IV. Evaluation

The story of Judith was preserved as an effort to encourage perseverance on the part of the Jewish people in the face of religious and military oppression. The focus is not on "strength in numbers" or "men of strength," but rather on faith in the "God of the lowly, helper of the oppressed, upholder of the weak, protector of the forlorn, savior of those without hope" (9:11).

As a personification of the Jewish people or "Everywoman," Judith demonstrates utter faithfulness to God and to her fellows; that she was a woman and a widow underscore her significance as the instrument of God in the history of his people (cf. v. 18). Despite her almost Pharisaic adherence to the requirements of ritual purity, Judith did not hesitate to employ acts of questionable morality to accomplish God's purpose (e.g., 11:5-8, 11-19; 13:6-10, 16). Complementing the theme of faithfulness is the notion of divine retribution for obedience to or rejection of the covenant stipulations (cf. 5:15-21; 8:17-20; 16:17).

Despite its basically orthodox views, the book was never accepted into the Hebrew canon, perhaps because of its conciliatory attitude toward the Samaritans (cf. 4:4-8; 15:3-5) and its acceptance of the proselyte Achior (14:7). Among Christians the book was accepted as inspired and canonical by Clement of Alexandria, Augustine, the First Council of Nicaea, and the Third Council of Carthage. Jerome included it in his Vulgate translation, and the book has thus come to be regarded as deuterocanonical.

Bibliography. M. S. Enslin, *The Book of Judith* (New York: 1973); C. A. Moore, *Judith.* AB 40 (1985).

JULIA [jōōl′yə] (Gk. *Ioulia*). A Christian woman in Rome (Rom. 16:15), perhaps the wife or sister of Philologus.

JULIUS [jōōl′yəs] (Gk. *Ioulios*). A Roman centurion of the Augustan cohort (Acts 27:1). Responsible for taking the prisoner Paul to Rome, he treated his charge kindly and permitted him to visit his friends when they harbored in Sidon (v. 3). During the storm off Crete he ignored Paul's warning (vv. 11, 21), but later heeded him (v. 31) with the result that all reached land safely. Julius protected the apostle when the other soldiers were intent on killing all prisoners to prevent their escape (vv. 42-44).

JUNIAS [jōō′nǐ əs] (Gk. *Iounias*).† A Jewish Christian in Rome, perhaps a female associate of Paul (the wife of Andronicus?) with whom the apostle had been imprisoned. Junias was a Christian before Paul was converted and was accorded a position of stature among the apostles (Rom. 16:7).

JUNIPER. *See* BROOM TREE.

JUPITER [jōō′pə tər] (Lat. *Iupiter*).† Chief of the Roman gods, identified with the Greek ZEUS (Acts 14:12-13). The KJV uses the Latin name, following the Vulgate.

JUSHAB-HESED [jōō′shǐb hě′sĕd] (Heb. *yûšab ḥeseḏ* "may steadfast love be returned"). A son of Zerubbabel (1 Chr. 3:20).

JUST (Heb. *ṣeḏeq, ṣaddîq*; Gk. *díkaios*), **JUSTICE** (Heb. *mišpāṭ*; Gk. *krísis, dikaiosýnē*).† Justice and righteousness (Heb. *ṣᵉḏāqâ*) are often used together (cf. 1 Kgs. 10:9; Ps. 33:5). While their meanings can overlap, justice properly is that action or legal decision which vindicates or establishes the right, and so expresses a person's righteousness. *See* RIGHTEOUSNESS.

The people of God share with others a common sense of justice (Phil. 4:8; cf. Job 19:7; Isa. 5:23; Matt. 27:19), as well as common standards: just weights (Lev. 19:36; Prov. 16:11; cf. Amos 8:5) and fair pay (cf. Matt. 20:4). A product of wise reflection

(Prov. 1:3ff.), justice is a frequent topic in Proverbs and other Wisdom Literature.

While Israel's elders and kings delivered justice in social contexts similar to those of other nations, the spiritual context was that of the covenant. The duty to execute justice was an integral part of God's law, founded upon his holiness, filled with his promise of security in the land. Its standards were plain: impartiality and the shunning of bribes and influence that would pervert justice (Exod. 23:1-3, 6-8; Lev. 19:15-16; Deut. 16:18-20). While they are to look impartially (cf. Exod. 23:3; Job 34:17-19), authorities are directed to watch for the rights of the poor, needy, fatherless, and afflicted (Ps. 72:2; 82:3; Jer. 5:28; cf. Job 24:2-12; Luke 18:2). To do justice is the hallmark of the righteous king (2 Sam. 8:15; 1 Kgs. 10:9; Ps. 72:1; Isa. 9:7 [MT 6]), proof that he walks in the way of God's wisdom (1 Kgs. 3:28; cf. v. 9; Prov. 8:15). Through his prophets, God held kings and judges accountable to this standard (e.g., Jer. 22:1-17; Ezek. 45:9). To ignore wisdom and not know justice is the foolishness that brings devastating judgment (Prov. 29:2, 4; Mic. 3).

Moreover, justice is the responsibility of all in the covenant community. Their experience of God's gracious salvation demands in response that they show justice to others (Deut. 10:17-19; cf. Lev. 19:36). Indeed, to do justice is part of walking with God and displaying the same steadfast, covenanting love (Mic. 6:8); it is inseparable from moral and cultic duty (Ezek. 18:5-9), which have their *raison d'être* in God's coming salvation (Isa. 56:1ff.). To do justice means to vindicate the cause of the poor and oppressed by heeding their cry (cf. Job 29:12; Ps. 18:6 [MT 7]), knowing their rights, and being their help (cf. Job 29:15-17; Prov. 29:7), to deal fairly in the marketplace (cf. Deut. 24:10-13), to show an impartiality not favoring the rich (cf. Jas. 2:1-7), and to care for the hungry, thirsty, and naked (cf. Matt. 25:31-46). Failure to do justice only blinds people to the merciful justice of God's salvation (Isa. 59:4, 9-11, 14; cf. Prov. 21:13; Jas. 2:13), yet with repentance God's glory can again shine in their lives (Amos 5:14-15). Justice is the proof of the covenant. It is better than sacrifices (Prov. 21:3; cf. Hos. 6:6), for without it sacrifices, sabbaths, and all other religious duties are worthless (Isa. 1:11-17; 58:1ff.; Matt. 23:23).

God is just (Heb. *ṣaddîq*; Deut. 32:4; cf. Isa. 45:21), for he executes justice for the poor and oppressed (Deut. 10:18; Ps. 103:6; 146:7), and brings salvation and restoration to Israel (Neh. 9:33; Isa. 30:18; cf. Ps. 35:27; Isa. 33:5). By doing justice, he shows faithfulness (Ps. 111:7; Rev. 15:3; cf. 1 John 1:9), and steadfast love (Heb. *ḥeseḏ*; Ps. 33:5; 89:14 [MT 15]; 119:149; Hos. 2:19 [MT 21]). As "Judge of all the earth" (Gen. 18:25; Rom. 3:6) God arbitrates justly (Jer. 11:20; Rev. 16:5, 7; cf. Jer. 10:24), and his punishment is just, as based upon his law (Rom. 3:8; Heb. 2:2) and wisdom (Prov. 2:9; 8:20). God reserves special condemnation for those who deny or pervert justice (Isa. 5:23; 10:1-2; cf. Jer. 5:1; Amos 5:6-7; 2 Thess. 1:6).

God's justice is also an object of hope. It is the promised work of the Spirit that walks in justice (Isa.

40:13-14), that will be poured out on a restored Israel (32:15-16), and will anoint the Messiah to "bring forth justice to the nations" (42:1-4) and establish a kingdom characterized by justice and righteousness (9:7; Jer. 23:5; cf. Isa. 11:4-5). Jesus fulfills this promise (Luke 4:18-21). By his death and resurrection he is proclaimed the Just (RSV "Righteous") One (Acts 3:14; 7:52; 1 John 2:1), through whom God justly deals with sin and displays saving mercy (1 Pet. 2:23-24; cf. Rom. 8:1-4).

People also may be called just or righteous (e.g., Joseph, Matt. 1:19; Joseph of Arimathea, KJV, Luke 23:50; cf. Noah, Gen. 6:9; Lot, 2 Pet. 2:7; Simeon, Luke 2:25).

At Acts 28:4 "Justice" (Gk. díkē; KJV "vengeance") is the name of a goddess, whom the people of Malta think has overtaken the shipwrecked Paul through a viper.

Bibliography. F. Büchsel and V. Herntrich, "κρίνω," *TDNT* 3 (1965): 923-954.

JUSTIFICATION (Gk. *dikaíōma*). † The presentation of justification by faith in Christ in the letters of Paul is slightly obscured in English versions by the dual terminology "just, justice, justify, justification" and "righteous, righteouness." Both sets of terms represent the one reality which is presented with the related Greek words *dikaióō* "justify, set right"; *dikíōma* "justification, judgment, righteous deed"; *dikaíōsis* "justification, acquittal." *See* RIGHTEOUSNESS.

Paul taught that the gospel is God's offer of righteousness to all who have faith in Jesus Christ and who give up reliance on human effort and "works of the law" in order to attain righteousness. Sin as a universal objective condition of humanity is the problem; God's justifying activity in Christ is the solution. Faith is the subjective human reception of God's objective offer of righteousness in Christ. "The righteousness of God" addressed in Romans is, therefore, not a quality of God, but God's activity of deliverance, of justification, of making right the relationship of human beings to himself. This righteousness and the ethical righteousness of humans are not entirely distinct from each other; they can, indeed, be spoken of in the same breath and with the same word (*dikaiosýnē*; Rom. 9:30; cf. 5:18-21). The basis of this relationship as it is known in Christian experience is seen at 8:3-4; Gal. 5:13-14 (cf. Rom. 13:8-10): God's objective is, as always, the fulfillment of the law, which is brought about by his justification of the sinner and by the life of the Spirit in the justified.

Paul's teaching, although of course dependent on the Christ event, sought its foundations in the Old Testament. The picture of Abraham as the man of faith, justified by that faith, is inspired mainly by Gen. 15:6 (Rom. 4; Gal. 3:6-9). The basic text of justification by faith is Hab. 2:4 (Rom. 1:17; Gal. 3:11). While the idea in Habakkuk is of faithful allegiance to God as constituting a person's righteousness, rather than of faith in justifying grace, the change is not as great as it might seem. Both in the Old Testament and in Christ the initiative is from God and the human part is the response of allegiance to the acting God. Paul also has in mind the thought repeated in the Psalms that God is the one who brings about righteousness by giving just verdicts as the bringing of justice for the oppressed (e.g., Ps. 9:4, 7-8 [MT 5, 8-9]; 17:1-15; 18:20, 24 [MT 21, 25]; 35:22-25). Despite the frequent claims to human righteousness in these Psalms, the thought has an important point of contact with Paul: God is still the one active to establish righteousness for and in his people. (The same can be said about the relationship between the teaching on justification in the Dead Sea Scrolls and that in Paul, although in the Scrolls it is the teachings of the "Teacher of Righteousness" by which righteousness is brought.) However, Ps. 143:2, in which the psalmist refuses to make such a claim before the divine judge, is also a significant part of the background of Paul's teaching, echoed at Rom. 3:20; Gal. 2:16. Another significant element in the background of Paul's teaching is the late prophetic expectation of the day when God would himself become the provider and guarantor of the righteousness of his people (Isa. 46:12-13; Jer. 31:31-34).

Paul's teaching on justification by faith in Christ became in the hands of Luther, Calvin, and others (following Augustine) the theological basis of the Protestant Reformation. It was especially underlined by Luther's insistence on "by faith alone" and "by grace alone," and by the Reformers' teaching on election. Some scholars have insisted against the prevailing tendency of Protestantism inherited from the Reformers that justification by faith should not be considered the center of Paul's theology (often with the added comment that it should not thereby be considered an unessential doctrine). Justification by faith appears fully only in connection with some controversy concerning the law and only where Paul bases an argument on the priority of Abraham's righteousness to his circumcision (i.e., in Galatians and Romans). Justification is brought into the argument in both letters because of what it is able to say about the situation of the law in the eschatological community, the Church. The law's function is not to justify the sinner, but to bring about "knowledge of sin." God's justification does not follow ethnic lines; Jew and Gentile are equal in justification by faith (Rom. 3:29-30). The setting of this teaching on the law is not an argument with Judaism, but rather with Jewish Christians who sought to give the law a role in eschatological salvation that Paul refused to give it.

The teaching of Paul appears to be contradicted by Jas. 2:18-26, which, like Paul, argues from the experience of Abraham and emphasizes Gen. 15:6. James asserts that faith lacking works is dead (Jas. 2:17); "faith," here meaning a mere intellectual assent to religion, is not sufficient (v. 19). True living faith manifests itself in acts of love to the needy (vv. 14-16). Justification "by works and not by faith alone" (v. 24) means that faith is "completed by works" in this way (v. 22). The contradiction is only apparent; Paul and James address different issues. Jas. 2:18-26 was apparently written to counteract a misunderstanding of Paul's teaching which separated "faith" from any moral obligation.

See GRACE; LAW.

JUSTUS [jŭs'təs] (Gk. *Ioustos*, from Lat. *Justus*).
1. The surname of Joseph Barsabbas, a candidate

to succeed Judas Iscariot among the disciples (Acts 1:23). *See* BARSABBAS **1**.

2. Titius (or Titus) Justus, a Corinthian citizen whose house was next to the synagogue (Acts 18:7; KJV "Justus"). He welcomed Paul and the Corinthian Christians after they had been opposed in the synagogue.

3. Jesus Justus, one of the few Jewish Christians to assist in Paul's work, and in whose name he greets the church at Colossae (Col. 4:11).

JUTTAH [jŭt′ə] (Heb. *yuṭṭâ* "stretched out, inclined"). A town in the hill country of Judah (Josh. 15:55; Heb. *yûṭṭâ*) later included among the levitical cities (21:16; some LXX versions include Gk. *Iota* in the parallel account, 1 Chr. 6:57). Eusebius (*Onom.* cxxxiii.10; clxvi.49) cites a large Jewish village by this name (Gk. *Iettan*) 18 Roman mi. from Eleutheropolis (Beit Jibrîn) in the southern Darome (Negeb); this would coincide with modern Yuṭṭā, 25 km. (15.5 mi.) south of Beit Jibrîn and 8.8 km. (5.5 mi.) south of Hebron.

One tradition, now generally abandoned, identified Juttah with the "city of Judah" where Mary visited Elizabeth and where John the Baptist was born (Luke 1:39).

KAB [kăb] (Heb. *qaḇ*, from Egyp. *kb*[?]). A unit of measurement for dry wares and liquids. According to 2 Kgs. 6:5 (KJV "cab"), during the Syrian siege of Samaria one-fourth of a kab of dove's dung sold for five shekels. The Mishnah recognizes the kab as one-sixth of a seah, an eighteenth of an ephah, or about 1.2 l. (1.3 liquid qt.). According to Josephus (*Ant.* ix.4.4), a kab would equal approximately 1.9 l. (2 qt.). *See* WEIGHTS AND MEASURES.

KABBALAH [kə bäl′ə] (Heb. *qabbalâ* "tradition").†
According to the Midrash, those books of the Hebrew scriptures contained in the Prophets and the Writings, as well as the corpus of oral law.

More commonly the term designates the system of Jewish theosophy and mysticism which developed after A.D. 1200, according to which God manifests himself through ten mysterious emanations. Of particular interest are aspects of creation and the visionary portions of Scripture. Abbreviations of words and the transposition of letters, with emphasis on their numerical values and symbolism, are the concern of gematria, a method of interpretation which seeks hidden meanings. In a less technical sense the Kabbalah comprises all esoteric Jewish doctrine from the beginning of the Christian era on.

KABZEEL [kab′zĭ əl] (Heb. *qaḇṣeˀ ēl* "may God gather"). A city in southern Judah, near the border of Edom (Josh. 15:21). It was the home of Benaiah, one of David's mighty men (2 Sam. 23:20 par. 1 Chr. 11:22). Following the Exile it was resettled under the name Jekabzeel (Neh. 11:25). The site may be identified with modern Khirbet Gharreh (Tell ˁIra), near Wâdī Mishash about 21 km. (13 mi.) northeast of Beersheba.

KADESH [kā′dĭsh] (Heb. *qāḏēš* "sacred, holy").
KADESH-BARNEA [bär′nĭ ə] (Heb. *barnēaˁ*). † The names Kadesh and KEDESH designate sites used as sanctuaries prior to the emergence of the Israelites. The names vary only in the Masoretic vowel pointing; the MT usually uses Kadesh for cities in the south and Kedesh for those in the north. Sanctuaries, and thus these sites, generally were located on the tops of mountains ("high places").

1. An oasis at the southern edge of Palestine (Josh. 15:3), probably modern ˁAin el-Qureirat; earlier known as En-mishpat ("spring of Mishpat"; Gen. 14:7). The spring at this site is presently the largest in the region and flows all year. Ruins of an eighth- to tenth-century B.C. fortress have been discovered nearby.

Kadesh, also called Kadesh-barnea, was located on the Israelite boundary from the patriarchal period on. Invading kings seized it as a part of their territory in the days of Abraham (Gen. 14:7), and Hagar bore Ishmael nearby (16:14). Subsequently Abraham settled between Kadesh and Shur (20:1). The Israelites used the area as a staging arena for their conquest of Palestine (Num. 13:26), encamping there while their spies scouted the land (13–14; Deut. 1). It was from here that Moses sought unsuccessfully to gain the king of Edom's permission for safe passage through that territory (20:14-21). After further wanderings the Israelites returned to Kadesh (33:36-37); it was here that Aaron died (v. 38).

It was at this place that the Israelites complained about the hardship of their wanderings, so angering Moses that he struck the rock (Num. 20:1-13; cf. Exod. 17:1-7). Moses renamed the spring Meribah, the "waters of contention" or "strife" (Heb. *mᵉrîḇâ*, perhaps a pun on *mirḇâ* "abundance"). This new name occurs in Ezekiel's vision of the new Israel (Ezek. 47:19; 48:28).

2. Kadesh (Aram. *qiḏsî*) on the Orontes, the site of Rameses II's defeat of the Hittites in 1288 B.C. This site, identified as modern Tell Nebī Mend, was strategically located at the intersection of the north-flowing Orontes river and a small western tributary, where it guarded the northern pass from the valley; thus for an army it was the only alternative to the narrower north-south road along the Phoenician coast. The name does not occur in the Bible, but it is found in the city lists of Thutmose III and the Amarna Letters.

KADMIEL [kăd′mĭ əl] (Heb. *qaḏmîˀ ēl* "God goes before"). The head of a levitical family who with his descendants returned under Zerubbabel from captivity in Babylon (Ezra 2:40; Neh. 7:43; 12:8, 24). He and his sons supervised those rebuilding the temple (Ezra 3:9), took part in the public confession of sin (Neh. 9:4-5), and signed the renewed covenant (10:9).

KADMONITES [kăd'mə nīts] (Heb. *qaḏmōnî* "Easterners").† A people listed among the pre-Israelite inhabitants of Canaan (Gen. 15:19). The name probably represents the same peoples as those called the "sons of Qedem" (RSV "people of the east"; e.g., 29:1; Judg. 6:3, 33; Job 1:3).

KAIN [kān] (Heb. *qayin* "edge, point, spear") (PEOPLE).† A collective term, singular in form, designating the KENITES (Num. 24:11; KJV "the Kenite"). At Judg. 4:11 the English versions read "the Kenite."

KAIN [kān] (Heb. *haqqayin*) (PLACE)* According to Josh. 15:57, a city in the southern hill country of Judah (KJV "Cain"). The name suggests that it might have been a Kenite possession. Some scholars would locate the city at modern Khirbet Yaqin, southeast of Hebron.

Following the LXX, some scholars suggest that the text of vv. 56-57 be emended to read "Zanoah of Kain . . . nine cities with their villages."

KAIWAN [kī'wən] (Heb. *kiyyûn*; Akk. *kaywânu*). The Babylonian name for the planet Saturn, which Amos calls a star-god (Amos. 5:26; NIV "pedestal"). Amos prophesied that since the Israelites worshipped a Babylonian deity God would send them to Babylon (presumably so they could be nearer the pagan god they wanted to worship). Stephen's quotation of this passage at Acts 7:43 follows the LXX, which reads "Rephan," apparently an error in transliteration.

KALLAI [kăl'ī] (Heb. *qallay* "light, swift"[?]). The head of the priestly family of Sallai at the time of the high priest Joiakim (Neh. 12:20).

KAMON [kā'mən] (Heb. *qāmôn* "station"). The place where Jair died and was buried after having judged Israel for thirty-two years (Judg. 10:5; KJV "Camon"). The city was one of the thirty cities belonging to Jair's descendants, known collectively as HAVVOTH-JAIR. The site generally is identified as modern Qamm, 20 km. (13 mi.) southeast of the Sea of Galilee; an alternate identification is Qumeim, 11 km. (7 mi.) east-northeast of Irbid (biblical Beth-arbel).

KANAH [kā'nə] (Heb. *qānâ* "reed").

1. Brook Kanah, modern Wâdī Qanah, which formed part of the border between Manasseh and Ephraim (Josh. 16:6; 17:9; KJV "river Kanah"). The stream, which begins at the watershed of Mt. Gerizim, becomes a tributary of the Yarkon, the largest river in Palestine, and flows into the Mediterranean Sea just north of Joppa. Some scholars speculate that the stream had a different course in biblical times, flowing independently all the way to the Mediterranean (E. Danelius, "The Boundary of Ephraim and Manasseh in the Western Plain," *PEQ* 90 [1958]: 32-43).

2. A city on the northern border of the tribal territory of Asher (Josh. 19:28). It has been identified with modern Qana, located 9.6 km. (6 mi.) southeast of Tyre.

KAREAH [kə rē'ə] (Heb. *qārēaḥ* "bald head"), The father of Johanan 1, a military leader in Judah who

escaped deportation after the Babylonian conquest of Jerusalem (2 Kgs. 25:23; KJV "Careah"; Jer. 40:8-16; 41:11-16; 42:1, 8; 43:25).

KARKA [kär'kə] (Heb. *haqqarqa'* "the floor"). A city on the southern border of the tribal territory of Judah, located between Addar and Azmon northwest of Kadesh-barnea (Josh. 15:3; KJV "Karkaa"). The site is perhaps to be identified with modern 'Ain el-Qoseimeh at the confluence of the Wâdī el-'Ain and Umm Has.

KARKOR [kär'kôr] (Heb. *qarqōr*). A city in eastern Gilead where Gideon defeated two Midianite kings in a surprise attack (Josh. 8:10-11). The ancient city was situated on a caravan route between Palestine and Dumah. It is almost certainly to be identified with modern Qarqar in the plain of Wâdī Sirḥân.

KARNAIM [kär nā'əm] (Heb. *qarnāyim* "two horns" or "peaks").† A fortress-city in Gilead. Located at modern Sheikh Sa'd, on a northern tributary of the middle Yarmuk river about 32 km. (20 mi.) east of the Sea of Galilee and 5 km. (3 mi.) north of Ashtaroth), it is identical with ASHTEROTH-KARNAIM (Gen. 14:5) and perhaps with postexilic Carnaim (1 Macc. 5:26, 43-44). At Amos 6:13 (KJV "horns") the prophet puns upon the names Karnaim (the "horns" of a bull, thus "strength"; cf. 1 Kgs. 22:11) and Lo-debar ("Nothing"), apparently cities captured by King Jeroboam II of Israel (2 Kgs. 14:28).

KARTAH [kär'tə] (Heb. *qartâ*).† A levitical city in the tribal territory of Zebulun, allocated to the Gershonite family (Josh. 21:34). The site has not been identified. Because the name is missing from the similar account at 1 Chr. 6, some scholars suggest the name here may be a scribal error stemming from Kartan at Josh. 21:32.

KARTAN [kär'tăn] (Heb. *qartān*). A levitical city in the tribal territory of Naphtali given to the Gershonites (Josh. 21:32). The parallel account at 1 Chr. 6:76 (MT 61) refers to the city as Kiriathaim (Heb. *qiryāṯayim*; KJV "Kirjathaim"). Modern Khirbet el-Qureiyeh, thought to be 11 km. (7 mi.) northwest of Kedesh in Upper Galilee, has been suggested as the site.

KATTATH [kăt'ăth] (Heb. *qaṭṭāṯ*). A city on the border of Zebulun (Josh. 19:15), probably the same as the Kitron from which the Canaanites could not be driven (Judg. 1:30). The site has not been identified, although Khirbet Qoṭeina, 8 km. (5 mi.) southwest of Tell Qeimûn (biblical Jokneam), is a possibility.

KEDAR [kē'dər] (Heb. *qēḏār* "dark" or "mighty").† The second son of Ishmael (Gen. 25:13 par. 1 Chr. 1:29) and the eponymous ancestor of the Kedarites (Isa. 21:17; 60:7). At some point the name became virtually synonymous with the gentilic "Arab" (e.g., Ezek. 27:21). Since at least part of the time the Arabs lived in tents made of black goats' hair (Cant. 1:5; cf. Ps. 120:5), the designation "sons of Kedar" or "sons of the dark" could have derived from their association with these tents.

The Kedarites were nomads in the Syroarabian desert (cf. Gen. 25:18; Isa. 21:13-17; Ezek. 27:21) whose primary weapons were the bow and arrow. They probably followed the seasonal pastures with their flocks and wintered in more permanent (though unwalled) villages (Isa. 42:11; Jer. 49:28-33). Anthropological models suggest a symbiotic relationship between the Kedarites and their environment. Mercenary service for local kings could be exchanged for winter pasture. The sheep would eat the stubble of the grain and simultaneously fertilize the fields. Moreover, wool, leather goods, and other materials related to the herd could be traded for products of the more settled villages: pottery, metal goods, and grain.

The Kedarites (or Arabs) were a powerful economic and military force in the east, but according to Isaiah their glory would be short-lived (Isa. 21:16-17). Jeremiah predicted their demise at the hands of Nebuchadnezzar (Jer. 49:28), a fate confirmed by the Babylonian historian Berossus (Josephus *Ap.* i.19).

These people are mentioned in various extrabiblical sources. The Assyrian annals record attempts by Sennacherib and Assurbanipal to subdue the Kedarites (Akk. *Qidri*). A fifth-century Aramaic stele discovered at Tell el-Maskhuta in Egypt also refers to Kedar, calling Geshem the Arab (cf. Neh. 2:19; 6:1-2, 6) the "king of Kedar."

KEDEMAH [kĕd'ə mə] (Heb. *qēḏᵉmâ*, from *qeḏem* "east"). A son of Ishmael whose descendants constituted an Arabian tribe (possibly to be reckoned among the Kadmonites) (Gen. 25:15 par. 1 Chr. 1:31).

KEDEMOTH [kĕd'ə mŏth] (Heb. *qᵉḏēmōṯ* "eastern region"). A levitical city in the tribal territory of Reuben (Josh. 13:18), allocated to the Merarite families (21:37; 1 Chr. 6:79 [MT 64]). Moses sent messengers from the nearby desert to King Sihon of Heshbon requesting permission to pass through the land (Deut. 2:26).

The city apparently was located on the northern shore of the Arnon river. There the remains of two Nabatean sites, Kaṣr ez-Zaʿferan and Khirbet er-Remeil, have been found, 4 km. (2.5 mi.) northwest of Khirbet el-Medeiyineh and 14 km. (9 mi.) southeast of Medeba. Another possibility is es-Saliyeh (R. G. Boling and G. E. Wright, *Joshua*. AB [1982], p. 342).

KEDESH [kē'dĕsh] (Heb. *qeḏeš* "holy place").† The names Kedesh and Kadesh generally designate sites where pre-Israelite sanctuaries were located. Distinguished only by the later Masoretic vowel pointing, sites named Kedesh generally are found in the north and those named Kadesh in the south.

1. A city listed among those conquered by Joshua (Josh. 12:22). It may be the same as the city in the territory of Issachar assigned to the Gershomite Levites (1 Chr. 6:72 [MT 57]), elsewhere known as Kishion (Josh. 19:20; 21:28). The site has been identified tentatively as Tell Abū Qudeis, 4 km. (2.5 mi.) southeast of Megiddo.

2. A city in southeastern Judah (Josh. 15:23), probably an alternate form of KADESH 1 (KADESH-BARNEA).

3. A city in the tribal territory of Naphtali (Josh. 19:37). Subsequently the city was appointed a city of refuge (Josh. 20:7) and given to the Gershonite Levites (21:32; 1 Chr. 6:76 [MT 61]).

Tiglath-pileser III conquered the city in 733 B.C. and deported the populace to Assyria (2 Kgs. 15:29). The region around Kedesh (but not the city itself) is mentioned in the list of Thutmose III.

The site can be identified with some certainty as modern Tell Qadesh, 11 km. (7 mi.) northwest of Hazor and 36 km. (22 mi.) east of Tyre; the site is comprised of two hills, one of which was inhabited from the third millennium to the close of the Israelite period.

4. Kedesh in Naphtali, the home of Barak, at which he assembled the Israelite forces to battle Sisera (Judg. 4:6; cf. vv. 9-11). The site is probably Khirbet Qedesh near the southwestern shore of the Sea of Galilee.

KEEPER.† The translation of a number of Hebrew words representing a variety of offices and responsibilities in Israelite society.

1. A guard or watchman over agricultural matters, thus a shepherd or herdsman (Heb. *rōʿēh ṣōʾn* "a tender of sheep"; Gen. 4:2; *šōmēr*; 1 Sam. 17:20; Jer. 4:17) or especially someone who protected the harvest of the field, vineyard, or orchard (*nāṭar*; Cant. 1:6; 8:11; *nāṣar*; Job 27:18; RSV "watchman"). Such watchfulness was vital to the welfare of a community because an entire year's produce could be stolen or destroyed by an enemy (cf. Judg. 15:1-5). The owner of a field and his family or hirelings often built a booth or temporary shelter and spent the entire harvest there to protect the crops. The custom was probably the precedent for the Feast of Booths (Lev. 23:33-44; Neh. 8:13-18).

These same terms are also used figuratively with regard to caring for one's own body (Eccl. 12:3; cf. Cant. 1:6), for protecting a brother (Gen. 4:9), and for Yahweh's protection of his people (Ps. 121:5).

2. An important temple official, the "keeper of the threshold" (Heb. *šōmrê hassap*), who was in charge of the temple treasury and the various chambers of the sanctuary, as well as opening it each morning (2 Kgs. 12:9; 22:4; Jer. 35:4). According to 1 Chr. 9:17-32, early in the Monarchy David and Samuel assigned some 212 individuals and their descendants as gatekeepers for the tabernacle (cf. 2 Chr. 23:4). These officials served a seven-day rotation, collecting money from the congregation as the worshippers entered the inner court. The gatekeepers were headed by four Levites, one responsible for each of the four gates.

Apparently duties were reassigned after Solomon built the temple, for 2 Kgs. 25:18; Jer. 52:24 list only three official "keepers of the threshold"–probably one in charge of each of the major temple entrances (the east gate was not used). These officials were in charge of temple income and disbursements, the latter primarily for upkeep of the building. They appear to have ranked just under the high priest and the priests of the second order (2 Kgs. 23:4). Later, when it became apparent that the temple was not being properly maintained, King Jehoash again shifted the responsibilities of these officials (12:4-6). He relieved them of overseeing temple repairs and diverted collection monies from the general fund and placed them into a special offering chest beside the altar; the king and high priest then took over regulation of building funds. In postexilic times the office probably became superfluous.

Ezekiel lists two "keepers" which may or may not be identical with the keeper of the threshold: the "keepers of the charge of the altar" (Ezek. 40:46, KJV) and the "keepers of my charge in my sanctuary" (44:8, KJV).

3. A prison guard or warden (Heb. *śar bêṭ-hassōhar*; Gen. 39:21-23).

4. Various palace officials, including the ranger in charge of the royal forests (Neh. 2:8) and the chamberlain responsible for the king's robes (2 Kgs. 22:14 par. 2 Chr. 34:22), as well as military personnel (1 Sam. 17:22).

KEHELATHAH [kē'ə lā'thə] (Heb. *qᵉhēlāṭâ* "assembly"). An unidentified place where the Israelites rested during the wilderness wanderings, located between Rissah and Shepher (Num. 33:22-23). It may be the same as MAKHELOTH (v. 25).

KEILAH [kē ī'lə] (Heb. *qᵉˁîlâ*) (PERSON). Keilah the Garmite, the grandson of Hodiah in the list of the descendants of Judah (1 Chr. 4:19).

KEILAH [kē ī'lə] (Heb. *qᵉˁîlâ*) (PLACE). A city in the Shephelah region of Judah (Josh. 15:44) which David defended against the Philistines before Saul forced him to flee into the Wilderness of Ziph (1 Sam. 23:1-13). After the Exile the city was resettled and divided into two half-districts (Neh. 3:17-18). The city, called Qilti in the Amarna Letters, was disputed territory during the reign of the Egyptian Akhenaten just as it was in the Philistine period. It can be identified as modern Khirbet Qîlā, located about 25 km. (15.5 mi.) southwest of Jerusalem and 13.6 km. (8.5 mi.) northwest of Hebron.

KELAIAH [kĭ lā'yə] (Heb. *qēlāyâ*). A Levite who was forced by Ezra to give up his foreign wife (Ezra 10:23); also known as KELITA.

KELITA [kĭlī'tə] (Heb. *qᵉlîṭāˀ* "dwarf, crippled" [?]). A Levite who had to divorce his foreign wife (Ezra 10:23); also known as Kelaiah. According to Neh. 8:7 he helped to explain (i.e., translated from Hebrew to Aramaic) the portions of the Law which Ezra read to the people. He was among those who set their seal to the renewed covenant under Nehemiah (10:10).

KEMUEL [kĕm'yŏŏ əl] (Heb. *qᵉmûˀ ēl* "God remains firm").

1. A son of Nahor and Milcah; the father of Aram and eponymous ancestor of the Aramean peoples (Gen. 22:21).

2. The son of Shiphtan; a chief of the Ephraimites and one of those responsible for dividing the land of Canaan (Num. 34:24).

3. The father of Hashabiah, who was the chief officer of the Levites at the time of David (1 Chr. 27:17).

KENAN [kē'nən] (Heb. *qênān* "acquired, bought"

or "metalworker").† A son of Enosh and father of Ma-halalel (Gen. 5:9-14; KJV "Cainan").

KENATH [kē'năth] (Heb. *qᵉnāṭ* "property"). A city in eastern Gilead. It was captured during the Conquest by the Manassehite chieftain Nobah, who renamed it after himself (Num. 32:42). But apparently the original name persisted when the city later fell into Syrian hands (1 Chr. 2:23). Known as Canatha in the Greco-Roman period, it was the easternmost city of the Decapolis.

The site is identified as modern Qanawat, approximately 97 km. (60 mi.) east of the Sea of Galilee on the outskirts of ancient Auranitis.

KENAZ [kē'năz] (Heb. *qᵉnaz*), **KENIZZITE** [kĕn'ə zīt] (*qᵉnizzi*).†

1. A son of Eliphaz and grandson of Esau (Gen. 36:11 par. 1 Chr. 1:36); a tribal chief in Edom (Gen. 36:15, 42; 1 Chr. 1:53) and eponymous ancestor of the Kenizzites (Gen. 15:19).

2. A Judahite, the son of Elah (1 Chr. 4:15) and grandson of Caleb the son of Jephunneh "the Kenizzite" (Num. 32:12; KJV "Kenezite"; Josh. 14:6, 14).

3. A Judahite, the father of Seraiah and the judge Othniel (1 Chr. 4:13), called the brother of Caleb the son of Jephunneh (Josh. 15:17; Judg. 1:13; 3:9, 11).

References to the Kenizzites suggest a complex social and political history, particularly if the name Kenaz represents not only persons but also social groups. These people are reckoned among the pre-Israelite inhabitants of Canaan (Gen. 15:19), having perhaps migrated earlier from Anatolia. Situated in southern Judah or the northern Negeb, they apparently allied first with the Edomites. That they are later listed as descendants of Judah may indicate that they joined with the mixed multitude (Exod. 12:38; Num. 11:4) of Israelites in the conquest of Canaan.

KENITES [kē'nīts, kĕn'īts] (Heb. *qênî* "metalworker, smith").† A tribe or guild of smiths whose eponymous ancestor was Cain (Heb. *qayin*; Gen. 4:1; cf. Tubal-cain, v. 22). The Kenites appear in Palestine long before the Conquest (Gen. 15:19; Num. 24:21-22) and are numbered among the allies of the invading Israelites (Judg. 1:16; 4:11, 17). The biblical account locates them in several geographical regions and among several tribes, prompting some scholars to identify them as traveling smiths or tinkers, on the order of modern gypsies.

Hobab, Moses' father-in-law, whom Moses requested to guide the Israelites through the wilderness, was a Kenite. That the text also identified him as a Midianite (Judg. 1:16) suggests a broader political configuration. Although the narrative never explicitly indicates that he accepted the invitation, it does record that some of his descendants did. These Kenites settled with the people of Judah in the Negeb near Arad (Num. 10:29-32; cf. Judg. 1:16). Still later they are identified as proper members of the tribe of Judah (1 Chr. 2:55).

Jair, who killed Sisera, was the wife of Heber the Kenite who lived in northern Israel near Kedesh (Judg. 4:11-24; 5:24). In return for previous kindness shown the Israelites during the wilderness wanderings, Saul warned those Kenites who had settled among the Amalekites to depart before he attacked the city (1 Sam. 15:6). The Kenites are reckoned among those peoples of the Negeb allied with Israel in Philistine times (27:10; 30:29; LXX "Kenizzites").

The Rechabites generally are considered a subgroup of the Kenites who camped in tents, abstained from agriculture, and kept the Nazirite vows (Jer. 35). They are portrayed as an ideal of faithfulness the Israelites could not attain (cf. 2 Kgs. 10:15-17).

Certain scholars have advanced the so-called Kenite hypothesis, according to which the Kenites were the original worshippers of Yahweh. Accordingly, Moses acquired his religious knowledge in Midian through his father-in-law Hobab, who was a priest. Thus it was this Kenite god whom Israel chose to worship at Sinai. While intriguing, the hypothesis lacks adequate textual support and must remain in the realm of speculation.

Bibliography. F. S. Frick, "The Rechabites Reconsidered," *JBL* 90 (1971): 279-287.

KENIZZITE. *See* KENAZ, KENIZZITE.

KENOSIS [kǐ nō'sǐs] (from Gk. *kenóō* "to be or make empty, without power or reputation").† A doctrine which attempts to reconcile the two natures of Christ by suggesting that he "emptied himself" of all divine powers and attributes. This view takes its name from Paul's use of the term at Phil. 2:7, referring to Christ's being born in human likeness. Careful exegesis of the passage, however, demonstrates that proponents of this view fail to take into account a corollary meaning of the term, namely "to be of no reputation." This alternate meaning better fits Paul's purpose in writing the letter and his appeal to the Philippians to "do nothing from selfishness or conceit" (v. 3) and to "have this [same] mind among yourselves" (v. 5). The Philippians could scarcely have had any divine attributes from which to rid themselves; they could, however, make themselves "of no reputation" and take on the attitude of a servant— a theme quite common in Pauline literature. *See* PHILIPPIANS, LETTER TO THE.

KERAK, KHIRBET [kĕr'bĕt kûr'äk].* An important archaeological site (lit. "ruins of the fortress") located on the southwestern shore of the Sea of Galilee near the mouth of the Jordan river. The ancient city, which is not mentioned in the biblical accounts, was situated at the intersection of two major trade routes.

The site covers nearly 24 ha. (60 a.). It was occupied from the Late Chalcolithic period through MB IIA (*ca.* 3700-1700 B.C.) and then left desolate until early Hellenistic times, when it was rebuilt as Philoteria. In the Talmud it is called Beth-yerah. A famous EB III style of pottery, "Khirbet Kerak" ware, was first discovered here.

KERE. *See* KETHIB AND QERE.

KEREN-HAPPUCH [kĕr'ən hăp'ək] (Heb. *qeren happûk* "horn for antimony [eye paint]," thus a powder box). The youngest of three daughters who were born to Job after his trials had ended (Job 42:14).

KERIOTH [kĕr'ĭ ŏth] (Heb. *qᵉrîyôt* "cities"). A fortified city in Moab (Jer. 48:24; Amos 2:2; KJV "Kirioth"; cf. Jer. 48:41; RSV, NIV "the cities"). According to the inscription on the Moabite Stone, the city contained a sacred shrine for Chemosh. The site remains uncertain.

KERIOTH-HEZRON [kĕr'ĭ ŏth hĕz'rən] (Heb. *qᵉrîyôt heṣrôn* "fortified cities"). A city in the southern region of Judah, also called Hazor (Josh. 15:25). Some scholars, following the KJV, identify two distinct sites here, Kerioth and Hezron. The modern site may be Khirbet el-Qaryatein, 7 km. (4.5 mi.) south of Maon.

Kerioth-hezron has been suggested by some as the birthplace of Judas Iscariot, based on the interpretation of the name Iscariot as "man of Kerioth" (from a Hebrew form *'îš qᵉrîyôt*; cf. some MSS of John 12:4; 13:2, 26; 14:22).

KEROS [kĭr'ŏs] (Heb. *qērōs, qêrōs,* perhaps from *qeres* "curtain hook [in the tabernacle]"). The head of a family of temple servants who returned with Zerubbabel from the Exile (Ezra 2:44 par. Neh. 7:47).

KERYGMA [kĭ rĭg'mə] (Gk. *kérygma* "preaching, proclamation").* The proclamation of the good news in the New Testament and later. The word has become a quasitechnical term for the content of early Christian polemic, the "gospel" par excellence.

KETHIB AND QERE [kə thĕv', kə rä'] (Heb. *kᵉtîb* "it is written," *qᵉrê* "to be read"). Forbidden to alter the sacred consonantal Hebrew text (Kethib), scribes added some 1300 variant readings (Qere) in the margins. Some such emendations are intended to correct obvious errors in the text as transmitted (e.g., Jer. 42:6; K *'ªnû*; Q *'ªnaḥnû*). Others signal a preferred reading for sacred names or indelicate or otherwise offensive words.

Generally, the Qere represents the consonants of the correct or preferred form, preceded by the sign [°], the "circle of the Masoretes." Some readings (Qere Perpetuum, "permanent qere") occur often and thus are not written in the margin; in such cases only the vowels of the word to be read are placed under the consonants of the word written in the text (e.g., MT *hiw'*; K *hw'*, Q *hî'*). The divine name Yahweh is such a Qere Perpetuum, with the vowels of the Qere indicating the reading "Lord" (Heb. *'ªdōnāy*).

KETURAH [kǐ tŏŏr'ə] (Heb. *qᵉṭûrâ* "incense").† Abraham's second wife (Gen. 25:1-6), with whom he produced six sons (1 Chr. 1:32-33).

Although the Genesis account reports that Abraham married Keturah (25:1) after it records the death of Sarah (23:1-2), it is probable that this marriage took place earlier. The biblical writers often concluded narratives of persons they considered primary with other less important material, including secondary genealogies. Recognition of such an arrangement, dictated by literary convention rather than strict chronology, helps explain how the birth of Isaac could be regarded as· a miracle even though Keturah bore Abraham six sons. Keturah is called Abraham's concubine (1 Chr. 1:32; cf. Gen. 25:6), an appellation more appropriate if Sarah were living when the second marriage occurred.

Genesis depicts Keturah's sons as the eponymous ancestors of Arab peoples living east of Palestine (Gen. 25:4-6). It is through them that Abraham became "the father of a multitude of nations" (17:4).

KEYS, POWER OF.* The symbol of apostolic authority granted by Jesus. A common view in the ancient world was that the earth was separated from the upper and lower worlds by locked doors, access to which was only through the angelic being or deity who held the keys (Gk. *kleís*). Figuratively, then, keys represent the power and authority to control access to whatever is behind the locked door (e.g., Rev. 9:1; 20:1).

In the New Testament, Jesus is the one par excellence who holds the keys. He is the scion of the royal house of David (Rev. 3:7; cf. Isa. 22:22) and has overcome Death and Hades (Rev. 1:18), thus stripping them of their authority and terror (cf. 1 Cor. 15:54-57). Moreover, he has the power to delegate authority (Matt. 16:19). Jesus accuses the scribes of withholding the key to understanding God's purpose (Luke 11:52).

At Matt. 16:19 Jesus grants to Peter "the keys of the kingdom of heaven," as well as the power to "bind" and to "loose." In accordance with Matthew's understanding of the kingdom of heaven (i.e., of God) as anywhere God reigns, the keys here represent authority in the Church. *See* BINDING AND LOOSING.

Bibliography. J. Jeremias, "κλεῖς" *TDNT* 3 (1965): 744-753.

KEZIAH [kĭ zī′ə] (Heb. *qᵉṣîᶜâ* "cassia, cinnamon"). The second daughter born to Job after his trials had ended (Job 42:14; KJV "Kezia").

KEZIZ, VALLEY OF (Josh. 18:21, KJV). *See* EMEK-KEZIZ.

KIBROTH-HATTAAVAH [kĭb′rŏth hə tā′ə və] (Heb. *qibrôt hatta'ᵃwâ* "graves of craving"). The first place that the Israelites stopped after leaving Sinai (Num. 11:34-35; 33:16-17). It was the gluttonous behavior of many of the Israelites here in response to the Lord's provision of quail meat that incurred his wrath and thus the plague in which many died (vv. 31-33; cf. Deut. 9:22); the name derives from their burial here. The site is tentatively identified as Rueis el-Ebeirij, about 50 km. (31 mi.) east of Mt. Sinai.

KIBZAIM [kĭb zā′əm] (Heb. *qibṣayim* "two mounds").† A city in the tribal territory of Ephraim allocated to the Kohathite family of Levites (Josh. 21:22). Some scholars believe it to be the same as JOKMEAM in the parallel account at 1 Chr. 6:68 (MT 53), but the names may represent two distinct sites. The location is uncertain.

KID (Heb. *gᵉdî*). A young goat. The meat of a kid was regarded as particularly savory (e.g., Gen. 27:9; cf. Luke 15:29) and perhaps for this reason was associated with ritual meals (Num. 11:15; Judg. 6:19; 2 Chr. 35:7). The biblical injunction against boiling a kid in its mother's milk (Exod. 23:19; 34:26; Deut.

14:21) may be a prohibition of a practice found in Canaanite worship (cf. *UT* 52:14); it constitutes the basis of the kosher law against eating meat and dairy products in the same meal. *See* GOAT.

KIDNEYS (Heb. *kᵉlāyôt*).† Animal kidneys, considered one of the choicest parts of the animal (cf. Deut. 32:14), were burned along with the fat and the liver as the part of the altar sacrifice presented as a gift to God (Exod. 29:13, 22).

The Hebrews considered the human kidneys, along with the heart, to be the seat of the emotions (Ps. 7:10; 26:2; Jer. 17:10; RSV "heart"; KJV "reins").

The Greek word for kidneys (*nephroí*) occurs only once in the New Testament (Rev. 2:23), where the RSV translates "mind." A semantically related term is Gk. *splánchnon* "inward parts," which occurs in the figurative sense of "bowels (of compassion)" (2 Cor. 6:12; RSV "affections"; 7:15; RSV "heart").

KIDRON [kĭd′rən] (Heb. *qiḏrôn* "murky, dark"; Gk. *Kedrōn*). A valley east of Jerusalem, known in modern times as Wâdī Sittī Maryam ("Valley of St. Mary") or Wâdī en-Nâr ("Valley of Fire"), which divides the city from the Mount of Olives. The Hebrew name derives from the stream which once flowed through the valley, called the "black brook" no doubt because of the dark color of the detritus it once carried. Although situated some 3-15 m. (10-50 ft.) above its ancient level, the Kidron brook is now only a dry creek bed except for brief periods following heavy rain.

In capturing the city from the Jebusites, David apparently proceeded from this valley through a water shaft connecting the city with the Gihon spring (2 Sam. 5:8). The overflow of that spring was originally directed to the brook Kidron, where it then flowed southeast through the valley to the Dead Sea. Along the way the stream irrigated gardens in the Kidron valley (also called the valley of Shaveh [Gen. 14:17] or the King's valley [18:18] because the royal house owned property there). Later King Hezekiah realized the defensive weakness posed by this water route and, fearing Assyrian attack, diverted Gihon's waters and sealed the tunnel.

The Kidron was considered the border of Jerusalem. David fled beyond this point during Absalom's rebellion (2 Sam. 15:23), and Shimei, who had insulted David, was later ordered to cross the brook under penalty of death (16:5-14; cf. 1 Kgs. 2:36-46).

From early times the valley was used as a burial ground for both rich and poor (2 Kgs. 23:6; cf. Jer. 31:40), and here some of Judah's kings burned idols (Asa, 1 Kgs. 15:13; Hezekiah, 2 Chr. 29:16; Josiah, 2 Kgs. 23:4). The third-century B.C. tombs traditionally associated with Jehoshaphat, Absalom, James the Less, and Zechariah are located here.

According to John 18:1, Jesus and his disciples crossed the Kidron valley on the night of his betrayal (KJV "Cedron").

KILAMUWA [kĭl′ə mŏŏ′wə] (Phoen. *klmw*) **INSCRIPTION.**† A Phoenician inscription, dated to *ca.* 825 B.C., discovered in 1902 at Zinjîrlî in northwestern Syria. Associated with a palace dedication, it is an autobiographical account of King Kilamuwa of Yaʾudi (*Yʾdy*, perhaps the capital of a region in Samʾal) describing his achievements in foreign and domestic affairs (*ANET*, pp. 654-55).

A brief inscription of Kilamuwa was found on a gold sheath at Zinjîrlî. Other texts discovered at the same site include a Phoenician inscription of King Barrākib (*ca.* 730) and two in the Yaʾudic (or Samʾal) dialect of Aramaic which are ascribed to Kings Panammuwa I (*KAI* 214) and Panammuwa II (*ca.* 733-727 B.C.; *KAI* 215).

KILL.† Both Hebrew and Greek employ a variety of words which the English versions render "kill," but Heb. *rāṣaḥ* and Gk. *phoneúō* are the primary terms meaning "to put to death unlawfully, to murder."

The Hebrew term, which occurs in the sixth commandment (Exod. 20:13; Deut. 5:17; cf. Jer. 7:9), does not specifically refer to premeditated murder, although it is used of such (e.g., 1 Kgs. 21:19; Job 24:14; Ps. 94:6; Hos. 4:2; 6:9). The participial form, which the RSV translates as "murderer" (Num. 35), "manslayer" (Deut. 4:42; 19:3ff.; Josh. 20:3), and "slayer" (v. 5; 21:13), can indicate the agent of either intentional or unintentional killing. At Ps. 62:3 (RSV "shatter") and Prov. 22:13 (RSV "slain") the verb indicates unlawful killing. It is never used of killing for juridical reasons or in war, for in biblical times such acts were considered justifiable; for these situations such words as *hārag*, *hēmît*, and *nākâ* were used. Thus the sixth commandment forbids unlawful homicide but does not address capital punishment or organized warfare.

Gk. *phoneúō* regularly (although not exclusively) translates Heb. *rāṣaḥ* both in the LXX (e.g., Exod. 20:13; Num. 35:6; Deut. 4:42) and in the New Testament (e.g., Matt. 5:21; Mark 10:19; Rom. 13:9) and carries the same meaning.

KILN.† A container used to concentrate the heat from a fire in order to bake bread, fire pottery, or smelt ore. In ancient times such devices were made by coiling long, thin rolls of clay to form a large, open bowl, which was then inverted and a hole made in the top; the oven or kiln (Heb. *tannûr* is used indiscriminately for both) was covered with broken pottery sherds and fired (e.g., Exod. 8:3; Lev. 23:26; cf. Gk. *klíbanos*; Matt. 6:30). Bread ovens were usually .6-.9 m. (2-3 ft.) in diameter, and pottery kilns larger.

The word "kiln" is found in the RSV only at Exod. 9:8, 10; 19:18, where it translates Heb. *kibšān* (KJV, NIV "furnace"; cf. Gen. 19:28), probably a true pottery kiln. Heb. *malʿbbēn*, translated "brickkilns" at 2 Sam. 12:31 (JB "brickmaking"), is better understood as a brick mold (so RSV, Nah. 3:14). *See* BRICKKILN.

KINAH [kī′nə] (Heb. *qînâ* "smith[ville]"). A city in the southern portion of the territory allotted to Judah (Josh. 15:22), probably associated with the Kenites. Although the site has not been determined, it is probably located along the Wâdī el-Qeini near Arad.

KINDNESS.† Basically, a benevolent attitude or action between individuals (Heb. *ḥeseḏ*; e.g., Gen. 20:13;

Ruth 2:20). The KJV frequently translates "lovingkindness" for this technical term designating the covenantal love between God and his people (e.g., Ps. 17:7; Jer. 9:24; RSV "steadfast love"); elsewhere the term may be used similarly with reference to God's "mercy" (e.g., Ps. 23:6; cf. Deut. 5:10, KJV).

In the New Testament kindness (Gk. *philanthrōpía*) means "love for mankind" demonstrated by people (Acts 28:2) as well as God (Tit. 3:4). Gk. *philadelphía* means not only "brotherly affection" (2 Pet. 1:7; KJV "brotherly kindness"; cf. 1 Pet. 1:22) but specifically Christian kindliness (Col. 3:12). A more general term is Gk. *chrēstótēs* (e.g., Rom. 2:4; 2 Cor. 6:6; Gal. 5:22; Eph. 2:7), also translated "good, goodness" (e.g., Rom. 3:12).

See LOVE.

KING, KINGSHIP (Heb. *mālak̲, māšal, melek̲*; Gk. *basileús, basileúō*).† A male ruler with supreme authority. Generally the king was sovereign over an independent state, although sometimes an emperor would allow a subordinate vassal to retain that title as an illusion of autonomy. In the ancient world a king usually gained the throne by hereditary succession and reigned for life. The king was often regarded as the personal representative of the god(s) and thus ruled by divine right. Kingship is the position, authority, and majesty of such a ruler.

I. Early Israel

Israel, in contrast to the surrounding ancient Near Eastern nations, was to be a theocracy— a kingdom whose ruler was God (Deut. 33:1-5). Thus it would be God who would establish the laws and statutes (Exod. 19–23) and who would make his will known through the Urim and Thummim (28:30; cf. Num. 27:21) as well as the prophets (Deut. 18:15-22). Yet when Moses and Joshua, the first prophets, died, Israel entered a period of apostasy when everyone "did what was right in his own eyes" (Judg. 17:6; 21:25; cf. 2:18-20, 23). After having conquered the Canaanite city-states and formed a confederacy with no human sovereign, Israel was to be truly the "kingdom of God." But the ideal of "Yahweh as king" was never realized. *See* JUDGE.

II. Israelite Monarchy

Israel rejected the theocracy outright during the days of the prophet Samuel. Although Samuel warned them of the dangers inherent in a monarchy, the people apparently were tired of the insecurity of charismatic leadership as exercised by the judges. Fearful of the future, the people insisted upon having a king, "that we also may be like all the nations" (1 Sam. 8). They ignored the poor example of Abimelech, who had set himself up as king at Shechem (Judg. 9). God granted the Israelite request and instructed Samuel to anoint Saul as king.

Saul's reign began inauspiciously. Chosen by lot, he protested his humble origins (1 Sam. 9:21; cf. Judg. 6:15) and hid among the baggage at his enthronement (1 Sam. 10:21-22). Only after he was summoned from behind his oxplow and delivered Jabesh-gilead from Ammonite attack did Saul prove himself as king (ch. 11). Yet although his monarchical abilities increased,

Saul's obedience to the Lord did not (13:7-15). Finally, Samuel was forced to strip him of his rule and anoint David instead (16:1-13).

David is portrayed as the ideal king, although his shortcomings both as a monarch and an individual are fully evident. Indeed, he was a powerful and crafty ruler who united both the northern and southern tribal configurations under a single (actually dual) crown. Because David desired to build a temple for God, the Lord promised that a member of David's house would rule Israel forever (2 Sam. 7:5-16)— a promise that eventually came to be interpreted messianically.

The monarchy remained united under the able administration of David's successor Solomon, who increased the sphere of Israelite "empire" and authorized an extensive building program, the crowning achievement of which was the temple at Jerusalem. Subsequent kings, however, were unable to retain control over the diverse and competing factions of north and south, and the union was severed. To the south, in Judah, the kingship was passed to David's descendants. In Israel to the north, almost constant turmoil gave rise to a number of lesser dynasties.

For specific kings of Israel and Judah see the individual entries. *See* MONARCHY.

III. Duties of the King

The king was responsible for raising an army (1 Sam. 11:5-7; 2 Sam. 24), collecting taxes and conscripting for governmental services (1 Sam. 8:10-22; cf. 1 Kgs. 9:15-22), and administering in general the civil, military, and religious affairs of the kingdom (1 Kgs. 4:2-19; 1 Chr. 23–27). In addition to promoting domestic building on a monumental scale (1 Kgs. 5:13–7:51; cf. Eccl. 2:4-6), the king maintained diplomatic relations (1 Kgs. 10:1-13; 2 Kgs. 18:9-37) and fostered international trade (1 Kgs. 9:26-28; 2 Chr. 9:28). Moreover, he was responsible for the administration of justice (Deut. 17:14-20) and represented in extreme circumstances the final appeal (2 Sam. 15:2-4; 1 Kgs. 3:16-28).

Most important to the biblical account is the performance of the king with regard to the divine covenant, particularly evident in the editorial evaluation of his reign (e.g., 1 Kgs. 16:25-26). As the Lord's anointed (Heb. *māšîaḥ*; e.g., 1 Sam. 9:16; 16:13), the king was regarded as enjoying a special relationship with God. Nevertheless, he himself was not considered divine as were other monarchs of the ancient Near East.

IV. The Queen

Marriages were a common means of sealing alliances in the ancient Near East. For example, David married Maacah, the daughter of the Aramean king of Geshur (2 Sam. 3:3), just as Omri married his son Ahab to Jezebel, the daughter of the king of Sidon (1 Kgs. 16:31). A powerful king with many allies would have a correspondingly large number of wives (cf. Solomon, with 700 wives and 300 concubines; 1 Kgs. 11:3). Yet although a large harem symbolized the king's wealth and power (cf. 2 Sam. 3:6-11; 16:21-22; 1 Kgs. 2:22), the numerous wives and concubines themselves had no official status; nevertheless, the daughter of a particularly important ally or a favorite wife might

exercise considerable political or cultural influence (cf. 11:1-8).

Apparently the queen mother (Heb. *geḇîrâ* "great lady") was a figure of some importance. She is named in the royal pedigree (e.g., 1 Kgs. 11:26; 14:21; 15:2, 10), suggesting a matrilineal factor in succession, and apparently served in an advisory or at least ceremonial capacity (e.g., 2:19; 2 Kgs. 10:13). King Asa of Judah dismissed the queen mother Maacah because she worshipped the Asherah (1 Kgs. 15:13).

Upon the death of her last surviving son, Athaliah 1, a descendant of Omri who through marriage alliance became queen mother of Judah, murdered her grandchildren (except the infant Joash) and established herself as monarch over the southern kingdom. She reigned six years (842-836 B.C.) before falling to a coup organized by the high priest Jehoiada (2 Kgs. 11:1-20).

V. Theological Implications

The institution of kingship afforded ample opportunity for theological amplification. An idealized king came to be viewed as the millennial or apocalyptic champion, the Messiah. Such a king would be the scion of David (Jer. 23:5-8; cf. 2 Sam. 7:11-16) and the savior of the people (Pss. 2, 20–21, 110). The importance given this figure increased as the political situation in Israel steadily worsened, especially during the intertestamental period. Ultimately the messianic king was identified as God Incarnate (Matt. 16:16; 21:9; Heb. 1–2).

Bibliography. B. C. Birch, *The Rise of the Israelite Monarchy*. SBL Dissertation 27 (Missoula: 1976); H. Frankfort, *Kingship and the Gods* (Chicago: 1948); T. Ishida, ed., *Studies in the Period of David and Solomon and Other Essays* (Winona Lake: 1982); G. E. Mendenhall, *The Tenth Generation* (Baltimore: 1973), pp. 1-31.

KINGDOM OF GOD, KINGDOM OF HEAVEN (Heb. *malkûṯ yhwh*; Aram. *malkûṯā' dismayyā'*; Gk. *basileía toú theoú, basileía tón ouranón*).† That realm ruled by God. Although the designation occurs infrequently outside the New Testament, the concept of a kingdom ruled by God was extremely complex and experienced a long history of development.

I. Ancient Israel

In the Old Testament the kingdom of God was identified with the people of Israel (1 Chr. 28:5). In the ancient Near East gods often were associated with particular places and peoples, so it is not surprising that Israel also had such a relationship. Just as Chemosh was the god of Moab and Molech was the deity of Ammon (1 Kgs. 11:7), so Yahweh was the god of Israel (Josh. 24:14-24).

In ancient, sedentary societies, in particular, it inevitably was difficult to distinguish between a people and the land in which they lived. Since the kingdoms of earthly rulers were usually marked by geographical boundaries, it was natural that the dominions of their gods would be equated with that same territory. This is certainly why Naaman the Syrian requested "two mules' burden of earth" so he might worship Yahweh upon his return to his native land (2 Kgs. 5:17-18).

Thus throughout the Old Testament the "kingdom of God" designated both the people of Israel and the land in which they lived.

A unique aspect in the development of Yahwism was its extreme exclusivism. Worshippers of Yahweh were not permitted to serve other gods— an idea unusual for this period and one that eventually resulted in a strong Jewish monotheism. Even at its inception (Exod. 20:3), the covenant between Yahweh and Israel stipulated that he be honored as the supreme deity (while not specifically denying the existence of other gods).

The exilic and postexilic periods brought an intensification of this idea. If Yahweh were indeed El Elyon ("God Most High," the head of the pantheon; Gen. 14:18ff.; cf. Deut. 32:8; Ps. 46:4), then his kingdom must encompass the entire earth and the cosmos (Isa. 40:18-26; Jer. 10:7-16). This growing universality portrayed Yahweh as the "great God, and a great King above all gods" (Ps. 95:3; cf. 89:6-8) and realized "his kingdom" over all (103:19).

But precisely because of this universality, it became necessary to differentiate between those subjects who were loyal to Yahweh, the "true Israel," the "remnant") and those who did not acknowledge him as the Most High God. In addition, the Hebrew people no longer lived exclusively in Palestine. Deported after the fall of the northern and southern kingdoms, they were now spread throughout much of the Near East. Consequently, the concept of the "kingdom of God" experienced a radical shift in interpretation. It became not a geographical area or a political entity but an allegiance of faithful individuals.

II. Intertestamental Period

The postexilic state of Israel never regained the glory of the former monarchy, and the resultant tension between the people's expectations and the political realities forced a reassessment of the Jews' understanding of the "kingdom of God." As the possibility of God's kingdom ever being realized upon earth diminished, that reign was relegated to a period distinct from history and time (the "end times"; Gk. *tó éschaton*) and reinterpreted as a spiritual reality. Apocalyptic literature represents the kingdom as a realm where God would rule personally over all "peoples, nations, and languages" (Dan. 7:13-14; cf. 2:44; Zech. 14:9). This new realm, which would be the climax of human history (1 En. 90:20-42), would be only for the saints (Dan. 7:27); the wicked would be judged for their deeds (1 En. 91:7-11). Nominally, this distinction was primarily between Jews and Gentiles (e.g., Zech. 14:12; Jub. 23:30; 50:5; but cf. Zech. 14:12; 1 En. 8; 48:4). Ultimately, membership in the kingdom seemed to depend more on lack of material possessions (48:8; cf. Matt. 5:3 par. Luke 6:20) than blood ties to Israel.

This kingdom would be ushered in personally by God or his Messiah, who in this period was viewed more as a demigod (1 En. 45:3–46:6; 48:2-10) than simply an exalted king or military leader.

III. New Testament

The kingdom of God is perhaps *the* central theme of the New Testament. As heir to all the preceding, the New Testament presents the kingdom as one of three interrelated concepts: a theocracy, an actual political kingdom ruled by God; a spiritual reality, an inner attitude of voluntary acceptance of the rule of God; and, par excellence, the individual who placed himself in total and perfect submission to God— namely Jesus Christ himself, who in fact personifies the kingdom.

The gospel of Matthew uses the expression "kingdom of God" only four times (Matt. 12:28; 19:24; 21:31, 43), preferring the alternate designation "kingdom of heaven." The latter usage occurs thirty-four times, often where the Synoptic parallels read "kingdom of God." Although not found elsewhere in the New Testament, "kingdom of heaven" is a literal translation of Aram. *malkûṭā' dismayyā'*, a circumlocution deriving from postexilic Judaism's reluctance to use the name of God (cf. Targ. Onk. Exod. 15:18; Targ. Isa. 24:23); Matthew employs the term out of sensitivity toward his Jewish-Christian audience.

The phrase "kingdom of God," a freer translation of the Aramaic expression, is regularly used by most of the other New Testament writers; it occurs fourteen times in Mark, twenty-two in Luke, twice in John, six times in Acts, eight in Paul's epistles, and once in Revelation.

The rabbis used the expression "taking on the yoke of the kingdom of God" to indicate one who was in perfect obedience to the law (Mishnah *Ber.* ii.2, 5); to them the kingdom of God was a spiritual reality rather than a political system. It is this understanding of the kingdom that predominates in Jesus' teachings as recorded by each of the Evangelists (e.g., John 18:36). The coming of the kingdom is likened to the growth of a garden herb (Matt. 13:31) or that of sown seed (Mark 4:3-20). The kingdom itself is a treasure, the value of which exceeds all other possessions (Matt. 13:44-46). It is this inner kingdom, this voluntary acceptance of the rule of God (cf. John 3:3, 5), of which Jesus speaks (cf. Mark 9:1; 10:14; 12:34).

By extension, the "kingdom of God" also refers to Jesus Christ, the One who was in perfect submission to God. It is as such that the kingdom is "at hand" (Matt. 3:2; Mark 1:15; Luke 10:9, 11). Some evidence suggests that from this perspective the phrase serves as a divine name; accordingly, Jesus' statement that the kingdom of God was present in him is a virtual declaration of divinity (Matt. 12:28; Luke 11:20; cf. Targ. Isa. 40:9).

Paul's epistles reflect identical concepts of the kingdom of God. The apostle refers to an inner, spiritual reality when he argues that the kingdom (in the sense of "perfect obedience to God," as in the rabbis) does not consist of food and drink (Rom. 14:17), and his frequent use of the expression "in Christ" may be an abbreviation of "in the kingdom of Christ" as a locative for believers (cf. Eph. 5:5). Nevertheless, Paul's assertion that the kingdom of God will not be inherited by the unrighteous (1 Cor. 6:9-10; Gal. 5:21) seems more in keeping with the apocalyptic writers' vision of a future kingdom. Indeed, his emphasis on the believer's "hope of glory" (Rom. 5:2) seems to indicate a future possibility realized only after suffering the suffering and persecution of this world (vv. 3-5).

The theme of the book of Revelation, which builds upon the apocalypticism of the intertestamental period, is the establishment of the kingdom of God upon earth as a political reality (Rev. 11:15). Even though the precise term occurs only once (12:10), other expressions convey the same concept (e.g., "kingdom"; 1:6; "throne"; 4:2; "reign"; 11:17; "King of kings and Lord of lords"; 19:16; cf. 17:14). Certainly the kingdom of God as depicted in Revelation enters the world with none of the subtlety suggested by other New Testament books. It appears suddenly and violently with war (9:1-12) and plague (vv. 13-19). Society is split into two opposing forces, the people of the kingdom of God (6:9; 7:9) and all other "inhabitants of the earth" (3:10; 6:10, 15).

The kingdom of God is thus a broad concept with many divergent strands. The writers of the New Testament synthesized to a great extent the prevailing views of their day. Like the rabbis, they perceived that the kingdom was present wherever people allowed God to rule in their hearts and minds. But the followers of Jesus were unwilling to settle for a simple spiritualization of the kingdom. Rather, the kingdom began as an inward reality that would grow to dominate the whole earth until ultimately the kingdom "of our Lord and of his Christ" would swallow up the kingdoms of the earth. Then God would dispense judgment and personally rule over his people, assisted by those who voluntarily accepted his kingdom: the poor, the weak—those who became Christians.

Bibliography. J. Bright, *The Kingdom of God* (Nashville: 1953); R. H. Hiers, *The Historical Jesus and the Kingdom of God* (Gainesville: 1973); N. Perrin, *The Kingdom of God in the Teaching of Jesus* (Philadelphia: 1963); R. Schnackenburg, *God's Rule and Kingdom*, trans. J. Murray (New York: 1963).

KINGS, BOOKS OF.†

I. Place in the Canon

In the Hebrew canon 1-2 Kings constitute the concluding portion of the Former Prophets, the narrative of Israel's history from the Conquest to the collapse of the divided monarchy. The books originally formed a unit with 1-2 Samuel; they were first divided by the LXX as 3-4 Kingdoms (Gk. *Basileiōn*; Vulgate Lat. *Regum*).

II. Contents

The books open with an account of the final days of David's reign (1 Kgs. 1-2), thus concluding the narrative begun at 1 Sam. 9. Solomon's reign is recorded in 1 Kgs. 3-11, including accounts of his administrative reorganization, the construction of the temple, and commercial ventures and foreign affairs. This is followed by the history of the divided monarchy, from the revolt of Jeroboam I through the fall of Samaria and the northern kingdom (1 Kgs. 12-2 Kgs. 17); included here are the ministries of the prophets Elijah and Elisha. 2 Kings concludes with a record of the final days of Judah (chs. 18-25), from Hezekiah's reforms through the Babylonian destruction of Jerusalem and the deportation of the people.

III. Composition

The books of Kings, as also 1-2 Samuel and 1-2 Chronicles, demonstrate reliance on a number of ancient historical sources. Specifically mentioned are

"the book of the acts of Solomon" (1 Kgs. 11:41) and official annals, the Book of the Chronicles of the Kings of Israel (e.g., 14:19; 2 Kgs. 15:31) and the Book of the Chronicles of the Kings of Judah (e.g., 1 Kgs. 14:29; 2 Kgs. 24:5). Other blocks of material, particularly the "cycles" of narrative concerning the activities of the prophets Elijah (1 Kgs. 17-19, 21; 2 Kgs. 1) and Elisha (chs. 2-13), suggest the author's reliance upon other, unnamed ancient sources. Some scholars contend that the account of Hezekiah's encounter with the prophet Isaiah (par. Isa. 36-39) derives from an independent prophetic collection.

Individual regnal accounts (including that of David's reign; 2 Sam. 5-1 Kgs. 2) follow a standard format (e.g., 1 Kgs. 14:21-31; 16:29-22:40). Each begins with the name and pedigree of the monarch, the date of his accession, the length of his reign and place of residence, and a concise theological appraisal (e.g., "he did what was evil in the sight of the Lord"); also included for the kings of Judah are the name of the queen mother and the king's age upon gaining the throne. Following the record of events within the monarch's reign is a concluding summary indicating annalistic sources, particulars regarding the king's death and burial, and indication of a successor. For the period of the divided monarchy the king's accession is correlated with the regnal year of his counterpart in the other kingdom; accounts are arranged in roughly chronological order, alternating between the northern and southern kingdoms.

Critical scholars have long held that the books of Kings represent the work of one, two, or more editors, thus accounting for passages which presumably indicate awareness of the Exile (cf. 1 Kgs. 9:1-9; 2 Kgs. 17:19-20) and those which do not (cf. 1 Kgs. 11:34-36). More recently the standard view of a double (i.e., prexilic and exilic) redaction has been challenged in view of the literary and thematic unity of the Former Prophets.

The prevailing view is that 1-2 Kings were composed during the Exile, perhaps at Babylon, by a scribe or other privileged individual with access to official sources, or by a group or "school" of such persons.

IV. Theology

In addition to recounting the events of Israel's history during the Monarchy, the books of Kings demonstrate a concern for two major Old Testament themes, the covenant relationship between God and his chosen people (e.g., 1 Kgs. 8:53) and the acts of God in history.

Faithfulness to the covenant is viewed primarily in terms of adherence to the law (e.g., 1 Kgs. 2:3; 2 Kgs. 17:13), particularly as demonstrated through purity of cultic observance. Thus Solomon's construction and dedication of the Jerusalem temple is regarded as the ultimate form of obedience (1 Kgs. 5-8). In extreme contrast is his tolerance of foreign cults (ch. 11) and the construction of high places and participation in pagan practices by later kings of both Judah and Israel (e.g., 12:31-32; 2 Kgs. 16:4).

God's activity in history is demonstrated through the fulfillment of prophecy (e.g., 1 Kgs. 11:29-40; 12:1-20). To a greater degree it is expressed in terms of divine retribution for violation of the covenant stipulations, most notably through destruction and exile (2 Kgs. 10:32-33; 17:7ff.; 24:2-4, 20).

Bibliography. J. Gray, *I & II Kings*, 2nd ed. OTL (1970); G. H. Jones *1 and 2 Kings*, 2 vols. NCBC (1984); B. O. Long, *1 Kings*. FOTL (1984); *2 Kings* (forthcoming); J. A. Montgomery and H. S. Gehman, *I and II Kings*. ICC (1951).

KING'S GARDEN (Heb. *gan hammelek*). A royal garden area outside the walls of Jerusalem near the pool of Siloam, irrigated during the early days of the Monarchy by the brook Kidron. A tunnel led from the city to the pool and then out into the valley (Neh. 3:15). King Zedekiah apparently used this route to escape the Babylonian siege; the narrative describes the entrance to the garden as outside Jerusalem "through the gate between the two walls" (Jer. 39:4; cf. 52:7; 2 Kgs. 25:4). See KIDRON.

KING'S GATE (Heb. *ša'ar hammelek*). A gate on the east side of Solomon's temple which connected the temple to the royal palace. Warded by a Levite gatekeeper (1 Chr. 9:18), it was open only on the Sabbath and the day of the new moon for use only by the king (Ezek. 46:1-3). King Ahaz apparently dismantled this gate, using its metal ornamentation as partial payment of tribute for the Assyrian king Tiglath-pileser III (2 Kgs. 16:18).

KING'S HIGHWAY (Heb. *derek hammelek*).† The main north-south thoroughfare running from Damascus to the Gulf of Aqabah, closely equivalent to the modern Tariq es-Sulṭānī ("the Sultan's Road"). The king of Edom and the Amorite king Sihon refused to permit the Israelites to pass along this highway (Num. 20:17-18; 21:22-23; Deut. 2:27-30). Chedorlaomer and his allies apparently followed this route into Palestine, for among the cities they captured are fortresses that guarded this route (Ashtaroth, Karnaim, Ham, and Kiriathaim; Gen. 14:5). After conquering the Nabateans the Roman general Trajan rebuilt this road (ca. A.D. 106).

KING'S POOL (Heb. *berēkat hammelek*). A pool presumably located in the King's Garden (Neh. 2:14), perhaps the same as the Pool of Shelah (3:15). Some would identify it with the pool of Solomon, which Josephus cites between the spring of Siloam and Ophel (*BJ* v.4.2 [145]). It is not clear whether this pool is the same as the "artificial pool" of Neh. 3:16.

KING'S VALLEY (Heb. *'ēmeq hammelek*). A valley in the vicinity of Jerusalem, apparently identical with the valley of Shaveh where Melchizedek and the king of Sodom greeted the victorious Abram (Gen. 14:17; KJV "king's dale"). Tradition places it in the Kidron valley, perhaps near the point where that valley meets the Hinnom valley south of David's city; Josephus indicates that it was two stadia (370 m. [400 yds.]) from Jerusalem. A portion of this region was probably royal property, much like the royal garden in the same vicinity (Neh. 3:15). It was here that Absalom erected a monument in his own honor (2 Sam. 18:18).

KINSHIP.* The Israelites reckoned and structured their society and the attendant interpersonal configu-

rations primarily in terms of consanguine and affine relationships. In standard practice the basic social unit was the father's house (or functionally the household, incorporating nonkin service personnel and guests), patripotestal in authority, patrilocal in residence, and patrilineal in descent; at least in the early stages of Israel's history this unit was also reasonably self-sufficient in production. Neighboring father's houses were aligned in a "clan" (Heb. *mišpāḥâ*), actually a jural association which provided a broader economic base as well as military self-defense (in turn part of the larger *'elep* "thousand") and a larger source from which to draw endogamous marriage partners. Perhaps fifty or more of these associations in turn made up the major organizational segment of Israel, the tribe (*šebeṭ, maṭṭeh*).

In addition to providing social identity for individuals and groups, kinship constituted the means for transferring property (inheritance) and rights and authority within the social unit (descent) from generation to generation. Regulations governing marriage patterns and sexual relations (incest taboos; cf. Lev. 18:6-18) were formulated in terms of kinship. Religious events, such as the annual festivals (1 Sam. 20:6, 28-29), were observed within kinship groups, and cultic leadership was performed and perpetuated by designated kinship units (e.g., the Levites and Aaronic priests). Accordingly, genealogies played an important role in determining status and maintaining relationships. Moreover, deviations from standard practice caused by death, mobility (including marriage of offspring and divorce), and accidents of birth (e.g., no sons) necessitated the flexibility to allow alternative social patterns (cf. Zelophehad's daughters; *see* LEVIRATE MARRIAGE).

Kinship terminology varies in definition and application from society to society, and Israelite usage frequently differs from modern Western usage. For example, Heb. *bēn* may mean not only the immediate male descendant but also a grandson or more distant male descendant; in a more general sense it designates a member of a geographical, political, ethnic, or professional group. Other terms are equally vague, such as *ḥāṭān* "bridegroom," more precisely "a person related through marriage" (i.e., to his wife's family), and *ṭap* "dependent," a member of the household.

As Israelite society became increasingly more complex from the time of the Exodus on, with the influx and incorporation of large segments of biologically non-Israelite peoples (cf. Exod. 12:38; Num. 11:4), the major social units ceased to be genuinely kinship groups (some scholars question whether they actually ever were). These new peoples expressed their solidarity with Israel in kinship terminology, acknowledging the fatherhood of Yahweh, their common heritage of oppression and deliverance, and their putative descent from the Hebrew patriarchs.

In addition to designating familial relationships, kinship terminology also occurs within the jural-political domain. A king may call another monarch "my son," whether he is his biological descendant or his political subservient; allies of equal rank are "brothers." A clan regarded as the "son" of another clan need have no biological bond but may be rather a cultural or political dependent, and a town described as the "daughter" of another may be its colony. Furthermore, the inviolability of the land (as the possession of Yahweh it could not be sold) led to fictive adoptions, hence the transference of property to one outside the social unit by means of legally sanctioned "inheritance" patterns.

See INHERITANCE; MARRIAGE. See further the individual entries.

KIR [kĭr] (Heb. *qîr* "wall, walled city").
1. A city in Moab (Isa. 15:1), probably the same as KIR-HARESETH.
2. A city or region in Mesopotamia where Tiglath-pileser III relocated the populace of Damascus after conquering the Syrian capital *ca.* 733 B.C. (2 Kgs. 16:9; Amos 1:5). According to 9:7 it was here that the Syrians' forebears had lived before migrating to Aram. At Isa. 22:6 Kir is named with Elam as an ally of Assyria against Judah.

The name has been identified with Mesopotamian Dēr (Akk. *dūru*, BÀD.DINGIR^ki "wall of the gods"), a city located on the main road between Elam and Babylon east of the Tigris river. Dēr itself had been captured by Tiglath-pileser and its inhabitants deported *ca.* 738.

KIR-HARESETH [kĭr här'ə sĕth] (Heb. *qîr ḥ^areśeṭ* "wall[ed city] of potsherds"), **KIR-HERES** [kĭr hĭr'ĭz] (Heb. *qîr ḥereś*). A fortified capital of Moab, located on its southwestern border at modern el-Kerak. The alternate form Kir-heres occurs at Isa. 16:11; Jer. 48:31, 36 (KJV "Kir-haresh"). The city is probably the same as the Kir (1) mentioned at Isa. 22:6. Jeremiah's comment that "every head is shaved and every beard cut off" may be a pun on the Moabite name of this city (cf. Heb. *qorḥâ* "bald").

Kir-hareseth was situated 915 m. (3000 ft.) atop a steep hill about 28 km. (17 mi.) south of the Arnon river and about 18 km. (11 mi.) east of the Dead Sea. It controlled trade routes linking Syria with Arabia and Egypt. Although separated from Kir-hareseth by steep valleys, the neighboring hills tower over the city; thus the Israelites were able to lay siege to the city with stones and slingshots (2 Kgs. 3:24-25; KJV "Kir-haraseth"). Faced with defeat, King Mesha of Moab sacrificed his oldest son upon the city wall; according to the text, there then "came great wrath upon Israel" and the Israelites were forced to retreat (vv. 26-27).

KIRIATH [kĭr'ī ăth] (Heb. *qiryaṭ* "city of ..."). A city in the tribal territory of Benjamin (RSV mg., Josh. 18:28; KJV "Kirjath"), also called KIRIATH-JEARIM.

KIRIATHAIM [kĭr'ī ə thā'əm] (Heb. *qiryāṭayim* "two cities").
1. A very ancient city of Moab. It was one of a line of fortresses which guarded the major north-south route east of the Jordan. The site is generally identified as Qereiyât el-Mekhaiyet, a ruin situated on two hills 9.6 km. (6 mi.) northwest of Dibon and about 15 km. (9 mi.) northeast of the mouth of the Arnon river. At Gen. 14:5 the city is called Shaveh-kiriathaim because of its location in the valley of Shaveh (cf. v. 17).

Chedorlaomer and his allies captured the city early in the second millennium B.C. (14:1-2). After Israel's victory over Sihon, the city was assigned to Reuben (Josh. 13:19; KJV "Kirjathaim"), who subsequently rebuilt it (Num. 32:37; RSV "built"). The Moabites reconquered the city, for the Moabite Stone records Mesha's claim to having rebuilt it. Later the Israelite prophets predicted a time when this Moabite possession would be levelled (Jer. 48:1, 23; cf. Ezek. 25:9-11; Heb. *qiryāṭām*).
2. A city in the tribal territory of Naphtali assigned to the Gershomite Levites (1 Chr. 6:76 [MT 61]). It is probably the same as KARTAN in the parallel list at Josh. 21:32.

KIRIATH-ARBA [kĭr'ī ăth är'bə] (Heb. *qiryaṭ 'arba'* "city of four"). The ancient name of the city of HEBRON (Josh. 15:54; KJV "Kirjath-arba"). The name could mean "city of four districts" (a tetrapolis) or "city of four famous persons," as Jerome assumed by citing Adam, Abraham, Isaac, and Jacob; Josh. 14:15 traces the etymology to Arba, a great hero among the Anakim (cf. 15:13; 21:11).

KIRIATH-ARIM [kĭr'ī ăth âr'ĭm] (Heb. *qiryaṭ 'ārim*). A city named in the list of those returning from exile (Ezra 2:25; KJV "Kirjath-arim"). The correct form of the name, KIRIATH-JEARIM, occurs in the parallel account at Neh. 7:29.

KIRIATH-BAAL [kĭr'ī ăth bā'əl] (Heb. *qiryaṭ ba'al* "city of Baal"). An alternate name of KIRIATH-JEARIM (Josh. 15:60; 18:14; KJV "Kirjath-baal"; cf. 15:9, "Baalah").

KIRIATH-JEARIM [kĭr'ī ăth jē'ərĭm] (Heb. *qiryaṭ ḥuṣôt* "city of streets"). A Moabite city to which Balaam accompanied Balak (Num. 22:39; KJV "Kirjath-huzoth"). There Balak sacrificed to Baal in an effort to coerce him to curse the Israelites (v. 40). The site is probably to be sought north of the Arnon river.

KIRIATH-JEARIM [kĭr'ī ăth jē'ə rĭm] (Heb. *qiryaṭ y^e'ārîm* "city of forests"). A city on the border of Judah and Benjamin, near where those territories adjoined Dan (KJV "Kirjath-jearim"). It was reckoned among the possessions of Judah (Josh. 15:9, 60; 18:14-15), although at v. 28 some versions assign it to Benjamin. Probably originally known as Kiriath-baal (Josh. 15:60; 18:14), the city is also referred to as Kiriath (18:28), Kiriath-arim (Ezra 2:25), Baalah (Josh. 15:9; 1 Chr. 13:6), and Baale-judah (2 Sam. 6:2). Some indication of the ethnic composition of the pre-Israelite city is suggested in the genealogy at 1 Chr. 2:50-53.

Kiriath-jearim was one of four Gibeonite cities spared by the Israelites during the Conquest (Josh. 9). Seeking to avoid the fate of Jericho and Ai, the Hivite inhabitants connived to gain a treaty with Israel, claiming to be immigrants from afar and showing decayed food and threadbare garments as evidence. When the deception was discovered, the Israelite leaders honored their oath to spare the cities but forced the Gibeonites to accept a role of virtual serfdom.

It was just west of the city that the Danites encamped as they prepared to take Ephraimite land as their inheritance (Judg. 18:12). The Philistines returned the ark of the covenant to the Israelite inhabitants of Kiriath-jearim, who enshrined it in the house of Adinadab under the care of his son Eleazar (1 Sam. 6:21–7:2); here it remained for twenty years before David transported it to Jerusalem. The prophet Uriah was from this city (Jer. 26:20), as were a number of the exilic returnees (Ezra 2:5 par. Neh. 7:29).

Most scholars identify the site as Tell el-ʿAzhar (Tel Qiryat Yeʿarim), 13 km. (8 mi.) north of Jerusalem. Some evidence suggests that the city may have been relocated at nearby Abu Ghosh during the Roman period.

KIRIATH-SANNAH [kir′ĭ ăth săn′ə] (Heb. *qiryaṯ sannâ*). Either an alternate name or a scribal error for Kiriath-sepher (Josh. 15:49; KJV "Kirjath-sannah"). This form, which occurs only in the MT, may be the result of dittography with the preceding site, Dannah.

KIRIATH-SEPHER [kir′ĭ ăth sē′fər] (Heb. *qiryaṯ sēper* "city of [the] book [or document]"). The ancient name of DEBIR 1 (Josh. 15:15-16; Judg. 1:11; cf. Josh. 15:49).

KIRIOTH (Amos 2:2, KJV). *See* KERIOTH.

KIRJATH (KJV). *See* KIRIATH and related forms.

KISH [kish] (Heb. *qîš*) (PERSON).
1. A Benjaminite from Gibeah; the father of Saul, the first king of Israel. According to 1 Chr. 8:29-33; 9:35-39 Kish was the son of Ner and grandson (or a descendant) of the Gibeonite Jeiel, but 1 Sam. 9:1 cites his descent as son of Abiel from the lineage of the Aphiah of Benjamin (cf. Acts 13:21; KJV "Cis"). Some scholars have attempted to reconcile the two genealogies by identifying Abiel (Heb. *ʾăḇîʾēl* "my father is God") and Jeiel (Heb. *yeʿîʾēl* "Yah[weh] is God"), though none of the other individuals listed at 1 Sam. 9:1 can be so reconciled. The issue is further complicated by the designation of Ner as the brother of Kish (and uncle of Saul) at 14:50-51 (cf. 1 Chr. 9:36 and 2 below).

Despite Saul's modest disclaimer (9:21), Kish was a wealthy man (v. 1), as shown by his ownership of servants and asses (v. 3). He was buried at Zela in Benjamin (2 Sam. 21:14).

2. A son of Jeiel 1 and Maacah (1 Chr. 8:30; 9:36), and uncle of King Saul.

3. A Levite; the second son of Mahli of the lineage of Merari (1 Chr. 23:21) and father of Jerahmeel (24:29). His sons married the daughters of his brother Eleazar (23:22).

4. A son of Abdi, a Merarite Levite (2 Chr. 29:12). He was among those who cleansed the temple during Hezekiah's reform.

5. A Benjaminite ancestor of Mordecai (Esth. 2:5; Add. Esth. 11:2; KJV "Cisai"). Some scholars identify him with 1 above; others suggest that it was he, rather than Mordecai, who had been deported to Babylon (Esth. 2:6).

KISH [kish] (Sum. KIŠ) (PLACE).† An important Early Dynastic city in northern Babylonia. According to the Sumerian King List, it was here that kingship was first "lowered" after the great Flood (*ANET*, p. 265). The city apparently exercised suzerainty over a number of neighboring city-states. Even though Kish was later incorporated into the kingdom of Babylonia, the title "king of Kish" (Akk. *šar kiššati*) came to be an official appellation of any king exercising dominion over all of that sphere (lit. "king of the world"). The site has been identified as Tell el-Uhaimer, northeast of Babylon.

KISHI [kish′ī] (Heb. *qîšî* "gift [?]").† An alternate form of the name KUSHAIAH (1 Chr. 6:44).

KISHION [kish′ī ən] (Heb. *qišyôn*). A levitical city in the tribal territory of Issachar (Josh. 19:20; 21:28; KJV "Kishon"). In the parallel account at 1 Chr. 6:72 (MT 57) the city is called Kedesh (1). It is mentioned in the list of towns conquered by Thutmose III (Egyp. *Qsn*). The site has not yet been identified; some scholars locate it at Khirbet Qasyun, a hill between Endor and Mt. Tabor, while others place it at Tell el-Muqarqash, east of Endor.

KISHON [kish′ŏn, kish′ŏn] (Heb. *qîšôn*). A brook in the western portion of the valley of Jezreel and the plain of Acco (Judg. 4:7, 13; Ps. 83:9 [MT 10]; KJV "Kison"), the modern Nahr el-Muqaṭṭaʿ. At Judg. 5:19 it is called "the waters of Megiddo."

In the Hebrew text Kishon is identified as a *naḥal*, which may be translated "brook," "river," or "torrent" but which primarily designates a wâdî, a ravine in which water flows only seasonally, depending upon the rainfall. Indeed, the upper course of the Kishon and the wâdîs which feed into it flow only during the rainy season. Much of the rainwater which falls in the valley of Jezreel does not reach the river but creates marshes in several areas; when the river swells in winter and early spring, the shores are especially swampy. The lower course of the river, fed by various springs as it crosses the plain of Acco, contains sufficient water to flow throughout the year (cf. Heb. *nāhār*).

It was in the vicinity of Taanach and Megiddo, where the several wâdîs join to form the river, that Deborah drew out Sisera's troops for battle with Barak (Judg. 4:7, 13; 5:19). Routed by a flash flood (vv. 20-21), the Canaanite chariots became mired in the soggy terrain and Sisera fled on foot before the lighter-armed Israelites (4:15-17; cf. Ps. 83:9). Some scholars regard Heb. *qedûmîm* at Judg. 5:21 (RSV "onrushing"; KJV "ancient") as an alternate name for the river (cf. Peshitta "the river Karmin").

Elijah's massacre of the prophets of Baal is traditionally located at Tell el-Qasîs ("Mound of the Priests") near Deir el-Muḥraq.

KISS (Heb. *nāšaq*, *nᵉšîqâ*; Gk. *philéō, kataphiléō, phílēma*). A sign of affection, salutation, or worship. Kissing was one of the many signs of greeting in the ancient Near East.

In ancient Israel the kiss was most often used as a salutation. Family members often greeted one another with a kiss (e.g., Gen. 48:10; Exod. 4:27; Ruth 1:9, 14). Acquaintances also saluted one another by kissing (1 Sam. 20:41), even when the act was a subterfuge for betrayal (2 Sam. 20:9; cf. Prov. 27:6). That the kiss was a common greeting is corroborated by the poetic parallelism at Ps. 85:10 (MT 11). Honesty and candor are likened to a kiss as the mark of true friendship (Prov. 24:26).

While a kiss on the cheek was often a sign of greeting between equals, a kiss could also be a gesture of submission, worship, or adoration (cf. Gen. 27:26-27; 50:1; Exod. 18:7). The phrase "may his enemies lick the dust" (Ps. 72:9) refers to captives who pressed their lips to the dusty ground upon which their conqueror had trod, thus acknowledging their status. The command to "kiss [the Lord's] feet, lest he be angry" (2:12; KJV, NIV "kiss the Son") is an exhortation to "pay homage in good faith" (so NJV). One could also show submission by kissing the outer garment of a prominent figure, as Saul was attempting when he tore Samuel's robe (1 Sam. 15:27). Samuel himself had kissed Saul to honor him as Israel's chosen king (10:1; cf. Absalom's response to those sought his judgment; 2 Sam. 15:5). In similar fashion, a kiss was apparently employed in the idolatrous worship of the local baals (1 Kgs. 19:18) as well as the Israelite images at Dan and Bethel (Hos. 13:2).

The erotic kiss is attested in the ancient Near East, although it did not predominate as in the modern West. The Bible contains only a single example of a kiss as an erotic gesture (Cant. 1:2).

The kiss as depicted in the New Testament conveys many of the same meanings demonstrated in the Old Testament. The prodigal son is kissed by his father (Luke 15:20), and the Ephesians weep and kiss the departing Paul (Acts 20:37). The "holy kiss" of the epistles (e.g., Rom. 16:16; 1 Thess. 5:26; 1 Pet. 5:14) is simply the traditional kiss of greeting. It is that kiss which Judas employed in betraying Jesus (Matt. 26:48-49 par. Mark 14:44-45). Jesus cites observance of the kiss of submission and adoration in contrasting the attitudes of the Pharisee Simon and a sinful woman (Luke 7:38, 45).

KITE (Heb. *'ayyâ, dā'â, dayyâ*). A predatory bird of the hawk (*Accipitridae*) family, of the genus Milvus. Three species have been attested in Palestine. The common kite (*Milvus milvus*) is a brown bird, about 60 cm. (2 ft.) long. It is most prevalent in the winter, when flocks are found along the Mediterranean coast, in southern Judah, west of the Dead Sea, and in the wilderness of Beer-sheba. The black kite (*Mivus migrans*; NIV, Deut. 14:13) is blackish-brown with a notched tail; it arrives in March and settles for the summer near villages, where it feeds on refuse (cf. Isa. 34:15; NIV "falcon"; NJV "buzzards"). The Egyptian kite (*Milvus aegypticus*) is found in southern Palestine as well as in Syria and Asia Minor. In addition, several species are known to breed during the summer in the vicinity of Mt. Carmel, Nâblus, and northern Galilee. As elsewhere in biblical usage, the terms designating these species are applied imprecisely by modern standards. The KJV translates "vultures" in each of the passages cited.

The kite feeds on small rodents such as rats, moles, and field mice, hence it is listed among the unclean birds (Lev. 11:14; Deut. 14:13). With its keen vision the kite can detect its victim from rather high altitudes and then swoop down for the kill. Thus the Hebrew term *dā'â*, which means literally "that which flies powerfully though gracefully," is an apt description of the soaring kite.

Bibliography. F. S. Bodenheimer, *Animal and Man in Bible Lands* (Leiden: 1960).

KITHLISH (Josh. 15:40, KJV). See CHITLISH.

KITRON [kĭt'rŏn] (Heb. *qiṭrôn*). A Canaanite city in the territory allotted to Zebulun which the Israelites were not able to capture initially (Judg. 1:30). It is probably the same as KATTATH. The location has not yet been identified; suggestions include Khirbet Qoteina, southwest of Jokneam, and Tell el-Far.

KITTIM [kĭt'ĭm] (Heb. *kittîm, kittîyîm*).† The Hebrew name for Cyprus, derived from Kition (modern Larnaca), an important Phoenician city (Phoen. *Kty*) on the southeast coast of the island. According to the Table of Nations (Gen. 10:4 par. 1 Chr. 1:7), Kittim was a descendant of Javan (Ionia), apparently reflecting the city's sizable Greek population.

The Hebrews associated the island of Kittim with ships (Isa. 23:1, 12; so JB, following MT; KJV "Chittim"; RSV "Cyprus") and was a source of pine for Phoenician shipbuilders (Ezek. 27:6). Jeremiah speaks of the land in terms which indicate that for the Hebrews it represented a westernmost boundary of civilization (Jer. 2:10).

As Cyprus came increasingly under Greek influence, the name Kittim was extended to include Greece proper (1 Macc. 1:1; 8:5; RSV "Macedonians") and ultimately Rome (Dan. 11:30; LXX Gk. *Rhōmaioi*).

The name is also found in extrabiblical sources. The Kittim are named at Jub. 24:28-29; 37:11, where the term seems to indicate the Seleucid Greeks. The Habakkuk Commentary (or Pesher) of the Dead Sea Scrolls (1QpHab) interprets the Chaldeans (Heb. *kaśdîm*) at Hab. 1:6 as the Kittim; here the description best fits the Romans, particularly in that they sacrificed to their military standards (cf. v. 15). The contemporary Dead Sea Nahum Commentary also applies the term to the Romans, citing "the kings of Greece from Antiochus until the rise of the rulers of the Kittim").

See CYPRUS.

KNEADING BOWL (Heb. *miš'eret*). A portable bowl (Exod. 12:34), shallow and usually made of wood; also called a kneading trough (Deut. 28:5, 17). It was a common household item throughout the ancient Near East (cf. Exod. 8:3; Deut. 28:5, 17). Flour and water were mixed in this bowl (e.g., Gen. 18:6; 1 Sam. 28:24) and the dough left there to leaven (cf. Hos. 7:4).

According to later Jewish custom, the kneading bowl was to be specially checked before Passover because dough could become lodged in cracks of the wooden bowl. Less than an "olive's bulk" in any single place was considered negligible according to the rabbis (Mishnah *Pesaḥ* iii.2). Since normally a piece of day-old bread was kneaded into the dough to aid leavening, larger portions remaining in the cracks apparently were thought to contribute to the fermentation process.

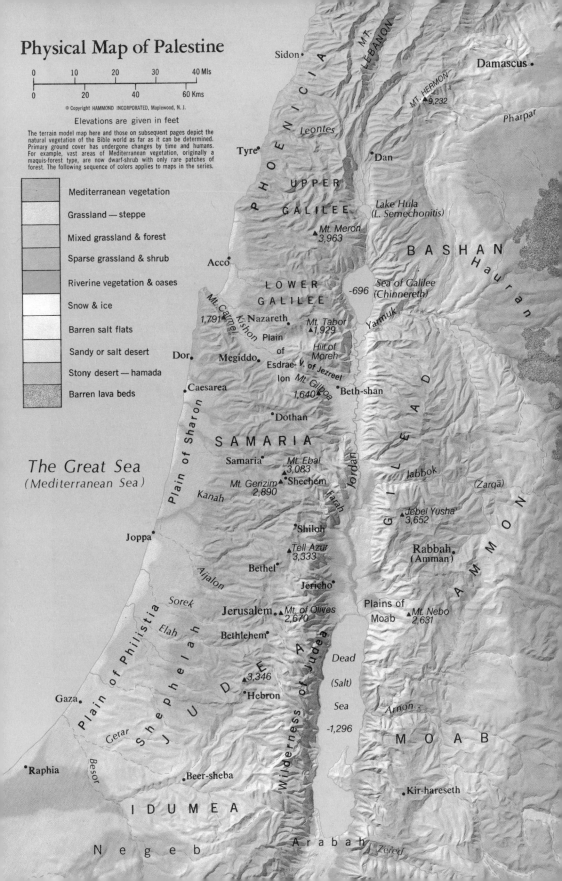

Physical Map of Palestine

0   10   20   30   40 Mls
0   20   40   60 Kms

Elevations are given in feet

The terrain model map here and those on subsequent pages depict the natural vegetation of the Bible world as far as it can be determined. Primary ground cover has undergone changes by time and humans. For example, vast areas of Mediterranean vegetation, originally a maquis-forest type, are now dwarf-shrub with only rare patches of forest. The following sequence of colors applies to maps in the series.

Mediterranean vegetation
Grassland — steppe
Mixed grassland & forest
Sparse grassland & shrub
Riverine vegetation & oases
Snow & ice
Barren salt flats
Sandy or salt desert
Stony desert — hamada
Barren lava beds

The Great Sea
(Mediterranean Sea)

Sidon
Damascus
MT. LEBANON
MT. HERMON
9,232
Pharpar
Leontes
Tyre
P H O E N I C I A
Dan
UPPER
GALILEE
Lake Hula
(L. Semechonitis)
Mt. Meron
3,963
B A S H A N
Hauran
Acco
LOWER
GALILEE
-696
Sea of Galilee
(Chinnereth)
Mt. Carmel
1,791
Kishon
Nazareth
Mt. Tabor
1,929
Plain
of
Esdrae-
Ion
Hill of
Moreh
V. of Jezreel
Mt. Gilboa
1,640
Yarmuk
G I L E A D
Dor
Megiddo
Caesarea
Beth-shan
Plain of Sharon
Dothan
S A M A R I A
Jabbok
(Zarqā)
Samaria
Mt. Ebal
3,083
Mt. Gerizim
2,890
Shechem
Jebel Yusha'
3,652
Kanah
Jordan
Jabbok
A M M O N
Shiloh
Tell Azur
3,333
Rabbah
(Amman)
Bethel
Jericho
Ajjalon
Sorek
Joppa
Plains of
Moab
Mt. Nebo
2,631
Jerusalem
Mt. of Olives
2,670
Elah
Bethlehem
J U D E A
Shephelah
3,346
Wilderness of Judea
Dead
(Salt)
Sea
-1,296
Gaza
Hebron
Arnon
Plain of Philistia
Gerar
Besor
Kir-hareseth
Raphia
Beer-sheba
M O A B
I D U M E A
N e g e b
Arabah
Zered

Ancient Canaan

——— Trade Routes

0 5 10 15 20 25 30 35 Mls
0   10   20   30   40   50   60 Kms
© Copyright HAMMOND INCORPORATED, Maplewood, N. J.

The Great Sea
(Mediterranean Sea)

Gebal
(Byblos)

Berytus

Dog R.

P H O E N I C I A

M O U N T   L E B A N O N

B E Q A 'A

A N T I - L E B A N O N

Kumidi

Sidon

To Tadmor

Damascus

MT. HERMON

Leontes

Tyre

Laish (Dan)

Hazor

B A S H A N

Acco

Sea of
Chinnereth

Ashtaroth

Mt. Carmel

Beth-yerah

Dor

Edrei

Megiddo

V. of Jezreel

Taanach

Beth-shan

Ibleam

Dothan

Tirzah

Farah R.

Penuel

Mahanaim

Shechem

Succoth
(Tell Deir 'alla)

Jabbok

A M O R I T E S

Joppa

Shiloh

Jordan R.

Bethel
(Luz)

Ai

Rabbah

A M M O N

Gezer

Gibeon

Jericho

Ashdod

Sorek

Heshbon

Jerusalem (Jebus)

Timnah

Bethlehem

Ashkelon

Salt

Lachish

Mamre

Eglon?
(Tell el-Hesi)

Gaza

Hebron

Sea

Arnon R.

Gerar

Debir?

Sharuhen

Arad

Beer-sheba

Ancient cemetery
(Bab edh 'Drah)

M O A B

Kir-hareseth

Sodom and
Gomorrah?

Zoar

Zered

N e g e b

E D O M

The Ancient World
at the Time of the Patriarchs

→ Route of Abraham and the Patriarchs
(Early 2nd Millennium B.C.)

▬ Areas of influence of major
powers about 1350 B.C.

© Copyright HAMMOND INCORPORATED, Maplewood, N.J.

Mls
0   50   100   150   200   250Mls
0   100   200   300   400Kms

Caspian Sea

Persian Gulf (Lower Sea)

Mediterranean Sea (Great or Upper Sea)

Red Sea

Dilmun?

MEDIA
ELAM
URARTU
KASHKA
HURRIANS
HORITES
ZAGROS MOUNTAINS
GUTIUM MOUNTAINS
MITANNI
ASSYRIA
BABYLONIA
KASSITES
SUMER
AMURRU
KEDAR
MIDIAN
EGYPT
LIBYAN Desert
ASSUWA
ARZAWA
LUKKA
HITTITE EMPIRE (HATTI)
TAURUS MOUNTAINS
KIZZUWATNA
MYCENAEAN DOMAIN
MINOAN
CAPHTOR (Crete)
ALASHYA, KITTIM (Cyprus)
SINAI
Lower Egypt

Mt. Ararat
L. Van
L. Urmia
Ecbatana
Tepe Giyan
Susa
Cyrus
Araxes
Sangarius
Hermes
Maeander
Hattusas
Alaca Huyuk
Ankuwa
Kanish
L. Tuz
Beycesultan
Karabel
Mersin
Troy
Rhodes
Knossos
Ugarit
Arvad
Gebal
Byblos
Sidon
Tyre
Dor
Hazor
Megiddo
Joppa
Gaza
Beer-sheba
Kadesh-barnea
Hebron
Jerusalem
Jericho
Shechem
Damascus
Kadesh
Hamath
Haleb
Ebla
Alalakh
Carchemish
Tadmor
Mari
Tell Halaf
Harran
Paddan-aram
Malatya
Tell Brak
Nineveh
Calah
Asshur
Arbela
Gozan
Tepe Gawra
Jarmo
Nuzi
Tigris
Euphrates
Diyala
Eshnunma
Akkad
Agade?
Sippar
Cuthah
Babylon
Nippur
Isin
Lagash
Erech
Ur
Eridu
Dumah
Tema
Dedan
Avaris (Zoan)
Memphis (Noph)
Heracleopolis
Hermopolis
Akhetaton (Tell el-Amarna)
Abydos
Nile

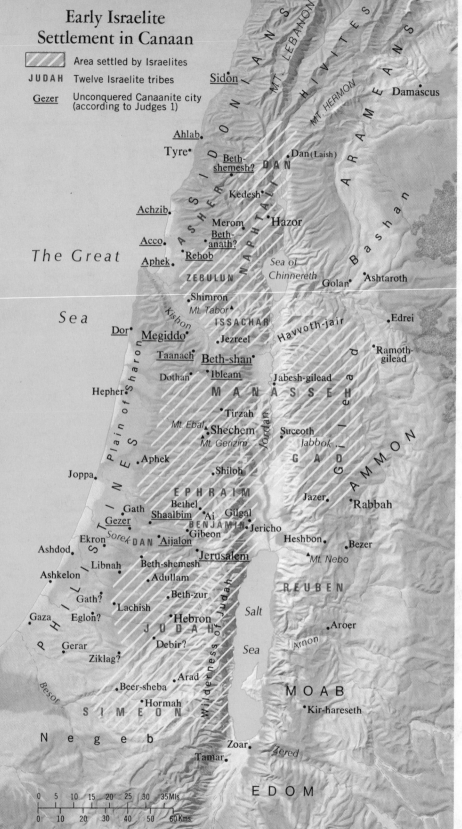

Early Israelite
Settlement in Canaan

/////	Area settled by Israelites
JUDAH	Twelve Israelite tribes
Gezer	Unconquered Canaanite city (according to Judges 1)

Sidon

MT. LEBANON

HIVITES

ARAMEANS

MT. HERMON

Damascus

Ahlab.

Tyre•

Beth-
shemesh?

DAN

Dan (Laish)

Kedesh•

Achzib.

Merom
Beth-
anath?

Hazor

Bashan

Acco.

Rehob

Aphek.

Rehob

ZEBULUN

Sea of
Chinnereth

Golan•

Ashtaroth

The Great

ASHER

NAPHTALI

Shimron•

Mt. Tabor ▲

ISSACHAR

Havvoth-jair

Edrei

Sea

Kishon

Dor•

Megiddo•

Jezreel•

Ramoth-
gilead

Taanach•

Beth-shan•

Dothan•

Ibleam

Jabesh-gilead

Hepher•

MANASSEH

Gilead

AMMON

Tirzah•

Mt. Ebal ▲

Shechem

Succoth

Plain of Sharon

Mt. Gerizim ▲

Jordan

Jabbok

GAD

Aphek•

Shiloh•

Joppa.

EPHRAIM

Jazer•

Rabbah•

Bethel•

Gath•

Ai

Gilgal

Shaalbim•

BENJAMIN

Jericho•

Heshbon•

Bezer•

Gezer•

Gibeon•

Ekron•

Sorek

DAN

Aijalon

Jerusalem•

Mt. Nebo•

Ashdod•

Libnah•

Beth-shemesh•

PHILISTINES

Ashkelon•

Adullam•

REUBEN

Gath?•

Beth-zur•

Lachish•

Salt

Gaza•

Eglon?•

JUDAH

Hebron•

Aroer•

P

Gerar•

Debir?•

Sea

Arnon

Ziklag?•

Besor

Arad•

MOAB

Beer-sheba•

Wilderness of Judah

Hormah•

Kir-hareseth•

SIMEON

N e g e b

Zoar•

Zered

Tamar•

E D O M

| 0 | 5 | 10 | 15 | 20 | 25 | 30 | 35 Mls. |
| 0 | 10 | 20 | 30 | 40 | 50 | 60 Kms. |

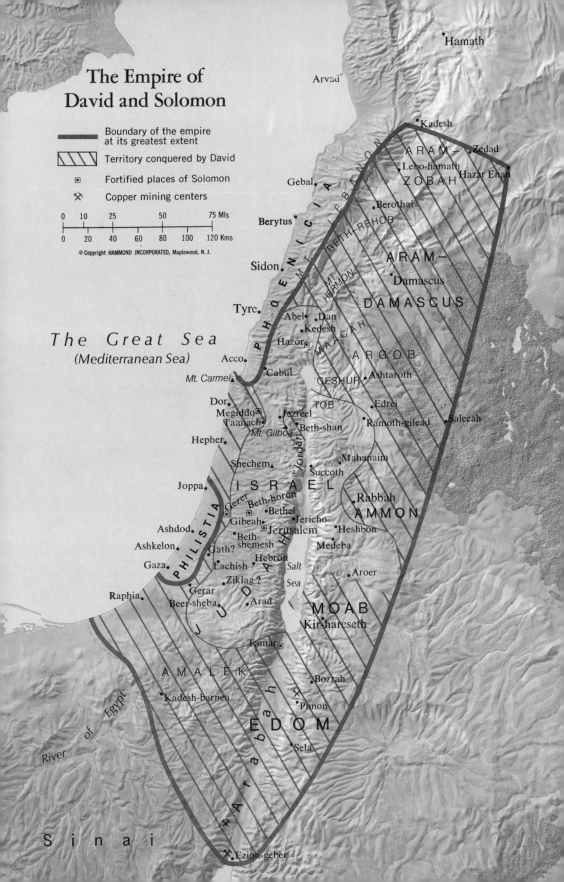

The Empire of
David and Solomon

Boundary of the empire
at its greatest extent

Territory conquered by David

Fortified places of Solomon

Copper mining centers

0   10   25   50   75 Mls

0   20   40   60   80   100   120 Kms

© Copyright HAMMOND INCORPORATED, Maplewood, N.J.

•Hamath

Arvad

•Kadesh

ARAM –   •Zedad

•Lebo-hamath   Hazar Enan

ZOBAH

Gebal•

•Berothai

Berytus•

ARAM –

Sidon•   •Damascus

DAMASCUS

Tyre•   Abel• •Dan

•Kedesh

Hazor•   ARGOB

Acco•   •Ashtaroth

•Cabul   GESHUR

The Great Sea   TOB   •Edrei

(Mediterranean Sea)   •Ramoth-gilead   •Salecah

Dor•   Jezreel•

Megiddo•   •Beth-shan

Taanach•

Mt. Gilboa

Hepher•   •Mahanaim

Shechem•

•Succoth

Joppa•   ISRAEL

Gezer• Beth-horon•   Rabbah•

Bethel•   AMMON

Gibeah•

Ashdod•   Beth-•Jerusalem •Heshbon

Ashkelon•   shemesh•

Gath?•   •Medeba

Gaza•   Lachish• Hebron•

Ziklag?•   Salt   •Aroer

Raphia•   Gerar•   Sea

Beer-sheba• •Arad

AMALEK   MOAB

Kadesh-barnea•   Kir-hareseth

•Bozrah

River   •Punon

of

Egypt   EDOM

Tamar•   •Sela

Ezion-geber

Sinai

Mt. Carmel▲

PHOENICIA

LEBANON

BETH-REHOB

MT. HERMON

MAACAH

Jordan

PHILISTIA

JUDAH

Arabah

The Kingdoms of Israel and Judah

- - - - Approximate frontiers
ISRAEL Hebrew kingdoms
AMMON Foreign kingdoms

0 10 20 30 40 Mls
0   20   40   60 Kms

© Copyright HAMMOND INCORPORATED, Maplewood, N.J.

The Great Sea
(Mediterranean Sea)

Damascus

PHOENICIA

SYRIA
(ARAM)

Sidon
Tyre
Acco

Leontes
Abel-beth-maachah
Ijon
MT. HERMON
Dan
Kedesh
Hazor
Merom
Galilee
Cabul
Chinnereth
Rumah
Hammath
Sea of Chinnereth
Bashan
Karnaim
Ashtaroth
Aphek

Dor
Megiddo
Plain of Kishon
Mt. Carmel
Mt. Tabor
Yarmuk
Havvoth-jair
Edrei

Shunem
Esdraelon
Jezreel
Taanach
Mt. Gilboa
Beth-shan
Ibleam
Dothan
Jabesh-gilead
Abel-meholah
Tishbe
Ramoth-gilead

ISRAEL
Socoh
Tirzah
Samaria
Mt. Ebal
Mt. Gerizim
Shechem
Succoth
Penuel
Mahanaim
Jabbok
Gilead

Plain of Sharon
Kanah
Aphek
Shiloh
Zeredah
Joppa

AMMON
Jazer
Rabbah

Lod
Gath
Bethel
Mizpah
Zemaraim
Geba
Gilgal
Jericho
Ramah
Shittim?
Heshbon

Jabneel
Gezer
Gibbethon
Aijalon
Gibeon
Zorah
Jerusalem
Ekron
Ashdod

Beth-shemesh
Bethlehem
Mt. Nebo
Medeba
Jahaz

Ashkelon
Socoh
Adullam
Etam
Tekoa
Mareshah
Beth-zur

PHILISTIA
JUDAH
Lachish
Adoraim
Hebron
Ziph
Debir?
Ziklag?

Gaza
Gerar
Wilderness of Judah
En-gedi
Salt Sea
Ataroth
Dibon
Aroer
Arnon

Raphia
Sharuhen
Arad
Beer-sheba

Ar?
MOAB
Kir-hareseth

Negeb
Ziph
Tamar
Zoar
Arabah
Zered
Ascent of Akrabbim
EDOM

Jordan

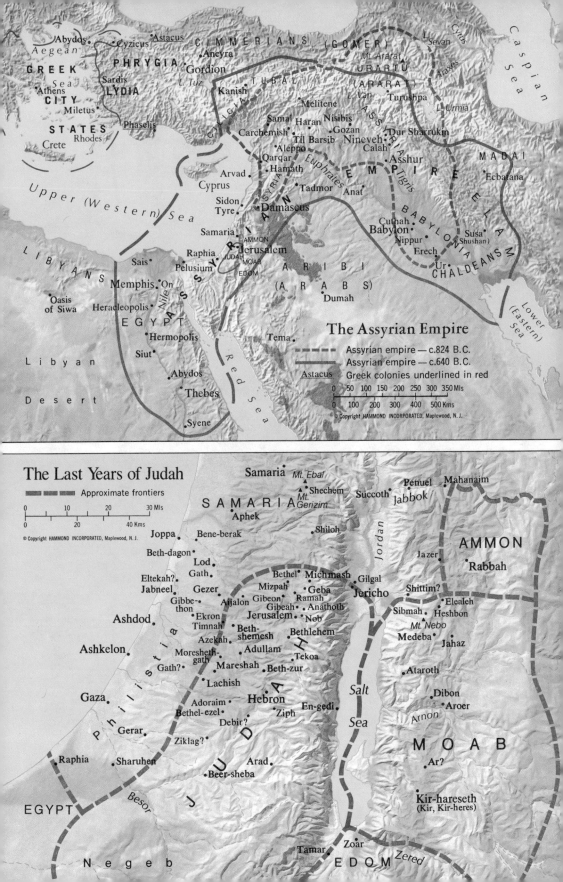

The Assyrian Empire

The Last Years of Judah

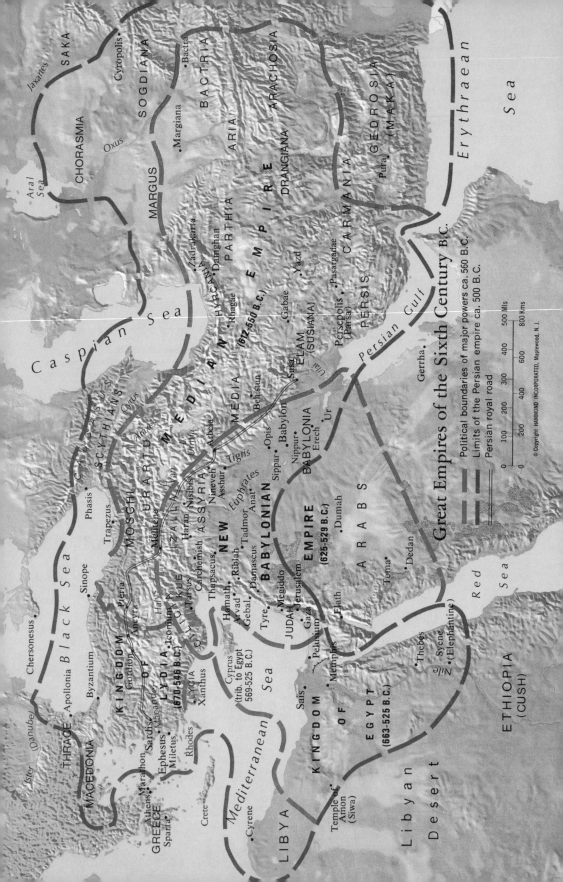

Great Empires of the Sixth Century B.C.

Political boundaries of major powers ca. 560 B.C.
Limits of the Persian empire ca. 500 B.C.
Persian royal road

| 0 | 100 | 200 | 300 | 400 | 500 Mls |
| 0 | 200 | 400 | 600 | 800 Kms | |

© Copyright HAMMOND INCORPORATED, Maplewood, N.J.

Erythraean Sea

GEDROSIA (MAKA)
• Pura

ARACHOSIA

DRANGIANA

CARMANIA

PERSIS
• Pasargadae
Persepolis •
(Parsa)

Persian Gulf
• Gerrha

ARIA

BACTRIA
• Bactra

SOGDIANA

MARGUS
• Margiana

CHORASMIA

SAKA
• Cyropolis

Jaxartes

Aral Sea

Oxus

PARTHIA

HYRCANIA
• Damghan
• Zadrakarta

Rhagae •
(612-550 B.C.)

MEDIA

Caspian Sea

MEDIAN EMPIRE

• Yazd
• Gabae

ELAM (SUSIANA)
• Susa

Ulai

ARABS
• Dumah
• Tema
• Dedan

Red Sea

ETHIOPIA (CUSH)

Nile
• Syene (Elephantine)
• Thebes

Libyan Desert

KINGDOM OF EGYPT
(663-525 B.C.)
• Memphis
• Sais
• Pelusium

Temple of Amon (Siwa) •
• Cyrene

LIBYA

Mediterranean Sea

NEW BABYLONIAN EMPIRE
(625-529 B.C.)

BABYLONIA
• Babylon
• Opis
• Sippar
• Nippur
• Erech
• Ur

Tigris
Euphrates

ASSYRIA
• Nineveh
• Asshur
• Arbela
• Carchemish
• Harran
• Nisibis

Urmia
• Van

URARTU

MOSCHI

SCYTHIANS

CAUCASUS

Araxes

Cyrus

KINGDOM OF LYDIA
(670-546 B.C.)
• Sardis
• Gordion
• Ancyra
• Iconium
• Tarsus

CILICIA

LYCIA
• Xanthus

Maeander
• Ephesus
• Miletus
• Rhodes

Halys

Cyprus
(trib. to Egypt 569-525 B.C.)

Hamath •
Arvad •
Gebal •
• Riblah
• Tadmor
• Anat
• Damascus

Thapsacus •

Megiddo •
Tyre •
JUDAH
• Jerusalem
• Gaza
• Elath

Crete

GREECE
• Athens
• Sparta
Marathon •

MACEDONIA

THRACE
• Apollonia

Black Sea
• Byzantium
• Chersonesus
• Sinope
• Trapezus
• Phasis
• Pieria
• Mitylene

Ister (Danube)

Palestine
Between the Testaments

- - - - Boundary of Judea before
the Maccabean revolt, 166 B.C.

──── Hasmonean domain at
maximum extent, 76 B.C.

| 0 | 5 | 10 | 15 | 20 | 25 | 30 | 35 Mls |

| 0 | 10 | 20 | 30 | 40 | 50 Kms |

© Copyright HAMMOND INCORPORATED, Maplewood, N.J.

Tyre

Paneas

MT. HERMON

Leontes

PHOENICIA

Ladder
of Tyre

Cadasa
(Kedesh)

Hazor

Seleucia

GAULANITIS

Ptolemais
(Acco)

Gamala

Arbela

Lake
Gennesaret

Carnaim

GALILEE

Sepphoris

Hippos

Dion

Philoteria

Abila

Mt. Carmel

Gaba

Plain of Esdraelon

Mt. Tabor

Yarmuk

Gadara

Edrei

Dora

Ephron

GALAADITIS

Strato's Tower

Scythopolis
(Beth-shan)

Pella

Plain of Sharon

Narbata

Jordan

The Great Sea

(Mediterranean Sea)

SAMARIA

Amathus

Gerasa

Samaria

Ragaba

Jabbok

Apollonia

Capharsaba

Sichem

Pharathon

Mt. Gerizim

Joppa

Alexandrium

Gedor

TOBIADS

Ramathaim

Beth-dagon

Timnah

Adida
(Hadid)

Gophna

Aphairema

Tyrus

Philadelphia
(Rabbah)
Free city state

Lydda
(Lod)

Modein Bethel

Dok

Jamnia
(Jabneh)

Beth-horon Elasa

Mizpah

Heshbon

Samaga

Gazara
(Gezer)

Caphar-
salama

Michmash

Jericho

Emmaus

Adasa

Cedron

Jerusalem

Azotus
(Ashdod)

Qumran

Medeba

Ekron

JUDEA

Hyrcania

Ascalon
Free city state

Beth-zacharias?

Bethbasi

PHILISTIA

Adullam

Tekoa

Machaerus

Marisa
(Mareshah)

Beth-zur

Anthedon

Adora

Hebron

En-gedi

Salt
Sea

Gaza

IDUMEA

Masada

Arnon

Raphia

Beer-sheba

Arad

NABATEANS

Charachmoba

AKRABATTENE

Zoara

Zered

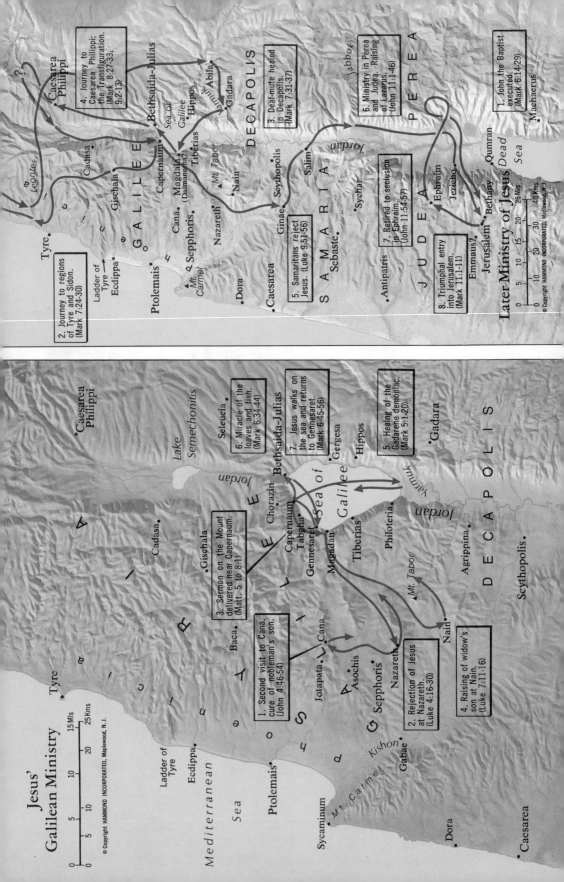

Jesus' Galilean Ministry

Mediterranean Sea

Ladder of Tyre

Tyre

Caesarea Philippi

Lake Semechonitis

Jordan

Cadasa

Gischala

Baca

Chorazin

Bethsaida-Julias

Capernaum

Tabgha

Gennesaret

Sea of Galilee

Gergesa

Hippos

Tiberias

Philoteria

Jordan

Yarmuk

Magadan

Jotapata

Cana

Asochis

Sepphoris

Nazareth

Mt. Tabor

Nain

Agrippina

D E C A P O L I S

Scythopolis

Gadara

Ecdippa

Ptolemais

Sycaminum

Gabae

Mt. Carmel

Kishon

Dora

Caesarea

1. Second visit to Cana, cure of nobleman's son. (John 4:46-54)

2. Rejection of Jesus at Nazareth. (Luke 4:16-30)

3. Sermon on the Mount delivered near Capernaum. (Matt. 5 to 8:1)

4. Raising of widow's son at Nain. (Luke 7:11-16)

5. Healing of the Gadarene demoniac. (Mark 5:1-20)

6. Miracle of the loaves and fish. (Mark 6:34-44)

7. Jesus walks on the sea and returns to Gennesaret. (Mark 6:45-56)

0 5 10 15 Mls
0 5 10 15 20 25 Kms

© Copyright HAMMOND INCORPORATED, Maplewood, N.J.

Later Ministry of Jesus

Tyre

Leontes

Cadasa

Gischala

Ladder of Tyre

Ecdippa

Ptolemais

Caesarea

Dora

Mt. Carmel

Sepphoris

Cana

Nazareth

Nain

Mt. Tabor

G A L I L E E

Capernaum

Magdala (Dalmanutha?)

Tiberias

Sea of Galilee

Bethsaida-Julias

Abila

Gadara

Hippos

D E C A P O L I S

Jordan

Ginae

Scythopolis

Salim

S A M A R I A

Sebaste

Sychar

Jordan

Jabbok

P E R E A

Antipatris

Ephraim

J U D E A

Emmaus?

Jerusalem

Bethany

Jericho

Qumran

Dead Sea

Machaerus

1. John the Baptist executed. (Mark 6:14-29)

2. Journey to regions of Tyre and Sidon. (Mark 7:24-30)

3. Deaf-mute healed in Decapolis. (Mark 7:31-37)

4. Journey to Caesarea Philippi; the Transfiguration. (Mark 8:27-33; 9:2-13)

5. Samaritans reject Jesus. (Luke 9:51-56)

6. Ministry in Perea and Judea. Raising of Lazarus. (John 11:1-46)

7. Retired to seclusion in Ephraim. (John 11:54-57)

8. Triumphal entry into Jerusalem. (Mark 11:1-11)

Caesarea Philippi

0 5 10 15 20 25 Mls
0 10 20 30 40 Kms

© Copyright HAMMOND INCORPORATED, Maplewood, N.J.

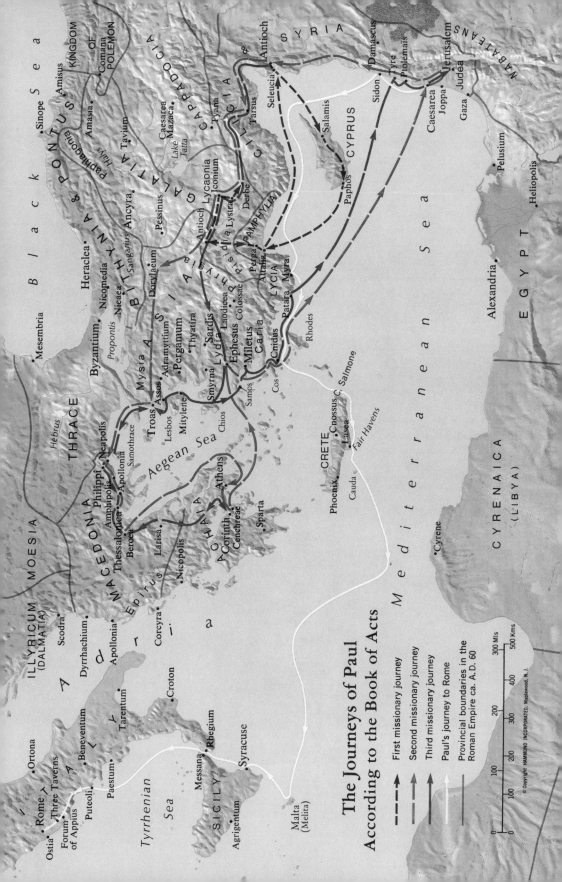

The Journeys of Paul
According to the Book of Acts

First missionary journey
Second missionary journey
Third missionary journey
Paul's journey to Rome
Provincial boundaries in the
Roman Empire ca. A.D. 60

300 Mls
400
500 Kms

© Copyright HAMMOND INCORPORATED, Maplewood, N.J.

B l a c k   S e a

Mesembria
Sinope
Amisus
Comana
KINGDOM OF
POLEMON
Heraclea
Nicomedia
Amasia
Tavium
PONTUS
Paphlagonia
Halys
Caesarea Mazaca
Lake Tatta
CAPPADOCIA
Tyana
Comana
Byzantium
Nicaea
Proponis
Pessinus
Ancyra
GALATIA
Dorylaeum
Sangarius
BITHYNIA & PONTUS
Tarsus
CILICIA
Antioch
SYRIA
Damascus
Seleucia
NABATAEANS
Tyre
Ptolemais
Sidon
Caesarea
Joppa
Jerusalem
Gaza
Judea
Pelusium
Heliopolis
Alexandria
EGYPT

THRACE
Hebrus
MOESIA
ILLYRICUM
(DALMATIA)
Scodra
Dyrrhachium
Apollonia
Corcyra
Epirus
MACEDONIA
Neapolis
Philippi
Amphipolis
Apollonia
Samothrace
Thessalonica
Beroea
Larisa
Nicopolis
ACHAIA
Athens
Corinth
Cenchreae
Sparta
Troas
Assos
Lesbos
Mitylene
Smyrna
Chios
Samos
Cos
Cnidus
Caria
Miletus
Ephesus
Lydia
Sardis
Laodicea
Colossae
Thyatira
Pergamum
Adramyttium
Mysia
ASIA
Phrygia
Antioch
Pisidia
Iconium
Lystra
Derbe
Lycaonia
PAMPHYLIA
Perga
Attalia
LYCIA
Myra
Patara
Rhodes
Salamis
Paphos
CYPRUS

A e g e a n   S e a
M e d i t e r r a n e a n   S e a

CRETE
Cnossus
Lasea
Fair Havens
Phoenix
Cauda
C. Salmone

CYRENAICA
(LIBYA)
Cyrene

A d r i a

Rome
Three Taverns
Forum of Appius
Ostia
Puteoli
Paestum
Beneventum
Tarentum
Ortona
Croton
Rhegium
Messana
Syracuse
Agrigentum
SICILY
Malta
(Melita)
Tyrrhenian Sea

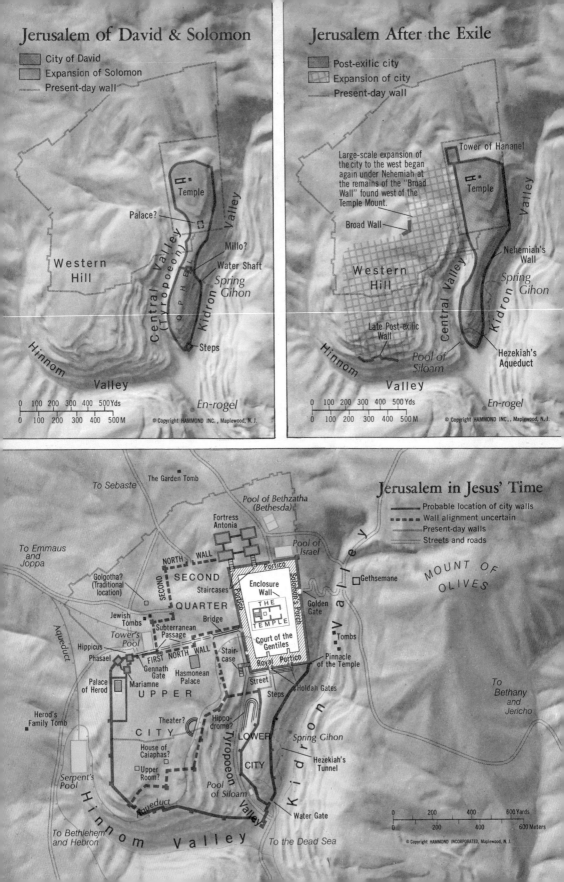

Jerusalem of David & Solomon

- City of David
- Expansion of Solomon
- Present-day wall

Temple
Palace?
Millo?
Water Shaft
Spring Gihon
Western Hill
Central Valley (Tyropoeon)
OPHEL
Kidron Valley
Steps
Hinnom Valley
En-rogel

| 0 | 100 | 200 | 300 | 400 | 500 Yds |
| 0 | 100 | 200 | 300 | 400 | 500 M |

© Copyright HAMMOND INC., Maplewood, N.J.

Jerusalem After the Exile

- Post-exilic city
- Expansion of city
- Present-day wall

Tower of Hananel
Temple
Large-scale expansion of the city to the west began again under Nehemiah at the remains of the "Broad Wall" found west of the Temple Mount.
Broad Wall
Nehemiah's Wall
Spring Gihon
Western Hill
Central Valley
Kidron Valley
Late Post-exilic Wall
Pool of Siloam
Hezekiah's Aqueduct
Hinnom Valley
En-rogel

| 0 | 100 | 200 | 300 | 400 | 500 Yds |
| 0 | 100 | 200 | 300 | 400 | 500 M |

© Copyright HAMMOND INC., Maplewood, N.J.

Jerusalem in Jesus' Time

- Probable location of city walls
- Wall alignment uncertain
- Present-day walls
- Streets and roads

To Sebaste
The Garden Tomb
Pool of Bethzatha (Bethesda)
Fortress Antonia
To Emmaus and Joppa
Golgotha? (Traditional location)
NORTH WALL
SECOND
SECOND
QUARTER
Staircases
Pool of Israel
Portico
Gethsemane
MOUNT OF OLIVES
Enclosure Wall
THE TEMPLE
Solomon's Portico
PORTICO
Golden Gate
Court of the Gentiles
Jewish Tombs
Bridge
Subterranean Passage
Tower's Pool
Hippicus
Phasael
FIRST NORTH WALL
Staircase
Gennath Gate
Hasmonean Palace
Mariamne
Palace of Herod
UPPER
Royal Portico
Street
Steps
Pinnacle of the Temple
Huldah Gates
Tombs
Aqueduct
Herod's Family Tomb
Theater?
CITY
Hippo-drome?
House of Caiaphas?
Upper Room?
Serpent's Pool
Tyropoeon Valley
LOWER
CITY
Spring Gihon
Hezekiah's Tunnel
Kidron
To Bethany and Jericho
Pool of Siloam
Aqueduct
Water Gate
Hinnom Valley
To Bethlehem and Hebron
To the Dead Sea

| 0 | 200 | 400 | 600 Yards |
| 0 | 200 | 400 | 600 Meters |

© Copyright HAMMOND INCORPORATED, Maplewood, N.J.

KNEELING (Heb. *bāraḵ*; Gk. *gonypeteō*). A position of submission adopted toward a superior person or deity for purposes either of petition or worship. Solomon prayed while kneeling (1 Kgs. 8:54; 2 Chr. 6:13), as did Ezra (Ezra 9:5) and Daniel (Dan. 6:10). This was also the posture taken during prayer by Jesus in Gethsemane (Luke 22:41), Stephen as he was martyred (Acts 7:60), and the believers of Tyre at Paul's departure (21:5). According to Ps. 95:6 kneeling followed the gesture of prostrating oneself. Usually the worshipper knelt with hands outstretched to heaven rather than folded, for the latter was considered a soporific gesture (cf. Prov. 6:10; 24:33).

The Hebrew word meaning "to kneel" also means "to bless," suggesting that a person receiving a blessing assumed that position. Accordingly, kneeling was a particularly appropriate position for making a petition (2 Kgs. 1:13; Matt. 17:14; Mark 1:40; Luke 5:8). The Roman soldiers mocked Jesus by kneeling before him (Matt. 27:29-30).

KNIFE.† A cutting utensil generally used for domestic purposes. Several Hebrew terms are represented by the English term.

Archaeological evidence indicates that the common knife (Heb. *mā'ăḵeleṯ*) was an instrument 15-25 cm. (6-10 in.) long. Stone knives were used until *ca.* 3500 B.C., copper until *ca.* 1220, and iron throughout the rest of the biblical period. These multipurpose implements were used for slaughtering (cf. Gen. 22:6, 10; Judg. 19:29), pruning trees, and as eating utensils (cf. Prov. 30:14).

God commanded Joshua to make flint knives (Heb. *hereḇ*, usually translated "sword") in order to circumcise the Israelites (Josh. 5:2-3; RSV "flint knives"). Ezekiel, also at the command of God, used a similar instrument to cut his hair to illustrate his prophecy of war (Ezek. 5:1-2; RSV, KJV "sword").

Heb. *ta'ar* is usually translated "razor" (Num. 6:5; Ps. 52:2 [MT 4]), but at Jer. 36:23 it designates a penknife. All occurrences suggest a rather small knife used for close work, such as that performed by a barber (Ezek. 5:1). This may be the instrument which Israelite scribes used to sharpen their reed pens.

Two terms occur only once in the Hebrew text. Heb. *śakkîn* (Prov. 23:2; perhaps a pun on *śāḵan* "incur danger") occurs in Aramaic texts as *śakkîn'ā*, meaning a sacrificial knife. Listed among the temple articles that Cyrus returned were twenty-nine *maḥălāpîm* (Ezra 1:9, KJV, NJV; RSV "censers," following LXX; NIV "silver pans"; cf. JB).

KNOW, KNOWLEDGE (Heb. *yāḏa'*, *da'aṯ*; Gk. *ginōskō*, *gnōsis*, *epígnōsis*).† To understand, to grasp or ascertain; especially to be familiar or acquainted with a person or thing.

I. Old Testament

Knowledge in the Old Testament connotes an intimate acquaintance with something. This is not so much knowledge "about," in the sense of an objective, mental apprehension. Rather, a personal relationship is implied between an individual and the object, whether a spiritual relationship as between worshipper and deity (Ps. 135:5; Isa. 1:2-3; Hos. 5:3), a social relation-

ship between two people (Gen. 29:5), or a sexual relationship between husband and wife (4:1; 1 Sam. 1:19).

For the Hebrews, knowledge was acquired through experience, as evident in the Hebrew concept of wisdom which gave high regard to the common sense attained throughout life. For example, mankind learned the difference between good and evil in the garden of Eden not by the ingesting of fruit mystically imbued with the essence of morality (in philosophical or theoretical terms) but by the very act of transgressing the law of God.

Knowledge was an important part of the relationship between mankind and God. Peoples of the ancient Near East often believed that gods could be persuaded by the proper combination of words and sacrifices (cf. Num. 23). Israel, however, understood that God is one, to be loved with all one's heart (the seat of the intellect; Deut. 6:4-5). Since Yahweh was all powerful and could not be opposed, then knowledge about him was the key to all wisdom (Ps. 111:10; Prov. 9:10). Yahweh is the source of all wisdom, and the one who searches for wisdom ultimately will find God (2:6).

Perhaps as a semantic extension of the intimate relationship between subject and object implicit in the Hebrew concept of knowledge, the verb "to know" occurs frequently in a technical sense for the covenantal bond. Thus "to know" God (e.g., Deut. 34:10; Judg. 2:10; Hos. 8:1-2) or another person (e.g., Deut. 28:33; Ruth 2:11; cf. the sexual bond; e.g., Judg. 21:12) means to enter into an intimate bond with that other.

II. New Testament

The New Testament authors employ the Hebrew understanding of knowledge to combat concepts prevalent in the Hellenistic world. In the classical Greek sense, knowledge was more an intellectual perception than the product of human experience. Thus Gk. *ginōskō* occurs with two technical meanings. First, the goal of the Hellenistic mystery religions was to acquire that secret knowledge necessary for salvation; this esoteric information was obtained through visions or an "inner illumination" which bypassed the normal rational processes. Second, in the world of Hellenistic magic knowledge of special words, rites, and symbols gave the initiate power to work miracles (cf. Simon the sorcerer; Acts 8:9-24).

The writers of the New Testament agreed with Gnosticism that there is a knowledge which leads to salvation. But this is not "philosophy and empty deceit . . . according to the elemental spirits of the universe" (Col. 2:8). Rather, it is the knowledge of Jesus Christ and his sacrificial death on behalf of the world. This knowledge is not secret or hidden, but is a "mystery" (Gk. *mystérion*) now revealed to all generations of mankind (Rom. 16:25; Eph. 6:19; Col. 1:26; cf. John 1:18; 1 Cor. 4:1).

This knowledge gives power to the believer—power over sin (Rom. 6) and power to become children of God (John 1:12). All power belongs to Christ (Matt. 28:18), but he has given it to those who follow him (Luke 10:19), to those who truly "know" him (John 10:14-15; cf. the technical Hebrew sense of knowledge as covenantal bond).

It is the New Testament's Hebraic background which most distinguishes it from the Hellenistic concepts of knowledge. To truly know something, according to the New Testament, is to act upon that knowledge. The teacher must not only communicate knowledge, but live out that knowledge as well (Matt. 5:19; Acts 1:1).

Bibliography. J. Bergman and G. J. Botterweck, "yāḏaʿ," *TDOT* 5 (1985): 448-481; R. Bultmann, "γινώσκω," *TDNT* 1 (1964): 689-719.

KOA [kōʹə] (Heb. *qôʿa*). An Aramaic tribe which probably lived east of the Tigris river and north of the territory occupied by Pekod (Ezek. 23:23). They are generally thought to be identical with the Guti familiar from various cuneiform texts.

KOHATH [kōʹhăth] (Heb. *qᵉhāṯ*). The second son of Levi (Gen. 46:11; Exod. 6:16). His sons were Amran, Izhar, Hebron, and Uzziel (v. 18; cf. Num. 3:27); among his descendants were Moses, Aaron, and Korah (Exod. 6:20-21). He died at age 133.

The families of the sons of Kohath (Kohathites) camped on the south side of the tabernacle (Num. 3:29). They were entrusted with the care of the tabernacle furnishings and were to carry the sacred things when Israel broke camp (Num. 4:1-20). Some of the Kohathites were also responsible for preparing the showbread on the Sabbath (1 Chr. 9:32). Later, during Josiah's reformation, some of Kohath's descendants were among those assigned to supervise the restoration of the temple (2 Chr. 34:12).

At the time of the first census taken in the wilderness the Kohathites numbered 2750 males between the ages of thirty and fifty (Num. 4:34-37), thus eligible for temple service. When the land of Canaan was divided, those who were descendants of Aaron received thirteen cities from the tribes of Judah, Simeon, and Benjamin; the remaining Kohathites received ten cities, some from Ephraim, some from Dan and the half-tribe of Manasseh (Josh. 21:1-45; 1 Chr. 6:61, 66-70 [MT 46, 51-55]).

KOHELETH. *See* QOHELETH.

KOINE. *See* GREEK.

KOLAIAH [kō lāʹyə] (Heb. *qôlāyâ* "the voice of the Lord").

1. A Benjaminite; an ancestor of Sallu (Neh. 11:7).

2. The father of the false prophet Ahab, an opponent of Jeremiah (Jer. 29:21).

KORAH [kôʹrə] (Heb. *qōrāḥ* "bald").

1. An Edomite chief; the third son of Esau and Oholibamah the Hivite (Gen. 36:5, 14, 18; 1 Chr. 1:35).

2. According to Gen. 36:16, an Edomite chief who was the son of Eliphaz and descendant of Esau. The name here is probably a scribal error (dittography) duplicating the name from the list which contained KORAH 1; it does not occur at vv. 11-12 (or at v. 16 in the Samaritan Pentateuch) or 1 Chr. 1:36.

3. The leader of an uprising against Moses and Aaron (Num. 16; Jude 11; KJV "Core"). According

to Exod. 6:21; Num. 16:1 he was a Levite, the son of Izhar and grandson of Kohath; 1 Chr. 6:22 calls him the son of Amminadab.

According to the biblical narrative, which critical scholars consider to be the conflation of two or more accounts, Korah, with the support of some 250 leaders from the Israelite assembly, challenged Moses concerning the limitation of the priesthood to Aaron's descendants (Num. 3:2-3, 10). The levitical sons of Kohath (including Korah) were to carry the most holy things from the tabernacle but could not offer the sacrifices (4:1-15). Related to these events was a civil revolt led by the Reubenites Dathan and Abiram. Moses responded by challenging his opponents to an ordeal the next day before the tabernacle. Korah and his followers (Korahites; KJV "Korathites," "Korhites," "sons of Kore") were to light the censers and offer incense before the Lord, allowing him to choose those acceptable to perform ceremonial functions (16:5-7). When Korah and his company neared the entrance of the tabernacle the "glory of the Lord" appeared to the entire congregation (v. 19). Moses and Aaron were instructed to withdraw, whereupon the ground split asunder and the rebels were swallowed into Sheol (vv. 31-32); those offering the incense were consumed by fire (v. 35). (If, as some scholars believe, this represents an ordeal by fire, the Korahites may have been required to walk on the burning incense; those who were unharmed would have been chosen while those who were burned were put to death, probably by fire). The rebels' censers were rescued from the blaze and beaten into a covering for the ark as a reminder of the incident (vv. 36-40).

The next day the Israelites accused Moses and Aaron of murder. God sent a plague to destroy them, and some 14,700 perished. Aaron offered atonement, thereby preventing further losses (vv. 46-50).

Among those who survived were Korah's three sons, Assir, Elkanah, and Abiasaph (Num. 26:11). Their descendants are mentioned as gatekeepers in the tabernacle and temple (1 Chr. 9:17-19; 26:1, 19) and as singers (2 Chr. 20:19, but cf. 1 Chr. 6:33-48 where Heman appears instead of Korah). A Korahite was also put in charge of making the flat sacrificial cakes (9:31). Many of the psalms bear a superscription ascribing them to the sons of Korah (Pss. 42, 44–49, 84–85, 87–88).

Bibliography. G. W. Coats, *Rebellion in the Wilderness* (Nashville: 1968).

4. A Judahite; the son of Hebron and descendant of Caleb (1 Chr. 2:43).

KORE [kôrʹī] (Heb. *qōrēʾ*, *qōrēʾ* "partridge").†

1. A Levite; the ancestor of Shallum (1 Chr. 9:19) and Meshelemiah (26:1), both of whom were gatekeepers at the temple.

2. (1 Chr. 29:19, KJV). *See* KORAH 3.

3. A Levite; the son of Imnah (2 Chr. 31:14). He was appointed by Hezekiah as keeper of the east gate of the temple (the king's gate) and was in charge of apportioning the freewill offerings. He may have been the same as **1.**

KOZ [kŏz] (Heb. *qôṣ* "thorn").*

1. A Judahite; the father of Anub and Zobebah

(1 Chr. 4:8; KJV "Coz"). He may have been the eponymous ancestor of the priestly house of Hakkoz.

   2. (KJV). *See* HAKKOZ.

KUE [kū′ĭ] (Heb. *qûh*; Akk. *Qaue*).* Ancient Adana (Hitt. *Adanawa*), a country in eastern Cilicia on the coastal plain of Asia Minor. It was one of the countries from which King Solomon imported horses (1 Kgs. 10:28 par. 2 Chr. 1:16; JB "Cilicia"). The KJV, following the Masoretic misreading of the text, renders it "linen yarn."

KUSHAIAH [kŏŏ shā′yə] (Heb. *qûšāyâ*). A Levite; one of the sons of Merari who ministered in song before the tabernacle at the time of King David (1 Chr. 15:17). He was the father of Ethan. At 1 Chr. 6:44 he is called Kishi.

KYRIE ELEISON [kîr′ĭ əlā′əsăn] (Gk. *Kýrie eléēson* "Lord have mercy").† A prayer for divine mercy, often spoken or sung responsively, attested from earliest times in the liturgy of the Church (e.g., Apost. Const. viii.6). It is reminiscent of the plea uttered by the Canaanite woman in Matt. 15:22 and the blind men in 20:30-33 (cf. Dan. 9:19).

L

L.

1. A designation for material found only in the gospel of Luke that cannot be accounted for by Luke's probable dependence on Mark or on Q, the non-Markan common source of Matthew and Luke.

2. The symbol designating Codex Leningradensis B 19ᵃ, which provides the basic text for modern editions of the Hebrew Old Testament. The L manuscript was completed at Cairo in 1008 A.D. and was supposedly copied from exemplars of Aaron ben Moses ben Asher.

LAADAH [lā'ə də] (Heb. *laʿdâ*). A Judahite of the lineage of Shelah, progenitor of the inhabitants of Mereshah (1 Chr. 4:21; cf. Josh. 15:44).

LAADAN (KJV). *See* LADAN.

LABAN [lā'bən] (Heb. *lāḇān* "white") **(PERSON).** An Aramean (Gen. 25:20; 28:5; 31:24) living in Paddan-aram, in Haran (29:4-5; 27:43); the son of Bethuel, grandson of Nahor (Abraham's brother), brother of Rebekah (24:29; 28:5), and father of Leah and Rachel (29:16).

Laban played a more important role in Rebekah's betrothal to Isaac than did their father (24:29-61). The importance given his household gods (*see* TERAPHIM) reflects pagan practices (31:19, 30). In his relationship with his nephew Jacob, who married his two daughters, Laban was both deceitful and greedy (29:1-30; cf. 24:30); yet the God of Israel kept Laban from harming Jacob, who had served him for twenty years (v. 24). Laban was a man of considerable means, but he had to acknowledge that it was only for the sake of Jacob that the Lord had blessed him (30:27). Yet outwitted by Jacob with regard to the cattle and deprived of the household gods by Rebekah, Laban found it necessary to make a covenant of mutual peace with Jacob at Mizpah (31:43-54).

LABAN [lā'bən] (Heb. *lāḇān* "white") **(PLACE).**† An unknown place east of the Jordan, perhaps in Moab, named in describing the Israelites' wilderness wanderings (Deut. 1:1). Laban has sometimes been identified with LIBNAH **1** (Num. 33:20), but the latter was probably in the wilderness of Paran between Mt. Sinai

and Ezion-geber; some relationship, however, may exist between the two names, since other unidentified places listed at Deut. 1:1 are also associated with locations connected in Numbers with the Sinai peninsula.

LABOR, WORK.† In creation God was the first laborer (Gen. 2:2-3; Heb. *mᵉlāʾḵâ*), and he continues to work in nature and human history (John 5:17; Gk. *ergázomai*). Humans first experienced labor as creatures involved in the work of creation (cf. Gen. 1:26, 28; 2:5, 15). Mankind's fall into sin did not in itself necessitate labor, but work thus became arduous and a painful necessity (3:16-19; *see* FALL, THE). Regulations were necessary to prevent oppressive treatment of laborers (Lev. 19:13; Deut. 24:14-15); later, relations between laborers and their masters became a concern for the early Church (Eph. 6:5-9; Col. 3:22–4:1).

Work was not despised but rather was honored by the people of God as good (Prov. 22:29; 31:13-27; 2 Thess. 3:6-12; cf. Prov. 6:6-11; 10:4-5; Eccl. 10:18), even though the pain and seeming futility of work was recognized (e.g., Eccl. 1:3; 2:11, 18-23; 5:15-17 [MT 14-16]; Heb. *ʿāmāl*). Only with God's blessing on it could work be productive (Ps. 127:1-2; cf. 107:35-38). In the early Church terms for manual labor were applied to work of religious value, such as preaching and other forms of ministry (1 Cor. 3:5ff.; 15:58; 1 Thess. 5:12; Rev. 2:2; Gk. *kópos*; cf. Gal. 6:7-10; *see* WORKS).

The Sabbath was established, not as a denigration of work, but as "an island in time," in recognition of the community's relationship to God and of the needs of the laborers within the community (Exod. 20:9-11; 23:12; Deut. 5:12-15; Heb. *ʿāḇaḏ*; *see* SABBATH). In the Sabbath commandment labor and rest are regarded as complementary (Exod. 31:15; 34:21; 35:2; Lev. 23:3). In the New Testament the contrast between labor and rest is an eschatological image (Matt. 11:28-29; Rev. 14:13); the age to come is like the Sabbath, when labor ceases.

For specific occupations see the individual articles. *See* FORCED; SERVANT.

LACEDAEMONIANS [lăs'ə dĭ mō'nĭ ənz] (Gk. *Lakedaimonioi*).† Inhabitants of Lacedaemon, the capital of Laconia, among whom the high priest Jason sought refuge (2 Macc. 5:9). *See* SPARTA.

LACHISH [lāʹkĭsh] (Heb. *lāḵîš*). An important fortified city of Judah, located at modern Tell ed-Duweir, 8 km. (5 mi.) southwest of Beit Jibrîn (ancient Eleutheropolis) and 45 km. (28 mi.) southwest of Jerusalem.

Evidence of settlement at Lachish may be traced to the Neolithic period (eighth millennium B.C.), and the surrounding hills were occupied by cave dwellers in the late fourth millennium. The site was abandoned sometime during the Early Bronze Age II period (*ca.* 2800-2600), but is mentioned in commercial texts from Ebla (*ca.* 2400). It was resettled and fortified during Middle Bronze II B by the Hyksos rulers of Egypt (*ca.* 1700-1600), and apparently continued to enjoy some prominence because of links with Egypt, as indicated by quantities of scarabs found on the site. Lachish is mentioned in the fourteenth-century Amarna Letters (Akk. *Lakisu, Lakišu*).

The combination of weakened Egyptian power in Palestine and the entry of the Israelites into the Judean hill country resulted in the destruction of Lachish and other cities in the late thirteenth century; the ferocious Israelite attack in defense of the Gibeonites, chronicled at Josh. 10, left Lachish uninhabited for some two centuries. It is named among the cities allotted to the tribe of Judah (15:39). The city was rebuilt in the Early Iron I C period (*ca.* 1025-950), at the time of the united monarchy. Lachish continued to be an important Judean city after the schism of 922, as its defenses were strengthened by Rehoboam (2 Chr. 11:9; perhaps also by Asa [cf. 14:7] and Jehoshaphat [17:2, 19]). King Amaziah fled to Lachish because of a conspiracy against him in Jerusalem, but was assassinated there (25:27-28).

Lachish was among forty-six cities captured and destroyed during the Assyrian Sennacherib's eighth-century campaign against Syria-Palestine (2 Kgs. 18:13). The siege of Lachish was mounted from the vulnerable southwest side, near the city gate and opposite the Assyrian camp. As depicted in a palace relief discovered at Nineveh, a wide siege ramp was built to permit a half-dozen battering rams to assault the wall under the covering fire of bowmen and slingers (*ANEP*, no. 372-73). The defenders piled up a counterramp to strengthen the wall, but the Assyrians prevailed. The inhabitants of Lachish were driven out, and the city was looted before being put to the torch (cf. *ANEP*, no. 374; *ANET*, p. 288). The excavation of Lachish uncovered the remains of some 1,500 people whose bodies were dumped into the Assyrian army's garbage pits. Sennacherib then established his headquarters at Lachish, and Hezekiah sent messengers to him, begging for mercy (2 Kgs. 18:14-16). The heavy tribute exacted by the Assyrians did not lessen their determination to take Jerusalem (vv. 17-37; Isa. 36), but some form of divine intervention—a message Sennacherib received (2 Kgs. 19:5-7) or a plague in the Assyrian camp (v. 35)—caused him to withdraw from Lachish. Some scholars contend that v. 8 implies a second invasion. Archaeological evidence indicates that Lachish was refortified after the Assyrian retreat, with a new wall and a double gate system better suited for defending the approach to the city.

Lachish was besieged and destroyed before Judah fell to the Babylonians in 587. The Lachish Letters, twenty-one inscribed clay ostraca (potsherds) discovered at the site in 1935, provide vivid insights into the deteriorating military situation as the Babylonians advanced (*ANET*, pp. 321-22).

Following the Exile, Judeans returning from Babylon resettled Lachish and the surrounding villages (Neh. 11:30).

A city gate in the ruins of Lachish (Institute of Archaeology, Tel-Aviv University; photo Avraham Hay)

Lachish Letter IV, side B (see *ANET,* p. 322) (by courtesy of the Israel Department of Antiquities and Museums)

LADAN [lā'dən] (Heb. *la'dān*).
1. An Ephraimite, and ancestor of Joshua (1 Chr. 7:26; KJV "Laadan").
2. A Levite of the lineage of Gershom (1 Chr. 23:7-8; 26:21; KJV "Laadan"). He is apparently the same as LIBNI **1** at Exod. 6:21; Num. 3:18.

LADDER (Heb. *sūllām*; Gk. *klímax*).* Ladders were used in construction, arboriculture (*ANEP*, no. 96), and siege warfare (1 Macc. 5:30; cf. *ANEP* nos. 311, 344, 359, 365).
The ladder (or stairway) seen by Jacob in a dream at Bethel (Gen. 28:12) may have been suggested by the naturally exposed rock strata nearby. The vision depicts contact between earth and heaven, the home of God and angels; cf. John 1:51.

LADDER OF TYRE (Gk. *klímax Tyrou*).* A land feature on the Palestinian coastline near Tyre, perhaps the ridge that extends the coastline out to a point about halfway between Ptolemais (Acre) and Tyre. Antiochus VI, one of the contestants for the Seleucid throne, appointed Simon Maccabeus governor "from the Ladder of Tyre to the borders of Egypt" (1 Macc. 11:59; *ca.* 145 B.C.), i.e., of the coast of Palestine.

LAEL [lā'əl] (Heb. *lā'ēl* "belonging to God"). A Gershonite Levite, father of Eliasaph (Num. 3:24).

LAHAD [lā'hăd] (Heb. *lahaḏ* "slow [?]"). A Judahite, and a son of Jahath (1 Chr. 4:2). His house was reckoned among the families of the Zorathites.

LAHAI-ROI (Gen. 24:62; 15:11, KJV). *See* BEER-LAHAI-ROI.

LAHMAM [lä'măm] (Heb. *lahmām*). A city in the Shephelah of Judah (Josh. 15:40; JB, NIV "Lahmas," following MT). The site is probably modern Khirbet el-Laḥm, 4 km. (2.5 mi.) south of Beit Jibrîn (Eleutheropolis) and near Lachish.

LAHMI [lä'mī] (Heb. *lahmî*).† The brother of the giant Goliath the Gittite, killed by Elhanan (1 Chr. 20:5). According to 2 Sam. 21:19 Elhanan's victim was Goliath himself. Some scholars regard the ac-

count in 1 Chronicles as an editorial attempt to reconcile 2 Sam. 21:19 and 1 Sam. 17:4. An alternate suggestion is that "Lahmi, the brother of Goliath" may reflect a scribal error ("Lahmi" with the sign of the direct object, as at 1 Chr. 20:5, is *'eṭ-laḥmî*; cf. *bêṭ hallaḥmî* "the Bethlehemite" at 2 Sam. 21:19). *See* ELHANAN **1**.

LAISH [lā'ĭsh] (Heb. *layiš* "lion") **(PERSON)**. The father of Palti (1 Sam. 25:44) or Paltiel (2 Sam. 3:15).

LAISH [lā'ish] (Heb. *layiš* "lion") **(PLACE)**.
1. A Canaanite city in northern Palestine, captured by the Danites and renamed DAN [PLACE] **(1)** (Judg. 18:7, 27, 29). At Josh. 19:47 it is called Leshem. The site has been identified as modern Tell el-Qâḍī, 17 km. (10.5 mi.) north of ancient Lake Huleh at the source of Nahr el-Leddan.
2. (Isa. 10:30, KJV). *See* LAISHAH.

LAISHAH [lā'ə shə] (Heb. *layšâ* "lion"). A village of the tribe of Benjamin northeast of Jerusalem (Isa. 10:30; KJV "Laish"), which Isaiah locates between Gallim and Anathoth. The site may be modern Khirbet el-'Isāwiyeh, 2 km. (1.2 mi.) southwest of 'Anâtâ (ancient Anathoth).

LAKKUM [lăk'əm] (Heb. *laqqûm* "obstacle"). A border city in the tribal territory of Naphtali (Josh. 19:33; KJV "Lakum"). The site is generally identified as modern Khirbet el-Manṣûrah, southwest of the point where the Jordan river flows out of the Sea of Galilee.

LAMB (Heb. *keḇeś, kiḇśâ*; Aram. *'immar*; Gk. *amnós, arḗn arníon*).† For ancient pastoralists sheep were the source of milk, food, wool, cloth, and skins for clothing and tents. Accordingly, the young and thus pure lambs were used extensively in sacrifice, symbolizing not only gentleness and innocence (e.g., 2 Sam. 12:3) but the offering to God of a creature essential to human existence. Lambs were offered by the Israelites in worship each morning and evening in the burnt offering (Exod. 29:38-42), at the beginning of every new month (Num. 28:11), each of the seven days of Passover (vv. 16-24), in observance of the Feast of Weeks (Pentecost; vv. 26-30) and the Day of Atonement (29:7-10, but cf. Lev. 16), and for peace offerings and sin offerings (e.g., 3:7; 4:32; 5:6).
Every use of "lamb" in the New Testament is figurative: twenty-eight times with reference to Christ (twenty-four in Revelation; Gk. *arníon*), twice for followers of Christ, and once in the description of the beast out of the earth (Rev. 13:11). This figurative usage is rooted in the Old Testament, where—as also in the New Testament—it may refer to the defenselessness of the lamb (Jer. 51:40; Heb. *kar*; cf. 50:17). The eschatological imagery of Isa. 11:6; 65:25 (*tāleh*) notes the incongruity of wolf and lamb together (as Luke 10:3). Isa. 53:7 (*śeh*; one of the Servant Songs, applied to Christ at Acts 8:32; Gk. *amnós*); Jer. 11:19 picture the lamb as not responding to its fate. These figures are part of a broader sheep imagery that emphasizes the defenselessness of sheep, which exist only to be slaughtered (e.g., Ps. 44:11, 22 [MT 12, 23]; Jer. 12:3; Rom. 8:36). Also, the people of God are

depicted as the flock under the charge of either God or human leaders (cf. John 21:15; *see* SHEEP).

The designation of Jesus as the Lamb of God derives from the sacrificial language of the Old Testament (John 1:29, 36; cf. 1 Pet. 1:19). At 1 Cor. 5:7 (where RSV supplies "lamb") the reference is specifically to the Passover. In the book of Revelation Christ is portrayed primarily as "the Lamb that was slain" (Rev. 5:6, 12; 13:8). The image is further developed in highly apocalyptic language in the throne-room scene of chs. 5–7. The Lamb is further depicted as a conqueror (17:14) and the groom at a wedding supper (19:7, 9; 21:9).

LAME (Heb. *pissēaḥ, ṣālaʿ*; Gk. *chōlós*), **CRIPPLED** (*nākeh, niŝberet*).† A congenital or acquired condition that impedes walking. Lameness was among the physical defects that disqualified priests from serving in the tabernacle and temple of Israel (Lev. 21:18; the same restriction applied to sacrificial animals [Deut. 15:21; Mal. 1:8, 13]). In other ways lameness was a handicap that set apart those so afflicted from society in general. The crippled were regarded with contempt because they were considered unable to perform military or other functions (cf. 2 Sam. 5:6, 8; Ps. 35:15; Isa. 33:23). Jesus warned that it was better to risk lameness by cutting off an offending foot than to endure the hell of fire (Matt. 18:8 par.). Yet it was the lameness of Mephibosheth that gained his preservation at David's court (2 Sam. 4:4; ch. 9). The righteous were expected to assist the lame (Job 29:15; Ezek. 34:4).

Prophetic eschatology cites the healing of the lame as one example of the restoration of Israel (e.g., Isa. 35:6; Ezek. 34:16). The lame are to be included in the eschatological ingathering of the people of God (Jer. 31:8; Mic. 4:6-7; Zeph. 3:19; cf. Luke 14:13, 21). The healings of the lame by Jesus (e.g., Matt. 15:30-31; 21:14) and leaders in the early Church (Acts 3:1-8; 4:7-10; 8:7; 14:8-10) were understood, in part, as representing the fulfillment of the Old Testament promises (cf. Matt. 11:5 par.). The Jews challenged Jesus' healing of the lame at Bethzatha (Bethesda) as a violation of the Sabbath (John 5:3; KJV "halt").

See DISEASE; HEALING; PARALYSIS.

LAMECH [lä′mək, lā′měk] (Heb. *lemek*; Gk. *Lamech*).
1. The son of Methushael and a descendant of Cain; husband of Adah and Zillah, and father of Jabal, Jubal, Tubal-cain, and Naamah (Gen. 4:18-24). The ancient song of Lamech (vv. 23-24) celebrates prowess in battle (cf. Judg. 15:16; 1 Sam. 18:7). The song reflects the increase in human pride and sin as recounted in Gen. 3–11.
2. The son of Methuselah, descendant of Seth, and the father of Noah (Gen. 5:25-31). He is named in the genealogy of Jesus (Luke 3:36), and is depicted also in extrabiblical writings such as Jubilees and the Dead Sea Genesis Apocryphon.

LAMENT.† A general term encompassing various literary forms whereby the speaker appeals to God for aid in overcoming present calamity.

The designation lament is perhaps best associated

with the dirge (Heb. *qînâ,* from its metric form), a funeral song bewailing the loss (generally introduced by the question *ʾêkâ* "How . . .?"; cf. 2 Sam. 1:19-27; Lam. 1–2, 4), recounting the attributes of the deceased, and inviting further mourning (e.g., 2 Sam. 1:19-27; Ezek. 19:2-14). Often accompanied by music, the dirge was sung by friends and family (e.g., 2 Sam. 1:17) or by professional mourners (e.g., Jer. 9:17). The form was adapted by the prophets, who applied it to the fall of mighty rulers (e.g., Isa. 14:4-21) and nations (e.g., Ezek. 27:32-36).

More frequently form critics label as lament the "complaint," wherein an individual (e.g., Job 3; Pss. 5, 7, 38, 140-143) or group (e.g., Pss. 44, 74, 79; Jer. 14:1–15:4) voice distress and implore God's deliverance. The book of Lamentations contains both the individual (ch. 3) and communal (ch. 5) forms.

See PSALMS, BOOK OF.

LAMENTATIONS, BOOK OF.† An Old Testament book mourning the destruction of Jerusalem and the temple by the Babylonians in 586 B.C.

I. Name

In the Hebrew Bible the book is entitled *ʾÊkâ* "How?", from its opening word and an expression characteristic of the dirge form of lamentation (e.g., Lam. 1:1; 2:1; 4:1). From the designation *Qînôt* "Lamentations" in rabbinic sources (*B. Bat.* 14b) derive the LXX (Gk. *Thrēnoi*) and Vulgate (Lat. *Threni*) translations, hence the English title.

II. Place in Canon

Lamentations is included in the Writings division of the Hebrew canon, and is generally third among the Megilloth or Scrolls (some manuscripts place it chronologically as fourth), the prescribed reading for the annual fast (Ninth of Ab) mourning the destruction of the temple and the Dispersion of A.D. 70. In the LXX canon the book is an appendix to Jeremiah, following Baruch; in the Vulgate the order is Baruch, Jeremiah, Lamentations.

III. Author and Date

The book itself contains no reference to authorship. Its association with the prophet Jeremiah is quite ancient, perhaps stemming from 2 Chr. 35:25, which notes Jeremiah's lament over Josiah; in many early lists of canonical works Jeremiah and Lamentations are counted as one (cf. Josephus *Ap.* i.8 [38]). Later editions add to the title the phrase "of Jeremiah," and the LXX prologue ascribes the laments to the prophet. Jeremianic authorship is supported by similarities of theme and style (cf. Lam. 1:17; Jer. 14:17). However, current scholarship in general rejects Jeremiah's connection with the book, not only because of its anonymity but largely on the basis of ideas seemingly contrary to those of the prophet (e.g., Lam. 1:21; 2:9; 4:12, 17, 20; cf. Jer. 2:18; 37:5-10, 17) or references that do not fit the details of his life (e.g., Lam. 4:19; cf. Jer. 38:28). Some suggest that, despite the unity of form and topic, the various chapters represent the work of several authors.

The intense grief expressed in the book suggests composition of at least chs. 1–4 shortly after the destruction of the city, and the lack of specific allusions to the plight of the exiles in Babylon or Egypt points to Palestine as the place of origin; ch. 5 may date from slightly later in the Exile (cf. Lam. 5:3, 7).

IV. Contents

Chs. 1–2 each comprise a dirge in the form of an acrostic poem of twenty-two three-line verses, each verse beginning with a successive letter of the Hebrew alphabet. Ch. 1 portrays Jerusalem as a widow, the "daughter of Zion" (1:6) bewailing her condition and eliciting the pity of "all you peoples" (v. 18) and the Lord (vv. 20-22). In the second acrostic the poet recounts the desolation of Jerusalem, whereby "the Lord has become like an enemy" and destroyed his people (2:5); addressing the city directly, he implores it to "cry aloud to the Lord" (vv. 18-19; cf. vv. 20-22). Ch. 3 also is an alphabetic acrostic, of three-line (verse) stanzas with each line beginning with the appropriate letter. The chapter is an individual complaint wherein the poet—speaking perhaps as "Everyman" or the personified community—depicts his personal suffering (3:1-18) and despair (vv. 19-20), yet still maintains trust in God (vv. 21-24). Recalling God's mercy, he implores the people to repent and return to God (vv. 25-41). The chapter concludes with further lamentation (vv. 42-54) and supplication that the Lord will grant vengeance upon the poet's enemies (vv. 55-66). Ch. 4 is another acrostic dirge of two-line stanzas, in which a survivor recounts the catastrophic siege and sack of Jerusalem; it concludes with an imprecation against Edom (4:21-22). The final chapter is a communal complaint; although of twenty-two verses, it is not an acrostic. The people describe vividly their plight and its causes (5:2-18) and petition God for restoration (vv. 19-21).

V. Theology

The intense pain and disillusionment that pervade Lamentations derive poignantly from the greatest tragedy that Israel had yet experienced. The destruction of Jerusalem and the dispersal of its people, as well as the breach of the supposedly inviolable Davidic covenant (cf. 2 Sam. 7:10, 15-16), constituted a major crisis of faith. Drawing upon the Hebrew understanding of the people's fortunes as directly reflecting God's pleasure or displeasure, these laments seek in fashion not unlike the wisdom writings to ascertain the meaning of these cataclysmal events, interpreted as the ultimate expression of God's judgment upon the covenant people (cf. Lam. 5:22). Indeed, nowhere do they question the motifs for or deny the justification of God's punitive actions (cf. 1:8-9, 18; 3:40-42). Yet in the midst of utmost despair the poet acknowledges God's past mercies and voices profound hope of forgiveness and restoration (e.g., 2:21-27; 3:31-36).

Bibliography. B. Albrektson, *Studies in the Text and Theology of the Book of Lamentations*. Studia Theologica Lundensia 21 (Lund: 1963); N. K. Gottwald, *Studies in the Book of Lamentations*, 2nd ed. SBT 14 (1962); D. R. Hillers, *Lamentations*. AB 7A (1972).

LAMP (Heb. *nēr*; Gk. *lýchnos, lampás*).† Originally a shallow clay or pottery bowl having a crimp in the rim to hold a wick fed by oil. By the fifth century B.C. metal lamps had been introduced. The form of the lamp evolved gradually, first by elongating the crimp, later by folding the edges together, leaving a hole in each end—one for the wick and the other for filling. Hellenistic lamps were round with a long neck for the wick and a circular filling hole. Roman lamps were characteristically covered saucers, often decorated, with an opening for receiving oil and a projection on the opening for the wick. In some Roman lamps more than one wick tube led from the oil chamber. Palestinian lamps often rested on lampstands (Matt. 5:15; Mark 4:21; Luke 11:33; *see* LAMPSTAND). Lamps were probably kept burning night and day, both because of the difficulty of lighting them and because interiors of Near Eastern buildings were usually dim even in daylight hours.

In the Old Testament, lamps appear in a variety of figurative usages. The extinguishing of a lamp is a common metaphor for destruction, e.g., of Judah (Jer. 25:10) and the wicked (Job 21:17; Prov. 13:9; 20:20). David is "the lamp of Israel" (2 Sam. 21:17), and his dynasty is a lamp for David (1 Kgs. 11:36; 15:4). More generally, the "spirit of man" is the "lamp of the Lord" (Prov. 20:27). God himself, as the source of all light, is a lamp (2 Sam. 22:29 par. Ps. 18:28 [MT 29]; 132:17), and thus so also is his word (119:105; cf. Prov. 6:23). In the New Testament lamps suggest the light of the coming Lord in the parable of the ten virgins; here, however, the intended image is probably torches, since lamps were for indoor use (Matt. 25:1-13; Luke 12:35). The eye is the lamp of the body (Matt. 6:22; Luke 11:34). In likening John the Baptist to "a burning and shining lamp" (John

Typical lamps of (clockwise from upper left) the Bronze Age, the Iron Age, the Roman Empire, and the Byzantine Empire (R. H. Johnston)

5:35), the evangelist probably intended a contrast to Christ, who is the light itself (1:7). This motif is repeated at Rev. 21:23, where the Lamb is the lamp, the sole illumination, of the heavenly Jerusalem. The lamp is also a metaphor for witness that proceeds through preaching of the gospel (as implied at Mark 4:21; Luke 8:16; 11:33) or through good works (specified at Matt. 5:15-16).

See LIGHT.

LAMPSTAND (Heb. $m^e n \hat{o} r \hat{a}$; Aram. $nebr^e \check{s}\hat{a}$; Gk. *lychnía*). A pedestal for oil-filled wick lamps, or a stand incorporating one or more such lamps into its structure. The simple household lamp, if not placed in a wall niche or hung from the ceiling, would be placed on a lampstand, in effect, a small, high table (2 Kgs. 4:10; RSV, JB, NIV "lamp"; Matt. 5:15 par.; cf. *ANEP*, nos. 519, 657-58, 857). Some lampstands were single-stemmed and held a single lamp; others, usually found in wealthy homes and public buildings, had several branches on one pedestal.

The menorah, a seven-branched lampstand, was specified in the lists of furnishings for the tabernacle (Exod. 25:31-37; 37:17-24; cf. 26:35; 40:24; Heb. 9:2), and ten such lampstands were crafted for Solomon's temple (2 Chr. 4:7; cf. 1 Chr. 28:15). That the lampstands of the late Solomonic (1 Kgs. 7:49; Jer. 52:19), restoration (Zech. 4:2), and Herodian temples (cf. Rev. 11:4) were similar to that of the tabernacle is suggested by the resemblance of the lampstand portrayed on Titus' triumphal arch in Rome, which celebrated his defeat of Jerusalem in A.D. 70, to the descriptions in Exodus. The seven branches and cups (small basins for oil) may be the basis of the seven lampstands that portray the seven churches of Asia in Revelation (1:12-13, 20; 2:1, 5) and the witness at 11:4. The tabernacle and temple lampstands do underlie much of the light symbolism of Judaism and Christianity (e.g., John 8:12). The feast of Hanukkah (*see* DEDICATION, FEAST OF) focuses on the progressive lighting of the eight branches of the candelabrum (in modern observances a ninth central candle is used for lighting the others).

LANCE. *See* SPEAR.

LAND (Heb. *'ereṣ;* Gk. *gḗ*).† In biblical usage "land" designates territory defined for political purposes, and represents the source of produce that sustains people and animals. In Hebrew cosmology land is the antithesis of "heaven," and it takes on special theological significance with regard to the history of Israel. Such wide-ranging definitions of land are mirrored in other ancient Near Eastern cultures. In Sumerian and Akkadian, *erṣetu* encompasses earth (in contrast to heaven), the Underworld, a defined territory, and ground. The Egyptian word for land, symbolized hieroglyphically by a flat floodland with grains of sand beneath, can mean earth, dust, dirt, ground, or land (nation). Consequently it is not always easy to determine whether *'ereṣ* means land, earth, or ground in the Old Testament. For example, the common phrase *kōl hā'āreṣ* can mean "all the land" (ground, Isa. 7:24; Judah, Jer. 4:20; Israel, 1 Sam. 13:3; territory,

Deut. 19:8; 34:1) or "all the earth" (Gen. 1:26; 2 Kgs. 5:15).

I. Old Testament

A. Cosmological Use. The account of creation at Gen. 1:1–2:4a contains details common to many ancient Near Eastern cosmologies. For example, the earth was believed to be surrounded by water, held back by a domed firmament, beyond which lay heaven (1:6-10). The division of the universe thus made "heavens and earth" a common formula which is used throughout the Bible. A variety of Hebrew verbs are employed to describe the earth's creation, including *bārā'* "create," *yāsadh* "lay the foundations," and *raqa'* "stretch out." God, as Creator, provides rain (Job 38:26-27) so the land could bring forth plants and trees to sustain life upon it (cf. Amos 7:2). *See* CREATION; EARTH.

B. Ground. Heb. *'ereṣ* is understood to mean "ground" when it appears in passages referring to the constitution of the earth, or its produce. The ground is the source of "fatness" (abundance) and fruitfulness (Lev. 26:4-5; Ps. 85:12 [MT 13]; cf. Gen. 27:28; Zech. 8:12). It brings forth a variety of foodstuffs: produce (Lev. 23:39; cf. Gen. 1:11), fruit (Lev. 19:23; cf. Isa. 61:11), bread and wine (cf. Ps. 104:14-15), and edible oils (cf. Deut. 7:13).

However, not all land is fruitful. There are dry and inhospitable deserts (Jer. 9:12 [MT 11]; cf. Deut. 8:15), and unproductive wildernesses inhabited by wild animals (29:23 [MT 22]; Jer. 2:2). Barren land can also be a sign of divine punishment (Lev. 26:19-20; Ps. 107:33-34; Jer. 12:11; 51:42-43; Ezek. 12:19-20; 32:15; Hag. 1:10-11). Heb. *'ereṣ* "ground" can also symbolize defeat (Isa. 14:12; 21:9; Obad. 3) or mourning (Job 2:13; Ezek. 26:16).

C. Defined Territory. **1.** Nations and Other Political Entities. Throughout their history Israel came into contact with political groups whose "lands" (i.e., territory) are mentioned in the Bible. These include Egypt (Gen. 41; Ps. 78:12), Moab (Judg. 11:15), Assyria (Isa. 7:18), Babylon (Jer. 25:12), the Hittites (Judg. 1:26), and Ammonites (Deut. 2:37). Reference is also made to the "land of the people of the east" (Gen. 29:1), the "land of the Hebrews" (40:15), and the "land of Israel" (1 Sam. 13:19).

2. Regions. "Land" also designates districts or regions whose names are derived from cities or prominent geographical features. Included are the land of Havilah (Gen. 2:11), Seir (32:3 [MT 4]), Ararat (2 Kgs. 19:37), Hamath (25:21), and Jordan and Hermon (Ps. 42:6 [MT 7]).

3. Tribal. The territories of the Israelite tribes also are referred to as "lands" (e.g., Deut. 34:2; 1 Sam. 9:4, 16; 13:7; 1 Kgs. 15:20).

D. Theological Use. From the beginning of Israel's history, the land of Canaan was one of the two elements of God's promise, the other being that of the people of Israel themselves—offspring for Abraham (nation). Abraham migrated to this land but lived there only as a nomad or transhumant. Other than the cave of Machpelah (23:3-20), Abraham owned no land in Canaan. According to the biblical account, it was not until after the Exodus that the descendants of Abraham through Isaac and Jacob actually came into possession of the land in any more meaningful way (*see* CONQUEST). "A wandering Aramean was my father" begins a recounting of this course into the land that was to be recited with every annual presentation of the firstfruits of the land to the Lord (Deut. 26:5-10). That the Exodus, the wilderness wanderings, and the Conquest were a course set toward possession of the land of promise is underlined by the story of the spies sent into the land (Num. 13) and its sequel, the rebellion of the people against that very promise (14:1-10).

However, the Conquest was not immediately completed; a number of peoples who were in the land before Israel were not driven out (Judg. 1:19ff.), causing further difficulties for the Israelites (2:1-4). The reigns of David and Solomon were remembered as a golden age in Israel's history—a time when the nation was politically united and in firm possession of the land as its borders were typically defined, "from Dan to Beersheba," (e.g., 2 Sam. 3:10) and from the Euphrates river to the land of the Philistines and the border of Egypt (1 Kgs. 4:21; 2 Chr. 9:26; cf. Num. 34:2-12; 1 Kgs. 8:65.; Ezek. 47:15-20).

With the end of the monarchies of Israel and Judah, the people's possession of the land came to an end. The biblical account suggests that Israel's course throughout the monarchic period was for the most part leading toward exile from the land (cf. 2 Kgs. 17:7-23; 24:3-4, 20). The curses of Deuteronomy (Deut. 28:15-68) had come to pass, and it seemed to some that the promises of God had reached their end (cf. Jer. 9:19 [MT 18]). Yet with the Exile came almost immediately the promise of a return to the land (31:17-18; Isa. 43:19-21; Ezek. 37:5-6).

In late Old Testament and later Jewish apocalyptic a two focal point of the expected salvation is restoration of the "lost" people of Israel—those in exile, the diaspora, or the "lost tribes." The land and the lost will be brought together in glory (e.g., Isa. 27:12-13; Ezek. 37:21-25; Zeph. 3:10; Tob. 14:4-5). The enemies of Israel will be destroyed (Isa. 63:1-6; Zech. 14:12-15; cf. Sib.Or. 5:225-227) or will make humble procession to the glorified holy city Jerusalem (Zech. 14:16-19; Isa. 60:1-3). Then will Israel live securely in the land centered around the temple (Isa. 26:1-2; 60:18; Jub. 50:5; cf. Jer. 31:40; Zech. 14:11).

The concept that the world and all within it is God's property (cf. Ps. 24:1) underlies biblical statements concerning property; therefore, whoever has property holds it only as a gift from God. Within the covenant between Yahweh and Israel, the people are considered to be God's property in a unique way (Exod. 19:5). On the basis of God's promise to Abraham (Gen. 13:14-17), Israel received the land of Canaan from God as their possession (Deut. 1:25). Each person within Israel received land of his (and occasionally her) own, but ownership was always contingent upon the solidarity of the individual with the people as a whole. Because property was governed by the covenant relationship between Yahweh and his people, rights of ownership were not transferable. The purpose of the pentateuchal regulations concerning redemption and the Year of Jubilee was to keep land perpetually

in the family to which it had been allotted. A person compelled by circumstances to sell his property regained possession of it in the Jubilee (Lev. 25:8-10, 13-16), although the first recourse in such a situation was for a relative of the impoverished to redeem it or, if the person's fortunes improved before the Jubilee, to redeem it himself (vv. 25-28; Ruth 4; Jer. 32:6-8). The account of Ahab and Jezebel's seizing of Naboth's vineyard (1 Kgs. 21) illustrates the erosion of these Israelite regulations concerning land tenure (cf. Naboth's appeal at v. 3) in the face of foreign influences, including royal absolutism (v. 7). As adherence to these principles dimished, the gaps between the landholding rich and the poor increased (cf. Isa. 5:8).

II. New Testament

Paul emphasizes Abraham's faith in the promise of offspring rather than the promise of the land (Rom. 4:17-21). In Acts the promise of the land is mentioned in two speeches, but does not become a matter of central concern (Acts 7:3-7; 13:17-19); in both places, the goal of the historical review does not involve the promise of land. In Hebrews Abraham's faith in the promise of land is recalled (Heb. 11:8-9), but the land, specifically "the city" (Jerusalem), becomes the symbol for a more transcendent reality (vv. 10, 13-16). At Gal. 4:25-26 Paul contrasts the Jerusalem that the Jews already possessed (though not freely, because of the Roman occupation) with the Jerusalem that the readers are yet to possess, "the Jerusalem above." (If Rom. 4:13 intends any more than an allusion to the promise given to Abraham in terms used in later Judaism [Gk. *kósmos* "world"; cf. Sir. 44:21], it would be such a symbolized understanding of the land.) The same contrast with the earthly Jerusalem is not far below the surface wherever the "new" or "heavenly" Jerusalem is mentioned in Christian contexts (Heb. 12:22; Rev. 3:12; 21:2–22:5)—the promise is renewed in such a different fashion that a contrast is inevitable. It is in this context that the destruction of Jerusalem in A.D. 70 can be understood as having a part in the unfolding of eschatological events (Luke 21:20-24), although a positive role of the earthly Jerusalem in the events surrounding the Parousia may be suggested (Luke 21:24; Rom. 11:26). Matt. 5:5, with its promise of "the land" (*gē;* usually "earth") alludes to Ps. 37:11 and may have begun as a restatement of the message given in different ways in the Old Testament: trust in God, not in human pride or strength, attains the promise. In the context of the New Testament, however, where the promises are not centered in Israel as a nation, this verse points to something broader than the promise of independent control of Canaan by Israel.

Bibliography. W. Brueggemann, *The Land* (Philadelphia: 1977); W. D. Davies, *The Gospel and the Land* (Berkeley: 1974); R. Gnuse, *You Shall Not Steal: Community and Property in the Biblical Tradition* (Maryknoll: 1985).

LANGUAGE.† Archaeological discoveries continue to provide inscriptional evidence for the vast multitude of languages and dialects employed throughout the ancient Near East. Awareness of this diversity is reflected in the biblical Table of Nations (Gen. 10:5, 20, 31; cf. Neh. 13:24), and explanation is offered in the account of the tower of Babel (11:1-9). Other nations are identified as peoples "of strange language" (Ps. 114:1), "whose language you do not understand" (Deut. 28:49; cf. Jer. 3:15; "nor can you understand what they say"). Frequent reference is made to words written or spoken in another language (Heb. *lāšôn* "tongue"; *śāpâ* "lip"; e.g., 2 Kgs. 18:26, 28 par.; Ezra 4:7; MT Dan. 2:4). Dialectical distinctions underlie the account of the incident wherein the fugitive Ephraimites were detected by their pronunciation "Sibboleth" (Judg. 12:6).

For specific biblical languages see the individual entries; *see also* ALPHABET; WRITING. For glossalalia *see* TONGUES.

LAODICEA [lāŏd'ə sē'ə] (Gk. *Laodikeia*). A city in Asia Minor (Rev. 1:11), rebuilt on the site of ancient Rhoas (Diospolis) *ca.* 250 B.C. by Antiochus II Theos and named after his wife Laodice. The ruins of the city are on the outskirts of modern Denizli, 10 km. (6 mi.) south of ancient Hierapolis and 18 km. (11 mi.) west of Colossae on the Lycus river, a tributary of the Maeander. The city was in the southwestern portion of Phrygia (some scholars would place it in Caria) and in the Roman province of Asia, on the heavily traveled road from Ephesus to Syria. Laodicea was known for its involvement in banking, its linen and wool industry, and its pharmaceutical skills, especially the preparation of eye salve. The city was sufficiently wealthy and its population energetic enough that without outside financial aid it recovered completely from a destructive earthquake in A.D. 60 with hardly any noticeable stagnation in its commerce and industry.

Epaphras labored in the Christian congregation of Laodicea, which was closely linked with the congregations of Hierapolis and Colossae (Col. 4:12-16). Although Paul himself not visit the congregation in Laodicea (2:1), he did write a letter to the Laodiceans (4:16), as did John later (Rev. 3:14-22). According to John's letter the wealth of Laodicea had adversely affected the spiritual condition of the Laodicean Christians.

LAODICEANS, LETTER TO THE.† Paul's letter to the Laodicean Christian congregation, referred to

at Col. 4:16. It was apparently a circular letter or at least an open letter, most likely lost at an early date. Marcion knew the Epistle to the Ephesians under the title "to the Laodiceans," but the identification of Ephesians as the letter to the Laodiceans has not been in great favor, especially as questions about the authorship of the canonical work and its relationship to Colossians have increased. Similarly, some scholars would identify it with Philemon. A sixth-century Vulgate manuscript contains a Letter to the Laodiceans that is merely a short assemblage of lines from the canonical Pauline epistles composed perhaps as late as the fourth century A.D.

LAPIS LAZULI (Heb. *sappîr*).* A deep blue stone marked with traces of iron pyrite ("fool's gold"), well-known and widely used in jewelry and small decorations in the ancient Near East (so RSV mg., e.g., Job 28:6, 16; Cant. 5:14; Isa. 54:11; Ezek. 28:13; RSV "sapphire[s]"). Because of the nature of ancient methods of classification, the precise type of stone intended cannot now be determined with certainty.

LAPPIDOTH [lăp'ə dŏth] (Heb. *lappîdôt* "torches, lightning flashes").† The husband of the prophetess and judge Deborah (Judg. 4:4). Some scholars suggest that the name is a hypocoristicon of the general Barak (cf. R. G. Boling, *Judges*. AB 6A [1975], p. 95).

LASEA [lə sē'ə] (Gk. *Lasaia*). A city on the southern coast of Crete (Acts 27:8), near Fair Havens. It is not mentioned elsewhere in ancient literature.

LASH (Gk. *mástix, phragéllion*; cf. Lat. *flagellum*).† A whip used in punishment. In Old Testament times the lash was used only on animals (cf. Prov. 26:3; Nah. 3:2; RSV "whip"); for punishment of humans, sticks and clubs were used (Exod. 21:20; Prov. 10:13; 26:3; *see* ROD). According to Mishnah *Mak.* iii.12, a triple-ended whip was used for the forty lashes of Deut. 25:2-3 (cf. LXX, which suggests that this change had come by the third century B.C.). The "whips" (Heb. *šôṭîm*) of 1 Kgs. 12:11, 14 par. 2 Chr. 10:11, 14 were normally used on animals; the reference may be figurative.

In Jewish practice the forty "stripes" (wounds of unspecified origin; e.g., Isa. 53:5) were reduced to "forty less one" (Josephus *Ant.* iv.238, 248; Mishnah *Mak.* iii:10), probably to allow for miscounting. Five times Paul had received this punishment by the time he wrote 2 Cor. 11:24 ("lashes" is supplied in the translations, as distinguished from beating with rods in the next verse; cf. Matt. 10:17; 23:34).

The Roman examination by scourging with whips was for non-citizens of Rome (Acts 22:24-25); Roman citizens could be beaten with rods only after they had been convicted and sentenced for certain crimes (cf. 16:22-23, 37; 2 Cor. 11:25). Non-Romans could also be whipped with the flagellum, which might have bits of bone, metal, or glass in the ends of its straps, as punishment rather than for examination, as was Jesus before being crucified (Matt. 27:26 par.); such scourging was sometimes fatal.

LASHA [lā'shə] (Heb. *lāša'*).† A city marking the limits of the territory inhabited by the Canaanites (Gen.

The ruins of the theater at Laodicea (Laval University Excavations, Quebec)

10:19). The location is unknown. On linguistic grounds some scholars have identified Lasha with Laish (Dan) in the far north of Palestine, but the context points rather toward the south, near the Dead Sea. Early tradition identified Lasha with Callirhoe (modern Zerqā Māʿîn; cf. Zereth-shahar at Josh. 13:19) on the east side of the Dead Sea, southwest of Medeba.

LASHARON [lă shârʹən] (Heb. *laššârôn*). In most English translations, a place conquered by Joshua (Josh. 12:18). On the basis of one recension of the LXX and some later manuscripts of the MT, the Hebrew term should be read "(belonging) to Sharon," thus describing APHEK 1 on the plain of Sharon (JB, NJV "the king of Sharon").

LAST DAY(S), LATTER DAYS.* In the Old Testament several constructions appear with Heb. *ʾaḥᵃrît* "latter, last" and related words, but only sometimes with a focus that could be called eschatological (e.g., Ezek. 38:8, 16; Hos. 3:5; Mic. 4:1; cf. Isa. 2:2). More often the "latter days" are simply "days to come" (e.g., Deut. 31:29; cf. 4:30; Num. 24:14) and the "latter (time)" is "the future" (e.g., Prov. 19:20; Jer. 31:17; so RSV). Some of these noneschatological passages (particularly in Deuteronomy) can, however, be seen as part of the background of the development of prophetic eschatology. "The end (*qēṣ*) of days" is another expression used eschatologically in the Old Testament (Dan. 12:13; simply "the end" in Ezekiel and Daniel), but more often noneschatological (e.g., 1 Kgs. 17:7; RSV "after a while"; Neh. 13:6; RSV "after some time"; Jer. 13:6; RSV "after many days").

In the New Testament Gk. *éschatos* "last" occurs in various ways with reference to the end and the time immediately before the end. The coming of Christ and the conditions brought on by his coming, including the experiences of the Church, are so indicated (e.g., Acts 2:17; Heb. 1:2; 2 Tim. 3:1; 2 Pet. 3:3; Jude 18; cf. 1 Pet. 1:20, "end of the times"; 1 John 2:18, "last hour"), as are events and conditions of the future (1 Cor. 15:26; 1 Pet. 1:5; Rev. 15:1; 21:9). Unique to the gospel of John is "the last day," which refers to the time of the coming general resurrection (John 6:39-40, 44, 54; 11:24) and judgment (12:48). Analogous terms are "the day of judgment" (1 John 4:17), "the day of the Lord" (1 Thess. 5:2; 2 Thess. 2:2), "the day of our Lord Jesus Christ" and similar expressions (1 Cor. 1:8; 5:5; 2 Cor. 1:14; Phil. 1:6, 10; 2:16), and "that Day" (2 Tim. 1:18).

See DAY OF THE LORD, ESCHATOLOGY.

LAST SUPPER.† The last evening meal that Jesus ate with the twelve apostles. The Last Supper is described by the Synoptic Gospels in connection with the betrayal of Jesus by Judas and the institution of the Lord's Supper (Matt. 26:20-29; Mark 14:17-25; Luke 22:14-30). The gospel of John gives additional information about what took place at the Last Supper: the washing of the disciples' feet, the explanation that the other disciples did not hear what was said to Judas, the "new commandment," the prediction of Peter's denial, the promise of the Comforter, and Jesus' prayer for the disciples (John 13–17). Paul alludes to the betrayal of Jesus and the institution of the Lord's Sup-

per as the main events of the Last Supper (1 Cor. 11:17-26). All four Gospels and the unanimous tradition of the Church hold that the Last Supper was eaten on a Thursday night and that the crucifixion occurred on Friday.

The Synoptic accounts suggest that Jesus was celebrating the Passover meal with his disciples (Matt. 26:18; cf. Luke 22:15, "this passover"). Indeed, the disciples made preparations for the Passover and the place it was to be celebrated (Matt. 26:17, 19). Yet Matthew's reference to the first day of "Unleavened Bread" (Matt. 26:17) actually denotes the day after the paschal lamb was killed; some scholars explain this discrepancy as a nontechnical, popular reference to a preliminary time of preparation for the feast when all leaven was removed from the houses. Similarly, Luke 22:7 is explained as referring to the entire period of time when the Passover was celebrated, during which the lamb was sacrificed. Moreover, John seems very clear in stating that the Last Supper was "before the feast of the Passover" (John 13:1). In John's account the disciples did not hear Jesus telling Judas to quickly execute his plan; they thought Jesus was giving Judas instructions to buy what was needed for the feast (vv. 28-29). Furthermore, at 18:28—after the Last Supper and before the Passover—some of the Pharisees did not enter the praetorium because they did not want to defile themselves and thus be unable to eat the Passover. One suggestion for reconciling the apparent discrepancies between John and the Synoptics is the use of different calendars by various sects, so that the Passover would have been celebrated on two separate days, first by Jesus and his disciples and then on the following day by the Pharisees.

The important elements of the Last Supper, according to the Synoptic Gospels, were the betrayal of Judas in contrast to the allegiance of the other disciples, the institution of the Lord's Supper with its continuing teaching of the cardinal importance of the atoning death of Jesus, the opportunity for the disciples' participation in the farewell meal and their sharing the sorrow over separation from Jesus, and the promise of resurrection and the kingdom. John does not mention the institution of the sacrament specifically, but adds Jesus' teaching on humility and the promise of the Holy Spirit, who will take the place of Jesus in encouraging the disciples.

See LORD'S SUPPER.

LASTHENES [lăsʹthə nēz] (Gk. *Lasthenēs*). A highly regarded official (perhaps a chief minister; cf. Diodorus *Hist.* xxxiii.4) under the Seleucid king Demetrius II Nicator, perhaps governor of Coele-Syria contemporary with the Hasmonean Jonathan. A Cretan, he had gathered mercenary troops and assisted Demetrius gain the throne (Josephus *Ant.* xiii.4.3 [86]). The terms "kinsman" (1 Macc. 11:31) and "father" (v. 32) were honorific titles rather than references to blood relationship.

At the suggestion of Jonathan (and for a sum of three hundred talents), Demetrius sent a letter to Lasthenes according to the Jews certain irrevocable privileges, transferring three districts (Apherema, Lydda, and Ramathaim) from Samaria to Judea, and ceding various revenues (vv. 30-37). Lasthenes was asked to make a public disclosure of these items, and a copy of the letter was sent to Jonathan.

LATIN (Gk. *Rhōmaïsti*).† The language of Rome and the Roman Empire, hence the official (although locally primarily military) language of the rulers of Palestine in the New Testament period (e.g., John 19:20; cf. Luke 23:38 mg.). The influence of Latin vocabulary is particularly apparent in the gospel of Mark (e.g., "denarius," "centurion," "legion," "Praetorium").

Attested first in the seventh century B.C., Latin was originally the language of Latium, a district encompassing the plain of the lower Tiber valley and the Alban hills in west central Italy. Itself a derivative of Indoeuropean, Latin adopted the Greek-type Etruscan alphabet. With the rise of Rome it replaced other local dialects and eventually became dominant throughout the western empire, although Greek remained dominant in the eastern portion and even Rome itself. Latin flourished as a living language for nearly one thousand years, provided the foundation for the various Romance languages, and continued as the ecclesiasical language of the Church.

For Latin versions of the Bible see OLD LATIN; JEROME; VULGATE.

LATRINE (Heb. *maḥᵃrā'ôṯ* "places of dung"). A toilet or privy, probably for public use. Using the demolished Baal temple as a latrine (or possibly a cesspool) (2 Kgs. 10:27; KJV "draught house"; Q *môṣā'ôṯ* "excrement") was an obvious sign of triumph and contempt, and an illustration of the severity of Jehu's prophet-backed rebellion against the house of Omri and its worship of foreign gods.

LATTER PROPHETS. In the Hebrew canon, those books representing the major or "classical" prophets Isaiah, Jeremiah, Ezekiel, and the twelve minor prophets. They are preceded by the Former Prophets: Joshua, Judges, Samuel, and Kings.

LAVER (Heb. *kîyôr*; Gk. *loutrón*). A large basin. Yahweh instructed Moses to make a large bronze laver and place it between the tent of meeting and the altar to hold the water Aaron and his sons would use to wash their hands and feet (Exod. 30:17-21; 38:8). The priests were to wash themselves as they approached the tabernacle and before making offerings on the altar. The precise form of this laver is not known, but because its base is described separately, it can be concluded that the tabernacle laver could be lifted from its base.

Solomon's temple had ten lavers, the bases of which are described in great detail (1 Kgs. 7:27-37; cf. 2 Kgs. 16:17). These lavers each held forty baths, i.e., about 880 l. (232.5 gal.) of water (1 Kgs. 7:38-39). These lavers did not have the same function as the single laver of the tabernacle, which was replaced by a bronze (molten) sea (vv. 23-26; 2 Chr. 4:6).

The Hebrew term was used also for other round objects, such as cooking pots (1 Sam. 2:14; Zech. 12:6) and some sort of platform or scaffold (2 Chr. 6:13).

The ritual purity called for by the precepts concerning the laver came to represent God's abhorrence of sin (cf. Isa. 52:11) and was the basis for the development of the Jewish practice of handwashing before certain prayers and before meals (cf. Mark 7:3-4; John 2:6). In New Testament usage the Greek term (RSV "washing") is used metaphorically for the Christian's spiritual cleansing through the word (Eph. 5:26) and "the washing of regeneration and renewal in the Holy Spirit" (Tit. 3:5).

LAW (Heb. *tôrâ*; also *miṣwâ* "commandment," *dābār* "word, commandment," *ḥōq* "statute, decree," *mišpaṭ* "ordinance, judgment"; Aram. *dāṯ* "law, regulation"; Gk. *nómos*).†

I. Old Testament and Judaism

For the formative period of Israelite history, before Moses and the Exodus from Egypt, the lives of God's people were regulated by the customs and traditions of tribal law. Such customs may underlie accounts of various encounters betwen the patriarchs and neighboring peoples, as in the establishment of covenants and redress for wrongs (e.g., Gen. 20:9-16; 21:25-32; 31:44-54; 34:8-10). Israelite law may also have been influenced by ancient Near Eastern law collections such as that of King Ur-nammu of Ur (*ca.* 2100 B.C.) and the Code of Hammurabi (eighteenth century). Such law codes are comprised of specific case laws, which prescribe the resolution of specified situations or the penalty for specified crimes. The Pentateuch contains both case (casuistic) laws (e.g., the Covenant Code; Exod. 20:22–23:33) and prescriptive (or apodictic) laws (e.g., the TEN COMMANDMENTS), which prescribe or forbid some deed or set of deeds in general terms but provide no penalty.

The laws of the Pentateuch are contained in two major collections, those associated with the events at Sinai (Exod. 19–Num. 10:10) and those given in Moses' farewell speeches on the plains of Moab (Deuteronomy). The context of both collections underscores their association with God's deliverance of Israel from slavery in Egypt, his sustaining of the people in the wilderness, and his establishment of them as a nation in the promised land. Yahweh, the deliverer, is the source of the laws; Moses is the human agent of both the salvation and the giving of the laws. The laws were given in the context of the covenant between Yahweh and Israel, and the people of Israel were thus bound to adhere to the laws (cf. Exod. 19:5). Indeed, the covenant was to be the means of life for the people of God when they obeyed the covenant stipulations; but when they disobeyed, whether through neglect or rebellion, disaster would follow (note the blessings and curses at Deut. 28). *See* COVENANT.

The pentateuchal laws encompass all areas of religious and social life, with no absolute demarcation between the two, and treat disparate matters with equal seriousness. Their intent is to establish and preserve the people of God as an ideal just and worshiping community. In this way the Israelite law codes resembled other ancient codes, which often stood not as guides for the actual practice of law but as statements of the ideal of an ordered community—the gift of kings who delivered peoples from oppression and established order.

The history of Israel's conquest and settled life shows

A fragment of the law code of King Lipit-Ishtar (early nineteenth century B.C.) (University Museum, University of Pennsylvania)

that the detailed codes of the Pentateuch were never completely known or followed. Numerous variations derived from local practices, and the covenant-legal traditions were challenged by forces within and outside Israel. The discovery of "the book of the law," perhaps closely akin to the book of Deuteronomy, in the reign of Josiah (2 Kgs. 22:8-20) brought about a limited reformation (23:1-25; cf. vv. 31-32), though it may have precipitated a penitential, Deuteronomistic rewriting of Israel's history (cf. 1–2 Samuel – 1–2 Kings) intended to demonstrate that the curses threatened by Deuteronomy had indeed come to pass on Israel and Judah.

The Pentateuch (called the Torah or Law) became permanently established as the central authority for the religion of the Jews after the return from exile, at the time of Ezra. Probably also at this time the contents and form of the Pentateuch were completed and established. In this context, the promises and threats of Deuteronomy had a particularly strong meaning to those who had returned: the curses had been carried out, but hope survived for blessings through strict adherence to the covenant stipulations.

Once the pentateuchal laws had become established as the focus of Jewish religion, the understanding and application of the laws—now the responsibility of the scribes—became a significant religious concern. Indeed, Ezra is depicted as the ideal scribe (Ezra 7:6, 10-12; Neh. 8:1-8, 13). The understanding of the law developed along with the desire to protect the distinctiveness of the people of Israel from syncretistic or assimilationist tendencies (cf. Ezra 9–10; 1 Macc. 1:11-15). Because violation of the covenant and the laws was such a serious matter (cf. Isa. 24:5; 1 Macc. 2:27), the question was now asked: what specific laws, what specific aspects of the covenant? This develop-

ment is reflected in the book of Jubilees, which reads an interpretation of certain laws back into the patriarchal period, as well as in the covenant-legal ideas and practices of Qumran, and the development of the centrality of HALAKHAH (detailed interpretation of the laws of the Pentateuch) in rabbinic Judaism. In somewhat parallel development, the ancient wisdom tradition came to celebrate the law (e.g., Pss. 1; 37:3-31; 119); eventually wisdom became virtually equated with the prescriptions of the Pentateuch (e.g., Wis. 6:1-11, 18; Sir. 24:8-12, 23-29).

For laws regarding worship and ritual see CLEAN AND UNCLEAN; Leviticus, BOOK OF; and the entries on individual feasts and offerings.

II. New Testament

In his statements about the law Jesus did not call for an end to the Mosaic prescriptions; in fact, he denied that such was his intention (Matt. 5:17-20). But he distinguished between the law of Moses and scribal Halakhah ("tradition," Mark 7:1-8 par.). Rather than calling for an end to the law, Jesus called for a deeper, more radical living by the law, which embodies that which the law intends to produce—justice, mercy, and self-denial (Luke 11:42 par.; 18:18-22 par.).

Jesus insisted that repentant sinners were more readily accepted by God than the "righteous," law-abiding people who were unaware of the eschatological situation that called for repentance and the deeper, more radical adherence to the law (5:32 par.; cf. 18:9-14). Therefore, he himself violated Halakhah by eating with prostitutes, tax-collectors, and other sinners (5:29-30 par.; 7:34 par.; 15:1-2; 19:7; cf. 7:39), and by healing on the Sabbath (6:6-11; 13:10-16). At other times when Jesus or his disciples violated scribal interpretation of the law the issue was simply the authority of Jesus (cf. Matt. 7:28-29)—"The Son of man is lord of the sabbath" (Luke 6:5 par.; cf. 5:24 par.). In the new eschatological situation brought in by the ministry of Jesus, the call to a more radical ethics and the question of authority could only provoke controversy, and the violation of scribal tradition became the catalyst for such controversies.

A certain detachment from orthodox living by the Torah might have characterized the Jewish "Hellenists" (Acts 6:1) within the early Church. Stephen, a leader among the Hellenists, was accused of predicting the alteration of the laws received from Moses (vv. 11-14), but he in turn accused the Jews who heard him of breaking the law (7:53).

The evangelistic energy of the early Church brought the teachings of Jesus to the "uncircumcised," including Samaritans and Gentiles who worshipped the God of Israel, and thus raised the question of adherence to the law (11:1-8). The existence of the church at Antioch and the mission of Paul and Barnabas to Cyprus and south-central Asia Minor forced a confrontation (15:1-5). The course followed in the APOSTOLIC COUNCIL was to require of Gentile Christians not full adherence to the law but only a certain amount of sensitivity to Jewish principles (vv. 19-21, 28-29). The disputed issues were apparently not resolved to the satisfaction of all, and Paul's letters suggest that the same and related issues remained alive. (Paul himself did not refer to the Council's decision in his letters, even at points where it might have been to the advantage of his argument to do so.) The events surrounding the Council and its unsatisfactory outcome probably represent the beginning of the division between what was to become the mainstream of Christianity, dominated by Gentiles, and Jewish-Christian sects such as the Ebionites.

Paul's teachings on the law, found particularly in Galatians and Romans, thus developed in the midst of controversy. The basic issue in Paul's view was the role of the law in eschatological salvation. With the coming of Christ righteousness is not a human quality to be attained by adherence to the law, but the activity of God for the deliverance from sin of those who believe in Jesus Christ (Rom. 1:16-17; 3:21-22). The law is fulfilled in this salvation (vv. 21, 31). Not the law but the Spirit is the means for the new life that is lived by those who have been saved (8:2-13; Gal. 3:2-3; 5:2-5, 16, 25). Although "the law is holy, and the commandment is holy and just and good" (Rom. 7:12), it becomes for the person who has not yet experienced salvation in Christ and life in the Spirit only that which exposes sin (3:20; 7:7, 22-23) and even an inducement to sin (5:20; 7:8-11). But it is as that which exposes sin that the law is able to lead to Christ (Gal. 3:23). Because justification is available through faith in Christ, "Christ is the end of the law," as a means of justification for everyone who has faith (Rom. 10:4). This is not to say that justification was ever attainable by adherence to the law; already in Abraham's case, justification was by faith (ch. 4; Gal. 3:6-7). See JUSTIFICATION.

Apparently Paul experienced personally a radical shift in practice with regard to the law. Before his conversion and call to be an apostle he was "as to the righteousness under the law blameless" (Phil. 3:6). He excelled at living by the Torah and was a Pharisee who zealously interpreted the law (Gal. 1:14; Phil. 3:5-6). Paul did not, on the basis of his views toward the role of the law in eschatological salvation, give up observance of the law; but he did vary his behavior because of the demands of his role as an evangelist (1 Cor. 9:20-21).

Bibliography. R. Banks, *Jesus and the Law in the Synoptic Tradition* (New York: 1975); G. E. Mendenhall, *Law and Covenant in Israel and the Ancient Near East* (Pittsburgh: 1955); M. Noth, *The Laws in the Pentateuch and Other Studies* (Philadelphia: 1967); E. P. Sanders, *Paul and Palestinian Judaism* (Philadelphia: 1977).

LAWLESS ONE. See ANTICHRIST.

LAWSUIT (Heb. *rîḇ* "controversy, dispute").† A literary form couched in language and forms stereotypical of legal proceedings (e.g., Gen. 13:7-9; 31:25-42; Deut. 25:1-3; Prov. 25:7b-9; cf. Judg. 11:12-28), particularly prevalent in the preexilic prophetic writings, wherein Yahweh contends with his covenant people (Jer. 2:9; cf. Isa. 1:18; Heb. *ykḥ niphal* "reprove each other"; RSV "reason together").

In the lawsuit the Lord brings a "controversy" (Hos. 4:1; Mic. 6:2) or "indictment" (Jer. 25:31; cf. Job 31:35; cf. Jer. 49:19) against the unfaithful nation and summons heaven to witness (Ps. 50:4; Isa. 1:2). Yahweh

lays out the charges (cf. Jer. 49:29), interrogates Israel (Isa. 1:4-9), exchanges arguments (3:13-14; cf. Job 13:3, 6-8, 17-19, 22), offers settlement (1:18-20), and pronounces judgment, "acquitting the innocent and condemning the guilty" (Deut. 25:1-3).

LAWYER (Gk. *nomikós*).† An expert in the law of Moses (Matt. 22:35 par.; Luke 7:30; 11:45-46). The term is equivalent to Gk. *grammateús*, the more usual translation of Heb. *sōp̄ēr* "scribe." Another equivalent term is Gk. *nomodidáskalos* "teacher of the law" (Luke 5:17; Acts 5:34; 1 Tim. 1:7). "Zenas the lawyer" (Tit. 3:13) may have been a practitioner of Greek or Roman civil law rather than a teacher and interpreter of Jewish law. See SCRIBES.

LAYING ON OF HANDS (Heb. *sāmaḵ yaḏ'al*; Gk. *[epi]títhēmi tás cheíras [ep']*).† A ceremonial act of consecration or identification.

I. Old Testament

The Pentateuch prescribes that laying one or both hands upon the sacrificial offering precede the twice-daily burnt offering (Exod. 29:15; Lev. 1:4; 8:18; Num. 8:12), peace offerings (Lev. 3:2, 8), sin offerings (ch. 4; 8:14; 2 Chr. 29:23), and offerings made upon the consecration of priests (Exod. 29:19; Lev. 8:14, 22) and Levites (Num. 8:12). Hands were also laid on the Levites themselves as part of their consecration (v. 10). Moses laid hands on Joshua in consecrating him as his successor (27:18, 23; Deut. 34:9).

Lev. 16:21-22, which specifies that on the Day of Atonement the high priest lay his hands on the goat to be released into the wilderness (see ATONEMENT, DAY OF), clearly implies that an idea of transference—indeed, substitutionary atonement—could be connected with the laying on of hands. Some interpreters contend that such a transference of sin should be envisioned in connection with all the offerings mentioned. Likewise, when all who heard a blasphemer laid their hands on his head before he was stoned, the guilt thus transmitted would be that incurred by hearing the blasphemy (24:14). Some scholars suggest further that the duty of service of firstborn sons (cf. Num. 3:40-41) was transferred by the laying of hands on the Levites, and that an impartation of Moses' wisdom or authority onto Joshua was effected or symbolized by the laying on of hands.

It is questionable, however, whether sin and guilt were so constantly in view in connection with the sacrifices. Philo (*De spec. leg.* i.203-4) regards the laying of hands on the sacrificial animal as the sign of a claim to a righteous use of the hands, but he may be influenced by Deut. 21:7 and his own concerns. In the incident of the blasphemer, a graphic identification of the accused by the accusers may be all that is intended. In the consecration of the Levites and of Joshua, a transference may be in mind, or again simply a graphic identification of the one consecrated, or a conveyance of blessing, as in Gen. 48:14, 17 (Heb. *šît*).

Heb. *šît* is also used in instances where God's hand is said to lay upon someone for blessing or judgment (Ps. 139:5) and in an apparent reference to a procedure followed in arbitration (Job 9:33). Where hands are laid on another for destruction the verb is *šālaḥ* (e.g., Gen. 22:12; Exod. 24:11) or *nāṭan* (e.g., 7:4).

II. New Testament

Apart from the passages that mention someone laying hands on another with hostile intent (Gk. *epibállō*; e.g., Matt. 26:50 par.; cf. Acts 4:3; RSV "arrest"), the laying on of hands (*epitíthēmi*) in the New Testament most often represents a channel of blessing, as in Jesus' blessing of the children (cf. Matt. 19:13-15; Mark 10:13-16).

Laying on of hands is an action often accompanying healings by both Jesus (e.g., Matt. 9:18 par.; Mark 6:5) and the leaders of the early Church (Acts 9:12, 17; cf. 28:8). At 4:30 God's hand is involved in healing; this anthropomorphism (cf. 14:3; 19:11) makes clear that the Church's representative is the channel for healing that is actually accomplished by God. With Jesus, however, the power of healing should probably be considered more direct, since it is in his own person that the power of the new age came (cf. Luke 11:20). In both cases, the touch typical of ancient healers became a means of expressing involvement and the authority to convey God's blessing. The hands represented the whole person, effective for healing (Acts 5:12).

When hands were laid on new believers in Samaria and they received the Holy Spirit, Simon assumed that a neutral power was involved that was effective through the hands of the apostles (8:17-19; cf. 9:17; 19:6), but the apostles' response shows that it was the attitude of the recipient's heart rather than the laying on of hands (8:20-21), that was instrumental for receiving the Holy Spirit (10:44-47). At Heb. 6:2 "the laying on of hands" denotes the receiving of the Holy Spirit, here listed among "the elementary doctrines of Christ" and taken by some as a reference to the rite of confirmation.

The pracitce of laying on of hands in connection with ordination was probably closely related to its use in connection with the giving of the Holy Spirit and its gifts to new believers (so esp. 1 Tim. 4:14; 2 Tim. 1:6; cf. Acts 6:6; 13:3; 1 Tim. 5:22).

LAZARUS [lăz'ə rəs] (Gk. *Lazaros*; cf. Heb. *ʾelʿāzmar* "God has helped").

1. In the parable of Lazarus and the rich man (Luke 16:19-31) the poor man who lay at the gate of the rich man to beg for scraps from the table. Both men die, and Lazarus is carried by angels into ABRAHAM'S BOSOM, but the rich man is tormented in Hades. This parable does not make poverty a virtue and wealth a vice, though the danger wealth poses for piety is definitely in mind. The chasm between the two realms of the dead (v. 26) underscores the need to heed the word of God in earthly life (cf. v. 31). Lazarus is the only character in a parable of Jesus given a proper name. ("Dives," the name traditionally given to the rich man in the same parable, is actually the Latin word for "rich.")

2. The brother of Mary and Martha, who lived in Bethany (John 11). The sisters had summoned Jesus to heal Lazarus, whom he loved (vv. 3, 5, 36), but by the time Jesus arrived Lazarus had been dead four days (v. 17). His death gave Jesus the opportunity to teach about the relationship of faith in himself to the

coming resurrection (vv. 25-26, 40). Jesus chose to raise Lazarus from the dead in order to reveal his power and to move people to faith in his divine origin (v. 42); some interpreters suggest that Jesus actually delayed his arrival in order to accomplish this goal (cf. vv. 4, 6ff., 21ff.). Some Jewish leaders persecuted Jesus on account of this miracle and plotted to kill Lazarus as well because of the miracle's effectiveness in producing faith (vv. 47-53, 57; 12:11). Lazarus was present at the meal given in Jesus' honor by Simon the leper (vv. 1-2). Despite a number of similarities in the accounts of this Lazarus and **1** above, no relationship between the two individuals has been demonstrated.

LEAD (Heb. *ʿôpereṭ*).† A malleable, blue-gray metal widely known and used in the ancient world. Lead was abundant and cheap (Sir. 47:18). Among the metal objects captured from the Midianites in battle in the Transjordanian plain were some made of lead (Num. 31:22). Tyre received imports of lead from "Tarshish" (Ezek. 27:12); lead was mined in a large number of locations around the Mediterranean Sea. The great weight of lead (cf. Exod. 15:10; Sir. 22:14) dictated some of its uses (e.g., Zech. 5:7-8). It was also used in the refining of silver (Jer. 6:29-30); on the refining of lead itself, among other metals, cf. Ezek. 22:18-22. Job 19:24 may refer to lead being poured into inscriptions cut into stone, or to its being the actual surface for inscriptions, both of which are known from archaeological finds.

LEAH (lē'ə] (Heb. *lēʾâ* "wild ox"). A daughter of Laban and elder sister of Rachel (Gen. 20:16). It was she rather than Rachel whom the crafty Laban gave Jacob as a wife after he had labored seven years (vv. 18-26). Leah is described as having "weak" eyes, meaning she was unattractive in contrast to the beautiful Rachel (v. 17). Because Jacob favored Rachel (v. 30), the Lord made Leah conceive while Rachel remained childless (v. 31). Leah's children were Reuben, Simeon, Levi, Judah, Issachar, Zebulun, and Dinah, the only daughter of Jacob (vv. 31-35; 30:18-21). Gad and Asher, the sons of Leah's maid Zilpah, were also considered among Leah's children (vv. 9-13). The loyal Leah (cf. Ruth 4:11) accompanied Jacob when he returned to his homeland (Gen. 31:4, 14), and upon her death he buried her in the cave of Machpelah (49:30-31).

LEATHER. (Heb. *ʿôr* "skin"; Gk. *dermátinos*).† The tanned skins of various animals were used for a wide variety of purposes, including clothing (2 Kgs. 1:8; Matt. 3:4; cf. Lev. 13:47-59; RSV "skin"), slings (cf. 1 Sam. 25:29), shepherds' bags (17:40), containers for liquids (Gen. 21:14; Matt. 9:17), sandals (Ezek. 16:10), and scrolls (such as the Dead Sea Scrolls). Untanned skins also might be used for clothing (Gen. 3:21; Heb. 11:37).

Almost all tanned hides were from domesticated livestock. The identity of the *taḥaš*, an animal whose skins provided coverings for the tabernacle and its utensils (Exod. 25:5; 26:14; 35:7, 23; 36:19; 39:34; Num. 4) and of which sandals were made (Ezek. 16:10), is unknown (cf. JB, "fine leather"). Badgers (so KJV) are widely-known in Palestine but not in Sinai; goats (RSV) are a possibility. Use of the Red Sea dugong, an aquatic mammal (NIV "sea cows"; NJV "dolphin"), for sandals has been confirmed.

Though the designation of Paul's profession is literally "tentmaker" (Gk. *skēnopoiós*; Acts 18:3), the sense of the term appears to have been leather-worker, or perhaps a maker of leather tents, which were common.

See TANNING.

LEAVEN (Heb. *ḥāmēṣ, śeʾōr*; Gk. *zýmē*).† Any substance added to dough to cause it to ferment. Leaven usually consisted of a bit of dough from an earlier batch.

The bread and meal sacrifices that went to the altar were to be unleavened (e.g., Exod. 23:18; Lev. 2:11; cf. Amos 4:5). Only two offerings, which were eaten before the altar, were to be leavened (Lev. 7:13; 23:17). Especially important was the prohibition of leaven during PASSOVER in commemoration of the haste with which Israel left Egypt (Exod. 12:15-20, 33-34; *maṣṣôt* "unleavened bread").

The New Testament figurative references to leaven have in mind that which is small, insignificant, or hidden, but which is of great effect. Paul links the proverb, "A little leaven leavens the whole lump" (Gal. 5:9), with the pre-Passover search for *ḥāmēṣ* that occurs in every observant Jewish home. "The leaven of the Pharisees and Sadducees," (or Herod; Mark 8:15; RSV mg. "the Herodians") (Matt. 16:6 par.), which is interpreted as "teaching" at v. 12 and "hypocrisy" at Luke 12:1, is also that which has effects greater than its appearance. Similarly, leaven is also used of that which is of beneficial effect, namely, the kingdom of heaven (Matt. 13:33 par.).

LEBANA, LEBANAH [lə bāʹnə] (Heb. *leḇānâ* "white"; Gk. *Labana*). The head of a family of temple servants whose descendants returned with Zerubbabel from captivity in Babylon (Ezra 2:45, "Lebana"; Neh. 7:48, "Lebanah"; 1 Esdr. 5:29; KJV "Labana").

LEBANON [lĕbʹə nŏn] (Heb. *leḇānôn* "white mountain"). A mountain range north of Israel and parallel to the Mediterranean Sea, named for its snowcapped peaks (Jer. 18:14). The range extends from the Nahr el-Kebir (the ancient Eleutheropolis river) near the Amanus mountains in the north nearly 160 km. (100 mi.) south to the Nahr el-Qāsimiyeh (the Litani river gorge) at the northern border of Palestine. The highest peak is Qurnat es-Sawda, 2088 m. (10,131 ft.) high. East of the Lebanon range, separated by the Beqaʿ (el-Biqāʿ) valley (cf. Josh. 11:17, "the valley of the Lebanon, below Mount Hermon"; 12:7), is the parallel Anti-lebanon range. At Judg. 3:3 Heb. *har hal-leḇānôn* (RSV "Mount Lebanon," may designate the adjacent region (cf. Josh. 9:1).

According to Josh. 13:5-7 "all Lebanon, from Baal-gad below Mount Hermon to the entrance of Hamath," was to be allotted to Israel. David and Solomon's kingdom did border on the Phoenicians at Lebanon.

In antiquity many species of plants and animals were native to the Lebanon (e.g., 2 Kgs. 14:9; Ps.

72:16; Isa. 40:16; Ezek. 17:3; Hab. 2:17). Its slopes were wooded with cedar (Isa. 2:13; cf. Ezek. 31:15), which was used in the construction of Solomon's temple (1 Kgs. 5:14 [MT 28]) and palace (7:2-5). Its beauty and fruitfulness were proverbial (Isa. 35:2; cf. Cant. 4:11; Hos. 14:6 [MT 7]).

LEBAOTH [lə bāʹŏth] (Heb. *leḇāʾōt* "lionesses"). A city in the extreme south of Judah (Josh. 15:32). At 19:6 it is called Beth-lebaoth and assigned to Simeon. *See* BETH-BIRI.

LEBBAEUS [lĕ bēʹəs] (Gk. *Lebbaíos*). According to the Western text at Matt. 10:3 (so KJV, RSV mg.); Mark 3:18, another name for the apostle Thaddeus. If, as the KJV reads at Matt. 10:3, the name is a surname it could refer to his place of origin. Some scholars derive the name from Heb. *lēḇ* "heart," taking it as an epithet of JUDAS (**8**) the son of James (Luke 6:16; Acts 1:13; cf. Syr.) distinguishing this apostle from Judas Iscariot (cf. John 14:22).

LEBONAH [lə bōʹnə] (Heb. *leḇônâ* "incense"). A city about 5 km. (3 mi.) northwest of Shiloh, on the road to Shechem (Judg. 21:19). The site has been identified as the modern village Khan el-Lubban.

LEB-QAMAI [lĕb kämʹī] (Heb. *lēḇ qāmāy*). A cipher for Chaldea (Jer. 51:1, RSV mg.). *See* ATHBASH.

LECAH [lēʹkə] (Heb. *lēḵâ*). A son of Er and descendant of Shelah (1 Chr. 4:21). The context, however, suggests that Lecah was a place in the tribal territory of Judah, founded by Er. Because Mareshah, mentioned in the same text, is located northwest of Hebron, Lecah would have been in the same region, though it cannot be identified more precisely.

LEECH. (Heb. *ʿalûqâ* "clinging"). A bloodsucking worm of the class *Hirudinea* (Prov. 30:15; KJV "horse-leech"). Various types of leech have been attested since ancient times in the stagnant or slow moving waters of Palestine. The Talmud warns against drinking water directly from a river or pond with the mouth or hands out of the fear of ingesting a leech (*ʿAbod. Zar.* 12b).

LEEK (Heb. *ḥāṣîr*).† An herb (*Allium porrum* L.) related to the onion and the garlic. In ancient times leeks were widely used in both Palestine and Egypt, where the Israelites became acquainted with them (Num. 11:5). Because the Hebrew term is otherwise translated more generally as "grass" (e.g., 1 Kgs. 18:5; cf. Job 8:12; KJV "herb"; RSV "plant"; Prov. 27:25; KJV "hay"), some scholars question whether leeks are in fact intended at Num. 11:5. In support of the reading are the ancient versions, including the LXX, and the association with onions and garlics. Other suggestions include fenugreek, which was also widely used in ancient Egypt and Palestine, and any green leafy vegetable.

LEES (Heb. *šemārîm*). The sediment formed in the fermentation of wine. Wine was left in the wineskin "on the lees" for a time to improve its flavor and richness, then strained before drinking (Isa. 25:6; cf. Zeph. 1:12). Jer. 48:11 apparently refers to a practice of pouring wine from container to container to keep the lees in suspension. *See* DREGS.

LEGEND.* A designation for a broad number of narrative forms. It does not necessarily imply denigration of the historical value of the narrative found in these forms. Included under the general designation of legends, as the term is used in a broad sense, are legends proper, ancestor sagas, cult etiologies, and other etiological tales. Each of these forms represent stories that were transmitted orally for some length of time before becoming incorporated into larger narratives.

The legend proper is a narrative of wondrous and miraculous deeds composed for the sake of edification and to celebrate the piety, virtue, or strength of its hero and not originally for its part in a larger narrative. The heroes of legends include Phinehas (Num. 25:6-18), Samson (e.g., Judg. 16) and other judges (e.g., 3:31; 9:26-49), Elijah (e.g., 2 Kgs. 2:23-24), Elishah (e.g., 6:1-7, 8-10a) and other prophets (e.g., 1 Kgs. 14:1-18), David (e.g., 2 Sam. 8:1-14), Solomon (1 Kgs. 3:16-28), Jesus (e.g., Mark 11:12-14, 20; Luke 2:41-51; 7:36-50), and Paul (e.g., Acts 19:12-13; 28:3-6).

Ancestor sagas were preserved by tribes, clans, and nations as statements of the antiquity, legitimacy, and character of themselves as a people. Among ancestor sagas are the stories of Lamech (Gen. 4:19-24), Judah and Tamar (ch. 38), and the other patriarchs.

Cult etiologies are narratives that explain the holiness of places such as Bethel (28:11-22) and the origin of institutions such as the Sabbath (1:1–2:3) and the ordination of the Levites (Exod. 32:25-29). Other etiological tales are focused on a variety of matters such as place names (e.g., Gen. 11:1-9; Exod. 17:7), ownership arrangements (Josh. 15:16-19), and the practice of not eating "the sinew of the hip which is upon the hollow of the thigh" (Gen. 32:24-32 [MT 25-33]).

LEGION (Gk. *legíōn*; Lat. *legio*).† The primary division of the standing citizen army of the Roman Empire. The number varied from time to time, but in New Testament times a legion consisted of theoretically 6000 men, in actuality about 5000 foot soldiers and 120 horsemen. A legion consisted of ten cohorts, and a cohort of six centuries. Legions were commanded by legates, cohorts by military tribunes, and centuries by centurions. From A.D. 9 into the second century there were twenty-five to thirty legions in the empire.

Auxiliary troops were divided into cohorts of theoretically 760 foot soldiers and 240 horsemen, commanded by tribunes as were legionary cohorts. Provincial fortresses, such as the Antonia in Jerusalem, would normally house one auxiliary cohort. The cohorts referred to in the New Testament (Matt. 27:27 par.; RSV "battalion"; Acts 10:1; 21:31; 27:1) all appear to have been auxiliary rather than legionary cohorts.

At Matt. 26:53; Mark 5:9, 15 par. "legion" is figurative for a large number.

LEHABIM [lə hā'bĭm] (Heb. *lᵉhābîm*). A people among the sons of Ham, named as offspring of Egypt (Heb. *miṣrayim*) (Gen. 10:13; 1 Chr. 1:11). They are generally identified with the Libyians (Lubim). *See* LIBYA.

LEHEM [lē'hĕm] (Heb. *leḥem*).* A possible place name at 1 Chr. 4:22 (RSV). Heb. *wᵉyāšubî lāḥem* is difficult, perhaps because the text derives from ancient records, and a number of translational and emendational possibilities exist. The KJV and NIV take the words as a personal name, "Jashubi-lehem." With slight emendations, "and they returned to themselves" (an idiom meaning simply "and they returned"), "and they returned to Lehem" (cf. JB), and "and (they were) inhabitants of Lehem" are possible. Lehem, if such a name is intended, could be a shortened form of Bethlehem (so JB), which would fit the Judahite context of the verse.

LEHI [lē'hī] (Heb. *lᵉḥî* "jawbone"). A place in the tribal territory of Judah where the Philistines camped and Samson killed a thousand of their number with the jawbone of an ass. It was called thereafter Ramath-lehi, "the hill of the jawbone" (Jgs. 15:9-17, 19). Lehi may have been the site of the incident recorded at 2 Sam. 23:11-12 (emending *laḥayyâ* "into a troop" [so KJV; NJV "in force"; cf. NIV] to *leḥyâ* "at Lehi" [RSV, JB]). Lehi may have been in the vicinity of Beth-shemesh, but the precise location remains uncertain.

LEMUEL [lĕm'yōō əl] (Heb. *lᵉmô'ēl* "belonging to God"). A king of MASSA (Prov. 31:1, 4; cf. 30:1). At Gen. 25:4; 1 Chr. 1:30 Massa is a place name, identifiable (with inscriptionary confirmation) as a north Arabian tribe. Heb. *maśśā'* may also be translated "oracle" (so RSV mg.; also "burden") or "prophecy" (so KJV), suggesting that the instructions that follow are wisdom imparted to the king by his mother.

LENDING (Heb. *lāwâ*; Gk. *daneízō*). An obligation in the Mosaic legislation intended to aid the poor (Deut. 15:7-11). No interest was to be charged to fellow Jews (Exod. 22:25 [MT 24]; Lev. 25:35-37; Deut. 23:19-20 [MT 20-21]; *nāšak*), although it was permissible to so charge foreigners (v. 20 [MT 21]). The taking of pledges for loans was strictly limited (Exod. 22:26-27 [MT 25-26]; Deut. 24:6, 17). During the Sabbatical Year all debts were to be canceled (15:1-6). One intention of the pentateuchal laws was to prevent debt slavery (cf. Exod. 21:1-2), which did, in fact, occur in postexilic Israel (Neh. 5:1-5; *nāšā'*). For faithful adherence to the covenantal stipulations, God would so bless Israel that they would "lend to many nations" but "not borrow" (Deut. 15:6).

Jesus' teaching went beyond the Old Testament precepts: one should always behave as if the Sabbatical Year had just begun and expect the return of neither interest nor principal (Luke 6:35).

See DEBT; INTEREST.

LENTILS (Heb. *'ᵃdašîm*).† A leguminous plant (*Lens esculenta* Moench; also called *Ervum lens* L.) grown for its seeds from very ancient times in Palestine and neighboring lands. The plants, which grow well even in poor soil, have slender stems, violet flowers and pinnate leaves, and produce flat round seeds about 1 cm. (.2 in.) across, one to a pod. Lentils (KJV "lentiles") were mainly cooked in stews (Gen. 25:34; cf. v. 30, "red pottage," a pun on Heb. *'ĕḏôm* "Edom") and could also be used in bread (e.g., Ezek. 4:9), though this was probably rare.

LEOPARD (Heb. *nāmēr*; Aram. *nᵉmar*; Gk. *párdalis*). *Felis pardus*, a large member of the cat family (Felidae), yellow with black spots (actually broken rings; cf. Jer. 13:23) arranged in a pattern. Leopards are now nearly extinct in Palestine, but their common occurrence in biblical times is reflected in the place names Beth-nimrah (Josh. 13:27; Nimrah at Num. 32:3) and "the waters of Nimrim" (Isa. 15:6).

"The mountains of leopards" (Cant. 4:8) probably refers to no specific place, but rather to the wildness of the Syrian mountains. Leopards were known as beasts of prey dangerous to both humans and flocks (hence Jer. 5:6 and the figures at Isa. 11:6; Hos. 13:7); cheetahs (*Acinonyx jubatus*) have been trained for hunting and are probably what is intended at Hab. 1:8. The fierce qualities of leopards also led to their figurative use in apocalyptic language (e.g., Dan. 7:6; Rev. 13:2).

LEPROSY (Heb. *ṣāra'aṯ*; Gk. *lepra*).† A broad generic term for any number of eruptive skin diseases and disorders. Indeed, specific identification of the disease so named in the biblical accounts with that now called leprosy (from the formerly more general Latin loanword *lepra*) or Hansen's disease was not made until the Middle Ages when the disease became widespread in Europe. The biblical descriptions of leprosy are not clinically precise, and the necroses associated with Hansen's disease are apparently not in view in the Bible. "Leprosy" in garments and buildings (Lev. 13:47-59; 14:33-57) was caused by mold, rot, or fungus.

The extensive code for dealing with "leprosy" at Lev. 13–14 is one means of stressing the separation of the people of God from any uncleanness, whether moral or physical. This does not mean that skin diseases were invariably thought of as punishment for sin, though they could be (Num. 12:10; 2 Kgs. 15:5; 2 Chr. 26:19-23). Jesus' healings of lepers (Matt. 8:2-4 par.; Luke 17:12-19) were among the signs of Jesus' messiahship relayed to John the Baptist (Matt. 11:5 par.). *See* CLEAN AND UNCLEAN *II.C.*

LESHEM [lēʹshəm] (Heb. *lešem*). The alternate form of LAISH 1, the ancient name of DAN (PLACE) 1 (Josh. 19:47).

LETHECH. [lēʹthĕk] (Heb. *leṯek̠*). A dry measure equivalent to one-half HOMER (Hos. 3:2).

LETTERS (Heb. *sēper*, *'iggereṯ*; Gk. *epistolḗ*, *grámmata*).† A broad designation for various types of written documents in biblical and ancient usage. Numbered among ancient letters are a great variety of business, government, and legal documents, political

and military reports, orders, and correspondence, as well as more personal correspondence.

I. General

Several letters or parts of letters are preserved in the Old Testament and Apocrypha (e.g., 2 Sam. 11:15; 1 Kgs. 5:2-6 [MT 16-20]; 21:9-10; 2 Chr. 2:11-16 [MT 10-15]; Ezra 4:11-22; 7:12-26; Neh. 6:6-7; Jer. 29; 1 Macc. 10–15). In addition, letters are often mentioned with a summary, rather than a quotation, of their significant content (e.g., 2 Kgs. 20:12; Neh. 2:7-8; 6:17, 19; Esth. 3:12-13; 8:9-11; 9:20-32; Jdt. 4:6-7; 1 Macc. 1:41-42, 44-50). Such letters preserved in historical narratives may be fictional, composed as appropriate to the situation narrated rather than retrieved from an official archive. In addition to the New Testament books written at least partly in letter form (all of those commonly designated "epistles" or "letters" with the exception of 1 John) and the letters of John to the seven churches of Asia (Rev. 1:4-8; chs. 2–3), letters are preserved at Acts 15:23-29; 23:26-30.

Numerous letters have been preserved from throughout the ancient world that in different ways clarify aspects of the Bible. The most important letters in cuneiform tablet form, primarily diplomatic, political, and military documents, are from Mari in Mesopotamia (eighteenth century B.C.) and Amarna in Egypt (fourteenth century). From Arad and Lachish in Palestine come inscribed ostraca (potsherds), including military and government documents in Hebrew from the late Judean monarchy, an important contribution to understanding the history of the Hebrew language and letter forms, and, from Arad, Aramaic letter-documents from *ca.* 400 relating to the Persian garrison on the site.

Thousands of papyrus letters have been unearthed, mostly from Egypt, including the fifth-century Aramaic Elephantine Papyri from a postexilic Jewish settlement in Egypt. Understanding of New Testament Greek and of Hellenistic letter conventions has been increased immeasurably by Greek papyri from Egypt. The papyrus letters of Bar Kokhba, leader of a Jewish rebellion in A.D. 132-135, found at Wâdī Murabba'at near the Dead Sea are significant for the history of Hebrew letter conventions (*see* DEAD SEA SCROLLS V).

Literary letters, written with wide publication in mind, were a significant literary form in the Hellenistic and Roman world, especially after the publication of Cicero's letters in the first century B.C. With the publication of letters came the concern for collecting letters. Already during Cicero's lifetime, collections of his letters were assembled and published by himself and others. In similar fashion, the letters of Paul and Ignatius came to be collected after their deaths; no letters of these men survive independent of collections.

Letters generally had a dual nature as written communication that bordered on spoken communication, and the distinction between written and oral was not absolute (cf. 2 Kgs. 10:2-8; 18–19; 2 Chr. 32:17-18). Letters could begin with oral dictation and usually were read to their addressees, even if the latter might include a scribe (e.g., Ezra 4:23; cf. Acts 15:31).

Even when the recipient read a letter for himself (2 Kgs. 5:7; Acts 23:34), the usual practice was to read aloud. Letters apparently began as an extension of the practice of sending messages by way of messengers.

Although regular postal systems met the administrative needs of large kingdoms and empires (cf. "couriers," 2 Chr. 30:6, 10; Esth. 3:13, 15; 8:10, 14; "messengers," 1 Macc. 1:44), no postal system ever existed for private correspondence. Paul's letters were delivered by his coworkers, whose personal contact with the addressees was significant in itself (Phil. 2:25-30; Col. 4:7-9; cf. Eph. 6:21-22).

II. Form and Style

Because many letters were written by professional scribes, the contents were prescribed as much by customary forms as by particular occasions. Ancient letters can be analyzed according to the general model of opening—body—closing (cf. 2 Chr. 2:11-16; Ezra 4:11, 17; 5:7; 7:12-26; Add.Esth. 13:1-7; 1 Macc. 10:18-20; 2 Macc. 1:1–2:18); unlike Greek and Aramaic letters, through the first century A.D. Hebrew letters lacked any sort of closing. Hellenistic Greek letters included in the opening: "A to B," a greeting, and sometimes an expression of desire for the recipient's good health coupled with "I myself am well," and in the closing: greetings, wishes, sometimes a prayer, and sometimes a date. Hellenistic letters were highly formalized, with each part more or less determined by convention, regardless of the occasion.

Paul's letters, while they fall within the designation of Hellenistic letters and are influenced by some Jewish conventions, show some development of the letter pattern based on Paul's creativity. The letter form as developed by Paul became established as a genre for the communication of ecclesiastical policy, instruction, and exhortation and for the binding together of churches separated by distance. In Paul's letters and other Christian letters written under the influence of his pattern, the openings follow the usual Hellenistic pattern of "A to B, greetings," but the specific purposes of the letters come even into the openings by way of expansions of this basic pattern (e.g., Rom. 1:1-7; Gal. 1:1-5; 1 Thess. 1:1; Tit. 1:1-4; Phlm. 1-3; Jas. 1:1; 1 Pet. 1:1-2; 2 Pet. 1:1-2; 2 John 1:1-3; Jude 1:1-2; Rev. 1:4-5; superscriptions to 1 Clement, Polycarp's Epistle to the Philippians). Identifications of the writer (coworkers are sometimes named) and addressees are followed by expanded descriptions of both parties in terms of their standing in relation to God in Christ (Ignatius especially expands the description of the addressees). The usual Hellenistic greeting *chaírein* is replaced by *cháris eirḗnē* "grace, peace" (which represents the Hebrew greeting *šālôm*) and sometimes Gk. *éleos* "mercy." This two- or threefold greeting becomes a benediction with the addition of "from God our Father and the Lord Jesus Christ" or the like.

Hellenistic letters sometimes include a section following the opening consisting of thanksgiving to the gods (cf. 2 Macc. 1:11-17). Paul's letters and others influenced by them generally have such a thanksgiving, usually including prayer for the addressees (e.g., 1 Cor. 1:4-9; Eph. 1:15-23; Phil. 1:3-11; 2 Thess.

1:3-12; 2:13-14; 2 Tim. 1:3-7) or corresponding sections of blessing to God, which are more related to Jewish liturgical traditions (2 Cor. 1:3-4; Eph. 1:3-14; 1 Pet. 1:3-5), or of rejoicing (2 John 4; 3 John 3-4; Barn. 1:2-3; Polyc.Phil. 1). Generally, Paul's thanksgivings are focused on the the addressees' faithfulness and reflect some of the concerns raised in the course of the letters. In this light, at Gal. 1:6 the substitution of "I am astonished that you are so quickly deserting ..." for the thanksgiving section is noteworthy.

A number of typical clauses are used to begin the bodies of these Christian letters and to signal transitions within the bodies. These include "I appeal to you, brethren" (e.g., Rom. 15:30; 16:17; 1 Cor. 1:10; cf. 2 Cor. 10:1; 1 Pet. 2:11), "I/we beg you" (2 Thess. 2:1; 2 John 5), "it is reported" (1 Cor. 5:1), "now concerning ..." (1 Cor. 7:1; 8:1; 12:1; 16:1), "now I would remind you" (15:1; cf. 2 Pet. 1:12; Jude 5), "I/we want you to know" (2 Cor. 8:1; Phil. 1:12), "for you yourselves know" (1 Thess. 2:1; cf. 2 Tim. 1:15), and "finally, brethren," sometimes a transition to the letter closing (e.g., 2 Cor. 13:11; Eph. 6:10; Phil. 3:1; 4:8; 1 Thess. 4:1). Sometimes a distinct transition from a more didactic section to a large section of parenesis is signaled by a closing doxology and one of the transitional formulas (e.g., Rom. 11:36–12:1; Eph. 3:21–4:1; 1 Thess. 3:11–4:1). Another typical feature of the bodies of Paul's letters is the "apostolic *parousia* (i.e., presence)," wherein Paul speaks of his travel plans (his intention to be with the addressees) and of his past and intended contacts with them through his coworkers (e.g., 1 Cor. 4:17-21; 16:5-12; Phil. 2:19-30; 1 Thess. 2:17–3:11; Phlm. 22; cf. Heb. 13:19).

Paul used the typical closing greetings of Hellenistic letters as another element linking the congregations and his own traveling ministry. Included are greetings relayed from others or the injunction to "greet one another" (e.g., Rom. 16:3-16, 21-23; 2 Cor. 13:12-13; Col. 4:10-15, 18; Tit. 3:15; cf. 1 Pet. 5:13-14; 3 John 15). Other significant elements in the closings of Paul's and other early Christian letters are final parenetic sections (e.g., Rom. 16:17-20; 1 Cor. 16:13-18; 2 Cor. 13:11; Heb. 13:22), benedictions (e.g., 1 Cor. 16:23; Gal. 6:16, 18; Eph. 6:23-24; 2 Thess. 3:16, 18), and doxologies (e.g., Rom. 16:25-27; Heb. 13:20-21; 1 Pet. 5:11; Jude 24-25).

Paul's letters exhibit a broad stylistic range, employing a variety of rhetorical features and traditional hymnic and confessional materials. He was not bound to any one stylistic convention, whether epistolary sermonic, or oratorical, but used a variety of approaches.The question-and-answer, forensic style in Romans is typical of Hellenistic rhetoric combined here with appeals to the authority of the Old Testament. Paul and others used traditional Christian hymnic and confessional materials (e.g., Rom. 1:3-4; 1 Cor. 15:3-7; 16:22; Col. 1:15-20; 1 Tim. 3:16; Ignatius Eph. 7:2; Trall. 9:1-2); such statements gave structure to the Church's thought world, and the writers could thus establish points of contact between their arguments and the addressees.

Some early Christian writings traditionally identified as letters are more likely sermons cast only partly in letter form. This follows Old Testament precedent, such as the letters of Jeremiah (Jer. 29), which are in the form of prophetic oracles rather than letters (so also the letter of Elijah at 2 Chr. 21:12-15; cf. the Epistle of Jeremiah). Letter conventions, except for the letter opening at Rev. 1:4-5, are absent from the letters to seven churches in chs. 2–3, but this may be explained by their apocalyptic context. More common are Christian sermons put into writing for a distant audience (e.g., Hebrews, James; cf. Ephesians). In all early Christian letters including Paul's, sermonic elements abound (cf. Col. 4:16).

Bibliography. W. G. Doty, *Letters in Primitive Christianity* (Philadelphia: 1973); D. C. Pardee, *Handbook of Ancient Hebrew Letters*. SBL Sources for Biblical Study 15 (Chico: 1982); J. L. White, *The Form and Function of the Body of the Greek Letter*. SBL Dissertation 1 (Missoula: 1975); ed., *Studies in Ancient Letter Writing*. Semeia 22 (1982).

LETUSHIM [lə tōō'shəm] (*leṭûšîm*). An Arabian people descended from Dedan, the grandson of Abraham and Keturah (Gen. 25:3).

LEUCIUS [lōō'shəs] (Gk. *Leukios*). A supposed disciple of John and author of the apocryphal Acts of John. After the fifth century four other books of acts — the Acts of Paul, Peter, Andrew, Thomas — were also ascribed to Leucius. The Manicheans evidently replaced the canonical book of Acts with these five. Probable references to the books by Clement of Alexandria and Tertullian, combined with the varying docetic and Gnostic elements of the books suggest that Leucius wrote in the late second century.

LEUMMIM [lē ŭm'ĭm] (Heb. *le'ummîm*). An Arabian people descended from Dedan, the grandson of Abraham and Keturah (Gen. 25:3).

LEVANT [lə vänt'].* A designation for the lands of the eastern Mediterranean (from Fr. *lever* "to rise" [i.e., the sun]), primarily Asia Minor and Syria-Palestine but often the entire coastlands from Greece to Egypt. In geological usage the Jordan valley is sometimes called the Levant Rift valley.

LEVI [lē'vī] (Heb. *lēwî*; Gk. *Leui*).
   1. The third son of Jacob and Leah (Gen. 29:34); father of Gershom, Kohath, and Merari (46:11). The name is associated with Heb. *lāwâ* "he who joins," reflecting his mother's wish that her husband Jacob love her for having borne three sons. Levi and his brother Simeon overtook the city of Shechem and killed all the male inhabitants in revenge for the dishonoring of their sister Dinah (34:25). Levi accompanied his brothers in their journey to Egypt (42:3). Levi died in Egypt at the age of 137 (Exod. 6:16).
   Jacob's blessing of Levi and Simeon is one of disapproval (Gen. 49:5-7), but the prediction that their descendants would scatter among the Israelites proved to be to Levi's advantage, as well as that of the whole nation when battle was to be done (cf. Exod. 32:26-29; Deut. 33:8-11). The statement may reflect the understanding of Levi as progenitor of the tribe of Levi and, through Aaron, of the priests and Levites, who sub-

stituted for the firstborn males as Yahweh's servants in specifically cultic matters (Num. 3:12-13, 41, 45). Accordingly, no specific territory was assigned to the Levites in Canaan (18:20, 24; Deut. 12:12; Josh. 13:14).
   2. The Hebrew name of the apostle Matthew, the former tax collector (Mark 2:14; Luke 5:27, 29).
   3. The great-great-grandfather, or a more distant relative, of Jesus (Luke 3:24).
   4. An ancestor of Jesus (Luke 3:29).

LEVIATHAN [lə vī'ə thən] (Heb. *liwyāṯān*, from *lāwâ* "turn, coil, twist"; cf. *liwyâ* "wreath").† A mythological chaos creature. According to 1 En. 60:7-10, Leviathan is a female monster associated with "the abyss of the ocean over the fountains of water" (cf. 2 Esdr. 6:49-52). At Ps. 74:14 the slaying of Leviathan is part of the picture of God's creation of the ordered world out of chaos (cf. Job 26:5-13; Ps. 89:10-12 [MT 11-13]). Leviathan here is a chaos monster similar to the dragon RAHAB and the Babylonian Tiamat, except that Leviathan is associated with the sea rather than dry ground. The "heads" of Leviathan have been crushed like the seven heads of Lotan (an etymologically related term), a chaos monster destroyed by Baal according to Ugaritic texts (cf. Hab. 3:13). At Job 3:8 those whose curses are especially effective are described as capable of reversing the defeat of Leviathan (KJV "their mourning") that occurred at creation. By contrast, Isa. 27:1 looks forward to the subjection of Leviathan, a figure for the future day when Yahweh will end the chaos of this present age (cf. 2 Bar. 29:4, where Behemoth and Leviathan are to be destroyed after they have been temporarily released.) The focus of these passages is God's power, whether as the creator of or the victor over Leviathan.
   At Ps. 104:26 the name of the chaos monster is applied to some otherwise undesignated sea creature, created by God for his own enjoyment. The Israelites were not knowledgable about the sea, and "Leviathan" may here represent large sea creatures in general, known only by hearsay (cf. 148:7). Job 41:1-34 (MT 40:25–41:26) is probably a description of the Egyptian CROCODILE, here perhaps influenced by both hearsay and mythology (*see also* BEHEMOTH).

LEVIRATE LAW [lĕv' ər ət] (Lat. *levir* "a husband's brother, brother-in-law").† The ancient Israelite law (Deut. 25:5-6) that when one brother in a family dies without fathering a son, his other brother shall marry his widow. The first male child resulting from such a union would carry on the deceased man's name in Israel, and the Israelite woman would find it unnecessary to marry a non-Israelite man for protection and economic security. Since a widow inherited her husband's property, this law was intended to retain the property in the deceased husband's family. A parallel to this practice exists in Hittite law, wherein a widow is taken in marriage by a relative of her deceased husband.
   The brother had the option of refusing to take his sister-in-law in levirate marriage. If this happened, the widow made a public declaration to the city's elders, who would attempt to change the brother's mind. If they were unsuccessful, the woman removed one

of the brother's sandals and spat in his face to signify that he was derelict in his duty (vv. 7-10).

A technical term, Heb. *yāḇām* "to act as a brother-in-law" is found not only in the legislation at Deut. 25 but also in the story of Judah and Tamar at Gen. 38. Here, Judah's son Er dies, and his brother Onan is invited to fulfil his duty to Tamar (v. 8). Onan's tactic of withdrawing before ejaculation (v. 9) is traced to his resentment over playing this part, but it costs him his life. Judah refuses his next son, Shelah, to Tamar, who thus masquerades as a cultic shrine prostitute to entice her father-in-law to impregnate her.

While some characterize the marriage of Ruth and Boaz (Ruth 4) as another example of levirate marriage, the marriage involves not a brother but rather a distant relative of Elimelech's; and it is not to the widowed Naomi, but to her widowed daughter-in-law.

LEVITES [lē'vīts] (Heb. *lᵉwî*; Gk. *leuítēs*). The descendants of Levi, the third son of Jacob and Leah; the assistants of the Aaronic priests in the tabernacle and temple worship. The Levites were divided into three clans named for Levi's sons: the Gershonites, Kohathites, and Merarites (Exod. 6:16-19; Num. 3:17-37; 1 Chr. 23:6-23).

At the time of the Exodus, Yahweh proclaimed his right to all firstborn Israelite males (Exod. 13:2), but in the wilderness he determined that the tribe of Levi be dedicated to his service in place of the firstborn (Num. 3:12-13, 41, 45). Within the tribe of Levi the descendants of Aaron were to be priests (Exod. 28:1), while those Levites not descended from Aaron were to assist in the tabernacle and temple worship, but not as priests (Num. 18:1-7). Following the apostasy of the golden calf the Levites sided with Yahweh (and Moses) and killed the rebels (Exod. 32:26-28); this show of loyalty was considered a reason for their ordination for assistance in worship (v. 29). Num. 8:5-22 describes the anointing of the Levites, who were presented before the Lord as a wave offering.

Because the tribe of Levi had not been alloted land within Canaan, the Levites had no direct means of support. Thus they were to receive a tenth of both the harvest and the livestock (Lev. 27:30-33; Num. 18:21, 24), of which they, in turn, were to give a tenth of the tenth to the priests (vv. 26-27). The Israelites were also to invite the Levites to the sacrificial meals (Deut. 12:12, 18; 14:27, 29; 16:11).

Levites could serve until age fifty (Num. 4:3). The beginning of their service is reckoned variously from ages twenty (1 Chr. 23:24, 27; 2 Chr. 31:17; Ezra 3:8), twenty-five (Num. 8:24), and thirty (4:3; 1 Chr. 23:3). During the wilderness wanderings the Levites had charge of the tabernacle and its furnishings (Num. 3:8, 25-26, 31, 36-37; 4:15, 25-26, 31-32) and assisted the priests in the tabernacle service (18:2-4, 6, 23; cf. the play on Heb. *lāwâ* "to be joined"). They were exempted from military duty so that they could carry on with these duties (1:47-54). The Levites' duties changed with their reorganization during the monarchy (1 Chr. 23:25-26). They were now to assist in the care of the temple and in the offerings (vv. 28-29, 32), stand with the priests at prayer and offering times (vv. 30-31), and take care of the temple treasuries (26:20-28; cf. 2 Chr. 8:15). Some were to be "officers

and judges" (1 Chr. 23:4; cf. 26:29-32), gatekeepers (23:5; cf. 16:38, 42; 26:1-19), and musicians (23:5; cf. 16:41-42; ch. 25; 2 Chr. 8:14).

At times Levite was apparently a functional designation rather than a genealogical designation. This is shown by the Judahite Levite of Judg. 17:7 (cf. 19:1) and possibly by the Ephraimite origin of Samuel (1 Sam. 1:1), who assisted the priests of Shiloh (2:11), and is to be expected as a result of the dispersion of the Levites throughout Israel.

See PRIEST.

LEVITICAL CITIES.† Forty-eight cities with adjoining pasture given as dwelling places for the Levites. The mandate for this provision was given shortly before the entry of Israel into Canaan (Num. 35:2-8; cf. Lev. 25:32-34). The six CITIES OF REFUGE were to be among the levitical cities (Num. 35:6). The actual allotment of the forty-eight cities is described twice (Josh. 21:1-42; 1 Chr. 6:54-81 [MT 39-66]), with differences between the two lists.

Some interpreters contend that a contradiction exists between the provision of the Levitical cities and the designation of the Levites as those who have no "inheritance" (territory) in Canaan. Because they had no inheritance they were to receive the tithe (Num. 18:20, 24; Deut. 10:9; Josh. 13:14). Moreover, they lived in the various towns of the other Israelites and were, therefore, to be invited to the sacrificial meals (Deut. 12:12, 18; 14:27, 29; 16:11) and guaranteed a place in the worship of the central shrine and the food that came with it (18:6-8). At 14:29; 16:11 the Levites are reckoned together with "the sojourner, the fatherless, and the widow."

Three general solutions to this problem have been offered. (1) Levitical cities as such never existed. The narratives represent two idealized interpretations of the dispersed condition of the tribe of Levi. (2) The levitical cities were part of the Davidic reorganization of the Levites (cf. 1 Chr. 13:2; 2 Chr. 11:14; 31:15, 19). (3) The lack of an "inheritance" meant the lack of a unified territory similar to the territories assigned the other tribes. Perhaps the levitical cities did not become the unimpeded possession of the Levites, or at least provision for the cities did not adequately meet the Levites' needs—hence references to Levites living in the towns of other Israelites and as wanderers and sojourners (e.g., Judg. 19:1).

LEVITICUS [lə vĭt'ə kəs], **BOOK OF.**† The third book of the Pentateuch and of the Old Testament.

I. Name

The English title is the same as that used in the Latin Vulgate, which is derived from the LXX Gk. *Leuitikon*, meaning "levitical" or "concerning the Levites"; the later rabbinic title "Instruction of the priests" (Heb. *tôraṭ kōhᵃnîm*) is more accurate. In the Hebrew canon the book is called *Wayyiqrāʾ* "and he called," from its opening word (Lev. 1:1).

II. Contents

Leviticus is basically a logically and topically arranged collection of instructions concerning various aspects of Israelite worship pertaining to the priests and the "priestly" nation as a whole.

The first seven chapters are comprised of laws concerning sacrifices. Instructions for the laity are presented in 1:1–6:7 (MT 5:27): regarding the burnt offering (ch. 1), cereal offering (ch. 2), peace offering (ch. 3), sin or purification offering (4:1–5:13), and guilt or reparation offering (5:14–6:7 [MT 5:26]). Lev. 6:8–7:36 contains details of importance to the officiating priests regarding these same sacrifices, in somewhat different order: burnt offering (6:8-13 [MT 1-6]), cereal offering (vv. 14-18 [MT 7-11]), the priests' cereal offering (vv. 19-23 [MT 12-16]), sin offering (vv. 24-30 [MT 17-23]), guilt offering (7:1-10), and peace offering (vv. 11-36). Vv. 37-38 provide a concluding summary. *See* SACRIFICES AND OFFERINGS; and the individual entries.

Chs. 8–10 recount the origins of Israel's priesthood. In ch. 8 Aaron and his sons are ordained in accordance with the procedures set forth in Exod. 29. Lev. 9 depicts the first sacrifices officiated by Aaron. Ch. 10 records the divine judgment upon Aaron's sons Nadab and Abihu for offering "unholy fire" (vv. 1-7); the remainder of the chapter contains a prohibition of the use of intoxicants by priests (vv. 8-11) and instructions regarding the eating of sacrificial meat (vv. 12-19).

Laws concerning individual purity are set forth in chs. 11–15. Ch. 11 distinguishes between clean and unclean animals (cf. Deut. 14:3-20). Lev. 12 indicates the procedure for purification of a woman following childbirth. Diagnosis and treatment of various skin diseases ("leprosy") are delineated in ch. 13, with instructions for ritual cleansing in ch. 14. Instructions for purification from various bodily discharges associated with the reproduction process appear in ch. 15. Ch. 16 outlines the ritual for the Day of Atonement; it is often grouped with the preceding chapters as depicting the process for purification of the tabernacle from defilements introduced by the worshiping community.

The remaining chapters contain various laws regulating Israel's life as a holy people; chs. 17–26 are commonly called the Holiness Code. Lev. 17 sets forth restrictions on sacrifice and the eating of meat, including proscription of eating blood (vv. 10-12). The acceptable bounds of sexual relations within the Israelite community are described in ch. 18, most notably those relationships considered incestuous (vv. 6-18). Ch. 19 encompasses a variety of cultic and ethical standards (e.g., hospitality, love of neighbor, conservation of natural resources, abstinence from pagan religious practices). Ch. 20 lists as capital offenses various violations that endanger the solidarity of the covenant community. Restrictions to ensure the purity of the priesthood are given in ch. 21, followed by rules about eating sacrifices (ch. 22) and the calendar of religious festivals (ch. 23). Ch. 24 contains laws regarding the tabernacle (the lampstand, vv. 1-4; the Bread of the Presence, vv. 5-9) and punishment of blasphemy and other offenses (vv. 10-23). Ch. 25 elaborates on the Sabbatical Year (vv. 2-7) and the Jubilee Year (vv. 8-24). The Code concludes with the standard covenantal sanctions, reward for obedience and punishment for disobedience (ch. 26). The book's

final chapter concerns religious vows (27:1-29) and tithes (vv. 30-33).

III. Composition

As with the other books of the Pentateuch, authorship of Leviticus traditionally is attributed to Moses. Frequent reference is made to God's speaking to Moses in the wilderness (e.g., 6:1 [MT 5:20]; 8:1; 22:1, 17, 26), commanding him to instruct the Israelites (e.g., 6:9; 8:4-5, 9, 34, 36). Indeed, the book is set within the larger narrative of Israel's wilderness experience, following construction of the tabernacle (Exod. 35–40) and preceding preparations for departure from Sinai (Num. 1–10).

Critical scholars by-and-large ascribe the entire book (at least in its canonical form) to the pentateuchal source P, the Priestly writer (much of the legal material would derive from earlier sources, and Lev. 17–26, the Holiness Code, may represent H, the Holiness source). Accordingly, the book is dated in the postexilic period and is viewed as reflecting practices and beliefs associated with the restored temple and worship community (sixth century or later). A conservative compromise accepts the religious practices delineated as reflecting an established sacrificial system, yet in the preexilic period (as early as the judges or Samuel or as late as the seventh or sixth century). The key to dating rests with one's understanding of the nature of the biblical account—whether a later reconstruction of "theological history" or the preserved record of Moses' actual words (cf. 27:34). *See* PENTATEUCH.

Diversity of form and vocabulary as well as the structure of the book suggest that Leviticus is a compilation of legal materials representing a variety of sources, much of which even critical scholars identify as quite ancient. Chs. 1–7 may be a collection of originally independent laws regarding sacrificial practices, set off by introductory (e.g., 6:9, 14, 24 [MT 2, 7, 17]) and closing (e.g., 7:37) formulas. Other major collections would be the purity laws (chs. 11–15) and the Holiness Code (chs. 17–26).

IV. Theology

The unifying theme of Leviticus is the holiness of God's covenant people: "You shall be holy; for I the Lord your God am holy" (19:2). As a "kingdom of priests" (cf. Exod. 19:6), Israel is "set apart" (Heb. *qāḏôš* "holy"; cf. Lev. 20:26) for a special relationship with God. Accordingly, they must be cleansed by ritual means (sacrifices and offerings, distinction between clean and unclean) from the moral impediments (sin) that separate mankind from God. Moreover, in order to maintain unbroken fellowship with God they must abide by definite ethical standards (the covenant stipulations; e.g., ch. 19; cf. the comparatively humane punishments at 24:17-21). By nature these religious and moral standards are essential to preservation of the fragile covenant community, whether in the formative stages or at the time of the restoration.

Christian interpreters frequently present Leviticus as the precedent (or "type") for Christ's atoning sacrifice (ch. 16; Heb. 8 — 10). Some also view it as typifying the contrast between "Old Testament law" and "New Testament grace" (cf. Heb. 10:4).

Bibliography. M. Noth, *Leviticus.* OTL (1965); G. J. Wenham. *The Book of Leviticus.* NICOT (1979).

LIBATION (Heb. *neseḵ*). A sacrifice of liquid, or drink offering. Libations were, along with livestock, grain, and oil, part of the regular offerings of the various classes of food products made by the Israelites every day and in larger quantities on fast days (Num. 28–29). "Strong (or intoxicating) drink" (*šēḵār*) was to be poured out as an offering in the "holy place" (28:7). Libations were the normal accompaniment of any offering of animals or grain (e.g., 6:15, 17; 1 Chr. 29:21; 2 Chr. 29:35; Ezra 7:17); the quantity was in proportion to the size of the animal offered (Num. 28:14). A libation had a part in Jacob's dedication of the altar at Bethel (Gen. 35:14).

Drink offerings were a widespread worship practice in different nations (e.g., Canaanite Ugarit) and thus were part of idolatrous worship engaged in by Israelites (Isa. 57:6; Jer. 7:18; Ezek. 20:28). Blood of sacrificial animals was poured out in the worship of Yahweh, but the use of blood as a libation was a practice associated only with worship of other gods (Ps. 16:4).

Paul used libations as a figure of speech for his own death in the service of the gospel (Phil. 2:17).

See SACRIFICES AND OFFERINGS.

LIBNAH [lĭb'nə] (Heb. *libnâ* "white").

1. A place where Israel camped during the wilderness wanderings after leaving the wilderness of Sinai (Num. 33:20-21). Some scholars would identify it with Laban (Deut. 1:1). The site is unknown.

2. A Canaanite city in the Shephelah, probably between Makkedah and Lachish near the Philistine border. It was captured (Josh. 10:29-30; 12:15) and included in the tribal territory of Judah (15:42), but subsequently was named a levitical city and assigned to the priests (21:13). When Joram was king in Judah, Libnah revolted (2 Kgs. 8:22); later the Assyrian king Sennacherib attacked the city after capturing Lachish (19:8; Isa. 37:8).

Libnah's precise location is unknown. It was formerly identified with Tell eṣ-Ṣâfī on the south bank of Wâdī Elah, now identified as the site of Philistine Gath. Tell Bornât, 10 km. (6 mi.) north-northwest of Lachish and 8 km. (5 mi.) south of Gath, is a better possibility.

LIBNI [lĭb'nī] (Heb. *libnī* "white" or "of Libnah").

1. A son of Gershon and descendant of Levi; a subgroup within the Gershonite clan of Levites (Exod. 6:17; Num. 3:18; 1 Chr. 6:17, 20 [MT 2, 5]). He was the eponymous ancestor of the Gershonite clan known as the Libnites (Num. 3:21; 26:58); some scholars associate this clan with LIBNAH 2 (cf. Josh. 21:13).

2. A Levite, descended from Merari (1 Chr. 6:29 [MT 14]).

LIBYA [lĭb'ĭ ə] (Heb. *lûbîm* Gk. *Libyē*).† The desert region of northern Africa west of the Nile valley of Egypt. Peoples from the Libyan desert fought periodically against Egypt from the third millenium B.C. In 950 the Libyan dynasty, which was to endure until 730, began with the accession of Shishak I (Sheshonq), who gave Jeroboam I refuge from Solomon (1 Kgs. 11:40) but who later fought and exacted tribute from Jerusalem (14:25-26; 2 Chr. 12:2-9; KJV "Lubims").

The inhabitants of Palestine apparently associated Libya with Egypt and Ethiopia (cf. the Israelite prophets; Ezek. 30:5; so RSV, following LXX; KJV "Chub"; Dan. 11:43; Nah. 3:9; cf. Jer. 46:7-9). Accordingly, the Libyans were probably among the forces led by Zerah (2 Chr. 16:8; cf. 14:9 [MT 8]) and may have been reckoned with Put, a supplier of mercenaries to Tyre (Ezek. 27:10; KJV "Phut"; cf. Gen. 10:6; 1 Chr. 1:8; Isa. 66:19; KJV "Pul"). The relationship of Libya to the Lehabim, perhaps a linguistic variant of the same name, remains uncertain (cf. Gen. 10:13).

In the Roman Empire the northern part of the Libyan desert constituted the province of Cyrenaica, named for city of Cyrene (Acts 2:10). Cyrenaica was administratively joined to the island of Crete.

LIDEBIR [lĭd ə bĭr] (Heb. *liḏᵉḇir*). A place in eastern Gilead (Josh. 13:26; so RSV mg., following MT). *See* DEBIR (PLACE) 2; LO-DEBAR.

LIFE.†

I. Terminology

The living organism is indicated by a variety of Hebrew and Greek words, representing different aspects of physical and spiritual existence. Heb. *ḥayyîm* and the verb *ḥāyâ* are abstract terms for human life in general (e.g., Deut. 30:19; Jer. 21:8) as well as the span of a person's existence (e.g., Gen. 23:1; cf. Gk. *zōḗ*; Luke 16:25). The related Hebrew term *ḥayyâ* designates animal life (e.g., Gen. 1:18; 8:1, 17), and *ḥay* "living (thing)" encompasses both humans and animals (e.g., v. 21). Heb. *nepeš* and Gk. *psychḗ*, usually translated "soul," represent that which animates the person and constitutes the individual's identity. Heb. *bāśār* "flesh" and Gk. *sárx* "flesh" and *sōma* "body" focus primarily on the physical being. Heb. *bāśār*, largely used for meat to be eaten and to be sacrificed, could also indicate human flesh, often in distinction to bones, the entire human body, the sexual organs, weak humanity as contrasted with God (e.g., Ps. 56:4 [MT 5]), and kinship relationships (cf. the modern usage, "blood"). In the New Testament Gk. *bíos* designates the manifestations and duration of earthly existence (e.g., 1 Tim. 2:2; 1 Pet. 4:3; 1 John 3:17; RSV "world's goods"). Gk. *sōma* is frequently used metaphorically (e.g., "body of Christ," "body of sin") in addition to being the normal word for animal and human bodies.

Gk. *pneúma*, usually translated "spirit," represents Heb. *rûaḥ* ("wind, breath, life, creative power [divine as well as human], authority, will, emotions") and *nᵉšāmâ* ("breath"; cf. Ps. 150:6, where it denotes all humanity). In the Old Testament, a number of words for physical organs are used to represent aspects of human mental and emotional capacities. Chief among these is "heart" (Heb. *lēb*, *lēbāb*; cf. Gk. *kardía* in the New Testament), which represents reason and will more than emotions. Other such terms are "liver"

(Heb. *kābēd*) and "kidneys" (*keelāyôt*), which are related to strong emotions. In the New Testament Gk. *splánchna* "bowels, entrails" is often used for "affection" and "compassion" (as it is usually translated in the RSV). In the New Testament especially, some of these terms for human beings considered in different aspects are used in tandem to represent the totality of the person (e.g., 1 Thess. 5:23; Heb. 4:12; cf. Deut. 6:5). But Paul's use of "flesh" and "spirit" (Rom. 8:4-13) contrasts these different terms as figures of speech for different patterns of life (cf. 7:23, "members" and "mind"; v. 25, "mind" and "flesh"). For specific terms see the individual entries.

II. Biblical Teachings

That God created by his word all plants and animals (Gen. 1:11-12, 20-25), "breathed the breath of life" into the first human (2:7; cf. Job 33:4; Isa. 57:16), and created the male and female ancestors of all mankind (Gen. 1:25-27) are ways of expressing the fact that God is the source of all life. God retains his sovereignty over life and the withholding of life (6:17; 7:23; 1 Sam. 2:6; Job 34:13-15; Ps. 104:29). Moreover, as Israel knew from experience, Yahweh was "the living God" (e.g., Deut. 5:26; Josh. 3:10; cf. 2 Sam. 22:47; Matt. 26:63); as a result, oaths were taken with the words "as the Lord lives" (Judg. 8:19; Jer. 5:2; cf. Num. 14:28; Deut. 32:40). Yahweh is, in contrast to any other object of worship, the God who lives (Ps. 115:3-13; Jer. 10:2-16; Dan. 5:23; Hab. 2:18-19; Acts 14:15; 1 Thess. 1:9).

Through the prohibition of murder (Exod. 20:13; Deut. 5:17) God protected human life from the violence that had soon become a part of human social existence (e.g., Gen. 4:8-12, 23-24). This respect for life was underscored by the penalty attached to murder (9:5-6; Num. 35:31-33; Deut. 19:11-13). The sanctity of life was also evident, in a more general sense, through the prohibition of eating blood (Gen. 9:4; Lev. 7:26-27; Deut. 12:23-25), which was equated with life (v. 23; cf. Gen. 42:22; Josh. 2:19; Judg. 9:24 where blood is used figuratively for murder and death).

Death was regarded as a certainty (Num. 16:29; 2 Sam. 14:14; Ps. 49:10-11 [MT 11-12]; cf. 1 Chr. 29:15) beyond which, as far as the earliest parts of the Old Testament are concerned, there was no real existence (cf. Ps. 88:11-12 [MT 12-13]; 115:17; Isa. 38:11; *see* HELL I). But the association of death with divine retribution against the wicked (Ps. 49:13-14 [MT 14-15]) and of the prolongation of life with God's mercy for the righteous (cf. Judg. 8:32) could lead to a hope for something beyond this life. This hoped-for continuation of life was not at first focused on the individual but only toward the continuation of the community of God's people (cf. Isa. 56:5). Such vague expressions of hope (e.g., Job 14:7-17; Ps. 49:15 [MT 16]; 139:8) did eventually develop into the expectation of an everlasting end to death (cf. Isa. 25:8, here concerning the community) and of resurrection (26:19; Dan. 12:2). In particular, the Jews' great turmoil and suffering, which appeared to indicate the failure of the old belief in this-worldly reward and retribution, and the influence of Persian religion fostered belief in resurrection (Pss.Sol. 3:12; 4 Ezra 7:32, 37) and the age to come (v. 50). These ideas, together with

those of eternal punishment (1 En. 10:13) and eternal life (Wis. 5:15; 2 Macc. 7:9; 1 En. 58:3) became widespread in Judaism and formed the background of Jesus' preaching and thus the Christian understanding of the future.

Jesus' teachings did not, however, simply reiterate a Jewish belief in the expectation of the age to come to be brought in by the victory over Israel's enemies obtained through the messiah and by the resurrection of the dead. Jesus attached significance to his own coming. The ages are still distinguished; eternal life is still a hope for the future (Matt. 25:46; Luke 18:29-30; John 5:25-29; 6:27; 1 John 2:25; Jude 21). But the close connection between Jesus and eternal life (John 3:15-16; 6:68; Rom. 5:21; 6:23) is such that in the Johannine literature it can be said that the follower of Jesus "has eternal life" (John 3:36; 5:24; 6:47, 54; cf. 10:28; 17:2-3; 1 John 5:11, 13), that Jesus is "life" (John 11:25; 14:6; cf. John 6:48; 1 John 1:2), and that he is, like the living God, the one who has life in himself (John 1:4; 5:26). Where life thus comes to stand for the experience in this age of the blessings of the age to come, it is used metaphorically. This metaphor is found also where Paul speaks of spiritual "death" and "life" (e.g., Rom. 6:3, 11, 16; 7:5-13, 24; 8:2, 6; 2 Cor. 7:10; Eph. 2:1, 5; cf. Luke 15:32; 1 John 3:14). But such metaphorical language is related to and sometimes overlaps with the belief, which began in the Old Testament, that literal death is the result of human sin (Gen. 2:17; Deut. 30:15-20 [here speaking of the community]; Ezek. 18:4) and the Christian confession that the resurrection will come through Jesus (Rom. 5:12-21; 6:23; 1 Cor. 15:20-22). The way to the tree of life, a symbol of the unending and harmonious life available for mankind in close relationship to God (i.e., before the fall), was blocked because of the sin of Adam and Eve, but will again be made open by Jesus in the age to come (Rev. 2:7; 22:2, 14).

Not only has earthly life come to be affected by the eternal life in the age to come, but its transitory nature is emphasized by the eternity to come. In this perspective to be a disciple of Jesus one must deny self (Luke 9:23), "hate ... his own life" (14:26), and "lose" his life for Jesus' sake (9:24; cf. 12:4-5). True "life" is not found in possessing much or in having food to eat (v. 15, 23). For the same reason, Paul could speak of the Christian as "dead to sin and alive to God in Christ Jesus" (Rom. 6:11; cf. Col. 3:3).

Bibliography. H. G. Link, "Life," *DNTT* 2:474-84; H. Ringgren, "ḥāyâ [chāyāh]," *TDOT* 4 (1980): 324-44; H. W. Wolff, *Anthropology of the Old Testament* (Philadelphia: 1974).

LIGHT (Heb. *'ôr*; Gk. *phōs*).† God's first acts of creation were the creation of light and the separation of light and darkness (Gen. 1:3-5). God maintains his creation by maintaining this separation of day and night (Ps. 104:19; 148:3-6; Jer. 31:35-36; 33:25). The heavenly bodies through which day and night are separated (Gen. 1:14-18; cf. Isa. 60:19) were worshiped by other peoples and sometimes by the Israelites (Deut. 4:19; 2 Kgs. 21:3, 5; Jer. 19:13). Light itself was used in a wide range of positive metaphors and identified as an essential aspect and symbol of the manifestation of God's presence and blessing (e.g., Ps. 44:3 [MT 4]).

Light occurs as a metaphor for life itself (e.g., Job 3:9, 16, 20; 18:5-6, 18; Ps. 49:19 [MT 20]; 56:13 [MT 14]; cf. Prov. 13:9). It can also represent what is good in life, whether prosperity, safety, salvation, and blessing (darkness representing calamity; e.g., Esth. 8:16; Job 30:26; Ps. 112:4; Isa. 9:2 [MT 1]; Lam. 3:2; Amos 5:18, 20; cf. Job 22:11, 28; Isa. 30:26). Light symbolizes truth and right guidance (Isa. 42:6; Luke 11:33-36 par.), often the word of God (Job 24:13; Ps. 43:3; 119:105; Prov. 6:23; Isa. 2:5; John 5:35; 2 Pet. 1:19). It also represents divine or human favor shown in facial expressions (Job 29:24; Ps. 4:6 [MT 7]; 89:15 [MT 16]; Prov. 16:15), understanding and wisdom (Dan. 5:11, 14), that which comes as surely as the sunrise (Ps. 37:6; cf. Jer. 31:35-36).

God himself is light (Ps. 27:1; Mic. 7:8), "the light of Israel" (Isa. 10:17), and uses light to expose that which would be hidden (Ps. 90:8; 139:11-12; Luke 12:3; cf. Dan. 2:22; 1 Cor. 4:5). The constant appearance of light as a characteristic of theophanies (e.g., Ps. 104:2; Hab. 3:4; Matt. 17:2 par.) is perhaps derived from the impressiveness of lightning, sometimes called simply "light" (Job 36:30, 32; 37:15; cf. Hab. 3:11). The light associated with the divine presence will be particularly evident at the eschaton (Isa. 60:19-20; Rev. 21:23; 22:5; cf. Zech. 14:7). But other passages associate the coming of the eschaton and final judgment with the cessation of light from the sun and moon (Isa. 13:10; Ezek. 32:7; Joel 2:10, 31; 3:15 [MT 4:15]; Matt. 24:29 par.; Rev. 6:12-14).

Part of the evidence of the new age having come in Christ is the presence of light. This positive imagery is especially important in John, where its eschatological meanings are similar to those found in the Qumran documents. Just as Jesus is the "true light" (John 1:9), the "light of the world" (8:12; 9:5; 12:46; cf. 1 John 1:5-7), so also are believers in him "sons of light" (John 12:36; also Luke 16:8; 1 Thess. 5:5; cf. Eph. 5:8, "children of light"; 1QS 1:9; 1QM passim).

See also DARKNESS; LAMP; LAMPSTAND.

LIGHTNING (Heb. *bārāq*; Gk. *astrapé*). Lightning was looked on as one of the more spectacular evidences of the power and wisdom of the creating God (Job 28:26; 36:30, 32; KJV "light"; 37:3-4, 11, 15; KJV "bright cloud"; Sir. 43:13), particularly as he is contrasted to useless idols (Jer. 10:13 par. 51:16; Ep.Jer. 6:61). Beyond this, lightning has a significant role in signaling the presence of God (Ps. 97:4; Ezek. 1:13; Rev. 4:5), as evidenced at Sinai (Exod. 19:16; 20:18) and his opening of the way through the Red Sea (Ps. 77:18 [MT 19]). Lightning goes out as a weapon of God against his enemies (2 Sam. 22:15 par. Ps. 18:14 [MT 15]; 144:6; cf. Hab. 3:4, 11; Zech. 9:14; 4 Macc. 4:10). Perhaps underlying these Old Testament theophanic passages are the characteristics of ancient Near Eastern storm gods such as Hadad (the Baal of 1 Kgs. 18; cf. v. 38; *see* THEOPHANY.). Lightning will also signal the approach of the eschaton (Rev. 8:5), and have a part in the final judgment (Rev. 16:18; 2 Esdr. 16:10; Wis. 5:21).

Lightning is also used in figures of speech to indicate great speed (Ezek. 1:14; Nah. 2:4 [MT 5]) and the bright or glittering flash of swords and spears (Deut. 32:41, RSV mg.; Ezek. 21:10, 15, 28 [MT 15, 20, 33]; cf. Job 20:25; Nah. 3:3; Hab. 3:11), usually with regard to theophany or eschatology. Similarly, lightning describes the swift dramatic downward movement of Satan from his place in the heavenly court, in a vision related to the exorcisms performed by Jesus' disciples (Luke 10:18). The phrase "appearance like lightning" signals that something more than human is seen, whether angels (Matt. 28:3; cf. 4 Macc. 4:10) or the transformation of the present disconsolate Jerusalem (symbolized by a woman) into the coming glorified Jerusalem (2 Esdr. 10:25). The coming of the Son of Man is likened to the flashing of lightning, to be accomplished in a manner immediately visible to all (Matt. 24:27 par. Luke 17:24).

LIGN ALOES (Num. 24:6, KJV). *See* ALOES.

LIGURE (Exod. 28:19; 39:12, KJV). *See* JACINTH.

LIKHI [lĭk´hī] (Heb. *liqhî*). A son of Shemida of the tribe of Manasseh (1 Chr. 7:19). The name may be a scribal error for Helek (cf. Num. 26:30; Josh. 17:2) and, like the accompanying names, may represent a place.

LILITH [lĭl´ĭth] (Heb. *lîlît*; cf. Phoen. *llyn*).† According to rabbinical tradition the first wife of Adam who left him because she was not granted full equality. Some scholars equate her with the Sumerian Belit-ili (Belili) or the Canaanite Baalat.

In later Jewish thought her descendants, the "daughters of Lilith," were lustful demons with whom men copulated in their dreams. Some scholars trace such figures to the single occurrence of the term in the Old Testament, supernatural female beings associated with beasts that haunt desolate places (Isa. 34:14; JB "Lilith"; cf. NJV; RSV "night hag"). *See* NIGHT HAG.

LILY (Heb. *šôšān, šûšan, šôšannâ*; Gk. *krínon*). As with a number of other botanical terms in the Bible, the Hebrew terms translated "lily" are less specific than modern terms (Egyp. *ššn*, the lotus or water lily, *Nymphaea lotus* L.). The only lily occurring naturally in Palestine, *Lilium candidum* L., is a white forest flower, which would not fit with the biblical references to lilies (cf. Akk. *šešanu*). A likely candidate in some passages is *Anemone coronaria*, a scarlet, purple, or white flower that appears in open fields and on hills throughout the Near East. Other passages may refer to flowers in general (cf. Cant. 2:1, where "lily of the valleys" cannot mean *Convallaria majalis* L.).

In the Song of Solomon a lily (2:1-2) and gazelles feeding among lilies (4:5) are images for the beauty of a young woman. The woman says that her lover's "lips are lilies" (5:13), perhaps thinking of the bright red color of many anemones. Pasturing a flock "among the lilies" (2:16; 6:3) and gathering lilies (v. 2) are images for sexual love. Fruitfulness is another idea in which lily imagery plays a part (7:2 [MT 3], for a woman's womb; Hos. 14:5, for Israel after it has repented; cf. 2 Esdr. 2:19; Sir. 39:14; 50:8).

Lilies figure in the descriptions of the capitals of the two pillars before Solomon's temple (1 Kgs. 7:19, 22 see LILY-WORK) and of the brim of the temple's "molten sea" (v. 26; 2 Chr. 4:5), which was perhaps gently curved outward. The superscriptions of Pss. 45, 69, 80 contain the phrase "according to Lilies" (so RSV; KJV "upon Shoshannim"), probably indicating a familiar melody. The superscription of Ps. 60 reads "according to Shushan Eduth" (so RSV); here the name of the melody might be "the decree is a lily" (JB) or "the lily of the covenant" (NIV). "The lilies of the field," with their beauty, are included in a group of parables spoken by Jesus for the abundant care of God (Matt. 6:28-30 par.).

LILY-WORK (Heb. *ma'ªśēh šûšan*).* The description of the shape (so JB, NIV) or decorations (or both; cf. NJV) of the capitals of the two bronze pillars set before the vestibule of Solomon's temple (1 Kgs. 7:19, 22). Analogies to these capitals may be present in two incense altars unearthed at Megiddo, both of which have bowls that suggest flowers and sculpted decorations that suggest leaves; one of these altars was painted with floral decorations.

LIME (Heb. *śîd*).* Quicklime (calcium oxide), a white, alkaline substance obtained by burning at high temperatures shells and limestone. The Moabites are condemned at Amos 2:1 for burning the bones of the king of Edom down to a similar-appearing substance (calcium phosphate) as a sign of victory and contempt. Isa. 33:12 may threaten the same fate, or it may threaten burning with caustic quicklime. Archaeological finds have identified the use of lime for plaster (cf. Deut. 27:2, 4), whitewash, and mortar.

LIMP (Heb. *pāsaḥ*). In their cultic dance the priests of Baal "limped about" (so RSV; KJV "leaped upon"; JB "performed their hobbling dance around"), alongside, or up the steps of the altar they had made (1 Kgs. 18:26). This limping dance would likely have been performed in a small procession rather than by all 450 priests simultaneously. A Baal Marqad ("Baal [or Lord] of the dance") was worshiped in locations in Lebanon. The etymology of the Hebrew term and its connection to *pesaḥ* "Passover" remains subject to debate.

LINEN. See FLAX.

LINTEL. A horizontal wooden or stone beam above a doorway. In preparation for the final plague (and subsequently to commemorate the Passover), the Israelites spread lambs' blood on the lintel (*mašqôp*) and doorposts of their houses (Exod. 12:7, 22-23; KJV "upper door post"). The lintel (*'ayil*) that framed the doorway to the inner sanctuary of the temple may refer to a pilaster (1 Kgs. 6:31; cf. Ezek. 40:9-41:3; RSV "jambs"; KJV "posts"); the text is obscure. At Amos 9:1; Zeph. 2:14 the KJV translates Heb. *kaptôr* as "lintel" (RSV "capitals").

LINUS [lī'nəs] (Gk. *Linos*). A man from whom greetings are relayed at 2 Tim. 4:21. According to tradition this Linus was the son of the Claudia mentioned in the same verse and bishop of Rome for twelve years, ordained to that office by Peter and Paul and preceding Clement in it (Irenaeus *Adv. haer.* iii.3.3; Eusebius *HE* iii.2, 13).

LION (Heb. *'ªrî, 'aryēh, kᵉpîr, lābî'*; Aram. *'aryēh*; cf. Akk. *arû, lābu*; Gk. *léōn*; cf. Lat. *leo*).† *Panthera leo* or *Felis leo*, a large carnivorous member of the cat family. The Asiatic lion, *Panthera leo persica*, was once common throughout the ancient Near East and the Mediterranean, but has been extinct in Palestine for centuries; in Mesopotamia, however, it survived until the nineteenth century A.D.

Lions were widely regarded as a threat to flocks (1 Sam. 17:34; Amos 3:12) as well as to humans (1 Kgs. 13:24; 20:36; Prov. 22:13; Amos 5:19), sometimes understood as agents of divine judgment (2 Kgs. 17:25; Isa. 15:9). Among the celebrated deeds of great heroes were lion-killings (Judg. 14:5-9; 1 Sam. 17:34-37; cf. 1 Chr. 11:22; RSV "ariels"; Sir. 47:3), further attested by Assyrian reliefs of kings hunting lions (cf. *ANEP*, no. 184). Reliefs and statues of lions were widely used in decoration, as in Nebuchadrezzar's palace and in Solomon's temple (1 Kgs. 7:29, 36; cf. Ezek. 41:19) and palace (1 Kgs. 10:19-20).

Regarded as fierce and dangerous animals, lions were used figuratively to portray warriors and armies (1 Chr. 12:8 [MT 9]; Isa. 5:29; Jer. 4:7; 50:17; 1 Macc. 3:4; cf. Rev. 9:17), enemies waiting in ambush (Ps. 10:9; 17:12), and wicked rulers (Prov. 28:15; Ezek. 22:25; Zeph. 3:3; cf. Jer. 50:17). The lion symbolized courage and boldness (Prov. 28:1), vengeance (Sir. 27:28), calamity (2 Esdr. 16:6), the ravages of locusts (Joel 1:6; Rev. 9:8), death (2 Tim. 4:17), and the devil (1 Pet. 5:8; cf. Sir. 21:2; 27:10), and the image was employed to depict God going in judgment against his people (Hos. 5:14). It was anticipated that lions would either be domesticated (Isa. 11:6-7; 65:25) or eradicated in the eschaton (35:9).

Victorious Israel and constituent tribes could be depicted with lion figures (Israel, Num. 23:24 [also *lābî'* "lioness"]; 24:9; cf. Mic. 5:8 [MT 7]; Dan, Deut. 33:22). Because of its ruling position through David and the Davidic dynasty, Judah in particular came to be regarded as "lion" or "lioness" (Gen. 49:9). By extension, the Davidic messiah was likened to a lion (Rev. 5:5, "the Lion of the tribe of Judah"; 2 Esdr. 11:37-46; 12:1, 31-32). Frequently a lion was included among four apocalyptic creatures, such as the four faces of the "living creatures" in Ezekiel's throne chariot vision (Ezek. 1:10) or cherubim (10:14), or the four beings around the throne of God (Rev. 4:7)—all of which communicate the universality of creation's praise to God—and, as one of four beasts symbolizing mighty empires, the winged lion representing the Babylonian Empire (Dan. 7:4).

See ARIEL.

LITHOSTROTOS [līth'ə strōt'əs] (Gk. *lithóstrōtos* "pavement").† The place of judgment in the courtyard of the Fortress Antonia where Jesus was condemned to death (John 19:13). *See* GABBATHA; PAVEMENT.

LITTER (Heb. *miṭṭâ* "bed"; Gk. *phórion*). Generally a covered bed or couch equipped with shafts for carrying. At Cant. 3:7 the bridegroom is portrayed as King Solomon coming up from the wilderness in a "litter" to greet his beloved (RSV, JB; NIV "carriage"; KJV "bed"; cf. Gen. 49:33; 2 Chr. 24:25; Amos 6:4). At 2 Macc. 9:8 the litter is a stretcher used to carry the ailing Antiochus V Eupator. The "litters" (Heb. *ṣabbîm*; NIV "wagons") at Isa. 66:20 are covered conveyances of some kind.

LIVER (Heb. *kābēd*).† The largest gland in vertebrates, which secretes bile. In sacrifices the "appendage of the liver" (RSV; KJV "caul above the liver"), i.e., the caudate lobe of the liver that is usually prominent in sheep, was set apart with the kidneys and sometimes other parts as a separate special sacrifice (Exod. 29:13, 22; Lev. 3:14-15; 4:8-10; 7:3-5). An arrow going into the liver (so KJV, JB; RSV "entrails") of a stag was known to cause a quick death and so was symbolic for the fate of a young adulterer (Prov. 7:23). The only mention of a human liver in the Bible, at Lam. 2:11 (RSV "my heart is poured out in grief"; KJV more literally "my liver is poured upon the earth"), is an example of the ancient Semitic understanding of internal organs as the seat of mental faculties and emotions.

Hepatoscopy, the examination of an animal's liver, was one of the methods of divination used by Nebuchadrezzar to determine which to attack, Rabbah of the Ammonites or Jerusalem of the Judahites (Ezek. 21:19-21 [MT 24-26]). Hepatoscopy was common in the ancient Near East, as seen in the number of textbooks of hepatoscopy and clay liver models found at Mari.

LIZARD.† A reptile, usually small, of the suborder *Lacertilia*, a wide variety of which are found in Palestine. Among the unclean "swarming things that swarm upon the earth" are various types of lizards designated by six different Hebrew words (Lev. 11:29-30), all of which appear as designations of lizards only in these verses. Because Hebrew zoological terms did not have the precision of modern scientific terminology, little is absolute about the meaning of these terms beyond the probability that they all stand for types of lizards. Thus the first and fourth of the six terms, *ṣāb* (RSV, NIV "great lizard"; KJV "tortoise"; JB "lizard" [taken as a general heading for the five terms that follow]) and *lᵉṭā'â* (RSV, KJV "lizard"; NIV "wall lizard"; JB "letaah"). The second term, *'ᵃnāqâ*, means "groaning, crying" and may stand for the gecko (so RSV, NIV, JB; KJV "ferret") because of the gecko's characteristic sound; several varieties of geckos are found in Palestine. The third term, *kōaḥ*, means "strength," and is probably used for the most powerful-appearing lizard; RSV "land crocodile" (NIV "monitor lizard"; KJV "chameleon"; JB "koah") could well be right because of the great length relative to other lizards attained by monitors (*Varanidae*). A suggested relation to Talmudic Heb. *ḥumṭôn* "sandy soil" has been suggested for the fifth term, *ḥōmeṭ*. This suggests some variety of skink (so NIV; KJV "snail"; JB "chameleon"); "sand lizard" (RSV) is a common name for skinks. The last term, *tinšemeṭ*, may be related to *nāšam* "pant," and is usually taken to represent the chameleon. The same

word is used for a variety of birds at Lev. 11:18; Deut. 14:16.

Heb. *ṣᵉmāmît* (Prov. 30:28; KJV "spider") is another word for some kind of lizard that appears only once. In Jewish Aramaic the word (spelled *sᵉmāmît* or *sᵉmāmîtā'*) was used for poisonous spiders as well as lizards.

LO-AMMI [lō ăm'ē] (Heb. *lō' 'ammî* "not my people"). A symbolic name that the prophet Hosea was commanded to give to his and Gomer's third child (Hos. 1:9; RSV "Not my people"; cf. v. 10; 2:1, 23 [MT 2:1, 3, 25]). See AMMI.

LOCUST (Heb. *'arbeh, yeleq*; Gk. *akrís*).† Flying and hopping insects of order *Orthoptera*, suborder *Saltatoria*, which includes grasshoppers, locusts or short-horned grasshoppers, crickets, and katydids. In addition to Heb. *'arbeh* and *yeleq*, a wide variety of other terms are used, probably not in a consistent manner; the variations in English translations illustrate the uncertainty regarding what exactly is designated. A variety of orthoptera are found throughout the Near East. The most frequently attested swarming orthopteran, hence true "locust," is the desert locust, *Schistocerca gregaria* Forsk.

Among winged insects, only these hopping insects were allowed for food in the Mosaic code (Lev. 11:20-23; see CLEAN AND UNCLEAN). John the Baptist's food was "locusts and wild honey," both easily obtained in the Judean wilderness (Matt. 3:4 par. Mark 1:6). The invasion of a locust swarm is graphically described at Joel 1:2-2:11. A variety of terms are used at 1:4 (the order is changed at 2:25) for different growth stages of the insect or more probably for successive swarms of slightly different appearance. Here, as in other passages (Deut. 28:38, 42 [*ṣᵉlāṣal*]; 2 Chr. 7:13 [*ḥāgāb*]; Amos 4:9 [*gāzām*]; 7:1 [*gōbay*]), the devastation of agriculture by locusts is regarded as the judgment of God. Locusts came as the eighth plague and destroyed the fields and orchards of Egypt (Exod. 10:1-20; Ps. 78:46; 105:34).

Figuratively locusts represent great numbers (Judg. 6:5; 7:12; Jer. 46:23; 51:14), eagerness (Isa. 33:4; *gēb*), and orderliness (Prov. 30:27). At Job 39:20 a leaping horse is compared to the locust. At Nah. 3:15-17, three Hebrew terms for locusts or grasshoppers occur six times in at least three distinct metaphors: for aggrandizement (v. 15b), destruction (v. 15a and possibly 16b), and leaders who disappear when difficulties arise (v. 17). Among the eschatological calamities of Rev. 8:6-9:21 are locusts who harm not plants but human beings (9:3-11), here probably representing a human army.

See GRASSHOPPER.

LOD [lŏd] (Heb. *lōḏ*). A city *ca.* 18 km. (11 mi.) southeast of Joppa near the Wâdî el-Kabir. Archaeological work has been limited by the presence of a modern city on the site.

Lod existed at least as early as the fifteenth century B.C., appearing in a list of Canaanite cities conquered by Pharaoh Thutmose III. Lod was rebuilt (or fortified) by Benjaminites ("the sons of Elpaal"), apparently sometime during the monarchic period (1 Chr.

8:12) and resettled after the Exile (Ezra 2:33; Neh. 7:37; 11:35). In the Hellenistic period the city was known in Greek as Lydda. As a result of the struggles within the Seleucid Empire the city-district of Lydda was taken from Samaritan control and ceded to Hasmonean Judea (1 Macc. 11:34; cf. 10:30, 38; Josephus *Ant.* xiii.4.9 [127]). *See* LYDDA.

LO-DEBAR [lō′ də bär] (Heb. *lô dᵉḇār, lō' dᵉḇār*). A city in northern Transjordan, probably the same as DEBIR **2**, and probably to be identified with Umm ed-Dabar, south of the Wâdī Arab, a tributary of the Jordan south of the Yarmuk. Machir of Lo-debar assisted both Jonathan's son Mephibosheth (2 Sam. 9:3-5) and David (17:27-29). It may be the same as the Lidebir named by the MT at Josh. 13:26 as a place on the border of Gad (RSV "Debir").

Heb. *lō' ḏāḇār* (lit. "a thing of nought") at Amos 6:13 (KJV, RSV mg.) differs from Lo-debar by only one vowel. This may be a reference to the same town (so RSV, JB), apparently recaptured from the Arameans by Israel at the time of Jeroboam II.

LOG (Heb. *lōg*). A unit of liquid measure, probably *ca.* .35 l. (.63 pt.), mentioned only with reference to the olive oil accompanying the leper's purification offering (Lev. 14:10, 12, 15, 21, 24).

LOGIA [lō′jē ə, lōg′ē ə] (Gk. *lógia* "sayings" or "pronouncements").† A technical term for the sacred utterances of deities. The term has been applied in technical usage to the sayings of Jesus, especially collections found in papyri fragments that may have been used by the writers of the Gospels.

The term, transliterated from Greek, means literally "little words." It usually refers to short sacred pronouncements, and is used in the New Testament for the sacred Word of God ("oracles," Acts 7:38; Rom. 3:2; 1 Pet. 4:11; cf. Heb. 5:12).

Considerable debate has focused on the meaning of the term as used by the Church Fathers. For example, Polycarp's reference to "oracles of the Lord" (Polyc.Phil. 7:1) could denote the sayings of Jesus. In connection with ancient tradition concerning the authorship of the gospel of Matthew, a statement of Papias recorded in Eusebius (*HE* iii.39) is often quoted: "Matthew compiled the Logia in the Hebrew tongue." This statement has been variously interpreted, but it could possibly refer to a collection of sayings of Jesus. If this statement of Papias does refer to such a collection, however, no other references to it survive in the Fathers.

In investigating the possible oral and written traditions and sources of the Gospels, some scholars have attempted to identify a sayings source (Logia), labeled Q (from Ger. *Quelle* "source"). This hypothesis has never been proven, however, and remains pure speculation.

Logia in the technical sense of sayings of Jesus have been discovered and studied in several papyri. Among the Oxyrhynchus papyri discovered by B. P. Grenfell and A. S. Hunt in Egypt at the turn of the twentieth century was Oxy. p. 1, which contains seven or eight sayings of Jesus that are uniformly introduced with the formula "Jesus says." This fragment is obviously part of a book, since it is given a page number (11) and is the right-hand page. These same eight sayings of Jesus have also been found in the Coptic gospel of Thomas discovered near Nag Hammadi in 1946. It has been debated whether or not Oxy. p. 1 is the original Greek form of the gospel of Thomas, which contains some 114 sayings ascribed to Jesus. Oxy. pp. 654, 655 also contain compilations of sayings of Jesus.

All the logia, or sayings of Jesus, that are not found in the four Gospels are called agrapha (a Greek transliteration meaning "noncanonical"). Two such "isolated" sayings of Jesus that are found within the New Testament itself are usually designated as agrapha because they do not occur in the canonical Gospels (Acts 20:35; 1 Thess. 4:15-17). The vast body of New Testament apocryphal literature also contains many agrapha as well as many sayings that are found in the Gospels.

Bibliography. J. Finegan, *Hidden Records of the Life of Jesus* (Philadelphia: 1969); E. Hennecke–W. Schneemelcher, *New Testament Apocrypha* 1 (Philadelphia: 1963).

LOGOS. *See* WORD.

LOINS (Heb. *moṯnayim, ḥᵃlāṣayim, kᵉsālîm*; Aram. *ḥᵃraṣ*; Gk. *osphýs*).† The waist and lower torso, usually more specifically the reproductive organs. The RSV and other modern translations usually translate references to the loins as the source of offspring in terms of the person of the parent or ancestor (e.g., "you" in Gen. 35:11; KJV "thy loins"; cf. NJV; NIV "your body"). Great fear is often described as accompanied by discomforts, variously described, of the loins (e.g., Ps. 38:7 [MT 8]; 69:23 [MT 24]; Isa. 21:3; cf. Jer. 30:6; Ezek. 21:6 [MT 11], KJV; RSV "heart"; Dan. 5:6, *qiṭrê ḥarṣēh*; KJV "joints of his loins"; RSV "limbs"). In the sacrificial legislation Heb. *kᵉsālîm* is associated with the kidneys of the respective animals (e.g., Lev. 3:4, 10, 15; KJV "flanks").

A belt or girdle of leather or cloth folded over was worn around the waist (e.g., Matt. 3:4; KJV "loins") by both men and women. The lower edge or folds of loose garments would be brought up under this belt or girdle for work or when haste was required (Exod. 12:11). This "girding (up) of the loins" became a figure of speech for preparedness (1 Kgs. 18:46; Job 38:3; 40:7; Jer. 1:17; cf. 1 Pet. 1:13). Sackcloth was worn on the loins (actually covering the entire torso) in times of mourning, repentance, and degradation (Gen. 37:34; 1 Kgs. 20:31-32; Isa. 32:11; Joel 1:8).

LOIS [lō′ĭs] (Gk. *Lōis*). The mother of Eunice and grandmother of Timothy (2 Tim. 1:5).

LOOM (Heb. *'ereg*).* A machine or simple frame for weaving (cf. *ANEP*, nos. 142-43). After Delilah attempted to bind him by weaving his hair into the cloth on a loom, Samson successfully freed himself from the loom (Judg. 16:14; KJV "beam"). At Job 7:6 the term is translated "weaver's shuttle." Heb. *dallâ* (Isa. 38:12; RSV, NIV, JB "loom"; KJV "pining sickness") is actually the thrum, the threads of cloth the warp left on the beam when the finished piece of cloth has been cut off. *See* WEAVING.

LORD, MASTER (Heb. 'āḏôn, 'ᵃḏōnāy, baʿal; Aram. mārēʾ; Gk. kýrios).† One who possesses and exercises power and authority and to whom respect is thus ascribed. Several Hebrew and Greek terms are represented in English translations by "lord" and "master," with reference to both human masters as well as God and Christ.

I. Human Masters

Heb. 'āḏôn is commonly used in addressing superiors and to indicate superior rank (e.g., Gen. 23:6; 24:9; cf. 18:12; RSV "husband"). Similarly, baʿal encompasses the meanings "owner, master, husband, lord" (e.g., Esth. 1:17; Eccl. 5:11 [MT 10]; cf. Prov. 1:19; RSV "possessors"). Gk. kýrios approximates these meanings (e.g., Matt. 20:8; Luke 13:8; Gal. 4:1; Eph. 6:5, 9; 1 Pet. 3:6). Gk. despótēs refers to rulers and to the head of a household, especially functioning as the master of slaves (1 Tim. 6:1-2; Tit. 2:9; 1 Pet. 2:18; cf. 2 Tim. 2:21).

The Old Testament laws dealing with the master-slave relationship show an acceptance of slavery (Lev. 25:44-46), and in the social stratification thus reflected masters enjoy a privileged position. Humane treatment of slaves is expected on the basis of the equality of all in God's acts of creation and redemption (cf. Deut. 5:14-15; Job 31:13-15), but in the laws dealing with bodily injuries (Exod. 21:18-36) masters who assault their slaves are not in as serious a position as others who commit assaults. Distinctions between social classes, between masters, slaves, and others, in the early Church are not often mentioned in the New Testament. The giving of reciprocal instructions to masters and slaves (Eph. 6:5-9; Col. 3:22–4:1; cf. Barn. 19:7; Did. 4:10-11) shows both an acceptance of the social forms and an underlying spiritual egalitarianism (1 Cor. 12:13; Gal. 3:28; Col. 3:11), which becomes a call to reverse the master-slave relationship only at Phlm. 15-17 (cf. 1 Tim. 6:2).

In the KJV "master" also represents Gk. didáskalos (RSV "teacher"), most often translating Heb. rabbî "rabbi."

II. God

Terms for human masters were applied without question to God. Difficulties arose not because of the use of the same terms for humans, but because some terms were in use in other religious contexts. God is often referred to by Heb. 'ᵃḏōnāy (lit. "my lords"), a plural of majesty, especially as a euphemistic substitute for the sacred name YAHWEH (YHWH). The term baʿal was rejected as a designation for Israel's God because of its use in non-Israelite religion (see BAAL).

In accordance with usual pattern among Greek-speaking Jews, the New Testament uses kýrios as a designation for God (e.g., Luke 2:9; Acts 7:33; Jas. 1:7). Gk. despótēs occurs only infrequently for God (Luke 2:29; Acts 4:24; Rev. 6:10; cf. 2 Tim. 2:21).

III. Jesus

Jesus is commonly referred to as "Lord," primarily by Paul and in the Lukan writings. This epithet is most generally a designation of the risen Lord known in the Church (e.g., Acts 7:59; Rom. 1:7; 8:39; 1 Cor. 7:35; 1 Thess. 4:16; cf. Matt. 7:22) rather than of

Jesus in his earthly ministry (but cf. Luke 18:6; 1 Cor. 7:10, "the Lord"). Christians are those who "call upon the name of the Lord" (Rom. 10:12-13; 1 Cor. 1:2; 2 Tim. 2:22; cf. Acts 9:14) and make the confession "Jesus is Lord" (Rom. 10:9; 1 Cor. 12:3; Phil. 2:11).

This designation of Jesus undoubtedly began with the simple use of the term as a form of address implying respect (cf. John 4:15, "Sir"). But Jesus was recognized before his crucifixion and resurrection as the one who is uniquely the master (even beyond the sense of "teacher") of the company of his disciples, who determined for them the course of their actions (Luke 5:5; 9:49; Gk. epistátēs "master," in the New Testament used only by Luke). The miracles of Jesus taught his disciples, though perhaps not fully, that his lordship was far broader than their own relationship to him (cf. 8:24-25). Indeed, the understanding of Jesus as Messiah already implied that he was much more than a teacher of a group of disciples.

At the heart of the Church's confession of Jesus as Lord is the simple fact of the authority of the risen Christ in the life of the Church and its members (cf. 1 Cor. 4:19; Jas. 4:15). Jesus' designation as Lord is attested early in the Church's existence, e.g., in the Aramaic prayer "MARANATHA" "Our Lord, come" (1 Cor. 16:22). In Hellenistic usage Gk. kýrios was applied to various deities, but always in conjunction with the name of the deity. While such Gentile cultic language should not be considered the source of the epithet as applied to Jesus, it is apparent that once the designation was established, comparison with other divine "lords" became possible. This was particularly true in connection with the differentiation between the Christian eucharist and the cultic meals of other groups (e.g., the dinner at the table of the Lord Serapis; cf. 1 Cor. 8:5-6; 11:20). The eucharist meal and the confession "Jesus is Lord" contributed significantly to the designation of Jesus as "Lord" among Christians, as did the frequent application of Ps. 110:1, interpreted messianically, to Jesus (Acts 2:34-35; cf. Matt. 22:41-45; Heb. 10:12-13).

Startling as it might have seemed to non-Christian Jews, the designation of Jesus as Lord did call to mind the Greek-speaking Jewish use of kýrios as an equivalent to Heb. YHWH, at least implying that Jesus shared in the authority of the God of Israel. Old Testament passages referring to Yahweh (LXX Gk. kýrios) could be applied to Jesus (1 Pet. 2:3, using Ps. 34:8 [MT 9]; 1 Pet. 3:14-15, possibly relying on Isa. 8:12-13). Furthermore, Christ, the risen and exalted Lord, was involved in the creation of the world (cf. John 1:3; Col. 1:16-17) and rules over all (Rom. 14:9; Phil. 2:9-11 [cf. Isa. 45:23]; Rev. 17:14).

Twice Jesus is called despótēs (2 Pet. 2:1; Jude 4), in both cases as the "Master" who is denied by false teachers.

LORD OF HOSTS (Heb. YHWH ṣᵉḇāʾôt; Gk. kýrios sabaóth).* A name of God, originally an epithet denoting his function as creator and divine warrior (lit. "he creates the [heavenly] hosts"; cf. Isa. 40:26). It designates Yahweh as the national God of Israel and is probably first associated with the shrine at Shiloh, locus of the ark of the covenant (1 Sam. 1:3, 11; 4:4; 2 Sam. 6:2; cf. Rom. 9:29; Jas. 5:4); here the name also suggests the role of Yahweh in directing the earthly armies of the Confederation (1 Sam. 17:45). An expanded form, "the Lord, the God of hosts" (Heb. YHWH *ᵉlōhê ṣᵉbā'ôt*), may be a later interpretation from a time when the verbal sense of the epithet had been forgotten (e.g., Jer. 5:14; Hos. 12:5 [MT 6]; Amos 6:14).

LORD'S DAY (Gk. *hḗ kyriakḗ* [*hēméra*]).† The first day of the week, Sunday, adopted by the early Christians as the day of worship. The full phrase "the Lord's day" (Gk. *hḗ kyriakḗ hēméra*) appears in the New Testament only at Rev. 1:10, but *hḗ kyriakḗ* (with "day" understood) soon became a technical term in the early Church for the day on which Christians observed the eucharist (Did. 14; Ignatius *Magn.* 9:1; Gospel of Peter 9:35; 12:50). In the mainstream of early Christianity, the Decalog's injunction against work on the Sabbath was spiritualized (Barn. 15; Justin Martyr *Dial.* xii; Irenaeus *Adv. haer.* iv.16.1; cf. Col. 2:16-17); it was not until the fourth century that the Sabbath commandment was applied to Sunday by Christians. Tertullian did briefly urge the cessation of business dealings on Sunday, but apparently with no thought of the Sabbath commandment (*De orat.* xxiii). The observance of worship on every seventh day—even if it were Sunday rather than the Sabbath (i.e., Saturday)—was, however, a recognition of the division of time into seven-day periods, a practice then just beginning to enter the Roman world from Judaism.

Christian worship on Sunday, "the first day of the week" (Acts 20:7; 1 Cor. 16:2), was based on the occurrence of Jesus' resurrection during the early morning hours of a Sunday (Matt. 28:1; Mark 16:2, 9; Luke 24:1; John 20:1, 19). Justin Martyr associates Sunday observance also with its being the first day of creation (*Apol.* i.67). The LORD'S SUPPER was celebrated on Sunday (Acts 20:7 [Saturday evening as the beginning of Sunday by Jewish reckoning, or Sunday evening, still part of Sunday by Roman reckoning]; Did. 14.1; cf. Luke 24:30). At the same gathering money for charitable purposes could be set aside (1 Cor. 16:2) and, as the practice developed later, collected from those attending worship (*Apol.* i.67), and teaching from the Scriptures could take place (i.67; cf. Acts 20:7, 9).

Bibliography. S. Bacchiocchi, *From Sabbath to Sunday* (Rome: 1977); D. A. Carson, ed., *From Sabbath to Lord's Day* (Grand Rapids: 1982); W. Rordorf, *Sunday* (Philadelphia: 1968).

LORD'S PRAYER.† The prayer taught by Jesus to his disciples (Matt. 6:9-13; Luke 11:2-4; Did. 8.2 [perhaps based on Matthew]). The address is followed first by petitions relating to God's name, kingdom, and will, and then by petitions relating to the physical and spiritual needs of those praying.

The address appears in a simple form, "Father," in Luke and a longer form in Matthew, lit. "Our father in the heavens" (Didache sing. "heaven"). The invocation of God as "Father" was known in Judaism (e.g., Isa. 63:16; Jer. 3:4). But Jesus, as one uniquely possessing sonship to God (Luke 2:49), spoke of and to God as "Abba" (Mark 14:36; cf. Rom. 8:15; Gal. 4:6) and here urges his disciples to use the same form

of address, which carries with it a strong sense of trust in God and of acceptance by him (cf. Matt. 6:8, 32; 1 Pet. 1:17).

The same link to the person and teachings of Jesus is found in the first group of petitions (often called the "thou" petitions). Luke's two (Luke 2:11b-d) and Matthew's three (Matt. 6:9d-10c) petitions are in the form of a Jewish liturgical blessing, and their content is not inconceivable in the context of Jewish blessings. But in the context of Jesus' focus on the coming of the kingdom in and through his own person (Matt. 4:17; Luke 11:20; 16:16), these petitions bring Jesus' disciples into close association with the kingdom's coming. The eschatological action of God's sovereignty is thus affirmed and made the hope of the disciples.

The word commonly translated "daily" (Gk. *epioúsios*) in the ("we") petition for bread is difficult and has been interpreted variously (e.g., "for the coming day" [RSV mg. "the morrow"], "for today," "for the future," "needed," "continual," and "sufficient for the day's needs"). At any rate, the basic physical needs of human existence are brought into the prayer rather than left solely to human effort (cf. Matt. 6:25-33).

Jesus' use of "debts" (v. 12a; Didache "debt") in the petition for forgiveness as a figure of speech for forgiven sins (as at 18:23-35; Luke 7:41-43, 47-48) is indeed translated "sins" in Luke's rendering of the first part of the petition (11:4a). The condition imposed on the receiving of God's forgiveness, underscored after the prayer at Matt. 6:14-15 (cf. 18:23-25; Mark 11:25-26) is, in effect, a commentary on the fifth beatitude (Matt. 5:7).

The next (7:13; Luke 11:4b) petition has been regarded as a difficulty since early in its history, when (in some ancient versions and liturgical documents) it was modified to "Do not allow us to yield to temptation" and the like. God has tempted people (Gen. 22:1; Exod. 17:7; Deut. 33:8; 2 Chr. 32:31) but does not entice them to commit evil (Jas. 1:13); rather, he tests them so as to disclose their faithfulness or lack thereof (Deut. 8:2). He limits the power of temptation (Job 1:12; 2:6; 1 Cor. 10:13; cf. 1 Kgs. 22:21-23). "Temptation" (Gk. *peirasmós*) is of broad significance, including within it "testing, trial, ordeal" or any experience that tests the disciple of Jesus (cf. 1 Pet. 4:12). The second part of this petition, "Deliver us from evil," does not occur in Luke's version. "Evil" (*ponērós* with a neuter or masculine article) may represent abstract "evil," "the evil one"—the devil or antichrist, "the evil inclination" (which Judaism saw existing in every person alongside the inclination to good), or the expected "evil" of the end of the age (which "temptation" may represent as well).

A concluding doxology (based on the blessing at 1 Chr. 29:10-13) has been added to some manuscripts of Matt. 6:13 (v. 13b in KJV; mg. in most modern translations) and appears in a shorter form in the Didache ("for thine is the power and the glory forever"). This addition and the differences between Luke's and Matthew's versions of the prayer are the best known evidences of the adoption of the Lord's Prayer into the Church's liturgical traditions and its consequent adaptation and development as part of those traditions. Other evidences of this adoption are the simple "Amen" appearing at the end of the prayer in some manuscripts of Matthew, the substitution of "May thy Holy Spirit come on us and purify us" for "Thy kingdom come" in some versions of Luke, and the adaptation of "deliver us from evil" into a prayer for the Church's sanctification (Did. 10:5).

Liturgical adaptation is not beyond the intention of the prayer, the purpose of which is to provide not one set prayer but an outline on which all prayer can be based. This is made clear by its context in Matthew, where it is offered as an alternative to the wrong kind of prayer based on wrong ideas about God, and in Luke, where it is given in response to a request not for a prayer but for teaching on how to pray. Thus, the Lord's Prayer can be considered an abstract of Christian prayer.

Bibliography. J. Jeremias, *The Prayers of Jesus* (Philadelphia: 1978); J. J. Petuchowski and M. Brocke, eds., *The Lord's Prayer and Jewish Liturgy* (New York: 1978).

LORD'S SUPPER.† One of the Christian sacraments, in which the Church gathers to participate in a ceremonial meal of bread and wine that symbolize the body and blood of Christ. The celebration of the sacrament proclaims the death of Christ as the source of life in him.

I. Institution

The Lord's Supper was instituted by Jesus on the night of his betrayal (Matt. 26:20-29; Mark 14:17-25; Luke 22:14-30). The name Lord's Supper occurs only at 1 Cor. 11:20, but the intention of a ceremony of memorial, fellowship, communion, proclamation, and anticipation is clear in the New Testament passages that deal with the institution and celebration of the meal. On the first day of Unleavened Bead, as he and his disciples were eating the last passover, Jesus announced that one of the twelve would betray him. He then blessed and broke the bread and said, "Take, eat; this is my body." Concerning the cup, he said, "Drink of it, all of you; for this is my blood of the covenant, which is poured out for many for the forgiveness of sins" (Matt. 26:26-28). *See* LAST SUPPER.

II. Significance

Several aspects of the institution of the Lord's Supper indicate its meaning. First, most modern interpreters agree that the literal elements are in some way symbolic of the atonement of Christ. The bread and wine are metaphors of the work of Christ on the cross. As bread is eaten for sustenance of life, so the offering of the body of Christ provides life for the Christian. As the wine is poured out and gives life, so Jesus poured out his life on behalf of many for their forgiveness. The elements of the Supper are then visible words that convey the teaching of Jesus concerning redemption.

The aspect of betrayal as the context of the institution of this sacrament in the Gospels is also referred to by Paul (1 Cor. 11:23). The followers of Jesus, in celebrating the Supper, show their allegiance to him in contrast to the treachery of Judas. By celebrating the Supper, Christians are not mourning Jesus' death or reenacting the emotions of the event, but are showing their appreciation of it as the basis of their life;

the Supper shows the Christian's relationship to Christ—fidelity to the Lord.

Another aspect of the Lord's Supper is its relationship to the Passover and the transition to the new covenant. The Supper was instituted during the Passover feast and was apparently intended as an extension of it. Paul suggests a reinterpretation of the Old Testament Passover when he says that the Church is unleavened, and that "Christ, our paschal lamb, has been sacrificed" (5:7). The Church no longer celebrates Passover because it now celebrates the Lord's Supper instead; the Supper is the sign of the blood (Exod. 12:13) and the mark of the distinct redemption of the Church on the basis of the death of Christ. The statement of Jesus, "This is my blood of the covenant," was taken to mean that with his death the new covenant would be established (Mark 14:24). The Supper portends the fulfillment and accomplishment of the primary purpose of Jesus' ministry; he was about to reach his goal—his hour had come (cf. John 12:23; 13:1; 17:1; cf. 7:6, 8), his "time" was "at hand" (Matt. 26:18).

In the institution of the Lord's Supper the participation of all of the disciples was emphasized in the words, "Drink of it, all of you." The intention of sharing, communion, and participation was identified and passed on as an integral part of the celebration, as can be seen from the statement of Paul, "The cup of blessing which we bless, is it not a participation (RSV mg. "communion") in the blood of Christ? The bread which we break, is it not a participation in the body of Christ" (1 Cor. 10:16)?

The substitutionary nature of the atonement and the forgiveness of sins are important aspects of the Lord's Supper as well. Jesus said that the blood of the covenant would be "poured out for many for the forgiveness of sins" (Matt. 26:28). Just as in the Old Testament the covenant was ratified by the shedding and sprinkling of blood, so the new covenant was established in the same way, and this is symbolized in the Supper: "without the shedding of blood there is no forgiveness of sins" (Heb. 9:22). Resurrection was an important aspect of the institution of the Lord's Supper; Jesus said, "I tell you I shall not drink again of this fruit of the vine until that day when I drink it new with you in my Father's kingdom" (Matt. 26:29). The apostles in particular understood this as a reference to the resurrection, and later they referred to the fact that God had made him manifest to those who "ate and drank with him after he rose from the dead" (Acts 10:41). This aspect of the celebration of the Supper looks forward with joy to the coming of the Lord, the resurrection, and the kingdom. The sacrament of the Lord's Supper is a proclamation of "the Lord's death until he comes" (1 Cor. 11:26).

III. Theological Reflection

The interpretation of the celebration of the Lord's Supper (Eucharist, from Gk. *eucharistéō* "be thankful, give thanks") involves a critical point of difference between Roman Catholic and Protestant theology. Roman Catholics take literally the phrases "This is my body" and "This is my blood." In this interpretation, the elements (bread and wine) are wondrously converted into the actual body and blood of Christ at each celebration of the Mass (transubstantiation) and then offered to God as a new sacrifice of Christ. In Roman Catholic theology, the sacrament of Holy Eucharist is an offering that accomplishes something—it is a means of grace. In Protestant theology, the body of Christ was offered to God once on the cross—a historic, never-to-be-repeated sacrifice. The Lord's Supper is therefore not a sacrifice but a symbolic celebration, a reminder, of the fact that on the cross Christ has already accomplished redemption for mankind.

Bibliography. J. Jeremias, *The Eucharistic Words of Jesus* (Philadelphia: 1977); I. H. Marshall, *Last Supper and Lord's Supper* (Grand Rapids: 1981); E. Schweizer, *The Lord's Supper According to the New Testament* (Philadelphia: 1967).

LO-RUHAMAH [lō'rōō hä'mə] (Heb. *lōʾ ruḥāmâ* "not pitied"). A symbolic name that the prophet Hosea was commanded to give to his and Gomer's daughter (Hos. 1:6; RSV "Not pitied"; cf. 2:1, 23 [MT 3, 25]).

LOT [lŏt] (Heb. *lôṭ;* Gk. *Lōt*). The son of Haran and nephew of Abraham (Gen. 11:27, 31).

Lot was born in Ur and taken to Haran by his grandfather Terah (v. 31) and then to Canaan by Abraham (Abram) (12:4-5). In Canaan Abraham and Lot were the chiefs of two allied pastoral clans. When the two groups became too large to live and travel together, Abraham proposed a separation and magnanimously gave to Lot the choice of direction (13:5-9). Lot took his flocks into the Jordan valley, apparently into part of the Arabah subsequently covered by the southern portion of the Dead Sea. The narrative makes an intentional contrast: Lot chose the green, well-watered valley, eventually making his way as far as the proverbially evil Sodom, the fate of which was well known (vv. 10-13; cf. Deut. 29:23 [MT 22]; 32:32; Isa. 1:9-10; 3:9), while Abraham moved into the highlands that were to be the land of promise (Gen. 13:14-17).

Lot was taken captive by the coalition headed by Chedorlaomer against cities in the Dead Sea–Arabah region, but was freed by Abraham (14.1-16). Later, Lot was spared by God from the destruction of Sodom (19:16; cf. v. 29); he and his two daughters fled to Zoar, but his wife looked back and was turned into a pillar of salt.

Lot went with his daughters to live in a cave in the hills above Zoar, apparently afraid to return to town life because of what had happened to Sodom and Gomorrah (v. 30). Being thus cut off from human society, his daughters feared the extinction of their family, and so arranged between themselves to have offspring by their father (vv. 31-36). The two sons thus produced were the eponymous ancestors of two Transjordanian peoples, the Moabites (v. 37; cf. Deut. 2:9) and Ammonites (19:38; cf. Deut. 2:19), future enemies of Israel (cf. Ps. 83:6-8 [MT 7-9]).

In later literature Lot is most remembered for the flight from Sodom and the attendant events. The destruction "in the days of Lot" was proverbial for judgment that is sudden and complete (Luke 17:28-30). Lot's neighbors became examples of sinners not spared (Sir. 16:8; cf. Wis. 10:7-8), Lot's wife of indecision (Luke 17:31-32) and unbelief (Wis. 10:7), and Lot

himself of a righteous person delivered through judgment (2 Pet. 2:7; Wis. 10:6).

LOTAN [lō'tăn] (Heb. *lôṭān*). A son of Seir (Gen. 36:20, 22; 1 Chr. 1:38-39), and a chief of Horite peoples who lived in Seir (Edom) before the entry of the Edomites (Gen. 36:29).

LOTS (Heb. *gôrāl*; Gk. *klḗros*). Objects cast or thrown to call upon God or gods (cf. Jonah 1:7) to render a decision either beyond human understanding or otherwise demanding impartiality—as in the division of land or goods. Used throughout the ancient world, Israel viewed lots in the context of faith in God's governance. Thus humans may cast the lot, but the Lord gives the decision (Prov. 16:33).

Lots were employed primarily for consultation (e.g., Lev. 16:8; 1 Sam. 10:20-21; Esth. 3:7; *pûr*; Ezek. 21:22 [MT 27]; Heb. *qesem*; cf. Josh. 7:16-18; Acts 1:26) and apportionment (Num. 33:54; Josh. 14:2; 1 Chr. 24:5ff.; Ps. 22:18 [MT 19]; cf. Luke 1:9). Some interpreters view the Urim and Thummim as a form of lots used for prediction, but the meaning and use of these two stones on the breastplate of the high priest remains uncertain (*see* URIM AND THUMMIM).

Lots were customarily stones or pebbles (cf. Arab. *ǧarwal* "gravel, small stone") but could also be little sticks or even arrows (cf. Ezek. 21:21 [MT 26]; Hos. 4:12). The verbs used with lots (Heb. *nāpal* "fall"; e.g., Ezek. 24:6; cf. RSV mg.; *yāṣāʾ* "come out"; e.g., Josh. 19:1) imply that they were kept in a container. The reference to casting lots in the lap (Prov. 16:33) alludes to the shaking of lots in the upper part of the outer garment, perhaps from a pocket (cf. Exod. 28:30).

The lot came to denote the land itself that had been divided by this means (e.g., Josh. 15:1; cf. Ps. 125:3). Figuratively, it represented the destiny appointed by God (16:5-6; Isa. 17:14; cf. Dan. 12:13). In the New Testament, Gk. *klḗros* is used of one's share or place in the gospel and its ministry (Acts 1:17; cf. 26:18; Col. 1:12; 1 Pet. 5:3).

See PURIM.

LOTUS (Heb. *ṣeʾĕlîm*). A plant mentioned only at Job 40:21-22 (KJV "shady trees"). The usual identification is with *Zizyphyus lotus* (L.) Lam., the thorny lotus, a member of the buckthorn family (*Rhamnaceae*). This shrub, which grows in dry places around the Mediterranean, has small greenish flowers and thorns at the base of its small leaves and reaches a height of about 1.5 m. (5 ft.). Whether this is indeed the plant named in Job is in doubt and depends partly on the identification of BEHEMOTH. The swampy setting of these verses makes the thorny lotus unlikely. The Egyptian lotus or water lily (*Nymphaea lotus* L.) fits the context but would not be a plant under which a large animal would find shade.

LOVE (Heb. *ʾāhaḇ, ḥesed*; Gk. *agapáō* [verb], *agápē* [noun], *philós*).† The basic aspect of relationships between humans and between God and humans, encompassing affection, loyalty, and responsibility. In biblical usage the emphasis is on the quality of the relationship.

I. Human Love

The Bible, and especially the Old Testament, refers to the love of human for human in a number of contexts, often that of sexual love. Sexual love is a mystery, a natural part of the created order (cf. Prov. 30:18-19), and a power as undeniable as death (Cant. 8:6), to be handled with care (2:7). It is characterized by mutuality and delight (vv. 3, 16), and is experienced with all the senses (e.g., v. 14; 3:1-5). Although its highest expression is in marriage (Eccl. 9:9), the term "love" is also used for the distortions of adultery, incest, and prostitution, so becoming a metaphor for apostasy (Jer. 2:25; Hos. 3; cf. 2 Sam. 13:15).

Love is expressed in families for wives (1 Sam. 1:5; Eph. 5:25), husbands (Tit. 2:4), children (Gen. 22:2; Prov. 13:24; Tit. 2:4), and in-laws (Ruth 4:15). In polygamous marriages love can lead to favoritism and strife (Gen. 29:30, 32; Deut. 21:15-17; 1 Sam. 1:4-8).

The devoted loyalty of a slave (Exod. 21:5) and the close bonds of friendship (2 Sam. 1:26; cf. Prov. 18:24) constitute love. By extension, "love" is used in a technical sense to indicate the covenant bond (e.g., Deut. 5:10; 7:7-9; Heb. *ḥeseḏ*; RSV "steadfast love"; Hos. 11:1). Accordingly, words for love also occur in the context of international relations (1 Kgs. 5:1 [MT 15]) or of loyalty to a leader (1 Sam. 18:16; 20:13-17). This love for a ruler is characterized by faithfulness and obedience (cf. Dan. 9:4), and is answered by the ruler's love, favor, and kindness toward the subject (1 Sam. 16:21; cf. 2 Sam. 9:1). To give this love to political enemies is to show disloyalty to one's first love (19:6 [MT 7]; 2 Chr. 19:2).

Love for abstract qualities or activities is also cited: for righteousness (Ps. 45:7 [MT 8]), wisdom (Prov. 4:6; cf. 8:36), farming (2 Chr. 26:10), foolishness (Prov. 1:22), wealth (Eccl. 5:10 [MT 9]), and pleasure (2 Tim. 3:4).

II. Divine Love

God is love (1 John 4:8), and his love is everlasting (Jer. 31:3). In the Old Testament God shows his love through his covenant with Israel (cf. Hos. 11:1), as demonstrated in mercy and forgiveness (Ps. 103:8; cf. Jer. 31:20) and displayed in deliverance (Deut. 4:37-38; 7:7-8; Ps. 18:50 [MT 51]; 107). God loves justice (99:4). Often this love is expressed in political terms as the love of the sovereign who expects love and obedience in return (cf. Deut. 6:5-9). God's covenant love (e.g., Ps. 115:1) is shown in his judgment and gracious blessing (Exod. 34:6-7; Ps. 62:12 [MT 13]; 106; Lam. 3:32; *see* GRACE). Hosea speaks of God's love as parental love (Hos. 11:1-4). Because the love between God and his people is also likened to that of man and wife, idolatry and the betrayal of the covenant for cultural or political advantage constitute adultery and prostitution (Jer. 5:7; Ezek. 23; Hos. 1-3). Nevertheless, God forgives and his love revives (Ps. 85:9-13 [MT 10-14]; Hos. 2:19-23 [MT 21-25]; Mic. 7:18-20; Zeph. 3:17). While Israel remains its primary object, God's love extends to all creation and the nations, even Israel's enemies (Ps. 117; 145:9-10; cf. Isa. 19:19-25).

In the New Testament God's love is known in and through Jesus. He is God's beloved (Gk. *agapētós*) Son (Mark 1:11; cf. Luke 20:13; Eph. 1:6), who was with the Father from the beginning in a relationship of mutual love (John 3:35; 14:31; 17:23; cf. 1:1) and was sent because of God's love for mankind (3:16). Jesus demonstrates love for people with acts of healing and forgiveness (cf. Mark 1:41; *splagchnizómai* "have pity") and by his grief for the hardness of human hearts (cf. Matt. 23:37). God's love is seen most fully in the salvation brought by Jesus in giving his life for his friends (John 15:13; Gal. 2:20; Eph. 5:2; 1 John 3:16).

God pours out his love through his Spirit (Rom. 5:5; cf. 15:30; 2 Cor. 13:14). The fruit of the Spirit's work is a love that marks believers before the world (John 13:35; Gal. 5:22; Phil. 1:9-11).

III. Love for God

In the Old Testament love for God is said to be evidenced in those who keep God's commandments, obey his voice, walk in his way, and cleave to him (Deut. 6:5-9; 11:22; 30:20). The New Testament shares the call to love God and keep his commandments (Mark 12:28-34; John 14:23; 15:9-10), understood now in terms of following Jesus (Matt. 10:37-39; cf. Phil. 2:1-11). Love for God is essential (1 Cor. 16:22). Two ways that God's people respond to his love are to love him in return and to love other humans; the two responses are inseparable (Matt. 22:37-40). Usually other words than "love" are used for this response to God's love: faith, knowledge, abiding, or simply being "in Christ."

In the Old Testament love for other people is part of the broader duty of keeping God's commandments. God's people are to love neighbors (i.e., their fellow Israelites) as well as sojourners or resident aliens (Lev. 19:18, 34; Deut. 10:19). This love is grounded in God's identity as the Lord, the covenant maker and keeper, and is displayed by those who protect the weak, give justice, and maintain peace (Lev. 19:9-18; Ps. 11:7; cf. Isa. 58:6-7). The New Testament gives special prominence to the love commandment. Like the rabbis, it views this love as the summary and fulfillment of the Torah (Matt. 22:35-40; Rom. 13:8-10). The love of Jesus for his followers becomes the pattern for their love for each other (John 15:12), just as God's mercy is the pattern for the mercy to be shown by the Christian (Luke 6:36). The Christian's love is to see in the other person one for whom Christ died (Rom. 14:15). It is not to stop with the neighbor, but is to extend to enemies and persecutors (Luke 6:27-36; cf. Rom. 12:14-21). Love is especially to be shown within the community of grace (1 Pet. 2:17; cf. Gal. 6:10). Love defines the life of the community (1 Cor. 16:14) and is constantly proven in good deeds and humility (Rom. 12:9-13; 1 Cor. 13:4-7; 1 Pet. 4:8-11; 1 John 3:10, 18).

Bibliography. J. Bergman, A. O. Haldar, and G. Wallis, "'āhaḇ ['āhabh]," *TDOT* 1, rev. ed. (1977): 99-118; V. P. Furnish, *The Love Command in the New Testament* (Nashville: 1972); L. Morris, *Testaments of Love* (Grand Rapids: 1981); G. Quell and E. Stauffer, "ἀγαπάω," *TDNT* 1 (1964): 21-55.

LOVE FEAST. *See* AGAPE.

LOWLAND (Heb. *šᵉpēlâ*). The foothills going down

westward from the Judean highlands to the coastal plain of Philistia. The Hebrew term is usually transliterated as a proper name, SHEPHELAH (KJV "vale," "valley[s]," "plain[s]"). The same word is used more broadly at Josh. 9:1; 11:2 (here probably referring to the coastal lowlands north of Carmel), 16; 12:8.

LUBIM, LUBIMS (KJV). *See* LIBYA.

LUCAS. *See* LUKE.

LUCIFER. *See* DAY STAR.

LUCIUS [lōō´shəs] (Gk. *Loukios*).
1. A Roman consul who addressed letters to a number of countries telling of a Roman protective alliance with the Jews of Judea (1 Macc. 15:15-24). If the text is taken at face value the letters were written in 139 B.C. and the consul was Lucius Calpurnius Piso. But the latter's praenomen was most likely not Lucius, but Cnaeus. Furthermore, the letters were written in response to the Jewish embassy under Numenius that went to Rome in 142 (14:24), the success of which is already mentioned at v. 40. This suggests that the text of the letters has apparently been misplaced, in which case Lucius the consul would be Lucius Caecilius Metellus, consul in 142.
2. Lucius of Cyrene, a Christian prophet and teacher in the church at Antioch (Acts 13:1). He was among those who received a command from the Holy Spirit to commission Paul and Barnabas for the first missionary tour. Lucius was probably one of the Jewish teachers who preached the word to the Greeks at Antioch (11:20-21).
3. A man whose greetings to the Roman church are conveyed at Rom. 16:21. If "kinsmen" (i.e., fellow Jews) applies only to Jason and Sosipater, then this Lucius might be the Gentile Luke mentioned at Col. 4:14. It has been suggested that he is Paul's companion Luke (2 Tim. 4:11; Phlm. 24; KJV "Lucas"), and thus possibly the author of the gospel of Luke and Acts.

LUD [lōōd] (Heb. *lûḏ*), **LUDIM** [lōō´dīm] (*lûḏîm*).†
A people variously identified as of Semitic ancestry (i.e., through Shem; Gen. 10:22 par. 1 Chr. 1:17) or as descendants of Ham through Egypt (Gen. 10:13 par. 1 Chr. 1:11). Elsewhere, they are connected with Egypt and northeastern African peoples such as Ethiopia and Put (Ezek. 30:5; Jer. 46:9). They are portrayed as mercenaries for Tyre (Ezek. 27:10) and possibly for Egypt (Jer. 46:9; Ezek. 30:5), and their skill as archers is proverbial (Isa. 66:19; Jer. 46:9).
The names themselves have been interpreted variously. They are linguistically similar to Akk. *Luddu*, the region of Lydia in western Asia Minor that included the cities of Thyatira, Sardis, and Philadelphia. An alternate suggestion is some otherwise unknown northeastern African people or perhaps the Libyans (Heb. *lûḇîm*). The names Lud and Ludim may actually represent in some of the passages a vague far-away people or, at least, different peoples known under the same names, as suggested by their association with lands and peoples known to Israel as simply remote and generally westward (Isa. 66:19; cf. Ezek. 27:10).

LUHITH [lōō´hĭth], **ASCENT OF** (Heb. *ma'ălēh hallûḥṯ*). A place or road going up into the heights of southern Moab (Isa. 15:5; Jer. 48:5). The location is otherwise unknown. Eusebius (*Onom.* cxxii.29) identifies Luhith with Loueitha between Ar (Areopolis) and Zoar.

LUKE [lōōk] (Gk. *Loukas,* a shortened form of *Loukios* or *Loukanos*).† A coworker and traveling companion of Paul, and the probable author of the gospel of Luke and the Acts of the Apostles.
A number of probable but not absolutely certain sources relevant to the person of Luke can be assembled. Tradition ascribes the authorship of the third Gospel and Acts to Luke (the so-called anti-Marcionite prologue to the gospel, the Muratorian Canon, Irenaeus, and Clement of Alexandria), who was from Syrian Antioch (anti-Marcionite prologue; cf. the Western text of Acts 11:28). Luke and Acts can then be a possible source regarding the person Luke, his theology, and inclinations. Moreover, if the "we" sections of Acts (16:10-17; 20:5-21:18; 27:1-28:16) are in fact a record of the author's involvement and neither a literary device nor inherited from a source used by the author, they shed light on his participation in the missionary journeys of Paul. They would place Luke with Paul shortly after the apostle left Achaia for the last time (20:5). Since it was at about this time that Paul wrote to the Christians of Rome (cf. Rom. 15:25-26; Acts 19:21), the LUCIUS **(3)** of Rom. 16:21 may be Luke. The author would then also be placed with Paul in Rome (Acts 28:16), from which "Luke the beloved physician" greeted the Colossian Christians (Col. 4:14) and Luke (KJV "Lucas"), one of Paul's "fellow workers," greeted Philemon (Phlm. 24). 2 Tim. 4:11, reflecting on the end of Paul's life in Rome, reports that "Luke alone is with me."
If all these factors are added together, the following picture emerges. Luke was a Gentile (cf. Col. 4:11) and a physician, making his home in Syrian Antioch. He may have been a brother of Titus (2 Cor. 8:16-18; 12:18), which would possibly explain why Titus is not mentioned in Acts (not even at 20:4), despite Titus' prominence in Paul's letters and his inclusion among those accompanying Paul to Jerusalem. Since already on Paul's second missionary journey Luke was a coworker of Paul (16:10), it is probable that he was among the earliest Gentile converts (cf. 11:19-21); he was not, however, the same person as Lucius **(2)** of Cyrene (13:1), with whom Luke was not identified until the fourth century. Luke went with Paul and Silas at least from Tarsus to Philippi (16:10-12) and was a witness of the first stage of their ministry in that city (vv. 13-17). Later Luke was with Paul on the last part of Paul's third missionary journey as it brought Paul from Macedonia to Troas, and down the coast of Asia Minor to Miletus, and then on through Tyre and Caesarea to Jerusalem (20:5-21:18). After Paul's arrest in Jerusalem and multiple hearings in Caesarea, Luke was one of Paul's traveling companions on the eventful journey to Rome (27:1-28:16), where he stayed on with Paul. Paul found Luke to be a dear friend and valuable coworker.
Something of the personality and theology of Luke

can be seen in his writings. He shows special interest in the spread of the gospel beyond the boundaries of Israel into the Gentile world (Luke 2:32; 4:25-27; Acts 11:18). Much of Jesus' ministry is on a course set for Jerusalem (Luke 9:51; 13:33), but the Church's course is set to begin in Jerusalem and make its way outward into the world (24:47; Acts 1:8), as portrayed particularly in Acts, which begins in Jerusalem and ends in Rome. Luke also shows a special interest in the repentance of sinners (e.g., Luke 5:8; 7:37-48; 13:1-5; 18:13-14) and in Samaritans (e.g., 9:51-56; 10:29-37; Acts 8:5-25). He demonstrates a greater concern than the other Gospel writers for including women in his story (e.g., Luke 1:24-56; 2:36-38, 51; 7:12-15, 37-38; 8:2-3; 10:38-42). He has a particular interest in the coming, the gift, the fullness, and the joy of the Holy Spirit (e.g., 4:1, 14; 11:13; Acts 2:1-21; 4:8, 31; 8:15-19). He also emphasizes the severe demands of discipleship, including the need for financial sacrifices and sharing (e.g., Luke 6:34-35; 12:13-21; 14:7-14, 25-35; 16:10-13; 17:7-10; Acts 2:44-45; 4:32-5:10).

Bibliography. H. Conzelmann, *The Theology of St. Luke* (Philadelphia: 1982); I. H. Marshall, *Luke: Historian and Theologian* (Grand Rapids: 1971).

LUKE, GOSPEL OF.† The third book of the New Testament, and the third Gospel.

I. Author

Tradition has been unanimous in attributing the third Gospel to Luke, the "beloved physician" (Col. 4:14). Although the author is not named or identified within the book, the tradition has survived critical challenge.

The author writes with remarkable precision and literary skill; he stays in the background and presents Jesus as the Redeemer. The Gospel is addressed to the "most excellent Theophilus," possibly a Roman official who had become a Christian. Comparison of Luke 1:1-4 and Acts 1:1-2 supports the widely accepted view that the same author wrote both books, addressed them to the same individual, and intended them as companion volumes. According to 16:10-40, Luke joined Paul at Troas, on his second missionary journey, and accompanied him to Philippi; he then stayed at Philippi until after the third journey and then went with Paul to Jerusalem (and Rome) (20:5-21:18; 27:1-28). Luke was the companion of Paul (cf. Irenaeus *Adv. haer.* iii.1.1; 3.3; 14.1) and is mentioned as being with him when Colossians, Philemon, and 2 Timothy were written (Col. 4:14; Phlm. 24; 2 Tim. 4:11). Although Luke's perspective on such matters as the Apostolic Council differs from that of Paul (e.g., Acts 15; cf. Gal. 2), his unique experiences provided valuable background for writing his two-volume work, which he apparently wrote with the Hellenistic Church in mind. He was the only Gentile author of a biblical book.

II. Sources

From the highly complex analysis of the relationships between the Gospels, the present text of Luke seems to have derived essentially from two sources: the gospel of Mark (considered by most scholars as the primary Gospel), and, somewhat less certainly, the

Luke 16:9-21 in Bodmer Papyrus XIV ($\mathfrak{p}^{75}$; second-third century) (Bodmer Library, Geneva)

hypothetical document Q. The existence of Q is posited by scholars as a plausible source for about two hundred verses that Matthew and Luke have in common; these verses are not found in Mark.

Luke omits material found in both Mark and Matthew, and adds material of his own that is not found in either of them. He also varies the arrangement of the material considerably. Whatever his exact sources, Luke had access to personal information about the parents of John the Baptist, the birth of Jesus, and other facts not found in the other Gospels.

The preface of the Gospel mentions that many had "undertaken to compile a narrative" of the gospel events, and that traditions had been handed down by "eyewitnesses and ministers of the word." Whether or not Luke considered such writings and traditions as his sources, he seems to have had considerable confidence in his own careful research and ability to organize the material so as to present "the truth" (Luke 1:1-4).

III. Date and Place

Assignment of an exact date for the writing of Luke

is difficult, but since the gospel of Mark was the primary source used by Luke, the work must have been written after Mark. It is to be assumed that the Gospel was written before Acts (cf. Acts 1:1). Within those limits, scholars have assigned dates between A.D. 63 and 80. Several precise predictions would seem to describe what actually happened in the destruction of Jerusalem (A.D. 70) and thus be more easily explained if they were written after that date. Accordingly, critical scholars for the most part date the book to the years A.D. 80-85, prior to the collection and distribution of Paul's letters (*ca.* 90). This would accord with Luke's indication that he was not himself an eyewitness to the events recorded in the Gospel (Luke 1:2). Conservative scholars, however, contend that Jesus' predictions of Jerusalem's destruction (cf. 19:41-44; 21:20-24) can be understood as supernatural prophecies prior to the actual event, and thus argue for a date around A.D. 70.

According to the anti-Marcionite prologue the Gospel was written in Achaia (cf. Gregory of Nazianzus *Orations* xxiii.11), but the view has little convincing support. More likely places of origin are Rome or Antioch.

IV. Purpose

The purpose of the Gospel is given in Luke's own preface (1:1-4). Luke intended to write "an orderly account," a literary narration based upon careful research rather than a casual letter. At Acts 1:1 Luke summarizes what was accomplished in this first volume as the beginning of what "Jesus began to do and teach," while the second volume was intended to continue the record of Jesus' work through his apostles after the resurrection. Luke's concern is that Theophilus (and many more in the Gentile world who had become Christians) may know the "truth" or reliability of the facts of the gospel. "The things of which you have been informed" are the basic facts of the gospel, and this phrase indicates that the readers are members of the Church who have been catechized. The purpose is then to write a basic, well-organized, authentic, confirming account of the deeds and words of Jesus.

V. Characteristics and Content

Luke's gospel reflects his missionary interest. It is a work of joy and salvation, and reflects both a profound respect for the aspect of fulfillment of prophecy in Jesus and a deep gratitude for the fact that Jesus came "to seek and to save the lost" (19:10). Luke expresses sincere interest in human sentiment and emotion with regard to the fulfillment of Scripture in the Christ event. He totally understands the emotion of the experiences of Zechariah and Elizabeth at the birth of John the Baptist and those of Mary at the birth of Jesus. These emotions are expressed poetically in the Magnificat (1:46-55) and the Benedictus (vv. 68-79). Luke's ability to empathize is also graphically portrayed in the story of the tax collector who "would not even lift up his eyes to heaven, but beat his breast, saying, 'God, be merciful to me a sinner'" (18:13).

Luke's genuine interest in people is apparent in his accounts of the Good Samaritan, the Prodigal Son, and the forgiven sinner who washed the Savior's feet

with her tears (7:36-50). Luke is the most clearly universal Gospel; forgiveness, redemption, and the joy of salvation are for all mankind—pagans and Samaritans, publicans and sinners.

This Gospel seems also to be the most comprehensive. The genealogy of Jesus (3:23-38) is traced back through Adam to God, and Luke is the only Gospel to describe the Ascension (24:13-51). The so-called great insertion (9:51–19:27) contains primarily material not found in the other Gospels; it includes the well-known accounts of the sending out of the seventy disciples, Mary and Martha, the Rich Fool, the Lost Sheep, Zacchaeus, and the Parable of the Pounds.

Luke is the Gospel of love. It portrays the great compassion of Jesus and shows his concern for the one lost coin (15:8-10; cf. 3-7, 11-32). It shows how the ideal father who gives good gifts to his children is symbolic of the heavenly Father who will "give the Holy Spirit to those who ask him" (11:13). Luke encourages his followers to show the same love, kindness, and forgiveness to others: "Love your enemies, . . . bless those who curse you . . . Give to every one who begs from you" (6:27-30).

Bibliography. E. E. Ellis, *The Gospel of Luke.* NCBC (1981); J. A. Fitzmyer, *The Gospel According to Luke I-IX.* AB 28 (1981); *The Gospel According to Luke X–XXIV.* AB 28A (1985); I. H. Marshall, *Commentary on Luke.* NIGTC (1978).

LUST (Gk. *epithymía* "desire").* The word "lust" has become more narrow in meaning since the time of the KJV; the RSV generally reserves the term for passionate evil desires, usually sexual (cf. the verb *epithymeín*; also LXX, Exod. 20:17; Deut. 5:21; *see* COVET). As in English, the Greek term is of wide meaning, with particular meaning dependent on the context. It can represent any strong desires, including those that are sinful (e.g., Eph. 4:22; 1 John 2:16-17; cf. Rom. 7:7, "covet") and those that are not (e.g., Luke 22:15; Phil. 1:23; 1 Thess. 2:17; RSV "desire"), and can be as broad as materialism (Mark 4:19; Rev. 18:14; RSV "longed for") or as specific as sexual passion or obsession (Matt. 5:28; Rom. 1:24; 1 Thess. 4:5).

LUTE. "Lute" appears in the RSV to translate Heb. *nēḇel* (Ps. 150:3; elsewhere "harp") and *ʿāśôr* (lit. "ten"; 92:3 [MT 4] KJV "instrument of ten strings"; JB "zither"), which may represent the same musical instrument as *nēḇel ʿāśôr* (33:2; RSV "harp of ten strings"; 144:9; RSV "ten-stringed harp"). The ancient lute, a two- or three-stringed instrument with skin head and long neck (predecessor of the modern banjo), is attested in a relief at Carchemish (*ANEP*, no. 200) and an Egyptian tomb painting (no. 208). "Lutes" (NIV) may have been, with timbrels (tambourines), what the Israelite women played in celebration of David's killing of Goliath (1 Sam. 18:6; *šālîš*; KJV, RSV "instruments of music"; JB "lyre"; NJV "sistrums"); the term may indicate a triangle or three-stringed instrument (cf. RSV mg.).

LUZ [lŭz] (Heb. *lûz* "turn aside" or "take refuge"[?]).
1. The original name of BETHEL (**1**), renamed by Jacob (Gen. 28:19; 35:6; 48:3; Josh. 18:13; Judg. 1:23).

The reading "from Bethel to Luz" at Josh. 16:2 is difficult; the names may have represented two neighboring cities for a period, or the text should perhaps be emended to read "from Bethel-Luz," so using both names to represent the one location.

2. A city built in "the land of the Hittites" by a man of Bethel, whom the spies of Joseph allowed to escape the utter destruction of that city (Judg. 1:26). The location of this city is unknown, but "the land of the Hittites" probably refers to Syria northeast of the Orontes rather than to the center of the Hittite Empire in Anatolia.

LXX. See SEPTUAGINT.

LYCAONIA [lĭk′ĭ ō′nĭ ə, lī′kə ō′nĭ ə] (Gk. *Lykaonia*). A region situated on the dry Anatolian plateau north of the Taurus mountains of Cilicia and Pamphylia, east of Phrygia and Pisidia, south of the region of Galatia proper, and west of Cappadocia. During the first century A.D. the greater part of Lycaonia was within the Roman province of Galatia. Lystra and Derbe were Lycaonian cities in the province of Galatia (Acts 14:6). Iconium (13:51; 14:1, 19) was sometimes considered part of Lycaonia (cf. Strabo *Geog.* xii.6.3), but, as apparently in Acts, was more often considered part of Phrygia since its people were Phrygians. The Lycaonian language was spoken by the natives of the region (v. 11), who also understood the Greek spoken by Paul and Barnabas.

Jews were among the populace at Iconium (14:1, 19) but apparently few or no Jews were at Lystra (here Paul and Barnabas did not go first to a synagogue, as was their custom). Timothy, whose mother was Jewish, did live at least for a time in Lystra (16:1-2). Paul is known to have passed through Lycaonia twice (ch. 14; 16:1-5), and most likely at least a third time (cf. 18:23). The Lycaonian churches were probably a significant product of the Pauline mission and were among the addressees of the letter to the Galatians, if the "South Galatian" theory is correct (*see* GALATIANS, LETTER TO THE); nonetheless, other than the story of Paul's initial visit to Lystra (14:8-20), few details are offered in Acts concerning the history of these churches.

LYCIA [lĭsh′ĭ ə] (Gk. *Lykia*; Akk. *Lukki*). A mountainous region on the southwestern coast of Asia Minor, bounded on the west by Caria, on the north by Phrygia and Pisidia, and on the east by Pamphylia. The principal city was Xanthus (modern Günük). Anatolian elements akin to the Hittites are attested as early as the Bronze Age, and linguistic and onomastic evidence indicates a relationship to the Luwians. Occasional references to the Lukka/Lukki are found in Egyptian, Akkadian, and Ugaritic texts, and Lycian deities occur in Greek mythology. The region was conquered by Cyrus' general Harpagus and subsequently was incorporated into Alexander the Great's empire. The Romans established Lycia as a province in A.D. 43, and in 74 it was combined with Pamphylia.

Paul, on returning from his third missionary tour, landed at Patara, a city of Lycia, from which he later sailed to Tyre (Acts 21:1-3). When Paul was sent to Rome, the ship on which he was traveling put in at Myra, a Lycian harbor popular for westward-sailing ships because of the prevailing west winds; here Paul and the other prisoners were transferred to an Alexandrian ship en route to Italy (27:1-8).

According to 1 Macc. 15:15-24, a substantial Jewish population was settled in Lycia at the time of the Hasmoneans. The Christian church, however, apparently developed slowly in the region and may have faced considerable opposition until at least the fourth century.

LYDDA [lĭd′ə] (Gk. *Lydda*). Old Testament LOD, a city *ca.* 18 km. (11 mi.) southeast of Joppa (cf. Acts 9:38). Resettled following the return from exile (Ezra 2:33; Neh. 7:37; 11:35), the city became known as Lydda in Hellenistic times (the name occurs in a conquest list of Thutmose III, *ca.* 1500 B.C.; *ANET,* p. 243). The Seleucid king Demetrius II gave the city and the surrounding district to the Hasmonean Jonathan Maccabeus *ca.* 145 B.C. (1 Macc. 11:34), and Julius Caesar later granted control to the Jews under John Hyrcanus. Cassius captured the city *ca.* 45 B.C. and ordered the inhabitants sold into slavery, but their release was granted by Marcus Antonius. It was destroyed in A.D. 66 by the forces of Cestius Gallus as they marched to attack Jerusalem and was resettled two years later during the campaign of Vespasian. It was made a Roman colony *ca.* 200 and renamed Diospolis.

Lydda was the home of a fledgling Christian community in New Testament times (Acts 9:32, 35). It was here that Peter healed the paralytic Aeneas (vv. 33-34). Following the A.D. 70 destruction of Jerusalem the city became a center of rabbinic learning.

LYDIA [lĭd′ĭ ə] (Gk. *Lydia*) (**PERSON**). A woman from Thyatira residing in Philippi, who became a Christian and opened her home to Paul and his coworkers (Acts 16:14, 40). The name Lydia may have derived from her designation as "a woman from Lydia," a region in western Asia Minor where Thyatira, a small city with numerous craft guilds, is located. As a seller of purple cloth, an especially prized commodity (cf. Mark 15:17-20; Luke 16:19), Lydia was probably wealthy. She was a "God-fearer" (RSV "a worshipper of God"), a Gentile who worshipped with Jews although not a full convert to Judaism. Lydia apparently had adopted Philippi as her home, since she had a house there. After her conversion and baptism and the baptism of those in her household, this house became the home base for Paul's mission in Philippi (Acts 16:15, 40).

LYDIA [lĭd′ĭ ə] (Gk. *Lydia*) (**PLACE**).† A region and country in southwestern Asia Minor, named after its Iron Age inhabitants, the Lydians (Gk. *Ludoi*), an apparently Indoeuropean people perhaps related to the Luwians. The territory was bounded on the north by Mysia, on the east by Phrygia, and on the south by the Meander (modern Büyük Menderes) valley and Caria. The western border was the Aegean Sea, along which Greek colonies impinged upon Lydian territory. Most Lydian cities were inland, including the capital Sardis, Thyatira, and Philadelphia, all along the Hermus (modern Gediz) valley.

The early history of Lydia remains obscure. The Heraclid dynasty, which may have arisen during the widespread turmoil at the close of the Late Bronze Age (*ca.* 1200 B.C.), was defeated *ca.* 700 by Gyges, founder of the militant Mermnad ("Hawk") dynasty (Herodotus *Hist.* i.13). Gyges (685-652) attacked the Ionian cities on the Aegean coast, establishing Lydia's reputation as a formidable power (cf. Jer. 46:9; Heb. *lûdîm*). Aided by the Assyrian Assurbanipal, Gyges (Akk. *Guggu*) repelled Cimmerian invasion *ca.* 668, but *ca.* 654 he allied with the Egyptian Psamtik I (Psammetichus) against Assyria (cf. Ezek. 30:5; Heb. *lûd*); Gyges died when the Cimmerians again invaded. Subsequent kings faced constant pressure from the Scythians and Medes. King Alyattes expanded Lydian influence and forged a treaty with the Mede Cyaxares *ca.* 580, establishing the Halys river as the boundary between the two powers; according to tradition, Alyattes' daughter married the son of Cyaxares, and their daughter Mandanes became the mother of Cyrus the Great. Lydian fortunes increased through trade, diplomacy, and conquest under Alyattes' son and successor Croesus (560-546), whose personal wealth was legendary. Sardis fell to Cyrus the Great in 546, who made Lydia a Persian satrapy. The region became part of Alexander the Great's empire, was subsequently ruled by the Seleucids and Pergamum (cf. 1 Macc. 8:8), and was later incorporated into the Roman province of Asia.

LYE (Heb. *neter, bōr*), **SOAP** (*bōrît*).† Potassium carbonate lye was refined from wood ashes and combined with oils to produce soap. Lye and soap are both mentioned only in figures of speech, primarily for thorough moral purification, as at Job 9:30 (Heb. *bōr*; KJV "never so clean"); Jer. 2:22 (*neter, bōrît*); Mal. 3:2 (*bōrît*; see FULLER). Vinegar poured on lye (RSV mg.; KJV "nitre") is a figure for the defeat given when one "sings songs to a heavy heart" at Prov. 25:20 (RSV "wound," following the LXX, a figure of exacerbation of sorrow). At Isa. 1:25 "thoroughly" (cf. KJV "purely") is preferable to the RSV "as with lye"; the JB emends *kabōr* (*bōr* with the preposition *kᵉ*) to *bakūr* "in the furnace" (cf. NJV).

LYING (Heb. *šeqer, šāqar, kāhaš, kahaš, kāzab, kāzāb, šāw', šeqer, šāw'*; Aram. *kidbâ*; Gk. *pseúdos, pseúdomai, apseúdēs, dólos*).† Lying is condemned in a number of ways in the Bible, and never commended as a general practice. It is directly prohibited in the Pentateuch (Lev. 19:11; cf. 6:2-7 [MT 5:21-26]), and considered to be an aspect of wickedness (Ps. 58:3 [MT 4]); God regards liars as an abomination (Prov. 6:16-19; 12:19, 22) and will destroy them (Ps. 5:6 [MT 7] [cf. v. 9 (MT 10)]; Prov. 19:5, 9). The prohibition of false testimony in the Decalog (Exod. 20:16; Deut. 5:20) has in mind legal testimony. Provision was made in the pentateuchal laws to guard against false accusations and false testimony and to deal with lying witnesses (19:15-21; cf. Exod. 23:1-3). Similarly, because of the vitality ascribed to the spoken word, oaths were to be upheld and not allowed to become lies (Lev. 19:12; Num. 30:2 [MT 3]; cf. Exod. 20:7; Deut. 5:11).

Jesus forbade oaths as incapable of insuring the truth that his followers are to speak (Matt. 5:33-37; cf. 23:16-22; Jas. 5:12). Lying is among the practices that Paul urges Christians to put aside thoroughly (Eph. 4:25; Col. 3:9).

Lying and deception are characteristic of human nature from the earliest times (e.g., Gen. 3:10; 4:9). Abram tells Pharaoh that Sarai is his sister (12:10-20 (cf. 20:2, 5; 26:7-11), and Jacob gains his brother's birthright through deception (27:19, 24). Through a ruse the Gibeonites gain alliance with Joshua (Josh. 9:3-13). Samson lies to Delilah about the source of his strength (Judg. 16:7, 11, 13). The pervasiveness of lying is a theme in Old Testament laments (Ps. 12:2 [MT 3]; Jer. 9:3, 5 [MT 2, 4]; cf. Ps. 62:4 [MT 5]). Yet sometimes the deliverance or very survival of God's people was brought about through deception (e.g., Exod. 1:19-21; Josh. 2:4-5 [cf. Heb. 11:31]; Judg. 4:18-21; 5:24-27); certain incidents in David's flight from Saul (1 Sam. 21:2, 8, 13 [MT 3, 9, 14]) and Absalom (2 Sam. 17:20) can perhaps be so regarded. The accusation of lying, consciously or unconsciously, is often part of the true prophets' indictments against those prophets who do not represent the truth because of their allegiance to the aims of the government (e.g., 1 Kgs. 22:19-23; Jer. 5:31; 14:14; 23:14, 25-27, 32; 27:10, 14-16; Ezek. 13:3, 6, 8-12).

In the New Testament lies are associated with the devil as "a liar and the father of lies" (John 8:44; cf. Gen. 3:4), and are part of the persecution expected against Jesus' followers (Matt. 5:11). False prophets are expected in the end times (24:11, 24; Mark 13:22; Rev. 16:13; 19:20); many will believe lies rather than truth (2 Thess. 2:9-12; Rev. 20:7-8). But those who are redeemed by Christ will be committed to the truth (14:5; 21:27; cf. 1 John 2:21-27), just as is Christ (1 Pet. 2:22). Liars will be destroyed (Rev. 21:8; 22:15), as will Satan the deceiver (20:10).

LYRE (Heb. *kinnôr;* Aram. *qaytᵉrôs*). A stringed instrument used on festive occasions (e.g., Gen. 31:27; Job 21:12; KJV "harp"), in public worship (e.g., Ps. 43:4; 98:5; Dan. 3:5), and as accompaniment to or inducement of ecstatic prophecy (cf. 1 Sam. 10:5; 1 Chr. 25:1; cf. Ps. 49:4 [MT 5]). Its use is traced to Jubal (Gen. 4:21). The term used most often in the LXX to translate Heb. *kinnôr* is Gk. *kithára*, the "harp" of the New Testament. The English terms "harp" and "lyre" are generally used for triangular and quadrilateral instruments, both of which were widely known in the ancient world (cf. *ANEP,* nos. 3, 191-93, 199, 205, 208, 796-97). Lyres generally had six to eight strings attached to a sounding-box and plucked with the fingers or with a small stick.

See HARP.

LYSANIAS [lĭ sā'nĭ əs] (Gk. *Lysanias*). Tetrarch of Abilene during the fifteenth year of Tiberius' reign (A.D. 28-29 or 27-28), the beginning of John the Baptist's ministry (Luke 3:1). It was formerly thought that this mention of a Lysanias, ruler of Abilene, was an anachronistic reference to King Lysanias of Chalcis (which included Abilene) executed by Mark Antony in 36 B.C. But Josephus identifies Abilene specifically with a ruler named Lysanias (e.g., *Ant.* xx.7.1 [138]). Furthermore, an inscription mentioning a tetrarch

Lysanias has been found at Abila, capital of Abilene.
Why Luke mentions the ruler of Abilene in his temporal and geographical orientation (3:1-2) is not clear;
Jesus himself apparently never entered Abilene. The
solution may lie in the later rule of Herod Agrippa I
and II over Abilene, which may have brought Abilene
into closer association with Jewish Palestine.

LYSIAS [lĭs′ĭ əs] (Gk. *Lysias*).

1. A Seleucid nobleman, appointed regent over Syria
and guardian of the royal son Antiochus V Eupator
while Antiochus IV Ephiphanes attacked Persia in
166-165 B.C. Lysias was given command over half
the Syrian army, together with the elephants, and told
to destroy the Jews as part of his assignment (1 Macc.
3:31-37). The large army he dispatched suffered resounding defeat (3:38–4:25), and the following year
Lysias himself encamped against Judea at Beth-zur
(vv. 26-29); whether he was defeated by Judas Maccabeus (vv. 34-35) or at most managed a standstill
(cf. 2 Macc. 11:6-12), the resultant treaty restored
Jewish worship and led to the purification of the Jerusalem temple. Lysias insured his further power by
establishing Antiochus V as king of Syria upon his
father's death (1 Macc. 6:14-17). Together they defeated Judas at Beth-zechariah, but were forced by his
rival Philip to withdraw their siege against Jerusalem.
Lysias later defeated Philip at Antioch but was assassinated in Demetrius I Soter's bid for the throne (6:28–
7:4).

2. *See* CLAUDIUS LYSIAS.

LYSIMACHUS [lī sĭm′ə kəs] (Gk. *Lysimachos*).

1. The reported translator of Esther into Greek—
either the LXX version or the Lucianic recension of
the book (Add. Esth. 11:1)—and the possible author
of some of the Greek additions to Esther. Lysimachus
was the son of a Ptolemy (not to be identified with
either Ptolemy mentioned earlier in the verse) and a
resident of Jerusalem. Several couples named Ptolemy
and Cleopatra ruled Ptolemaic Egypt; the most likely
candidates are Ptolemy VIII Soter II and his wife, which
would date the fourth year to 114 B.C.

2. The brother of Menelaus, who outbid Jason the
high priest to obtain the high priesthood from Antiochus IV Epiphanes (171 B.C.) and who appointed
Lysimachus deputy high priest in his absence (2 Macc.
4:29). With his brother's aid, Lysimachus stole and
sold a number of the sacred gold vessels of the temple

and was then obliged to asemble a force of three thousand soldiers to defend himself from the enraged people. The mob routed this bodyguard with hastily
improvised weapons and killed Lysimachus (vv. 39-42).

LYSTRA [lĭs′trə] (Gk. *Lystra*). A city in the region
of Lycaonia and the province of Galatia some 20 mi.
(30 km.) south-southwest of Iconium (modern Konya)
near modern Hatunsaray (Khatyn Serai). The site may
have been inhabited as early as the third millennium
B.C. and was a rural settlement in Hellenistic times.
It was colonized by Caesar Augustus *ca.* 6 B.C. for
military purposes as a stronghold against the tribes of
the Taurus mountains to the south. A Roman road that
ran close to Iconium connected Lystra with Pisidian
Antioch and, in the other direction, with Cilicia and
Syria.

There were apparently few Jews at Lystra, inasmuch as Paul and Barnabas did not go first to a synagogue there as was their custom. Instead they spoke
immediately to the Gentile population, which, because
of a healing performed by Paul, took the two men to
be divine visitors, namely Zeus and Hermes (Acts
14:8-13). Paul and Barnabas did not understand the
Lycaonian language spoken by the people, but when
they realized that preparations were under way to accord them divine honors they intervened and instead
proclaimed the gospel (vv. 14-18). The Jews from
whom the two had escaped in Pisidian Antioch and
Iconium (13:50; 14:2-6) came into Lystra and persuaded the people of Lystra to oppose Paul and attempt to kill him (v. 19; cf. 2 Tim. 3:11). When Paul
and Silas later passed through Lystra, Timothy, a resident of the city, joined them (Acts 16:1-3).

The city mound of Lystra (W. S. LaSor)

M

M. A source-critical designation for material found only in the gospel of Matthew and therefore arising from neither Mark nor Q, the two common sources of Matthew and Luke.

MAACAH [mā′ə kə] (Heb. *maʿăkâ* "stupid [?]") (**PERSON**).

1. A son of Abraham's brother Nahor and Reumah (Gen. 22:24; KJV "Maachah"), perhaps to be identified as the eponymous ancestor of the kingdom of Maacah.

2. The mother of David's son Absalom and the daughter of Talmai, king of Geshur (2 Sam. 3:3; KJV "Maacah"; 1 Chr. 3:2; KJV "Maachah").

3. The father of King Achish of Gath, a contemporary of King Solomon (1 Kgs. 2:39; cf. "Maoch" at 1 Sam. 27:2).

4. The favorite wife of King Rehoboam of Judah, and the mother of King Abijam (1 Kgs. 15:2-3). At 2 Chr. 13:2 the mother of Abijam (Abijah) is called Micaiah, probably only an alteration of the name by scribal error. A more serious difficulty arises with regard to the identity of Abijam's maternal grandfather (i.e., Maacah's father), who is called Uriel of Gibeah at 2 Chr. 13:2 but Abishalom (i.e., Absalom the son of David and Maacah **2**) at 1 Kgs. 15:2; 2 Chr. 11:20-21. A more reasonable chronology is constructed if, as is usual, it is assumed that Maacah, Abijam's mother, was the daughter of Uriel and Tamar (1 Sam. 14:27) and therefore Absalom's granddaughter. Asa, Abijam's son (1 Kgs. 15:8), is also called the son of Maacah the (grand)daughter of Abishalom (v. 10); he was, in fact, her grandson. During Asa's reign Maacah was prominent in her role as queen mother until her deposition as part of Asa's reforming reaction against Canaanite fertility cults (v. 13; 2 Chr. 15:16).

5. A concubine of Caleb **2** (1 Chr. 2:48).

6. According to the apparently garbled text 1 Chr. 7:14-19, the sister (v. 15) or wife (v. 16) of Machir, the son of Manasseh and father of Gilead (cf. Num. 26:29).

7. The wife of Jeiel, ancestor of the Benjaminites of Gibeon and of King Saul (1 Chr. 8:29; 9:35).

8. The father of Hanan, one of David's mighty men (1 Chr. 11:43).

9. The father of Shephatiah, commander of the tribe of Simeon during David's reign (1 Chr. 27:16).

MAACAH [mā′ə kə] (Heb. *maʿăkâ*) (**PLACE**). A small Aramean (Syrian) kingdom in the Golan Heights south of Mt. Hermon, west of Bashan, east of the sources of the Jordan, and north of Geshur, another small kingdom with which it partly withstood the attempted Israelite conquest (Deut. 3:14; Josh. 12:5; 13:11); the form Maacath occurs at v. 13 (Heb. *maʿăkāṯ*). Maacah was again an independent kingdom at the time of David, when it allied with other Aramean kingdoms and the Ammonites. This alliance was defeated by Israel (2 Sam. 10:6 [KJV "king Maacah" should read "the king of Maacah"], 8; 1 Chr. 19:6 [RSV "Aram-maacah"; KJV "Syria-maacah"], 7). Individuals referred to as Maacathites (2 Sam. 23:34; 2 Kgs. 25:23; 1 Chr. 4:19; Jer. 40:8; KJV "Maachathites") are associated with the kingdom of Maacah or with the nearby city of Abel-beth-maacah, which was apparently associated with or part of the kingdom of Maacah at an early time but later regarded as a long-time Israelite possession (2 Sam. 20:15-19).

MAADAI [mā′ə dī] (Heb. *maʿăday*). An Israelite required to divorce his foreign wife (Ezra 10:34); called Momdius at 1 Esdr. 9:34.

MAADIAH [mā′ə dī′ə] (Heb. *maʿaḏyâ*). A priest or family of priests who returned with Zerubbabel from captivity in Babylon (Neh. 12:5). He may be the same as Moadiah at v. 17 or Maaziah at 10:8 (so one recension of the LXX at 12:5).

MAAI [mā′ī] (Heb. *māʿay*). A musician in the procession during the dedication of the walls of Jerusalem (Neh. 12:36).

MAALEH-ACRABBIM (Josh. 15:3, KJV). *See* AKRABBIM.

MAARATH [mā′ə răth] (Heb. *maʿărāṯ* "barren place"). A city in the tribal territory of Judah linked with other cities north of Hebron. It is probably to be identified with Khirbet Qufin, a site adjacent to modern Beit Ummar (Josh. 15:59), 10.5 km. (6.5 mi.) north of Hebron. Maroth (Mic. 1:12) may be the same city.

MAASAI [mā'ə sī] (Heb. *ma'śay* "the work of Yahweh"). A priest in postexilic Jerusalem and a descendant of Immer (1 Chr. 9:12; KJV "Maasiai"). He may be the same as Amashsai (Neh. 11:13).

MAASEIAH [mā'ə sē'yə] (Heb. *ma'ăśēyâ, ma'ăśēyāhû* "work of Yahweh").
1. A Levite musician who performed when the ark was taken to Jerusalem (1 Chr. 15:18, 20).
2. A commander who supported the priest Jehoiada in the overthrow of Queen Athaliah of Judah, resulting in the enthronement of Joash (2 Chr. 23:1).
3. An official of King Uzziah who, with Jeiel the secretary and Hanaiah the commander, organized the army of Judah (2 Chr. 26:11).
4. A son of King Ahaz of Judah killed by Zichri of Ephraim during the invasion by King Pekah of Israel (2 Chr. 28:7).
5. A governor of Jerusalem appointed by King Josiah as one of the overseers for the repair of the temple (2 Chr. 34:8).
6. A priest of the "sons of Jeshua" (5) whom Ezra required to divorce his foreign wife (Ezra 10:18; 1 Esdr. 9:19; KJV "Matthelas").
7. A priest of the family or guild of Harim among those required to divorce their foreign wives (Ezra 10:21; 1 Esdr. 9:21; KJV "Eanes").
8. A priest, descendant or follower of Pashhur, who pledged to divorce his foreign wife (Ezra 10:22; 1 Esdr. 9:22; KJV "Massias").
9. An Israelite of the lineage of Pahath-moab who was required to divorce his foreign wife (Ezra 10:30). He may be the same as Moossias at 1 Esdr. 9:31. He may be the same as **11** or **13**.
10. The father of Azariah **20**, who helped repair the walls of Jerusalem (Neh. 3:23).
11. One of those standing on the platform with Ezra as he read the Book of the Law (Neh. 8:4; cf. 1 Esdr. 9:43, "Baalsamus"). He may be the same as **9** or **13**.
12. An Israelite who participated in the sealing of plained) the law to the people after Ezra's reading (Neh. 8:7; 1 Esdr. 9:48; RSV mg. "Maiannas"; KJV "Maianeas").
13. An Israelite who participated in the sealing of the new covenant under Nehemiah (Neh. 10:25); perhaps the same as **9** or **11**.
14. A man from Judah who lived in Jerusalem after the Exile (Neh. 11:5). At 1 Chr. 9:5 he is called Asaiah (**4**).
15. An ancestor of a Benjaminite clan head contemporary with Nehemiah (Neh. 11:7). He is not mentioned in the account at 1 Chr. 9:7-8.
16. A priest who played the trumpet at the dedication of the walls of Jerusalem (Neh. 12:41). He may be the same as **6**, **7**, or **8**.
17. A musician who participated in the dedication of the rebuilt walls (Neh. 12:42). It was apparently a priest, perhaps the same as **6**, **7**, or **8**..
18. The father of Zephaniah the priest, a contemporary of Jeremiah and King Zedekiah (Jer. 21:1; 29:25; 37:3).

19. The father of the false prophet Zedekiah (Jer. 29:21).
20. (Jer. 32:12; 51:59, KJV). *See* MAHSEIAH.
21. A temple doorkeeper during the days of Jeremiah (Jer. 35:4).

MAASIAI (1 Chr. 9:12, KJV). *See* MAASAI.

MAATH [mā'ăth] (Gk. *Maath*). A postexilic ancestor of Jesus (Luke 3:26).

MAAZ [mā'ăz] (Heb. *ma'aṣ*). A Judahite, son of Ram and grandson of Jerahmeel (1 Chr. 2:27).

MAAZIAH [mā'ə zī'ə].
1. The eponymous founder of the twenty-fourth division of priests during the reign of David (1 Chr. 24:18; Heb. *ma'azyāhû*).
2. A priest who participated in the sealing of the new covenant under Nehemiah (Neh. 10:8 [MT 9]; Heb. *ma'azyâ*).

MACCABEES [măk'ə bēz].† The family and immediate successors of Mattathias, who in 167 B.C. initiated the Jewish revolt against the Hellenistic abuses of Antiochus IV Epiphanes. The appellative, presumed to derive from the epithet of Mattathias' son Judas Maccabeus (Gk. *Makkabaios*, from Heb. *maqqābî* "hammerlike" or "hammerhead"; cf. 1 Macc. 2:4), is applied primarily to Judas and his brothers Jonathan and Simon.

Later tradition also identifies as Maccabees the seven brothers who with their mother were martyred for refusing "to partake of unlawful swine's flesh" (2 Macc. 7; cf. 4 Maccabees).

See HASMONEANS and the individual entries.

MACCABEES, BOOKS OF.† Four apocryphal or deuterocanonical (1 and 2 Maccabees) and pseudepigraphal (3 and 4 Maccabees) books, independent in origins yet concerning the struggle of the Jews against Hellenism during the intertestamental period.

I. 1 Maccabees

A history of the Jews under the Hasmonean dynasty, from the accession of Antiochus IV Epiphanes and the Maccabean revolt to the death of Simon and the accession of John Hyrcanus I (175-135 B.C.). Its original title may have been "The Scroll of the Hasmonean House" or "The Book of the House of the Princes of God."

A. *Contents*. 1 Macc. 1 provides the historical background for the Maccabean revolt: the conquests of Alexander the Great, division of his empire, the rise of Antiochus IV and his paganizing influence, invasion of Egypt and Palestine, and the deliberate desecration of the Jerusalem temple, depicted as an effort to establish a Hellenistic state religion. Ch. 2 records the revolt by Mattathias and his sons (2:1-48), the death of the aged priest, and the succession of his son Judas (vv. 49-70).

Judas' military and political fortunes are set forth at length in 3:1–9:22. Included are accounts of his early victories over Apollonius and Seron (3:1-26), his defeat of Lysias at Emmaus and Beth-zur (3:27–

4:35), the restoration of the temple (vv. 36-61), and various campaigns against Idumea, Ammon, Gilead, Galilee, and the coastal plain (ch. 5). Ch. 6 narrates the death of Antiochus IV, the accession of Antiochus V Eupator, his attack on the citadel at Jerusalem, Judas' second battle at Beth-zur, and Lysias' offer of peace, prompted by the return of the coregent Philip. The following chapter recounts Demetrius I Soter's usurpation, his appointment of Alcimus as high priest, and Judas' last great victory, his defeat of Nicanor. Judas' alliance with Rome is delineated in ch. 8. His death in battle with Bacchides is recorded in 9:1-22.

The career of Judas' brother Jonathan is summarized in 9:23-12:53, beginning with his succession (9:23-31) and victory over Bacchides (vv. 32-73). Ch. 10 depicts Alexander Balas' claim of kingship and his appointment of Jonathan as high priest (10:1-21), Demetrius' overtures to the Jews and his defeat by Jonathan ca. 150 (vv. 22-50), and the strengthening of Alexander's relations with Egypt and Judea (vv. 51-66); vv. 67-89 record the challenge to succession by Demetrius II and Jonathan's defeat of Apollonius at Azotus. Ch. 11 records the invasion of Ptolemy VI Philometor, his defeat of Alexander, the triumph of Demetrius (11:1-19), Jonathan's siege of the Jerusalem citadel, his pact with and aid to Demetrius (vv. 20-52), and their subsequent falling out (vv. 53-74). Jonathan's exploits conclude with accounts of his alliances with Rome and the Spartans (12:1-23) and his capture by the Syrian general Trypho (vv. 24-53).

The concluding chapters concern events during the leadership of Simon, Mattathias' last surviving son (13:1-16:24). Assuming that Jonathan was dead, Simon gathers troops to withstand Trypho's invasion; in the meantime the Syrian kills Jonathan in Galilee (13:1-30). Threatened by Trypho's claim to power after assassinating Antiochus VI, Demetrius names Simon high priest (vv. 36-40); Simon captures the citadel and gains political independence for Judea (vv. 43-53). Ch. 14 records the Parthians' defeat and capture of Demetrius (14:1-3) and summarizes Simon's beneficent rule as high priest, military commander, and ethnarch (vv. 4-49). The subsequent narrative relates the overture of Antiochus VII Sidetes, Simon's renewal of relations with Rome, and the outbreak of war with Antiochus (15:1-16:10). The book concludes with the death of Simon at the hand of the Galilean governor Ptolemy and the accession of John Hyrcanus as high priest (vv. 11-24).

B. Origins. Although the oldest extant text is that of the LXX, underlying Semitic idioms suggest that 1 Maccabees was first composed in Hebrew. The anonymous author was apparently a Palestinian Jew, writing to advance the Hasmonean cause ca. 100 B.C., at the time of Alexander Jannaeus; some scholars would place it during the reign of Hyrcanus, perhaps a decade or so earlier or as early as 135.

The author or compiler of this "official history" of the rise of the Hasmonean dynasty employed a number of sources, including royal epistles (e.g., 8:20-32; 10:23-45; 15:2-9), temple documents (cf. 14:23, 49), chronicles (16:23-24), and other archival sources (cf. 11:37; 15:24). In addition, the book contains poetic materials, some of which may be contemporary with the events (e.g., 1:24-28, 36-40; 2:7-13; 3:3-9, 45,

50-53; 14:4-15). Claiming that Josephus did not rely on chs. 14-16 for his *Jewish Antiquities,* some scholars have suggested that these chapters are a later addition, but the argument is now generally discounted.

C. Evaluation. Despite certain errors or anachronisms (e.g., 5:6, where more than one Timothy may be involved; 6:20, where the dating is in question [cf. 2 Macc. 13:1]; 1 Macc. 6:55-66, where the wrong Philip is noted) and omissions (cf. 9:22), 1 Maccabees is regarded as a reliable, albeit partisan, source for the period represented. In similar fashion to the canonical history (e.g., 1-2 Samuel, 1-2 Kings), 1 Maccabees depicts the Hasmoneans as God's chosen agents of salvation (cf. 5:62; 9:21), rewarded for their faithfulness to the law (cf. 2:67-68; 14:14), although neither the name of God nor his biblical epithets are cited (cf. 3:18-19, 50; 12:15, "Heaven").

Bibliography. J. A. Goldstein, *I Maccabees.* AB41 (1976).

II. 2 Maccabees

A history of the Maccabean revolt through the defeat of Nicanor (ca. 180-161 B.C.), thus parallel to 1 Macc. 1:10-7:50. It is an abridgment or epitome of a five-volume history by Jason of Cyrene (2 Macc. 2:23).

A. Contents. The history is prefaced by two letters from the Jews in Jerusalem and Judea to those in Egypt (1:1-9) and the priest Aristobulus (1:10-2:18), urging celebration of the Feast of Hanukkah and a prologue by the author or epitomist (vv. 19-32).

Events and conditions leading to the revolt are elaborated upon in chs. 3-7. Simon, captain of the temple and a descendant of Tobias, plots against the pious high priest Onias III and incites the greed of King Seleucus IV; Heliodorus, ordered by the king to loot the temple treasury, is impeded by an apparition and scourged by God's power. Although Simon perpetrates further intrigues, Onias is replaced by his brother Jason, who attains the high priesthood by bribing the new king Antiochus IV (4:1-22); he in turn is supplanted by Menelaus, who arranges the murder of Onias and continues the Hellenization sponsored by Jason (vv. 23-50). Ch. 5 portrays Antiochus' desecration of the Jerusalem temple as retaliation for Jason's attempt to overthrow Menelaus; in the meantime, "Judas Maccabeus, with about nine others," escapes to the wilderness (v. 27). Antiochus now seeks to obliterate Jewish practices (6:1-6), and many of the faithful are martyred (6:7-7:42).

2 Macc. 8-15 depict the career of Judas Maccabeus. With prayerful consideration (8:1-4), he organizes an army (vv. 5-7) and repels Nicanor's invasion (vv. 8-29); other victories follow (vv. 30-36). Antiochus becomes mortally ill (9:1-12), but repents before his death (vv. 13-29). Judas and his forces then recover the temple and purify it (10:1-9). Judas' many victories during the reign of Antiochus V are recorded in 10:10-12:45; ch. 13 narrates the death of Menelaus and the unsuccessful attack of Antiochus and Lysias on Beth-zur. Following the accession of Demetrius I, Nicanor (now governor of Judea) again invades; bolstered by a vision of Onias III in which he is given a sword from God, Judas is victorious (14:1-15:36). An epilogue by the epitomist is appended at vv. 37-39.

B. Origins. Apart from this abridgment, nothing is

known of Jason of Cyrene. The abridger, who not only condensed but also embellished Jason's weighty account (cf. 2:23-31), wrote in highly literate Greek apparently for the Jewish community at Alexandria, of which he himself may have been a member (cf. indications that he was unfamiliar with the geography of Palestine; e.g., 12:21; 15:7-30). This condensation may be dated to the reign of Alexander Jannaeus (103-76 B.C.), and certainly before Jerusalem fell to Pompey in 63 B.C. (cf. 2 Macc. 15:37). Jason's history itself was composed after 1 Maccabees, and probably before 86 B.C.

C. *Evaluation*. Classified as sensational or "pathetic" history typical of contemporary Greek writers, 2 Maccabees includes highly emotional accounts of the early martyrs (e.g., 6:7-7:42; 14:37-46; cf. Heb. 11:35-37) and vivid depictions of heroic feats (e.g., 8:8-29; 11:6-15) and horrendous atrocities (e.g., 1:16; 14:41-46; cf. 9:5-12). Although occasionally correcting the record of 1 Maccabees (cf. 13:1), 2 Maccabees is clearly "theological history," conscientiously demonstrating the role of God in behalf of his people (e.g., 10:1; 15:27), frequently portrayed through apparitions and other suprahuman manifestations (e.g., 3:24ff.; 5:2-4; 10:29-31). Piety and obedience to the law are rewarded by success (e.g., 8:36), and disobedience provokes calamity, divine punishment "designed not to destroy but to discipline our people" (6:12-16). Accordingly, the early Hasmoneans are portrayed here as less than ideal figures (e.g., 10:19-22; cf. 12:40; 14:17).

An important theme is the sanctity of "the most holy temple in all the world" (e.g., 2:19, 22; 5:15; 14:31, 35-36), the "greatest and first fear" of the Jews (15:18). Other distinctive concepts include God's creation of the world ex nihilo (7:28), the resurrection of the dead (e.g., 7:9, 14, 23, 29, 36; 14:46), intercession of the saints (15:11-16), and sacrifices in behalf of the dead (12:43-45).

Bibliography. J. A. Goldstein, *II Maccabees*. AB 41A (1983).

III. 3 Maccabees

A polemical account of Ptolemy IV Philopator's persecutions of the Jews *ca.* 217 B.C., one-half century prior to the Maccabean revolt. Despite similarities of theme (Hellenistic assault on Jewish practice) and incidents recorded (attempted violation of the temple, divine intervention; cf. 2 Macc. 3), the book may more properly be titled "Ptolemaica."

Presumably composed in Greek, the book was included in Codex Alexandrinus and the Syriac Peshitta, and exists in a later Armenian version. Although intended to provide inspiration to the Jewish community in time of crisis, its lack of clear historical allusions preclude dating the book more precisely than after the battle of Raphia (217 B.C.) and before the destruction of the temple (A.D. 70); scholars have sought to associate it with the Roman annexation of Egypt in 24 B.C. or the persecutions of Caligula (A.D. 40). Language and style, as well as content suggest that the work originated among the Jews of Alexandria.

Spared from attempted assassination by the Jew Dositheos, Ptolemy defeats the Seleucid Antiochus III

at Raphia (3 Macc. 1:1-5). Passing through Jerusalem on his return home, the triumphant king seeks to enter the temple (vv. 6-16), to the great consternation of the Jews (vv. 17-29). In response to the supplication of the high priest Simon, Ptolemy is thwarted by sudden paralysis (2:1-20). Upon his return to Alexandria, he restricts the civil and religious freedom of all Jews who refuse to acknowledge Dionysius (vv. 21-31). When most of the Jews resist, Ptolemy orders the arrest and annihilation of all Jews in his kingdom (chs. 3-4). Five hundred drunken elephants are to trample the recalcitrant Jews, but twice the intended victims are spared by divine intervention; instead, the herd turns upon the king and his army (5:1 — 6:29). Ptolemy repents and decrees for the Jews a seven-day thanksgiving feast (vv. 30-41), instructing his governors to protect them (7:1-9). The Jews are permitted to execute those who had abandoned the faith and to return home (vv. 10-23).

IV. 4 Maccabees

A discourse or treatise on the supremacy of inspired (or religious) reason over the passions (e.g., 4 Macc. 1:30, "For reason is the guide of the virtues and the supreme master of the passions"). Called "On the Supremacy of Reason" by Eusebius (*HE* iii.10.6) and Jerome (*De vir. ill.* 13), who attribute it to Flavius Josephus, the work advocates faithfulness to the Jewish law, which is the sole means of fulfilling the Greek ideal of virtue. It was written in Greek by a faithful Jew well acquainted with Greek philosophy, presumably at Alexandria or perhaps Antioch of Syria in the period between Pompey's conquest of Jerusalem (63 B.C.) and Hadrian's destruction of the temple (A.D. 70). The text is preserved in Codex Sinaiticus and the Syriac Peshitta.

The author immediately sets forth his premise (1:1-6), which he contends is best demonstrated by the early martyrs under Antiochus IV Epiphanes (vv. 7-12)—hence the book's association with the Maccabees). He then expounds upon the relationship of reason and emotion (vv. 13-35), the compatibility of reason and the law (as illustrated in the lives of the patriarchs; ch. 2), and the conquest of the passions by reason (as demonstrated by David; ch. 3). Following an account of the thwarted violation of the temple by Apollonius (4:1-14; cf. 2 Macc. 3:7-34, "Heliodorus") and the abuses of Antiochus IV (4 Macc. 4:15-26), the author intersperses lurid descriptions of the torture of Eleazar (cf. 2 Macc. 6:18-31), the seven brothers, and their mother (cf. 2 Macc. 7) and speeches of the martyrs' triumph through devout reason (4 Macc. 5:1-17:6). The work concludes with an assessment of the martyrdoms' effect (17:7-18:5), the mother's address to her children (vv. 6-19), and a doxology (vv. 20-24).

Of theological interest are indications of the author's belief in the immortality of the soul (e.g., 16:13; 17:12; 18:23; cf. 14:5-6) and the vicarious atonement of the righteous martyrs, "a ransom for the sin of our nation" (6:28-29; 17:21-22).

MACEDONIA [măs´ə dō´nĭ ə] (Gk. *Makedonia*).†
The region of the Balkan peninsula north of Achaia. The region had long been the major land route from Asia Minor to the West when the Egnatian Way was

constructed in 146 B.C.; this road went from Byzantium in the East through the Aegean ports of Macedonia (Neapolis [near Philippi], Amphipolis, and Thessalonica) to Dyrrhachium and Apollonia on the Adriatic.

Displacing the indigenous tribes at the beginning of the seventh century B.C., the Macedonians established an independent monarchy under King Perdikkas I. Skirmishes with neighboring peoples such as the Thracians and Illyrians and alliance with or vassalage to Athens, Sparta, and Persia characterized much of the state's early history. In 359 Philip II consolidated the army and political factions and quelled neighboring tribes; through diplomacy and military action he extended Macedonian dominion throughout Greece and into Asia Minor. After Philip's assassination in 336, his son Alexander ("the Great") conquered the Persian Empire and subdued territory as far as the Nile and the Indus rivers. Alexander's death in 323 led to an intense and extended power struggle, with the conquered eventually divided among the Antigonids, Ptolemies, and Seleucids. In 276 Antigonus II Gonatus established control over Macedonia, but after decades of struggle against the rising Roman power Macedonia fell at Pydna in 168. Although regarded as free, Macedonia was divided into four separate republics (Pella, Thessalonica, Amphibolis, and Pelagonia). Responding to a revolt incited by a pretender to the line of Perseus, the Romans in 148 B.C. incorporated Macedonia into a protectorate encompassing all Greece. In 27 B.C. Augustus divided Macedonia and Greece (Achaia) into two separate provinces. Claudius made it a senatorial province in A.D. 44.

Responding to his vision of "a man of Macedonia" (Acts 16:9-10), Paul crossed over to Neapolis and founded churches in Macedonia at Philippi, Thessalonica, and Beroea (Acts 16:11–17:13). He later passed through Macedonia at least twice (19:21; 20:1, 3; cf. 1 Cor. 16:5; 2 Cor. 1:16; 2:13; 7:5). The churches of Macedonia quickly became quite significant in the spread of the gospel, in cooperation among churches, and in the support of Paul's mission work (Acts 19:29; 20:4; Rom. 15:26-27; 2 Cor. 8:1; 11:9; Phil. 1:5-6; 4:10-18; 1 Thess. 1:8).

See Greece.

MACHAERUS [mə kîr'əs] (Gk. *Machairous*). A fortress in the hills of Moab near the Dead Sea, located at modern Mukâwer (Mukâwer), east of Callirrhoe. The fortress was built by Alexander Jannaeus, destroyed by the Romans, and rebuilt by Herod the Great. After the death of Herod, Machaerus became the property of Herod Antipas, who had John the Baptist beheaded there (Josephus *Ant.* xviii.5.2 [119]; cf. Mark 6:14-29). Machaerus was one of the three fortresses which were held by Jewish rebel forces even after the fall of Jerusalem during the war with Rome which began in A.D. 66; the Jewish defenders surrendered the fortress in 71.

MACHBANNAI [măk băn'ī] (Heb. *makbannay*). One of the Gadite "mighty and experienced warriors" who joined David's rebel band at Ziklag and became officers in his army (1 Chr. 12:13 [MT 14]; KJV "Machbanai").

MACHBENAH [măk bē'nə] (Heb. *makbēnâ*). A name in a Judahite genealogy collection probably representing a town in Judah (1 Chr. 2:49). No location has been identified with this name, though identifications with Cabbon (Josh. 15:40) and with Meconah (Neh. 11:28) have been suggested.

MACHI [mā'kī] (Heb. *māki*). The father of the spy Geuel, of the tribe of Gad (Num. 13:15).

MACHIR [mā'kîr] (Heb. *mākîr*).†

1. The firstborn son of MANASSEH 1 and his Aramean concubine Asriel (Josh. 17:1; cf. 13:31; Num. 26:29). He was the eponymous ancestor of the Machirites (usually called simply Machir), and the father of Gilead, the ancestor of the Gileadites (Gen. 50:23; Num. 26:29; 1 Chr. 7:14).

Two aspects of the settlement of the Machirites receive repeated notice: they conquered and received permission to inhabit part of the Amorite region of Gilead (Num. 32:39, 40; Deut. 3:15; Josh. 13:31; 17:1; cf. 1 Chr. 2:21-23); Zelophehad, the grandson of Gilead, had daughters only, and provision was made for them to receive land (Num. 26:33; 27:1-11; 36:1-12; Josh. 17:3-6; 1 Chr. 7:15). At Judg. 5:14 Machir is a place name referring to some part of the territory of the Machirites, here west of the Jordan river (cf. 27:1, where some of Zelophehad's daughters may represent names of places west of the Jordan; cf. R. G. Boling and G. E. Wright, *Joshua.* AB [1982], pp. 347, 410).

2. A resident of Lo-debar in whose house Mephibosheth, the son of Jonathan, lived for a time (2 Sam. 9:4-5). Later he assisted David during his flight from Absalom (17:27).

MACHNADEBAI [măk năd'ə bī] (Heb. *maknadᵉbay*).† An Israelite required to divorce his foreign wife (Ezra 10:40). The RSV reads the name in the parallel account at 1 Esdr. 9:34 (Gk. *Mamnitanaimos*; KJV "Mamnitanaimus"; cf. RSV mg.).

MACHPELAH [măk pē'lə] (Heb. *makpēlâ* "double"). A cave which Abraham purchased from Ephron the Hittite in order to bury Sarah (Gen. 23:19). Abraham himself (25:8-9), Isaac, Rebekah, Leah (49:31), Jacob (50:13), and possibly others (cf. Jub. 46:9; T. Jos. 20:6) were buried there as well.

The name may have been applied first to the cave, apparently a "double" cave, and then extended to the field adjacent to or around the cave (Gen. 23:19; 50:13) and to the surrounding area (23:17; 49:30). The purchase of the cave and the field by Abraham from Ephron the Hittite is carefully related (ch. 23) and repeatedly referred to (25:10; 49:30; 50:13) because it marked the first Israelite ownership of land in Palestine; as such, it was a unique prefiguration of the fulfillment of the promises of God (cf. 12:7). According to later Jewish tradition, the path to the garden of Eden begins within the cave.

The traditional site of the cave is marked by a primarily Herodian enclosure, the Ḥaram el-Khalil, and a mosque (originally a Byzantine church) at Hebron (cf. 23:19).

MACRON. *See* Ptolemy 12.

MADAI [mā'dī] (Heb. *māḏay* "Media"). A son of Japheth (Gen. 10:2; 1 Chr. 1:5), eponym of Media (cf. 2 Kgs. 17:6; Isa. 21:2).

MADIAN (Acts 7:29, KJV). *See* MIDIAN.

MADMANNAH [măd măn'ə] (Heb. *maḏmannâ*). According to a Judahite genealogy (1 Chr. 2:49), the son of Shaaph, a descendant of Caleb through his concubine Maacah. The name represents a town in Judah's tribal allotment among the towns "toward the boundary of Edom in the Negeb" (Josh. 15:21, 31; RSV reads "extreme south" for "Negeb"). In the parallel list at 19:5, here attributed to Simeon, Madmannah is replaced by Beth-marcaboth; some would also identify it with Meconah in the Judahite list at Neh. 11:28, but this town has also been identified with Machbenah in 1 Chr. 2:49. Some scholars have suggested that the four names may indeed represent the same site.

Although a location near Beersheba and Ziklag is required, the various names have not been identified conclusively with any site. Possibilities include Khirbet Umm ed-Deimneh, *ca.* 16 km. (10 mi.) northeast of Beersheba, and the nearby Khirbet Tatrît.

MADMEN [măd'mĕn] (Heb. *maḏmēn*). A city in Moab (Jer. 48:2). It is probably the same as Dimon and thus identified with Khirbet Dimneh, *ca.* 13 km. (8 mi.) east of the Dead Sea, south of the Arnon river and north of Kir-haresheth.

MADMENAH [măd mē'nə] (Heb. *maḏmēnâ* "dunghill"). A city north of Jerusalem, along the route by which Isaiah prophesied the Assyrians would attack (Isa. 10:31). It is perhaps located at modern Shu'fat, *ca.* 3 km. (2 mi.) north of Jerusalem.

MADNESS.* In English usage, "madness" and related terms ("mad," "madman") designate a number of human conditions, most basic of which is unusual or bizarre behavior. This is represented in the biblical accounts primarily by Heb. *šāgaʿ*, *šiggāʿôn*; Gk. *maínomai*, *manía*. Ecstatic prophecy is associated with madness in this sense, generally where a negative view of the prophet(s) is taken (e.g., 2 Kgs. 9:11; Jer. 29:26; Hos. 9:7; cf. 1 Sam. 10:10-12; 19:20-24; 1 Kgs. 18:28). David acted the part of a madman when he realized that his life was in danger in the court of Achish ("he changed [i.e., disguised] his judgment"; 1 Sam. 21:13-15 [MT 14-16]; cf. Ps. 34 superscription). In the New Testament madness is ascribed to a person or a group because of the manner or message of their speaking, sometimes with hostility in the accusation (John 10:20; Acts 12:15; 26:24-25; 1 Cor. 14:23).

Bizarre behavior is often associated with the activity of supernatural beings, including God. This is in keeping with the ancient worldview, evidenced in the Old Testament, which saw intense emotion, great skill, ecstatic speech, and sickness as manifestations not of forces within a person but of forces working upon a person from the outside. So it was with the ecstatic prophets, and David's ploy was probably effective because it was perceived as involving such powerful su-

pernatural forces. Saul's moody, sometimes violent, behavior, beginning after his rejection by Samuel and exacerbated by his jealousy of David, was initiated by the substitution of an evil spirit from God for the Spirit of the Lord which had been upon him (1 Sam. 16:14-23; 18:10-11; 20:30-33). The main message is God's sovereignty in the downfall of Saul, but the underlying idea is the ascription of strange behavior to supernatural forces. God himself can be, in his judgment of sin, the being who brings about madness, whether directly or indirectly, as the punishments he brings drive people to madness (Deut. 28:28, 34; Dan. 4:23-37; Zech. 12:4). The seemingly inflated claims of Jesus led some to the dismissal, "He has a demon, and he is mad," two statements nearly equivalent in meaning (John 10:20). New Testament demonology exhibits development beyond the Old Testament concept: the forces (demons and spirits) that cause insanity and disease are in the New Testament entirely malevolent; the "madness" of prophets is closer to acceptance in the Old Testament than in the New Testament.

A different kind of "madness," the madness not of a person acting strangely but of the FOOL, the person characterized by stupidity and wickedness, is commonly designated by forms of Heb. *hālal* and related words (Eccl. 1:17; 2:2, 12; 7:7, 25; 9:3; 10:13; Isa. 44:25) and by Gk. *paraphronía* and *paraphronéō* (2 Cor. 11:23; 2 Pet. 2:16).

MADON [mā'dŏn] (Heb. *māḏôn*). A Canaanite city which joined in an ill-fated alliance against the Israelite conquest (Josh. 11:1; 12:19). Qarn Ḥaṭṭîn, *ca.* 8.5 km. (5.5 mi.) northwest of Tiberias, has been suggested as the site.

MAGADAN [măg'ə dăn] (Gk. *Magadan*).* A region on or near the Sea of Galilee (Matt. 15:39). Neither Magadan nor Dalmanutha, which appears in the Markan parallel (Mark 8:10), are known place names; indeed, Magadan has been located variously on the eastern and western shores of the Sea. KJV "Magdala" at Matt. 15:39 represents a variant reading which is not to be preferred. Gk. *Magada* represents Heb. *migdāl* "tower" in one recension of the LXX at Josh. 15:37 (RSV "Migdal-gad"); this suggests that "Magadan" may have been the name of some region named for a tower or that it may be an alternative Greek representation of the name of the town Magdala. *See* MAGDALENE.

MAGBISH [măg'bĭsh] (Heb. *magbîš*). A place in Judah settled by those who returned with Zerubbabel from exile (Ezra 2:30). The site may be modern Khirbet el-Mahbiyeh, 5 km. (3 mi.) southwest of Adullam.

MAGDALENE [măg'də lēn] (Gk. *Magdalēnē* "from Magdala"). A gentilic, from Magdala (cf. Matt. 15:39, KJV; RSV "Magadan"), designating MARY 2, a principal follower of Jesus (e.g., 27:56, 61 par.; 28:1; Mark 16:9; Luke 8:2; 24:10 par.). Magdala (Aram. *migḏelā'* "tower"), also known as Tarichaea, was northwest of Tiberias at the western tip of the Sea of Galilee. A modern town, Mejdel, is on the site.

MAGDIEL [măg'dĭ əl] (Heb. *magdîʾēl*). A tribal

chief of Edom and descendant of Esau (Gen. 36:43; 1 Chr. 1:54).

MAGGOT. *See* WORM.

MAGI [mā'jī].† Gk. *mágos* (pl. *mágoi,* translated "magi" or "wise men"), designated originally a type of Median or Zoroastrian priest (cf. Herodotus *Hist.* i.101). By New Testament times the term was used quite broadly for persons adept in any of a number of secret arts, including dream interpretation, mediation of divine messages, astrology, fortune-telling, magic, and divination (cf. Philo *De spec. leg.* iii.18.100-101), whether such persons were regarded positively or negatively. The Greek term is applied to the "magi from the East" who came to pay homage to Jesus (Matt. 2:1, 7, 16) and to Elymas Bar-Jesus, apparently a magician-prophet in the employ of Sergius Paulus (Acts 13:6, 8; RSV "magician"; KJV "sorcerer"). A participle of the related verb *mageúō,* lit. "function as a *magos,*" and the noun *mageía* "activity of a *magos*" (RSV "magic," "sorceries") are used with reference to Simon Magus (Acts 8:9, 11), who was not only a simple magician but a man with considerable claims and a large following.

See WISE MEN.

MAGIC.† The attempted manipulation of events through charms, amulets, incantations, and the like. In the ancient world, magic was not sharply distinguished from religion. In polytheistic religion no power is thought of as having final control over all things; magic is the attempt to affect events within this situation of multiplicity. Inded, in Mesopotamian and Canaanite religious texts, as also in Homer, the gods themselves are portrayed as using magic and wearing amulets.

Magic was quite widespread in the ancient world—both the Old and New Testament exhibit extensive vocabulary for the various aspects of magic, their practitioners, and adherents. Yet magic was also often proscribed by the opinion of society and sometimes by law (cf. *ANET,* pp. 166, 184; *OCD,* p. 638). The Old Testament is quite definite in its prohibition of a wide range of magical practices, sometimes linking them with human sacrifice (Lev. 19:26; Deut. 18:10-14; cf. 2 Kgs. 23:24). That the prohibitions were made indicates that such practices were engaged in not only by neighboring peoples, but by Israelites as well (cf. 1 Kgs. 17:17; 2 Chr. 33:6; Isa. 3:2-3; Mic. 5:12). Among the practices specifically mentioned are the wearing of amulets (Isa. 3:20; KJV "earrings") and of "magic bands," charms associated with witchcraft (Ezek. 13:18, 20).

This entirely negative attitude toward magic is maintained in the New Testament (Acts 13:10; Gal. 5:20; Rev. 9:21; 18:23; 21:8; 22:15). The sometimes close relationship of magical powers and of religion is especially evident in the case of Simon Magus, who inspired religious devotion by magic (Acts 8:9-11), then attempted to buy divine power as if it involved only a simple incantation (vv. 18-21). The power of Jesus over diseases and spirits might adhere to Paul's handkerchiefs (19:11-12), but this did not mean that the name "Jesus" could become a neutral incantation

An amulet depicting Horus as a protector against animal bites; from Twenty-fourth or Twenty-fifth Dynasty Egypt (by courtesy of the Oriental Institute, University of Chicago)

(vv. 13-16). A wide variety of incantations were used in the Hellenistic world, some derived from Old Testament names of God; they were highly prized secrets and available for a price in scrolls sometimes called "Ephesian letters" because of the association of magic with Ephesus (cf. v. 19).

See DIVINATION; MEDIUM.

MAGISTRATE.† A judicial official, or a government official of wider responsibilities viewed in relation to his judicial function. The highest officials in Roman colonies such as Philippi were called in Latin *duumviri* or (an older term) *praetores.* The usual Greek equivalent was *stratēgoí* "magistrates," as at Acts 16:20, 22, 35, 36, 38. *Stratēgós* was a broad term for different types of government officials, including the Jerusalem temple police (Luke 22:4, 52) and their captain (Acts 4:1; 5:24, 26). Because of context, "magistrate(s)" is used to represent two even broader terms in Luke 12:11 (so KJV, JB; *arché,* RSV, NIV "rulers"), 58 (*árchōn* "ruler"; JB "court"); in the latter, the "magistrate" is probably the same official as the "judge" (*kritḗs*) mentioned in the same verse. Ezra was directed by Artaxerxes to appoint "magistrates" (Aram. *šāpṭîn,* pl. peal participle of *šᵉpaṭ* "to judge";

JB "scribes"), and "judges" (*dayyānîn*), perhaps two names for one office (Ezra 7:25). In a list of Babylonian imperial officials (Dan. 3:2-3), the "magistrates" (RSV, NIV; **K** *tiptāyēʿ*; **Q** *tiptaʿê*; KJV "sheriffs," JB "men of law") are named last; the meaning of the term is uncertain.

The KJV's use of "magistrate" at Judg. 18:7 is but one conjecture, and not the most likely, concerning this difficult verse (RSV "lacking nothing"; NJV "hereditary ruler"). The KJV supplies "magistrates" at Titus 3:1.

MAGNIFICAT [măg nĭf'ə kăt].† The name commonly given to Mary's song of praise (Luke 1:46-55), from the first word of the Latin translation of the song: "Magnificat anima mea Dominum...."

Like the related songs in 1:68-79; 2:29-32, the Magnificat represents what would be expected of common Palestinian Jews such as the speakers are portrayed. What is hoped for is the fulfillment of the covenant with Abraham (1:55; cf. vv. 72-73) and Israel's salvation (v. 54; cf. 2:25), in which Gentiles may, however, participate (vv. 31-32). This salvation is envisioned at least partly in military terms (1:51-52). While these ideas are elsewhere put to use in Christian teaching and imagery, in the Magnificat they appear as an unqualified expression of the eschatological and nationalistic piety common in Judaism from *ca.* 200 B.C. to A.D. 100. But in the present context of the song, namely the gospel of Luke, the salvation spoken of is that which has come in Jesus and is not bound to any nation (cf. vv. 69, 77; 2:11, 30-32).

The content of the Magnificat is not specifically linked to the situation of Mary, except at 1:48 (cf. vv. 38, 42, 45). In that verse (cf. 2 Esdr. 9:45) and with every line in Mary's song, there are close relations—sometimes word for word—to several of the Psalms and poetic passages elsewhere in the Old Testament and later Jewish literature, particularly the song of Hannah (1 Sam. 2:1-10). The lack of specificity and the parallel between Elizabeth's story and Hannah's story suggest that the song was Elizabeth's and not Mary's. Indeed, a small possibility exists that the song was originally ascribed to Elizabeth at Luke 1:46, either by the appearance of her name there in place of Mary's (as in three Latin manuscripts and three references to the song in the Church Fathers) or by the absence of any name ("And she said..."; cf. vv. 41-44, 56). But because of the connections of v. 48 and the overwhelming manuscript evidence, Mary's name should be retained at v. 46.

MAGOG [mā'gŏg] (Heb. *māgôg*; Gk. *Magōg*).* A son of Japheth and eponym of an unidentified people (Gen. 10:2; 1 Chr. 1:5) which became linked with Gog as a cryptic name in apocalyptic texts (Ezek. 38:2; 39:6; Rev. 20:8; Sib.Or. 3:319, 512). Identifications of Magog have included the Scythians (Josephus *Ant.* i.6.1 [123]), Ethiopia (Sib.Or. 3:319), and, in recent scholarship, the land of King Gyges of Lydia (seventh century B.C.), and the Gagaia, a people mentioned in the Amarna Letters; some scholars suggest that it is a variant form of Gog (cf. Akk. *māt gugu* "land of Gog"). In eschatology, Gog and Magog are general symbols of the enemies of God (or the

Messiah; Rev. 20:8) and his people; any attempt at definite identification is beside the point.

See GOG 2.

MAGOR-MISSABIB [mā'gôr mĭs'ə bĭb].* KJV and NIV transliteration of Heb. *māgôr missābîb* "terror on every side" (Jer. 20:3; so RSV). The phrase, which appears elsewhere (Ps. 31:13 [MT 14]; Jer. 6:25; 20:10; 46:5; 49:29; Lam. 2:22), is given by Jeremiah to Pashhur as a name to represent what was about to come upon Judah.

See PASHHUR.

MAGPIASH [măg'pĭ ăsh] (Heb. *magpîʿāš*). An Israelite who participated in the sealing of the new covenant under Nehemiah (Neh. 10:20 [MT 21]).

MAHALAB [mā'ə lăb].* Of the several proposals concerning interpretation of the last two words of Josh. 19:29 (Heb. *mēḥebel 'akzîbâ*), that most commonly accepted emends the text to read (*û)maḥᵃlēb (wᵉ)'akzîb* "(and) Mahalab (and) Achzib" (so *BH, BHS,* RSV, JB; cf. NEB "Mehalbeh, Achzib"; LXX B "and from Leb and Echozob"). According to this view, Mahalab is identical with Ahlab (Judg. 1:31), and both are the same as the Maḥalib mentioned in the annals of Sennacherib, and thus identified with Khirbet el-Maḥâlib on the Litani river, 6.4 km. (4 mi.) northeast of Tyre. It is, however, altogether possible to take the Hebrew text as it stands (perhaps dropping *he*-locale from "Achzib"), translating "from the region [*hebel*] of Achzib" (cf. KJV, NIV, NEB mg., Vulg., LXX A).

MAHALAH (1 Chr. 7:18, KJV). *See* MAHLAH **2**.

MAHALALEL [mə hăl'ə lĕl] (Heb. *mahᵃlal'ēl*).
1. A son of Kenan and the father of Jared in the lineage of Seth (Gen. 5:12-17; KJV "Mahalaleel"). He is called Mahalaleel in Luke's genealogy of Jesus (Luke 3:37; Gk. *Maleleēl*; KJV "Maleleel").
2. A Judahite of the family of Perez (Neh. 11:4; KJV "Mahalaleel").

MAHALATH [mā'ə lăth] (Heb. *mahᵃlat*).
1. The daughter of Ishmael, sister of Nebaioth, and third wife of Esau (Gen. 28:9). She is called Basemath (**2**) at 36:3.
2. David's granddaughter, the daughter of Jerimoth and Abihail, and one of the wives of King Rehoboam (2 Chr. 11:18).
3. A term in the superscriptions of Pss. 53, 88 possibly meaning "sickness" (from Heb. *ḥālâ* "be sick"). Leannoth (Heb. *lᵉʿannôt*), which appears with Mahalath at Ps. 88, is even more obscure, possibly meaning "for humiliation" (from *ʿānâ* "be afflicted"), thus suggesting penitence or purification from disease. "According to Mahalath" and "according to Mahalath Leannoth" are musical directions, perhaps references to well-known melodies.

MAHALI (Exod. 6:19, KJV). *See* MAHLI **1**.

MAHANAIM [mā'ə nā'əm] (Heb. *mahᵃnayim* "two camps"). A place near the Jabbok river where the angels of God met Jacob on his return to Canaan from Haran (Gen. 32:2 [MT 3]; cf. v. 10 [MT 11]). Mahanaim is mentioned as a Gadite city on the border with Manasseh (Josh. 13:26, 30) and as a levitical city of refuge assigned to the Merarite clan (21:38; 1 Chr. 6:80). The city, which was apparently a fortress, served as Ishbosheth's capital (2 Sam. 2:8, 12, 29) and later as David's refuge when he fled from Absalom (17:24, 27; 19:32; 1 Kgs. 2:8). Later it was the center of one of Solomon's administrative districts (4:1). A number of sites have been proposed, including Khirbet Maḥneh, near ʿAjlûn, and the twin sites Tulul edh-Dhahab (ancient Penuel) and Tulul el-Gharbiyeh.

MAHANEH-DAN [māʹ nə dănʹ] (Heb. *maḥᵃnēh-ḏān* "camp of Dan"). A place west of Kiriath-jearim and between Zorah and Eshtaol. Here the Spirit of the Lord "began to stir" Samson (Judg. 13:25). An armed group of Danites camped here as their tribe migrated northward (18:12).

MAHARAI [māʹə rī] (Heb. *mahᵃray*). One of David's mighty men. A native of Netophah in Judah (2 Sam. 23:28; 1 Chr. 11:30) and reckoned among the clan of the Zerahites, he was commander of the tenth monthly levy of David's army (27:13).

MAHATH [māʹhăth] (Heb. *mahaṭ*).
1. A Kohathite Levite, son of Amasai and ancestor of Samuel and the temple singer Heman (1 Chr. 6:35 [MT 20]).
2. The son of Amasai; a Kohathite Levite who participated in Hezekiah's cleansing of the temple (2 Chr. 29:12). He was an overseer of the temple contributions (31:13).

MAHAVITE [māʹə vīt] (Heb. *mahᵃwîm*). A gentilic associated with Eliel, one of David's mighty men (1 Chr. 11:46). The term makes little sense as it stands and has been emended to *mahᵃnî* or *mahᵃnaymî* "Mahanaimite."

MAHAZIOTH [mə hāʹzī ŏth] (Heb. *mahᵃzîʹôt*).† A son of Heman and leader of the twenty-third division of levitical temple musicians (1 Chr. 25:4-6, 30).

MAHER-SHALAL-HASH-BAZ [māʹər shălʹəl hăshʹbăz] (Heb. *mahēr šālāl ḥāš baz* "the spoil speeds, the prey hastes" [so RSV mg.]). The portentous name given to Isaiah's third son to symbolize the coming Assyrian defeat of the kingdoms of Syria and Israel (Isa. 8:1-4, cf. v. 18).

MAHLAH [mäʹlə] (Heb. *mahlâ* "weak").
1. One of the daughters of Zelophehad for whom special provision was made so that they might be his heirs (Num. 26:33; 27:1; Josh. 17:3). She may be the eponymous ancestor of a clan or town in Manasseh.
2. A son or daughter of Hammolecheth of the tribe of Manasseh (1 Chr. 7:18; KJV "Mahalah").

MAHLI [mäʹlī] (Heb. *mahlî*).
1. A Levite, son of Merari and brother of Mushi (Exod. 6:19 [MT 4]; KJV "Mahali"; Num. 3:20; 1 Chr. 23:21). He is the ancestor of the Mahlites (Num. 3:33; 26:58; 1 Chr. 6:29 [MT 14]).

2. A Levite, son of Mushi and grandson of Merari (1 Chr. 6:47 [MT 32]; 23:23; 24:30).

MAHLON [mäʹlən] (Heb. *mahlôn*). The husband of Ruth, a son of Elimelech and Naomi who died without heirs (Ruth 1:2, 5; 4:9-10).

MAHOL [māʹhŏl] (Heb. *māhôl* "dancing").† The father of Heman, Calcol (KJV "Chalcol"), and Darda (and perhaps also of Ethan the Ezrahite; cf. the superscriptions of Pss. 88–89), wise men with whom Solomon is compared and found superior (1 Kgs. 4:31 [MT 5:11]). The "sons of Mahol" here probably represent members of a musicians' guild (cf. JB "cantors"); Heman was among the temple musicians (1 Chr. 6:33), and Ethan, Heman, Calcol, and Dara are listed among the sons of Zerah at 2:6.

MAHSEIAH [mä sēʹyə] (Heb. *mahsēyâ* "Yahweh is my refuge"). The grandfather of Jeremiah's secretary, Baruch (Jer. 32:12; KJV "Maaseiah"), and of Seraiah, King Zedekiah's quartermaster (51:59).

MAKAZ [māʹkăz] (Heb. *māqaṣ* "end, border," from *qāṣâ* "cut off" [?]). A city in the second district of Solomon's kingdom (1 Kgs. 4:9). The site may be Khirbet el-Mukheizin, 6 km. (4 mi.) south of Ekron.

MAKHELOTH [măk hēʹlŏth] (Heb. *maqhēlōt* "assemblies"). A place where the Israelites stopped during the wilderness wanderings, situated between Haradah and Tahath (Num. 33:25-26). Some scholars associate this site with the similar name Kehelathah at vv. 22-23.

MAKKEDAH [mə kēʹdə] (Heb. *maqqēḏâ*). A Canaanite royal city to which Joshua pursued the army of the Amorite alliance after their unsuccessful assault on Gibeon, killing the five kings who had hidden in a nearby cave and annihilating the city's entire population (Josh. 10:10-28; 12:16). The precise location of Makkedah, which was later assigned to Judah (15:41), is uncertain, though it was in the southern Shephelah region near Azekah. Eusebius locates it 8 Roman mi. (12 km. [7.3 mi.]) east of Eleutheropolis (Beit Jibrîn); recent scholars suggest rather Tell eṣ-Ṣâfî or another site north of Beit Jibrîn..

MAKTESH (Zeph. 1:11, KJV). *See* MORTAR, THE.

MALACHI [mălʹə kī] (Heb. *malʾāḵî* "my messenger" or "angel").† The last of the Minor Prophets. No personal information is recorded about this prophet (Mal. 1:1), and even his name is uncertain. Although Malachi (or a similar form, such as Malachiah) could well be a proper name, most scholars agree that it is a title or symbolic name (LXX Gk. *angélou autoú* "his messenger"; cf. 3:1, "my messenger"). Rabbinic tradition suggests identifying him with Ezra the scribe (Targ. Mal. 1:1) or Mordecai (cf. Talmud *b. Meg.* 15a).

MALACHI, BOOK OF.† The last of the Minor Prophets and the final book in the Old Testament.

I. Contents

On the basis of form and content the book divides into six distinct oracles. Each follows a basic dialectical pattern of statement, objection ("prophetic disputation"), and substantiation of the statement. In each oracle the Lord, through the prophet, responds to the people's skeptical questioning ("You say, 'How...?'"), occasionally posing a question of his own (cf. Mal. 1:6, 8; 3:8).

Following the superscription to the work (1:1), the book opens with the prophet's declaration of Yahweh's love for Israel (Jacob); although not readily apparent in their current political and economic circumstances, God's favor may be perceived in contrast to his angry treatment of the recalcitrant Edomites (Esau) (vv. 2-5).

In the second oracle the Lord denounces the lack of proper respect shown by the priests: "Where is my honor? . . . where is my fear?" (1:6—2:9). Weary of their responsibilities (1:13), they lackadaisically offer impure food and blemished sacrifices (vv. 7-8, 12-14); indeed, even the nations honor him more (v. 11). Moreover, the priests fail to properly instruct the people in the law (2:8-9; cf. vv. 6-7). How then can Israel expect God's favor (1:9)?

The third oracle (2:10-16) scores the laity for entering into mixed marriages, "profaning the covenant of our fathers" by being "faithless to one another" and thus to God (v. 10). Only if they remain faithful to their Jewish wives (rather than "the daughter of a foreign god," v. 12) and eschew divorce (v. 16) will God accept their offerings (v. 13).

The prophet then announces the Lord's coming in judgment (2:17–3:5). Israel has wearied God, saying that he does not exercise judgment against the wicked (2:17). But his messenger will prepare the way for God's day of judgment (3:1-2), when the Lord will "refine" the priesthood and judge those who oppress the unfortunate, and thereby purify the nation (vv. 3, 5).

In the fifth oracle (vv. 6-12) Malachi enjoins the people to repent of their obstinacy, typified by their refusal to contribute the proper tithe (vv. 8-10). When they do, they will again be "a land of delight" (v. 12): "Return to me, and I will return to you" (v. 7).

The final oracle (3:13–4:3 [MT 3:21]) rebuffs those who question the benefit of obedience to God ("it is vain to serve God"), charging that evildoers prosper with no fear of redress (3:13-15). Yet the truly faithful find encouragement in the Lord's promise of a book of remembrance, whereby at the time of judgment he would distinguish between the righteous and the wicked (3:16–4:3 [MT 3:21]).

Malachi concludes with a challenge to "remember the law of my servant Moses" (4:4 [MT 3:22]) and prepare for Elijah, who precedes the terrible day of the Lord (4:5-6 [MT 3:23-24]).

II. Origins

Although the biblical account provides no direct information concerning the anonymous author of Malachi (see MALACHI), the book does provide insight into conditions in Palestine at the time of his prophecy sufficient to posit something of his date and background. Israel is ruled by a governor (Heb. peḥâ; 1:8), thus placing the book in the Persian period. From the

prophet's concern with priestly indifference to matters of ritual, it appears that the temple had been rebuilt far enough in the past (515 B.C.) to permit enthusiastic observance to decline. The problem of mixed marriages reflects circumstances addressed by Ezra and Nehemiah. Accordingly, most scholars date the prophet and his utterances to the mid-fifth century, either in the decades before Nehemiah (thus ca. 460) or just prior to his second administrative term (ca. 432); some would place him somewhat later, arguing that conditions recorded indicate decreased effectiveness of Nehemiah's reforms. Others date him as late as the early third century.

The designation of this collection of prophecies as an "oracle" (Heb. maśśā᾽; KJV "burden") has prompted some scholars to group the book of Malachi with similar "oracles" in the preceding book (cf. Zeph. 9:1; 12:1) and to regard all three as the work of a single author.

III. Theology

Rabbinic tradition regards Malachi as among the last—if not the very last—of the Israelite prophets, the demise of which contributed to great distress among the people (cf. 1 Macc. 9:27). The issues and circumstances this anonymous prophet addresses indicate that already in his day Israel was experiencing dissatisfaction with their political, economic, and even natural fortunes. Lacking sound religious instruction (Mal. 2:8-9), they acted out their despair through moral decay and cultic apathy. Even the faithful were perplexed, as evident from the skepticism voiced as they tried to understand the ways of their Lord. In response to this situation, Malachi proclaims Yahweh's faithfulness to his chosen people, expressed in terms of their historic covenantal relationship (e.g., 2:11; 3:1; cf. the ancient name of God, "the Lord of hosts"; e.g., 1:6, 9, 14). If the intimacy of this relationship is to be restored, the people must repent (Heb. šûb "turn, return") from their deceitful ways (3:7, 10).

The terrible day of the Lord, his coming in judgment, permeates Malachi's thinking. He reiterates the standard prophetic view of this day as a time of wrath for "the arrogant and all evildoers" (3:5; 4:1 [MT 3:19]; cf. Amos 5:18-20; Zeph. 1:7-18). Yet on this day, he declares, the righteous who revere and serve God (some interpret Mal. 1:11 to mean here even those beyond Israel) will be spared; indeed, for them "the sun of righteousness shall rise, with healing in its wings" (4:2 [MT 3:20]; cf. 3:16-18). Unique to Malachi's eschatology is the concept of a "messenger" (3:1), a forerunner who will prepare the way of the Lord. Although some interpret this figure as the prophet whose words are recorded here, later tradition identifies him as "Elijah the prophet" (cf. 4:5 [MT 3:23]; Matt. 11:14; 17:10-12 par.; John 1:21).

Bibliography. J. G. Baldwin, *Haggai, Zechariah, Malachi.* Tyndale (1972); R. A. Mason, *The Books of Haggai, Zechariah, and Malachi.* CBC (1977).

MALCAM [măl′kăm] (Heb. *malkām*). A Benjaminite, the son of Shaharaim and Hodesh (1 Chr. 8:9; KJV "Malcham").

MALCHAM (Zeph. 1:5, KJV). *See* MILCOM.

MALCHIAH [măl kī'ə] (Heb. *malkîyâ, malkîyāhû* "Yahweh is king").†

1. The father of Pashhur the priest and chief officer of the temple in the time of Jeremiah (Jer. 21:1; KJV "Melchiah"; 38:1). He is generally distinguished from MALCHIJAH **2**.

2. A member of Judah's royal family and owner of the cistern into which Jeremiah was thrown (Jer. 38:6). Some scholars identify him with **1**.

MALCHIEL [măl'kī əl] (Heb. *malkî'ēl* "God is king"). A son of Beriah and grandson of Asher (Gen. 46:17; 1 Chr. 7:31). He was ancestor to the Malchielites (Num. 26:45).

MALCHIJAH [măl kī'jə] (Heb. *malkîyâ, malkîyāhû* "Yahweh is king").

1. A Gershonite Levite; ancestor of Asaph **1** (1 Chr. 6:40 [MT 25]; KJV "Malchiah").

2. An ancestor of the priest Adaiah, who was among those who went to live in Jerusalem after the Exile (1 Chr. 9:12; Neh. 11:12; KJV "Malchiah").

3. The leader of the fifth division of priests in David's time (1 Chr. 24:9). He is probably the same as **2**.

4. A postexilic Israelite among the sons of Parosh required to divorce his foreign wife (Ezra 10:25a; KJV "Malchiah").

5. (Ezra 10:25b, KJV). See HASHABIAH **8**.

6. One of the sons of Harim who had to divorce his foreign wife (Ezra 10:31; KJV "Malchiah").

7. A son of Harim who assisted in rebuilding Jerusalem's walls (Neh. 3:11). He is perhaps the same as **6**.

8. A son of Rechab (perhaps a Rechabite) who helped rebuild the walls (Neh. 3:14; KJV "Malchiah").

9. A goldsmith who repaired a portion of the city walls (Neh. 3:31; KJV "Malchiah").

10. One of the men standing on the platform to the left of Ezra while he read the Book of the Law (Neh. 8:4; KJV "Malchiah"). He may be the same as **4, 6, 8,** or **9**.

11. A priest who participated in the sealing of the new covenant under Nehemiah (Neh. 10:3 [MT 4]).

12. A musician who participated in the dedication of the walls of Jerusalem (Neh. 12:42).

MALCHIRAM [măl kī'rəm] (Heb. *malkîrām* "my king is exalted"). A son of King Jeconiah (1 Chr. 3:18).

MALCHISHUA [măl'kə shoo'ə] (Heb. *malkîsûaʿ* "my king saves"). A son of King Saul, killed in the battle with the Philistines on Mt. Gilboa (1 Sam. 14:49; 31:2; KJV "Melchishua"; 1 Chr. 8:33; 9:39; 10:2).

MALCHUS [măl'kəs] (Gk. *Malchos,* from Sem. *mlk* "king"). A servant (perhaps a Nabatean) of the high priest Caiaphas whose right ear Peter inexplicably cut off at Gethsemane (John 18:10). According to Luke 22:51 Jesus restored the ear.

MALELEEL (Luke 3:37, KJV). See MAHALALEL **1**.

MALLOTHI [măl'ə thī] (Heb. *mallôṯî*). A son of Heman; chief of the nineteenth division of temple singers (1 Chr. 25:4, 26).

MALLOW (Heb. *mallûaḥ*).† Job's belittling description of his critics (Job 30:1-8) includes their eating the leaves of the mallow, a sign of abject poverty (v. 4; KJV "mallows"; NIV "salt herbs"). Here the "mallow" (LXX Gk. *hálimon*; cf. Heb. *melaḥ* "salt") is not the common mallow (*Malva sylvestris* L.), but the sea orache (*Atriplex halimus* L.), a shrub in the goosefoot family (*Chenopodaciae,* which includes spinach) found in the Dead Sea region. At 24:24 the LXX reads "like the mallow" (Gk. *hósper moloché*), referring to the common mallow (so RSV and JB); the MT has "like all" (Heb. *kakōl;* RSV mg.; KJV "as all other"; NIV "like all others"). Here the withering of the mallow's showy flowers has a part in a description of the wicked's inevitable fading away.

MALLUCH [măl'ək] (Heb. *mallûḵ*).

1. A Merarite Levite and ancestor of Ethan (1 Chr. 6:44 [MT 29]).

2. One of the sons of Bani required to divorce their foreign wives (Ezra 10:29; 1 Esdr. 9:30; KJV "Mamuchus").

3. An Israelite among the sons of Harim who was compelled to "put away" his foreign wife (Ezra 10:32).

4. A priest who participated in the sealing of the new covenant under Nehemiah (Neh. 10:4 [MT 5]).

5. One of the chiefs of the people who with Nehemiah signed the covenant (Neh. 10:27 [MT 28]). He may be the same as **2** or **3**.

6. A priest who returned with Zerubbabel from Babylon (Neh. 12:2). He is perhaps the same as **4**.

MALLUCHI [măl'loo kī] (Heb. K *malûḵî,* Q *malîḵû;* LXX Gk. *Malouch*). A priestly household headed by Jonathan at the time of the high priest Joiakim (Neh. 12:14; KJV "Melicu"). It may be associated with MALLUCH **6** (cf. NIV).

MALLUS [măl'əs] (Gk. *Mallōtēs*).* A Cilician city whose people revolted when Antiochus IV Epiphanes gave it and nearby Tarsus to his concubine Antiochis (2 Macc. 4:30; KJV "Mallos"). Overlooking the Pyramus (modern Ceyhan) river delta, the city is situated on the route taken by Alexander the Great.

MALTA [môl'tə] (Gk. *Melitē*). Ancient Melita, the largest of the Maltese islands, *ca.* 96 km. (60 mi.) south of Sicily. The island is believed to have been colonized by the Phoenicians *ca.* the ninth century B.C. (cf. Diodorus *Hist.* v.12). Some accounts indicate Greek occupation as well. The island came under Punic control in the sixth century. Although Malta passed into Roman hands in the Second Punic War (218) and with the other islands was later governed by a procurator, its Punic character seems to have continued into New Testament times.

En route to Rome the ship carrying Paul was destroyed and all the travelers landed on Malta (Acts 28:1; KJV "Melita"). The traditional location of their landing is St. Paul's Bay on the northern side of the island, 13 km. (8 mi.) northwest of modern Valletta. During his three-month stay the apostle miraculously avoided attack by a viper, leading the natives to regard him as a god (vv. 3-6). He also cured the father of the "chief man" Publius, along with several others (vv. 7-10).

MAMERTINE [măm′ər tĭn] **PRISON.**† A prison in Rome on the east side of the Capitoline Hill and adjacent to the Forum. According to early Church tradition, Peter and Paul were held prior to their execution in this small building consisting of only two cells, one above the other. Although its name is medieval, the prison is known to have existed in the early first century A.D. and was possibly the oldest in the city.

MAMMON [măm′ən] (Gk. *mamōnás*).† The Greek transliteration of Aram. *māmônā'*, apparently widely enough known to need no translation in Greek Christian documents, designating wealth in any form—including money, cattle, and land.

Jesus frequently refers to mammon. Though "unrighteous," it can, by generosity, be used in winning that which is eternal (Luke 16:9; cf. 12:33, 34). In an a fortiori argument he cites mammon as faithfulness in dealing with earthly possessions (16:11). Finally, he personifies the "master" mammon in stark contrast with God, who requires loyal service: "You cannot be a slave to (both) God and mammon" (v. 13 par. Matt. 6:24).

MAMRE [măm′rĭ] (Heb. *mamrē'*) (PLACE). A place Amorite from the vicinity of Hebron. He and his brothers, Eshcol and Aner, were allies of Abraham in the battle against the four eastern kings (Gen. 14:13, 24).

MAMRE [măm′rĭ] (Heb. *mamrē'*) (PLACE). A place near Hebron distinguished by a prominent tree (so LXX, Syr.) or group of trees (so MT; RSV "oaks"; NIV "great trees"; RSV mg. "terebinths"), apparently named after Abram's ally (14:13). The traditional site is Râmet el-Khalîl, *ca.* 3 km. (2 mi.) north of Hebron. Here Abraham established a shrine, and he and his son Isaac often lived in the grove (Gen. 13:18; 14:13; 18:1; 35:27; KJV "plain[s]"). The patriarchal burial site at Machpelah was east of Mamre (23:17, 19; 25:9; 49:30; 50:13).

MAN OF GOD (Heb. *'îš (hā)'ĕlōhîm*).* A designation for early prophets in Israel, used particularly where the giving of oracles (sometimes almost after the manner of divination) and the working of wonders are in view. The term is used of unnamed prophets (1 Sam. 2:27; 1 Kgs. 13; 2 Chr. 25:7, 9), Moses (Deut. 33:1; Josh. 14:6; 1 Chr. 23:14; 2 Chr. 30:1; Ezra 3:2), the angel of the Lord—thought to be a prophet (Judg. 13:6, 8), Samuel (1 Sam. 9:6-10), Shemaiah (1 Kgs. 12:22; 2 Chr. 11:2), Elijah (1 Kgs. 17:18, 24), and Elisha (e.g., 2 Kgs. 1:9-13; 5:8-15). In later periods the term apparently came to be applied to some, other than prophets, who were thought of as bearing some special relationship to God, such as David (Neh. 12:24, 36; cf. Jer. 35:4). Christian piety is most in mind where the term is used at 1 Tim. 6:11 (Gk *ánthrōpos theoú*) and 2 Tim. 3:17 (*ho toú theoú ánthrōpos*).

See PROPHECY.

MAN OF LAWLESSNESS. *See* ANTICHRIST.

MAN OF SIN (2 Thess. 2:3, KJV). *See* ANTICHRIST.

MANAEN [măn′ĭ ən] (Gk. *Manaén*, from Heb. *mᵉnāḥēm* "comforter"). A Christian prophet-teacher in Antioch (Acts 13:1). Manaen was a "foster brother" (Gk. *sýntrophos*; RSV "member of the court") of Herod Antipas, tetrarch of Galilee and Perea; the title was given to boys raised as companions to royal princes (cf. KJV, NIV) and was retained in adulthood.

MANAHATH [măn′ə hăth] (Heb. *mānaḥaṭ* "rest, settlement") (PERSON). A son of Shobal and descendant of the Horite Seir (Gen. 36:23; 1 Chr. 1:40).

MANAHATH [măn′ə hăth] (Heb. *mānaḥaṭ* "rest, settlement") (PLACE). A place to which Benjaminite inhabitants of Geba were exiled (1 Chr. 8:6). The circumstances of this exile are unknown. If associated with the Horite descendant of the same name, Manahath may have been in Edom; more likely, it is related to the Manahathites, and would thus be located in Judah, perhaps at modern Mâlḥa, about 5 km. (3 mi.) west-southwest of Jerusalem.

MANAHATHITES [măn′ə hăth′īts] (Heb. *manāḥtî*). A Judahite clan, half of which was descended from Salma, a son of Hur (1 Chr. 2:54; KJV "Manahethites"). The other half of the clan is probably mentioned at v. 52 (so KJV, NIV, JB, following LXX); the RSV, following the MT, reads "half of the Menuhoth" (Heb. *mᵉnuḥôṭ*). The gentilic probably refers to a town of Manahath in Judah.

MANASSEH [mə năs′ə] (Heb. *mᵉnaššeh* "causing to forget").

1. The older son of Joseph and Asenath (Gen. 41:51) and eponymous ancestor of the tribe of Manasseh. The dying Jacob adopted Joseph's sons Manasseh and Ephraim and, after the fashion of his own father Isaac, gave the greater blessing of the firstborn to Manasseh's younger brother Ephraim (48:14-20; cf. ch. 27). Some scholars interpret this account as a later explanation for the greater importance of Ephraim within the tribal confederation. No further details of his life are preserved.

According to the first census in the wilderness, the tribe of Manasseh numbered 32,200 military men (Num. 1:34-35); by the time of the second census at the end of the wilderness journeys, the tribe had grown to 52,700 men (26:34). Half of the tribe, particularly the Machirites, settled in the Transjordan, specifically in the northern part of Gilead and in Bashan north of Gad's territory (32:33-42; 34:14-15; Deut. 3:13-15; 29:7-8; Josh. 12:4-6; 13:8-12). The Transjordanian Manassites, with Gad and Reuben, crossed the Jordan to help the other tribes conquer Canaan (Num. 32:20-27; Josh. 1:12-18; 4:12-13; 22:1-34).

The other "half-tribe" of Manasseh received territory west of the Jordan, north of Ephraim, south of Asher, Zebulun, and Issachar, extending to the Mediterranean Sea (17:5-10). The Ephraimites possessed certain cities on Manasseh's side of their mutual border with this western territory (16:9). The Manassites themselves were granted claim to cities within the territories of Issachar and Asher, but were unable to conquer them (17:11-13; 1 Chr. 7:29; cf. R. G. Boling and G. E. Wright, *Joshua*. AB 6 [1982], pp. 407, 413, "near Issachar and Asher . . . ''); later, however, they did subject the non-Israelite inhabitants to forced labor (Josh. 17:12-13; Judg. 1:27-28). The Kohathite Levites were assigned cities in the western portion of Manasseh and the Gershonites in the eastern portion (Josh. 21:5-6).

The judge Gideon was from a lesser Manassite clan (Judg. 6:15), and Jephthah also may have traced his lineage to this tribe through Gilead (11:1). David received help from Manasseh when he dwelled at Ziklag and Hebron (1 Chr. 12:19-22, 31, 37). According to 2 Chr. 15:9, many from Ephraim and Manasseh went over to King Asa of Judah when they saw that the Lord favored him. Some from Manasseh worshiped at the Jerusalem temple after the fall of the northern kingdom of Israel, of which the tribe had been a part (2 Chr. 30:1, 10-11, 18; 31:1; 34:6, 9). Some Manassites are numbered among those settling in Jerusalem after Judah's return from exile (1 Chr. 9:3).

2. "Manasseh" at Judg. 18:30 (KJV, following MT) reflects an early scribal error for "Moses" (Heb. *mōšeh*; so RSV; cf. Exod. 2:22).

3. The son of Hezekiah **1** and Hephzibah; king of Judah *ca.* 687-642 B.C. His reign, including a coregency with his father beginning in 696, was the longest of any Judahite king. Unlike his father, Manasseh led Judah into a variety of idolatrous practices (2 Kgs. 21:1-9 par. 2 Chr. 33:1-9). Moreover, he killed many innocent people in Jerusalem (2 Kgs. 21:16), apparently including prophets who forecast disaster for Judah because of Manasseh's idolatry (vv. 10-15; according to later traditions Isaiah was among the victims).

The portrayal of Manasseh's reign in 2 Kgs. 21:1-18 is unvaryingly negative, and Judah's destruction is repeatedly blamed on Manasseh (vv. 10-15; 23:12, 26; 24:3; cf. Jer. 15:4). The version presented in 2 Chr. 33:1-20, on the other hand, does not attach blame in this way to Manasseh. Furthermore, 2 Chronicles depicts Manasseh's repentance, an incident not recorded in 2 Kings. According to this account, Manasseh, who apparently continued at least in part his father's policy of rebellion against Assyria, was taken in chains to Babylon, where he turned to Yahweh (2 Chr. 33:11-13). Upon his return to Jerusalem, Manasseh fortified Jerusalem (v. 14; perhaps for a further rebellion) and put an end to idolatry there (vv. 15-16). He is named among the ancestors of Jesus (Matt. 1:10; KJV "Manasses"). *See* MANASSEH, PRAYER OF.

4. A postexilic Israelite "of the sons of Pahathmoab" required to divorce his foreign wife (Ezra 10:30; 1 Esdr. 9:31 "Manasseas"; KJV "Manasses").

5. One of the sons of Hashum who divorced his non-Israelite wife (Ezra 10:33).

6. The husband of Judith, a wealthy Simeonite who apparently died of sunstroke (Jdt. 8:2-3, 7).

MANASSEH, PRAYER OF.† A book of the Apocrypha, purportedly the penitential prayer uttered by the infamous King Manasseh of Judah while exiled in Babylon (2 Chr. 33:12-13; cf. 2 Bar. 64:8). Although only fifteen verses long, it is recognized as one of the finest examples of Jewish devotional writing.

Most scholars believe that the work is pseudepigraphal, written by a pious Jew of the Hellenistic or Roman period (second century B.C.–first century A.D.), perhaps at Jerusalem or Alexandria. Partly because it lacks specific reference to the sins of Manasseh reported in the canonical accounts, few would identify it as the actual words of the king, according to 2 Chr. 33:18-19 recorded in the long-lost Chronicles of the Kings of Israel and Chronicles of the Seers (so RSV; JB "Annals of Hozai"). Because of its brevity scholars cannot determine with certainty whether it was composed originally in Hebrew (or Aramaic) or Greek. The earliest version extant is the third-century A.D. Syriac Didascalia. It does not appear to have been included in the earliest versions of the LXX but is found in Codex Alexandrinus, appended to the Psalms as Ode 8. Jerome did not include the book in his Vulgate and it was not approved as canonical by the Council of Trent (1546), but it did appear in the 1540 and 1592 Vulgate editions. The Prayer has been placed variously as an appendix to 2 Chronicles, 4 Maccabees, and the New Testament.

The Prayer opens with an invocation to the "God of our fathers" (Pr.Man. 1) and an expression of praise to God as majestic in creation and merciful to the repentant (vv. 2-8). The poet confesses his numerous transgressions, which have provoked God's wrath (vv. 9-10), and beseeches pardon of "the God of those who repent" (vv. 11-15a). It concludes with a doxology (v. 15b).

MANDRAKE (Heb. *dûḏay*). *Mandragora officinarum* L., an herb in the nightshade family (*Solanaceae*) common in Syria and Palestine, as throughout the Mediterranean region. The mandrake is nearly stemless with oval leaves, purple flowers, and fruits that ripen to bright yellow or orange during May, "the days of wheat harvest" (Gen. 30:14). The fruits and the fleshy forked root, which resembles the form of the human body, have been used traditionally to induce amorous responses and to promote conception (hence the common name "love-apple"; cf. vv. 14-16, 22). The odor of the mandrake is disagreeable to most Westerners but apparently was thought pleasant in Old Testament times (Cant. 7:13).

MANGER (Gk. *phátnē*).† A box or trough in a stable for holding feed for livestock. Mangers were made of stone or masonry or might be carved into the stone walls of caves used as stalls (a meaning encompassed by the Greek term; cf. LXX, 2 Chr. 32:28; Hab. 3:17; so KJV, NIV, Luke 13:15; RSV "manger").

The manger in which Jesus was laid after his birth (Luke 2:7, 12, 16) represents not poverty or the heartlessness of an innkeeper, but the unusual circumstances of Jesus' birth brought about by the census decree of Augustus (v. 1). The manger is not only mentioned three times, but is also made part of a "sign" (v. 12). Perhaps Isa. 1:3 is in mind here—the Lord (*kýrios* at Luke 2:11) in a manger (cf. LXX Isa. 1:3, "the manger of his *kýrios*''; RSV "his master's crib") is the sign that God is giving back to Israel the knowledge of him that they had lost.

MANICHAEISM [măn'ĭ kē ĭzm'].* The religion founded in the second century A.D. by Mani (or Manes; *ca.* A.D. 216-277), which survived into the late Middle Ages. Mani was a Parthian who at an early age broke from the baptizing sect of which his father was a member and began to preach his own beliefs, which combined elements of Christianity, Judaism, Zoroastrianism, Buddhism, and Hinduism in an elaborate mythology largely determined by Gnostic and Zoroastrian dualism. He taught that the two opposing forces of God (light) and matter (darkness) in the universe were originally separated, but now are commingled in the present world, including humanity. Human deliverance from evil comes by way of knowledge of this dualism. Humans have the responsibility of protecting the spark of light within them so that it might pass into the realm of light at the death of the body, rather than passing into another body. The present age of mixed light and darkness will be followed by the final judgment and the burning of the world, after which light and darkness will be eternally separated.

Mani regarded himself as the Paraclete promised by Jesus and as the final mediator of revelation pointed to by Abraham, Buddha, Jesus, and Zoroaster. The "elect" were Manichaeans who lived a strict monastic life that required celibacy, vegetarianism, and abstention from alcohol and agricultural work. "Hearers," who could only hope to enter the next life as the "elect," lived a religiously and morally strict, but more normal life.

Despite his execution, instigated by Zoroastrian religious leaders, Mani's syncretistic religion quickly became widespread and influential. His immediate disciples traveled from Egypt to China and India spreading their faith, and some medieval European sects (often referred to as "Manichaean" by their Christian opponents) may have been influenced by Manichaeism. Augustine of Hippo was a Manichaean "hearer" for nine years before his conversion to Christianity and then became a major voice in Christian anti-Manichaean polemics.

A number of Manichaean texts, some composed by Mani himself, are extant, some of which have come to light only in the last century.

Bibliography. F. C. Burkitt, *The Religion of the Manichees* (1925; repr. New York: 1978); H. Jonas, *The Gnostic Religion*, 2nd ed. (Boston: 1963), pp. 206-236; K. Rudolph, *Gnosis* (San Francisco: 1984), pp. 326-342.

MANKIND (Heb. *'āḏām*).† Although neither the Old nor the New Testament contains a systematic anthropology, various accounts reveal much concerning the underlying conception(s) of human nature.

I. The Human Condition

As with all that exists (except for God), the origin of mankind (Heb. *'āḏām* "Adam, a man, mankind") is in God's act of creation. Genesis preserves two distinct accounts with significantly different anthropological perspectives. The first, Gen. 1:1–2:4a, attributed by critical scholars to the later Priestly source, is the more optimistic. God intends humanity to share his own "image" and "likeness" from the very beginning (v. 26); no reference is made to human usurpation of God's knowledge or image as the cause of evil or the fall (but cf. 6:11-12, also ascribed to "P"). Mankind, created on the sixth day, is to exert dominion over other aspects of creation (vv. 26, 28; cf. Ps. 8:3-8 [MT 4-9]); work (here agricultural) is presented as a sacred trust from God, not as a burden or punishment (Gen. 1:29). The second account, 2:4b–3:24, addresses the dreary and futile human condition, viewing the fall as another stage of the creation; indeed, humanity as it is now known is a product of both creation and fall. Mankind is formed (first, according to this account) "of dust from the ground" (2:7). Humans are able to attain knowledge, and thus likeness to God (3:22) and differentiation from dumb animals (contrast 2:25 with 3:7), by usurping it from God who had jealously guarded it. And this step forward cost dearly: humanity is condemned to a painful, futile, and brief life. Men will be required to farm, and do so with back-breaking toil (vv. 17-19); women will experience agony in childbirth and be subjected to their husbands (v. 16). Humanity is cheated of eternal life: if they have knowledge like God, they cannot be trusted to live forever like God as well (vv. 22-23). The entire human condition, according to this account, is a punishment from God (cf. Ps. 90:7-10).

Because the creation of humanity is viewed as a single act of creation, a basic unity transcends the distinctions of race, nation, and class (Acts 17:26-28). Yet one distinction depicted as arising directly from this single act of creation is the distinction between male and female. Mankind cannot be said to exist apart from this distinction, which is shared with the rest of animal creation, but which becomes for mankind the basis for human interrelationship (Gen. 2:20-23). Presupposing rigid sex roles as the divine order for men and women (cf. 3:16-19), this distinction is seen as the basis for the normativity of permanent heterosexual monogamy (Matt. 19:5-6, citing Gen. 2:24; Rom. 1:26-27).

See CREATION.

II. Human Constitution

In Old Testament times people did not think of themselves as divided into a body and a soul. As is often said, the Hebrews regarded a human being not as an incarnated soul (the Platonic view) but, rather, as an animated body. The "soul" (Heb. *nepeš*) was understood as the animating breath of life (Gen. 2:7; 1 Kgs. 17:22). Even various aspects of the inner life were associated with parts of the body: thought was centered in the heart (not the brain), the emotions in the kidneys, bowels, or liver. Heb. *rûaḥ* "spirit" was at first used only of God's Spirit or various spirits sent by him (e.g., the spirit of madness sent upon Saul; 1 Sam. 16:14). Later it came to be used of mortals, denoting that part of the human psychology especially sensitive to God. So little did the ancient Hebrews presuppose a body-soul dualism that they did not even have a word for "living body" as opposed to "soul." Indeed, the entire human entity might be referred to as a "living soul" (= living being). The only words for body apart from soul were, as is literally appropriate, those which designate "corpse."

In the New Testament a body-soul dualism is implicit, perhaps having derived from Greek or later

Jewish thought. Jesus warns his disciples not to fear "those who kill the body but cannot kill the soul"; rather, they should fear God, who can "destroy both soul and body in hell" (Matt. 10:28). Here to take "soul" (Gk. *psyché*) simply as "the life of the body" would be absurd. Moreover, Paul describes a dramatic ethical conflict between the mind which serves the law of God and the flesh or bodily members which are slaves to sin (Rom. 7:14-25). Similarly, Paul sees an unending opposition between God's spirit and human "flesh" (*sárx*; Gal. 5:16-25); it is easy to see how early Gnostic Chrisitians such as Marcion could consider themselves Paulinists at this point. More world-affirming moderns would rather see greater continuity between Paul and the Old Testament, and thus often translate Paul's *sárx* abstractly as "sinful nature," as if to downplay the sinfulness Paul ascribed to the physical flesh (cf. also his implied denigration of sexual relations as inhibiting spirituality; 1 Cor. 7:1, 5). Indeed, it is no surprise that Paul regarded all (fleshly) mortals as having fallen into sin (Rom. 3:23).

III. Divisions of Humanity

The Old Testament demonstrates a genuine, albeit prescientific, concern for ethnography. The Table of Nations (Gen. 10) apparently traces all ethnic and racial groups of whom any knowledge or tradition existed (included primarily are those ancient Near Eastern peoples with whom the Hebrews had contact) back to Noah, from whom the replenished human race was considered to have derived. Genealogical connections between the various groups may be inferred largely from what the Hebrews knew of geographical proximity and the political and economic relations of these people, often interpreted as resulting from fortuitous events involving the eponymous ancestors of these peoples (cf. 9:20-27; 19:30-38; 25:29-34). Moreover, 11:1-9 traces the beginnings of differences between nations and peoples to the divine retribution which followed a particular act of hubris engaged in by all of mankind together. Indeed, the beginnings of sin as depicted with regard to the tower of Babel (v. 4) and earlier in the garden of Eden (3:7) and God's retribution for sin work against the unity of mankind (cf. vv. 12, 16; 4:8, 14, 23-24; 11:8).

Racial and ethnic divisions were at first of utmost importance to the ancient Hebrews, who understood themselves as God's chosen nation (beginning at first with just one man, Abraham; Gen. 12). Yet the objective of God's choice was the blessing of "all the families of the earth" (v. 3; cf. Rom. 4:16-17; Gal. 3:29). Moreover, voices from the prophets began to suggest that God could also choose other peoples (e.g., Isa. 19:25; Amos 9:7). In the Wisdom Literature the distinction of nationality is abandoned, replacing the Jew/Gentile distinction with that between "wise" and "fool" (e.g., Prov. 12:15-16; 14:16).

The older dichotomy did not disappear, and Paul and other New Testament writers attempt to supplant it with the distinction between "believer" and "unbeliever." For Luke devout Gentiles who believe in Jesus are to be favored, while devout Jews who do not accept him are not (Acts 10:34ff.; cf. 3:19-23). For Paul "there cannot be Greek and Jew, circumcised and uncircumcised, barbarian, Scythian, slave, free man,

but Christ is all, and in all" (Col. 3:11). For John of Patmos the only relevant division of humanity is that between those who take the mark of the beast (Rev. 13:16-17) and those who bear the seal of the Lamb (7:3-9). Because of the universal focus of salvation it can be said that there is in the community of salvation "neither Jew nor Greek, . . . neither slave nor free, . . . neither male nor female," but the beginning of a new humanity in Christ in which such distinctions are not barriers to unity (Gal. 3:28; cf. Eph. 1:9-10; 2:14-16). Indeed, Jesus himself said "men will come from east and west, and from north and south, and sit at table in the kingdom of God" (Luke 13:29).

Bibliography. W. G. Kümmel, *Man in the New Testament*, rev. ed. (Philadelphia: 1963); L. Verduin, *Somewhat Less Than God: The Biblical View of Man* (Grand Rapids: 1970); H. W. Wolff, *Anthropology of the Old Testament* (Philadelphia: 1974).

MANNA [măn′ə] (Heb. *mān*; Gk. *mánna*). "Bread from heaven" which sustained the Israelites during their entire time in the wilderness until they had entered the land of Canaan (Exod. 16:35; Josh. 5:12). The Lord promised the demoralized people that he would "rain" for them with the morning dew a portion that each person was to gather every day except the Sabbath (Exod. 16:4-5, 22). They were to have faith that the manna would come as promised every morning and were not to gather more than they could use in the same day except when the day following was the Sabbath; if an excess was gathered it would spoil (vv. 16-30).

Manna is described as "a fine flake-like thing on the face of the wilderness, as fine as hoarfrost on the ground" (v. 14), "like coriander seed, white" (v. 31) and gummy, "like . . . bdellium" (Num. 11:7). It could be boiled like porridge (cf. Exod. 16:23) or ground up and baked into cakes (v. 8) or wafers tasting "like . . . honey" (Exod. 16:31). Several suggestions have been made identifying manna (cf. Heb. *mān hū'* "what is it?"; v. 15) with various natural substances, including lichens carried by the wind, resinous exudations from a number of different kinds of plants (including tamarisk "manna"), and secretions of scale insects and cicadas.

The important aspect of the phenomenon was that it was provided miraculously by God and, as such, represented God's miraculous and saving provision for his people (Deut. 8:3, 16; Neh. 9:20; Ps. 78:24; 105:40; John 6:31). A container of manna was to be kept in the ark of the covenant as a reminder of this divine provision (Exod. 16:32-34; Heb. 9:4). But Jesus compared this temporal and temporary provision with God's eschatological gift of the bread of heaven (John 6:49, 58; cf. Rev. 2:17). Paul saw the manna as a part of the presence of Christ ("the supernatural Rock") with the people of Israel in the wilderness (1 Cor. 10:3-4).

MANOAH [mə nō′ə] (Heb. *mānôaḥ* "rest, resting-place").† A Danite living in the town of Zorah; the father of Samson (Judg. 13; 16:31). As with other important figures, the birth of the hero Samson was announced beforehand to pious but childless parents (13:2-3; cf. 1 Sam. 1:5, 9-17; Luke 1:5-17), and Manoah and his wife conscientiously carried out the instructions given them to prepare Samson for his task (Judg. 13:4-5, 7, 14). The parents did not recognize the messenger as the angel of the Lord until his ascent in the flame of Manoah's sacrifice to God (v. 20); the implications of these events then became clear—the Lord truly was about to show his favor (vv. 21-23).

MANTLE. See CLOTHING.

MANUSCRIPTS (from Lat. *manus* "hand" and *scriptus* "written").† Handwritten documents, in a particular sense early copies of biblical books in scroll or codex form. Biblical texts are represented by thousands of manuscripts in a number of languages and by numerous quotations in ancient authors.

Before the development of practical typographic printing in the fifteenth century A.D., the method for duplicating books was copying by hand, generally by professional scribes. Since books were produced one-by-one, unconscious errors and conscious changes regarded by copyists as improvements easily crept in. Textual criticism, the comparison of manuscripts in order to ascertain the readings most likely to be original, is therefore important when any ancient text (except those represented by only one manuscript) is studied.

Originally books were produced in rolled scroll form, but the more easily handled codex form, in which sheets of papyrus or parchment were stacked or folded together in quires and sewn together much like modern books, gradually displaced the scroll in the first to third centuries A.D. Palimpsest manuscripts are those from which one text has been been erased so that the parchment or vellum might be reused. Ultra-violet photography is now used to enable the reading of the erased text. From the third century B.C. to the tenth century A.D. uncial (majuscule or upper-case) letters were used in Greek manuscripts. From *ca.* A.D. 800 up to the time of printed books, minuscule letters developed from nonliterary cursive script were used.

Bibliography. J. Finegan, *Encountering New Testament Manuscripts* (Grand Rapids: 1974).

MANY WATERS (Heb. *mayim rabbîm*).* A frequent image in Hebrew poetry, presumably derived from the ancient Canaanite (Ugaritic) myth of Baal's battle with the sea (Yamm; cf. *ANET*, pp. 129-132; cf. Marduk and Tiamat). It appears in the earliest examples of Hebrew verse (e.g., 2 Sam. 22:17 par. Ps. 18:16 [MT 17]) and archaizing poetry (e.g., Hab. 3:15; RSV "mighty waters"; cf. Ps. 77:19 [MT 18]; RSV "great waters"; Isa. 51:9-10) among the forces of nature (later used figuratively of Israel's enemies; e.g., Isa. 17:12-13) vanquished by Yahweh as he appears in theophany (cf. Ezek. 1:24; 43:2; Rev. 1:15). In other archaic passages the "many waters" are Yahweh's weapon against his enemies (cf. Exod. 15:10) or a vehicle of creation (Num. 24:7). The figure may denote paradisiacal conditions (Jer. 51:13; cf. Ezek. 17:5; 19:10; 31:5, 15) or danger and destruction (Ps. 144:7; cf. 32:6; Ezek. 26:19).

MAOCH [mā'ŏk] (Heb. *mā'ôk*). The father of King Achish of Gath (1 Sam. 27:2). At 1 Kgs. 2:39 he is called Maacah (3).

MAON [mā'ŏn] (Heb. *mā'ôn* "dwelling") (PERSON).† A Calebite, the son of Shammai and father of Bethzur (1 Chr. 2:45). The name may designate here a clan or village.

MAON [mā'ŏn] (Heb. *mā'ôn* "dwelling") (PLACE). A city in the Shephelah of Judah (Josh. 15:55), identified with modern Tell Ma'în, *ca.* 13.6 km. (8.5 mi.) south of Hebron. Maon was among those towns associated with the descendants of Caleb (1 Chr. 2:45). It was the home of the wealthy Calebite Nabal and his wife Abigail who denied hospitality to David and his followers (1 Sam. 25:2). Earlier the "wilderness of Maon," a desert region east of the town, served as a hiding place for David and his forces when he fled from Saul (23:24-25).

MAONITES [mā'ə nīts] (Heb. *mā'ôn*).† A people from whom, along with the Sidonians and Amalekites, God had delivered the Israelites (Judg. 10:12). The Maonites may be connected with the MEUNIM (cf. 2 Chr. 26:7, "Meunites"), from Mā'an near Petra. The two primary recensions of the LXX read "Midianites" (Gk. *Madiam*, for Heb. *midyān*), people from the same region with whom the Maonites were allied.

MARA [mâr'ə] (Heb. *mārā'* "bitter"). A name taken by Naomi (rather than her own, which means "my pleasant one") after God had "dealt bitterly" with her, that is, after her husband and two sons had died (Ruth 1:20; cf. v. 13).

MARAH [mâr'ə] (Heb. *mārâ'* "bitterness"). A spring, the first source of water found by the Israelites after the Red Sea crossing, three days' journey in the wilderness of Shur (Exod. 15:23; Num. 33:8, "wilderness of Etham"). The water proved to be "bitter," but God showed Moses how to make it sweet (Exod. 15:25). As with other places in the Sinai peninsula named in the accounts of the Exodus, Marah cannot be located with any certainty. 'Ain Hawârah, *ca.* 72 km. (45 mi.) south of the northern end of the Gulf of Suez and about 11 km. (7 mi.) inland, is frequently suggested.

MARALAH (Josh. 19:11, KJV). See MAREAL.

MARANATHA [măr'ə năth'ə] (Gk. *maranathá*). The representation in Greek of an Aramaic expression, most likely "Our Lord, come!" (Aram. *māranā' tā'*; so RSV, 1 Cor. 16:22; KJV "Maranatha"; cf. Rev. 22:20; RSV "Come, Lord Jesus") or possibly "our Lord has come" (*māran 'ᵃtâ*; cf. JB, 1 Cor. 16:22). The expression was in use in the Aramaic language in Greek-speaking Christian congregations (Did. 10:6), reflecting the Palestinian Jewish origin of some of the liturgical language of Greek Gentile congregations (cf. "Amen"; e.g., Gal. 1:5).

MARBLE (Heb. *šēš, šayiš*; Gk. *mármaros*). Limestone (calcium carbonate) crystalized by metamorphism (heat and pressure) into a stone that polishes well and is found in a great variety of colors. As today, marble was used in the ancient Near East in buildings and was a mark of wealth and opulence. According to 1 Chr. 29:2, David gathered marble (JB "masses of alabaster") and other precious materials for use in the construction of the temple; this marble may have been from the limestone-rich hill of Bezetha, north of the temple site. Marble columns and a pavement made of marble and other materials adorned the garden court for the luxurious banquet given by Ahasuerus (Esth. 1:6; the third instance of "marble" in the KJV of this verse represents Heb. *sōheret*; RSV "precious stones"). According to Rev. 18:12, part of the luxurious cargo of the merchants weeping for "Babylon," their former customer, is marble. At Cant. 5:15 marble (RSV, JB "alabaster") columns are symbolic of the lover's physical beauty.

MARCION [mär′shən] (Gk. *Markiōn*), **GOSPEL OF.**† An abridged version of the gospel of Luke by the second-century heretic Marcion of Sinope. It lacks chs. 1–2 of the canonical gospel as well as other "accretions," and revises passages offensive to his particular views.

Troubled by the fourfold account of the good news, Marcion reduced the account to a single book. It is not certain how much of the editing of Luke was actually done by Marcion and how much he received from earlier "ecclesiastical texts." Extremely hostile to Judaism, Marcion rejected the entire Old Testament. His Bible included the "Gospel," this truncated form of Luke (chosen perhaps because he associated Luke with Paul, according to Marcion the only apostle truly faithful to the good news), and "Apostle," ten of the Pauline epistles.

Often labeled a Gnostic, Marcion professed a Docetic christology (he denies the incarnation; Tertullian *Adv. Marc.* iii.8) and practiced an Encratic lifestyle, eschewing meat and marriage. His central focus was the gospel of love as opposed to the (Old Testament) gospel of law (i.27). Marcion was excommunicated in A.D. 144 for his heretical views, but his following thrived until *ca.* the fourth century, particularly in the East.

MARCUS (Col. 4:10; Phlm. 24; 1 Pet. 5:13, KJV). *See* MARK, JOHN.

MARDUK [mär′dûk] (Akk. ᵈAMAR.UTU "calf of the sun [?]," ᵈ*Ma-ru-du-uk-ku*).† The chief god of Babylon and later the state god of Babylonia; son of Ea (Enki). From obscure origins as a local deity perhaps at Eridu and then at Babylon, Marduk gained supremacy as creator god and chief of the pantheon, supplanting Enlil (and assuming his epithet, BEL) following Hammurabi's political successes (*ca.* 1750 B.C.). In the biblical accounts his name is hebraized as Merodach (Jer. 50:2) and as such is compounded in the names Merodach-baladan and Evil-merodach (cf. Mordecai).
See BABYLONIA *II*.

MAREAL [mâr′ĭ əl] (Heb. *marʿălāh*). A city marking a border of the tribal territory of Zebulun (Josh. 19:11; KJV, NIV "Maralah"; JB "Maraalah"; RSV "Mareal" takes the final letter he as locative). From the context, the location must have been slightly north of Megiddo. Tell Ghalta, *ca.* 10 km. (6 mi.) southwest

of Nazareth in the valley of the Kishon river ("the brook which is east of Jokneam"), is a possible site.

MARESHAH [mə rē′shə] (Heb. *mārēšâ*) (**PERSON**).†
1. The firstborn son of Caleb and the father of Ziph (1 Chr. 2:42, following LXX Gk. *Marisa*; MT Heb. *mêšāʿ* "Mesha"; so KJV, NIV) and Hebron. If the second occurrence is read "the father of," following MT (so KJV, NIV, RSV mg.), it may be understood as "the founder of (the town[s] named)," the meaning generally found in this Calebite genealogy. If, however, the first of these two names is taken as "Mesha," then either Mesha was the father of Ziph, who was the father of Mareshah and grandfather of Hebron (so JB; KJV and NIV are less clear), or Mesha and Mareshah were the founders, respectively, of the towns of Ziph and Hebron (so NEB).
2. The son of Laadah, of the tribe of Judah (1 Chr. 4:21).

MARESHAH [mə rē′shə] (Heb. *mārēšâ, mārēʾšâ*) (**PLACE**). A city in the tribal territory of Judah (Josh. 15:44; Mic. 1:15), among the cities fortified by King Rehoboam (2 Chr. 11:8). The city was the site of the battle between King Asa and Zerah the Ethiopian (14:9) and the home of the prophet Eliezer, who prophesied against King Jehoshaphat of Judah for concluding a treaty with King Ahaziah of Israel (20:37). During the Exile the city was annexed by the Idumeans. Called Marisa in the Hellenistic period, it alternated between Seleucid and Ptolemaic control. Judas Maccabeus captured and burned the city (Josephus *Ant.* xii.8.6 [353]; cf. 1 Macc. 5:66), where the Idumean governor Gorgias had fled (2 Macc. 12:35). Pompey restored Marisa to the Idumeans in 63 B.C.; in 47 Julius Caesar annexed it to Judea under the Idumean procurator Antigonus. When Herod the Great took refuge within its walls, Antigonus solicited aid from the Parthians, who destroyed the city in 40 B.C.

Mareshah has been identified with Tell Sandahannah, 1.6 km. (1 mi.) south of Beit Jibrîn (Eleutheropolis).

MARI [mä′rē] (Akk. *Ma-ri*).† An ancient Mesopotamian city situated at Tell Ḥarīrī on the west bank of the Euphrates river near modern Abu Kemal, Syria. More than twenty thousand cuneiform texts discovered in the palace archives of King Zimri-lim thoroughly document the city's history and socioeconomic life in the Old Babylonian period (early second millennium B.C.). Three palaces, built in succession on the same site, date from the early third millennium B.C. (pre-Sargonic II) to the reign of Zimri-lim, the last king of Mari in the Old Babylonian period. Other discoveries include temples to Šamaš, Ishtar, and Dagan. The city is not mentioned in the Bible.

Excavations at the site since confirmation of its identity in 1933 indicate that the city was a thriving commercial center in the early third millennium. Conquered by Sargon of Akkad *ca.* 2300, it remained in Mesopotamian control until Ishbi-erra of Mari overthrew the Third Dynasty of Ur in the early twentieth century. Among the early rulers of the Amorite dynasty of Mari was Iaggid-lim, who fought against the neighboring city of Terqa. His son Iaḫdun-lim fortified cities throughout the Middle Euphrates region and

campaigned as far as the Mediterranean. Local rule
was halted when King Šamši-adad of Assyria, a native
of the rival Terqa, conquered the region; rumored to
have instigated the assassination of Iaḫdun-lim, he installed his son Iasmaḫ-adad as ruler of Mari. Upon
the death of Šamši-adad *ca.* 1780, the legitimate heir
Zimri-lim regained control of Mari, aided by his
father-in-law, King Iarim-lim of Iamḫad (Aleppo).
Iarim-lim's successor, Hammurabi, favored relations
with Babylon over Mari, and Zimri-lim in turn became lax as vassal of Iamḫad. Consequently, Hammurabi destroyed Mari *ca.* 1757.
1757.

Although the Mari texts—correspondence as well
as administrative documents—were written primarily
in standard Akkadian, the official or imperial language, their syntax and vocabulary reflect Northwest
Semitic characteristics; of particular importance to
linguistic study are the Amorite personal names. The
extensive royal correspondence includes diplomatic
exchanges, military directives, and various administrative matters. Of particular historical interest are
letters between the regent Iasmaḫ-adad and the Assyrian kings Šamši-adad and Išme-dagan, and between Zimri-lim and Hammurabi. Administrative and
economic texts concern juridical matters, building
activities, and procurement of food and supplies.

Because the Mari texts represent the approximate
period to which the biblical patriarchs have been dated,
they have been examined extensively for possible correlations with the biblical accounts. Numerous texts
refer to prophetic activity, citing various types or classes
of prophets who receive communications from the
deities, primarily in ecstatic form (such as dreams)
but also through divination. The documents also provide insight into nomadism and transhumance as well
as aspects of social organization (e.g., tribal and clan
organization, inheritance); the connection between the
"sons of the right hand (South)" (Akk. TUR^{MEŠ}.*Ia-
mi-na*) at Mari and the biblical Benjaminites remains
uncertain. Among the possible similarities are the
military "thousand" (Sem. *'lp*), the census, the institution of the "ban" (cf. Heb. *ḥerem*; *see* DEVOTED),
and the military title *dawidum* "commander" (*see*
DAVID). *See* ARCHAEOLOGY, BIBLICAL *V.*

Bibliography. BA 47/2 (1984): 70-120; A. Malamat,
Mari and the Bible, 2nd ed. (Jerusalem: 1980).

MARIAMNE [mărĭ ăm'nē] (Gk. *Mariamne*).† The
name of two of Herod the Great's ten wives. The first,
his second wife, was the daughter of the Hasmonean
ruler Hyrcanus II and Alexandra; their offspring were
sons Alexander and Aristobulus and daughters Sa-
lampsio and Cypros. At her insistence Herod named
her brother Aristobulus high priest. Incited by his sister Salome and Mariamne's mother, Herod had Mariamne assassinated in 29 (some accounts date her
murder to 35 or 34) B.C. The second Mariamne was
the daughter of the high priest Simon and the mother
of Herod's half-brother Philip; she and Herod produced a son, Herod Boethus. It was apparently this
wife for whom Herod named one of the three towers
of his palace at Jerusalem.

MARISA. *See* MARESHAH (PLACE).

MARK.† The common noun "mark" represents a target or goal (e.g., 1 Sam. 20:20; Phil. 3:14; RSV "goal")
or a scar on a person's body, usually one deliberately
made so as to identify or stigmatize that person.
Marking the body with tattoos (Heb. k^e*ṭōbet qa*$^{⊂a}$*qa*$^⊂$)
was among mourning rites involving physical disfig-
urement prohibited to Israelites (Lev. 19:28; cf. 21:5;
Deut. 14:1). Similarly, the worship of Yahweh did not
follow the practice of gashing the body (1 Kgs. 18:28).
Circumcision, however, was recognized as a marking
of the body that was legitimate in the context of Israelite worship as "the sign (*'ôt*) of the covenant"
(Gen. 17:11). The use of phylacteries (Exod. 13:9,
16; Deut. 6:8; 11:18) might have arisen from a custom
of ritual marking or tattooing of the body (*see*
PHYLACTERY).

In Ezekiel's vision of idolatry in the temple and the
resultant punishment (Ezek. 8–11), a mark in the
form of the letter tau (Heb. *tāw*)—at that time like
the letter *X,* not in the form of a cross (as assumed by
JB)—is set on the foreheads of those grieving because
of the idolatry; thus the executioners seen in the vision
will know to spare them (9:4, 6; cf. Exod. 28:36-38;
and the "sign" in the Passover story; 12:3). The "mark"
placed on Cain (Gen. 4:15) was also a protective sign,
reminiscent of brands placed on Sumerian slaves to
hinder their running away; here apparently it was related to Cain's transition from sedentary, civilized life
to nomadic life. The mark (Gk. *cháragma* of "the
beast" (Rev. 13:16-17; 19:20) is intended by the forces
of evil as a protective and authorizing sign; under
God's sovereignty it becomes a mark of those to be
destroyed (14:9-11; 16:2; 20:4), in contrast to the
mark of those who persist in their faith in Christ
(14:1; cf. 7:3-4).

Paul speaks of the "marks (*stígmata*) of Jesus" that
he has on his body (Gal. 6:17). Although the apostle
may well have known of specific scars resulting from
Jesus' crucifixion, such as the mark (*týpos*) of the nail
driven through each hand (John 20:25), he probably
has in mind here scars he himself had received in the
course of his mission work (cf. 2 Cor. 11:23-25).

MARK, GOSPEL OF.† The second book of the New
Testament and the second (in canonical order) of the
four Gospels.

I. Authorship

A strong tradition in the early Church affirms that
Mark (John Mark) is the author of the gospel bearing
his name and that the book represents the preaching
of the apostle Peter. According to Papias (Eusebius
HE iii.39.15; cf. ii.15; v.8.3), Mark was "the interpreter of Peter" and "accompanied Peter." Indeed, the
gospel does reflect an acquaintance with Peter and
recount details of Jesus' ministry (e.g., his healings
of a leper [Mark 1:40], a man with a withered hand
[3:5], and a demoniac [5:4-6]), in a way suggestive
of contact with an eyewitness. The influence of the
Aramaic language on the syntax and usage of Mark's
Greek may derive from the gospel's relation to the
preaching of Peter. A concern for the coming of the
gospel to the Gentiles is occasionally evident (e.g.,
7:19, 24-29), as would be expected from a coworker
of Paul such as Mark (Acts 12:12, 25; Phlm. 24).

Mark 1 in Codex Sinaiticus (by courtesy of the Trustees of the British Museum)

Mark could have written his gospel at Rome (called "Babylon" at 1 Pet. 5:13, which may place Mark there), perhaps shortly after Peter's death (probably during the Neronian persecution in A.D. 64-65). The gospel was certainly written not long after, although some interpret Mark 13:2 as a reference to the fall of Jerusalem in A.D. 70.

II. Addressees and Purpose

Mark addressed his gospel to Gentile Christians who had no close acquaintance with Jewish customs, some of which he explains in the course of his account (e.g., 7:3; 14:12; 15:42). For the same reason he provides a translation of Semitic words and phrases as they arise in his narrative (3:17; 5:41; 7:11, 34; 10:46; 14:36; 15:22, 34).

Mark also uses transliterations (rather than translations) of several Latin terms, such as *praetorium* (15:16; Gk. *praitórion*), *centurio* (15:39, 44-45; *kenturíōn*), *denarius* (12:15; *dēnárion*; RSV "coin"), *quadrans* (v. 42; *kodrántēs*; RSV "penny"), and *speculator* (6:27; *spekoulátōr*; RSV "soldier"). Although these Latin words are typical loanwords, they do suggest the concern of a Palestinian Jew to speak properly to a Roman Gentile audience. Indeed, Mark's primary aim was to make the gospel concerning "Jesus Christ, the Son of God" (1:1) understandable to a Gentile audience.

III. Mark and the Synoptics

For centuries Mark's gospel was virtually ignored, overshadowed as it was by Matthew's and John's gospels. In recent years interest in Mark has grown as a result of the Markan or two-source hypothesis, according to which Mark is one of the two main sources of Matthew and Luke, the other two Synoptic Gospels. This view contrasts with the long-held view that Mark was essentially a later abbreviation of Matthew. But the priority of Mark is not without challenge.

See SYNOPTIC GOSPELS.

IV. Contents

If the usual view, which holds that Mark was the earliest of the Synoptic Gospels and a source of Matthew and Luke, is correct, then Mark was apparently the creator of the "gospel" genre as a literary means of Christian teaching. While the overall outline of Mark and the other Gospels—the coming of Jesus (1:2-15), his teaching and attestation as God-sent by miracles (1:16-13:37), and his death and resurrection at Jerusalem (14:1-16:8)—is apparently based on the form given to proclamation of the good news in early sermons (e.g., Acts 2:22-24; 10:36-40), the story is filled out considerably by Mark.

Mark announces his theme as "the gospel of Jesus Christ, the Son of God" (Mark 1:1). Jesus' identity, thus announced at the outset, is the primary focus of Mark's gospel. Jesus' commands for silence with regard to his messiahship (1:25, 34; 3:12; 8:30) and miracles (1:43-45; 5:43; 7:36; 8:26; cf. 9:9) have been considered by some an effort by the gospel writer to reconcile the Church's belief in Jesus as Messiah with the factual history of Jesus' ministry, in which (it is assumed) Jesus was not identified as the Messiah. But these commands were more likely the result of Jesus' concern that "Messiah" and other titles would elicit incorrect understandings of his mission. Jesus was not simply the "Messiah," with all that the term might mean. He was the Messiah whose course was set toward suffering.

A. The Coming of Jesus. Jesus comes, heralded by John the baptizer, and his ministry is prefaced by his baptism by John, the descent of the Spirit on him, and his temptation in the desert (1:2-13). As Jesus enters into Galilee, the main scene of his ministry, a summary of his preaching of the gospel is given: "The time is fulfilled, and the kingdom of God is at hand; repent and believe in the gospel" (vv. 14-15).

B. The Ministry of Jesus. Jesus teaches, heals, and calls disciples to himself, and in so doing gains fame (1:16-45). He also comes into conflict with Pharisees and pharisaic scribes; five accounts of such confrontations (2:1-3:5) culminate with a plot on Jesus' life (3:6).

From this point, Jesus' ministry becomes more focused on the twelve disciples, and the gospel describes his teaching more broadly (3:7-6:13). The twelve are chosen so that they can preach and exorcise demons as Jesus has been doing (3:13-19). They do set forth on such a mission (6:7-13), but only after accounts of various matters: controversy concerning the nature of Jesus (3:20-35; 6:1-6; cf. vv. 14-16; 8:27-30); Jesus' teaching in parables, by which he makes a distinction between those who only hear him and those who seek out the meaning of what he is saying (4:1-34); and miracles which especially show the power associated with Jesus' person (4:35-5:43). After the death of John the baptizer and the return of the twelve from their mission (6:14-30), Jesus' ministry extends beyond Galilee (6:34-8:30).

Peter's identification of Jesus as "the Christ" (i.e., the Messiah; 8:30) marks the beginning of a quite different phase of Jesus' ministry in which he is depicted as the Messiah who is on a course toward suffering, and discipleship to Jesus is depicted as involving suffering. From this point, Jesus predicts his own execution and resurrection at Jerusalem (vv. 31-33; 9:30-32; 10:32-34; cf. 9:12), focusses his teaching on the cost of being his disciple (8:34-38; 9:33-37, 43-50; 10:17-31, 35-45), and sets his course toward Jerusalem (vv. 1, 32). The transfiguration of Jesus in the presence of Moses and Elijah (9:2-8) places the identification of Jesus as Messiah in the broader context of salvation history.

Jesus' entry into Jerusalem, a deliberate fulfillment of Zech. 9:9 (though Mark does not point this out), is the occasion of his acclamation as "he who comes in the name of the Lord" and as at least the herald of "the kingdom of our father David," probably the king himself (Mark 11:1-10). Jesus' few days of ministry in and near Jerusalem (11:11–13:37) are a tale of mounting controversy and tension. The plot against Jesus' life starts moving after he drives money-changers and animal-sellers out of the outer courts of the temple (11:15-18) and proceeds through an interrogation concerning the authority for Jesus' actions (vv. 27-33); a clearly understood parable against his interrogators (12:1-12); questions concerning tribute (vv. 13-17), the resurrection (vv. 18-27), and, again, the nature of the Messiah (vv. 35-37); and Jesus' drawing of a contrast between his opponents, the scribes (vv. 38-40) and a more humble Jew (vv. 41-44, cf. v. 37b). The apocalyptic discourse of ch. 13 serves, in effect, as a final warning to both the disciples and to the Church (note especially v. 37; cf. 14:38).

C. Crucifixion and Resurrection. The plot against Jesus then becomes a definite plan (14:1-2, 10-11). The anointing of Jesus at Bethany (vv. 3-9) and his final Passover meal (14:12-21) are both done with Jesus fully aware of the plot and the outcome it will have. After the institution of the Lord's Supper (vv. 22-25), Jesus' prediction of the scattering of the disciples and of his own resurrection (vv. 26-31), and Jesus' prayer in Gethsemane (vv. 32-42), the plot begins to take control—Jesus is betrayed and arrested (vv. 43-50). The account of Jesus' trials (14:53-65; 15:1-15) emphasizes the difficulty with which the case was made against Jesus (14:55-61a) and Pilate's unwillingness to endorse Jesus' condemnation, despite his carrying it out (15:5, 9-15). The predicted scattering of the disciples finds its confirmation in Peter's threefold denial of Jesus (14:66-72). Again, during the trial, the question of Jesus' identity arises and is answered: "the Christ, the Son of the Blessed [i.e., of God]" (14:61-62) and "the King of the Jews" (15:2).

The account of Jesus' crucifixion (15:16-41) emphasizes the suffering of Jesus and, on the one hand, the mocking of his identity (vv. 17-19, 26, 29-32, 35) and, on the other hand, the affirmation of his identity even at the point of his death (vv. 38-39). The body of Jesus is laid in a tomb (vv. 42-47). Two days later, three women go to the tomb. Jesus' body is not found, but his resurrection is announced to the women (16:1-8).

As it now stands, the gospel may be missing its original ending, although a good case can be made for it ending with 16:8. In any case, the textual evidence is strongly against the inclusion of either the "longer ending" (16:9-20) or any of the shorter endings (the most common of which appears in the RSV mg. at v. 20). While a gospel account without resurrection appearances is difficult to explain, it is certain from the predictions of the event recorded in Mark's gospel that Jesus' resurrection at Jerusalem was considered an essential part of the gospel, and from 1 Cor. 15:3-8 that specific resurrection appearances were ordinarily part of Christian teaching of the gospel before Mark was written.

Bibliography. C. E. B. Cranfield, *The Gospel According to St. Mark,* rev. ed. CGNTC (1977); S. Kealy, *Mark's Gospel: A History of its Interpretation* (New York: 1982); W. L. Lane *The Gospel According to Mark.* NICNT (1974); R. P. Martin, *Mark: Evangelist and Theologian* (Grand Rapids: 1972); V. Taylor, *The Gospel according to St. Mark,* 2nd ed. (Grand Rapids: 1981).

MARK, JOHN (Gk. *Iōannēs Markos*).† The son of Mary of Jerusalem (Acts 12:12); a companion of the apostles Paul and Peter, believed to be the author of the gospel of Mark.

The family of John Mark was apparently of some importance to the early Church in Jerusalem since Peter, after his miraculous escape from jail, went to the house of Mark's mother, where he knew that many Christians would be gathered to pray (Acts 12:12). This house was a center for Christian gathering; that it also contained the upper room, the setting for the institution of the Lord's Supper and the Pentecost event, as is often suggested, is far from certain.

Mark went with Barnabas and Paul first to the Gentile Christian community at Antioch (v. 25) and then to Cyprus, where Paul's first missionary journey began (13:5; "John"). But when Barnabas and Paul began to enter the interior of Asia Minor, Mark left them and returned to Jerusalem (v. 13). Mark's departure later caused a dispute between Barnabas and Paul; Barnabas wanted Mark to accompany them on a new journey, but Paul did not. Paul took a new companion, Silas, and went into Asia Minor, while Barnabas and Mark went to Cyprus (15:36-41). John Mark, though perhaps not a central character in the early mission to the Gentiles, was, like Barnabas and Silas, one of those by whom the church of Jerusalem and the Gentile churches beyond Syria were linked together.

Twice in Acts Mark is referred to as "John whose other name was Mark" (Acts 12:12, 25; cf. 15:37) because of possible confusion with John the son of Zebedee and because John was a common name among Jews. Twice he is called John (13:5, 13) and once Mark (15:39), but confusion is ruled out by links made in the course of the narrative. What is not so certain is that all of the other references to Mark in the New Testament refer to the same person. Marcus was a very common Latin name.

It is, nonetheless, quite likely that "Mark the cousin of Barnabas" (Col. 4:10; KJV "sister's son") was the same person as John Mark. Barnabas' cousin was with Paul, probably at Rome, when Paul wrote to the Colossians, and it was expected that he might go to Colossae. This Mark is in all likelihood the Mark named at Phlm. 24; both are named with Aristarchus, and the two letters were written to the same city probably about the same time. It is possible that John Mark overcame his fear of venturing beyond the familiarity of Judea, Syria, and Cyprus (if that is what caused his turning back) and was reconciled to Paul. 2 Tim. 4:11 asks the recipient of the letter to send Mark, "for he is very useful in serving me."

1 Pet. 5:13 probably places "my son Mark" at Rome ("Babylon") with Peter. If John Mark was in Rome with Paul, he may well have been in the same city with Peter. "Son" here certainly refers to a spiritual relationship (cf. Phil. 2:22; 1 Tim. 1:18) rather than to literal parentage. According to early Church tradition Mark accompanied Peter, for whom he was the "interpreter" (Eusebius *HE* iii.39.15), and wrote the gospel of Mark at Rome.

The reference to the "young man" who fled naked from Gethsemane (Mark 14:51-52) has been thought of as a reference by the author of the gospel to himself, but there is no real ground for this; the young man's flight is mentioned to emphasize that "all forsook [Jesus] and fled" (v. 50).

Church tradition also speaks of Mark as the first Christian preacher in Alexandria (Eusebius *HE* ii.16.1; ii.14), and later associates him with Venice.

MARKETPLACE (Heb. *rᵉḥôḇ*; Gk. *agorá*). In the typical ancient town, a place not only for buying and selling but also for public assembly and debate (Matt. 11:16 par.; 20:3; 23:7; Mark 6:56 [KJV "streets"]; 7:4). In Hellenistic cities the central square served as the marketplace; in older Palestinian cities it was the city gate (cf. Ps. 55:11 [MT 12]; Prov. 1:20; 7:12). At Philippi the local magistrates held a court session in the marketplace, to which irate citizens brought Paul and Silas (Acts 16:19ff.). In the marketplace of Athens Paul argued daily with whomever he encountered (17:17).

MAROTH [mârʹōth] (Heb. *mārôṯ* "bitterness"). A town in Judah (Mic. 1:12), possibly the same as Maarath (Khirbet Qufin; Josh. 15:59).

MARRIAGE.† Marriage is presented in the Bible as an essential aspect of social life. It is the outcome and intention of God's creation of mankind as male and female, counterparts of each other, capable of reproduction and indeed commanded to reproduce (Gen. 1:27-28; 2:18-24). Much of the Bible is given over to regulating and teaching about marriage, especially in view of the contrast between the attitudes required of God's people toward sex and human relationships and the attitudes of surrounding peoples (e.g., Lev. 18:1-5; 1 Thess. 4:3-6).

I. Old Testament

To remain unmarried was considered a disgrace by the Hebrews, largely because the production of offspring was viewed as essential for the perpetuation of the covenant community. For women not to marry made life tenuous, because necessities of life normally came from a husband's support (cf. Isa. 4:1; cf. provisions for the care of widows; e.g., Deut. 14:29; 24:19-21). Since having no descendants was a disgrace for a man (cf. Ps. 127:3-5), a wife who failed to bear children was of less value than one who did (Gen. 16:4; 1 Sam. 1:5-6).

Weddings were celebrated with feasting (Gen. 29:22; Judg. 14:10), special adornment of bride and groom

(Cant. 3:11; Isa. 61:10), and music (Jer. 16:9). Ps. 45 is a song for a royal wedding procession (cf. 1 Macc. 9:37, 39).

Generally a woman would leave her own community to join that of her husband (Gen. 24:5-8, 58-61), but sometimes the reverse may have been the case (cf. 2:24). It was when the man brought the woman into his home that the couple actually was considered married (24:67). A newly married man was to be free from military service for one year (Deut. 24:5). Brothers would sometimes continue after marriage to live together, so that, with their wives and children, they formed a large family unit; underlying Ps. 133 may be a protest against the erosion of such a system, which was of importance for the consolidation and maintenance of property in the family. The same objective was served by the institution of LEVIRATE MARRIAGE.

Although polygyny is recognized and not condemned, the Old Testament assumes that monogamy is the basic form of marriage, or at least that a man should be faithful above all to "the wife of his youth" (Prov. 5:18-19; Mal. 2:14-15). It may be that the two wives of Lamech are emphasized (Gen. 4:19) to associate the origin of polygyny with the evil line of Cain. Concubines and secondary wives are associated mostly with, though by no means restricted to, the patriarchal period and royalty.

The tendency toward monogamy or the preference of a primary wife was reinforced most of all by love, which was acknowledged as a significant—though certainly not the only—force in the initiation and nature of marriage relationships (e.g., Gen. 24:67; 1 Sam. 18:20). Recognition of the dangers into which sexual attraction could lead (Prov. 7:6-27) did not draw the people of Israel into a harsh puritanism, but rather into a celebration of the pleasures of faithful marriage (ch. 31; Eccl. 9:9; Cant. 8:12).

In ancient Hebrew practice the wife was little more than the property of her husband (cf. Exod. 20:17). Although marriage might be called a "covenant" (Heb. *bᵉrîṯ*; Mal. 2:14; cf. Ezek. 16:8), this does not imply equality. The common Hebrew word for husband (*bāʿal*) means "owner, master" (e.g., Exod. 21:22; 2 Sam. 11:26; cf. Gen. 20:3, MT). A man entered into marriage by paying a marriage present (*mōhar*) to the bride's father, not so much a purchase price as compensation for his clan's loss of her offspring (34:12; 1 Sam. 18:25; cf. Gen. 29:18). A father could sell his daughter as a concubine, but the law did seek to protect the status of such women (Exod. 21:7-11). If a man raped or seduced an unmarried woman, he was required to pay the marriage gift to her father and take her as his wife (22:16-17; Deut. 22:28-29). Yet because the husband was regarded as master over his wife, adultery was a crime only against the man whose wife or fiancée had been unfaithful; there was no sense in which it could be a crime against the woman (Lev. 20:10; Deut. 22:22-24). But that marriage was not as simple as an owner-property relationship is shown by the contrast in penalties for intercourse with a betrothed female slave (Lev. 19:20-22) and for adultery.

Specific relationships are forbidden as incestuous (Lev. 18:6-18), punishable by death (20:11-12, 14, 17). Some consanguineous unions proscribed in Israel were permitted among the Egyptians and Canaanites (18:3), and indeed were entered into from the time of the Israelite patriarchs on (cf. Gen. 20:12; Lev. 18:9; cf. Amos 2:7). Priests were more stringently restricted than other Israelites in whom they could marry; they had to marry virgins, never women that had been raped, divorced, or served as prostitutes (Lev. 21:7).

At the same time, marriage outside the Israelite nation was forbidden, ostensibly to guard against religious corruption but also to prevent alienation of the land allotted to Israel by its actual owner, Yahweh (Exod. 34:12-16; Deut. 7:3-4; Josh. 23:12-13; cf. Num. 36:1-12). Kings, however, frequently entered into marriage alliances with foreign peoples (cf. 1 Kgs. 11:1-11). With the social upheaval following the Exile, Ezra and Nehemiah found it necessary to reinstate the requirement of strict national endogamy (Ezra 9–10; Neh. 10:30; 13:23-27).

Divorce initiated by men was permitted and regulated with a view to stabilizing society, preventing unrestrained exchanging of partners, and protecting women by requiring a written document of divorce (Deut. 24:1-4). Women who were full wives could not initiate divorce, but under certain conditions concubines could leave their owner-husbands (Exod. 21:7-11).

II. New Testament

Monogamy continued as the norm in New Testament times; it was only the few who could afford to be polygamous. Among their contemporaries in the ancient world, the Greeks also were for the most part monogamous, as were the Romans.

Jesus' teaching on marriage and divorce surpasses the Old Testament's more legalistic regulation of divorce. He sees in Gen. 1:27; 2:24 evidence that God intended marriage to be permanent (Mark 10:6-9; cf. Mal. 2:14-16). Only at Matt. 5:32; 19:9 is an exception to his rejection of divorce made "on the ground of unchastity" (Gk. porneía); otherwise, divorce itself can be regarded as the cause of adultery (5:32 par.; Mark 10:2-12 par.). The exception may have been added by a conservative Church which wished to retain adultery as grounds for divorce; or perhaps porneía, a general word for any unlawful sexual intercourse, may here refer only to cases where the marriage itself was discovered to be illegal because of consanguinity.

The rights of men over their wives are reduced by the rejection of divorce, and the position of women is improved by the redefinition of adultery. Through divorce and remarriage a man can commit adultery against his wife (Mark 10:11). Similarly, Jesus' extension of what constitutes adultery (Matt. 5:27-28) shifts the focus away from a man's rights over his wife to the mental attitude of one who even entertains the thought of adultery.

Paul reiterates Jesus' rejection of divorce (1 Cor. 7:10-11) and applies it to situations that arise when individuals become Christians and their spouses do not. Because the marriage relationship is to be one of "peace" or "wholeness," Paul does not consider such situations grounds for divorce—yet neither does he deter non-Christian spouses from seeking divorce for that reason (vv. 12-16; cf. 2 Pet. 3:1-2). Nonetheless,

marriage by Christians is to be endogamous; Christians faced with the possibility of marriage should marry "only in the Lord" (1 Cor. 7:39)—a point that needed little emphasis in view of the Corinthians' belief that non-Christian spouses should be divorced.

The traditional interpretation of Paul's teachings on marriage is that Christians should adhere to the pattern of the husband's leadership and the wife's submission (Eph. 5:22; Col. 3:18; cf. 1 Pet. 3:1-2; 1 Cor. 11:3). It has been suggested, however, that Paul may be encouraging the mutual subjection of spouses to each other (Eph. 5:21). Indeed, the pattern of dominance by an owner-husband had been broken and salvation been given equally to men and women (Gal. 3:28).

Jesus accepts celibacy as a voluntary response to the kingdom of God, but he restricts it to those who are not "able to receive" what he has taught about the indissolubility of marriage (Matt. 19:10-12). This teaching assumes that in a community with an eschatological focus, such as the early Church or the Qumran community (where celibacy was required of some), some will think it best to abstain from marriage. Indeed, at Corinth some Christians thought it best to adopt celibacy even though they were married—a radical position that Paul rejects as dangerous, though he does allow for temporary abstention from sex (1 Cor. 7:2-6). For persons who are not already married, he recommends remaining unmarried because of the eschatological focus that the Christian should have; exception could be made in the case of those for whom not being married would pose the danger of temptation to immorality (vv. 7-9, 25-38, 40). Paul refuses to set an absolute rule, either for laypeople or apostles (cf. 9:5), even though he considers his view the best (7:28, 36, 39, 40; cf. 1 Tim. 4:1-3).

III. Figurative Use

Frequently the relationship between God and his people is depicted as that between husband and wife. This imagery is particularly developed in the prophets, which often employ the entire history of a marriage relationship (Jer. 3:1-14; Ezek. 16; Hos. 1–3). Among the points so illustrated by the prophets are: the good that befalls the homeless or childless woman when her husband receives her (Isa. 54:1-3; Ezek. 16:8-14); the unfaithful wife's entering into prostitution, a metaphor for idolatry (Jer. 3:1-2; Hos. 1:2); the unfaithful spouse's misuse in her prostitution and adultery of the good things provided by her faithful spouse (Ezek. 16:15-26, 30-34; Hos. 2:8); the unfaithful spouse's desire to remain on friendly terms with her spouse without becoming faithful herself (Jer. 3:3b-5); the rejection of the unfaithful one (God's judgment of his people—Ezek. 16:27, 35-63; Hos. 2:2 [which contains the text of a bill of divorce], 3-13); the true lover's seeking for his unfaithful beloved (Jer. 3:6-14; Hos. 2:14-20; 3:1-5); and reconciliation, restoration, and rejoicing (Isa. 54:1-8; 62:4-5).

At Eph. 5:22-30, within the context of the ethical code of the ideal household (cf. Col. 3:18-19; 1 Pet. 3:1, 7), the husband-wife relationship is metaphorically applied to the relationship of Christ and the Church; Gen. 2:24 is cited as the foundation for the unity of Christ and the Church (Eph. 5:31-33). At

Rev. 19:7-9 the messianic banquet of Christ at the end of the age is depicted as a wedding feast in which the marriage of the Lamb (Christ) and his bride (the Church) is celebrated (cf. Matt. 22:2-14; Luke 14:15). *See* BRIDE OF CHRIST.

Bibliography. O. A. Piper, *The Biblical View of Sex and Marriage* (New York: 1960); H. Thielicke, *Theological Ethics.* Vol. 3: *Sex* (Grand Rapids: 1975).

MARRIAGE PRESENT. *See* DOWRY.

MARS' HILL (Acts 17:22, KJV). *See* AREOPAGUS.

MARSENA [mär sē'nə] (Heb. *mars^enā'*). One of the seven nobles of King Ahasuerus who had most direct access to the king (Esth. 1:14).

MARSH (Heb. *biṣṣâ*).* Soft wet land. The marshes of Job 8:11 (KJV "mire"), supporting the growth of papyrus, and 40:21 (KJV "fens"), where Behemoth lies among the lotus plants and reeds, are those of the Nile valley. The river flowing from the temple in the vision of Ezek. 47:1-12 turns the Dead Sea into fresh water; only the swamps (*biṣṣâ*; KJV "miry places") and marshes (*gebe'*; KJV "marshes") south of the Sea will remain salty to provide the salt needed for life. These salt marshes, known as es-Sebkha, are a mineral-rich "land possessed by nettles and salt pits" (Zeph. 2:9).

MARSHAL. The organization of war against Babylon foreseen at Jer. 51:27 includes the summoning of a "marshal" (Heb. *ṭipsār*; KJV "captain"), probably a military official responsible for mustering troops. (The same Hebrew word is used at Nah. 3:17 of government officials in Nineveh; RSV "scribes"; RSV mg. "marshals"; KJV "captains.") In the song of Deborah and Barak, "those who bear the marshal's staff" (so RSV; KJV "they that handle the pen of the writer") are mentioned (Judg. 5:14). Here it would appear that the "marshal" (*sōpēr* "scribe") has clerical duties involving the census of the troops (but cf. R. G. Boling, *Judges.* AB 6A [1975]: 103, 112, "bearers of the ruler's scepter"); the same function is held by the "secretary" (*sōpēr*; KJV "scribe") at 2 Kgs. 25:19; Jer. 52:25.

MARTHA [mär'thə] (Gk. *Martha,* from Aram. *mārṭā'* "mistress, hostess" [fem. form of *mar* "lord, master"]).† The sister of Mary and Lazarus (Luke 10:38-39; John 11:1, 21). In all three accounts of visits of Jesus with Martha, she takes a leading role—as a homeowner and hostess (Luke 10:38-40; John 12:2) and as the one who goes out to meet Jesus and deals most directly with him (John 11:20-28, 39). Martha's role as a busy hostess is set in contrast with Mary's attention to the teaching of Jesus, and leads to Martha's complaint against her sister directed to Jesus (Luke 10:39-40). Jesus rebukes Martha's anxiety and commends Mary's attention to his teaching, in effect, to the kingdom of God (vv. 41-42; cf. 12:22-31).

After the death of Lazarus, Martha shows the same willingness to speak boldly to Jesus, but also considerable faith in him (John 11:21-22). She believes that Jesus intends to console her with the hope of the final resurrection (vv. 23-24), but he links himself with the resurrection as the giver of life itself (vv. 25-26). This elicits a confession from Martha that Jesus is the promised Messiah (v. 27; cf. Matt. 16:16). Jesus does not clearly say that he intends to raise Lazarus from the dead, so his request to have the tomb opened is misunderstood by Martha, who is the one to remind him that Lazarus had been dead long enough for decomposition to set in (John 11:39).

If the meal of 12:1-7, at which Martha was the hostess, is the same as the meal at the house of Simon the leper (Matt. 26:6-13; Mark 14:3-9), Martha may have been the daughter or wife (perhaps widow) of Simon. John places Martha's home at Bethany 1 near Jerusalem (John 11:1, 18; 12:2). If Luke's gospel is taken as a chronologically ordered account, Martha's home could hardly be at Bethany, since at the time of his visit Jesus is resolutely headed toward Jerusalem, has entered but not yet gone beyond Samaria, and has certainly not yet gone as far as Jericho (Luke 9:51-53; 13:22, 33; 17:11; 18:31, 35; 19:1). Luke's account probably does not, however, place all incidents in strict chronological order.

MARTYR. The meaning of Gk. *mártys* at the time of the New Testament was simply "witness." The word is frequently used in Acts to designate the apostles, considered "witnesses" of the resurrected Jesus (so RSV; e.g., Acts 1:8, 22; 2:32). Willingness to suffer was to be an integral part of their testimony (5:40-42; 9:15-16). Other Christians who suffered death for their witness came in time to be called *mártyres* (22:20; Rev. 2:13; 17:6), but the Christian use of the word specifically for those who had died for the faith did not come until later than the New Testament, with the veneration of Christian martyrs (cf. Ignatius *Rom.* 2; Mart.Pol. 14:2; 17:3).

MARY (Gk. *Mariam, Maria,* from Heb., Aram. *miryām* "Miriam").

1.† The mother of Jesus and wife of Joseph (Matt. 1:16).

I. New Testament

Mary lived in Nazareth where she was betrothed to Joseph, a carpenter. Before the consummation of their marriage, the angel Gabriel appeared to her at her home with the message that she would bear a son, who was to be God's own Son (Luke 1:26-28; cf. Matt. 1:18). Shortly thereafter she traveled to the home of her relative Elizabeth in the hills of Judea (Luke 1:39-40), where Elizabeth confirmed the angel's message (vv. 41-45). Before the birth of her son, Mary traveled again to Judea with Joseph, this time because of a census ordered by Emperor Caesar Augustus. She gave birth to Jesus at Bethlehem under unusual circumstances—in a stable—because the inns were crowded by those responding to the census (2:1-7). Forty days later Mary and Joseph accompanied the child to Jerusalem to present him to God and to purify Mary after childbirth in accordance with the law (vv. 22-24; cf. Lev. 12). It was apparently after this that the couple escaped to Egypt to escape Herod's massacre of young boys in the region of Bethlehem (Matt. 2:16-18). After returning from Egypt, the family returned to Nazareth, which became the home of Jesus (vv. 19-23; cf. Luke 2:39).

When Jesus was twelve years old, Mary and Joseph took him to Jerusalem to celebrate the Passover. When they discovered that Jesus had not accompanied them as they left the city, they became worried, turned back, and three days later found him in the temple (vv. 41-47). Jesus' answer to Mary's rebuke, which shows considerable awareness of his identity as God's Son, was not really understood by his parents (vv. 48-49). Mary had heard much about the role Jesus was to play (including how it would affect her; v. 35) and may have become increasingly aware of it (vv. 19, 51 are merely hints), but much confusion no doubt remained (cf. vv. 33, 50). Some interpreters suggest that, as Jesus' fame grew during his ministry, she was confronted with the rumor that he was an illegitimate child (cf. John 8:41).

After the incident in the temple, Joseph does not appear in the gospels again; perhaps Mary was widowed before Jesus' ministry began (but cf. 6:42). Mary was with Jesus and his disciples at Cana at the outset of his ministry and there called on Jesus to perform his first miracle (2:1-11); Jesus apparently remained with his family for some time after this miracle (v. 12). Later, Mary and the brothers of Jesus once sought to extricate him from the crowds which had become typical of his Galilean ministry (Matt. 12:46 par. Mark 3:31-32 [cf. v. 20]; Luke 8:19); their concern was that he had gone mad (Mark 3:21). On hearing of his family's request, Jesus in effect separated himself from them by expressing a closer relationship to his disciples, "whoever does the will of God" (vv. 33-35; cf. Luke 11:27-28). Beyond the accounts of this incident, no indication is given of whether Mary became an actual disciple prior to the crucifixion; his brothers did not (John 7:3-5). Mary was present when Jesus was crucified, and he committed her to the care of John, "the disciple whom he loved" (19:25-27). After Jesus' resurrection and ascension, Mary and Jesus' brothers were among the disciples who "with one accord devoted themselves to prayer" in the upper room (Acts 1:14).

See also MAGNIFICAT.

II. Theological Significance

Mary has a special role in Roman Catholicism which she does not have among Protestants. Aspects of this special role are the perpetual virginity of Mary and an expanded understanding of her role in salvation as "mother of God" (Gk. theotókos)—the one through whom God became human—and as a primary intercessor before God for Christians.

The view that Mary remained a virgin even as she conceived Jesus is derived from the New Testament (Matt. 1:18-23; Luke 1:31-35; cf. Gal. 4:4). The belief that she, as "the handmaid of the Lord" (Luke 1:38), remained a virgin all her life began early in the Church and has continued to be a focus of Roman Catholic teaching. Accordingly, the "brothers" of Jesus (Matt. 12:46 par.; 13:55 par.; John 2:12; 7:3-5, 10; Acts 1:14; 1 Cor. 9:5; Gal. 1:19) were not sons of Mary born after Jesus her "firstborn" (Luke 2:7; cf Matt. 1:25) but rather cousins of Jesus or sons of Joseph by an earlier marriage. See BROTHERS OF THE LORD; VIRGIN; 3 below.

As the mother of sinless Jesus, Mary could not have been a transmitter of inherited sin to her son. Thus she has been presented in Roman Catholic doctrine as sinless by a special grace (this as early as 1439) and herself born as the result of an Immaculate Conception (this received papal approval in 1483 and papal definition in 1854). According to this teaching, Jesus received his sinless nature from his mother. It has also come to be Roman Catholic teaching that Mary was preserved from the corruptions of the grave and taken up body and soul into heaven (this is found as early as the fourth century and was given papal definition in 1950).

Furthermore, Mary is held in Roman Catholic teaching to have a unique and essential role in the coming of salvation, in that her obedient cooperation with God's intention (Luke 1:38, taken as a model for the obedience of the Church) paved the way for carrying out that intention. In this sense and because all Christians were "in Christ" before his birth, Mary is believed to be the "mother of all Christians." Because of the union of mother and son, Mary is believed to hold a unique role as mediatrix and intercessor for mankind, but not in such a way that the unique role of Jesus is diminished.

The recent tendency in Roman Catholicism, as signaled in particular by the Second Vatican Council, has not been to expand the definition of Mary's role, but to attempt to hold together traditionalist and critical approaches to Mariology within Catholicism while evidencing sensitivity to today's ecumenical atmosphere. While the elaboration of Mary's role and nature has little strictly biblical warrant, Protestants can nonetheless look to Mary as a significant example of one uniquely "favored" and "blessed among women" in her role in salvation history (vv. 28, 42) and obedient in the face of certain ridicule and misunderstanding.

Bibliography. T. A. O'Meara, *Mary in Protestant and Catholic Theology* (New York: 1966); R. E. Brown et al., eds., *Mary in the New Testament* (Philadelphia and New York: 1978).

2.† A woman, called "Mary Magdalene," from Magdala on the Sea of Galilee (*see* MAGDALENE). She was one of the women who "ministered" to Jesus and contributed financially to him and his disciples (Matt. 27:55-56 par.; Luke 8:3). Mary Magdalene was present at the crucifixion and burial of Jesus (Matt. 27:56, 61 par.), and was among the women who went to visit the tomb on Easter morning (28:1 par.). It was she who reported his resurrection to the apostles (Luke 24:10; John 20:18). Identified as one "from whom seven demons had gone out" (Luke 8:2), Mary has traditionally been identified with the sinful woman (by tradition, a prostitute) of 7:36-50; however, this is very unlikely because of the way Mary is introduced as a new character at 8:2. Tradition has also identified the Magdalene with Mary of Bethany (**4** below), but this also is very unlikely.

3. The mother of James the younger and Joseph (or Joses), one of the women present when Jesus was crucified and buried, and who went on Easter morning to visit his tomb (Matt. 27:56, 61 ["the other Mary"];

28:1; Mark 15:40, 47; 16:1) and who reported the resurrection of Jesus to the apostles (Luke 24:10). It is possible but not likely that this Mary was the same person as the mother of Jesus (1 above; cf. Matt. 13:55; Mark 6:3). It is also possible, but again hardly likely, that she is the same as the sister of Jesus' mother, who was with Mary at the crucifixion (John 19:25); if so, James, Joseph, Judas, and Simon, the "brothers of Jesus," would instead be his cousins. James (Gk. *Iakobos*) and Joseph were very common names among Jewish men, so there is little reason to identify the two sons of this Mary with two of the "brothers of Jesus."

4. Mary of Bethany, the sister of Martha and Lazarus. In all three stories in which Mary and Martha appear, the two sisters are contrasted with each other. Mary sits at Jesus' feet to listen to his teaching (Luke 10:39) or anoints his feet (John 12:3), while Martha is the active homeowner and hostess (Luke 10:38, 40; John 12:2). After the death of their brother Lazarus, Martha goes out to meet and speak with Jesus, but Mary remains in the house until called (11:20, 28-31); yet she, like Martha, boldly voices her grief (vv. 32-33). It is probable that the anointing at Bethany recorded at Matt. 26:6-13 (par. Mark 14:3-9) is the same as Mary's anointing of Jesus (John 12:3), but the anointing by a notoriously sinful woman (Luke 7:36-50) is probably not the same incident. On the traditional identification of Mary of Bethany with Mary Magdalene, see 2 above.

5. Mary of Clopas (or Cleophas), one of the women present at the crucifixion of Jesus (John 19:25). Mary was probably the wife of Clopas, who is not otherwise mentioned in the New Testament (Cleopas at Luke 24:28 is a different name). If, following ancient tradition, Clopas is to be identified with Alphaeus, the father of the apostle James (Matt. 10:3; Mark 3:18; Luke 6:15; Acts 1:13), this Mary might be the same as 3, the mother of James and Joseph. The historian Hegesippus, cited by Eusebius (*HE* iii.3; iv.22), suggests that Clopas was Joseph's brother, which would make this Mary the sister-in-law of 1.

6. The mother of John Mark, and owner of a house which was a significant meeting place for the early Church (Acts 12:12). Mary must have been a person of some wealth; her house was large enough for church meetings and had at least one servant (v. 13). That this house was also the scene of the institution of the Lord's Supper and of the Pentecost event is often suggested, but far from certain.

7. An otherwise unknown Christian in Rome, greeted by Paul and commended for her considerable work in that church (Rom. 16:6).

MARY, GOSPEL OF.† An apocryphal writing, probably associated with Mary Magdalene rather than Mary the mother of Jesus. Generally identified as a Gnostic writing of the second century A.D., the book is apparently a compilation of two originally independent works. The first portion is a conversation between the risen Christ and his disciples concerning the future of creation and the nature of sin. In the second part Mary describes to Peter and the disciples visions of Jesus related to the soul's journey through the planetary

spheres. The work survives in fragments dated to the third and fifth centuries A.D.

MARY, GOSPEL OF THE BIRTH OF (Lat. *Genna Marias* "Genealogy" or "Descent of Mary").* A hostile anti-Jewish apocryphal book of the second century A.D., attributed to the Gnostics. It is known only from the reference in Epiphanius *Haer.* xvi.12.1-4.

MARY, REVELATION OF.† A New Testament apocryphal apocalypse in which Mary, the mother of Jesus experiences a vision of the punishments of the damned and prays to the Son that they may have respite from that torment. Among the sins for which the damned suffer in hell are such atrocities as lying in bed late on Sunday and refusing to rise when a priest enters the room. This book is preserved in Greek, Armenian, Ethiopic, and Old Slavonic versions. It was probably written in the ninth century A.D., and is dependent on the apocalypses of Peter and Paul.

An Ethiopian apocalypse from the seventh century or later, purporting to be a vision of the Virgin Mary, is even more dependent on the apocalypse of Paul (Apoc.Paul 13-44).

A work cited by Epiphanius (*Haer.* xxvi.8.2-3), the Great Questions of Mary (Gk. *Erōtēseis Marias*), is a Gnostic gospel, actually an apocalypse wherein the risen Christ imparts to Mary Magdalene secret instruction regarding sexual enactment of the Eucharist among various Gnostic sects. The Little Questions of Mary (*Mikrai Erōtēseis*), also cited by Epiphanius, is similar to portions of the Pistis Sophia.

MASADA [mə sä′də] (Aram. *mᵉṣāḏâ* "fortress"; Gk. *Masada*).† A nearly impregnable wilderness fortress near the west shore of the Dead Sea *ca.* 33 km. (21 mi.) southeast of Hebron. The rock of Masada rises with sheer cliffs some 180 to 250 m. (600 to 820 ft.) above the surrounding low ground to an irregularly shaped flat top some 600 m. (656 yds.) long north to south and 316 m. (346 yds.) at the widest point.

Masada was used as a fortress as early as the mid-second century B.C., but Herod the Great was the earliest known builder on the site. He constructed most of the buildings and defensive walls, including his main residence, the large western palace. An even larger complex of buildings at the northern end of the rock features extensive storerooms and a palace built on three terraces descending *ca.* 35 m. (115 ft.) from the top of the rock. These structures and other buildings constructed during the time of Herod required extensive waterworks, which included huge cisterns cut into solid rock. Herod surrounded the whole of the top of the rock, except for the northern end, by a double wall with thirty towers.

After Herod's death Masada was used as a Roman border fortress. In the summer of A.D. 66, as the great Jewish revolt was beginning, the fortress was taken by rebel forces. Even after the Romans had taken all the rest of Judea, including Jerusalem (A.D. 70) and the fortresses of Machaerus (71) and Herodium (72), Masada held on. Masada fell before an elaborate Roman assault in April of 73 or 74. But before the Roman soldiers entered, all but seven of

Masada, with Herod's temple complex on the northern end of the rock in the foreground (W. Braun)

the 960 Jews on Masada had committed mass suicide rather than be killed by Romans (Josephus *BJ* vii.8.1– 9.2 [252-406]). For about forty years Roman forces occupied the rock, which was not again inhabited until Byzantine times.

Extensive archaeological work on Masada has uncovered and reconstructed the Herodian buildings and walls and the buildings from other periods. Evidence has been found of the occupation by Jewish rebel forces, including scrolls of biblical, apocryphal, and cultic texts, two ritual baths, a synagogue (the oldest yet found), modifications of the earlier buildings, pottery, clothing, and ostraca inscribed with names.

Bibliography. Y. Yadin, *Masada* (New York: 1966).

MASH [măsh] (Heb. *maš*). A son of Aram (Gen. 10:23; LXX Gk. *Mosoch*). He was the eponymous ancestor of an Aramaic tribe perhaps to be associated with the Mons Masius (now called Keraga Dag), a mountain range near the headwaters of the Euphrates river, or with Akk. *Māšu*, the Lebanon and Anti-

lebanon ranges. The parallel passage (1 Chr. 1:17) reads Meshech (2) (Heb. *mešek*).

MASHAL. A levitical town in Asher (1 Chr. 6:74 [MT 59]). *See* MISHAL.

MASKIL [măs'kĭl] (Heb. *maśkîl*).† A term, apparently designating a type of psalm, appearing in the superscriptions of Pss. 32; 42; 44–45; 52–55; 74; 78; 88–89; 142 (KJV "Maschil"; JB "Poem"). Various meanings have been suggested, including "efficacious song," "didactic poem," and "meditation."

MASONS (forms of Heb. verbs *gāḏar* "make a wall or hedge," *ḥāraš, ḥāṣab* "hew"). Workers skilled in building walls and structures of stone, particularly the large, lavish, or monumental buildings and defensive walls around cities built of dressed stones. Hiram of Tyre sent skilled masons from Phoenicia to build David's palace in Jerusalem (2 Sam. 5:11 par. 1 Chr. 14:1), and it is likely that for some time masons continued to be brought from Phoenicia. Solomon, however, did have his own stone quarries (1 Kgs. 5:15 [MT 39]; 2 Chr. 2:18 [MT 17]). Since the temple at Jerusalem was the most significant building for the people of Israel and Judah, its construction (1 Chr. 22:2, 15), repair (2 Kgs. 12:12 [MT 13]; 22:6; 2 Chr. 24:12), and reconstruction (Ezra 3:7) are the concerns most often mentioned in connection with the need for masons. But the numerous other government and monumental buildings and the extensive use of walls around cities, both of which are confirmed by archaeological evidence, claimed much of the work of masons.

MASORETIC [măs′ə rĕt′ĭk] **TEXT.**† The standard text of the Hebrew Bible and the basis of printed Hebrew Old Testaments (abbreviated MT).

Hebrew texts were originally written with consonants only, with some long vowels indicated by the use of the consonants aleph, he, waw, and yodh. The consonantal text was relatively fixed *ca.* A.D. 100. As Hebrew had ceased to be the language of everyday life for Jews, efforts were made to retain the traditional vocalizations of the words of the biblical text by the use of signs added to the consonantal text. Eventually three systems of vocalization developed: the Babylonian and Palestinian, which place the vowel points above the consonants, and the Tiberian, which places most of the vowel points below the consonants. The Tiberian system as it was finally established in the tenth-century school of ben Asher is represented in printed Hebrew Bibles. The two most recent editions published by the United Bible Societies, *Biblia Hebraica (BHK)* and *Biblia Hebraica Stuttgartensia (BHS)*, are based on the Leningrad Codex (written out in 1008), but have textual notes drawing on other manuscripts and the versions.

The name derives from the Masora (Heb. *māsôreṭ* "tradition"), the textual tradition attributed to the Masoretes, Jewish scholars who guarded the transmission of the consonantal text and developed the vocalization signs and other parts of that particular apparatus. The full Masoretic apparatus includes vowel points, indications of Qere readings (*see* KETHIB AND QERE), use of the dagesh to indicate doubled consonants and stopped pronunciation of consonants which are otherwise spirantized, a number of different accent marks, the marginal and final Masora, and numerous other signs—a few of which are not now understood.

Before the establishment of the standard consonantal text that became the basis for the Masoretes' work, a variety of textual traditions existed. Three groups of these can now be identified, represented by the Samaritan Pentateuch, the LXX, and the MT; all are present in the Qumran biblical scrolls. Textual criticism of the Old Testament must, therefore, be concerned with a wide variety of materials in addition to manuscripts of the MT.

See also BIBLE, TEXT OF THE *I*.

Bibliography. E. Würthwein, *The Text of the Old Testament* (Grand Rapids: 1979).

MASREKAH [măs′rə kə] (Heb. *maśrēqâ* "vineyard [?]"). A city in Edom, the home of King Samlah (Gen. 36:36; 1 Chr. 1:47). The name of the city is preserved in modern Jebel el-Mushraq, 32 km. (20 mi.) south-southwest of Maʿan.

MASSA [măs′ə] (Heb. *maśśāʾ* "burden, oracle").† A son of Ishmael and eponymous ancestor of a north Arabian tribe (Gen. 25:14; 1 Chr. 1:30). Assyrian inscriptions name Masʾa with some of the other tribes of Ishmael, and the second-century A.D. geographer Ptolemy (*Geog.* v.18.2) mentions the Masanoi; both may be placed in the general area assigned to the Ishmaelites, the north-central region of the Arabian desert.

Massa at Prov. 30:1; 31:1 may have its literal meaning of "oracle," in which case the two verses could be translated "The words of Agur son of Jakeh, the oracle," and "The words of King Lemuel, the oracle which his mother taught him."

MASSAH [măs′ə] (Heb. *massâ* "temptation, testing"), **MERIBAH** [mĕr′ə bə] (Heb. *mᵉrîbâ* "strife, contention"). Place names associated with the Israelites' wilderness wanderings.

Although some interpreters view the two names as designating a single site (*massâ ûmᵉrîbâ*), recent scholarship favors identifying accounts of two similar incidents in which the Israelites "put the Lord to the proof" (cf. Deut. 33:8; Ps. 95:8, where the two names occur in parallel); in both instances God commands Moses to strike a rock, which then issues forth water (Exod. 17:5-6; Num. 20:5, 8-9). The first occasion is set toward the outset of the wanderings, at Rephidim (renamed Massah and Meribah) in the wilderness of Sin close to Mt. Horeb (Exod. 17:1-7; called only Massah at Deut. 6:16; 9:22). The second instance takes place at Meribah, which may be identified with Kadesh-barnea, in the wilderness of Zin near the end of the wilderness period (Num. 20:1-13; cf. Deut. 9:23).

According to Deut. 33:8, it was God who tested and strived with the Levites at Massah/Meribah (cf. Ps. 81:7 [MT 8]). Because of Israel's rebellion and Moses' failure to stand firm "by the waters of Meribah," Aaron and Moses were not able to enter the Promised Land (Num. 20:12, 24; 27:14; Deut. 32:51; RSV "Meribath-kadesh"; KJV "Meribah-Kadesh"; cf. Ps. 106:32-33).

MATHUSALA (Luke 3:37, KJV). *See* METHUSELAH.

MATRED [mā′trĭd] (Heb. *maṭrēḏ*). The daughter of Mezahab and mother of Mehetabel, the wife of King Hadad (Hadar) of Edom (Gen. 36:39; 1 Chr. 1:50; so MT; according to LXX and Syr., the father of Mehetabel; cf. JB).

MATRITES [mā′trīts] (Heb. *maṭrî*). The subgroup (*mišpāḥâ* "family") within the tribe of Benjamin of which Saul was a member (1 Sam. 10:21; KJV, NIV, JB "Matri").

MATTAN [măt′ən] (Heb. *mattān* "gift").
1. A priest of Baal slain in the coup against Queen Athaliah of Judah (2 Kgs. 11:18; 2 Chr. 23:17).
2. The father of Shephatiah, a contemporary of Jeremiah (Jer. 38:1).

MATTANAH [măt'ə nə] (Heb. *mattānâ* "gift"). A place between the Arnon river and Nahaliel where the Israelites stopped while journeying northward on the east side of Moab (Num. 21:18-19). A possible location for Mattanah is modern Khirbet el-Medeiyineh on the Heidan (a tributary of the Arnon) *ca.* 35 km. (22 mi.) east of the Dead Sea.

MATTANIAH [măt'ə nī'ə] (Heb. *mattanyâ, mattanyāhû* "gift of Yahweh").
1. The last king of Judah; son of King Josiah and uncle of Jehoiachin. Nebuchadrezzar in lled Mattaniah on the throne in place of his nephew and renamed him ZEDEKIAH (**2**) (2 Kgs. 24:17).
2. The son of Mica; an Asaphite Levite living in postexilic Jerusalem (1 Chr. 9:15). The leader of the temple choir, he was among those who returned with Zerubbabel (Neh. 11:17; 12:8, 35 ["son of Micaiah"]).
3. A son of the seer Heman, and leader of the ninth division of levitical musicians during David's reign (1 Chr. 25:4, 16).
4. An Asaphite Levite; ancestor of the ecstatic prophet Jahaziel (2 Chr. 20:14).
5. An Asaphite Levite who participated in the cleansing of the temple ordered by King Hezekiah (2 Chr. 29:13).
6. An Israelite of the sons of Elam who divorced his foreign wife (Ezra 10:26; 1 Esdr. 9:27; KJV "Matthanias").
7. One of the sons of Zattu required to divorce his foreign wife (Ezra 10:27; 1 Esdr. 9:28, "Othoniah").
8. An Israelite among the sons of Pahath-moab who divorced a foreign wife (Ezra 10:30; 1 Esdr. 9:31; RSV, KJV "Mathanias"; "Bescaspasmys," following LXX).
9. An Israelite, a son of Bani required to put away his foreign wife and children (Ezra 10:37; 1 Esdr. 9:34; KJV "Mamnitanaimus"; RSV "Machnadebai").
10. An ancestor of Uzzi, who was overseer of the Levites in postexilic Jerusalem (Neh. 11:22).
11. A postexilic Levite who guarded the storehouses of the gates (Neh. 12:25).
12. An Asaphite Levite, ancestor of the priest Zechariah (**28**) (Neh. 12:35).
13. An ancestor of Hanan, an assistant to the keepers of the Levites' storehouses in the time of Nehemiah (Neh. 13:13).

MATTATHA [măt'ə thə] (Gk. *Mattatha*). An ancestor of Jesus; grandson of King David (Luke 3:31).

MATTATHIAS [măt'ə thī'əs] (Gk. *Mattathias,* from Heb. *mattityâ* "gift of Yahweh").† A common Jewish name in the Hellenistic and Roman periods.
1. A priest whose killing of a compliant Jew and a royal officer at Modein touched off the Maccabean revolt against Antiochus IV Epiphanes (1 Macc. 2). The Hasmonean rulers were descendants of Mattathias. *See* HASMONEANS.
2. The son of Absalom; one of only two officers who did not flee when Jonathan was ambushed near Hazor (1 Macc. 11:70).
3. A son of Simon Maccabeus and grandson of Mattathias 1. During a banquet he and his father were murdered by his brother-in-law, the governor Ptolemy (1 Macc. 16:14-16).

4. An envoy sent to Judas Maccabeus by Nicanor (2 Macc. 14:19).
5. An ancestor of Jesus; son of Amos (**2**) and father of Joseph (**13**) (Luke 3:25).
6. An ancestor of Jesus; son of Semein and father of Maath (Luke 3:26).

MATTATTAH [măt'ə tə] (Heb. *mattattâ* "gift"). An Israelite required to divorce his foreign wife (Ezra 10:33; KJV "Mattathah"; some Hebrew manuscripts read *mattityâ*).

MATTENAI [măt'ə nī] (Heb. *matt^enay* "gift").
1. An Israelite among the sons of Hashum required to divorce his foreign wife (Ezra 10:33).
2. One of the sons of Bani who divorced his foreign wife (Ezra 10:37).
3. Head of the priestly father's house of Joiarib at the time of the high priest Joiakim (Neh. 12:19).

MATTHAN [măth'ăn] (Gk. *Matthan,* from Heb. *mattān* "gift"). A postexilic ancestor of Jesus; grandfather of Joseph (Matt. 1:15; cf. Matthat at Luke 3:24).

MATTHAT [măth'ăt].
1. (Gk. *Maththat,* from Heb. *mattāṯ*). An ancestor of Jesus; according to Luke 3:24 the grandfather of Joseph (cf. Matt. 1:15, "Matthan").
2. A postexilic ancestor of Jesus (Luke 3:29).

MATTHEW [măth'ōō] (Gk. *Maththaios, Matthaios,* from Heb. *mattityâ* "gift of Yahweh"). One of the twelve apostles, also called Levi, and traditionally identified as the author of the gospel of Matthew. Matthew is the name given in all of the lists of apostles (Matt. 10:3; Mark 3:18; Luke 6:15; Acts 1:13); the identification of Matthew with Levi is possible only because both names are associated with the story of the call of a tax collector in Capernaum (Matthew at Matt. 9:9; Levi at Mark 2:14; Luke 5:27, 29). Perhaps the apostle adopted one of the names at the time of his call (cf. Simon Peter).

Levi's father was Alphaeus (Mark 2:14), whom some would identify with Alphaeus the father of James, another of the apostles. However, Matthew and James are not associated with each other in the lists of the apostles, as are those pairs known to be brothers (Peter and Andrew, James and John the sons of Zebedee).

Matthew was a tax collector (KJV "publican"), involved in tax collecting at the very moment that Jesus called him to be a follower (Luke 5:27; cf. Matt. 10:3). Tax collectors were despised among the Jews as those who profited by collaborating with the occupying Roman forces and by engaging in legalized robbery of their own people. Matthew responded immediately to Jesus' call; the implication is that he never returned to tax collecting (Luke 5:28). The feast which ensued in Matthew's house typified Jesus' ministry: "not to call the righteous, but sinners" (Mark 2:17).

MATTHEW, GOSPEL OF.† The first book of the New Testament and the first (in canonical order) of the four Gospels.

I. Authorship and Sources

Although the gospel itself provides no indication of authorship, tradition dating to at least the early second century A.D. ascribes the work to the apostle Matthew, identified only in Matthew with the tax collector Levi (Matt. 9:9; 10:3). Yet it has been questioned why one of the Twelve, an eyewitness to the events recorded, would seemingly base his account on that of the later Mark (some would object, however, that Mark's gospel represents the preaching of the apostle Peter). Recent scholarship attributes Matthew to a Greek-speaking Jewish Christian living in (Gentile) Syria (probably Antioch) toward the end of the first century (*ca.* 90). Indeed, possible references to the destruction of Jerusalem (Matt. 22:7) and to the temple tax being collected by "the kings of the earth" (17:24) make a date after the Roman destruction of the city in A.D. 70 likely; the Jewish temple tax had then become a Roman tax to support the temple of Jupiter Capitolinus). The contents of the gospel suggest conflict within a previously secure Jewish community; some posit Matthew as the founder of the church at this place.

According to Papias, writing in the first third of the second century A.D., "Matthew wrote the *lógia* in the Hebrew language, and everyone interpreted them as he was able" (Eusebius *HE* iii.39.16). Gk. *lógia* normally would be expected to refer to sayings and discourses, but not to the narrative of deeds and events that occupies much of the gospel of Matthew. Possibly Matthew was the compiler of some collection of sayings material (or of Old Testament messianic texts, as are cited frequently in Matthew) in the Hebrew or Aramaic language. Such a collection then might have been incorporated into a gospel in Greek that included narrative material by one of those who "interpreted" (i.e., translated) the collection. At any rate, the traditional identification of Papias' Hebrew *lógia* of Matthew with the canonical gospel cannot be correct, since the gospel was written in Greek and is not a translation from a Hebrew or Aramaic original. However, this does not rule out some connection between the two.

Traditionally, Matthew has been regarded as the first gospel written and the source of the gospel of Mark. Most scholars now regard Mark as one of the sources of Matthew, which also draws on at least two other sources, oral or written—one a sayings source (called Q; Ger. *Quelle* "Source") also used by Luke, and the other (M) represented by material peculiar to Matthew. The hypothesis of Mark's priority has not remained unchallenged, but remains the most probable way to account for the evidence. *See* SYNOPTIC PROBLEM.

II. Contents and Purpose

A. *Primary Concerns.* Matthew appears to be a gospel designed primarily for instruction of persons new to Christian faith, of missionaries, and of the Church in general. The organization of Jesus' teaching into five discourses with distinct concerns is evidence of this, as is the special interest in the operation of the Church (16:17-19; 18:15-20). Numerous quotations from the Old Testament are included, some of which are given as testimonies that the coming and ministry of Jesus are the fulfillment of the hope of Israel.

Matthew clearly was written for a Jewish Christian congregation. The positive relationship of Jesus to the law of Moses is emphasized (5:17-19), but a critique is sustained against pharisaic Judaism, the early rabbinic Judaism that was the main competitor of Jewish Christianity in the decades immediately after the war of A.D. 66-70 (e.g., 5:20; 12:1-20; 21:43; ch. 23; 28:11-15). A number of Jewish terms and customs are mentioned without explanation (e.g., 5:22; 15:2; 23:5). The readers were probably among those obligated to pay the temple tax which only Jews paid (17:24-27). That the mission of Jesus and his disciples was limited to Jews is made explicit in Matthew (10:5-6; 15:24), but the extension of the gospel to all nations is anticipated at certain points (13:38; 22:9; 24:14) and expressly commanded at the climax of Matthew's gospel (28:18-20).

The basic threefold structure of the gospel of Mark is preserved in Matthew: the coming of Jesus (Matt. 1:1-4:16), his teaching and attestation as God-sent by miracles (4:17-25:46), and his death and resurrection at Jerusalem (26:1-28:20). This division of the book is marked by the clause "From that time Jesus began to . . ." (4:17; 16:21). As in Mark, Peter's confession of Jesus as Messiah (16:13-20) represents a turning point in Jesus' ministry.

B. *The Coming of Jesus.* Matthew begins with a genealogy tracing the ancestry of Joseph (i.e., Jesus' legal ancestry) from Abraham through three groups of fourteen generations (actually thirteen in the third group; 1:1-17). The description of the circumstances of the beginning of Jesus' life (1:18-2:23) is focused on Jesus' conception by a virgin, the homage paid to him by Gentile visitors from far away, and the threat sensed by Herod the Great because of him. A scriptural testimony (introduced by the formula "in order to fulfill what was spoken by the prophet[s]") is attached to each of these themes (1:23; 2:5-6, 17-18; cf. 2:15, 23). Throughout the narrative, God's protection of his new work is expressed in angelic visitations and warning dreams (1:20-23; 2:12-13, 19-20, 22).

As in the other Synoptic Gospels, the ministry of Jesus is preceded by that of John the baptizer (3:3; cf. 11:10); Jesus' baptism by John (3:14-15 does not mean that Jesus is subordinate to John), and Jesus' temptation in the wilderness (Matt. 3:1-4:11). The mention of Jesus' return to Galilee and the initiation of his preaching there (4:12, 17) are also shared with the other Synoptics, here reinforced by a formula quotation (vv. 13-16).

C. *The Ministry of Jesus.* In the presentation of Jesus' ministry of gathering disciples, teaching, and healing (4:17-25:46), most of the sayings material is organized into five discourses (chs. 5-7, 10, 13, 18, 24-25), each with a distinct theme or orientation and each ending with "when Jesus had finished these sayings . . ." or a similar clause (7:28; 11:1; 13:53; 19:1; 26:1). But a more significant structural feature in terms of the overall outline of Matthew is the turning point at 16:13.

The "kingdom of heaven" is introduced as the focus of Jesus' preaching (4:17; cf. 3:2), followed by an account of Jesus' calling individuals to follow him (4:18-22). The Sermon on the Mount (chs. 5-7) comprises a variety of material focused on the spiritual and ethical nature of the people who are in the kingdom. The people of the kingdom are those who are meek, poor in spirit, and persecuted (5:3-12, the Beatitudes), but whose righteousness exceeds that of the scribes and Pharisees (v. 20), going beyond the letter of the law to the full intention of the law (vv. 21-48). The people of the kingdom are spiritually sincere and simple (6:1-18), oriented toward the kingdom rather than toward insuring their own material security (vv. 19-34), and more mindful of their own judgment before God than of judging other people (7:1-5, 13-14, 24-27).

Jesus' active ministry to the crowds, depicted in chs. 8–9 (which include ten accounts of miracles) and summarized at 9:35-36, leads to the mission of the Twelve (9:37–10:5a). As the disciples set out they are given instructions concerning the method of their mission and what they can expect of it (10:5-42). Their presence as preachers of the kingdom is itself a sign wherever they go of the kingdom's presence; the response given them will be determinative in the final judgment (vv. 7, 11-15, 40-42). They can expect persecution (vv. 16-18, 24-25, 34-39), but also God's providence in the midst of that persecution (vv. 19-22, 26-33).

Most of chs. 11–12 represent stories concerned with acceptance of Jesus and opposition to him. This focus is summarized at 11:25-30 and becomes the context of the discourse in parables of ch. 13. In addition to material drawn from Mark 4 (Matt. 13:1-13, 18-23, 31-32, 34), the discourse includes additional parables found only in Matthew's gospel (vv. 24-30, 36-52). Two formula quotations underscore Jesus' parables and the people's response as fulfillment of the Old Testament (vv. 14-15, 35).

The major turning point in the account of Jesus' ministry is marked by Peter's confession of Jesus as "the Christ, the Son of the living God" (16:16), Jesus' initial statements concerning what specifically awaits him in Jerusalem (v. 21; 17:12, 22-23), and his transfiguration before the disciples (vv. 1-9). Henceforth Jesus' teaching features a stronger emphasis on the nature of discipleship as following him in suffering. Accordingly, Jesus' fourth discourse (ch. 18) focuses on discipleship, particularly discipline and forgiveness in the community of disciples (cf. 16:18-19, 22-28).

Jesus now leaves Galilee and begins his journey toward Jerusalem (19:1). The teachings stressing the commitment required of disciples continue, as do the stories concerning opposition to Jesus (chs. 19–20; cf. ch. 12). Jesus' entry into Jerusalem is underscored by a formula quotation (21:4-5), as is the crying out of the children in the temple (v. 16). Matthew augments material used by Mark to show how increasing conflict led to Jesus' crucifixion and to distinguish between the common Jews and the opponents of Jesus (Mark 11:27–12:44) with two parables (Matt. 21:28-32 [cf. 20:1-16]; 22:1-14) and the woes against the scribes and Pharisees (ch. 23).

Matthew, like Mark, concludes the record of Jesus' ministry and introduces the account of his death and resurrection with an extended collection of eschatological warnings, here comprising the fifth discourse (chs. 24 [except for vv. 26-28, 37-51 based on Mark 13]–25).

D. Death and Resurrection. Matthew's portrayal of the Last Supper and the betrayal, trial, and crucifixion of Jesus follows Mark, with the simplifications and clarifications typical of Matthew's handling of that material. Matthew places greater emphasis on the events' fulfillment of Scripture (26:52-54; cf. v. 56), and depicts the trial before the high priest and the council of elders more as a legal trial (cf. numbering of the witnesses, v. 60; omission of the witnesses' disagreement [cf. Mark 14:59]; high priest's oath and statement, Matt. 26:63, 65). Matthew, nonetheless, suggests that the trial was illegal in a number of ways, and his account of the trial before Pilate implies the responsibility of the Jewish crowd for Jesus' death and thus Pilate's innocence (27:19, 24-25). The only substantial non-Markan materials are the accounts of Judas' death (vv. 3-10), the earthquake and opening of the tombs accompanying Jesus' death (vv. 51-54), and the posting of a guard at Jesus' tomb (vv. 62-66; cf. 28:11-15).

The account of the women's early morning visit to the tomb is taken substantially from Mark, but is more vivid (note esp. vv. 2-4). The meeting of Jesus with the disciples in Galilee, mentioned at Mark 16:7, is set forth in Matthew as the commissioning of the apostles for world mission (Matt. 28:16-20).

Bibliography. G. Bornkamm, G. Barth, and H.-J. Held, *Tradition and Interpretation in Matthew.* NTL (1963); F. V. Filson, *The Gospel According to St. Matthew,* 2nd ed. HNTC (1971); R. H. Gundry, *Matthew: A Commentary on His Literary and Theological Art* (Grand Rapids: 1982); J. D. Kingsbury, *Matthew: Structure, Christology, Kingdom* (Philadelphia: 1975); E. Schweizer, *The Good News According to Matthew* (Atlanta: 1975).

MATTHIAS [mă thī'əs] (Gk. *Maththias, Matthias,* from Heb. *mattiṯyâ* "gift of Yahweh"). The man chosen by lot to succeed Judas Iscariot among the twelve apostles (Acts 1:23, 26). Because Matthias had accompanied Jesus' disciples from the beginning of his ministry through the ascension, he was qualified to witness to the resurrection (vv. 21-22). Although others may have been similarly qualified, only Matthias and Justus were put into the lot, perhaps because they met other unspecified qualifications. The apostleship of Matthias is attested elsewhere only in unreliable legends.

MATTITHIAH [măt'ə thī'ə] (Heb. *mattiṯyâ, mattiṯyāhû* "gift of Yahweh").

1. A postexilic Levite in charge of baking the temple bread; a son of Shallum and descendant of Korah (1 Chr. 9:31).

2. A levitical temple musician of David's time who played the lyre when the ark was brought to Jerusalem (1 Chr. 15:18, 21; 16:5).

3. A levitical temple musician who played the lyre and was leader of the fourteenth division of temple musicians at the time of David (1 Chr. 25:3, 21). He may be the same as **2**.

4. A postexilic Israelite required to divorce his foreign wife (Ezra 10:43; 1 Esdr. 9:35; KJV, RSV mg. "Mazitias").

5. One who stood at Ezra's right hand as he read the Book of the Law (Neh. 8:4).

MATTOCK (Heb. *'ēṯ*). A tool consisting of a long wooden handle with a metal blade at the end used for breaking up soil (1 Sam. 13:20-21; the KJV here renders *maḥᵃrēšeṯ* as "mattock"; RSV "plowshare"). KJV "with their mattocks round about" at 2 Chr. 34:6 is one rendering of a difficult text; a more likely reading is "in their ruins round about" (so RSV; cf. NIV, JB). For Isa. 7:25 (KJV) *see* HOE.

MAUNDY [mŏn′dē] **THURSDAY.*** The Thursday preceding Easter, according to early tradition the date of the Last Supper and the institution of the Eucharist. The name is traced to Lat. *mandatum* "commandment" (Vulg. John 13:34), from the Roman Catholic ceremony of footwashing commemorating the occasion. Popular tradition also associates the name with Jesus' instructions regarding the Lord's Supper (cf. Matt. 26:26-27 par.).

MAZZAROTH [măz′ə rŏth] (Heb. *mazzārôṯ*). A star or constellation (Job 38:32; NIV "constellations"; cf. 2 Kgs. 23:5, *mazzālôṯ*). Several suggestions have been made as to the identity of Mazzaroth (e.g., Corona Borealis, from *nēzer* "crown"; the Zodiac, from *'āzar* "gird, encompass"; JB, NIV mg. "morning star"), but none is certain.

MEAH (KJV). *See* HUNDRED, TOWER OF THE.

MEAL. Grains ground coarse from the whole kernels with the bran, thus distinguished from flour which was ground fine from only the inner kernels. Meal was apparently used more commonly than flour (1 Kgs. 4:22; Heb. *qemaḥ*, the most general term for meal). Generally meal was ground from wheat, although barley was also used (Num. 5:15; cf. 15:20-21; *ʿᵃrîsâ*; RSV "coarse meal"; KJV "dough"). More finely ground meal (*sōleṯ*) was expensive (cf. 2 Kgs. 7:1, 16, 18) and was reserved for special occasions (Gen. 18:6; KJV "fine flour"), including perhaps the meal offering (*minḥâ*; Ezek. 46:15).

Ground anew each day (cf. Prov. 31:15), meal (along with oil) was among the last food left in a widow's house in time of serious drought (1 Kgs. 17:12). The task of grinding meal between stones was difficult and noisy, and was considered women's work (Isa. 47:1-2; cf. Exod. 11:5; Matt. 24:41; cf. also Lam. 5:13; Judg. 16:21).

Poorly developed grain from which no meal can be produced is a sign of judgment (Hos. 8:7). The silence of the grinding stones is symbolic of the destruction of a city (cf. Jer. 25:10; Rev. 18:22). Jesus compares the kingdom of God to the leavening of meal (Gk. *áleuron* "wheat flour"; Matt. 13:33 par.).

See also BREAD; CEREAL OFFERING; FLOUR.

MEALS.† In the ancient Near East the one substantial meal of the day was eaten at sunset, after the day's work was over and after travelers had stopped for the night (cf. Luke 17:7; 24:29-30). The midday meal was small and was normally the first of the day (cf. Gen. 43:16; Ruth 2:14). Those who did not eat at midday

were considered to be fasting (cf. Judg. 20:26; cf. 1 Sam. 14:24), while feasting in the morning was considered decadent (Eccl. 10:16). Eating was nearly always an occasion for people to meet together, whether just with family members or coworkers or in more formal social settings.

Furniture might be reserved specifically for dining (cf. 1 Sam. 20:25), and apparently symbolic meaning was attached to the seating arrangement (1 Sam. 9:22; Luke 14:7-10). The practice of reclining on couches while eating (Luke 5:29, RSV mg.; John 13:23; cf. Amos 6:4; Ezek. 23:41), typical of the Greek and Roman periods, was introduced from the East. Often, each person would dip with bread from a common bowl (Ruth 2:14; Mark 14:20).

In wealthy homes, particularly that of the king, feasting could be lavish, involving many guests (cf. 2 Sam. 9:7, 13; 1 Kgs. 25:29; Luke 14:21), numerous servants (1 Kgs. 10:5), music (Isa. 5:12), dancing (cf. Luke 15:25), and much expensive food, including meat, which was rarely eaten by ordinary people (1 Kgs. 4:22-23). Royal feasts, such as Ahasuerus' consecutive banquets lasting 187 days (Esth. 1:3-9), could be boldly elaborate; to absent oneself from a king's table could be a serious offense (1 Sam. 20:25-29; Esth. 1:10-19). As a special honor, dinner guests might be anointed (Mark 14:3; John 12:3; cf. Luke 7:46).

Because eating was a vital necessity common to all mankind, shared meals developed special significance in symbolizing a bond between individuals, peoples, and with God. Religious meals with a memorial or sacramental focus were a part of Israel's worship from the earliest times, generally associated with sacrificial worship. Ceremonial meals, often focusing on the Sabbath, were significant in the Gospels (Luke 11:37; 14:1; cf. 7:36). The Lord's Supper, derived from the Passover meal, continued the significance of meals as worship (1 Cor. 11:20-34), as did the love feast (Jude 12); also underlying both may be the portrayal of the future messianic kingdom as a banquet (Luke 13:29; Rev. 19:9; cf. Mark 14:25). Paul's concern to distinguish between cultic meals in pagan temples and innocent meals which did, nonetheless, include meat from sacrificial animals (1 Cor. 10:25-27), and also between the meaning of pagan cultic meals and that of the Lord's Supper (vv. 14-21) reflects the covenantal significance of shared eating.

See FOOD.

MEARAH [mē âr′ə] (Heb. *mᵉʿārâ* "cave").† A place belonging to the Sidonians (Josh. 13:4). A number of suggestions have been made with regard to the nature and location of Mearah, including modern Mogheiriyeh, north of Sidon; the caves of Mughar Jezzin, east of Sidon; and a location along the Wâdî ʿAra in the plain of Megiddo (emending *mᵉʿārâ* to *mēʿārâ* "from ʿAra"; JB, NIV "from Arah"). Another suggestion is to read *mēʿārîm* "from the cities."

MEASURE.* A term representing various units of capacity, including Heb. *'êpâ* (also translated "ephah"), *kōr* ("cor"), *sᵉʾâ*; Gk. *bátos*, *kóros*, *sáton*, and *choínix* (KJV; RSV "quart"). The RSV supplies "measure(s)" at Exod. 29:40 (KJV "deal"); Ruth 3:15,

17; Hag. 2:16 (KJV "vessels"). *See* WEIGHTS AND
MEASURES.

MEAT (Heb. *bāśār, ṭibḥâ, šᵉʾēr*; Gk. *kréas*). The
flesh (*bāśār*) of animals. In biblical times meat was
used primarily in sacrifices. Because it was expensive,
meat was eaten primarily by the wealthy, including
the king (1 Kgs. 4:23); the common people had meat
only on feast days or in times of great prosperity (cf.
Amos 6:4). Meat was most often roasted on a spit,
but it might also be boiled (1 Sam. 2:13; cf. Judg.
6:19).

The question at issue in 1 Cor. 8:1–11:1 is "food
offered to idols" (8:1, 4, 10; 10:19). Since almost all
meat sold in the meat market (v. 25; Gk. *mákellon,*
from Lat. *macellum* "butcher shop, meat market") had
been slaughtered with a modicum of pagan ritual and
could therefore be considered "food offered to idols,"
some Christians could not in good conscience eat any
meat. Paul here sets consideration for the conscience
of others above other factors in the issue (8:7-13;
10:23-24, 28–11:1), but encourages his readers not
to raise for themselves any question of conscience
(10:25-27).

MEBUNNAI [mĭ bŭn'ī] (Heb. *mᵉbunnay*). One of
David's mighty men, surnamed the Hushathite (2 Sam.
23:27). Elsewhere he is called Sibbecai (21:18; 1 Chr.
11:29; 20:4; 27:11; KJV "Sibbechai").

MECHERATHITE [mĭ kĕr'ə thīt] (Heb. *mᵉkērāṯî*).
A gentilic applied to Hepher, one of David's mighty
men (1 Chr. 11:36). It is probably a scribal error for
Maacathite (*maʿᵃkāṯî*; cf. 2 Sam. 23:34; *see* MAACAH
(PLACE).

MECONAH [mĭ kō'nə] (Heb. *mᵉkōnâ* "base, foundation, resting-place"). A city in the southern part of
Judah (Neh. 11:28; KJV "Mekonah"), possibly identical with Madmannah.

MEDAD [mē'dăd] (Heb. *mêḏāḏ* "beloved"). An elder
who, with Eldad, prophesied in the wilderness camp
outside the tent of meeting (Num. 11:26-29).

MEDAN [mē'dăn] (Heb. *mᵉḏān*). A son of Abraham
and Keturah (Gen. 25:2; 1 Chr. 1:32), presumably the
eponymous ancestor of an Arabian group. Some
scholars suggest that the name represents a scribal
error from Midian, which follows.

MEDEBA [mĕd'ə bə] (Heb. *mêḏᵉḇāʾ*). A city, modern Mâdebā (Madaba), *ca.* 21 km. (13 mi.) east of
the Dead Sea and 30 km. (18.5 mi.) north of the
Arnon river. It is 11.2 km. (7 mi.) south of Heshbon.

Medeba may have been among the cities destroyed
when the Israelites defeated the Amorite kingdom of
Sihon (Num. 21:30). With the other cities of Sihon,
"the tableland of Medeba" was assigned to the tribe
of Reuben (Josh. 13:9-10, 16). According to 1 Chr.
19:7, Joab's battle against the Ammonites and Syrians
began at Medeba, where the Ammonites had encamped (cf. 2 Sam. 10). Following Solomon's reign

the Moabites gained control of Medeba (cf. Moabite
Stone). Omri retook the city for Israel, but it was lost
again to King Mesha of Moab some forty years later
(cf. 2 Kgs. 3:4-27). In a lament over Moab, Isaiah
mentions Medeba's defeat, probably by Assyria (Isa.
15:2). The sons of Jambri, who ambushed and murdered John (Gaddi), the son of Mattathias, were from
Medeba (1 Macc. 9:35-42; KJV "Medaba").

Among the archaeological finds at the site is a sixth-
century A.D. mosaic floor featuring the oldest extant
map of Palestine.

MEDES [mēdz], **MEDIA** [mē'dĭ ə] (Heb., Aram.
māḏay; cf. Akk. *ma-da-a-a*; O.Pers. *māda*; Gk. *Mē-
doi*). An Indoaryan people living in the mountains of
Iran east of Armenia, northeast of Mesopotamia, and
south of the Caspian Sea.

The early history of the Medes remains obscure.
Archaeological evidence suggests that they entered
Iran as nomads or transhumants at the beginning of
the tenth century B.C. Frequent references in Assyrian cuneiform texts from the mid-ninth century on
suggest a loose confederation of autonomous tribes.
Tiglath-pileser III captured some of the Median territory *ca.* 740, and Sargon II subdued Median factions
and their allies. After Assyria defeated Israel in 722,
some of the populace was resettled in "the cities of
the Medes" (2 Kgs. 17:6; 18:11). Threatened by
neighboring peoples *ca.* 676, various Median tribes
sought Assyrian aid and soon thereafter were subjugated through vassal treaties. In the seventh century,
however, a number of the tribes were unified by the
chieftain Deioces, who ruled from Ecbatana, and the
Medes became increasingly powerful. Deioces' son
Phraortes conquered the Persians as well as much of
Anatolia. Joining with Babylon, the Medes under
Cyaxares II destroyed the Assyrian capital Nineveh in
612. Subsequently Cyaxares extended Median control
over Parthia and Anatolia as far as Lydia. Cyaxares'
son Astyages was overthrown by the vassal king of
Persia, Cyrus II the Great, son of Cambyses I and Astyages' daughter Mandane. Cyrus made Media the
first satrapy of his (Medo-)Persian Empire, which he
ruled from Ecbatana. The territory, along with the
entire Persian Empire, fell to Alexander the Great in
331 (Dan. 8:1-8, 20-21) and subsequently came under
Seleucid (1 Macc. 6:56) and Parthian (14:1-3) rule.
Although Cyrus had permitted the return of Judahites
deported by Babylon and the rebuilding of Jerusalem,
Media remained home to some Diaspora Jews in the
first century A.D. (Acts 2:9).

In the Old Testament "the Medes (and Persians)"
are cited primarily for their conquest of the Neo-
Babylonian Empire in 539 (Isa. 13:17; 21:2; Jer. 51:11,
28; Dan. 5:28). The immutability of their law is proverbial (Dan. 6:8, 12, 15; cf. Esth. 1:19).

See MADAI; ZOROASTRIANISM. For Darius the Mede
(Dan. 5:31; ch. 6; 9:1; 11:1), *see* DARIUS 1.

MEDIATOR (Heb. *mēlîṣ*; Gk. *mesítēs*).† Fundamental to the idea of Jesus as mediator between God and
humanity (1 Tim. 2:5) is the estrangement caused by
sin. A "mediator" is normally the third party through
whom agreement is reached between two parties pre-

viously in conflict with each other; though this idea is present, it must be understood as one among other legal and social metaphors for the work of atonement, most notably "ransom" (v. 6).

The basis for the idea of Christ's mediation is found in Old Testament indications of the need for mediation in the inapproachability of God and sin of humanity. Admonishing his sons, Eli denies the possibility of mediation between them in their grievous sins and God (1 Sam. 2:25). Speaking from a very different situation, Job desires a mediator between himself and the God of the orthodoxy defended by his comforters, who tortures him (Job 9:33; RSV "umpire"; cf. RSV mg.; 13:3); he concludes that God himself will be his representative (19:25-27).

Moses mediated the covenant between God and the people, and communicated to them the messages of God's judgment (Exod. 20:18-21; 21:1; Deut. 5:4-5). His contact with God was as unique as his position of leadership over the people (Exod. 33:7-11); he was privileged with a unique vision of God (vv. 12-23) and, if permitted, would have offered himself to God's judgment in substitution for the people (32:30-34; cf. Rom. 9:3). Isaiah, himself deeply aware of the holiness of God and his own sin, is—like the other prophets—commissioned to be a mediator of God's message to the people (Isa. 6). The mediatorial role of the prophet becomes sufficiently developed in Jeremiah and the servant songs of Isaiah that the prophet's suffering becomes a focus of the message. The servant of the Lord is the mediator of God's revelation (Isa. 42:1-4) and salvation (49:1-6), and becomes the one who suffers on behalf of others (52:13–53:12). With this, the way is prepared for the understanding of Christ as the mediator, intercessor, and even substitute for the guilty.

In Hebrews, Christ is the mediator of the new covenant, the one whose action makes the covenant possible and who is the guarantor of its execution (Heb. 8:6; 9:15; 12:24; cf. 7:22). In Galatians the fact that the law of Moses was given not directly to the people but through a mediator (Gal. 3:19-20; RSV "intermediary")—i.e., through Moses—is one aspect of the law that implies its subordination to the promises given to Abraham and their fulfillment in Christ (cf. John 1:17).

See ATONEMENT; RECONCILIATION.

MEDICINE. * Like other ancient peoples, premonarchic Israel relied mainly on priests who functioned as medical practitioners. Accordingly, the varied purification procedures that involve the activity of the priests (Lev. 12–15) should be viewed in terms of this conjunction of medical and religious authority. In comparison with Egypt and Mesopotamia, the medical practices of Israel's priests were relatively free of magical elements, though some of the procedures for ritual purification (e.g., 14:49-53) may have originated in magic. The main concerns were physical and ritual purity, the former served by such elements as quarantining, washing of clothes, and bathing (e.g., 13:4, 6; 14:9). Prophets sometimes gave medical prognoses (2 Sam. 12:14; 1 Kgs. 14:5, 12; 2 Kgs. 1:4; 8:7-10; 20:1) and were sometimes the agents of miraculous healings (1 Kgs. 17:17-23; 2 Kgs. 5:3-14),

but seldom could their activity be called "medical" (cf. 20:7).

Not until the Monarchy are persons who function specifically as physicians encountered (e.g., 2 Chr. 16:12). Among the main duties of physicians were binding external wounds (cf. Isa. 1:6; Hos. 6:1), applying ointments (Jer. 8:22), and bandaging (possibly splinting) broken limbs (cf. Ezek. 30:21; 34:4). The reputation of physicians and their distinction from those occupying other roles grew in time (Sir. 38:1-15), though skepticism with regard to the efficacy of their treatments may be reflected in the story of a woman healed by Jesus (Mark 5:26; Gk. *iatrós*) and in a proverb quoted by Jesus (Luke 4:23). The most common medical procedures were administered without the aid of a physician (e.g., Mark 15:23 [probably administration of laudanum]; Luke 10:34; 1 Tim. 5:23).

See BIRTH; DISEASE; HEALING.

MEDITERRANEAN SEA. See GREAT SEA.

MEDIUM (Heb. *'ôḇ*), **WIZARD** (*yiddeʿōnî*).† A person who engages in necromancy, divination by consulting the spirits of the dead who are presumed to have information about the future and an ability to give useful counsel (Isa. 8:19). The Hebrew term for "wizard(s)" as translated by RSV and KJV is derived from *yāḏaʿ* "know" and alludes to either the knowledge possessed by the practitioner of secret arts or the intimacy of the spirits consulted with the practitioner. A medium is one who "has" or consults an *'ôḇ* (KJV "familiar spirit"). The Hebrew term may be related to *'āḇ* "father, ancestor" or to Sum. *ab* and Akk. *aptu* "opening, pit"; nonbiblical stories of consultation with the deceased sometimes involve the digging of a pit out of which the spirit is called (cf. 1 Sam. 28:13; Isa. 29:4; RSV "ghost"). The term for medium always appears in conjunction with that for wizard, once also with *dōrēš 'el-hammēṯîm* "one who inquires of the dead" (Deut. 18:11; RSV, KJV "necromancer").

The law of Moses prohibited necromancy (Lev. 19:31; 20:6), imposing the penalty of death (v. 27). The reasons were the association of such divination with the practices of the nations being ousted by Israel from the promised land (Deut. 18:9-14; perhaps also Egypt [cf. Isa. 19:3]) and the distinction between prophecy and necromancy (with other forms of divination; Deut. 18:9-22). One might seek a word about the future from both prophets and mediums, but the necromancer's report was not to be trusted (Isa. 8:16-20). When Saul could not obtain an oracle from the Lord through prophets and other proper means (1 Sam. 28:6), he contacted the deceased Samuel through a medium (vv. 7-14); but Samuel refused to give neutral advice, speaking instead as a prophet and confirming the repudiation implied in the failure to obtain a word from the living prophets (vv. 15-19; cf. 13:13-15; ch. 15).

Occasionally necromancers were purged in Israel and Judah (1 Sam. 28:3; 2 Kgs. 23:24), but obviously their arts were not entirely abrogated (21:6). Apparently both men and women engaged in necromancy (Lev. 20:27), but Saul specifically sought a female medium (1 Sam. 28:7).

See DIVINATION.

Reconstructed fortifications at Megiddo (by courtesy of the Oriental Institute, University of Chicago)

MEGIDDO [mə gǐd'ō] (Heb. *mᵉgiddô*). A very ancient fortified Canaanite and Israelite city, the ruins
of which (modern Tell el-Mutesellim) are *ca.* 16 km.
(10 mi.) southwest of Nazareth on the northeastern
slope of the Mt. Carmel ridge, on the edge of the
Jezreel valley (the plain of Esdraelon). The city was
strategically located near the intersection of two important ancient trade routes. Zech. 12:11 (*mᵉgiddôn*;
KJV "Megiddon") may refer to the numerous battles
fought in the plain (KJV "valley") of Megiddo, i.e.,
in the Jezreel valley near Megiddo (cf. ARMAGEDDON).

According to archaeological exploration, Megiddo
was occupied before the thirty-third century B.C. and
was heavily fortified by the early part of the third
millennium. Texts indicate that the city was subject
to Egypt as early as the first half of the nineteenth
century; it took an important role in anti-Egyptian resistance prior to its defeat by Thutmose III *ca.* 1468.
Megiddo was assigned to the Israelite tribe of Manasseh, but despite an early victory (Josh. 12:21; cf. Judg.
5:19) the Israelites did not completely expel the Canaanites from this and other cities in the valley of
Jezreel (Josh. 17:11-12; Judg. 1:27-28). The city was
in Israelite hands at the time of Solomon (1 Kgs. 4:12;
9:15), who rebuilt it as an administrative and military
center. It was to Megiddo that King Ahaziah of Judah
fled from King Jehu of Israel (2 Kgs. 9:27); the city
was then under Egyptian control, having been conquered along with other towns in Judah and Israel by
Pharaoh Shishak (Sheshonq I) *ca.* 925. In 733 the
Assyrians defeated Megiddo and established it as a
provincial capital. In 609 King Josiah of Judah battled
Pharaoh Neco at Megiddo and died there (23:29-30;
2 Chr. 35:22-24). Use of Megiddo as a fortress ended

at that time. In the second century A.D. Legio (modern el-Lejjun), a Roman camp, was established south
of and adjacent to Megiddo.

The large Megiddo mound, covering *ca.* 6 ha. (15
a.), has been subject to more extensive archaeological
excavations than any other site in Palestine. Some
twenty strata have been determined. Among the finds
are city walls and gates built at the time of Solomon,
a huge grain storage pit dug during Israelite occupation, and the seal of Shema servant of King Jeroboam
(probably Jeroboam I) bearing the image of a roaring
lion. Structures originally identified as stables dating
to Solomon's time have more recently been assessed
as storehouses contemporary with the Omride dynasty
of Israel. A water system consisting of a vertical shaft
extends down into bedrock, and a tunnel leads from
the shaft to a spring at the foot of the mound so water
might be obtained during sieges.

Bibliography. Y. Aharoni and Y. Yadin, "Megiddo," *EAEHL* 3:830-856.

MEGILLOTH [mǐ gǐl'ŏth] (Heb. *mᵉgillôṯ* "scrolls").
The five books of the Hebrew Bible read in synagogues on five of the annual holidays: Ecclesiastes
during the Feast of Booths; Esther, Purim (cf. Esth.
9:23-28); Song of Solomon, Passover; Ruth, Pentecost;
and Lamentations, the Ninth of Ab (the day of mourning for the destruction of the temple). These books
appear together in the third division (the Writings)
of the Hebrew canon in this order: Ruth, Song of
Solomon, Ecclesiastes, Lamentations, Esther.

MEHETABEL [mǐ hět'ə běl] (Heb. *mᵉhêṭab'ēl* "God
does good").

1. The wife of King Hadar (Hadad) of Edom; daughter of Matred and descendant of Mezahab (Gen. 36:39; 1 Chr. 1:50).

2. An ancestor of the false prophet Shemaiah (Neh. 6:10; KJV "Mehetabeel").

MEHIDA [mĭ hī'də] (Heb. *mᵉḥîḏāʾ*). A temple servant whose descendants returned with Zerubbabel from captivity (Ezra 2:52; Neh. 7:54).

MEHIR [mə hĭr', mē'hər] (Heb. *mᵉḥîr*). A Judahite; son of Chelub and father of Eshton (1 Chr. 4:11).

MEHOLATHITE [mĭ hō'lə thīt] (Heb. *mᵉḥōlāṯî*). A gentilic ascribed to Adriel, the husband of Saul's daughter Merab (1 Sam. 18:19; 2 Sam. 21:8). It apparently indicates that he was from Abel-meholah.

MEHUJAEL [mĭ hoo'jĭ əl] (Heb. *mᵉḥûyāʾēl, mᵉḥîyāʾēl*). An ancestor of Lamech; the son of Irad and father of Methushael (Gen. 4:18). Some scholars identify him with MAHALALEL (5:12-13, 15-17).

MEHUMAN [mĭ hoo'mən] (Heb. *mᵉhûmān*). One of the seven eunuchs who served as chamberlains for Ahasuerus (Esth. 1:10).

MEHUNIM (Ezra 2:50, KJV), **MEHUNIMS** (2 Chr. 26:7, KJV). *See* MEUNIM, MEUNITES.

ME-JARKON [mē jär'kŏn] (Heb. *mê hayyarqôn* "waters of the Jarkon" or "pale green waters").† A place in the original tribal territory of Dan, probably near Joppa (Josh. 19:46; cf. R. G. Boling and G. E. Wright, *Joshua*. AB 6 [1982], pp. 462-63: "on the west: from the Yarkon . . . ," following LXX). Mejarkon is probably a body of water, perhaps the Nahr el-ʿAujā, a stream flowing into the Wâdī Kanah (cf. 16:8; 17:9).

MEKONAH (Neh. 11:28, KJV). *See* MECONAH.

MELATIAH [mĕl'ə tī'ə] (Heb. *mᵉlaṭyâ* "Yahweh has delivered"). A Gibeonite of Nehemiah's time who worked on the reconstruction of the walls of Jerusalem (Neh. 3:7).

MELCHI [mĕl'kī] (Gk. *Melchi*, from Heb. *malkî* "my king" or *malkîyâ* "Yahweh is king").†

1. An ancestor of Jesus; son of Jannai and father of Levi (Luke 3:24).

2. A late exilic or postexilic ancestor of Jesus; son of Addi and father of Neri (Luke 3:28).

MELCHIAH (Jer. 21:1, KJV). *See* MALCHIAH 1.

MELCHIOR [mĕl'kī ôr] (Lat. *Melchior*, from Heb. *melek ʾōr* "king of light").* According to Western church tradition, the first of the Magi who brought the infant Jesus gold (*Excerpta Latina Barbari, ca.* sixth century A.D.; cf. Matt. 2:11). He is described as an old man with white hair and long beard (*Excerpta et Collectanea*; PL 94:541CD; *ca.* 700?), perhaps representing the descendants of Shem (cf. Bede *In Matthaei Evangelium Expositio* i.2). Other ancient sources identify him as Hor (Ethiopic Book of Adam

and Eve iv.15) or Hormizdah, king of Persia. He is called Melkon in the fourteenth-century Armenian Infancy Gospel, which records that he presented Jesus with a letter from God to Adam.

MELCHIZEDEK [mĕl kĭz'ə dĕk'] (Heb. *malkî-ṣedeq*; Gk. *Melchisedek*).† The king of Salem and priest of God Most High at the time of Abraham (Gen. 14:18). His name means "my king is Ṣedeq," perhaps referring to a deity (lit. "righteousness"; cf. "Adonizedek," a later king of Jerusalem; Josh. 10:1). Heb. 7:2 interprets the name as "king of righteousness" and the title king of Salem as "king of peace" (cf. Philo *Legum allegoriae* iii.79).

The king-priest of the city of Salem, which later became Jerusalem, met Abram (Abraham) at the valley of Shaveh (the King's valley; Gen. 14:17-18), which may have been near Jerusalem and possibly identical to Kidron (cf. 2 Sam. 18:18). Melchizedek brought out bread and wine, probably a meal for Abram's victorious army (Gen. 14:18), and gave Abram the blessing of God Most High. In response to the blessing and in recognition of Melchizedek's priestly role, the patriarch then gave Melchizedek a tithe of the booty taken in battle (vv. 19-20). Thus Abram acknowledged that "God Most High" was the same as Yahweh, the God already revealed to him (cf. "the Lord God Most High" at v. 22).

Ps. 110:4 sees the Judahite king in Jerusalem as the successor of Melchizedek—not simply as king of the city ("Zion," v. 2), but as king-priest. This suggests the priestly role assumed by David (2 Sam. 6:12-19; cf. 1 Kgs. 8:14, 22-23, 54-56) and his probable attempt to maintain continuity between the old Canaanite institutions of Jerusalem and their Judahite and Israelite successors.

Within the interpretation of Ps. 110 that occupies much of the Epistle to the Hebrews, Heb. 7 builds on Gen. 14:18-20. Abraham's acknowledgment of the legitimacy of Melchizedek's priesthood becomes an argument for the priority of that priesthood over the "descendants of Levi" (vv. 4-10). The messianic ruler of Ps. 110 is, therefore, a priest of a line prior to the levitical priesthood ("after the order of Melchizedek"; Heb. 7:11-19; KJV "Melchisedec"; cf. 5:6, 10; 6:20). That the narrative of the king-priest Melchizedek is introduced so abruptly into Genesis becomes an argument for Melchizedek's being "without father or mother or genealogy," i.e., beginning or end (7:3), and so not only a predecessor but also a type of Christ as "a priest for ever" (cf. Ps. 110:4). The legitimacy of the levitical priesthood depends on its descent from Levi; as it has a beginning, so it has an end in the understanding of the author of Hebrews.

Melchizedek was a figure of considerable interest for various strands of Judaism, including the Qumran community, which viewed him as a heavenly judge (11QMelch). He also figures in the book of Jubilees, the Testaments of the Twelve Patriarchs, the writings of Philo, Josephus, and the Talmud, as well as Christian and Gnostic works.

Bibliography. J. A. Fitzmyer, *Essays on the Semitic Background of the New Testament*. SBL Sources for Biblical Study 5 (1974), pp. 221-267; F. L. Horton, *The Melchizedek Tradition*. NTSMS 30 (1976).

MELEA [mē'lĭ ə] (Gk. *Melea*). An ancestor of Jesus, apparently from the time of the divided monarchy (Luke 3:31).

MELECH [mē'lĕk] (Heb. *melek* "king"). One of the sons of Micah (3) grandson of Meribaal and great-grandson of Saul's son Jonathan 2 (1 Chr. 8:35; 9:41).

MELICU (Neh. 12:14, KJV). See MALLUCHI.

MELITA (Acts 28:1, KJV). See MALTA.

MELONS (Heb. *'ªbaṭṭiḥîm*; cf. Arab. *baṭîḥ*).† The melons of Egypt for which the Israelites longed in the wilderness (Num. 11:5) may have been of more than one variety. Muskmelons (*Cucumis melo* L.) as well as watermelons (*Citrullus vulgaris*) have been cultivated in Egypt since the earliest times.

MELQART [mĕl'kärt] (Phoen. *milk qart* "king of the city").† The chief god of Tyre, whose worship the Phoenicians subsequently spread as founder and patron of their colonies at Cyprus, Sicily, Sardinia, and Spain, as well as Carthage where he was known as Baal Melqart. Herodotus identifies him with Heracles (*Hist.* ii.44; cf. *KAI* 47). Melqart is associated primarily with the sea and navigation, and later with the sun and the underworld (perhaps as a dying and rising god). He is symbolized by the eagle and lion. Although not mentioned by name in the Bible, Melqart is probably the "Baal" introduced at Samaria by Ahab and the Tyrian Jezebel (1 Kgs. 8:31-32) and fostered at Jerusalem by Athaliah (2 Kgs. 11:18; perhaps introduced by Jehoram; cf. 8:18) and Manasseh (21:3).

MELZAR [mĕl'zär] (Heb. *hammelṣar*). This word, taken as a proper noun in KJV (Dan. 1:11, 16, following LXX, Syr., Vulg.), was actually a title, possibly "steward" (so RSV, following MT) or "guard" (JB, NIV).

MEMORIAL PORTION (*'azkārâ*).† A handful taken from a grain offering, with the accompanying frankincense (cf. Isa. 66:3; Heb. *mazkîr lᵉḇōnâ*), burned on the altar as a token of the fact that the whole offering was indeed God's even though the rest went to the priests for their consumption (Lev. 2:2, 9, 16; 5:12; 6:15 [MT 8]; 24:7; Num. 5:26). It is possible that the superscriptions of Pss. 38, 70 are intended to associate these psalms with the offering of memorial portions (*lᵉhazkîr*; RSV "for the memorial offering"; KJV "to bring to remembrance").

See CEREAL OFFERING.

MEMPHIS [mĕm'fĭs] (Heb. *nōp, mōp*; from Egyp. *Mn-nfr*). The chief city of Lower (northern) Egypt, located at modern Mīt Rahīnah, ca. 19 km. (12 mi.) south of Cairo on the west side of the Nile at the ancient border between Upper and Lower Egypt. The name of the city (lit. "the goodness [of Pharaoh Pepi I] endures") was originally that of the pyramid of Pepi I, built at Memphis ca. 2300. It was also called *Ht-kœ-ptḥ* (from which comes Gk. *Aigyptos* "Egypt"), "the abode of the spirit (*Ka*) of (the god) Ptah," after the great temple erected by Menes ca. 3100 B.C.

According to Egyptian tradition, Menes (ca. 3200-3100), the first king of united Egypt and founder of the First Dynasty, established the city. Memphis was the capital of Egypt during much of the Old Kingdom period (ca. 2700-2200), but was superseded by Thebes in the Middle Kingdom; it never regained its former political importance, though it was sometimes a force to be reckoned with.

Memphis is mentioned in prophetic oracles against Egypt (Isa. 19:13; Jer. 46:14, 19; Ezek. 30:13; KJV "Noph"), in a lament over Israel (Jer. 2:16), and in an oracle against Israel (Hos. 9:6), of which Egypt was an archenemy. Some of the Jews who fled Babylon's assault on Judah established residence at Memphis (Jer. 44:1).

See EGYPT.

MEMUCAN [mĭ moo'kən] (Heb. *mᵉmûḵān*). One of the seven princes who acted as legal advisers for Ahasuerus, apparently the spokesman for the group (Esth. 1:14, 16, 21).

MENAHEM [mĕn'ə hĕm] (Heb. *mᵉnaḥēm* "comforter"). King of Israel ca. 745 to 738 B.C.; the son of Gadi, perhaps of the tribe of Gad (2 Kgs. 15:14-22). Menahem was accorded the formulaic denunciation of Israel's evil kings who continued the evil ways of Jeroboam I (v. 18).

Menahem's reign began during a period of turmoil. Zechariah, the son of Jeroboam II, was murdered after a reign of six months by Shallum, who reigned one month before he in turn was murdered by Menahem at Samaria (v. 14). Based at Tirzah, the former capital of the northern kingdom, Menahem first had to quell resistance by rival factions seeking the throne (v. 16). His reign of several years (v. 17 reads "ten," but this is problematic), followed by his apparently peaceful death and the succession of his son Pekahiah (vv. 22-23), indicates that some stability had been established. But Israel was already subject to Assyria and approaching its demise. That Tiglath-pileser III (Pul) "might help him to confirm his hold of the royal power," Menahem found it necessary to pay tribute to the Assyrian king (vv. 19-20; *ANET*, pp. 283-84).

MENAN (Luke 3:31, KJV). See MENNA.

MENELAUS [mĕn'ə lā'əs] (Gk. *Menelaos*). High priest in Jerusalem from 171 B.C. Jason, the previous holder of the office, had bought it from the Seleucid ruler Antiochus IV Epiphanes, thus supplanting his brother Onias III (ca. 174 B.C.), and had begun the radical hellenization of Jerusalem (2 Macc. 4:7-22). Menelaus, brother of Simon (the chief administrator of the temple and an opponent of the deposed Onias), was sent by Jason to carry money to Antiochus. Taking advantage of the circumstances, Menelaus outbid Jason for the high priesthood and was granted the office by Antiochus (vv. 23-25). For the first time, the high priesthood was held by a person who was not a descendant of Zadok, perhaps not even a descendant of Aaron (v. 23; according to 3:4, a Benjaminite; LXX "Bilgah," a priestly clan). The high priest was no longer an official representing the Jewish people, but a royal official representing the interests of the Seleucid crown in Jerusalem. Jason fled into Transjordan (4:26).

Menelaus, summoned to the Syrian capital for failure to make regular payments to Antiochus, left his brother Lysimachus as deputy high priest (vv. 27-29). Desiring to insure his own continuation in office, Menelaus bribed Andronicus, the king's deputy, with treasures stolen from the temple and thus persuaded him to kill Onias (vv. 30-38). Back in Jerusalem, Lysimachus (with Menelaus' compliance) robbed the temple treasures and was killed in the riot that ensued (vv. 39-42). Nevertheless, Menelaus was able to remain in the priestly office by bribing the appropriate officials (vv. 43-50). When Antiochus attacked Jerusalem and entered and defiled the temple itself to rob it, he had the cooperation of Menelaus (5:11-20). The Seleucid's forced hellenization of Judea touched off the Maccabean revolt (6:1-2; cf. 1 Macc. 1:41-51; 167 B.C.). Although still alive at the time, Menelaus was no longer high priest when temple worship was restored in 164. He was executed by Antiochus V in 162 (2 Macc. 13:3-8).

MENE, MENE, TEKEL, AND PARSIN [mē'nĭ, tē'kəl or tĕk'əl, pär'sĭn] (Aram. *mᵉnē᾽ mᵉnē᾽ tᵉqēl ûparsîn*).† The inscription made on the wall of the Babylonian king Belshazzar's banqueting hall by a mysterious disembodied hand (Dan. 5:5, 24-25; KJV "Mene, Mene, Tekel, Upharsin"). The Aramaic words, translatable as "numbered, numbered, weighed, and divided" or "mina, mina, shekel, and half-minas [or half shekels]'"), were probably a well-known proverbial saying. They are interpreted by Daniel in three sentences referring to the divine judgment on Belshazzar in the form of the defeat of the Babylonian Empire by the Medo-Persian Empire, which occurred in 539 B.C. (vv. 26-28). In the last sentence of the interpretation (v. 28) sing. "peres" (*pᵉrēs*) is substituted for pl. *parsîn* of the proverb because of its similarity to *pāras* "Persia."

MENNA [mĕn'ə] (Gk. *Menna*). An ancestor of Jesus (Luke 3:31; KJV "Menan," representing the variant reading *Mainan*).

MENORAH. *See* LAMPSTAND.

MENSTRUATION. *See* BLOOD, FLOW OF; CLEAN AND UNCLEAN *II D.*

MENUHOTH. *See* MANAHATHITES.

MEONENIM, PLAIN OF (Judg. 9:37, KJV). *See* DIVINERS' OAK.

MEONOTHAI [mē ŏn'ə thī] (Heb. *mᵉ῾ōnōṯay*). A Judahite, the son of Othniel and father of Ophrah (1 Chr. 4:13-14).

MEPHAATH [mĕf'ĭ ăth] (Heb. *mêpā῾aṯ, mēpā῾aṯ, mēpa῾aṯ*).† A levitical city in the tribal territory of Reuben which belonged to Moab at the time of Jeremiah (Josh. 13:18; 21:37; 1 Chr. 6:79 [MT 64]; Jer. 48:21 [K *môpā῾aṯ*]). The location most often suggested for Mephaath is Tell ej-Jâwah, *ca.* 10 km. (6 mi.) south of Amman.

MEPHIBOSHETH [mĕ fĭb'ə shĕth] (Heb. *mᵉpîbōšeṯ* "scatterer of shame").

1. A son of Saul and his concubine Rizpah, whom David handed over along with his brother and five grandsons of Saul to be hanged by the Gibeonites as expiation for the bloodguilt incurred when Saul violated his covenant with Gibeon (2 Sam. 21:1, 8-9; cf. Josh. 9).

2. The son of King Saul's son Jonathan; father of Mica (also called "Micah"; KJV also "Micha"). At 1 Chr. 8:34; 9:40 he is called Meribbaal (Heb. *mᵉrîb bā῾al* "Baal contends" or "Baal is advocate"), and in the second instance in 9:40, Meribaal (*mᵉrî-ba῾al* "hero of Baal"), the difference usually obscured in translations. Meribaal was probably Mephibosheth's original name, changed because the theophoric element *ba῾al* "lord" (here applied to Yahweh?) might be taken as a reference to the rejected Baal cult (cf. Eshbaal/Ishbosheth; cf. P. K. McCarter, *II Samuel*. AB 9 [1984], pp. 124-25, 128).

When Mephibosheth was five years old his feet became paralyzed when he fell (or was dropped) as he fled at the report of Saul and Jonathan's deaths (2 Sam. 4:4). David brought Mephibosheth from Lo-debar in Transjordan to Jerusalem and gave him Ziba, who had been a servant in the house of Saul; David returned to him Saul's family lands, which he then committed to Ziba's care, and gave Mephibosheth a regular place at the king's table (ch. 9). When David fled Jerusalem during Absalom's revolt, Ziba accused Mephibosheth of unfaithfulness to the king, so David gave all Mephibosheth's possessions to the servant (16:1-4). But when David returned to Jerusalem, Mephibosheth protested that Ziba had slandered him; David decided that the land should be divided between the two (19:24-30), each of whom apparently was eager to represent himself as loyal to David at the other's expense. When David handed over two sons and seven grandsons of Saul to the Gibeonites (cf. **1** above), he spared Mephibosheth out of consideration for the covenant he had made with Jonathan (21:7; cf. 1 Sam. 20:14-17).

MERAB [mē'răb] (Heb. *mērab*). A daughter of Saul (1 Sam. 14:49), whom he promised to David but then gave to Adriel the Meholathite (18:17-19). The five sons of Adriel and Merab were handed over by David to the Gibeonites to be hung (2 Sam. 21:8-9; KJV "Michal," following most MT MSS).

MERAIAH [mĭ rā'yə] (Heb. *mᵉrāyâ*). The head of the priestly family of Seraiah at the time of the postexilic high priest Joiakim (Neh. 12:12).

MERAIOTH [mĭ rā'yŏth] (Heb. *mᵉrāyôṯ*).

1. A Levite; descendant of Aaron and ancestor of the high priest Zadok (1 Chr. 6:6-7, 52 [MT 5:32-33; 6:37]) and the postexilic leader Ezra (Ezra 7:3).

2. A priest, the son of Ahitub and father of Zadok, and an ancestor of Azariah (1 Chr. 9:11) or Seraiah (Neh. 11:11). Some scholars identify him with **1**.

3. A priestly family headed by Helkai at the time of the postexilic high priest Joiakim (Neh. 12:15; one recension of the LXX reads *Mariôth*). In the corresponding list v. 3 he is called Meremoth (*see* MERE-MOTH **4**).

MERARI [mə râr′ī] (Heb. *mᵉrārî* "bitterness").
1. The third son of Levi (Gen. 46:11; Exod. 6:16; Num. 3:17; 1 Chr. 6:1, 16 [MT 5:27; 6:1]), father of Mahli and Mushi (Exod. 6:19; Num. 3:20, 33; 1 Chr. 6:19, 29 [MT 4, 14]), and eponymous ancestor of the Merarites (*bᵉnê mᵉrārî*; Num. 26:57). During the wilderness journeys of the Israelites, the sixty-two hundred Merarites encamped on the north side of the tabernacle and were charged with the care of "the frames of the tabernacle, the bars, the pillars, the bases, and all their accessories," and "the pillars of the court . . . with their bases and pegs and cords" (Num. 3:33-37; 4:29-33; cf. vv. 42-45; 7:8; 10:17). The Merarites were alloted twelve cities in Palestine — four each in the tribal territories of Zebulun, Reuben, and Gad (Josh. 21:34-40; 1 Chr. 6:63, 77-81 [MT 48, 62-66]).

Groups of Merarites assisted in bringing the tabernacle to Jerusalem (1 Chr. 15:6) and were responsible for the music of the tabernacle worship (6:44-47 [MT 29-32]; 15:17). The descendants of the Merarite Hosah were gatekeepers in the temple (26:10-11). Two Merarites participated in the cleansing of the temple during Hezekiah's reign (2 Chr. 29:12), and two were given oversight for repair of the temple at the time of King Josiah (34:12). Representatives of the Merarites were among the group returning with Ezra from exile (Ezra 8:18-19) and resettled in postexilic Jerusalem (1 Chr. 9:14).
2. The father of Judith; son of Ox (Jdt. 8:1; 16:7 [LXX 6]).

MERATHAIM [mĕr′ə thā′əm] (Heb. *mᵉrāṯayim*). The southern region of Babylonia where the Tigris and Euphrates rivers merge and empty into the Persian Gulf (Jer. 50:21). The Hebrew representation of the Akkadian name of the region, *māt marraṯim* (taken from the name of the Persian Gulf, *nar marrâtu* "bitter river"; cf. Heb. *mrr*), is a play on words that means "double rebellion" (*mrh*).

MERCURIUS (Acts 14:12, KJV). *See* HERMES (DEITY).

MERCY (Heb. *rāḥam, raḥᵃmîm ḥānan*; Gk. *éleos, oiktirmós*).† In the Old Testament, the basis of God's mercy toward Israel is his covenant with Israel. Having established his covenant, he maintains it by his covenant love (Heb. *ḥeseḏ*; RSV usually "steadfast love"; KJV usually "lovingkindness") and mercy (Exod. 33:19; Isa. 63:7-9), as well as by his judgments (Hos. 2:19 [MT 21]). Since the covenant is established and maintained in history, God's mercy is known in specific historical acts (e.g., Neh. 9:27-28; Isa. 30:18-26; Jer. 33:24-26; Ezek. 39:25-29). Because God is known as merciful by his past acts of deliverance, his people can have confidence to call on him for deliverance in the present (e.g., Ps. 57:1 [MT 2]; 123:1-4; Dan. 9:18). God's forgiving of his people's sins is a fundamental manifestation of his mercy (Ps. 25:6; 51:1-19 [MT 3-21]). The reversal from being forsaken by God to being received by his mercy is

fundamental to the beginnings of biblical eschatology (cf. Hos. 1:6-7; 2:1 [MT 3]). God's mercy toward his covenant people is sometimes portrayed as the love of a parent (Ps. 103:13; Isa. 49:15; Jer. 31:20) or a husband (Hos. 3:1-3).

It is within family relationships that human mercy was most experienced and expected as a duty by the people of the Old Testament (cf. Amos 1:11; Zech. 7:9-10). But human mercy was to extend to neighbor and even stranger, especially the needy and oppressed (Prov. 21:10; cf. Job 19:21; Ps. 72:12-14; RSV "pity"; Exod. 22:21-22 [MT 20-21]), just as does God's mercy (cf. Deut. 10:18-19). In the New Testament also, God's mercy is to be the model of the human mercy of his people (Luke 6:36; cf. Eph. 4:32).

A significant aspect of Jesus' ministry was his active compassion toward the suffering (Matt. 20:34; Mark 1:41; RSV "pity"; Luke 7:13; RSV "compassion") and toward the leaderless (cf. Matt. 9:36). He developed a reputation for his healing powers, so that those who were suffering often took the initiative in seeking his merciful help (e.g., v. 27; 15:22; 17:15). The mercy of Jesus also gives forgiveness and eternal life (2 Tim. 1:18; Heb. 2:17; 1 Pet. 1:3; Jude 21).

The divine covenant love of the Old Testament is carried into the New Testament, but is known mainly in God's gift of Jesus Christ to those who have not been his covenant people (Rom. 9:23-26; 11:30-32; Eph. 2:4-5; 1 Tim. 1:13). Paul is particularly insistent that God's mercy is independent of human will and exertion (Rom. 9:15-18). According to Jesus, the one who refuses to show human mercy will not receive God's mercy (Matt. 6:14-15; 18:23-35; cf. 5:7).

MERCY SEAT (Heb. *kappōreṯ*). A rectangular slab of pure gold that covered the ark of the covenant (Exod. 25:17-22). *See* ARK OF THE COVENANT.

MERED [mĭr′ĕd] (Heb. *mereḏ* "rebel"). A son of Ezrah of the tribe of Judah who married both an Egyptian ("daughter of Pharaoh") and a Jew (1 Chr. 4:17-18).

MEREMOTH [mĕr′ə mŏth] (Heb. *mᵉrēmôṯ*).
1. A priest, the son of Uriah and grandson of Hakkoz, responsible for weighing silver and gold in the temple treasury (Ezra 8:33). He also worked on the repair of the walls of Jerusalem (Neh. 3:4, 21; cf. Ezra 2:61).
2. An Israelite required to divorce his foreign wife (Ezra 10:36).
3. A priest who participated in the sealing of the new covenant under Nehemiah (Neh. 10:5 [MT 6]). He may be the same as **1**.
4. A priestly family who returned from Babylon with Zerubbabel (Neh. 12:3), probably the same as MERAIOTH **3** (v. 15; cf. LXX, Syr.).

MERES [mĕr′əz] (Heb. *meres*). One of the seven princes who acted as advisers for Ahasuerus (Esth. 1:14).

MERIBAH. *See* MASSAH, MERIBAH.

MERIBATH-KADESH [mĕr′ə băth kā′dĭsh] (Heb. *mᵉrîḇaṯ qāḏēš* "strife of Kadesh"). A name given to

Kadesh-barnea because of the Israelites' testing of God during their wilderness journeys (Deut. 32:51; KJV "Meribah-Kadesh"; cf. Num. 20:1-3; 27:14; cf. also BHS, Deut. 33:2). This new name occurs in Ezekiel's descriptions of the southern borders of the land of the new Israel (Ezek. 47:19; 48:28).

See KADESH, KADESH-BARNEA 1; MASSAH, MERIBAH.

MERIBBAAL. *See* MEPHIBOSHETH 2.

MERODACH [mĕr′ə dăk] (Heb. *mᵉrôḏāḵ*). Hebrew form of MARDUK (Jer. 50:2).

MERODACH-BALADAN [mĕr′ə dăk băl′ə dən] (Heb. *mᵉrôḏāḵ balʾᵃḏān*; from Akk. *marduk-apla-iddina* "Marduk has given a son"). Merodach-baladan II, king of Babylon 721-710, 704-703 B.C. A chieftain of the Chaldean tribe Bīt Yakin, Merodach-baladan was able in 721 to become king of Babylon. He claimed descent from Erība-Marduk, king of Babylon 782-762, but his power was based primarily on military aid from Elam. Sargon II (722-705), ruler of the Assyrian Empire, successfully ousted Merodach-baladan in 710, but the Chaldean returned to the throne of Babylon in 704. During his later brief reign, Merodach-baladan attempted to incite wide rebellion against the Assyrian Empire; his embassy to King Hezekiah of Judah was part of this attempt (2 Kgs. 20:12; KJV "Berodach-baladan," following MT; Isa. 39:1). Merodach-baladan was again ousted from Babylon, this time by Sennacherib (705-681), who exiled him to Elam.

MEROM [mĭr′əm], **WATERS OF** (Heb. *mê mērôm*).† The place where the Israelites under Joshua won a battle against an alliance of northern Canaanite rulers headed by Jabin of Hazor (Josh. 11:5, 7). This place, formerly identified with Lake Huleh, cannot yet be identified with certainty. Some scholars favor Wâdī Meirôn, which flows into the Sea of Galilee from the northwest, as the site, but the topography of Birket el-Jish (also called ʾAgam Daltōn), a small lake 4 km. (2.5 mi.) northeast of Meirôn, better fits the biblical account.

MERONOTHITE [mə rŏn′ə thīt] (Heb. *mērōnōṯî* "from Meronoth").† A gentilic designation of Jehdeiah, chief herder of David's she-asses (1 Chr. 27:30), and Jadon, one of the postexilic rebuilders of the walls of Jerusalem (Neh. 3:7).

MEROZ [mĭr′ŏz, mē′rŏz] (Heb. *mērôz* "calamity" [?]). A city (or clan) cursed in the Song of Deborah for its failure to aid the Israelites in the battle against Sisera (Judg. 5:23). A number of locations have been suggested for Meroz, among them Khirbet Mārûs, located near Hazor, the city whose forces Sisera commanded (4:2, 17). The battle itself took place in the valley of Jezreel.

MESECH (Ps. 120:5, KJV). *See* MESHECH 1.

MESHA [mē′shə] (PERSON).
  1. (Heb. *mêšaʿ*).† The king of Moab who fought against Israel, Judah, and Edom in the ninth century

B.C. (2 Kgs. 3:4). *Ca.* 865 Mesha seized control of Moab, which was then in the hands of the Israelite king Ahab, but he was then obligated to pay tribute to Israel from his personal wealth as a sheep breeder. Mesha's cessation of tribute after Ahab's death (2 Kgs. 1:1; 3:4-5) led to war (vv. 6-27). According to Mesha's own report of the war, inscribed on the MOABITE STONE, he won a decisive victory over Israel. The biblical account, which covers only one campaign in the war, tells of a battle that went badly against Mesha (vv. 24-26) but in the end led to Israel's retreat, in some way the result of Mesha's sacrificing his heir to the god Chemosh (v. 27). The battle between Judah and the alliance of Moabites, Ammonites, and Meunites reported in 2 Chr. 20 may be part of the same war; there the allies turn against each other, leaving Judah to gather the spoils of battle.
  2. (Heb. *mêšaʿ*; 1 Chr. 2:42, KJV). *See* MARESHAH (PERSON) 1.
  3. (Heb. *mêšaʾ*). A Benjaminite, son of Shaharaim and Hodesh (1 Chr. 8:9).

MESHA [mē′shə] (Heb. *mêšaʾ*) (PLACE). A boundary of the region inhabited by the descendants of Joktan (Gen. 10:30). Mesha was most likely a location in the desert of Syria or Arabia; indeed, several of the Joktanite names suggest a south Arabian origin. Some scholars identify Mesha with MASSA (Gen. 25:14).

MESHACH [mē′shăk] (Heb., Aram. *mêšaḵ*). The Babylonian name (Akk. *Mîsha-aku* "Who is that which Aku [a Sumerian lunar deity] is?") given to one of Daniel's companions (Dan. 1:7; 2:49; 3:12-30). Meshach's Hebrew name, Mishael (*mîšāʾēl*) means "Who is what God is?" *See* ABEDNEGO.

MESHECH [mē′shĕk] (Heb. *mešeḵ*).
  1. A son of Japheth and eponymous ancestor of an Anatolian people (Gen. 10:2 par. 1 Chr. 1:5). His descendants are probably to be identified with those known in Akkadian sources as Muški (cf. Gk. *Moschoi*), a people known for metallurgy and military ability who lived southeast of the Black Sea.
  At Ezek. 27:13 Meshech appears together with Tubal (cf. Akk. *Tabal*, associated with *Muški*) and Javan (Greeks) as traders supplying slaves and bronze vessels to Tyre. At 38:2; 39:1 Meshech and Tubal appear together as peoples subordinate to "Gog, of the land of Magog." Here Meshech, as other names in this context, is probably chosen to represent an unknown, distant people, thus representing the enemies of God and his people in general. Similarly, at Ps. 120:5 (KJV "Mesech"), Meshech is proverbial for a distant place (both from Jerusalem and from Kedar, named in the same verse) and a hostile people.
  2. A son of Aram and eponymous ancestor of an Aramean tribe (1 Chr. 1:17). At Gen. 10:23 he is called Mash.

MESHELEMIAH [mə shĕl′ə mī′ə] (Heb. *mᵉšelemyâ*, *mᵉšelemyāhû* "Yahweh rewards"). A Korathite Levite who was a temple gatekeeper at the time of David; the father of Zechariah, also a temple gatekeeper (1 Chr. 9:21; 26:1, 2, 9). Meshelemiah may also be called Shelemiah (26:14) and possibly Shallum (9:17, 19, 31; Ezra 2:42).

MESHEZABEL [mə shĕz'ə bĕl] (Heb. *mᵉšêzaḇ'ēl*
"God delivers").
1. An ancestor of Meshullam (**13**), who worked on
rebuilding the walls of Jerusalem (Neh. 3:4).
2. An Israelite who participated in the sealing of
the new covenant under Nehemiah (Neh. 10:21 [MT
22]).
3. The father of Pethahiah of the Judahite family
of Zerah (Neh. 11:24).

MESHILLEMOTH [mə shĭl'ə mŏth] (Heb. *mᵉšillēmôṯ*).
1. The father of Berechiah of the tribe of Ephraim
(2 Chr. 28:12).
2. A priest and descendant of Immer (Neh. 11:13).
At 1 Chr. 9:12 he is called Meshillemith (Heb. *mᵉšillē-
mîṯ*).

MESHOBAB [mə shō'băb] (Heb. *mᵉšôḇāḇ* "returned"). One of twelve princes of the tribe of Simeon
who took possession of the pastures at Gedor during
the days of King Hezekiah (1 Chr. 4:34-41).

MESHULLAM [mə shoōl'əm] (Heb. *mᵉšullām*).
1. An ancestor of Shaphan, secretary during the
reign of King Josiah of Judah (2 Kgs. 22:3).
2. A son of Zerubbabel (1 Chr. 3:19).
3. The head of a Gadite father's house in Bashan
(1 Chr. 5:13).
4. A Benjaminite, and son of Elpaal (1 Chr. 8:17).
5. The father (or an ancestor) of Sallu of the tribe
of Benjamin (1 Chr. 9:7; Neh. 11:7). He may be the
same as **4**.
6. The son of Shephatiah; a Benjaminite, among
the first to return from the exile (1 Chr. 9:8).
7. The son of Zadok the high priest; ancestor of the
priest Azariah (**8**) (1 Chr. 9:11) and Seraiah (**8**) (Neh.
11:11). He may be the same as Shallum (**9**) (1 Chr.
6:12-13; Ezra 7:2).
8. A priest of the house of Immer (1 Chr. 9:12).
9. A Kohathite Levite; one of the overseers of the
temple repairs made by King Josiah (2 Chr. 34:12).
10. One of the "leading men" sent by Ezra to Iddo
at Casiphia to obtain Levites for service in the postexilic temple worship (Ezra 8:16).
11. One who supported the opposition to Ezra's
dissolution of marriages to foreign women (Ezra
10:15). He may be the same as **10**.
12. An Israelite required to divorce his foreign wife
(Ezra 10:29). He may be the same as **10** or **11**.
13. The son of Berachiah (**6**); one of those who
worked on the walls of Jerusalem at the time of Nehemiah (Neh. 3:4, 30). His daughter married Tobiah's
son Jehohanan (**6**) (6:18).
14. The son of Besodeiah; one of those who repaired the Old Gate of Jerusalem (Neh. 3:6).
15. One of those who stood on the platform with
Ezra during the reading of the law (Neh. 8:4).
16. A priest who participated in the sealing of the
new covenant under Nehemiah (Neh. 10:7 [MT 8]).
17. An Israelite chief who sealed the new covenant
with Nehemiah (Neh. 10:20 [MT 21]).
18. The head of the priestly house of Ezra at the
time of the postexilic high priest Joiakim (Neh. 12:13).
19. The head of the priestly house of Ginnethon at

the time of the postexilic high priest Joiakim (Neh.
12:16).
20. A postexilic gatekeeper; one of those who
guarded the storehouses of the gates (Neh. 12:25; cf.
Shallum at 1 Chr. 9:17; *see* MESHELEMIAH).
21. One who participated in the postexilic dedication of the walls of Jerusalem (Neh. 12:33).

MESHULLEMETH [mə shoōl'ə mĕth] (Heb. *mᵉšul-
lemeṭ*). The daughter of Haruz of Jotbah, wife of
King Manasseh of Judah, and mother of King Amon
(2 Kgs. 21:19).

MESOBAITE (1 Chr. 11:47, KJV). *See* MEZOBAITE.

MESOPOTAMIA [mĕs'ə pə tā'mĭ ə] (Heb. *'ᵃram
naḥᵃrayim* "Aram of two rivers"; Gk. *Mesopotamia*
"[the land] between the rivers").† The region between
the Tigris and Euphrates rivers (e.g., Gen. 24:10;
Deut. 23:4 [MT 5]), roughly equivalent to modern
Iraq and northeastern Syria.
By the fourth millennium B.C. village populations
existed throughout Mesopotamia. The literate culture
of the Sumerians was established *ca.* 3000. Mesopotamia became the center of successive powerful empires from *ca.* 2350.
Despite their early relation to both Palestine and
Egypt, the people of Israel were aware of their ultimate Mesopotamian origin (Gen. 11:26-31; cf. 24:10;
Acts 7:2).

See ASSYRIA; BABYLONIA.

MESSIAH [mə sī'ə] (Gk. *Messías*; from Heb. *māšîaḥ* "anointed [one]").† God's anointed king; in the
Old Testament specifically the expected Jewish Messiah, in the New Testament Jesus Christ.
In its basic sense the term "messiah" refers to a
person who has been consecrated to a high office by
ceremonial anointing with oil. In the ancient world
priests and kings were so anointed, a practice reflected
at 1 Kgs. 19:16; Ps. 133:2. The anointing to an office
gave a person high and sacred status and assured authority, reverence, and respect.

I. Old Testament

Aaron and his sons were anointed as priests to serve
Yahweh (Exod. 30:22-30); the oil used in consecrating
them was a special formula made by Moses for this
sacred purpose. Saul was chosen by God as king and
referred to as the Lord's anointed (1 Sam. 12:3, 5).
David was careful not to lift his hand against Saul
because he respected as sacred the office of the
anointed.
Following Saul David became God's king. David
was conscious of being chosen by the Lord to replace
Saul, and he respected the office, considering it a
sacred destiny. God promised David that through his
offspring his kingdom and throne would endure forever (2 Sam. 7:1-17). This promise is known as the
Davidic covenant or the divine charter, and is the
source of the Jewish expectation of the Messiah; an
anointed one of God from the line of David would
always rule over God's people.
David is considered a "type" of Christ, God's ul-

timate anointed one. The history and memory of David were revered for centuries during the development of the messianic ideal. Many important prophetic constructs came into being that were applied in the expectation of the Coming One. He would be the son of David, the root of Jesse, a righteous branch, the servant of the Lord, and the anointed one on whom the spirit of the Lord would rest. Such images of the Messiah represent themes of many Old Testament books, apocryphal writings, and Jewish apocalyptic texts. The Psalms and the Prophets are filled with messianic vision. The anointed would come with authority, glory, and sovereign power; all people everywhere would worship him—his kingdom would never end (Dan. 7:14). Isaiah specifically identified the coming Messiah as the Servant who would bring salvation to God's people through his vicarious suffering and death (Isa. 53:10).

The coming of the Messiah is also an important motif in extrabiblical Jewish apocalyptic literature. Often the expectation was a poorly understood national optimism—an earthly political hope. Some writers perpetuated an idealistic, cosmic concept of a new world of peace and tranquility with Israel as God's people on earth. Judith, the Wisdom of Solomon, 1-2 Maccabees, Tobit, and Baruch concentrate on hopes for this world; later writings contrast this world and the next, and view the coming of the Messiah as the beginning of the new age (cf. 2 Bar. 40:3; 1 En. 38).

The Dead Sea Scrolls provide information that indicates a belief in two Messiahs, one who would be a military and political leader and an Aaronic descendant who would be the spiritual leader (e.g., 1QS 9:11; CD 20:1).

II. New Testament

By the Roman times the focus of Jewish hope had become mainly political. Many Jews expected a Messiah who would deliver them from their Roman oppressors and reduce the burden of taxation.

Jesus of Nazareth, whom many would come to recognize as the Messiah, taught and performed miracles both publicly and privately for the three years of his ministry in Galilee and Judea. His primary claim was that he was the Messiah of the Old Testament prophecies. Jesus persistently clarified the prophecies, answered criticisms, corrected false ideas about the messianic kingdom, and demonstrated in many indisputable ways that he was the promised Messiah.

Because Jesus, in his early public ministry, often commanded people to keep silent about his messianic miracles (e.g., Mark 1:43; 5:43; 7:36; cf. 8:26), some scholars have sought by means of a "messianic secret" to explain the difference between the "historical Jesus" and the Church's dogma of the Messiah. The commands to silence, however, were simply a means of expediting the full exposition of the Messiah's mission—it was a matter of timing.

The Hebrew term for Messiah (māšîaḥ) occurs twice in transliterated form (John 1:41; 4:25). In both passages the Greek translation "Christ" also appears.

Jesus clearly claimed to be the promised Messiah or Christ (v. 26). He explained to his followers the full meaning of his coming as the Anointed (Mark 10:32-45), and he accomplished the promised salvation through his death on the cross. After the resurrection Jesus showed himself alive to the apostles over a period of forty days, and taught them still more about the nature of the messianic kingdom of God before ascending into heaven (Acts 1:1-11). The Gospels were written to address what scholars call the christological question; the answer they provide is that Jesus is indeed the Messiah (John 20:31).

See CHRIST.

Bibliography. W. Manson, *Jesus the Messiah* (New York: 1946); S. Mowinckel, *He That Cometh* (Nashville: 1956); G. G. Scholem, *The Messianic Idea in Judaism* (New York: 1971).

METHEG-AMMAH [mĕ'thĕg ăm'ə] (Heb. *meṯeg hā'ammâ*).† Apparently a place that David took "out of the hand of the Philistines" (2 Sam. 8:1). Heb. *meṯeg* means "bridle," and *'ammâ* can be taken in a number of ways. Two general routes have been followed in interpretation of the phrase. One approach takes *'ammâ* as "mother" (as a feminine form of *'ēm*), here used metaphorically for "metropolis" or "capital city"; *meṯeg* is taken in a figurative sense as "control," thus "control of the chief city" (so NASB; cf. JB mg.). The more frequent approach takes *meṯeg hā'ammâ* as the actual name of an otherwise unknown city (so RSV, KJV). The parallel at 1 Chr. 18:1 reads "Gath and its villages (lit. "daughters")" (*gaṯ ûḇᵉnōṯeyhā*), either an attempt to explain what appears at 2 Sam. 8:1 or a preservation of the reading from which *meṯeg hā'ammâ* originated.

METHUSELAH [mə thoo'zə lə] (Heb. *mᵉṯûšelaḥ* "man of the javelin" or "worshipper of [the god] Šelaḥ"; Gk. *Mathousala*). The son of Enoch and father of Lamech in the lineage of Seth (Gen. 5:21-27; 1 Chr. 1:3). Of the extremely long-lived people before the Flood, Methuselah is credited with the longest life, 969 years. He is named among the ancestors of Jesus (Luke 3:37; KJV "Mathusala").

METHUSHAEL [mə thoo'shə ĕl] (Heb. *mᵉṯûšā'ēl*). The son of Mehujael and father of Lamech in the lineage of Cain (Gen. 4:18; KJV "Methusael"). Some critics regard him as the Yahwistic (J) source's counterpart to the Priestly (P) account's Methuselah.

MEUNIM [mə ū'nĭm], **MEUNITES** [mə ū'nīts] (Heb. *mᵉ'ûnîm*).* An Arab people from the vicinity of Māʿan southeast of Petra (or possibly associated with Maon, south of Hebron; cf. the MAONITES at Judg. 10:12). They were among the pastoral groups attacked by King Hezekiah of Judah (1 Chr. 4:41, Q; so RSV; KJV "habitations"; cf. JB) and later engaged in battle by King Uzziah (2 Chr. 26:7; KJV "Mehunims"). The second mention of the Ammonites at 2 Chr. 20:1 (Heb. *'ammônîm*; so KJV) should probably be corrected to Meunites (so RSV, NIV; LXX Gk. *Minaioi* as at 26:7), which would accord with their identification as "inhabitants of Mount Seir" (20:10, 22-23). At Ezra 2:50 (KJV "Mehunim"); Neh. 7:52 the Meunim are mentioned among the postexilic temple servants (KJV "Nethinims").

MEZAHAB [mĕz'ə hăb] (Heb. *mê zāhāḇ* "waters of gold"). The grandmother or grandfather of Mehetabel, the wife of King Hadar (Hadad) of Edom (Gen. 36:39; 1 Chr. 1:50). Some scholars suggest that the name represents a place.

MEZOBAITE [mə zō'bĭ ĭt] (Heb. *hammᵉṣōḇāyâ*). A gentilic ascribed to Jaasiel, one of David's mighty men (1 Chr. 11:47; KJV "Mesobaite"). It should perhaps be emended to *miṣṣōḇâ* "from Zobah" (cf. 18:3).

MIAMIN (Ezra 10:25; Neh. 12:5, KJV). *See* MIJAMIN 2, 4.

MIBHAR [mĭb'här] (Heb. *miḇḥār* "chosen, best"). One of David's mighty men; son of Hagri (1 Chr. 11:38).

MIBSAM [mĭb'săm] (Heb. *miḇśām*).
1. A son of Ishmael, and eponymous ancestor of an Arabian people (Gen. 25:13; 1 Chr. 1:29).
2. A Simeonite, the son of Shallum and father of Mishma (1 Chr. 4:25). The mention of Mibsam and Mishma also at 1:29-30 may suggest some relationship between a Simeonite clan and an Ishmaelite tribe.

MIBZAR [mĭb'zär] (Heb. *miḇṣār* "fortress"). A chief of Edom (Gen. 36:42; 1 Chr. 1:53). The name probably represents a place, perhaps Mabsara in northern Edom (cf. Eusebius *Onom.* cxxiv.20-21, in the region of Gebalena and subject to Petra) or Bozrah in Moab.

MICA [mī'kə] (Heb. *mîḵā'* "Who is like [God]?").
1. The son of Mephibosheth (Meribbaal) and grandson of Jonathan (2 Sam. 9:12; KJV "Micha"). He is called Micah (3) at 1 Chr. 8:34-35; 9:40-41.
2. The father of Mattaniah, a postexilic Levite of the lineage of Asaph (1 Chr. 9:15; KJV "Micah"; Neh. 11:17; KJV "Micha").
3. A Levite who participated in the sealing of the new covenant under Nehemiah (Neh. 10:11 [MT 12]; KJV "Micha").
4. The father of Mattaniah and ancestor of Uzzi, a postexilic Levite of the lineage of Asaph (Neh. 11:22; KJV "Micha"). He may be the same as 2 above or MICAIAH 5.

MICAH [mī'kə] (Heb. *mîḵâ*; shortened form of *mîḵāyāhû* "Who is like Yahweh?").
1. A man of the hill country of Ephraim during the period of the judges (Judg. 17–18; *mîḵāyᵉhû* at 17:1, 4). Micah stole eleven hundred pieces of silver from his mother, but when he returned them she provided two hundred pieces of the silver to make an idol ("a graven and molten image"; vv. 1-4). Micah made an ephod and teraphim and appointed first one of his sons and then a young Levite from Bethlehem (or perhaps only the Levite, whom he had adopted as his son; cf. vv. 10-11) priest in a shrine for the idol (vv. 5-13). A contingent of Danites searching for a place to resettle their tribe stopped at Micah's house and found the young Levite, with whom they were previously acquainted (18:1-4). When the Danites returned with troops en route to Laish, they stole the ephod, teraphim, and idol and convinced the Levite to go with

them (vv. 14-20). Micah pursued, but retreated before their superior forces (vv. 21-26). The Danites conquered Laish and established the idol in a shrine there with Jonathan the son of Gershom (perhaps the young Levite) as priest (Judg. 18:27-31).

The background of Micah's story is the nature of Yahweh worship at a time when there was a central shrine but no exclusive shrine (v. 31). Micah's supposition that he could guarantee Yahweh's favor by maintaining a personal shrine (17:13) is shown to be false as the Danites execute divine judgment upon him.

2. A Reubenite; the son of Shimei and father of Reaiah (1 Chr. 5:5).
3. The son of Mephibosheth (Meribbaal) and grandson of Jonathan (1 Chr. 8:34-35; 9:40-41). At 2 Sam. 9:12 he is called Mica (KJV "Micha").
4. (1 Chr. 9:15, KJV). *See* MICA 2.
5. A Kohathite Levite; chief of the sons of Uzziel (1 Chr. 23:20; 24:24-25; KJV "Michah").
6. The father of Abdon (2 Chr. 34:20). *See* MICAIAH 2.
7. Micah of Moresheth (cf. v. 14, "Moresheth-gath"), a prophet whose utterances are recorded in the book of Micah (Mic. 1:1; Jer. 26:18, Q; K *mîḵāyâ*). He prophesied during the second half of the eighth century B.C. and the early seventh century.

MICAH, BOOK OF.† The sixth book of the twelve Minor Prophets (third in the Greek canon).

I. Author and Date

According to the superscription (Mic. 1:1), the book comprises the utterances of Micah of Moresheth during the reigns of Judahite kings Jotham, Ahaz, and Hezekiah, *ca.* 740-687 B.C. Jer. 26:18-19 records Micah's judgment against Jerusalem during the time of Hezekiah (Mic. 3:12). Yet other than his hometown, generally identified with Moresheth-gath (modern Tell ej-Judeideh) in the Shephelah of Judah near Philistine Gath (cf. 1:14), no specifics are known concerning the prophet Micah. It is generally presumed that he was not a professional prophet and that his background was agricultural.

Micah is regarded as a contemporary of Isaiah of Jerusalem. His ministry witnessed the increasing might of the Assyrian Empire, which precipitated the Syro-Ephraimite war of rebellion in 734 and was felt most vividly in the fall of Israel to Sargon II in 722/721 and the dispersal of the northern tribes. Judah itself was invaded in 701 but was spared more than payment of tribute to Assyria and some loss of territory to the Philistines. The influx of refugees, first from Samaria and later from territory ceded to Philistia, widened the economic gap between rich and poor.

II. Contents and Composition

As with other prophetic books, Micah is a compilation of various oracles, and perhaps a compilation of compilations. Numerous attempts have been made to discern the overall structure of the book, with varying degrees of success. Most scholars see it as comprised either of two (generally chs. 1–5 and 6–7) or three (chs. 1–2, 3–5, 6–7 or 1–3, 4–5, 6–7) main sections, alternating in various combinations threats of doom and promises of salvation. Yet no clearly convincing chronological or even topical arrangement is apparent, and many scholars view this as evidence for later editing and supplementation of the basic collection. This is further complicated by abundant textual difficulties.

Following the superscription (1:1), the prophet pronounces judgment against Samaria for idolatrous worship (vv. 2-7), punishment of which he laments will reach as far as Jerusalem (vv. 8-9). Moreover, Jerusalem's corruption will doom the cities of Judah (vv. 10-16); extensive wordplay on various place names has contributed to considerable textual difficulty. Micah employs an oracle of woe to delineate the causes of punishment: the greed of the rich and powerful, their scorn for social justice as guaranteed by the ancient Israelite covenant, and their resistance of true prophecy (2:1-11). In stark contrast, vv. 12-13 promise salvation for "the remnant of Israel"; some scholars see here reference to Sennacherib's invasion of 701. Ch. 3 returns to prophecy of doom: because of the cannibalistic mistreatment of the poor by Judah's rulers and judges (RSV "heads" and "rulers") and the commercialism of the prophets, the temple mount "shall be plowed as a field" and Jerusalem itself "shall become a heap of ruins" (v. 12).

In chs. 4–5 the emphasis is on hope. Zion, "the mountain of the Lord," shall be exalted, and all peoples shall come in peace to Jerusalem for instruction (Heb. *tôrâ*; 4:1-5; cf. Isa. 2:2-4). Yahweh will establish as "the remnant" his afflicted people (Mic. 4:6-7) and restore the Davidic kingdom (v. 8); despite a period of travail (the Exile; vv. 9-10; cf. 5:1 [MT 4:14]), Israel will triumph ultimately over "many nations" (4:11-13). Again the prophet proclaims an era of peace for a reunited Israel under the messianic king, who is to be a descendant of David (5:2-15 [MT 1-14]).

In the final section of the book the prophet again warns of impending doom (chs. 6–7). Using the form of a prophetic lawsuit, he recalls Yahweh's past acts of deliverance and charges the people to emphasize justice and kindness rather than ritual (6:1-8). He pronounces the Lord's judgment against "the city" (presumably Jerusalem), for the corrupt rich follow the wicked precedent of Omride Samaria (vv. 9-16). Micah laments his decadent society, in which "there is none upright among men" and not even one's family can be trusted (7:1-7). Yet the book concludes with a promise of redemption, a psalm or "prophetic liturgy" affirming that Yahweh will pardon Israel and compassionately shepherd his chastened people (vv. 8-20).

III. Theology

Underlying Micah's prophecies of doom as well as his proclamations of salvation is the historic covenant relationship between Yahweh and his chosen people (cf. 2:8-9; 6:2-3, 5, "my people"). Because the people have forsaken their obligation to safeguard the community's survival as stipulated in the Sinai covenant, God must execute judgment upon Israel/Judah (e.g., 1:5; 3:8; 6:13). Yet even though they must first "writhe and groan . . . like a woman in travail" (4:9-10), Israel will be restored; Yahweh will uphold his covenantal responsibility to protect and foster his children

(e.g., 5:2-4 [MT 1-3]), and they shall be vindicated before the nations (vv. 7-9 [MT 6-8]; 7:8-10, 16-17).

The essence of the covenant stipulations is that God's people demonstrate justice and compassion for their fellows: "what does the Lord require of you but to do justice, and to love kindness, and to walk humbly with your God?" (6:8; cf. Hos. 6:6). Micah's indictments of Israel's transgressions are among the most vivid prophetic depictions of the lack of social justice (e.g., Mic. 2:1-2, 6-11; 3:1-11; 6:9–7:6).

Two significant themes in Israelite prophecy figure prominently in Micah's words of hope. First, the Lord will lift up from among the most despised of his people a remnant who under his perpetual rule will come to be a "strong nation" (4:6-7) that will prevail over the nations (5:7-9 [MT 6-8]). Second, the restored community will be guided by a scion of the house of David, a messianic figure who "shall stand and feed his flock in the strength of the Lord" (5:2-4 [MT 1-3]; cf. 2:12-13, where Yahweh is portrayed as the shepherd-king).

Not only does Yahweh actively direct events and circumstances concerning his covenant people (e.g., 1:6-7, the fall of Samaria; 4:9-10, the Exile; 6:3-5, deliverance of Israel; cf. 1:10-16), but he also includes the fortunes of the nations in his divine plan for history (e.g., 4:11-13; 7:11-13; cf. 1:2). His power is universal (5:4 [MT 3]), and all peoples may come to know and worship him (4:2-3; 7:16-17).

Bibliography. L. C. Allen, *The Books of Joel, Obadiah, Jonah and Micah.* NICOT (1976), pp. 237-404; D. R. Hillers, *Micah.* Hermeneia (1984); J. L. Mays, *Micah.* OTL (1976); H. W. Wolff, *Micah the Prophet* (Philadelphia: 1981).

MICAIAH [mĭ kā′yə, mĭ kā′yə] (Heb. *mîk̄āyâ, mîk̄āyāhû, mîk̄ayᵉhû* "Who is like Yahweh?").

1.† The son of Imlah; a prophet who informed King Ahab of Israel that the monarch would die in battle at Ramoth-gilead (1 Kgs. 22; 2 Chr. 18:4-27 [called *mîk̄â* at v. 14]).

Largely influenced by Queen Jezebel, daughter of the king of Tyre, the northern kingdom became increasingly paganized under Ahab, as manifested in the killing of many prophets of Yahweh (19:10) and the disregard for the covenantal ideal of Israel as steward of the land, which was ultimately owned by God (ch. 21). In this atmosphere the prophets' enthusiastic support for Ahab's war policy (22:6, 10-13 par.) was understandable. King Jehoshaphat of Judah, Ahab's ally, apparently understood such loyalties and insisted on being assured of God's intent (vv. 7-8). Micaiah was summoned and first echoed the other prophets; but at Ahab's prodding (based on the king's prior experience with Micaiah; cf. v. 8) he spoke of Ahab's death (vv. 13-17). Although Micaiah was jailed, his prophecy was fulfilled (vv. 26-37).

2. The father of Achbor, an official of King Josiah (2 Kgs. 22:12; KJV "Michaiah"). At 2 Chr. 34:20 Micaiah is called Micah (**6**) and Achbor is called Abdon.

3. The mother of King Abijah (Abijam) of Judah; daughter of Uriel of Gibeah (2 Chr. 13:2; KJV "Michaiah"). See MAACAH **4**.

4. One of the princes whom King Jehoshaphat sent

to instruct the people of Judah from the book of the law (2 Chr. 17:7; KJV "Michaiah").

5. The father of Mattaniah, and an ancestor of Zechariah (**30**), a priestly musician who participated in the postexilic dedication of the walls of Jerusalem (Neh. 12:35; KJV "Michaiah"). He may be the same as Mica **2** and/or **4**.

6. A priest who participated in the postexilic dedication of the walls of Jerusalem (Neh. 12:41; KJV "Michaiah").

7. A member of a highly placed Jerusalem family who reported to the princes of Judah the words of Jeremiah that Baruch had read from the scroll (Jer. 36:11-13; KJV "Michaiah").

MICHA (KJV). *See* MICA **1, 2, 4.**

MICHAEL [mī'kəl] (Heb. *mîḵā'ēl* "Who is like God?"; Gk. *Michaēl*).

1. An Asherite, the father of Sethur whom Moses sent to spy out Canaan (Num. 13:13).

2. The head of a father's house in the tribe of Gad (1 Chr. 5:13).

3. An ancestor of the Gadite Abihail (1 Chr. 5:14).

4. A Levite and ancestor of Asaph (1 Chr. 6:40 [MT 25]).

5. A son of Izrahiah of the tribe of Issachar (1 Chr. 7:3).

6. A son of Beriah of the tribe of Benjamin (1 Chr. 8:16).

7. A chief of a thousand from the tribe of Manasseh, among those who joined David's rebel forces at Ziklag and became a commander in his army (1 Chr. 12:20-21).

8. The father of Omri **4** (1 Chr. 27:18).

9. A son of King Jehoshaphat who, with his brothers and several princes of Israel, was murdered when his brother Jehoram became king of Judah (2 Chr. 21:2-4).

10. The father of Zebadiah (**8**), who returned from exile in Babylon with Ezra (Ezra 8:8).

11.† The celestial guardian "prince" (Heb. *śar*; LXX *ángelos* twice) of the Jews (Dan. 10:13, 21; 12:1). The central part of Daniel's final vision (chs. 10–12) is concerned with the course of eastern Mediterranean political history from the fall of the Persian Empire (11:2-3) through the reign of the Seleucid emperor Antiochus IV Epiphanes (vv. 21-45). Michael fights in heaven against the patron "princes" of Persia and Greece, who rule over Judea (10:13, 20-21). The transition from the chaos of conflict between the Ptolemaic and Seleucid Empires (11:40-45) to the deliverance of the Jews is marked by the coming of Michael (12:1). The point is that heaven is involved in the battles and sufferings of people, with God's chosen people having the strongest advocate in heaven.

In postbiblical Jewish writings Michael is one of the seven archangels (1 En. 20:4; cf. Rev. 8:2), "who is set over all disease and every wound of the children of the people" (1 En. 40:9). He appears frequently as the advocate and protector of Israel who intercedes for Israel (cf. T.Levi 5:6) and will avenge the people on their enemies at the end of the present age (cf. T.Dan 6). He is the gatekeeper of paradise (4 Bar. 9:5)

and guardian of "the hidden things" that order heaven and earth (cf. 1 En. 60:11ff.; Asc.Isa. 9:22).

Jude 9 alludes to a Jewish tradition concerning a dispute between the devil and "the archangel Michael" over the body of Moses (for the statement attributed to Michael, cf. Zech. 3:2); according to Origen (*De prin.* iii.2.1) this tradition was found in the Assumption of Moses, but it is not contained in any part of that work which has survived. At Rev. 12:7-9 Michael is the leader of the angels who engage in battle against the dragon (Satan) and his angels. Michael was sometimes spoken of as the angel who mediated between God and Moses in the giving of the law at Sinai (cf. Jub. 1:27; 2:1) and so may be the angel mentioned at Acts 7:38.

MICHAH (1 Chr. 24:24-25, KJV). *See* MICAH **4.**

MICHAIAH (KJV). *See* MICAIAH.

MICHAL [mī'kəl, mē'kăl] (Heb. *mîkal*, from *mîḵā'ēl* "Who is like God?"). A daughter of King Saul, the younger sister of Merab, and one of King David's wives (1 Sam. 14:49; 18:20ff.). She died childless (2 Sam. 6:23).

When Saul learned that Michal loved David, he promised her to him as his wife in exchange for a brideprice of one hundred Philistines' foreskins taken in battle, hoping thereby to end his young rival's life (1 Sam. 18:20-21, 25). But David delivered twice the number of foreskins required and thus was granted Michal as his wife (v. 27). Some time later Mical demonstrated greater love for her husband than her father, helping David to escape the jealous Saul (19:11-17).

In an attempt to weaken David's claim to succeed him, Saul gave Michal as a wife to Palti(el) the son of Laish (25:44). After Saul's death David demanded Michal's return, no doubt to strengthen his bid to succeed Saul among the northern as well as the southern tribes (2 Sam. 3:12-16). David subsequently defended himself as the one chosen by the Lord over her father (2 Sam. 6:21-22).

When the ark was brought into Jerusalem, David's dancing before it caused Michal to despise and mock him (6:16, 20; 1 Chr. 15:29).

At 2 Sam. 21:8 the name Michal (so KJV and most MT manuscripts) should be read "Merab" (so RSV, following LXX).

MICHMASH [mĭk'măsh] (Heb. *miḵmās, miḵmāś, miḵmāš, miḵmas*). A Benjaminite city in the hill country of Bethel, overlooking the pass leading to the Jordan valley. It is identified with modern Mukhmâs, *ca.* 12 km. (7.5 mi.) northeast of Jerusalem and 17.4 km. (11 mi.) west of Jericho near the Wâdī eṣ-Ṣuweinîṭ. It was at Michmash that Saul and Jonathan defeated the Philistines (1 Sam. 13:2–14:31). Michmash is one of the cities north of Jerusalem mentioned in Isaiah's description of an Assyrian advance from the north toward the capital city (Isa. 10:28; cf. Heb. *kāmas* "store up"). Groups of Benjaminites among those who returned from the Exile with Zerubbabel resettled the city (Ezra 2:27 par. Neh. 7:31; KJV, RSV "Michmas"; 11:31). After forcing Bacchides to flee to Antioch, the

Hasmonean Jonathan took up residence for a time at Michmash (1 Macc. 9:73; Gk. *Machmas*; KJV "Machmas").

MICHMETHATH [mĭk'mə thăth] (Heb. *hammiḵ-mᵉṭāṯ*). A place on the northern border of Ephraim (Josh. 16:6), also depicted in delineating the border of Manasseh as east of Shechem and north of Entappuah (17:7). Coordinating these seemingly contradictory locations for "the Michmethath" (so MT) is difficult. Two frequently suggested locations are Khirbet Makhneh el-Fôqā (also called Khirbet en-Nebi), *ca.* 8 km. (5 mi.) southeast of Shechem, and Khirbet Juleijil, east of Shechem.

MICHRI [mĭk'rī] (Heb. *miḵrî*). An ancestor of Elah, a postexilic Benjaminite (1 Chr. 9:8).

MICHTAM (KJV). *See* MIKTAM.

MIDDIN [mĭd'ən] (Heb. *middîn*).† A city or town in the wilderness of Judah (Josh. 15:61), usually identified with Khirbet Abū Ṭabaq in the valley of Achor west of the northern end of the Dead Sea.

MIDDLE COURT (Heb. *ḥāṣēr hattîḵōnâ*).† The enclosure or area between the royal palace and the temple in Jerusalem (2 Kgs. 20:4, Q; K *hāʿîr* "the city"), probably the same as the "other court" where the royal residence was located (1 Kgs. 7:8).

MIDDLE GATE (Heb. *šaʿar hattāweḵ*). A gate in the wall of Jerusalem (or possibly in a wall within the city), usually identified with the EPHRAIM GATE (Jer. 39:3).

MIDIAN [mĭd'ĭ ən] (Heb. *miḏyān*).† The fourth son of Abraham and his third wife (or concubine), Keturah; eponymous ancestor of the Midianites (Heb. *miḏyānî, miḏyānîm*; Gen. 25:1; 1 Chr. 1:32). Along with the other sons of Abraham's concubines, Midian was sent "eastward to the east country," which is interpreted as the Arabian desert (Gen. 25:6).

The territory in which Midian's descendants settled is usually identified as the eastern shore of the Gulf of Aqabah, but no definite borders for Midian are described in the Bible. Midianites are noted in Moab (36:35; 1 Chr. 1:46), the eastern Jordan valley (Num. 25:1-8; Judg. 7:25), the Sinai peninsula (Exod. 2:15ff.), and Canaan (Judg. 6:1-6, 33). References to the Midianites suggest that they were both nomads and city-dwellers, which combined with the lack of specific territoriality implies that they were seasonal transhumants (Num. 31:10). Some scholars suggest that Midian comprised a confederation of desert peoples (cf. Num. 31:8; Josh. 13:21).

In the biblical account Midianites are first encountered as traders to whom Joseph is sold by his brothers (Gen. 37:28); their association with the Ishmaelites is unclear (cf. vv. 25, 27; Judg. 8:24).

Moses flees to Midian after killing an Egyptian who was beating a Hebrew slave (Exod. 2:15-21; 4:18; cf. Acts 7:29; KJV "Madian"). He is given sanctuary by one Jethro (or Reuel), who is identified as the "priest of Midian" (but at Judg. 1:16; 4:11 he is called a Kenite). Moses marries Jethro's daughter Zipporah and they have two sons, Gershom and Eliezer (2:20-21). While tending Jethro's flocks near Horeb Moses encounters Yahweh in the burning bush (ch. 3).

The Midianites are numbered among those peoples in Canaan who viewed the Israelites as a threat to their hold on the land. The elders of Midian and Moab conferred and enlisted the diviner Balaam, to curse the Israelites (Num. 22:4-7). Once the Israelites settled in the land they became prey to the variety of pagan practices commonplace among the indigenous population of Canaan. The incident at Baal-peor (ch. 25), in which the priest Phinehas killed an Israelite and a Midianite woman who were engaged in sexual intercourse, is typical of the conflict that existed between worshippers of Yahweh and the neighboring peoples. Such tensions led to ferocious warfare between Israel and Midian (ch. 31; cf. Josh. 13:21-22). Each Israelite tribe supplied a military unit (called a thousand) for the war, which saw Midianite cities and camps destroyed, and the death of every Midianite man. Women and children were taken prisoner, and considerable booty was acquired; only virgin women were spared the sword.

During the period of the Israelite confederacy the Midianites invaded Palestine, where they oppressed the Israelites for seven years. The high mobility they enjoyed because of their camels contributed to Midianite military success in league with the Amalekites and the nomadic "people of the East" (Judg. 6). The judge Gideon (Jerubbaal) organized an Israelite counterattack and pursued them across the Jordan (chs. 7–8). In his surprise attack on the Midianite camp at Karkor, Gideon routed their army and captured the Midianite kings Zebah and Zalmunnah, who died at his own hand (8:21). The victory was long remembered in Israel (Ps. 83:9, 11 [MT 10, 12]).

Midian is mentioned in the prophecies of Isaiah as an example of Yahweh's ability to crush oppressors (Isa. 9:4). Midian is also to supply camels to the glorified Zion as a sign of the restored city's wealth (60:6).

MIDRASH [mĭd'răsh] (Heb. *miḏrāš*, from *dāraš* "to seek, investigate").† A form of biblical interpretation, largely philological and expository, typical of the rabbinic schools in Palestine during the early centuries A.D. *See* COMMENTARY.

MIDWIFE (Heb. *mᵉyaleḏeṯ*).† A woman who assists at childbirth (Gen. 35:17; 38:27-30). It is unclear whether midwives constituted a professional class. *See* BIRTH.

MIGDAL-EL [mĭg'dăl ĕl'] (Heb. *migdal-ʾēl* "tower of God" [or "El"]).† A fortified city in the tribal territory of Naphtali (Josh. 19:38). The site may be modern Mejdel Islim, 26 km. (16 mi.) east-southeast of Tyre.

MIGDAL-GAD [mĭg'dăl găd'] (Heb. *migdal-gāḏ* "tower of Gad"). A city in the vicinity of Lachish, in the lowland of the tribal territory of Judah (Josh. 15:37).

The site is generally identified as Khirbet el-Mejdeleh, 8 km. (5 mi.) south of Beit Jibrîn (Eleutheropolis).

MIGDOL [mĭg′dŏl] (Heb. *migdōl* "tower, fortress").† One or more Egyptian fortress cities. The city called Migdol with a Jewish population addressed by Jeremiah (Jer. 44:1; 46:14; *migdôl*) is probably to be identified with Tell el-Ḥeir, near Pelusium in the northeastern part of the Nile Delta, and may be the Ma-ag-da-lí referred to in one of the Amarna Tablets. The expression "from Migdol to Syene [Aswan]" (Ezek. 29:10; 30:6; KJV "from the tower of Syene") indicates the whole of Egypt from north to south. Ezekiel's "Migdol" is therefore in the north, and is probably to be identified with Tell el-Ḥeir. The same location again or another Migdol also in the delta region is referred to in the description of the place the Israelites stopped immediately before crossing through the Sea of Reeds (Exod. 14:2; Num. 33:7).

MIGHTY MEN (Heb. *gibbôrîm*, sing. *gibbôr*).* Originally a term used generally for battle-heroes and others renowned for strength (e.g., Gen. 6:4; 10:8; 2 Chr. 32:3; cf. Josh. 1:14; RSV "men of valor"). It is used primarily in a technical sense (lit. "warriors") to designate members of King David's mercenary forces, many of whom were non-Israelites. The "mighty men" were under the command of Joab (2 Sam. 10:7) and may have included the Cherethites and Pelethites, the royal bodyguard under the command of Benaiah (cf. 8:18; 1 Kgs. 1:10, 38). The heroic deeds of three particular "mighty men" (Joshebbasshebeth, Eleazar, and Shammah; "the three," apparently officers of the highest order) are recounted (2 Sam. 23:8-12; cf. v. 23), followed by the names of a group of thirty "mighty men" (or "the thirty," a most select unit) with the deeds of two of their leaders, Abishai and Benaiah (vv. 18-39).

MIGRON [mĭg′rŏn] (Heb. *migrôn*). A place on the outskirts of the territory controlled by the Benjaminite city of Geba (the text reads "Gibeah," probably incorrectly) where Saul and his men were stationed during a time of war with the Philistines (1 Sam. 14:2; cf. P. K. McCarter, *I Samuel*. AB 8 [1980], pp. 232, 235, 238-39, "on the threshing floor"). It was also one of the places north of Jerusalem mentioned in Isaiah's description of an Assyrian advance toward the capital (Isa. 10:28). Migron can probably be identified with Tell Miriam, southwest of Michmash and north of Geba on the northern side of Wâdī eṣ-Ṣuweinîṭ. However, because the context in Isaiah suggests that Migron was north of Michmash (not a necessary conclusion), some would identify it with sites north of Michmash.

MIJAMIN [mĭj′ə mĭn] (Heb. *mîyāmin, mîyāmîn*).
1. The leader of the sixth division of priests during the time of King David (1 Chr. 24:9).
2. An Israelite who was required to divorce his foreign wife (Ezra 10:25; KJV "Miamin").
3. A priest who participated in the sealing of the new covenant under Nehemiah (Neh. 10:7 [MT 8]). He may be the same as Miniamin 3 (cf. 2).
4. A chief of the priests among those who returned

from exile with Zerubbabel (Neh. 12:5; KJV "Miamin").

MIKLOTH [mĭk′lŏth] (Heb. *miqlôt*).
1. A Benjaminite who lived at Gibeon; a descendant of Jeiel and father of Shimeah/Shimeam (1 Chr. 8:32; 9:37-38).
2. The chief officer under Dodai the Ahohite of the second monthly division of David's army (1 Chr. 27:4; RSV mg., following MT).

MIKNEIAH [mĭk nē′yə] (Heb. *miqnēyāhû* "Yahweh possesses"). A levitical musician at the time of David (1 Chr. 15:18, 21).

MIKTAM [mĭk′təm] (Heb. *miḵtām*). A term found in the headings of Pss. 16, 56–60 (KJV "Michtam"), the meaning of which is not certain. It may mean "psalm of expiation" (cf. Akk. *katāmu* "cover"). Earlier commentators related it to Heb. *keṯem* "gold." The LXX reads Gk. *stēlographía* "document inscribed on a stele." Heb. *miḵtāḇ* "writing" at Isa. 38:9 may be a scribal error for *miḵtām*.

MILALAI [mĭl′ə lī] (Heb. *milʿalay*). A levitical musician who participated in the postexilic dedication of the walls of Jerusalem (Neh. 12:36).

MILCAH [mĭl′kə] (Heb. *milkâ* "queen").
1. The daughter of Haran, sister of Lot and Iscah, wife of Nahor, mother of eight, and grandmother of Rebekah (Gen. 11:29; 22:20-23; 24:15, 24, 47).
2. One of the five daughters of Zelophehad for whom special provision was made that they might be his heirs (Num. 26:33; 27:1; 36:11; Josh. 17:3). The name may actually represent a town or tribal unit.

MILCOM [mĭl′kŏm] (Heb. *milkōm*; Ugar. *mlkm*).† The principal Ammonite deity (cf. *UT*, no. 1483; inscriptional evidence for Milcom as the name of an Ammonite deity has been found at Amman [Rabbah]). In the Hebrew text Milcom is sometimes vocalized as *malkām* "their king" (Jer. 49:1, 3; Zeph. 1:5; KJV "Malcham"; cf. *meleḵ* "king"), making it difficult to determine whether the deity or a human king is intended (cf. *UT*, no. 1483). When Joab defeated Rabbah, the Ammonite capital, the crown of Milcom (so JB, RSV mg.) or of "their king" (that is, the king of the Ammonites; so RSV, KJV) was placed on David's head (2 Sam. 12:30; 1 Chr. 20:2); if the deity is intended, the crown was probably one made for a statue. Among the foreign deities worshipped by Solomon was Milcom of the Ammonites (1 Kgs. 11:5, 33). Zeph. 1:5 speaks of seventh-century Judahites swearing by both Yahweh and Milcom (or "their king"—a human king or a deity addressed as "king," perhaps Baal as at v. 4).

Like other national deities, Milcom was closely identified with the fate of his nation; Milcom (that is, the Ammonites) drove out the Gadites, but according to Jer. 49:1, 3, Milcom (KJV "their king") would himself go into exile with the defeat of Rabbah. Amos 1:15 may also imply the exile of Milcom upon the defeat of Rabbah (so some Gk. MSS; Eng. versions generally "their king").

It is generally assumed that Molech (Heb. *mōlek*) is a deliberately distorted form of Milcom's name. Indeed, in reference to Solomon's worship, Milcom is once called Molech (1 Kgs. 11:7; the LXX suggests Heb. *'elōhê* "gods" as at v. 2). But at 2 Kgs. 23:10, 13, the people's worship of Molech and the Milcom sanctuary of Solomon are mentioned separately. *See* MOLECH.

MILDEW (Heb. *yērāqôn*). Some form of agricultural disaster, the exact identification of which is uncertain. The Hebrew term has the literal meaning of "paleness" (cf. its use in the last clause of Jer. 30:6). Most likely it refers to the effects of some type of fungus on grain crops (e.g., *Erysiphe graminis*). Mildew and blight (*šiddāpôn*; KJV [and RSV once] "blasting") are, however, always mentioned together; mildew may be the visible effects of blight, actually the strong, hot east wind.

Mildew and blight are mentioned only in lists of potential disasters. In Solomon's prayer during the dedication of the temple (1 Kgs. 8:37 par. 2 Chr. 6:28), such disasters are foreseen as reasons for the prayers of the people, which God is asked to hear and answer. Another such disaster list including blight and mildew is part of threatened divine judgment for covenant disobedience (Deut. 28:22). At Amos 4:9; Hag. 2:17 past disasters are interpreted as divine judgment.

MILE (Gk. *mílion*). A Roman measure of distance (Matt. 5:41) equivalent to *ca.* 1480 m. (1618 yds.; the modern mile is 1760 yds.). Some English versions translate other ancient measurements into miles (particularly the *stádion*, equivalent to one-eighth Roman mile).

MILETUS [mī lē'təs] (Gk. *Milētos*). A city on the western coast of Asia Minor, on the south side of the estuary of the Maeander river. In ancient times Miletus was an important port with four harbors, but the harbors have long since been silted up. The remains of the city are now several kilometers from the coast.

Miletus had already been in existence for more than a millennium when in the sixth century B.C. it became a center of Greek art and philosophy. Milesians had established trading colonies as far away as the Black Sea and Egypt. The city was destroyed by the Persians in 494, but was soon rebuilt and continued to be an important commercial center through the Roman period.

The ship boarded by Paul and his companions at Philippi, which took them as far as Patara in Lycia, touched at Miletus among other ports (Acts 20:15). There Paul met with the elders of the Ephesian church (vv. 17-38). It was apparently on a later journey that Paul passed through or near Miletus and left there Trophimus, a traveling companion who had become ill (2 Tim. 4:20; KJV "Miletum"; cf. Acts 21:29).

MILK (Heb. *ḥālāb*; Gk. *gála*).* From their beginnings the Israelites kept livestock and obtained milk from goats, sheep, and cows. Normally, milk was not drunk but was eaten in the form of butter, cheese, and curds (cf. Deut. 32:14; *see* DAIRY PRODUCTS). Milk was kept in skins, like other liquids (Judg. 4:19).

The prohibition of boiling "a kid in its mother's milk" (Exod. 23:19; Deut. 14:21), which led to the distinction between milk meals and meat meals among observant Jews, began as a prohibition of specific Canaanite sacrificial customs (cf. *UT,* 52:14).

An abundance of milk was a sign of great fruitfulness, whether in statements about the land the Israelites were to enter and possess ("a land flowing with milk and honey"; e.g., Exod. 3:8; cf. Gen. 49:12), in a statement about a lover (Cant. 4:11), or in eschatological statements (Isa. 7:21-22; 60:16; Joel 3:18 [MT 4:18]). Milk could also represent whiteness (Lam. 4:7) and the refreshing and reviving quality of the proclamation of eschatological restoration (Isa. 55:1). On the other hand, strife between individuals is akin to pressing milk into curds (Prov. 30:33).

Human milk was the normal food of infants and of children even as old as three years of age (cf. 2 Macc. 7:27). A significant aspect of a people's happy state of affairs was the abundant flow of mother's milk (Gen. 49:25; cf. Hos. 9:14; Luke 23:29). Nursing and mother's milk are used figuratively to represent communication of basic teachings and insights (Isa. 28:9; 1 Cor. 3:2; Heb. 5:12-13) and for unadulterated and beneficial truth (1 Pet. 2:2).

MILL (Heb. *rēḥayim*; Gk. *mýlos*). An implement for grinding grain into meal or flour, consisting of two stones—often of black basalt—rubbed or turned against each other. Early types of mill consisted of a lower stone (Heb. *pelaḥ taḥtît*), rectangular with a concave upper surface, and a semicylindrical upper stone (*pelaḥ rekeb*; cf. Judg. 9:53), which was rubbed (not rolled) against the lower stone to grind grain. A later type of mill, which made grinding a less time-consuming though still a laborious task, consisted of two round stones—the lower, with a convex upper surface, fixed to the ground and the upper, with a concave lower surface, turned against the lower stone.

The grinding of grain, which had to be done every day (cf. Prov. 31:15), was difficult and noisy. It was considered women's work (Exod. 11:5; Isa. 47:1-2; Matt. 24:41; cf. Judg. 16:21; Lam. 5:13), though by the Late Bronze Age beasts of burden were used at large mills (cf. Gk. *mýlos onikós* "large millstone turned by a donkey"). The silence of the mills was symbolic of the destruction of a city (Jer. 25:10; Rev. 18:22). Because grain had to be ground in order for life to go on, it was prohibited from receiving a millstone as a guarantee for a loan (Deut. 24:6).

MILLENNIUM [mə lĕn' ē əm] (Gk. *chília étē* "one thousand years"; Lat. *mille* "thousand" plus *annus* "year").† The "thousand years" of Christ's eschatological reign (Rev. 20:2-7). Numerous interpretations have been offered.

According to Rev. 20, the thousand-year period is inaugurated by the following events: Satan is chained and imprisoned in "the bottomless pit" for a thousand years (vv. 1-3; cf. 9:2), "those to whom judgment was committed" are enthroned (20:4), and Christian martyrs are raised to life and begin a thousand-year reign with Christ (vv. 4-6). When this period has ended, Satan is released to bring together God's enemies for battle; they are defeated, and his eternal punishment begins (vv. 7-10), after which the general resurrection of "the rest of the dead" occurs, followed by judgment (vv. 5a, 11-15). Then "a new heaven and a new earth" are experienced (21:1).

The idea of such an interim period of earthly peace and righteousness is found in some Jewish apocalypses (e.g., 2 Esdr. 7:28; 1 En. 91:14; 2 En. 32–33; cf. Barn. 15) as the reconciliation of earthly messianic hopes for the future with more transcendent hopes centered on "new heavens and a new earth" (Isa. 65:17). In some rabbinic discussions the issue was not whether such an interim would be, but how long it would last.

Rev. 20 portrays a two-stage victory over death and the forces of evil. Both stages involve a defeat of Satan, a resurrection, and possibly (depending on interpretation of the first sentence in v. 4) a judgment. The two stages are separated by a thousand-year period wherein those who did not worship "the beast" or bear its mark reign victorious with Christ. At the second stage the forces of evil are released only to be thrown into "the lake of fire" for eternal punishment (vv. 10, 14-15).

The different views concerning this thousand-year period arise from different answers to these questions: (1) What is the nature and location (earth or heaven) of the reign of the Christian martyrs? (2) In what sense is Satan bound? To what degree is he prevented from being active? (3) What relation does the millennium bear to the present and to the Parousia? (4) Is "one thousand" a literal measure of time, or a symbol like many of the other numbers in the book of Revelation? (5) What is the relation, parallel or subsequent, of the events portrayed in Rev. 20 to those portrayed in 19:11-21 and other parts of the book?

The "amillennial" viewpoint interprets Rev. 20 symbolically rather than literally. According to this position, Satan is bound in the abyss already in the present age, in that he is unable to prevent the Church's extension of the gospel to all nations (cf. John 12:31). The Christians who have come to life and reign are those who are now in triumph with Christ and waiting for his coming, or those who experience the "resurrection" of the new birth of faith in Christ and the activity of his kingdom in this age (cf. Rev. 1:6, 9). "One thousand" is, like other numbers in the book of Revelation and like much of the rest of the language of ch. 20, of metaphorical or symbolic, not literal, value.

"Postmillennialists" think of a period before the Parousia during which the steady transformation of the world through Christ's rule in his kingdom (cf. Matt. 13:31-33) will be great enough to be regarded in terms of Satan's imprisonment. The world will be essentially "christianized," after which Christ's Parousia will occur.

The "premillennial" position interprets Rev. 20 literally. Its adherents consider Satan extremely active in the present age (cf. 1 Pet. 5:8), but he is to be rendered entirely inactive as outlined at Rev. 20:1-3. Hence the "thousand years" is yet to come and will, in fact, follow the Parousia. Christ and his followers will, it is held, rule directly on earth in a thousand-year period of worldwide justice and peace. This messianic reign of limited duration is, according to some premillennialists, referred to at 1 Cor. 15:23-26.

Bibliography. R. G. Clouse, ed., *The Meaning of the Millennium: Four Views* (Downers Grove: 1977).

MILLET (Heb. *dōḥan*). A grain, *Sorghum vulgare* Pers. (sorghum) or *Panicum miliaceum* L. (millet) or some other grain or variety of grains. Millet is mentioned only at Ezek. 4:9, and there its significance is apparently that it is unusual as human food. Siege conditions brought about the scarcity of food represented by the prophet's bread (cf. v. 16).

MILLO [mĭl′ō] (Heb. *millô*').

1. "The house of Millo" (Judg. 9:6, 20, KJV). *See* BETH-MILLO.

2. Perhaps an earthwork fill (cf. Heb. *mālē*' "fill") between the temple area and the city of David (south of the temple area, farther down the slope of the eastern hill of the city) or a fortified tower in the same approximate location. The identification now most commonly advocated is the Jebusite terraces on the eastern side of the city of David, descending the steep slope into the Kidron valley and supported by retaining walls that may have been augmented by Solomon.

Though it is mentioned in the account of David's rebuilding of Jebus at 2 Sam. 5:9 par. 1 Chr. 11:8, some contend that the Millo actually was not built until Solomon's time (1 Kgs. 9:15, 24); yet although the description of David's building projects may reflect features present at the time of a later writer, 1 Kgs. 9 may also represent a rebuilding or expansion at the time of Solomon. David built his city "from the Millo inward" (cf. 1 Chr. 11:8, "in complete circuit") or, possibly, "from the Millo to the house (i.e., the temple, which also did not yet exist)." Solomon built (or augmented) the Millo to close a gap in the defenses of the city of David (1 Kgs. 11:27). Centuries later, in preparation for the Assyrian invasion, Hezekiah strengthened the Millo (2 Chr. 32:5).

3. The place where King Joash of Judah was murdered (2 Kgs. 12:20 [MT 21]; Heb. *millô*'), "on the way that goes down to Silla" (cf. Syr., "as he [i.e., Joash] was going down"). The reference may be to a specific structure, such as a barracks, or to the general vicinity of the Millo (NIV, JB "Beth-millo").

MINA [mī′nə] (Heb. *māneh*; cf. Ugar. *mn*). A unit of weight (1 Kgs. 10:17; Ezra 2:69; Neh. 7:71-72; KJV "pound") approximately equal to 571 gm. (1.26 lb.). *See* WEIGHTS AND MEASURES.

MIND (Heb. *lēḇ*, *lēḇāḇ*, *rûaḥ*, *nepeš*; Gk. *noús*, *phrónēma*, *diánoia*).* As with similar concepts (*see* HEART; LIFE; SOUL), the "mind" in Hebrew usage, as rendered in English translations, represents a variety of human qualities and functions (cf. Deut. 6:5). The terms most often used are Heb. *lēḇ* and *lēḇāḇ*, regarding the heart as the seat of human emotion, intellect, and volition or will (e.g., Jer. 19:5). Accordingly, people remember God's actions (e.g., Isa. 65:17) or the covenant ideals (cf. Deut. 30:1). Through the mind one exhibits wisdom (1 Kgs. 3:12) or skill (*rûaḥ*; e.g., Exod. 28:3). The mind enables a person to direct his life (e.g., 1 Sam. 2:35; 1 Kgs. 8:48; *lēḇ* and *nepeš* "heart" and "mind").

In the New Testament the various Greek words translated "mind" stand for aspects of human existence, consciousness, and functioning. The use of several different Greek terms does not, as it might appear, represent any great precision. Indeed, the whole person is represented emphatically by the use of more than one term (e.g., Matt. 22:37; Eph. 2:3; Phil. 4:7; Rev. 2:23); on the other hand, the human dilemma is represented by setting the various terms in contrast to each other (e.g., Rom. 7:22-25; 8:5; 1 Cor. 14:14).

The mind (*noús*), as the thinking, reasoning, and planning aspect of human existence and awareness, is particularly prominent in Paul's letters, here representing simply the whole of human existence and experience, considered from one particular aspect. The mind is corrupted by sin just as are other aspects of human existence (Rom. 1:28; Eph. 4:17-19; Col. 2:18; cf. 1 Tim. 6:5; 2 Tim. 3:8). As such, it is capable of comprehending the good but not of ensuring its accomplishment (Rom. 7:22-25). The mind's transformation is at the heart of the renewal of the person into life lived in accordance with God's will (12:2; Eph. 4:23). The mind can, indeed, become conformed to Christ's "mind"; through the risen Lord the follower of Christ can experience the power and wisdom of the Lord (1 Cor. 2:16). The rational operations of the mind are transcended by the spiritual experience of glossolalia, but they ought not be overcome or replaced by it (1 Cor. 14:13-19).

MINIAMIN [mĭn′yə mĭn] (Heb. *minyāmin, minyāmîn* "from the right hand," i.e., "fortunate").

1. A Levite who assisted in the distribution of the offerings among the levitical cities at the time of King Hezekiah (2 Chr. 31:15).

2. A priestly father's house represented at the time of the high priest Joiakim (Neh. 12:17).

3. A priest and musician who participated in the postexilic dedication of the walls of Jerusalem (Neh. 12:41). He may be the same as Mijamin 3 (10:7 [MT 8]).

MINING.† The principal biblical reference to mining is at Job 28:1-11. A number of Hebrew terms relating to mining and refining appear in vv. 1-4 of that passage: *môṣā'* "source, mine" (v. 1a); *zāqaq* "wash the ore (from)" (v. 1b; RSV "refine"); *lāqaḥ mē'āpār* "take from the dry earth" (v. 2a); *ṣûq 'eḇen* "smelt from ore" (lit. "melt rock"; v. 2b); *ḥāqar 'eḇen* "search for ore" (v. 3); and *pāraṣ naḥal* "open a shaft" (v. 4). Descriptions follow of the disturbance of the natural state of things underground which results from mining (vv. 5, 9-10), the hiddenness of underground mines (vv. 7-8), and the damming of streams to prevent flooding of mines (v. 11). This extended description represents the considerable human labor expended in the quest for metals and gems, but the point is that wisdom cannot be obtained even with a comparable expenditure of human effort (vv. 12-22).

As part of a hyperbolically glowing description of the land of promise, it is said that the stones of that rocky land are iron and that one can mine (*ḥāṣaḇ* "hew, dig") copper from its hills (Deut. 8:9). Yet archaeological and geological studies indicate the rela-

tive scarcity of mineral resources in Palestine proper. It was probably shortly before iron tools began to be used in that region of the ancient world (*ca.* 1200 B.C.) that Israel entered Canaan, but for some time the Israelites apparently lagged far behind the Philistines in the use of iron (1 Sam. 13:19-22). The Egyptians mined copper in the Sinai peninsula as early as predynastic times. Copper deposits in the Arabah and Edom began to be exploited *ca.* 2000 and were mined especially from 1200 to 600. Iron was also mined in the Arabah and in northern Transjordan (cf. Deut. 3:11). But other than obtaining iron and copper from the Arabah—the desire for which was probably often cause of war between Israel and Edom—the Israelites were little engaged in mining. Israel did import such mined products as gold and gems from southern Arabia (1 Kgs. 10:2, 10; Ps. 72:15).

MINISTER (Heb. piel *šārat*, ptcp. *mᵉšārēṭ*; Gk. *diákonos, leitourgéō, leitourgós*), **MINISTRY** (Gk. *diakonía, leitourgía*).* Nearly half of the occurrences of the Hebrew verb in the Old Testament refer to some form of priestly service and are translated "minister" in the KJV and RSV. Included are the work which the Aaronic priests perform as they offer sacrifices at the altar (e.g., Exod. 28:43; Deut. 17:12; 1 Chr. 16:37; Ezek. 40:46), the work of the Levites as assistants to the priests (Num. 3:6; 8:26; 18:2), and the Levites' service before the Lord, described in such a way that they are given almost independent priestly status (e.g., Deut. 10:8; 1 Chr. 15:2; Jer. 33:21-22). Secular uses of *šārat* suggest that part of what the word conveys is the intimacy between the servant and the master who is served (e.g., Num. 11:28; cf. Gen. 39:4; 2 Chr. 22:8; RSV "attended"), an intimacy not known in the usually more menial work of the *'eḇed* "servant" (though the related verb *'āḇad* is sometimes used of the work of the priests; e.g., Exod. 13:5; RSV "service").

The Greek terms are used in the New Testament (as in the LXX, where this word group is the most common translation of Heb. *šārat*) for Jewish priestly worship (Luke 1:23; cf. Heb. 9:21; RSV "worship"; 10:11; RSV "service"), and in comparing Christ's "ministry" with that of the Old Testament priesthood (8:2, 6). Once *leitourgía* is used for acts of Christian worship (Acts 13:2; RSV "work"). Paul also applies this word group to material assistance given by Christians to other Christians (Phil. 2:25; cf. v. 30; Rom. 15:27; 2 Cor. 9:12; RSV "service"), and to his own apostolic ministry to Gentiles, in both cases often in the metaphorical sense of Jewish priestly service (Rom. 15:16). Similarly, Gk. *latreúō* "serve" and *latreía* "service" also reflect a background of use for Old Testament and Jewish worship (e.g., 9:4; RSV "worship"; Heb. 8:5; RSV "serve"), with the additional thought of specific acts being a "service" for God (e.g., John 16:2; Rom. 1:9; Heb. 9:14; cf. Rom. 12:1; Phil. 3:3).

Gk. *hypērétēs* "servant" is used of those through whom God's word is made known (Luke 1:2; cf. the cognate verb *hypēreteō* "work for, wait on, assist"; Acts 13:36).

The word group most commonly translated "minister" and "ministry" in the New Testament is *diá-*

konos "servant," *diakonía* "service, task," *diakonéō* "serve." Although these terms came to be used among Christians for the particular office of deacon or deaconess (Rom. 16:1; 1 Tim. 3:8-13; cf. Acts 6:1; also Phil. 1:1; RSV "servants"), they were also used more widely for Christian ministries in general, especially the apostolic ministry of gospel preaching (e.g., Acts 1:25; 6:4; 20:24; 2 Cor. 3:6; Col. 1:23, 25), as well as visiting and providing for physical needs (Matt. 25:44), administration and teaching (1 Tim. 4:6), specific tasks given to individuals by God (Col. 4:17), and the Church's work and mission as a whole (Eph. 4:12). The secular uses of these words most often have to do with providing for physical needs (including provision of finances, as in Luke 8:3; RSV "provided for"), and waiting on guests (as in Matt. 8:15; Luke 10:40; RSV "serve[d]").

For offices in the early Church, *see* CHURCH *IV*.

MINNI [mǐn'ī] (Heb. *minnî*). A region south of Lake Urmia in modern Iran, and an ancient people, the Manneans (Akk. *Mannay, Mannaya*), living in that region. These people were among the reluctant and often rebellious subjects on the borders of the Assyrian Empire. After the defeat of the Assyrians in 612 B.C., Minni came under Median and then Persian control. The kingdom of Minni is among those subjects of Persia summoned to war in Jeremiah's oracles against Babylon (Jer. 51:27).

MINNITH [mǐn'ǐth] (Heb. *minnîṯ*).† A region or city in Ammonite territory that marked the limit (probably the southwestern limit) of the "twenty cities" conquered by Jephthah (Judg. 11:33). A possible identification is with Khirbet el-Hanafish, *ca.* 7 km. (4.3 mi.) northeast of Heshbon and *ca.* 15 km. (9 mi.) southwest of Amman (cf. Eusebius *Onom.* cxxxii.2).

At Ezek. 27:17 the MT reads *ḥiṭê minnîṯ*, perhaps "wheat of (i.e., from the place called) Minnith" (so KJV; cf. NIV, JB). Other interpretations involve a simple emendation to *ḥiṭṭîm zayiṯ* "wheat and olives" (so RSV) or a more extensive emendation, *ḥiṭṭîm ûneḵōʾṯ* "wheat and gum" (cf. LXX *mýron* "perfumed oil").

MINT (Gk. *hēdýosmon*). Any of several herbs of the genus *Mentha* (family *Labiatae*), a number of which grow in Palestine. Tithing garden herbs such as mint is not explicitly required by the Pentateuch, but was considered a requirement by scribal interpretation (cf. Deut. 14:22-23). Jesus condemned not this attention to detail, but the neglect of "justice and mercy and faith" that could coexist with it (Matt. 23:23 par. Luke 11:42).

MINISCULE [mǐ nŭs'kyōōl]. *See* UNCIAL.

MIPHKAD (Neh. 3:31, KJV). *See* MUSTER GATE.

MIRACLE.† An event remarkable in that it goes contrary to the laws of nature, that is, to the usual course of events. The direct action of God or some other being whose existence lies outside the natural universe is assumed to be the cause of miracles, so that they are commonly taken as attestation of the claimed divine origin of a message or messenger. Biblical miracles are never just conjuring tricks, but are bound up with the work of God in history for his people's salvation and with the understanding and acceptance of his message. As such, each is in some way a "sign" (Heb. *ʾôṯ*; Gk. *aēmíon*).

I. Old Testament

Most Old Testament reports of miracles are associated with Israel's deliverance from Egypt, their subsequent time in the wilderness, and entry into the land of promise. This period of the people's deliverance and establishment is considered the primary setting of miracles (cf. Pss. 105–106). The only other Old Testament setting in which miracles appear in any quantity is the activities of the prophets Elijah and Elisha (1 Kgs. 17–2 Kgs. 8). In the Old Testament "signs" are given and "wonders" (*môpēṯ*) worked by God as manifestations of his saving power and covenant faithfulness on behalf of his people. Some signs and wonders given by God actually do not fit in the category of miracle, but a clear distinction is not made; the manifestation of God's faithfulness to his people does not require a distinction between miracles, predictions, and natural events.

A prophet might give a miraculous or predictive authenticating sign or wonder (Deut. 13:1-2 [MT 2-3]; 2 Kgs. 20:8-11; Isa. 7:10-14; cf. 44:25). At Joel 2:30 (MT 3:3) *môpēṯ* refers to eschatological cosmic signs (RSV "portents").

II. New Testament

Three kinds of miracles (Gk. *dýnamis* "power," *érgon* "work") are attributed to Jesus and his disciples: healings, exorcisms, and what are usually called "nature miracles," the latter performed by Jesus only. The accounts of healings (e.g., Matt. 8:14-17 par.; 9:20-22 par.; John 4:46-54; Acts 3:1-10) follow a basic outline: the person to be healed and the healer meet through some means; a statement about the nature and severity of the illness is sometimes made; the healer heals the person by speaking, by some physical action in connection with the person, or by both; and the success of the healing and the reaction of witnesses are described. The instances in which a person is raised from the dead (Matt. 9:18, 23-26 par.; Luke 7:11-17; John 11; Acts 9:36-42; cf. 20:9-12) are healing stories on the basis of their literary form.

The exorcism stories (e.g., Matt. 8:28-34 par.; 12:22-37 par.; Mark 1:23-28 par.; Acts 16:16-18) follow an outline similar to that of the healings: the meeting of Jesus or the disciple with the possessed person, the demon's recognition of Jesus' power, the exorcism of the demon, and the demonstration of accomplishment of the exorcism and its recognition by witnesses.

The nature miracles are: Jesus' turning water into wine (John 2:1-11), his walking on the sea (Matt. 14:22-33 par.), stilling of the storm on the sea (8:23-27 par.), multiplications of food to feed crowds (14:15-21 par.; 15:32-39 par.), discovery of the temple tax in the fish's mouth (17:24-27), cursing of the fig tree (21:18-22 par.), and miraculous catches of fish (Luke 5:1-11; John 21:5-6). These do not follow an outline to the same degree as the healings and exorcisms.

Jesus' disciples, not the crowds, are the witnesses to the nature miracles, which are usually accomplished in response to some human difficulty, whether of the crowds or the disciples.

Parallels to the miracles recorded in the Gospels and Acts are easily found in other ancient literature—pagan, Jewish, and Christian. The most apparent differences from these parallels are the New Testament miracle accounts' simplicity and lack of embellishment, particularly with regard to the healing process.

III. Meaning

It is assumed in the Bible that miracles will be taken as attestation or authorization of a message or messenger. If miracles are part of a series of events, then that larger series of events—whether the Exodus, the ministry of Jesus, or something else—is considered to be the work of God (cf. Exod. 4:1-5; 1 Kgs. 18:38-39; John 2:23; 3:2; 20:30-31).

Attestation becomes a problem when the existence of God is itself in question. The attestation given to the people of biblical times by miracles was given within an assumptive framework or worldview that included the possibility of supernatural beings. At question was, e.g., Yahweh's claim to an authority that excluded worship of Baal (1 Kgs. 18:21-40), a prophet's claim to speak a true word from God, or the claim of Jesus to be the Messiah. God's existence cannot be proved in any conclusive way by miracles, but for one who believes in God as Creator and Sustainer of the universe, belief in the possibility of miracles poses no difficulties.

The Bible does not consider miracles an unquestionable attestation or authorization in whatever context they might appear. The appearance of miracles was created by mechanical means in some temples of the Hellenistic age (cf. Rev. 13:13-14). It is also acknowledged that genuinely supernatural acts can be performed by those making dangerously false claims (Matt. 24:24). Miracles can lead to faith, but they do not make faith inescapable, even if they are acknowledged to be miracles (cf. John 11:47-48). The demand for attesting miracles is not seen as openness to the message, but as resistance against the message (Matt. 16:1-4; 1 Cor. 1:22-24; cf. Matt. 12:24). That prophets will come with attesting miracles is not in itself taught by the Bible, but is rather the assumption within which caution concerning prophets is taught; the criterion of truth is not miracles but adherence to the true God and his will (Deut. 13:1-3; Matt. 7:21-23). Disagreement with a form of Christianity that emphasized attestation by miracles and "power" rather than "weakness" is reflected in the Gospels' emphasis on the crucifixion of Jesus as a fact of primary importance in his ministry, in the records of Jesus' caution with regard to the faith brought about by miracles (e.g., Mark 1:34; 3:11-12), and in Paul's defense of his apostleship at 2 Cor. 10–13.

See HEALING; EXORCISM.

Bibliography. C. Brown, *Miracles and the Critical Mind* (Grand Rapids: 1984); R. H. Fuller, *Interpreting the Miracles* (Philadelphia: 1963); G. Theissen, *The Miracle Stories of the Early Christian Tradition* (Philadelphia: 1983).

MIRIAM [mĭr′ĭ əm] (Heb. *miryām*).

1. The sister of Moses and Aaron (Num. 26:59). When Moses was found in a basket by Pharaoh's daughter, it was probably Miriam who arranged for Moses' own mother to become his wet nurse (Exod. 2:4-9).

Miriam, together with Aaron, later claimed to be a mediator of God's messages on a par with Moses (Num. 12:2). The Lord's response to this situation indicated that though he did communicate to prophets, he spoke more directly to Moses (vv. 6-8). As punishment for so challenging Moses' authority as leader of the people Miriam was afflicted with leprosy (vv. 9-10). Despite Moses' pleading with God on her behalf, she was still subject to the restrictions normally placed on lepers (vv. 13-15; cf. 5:2-3; Lev. 13:2-8; Deut. 24:8-9). Miriam died at Kadesh in the wilderness of Zin and was buried there (Num. 20:1). She is remembered as having a role next to her brothers in the Exodus (Mic. 6:4).

The brief poem in response to Moses' song of praise after the Israelites had crossed through the sea is ascribed to Miriam (Exod. 15:21). This ancient song, variously dated to the thirteenth or twelfth centuries, is the simplest and perhaps one of the earliest accounts of the miracle at the sea; some scholars see it as a concluding portion of the larger Song of the Sea (vv. 1-18; cf. v. 1). On account of her connection with this song Miriam is called a "prophetess" (v. 20), probably because of the relationship between ecstatic prophecy and music (cf. 1 Sam. 10:5-6).

2. A Judahite, among the descendants of Ezrah (1 Chr. 4:17). According to the most likely reconstruction of the text, Miriam was a son or daughter of Bithiah, the daughter of Pharaoh, and Mered (so RSV).

MIRMAH [mûr′mə] (Heb. *mirmâ*). A son of Shaharaim and Hodesh of the tribe of Benjamin (1 Chr. 8:10; KJV "Mirma").

MIRROR (Heb. *mar'â*, *rᵉ'î*; Gk. *ésoptron*).† Mirrors are attested as early as the third millennium B.C. Despite the KJV translations "glass" (1 Cor. 13:12; Jas. 1:23) and "looking glass" (Exod. 38:8; Job 37:18), mirrors were made of polished metal, often bronze (Exod. 38:8), and were not yet glass-covered. Generally they were disk-shaped and hand-held with handles of sculpted or decorated metal, bone, or ivory. Naturally, such mirrors gave only a dim image (cf. 1 Cor. 13:12).

Elihu's comparison of the sky's hardness to that of a mirror (Job 37:18) has in mind the conception of the sky as a hard firmament (cf. Gen. 1:6-8) that will not let rain through during time of drought (cf. Deut. 28:23). The reading "mirrors" at Isa. 3:23 (so JB, NIV; KJV "glasses") is but one possibility for a difficult text; RSV "garments of gauze" (NJV "lace gowns") follows the LXX.

MISCARRIAGE. See BIRTH.

MISGAB [mĭs′găb] (Heb. *hammiśgāḇ*). According to the KJV (cf. NIV mg.), a place in Moab (Jer. 48:1). The RSV and JB translate "the fortress" (cf. NIV, NJV).

MISHAEL [mǐsh′ĭ əl] (Heb. *mîšā᾽ēl* "Who is what God is?").

1. A Kohathite Levite, the son of Uzziel (Exod. 6:18, 22). He and his brother Elzaphan carried out of the camp the bodies of Nadab and Abihu, who had been struck dead by God (Lev. 10:4-5).

2. One who stood at the left hand of Ezra as he read the Book of the Law (Neh. 8:4).

3. One of Daniel's three companions, whose name was changed to MESHACH (Dan. 1:7). Together with Shadrach and Abednego, Mishael was appointed to a significant government position in the province of Babylon (3:12). After they refused to worship a huge golden image erected by Nebuchadnezzar, the three men were thrown into a furnace, in which they were preserved by God's angel (ch. 3).

MISHAL [mī′shəl, mǐsh′ăl] (Heb. *miš᾽āl*). A levitical city in the tribal territory of Asher (Josh. 19:26; KJV "Misheal"; 21:30). It is called Mashal (*māšāl*) at 1 Chr. 6:74 (MT 59). The location of Mishal is not known, but it was somewhere near the Carmel ridge, probably in the plain of Acco. Tell Kīsân, 9.6 km. (6 mi.) southeast of Acco, is a leading possibility as the site.

MISHAM [mī′shăm] (Heb. *miš᾽ām*). A son of Elpaal of the tribe of Benjamin (1 Chr. 8:12).

MISHMA [mǐsh′mə] (Heb. *mišmā῾* "that which is heard").

1. A son of Ishmael, and eponymous ancestor of an Arabian people (Gen. 25:14; 1 Chr 1:30).

2. A Simeonite, the son of Mibsam (1 Chr. 4:25-26). The presence of Mibsam and Mishma at both 1:29-30 and 4:25 may suggest some prior relation between a Simeonite clan and what may originally have been an Ishmaelite (i.e., Arabian) tribe.

MISHMANNAH [mǐsh măn′ə] (Heb. *mišmannâ*). One of the Gadite "mighty and experienced warriors" who joined David at Ziklag and became officers in his army (1 Chr. 12:10 [MT 11]; some MSS read *mašmannâ*).

MISHNAH [mǐsh′nə] (Heb. *mišnâ* "repetition").* The basic authoritative document of rabbinic Judaism, compiled *ca.* A.D. 200 by Rabbi Judah ha-Nasi (the Prince, or the Patriarch). A corpus of law—regarded as the "second Torah" given to Moses—transmitted orally (i.e., by repetition), the Mishnah consists almost entirely of HALAKHAH. It consists of six orders (Heb. *s*e*ḏārîm*) divided into sixty-three tractates (*massek̲tôt̲*), which are themselves divided into chapters. The orders of the Mishnah concern agricultural law (*Zera῾im*), Sabbath and festival law (*Mo῾ed*), family law (*Našim*), civil and criminal law (*Neziqin*), sacrifices (*Qodašin*), and ritual purity (*Ṭoharoth*). Subsequently the Mishnah was augmented with later commentaries and expansions (the Gemara) to produce the Babylonian and Palestinian (Jerusalem) Talmuds.

MISHRAITES [mǐsh′rə īts] (Heb. *mišrā῾î*). A Judahite family of Kiriath-jearim, among the ancestors or predecessors of the Zorathites and Eshtaolites (1 Chr. 2:53).

MISPAR [mǐs′pär] (Heb. *mispār* "number"). One of the leaders who returned with Zerubbabel from Babylon (Ezra 2:2; KJV "Mizpar"). At Neh. 7:7 he is called Mispereth.

MISPERETH [mǐs′pə rĕth] (Heb. *misperet̲*). Alternate form of MISPAR (Neh. 7:7).

MISREPHOTH-MAIM [mǐz′rə fŏth mā′əm] (Heb. *miśr*e*p̲ôt̲ mayim* "lime-burning [?] at the waters" or "from the west").† A place on the coast of Phoenicia. It is identified by some with the warm springs at ῾Ain Mesherfi or the ruins of Khirbet el-Musheirefeh on the Mediterranean Sea a short distance south of the modern Israel-Lebanon border and at the northern end of the plain of Acco, and by others with the ancient southern boundary of Sidon's territory (cf. Josh. 13:6), perhaps the Litani river. It is mentioned in connection with an Israelite victory over the coalition headed by King Jabin of Hazor (11:8) and in a description of territory still not conquered by the Israelites (13:6). Both texts seem to speak of a place just beyond the borders of Israelite control to the north.

MIST. Subterranean waters (Heb. *᾽ēḏ*; cf. Akk. *edû*; Sum. *a-dé-a* used by God in the creation of plant and subsequently human life (Gen. 2:6; KJV "flood"). According to Job 36:27, God distils the mist to produce rain. Elsewhere Heb. *n*e*śi᾽îm* designates the vaporous mist, one of many forms of water and precipitation under God's control of the elements (e.g., Jer. 10:13; 51:16).

Often references to mist are figurative, depicting the transitoriness of life (Gk. *atmís*; Jas. 4:14; KJV "vapor"), idols (Hos. 13:3) and false teachings (*hómichlē*; 2 Pet. 2:17), and God's forgiveness of sins (Heb. *῾āmān*; Isa. 44:22). At Acts 13:11 Gk. *achlýs* describes Paul's temporary blindness.

MITANNI [mĭ tăn′nē]. A powerful kingdom and empire in northern Mesopotamia during the Late Bronze Age (fifteenth-fourteenth centuries B.C.). At its height in the mid-fifteenth century Mitanni (also called Ḥanigalbat, Ḥurri, and Naharina) dominated peoples as far away as Syria, Adaniya in southeastern Asia Minor, and Lake Urmia in northern Iran. Although apparently ruled by an Indoeuropean minority, the Mitannians were an important force in the spread of Hurrian culture, as well as the use of horses and chariots, among the Hittites and in Syria-Palestine. *See* HURRIANS.

MITE (Mark 12:42; Luke 12:59; 21:2, KJV). *See* COPPER; MONEY.

MITHKAH [mǐth′kə] (Heb. *miṭqâ* "sweetness"). A place where the Israelites stopped between Terah and Hashmonah during the wilderness wanderings (Num. 33:28-29; KJV "Mithcah"). Its location is unknown.

MITHNITE [mǐth′nīt] (Heb. *miṯnî*). A term designating Joshaphat, one of David's mighty men (1 Chr. 11:43). The gentilic may indicate that he was from a place called Meten, which is not otherwise known.

MITHREDATH [mĭth′rə dăth] (Heb. *miṯrᵉḏāṯ*, from Pers. "given by [the deity] Mithra").

1. The treasurer of King Cyrus of Persia who restored to Sheshbazzar the temple treasures (Ezra 1:8; 1 Esdr. 2:11, "Mithridates").

2. One of three Persian officials who wrote to King Artaxerxes I (465-424 B.C.) opposing the rebuilding of Jerusalem (Ezra 4:7; 1 Esdr. 2:16, "Mithridates").

MITRE (KJV). *See* TURBAN.

MITYLENE [mĭt′ə lē′nĭ] (Gk. *Mitylēnē*).† A port and the major city of the island of Lesbos, which lies in the Aegean Sea off the west coast of Asia Minor. The city is *ca.* 10 km. (6 mi.) northwest of the eastern tip of the island. Colonized by the Aeolians *ca.* 1000 B.C., the city came under Persian control and subsequently was liberated by the Athenians in 479. It joined the Delian league and later allied with Athens. In the Roman period it was a popular resort for the Roman aristocracy. In 80 B.C. much of the city was destroyed in Roman reprisal against a tax revolt, and in A.D. 181 it was leveled by an earthquake.

The ship boarded by Paul and his companions at Philippi, which took them as far as Patara in Lycia, touched at Mitylene among other ports (20:14).

MIXED MULTITUDE (Heb. *ʿēreḇ raḇ*). That the company of those who left Egypt under the leadership of Moses was not as homogeneous as might be thought is suggested in two texts. At Exod. 12:38 it is reported that "a mixed multitude" (NIV "many other people"; JB "people of various sorts") went out of Egypt with the Israelites. Heb. *ʿēreḇ* here, as elsewhere (Neh. 13:3; Jer. 25:20; RSV "foreign folk"; 50:37), designates those of a different ethnic stock who have attached themselves to an established national people. At Num. 11:4 the "rabble" (*ᵃsapsup*; KJV "mixed multitude"; NJV "riffraff") that were among the Israelites are said to have taken part in Israel's murmuring against Moses' leadership. These texts may imply the actual ethnic diversity of those who comprised the formative Israelite state and may suggest some relationship between the Hebrews of the Exodus with the HABIRU (ʿAPIRU) movement. At the least it can be concluded that some non-Israelite slaves in Egypt took the chaos engendered by the death of the Egyptian firstborn (Exod. 12:29-30) and the subsequent departure of the Israelites (vv. 31-36) as an opportunity for their own escape, and were later incorporated into the people of Israel.

MIZAR [mī′zär] (Heb. *miṣʿār* "little").† A mountain (*har*; KJV "hill") mentioned at Ps. 42:6 (MT 7) but not otherwise attested, at least by this name. It may be Khirbet Mazârâ near the sources of the Jordan below Hermon. On the other hand, the literal meaning "small" may be a description rather than a name; if so, Mt. Zion, much smaller than Hermon, may be in view. The psalmist would then be an exile "away from the land of the Jordan, from Hermon, and from (Zion) the small mountain" longing for the presence of God in Israel's homeland (cf. vv. 1-4), or a person remembering Zion ("the small mountain") "from the land of Jordan and of Hermon." In the latter case the

prepositional *mem* ("from") with *har* ("mountain") is considered an extraneous dittograph.

MIZPAH [mĭz′pä] (Heb. fem. *miṣpâ* "lookout, watchtower"), **MIZPEH** [mĭz′pə] (masc. *miṣpeh*).

1. The name given by Jacob as a sign of the covenant between himself and Laban (Gen. 31:49). According to the MT the name was given to the heap of stones (so KJV), but the Samaritan text (followed by RSV) adds "the pillar" at the beginning of v. 49 so that Mizpah is taken as the name of the pillar mentioned at v. 45 (cf. v. 49, where "pillar" [*mṣṣbh*] could be a dittograph). The so-called Mizpah benediction (31:49) is associated with these events. Since Jacob had not yet crossed the Jabbok (32:22), Jacob's naming of Mizpah took place in northern Gilead.

2. "The land of Mizpah" (Josh. 11:3) or "the valley of Mizpeh" (v. 8). At such a place in Upper Galilee near the foot of Mt. Hermon dwelled some Hivites who joined the unsuccessful anti-Israel alliance headed by Jabin of Hazor. It was apparently just beyond the northern limits of Israel's control, but the precise location is not known.

3. A city in the Shephelah region of Judah (Josh. 15:38; cf. Eusebius *Onom.* cxxx.2-3). The location of the city is not known with certainty; it has sometimes been identified with Tell eṣ-Ṣâfî, which is more likely the site of Gath.

4. A city in the tribal territory of Benjamin (Josh. 18:26). It was at this Mizpah that the Benjaminites raped and murdered the Levite's concubine, and here the forces of Israel assembled to retaliate (Judg. 20:1, 3; 21:1, 5, 8). Later Mizpah was one of the three centers from which Samuel "judged" Israel (1 Sam. 7:16). It was here that he assembled Israel's forces to prepare for battle against the Philistines (vv. 5-12). King Asa of Judah "built" (i.e., fortified) Mizpah (1 Kgs. 15:22 par. 2 Chr. 16:6), thus moving his northern border somewhat farther north. Mizpah was the capital of Judah during Gedaliah's brief governorship under Babylonian hegemony (2 Kgs. 25:23, 25; Jer. 40-41). Mizpah supplied as workers on the postexilic rebuilding of the walls of Jerusalem some who were apparently local officials under the Persian government (Neh. 3:7, 15, 19). In Hasmonean times Mizpah was known as a center for community prayer (1 Macc. 3:46; KJV "Maspha"; Gk. *Massēpha*), perhaps partly because of the nature of Samuel's assembly of Israel there.

The site is identified by many with Tell en-Naṣbeh, *ca.* 12 km. (7.5 mi.) north of Jerusalem; others suggest Nebī Ṣamwil, *ca.* 8 km. (5 mi.) northwest of Jerusalem. Excavations at Tell en-Naṣbeh have shown that it was a very heavily fortified settlement, particularly at the time of Asa. The seal of a Jaazaniah, perhaps the one mentioned at 2 Kgs. 25:23; Jer. 40:8, was found at Tell en-Naṣbeh. In general, the pattern of occupation at Tell en-Naṣbeh fits well the events associated with this Mizpah.

5. Mizpah of Gilead. Israel's forces assembled here in preparation for war against Ammon, and Jephthah, recalled to Gilead to head the war effort, made his home here (Judg. 10:17; 11:11, 29, 34).

Ramath-mizpeh (Josh. 13:26) could fit the Mizpah associated with these events but is unlikely to agree with those concerning Jacob (**1** above), since it was evidently south of the Jabbok river.

6. Mizpeh of Moab. Here David met with the king of Moab during his flight from Saul and requested that his parents be allowed refuge in Moab (1 Sam. 22:3). The location of this Mizpah is not known, although it has been identified with the Rujm el-Mesrife, a prominent height southwest of Medeba.

7.* A place mentioned at Hos. 5:1. It may be the same as any of the places so named; **4** or **5** would be the most likely candidates because of their significance in Israel's memory.

MIZPAR (Ezra 2:2, KJV). See MISPAR.

MIZRAIM [mĭz´rǎ əm] (Heb. *miṣrayim*; cf. Egyp. *mṣrym*). The Hebrew word for Egypt, the people of which are represented as descended from Ham (Gen. 10:6, 13; RSV "Egypt"). See EGYPT *I*.

MIZZAH [mĭz´ə] (Heb. *mizzâ*). A son of Reuel (**1**), grandson of Esau, and Edomite chief (Gen. 36:13, 17; 1 Chr. 1:37).

MNASON [nā´sən] (Gk. *Mnasōn*).† A Christian originally from Cyprus at whose house in Jerusalem Paul lodged during his final stay in the city (Acts 21:16). Mnason's description as "an early disciple" may mean that he was a founding member of the church in Jerusalem.

MOAB [mō´ăb] (Heb. *mô´ăb*).† The son of Lot by his older daughter (Gen. 19:37; cf. LXX "saying, from my father"); fearing the lack of eligible mates would leave them childless, both of Lot's daughters entered incestuous relations with their father (vv. 30-38). Moab was the eponymous ancestor of the Moabites, a people and state in Transjordan.

Moab was located on a high plateau on the southeastern coast of the Dead Sea, approximately 915 m. (3000 ft.) above sea level. Moab's northern, western, and southern borders were defined by the terrain. The western border descended to the Dead Sea and the Jordan Rift valley. What arable land existed in Moab was found along the Arnon river (modern Wâdī el-Môjib, generally the northern border, although when political fortunes permitted it might extend as far north as Heshbon) and along a north-south strip in the western part of the plateau. The southern border was the brook Zered (modern Wâdī el-Ḥesā), whose steep banks made it a defensible border. The land becomes increasingly dry to the east—where the Moabites maintained large sheep herds (cf. 2 Kgs. 3:4)—eventually becoming desert.

Traces of at least temporary settlement have been found for Paleolithic and Chalcolithic times, and the roots of urbanization are evident in the Early Bronze Age (*ca.* 3000-2300 B.C.). Like most of Transjordan, Moab was well populated by the end of the Early Bronze Age (*ca.* 2300-2100; cf. Deut. 2:10-11). Strongly walled cities were built on hills near water supplies, with agricultural areas located outside the walls; the most notable to date is Bâb edh-Dhrâ´ on the Lisan peninsula at the southern end of the Dead Sea. Moab undoubtedly benefited from the network of north-south

trade routes that existed through Palestine from ancient times.

Much of Moab appears to have been unoccupied toward the end of the second millennium. But by the advent of the Iron Age (*ca.* 1200) independent kingdoms had been established in Moab as well as Edom and Ammon, no doubt aided by the decline in Egyptian power *ca.* 1300. Moab is named in a topographical list of Pharaoh Rameses II (*ca.* 1290-1224) at Luxor. Iron Age Moab was defended by a system of fortresses, particularly on its southern and eastern borders. The introduction in Palestine of slaked lime plastered cisterns and the practice of hewing cisterns from rock allowed Moabite settlements to flourish away from natural water sources, especially toward the eastern desert.

Israel's advance toward Canaan was viewed by rulers of the small neighboring kingdoms as a definite threat to their power, even though the Israelites had been forbidden by God to harass Moab, which was to be Lot's possession (Deut. 2:8-9). The Amorite king Sihon, who had conquered the Moabites and gained control of their land, denied Israel permission to pass through his territory (Num. 21:21-30). Later King Balak of Moab joined with the elders of Midian in enlisting the diviner Balaam to curse the advancing Israelites, a plan that failed (chs. 22–24; cf. Josh. 24:9; Judg. 11:25). In time Israelite contact with Moabite religion led them to apostasy and immorality (Num. 25). Before his death, Moses surveyed the Promised Land from Mt. Nebo, in Moabite territory northeast of the Dead Sea; he was buried opposite Beth-peor (Deut. 32:48-49; 34:1-6).

Although the portrayal of Israelite-Moabite relations in the book of Ruth suggests relative peace, elsewhere it is apparent that animosity continued between the peoples during the period of the Israelite confederation. According to Judg. 3:12-30, because of their apostasy Israel "served" Moab for eighteen years until the Benjaminite judge Ehud assassinated the Moabite king Eglon and gained "rest" for the Israelites.

Moab was among the nations defeated by Saul while establishing his kingdom (1 Sam. 14:47). Although David appealed to the king of Moab to shelter his parents at Mizpeh as he himself fled from Saul (22:3-4), he later subdued Moab, took silver and gold as spoil (2 Sam. 8:11-12; 1 Chr. 18:11), and demanded tribute (v. 2). During Solomon's cosmopolitan reign he entered numerous alliances by marrying foreign princesses, including one from Moab (1 Kgs. 11:1). As such wives were customarily permitted to worship their own gods, Solomon built a "high place" on a mountain east of Jerusalem for the Moabite god Chemosh (v. 7), and he himself may have participated in worship of Chemosh (v. 33).

Israel's control over Moab lasted for another century, until the reign of the Omride king Ahab (*ca.* 869-850). The MOABITE STONE records that during this period King Mesha of Moab successfully revolted against Israel. According to the biblical account, King Jehoram of Israel, aided by Judah and Edom, marched on Moab (2 Kgs. 3:4-27). As the prophet Elisha declared, Moab would be utterly destroyed and the land despoiled. A Moabite attack on the Israelite camp failed, and Mesha was surrounded; in desperation he

Crusaders' castle at Kir-heres (Kir-hareseth), a principal city of Moab (A. D. Baly)

offered his eldest son as a burnt sacrifice to Chemosh. Whatever happened next, Israel withdrew and returned home (v. 27). 2 Chr. 20 apparently records a separate attack by a Moabite alliance on the region south of Bethlehem; the allies were routed and took to fighting among themselves.

Like other contemporary Palestinian states Moab chafed under the successive rule of the Assyrians and Babylonians, and actively joined the plots and rebellions of which Judah and Israel were part. The oracles of Isaiah and Jeremiah depict Moab as a conquered people, full of wailing and despair (e.g., Isa. 15–16; Jer. 48). This view of Moab is maintained as well in the utterances of Amos (Amos 2:1-3), Zephaniah (Zeph. 2:8-9), and Ezekiel (Ezek. 25:8-11).

In postexilic times the Israelites were required to abandon marriages with Moabite women in order to stabilize the fragile restoration community (Ezra 9:1-2; Neh. 13:1-3, 23-27). Subsequently Moabite territory fell under Nabatean control.

MOABITE STONE. † A black basalt stele bearing an inscription celebrating the victory of King Mesha of Moab over Israel in the ninth century B.C.; also called the Mesha stele. Its dimensions are 112 cm. (44 in.) high by 71 cm. (28 in.) wide by 36 cm. (14 in.) thick.

The stele was discovered in 1868 at Dhîbân (biblical Dibon) in Transjordan just north of the Arnon river by the Prussian missionary F. A. Klein, and the French orientalist C. S. Clermont-Ganneau obtained copies of some of the inscription's lines and a squeeze (facsimile impression) of its surface. Recognizing the European archaeologists' interest in the stele, its Arab keepers broke it up, apparently in hope of selling it piecemeal for a great profit. Most of the fragments have been recovered by the Louvre, and Clermont-Ganneau's squeeze made it possible to reconstruct the entire text by 1873.

The historical background of the inscription is rooted in the long-standing enmity between the Israelites and the neighboring Moabites. Not long after the schism between the northern and southern tribes in 922 B.C. the Israelite king Omri conquered northern Moab, including the region around Medeba. Israel held this territory until the death of Omri's son Ahab, *ca.* 850. It was common in the ancient Near East for a people to revolt when the king to whom they had been vassal died, and Moab was no exception (2 Kgs. 1:1; 3:5). King Mesha soon faced a coalition of armies under Jehoram of Israel, Jehoshaphat of Judah, and the king of Edom (vv. 4-27; cf. 2 Chr. 20:1-28).

The thirty-four line inscription (*ANET,* pp. 320-21) constitutes the only major text yet discovered in the Moabite language, a Canaanite dialect of Northwest Semitic. It is typical of ancient Near Eastern royal inscriptions in recording its patrons' successes (Medeba, Ataroth, Nebo, Yaḥaṣ) while ignoring his defeats (cf. 2 Kgs. 3). The text is dedicated to the god Chemosh, whose discontent with his people reportedly led to their subjugation by Israel but who later guided

The Moabite Stone (by courtesy of the Oriental Institute, University of Chicago)

them over the oppressor. The remainder of the inscription outlines Mesha's building activities and a campaign against Ḥauronen. Of particular interest for biblical studies are mention of Yahweh as Israel's God and reference to the ban or "devotion to destruction" (cf. Heb. *ḥerem*).

MOADIAH [mō'ə dī'ə] (Heb. *môʿaḏyâ* "Yahweh promises"). A family of priests of the time of the high priest Joiakim (Neh. 12:17). *See* MAADIAH.

MODEIN [mō'dēn] (Gk. *Modein*; from Heb. *môḏāʿîm*, Aram. *môḏāʿîn*).† The ancestral home of the Hasmoneans, located at el-Arbaʿîn (Ras Medieh), in a mountainous region 29 km. (18 mi.) northwest of Jerusalem and 9 km. (6 mi.) east of Lod (Lydda). It was here that the Maccabean revolt was initiated by Mattathias' killing of a Jew who complied with Antiochus' order to offer non-Jewish sacrifice and of the royal officer sent to enforce the order (1 Macc. 2:1, 15-25). The Hasmonean family tombs were at Modein (2:70; 9:19; 13:25-30).

MOLADAH [mŏl'ə də] (Heb. *môlāḏâ* "childbearing, parentage"). A town in the tribal territory of Simeon (Josh. 19:2; 1 Chr. 4:28), apparently later reckoned among the territory of Judah (Josh. 15:26). It was resettled after the Exile (Neh. 11:26). Its location is unknown, but both modern Khirbet el-Waṭen, *ca.* 12 km. (7.5 mi.) east-northeast of Beersheba, and Tell el-Milḥ, *ca.* 24 km. (15 mi.) east of Beersheba, have been suggested.

MOLE. * At Isa. 2:20 it is said that idolaters facing God's judgment will throw their idols to bats and Heb. *laḥpōr pērôṯ*. The Hebrew is generally read as *ḥᵃparpārôṯ* "diggers" (following Theodotion, Gk. *pharphárōth*), that is, moles (so RSV) or some similar animals (NIV "rodents"; NJV "flying foxes"). The context suggests some kind of animal considered unclean (cf. Lev. 11:19) and living underground. Asian mole rats (genus *Spalax*) are larger than European and North American moles, reaching 20 cm. (8 in.) in length, and are common in Palestine.

At 11:30 the KJV reads "mole" for *tinšemeṭ*, usually understood in this passage as "chameleon" (so RSV, NIV; cf. v. 29, JB).

MOLECH [mō'lĕk] (Heb. *mōlek*).† Usually understood as the name of a deity *melek* "king," deliberately distorted in the Hebrew text by use of the vowels for *bōšeṯ* "shame." However, sacrifice "to *mlk*" may have originally meant sacrifice "as a votive offering," and *mōlek* may have come to be understood only later as the name of a deity. Indeed, various deities—including Yahweh—were addressed as "king"; *melek* at Isa. 57:9 is probably such a divine title (KJV, RSV mg. "the king") rather than a reference to Molech (as RSV). It is also often assumed that Molech bore some relation to the Ammonite deity MILCOM, but the two are spoken of separately at 2 Kgs. 23:10, 13.

Child sacrifice was sometimes practiced in Israel and Judah, especially in the valley of Hinnom adjacent to Jerusalem (2 Chr. 28:3; 33:6; Jer. 7:31; 19:5-6), and was sometimes associated with the name of Molech (2 Kgs. 23:10; Jer. 32:35), a practice specifically prohibited in the Pentateuch (Lev. 18:21; 20:2-5).

The LXX reads *Moloch*, one of its renderings of *mōlek*, at Amos 5:26 (so KJV; RSV "your king"), followed by Acts 7:43 (Gk. *Moloch*; RSV "Moloch").

MOLID [mō'lĭd] (Heb. *môlîḏ* "one who begets"). A Judahite; the son of Abishur and Abihail (1 Chr. 2:29).

MOLOCH. *See* MOLECH.

MOLTEN IMAGE. *See* IDOLATRY.

MOLTEN SEA. *See* SEA, MOLTEN.

MONEY.† Until the introduction of coins the most common media of exchange in ancient societies were metals measured by weight. For this reason, Old Testament references to units of exchange are almost all to units of weight and not to coins. Coins were first minted in Asia Minor in the seventh century B.C. and gradually gained acceptance, first in Greece, as a means of standardizing and guaranteeing the weights of currency metals. The weight of a coin was still the fundamental measure of its value. Barter and other forms of nonmonetary exchange were never entirely dispensed with, and times of rapid inflation (divergence between face values of coins and their actual buying

Bronze lepton of Herod the Great. Tripod and bowl with Greek inscription; incense altar and palm branches (by courtesy of the Trustees of the British Museum)

Silver denarius of Tiberius. Head of Tiberius with Lat. inscription "Tiberius Caesar, son of the divine Augustus" (cf. Matt. 22:19-21); Livia seated with branch and scepter (by courtesy of the Trustees of the British Museum)

value) sometimes encouraged reversion to primitive methods of exchange.

I. Old Testament

In Old Testament times silver (Heb. *kesep,* often omitted with expressions of quantity and often translated "money") was the metal most commonly used for exchange. The units of weight most frequently used to measure currency metals were the shekel (*šeqel*), about 11.4 gm. (0.4 oz.), and the talent (*kikkār*), about 34.27 kg. (75.6 lb.). An unknown amount of currency metal is represented by *qᵉśîṭâ* (Gen. 33:19; Josh. 24:32; Job 42:11; KJV, RSV "piece [of money/silver]"). *See also* WEIGHTS AND MEASURES.

Hag. 1:6 may allude to the use of coins. The shekel of Neh. 5:15; 10:32 may be a Persian coin of the old shekel weight. The Hebrew terms *darkᵉmônîm* (Ezra 2:69; Neh. 7:70-72) and *'ᵃḏarḵōnîm* (1 Chr. 29:7; Ezra 8:27) are probably equivalent (RSV "darics"; KJV "drams"), although it is possible that two different kinds of coins are intended (JB, NIV "drachmas" for *darkᵉmônîm* and "darics" for *'ᵃḏarḵōnîm*). The Persian gold daric of 8.4 gm. (0.3 oz.) was first issued by Darius I in 515 B.C. and so at 1 Chr. 29:7 is an anachronistic representation of an earlier system.

II. New Testament

In the New Testament, in contrast to the Old Testament, coins are mentioned often. The basic monetary units of the Greco-Roman world were the Greek drachma (Gk. *drachmḗ*; Luke 15:8-9; RSV "coin"; KJV "pieces [of silver]") and its near equivalent, the Roman denarius (Gk. *dēnárion*; Matt. 18:28; KJV "pence"; 20:2-13; KJV "penny"; 22:19 par.; RSV "coin"; Mark 6:37 par.; 14:5 par.; Luke 7:41; 10:35; Rev. 6:6). These weighed 3–4 gm. (0.1 to 0.14 oz.) of silver and were considered equivalent to one day's wage for a laborer (Matt. 20:2).

Greek monetary units of value greater than a drachma had names derived from the ancient Mesopotamian system of weights. A Greek talent (*tálanton*; Matt. 18:24; 25:15-28) was equal in value to about six thousand drachmas. Talents were a monetary unit, but no coin of such high value was ever minted. A mina (*mná*; Luke 19:13-25; RSV, KJV "pound") was equal in value to about one hundred drachmas. A shekel or tetradrachma (*statḗr*; Matt. 17:27; KJV "piece of

money") was equal in value to four drachmas (but Antiochene tetradrachmas were devalued to only three denarii). The didrachma (*dídrachmon*; two drachmas or half a shekel) was not a coin issued in New Testament times but a term for the annual temple tax paid by Jews (Matt. 17:24; KJV "money"; cf. Exod. 30:13; 38:26). The "gold" of Matt. 10:9 may be the Roman gold aureus, worth about twenty-five denarii.

Copper and bronze coins of small value included the Roman *as* or assarion (Gk. *assárion*; Matt. 10:29 par.; RSV "penny"; KJV "farthing"), equal in value to one-sixteenth denarius; the Roman quadrans (*kodrántēs*; 5:26; Mark 12:42; RSV "penny"; KJV "farthing"), equal in value to one-fourth *as*; and the locally produced lepton (v. 42 par.; Luke 12:59; RSV "copper [coin]"; KJV "mite"), half the value of a quadrans.

The value of the thirty pieces of silver with which Judas was paid for his betrayal of Jesus (Matt. 26:15; 27:3-6) is not specified. If the amount was settled on the basis of Exod. 21:32, then the coins were probably Tyrian shekels, the coins used in the treasury of the Jerusalem temple. Gk. *nómisma* (Matt. 22:19; RSV, KJV "money") and *kérma* (John 2:15) are general terms for "coin(s)" (so RSV; KJV "money").

III. Jewish Coins

Rights of coinage were closely controlled by imperial authorities, whether Persian, Greco-Macedonian, or Roman. The first coins of Judea were not Jewish coins,

Silver shekel from the Jewish revolt, A.D. 66. Chalice with Heb. inscription "shekel of Israel"; flowers with Heb. inscription "Jerusalem the holy" (by courtesy of the Trustees of the British Museum)

but silver coins of the Persian province of Judea made in Greek style. Among his efforts to gain Jewish loyalty, the Seleucid emperor Antiochus VII Sidetes gave rights of coinage to Simon the Hasmonean high priest (1 Macc. 15:6; 139 B.C.), but Antiochus later reneged on his promises and Simon probably never produced coins. Simon's successor, John Hyrcanus I, began minting what were probably the first Jewish coins *ca.* 111-110 at a time of weakness in the Seleucid Empire. These were not silver coins (which to issue would have been too bold a declaration of independence), but small bronze coins. Such coins continued to be minted by Jewish rulers, Hasmonean and Herodian. After Judea came under direct Roman procuratorial rule, similar coins—but with the name and regnal year of the emperor—were issued by the procurators. The silver coins issued by Jewish governments during the rebellions of A.D. 66-70 and 132-135 were an important declaration of rebellion.

Bibliography. F. Banks, *Coins of Bible Days* (1955); Y. Meshorer, *Ancient Jewish Coinage*, 2 vols. (New York: 1982); *Jewish Coins of the Second Temple Period* (Tel Aviv: 1976); A. Reifenberg, *Ancient Jewish Coins*, 2nd ed. (Jerusalem: 1947).

MONEY BOX (Gk. *glōssókomon*). A small container for carrying coins. Judas Iscariot took care of the common money box of Jesus and the disciples (John 12:6; 13:29; KJV "bag"). The same word is used in the LXX at 2 Chr. 24:8-11 for the chest made to receive the temple tax at the time of King Joash.

MONEY-CHANGER (Gk. *kollybistḗs, kermatistḗs*).† In ancient Palestine, the banker who exchanged local currency for that of a different country or province. The work of the money-changers in the Jerusalem temple (Matt. 21:12 par. Mark 11:15; John 2:14-15) was necessary so that coins from various mints brought by pilgrims could be changed into the Tyrian coins accepted for contributions to the temple treasury and for the annual half-shekel temple tax (cf. Matt. 17:24). The money-changers normally carried on their business outside the temple premises, but were admitted to the temple's Court of the Gentiles before feast days when many pilgrims were present.

While the money-changers' surcharges may have become exploitative at times, Jesus' basic objection to their presence was not with regard to exploitation or dishonesty; by "a den of robbers" (Matt. 21:13 par.; cf. Jer. 7:11) he means not a place where crimes are committed but a place of refuge for the offenders. Rather, Jesus objected that by carrying on their business in the Court of the Gentiles the money-changers thwarted Gentile worship of the God of Israel at the temple (Mark 11:17; cf. Isa. 56:7).

MONSTER. *See* DRAGON; SEA MONSTER.

MONTH. *See* YEAR.

MOON (Heb. *yārēaḥ, lᵉḇānâ*; Gk. *selḗnē*). Worship of the moon was practiced throughout ancient Palestine, Syria, Mesopotamia, and Anatolia. But Hebrew theology clearly regarded the moon as among those things created by God to serve circumscribed func-

tions (Gen. 1:16; Ps. 8:3 [MT 4]; 104:19; 136:7-9; Jer. 31:35; 2 Esdr. 6:45-46; Sir. 43:6-7; Ep.Jer. 6:60) and thus under his direct control (Josh. 10:12-13; Hab. 3:11). Worship of the moon and other heavenly bodies was specifically prohibited (Deut. 4:19; 17:3; cf. Job 31:26), although the practice is sometimes attested among the Israelites (2 Kgs. 23:5; Jer. 8:2).

The moon was a symbol of permanence (Ps. 72:5, 7; 89:37 [MT 40]; Isa. 60:20; Jer. 31:35-36). It was on this basis that changes in the moon or its disappearance became a significant symbol of the end in apocalyptic language (Isa. 13:10; 24:23; Joel 2:10, 31 [MT 3:4]; 3:15 [MT 4:15]; 2 Esdr. 5:4; 7:39; Matt. 24:29 par.; Acts 2:20; Rev. 6:12; 8:12).

For Heb. *ḥōḏeš* "new moon," *see* NEW MOON; FEASTS *I.A.2. See also* YEAR.

MORASTHITE (Jer. 26:18; Mic. 1:1, KJV). *See* MORESHETH.

MORDECAI [môr′də kī] (Heb. *mordᵃḵay, mordᵉḵay*; from Akk. *Marduk*).

1. An Israelite who returned from exile with Zerubbabel (Ezra 2:2; Neh. 7:7).

2. A Jew of the tribe of Benjamin living in the Persian capital of Susa at the time of King Ahasuerus (Xerxes I, 485-465 B.C.; Esth. 2:5). His cousin Esther, whom he had adopted as his daughter, succeeded the deposed Queen Vashti. When Mordecai overheard a plot against Ahasuerus Esther communicated it to the king (vv. 21-22), for which he was later rewarded (ch. 6). Mordecai's refusal to bow before Haman the Agagite antagonized the vizier, who then sought to annihilate the Jews throughout the empire (ch. 3). Again Mordecai enlisted Esther to inform the king of the plot, and thus they thwarted Haman's plans (chs. 4–5). Mordecai then led the Jews in annihilating their opponents (ch. 9) and subsequently was accorded a place next in rank to the king (10:3).

MOREH [môr′ə] (*môreh, mōreh* "teacher, instruction").

1. A place at Shechem distinguished by a prominent tree where Yahweh first spoke to Abraham (Gen. 12:6) and where Abraham established a shrine (vv. 7-8). At this shrine Jacob buried small cult objects that Leah and Rachel had brought into the land (35:4). There also Joshua erected a memorial stone after the covenant renewal at Shechem (Josh. 24:26; cf. Judg. 9:6). At Deut. 11:30 the MT refers to the same place, again probably in connection with covenant renewal; in this passage the MT speaks of a group of trees.

See also DIVINERS' OAK.

2. A hill in the Jezreel valley where the Midianites camped in preparation for battle against the Israelites under Gideon (Judg. 7:1; cf. R. G. Boling, *Judges.* AB 6A [1975], pp. 142, 144, "Teacher's Hill"). The hill is probably to be identified with Nebī (or Jebel) Daḥī, east-northeast of modern ʿAfula.

MORESHETH [môr′ə shĕth], **MORESHETH-GATH** [môr′ə shĕth gäth′] (Heb. *môrešet gaṯ* "property of Gath"). The home of the prophet Micah (Jer. 26:18; Heb. *môraštî*; Mic. 1:1; *môraštî*; RSV "of Moresheth"; KJV "Morasthite"). Moresheth-gath is mentioned by the prophet as one of a series of towns that will experience disaster; accordingly, its residents will receive "parting gifts" (*šillûḥîm*; v. 14; cf. 1 Kgs. 9:16, "dowry"; perhaps here a pun on *mᵉ'ōrāśāṯ* "betrothed" at Deut. 22:23).

The site is generally identified with Tell ej-Judeideh, *ca.* 2.5 km. (1.5 mi.) north-northeast of Beit Jibrîn (ancient Eleutheropolis) and 9.7 km. (6 mi.) northeast of Lachish. This city may be the Gath mentioned at 2 Chr. 11:8.

MORIAH [mō rī'ə] (Heb. *môrîyâ*).†
1. "The land of Moriah," on one of whose mountains Abraham was commanded by God to sacrifice his son Isaac (Gen. 22:2). The identification of this place, three days' journey from Beer-sheba, has long been a difficulty; Syr. reads "the land of the Amorites," LXX "the hill country," and Vulg. "the land of vision." Sam. has *mwr'h*, thus identifying Moriah with Moreh **1**, which is near the Samaritan place of worship on Mt. Gerizim.
2. Mt. Moriah, according to 2 Chr. 3:1 the location of the Jerusalem temple. The site was formerly the threshing floor of Ornan the Jebusite (cf. 21:16-26; called Araunah at 2 Sam. 24:16-25).

MORNING STAR (Gk. *phōsphóros*). The planet Venus, symbolic of the coming of Jesus as the beginning of the new age (2 Pet. 1:19; KJV "Day Star"; Rev. 2:28; 22:16; KJV "[bright and] morning star"). *See* DAY Star.

MORTAR.†
1. A vessel in which material such as grain or pigmentation is crushed and ground with a pestle. Specifically mentioned in the Bible are the manna (Num. 11:8; Heb. *mᵉḏōk̲â*) and grain (Prov. 27:22, here figurative of the punishment due a fool; *maktēš*).
2. A plastic building material (Heb. *ḥōmer* "clay, mortar") used to bind bricks (e.g., Exod. 1:14; Nah. 3:14) or stones (Jer. 43:9; *meleṭ*). It was usually made of the same clay used for bricks, with the addition of straw or sand. It was mixed with the feet (Isa. 41:25; Nah. 3:14) and applied while wet. Bitumen was used in construction of the tower of Babel (Gen. 11:3).

MORTAR, THE (Heb. *hammaktēš*). A trading district in Jerusalem (Zeph. 1:11; KJV "Maktesh"; NIV "the market district"). It was named, probably for its topography (cf. Judg. 15:19; RSV "hollow place"), after the common mortar used with a pestle for grinding (cf. Prov. 27:22). The northern part of the Tyropoean valley has been suggested as its location.

MOSERAH [mō'sə rə] (Heb. *môserâ* "bond"), **MOSEROTH** [mō'sə rŏth] (*môsērôṯ* "bonds"). An unidentified place where the Israelites stopped during the wilderness wanderings (Num. 33:30-31, "Moseroth") and where Aaron died and was buried (Deut. 10:6, "Moserah"; KJV "Mosera"). According to Num. 20:22-28; 33:38; Deut. 32:50, however, Aaron's death occurred on Mt. Hor, which may suggest that Moserah was in the vicinity of Mt. Hor. An additional difficulty is raised by the relation of Moserah/Moseroth to (Beeroth) Bene-jaakan; according to Num. 33:31, the Israelites went from Moseroth to Bene-jaakan, but

according to Deut. 10:6, they went from Beeroth Benejaakan (RSV mg. "the wells of the Bene-jaakan") to Moserah.

MOSES [mō'zəz] (Heb. *mōšeh*; cf. Egyp. *mśy* "to be born" or "son").† The first great leader of the Hebrew people, regarded as author of the first five books of the Old Testament. Moses is revered by Jews, Christians, and Muslims for his daring leadership and diplomacy as well as his promulgation of the divine law.

According to the biblical record, Moses was born in Egypt when the Hebrews were enslaved to Pharaoh, apparently during the early to middle centuries of the New Kingdom period (*ca.* 1550-1085 B.C.). His parents (or perhaps ancestors) were Amram and Jochebed of the tribe of Levi (Exod. 2:1; 6:20).

The account of Moses' birth and his rescue from the drowning decreed by Pharaoh is presented at Exod. 2:1-10. Believing that God had chosen him (cf. Heb. 11:23), Moses' parents hid him for three months and then placed him in a papyrus basket among the reeds at a bathing spot in the Nile river. Moses was found and, although his mother was permitted to rear him for a time, later adopted by a daughter of Pharaoh. The narrative associates his name with being "drawn out" (Heb. *māšâ*) of the water. Similarities to birth accounts of other ancient Near Eastern figures have been noted (e.g., Sargon of Akkad).

Accordingly, Moses was raised in the royal household and received all the benefits of education and luxury then available; he was well-trained, eloquent, and powerful (Acts 7:22). Yet he was aware of his roots and the plight of his fellow Hebrews, and thus seemed to be conscious of a divine calling to aid and deliver them. When he was forty years old he witnessed an Egyptian beating a Hebrew and avenged the attack by killing the Egyptian (Exod. 2:11-12). Yet his fellow Hebrews resented what appeared to them an arrogant usurpation of power (v. 14). Fearing reprisal by Pharaoh, Moses fled to Midian (v. 15).

In Midian Moses again assumed the role of deliverer, rescuing the seven daughters of the priest Reuel (also called Jethro and Hobab) from hostile shepherds (vv. 16-17). Subsequently he sojourned with Reuel, marrying his daughter Zipporah. Together they had two sons, Gershom and Eliezer (**2**) (v. 22; 18:3-4; 1 Chr. 23:15).

Moses' call and commission came while he was tending Jethro's sheep in the desert near Horeb. He was attracted to a burning bush that was not consumed by the fire, where the angel of the Lord and then God spoke to him and at length convinced him to become the deliverer who would lead the Hebrews out of Egypt (Exod. 3:1–4:17). It was in this setting that God revealed to Moses the name Yahweh (3:14ff.; *see* I AM WHO I AM; Yahweh). Moreover, God chose Moses' brother Aaron to assist as spokesman (some suggest because Moses had a speech impediment; cf. 4:10).

Yahweh had instructed Moses to perform miracles before Pharaoh and to request the people's release, but he also promised to harden Pharaoh's heart so he would not let them go. When Moses sought a three-day release for the Hebrews to offer sacrifices to Yahweh their plight became even more intolerable; Pharaoh refused and commanded them to gather their own straw and yet produce the same quantity of bricks (5:1-19). Moses became discouraged, but God again promised to bring the Israelites out from under the Egyptian yoke with mighty acts of judgment, thereby making them his own miraculously redeemed people and giving them the promised land (5:22–6:8).

Through a series of ten miraculous plagues Yahweh did indeed crush the Egyptians and liberate the Hebrews from slavery. Each time Moses and Aaron asked Pharaoh to release the people the Egyptian refused. Ten times Moses stretched out his hand and brought a devastating plague (7:8–11:10; 12:29-32; *see* PLAGUES OF EGYPT, THE). The occasion of the final plague, the death of the firstborn of Egypt, is associated in the biblical account with the institution of the feast of Passover commemorating God's mercy in "passing over" the Israelites (vv. 1-28).

The deliverance from Pharaoh and the miraculous crossing of the Red Sea (or Sea of Reeds; chs. 14–15) marked only the beginning of the Israelites' arduous journey to the promised land led by Moses. When the people grumbled against Moses and God at Marah because of the bitter water, Moses made the water sweet (vv. 22-25). Yet because of their continued resistance (e.g., 17:1-4; Num. 14:1-4), this entire generation of Israelites, including Moses, were destined to die in the wilderness without entering the promised land (vv. 26-35; cf. Heb. 3:7-19).

Of particular importance is Moses' role as Israel's law giver. It was at "the mountain of the Lord," Sinai or Horeb, that he experienced a theophany and received from Yahweh the TEN COMMANDMENTS or Decalog (Exod. 19:1–20:17; Deut. 5). It is traditionally held that at this time he also received the diverse laws of the Covenant Code (Exod. 20:22–23:33), the cultic regulations contained in the book of Leviticus (cf. Num. 5:1–6:21; chs. 15, 18–19), the so-called Deuteronomic legislation (e.g., Deut. 12–26), and the oral laws contained in the Mishnah and Talmud.

Although Moses was not allowed to enter the promised land, he was permitted to view it from atop Mt. Nebo (Deut. 34:1-4). He died in Moab at the age of 120 and was buried at an unknown site opposite Bethpeor (vv. 5-7).

Apparently because of his role as intercessor between Yahweh and the Israelites Moses is regarded as the first and one of the greatest Hebrew prophets (v. 10; 18:15-18; cf. Exod. 20:19; Num. 11:25; 12:7-8). Moreover, he interceded among the Israelites themselves as judge (e.g., Exod. 18:13-16; cf. Num. 27:1-11; 36:1-12). Moses is also credited with military leadership (e.g., Exod. 17:8-13; Num. 31), conducting various censuses (chs. 1, 4, 26), the allotment of tribal territories (e.g., ch. 32), and construction of the tabernacle (Exod. 25–31). Two of the oldest examples of Hebrew poetry, the Song of Moses (Deut. 32:1-43; variously dated to the eleventh-ninth centuries; cf. 2 Macc. 7:6) and the Blessing (or Testament) of Moses (33:2-29; eleventh century), are attributed to Moses; Exod. 15:1-18, the Song of the Sea (or, according to some scholars, the Song of Miriam) also is occasionally called the Song of Moses (cf. Rev. 15:3). For other references to Moses' writing activity, *see* PENTATEUCH *III*.

In addition to numerous references to Moses, his activities, and particularly the "law of Moses" throughout the Old Testament, he is frequently mentioned in later writings. Many of his deeds are recounted and embellished in intertestamental literature (e.g., 1 En. 89:16-40; As.Mos.), the Dead Sea Scrolls, and such Jewish writers as Philo and Josephus. In the New Testament Moses is frequently presented as a forerunner or "type" of Christ, the "second Moses" (e.g., John 1:17; Heb. 3:1-6; 11:23-28) and the events of the Exodus compared to the redemption through Christ (cf. Acts 7:17-44; 1 Cor. 10:1-10).

Bibliography. D.M. Beegle, *Moses, the Servant of Yahweh* (Grand Rapids: 1972; J.G. Gager, *Moses in Greco-Roman Paganism*. SBL Monograph 16 (Nashville: 1972); H.M. Teeple, *The Mosaic Eschatological Prophet*. JBL Monograph 10 (Philadelphia: 1957).

MOSES, ASSUMPTION OF.† A Jewish apocalyptic writing dating to the first half of the first century A.D., purportedly Moses' farewell exhortation to Joshua. The single surviving text is a fragmentary sixth-century Latin palimpsest translated from Greek, apparently itself a translation of a Hebrew or Aramaic original. Although the work at hand has been known for more than a century as the Assumption of Moses, the extant text contains no reference to or description of Moses' postmortem ascension to heaven but only his burial; it constitutes, rather, a retelling of the biblical account at Deut. 31–34; consequently, it is becoming more commonly known as the Testament of Moses. Yet ancient Jewish and Christian lists of apocryphal works associated with Moses include both an Assumption of Moses and a Testament of Moses. Because the text breaks off midsentence and on the basis of the ancient references, some scholars contend that the complete original may have contained both works.

Here Moses predicts Israelite history from the entrance into Canaan until the end of days, which the author understands to refer to his own troubled time. This work, like much Jewish apocalyptic literature, was written to encourage people enduring great hardships to remain faithful to the Lord's commandments in the midst of their trials, which it claims are soon to end. Thus the author explains the certainty that God's covenant promises will be kept, the imminence of divine intervention on behalf of the suffering righteous, and the terror surrounding his vengeance upon their idolatrous Gentile oppressors.

The writer was almost certainly a Palestinian Jew, although it is impossible to determine of which particular group or sect. Although the work contains certain affinities with the Essenes and their writings, the complexity of Judaism in this period precludes any absolute identification.

MOST HIGH (Heb. *'elyôn*). An epithet of God. Similar to forms attested in Ugaritic literature (Ugar. *'ly*; cf. *UT,* no. 1855), it occurs in the most archaic Hebrew poetry within the patriarchal accounts (e.g., Num. 24:16; Deut. 32:8; cf. 2 Sam. 22:14 par. Ps. 18:13 [MT 14]; cf. Acts 7:48). It appears also in the compound form God Most High (*'ēl 'elyôn*; e.g., Gen.

14:18-20, in the encounter between Abram and Melchizedek; cf. v. 22; Mark 5:7).

MOST HOLY PLACE (Heb. *qōḏeš haqq°ḏašîm* "holy of holies"; Gk. *hágia hagíōn*). The innermost sanctuary of both the tabernacle and the Jerusalem temple. The most holy place was not to be entered except by the high priest, himself permitted to enter only on the Day of Atonement and only with the proper precautions (cf. Lev. 16:2; RSV "holy place [within the veil]"; cf. vv. 4-5). The reference at Num. 18:10 to "a most holy place" where the priests were to eat their portions of the offerings probably indicates the "holy place" before the veil and outside what is usually called "the most holy place" (cf. v. 7). In later usage the designation "most holy place" (*qōḏeš qoḏāšîm*) is also used for places other than the inner sanctuary at Ezek. 45:3 (the temple as a whole); 48:12 (the land assigned to the priests); and Dan. 9:24 (perhaps rather a person [cf. v. 25] or object; cf. RSV mg.).

In the tabernacle, a heavily decorated veil separated the (inner) most holy place from the (outer) holy place. The only tabernacle furnishings in the most holy place were the ark with the mercy seat (Exod. 26:31-34) and possibly the altar of incense (Heb. 9:3-4; RSV "Holy of Holies"; cf. Exod. 30:1-6; Lev. 16:18).

The most holy place of Solomon's temple was also called the "inner sanctuary" (Heb. *ḏᵉḇîr*; 1 Kgs. 6:16; KJV "oracle"). Although problems of text and translation arise at a number of points in the description of the Solomonic most holy place, it appears to have been a cube, twenty cubits on a side, with its cedar walls overlaid with gold. In it was the ark and two large statues of cherubim whose wings were above the ark (vv. 19-28; 8:6-7; cf. Ezek. 41:4). It is possible that the incense altar was inside the most holy place (1 Kgs. 6:22). Gold chains and two highly decorated doors overlaid with gold separated the most holy place from the rest of the temple (vv. 21, 31-32).

Although the ark could no longer be part of the postexilic temples of Zerubbabel and Herod (cf. Jer. 3:16), the most holy place remained an important part of observances of the Day of Atonement. The position previously occupied by the ark was marked by a slab of stone, the "foundation" (*šᵉṭîyâ*), three finger-breadths high (Mishnah *Yoma* v. 2). The most holy place was now marked off from the main sanctuary by a curtain. The incense altar was in the temple sanctuary but outside the most holy place.

At Heb. 9:3, 11-28 the high priest's annual entry into the most holy place of the tabernacle, here called "the holy place," is a symbol of Christ's work of atonement.

MOTH (Heb. *'āš*; cf. Akk. *ašašu*; Gk. *sés*). The Palestinian clothes moth, *Tineola biselliella* of the order *Lepidoptera*, whose larvae feed on wool and fur. The moth is pictured as frail, but the human being, considered hyperbolically, is even more frail (Job 4:19). Similarly, a moth-eaten garment also illustrates the frailty of human existence (13:28; Isa. 50:9; 51:8). God himself is pictured as a consuming moth, e.g., the moth's larva (Ps. 39:11 [MT 12]; Hos. 5:12; NEB "festering sore"). The destruction of garments by moths

is an indication of the temporariness of earthly possessions (Matt. 6:19-20; Luke 12:33; Jas. 5:2). At Job 27:18, LXX and Syr. read "spider" (so RSV, JB; cf. 8:14), probably correctly, in place of MT "moth" (so KJV, RSV mg., NIV).

MOTHER (Heb. *'ēm*; Gk. *mḗtēr*).* Since the leading roles in Israelite families were generally taken by men, the primary function of women was to bear and raise children. Accordingly, childbearing was an occasion for great joy (Ps. 113:9; Isa. 54:1), and the childless woman had a difficult life (cf., e.g., 1 Sam. 1:4-11). While patrilineality was almost entirely the rule in ancient Israel, some evidence does exist for matrilineal reckoning in the tribal lists (cf. the female ancestors Leah and Rachel and different treatment of those tribes descended from the concubines Bilhah and Zilpah; e.g., Gen. 46:8-25; 49:3-27; Num. 1:5-15, 20-43; 2:3-31; 26:5-50; but cf. Deut. 27:12-13; 33:6-21). Heb. *'ēm* is used not only of biological mothers, but also of a grandmother (1 Kgs. 15:10 [MT 24]; so NIV), a female ancestor (Gen. 3:20; cf. 24:60, where translations supply "mother"), or a female military leader (Judg. 5:7).

While the Bible does not use "mother" for God as it does "father," it does use maternal imagery in speaking of God, although with reserve (e.g., Ps. 131:2; Isa. 49:15; Matt. 23:37), perhaps to avoid confusion with the maternal goddesses of fertility cults. More frequent is the application of feminine imagery to the people of God, which includes the portrayal of Israel as a mother (e.g., Isa. 50:1; Rev. 12; cf. Gal. 4:26).

MOTHER OF PEARL (Heb. *dar*; cf. Arab. *durr* "pearl").* The iridescent inner layer of mollusk shells, one of the materials used in the mosaic pavement at Ahasuerus' extravagant banquet (Esth. 1:6; KJV "white [marble]").

MOUNT EPHRAIM (KJV). See EPHRAIM, HILL COUNTRY OF.

MOUNT OF ASSEMBLY (Heb. *har-mô'ēḏ*). A mythical mountain "in the far north" where the gods were thought to assemble (cf. NEB) and where the king of Babylon claimed he would be enthroned (Isa. 14:13; KJV "mount of the congregation"). The mountain dwelling of the gods is portrayed in Ugaritic and Akkadian literature (cf. Ps. 89:5-7; also 48:2, where Zion is identified with the mythical mountain).

MOUNT(AIN) OF GOD (Heb. *har hā'ᵉlōhîm*), **MOUNT(AIN) OF THE LORD** (*har YHWH*).† Reminiscent of Canaanite and Mesopotamian beliefs concerning the dwelling place(s) of the gods, the dwelling place of Israel's God or the place where he made his presence known to his people is often depicted as a mountain (Heb. *har*), though not always the same mountain. The commanders of the Syrian army advised Ben-hadad that their loss to the Israelites in the hill country stemmed from the fact that Israel's God, like the Canaanite deities, was a mountain deity (1 Kgs. 20:23). In the ancient world mountains, as homes of deities, were regarded as places of worship (e.g., Deut. 12:2); similarly, in Israel, the mountains associated with God were places of worship and pilgrimage as well as the scene of theophanies.

In the Old Testament two mountains are known as "the mountain of God" or "the mountain of the Lord": Sinai/Horeb (Exod. 3:1; 4:27; 18:5; 24:15; Num. 10:33; 1 Kgs. 19:8) and the temple mount in Jerusalem (Gen. 22:14; see MORIAH; Isa. 2:3 par. [cf. v. 2, "mountain of the house of the Lord"]; 30:29; cf. Ps. 24:3; RSV "hill of the Lord"). The latter is also called "his/my [i.e., God's] holy mountain" (48:1 [MT 2]; Isa. 65:11), but this terminology also designated the whole land of Israel (v. 25; Ezek. 20:40; cf. Exod. 15:17). Ps. 68:15-16 [MT 16-17] describes the envy of Bashan, a "mountain of gods" (RSV "mighty mountain"), directed toward the temple mount in Jerusalem, "the mount which God desired for his abode" (cf. v. 17 [MT 18]).

For a people who associated worship of God with a mountain, it was essential that they not worship Yahweh on any mountain associated with any other deity (Deut. 12:2). The mountain on which God was to be worshipped (i.e., Zion or Gerizim) was a major issue dividing the Jews and the Samaritans, and Jesus sought to resolve the issue (John 4:20-24).

Some Greek recensions, followed by RSV, JB, suggest a "mountain of Yahweh" in Gibeon at 2 Sam. 21:6; cf. v. 9), but "Saul the chosen of the Lord" is probably the correct reading (so MT, KJV, NIV, RSV mg.).

MOUNTAIN-SHEEP (Heb. *zemer*).* One of the animals permitted for eating according to the pentateuchal food laws (Deut. 14:5). "Mountain-sheep" (*Ovis tragelaphus*) is a reasonable possibility for the identity of this animal (cf. NEB "rock-goat"); the "chamois" (KJV) is not attested in Palestine or nearby areas.

MOURNING.† Because of the conservatism that generally attaches to such matters, Jewish mourning customs exhibited little change through the Old and New Testament periods. Mourning was an important way of showing respect for the dead; the omission of such observances was a sign of unusual or difficult

circumstances (Jer. 16:4-7; Ezek. 24:15-27) or of disrespect (Jer. 22:18-19). The employment of professional mourners (Eccl. 12:5; Matt. 9:23-24; cf. *ANEP*, nos. 459, 634, 638) underscores its importance. Such mourners along with family members would wail and weep for the dead (1 Kgs. 13:30; Jer. 9:17-18 [MT 16-17]; 22:10, 18; 34:5; Amos 5:16; Matt. 11:17), as well as sing and play both traditional and specially composed songs of mourning (2 Sam. 1:17-27; 3:33-34; Jer. 9:20-22 [MT 19-21]; see LAMENT). Tearing of garments (2 Sam. 1:11) and wearing of sackcloth (Gen. 37:34; 2 Sam. 3:31) were also customary. Mourning generally continued for a specified period of time (Gen. 50:10; cf. 2 Sam. 1:12).

Self-mutilation, including shaving the head (cf. Job 1:20; Isa. 22:12; Jer. 7:29; Mic. 1:16) and gashing the body (Jer. 41:5), typified some ancient Near Eastern cultures but was forbidden to the Israelites as a "holy people" (Lev. 19:27-28; Deut. 14:1). Greater restrictions with regard to mourning were placed on priests because of their need to maintain ritual purity (Lev. 21:1-5, 10-12).

See BURIAL.

MOUSE (Heb. *'akbār*). In biblical usage, any of a number of rodents of family *Muridae,* including mice, rats, and field mice. Such creatures were not acceptable according to the Pentateuchal food laws (Lev. 11:29; cf. Isa. 66:17, which depicts pagan observances). In answer to a divinely sent invasion of mice the Philistines included five golden mice as part of a guilt offering when they returned the ark of the covenant to Israel (1 Sam. 6:4-18).

MOZA [mō′zə] (Heb. *môṣā'* "departure, origin").

1. A son of Caleb and his concubine Ephah (1 Chr. 2:46).

2. A son of Zimri and father of Binea; descendant of King Saul through his son Jonathan (1 Chr. 8:36-37; 9:42-43).

MOZAH [mō′zə] (Heb. *môṣâ*). A city assigned to the tribe of Benjamin (Josh. 18:26). Later, as Colonia Emmaus, it was colonized in A.D. 75 by Roman veterans of Vespasian's war against Jerusalem. The site

Mourners depicted in a thirteenth-century B.C. relief at Memphis (MARBURG/Art Resource, N.Y.)

is modern Qalôniyeh (Qâlunyah), *ca.* 6.5 km. (4 mi.) northwest of Jerusalem.

MULBERRY (Gk. *móron*).† The black mulberry (*Morus nigra* L.), the juice of which was used to arouse the elephants of Antiochus V's army for battle against Judas Maccabeus (1 Macc. 6:34). For the KJV usage at 2 Sam. 5:23-24; 1 Chr. 14:14-15, *see* BALSAM TREES.

MULE (Heb. *pered, pirdâ*). The hybrid offspring of a female horse and a male ass. Since crossbreeding of animals was forbidden in Israel (Lev. 19:19), the Hebrews presumably obtained nearly all their mules from Gentiles (cf. 1 Kgs. 10:25). Mules were considered especially appropriate transportation for royalty (2 Sam. 13:29; 18:9; 1 Kgs. 1:33, 38, 44; cf. Zech. 9:9; Matt. 21:5), but might also be ridden by others (Isa. 66:20) and used for transporting goods (2 Kgs. 5:17; 1 Chr. 12:40 [MT 41]). The mule's petulance is proverbial (cf. Ps. 32:9).

The RSV rendering "swift horse" for Heb. *rekeš* at Esth. 8:10, 14 is more correct than the KJV's "mule." At Gen. 36:24 the KJV translates the difficult *yēmim* as "mules" (RSV "hot springs," following Vulg.); the Hebrew original may have been *mayim* "waters."

MUPPIM [mŭp'ĭm] (Heb. *muppîm*). A son of Benjamin (Gen. 46:21). He is called Shephupham (cf. 1 Chr. 8:5, "Shephuphan") and his descendants Shupamites at Num. 26:39. The plural form of Muppim and Huppim suggests that they might actually have been populations that joined themselves to the tribe of Benjamin (cf. 1 Chr. 7:12, 15).

MURATORIAN [mŏōr'ə tôr'ĭ ən] **FRAGMENT.*** A fragmentary Latin manuscript containing a list of New Testament books, discovered at Milan in the eighteenth century by L. A. Muratori. The document's original language was probably Greek. A date near A.D. 200 and origin in the city of Rome are made probable by information in the document.

The original document described the four Gospels, though the names of the first two canonical Gospels have not survived. Other books of the full New Testament canon not mentioned in the fragment are the Epistle to the Hebrews and those of James and Peter. Also included in the fragment's canonical New Testament books are the Wisdom of Solomon, ascribed to "friends of Solomon," and an apocalypse of Peter that is said to be rejected by some. The Shepherd of Hermas is recommended for private reading but not considered canonical. The pseudo-Pauline letters to the Laodiceans and Alexandrians are rejected and ascribed to Marcionites. Also rejected are Gnostic, Marcionite, and Montanist writings in general. The fragment reinforces the conclusion that the existence of such heretical writings caused the Church to move toward definition of a New Testament canon.

See also CANON *III. C.*

MURDER.† Under the basic prohibition of taking human life (Exod. 20:13), the pentateuchal codes distinguish homicide punishable by death (cf. Gen. 9:5-6) from accidental and justified homicide. Murder was punishable by death if an object was intentionally struck against or thrown at the victim, if hostility had existed between the two parties, or if the murderer lay in wait for the victim (Exod. 21:12-14; Num. 35:16-23). While some other nations made provision for monetary settlements, Israelite law allowed for no alternative to the death penalty in such cases (cf. Deut. 19:13; in situations such as when an ox known to be dangerous killed a person, the prescribed penalty was the owner's death, but a money settlement was possible; Exod. 21:28-30). The killing of a murderer was done by the "avenger of blood," a close relative of the victim (Num. 35:19; Deut. 19:12) or by some other person (cf. 2 Sam. 4:1).

If the killing of a person did not meet the judicial requirements of capital homicide and was thereby ruled accidental, the killer could flee to a city of refuge to escape the avenger of blood (Exod. 21:13; Num. 35:9-15; Deut. 19:1-10). If a killing was in self-defense (e.g., as was presumed when a thief who came at night was killed), the killer was not considered guilty (Exod. 22:2-3 [MT 1-2]). Killing in battle also was not subject to blood revenge (cf. 1 Kgs. 2:5).

While the objective of the pentateuchal laws was in part the amelioration of conditions brought about by unrestricted exercise of blood revenge customs, Jesus' teachings sought to abolish among his followers the concept of human revenge—even revenge regulated or carried out by the state (Matt. 5:38-39; cf. Rom. 12:17-19). Unrepentant murderers are excluded from God's people, the Church (Rev. 21:8; 22:15). Even the attitude of hate toward others is regarded in the New Testament as tantamount to murder (1 John 3:15; cf. Matt. 5:21-22).

See AVENGER OF BLOOD; CITIES OF REFUGE.

MURMURING.* A repeated theme in the narratives of the Exodus is the complaining (Heb. *teˈlunnôt* "murmurings"; cf. *lûn* "murmur, complain") of the people concerning the conditions into which they had been brought in the wilderness after their departure from Egypt (Exod. 15:22-25; 16:1-36; 17:1-7; Num. 11:1-34; 20:1-13; 21:4-9). Typical elements in the murmuring accounts are: travel to the place where the incident occurs (Exod. 15:22; 17:1; Num. 20:1; 21:4); description of the condition, usually related to water or food, which brings about the complaint (Exod. 15:22-23; 17:1; Num. 11:1); the complaint of the people directed against (Exod. 15:24; 16:2-3; 17:2-3; Num. 20:2; 21:4-5) or to (Num. 11:2; cf. vv. 4-6; 21:7) Moses and Aaron; Moses and Aaron's directing the complaint to God (Exod. 17:4; Num. 11:2, 11-15; 20:6; 21:7); the divine provision of a remedy for the condition through Moses (Exod. 15:25; 16:4-5, 11ff.; 17:5-6; Num. 11:2, 16-33; 20:7-11; 21:8-9); and the naming of the place in commemoration of the incident (Exod. 15:23; 17:7; Num. 11:3, 34; 20:13). Other themes, such as the Sabbath (Exod. 16:22-30), are sometimes associated with these stories.

The considerable variations in the narratives at the point of Moses and Aaron's directing the complaint to God are related to the difficulties of the relationship between the leadership of the two men and that of God. Indeed, the problem of the people's incomplete acceptance of Moses and Aaron as Yahweh's representatives and even of Yahweh as Israel's God, which recurs in other forms in the narratives (e.g., 5:20-21; Num. 12; cf. Josh. 9:18), can be considered the focal concern of the mumuring stories. The climax of these incidents occurs with the crisis brought about by the spies' report (Num. 14) and in the challenge to Moses and Aaron's authority initiated by Korah (chs. 16-17).

Later references to the murmuring incidents emphasize the people's rebelliousness and apostasy (Deut. 9:6-29; Neh. 9:16-20; Pss. 78, 106; Ezek. 20; 1 Cor. 10:9-10). This wilderness tradition was to be important in later interpretations of the occupation of the land and the days leading to Israel's destruction (e.g., Neh. 9:26-31).

Bibliography. G. W. Coats, *Rebellion in the Wilderness* (Nashville: 1968).

MUSHI [mōō'shī] (Heb. *mûšî, mušî*). A Levite, the second son of Merari (Exod. 6:19; Num. 3:20; 1 Chr. 6:19, 47 [MT 4, 32]; 23:21, 23; 24:26, 30). He was the eponymous ancestor of a levitical family, the Mushites (Num. 3:33; 26:58).

MUSIC.* Biblical references to music are numerous because of the essential role it played in all aspects of the life of the people of the Bible. While the music of worship is a major focus, music concerned with matters of everyday life is also represented.

The origin of music, or at least instrumental music, is ascribed to Jubal (Gen. 4:21), whose kin are regarded as originators of various aspects of human culture (vv. 17, 20, 22). Singing is associated with Jubal's father Lamech, to whom is ascribed a song of boasting revenge (vv. 23-24), and may have been as ancient as mankind itself (cf. 2:23). The shaping of human speech to melodies and rhythms, which is the beginning and basis of singing, is natural when the voice is used in expressing emotion, in prayer, or in ritual, and all biblical poems can be considered songs at least at this initial level. Recitation, such as the public recitation of the law before the postexilic community (Neh. 8:8-9) and private recitation of the law (e.g., Ps. 119:23; cf. 63:5-7 [MT 6-8]), was also performed in a chant or melodic pattern.

It is, of course, impossible to know for certain how ancient Israel's music sounded, but certain observations have been possible. Ancient Israelite music did not constitute fully developed melodies in the modern Western sense, but rather simple melodic patterns around which music was structured; thus, Israelite songs were similar to Indian ragas and Gregorian chant. Two further characteristics were homophony—harmony being a relatively modern (and Western) development—and the use of microtonic intervals, typical of oriental music to this day. The similarity of Christian liturgical chants of the late Roman period and early Middle Ages to the cantillation of Yemenite, Mesopotamian, and Persian Jews is taken as evidence that both contain survivals of ancient Israelite and Jewish melodic patterns.

Some of Israel's songs of corporate praise to God were sung antiphonally, as evident, for example, in the repetition of the Song of Miriam in the first lines of Moses' Song of the Sea (Exod. 15:1, 21), in the repeated refrains of Pss. 80; 118:1-4; 136, and in the responsive singing of the angels in Isaiah's vision (Isa. 6:3). Antiphony is explicitly mentioned in connection with the postexilic community (Ezra 3:11; Neh. 12:24) and in rabbinic literature. Secular singing could also be antiphonal (1 Sam. 18:7).

David may be the earliest professional musician specifically named in the Bible (1 Sam. 16:23; 18:10), though professional "ballad singers" (Heb. *yō'mᵉrû hammōšlîm*; KJV "they that speak in proverbs"; JB, NIV "poets"; NJV "bards") are mentioned at Num. 21:27, and early song collections are noted (v. 14; Josh. 10:13; 2 Sam. 1:18; cf. Exod. 17:14; 2 Chr. 35:25). Professional mourners also employed music (*see* LAMENT; MOURNING). The advent of monarchy in Israel increased the importance and numbers of professional musicians (cf. Eccl. 2:8), and it is to David's name that musical traditions of the Old Testament have attached themselves (cf. 2 Sam. 23:1). David did compose some songs (1:17-27; 3:33-34; 22:1-51). However, the designation "of David" in the superscriptions to seventy-three psalms was not originally an ascription of authorship, but is a statement that these psalms should be considered among the Davidic class or type of songs.

David is also remembered for organizing the temple musicians (1 Chr. 25; 2 Chr. 29:30; Ezra 3:10; Neh. 12:24, 45-46) and providing musical instruments for the liturgy (1 Chr. 23:5; Neh. 12:36; Amos 6:5). He himself participated in liturgical music (2 Sam. 6:5; cf. v. 15). Indeed, the kingdom of David and Solomon, larger, stronger, more centralized, and more culturally eclectic than Israel had been earlier, experienced the transformation of liturgical music through the institution of levitical temple musicians (1 Chr. 6:31-48 [MT 16-33]). Musicians were organized into guilds such as "the sons of MAHOL" (1 Kgs. 4:31 [MT 11]) and "the sons of Korah" (superscriptions to Pss. 42, 44–49, 84–85, 87–88). A "choirmaster" was designated (superscriptions to fifty-five psalms; KJV "chief Musician"; Hab. 3:19; KJV "chief singer"). It became possible for individual musicians to gain renown, e.g., Heman (1 Chr. 6:33 [MT 18]; superscription to Ps. 88) and Asaph (1 Chr. 16:7; superscriptions to Pss. 50, 73–83).

Evidence of the degree of development of religious song is found in the varied collection represented by the book of Psalms. Even the directions in the superscriptions to the psalms are indicative of their great variety: e.g., the type of song, including psalm, song, prayer, shiggaion, miktam (KJV "michtam"), maskil (KJV "maschil"), praise song, love song, and song of ascents (i.e., of pilgrimage to Jerusalem); the place of the various songs in the liturgy, including association with the thank offering (KJV "of praise"), the memorial offering (KJV "to bring to remembrance"), the dedication of the temple (KJV "... of the house of David"), "for instruction" (KJV "to teach"), and "for the Sabbath"; musical directions, including "to the choirmaster," "with stringed instruments" (KJV "on Neginoth"), "for the flutes" (KJV "upon Nehiloth"); and indications of melodic patterns to be used, e.g., "The Hind of the Dawn" (KJV "Aijeleth Shahar"), "Lilies" (KJV "Shoshannim"), "The Dove on Far-off Terebinths" (KJV "Jonath-elem-rechokim"), and possibly also "Do Not Destroy" (KJV "Al-taschith"), "Mahalath," "Mahalath Leannoth," "Muth-labben," "Gittith" (perhaps the name of a musical instrument: "lyre"), "Sheminith," and "Jeduthun." *See also* the individual articles.

Nonliturgical music, the popular song of everyday life, is of great variety: songs of family celebrations (Gen. 31:27; Luke 15:25), children's songs (Matt. 11:16-17; cf. Job 21:11-12; Zech. 8:5), love songs (Song of Solomon; e.g., Cant. 2:8-14), wedding songs (Ps. 45; Jer. 16:9; Rev. 18:23), royal acclamations (1 Kgs. 1:39-40), marching songs (Num. 10:35-36; 2 Chr. 20:21) the luxurious music enjoyed by the royal and the wealthy (Eccl. 2:8; Amos 6:5), mocking songs (Num. 21:27-30; 1 Kgs. 12:16), triumphant songs (Judg. 5; Amos 2:2), songs of mourning and lament (2 Chr. 35:25; Amos 5:16-17), banqueting songs (Isa. 5:12; 24:8-9; Amos 8:10), songs for the laying of a cornerstone (Zech. 4:7; cf. Ezra 3:10-11), songs of the watchmen on the city walls (Isa. 21:11-12), work songs (Num. 21:17-18; Jer. 48:33), and songs of harvest (Isa. 16:10). The social importance of secular music is seen, for example, in the recurrent use of a song celebrating David's prowess in battle and thus helping to establish his reputation (1 Sam. 21:11 [MT 12]; 29:5).

Music was also important in the worship of the early Church. As Christian communities became less associated with the Jewish temple and synagogues, they not only retained the forms and sounds of Jewish worship music but also developed new forms. In the earliest Christian communities music was not set within regular and repeated patterns of worship but was, rather, allowed some spontaneity (1 Cor. 14:26; Eph. 5:19; Col. 3:16; Jas. 5:13). Some early Christian hymns consisted of Old Testament psalms and parts of psalms, sometimes interpreted christologically (Acts 4:24-26; Rev. 15:3-4). Other early Christian hymns were perhaps inherited from the synagogues (Rom. 11:33-36; Rev. 4:11), while others could only have been specifically Christian compositions (cf. 1 Tim. 3:16; Phil. 2:6-11; Col. 1:15-20).

Bibliography. R. P. Martin, *Worship in the Early Church* (Grand Rapids: 1975), pp. 39-52; A. Sendrey, *Music in Ancient Israel* (New York: 1969); W. S. Smith, *Musical Aspects of the New Testament* (Amsterdam: 1962)..

MUSICAL INSTRUMENTS.† Musical instruments mentioned in the Bible can be divided into three general groups: instruments with strings plucked by fingers or a plectrum, wind instruments, and percussion instruments, including those shaken or rattled. String instruments (a generic term is Heb. *mēn*; Ps. 45:8 [MT 9]; 150:4) included harps (*nēḇel*) and lyres (*kinnôr*; Gk. *kithára*; both often translated "harp"). Among wind instruments were pipes, often double pipes (Heb. *ḥālîl*, *ʿûgāḇ*; Gk. *aulós*), metal trumpets (Heb. *ḥᵃṣōṣᵉrâ*), rams' horns (*šôpār*, *yôḇēl*), and cattle horns (*qeren*; both trumpets and horns are represented by Gk. *sálpinx*). Percussion instruments included hand drums (Heb. *tōp*, often translated "tambourine"), paired cymbals (*ṣelṣelîm*, *mᵉṣiltayim*), single cymbals (Gk. *kýmbalon*), and sistrums (Heb. *mᵉnaʿanʿîm*; 2 Sam. 6:5; RSV "castanets"; KJV "cornets"); bells (*paʿᵃmôn*, *mᵉṣillôṯ*) were used as noise-making ornaments rather

Musicians playing a double flute, lute, and harp. From an Egyptian tomb painting of the Eighteenth Dynasty (by courtesy of the Oriental Institute, University of Chicago)

than as musical instruments (Exod. 28:33-34; Zech. 14:20). The *šālîš* (1 Sam. 18:6) has been variously identified as a lute, hand drum, triangle, or sistrum (RSV, KJV "instrument of music").

Various instruments used in the Babylonian court of Nebuchadnezzar appear at Dan. 3:5, 7, 10, 15. Included are harp- and lyre-type instruments (Aram. *qîṯᵉrōs/qîṯārōs*, *śabbᵉḵāʾ/sabbᵉḵāʾ*, and *pᵉsantērîn*, the latter possibly more like a hammered dulcimer or hackbrett), a pipe or flute, possibly a panpipe (*mašrôqîṯāʾ*), and a horn (*qarnāʾ*). The additional term *sumpōnyâ* (probably from Gk. *symphōnía*) has been thought to designate a type of instrument (RSV "bagpipe"; KJV "dulcimer"), but actually may refer to the orchestra as a whole. The unusual names of these musical instruments, which except for *qarnā* ʾ (cf. Heb. *qeren*) are not cognates of Israelite terminology, underscore the alien quality of the festivities recorded in this passage.

Just as today, different musical instruments were associated with different aspects of culture. For instance, both harps and lyres are mentioned repeatedly in connection with the temple worship of Jerusalem, usually along with cymbals (e.g., 1 Kgs. 10:12; 1 Chr. 25:1; 2 Chr. 29:25). Lyres had the greatest variety of uses: e.g., by David (1 Sam. 16:23), in temple worship, and as a prostitute's instrument (Isa. 23:16). Pipes, especially the *ʿûgāḇ*, were often associated with revelry and eroticism (e.g., Isa. 5:12) and thus were not used in the ritual music of the Jerusalem temple; they were employed especially in mourning (e.g., Jer. 48:36; Matt. 9:23; RSV "flute"). Hand drums (RSV "tambourines, timbrels") were generally used in celebrations and acclamations and were most often played by women (Gen. 31:27; Exod. 15:20; Judg. 11:34; 1 Sam. 18:6). The lists of instruments at 10:5; 2 Sam. 6:5; Ps. 150 represent broad mixtures; here pipes and hand drums are acceptable in religious contexts where either prophetic ecstasy (cf. 2 Kgs. 3:15) or group celebration rather than ordered ritual was the aim.

Horns and trumpets were used more for giving signals than as musical instruments properly speaking. Trumpets sounded the call to battle (Num. 31:6; Judg. 7:19-20; 2 Chr. 13:12, 14; 1 Cor. 14:8) and heralded every major step of ritual in the temple (cf. Num. 10:2, 7-8). They are mentioned as instruments for signalling in eschatological texts as well (Matt. 24:31; 1 Cor. 15:52; 1 Thess. 4:16). The ram's horn shofar was used in connection with particularly significant worship events, such as the movement of the ark into Jerusalem (2 Sam. 6:15) and an oath of covenant renewal (2 Chr. 15:14). The ritual significance of the shofar was such that it alone of Old Testament musical instruments has survived in Jewish religious ceremony.

For specific instruments see the individual articles.

Bibliography. A. Sendrey, *Music in Ancient Israel* (New York: 1969).

MUSTARD (Gk. *sínapi*). A plant cultivated in both gardens and fields for its seeds, ground for spice, and for the oil in the seeds (Matt. 13:31-32 par.; 17:20 par.). The variety grown in Palestine was black mustard (*Brassica nigra* Koch or *Sinapis nigra* L.), which can grow to 3 m. (10 ft.) in height but which had the smallest seed of plants then cultivated.

MUSTER GATE (Heb. *šaʿar hammipqāḏ*). A gate in Jerusalem's city wall or in the wall around the temple court, probably near what was then the northeastern corner of Jerusalem (Neh. 3:31; NIV "Inspection Gate"; JB "Watch Gate"; KJV "the gate Miphkad"; cf. RSV mg.). It may be the same as the Gate of the Guard (12:39) or the Benjamin Gate.

MUTH-LABBEN [mōōth lăb′ən] (Heb. *mût labbēn*). A term in the superscription of Ps. 9 (MT v. 1), meaning "death of a son" (NJV mg. "over the death of the son"; cf. NIV). It may be the name of a well-known melody to which the psalm was to be sung.

MYRA [mī′rə] (Gk. *Myra*). A city in Lycia on the Andriacus river, 4 km. (2.5 mi.) from the Mediterranean coast; modern Dembre. Myra was an important trading center through its adjacent port of Andriaca. At the time of the Roman Empire (as later also in Byzantine times) Myra was capital of the province of Lycia. The party that included Paul, a prisoner at the time, changed ships at Myra (Acts 27:5). St. Nicholas was bishop of Myra in the fourth century.

MYRRH [mûr] (Heb. *lōṭ, mōr, môr*; cf. Ugar. *mr*; Akk. *murru*; Gk. *smýrna*). Aromatic resinous gum, usually from the bark of trees and shrubs of genus *Commiphora* (*Balsamodendron*), in biblical times obtained from Arabia, Abyssinia, and India. Myrrh has long been a luxury item valuable as a perfume (cf. Cant. 1:13) and therefore an important item of trade, thus its significance as one of the gifts of the Magi to the infant Jesus (Matt. 2:11). To be heavily perfumed with oil containing myrrh and other perfumes thus connoted luxury and beauty (Esth. 2:12; Ps. 45:8 [MT 9]; Prov. 7:17; Cant. 3:6; 4:14; 5:13); the "mountain of myrrh" and "hill of frankincense" (4:6) is not a geographical location, but the lover's figure of speech for a woman's breasts (cf. v. 5). Myrrh was also used in Jewish burial (John 19:39). "Liquid myrrh," which was part of the recipe for the anointing oil of the tabernacle (Exod. 30:23; cf. Cant. 5:5), was the finest form of myrrh, which normally hardened quickly when exposed to air. "Wine mingled with myrrh" was offered to Jesus as a narcotic just before he was crucified (Mark 15:23).

Heb. *lōṭ* at Gen. 37:25; 43:11 probably designates a particular variety of resin (NJV "ladanum"; cf. JB), obtained from the cistus or "rock rose" (*Commiphora villosus* or *Commiphora salviaefolius*) common to Palestine. Heb. *nešeq* may refer to myrrh at 1 Kgs. 10:25 par. 2 Chr. 9:24 (so RSV); elsewhere, however, it means armor or weapons (so JB, NIV; cf. KJV). Gk. *mýron* normally represents "ointment" and should probably be so translated at Rev. 18:13 (so KJV, JB; RSV, NIV "myrrh"). Hadassah, the Hebrew name of Esther, is derived from the term for myrtle (Esth. 2:7).

MYRTLE (Heb. *hᵃdas*). *Myrtus communis* L., a fragrant evergreen shrub with dark oval leaves, white or pink flowers, and black berries common in Syria and Palestine and elsewhere in the Mediterranean region (Zech. 1:8, 10-11). The myrtle is mentioned in connection with the eschatological transformation of the desert into a well-watered place (Isa. 41:19; 55:13). In the postexilic restoration of the Feast of Tabernacles, myrtle branches were used in constructing the booths (Neh. 8:15).

MYSIA [mĭsh′ĭ ə] (Gk. *Mysia*). A region of northwestern Asia Minor included in the Roman province of Asia and adjacent to the province of Bithynia and Pontus. The boundaries of Mysia were never precisely defined and vary over time and according to different sources (cf. Strabo *Geog.* xii.4.10). Paul's route as described at Acts 16:6-8 apparently took him north along the boundary of the provinces of Galatia and Asia when his intention had been to go west into Asia, and then west across Asia to the Aegean coast at Troas when his intention had become to continue north into Bithynia.

MYSTERY (Aram. *rāz*; Gk. *mystḗrion*).† That which is unknown or which was unknown prior to or apart from its disclosure in divine revelation. At Dan. 2; 4:9 (MT 6), "mysteries" (KJV "secrets") are things unknown except by God's disclosure to his designated intermediary (cf. Rev. 1:20; 17:5, 7). More specifically, they are the meaning of symbolic revelatory dreams, the interpretation of which has an eschatological focus (Dan. 2:28). In apocalyptic writings "mystery" continued to have this eschatological focus (e.g., 1 En. 38:3) as well as indicating heavenly secrets in general as revealed to a visionary (e.g., ch. 71). At Rev. 10:7 the disclosure of the mystery is the eschatological fulfillment of the predictive words of the prophets.

It is primarily this eschatological focus of the Jewish use of "mystery," rather than that of the Greek mystery cults, that generally forms the basis for Paul's use of the term (1 Cor. 4:1; 13:2; 14:2; cf. Col. 2:2-3). Paul refers to marriage as mystery in a symbolic sense, as the union between Christ and the Church (Eph. 5:32). The more specifically Pauline use is for items of revelation disclosed at the same time that Paul identifies them as mysteries. Generally, these are matters of future eschatology, such as the salvation of Israel by way of its "hardening" (Rom. 11:25), the general resurrection (1 Cor. 15:51), and God's plan to unite all things in Christ (Eph. 1:9)—a secret decreed long before (cf. 1 Cor. 2:7; Col. 1:26). Indeed, Paul depicts as "mystery" the gospel, which has been "kept secret for long ages" but is now revealed, proclaimed, and believed (Rom. 16:25; 1 Cor. 2:1 [RSV "testimony"; cf. RSV mg.]; Eph. 3:3-4, 9; 6:19; Col. 2:2; cf. 1 Tim. 3:9; 1 En. 46:2). He speaks also of "the mystery of lawlessness" (2 Thess. 2:7), probably the activity of evil in general, which should not lead to alarm or thoughts that the end is near since "the man of lawlessness" has not yet come (v. 3).

An eschatological focus is also present where Jesus speaks of "the mystery [or mysteries] of the kingdom of God" given to his disciples while for others "everything is in parables" (Matt. 13:11; Mark 4:11; Luke 8:10; RSV "secret[s]). The parables to which this statement of Jesus is attached (especially the largest group at Matt. 13) show that "the mystery of the kingdom" is its coming in a concealed form. The disciples who ask for and receive the explanation of the parables learn about the hidden nature of the kingdom in its coming in Jesus' ministry, while for others, the parables remain misunderstood. *See* MESSIAH *II*; SECRET.

MYTH (Gk. *mýthos*).* The "myths" of the false teachings warned against in the Pastoral Epistles are mentioned in connection with speculative doctrines and "endless genealogies" (1 Tim. 1:4; cf. Tit. 3:9) and "commands of men who reject the truth" (1:14). Moreover, they are described as "godless and silly" (1 Tim. 4:7) and "Jewish" (Tit. 1:14). The picture of the false teachings that emerges from these and other passages in the Pastorals most clearly includes the combination of Jewish (1 Tim. 1:7; Tit. 1:10) and Gnostic-ascetic (1 Tim. 4:3; 6:20; 2 Tim. 2:18) elements. Such "myths" may be, like "genealogies," a term for Gnostic accounts of the aeons thought to exist between earth and the true God. "Myths" are also cited negatively at 2 Pet. 1:16 (KJV "fables"; NIV "stories"); not "cleverly devised myths" but eyewitness reports concerning Jesus were the basis for the preaching of the gospel. Here the gnostic preference for cosmological myths appears to be set in opposition to an insistence on revelation occurring in history.

In these New Testament uses of "myth" the term is used, as it commonly is today, to represent that which is assumed by the very use of the term to be not true, but which has been devised or developed to account for some state of affairs or to reinforce some system of belief or teaching. The term can also be used for that which, whether true or false, is nonessential to the teaching in connection with which it is found, possibly borrowed from the outside, and at any rate representative not of what is explicitly taught but of the very thought-world in which the teaching was originally expressed. With this definition, one can speak of mythic elements contained in the Bible, particularly the Old Testament, which may be expected in a collection of documents that is the total literary deposit of a people with a long history. Among such mythic elements are narratives concerning the origins of aspects of civilized existence (Gen. 4:17, 20-22), an account of the origin of distinctions among peoples (11:1-9), a reference to the mountain "in the far north" where the gods assembled (Isa. 14:13), and references to the monster(s) subdued at the time of creation (Job 26:12; Ps. 74:13-14; Isa. 51:9; cf. Hab. 3:8, 15). Along with these reflections of developed myths are simple figurative expressions that make use of mythical language, such as the voice of God for thunder (2 Sam. 22:14), the parallel of the earth and mother's womb (Job 1:21; Ps. 139:15), and the book of days (v. 16). These mythic elements can be closely paralleled in the literatures of other ancient Near Eastern peoples.

The distinction between mythic elements and essential content often becomes an important question for the interpreter. The worldview of the interpreter is itself a factor in interpretation, especially when the question arises whether particular mythic stories represent real events or not. For example, a person who lives within a worldview that excludes the possibility of demons might interpret the exorcisms performed by Jesus as portrayals in story form of Jesus' abstract power over evil in all its forms. But the interpreter has thereby proved neither the existence nor the nonexistence of demons of the sort believed in by the contemporaries of Jesus.

An important development in modern biblical studies has been the use of the concept of myth as a hermeneutical key; with this has come the concern with "demythologizing," a basic assumption of which is that the mythic elements in the Bible cannot be accepted by people living in a scientific age and therefore make incomprehensible or unacceptable the true message to which they are attached in the Bible. Myths must, therefore, be interpreted and presented in a new form receivable by modern mankind. The question arises, however, whether it is suitable to speak of the truth represented by, e.g., the virgin birth of Jesus, without also retaining the objectivity of the event itself. It is, furthermore, impossible to state the irreducible minimum of Christian teaching and, thereby, the limits of the demythologizing enterprise without subjectivity. Furthermore, the assumption that religious language is possible without the genres of myth, symbol, and story has been questioned.

NAAM [nāʹəm] (Heb. *naʿam*). A son of Caleb and grandson of Jephunneh in the tribal list of Judah (1 Chr. 4:15).

NAAMAH [nāʹə mə] (Heb. *naʿămâ* "pleasant") **(PERSON)**.

1. The daughter of Lamech and Zillah, and the sister of Tubal-cain in the lineage of Cain (Gen. 4:22).

2. The Ammonite woman who married Solomon and bore him Rehoboam (1 Kgs. 14:21, 31; 2 Chr. 12:13).

NAAMAH [nāʹə mə] (Heb. *naʿămâ* "pleasant") **(PLACE)**. A city in the Shephelah of Judah (Josh. 15:41). The name may be preserved in modern ʿArâq Naʿaman (an ʿarâq is a steep precipice) and Deir Naʿaman, but the actual site may be Khirbet Fered, situated on the Wâdî eṣ-Ṣarâr (Nahal Soreq) near TIMNAH **(1)**, 7 km. (4 mi.) northwest of Beth-shemesh.

NAAMAN [nāʹə mən] (Heb. *naʿămān* "pleasantness"; Gk. *Naiman*).

1. A Benjaminite who settled in Egypt (Gen. 46:21), also called a son of Bela (1 Chr. 8:3-4; cf. v. 7). He was the eponymous ancestor of the Naamites (Num. 26:40).

2. The leprous "commander of the army of the king of Syria" (2 Kgs. 5). Informed by an Israelite slave girl that his leprosy could be cured by the prophet Elisha in Samaria, Naaman embarked with gifts and a letter from the unspecified king of Syria. The king of Israel, identified by some scholars as Jehoram, tore his garments in despair, thinking that the Syrians were merely seeking an opportunity to invade. Elisha requested that the king send the Syrian to him, but then merely instructed Naaman through a messenger to immerse himself in the Jordan river seven times. Although he felt slighted, Naaman heeded his servants' pleas and complied with the prophet's directive, and his leprosy vanished.

The commander praised the God of Israel and, believing that he could only worship Yahweh on Israelite soil, requested two baskets of dirt to take back to Syria. Elisha himself refused compensation, but his servant Gehazi saw the opportunity for personal gain. Telling Naaman that the prophet had reconsidered, he took the Syrian's gifts for himself. For this infelicity Elisha cursed Gehazi and his descendants to be lepers forever.

Jesus recalled the incident as an example of God's care for a Gentile (Luke 4:27).

NAAMATHITE [nāʹə mə thīt] (Heb. *naʿămātî*). A gentilic attributed to Job's friend Zophar (Job 2:11; 11:1; 20:1; 42:9; cf. LXX "the Minean," "king of the Mineans"). It apparently derives from Naamah or Naameh, a city (or district) in northwest Arabia (possibly Jebel el-Naʿameh) or Edom.

NAAMITES [nāʹə mīts] (Heb. *naʿămî*). A clan of the Benjaminites, the descendants of NAAMAN (Num. 26:40).

NAARAH [nāʹə rə] (Heb. *naʿărâ* "girl") **(PERSON)**. One of the two wives of Ashhur, the father of Tekoa. She was the mother of Ahuzzam, Hepher, Temeni, and Haahashtari (1 Chr. 4:5-6).

NAARAH [nāʹə rə] (Heb. *naʿărâ* "girl") **(PLACE)**. A city on the boundary between Ephraim and Benjamin (Josh. 16:7; KJV "Naarath"). At 1 Chr. 7:28 it is called Naaran (Heb. *naʿărān*). It was called Naara by Josephus (*Ant.* xvii.13.1 [340]), Noaran during the New Testament period, and Noarath by Eusebius (*Onom.* cxxxvi.24), who locates it 8 km. (4.5 mi.) from Jericho. It has been identified variously as Khirbet el-ʿAyâsh near Wâdî el-ʿAujã; ʿAin Dûq, where an early synagogue has been found; and the nearby Tell el-Jisr, 6 km. (3.5 mi.) northwest of Jericho.

NAARAI [nāʹə rî] (Heb. *naʿăray,* "servant of Yahweh [?]"). The son of Ezbai; one of David's mighty men (1 Chr. 11:37). He may be the same as Paari the Arbite at 2 Sam. 23:35.

NAARAN [nāʹə răn] (Heb. *naʿărān*). Alternate form of NAARAH (1 Chr. 4:5-6; KJV, 7:28).

NAASHON (Exod. 6:23, KJV). *See* NAHSHON.

NAASSON (KJV). *See* NAHSHON.

NABAL [nā′bəl] (Heb. *nāḇāl* "fool"). A wealthy Calebite, a resident of Maon, who refused to grant David and his mercenary band compensation for their protection at the time of David's estrangement from Saul (1 Sam. 25). Encamped in the wilderness of Paran near Nabal's large flocks, David and his band not only refrained from helping themselves to the flock but apparently by their presence discouraged others from raiding (vv. 1-3, 7, 15-16, 21).

At festival time David dispatched messengers to ask Nabal for a gift of food, but the churlish Calebite adamantly refused, apparently pretending not to recognize the former commander of Israel's army whom he slandered as one of "many servants nowadays who are breaking away from their masters" (v. 10). In a society that placed high value on hospitality, such an action was completely inexcusable. David swore to avenge himself, and advanced with four hundred men toward Carmel, Nabal's place of business. Nabal's wife Abigail met him with generous gifts and asked David to forgive her husband, who had indeed lived up to his name (vv. 3, 17, 25).

When Abigail told Nabal, who was hosting a great banquet "like the feast of a king," what had transpired, he became so enraged that he suffered an apparent heart attack or stroke and died ten days later (vv. 36-38). David then took as wife Abigail, whom he credited for preventing his usurping the Lord's responsibility for vengeance (vv. 39-42; 2 Sam. 2:2; 3:3).

NABATEANS [năb′ətē′ənz] (Gk. *Nabataioi*).† An originally nomadic South Semitic people who settled in southeastern Transjordan in the fourth century B.C. Until the discovery of the Nabatean capital of Petra and its inscriptions early in the nineteenth century, little was known about them except for often inaccurate references from such ancient writers as Diodorus Siculus, Pliny the Elder, and Josephus. The earlier identification of the Nabateans with the Ishmaelite NEBAIOTH has been rejected on linguistic grounds.

Archaeological evidence from the region some 460 km. (285 mi.) southeast of Petra suggests that the Nabateans were originally from northwest Arabia. While the exact sequence of events remains a mystery, by the second century the Nabateans apparently had made the transition to sedentary life. They controlled Edomite and Moabite territories and the important international trade routes to Arabia, Egypt, Damascus, and beyond that passed through them. Consequently, the Nabateans became an important commercial power in the ancient Near East.

Their capital Petra ("the rock") is situated in the Wâdī Mûsā ("valley of Moses") some 80 km. (50 mi.) south of the Dead Sea. It can be reached only by ascending the wâdī and passing through the Siq, a narrow gorge. Here the Nabateans hewed magnificent tombs, temples, and dwellings from the red sandstone cliffs that protected their stronghold. They employed irrigation for agricultural purposes and mined copper from the former Edomite mines.

What is known of Nabatean history is set in the context of the Seleucid and Hasmonean dynasties and the Roman Empire. Shortly before the Jewish rebellion against the Seleucid king Antiochus IV Epipha-

nes, the Nabatean tyrant Aretas I held Jason captive after the latter unsuccessfully attempted to win the Jewish high priesthood by force (2 Macc. 5:8; cf. 1 Macc. 5:25; 9:35). Capitalizing on declining Seleucid power, the Nabateans strengthened their hand in northern Transjordan. Although Aretas II Erotimus and his successors opposed Alexander Janneus, Aretas III Philhellene did support Hyrcanus II against Aristobulus. The Herodian dynasty was of Nabatean origin, but Malichus I refused Herod the Great sanctuary *ca.* 40 B.C., and Malichus and his successors remained openly hostile to Herod. Aretas IV extended Nabatean influence to Damascus (cf. 2 Cor. 11:32), but the kingdom's power declined drastically under his successors. In A.D. 106 Trajan seized Nabatean territory and incorporated it into the province of Arabia.

Bibliography. G. W. Bowersock, *Roman Arabia* (Cambridge, Mass.: 1983); J. I. Lawler, *The Nabataeans in Historical Perspective* (Grand Rapids: 1974).

NABLUS [năb′lo͞os] (Arab. *Nablus*; from Gk. *Neapolis* "new city").† A city just west of Tell Balâṭah (biblical Shechem), founded by Vespasian in A.D. 72 as Flavius Neapolis, a settlement for Roman army veterans. Justin Martyr was born nearby *ca.* A.D. 100. The city is home to the modern Samaritan community.

NABONIDUS [năb′ō nī′dəs] (Akk. *Nabû-na'id* "Nabu is exalted").† The last king of the Chaldean dynasty and the last king of the Neo-Babylonian Empire (556-539 B.C.). He was probably born at Haran before 610, the son of Nabû-balātsu-iqbi, Assyrian-appointed governor of the district, and Adad-guppi, thought to be a priestess of the moon-god Sin.

Nabonidus' career apparently began in the service of Nebuchadnezzar, for whom he is believed to have negotiated treaties with the Medes and Libyans (cf. Herodotus *Hist.* i.74, 77, 188-191; Gk. *Labynētos*). He gained the throne in 556 through an apparent coup. Following military campaigns in Syria, Cilicia, and Arabia he turned his attention to restoring the temples of various deities throughout his realm. Shortly thereafter Nabonidus abandoned Babylon and established his capital at Tema (modern Teimā) in the middle of the Arabian peninsula, remaining there perhaps ten years (*ANET*, p. 562) and leaving Babylon in the control of his son Belshazzar (cf. Dan. 5); this move may have been based on political or commercial motives as well as conflict with the Marduk priesthood. Nabonidus returned to Babylon in 542 or 540 in a futile attempt to stave off the advancing Persian forces, but was captured (or perhaps killed) when Babylon fell to Cyrus without a battle in 539.

Several ancient texts document the reign of Nabonidus, including the so-called Nabonidus Chronicle (*ANET*, pp. 305-7), an account of his rise to power (pp. 308-11), a verse account of his relationship to the Babylonian priesthood (pp. 312-15), and inscriptions depicting his loyalty to the moon-god (pp. 562-63), as well as memorial inscriptions for his mother (pp. 311-12, 56-62). The Prayer of Nabonidus (4QPrNab), a fragmentary Aramaic text from Qumran, depicts the king's conversion from idolatry.

The antics of the mad "Nebuchadnezzar" at Dan. 4 may derive from a polemical tradition concerning Nabonidus' indifference toward Marduk and Babylon.

NABOTH [nā′bŏth] (Heb. *nāḇôṯ* "sprout [?]"). A Jezreelite who owned a vineyard located next to the palace of King Ahab. When Ahab wanted to buy the vineyard Naboth refused on the grounds that it was his family inheritance (Heb. *naḥ°lâ*; v. 3) and, as an inalienable trust from the ultimate landowner Yahweh, could not be sold under Israelite law (Lev. 25:23 cf. Num. 36:5-9). Queen Jezebel, who fostered Tyrian religion in Samaria and scorned such Yahwistic sensitivity, arranged for two men to falsely accuse Naboth of blasphemy. The people, believing the report, stoned him outside the city gate and left his body for the dogs to eat—thus allowing Ahab to take possession of the vineyard (1 Kgs. 21:8-16; cf. 2 Kgs. 9:26, which suggests that Naboth's sons and heirs were also eliminated).

Elijah prophesied to Ahab that because of his actions he and all his house would suffer the same fate as Naboth: they would die and be eaten by the beasts of the field (1 Kgs. 21:17-24; 2 Kgs. 9:26, 30-37).

NACHOR (2 Sam. 6:6, KJV). *See* NAHOR.

NACON [nā′kŏn] (Heb. *nāḵôn*). The owner of a threshing floor near Jerusalem where the ark of the covenant nearly fell from an ox cart (2 Sam. 6:6; KJV "Nachon," following LXX A; but cf. par. 1 Chr. 13:9, where the owner is called Chidon). The oxen stumbled, and when Uzziah tried to restrain it he was struck dead, for no one but a priest was permitted to touch the ark (even the Levites were only permitted to carry it by its poles; Num. 4:15; cf. Exod. 25:12-14). David called the place Perez-uzzah (Heb. *pereṣ ʿuzzâ* "the outbreak against Uzziah") because here the anger of the Lord "broke out" against Uzziah (2 Sam. 6:8; 1 Chr. 13:11).

NADAB [nā′dăb] (Heb. *nāḏāḇ* "generous"; Gk. *Nadab*).

1. The eldest of Aaron's four sons (Exod. 6:23; 28:1; Num. 3:2; 1 Chr. 6:3 [MT 5:29]) who with Moses, Aaron, his brother Abihu and seventy elders of Israel ratified the covenant with Yahweh at Sinai (Exod. 24:1-11). Later, after being ordained as a priest (Num. 3:2-3), he and his brother Abihu offered "unholy" (Heb. *'ēš zārâ*; KJV "strange") fire to Yahweh and subsequently died without offspring (Lev. 10:1-2; Num. 3:4; 26:61). Apparently the incense itself, consecrated to Yahweh and thus holy (*qōḏeš* "set apart," perhaps by extension "alien"; cf. Num. 16:37 [MT 17:2]), may not have been the problem, but rather the manner in which it was offered (Lev. 10:1; cf. v. 9).

2. King of Israel (901-900 B.C.); son and successor of Jeroboam I. Baasha of Issachar killed Nadab during the siege of Gibbethon and, upon assuming kingship, exterminated the rest of the house of Jeroboam, thus fulfilling the prophecy of Ahijah (1 Kgs. 14:20; 15:25-32; cf. 14:1-16).

3. A Judahite of the line of Jerahmeel, son of Shammai and father of Seled and Appaim (1 Chr. 2:28, 30).

4. A Benjaminite, son of Jeiel (**2**) and Maacah (1 Chr. 8:30; 9:36). He was the uncle of King Saul.

5. The nephew of Ahikar, and one of the guests at the wedding of Tobias (Tob. 11:17-19; KJV "Nasbas"). He is probably the Nadab mentioned by Tobias on his deathbed as having come to an untimely end (14:10; KJV "Aman'').

NADABATH [năd′ə băth] (Gk. *Nadabath*). A Transjordanian city, the home of the bride whose wedding procession was ambushed by Jonathan and Simon Maccabeus in retaliation for the Jambrite murder of their brother John (1 Macc. 9:37; KJV "Nadabatha"). It has been identified with both modern en-Nebâ (ancient Nebo), northwest of Medeba, and Khirbet et-Teim, 2 km. (1.2 mi.) south of Medeba.

NAG HAMMADI [näg həm mä′dē].† A site at the foot of the Jebel et-Tarif, across the Nile from the modern town of Nag Hammadi, in Upper Egypt where in 1946 was found a corpus of Christian and non-Christian Gnostic documents in the Coptic language. Discovery of these texts has increased significantly the number of primary documents available for the study of Gnosticism.

Twelve papyrus codices with leather covers are represented in widely varying states of preservation, and a few pages that were probably once bound in a thirteenth were found placed inside one of the codices. The codices were bound in the mid-fourth century A.D., but some of the tractates may have been translated from their Greek originals in the third century. The forty-five separate tractates, six represented by more than one version, are on 1153 extant pages or parts of pages, and consist of Gnostic Christian writings, Christian writings with no specifically Gnostic content, and writings with no specifically Christian content. They encompass a wide range of ideas and sources, and were apparently a library assembled for the use of a monastic community. Except for a small section of Plato's *Republic*, the composition of the tractates in Greek can be assigned to the second and third centuries A.D. The genres represented include

Nag Hammadi codex VII open to the first page (the beginning of the Paraphrase of Shem) (Photo by Jean Doresse, by courtesy of the Institute for Antiquity and Christianity, Claremont, California)

The seventieth page of Nag Hammadi Codex VII — the end of the Second Treatise of the Great Seth and the beginning of the Apocalypse of Peter (by courtesy of the Institute for Antiquity and Christianity, Claremont, California)

sayings collections, prayers, dialogues, speculative treatises, literary letters, apocalypses, and sermons. Though some of the tractates are designated "acts of apostles" and "gospels," they are not of the same genres as the canonical Gospels and Acts.

Before the Nag Hammadi discovery, only a few Gnostic writings were available, and studies of Gnosticism were more dependent on the reports in anti-heretical writings of Church Fathers. Only six of the Nag Hammadi tractates were known previously, two from the Berlin Gnostic Codex (Papyrus Berolinensis 8502), which though discovered in Egypt in 1896 was not published until 1955.

The discovery and availability of the Nag Hammadi codices have made possible a more distinct picture of the contrast between Christian Gnosticism and orthodox Christianity. The two developed from the same Christian beginnings, but with differing influences and solutions. The speculative, esoteric, and ascetic characteristics of the codices contrast to the conservatism, historical focus, practical, more "worldly" ethicism, and tendency toward institutionalism found in some of the New Testament and in patristic writings. The

codices have demonstrated that Gnostic as well as orthodox theologies were associated with the fourth-century Egyptian beginnings of Christian monasticism. A more liberal view of women's roles in the worshiping community is generally reflected in the codices, which suggests that attitudes toward women may have stimulated some of the division between the two forms of Christianity.

The diversity of Gnosticism is apparent in the codices, and the different ideas of some specific Gnostic groups and teachers have been somewhat clarified. The anti-Judaism that has usually been associated with Gnosticism is sometimes evident, but the codices have shown that the acceptance of Jewish elements was more possible in Gnosticism than previously thought. A closer relationship between apocalyptic thought and Gnosticism is also seen. The docetism of typical Gnosticism is represented, but non-docetic strains are also present. Moreover, the codices have made more certain the existence of non-Christian forms of Gnosticism.

The gospel of Thomas, the contents of which were previously known in part from some of the Oxyrynchus papyri, has become the best known of the Nag Hammadi tractates. It consists of 114 sayings of Jesus and has been particularly important for study of the history of the transmission of Jesus' sayings and the gnosticization of the tradition of those sayings.

See GNOSTICISM.

Bibliography. J. M. Robinson, ed. *The Nag Hammadi Library* (San Francisco: 1981); K. Rudolph, *Gnosis* (San Francisco: 1984).

NAGGAI [năg′ī] (Gk. *Naggai*). An otherwise unknown ancestor of Jesus (Luke 3:25; KJV "Nagge").

NAHALAL [nā′ə lăl] (Heb. *nahªlāl* "watering place [?]"). A levitical city in the tribal territory of Zebulun (Josh. 19:15; KJV "Nahallal"; 21:35) where the Israelites had failed to drive out the original inhabitants (Judg. 1:30, "Nahalol"; *nahªlōl*). Some scholars have identified the site as modern Tell en-Naḥl, located in a valley 11 km. (7 mi.) south of Acco. Others suggest a location in the vicinity of modern Nahalal, including Maʿlûl, 4 km. (2.5 mi.) northeast (cf. Talmud *b. Meg.* 77a), and Tell el-Beiḍā to the south.

NAHALIEL [nə hā′lī əl] (Heb. *nahªlîʿēl* "wâdī of El"). A place where Israel camped during the wilderness wanderings (Num. 21:19), between Mattanah and Bamoth. According to some scholars, the Wâdī Zerqā Māʿîn flowed through this valley to the Dead Sea 17 km. (10.5 mi.) north of the Arnon; others believe it to be the Wâdī Wâlā, a northern tributary of the Arnon river.

NAHAM [nā′hăm] (Heb. *naham* "comfort"). The sibling of Hodiah's wife (1 Chr. 4:19). The KJV incorrectly calls Hodiah the sister of Naham.

NAHAMANI [nā′ə mā′nī] (Heb. *nahªmānî*, from *nªhemyâ* "Yahweh has comforted"). One of the leaders of the Israelites who returned with Nehemiah from exile in Babylon (Neh. 7:7).

NAHARAI [nā′ə rī] (Heb. *nahªray*). One of David's mighty men and Joab's armor-bearer, whose hometown was Beeroth (2 Sam. 23:37; KJV "Nahari"; 1 Chr. 11:39).

NAHASH [nā′hăsh] (Heb. *nāḥāš* "serpent"; cf. Akk. *nuḥšu* "magnificence").

1. The king of Ammon during the reigns of Saul and David. Having besieged Jabesh-gilead, he was willing to conclude a treaty with its inhabitants only upon the condition that he gouge out every person's right eye. The city elders asked for a seven-day respite in hope that they could summon help. Confident of his ultimate victory and anxious to humiliate Israel, Nahash agreed. But Saul, as newly appointed king, was able to rally enough troops to defeat Nahash; the victory sealed Saul's claim to the throne (1 Sam. 11:1-11; 12:12).

David apparently had no such problems with Nahash. In fact, he sent a delegation to console Hanun, Nahash's son and successor, upon the death of his father. But Hanun treated them shamefully, and the incident led to war (2 Sam. 10:1-19; 1 Chr. 19:1-18). Another of Nahash's son's, Shobi, aided David when he fled from Absalom (2 Sam. 17:2-29).

2. An ancestor of Abigal (KJV "Abigail"), the mother of Absalom's new army commander, Amasa (2 Sam. 17:25). According to 1 Chr. 2:16, Zeruiah and Abigail were David's sisters, daughters of Jesse; scholars have suggested that Nahash is either the mother of Zeruiah and Abigail or a previous husband of Jesse's wife.

3. *See* IR-NAHASH.

NAHATH [nā′hăth] (Heb. *nahat* "descent, rest" or "pure, clear").

1. An Edomite chief, the son of Reuel (Gen. 36:13, 17; 1 Chr. 1:37; cf. LXX Gk. *Nachoth, Nachom, Nacheth, Naches, Nachōr*).

2. A Levite of the house of Kohath (1 Chr. 6:26 [MT 11]; LXX Gk. *Naath, Kainath*). He is thought to be the same as Toah (v. 34 [MT 19]) and Tohu (1 Sam. 1:1).

3. A Levite appointed by King Hezekiah to assist the chief officers of the temple in supervising the temple tithes (2 Chr. 31:13; LXX Gk. *Naeth, Maeth*).

NAHBI [nä′bī] (Heb. *naḥbî* "hidden [?]"). A Naphtalite, the son of Vophsi. He was one of the twelve spies Moses sent into Canaan (Num. 13:14).

NAHOR [nä′hôr] (Heb. *nāḥôr* "the angry one [?]"; Gk. *Nachōr*) (**PERSON**).

1. The father of Terah and grandfather of Abraham; a son of Serug of the line of Shem. He lived to be 148 years old (Gen. 11:22-25; cf. Josh. 24:2; Luke 3:34; KJV "Nachor").

2. One of three sons of Terah, and the brother of Abraham and Haran (Gen. 11:27). His wife was Milcah, daughter of Haran and sister of Lot (v. 29), and his concubine was Reumah (22:24); he fathered twelve children (vv. 20-24). Isaac's wife, Rebekah, was the daughter of Bethuel, the son of Nahor and Milcah (24:15), and Jacob's wives Rachel and Leah were also

descendants (granddaughters) of this Nahor (29:4-6; cf. 25:20).

NAHOR [nä′hôr] (Heb. *nāḥôr* "the angry one [?]"; Gk. *Nachōr*) (**PLACE**). A city in northwest Mesopotamia to which Abraham sent his servant to obtain a wife for Isaac (Gen. 24:10). The Mari letters mention a Naḥur situated east of the upper Baliḫ river near Haran.

NAHSHON [nä′shŏn] (Heb. *naḥšôn* "snake [?]"). A son of Amminadab and brother of Elisheba the wife of Aaron (Exod. 6:23; KJV "Naashon"). He represented Judah in assisting Moses with the first census (Num. 1:7) and led that tribe during the wilderness wanderings (2:3; 10:14; cf. 7:12, 17). He is reckoned among the ancestors of David (Ruth 4:20; 1 Chr. 2:10-11) and Jesus (Matt. 1:4; Luke 3:32; KJV "Naasson").

NAHUM [nā′həm, nā′hōōm] (Heb. *naḥûm* "comfort, compassion"; Gk. *Naoum*).

1. One of the twelve minor prophets, whose words are recorded in the book of Nahum. He was a native of Elkosh (Nah. 1:1), a village in southern Judah.

2. A son of Esli, listed among the ancestors of Jesus (Luke 3:25; KJV "Naum").

NAHUM, BOOK OF.† The seventh book of the twelve Minor Prophets.

I. Origins

Other than his place of origin, Elkosh, a town near the Philistine frontier of Judah (Nah. 1:1), little is known of the prophet Nahum, whose vision the book preserves. Primarily on the basis of v. 15 and the book's possible liturgical use, a number of scholars contend that Nahum was a cult prophet, but the book lacks references to Jerusalem or standard cultic concerns.

The prophecy has been dated, by most scholars, to the seventh century B.C. The reference at 3:8-10 to the fall of Thebes to the Assyrian Assurbanipal would place it after 663. The focus of the "vision" (1:1) is the destruction of Nineveh in 612 by Nabopolassar, founder of the Neo-Babylonian Empire. Those who view the prophecy as predictive date it shortly before, when the fall of Assyria was imminent, or even before the restoration of Thebes in 654, when Judah fully felt the threat of the brutal Assyrians and accordingly sought release or even retaliation; others place the book's composition in the years immediately following 612, or suggest that an earlier pronouncement was revised in terms of the actual events (cf. 2:6 [MT 7]). A few scholars interpret the events in the context of the Maccabean (Hellenistic) period (cf. the Dead Sea Nahum commentary [4QpNah], which interprets Nah. 2:11-13 [MT 12-14] in terms of Demetrius III and Antiochus IV Epiphanes).

II. Contents

Following the superscription (1:1), the "oracle" (Heb. *maśśā'*; KJV "burden") begins with an incomplete acrostic poem depicting the advance of Yahweh in theophany to wreak vengeance upon his enemies (vv.

2-8). Each line begins with the successive letter of the Hebrew alphabet, aleph through kaph; largely through emendation, some scholars have attempted to extend the acrostic through nun (v. 9), samech (v. 10), or even the entire alphabet (2:3-4). The following section (1:9–2:2 [MT 3]) alternates words of condemnation upon Assyria (1:9-11, 14; 2:1 [MT 2]) and hope to Judah (1:12-13, 15 [MT 2:1]; 2:2 [MT 3]).

As a unit, chs. 2–3 may be considered a taunt song against Assyria. Nah. 2:3-12 (MT 4-13) is comprised of two poems proclaiming the defeat of Nineveh. Vv. 3-9 (MT 4-10) graphically depict the forces of Yahweh, the divine warrior, breaking into and plundering the city; other ancient accounts corroborate the miraculous flooding of the Tigris river that coincided with and aided the attack (vv. 6-8 [MT 7-9]). Vv. 10-12 (MT 11-13) describe the desolation of Nineveh, the lair of the predatory lion; the figure continues in v. 13 (MT 14), a prose oracle pronouncing the judgment of the Lord of hosts against the city. Ch. 3 begins with an oracle of woe (Heb. *hôy*) against the "bloody city" (v. 1-7), portrayed as a harlot whom Yahweh and then the nations will treat with contempt. Nineveh's fate is that of Thebes, whom the Assyrians themselves had sacked (vv. 8-9); the populace will suffer brutality akin to that for which Assyria was notorious—captivity and carnage (vv. 10-13). The prophet sarcastically enjoins the Assyrians to prepare for the siege by which they will be destroyed (vv. 14-17). All who hear of Nineveh's fate rejoice (vv. 18-19).

III. Theology

The theme that pervades Nahum's prophecy is the absolute sovereignty of Yahweh, here expressed in terms of his announced (and executed) judgment upon the Assyrian Empire, a powerful and loathsome force in the lives of his chosen people. As in other collections of "oracles against foreign nations" (e.g., Isa. 13–21; Jer. 46–51; Ezek. 25–32), the prophet proclaims the supremacy of Israel's God over the history and gods of Israel's enemies (e.g., 1:2-8). Some scholars contend that the book was composed as a liturgy for the annual New Year festival, thus celebrating Yahweh's sovereignty over the nations.

The overarching concern for God's exercising vengeance upon Assyria (e.g., 2:13 [MT 14]–3:5)—an embarrassment for many interpreters—actually underscores his role as the universal judge. Although "slow to anger," the Lord can "by no means clear the guilty" (1:3). The message is one of hope to Judah, who had known firsthand the Assyrians' "unceasing evil" (3:19). God speaks comfort (cf. Heb. *naham*) through Nahum to his longsuffering but discouraged people to maintain faith (cf. 1:15 [MT 2:1]), for they would be afflicted by Assyria no more (vv. 12-13).

Uniquely, the book lacks any direct challenge to the moral or spiritual character of Judah, perhaps because of Josiah's recent reforms (*ca.* 622/621).

Bibliography. R. J. Coggins and S. P. Re'emi, *Israel Among the Nations.* ITC (1985), pp. 1-63; W. A. Maier, *The Book of Nahum* (St. Louis: 1959); J. D. W. Watts, *The Books of Joel, Obadiah, Jonah, Nahum, Habakkuk and Zephaniah.* CBC (1975).

NAIN [nān] (Gk. *Nain*; perhaps from Heb. *nāʿîm*

"lovely, pleasant"). A city in Galilee where Jesus raised from the dead a widow's only son (Luke 7:11-17). The site is modern Nein, a small village on the slopes of Mt. Moreh (modern Jebel ed-Dahi), 9 km. (5.5 mi.) southeast of Nazareth. It overlooks the beautiful plain of Esdraelon, perhaps the reason it was named "lovely" (*Gen. Rab.* xc111.12).

NAIOTH [nā′ ŏth] (Heb. Q *nāyôṯ*, K *nāwyôṯ* "dwellings"). The place in Ramah to which David went when he fled from Saul (1 Sam. 19:18-24). A company of prophets lived there, headed by Samuel. When Saul sent messengers to seize David, three times they prophesied instead of returning with him. Finally, Saul himself went in person, but he too stripped off his clothing and prophesied. The story spread throughout Israel and became a heavily ironic saying "Is Saul also among the prophets?" (v. 24).

Since Naioth is mentioned only here—in connection with a group of prophets—scholars have argued that Naioth was actually a designation for a prophetic community rather than a separate city. The Targums translate the name as "house of instruction."

NAKEDNESS (Heb. *ʿerwâ*; Gk. *gymnótēs*).† A term used in the Bible to indicate various stages of undress, from being inappropriately clad to being totally nude.

The naked body was taboo in Hebrew society, perhaps in part because the bodily fluids were considered unclean (e.g., semen; Lev. 15:2-18; blood from either the menstrual cycle [vv. 19-24] or a consistent discharge [vv. 25-30]; even spittle under certain circumstances; v. 8). Clothing confined the fluids and prevented them from contaminating public areas.

In Hebrew usage "nakedness" is often an euphemism for sexual relations (e.g., the prohibitions at Lev. 18; cf. Ezek. 16:8, "covered your nakedness"). This usage helps explain the incident at Gen. 9:20-27, where Ham apparently took advantage of his father's drunken state and had sexual relations with him (vv. 21-22; Heb. *ʿerwaṯ ʾābîw*; RSV "saw the nakedness of his father"). Noah's curse of Ham's son Canaan, rather than Ham, may allude to the sexual practices of the Canaanites who used male cult prostitutes.

Public nakedness was normally considered an occasion for shame—a characteristic of the prostitute or the adulteress (1 Sam. 20:30; Rev. 17:16). The prophets often used the image of the lascivious, naked prostitute as a visual symbol of Israel's apostasy (Ezek. 16:15-43; ch. 23; Hos. 2:1-13 [MT 1:10–2:11]). But nakedness might also be a result of extreme poverty (Deut. 28:48; [figuratively] Rev. 3:17-18) and therefore an opportunity for good works (Ezek. 18:7, 16; Matt. 25:36-44; cf. Jas. 2:15-16). Paul says that the apostles were often in such extreme circumstances (1 Cor. 4:11; 2 Cor. 11:27; RSV "ill-clad"; KJV "naked"; cf. John 21:7).

Nakedness was forbidden in Israelite religious ceremonies, largely because of its association with Canaanite rites (cf. Lev. 20:23). The priests wore linen garments to cover themselves (Exod. 28:42), and altars were to be built without steps lest the priests' nakedness be exposed to the crowd below (20:26). Yet while Moses was on the mountaintop receiving the commandments, Aaron under the people's influence had made a calf before which the people danced naked (32:25, KJV; RSV "break loose"). Saul lay naked all night and prophesied ecstatically (1 Sam. 19:24), while Isaiah had to walk naked for three years as a visual prophecy of doom against Egypt (Isa. 20:2-4). David, wearing a linen ephod, danced so enthusiastically before the returning ark that he became "uncovered" (*niglâ*; 2 Sam. 6:20).

Generally neither the Hebrew nor the Greek terminology is specific enough to distinguish between various stages of undress. Yet three of the four Gospel accounts of the crucifixion record that the soldiers who crucified Christ divided his garments (pl.) between them (Matt. 27:35; Mark 15:24; John 19:23). Judging from historical parallels, it seems probable that Jesus was completely naked, not partially clothed as in most modern portrayals; some interpreters view this as the "shame" of the cross (Heb. 12:2).

In some instances, however, nakedness characterized the innocence and dependence of birth (Job 1:21; Eccl. 5:15; cf. Ezek. 16:7, 22 [MT 6, 23]). Adam and Eve were naked and unashamed in the garden of Eden before the fall, a state of "innocence" (Gen. 2:25); having eaten from the tree, they became aware of their nakedness and covered themselves (3:7).

NAME (Heb. *šēm*; Gk. *ónoma*).† The designation of a person or place. Names carry more value and importance in biblical than in modern usage. Not only may a name identify, but it frequently expresses the essential nature of its bearer; to know the name is to know the person (cf. Ps. 9:10 [MT 11]).

I. Naming Practices

Hebrew names are classified by syntax as either simple, with one element, or compound, with two or three elements in a phrase or sentence. Compound names customarily include either a kinship or divine (theophoric) name. Kinship elements include Heb. *'āḇ* "father, ancestor" (e.g., Abimelech), *'āḥ* "brother" (e.g., Ahihud), *bēn* "son" (e.g., Benjamin), *baṯ* "daughter" (e.g., Bathsheba), and *'am* "kinsman" (e.g., Ammiel). Theophoric names contain either the common Semitic word for God, El (e.g., Ezekiel, Eliezer), or an abbreviated form of Yahweh, such as *yô*, *yᵉhô* (e.g., Jehonathan, Joel) or *yāhû, yāh* (e.g., Adonijah, Shemaiah).

Among the Israelites names were customarily given at birth. Normally the mother would give the name, but the father held the final say (cf. Gen. 35:18; Luke 1:60). Occasionally others could also provide the name (Exod. 2:10; Ruth 4:17; 2 Sam. 12:25). In New Testament times boys received their names at circumcision on the eighth day after birth (Luke 1:59-60; 2:21).

Names were chosen for various reasons, such as to express religious convictions or hopes or some to describe a physical characteristic or some circumstance of birth. Many represent a creedal statement (e.g., Uzziah, "Yahweh is my trust"), express gratitude or a similar emotion (e.g., Saul, "asked [of God]"; Elishama, "God has heard"; Joshua/Jesus, "Yahweh will save"), or function as prophecy (cf. Isa. 8:3-4; Hos. 1:4-11 [MT 2:2]). Other names derive from national, familial, seasonal, or physical circumstances (e.g., Ichabod, "the glory has departed"; Becher, "first-

born"; Haggai, "festal [i.e., born at feast time]"; Laban, "white") or from nature (e.g., Jonah, "dove"; Deborah, "bee"; Hadassah, "myrtle"). Some names are apparently abbreviations (e.g., Ahaz for Jehoahaz, Jonathan for Jehonathan).

Occasionally the biblical account provides an explanation for a name. Not strictly an etymology, this may represent a wordplay alluding to the bearer's character (Jacob; Gen. 27:36), circumstance (Isaac; 17:17), history (Noah; 5:29), or prophecy (Hos. 1:9). Such wordplays are built on a shared root (e.g., Seth and *šîṯ* "put, set"; Gen. 4:25), a cognate root (Cain [*qayin*] and *qānâ* "obtain"; 4:1), assonance (Babel and *bālal* "confuse"; 11:9), or meaning (Zerah, "scarlet"; 38:30).

In postexilic times children were often named after an illustrious person. In priestly and dynastic (royal) circles especially, papponymy was practiced, wherein the child was named after a grandparent (e.g., Johanan, Tobiah/s). Foreign influence was also apparent in this period (e.g., Esther).

In New Testament times double names were common, including a formal Greek or Roman name (the cognomen) and a familiar Semitic name (the signum) used with one's intimates (e.g., Saul/Paul; Acts 13:9; John Mark; 12:12). Some names are translations (e.g., Theodotus for Mattaniah, "gift of Yahweh") or transliterations (Jesus for Joshua).

II. Significance

In the Bible, as throughout the Semitic world, a name carries significance beyond that of its meaning or its use as a title. Because of the vitality ascribed to words, a name signifies first and foremost existence. Everything and everyone has a name (Eccl. 6:10), and the very naming brings them into being (Isa. 40:26; cf. Gen. 2:19). The name represents the person (Num. 1:2; cf. Acts 1:15, KJV; RSV "persons") and the personality (e.g., Nabal, "fool"; 1 Sam. 25:25). Because a name is a social reality, kept by memory and through posterity (cf. Ps. 72:17), to cut off a person's name means not only death but the very obliteration of one's existence (e.g., 1 Sam. 24:21 [MT 22]; Ps. 9:5 [MT 6]; 109:13). See WORD.

The name conveys the authority of the person even when absent. To speak or act in another's name is to participate in that person's authority (1 Sam. 17:45; 25:9; Acts 4:7). The principle is that of prophecy and revelation (Exod. 3:13-14; Deut. 18:19; John 5:43). God's name reveals his character and salvation in which people may take refuge (Ps. 20:1 [MT 2]; cf. Isa. 25:1; 56:6); to treat God's name as empty is to despise his person (Exod. 20:7). Similarly, to act in the name of Christ is to participate in his authority (Acts 3:6; 1 Cor. 5:4; 2 Thess. 3:6; Jas. 5:14) as well as to share in his contempt (Luke 21:12-19; Acts 5:41). Elsewhere the name of Christ stands for the whole of his salvation (4:7; 1 Cor. 6:11).

By extension, a person's character is his name, whether for good (Prov. 22:1; Eccl. 7:1) or ill (Job 30:8; *bᵉlî-šēm*; NIV "nameless"; RSV "disreputable"). It is the equivalent of fame or renown (Gen. 11:4; 1 Sam. 18:30).

To bestow a name is an act of authority, denoting possession, responsibility, and protection for some person or object (2 Sam. 12:28; Ps. 49:11; Isa. 4:1).

The naming of creation is thus an exercise of dominion, part of the "image of God" (Gen. 2:19-20; cf. 1:28). Changes of name confer new status, either greater or lesser (32:28; 2 Kgs. 24:17). Similarly, baptism into (Gk. *eis*) Christ's name signifies a new status, from death into life (Rom. 6:2ff.), and a new Lord (1 Cor. 1:2). Believers are not given a new name, but bear Christ's name (Acts 11:26; 1 Pet. 4:16; Rev. 14:1); their names are known by God (13:8).

Bibliography. H. Bietenhard, "ὄνομα," *TDNT* 5 (1967): 242-283.

NANEA [nə nē′ə] (Gk. *Nanaia*). A Syrian deity, presumably identified with the Sumerian love and fertility goddess Inanna (Babylonian Ishtar, Phoenician Ashtoreth), Greek Artemis, Persian Ardi Sura Anahita, and Roman Venus.

According to 2 Macc. 1:13-17, the priests of Nanea's temple in Persia deceived and murdered Antiochus, who sought to plunder the temple treasure as "dowry" for his marriage with the goddess. Apparently the practice was related to the annual New Year marriage of Inanna and Dumuzi, ritually celebrated by the Sumerian king and priestess of Inanna as a guarantee of fertility in the upcoming year. If this account refers to the same incident as 1 Macc. 6:1-16, the treasure included the golden arms and shields of Alexander the Great. The latter account may concern Antiochus III the Great, who died at the temple of Bilus in Elymea, while according to some scholars the narrative at 2 Macc. 1 involves Antiochus VII Sidetes, who died at the hands of the Parthians in 129 B.C. (reading "Persis" at v. 13, a reference to territory controlled by the Parthians; Heb. *pāras*). The author of 2 Maccabees may actually have in mind Antiochus IV Epiphanes, here punished for his desecration of the temple at Jerusalem.

NAOMI [nā ō′mĭ] (Heb. *noʿomî* "my joy, my pleasant one"). The wife of Elimelech, and the mother of Mahlon and Chilion; an important figure in the book of Ruth.

At some point during the period of the judges, Judah was struck by famine, and Elimelech and Naomi left Bethlehem for eastern Moab in order to provide for the family's physical needs (Ruth 1:1-2). Sometime thereafter Elimelech died, and then their two sons. The widow was left with only two Moabite daughters-in-law, Orphah and Ruth (vv. 4-5). After ten years of hardship (cf. her new name Mara, "bitter"; vv. 19-21), Naomi learned that the famine had ended, and she decided to return to Bethlehem. Though she was able to persuade Orphah to return to the house of her father, Ruth refused, returning instead with Naomi to Bethlehem (vv. 6-18).

Naomi's daughter-in-law initially supported the two of them by gleaning in the barley fields of Boaz (2:1-23). But Naomi convinced Ruth to approach Boaz, a relative of Elimelech, as next of kin and a potential redeemer for the family's property (3:1-4). Moreover, their son Obed preserved Elimelech's family line (4:13-17).

NAPHATH [nā′făth] (Heb. *nāpet* "heights").† Apparently an alternate designation for Dor, distinguish-

ing it from En-dor at Josh. 17:11. The Hebrew text is obscure.

NAPHATH-DOR [nā′făth dôr′] (Heb. *nāpat dôr, nāpôt dôr, nāpat dōʾr* "hills" or "heights of Dor"). Probably a region of low narrow hills that border the Palestine coast from Joppa to the north; the fortified port city of Dor seems to have been its capital. A coalition of Canaanite kings, including the king of Naphath-dor, was defeated by Joshua (Josh. 11:2, "Naphoth-dor"; KJV "borders of Dor"; 12:23; KJV "coast of Dor"). Later the region became one of Solomon's administrative districts (1 Kgs. 4:11; KJV "region of Dor"). See Dor.

NAPHISH [nā′fĭsh] (Heb. *āpîš*). A son of Ishmael (Gen. 25:15). His descendants were an Arabian tribe that fought the Reubenites and Gadites (1 Chr. 5:19; KJV "Nephish").

NAPHOTH-DOR [nā′fŏth dôr′] (Heb. *nāpôt dôr*). Alternate form of NAPHATH-DOR (Josh. 11:2; KJV "borders of Dor").

NAPHTALI [năf′tə lē] (Heb. *naptālî* "wrestler").† The sixth son of Jacob, and his second son by Bilhah, Rachel's maid (Gen. 30:7-8); father of Jahzeel, Guni, Jezer, and Shillem (46:24). Jacob's blessing ("a hind let loose..."; EB "a spreading terebinth") alludes to the beauty and fruitfulness that his descendants, the tribe of Naphtali, would enjoy (49:21).

During the wilderness wanderings the people of Naphtali marched with the tribe of Asher under the standard of Dan to comprise Israel's rear guard, and camped north of the tabernacle (Num. 2:25-31). Moses' first census counted 53,400 men capable of bearing arms (1:43); another census at the end of the wanderings numbered 45,400 soldiers (26:50).

Naphtali's patrimony lay in the north of Canaan. The Song of Moses (Deut. 33:23) tells of its abundance ("full of the blessing of the Lord") and describes its location as "the lake (i.e., Chinnereth) and the south," although the latter point is unclear (cf. NIV). After Israel's initial victories, Naphtali received territory bounded on the east by the upper Jordan river and Lake Chinnereth, on the south by the territories of Issachar and Zebulun, and on the west by Asher (Josh. 19:32-34). A fertile region with abundant springs, it included nineteen walled cities (vv. 35-38), including Hazor (cf. 11:1), the city of refuge Kedesh (20:7, "Kedesh in Galilee in the hill country of Naphtali"; KJV "... mount Naphtali"), and two levitical cities (21:6, 32). Under Solomon the region became an administrative district (1 Kgs. 4:15). Later the name Naphtali apparently designates the whole of northern Israel, captured by the Assyrian Tiglath-pileser III *ca.* 733-732 B.C. (2 Kgs. 15:29; cf. 1 Macc. 5:15; Matt. 4:12-16).

While the defeat and sack of Hazor enabled Naphtali to enter the land (Josh. 11:1-15), the tribe was unable to drive the Canaanites from the fortified cities of Beth-shemesh and Beth-anath, settling instead for assimilation and eventually political control (Judg. 1:33). When Sisera and resurgent Canaanite forces threatened Israel, Naphtali followed Barak of Kedesh into battle and subsequently victory, gaining fame for their valor (4:6, 10; 5:18). Later the tribe also rallied to Gideon to repel the Midianites (6:35; 7:23). Naphtali sent a thousand officers, thirty-seven thousand troops, and abundant provisions to David at Hebron (1 Chr. 12:33, 40 [MT 34, 41]). Despite their might, Naphtali's position in the north proved precarious. The Syrians under Ben-hadad ravaged the land during the reign of Baasha (*ca.* 885; 1 Kgs. 15:20). Then during the reign of Pekah, Tiglath-pileser annexed the territory and sent the people into captivity, the first province west of the Jordan to fall to Assyria (2 Kgs. 15:29).

For the people of Naphtali, who suffered the gloom of exile, Isaiah prophesied that they would see the light of salvation (Isa. 9:1-2 [MT 8:23–9:1]), fulfilled in Jesus' public ministry in Galilee (Matt. 4:12-16). The tribe is also listed among the 144,000 sealed for salvation (Rev. 7:6), a figure for the full number of the faithful.

NAPHTHA [năf′tə] (Gk. *náphtha*). An inflammable substance (Sg.Three 23), an ancient name for petroleum. It is described as a "thick liquid" that caught fire after the sun shone on it (2 Macc. 1:20-22). The term is linked with "purification" through a strained derivation from Heb. *niptār* (1:36, "nephthar"; KJV "naphthar"; cf. Num. 31:23).

NAPHTUHIM [năf′tə hĭm] (Heb. *naptuḥîm*). A descendant of Egypt (Mizraim) listed in the Table of Nations (Gen. 10:13 par. 1 Chr. 1:11). Some scholars believe them to be the inhabitants of the Nile Delta (cf. Egyp. *na-patoḥ* "dwellers of the Delta").

NARCISSUS [när sĭs′əs] (Gk. *Narkissos*). The head of a household in Rome in which some of the members were Christians. They are greeted by Paul at the end of his epistle to the Romans (Rom. 16:11).

NARD [närd] (Heb. *nērd, nᵉrādîm*; Gk. *nárdos*). An expensive ointment prepared from the roots and stems of the *Nardostachys jatamansi* Wall., a plant belonging to the family of the Valerianaceae. The plant, native to the Himalaya mountains in India, has several vertical stems with lanceolate leaves and clusters of reddish-purple flowers. At Cant. 1:12; 4:13-14 (KJV "spikenard") the ointment is mentioned with myrrh, frankincense, cinnamon, and other aromatic herbs. Jesus was anointed with nard while he ate at the house of Simon the leper (Mark 14:3) and at that of Lazarus in Bethany (John 12:3); here a small flask of the pure ointment (Gk. *nárdos pistikós*) is valued at more than 300 denarii—about the annual salary of a day laborer.

NASH PAPYRUS. A Hebrew papyrus dating to the Maccabean period (first or second century B.C.), until the discovery of the Dead Sea Scrolls the earliest witness to the Hebrew text of the Old Testament. The twenty-four line text contains the Decalogue (following primarily Exod. 20:2-7 but with some preference for Deut. 5:6-21; the sixth and seventh commandments are in reversed order) and the Shema (6:4-5). The document is named after W. L. Nash, who obtained it in Egypt in 1902; it is presently in the Cambridge University Library.

NATHAN [nā′thən] (Heb. *nāṯān* "gift"; Gk. *Nathan*).

1. A prophet and historian of the Davidic and Solomonic courts (2 Sam. 7, 11; 1 Kgs. 1; 1 Chr. 29:29; 2 Chr. 9:29).

When David first announced his plan to build the temple, Nathan approved wholeheartedly. Later however, the prophet communicated a word from the Lord that the temple would not be built by David but by his son and successor. The same prophecy promised that David's dynasty would endure forever (2 Sam. 7).

David committed adultery with Bathsheba and then had her husband, the Hittite Uriah, murdered (ch. 11). Nathan approached the king with a hypothetical case wherein a rich man robs a poor man of his only lamb. When King David ordered that the man be put to death, Nathan identified David himself as the man. The king repented of his actions, but the first son of that union died shortly after birth (12:1-23).

When David lay on his deathbed, his son Adonijah plotted to become king. Nathan and Bathsheba interceded in behalf of Solomon; Nathan urged Bathsheba to remind the ailing king of his promise to Solomon and to inform him of Adonijah's actions. The plan worked, and David declared Solomon his successor (1 Kgs. 1).

Nathan and Gad, another of David's court prophets, communicated Yahweh's word concerning the placement of the levitical singers and musicians (2 Chr. 29:25). Nathan also compiled a history of the reigns of David and Solomon (9:29), but it is possible that the prophet died before Solomon and so did not complete the history.

2. The father of Igal of Zobah, one of David's mighty men (2 Sam. 23:36). He may be the brother of Joel, another of the mighty men (1 Chr. 11:38).

3. The father of Azariah, commander of the army officers, and of Zabud, the priest and "friend of the king" (1 Kgs. 4:5). He may be the same as either 1 or 5.

4. A Judahite of the line of Jerahmeel; the son of Attai and father of Zabad (1 Chr. 2:36). He may be the same as 1.

5. One of the four sons of Bathsheba (Bath-shua) born to David in Jerusalem (1 Chr. 3:5; cf. 2 Sam. 5:14; 1 Chr. 14:4; Zech. 12:12). He is named among the ancestors of Jesus at Luke 3:31.

6. One of the "leading men" whom Ezra sent to Iddo at Casiphia to ask the Levites to return to Jerusalem (Ezra 8:15-17). He is probably to be identified with the son of Binnui (or Bani; cf. RSV mg.) who was forced to divorce his foreign wife (10:39).

NATHANAEL [nə thăn′ĭ əl] (Gk. *Nathanaēl*; from Heb. *nᵉtan'ēl* "God has given").

1. A priest ordered to divorce his non-Israelite wife (1 Esdr. 9:22).

2. An ancestor of Judith (Jdt. 8:1).

3. An Israelite of Cana, according to Jesus "in whom is no guile" (John 1:47). Nathanael is first introduced to Jesus by Philip (vv. 45-46). When Jesus remarks that he had already seen the man under a fig tree before the apostle called him, Nathanael acknowledges Jesus as the Son of God and King of Israel (vv. 48-51)

Nathanael also appears in the company of Peter and

several other disciples when Jesus revealed himself as they were fishing on the Sea of Tiberias after his death and resurrection.

Scholars have speculated that Nathanael may be found in the Synoptic Gospels under another name. He has been variously identified as Matthew, John the son of Zebedee, Simon the Canaanean, James the son of Alphaeus or (most often) Bartholomew.

NATHAN-MELECH [nā'thən mē'lĭk] (Heb. *nᵉtan-melek* "the king has given"). A chamberlain during the reign of Josiah (2 Kgs. 23:11). The name may refer to Molech or the Ammonite deity Milcom. Josiah removed the horses dedicated to the sun-god Šamaš, which were quartered near the chambers of Nathan-melech. Though his chamber could have been in the temple dedicated to the sun-god, the phrase in the "precincts" (Heb. *parôrîm*; cf. parbār at 1 Chr. 26:18; NIV "court"; NJV "colonnade") suggests that the location was probably in the temple of Solomon.

NATIONS (Heb. *gôyim*, *'ammîm*; Gk. *éthnē*).† Specific cohesive groups of people, generally bonded by political or geographical considerations. In the ancient world the history and relationships of nations frequently are expressed through genealogies; such reckonings often reflect ethnic and linguistic factors as well (cf. the Table of Nations, Gen. 10). The Hebrew and Greek terms are generally rendered "Gentiles" when specifying non-Jews and "nations" when all peoples are designated. *See* TABLE OF NATIONS.

Yahweh is the Lord and Judge of all nations, not merely Israel (e.g., Ps. 22:28 [MT 29]; Isa. 2:4; 34:1-2; Jer. 1:10). God chose Abraham for two purposes: to make of him a great nation and to make his descendants a blessing to all other nations (Gen. 12:1-3; 18:18). The divine purpose behind the Exodus was to fulfill the promise to Abraham, and to make of Israel an instrument by which to bless the nations; Israel was to be a special, elect nation whose purpose was, in part, to declare the name and will of Yahweh to all other nations: to be a kingdom of priests (Exod. 19:3-6; Deut. 4:5-8; 1 Kgs. 8:60; Ps. 67; Isa. 9:3 [MT 2]), "a covenant to the people, a light to the nations" (42:6). Israel failed in this task and thus was scattered among the nations (Deut. 4:27; Amos 9:9). Israel was also to be an instrument of destruction and judgment upon the nations living in Palestine (cf. Exod. 34:24; Deut. 4:38).

In the New Testament Jesus becomes the "light for revelation to the Gentiles" (Luke 2:32). His ministry was primarily to Israel but also included non-Jews (e.g., Mark 7:24-30); his death was not merely for Jews but for all nations (John 11:50-52). He sent his disciples into all the earth, to preach the good news and make disciples of all nations (Matt. 24:14; 28:19; cf. Acts 1:8). A common theme in Revelation is that at the end of the present age people from "every tribe and tongue and people and nation" will participate in the kingdom of God and share in the praise of Christ (e.g., Rev. 5:9-10).

See GENTILES.

NAUM (Luke 3:25, KJV). *See* NAHUM 2.

NAVE [nāv].*
1. (Heb. *hêkal*). The main room of the temple, between the vestibule (KJV "porch") and the holy of holies (1 Kgs. 6 *passim*; 7:50; 2 Chr. 3:4-5, 13; KJV "(greater) house"; 4:22; Ezek. 41 *passim*). The Hebrew term can refer to either this room or the entire temple (cf. Sum. *e-gal* "great house").
2. (Heb. *gab*). Probably the hub of a wheel (KJV, 1 Kgs. 7:33; RSV "rim").

NAZARENE [năz'ə rēn] (Gk. *Nazarēnos, Nazōraios*). A gentilic ascribed to Jesus (Matt. 2:23; Mark 14:67) and once, by extension, to his followers (Acts 24:5). Even though the term Nazarene occurs only three times in most English versions, the Greek form occurs in all four Gospels (Gk. *Nazōraios*, Matt. 26:71; Luke 18:37; John 18:5, 7; 19:19; *Nazarēnos*, Mark 1:24; 10:47; 16:6; Luke 4:34; 24:19), translated "of Nazareth."

The derivation of the term, complicated by the different spellings, is variously disputed. Some scholars derive the term from Nazareth (Gk. *Nazara, Nazarat[h], Nazaret, Nazareth*), the town in which Jesus grew up. Matthew explicitly states that Jesus "went and dwelt in a city called Nazareth, that what was spoken by the prophets might be fulfilled, 'He shall be called a Nazarene'" (Matt. 2:23). But *Nazōraios* is not easily explained as a derivation of the place name (although some argue that a derivation from Aram. *nāṣᵉrāyā* is possible). More importantly, the gentilic may not be more than a play on Isaiah's prophecy that "there shall come forth a shoot from the stump of Jesse, and a branch (Heb. *nēṣer*) shall grow out of his roots" (Isa. 11:1).

Nazarene does appear to be closely linked to the term Nazirite (Heb. *nāzîr*; Gk. *nazeiraíos*). Accordingly, some scholars suggest that the source of Matthew's prophecy was actually Judg. 13:3-7. But Jesus is never referred to in the New Testament as a Nazirite. No specific reference is made to his hair being cut, but he did touch at least one dead body (Matt. 9:18-25) and drink wine (26:26-29; Luke 7:34)—both of which are prohibited by the Nazirite vow. So while the attempt to link Nazarene to Nazirite is etymologically possible, it is denied by the actions of Jesus, "the Nazarene."

Finally, some scholars trace the term to a supposedly pre-Christian cult, citing Acts 24:5, which refers to a "sect of Nazarenes," and a puzzling fourth-century reference to a cult of *Nasaraioi* (Epiphanius *Haer.* i.18; xxix.6). The twelfth section of the Palestinian recension of the Eighteen Benedictions, used at the close of the synagogue service, also apparently cursed "the Nazarenes"—and was directed against Jewish Christians. Some early Christian groups also labeled themselves "Nazarenes," despite the once derogatory connotation (cf. John 1:46). No evidence survives, however, that this group existed before the birth of Jesus, and it cannot therefore account for the source of the term with regard to him.

In summary, there is no unassailable explanation of the term Nazarene. The New Testament authors obviously linked it to Jesus' hometown, Nazareth. That the term carried a more powerful connotation cannot be doubted, but what that connotation was remains in doubt.

NAZARENES, GOSPEL OF.* A targum, or paraphrastic translation, of the canonical gospel of Matthew. This Jewish-Christian gospel has been confused with the gospel of the Hebrews and also mistakenly identified as the Hebrew original of Matthew. Scholars now believe it to be simply a translation of the Greek canonical Matthew into Aramaic. Jerome's unwarranted claims to having translated for the first time a "Gospel According to the Hebrews" and his many citations from Apollinaris contributed to the development of a general confusion regarding this targum, the canonical Matthew, and another Jewish-Christian Gospel According to the Hebrews.

This Aramaic translation must, of course, be dated subsequent to the canonical Matthew from which it is taken. It must also have been completed by the time of Hegesippus (A.D. 180), who is the earliest to note its existence. A date in the early second century seems most suitable.

NAZARETH [năz'ə rĕth] (Gk. Nazara, Nazarat[h], Nazaret, Nazareth; perhaps from Heb. nāṣar "watch, guard, observe" or nēṣer "sprout, descendant"). A city in Galilee where Jesus grew up.

The location of Nazareth at modern en-Nâṣirah is generally accepted. The village is situated on the side of a hill some 350 m. (1150 ft.) above sea level, 24 km. (15 mi.) from the Sea of Galilee and 3 km. (2 mi.) south of Sepphoris. Toward the south and southeast Nazareth commands the view of the entire valley of Jezreel as well as Mt. Carmel and Mt. Tabor. Nathanael's comment to Philip, "Can anything good come out of Nazareth" (John 1:46), probably only indicates that the village was small. The city is not mentioned in the Old Testament.

Although some scholars are skeptical because of difficulties in correlating the two accounts of Jesus' birth and infancy, Mary and Joseph apparently lived in Nazareth before their journey to Egypt (Luke 1:26; 2:4-5) and settled there when they returned from Egypt (Matt. 2:23). Jesus lived in the village as a boy (Luke 2:39, 51; cf. 4:16), coming from there to be baptized by John the Baptist (Mark 1:9). Jesus apparently moved from Nazareth to Capernaum at the beginning of his public ministry (Matt. 4:12-13). He returned at least once to his boyhood home, where his message was rejected (Mark 6:1; Luke 4:16-24; cf. Matt. 13:53-58).

Modern Nazareth features a number of shrines. Nearby is a spring, according to tradition Mary's well, at which Mary and her son may have gone daily to draw water, and several other sites within the town are traditionally associated with the Holy Family: the Annunciation church, supposedly built on the site of Jesus' home; to the north a church dating from the Crusades; a Greek church, said to be the site of the synagogue where Jesus spoke of the fulfillment of Isa. 61:1-3 (Luke 4:18-21); and to the south Mons Saltus Domini, purportedly the hill from which the Jews sought to throw Jesus (v. 29).

NAZIRITE [năz'ə rīt] (Heb. nazîr "consecrated" or "devoted one"; from nāzar "to consecrate" or "separate [oneself]"). An individual who made a vow to separate himself to Yahweh. The vow consisted of three important abstentions: from consuming any products of the vine, from touching dead bodies, and from cutting one's hair (Num. 6:1-21; KJV "Nazarite"). The vows are further refined and defined in the Mishnah.

The vow of the Nazirite could be taken by a man or a woman (v. 2), or even a slave, but not a Gentile (Mishnah Nazir ix.1). It could be made for a specific period (a minimum of thirty days) or be a lifelong commitment (i.3-5). If taken for a specific period, certain sacrificial offerings were required at the end of the period, including offering the hair that had grown during the vow as a burnt offering (Num. 6:13-20). Similar sacrifices were required for a Nazirite who broke one of the conditions of the vow (vv. 9-12).

A general view of Nazareth (by courtesy of the Oriental Institute, University of Chicago)

Some scholars see in the Nazirite vow a refutation of the influence of the Canaanite nature religions. Certainly the prohibition against the products of the vine may be linked to the excesses encouraged by wine and strong drink (Lev. 10:8-11; cf. Gen. 9:20-21; Prov. 20:1; Hos. 4:11). Amos links the demise of Nazirites and the prophets in Israel to the apostasy in the land (Amos 2:11-12), and Lamentations mourns the death of the Nazirites (so KJV; RSV "princes") in the conquest of Jerusalem (Lam. 4:7).

Samson is the earliest biblical example of the Nazirite (Judg. 13:2-7; cf. 16:17). His great strength, charismatic leadership, and victory in battle as a Nazirite exemplify the Israelite concept of holy war. Yet Samson broke at least two of his vows, eating honey from the carcass of a dead lion (i.e., the prohibition against touching dead bodies; 14:8-9) and allowing Delilah to cut his hair (16:15-19).

Samuel also was a Nazirite, according to Rabbi Nehorai (Mishnah *Nazir* ix.5), who cites as proof Hannah's vow that "no razor shall touch his head" (1 Sam. 1:11; cf. Judg. 13:5).

The word Nazirite does not occur in the New Testament, nor does there appear to be any evidence that Jesus was a Nazirite. On the contrary, he touched dead bodies (Matt. 9:18-25) and drank wine (Matt. 26:26-29; Luke 7:34). *See* NAZARENE.

NEAH [nē′ə] (Heb. *nē′â*). A boundary city of the tribal territory of Zebulun, located somewhere between Rimmon and Hannathon (Josh. 19:13). The city may be the Noa mentioned on Samarian pottery fragments dating from the time of King Ahab.

NEAPOLIS [nē ăp′ə lĭs] (Gk. *hēá Néa pólis, Neapolis* "new city"). The seaport of the city of Philippi (Acts 16:11) where Paul landed on his second missionary journey. The port is located at modern Kavalla on the northern shore of the Aegean Sea about 16 km. (10 mi.) from Philippi. The city was known as Christoupolis during the Byzantine period.

Modern archaeological excavations have unearthed the remains of a village dating to the Hellenic period and a structure identified as a temple to the city god of Parthenos.

When Paul left the port for Philippi, he would have taken the famous Roman road, Egnatian Way, which cut through the rocks of the coastal Pangaeus mountain range.

See NABLUS.

NEARIAH [nē′ə rī′ə] (Heb. *nᵉʿaryâ* "servant" or "young man of Yahweh").

1. A descendant of Solomon; the son of Shemaiah and father of Elioenai, Hizkiah, and Azrikam (1 Chr. 3:22-23).

2. One of the four sons of Ishi who led the five hundred Simeonites to victory over the remnant of Amalekites at Mt. Seir (1 Chr. 4:42-43).

NEBAI [nē′bī] (Heb. K *nôḇāy*, Q *nêḇāy* "a native of Nebo [?]"). One of the "chiefs of the people" who set his seal to the new covenant under Nehemiah (Neh. 10:19 [MT 20]).

NEBAIOTH [nə bā′yŏth] (Heb. *nᵉḇāyôṯ, nᵉḇāyōṯ*). The oldest son of Ishmael (Gen. 25:13), noted as the brother of Mahalath (28:9) and Basemath (36:3). He was apparently the eponymous ancestor of an Arab tribe (cf. Isa. 60:7), mentioned in extrabiblical sources as the Nabaiati defeated by Tiglath-pileser III.

The proposal that this people were the founders of the Nabatean kingdom is generally regarded as unlikely; Nebaioth is spelled with the Hebrew tau, while Nabatean is spelled with teth.

NEBALLAT [nə băl lət] (Heb. *nᵉḇallaṭ*). A city in which the Benjaminites settled following the Exile (Neh. 11:34). It has been identified with modern Beit Nabala, 32 km. (20 mi.) west of Hazor and 7 km. (4.3 mi.) northeast of Lod.

NEBAT [nē′băt] (Heb. *nᵉḇāṭ*). The father of Jeroboam I; an Ephraimite from Zereda (1 Kgs. 11:26). The appellative "son of Nebat" occurs frequently in the Old Testament to distinguish between Jeroboam I and Jeroboam II, the son of Joash.

NEBO [nē′bō] (Heb. *nᵉḇô*; Akk. *Nabû* "to call, announce") (**DEITY**). Hebrew form of Nabû, a prominent Babylonian deity, the son of Marduk. Associated with the planet Mercury, he was the god of writing, and by extension of wisdom, trade and commerce, and prophetic omens. His major temple was Ezida, located in Borsippa.

Nebo and Bel (another name for Marduk) were carried in procession together as a major part of the New Year's (Akītu) ceremony in Babylon. Isa. 46:1 refers to such a procession, remarking that the idols of these gods could not even determine which direction they themselves were carried, but had to be carried by dumb animals. Nebo may have been one of the Babylonian gods worshipped by the Israelites.

This divine name occurs as an element in several personal names in the biblical record (Nebuchadnezzar, Nebushazban, Nebuzaradan) as well as those of the Neo-Babylonian kings Nabopolassar and Nabonidus.

NEBO [nē′bō] (Heb. *nᵉḇô*) (**PLACE**).

1. A city in Transjordan conquered by the Israelites, assigned to and rebuilt by the tribe of Reuben (Num. 32:3, 38; 1 Chr. 5:8). In the Moabite Stone King Mesha claims to have retaken it and slain its seven thousand Israelite inhabitants *ca.* 830 B.C. (*ANET*, p. 320). Isaiah and Jeremiah both record that the Moabite city was later destroyed (Isa. 15:2; Jer. 48:1, 22).

The site may be modern Khirbet el-Mekhaiyeṭ, 8 km. (5 mi.) southwest of Heshbon. Excavators at the site have discovered large quantities of Moabite pottery and the remains of a fortress.

2. A city in the tribal territory of Judah, to which fifty-two "sons of Nebo" returned from exile (Ezra 2:29). In the parallel list at Neh. 7:33, it is called "the other Nebo," perhaps to distinguish it from **1**. Some commentators believe Nebo here is actually a family name (cf. Ezra 10:43). Others suggest that this "other Nebo" be identified with NOB.

NEBO [nē'bō], **MOUNT** (Heb. *har-nᵉbô*; cf. Akk. *Nabû*; cf. Arab. "the height"). A mountain in the Abiram range (Num. 33:47), modern Jebel Nebā, 19 km. (12 mi.) east of the place where the Jordan enters the Dead Sea. Immediately to the south is Khirbet el-Mekhaiyeṭ, the presumed site of NEBO 1, and Râs es-Siâghah, Mt. Pisgah, is just to the northwest. Moses surveyed the promised land from atop Mt. Nebo (Deut. 32:49; 34:1), which rises more than 1200 m. (4000 ft.) above the level of the Dead Sea.

The traditional burial place of Moses, still identifiable in Byzantine times, is in the vicinity. Excavated remains on the slopes of Nebo include a possible Nabatean fortification, a Byzantine church and monastery complex, and numerous tombs from the Israelite through Byzantine periods. Several Samaritan, Greek, and Christian Palestinian Aramaic inscriptions have also been found.

NEBUCHADNEZZAR [nĕb'ə kəd nĕz'ər, nĕb'ōō kəd nĕz'ər] (Heb. *nᵉbûkadne'ṣṣar*), **NEBUCHADREZZAR** [nĕb'ə kəd rĕz'ər, nĕb'ōō kəd rĕz'ər] (*nᵉbûkadre'ṣṣar*; Akk. *Nabûkudurri-uṣur* "may Nabû protect the boundary" or "succession").†

1. Nebuchadrezzar I, most important king of the Babylonian Second Dynasty of Isin (1124-1103 B.C.). Benefitting from the strong central government established by his predecessors, he concentrated on foreign affairs, invading and annihilating Elam, which had long oppressed Babylonia. He also subdued the Lullubi and Kassites and established suzerainty over Assyria.

2. Nebuchadrezzar II, king of Babylonia 605-562 B.C.; eldest son of Nabopolassar, founder of the Chaldean dynasty; father of Amēl-marduk (biblical "Evil-merodach"), Marduk-šum-uṣur, and Marduk-nadin-audhi, and husband of Amytis, daughter of King Astyages of Media.

As crown prince Nebuchadrezzar accompanied his father in attacks against various peoples of surrounding mountain territories. In 605 he handily defeated Necho II and the Egyptians at Carchemish, thus gaining control of Syria and Palestine (Ḥatti-land); later that year he succeeded his father as king. Nebuchadrezzar's early reign included annual campaigns against Palestine, sacking Ashkelon in 604. In 601 he suffered a setback at the hands of Egyptian pharaoh Hophra (Apries), but by 597 he had recovered sufficiently to besiege Jerusalem, capturing King Jehoiachin and enthroning in his place Mattaniah (Zedekiah), who was more sympathetic to Babylonian policy (2 Kgs. 24:10-17, "Nebuchadnezzar"; cf. LXX Gk. *Nabouchodonosor*). At about the same time the Babylonians began a thirteen-year siege of Tyre (cf. Josephus *Ap* i.21 [156, 159]). In 589 Nebuchadrezzar laid waste to Jerusalem in retaliation for Zedekiah's Egyptian-sponsored rebellion, and three years later deported its populace (2 Kgs. 24:20–25:21; Jer. 52:3-34, "Nebuchadrezzar"; Ezek. 24:1-2; cf. Jer. 37:5; Ezek. 17:15), thus ending Judah's political independence as well as the Davidic dynasty.

In addition to military enterprise, Nebuchadrezzar engaged in extensive building activities, fortifying and embellishing the capital and other cities. At Babylon he renovated the palace and Esagila, the temple of Marduk, and constructed the famed hanging gardens in honor of Amytis. Upon his death Nebuchadrezzar was succeeded by Amēl-marduk.

Scholars now associate the account of Nebuchadnezzar's madness at Dan. 4 with NABONIDUS, the last king of Babylonia.

3. Nebuchadrezzar III, the name assumed by Nidintu-bēl who usurped the Babylonian throne from Darius I for three months in late 522 B.C.

4. Nebuchadrezzar IV, the name ascribed to Arakha, who reigned for three months following his revolt in August 521 B.C. Some scholars question the historicity of this individual.

NEBUSHAZBAN [nĕb'ə shăz'băn, nĕb'ōō shăz'băn] (Heb. *nᵉbûšazbān*; Akk. *Nabû-šúzibanni* "Nabû, save me"). The Rabsaris, or chief eunuch, of Nebuchadrezzar, dispatched by the Babylonian king to protect Jeremiah after the fall of Jerusalem (Jer. 39:13).

NEBUZARADAN [nĕb'ə zə rā'dən, nĕb'ōō zə rā'dən] (Heb. *nᵉbûzar'ᵃdān*; Akk. *Nabû-zēr-iddin* "Nabû has granted descendants"). Nebuchadrezzar's captain of the (body)guard, a high-ranking official (Heb. *rab ṭabbāḥîm*, perhaps "chief cook" or "chief executioner") responsible for the occupation of Jerusalem and the deportation of the Israelites (2 Kgs. 25:8-12; Jer. 39:9-14). Nebuzaradan took the leaders of the Judean resistance to Riblah, where they were put to death before the king of Babylon (2 Kgs. 25:18-21; Jer. 52:12-16, 24-27). Then he installed Gedeliah as governor of the city (v. 22 cf. Jer. 41:10; 43:6). According to Jeremiah, four years later the captain deported an additional group of Israelites (52:12-30).

NECO [nē'kō] (Heb. *nᵉkōh, nᵉkô*; Egyp. *Nk'w*).†

1. Neco I, installed by the Assyrian king Esarhaddon *ca.* 670 B.C. as prince of Saïs and Memphis in the Nile delta; father of Psamtik (Psammetichus) I.

2. Neco II (Wahibre), second king of the Egyptian Twenty-sixth (Saïte) Dynasty (610-595 B.C.).

With Egypt reunited and stabilized domestically during the fifty-five-year reign of his father Psamtik I, Neco sought to renew Egyptian strength abroad in the face of the rising Neo-Babylonian and Median powers. Advancing eastward to aid Aššur-uballiṭ II's vain attempt to reestablish the Assyrian state at Haran, he captured Gaza and Ashkelon (cf. Jer. 47:1, 5). King Josiah of Judah engaged Neco and his Greek mercenaries in battle at Megiddo in 609; Josiah died in battle (2 Kgs. 23:29; KJV "Pharaoh-nechoh"; 2 Chr. 35:20-24; KJV "Necho"), but the skirmish prevented the Egyptians from reaching the Assyrians in time. Nevertheless, Egypt dominated Syria-Palestine, imposing heavy tribute and deposing Josiah's successor, the anti-Egyptian Shallum (Jehoahaz), with his more amenable brother Eliakim (Jehoiakim) (2 Kgs. 23:31-35; 2 Chr. 36:1-4). In 605, however, shortly before his succession the Babylonian Nebuchadrezzar II routed the Egyptian garrison at Carchemish and pursued the retreating Neco to the "brook of Egypt" (2 Kgs. 24:7; Jer. 46:2). The two forces both sustained heavy losses at the Egyptian border in 601. Neco died in 595 and was succeeded by his son Psamtik II.

Neco promoted Egyptian trade along the Red Sea. He directed construction of a canal through the eastern Nile Delta connecting the Mediterranean and Red Seas and commissioned a Phoenician fleet to circumnavigate Africa (Herodotus *Hist.* ii.158; iv.42; Diodorus *Hist.* i.33).

NECROMANCY. *See* DIVINATION; MEDIUM, WIZARD.

NEDABIAH [nĕd'ə bī'ə] (Heb. *n^eḏaḇâ* "Yahweh has incited" or "compelled"). A son of King Jeconiah (Jehoiachin) (1 Chr. 3:18).

NEEDLE (Gk. *hraphís, belónē*). A slender implement, sharp at one end, with an eye for thread or a leather thong. In the ancient Near East needles were made of bone, ivory, and bronze. Found at excavation sites throughout Palestine, ancient needles ranged in size from 3.8 to 14 cm. (1.5 to 5.5 in.). Needles were used both in hand sewing and loom weaving ("needlework"; Heb. *ma^ʿăśēh rōqēm*, Exod. 26:36; 38:18; *riqmâ*, Judg. 5:30; Ps. 45:14 [MT 15]).

In biblical usage "needle" occurs in Jesus' saying that "it is easier for a camel to go through the eye of a needle than for a rich man to enter the kingdom of God" (Gk. *hraphís*, Matt. 19:24; Mark 10:25; *belónē*, Luke 18:25). This expression contrasts the size of the largest animal on Palestinian soil (the camel) with the smallest familiar opening (the eye of a needle); a rabbinic parallel uses an elephant in the same context (Talmud *b. Ber.* 55b; *B. Meṣ.* 38b). In contrast to the Western literal sense, this example of typical oriental hyperbole employs the absurd to heighten tension and make the statement emphatic (cf. Matt. 5:29-30).

While early Palestinian Christianity was in complete agreement with the spirit of the statement, later, more affluent Christianity found it difficult. Some late Greek manuscripts attempted to reduce the harshness by reading *kámilos* "cable" for *kámēlos* "camel." Still later, some scholars speculated that the phrase "eye of the needle" might have meant a low, small gate next to the main city gate, through which a camel was just able to enter the city. However, Jesus is simply indicating that those who have large vested interests in this world (i.e., the rich) are highly unlikely to seek fulfillment in the world to come. Those who have greater wealth will find it correspondingly harder to become a disciple—leaving all to follow Christ (19:27-30).

NEGEB [nĕg'ĕv, nĕg'ĕb] (Heb. *negeḇ* "southward" or "south country").† A triangular desert area southwest of the Dead Sea. Framed by the Judean hill country to the north, the Arabah to the east, and the Mediterranean coastal strip to the west, it is the southernmost district of Judah (cf. Josh. 10:40; 11:16). In biblical times several trade routes, including the east-west route to Egypt via Kadesh-barnea and another linking Egyptian On to the Arabian desert city of Tema via Elath and the north-south King's Highway, ran through and intersected in the Negeb.

Abraham passed through the Negeb as he journeyed from Haran to Egypt (Gen. 12:9) and returned to settle there after the destruction of Sodom and Gomorrah (20:1). Isaac was dwelling in the south country when he first met Rebekah (24:62).

The Israelites spied out the Negeb before entering the promised land (Num. 13:17), and the region was included in the territory that the people were to possess (Deut. 1:7; 34:1-3). Joshua led the military expeditions that wrested control of the Negeb from the indigenous peoples (Josh. 10:40; 11:16; 12:8). The region eventually became the possession of the tribes of Judah and Simeon (ch. 15; 19:1-9; Judg. 1:9).

The king of Gath gave David the city of Ziklag in the south country as a possession after the young officer fled from Saul (1 Sam. 27:5-7). The Amalekites raided Ziklag and the "Negeb" of Judah, Caleb, and the Cherethites (30:1, 14). Other territories so named include the Negeb of Arad, the Kenites, and the Jerahmeelites.

After the fall of Jerusalem in 587 B.C. the Negeb came under the control of EDOM, IDUMEA, and the NABATEANS.

In an oracle concerning Judah's reliance on Egyptian aid, Isaiah surveys "the beasts of the Negeb," a "land of trouble and anguish" (Isa. 30:6-8). Jeremiah remarks that were the Sabbath to be observed, people would come from many places—including the Negeb—to offer sacrifices in Jerusalem (Jer. 17:26). Obadiah proclaims that the postexilic restoration would see the inhabitants of the Negeb possessing the "Mount Esau," and the exiles of Jerusalem "the cities of the Negeb" (Obad. 19-20).

NEGINAH [nĕg'ī nə] (Heb. *n^egînâ*), **NEGINOTH** [nĕg'ī nŏth] (*n^egînôṯ*). A technical term in the superscripts to Pss. 4, 6, 54-55, 61, 67, 76 (RSV "with stringed instruments").

NEHELAM [nə hĕl'əm] (Heb. *hanneḥ^elāmî* "the Nehelamite"). An appellative of the false prophet Shemaiah who opposed Jeremiah (Jer. 29:24, 31-32; RSV "of Nehelam"; KJV, NIV "the Nehelamite"). The term, otherwise unattested, may be either a family name or a location. Some scholars suggest that it represents a wordplay on Heb. *ḥālam* "dream" and so means "Shamaiah the dreamer."

NEHEMIAH [nē'ə mī'ə] (Heb. *n^eḥemyá* "Yahweh has comforted").

1. A leader of the Israelites, who returned with Zerubbabel from captivity in 538 (Ezra 2:2; Neh. 7:7).

2. The son of Hacaliah (Neh. 1:1); postexilic governor of Jerusalem, whose public ministry is recorded in the book of Nehemiah.

Nehemiah served as cupbearer to the Persian king Artaxerxes I Longimanus (464-424 B.C.), who sent him at his own request to Jerusalem in 445, the twentieth year of the king's reign (2:1). Artaxerxes commissioned him as governor, providing letters to the governors of the province Beyond the River for his safe passage and for building supplies for the temple and the city walls (vv. 7ff.). Under the protection of Persian officers and horsemen, Nehemiah reached Jerusalem, despite stiff resistance by Sanballat the Horonite and Tobiah the Ammonite (v. 10; cf. v. 19; chs.

4, 6, 13). Shortly after his arrival, Nehemiah secretly inspected the city walls at night. In the face of continued opposition by Israel's enemies, he persisted in his plans and completed the restoration of the city walls in fifty-two days (6:15). In order to bolster the city's strength, Nehemiah resettled one-tenth of the Jewish population there (11:1-2).

In addition to the administrative abilities demonstrated in the completion of the walls, Nehemiah ably resolved economic and social problems affecting the well-being of his countrymen (ch. 5). His concern for the religious life of the postexilic community is seen in the reading of the law by Ezra (7:73b–8:12) and the reintroduction of the Feast of Booths (vv. 13-18), followed by a day of penance and prayer (ch. 9). In addition, Nehemiah sponsored a written covenant supporting the rebuilt temple and various religious reforms (ch. 10).

Nehemiah returned to Susa in 433, perhaps leaving the city under the control of his brother Hananiah (cf. 7:2). In the years that followed, many of the religious and social abuses reappeared, and Nehemiah returned to Jerusalem "after some time" (13:6-7). Among the reforms of his second period of administration were the exclusion of foreigners from worship, the expulsion of Tobiah the Ammonite from his chamber within the temple quarters, the renewal of support for the Levites, the institution of regulations for Sabbath observance, and the abolition of mixed marriages (ch. 13). The length of Nehemiah's second term is uncertain, and it is possible that he died in office; according to the Elephantine papyri, a certain Bagohi was governor of Judah in 411.

Nehemiah's work was of the utmost significance for the life of God's covenant people, contributing to the political, social, economic, and religious well-being of the fragile postexilic community.

3. The son of Azbuk, ruler of half the district of Beth-zur, who helped repair the walls of Jerusalem (Neh. 3:16).

NEHEMIAH, BOOK OF. †

I. Origin and Place in Canon

According to the Talmud (*B. Bat.* 15a), the book of Nehemiah was part of a single unit with the books of Ezra and Chronicles, written by Ezra but completed by Nehemiah. Most scholars now acknowledge, however, that the writings of Nehemiah (at least parts of his memoirs, Neh. 1-7, 11-13) were in circulation prior to the completion of Ezra. The book does form a unit with Ezra in the Hebrew canon and the LXX (Esdras B), but it was known as 2 Ezra (2 Esdras) by the time of Origen (third century A.D.) and Jerome (fourth century), a division adopted in the Vulgate and eventually in a fifteenth-century Hebrew manuscript.

In the English canon Nehemiah follows Ezra in the historical writings; the Hebrew canon assigns it to the third division, the Writings, and places it out of proper chronological order before Chronicles.

II. Contents

The book of Nehemiah records the events of Nehemiah's return from the Exile and his two terms as governor over the province of Judah during the reign of the Persian king Artaxerxes I Longimanus. Neh. 1:1–2:10 recounts Nehemiah's distress at learning the conditions in Jerusalem, his request and royal commission to return and rebuild the city, and his return as governor. His secret inspection of the city walls, his decision to rebuild them, and the beginnings of construction despite opposition are recounted at 2:11–4:17. Following an account of Nehemiah's efforts to resolve economic difficulties among the people and his administrative activities (ch. 5), the narrative depicts various plots against Nehemiah and the building activity and the actual completeion of the work in fifty-two days (6:1–7:4). A list of the returned exiles is given at 7:5-73a (cf. Ezra 2). Ezra's public reading of the Law, the celebration of the Feast of Booths, and a day of penance and prayer are recorded at 7:73b–9:37. The covenant ratifying the law and the list of signers are given at 9:38–10:39 (MT 10:1-40). Ch. 11 reports Nehemiah's efforts to strengthen the city by resettling one-tenth of the Jewish population there. Lists of priests and Levites who returned with Zerubbabel are given at 12:1-26, followed by an account of the dedication of the walls (vv. 27-43) and provision for temple worship, including the expulsion of foreigners (12:44–13:3). Various reforms during Nehemiah's second term of administration are described at 13:4-31, including the eviction of Tobiah the Ammonite from his spacious chambers in the temple precincts, resumption of collections for the Levites, enforcement of regulations regarding the Sabbath, and stringent measures against mixed marriages.

III. Literary Aspects

Like its counterpart Ezra, the book of Nehemiah is comprised of a variety of literary materials and documents. The core of the book is the collection commonly known as Nehemiah's memoirs, although the precise extent of this material is subject to debate. The memoirs are primarily first-person narrative (1:1–7:5; 12:32–13:31), but ch. 3; 7:6-73; 11:1–12:30 are third-person. The Ezra memoirs in 7:73b–10:30 (MT 40) continue the account of Ezra's work interrupted at the end of the book of Ezra; some scholars would attribute this material also to the hand of Nehemiah.

A considerable portion of the book is comprised of lists, probably drawn from administrative records or the temple archives. Included are lists of those who returned with Zerubbabel 7:6-72a; cf. Ezra 2:1-70); builders of the walls (3:1-32); signatories to the covenant (9:38–10:27 [MT 1-28]); inhabitants of Jerusalem (11:3-24); town lists of Judah and Benjamin (vv. 25-36); and priests and Levites (12:1-26). Other sources include portions of messages between Sanballat and Nehemiah (6:2-9), the text of the covenant stipulations (10:28-39 [MT 29-40]), and the account of the dedication of the walls (12:27-43).

IV. Historical Aspects

The activity of Nehemiah can now be dated with certainty during the reign of Artaxerxes I (461-424 B.C.) and his arrival in Jerusalem in 445, the twentieth year of that Persian ruler. Supportive evidence comes from the Elephantine papyri, which help to date Sanballat the Horonite and the high priest Eliashib (3:1, 20-21); the Samaritan papyri from Wâdī Dâliyeh, which aid in establishing the succession of Samaritan governors from Sanballat until the time of Alexander the Great (332); a silver bowl from the Egyptian delta, which places the time of Geshem the Arab (2:19; 6:1-6); as well as a number of seals and jar handle stamps. (On the question of the relationship between Nehemiah and Ezra, *see* EZRA, BOOK OF *IV*.)

Nehemiah completed his first term as governor in 433 and returned to Susa. The length of his absence from Jerusalem is uncertain (cf. 13:6-7), as is also the extent of his second term. The Elephantine papyri mention a Bagohi as governor of Judah in 411.

As with the book of Ezra, the arrangement of material in Nehemiah occasionally reflects the author-compiler's preference for topical rather than chronological organization. An example of the author's use of sources is the list of those who returned with Zerubbabel (7:6-73a), intended here as the basis for Nehemiah's repopulation of Jerusalem; in the parallel version of Ezra 2:1-70, the list serves to legitimate the returnees as the continuation of the "true Israel."

V. Theological Significance

In addition to advancing the physical and economic security of the postexilic community, Nehemiah supported its religious revitalization through various reforms. His profound faith is evident throughout the book in his acknowledgment of God's guidance (2:8, 18), his concern for divine blessing on his own work and that of others (5:19; 6:14; 13:14, 22, 29, 31), and his frequent prayers (1:5-11; 2:4; 4:4-5, 9; 6:9).

See also CHRONICLES, BOOKS OF; EZRA, BOOK OF.

Bibliography. E. Bickermann, *From Ezra to the Last of the Maccabees* (New York: 1947); J. M. Myers, *Ezra-Nehemiah.* AB 14 (1965); E. M. Yamauchi, "The Archaeological Background of Nehemiah," *Bibliotheca Sacra* 137 (1980): 291-309.

NEHILOTH [nē'ə lŏth] (Heb. *nᵉḥîlôṯ*). A technical term in the KJV superscription to Ps. 5. The RSV correctly translates "for the flutes," probably indicating that flutes were to be played as an accompaniment to the chanting of the psalm.

NEHUM [nē'hŭm] (Heb. *nᵉḥûm* "comfort"). One of the leaders who returned with Zerubbabel from captivity in Babylon (Neh. 7:7). At Ezra 2:2 he is called Rehum.

NEHUSHTA [nə hŏŏsh'tə] (Heb. *nᵉḥuštaʾ* "copper" or "serpent"). The daughter of Elnathan of Jerusalem, wife of Jehoiakim and mother of Jehoiachin, kings of Judah (2 Kgs. 24:8). She was taken captive to Babylon by Nebuchadrezzar in 597 B.C. (vv. 12, 15).

NEHUSHTAN [nə hŏŏsh'tən] (Heb. *nᵉḥuštān* "made of copper"). The bronze serpent destroyed during Hezekiah's reform (2 Kgs. 18:4). It had been fashioned by Moses at Yahweh's command, in response to a plague of fiery serpents sent upon the Israelites as punishment for their impatience during the wilderness wanderings (Num. 21:4-9). Hezekiah's destruction of the serpent suggests that it had become the object of cultic worship.

Some scholars have speculated that the "fiery snakes"

of Num. 21 were actually guinea worms (*Dracunculus medinensis*), a human parasite whose larva enter the human body through contaminated drinking water and may attain a length of nearly 1 m. (3 ft.). The worm may be extracted with great difficulty, but the infected area burns intensely and death can result if the worm is broken. The bronze serpent on the pole, reminiscent of the physician's caduceus wound about the wand of Mercury, may be derived from the process of removal.

Jesus compared his "lifting" on the cross to the "lifting up" of the serpent in the wilderness (John 3:14-15). As looking upon the bronze serpent brought life to the people of Israel, so looking upon the crucified Son would bring eternal life to the believer.

NEIEL [nē ī'əl] (Heb. *nᵉʿîʾēl* "God's dwelling place"). A border city in the tribal territory of Asher (Josh. 19:27), called Inhi in the Egyptian text of Seth. The city has been identified as modern Khirbet Yaʿnîn, 3 km. (2 mi.) north of Cabul on the edge of the plain of Acco. Cultural remains from the Bronze and Iron ages have been excavated at the site.

NEIGHBOR (Heb. *ʿāmîṯ, qārôḇ, rēaʿ*; Gk. *geítōn, períoikos, hó plēsíon*).

I. Old Testament

"Neighbor" in the Old Testament specifies a much closer relationship than the simple coincidence of living next to an individual. Since land was originally assigned by tribe (Josh. 13–21) and then passed from parent to child (Num. 33:54; cf. Lev. 25:25), subclans and families normally remained tied to the same parcel of land generation after generation (i.e., 1 Kgs. 21:3). Thus Israelites generally had, if not a blood relationship, a long-term covenant relationship with their neighbors.

In terms of the Israelite covenant, the terms "neighbor" and "brother" (Heb. *ʾāḥ*; Gk. *adelphós*) are virtually synonymous (e.g., Lev. 19:17-18); either term describes the resident Israelite who was also a fellow member of the covenant, the closest social relationship defined by that bond. More distant was the relationship of the sojourner (Heb. *gēr, tôšaḇ*; Gk. *pároikos, prosélytos*), the non-Israelite (including the pre-Conquest indigenous population of Canaan) who took up residence in Israel; the sojourner was not related by blood, but was subject nevertheless to the laws of the land (Exod. 12:19; Lev. 24:22). Most distant were the "foreigner," "stranger," or "alien" (Heb. *zār, nāḵrî*; Gk. *allótrios, allogenḗs*), the nonresident non-Israelite; such relationships were not governed by the covenant (Deut. 14:21; 15:3; 23:20 [MT 21]) but by the more general customs of hospitality (Gen. 18:1-8; 24:14ff.; cf. Judg. 19:15-20:48; Ezek. 16:48-49).

Foreigners and resident aliens, therefore, are not covered by the biblical commands concerning relationships with neighbors. Loving one's neighbor (Lev. 19:18), not bearing false witness against one's neighbor (Exod. 20:16), and not coveting one's neighbor's possessions (v. 17) are all commands that encompassed only relationships with fellow Jews. Later these were extended to include the proselytes, who were completely incorporated into the Jewish nation through baptism and circumcision.

II. New Testament

In the New Testament "neighbor" occurs primarily in references to or quotations from the Old Testament (e.g., Matt. 5:43; 19:19; 22:39; Mark 12:31-33; Luke 10:27; Rom. 13:9-10; Gal. 5:14; James 2:8, citing Lev. 19:18; Acts 7:27, citing Exod. 2:13; Heb. 8:8-11, citing Jer. 31:31-34; cf. Eph. 4:25, referring to Lev. 19:11).

Jesus recognizes the narrowness of the definition of neighbor when he points out that the command permitted one to "hate your enemy" (Matt. 5:43). He intensifies the ethic, fulfilling rather than destroying the law as stressed throughout Matthew; Christians are to love their enemies and pray for those who persecute them (vv. 43-46).

Jesus quotes Lev. 19:18 with approval, calling it the second greatest commandment (Matt. 22:39; Mark 12:31). But the ethical dilemma in Judaism was, as the lawyer recognized, "Who is my neighbor?" (Luke 10:29). According to the Old Testament the answer was a fellow member of the covenant, but the various Jewish sects tended to exclude all outside the particular group. The Pharisees exempted a number of ordinary people from the definition, including all who worked certain "despised" trades, and the Qumran community excluded "the sons of darkness" (1QS 1:10; 9:21-22).

Jesus' response is to redefine the relationship between love and neighbor in the parable of the Good Samaritan (Luke 10:29-37). The priest and the Levite are both fellow members of the covenant and therefore "neighbors" in the Old Testament sense, but they ignore the injured man; the Samaritan is neither a resident nor a Jew, but he shows compassion to the helpless victim. Jesus' point is that neighborliness is not a precondition of love but a consequence of it: the one who "proved [to be a] neighbor" was "the one who showed mercy" (v. 36).

NEKEB (Josh. 19:33, KJV). See ADAMI-NEKEB.

NEKODA [nə kō'də] (Heb. neqôḏā').
1. The head or founder of a family of temple servants who returned with Zerubbabel from captivity in Babylon but could not prove their ancestry (Ezra 2:48 par. Neh. 7:50).
2. The head of a family who returned from Exile but were unable to prove their Israelite ancestry (Ezra 2:60 par. Neh. 7:62).

NEMUEL [nĕm'yŏŏ əl] (Heb. nᵉmû'ēl).
1. A Reubenite; the elder brother of Dathan and Abiram, who sided with Korah against Moses and Aaron (Num. 26:9).
2. A Simeonite, eponymous ancestor of the Nemuelites (Num. 26:12; 1 Chr. 4:24). At Gen. 46:10; Exod. 6:15 he is called Jemuel (Heb. yemû'ēl).

NEPHEG [nĕf'ĕg] (Heb. nepeg).
1. A Levite, son of Izhar and brother of Korah (Exod. 6:21).
2. A son of David who was born in Jerusalem (2 Sam. 5:15; 1 Chr. 3:7; 14:6).

NEPHILIM [nĕf'ə lĭm] (Heb. nᵉpîlîm).* A prede-

luvial people, the children of the "sons of God" and the "daughters of men" (Gen. 6:1-4). The term, of uncertain etymology, is rendered "giants" by the KJV, but appears to be distinct from the standard Hebrew term rᵉdupā'îm). Their depiction as "mighty men ... of old, the men of renown" (v. 4) suggests a legendary people of the distant past, portrayed as the gigantic offspring of an unnatural union between humans and divine beings in an attempt to bring moral indictment against the generations prior to the Flood. An alternate interpretation regards the Nephilim as the product of marriage between the righteous offspring of Seth and ungodly women in general, thus leading to a moral degeneration of the righteous line of Seth.

At Num. 13:33 the spies report that they have seen the Nephilim, here called "the sons of Anak, who come from the Nephilim." The context (v. 32, "men of great stature") clearly suggests a type of giant familiar to the Israelites (cf. the Anakim [Deut. 9:2; Josh. 15:14; Judg. 1:20], David and Goliath).

NEPHISH (1 Cor. 5:19, KJV). See NAPHISH.

NEPHISIM [nə fī'sĭm] (Heb. K nᵉpîsîm, Q nᵉpûsîm). The head of a family of temple servants who returned with Zerubbabel from captivity (Ezra 2:50; KJV "Nephusim"). In the parallel list at Neh. 7:52 he is called the "Nephushesim" (KJV "Nephishesim").

NEPHTOAH [nĕf tō'ə], **WATERS OF** (Heb. mê neptôaḥ). A place on the boundary between the tribal territories of Judah and Benjamin (Josh. 15:9; 18:15). The name may derive from the Egyptian pharaoh Merneptah (1224-1214 B.C.) (cf. ANET, p. 258). The site is generally identified as the spring of modern Liftā, 2 km. (3 mi.) northwest of Jerusalem.

NEPHUSHESHIM [nə fŏŏsh'ə sĭm] (Heb. K nᵉpûšesîm. Q nᵉpûšesîm). Alternate form of NEPHISIM (Neh. 7:52; KJV "Nephishesim").

NEPHUSIM (Ezra 2:50, KJV). See NEPHISIM.

NER [nûr] (Heb. nēr "lamp"). The name of either one or two Benjamites related to Saul. The textual evidence seems to be contradictory.
1. The son of Maacah and Jeiel (2) (called Abiel at 1 Sam. 14:51), and therefore a brother of Kish (1 Chr. 9:36; the parallel list at 8:30 omits his name). He was the father (or perhaps the grandfather) of Abner and Saul's uncle (1 Sam. 14:51).
2. The son of Jeiel (2) and the father of Kish (1 Chr. 8:33; 9:39). The name is omitted from the list of Jeiel's sons at 8:30; 9:36, where Kish is called the son of Jeiel.

NEREUS [nĭr'ĭ əs] (Gk. Nēreus). A Christian in Rome to whom Paul sent his greetings (Rom. 16:15). According to some scholars, he was the son of Philologus and Julia and the brother of Olympas, also greeted by Paul.

NERGAL [nûr'găl] (Heb. nērgal; Akk. Ne-uru-gal "lord of the great city"). A Babylonian deity whose cult was centered at Cutha (biblical Cuth; 2 Kgs. 17:30); he was worshipped by some who colonized Samaria after its fall in 722 B.C. Nergal ruled the underworld with his consort Ereshkigal (lit. "lady of the great land") and was the source of plague. He was the god of the scorching, destructive afternoon and summer sun, of the hunt and of war. His symbol was the lion. A myth found at Amarna and Sultantepe recounts his marriage to Ereshkigal and accession to power in the underworld (*ANET*, pp. 103-4, 507-512).

NERGAL-SHAREZER [nûr'găl shə rē'zər] (Heb. *nērgal šar-'eṣer*; Akk. *Nergal-šar-uṣur* "may Nergal preserve the king").† The Rabmag (an official) of Nebuchadrezzar II, one of the "princes" present during the Babylonian siege and capture of Jerusalem (Jer. 39:3, 13). Some scholars identify him with the nobleman Neriglissar, who gained the throne (560-556 B.C.) when his brother-in-law Amēl-Marduk (Evil-merodach) died in a coup. Despite initial success, he conducted a disastrous campaign across the Taurus mountains into Cilicia seeking to head off the advancing Medes. His son and successor Labāši-Marduk was deposed after nine months in favor of Nabonidus.

The two occurrences of the name at v. 3 may indicate two separate individuals (so LXX).

NERI [nĭr'ī] (Gk. *Nēri*; from Heb. *nēr* "lamp"). The father of Shealtiel in Luke's genealogy of Jesus (Luke 3:27).

NERIAH [nə rī'ə] (Heb. *nērîyâ, nērîyāhû* "Yahweh is light"; Gk. *Nērias*). The son of Mahseiah (Jer. 32:12), and father of Baruch, Jeremiah's scribe (v. 16; 36:4, 8; 43:3; 45:1; Bar. 1:1; KJV "Nerias"), and the prophet's quartermaster Seraiah (Jer. 51:59).

NERO [nē'rō] (Gk. *Nerōn*; Lat. *Nero*).† Nero Claudius Caesar, last Roman emperor of the Julian-Claudian house (A.D. 54-68); son of Cnaeus Domitius Ahenobarbus and Agrippina, great-granddaughter of Augustus.

Originally named Lucius Domitius Ahenobarbus, he was renamed Nero Claudius Caesar Drusus Germanicus in 50, when at his mother's urging her husband, the Emperor Claudius, adopted Nero and made him guardian of his own son Britannicus. In 53 Nero married Claudius' daughter Octavia.

After Claudius died, reputedly poisoned by Agrippina in 54, Nero's mother arranged for the Praetorian Guard to proclaim him emperor. At first Burrus, the chief of the Guard, and the philosopher Seneca administered Nero's government, while the emperor's private life became increasingly dissipated. Agrippina, losing control over her son, intrigued in favor of Britannicus, whom Nero poisoned in 55. Subsequently Nero murdered his mother in 59 and his wife in 62, marrying Poppaea Sabrina, the ambitious wife of Nero's companion Otho; in the same year Burrus died and Seneca retired.

Ca. A.D. 60 the apostle Paul, tried before Felix the procurator of Caesarea, appealed to "Caesar" (Acts 25:10-12, 21, 25; 28:19), i.e., Nero, who was an unlikely protector of Christians. In 64 a fire destroyed half of Rome, and rumors accused Nero of setting it

as a dramatic backdrop for his recital of the fall of Troy. For his part, Nero accused the Christians of the arson and instituted the first Roman persecution. Universal Christian tradition reckons the apostles Peter and Paul among Nero's victims (Tertullian *Scorpiace* xv.3; Eusebius *HE* i.25; Sulpicius Severus *Chronicorum* ii.39), commemorating their martyrdom on June 29.

Although Nero rebuilt the city magnificently, Rome had tired of him. When he discovered in 65 a widespread conspiracy to make Gaius Calpurnius Piso emperor, Nero had many Romans murdered, including Seneca. In 67, fancying himself a great artist in the Hellenistic tradition, Nero visited Greece and competed for prizes at festivals. After returning to Italy in 68, Nero was faced by a series of revolts. When the Praetorian Guard recognized Servius Sulpicius Galba as emperor and the Senate declared Nero a public enemy (Lat. *hostis*), Nero committed suicide.

A legend arose that Nero had fled to the Parthians and would return at their head to punish Rome. The mythologization of this story took various forms. The monstrous return of Nero from the dead (*Nero redivivus*) is implied at Rev. 13:3. The number of the beast, 666, at v. 18 is believed to allude to "Nero Caesar" in Hebrew numerology. Asc.Isa. 4:2-12 predicts the second coming of a matricidal king in terms reminiscent of the antichrist in Revelation; the passage also alludes to the martyrdom of one of "the Twelve" under that king's reign. The Sibylline Oracles transmit the popular legend of Nero's eschatological return (e.g., Sib.Or. 3:63-74; 4:119-24, 137-39; 5:28-34, 93-110, 137-54, 214-37, 361-85; 8:68-72, 139-59; 12:78-94). Their account of the Roman traitor who attempted to invade the empire from Parthia, Mareades, or Kyriades (13:89-99, 119-30) was also modeled on the Nero legend. The theme also occurs in inverted form in the early ninth-century A.D. Byzantine Apocalypse of Daniel, which describes a Roman king revived by God to save the empire (Apoc.Dan. 3:10).

NET. A loosely woven mesh fabric made of flax, palm fiber, hemp, or papyrus and used for trapping game or fish.

The frequency with which "net" and "pit" occur together in biblical usage (Heb. *rešeṭ*; e.g., Job 18:8-10; Ps. 9:15 [MT 16]; 35:7-8; 57:6 [MT 7]; Ezek. 19:8) suggests that these devices were used in combination to conceal the cord snares from wary game. Pits were probably dug along game trails and then nets stretched over the opening, camouflaged with grass or brush. When prey (such as an antelope; Isa. 51:20; KJV "wild bull") stepped into the net (*mikmār*), their weight would collapse the net; struggling would only further entangle the prey. Nets could also have been hidden in the brush along a trail where the game could be driven into them; others were undoubtedly disguised under a thin layer of soil where an operator could pull them tight around the unsuspecting animal (i.e., a snare; Ps. 140:5 [MT 6]; Prov. 29:5; Isa. 51:20; cf. Ps. 141:10, *makmôr*).

The Israelites also caught birds with traps that closed over them (*mᵉṣôḏâ*; Eccl. 9:12; Prov. 1:17). The

Egyptians used a similar claptrap for waterfowl (cf. Hos. 7:12, *rešeṭ*). An alternate method was to throw or drop a casting net over the quarry (Ezek. 12:13).

Nets were the most common method of catching fish in ancient times (*ḥērem*, Hab. 1:15-17; Ezek. 26:5, 14; 47:10; *miḵmōreṭ*, Isa. 19:8). A cone-shaped circular net, 3-5 m. (10-16 ft.) in diameter, was thrown into the water. Weights attached to the rim caused the net to sink, trapping any fish below it (Gk. *amphíblēstron*, Matt. 4:18; Mark 1:16; *díktyon*, Matt. 4:20-21; Luke 5:2-6; John 21:6-11). Fishermen also used the large dragnet or seine (*sagḗnē*, Matt. 13:47-50), a net 200-250 m. (650-800 ft.) long with a width of about 5 m. (16 ft.). It was pulled through the water between two boats and the net then dragged up on shore in a wide semicircle together with any fish trapped in it.

In the Bible "net" occurs primarily in a figurative sense (e.g., Job 19:6; Ps. 25:15). It frequently symbolizes potential entrapment (104:5 [MT 6]; Eccl. 7:26; Hos. 7:12), in particular a trap that is devious or concealed (Ps. 31:4 [MT 5]; 35:7-8; Prov. 1:17). Nets, particularly dragnets, need a large flat place in which to be spread to dry; hence, Ezekiel's prophecy that Tyre would be such a place signifies the extent of the city's future desolation (Ezek. 26:5, 14; 47:10). In a parable of the kingdom of God, Jesus likens the net's indiscriminate catch to the harvest of the kingdom; people, like fish, must be judged profitable or worthless (Matt. 13:47-50).

NETAIM [nə tāəm] (Heb. *nᵉṭā'îm* "plantings"). A place in Judah where the royal potters lived and worked (1 Chr. 4:23; KJV "plants"). Khirbet en-Nuweiti', south of Wâdî Elah, has been suggested as the site.

NETHANEL [nə thăn'əl] (Heb. *nᵉṭan'ēl* "God has given").

1. The son of Zuar; the chief responsible for the tribe of Issachar during the wilderness wanderings (Num. 1:8; 2:5; 10:15; KJV "Nethaneel"). He made a large offering for the tabernacle (7:18, 23).

2. The fourth son of Jesse, and the older brother of David (1 Chr. 2:14).

3. A priest who was to blow the trumpet before the ark of the covenant when it was brought to Jerusalem at the time of David (1 Chr. 15:24).

4. A Levite; the father of the scribe Shemaiah (1 Chr. 24:6).

5. The fifth son of the gatekeeper Obed-edom; a Korahite Levite contemporary with David (1 Chr. 26:4).

6. One of the princes of King Jehoshaphat, sent to the cities of Judah to instruct the people in the law (2 Chr. 17:7).

7. A chief of the Levites who gave offerings for a passover celebration during the reign of Josiah (2 Chr. 35:9).

8. A priest of the house of Pashhur who was forced to divorce his foreign wife (Ezra 10:22).

9. Head of the priestly household of Jedaiah at the time of Joiakim (Neh. 12:21).

10. One of the priestly descendants of Asaph who blew a trumpet at the dedication of the rebuilt walls of Jerusalem (Neh. 12:36).

NETHANIAH [nĕth'ə nī'ə] (Heb. *nᵉṭanyâ*, *nᵉṭanyāhû* "Yahweh has given").

1. The father of Ishmael, one of the men who murdered Gedaliah (2 Kgs. 25:23, 25; Jer. 40:8, 14-15; 41:1-9).

2. A Levite of the line of Asaph who prophesied with lyres, harps, and cymbal (1 Chr. 25:2). He led the fifth division of levitical singers (v. 12).

3. A Levite sent to teach in the cities of Judah during the reign of King Jehoshaphat (2 Chr. 17:8).

4. The father of Jehudi, who conveyed Jeremiah's scroll to Jehoiakim (Jer. 36:14).

NETHINIM. *See* TEMPLE SERVANTS.

NETOPHAH [nə tō'fə] (Heb. *nᵉṭōpâ* "dropping, flowing"; Gk. *Netebas*). A town in the hill country of Judah, probably identical to modern Khirbet Bedd Fālûḥ, 2 km. (3.5 mi.) southeast of Bethlehem. According to 1 Chr. 2:54, the village was settled following the Exile by the descendants of Salma of the clan of Caleb. The nearby spring 'Ain en-Natûf preserves the ancient name.

Maharai and Heleb, two of David's mighty men, came from Netophah (2 Sam. 23:28-29; 1 Chr. 11:30; 27:13, 15). Other Netophathites (Heb. *nᵉṭōpāṭî*), Seraiah the son of Tanhumeth and the sons of Ephai the Netophathite, were among the captains of the forces that opposed Nebuchadrezzar at the destruction of Jerusalem; they later swore allegiance to Gedaliah, the puppet governor of Judea (2 Kgs. 25:23; Jer. 40:8-9). Descendants of the Netophathites are numbered among those who returned from captivity with Zerubbabel (1 Chr. 9:16; Ezra 2:22; Neh. 7:26; cf. 12:28 [KJV "Netophathi"]).

NETTLES (Heb. *qimmôś*, *ḥārûl*). Any of the coarse herbs of the genus *Urtica*, having leaves covered with hairs that secrete a fluid that stings the skin on contact.

Stinging nettles grow throughout Palestine, particularly *Urtica ureus* L. and *Urtica pilulifera* L. They are common in fallow fields, unkempt gardens, and on ruins. In ancient times nettles were viewed as a sign of desolation (Isa. 34:13; Hos. 9:6; Zeph. 2:9).

Some scholars contend that Heb. *ḥārûl* (Zeph. 2:9; Job 30:7) is actually a general term for weeds, or perhaps a specific term for wild mustard (*Brassica nigra* [L.] Koch or *Sinapis arvensis* L.), which tends to grow on abandoned sites. This view is supported by parallel occurrences of the two terms (cf. Prov. 24:31).

NETWORK (Heb. *śᵉḇāḵâ*, *rešeṭ*). Any pattern with a "netlike" reticulation, primarily associated with the embellishments of the tabernacle and temple. Heb. *rešeṭ* designates the bronze latticework that covered the ark of the covenant, extending from just below the ledge to halfway down the side. Four rings were fastened to this grating at the corners, and poles were inserted through these rings when the ark had to be carried (Exod. 27:4-5; 38:4). A "network (*śᵉḇāḵâ*) of interwoven chains" (1 Kgs. 7:17, NIV; RSV "nets of checker work") adorned the capitals of the two pillars that stood in front of the temple; the capitals were further decorated with pomegranates and lilies (vv. 17-42; 2 Kgs. 25:17; 2 Chr. 4:12-13; Jer. 52:22-23; KJV "wreath[en work]").

The KJV translates *ḥôr* as "network," representing a type of woven cloth (Isa. 19:9; RSV "white cotton"; NIV "fine linen").

NEW (Heb. *ḥāḏaš*; Gk. *kainós*, *néos*). The quality of being fresh or recent. In apocalyptic and related world views (including Christianity), the "new" is the final stage of being for creation and creature alike. The concept of newness is one of the central themes of the New Testament.

I. Terminology

Heb. *ḥāḏaš* generally conveys the sense of "brand new, having never previously existed" (e.g., Exod. 1:8; Lev. 26:10; Deut. 20:5, 8; cf. Gk. *prósphatos*, which appears only at Heb. 10:20). Gk. *néos*, primarily "younger, more recent," is less technical; it describes "young" people (so RSV, Tit. 2:4), a more recent covenant (Heb. 12:24), and freshly pressed wine (Matt. 9:17; Mark 2:22; Luke 5:37-38).

Gk. *kainós* is richest in meaning by far ("unused, previously unknown, remarkable"). The LXX uses this broad word to translate Heb. *ḥāḏaš* in virtually all cases. By New Testament times, this word had become "the epitome of the wholly different and miraculous thing which is brought by the time of salvation . . . a leading teleological term in apocalyptic promise" (J. Behm, "καινός," *TDNT* 3 [1965]: 449). The New Testament writers use *kainós* to characterize all of the changes brought about by Jesus Christ.

Since the "new" implies a displacement of the "old," *kainós* can be synonymous with *deúteros* "second" (e.g., "new covenant," Heb. 8:8, 13; 9:15; cf. 8:7; "second" coming of Christ, 10:9; "second death," Rev. 2:11; 20:6, 14; 21:8), *ánōthen* "again, anew" (John 3:3, 7; cf. v. 4), and similar terms.

II. Old Testament Prophets

The biblical promise of a new age first appears in the major prophets. The destruction of Jerusalem and the temple had also destroyed the dominant ideology. Obviously the original covenant had failed; it was now obsolete. But even before the dust had settled from the conquerors' feet, Yahweh began to speak to Israel about a second opportunity. He would make a new covenant with them (Jer. 31:31). He would gather them again out of captivity, this time out from Babylon, not Egypt (Isa. 43:14-21; "a new thing," v. 19). This return of Israel is described in glowing, otherworldly terms: it would be like "new heavens and a new earth" (65:17-25); a new temple would be rebuilt—superior to the old (Ezek. 40:4-47:12)—and the boundaries of Israel would be restored to their greatest extent (47:13-48:35). Even the people themselves would be different; they would have a new heart and a new spirit (11:17-20; 18:31; 36:24-29) and sing "a new song" (Isa. 42:10).

III. Apocalyptic Literature

Unfortunately, the return from exile in Babylon failed to meet these high expectations. As the political sit-

uation grew progressively worse, so did Israel's hope of achieving any of these utopian goals. The tension between these high expectations and the grim realities of the present forced a reinterpretation of the new age. The past and the present were regarded with a dour pessimism—the old was totally under the control of the Evil One.

The only hope lay beyond this present time in the possibility of a new age. If utopia could not be gained by natural processes here on earth, perhaps it could be gained by supernatural means. The theme of apocalyptic literature is that God (and/or his appointed representative, the Messiah) would break into this world to establish justice. In the process the old heavens and earth, with all their wicked inhabitants, would be physically destroyed. Then God and his Messiah would establish and rule a new world, one now populated only by the righteous (e.g., 1 En. 45:4-5; 72:1; 91:16; Jub. 1:29; 2 Bar. 32:6; 57:2; 4 Ezra 7:75).

IV. New Testament

Jesus speaks to an audience thoroughly rooted in apocalyptic thought. They hailed him as the Messiah, who would usher in the age in which "the old has passed away" and "the new has come" (2 Cor. 5:17; Rev. 21:5).

A. New Covenant. Just as the old covenant established the respective obligations of Israel and Yahweh, so also does the new. But where the old required the sacrifice of an animal as the penalty for breakage, the new covenant demands no such sacrifice. God has already paid the penalty for sin through a more perfect sacrifice, the death of the Son, which the New Testament writers identify with Jeremiah's "new covenant (Matt. 26:28; Mark 14:24; Luke 22:20; 1 Cor. 11:25; Heb. 8:7-13; 9:11-15).

B. New Creature. Just as Adam was the first person of a race of humans, so Jesus Christ is the first of a new race. He is the Adam of the new age (cf. Rom. 5:14-21) and the "firstborn of the dead" (Rev. 1:5). The one who has accepted this new covenant becomes a "new creation" (Gal. 6:15). He has a "new nature" (Col. 3:10; cf. "new spirit"; Ezek. 11:19; 18:31; 2 Cor. 3:3). He is given a "new name" (Rev. 2:17; 19:12; cf. Isa. 62:2) to signify his new character. He has been "born anew" (Gk. *gennēthḗ ánōthen*, John 3:3) and is thus a member of the second age; his renewal is external, awaiting only the resurrection of the physical body (1 Cor. 15:52).

C. New Heavens and Earth. While the new heavens and new earth of Isaiah (Isa. 65:17; 66:22) may appear somewhat ambiguous and perhaps figurative, the new heavens and the new earth of the New Testament are unabashedly literal. The old heaven and earth will be abolished (2 Pet. 3:13; cf. Heb. 12:25-27); even now the earth is groaning as in labor (cf. Rom. 8:19-23). Only the righteous will inhabit this new creation (Rev. 21:1-8).

D. New Jerusalem. The new Jerusalem pictured at Rev. 21-22 is a not a new theme, but one borrowed from the Old Testament and later Jewish literature (Isa. 54:11-14; 60:15-22; Ezek. 40-48). The new Jerusalem in Revelation, however, figuratively represents the body of Christ; the identification is certain. The city is "prepared as a bride adorned for her husband" (Rev. 21:2). It is what John sees when the angel promises to show him "the Bride, the wife of the Lamb" (vv. 9-10). The new Jerusalem is the antithesis of "Babylon," which city represents the worldly system (16:19–18:24).

E. New Song. In the light of all this, the redeemed now sing a "new song" of praise to God. He is the one who has established justice and delivered them from oppression (Rev. 14:3; cf. Ps. 33:3; 40:3 [MT 4]; 96:1; 98:1; 144:9; Isa. 42:10).

Bibliography. J. Behm, "καινός," *TDNT* 3 (1965): 447-454; "νέος," 4 (1967): 896-901; R. H. Charles, *A Critical and Exegetical Commentary on the Revelation of St. John,* ICC (1920) 2:200-204; R. North, "ḥāḏāš [chādhāsh], *TDOT* 4 (1980); 225-44.

NEW GATE (Heb. *iiśaʿar[bêṭ-YHWH] heḥāḏāš*).* A gate of the Jerusalem temple, at the entry to which the "princes of Judah" heard the priests' and prophets' sentence of death upon Jeremiah (Jer. 26:10). Here also Baruch read publicly from the prophet's scroll (36:10). The location of the gate is uncertain, but it may have been in the upper court (cf. 20:2).

NEW MOON (Heb. *[ha]hōḏeš* "new moon, month"; Gk. *neomēnía*).† The beginning of the lunar month, the appearance of the crescent moon, which the Israelites regularly celebrated with a festival (cf. Gen. 1:14).

The festival of the new moon is named with the appointed feasts as a time of rejoicing in which the Israelites were to blow the trumpet and offer sacrifices (Num. 10:10); the nature of these offerings is detailed at 28:11-15, including animal, drink, and cereal offerings, and a male goat specified as a sin offering. In Ezekiel's portrayal of the restored temple the prince was to stand at the east gate of the inner court on the day of the new moon; from there he could observe the sacrifices conducted therein (Ezek. 45:17; 46:1-6). Cultic celebration of the new moon is reckoned among postexilic observances (1 Chr. 23:31; 2 Chr. 2:4; 8:13; 31:3; Ezra 3:5; Neh. 10:33), often in association with the Sabbath.

The festive nature of the new moon is suggested by the two days of feasting hosted by Saul (1 Sam. 20:5, 18, 24-27), the rest from work (Amos 8:5, although not prescribed in the Pentateuch), and its description as a time of rejoicing (Num. 10:10). The common people seem to have regarded it as an occasion upon which to consult prophets (2 Kgs. 4:23). According to the latter prophets the day was subject to abuse (Isa. 1:13-14; Amos 8:5). In the eschaton the new moon and Sabbath would be redeemed to mark the times of universal praise (Isa. 66:23).

The focus of the day was the offering of thanksgiving to Yahweh rather than adulation of the moon itself. Unlike the surrounding peoples, Israel was to avoid worshipping the moon or any other heavenly bodies (Deut. 4:19; 17:3), though such practices are attested (2 Kgs. 21:3, 5; 23:5; Jer. 8:2; 19:13). Worship of the moon was nearly universal in the ancient world, and to it was ascribed the power of growing and ripening the fruit of the soil and the bestowal of life and happiness upon men and women. In Palestine Jericho was named after the moon-god (*yārēaḥ*), and tablets from

Ras Shamra note a special offering "on the day of the new moon."

In particular the Old Testament stresses the importance of observing the new moon of the seventh month, Tishri (Sept./Oct.). Whether of not this celebration marked the beginning of the lunar new year as it did in later Judaism (Rosh Hashanah) is widely debated. According to Exod. 12:2, the month of Abib, later called Nisan (Mar./Apr.), was to mark the new year. The care taken in postexilic Judaism to establish the precise arrival of the new year is attested in the Mishnah; witnesses of the arrival of the crescent moon were closely questioned and the beginning of the feast signaled by fires and wind instruments.

The new moon celebration mentioned at Col. 2:16 probably refers to a syncretistic practice at Colossae the motivation for which was fear of the "elemental spirits of the universe" (v. 20). Paul does not condemn the keeping of holy days as such but urges believers to claim their liberation in Christ from the powers of this age (cf. Gal. 4:3-11).

NEW YEAR (Heb. *rōʾš haššānâ* "head of the year").† The day (and often by extension the season) marking the beginning of a new calendar year, widely observed throughout the ancient Near East by a variety of elaborate festivals.

In Egypt the statue of the god Horus was brought forth from his temple in order that exposure to the sun's rays might reunite his soul and body. In Babylon (and similarly in Assyria) the spring *akītu* festival began with the new year. During this eleven-day event Marduk's supremacy was celebrated, the temple purified, and the king's authority renewed; the Babylonian creation epic was recited before Marduk, and events of the coming year were foretold. The Canaanite myth (as found in the Ras Shamra texts) of the death and resurrection of the fertility-god Baal has been linked by some scholars to the autumn celebration of the new year.

Much scholarly debate has surrounded the question of the nature and date of a new year festival in Israel, impeded largely by the scarcity of biblical references to such an observance. Some scholars seek to identify the new year observance as an agricultural festival, noting particularly autumn celebrations associated with the harvest (e.g., the festival of trumpets, Lev. 23:23-25; Num. 29:1-6). Others suggest that certain "enthronement" Psalms (e.g., Pss. 47, 93, 96-100) represent part of a liturgy for annual celebration of Yahweh's enthronement. Too many gaps exist in current knowledge of both ancient Near Eastern and Israelite festivals to speak confidently of any patterning or borrowing from the observances of neighboring peoples.

Similarly, debate rages concerning whether the Israelite new year was observed in the autumn (first of Tishri, Sept./Oct.) or spring (first of Nisan, Mar./Apr.). At Exod. 12:2 God tells Moses and Aaron that Abib (Nisan) is to be the first month of the year ("the beginning of months"; cf. 13:4; 23:15; 34:18; Deut. 16:1; also Exod. 40:2, 17). At 1 Kgs. 6:1 Ziv (Iyyar; Apr./May) is indicated as the second month, which would necessitate Nisan's being the first; similarly, at Jer. 36:22 Chislev (Nov./Dec.) is mentioned as the ninth month. Ezek. 40:1 contains the sole biblical reference to Rosh Hashanah (the later Jewish designation of the holiday), and Ezekiel's regular calendrical understanding includes a Nisan new year; here the term means simply "the beginning (lit. "head") of the year." Lev. 25:9, however, refers to the advent of the Year of Jubilee in the fall, and Neh. 1:1; 2:1 put Chislev (ninth month) before Nisan (first) in the same year, perhaps implying an autumn new year. The Year of Jubilee does seem to reflect an agricultural calendar that may not be perceived as official, much like the modern fiscal or academic year (cf. Exod. 34:22b, which probably also reflects an agricultural cycle). Neh. 8:2, 14-15, by placing the autumn Feast of Booths in the seventh month, suggests that at that time the Israelites employed a calender that began in the spring. In sum, the Old Testament references to the new year appear to be ambiguous and/or imprecise, although the scant concrete evidence leans toward a first of Nisan observance. It would appear, then, that in Israel the more significant religious celebrations so overshadowed any new year festival that few records survive. See YEAR.

The New Testament is devoid of references to the new year. In postbiblical Judaism the first of Tishri was observed as the new year (Mishnah Roš Haššanah), a solemn occasion commemorating God's creation and a time for personal reflection (Yom ha-Zikkaron "Day of Remembrance") and repentance.

NEZIAH [nə zī'ə] (Heb. nᵉṣîaḥ "faithful"). A temple servant whose descendants returned with Zerubbabel from captivity in Babylon (Ezra 2:54; Neh. 7:56).

NEZIB [nē'zīb] (Heb. nᵉṣîḇ "garrison, outpost"). A city in the Shephelah of Judah (Josh. 15:43), generally identified with modern Khirbet Beit Neṣîb, 13 km. (8 mi.) north of Hebron.

NIBHAZ [nīb'hăz] (Heb. niḇaz). One of two gods worshipped by the Avvites, a Syrian people whom the Assyrians resettled at Samaria (2 Kgs. 17:31). He has been identified variously as "Nebo the Seer" or "Nebo of the face," a Babylonian deity revered in Syria, or an Elamite deity Ibnakhaza.

NIBSHAN [nīb'shăn] (Heb. hanniḇšān). A city in the wilderness of Judah (Josh. 15:62). The site has been as modern Khirbet el-Maqârî in the valley of Achor, identified 17 km. (10.5 mi.) southeast of Jerusalem.

NICANOR [nī kā'nər, nĭ kä'nôr] (Gk. Nikanōr "conqueror").†
1. A Syrian general under Lysias and friend of the Seleucid king Antiochus IV Epiphanes (1 Macc. 3:38). In 166 B.C. he was commanded to invade and destroy Judea (vv. 31-41), but Judas Maccabeus defeated the Seleucid forces at Emmaus the following year (4:1-15). Following the death of Antiochus IV and the murder of Lysias and Antiochus V, Demetrius I Soter named Nicanor governor of Judea and dispatched him to seize Judas and install Alcimus as high priest (2 Macc. 14:12-13). In 161 this bitter enemy of the Jews was again defeated at Beth-horon; all of his troops perished, and Nicanor's head and right hand were cut off

and displayed in Jerusalem. The event was commemorated as an annual celebration (1 Macc. 7:43-50; 2 Macc. 15:25-36).
2. One of the seven chosen to distribute food to the needy and disenfranchised ("serve tables"), thus freeing the apostles for preaching and other responsibilities (Acts 6:5).

NICANOR GATE. One of the gates leading to the courtyard of the temple. According to an inscription on a sarcophagus discovered in a cave on Mt. Scopus, it was named for the first-century A.D. Alexandrian craftsman who made the gates. It was the only gate in the temple courtyard that was not gilded, formed of "Corinthian copper that shone like gold."

The location of the gate remains subject to debate, focused largely on interpretation of Josephus BJ v.5.3. Some scholars would place it on the western side of the Court of the Women, to the east of the Court of the Israelites. Others would place it on the eastern side of the Court of the Women, beyond the entrance to the sanctuary and facing the larger gate.

If the gate was located on the west side of the Court of the Women in Herod's temple complex, then Mary would have brought the infant Jesus up the semicircular stairway of fifteen steps that led into the Court of the Israelites (Luke 2:22-23), and here both Simeon and Anna would have prophesied that through Mary's child would come deliverance for Israel (vv. 27-38).

NICODEMUS [nĭk'ədē'məs] (Gk. Nikodēmos "conqueror of the people"). A Pharisee and member of the Sanhedrin who came to Jesus during the night. Recognizing Jesus' greatness, Nicodemus asked to be instructed more fully by him (John 3:1-2). Although he did not immediately understand Jesus' words about the necessity of regeneration (vv. 3-36), he eventually did comprehend and become a disciple (7:50). He argued that Jesus be given a fair hearing before the Sanhedrin (v. 51). Nicodemus also aided Joseph of Arimathea in burying the body of Jesus (19:38-42).

Nicodemus is an important exception to John's categorization of "the Jews" as a group that as a whole opposed Jesus (cf. 1:11; 9:39-41) .

NICODEMUS, GOSPEL OF. The name ascribed by Latin traditions of the thirteenth-fourteenth centuries A.D. to the Acts of Pilate. See PILATE, ACTS OF.

NICOLAITANS [nĭk'ə lā'ə tənz] (Gk. Nikolaïtēs). A party or sect present in the churches of Ephesus and Pergamum (Rev. 2:6, 15).

Little is known about this group aside from the biblical references. Some scholars suggest that the Nicolaitans and the followers of Balaam (v. 14) were one and the same, a theory based largely on the similar etymology "to conquer the people" ascribed to both names (Gk. niká laón, Heb. bālaʿ ʿām); the LXX, however, never uses Gk. nikáō to translate Heb. bālaʿ. Others speculate that the Nicolaitans were followers of Nicolaus (Nikolaos) of Antioch, one of the seven original elders (Acts 6:5), but again there is no evidence other than a similarity of names (cf. Irenaeus Adv. haer. i.26.3; iii.11.1).

The Nicolaitans may have practiced idolatry (especially eating meat offered to idols) and immorality (Tertullian *Adv. Marc.* i.29; *De praesc. her.* 33; *De pudic.* 19; Clement of Alexandria *Strom.* ii.20; iii.24), like other sects mentioned by name such as the followers of Balaam (Rev. 2:14) and Jezebel (vv. 20-24). Accordingly, some scholars have sought to establish a connection between this sect and the later Gnostics (cf. Hippolytus *Ref.* vii.36; Eusebius (*HE* iii.29).

NICOLAUS [nĭk'ələ'əs] (Gk. *Nikolaos* "conqueror of the people"). A proselyte from Antioch of Syria; one of seven deacons appointed in response to a complaint that the Church was neglecting the Greek-speaking widows in the distribution of food (Acts 6:5; KJV "Nicolas"). As did the other six, Nicolaus had a Greek name, prompting the suggestion that all of the deacons were proselytes.

Some of the Church Fathers suggest that Nicolaus later fell from the faith and became the leader of the heretical Nicolaitans.

NICOPOLIS [nĭ kŏp'ə lĭs] (Gk. *hē Nikopolis* "city of victory"). A name given to many ancient towns; in the New Testament probably Nicopolis in Achaia, a Roman colony in Epirus on the Ambracian gulf, just north of Greece. Founded by Octavian in honor of his victory against Antony and Cleopatra at Actium in 31 B.C., it was later the home of the philosopher Epictetus. According to Josephus (*Ant.* xvi.5.3 [147]), Herod the Great built many of the public buildings. The apostle Paul intended to spend the winter here (Tit. 3:12), perhaps so he could travel through Illyricum en route to Rome.

NIGER [nī'jər] (Gk. *Niger*; from Lat. *niger* "black"). The surname of Simeon, a prophet and teacher who lived in Antioch (Acts 13:1). Some scholars identify him with Simon of Cyrene (Mark 15:21).

NIGHT (Heb. *laylā, lāyil*; Gk. *nýx*). The period of darkness between sunset and sunrise, the length of which varies according to the season.

The Hebrews originally divided the night into three equal periods or "watches" (Heb. *'ašmûrâ*), based on the period assigned to a guard detail (Ps. 63:6 [MT 7]; cf. Exod. 14:24; Judg. 7:19). Technical terms distinguished the beginning of the night, "evening" (*'ereḇ*), from the end, "dawn" (*šaḥar*); the period of semidarkness immediately following sunset and prior to dawn was called "twilight" (*nešep*). By New Testament times they had adopted the Greco-Roman standard of four watches (Gk. *phylakḗ*), each approximately three hours long: "evening" (*opsé*), "midnight" (*mesonýktion*), "cockcrowing" (*alektorophōnías*) and "morning" (*prōóï*) (Mark 13:35; cf. Matt. 14:25; Luke 12:38).

Night was a particularly significant time for dreams (Gen. 20:3; 31:24; 2 Chr. 1:7) and therefore esoteric knowledge (Ps. 19:2 [MT 3]). The only mention even closely resembling chthonian deities, typically associated with the dark in other cultures, is the spirit of Samuel invoked by the witch of Endor "by night" (1 Sam. 28:8-25); even here the emphasis is not on the fact that the séance took place at night but rather that Saul felt compelled to keep his visit secret and so

waited until dark (witches were outlawed in Israel; Exod. 22:18).

Only a few figurative uses are apparent in the Old Testament. Night is the antithesis of day (cf. Job 26:10, KJV; Heb. *ḥōšeḵ*; RSV "darkness"), so "a night and a day" mean a twenty-four-hour period (Jonah 1:17 [MT 2:1]; cf. 2 Cor. 11:25) or "all of the time, constantly" (cf. Ps. 32:4; 55:10 [MT 11]). Such usage is typical of Hebrew thought, where the whole is indicated by its polar opposites (cf. "from Dan to Beersheba," meaning "all of Israel"; 1 Sam. 3:20; 1 Kgs. 4:25 [MT 5:5]; "knowledge of good and evil," meaning "all knowledge"; Gen. 2:9). Night is most powerful as a symbol in the book of Job. Here night is a time of gloom and darkness (Job 3:3-10). It is the time when Job is visited by a wise spirit (a variation on the dream) that terrifies him (4:12-21, "visions of the night"; cf. 20:8; 33:15). Because of his suffering the nights are long and full of misery (7:2-4). They are times of murder, theft, and adultery (24:13-17; 36:20). Nevertheless, night is a time when God will execute judgment upon the wicked (34:21-30) and give songs to the just (35:10).

Night is a powerful symbol in apocalyptic literature, later Judaism being influenced by apocalyptic, and the gnostic cults, all of which feature an extensive demonology and sharp, mutually exclusive categories of opposites (e.g., black/white, darkness/light, good/evil, day/night). Here night is the time of demons and evil (e.g., Mic. 3:6; Wisd. 17:2-21). Night is also associated with the judgment to accompany the end of the age (e.g., 2 Esdr. 5:4, 7).

In the New Testament night is again the time for dreams, visions, and apparitions (Matt. 2:13-14; 14:25-26; Luke 2:8ff.; Acts 5:19; 16:9; 18:9). It is symbolic of the sudden return of the Lord (Matt. 24:43) and in John's gospel is associated with spiritual darkness (John 11:10; of Nicodemus, 3:2; 19:39; cf. 7:50, KJV; of Judas, 13:30; and of the disciples before they saw the resurrected Christ, 21:3). In Revelation the heavenly city of Jerusalem (metaphorically the Church) needs no external source of light because God is its light; thus "night" will never come (Rev. 21:23-25; 22:5).

NIGHT HAG (Heb. *lîlîṯ*). In English translations a female demon that inhabits deserted places (Isa. 34:14; KJV "screech owl"). Such renderings seek to derive the term from Heb. *laylâ* "night," but more likely it stems from Akk. *lilîtu* (Sum. *lil* "wind"), a female demon presumed to steal children according to late Jewish literature. In his description of the destruction of Edom Isaiah pictures this creature haunting ruins in the company of jackals, hyenas, owls, and ravens—all unclean animals. *See* LILITH.

NIGHTHAWK (Heb. *taḥmas* "violent one [?]"). A fowl numbered among the unclean birds (Lev. 11:16; Deut. 14:15). The nighthawk (Lat. *Chordeiles*) is a small nocturnal bird of prey related to the owl and the hawk. Also called the night jar or "goatsucker," one variety (*Caprimulgas europaeus*) ranges over all of Europe below sixty-four degrees north latitude. It is also attested in Asia from the northern edge of the wooded regions south to middle Asia, but is rarer in southern Asia. In North Africa the *Caprimulgas nubicus* is found for the most part only as it migrates.

Heb. *taḥmas,* however, does not properly designate a nighthawk but more probably a small predator owl (cf. JB, NIV "screech owl"). These birds live in the forests of Galilee, roosting during the day, at times in a row on a single thick branch. Their grey excrete, "owlballs," is distinctive and betrays their presence; it is composed mostly of the hair and skeletons of their prey.

NILE [nīl] (Heb. *yeʾôr;* cf. Egyp. *aiitrw, ʾrw*).† The river that flows more than some 6500 km. (4000 mi.) in an irregular course winding from the highlands of East Central Africa to the shores of northern Egypt, where it empties into the Mediterranean Sea. Comprised of two major tributaries, the Blue Nile and the White Nile, with a total estimated watershed in excess of 2.6 million sq. km. (1 million sq. mi.)—nearly one-tenth the area of Africa—the Nile is not only one of the longest rivers in the world (the Amazon may be longer, but the dispute awaits further detailed mapping of the region) but also the single most dominant influence upon the terrain and environment of northeastern Africa.

The origin of the Greek name for the river (Gk. *Neilos;* Lat. *Nilos*) remains obscure. Its ancient name appears to have been Egyp. *ḥʿpy,* which served also to designate the Nile god Haʿpy. By the time of the Middle Kingdom (*ca.* 2000 B.C.) Egypt. *trw,* at first meaning simply "river," had become the common appellation, continuing in use until the Greco-Roman period. The Hebrew adaptation of this form occurs in both singular and plural, apparently referring to the several branches that course through the delta (but cf. Job 28:10; Isa. 33:21, where the plural designated not the Nile but rivers or streams in general).

Originating on the northern shore of Lake Victoria in Uganda and Tanganyika near the Ripon Falls where it is known as Kagewra, the White Nile (al-Baḥr al-Abyad) flows northwest (downstream) to Lake Albert, flowing through the wild swamplands of the Sudan where the water is increasingly filtered, giving its waters the lighter appearance from which its name derives. Near the northern reaches of the swamplands the White Nile is joined by the Sobat before flowing northward toward Khartoum, where it merges with the Blue Nile.

The source of the Blue Nile (al-Baḥr al-Azraq) lies in western Ethiopia at Lake Tana, where it is called Abbai. Flowing through the center of the Ethiopian plateau and then northwest to Khartoum in modern Sudan, the dark, turgid waters of the Blue Nile join the lighter waters of the White Nile just south of the sixth cataract near Khartoum to form the main body of the Nile river. The Nile is then joined on its northerly course by another important tributary, the Atbara or al-Baḥr al-Aswad, which enters about 320 km. (200 mi.) north of Khartoum between the fifth and sixth cataracts.

Between Khartoum and Wâdī Halfa the Nile winds in an S-course, in which the river is disrupted by several series of rapids known as cataracts (the sixth through second, proceeding northward) making it navigable for only relatively short stretches. Just north of modern Cairo the apex of the Delta juts out, dividing the river into two main branches, the Rosetta to the west and the Damietta to the east, which in turn flow into the Mediterranean.

From early times until the present, an arid climate has assured the Nile's paramount role in the life of Egypt. Both its annual flooding and the rich alluvium carried downstream that provides rich silt for the adjacent fields have been the mainstay of Egyptian agriculture since antiquity. Excessive seasonal rainfall on the plateau region of Ethiopia from June to September swells the waters of the Blue Nile and the Atbara as the rivers take with them enormous amounts of silt that are later deposited in the fields of the Nile valley and the delta. In turn the soil yields a rich harvest in April and May, after which farmers in earlier times could plant seeds near the river bed or irrigation devices (cf. Deut. 11:10). In modern times a complex system of dams, barrages, and canals regulate the flow of water, enabling three crops a year to be raised through perennial irrigation.

The regular flooding of the Nile also spawned such innovations as a sophisticated calendar, hydraulic engineering and surveying as well as irrigation as early as 4000 B.C. Ancient trade routes followed the course of the Nile, also using the river for transportation of such materials as the large blocks employed in the construction of the numerous massive monuments that dot the Egyptian landscape.

Archaeological remains attest to the river's central cultural role as well. Lyrical references as early as the Pyramid Texts (early third millennium) point to annual celebrations greeting the innundation of the river, whose source the ancient Egyptians believed to be the underworld (Nun). Most famous is "The Adoration of the Nile," which survives in copies dating as early as the Nineteenth Dynasty (thirteenth century). Such a central role in agriculture and trade led to personification of the river as the god Haʿpy; although he never gained a central role in the Egyptian pantheon (partly due to the association of the prominent Osiris with the innundation), Haʿpy is frequently portrayed as providing offerings of food and drink for other deities.

Despite the certain importance of the Nile to the Israelites during their sojourn in Egypt, biblical references to it are scant. Ezekiel sketches Egypt's pride with the pharaoh's claim, "My Nile is my own; I made it" (Ezek. 29:3), while Isaiah prophesies doom, threatening that the river's waters would be dried up and its bed parched and dry (Isa. 19:5; cf. Ezek. 30:12).

NIMRAH [nĭm′rə] (Heb. *nimrâ*). Alternate form of BETH-NIMRAH (Num. 32:3).

NIMRIM, WATERS OF [nĭm′rĭm] (Heb. *mê nimrîm* "water of leopards [?]"). A place in Moab, whose waters the prophets Isaiah and Jeremiah prophesied would become desolate (Isa. 15:6; Jer. 48:34). The desolation was especially significant because it caused the surrounding crops to wither.

Most scholars identify the site with modern Wâdī en-Numeirah, a stream in a swampy area on the east side of the Dead Sea, 14 km. (8.5 mi.) north of the southern tip. The site is marked by the Rudshim en-Numeira (a "heap of stones" discovered at en-Numeira), 1 km (.5 mi.) south of the river near an ancient building thought to be of Nabatean origin. West of the swamp as far as the Dead Sea the terrain shows traces of the brook's former course, while to the east is a foothill, perhaps formed by silt deposits from the waters of the brook.

Other scholars support the identification of Nimrim with Wâdī Nimrîm in the plains of Moab. This stream joins the Jordan 13 km. (8 mi.) north of the point where the Jordan flows into the Dead Sea.

NIMROD [nǐm'rŏd] (Heb. *nimrōḏ, nimrôḏ*; from *māraḏ* "to rebel [?]"; LXX Gk. *Nebrōd*). The son of Cush, and the first mighty man and hunter (Gen. 10:8-9; 1 Chr. 1:10, "a mighty one in the earth"). Nimrod's kingdom began with Babel, Erech, and Accad in the land of Shinar; he then expanded to Assyria, building Nineveh, Rehoboth-Ir, Calah (modern Nimrûd), and Resen (Gen. 10:11-12). The prophet Micah refers to Assyria as "the land of Nimrod" (Mic. 5:6 [MT 5]).

Since such an outstanding person would have been widely known, many scholars have sought to link him with other famous Near Eastern figures, including Tukulti-Ninurta I, king of Assyria *ca.* 1250-1200 B.C.; Amenophis III, king of Egypt *ca.* 1400-1375; and the Babylonian war-deity Ninurta.

NIMSHI [nǐm'shī] (Heb. *nimšî* "pulled out"). The father of Jehoshaphat and grandfather (or "ancestor") of King Jehu of Israel (2 Kgs. 9:2, 14).

NINEVEH [nǐn'ə və] (Heb. *nînᵉwēh*; Gk. *Nineui*; Akk. *Ninua, Ninuwa*).† One of the earliest Mesopotamian cities, and capital of the Assyrian Empire. Situated on the eastern bank of the Tigris river opposite modern Mosul, some 350 km. (220 mi.) northwest of Baghdad, the city's ruins are marked by two large mounds divided by the Khoser river: Kuyunjik, 30 m. (98 ft.) high and long uninhabited, and Tell Nebi Yûnus ("hill of the prophet Jonah"), 15 m. (49 ft.) high. Kuyunjik was excavated from 1820 to 1932, but the presence of a village and mosque has limited exploration of Nebi Yûnus to a few test shafts. The mounds are surrounded by a rectangular wall some 13 km. (8 mi.) in circumference, enclosing some 730 ha. (1800 a.). The statement at Jonah 3:3 that Nineveh was "three days journey in breadth" attests to the size of the city and its environs.

The cuneiform name *Ninua* derives from the older form *Ninuwa*, which survived as late as the Mari texts (eighteenth century B.C.). The name may be Hurrian in origin. Some cuneiform texts employ the logogram *Ninā*, which portrays a fish (the sign *ḫa*) inside an enclosure (*AB*), a link with the river-goddess Nina.

Archaeological evidence indicates that the site has been occupied from prehistoric times. An inscription of King Naram-Sin of Akkad (2360-2180) has been discovered, and Maništusu, successor to Sargon I (nineteenth century), erected a temple to Ishtar that may be the oldest building on the site. The city is named in the prologue to the Code of Hammurabi.

In the Middle Assyrian period (fourteenth-twelfth centuries) Nineveh was the palace-city for many Assyrian kings, and most conducted extensive building programs there. The Ishtar temple constructed by Maništusu was rebuilt and refurnished several times.

Sennacherib (705-681) razed the old royal palace in the southern corner of Kuyunjik and replaced it with a massive structure of more than seventy rooms, with walls covered with slabs of sculptured stone and gateways flanked by winged bulls and lion-sphinxes. Sennacherib also enlarged the city, widened its streets, and built an aqueduct to carry fresh water from the mountains.

The northern portion of Kuyunjik was the site of Assurbanipal's (669-633) palace, which featured an extensive royal library. Found in two large deposits, some twenty-six thousand cuneiform tablets encompass historical, legal, philological, religious, and scientific texts and provide evidence of Assyrian royal and literary accomplishments.

Yet as magnificent as Nineveh was it did not survive the fall of the Assyrian Empire. The city was captured in August 612 by a combined force of Babylonians under Nebuchadrezzar II and Medes commanded by Cyaxares. The site remained unoccupied for three centuries, with only brief intervals of settlement during the Seleucid, Roman, and Sassanian periods.

The biblical account names Nineveh among the cities founded by Nimrod, the son of Cush (Gen. 10:11; "great city" here probably refers to Calah). The parallel accounts 2 Kgs. 19:36-37; Isa. 37:37-38 note that Sennacherib returned to the capital after abandoning his siege of Jerusalem and was assassinated there by his sons; the deity Nisroch, in whose temple the murder occurred, does not appear in Assyrian records. The reluctant prophet Jonah was instructed to journey to Nineveh and preach against that wicked city (Jonah 1:2; 3:2). The account records the king and citizenry as responding to the prophet's warning by fasting and turning to Yahweh (vv. 4-10; cf. 4:11). The prophet Nahum proclaimed the fall of Nineveh as divine retaliation for plotting evil against the Lord (Nah. 1:11), cruelty and plundering in wartime (2:12-13; 3:1, 19), prostitution and witchcraft (v. 4), and commercial exploitation (v. 19). Nahum's contemporary Zephaniah assails the inhabitants' arrogance (Zeph. 2:13-15). Jesus responds to the request for a miraculous sign by declaring that at the final judgment the Ninevites (Gk. *Nineuitai*) would rise in condemnation of the Pharisees' generation (Matt. 12:41 par. Luke 11:32 [KJV "Nineve"]).

NISAN [nī'săn, nē'sän] (Heb. *nîsān*; Gk. *Nisan*; Akk. *nisānu*). The first month of the Hebrew calendar (Mar./Apr.) (Neh. 2:1; Esth. 3:7), called ABIB in preexilic times.

NISROCH [nǐs'rŏk] (Heb. *nisrōḵ*). The deity in whose temple the Assyrian king Sennacherib was murdered (2 Kgs. 19:37; Isa. 37:38). Because the term Nisroch occurs in no other ancient Near Eastern literature, some scholars speculate that the present form may be a result of an early scribal error (cf. LXX Gk. *Esdrach, Esthrach, Asrach*). Alternate readings include Marduk, the city-god of Babylon; Nusku, the Assyrian fire-god; and the national god Assur.

NITRE. *See* LYE.

NO (KJV). *See* THEBES.

NOADIAH [nō'ə dī'ə] (Heb. *nô'aḏyâ* "Yahweh has gathered together" or "Yahweh has met by appointment").

1. The son of Binnui; a Levite to whom the temple vessels were returned after the Exile (Ezra 8:33).

2. A prophetess among those who tried to discourage Nehemiah from rebuilding Jerusalem's walls (Neh. 6:14).

NOAH [nō'ə].

1. (Heb. *nōaḥ*; Gk. *Nōe*). The son of Lamech and father of Shem, Ham, and Japheth; builder of the ark who with his family escaped the Flood (Gen. 5–10).

I. Name

The origin of the name Noah has been widely disputed. According to the text, it is related to Heb. *nāḥam* "to comfort, cheer," apparently because the fruit of Noah's planting the first vineyard (9:20) "shall bring us relief (*yenaḥamanû*) from our work and from the toil of our hands" (5:29). The LXX here substitutes Gk. *dianapaúsei* "cause (us) to rest," perhaps from Heb. *nûaḥ* "to rest," a derivation accepted by some early rabbis (*Gen. Rabb.* xxv). Some scholars suggest a relationship to Akk. *Nâḥ*, possibly a divine name. None of these readings is without problems.

II. First Tiller of the Soil

Noah was the first to farm the soil and plant a vineyard. He then partook of the fruit of his labors and became drunk (9:20-27).

The story of Noah as the first farmer forms a counterpoint to that of the first sin, committed by Adam (3:17); Adam eats forbidden food and so God curses the soil so food can only be obtained by much hard work (vv. 1-19). By contrast, Noah, the first to be called righteous (6:9), is also the first who tills the earth to obtain food; he is then rewarded with a product (wine) that mitigates the curse and provides relief for those tilling the soil.

The discovery of wine is clouded by Ham's actions. After becoming drunk, Noah lay in his tent uncovered. Ham "saw the nakedness of his father" and informed his brothers, who covered Noah. When their father awoke he knew what Ham his son had "done to him." Surprisingly, Noah did not curse Ham for his actions, but Ham's youngest son Canaan (*see* NAKEDNESS). The curse of Canaan (9:25-27) may be recorded to explain why the Israelites (sons of Shem) had to share Palestine (or Canaan) with the Philistines (sons of Japheth).

III. Flood Narrative

Noah is the leading figure in the biblical story of the Flood (6:5–8:22). When Noah was six hundred years old (7:11), God realized that the heart of mankind was bent on evil and resolved to destroy his creation. Yet he revealed his intentions to the righteous Noah, instructing him to build an ark and thus save himself and his family (6:5-22); Noah was to take at least two of every animal in order to preserve the various species. Noah heeded God and built the ark, and when the rains came he, his family, and the animals were all safe. After the Flood subsided the ark came to rest on the "mountains of Ararat," where Noah and his

shipmates disembarked (6:22–8:19). *See* ARK OF NOAH; FLOOD.

Noah immediately offered burnt offerings to the Lord for rescuing him from the Flood, and God promised in return never again to curse the ground or destroy every living creature (vv. 20-22). In this new covenant the Lord blessed Noah and his descendants, repeating his command to be fruitful, multiply, and exercise dominion over the animals (9:1-7; cf. 1:28); here they were specifically given to mankind for food, and would therefore regard them with fear and dread. In addition, God instituted new stipulations concerning murder and proper drainage of blood from animal carcasses intended for food (vv. 3-6). The Babylonian Talmud (*Sanh.* 56a; cf. Pseudo-Phocylides *Sentences*) cites seven more "Noachian laws" that were to be binding upon all people: they were to recognize government, avoid blasphemy and idolatry, refrain from adultery, refrain from bloodshed, resist robbery, and abstain from eating any flesh cut from a living animal. God then signified his promise, sealing the covenant with a rainbow (Gen. 9:8-17).

IV. Later References

In later literature Noah is primarily remembered for his faith. Ezekiel lists Noah as one of three persons (with Daniel and Job) who could have saved himself (but no others) by his own righteousness (Ezek. 14:14, 20; cf. Sir. 44:17-18). The author of Hebrews concurs, calling Noah "an heir of the righteousness which comes by faith" because he heeded God (Heb. 11:7), and 2 Pet. 2:5 identifies Noah as a "herald of righteousness." It is remarkable, then, that the apostle Paul does not mention Noah as an example of the righteousness that comes from faith, nor does he link Noah's preservation in the ark to baptism as he did Moses' crossing of the Red Sea (1 Cor. 10:2; cf. 1 Pet. 3:20).

Elsewhere the prophet Isaiah recalls God's covenant with Noah (Isa. 54:9). Jesus likens the lifestyles of his contemporaries to the "the days of Noah" preceding the Flood (Matt. 24:37-38 par.; KJV "Noe"; cf. 1 Pet. 3:20). Luke lists Noah among the ancestors of Jesus (Luke 3:36).

Bibliography. H. H. Cohen, *The Drunkenness of Noah* (University, Ala.: 1974): pp. 1-17; A. Heidel, *The Gilgamesh Epic and Old Testament Parallels*, 2nd ed. (Chicago: 1949).

2. (Heb. *naō'â*). The second of the five daughters of Zelophehad (Num. 26:33). She and her sisters successfully petitioned Moses for an inheritance because her father had no sons (27:1-11; cf. Josh. 17:3-6). Noah and her sisters each eventually married one of their father's kinsmen (Num. 36:10-12). The name is thought to be a place name, presumably associated with a Manassite clan.

NOAH, APOCALYPSE OF.† A pseudepigraphical writing noted at Jub. 10:13; 21:10, hence written before the mid-second century B.C. Passages from this work, more properly titled "Book of Noah" (cf. 10:13), are thought to be preserved in Jubilees and 1 Enoch (e.g., 7:20-39; 10:1-17; 1 En. 6–11; 54:7–55:2; 65:1–69:25) and the Dead Sea Scrolls. Its primary concerns appear to be legends surrounding "the sons of God" and "the daughters of men" and their offspring (Gen.

6:1-2) and the marvelous birth and subsequent death of Noah.

NO-AMON [nō ăm'ən] (Heb. *nō' 'āmôn*). A longer form of the Hebrew name for THEBES (Heb. *nō'*; Nah. 3:8; so JB, RSV mg., NIV mg.), intermittently the capital of Egypt *ca.* 2000-661 B.C. The KJV translates "populous No," assuming Heb. *'āmôn* to be related to *'ōm* "people"; actually *'āmôn* designates the Egyptian sky-god Amon, whose cult was centered at Thebes.

NOB [nŏb] (Heb. *nōḇ*). A town in Benjamin to which David fled from Saul (1 Sam. 21:1-11 [MT 2-12]). After the Philistine destruction of Shiloh Nob was apparently a significant cultic center attended by at least eighty-five priests (22:18; cf. v. 19, "the city of the priests"); here were the Bread of the Presence (21:4, 6 [MT 5, 7]), the ephod, and the sword of Goliath (v. 9 [MT 10]).

Claiming to have been dispatched by the king, David asked the priest Ahimelech for provisions and a weapon; Ahimelech gave him the sword of Goliath and five loaves of the holy bread (vv. 3-9 [MT 4-10]), which could legitimately be eaten only by the priests (cf. Lev. 24:8-9; Jesus refers to this incident when challenged about his disciples activities on the Sabbath [Matt. 12:4; Mark 2:26; Luke 6:4]). When Saul heard of the incident, he ordered that the inhabitants of Nob be put to death for treason. Saul's Israelite soldiers refused to harm the priests, but Doeg the Edomite (Saul's chief herdsman), carried out the king's orders, slaughtering the entire city, eighty-five priests, their families and livestock (22:11-19). Abiathar, one of the sons of Ahimelech, escaped and related the entire incident to David, who then offered him sanctuary (vv. 20-23).

The location of Nob is uncertain. Postexilic references imply that Nob was in Benjamin, between Anathoth and Jerusalem, on a hill overlooking Jerusalem (Neh. 11:32; Isa. 10:32). Several locations fit these criteria, including eṭ-Ṭôr on the Mount of Olives; Mt. Scopus, 2 km. (1 mi.) northeast of Jerusalem; or various slopes in the vicinity of Mt. Scopus (e.g., Quʿmeh, Râs el-Mesharif, Râs Umm et-Tala).

NOBAH [nō'bə] (Heb. *nōḇaḥ* "a dog's bark") (PERSON). A Manassite who captured Kenath and its villages in Transjordan and renamed the city after himself (Num. 32:42).

NOBAH [nō'bə] (Heb. *nōḇaḥ* "a dog's bark") (PLACE).

1. A city in Transjordan, formerly called KENATH, renamed by the Manassite who captured it (Num. 32:42).

2. A place near Jogbehah in Transjordan, west of the caravan along which Gideon pursued the Midianites (Judg. 8:11). The site is unknown, although some scholars suggest it may be the same as NOPHAH, the site of which is also unknown. It may also be the same as **1**, and hence modern Qanawat.

NOD [nŏd] (Heb. *nôḏ* "wandering, banishment"). The land east of Eden to which Cain moved (Gen. 4:16).

The name is probably symbolic, playing on Cain's punishment.

NODAB [nō'dăb] (Heb. *nôḏāḇ* "noble"). A clan attacked by the Transjordanian tribes of Israel (1 Chr. 5:19). Associated with Jetur and Naphish, Ishmaelite groups descended from Hagar, they may be the same as Kedemah named at 1:31; Gen. 25:15.

NOE. *See* NOAH 1.

NOGAH [nō'gə] (Heb. *nōgah* "brightness, splendor"). A son of David, born in Jerusalem (1 Chr. 3:7; 14:6). Since the name is missing in the parallel list at 2 Sam. 5:15, scholars suspect that the name may be a dittographical error for Nepheg.

NOHAH [nō'hə] (Heb. *nôḥâ* "rest") (PERSON). The fourth son of Benjamin (1 Chr. 8:2). The name is missing from the list at Gen. 46:21.

NOHAH [nō'hə] (Heb. *nôḥâ* "rest") (PLACE). A place inhabited by the descendants of Nohah, from which the other tribes pursued the Benjaminites (Judg. 20:43; Heb. *mᵉnûḥâ*; RSV mg. "resting place"; KJV "with ease," following LXX).

NOMADISM.* For the biblical period specifically pastoral nomadism, a cultural and socioeconomic pattern of subsistence involving the domestication and herding of animals, and periodic movement determined by economic and especially ecological conditions, including climate and the availability of water and fodder. Rather than the random movement of entire nomadic societies, pastoral nomadism generally involves the seasonal movement of only segments of a society within a somewhat fixed geographical area It is often imprecisely called "seminomadism."

Largely influenced by the nineteenth-century nomadic ideal, in part derived from observation of modern bedouin, interpreters long assumed that initially pastoral Israelites gradually settled and became agriculturalists, eventually forming villages and then towns and cities. But recent comparative ethnological study, supported by archaeological evidence, indicates that (with occasional variation) ancient peoples typically advanced from plant collecting and the hunting and gathering of animal products by first domesticating plants and then animals (goats *ca.* 6000 B.C., sheep *ca.* 5000), banding together in agricultural villages, and in time urbanizing. "Full" or "true" (i.e., desert) nomadism did not appear until much later, enabled by domestication of the camel *ca.* 1200.

Pastoral nomadism, then, is seen as a relatively late development of agricultural village life occupying only a small portion of Israelite society. The early Israelites may be classified as transhumants, primarily agriculturalists (cf. Gen. 26:12-14; 27:27-28; 37:5-8; 43:11; Num. 11:5) of whom a certain segment was responsible for grazing, in winter on the steppes to the south and east and in late spring and summer on the highlands (e.g., Gen. 37:12-17; Exod. 3:1; cf. Gen. 38:12-13). Such an arrangement necessitated a symbiosis between agriculturalists and pastoralists (cf. 13:12; 33:18-20; ch. 23; 47:4-9; Num. 20-23); various degrees of clientage were arranged, largely based on the exchange of water or grazing rights in return for the flocks' fertilizing the land. These relationships were not without strife, among neighboring transhumant segments as well as between agriculturalists and pastoralists (e.g., Gen. 13:5-7; 26:17-22). By necessity the Israelite pastoralists were highly adaptable; variations in the patterns of transhumance were determined by ecological concerns as well as such factors as the variety and number of animals herded (e.g., sheep and goats have limited endurance without water, hence restricting movement of herds), and the proportion of the social unit's dependence on livestock.

Israelite involvement in pastoral nomadism, as elsewhere in the ancient world, was fluid, influenced in part by restrictions imposed by the central authority and economic variables (e.g., greater market for wool than mutton). Pastoral as well as nonpastoral or predatory nomadism had particular appeal in times of heightened social stress; see HABIRU ('APIRU).

In interpreting the biblical accounts caution must be exercised to avoid confusing nomadism with migrations of large groups of peoples as the result of natural disaster (e.g., famine; Gen. 12:10ff.; 46) or for political or religious reasons (12:4-8; the wilderness wanderings).

Bibliography. N. K. Gottwald, "Were the Early Israelites Pastoral Nomads?" *BAR* 4/2 (1978): 2-7; W. Irons and N. Dyson-Hudson, eds., *Perspectives on Nomadism.* International Studies on Sociology and Social Anthropology 13 (Leiden: 1972); V. H. Matthews, *Pastoral Nomadism in the Mari Kingdom (ca. 1830-1760 B.C.).* ASOR Dissertation 3 (Cambridge, Mass.: 1978).

NON (1 Chr. 7:27, KJV). See NUN.

NOPH (KJV). See MEMPHIS.

NOPHAH [nō'fə] (Heb. *nōpaḥ*). According to the MT, a city in Moab north of Dibon (Num. 21:30; so KJV; RSV "fire spread," following LXX, Sam.).

NORTH (Heb. *ṣāpôn* "hidden, dark"; *śᵉmō'l* "left"; Gk. *borrás*). The ancient Hebrews based their directions on the position of the rising sun, hence east was "front" (Heb. *qedem*) and north was "left" (*śᵉmō'l*; Gen. 14:15; cf. KJV).

Palestine was protected by the Mediterranean Sea on the west and the Arabian desert in the east, so even though Damascus, Assyria, Babylon, Media, and Persia were all to the east they had to attack Israel from the north (Isa. 14:31; Jer. 25:9; Ezek. 26:7). Accordingly, the Israelites called these peoples of the east "northerners" (Joel 2:20; cf. Isa. 41:25).

In ancient Near Eastern mythology the various deities assembled for council at the mountain of the gods, which was located to the north (14:13; cf. Ps. 82). Mons Casius, 40 km. (25 mi.) north of Ugarit, was the locus of the Canaanite deity Baal-zephon ("lord of the north"), whose name is preserved in the place name BAAL-ZEPHON (Exod. 14:2, 9; Num. 33:7). Ps. 48 identifies Mt. Zion as this "mount of assembly" situated "in the far north" (KJV "on the sides of the north," v. 2 [MT 3]), although it is actually in southern Palestine. The north was also the region from which God would come in theophany, "clothed with terrible majesty" as a "golden splendor" (Job 37:22).

The north wind (*rûaḥ ṣāpôn*), according to Prov. 25:23, "brings forth rain." Actually, while the north wind in much of the Mediterranean region does bring rain, such is not the case in Palestine; the northerly jetstream is diverted around the island of Cyprus so that it blows across Palestine from the west, bringing rain with it. The fact that the north wind does bring rain in Egypt has led some scholars to postulate that the proverb may have originated there (*see* WISDOM).

At Job 37:9 the KJV translates *mᵉzārîm* (from *zārâ* "to scatter") as "north" (RSV "scattering winds").

NORTHEASTER (Gk. *eurakýlōn*; from *euros* "east wind" and Lat. *aquilo* "northern wind," hence "northeastern wind"). A tempestuous wind that blows from the east-northeast. Such a wind caused the ship carrying Paul and other prisoners to be thrown off its western course along the south side of the island of Crete (Acts 27:14-15; KJV "Euroclydon"). The ship on which Paul sailed left Crete after "the fast" (the Day of Atonement; v. 9), i.e., after autumn began, a particularly dangerous time for sailing because of the strong east wind (Ps. 48:7 [MT 8]; Ezek. 27:26; cf. Gk. *euroklýdōn* in some MSS of Acts, from *euros* "[south]east wind" and *klýdōn* "rough waves").

NOSE RING (Heb. *nizmê hā'ap* "rings of the nose"). One of various types of finery that the Lord intended to take from the haughty Jerusalem (Isa. 3:21; KJV "nose jewels"). Such ornaments were worn in the right nostril and reached below the mouth, so the wearer had to lift it up when eating. The more general Hebrew term *nezem* "ring" may also designate a nose ring (e.g., Ezek. 16:12; KJV "a jewel on thy forehead"). Abraham's servant gave Rebekah a ring, which the text specifically notes she placed in her nose (Gen. 24:22, 30, 47). "A beautiful woman without discretion" is likened to "a gold ring in a swine's snout" (Prov. 11:22).

NOT MY PEOPLE (Heb. *lō' 'ammî*). The name of Hosea's third child, a son. God told the prophet to name his son accordingly because "you are not my people and I am not your God" (Hos. 1:9; KJV "Loammi"), thus symbolizing the broken covenant. When Yahweh later promises to restore Israel he will say paranomastically, "You are my people" (2:23 [MT 25]).

NOT PITIED (Heb. *lō' ruḥāmâ*). The symbolic name given to Hosea's second child, a daughter, indicating that Yahweh would no longer forgive the house of Israel (Hos. 1:6; KJV "Lo-ruhamah"). When the covenant is later restored God will again "have pity" on Israel (2:23 [MT 25]).

NUMBERS.† Although for the most part numbers in the Bible have literal value, they often also have symbolic or idiomatic application, connoting completion, limitation, or magnanimity. Carrying this recognition to an extreme, some early twentieth-century interpreters were obsessed with numerology, believing that certain numbers had symbolic value even apart from the obvious meaning of the context. The idea that numbers had mystical or magical meaning may be traced to the gematria of the Hellenistic period, which ascribed hidden meaning based on the numerical value of individual letters; later the Masoretes would employ these symbolic values in an elaborate system for checking the accuracy of their copies.

In biblical usage the number four (Heb. 'arbaʿ; Gk. téssares) is often used to indicate complete representation: four rivers in Eden, representing all of creation (Gen. 2:10-14), four corners of the earth (Rev. 7:1), four winds of heaven (Dan. 7:2). The number is also frequent in apocalyptic literature: e.g., four kingdoms (2:37-45), four horns (Zech. 1:18 [MT 2:1]), four beasts (7:3), four living creatures with four faces and wings (Ezek. 1:5-10; cf. Rev. 4:6; 5:6, 8, 14). In the concrete simplicity of Semitic thought the notion derives from the four points of the compass.

The most important symbolic number is seven (Heb. šebaʿ; Gk. heptá), itself the sum of four ("completeness") and the sacred number three (encompassing beginning, middle, and end). The creation event embraced seven days; having completed the work of creation in six days, God rested on the seventh, blessing that day and making it holy (Gen. 2:3; Exod. 20:8-11). The number has particular importance for ritual and oath-taking (cf. Heb. šābaʿ "swear"). After six years of production the Hebrews were to observe the seventh year as "a sabbath to the Lord" and after seven sabbatical years a Year of Jubilee (Lev. 25). The Feast of Unleavened Bread (34:18) and the Feast of Tabernacles (23:34) were seven-day events. The menorah in the tabernacle had seven branches (Exod. 25:32). The leper Naaman was instructed to dip himself seven times in the Jordan river to show his complete compliance (2 Kgs. 5:10). The multiple seventy (seven times ten) compounds the significance: seventy elders appointed by Moses (Num. 11:16), seventy disciples commissioned by Jesus (Luke 10). Total forgiveness is demonstrated not by forgiving once or even seven times, but seventy times seven (Matt. 18:21-22).

Ten (Heb. 'eśer; Gk. déka) indicates simple completion, the total of fingers on both hands and a convenient rounded number, thus the basis for the decimal system. The Bible records ten plagues against Egypt (Exod. 7:8-11:10), the Ten Commandments of the covenant (20:2-17; Deut. 5:6-21), and the tithe, the offering of one-tenth of all produce (Deut. 26:12; cf. Gen. 14:20). God promised not to destroy Sodom if ten righteous people could be found in it (18:32), and Laban angered Jacob by changing his wages ten times (31:41).

Forty (Heb. 'arbāʿîm; Gk. tessarákonta) is idiomatic for any period of time regarded as a complete event. It is the standard figure for a complete generation; Moses' life is divided into three distinct periods of forty years each (Deut. 34:7). Israel wandered in the wilderness for forty years until the entire unbelieving generation had perished (e.g., Exod. 16:35; Deut. 29:5 [MT 4]; Josh. 5:6). The periods of oppression and deliverance in the book of Judges often comprise forty years (Judg. 3:11; 5:31; 8:28; cf. 3:30). The reigns of Saul and David each totaled forty years (2 Sam. 5:4; Acts 13:21). The period of the rain during

the flood was forty days and forty nights (Gen. 7:4). Moses remained on Mt. Sinai for forty days to receive the details of the tabernacle (Exod. 24:18). Jesus was tempted by Satan in the desert for forty days (Matt. 4:2 par.), and his postresurrection appearances lasted forty days (Acts 1:3).

One thousand (Heb. 'elep; Gk. chilías, chílioi) represents a very large group or entity, especially one so large that it cannot be numbered (e.g., Deut. 5:10; Ps. 84:10 [MT 11]; 2 Pet. 3:8). In the New Testament it indicates the MILLENNIUM, the thousand-year period during which Satan is bound preceding the final battle (Rev. 20:2-7). Heb. 'elep is a technical term for a social unit, perhaps equivalent to the clan or a similar association of fathers' houses (e.g., Exod. 18:27; 1 Sam. 10:19; cf. Judg. 6:15; Isa. 60:22; Mic. 5:2 [MT 1]; RSV "clan"); it occurs particularly in military contexts, perhaps as a unit of somewhat variable size mustered from the various tribes (e.g., Judg. 5:8; 1 Sam. 17:18; 1 Chr. 13:1; and especially the "thousands" in the census lists of Num. 1, 26).

NUMBERS, BOOK OF.† The fourth book of the Pentateuch.

I. Name

The name "Numbers" derives from the LXX (Gk. Arithmoi) by way of the Vulgate (Lat. Numeroi). In modern printed editions the name of the book in Hebrew is bemidbār "In the wilderness," although other Hebrew names are attested (e.g., wayeuldabbēr "And [Yahweh] said," from the book's opening word in the MT).

II. Contents and Form

Numbers is in every way a part of its larger literary and historical context. It must be interpreted as literature in the context of the Pentateuch, and as a historical source in the context of Israel's early history. Indeed, the very value of the book derives from its context, for it was never intended to be interpreted as an independent document.

A. Outline. Numbers may be divided into two main units. The first, Num. 1:1-10:10, constitutes the final section of the larger "Sinai pericope" (Exod. 19:1-Num. 10:10). It presupposes the completed construction of the central sanctuary (Exod. 35-40; cf. Lev. 1:1; Num. 1:1), specifically depicted in Numbers as a portable shrine (9:15-23). This unit narrates the final organization of the camp around this central sanctuary in view of the impending continuation of the pilgrimage to Canaan. It begins in chs. 1-4 with the organization of the nonlevitical (chs. 1-2) and levitical (chs. 3-4) tribes, and continues with a variety of divine ordinances (5:1-6:27; 7:89-9:14) and the offering for the dedication of the altar (7:1-88). It concludes with two pericopes concerning the impending pilgrimage (9:15-10:10).

The second major unit, 10:11-36:13, resumes the narration of the pilgrimage that began in Exod. 1-18. The sacral community leaves Mt. Sinai and eventually arrives in Moab (Num. 22-36), with major stops at Hazeroth (10:11-12:15), Paran (12:16-19:22), and Kadesh (20:1-21:4). Moab is the final stop recorded in Numbers and provides the setting for Moses' last

Greek text of Num. 5:22-64 in Chester Beatty papyrus VI (Chester Beatty Library; photo Pieterse Davison International Ltd.)

will and testament, the book of Deuteronomy. However, this unit not only narrates the community's pilgrimage; it also records a variety of divine ordinances (chs. 15, 18-19, 27-30, 35-36) and other traditions imbedded within the pilgrimage (e.g., chs. 13-14, 16). Numbers incorporates both narrative and legal genres and traditions, but the interpretation of the relationship between the narrative and legal traditions remains uncertain.

B. *Context.* The Sinai pericope itself may be divided into two parts, the first of which (Exod. 19-40) is concerned with the construction of the tabernacle. Here the focus is on the instructions for construction of the tabernacle (chs. 25-31) and the subsequent construction itself (chs. 35-40; the various parts are created in chs. 35-39 and, following a new instruction from Yahweh, assembled in ch. 40). The preceding material (chs. 19-24) represents the necessary conditions established by Yahweh to which Israel must agree before the sanctuary can be constructed. The significance of the tabernacle derives from its role as the permanent locus of divine revelation (at Exod. 40:34-38 the glory of Yahweh fills the tabernacle; at Lev. 1:1; Num. 1:1 he speaks from the tabernacle and not from Mt. Sinai). No longer need the Israelites travel back to Sinai to receive the divine will; henceforth they would receive divine revelation from the tabernacle with its priestly hierarchy.

In the second portion of the Sinai pericope (Lev. 1:1-Num. 10:10) the Israelite migration to Canaan becomes the sacral journey of Yahweh from Mt. Sinai to Palestine. No more is Israel another wandering people; they accompany Yahweh to Palestine, but their migration is no longer the dominant feature. Clearly the construction of the tabernacle is crucial to the intention of the Sinai pericope and, thereby, to that of the Pentateuch as a whole. But the construction of the tabernacle (Exod. 19-40) and the constitution of the sacral community (Num. 1:1-10:10) are important only in the context of the migration of Yahweh— and Israel—from Egypt to Palestine. Leviticus, from structural considerations the focus of the pericope, represents Yahweh's intention—the divine ideal— for Israel's settled life.

Num. 10:11-36:13 relates directly to the Sinai pericope by narrating the failure of the Israelites vis-à-vis the Sinai legislation, especially through their MURMURING against God (ch. 16). Their very failure to respond appropriately to the implications of the Exodus and Sinai events underscores the continuing validity of the Sinai legislation, which constitutes a program for the ideal existence of Israel in the promised land.

III. Interpretation

Like other Old Testament documents, Numbers presents the interpreter with certain critical problems. One such difficulty is the use of large numbers, as typified in the census reports of Num. 1, 26. According to 1:46, the number of adult male Israelites (excluding Levites) over twenty years of age was 603,550; at 26:51—a census necessitated by the death of the wilderness generation—the number is cited as 601,730, which would suggest a total population of some two to three million Israelites. But research concerning population density estimates the total population of Palestine during the United Monarchy to be approximately one million; furthermore, in view of the conflicting tradition of Israel's small size vis-à-vis the Canaanite population (Exod. 23:29; Deut. 7:7), it is difficult to regard Num. 26:51 as a historically accurate report of the number of Israelites in the wilderness camp. Various attempts have been made to reinterpret the word "thousand" (Heb. *'elep*) as meaning "tribal chief" or "military unit," but the extant text of Numbers clearly presupposes the meaning "thousand." (See W. S. LaSor, D. A. Hubbard, and F. W. Bush, *Old Testament Survey* (Grand Rapids: 1982), pp. 166-70).

Also problematic are the conquest and settlement of Transjordan. Num. 21:1-3, 21-35 narrates the conquest of the area east of the Jordan river, and ch. 32 relates the subsequent settlement of the tribes of Reuben, Gad, and the half-tribe of Manasseh in the conquered area. However, archaeological research continues to confirm Nelson Glueck's earlier view that, although Moab, Edom, and Ammon were settled in the thirteenth century, these settlements did not constitute a powerul nation as presupposed by the Old Testament text (this is not true of Midian). (If one chooses the alternate, fifteenth-century B.C. date for the Exodus and Conquest, there is no evidence of any settlement in these areas.) The view presented in Numbers accords with the tradition of a complete military conquest of the promised land (cf. Josh. 1–12), but in view of this and similar archaeological evidence, and in view of other conflicting conquest/settlement traditions (e.g., Judg. 1:1–2:25), the military conquest interpretation is generally held to be a theological idealization. Recent scholarship generally favors either a peasant revolt model or a combined military conquest-peaceful settlement view. (See R. de Vaux, *The Early History of Israel* (Philadelphia: 1978) 2:475-592; J. H. Hayes and J. M. Miller, eds. *Israelite and Judean History.* OTL (1977), pp. 213-84.)

The BALAAM pericope, delineated by the itinerary notice at Num. 22:1 and the departure rubric at 24:25, includes the request by Balak for Balaam to come in order to curse Israel and the four subsequent oracles of that Syrian prophet. On each occasion, however, Balaam blesses Israel. The first three times Balak attempts to manipulate a curse, but in no case is he successful; the fourth oracle is apparently uninitiated. Balaam is thus presented as a non-Israelite prophet who blesses Israel at Yahweh's instigation (e.g., 22:12; 23:11-12, 25-26; cf. Deut. 23:5-6; Josh. 24:9-10; Neh. 13:2). Another tradition about Balaam is attested at Num. 31:16, which blames Balaam for the sin at Baal-peor (ch. 25), although Balaam is not mentioned in that chapter. Presumably, the tradition of Balaam's death at the hands of the Israelites (31:8; Josh. 13:22) belongs here also. It is this tradition that later Judaism and the New Testament would emphasize (2 Pet. 2:15; Jude 11; Rev. 2:14). A variant Balaam tradition, written in Aramaic and discovered at Deir ʿAllâ in 1967, has virtually nothing in common with the biblical tradition.

IV. Origins

Such problems, which are specific to Numbers, and similar critical problems throughout the Pentateuch, have led the majority of modern scholars to deny the Mosaic authorship of the book, preferring in its place the JEDP hypothesis. The question of the independent existence of the "Elohistic" source has been answered variously by critical scholars. Generally, scholars now speak of an Elohistic redaction of the earlier "Yahwistic" tradition or of Elohistic fragments. Those who favor Mosaic authorship generally emphasize the desert milieu of the material, seeking to buttress this traditional view by appealing to the archaeological and ancient Near Eastern evidence (cf. R. K. Harrison, who argues that nothing in Numbers demands a post-Mosaic date, except a few glosses that may be attributed to Joshua; *Introduction to the Old Testament* [Grand Rapids: 1969], p. 622). See PENTATEUCH.

Bibliography. P. J. Budd, *The Book of Numbers.* WBC 5 (1984); G. W. Coats and R. Knierim, *Numbers.* FOTL 4 (1987); M. Noth, *The Book of Numbers.* OTL (1969); D. T. Olson, *The Death of the Old and the Birth of the New.* BJS 71 (Chico: 1985).

NUMENIUS [noo mēn′ĭəs] (Gk. *Nouménios*).* The son of Antiochus, chosen by the Maccabean high priest Jonathan as a Jewish ambassador to Rome and the Spartans (1 Macc. 12:16). The high priest Simon later dispatched him to Rome with a large shield to confirm the alliance (14:24). He returned with letters from the consul Lucius detailing the Romans' support (15:15-24; cf. Josephus *Ant.* xiv.8.5 [143-48]).

NUN [nŭn] (Heb. *nûn* "fish")). An Ephraimite, the father of Joshua (Exod. 33:11; Josh. 1:1; 1 Chr. 7:27; KJV "Non"; cf. Num. 13:8, 16).

NUNC DIMITTIS [nŭnk′ dĭ mĭt′əs].† The traditional name given to the brief psalm of praise of Simeon (Luke 2:29-32), derived from the first two words of the Latin Vulgate text ("now let depart"). The setting for the song is the temple, where Simeon encounters Mary and Joseph who have brought their infant son Jesus to be dedicated (v. 27).

Simeon, portrayed as a servant-watchman instructed by his master to await a sign, has been told by the Holy Spirit that he will not die until he has seen the Messiah (v. 26). Accordingly, the song opens with his request that the Lord allow him to die in peace, for his eyes have seen the Messiah (v. 30), whose salvation God has prepared in the presence of all people (i.e., Jew and Gentile; vv. 32-33).

Except for the brief prophecy in vv. 34-35, nothing else is known of Simeon. Some scholars see a connection between the Nunc Dimittis and a first-century A.D. group of nonviolent Jews (the "Quiet of the Land") who waited patiently for the Messiah. The psalm has been associated with Christian worship since the fourth century (cf. Apost. Const. vii.48).

NURSE (Heb. *mēneqeṭ, ʾōmeneṭ*; Gk. *trophos*). In biblical usage a woman charged with caring for, and often suckling, a child other than her own. Since the Old Testament is primarily concerned with the activities of wealthy and/or royal families, most examples of nurses are for this upper class; here the nurse was normally a servant hired to care for the infant (thus the incongruity of Isa. 49:23). Pharaoh's daughter hired Moses' own mother as a wet nurse (Exod. 2:7-9). When his life was threatened the royal heir Joash was hidden with his nurse (2 Kgs. 11:2 par. 2 Chr. 22:11). Jonathan's son Mephibosheth was dropped by his nurse as a child and was crippled for life (2 Sam. 4:4).

The nurse was entrusted with great responsibility and so often became a permanent member of the household (if was not already a family member). Deborah, Rebekah's nurse, left Nahor with her (Gen. 24:59) and stayed with Rebekah as a servant until her death at Bethel (35:8). A more typical example is probably Naomi, who nursed her own grandson (Ruth 4:16).

Both Moses (Num. 11:12) and Paul (1 Thess. 2:7) use the term "nurse" figuratively to describe their responsibility in caring for God's people.

NUTS. Walnut trees (*Juglans regia* L.) are native to the region from what is now southern Hungary east as far as Persia, and were imported into other regions as well. They require cool, moist soil, and thus were common in the hills of Palestine and around Lake Gennesaret and the upper course of the river Jabbok. In biblical times the walnut usually grew wild, although it was also cultivated (cf. Cant. 6:11; Heb. *ʾegôz*; RSV "nut orchard"). Walnut trees are far less abundant than in ancient times, but beautiful specimens are still attested on the slopes of the Lebanon mountains.

The "nuts" of Gen. 43:11 (*boṭnâ*) are certainly one of the varieties of pistachio (*Pistacia vera* L.; cf. RSV), although the Hebrew term can refer to other kinds of nuts. Pistachio nuts are considered delicacies in the Near East and hence, particularly appropriate for a gift of the "choice fruits of the land." Syria is a great source of supply for these nuts. The LXX reads here Gk. *terébinthos* "terebinth" (*Pistacia palaestina* [Boiss.] Post or *atlantina*; KJV "oak").

The ALMOND (*Amygdalus communis* L.) is also native to Palestine, but the hazel nut is not (cf. Gen. 30:37; Heb. *luz*; KJV "hazel"). Heb. *šāqēḏ* probably also refers to the almond (Gen. 43:11).

NUZI [nōō′zī] (Akk. *Nuzi*).* An ancient Mesopotamian city situated east of Assur and 15 km. (9 mi.) southwest of Arrapḫa (modern Kirkûk). Excavations at the site, modern Yorghan (or Yoghlan) Tepe, have yielded remains from the fourth millennium B.C. through the Roman period. Finds include cuneiform texts from the Old Akkadian and Ur III (late third millennium) and Old Assyrian (early second millennium) periods, during which the primarily Akkadian city was known as Gasur. Most importantly for biblical studies, some five thousand tablets have been found dating to the late fifteenth–early fourteenth centuries, during which period the city was part of the kingdom of Mitanni and was dominated by Hurrians. Nearly one thousand similar texts have been discovered at Tell el-Faḫḫār, 30 km. (19 mi.) to the southwest.

The large corpus of texts, written in an Akkadian dialect strongly influenced by Hurrian, is comprised of administrative texts and, in particular, family archives. The bulk of the texts concern various aspects of family law and illuminate such practices as marriage, adoption (here often a fictive means of transferring title to land), civil and criminal lawsuits, and the sale and exchange of persons, goods, and land. Because recovery of such an extensive archive is rare, scholars are uncertain whether the customs recorded are uniquely Hurrian or representative of Mesopotamian practice in general.

Since discovery of the texts in 1925-1931 scholars have sought parallels between Nuzi social customs and those of the biblical patriarchs, whose homeland was the nearby Hurrian-influenced region of Haran and Nahor. Indeed, such practices as the eldest son's receiving a double share of inheritance (Deut. 21:15-17), adoption in the absence of a son to keep inheritance within a family (Gen. 15:2ff.), and provision of a concubine for the purpose of obtaining an heir (16:1-4; 30:1-13) are attested in Nuzi texts. Recent study has discredited other suggested parallels, such as adoption of a wife as sister and the resultant creation of a fratriarchy (cf. ch. 24 and the role of household gods as symbolizing inheritance rights (chs. 29-31).

See ARCHAEOLOGY, BIBLICAL *V*; HURRIANS *II*.

NYMPHA [nĭm′fə] (Gk. *Nympha* [fem.] or *Nymphas* [masc.]). A Christian in Laodicea to whom Paul sends his greetings (Col. 4:15) and who owned the house in which the congregation met. The name occurs in the Greek text in a form that makes it impossible to determine whether it is Nympha (feminine; so RSV) or Nymphas (masculine; so KJV).

O

OAK (Heb. *alēlâ*, *'allâ*, *'allôn*). A tree (genus *Quercus* or *Lithocarpus*) of the beech family. More than three hundred species have been attested, including both evergreen and deciduous varieties. The oak is the most common leaf-bearing tree of Palestine and the surrounding region; the two most prevalent species here are the kermes and the valonea.

The kermes oak (*Quercus coccifera* L.) is a hardwood evergreen tree with thickly-leafed branches. The leaves are undivided and are serrated along the edges. The acorns are rather small, pointed at the ends and seated in a scaled cupule. The name of this species is derived from a variety of scale insect (*Kermes nahalali* or *Coccus ilicis*) that feeds upon its branches and leaves.

The valonea oak (*Quercus aegilops* L.) is very common in the Transjordan and in large forests in Galilee, but it does not grow south of Mt. Carmel. The "oaks of Bashan" (Heb. *'allônê habbāšān*) mentioned at Isa. 2:13; Ezek. 27:6; Zech. 11:2 were probably of this species. The valonea oak is a deciduous tree, the leaves of which are larger than those of the kermes oak and are somewhat indented. The acorns are remarkably long, and the scales that form their cupules are ligulate, creating the hairy appearance that gave the tree the nickname "goat's-beard oak." The acorns are edible when roasted; the cupules and bark provide tanin, which is used to tan leather. The trunk of the valonea oak has a thick bark that is often overgrown with lichen. Its wood is softer and not as smooth as that of the kermes oak.

Various other less common species of oak also grow in Palestine. The holm oak or evergreen holly oak (*Quercus ilex* L.) grows high on Mt. Tabor, often attaining great age. The Turkey oak (*Quercus cerris*, native to the Taurus mountain range) covers the lower mountain slopes. Magnificent specimens of durmast (*Quercus sessiliflora*) are found in the upper regions of the mountains of Lebanon.

Several Hebrew terms are translated "oak" in the various translations, perhaps reflecting the imprecision of ancient usage. For example, both *'ēlâ* and *'allôn* occur at Isa. 6:13; Hos. 4:13, where they apparently indicate different varieties of trees (RSV "terebinth, oak"; KJV "teil tree, oak"); the sacred tree (RSV "oak") at Shechem is called *'ēlâ* at Gen.

35:4, *'allâ* at Josh. 24:26. Most scholars agree that *'allôn* should always be translated "oak" (e.g., Gen. 35:8). The other terms could probably better be rendered "TEREBINTH" (e.g., 13:18, RSV mg.).

The wood of an oak is used to make an idol at Isa. 44:14-17. At Amos 2:9 the strength of the Amorites is compared to that of the oak.

OATH (Heb. verb *šāba'*; noun *šᵉbû'â*, *'ālâ*; Gk. verb *hórízō*, *anathematízō*; noun *hórkos*, *horkōmosía*).† A declaration or solemn promise in which one invokes God (or gods) as witness(es); a profane exclamation; a careless use of the name of God and therefore blasphemy.

I. Old Testament

The oath was a manner of guaranteeing a promise in Israelite society and the ancient Near East. The parties of the covenant invoked their deity (or deities) to witness the agreement, then bound themselves with specific sanctions (curses and blessings), symbolized by melting substitutionary wax figures or cutting animals in half (e.g., 1 Sam. 11:7). The one taking the oath would normally raise (Heb. *nāśā'*) his right hand toward heaven (Deut. 32:40; KJV, NIV, Gen. 14:22; RSV "swore"; cf. Dan. 12:7 [both hands]); God is also portrayed as using this gesture (Isa. 62:8; NIV, Exod. 6:8; KJV, Ezek. 20:5). God (or the gods) was expected to enforce the agreement by inflicting the curses upon either party that broke the covenant (e.g., Josh. 9; cf. 2 Sam. 21:1-9).

The Israelites were permitted to swear by Yahweh, and so invoked his name frequently (e.g., "God do so to me and more also," 1 Sam. 14:44; or more commonly "as the Lord lives," Judg. 8:19; 1 Sam. 19:6; 2 Kgs. 5:16, 20). Typical Near Eastern international treaties required that both parties swear by the deities of each nation. However, the swearing of an oath by the name of a god implied a recognition of that god and his power, which created a problem for the monotheistic Israelites. The prophets in particular overwhelmingly condemned those who swore by any other god (Jer. 5:7; 12:16; Amos 8:14; Zeph. 1:4-6) *See* COVENANT.

Oaths were solemn commitments and not to be undertaken lightly. The third commandment of the

Decalog forbids oaths that are made thoughtlessly (Exod. 20:7; Deut. 5:11); the ninth commandment forbids perjury (Exod. 20:16; Deut. 5:20; cf. Jer. 7:9). An oath must be fulfilled (Judg. 11:30-32 [!]; Eccl. 5:4-5 [MT 3-4]), though under certain conditions it could be nullified (Num. 30:1-15 [MT 2-16]). An oath could also bind one's descendants (e.g., Gen. 50:25-26; Josh. 9); this is probably the symbolism underlying the act of placing one's hand on another's genitals before swearing an oath (Gen. 24:9; 47:29-31).

Oath-taking became quite complicated in intertestamental Judaism. Oaths were important to the Qumran community, and the Mishnah contains an entire tractate on the subject (*Šebuʿoth*). Here the form of the oath took precedence over any other element. The system of binding vows was so complicated as to allow the initiate to deceive anyone not familar with the system. The net result was that the oath became a primary means of defrauding outsiders, hence Jesus' condemnation of the system (Matt. 5:33-34).

II. New Testament

Only Matthew's gospel is much concerned about oath-taking, as it is about other questions of Jewish law. Matthew alone records Jesus' attack of the complicated Pharisaic system of graded oaths (Matt. 23:16-22; cf. Mishnah *Šebu*. iv.13). In the discourses concerning fulfillment of the law (Matt. 5:17-48) Jesus admonishes his followers not to swear oaths (vv. 33-34; cf. Jas. 5:12); rather, their speech should be so trustworthy that a simple "yes" or "no" would suffice. Nevertheless, Peter swears three times that he did not know Jesus (Matt. 26:69-75 par. Mark 14:66-72; Luke 22:54-62).

Jesus' use of "truly" in the Synoptic gospels (Matt. 5:18; 6:2; Mark 3:28; 8:12; Luke 4:24; 12:37) is a mild oath of confirmation that fits within the guidelines recorded by Matthew. John uses the more emphatic "truly, truly" in his gospel (John 1:51; 3:3; 6:26). Paul also uses mild oath formulas to indicate earnestness (2 Cor. 1:23, "I call God to witness against me"; Gal. 1:20, "before God"; Phil. 1:8, "For God is my witness").

Bibliography. J. Behm, "ἀνατίθημι," *TDNT* 1 (1964): 353-56; J. Scharbert, "ʾālâ [ʾālāh]," *TDOT* 1, rev. ed. (1977); 261-66; K. L. Schmidt, "ὁρίζω," *TDNT* 5 (1967): 452-56.

OBADIAH [ōʹbə dīʹə] (Heb. *ʿōḇaḏyāhû, ʿōḇaḏyâ* "worshipper" or "servant of Yahweh").

1. (Heb. *ʿōḇaḏyāhû*). King Ahab's major domo who hid and fed one hundred prophets of Yahweh during Jezebel's persecutions. Sent by Ahab to find feed for the animals during the drought, Obadiah met Elijah, who told him to inform the king where the prophet could be found (1 Kgs. 18:3-16).

2. (Heb. *ʿōḇaḏyâ*). One of the sons of Hananiah, the son of Arnan, and a descendant of Zerubbabel (1 Chr. 3:21).

3. The second son of Izrahiah of the tribe of Issachar (1 Chr. 7:3).

4. The fifth son of Azel; a Benjaminite and descendant of Saul (1 Chr. 8:38; 9:44).

5. A Levite; the son of Shemaiah who returned from captivity in Babylon (1 Chr. 9:16). He is called

Abda (Heb. *ʿaḇdāʾ*) the son of Shammua at Neh. 11:17.

6. One of the Gadite men of war who came to David's stronghold at Ziklag (1 Chr. 12:9 [MT 10]).

7. (Heb. *ʿōḇaḏyāhû*). The father of Ishmaiah, who was military chief of Zebulun during the reign of David (1 Chr. 27:19).

8. (Heb. *ʿōḇaḏyâ*). One of the princes whom King Jehoshaphat sent to instruct the people of Judah in the Law (2 Chr. 17:7).

9. (Heb. *ʿōḇaḏyāhû*). A Merarite Levite who supervised the restoration of the temple during the reign of King Josiah (2 Chr. 34:12).

10. (Heb. *ʿōḇaḏyâ*). The son of Jehiel (**10**), a descendant of Joab who returned from Babylon (Ezra 8:9).

11. A priest who set his seal to the new covenant under Nehemiah (Neh. 10:5 [MT 6]).

12. A Levite, and one of the gatekeepers of the storehouses (Neh. 12:25).

13. The prophet whose vision is recorded in the book of Obadiah (Obad. 1).

OBADIAH, BOOK OF.† The fourth book of the Minor Prophets (fifth in the LXX canon). Numbering twenty-one verses, it is the shortest of the Old Testament writings.

I. Origins

No pedigree is provided for the Obadiah whose vision is recorded here (Obad. 1), nor do any internal allusions support identification with any of the persons so named in the Old Testament. A rabbinic tradition associates him with OBADIAH **1**, the chief officer of King Ahab's household (1 Kgs. 18:3-16), and the early Christian writer Pseudo-Epiphanius identified him as an officer of Ahab's son Ahaziah.

The book's focus as an extended oracle (or a compilation of oracles) against Edom suggests that it is directed primarily at the Edomites' early capitulation to the Chaldeans and alleged participation in the sack of Jerusalem in 587 B.C. (cf. vv. 11-14). However, the centuries-long conflict between Israel and Edom has prompted scholars either to propose multiple sources for the book or to date it variously from *ca.* 850 (the reign of Jehoshaphat; cf. 2 Chr. 20:10-11) to 312 (the Nabateans).

II. Contents and Form

Following the superscription (Obad. 1a) the "vision" (Heb. *ḥāzôn*) begins with an oracle (vv. 1b-10) proclaiming the humbling (vv. 2-4) of Edom, the abandonment of its allies (vv. 5-7). and the thoroughness of its destruction (vv. 9-10). Vv. 11-14 delineate the wrongs committed by Edom: remaining aloof when "brother Judah" was under siege (v. 11), gloating over Jerusalem's misfortune (v. 12), even joining those who looted the broken city (v. 13) and otherwise abetting the Babylonians (v. 14); vv. 12-14 consist of eight specific indictments ("you should not have . . ."). The remaining verses concern the "day of the Lord," when judgment will befall Edom and "all the nations" (vv. 15-16); the remnant of Judah will be delivered (vv. 17-20 and the kingdom of Yahweh established (vv. 20-21).

Some scholars view the component oracles as indication of the book's compilation from a variety of sources representing distinct historical settings. For the most part, however, Obadiah is regarded as a unified composition. On the basis of stanza form and thematic arrangement some label it a prophetic liturgy.

Obadiah demonstrates parallels of thought and expression with other prophetic works, notably Obad. 1-9 with Jer. 49:7-22, particularly Obad. 1-4 with Jer. 49:14-16 and Obad. 5 with Jer. 49:9. Scholars have argued variously for the priority of each (and thus the dependence of the other prophet), but most likely both Obadiah and Jeremiah have drawn independently from an earlier prophecy against Edom. Some have suggested Joel 2:32 (MT 3:5) as an allusion to Obad. 17, but this and other instances (e.g., v. 10 and Joel 3:19 [MT 4:19]; Obad. 15 and Joel 3:4, 7 [MT 4:4, 7]) probably represent merely similarity of expression.

III. Theology

Obadiah's utterances against Edom reflect similar pronouncements among the Hebrew prophets (e.g., Isa. 21:11-12; 34:5ff.; Ezek. 25:12-14; Amos 1:11-12). Reputed for wisdom (Obad. 8), Edom historically had a close (cf. Deut. 23:7; Amos 1:11) yet tempestuous (e.g., 2 Sam. 8:13-14; 2 Kgs. 14:7) relationship with Israel. Thus it was a particularly effective focus for impressing upon Israel the fate of all who oppose Yahweh (cf. Isa. 63:1-6).

The impending day of the Lord is a theme prominent in prophetic eschatology. Obadiah portrays the havoc of this day as just retribution for injustices committed against Yahweh's chosen people (Obad. 15; cf. vv. 10ff.). Underlying this theme is the recognition of Yahweh as sovereign (v. 21) over not only Israel but Edom and "all the nations" (v. 15), whom he employs as an instrument against Israel (cf. v. 16) yet upon whom he wreaks vengeance for wrongdoing (vv. 15-21).

Bibliography. L. C. Allen, *The Books of Joel, Obadiah, Jonah and Micah.* NICOT (1976), pp. 127-72; R. J. Coggins and S. P. Re'emi, *Israel among the Nations.* ITC (1985), pp. 65-102; J. D. W. Watts, *Obadiah* (Grand Rapids: 1969).

OBAL [ō′bəl] (Heb. *'ôḇāl*). One of the sons of Joktan, and the eponymous ancestor of an Arabian tribe (Gen. 10:28). He is called Ebal at 1 Chr. 1:22.

OBED [ō′bĕd] (Heb. *'ôḇēḏ 'ōḇēḏ* "worshipper" or "servant"; Gk. *'lōbēd*).

1. The son of Boaz and Ruth, the grandfather of David, and an ancestor of Jesus (Ruth 4:17, 21-22; 1 Chr. 2:12; Matt. 1:5; Luke 3:32).

2. A Judahite, the son of Ephlal and a descendant of Jerahmeel (1 Chr. 2:37-38).

3. One of David's mighty men (1 Chr. 11:47).

4. A levitical gatekeeper, presumably a Korahite; one of the sons of Shemaiah (1 Chr. 26:7).

5. The father of the commander AZARIAH (**15**), who took part in the conspiracy against Queen Athaliah and Jehoiada (2 Chr. 23:1).

6. The son of Jonathan, one of the sons of Adin who returned with Ezra to Jerusalem (1 Esdr. 8:32; KJV "Obeth"). He is called Ebed (**2**) at Ezra 8:6.

OBED-EDOM [ō′bəd ē′dəm] (Heb. *'ōḇēḏ 'eḏōm, 'ōḇēḏ 'eḏôm* "servant of Edom").

1. A man from the city of Gath ("a Gittite," 2 Sam. 6:10-11; 1 Chr. 13:13-14) in whose house David placed the ark for three months after the death of Uzzah. When David saw that the Lord blessed Obededom and his family, he felt it safe to move the ark to the temple (2 Sam. 6:12; 1 Chr. 15:25).

2. A levitical musician assigned to the second order under David (1 Chr. 15:18, 21). The son of the musician Jeduthun (16:38), he was also one of the gatekeepers for the ark (15:24). He and his descendants (or followers) were also assigned to minister before the ark (16:5, 38). Some scholars contend that he is the same as **1**, or that the gatekeepers chose the Philistine as their eponymous ancestor.

3. A Korahite Levite, head of the guild that guarded the south gate of the temple and the storehouse (1 Chr. 26:4-8, 15). He may be the same as **2**.

4. The gatekeeper of the temple treasures during the reign of the Judahite king Amaziah, taken captive when King Joash of Israel seized the temple treasures *ca.* 790 B.C. (so RSV, 2 Chr. 25:24; cf. 2 Kgs. 14:14). According to the MT, these treasures were those that had been "in the care of" (so NIV; KJV, JB "with") Obed-edom.

OBEDIENCE (Heb. *šāma'*; Gk. verb *hypakoúō, hypotássō*, pass.; noun *hypakoē*; adj. *hypēkoos*).† The key to the biblical concept of obedience is Heb. *šāmā'*, which means both "listen to" and "act upon, obey." The term occurs in (and gives its name to) the Shema, Israel's confession of faith: "Hear, O Israel" (Deut. 6:4; cf. Matt. 22:37; Mark 12:30; Luke 10:27). True "hearing," or obedience, involves the physical hearing that inspires the hearer, and a belief or trust that in turn motivates the hearer to act in accordance with the speaker's desires.

In the New Testament Christ embodies this quality of perfect obedience to God (John 6:37-38). His obedience, the antithesis of Adam's disobedience, provided for mankind's atonement (Rom. 5:18-21). It began at the incarnation (Heb. 10:5-10) and continued throughout his life on earth, including ultimately his death on the cross (Phil. 2:6-11). His obedience thus became an example for those who would become his disciples (Matt. 16:24).

OBELISK [ō′bə lĭsk] (Heb. *maṣṣēḇâ* "pillar, standing stone, image"). A monument shaped like a four-cornered pillar that rises to a pyramidal point. The sides are often covered by inscriptions commemorating the actions of a god or king.

Such monuments may have originated in the Egyptian city of Heliopolis (or ON), the cult center of the sun-god Atum-Re. One such obelisk, the lone survivor of a group that stood in front of the temple of Atum-Re, stands about 19 m. (62 ft.) high and bears an inscription to Horus, "the son of Re."

The sole biblical reference to an obelisk is at Jer. 43:13 (KJV "image"), where Jeremiah prophesies that Nebuchadrezzar would break the obelisks of Heliopolis (KJV "Beth-shemesh"). This prophecy was fulfilled in 568 B.C. during Nebuchadrezzar's expedition to Egypt.

Heb. *maṣṣēḇâ* is the common word for "pillar" (e.g., Gen. 28:18; Exod. 24:4), here rendered "obelisk" by the RSV because of its location in Egypt.

OBIL [ō'bĭl] (Heb. *'ôḇîl* "camel driver"). An Ishmaelite who was the overseer of King David's camels (1 Chr. 27:30).

OBLATION (Heb. *minḥâ*). The evening temple sacrifice (so KJV, NIV; 1 Kgs. 18:29, 36). See SACRIFICES AND OFFERINGS.

OBOTH [ō'bŏth] (Heb. *'ōḇōṯ* "waterskins"). A place between Punon and Iye-abarim where the Israelites camped during the wilderness wanderings (Num. 21:10-11; 33:43-44). Some scholars believe it to be one of two modern oases, either ʿAin el-Weiba, just west of Punon (modern Feinân), or ʿAin Hoṣob, 19 km. (12 mi.) farther north.

OCHRAN [ŏk'rən] (Heb. *'oḵrān* "trouble, affliction"). The father of Pagiel, chief of the tribe of Asher (Num. 1:13; 2:27; 7:72, 77; 10:26; KJV "Ocran").

OCINA [ō sī'nə] (Gk. *Okina*). A coastal town south of Tyre (Jdt. 2:28). Its exact location is unknown, although some scholars have suggested modern Acco, largely on the basis of name similarity and general location.

ODED [ō'dĕd] (Heb. *'ôḏeḏ* "restorer").
1. The father of the prophet Azariah (**11**) (2 Chr. 15:1, 8).
2. A prophet of Yahweh at Samaria who ordered the victorious Israelite army of King Pekah to free their Judahite prisoners. Oded rebuked the soldiers for their slaughter and reminded them of their own sins toward God, whereupon they fed, clothed, and released their captives (2 Chr. 28:8-15).

ODES OF SOLOMON. See SOLOMON, ODES OF.

ODOR (Heb. *rêaḥ*).† The smell of a burnt offering, in popular belief supposed to please the deity and give him sustenance (cf. "my food," Num. 28:2). The relationship between the burnt offering and its odor was so close that the expression "pleasing odor" (so RSV; KJV "sweet savor") is often used as a euphemism for the burnt offering (e.g., Lev. 23:18; 26:31).

The designation "pleasing odor" is used of sacrifices of meat (Exod. 29:18, 25, 41; Lev. 1:9, 13, 17) and grain (2:2), but not honey or other leaven (vv. 11-12). Offerings were often mixed with other fragrant ingredients such as frankincense or fine oil (ch. 2). Such aromatic woods as walnut, pine, fig, and cedar added their own characteristic aroma to the blaze (cf. Mishnah *Tamid.* ii.3; *Parah* iii.8, 10).

This expression and its Greek equivalents were also used figuratively for other "offerings": the people of Israel (Ezek. 20:41), financial support for Paul's ministry (Phil. 4:18; *osmḗn* [*euōdías*]; RSV "fragrant [offering]"), the death of Jesus Christ (Eph. 5:2), the life of the Church (2 Cor. 2:14-16), and the prayers of the saints (*thymíama* "incense, incense offering," Rev. 5:8)

OFFENSE (Heb. *miḵšôl, ḥēṭeʾ*). The act of offending, of transgressing a moral or divine law. In biblical usage "offence" can imply an act of stumbling, an occasion for sin, or a cause of sin. The English word "offense" is almost obsolete and often ambiguous, thus more recent versions have substituted more precise translations.

"Offense" may refer to the sin itself (usually Gk. *paráptōma*). The transgression (RSV usually "trespass") might be against either fellow humans (Matt. 6:14-15; cf. Jas. 5:16; RSV "sins") or God (Rom. 5:17; Eph. 1:7). With this sense the KJV renders *hamartía* "sin" as "offense" at 2 Cor. 11:7.

More often, the term means a stumbling block—an obstacle placed in someone's path causing him to loose his footing and fall (e.g., Heb. *miḵšôl*; Isa. 8:14). In the New Testament, this stumbling (Gk. *skandalízō*) over stumblingblocks (*skándalon, próskomma, proskopḗ*) always refers to a moral shortcoming. That which causes a person to stumble, or sin, might be a part of the human body (Mark 9:42-47), another person (Matt. 18:7; cf. Rom. 16:17; 1 Cor. 8:13), and even the inward condemnation brought by the revelation of Jesus Christ (John 6:61; Rom. 9:32-33; 1 Pet. 2:8) or God himself (cf. Isa. 8:13-15). By contrast, Gk. *apróskopos*, means "without offense, blameless" (1 Cor. 10:32; cf. Acts 24:16; Phil. 1:10).

OFFERING. See SACRIFICES AND OFFERINGS.

OFFICE.† An official position or responsibility, usually of some importance, conferred by a government, religion, or organization. Various Hebrew and Greek words are rendered "office" in English translations. At Gen. 40:13; 41:13 the RSV so translates Heb *kēn*, with the connotation "position" or "station"; elsewhere the term is translated "base" (e.g., Exod. 30:18, 28; 31:9) and "place" (Dan. 11:7), indicating the point from which something rises. Heb. *'emûnâ* is translated "office of trust" at 1 Chr. 9:22; the word appears primarily with the meaning "reliability, faithfulness" (e.g., 2 Chr. 31:18; Prov. 14:5; Deut. 32:4; Ps. 33:4; cf. 1 Chr. 9:31). "Office" can also simply refer to the station in life that a person might occupy (*pᵉqûddâ*; Ps. 109:8). Alternate translations for the various terms include "ministry," "service," "duties," "responsibilities" and "functions."

Among offices specified in the Old Testament are the positions of the priests (Heb. *mišmeret* "watch, guard," 2 Chr. 7:6; RSV "posts"; *pᵉqûddâ* "inspection, charge," Num. 4:16; RSV "oversight"; 1 Chr. 24:3; RSV "appointed duties"; cf. 2 Chr. 23:18; cf. Heb. 7:5; Gk. *hierateía*; RSV "office"), the duties of the Levites (Heb. *maʿᵃmār* "standing, station," 1 Chr. 23:28; RSV "duty"), the ministry of the temple singers (*'ᵃḇōḏa* "service," 6:32 [MT 17]; RSV "in due order"), the gatekeepers of the temple (*'ᵉmûnâ* "office of trust," 9:22) and other temple positions in general (*mišmār* "watch, guard," Neh. 13:14; RSV "service"). Government offices are also mentioned: the position of cupbearer to the Egyptian pharaoh (Gen. 41:13) and treasury officers of the Israelite king (2 Chr. 24:11).

In the New Testament "office" occurs only in reference to the duties or function of apostle (Gk. *epis-kopé*; Acts 1:20; KJV "bishoprick"; citing Ps. 109:8, Heb. *p^equddâ*; RSV "goods") or bishop (1 Tim. 3:1) or of the high priest (*hierateía*; Heb. 7:5; cf. Num. 3:3). Paul uses Gk. *diakonía* to describe his own responsibilities as an apostle (Rom. 11:13; KJV "office"; RSV "ministry"); at 12:4 he reminds his readers that each has specific work to perform (*práxis*; KJV "office"; RSV "function").

"Office" does not occur in the Bible with the sense of a ceremony prescribed by liturgy, as it has come to mean in theological and ecclesiastical circles.

OFFICER, OFFICIAL (Heb. *sārîs, pāqîd, rab, śar*; Gk. *práktōr, hypérétēs*).† A person imbued with civil, political, military, or religious responsibility.

Heb. *sārîs* designates a eunuch or someone who has been castrated, originally a precaution taken for one who would guard the king's harem. Later, these servants occupied other key positions (Gen. 37:36; 40:2; 2 Kgs. 23:11; 24:12, 15), perhaps eventually including key servants of all types, whether castrated or not. *See* EUNUCH.

Heb. *šāṭar* is used of the taskmasters in Egypt (Exod. 5:6, 10, 14-15, 19; RSV "foremen") as well as subordinate officers in Israel (Num. 11:16; Deut. 16:18; Josh. 1:10). The exact staus of such officers is unknown, but the Hebrew term is related to Akk. *šatāru* "scribe," suggesting that they may originally have been civil functionaries whose job it was to keep lists or perform other secretarial tasks.

Solomon reorganized Israel into twelve administrative districts, each headed by an officer (Heb. *niṣṣab*) in charge of the taxation of foodstuffs (1 Kgs. 4:5, 7, 27 [MT 5:7]) and the involuntary labor force used for public works ("chief officers"; 5:16 [MT 30]; 9:23; 2 Chr. 8:10).

Several generic Hebrew terms designate with no real precision officers and officials of all types (e.g., verbal forms of *pāqad* "appoint, muster" and related nouns such as *p^equddâ, pāqîd; śar*). The title *rab* "great one" (Esth. 1:8; 41:1) and related compounds (2 Kgs. 18:17; Jer 39:13; Dan. 1:3; Jonah 1:6) and *'āśâ melā'kâ* (lit. "doer of work"; Esth. 3:9; cf. *'ōśeh hamm^elā'kâ* 9:3) are commonly used of foreign officials, especially those of the lands east of Israel; little else is known about these functionaries.

Gk. *hypérétēs* is a generic term designating either the deputies of the scribes and Pharisees (e.g., John 7:32; 18:3; 19:6; Acts 5:22, 26) or the "ministers" of the gospel (Luke 1:2; cf. 1 Cor. 4:1). It can also refer to a servant of the court as at Matt. 5:25 (RSV "guard"), though the parallel passage at Luke 12:58 uses the more specific *práktōr*, a technical term for the baliff in charge of the debtor's prison.

The RSV also translates *basilikós* as "official" at John 4:46, 49 (KJV "nobleman"; NIV "royal official"). Elsewhere the term is rendered as an adjective, "royal" or "king's" (Acts 12:20-21; Jas. 2:8).

OG [ŏg] (Heb. *'ōg, 'ōg*). An Amorite king of Bashan, the last of the Rephaim (Deut. 3:11), defeated by the Israelites under Moses.

Og controlled sixty fortified cities in the northern region of the plain east of Jordan (vv. 1-10). The Israelites defeated and killed him at Edrei (Num. 21:33-35; Deut. 1:4), dividing his territory among the tribes of Reuben, Gad, and Manasseh (Num. 32:33). Og and the Amorite king Sihon were remembered as the most famous of the Caananite kings (Ps. 135:10-12; 136:18-21).

According to Deut. 3:11, Og's bedstead was made of iron and measured 9 common cubits (4 m. [13 ft.]) long and 4 cubits (1.8 m. [6 ft.]) wide. Some scholars have suggested this was actually a sarcophagus of basalt (cf. NEB).

OHAD [ō'hăd] (Heb. *'ōhaḏ*). The third son of Simeon (Gen. 46:10; Exod 6:15). He is not mentioned in the genealogies at Num. 26:12-14; 1 Chr. 4:24-25.

OHEL [ō'hĕl] (Heb. *'ōhel* "tent"). A descendant (perhaps a son) of Zerubbabel (1 Chr. 3:20).

OHOLAH [ō hō'lə] (Heb. *'oh^olâ* "she who has a tent" or "her tent"). The elder of two sisters in the allegory of Ezek. 23 (KJV "Aholab"), representing Samaria. Both sisters were promiscuous (i.e., idolatrous), plying their trade as a prostitutes first in Egypt and afterward with the Assyrians (vv. 4-11). As punishment Yahweh turned Oholah over to the Assyrians for destruction (vv. 9-10).

OHOLIAB [ō hō'lĭ ăb] (Heb. *'oh^olî'āḇ* "tent of the father"). The son of Ahisamach of the tribe of Dan, a craftsman and designer. He and Bezalel were responsible for construction of the tabernacle (Exod 31:6; 35:34; 36:1-2; 38:23; KJV "Aholiab").

OHOLIBAH [ō hō'lĭ bə] (Heb. *'oh^olîbâ* "my tent is in her"). A name given to Jerusalem in the allegory of Ezek 23 (KJV "Aholibah"). The younger of two sisters, Oholibah continued in her corruption and adultery (vv. 11-21). Therefore Yahweh would turn Oholibah over to her lovers for punishment, stripping and disfiguring her and slaying her sons and daughters; she would suffer the consequences of her lewdness and harlotry and so come to know that the Lord was truly God (vv. 22-35, 46-49).

OHOLIBAMAH [ō hō'lĭ băm'ə] (Heb. *'oh^olîḇāmâ* "tent of the high place").

1. A wife of Esau, and the daughter of Anah the son of Zibeon the Hivite (Gen. 36:2, 25; KJV "Aholibamah"). She bore three sons (vv. 5, 14, 18). Oholibamah is not named among Esau's wives at 26:34; 28:9.

2. The chief of an Edomite clan (Gen. 36:41; 1 Chr. 1:52; KJV "Aholibamah").

OIL (Heb. *šemen, yiṣhār*; Aram. *m^ešaḥ*; Gk. *élaion*), **OINTMENT** (Heb. *merqāḥaṭ*; Gk. *mýron*).† A fluid applied to the skin to prevent its desiccation in hot, dry climates, sometimes also mixed with aromatic substances to make perfume. Olive oil, the most common oil in Palestine, is also used as a cooking oil, a dietary supplement, a medicinal balm, a lighting fluid, and as a base for the ceremonial oil of anointing (Heb. *šemen hammišḥâ*).

Oil constitutes more than 50 percent of the ripe olive. The Israelites extracted it from the fruit in two separate pressings, the first of which yielded the best oil. The olives were placed in a stone press, where they were either tromped with the feet or pressed with a large stone. The olive pulp was then placed into baskets and the oil gently strained through the open weave. This oil, called pure (*tôḇ* "good") or beaten (*kāṯîṯ*), was used in religious services (Exod. 29:40; Ps. 133:2) and for trade (1 Kgs. 5:11 [MT 25]; 2 Kgs. 20:13; cf. Ezra 3:7; Ezek. 27:17; Rev. 18:13; cf. Prov. 21:17. "he who loves wine and oil will not be rich").

The remaining olive mash was then heated for the second pressing and placed back into the vat. The lesser grade of oil was squeezed from the pulp with the aid of a lever; a beam was inserted into a niche in the wall and loaded with heavy stones to help force the oil from the olives. This pressing yielded an oil clouded with bits of pulp and seeds; it had to stand until the sediment settled, though salt could be added to clarify it. The Israelites used this type of olive oil for their daily use. During biblical times, it was stored in earthen jars and vessels (1 Kgs. 17:12; 2 Kgs. 4:2-6).

Olive oil was used as shortening for cooking (Num. 11:8). It also frequently replaced butter as a complement for bread in the Mediterranean world. Likewise, beaten oil mixed with flour was a required ingredient in the daily morning sacrifice (Exod. 29:40; Num. 28:5).

The Bible mentions oil most frequently in connection with anointing. Daily anointing was an accepted practice (Ruth 3:3; 2 Sam. 12:20), so much so that its omission was considered a deprivation (Deut. 28:40; Matt. 6:16-18). A good host would offer guests water to wash their feet and oil with which to anoint themselves (Ps. 23:5; Luke 7:46). Anointing with oil could also be a mark of divine favor and thus a means of ordaining a person for a special task. Oil was used to anoint priests (Exod. 29:7; Lev. 8:30; Ps. 133:2), kings (1 Sam. 10:1; 16:1-13), and prophets (1 Kgs. 19:16; Ps. 105:15; Isa. 61:1; cf. Luke 4:18). The term Messiah (*māšîaḥ*) means "anointed one." Ordinary olive oil was probably used for daily anointing, except by the very rich (Amos 6:6). Costly aromatics could be added to the oil to enhance its odor. The anointing oil of the temple for example, its use restricted to the temple and probably the king, was mixed with myrrh, cinnamon, aromatic cane, and cassia (Exod. 30:25-33). Other substances could be used instead of olive oil. Mary, for example, anointed Jesus with pure nard (Mark 14:3; John 12:3; KJV "spikenard"). *See* ANOINT, PERFUME.

Olive oil burns brightly, making it a suitable fuel for lamps, which had to be kept burning continually (Zech. 4:2-3; Matt. 25:1-13). The lamps of the tabernacle and temple were to be kept supplied with pure oil (Exod 27:20; Lev. 24:2). Hanukkah, the Feast of Lights, is associated with Judas Maccabeus' discovery of a single day's supply of oil that miraculously lighted the temple for eight days (Talmud *b. Šabb.* 21b).

Olive oil was also commonly used as an unguent to keep wounds soft and thus aid healing (Isa. 1:6; Luke 10:34). There is no record that ancient Israelites used ceremonial oiling in a healing ritual, but the disciples did anoint the sick with oil as they prayed for them (Mark 6:13; Jas. 5:14). See Medicine.

OLD GATE (Heb. *ša'ar hayᵉšānâ*).† A gate repaired during Nehemiah's rebuilding of Jerusalem's walls (Neh. 3:6; 12:39). Attempting to identify the gate and its location, commentators have proposed various readings or emendations of the text: taking *ša'ar* as a construct, thus "Gate of the Old (City?)"; reading *yᵉšānâ* "old" as "Jeshanah," a small city located north of Jerusalem on the border of Judea and Samaria (2 Chr. 13:19), in which case the gate would have opened onto the road leading to that city; emending *yšnh* to *mšnh* "second," thus Mishneh Gate, which would suit nicely the gate's location as an entrance to the Mishneh (or Second) Quarter of Jerusalem (2 Kgs. 22:14; 2 Chr. 34:22). Some scholars identify the Old Gate with the Corner Gate mentioned at 2 Kgs. 14:13; 2 Chr. 26:9.

OLD LATIN VERSIONS.† Vetus Latina, the collective designation for a comparatively colloquial Latin textual tradition, the Old Testament portion of which is based on the LXX rather than the MT. It apparently originated during the second century A.D. in North Africa, where Latin was the primary language of the Church, but versions are known to have circulated in Europe by the third century (*see* ITALA). Scholars suggest that the Old Latin represents the conflation of several versions rather than a single translation (cf. Augustine *De doctr. christ.* ii.11, 13). By the eighth or ninth century the Old Latin had been supplanted by the Vulgate.

OLIVE, OLIVE TREE (Heb. *zayiṯ*; Gk. *elaía*).† Any tree of the species *Olea,* but particularly the cultivated variety *Olea europaea* L.

The olive tree is a small evergreen native to Asia Minor and southern Europe. It stands no more than 10 m. high (33 ft.) and has a grayish trunk and bark. Its leaves are 6-8 cm. (2-3 in.) long and 1.5 cm. (.5 in.) wide and resemble the leaves of a willow; the upper surface of the leaf is dull green and leathery, and the lower surface is covered with fine white hairs. Olive trees grow best in the Mediterranean climate, which can have less than 200 mm. (8 in.) of annual rainfall. Although olive trees grow nearly everywhere in Palestine (Deut 28:40; cf. 8:8), they are cultivated especially in Gilead and the region west of the Jordan, where the lime and basalt of the region's soil are exceptionally well suited to them. Since the best ground is usually reserved for wheat, olive trees—which can take root in very shallow soil—are planted in particularly rocky soil or on mountain slopes (cf. "Mount of Olives"; e.g., 2 Sam. 15:30; Matt. 21:1).

The olive tree blossoms in early May, when the small, white, clustered flowers are vulnerable to the hot winds of the sirocco (Job 15:33). The fleshy, oval-shaped fruit, which is rich in oil, is green when immature and blue-black or dark green when ripe. Each berry is about 2 cm. (1 in.) long and 1.5 cm. (.6 in.) wide. Olives are harvested along with the grapes in the early fall (Isa. 32:10); the olives are gathered by beating the trees with sticks (Deut. 24:20). They can be eaten while still green, if first heated in lye and

A branch of olive with flowers

soaked in brine to remove the bitterness. *See* OIL,
OINTMENT.

New olive shoots may spring up around an old stump
(Ps. 128:3). More typically, new olive trees are grown
by grafting an olive branch from a productive tree to
a wild olive tree (Heb. *ʿēṣ šemen*; cf. RSV, Neh. 8:15;
sometimes incorrectly called an oleaster, *Elaeagnus
angustifolia* L.), a practice originating with the Phoenicians. Seeking to humble his Gentile readers, the
apostle Paul compares them to a shoot taken from a
wild olive tree (Gk. *agriélaios*) and grafted onto a
cultivated olive tree (*kalliélaios*; Rom. 11:17, 24); the
graft is "contrary to nature" because it does not follow
the usual procedure of grafting a good branch to a
wild tree.

Although olive trees can attain a very old age and
are able to bear fruit for several hundred years, they
take a long time to grow. The early Palestinian olive
groves dated to pre-Israelite times (Deut. 6:11), and
some modern trees are estimated to be more than one
thousand years old. Because olive trees take so long
to mature, they were protected in biblical times, even
during war (cf. 20:19-20; 2 Kgs. 3:25). The wood of
the cultivated olive was not even acceptable fuel for
burning a sacrifice, unlike that of the wild olive (Mishnah *Tamid.* ii.3).

The exact species of the Heb. *ʿēṣ šemen* (lit. "oil
tree"; so KJV, Isa. 41:19) is uncertain. It may designate either the cultivated olive (1 Kgs. 6:23, 31-33)
or the wild olive (Neh. 8:15); but oil, in the form of
turpentine and tar, can also be obtained from the pine
(*Pinus halepensis* Mill. or *bruttia*; cf. KJV, JB, Neh.
8:15).

OLIVES, MOUNT OF (Heb. *har hazzēṭîm*; Gk. *tó
óros tṓn elaiṓn*).† A high ridge about 4 km. (2.5 mi.)
in length, part of the central north-south mountain
range that runs through Palestine. It is characterized
by three distinct summits overlooking Jerusalem across
the Kidron valley, each with distinct names and histories. The ridge not only provides a windbreak from
the eastern and northern winds, but causes the mois-
ture-laden air of the western Mediterranean breeze to
condense as it rises up its slopes, thus insuring Jeru-

salem an ample water supply. By virtue of this same
abundant water supply, it supported dense groves of
olive trees thoughout antiquity, hence the name (e.g.,
2 Sam. 15:30; cf. Lat. *olivetum* "olive grove," hence
"Olivet"); much of this growth was destroyed during
Titus' sack of the city in A.D. 70.

The northernmost peak is Ras Abū Kharnub, often
imprecisely called Mt. Scopus ("lookout"). It is the
highest of the three peaks, rising some 903 m. (2963
ft.) above the level of the Mediterranean Sea. The
Galileans who attended the great pilgrimage feasts are
said to have camped at this high altitude, thus its
alternate name Viri Galilaei (cf. Acts 1:11, "men of
Galilee"). A Greek Catholic tradition suggests that
this was also the site from which Jesus delivered his
Great Commission (Matt. 28:10, 16). Today a German
hospice is located on this site.

To the south is Jebel eṭ-Ṭûr, located directly across
from the temple area (Ḥaram esh-Sharif). Reaching
818 m. (2684 ft.) above sea level, it is the traditional
site of Jesus' ascension (Luke 24:51; Acts 1:12; Gk.
toú elaión; RSV "Olivet"). The modern Jerusalem-
Jericho highway passes just south of here.

Jebel Bāṭn el-Hawā ("mountain of the womb of the
wind"), the southernmost of the three summits, is the
lowest in height. It is also called Mons Scandali ("the
mountain of offense"), a reference to the idolatrous
temples built here by Solomon (1 Kgs. 11:7; 2 Kgs.
23:13-14). The name Mount of Corruption (Heb. *har
hammašḥît*; v. 13) is probably a pun on "mount of
ointment (of olive oil)" (*hammašḥâ*).

Forced to flee Absalom's rebellion, David escaped
across the Kidron valley and up the ascent of the
mount of Olives (2 Sam. 15:23, 30; 16:1). The summit apparently was a cultic site at the time (15:32).
According to the Talmud (*Parah* iii.6), the Mount of
Olives was also the place where the red heifer was
slain in ritual purifications (Num. 19).

The Mount of Olives is closely associated with the
Feast of Booths. It was probably here that the returned
exiles gathered the olive branches for their first celebration of the feast (Neh. 8:15). Zechariah mentions
the mount as the site of the coming of the Messiah on
the day of the Lord. The mountain would be split in
two, and "living waters" would flow from Jerusalem
to the eastern and western seas; then all of the remaining nation would go up to Jerusalem to celebrate
the Feast of Booths (Zech. 14). This is also where
"the glory of the Lord" rested upon departing from
the temple in Ezekiel's vision (Ezek. 11:23).

The Mount of Olives figures even more prominently
in the New Testament. Bethany and Bethphage were
both located on or near the mountain as was Gethsemane (Aram. *gaṯ šᵉmānîm* "[olive] oil press"). Looking over Jerusalem from this vantage point, Jesus wept
(Luke 19:28-44). Many of his prophecies are associated with the Mount of Olives (Matt. 24:3–25:46;
Mark 13:3-37).

Stemming from the many rich and varied traditions
associated with the Mount of Olives, Jewish, Christian, and Moslem shrines have been established at several sites over the centuries. An extensive Jewish
cemetery is located here in anticipation of the final
judgment (Zech. 14; cf. Joel 3:2 [MT 4:2]). Among

The Mount of Olives from the Temple Mount. In the center are the Garden of Gethsemane with the onion-domed Church of Mary Magdalene and the Church of the Ascension at the top of the hill. On the right are the Chapel of Dominus Flevit and, on the ridge, the Carmelite Monastery (KLM)

the shrines are the Christian church of the Ascension, the tomb of Mary beneath the church of St. Mary of Josaphat, the Dominus Flevit ("the Lord wept") chapel, the Pater Noster church on the site where Jesus is said to have taught the Lord's Prayer, the basilica of the Agony (Church of All Nations) in the traditional garden of Gethsemane, and the Moslem mosque of the Ascension.

OLIVET [ŏ lĭ vĕt'] (Gk. *elaiōn* "of olive trees," *toú elaiōnos* "of the olive grove"; from Lat. *olivetum* "olive grove"). Alternate name for the Mount of Olives (Luke 19:29; 21:37; Acts 1:12). *See* OLIVES, MOUNT OF.

OLYMPAS [ō lĭm'pəs] (Gk. *Olympas* "celestial"). A Christian at Rome to whom Paul sent his greetings (Rom. 16:15).

OMAR [ō'mär] (Heb. *'ômār* "word, song, praise"). An Edomite chief, the second son of Eliphaz and grandson (or descendant) of Esau (Gen. 36:11, 15; 1 Chr. 1:36).

OMEGA [ō mĕg'ə] (Gk. *Ō*). The twenty-fourth and last letter of the Greek alphabet. Phonetically it represents a long "o" sound; its numerical value is eight hundred. It is used figuratively with Alpha, the first letter of the Greek alphabet, to signify God (Rev. 1:8; 21:6) and Christ (22:13) as "the beginning and the end" (cf. 1:17; 2:8). *See* ALPHA AND OMEGA.

OMER [ō'mər] (Heb. *'ōmer*). A dry measure equal to one-tenth of an ephah (Exod. 16:16-36). The measure was probably not exact, indicating basically the capacity of a common-sized bowl. Heb. *'ōmer* originally meant a sheaf of grain (so Lev. 23:11, 12, 15; Deut. 24:19). The probable measure was 2.2 l. (2.3 qts.), although suggestions range as high as 4 l. (4 qts., about one-half of a peck basket).

OMRI [ŏm'rē] (Heb. *'omrî*).

1. One of the ablest kings to rule the northern kingdom of Israel (876-869); father of Ahab and founder of the Omride dynasty. That Omri's ancestry is not given is an almost certain indication that he was a foreigner.

Omri was a commander of Israel's army during the brief reign of King Elah, son of Baasha. While Omri and his troops were engaged against the Philistines at Gibbethon *ca.* 876, Zimri, commander of half of the chariots, assassinated Elah and his family at the capital

Tirzah. "All Israel" then proclaimed Omri king, and he turned his army on Tirzah. When Zimri realized all was lost, he committed suicide, having reigned only seven days (1 Kgs. 16:8-18).

The country, however, remained in a state of civil war. Half of the Israelites supported Omri, but the other half turned to Tibni the son of Ginath. The two factions warred until Tibni died *ca.* 872. Omri then reigned uncontested until his death in 869 (vv. 21-23).

Omri's accomplishments as king are impressive. He established a new northern capital on the hill of Samaria, purchased from Shemer for two talents of silver (v. 24). The move was propitious, giving Israel a capital that remained virtually impregnable for more than one hundred years. Moreover, the purchase of Samaria gave Omri land with which to conscript an army. (Elsewhere in the ancient Near East land was granted primarily in exchange for military service. But since in Israel the land was viewed ultimately as Yahweh's possession divided among the tribes, the king was dependent upon the good will of the tribes to constitute his army. As a private purchase, Samaria became a royal city, and Omri thus could grant land directly to his army, bypassing the tribal authorities and increasing his power enormously [cf. David's acquisition of Jerusalem, 2 Sam. 5:6-10]).

Freedom from domestic conflict enabled Omri to carry out a comprehensive foreign policy. Realizing that the constant friction between Israel and Judah was sapping the strength of both nations, he refrained from attacking Judah. The marriage of his daughter (or granddaughter) Athaliah to Jehoram son of Jehoshaphat of Judah formally repaired the breach (2 Kgs. 8:18; 2 Chr. 21:6; cf. 2 Kgs. 8:26; 2 Chr. 22:2). Omri concluded a treaty with King Ethbaal of Sidon by marrying his son Ahab to Ethbaal's daughter Jezebel (1 Kgs. 16:31). Although he apparently relinquished some northern territory to Ben-hadad of Syria (20:34), Omri succeeded in conquering Moab and making it a vassal state (Moabite Stone; *ANET*, p. 320; cf. 2 Kgs. 3:4). Omri's international reputation is underscored by Assyrian texts more than a century later referring to Israel as the "house of Omri" (Akk. *Bīt Ḥumria*; Tiglath-pileser III, *ANET*, pp. 284-85) and Jehu, who supplanted the Omride dynasty in 842, as the "son of Omri" (*mâr Ḥumri*; Shalmaneser III, *ANET*, p. 280).

Omri was succeeded in 869 by his son Ahab (1 Kgs. 16:28). The author of 1 Kings accords Omri only a scant fourteen verses, concluding that he "did what was evil in the sight of the Lord, and did more evil than all who were before him" (v. 25). This evaluation is supported by onomastic evidence suggesting that syncretistic religious practices permeated Samaria during Omri's reign.

2. A Benjaminite; the son of Becher and grandson of Benjamin (1 Chr. 7:8).

3. The grandfather of Uthai, a Judahite who returned to Jerusalem after the Exile (1 Chr. 9:4).

4. The son of Michael; chief officer of Issachar during the reign of David (1 Chr. 27:18).

ON (PERSON) [ŏn] (Heb. *'ôn* "vigor, wealth"). A Reubenite, the son of Peleth who joined with Korah in rebelling against Moses (Num. 16:1).

ON (PLACE) [ŏn] (Heb. *'ôn*; Egyp. *iwnw*). The Egyptian city of HELIOPOLIS (1) (lit. "house of the sun"; Jer. 43:13; KJV "Beth-shemesh"). Located at the southern tip of the Nile delta, the city was the capital of an Egyptian district and the cult center of the sun-deity Atum-Re, in honor of whom the Egyptians erected a number of obelisks. Potiphera, Joseph's father-in-law, is called "priest of On," presumably associated with this cult (Gen. 41:45, 50; 46:20).

The Hebrew prophets also refer to this city as Aven (Heb. *'āwen* "evil"; so KJV, Ezek. 30:17).

See CITY OF THE SUN.

ONAM [ō'nəm] (Heb. *'ônām* "vigorous").

1. The fifth son of Shobal, and ancestor of a Horite clan (Gen. 36:23; 1 Chr. 1:40).

2. The son of Jerahmeel and Atarah (1 Chr. 2:26, 28).

ONAN [ō'nən] (Heb. *'ônan* "vigorous, wealthy"). The second son of Judah and the Canaanite (Bath-) Shua (Gen. 38:4, 8-9; 46:12; Num. 26:19; 1 Chr. 2:3). When his wicked older brother Er died without leaving an heir, Onan was obligated to father a son by his brother's widow, Tamar (Gen. 38:7-8; cf. Deut. 25:5-10). Onan slept with Tamar, apparently fulfilling his fraternal obligation, but realizing that the child would be heir to his brother's double portion of the patrimony, whenever Onan and Tamar had intercourse he would spill his sperm on the ground to prevent her from conceiving; for this the Lord slew him (Gen. 38:9-10). *See* LEVIRATE LAW.

ONESIMUS [ō nĕs' məs] (Gk. *Onēsimos* "useful"). A slave, presumably of Philemon, who apparently stole from his master and fled to Rome, where he met Paul (Phlm. 10). There Onesimus became a Christian and a "son" to the imprisoned apostle, who later returned him to Philemon with a letter (the epistle to Philemon). In the letter Paul commends Onesimus, offers to personally compensate Philemon for his loss, and conveys his hope that Onesimus can continue to serve him (vv. 10-20). Playing on the name Onesimus, Paul writes that the slave formerly "useless" to Philemon had become "useful" to both (v. 11). Onesimus is mentioned also at Col. 4:9 as "one of yourselves" among those whom Paul sent to bear the epistle.

Employing the same pun as Paul, Ignatius of Antioch commends in a letter to Ephesus *ca.* A.D. 115 a bishop named Onesimus. The name, however, appears to have been common, first among slaves and then among Christians commemorating Paul's associate. It is not impossible that the person named by Ignatius was the biblical figure, but were he still alive he would have been a very old man.

Some scholars suggest that Onesimus is to be identified with ONESIPHORUS, of which his name could be a shortened form (cf. *Onēsiphoros* "profit-bearing"). Like Onesimus, Onesiphorus ministered to the imprisoned Paul at Rome (2 Tim. 1:16-17). He also apparently was active at Ephesus (v. 18).

ONESIPHORUS [ŏnə sĭf'ərəs] (Gk. *Onēsiphoros* "profit-bearing"). A Christian who sought out the imprisoned Paul in Rome and ministered to him without being "ashamed of [Paul's] chains" (2 Tim. 2:16-17). He also performed at Ephesus some unspecified service of which Timothy was aware (v. 18). 2 Timothy twice greets "the household of Onesiphorus" (v. 16; 4:19). *See* ONESIMUS.

ONIAS [ō nī′əs] (Gk. *Onias*).† A common name among members of the wealthy high priestly family during the Maccabean period. The Oniads traced their descent from Zadok (cf. 1 Kgs. 2:35). Their primary opponents were the Tobiads, a family of merchants and the financial administrators of Jerusalem.

1. Onias I or Johanan IV (b. *ca.* 345 B.C.); son of Jaddua and father of Simon I the Just. He was high priest in Jerusalem from *ca.* 320, about the time of the death of Alexander the Great (Josephus *Ant.* xi.8.7 [347]), until 290. He concluded an alliance with King Arius I of Sparta (1 Macc. 12:7-23; Josephus *Ant.* xii.4.10 [225] attributes this treaty to Onias III).

2. Onias II, son of Simon I. He succeeded his uncle Eleazar (Josephus *Ant.* xii.2.5 [40-50]) and great uncle Manasseh (4.1 [156-58]) as high priest. Seeking to increase his own power, in the Third Syrian War (246-241 B.C.) Onias sided with the more lenient Seleucids against the Ptolemies, who exercised tight fiscal control over the Palestinian temple cities. But when Onias refused to pay the tribute to the Egyptian king Ptolemy III Euergetes, Seleucis II failed to support him. The Tobiad Joseph, Onias' nephew and the chief tax collector for the region, intervened to halt Egyptian retaliation, and Ptolemy granted him Onias' civil authority (*Ant.* xii.2.4.1-6). This loss of political rule was a severe blow both to the office of high priest and the fortunes of the Oniads.

Onias was succeeded by his son Simon II the Just, who managed to regain some of the prestige of the high priestly office.

3. Onias III, son of Simon II; high priest at the time of Seleucus IV Philopater (187-175 B.C.). Partly because of the current ineffectiveness of Seleucid rule Onias allied with the Ptolemies, who saw also opportunity to attract wealthy pilgrims from Alexandria in Egypt to the Jerusalem temple.

The Tobiads, secure in their relationship as financial administrators for the Seleucid crown, accused Onias III of unjustly withholding monies. Seleucus sent his minister Heliodorus to investigate the charges. Heliodorus gained entrance to the temple despite Onias' objections, only to swoon at the sight of a fearful apparition. While Heliodorus lay near death, his friends convinced the pious Onias to intercede with God for his life, whereupon Heliodorus recovered and returned to his king (2 Macc. 3).

Simon, scion of the Tobiads and temple captain, accused Onias of responsibility for Heliodorus' affliction. Onias journeyed to Antioch to defend himself before the king. Meanwhile however, Heliodorus murdered Antiochus III, who was succeeded by his brother Antiochus IV Epiphanes. Onias apparently fled to Egypt, where Josephus reports that he founded a rival temple in Heliopolis (*BJ* i.1.1 [33]; vii.10.2-3 [421-432]); perhaps at the instigation of the rival Tobiads, Onias' brother Jason (Joshua) offered Antiochus money to gain the high priesthood. According to 2 Maccabees, Onias later sought to expose the em-

bezzlement of temple treasures by Jason's successor, the non-Zadokite Menelaus (see 5 below), who had him imprisoned and murdered (4:1-34; cf. Dan. 9:26).

Some scholars identify Onias III as the "Teacher of Righteousness" alluded to at Hos. 10:12; Joel 2:23.

4. Onias IV, son of Onias III. When Antiochus V had the high priest Menelaus murdered and installed in his place Alcimus, the rightful appointee Onias fled to Egypt (*ca.* 163 B.C.). Here he founded a military colony at Leontopolis and, according to Josephus (*Ant.* xii.9.7 [388]; xiii.3.1-3 [62-73]), a temple. His sons became generals under Cleopatra III.

5. Onias Menelaus, successor to Jason as high priest. He is variously identified as the brother of the temple captain and a cousin of Jason and Onias III. *See* MENELAUS.

ONION (Heb. *bāṣal*). One of the vegetables for which Israel longed in the wilderness (Num. 11:5). Onions (*Alium cepa* L.) were grown all over the ancient Near East, but obviously the Israelites could not cultivate even the simplest vegetables during their wanderings.

Egyptian onions were reputedly among the most flavorful. The Egyptians ate them raw, boiled, and as a condiment in lentil dishes. In Palestine the Israelites ate the mature onions, but not the leaves, which they considered to be harmful.

ONLY BEGOTTEN. The KJV translation of Gk. *monogenḗs* "only, unique, one of a kind," used (following Vulg. Lat. *unigenitus*) with reference to both Jesus Christ (John 1:14, 18; 3:16, 18; 1 John 4:9) and Issac (Heb. 11:17). Most other translations consistently read "only," while the NIV translates "the one and only" with regard to Jesus. In English "only begotten" implies a created being, an implication not conveyed by the Greek term (cf. Luke 7:12; 8:42; 9:38).

ONO [ō′nō] (Heb. *'ônô* "vigorous"). A Benjamite city (modern Kefr ʿAnā) located 12 km. (7 mi.) east-southeast of Joppa (cf. Neh. 11:35). Thutmose III claimed to have conquered the city *ca.* 1468 B.C. (Karnak inscription; *ANET*, p. 243). 1 Chr. 8:12 credits "the sons of Elpaal" with the (re)construction of Ono and Lod and their outlying towns. The city was repopulated after the Exile (Ezra 2:33; Neh. 7:37; 11:35). It was the nearby plain of Ono to which Sanballat and Geshem attempted to lure Nehemiah to harm him (6:2; cf. 11:35, "the valley of craftsmen").

ONOMASTICON [ŏn′ə măs′tĭ kŏn] (Gk. *Onomastikon* "consisting of names").† Generally, a learned term describing a philological aid purporting to supply the meaning and etymology of a list of proper names. Often in antiquity such lists were somewhat arbitrary and fanciful.

Specifically, the name is attributed to the last section of a four-part geographical work by the fourth-century Church historian Eusebius of Caesarea. The Onomasticon listed, in Greek alphabetical order, the geographical location of nearly one thousand sites, whether towns, districts, deserts, wâdīs, rivers, mountains, or tombs. Of these, four hundred are described fully enough to attempt to locate them. Most of these sites are known from the Bible, particularly the Old Testament, and the great majority are to be found in Palestine. This list also provided corresponding fourth-century Roman place names, and often included the mileage along the Roman roads from one place to another. Although excavation of many of the sites in modern times has expanded upon or corrected material from the Onomasticon, it remains a very important source for the study of Palestinian topography.

ONYCHA [ŏn′ĭ kə] (Heb. *šᵉ ḥēleṭ*). One of the ingredients of the incense for the tabernacle (Exod. 30:34), most probably the powdered nail-shaped shell of a certain mollusk that gives off a sharp, pungent odor when burned. According to the Talmud, the smell of burning onycha is initially similar to fried shrimp, then changes to an oil-like odor. The powder was said to foster power and stamina when burned with scented spices.

Some scholars suggest that the ingredient was actually cloves (*Eugenia aromatica*), a scented spice like the other ingredients of the list. In addition, certain versions of the LXX translate the word as Gk. *ónyx* rather than *ónycha*, fallaciously giving rise to the speculation that the ingredient was onyx (an obsolete, secondary meaning of "onycha"), a variety of the mineral chalcedony.

ONYX (Heb. *šōham*). A form of banded chalcedony, imported in biblical times as a precious stone comparable in value to gold and sapphire (Gen. 2:12; Job 28:16). The variously colored bands of onyx make it an excellent material for carving—a careful engraver can carve the stone so that the engraving is in a completely different color than the background—thus a highly suitable material for signets and seals. The names of the twelve tribes of Israel were carved in two pieces of onyx and the stones placed in gold settings on either shoulder of the high priest's ephod (Exod. 28:9-13; 39:6-7); another onyx was engraved with the name of an Israelite tribe and fastened to the breastplate (39:13; cf. Ezek. 28:13).

The LXX understands Heb. *šōham* to mean a gemstone of any of a number of shades of green, variously translating it as "sardius" (Exod. 25:7), "emerald" (Exod. 28:9), or even "leek-green stone" (Gen. 2:12). At Rev. 21:20 the RSV reads "onyx" for Gk. *sardónyx* "sardonyx" (JB "agate").

OPHEL [ō′fĕl] (Heb. *hā ʿōpel* "swelling, lump"). The ridge between the Kidron and Tyropoeon valleys, some 600 m. (2000 ft.) above sea level, fortified by David as his capital (cf. 2 Sam. 5:7, 9; 1 Chr. 11:5, 7; see DAVID, CITY OF; cf. Josephus *BJ* v.4.2 [142-45], "Ophlas"). An important part of the defenses of Jerusalem, Jotham (2 Chr. 27:3) and Manasseh (33:14) both reinforced the walls of this part of the city during their reigns. After the Exile Ophel was the residence of the temple servants (Neh. 3:26-27; 11:21). Some scholars would restrict the name to the northern portion of the city of David, the area immediately south of the present Haram esh-Sharif. The northern conitnuation of the ridge, Mt. Moriah, was the site of Solomon's temple. See JERUSALEM.

The Old Testament also refers to an Ophal in Samaria (2 Kgs. 5:24; KJV "tower"; RSV "hill"). Elsewhere the Hebrew term is taken simply as "hill" (Isa. 32:14; Mic. 4:8).

OPHIR [ō′fər] (Heb. *ʾôpîr*) (PERSON).† According to the Table of Nations, a descendant of Shem, the son of Joktan and brother of Havilah (Gen. 10:29; 1 Chr. 1:23). He is presumably the eponymous ancestor of the region of Ophir.

OPHIR [ō′fər] (Heb. *ʾôpîr*) (PLACE).† A region from which the trade ships of Solomon and Hiram imported gold, almug wood, and precious stones (1 Kgs. 9:28; 10:11; 2 Chr. 8:18; 9:10; cf. 1 Kgs. 22:48). The gold of the region was so pure that "gold of Ophir" became a synonym for high quality gold (1 Chr. 29:4; Job 22:24; 28:16; Ps. 45:9 [MT 10]; Isa. 13:12). An eighth-century B.C. pottery fragment discovered at Tell Qasileh bears the inscription "gold from Ophir for Beth-horon, 30 shekels."

The location of Ophir remains uncertain. India, Africa, and Arabia are the most common suggestions, and a few scholars have even argued for a location in South America. Attempts to locate the region are based on either linguistic similarity of place names or suitability of climate for the indicated products: gold and almug wood (probably sandlewood [*Pterocarpus santalihus* L.]), indigenous to India and Ceylon. Ophir is commonly associated with the "ships of Tarshish" with which Solomon also imported silver, ivory, apes, and peacocks (1 Kgs. 10:22; 2 Chr. 9:21); these products would seem to favor a location in Africa (or even South America), but scholars argue the phrase "ships of Tarshish" designates not a trade route but a size or type of sailing vessel.

OPHNI [ŏf′nē] (Heb. *ʿopnî*). A city in the tribal territory of Benjamin (Josh. 18:24), perhaps to be identified with modern Jifna, 21 km. (13 mi.) north of Jerusalem and 5 km. (3 mi.) north-northwest of Bethel. Josephus calls the town Gophna, which he indicates was the capital of its toparchy (*BJ* iii.3.5 [55]); the Tabula peutingeriana, an ancient Roman map, locates Gophna 25.5 km. (16 mi.) from Aelia Capitolina.

OPHRAH [ŏf′rə] (Heb. *ʿoprâ* "young hart, stag") (PERSON). The son of Meonothai of Judah (1 Chr. 4:14).

OPHRAH [ŏf′rə] (Heb. *ʿoprâ* "young hart, stag") (PLACE).

1. A city situated at the fork in the road leading from Lebanon to either Michmash or Jericho. It was allocated originally to the tribal territory of Benjamin (Josh. 18:23; 1 Sam. 13:17). Ophrah is probably identical with the city bearing the tribal name of Ephraim (2 Sam. 13:23 [near Baal-hazor, where Absalom avenged Amnon's rape of Tamar]; John 11:54; 1 Macc. 11:34 "Aphairema"), as well as Ephron (2 Chr. 13:19; KJV "Ephraim"); like Bethel to the south, this city was probably lost to the Canaanites very early, then recaptured by the Ephraimites, who subsequently claimed it (cf. Judg. 4:5; 1 Kgs. 12:29). Modern eṭ-Ṭaiyibeh, 6.5 km. (4 mi.) northeast of Bethel, is the most likely site.

During the reign of Saul, one of the three raiding parties that went out from the Philistine camp at Michmash traveled north along the road toward Ophrah and the land of Shual (1 Sam. 13:17). The city was among those that King Abijah of Judah recaptured from Jeroboam I (2 Chr. 13:19). Jesus retreated to the isolation of Ephraim at the beginning of his period of persecution (John 11:54); the city was the capital of one of the three Samaritan districts given to Jonathan Maccabeus by Demetrius II (1 Macc 11:34). Vespasian later conquered this city and Bethel en route to Jerusalem (Josephus *BJ* iv.9.9).

2. Ophrah of Abiezer, a city mentioned only in the story of Gideon (Judg. 6–9). The designation "of Abiezer" indicates the city was part of the tribal territory of Manasseh (cf. Josh. 17:2; 1 Chr. 7:18); it was located somewhere in the region around Moreh, Mt. Tabor, and the Jezreel valley (perhaps at modern ʿAffuleh). Gideon's family home was situated here (Judg. 6:11; 9:5), and here Gideon was buried in the tomb of his father (8:32). Gideon built an altar inscribed "The Lord is peace" to commemorate the appearance of the angel at Ophrah, and the monument was still standing when the book of Judges was compiled (6:24, "to this day"). Gideon also erected an ephod here that the Israelites began to worship (8:27). After Gideon's death, his son Abimelech killed all but one of his seventy brothers here in his bid for kingship (9:5).

ORACLE (Heb. *maśśāʾ* "burden," *nᵉʾum* "utterance"; Gk. *lógion* "word"). A communication from a deity. Heb. *nᵉʾum* is the most common term, designating the actual words of the divine speech (e.g., Num. 24:3-4, 15-16; 2 Sam. 23:1; KJV "[hath] said") or the act of speaking prophetically (Jer. 23:31; RSV "say"). Heb. *maśśāʾ* often has a negative connotation and occurs largely as a designation for proclamations against foreign nations (e.g., Isa. 13:1; Hab. 1:1; Zech. 9:1; KJV "burden") or denunciations of evildoers in Israel (e.g., 2 Kgs. 9:25; Zech. 12:1). At 2 Sam. 16:23 Ahithophel consults the "oracle" (*dāḇar* "word") of God. In the New Testament Gk. *lógion* indicates the word of God communicated to his people (Acts 7:38; Rom. 3:2) and the authority of the gospel as preached by the apostles (1 Pet. 4:11).

The KJV also sometimes uses "oracle" in the sense of the place or means by which God speaks, referring specifically to the inner sanctuary of the temple (e.g., 1 Kgs. 6:5, 16, 19-23, 31; 2 Chr. 5:7, 9; Ps. 28:2; Heb. *dᵉḇîr*; RSV "inner sanctuary").

See PROPHECY.

ORAL TRADITION.† Any materials passed on solely by word of mouth, and the process by which they are preserved. It is during this process that these materials are most fluid and subject to reinterpretation. In biblical studies the term particularly refers to the legends, revelations, histories, prophecies, and other elements that later became a part of written Scripture.

There can be no doubt that most of the Bible existed first in oral form. The oracles of the prophets, the psalms of the Jerusalem cult, the parables and teachings of Jesus all were first delivered verbally. The major dispute among scholars concerns the length of time between the first verbal delivery and the time when the material was written down.

At one time scholars were divided into two firmly established camps. Liberal scholars held that most of the material was written down very late (exilic or postexilic period for the Old Testament) and primarily reflect the concerns of this later period. Conservative scholars argued that these materials were written down early, close to the time they purport to cover, and reflect early concerns. Modern research has broken down these iron-clad positions and spurred dialogue between both groups.

Scholars use a distinct method of analysis known as "tradition criticism" to investigate oral tradition. This approach involves first retracing the history of the evolution of a particular text. At each stage certain persons were responsible for preserving the tradition. Identifying their concerns or prejudices helps the exegete understand the ways in which the tradition might have been shaped or used. A second approach is comparison of the tradition under study with other similar traditions to highlight its similarities and differences. Such comparison can, in turn, help the exegete identify common themes, motifs, or even mutual dependencies.

The study of the oral traditions underlying the text has proven quite valuable for biblical studies, particularly where adequate parallels exist (e.g., Psalms and Gospels). This discipline allows the interpreter to see the different ways the community (Israel or the Church) understood the text throughout its history. Hermeneutically, this also permits the modern interpreter a wider range of applications featuring a greater depth of understanding.

Bibliography. D. A. Knight, *Recovering the Traditions of Israel.* SBL Dissertation 9 (Missoula: 1973); K. Koch, *The Growth of the Biblical Tradition* (New York: 1969); M. Noth, *A History of Pentateuchal Traditions* (1972; repr. Chico: 1981); W. E. Rast, *Tradition History and the Old Testament* (Philadelphia: 1972).

ORDER.* A society or class of people united by certain common characteristics. According to 1 Chr. 6-7, 24, David arranged the priests and Levites into certain labor divisions based on family units (cf. 2 Kgs. 23:4; 1 Chr. 15:18). The "order of Melchizedek" (Heb. *diḇrâ*; Ps. 110:4; Gk. *táxis*; Heb. 5:6, 10; 6:20; 7:11, 17) is an appeal to a tradition of legitimate priests outside of the levitical ranks; it refers to not only the position of Melchizedek but also to the distinctive nature of his (and thus Christ's) priesthood. *See* MELCHIZEDEK.

OREB [ôʹrəb] (Heb. *ʿōrēḇ, ʿōrēḇ* "raven"). One of two Midianite princes beheaded by the Ephraimites at the time of Gideon (Judg. 7:25; 8:3; cf. Ps. 83:11 [MT 12]). Subsequently his name was given to the rock where he was killed (Judg. 7:25).

OREN [ôrʹən] (Heb. *ʿōren* "laurel"). A Judahite, son of Jerahmeel (1 Chr. 2:25).

ORION [ō rīʹən] (Heb. *kᵉsîl*).† A constellation of stars in the form of a warrior, named for the mighty hunter of Greek mythology who was changed into a constellation after Artemis slew him. Located east of Taurus, the configuration includes yellowish-red Betelgeuse at the top, with blue-white Rigel below and to the right; a line of three stars forms the belt, and another the sword attached to it. Orion is mentioned at Job 9:9; 38:31; Amos 5:8 as testimony to the creative power of God.

Other than the plural "constellations" at Isa. 13:10, in other contexts the Hebrew term means "fool" (Ps. 49:10 [MT 11]; 92:6 [MT 7]; 94:8; cf. Prov. 26:7, 9; Eccl. 7:4), perhaps reflecting a theological contrast of the relative ineffectiveness of the mighty Orion or an implicit judgment upon nations that worshipped celestial bodies.

ORNAMENTS (Heb. *ʿaḏî* "adornments").† Jewelry and other decorative accessories, well attested by archaeological excavations throughout Palestine and the ancient Near East. Among the Israelites ornaments were a statement of wealth and prosperity (cf. 2 Sam. 1:24; Ezek. 16:11) and considered especially appropriate for special occasions (cf. Isa. 49:18; Jer. 2:32). They might be worn daily, but were considered out of place for those in mourning (Exod. 33:4-6). Typical Israelite ornaments included rings for the nose, ears, fingers, arms, and ankles (e.g., Prov. 25:12; Heb. *ḥalî*; cf. Cant. 7:1 [MT 2]; RSV "jewels"), elaborate necklaces, and headdresses (cf. KJV, Prov. 1:9; 4:9; *liwyâ*; RSV "garland"). The best comprehensive listing of the various kinds of finery of the rich is Isa. 3:18-23; Ezek. 16:10-13 lists of typical bridal ornaments. Even idols might be decked out with expensive clothing and jewels (vv. 16-18; cf. KJV, Isa. 30:22; *ʾapuddâ*; RSV "gold-plated").

See also the individual entries.

ORNAN [ôr′nən] (Heb. *ʾornān*).† An alternate form of AROUNAH.

ORONTES [ôr ŏn′tēz].† The major river of western Syria, the modern Nahr el-ʿAṣī. Originating north of Baalbek, it flows northward some 300 km. (186 mi.) between Lebanon and the Anti-lebanon mountains; at Jisr al-Hadid near Antioch (modern Anṭâkiyeh) it bends sharply to the west and flows into the Mediterranean Sea at Seleucia (modern Samandag). In ancient times a major trade and military road connected the river valley with Nineveh and the Tigris river; branches of the road led to the Mediterranean coast, central Syria, and Anatolia. In 853 B.C. an alliance of Ben-hadad II of Damascus, Irḥuleni of Hamath, and Ahab of Israel battled to a standstill the Assyrian king Shalmaneser III at Qarqar on the lower Orontes (*ANET*, pp. 278-79), and here *ca.* 720 Sargon II routed the rebels of Hamath and Damascus.

ORPAH [ôr′pə] (Heb. *ʿorpâ* "neck" or "cloud" [?]). A Moabite woman, daughter-in-law of Naomi. After her husband Chilion died, Orpah sought to accompany Naomi to Bethlehem, but at her mother-in-law's insistence returned to her kin in Moab (Ruth 1:4-14).

ORPHAN (Heb. *yāṯôm* "fatherless"; Gk. *orphanós*)

Together with the widow and the alien, the orphan was a particularly vulnerable member of Israelite society (cf. Deut. 10:18; 14:29; RSV "fatherless").

In Old Testament usage "orphan" does not necessarily imply that both of the child's parents were dead (cf. Job 24:9), as reflected in the frequent RSV rendering of the word as "fatherless." Orphans are mentioned most often with "widows," which would thus encompass all members of bereaved families. In ancient Israel, men, through whom inheritance generally was passed, were the most frequent casualties of war; thus a husbandless family was left not only without a family provider but also with no one to defend their rights before the clan. In addition, some scholars believe many "orphans" were the illegitimate offspring of the various shrine prostitutes; these, with no hope of an inheritance, must have lived a particularly precarious existence.

Many of these children must have been very poor (cf. 1 Kgs. 17:8-24; 2 Kgs. 4:1-7; Lam. 5:1-5), so it is not surprising that the Mosaic law contains special provisions for the orphan and the widow (e.g., Exod. 22:22 [MT 21]; cf. Num. 27:7-11). A creditor could not take one of their garments as a pledge (cf. Deut. 24:17). A sheaf of grain dropped in the field must be left for them (cf. Ruth 2), and grapes and olives could only be harvested once a season—fruit that ripened late belonged to the poor (Deut. 24:19-21). The special tithe of the third year was designated for the aid of the widow, the orphan, the sojourner, and the Levites, all of whom had no land of their own (14:29; 26:12-13).

These most vulnerable members of society often had no recourse to justice. Job noted caring for orphans and widows as one of the proofs of his righteousness (Job 29:12), but not everyone was so conscientious (6:27; 22:9; 24:3; Deut. 27:19; Ps. 94:6). The prophets also frequently appealed for better treatment of orphans and widows (Isa. 1:17, 23; 10:2; Jer. 5:28; Ezek. 22:7; Zech. 7:10; Mal. 3:5). God himself promised to be their protector (Exod. 22:23-24 [MT 22-23]; Deut. 10:18; Ps. 10:14, 18; Prov. 23:10-11; cf. Isa. 9:17 [MT 16]). According to James, ministering to orphans was a characteristic of "pure and undefiled" religion (Jas. 1:17).

OSEE (Rom. 9:25, KJV). *See* HOSEA.

OSHEA (Num. 13:8, 16, KJV). *See* HOSHEA 1.

OSIRIS [ō sī′rəs].† Egyptian god of vegetation and the underworld, brother and husband of ISIS and father of Horus. Held by tradition to have taught mankind the arts of civilization, he may have been originally an early Egyptian king or the eponymous ancestor of a conquering clan. He is represented in Egyptian art as a human king bearing a long crooked scepter and whip as symbols of authority.

Drowned and dismembered by his evil brother Seth, the kindly King Osiris was resurrected through the perseverance of the faithful Isis. Hence he came to be associated with the seasonal death and return to life of nature. Aided by Thoth and Anubis, Osiris (depicted as a mummified king) judged the dead, who might accompany him in the blissful existence of the afterworld. The Egyptian pharaoh, identified in life as the god Horus, would after death rule the underworld as Osiris; in time, the name Osiris became the vernacular designation for all deceased persons (Osiris X, "the late X").

At Abydos, where tradition held that Osiris' head had been buried, an annual festival recreated the Osiris legend. Assimilated with the sacred bull Apis (in whom he was held to be incarnate) as Serapis, Osiris was worshipped throughout the Greco-Roman world.

OSNAPPAR [ŏs nǎp'ər] (Aram. *'osnappar*). An Assyrian king who deported conquered peoples and resettled them at Samaria (Ezra 4:10; KJV "Asnapper"). He is generally identified as ASSURBANIPAL (so JB, NIV).

OSPREY [ŏs'prĭ] (Heb. *'oznîyâ*). A bird of prey mentioned only in the lists of unclean animals (Lev. 11:13; Deut. 14:12; KJV "ospray"). The exact species is impossible to identify based on the scant biblical references, but a strong Talmudic tradition supports the bird's identification as the osprey (*Pandion haliaëtus*), a large fish-eating hawk. Other possible candidates are the harrier (or short-toed) eagle (*Circaëtus gallicus*; cf. Aram. *'ûzyā'* "sea-eagle"; so LXX), the bearded vulture (*Gypaëtus barbatus aureus*; so NEB), or the black vulture (*Aegypius* [or *Vultur*] *monachus*; so NIV, NJV).

OSSIFRAGE (KJV). See VULTURE.

OSTRICH (Heb. *baṭ hayya'ᵃnâ* "daughter of greed" or "daughter of the desert"), A large, swiftly running bird (*Struthio camelus* or *syriacus*) considered unclean for food in the Old Testament (Lev. 11:16; Deut. 14:15; KJV "owl"). Because it can attain speeds close to 130 km. per hour (80 mph) (cf. Job. 39:13; Heb. *rᵉnānîm*; KJV "peacock"), this bird is most at home in the desolate, relatively barren plains (Isa. 13:21; 34:13; 43:20; Jer. 50:39), hence the etymology "daughter of the desert." Its mournful cry seemed particularly suited to these places (Mic. 1:8). The bird was still common in the Syrian desert and the extreme southern part of the country as late as the nineteenth century A.D., but now is found in the wild only in Africa.

A second possible etymology for the name is "daughter of greed," again a most apt characterization of its habits. The ostrich is omnivorous, consuming all manner of grass, fruit, snakes, lizards, small animals—seemingly whatever it can manage to swallow. The fact that its diet included other animals is probably why the Hebrews considered it unclean. Most other peoples of the ancient Near East hunted it for food. Ostrich hunts are a recurring theme in Assyrian artwork.

The ostrich lays its eggs in the sand where they are warmed by the sun during the day. While the eggs have especially hard shells, this habit seemed to the Hebrews akin to desertion (Lam. 4:3; Job 39:14-17). Thus the ostrich was, for the Hebrews, symbolic of stupidity, apathy, and desolation.

OTHNI [ŏth'nĭ] (Heb. *'otnî*). The eldest son of She-

maiah; a levitical gatekeeper during the reign of King David (1 Chr. 26:7).

OTHNIEL [ŏth' nĭ əl] (Heb. *'otnî'ēl*).
1. The son of Kenaz and nephew (or younger brother) of Caleb (Josh. 15:17; Judg. 1:13; 3:9; 1 Chr. 4:13); Israel's first judge. He conquered Debir and claimed as his wife Caleb's daughter Achsah, who had been offered as a reward (Josh. 15:16-17; Judg. 1:13). Othniel later delivered Israel from the eight-year rule of the Mesopotamian king Cushan-rishathaim (Judg. 3:7-11). Some scholars see the various relationships of Othniel and Caleb as reflecting the social history of Judahite or Kenizzite clans.
2. A military division during the reign of David (1 Chr. 27:15), perhaps a clan who traced their ancestry to **1**.

OVEN (Heb. *tannûr*; Gk. *klíbanos*). An enclosed or semi-enclosed stone, earthen, or pottery structure used for baking. Because such a device provides a higher temperature and a more even heat than an open flame, it is particularly suitable for baking bread (Lev. 2:4; 7:9; 26:26). Grass (Matt. 6:30; Luke 12:28) is burned to heat the stone floor, the ashes are swept away, and the dough is laid on the floor or stuck to the oven walls to bake. Accordingly, the oven provided an apt image for intense heat (Ps. 21:9 [MT 10]; Lam. 5:10; Hos. 7:6-7; Mal. 4:1 [MT 3:19]).

Excavations in Israel, Egypt, and Mesopotamia have uncovered the remains of ovens similar to those still used in modern rural Palestine. Cylindrical, they often take the form of clay chimneys, 600-900 cm. (2-3 ft.) across and as much as 1 m. (2-4 ft.) high, but tapering toward the top. According to tradition, one of the rooms of Herod's temple contained a metal oven for baking the showbread. Portable ovens are attested, such as those that may have been used in the Israelite encampments.
See KILN.

OVENS, TOWER OF THE (Heb. *migdal hattannûrîm*).† A tower defending the northwestern angle of Jerusalem's city wall, possibly constructed first by King Uzziah (cf. 2 Chr. 26:9) and later rebuilt by Nehemiah (Neh. 3:11; 12:38; KJV "tower of the furnaces"). The precise location of the tower, as well as its position relative to the Corner Gate, is a matter of dispute. According to Nehemiah it was situated somewhere south of the Broad Wall and north of the Valley Gate. The name may point to a location near the "bakers' street" of Jer. 37:21, although this reference dates before the time of Nehemiah.

OVERSEER. A leader or supervisor. Various Hebrew terms are employed to designate the major domo of the Egyptian pharaoh's household (Gen. 39:4-5; Heb. *pāqaḏ* "visit, muster" hiphil), foremen responsible for agricultural production (41:34; *pāqîḏ*) or forced labor (2 Chr. 2:2, 18 [MT 1, 17]; *nāṣaḥ*, piel), and those in charge of the operation (KJV, Neh. 12:42; RSV "leader"; cf. *nāṣaḥ*, piel in the superscriptions to the Psalms; RSV "choirmaster") and restoration of the temple (2 Chr. 31:13; *mišmereṭ*; 34:17). According to Prov. 6:7, the diligent ant works without an overseer (so KJV; *šōṭēr* "scribe"; RSV "officer").

At Acts 20:28 the KJV translates as "overseer" Gk. *epískopos*, a term referring to the chief official (pastor or elder) of a church (Phil. 1:1, RSV mg.; 1 Tim. 3:2; Titus 1:7; RSV "bishop"; cf. 1 Pet. 2:25, with reference to Christ; RSV "Guardian").

OWL (Heb. *kôs, yanšûp, yanšôp*).† A nocturnal bird of prey of the order *Strigiformes*, listed among the unclean birds ("birds of abomination"; Lev. 11:17; Deut. 14:16). The owl is characterized by exceptionally large eyes that are directed forward rather than to the sides. The feathers around the eyes radiate from a common center and enhance the apparent size of the eyes. Yet in spite of this owls trust their ears far more often than their eyes in their search for prey. They fly extremely quietly, though slowly, and surprise their prey by descending from above. Their sharp talons and short, hooked beak are extremely powerful and make escape difficult. Owls swallow their prey whole and regurgitate the indigestible parts in pellets known as "owl balls."

At least seven of the more than two hundred known varieties of owl can be found in Palestine at the present: the little owl (*Athene noctua*), eagle owl (*Bubo bubo*), scops owl (*Otus scops*), tawny owl (*Strix aluco*; cf. RSV "great owl"), screech owl (*Otus asio*), short-eared owl (*Asio otus*), long-eared owl (*Asio flammeus*), and barn owl (*Tyto alba*). Attempts to associate the Hebrew terms with particular species is extremely problematic and may never be accomplished. Heb. *qippôz* (Isa. 34:15) is considered by some to be a variety of snake (NJV "arrow-snake"; cf. JB "viper"). The KJV rendering "screech owl" for Heb. *lîlît* at v. 14 designates a nocturnal creature, whether real or mythical (cf. NIV; RSV "night hag"). Heb. *baṭ hayyaʿᵃnâ* (KJV, Lev. 11:16; Deut. 14:15) is an OSTRICH (so RSV).

OX (ANIMAL). A domesticated adult bovine, especially a bull that has been castrated to make it a more docile draft animal. The biblical terms "ox" and "oxen" however, often are used in a much broader sense to indicate cattle of either sex and various ages, often in the collective sense (Heb. *šôr*; e.g., Deut. 14:4; *bāqār*; e.g., Gen. 12:16; 20:14; *'elep*, Ps. 8:7 [MT 8]; Aram. *tôr*; e.g., Dan. 4:5 [MT 2]; Gk. *boús*; e.g., Luke 13:15). *See* CATTLE.

The modern ox is probably a descendant of the wild ox (*Bos promigenius*; Heb. *reʾēm*; KJV "unicorn"), with which the Hebrews were apparently rather familiar. The indomitable spirit and strength of the wild ox were proverbial (Job. 39:9-12), and its horns symbolized strength (Num. 23:22; 24:8) and majesty (Deut. 33:17; Ps. 92:10 [MT 11]). Isaiah prophesied that God's judgment of Edom would extend to even the wild ox (Isa. 34:7). In Assyrian reliefs of hunting scenes the animal's two horns are superimposed, giving the appearance of only one (cf. LXX Gk. *monókerōs* "one-horned," hence KJV "unicorn"). At Deut.

14:5 the KJV translates Heb. *tᵉʾô* "antelope" as "wild ox."

A single bull could propagate an entire herd of cattle, so the Israelites often castrated additional or lesser bulls to make them a more suitable draft animal (an "ox," in the more specific modern sense). Such oxen pulled plows (Deut. 22:10; 1 Sam. 11:5; Luke 14:19), wagons (Num. 7:3; 2 Sam. 6:6), and threshing sleds (Deut. 25:4; 1 Cor. 9:9; 1 Tim. 5:18). Oxen (perhaps in the generic sense of "cattle" or less precisely meaning "bull") were specified for certain forms of sacrifice (Exod. 24:5, par "young bull"; Deut. 17:1, *šôr* "bull"; 2 Sam. 24:22-25, *bāqār*; John 2:14-15; Acts 14:13, *taúros* "bull"), but by levitical standards a castrated beast would have been regarded as unsuitable for such a purpose (Lev. 22:17-25). Twelve bronze oxen supported the molten sea of Solomon's temple (1 Kgs. 7:25; cf. Ezek. 1:10, where each living creature had one face like that of an ox; Rev. 4:7).

OX (PERSON) [ŏx] (Gk. *Ōx*). The paternal grandfather of Judith; father of Merari and descendant of Israel (Jdt. 8:1; cf. LXX, Gen. 22:21; MT "Uz").

OXYRHYNCHUS FRAGMENTS.† Among the numerous manuscript fragments found at Oxyrhynchus (modern Behnesa, *ca.* 185 km. [115 mi.] south of Cairo) are fragments of several New Testament books as well as four fragments preserving parts of apocryphal Gospels. Of the latter, three (Oxy. p. 1, 654, and 655, probably dating to the third century A.D.) are papyrus fragments in Greek of noncanonical sayings of Jesus included in the GOSPEL OF THOMAS, more recently recovered in full in a Coptic translation among the Nag Hammadi codices.

Oxy. p. 840 is a fourth- or fifth-century parchment fragment that tells of Levi, "a Pharisaic chief priest" who challenged Jesus and his disciples in the temple court because they had not carried out the purification procedures required for entry. Jesus' response contrasts the water with which Levi has bathed with "living water." The story resembles Synoptic accounts of Jesus' disputes with the scribes concerning the Pharisees' traditional interpretations of the law (e.g., Mark 2:23-28; 7:1-23).

OZEM [ŏ'zəm] (Heb. *'ōṣem*).
1. The sixth son of Jesse, and the brother of King David (1 Chr. 2:15).
2. A Judahite, the fourth son of Jerahmeel (1 Chr. 2:25).

OZIAS (Matt. 1:8-9, KJV). *See* UZZIAH 1.

OZNI [ŏz'nĭ] (Heb. *'oznî* "my ear [?]"). A son (or descendant) of Gad, and the eponymous ancestor of the Oznites (Num. 26:16). He is called Ezbon in the parallel list at Gen 46:16.

P. A designation of the PRIESTLY DOCUMENT, one of the hypothetical sources of the Pentateuch ascribed by critics.

PAARAI [pă′ə rī] (Heb. *pa‘ăray*). An Arbite; one of David's mighty men numbered among "the thirty" (2 Sam. 23:35). At 1 Chr. 11:37 he is called "Naarai the son of Ezbai."

PACATIANA [păk ə tī′ə nə, pă kā tĭ ā′nə] (Gk. *Pakatianēs*).* Phrygia Prima or Greater Phrygia, a province formed by Diocletian's sevenfold division of the Roman province of Asia *ca.* A.D. 300. According to the late Greek subscription to 1 Timothy, Laodicea was its "chiefest city" (so KJV).

PADDAN [păd′ən] (Heb. *paddan*). A short form of the name of PADDAN-ARAM (GEN. 48:7; KJV "PADAN").

PADDAN-ARAM [păd′ən âr′əm] (Heb. *paddan ’ărām*). A region in northern Mesopotamia centered around the city of Haran; according to critical scholars the term used by the Priestly source for ARAM-NAHARAIM. The inhabitants are identified as Arameans (Gen. 25:20; KJV "Padan-aram"; 31:24; RSV "Mesopotamia") and their language as Aramaic (v. 47).

Jacob went to Paddan-aram to the home of his grandfather, Bethuel, Rebekah's father (25:20), for safety from Esau and to seek a wife among his relatives (28:2-7; cf. 27:42-45). There he was married to Rachel and Leah (ch. 29), children were born to him (35:23-26; 46:15), and he became wealthy.

PADON [pă′dŏn] (Heb. *pāḏôn*). A temple servant whose descendants returned with Zerubbabel from captivity in Babylon (Ezra 2:44 par. Neh. 7:47).

PAGANS (Gk. *éthnē* "Gentiles").* At 1 Cor. 5:1; 10:20 a designation for non-Christian Gentiles in contrast to the Christian Gentiles addressed by Paul (so RSV, NIV; KJV "Gentiles").

PAGIEL [pā′gĭ əl] (Heb. *pag‘î’ēl* "destiny of God [?]"). The son of Ochran; a chief of Asher who assisted Moses in the census in the wilderness and who brought an offering for the tabernacle (Num. 1:13; 2:27; 7:72, 77; 10:26).

PAHATH-MOAB [pā′hăth mō′ăb] (Heb. *paḥaṯ mô’āḇ* "governor of Moab"). An Israelite whose descendants returned with Zerubbabel (Ezra 2:6; Neh. 7:11) and with Ezra (Ezra 8:4) from exile in Babylonia. Some of this clan were among those who divorced their foreign wives (10:30), others set their seal to the new covenant under Nehemiah (Neh. 10:14 [MT 15]), and one, Hasshub, helped repair the walls of Jerusalem (3:11).

PAI [pā′ī] (Heb. *pā‘î*). Alternate form of PAU (1 Chr. 1:50).

PALACE (Heb. *bayiṯ* "house, temple, palace," [also Aram.] *hêḵāl* "temple, palace," *’armôn* "fortress, palace"; Gk. *aulḗ* "courtyard, palace").† Primarily the dwelling of a king or other noble personage. The Bible refers to palaces in Egypt (Gen. 12:15; Exod. 7:23; RSV "[Pharaoh's] house"; cf. Egyp. *pr-‘3* "Pharaoh," lit. "Great House"), Judah (cf. 2 Sam. 7:1-2; 1 Kgs. 9:1; Jer. 22:1; RSV "[king's] house"), Israel (1 Kgs. 4:6; cf. 16:18), Babylon (Dan. 4:4, 29 [MT 1, 26]; cf. Akk. *ekallum*; Sum. *é-gal* "big house"), and the Persian Empire (Esth. 1:5-9). Excavations in Palestine have uncovered foundations of Bronze Age structures at Lachish and Ai large enough to be palaces of rulers. Other Near Eastern palace remains, some as large as 12.4 ha. (5 a.), have been found at Mari, Nineveh, and Babylon.

David's palace in Jerusalem was the first royal palace in Israel's history. It signified to David that Yahweh had established him as king over Israel (2 Sam. 5:11-12; cf. 19:11). Much more elaborate was Solomon's massive and splendid temple and palace complex. After taking seven and one-half years to build the temple (1 Kgs. 6), he spent thirteen more years building his palace (7:1; 9:10); in addition to his own dwelling, it included the House of the Forest of Lebanon, the Hall of Pillars, a throne room and Hall of Judgment, and a residence for Pharaoh's daughter (7:1-8; cf. 2 Chr. 8:11). How these buildings were arranged relative to one another is not known, but it is thought that the palace complex may have been south of the temple.

Aerial view of the northern wing of Herod's palace complex at Jericho (cf. *EAEHL*, p. 567) (site excavated by Dr. Ehud Netzer on behalf of the Hebrew University in Jerusalem; photo E. Netzer)

When Nebuchadrezzar defeated Judah, he despoiled the palace and burned it with the rest of.the significant buildings of Jerusalem (2 Kgs. 24:13; 25:9). Some remains of the palace apparently existed when Nehemiah was rebuilding the city wall (Neh. 3:25).

At Samaria, which Omri established as the royal residence of the northern kingdom (1 Kgs. 16:24), Ahab built an elaborate palace known especially for the ivory inlays in its walls and furniture (22:39; cf. Amos 3:15; 6:4). This palace was destroyed by Sargon II of Assyria in 722-721 B.C. Ahab may have had another palace in Jezreel (1 Kgs. 21:1; but cf. v. 19; 22:38, which may place this palace in Samaria).

Herod the Great was known for his tremendous building projects, including a number of palaces. His primary residence in Jerusalem had enough banquet halls and bedrooms for one hundred guests, as well as beautiful colonnades, pools, and gardens. The foundation platform of this palace, covering more than 11 ha. (4.5 a.), has been discovered, and portions remain of the Phasael tower, one of the three guard towers north of the palace. Excavations near Jericho have uncovered remains of Herod's beautiful winter palace built near an earlier Hasmonean palace. Two of Herod's border fortresses, Herodium and Masada, also included palaces.

The palace of the high priest Caiaphas in Jerusalem was where the chief priests gathered to prepare for the trial of Jesus (Matt. 26:3-4; cf. Mark 14:53-54). The site of Jesus' trial before Pilate (Mark 15:16; John 18:28) may have been Herod's Jerusalem palace, or, in accord with tradition, the fortress of Antonia, which Herod had built northwest of the temple complex. A palace of Herod at Caesarea became the usual residence of the Roman governors of Judea; it was there that Paul was kept under guard for two years by Felix (cf. Acts 23:33-35; 24:27).

On Phil. 1:13, KJV, *see* PRAETORIAN GUARD.

PALAL [pā'lăl] (Heb. *pālāl* "judge"). The son of Uzai who participated in Nehemiah's rebuilding of the walls of Jerusalem (Neh. 3:25).

PALESTINE [păl'ə stīn].† A geographical designation used by biblical scholars and archaeologists for the region inhabited by the people of Israel. The name Palestine (from Heb. *p*lešeṭ* "Philistia," *p*lištî* "Philistines," derived from a component of the Sea Peoples who overran the eastern Mediterranean in the twelfth century B.C.; cf. Egyp. *prst*; Akk. *palaštu*) does not occur in the Bible, which prefers simply "the land" (*hā'āreṣ*; e.g., Num. 26:55; Deut. 5:31; Ruth 1:1; cf. 1 Sam. 13:19, "the land of Israel"; Gen. 40:15, "the land of the Hebrews") or "Canaan" (e.g., Gen. 12:5; Num. 33:51; cf. Deut. 1:7, "land of the Canaanites"). Gk. *Palaistinē* occurs first in the writings of Herodotus, who uses it imprecisely for the Philistine coast from Syria to Egypt (*Hist.* vii.89). Josephus distinguishes Palestine from Coelesyria (*Ant.* i.6.4 [145]) and identifies it as the region inhabited by the Jews (*Ap.* i.22 [171]). *See* PHILISTINES.

The general limits of Palestine are described in the biblical account as stretching (north to south) "from Dan to Beer-sheba" (e.g., Judg. 20:1; 1 Sam. 3:20) or from the entrance of Hamath to the wilderness of Zin (Num. 13:21), and (west to east) from the river of Egypt to the Euphrates (Gen. 15:18). The ideal boundaries of the promised land are set forth at Num. 34:1-12.

Palestine is naturally divided into five geographical or topographical regions: the coastal, littoral plain, often subdivided into the plain of Asher (or Zebulun), the plain of Sharon (cf. Isa. 33:9), and the Philistine plain (cf. Judg. 1:19, 34); the Shephelah or lowland, the fertile foothills that separated Philistine and Israelite territory (e.g., Josh. 11:16); the rugged central mountain range, a continuation of the Amanus-

Lebanon mountains, comprising Galilee, Samaria, and Judah, the primary areas of Israelite settlement; the Jordan (or Rift) valley, a major geological fault dividing Palestine geographically and politically from the Huleh valley to the Arabah; and the high Transjordan plateau encompassing Bashan, Gilead, Ammon, Moab, and Edom. See further the individual articles.

Strategically located at the southwestern end of the Fertile Crescent, Palestine forms a land bridge connecting Anatolia and Mesopotamia with North Africa. In ancient times it was traversed by important commercial and military roads, including the coastal Way of the Sea and the Transjordanian King's Highway.

Palestine experiences primarily two seasons (cf. Gen. 8:22; Ps. 74:17), summer (June-September), which is sunny, warm, and dry (Ps. 32:4), and winter (November-March), marked by cooler weather and violent rainstorms (Deut. 11:14; Cant. 2:11), with 70 percent of the rainfall between November through February. During the transitional periods between the seasons hot, dry winds (sirocco; Arab. ḥamsin) blow from the southeast (Jer. 4:11; Jonah 4:8; Luke 12:55).

Bibliography. D. Baly, *The Geography of the Bible*, rev. ed. (New York: 1974); M. Noth, *The Old Testament World* (Philadelphia: 1966).

PALLU [păl′oo͞] (Heb. *pallû'* "excelling"). A son of Reuben (Gen. 46:9; KJV "Phallu"; Exod. 6:14; 1 Chr. 5:3). He was the father of Eliab (Num. 26:5) and ancestor of the Palluites (v. 5).

PALM TREE (Heb. *tāmār, timōrâ*; Gk. *phoínix*). The date palm (*Phoenix dactylifera* L.). Consisting of a branchless trunk, it reaches a height of 18-24 m. (60-80 ft.) when mature, with a crown of dark green pinnate leaves (referred to as "branches" in the Bible) measuring 3-6 m. (10-20 ft.) in length. Ancient Egyptian, Mesopotamian, and Levantine texts reveal the importance of the date palm as a source of food as well as its economic and ornamental value in the ancient world. The tree's most dense areas of growth in Palestine were the lower Jordan valley, the Arabah, and certain portions of the coastal plain.

The palm tree held an important place in the lives of the Hebrew people, for they literally put the entire tree to use. Its sweet fruit provided a nourishing form of refreshment. The smaller leaves were used to make household items, such as baskets or mats, while the larger ones served as a coverings for roofs or sides of houses. The leaves were also used to build the booths of the Feast of Tabernacles (Lev. 23:40; Neh. 8:15). The trunk was a source of timber, and the seeds were used as food for animals. A number of ancient authors (including Josephus and Herodotus) substantiate the claim that the date palm was used in the manufacture of wine and honey; "strong drink" (Heb. *šēḵār*; e.g., Lev. 10:9; Num. 6:3; Deut. 14:26; 29:6 [MT 5]; Judg. 13:4) may refer to the syrupy drink obtained from the tree, while *dᵉḇaš* "honey" may refer not only to honey from bees but also to "honey" derived from various types of plants such as dates or figs (e.g., Gen. 43:11; 1 Sam. 14:25; Isa. 7:15).

A number of places in the Old Testament are named or identified by their abundance of palms or by a prominent palm in their vicinity, including the "city of palms" (i.e., Jericho; Deut. 34:3; 2 Chr. 28:15), Elim, a town identified by its "twelve springs of water and seventy palm trees" (Exod. 15:27; Num. 33:9), Tamar (1 Kgs. 9:18; Ezek. 47:19), the "palm of Deborah" (Judg. 4:5), Hazazon-tamar (identified with Engedi at 2 Chr. 20:2), and Baal-tamar (lit. "Lord of the palm"; Judg. 20:33). Heb. *tāmār* also appears as a feminine proper name (Gen. 38:6; 2 Sam. 13:1; 14:27).

As a result of its impressive appearance and fruitfulness the palm became a symbol of prosperity (Ps. 92:12 [MT 13]), beauty (Cant. 7:7-8), and victory (1 Macc. 13:51; 2 Macc. 10:7; 14:4; John 12:13; Rev. 7:9). At Isa. 9:14 (MT 13) (cf. Joel 1:12) the destruction of a palm tree is a metaphor for divine destruction of the upper levels of society along with the lower levels (the reed). The palm became a common ornament in ancient Near Eastern art, employed on cylinder seals, in temple architecture, and on coins. Both Solomon's temple (1 Kgs. 6:29, 32, 35; 7:36; *timōrâ*) and the temple of Ezekiel's vision (Ezek. 40–41) made frequent use of this motif.

PALMERWORM (Joel 1:4; 2:25; Amos 4:9, KJV). *See* LOCUST.

PALSY (KJV). *See* PARALYSIS.

PALTI [păl′tī] (Heb. *palṭî* "my salvation").
1. The son of Raphu of the tribe of Benjamin; one of the twelve Israelite spies sent into Canaan (Num. 13:9).
2 A Benjaminite from Gallim, the son of Laish, to whom Saul punitively gave David's wife Michal as his own wife (1 Sam. 25:44; KJV "Phalti"). According to 2 Sam. 3:15-16, where he is called Paltiel (KJV "Phaltiel"), when Abner and Ish-bosheth took her from him to return her to David, he followed Michal, weeping, as far as Bahurim.

PALTIEL [păl′tī əl] (Heb. *palṭî'ēl* "God is salvation").
1. The son of Azzan; a leader of Issachar who assisted Moses in the division of Canaan (Num. 34:26).
2. Alternate form of PALTI 2.

PALTITE [păl′tīt] (Heb. *palṭî*). A gentilic ascribed to Helez, one of David's mighty men (2 Sam. 23:26). The name may indicate that Helez was from Bethpelet (Josh. 15:27; Neh. 11:26) or that he was a descendant of the Calebite Pelet (1 Chr. 2:47) or perhaps Palti. At 1 Chr. 11:27; 27:10 Helez is called "the Pelonite."

PAMPHYLIA [păm fĭl′ĭ ə] (Gk. *Pamphylia*).† A district on the southern coast of Asia Minor bounded by Lycia on the west, Pisidia on the north, and Cilicia on the east. This narrow coastal region boasts a somewhat variegated history, having been ruled successively by the Persians, Macedonians, Seleucids, Attalids (thus the port city named Attalia), and Romans. It was joined with Lycia in a single Roman province during the time of Paul's journeys, but at other times was attached to Cilicia, Asia, or Galatia.

At Acts 2:10 Pamphylia is included in the geographical list of nations represented by the Jews who had made the pilgrimage to Jerusalem for the Feast of Pentecost. On Paul's first missionary journey into Asia Minor he, Barnabas, and John Mark sailed from Cyprus "and came to Perga in Pamphylia," probably by way of the port of Attalia (13:13). John Mark left from Perga to return to Jerusalem, and Paul and Barnabas quickly made their way through Pamphylia toward Antioch of Pisidia. Various solutions have been offered to account for this seemingly sudden departure from Perga. Possibly Paul contracted malaria and fled inland toward higher ground for relief (cf. Gal. 4:13-14). On their return journey, however, Paul and Barnabas did remain in Perga long enough to engage in evangelistic work before setting sail from Attalia for Syrian Antioch (Acts 14:24-26). Luke also makes passing reference to Pamphylia in connection with Paul's voyage to Rome (27:5).

PANNAG [păn'ăg] (Heb. *pannag*).† According to the KJV, a place from which Judah and Israel obtained wheat for export to Tyre (Ezek. 27:17). The term might also designate a product imported by Tyre, perhaps "early figs" (RSV, reading *paggag*; cf. Cant. 2:13), some sort of baked "confections" (NIV; cf. Akk. *pannig*), an unidentified food product (cf. RSV mg. "wheat of minnith and pannag," following MT), or "wax" (JB, emending to *dônāg*).

PAPER. See PAPYRUS.

PAPHOS [pā'fŏs] (Gk. *Paphos*). A city on the southwest coast of the island of Cyprus, visited by Paul and Barnabas on their first missionary journey (Acts 13:6-13). Their visit was actually to New Paphos, established in the fourth century B.C. as a port town at the site of modern Baffo, some 15 km. (9 mi.) distant from the older inland city (modern Kouklia). When Cyprus became part of the Roman Empire in 58 B.C., New Paphos became the capital of the island. At the time of Paul it was the most important city on Cyprus.

Old Paphos was renowned in antiquity for its temple of Aphrodite. According to legend, it was off the coast near Paphos that this goddess first appeared to humankind. Traveling on the Roman road from Salamis to Paphos, Paul and Barnabas would have descended from the hills of central Cyprus to a view of the temple and the two towns with the sea beyond. Paphos retained its importance until the Byzantine era when Salamis, rebuilt as Constantia, became the island's capital.

PAPIAS [pā'pĭ əs].* The bishop of Hierapolis in Phrygia in the first half of the second century A.D. Papias was reputed to be a disciple of the apostle John, but Eusebius concluded that Papias had no direct contact with any of the apostles (*HE* iii.39.1-7). Of Papias' five-volume *Expositions of Oracles of the Lord* nothing is extant except what is quoted by other authors. This work apparently consisted largely of traditional (rather than written) stories and sayings of Jesus, the apostles, and other significant persons of the apostolic generation. Statements by Papias that relate Mark's gospel to Peter's teaching and "the oracles in the Hebrew" to the apostle Matthew (*HE*

iii.39.15-16; cf. ii.15) have been important in discussion of the origins of the first and second Gospels.

PAPYRUS (Heb. *gōme'*; Gk. *býblos*). A tall aquatic plant, *Cyperus papyrus* L., a member of the sedge family, and the writing material manufactured from it or any manuscript written on this material. Growing in river shallows or in marshes, the plant is associated with abundant water (Job 8:11; KJV "rush"; cf. Isa. 35:7; KJV, RSV "rushes"). In the ancient world papyrus grew in Syria, Sicily, Palestine, and especially in Egypt. Although the plant is now extinct in lower Egypt, it can still be found in Israel in the marshes between Haifa and Mt. Carmel, and in the Huleh region.

Every part of the plant could be used: the flowers for sacred garlands; the roots for firewood; the stalks for roping, roofing, small boats (Isa. 18:2; KJV "bulrushes"), and baskets (Exod. 2:3; KJV, RSV "bulrushes"); and the pith for food and sandals. However, the chief use of papyrus was in the manufacture of paper from the pith of Egyptian papyrus.

To make paper, the heavy, triangular stem was first pared, then the pith sliced into thin strips. These were laid horizontally to the required width, each strip slightly overlapping the other. A second layer was then added crosswise to the first. The two layers were soaked, pressed together or pounded, and dried. Once dry, the sheet was finished by scraping off irregularities, and then trimmed.

The finished sheet of paper (Gk. *chártēs*; 2 John 12) varied in width and grade according to its intended use: larger sizes for business or imperial documents, smaller ones for literary compositions. Sheets were either joined together to form a continuous roll, or folded to form a codex.

Because of the dry conditions there, papyri have been best preserved in upper (southern) Egypt. Recovered Egyptian papyri date from as early as the twenty-seventh century B.C. and have been quite important for understanding Egyptian history. Greek papyri found in Egypt date from the fourth century B.C. to the eighth century A.D. The greatest number of Greek papyri from the Roman period have been found at Oxyrhynchus in Egypt. The thousands of extant Greek papyri include a number of important literary

Egyptian tomb model of two papyrus fishing boats from the Eleventh Dynasty (The Metropolitan Museum of Art; photo by the Egyptian Expedition)

Papyrus as a writing material: part of the teaching of Amenemope written in Egyptian hieratic script (tenth to sixth centuries B.C.) (by courtesy of the Trustees of the British Museum)

manuscripts, but most are not literary but consist of every kind of personal, commercial, and legal document. These have increased the knowledge of the Hellenistic and Roman worlds greatly and have proven invaluable for establishing the linguistic world of the New Testament, documenting usage and vocabulary once known only from the Bible.

Greek papyri of both the LXX and the New Testament have been of importance in text criticism of both the Old and New Testament. Some of the small papyrus fragments of portions of the New Testament are the earliest such manuscripts extant. The oldest is p⁵² (John 18:31-33, 37-38), dating from *ca.* A.D. 125. Among the most important New Testament papyri for their age and completeness are three third-century manuscripts in the Chester Beatty Library in Dublin: p⁴⁵ (portions of the Gospels and Acts); p⁴⁶ (the letters of Paul), which is significant for containing the concluding doxology of Romans at the end of ch. 15; and p⁴⁷ (a large part of the book of Revelation).

The total of eighty-eight Greek New Testament papyri constitute together a significant factor in New Testament textual criticism.

Greek papyri of Christian documents outside the New Testament, many from Oxyrhynchus, have contributed to the knowledge of early Christianity in other ways, as have early Christian papyri in the Coptic language, especially the Nag Hammadi codices. Also surviving are a large number of biblical papyri in Coptic.

The Aramaic papyri from Elephantine have given much knowledge of a significant Jewish diaspora community. Most of the manuscripts from the caves at Qumran and at other Judean wilderness locations are on leather, but a number of Hebrew and Aramaic papyri have also been found, including the Bar Kokhba letters.

PARABLE (Gk. *parabolḗ*).† The parables of Jesus in the Synoptic Gospels are similes or metaphors, sometimes extended into narratives, which involve everyday life and objects and typical events of households, farms, and royal courts. They are a primary means of Jesus' teaching, closely connected to the main focus of his teaching, the coming of the kingdom of God.

Modern study of the parables was initiated by A. Jülicher (1899), who argued that each parable has only one point of contact with the teaching that it seeks to convey. Earlier treatment of the parables had usually seen them as allegories, seeking to discover a symbolical significance or hidden meaning for every detail mentioned in each parable (e.g., identifying the beast of burden at Luke 10:34 with the body of Christ). This approach yielded interpretations removed from the context of Jesus' teaching and set in competition with each other.

Jülicher's interpretations of the parables tended to assign moralistic motives to the parables and so obscure their connection to Jesus' teaching concerning the coming of the kingdom. Nevertheless, his basic argument against allegorical interpretation has continued to be of importance with some modification. Some parables do have more than one point of contact with the teaching they seek to convey, but these are only to be read from the text (as in Mark 4:14-20). In every case, the movement of the overall story matters more to interpretation than the details that make up the story and give it verisimilitude.

Form-critical study has clarified the structure of the parables. It has also raised questions concerning their modification in the course of their being brought from their original setting in the proclamation of Jesus to the Gospels, where they are, so it is thought, directed more to meeting Church needs. In particular, it has been debated whether the narrative settings given to the parables (e.g., Luke 18:1, 9; 19:11) and interpretational comments attached to them (e.g., Mark 4:14-20; Luke 10:37b; 18:8, 14) were originally attached to the parables or were later additions.

Recent study of the parables has concentrated on their nature and structure as literature rather than on the history of their transmission from the teaching of Jesus to the writing of the Gospels. Among the values of this research has been the understanding of the parables as "language events" that have their effectiveness in the very act of their being heard. For instance, the conjunction of "neighbor," "one who has mercy," and "Samaritan" in the parable at 10:29-37 is itself an event in which barriers are broken down so that the grace of God can be received. Some parables are purposely obscure so that the gradual realization of their point becomes part of the experience of hearing them. Some, however, use shocking elements (often not seen as such by the modern reader) to make their point clear.

The primary purpose of the parables is to reveal some aspect of the coming of the kingdom of God in the person and teaching of Jesus. But Jesus also intended that the parables conceal his teaching while being a vehicle for it (Mark 4:11-12). Even the disciples of Jesus did not understand the parables without fail (v. 13). But their adherence to Jesus caused them to seek (v. 10) and to receive (vv. 14-20) understanding of the parables. Understanding is made subject to whether a listener is willing to identify with Jesus or wishes to remain "outside" (i.e., to hold Jesus and his claims at arm's length). The disciples' inquiry arose from commitment and was itself hearing (Matt. 13:16), which was in contrast with others' failure to hear (vv. 14-15).

An additional significant factor was brought into study of the parables by the discovery and publication of the Nag Hammadi gospel of Thomas. This collection of sayings attributed to Jesus contains versions of eleven of the canonical parables that are simpler than the canonical versions. Some scholars regard these simpler versions as closer to the actual words of Jesus than the canonical versions; others regard them as dependent on the Synoptic parables. The gospel of Thomas also has two other parables attributed to Jesus that are not paralleled in the Synoptics.

A general classification of the canonical parables according to their relative complexity can be made: metaphors and similes that are only simply extended (e.g., Matt. 5:14-16; 13:31-32; Luke 7:41-43); more extended illustrations (e.g., Matt. 13:3-8; 21:28-32; Mark 4:26-29; Luke 12:16-21; 17:7-10); and stories with plot, characters, and action (Matt. 21:33-41; 25:14-30; Luke 14:16-24; 16:1-9).

It is more difficult to classify the parables according to their structure or the content of their teaching. Some specific groups can, however, be discerned, such as parables in which losing and finding is an illustration of the gospel's availability to sinners (Luke 15), parables that speak of the hidden growth of the kingdom (Matt. 13:31-33; Mark 4:26-32), those that contrast what is old with the newness of the kingdom in its coming (Matt. 9:16-17; 13:44-46, 52), parables that find their point in a contrast between the expected and the unexpected (20:1-15; Luke 10:25-37; 18:9-14), those in which the contrast stands outside the parable itself, between God's activity and the activity of a person in the story (11:5-8, 11-12; 18:2-6; cf. 14:5), parables speaking of the nearness or unexpectedness of the coming of the Son of Man (Matt. 24:32; 25:1-13; Mark 13:34-36; Luke 12:36-39), and parables of judgment (e.g., Matt. 7:24-27; 13:24-30, 47-48; 22:2-13;

24:45-51; Mark 12:1-9; Luke 12:42-48; 13:6-9; 16:19-31).

Rather than the longer parables such as occur in the Synoptics, the gospel of John distinctively uses a different form of extended metaphor (e.g., "bread," John 6:22-71; "vine," 15:1-8). The closest John comes to a narrative parable is the contrast between thieves, robbers, strangers, and hirelings on the one hand, and the good shepherd and the door of the sheepfold on the other (10:1-16). This use of metaphorical language is called a "figure" (v. 6; Gk. *paroimía*; KJV "parable"), a term used elsewhere in John for obscure metaphorical language as used by Jesus (16:25, 29).

While Jesus' use of parables (as represented in the Synoptics) is unique, particularly in that it is linked with his teachings concerning the kingdom, it does have antecedents in the Old Testament (Judg. 9:8-15; 2 Sam. 12:1-6; 2 Kgs. 14:9; Isa. 5:1-7) and parallels in rabbinic literature. The latter are directed to explanation of Scripture passages rather than serving as the vehicle of a new proclamation as with Jesus. Heb. *māšāl*, sometimes translated "parable" in the Old Testament (eighteen times in KJV; RSV only Ps. 78:2), is a broad term for any kind of saying, formalized discourse, proverb, or taunt.

Bibliography. G. E. Ladd, *A Theology of the New Testament* (Grand Rapids: 1974), pp. 91-104; N. Perrin, *Jesus and the Language of the Kingdom* (Philadelphia: 1976), pp. 89-193.

PARACLETE [păr'ə klēt] (Gk. *paráklētos* "one called to the side of"). *See* ADVOCATE; HOLY SPIRIT *III.B.* 2.

PARADISE (Heb. *pardēs*; Gk. *parádeisos*; from O.Pers. *pairi-daēza* "enclosure").† A term introduced into Greek by Xenophon to indicate the game parks and pleasure gardens of Persian kings and nobles. By the third century B.C., it came to mean any park or garden. The three occurrences of *pardēs* in the Old Testament are all late and all have a literal, secular meaning (Neh. 2:8; RSV "forest"; Eccl. 2:5; RSV "parks"; Cant. 4:13; RSV "orchard"). The LXX uses *parádeisos* to translate Heb. *gan, gannâ* "garden," including references to the garden of Gen. 2–3, as does Philo.

Speculations about Paradise/Eden, envisioned as hidden in some terrestrial or celestial location, were common in post-Old Testament Jewish writings (e.g., 2 Esdr. 4:7; 7:36; Adam and Eve 25, 29, 37ff.). Descriptions of revelatory journeys to Paradise also appeared in the literature (e.g., 2 En. 8; Apoc.Abr. 21:6). Paul's rapture into the third heaven and Paradise (2 Cor. 12:2-4) is related to such speculations. According to the Talmud (*Ḥag.* 14b), four rabbis are said to have entered Paradise, usually interpreted as a metaphor for mystical or philosophical speculation; this is as close as rabbinic literature comes to a use of *pardēs* as a religious technical term, and even this instance may be a product of Hellenistic influence.

Along with "spatial" concerns with Paradise, eschatological ideas arose. Isa. 51:3; Ezek. 36:35 compare the restoration of Israel to the garden of Eden (LXX *parádeisos* for Heb. *ʿēḏen* at Isa. 51:3). Some apocalyptic writings identified the messianic age with the original Paradise/Eden (e.g., T.Levi 18:10; T.Dan 5:12; 1 En. 25:4-6; Rev. 2:7). Paradise was also identified as the abode of the righteous dead (1 En. 70:4; 2 En. 42:3). As such it replaced Sheol/Hades, which came to be reserved for the wicked, as in the story of the rich man and Lazarus (Luke 16:22-26). One of the thieves crucified with Jesus asked to be remembered when Jesus came in his kingship, to which Jesus replied that the thief would that day be with him in Paradise (Luke 23:42-43). In this way it is said that Jesus is the one who makes Paradise accessible to human beings once more.

PARAH [pâr′ə] (Heb. *pārâ* "heifer"). A city in the tribal territory of Benjamin (Josh. 18:23), identifiable with Khirbet el-Fârah, 8 km. (5 mi.) northeast of Jerusalem.

PARALYSIS (Gk. *paralýō, paralytikós*).* The descriptions of paralyzed persons healed by Jesus (Matt. 4:24; 9:2-7 par.; KJV "palsy") and leaders of the early Church (Acts 8:7) are too general to lead to any idea of the actual disability involved. In one case a person is described as not only paralyzed but also "in terrible distress," perhaps meaning that his respiration was affected as well (Matt. 8:6; cf. Luke 7:2; John 4:46, 52). A paralyzed man healed by Peter had been bedridden for eight years (Acts 9:33).

PARAN [pâr′ən] (Heb. *pā′rān*).† The eastern side of the Sinai peninsula, usually called the "wilderness of Paran." After receiving the law at Sinai the Israelites encamped at Hazeroth before crossing Paran (Num. 10:12; 12:16). Kadesh, to which the spies returned after scouting Canaan, was apparently in Paran (13:3, 26; cf. 33:36, where the LXX identifies Kadesh with the wilderness of Zin). In poetic references to the wilderness theophanies, "Mount Paran," the hilly region west of the Gulf of Aqaba, is part of a general designation of the lands beyond the borders of Israel to the south (Deut. 33:2; Hab. 3:3).

Ishmael lived in Paran (Gen. 21:21), and there David obtained his wife Abigail (1 Sam. 25:1, unless the LXX is correct in reading "Maon"; cf. P. K. McCarter, Jr., *I Samuel*. AB 8 [1980], p. 388). Hadad crossed Paran as he fled to Egypt from Edom (1 Kgs. 11:18).

PARAPET (Heb. *ma'ªqeh*).* A low wall built around the outer edge of a roof to prevent people from falling (Deut. 22:8; KJV "battlement"). The flat roof of a house was commonly used as part of the living and working quarters (cf. Josh. 2:6; 1 Sam. 9:25-26; 2 Sam. 11:2; 16:22).

PARBAR [pär′bər] (Heb. *parbār*).† A word of non-Hebrew origin designating a structure to the west (i.e., behind) the main temple building (1 Chr. 26:18; NIV "court"; NJV "colonnade"), so that it corresponds to the building spoken of in Ezek. 41:12, the purpose of which is unknown. Heb. *parwārîm* at 2 Kgs. 23:11 (RSV "precincts"; KJV "suburbs") may represent the plural form; it occurs here in a description of the place where horses dedicated to the worship of the sun were

kept until their removal by Josiah, but represents a location in front of rather than behind the temple. Suggested derivations of *parbār/parwārîm* include Pers. *parwār* "open summer house," *frabada* "court," Akk. *ê-bar-bar* "shining house" (i.e., "sun temple"), and Egyp. *pr wr* "great house" (again, "sun temple").

PARCHMENT (Gk. *membrána*). A writing material made from the skins of sheep or goats. The skins are soaked in a lime solution, the hair scraped off, and the skins stretched on frames and smoothed with chalk and pumice. The English term "parchment" is derived from Gk. *pergamēnḗ*, referring to Pergamum, where production of parchment was developed.

Parchment was an expensive material. Therefore, the parchments that Paul asked Timothy to bring to him (2 Tim. 4:13) were more likely the Old Testament or parts of it rather than blank sheets to be used for taking notes, as some scholars have suggested.

PARMASHTA [pär mȧsh′tə] (Heb. *parmaštā'*). One of the ten sons of Haman killed by the Jews after their father was hanged (Esth. 9:9).

PARMENAS [pär′mə nəs] (Gk. *Parmenas*; cf. *Parmenidēs* "persistent"). One of the seven chosen to assist the apostles in the distribution to the widows of the Church (Acts 6:5).

PARNACH [pär′năk] (Heb. *parnāk̠*). The father of Elizaphan, who led the tribe of Zebulun during the time of Moses (Num. 34:25).

PAROSH [pâr′ōsh] (Heb. *par'ōš* "flea").

1. A person whose descendants returned with Zerubbabel (Ezra 2:3; Neh. 7:8) and Ezra from exile in Babylon (Ezra 8:3; KJV "Pharosh"). Among the descendants of Parosh were some of the men who divorced their foreign wives (10:25) and one of those who repaired the walls of Jerusalem (Neh. 3:25).

2. A chief of the people who participated in the sealing of the covenant under Nehemiah (Neh. 10:14).

PAROUSIA [pär ōō sē′ə, pə rōō′ zĭ ə] (Gk. *parousía* "arrival, presence"). A technical term for the eschatological coming of Christ, generally envisioned as his imminent return to inaugurate the new age. *See* SECOND COMING.

PARSHANDATHA [pär shăn′də thə] (Heb. *paršandāṭā'*). One of the ten sons of Haman killed by the Jews after their father was hanged (Esth. 9:7).

PARTHIANS [pär′thĭ ənz] (Gk. *Parthoi*; O.Pers. *Parthava*). Inhabitants of Parthia, a region southeast of the Caspian Sea and corresponding to modern Khorasan (northeastern Iran). Long dominated by the Assyrians, Medes, Persians, and Greeks under Alexander the Great, Parthia became independent of the Seleucid Empire in the third and early second centuries B.C., and under the Arsacid (or Parni) dynasty became itself a large empire stretching across Mesopotamia and Persia from the Euphrates river to the Indus. The Parthians became also a major threat to the Seleucid Empire and an important factor in the Seleucid weakness that made Hasmonean independence possible. When Rome replaced the Seleucids as the power in the eastern Mediterranean, Parthia became Rome's main rival for control of the Near East. A Parthian invasion of Syria was the basis for the departure from Roman rule under Antigonus II, who ruled Judea 40-37 B.C. Parthia fell to the Persian Sassanid dynasty in the third century A.D.

Jews and proselytes from Parthia were among the pilgrims to Jerusalem for Pentecost who witnessed the coming of the Holy Spirit on the Church (Acts 2:9).

PARTRIDGE (Heb. *qōrē'* "caller"). Any of a number of medium-sized thick-set gallinaceous birds of genera *Alectoris, Ammoperdix, Perdix,* and *Caccabis*. Partridges found in Palestine include chukars (*Caccabis chukar* and varieties of *Alectoris graeca*), which lives in rocky terrain; the sand (or desert) partridge (*Ammoperdix heyi*); and the black partridge (*Francolinus francolinus*), found in the marshy regions of the coastal plain and the northern Jordan valley. The Hebrew name derives from the bird's characteristic clucking.

Partridges seldom resort to flying to escape when pursued; 1 Sam. 26:20 refers to a hunting method in which one pursued a partridge until it was exhausted and could easily be caught. Sir. 11:30 notes the use of caged partridges as decoys. The proverb at Jer. 17:11 is based on a belief that partridges steal eggs from other birds and hatch them out; unjustly gained wealth is said to be like a bird leaving because it recognizes that it does not really belong where it is.

PARTY (SPIRIT). *See* HERESY.

PARUAH [pə rōō' ə] (Heb. *pārûaḥ*). The father of Jehoshaphat, Solomon's officer in Issachar (1 Kgs. 4:17).

PARVAIM [pär vā'əm] (Heb. *parwāyim*). A region from which Solomon imported gold for the temple (2 Chr. 3:6). Though some scholars believe it was located in Yemen or Middle Arabia, the exact site is unknown.

PASACH [pā'săk] (Heb. *pāsak*). A son of Japhlet of the tribe of Asher (1 Chr. 7:33).

PASCHAL [păs'kəl] **LAMB** (Gk. *páscha*). The lamb slain for the Passover, referred to as a metaphor for the death of Christ (1 Cor. 5:7; KJV "passover"). *See* PASSOVER.

PAS-DAMMIM [păs dăm'ĭm] (Heb. *pas dammîm*). A place where David's forces defeated the Philistines (1 Chr. 11:13). *See* EPHES-DAMMIM.

PASEAH [pə sē'ə] (Heb. *pāsēaḥ* "one who limps").
1. A son of Eshton of the tribe of Judah (1 Chr. 4:12).
2. A temple servant whose descendants returned from exile with Zerubbabel (Ezra 2:49 par. Neh. 7:51; KJV "Phaseah").

3. The father of Joiada, who repaired the Old Gate of Jerusalem (Neh. 3:6).

PASHHUR [păsh'ər] (Heb. *pašḥûr*; cf. Egyp. *Pš Ḥōr*). Some or all of the individuals bearing this name may actually be the same person. The name arises in two contexts, among the names of ancestors of postexilic priests (**1, 2**) and among names of opponents of the prophet Jeremiah (**3-5**). One in each of these two groups is a descendant (or "son") of Immer (**1, 3**); one in each group is the son of Malchijah/Malchiah (**1, 4**).

1. A priest, the son of Malchijah (1 Chr. 9:12; Neh. 11:12) and a descendant of Immer (1 Chr. 9:12). Among Pashhur's postexilic descendants were a group of priests who returned from exile with Zerubbabel (Ezra 2:38 par. Neh. 7:41), some of the priests who divorced their foreign wives (Ezra 10:22), and a priest named Adaiah (1 Chr. 9:12; Neh. 11:12).

2. A priest who participated in the sealing of the covenant under Nehemiah (Neh. 10:3 [MT 4]).

3. A priest, the son (or descendant) of Immer and chief officer in the temple in Jeremiah's time. Pashhur beat Jeremiah and put him in stocks overnight in response to his prophecy against Jerusalem. Jeremiah then prophesied against Pashhur himself and said that he would go into exile (Jer. 20:1-6).

4. The son of Malchiah who was sent by King Zedekiah to Jeremiah to request a word from God against Nebuchadrezzar (Jer. 21:1). He was among the opponents of Jeremiah who threw the prophet into a muddy cistern (38:1). Some scholars identify him with **1**.

5. The father of Gedeliah, another of those who threw Jeremiah into the cistern (Jer. 38:1).

PASSION, THE.† Christ's redemptive suffering during the last days of his earthly life, specifically the events leading up to and including his crucifixion. The RSV and KJV read "passion" at Acts 1:3 (cf. Vulg. Lat. *passionem*) to translate Gk. *patheín*, from *páschō* "suffer." The early Church applied the term also to those Gospel passages concerned with Jesus' final days (esp. Matt. 26–27; Mark 14–15; Luke 22–23; John 18–19) and the liturgical (musical) settings for these Gospel readings, as well as to observances of the second Sunday before Easter (the traditional [pre-Vatican II] Passion Sunday), the combined observances of Good Friday and Easter, and Passiontide, the two weeks between Passion Sunday and Holy Saturday.

Jesus predicted his passion and resurrection three times (Matt. 16:21 par.; 17:22-23 par.; 20:17-19 par.; cf. 17:12 par.; Luke 13:33; 17:25; 22:15), and was aware of the redemptive significance it would have (Mark 10:45). Jesus' followers were bewildered by these predictions (Matt. 16:22 par.; 17:23) and were dispersed by his arrest (26:31, 56b par.). It was only his resurrection that opened the door to their understanding of his death as a redemptive event.

The Old Testament provided most of the concepts that were used in reflection on the significance of Jesus' death, in particular the Passover, since it was during that feast that Jesus' arrest, trial, and crucifixion occurred (Matt. 26:2, 18 par.; Luke 22:15; John 11:55-57; 13:1; 19:14; 1 Cor. 5:7). Other Old Testament contributions included references to the sacrificial system (e.g., Eph. 5:2; Heb. 9:26), and glimpses of a person whose suffering has redemptive significance, especially Ps. 22 (e.g., Matt. 27:39, 46; John 19:24; cf. v. 28) and Isa. 53 (e.g., Matt. 8:17; Luke 22:37; Acts 8:32-35; 1 Pet. 2:23-25). In short, Jesus' death came to be understood as it is in a traditional statement cited by Paul: "Christ died for our sins in accordance with the scriptures" (1 Cor. 15:3).

See ATONEMENT *II.B.*

PASSOVER (Heb. *pesaḥ;* Gk. *páscha;* cf. Aram. *pisḥā'*),† The spring festival of the Jewish liturgical calendar that commemorates God's deliverance of the Israelites from Egyptian bondage.

I. Terminology

The noun *pesaḥ* is derived from the verb *pāsaḥ,* which appears in a number of contexts in the Old Testament, thus giving rise to various theories of its meaning and etymology. It may derive from a Hebrew root meaning "pass" or "leap over," "spare," as in the translation of Exod. 12:13 (RSV "I will pass over you"; cf. vv. 23, 27); it is this usage that accounts for "passover" as the rendering of the noun *pesaḥ* at v. 11. But in this context the root can also mean "defend, protect," as it does at Isa. 31:5. Other scholars have suggested an etymology based on Old Testament passages unrelated to Passover where the verb comes from a root meaning "hop, skip," or "limp, be lame" (e.g., 1 Kgs. 18:21, 26; cf. Lev. 21:18; 2 Sam. 4:4; 9:13; Isa. 35:6). On the other hand, attempts to derive *pesaḥ* from Akkadian, Egyptian, or Arabic loanwords have been unconvincing.

In the Old Testament, the term can refer to the festival in general (Exod. 12:48; 2 Kgs. 23:21) or, more specifically, to the eating of the Passover sacrifice (Exod. 12:11; 2 Chr. 30:18) or to the victim itself, the Passover lamb (Exod. 12:21; 2 Chr. 30:15). In later Judaism Passover designated the entire range of observances related to the season (Mishnah *Pesaḥim;* cf. Josephus *Ant.* xiv.2.1; xvii.9.3; xx.5.3; *BJ* ii.14.3; vi.9.3), including those of the Feast of Unleavened Bread (*ḥag hammaṣṣôt*). This had not always been the case. In ancient Israel, Passover and Unleavened Bread referred to distinct festivals that were celebrated in immediate succession, the former on the eve of the fourteenth day of the month (Exod. 12:6) and the latter for the seven days that followed (v. 15; Lev. 23:5-6; Num. 28:16-17; 2 Chr. 35:1, 17). This distinction continued to an extent even into the New Testament period, although by this time either Passover or Unleavened Bread could serve as a denominator of the observances pertaining to both festivals (Matt. 26:17; Mark 14:1; Luke 22:1, 7).

II. Background and History

Some scholars believe that these distinctive though closely related festivals originated in different pre-Israelite spring rites, one a sacrificial rite of transhumant shepherds petitioning the deity for protection when feeding grounds for the flock were changed (cf. Exod.

5:1; 10:9), the other a Canaanite agricultural festival related to the spring barley harvest. A more controversial issue concerns the history of the festival in Israel, some scholars holding that it was not until late in the Monarchy or as late as the exilic and postexilic periods that elements of the rites taken over by Israel were combined and celebrated in connection with the Exodus from Egypt as the redemptive event par excellence in the history of God's people. However, the linking of agricultural and pastoral elements with the event of the Exodus and the close association of *pesaḥ* and *maṣṣôt* (the sacrificial meal of the Passover lamb and the eating of unleavened bread) are characteristic of the Old Testament sources as a whole.

The major account of the Passover at Exod. 12:1–13:16 has as its obvious intent the rooting of the annual observances of both festivals in the events of the slaying of the firstborn of the Egyptians on "that night" (12:12; cf. 1 Cor. 11:23) and the departure of the Israelites "on this very day" (Exod. 12:17; cf. 13:3-4). Unlike other Old Testament accounts, however, 12:1–13:16 completely lacks a temple ceremony, presupposing a wholly domestic setting. This may preserve archaic features from premonarchic Israel (cf. Num. 9:1-5; Josh. 5:10-12; 2 Kgs. 23:21-23) and at the same time reflect the adaptation of a national pilgrimage during the Monarchy (Exod. 23:14-17) to an exilic setting. (For references to the celebration of Passover in the setting of a central sanctuary or carried out by priests and Levites at the Jerusalem temple, see Deut. 16:2, 5-7; 2 Kgs. 23:21-23; 2 Chr. 8:12-13; 30:1-27; 35:1-19; Ezra 6:19-22).

The Passover was observed on the first month in the spring (Exod. 12:2), the month of Abib (13:4; Deut. 16:1; later called Nisan), at the beginning of the barley harvest. A year-old male lamb without blemish was selected on the tenth day of the month according to the size of the household (Exod. 12:3-5). The lamb was killed at dusk on the fourteenth of the month (v. 6), its blood applied to the doorposts and lintel of the house (vv. 7, 22); without breaking its bones (v. 46), it was roasted (v. 9; 2 Chr. 35:13; cf. Deut. 16:7, "boil") and eaten together with unleavened bread and bitter herbs (*merôrîm*, Exod. 12:8). The meal was to be eaten in haste (v. 11) with slaves and resident aliens taking part, provided they had been circumcised (vv. 44, 48). On the following day, the Feast of Unleavened Bread began. During the seven days on which it was held only bread made without yeast was eaten (vv. 15, 17-20; 13:6-7). No work was done on the first and seventh days, which were set aside as holy convocations (12:16). The observances were to be an ordinance for every generation (vv. 14, 24, 42). As a family celebration, Passover gave opportunity for the father to answer the children's questions and explain the ceremony (vv. 26-27; 13:8, 14-16). From the practice of ritual questioning, the Haggadah (lit. "telling, explaining") developed in later Judaism (i.e., the recital of the Passover narrative and explanations of the ritual that accompany the Passover meal).

The Passover began its long history in the setting of the household, and it has remained in Judaism a festival centered on the home. From the time of the destruction of the temple in A.D. 70, it ceased to be a pilgrimage festival celebrated at the central sanctuary and featuring the Passover sacrifice, as it still was in the time of Jesus. (Only the small Samaritan community near Shechem [modern Nablus] still observes the sacrifice of the Passover lamb; in modern Judaism, the Passover meal or seder [sĕḏer "order"] calls to mind the sacrificial lamb by placing a shankbone and roasted egg on the seder plate.) The sacrificial and sacramental aspects of Passover consequently declined in importance, and it has become preeminently Israel's festival of freedom, the memorial celebration of God's great act of redemption that awakens the hope for final redemption in the future. The New Testament takes up this same structure of past and future redemption along with elements of a Passover seder in the description of Jesus' last meal with his disciples (Matt. 26:26-30; Mark 14:22-26; Luke 22:14-20; 1 Cor. 11:23-26). But the sacrificial rite of Passover remains central to the significance of the Lord's Supper and Christ's death, for Jesus is identified with the Passover lamb that is sacrificed (John 1:29, 36; 19:36; 1 Cor. 5:7; 1 Pet. 1:18-19; cf. Rev. 5:12).

Bibliography. B. S. Childs, *The Book of Exodus.* OTL (1974), pp. 178-214; J. Jeremias, *The Eucharistic Words of Jesus* (Philadelphia: 1977); H. Schauss, *The Jewish Festivals* (New York: 1973), pp. 38-85; J. B. Segal, *The Hebrew Passover from the Earliest Times to A.D. 70* (London: 1963); R. de Vaux, *Ancient Israel* (New York: 1965) 2:484-493.

PASTORAL EPISTLES.† The two letters of Paul (but see below on the problem of authorship) to Timothy and his one letter to Titus, usually considered together because of their similarities and common concerns. All three letters are ostensibly at least from the apostle to two church leaders, both coworkers of Paul on other occasions. Both addressees are given specific instructions relating to their specific situations of ministry (1 Tim. 1:3, 18-20; 2 Tim. 4:9, 19, 21; Titus 1:5; 3:12-13), other instructions, and numerous exhortations with regard to their ministries.

I. Primary Concerns and Value

Major areas of concern shared by the three letters are doctrinal controversies and false teachings that had arisen (1 Tim. 1:3-7; 4:7; 6:3-5, 20-21; 2 Tim. 2:14, 16-18, 23-26; 3:6-9; 4:3-4; Titus 1:10-16; 3:9-11). What is confronted is apparently a speculative and ascetic (1 Tim. 4:3-5) movement for which elements of Judaism (1:8-9; Titus 1:10, 14) provide an esoteric base.

In contrast to this movement, a respectable, quiet, and modest life is to be held up as an ideal (1 Tim. 2:1-2, 8-10, 15; 3:2-4, 7-13; 4:12; 5:14; 6:1, 6-10; Titus 2:7-8, 12; 3:1-2). The addressees are to speak to church members in accordance with their various positions in life and are to urge them to follow out the role that they already have (1 Tim. 5:1-8; 6:1-2; Titus 2:2-6, 9-10). Women especially are to be urged to live out their role, which is presented as definitely subordinate to that of men (1 Tim. 2:11-15; Titus 2:5). Church officers are to be appointed with regard to their ability to exemplify a respectable life (1 Tim. 3:1-13; 5:17-18, 22; Titus 1:5-9).

The Pastorals thus exemplify a shift of focus from apocalyptic immediacy (as in, e.g., 1 Cor. 7) to an interest in maintaining an ongoing community life, though eschatology is not simply done away with (2 Tim. 4:1, 8). This ideal community life is one in which ordered family life prevails and its pleasures are hallowed by a pious life (1 Tim. 4:4-5), in which all that is sought from political leaders is the opportunity to live a peaceable life (2:1-2), and in which argument and speculation are disliked and simple and traditionally formulated doctrinal standards are adhered to.

II. Authorship and Situation

A number of difficulties have caused a majority of scholars to regard the Pastoral Epistles as the product, not of Paul's authorship, but of a later generation.

A. *Late Inclusion in the Pauline Corpus.* There are a number of indications that the Pastorals came into the collection of Pauline canonical writings only gradually through the second and third centuries. The Pauline corpus known to Marcion probably did not include the Pastorals. Of the three letters, Tatian accepted only Titus. The earliest explicit quotations from the Pastorals are in the writings of Irenaeus (*ca.* A.D. 185). Possible earlier quotations in patristic writings that have been suggested are probably to be accounted for in other ways. The Chester Beatty Codex of the Pauline letters ($\mathfrak{p}^{46}$) of *ca.* A.D. 250 probably never contained the Pastorals.

B. *Vocabulary and Style.* A large number of words used in the Pastorals are not found in the unquestioned letters of Paul, some of them frequent and some of them important to the theology of the Pastorals. Most of these appear, however, in literary Greek by the mid-first century. Half of them are in the LXX. Paul's style was quite adaptable in his letters to churches; it may have changed considerably when he addressed not entire Christian communities, but key leaders. A number of the differences in terminology (and style as well) can be accounted for by reference to the extensive use of traditional material in the letters. For these and other reasons, word statistics are not considered as important as they formerly were by those who argue for non-Pauline authorship.

C. *Biographical Allusions.* The letters to Timothy provide biographical information with regard to Paul and Timothy. Some of this is of a general enough nature to represent the sort of testimony to the apostle's faithfulness that might be composed by an admirer after his death (e.g., 1 Tim. 1:12-16; 2:7; 2 Tim. 1:11-12; 2:9; 4:6-8). Some represents statements such as might be composed about a typical young local leader represented by "Timothy" (1 Tim. 1:18; 4:12; 6:12; 2 Tim. 1:6; 2:2; 3:14-15). The other biographical notes, including two in Titus, might have been included for the sake of adding verisimilitude and liveliness to what is intended to be received consciously as pseudepigraphal writing (1 Tim. 1:3; 5:23; 2 Tim. 1:5, 15-18; 3:11; 4:10-17; Titus 1:5; 3:12-13). These biographical notes include specific details of persons and locations that are not easily set into the context of Paul's career as it is known from Acts and the other letters.

If Paul wrote 1 Timothy and Titus, he was probably away from the East and so able to arrange for the functioning of the churches of Ephesus and Crete only through his assistants (1 Tim. 1:3; Titus 1:5; cf. 1 Tim. 3:14-15). Unfortunately, Nicopolis, given at Titus 3:12 as the apostle's location, was the name of several ancient cities. While he is probably free in both 1 Timothy and Titus (1 Tim. 3:14; Titus 3:12), 2 Timothy places Paul in prison, in a stricter imprisonment than that at Rome described at the end of Acts (2 Tim. 2:9; Acts 28:16, 30-31). Paul has had to defend himself in court more than once (2 Tim. 4:16) and expects to be executed (v. 6); he reflects on his past life as one about to die (3:10-12; 4:7-8).

D. *Nature of the Heresy.* The heresy confronted in the Pastorals is no more developed than that confronted in Colossians, but Paul's authorship of Colossians is also questioned, and the letters of Ignatius of Antioch (A.D. 107) could as easily be brought as a parallel with regard to the heresy confronted. However, the heresy addressed in the Pastorals is certainly not like the fully developed Gnostic systems of the second century. The denial of the coming resurrection (2 Tim. 2:18) appeared in a different form in Corinth during Paul's career (1 Cor. 15:12), as did the emphasis on "knowledge" (8:1-2; cf. 1 Tim. 6:20; Titus 1:16). Furthermore, the heresy confronted in the Pastorals is still within the Church, not yet a rival to the Church.

E. *Church Organization.* The degree of definition given to church offices and hierarchical relationships in the Pastoral Epistles has been associated with what is found in second-century documents such as the letters of Ignatius. The Pastorals may not, on the other hand, presuppose any more church structure than do Acts (e.g., Acts 20:28), which may, however, represent late first-century conditions, and Phil. 1:1. The Pastorals do not speak of the single authoritarian bishop advocated by Ignatius. Ordination is by "the elders" (1 Tim. 4:14). The greater degree of institutionalization as opposed to the charismatic leadership pattern reflected in 1 Corinthians is to be accounted for by reference to a change in time and situation, perhaps within Paul's career.

F. *Theology and Tradition.* A different attitude toward tradition than is usually found in Paul is seen in the Pastorals' understanding of the gospel as a pattern of teaching handed down (2 Tim. 1:13). The embodiment of truth in "sure sayings" and "sound words" (1 Tim. 1:15; 3:1; 4:9; 6:3; 2 Tim. 2:11; Titus 1:9; 3:8), the use of proverbial sayings (e.g., 2 Tim. 2:4-6, 19-20), and the appearance of christological statements which show that an interval of tradition-building in the Church has passed (1 Tim. 2:5-6; 3:16; 6:13-16; 2 Tim. 1:10; 2:8; Titus 2:13-14; 3:5-7) are evidence of this different attitude. Traditional materials are interpreted by Paul in the unquestioned letters and appropriated for the sake of his arguments, but in the Pastorals traditional materials are recited as authoritative lessons. The emphasis is not on "faith" (e.g., Rom. 4; Gal. 3), but on "the faith" (1 Tim. 3:9; 4:1)—on a body of doctrine handed down. The differences in theological terminology between the unquestioned letters of Paul and the Pastorals are considerable, and where the Pastorals use an expression found in the unquestioned letters, it is often with a different meaning or focus.

But even in the unquestioned letters, Paul displays considerable flexibility in his theological terminology and methods. The differences in theological focus and the emphasis on authoritative tradition are differences in degree, not substance. Like Paul, the writer of the Pastorals believes in human renewal understood as justification by God's grace (2 Tim. 1:9-10; Titus 3:3-7) received through faith in Christ (2 Tim. 3:15). The objectification of "the faith" in traditional "sure sayings" and orderly church organization may have been Paul's response to a volatile situation that arose in some churches late in his life.

G. *Views of the Pastorals.* A common response to these difficulties has been to conclude that the Pastoral Epistles were pseudonymously written in the first half of the second century (or earlier), to attach the views expressed in the letters to the authority of Paul's name. Paul's memory is venerated, but second-century problems, including an early form of Gnosticism, are given second-century solutions. As Gnosticism has become better known through the Nag Hammadi codices, it has been noted also that the Pastorals represent one side of a conflict in which the role of women was a major issue.

The traditional view of the Pastoral Epistles is that Paul composed them in a period of his life later than the events described in the book of Acts. It is assumed that Paul went to Rome for trial as described in Acts, was released, and had further travels in both West and East, during which he wrote 1 Timothy and Titus. (But Acts 20:25, 38 appear to imply that Paul never returned to the East.) He was then, as the hypothesis goes, arrested again, taken for trial to Rome (where he wrote 2 Timothy), and executed.

Other views of the letters have held them to be based on notes composed by Paul, but edited into their final state by another person, perhaps shortly after his death; or composed on the basis of Pauline fragments by a second-century writer; or written by Paul during the same period as his other letters, the release and second Roman imprisonment being rejected because of lack of evidence outside the traditional hypothesis regarding the Pastorals.

An underlying question that affects conclusions with regard to other documents as well as the Pastorals is that of the possibilities of pseudepigraphy in the early Church—the degree to which documents bearing the name of Paul (or some other significant figure of the apostolic generation) could have been written and could have been received by the Church. It is clear that some pseudepigraphal documents were, in fact, written and received, but there is still considerable disagreement concerning the extent to which this could be taken.

Bibliography. M. Dibelius and H. Conzelmann, *The Pastoral Epistles.* Hermeneia (1972); A. T. Hanson, *The Pastoral Epistles.* NCBC (1982); J. N. D. Kelly, *A Commentary on the Pastoral Epistles* (1963; repr. Grand Rapids: 1981).

PATARA [păt'ə rə] (Gk. *tá Patara*). The major port of Lycia situated on the southwest coast opposite Rhodes, 9.6 km. (6 mi.) east of the mouth of the

Xanthus river. A prosperous city, Patara was one of the six largest cities of the Lycian league (Strabo *Geog.* xiv.3.2-3). Here Paul changed ships to sail to Phoenicia during his final journey to Jerusalem (Acts 21:1; some texts read "Patara and Myra").

PATER NOSTER [păt′ər nŏs′tər] (Lat. "Our Father"). The opening words of the Lord's Prayer as translated by Jerome in the Vulgate, adopted by Roman Catholics as the prayer's title. In English the prayer is often called the "Our Father." *See* LORD'S PRAYER.

PATHROS [păth′rŏs] (Heb. *paṯrôs*; Egyp. *p3-t3-rsy* "southern land"). Upper Egypt, i.e., the southern part of Egypt from just south of Memphis to the first cataract at Syene, to which some of the exiled Israelites fled (Isa. 11:11; Jer. 44:1, 15; Ezek. 30:14). According to 29:14, "the land of Pathros" was the original home of the Egyptians.

PATHRUSIM [pə thrōō′ zĭm] (Heb. *paṯrusîm*). The inhabitants of Pathros, identified in the Table of Nations as descendants of Egypt (Gen. 10:14; 1 Chr. 1:12).

PATIENCE (Heb. *′ereḵ ′appayim* "slow to anger"; Gk. *makrothymía, hypomoné, anoché*).† In addition to "patience" and related forms, the concept is expressed by a number of English words: "forbearance," "longsuffering" (KJV), "slow to anger," "endurance," "tolerance," and "steadfastness."

God's forbearance toward sinners is insisted on in related Old Testament texts (Exod. 34:6-7; Num. 14:18; Neh. 9:17; Ps. 86:15; 103:8-18). In the New Testament, this divine patience is often perceived differently in view of the eschatological situation in which those books were written (Rom. 2:4; 9:22; 2 Pet. 3:9, 15) and in view of reflection on the past, whether of mankind in general (Rom. 3:25; 1 Pet. 3:20), or of individuals (1 Tim. 1:16).

Patience, forbearance, and tolerance of other people are fundamental ethical qualities taught in the Bible (e.g., Prov. 14:29; 19:11; 1 Cor. 13:4; Eph. 4:2; Col. 3:12-13; 1 Thess. 5:14). At Eccl. 7:8 "patient in spirit" suggests humility in contrast to a proud or haughty spirit. Divine forbearance toward sinners is made a motivation for human patience and mercy in the teachings of Jesus, especially at Matt. 18:23-34. Such steadfast endurance finds its source neither in personal bravery nor a stoic attitude, but in religious faith and Christian hope (e.g., 1 Pet. 2:20); by contrast, Greek ethics would regard such inner bravery as shameful and even servile.

"Patience" and its cognates also describe the believer's waiting persistently for God to act (e.g., Ps. 37:7; 40:1 [MT 2]; cf. LXX Gk. *hypomoné*, 1 Chr. 29:15; RSV "hope"). The eschatological situation of the New Testament is the basis for repeated calls for patient endurance and perseverance, especially when confession of Christian belief leads to suffering (e.g., Luke 21:19; Rom. 8:25; 15:4-5; 2 Thess. 3:5; Heb. 12:1-3; Jas. 5:7-11; Rev. 13:10). Patience in the sense of "enduring" or "standing fast" against the world does figure in the book of Job with its theme of pious endurance, the source of which is ultimately God (e.g., Job 6:11).

PATMOS [păt′məs] (Gk. *Patmos*). A rocky, barren island in the Aegean Sea, about 90 km. (56 mi.) southwest of Ephesus and 45 km. (28 mi.) south-southwest of Samos. Some 16 km. (10 mi.) long and 10 km. (6 mi.) at its widest point, Patmos was primarily a place of exile for Roman political prisoners.

John, the author of the book of Revelation, was exiled to Patmos "on account of the word of God and the testimony of Jesus" (Rev. 1:9). Some of the visions of John reflect their occurrence on the island (10:2; 19:6). John felt intensely his separation from the mainland, and so symbolized the removal of boundaries and enclosures as the disappearance of the sea (21:1).

Among the island's numerous shrines is the grotto where tradition holds that John experienced his visions. In 1088 the famous monastery of St. John the Theologian was founded on Patmos.

PATRIARCHS.† The forefathers of the Israelites. Gk. *patriárchēs* (pl. *patriárchai*) is used in the LXX for prominent members of tribe and clan groups who serve some sort of administrative or judicial function (1 Chr. 24:31; 27:22; 2 Chr. 19:8; 23:20; 26:12). In 4 Maccabees, however, the term is applied to Israel's ancestors, Abraham, Isaac, and Jacob (4 Macc. 7:19; cf. 16:25). In the New Testament "patriarch" is used of David (Acts 2:29), the twelve sons of Jacob (7:8-9), and Abraham (Heb. 7:4). Heb. *′āḇ* "father" is used for more than just a male parent (*see* FATHER) and can represent a distant tribal ancestor (e.g., Gen. 10:21; Deut. 8:1; Ezek. 20:30; cf. Gen. 4:20). Similarly Gk. *patḗr* "father" can be used of ancestors, including the patriarchs of Israel (Rom. 9:5; RSV "patriarchs"; 11:28; RSV "forefathers"; 15:8; cf. 1 Macc. 2:51-60). The God of the Bible is often referred to as "the God of my/our/the father(s)" (e.g., Gen. 31:5; Dan. 2:23; Acts 5:30) or with similar formulas that use the names of the patriarchs (e.g., Gen. 28:13; 31:42, 53; Exod. 3:6).

The patriarchal narratives in Genesis may be divided into three story cycles, dealing with Abram/Abraham and Isaac (Gen. 11:27–25:18), Jacob/Israel and Esau (25:19–37:1), and Joseph and his brothers (37:2–50:26). The divine call to which the patriarchs responded was usually given in the context of promises of land (e.g., 26:3; 28:4) and descendants (e.g., 12:2; 17:16; 22:17) and promises that the patriarchs would be a channel of blessing for all mankind (12:3; 26:4; 28:14). But the narratives begin with the patriarchs' entry into Canaan, only to end with them sojourning in Egypt, with the promises yet to be fulfilled. The patriarchs came to know God as one who made covenants with them. In the two occasions on which God established his covenant with Abraham (Gen. 15, 17) God lays himself under obligation. These covenant ceremonies are the first forms of the covenant of God with the nation of Israel (cf. 17:7; Exod. 2:24; 34:10; Josh. 24; 2 Sam. 23:5).

The patriarchs are portrayed as transhumants, tent-dwelling herdsmen possessing sheep, goats, and cattle (Gen. 13:5-7; 18:7; 30:29-43; 37:2), yet they also dug wells (21:30), grew crops (26:12), and settled near towns. They built altars (13:18; 26:25) and offered sacrifices (31:54; 46:1). Their manner of life is thought to resemble in many ways patterns recorded in second-millennium B.C. texts from MARI on the upper Euphrates; parallels with practices attested in the NUZI texts are now largely discredited. Scholars still disagree, however, on during precisely which centuries in the Middle Bronze Age (the first half of the second millennium) the patriarchs are most likely to have lived. *See* ABRAHAM *II*; NOMADISM.

The very historicity of the patriarchal narratives has been hotly debated. J. Wellhausen's documentary hypothesis, developed during the last decades of the nineteenth century, regarded the narratives as of little direct historical worth. Without the information on the second millennium B.C. available today, Wellhausen viewed the patriarchs as figures created out of folklore or mythology, most likely personifications of the tribes said to be descended from them. During the early decades of the twentieth century the discovery in Mesopotamia of cuneiform texts and other evidence shed light on customs found in Genesis. This made it necessary for scholars such as A. Alt and M. Noth to reexamine the narratives. However, they remained skeptical about the historical worth of Gen. 12–50, and their application of form and redaction criticism reduced the patriarchs to shadowy figures. Archaeological finds in Palestine led W. F. Albright, J. Bright, R. de Vaux, and others to assert that the biblical accounts were essentially reliable historical documents and that the narratives were indeed rooted in historical conditions. In the mid-1970s, however, a new generation of scholars, including J. Van Seters and T. L. Thompson, attacked this consensus on the basis of literary analysis of the Genesis material and a review of the extrabiblical evidence. The result has been a careful reevaluation of the evidence that is said to support the consensus, with some scholars moving away from it and others continuing to support it in a modified form.

Bibliography. A. R. Millard and D. J. Wiseman, eds., *Essays on the Patriarchal Narratives* (Winona Lake: 1983); J. Van Seters, *Abraham in History and Tradition* (New Haven: 1975); T. L. Thompson, *The Historicity of the Patriarchal Narratives*. BZAW 133 (1974); R. de Vaux, *The Early History of Israel*, 2 vols. (Philadelphia: 1978).

PATROBAS [păt′rə bəs] (Gk. *Patrobas*, abbreviated form of *Patrobios*). A Christian in Rome to whom Paul sent his greetings (Rom. 16:14).

PAU [pô] (Heb. *pāʿû*). An Edomite city, the capital of King Hadad (Gen. 36:39), called PAI at 1 Chr. 1:50. Its location is unknown. The LXX reads *Phogōr*, its usual designation for Peor.

PAUL [pôl] (Gk. *Paulos*).† A leading persecutor of Christians who became the Christian apostle to the Gentiles, known through his letters and the Acts of the Apostles.

I. Life

A. Early Life. Paul was from Tarsus, a prosperous city and center of education in the Cilician plain of southeastern Asia Minor (Acts 9:11; 21:39; 22:3). His family may have moved to Tarsus from Gischala in Galilee in 4 B.C. (cf. Jerome *De vir. ill.* 5). Paul inherited Roman citizenship (Acts 22:25-28), which was widely granted during the latter part of the Roman republic, and was also a citizen of Tarsus (21:39). His two names, Saul (Heb. *šāʾûl*) and Paul (Lat. *Paulus*, the source of Gk. *Paulos*), reflect the bicultural nature of Hellenistic Diaspora Judaism. Paul received rabbinic training in Jerusalem, but how early this training began is not certain ("this city" at 22:3 may refer to Tarsus or to Jerusalem). Paul was a "tentmaker" (18:3); the trade may well have been that of his family.

Despite the relative liberalism of his teacher Gamaliel, Paul was, according to his own reports a strict rigorist among Pharisees (Gal. 1:14; Phil. 3:5-6). This zealous strictness included his response to the gospel; Paul sought to destroy the Church (1 Cor. 15:9; Gal. 1:13, 23). Even in the retrospect of Christian faith and apostleship Paul was able to say that he was before his conversion "as to the righteousness under the law blameless" (Phil. 3:6). He was not converted because of a sense of religious failure; Rom. 7:7-25 is not so much a reflection of Paul's past as a statement of the condition of mankind in general under the law and not freed by Christ.

B. Beginning of Paul's Apostleship. Paul's conversion and call took place in and near the city of Damascus in Syria. Four features stand out in the accounts of this event (Acts 9:1-9; 22:4-16; 26:9-17). (1) Paul was actively engaged in persecuting Christians and did not anticipate that such an event would occur. (2) That which initiated and controlled the unexpected change of course was a revelation of Jesus made in a clear fashion to Paul alone. (3) Soon after this revelation Paul had contact with at least one Christian in Damascus who recognized Paul as a believer in Christ by baptizing him. (4) Paul was immediately called by Jesus to take the gospel to the Gentiles. This broad picture is confirmed by what Paul writes of his conversion to Christian faith and his call to be apostle to the Gentiles (1 Cor. 9:1; 15:8-9; Gal. 1:15-16; cf. Eph. 3:1-6).

Paul's preaching of Jesus as "Son of God" began immediately after his call (Acts 9:20). He then went into "Arabia" (the Syrian desert near Damascus; Gal. 1:17), and probably preached there too; whatever he did there caused the Nabatean king Aretas IV to attempt to have Paul arrested (2 Cor. 11:32). After three years in and around Damascus, Paul went to Jerusalem, where he stayed for fifteen days (Acts 9:22-26; Gal. 1:18). There Paul attempted to join with the Christians, but apparently met only with some of the apostles (Acts 9:26-27; Gal. 1:18-19; vv. 22-23 are apparently an overstatement intended to emphasize Paul's independence from Jerusalem). From Jerusalem Paul went to Tarsus, where he stayed for an unstated length of time. He then went to Antioch in Syria, where he stayed for one year and was quickly drawn into the Hellenistic Jewish Christians' first mission to Gentiles, probably because he had already shown himself suitable for such work (Acts 9:30; 11:20-26).

From this point the relationship of the events as described in Acts and those described in Galatians is not clear. According to Acts, during the year in Antioch Paul, Barnabas, and John Mark visited Jerusalem at least briefly, to bring famine relief money from

Antioch (Acts 11:27-30; 12:25); at the end of the one-year period they were sent out by the church in Antioch on Paul's "first missionary journey" (13:1-5). According to Galatians, Paul, Barnabas, and Titus went to Jerusalem after a fourteen-year period that probably began with Paul's conversion at Damascus (Gal. 2:1). This visit to Jerusalem was undertaken because of a "revelation"; it was of a serious and significant nature (vv. 2-10) and was followed by a difficult conflict between Peter ("Cephas") and Paul at Antioch (vv. 11-14). Paul is apparently silent about the famine relief visit of Acts 11 to Jerusalem, unless those who have identified it with the visit of Gal. 2 are correct. But if Paul considered the famine relief visit of too little significance to mention, the more usual identification of the visits of Acts 15:1-29 (the "APOSTOLIC COUNCIL") and Gal. 2 may be retained. Indeed, the persons present, the issues discussed, and the course of events at the meeting all suggest that the visits of Gal. 2 and Acts 15 are the same.

C. *First Missionary Journey.* The commissioning of Paul and Barnabas by the church in Antioch (Acts 13:1-3) marked the beginning of Paul's career as a planter and leader of churches in Asia Minor and Greece. His journeys from that point up to his arrest in Jerusalem (21:27–22:29) have been referred to as his "three missionary journeys." While Antioch was in some sense a home base, Paul spent at least eighteen months at Corinth in the course of the "second" journey (18:11) and was based in Ephesus for more than two years during the "third journey" (19:8, 10). The usual division of Paul's journeys is, however, useful as an outline.

The preaching work of Paul, Barnabas, and John Mark began at Salamis on the east coast of Cyprus after a sailing journey from Seleucia, a port near Antioch, and continued across to Paphos on the west coast of the island (13:4-6). Perhaps some reputation from this preaching tour preceded the three men so that the magician Elymas and the proconsul Sergius Paulus became interested in them; it is with this encounter that the story of Paul's apostolic ministry in Acts really begins (vv. 6-12). It may be more than coincidence that the shift from the use of "Saul" to that of "Paul" occurs where he first speaks as an apostle (vv. 9-10).

Acts omits incidents that may have been significant at the time of their occurrence in order to concentrate on a small number of typical events. General features that continue to be of importance in the account of Paul's work are present already in the narrative of the incident at Paphos. (1) Paul's ministry brings him into contact with government officials. (2) Paul is in the center of the action; his coworkers are barely more than mentioned. (3) Paul is characterized by his bold directness of speech. (4) Opposition is often defeated in one way or another; Paul's speech is not only bold but effective. (5) Faith usually results from Paul's preaching.

After Paul and his coworkers sailed to Asia Minor, John Mark left Paul and Barnabas (13:13), who then went inland to Antioch of Pisidia. The account of events there (vv. 14-51) is one of several in Acts that show, with typical features, Paul in dispute with Jews. (1) The apostle's preaching of Christ begins in the

synagogue and is based on the reading of Scripture in the Sabbath services (9:20; 13:5, 14-16; 14:1; 17:1-2, 10, 17; 18:4, 19; 19:8). (2) There might be repeated visits to the same synagogue (13:42; 17:2; 18:4; 19:8), but eventually violence against Paul originating from Jews drives him out of the synagogue and usually out of the town (9:23-25; 13:45, 50-51; 14:2, 4-6; 17:5-10, 13-14; 18:6-7; 19:9). (3) Among those converted are often Gentile proselytes and "God-fearers" (13:48; 14:1; 16:14; 17:4, 12; 18:4, 7). Perhaps as Gentile worshippers of the God of Israel were drawn away from the synagogues by Paul's preaching Jews were spurred to incite violence against Paul and his coworkers.

At Lystra (14:8-20) the encounter was not immediately with Jews but with adherents of the Hellenized local paganism. Therefore, Paul's sermon does not begin from the Jewish Scriptures but from a call to recognize the evidence in nature for the one "living God" of the Jewish people and to turn to him (vv. 15-17). If 17:22-31; 1 Thess. 1:9-10 are any indication, Paul's intention was to complete this message of the unity, universality, and forbearance of God by telling of Jesus' resurrection and the coming judgment and by giving a call to repentance. Paul's ministry in Lystra was cut short by opposition stirred up by Jews from Antioch and Iconium who had followed Paul there (Acts 14:19). After a successful preaching visit to Derbe, Paul and Barnabas turned back to strengthen the new Christian communities they had planted. If the "South Galatian" hypothesis for the letter to the Galatians is correct, then these Christian groups begun in Asia Minor during the first missionary journey are those addressed in the letter. Paul and Barnabas departed from Asia Minor for Syrian Antioch, stopping on the way to preach in Perga (vv. 24-26).

D. *Apostolic Council.* Though those who "came down from Judea" to Syrian Antioch (15:1) probably did not realize it at first, more than just Antioch was at stake in their insistence that Gentile Christians be circumcised. It is hardly surprising that "Paul and Barnabas had no small dissension and debate with them," given the work the two had been doing in Cyprus and Asia Minor. The result of this debate was the Apostolic Council, a pivotal event in the history of the early Church (vv. 4-29). The issue was simply whether or not Gentile Christians should become full converts to Judaism (vv. 1, 5). The course followed in the Council, which was to require only a minimal sensitivity to Jewish scruples on the part of the Gentiles (vv. 19-21, 28-29), was set both by the reports by Paul and Barnabas of what had happened beyond Antioch (vv. 4, 12) and by the arguments of Peter and James (vv. 7-11, 13-21). The decision of the Council allowed for some measure of unity between the Judean churches and the predominantly Gentile churches of Syria, Asia Minor, and Greece, a unity that Paul later sought vigorously to strengthen (Rom. 15:25-27, 30; Gal. 2:10).

The Council was not successful in resolving the disputed issues to the satisfaction of all. Agitation to have Gentile Christians circumcised continued (Galatians is evidence of this, unless it was written before the Council; cf. Rom. 2:25-29; Phil. 3:1-2), as did efforts to bring them under submission to what some viewed as properly constituted authorities, probably the leaders of the church at Jerusalem (2 Cor. 11:5; 12:11; cf. 1 Cor. 15:9-11), and to drive a wedge between Paul and those concerned for the Old Testament and Jewish heritage of Christianity (Rom. 3:8; 9:1-5; 10:1; 11:1). Paul did not refer to the Council's decision in his letters, even where it might have aided his argument to do so. He was later reminded of the Council's decision by the leaders of the Jerusalem Christians (Acts 21:25). Perhaps he was perceived at least as a not too enthusiastic supporter of its authority, though he did carry its decision to churches in Asia Minor that had been founded before the Council (16:4).

If Gal. 2:1-10 represents the same meeting, then to Paul the significant aspects of the Council were the reception of uncircumcised Gentile Christians (v. 3), the recognition given by James, Peter, and John to the validity of Barnabas and Paul's work, the fact that the three Jerusalem leaders had nothing to add to his message, and their arrangement with Paul and Barnabas of a division of labor in the spread of the gospel (vv. 6-9).

E. Second and Third Missionary Journeys. The Council's decision was received with rejoicing in Antioch, where for a time Paul and Barnabas joined in the preaching and teaching work (Acts 15:30-36). They planned a tour of the churches in Cyprus and south-central Asia Minor, but were divided over whether to take John Mark, who had left them before. Two parties were formed (vv. 36-41), Barnabas accompanying John Mark into his home territory (cf. 4:36) and Paul traveling into his. Paul's new coworker was Silas ("Silvanus" in the letters) from the Jerusalem church (15:22); they were joined by Timothy when they arrived to preach to the inland Asia Minor churches (16:1-3; cf. 2 Cor. 1:19). It was not until the three had crossed Asia Minor and gone to Philippi in Macedonia that they resumed organizing new churches (Acts 16:6-12; cf. Rom. 15:19).

Acts 16:12–19:41 stresses Paul's activity as bringer of the word to new territory. As before, in each city he generally began by teaching Jews and Gentiles who joined in the Jewish worship (16:13; 17:1-2, 10, 17; 18:4, 19; 19:8). At Athens he also spoke to Gentiles not influenced by Judaism, but apparently with little success (17:18-34). Above all, Paul's work attracted attention (including supernatural attention; 16:16-18; 19:15), which sometimes led to encounters with legal authorities in which Paul was vindicated and the blame placed on others (16:19-39; 18:12-16; 19:29-41; cf. 17:6-9).

From the beginning of ch. 20 (cf. 19:21-22), Acts leaves aside its concentration on the spectacular confrontations involved in the spread of the gospel and gives more attention to Paul's encouragement of established churches, mentioned only briefly up to that point (16:4-5; 18:23; 20:2). The focus changes in order to give emphasis to Paul's departure from the churches in eastern Asia Minor, Macedonia, and Greece. The farewell speech to the Ephesian elders (20:17-38) and the detailed description of the journey to Jerusalem, during which Paul's arrest is predicted (21:1-15), especially emphasize this departure.

Rom. 15, probably written from Corinth shortly before Paul's final departure from Greece (cf. Acts 20:1-3), contains a reflection on the past and anticipation of a future that includes Jerusalem, Rome, and Spain (Rom. 15:17-32; cf. Acts 19:21). In the past Paul has sought always to take the gospel where no one else has before (Rom. 15:19-21; cf. 2 Cor. 10:13-16), with the objective of winning "obedience [to Christ] from the Gentiles" (Rom. 15:18; cf. 1:5). He now proceeds to Jerusalem with relief money for the Christians there from the Christians of Greece and Macedonia (15:25-26; cf. 1 Cor. 16:1-3; 2 Cor. 8–9); he regards this money as representing the Gentile churches, the fruits of his work and of the growth of the Church beyond its beginnings in Jerusalem (Rom. 15:16, 27).

In the work of building up and encouraging the established churches (cf. 1:14; 2 Cor. 11:28-29), Paul considered both his letters and his personal presence essential (1:23–2:4, 9; 13:1-2; Phil. 1:27; Rom. 1:11-13). He was, to this same end, the chief administrator of a group of coworkers through whom he could transmit messages to churches and receive reports concerning churches (e.g., Acts 17:14-16; 19:22; 1 Cor. 16:10-11; 2 Cor. 7:6-7; Phil. 2:19-24).

F. Arrest and Trial. Paul and his traveling companions were received gladly in Jerusalem by "the brethren" (Acts 21:17), who were, however, concerned about rumors that Paul had been teaching Diaspora Jews to give up observance of the law, even though they recognized the exemption from total adherence granted Gentile Christians by the Jerusalem Council (vv. 20-22, 25). They proposed that Paul take part in a particular expression of Jewish piety in order to squelch the rumors; to do so was well within Paul's own policy as an apostle (1 Cor. 9:9). At their suggestion he agreed to meet the expenses of and participate in the purification ritual of four Jews who had made a Nazirite vow (Acts 21:23-24, 26; Paul himself had earlier made such a vow; 18:18).

The rumors of Paul's teaching against the law circulated among Christian Jews (21:20-21) and perhaps also among non-Christian Jews (cf. vv. 27-28; 20:18-19). The "brethren's" plan failed, and the Je-

The traditional site of Paul's imprisonment in Philippi (Acts 16:23) (W. S. LaSor)

rusalem Christians apparently made no further effort in defense of the apostle; they are not mentioned in Acts after 21:26. Ostensibly because he taught against the law, the Jewish people, and the temple, Paul was assaulted by an angry mob provoked by charges that he had brought Trophimus, a Gentile representative of the Ephesian church, into the sacred precincts (21:28-29). When the disturbance came to the attention of the military tribune in the Fortress Antonia adjoining the temple grounds, Paul was arrested as the source of the trouble and protected from the crowd.

Since little was learned about the disturbance by permitting Paul to speak to the crowd (21:39-22:21), the tribune sought to obtain information from him by torture (22:24). Thwarted by Paul's Roman citizenship (vv. 25-29), the tribune took him before the Sanhedrin for a coherent accusation (v. 30), but this also failed. A conspiracy to kill Paul became known, forcing the tribune to send the prisoner to the provincial capital of Caesarea—under a heavy protective guard and without an accusation (23:12-33).

In the accusation brought before Felix the governor by a segment of the Jewish leadership led by the high priest, the most concrete charge was profanation of the temple; with this were hints of seditious agitation (24:5-6). After Paul's defense (vv. 10-21), Felix adjourned the trial until the tribune in Jerusalem could report on the circumstances of Paul's arrest (v. 22). The adjournment extended to the end of Felix's time as procurator, two years after Paul's arrest or after the beginning of the trial (v. 27).

When some Jewish leaders petitioned Festus, Felix' successor, to have Paul's case moved to their jurisdiction, the governor asked instead that they bring their accusation to him at Caesarea (25:1-5; cf. v. 16). After he heard the accusations and Paul's defense, Festus did decide to let the case go to Jerusalem; but Paul, aware of how such a decision would end and determined to go to Rome (19:21; 23:11; Rom. 15:23-24), appealed to Nero ("Caesar," Acts 25:7-12). Festus called in Herod Agrippa II, king of Galilee, Perea, and other territories, to assist in composing a report for the emperor (vv. 26-27). After Paul's defense before Agrippa, the report was prepared, but with the recognition that there was really no case against Paul (26:30-32).

Although the case was brought before Roman officials, Paul sought to portray it as a dispute within Judaism concerning resurrection, and thus beyond their competence (23:6; 24:20-21). But when the danger arose that as a Jewish case it would probably lead to Paul's death, he said explicitly that it was a Roman case (25:8, 10). Only when his case had been committed to Rome and the direct danger of Jerusalem had thus been removed did Paul link it explicitly with the proclamation of Christ's resurrection (26:8, 22-23).

Fundamental to Paul's defense was his self-identification as a good Jew of clear conscience (22:3; 23:1; 24:14, 16-17; 26:4-7). It was not his mention of Jesus (22:8) but his call to preach to Gentiles (vv. 21-22) and, so it was thought, his bringing Gentiles into the temple that angered Paul's accusers. He did not mention his call to the Gentiles again, nor did he mention faith in Christ (except, in response to a formal accusation, a brief reference to the Jewishness of the Chris-

tian "Way"; 24:5, 14), until his case was safely out of Jewish hands (26:17-18, 20). Behind all this was Paul's desire to go to Rome.

G. *Journey to Rome and End of Paul's Life.* The voyage to Rome apparently began late in the sailing season. When the Day of Atonement ("the fast"), in late September or early October, had passed and the ship that had taken on Paul and his fellow travelers at Myra was only just south of Crete, the decision was made to winter further west on the island (27:9-12). But a severe storm arose, eventually taking the ship to Malta, where it was destroyed (27:14-28:1). When the sailing season began again in February or March, the party continued on to Puteoli and from there to Rome (28:11-14). *See* SHIPS AND SAILING.

On this journey Julius, the centurion escorting Paul and a number of other prisoners (27:1), "treated Paul kindly" (v. 3; cf. v. 43) and allowed him considerable freedom while on land (28:7, 14). It has been suggested that Paul's traveling companions, including Aristarchus (27:2; cf. 19:29; 20:4; Col. 4:10; Phlm. 24) and perhaps Luke and Titus (as far as Crete; Titus 1:4), traveled as Paul's servants; this would help to account for the high honor in which he was held despite his being a prisoner. Paul's conviction, once they had gone beyond Crete, was that God would bring him to Rome and that for his sake all those accompanying him would also be safe (Acts 27:21-24, cf. v. 10).

At Rome, though a prisoner, Paul was able for two years to teach quite freely all who came to him (28:30-31). At this point the Acts narrative ends. It is possible that Paul was released on the emperor's authority, but the vision of 27:23-24 would most likely not have been recorded had Paul never come to trial. Paul's trial was probably not actually conducted by Nero, whose habit was to delegate judicial responsibilities and merely confirm sentences. If Paul was tried, convicted, and executed at the end of the two-year period mentioned in Acts, then he died *ca.* A.D. 62. Early Church traditions say Paul was executed at Rome, but connect his execution not with the apostle's case that began at Jerusalem but with Nero's killing of many Christians in Rome in A.D. 64. Other statements from the early Church indicate that Paul was released and imprisoned again, which is a possibility. He may have gone to Spain, but the closest substantiation of such a report is Clement's statement that Paul preached "to the limit of the West," which need not imply Spain and may simply be a surmise based on Rom. 15:24.

See CHRONOLOGY, BIBLICAL.

II. Theology

Paul never wrote a comprehensive doctrinal statement detached from the life of specific churches. His letters were always written in response to the specific needs, problems, and questions of Christians in particular locations. Therefore, the various letters have differing vocabularies, argue differently, and insist on different conclusions. Also, development can be detected in certain aspects of Paul's thought. Nevertheless, all of what Paul wrote in his letters can be considered clarifications of what the eschatological salvation that has come in Christ does and does not mean. Certain

The end of Paul's Letter to the Ephesians and the beginning of his letter to the Galatians in p46 (ca. 200) (University of Michigan Library)

fundamental pastoral-theological concerns arise more than once, including Paul's concerns that adherence to the Jewish law not be required of Gentiles who receive salvation in Christ, that the continuity of salvation in Christ with the Old Testament be remembered, and that triumphalism and licentiousness not be considered results of this salvation.

A. Justification and Reconciliation. Paul's teaching on justification by faith in Christ is found in Galatians and Romans as a statement about the position of the Gentiles in the Church. The gospel is God's offer of righteousness to all who have faith in Christ and give up reliance on human effort and on adherence to the Mosaic Law in order to attain righteousness. God's justifying activity in Christ delivers from sin those who have such faith; this activity is "the righteousness of God . . . manifested apart from law," "the righteousness of God through faith in Jesus Christ for all who believe" (Rom. 3:21-22).

This divine justifying activity is not detached from the Old Testament. "The law and the prophets bear witness to it" (v. 21), and Abraham himself is the archetypal person of faith, justified by that faith (ch. 4; Gal. 3:6-9). In no other letter does Paul refer to the Old Testament more than in Romans. The Old Testament is always a positive and essential witness to what God is doing now in Christ and the Church. Israel has a central place in salvation history that is not destroyed by their not believing in Christ, and it will yet lead to salvation (Rom. 11:11-26).

With Paul's use of the term "reconciliation," the emphasis is usually, as with justification, on what has already been accomplished (5:10-11; Col. 2:20-22; cf. Eph. 2:1-6). The line between the reconciliation of God and the world (Rom. 11:5; 2 Cor. 5:19-20) and reconciliation among human beings is not definite.

God's act of reconciliation brings together diverse elements in the Church (Eph. 2:14-16) and prepares the way for the renewal of proper relations among Christians (2 Cor. 5:18-20; 6:11-13; 7:2).

B. Triumphalism and Ethics. Even as a believer in the eschatological salvation that has already come, Paul strongly warns against extremes and overstatements of such eschatological faith. He confronts those who consider themselves already saved and therefore beyond such mundane concerns as morality (1 Cor. 5:1-8; cf. 4:8; Gal. 5:13). Slogans such as "all things are lawful for me" (1 Cor. 6:12), "food is meant for the stomach and the stomach for food" (v. 13), and "all of us possess knowledge" (8:1) Paul affirms, but only as of less importance than pure living and concern for others (6:12-20; 8:1, 7-13). He also stands against excessive admiration of spectacular spiritual gifts at the expense of the upbuilding of God's people (chs. 12–14; esp. 14:12; 2 Cor. 11:5-6), an abandonment of hope for the coming resurrection based on the idea that it was already in some sense experienced (1 Cor. 15:12, 19, 23-26; 2 Thess. 2:2; 2 Tim. 2:18), and the idea that suffering, regarded as "weakness," ought not be part of Christian experience (1 Cor. 15:12; 2 Cor. 11:23-30; 13:4). For Paul, a future-oriented hope is just as much a part of faith as is possession in the present. Because of the salvation that has come in Christ—because there are those who are "in Christ"—God's new act of creation has begun (5:17). But much is still awaited (vv. 2-4; Rom. 8:18-25).

The ethical life of Gentile Christians ought not be destroyed in licentiousness or based on adherence to the Mosaic law, but should be an outgrowth of the redemption won in Christ. God's objective in Christ is, as always, fulfillment of the law, which is brought about by the justification of the sinner by God's grace and by the life in the Spirit lived by the justified (vv. 8-13; Gal. 5:13-26).

C. The Church. Paul's most significant contribution to a theology of the Church comes with his use of "the Body of Christ" for the entire Church, all local churches considered as a whole (Rom. 12:5; Eph. 1:23; 2:16; 4:4). This term assumes the unity of Christians in their participation in Christ's death, resurrection, and ascension (Rom. 6:3-4; 1 Cor. 12:13; Eph. 2:5-6, 14-16) and in their experience of his lordship over them (1 Cor. 12:5; Eph. 1:22-23; 4:5; Col. 1:18; 2:19). This unity in Christ means that the Church functions as a unified organism, not by requiring uniformity of function but by receiving and allowing the function of diverse spiritual gifts (Rom. 12:4-7; 1 Cor. 12:4-30; Eph. 4:4-16).

D. Eschatology and the Later Letters. The certainty of the contrast between the present and the time to come ushered in by Christ's future triumph (e.g., Rom. 8:18-25; 1 Cor. 15:24-25) was fundamental to Paul's understanding of situations that arise in the present. The expectation of the imminent return of Christ proved confusing to the Thessalonian Christians, to whom Paul responded by showing the connection between the expectation of the resurrection and that of Christ's return (1 Thess. 4:13-17; cf. 1 Cor. 15:20-28). Shortly after his first letter to the Thessalonians, Paul had reason to teach that there were yet events to happen before Christ's return (2 Thess. 2:1-12). Later he was concerned with the return and triumph of Christ and with the future of believers (2 Cor. 5:1-5; Phil. 1:21-26), but less with the connection between the two (but cf. Phil. 3:20-21). Perhaps his own experiences, in particular the "sentence of death" in Asia (2 Cor. 1:9), had convinced Paul that he was not likely to live until Christ's return. But even in Ephesians and Colossians, where Paul discusses more simply and directly than before the spiritual experience of Christians as a resurrection that has already happened (Eph. 2:5-6; Col. 3:1), the distinction of this age from the next and the hope of the future return of Christ remains essential (Eph. 1:21; 6:12; Col. 3:4).

Even so, the last part of this shift in eschatological focus has, with other factors, cast doubt on the authorship of Colossians and especially Ephesians. Ephesians shows the beginnings of a tendency toward greater emphasis on church authority structures, a tendency that is even clearer in the Pastoral Epistles, where the doubts concerning authorship are greater. In the undoubted letters, Paul frequently made use of traditional expressions of the Christian faith—e.g., hymns, confessions, and hortatory material (e.g., Rom. 1:3-4; 10:9; 1 Cor. 11:23-25; 15:3-7; 16:22; Gal. 6:7-8; Phil. 2:6-11). He had also been concerned for church order (1 Cor. 11:17-34; 14:40) and the recognition due to church leaders (Rom. 16:2; 1 Cor. 9:1-12; Gal. 6:6; Phil. 1:1). But if Paul wrote Ephesians, he had apparently begun to see authoritative church offices as an essential aspect of the redemptive work of Christ (Eph. 2:20; 3:5; 4:11; cf. 1 Cor. 12:28-30). Furthermore, if he did write the Pastoral Epistles he had begun to insist on properly examined and appointed church officers (1 Tim. 3:1-13; Titus 1:5-9), a traditional structure of worship (1 Tim. 2), and "sure sayings" (1:15; 3:1; 4:9; 2 Tim. 2:11; Titus 1:9; 3:8; cf. 1 Tim. 6:20) as stabilizing responses to threats of heresy facing the churches (1:3, 19-20; 4:1-7; 6:20-21; 2 Tim. 2:16-18; 3:2-9; Titus 1:10-16). Such changes are conceivable for a pastor and theologian like Paul, always concerned to respond to the immediate need. But the problems involved with these letters should not be minimized.

For specific letters see the individual entries.

Bibliography. J. C. Beker, *Paul the Apostle* (Philadelphia: 1980); F. F. Bruce, *Paul: Apostle of the Heart Set Free* (Grand Rapids: 1977); W. D. Davies, *Paul and Rabbinic Judaism,* 4th ed. (Philadelphia: 1980); E. Käsemann, *Perspectives on Paul* (Philadelphia: 1971); H. N. Ridderbos, *Paul: An Outline of His Theology* (Grand Rapids: 1975); E. P. Sanders, *Paul and Palestinian Judaism* (Philadelphia: 1977).

PAUL, ACTS OF.† An apocryphal account of the travels of Paul dating to the late second century A.D. According to Tertullian (*ca.* 200), the author was a presbyter from Asia Minor who was deposed from office for his efforts, despite his claim to write "out of love for Paul" and despite his apparent orthodoxy. The author's primary purpose was to edify and entertain, but his emphasis on sexual abstinence (e.g., AP 3:5) reveals a didactic intent as well. The book, written in Greek, traces Paul's ministry and miracles from Damascus through ten or more cities before ending in Rome.

Although much of the text has been lost, three sections were detached and circulated independently and have been preserved virtually intact. The first, the Acts of Paul and Thecla, offers the virgin Thecla as an exemplar of sexual abstinence and of a female teaching ministry. The second purports to be an exchange of letters between Paul and the Corinthians, and includes the so-called "3 Corinthians." It is, more than the rest of the Acts, written to combat a form of Gnosticism. The third, the Martyrdom of Paul at Rome, presents a confrontation between Paul and the Roman emperor; Nero has Paul beheaded, but afterwards Paul appears to him for a final word of doom.

The Acts of Paul as a whole was never accepted as authoritative, but portions were widely read and influential. 3 Corinthians appears in some Syriac and Armenian Bibles. The Acts of Paul provides this description of the apostle: "of small stature, bald, with crooked legs, in a good state of body, with eyebrows meeting and nose somewhat hooked, and full of graciousness; for sometimes he appeared like a man, and sometimes had the face of an angel" (3:3).

PAUL, APOCALYPSE OF.† A title apparently given to several apocryphal accounts of Paul's experience when he was "caught up to the third heaven" (2 Cor. 12:2-4). Two such works survive. One, preserved in full in Latin only, relates Paul's tour of paradise and hell, and was probably written in the late fourth century A.D. The other, which appears in the Nag Hammadi codices, incorporates Gnostic themes in its account of Paul's ascent from the third to the tenth heaven.

PAUL, PRAYER OF THE APOSTLE.* A brief Gnostic writing dating from the second or third century A.D. and found on the front flyleaf of Codex I (the Jung Codex) of the Nag Hammadi codices. It is related to other Gnostic texts and to Hermetic and magical texts, and draws some of its contents from Psalms and the epistles of Paul.

PAUL AND SENECA [sĕn'ə kə], **LETTERS OF.**† A collection of fourteen spurious letters between Seneca and the apostle Paul. A Spanish-born and Roman-educated Stoic philosopher and statesman, Lucius Annaeus Seneca was the teacher and trusted advisor of the emperor Nero. Suspected by Nero of participating in an unsuccessful plot against his life, Seneca was forced to commit suicide in A.D. 65. This contemporary of Paul was known for his ethical teachings in which moral law was viewed as identical with the will of God, who is the highest reason and father of humanity. Seneca was held in respect by several of the Church Fathers for his near-Christian insights (cf. Jerome *De vir. ill.* xii).

In these letters the two correspondents praise one another and form a bond of friendship. Seneca alludes to the divine inspiration of Paul's canonical letters, despite their lack of literary elegance, and wishes to produce an edition of them for the emperor. Written in the third or fourth century, probably in Italy, the letters of Paul and Seneca represent a popular literary attempt to commend the letters of Paul to a Roman audience.

PAUL AND THECLA [thĕk'lə], **ACTS OF.** One of three sections of the Acts of Paul that were separated from that work at an early stage and circulated independently.

Thecla rather than Paul is the central character. As Paul is preaching in Iconium "concerning continence and the resurrection," Thecla hears and responds by breaking her engagement to Thamyris. The enraged fiancé stirs up the crowd, and Paul is imprisoned. Thecla visits Paul, is discovered and condemned to burn, and Paul is expelled. Several miracles enable her to follow Paul from place to place, and at length Paul commissions her to preach. This she does in Iconium and Seleucia, where she enlightens many and dies a peaceful death. Later additions to the story describe her further search for Paul and her death in Rome.

It appears that the author of the Acts of Paul introduced Paul into independent Thecla traditions. The emphasis is on sexual abstinence and the virtues of the celibate life. The example of a woman commissioned by Paul to preach the word of God made the work particularly distasteful to Christians such as Tertullian who were uncomfortable with women in such roles. Nevertheless, the work was widely read in the early Church, and may reflect the mores of some groups of second-century Christians.

PAVEMENT, THE (Gk. *lithóstrōtos* "paved area"). The place of judgment outside the Praetorium where Pilate tried Jesus (John 19:13). *See* GABBATHA.

PEACE (Heb. *šālôm*; Gk. *eirḗnē*)†. A state of wholeness (Heb. *šālôm* "well-being") and security embracing both the physical and spiritual dimensions and relating not only to the individual, but also to entire communities and relationships among persons. "Peace" as experienced by communities includes economic prosperity (Ps. 147:14; cf. 37:11; Hag. 2:9) and political security (2 Kgs. 20:19; 1 Chr. 22:9; Isa. 32:18). Although peace may be attained through either military victory (Judg. 8:9; 1 Kgs. 22:27-28) or surrender (2 Sam. 10:19; 1 Kgs. 20:18), peace in the biblical sense often involves more than simply the Classical Greek connotation of *eirḗnē* as the cessation or absence of hostility. A warrior returning safely from battle has preserved health and so is truly "in peace" (KJV, Josh. 10:21; RSV "safe"; 1 Kgs. 22:17; KJV, Ps. 55:18 [MT 19]; RSV "in safety"). "Go in peace" is a common farewell to persons going on a journey that might involve difficulty (Exod. 4:18; Judg. 18:6); it occurs also with the sense of restoration to wholeness, of a relationship (1 Sam. 1:17; 2 Kgs. 5:19) or health (Mark 5:34), or of forgiveness (Luke 7:50).

All peace is said to come from the sovereign God (Isa. 45:7; RSV "weal"; cf. Num. 6:26; 1 Chr. 23:25; Ps. 147:14). For this reason, the experience of peace is dependent on righteousness, obedience, and justice (Ps. 119:165; Isa. 32:17; 48:18; 59:8). God's covenant with his people is sometimes called a "covenant of peace" (Num. 25:12; Isa. 54:10; Ezek. 37:26; cf. Mal. 2:5, "covenant of life and peace").

The fundamental quality of eschatological hope is peace like that which is not experienced in the present age (e.g., Ps. 72:7; 85:8, 10 [MT 9, 11]; Isa. 55:12).

The coming Deliverer is called "the Prince of Peace" (9:6 [MT 5]). As sin originating in the human heart disrupts the entire creation, so in the age to come all of life will be reconstructed in peace (v. 7 [MT 6]; cf. 2:1-4; 11:6-9).

The coming of Christ and the sending of the Spirit are interpreted as the coming of eschatological peace (John 14:27; 16:33; Acts 10:36; Rom. 8:6). The gospel is "the gospel of peace" (Eph. 6:15). In it "peace with God" is made available (Rom. 5:1; cf. 2 Cor. 5:19), and God is known as "the God of peace" (Rom. 15:33; Phil. 4:9; 1 Thess. 5:23; Heb. 13:20; cf. 2 Cor. 13:11). But conflict and insecurity are expected to continue on earth until the consummation of this peace with the return of Christ (Luke 12:51-53; 1 Thess. 5:3).

Christ is "our peace" (cf. John 20:19, 21) in that he has created the environment in which hostility can be replaced by new relationships (Eph. 2:14). Those who establish peace will be called "sons of God" (Matt. 5:9). Peace is a goal of Christian relationships with all people (Rom. 12:18; 1 Cor. 7:15; Heb. 12:14), including fellow Christians and the Church at large (Mark 9:50; 2 Cor. 13:11; Col. 3:15; 1 Thess. 5:13).

PEACE OFFERING.† Heb. *(zebaḥ) šelem* is customarily rendered "peace offering" (so RSV, KJV), but perhaps the best translation is "sacrifice of communion," since the apparent purpose of such offerings was communion between God and the worshipper in the ceremonial meal (Lev. 7:15-18; 19:5-8) that was the focus of these offerings. The animals sacrificed could be female or male and were to be, like all sacrificial animals, without blemish (3:1, 6). The blood was thrown against and around the altar (vv. 2, 8, 13). Certain organs of peace offerings, as with all sacrificial animals, were burned on the altar (vv. 3-5, 9-11, 14-16). The right thigh and the breast went to the priests for their consumption (Exod. 29:27-28; Lev. 7:31-36). Grain and oil offerings accompanied peace offerings (vv. 12-14; Num. 15:8-10).

Peace offerings were offered both from devotion free from any particular obligation and in fulfillment of vows made in time of trouble (Lev. 7:16; 22:21). They were also offered during the consecration of priests (9:4, 18, 22), on feast days (23:19), on completion of Nazirite vows (Num. 6:14, 17), and on other occasions that called for particular thanks or attention to God (7:88; Josh. 8:31; Judg. 20:26; 21:4; 1 Sam. 11:15; 1 Kgs. 8:63-64; Ezek. 43:27). The thank, freewill, and votive offerings apparently were categories of peace offering (Lev. 7:11-18; cf. Ps. 54:6-7 [MT 8-9]).

PEACOCK (Heb. pl. *tukkîyîm, tûkkîyîm*). *Pavo cristatus*, a large member of the pheasant family native to the jungle and mountain areas of India and Ceylon. The female is nondescript, but the male is strikingly beautiful with blue and green feathers and a crest and long tail distinguished by eyelike iridescent spots.

Though the meat of the peacock is edible and its brains and tongue were considered a delicacy among the Romans, in Israel this bird could certainly never have been more than ornamental. Actually, scholars question whether Solomon's fleet actually imported peacocks into Jerusalem (1 Kgs. 10:22; 2 Chr. 9:21); some translations render Heb. *tukkîyîm* (cf. Tamil *tokei* "peacock") as "baboons" (so RSV mg., JB, NIV; cf. Egyp. *ky* "baboon").

For Job 39:13, KJV, *see* OSTRICH.

PEARL (Heb. pl. *pᵉnînîm*; Gk. *margarítēs*). A smooth, lustrous deposit formed around a grain of sand or similar irritating foreign material in the shells of certain mollusks. In biblical times pearls were worn for adornment by affluent women (1 Tim. 2:9; Rev. 17:4; 18:16) and were important items of trade (v. 12). They are compared to wisdom and found to be of less value (Job 28:18b; KJV "ruby"; cf. Matt. 7:6; 13:45-46). Pearls have a part in the portrayal of the great beauty and preciousness of the new Jerusalem (Rev. 21:21).

For Job 28:18a, KJV, *see* CRYSTAL.

PEASANTRY (Heb. *pᵉrāzôn*).* In the anthropological sense, a class of rural cultivators whose surpluses are exploited by the dominant class(es). Characterized as autonomous/independent and traditional/conservative, they embody the transition and contradiction between two opposing types of social formation: "feudalism" and the nation-state.

Largely because they are the product of the scribal class as a subsidiary of the royal court, ancient sources, including the Bible, lack adequate documentation of the peasantry. Heb. *pᵉrāzôn* at Judg. 5:7, 11 (RSV "peasantry") probably represents the inhabitants of unfortified villages (Esth. 9:19; cf. Deut. 3:5; 1 Sam. 6:18; RSV "unwalled cities") in the open country (*pᵉrāâ*; Ezek. 38:11; RSV "land of unwalled villages") surrounding walled cities; in time of warfare these people were permitted refuge within the walls and in exchange might be called upon to serve as warriors (cf. Hab. 3:14; *przw*; LXX Gk. *dynatoí*).

A peasant revolt model explains the Israelite conquest of Canaan as a massive uprising of such peoples (generally associated with the ʿApiru movements) against the oppressive Canaanite overlords, precipitated by the influx of a "mixed multitude" (Exod. 12:38; cf. Num. 11:4; Heb. *ʾᵃsapsup*; RSV "rabble") that had escaped bondage in Egypt. *See* CONQUEST; HABIRU (ʿAPIRU).

Bibliography. R. A. Horsley and J. S. Hanson, *Bandits, Prophets, and Messiahs: Popular Movements at the Time of Jesus* (Minneapolis: 1985); E. R. Wolf, *Peasants* (Englewood Cliffs: 1966).

PEDAHEL [pĕdʹə hĕl] (Heb. *pᵉdahʾēl* "God has delivered"). A leader of the tribe of Naphtali who helped Moses divide the land of Canaan (Num. 34:28).

PEDAHZUR [pə däʹzər] (Heb. *pᵉdâṣûr* "the Rock [God] has delivered"). The father of Gamaliel (1), who led Manasseh in the wilderness journeys (Num. 1:10; 2:20; 7:54, 59; 10:23).

PEDAIAH [pə däʹyə] (Heb. *pᵉdāyâ*, *pᵉdāyāhû* "Yahweh has delivered").

1. (Heb. *pᵉdāyâ*). The maternal grandfather of King Jehoiakim of Judah (2 Kgs. 23:36).

2. One of the sons of Jeconiah (1 Chr. 3:18), called the father of Zerubbabel (v. 19; but cf. Neh. 12:1; Hag. 1:1).

3. (Heb. *pᵉdāyāhû*). The father of Joel, leader of the half-tribe of Manasseh during the days of David (1 Chr. 27:20).

4. (Heb. *pᵉdāyâ*). The son of Parosh who assisted in the postexilic repair of the walls of Jerusalem (Neh. 3:25).

5. One of those standing on the platform with Ezra as he read the Book of the Law (Neh. 8:4).

6. An ancestor of Sallu, a postexilic Benjaminite living in Jerusalem (Neh. 11:7).

7. A Levite among those appointed by Nehemiah as temple treasurers (Neh. 13:13).

PEKAH [pēʹkə] (Heb. *peqaḥ* "opening"). The son of Remaliah; king of Israel *ca.* 737-732 B.C. As "captain" (or general) of the Israelite forces, Pekah led a coup against King Pekahiah, whom he killed and succeeded as king (2 Kgs. 15:25). His reign is said to have been twenty years (v. 27), but this apparently includes a period before the coup when as general he was de facto ruler of portions of Israel.

Pekah apparently reversed the policy of Menahem, Pekahiah's father, which was to pay tribute to Assyria (vv. 19-20), but still lost substantial territories to Assyria (v. 29). Together with King Rezin of Syria, Pekah unsuccessfully attempted to displace Ahaz from the throne of Judah (v. 37; 16:5; Isa. 7:1, 5-6; cf. 2 Chr. 28:6), apparently because of Ahaz' pro-Assyrian policy (2 Kgs. 16:7-9). Pekah was killed and succeeded by Hoshea (15:30).

PEKAHIAH [pĕkʹə hīʹə] (Heb. *pᵉqaḥyâ* "Yahweh has opened"). The son and successor of Menahem as king of Israel (*ca.* 738-737 B.C.; 2 Kgs. 15:23). Like many of the kings of Israel, Pekahiah is said to have perpetuated the sins of Jeroboam I (v. 24). Perhaps because he continued his father's pro-Assyrian policies, Pekahiah was assassinated in a coup led by his captain Pekah (v. 25).

PEKOD [pēʹkŏd] (Heb. *pᵉqôḏ*; Akk. *puqûdu*). An Aramean tribe inhabiting the plain east of the lower (southern) Tigris river. Recorded among the conquests of various Assyrian kings, Pekod is associated with Babylonia in the oracles of Jeremiah (Jer. 50:21; cf. RSV mg. "Punishment") and Ezekiel (Ezek. 23:23).

PELAIAH [pə lāʹyə] (Heb. *pᵉlāyâ* "Yahweh is wonderful").

1. A son of Elioenai, and descendant of David (1 Chr. 3:24).

2. A Levite who interpreted the Book of the Law for the people as Ezra read it (Neh. 8:7). He was among the participants in the sealing of the covenant under Nehemiah (10:10 [MT 11]).

PELALIAH [pĕlʹə līʹə] (Heb. *pᵉlalyâ* "Yahweh judges"). An ancestor of Adaiah, a priest during Nehemiah's time (Neh. 11:12).

PELATIAH [pĕlʹə tīʹə] (Heb. *pᵉlaṭyâ*, *pᵉlaṭyāhû* "Yahweh has delivered").

1. (Heb. *pelatyâ*). A postexilic descendant of David (1 Chr. 3:21).

2. A leader of the Simeonites who at the time of King Hezekiah drove the Amalekites from the region of Mt. Seir and settled in their territory (1 Chr. 4:42).

3. A chief of the people who participated in the sealing of the covenant under Nehemiah (Neh. 10:22 [MT 23]).

4. (Heb. *pelatyāhû*). The son of Benaiah, and one of the "princes of the people" condemned by Ezekiel (Ezek. 11:1). He died while Ezekiel was prophesying against him (v. 13).

PELEG [pē'lĕg] (Heb. *peleg* "canal, division"; Gk. *Phalek*). A son of Eber, and an ancestor of the Israelites (Gen. 10:25; 11:16-19; 1 Chr. 1:19-25; Luke 3:35; KJV "Phalec"). The etymological remark that "in his days the earth was divided" (Gen. 10:25; 1 Chr. 1:19) may refer to the dispersion of mankind following the building of the tower of Babel (Gen. 11:8-9), or perhaps to irrigation practices or a form of geographical or political organization associated with his descendants.

PELET [pē'lĕt] (Heb. *pelet* "rescue").

1. A Calebite, son of Jahdai (1 Chr. 2:47).

2. One of the two sons of the Benjaminite Azmaveth who joined David at Ziklag (1 Chr. 12:3).

PELETH [pē'lĕth] (Heb. *pelet* "swift").

1. A Reubenite, the father of On, who participated in Korah's rebellion (Num. 16:1). He may be the same as Pallu (26:5, 8-10).

2. One of the two sons of Jonathan, a descendant of Jerahmeel of the tribe of Judah (1 Chr. 2:33).

PELETHITES [pĕl'ə thīts] (Heb. *peletî*).* The designation of a military unit in Israel, presumably mercenaries, who comprised David's bodyguard (2 Sam. 8:18; 20:23; 1 Chr. 18:17). Always named with the Cherethites, the Pelethites remained loyal to David during Absalom's rebellion (2 Sam. 15:18), aided in the pursuit of Sheba (20:7), and supported the crowning of Solomon against Adonijah's attempted coup (1 Kgs. 1:38, 44). Although the Pelethites cannot be identified with certainty, they are thought to be a component of the Sea Peoples, and thus related to the Philistines (Heb. *pelištîm*), the name may here be slightly modified to resemble "Cherethites."

PELICAN (Heb. *qā'āt, qā'at*). Any of the large web-footed birds of genus *Pelecanus* that have pouches in their lower bills used in catching fish. The Hebrew term represents some unclean bird (Lev. 11:18; Deut. 14:17; NIV "desert owl") that is said to live in the desert (Ps. 102:6; RSV "vulture") or in ruined cities (Isa. 34:11; RSV "hawk"; Zeph. 2:14; KJV "cormorant"). As a fish-eating bird, the pelican would have been considered unclean, and its identification with the *qā'āt* is attested as early as the LXX. The wilderness home of the *qā'āt* does not rule out the pelican, even though it is a water bird, since pelicans are often seen far from water. Heb. *qā'āt* is thought to mean "vomiter" (from *qû'* "vomit"), deriving from

the pelican's supposed habit of feeding its young from food thrown up from its pouch.

PELLA [pĕl'ə] (Gk. *Pella*). A city in Transjordan, located 3 km. (2 mi.) east of the Jordan river at modern Tabaqat Faḥil, on Wâdî Jurm about 6.5 km. (4 mi.) north of Wâdî Yābis. First settled in prehistoric times, the city is mentioned in the Amarna Letters (Akk. *Piḥilum*) and records of the Egyptian pharaohs Thutmose III and Seti I (fifteenth-fourteenth centuries B.C.). Excavations indicate that it was occupied throughout the Bronze and Iron ages, coinciding with the Israelite conquest and monarchy. In the late fourth century Macedonian colonists settled there, renaming it Pella after the ancestral home of their kings. The city is believed to have been destroyed by Alexander Jannaeus in 83-82 B.C., but was rebuilt by Pompey and became one of the cities of the Decapolis. During the siege of Jerusalem by the Romans in A.D. 70 the Christians of Jerusalem reportedly escaped to Pella, which became an important Christian center in succeeding centuries.

PELONITE [pĕl'ə nīt] (Heb. *pelônî, pelōnî*). A gentilic designating Helez and Ahijah, two of David's mighty men (1 Chr. 11:27, 36; 27:10). The term probably arises from separate errors; Helez is called "the Paltite" at 2 Sam. 23:26, and Ahijah is called "Eliam the Gilonite" at v. 34.

PELUSIUM [pə lōō'shĭ əm] (Heb. *sîn*; Gk. *Pēlousion*). An Egyptian border fortress, the "stronghold of Egypt" (Ezek. 30:15-16; KJV "Sin"; Egyp. *Sîn*). Situated in the northeastern Nile delta at Tell el-Faramâ, the site was originally a center of viticulture. But because of its strategic location 1.5 km. (1 mi.) inland on the Way to the Land of the Philistines that passed through the northeastern frontier, Pelusium was given over to military purposes. The importance of this fortress is reflected in its mention in Ezekiel's prophecy against Egypt (vv. 1-26).

The LXX version of Ezekiel's prophecy substitutes the names of two other places. Gk. *Sain* in v. 15 may represent Sais, the capital of the Twenty-sixth Dynasty, which was in power at the time of Ezekiel; *Syēnē* (v. 16) was a southern border fortress at modern Aswan (cf. Aram. *seyān* "clay"; Gk. *pēlós* "clay").

PENIEL [pĕn'ĭ əl] (Heb. *penî'ēl* "face of God"). The place where Jacob wrestled with a divine being and "saw God face to face" and yet survived (Gen. 32:30 [MT 31]). Elsewhere the name occurs as PENUEL.

PENINNAH [pĭ nĭn'ə] (Heb. *peninnâ* "coral"). One of Elkanah's two wives; because she had borne children, she taunted Elkanah's other wife Hannah, who was barren (1 Sam. 1:2-6).

PENNY. In the RSV "penny" represents two Greek words, both specifying Roman bronze coins: the *kodrántēs* (Matt. 5:26; Mark 12:42; Lat. *quadrans*) represented a value of one sixty-fourth of a denarius, and the *assárion* (Matt. 10:29; Luke 12:6; Lat. *as*), one sixteenth of a denarius. In the KJV "penny" (and "pence") represents Gk. *dēnárion* "denarius" (e.g., Matt. 18:28; 20:2; Rev. 6:6). *See* MONEY.

PENTATEUCH [pĕn' tə tōōk].† The first five books of the Old Testament (Genesis, Exodus, Leviticus, Numbers, Deuteronomy), constituting the first and most important of the three divisions of the Hebrew canon.

I. Name

The name Pentateuch does not occur in the Bible. The MT refers to these books as the Torah (Heb. *tôrâ*, lit. "teaching" or "instruction"), in English commonly rendered "law," following the LXX (Gk. *nómos*). This designation appears in the Old Testament in such phrases as "the law of Moses" (e.g., 2 Kgs. 23:25), "the book of the law of Moses" (Josh. 8:31; 23:6; 2 Kgs. 14:6), "the book of the law" (2 Kgs. 22:8), "the law" (Josh. 8:34; 2 Chr. 25:4), and "the book of the law of the Lord" (2 Chr. 34:14); in the New Testament it generally is called "the law" (e.g., Matt. 5:17; Luke 16:17; Acts 7:53; 1 Cor. 9:8). Rabbinic sources, such as the Talmud and other writings as early as A.D. 160, use the expression "the five-fifths of the law," hence Gk. *hē pentateúchos bíblos* "the five-volumed book."

II. Unity

The division of the Pentateuch into five distinct books is evident as early as the Samaritan Pentateuch and the LXX. Scholars in general accept this division as a secondary development that resulted mainly from purely practical considerations, namely the limits of papyrus scrolls. However, along topical lines the books are separate entities. For example, several centuries intervene between the death of Joseph at the end of Genesis and the period of bondage in Egypt at the beginning of Exodus; some would also see here a transition from the history of the patriarchs to the history of the people of Israel in its formative stages. Exodus ends with the building of the tabernacle, and Leviticus consists primarily of prescripts for religious practices and for Israel's life as God's holy people. Numbers resumes the narrative of the wilderness wanderings, and Deuteronomy records three addresses by Moses.

On the basis of literary or source criticism and tradition history, several scholars during the past century or so have abandoned the traditional five-part Pentateuch in favor of various other combinations of writings, primarily a Hexateuch (six books, Genesis–Joshua) but also a Tetrateuch (four books, Genesis–Numbers), Heptateuch (seven books, Genesis–Judges), Octateuch (eight books, Genesis–Samuel), and Enneateuch (nine books, Genesis–Kings). Indeed, the Pentateuch as it now stands appears to form part of a larger "Primary History" encompassing the beginnings of Israel from primordial times through the fall of the southern kingdom; this larger work (Genesis–Kings) is viewed as paralleling (although with different emphases and time limits) the so-called Chronicler's History (Chronicles–Ezra–Nehemiah). Nevertheless, most scholars still favor the basic unity of the Pentateuch as a historical narrative describing the origins of Israel from creation through the death of Moses.

III. Composition

The limitations of current resources and methodologies make it impossible to ascertain the precise origins of the Pentateuch. With ample support from the biblical account, both Jewish and Christian tradition associate Moses with the formation of these books, although the Pentateuch itself nowhere asserts that he is the author of the entire division. This position is recorded first in the preexilic historical books (e.g., Josh. 8:30-35; 23:6; 2 Kgs. 14:6) and receives its fullest biblical support in the postexilic Chronicler's History (e.g., 2 Chr. 25:4; Ezra 6:18; Neh. 13:1), quite likely composed shortly after the Pentateuch reached canonical form.

That Moses himself is responsible for at least portions of the Pentateuch is reinforced by a number of references to his literary activity. At Exod. 17:14 Yahweh commands Moses to record "as a memorial in a book" the Israelites' victory over the Amalekites, apparently the basis of the account in vv. 8-16. Exod. 24:4 indicates that Moses "wrote all the words of the Lord" as contained in the Book of the Covenant (20:22–23:33). In addition he is depicted as having recorded the covenant renewal depicted at 34:10-27, kept a journal of the wilderness wanderings (Num. 33:2), and composed the song preserved at Deut. 32:1-43 (31:22; cf. the Song of the Sea, Exod. 15:1-18). He is known best as having written down the Ten Commandments (34:28) and various other laws or instruction (Deut. 31:9, 24). Moses' intimate connection with many of the significant events of the Pentateuch account suggests that he may have played a prominent role in transmitting much of the material included in the books (note the frequent literary formulas "as the Lord had commanded Moses," Exod. 39:1, 7, 21; "the Lord said to Moses," Lev. 4:1; Num. 1:1; "the Lord said to Moses and Aaron," Lev. 11:1; 13:1; Num. 2:1).

Since the late nineteenth century biblical scholars have been strongly influenced by the documentary hypothesis, an attempt to demonstrate the compilation of the Pentateuch from a variety of ancient sources through a long and complex process of editing and transmission. This approach stems from scholarly concern for various literary characteristics such as the use of divine names, differences in diction and style, doublets or duplicate narratives, discrepancies in facts or descriptions, and alleged incongruities in historical or geographical perspective. The classic position, largely associated with Julius Wellhausen, identifies four main sources that may be characterized by particular historical and cultural concerns; some scholars have identified various combinations and substrata of these primary strands. More recently scholars have modified the original theory, seeing the complexities of the "documents" as representing schools of tradition and acknowledging their development as parallel rather than consecutive. Moreover, the attempt to assign every verse or fragment to a particular source has been abandoned. Yet despite heated debate and constant objection by more conservative scholars, the basic insights of literary criticism and tradition history are generally recognized as significant to the quest for understanding the formation and growth of the Pentateuch.

See also BIBLICAL CRITICISM.

IV. Theology

The Pentateuch sets forth the most basic components of Israel's faith, recording the very beginnings of the process of redemptive history. Among the significant theological concepts introduced are God's promise of land and posterity (Gen. 12:1-3; 15:18-21; Deut. 1:11; 6:23); election, God's choosing Israel as his "own possession among all peoples" (Exod. 19:5; Deut. 7:6; 14:2; 26:18); deliverance, demonstrated dramatically in the Exodus events (Exod. 14–15); and the covenant that bound Israel to God and the stipulations of the law that accompanied it (Exod. 19:1–Num. 10:10; Deut. 5–6; 10:12–11:32).

Bibliography. O. T. Allis, *The Five Books of Moses*, 2nd ed. (Philadelphia: 1949); D. N. Freedman, "Pentateuch," *IDB* 3:711-727; G. H. Livingston, *The Pentateuch in Its Cultural Environment* (Grand Rapids: 1974); G. E. Wright, *The Old Testament Against Its Environment*. SBT 2 (1950); J. A. Sanders, *Torah and Canon* (Philadelphia: 1972); D. J. A. Clines, *The Theme of the Pentateuch*. JSOTS 10 (1978).

PENTATEUCH, SAMARITAN. *See* SAMARITAN PENTATEUCH.

PENTECOST [pĕn'tə kôst] (Gk. *pentēkostē* "fiftieth [day]").† The Old Testament and Jewish Feast of Weeks (Lev. 23:15-21) is referred to under its Greek name three times in the New Testament, twice simply as an indication of date (Acts 20:16; 1 Cor. 16:8). These and other texts (cf. Acts 18:21 [the Western text]; 20:6; 27:9) show that Paul thought of the year and seasons according to the Jewish calendar.

At 2:1 "Pentecost" is again an indication of date, and also a means of accounting for the large crowd gathered from far away places in Jerusalem that witnessed the events associated with the coming of the Spirit on the Church (vv. 5-11). The Jewish Feast of Pentecost came to be a commemoration and celebration of the giving of the law at Sinai, but this change in the understanding of the Feast does not appear to be reflected in the record in Acts of the Church's Pentecost experience and, at any rate, probably arose only in the second to fourth centuries A.D.

Two factors involved in the interpretation of the Pentecost event of Acts 2 are Jesus' promise of the giving of the Holy Spirit (Luke 11:12; Acts 1:8) and the prophetic view of the future age of the Spirit and of salvation (represented by the quotation of Joel 2:28-32 [MT 3:1-5] at Acts 2:17-21). Another important factor that shapes the report of this event is the understanding of it as the initiation of the Church's worldwide preaching of the gospel. The report includes, therefore, the first post-Easter gospel sermon (vv. 22-36, 38-40), a report of the resultant great augmentation of the original community (v. 41), the establishment of the community in a pattern of liturgy, teaching, sharing of goods, miracles, and numerical

growth (vv. 41-47), and a prefiguration of the worldwide aspect of the spread of the gospel (vv. 5-11). The miracle of "other tongues" (v. 4) is of significance with regard to the last of these—whatever the nature of the speaking, the miracle was mainly one of hearing (vv. 8, 11).

See WEEKS, FEAST OF.

PENUEL [pə n̄oo'əl] (Heb. *pᵉnûʾēl* "face of God'') **(PERSON).**
1. A son of Hur, and grandson of the patriarch Judah (1 Chr. 4:4).
2. A son of Shashak of the tribe of Benjamin (1 Chr. 8:25).

PENUEL [pə n̄oo'əl] (Heb. *pᵉnûʾēl* "face of God'') **(PLACE).** A town in Transjordan, located at the eastern mound of modern Tulûl edh-Dhahab on the Jabbok river (modern Nahr ez-Zerqâ) east of Succoth. Here Jacob wrestled with God (Gen. 32:30-31 [MT 31-32], "Peniel"). Gideon demolished the tower at Penuel and killed all the soldiers of the town because the inhabitants refused to help him pursue the Midianites (Judg. 8:8-9, 17). Penuel was one of the towns fortified by Jeroboam I at the beginning of his reign (1 Kgs. 12:25).

PEOPLE OF THE LAND (Heb. *ʿam hāʾāreṣ*).* Although seemingly a designation for the general population of a given area, more likely a technical term indicating the responsible (male) citizens. Some scholars suggest that the term specifies a lower social class, perhaps a peasant level, but such an interpretation does not appear defensible in Jeremiah and Ezekiel (Jer. 1:18; 37:2; 44:21; Ezek. 7:27; 22:29), particularly at Jer. 34:19 where the people of the land owned slaves. Others suggest that they were representatives of the people as a political body at the time of the monarchy (cf. 2 Kgs. 11:18-20). The view that they were landowners ("freemen") who possessed civic responsibilities in a certain territory best fits the biblical evidence.

The meaning of the expression varies somewhat in the biblical record, depending upon who is addressed as the primary resident of the territory. Thus the people of the land may be Hittites (Gen. 23:12-13), Egyptians (42:6), Canaanites (Num. 14:9), Israelites (Lev. 4:27; so KJV mg., following MT; RSV "common people"; NIV "member of the community"), or non-Israelite inhabitants of Palestine (cf. Ezra 10:2, 11); each such group represents the primary residents in that context from the perspective of the author or protagonist. The term occurs most often in 2 Kings, Jeremiah, and Ezekiel, in which it clearly refers to the Israelites. After the return from captivity it refers to those who had not been exiled and had remained in Palestine (e.g., Ezra 4:4; "peoples of the land," 3:3; 10:2, 11; Neh. 9:30; 10:29, 31-32 [MT 30, 32-33]; cf. 9:1-2, 11, "peoples of the lands"). From the perspective of the returnees, those who had remained were the people of the land, even though they were "foreigners" (cf. Ezra 10:11).

Only in the rabbinical period, which coincided with the public ministry of Jesus and the early years of the

Church, did the term carry a negative connotation, referring to those who were ignorant of the law or who chose not to practice the commandments (cf. John 7:49).

PEOR [pē′ôr] (Heb. *pᵉʿôr* "opening").† A mountain peak (Num. 23:28) in Moab, also called Baal-peor (Deut. 4:3; Hos. 9:10), where a local manifestation of the deity Baal, known as "Baal of Peor" (KJV "Baal-peor"), was worshipped. Eusebius places Peor 9 km. (5.5 mi.) west of Heshbon (*Onom.* xlviii.4), but the specific location is uncertain. *See* BETH-PEOR.

According to 25:3, 5, 18; 31:16, a number of Israelites strayed into worship of this Baal. The incident was a serious threat to the Israelites on the eve of their entry into Canaan and thus became a significant memory of their early history (Deut. 4:3; Josh. 22:17; Ps. 106:28-31; Hos. 9:10). A key factor in the incident was enticement of the Israelite men by Midianite women (thought by some scholars to be cultic prostitutes; Num. 25:1-2; cf. 31:15-16); but behind the beginnings of the incident were the efforts of Balaam (v. 16), who had just before been unable to place a curse on the Israelites (chs. 22–24). A plague broke out in the Israelite encampment as a divinely sent result of the apostasy (25:8-9; 31:16). The response by Moses and other leaders was to execute quickly those men who had been involved (25:4-5); the slaying by the priest Phinehas of such a man and a Midianite woman he had brought into the Israelite camp is recorded as a particularly dramatic instance of this response (vv. 6-15). The Israelites' strong enmity toward the Midianites was regarded as a result of the Peor incident (vv. 17-18).

PERAZIM [pə rā′zĭm], **MOUNT** (Heb. *har-pᵉrā-ṣîm*). A mountain named in Isaiah's oracle against the leaders of Jerusalem (Isa. 28:21). *See* BAAL-PERAZIM.

PEREA [pə rē′ə] (Gk. *Peraia*). A Transjordanian territory paralleling the Jordan river and the Dead Sea from Machaerus and the Arnon river in the south to the Decapolis cities of Philadelphia (biblical Rabbath-ammon, modern ʿAmmân) and Gerasa (and just south of Pella) in the east and north (Josephus *BJ* iii.3.3 [46]). Perea was included in the kingdom of Herod the Great (37-4 B.C.) and, together with Galilee, from which it was separated by part of the Decapolis region, it constituted the territory ruled by the tetrarch Herod Antipas (4 B.C.-A.D. 39).

The name Perea does not appear in the New Testament, where the region is called "beyond the Jordan" (Matt. 4:25; Mark 3:8). The common route of Jews from Galilee to Judea was through Perea (cf. 10:1) rather than through Samaria (cf. John 4:4).

PERESH [pĕr′ĕsh] (Heb. *pereš*). A Manassite, son of Machir and Maacah (1 Chr. 7:16).

PEREZ [pĕr′ĕz] (Heb. *pereṣ* "breach"; Gk. *Phares*). A son of Judah and Tamar, the twin brother of Zerah, and an ancestor of David and Jesus (Gen. 38:30; 46:12; KJV "Pharez"; Matt. 1:3; Luke 3:33; KJV "Phares"). He was the eponymous ancestor of the Perezites (Num. 26:20; KJV "Pharzites").

PEREZ-UZZA [pĕr′ĕz ŭz′ə] (Heb. *pereṣ ʿuzzāʾ*, *pereṣ ʿuzzâ* "breach of Uzzah"). The name given to the place where Uzzah was killed by Yahweh after having taken hold of the ark of the covenant to keep it from falling as it was transported to Jerusalem (2 Sam. 6:8; 1 Chr. 13:11). Located somewhere west of Jerusalem, it is presumably to be identified with the threshing floor of Nacon/Chidon.

PERFECTION (Heb. *tām, kālîl, šālēm*; Gk. *téleios*).† The various Hebrew and Greek terms for moral and cultic perfection connote a state or condition consisting not only in the absence of blemishes, but also in completeness appropriate to function. Such language is used of sacrificial animals (Lev. 22:21), persons (KJV, Gen. 6:9; Job 1:1; RSV "blameless"), the law (Ps. 19:7 [MT 8]; Jas. 1:25), hatred (Ps. 139:22), physical beauty (Ezek. 16:14), cities (28:12), and weights (KJV, Deut. 25:15; RSV "full").

Christ is characterized as perfect in that he was innocent of specific accusations made against him (John 8:46; 9:24), ultimately of the charges that led to his execution (Luke 23:47; 1 Pet. 2:22). Moreover, since he was the ultimate sacrifice for sin, the cultic perfection required of sacrificial animals could be a metaphor for his sinless acceptability before God (2 Cor. 5:21; Heb. 9:14; 1 Pet. 1:19). Finally, he was morally perfect (Heb. 4:15; cf. Matt. 3:14; 119:17).

An important basis of biblical ethics is the perfection of God that is to be reflected in the perfection of his people (5:48; cf. Lev. 19:2; Deut. 18:13). This perfection to be sought by God's people is not an abstract quality, but is connected with specific needs, such as the need to imitate God in having love for all (Matt. 5:48), not just specific classes of people (cf. vv. 43-47; Luke 6:36; 1 John 4:18), and the need to go beyond the specific requirements of the law to a life fully given to being a disciple of Jesus (Matt. 19:21).

The Church has experienced controversy regarding the possibility of sinless perfection of Christians. In the early Church this controversy was focused on the possibility of repentance after postbaptismal sin, and more recently it has been focused on the possibility of a sanctification that takes the believer beyond the experience of conscious sin. The ambiguity of the New Testament on such issues has itself given rise to these controversies. Some texts speak of perfection, not in the sense of the absence of all sin, but in more specific senses, e.g., of a positive readiness for whatever task is at hand for the Christian (KJV, Eph. 4:13; Col. 1:28; 4:12; RSV "mature"; 2 Tim. 3:17; RSV "complete"; Jas. 1:4), an ability to receive teaching concerning God's purposes (KJV, 1 Cor. 2:6; Heb. 5:14; RSV "mature"), an ability to make mature judgments concerning specific issues in the Church (KJV, Phil. 3:15; RSV "mature"; cf. 1 Cor. 14:20; KJV mg. "perfect," "of a ripe age"), and self-control in speaking (Jas. 3:2).

Paul assumes that the experience and knowledge of Christians are not perfect, that "the perfect" is yet to come (1 Cor. 13:9-10; cf. Phil. 3:12). 1 John, on the other hand, is willing to speak of a perfected Christian experience (1 John 2:5; 3:9; 4:12, 17; 5:18), but not without qualification (1:8-10; 5:16). Hebrews also appears to imply a perfected Christian experience, mainly because of its insistence on the once-for-all efficacy of Christ's sacrifice (Heb. 9:26; 10:14-18, 26-29).

PERFUME (Heb. *rōqēaḥ, rāqaḥ, qᵉṭōreṭ, bōśem*).†
In biblical times perfumes derived from a number of plants were used in the manufacture of cultic incense (Exod. 30:34-38; Heb. *rōqēaḥ*; cf. Isa. 57:9; *riqqûaḥ*), to adorn one's body (Prov. 27:9; *qᵉṭōreṭ*; Isa. 3:24; *bōśem*), and to sweeten rooms (Prov. 7:17; *nûp*). The pleasing effect of perfume is proverbial (27:9), and occurs in erotic imagery (e.g., Cant. 3:6; *mᵉquṭṭereṭ*). The blending of perfumes required the skill of a professional (Exod. 30:35; 37:29; Eccl. 10:1; cf. 1 Sam. 8:13; Neh. 3:8; *rāqaḥ*).

At Isa. 3:20 Heb. *bātê hannepeš*, lit. "houses of the soul," is often taken as "perfume boxes" (so RSV) or "perfume bottles," but other interpretations are possible, including "lockets" (NEB).

See also INCENSE; SPICES.

PERGA [pûrʹ gə] (Gk. *Pergē*). An important city in Pamphylia (southern Asia Minor) near the modern village of Murtana, east-northeast of the seaport of Antalya (biblical Attalia) about 12 km. (8 mi.) from the coast and 8 km. (5 mi.) west of the Cestrus river. Perga was located on the main trade route of Pamphylia paralleling the coast; the nearby Cestrus provided a passage for travel inland through the mountains. The city was safe from the occasional coastal raids of pirates and was known for its large shrine to Artemis

The theater at Perga (B. K. Condit)

Pergaia. The Romans rebuilt Perga with baths, a theater, and a stadium with a capacity for 12,000 spectators.

Paul's first missionary journey brought him from Cyprus by sea to Perga (Acts 13:13). He and his companions may have arrived at the port of Attalia and traveled overland to Perga, or they may have disembarked at the mouth of the Cestrus and transferred to a riverboat to go to Perga. At Perga John Mark left Paul and Barnabas and returned to Jerusalem; Paul and Barnabas continued inland (v. 14). Paul "spoke the word" in Perga as he returned from establishing churches in Pisidian Antioch, Iconium, Lystra, and Derbe (14:24-25), but probably established no lasting Christian community there. The city was an important Christian center in later centuries.

PERGAMUM [pûrʹgə məm] (Gk. *Pergamon* "fortress," *Pergamos*). A city in western Asia Minor, modern Bergama, Turkey, about 26 km. (16 mi.) from the Aegean coast near the island of Lesbos. Located in the southern part of the ancient district of Mysia, Pergamum was one of the most important cities of Asia Minor. Archaeological evidence can be dated as early as the Bronze Age. The peak of Pergamum's glory came during the Hellenistic period when it became an independent kingdom under the Attalid dynasty (282-133 B.C.). Great wealth was accumulated and buildings of world renown were constructed during this period. The library was the second largest in the world; from the extensive local use of goatskin sheets in place of papyrus came the term *pergamēnē* "parchment." "Bequeathed" to the Romans by Attalus III, Pergamum became the capital of the province of Asia. Signs of its splendor included a theater, Asclepium (healing center), gymnasium, and several famous temples including those of Augustus, Athena, Polias, and most notably the splendid temple of Zeus Soter. The construction of the city on mountain terraces, surrounded by natural theaters with spectacular views of the valley below, made Pergamum one of the most beautiful places in Asia Minor.

According to the Revelation of John, the city posed many difficulties to the Christians living there (Rev. 2:12-17; KJV "Pergamos"). "Satan's throne" (v. 13) is probably a reference to the imperial cult, which had an important center in Pergamum. Antipas, a member of the congregation, had already been martyred (v. 13), and the false teachings of the Nicolaitans and others were a problem in this church (vv. 14-16).

PERIDA [pə rīʹdə] (Heb. *pᵉrîdāʾ*). The head of a family or guild of Solomon's servants who returned from exile with Zerubbabel (Neh. 7:57). In the parallel account (Ezra 2:55) the name occurs as Peruda.

PERIZZITES [pĕrʹə zīts] (Heb. *pᵉrizzî* "villagers"). One of the earliest groups of inhabitants of Canaan, apparently long-established in Abraham's day (Gen. 13:7; 15:20; cf. 34:30). When the Israelites entered Canaan, the Perizzites were living in the hill country in parts of the territories that came to be assigned to Ephraim, Manasseh, and Judah (Josh. 11:3; 17:15; Judg. 1:4-5). Later generations of Perizzites intermarried with Israelites (3:5-6). During Solomon's reign the surviving nonassimilated Perizzites were forced into slavery (1 Kgs. 9:20-21 par. 2 Chr. 8:7-8). Some still survived in the postexilic period (Ezra 9:1).

Attempts to identify the Perizzites with the Hurrians or Amorites remain inconclusive. If not an ethnic term, at some point the name may be related to Heb. *p⁰rā-zôn* "peasantry" (*see* PEASANTRY). These people may also have been part of the larger Amorite (generically "westerner") movements at the beginning of the Middle Bronze Age.

PERSECUTION (Gk. *diṓkō*). The use of forcible means to inhibit the spread or practice of a religious faith. In the Old Testament, Haman is the premier persecutor of Jews, as his ill feelings toward Mordecai prompt him to plot the destruction of all Jews (Esth. 3:6).

A different approach was taken by the Syrian king Antiochus IV Epiphanes (175-164 B.C.) who determined to end Jewish resistance to his rule and to force the spread of Hellenistic culture by proscribing all practice of Jewish rites, forcing Jews to eat unclean swine's flesh, and defiling the Jerusalem temple in 167 B.C. by sacrificing a pig upon the altar. His rule was terrible, but brief; within three years the successful revolt led by the Maccabees enabled the Jews to renew worship in a repurified temple. The Jewish martyrs of this period (e.g., 2 Macc. 6–7) became paradigmatic for Jewish and Christian response to persecution in succeeding centuries.

Jews had a generally secure position in the early decades of the Roman Empire, but conflict with the Greeks of Alexandria had long been brewing and was ignited by specific incidents. The city saw anti-Jewish riots in A.D. 37-38 during the reign of Caligula. Troubles in Judea, exacerbated by insensitive Roman governors, led to the Jewish revolt of 66-70, which ended in the destruction of Jerusalem and the temple and was the occasion for pogroms in Syria and Alexandria. The revolt of 132-135 led by Simon bar Kokhba, whom many Jews regarded as the Messiah, also brought disaster, as the Jews' defeat by the Romans under Hadrian resulted in the loss of Jerusalem and the suppression of Judaism in Palestine.

Persecution of Christians is a frequent theme in the New Testament. It is predicted in the Gospels (Matt. 5:10-12; 24:9-14; Luke 21:12-19; John 16:2), and is a recurrent theme in Acts (Acts 4:17-18; 5:17-42; 7:54–8:3; 12:1-5) and the letters of Paul (e.g., 2 Cor. 11:23-26; 1 Thess. 2:14-16; cf. 2 Tim. 3:11-12). It appears to be part of the occasion of the writing of Hebrews (Heb. 12:1-11) and 1 Peter (1 Pet. 1:6-7; 4:12-16; 5:9-10).

In Revelation persecution seems more a part of the crisis that is predicted than the present experience of the original readers (Rev. 2:10; 6:9-11; 13:7, 15-17; 17:6). One martyrdom is mentioned, but it appears to have been an unusual event that occurred sometime in the past (2:13). Revelation may well have been written when Domitian was emperor (A.D. 81-96), and there is little evidence of a general persecution of Christians during his reign.

From Nero's killing of Christians in Rome in A.D. 64 until 250, persecution of Christians was mostly local, including the persecutions of Hadrian (117-138) and Marcus Aurelius (176-180). The correspondence between Pliny the Younger and the Roman emperor Trajan (111-112) shows that although Christianity was illegal, the law was not routinely enforced. After 250 the persecutions were empire-wide, with the objective of ridding the domain of all Christians; included were persecutions under Decius (250), Gallus (251-253), Valerian (257-260), and the extended persecution begun by Diocletian in 303. The accession of Constantine to a share of the throne in 306 (sole emperor in 323) marked the beginning of a new experience of toleration and even power for Christians in the Roman world.

PERSEPOLIS [pər sĕp'ə lĭs] (Gk. *Persepolis* "city of Parsa"; O.Pers. *Pārsa*).† Ceremonial capital of the Persian Achaemenids from Darius I the Great, who founded it *ca.* 520 B.C., to Darius III Codomannus, who died fleeing Alexander the Great, ending the dynasty in 330. It was here that the king received dignitaries and celebrated the New Year festival. (The Persian administrative capitals were Susa in winter and Ecbatana in summer, with additional royal residences at Babylon.) The site is modern Takht-i-Jamshīd ("throne of Jamshīd"), on the plain of Marvdasht 50 km. (31 mi.) northeast of Shiraz.

The ruins of Persepolis occupy a large platform, 452 m. (1485 ft.) by 352 m. (1155 ft.) and 12 m. (40 ft.) at the highest point, built of limestone quarried from adjoining mountains and reached by an enormous stairway. Among the colossal remains are the Apadana, Darius the Great's audience hall; another hall, Sad-sutun ("hundred columns"); royal palaces; and the harem. In the Treasury building were discovered several thousand tablets, primarily Elamite, detailing aspects of the extensive royal building program at Persepolis.

In 330 Alexander the Great burned and looted the city, which deteriorated further under Seleucid and Parthian rule. According to 2 Macc. 9:2, Antiochus IV Epiphanes sought to rob the temple at Persepolis but was evicted by the irate populace. Some authorities dispute the historicity of this account, which implies the previous rebuilding of the city and is suspiciously parallel to Antiochus' behavior in Jerusalem; Gk. *persépolin* may also be a common noun, "(a) Persian city" (cf. O.Pers. *Pārsa* "Persis," modern Fārs).

PERSEUS [pûr'sĭ əs] (Gk. *Perseus*).† The last king of Macedonia, successor of Philip V (*ca.* 212-162 B.C.). His perceived aggression precipitated in 171 the Third Macedonian War with Rome. After the battle of Pydna in Thessaly (168), Perseus was removed from power and his kingdom became a Roman province (1 Macc. 8:5; RSV mg. "king of Kittim").

PERSIA [pûr'zhə] (Heb. *pāras*; Gk. *Persis*; O.Pers. *Pārsa*; Akk. *Parsu*).† The largest empire of the ancient Near East, which, at the height of its power, spanned from the borders of India in the east to Ionia in the west. The people themselves called the empire Aryana, from a term in the Zoroastrian scriptures derived from Sanskrit *arya* "noble" (cf. "Iran," "Aryan").

I. Geography

The area in which Persia was established is a plateau

of some 777,000 sq. km. (300,000 sq. mi.), consisting of a series of high valleys and dry basins, approximately 900-2500 m. (3000-8000 ft.) above sea level. The plateau is ringed by a variety of mountain ranges (the Kurdistan and Zagros on the west, the Elburz on the north, and the Hindu Kush to the east). To the south, along the Persian Gulf and Gulf of Oman, lie inhospitable plains. Two vast, salt-caked deserts, the Dasht-i-Kavir and Dasht-i-Lut, occupy most of central eastern Persia.

Rainfall is meager, except in the north, averaging 20 cm. (8 in.) or less in the eastern portion of the plateau and 38 cm. (15 in.) in the western portion. Accordingly, large-scale farming demanded the use of irrigation technology; wheat and barley were cultivated, and sheeps and goats were first raised during the Neolithic period (*ca.* 9000 B.C.). Temperatures range from -18°C. (0°F.) to 20-32°C. (70-90°F.) in the central plateau and as high as 50°C. (120°F.) along the Persian Gulf coast. The climate is subtropical near the Caspian Sea to the north, where rain forests called *janqal* (cf. "jungle") grow.

II. History

A. Early Period. Archaeological evidence indicates that plants and animals were domesticated at several sites in the Zagros mountain region as early as 9000 B.C. ("the Neolithic Revolution") and that here were formed the earliest village civilizations relying on irrigation agriculture.

The kingdom of ELAM, which predated the formation of the Persian Empire, was located in southwestern Iran along the northern coast of the Persian Gulf. It supplied Sumer with such minerals as copper, tin, silver, lead, and alabaster. Precious gems, timber, and horses were also exported from Elam.

Toward the end of the second millennium ethnic groups from south and east of the Caspian Sea entered Elam. This wave of Aryan peoples included Cimmerians, Scythians, Medes, and Persians. By the ninth century the latter two groups had settled in northwest Iran, but they were hemmed in by the power of Urartu, Assyria, Elam, and Babylonia. An inscription of the Assyrian king Shalmaneser III (859-825) includes the first reference to Medes (Akk. *Madai*) and Persians (*Parsua*), whom he deported in large numbers in 837. These peoples also paid tribute to Tiglathpileser III (745-727) and Sargon II (721-705).

Attacks by the Assyrians and Urartians in the seventh century forced the MEDES to unite, founding a capital at Ecbatana (modern Hamadân). Their leader was one Deioces (or Dayakku), who was taken to Assyria in 715 and thence exiled to Hamath in Syria. His successor, Phraortes (Khshathrita), who ruled from 675-653, lost his life while conquering the Persians in the southwest. The Medians lived under Scythian rule for twenty-eight years, until Cyaxares (Uvakhshtra; 653-585) liberated them. Allied with the Babylonians and Scythians, Cyaxares participated in the siege and destruction of Nineveh. He then concluded a treaty with Babylon and married his granddaughter Amytis to Nabopolassar's son Nebuchadrezzar II (605-562); it was for Amytis that the famous "Hanging Gardens" of Babylon were built.

The Persians gradually settled east of Elam, led by a dynasty founded by Achaemenes (Hakhamanish) *ca.* 700. His successor Teispes added Anshan to Persian territory; his sons Ariaramnes (Ariyaramna; 640-590) and Cyrus I (Kurash; 640-600) annexed lands in the west. Cambyses I (Kanbujiya; 600-559) married Mandane, daughter of Astyages, who bore him Cyrus II. As with Moses, a legend about Cyrus depicts his birth and rescue by a shepherd after Astyages ordered the infant abandoned (Herodotus *Hist.* i.108-122). The

Persia: stairway and relief in the palace complex of Darius I (522-486 B.C.) at Persepolis (by courtesy of the Oriental Institute, University of Chicago)

Achaemenid dynasty was founded when Cyrus II successfully revolted against Astyages in 549.

B. *Persian Empire*. 1. Cyrus II (*ca.* 559-530). Babylonian preoccupation with westward expansion gave Cyrus time to add Assyria, Cilicia, Sardis, and the Ionian Greek cities to his realm. Newly acquired lands were organized into satrapies, initially approximately twenty administrative units headed by royal appointees from noble families. King Nabonidus' unpopular decision to remove the images of most of the deities of Babylon to the capital paved the way for Cyrus' conquest of Babylonia, and the Persian (aided by disgruntled Babylonians) entered the city on October 13, 539.

The Persian king was an autocrat. Edicts sealed with his ring had the force of law (Esth. 3:12; 8:8). Six prominent families called *vispati* held hereditary positions in the court; the commander of the "Immortals," the king's bodyguard, may have been the most distinguished such figure. Unfortunately, relatively little is known about the administration of the immense empire; although a large number of archival texts have been recovered, they concern primarily local matters.

In a stroke of diplomatic genius Cyrus returned the images to their temples and decreed that all subject peoples of the Babylonians return to their own homelands (2 Chr. 36:23; Ezra 1:1-4). The joy with which the deportees from Judah greeted this news (cf. Isa. 44:28; 45:1, 13) was undoubtedly expressed by other peoples as well. Persian rulers were careful to be crowned king of conquered lands in accordance with local customs and traditions; the Babylonian "Cyrus cylinder" depicts Cyrus as chosen by the god Marduk to topple Nabonidus, and praises him for not looting the temples in Babylon (*ANET*, pp. 15-16). Cyrus died in battle against the Massagetae on the northeastern frontier in 530.

2. Cambyses II (529-522). Cambyses, Cyrus' eldest son, was quick to continue the expansion of the empire. Egypt, Cyprus, and the Greek islands fell in quick succession, but the Persians were stopped at Nubia. At this juncture the throne was seized by Gaumata ("Pseudo-Smerdis"), a member of the *magi* who masqueraded as Cambyses' younger brother Bardya (killed by Cambyses in 526). Revolts broke out in Media, Armenia, and Babylonia. Gaumata hastened to consolidate his position by offering exemptions from military service and tax exemptions, but his rule lasted only six months. Cambyses died under mysterious circumstances, perhaps by suicide, as he returned to Babylon.

3. Darius I (Daryavaush; 522-486). Darius, son of Hystaspes (Vishtaspa), and satrap of Parthia and Hyrcania, took Gaumata prisoner and executed him at Ecbatana in 522. Consequently, he was proclaimed king. It took Darius two years to put down the revolts around the empire, but by 518 satrapies as distant as Ionia and Egypt acknowledged Darius' rule. Persian troops campaigned as far west as the Danube river, but they were defeated by Greek forces at Marathon in 490. A huge bas-relief on a high cliff at Behistun (modern Bisitun) on the Ecbatana-Babylon trade route commemorates Darius' victory. It depicts Darius, under the protection of the god Ahura-mazda, trampling Gaumata, with nine rebel leaders in attendance. The inscription in Old Persian, Akkadian, and Elamite proved invaluable in deciphering these ancient languages. Subsequently peace prevailed throughout the empire until the first Ionian revolt (500-494), which ended with the destruction of Miletus.

It was during Darius' reign that reconstruction of the temple in Jerusalem finally was undertaken by the exiles who had returned to Judah. Zerubbabel "prince of Judah" was in charge, and the prophets Haggai and Zechariah encouraged the people in their work. When the construction aroused the suspicion of satrap Tattenai and others, a letter was sent to Darius requesting confirmation of the Jews' assertion that Cyrus had given permission to rebuild the temple (Ezra 5). The search turned up a copy of Cyrus' decree, and Darius commanded that the work continue (ch. 6).

Darius was an able administrator who reorganized the empire into twenty-two satrapies, with delegates from the central government (the "eyes" and "ears" of the king) checking up on the satraps. A good road network, a royal mail service, and the use of Aramaic as the language of government (replacing Elamite, which had long served in this capacity) served to promote efficiency. Darius set up a uniform tax system and introduced uniform weights and measures. In 517 he unified the monetary system by introducing the gold daric (weighing 8.4 gm. [.3 oz.]) and silver shekel (5.6 gm. [.2 oz.], worth 1/20th of a daric).

Trade flourished, banking houses were established, and Darius had a canal dug linking the Nile river and Red Sea. Greek scientists, artists, and physicians were employed in the Persian court. An opulent new palace was built at Susa in 521, and work was started on the new capital at Persepolis (Pārsa) in 518. Darius constructed the so-called "royal" section of Persepolis, a large artificial terrace rising 12 m. (40 ft.) above the plain. The principal access to the platform was via a gradual stairway that could be ascended on horseback; official buildings and residential buildings shared the terrace.

Foreign ambassadors were received at Susa and Ecbatana, but apparently never at Persepolis. The royal court left Susa and journeyed to Persepolis to celebrate the New Year's festival (March 21), when the king received delegations from all parts of the empire.

When Darius died Persia was at the height of its territorial expansion and material wealth. Its borders ranged from the Indus and Jaxartes rivers in the east to Egypt and the Aegean in the west, and from the Persian Gulf in the south to the Caspian and Black seas in the north. All Persian kings after Darius were involved in maintaining the size and prestige the empire had achieved in his reign.

4. Xerxes I (485-465). Formerly viceroy of Babylon, Xerxes (called Ahasuerus in Ezra and Esther) ruled Egypt and Babylon with a heavy hand, and vigorously took up warring against the Greeks. In 480 a Persian army, accompanied by ships served by Phoenicians, Egyptians, Ionians, and Cypriots, moved against Greece. After a temporary delay at Thermopylae, the Persians took Thebes and Athens. However, the reverses suffered by the Persians at Salamis, Mi-

letus, Plataea, and Mycale forced Xerxes to relinquish control of all lands beyond Asia Minor. He was assassinated in 465 and succeeded by Artaxerxes I.

5. Artaxerxes I (465-425). During much of his early reign Artaxerxes was plagued by revolts in Egypt (460-454), encouraged by the Greeks. Other rebellions resulted in the loss of some eastern territories. Peace with Athens was restored by the treaty of Callias in 449.

Ca. 450 Rehum, the governor of Samaria, complained to Artaxerxes about repairs to the walls of Jerusalem (Ezra 4). This time a search of the royal archives yielded reports of Judean intrigue, and Artaxerxes put a halt to the restoration of Jerusalem; work did not resume until Nehemiah arrived from Susa in 455, and the city walls were not completed until 433.

6. Darius II (423-404). Darius ascended the throne as Greece was rent by the Peloponnesian War. Despite interference by his consort Parysatis, by siding with the Spartans he was able to recapture various Greek cities in Asia Minor.

In 419 the Egyptians, aided by the Persian governor Vidranga, destroyed the Yahu temple at Elephantine; a series of letters from the community of Jewish mercenaries to the Persian court details their efforts to receive permission to rebuild the temple.

7. Artaxerxes II Mnemon (404-359). A weak ruler, Artaxerxes II faced a revolt in Egypt that lasted for sixty years and involved the Egyptians in anti-Persian activities along with Sparta, Athens, and Cyprus. Artaxerxes made peace with the Greeks in 386, but his subsequent invasion of Egypt was blunted by the skillful defense of Pharaoh Nectanebo I.

8. Artaxerxes III Ochus (359-338). A brutal but ambitious ruler, Artaxerxes III mounted another expedition against Egypt. Nectanebo II repelled his forces in 351, and the Egyptians continued their tradition of stirring up unrest against Persia by supporting a revolt in Phoenicia. Artaxerxes finally succeeded in defeating the Egyptians in 343. He was murdered in 338 by Bagoas, his vizier and eunuch.

9. Darius III Codomannus (336-330). His troops defeated by Alexander the Great at Issus, Darius fled to Bactria, where he died, the last of the Achaemenid dynasty. Alexander captured Persepolis in February 330, and sent its treasures to Ecbatana.

C. Post-Achaemenid Persia. Alexander's death in 323 loosened Persia from Greek domination. The Seleucids retained control of the region but briefly. Parthians from eastern Iran established their capital at Ctesiphon (Casiphia) and under the Arsacid dynasty gradually took over the country. The Parthians revived trade in Iran, and served as intermediaries in commerce between the Mediterranean and Far East, which was centered at the mid-Euphrates city of Dura-Europus.

Roman absorption of Syria led to several unsuccessful attempts to extend Roman influence into Persia. In 40 B.C. the Parthians, who invaded the Roman province of Syria, were considered liberators by the Jews. They placed Antigonus, son of Aristobulus, on Jerusalem's throne (40-37), and gave military support to that city during Titus' siege. Jews and Parthians worked together against Rome during the reigns of Trajan and Hadrian.

The Parthians were succeeded by the Sassanians (A.D. 223-651), who annexed part of northwest India, northern Mesopotamia, and Armenia. In their battles with Rome they once captured the emperor Valerian (260). Like the Parthians, the Sassanians were able traders, linking the Near and Far East.

For the various rulers, see further the individual entries.

III. Religion

Initially, India and Persia shared a number of deities, as was common throughout the ancient Near East. At some point the god Ahura Mazdā was elevated to a supreme position. Other deities (*yazata*) included Mithra (lit. "agreement"; Indian *Mitra*; god of the contract and of war), Haoma (*Soma*; personification of an intoxicating drink), Anahita (goddess of rivers and fertility), and Tishtrya (bringer of rain).

In the sixth century the prophet ZARATHUSHTRA (perhaps "he who drives [or manages] camels") appeared on the scene. According to Zoroastrian tradition, he enjoyed the patronage of his convert, the local chief Vishtāspa. Zarathushtra's teachings, preserved in the Gāthās (the earliest portion of the Avesta), admonish persons to side with good against evil by exercising free choice. Other topics, such as the merits and benefits of animal husbandry and cattle breeding, are found in Zarathushtra's discourses.

While Zoroastrianism leans toward monotheism in the figure of Ahura Mazdā, it contains strong elements of dualism, as *aša* "truth" stands in opposition to *druj* "falsehood." How pervasive Zoroastrianism was in the Achaemenid dynasty is unclear, but Ahura Mazdā appears in many reliefs and inscriptions. *See* ZORO-ASTRIANISM.

Bibliography. G. G. Cameron, *History of Early Iran* (1936; repr. Chicago: 1976); A. T. Olmstead, *History of the Persian Empire* (Chicago: 1948).

PERSIS [pûr'sĭs] (Gk. *Persis* "Persian woman"). A Christian in Rome to whom Paul sends his greetings (Rom. 16:12). The name was a frequent appellative for Roman freedwomen and female slaves.

PERUDA [pə rōō'də] (Heb. *pᵉrûḏā'*). Alternate form of PERIDA (Ezra 2:55).

PESHITTA [pə shē'tə].† The most widely distributed and known Syriac translation of the Bible. The name means "the simple (version)" and refers to the plain, easily understood translation that lacks the technical textual notes and apparatus characterizing other, more scholarly versions.

Probably the work of Jewish Christians, the Peshitta translation of the Hebrew Bible existed already at the close of the second century A.D. During the fourth century all the books of the Hebrew Bible, including the Apocrypha, were incorporated into this translation. The Peshitta version of the New Testament, which dates from the final decades of the fourth century, is distinctive in that it does not contain 2 Peter, 2-3 John, Jude, or Revelation.

See SYRIAC VERSIONS.

PESTILENCE (Heb. *deḇer*; Gk. *loimós*). A fatal disease sent as punishment by God. It is mentioned with other typical forms of divine punishment, including the sword (e.g., Exod. 5:3; Lev. 26:25), famine (e.g., 2 Sam. 24:13; Jer. 34:17), and various other diseases (1 Kgs. 8:37; Hab. 3:5) and afflictions (e.g., Deut. 32:24; Ezek. 38:22; Amos 4:6-11). The usual combination is sword, famine, and pestilence, which suggests that *deḇer* most often represents diseases brought on by battle and siege conditions. The background of such lists of calamities includes, on the one hand, lists of curses attached as a form of guarantee to ancient Near Eastern contracts and treaties and, on the other hand, mythological concepts of deities accompanied by their destroying servants (cf. 2 Sam. 24:15-17; Hab. 3:5). Heb. *māweṯ* "death," where it is translated "pestilence" by RSV (Job 27:15; Jer. 15:2; 18:21; 43:11), is another term for fatal disease considered as a divine punishment. The two terms are reflected in New Testament uses of Gk. *loimós* (Luke 21:11) and *thánatos* "death" (Rev. 6:8; 18:8), both rendered "pestilence" by the RSV.

PETER [pē′tər] (Gk. *Petros*).† Simon Peter, the most prominent of Jesus' twelve disciples.

I. Name and Background

Peter's original name was Simon (Aram. *šim‘ôn*, represented in Greek by *Simōn* and *Symeōn*). Jesus gave him the Aramaic name *kêp̄ā'* "rock" (Matt. 16:18; Luke 6:14 par.; John 1:42), which is in Greek both transliterated (*Kēphas*; Eng. Cephas) and translated (*Petros*). Peter is also called "son of John" (v. 42; KJV "Jona"; 21:15-17; KJV "Jonas") and Bar-Jona (Matt. 16:17; from Aram. *bar-yônâ* "son of Jonah").

Peter's original home was Bethsaida (John 1:44), and he later lived in Capernaum (Matt. 8:5, 14; Mark 1:21). He was married (Matt. 8:14; 1 Cor. 9:5). He and his brother Andrew were partners in a fishing business with James and John the sons of Zebedee (Luke 5:10). According to the assessment of the leading priests of Jerusalem Peter had only the fundamental education in Judaism of the common people (Acts 4:13). Marked as a Galilean by his accent (Matt. 26:73; Mark 14:70), his background in that partly Gentile region later enabled him to work among Greek-speaking Gentiles (1 Cor. 1:12; Gal. 2:11-12).

Peter and Andrew were followers of John the Baptist and had their first contact with Jesus through John (John 1:35-42). When Jesus called Peter to follow him, Peter was still working as a fisherman (Mark 1:16-17), but had already respected Jesus as "Master" for some time (Luke 5:5).

II. Jesus' Disciple

Peter is first in every list of Jesus' twelve disciples (Matt. 10:2; Mark 3:16; Luke 6:14; Acts 1:13) and is the disciple most often mentioned in the Gospels. He, James, and John were the disciples closest to Jesus (Mark 5:37; 9:2; 13:3; 14:33; Luke 22:8). The prominent role of Peter among the disciples is acknowledged by Jesus (Matt. 16:16-19) and by an angel (Mark 16:7).

Peter is portrayed as a fervent person, always ready to speak or act in response to his loyalty to Jesus (Matt. 14:28-29; 17:24-25; Mark 10:28; 11:21; 14:29-31; Luke 5:8; 8:45; John 6:68-69; 18:10; 21:7). But he also misunderstood Jesus and was rebuked by the Master, often because of what his loyalty had led him into (Matt. 15:15-17; Mark 8:29-33; 9:5-6; 14:37-38; John 13:6-11; 18:10-11). Peter's loyalty failed at the point of greatest strain, during the trial of Jesus, while Peter was being pressed by outsiders (Mark 14:66-72 par.). Afterwards, he was the first of the apostles to see the risen Jesus (Luke 24:34; 1 Cor. 15:5), but returned to fishing in Galilee and had to be coaxed out of this decision by Jesus (John 21).

III. Leader of the Church

After the ascension of Jesus Peter was the main leader of the Church in Jerusalem (Acts 1:13-14). He initiated the replacement of Judas (vv. 15-26), showing by this that he was in some sense aware of the future mission of the apostles (v. 22). When the Church's growth was initiated by Pentecost, he stepped forward as interpreter of the event and the preacher of the gospel to the crowd that assembled (ch. 2). From that time until he had to go into hiding (12:17-19), Peter played a significant part in the Church in Palestine. He healed people (3:1-10; 5:15-16; 9:32-43), preached to crowds (3:12-26; 5:21, 42), was jailed (4:1-3; 5:17-18, 26; 12:3-5) and miraculously released (5:19-20; 12:6-17), and spoke to government authorities about Jesus (4:5-12; 5:27-32).

Peter played a central role in some of the events that took the Church beyond its original limitation to Judean Jews (8:14-25; 10:1–11:18; cf. Gal. 1:18-19). At the APOSTOLIC COUNCIL, which took place after he could safely return to Jerusalem, Peter took a leading part in the defense of evangelism of Gentiles, which did not require conformity to Judaism (Acts 15:7-11; cf. Gal. 2:8-10). Shortly after the Council, however (according to the most likely understanding of the relationship of Acts and Galatians), Peter bowed to pressure from more conservative Jewish Christians and withdrew from table fellowship with Gentile Christians, for which he was sharply rebuked by Paul (vv. 11-14).

Peter is not mentioned in Acts after the account of the Council. It appears, however, that after Antioch (Gal. 2:11-14) he went on missionary journeys farther into the Gentile world (1 Cor. 1:12; 3:22; 9:5). According to strong evidence from the early Church, Peter went to Rome ("Babylon" at 1 Pet. 5:13) and died as a martyr there under Nero. He was later called a founder (with Paul) and a bishop of the church in Rome, but it is unlikely that he was recognized as either during his lifetime.

A "theology of Peter" cannot be reconstructed. The only materials that could be drawn on would be his speeches (Acts 2:14-40; 3:12-26; 4:8-12; 5:29-32; 10:34-43), which reflect the beliefs of the early Church for whom he spoke and the interests of the writer of Acts more than any distinctive ideas of Peter; possibly 1-2 Peter (but see the respective articles with regard to the question of authorship); and the gospel of Mark, which was associated with Peter at an early date but does not necessarily reflect his particular concerns.

Bibliography. R. E. Brown, K. P. Donfried, and J. Reumann, eds., *Peter in the New Testament* (Minneapolis and New York: 1973); F. F. Bruce, *Peter, Stephen, James, and John* (Grand Rapids: 1980); O. Cullmann, *Peter: Disciple–Apostle–Martyr,* 2nd ed. (Philadelphia: 1962).

PETER, ACTS OF.† A New Testament apocryphon written *ca.* A.D. 185 and devoted to Peter's arrival and activity in Rome, particularly his contest with Simon Magus and his eventual martyrdom. The work is often identified as a romance, due to its inclination toward the magical and peculiar. Two-thirds of the work, originally composed in Greek, is extant in a Latin version known as the *Actus Vercellenses.* In addition, the account of Peter's martyrdom is preserved separately in the original Greek and in other languages, while other apocryphal stories from Peter's life, perhaps derived from the Acts of Peter, are also extant in various sources.

The heart of the work concerns Peter's encounter with his old adversary, Simon Magus (cf. Acts 8:9-24), who has led astray most of the Roman church by his magical power and defamation of Paul. Peter brings Simon to his death, having overcome the power of Simon's magic with the greater power of prayer. Peter's own martyrdom is brought about as a result of his ascetic ideals.

PETER, APOCALYPSE OF.† Two independent and dissimilar works are extant under this title: one an orthodox pseudonymous apocalypse written *ca.* A.D. 110-140, the other a Gnostic pseudonymous apocalypse written in the third century.

The orthodox Apocalypse of Peter was highly regarded by many Christians of the second century and was read in Palestinian churches still in the fifth century. It is known mainly through an Ethiopic translation and Greek fragments. The apocalypse combines an embroidered account of the transfiguration with an apocalypse like that at Mark 13. The center of interest is a vision of the torments of hell and the pleasures of paradise. Some dependence upon the canonical 2 Peter may be discerned in the development of the theme of eschatological judgment.

The Gnostic Apocalypse of Peter is explicit in its Gnostic themes and its polemic against orthodox Christianity. It is part of the collection of Coptic Gnostic texts found near Nag Hammadi. In this account, Peter has three visions in which the Savior serves as an interpreter. In the first vision the opponents of Jesus appear to be representatives of the orthodox Church. In the second the physical form of Jesus is crucified while "the living Jesus" stands nearby laughing. The third vision is a Gnostic reinterpretation of the resurrection in which the spiritual Jesus is reunited with the radiant light of the intellectual pleroma. A Gnostic christology of a docetic savior is clearly presented.

PETER, FIRST LETTER OF.† One of the Catholic Epistles and the twenty-first book of the New Testament; a letter from Peter (or someone writing in Peter's name) to Christians of Asia Minor.

I. Author

Peter is not mentioned in Acts after the description of the Apostolic Council (Acts 15). It appears, however, that after his stay in Antioch (Gal. 2:11-14), Peter's missionary journeys (cf. 1 Cor. 9:5) might have taken him deep into Gentile territory (despite Gal. 2:7; cf. 1 Cor. 1:12; 3:22). The tradition that Peter spent his last days in Rome and was martyred there (1 Clem. 5:4; Ignatius *Rom.* 4:3) may well be true.

1 Peter claims to have been composed by Peter (1 Pet. 1:1) with the assistance of Silvanus (5:12), quite possibly Paul's fellow missionary after the Jerusalem council (2 Cor. 1:19; cf. Silas, Acts 15:40; 16:19; 17:4). The letter may have been sent from Rome, cryptically referred to as "Babylon" (1 Pet. 5:13) as at Rev. 17:5 and some first-century Jewish documents. A greeting is passed on to the addressees from the author's "son" (probably meaning "close disciple") Mark (1 Pet. 5:13), probably the author of the gospel of Mark, whom Papias referred to in the second century as "Peter's interpreter" (Eusebius *HE* iii.39.15). The frequent mention of suffering (1 Pet. 1:6; 3:14; 4:1, 12-19) might well reflect the experience of an author who expects soon to be executed for the faith. He calls himself "a witness of the sufferings of Christ" (5:1), perhaps a claim to have been an eyewitness of Jesus' crucifixion or merely that he gives testimony in preaching to the sufferings of Christ.

The ascription of 1 Peter to the apostle Peter has been questioned for two main reasons. One is the letter's apparent similarity to parts of Paul's letters, including the conjunction of Isa. 8:14-15; 28:16 (1 Pet. 2:6, 8; Rom. 9:33); the picture of the Church as a temple being built on Christ the cornerstone (1 Pet. 2:4-5; Eph. 2:19-22); Christ's present position "at the right hand of God" and his rule over "angels, authorities, and powers" (1 Pet. 3:22; cf. Eph. 1:20-21); and the series of instructions for various members of a typical household (1 Pet. 2:18; 3:1, 7; cf. Eph. 5:22, 28; 6:1, 4-5, 9; Col. 3:18-22; 4:1). 1 Peter also resembles the letters of Paul in some matters of form (see below) and in the use of the common Pauline expression "in Christ" (1 Pet. 3:16; 5:10, 14). These and other similarities to the contents of Pauline letters may simply reflect traditional ways of speaking in the Church that both Paul and the writer of 1 Peter drew on, or perhaps direct contact with Paul or some of his letters on the part of the author of 1 Peter.

The second argument against Petrine authorship of 1 Peter is the author's excellent command of written Greek, which is not likely to have been possessed by Peter (cf. Acts 4:13). One aspect of this argument is the question of whether the LXX would be used consistently in a document written by a Palestinian Jew, as it is in 1 Peter. The education and familiarity with Greek reflected in the letter may, however, have been possessed by Silvanus or others assisting Peter in the writing.

The arguments for and against Petrine authorship must be assessed on the basis of the likelihood of the pseudonymous production of a document in the early Church and of such a pseudonymous document being accepted in the Church. These questions have themselves received varying answers. The letter, if not of direct Petrine authorship, was probably written by some person or group in contact with Peter during his lifetime or standing in the Petrine tradition but at a further remove from the apostle himself.

The end of 1 Peter and beginning of 2 Peter in Papyrus Bodmer VII (p72, *ca.* 300) (Vatican Library)

II. Addressees

The author of the letter does not appear to have had any special relationship to his addressees, who live in provinces in northern, central, and western Asia Minor (1 Pet. 1:1). The letter is apparently intended to be a circular document with wide distribution.

The addressees are called "the exiles of the Dispersion [Gk. *diasporá,* the usual word for Jews not resident in their ancestral land; cf. Jas. 1:1]." The distinction of the addressees from "the Gentiles" (1 Pet. 2:12; 4:3) might appear to imply that the addressees were Jews, but it is clear that the distinction is between the addressees and their (Gentile) neighbors and countrymen whose way of life the readers once fully shared (cf. the distinction between past and present at 1:14; 4:2-3; cf. 1:18). "Diaspora," like "exile" (1:1, 17; 2:11), is figurative for the temporary separation on earth of the Christian communities from their true, heavenly home (cf. Heb. 11:13; 13:14). Some commentators have suggested that the references to "exile" are literal indicators of the social standing of the addressees and not metaphors for the Christian's relationship to the world; but at 1 Pet. 2:11 it appears clear that the writer is insisting on an attitude, not referring to the addressees' social status.

Because of the frequent exhortations to proper conduct in the face of suffering, and because these exhortations show fewer marks of being generalized traditional material than much of the rest of the letter, it is possible that the addressees were undergoing persecution. However, the passages on suffering are not consistent enough with each other to indicate for certain that such was the case. Moreover, the Neronian persecution of A.D. 64-65 in which Peter is said to have died may not have spread beyond the city of Rome. Furthermore, the use of "Babylon" for Rome is, as noted, paralleled in the Revelation of John, which is usually associated with persecutions occurring three decades later that may have been particularly severe in Asia Minor (some have dated 1 Peter to the persecutions under Trajan that occurred yet later in A.D. 112). Here "Babylon" may be not a cryptic reference to Rome, but rather a contribution to the "exile" figure of speech that permeates the letter.

Nevertheless, localized persecutions may have occurred for which no information is available at present. The seemingly most specific section on suffering (4:12-19) appears immediately after a closing doxology (v. 11; cf. 5:11) and apparently reflects less settled conditions than are taken for granted by the earlier exhortations (esp. 2:13-17). It may be, therefore, that information concerning the situation of the addressees came to the writer during the composition of the letter, which would cause him to anticipate in an expansion of the letter that their suffering would increase.

III. Contents

1 Peter is a letter only with regard to its use of epistolary conventions for its opening (1:1-2) and closing (5:12-14). It is composed almost entirely of homiletical materials that had come to be used repeatedly in the Church. No definite outline is given to these traditional materials, though some thematic grouping is evident. At v. 12 the author describes his purpose, which is to give broad-ranging exhortations and to affirm what God in his grace has done. "Grace" is, indeed, an important term in the letter, bringing together what "the God of all grace" (v. 10) has done for salvation in the past (1:10; 4:10; cf. 5:5) and what will be experienced "at the revelation of Jesus Christ" (1:13; cf. 3:7; 5:10). The theological focus of the letter is on the polarity between this salvation and the suffering that Christians experience as strangers in this world. Both behavior and eschatological hope are focused on this polarity.

The epistolary opening (1:1-2) is influenced by similar forms in Paul's letters. Following it is a collection of catechetical materials (1:3–2:3), which begins with a blessing to God much like those at 2 Cor. 1:3; Eph. 1:3. These materials have a distinct break into two parts, the first speaking of what God has done in Christ (1 Pet. 1:3-12) and the second exhorting the readers to make the appropriate responses to what God has done (1:13–2:3). Next comes a collection of testimonies appealing to the Old Testament with reference to the nature of Christ and the Church (2:4-10). The next section (2:11–3:12) is a complex collection of materials on conduct, focused mainly on three expanded exhortations to "be subject" or "submissive" (2:13, 18; 3:1). Instructions regarding conduct in the face of suffering (3:13–4:7; 4:12-19; 5:6-11) then appear, combined with other materials mainly on the functioning of the churches (4:8-11; 5:1-5). The epistolary closing follows (vv. 12-14).

Bibliography. F. W. Beare, *The First Epistle of Peter,* 3rd ed. (Naperville: 1970); E. Best, *1 Peter.* NCBC (1971; repr. 1982); J. H. Elliott, *A Home for the Homeless: A Sociological Exegesis of 1 Peter* (Philadelphia: 1981); J. N. D. Kelly, *A Commentary on the Epistles of Peter and Jude.* HNTC (1969; repr. 1981); E. G. Selwyn, *The First Epistle of St. Peter,* 2nd ed. (1946; repr. Grand Rapids: 1981).

PETER, GOSPEL OF.† An apocryphal gospel written about A.D. 150. It is mentioned by Origen, Jerome, and Eusebius, but it is unlikely that they actually had direct access to it. Part of its contents is now known through one eighth-century Greek fragment.

The writer of this account of the death of Jesus seems to have drawn from all four canonical Gospels, but most of the contents are new and are mainly directed to placing the blame for the crucifixion entirely upon the Jews, exonerating Pilate entirely. The resurrection is portrayed as having occurred openly before the enemies of Jesus. The work also portrays a docetic Christ whose deity overshadows his humanity; Jesus is depicted as "suffering no pain" and, rather than dying on the cross, as "taken up" from there to heaven.

Serapion, bishop of Antioch from 199 to 211, first gave permission for the gospel of Peter to be read by Christians, but then upon further study published a treatise condemning its doctrinal tendencies.

PETER, PREACHING OF.† The *Kerygma Petrou* (not to be confused with the syncretistic Jewish-Christian *Kerygmata Petrou* [the "Preachings of Peter"] associated with the Clementine school), an early second-century Christian writing probably from Egypt and ascribed to Peter. The work is known primarily from quotations in Clement of Alexandria *Stromata* that resemble both early missionary preaching and the writings of the second-century apologists. Included are Jesus' sending of the apostles to preach to all nations, a distinguishing of Christian worship from both pagan and Jewish worship, and the apostles' discovery that the Hebrew prophets predicted the coming, death, resurrection, and ascension of Jesus.

PETER, REVELATION OF. *See* PETER, APOCA-LYPSE OF.

PETER, SECOND LETTER OF.† One of the Catholic Epistles, the twenty-second book of the New Testament, in the form of a letter from the apostle Peter or someone writing in his name.

I. Contents

2 Peter is a letter, but since its epistolary form is signaled only by the salutation (2 Pet. 1:1-2), and since the addressees are not specified in the salutation and greetings are not exchanged at the close of the letter, it was probably intended for wide circulation.

A summary statement of the gospel is given at 1:3-11, focused on the relationship between God's goodness in providing a way of escape from the mortality that results from sin (vv. 3-4, 9) and the ethical qualities that ought to follow in response to God's action (vv. 5-8, 10). Where both faith and virtue exist the gift of entry into Christ's eternal kingdom is to be given (v. 11). The transition that follows in vv. 12-21 shows that this statement of the gospel is offered as a reminder of what is already known (vv. 12-13), underscored as the truthful and authoritative teaching of the apostle (the "I" of vv. 12-15), who witnessed the transfiguration of Jesus (vv. 16-18; cf. Matt. 17:1-8 par.), and the last testament of one who is about to die (2 Pet. 1:14).

The implications in ch. 1 (vv. 16, 20) that the writer opposes a false teaching are confirmed in chs. 2-3. Yet for all that is said against the false teachers, little specific information is supplied concerning their practices and teachings. Licentiousness and greed are attributed to them (e.g., 2:2-3), but these resemble the standard charges leveled against teachers considered wrong; however, the strong ethical tone of 1:5-9 may serve as confirmation that this was a particular concern. The false teaching involved in some way a "denying (of) the Master" (2:1), and included a (perhaps ritual) reviling of "the glorious ones" (v. 10b), i.e., unrighteous spiritual beings and powers (vv. 11-13). It centered its teaching to noninitiates on "freedom" (vv. 18-19), denied the second coming of Christ (3:4-5), and misused the letters of Paul (vv. 15-17).

The combination of the "freedom" theme in the false teaching, the false teachers' sense of superiority to spiritual powers, and the rejection of future eschatological hope (cf. 1 Cor. 15:12; 2 Tim. 2:18) points to some form of Gnosticism or gnosticizing trend. Some Gnostics made much use of the Pauline letters. The denial of "the Master" may point to a docetic tendency, i.e., a denial of the humanity and physicality of Jesus (cf. 1 John 4:2-3), or to an antinomian tendency that denied responsibility for commands given by Jesus.

A main focus of the writer's response to this false teaching is the final eschatological judgment. Though the judgment day will be, above all, the time when some are destroyed (2 Pet. 3:7; cf. 2:1), and when the wicked will go to "the nether gloom of darkness" (2:17), it remains true that God desires the destruction of none (3:9; cf. v. 15). The condemnation and destruction of the unrighteous are already prepared "from of old" (2:3; cf. v. 9). Mirroring their destruction will be the rescue of the godly; judgment will, therefore, be a time of dividing between righteous and unrighteous (vv. 4-10). The present heavens and earth, since they are corrupted by the unrighteousness that goes on in them, are "stored up for fire" (3:7; cf. vv. 10, 12) and will be replaced by "new heavens and a new earth in which righteousness dwells" (v. 13). Christians face judgment in a position different from others—they will be judged more severely if they apostatize than if they had never heard the gospel or believed (2:20-21). Thought of judgment day should be an inducement to right living and faithfulness to the gospel (3:11, 14).

II. Authorship

Taken strictly at face value, 2 Peter is a letter from the apostle Simon Peter (1:1), an eyewitness of the transfiguration of Jesus (1:16; cf. Matt. 17:1-8 par.), who believes that his death will occur soon in keeping with a word from Jesus (2 Pet. 1:14; cf. John 21:18-19). He has written a previous letter to the unidentified addressees (2 Pet. 3:1) and is acquainted with some letters of Paul, which he acknowledges as "scriptures" (vv. 15-16). If this claimed authorship is accepted, then a date late in Peter's life—probably shortly before his martyrdom in Rome under Nero—is most likely. The addressees might, in this view, be the Gentile Christians of Asia Minor who received 1 Peter (1 Pet. 1:1).

But 2 Peter's claim to have been written by the apostle Peter is doubted more than the claimed authorship of any other New Testament document. A number of reasons exist for this consensus against Petrine authorship. Ch. 2 is quite similar to the letter of Jude. Analysis shows that the source of the letter is most likely to be Jude, and that 2 Peter 2 is a recasting for a different situation of Jude's attack on heretics. Much of the rest of the letter also appears to have borrowed from Jude, which is almost invariably given a date after Peter's death under Nero.

Other internal marks indicate a late date. One is the probability that it is the collection of Pauline letters spoken of in 3:16. Furthermore, that all the members of the first generation of Christians have died seems to be assumed by v. 4. The emphasis on correct interpretation of Scripture (1:20-21; 3:15-16) and adherence to apostolic tradition (1:13-14; 2:21; 3:2) are also considered pointers to a time when the apostles had all died, their memory was venerated, and theological creativity was less accepted.

The letter was accepted in the early Church with greater difficulty than any other New Testament document. It was not until the second half of the fourth century that it was even mentioned in the West, and then its authenticity was still contested by some. In the East it was better known but not unhesitatingly accepted. The book won a place in the canon largely on the basis of its contents rather than any certainty concerning its authorship.

As a result of these factors the conclusion is generally made that 2 Peter was written in the early- to mid-second century as one of the earliest documents in the pseudo-Petrine tradition that came to include the apocryphal Apocalypse, Gospel, and Preaching of Peter and other works written in the second and third century. On this view, the author of 2 Peter knew 1 Peter, a collection of Pauline letters, and a gospel narrative that included the transfiguration (perhaps one of the extant written Gospels), and accepted all these documents as authoritative. He also knew and used the letter of Jude, but probably did not regard it as authoritative in the same way. He stands as a mediator and advocate of the apostolic tradition to a new generation.

Bibliography. R. J. Bauckham, *Jude, 2 Peter*. WBC (1983); J. N. D. Kelly, *A Commentary on the Epistles of Peter and Jude*. HNTC (1969; repr. 1981); E. M. Sidebottom, *James, Jude, 2 Peter*. NCBC (1967; repr. 1982)

PETER AND PAUL, PASSION OF.* An orthodox writing of the fifth century A.D. depicting the close relationship of the apostles Peter and Paul, their continuing opposition to Simon Magus, and their eventual martyrdoms. Attributed to Marcellus, it is extant in both Greek and Latin.

The work is preserved almost verbatim in the Greek Acts of Peter and Paul, also ascribed to Marcellus, prefaced by chapters embellishing with legendary accounts the canonical book of Acts and the Acts of Peter and detailing the journey of Paul to Rome. Another work entitled the Passion of Peter and Paul exists only in Latin.

PETER AND THE TWELVE APOSTLES, ACTS OF.* A second- or third-century writing contained in the Coptic Gnostic library found near Nag Hammadi, Egypt. Although Gnostics may have found themes in this document useful for describing their own ideas, the work itself contains little or nothing to mark it clearly as a Gnostic document.

According to the narrative, after the resurrection of Jesus Peter and the rest of the Eleven sail to a city called Habitation where they meet Lithargoel, a pearl merchant. Lithargoel tells them that, although they will encounter hardships on the journey, they should travel to his city so that they can receive a pearl for nothing. When they arrive successfully at his city, Lithargoel comes to them disguised as a physician. He reveals that he is Christ (cf. Rev. 2:17) and gives them an ointment, instructs them in healing, and sends them back to Habitation for their ministry. The document's repeated emphasis on poverty in ministry and polemic against the rich have their roots in such New Testament passages as Matt. 10:9-10; Mark 10:17-31; Jas. 2:1-9.

PETER TO JAMES, LETTER OF.† Also called the Epistle of Peter, a portion of the Preachings of Peter (*Kerygmata Petrou*), a series of manifestations of the "true prophet" to Adam through Moses and Jesus. It was composed in Greek, probably in Syria during the third century, and is included in the Muratorian Canon. As the introduction to the Preachings, this purported letter to the head of the Jerusalem church exploits the authority of the apostle Peter to promote observance of the Jewish law by Christians and oppose Paulinism. Peter, portrayed as a consistent observer of the law from the beginning, warns James not to let these writings fall into any but the most carefully instructed hands, lest falsification occur.

PETER TO PHILIP, LETTER OF. One of the documents contained in the Nag Hammadi Gnostic library, dating from the late second or third century A.D. The tractate receives its title from the letter with which it begins. After Philip reads the letter the apostles assemble. In a dialogue with Jesus, who appears in a vision of light, they question him concerning basic matters of Gnostic belief, "the deficiency of the Aeons and their Pleroma" and the manner in which they are to fight the lawless Archons ("rulers"). The apostles, with Peter as leader, then discuss among themselves the necessity of suffering, experience a final vision of Jesus, and then disperse to enter into their ministries.

PETHAHIAH [pĕth'ə hī'ə] (Heb. *pᵉṭaḥyâ* "Yahweh opens").

1. The leader of the nineteenth priestly division during the days of David (1 Chr. 24:16).

2. A Levite among those who divorced their foreign wives at Ezra's direction (Ezra 10:23).

3. A Levite who participated in the corporate confession of sins under Ezra (Neh. 9:5). He may be the same as **2**.

4. The son of Meshezabel of the tribe of Judah. He was a postexilic administrator for the king of Persia in Judea, perhaps governor of the province sometime after Nehemiah (Neh. 11:24).

PETHOR [pē'thôr] (Heb. *pᵉṯôr*). A place on the western shore of the Euphrates river in northern Mesopotamia, the home of Balaam (Num. 22:5; Deut. 23:4). It is mentioned in a list of Pharaoh Thutmose III and is probably the same as Pitru, which Shalmaneser III conquered in 856 B.C.; if so, the location is probably Tell el-Aḥmar, 19 km. (12 mi.) south of Carchemish.

PETHUEL [pə thōō′əl] (Heb. *p°ṯûʾēl*). The father of the prophet Joel (Joel 1:1).

PETRA [pē′trə, pĕt′rə] (Gk. *Petra* "rock"). The capital of the Nabatean kingdom, about 75 km. (46.5 mi.) south of the Dead Sea. The city was built where a number of narrow wâdīs bound by high cliffs converge in a small valley, Wâdī Mûsā; access to the city is by the Siq, a narrow gorge through the eastern ridge. A number of spectacular Nabatean tombs, such as the Khazneh Farʿun ("treasury of the pharaoh"), are carved into the red sandstone cliffs in the vicinity of the city, and remains from the Roman period, including a theater, marketplace, and temple, have been discovered. A well-preserved Nabatean high place (modern Zibb ʿAtuf) has provided insights into the cultic practices of the ancient Israelites and their neighbors. Until J. L. Burckhardt identified its ruins in 1812, Petra lay deserted and forgotten for centuries.

Archaeologists have discovered evidence of settlement in the region as early as the Paleolithic period and including the period of the Edomite kingdom. One or more of the sites named "Sela" in the Old Testament (Judg. 1:36; 2 Kgs. 14:7; Isa. 16:1; 42:11) may have been located at Petra, as also the city named Rekem after its founder, one of the five Midianite kings defeated by the Israelites (Num. 31:8; so Josephus *Ant.* iv.7.1 [161]). The city on the floor of the valley, Petra proper, was not, however, founded until the third century B.C. It had its greatest prosperity in the late first century B.C. and the early first century A.D., despite the Nabatean kingdom's subjection to

The Roman temple ed-Deir cut into a sandstone cliff at Petra (Jordan Information Bureau, Washington, D.C.)

Rome; this prosperity was based on control of caravan routes. Rome gradually gained control of these routes and annexed the kingdom to the province of Arabia (A.D. 106), but Petra continued to be of importance into the sixth century.

PEULLETHAI [pē ŭl′ə thī] (Heb. *p°ʿullᵉṯay* "Yahweh's reward"). The eighth son of Obed-edom, a gatekeeper, whose family was assigned to the South Gate of the temple and the temple storerooms (1 Chr. 26:5, 15).

PHALEC (Luke 3:35, KJV). *See* PELEG.

PHALLU (Gen. 46:9, KJV). *See* PALLU.

PHALTI (1 Sam. 25:44, KJV). *See* PALTI **2**.

PHALTIEL (2 Sam. 3:15, KJV). *See* PALTIEL **2**.

PHANUEL [fə nōō′əl] (Gk. *Phanouēl*; cf. Heb. *p°nûʾēl* "face of God"). The father of the prophetess Anna of the tribe of Asher (Luke 2:36).

PHARAOH [fâr′ō] (Heb. *parʿōh*; Gk. *Pharaō*; Egyp. *pr-ʿȝ* "great house, palace"). Title of the Egyptian monarch. During the New Kingdom (fourteenth-tenth centuries B.C., roughly parallel to Moses and the Exodus), the title is used as if it were a personal name (e.g., Gen. 12:15-20; Exod. 6:11; cf. "the White House," "Buckingham Palace"). The actual names of only four pharaohs appear in the Bible: Neco (2 Kgs. 23:29, 33-35; Jer. 46:2) and Hophra (44:30), where again biblical usage reflects that of Egypt, in that after the tenth century rulers were called "Pharaoh X"; Shishak (1 Kgs. 11:40; 14:25; 2 Chr. 12:1-9), and So (2 Kgs. 17:4). *See* EGYPT *III*.

For the pharaoh who oppressed the Israelites and the pharaoh of the Exodus *see* EXODUS *III*.

PHARATHON [fâr′ə thŏn] (Gk. *Pharathōn*).† A city in Judea, one of those fortified by Bacchides, Seleucid governor of the province Beyond the River (1 Macc. 9:50; KJV "Pirathoni," following LXX). The city is often but should not be identified with Ephraimite Pirathon (Judg. 12:13-15).

PHARES, PHAREZ (KJV). *See* PEREZ.

PHARISEES [fâr′ə sēz] (Gk. *Pharisaíoi*).† One of the parties or movements within Judaism of the late Second Temple period (*ca.* 150 B.C.–A.D. 70). The Pharisees were noted most for their exact observance of the Jewish religion, their accurate exposition of the law, their handing down of extrabiblical customs and traditions, their moderate position with regard to the interplay of fate and free will, and their belief in the coming resurrection and in angels (Josephus *BJ* i.5.2 [110]; ii.8.14 [162-63]; *Ant.* xiii.10.6 [297]; xviii.1.3 [13-14]; Mark 7:3; Acts 23:6-9; Phil. 3:5; cf. Gal. 1:14). The ancient sources variously describe the Pharisees as a political party, a philosophical school and scholarly class, or a sect or voluntary association (Heb. *ḥaḇᵉrôṯ*) devoted to ritual purity.

Gk. *Pharisaíoi* derives from Heb. *p°rûšîm* "separated ones" (and the related Aramaic form). The Hebrew term appears a number of times in the rabbinic literature, but not every instance can be taken as a reference to the *Pharisaîoi* of Josephus and the Gospels. Since "separated ones" may be understood in either a favorable or unfavorable sense, it is not certain whether the name originated with the Pharisees or with their opponents.

The Pharisees may have begun as a faction of the HASIDIM, a religious reform movement of the time of the Maccabean revolt (1 Macc. 2:42; 7:13; 2 Macc. 14:6; RSV "Hasideans"; KJV "Assideans"). They came to prominence as an opposition party during the reign of the Hasmoneans John Hyrcanus (134-104 B.C.) and Alexander Jannaeus (103-76), and had great influence over Alexandra Salome (76-67; *Ant.* xiii.10.5-6 [288-296], 15.5-16.1 [401-6]; *BJ* i.5.2-3 [110-114]). With the reign of Herod (37 B.C.-A.D. 4) and direct Roman rule in Judea (from A.D. 6), the political influence of the Pharisees appears to have declined, although the extent to which they eschewed political activity during this period is debated.

During the time of Jesus and the first generation of the Church, the temple was essentially controlled by the Sadducean aristocracy and was the center of the religious life of the Jews. But through Pharisaic scribes the synagogues often became points of Pharisaic influence on the common people. Still, the enduring significance of the Pharisees for Judaism lies less in their direct impact on Second Temple Judaism than in their survival as the most viable leadership after the destruction of the temple. Almost all forms of modern Judaism trace their lineage through the Pharisees.

Jesus' harsh attacks against the Pharisees (esp. Matt. 23) may have been preserved or even intensified by the early Church because the Pharisees had emerged as the Church's major rival for Jewish allegiance. In the Gospels "Pharisees" has become one of the generalized designations for the opponents of Jesus (e.g., 27:62; John 7:32; 18:3). This negative view of the Pharisees can obscure the fundamental agreement of Jesus with them on a number of points, including resurrection (cf. Matt. 22:23-33) and the validity of the Pharisees' interpretation of the precepts of the Torah (23:1-2), although it is likely that the points on which Jesus and the Pharisees agreed are those held in common by all Jews. The presence in the rabbinic literature of attacks on certain kinds of Pharisees shows that Jesus' attacks reflect intra-Jewish conflict as much or more than Christian anti-Judaism.

The sources of the conflict that developed between Jesus and the Pharisees appear to have been Jesus' toleration of ritual uncleanness among his meal companions (Mark 2:15-17; 7:1-2; Luke 15:2), his disciples' neglect of regular fasting (Mark 2:18), his failure to insist on the Pharisees' applications of the law among his disciples (vv. 23-24; 7:1-4), his public critique of their understanding of the Sabbath regulations and of other parts of the law (3:4-6; 7:6-23), and their concern that he vindicate his claims (8:11-12; Luke 5:21; John 8:13). Jesus gave reasons for his behavior and views which show that the conflict extended to deep underlying concerns. Where the distinctive message, activity, and style of Jesus may have been offensive to the Pharisees, it is likely also to have been offensive

to other Jews. Other Jews were as far from the Pharisaic ideal as Jesus was, but his prominence as a teacher and his basing his deviation on his self-understanding made argument against him necessary from the standpoint of the Pharisees. Nevertheless, occasionally the Pharisees showed some positive interest in Jesus (Matt. 22:34-40; John 3:1-2).

The conflict appears not to have been carried over into the period of the Church's history covered by the book of Acts. Pharisees appear as defenders of the Church (Acts 5:34-39; 23:6-9) and as conservative members of the Church (15:5). When Paul speaks of his background as a Pharisee, he does not denigrate Pharisaism per se, even as he regards his former life focused on fulfillment of the precepts of the law as replaced by his life as apostle to the Gentiles (23:6; 26:5; 1 Cor. 9:20-21; Gal. 1:13-16; Phil. 3:4-11).

Bibliography. J. Bowker, *Jesus and the Pharisees* (Cambridge: 1973); J. Neusner, *From Politics to Piety: The Emergence of Pharisaic Judaism* (Englewood Cliffs: 1973); E. Rivkin, *A Hidden Revolution: The Pharisees' Search for the Kingdom Within* (Nashville: 1978); E. P. Sanders, *Jesus and Judaism* (Philadelphia: 1985); E. Schürer, *The History of the Jewish People in the Age of Jesus Christ*, rev. ed. 2 (Edinburgh: 1979): 381-403.

PHAROSH (Ezra 8:3, KJV). See PAROSH 1.

PHARPAR [fär′pär] (Heb. *parpar*). A river in Syria mentioned with the Abana at 2 Kgs. 5:12. It is generally thought to be the modern Nahr el-Aʿwaj, 13 km. (8 mi.) south of Damascus.

PHARZITES (Num. 26:20, KJV). See PEREZ.

PHASAEL [făz′ə ĕl] (Gk. *Phasaélos*). The largest of the three towers at the northern end of the palace of Herod the Great in Jerusalem, also known as David's Tower. Phasael was named after Herod's older brother. One of the few structures to survive Titus' destruction of the city in A.D. 70, Herodian blocks form the lower level of the present tower; the upper levels are Turkish.

PHASAELIS [fă sə ē′lĭs] (Gk. *Phasaélis*).* A town in the Jordan valley, built by Herod the Great in memory of his brother Phasael and bequeathed to his sister Salome. The site is modern Khirbet el-Fasayil, 16 km. (10 mi.) north of Jericho.

PHASEAH (Neh. 7:51, KJV). See PASEAH.

PHASELIS [fə sē′lĭs] (Gk. *Phasélis*).* A city on the Lycian coast of southern Asia Minor, modern Tekrova south of Perga. Founded in the seventh century B.C., Phaselis had long prospered as a commercial city because of its three harbors. It was one of the recipients of a letter from Rome warning against aggression against Hasmonean Judea (1 Macc. 15:23; 139-138 B.C.), probably because it had a substantial Jewish community.

PHEBE (Rom. 16:1, KJV). See PHOEBE.

PHENICE (Acts 27:12, KJV). See PHOENIX.

PHENICE (Acts 11:19; 15:3, KJV), **PHENICIA** (Acts 21:2, KJV). *See* PHOENICIA.

PHICOL [fī′kŏl] (Heb. *pî̱k̲ōl*). The Philistine commander-in-chief who witnessed Abimelech's covenants with Abraham at Beer-sheba (Gen. 21:22, 32; KJV "Phichol") and Isaac at Gerar (26:26). The name may be a title rather than a personal name.

PHILADELPHIA [fīl′ə dĕl′fī ə] (Gk. *Philadelphia, Philadelpheia* "love[r] of brother").

1. A city of Lydia in the valley of the Cogamis river (a tributary of the Gediz [ancient Hermus] river), located at modern Alaşehir, about 120 km. (74 mi.) east of Smyrna. Founded by Attalus II Philadelphus of Pergamum (159-138 B.C.) on the site of an earlier village called Callatebus, the city was strategically located at the junction of trade routes, and its geographic situation on the lower slopes of the Tmolus mountains made it easily defensible in war.

Philadelphia was of commercial importance and intended by the Pergamenes to bring Greek civilization and culture to the newly acquired areas of Lydia and Phrygia, but frequent earthquakes inhibited its development. In A.D. 17, the worst of these earthquakes levelled Philadelphia, and continuing tremors drove much of the populace to settle in the safer surrounding countryside. After Tiberius provided for the reconstruction of the city, the city took the name Neocaesarea. Coins show that the name Flavia was later used in honor of Vespasian. In the third century a temple for the emperor cult was built, and the city became Neokoros ("temple warden"). It gained the appellation "little Athens" in the fifth century because of the great number of pagan temples. Until 1391 Philadelphia stood alone in the region against Ottoman power.

According to John's letter to the church at Philadelphia (Rev. 3:7-13) the Christian community there was not strong, but could be singled out in particular for its faithfulness. The Jewish community in the city apparently caused difficulties for the Christians (v. 9).

2. A city of the Decapolis, modern ʿAmmân. *See* RABBAH 1.

PHILEMON [fī lē′mən] (Gk. *Philēmōn*). A Christian in Colossae to whom Paul wrote a letter in connection with his runaway slave Onesimus (cf. Col. 4:9). Since the apostle had probably not been in Colossae (2:1), he and Philemon must have met elsewhere, perhaps during Paul's extended ministry in Ephesus (Acts 19:8-10). Paul brought Philemon to conversion (the probable meaning of Phlm. 19). Philemon's owning at least one slave and a house in which a Christian group met (v. 2) and in which he could accommodate traveling preachers (v. 22) suggests that he was wealthy.

PHILEMON, LETTER TO.† The eighteenth book of the New Testament, a letter from the apostle Paul to Philemon, a Christian of Colossae.

Paul writes this letter as a prisoner (Phlm. 1, 23), probably while he is under house arrest in Rome and able to receive visitors with few restrictions (Acts 28:30; *ca.* A.D. 61-63). Onesimus, a slave owned by Philemon, has run away, perhaps robbing Philemon in the process (Phlm. 18-19), and has come into contact with Paul in Rome, perhaps as a fellow prisoner. He has

become a Christian under Paul's leading (v. 10) and has been working for Paul (vv. 11, 13). Paul sends Onesimus back to Philemon with the letter. It may be that Paul's letter to the Colossian church was sent at the same time (cf. Col. 4:9).

As Onesimus' owner, Philemon has full powers of life and death over the runaway. Paul asks Philemon to receive Onesimus back as a fellow Christian (Phlm. 16), even as Philemon would receive Paul himself (v. 17). The apostle reminds Philemon that he owes him some great debt of gratitude, probably because Paul brought the gospel to him (v. 19). Paul makes some further requests with regard to Philemon's handling of the case of the runaway, but it is not entirely clear what Paul hopes for, because of the careful obliqueness of his language (esp. v. 21, "even more than I say"). It is apparent that Paul does not wish Onesimus to be punished—his promise to repay anything Onesimus might have stolen or owes to Philemon in lost work is made quite emphatically (vv. 18-19). It is probable that Paul hopes Onesimus will be freed from slavery (vv. 16-17) and will be returned to him (vv. 13-14).

Paul exerts some pressure on Philemon by recognizing in his epistolary thanksgiving Philemon's standing in Christian faith (vv. 4-7), by mentioning his own position as *presbýtēs* ("elder" or "ambassador," v. 9), by involving other Christian leaders in both the sending and receiving of the letter (vv. 1-2, 23-24), and by mentioning the prospect of his own presence (v. 22). But Paul's ultimate appeal is not to any of these forms of pressure, but to Christian principles.

Paul does not make any comment to Philemon either in favor of or in opposition to the institution of slavery. Because of the recognized legal rights of Philemon, such a comment might be of little effect in this case. Furthermore, interference with the rights of slaveholders was severely punished. What Paul does mention as a motivation for mercy toward Onesimus is, however, that which eventually made slaveholding impossible for Christians: the equality in faith and service of every Christian because of which every fellow Christian is recognized as kin (cf. Gal. 3:28; Col. 3:11). A close relationship has developed between Paul and the slave, in which Onesimus was like both a son (Phlm. 10) and a "useful" subordinate worker (v. 11, perhaps a pun on Onesimus' name, Gk. *Onēsimos* "useful, worthwhile"). This relationship is probably described to Philemon as a model of the love, partnership, and acceptance that Paul hopes will exist between Philemon and Onesimus.

Bibliography. F. F. Bruce, *The Epistles to the Colossians, to Philemon, and to the Ephesians.* NICNT (1984); E. Lohse, *Colossians and Philemon.* Hermeneia (1971); R. P. Martin, *Colossians and Philemon.* NCBC (1981); P. T. O'Brien, *Colossians, Philemon.* WBC 44 (1982).

PHILETUS [fī lē′təs] (Gk. *Philētos* "beloved"). One who, with Hymenaeus, taught that the resurrection had already taken place (2 Tim. 2:17-18).

PHILIP [fīl′ĭp] (Gk. *Philippos*).†

1. Philip II of Macedonia (ruled 359-336 B.C.), father of Alexander the Great (1 Macc. 1:1; 6:2). Under

Philip the Macedonian tribes were unified, and Greece (except for Sparta) was for the first time brought under a single government. Although accomplished by force of arms, this Hellenic League enabled the Greeks to confront more effectively the Persian threat. Philip was assassinated before he could join his troops in confronting the Persians, but Alexander led the Greeks and Macedonians to victory over Persia and to the rapid establishment of a Greek empire in the Near East (cf. 1:1-4).

2. Philip V, king of Macedonia 220-179 B.C. An ally of Carthage, he was defeated by the Romans at Cynoscephalae in 197. His son Perseus was the last king of Macedonia before its annexation as a Roman province (1 Macc. 8:5).

3. A Phrygian, noted for his cruelty, appointed by the Seleucid emperor Antiochus IV Epiphanes as governor of Jerusalem ca. 170 B.C. (2 Macc. 5:22; 6:11; 8:8).

4. A courtier of the Seleucid emperor Antiochus IV Epiphanes (thought by some to be Antiochus' foster brother; cf. 2 Macc. 9:29, Gk. *sýntrophos*), appointed shortly before Antiochus' death as regent and guardian of the emperor's son, the future Antiochus V Eupator (1 Macc. 6:14-15; Josephus *Ant.* xii.9.2 [360]). Lysias, another courtier who had earlier been appointed regent over the western part of the kingdom and guardian of the young Antiochus (1 Macc. 3:32-33; *Ant.* xii.7.1 [295-96]), kept control of the young emperor after the death of Epiphanes and set himself up as regent (xii.9.2 [361]). Philip attempted to lead a revolt against Lysias (1 Macc. 6:55-56; 2 Macc. 13:23; *Ant.* xii.9.6 [379-380]), but either was killed in Antioch (7 [386]); cf. 1 Macc. 6:62-63) or was forced to flee to Egypt (2 Macc. 9:29). The revolt of Philip forced Lysias to lift a siege of Jerusalem and concede certain rights to the Jews (1 Macc. 6:55-62; 2 Macc. 13:23).

5. A son of Herod the Great and Mariamne the daughter of the high priest Simon, and half brother of Herod Antipas. He is called Philip only in the New Testament (Matt. 14:3; Mark 6:17; some texts of Luke 3:19) and is otherwise known as Herod, thus often Herod Philip. He was designated heir to all of his father's kingdom in his father's first will, but only in the event of the death of Antipater, the primary heir. He was married to Herodias, a granddaughter of Herod the Great and Mariamne the Hasmonean princess. He and Herodias had a daughter, Salome, who was married to his half brother Philip the tetrarch (6); that his half brother thus became his son-in-law may be the source of confusion regarding the name of Herod Philip reflected in the Gospels.

When Herod Antipas visited Herod Philip on his way to Rome, Antipas arranged with Herodias to take her as his own wife as soon as he was able to divorce the daughter of King Aretas of Nabatea (Josephus *Ant.* xviii.5.1 [109-110]). John the Baptist's reproof of this behavior led to John's imprisonment by Antipas and his death, in which Herodias and Salome were involved (Matt. 14:3-11; Mark 6:14-28; Luke 3:19-20).

6. Philip the tetrarch, son of Herod the Great and Cleopatra of Jerusalem. Philip's rule (4 B.C.-A.D. 34) extended over a sparsely populated, primarily Gentile territory northeast of the Decapolis and the Sea of Galilee, east of the upper Jordan, and south of Damascus and included the eastern slope of the Antilebanon range. The regions encompassed in this tetrarchy were Gaulanitis, Auranitis, Batanea, Trachonitis, and Ituraea (Luke 3:1). Its capital was Paneas (modern Bânîyâs), renamed Caesarea and called Caesarea Philippi to distinguish it from Caesarea Maritima on the Mediterranean coast south of Mt. Carmel. Popular among his subjects (Josephus *Ant.* xviii.4.6 [106-8]), Philip was married to Salome, the daughter of Herod Philip (5) and Herodias.

7. Philip the apostle, who, like Andrew and Peter, came from the city of Bethsaida (John 1:44). Jesus called Philip in Galilee (v. 43), and Philip brought Nathanael to Jesus (vv. 45-51). Before the first miraculous feeding of a large crowd, Jesus tested Philip, who was apparently well acquainted with the Scriptures, by asking him a question (6:5-7). A group of Gentiles ("Greeks") who wished to see Jesus approached Philip first (12:21-22). Philip's misguided request that Jesus "show us the Father" prompts a response in the upper room discourses (14:8-9). Philip's name appears in all four lists of apostles, at least three times joined with that of Bartholomew (Matt. 10:3; Mark 3:18; Luke 6:14; Acts 1:13).

8. Philip the evangelist, one of "the seven" chosen to assist the apostles in the distribution to the widows of the Church (Acts 6:1-5; 21:8). Philip was the first to take the gospel to Samaritans (8:5-8); one of the converts on that occasion was Simon Magus (vv. 9-13). Philip was then sent by an angel to take the gospel to an Ethiopian official who was returning home from a pilgrimage to Jerusalem (vv. 26-39). He then preached in the coastal cities from Azotus to Caesarea, where he settled (v. 40; 21:8). He was thus significant in the initial steps of extending the gospel beyond the Jews of Judea and Galilee. His four daughters were Christian prophetesses (v. 9).

PHILIP, ACTS OF. A fourth- or fifth-century compilation of legendary adventures of the apostle Philip and the evangelist Philip (understood as one person) in Greece, Parthia, and Carthage. Much of Philip's success as an evangelist is ascribed to the remarkable miracles he performed (e.g., raising from the dead, restoring sight). The document is extant only in fragments preserved in other writings.

PHILIP, GOSPEL OF. † One of the Gnostic writings in the Nag Hammadi codices. Epiphanius (*Haer.* xxvi.13.2-3) quotes an Egyptian Gospel of Philip used in the fourth century, but the words he cites are not in the Nag Hammadi gospel. Some scholars have suggested that the appended ascription, "The Gospel according to Philip," of the Nag Hammadi gospel is secondary, but Philip is the only apostle named in the work and is one of three charged in the Gnostic Pistis Sophia with writing down all that Jesus said and did.

The gospel of Philip was composed in Greek in the late second or third century, probably in Syria, and translated into Coptic ca. 400. It is not a gospel in the sense of a narrative of Jesus' life and teaching. Its numerous theological statements or sections expounding sacramental and ethical themes lack any clear outline, but some of the recurring motifs suggest that it may derive from a Christian Gnostic sacramental catechism. It locates the source of the fundamental human problem in the separation of the originally androgynous Adam/Eve, and teaches that now Christ has come to effect the reunion of male and female, which takes place between husband and wife in the sacramental bridal chamber—a foretaste of a heavenly union. Imagery of the bridal chamber and other sexual imagery used to depict sacramental initiation into the Gnostic mysteries is blended with literal teaching on the origin and meaning of mankind in two genders. The work teaches a docetic christology, and clear arguments are presented against the virgin birth, the orthodox understanding of Christ's resurrection, and the idea of a coming general physical resurrection.

The gospel of Philip is significant for its contribution to an understanding of Valentinian Gnosticism. While Valentinian sacramental practice still had at least some things in common with that of orthodox Christianity, the interpretations placed on the sacraments were distinctively Gnostic. The frequent use of New Testament quotation and paraphrase in the gospel clarifies the manner in which the Valentinians made use of New Testament documents.

PHILIPPI [fǐl′ə pī] (Gk. *hoi Philippoi*). A city in eastern Macedonia, situated in a fertile plain on the Roman military and commercial highway known as the Via Egnatia. Some of the city's prosperity came from gold in the mountains surrounding the city. Philippi was in the first district of the Roman province of Macedonia (as one possible reading of Acts 16:12 notes). It received its name from Philip II of Macedonia, but Greek and Thracian settlements had been located here before its refounding of the city. Its greatest growth came with its designation as a Roman colony in 42 B.C. and the settlement of Roman veterans there. Philippi was inhabited until the late Middle Ages, and extensive ancient and medieval ruins survive.

Paul visited Philippi during his second missionary journey after crossing the Symbolon mountains en route from Philippi's port city of Neapolis, 15 km. (9 mi.) to the south (vv. 11-12). After they arrived in Philippi, Paul, Silas, Timothy, and possibly Luke preached on the Sabbath to a group of women from the city at a "place of prayer" located "outside the gate" by the Gangites (Gangas) river (v. 13). One of their first converts was Lydia, a seller of purple fabric and apparently a prosperous woman (vv. 14-15). Sometime later Paul and Silas were arrested, beaten, and imprisoned (vv. 16-24; cf. 1 Thess. 2:2). They were set free at night when the prison was shaken by an earthquake that opened the doors and broke loose the prisoners' chains; the next day they were released and asked to leave the city (Acts 16:25-40). On a later occasion Paul and his traveling companions stopped at least briefly at Philippi (20:6). The Christian congregation that Paul and his coworkers founded there was notable for its generosity (Phil. 1:5; 4:10, 14-18; cf. 2 Cor. 8:1-5). It remains uncertain at what stage of his ministry Paul wrote his epistle to the Philippians.

PHILIPPIANS, LETTER TO THE.† The eleventh book of the New Testament, a letter from the apostle Paul to the Christians of the Macedonian city of Philippi.

I. Background and Composition

The church at Philippi began with Paul's preaching to a small group, probably of Gentile "God-fearers," which met on a riverbank to worship the God of Israel (Acts 16:11-13). As he writes to the Christians of Philippi, Paul is in prison under a military guard (Phil. 1:7, 13-14) and believes that his circumstances will lead to his death apart from God's deliverance (vv. 19-26; 2:17). Epaphroditus had been sent to Paul by the Philippians with a gift of money and become very ill; having recovered, he is returning to them with Paul's letter (vv. 25-30; 4:10, 14-18). Because of their gift and their previous relationship with Paul the Philippian Christians have a share in his ministry, which now consists not only of the defense of the gospel but also Paul's legal defense (1:7).

It is usually thought that Philippians was written while Paul was in Rome as recorded at the end of Acts (A.D. 61-63), but the references to the praetorian guard and to Caesar's household (Phil. 1:13; 4:22) do not make that conclusion necessary. Another suggestion, perhaps more likely because of the greater similarity of Philippians to earlier letters (Romans, 1 and 2 Corinthians, Galatians) than to the late "Prison Letters," places Paul in Ephesus when he wrote Philippians (*ca.* 55; cf. Acts 20:18-19; 1 Cor. 15:32; 2 Cor. 1:8-10). An advantage of the Ephesian hypothesis is that considerably less time needs to be allowed for the journeys between Paul's prison and Philippi mentioned in the letter (Phil. 1:26-27; 2:19, 23-25, 29-30; 4:18). Another less likely suggestion is that the letter was written in Caesarea, where it does not appear, however, that Paul was in immediate danger of death (Acts 24:26-27).

Some scholars have regarded Philippians as a composite document because of the sudden changes in tone and subject at Phil. 3:2; 4:10 and the repeated transition to final exhortations (3:1; 4:8). Some have concluded that the earlier of two letters is represented by 3:2 (or 3:1b)–4:23 and a later letter (which mentions the earlier one at 2:26) by 1:1–3:1(a). It is also sometimes held that a non-Pauline polemic has been interpolated into the Pauline material, beginning at 3:2 and extending to v. 16, v. 19, or into ch. 4. A fragment of an earlier short letter acknowledging the Philippians' gift is seen by some at 4:10-20 (or vv. 10-23). A large number of scholars, nevertheless, regard Philippians as a single composition by Paul.

II. Contents and Teaching

The letter speaks to three different interrelated situations, that of Paul, that of the Philippian Christians, and that of the threat posed by the false teachers.

A. Paul in Prison. Paul is confident and positive about his own circumstances because of his belief that God works out his will in whatever circumstances might arise. He is not sorry for his own imprisonment even though it allows the free operation of preachers opposed to him (1:15-17); both his being under guard and the preaching by others, despite their motives, have led to Christ's being heard of by more people (vv. 12-14, 18).

Paul is aware that his case might lead to death, but he hopes that he will be released because of the Philippians' prayers and because that is how God can best accomplish his purposes (vv. 19, 24-26). This is true even though Paul would rather die because his death would be his introduction into Christ's presence (vv. 21-23). But he remains confident that whether he lives or dies, Christ will be glorified (v. 20; cf. v. 27; 2:17). He asks the Philippians to join him in rejoicing concerning his situation (v. 18). Yet even though he is thankful for their financial assistance, he refuses to base his ability to continue functioning on what is provided in his external circumstances (4:11-13).

B. The Philippian Christians. Much of what Paul says about the situation of the Philippian Christians is based on the affectionate relationship and sharing of concerns that has existed between them and Paul and his associates, recently evidenced by their gift to him. His usual epistolary thanksgiving (cf. 1 Cor. 1:4-9) is focused on this relationship (Phil. 1:3-11). It is, as has been seen, partly from the standpoint of this relationship that Paul interprets his own perilous situation (vv. 19-26). That the Philippians are now also suffering because of their Christian faith strengthens the relationship (vv. 29-30). Paul interprets their suffering from an eschatological standpoint as that which leads to their salvation and to their opponents' destruction (vv. 27-28).

One striking characteristic of Philippians is the frequent mention of joy and rejoicing. This emphasis on joy is focused on the relationship between the Philippian Christians and Paul and his coworkers, and on the effectiveness of the gospel in the world and in believers. Paul rejoices with regard to his circumstances because Christ is proclaimed (1:18) and because of his hope that he will be released (v. 19). He rejoices because of the Philippian Christians (1:4; 4:1) and their gift to him (v. 10), and invites them to join with him in rejoicing over his circumstances (2:18). He wants them also to rejoice because Epaphroditus is restored to them after being ill (vv. 28-29). He exhorts them to "rejoice in the Lord" (3:1; 4:4). Joy is a feature of the Christian life that will be encouraged among them by his ministry with them (1:25) and will be encouraged in him by their moving toward a greater unity (2:2).

Paul is aware of friction among the Philippian Christians and urges them to every kind of emotion, attitude, and action that would counter rivalry and conflict (2:1-4, 12-14). He names two women whose disagreement may have been a root of the problems (4:2). He recognizes the importance of these women in the church's work and urges a particular unnamed person (possibly Luke) to assist them (v. 3).

As part of his exhortation to unity and humility, Paul reproduces at 2:6-11 a theologically rich hymn to Christ that may or may not have been composed by the apostle. His introduction to this hymn (v. 5) calls on the Philippian Christians to appropriate it as a lesson. Uncertainty concerning the way in which this appropriation is to be understood has made this one of the most debated passages in New Testament stud-

ies. According to the most likely view, Paul tells the Philippians to let the attitude that is theirs because they are "in Christ"—i.e., because they are Christians—be the one controlling attitude of their fellowship together. The attitude they have "in Christ" is determined by the course of Christ's experience: as his exaltation (vv. 9-11) came by means of his humiliation, so Christians can be patient and humble because they await the eschatological fulfillment (cf. 4:5).

C. The Opponents. Paul is aware that a false teaching faces the Philippian Christians that apparently seeks to bring them to an appreciation of the law of Moses as the way to righteousness and resurrection from the dead (3:2-11). The promoters of this teaching are apparently not simply teachers of Judaism or judaized Christianity, to judge from Paul's statement that "they glory in their shame" (v. 19); they may have been libertines with regard to some aspects of morality while being rigorists with regard to some aspects of the law.

His response to these teachers understands their emphasis on the law as "confidence in the flesh" (vv. 3-4). His own background is greater ground for such confidence than they can boast of (vv. 4-6; cf. 2 Cor. 11:16-22), but he sets that aside for such purpose because righteousness and resurrection are to be based on faith in Christ rather than on personal fulfillment of the law (Phil. 3:7-11).

Paul wants the Philippians especially to know that his own fulfillment will come only with the future resurrection. He is not perfected yet (vv. 12-13, 20-21). Perhaps the false teachers taught that full perfection was already available so that there was no need to await an eschatological fulfillment (cf. 1 Cor. 4:8; 15:12, 23-28; 2 Tim. 2:18). At any rate, Paul emphasizes a different understanding of the Christian life, one which does not simply rely on a fulfillment already obtained, but in which great energy is expended to move forward toward the eschatological goal (Phil. 3:12-17).

Bibliography. F. W. Beare, *The Epistle to the Philippians,* 2rd ed. BNTC (1969); J.-F. Collange, *The Epistle of Saint Paul to the Philippians* (London: 1979); G. F. Hawthorne, *Philippians.* WBC (1983); J. B. Lightfoot, *St. Paul's Epistle to the Philippians,* rev. ed. (1913; repr. Grand Rapids: 1953); R. P. Martin, *Carmen Christi: Philippians 2:5-11,* rev. ed. (Grand Rapids: 1983); *Philippians.* NCBC (1980).

PHILISTINES [fĭl'ə stēnz] (Heb. *pᵉlištîm*).† A people who migrated to the coast of Canaan (Philistia; Heb. *pᵉlešet,* from which is derived the name Palestine; Egyp. *prst;* Akk. *pilisti, palastu*) in the thirteenth or early twelfth century B.C. They became a major threat to early Israel's existence and the catalyst for the rise of monarchy in Israel.

I. Origins and Settlement

The thirteenth century B.C. was a period of major upheaval in the ancient Near East, characterized by the collapse of existing political systems and massive migrations of peoples from the Aegean area through Asia Minor, Syria, and Canaan to the Egyptian frontier. The "Sea Peoples," coming apparently from Greece, the Balkans, and even farther north, migrated south, destroying the Hittite Empire and threatening

Egypt. The Philistines were among these groups that surged toward Egypt. At Jer. 47:4; Amos 9:7 they are said to be from Caphtor, i.e., Crete and islands to the north of it in the Aegean Sea or the southern coast of Asia Minor.

First rebuffed by the Egyptian pharaoh Merneptah *ca.* 1224-1211, apparently the Philistines began to settle on the Palestinian coastal plain after being defeated by Ramses III in a combined land and sea battle near the beginning of the twelfth century. Their territory eventually extended from Joppa to the Wâdī Ghazzeh. The coastal cities of Ashdod, Ashkelon, and Gaza, and the inland cities of Ekron and Gath were the major Philistine population centers. The Philistines served as Egyptian mercenaries in the Nile delta, Nubia, and southwest Canaan, and apparently represented Egyptian power in Palestine until they became independent with the waning of Egyptian power in Asia in the eleventh and later centuries.

The Philistines were primarily warriors and did not displace the Canaanites whose territory they settled in. Instead, they adopted the culture of the Canaanites and became their rulers. Philistia was ruled by officials called *sᵉrānîm* (RSV "lords"; e.g., 1 Sam. 29:2). Most Philistine personal names in the Bible are Canaanite, as are the names of their deities, Dagon, Ashtaroth (perhaps ʿAnat), and Baalzebub (Judg. 16:23; 1 Sam. 5:2-5; 31:10; 2 Kgs. 1:2). Much of current knowledge of Philistine material culture comes from reliefs at Medinet Habu, Egypt, including the use by Philistine warriors of kilts, feathered headdresses, and curved-keel sailing vessels with high sterns and bows. Unlike the Canaanites, Israelites, and Egyptians, the Philistines did not practice circumcision (Judg. 14:3; 15:18; 1 Sam. 17:26). The biblical record attests to Philistine military prowess. They had iron weapons before the Israelites did (13:19-22), and effectively employed chariots and heavy infantry on the battlefield. According to Amos, they sold their captives into slavery (Amos 1:6-8).

II. Israel and the Philistines

The references to the Philistines at Gen. 10:14; 21:32, 34; 26:1-18; Exod. 13:17; 15:14; 23:31 are anachronistic. The Philistines probably arrived in Palestine not long after the Exodus and successfully resisted Israelite efforts to dislodge them (Josh. 13:2-3; Judg. 3:3; 10:6-7; chs. 13–16). By the time of Samuel it had become apparent that the Philistines were the greatest military threat faced by the Israelite tribal confederacy. The defeat experienced by Israel at Aphek, including the loss of the ark of the covenant (1 Sam. 4), showed that old patterns of leadership were ineffective. The Israelites demanded a king to lead them.

Having Saul as king did not prove to be a quick solution to the Philistine problem, but the Israelites did gain some victories over the Philistines (13:3; chs. 14, 17; 23:1-5). Saul died in battle at Mt. Gilboa (ch. 31), and it was left to David, as Saul's successor, to decisively defeat the Philistines. He fought them twice in the valley of Rephaim near Jerusalem and pursued them to Gezer (2 Sam. 5:17-25). Later victories were at Gob and Gath (21:18-22). Events of this period gave rise to the stories of the exploits of David's "mighty men" (vv. 16-22; 23:8-19). Solomon appar-

ently had no trouble at all from the Philistines (cf. 1 Kgs. 4:21 [MT 5:1]).

III. Divided Monarchy

The collapse of the Solomonic empire allowed many nations to revive their former territorial ambitions, and renewed pressure was felt from Egypt. An unnamed pharaoh of the Twenty-first Dynasty campaigned against the Philistines at Gezer (1 Kgs. 9:16-17), and Sheshonq I (biblical Shishak) launched a campaign into Palestine *ca.* 917 beginning at Gaza. The Philistines had adopted the Canaanite city-king (Heb. *melek*) political organization (Jer. 25:20; Zech. 9:5) and were, therefore, less cohesive in their competition with Israel and Judah. The early decades of the northern kingdom of Israel were marked by border battles with the Philistines (1 Kgs. 15:27; 16:15).

During the strong and prosperous reign of Jehoshaphat of Judah Philistines were among those who paid tribute to the southern kingdom (2 Chr. 17:11), but they raided the royal household during the reign of Jehoshaphat's successor Jehoram (21:16-17). King Uzziah had considerable military success against the Philistines, destroying the walls of Gaza, Jabneth, and Ashdod (26:6-7). Ahaz' submission to Tiglath-pileser III of Assyria was a response partly to Philistine raids on and occupation of Judean towns (28:16-21). Philistia was the subject of a number of prophetic oracles (Isa. 14:28-31; Jer. 25:20; ch. 47; Ezek. 25:15-17; Amos 1:6-8; Obad. 19; Zeph. 2:4-7; Zech. 9:5-8).

During this period, the Philistines, like the people of Israel and Judah, had increasingly to take Assyria into account. Adad-nirari III of Assyria (late ninth century) boasted that he had collected tribute from the Philistines (*ANET*, p. 282). Tiglath-pileser III attacked Ashkelon and Gaza for treasonous activity in 734, and Sargon II destroyed Gath in 715 and took control of Ashdod in 712. After other experiences of Assyrian force, the remaining Philistine cities were eventually willing to accept Assyrian domination. Yet it was not Assyria, or even the brief invasion of Philistine territory by Pharaoh Neco II after the fall of Assyria in 612, but the Palestinian campaign of Nebuchadrezzar of Babylon (604), in which mass deportations were employed, that ended the history of the Philistines.

Bibliography. T. Dothan, *The Philistines and Their Material Culture* (New Haven: 1982); E. E. Hindson, *The Philistines and the Old Testament* (Grand Rapids: 1972).

PHILO [fī′lō].† Philo Judaeus, a Jewish philosopher of Alexandria, Egypt, and a contemporary of Jesus. He is the outstanding example of an attempt within first-century Judaism to harmonize its traditions with Hellenistic philosophy and culture, an effort that was to pave the way for the spread of Christianity in the Graeco-Roman world. Philo's residence in a non-Jewish city (though one with a large Jewish population) and his huge literary output make him a prime subject for the study of this movement.

Not much is known about the details of Philo's life. He lived *ca.* 10 B.C.-*ca.* A.D. 45 and was a member of one of the wealthiest families in the Roman Empire. Emerging as an important public figure, he led a delegation of Alexandrian Jews to Rome in A.D. 39, and was able by his diplomacy to avert the wrath of the emperor Caligula against those Jews who refused to worship images of Caligula set up in Alexandria.

Philo's writings further reflect his allegiance to his Jewish heritage. He brings his traditional faith into a confident search for Hebrew values in Greek literature, philosophy, and history. His writings include philosophical works probing the nature of the cosmos and of human responsibility, apologetic treatises that present the history and faith of Israel in a way that would be attractive to a Gentile readership, and exegetical writings that feature a fully developed allegorical method of interpretation, allowing sweeping application of Stoic and Platonic insights to the Old Testament material. This allegorical approach became significant in the early and medieval Church's approach to the Old Testament. Philo's tracing of the best in non-Jewish thought to a Hebrew origin set the course for much of early Jewish and Christian apologetics.

Philosophically, Philo's significance lies in his attempt to introduce the idea of the self-revelation of God into the debate about how knowledge is possible. For biblical studies, the most important aspects of Philo's teachings are his attempt to bridge the Semitic and Hellenistic conceptual worlds, with results that were adopted by the early Christian Fathers in their theology, and his use of the neo-Platonic idea of the Logos as an intermediary figure between God and the world. Philo's portrait of the Logos is not consistent; at times he describes a personalized figure working in creation and in the illumination of humankind; at other times Logos is simply the inherent rationality of the world reflecting the rationality of its Creator God.

An unresolved debate concerns how far Philo's Logos has influenced the prologue of John's gospel (John 1:1-18). It was probably not a case of direct influence; the most that can be confidently asserted is that Philo wrote in a philosophical climate that pervaded the eastern Mediterranean, and that John's gospel was written a few decades later in the same cultural climate.

The allegorical and typological methods, patterns of thought, and literary style of Philo are reflected in the letter of Hebrews more than in any other New Testament book. Here too it is probably not a matter of literary dependence but of common background, striking enough that Hebrews is often thought to have been written by another Alexandrian.

PHILOLOGUS [fĭ lŏl'ə gəs] (Gk. *Philologos* "fond of learning"). A Christian in Rome greeted by Paul (Rom. 16:15).

PHILOSOPHY (Gk. *philosophía*).* In Classical Greek "philosophy" could refer either to the pursuit of wisdom and scientific knowledge or such knowledge itself. In the Hellenistic age the term took on a more generalized meaning, encompassing moral philosophy, religious speculation, and even magic. The Jewish historian Josephus used the term in its general meaning when he introduced the three sects of Judaism as philosophical schools. It is within this broader range of meaning that the terms "philosophy" (Col.

2:8) and "philosopher" (Gk. *philósophos*; Acts 17:18) are used in the New Testament.

In his warning against philosophy (Col. 2:8) Paul does not have in view the philosophical pursuits of a Socrates or Aristotle, but a particular religious group that offered the Colossian church a syncretism of Hellenistic religion and Jewish-Christian ideas, all under the label of philosophy. In contrast to the claims of the false teachers, Paul calls this teaching "empty deceit." While such religious philosophies might claim a venerable tradition and harmony with the true structure of the universe, Paul counters with the polemical charge that their teachings are based upon mere human tradition and are aligned with the inferior spirits of the universe. The root of the error is that this teaching is "not according to Christ." Paul has already demonstrated the supremacy of Christ over all powers (1:15-20); cf. 2:14-15) and will go on to show that Christ has invalidated the demands of human precepts and doctrines (vv. 20-23).

At Acts 17:18 Paul is confronted at Athens with Epicurean and Stoic philosophers who perceive him to be a "preacher of foreign divinities." Paul's Areopagus address treats his audience of philosophers with respect and seeks common ground in an altar "to an unknown god" (v. 23) and a quotation from two Greek poets, Epimenides and Aratus (v. 28). His message climaxes with a reference to Christ's resurrection (v. 31) and is rejected outright by most of the philosophers. While the Stoics might have accepted a message of the immortality of the soul, the Epicureans, with their materialist view of reality, would have rejected that also.

PHINEHAS [fĭn'ĭ əs] (Heb. *pînᵉḥas*; from Egyp. *p'nhsy* "Nubian").

1. The son of Eleazar and Putiel, and grandson of Aaron (Exod. 6:25). His slaying of an Israelite man and the Midianite woman he had brought into the Israelite camp was recorded as a particularly dramatic episode in the reaction of Israel's leaders to the crisis at Peor (Num. 25:7-11). As a result of this incident Phinehas' descendants were confirmed in the priesthood perpetually (vv. 12-13), and he became for Judaism the most significant hero of "zeal" that seeks at all cost to preserve the observance of the law and the purity of Israel (Ps. 106:30-31; Sir. 45:23-24; 1 Macc. 2:26 [KJV "Phinees"], 54; 4 Macc. 18:12). As priest, Phinehas accompanied Israel's army into battle against Midian (Num. 31:6) and later received from God a call to go to battle against the Benjaminites (Judg. 20:28). He headed a delegation from the Israelites west of the Jordan to the Reubenites, Gadites, and Manassites who had built a altar near the Jordan; this delegation sought successfully to prevent the eastern tribes from regarding themselves as separate from the rest of Israel (Josh. 22:10-34). When Israel settled in the land, Phinehas was given a town in the hill country of Ephraim (24:33). According to 1 Chr. 9:20 he was the chief of the gatekeepers of the tabernacle.

2. A son of Eli; with his brother Hophni, a priest at the shrine at Shiloh (1 Sam. 1:3; 14:3). Both brothers are condemned for their greedy disregard for the customs of the Shiloh cult (2:12-17) and for having sexual intercourse with the women who assisted at the shrine (vv. 22-25). The death of the two men was predicted (v. 34; cf. v. 25) and occurred when they were in battle at Aphek, where the Philistines captured the ark of the covenant (4:11).

3. The father of Eleazar, a postexilic priest who accompanied Ezra in the return from exile (Ezra 8:33).

PHLEGON [flĕg'ŏn] (Gk. *Phlegōn* "burning"). A Christian in Rome to whom Paul sent his greetings (Rom. 16:14).

PHOEBE [fē'bē] (Gk. *Phoibē* "bright, radiant"). A "deaconess" of the church at Cenchreae, the eastern port of Corinth, who is commended by Paul to the Christians of Rome and who probably delivered his letter to them (Rom. 16:1-2; KJV "Phebe"). *See also* DEACONESS.

PHOENICIA [fə nĭsh'ə] (Gk. *Phoinikē*).† A region on the Mediterranean coast extending roughly from the Carmel ridge in the south to Arvad in the north, nearly equivalent to the coast of modern Lebanon. Phoenicia was famous in ancient times for its active role in Mediterranean maritime shipping.

I. Name and Territory

The land was first designated as Phoenicia (and the people Phoenicians) in the eighth century B.C. by the Greeks, based on Gk. *phoínix*, a red-purple dye obtained from the Phoenicians, who manufactured it from the shells of the snails *murax brandaris* and *murax trunculus*. The Phoenicians were commonly called by their Near Eastern neighbors (and may have called themselves) "Sidonians" (e.g., Deut. 3:9; 1 Kgs. 5:6 [MT 20]), a narrower term referring most specifically only to the inhabitants of the city of Sidon, and "Canaanites," a broader term for all the peoples of Palestine and Syria speaking western Semitic languages—except for the Israelites (thus RSV "Phoenicia" for $k^ena^{'a}nîm$ "Canaanites" at Obad. 20).

Phoenicia extended along a narrow strip of coastal land about 300 km. (185 mi.) long. Its terrain alternates between coastal plains, hills, and mountainous areas that extend to meet the sea at some points. This varied topography made communications difficult both with the interior of Canaan and between the cities of Phoenicia themselves. As a result, the cities were always divided politically, and were as likely to act independently as in concert. All the major Phoenician cities were on the coast, on rocky promontories (Byblos, Sidon, and Acco) or on islands near the coast (Tyre and Arvad). The Phoenician cities included all the few good natural harbors of the eastern Mediterranean coast (Byblos, Berytos, Sidon, Tyre). The coastal plains were fertile enough to support extensive agriculture. The mountains supplied timber.

II. Trade

As early as the Late Bronze Age the Phoenicians traversed the Mediterranean in broadbeamed ships with high sterns and bows propelled by sails or oarsmen. Growing competition from Greeks beginning in the ninth century B.C. led the Phoenicians to found trading colonies in Spain, Cyprus, Malta, Sicily, and northern Africa (prominently Carthage). The lament for Tyre at Ezek. 27 is a good indication of the far-flung trade routes serviced by Phoenician sailors.

Phoenician merchants sold raw materials and finished luxury goods alike. Timber, dyed goods, foodstuffs, wine, glassware, and metal products were exported. Phoenicians served as middlemen in the ivory and papyrus trade. Financial success meant a high standard of living for some Phoenicians, and archaeologists have discovered Egyptian alabaster, fine pottery, furniture, and other evidences of a high culture in Phoenician cities. An export of major significance was the Phoenician alphabet, adopted by the Greeks in the ninth or eighth century.

III. History

Settlements existed on the sites of the Phoenician cities long before the historical period; at Byblos circular mud huts on stone bases and evidence of burial in earthenware pots have been discovered dating to the Neolithic period, and pottery has been found at Byblos and Ugarit dating to the late fifth millennium B.C. Urban culture began in the late fourth millennium, with evidence discovered of walled cities and bronze weaponry. Widespread destruction of Phoenician cities is indicated for the third millennium, with the influx of waves of Amorites and Hurrians throughout the land.

Contacts with Egypt existed from the earliest historical times, and extensive trade with Egypt was carried on by the eighteenth century. From that time, Phoenician colonization began along the Syrian and Palestinian coast. Egyptian control of Phoenician cities waxed and waned during this period.

When the Sea Peoples came into the area *ca.* 1200, Phoenician life was disrupted. The inhabitants of Sidon, until then the principal Phoenician city, fled, and Tyre became dominant. Egyptian control had been broken (cf. the Egyptian Tale of Wen-amon; *ANET*, pp. 25-29), and the period of greatest Phoenician prosperity began from this time. Hiram I, a significant ruler of Tyre, had close commercial relations with kings David and Solomon of Israel, supplying building materials for the palace and temple at Jerusalem (2 Sam. 5:11; 1 Kgs. 5:1-12, 18 [MT 15-26, 32]; 2 Chr. 2:13-16 [MT 12-15]). Solomon became the dominant partner, but Phoenician resources and expertise were essential (9:11-14, 27; 10:11, 22).

The religion of the Phoenicians was essentially that of Late Bronze Age Canaanite practice, although with some primarily local modifications. With the division of the monarchies, Phoenician religion became increasingly a threat to the Israelites, although it had already been such during the reign of Solomon (1 Kgs. 11:5; 2 Kgs. 23:13). King Ahab of Israel furthered the policy of alliance by marrying Jezebel, the daughter of Hiram's successor Ethbaal (1 Kgs. 16:31). Jezebel's zealous promotion of her native religion and culture (primarily the worship of the Tyrian Baal Melqart), together with Ahab's partial compliance with her aims and the threat posed by Phoenician prosperity, led the radically Yahwistic prophets, mainly Elijah at first, to battle against the inroads of Phoenician religion (vv. 32-33; ch. 18). The conflict continued on and eventually led to Israelite expressions of contempt for the Phoenicians (Ezek. 26–28; Joel 3:4-8 [MT 4:4-8]).

From the ninth century and especially the eighth century, Phoenicia suffered attacks and dominance by large empires—the Assyrian, Neo-Babylonian, Persian, and Greco-Macedonian empires in succession. Assurnasirpal II (884-859) attacked the Phoenician cities, and Shalmaneser II defeated a Syrian-Phoenician coalition at Qarqar in 853. In 743 Tiglath-pileser III established northern Phoenician (except Byblos) as the Assyrian province of Ṣimirra. Sennacherib seized Sidon from King Lulli of Tyre in 700 and installed an Assyrian vassal there. Sidon rebelled in 677, only to be destroyed by Esarhaddon and made an Assyrian province. Tyre revolted in 671, providing the Assyrians with the opportunity to carve out a third Phoenician province, Ushu, to the south. By the time the Assyrian Empire collapsed in 612, the only Phoenician city-states retaining a semblance of autonomy were Arvad, Byblos, and Tyre. Tyre stubbornly resisted a thirteen-year siege by Nebuchadrezzar, but the island fell to the Babylonians in 572. Persia's conquest of Babylon in 539 brought limited independence for the Phoenician cities; Sidon again gained dominance, and in the fifth century Phoenician ships took part in the Persian wars with Greece. In the fourth century both Tyre and Sidon revolted against the Persians; Artaxerxes III besieged Sidon and reduced it to ruins in 351. Tyre stood fast for seven months against the forces of Alexander the Great, but fell in 332 when Alexander used the rubble of monuments and houses to construct a causeway to the fortified island. Macedonian armies occupied Phoenicia for twenty years after Alexander's death until the southern area was annexed to Egypt under Ptolemy in 301; the northern region came under Seleucid dominance.

Greek culture took root throughout Phoenicia, and under the Pax Romana Phoenicia continued its commercial importance. Jesus spent a brief period in Phoenicia during his Galilean ministry (Mark 7:24-31). Some of the early spread of the gospel among Gentiles took place in Phoenicia (Acts 11:19; 15:3; KJV "Phenice"; 21:2; KJV "Phenicia").

Bibliography. D. Harden, *The Phoenicians,* 3rd ed. (New York: 1980); H. J. Katzenstein, *The History of Tyre* (Jerusalem: 1973); S. Moscati, *The World of the Phoenicians* (London: 1968); W. A. Ward, *The Role of the Phoenicians in the Interaction of Mediterranean Civilizations* (Beirut: 1968).

PHOENIX [fē'nĭks] (Gk. *Phoinix*). A harbor on the southern side of the island of Crete, possibly the one now called Loutro. On Paul's voyage to Rome, after the fast of the Day of Atonement, the captain of the ship chose to try to sail from the harbor of Fair Havens to spend the winter at Phoenix, a harbor farther to the west (Acts 27:12; KJV "Phenice"); this gamble resulted in shipwreck.

PHRYGIA [frĭj'ĭ ə] (Gk. *Phrygia*).† A region of inland Asia Minor. Phrygia's borders were not exact and varied from time to time. It can be identified generally as the region east of the coastal region of Lydia and

north of Pisidia. In New Testament times Phrygia was divided between the Roman provinces of Asia and Galatia. The cities of Pisidian Antioch and Iconium were sometimes considered to be within the limits of Phrygia, though the latter was more often considered part of Lycaonia; in the southwest, Colossae, Laodicea, and Hierapolis were sometimes included in Phrygia.

The Phrygians, a Thracian people for whom the region was named, probably came into Asia Minor from the northwest *ca.* 1500 B.C. As an independent kingdom Phrygia flourished in the eighth century under a succession of kings alternately named Gordius and Midas. Phrygian independence was ended abruptly after 700 by the invading Cimmerians, and the region was ruled successively by the neighboring Lydians, Persia, and Macedonia. In 301 it was annexed to the Seleucid kingdom of Syria. After 275 the western portion became part of Pergamum and subsequently the Roman province of Asia.

Jews from Phrygia were present in Jerusalem for the Feast of Pentecost when the Holy Spirit came upon the Church (Acts 2:10). Paul, Silas, and Timothy traveled northward through Phrygia toward Bithynia (16:6). At the beginning of a later journey (18:23), Paul again passed through Phrygia.

PHURAH (Judg. 7:10-11, KJV). *See* PURAH.

PHUT (Gen. 10:6; Ezek. 27:10, KJV). *See* LIBYA.

PHUVAH (Gen. 46:13, KJV). *See* PUAH **3.**

PHYGELUS [fī'jə ləs] (Gk. *Phygelos* "fugitive"). A Christian from the province of Asia who, together with Hermogenes and other Asian Christians, abandoned the imprisoned Paul (2 Tim. 1:15; KJV "Phygellus"). The reason for this desertion was probably fear of being associated with a notorious prisoner; Onesiphorus is held up as a person who "was not ashamed of my chains" and who was, indeed, eager to be with Paul (vv. 16-17).

PHYLACTERIES [fĭ lăk'tə rēz] (Gk. *phylaktéria*). Two small receptacles, generally called "tefillin" (from Aram. *rᵉpillîn*; cf. Heb. *rᵉpillâ* "prayer"), worn by Jewish men during prayer except on the Sabbath and feast days. Both tefillin contain tiny parchment scrolls with the Hebrew texts of Exod. 13:1-10, 11-16; Deut. 6:4-9; 11:13-21 inscribed on them as a reminder of the whole of the Torah. The tefillin are fitted with leather straps and are attached above the forehead and on the left upper arm (or right, for a left-handed person) according to a prescribed ritual. This practice, which was observed in the time of Jesus much as it is now, is based on Exod. 13:9, 16; Deut. 6:6, 8; 11:18.

In New Testament times, some Jews regarded phylacteries as amulets to ward off evil. Jesus criticized the Pharisees for using large phylacteries in order to draw attention to their piety (Matt. 23:5).

PHYSICIAN. *See* MEDICINE.

PIBESETH [pī bē'zĭth] (Heb. *pî-ḥeseṯ*; Egyp. *Pr-Bȝst*

"home of Bastet [the cat-goddess]"). A city in Lower Egypt on the easternmost branch of the Nile Delta, at modern Tell Basṭa 1.5 km. (1 mi.) southeast of modern Zagazig. Pibeseth is mentioned with On, another city in Lower Egypt, in an oracle against Egypt (Ezek. 30:17).

PIGEON. Any of several birds of the family Columbidae. The RSV and KJV so translate Heb. *yônâ* and Gk. *peristerá* when they refer to sacrificial animals (otherwise "dove").

Birds were usually offered for sacrifice as an alternative to larger animals; their use for sacrifice is, therefore, an indication of relative poverty (e.g., Lev. 1:14 [cf. vv. 3, 10]; 5:7; Luke 2:24), though a cereal offering might be an even greater indication of poverty (Lev. 5:11). Pigeons were sold in the outer courts of the Herodian temple so that sacrifice could be offered by pilgrims who had come a long distance (Matt. 21:12 par.).

Among the animals cut in half as part of the covenant ritual of Gen. 15 is a "young pigeon" (Heb. *gôzāl,* v. 9).

PI-HAHIROTH [pīʹə hīʹrŏth] (Heb. *pî-haḥîrôṯ*; cf. Egyp. *pr-Ḥrt* "house of [the deity] Ḥrt"). The last place the Israelites camped before they marched through the Reed Sea (Exod. 14:2, 9; Num. 33:7); at v. 8 it is called "Hahiroth." The location of (Pi-)Hahiroth is unknown, but must have been in the extreme eastern part of the Nile Delta.

PILATE, ACTS OF.† An apocryphal gospel also known as the Gospel of Nicodemus. The account of Jesus' trial (Acts Pil. 1–9) makes of it a dispute between Pilate, who defends Jesus' innocence, and Jesus' Jewish accusers, with certain Jews testifying in Jesus' defense. After Jesus has been crucified and his body placed in a tomb by Joseph of Arimathea, "the Jews" imprison Joseph, but he miraculously escapes (ch. 12). A number of witnesses appear before the Sanhedrin with conclusive testimony of Jesus' resurrection (chs. 12–16).

Chs. 17–27 are an imaginative attempt to provide details of Jesus' descent to "the spirits in prison" (1 Pet. 3:19) and the raising of "many bodies of the saints" at the time of Jesus' death (Matt. 27:52-53). The appearance of Christ causes great dismay for Satan and Hades, but joy for the souls there, as Christ raises the dead from Adam to the penitent thief who had been crucified. All this is presented as testimony given by Simeon (Luke 2:34) and his sons, who are among those who have been raised from the dead.

These two parts of this gospel (Acts Pil. 1–16, 17–27) originated separately, probably in the fourth century, and were joined together probably in the fifth century. They may contain traditions reaching back into the second century. The first part may have been penned as a response to "Acts of Pilate" circulated by pagan opponents of Christianity, including the Emperor Maximinus (cf. Eusebius *HE* i.9.2-3; ix.5). It is largely dependent on the canonical Gospels but offers many amplifications, including a strong emphasis on the innocence of Pilate with regard to Jesus' death and the consequent guilt of the Jewish leaders who forced

Pilate to do their will. Both parts of the Christian Acts show an interest in attaching names to persons who appear but are unnamed in the canonical Gospels. A number of expansions and appendixes exist in some recensions of the Acts, including a letter from Pilate to Emperor Claudius blaming the Jews for Christ's death and testifying to his resurrection, and the introduction of eyewitnesses to the betrothal of Joseph and Mary and Jesus' postresurrection commission to his disciples and his ascension from the mountaintop.

Pilate is described as "uncircumcised in the flesh, but circumcised in the heart" (Acts Pil. 12:1). Texts of the Acts are extant in Latin, Greek, Syriac, Coptic, and Armenian; the wide dissemination of the Acts, together with other traditions, led to the canonization of Pilate's wife in the Greek Orthodox Church and to the acceptance of Pilate as a saint and martyr by the Coptic Church. The work achieved considerable popularity as the inspiration for medieval mystery plays on the harrowing of hell, and remained popular among some Old Order Mennonites into the twentieth century.

PILATE, PONTIUS [pŏnʹtī əs pīʹlət] (Gk. *Pontios Pilatos*; Lat. *Pontius Pilatus*).† The fifth Roman governor of Judea (A.D. 26-36) who presided at Jesus' trial and authorized his execution. An upper-middle-class Roman equestrian of the Samnite clan of the Pontii, Pilate arrived in Palestine with the title of *praefectus* shortly before the ministry of John the Baptist (Luke 3:1). He was given full charge of the military operation of Judea, Samaria, and Idumea under the Roman legate of Syria. The title of *procurator* was

Inscription from Caesarea which includes the name of Pontius Pilate in the second line (by courtesy of the Israel Department of Antiquities and Museums)

used later of governors of equestrian provinces like Judea and is sometimes applied anachronistically to Pilate.

There is little mention of Pilate in non-Christian sources. Writing *ca.* 115, Tacitus (*Ann.* xv.44.4) mentions him only in connection with the death of Christ, as do all New Testament references outside the Gospels (Acts 3:13; 4:27; 13:28; 1 Tim. 6:13). Philo (*Leg. ad Gaium* xxxviii [299-305], quoting a letter of Agrippa I) and Josephus (*BJ* ii.ix.2-4 [169-177]; *Ant.* xviii.3.1-2 [55-59]) tell of his offenses against Jewish religious sentiment, specifically his bringing into Jerusalem military insignia bearing the emperor's image and, on another occasion, ornamental shields bearing his own and the emperor's names. Pilate also financed an aqueduct with money confiscated from the temple treasury. Philo and Josephus portray him as inflexible, corrupt, and cruel. Luke 13:1 mentions "the Galileans whose blood Pilate had mingled with their sacrifices." According to the Gospel accounts of Jesus' trial (Matt. 27; Mark 15; Luke 23; John 18:28–19:42) Pilate was swayed by pressure from the crowd led by the Jewish leaders in Jerusalem.

Pilate's tendency to react with force led to his removal from office. A Samaritan prophet said that he would produce the temple vessels which the Samaritans believed were buried on Mt. Gerizim. The crowd assembled to see this wonder was attacked, and some were executed later. Vitellius, legate of Syria, ordered Pilate recalled to Rome in A.D. 36 to answer for the incident.

Nothing certain is known about Pilate's later life and his death. There are late reports that he was ordered to commit suicide under Emperor Gaius Caligula (Eusebius *HE* ii.7) and also that he was beheaded under Emperor Nero (John Malalas *Chronography* x). The paucity of historical data did not discourage the formation of Christian legends. The shift of responsibility for Jesus' death from Pilate wholly to the Jewish leaders was a common theme in the developing Christian traditions, particularly as antagonism between Christians and Jews increased. Tertullian (*Apol.* xxi) went so far as to call Pilate "Christian before his own conscience." In adition to the Gospel of Peter and the Acts of Pilate, Pilate apocrypha included forged correspondence between the governor and both Herod and the Emperor Tiberius. Perhaps most interesting are the Anaphora of Pilate, a more detailed version of the letter of Pilate to Claudius, and the Paradosis of Pilate often joined to it, in which Pilate dies as a Christian martyr. Some legends also sanctified his wife; unnamed at Matt. 27:19, she is called Prokla in Greek, Procla or (Claudia) Procula in Latin. Both Pilate and his wife are honored with a feast day by the Ethiopian church, Prokla also by the Greek Orthodox. *See* PETER, GOSPEL OF; PILATE, ACTS OF.

PILDASH [pĭl′dăsh] (Heb. *pildāš*). A son of Abraham's brother Nahor and Milcah (Gen. 22:22).

PILGRIMAGE. A journey to a central sanctuary. All male Israelites were commanded to appear before the Lord three times each year: for Passover, for the Feast of Weeks, and for the Feast of Tabernacles (Exod. 23:14-17; 34:23-24; Deut. 16:1-17). Although this

commandment applied only to men, women and children also went if possible (cf. 1 Sam. 1:3-5; Luke 2:41-42). A specific group of psalms, the "Songs of Ascents" (Pss. 120–134), were probably sung by pilgrims on their way to Jerusalem.

Jeroboam I, the first king of the separate northern kingdom of Israel, wished to end the pilgrimages of his subjects to Jerusalem and so set up alternative shrines at Dan and Bethel (1 Kgs. 12:28-30). Pilgrimage to these shrines was criticized by the prophet Amos (Amos 4:4-5; 5:5-6; 8:14), not because they were an alternative to Jerusalem, but because pilgrimage had become a religious substitute for obeying God. King Hezekiah's efforts to gather all the inhabitants of Judah and the defunct northern kingdom to one Passover celebration in Jerusalem were partly successful (2 Chr. 30:1-13). One of the aims of King Josiah's reforms was to emphasize the Passover pilgrimage to Jerusalem (2 Kgs. 23:21-23; 2 Chr. 35:1ff.). After the Exile, pilgrimages were usually limited to the Passover (cf. Luke 2:41).

At Ps. 119:54 Heb. *māgôr* refers metaphorically to the human's transient life on earth (RSV elsewhere "sojourning"; cf. v. 19, *gēr* "sojourner").

PILHA [pĭl′hä] (Heb. *pilḥā'* "millstone"). One of the chiefs of the people who set his seal to the new covenant under Nehemiah (Neh. 10:24; KJV "Pileha").

PILLAR. Heb. *maṣṣēḇâ* (KJV sometimes "image") is used of stones set up as memorials, usually during the era of the patriarchs (Gen. 28:18; 31:45-52; 35:14, 20; Exod. 24:4; 2 Sam. 18:18). Such memorial stones might be intended to represent God's dwelling (Gen. 28:22).The places where they were erected generally became established in tradition as shrines (cf. v. 19; 31:13; 35:15). Pillars were also part of the cultic installations of the northern kingdom of Israel (Hos. 3:4; 10:1-2) and a later Jewish worship center in Egypt (Isa. 19:19).

The Hebrew term is also used of stones set up to represent Canaanite deities, sometimes adopted by Israelites (e.g., Exod. 23:24; Lev. 26:1; 1 Kgs. 14:23; 2 Chr. 31:1). These stones may have been thought of as crude statues, but their association with Baal (2 Kgs. 3:2; 10:26-27) and their placement usually with Asherim (i.e., representations of a female deity; e.g., Exod. 34:13; 1 Kgs. 14:23; 2 Kgs. 17:10; Mic. 5:13-14 [MT 12-13]) suggest that the sacred pillars were sometimes phallic symbols. Heb. *maṣṣēḇâ* is also used of later non-Canaanite cultic pillars, including Egyptian "obelisks" (so RSV, Jer. 43:13).

Heb. *'ammûḏ* is used of architectural pillars and columns (e.g., Exod. 38; 1 Kgs. 7; cf. *maṣṣēḇâ* at Ezek. 26:11) and of the pillar of fire and pillar of cloud that accompanied the Israelites in their flight from Egypt and journey through the wilderness (*see* PILLAR OF CLOUD, PILLAR OF FIRE).

Gk. *stýlos* is used figuratively in the New Testament—of the Church as that which upholds the truth (1 Tim. 3:15), of significant church leaders (Gal. 2:9), and of those who will be permanently established in the heavenly temple (Rev. 3:12).

PILLAR OF CLOUD (Heb. *'ammûḏ 'ānān*),

PILLAR OF FIRE (*'ammûḏ 'ēš*). The means by which God made his presence known and led and protected the Israelites during their escape from Egypt (Exod. 13:21-22; 14:19-20, 24) and their journeys in the wilderness (e.g., 40:38; Num. 14:14; Neh. 9:12, 19; cf. Ps. 78:14). The raising of the pillar of cloud was the signal for the people to resume their journey after a stop (Exod. 40:36-37). The pillar of cloud also revealed God's presence at the tent of meeting when Moses interceded for the people (33:9-10), when God intervened in the dispute of Moses with Miriam and Aaron (Num. 12:5), and as Moses' death approached (Deut. 31:15).

Related manifestations of God's presence involve a cloud, not necessarily the pillar of cloud (e.g., Exod. 16:10; Lev. 16:2; Num. 11:25; 1 Kgs. 8:10-11; Ezek. 1:4). Attempted naturalistic explanations of the pillar of cloud and the pillar of fire have focused on volcanic activity in the Sinai peninsula and on the use of fire and smoke signals to guide caravans. Another interpretation is that the fire represents the dazzling aura surrounding the divine king, depicted in Mesopotamian art as a garment of flame, and the cloud the covering of the deity that protects the onlooker from his might; it may also represent the voice of God as it thunders forth in theophany.

PILTAI [pĭl'tī] (Heb. *pilṭay* "[Yahweh] is deliverance"). The chief of a priestly family during the time of the postexilic high priest Joiakim (Neh. 12:17).

PIM [pĭm] (Heb. *pîm*).* A unit of weight equal to two-thirds of a shekel or about 7.6 gm. (0.27 oz.) (1 Sam. 13:21).

PINE.† Any of the various species of coniferous evergreen trees with long slender needles, of the genus *Pinus*. A number of pines are native to Palestine and Lebanon, including the Aleppo pine (*Pinus halepensis* Mill.) and the brutian pine (*Pinus brutia*).

Identification of trees mentioned in the Old Testament involves a number of difficulties and uncertainties, especially in regard to the conifers, except for cedar. At Isa. 41:19; 60:13 Heb. *tᵉʾaššûr* is translated "pine" in the RSV (KJV "box tree"; JB "cypress," "box"); in the same two verses the KJV renders "pine" for *tiḏhār* (RSV, JB "plane"; NIV "fir"). Heb. *tᵉʾaššûr* is probably the Italian cypress (*Cupressus sempervirens* L.); *tiḏhār* is evidently some other conifer, perhaps the fir. Heb. *tᵉʾaššûr* is probably also mentioned at Ezek. 27:6, where RSV "decks of pines" is based on an emendation of *baṯ-ʾašurîm* "daughter of Ashurites" (cf. KJV "company of the Ashurites") to *biṯ'aššurîm*, following the Targum (JB "cedar"; NIV "cypress").

Heb. *bᵉrôṯ* appears only at Cant. 1:17 (KJV "fir"; JB "cypress") and may be a variant form of *bᵉrôš*. *See* CYPRESS.

The KJV and JB translate *'ēṣ šemen*, lit. "tree of oil," as "pine" at Neh. 8:15, but it probably represents the oleaster or "wild olive" (so RSV).

PINNACLE (Gk. *pterýgion*).† The traditional location of the pinnacle of the temple on which Jesus stood while being tempted to throw himself down (Matt. 4:5; Luke 4:9) is the southeast corner of the temple enclosure. The retaining walls of that corner of the temple mount are in essentially the same location and form they were in the first century A.D., but they were at that time topped by a portico. A fall from the portico or its roof down into the Kidron valley would certainly be fatal apart from angelic intervention. Since it has been discovered that the height of the southwest corner of the temple enclosure would have been as high, some have suggested that the "pinnacle" was at that corner instead, since a fall from it would have put Jesus into the crowded city, rather than into the Kidron, outside the city. Other locations on the temple mount have also been suggested.

At Isa. 54:12 Heb. *šimšōṯ* represents the gleaming surfaces of buildings in the restored Jerusalem (KJV "windows"; NIV "battlements").

PINON [pī'nŏn] (Heb. *pînōn*). The name of a clan chief of Esau (Edom) or, more likely, of the geographical area that was under one such Edomite ruler (Gen. 36:41; 1 Chr. 1:52). Pinon should perhaps be associated with PUNON, a place where the Israelites encamped shortly before entering the plains of Moab (Num. 33:42-43).

PIPE.† Heb. *ḥālîl* (1 Sam. 10:5; 1 Kgs. 1:40; Isa. 5:12; 30:29; Jer. 48:36; RSV "flute" except at 1 Kgs. 1:40) and Gk. *aulós* (1 Cor. 14:7; related words at Matt. 11:17; Rev. 18:22) represent double-piped reed instruments. The identification of Heb. *'ûgāḇ* (Gen. 4:21; Job 21:12; 30:31; Ps. 150:4; KJV "organ") is not certain, but it may have been a single reedless pipe. Among the instruments used in the court of Nebuchadnezzar (Dan. 3:5, 7, 10, 15) was the Aram. *mašrôqî*, possibly a panpipe or multiple reed pipe (so RSV; KJV "flute").

Pipes and flutes, especially the *'ûgāḇ*, were often associated with eroticism and were generally not used in the music of the Jerusalem temple. They were used particularly in mourning (e.g., Jer. 48:36; Matt. 9:23; RSV "flute").

PIRAM [pī'rəm] (Heb. *pirʾām* "wild ass"). The Amorite king of Jarmuth at the time of the conquest of Canaan (Josh. 10:3). Along with the other allies of King Adonizedek of Jerusalem who attacked Gibeon, he was defeated and killed by Joshua (vv. 23-26).

PIRATHON [pĭr'ə thŏn] (Heb. *pirʿāṯôn*). The home of the judge Abdon (Judg. 12:13-15) and of Benaiah, one of David's mighty men (2 Sam. 23:30; 1 Chr. 11:31). Situated "in the land of Ephraim" (Judg. 12:15; cf. 1 Chr. 27:14), Pirathon has been identified with modern Far'âtā, about 10 km. (6 mi.) west-southwest of Nablus.

PISGAH [pĭz'gə] (Heb. *happisgâ*). A mountain in the land of Moab, opposite Jericho (Deut. 34:1) and near the Dead Sea (3:17; Heb. *'ašdōṯ happisgâ* "the slopes of Pisgah"; KJV "Ashdoth-pisgah"; cf. Josh. 12:3; 13:20). Balak built seven altars on Pisgah (Num. 23:14). It was from Pisgah (*rōʾš happisgâ*, lit. "the top of Pisgah"; cf. Num. 21:20; 23:14) that Moses looked out over the promised land (Deut. 3:27), and there he died (34:1-5). Pisgah is identified with modern Râs es-Siâghah, adjacent to Mt. Nebo and about 27 km. (17 mi.) east-southeast of Jericho.

PISHON [pī'shŏn] (Heb. *pîšôn*). One of the four rivers of Eden, said to have flowed around the land of Havilah (Gen. 2:11; KJV "Pison"). The Pishon has been identified with the Ganges, the Indus, tributaries of the Euphrates, and with other rivers. Each opinion depends on a particular view of the location of Eden, and none has any great advantage over the others.

PISIDIA [pĭ sĭd'ĭ ə] (Gk. *Pisidia*). A mountainous region in Asia Minor east of Lycia and Caria, south of Phrygia, and north of Pamphylia. Because of the rugged terrain and the general inaccessibility of the region, the inhabitants were fiercely independent and effectively resisted rule by conquerors from Alexander the Great through King Amyntas of Galatia.

At the time of Paul Pisidia was allotted to the Roman province of Galatia. Antioch of Pisidia, where Paul and Barnabas preached (Acts 13:14-50), was a Hellenized Roman city with a large Jewish population, one of several military colonies established by Augustus.

PISPA [pĭs'pə] (Heb. *pispâ*). A son of Jether of the tribe of Asher (1 Chr. 7:38; KJV "Pispah").

PISTACHIO NUTS (Heb. *boṭnîm*). The edible fruit of *Pistacia vera* L., a small tree native to Asia Minor, Syria, and Palestine. These nuts have long been valuable in trade, as they were in the time of the patriarchs (Gen. 43:11; KJV "nuts").

PISTIS SOPHIA [pĭs'tĭs sō fī'ə] (Gk. *Pistis Sophia* "faith-wisdom," here the name of a spiritual being).* A Gnostic writing divided into four sections, the first three of which date from the late third century A.D. and form one treatise, the Pistis Sophia proper. The fourth section is a separate treatise composed a few decades earlier. Both were apparently composed in Greek in Egypt and translated into Coptic, the language of the surviving manuscript. They are important as direct sources of information about one form of Gnosticism.

Like other Gnostic gospels both parts consist of a dialogue between the risen Christ and his disciples, in which he provides esoteric teachings in response to their questions. Set in the twelfth year after the resurrection, the three-part treatise emphasizes the role of Mary Magdalene and claims to have been written by Philip. The second treatise is set immediately after the resurrection.

PIT (Heb. *bôr*, *bᵉʾēr*, *šaḥaṭ*; *paḥaṭ*; Gk. *phréar*, *bóthymos*). Pits, whether natural (Gen. 14:10, "bitumen pits"; 37:22; Ps. 40:2 [MT 3]) or dug to collect rain water, to trap people or animals (cf. 35:7; 57:6 [MT 7]; Ezek. 19:4), or to hold prisoners (Isa. 24:22), constituted a danger addressed by provisions of the Covenant Code (Exod. 21:33-34). Most often pits occur metaphorically to represent destruction caused, e.g., by evil plots (Ps. 7:15 [MT 16]; Prov. 26:27; Jer.

18:20), association with "a loose woman" or a harlot (Prov. 22:14; 23:27), or divine judgment (Isa. 24:17-18).

"The Pit" can be, in particular, a synonym for death and Sheol (e.g., Job 17:14; Ps. 16:10; Prov. 1:12). The source of eschatological destruction on the earth and the place of eternal judgment of the devil is portrayed as an *ábyssos* "bottomless pit" (Rev. 9:1-11; 11:7; 17:8; 20:1-3).

PITCH (Heb. *kōper*, *zepeṭ*). A flammable liquid hydrocarbon distilled from plant resins or occurring with natural asphalt. In ancient times pitch was used to seal boats and baskets (Gen. 6:14; Exod. 2:3) and for mortar. Eruptions of pitch are part of a portrayal of judgment at Isa. 34:9. *See* BITUMEN.

PITHOM [pī'thəm] (Heb. *piṯōm*; Egyp. *pr-ỉtm* "house of [the deity] Atum").† An Egyptian store-city built by the enslaved Israelites (Exod. 1:11). Two sites are suggested for Pithom at the eastern end of Wâdī Tumilât in the area between the modern city of Zagazig and Lake Timsâḥ: modern Tell el-Maskhûṭah and, more likely, Tell er-Reṭâbeh, 14 km. (9 mi.) to the west.

PITHON [pī'thŏn] (Heb. *pîṯôn*). A son of Micah and descendant of Saul, of the tribe of Benjamin (1 Chr. 8:35; 9:41).

PLAGUE (Heb. *maggēpâ*, *negep*, *makkâ*, *negaʿ*; Gk. *mástix*, *plēge*).* Sudden disease, sometimes fatal, sent or threatened as punishment by God. On most occasions the nature of the disease is not specified (e.g., Gen. 12:17; Exod. 30:12; 32:35; Num. 11:33; 16:46-50 [MT 17:10-15]; cf. 25:8), but in some cases a "plague" might be associated with specific symptoms (1 Sam. 6:4; cf. 5:6). *See* PESTILENCE.

PLAGUES OF EGYPT.† Miraculous judgments that God performed against Egypt in order to effect the release of the enslaved Israelites (Exod. 7:8-11:10; cf. 3:20). The term "plagues" for this series of miracles originated with the use of various Hebrew terms translated "plague": *nāgap* (8:2 [MT 7:27]; Josh. 24:5), *deber* (Exod. 9:3; KJV "murrain"), *maggēpâ* (v. 14), and *negaʿ* (11:1).

In the first plague (7:14-24), the water of the Nile, and thus water throughout Egypt, was "turned to blood" (probably a metaphor) and became polluted and undrinkable. In the second, third, and fourth plagues (7:25-8:32 [MT 28]), frogs, gnats, and flies (all usually present in Egypt) overran the country in exceptionally large numbers. The next three plagues fell first on the livestock of the Egyptians (fatal disease, 9:1-7), then on the people and their livestock (boils, vv. 8-12), and then on the crops as well as the people and livestock (hail, lightning, and rain, vv. 13-35). The Israelites, however, were not affected (vv. 4, 6-7, 26).

The eighth plague was an intensification of what was a frequent problem for farmers in the Near East: locusts (10:1-20). The ninth plague, a "darkness to be felt" (vv. 21-29), may also have been an intensification of a natural occurrence—desert dust and sandstorms obscuring the light of the sun. The last plague, the death of the firstborn males of the Egyptians and of their livestock, led to the institution of the Passover and the release of the Israelites from Egypt (11:1–12:32). Attempts to link together some of the plagues as natural occurrences leading from one to the next may be of some value, but the text itself emphasizes the miraculous nature of the plagues and the role of Moses (e.g., 8:16 [MT 12]).

The plagues are referred to frequently in later biblical accounts (e.g., Deut. 6:22; Neh. 9:10; Ps. 106:21-22; Jer. 32:20-21; Acts 7:36). Ps. 78:43-51; 105:28-36 list the plagues, but both with considerable differences in order from the Exodus account, and both omitting more than one of the plagues mentioned in Exodus. The plagues of Egypt entered into the language of apocalyptic literature and inspired parts of the descriptions of eschatological judgments in the book of Revelation (Rev. 8:7-11; 11:6; 16:2-4, 10, 21).

PLANE TREE (Heb. *'armôn*). Trees of the genus *Platanus*, which can reach a large size and have rounded spiked fruits and large leaves shaped like those of grapevines (Gen. 30:37; Ezek. 31:8; KJV "chestnut"). Plane trees annually shed sheets of bark (cf. the Hebrew term *'armôn*, which is related to *'ārôm* "naked"). In *Plantanus orientalis* L., the species that grows in Palestine and Mesopotamia, the pieces of shed bark are larger, the flower heads smaller, and the leaves more deeply incised than in the plane or "sycamore" of the western hemisphere (*Plantanus occidentalis*). Generally in the Near East the plane is found near water.

At Isa. 41:19; 60:13 the KJV translates "plane" for Heb. *tidhār* (*see* PINE).

PLANTS.* Identifying the many plants named in the Bible (primarily the Old Testament) is difficult, and conflicting identifications exist for many plant names. A considerable number of names occur for which no sure identification is ever likely to be made. Furthermore, the people of the Bible did not distinguish plants as do modern botanists. Rather, plants were classified according to environment or function, often in general groups rather than as specific species. In this framework, plant names could change their meaning through time and with differences in environment experienced by a single language group. Changes in the ecology of the Bible lands since the time of the Bible also complicate the process of identification. Refinement in modern translations of the Bible has involved new identifications of many plants named in the Bible, particularly as the greater knowledge of the Bible lands has shown that earlier translations placed in those lands plants known elsewhere but not there. Still, a large number of uncertainties remain.

For specific plants see the individual articles.

PLEIADES [plē'ə dēz] (Heb. *kîmâ*).† A cluster of stars (so Heb. *kîmâ*, from *kûm* "accumulate"), generally identified with the Pleiades (so LXX), a grouping in the constellation of Taurus near that of Orion (Job 9:9; 38:31; Amos 5:8; KJV "the seven stars").

According to Greek mythology, the Pleiades were the seven daughters of Atlas and Pleione, pursued for five years by the hunter Orion and transformed by Zeus into stars just as Orion was about to molest them.

PLUMB LINE, PLUMMET.† A cord with a weight at one end used by masons to check if walls are vertical. All biblical references to plumb lines are metaphorical.

Justice and righteousness are to be the measuring line and the plummet (Heb. *mišqōleṭ*) by which rebuilt Jerusalem will be tested (Isa. 28:17). Many buildings in ancient cities were built with no foundation, so that periodic testing of walls with a plummet would lead to deliberate destruction of some walls that had gone too far from the vertical. According to 2 Kgs. 21:13 the destruction of Samaria that followed the application of God's standards (the measuring line and the plummet) will also come on Jerusalem. Amos 7:7-8 also speaks of a destruction that will come after the use of God's plumb line (Heb. *'ᵃnāḵ*, lit. "lead weight").

At Isa. 34:11, those things that should enable order, the measuring line and the plummet (*'ᵃḇānîm*, lit. "stones"; so KJV), will instead in God's judgment bring the emptiness and chaos of the time before the creation (cf. Gen. 1:2); everything will be disordered in the kingdom of Edom. Heb. *hā'eḇen habbᵉḏîl* (lit. "stone of tin") at Zech. 4:10 is understood by the LXX as a "plummet" in the hand of Zerubbabel (so RSV), an expression of hope regarding the reconstruction of the temple.

POCHERETH-HAZZEBAIM [pŏk'ə rĕth hăz'ə bā'əm] (Heb. *pōḵereṭ haṣṣᵉḇāyîm*). The progenitor of a family of Solomon's servants whose descendants returned from exile (Ezra 2:57 par. Neh. 7:59). While Zebaim could be an otherwise unknown place name (KJV "Pochereth of Zebaim"), the entire Hebrew expression appears to be a proper name (or the name of an office) meaning "gazelle hunter."

POETRY.†

I. Old Testament

As much as one-third of the Old Testament may be poetry. Perhaps only the books of Leviticus, Ruth, Ezra, Nehemiah, Esther, Haggai, and Malachi contain no poetry, and even in those books the manner of expression is often strongly affected by poetic forms. At any rate, the distinction between poetry and prose in the Old Testament is not absolute. Unlike its classical or European counterpart, ancient Hebrew poetry has no distinctive schemes of accentuation, meter, or rhythm to differentiate it from ordinary prose. Thus it is not clear whether some passages should be considered poetry or prose; there is often an alternation between poetry and prose, and it is necessary to speak of "oracular prose" bearing the characteristics of poetry in a prose form. The fundamental characteristic that can be said to define which passages are poetic is parallelism of thought within distichs (sometimes tristichs; i.e., the basic two- or occasionally three-part line or sentence); rhythm of thought rather than rhythm of sound distinguishes Old Testament poetry, though the latter has a place.

Poetry in the Old Testament ranges from brief extracts (e.g., Gen. 4:23-24; Num. 21:18; 1 Sam. 18:7) to longer odes and poetic sections (e.g., Gen. 49:2-27; Exod. 15:1-18; 1 Sam. 2:1-10; 2 Sam. 1:19-27), lengthy and ornate poetic compositions such as Job 3:1–42:6 and the Psalter, and the graphic oracular prose of Isa. 40–66, Nahum, and Habakkuk.

A. Background. Ancient Israel was the beneficiary of a long- and well-developed literary tradition in the ancient Near East. While the earliest written Hebrew poetry has been dated to the thirteenth or twelfth century B.C., the rudiments of Egyptian poetry can be traced as early as a triumph hymn for the pharaoh dated *ca.* 3200. Poetic parallel couplets occur in the Pyramid Texts of the Fifth Dynasty (*ca.* 2350), and matching couplets appear as early as 2300 in the victory hymn for Pepi I. Scholars have long noted similarities between Ps. 104 and the sun hymn of Akhenaten, and the love songs of the New Kingdom (*ca.* 1570-1085) show considerable affinity to the biblical Song of Solomon.

Similar poetic traditions developed concurrently in ancient Mesopotamia. Parallel couplets occur already in the building inscription of Gudea, prince of Lagash (*ca.* 2100). Old Babylonian kingdoms (*ca.* 1800-1500) canonized earlier Sumerian literature, including poetic hymns and prayers such as the Prayer to Any God. This period also saw the composition of Neo-Sumerian prayers and hymns such as the lengthy Hymn to Šamaš. Perhaps the most notable Old Babylonian poetic literature includes Enuma Elish, the creation epic, and the Gilgamesh epic.

Although Egyptian and Mesopotamian culture influenced the Levant, the most important ancient parallels to biblical poetry can be found in the Canaanite literature discovered at Ugarit (Ras Shamra). Dated to *ca.* 1400-1200, the written poetry of Ugarit probably follows some two centuries of orally composed precursors. Ugaritic poetry is similar to its biblical counterpart in vocabulary and style. For example, the discovery of hundreds of pairs of parallel (or A/B) word pairs that also occur in Hebrew poetry, usually in the same sequence, suggests that Hebrew poets were heir to a common parallelistic poetic tradition. The Ugaritic epics of Baal, Aqhat, and Keret also feature poetic devices such as chiasmus, numerical climax, and synonymous and synthetic parallelism. As in the Hebrew Psalter, Ugaritic hymns include superscriptions, subheadings, colophons, and occasional musical notations. More than mere cultural borrowing, the striking similarities between Ugaritic and Hebrew poetry suggest a common West Semitic linguistic and literary heritage.

B. Forms. 1. Rhythm of Thought. a. Parallelism. Parallelism of members (Lat. *parallelismus membrorum*) is the fundamental formal feature that distinguishes poetry from prose in the Old Testament. It is also that which most unites sound and thought in Hebrew poetry, balancing ideas in a structured or systematic form. Particular instances of Old Testament poetic parallelism can be classified as antithetic, emblematic, synthetic, synonymous, or chiastic, but the distinctions among these types of parallelism cannot

completely account for the freedom and variety with which the distichs are constructed.

In antithetic parallelism the second stich of a distich states the opposite or contrasting side of the truth of the first (e.g., Ps. 1:6; Prov. 14:21; 15:1). Emblematic parallelism is the use of a simile in one stich of a distich with the intended literal meaning stated in the other stich (e.g., Ps. 103:11, 12, 13; Jer. 17:11). In synthetic or climactic parallelism the second stich completes a thought begun in the first (e.g., Ps. 37:3; Prov. 4:23). Occasionally synthetic parallelism consists of a tiered structure in which each stich might begin from the same point but goes beyond the thought of the preceding stich (e.g., Judg. 5:27; Ps. 29:1-2; 94:1, 3).

Synonymous parallelism, sometimes called identical or complete parallelism, is the statement in the two stichs of the same thought in different terms but the same or similar grammatical structure (e.g., Ps. 15:1; 49:1 [MT 2]; Eccl. 11:4). Sometimes in synonymous parallelism a word or words that would complete a parallel construction are omitted (e.g., Ps. 115:5-7); called ellipsis, this is one criterion for distinguishing Hebrew poetry from prose. In chiastic parallelism the second stich agains restates the idea of the first, but inverts the word order of the first (e.g., 51:3 [MT 5]; Isa. 11:13b). Sometimes two distichs that each use synthetic parallelism internally are in synonymous parallelism in regard to each other (e.g., Ps. 27:1) or form a chiastic structure (e.g., Prov. 23:15-16).

b. Strophe. Larger structures in Old Testament poetic texts are often not readily identifiable, but are sometimes indicated by large-scale acrostic patterns, refrains, and the use of inclusio. An acrostic pattern is a particularly obvious indicator of structure in the Hebrew text of Ps. 119, where the lines of each successive strophe begin with the next letter of the Hebrew alphabet. The sections of Lamentations (corresponding to the book's five chapters) represent individual acrostics. Other acrostics include Pss. 9–10, 25, 34, 37, 111, 112, 145; Prov. 31:10-31. In part intended as a mnemonic tool in the ancient scribal school, the acrostic was also a somewhat artificial literary device to convey ideas of order, progression, and completeness within the poetic message and perhaps to aid memorization.

Refrains indicate strophic structure in, for example, Pss. 42–43 (cf. 42:5, 11 [MT 6, 12]; 43:5), 107 (vv. 8, 15, 21, 31). Inclusio, sometimes called an "envelope figure," is the repetition of elements from the beginning of a poem at its end (e.g., 118:1, 29; 136:1, 26).

2. Rhythm of Sound. Sound and thought cannot be entirely separated when Old Testament poetry is discussed, but certain features are indeed more closely related to the way in which the sound of the poetry contributes to its communication of meaning. These are meter, alliteration, paronomasia, and onomatopoeia.

a. Meter. Old Testament poetry uses syllabic or accentual meter (as does English poetry) rather than quantitative meter, but the way in which it does so remains a matter of dispute. Some metrical patterns apparently were associated with particular kinds of content or mood. Usually the two stichs of a line have the same number of accented syllables (most often two or three each), called balanced meter. A decrease in the number of accented syllables from the first stich to the second (usually from three to two) is called echoing or *qînâ* "dirge" meter, as used in Lamentations and, e.g., Amos 5:2. The two common methods of gauging Hebrew meter (counting the stressed or accented syllables in distichs, or counting total syllables in distichs) do not describe meter so much as they provide a guide to its structure. Recent studies employing syntactical and statistical analysis and modern linguistic methodology offer the greatest promise for unraveling the complexities of Hebrew poetic meter.

b. Alliteration, Assonance, and Rhyme. Alliteration is the consonance of sounds at the beginnings of words or syllables. A translation cannot represent the recurrence of *š* and *l* at Ps. 122:6a: *ša'ălû šelôm yerûšālāim*. Like alliteration, assonance may serve as a literary means of emphasizing an idea or theme or to set a certain tone for the poem. A parade example is the multiple repetition of the *a, e,* and *i* vowel sounds at Ezek. 27:27. Rhyming, the correspondence of sounds together at the ends of words, never functioned in Old Testament poetry as it has in English poetry. When rhyming does occur, it is usually the result of the same suffix appearing in several words in a verse (e.g., -*k* "your," also at Ezek. 27:27).

c. Paronomasia. Paronomasia or word play, the use in the same context of words similar in sound but not necessarily in meaning, is found especially in the prophets, who used it to heighten the impact of their messages. Amos saw a basket of summer fruit (*qāyiṣ*) and heard God announce the end (*qēṣ*) of Israel (Amos 8:2). Jacob says to Judah (*yehûdâ*) that his brothers "will praise you" (*yôdûkâ*; Gen. 49:8). A similar correspondence exists between "justice" (*mišpāṭ*) and "bloodshed" (*mišpāḥ*) and between "righteousness" (*ṣedāqâ*) and "a cry" (*ṣeʿāqâ*) at Isa. 5:7.

d. Onomatopoeia. The use of words that sound like what they describe, onomatopoeia, was an important feature of the Hebrew oral poetic tradition. Examples include the simple interjection "woe" (*'ôy*) at Isa. 24:16 and "galloping, galloping" (*dahărôt dahărôt*) at Judg. 5:22.

3. Setting and Typical Forms. Like all poetry, that of the Bible responds to and gives expression to a wide variety of experiences of life (e.g., birth, Gen. 25:23; the "seasons" of life, Eccl. 3:1-9; marriage, Gen. 24:60; death, 2 Sam. 1:19-27; blood revenge, Gen. 4:23-24; war, Josh. 10:12-13). Israel's poetry was shaped further by an intense faith in Yahweh for having acted in history on behalf of his people (e.g., Exod. 15:1-18, 21; Judg. 5:2-31), and a penchant for celebrating the worth and meaning of human existence (e.g., Pss. 92, 112, 127-28). Accordingly, Old Testament poetry transcends the historical setting of ancient Israel and touches the very fabric of modern culture (perhaps explaining the continued popularity of the Psalms).

The poetry of the Old Testament is musical in nature, intended to be sung or chanted and likely accompanied by musical instruments (e.g., Exod. 15:1-18, 21, the Song of the Sea and Song of Miriam; Deut. 32:1-43, the Song of Moses; Judg. 5:1-31, the Song of Deborah; Pss. 5–6). Vestiges of the musical char-

acter of the poetry remain, particularly in the Psalter and other works intended or adapted for liturgical use. The Psalter retains superscriptions denoting accompanying instrumentation (e.g., Pss. 4–5, 54–55, 67; cf. 150), the composer or recipient (e.g., 70, 72–73, 77, 81), the occasion (e.g., 45, 70, 92, 100), and the tune or arrangement (e.g., 6, 12, 22, 39, 57–58, 80, 88). *See* PSALMS, BOOK OF; MUSIC.

Form criticism has sought to classify typical forms of Hebrew poetry and to describe the settings or life situations in which they developed and were used. Several basic poetic types have been identified, including celebrations of past events (Num. 21:17-18; cf. v. 14; Josh. 10:12-13), victory songs (Exod. 15:1-18, 21; Judg. 5), curses (Josh. 6:26), taunt songs (Num. 21:27-30), dirges and funeral laments (2 Sam. 1:19-27; Isa. 14:4-20; 47; Jer. 9:17-22 [MT 16-21]; Lam. 1–5), wisdom songs (Ps. 36:1-4 [MT 2-5]; 37), coronation songs (21), hymns (8, 29, 47), thanksgiving songs (18, 30, 65, 75), penitential poems (51), songs of litigation (Isa. 45:20-21; Mic. 1:2), love songs (Song of Solomon), and wedding songs (Gen. 24:60; Ps. 45).

Efforts at classification have also focused on author (e.g., individual or comunity) and date, though the emphasis here concerns largely fixing the place of specific poems in the context of Israel's religious cult (e.g., Hab. 3). Recent scholars have sought to classify poetry on the basis of philological and historical considerations. For specific early poems see the individual entries (e.g., DEBORAH; HANNAH).

II. New Testament

Much of what can be called poetry in the New Testament consists of quotations from the Old Testament and passages in the style of the Old Testament. Jesus especially identified with the poetry of the book of Psalms (Matt. 3:17 [cf. Ps. 2:7]; 5:5 [cf. Ps. 37:11]; 27:46 [cf. Ps. 22:1 (MT 2)]). Passages in the style of Old Testament poetry include the songs at Luke 1:46-55, 68-79; 2:14, 29-32, where the forms of parallelism found in Old Testament poetry are strongly reflected, and the hymns in the book of Revelation (e.g., Rev. 11:17-18; 15:3-4). See further the individual entries (e.g., BENEDICTUS; MAGNIFICAT; NUNC DIMITTIS).

Paul occasionally quotes Greek poets (Acts 17:28, Epimenides and Aratus; 1 Cor. 15:33, Menander; cf. Titus 1:12, Epimenides). Several passages in New Testament letters are poetic in form and reflect early Christian hymnody (e.g., 1 Cor. 13; Eph. 5:14; Phil. 2:6-11; Col. 1:15-20; 1 Tim. 3:16; 2 Tim. 2:11-13; 1 Pet. 1:20). Some of these passages reflect clearly use of Greek rhetorical forms.

Bibliography. F. M. Cross and D. N. Freedman, *Studies in Ancient Yahwistic Poetry.* SBL Dissertation 21 (Missoula: 1975); S. Gevirtz, *Patterns in the Early Poetry of Israel,* 2nd ed. SAOC 32 (1973); G. B. Gray, *The Forms of Hebrew Poetry* (1915; repr. New York: 1972); J. L. Kugel, *The Idea of Biblical Poetry* (New Haven: 1981); M. P. O'Connor, *Hebrew Verse Structure* (Winona Lake: 1980).

POLYCARP, EPISTLE OF. * A letter by Polycarp, bishop of Smyrna, to the church at Philippi *ca.* A.D. 11, the only writing of Polycarp that has survived. The letter served a dual purpose: first, as a cover letter for some correspondence of Ignatius that the Philippian church had requested, and second, as an opportunity for Polycarp to extend pastoral advice and exhortation. In his letter Polycarp warns against the love of money and against heretics, and offers counsel regarding duties of church leaders and laity. The letter is earnest but conventional, and much of its content comes from a variety of New Testament books (although there is no indication that he considered them authoritative Scripture).

Polycarp was born *ca.* A.D. 70 and grew up in the church of the apostle John, so that he served as a link between the apostolic and postapostolic generations. For more than half a century he was bishop at Smyrna, standing firmly on the foundation of apostolic tradition, teaching it clearly, and tolerating no deviation from it, particularly from Gnostics. His role in the burgeoning Church was not primarily that of theologian.

The letter exists in nine very similar Greek manuscripts, each breaking off after ch. 9. The rest is known from a complete Latin version.

POLYCARP, MARTYRDOM OF.* The oldest of the Christian martyrdom accounts, depicting the fate of Polycarp, bishop of Smyrna, who was burned at the stake in Smyrna in A.D. 155 at the age of eighty-six. This moving account of his death was written within a year of the event by an eyewitness. The work is extant in six Greek manuscripts and through Eusebius.

Composed in the form of a letter from the church at Smyrna to that at Philomelium, the account begins with a summary of other martyrdoms, but moves quickly to the story of Polycarp. After one brief attempt to elude capture, Polycarp soon gives himself up rather than continue a pointless flight. The steadfast character and piety of the man are evident throughout his questioning, and in spite of all attempts to make him recant he holds fast to his faith, an example of the remarkable courage of many early Christians.

The miraculous element so prevalent in later martyr stories is more restrained here. After the fire fails to destroy the old man, he is killed with a dagger and his body burned. His bones are rescued by the Christians. Polycarp was greatly beloved by the people he had served; in memory of his martyrdom they established the tradition of an annual festival that spread well beyond Smyrna.

POLYGAMY. *See* MARRIAGE.

POMEGRANATE (Heb. *rimmôn*). *Punica granatum* L., a small semitropical tree or shrub and its fruit. Although not native to Palestine but to Persia and the surrounding countries, pomegranates were already present in Palestine when the Israelites entered the land (Deut. 8:8). The dissemination of the tree must have begun early, for discoveries made in the pyramids have revealed that it has been cultivated in Egypt since most ancient times. The numerous references to the pomegranate in the Old Testament suggest that it grew

throughout Palestine, implied further by the occurrence of Heb. *rimmôn* in several place names (e.g., Josh. 15:32; 19:45; 21:25).

The early blossoming of the pomegranate was one of the signs of the arrival of spring (Cant. 7:12 [MT 13]). It seldom grows to a height of more than 4.5 m. (15 ft.). The leaves are narrow and bright green in color, and the orange-red flowers are somewhat bell-shaped. The large red fruit is covered by a thick, leather-like rind. The numerous seeds are the size of grains of wheat and are each surrounded by a juicy red pulp that varies in taste from sweet to somewhat sour. In a country as hot as Palestine, pomegranates offered a delicious source of refreshment, both as a fruit and as a beverage (8:2).

The shape of some of the ornaments of the high-priestly garments (Exod. 28:33-34) and of some of the furnishings of the temple (1 Kgs. 7:18, 20, 42; 2 Kgs. 25:17) were inspired by pomegranates. In figurative language the pomegranate indicates physical beauty (Cant. 4:3). The withering of the pomegranate (Joel 1:12) and its restoration (Hag. 2:19) characterize the Exile and restoration.

PONTUS [pŏn′təs] (Gk. *Pontos* "sea"). A region in northeastern Asia Minor along the Black Sea, extending from the Halys to the Colchis river and southward to Cappadocia. Only a small part of Pontus was in the Roman province of Bithynia and Pontus; most was in the province of Galatia.

Although remains indicate Assyrian influence as early as the third millennium B.C. and Hittite occupation in the second, the region was largely inhabited by peoples such as the Tibareni, Mosynoeci, and Chalybes, the latter said to have been the first workers of iron. Greeks from Miletus colonized Sinope and other coastal sites in the seventh century. Following the Wars of the Diadochi (late fourth century) Pontus gained prominence as an independent kingdom under a dynasty founded by Mithridates I; it reached its greatest power under Mithridates VI, who checked the advance of Rome in Anatolia and extended Pontus' control as far as the Greek colonies in the modern Ukraine and Crimea. Pontus fell to the Roman Pompey at the end of the Third Mithridatic War in 66 B.C.

From Pontus Jews came to celebrate Pentecost in Jerusalem (Acts 2:9). Aquila was born in Pontus (18:2), and Peter addressed "the exiles of the Dispersion" in this region (1 Pet. 1:1).

POOL.† Eng. "pool" is the translation of a number of terms (e.g., Heb. *berēḵâ*, *ʾaḡam*; Gk. *kolymbḗthra*) that represent natural ponds (e.g., Ps. 114:8; KJV "standing water") and, more often, cisterns and reservoirs constructed to collect and hold rainwater. Because of the need for a constant water supply, cities of Palestine normally had one or more pools (e.g., 2 Sam. 2:13; 4:12; 1 Kgs. 22:38). At Jerusalem, the "upper pool" (2 Kgs. 18:17; Isa. 7:3; 36:2) and the "lower pool" (22:9) were two such reservoirs. The upper pool may be in the vicinity of the pool of Siloam (John 9:7) or near the spring of Gihon in the Kidron valley. Some scholars identify the lower pool with what is now known as Birket el-Hamra at the southern end of the Ophel spur. At Cant. 7:4 (MT 5) the pool of the city of Heshbon is an image for beautiful eyes. *See also* CISTERN.

POOR (Heb. *'ebyôn, dal, 'ānî, rā'š*; Gk. *ptōchós, pénēs, penichrós*).† Poverty (Heb. *rêš*) is identified as a result of sin (Prov. 10:4; 13:18; 21:17; 24:30-34; cf. 19:15), but more often it is mentioned in connection with the obligations of those who are not poor and their failure to live by those obligations. Poverty became an issue only after Israel attained a settled existence in the land of Canaan; all the people of Israel had been slaves in Egypt, and during their period in the wilderness they were essentially equal.

When the law was given to Israel, God made special provisions for specific groups of poor people (Exod. 23:6; Lev. 19:9-10; Deut. 15:11; cf. 24:19-22; Prov. 22:22-23; Isa. 25:4). The plight of the poor was taken into consideration in the instructions for sacrifices (Lev. 5:7; 12:8; 14:21). The regulations concerning the Sabbatical Year and the Year of Jubilee were intended to prevent any person from oppressing or gaining advantage over another. The unity of the people of Israel was a basic assumption of these provisions. Poverty was not to be considered the concern of individuals alone; the promise that the people would know no poverty if they were obedient (Deut. 15:4-5) was given to the people as a whole, not to individuals.

Religious decline and changes in social structure during the time of the Monarchy caused poverty and social inequality to increase. The seizure of Naboth's vineyard by Jezebel and Ahab (1 Kgs. 21) demonstrates the replacement of the old laws that kept property in a family (v. 3; cf. Lev. 25:23-25) by foreign concepts of absolute monarchy. Such changes made increasing social stratification inevitable. The prophets spoke strongly against the injustices involved in these changes (e.g., Isa. 5:8; Jer. 34:13-17; Amos 2:6-8; 3:15; 4:1; 5:11-12).

Because of the resultant need of the poor to depend on God alone, the poor and oppressed came to be identified as God's righteous people in a unique sense (Ps. 9:9-10 [MT 10-11]; 14:4-6; 37:14-15; 69:33 [MT 34]; Isa. 3:15; Hab. 3:13-14). The Christians of Jerusalem, who did indeed suffer from poverty, may have called themselves "the poor" in this sense as well (Rom. 15:26; Gal. 2:10); the name was adopted by the second-century A.D. EBIONITES (from Heb. *'ebyôn*), who considered themselves descendants of the Jerusalem church.

The hope of the coming age is of special meaning to the poor (Isa. 11:4; 29:19; 41:17). Jesus' pronouncement of the blessing of God's kingdom on the poor (whether with emphasis on their spiritual experience, as at Matt. 5:3-12, or with emphasis on their material deprivation, as at Luke 6:20-21) is based on the identification of the humble poor as God's people and on the reversal of "first" and "last" that is fundamental to Jesus' eschatological teachings (e.g., Matt. 19:30-20:16).

POPLAR. Any of several trees of the genus *Populus*, including the cottonwoods and aspens, which reach great heights quickly (cf. Hos. 14:5).

Heb. *libneh* (Gen. 30:37; Hos. 4:13) is usually identified as the poplar (so KJV, RSV; RSV, 14:5; KJV "Lebanon," following MT), but has also been identified as the storax (*Styrax officinalis* L.), an eastern Mediterranean shrub. The derivation of the Hebrew name from *lābān* "white" may suggest the white flowers of the storax or the gray-white bark and the leaves, white on the underside, of the white poplar (*Populus alba* L.), a large poplar common in wet places throughout Syria and Palestine. The reference to the shade provided by the tree (Hos. 4:13) favors the white poplar.

Heb. *'arābâ* (Lev. 23:40; Job 40:22; Isa. 15:7; 44:4) is usually taken as "willow" (so KJV, RSV), but has also been identified with *Populus euphraticus* L., which is common in river valleys of Palestine, Mesopotamia, and surrounding countries (cf. RSV mg., Ps. 137:2).

PORATHA [pō rā'thə] (Heb. *pôrātā'*). One of Haman's ten sons who were slain by the Jews (Esth. 9:8).

PORCIUS FESTUS. *See* FESTUS, PORCIUS.

PORCUPINE. *See* HEDGEHOG.

PORPHYRY [pôr'pə rī] (Heb. *bahaṭ*).* A red or purple stone consisting of white or pink feldspar crystals in a dark red groundmass. In biblical times porphyry usually was brought from the Red Sea coast of Egypt and cut and polished for ornamental purposes (Esth. 1:6; KJV "red . . . marble").

PORTICO OF SOLOMON. *See* SOLOMON'S PORTICO.

PORTION, SHARE (Heb. *ḥēleq, ḥebel, mānâ*; Gk. *méros, merís*). That which is distributed and received, e.g., spoils of war (Gen. 14:24; 1 Sam. 30:24) and food eaten in ceremonial meals (Exod. 29:26; Lev. 7:33; 1 Sam. 1:4-5). The terms are used in a technical sense with regard to inheritances (Gen. 31:14; Luke 15:12) and land (Deut. 10:9) as that entrusted or allotted to Israel by Yahweh, the true owner of the land. Expressions such as "to have a portion in (someone)" mean to be affiliated with that person or to belong to that person's company or community (2 Sam. 20:1; 1 Kings 12:16; cf. John 13:8). Words translated "portion" can also be used with reference to that which is dear and close to a person; thus Israel is called the portion of the Lord (Deut. 32:9), as the Lord is likewise Israel's portion (Ps. 16:5; 73:26; 119:57; 142:5; Jer. 10:16; Lam. 3:24). "Portion" can also refer to the lot or fate that befalls a person at the hand of the Lord (Job 31:2; Jer. 13:25; Rev. 21:8; RSV "lot"). At Luke 10:42, the "good portion" chosen by Mary is the attention she gives to Christ's teaching. *See* LOTS.

POSIDONIUS [pŏs'ĭ dō'nĭ əs] (Gk. *Posidōnios*).* An envoy sent by Nicanor in the face of certain defeat to negotiate a truce with Judas Maccabeus (2 Macc. 14:19).

POST. *See* DOOR.

POTIPHAR [pŏt'ə fär] (Heb. *pôṭîpar*; Egyp. *p3-dì-p3-Rᶜ* "the one given [sent] by Re [the sun-deity]"). The officer and captain of Pharaoh's guard who purchased Joseph from the itinerant Midianites/Ishmalites and became his master (Gen. 37:36; 39:1-6a). He later imprisoned Joseph after his wife falsely accused the Hebrew of improper advances (vv. 6b-20).

POTIPHERA [pŏ tǐf'ə rə] (Heb. *pôṭî peraᶜ*; cf. Egyp. *p3-dì-p3-Rᶜ* "the one given [sent] by Re [the sun-deity]"). A priest in the Egyptian city of On (Heliopolis, "city of the sun"), whose daughter Asenath became Joseph's wife (Gen. 41:45, 50; 46:20; KJV "Potipherah").

POTSHERD GATE (Heb. Q *šaᶜar haḥarsîṯ*).* A gate in the city wall of Jerusalem adjoining the Hinnom valley and, therefore, on the southern side of the city (Jer. 19:2; KJV "East Gate"). It has been identified with the Dung Gate (Neh. 2:13) and was probably near the southeastern corner of the city.

POTTAGE (Heb. *nāzîd* "boiled [food]"). A thick stew of lentils and other vegetables (Hag. 2:12), cooked by boiling. Esau sold his birthright to Jacob for pottage (Gen. 25:29-34; cf. v. 29, RSV "red pottage"). Elisha's disciples discovered that a pottage made for them was poisonous; the prophet ordered that meal be thrown into the pot, and the pottage was then edible (2 Kgs. 4:38-41).

POTTER'S FIELD. *See* AKELDAMA.

POTTERY.† Earthenware formed and hardened by fire so as to be distinguished at once from stoneware or porcelain at the one extreme, and brick or tile at the other.

I. Manufacturing Techniques

Pottery ware of the ancient Near East was constructed primarily from local clays, of which red clay is the most readily available in Palestine. The clay was dug, kneaded, or treaded (cf. Isa. 41:25; Nah. 3:14), separated from stones and mixed with water until it reached the desired consistency. Grit, dung, ashes, and straw (cf. Exod. 1:14; 5:7-14) were often added to aid in tighter binding of the material and to prevent shrinking and cracks. Once the desired consistency was attained, excess water and air pockets were removed. The clay then was allowed to age for several days, after which it was sun-dried and fired using various methods in a kiln, though this last step does not appear in the production of earliest pottery ware.

Earliest examples of clay vessels were handmade. These were often shaped with sticks or bones and polished until extremely hard. Decorative designs were simple. A common technique for producing larger jars was the stacking of clay coils, which were subsequently smoothed into a consistent shape. Slips, produced from fine clays of varying colors, were often added to give vessels individual decorations and designs. Burnishing was accomplished by rubbing the outside of the vessel.

The earliest form of the potter's wheel for which evidence survives was the tournette, a simple two-

Middle and Late Bronze Age pottery from Megiddo (by courtesy of the Oriental Institute, University of Chicago)

wheeled mechanism on which pottery pugs could be fashioned while in motion, usually by an assistant. Use of the tournette greatly increased mass production of simple pottery shapes and led to a certain degree of standardization. The subsequent appearance of a faster power wheel contributed to significant efficiency in pottery manufacture (Sir. 38:29-30; cf. Jer. 18:3). This device permitted the potter to turn by foot a large wheel, from which a shaft subsequently rotated a smaller wheel bearing the clay to be shaped.

Other methods of pottery construction included the use of press molds, particularly to produce unusual designs and shapes such as seals (Job 38:14) or lamps (Matt. 25:1-13). The variety of forms that potters were able to produce through their knowledge and craftsmanship often provided them with an elevated social status (1 Chr. 4:23; Sir. 38:31-34).

The ancient Israelites produced a variety of clay vessels, used primarily for utilitarian purposes. Most common of ceramic forms was the bowl, ranging in size and style from the four-handled great banquet bowl (Cant. 7:2 [MT 3], here used for mixing wine; cf. Exod. 24:6; RSV "basin"; Isa. 22:24) to smaller table bowls (for bread, Deut. 28:5; coals, Zech. 12:6; salt, 2 Kgs. 2:20). Also common were earthenware dishes (Exod. 25:29), cups (Luke 11:39), cooking pots (Zech. 14:21), pitchers (Jer. 35:5), jars (1 Kgs. 17:12), lamps (Matt. 25:1), and spindles (2 Sam. 3:29). Jer. 32:14 refers to a pottery container in which a deed of purchase was stored.

II. Archeological Significance

The value of ceramic ware for dating stratigraphic layers at excavation sites was first recognized by W. M. F. Petrie during work at Tel el-Ḥesi in 1890. Subsequent contributions by archaeologists at other excavations, such as C. S. Fisher, W. F. Albright, and K. M. Kenyon, soon produced a rough chronological scale whereby Palestinian pottery ware could be implemented to date early cultures and their geographic movements. Analysis of individual pieces ("potsherds") by methods such as carbon-14 dating, thermoluminescent testing, neutron activation, and petrographic microscopy have further served to advance the value of ancient pottery for the archaeologist apart from the mere analysis of shapes and designs.

Investigation of Palestinian pottery permits a classification of forms and styles into general historical periods. Vessels from the Pottery Neolithic period (ca. 5000-4000 B.C.) are handmade, usually crude and simple; a burnished red slip is common, as are zoomorphic shapes and flat bases. The Chalcolithic period (ca. 4000-3200) shows thinner ware with more advance firing. The Early Bronze Age (ca. 3200-2100) reveals complex development; both handmade and tournette-produced ware are found, featuring variously colored burnished slips, extensive decorative patterns, ledge and loop handles, spouts, and imaginative forms. Common to the Middle Bronze Age (ca. 2100-1550) is wheel-made, homogenous ware; vessels tend toward rounded, graceful shapes with less emphasis on shoulders, handles, and bases. Imported vessels from Cyprus and Greece appear in the Late Bronze Age (ca. 1550-1200). Egyptian forms are also apparent, with local imitations reflecting both

Two Middle Bronze Age jugs from Tell el-'Ajjûl (southwest of Gaza) (by courtesy of the Israel Department of Antiquities and Museums)

Greek and Egyptian influences; bichrome painted ware with animal and geometric patterns is common.

Pottery vessels from Iron I (ca. 1200-900) generally reflect previous Bronze Age styles, though individual pieces are usually of poorer quality. A mixture of Philistine and Israelite ware typically reveals bichrome bowls with alternating red and black bands, collared rims on larger jars, hand burnishing, and both red/black and yellow/brown slips. Mass production, made possible by use of the wheel, led to standardization during the divided monarchy (Iron II, ca. 900-600) and the use of cheaper materials (cf. Jer. 18:3-4). Wheel burnishing is prevalent, and though glazes are not used, artistic creations are common. Trademarks also appear with regularity. Both the Iron III (ca. 600-300, paralleling the Persian period) and Hellenistic periods (ca. 300-63) produced black ware with some modification of earlier pottery shapes and sizes. Closed lamps and Rhodian jars with stamped handles appear. Local imitations of foreign styles also became common in this period, though again with less degree of quality. Roman ware (ca. 63 B.C.-A.D. 323), the pottery of the New Testament period, includes standardized pottery produced commonly throughout the Mediterranean (terra sigillata), detailed shoulders and bases, elaborate designs, and ribbed ware. Better imitations of Italian imports appear in Palestine during this period.

III. Significance for Biblical Interpretation

The appearance of varying pottery styles at archaeological sites provides evidence for both dates and historical migrations among cultures. This is most significant in Palestine where permanent monuments, inscriptions, and coins are not in abundance. Imported ware and pottery styles, which typically develop along chronological lines, commonly indicate the influence of non-Palestinian civilizations and provide supportive evidence for those biblical passages that reflect foreign parallels or historical references (e.g., portions of Genesis, Proverbs, Psalms). Furthermore, changing pottery styles indicate the advance of technology among cultures and serve as a type of "cultural ecology" relating a potter's material and knowledge to the cultural implementation of his wares.

Finally, ceramic forms provide additional clues to

such matters as diet, weaponry, and produce. Specifically, Hebrew dietary laws reflect the danger of storing milk in porous pottery vessels where bacteria may quickly develop and flourish. Though it is widely known that ceremonial ware was typically made of metal (cf. Zech. 14:20-21), pottery vessels are often cited for specific uses (e.g., Lev. 11:32-35; 14:5; Num. 5:17). The creative use of pottery appears in symbolic images of creation and divine interaction with humanity (Gen. 2:7; Isa. 29:16; 45:9; 64:8 [MT 7]; Jer. 18:1-6; Lam. 4:2; Rom. 9:20-24). In this respect, the imagery of light, both physical and symbolic, produced from the ceramic lamp appears throughout the Bible (e.g., 2 Chr. 21:7; Job 29:3; Ps. 119:105; Prov. 20:20; Rev. 21:23). While intact pottery vessels reveal evidence of these and other cultural developments, the various functions of potsherds themselves give witness to the significance of pottery during the biblical period (cf. Job 2:8; 41:30 [MT 22]; Isa. 30:14).

Bibliography. R. Amiran, *Ancient Pottery of the Holy Land* (New Brunswick: 1970); K. M. Kenyon, *Archaeology in the Holy Land*, 4th ed. (New York: 1979); P. W. Lapp, *Palestinian Ceramic Chronology, 200 B.C.-A.D. 70* (New Haven: 1961); G. E. Wright, *The Pottery of Palestine from the Earliest Times to the End of the Early Bronze Age* (New Haven: 1937).

POUND. Gk. *mná* (Luke 19:13-25; NIV "mina") represents a unit of money equivalent to about one hundred drachmas or three months' wages for a laborer. Gk. *lítra* (cf. Lat. *libra*) represents both a unit of weight, about 326 gm. (11.5 oz.), and a unit of capacity, about .5 l. (.53 qt.); either measure may be in view in the two instances of the term (John 12:3; 19:39). For KJV "pound" at 1 Kgs. 10:17; Ezra 2:69; Neh. 7:71-72, *see* MINA.

POVERTY. *See* POOR.

POWER (Heb. *ḥayil, ḥāzāq, yāḏ*; Gk. *dýnamis, exousía*).† The actual or potential possession of control, authority, or influence over others. True power, which includes the effective exercise of authority, belongs only to God (1 Chr. 29:11-12; Jer. 10:6; Rev. 5:13; RSV "might"; 7:12).

In the Old Testament the power of God is revealed in nature (Ps. 65:5-13 [MT 6-14]), especially in creation (Jer. 10:10-12), and in history, particularly in God's act of redemption at the Exodus (Exod. 15:6, 13; 32:11) and in his giving to Israel the promised land (Ps. 111:6). God's intervention in history should remind people that human power is only delegated (Gen. 1:26, 28; Ps. 8:5-8 [MT 6-9]; 115:16) and, when compared to God's power, it fades into insignificance (cf. Ps. 33:16-17).

The basic meaning of Heb. *ḥayil* is "strength," from which come the derived meanings of "army" and "wealth." When used of God, *ḥayil* may refer to strength from God (18:32 [MT 33]; cf. 2 Sam. 22:33) or to the power of God (Ps. 59:11 [MT 12]). The term is used more than eighty times in the Old Testament as an attribute of people in the sense of "strength," "power," or "might." Wealth is often related to power, and *ḥayil* occurs with that meaning nearly thirty times.

The adjective *ḥāzāq* occurs fifty-seven times in the

Old Testament, twenty-three of which refer to a "strong hand," most frequently to God's power, as in the Exodus. The term includes the idea of the power to resist (Ezek. 2:4; RSV "stubborn"; 3:7-8, lit. "hard of forehead"), and with reference to sickness (1 Kgs. 17:17) or famine (18:2) may mean "severe" (KJV "sore"). As a substantive the term means "mighty one" or "strong one" (Job 5:15; Ezek. 34:16).

While *yāḏ* is used literally of the human hand as performing normal work functions (e.g., Gen. 5:29), it frequently appears idiomatically in phrases that convey the idea of authority involving responsibility, care, and dominion over someone or something (e.g., 16:6 [RSV "in your power"], 9 ["submit"]; 39:3-8). The psalmist entrusts his heart and spirit into the care, sovereignty, and judgment of God (Ps. 31:5, 15 [MT 6, 16]); 89:13 (MT 14) states that power and might are in the hand of God. The term is also used with the derivative senses of possession (Gen. 39:1) and submission (1 Chr. 29:24; RSV "pledge . . . allegiance").

In the New Testament the idea of power is rendered chiefly by Gk. *exousía* and *dýnamis*. Gk. *exousía* means either conferred or derived authority, indicating the warrant or right to do something (Matt. 21:23-27; RSV "authority"). From this basic meaning the term comes to denote one who bears authority on earth (Rom. 13:1-3) or in the spiritual realm (Col. 1:16). All authority was given to Christ by the Father (Matt. 28:19); with this authority Christ forgave sins (9:6) and cast out demons (10:1). To his disciples he gave authority to become children of God (John 1:12) and to carry on his work (Mark 3:15).

Gk. *dýnamis* implies ability (2 Cor. 8:3; RSV "means") or strength (Eph. 3:16). It may also mean a powerful act (Acts 2:22; RSV "mighty works"). The Gospels affirm that Jesus began his ministry "in the power of the Spirit" (Luke 4:14) and that his power was operative in miracles of healing (Matt. 11:20). The power of the Spirit is seen as operative in the life of the Church (Acts 4:7, 33; 6:8). Paul views the resurrection of Jesus as the primary evidence of God's power (Rom. 1:4; Eph. 1:19-20). He sees the gospel as God's instrument by which that power comes to work in human lives (Rom. 1:16).

The plural of *dýnamis*, with the basic meaning "powers," is used in the New Testament in a variety of ways. At Matt. 7:22; Luke 10:13; Acts 2:22 it is rendered "mighty works" and describes concrete manifestations of supernatural power, or miracles (8:13). At Matt. 24:29; Mark 13:25 some understand "the powers of/in the heavens" to be inherent forces in the celestial bodies by which they rule over the day and over the night (cf. Gen. 1:18); others interpret these heavenly powers as the starry hosts themselves, viewed either as the armies of the heavens or the actual beings that control them. The phrase "principalities and powers" (e.g., Eph. 3:10; 6:12; cf. 1:21, "power and dominion"; Col. 1:16) designates both good and evil angels, the identification of which is determined by the context (*see* PRINCIPALITY). At Rom. 13:1 civil magistrates (RSV "governing authorities") are called "higher powers" (so KJV) because of their rank, authority, and influence as ones ordained by God to adminster justice among mankind. "The powers of the age to come" at Heb. 6:5 may be understood of all supernatural gifts and spiritual forces that belong to the age of the new covenant, of which Jesus is the mediator (9:15).

For the "power of keys" see KEYS, POWER OF.

Bibliography. G. B. Caird, *Principalities and Powers* (Oxford: 1956); D. M. Lloyd-Jones, *Authority* (Chicago: 1958); C. H. Powell, *The Biblical Concept of Power* (London: 1964).

PRAETORIAN [prī tôr′ĭ ən] **GUARD.*** Gk. *praitórion* was a term for any official government residence (see PRAETORIUM). Its use at Phil. 1:13 has been a significant factor in discussion of where Paul was when he wrote Philippians. The traditional view is that the letter was written at Rome; the most likely alternative is that it was written at Ephesus. No certain evidence has been marshalled to prove an Ephesian imprisonment, but Philippians does appear to be more closely allied with the letters written before Paul had gone to Rome than with the other "prison epistles."

It is sometimes argued that *praitórion* at Phil. 1:13 indicates a location in or near Rome. But it is likely that the term represents not just a location, but the people (i.e., the guards) at such a place, since the *praitórion* is contrasted with "all the rest," i.e., with people who are elsewhere but also know of Paul's case. This justifies the translation "praetorian guard" (RSV; KJV "palace"; NIV "palace guard") but does not answer the question of location. A provincial governor's residence in which Paul might have been imprisoned (cf. Acts 23:35, "Herod's praetorium") would fit the use of *praitórion* at Phil. 1:13 as well as any location in Rome.

The reference to "Caesar's household" (4:22) may be taken as reinforcement of the traditional view that Philippians was written from Rome, but it need not be. Slaves and associates of the emperor in numerous places in the Roman Empire might have merited such a designation.

PRAETORIUM [prī tôr′ĭ əm] (Gk. *praitórion*; Lat. *praetorium*).† Originally the tent of the general (Lat. *praetor*) in a Roman army camp, the term came to be designate the residence of any provincial governor (or "magistrate") or, by extension, any magnificent building.

Jesus' trial before Pilate took place in "the praetorium" in Jerusalem (Matt. 27:27; KJV "common hall"; NIV "Praetorium"; Mark 15:16; KJV "Praetorium"; John 18:28, 33; 19:9; KJV "hall of judgment," "judgment hall"; NIV "palace") where the governor resided whenever he was in the city. Two competing identifications of this praetorium exist, one the Antonia fortress located just outside the northwest corner of the temple area, the other Herod the Great's magnificent palace on the extreme western side of the ancient city. The identification of the praetorium as "the palace" (Gk. *hē aulé*) at Mark 15:16 favors the latter view. Josephus never refers to Antonia as an *aulé*. On the other hand, tradition favors the Antonia, and it is possible that Pilate might have chosen that fortress as a better location from which to watch the city. "The Pavement" outside the praetorium to which Pilate came so that Jews who for reasons of ceremonial cleanness would not enter the praetorium could witness the proceedings (John 19:13) is commonly, but probably erroneously, identified with a stone pavement beneath the modern Convent of the Sisters of Zion, near where the Antonia stood.

The residence of the Roman governor of Judea in Caesarea, the capital of the province, was a palace built by Herod the Great. Paul was kept under guard in this palace while Felix the governor awaited a formal accusation against the apostle (Acts 23:35; KJV "judgment hall").

For Phil. 1:13, see PRAETORIAN GUARD.

PRAISE (Heb. piel *hālal*, hiphil *yāḏâ*, piel *zāmar*, piel *šāḇaḥ*; Gk. *ainéō*, *doxázō*, *epainéō*, *exomologéō*, *hymnéō*, *psállō*).* To honor and ascribe worth to God. Praise is regarded by the Bible as the response due to God from all creation because of his majesty and saving actions; it is the dominant characteristic of true piety.

While the summons to praise God is addressed mainly to God's people (Ps. 22:23 [MT 24]; Rev. 19:5; cf. Ps. 135:19-21; Isa. 12:6), God is clearly worthy of praise from all peoples (Ps. 67:3-5 [MT 4-6]; 117). Indeed, the fundamental sin of the Gentiles is said to be their failure to "honor him as God or give thanks to him" (Rom. 1:21). The human obligation to praise God is underlined by the praise bestowed by the rest of creation, by the mountains (Ps. 89:12 [MT 13]), by the cycles of day and night in the heavens (19:1-2 [MT 2-3]), and by all nonhuman creatures (Rev. 5:13-14).

The praise offered by inanimate creation is not, of course, like that given by human beings. It is not expressed in speech as is that of humans (Ps. 19:3-4 [MT 4-5]). But since the order and majesty of creation display so clearly the greatness of the creator, human praise should be inspired by what is evident in the world (Rom. 1:19-21). Thus those parts of creation that are worshipped as gods by those who are not aware of who has made them are themselves contributors to the praise of the One who is creator and ruler of all (1 Chr. 16:26; Ps. 89:5-7 [MT 6-8]; 95:3-5).

God is to be praised for his deliverance of his people as well as for his actions as creator. Repeatedly the people of God are called on to praise God in response to his saving actions on behalf of the whole people, whether the people of Israel in the Old Testament (1 Chr. 16:8-22; Ps. 22:23-24 [MT 24-25]; Isa. 63:7-9), or the Church in the New Testament (2 Cor. 9:15; Heb. 13:15). They are also to praise him for his actions on behalf of them as individuals (Ps. 107; Jer. 20:13; Jas. 5:13). Even inanimate creation can respond in praise for God's salvation of his people (Ps. 69:34-35 [MT 35-36]).

Because God's salvation came particularly in the person of Jesus, praise was heard on the occasion of Jesus' birth (Luke 2:13-14, 20), when he healed (13:13; 17:15; 18:43), when he entered Jerusalem (19:37-38) and died (23:47), and after he had risen in triumph (cf. Rev. 5:9-10). Praise of God characterized the early Christian community (Acts 2:47), and what was accomplished through Christian leaders caused others to praise God (4:21). The eventual outcome of the salvation that came through Christ is to be praise of God by all people and by all of creation (Rom.

14:10-11; Phil. 2:9-11). Even now, however, the purpose of God's people is to praise God (Eph. 1:11-14; Heb. 13:15) and to live the life he has given in such a way that he is praised (Phil. 1:9-11).

PRAYER (Heb. *tᵉpillâ*; Gk. *proseuchḗ, déēsis, aítēma*).† Any form of communication with God on the part of believing people in response to situations that may arise in life. Prayer is marked, therefore, by variety and encompasses petition (including intercession for others), complaint, praise, thanksgiving, confession, imprecation (e.g., Num. 16:15; Ps. 69:22-28 [MT 23-29]), nonverbal communication (Rom. 8:26), and glossolalia (1 Cor. 14:14-15). As speaking to God rather than about God, prayer expresses most clearly what is believed about God and serves to effect the personal relationship that exists between God and his people.

The two poles around which all forms of prayer turn are praise and petition. Petition assumes that God hears requests made, that he cares, and that he is able to act in accord with the petition. Prayer is a nearly universal religious practice; the same assumptions are made regarding other gods by those who pray to them as must be made regarding the God of the Bible by those who pray to him. But the Bible both rejects such assumptions as groundless in the case of other gods and sees differences between prayer to other gods and prayer to the true God based on this rejection. The most important of these differences is the simplicity that characterizes prayer to the God of the Bible (1 Kgs. 18:26-38; Matt. 6:7-8). Praise assumes that God is worthy to be praised, both as the creator (Ps. 104) and as the savior of his people (1 Chr. 16:8-22). *See* PRAISE.

Petitionary prayer is first and foremost prayer for the coming of the kingdom and justice of God (Matt. 6:9-10, 25-33; Luke 18:1-8). It also includes prayer for the receiving of the Holy Spirit (11:13). None of this can, however, be taken to exclude prayer for the needs of daily life (Matt. 6:11-13) and for "the desires of your heart" (Ps. 37:4).

Prayer is the primary activity involved in the worship of God, and as such is commonly experienced as a corporate activity. Nevertheless, prayer of individuals was not only a possibility but also an actuality in every phase of biblical history. Prayers of individuals often precede turning points in Israel's history. Such significant prayers include those of Abraham (Gen. 18:22-32), Jacob (32:9-12 [MT 10-13]), Moses (Exod. 32:11-13; Num. 14:13-19), Gideon (Judg. 6:36-39), Hannah (1 Sam. 1:10-11), and Elijah (1 Kgs. 18:36-37). Jesus, in particular, is depicted as one who prayed (e.g., Mark 1:35; 14:35-39; Luke 5:16; 6:12; 22:32; John 17), who taught about prayer (e.g., Matt. 6:5-15; Luke 11:1-13), and who not only considered prayer efficacious (Mark 9:29) but gave promises regarding its efficacy (e.g., Matt. 6:6, 8; 7:7-11; 18:19; 21:22; Mark 11:24; John 14:13-14).

In the preexilic Old Testament community corporate prayer came to be focused on specific locations, ultimately and primarily the temple of God in Jerusalem (1 Kgs. 8:28-30). Significant corporate penitential prayers of the postexilic community who rebuilt the temple also are recorded (Ezra 9:6–10:5; Neh.

9:1-37). While postexilic Jews once again had the temple, corporate prayer came to be experienced to a large extent in synagogues because of the scattering of the people throughout the Diaspora; where such a building was not available but people still wished to pray to the God of Israel, another "place of prayer" might be used (Acts 16:13). Although the Church's activities, including prayer, were initially centered in particular residences in Jerusalem (1:13-14; 12:12; cf. 2:2), the Church's rapid spread took prayer wherever the new faith went (cf. Acts 18:7; Rom. 16:5; 1 Cor. 16:19; Col. 4:15; Phlm. 2).

The posture assumed by people in prayer is frequently mentioned in the Bible, but never in such a way as to prescribe any particular position (e.g., kneeling with arms outstretched, 1 Kgs. 8:54; Ezra 9:5; head bowed and hands lifted, Neh. 8:6; cf. 1 Tim. 2:8; prostrate, Matt. 2:11; standing, 6:5; Luke 18:11, 13).

The unqualified completeness of some promises regarding prayer (e.g., Matt. 18:19; John 16:23; Jas. 1:5; 1 John 5:14-15) appears to run counter to the experience of "unanswered prayer," that which does not lead to reception of what has been prayed for (cf. Luke 22:42a; 2 Cor. 12:7-9). It is prayer made in submission to God's will (Luke 22:42; Rom. 8:26-27; 1 John 5:14) that is efficacious; it is within this framework of acceptance of God's will as the primary goal of prayer and life that the promises are to be read. To pray "in my [Jesus'] name" (Matt. 18:20; John 14:13-14; 15:16; 16:23-24, 26) is, in intention, to accept the same condition. On the same basis, faith (Matt. 21:22; Heb. 11:6) and righteousness (John 9:31; Jas. 4:3; 5:16; 1 John 3:22) are cited as conditions that precede prayer.

The question of how prayer can be considered efficacious in view of the foreknowledge of God is not discussed in the Bible (though it quickly comes to mind from Matt. 6:8). But God's knowledge of the needs of his people is taken as an encouragement to pray, not as a reason to refrain from so doing (7:7-11). Even if God does good things for the person who does not ask, that person cannot receive those good things as an answer to prayer, i.e., as a result or evidence of an intimate relationship between himself and God. To not pray, even out of respect for the foreknowledge of God, is to remove oneself from that relationship. Indeed, prayer can be taken seriously only where the covenant relationship between free human beings and the powerful God is fundamental in the understanding of the faith.

That God's power is without limit means that his love for his people is unfailing. Because of this, where Jesus has been thought to be teaching persistence or importunity in prayer (Luke 11:5-13; 18:1-8), his teaching is actually focused more on the difference from human love or justice in the way that God's love responds to the needs of his people. (This does not mean that persistent prayer is ruled out.)

See LORD'S PRAYER.

PREACHING, PROCLAMATION.† The act of communicating (Gk. *angéllō* "announce, proclaim"; *kērýssō*, originally the activity of an official herald but later used more broadly) the good news of salvation through Jesus Christ (esp. *euangelízō* and related verbs). Related nouns indicate the person who preaches (*euangelistḗs, kḗryx*) and the activity or content of preaching (*euangélion* "gospel, good news," *kḗrygma, lógos* "word, message, preaching").

One constant feature of the message of Jesus and the early Church is its expression and embodiment most of all as preaching. Indeed, the message has its power only as that which is publicly preached (Rom. 10:14).

An absolute distinction cannot be made between public "preaching" and private "teaching" in the ministry of Jesus. However, he did give only to his close disciples instruction concerning what he was to experience in Jerusalem (Mark 8:31), explanations of his parables (4:10-12), and instruction for their missionary work (Matt. 10). His public preaching was centered on the proclamation of the coming of the kingdom and the call to repentance (4:17). In the early Church also was evident a distinction between, on the one hand, the proclamation of the resurrection of Jesus, God's work of salvation in him, and the call to repentance (Acts 2:22-39; 17:30-31; 1 Cor. 2:1-5) and, on the other hand, the teaching of those who have responded to the call and joined the Christian community (Acts 2:42; 1 Cor. 2:6-7). These two tasks did overlap considerably, depending on the needs of the community (3:1-3; Col. 1:28; Heb. 6:1-2).

Questions arise repeatedly in the New Testament concerning the authority upon which preachers act. Jesus and the apostles faced such questions from the Jewish leadership (Matt. 21:23; Acts 4:7). Paul faced such questions in the Church, even in congregations that he had founded (2 Cor. 12:11-12). Such authority could be charismatic (Matt. 10:1; Luke 24:49) or institutional (Titus 1:5). With all this it appears that Jesus and the Church generally had little concern for the proper authorization of preachers; he deflected such questions when put to him by his disciples (Mark 9:38-40). When preachers set themselves up in competition with Paul, he did not inquire as to the source of their authority, but was merely pleased that they proclaimed Christ (Phil. 1:15-18); he saw his authorization in God rather than anything human (2 Cor. 10:8; 13:10; Gal. 1:1). Nonetheless, Jesus did authorize particular persons to preach (Matt. 10:1-5; Luke 10:1), and Paul did assume that preachers were "sent" (Rom. 10:15).

PRECINCTS. *See* PARBAR.

PRECIOUS STONES. *See* JEWELS.

PREDESTINATION (Gk. *proorízō*).* The divine determination of human beings to eternal salvation or eternal damnation. The doctrine of predestination is a branch, so to speak, of the doctrine of election; God's predestinating activity is a function of his existence as the electing God. Though expressed in the Old Testament primarily as the corporate election of the people of Israel (cf. Deut. 7:6-8), some also extend predestination to include God's having decided in advance the events of each day in an individual's life (e.g., Ps. 139:13-16).

The variety of views that have arisen with regard to predestination arises from the ambiguity of the New Testament itself, the positive teachings of which are seldom expressed in such a way as to answer unambiguously the detailed doctrinal questions of later generations of the Church. The interpretation of Rom. 9:6-24 can be considered pivotal in shaping a view of predestination. Paul is clearly, in this text, defending both God's freedom to determine human destinies and the understanding of election as a narrowing process, but interpreters do not agree on what application Paul intends this to have with regard to eternal salvation.

A defense of a strong view of predestination—a view that God determines which individuals are to be saved eternally and which are to be lost eternally—would regard those named at vv. 7-13 (Isaac and [implied] Ishmael, Jacob, and Esau) as examples of how God deals with human individuals; God determines the relationship of each individual to his promise. A defense of a less strong view of predestination would regard those named as examples of the rejection of human qualifications and claims, or as types or examples of God's freedom to accept or reject some ways to salvation, or as nations rather than individuals (cf. the context of the source of v. 13 at Mal. 1:2-3), functioning here as types of the spiritual condition of Jews and Christians.

Within the context of one's interpretation of Rom. 9, then, the election and predestination of Christians (Acts 13:48; Rom. 8:28-30 ["foreknew," taken by some to mean "chose beforehand"; cf. Jer. 1:5; Gal. 1:15]; Eph. 1:4-5; 1 Thess. 5:9; 2 Thess. 2:13; Rev. 13:8 [cf. 3:5]; 17:8) can be thought of as God's choice of specific individuals to salvation, or as God's choice of faith in Christ as the means to human salvation and of the company of those who follow this means as those who will be saved. It is clear that God draws persons to faith in Christ (John 6:44), but it is not unambiguously stated whether or not this call is irresistible (cf. Matt. 22:14; Luke 7:30; John 6:45 [cf. R. Bultmann, who sees here a "dualism of decision," the leading to Christ of those already inclined to love the Father and do the truth]; 1 Pet. 2:8; 2 Pet. 1:10).

In the eighth century John of Damascus formulated what would become the Eastern Orthodox view, that God simply knows in advance who will be worthy and predestines them to salvation. Augustine had accepted a similar view until 397, when he came to see faith as a divine gift. Thereafter he felt that God predestined some to salvation, "passing over" others who would be damned; still later he came to believe that God predestined to their respective fates both the saved and the lost, stopping short of believing that God had predestined the fall itself. Medieval Roman Catholics were divided between Thomas Aquinas' "middle-Augustinian" contention that God predestined the saved but merely permitted the remainder to be lost and Luis de Molina's doctrine that God predestines salvation based on his prescience of merit and faith (i.e., divine foreknowledge of free human cooperation with the gift of grace). Luther, Zwingli, and Calvin believed not only in double predestination (of the elect and the reprobate) but also in supralapsarianism (i.e., God predestined the fall). Later most Lutherans and some Calvinists moderated (infralapsarians: God elects after the fall, which he did not cause) or rejected (Arminians) predestination; other Calvinists strengthened their position, broadening predestination into a universal determinism stemming from the nature of God. Neo-orthodoxy rejects individual election and reprobation; K. Barth taught that all people are both elect and reprobate in Christ, perhaps implying a doctrine of universal salvation.

See ELECTION.

PREPARATION, DAY OF (Gk. *paraskeuḗ*). The day before the Sabbath or before one of the Jewish feasts on which the Sabbath rules applied. On this day observant Jews prepare all food to be eaten on the next day (which begins in the evening), so that the Sabbath or feast day need not be violated by the work involved in preparing food. Apparently the day on which Jesus was crucified was the day before a Passover that fell before a regular weekly Sabbath (Matt. 27:62; Mark 15:42; Luke 23:54; John 19:14, 31, 42),

PRESBYTERY. The KJV rendering of Gk. *presbytérion* (1 Tim. 4:14; RSV "council of elders"). *See* ELDER.

PRESENCE.† Christian theology envisions God as omnipresent, either present everywhere, or available to everyone wherever they are though not spatially distributed himself.

Especially in the early episodes of the Pentateuch, God is depicted as "present" in very anthropomorphic terms. He walks in the cool of the day with Adam and Eve (Gen. 3:8) and must look for them when they do not appear as usual (v. 9). God wrestles with Jacob on the riverbank (32:22-32 [MT 23-33]) and talks with Abraham in the shade of the oaks (18:1-8), with Hagar beside a well (16:7-13), with Manoah and his wife in the field outside their house (Judg. 13:2-20), and with Gideon at the wine press (6:11-24). In many of these instances, despite occasional terminology for "the angel of Yahweh" or "the angel of God," the humans are understood to have seen the very face of God (indeed, they do not expect to survive the seeing; Gen. 16:13; Exod. 3:6; Judg. 6:22-23; 13:22-23). In all these accounts God is spatially localized as a human being.

Other early biblical stories connect God with certain tracts of "sacred space," as when Abram goes to the oracle oak of Moreh at Shechem (Gen. 12:6-7; cf. 13:18) and when Jacob happens upon the very "house of God" at Luz (28:10-22). Moses meets Yahweh on a plot of sacred ground (Exod. 3:5), on Horeb, "the mountain of God" (v. 1). Sinai/Horeb becomes the most important place of God's presence. From there he may depart temporarily to come to Israel's aid (cf. Judg. 5:4-5) or to give the Torah (Deut. 33:2-5; cf. Exod. 15:25b). According to one account, God refuses to accompany the people from Sinai to the promised land and they undertake the journey in mourning (33:3-6); another account has God travel with Israel in the ark of the covenant (Num. 10:33-36).

For a long time the Ark remained the localized presence of God. He himself was within it. The men of Beth-shemesh look inside and die (1 Sam. 6:19; cf. Exod. 33:20); Uzzah touches the ark and dies (2 Sam. 6:6-7). The Ark was carried into battle with the ex-

pectation that Yahweh within would fight for Israel (Num. 10:35; Josh. 6:1-16; cf. Ps. 24:8-10).

Eventually King David thought it hardly fitting that God be housed in a mere "tent" (the tabernacle) and undertook to build a temple to serve as the divine palace on earth (2 Sam. 7:2). His son Solomon carried out the work, and God was believed to live in this "house of Yahweh," too (1 Kgs. 7:51; 8:29). To enter the temple courts was to "come into his presence" (Ps. 100:2). So firm was the conviction that God dwelt in the temple that many in Jeremiah's day could not believe the city housing the temple could ever be overthrown (Jer. 7:4). After the Babylonian conquest Ezekiel envisioned the glorious presence departing from the temple (Ezek. 9:3; 10:18; 11:23).

The perhaps surprising corollary to the belief that God was present in Israel was that he was not present outside Israel. Most striking is the plea of Naaman the Syrian that Elisha permit him to take two muleloads of Israelite soil back to Syria so that he might worship Yahweh there, something one could not otherwise do on Syrian soil (2 Kgs. 5:17).

Political events such as the fall of Israel and Judah and the succession of Assyrian, Babylonian, and Medo-Persian empires convinced the Hebrew prophets that if their God could thus move the nations like mere game pieces, he must be no mere national deity—even the greatest of them (Exod. 18:11)—but rather the only God, and therefore present everywhere (cf. Isa. 43:11; 44:6, 8; 45:5-6, 21; 47:8-10). Thus the psalmist knows that wherever one might flee there is no escaping God's presence, not even in Sheol (Ps. 139:7-10).

According to the New Testament, God is clearly omnipresent (e.g., Rom. 1:20). In particular, God is present in a new way through the compassionate and powerful ministry of Jesus of Nazareth (e.g., Emmanuel, "God with us"; Matt. 1:23; Luke 7:16; 2 Cor. 5:19). The Fourth Gospel makes the even more radical claim that God is present in Jesus in such a way (John 14:9-10) as to amount to an incarnation of God (1:14; cf. 20:28). Not only is God present among humanity in a special mode in Jesus, but John promises that the Father will come to dwell with anyone who loves Jesus (14:23). Finally, John of Patmos predicts that in the end times the unveiled presence of God will leave heaven and come to dwell on earth among the redeemed (Rev. 21:3; 22:3).

See BREAD OF THE PRESENCE.

Bibliography. T. W. Mann, *Divine Presence and Guidance in Israelite Traditions* (Baltimore: 1977); W. J. Phythian-Adams, *The People and the Presence* (New York: 1942).

PRIEST.† In the Old Testament the function of a priest was that of a mediator between God and mankind. As God's covenant people, Israel was to be "a kingdom of priests and a holy nation" among the peoples of the earth (Exod. 19:5-6). In the representative office of priest, the ideal state of holiness and the role of mediation were focused and maintained in order to preserve and facilitate Israel's service before God.

The most frequent Hebrew term for "priest," *kōhēn,* reflects a common West Semitic word designating priests of any religion. It may have been derived originally from the verb *kāhan* "stand," so that it refers to someone who stands before a deity in a serving capacity (cf. Deut. 10:8). That *kōhēn* is related to Arab. *kahîn* "soothsayer" has also been suggested. Ultimately, the meaning of the term must be sought in the role and function of a priest in Israel.

I. The Priestly Office

A. Descendants of Aaron. In the Genesis accounts the role of a priest was assumed by the head of the clan (e.g., Noah, Abraham, Isaac, Jacob). The first Israelites to be formally identified as priests were Aaron and his sons Nadab, Abihu, Eleazar, and Ithamar (Exod. 28:1). Yet upon Israel's arrival at Sinai, unidentified priests are recorded among the Israelites (19:24), perhaps from among the firstborn offered to Yahweh (13:12-13; cf. 24:5).

Aaron and his sons were of the tribe of Levi. While the origin of the Levites and their historical relationship to the priestly class has posed complex problems for biblical scholarship, the canonical text presents the Levites as a tribe set apart for cultic service. From the period of the wilderness wanderings through the postexilic era, the Levites were given the task of assisting the priests in place of the "firstborn in Israel" who were to have been set apart for Yahweh's service (Num. 3:5-13). Yet it was the privilege of the Aaronic house alone to serve in the official capacity as priests.

In spite of this ideal, certain anomalies appeared in practice. As an example of the disorder in worship prior to the establishment of a central sanctuary in Jerusalem, Judg. 17–18 mentions a young Levite, a descendant of Moses, who acts as a household priest and is later pressed into service as priest for the tribe of Dan. Samuel himself is introduced as an Ephraimite (1 Sam. 1:1) who is dedicated to Yahweh and priestly service (cf. 1 Chr. 6:25-28). Both Samuel, who would serve as prophet, judge, and priest after the fall of the house of Eli (1 Sam. 4), and the prophet Elijah, who would perform a sacrifice in the midst of the idolatrous northern kingdom (1 Kgs. 18), are evidence for the circumvention of the established priesthood during times of crisis.

B. Other Requirements and Provisions. Besides being descendants of Aaron, Israelite priests were to be free from physical deformities (Lev. 21:17-23) and were to meet stringent demands regarding marriage and cultic purity (chs. 21–22). The high priest was subject to even more demanding regulations (21:10-15). The impact of the holiness laws was to reinforce the holiness of God before Israel, just as the institution of the priesthood underscored the need for a mediator between God and Israel.

The priestly class, as members of the tribe of Levi, were not allotted a territory in Canaan (Num. 18:20, 23-24), but were given residence in thirteen of the forty-eight cities set aside for levitical use. Their support was not taken directly from the land but was received through a tenth of the tithes of the people (vv. 26-28), portions of sacrifices not consumed upon the altar (Lev. 5:13; 6:26 [MT 19]; 7:31-34; 10:14-15), the firstborn of flock and herd, the firstfruits of the harvest, the redemption money for Israel's firstborn sons (Num. 18:12-19), and the Bread of the Presence (Lev. 24:5-9). In addition, houses and land were provided for priests residing in Jerusalem and its environs (Neh. 11:3; cf. 1 Chr. 9:2).

C. Vestments and Investiture. The priestly vestments consisted of an undergarment of fine linen, a girdle embroidered in blue, purple, and scarlet, linen breeches, a white turban, and a sash (Exod. 28:40-43). The high priest wore a robe woven in blue from which golden bells and alternating scarlet, purple, and blue pomegranates were suspended around the hem. Over his robe he wore a set of shoulder pieces, the ephod, woven of gold, scarlet, purple, and blue and set with two onyx stones, one on each shoulder. Upon these stones were inscribed the names of the tribes of Israel, six on each stone. Suspended from the ephod by golden braids and fastened around the waist was a breastpiece set with four rows of three precious stones, each inscribed with the name of one of the twelve tribes. This breastpiece also had a pouch that held the sacred lots called Urim and Thummim. On the Day of Atonement, when the high priest would enter the holy of holies to make atonement for the nation, he would wear only his linen garments.

During the wilderness period the sons of Aaron were anointed when they were installed as priests (v. 41; 40:15; Lev. 8:30). Later, the high priest alone may have been anointed when he assumed office. This anointing was to signify consecration to holy service.

D. Duties. In their sanctuary service the priests were charged with maintaining holiness. They alone were to tend to the golden incense altar, the lamps, the Bread of the Presence, and the altar of sacrifice. But the primary role of a priest was that of a mediator representing God before mankind, and mankind before God.

Representing God before mankind, the priest instructed the people in God's laws concerning conduct and worship (Deut. 33:11; cf. 2 Chr. 17:7-9), a role that would expand during the exilic and postexilic periods. In difficult legal decisions the priests were to be consulted as a kind of higher court (Deut. 17:8-13; 19:16-17; 2 Chr. 19:8-10). They were authorized to pronounce God's blessing upon the people (Num. 6:22-27) and to judge ritual cleanness (Lev. 13). In addition, they were given the responsibility of consulting Yahweh on specific matters by means of the sacred lots, the Urim and Thummim.

Representing mankind before God, priests officiated in the offering of sacrifices. They alone were permitted to handle the blood of sacrificial victims and place the sacrifices upon the altar, both animal (4:30-31) and cereal (5:11-12) offerings.

The service of priests was regulated according to their divisions. 1 Chr. 24:7-18 lists twenty-four such divisions, though the origin of these divisions during David's time has been questioned. This arrangement allowed each division the privilege of temple service during two one-week periods each year (cf. Luke 1:5, 8).

II. Developments in the Priesthood

With the rise of the monarchy and the centralization of worship in Jerusalem, the priesthood came under the control of the king. Under David the office of priest was centered in Abiathar of the house of Eli, and Zadok, a descendant of Eleazar (2 Sam. 8:17;

15:24-29, 35). From the reign of Solomon until the restoration, the house of Zadok was the established high priesthood in Jerusalem (1 Kgs. 2:26-27, 35). In the postexilic period the high priesthood remained in the Zadokite family, but there was a shortage of priests because of the reluctance of many to leave Babylon. With the absence of a Davidic king the high priest gained in stature and autonomy, until his influence and power were at least equal to that of the descendant of the royal house. This was to set the stage for the priestly hierarchy that was to dominate the temple-state of Jerusalem. The house of Zadok was not deposed until the Seleucid king Antiochus IV Epiphanes appointed a priest of non-Zadokite lineage, Menelaus (171 B.C.). By A.D. 6 the high priests were chosen from the wealthy priestly families of the Sadducean party.

III. New Testament

Neither Jesus nor his disciples rejected the legitimacy of the priesthood and sacrifices, though they themselves were denounced by the Sadducean priesthood. Yet from a relatively early period the Church came to view the atoning death of Jesus in sacrificial terms (Mark 10:45; Rom. 3:25; 8:3; 1 Cor. 5:7), and the exalted Christ as a mediator (Rom. 8:34). The doctrine of Christ's priesthood was most fully elaborated by the author of the Epistle to the Hebrews, in which Christ is said to fulfill the role of a perfect high priest and sacrificial victim who brings to a close the Old Testament priesthood and sacrifice (e.g., Heb. 8:1-6); on the basis of Ps. 110:4 Christ is identified as a priest after the order of Melchizedek, thus superseding the order of Aaron (Heb. 7:11-19). Elsewhere, believers themselves are said to constitute "a spiritual house, . . . a holy priesthood" (1 Pet. 2:5, 9; Rev. 1:6; 5:10; 20:6), the typological fulfillment of the Old Testament people of God (Exod. 19:6).

Bibliography. A. Cody, *A History of Old Testament Priesthood.* AnBib 35 (1969); R. de Vaux, *Ancient Israel* (New York: 1965) 2:345-405.

PRIESTLY DOCUMENT. One of the hypothetical sources of the Pentateuch, commonly referred to as "P." To the Priestly Document are ascribed the first creation account (Gen. 1:1–2:4), the genealogies in the Pentateuch, and the largest part of the laws pertaining to the priestly and sacrificial system in Exodus, Leviticus, and Numbers. It has been dated to the Exile or thereafter. *See* BIBLICAL CRITICISM.

PRINCIPALITY (Gk. *archē* "beginning, first cause").* A cosmological power whose authority can work with or against the lordship of Christ. A "principality" can be a civil authority before which Christians may be brought for judgment (Luke 12:11; RSV "rulers"; KJV "magistrates"; cf. 20:20; RSV "authority") but to which they must nevertheless submit (Titus 3:1). In the Pauline literature *archē* is most often found in the plural paired with *exousíai* ("principalities and powers"), referring to aspects of a complex structure of primal forces that include "thrones," "dominions," and "authorities" (Rom. 8:38; 1 Cor. 15:24; Eph. 1:21; 3:10; 6:12; Col. 1:16; 2:10, 15; KJV, RSV sometimes "rule"); according to a wide-

spread first-century viewpoint, this structure stands behind natural and human events and influences them.

While first-century A.D. non-Christian writings on the "principalities and powers" are concerned to define the various cosmological factors and to relate them to each other, Paul mentions them only in establishing the absolute superiority of the dominion of Jesus Christ. Whatever principalities his Gentile converts believe to exist, they must now recognize the incomparably higher authority of Christ. Christ's supremacy has a double basis: he had a part in the creation of the principalities and powers (Col. 1:16), and he confronted and "disarmed" the rebellious principalities on the cross (2:15; cf. RSV mg.). Their potency remains, however; it is against these principalities that Christians struggle (and not against the human agencies under their sway, Eph. 6:12). But the conquest Christ has already achieved supplies daily assurance and effectiveness to the Christian (Rom. 8:38-39; Eph. 6:13) even as it is bringing about the final universal acknowledgment of the lordship of Jesus Christ "to the glory of God the Father" (Phil. 2:9-11).

PRISCA [prĭs'kə] (Gk. *Priska*), **PRISCILLA** [prĭsĭl'ə] (*Priskilla*). A "tentmaker" (possibly leather-worker) known both as Prisca (Rom. 16:3; 1 Cor. 16:19; 2 Tim. 4:19) and Priscilla (a diminutive form, used in Acts), the wife of Aquila, also a "tentmaker." It has been suggested that Prisca was connected with the *gens Prisca*, a noble Roman family. She and Aquila left Rome because of Claudius' expulsion of the Jews from Rome and went to Corinth, where they hosted and worked with Paul (Acts 18:2-3). From Corinth they went with Paul to Ephesus where they explained "the way of God more accurately" to Apollos (vv. 18-26). After the death of Claudius they went back to Rome, where she and Aquila were the first to receive Paul's greetings from Corinth (Rom. 16:3).

PRISON (Heb. *bêṯ (hak)keleʾ, bêṯ hassōhar, mišmār*; Gk. *phylakē, desmōtérion*).† Imprisonment was used for confinement of offenders awaiting trial (e.g., 1 Kgs. 22:27; Acts 5:21; 12:4; cf. Lev. 24:12; RSV "custody"), undergoing trial (e.g., Acts 24:27), or awaiting corporal or capital punishment (e.g., Isa. 24:22; Matt. 14:3-5), and for coercion of those owing debts or fines (e.g., 5:25-26; 18:30). The use of imprisonment solely as punishment in itself did not exist in Roman law and is for the most part a relatively modern idea, although it was apparently occasionally so used in early Egypt (Gen. 39:20-23) and in Judah (2 Chr. 16:10; Jer. 37:18); imprisonment might accompany forms of corporal punishment (v. 15; 20:2). Joseph's brothers were, as far as they knew, imprisoned pending the arrival of evidence (Gen. 42:16-17). The main reason for the Philistine imprisonment of Samson was apparently the humiliation of an enemy (Judg. 16:21-25), though he was probably awaiting execution as well; for similar reasons the Babylonians imprisoned the kings of defeated nations (Jer. 52:11).

The cry of the prisoner is included among the human pleas to God in the Psalms (Ps. 142:7 [MT 8]) and is answered by Jesus' mission to "those who are bound" (Luke 4:18, citing Isa. 61:1; cf. 42:7).

PRISON GATE (Neh. 12:39, KJV). *See* GUARD, GATE OF THE.

PRISON LETTERS. Four letters of Paul—Ephesians, Philippians, Colossians, and Philemon—are linked with each other because they were written while the apostle was in prison (Eph. 3:1; Phil. 1:13-14; Col. 4:3; Phlm. 1). All four are traditionally assigned to Paul's imprisonment at Rome (Acts 28; A.D. 61-63); but an earlier imprisonment of at least two years at Caesarea is known (23:33–26:32), and certain references suggest a yet earlier imprisonment at Ephesus (20:18-19; 1 Cor. 15:32; 2 Cor. 1:8-10). While the links of Colossians with Ephesians, on the one hand, and with Philemon, on the other, suggest that the three letters are to be dated together (if they may all be assigned to Paul's authorship), Philippians seems to be more closely linked with earlier letters (Romans, 1-2 Corinthians, and Galatians) as far as situation and language are concerned. One solution to the questions raised is to assign Philippians not to Rome but to the possible Ephesian imprisonment. 2 Timothy was also written from prison (2 Tim. 1:8), but is more closely linked with 1 Timothy and Titus. See the articles on the individual letters.

PROCHORUS [prŏk′ə rəs] (Gk. *Prochoros*). One of the seven charged with the care of the Greek-speaking widows in the early Church (Acts 6:5). His name indicates he was probably a Greek-speaking individual himself.

PROCONSUL [prō′kŏn səl] (Gk. *anthýpatos*). A title originally given to a Roman consul after his term of office in Rome, but eventually to governers of senatorial provinces regardless of whether they had served as consuls. These governers had both military and judicial authority in the provinces. In the New Testament (KJV always "deputy") Sergius Paulus in Cyprus (Acts 13:7-8) and Gallio in Achaia (18:12) bear this title. The proconsul of Asia is also alluded to, not by name and with the plural "proconsuls," probably because more than one person was bearing the duties of proconsul during an interregnum (19:38).

PROCURATOR [prŏk′yə rā′tər] (Gk. *hēgemón*; Lat. *procurator* "agent").† A title applied to different types of officials in the Roman Empire, including governors of minor provinces (Lat. *procurator pro legato*) such as Judea. Procuratorial governors were members of the Roman equestrian class. Such governors were originally called "prefects," the term "procurator" being ascribed to them after the time of Pilate; later writers, however, often referred to Pilate and earlier governors of Judea as "procurator."

Judea came under procuratorial rule after Herod's son Archelaus had been deposed in 6 B.C. and, except during the reign of Herod Agrippa I (A.D. 41-44), remained under procuratorial rule until the revolt in 66. Pontius Pilate was Judea's fifth governor (26-36), appointed and later deposed by Emperor Tiberius. Subsequent governors of Judea included Antonius Felix (appointed by Claudius, *ca.* 52; Acts 23:24) and Porcius Festus (appointed by Nero, *ca.* 58; 24:27). The governors of Judea were generally subject to those of Syria.

PROMISE.† "Promise" in English versions of the Old Testament represents a number of Hebrew words of broader meaning, principally *dāḇār* "word, matter, thing" (e.g., Josh. 21:45; 2 Sam. 7:21) and *'āmar* "say, speak" and related words (e.g., 2 Chr. 6:20; Ps. 77:8 [MT 9]; 119:38). God's promise is present in his word, which speaks of the blessings he intends to give to his people. Through covenants with mankind (represented by Noah, Gen. 8:21-22), with Israel (in the person of Abraham, 12:2-3; 15:18-21), and with the people of Israel assembled at Sinai (Exod. 19:5-6), God made the fundamental promises on which the further existence of the people of God is built. In promising a "new covenant" (Jer. 31:31-34) God promised to address those problems that were greatest for mankind by dealing directly with the hearts of persons.

In the New Testament "promise" represents Gk. *epangelía* and related words, which often refer to the Old Testament promise of the coming of Christ and of salvation in him. Indeed, the New Testament conception of the Old Testament is that of promise which has now been fulfilled. While specific Old Testament passages might be referred to as instances of promises that have been fulfilled (e.g., Isa. 7:14 at Matt. 1:22-23), sometimes the Old Testament as a whole is referred to as fulfilled promise (as at Luke 1:72; 24:27). An emphatic christocentricity is reflected in Paul's statement regarding Christ, that "all the promises of God find their Yes in him" (2 Cor. 1:20).

In the New Testament, God also continues to be the one who gives promises concerning the blessings he will bestow on his people, such as the promise of release from the power of sin (2 Pet. 1:4) and "the promise of the Spirit," i.e., the promise that the Holy Spirit would be given (Acts 2:33; cf. Luke 11:13). The latter is the same as "the promise of the Father" (24:49; Acts 1:4), that is, the promise given by the Father that the Spirit would be given.

PROPHECY, PROPHET.† Communication of a divine message (lit. "a word/matter [Heb. *dāḇār*] of/from God," "an oracle [*nᵉ'um* "utterance"] of Yahweh") through a human messenger (cf. Gk. *prophētēs*, one who proclaims (lit. "speaks for") and interprets divine revelation.

I. Terminology and Background

Various Hebrew terms are employed to designate the person and office of the prophet, providing insight into the functions of and perhaps distinctions between prophets. Most common is Heb. *nāḇî'* (fem. *nāḇî'â*), a general term thought to be derived from a root "to call," thus "one who calls (or announces)" or "one (who is) called." A distinct role is often suggested for the *rō'eh* or *ḥōzeh*, both rendered "seer" (cf. 1 Sam. 9:9), one who experiences and reports or interprets a dream or vision; such figures are frequently associated with ecstatic states. Other terms include "man of God" (*'îš hā'ᵉlōhîm*; e.g., 1 Kgs. 17:18, 24), "messenger" (*mal'āḵ*), and "(his) servant" (*'eḇeḏ*).

Portrayals of various classes of prophets among other ancient Near Eastern peoples has prompted scholars to posit parallels between and influence on Hebrew prophecy. Hittite texts of the mid-second millennium

CHRONOLOGY OF THE PROPHETS

Prophet	Approximate Dates B.C.	King(s)	Kingdom
EARLY PROPHETS:			
Samuel (1 Samuel)	1050-1000	Saul, David	United Israel
Elijah (1 Kgs. 17– 2 Kgs. 2)	870-852	Ahab, Ahaziah	Israel
Elisha (1 Kgs. 19; 2 Kgs. 2–13)	852-795	Jehoram-Jehoash	Israel
Micaiah (1 Kgs. 22)	853	Ahab	Israel
"WRITING PROPHETS" OF THE MONARCHIC PERIOD:			
Amos	760	Jeroboam II	Israel
Jonah	760	Jeroboam II	Israel
Though Jonah was active during the reign of Jeroboam II (2 Kgs. 14:25), the book of Jonah was probably written during the postexilic period.			
Hosea	760-722	Jeroboam II-Hoshea	Israel
Isaiah (Isa. 1–39)	740-700	Uzziah-Hezekiah	Judah
Micah	740-687	Jotham-Hezekiah	Judah
Zephaniah	640-610	Josiah	Judah
Nahum	630-612	Josiah	Judah
Jeremiah	626-580	Josiah-The Exile	Judah
Habakkuk	600	Jehoiakim	Judah
EXILIC AND POST-EXILIC PROPHETS:			
Ezekiel	592-570		
*Obadiah	587-early fifth century		
Deutero-Isaiah (Isa. 40–55)	550-539		
Haggai	520		
Zechariah (Zech. 1–8)	520-518		
*Trito-Isaiah (Isa. 56–66)	540-450		
*Malachi	500-400		
*Deutero-Zechariah (Zech. 9–14)	fourth-third centuries		

*Dates can be assigned to Obadiah, Joel, Trito-Isaiah, Malachi, and Deutero-Zechariah only speculatively. Joel has been assigned dates from the ninth to the fourth centuries B.C.

refer to "men of God," inspired speakers who interpreted events for the king. Here, as also in Egypt and Mesopotamia, diviners sought divine revelations through dreams (cf. Gen. 41; Dan. 2) and a variety of omens. Of particular interest are the eighteenth-century Amorite texts from Mari, which mention both professional and lay prophets who received divine messages in public contexts as well as privately. Represented are the Akk. *āpilu/apiltu* "one who answers (generally a particular deity)," men and women who related oracles to the king; *assinnu*, ecstatic cultic personnel, perhaps eunuchs; *muḫḫu/muḫḫûtu*, cultic prophets who attained an ecstatic state through ritual, similar to the Canaanite prophets of Baal and Asherah (Heb. *nᵉbîʾîm*) at 1 Kgs. 18:19. *See* DIVINATION.

II. Historical Development

A. *Premonarchic Period.* Before the monarchic period and in the early generations of the Monarchy, the terms "prophet" and "prophetess" were applied to individuals who gave significant military and judicial leadership (e.g., Moses, Deut. 18:15, 18; Deborah, Judg. 4:4; Samuel, 1 Sam. 3:20; cf. 17:15-17), who had ecstatic experiences of contact with God (Num. 11:24-29; 1 Sam. 19:20-24; 2 Kgs. 3:15; cf. 1 Kgs. 18:26-29), often through the playing and singing of liturgical music (Exod. 15:20; 1 Chr. 25:1-5). Some were organized in professional guilds (1 Sam. 10:5-12; 19:20). The term "prophet" was also applied to those protected by God in a special way (Abraham, Gen. 20:7; Ps. 105:15). Even though some of these early prophets were quite different from the later classical prophets, the understanding that prophets gave messages from God was always present, and these earlier conceptions of prophetism were never entirely forgotten.

B. *Monarchy.* With the beginning of Israel's monarchy, prophecy became more clearly recognizable as the movement that included the names of most of those called "prophets" in the Old Testament (e.g., Elijah, Elisha, Nathan). It would come to have a major role in shaping the development of Old Testament religion, and produce the canonical books of the prophets. Under the Monarchy prophets took an official role as advisors of kings (Gad, 1 Sam. 22:5; Isaiah, Isa. 37:1-4; Jeremiah, Jer. 37:16-17). Prophecy was institutionalized sufficiently that large numbers of recognized prophets could be summoned when the occasion demanded (1 Kgs. 18:4; 22:6). Within prophecy a movement would develop, particularly from the eighth century on, expressing opposition to kings, and thus would keep alive the classic faith in Israel's God even in difficult times. Yet although friction existed between prophets and kings from the beginning of Israel's monarchy (1 Sam. 13:13-14), nevertheless a fundamental assumption remained that kings needed and respected the free operation of the prophets.

Jezebel's importation of foreign absolutist ideas of monarchy and her opposition to Israel's native religion made royal opposition to prophets a dangerous possibility (1 Kgs. 18:4). Although commonly thought to represent a misplaced account from the time of Jeroboam II, ch. 13 probably indicates the roots of monarchic opposition, to prophets even prior to Jezebel's time. Such deliberate opposition, both official (22:26-27; Jer. 20:1-2; 36:23-26; 37:11-21; 38; Amos 7:10-13, 16) and popular (Isa. 30:9-11; Jer. 26:7-11; Amos 2:12; Mic. 2:6, 11), continued throughout the monarchic period. But the kings could not abolish Yahwistic prophecy as a whole, even if they would—and did—seek to control it by force.

While Gk. *pseudoprophḗtēs* "false prophet" occurs in the LXX, no equivalent term is found in the Hebrew Old Testament; "false prophets" are simply called "prophets." It is clear, however, that prophecy became divided between those more ready to oppose monarchs and others who accommodated their message to the optimistic hopes and desires of the monarchs. The latter included the prophets who advised Ahab and Jehoshaphat to go to war against Syria (1 Kgs. 22:6, 10-12) as well as prophets opposed by "true" prophets (Jer. 6:13; 23:9-40; 27:9; 28; Ezek. 13:2-10; Mic. 3:5). While accommodation to the aims of the monarchs was the main characteristic of false prophecy, it could also be recognized by its failure to predict what God would bring about in the future (Deut. 13:1-5 [MT 2-6]; 18:20-22; cf. Jer. 27:14-15).

Opposition isolated the "true" prophets and encouraged their close and sensitive identification with God's passionate response to the injustices and unfaithfulness of the people to the historic tenets of the covenant. A prophet's lament (e.g., 4:19-22) could itself be an expression of God's lament (vv. 11-18). This identification of the messenger with the message increased in the experiences of Jeremiah, but it can be seen already with Samuel (1 Sam. 8:7) and Elijah (1 Kgs. 19:10). The symbolic acting-out of prophecies in the prophets' lives (Isa. 7:3; 8:1-4; ch. 20; Jer. 27:1-15; 32:9-15; Hos. 1-3), the preservation of written collections of oracles associated with individual prophets (resulting in the canonical books of the prophets, the "Latter Prophets"), and the interest in the personal crisis experienced in the call of the individual prophet (1 Sam. 3; Isa. 6; Jer. 1) are aspects of this identification of the messenger with the message. An important climax of this identification is found in the Suffering Servant songs of the book of

Isaiah, where the prophet's sufferings are themselves his message. The culmination of this development was the early Church's teaching about Jesus—the prophet is the message, "the Word."

C. *Exile and Restoration.* The conflicts of the monarchic era are interpreted in the exilic and postexilic historical writings of the Old Testament as evidence of rebellion against God. The culmination of interest in the prophetic experience of the preceding centuries was the statement that Israel had persecuted or even killed the prophets, which would become a common element in Jewish and Christian understanding of the Old Testament past (e.g., Neh. 9:26; Jub. 1:12; T.Levi 16:2; 1 En. 89:51; Matt. 5:11-12; 23:29-37; Acts 7:52; 1 Thess. 2:15).

In the Hellenistic era a tradition arose that after Haggai, Zechariah, and Malachi Israel had no more prophets (2 Esdr. 12:42; Pr.Azar. 15; 1 Macc. 4:46; 9:27; 14:41). This tradition was itself based on the existence of the written canon; evidence exists within the prophetic books themselves that there was no definite end to the prophetic movement, but rather continuing developments on the basis of earlier prophetic materials. Apparently late productions of the prophetic movement, such as Zech. 9–14 and exilic and postexilic materials in the book of Isaiah, have been ascribed to books bearing the names of earlier prophets. Such a practice of attaching new prophecies to older prophetic material suggests a growing sense of the timeless authority of the old.

III. Present and Future

Distinction is frequently sought in understanding the content and function of prophecy as "foretelling," or prediction, and "forthtelling," or application of God's word to contemporary circumstances. Indeed, the prophets were deeply involved in the life and often the death of their own people and nation. The issues that they address with messages of judgment and hope were raised by the experience of the people of God at the time of the prophets' ministries. Nonetheless, the prophets were expected to say something significant concerning what the future would bring (Deut. 18:21-22; Amos 3:7). This expectation sometimes placed prophets little higher than diviners. But in the prophetic movement's confrontation of the nation, this predictive aspect of prophecy served the strong ethical and religious message of the prophets. What was said about the future was intended to call forth repentance. Hope was contingent on repentance and predicted destruction could be averted by repentance.

A longer look into the future was sometimes taken. As king after king failed to measure up to the prophets' ideals and as the Exile and the difficulties of the postexilic period postponed hope, messages of both hope and judgment became expanded to involve the whole world and to become total and irreversible (e.g., Isa. 2:2-4; 24:1-3). Predictions of the Messiah became part of these messages (e.g., 9:6-7; ch. 11). But the idea that a primary concern of the prophets was prediction of events concerning the Church and the end times arises from a misunderstanding of the prophets as apocalyptists. The value of the prophets for today, as for their original audiences, is primarily in their preaching of repentance, judgment, and hope for salvation, which their predictions of the future serve. *See* APOCALYPTIC.

III. Prophets in the Church

Part of the early Church's involvement in a new movement of God's Spirit was its exercise of prophecy (Acts 2:17-18). Both men and women were prophets in the churches (21:9; 1 Cor. 11:4-5). A class of itinerant prophets developed quickly in the Church (Did. 11:3-12).

According to Paul, prophecy is a gift of the Spirit given to particular individuals for the Church's benefit (Rom. 12:6; 1 Cor. 12:10, 28-29; Eph. 4:11; 1 Thess. 5:20), one that will pass away when knowledge is made complete by the coming of Christ (1 Cor. 13:8-10). Prophecy, unlike glossolalia, takes the form of a known language and is, therefore, more valuable to the Church than uninterpreted glossolalia (14:1-6, 23-25). Prophecy is, indeed, considered basic to the structure and operation of the Church (Eph. 2:20; 3:5).

Prophecies were made concerning the ministry of Timothy, perhaps before it began (1 Tim. 1:18) and again when he was ordained (4:14). Agabus, a prophet, foretold a famine (Acts 11:28) and Paul's arrest in Jerusalem (21:10). Apparently exhortation and encouragement, often based on prediction of the future, were the keynotes of early Christian prophecy. Also, the Church most often viewed the function of the Old Testament prophets as similar to that of the Christian prophets: predicting what was now fulfilled in Christ and in the Church, and providing a basis for exhortation and encouragement of Christians (e.g., 1 Pet. 1:10-12).

The book of Revelation is presented as prophecy (Rev. 1:3; 10:11; 22:7, 10) and can be considered as an embodiment of a Christian prophetic ministry. The suffering of the prophets, which was important in reflection on the Old Testament prophets, is brought into play in relation to the Church's prophets in Revelation's encouragement to persecuted Christians (11:3-12, 18; 16:6; 18:20, 24).

Bibliography. D. E. Aune, *Prophecy in Early Christianity and the Ancient Mediterranean World* (Grand Rapids: 1983); J. Blenkinsopp, *A History of Prophecy in Israel* (Philadelphia: 1983); W. Brueggemann, *The Prophetic Imagination* (Philadelphia: 1978); K. Koch, *The Prophets,* 2 vols. (Philadelphia: 1983-1984); J. Lindblom, *Prophecy in Ancient Israel* (Philadelphia: 1962); R. R. Wilson, *Prophecy and Society in Ancient* (Philadelphia: 1980).

PROPHETS, THE (Heb. *nᵉbîʾîm*).† The second of the three divisions of the Hebrew canon, subdivided into the "Former Prophets," which include Joshua, Judges, 1-2 Samuel, and 1-2 Kings (placed among the "historical books" in the LXX and Christian versions of the Old Testament), and the "Latter Prophets," comprised of Isaiah, Jeremiah, Ezekiel, and the Book of the Twelve (Hosea, Joel, Amos, Obadiah, Jonah, Micah, Nahum, Habakkuk, Zephaniah, Haggai, Zechariah, and Malachi, often called the "Minor Prophets"; cf. Sir. 49:10).

PROPITIATION. *See* EXPIATION.

PROSELYTE (Gk. *prosḗlytos*). A religious convert; in biblical usage primarily a Gentile who adopted the Jewish religion by submitting to circumcision, immersion, or "baptism" (from some time in the first century A.D.), the offering of a special sacrifice, and adherence to the law of Moses. Proselytes were full converts, unlike the "God-fearers," Gentiles who worshipped the God of Israel but did not submit to circumcision.

The LXX uses Gk. *prosḗlytos* (originally "newcomer," "visitor") to render Heb. *gēr*, in the Old Testament indicating primarily the "resident alien" or "sojourner," a non-Israelite who for various reasons had established extended if not permanent residence in Israel. Such persons were, with other vulnerable people such as widows and orphans, protected by Mosaic law (e.g., Lev. 19:10; 23:22; Deut. 24:14, 19-22; 27:19). They were permitted to offer sacrifices and, if circumcised, participate in the Israelite feasts (e.g., 16:11, 14; cf. Exod. 12:45, 48), and were reckoned among the congregation in observance of the covenant renewal (Josh. 8:33, 35). The term began to take on the meaning of religious convert perhaps as early as the divided monarchy (cf. 2 Kgs. 5:15-19) largely as a result of the upheaval and social mixing brought on by foreign conquest and resettlement of Israel and other peoples (cf. Ezra 9–10; Neh. 13:23-27; Esth. 8:17). The changed circumstances of exile and resettlement encouraged in Hebrew thought a new universalism (cf. Isa. 56:1-8). *See* SOJOURNER.

The Jewish dispersion was the basis of concerted efforts to bring knowledge of Israel's faith to Gentiles (cf. Matt. 23:15), and proselytism flourished especially from the intertestamental period on (cf. 2 Macc. 9:17). Proselytes were found everywhere Jews were located and among all social classes. *Ca.* A.D. 50 King Izates of Adiabene became a proselyte with his mother, Helen, his brother, and five of his sons. Both native Jews and proselytes were among pilgrims from Rome to Jerusalem for the Feast of Pentecost when the Holy Spirit came upon the Church (Acts 2:10). One of the seven chosen by the early Jewish Church to assist in the distribution to widows was a proselyte (6:5). In Pisidian Antioch, as no doubt in other places, many proselytes were attracted by the preaching of Paul (13:43; RSV "converts"), who may have been a preacher of Judaism to Gentiles before he became a Christian (cf. Gal. 5:11). It was mainly the attraction of Christian faith that after the first century A.D. decreased the number of Gentiles turning to Judaism.

PROSTITUTION. *See* CULT PROSTITUTE; HARLOT.

PROVERB (Heb. *māšal, māšāl*).† Basically a saying concerned with making an instructive comparison, in form-critical usuage called a mashal. The Hebrew noun is usually thought to be derived from a verbal root *mšl* "be like, be equal to" but includes a variety of related nuances.

In its most general usage, a mashal is described as a popular saying—sometimes with ancient roots—as at 1 Sam. 24:13 (MT 14) (cf. NIV, "As the old saying goes . . ."; cf. 2 Pet. 2:22; Gk. *paroimía*). Elsewhere such sayings are closely associated with the teaching of the wise men (1 Kgs. 4:32 [MT 5:12]; Prov. 26:7, 9; Eccl. 12:9). At Prov. 1:6 they are poetically paralleled with the phrase "the words of the wise(men)" as the most general and overarching of several characteristic forms of wisdom speech (proverbs, parables, riddles); in this connection, the term is employed in the title of the book of Proverbs (1:1) and appears in subsequent headings within the book (10:1; 25:1). A number of instances (all in Ezekiel) join the noun *māšal* with the verb of the same root, with the resulting construction "to utter a proverb" (Ezek. 12:22-23; 17:2; 18:2-3; 20:49 [MT 25:5] [RSV "allegories"]; 24:3).

In certain circumstances the term loses its neutral sense of proverb/saying and becomes more specifically a source of negative comparison. A regular formal construction accompanies this special understanding of mashal: verb + preposition (*le-*) + *māšal*. With the verb "be, become" (*hāyâ*) the construction is rendered "become a mashal" (Deut. 28:37; 1 Sam. 10:12; 1 Kgs. 9:7; cf. Ps. 69:11 [MT 12]; RSV "byword"). with the verbs "give" (*nātan*) and "set" (*śym*) the translation becomes "make someone/something into a mashal" (2 Chr. 7:20; cf. Ps. 44:14 [MT 15]; Jer. 24:9; Ezek. 14:8). The tendency in translating the term in this context is to follow the neutral rendering "proverb" (so usually RSV); but since proverbs can be either positive or negative, the use of the term in this particular construction can obscure the consistently negative connotation of the mashal here. In some cases the synonym "byword" has been employed, interpreting the mashal as a mocking taunt; this disregards the basic idea of comparison that is inherent in the mashal and should be preserved. Analysis of the passages in which this construction occurs makes it clear that the import of the phrase is not so much that someone or something is being mocked, but that the object is becoming or being made into an negative example so others will not follow the same path. It is easy to see how such an understanding of the mashal is closely related to the biblical proverbs where admonition by example is one of the key methods of the wisdom teacher's instruction (e.g., Prov. 17:19-21). It is also clear how such an example would become the object of mockery and taunt. Perhaps it is best in these circumstances to translate the term "example" since the English idiom "to make an example of someone/something" makes clear both the comparative and negative content of the phrase.

A further development in the meaning of the proverb takes place in prophetic contexts. Again the variation in meaning is signaled by a distinctive construction: verb (*nāśā'* "lift, raise") + *māšal* + verb (*'mr*) "he lifted up his mashal and said ..." (Num. 23:7; RSV "took up his discourse"). This construction occurs a number of times within the Balaam narrative (also v. 18; 24:3, 15, 20-21, 23), in prophetic contexts (Isa. 14:4; Mic. 2:4; Hab. 2:6; RSV "take up a taunt [song]"), and Job (Job 27:1; 29:1). The precise meaning of *māšal* in these contexts is not immediately clear; the term is variously translated "oracle, prophecy, discourse, parable, taunt." When the sayings introduced by this phrase are studied, a common thread appears. With the exception of the two

passages from Job, all are warnings. It seems that the function of the mashal as a negative example, cautioning the hearers against following similar paths, has developed into a prophetic warning in which the negative "example" is no longer clearly discernible. The meaning of the term in Job and its relation to prophetic usuage remain elusive, but it may be that admonition correctly characterizes these passages as well (cf. Luke 4:23; Gk. *parabolē*).

PROVERBS, BOOK OF.† The twentieth book of the Old Testament according to the Christian canon and third of the poetical books (Job, Psalms, Proverbs) in the Hebrew canon included among the Writings. The book of Proverbs is a collection of largely proverbial Wisdom Literature traditionally associated with Solomon, the Israelite king famed for his divine gift of wisdom (1 Kgs. 3-4); the Hebrew title for the book (Heb. *mišlê*; Prov. 1:1) reflects this association. It is clear from literary analyses and internal evidence that the contents of the book must be attributed to a variety of authors over an extended period of time. At least three authors are named in headings (Solomon, 1:1; 10:1; 25:1; Agur, 30:1; Lemuel, 31:1), and other segments are attributed anonymously to "the wise" (22:17; 24:23). The designation of the whole collection as "proverbs" (LXX Gk. *Paroimiai*; Vulg. Lat. *Liber Proverbiorum*) is not entirely apt since large portions of the contents (primarily the discourse material of chs. 1-9) do not fit this description. Many scholars contend the present introductory verse (1:1) originally stood as the heading of the Solomonic proverbs at 10:1-22:16, before chs. 1-9 were placed in their present position, and was only later moved to serve as the title of the composite book.

I. Collection and Dating

The process by which the various components of the book were brought together into a whole remains obscure. It is known that wisdom teachers employed brief proverbial sayings as well as longer discourses to instruct their pupils. According to Ecclesiastes, an important part of the wise man's task was "weighing and studying and arranging proverbs" for the edification of the people (Eccl. 12:9). Collections of sayings served as incentives to right action and fixed points of reference within the turmoil of life (v. 11). Whether or not the notice at Prov. 25:1 is accepted, the composition of the whole book could not have taken place before the reign of Hezekiah (*ca.* 715-687 B.C.) and may have continued long after this date.

II. Background

Wisdom in the ancient Near East can be characterized as a way of approaching life based on experience and observation and seeking to uncover the underlying principles of life as a source of guidance. As such, biblical wisdom is not unique, but part of a widespread, international phenomenon. Archaeology has discovered comparable wisdom texts in Egypt, Phoenicia (Ugarit), and Mesopotamia. The primary means for the transmission of wisdom insights was the proverb: a brief, pithy maxim, easily remembered, in which the distilled truths of observation and experience are encapsulated. While the origin of proverbial wisdom is probably popular (in the interaction between parent and child), the wisdom enterprise was ultimately elevated to a science by schools of skilled, professional wise men (Heb. *ḥᵃkāmîm*) who produced extensive collections of proverbs for their own study and the instruction of their students. In Egypt schools were located at the pharaonic court and served to advise the king. The same is likely the case in Israel, as suggested by the reference to the "men of Hezekiah king of Judah" who copied proverbs (Prov. 25:1).

III. Contents

In addition to the primary form of wisdom speech, the PROVERB (*māšal*), a number of other forms appear in the book of Proverbs.

A. *Two-lined Proverb*. Some scholars have suggested that the original form of wisdom speech was the brief proverb of one line (e.g., "Is Saul also among the prophets?"; 1 Sam. 10:11-12). Later this simple form was refined by the addition of a second line roughly paralleling the first in one of the following ways. (1) Synonymous parallelism. In this type of proverb, the first line states an idea that is repeated in the second, but using different words (e.g., Prov. 11:25; 16:20). (2) Antithetical parallelism. Here the first line is repeated, but in a way that reverses the original idea (e.g., 10:15; 14:31; 15:29). By far the most common form used in chs. 10–31 is the antithetical proverb. The wise and the fool, the righteous and the wicked are placed in close comparison so that the hearer sees at once the contrasting results of their lives. (3) Synthetic parallelism. In this type, the second line does not repeat the first, but advances the thought in some way (e.g., 13:14; 14:7; 16:29).

B. *Extended Sayings*. Further expansion of the proverbial saying resulted in extended sayings of several lines in which the proverbial flavor is lost. Several of these are collected in chs. 30–31 (e.g., 30:7-9; cf. vv. 1-4, 11-14; 31:1-9).

C. *Numerical Sayings*. Closely related to the extended saying are wisdom compositions in which several apparently unrelated phenomena are brought together in such a way as to reveal some illuminative similarity. Because of their introductory emphasis on numbers, these are commonly known as numerical sayings (e.g., 30:18-19, 24-28).

D. *Acrostic Poems*. Another carefully crafted literary composition employed by the wise men is the acrostic poem, in which each successive line or stanza begins with sequential letters of the Hebrew alphabet. A beautiful example honors the good wife at 31:10-31.

E. *Discourse*. A very different form of wisdom speech dominates chs. 1–9. Here, rather than brief compositions of only a few lines, one encounters much more extensive discourses. Despite considerable disagreement as to the number of poems comprising these nine chapters (some find nine or more, while others affirm the whole as a unity), it is clear that this material represents a marked advance beyond the rather limited sayings in chs. 10–31. The whole segment sustains a consistent theme and is able to develop complexities of thought unexampled in the remainder of Proverbs. Similar wisdom discourse is found in Ecclesiastes and parts of Job.

IV. Structure

As has been seen, the book of Proverbs falls readily into two major sections: the proverbial collections of chs. 10–31 and the discourse material in chs. 1–9. It is generally accepted that the proverbial collections are earlier than the discourses and may even have circulated as an independent unit before the inclusion of chs. 1–9. This may explain the title "proverbs of Solomon. . . ," which seems more applicable to chs. 10-31 than to the whole. In the canonical form, chs. 1–9 serve as an introduction to the succeeding proverbial collection and provide certain interpretive controls for the reader. The following segments are observed.

A. *Prov. 1:1-7*. The first seven verses of the book stand as an introduction to the whole. They set out the purpose of the unified collection, its expected audience, and some interpretive principles to guide the reader. According to these verses, the book is to provide guidance to right understanding of the words of the wise (i.e., the proverbial sayings of chs. 9–10) for all, from the untutored youth to the most experienced sage. The section concludes with a guiding principle: true wisdom must begin with "the fear of the Lord" (v. 7). This insight returns repeatedly in the discourse of chs. 1–9.

B. *Chs. 1–9*. In this section a series of discourses contrast the opposing ways of wisdom/righteousness and folly/wickedness with their respective ends: Life vs. Death. Wisdom is personified as a woman who competes with Dame Folly for the attention of men (chs. 7–9). Throughout the reader is counseled to follow the way of true wisdom. Early wisdom felt that it was possible, through the unbridled exercise of the human intellect in the observation and experience of life, to discover the basic principles of a successful life. At this stage wisdom was confident that wisdom/righteousness would prosper while folly/wickedness would perish. For the most part, the sayings of chs. 10–31 reflect this viewpoint. Later authors were pessimistic of the conclusions of early wisdom. In Ecclesiastes and Job, such easy solutions to the complexities of life were scrutinized and found wanting. Ecclesiastes holds rather bleakly to a distant God, while Job turns to an experience of God that obliterates any question of his justice.

In these first nine chapters of Proverbs, two corrective insights are offered to preserve the valuable guidance available in the proverbial literature while avoiding the pessimistic conclusions of the critical sages. Both are encapsulated in the exhortation: "The fear of the Lord is the beginning of knowledge; fools despise wisdom and instruction" (1:7). The value of wisdom is not in question; the basis of wisdom is. The first corrective insight questions the ability of the unaided human intellect to arrive at true wisdom (vv. 4-6, 5-7); wisdom that relies on human reason alone will come to distorted conclusions; true insight comes from God himself.

The second corrective insight concerns the relationship of wisdom to the traditional covenantal religion of Israel. It has long been recognized that biblical Wisdom Literature ignores the traditional forms of Israel's faith. There is no reference to the sacrificial system or any obligation to keep the commandments.

Here the omitted connection is supplied by grounding true wisdom in the "fear of the Lord"; Yahweh is the source of true wisdom and none other. In more subtle fashion, the reader is called to submit to the divine commandments. Throughout these chapters the commandments of the sage are described in terms clearly connected with the divine commandments in Deuteronomy (esp. 6:20-23; cf. Deut. 6:4-9). Proverbial wisdom is valid and valuable when it begins and is interpreted in light of Israel's covenantal faith in Yahweh.

C. *Prov. 10:1–22:16*. This major collection contains proverbs attributed to Solomon. There is no clear method of arrangement, although isolated groups of proverbs share common themes or key word connections. The primary form used is the proverb of two lines, the majority being antithetical parallelism.

D. *Prov. 22:17–24:22*. Various attempts have been made to delineate the "thirty sayings" mentioned at 22:20. Most scholars understand this section to be related in some way to the Egyptian *Instruction of Amen-em-opet* (*ANET*, pp. 421-25), which may antedate the ninth century B.C. The Egyptian text also has thirty sections, ten of which have close parallels in this segment of Proverbs. As noted, wisdom was an international phenomenon, and it is certain Israel was familiar with the wisdom of other peoples (cf. 1 Kgs. 4:30; some scholars suggest the sayings of Agur and Lemuel at Prov. 30-31 are examples of non-Israelite, perhaps Arabian wisdom); evidence of such cross-cultural contacts would not be unexpected in the book of Proverbs.

E. *Prov. 24:23-34*. An additional collection of sayings attributed at v. 23 to the anonymous "wise," this section is comprised largely of extended sayings of several lines concerned with impartiality in judgment (vv. 23-26), false testimony (vv. 28-29), and sloth (vv. 30-34).

F. *Chs. 25–29*. Included here are further sayings attributed to Solomon and said to have been collected or copied by "the men of Hezekiah." The section begins with an extended saying about kings and proper posture toward them (25:2-7). Its final chapter (ch. 29) also reflects concern with the proper conduct of kings and those in authority (vv. 4, 12-16, 26). In between there is no obvious method of arrangement.

G. *Ch. 30*. Agur, son of Jakeh of Massa, is not identified. Some take Massa as the name of a tribe in Arabia (Gen. 25:14; 1 Chr. 1:30); others understand the word, from its use in prophetic texts, as "oracle." The contents are largely numerical sayings, some quite beautiful and artistic.

H. *Ch. 31*. This final chapter, attributed to the otherwise unidentified Lemuel, is divided into an extended saying on the proper conduct of kings (vv. 2-9) and the classic acrostic poem on the good wife (vv. 10-31). As in ch. 30, there is no certainty as to the meaning of the word Massa in this context; it is variously understood as "oracle" or a tribal name.

Bibliography. D. Kidner, *The Proverbs*. Tyndale (1964); W. McKane, *Proverbs*. OTL (1970); R. N. Whybray, *The Book of Proverbs*. CBC (1972).

PROVIDENCE. God's action in providence is the continuation of his role as creator. He maintains and preserves the order that is fundamental to the heavens and earth as he created them, and he is bringing to completion his purposes for mankind and the rest of creation. There are, therefore, two aspects of providence, one oriented toward the continuation of life and order in the present and the other oriented toward the eschaton, the completion of what God intended when he created.

A fundamental assumption of providence viewed as God's preservation of the created order is that the created order is not self-sustaining, but requires God's will and action for the continuation of its processes (Ps. 104:29; Col. 1:17; Heb. 1:3). This maintenance of creation is thought of most in relation to phenomena of weather because of their importance for the pastoral and agricultural societies in which faith in God came to expression (Job 36:27-31; 37:2-13; 38:22-30). It is also affirmed in relation to God's utilization of human evil to provide for his people in time of need (Gen. 50:20), to the courses of the heavenly bodies (Job 38:31-33; Ps. 19:1-6 [MT 2-7]), and to the smallest calamity (Matt. 10:29).

Fundamental questions are, of course, raised by natural calamities. The people of the Bible did not usually experience these questions in terms of the existence of God or his fundamental character as the creator who cares for his creation. Suffering as well as sustenance comes from God (Exod. 4:11; Job 2:10; Isa. 45:7; Amos 3:6); God's maintenance and control of the created order sometimes functions for the judgment of human beings (Job 36:29-33; 37:13; Lam. 3:37-39). But generally it is said that God disregards the righteousness or unrighteousness of the human recipients as he gives the good things of creation (Ps. 145:9, 15-16; Matt. 5:45).

Because enjoyment of the good things of creation is subject to God's sovereignty, he alone can be trusted, in a final sense, with their provision (6:25-33), and even the suffering of his people can be viewed as part of his grace toward them (10:28-31; Rom. 8:28; 2 Cor. 12:7-10; Heb. 12:11; Jas. 1:2-3; 1 Pet. 1:6-7).

When providence is viewed as God's bringing to completion the purposes for which he created the world, questions concerning the existence of evil in the world created by God can receive in part their answer. There is evil in this world, even an organized realm of evil in revolt against the creator and against which the creator and his people struggle (Eph. 6:12; 1 John 5:19). But the outcome is not in doubt. All enemies will be defeated (John 12:31; 1 Cor. 15:24-26; Rev. 11:15) so that God may be "everything to every one" (1 Cor. 15:28). The length of the time remaining before the end is itself subject to God's sovereign control (Mark 13:20). During that time, God retains control of empires and nations (Dan. 2:37-39; 4:24-26 [MT 21-23]), and his purposes of salvation and judgment are brought about through the actions of sinful human beings (Isa. 10:5-6, 15; Acts 2:23; 4:27-28; 13:27).

God's providence is neither impersonal fate nor a determination of every event. Human freedom and natural processes have real existence within divine providence. God is not experienced by his people primarily as a governing force, but as the Lord who addresses persons with his grace and whose lordship can be resisted—though not in any complete or final way—or accepted. The real efficacy of prayer shows, not a limitation in God's governance and providence, but that even as Lord of all he is in gracious dialogue with his creation and able to respond as Lord. The final affirmation with regard to God's providence must be the same as the first: "The earth is the Lord's" (Ps. 24:1).

PSALMS, BOOK OF.† The first book of the third division of the Hebrew canon, the Writings; a varied collection of prayer, poetry, and songs of faith. In the Hebrew Bible the book is entitled *t^ehillîm* "praises" or "songs of praise." The English title derives from the Gk. title (LXX) *Psalmoi* "songs."

I. Formation and Division

In its present canonical form, the book of Psalms is the product of a long history of use, collection, adaptation, and reinterpretation of Israel's liturgical and devotional poetry. Evidence for the complex history of this anthology may be found even on the surface of the canonical text, yet the history of songs and their collection in Israel is older than what is represented by the Psalter.

A. Origins of Psalmody. Outside the Psalter ancient songs of Israel are embedded in narrative texts describing Israel's formative period. Recent studies in Hebrew and comparable poetry of the ancient Near East have emphasized the antiquity of compositions such as the Song of the Sea (Exod. 15:1-18), the Song of Moses (Deut. 32), the Song of Deborah (Judg. 5), and the Song of Hannah (1 Sam. 2:1-10). Evidence for early collections of songs is found in quotations from "the Book of the Wars of the Lord" (Num. 21:14) and "the Book of Jashar" (Josh. 10:13; 2 Sam. 1:18).

B. Compilation of the Psalter. While it is not possible to detect the precise history of the compilation of the Psalter, certain collections that have been incorporated into the present book are evident.

Seventy-three psalms are said to be "of David" (Heb. *l^edāwiḏ*). The Hebrew preposition *l^e-*, translated "of," is ambiguous and suggests several possible meanings: "for David," "by David," "to David" (e.g., "dedicated to David"), "about David," and "for the use of David." While it may be assumed that David, known for his musical ability (1 Sam. 16:17-23; 18:10; 2 Sam. 1:17-27; 3:33-34; 23:1-7; Amos 6:5), did indeed compose some of the psalms associated with his name, it is by no means clear that he authored them all. Eleven psalms (Pss. 42, 44–49, 84–85, 87–88) are associated with the sons of Korah, a family of levitical temple singers (Exod. 6:24; 2 Chr. 20:19). Twelve psalms (Pss. 50, 73–83) are attributed to the levitical musician Asaph, who ministered during the reign of David (1 Chr. 15:17-19; 16:4-5), and whose descendants continued in that role into the postexilic period (Ezra 2:41). Individuals associated with other psalms are Solomon (Pss. 72, 127), Heman the Ezrahite (88), Ethan the Ezrahite (89), Moses (90), and Jeduthun (if indeed a personal name; 39, 62, 77). Whether these are introduced as claims of authorship is unclear.

The Songs of Ascent are a group of fifteen psalms (120–134), varied in content and form, but all apparently associated with pilgrimage to Jerusalem, perhaps for the Feast of Tabernacles. A group of five

psalms (146–150), each distinguished by an opening and closing cry of "Praise the Lord" (*hal^elû-yāh*), may have originally formed a separate collection. A group of psalms overlapping several of the previously mentioned categories is the so-called "Elohistic Psalter" of Pss. 42–83, distinguished by their frequent use of the divine name *'elōhîm* "God" rather than *YHWH* "Yahweh" or "Lord," suggesting a collection made during a period when the covenant name Yahweh was used with caution (cf. the duplicate psalms, 14 and 53).

The final editor(s) of the Psalter presented the collection in five books, each ending with a doxology, the final psalm (150) serving as a closing doxology for the entire collection. This fivefold division (1–41; 42–72; 73–89; 90–106; 107–150) has led to the hypothesis that the editor(s) may have had in mind the analogy of the five books of Moses, the Torah. Ps. 1, serving as a preface to the entire collection, underscores the importance of meditation upon God's Torah for those on the path of righteousness.

C. Superscriptions. The superscriptions or "titles" found at the head of 116 of the psalms are usually held to have been added at a later stage in the compilation of the Psalter. However, the presence of notations accompanying psalms outside the Psalter (2 Sam. 22:1; Isa. 38:9; Hab. 3:1, 19) suggests that some of the superscriptions may have accompanied the psalms from an early stage of their history.

Five types of information are found in the superscriptions, much of which is obscure. (1) The psalm may be identified with a person or persons. (2) A note concerning the historical setting of the psalm may appear. Thirteen of the psalms related to David have such notes. The historical accuracy of these annotations and their role in the canon are questioned by modern scholarship. (3) Some psalms are classified according to their type: psalm (*mizmôr*), song (*šîr*), prayer (*t^epillâ*), instruction (*maśkîl*), or praise (*t^ehillâ*). The distinction between these terms is obscure, as is the meaning of other types (*miḵtām, šiggāyôn*). (4) A few psalms have notations indicating liturgical use. Ps. 30 is "A Song at the dedication of the Temple," Ps. 70 is "for the memorial offering," Ps. 92 "for the Sabbath," and Ps. 100 "for the thank offering." (5) The musical notations that accompany some psalms are the least understood. While certain instructions concerning musical accompaniment are reasonably clear (e.g., *bin^eḡînôṯ* "with stringed instruments," *el-hann^eḥîlôṯ* "for the flute"), others including the frequent "Selah" (*selâ*), continue to elude definition.

II. Literary Types and Settings

Psalms research in the twentieth century has turned its attention from historical questions of authorship, date, place of origin, and sources toward an investigation of the literary forms or genres within the Psalter and their place within the worship and piety of Israel. On the premise that religious literature tends to take on formal characteristics that are resistant to change, and that forms of like pattern were used in like settings, H. Gunkel (his studies were published 1926-1933) placed the psalms into categories that continue, with some refinements, to guide psalm research.

A. Psalms of Lament. Approximately fifty-eight

psalms may be classified as laments. Of these, forty-two are laments of an individual, while the remainder are laments of the community. Arising from corporate or individual experiences of disorientation, these psalms contain the most poignant expressions of human pain and hope in the Psalter. Communal laments (e.g., 12, 44, 58, 60, 74, 80, 83, 85, 90) were used during times of national distress such as defeat in battle, foreign domination, plague, and famine (cf. the summary lament of Joel 2:17b, an abbreviated version of the lengthier laments found in the Psalter and preceded by the assembly of the people [vv. 15-17a] and followed by an oracle of salvation [vv. 18-20] and a song of thanksgiving [vv. 21-24]). Such psalms of lament, like most of the psalms, have lost their historical specificity through repeated use and application in changing contexts. The individual laments (e.g., Pss. 3–4, 13, 22, 31, 39, 57, 69, 88, 139) arose from individual experiences of suffering in situations of sickness, injustice, oppression, or the consequences of personal sin. The "penitential psalms" (6, 38, 51, 102, 130, 143) belong to this category.

The form of the communal and individual laments is roughly the same, though a great deal of variation can be observed in order and emphasis: (1) an address to God with an introductory cry for help; (2) a complaint in which the nature of the distress is indicated and the party's innocence or guilt is stated; (3) a confession of trust in God's power to deliver; (4) a petition calling upon God to intervene, sometimes accompanied by motivations for God to act; (5) an assurance of being heard by God, perhaps echoing the words of a priest or prophet; and (6) a vow of praise in which the supplicant promises to give public praise to Yahweh when deliverance comes. All of the laments include the recognition that God is the only one capable of transforming the situation, and praise for God's intervention is anticipated.

B. Psalms of Thanksgiving. The psalm of thanksgiving (*tôḏâ* "praise") begins where the lament ends. Beyond the experience of disorientation, after God has intervened, the psalmist sings thanks to God and offers his sacrifice of thanksgiving. Two types of praise can be discerned in the Psalms, one praising God for who he is (descriptive) and the other praising God for what he has done in concrete circumstances, such as a bountiful harvest or deliverance from enemies (narrative). Among Israel's neighbors narrative songs of thanksgiving were reserved for personal, family gods and hymns for high gods, but Yahweh had shown himself to be both sovereign and personal. Thus in Israel's psalms the distinction between narrative praise (thanksgiving) and descriptive praise (hymn) was not hard and fast.

Few community psalms of thanksgiving have survived in the Psalter (65, 67, 75, 107, 124), though the salvation history psalms (78, 105-6, 135-36) with their narrative characteristics bear a close resemblance. The individual song of thanksgiving is better represented (18, 30, 32, 34, 92, 116, 118, 138; also 40:1-10 [MT 2-11]; 66:13-20), and a general structure may be discerned: (1) an announcement of praise and address to the Lord; (2) a central section reiterating the lament, the cry for help, and God's intervention; and (3) a conclusion of varied form, often renewing the vow of praise and calling upon God for future help.

C. Hymns. The hymn of descriptive praise has its setting in congregational worship and was not tied to a specific event. The hymn praises God in his relationship to the universe, the kingdoms of the earth, and Israel in particular. The essence of these psalms can best be described as an exposition of the dual themes of God's exalted majesty as creator and Lord and his gracious involvement with the humble and weak. The structure of the hymn is relatively simple: (1) an introductory call to praise given in the imperative; (2) the main part of the psalm, often introduced by "for" or "who," developing the themes of God's majesty and grace; and (3) a conclusion, frequently renewing the call to praise.

The hymns may be categorized according to their emphases; God may be praised as the creator of Israel (66:1-12; 100; 111; 149), the creator of the world (8; 19:1-6 [MT 2-7]; 104; 148), or the creator and ruler of history (33, 113, 145–47).

D. Enthronement Psalms. Beyond the basic categories of lament, thanksgiving, and hymn are several classifications of psalms that are hybrid in form and are classified according to characteristics of subject matter or liturgical use. Israel's earliest songs were narrative songs of victory in which Yahweh was described as the divine warrior who had delivered his people. Often incorporating imagery borrowed from the mythology of Israel's neighbors, such psalms are encountered also outside the Psalter (Exod. 15; Deut. 33:2-5, 26-29; Judg. 5; Hab. 3:3-15), and may be represented in Pss. 18:6-19 (MT 7-20) (par. 2 Sam. 22:7-20); 29; 68.

Closely related to the theme of God as a warrior is the affirmation of his reign over Israel and the nations. Psalms that affirm God's kingship with the characteristic words *YHWH mālaḵ* "Yahweh is/has become king" (47, 93, 96–99; RSV "the Lord reigns") have been labeled enthronement psalms.

A noteworthy debate has taken place concerning the possible use of these psalms in Israel. S. Mowinckel proposed the existence of an autumn New Year festival established during the Monarchy, along the lines of similar celebrations in Babylonian and Canaanite royal cults. In this festival the annual victory of Yahweh over cosmic and historical powers was reenacted, along with his enthronement once again as king over all creation. This was celebrated with the cry, "Yahweh has become king." A. Weiser, on the other hand, argued for an autumn covenant festival based upon Israel's historical traditions and the renewal of their covenant with Yahweh. These and other approaches have been widely discussed in Psalms studies. It seems unlikely that Israel would have adopted their neighbors' cyclic view of history, as Mowinckel suggested, or would imply that their eternal king (93:2) need once again be enthroned. The possibility of a celebration of Yahweh's kingship at the autumn Feast of Tabernacles should not be dismissed, however. Looking back on Yahweh's past victories (96:2-3) Israel would have praised God as their present king (vv. 7-10) and anticipated the future establishment of his rule among the nations (v. 13).

E. Royal Psalms. Closely related to the confession

of Yahweh's kingship are the psalms associated with the Davidic dynasty, all of which bear some reference to the king, though they are diverse in statement and use. Pss. 2, 72, 101, 110 may have been used in coronation ceremonies. In 20, 89, 144 God is asked to give the king victory in battle, and in 18, 21 the king thanks God for victory. Ps. 45 seems to have been composed for a royal wedding and reflects aspects of the ceremony.

These psalms, which emphasize the close association of the Davidic king with the heavenly king as the latter's son (2:7), as the lord at God's right hand (110:1), and as "anointed one" (māšîaḥ, 18:50 [MT 51]; 20:6 [MT 7]), were understood by the early Church to speak of Christ. Their fulfillment in Christ is rightly emphasized by Christians, yet not at the expense of overlooking their origin and use in Israel's royal theology and ceremonies.

F. Liturgical Psalms. A number of psalms can be linked to liturgical activity by their antiphonal dialogue or allusions to liturgical actions. Pss. 15, 24 are liturgies of entrance to the temple, with Ps. 24 suggesting a procession with the ark. Ps. 115 is liturgical in its format of question and answer, address and response. Of the Songs of Ascent (120–134), only 122 appears to have been composed originally for a pilgrimage, while 134 reflects the high point of temple worship in its call to praise and priestly benediction. The Songs of Zion (46, 48, 76, 84, 87, 122) focus on the glory of Jerusalem and the holy mountain, Zion, which God chose for his dwelling place.

G. Wisdom and Torah Psalms. A handful of psalms may not be classified as songs or prayers, but are literary in composition and are distinguished by their instruction given in the form of wisdom. Although scholars differ over classification, Pss. 36–37, 49, 73, 112, 127–28, 133 seem to bear characteristics of Israel's wisdom teachings. Closely related to these psalms in subject matter are the three Torah psalms (1; 19:7-14 [MT 8-15]; 119), which extol the glories of God's law or inspire the reader to righteous obedience.

III. Theological Contribution

In the prayers, laments, and praises of Israel the depth of the people's knowledge of God received its surest expression, for in the presence, and even the felt absence of God, Israel's poets were able to forge new expressions of faith hitherto unexplored. Theology was doxology, and on the praises of his people Yahweh was enthroned (Ps. 22:3 [MT 4]).

God's majesty and grace were not reduced to an abstraction, but were refracted through the concrete images of Israel's culture and institutions. God was not to be known in himself, but in relationship to his people. He ruled as a king, saved as a warrior, meted out justice as a judge, and cared as a shepherd. Israel could register their awe before his majesty and grace, and yet voice intimacy and boldness in the pained probings and challenges of the lament. The Psalms bear testimony to the strength of the covenant bond between God and people, as well as to the character of the God who upheld it.

From creation to re-creation, no theological theme of significance is missing from the Psalter. Yet its strength and purpose is not as a theological text, but

as a richly varied guide to the perception, experience, and worship of God. Israel's response to its creator and redeemer was a God-authorized response, and the timeless nature of this response is witnessed in the long history of the Psalter, the reapplication of its message by the early Church (particularly Pss. 2, 22, 110, 118), and its continued use and interpretation by Jews and Christians throughout the centuries. In their concrete images and depth of expression, the Psalms have formed the bedrock of faith and worship.

Bibliography. L. C. Allen, *Psalms 101–150.* WBC (1983); A. A. Anderson, *Psalms,* 2 vols. NCBC (1972; repr. 1981); P. C. Craigie, *Psalms 1–50.* WBC (1983); S. Mowinckel, *The Psalms in Israel's Worship* (Nashville: 1962); A. Weiser, *The Psalms.* OTL (1962); C. Westermann, *Praise and Lament in the Psalms,* rev. ed. (Atlanta: 1981).

PSALMS OF SOLOMON. *See* SOLOMON, PSALMS OF.

PSALTERY (KJV). *See* HARP.

PSEUDEPIGRAPHA [sōō′də pĭg′rə fə].† A general term for Jewish writings of approximately the second century B.C. through the second century A.D. not included in either the Bible, the Apocrypha, the documents found only among the Dead Sea Scrolls, the rabbinic literature, or works attributable to a known author. The term arises from the frequently pseudonymous authorship of these works (Gk. lit. "false [i.e., falsely attributed] writings"); the presentation of these writings as those of great persons of the Old Testament past is, with most of the Pseudepigrapha, linked to their nature as revelatory documents in apocalyptic or testamentary form.

Which documents ought to be included in the Pseudepigrapha is not an easily settled matter. Those writings generally so designated include a broad range of literary genres, including apocalypses attributed to Abraham, Adam, Daniel, Elijah, Enoch, Zephaniah, Ezra, Sedrach (i.e., Shadrach), and Baruch; testaments of the twelve patriarchs and of Job, Abraham, Isaac, Jacob, Moses, Solomon, and Adam; legendary expansions of parts of the Old Testament (e.g., Jubilees, the Martyrdom of Isaiah, the book of Joseph and Asenath, the Life of Adam and Eve, and the Lives of the Prophets); psalms and prayers attributed to Old Testament figures (e.g., Psalms of Solomon, Prayer of Manasseh, Odes of Solomon); wisdom writings (e.g., Ahikar, 3-4 Maccabees); and fragments of works written according to Hellenistic literary genres by Jewish authors (e.g., Aristobulus, Orphica, Eupolemus), primarily lost works preserved only in citations by Church Fathers.

Many of the Pseudepigrapha are of great importance for understanding Judaism of the time of Jesus and the writers of the New Testament, in many respects of equal value to the books of the Apocrypha. Some of the Christian interpolations present in certain of these works are significant for the history of early Christian literature.

See APOCALYPTIC and articles on the individual works.

Bibliography. J. H. Charlesworth, ed., *The Old*

Testament Pseudepigrapha, 2 vols. (Garden City: 1983-1985); *The Pseudepigraph and Modern Research*. SBL Septuagint and Cognate Studies 7 (Missoula: 1976); G. W. E. Nickelsburg, *Jewish Literature Between the Bible and the Mishnah* (Philadelphia: 1981).

PSEUDO-MATTHEW, GOSPEL OF. A Latin infancy gospel from the eighth or ninth century A.D. The work is basically a rewriting of two other apocryphal works, the Protevangelium of James and the Infancy Gospel of Thomas, but with substantial omissions, additions, and expansions. From this work, very popular in the Middle Ages, tales from its sources made their way into ecclesiastical art and legend.

PTOLEMAIS [tŏl'ə mā'ĭs] (Gk. *Ptolemaïs*).† Another name for the ancient southern Phoenician city of Acco. Renamed Ptolemais in honor of Ptolemy II Philadelphus (285-246 B.C.), the city fell under Seleucid control in 210 B.C. It became a Roman colony at the time of Emperor Claudius (A.D. 41-54). After Roman rule came to an end, the city was again known as Acco.

Informed that troops from Ptolemais were among the coalition seeking to annihilate the Jews in Galilee, Judas Maccabeus dispatched his brother Simon against them (1 Macc. 5:15, 22, 55). Ca. 163 B.C. Antiochus V appointed Hegemonides governor of the region from Ptolemais to Gerar (2 Macc. 13:24-25). In 149 Alexander Balas occupied the city (1 Macc. 10:1), which Demetrius II then offered as a gift to the Jerusalem temple in hopes of enlisting the Jews to help him recapture it (v. 39). Here Jonathan was ambushed and imprisoned by Trypho (12:45, 48). The apostle Paul, at the end of his third missionary journey, stopped briefly at Ptolemais to visit a group of Christians (Acts 21:7).

PTOLEMY [tol'ə mē] (Gk. *Ptolemaios*).†

1. Ptolemy I Soter (367-283 B.C.), founder of a dynasty of Hellenistic kings who ruled Egypt 323-30 B.C. The son of Lagos of Eordaea, he was one of Alexander the Great's most trusted generals in the conquest of Afghanistan and India, and one of Alexander's seven bodyguards. Named satrap of Egypt in 323, he conquered Cyprus and annexed Palestine (then under Seleucid control) in 320 but retreated before the Seleucid general Antigonus, bringing numerous Jewish prisoners of war to Alexandria. In 315 he joined a coalition to halt the encroachment of Antigonus and, allying with the Babylonian satrap Seleucus, in 312 again invaded and captured Palestine. Relinquishing control of Syria-Palestine through a peace treaty in 311, Ptolemy concentrated on conquering parts of the Greek mainland and Asia Minor. He lost Cyprus to Demetrius in a naval battle at Salamis in 306, but named himself king of Egypt (cf. Dan. 11:4) and a year later withstood Antigonus' invasion of Egypt. For aiding Rhodes against Demetrius in 305 he was accorded the eponym Soter (Gk. "Savior"). In 302 Ptolemy joined a coalition against Antigonus and invaded Palestine a third time; responding to erroneous reports of Antigonus' death, he withdrew from Palestine, and his allies, taking this to be desertion, gave control of

the region to Seleucus, precipitating a century-long conflict between the two factions. Ptolemy abdicated to his son Ptolemy II in 285 and died two years later. His son Ptolemy Ceraunus ruled as king of Macedonia 281-279.

Ptolemy I was an able ruler, whose civil and military organization of Egypt were exemplary. He promoted Hellenism and was a patron of letters, establishing the great library at Alexandria and himself writing a history of Alexander the Great's campaigns. Ptolemy is also credited with fostering the syncretistic cult of Serapis.

2. Ptolemy II Philadelphus (309-246), ruler of Egypt 283-246. Divorcing his first wife Arsinoë I, daughter of King Lysimachus of Thrace, he followed pharaonic custom in marrying his sister and former mother-in-law, the ambitious and capable Arsinoë II (properly speaking, the surname Philadelphus "brother-loving" was first ascribed to her). Victories over the Seleucid Antiochus I in 280-279 and 276-271 established Ptolemaic naval supremacy over the eastern Mediterranean, and Ptolemy II solidified his control over Phoenicia and Judea, rebuilding as Hellenized cities Rabbath-ammon (Philadelphia) and Acre (Ptolemaïs). Ca. 250 he concluded a marriage alliance between Antiochus II and Ptolemy's daughter Bernice, with the stipulation that Bernice's son inherit the kingdom (Dan. 11:6). Trade flourished, helping to support Ptolemy's lavish and rather decadent court. He increased the library at Alexandria and fostered scientific research, including the establishment of a zoo. According to tradition the translation of the Hebrew scriptures in Greek (the LXX) was initiated during his reign (Letter of Aristeas).

3. Ptolemy III Euergetes (ruled 246-221), son of Ptolemy II and Arsinoë II. When Antiochus II's first wife Laodice murdered Bernice and her infant son, her brother Ptolemy III attacked Syria (with little popular resistance; Dan. 11:7-8; cf. 1 Macc. 11:8) to prevent Seleucus II from usurping the Ptolemaic kingdom. Conquering territories as far as Babylon and Thrace, and recapturing the Aegean lands lost by Ptolemy II, he extended Ptolemaic dominion to its greatest reaches. His treaty with Seleucus II in 214 assured peace between the rival dynasties for some two decades (Dan. 11:9).

4. Ptolemy IV Philopator (ruled 221-204), son of Ptolemy III and Bernice II, who was murdered soon after he gained the throne. Characterized by Ptolemy's personal debauchery and manipulation by advisers and courtiers, his reign initiated the decline of Ptolemaic fortunes. Ptolemy halted the advance of Antiochus III at Raphia in 217 (Fourth Syrian War), securing Ptolemaic control over Palestine, but the condfidence gained by his Egyptian forces prompted nearly continuous rebellion for some thirty years (cf. Dan. 11:10-11).

5. Ptolemy V Epiphanes (ruled 204-181), son of Ptolemy IV and his sister Arsinoë III. The Seleucid Antiochus III and Philip V of Macedonia took advantage of the series of regents who dominated the young Ptolemy V (five years old when he ascended to power), seizing Egypt's Aegean and Anatolian holdings and, following victory at Panias (New Testament Caesarea Philippi) in 198, giving Palestine over to the Seleucids. In 197 Ptolemy was crowned king in ancient Egyptian rites commemorated in the Rosetta Stone. Through a treaty formed in 192 he married Antiochus' daughter Cleopatra (Dan. 11:13-18).

6. Ptolemy VI Philometor (ruled 181-145), elder son of Ptolemy V. The death of his mother (hence the eponym Philometor "mother-loving") and regent Cleopatra in 176 reopened Ptolemaic-Seleucid conflict over Palestine. Seeking to thwart Egyptian hopes of recapturing Palestine, Antiochus IV Epiphanes invaded Egypt and captured Ptolemy VI in 170, whereupon the Alexandrians installed his younger brother Ptolemy VII (7) as king. After Antiochus withdrew, the two ruled jointly with their sister Cleopatra until 164; the arrangement was marked by constant discord, which surfaced even later with Philometor's defeat and capture of his brother when the latter invaded Cyprus in 154. At approximately this time he permitted the fugitive high priest Onias IV to establish a Jewish temple at Leontopolis. In 152 Ptolemy VI joined a coalition against the Seleucid Demetrius I. He and his son-in-law Alexander Balas died in battle against Demetrius II near Antioch (1 Macc. 11:18).

7. Ptolemy VIII Euergetes II (also called Physkon "fat paunch" because of his bloated physique; reckoned by some scholars as Ptolemy VII, with renumbering of successive kings), brother of Ptolemy VI. He ruled jointly with Ptolemy VI from 170 to 164, when he was became king of Cyrenaica. He usurped kingship over Egypt in 145 by murdering Ptolemy VI's infant son Ptolemy VII and marrying his sister and former sister-in-law Cleopatra II. In stark contrast with his brother, the amenable Philometor, Euergetes displayed a loathsome personality and extreme cruelty, murdering his own son Ptolemy Memphites and massacring countless Alexandrians. He named his illegitimate son Ptolemy Apion his successor over Cyrenaica, and his second wife Cleopatra III Kokke (daughter of Cleopatra II) and her heir over Egypt and Cyprus.

8. Ptolemy IX Soter II (also called Lathyros), eldest son of Ptolemy VIII and Cleopatra III. His coregency over Egypt 116-180 was marked by domestic strife, climaxed by his mother's supplanting him with her favorite son, the younger Ptolemy X, whereupon Soter seized his brother's domain, Cyprus. Despite Soter's aid to the Seleucids, Samaria fell to John Hyrcanus *ca.* 107. When Ptolemy X died in 88 B.C. Soter was reinstated by the Egyptians, reigning with his daughter (and Alexander's widow) Bernice over both Egypt and Cyprus until 80 B.C. A local rebellion in 85 resulted in the destruction of Thebes.

9. Ptolemy XII Philopator Philadelphus Neos Dionysus (more comonly called Auletes "flute-player"), illegitimate son of Ptolemy IX. Successor to the last legitimate Ptolemaic heir, Ptolemy XI Alexander II who was assassinated after ruling but twenty days, Auletes spent much of his early reign currying Roman support. Exiled 58-55 because of his associations with Rome, he returned to Egypt, murdered his daughter Bernice, and reigned until 51 B.C.

10. Cleopatra VII Philopator (69-30 B.C.), daughter of Ptolemy XII, coregent with her brothers Ptolemy XIII Philopator (51-47) and Ptolemy XIV Philopator (47-44) and her son (purportedly by Julius Caesar) Ptolemy XV Philopator Philometor Caesar

(44-30; also called Caesarion). She committed suicide after she and her consort Mark Antony were defeated at Actium by Octavian, whereupon Egypt became a Roman province.

11. The son of Dositheus and father of Lysimachus who, during the reign of Ptolemy IX (8) and Cleopatra III, brought to Alexandria the Letter of Purim (Ad.Esth. 11:1).

12. The son of Abubus and son-in-law of the high priest; governor of the region north of the Dead Sea. His ambitions led him to ambush and murder his son-in-law Simon Maccabeus and the latter's sons Mattathias and Judas during a feast at Dok (1 Macc. 16:11-17). Enraged at this vile act and the perpetrator's boastfulness, the enraged John Hyrcanus retaliated, slaying Ptolemy and his cohorts (vv. 18-22).

13. Ptolemy Macron (Gk. *Makrōn*), son of Dorymenes. Appointed governor of Cyprus by Ptolemy VI (6), he transferred his loyalties to the Seleucid Antiochus IV Epiphanes (2 Macc. 10:12-13). Bribed by Menelaus, he convinced Antiochus IV to clear the high priest of complicity in Lysimachus' plundering of the temple (4:45-47). According to 6:8 he decreed that Jews participate in the Greek feast of Dionysus. Named by Antiochus V as governor of Coelesyria and Phoenicia, he dispatched Nicanor to annihilate the Jews (8:8-9; cf. 1 Macc. 3:38-41, where he is among those commissioned to attack Judas Maccabeus). According to 2 Macc. 10:12-13, however, he was regarded as a traitor for his pro-Jewish stance.

14. Claudius Ptolemaus, second-century A.D. Alexandrian astronomer, geographer, and mathematician.

PUAH [pōo′ə].

1 (Heb. *pûʿâ*; cf. Ugar. *pġt* "girl"). One of the two Hebrew midwives in Egypt ordered by Pharaoh to kill all male Hebrew children (Exod. 1:15).

2 (Heb. *pûʾâ*). The father of the judge Tola of the tribe of Issachar (Judg. 10:1). Some scholars think the name designates a clan.

3. Alternate form of PUVAH, one of Issachar's four sons (1 Chr. 7:1).

PUBLICAN. *See* TAX.

PUBLIUS [pŭb′lĭ əs] (Gk. *Poplios*; Lat. *Publius*). The leading Roman official (RSV "chief man") on the island of Malta, where Paul landed after surviving a shipwreck. Publius provided lodging for Paul and his companions and acted kindly to them during their three-day stay (Acts 28:7). Paul cured Publius' father of a fever and dysentery (v. 8).

PUDENS [pōo′dĕnz] (Gk. *Poudēs*; Lat. *Pudens* "modest"). A Christian in Rome who, with Paul, sent greetings to Timothy (2 Tim. 4:21).

PUHITES (1 Chr. 2:53, KJV). *See* PUTHITES.

PUL [pŏol] (Heb. *pûl*).

1. Another name for TIGLATH-PILESER III, king of Assyria (2 Kgs. 15:19; 1 Chr. 5:26). Although the name occurs in the Babylonian King List A (Akk. *Pulu*; *ANET*, p. 219), it is not attested in cuneiform sources contemporary with Tiglath-pileser's reign. Some scholars consider it to be either his original name or a throne name.

2 (Isa. 66:19, KJV). *See* LIBYA.

PUNITES [pōō'nīts] (Heb. *pûnî*). The descendants of PUVAH (Num. 26:23; some versions suggest *pû'î*).

PUNON [pōō'nŏn] (Heb. *pûnōn*). A place between Zalmonah and Oboth where the Israelites encamped shortly before entering the plains of Moab (Num. 33:42-43). The identification of the site as modern Feinân, the ruins of an ancient copper-mining center about 35 km. (22 mi.) north of Petra, might accord with the suggestion of Punon as the place where Moses made the bronze serpent (21:4-10). The clan name Pinon (Gen. 36:41; 1 Chr. 1:52) may be related to this place.

PUR. *See* PURIM.

PURAH [pōōr'ə] (Heb. *purâ*). Gideon's servant who accompanied him in spying on the camp of the Midianites (Judg. 7:10-11; KJV "Phurah").

PURIM [pōō'îm] (Heb. *pûrîm* "lots"; Akk. *pūrû*).†
An Israelite feast celebrating Esther and Mordecai's foiling of Haman's attempt to destroy all the Jews of the Persian Empire. The name derives from Haman's use of lots (Heb. *pûr*) to determine the day for the pogrom (Esth. 3:7; 9:24-28). Suggestions that the festival derives from the Babylonian or Assyrian New Year (Akk. *puḫru*; cf. the equation of Mordecai with Marduk and Esther with Ishtar) or a Greek bacchanalian celebration are now largely discredited.

The feast is celebrated on the fourteenth and fifteenth days of Adar (Feb.–March), which according to practices "fixed" by Queen Esther (vv. 31-32) are days of feasting and merry-making—often to condoned excess—and the sharing of gifts and food with friends and the poor (vv. 20-23; cf. Mishnah *Megillah*). The book of Esther is read in synagogues on the evening preceding Purim (thirteenth of Adar), itself a day of fasting, and again on the first of the two days of Purim (cf. 2 Macc. 15:16, "Mordecai's day").

PURPLE (Heb. *'argāmān*, [also Aram.] *'arg^ewān*; Gk. *porphýra*). A highly valued dye obtained from the Mediterranean snail (genus *Murex*) and mainly a Phoenician product (cf. Ezek. 27:16; RSV "Edom"; RSV mg. "Aram"). Purple fabrics were an expensive luxury (cf. Luke 16:19); Lydia was a seller of purple and (apparently as a result) a wealthy woman, whose home was in Thyatira but who maintained a house in Philippi in Macedonia (Acts 16:14-15). The wearing of purple was associated particularly with royalty and the highest officials (Judg. 8:26; Esth. 1:6; 8:15; Cant. 3:10; Ezek. 23:6; Dan. 5:7, 16, 29; KJV "scarlet"; cf. the mocking of Jesus, Mark 15:17; John 19:2-3). Purple fabrics were much used in the tabernacle (numerous references at Exod. 25–28; 35–39; Num. 4:13)

and in Solomon's temple (2 Chr. 2:7, 14 [MT 6, 13]; 3:14). At Cant. 7:5 (MT 6) "purple" is a figure of speech for rich beauty. The RSV reads "purple" for Heb. *tôlā'*, usually translated "scarlet," at Lam. 4:5 and for *t^eḵēleṭ*, usually "blue," at Ezek. 23:6.

See also COLOR; SCARLET, CRIMSON.

PURSLANE [pûrs'lĭn].* The meaning of Heb. *ḥallāmûṭ*, found only at Job 6:6, is unclear. KJV, JB, NIV "white of an egg" for the entire phrase *b^erîr ḥallāmûṭ* is based on the Targum. RSV "slime of the purslane" is based on the Syriac version. The idea of a plant or herb that exudes a tasteless, bland mucilage is often given as a possible meaning. Suggestions other than the purslane plant (*Portulaca oleracea* L.) are the mallow (*Atriplex halimus* L.; cf. NJV) and bugloss (*Anchusa officinalis* L.). Whatever the precise reference, Job hereby rejects the counsel of Eliphaz (chs. 4–5) as his appetite would reject insipid food.

PUT [pŏŏt] (Heb. *pûṭ*). According to the Table of Nations, the third son of Ham (Gen. 10:6; KJV "Phut"; 1 Chr. 1:8). His descendants are generally identified as the inhabitants of a region in Africa, perhaps part of LIBYA (KJV, Ezek. 30:5; 38:5; Jer. 46:9; cf. LXX Gk. *Libyes*; O.Pers. *Putāyā*). Renowned for their skill in battle (Jer. 46:9), warriors from Put are cited (perhaps as mercenaries) in the service of Tyre (Ezek. 27:10; KJV "Phut"). Put is named in Ezekiel's oracles against Egypt (30:5) and "Gog" (38:5).

Earlier scholars' identification of Put with Punt (Egyp. *pwn.t*), modern Somaliland, has been discredited on linguistic as well as historical grounds.

PUTEOLI [pōō tē'ə lē] (Gk. *Potioloi*; Lat. *Puteoli* "sulfur springs"). A major port on the Gulf of Naples, modern Pozzuoli, west of Naples. Founded in the sixth century B.C. as the Greek colony Dicaearchia, Puteoli had a long breakwater that permitted grain ships to move into protected waters. Paul visited the city, where he stayed for seven days with a group of Christians while en route to Rome (Acts 28:13-14).

PUTHITES [pōō'thīts] (Heb. *pûṭî*). A family who lived in the region of Kiriath-jearim, mentioned in a Judahite list (1 Chr. 2:53; KJV "Puhites").

PUTIEL [pōō'tĭ əl] (Heb. *pûṭî' ēl*; Egyp. *p3-dî-* + Heb. *' ēl* "the one given by God" [?]). The father-in-law of Aaron's son Eleazar (Exod. 6:25).

PUVAH [pōō'və] (Heb. *puwwâ*). The second son of Issachar (Gen. 46:13; KJV "Phuvah"; Num. 26:23; KJV "Pua"), called PUAH (**3**) at 1 Chr. 7:1. He was the ancestor of the Punites (Num. 26:23).

PYGARG (Deut. 14:5, KJV). *See* IBEX.

PYRRHUS [pĭr'əs] (Gk. *Pyrros* "fiery red"). The father of Sopater, one of Paul's companions (Acts 20:4; KJV omits, following late manuscripts).

Q

Q. The Gospels of Matthew and Luke have considerable material in common, some of which is also found in Mark but some only in Matthew and Luke. A common explanation is that Matthew and Luke both drew on Mark as a source in their writing and on another source as well, called "Q" (from Ger. *Quelle* "source"). This source may have been a written document, but if so, is not now extant. It might also have been a relatively stable collection of oral traditions to which both Gospel writers had access. The Q material consists almost entirely of discourses and sayings of Jesus. Some scholars reject the ideas that Q existed in any form and that Mark was a source for Matthew and Luke.

QERE. *See* KETHIB AND QERE.

QESITAH [kə sē'tə] (Heb. *qᵉśîṭâ*).† A unit of weight of unknown quantity used to measure currency metal before coins were minted (Gen. 33:19; Josh. 24:32; Job 42:11; KJV, RSV "piece [of silver/money]").

QOHELETH [kō hĕl'əth] (Heb. *qōhelet̠*). The pseudonym assumed by the author of the book of Ecclesiastes (KJV, RSV "the Preacher"). The word is the feminine participle of Heb. *qhl* "assemble a congregation," a grammatical form commonly used to designate an office or one who held such an office. Its use in Ecclesiastes (Eccl. 1:1-2, 12; 7:27; 12:8-10) indicates that it is indeed a title, not a name. An alternate English spelling is Koheleth. *See* ECCLESIASTES, BOOK OF.

QUAIL (Heb. *śᵉlāw*). *Coturnix coturnix*, a thickset bird with a short tail, similar in shape to the partridge but smaller in size, about 19 cm. (7.5 in.) long. The quail is also quicker and more adroit than the partridge. It is mottled brown and buff on its back, with black and light brown streaks, and lighter on its underparts.

Quails are found nearly everywhere in Europe but are more common in the southern regions. In summer they are found in grainfields. As winter approaches, they migrate to Ethiopia and Sudan. In mid-March the spring migration via Palestine, Sinai, and Egypt begins. Breeding takes place in Europe and Central Asia.

God's sending of quails to feed the Israelites in the wilderness is viewed both as a blessing (Exod. 16:9-13; Ps. 105:40) and a judgment (Num. 11:31-34; Ps. 78:26-31).

QUARTERMASTER (Heb. *śar mᵉnûḥâ*). The title of Seraiah, one of Zedekiah's officers (Jer. 51:59), is difficult to interpret. The Hebrew term, lit. "officer of rest" or "officer of the resting place," is taken as "quiet prince" by the KJV. RSV "quartermaster" is probably based on emendation to *śar maḥᵃneh* "officer of the camp," suggested by the Syriac text. The LXX and Targum reflect *śar mᵉnāḥôt̠* "officer of tribute." The task given to Seraiah by Jeremiah (vv. 61-64) does not appear to be related to Seraiah's office.

QUARTUS [kwôr'təs] (Gk. *Kouartos*; Lat. *Quartus* "the fourth"). A Christian in Corinth whose greetings to the Roman Christians are passed on in Paul's letter (Rom. 16:23). The epithet "the brother" identifies him as a fellow Christian rather than as a sibling of Erastus or Paul.

QUEEN (Heb. *malkâ*, *šēgal*; Gk. *basílissa*).* Although kings in the ancient Near East, including those of Israel and Judah, almost always had more than one wife and a number of concubines, it was normal for every royal harem to have one woman with a leading role, the "queen," who would be the mother of the heir to the throne and who would possess considerable power in the royal household. Among those named in the Bible are Jezebel, consort of Ahab (1 Kgs. 16:31; 19:1-3; ch. 21), and Maacah, consort of Rehoboam (2 Chr. 11:21-22). Esth. 1–2 recounts the replacement of a queen in the Persian court. The queen was often the daughter of a foreign monarch, married to formalize a political alliance (e.g., 1 Kgs. 3:1; 16:31).

Another position of authority in royal courts was the *gᵉb̠îrâ* "great woman," who was sometimes the queen (Tahpenes in Egypt, 1 Kgs. 11:19; RSV "queen") but in Judah and Israel apparently was always the mother or grandmother of the king (15:13 par.; 2 Kgs. 10:13; Jer. 13:18; 29:2 [cf. 2 Kgs. 24:15]; KJV "queen"). Bathsheba apparently held such a role in Solomon's court (1 Kgs. 2:19). The usual identification of the mothers of the kings of Judah in the accounts of their reigns (e.g., 11:26; 2 Kgs. 21:1) suggests that the "queen mother" had an important role not only in the court (cf. 1 Kgs. 2:19) but perhaps also in the royal succession. The queen mother Athaliah, granddaughter of King Omri of Israel (2 Kgs. 8:26), usurped the throne following the death of her son Ahaziah and reigned for seven years (11:1-4).

QUEEN OF HEAVEN (Heb. *malkat haššāmayim*). A fertility deity worshipped by people of Judah in disobedience to the commandments of God (Jer. 7:18; 44:17-19, 25). Women in particular seem to have been involved in veneration of the queen of heaven, offering cakes and libations and burning incense, but men and children participated as well.

Some manuscripts read Heb. *m^ele'ket haššāmayim* "cultic service of heaven." The LXX (Jer. 44 [LXX ch. 51]) and Vulg. (Gk. *hē basílissa toú ouranoú*; Lat. *Regina caeli*) show that MT Heb. *m^eleket* should be understood as a Masoretic distortion of *malkâ* "queen."

The queen of heaven can be related to a number of ancient Near Eastern female deities, but the clearest connection is with the Assyrian ISHTAR. Worship of Ishtar may have been introduced into Judah by Manasseh (cf. 2 Kgs. 21:3, 5; RSV "Asherah"), but even so it may have coincided with what had long been observed in private worship in Israel and Judah; worship of the queen of heaven apparently took place in homes. Josiah's reform had brought an end to worship of foreign deities, including the queen of heaven (chs. 22–23). The view of the Judahites of Jeremiah's day was that this was to blame for the troubles that had befallen Judah (Jer. 44:17-19).

QUIRINIUS [kwĭ rĭn'ĭ əs] (Gk. *Kyrēnios*; Lat. *Quirinius*). Publius Sulpicius Quirinius, governor of the Roman province of Syria from A.D. 6 or 7 and for a few years afterward. The census that forced Joseph and Mary to journey from their home in Nazareth to Bethlehem, where Jesus was then born, is said by Luke to have occurred when Quirinius was governor of Syria (Luke 2:1-5; KJV "Cyrenius"). For the difficulties posed by this report, *see* ENROLLMENT.

QUMRAN [kŏŏm'rän]. Khirbet Qumrân, 14 km. (8.5 mi.) south of Jericho overlooking the western shore of the Dead Sea, ruins of the site inhabited by the community that produced the DEAD SEA SCROLLS.

QUOTATIONS.† The Old Testament has a number of direct quotations, all poetic, from books no longer extant, including the Book of Jashar (Josh. 10:12-13; 2 Sam. 1:18-27) and the Book of the Wars of the Lord (Num. 21:14-15). Indirect quotations from such works also appear. The books of the Chronicles of the Kings of Israel and Judah are major sources for 1-2 Kings (e.g., 1 Kgs. 14:19; 2 Kgs. 24:5). 1 Kgs. 11:41 refers to a book of the acts of Solomon. A genealogical Book of the Kings of Israel was used by the Chronicler (1 Chr. 9:1), as were a Commentary on the Book of

the Kings (2 Chr. 24:27) and other works (1 Chr. 27:24; 29:29; 2 Chr. 12:15; 33:18-19). The Chronicler also drew on the Pentateuch and the books of Samuel and Kings (perhaps referring to the latter by name at, e.g., 16:11; 32:32). A shorter quotation of a canonical book is the quotation of Mic. 3:12 at Jer. 26:18.

The New Testament contains more than one thousand quotations from and allusions to each of the three divisions of the Old Testament, the Torah, the Prophets, and the Writings. These quotations and allusions function in a variety of ways, largely to underscore the authority of a New Testament statement or to show an event as divinely ordained. The fundamental assumption underlying such quotations is that the divine origin of the salvation in Jesus and of the proclamation and possession of that salvation by the Church is recognizable only because in the events so noted has the Old Testament reached its fulfillment; the quotation formulas (e.g., ". . . to fulfill what the Lord had spoken by the prophet," Matt. 2:15) make this clear. Elsewhere the teaching of the Hebrew Bible is held up as exemplary moral teaching (e.g., Mark 10:19), or it may be cited only for the sake of criticism and revision (e.g., vv. 2-9).

The New Testament quotes the Old Testament most often according to the LXX. Matthew is the most significant exception to this rule; thirty-two of his quotations differ from the LXX; this may indicate that he used the MT or that he had access to a now lost Greek version of the Old Testament. Some quotations are Targumic in style (e.g., Rom. 12:19, quoting Deut. 32:35), while others join interpretation closely to quotation in a manner somewhat like that of the Qumran commentaries (e.g., Mark 1:2-4, quoting Mal. 3:1; Isa. 40:3). Effort generally is made in the choice of text and in its presentation to show clearly the correspondence between the Old Testament text and that aspect of the coming of redemption in Christ that constitutes fulfillment of the particular text. Sometimes the meaning of an Old Testament passage in its original historical context is set aside in its application to a new situation in the New Testament; e.g., what is said of Solomon at 2 Sam. 7:14 is applied to believers in Christ at 2 Cor. 6:18. In such cases, a typological correlation between the original focus of the statement and the new focus is assumed, as is the underlying continuity of salvation history.

The pseudepigraphal book of 1 Enoch is quoted at Jude 14-15 (1 En. 1:9). Greek poets are quoted in the epistles: the Cretan Epimenides at Titus 1:12, Epimenides and Aratus of Cilicia at Acts 17:28, and the Athenian Menander at 1 Cor. 15:33.

Each of the gospel writers was dependent upon earlier sources, both oral and written, as the basis for his work. These sources were quoted liberally, as can be seen in the way in which Mark serves as a source for Matthew and Luke, at times quoted verbatim and at others changed significantly by the later Gospels. Authors apart from the evangelists quote liberally from hymnic and poetic sources, such as Phil. 2:6-11; 1 Tim. 3:16; and hymns found in the book of Revelation. Some later New Testament books were written with knowledge of others written earlier, and contain a development of the thinking found in the earlier works.

2 Peter, for example, is partly based on the Epistle of Jude, and Ephesians is apparently a development of the thought of Colossians and its application to a new situation.

Bibliography. J. M. Efird, ed., *The Use of the Old Testament in the New* (Durham: 1972); R. H. Gundry, *The Use of the Old Testament in St. Matthew's Gospel.* NovTSup 18 (1967).

R

RAAMA [rā′ə mə] (Heb. *raʿmāʾ*), **RAAMAH** (*raʿmâ*). A son of Cush (Gen. 10:7; 1 Chr. 1:9). The descendants of Raamah are associated with those of Sheba, another son of Cush, and lived somewhere in southwestern Arabia in a place rich in spices, gems, and gold (Ezek. 27:22). The city or region of Raamah is mentioned in an inscription and by Strabo.

RAAMIAH [rā′ə mī′ə] (Heb. *raʿamyâ*). An Israelite who returned with Zerubbabel from exile (Neh. 7:7). *See* REELAIAH.

RAAMSES [rā ăm′sēz] (Heb. *raʿamsēs*). Alternate form of the name of the Ramesside capital (Exod. 1:11). *See* RAMESES (PLACE).

RABBAH [răb′ə] (Heb. *rabbâ* "large city").

1.† A city in the tribal territory of Judah near Kiriath-jearim (Josh. 15:60), generally identified with a city named Rubutu mentioned in the Amarna Letters and Rubute in Egyptian texts. It is likely that Rabbah/Rubutu was at Khirbet Bîr el-Hilu (Khirbet Hamîdeh), a short distance south of Emmaus (Nicopolis/ʿAmwâs).

2. Rabbah of the Ammonites (Rabbath-ammon), capital of the Ammonite kingdom; modern Amman, located in the Transjordanian highlands at one of the major sources of the Jabbok river. Settled during the early second millennium B.C., it was conquered by Israel under Joab and David (2 Sam. 11:1; 12:26-29; 1 Chr. 20:1-3). Two districts within the city are mentioned, the "royal city" and the "city of waters" (2 Sam. 12:26-27), the latter probably on low ground near springs and watercourses; but the greater part of the city lay outside these two districts (cf. vv. 28-29). The Israelite conquest was not permanent; presumably after the division of the Israelite kingdom Rabbah again became an Ammonite city and oppressed the Transjordanian Israelites (Jer. 49:1-3; Ezek. 21:20 [MT 25]; KJV "Rabbath"; 25:1-7; Amos 1:13-15).

Rabbah came under the dominance successively of Assyria, Babylon, and Persia. Ptolemy II Philadelphus (285-246) enlarged and embellished the city and gave it the name Philadelphia. Under Rome it was one of the cities of the Decapolis.

RABBI.† An honorific form of address derived from Heb. *rab* "great one, master, lord." In the Old Testament, *rab* designates a person of high rank ("chief" or "officer"; e.g., 2 Kgs. 25:8; Esth. 1:8; Jer. 39:13; Dan. 1:3). This broader usage continued into the rabbinic period, especially in connection with the master/slave relationship. Nevertheless, at least by the second century A.D. the suffixed form *rabbî* "my teacher" had established itself as a title for an officially ordained teacher and master of the law.

Since Jesus taught in parables and well-formed sayings, gathered disciples, spoke in synagogues and debated opponents, it is not surprising that he was addressed as "rabbi." During his lifetime the term was still a broadly used honorific form of address and not yet restricted to those trained in schools of scribes and scholars or ordained as rabbis. Thus, the title is hardly definitive for the authority or style of religious leadership with which Jesus may have been identified. In Jesus' diatribe against the scribes and Pharisees he rejected the use of "rabbi" as a title for those within the community around him (Matt. 23:7-10).

The New Testament uses two forms of Greek transliteration of the term, *rhabbí, rhabbeí* (e.g., 26:25; Mark 9:5; RSV "Master"; John 1:38) and *rhabboun[e]í, rhabbon[e]í* "Rabboni" (Mark 10:51; RSV "Master"; John 20:16). The latter is derived from *rabbān,* an intensive form, just as *rhabbí* is derived from *rab.* These Hebrew and Aramaic terms are also represented in the New Testament by Greek translations: *didáskalos* "teacher" (e.g., Matt. 8:19; Luke 10:25; John 11:28) and *epistátēs* "master" throughout Luke. Gk. *kýrios* "lord" may sometimes also represent *rabbî* (e.g., Matt. 7:21).

RABBITH [răb′ĭth] (Heb. *rabbît*). A city in the tribal territory of Issachar (Josh. 19:20; LXX B Gk. *Dabirōn*). It is probably to be identified with Daberath, a levitical town (21:28) on the border of Zebulun (19:12).

RABBONI. *See* RABBI.

RABMAG [răb′măg] (Heb. *rab-māg*). The title of Nergal-sharezer, one of Nebuchadrezzar's officials (Jer. 39:3, 13). The term is probably derived from Akk. *rab-mūgi,* an Assyrian title, the exact meaning of which is unknown.

RABSARIS [răb sär′ĭs] (Heb. *rab-sārîs*).† The title of an important Assyrian (2 Kgs. 18:17) and Babylonian (Jer. 39:3, 13) official, it is derived from Akk. *rab-ša-rēši* "chief of the eunuchs" (so Dan. 1:3).

RABSHAKEH [răb′shə kə] (Heb. *rab-šāqēh*; Akk. *rab šāqū*).† A title for an important official in the Assyrian government. While "chief cupbearer" is the literal meaning of the term, it is evident from 2 Kgs. 18:17–19:8 (par. Isa. 36:2–37:8) and from Assyrian records that it came to be the designation for an important military position.

RACA [rä′kä] (Gk. *rhaká, rhachá*).† An expression of contempt, perhaps a transliteration or derivative of Aram. *rêqā'* "stupid fool" (KJV, NIV, Matt. 5:22; RSV paraphrases; cf. JB).

RACAL [rä′kăl] (Heb. *rākāl* "market"). A place in Judah to which David sent a portion of the spoil taken in a battle against Amalekite raiders (1 Sam. 30:29; KJV "Rachal"). The LXX reading "Carmel" is probably correct (*see* CARMEL 1).

RACHAB (Matt. 1:5, KJV). *See* RAHAB 1.

RACHEL [rä′chəl] (Heb. *rāḥēl* "ewe"; Gk. *Rhachēl*). The daughter of Laban, wife of Jacob, and mother of Benjamin and Joseph. Jacob worked seven years for Laban to earn the right to marry his beautiful cousin Rachel (Gen. 29:17-20), but Laban duped Jacob into marrying the older and less attractive Leah, so that Jacob had to work another seven years to marry Rachel (vv. 21-30). Jealous of her sister who had children while she did not, Rachel gave Jacob her handmaid, Bilhah, so that she might claim children born of the slave (29:31–30:8; this ancient Semitic custom finds parallels in the Nuzi texts). God later favored Rachel with her own first son, Joseph (vv. 22-24). When Jacob returned to Palestine, Rachel stole her family's household gods in order to secure a part in the family inheritance (31:19-35). She died while giving birth to Benjamin as the family traveled from Bethel to Ephrath-Bethlehem (35:16-20).

Rachel and Leah are viewed as mothers (matriarchs) of Israel (Ruth 4:11). Jer. 31:15 (KJV "Rahel") speaks of her haunting her tomb (*see* EPHRATHAH [PLACE]), weeping for her lost descendants through Joseph, i.e., the northern kingdom of Israel (Ephraim), which had been destroyed by Assyria (cf. Matt. 2:18, with regard to Herod's slaughter of the children of Bethlehem).

RADDAI [răd′ī] (Heb. *radday*). The fifth son of Jesse, and a brother of David (1 Chr. 2:14).

RAGAU (Luke 3:35, KJV). *See* REU.

RAGES [rä′jēz] (Gk. *Rhagoi*; O.Pers. *Râgâ*).† A city in Media where Tobit hid ten talents of silver at the home of his kinsman Gabael (Tob. 1:14; 4:1, 20). The angel Raphael guided Tobit's son Tobiah to and from this city to retrieve the money (5:5; 6:12; 9:2). According to Jdt. 1:5, 15, Nebuchadrezzar waged war against Arphaxad in the mountainous region of "Ra-

gae" (KJV "Ragau"). The ruins of Rages are immediately south of modern Tehran.

RAGUEL [răg′yo̅o̅ əl].*
1. (Num. 10:29, KJV). *See* REUEL 2.
2. (Gk. *Rhagouēl*). The father of Sarah (2) and father-in-law of Tobias (1) (Tob. 3:7).
3. An archangel (1 En. 20:4; 23:4).

RAHAB [rä′hăb].
1. (Heb. *rāḥāb* "wide, extended"; Gk. *Rhaab, Rhachab*). A prostitute in Jericho in whose house on the city wall stayed two of the spies sent by Joshua (Josh. 2). After hiding the spies on the roof and helping them escape, Rahab asked that in return she and her family might be spared when Israel took the city. She marked her house by tying a scarlet cord in its window so that this might be accomplished. Joshua kept this promise, and only Rahab and her family survived the conquest of Jericho (6:17, 22-25).

In Jesus' genealogy Rahab is credited with being the wife of Salmon and the mother of Boaz (Matt. 1:5; KJV "Rachab"); Salmon's wife is not named in the Old Testament (cf. Ruth 4:20-21; 1 Chr. 2:11). Matthew probably includes Rahab (one of only four women mentioned in the Matthean genealogy of Jesus) as a reminder of God's inclusion of Gentiles in salvation history. Rahab's actions in protecting the spies and the reward she received are remembered at Heb. 11:31; Jas. 2:25.

2. (Heb. *rahab* "arrogant" or "one who rages"). A mythological chaos monster whose defeat by God or the gods was part of the creation of the ordered world. Such myths of creation through conflict were significant in Babylonian and Canaanite religion and are alluded to in the Old Testament as a means of speaking of the sovereign power of the God of Israel (Job 9:13; 26:12; KJV "proud"; Ps. 89:10 [MT 11]; Isa. 51:9). Because the Exodus also was a dramatic defeat of God's enemies, Egypt is called "Rahab" at Ps. 87:4; Isa. 30:7. *See* DRAGON.

RAHAM [rä′hăm] (Heb. *raham* "mercy"). The son of Shema and a descendant of Judah (1 Chr. 2:44).

RAHEL (Jer. 31:15, KJV). *See* RACHEL.

RAINBOW (Heb. *qešeṭ*; Gk. *íris*). An arc of colored bands in the sky opposite the sun produced by the double refraction and single reflection of the sun's rays by mist or rain. The rainbow is mentioned in visions of the heavenly throne room as a symbol of the majesty of God (Ezek. 1:28; Rev. 4:3; cf. 10:1). After the Flood God established the rainbow as a sign of his covenant with mankind and as a symbol of his promise never again to destroy the earth with a flood (Gen. 9:13-17; *see* BOW AND ARROW).

RAISIN CAKES. Raisins were produced by soaking grapes in a mixture of oil and water and drying them in the sun, thus producing a nonperishable food with high sugar content. Raisin cakes were simply masses of raisins pressed into an easily transportable form. Heb. *ṣimmûqîm* may represent "bunches" or "clusters" of raisins (so RSV, KJV) or "cakes of raisins" (so NIV); they were, at any rate, served as part of luxurious or joyous meals (1 Sam. 25:18; 2 Sam. 16:1; 1 Chr. 12:40 [MT 41]) and on more humble occasions as well (1 Sam. 30:12). Heb. *'ašîšâ* is a term for cakes of raisins that were eaten as a luxury food, perhaps most often on cultic occasions (2 Sam. 6:19; 1 Chr. 16:3; Cant. 2:5; Hos. 3:1; KJV "flagon[s] [of wine]"; Isa. 16:7; KJV "foundations"). The "cakes" (*kawwānîm*) offered to the Queen of Heaven (Jer. 7:18; 44:19) may have been raisin cakes.

RAKEM [rā'kĕm] (Heb. *rāqem*). A son of Sheresh, and descendant of Manasseh (1 Chr. 7:16).

RAKKATH [răk'əth] (Heb. *raqqaṯ*).† A fortified city in the tribal territory of Naphtali (Josh. 19:35). Talmudic tradition associated it with the site of later Tiberias, but some scholars now place it 2.4 km. (1.5 mi.) north of Tiberias but still on the shore of the Sea of Galilee at Tell Eqlāṭîyeh or Tell Rakkath.

RAKKON [răk'ŏn] (Heb. *raqqôn*). A city in the original southern tribal territory of Dan (Josh. 19:46), located perhaps at Tell er-Reqqeit, a short distance north of the Nahr el-ʿAujā on the Mediterranean north of Joppa (cf. R. G. Boling and G. E. Wright, *Joshua*. AB 6 [1982]: Heb. *hyrqwn* "the Yarqon [river]").

RAM (Heb. *'ayil*) (ANIMAL). A male sheep, frequently used in sacrifices (e.g., Lev. 5:15; 6:6; cf. 1:10). Rams' skins were used as a covering for the tabernacle (Exod. 36:19), and their horns (Heb. *šôpār*) were used to signal in worship and battle (e.g., Josh. 6; 2 Sam. 6:15; *see* TRUMPET). When the obedient Abraham attempted to sacrifice Isaac, the Lord provided a ram as a substitute burnt offering (Gen. 22:13). *See* SHEEP.

RAM [răm] (Heb. *rām* "exalted") (PERSON).
1. A son of Hezron, and ancestor of David (Ruth 4:19; 1 Chr. 2:9-10) and Jesus (Matt. 1:3-4; Gk. *Aram*; KJV "Aram"; cf. Luke 3:33).
2. A son of Jerahmeel of the tribe of Judah (1 Chr. 2:25, 27).
3. An ancestor of Elihu (Job 32:2).

RAMAH [rā'mə] (Heb. *[hā]rāmâ* "[the] height"; Gk. *Rhama*).
1. A town in the tribal territory of Benjamin (Josh. 18:25), near Saul's home, Gibeah (Judg. 19:13). Ramah of Benjamin is usually identified with er-Râm, *ca.* 8 km. (5 mi.) north of Jerusalem, 3 km. (2 mi.) north of Gibeah, and 7 km. (4 mi.) south of Bethel (cf. 4:5).
Ramah was one of a group of towns whose position north of Jerusalem made them of military significance. King Baasha of Israel began to fortify Ramah in an attempt to halt the flow of traffic to and from Jerusalem (1 Kgs. 15:17 par.). After Asa of Judah had bought an alliance with Syria, Israel's neighbor to the north, and Syria began to invade Israel's northern territories, Baasha left Ramah to Asa, who used Baasha's building materials to fortify other cities (vv. 18-22 par.). When the Assyrians invaded Judah, Ramah was probably one of the places through which they passed

as they approached Jerusalem (Isa. 10:29; Hos. 5:8).
The prophet Jeremiah was released at Ramah following the fall of Jerusalem to Babylonia (Jer. 40:1, 4). After the Exile returning Benjaminites repopulated the town (Ezra 2:26; Neh. 7:30; 11:33). The traditional site of Rachel's tomb was near Ramah (Jer. 31:15; Matt. 2:18; KJV "Rama"; cf. 1 Sam. 10:2).
2. "Ramah of the Negeb" (Heb. *rā'maṯ negeḇ*; KJV "Ramath of the south"), a Simeonite town also known as Baalath-beer (Josh. 19:8). David gave part of the spoil captured from the Amalekites to the people of this town (1 Sam. 30:27; *rāmôṯ-negeḇ* "Ramoth of the Negeb" or the "southern heights"; KJV "south Ramoth"). Its location is unknown. One suggested site is Khirbet Ghazza, *ca.* 45 km. (28 mi.) south-southeast of Hebron.
3. A town on the boundary of the tribal territory of Asher (Josh. 19:29). It is sometimes identified with Ramieh, 21 km. (13 mi.) south-southeast of Tyre, although some scholars consider it the same as Ramah of Naphtali (4 below).
4. A fortified town in the tribal territory of Naphtali (Josh. 19:36). Some scholars identify it with 3 above, though it is more probably modern er-Râmeh, a village *ca.* 24 km. (15 mi.) west-southwest of Safed.
5. The home of Samuel, a town in the hill country of Ephraim (1 Sam. 1:19; 2:11). According to 1:1 Samuel's parents lived at Ramathaim-zophim (Heb. *rāmāṯayim ṣôpîm* "the two heights of Zophim"; LXX *Armathaim Sipha*); "Zophim" should probably be emended so that Elkanah is identified as "a certain man from Ramathaim, a Zuphite (*ṣûpî*) from the hill country of Ephraim" (so NIV; cf. "Zuph" later in the verse and at 9:5).
From Ramah Samuel administered justice to Israel when he was not on his annual circuit of Bethel, Gilgal, and Mizpah (7:15-17). Saul was anointed as Israel's first king at Ramah after the elders of the nation had gathered there to petition Samuel to give them a monarch (8:4–10:1). Later David, also anointed king by Samuel, sought refuge from Saul at Ramah (19:18). A group of prophets had attached themselves to Samuel in the city (v. 20). When Samuel died he was buried at Ramah (25:1, "in his house"; 28:3).
Eusebius (*Onom.* xxxii.21-23) identified Ramah with Arimathea (Rentîs), *ca.* 14 km. (9 mi.) northeast of Lydda (Lod), and this site is still advocated by some. Others locate Samuel's home *ca.* 8 km. (5 mi.) farther east at Beit-rima.
6. (2 Kgs. 8:29; 2 Chr. 22:6). *See* RAMOTH-GILEAD.

RAMATH OF THE SOUTH (Josh. 19:8, KJV). *See* RAMAH 2.

RAMATHAIM-ZOPHIM (1 Sam. 1:1). *See* RAMAH 5.

RAMATHITE [rā'mə thīt] (Heb. *rāmāṯî*). The gentilic designation of Shimei (13), overseer of David's vineyards, indicating that he was from one of the places named Ramah (1 Chr. 27:27).

RAMATH-LEHI [rā'məth lē'hī] (Heb. *rāmaṯ leḥî* "hill of the jawbone"). A place where Samson killed a thousand Philistines using a jawbone as a weapon (Judg. 15:17). *See* LEHI.

RAMATH-MIZPEH [rā′məth mĭz′pə] (Heb. *rāmaṯ hammiṣpeh* "Lookout Height"). A town that marked one of the limits of Gadite settlement in Transjordan (Josh. 13:26). It is usually identified with Mizpah of Gilead (*see* MIZPAH, MIZPEH 5). A suggested site is Khirbet Jelʿad, *ca.* 8 km. (5 mi.) south of the Jabbok river and 23 km. (14 mi.) from the Jordan.

RAMESES [răm′sēz, rə mĕs′ēz] (Egyp. *Rʿ-ms-sw* "Ra [the sun-god] begot him") (**PERSON**).† The name of eleven pharaohs of the Nineteenth and Twentieth Dynasties (1319-1085 B.C.), the "Ramesside era" in which Egyptian government was moved back to the delta region after the Amarna period. The name is also rendered Ramses and Ramesses.

1. Rameses I (Peraʿmessu), vizier and successor to Horemheb; founder of the Nineteenth Dynasty. Already aged at his accession to the throne in 1319, he died a year later and was succeeded by his son Seti I.

2. Rameses II (sometimes called "the Great"), who reigned sixty-seven years (1299-1232 B.C.). He warred with Nubians, Libyans, Syrians, and Hittites, but in his twenty-first year made peace with the Hittite king Hattusilis because they faced a common enemy in the Sea Peoples (*ANET*, pp. 199-203). Rameses built numerous monuments and buildings, including temples at Abu Simbel and Karnak, and a royal residence at Pi-Raʿmesse (Egyp. *Pr-rʿ-ms-sw*; biblical Raamses; Exod. 1:11). Because of this building activity, he is often identified as either the pharaoh who oppressed the Israelites or the pharaoh of the Exodus. Many scholars disregard 2:23, which refers to the death of one pharaoh and the accession of the pharaoh of the Exodus, and regard Rameses II as the pharaoh of both the oppression and the Exodus. But Raamses was an old city when Rameses built there and renamed the city for himself. Most likely the pharaoh of the oppression was Rameses' predecessor Seti I, under whom considerable building took place at Raamses, and the pharaoh of the Exodus was Rameses. *See* EXODUS.

3. Rameses III, second king of the Twentieth Dynasty (1198-1167 B.C.). Initially highly imitative of Rameses II, he successfully withstood incursions by a Libyan alliance to the west and Sea Peoples/Philistine movements from the east. He was assassinated as the result of palace intrigue.

4. Rameses IV–XI, throne names assumed by the final eight weak kings of the Twentieth Dynasty (1167-1085 B.C.) and of the New Kingdom, overthrown by Herihor and Pinhasy.
See EGYPT *III*.

RAMESES [răm′ə sēz] (Heb. *raʿmᵉsēs*; Egyp. *Pr-rʿ-ms-sw* "house of Rameses") (**PLACE**). A city in the northeastern Nile delta region of Egypt, capital during the Ramesside era (Nineteenth-Twentieth Dynasties, 1319-1085 B.C.). It was renamed after Pharaoh Rameses II, who, together with his predecessor Seti I, conducted extensive building projects there. The city had been in existence for more than four hundred years before being refounded as the capital following the Amarna period. The exact location of the city remains subject to debate; scholars long identified it with Tanis (Zoan), but Qanṭîr, *ca.* 24 km. (15 mi.) to the south, is more likely. Rameses may have been an adminis-

trative district encompassing both cities (cf. Gen. 47:11).

The region around Rameses was given to the Israelite patriarchs by their brother Joseph (Gen. 47:11; Heb. *raʿamsēs*; RSV, KJV "Raamses"; cf. "Goshen," v. 6). It was one of two store cities which Israelite slaves built for the pharaoh of the oppression (Exod. 1:11), and it was the place from which the Israelites began their journey from Egypt (12:37; Num. 33:3, 5).

RAMIAH [rə mī′ə] (Heb. *ramyâ* "Yahweh is exalted"). One of the returnees from exile who were compelled to divorce their foreign wives (Ezra 10:25).

RAMOTH (**PERSON**) (Ezra 10:29, KJV). *See* JEREMOTH **8**.

RAMOTH [rā′mŏth] (**PLACE**).

1. (Heb. *rāʾmōṯ, rāmōṯ, rāʾmōṯ*). Ramoth in Gilead (Deut. 4:43; Josh. 20:8; 21:38; 1 Chr. 6:80 [MT 65]). *See* RAMOTH-GILEAD.

2. (Heb. *rāmōṯ*). Ramoth of the Negeb (1 Sam. 30:27). *See* RAMAH **2**.

3. (Heb. *rāʾmōṯ*). A levitical city in the tribal territory of Issachar, assigned to the Gershomites (1 Chr. 6:73 [MT 58]). It was probably the same as JARMUTH **2** (Josh. 21:29) and Remeth (19:21).

RAMOTH-GILEAD [rā′mŏth gĭl′ĭ əd] (Heb. *rāmōṯ, rāʾmōṯ, rāmōṯ [bag]gilʿāḏ*). A city in the tribal territory of Gad that served as one of the three Transjordanian cities of refuge (Deut. 4:43; Josh. 20:8) and as a levitical city for the Merarites (Josh. 21:38; 1 Chr. 6:80 [MT 65]). During Solomon's reign Ramothgilead was the seat of one of the king's administrative districts (1 Kgs. 4:13).

After the division of Israel and Judah Ramothgilead came under Syrian control. The effort to regain the city was a major concern of Israel during the last decade of the Omride dynasty. The expedition of kings Ahab of Israel and Jehoshaphat of Judah against the city failed, and Ahab died in the combat (1 Kgs. 22). A few years later Joram of Israel and Ahaziah of Judah succeeded in taking the city (2 Kgs. 8:28; v. 29, "Ramah"). Shortly after this victory Jehu, Joram's general, was anointed and acclaimed king at Ramothgilead (9:1-13).

Tell Rāmîth, the probable site of Ramoth-gilead, is located *ca.* 45 km. (28 mi.) east of the Jordan and *ca.* 66 km. (41 mi.) north of Amman (Rabbathammon) on the Wâdī Shomer. Pottery evidence suggests that it was occupied between 950 and 733 B.C., when it was destroyed by Tiglath-pileser III.

RANSOM (Heb. *kōper*; Gk. *lýtron*).† A price paid to release a captive or seized property, or the act of procuring release in this manner. Heb. *kōper* (from *kpr* "to cover"; cf. Akk. *kapāru* "wipe off") is most often used in the positive sense of ransom money (e.g., Exod. 21:30; KJV "sum of money"; NIV "payment"; Num. 35:31-32; KJV "satisfaction"; Isa. 43:3; cf. Ps. 49:7-8 [MT 8-9]; Heb. *[pāḏōh] yipdeh*; KJV "redeem"). Negatively, the term can refer to a "bribe" (so RSV, 1 Sam. 12:3; Amos 5:12). Though among the Greeks Gk. *lýtron* could refer to the redemption of a slave, in New Testament usage it specifies also "atonement money." Matt. 20:28 par. Mark 10:45 clarify the substitutionary nature of Christ's atonement as "a ransom for many" (cf. Exod. 21:30; Isa. 53:4-12). The compound noun *antílytron* (1 Tim. 2:6) makes this concept even stronger.

See REDEMPTION.

RAPHA [rǎ'fə] (Heb. *rāpā'* "[God] heals"). The fifth son of Benjamin (1 Chr. 8:2). Rapha is omitted from the genealogy at Gen. 46:21. Born perhaps in Egypt, he had either no descendants or only a few who came to be included among the descendants of other sons of Benjamin.

RAPHAEL [rǎf'ī əl] (Gk. *Raphaḗl,* from Heb. *rᵉpā'ēl* "God heals"). One of the angels named in post-Old Testament Jewish literature. In 1 Enoch Raphael is one of "the holy angels who watch," i.e., the leading angels set over different aspects of the working of the universe (1 En. 20; cf. 40:9; 71:8-9, 13). He also casts Azazel into darkness to be held until the day of judgment (10:4-6; cf. Jude 6), gives explanations of visions to the seer (1 En. 32:6), and is among the angels who will execute God's final judgment (54:6; cf. ch. 68). In the book of Tobit Raphael, disguised as Azarias, accompanies Tobias on his journey to Rages in Media and directs him in the healing of Sarah and Tobit.

RAPHAH [rǎ'fə] (Heb. *rāpâ*). A descendant of King Saul (1 Chr. 8:37; KJV "Rapha"). At 9:43 he is called Rephaiah.

RAPHON [rǎ'fŏn] (Gk. *Raphṓn*). A city near one of the major sources of the Yarmuk river, *ca.* 55.5 km. (34.5 mi.) directly east of the upper Jordan as it enters the Sea of Galilee; modern er-Râfeh. The Ammonite general Timothy encamped with his forces across a seasonal stream from the city before a battle with Jewish forces under Judas Maccabeus (1 Macc. 5:37).

RAPHU [rǎ'fū] (Heb. *rāpû'* "healed"). The father of Palti of the tribe of Benjamin, one of the twelve spies appointed by Moses (Num. 13:9).

RAPTURE.† The rapture (from Lat. *rapio* "seize, carry away") is to be the eschatological event in which Christians still living on the earth will be "caught up together with them [deceased Christians who have been resurrected] in the clouds to meet the Lord [Christ] in the air" (1 Thess. 4:17). The rapture contains within it several aspects of eschatological expectation, including the hope for the gathering together of God's people, who have been separated by death, geography, or circumstances, and their being united with their Lord (Matt. 24:31; 1 Thess. 3:13; 4:16-17); the hope for God's vindication of his people and judgment of their enemies (Luke 18:7-8; 2 Thess. 1:6-10); the hope for unending life (1 Cor. 15:51-56); the expectation of sudden judgment (Matt. 24:36-44); and the hope of the release of the righteous from a troubled world (Rev. 3:10).

Considerable disagreement exists among certain in-terpreters over whether the rapture will take place immediately prior to, at the midpoint of, or after the eschatological "great tribulation." This dispute is confined to premillennialism, in which Christ's return is thought of as preceded by a definite seven-year period of tribulation and followed by the millennium. Pre- and midtribulation views of the rapture tend to think of that event mainly as the escape provided for believers from the troubled world of the end times. Pretribulationism posits, in effect, two second comings of Christ, the first an invisible "secret rapture" (of Christians) before the tribulation, the second a return with the previously raptured saints to judge the wicked (i.e., a chastisement of the Jews) and inaugurate the millennium (cf. dispensationalism, which distinguishes Jews and Christians as distinct covenant peoples). Partial rapturism, another variant of pretribulationism, warns that only those in a sanctified state will be caught up before the tribulation; backsliders must endure the tribulation which will serve as a kind of Purgatory to make them fit for the final coming of Christ (1 Pet. 1:6-7; cf. Matt. 6:13; Luke 21:34-36; Rev. 3:10). Nevertheless, the rapture, as an aspect of the eschatological gathering of God's people, can still be thought of where there is no conception of a definite period of eschatological tribulation.

Bibliography. G. L. Archer et al., *The Rapture: Pre-, Mid-, or Post-Tribulation?* (Grand Rapids: 1984); R. Jewett, *Jesus Against the Rapture* (Philadelphia: 1979); J. F. Walvoord, *The Rapture Question* (Findlay, Ohio: 1971).

RAS SHAMRA. *See* UGARIT.

RASSIS [rǎs'ĭs] (Gk. *Rhassis*).* A place or region that was plundered by the army of Holofernes (Jdt. 2:23). Some support exists for the view that this region is to be identified with the environs of the city of Tarsus (cf. "Cilicia," v. 25).

RATHAMIN [rǎth'ə mĭn] (Gk. *Rhathamin*). One of the districts taken from Samaria and given by Demetrius to Jonathan Maccabeus *ca.* 150 B.C. (1 Macc. 11:34; KJV "Ramathem"). The place is otherwise unknown, but some scholars identify it (through a transposition of consonants) with Ramathaim (-zophim), the birthplace of Samuel (*see* RAMAH 5).

RAVEN (Heb. *'ōrēḇ*; Gk. *kórax*). A bird of the Corvidae family (cf. Cant. 5:11), black with a purple sheen. Averaging 62 cm. (24.5 in.) in length, it is the largest of the order *Passeres*. Among the species of raven indigenous to Palestine are the common raven (*Corvus corax*), which lives throughout Palestine and Transjordan, and the brown-necked raven (*Corvus umbrinus*), found only in the Jordan valley. Ravens are practically omnivorous, feeding on fruits and grains, insects, snails, worms, and small mammals, and even on carcasses or weakly birds or animals larger than ravens themselves.

Ravens were known as carrion eaters (Prov. 30:17) and birds of prey (Job 38:41). As such they were considered "unclean," i.e., unsuitable for human consumption or sacrifice (Lev. 11:15; Deut. 14:14). Because a carrion-eating bird would be able to survive on floating corpses, the raven sent out by Noah did not return (Gen. 8:7).

Elijah was miraculously fed by ravens as he hid from King Ahab (1 Kgs. 17:1-6; some commentators read Heb. *'arḇîm* "Arabs"). Ravens were among the wild animals that could be expected to come to live in a ruined city (Isa. 34:11; Zeph. 2:14; KJV "desolation," from MT *ḥōreḇ*; cf. LXX Gk. *kórax*, Vulg. Lat. *corvus*).

RAZOR (Heb. *taʿar, môrâ*). A barber's tool used to trim and shave hair. The use of razors is mentioned in connection with prohibitions for Nazirites (Num. 6:5; cf. Judg. 13:5; 16:17; 1 Sam. 1:11) and consecration of Levites (Num. 8:7). Razors and their use are mentioned in figurative language to describe deceitful talk (Ps. 52:2 [MT 4]) and thorough destruction (Isa. 7:20; cf. Ezek. 5:1-8).

REAIAH [rē ā'yə] (Heb. *rᵉʾāyâ* "Yahweh sees").
1. A Judahite, the son of Shobal (1 Chr. 4:2). He is called Haroeh at 2:52.
2. The son of Micah of the tribe of Reuben (1 Chr. 5:5; KJV "Reaia").
3. A temple servant whose descendants returned with Zerubbabel from exile in Babylon (Ezra 2:47 par. Neh. 7:50).

REBA [rē'bə] (Heb. *reḇaʿ* "fourth"). One of the five kings of the Midianites, all vassals of King Sihon of the Amorites, who were killed by the Israelites in war (Num. 31:8; Josh. 13:21). His territory was later assigned to the Reubenites.

REBEKAH [rə běk'ə] (Heb. *riḇqâ*).† The daughter of Bethuel and sister of Laban, who became the wife of Isaac and mother of Jacob and Esau.

Abraham sent his chief servant to the patriarch's northern Mesopotamian homeland to find a wife for his son Isaac (Gen. 24:1-10). In accordance with the servant's prayer for a sign, Rebekah came to the well outside the city where Abraham's relatives lived to draw water and offered water for the servant and his camels (vv. 11-21). She was a beautiful virgin (v. 16). Rebekah's father and brother heard the servant explain his mission, agreed that the choosing of Rebekah for Isaac was from the Lord, and sent her with the servant (vv. 34-61). Rebekah and Isaac were married as soon as she arrived where he was living in the Negeb (vv. 62-67). Like Abraham before him, Isaac later protected himself from potential rivals for possession of Rebekah by lying, saying that she was his sister, not his wife (26:7-11; cf. 12:11-20; 20:2-18).

For the first twenty years of their marriage, Rebekah was unable to bear children. Isaac prayed on her behalf, and Rebekah gave birth to twins, Jacob and Esau (25:19-26). The rivalry of the two sons began even before their birth, causing Rebekah considerable distress during pregnancy (v. 22). God's prediction that the second child would dominate the firstborn (v. 23) came to be reflected in the history of the two nations descended from the two sons; Paul views this as evidence of God's electing purpose (Rom. 9:10-13). Isaac favored Esau, and Rebekah favored Jacob (Gen. 25:28). Rebekah's support of Jacob was

eventually decisive in establishing him as Isaac's primary heir in place of Esau (27:1-40). Both Jacob and Rebekah were displeased with Esau's wives (26:34-35); it was on Rebekah's insistence that Jacob was sent to Mesopotamia to obtain his wives, though her primary motive in sending Jacob away was to prevent Esau from killing him (27:41–28:5).

When she died Rebekah was buried in Abraham's family burial place, the cave of Machpelah (Gen. 49:31).

RECAH [rē'kə] (Heb. *rᵉkâ*).* The home of a branch of the Judahites (1 Chr. 4:12; KJV "Rechah"). The location of this place is unknown, and the text may well be corrupt. A major recension of the LXX suggests that the name referred to is Rechab, in which case it might be not a place name but a gentilic form designating those listed here as Rechabites (cf. 2:55).

RECHAB [rē'kăb] (Heb. *rēḵāḇ* "charioteer" [?]).
1. A son of Rimmon of Beeroth who with his brother Baanah murdered Ishbosheth the son of Saul (2 Sam. 4:2, 5-8). For this act Rechab and Baanah were executed by David (vv. 9-12).
2. The father of Jehonadab/Jonadab, whose descendants were the RECHABITES (2 Kgs. 10:15, 23; 1 Chr. 2:55; Jer. 35).
3. The father of Malchijah, the postexilic ruler of the district of Beth-haccherem (Neh. 3:14). This Rechab may be the same as **2** above, so that Malchijah, as "the son of Rechab," would be a Rechabite.

RECHABITES [rěk'ə bīts] (Heb. *rēḵāḇîm*). A people or sect in Israel commended by Jeremiah for their obedience to instructions given by Jonadab, the son of Rechab (Jer. 35). Jonadab (Jehonadab) was the "father" or founder of the Rechabites (v. 6) and supported Jehu in his rebellion against King Ahab (*ca.* 840 B.C.; 2 Kgs. 10:15-17, 23).

A commonly held view of the Rechabites is that they exemplified a "nomadic ideal" seen also in some of the prophets. According to this view, adherence to Jonadab's instructions, which prohibited drinking wine, planting crops, and living in permanent structures (Jer. 35:6-7), constituted the Rechabites as a subgroup that sought to live a nomadic way of life in protest against religious practices in Israel's cities. It is also thought that an idealization of Israel's experience in the wilderness before its entry into the land of Canaan was behind the Rechabites' practices.

However, clearly more than a nomadic or wilderness ideal was involved in the Rechabite way of life. Abstinence from wine was a Nazirite practice. Every mention of the Rechabites finds them in or near a city (though v. 11 may regard this as an unusual situation). Jonadab's designation as the "son of Rechab" may indicate not his ancestry but his membership in an occupational guild (cf. the possible derivation of Heb. *rēḵāḇ from reḵeḇ* "chariot"). Connections existed between the Rechabites and the Kenites, a group of metalworkers (1 Chr. 2:55), and possibly between the Rechabites and Irnahash, the "city of copper" (4:12; *see* RECAH). Some scholars have proposed that the Rechabites were itinerant metalworkers involved in the manufacture of chariots and weaponry.

Jeremiah spoke of the Rechabites as an example for the people of Jerusalem, not as though the people of Jerusalem should adopt the Rechabite way of life, but because the Rechabites were faithful to the instructions they had received, just as the people of the city should be faithful to the instructions they had received from God (Jer. 35:12-17). Because of their faithfulness, the Rechabites received a promise that they would continue as a group in the midst of the calamities about to come on Judah (vv. 18-19). Neh. 3:14 may attest to a postexilic continuation of the Rechabites.

RECHAH (1 Chr. 4:12, KJV). *See* RECAH.

RECONCILIATION.* The restoration of a harmonious relationship between two parties; in the New Testament the term refers most often to God's restoration of his relationship with sinful humanity through Jesus Christ.

I. Terminology

The restoration of the divine-human relationship is the central theme of the Bible. But in the Old Testament this restoration of relationship is expressed in terms of blood atonement; there is no word for this restoration of relationship that may be properly represented in English by "reconcile" or any similar word. Where the KJV has "reconcile" and "reconciliation" for Heb. *kāpar* the RSV reads "atone" or "atonement" (e.g., Lev. 6:30 [MT 23]; Ezek. 45:15; Dan. 9:24).

2 Maccabees speaks of God being reconciled (Gk. *katallássō*) to his people through their prayers (1 Macc. 1:5; 8:29; cf. 7:33). In Paul a doctrine of reconciliation is developed; the apostle sees God in the role of the one who reconciles (*katallássō, apokatallássō*) or who makes reconciliation (*katallagé*) through Jesus Christ. "Reconciliation" is also used in the New Testament for the restoration of relationships between humans (Matt. 5:24, *diallássomai*; Acts 7:26, *synallássō*; 1 Cor. 7:11, *katallássō*).

II. Divine Reconciliation in Paul

Although "reconciliation" and related terms are rare in Paul's letters, reconciliation is a central concept in his understanding of the gospel. At 2 Cor. 5:18-21 the words for reconciliation appear five times in a theologically charged passage that is the heart of Paul's appeal to the recalcitrant Corinthians. The whole of God's activity in the history of salvation is captured in the statement that "God was in Christ reconciling the world to himself" (v. 19; cf. Rom. 11:15). It is probable that this basic statement (and perhaps more of 2 Cor. 5:18-21) was a typical evangelistic abstract of the gospel used here by Paul in a different context. At Rom. 5:10-11 reconciliation is as key a concept as justification by faith is elsewhere in Romans. Paul's use of reconciliation as a concept by which to understand God's work of salvation is developed yet further at Eph. 2:16; Col. 1:20-22.

God is the initiator and executor of reconciliation. This is consistent with the Old Testament themes of the mercy of God (Exod. 34:6-7; Ps. 103:8-14; Isa. 43:25) and his gift of the covenant to his people (Jer. 31:31-34). The reconciliation accomplished by God stands as a completed act, which alone makes possible human contact with God (Rom. 5:10). The assurance that God has taken the matter in hand is the ground of the believer's joy (v. 11).

Christ has not simply eliminated a hostility that existed on God's side, thereby allowing God to participate in human affairs. Human hostility confronts God as he begins the reconciliation process (v. 10; Col. 1:21). At the same time, the death of Jesus on the cross did effect atonement through his becoming a sin offering for believers (2 Cor. 5:21) and thereby made possible God's entry into the sinful human condition (Rom. 5:10; Eph. 2:13; Col. 1:20-22).

Divine reconciliation has effects beyond just the relationship of the individual believer to God. Christ's death is also the basis for the restoration of human relationships, since the enmity between human groups has been "slain" by God's action of reconciliation (Eph. 2:16). Therefore, Christ "is our peace," whether in relation to God or to other humans (v. 14). Paul's appeal to the Corinthians that they be reconciled to God (2 Cor. 5:20) arises from his concern for their alienation from himself and their misunderstanding of his ministry (1:23–6:13); he expects that a renewal of their relationship with God on the basis of divine reconciliation in Christ will resolve the problems existing between humans.

Col. 1:19-20 applies divine reconciliation even more broadly. Jesus' death has reconciling significance for the whole cosmos. Since "in him all the fulness of God was pleased to dwell" (i.e., because God was fully present in Christ; cf. v. 9), not only humanity but all of creation has been put back into its proper relation to God "by the blood of his cross."

Bibliography. K. Barth, *Church Dogmatics* IV/1 (Edinburgh: 1956): 3-78; G. C. Berkouwer, *The Work of Christ* (Grand Rapids: 1965), pp. 254-294; J. Denney, *The Christian Doctrine of Reconciliation* (London: 1917); repr. *The Biblical Doctrine of Reconciliation* (Minneapolis: 1985); R. P. Martin, *Reconciliation* (Atlanta: 1981).

RECORDER (Heb. *mazkîr* "one who remembers"). A high office in the monarchies of united Israel and of Judah. Three individuals who held this office are mentioned: Jehoshaphat, under David and Solomon (2 Sam. 8:16; 20:24; 1 Kgs. 4:3; 1 Chr. 18:15); Joah, under Hezekiah (2 Kgs. 18:18, 37 par. Isa. 36:3, 22); and another Joah, under Josiah (2 Chr. 34:8). The task of the recorder is not described but may have included the duties of archivist or chronicler (lit. "remembrancer"). The recorder could perhaps also represent the king in foreign affairs (2 Kgs. 18:18).

RED.* In Old Testament usage the basic designation of red and brown colors is Heb. *'āḏōm* and related terms, perhaps associating these colors with "earth" (*'āḏām*). Colors tending more toward brown and even yellow rather than pure red are designated by *'āḏōm*, as in the reference to the colors of Jacob's lentil stew (Gen. 25:30, 34), of the heifer to be slaughtered for the purification of a person defiled by a corpse (Num. 19:2), and of the horses in Zechariah's visions (Zech. 1:8; 6:2), which were probably bay-colored. Wine could also be thought of as "red" (Prov. 23:31; cf. Isa. 63:2), as could the skin of healthy young men

(Cant. 5:10; Lam. 4:7; RSV "ruddy"). But a pure red was also included in *'āḏōm*, red like blood (*dām*; 2 Kgs. 3:22) or crimson dye (Isa. 1:18; *see* SCARLET, CRIMSON); when the unnatural conditions of the end of the age are spoken of, it is sometimes said that the moon will be turned to blood or will become like blood (Joel 2:31 [MT 3:5]; Acts 2:20; Rev. 6:12).

The quality given to eyes by wine (Gen. 49:12, *ḥaḵlîlî*; Prov. 23:29, *ḥaḵlîlûṯ*) is traditionally interpreted as "redness," but this identification is not certain. Other suggested translations include "sparkling," "dull," and "dark."

Rev. 6:4 refers to another "red" horse seen in an apocalyptic vision, this one representing war. The same color is given to a destructive and warlike dragon (12:3). In both instances Gk. *pyrrós* (from *pýr* "fire") is used. A related verb, *pyrrázō* "be red, fiery," is used of natural sky conditions (Matt. 16:2-3).

RED SEA.† The large body of water extending from the straits of Bab el-Mandeb in the south to the Sinai peninsula in the north and separating northeastern Africa from the Arabian peninsula. In the north it branches into the Gulf of Suez to the west and the Gulf of Aqabah to the east. Ancient Greek authors used the name "Red Sea" to denote not only the Red Sea proper, but the Arabian Gulf and the Indian Ocean as well.

In the Old Testament Heb. *yam sûp* is used for the Gulf of Aqabah (e.g., Exod. 23:31; Num. 21:4; Deut. 1:40; 1 Kgs. 9:26; cf. Judg. 11:16), the Gulf of Suez (Exod. 10:19; 13:18; Num. 33:10-11), and the sea crossed by the Israelites as they left Egypt (e.g., Exod. 15:4, 22; Deut. 11:4; Josh. 4:23; 24:6; Neh. 9:9; Ps. 136:13, 15). The exact location of the last of these is uncertain, and scholars have variously proposed the Bitter Lakes region, Lake Menzaleh, Lake Sorbonis, and the Gulf of Suez as possible sites.

"Sea of reeds," the translation of *yam sûp* that has come to be commonly accepted, is based upon the derivation of *sûp* from Egyp. *ṯwfi* "papyrus, reed." This use of *sûp* does appear in the Old Testament (Exod. 2:3, 5; Isa. 19:6; cf. Jonah 2:5). An Egyptian text refers to the "papyrus marsh" (Egyp. *p3-ṯwf*) near the city of Rameses, which is thought by many to be the body of water crossed by the Israelites (cf. Num. 33:5-8). But the name was apparently a general designation for marshes in more than one part of Lower Egypt.

The identification of *sûp* in *yam sûp* with Egyp. *ṯwfi* has, moreover, been challenged with arguments that relate it instead to Heb. *sôp* "end, conclusion, annihilation" and the related verb *sûp*. There may be some influence on the designation of the sea of the Exodus as *yam sûp* from the possible use of these words in descriptions of the primeval sea and God's triumph over it (suggested in the case of Jonah 2:5; RSV "weeds"), which were influential in other ways on the language used to describe the Exodus (cf. Ps. 18:4-5, 15 [MT 5-6, 19] with Exod. 15:4-5). Despite the possibility of such influence, it is nevertheless likely that *yam sûp* in *all* of its Old Testament uses is simply the sea at the "end" (*sôp*) of the earth, i.e., the large connected bodies of water beyond Palestine and Arabia to the south. This would be in accord with many other Old Testament occurrences of *sôp* that have a spatial rather than a temporal or eschatological focus.

See EXODUS *IV*.

REDEMPTION.† Release from bondage, usually by means of a price paid, though in some instances biblical usage focuses on the aspect of liberation alone.

I. Old Testament

Heb. *pāḏâ* and related words are used most often with reference to redemption of the firstborn of humans or animals that, according to law, belonged to God (e.g., Exod. 13:13). Sometimes *pāḏâ* refers to the ransom given for a forfeited life (e.g., 21:30; 1 Sam. 14:45; cf. Exod. 30:12, *kōper*). When God himself is the subject of *pāḏâ*, the Exodus event is usually in view (e.g., Deut. 7:8; 9:26; 2 Sam. 7:23; Ps. 78:42). In these cases the emphasis lies upon God's powerful act of deliverance rather than on payment of a price.

The verb *gā'al* and the noun *ge'ullâh* are used in reference to the situation in which the closest relative was under obligation to redeem an impoverished family member who had sold himself into slavery (Lev. 25:47-49) or to regain possession of family land that had been sold (vv. 25-26, 33; Ruth 4:4, 6). The one who carried out this redemption was the redeemer (*gō'ēl*). The redeemer might also deal out vengeance for the death of a family member. Job's affirmation, "I know that my redeemer lives" (Job 19:25), refers to one who would avenge his shameful death should it come. The larger context for these familial obligations was God's redemption of his people from slavery in Egypt, and his gift of the land that was to be theirs in perpetuity. When God is said to be the redeemer, as in Isaiah (e.g., Isa. 41:14; 47:4), the emphasis is placed upon his mighty act of deliverance that will be like the Exodus. Here, as elsewhere, one must be careful to observe the operation of these words in context, for they do not carry a prescribed, unchanging meaning such as "ransom" in every setting.

II. New Testament

In the New Testament the concept of redemption is conveyed primarily by words of the Gk. *lytro-* group (nouns *lýtron*, *lýtrōsis*, *apolýtrōsis*, *antílytron*; verb *lytróomai*). These words cannot be assumed to carry the full meaning of the Old Testament redemption laws and customs. In secular Greek the terms implied recompense and could refer to a gift of money offered to a god in a cultic ceremony in order to obtain the freedom of a slave or to a ransom paid for prisoners. This meaning, parallel in many ways with the Hebrew idea of redemption, would also have shaped the understanding of redemption in the Greco-Roman world.

Gk. *lytro-* words are used in Luke for God's deliverance of Israel (Luke 1:68; 2:38; 24:21) and for the eschatological deliverance awaited by Jesus' disciples (21:28). Jesus interpreted his death as a "ransom (*lýtron*) for many" (Mark 10:45); against the background of Isa. 53:10-12 he views his coming death as a substitutionary payment for those who live in bondage to sin and death. These Greek words also refer to the saving significance of Jesus' death at Titus 2:14; Heb. 9:12, 15; 1 Pet. 1:18-19. In Paul's letters *apolýtrōsis* is used of present redemption from sin through Christ's death (Rom. 3:24; Eph. 1:7; Col. 1:14; cf. 1 Cor. 1:30) and of the future aspect of redemption (Eph. 1:14 [RSV takes this as a verbal noun describing the action of God's people]; 4:30), which may include cosmic redemption (Rom. 8:22-23). This noun is also used at Heb. 11:35 in a secular sense of release (so RSV) from torture.

The verb "to buy" (Gk. *agorázō*) is taken from the language of the marketplace and most often is used literally in the New Testament. In Hellenistic usage the term could refer to the purchase of slaves, a meaning that provided a ready bridge for its use as a term for God's redemption of Christians (1 Cor. 6:20; 7:23; 2 Pet. 2:1; Rev. 5:9; 14:3). In this case the emphasis is on the change of ownership from one master to another, occasionally linked to the price paid, Christ's blood (e.g., 5:9). (As later Church Fathers would demonstrate in elaborate theories of atonement, the meaning of the metaphor of redemption becomes strained if the question is asked to whom the price was paid.) The intensive form, *exagorázō*, is used at Gal. 3:13; 4:5 to speak of redemption in Christ from the curse of or bondage to the law; that the cross is the turning point in redemption is spelled out at 3:13, and implied at 4:4-5.

In the New Testament the title "redeemer" is not used of Christ, although the term has proven useful in subsequent theological discussion. The only occurrence of the term in the New Testament is at Acts 7:35 where Stephen refers to Moses as a deliverer (Gk. *lýtrōtēs*) sent by God.

Bibliography. I. H. Marshall, "The Development of the Concept of Redemption in the New Testament," pp. 153-169 in R. J. Banks, ed., *Reconciliation and Hope* (Grand Rapids: 1974); L. Morris, *The Apostolic Preaching of the Cross*, 3rd ed. (Grand Rapids: 1965), pp. 11-64; W. Mundle, J. Schneider, and C. Brown, "Redemption," *DNTT* 3 (1978): 177-223.

REED, RUSH. Reeds are tall marsh grasses with jointed hollow stalks. Palestine, Egypt, and other countries of the ancient Near East knew two species of reeds: the common reed (*Phragmites communis* Trin.) and arrow reed (*Arundo donax* L.). Both are tall, arrow reeds sometimes reaching a height of 5 m. (15 ft.). Rushes are also marsh plants, shorter than the large reeds and also distinguished by generally having hollow leaves. The Near East has a number of rushes of genera *Juncus* and *Scirpus*. Biblical terminology does not distinguish clearly between reeds and rushes (*see* PAPYRUS).

Heb. *qāneh*, which carries the more general meanings "stalk, stick, rod, branch," is used of reeds employed measuring sticks (e.g., Ezek. 40:3) and in their watery natural setting (e.g., 1 Kgs. 14:15; 2 Kgs. 18:21 par.; Job 40:21; Isa. 42:3). Other less common Hebrew words for reeds and rushes are *'agmôn*, *'āḥû*, *'ēḇeh* (only at Job 9:26, where it refers to vessels made of papyrus; KJV "swift"), and *sûp*. Gk. *kálamos* is used in the New Testament.

These marsh plants were known as the home of "Behemoth," perhaps the hippotamus (Job 40:21; cf. RSV, Ps. 68:30 [MT 31]), and as plants that were dependent on abundant water for life (Isa. 19:6; KJV

"flags"). Job 41:2 (MT 40:26) refers to the custom of running a reed stalk (RSV "rope"; KJV "hook") through the gills of a large fish to keep it near the shore but still alive after it was caught. Pieces of reed were used as simple writing pens (3 John 13), and dried reeds and rushes could be used as fuel (Job 41:20 [MT 12]; KJV "caldron"). Reeds and rushes were also woven into baskets.

Reeds are used in figurative language for that which is easily shaken (1 Kgs. 14:15; Matt. 11:7) and easily broken (Isa. 42:3), making it sharp-pointed (2 Kgs. 18:21 par. Isa. 36:6). Similarly, the fragile rush pictures vulnerability (58:5; KJV "bulrush").

REEDS, SEA OF. *See* RED SEA.

REELAIAH [rē'ə lī'ə] (Heb. *rᵉʿēlāyâ*). A prominent Israelite who returned from captivity with Zerubbabel (Ezra 2:2). At Neh. 7:7 he is called Raamiah.

REFUGE (Heb. nouns *maḥseh*, *mānôs*, *māʿôz*, verb *ḥāsâ*).† Shelter or protection from danger or distress. The main thought underlying the Hebrew terms translatable as "refuge" is security. Such words are applied in the Old Testament to places of physical shelter, as for those seeking protection from rain (Job 24:8; RSV, KJV "shelter"), wind (Isa. 32:2; Heb. *maḥᵃḇēʾ*; RSV, KJV "hiding place"), or enemy armies (14:32; Nah. 3:11). Figuratively, a strong ruler or ally could be called a "refuge" (Judg. 9:15; Isa. 30:2), as could, temporarily, false assurances (28:15).

God is depicted numerous times as the "refuge" of his people, most often in the Psalms (e.g., Ps. 7:1 [MT 2]; 46:1 [MT 2]; 59:16 [MT 17]; 94:22; Jer. 16:19). It is definite dangers, sometimes named, that cause God's people to take refuge in him. These are most often enemies (e.g., Ps. 17:7; 37:40), but also the oppression suffered by the poor (Ps. 14:6; Isa. 25:4; cf. Ruth 2:12). To seek refuge in something other than God, such as wealth, is foolhardy (Ps. 52:7 [MT 9]).

See CITIES OF REFUGE.

REGEM [rē'gəm] (Heb. *regem* "friend"). A son of Jahdai of the Calebite clan of Judah (1 Chr. 2:47).

REGEM-MELECH [rē'gəm měl'ek] (Heb. *regem melek* "friend of the king"). An inhabitant of Bethel who was sent with Sharezer to Jerusalem to ask the priests and prophets whether certain days of fasting and repentance were still in effect (Zech. 7:2-3). Syr. suggests an original Hebrew form *raḇ-mag hammelek*, a title adapted from Akkadian (cf. Jer. 39:3, 13).

REGENERATION.† Protestant soteriology distinguishes between justification, regeneration, and sanctification. Justification is God's decree whereby believers are set right with him "positionally" and whereby he imputes the merits of Christ to them by grace. It is, so to speak, the objective side of an individual's salvation (the ultimate objective basis being the death of Jesus on the cross). The subjective side is regeneration, the experience of being born again as a new creature, a child of God. Sanctification is the process whereby that new life is nourished and matures into conformity with one's justified "positional" status.

The concept of regeneration as it is found in the Bible is first of all eschatological and cosmic rather than being focused on individual salvation. Isa. 65:17; 66:22 predict the creation of a new heaven and earth. Rev. 21:1-4 elaborates this prediction, and Matthew makes passing reference to the same "regeneration" (Matt. 19:28; Gk. *palingenesía*; RSV "new world"). The future participation of God's people in this cosmic regeneration is made clear at Rom. 8:19-23 (cf. Jas. 1:18).

It is Paul who first makes regeneration something experienced by believers already in the present. The Christian is already initiated into the new age (2 Cor. 5:17, lit. "If any one is in Christ, there is a new created order"; cf. Gal. 6:15). The Spirit is received as the "guarantee" (2 Cor. 1:22; 5:5; Eph. 1:13-14) or "first fruits" (Rom. 8:23) of the resurrection that is yet to come. In baptism believers experience a kind of anticipatory resurrection (6:3-4; Col. 2:11-13; 3:1, 9-14). Titus 3:5, which includes the word "regeneration" (*palingenesía*), also associates this new reality with both water baptism and with the Spirit, as do 1 Pet. 3:21 (cf. 1:3) and the classic text concerned with rebirth, John 3:3-8. A number of other texts speak, directly or obliquely, of regeneration (Matt. 18:3; John 1:13; 1 Pet. 1:23; 1 John 2:29 and passim).

REHABIAH [rĕ′ə bī′ə] (Heb. *rᵉḥaḇyâ, rᵉḥaḇyāhû* "Yahweh has enlarged"). The son of Eliezer and grandson of Moses (1 Chr. 23:17; 24:21; 26:25).

REHOB [rĕ′hŏb] (Heb. *rᵉḥôḇ, rᵉḥōḇ* "open place, plaza") (**PERSON**).
1. The father of King Hadadezer of Zobah, who was defeated by David (2 Sam. 8:3, 12; Heb. *rᵉḥōḇ*). "Son of Rehob" may mean "of the house (i.e., dynasty) of Rehob," indicating that a relationship existed between the two Aramean states of Beth-rehob and Zobah.
2. A Levite listed among those who placed their seal on the covenant under Nehemiah (Neh. 10:11 [MT 12]; Heb. *rᵉḥōḇ*).

REHOB [rĕ′hŏb] (Heb. *rᵉḥôḇ, rᵉḥōḇ* "open place, plaza") (**PLACE**).
1. An Aramean stronghold (Num. 13:21; 2 Sam. 10:8). See BETH-REHOB.
2. A city in the plain of Acco allotted by Joshua to the tribe of Asher (Josh. 19:28, 30). Rehob was one of the cities assigned to Asher that withstood the Israelite attack and retained their Canaanite population (Judg. 1:31). It was later designated a levitical city (Josh. 21:31; 1 Chr. 6:75 [MT 60]). Scholars have tentatively identified Rehob with Tell el-Gharbī (Tel Bira), *ca.* 11 km. (7 mi.) east-southeast of Acco.
3. The principal city of the Beth-shean valley during the Canaanite and Israelite periods, located *ca.* 5.3 km. (3.3 mi.) south of the ancient city of Beth-shean. Although it is not mentioned in the Bible, references to Rehob are found in a number of Egyptian documents. Excavations at the site (Tell eṣ-Ṣârem) have

unearthed Israel's longest Hebrew mosaic inscription to date.

REHOBOAM [rē′ə bō′əm] (Heb. *rᵉḥaḇᵉʿām* "The people are numerous"; Gk. *Rhoboam*). A son of Solomon and Naamah the Ammonitess, and the first king of the southern kingdom of Judah after the division of Israel and Judah (*ca.* 922-915 B.C.). He is listed among the ancestors of Jesus (Matt. 1:7; KJV "Roboam").

Rehoboam was forty-one years old when he began to reign over Judah after the death of Solomon (1 Kgs. 14:21). He was initially to be king of all Israel (12:1 par. 2 Chr. 10:1), but because he refused to reduce the burden of forced labor that Solomon had imposed, the northern tribes revolted (1 Kgs. 12:3-16). Their representatives killed his taskmaster, Adoram, and proclaimed Jeroboam I king of Israel. Only Judah and a part of the tribe of Benjamin supported Rehoboam, who fled to Jerusalem (vv. 18-21). But his army accepted the counsel of the prophet Shemaiah and did not seek to retaliate against the northern tribes (vv. 22-24). The division of the kingdom came to be regarded as God's response to Solomon's idolatry, in fulfillment of what had been spoken earlier through the prophet Ahijah (11:29-36; 12:15).

The priests and the Levites in the north came south to live in Judah, but Rehoboam was faithful to the God of Israel for only the first three years of his reign (2 Chr. 11:13-17). Thereafter, Rehoboam and the people of Judah engaged in idolatry (1 Kgs. 14:22-24; 2 Chr. 12:1). In response God punished Rehoboam by sending the Egyptian pharaoh Shishak, who took the temple treasures of Jerusalem, and by causing continuous conflict between Rehoboam and Jeroboam (2 Chr. 12:2-4, 9). The people of Judah repented as a result of Shemaiah's preaching (vv. 5-8).

Rehoboam had eighteen wives, sixty concubines, twenty-eight sons, and sixty daughters (11:21). He provided well for all his sons and appointed them to rule over distinct parts of his territory. In accordance with his wishes, Abijah (5)/Abijam, his son by Maacah/Micaiah, succeeded him as king (vv. 22-23).

REHOBOTH [rə hō′bŏth] (Heb. *rᵉḥōḇōṯ, rᵉḥōḇōṯ* "open places").
1. (Gen. 10:11, KJV). *See* REHOBOTH-IR.
2. (Heb. *rᵉḥōḇōṯ*). A well dug by Isaac in the valley of Gerar (Gen. 26:22). The name is preserved in modern Khirbet Ruḥeibeh, *ca.* 33 km. (21 mi.) southwest of Beersheba, but it is unlikely as the biblical site; a number of large cisterns there date only from the Middle Ages.
3.† (Heb. *rᵉḥōḇōṯ hannāhār*). "Rehoboth on the river," the home of Shaul, one of the early kings of Edom (Gen. 36:37; 1 Chr. 1:48). "The river" is usually taken to be the Euphrates (so RSV), and does, in fact, carry that meaning elsewhere (e.g., Gen. 31:21). But in this case "the river" is perhaps to be found in Edom; it is, indeed, often identified with the brook Zered, which marked the boundary between Moab and Edom (cf. Deut. 2:8-14). Nothing more can be said about the location of Rehoboth.

REHOBOTH-IR [rə hō'bŏth ĭr'] (Heb. *rᵉhōḇōṯ 'îr* "open places of the city").† A city built in Assyria by Nimrod (Gen. 10:11; KJV "the city of Rehoboth"), or, if the Hebrew term is not taken as a place name, a designation for part of the city of Nineveh (NIV mg., "Nineveh with its city squares") or for open areas within the limits of Nineveh (which are mentioned in Assyrian documents).

REHUM [rē'əm] (Heb. *rᵉhûm, rᵉhum* "mercy").
1. A prominent person among those who went back to Judah from Babylon with Zerubbabel after the Exile (Ezra. 2:2). At Neh. 7:7 the name occurs as Nehum.
2. A Persian official (RSV "commander") in Samaria who, by means of a letter to King Artaxerxes, managed to delay the rebuilding of the walls of Jerusalem (Ezra 4:8-24).
3. A Levite who participated in the rebuilding of the walls of Jerusalem (Neh. 3:17).
4. One of those who put their seals to the covenant under Nehemiah (Neh. 10:25 [MT 26]). He may be the same as **3**.
5.† The ancestor of a priestly family, some of whom returned with Zerubbabel from Babylon after the Exile (Neh. 12:3). He is probably to be identified with Harim (**1**) (v. 15).

REI [rē'ī] (Heb. *rē'î* "friendly"). One of the group who continued to support David when Adonijah's revolt was under way (1 Kgs. 1:8).

REKEM [rē'kəm] (Heb. *reqem*) (**PERSON**).
1. One of the five kings of Midian who were vassals of King Sihon of the Amorites and were killed by the Israelites in war (Num. 31:18; Josh. 13:21).
2. A son of Hebron of the tribe of Judah (1 Chr. 2:43-44).

REKEM [rē'kəm] (Heb. *reqem*) (**PLACE**).† A city in the tribal territory of Benjamin (Josh. 18:27). It was in the western group of Benjaminite cities (vv. 25-28), but little else can be said about its location.

RELEASE, YEAR OF.* In English translations, an alternate name for the SABBATICAL YEAR, following LXX Gk. *étos tḗs aphéseōs* (Deut. 15:9; 31:10; JB NJV "year of remission," following Vulg. Lat. *annus remissionis*; cf. NIV).

REMALIAH [rĕm'ə lī'ə] (Heb. *rᵉmalyāhû*). The father of King Pekah of Israel (2 Kgs. 15:25; Isa. 7:1).

REMETH [rē'mĕth] (Heb. *remeṯ* "height"). A city in the tribal territory of Issachar (Josh. 19:21). Also known as "Ramoth" (1 Chr. 6:73 [MT 58]), it is probably to be identified with JARMUTH **2** and RAMOTH **3**.

REMMON (Josh. 19:7, KJV). *See* RIMMON (PLACE) **1**.

REMMON-METHOAR (Josh. 19:13, KJV). *See* RIMMON (PLACE) **2**.

REMNANT (Heb. nouns *šᵉ'ār, šᵉ'ērîṯ, yeṯer, pᵉlēṭâ,*

śārîḏ and related verbs; Gk. *leímma, hypóleimma, loipós*).† What remains of a group of people after most of that group has been destroyed or lost through dispersal. The term has particular theological significance with regard to the people of God.

Among the remnants of Gentile nations or groups were the Gibeonites, who were among the Amorites that survived the Israelite conquest of Canaan (2 Sam. 21:2); Og, the last of the Rephaim (Deut. 3:11); and the remaining representatives of other groups in Canaan (Josh. 23:12). In the story of the Flood the remnant is what remains of all mankind (Gen. 7:23). But it is in relation to the people of Israel remaining after God's judgment has come on them or after apostasy has taken the people away from God that "remnant" as a concept in biblical theology is developed.

The depletion of God's people by his judgment (generally through war) is a primary theme in the Old Testament; indeed, the difficult history of Israel made possible frequent reference to the remnant of the people after God's judgment. Those who survived the wilderness wanderings to enter the promised land were such a remnant, as were the inhabitants of the former northern kingdom of Israel who escaped the Assyrian deportation (2 Chr. 30:6; 34:9), those whom the Babylonian conquerors left in Judah and who then migrated to Egypt (Jer. 40:11, 15; 42:15, 19; 43:5; 44:12, 14), those who returned to Judah after the Babylonian Exile (Hag. 1:12, 14; Zech. 8:6; cf. Neh. 1:2-3, "survivors"), and those to be brought back from the Dispersion into the land of Israel (Isa. 11:11, 16; Mic. 2:12).

A faithful remnant could also be identified in the setting of national apostasy. Elijah considered himself the sole survivor of national apostasy and persecution of the faithful (1 Kgs. 19:10). That a remnant could be spoken of in such a situation meant that a distinction could be drawn between the people of Israel as a whole and the remnant, here specifically those who had remained faithful to God. In such a situation the remnant is the often small (Isa. 10:22; cf. 6:13; Ezek. 5:3; Zech. 13:9) segment of God's people that survives through the ages. The remnant as that which survives apostasy is the same as the remnant that survives divine judgment when God eliminates those who are not faithful to him; thus those who remain can be a purified people (Isa. 1:24-26; Zeph. 3:11-13; Matt. 3:12).

The distinction between the people as a whole and the faithful remnant comes to the forefront in the few references to the concept in the New Testament (Rom. 9:27-29; 11:2-5, 7; Rev. 12:17; cf. Matt. 7:14). For Paul the existence of a remnant is evidence of both the apostasy of the people and the judgment of God; the sovereignty of God in determining the limits of his people is communicated by Paul in terms of a constant narrowing of the people, which takes place apart from their merits (Rom. 9:6-29).

The concept of the remnant of God's people functions in two fundamental ways, as expression of both warning and hope. On the one hand, the survival of "only a remnant" indicates how severe God's judgment (or the apostasy of the people) has been (Isa. 10:22-23). The use of the remnant concept as an expression of warning receives special emphasis when it is said that even the remnant of a group will be destroyed—i.e., that the group will utterly cease to exist (14:30; 15:9; 17:3; Amos 1:8; Zeph. 1:4). On the other hand, that a remnant exists at all shows that God does not abandon his people, but preserves their existence and integrity as a whole (Gen. 45:7; cf. Isa. 1:9). The survival of God's people is required by his election of and promises to them, promises impossible to keep if they were destroyed (cf. Rom. 11:1-2, 28).

Bibliography. G. F. Hasel, *The Remnant,* 2nd ed. AUM 5 (1974).

REMPHAN (Acts 7:43, KJV). See REPHAN.

REPENTANCE.† "Repentance" may represent only regret or remorse over a past thought or action (Heb. *nāḥam*; Gk. *metamélomai*), but in its fullest sense it is a term for a complete change of orientation involving a judgment upon the past and a deliberate redirection for the future (Heb. *šûḇ* "return, turn back"; Gk. *metanoéō* "have a change of heart, repent," *metánoia* "repentance"). As such it is the subjective human experience involved in conversion (*epistréphō*).

I. Old Testament

The Old Testament concept of repentance appears as both ritual action meant to demonstrate repentance, and the prophetic call for repentance. Rituals such as fasting, dressing in sackcloth, sitting in ashes, and wailing were characteristic expressions of repentance. In addition, the liturgical form of the lament might be employed by individuals or the community to express a strong sense of sin. Although such rituals were expected to be accompanied by authentic repentance, they could also represent simple remorse and a desire to escape the consequences of past actions, rather than a commitment to establish a new relationship with God and walk a path of righteousness.

The prophetic call for repentance was a summons for a complete turnabout that was to arise from the heart, the seat of the will (Joel 2:12-13). This call for conversion stressed the basic question of human existence, and the human's standing before God. It summoned people to a relationship in which God exercised sovereignty over all of life. Although in the historical books Israel as a nation was called to repentance, the prophets (particularly Jeremiah and Ezekiel) urged individuals to turn from ungodly living to a life of obedience and trust in Yahweh (Jer. 4:1; 26:3; 36:3; Ezek. 18:21-28; Hos. 6:1-6).

The Old Testament frequently refers to God as repenting (e.g., Exod. 32:14; 1 Sam. 15:11, 35; 2 Sam. 24:16). These passages depict God's departure from a course of action that he had followed earlier or had said that he would follow, the change coming as he responds to human conduct, either in mercy or judgment.

II. New Testament

The prophetic call for repentance is echoed in the preaching of John the Baptist, who called Israel to repentance. The motivation for repentance spoken of by John was the imminent arrival of the kingdom of God (Matt. 3:2). This call to repentance was reissued

in the proclamation of Jesus (4:17), which became with him a call to discipleship. The same call could be expressed in other terms, such as the command to become like children (18:3) or the call to renounce all that one has (Luke 14:33).

The missionary preaching of the early Church restated the call to repentance (e.g., Acts 3:19; 26:20). Such repentance not only brought one into faith, but was also demonstrated outwardly in baptism (2:38).

In missionary preaching to Gentiles repentance was understood as a change of lordship that could be depicted as a reorientation from darkness to light (26:18). Evidence for such a theme of repentance in Paul's missionary preaching is found at 1 Thess. 1:9, where he writes that the Thessalonians "turned to God from idols." Generally, however, words for "repentance" are infrequent in Paul's letters. Some scholars have viewed this as evidence for the eclipse of the idea of repentance in Paul. The apostle seems to have employed the word "faith" (Gk. *pístis*) when speaking to believers of the act of repentance and coming to Christ (e.g., Rom. 11:20; Gal. 3:25-26; Eph. 4:5).

The writer of Hebrews takes up an issue of the Church in his day: the possibility of a second repentance after apostasy (Heb. 6:4-8). He emphasizes the absolute nature of repentance, along with the alternative of God's judgment against sin. For the writer of this epistle, as with Scripture as a whole, true repentance means a complete and irrevocable about-face from the past to a future shaped by the demands of God's reign.

REPHAEL [rĕf′ĭ əl] (Heb. *rᵉpā′ēl* "God cures"). A levitical temple gatekeeper, the son of Shemaiah of the family of Obed-edom (1 Chr. 26:7).

REPHAH [rē′fə] (Heb. *repaḥ*). An Ephraimite, and an ancestor of Joshua (1 Chr. 7:25).

REPHAIAH [rə fā′yə] (Heb. *rᵉpāyâ* "Yahweh cures").

1. A descendant of Zerubbabel (1 Chr. 3:21).

2. One of the sons of Ishi who led five hundred Simeonites in the defeat of the Amalekite remnant on Mt. Seir (1 Chr. 4:42-43).

3. A son of Tola of the tribe of Issachar (1 Chr. 7:2).

4. A descendant of Saul through Jonathan (1 Chr. 9:43). He is also called Raphah (8:37).

5. The son of Hur, and chief of half of the district of Jerusalem in the days of Nehemiah (Neh. 3:9).

REPHAIM [rĕf′ĭ əm] (Heb. *rᵉpā′îm*).*

1. Early inhabitants of Palestine, often called "giants" (RSV, 1 Chr. 20:4; KJV passim), perhaps in part because of megalithic structures of the Neolithic period found in Transjordan. The Rephaim are identified with the Anakim, and were known to the Moabites as Emim and to the Ammonites as Zamzummim (Deut. 2:10-11, 20-21; cf. Gen. 14:5). See **2** below.

The Rephaim are mentioned as inhabitants of Transjordan, but their descendants were found in Philistia, and a valley near Jerusalem is named for them. Josh. 17:15 may refer to a Transjordanian home of the Rephaim, but this is not certain. The whole region of Bashan in northern Transjordan was known as a "land of Rephaim" (Deut. 3:13; Heb. *'ereṣ rᵉpā'îm*), as was Ammon (2:20); King Og of Bashan is called the last of the Rephaim (3:11; Josh. 12:4; 13:12). Some Philistine heroes slain by David and his men were descendants of Rapha (so JB, NIV; NJV "the Raphah"), a corresponding singular form of this name (2 Sam. 21:16-22, *hārāpâ*; 1 Chr. 20:4-8, *hārāpā'*; RSV "giants"; KJV "giant").

The "valley of Rephaim" (*'ēmeq rᵉpā'îm*), southwest of Jerusalem, was on the border between Judah and Benjamin (Josh. 15:8) and not far from Bethlehem (2 Sam. 23:13-14 par. 1 Chr. 11:15-16). In this valley David met the Philistines in battle on more than one occasion (2 Sam. 5:17-18; 23:13-14; 1 Chr. 14:8-9). It may have received its name from these encounters. It was known as a fertile agricultural area (Isa. 17:5). The modern name of the valley is el-Baqaʿ.

2. The dead, those who inhabit Sheol (RSV "shades," "dead"; KJV usually "dead"). The derivation of *rᵉpā'îm* as used in this sense may be from Heb. *rāpâ* "to sink down, relax," referring to descent to Sheol and to the weak, shadowy existence of the underworld. A more likely derivation, however, is from *rāpā'* "to heal" in the sense of mending or stitching together, thus to bind together as a community in a common existence in Sheol. Rephaim live an uninviting existence at the lowest ebb of life. They cannot praise God (Ps. 88:10 [MT 11]), and their assembly is not a place of understanding (Prov. 9:18; 21:16). They are sometimes represented as a company of once mighty rulers who have descended to the underworld (Isa. 14:9; 26:13-14; cf. v. 19 for the hope of return from death for the righteous of Israel who have died).

Discussion of the origin and relationship of the two uses of *rᵉpā'îm* has been focused on the Ugaritic texts from Ras Shamra that provide the earliest and most numerous references to Rephaim (Ugar. *rpùm*). Some scholars regard the *rpùm* as, first of all, the dead who have been deified and are possessed of special powers of healing and quickening. Israel, it is thought, took over this primary reference to the dead, depriving them, however, of their special powers. The ethnic use would be a secondary application to an ancient and legendary race of giants on earth. According to another view, the "divine ones" are the deceased members of a legendary, aristocratic warrior guild headed by the king. This is, so it is thought, the source of the ethnic use of Rephaim in the Old Testament, while reference to the guild's deceased members has been generalized to refer to all the dead (cf. Isa. 14:9; 26:13).

REPHAN [rē'făn]. The corruption of the Hebrew name of a deity worshipped by the Israelites during their wilderness wanderings (Acts 7:43; KJV "Remphan"; Gk. *Rhaiphan* from the LXX of Amos 5:26). *See* KAIWAN.

REPHIDIM [rĕf'ə dĭm] (Heb. *rᵉpîḏîm*).† An Israelite encampment en route to Sinai where Moses struck a rock to provide water for the thirsty Israelites and where they were attacked by Amalekites (Exod. 17; 19:2; Num. 33:14-15). Other than noting its nearness

to Mt. Sinai, little can be said about the location of Rephidim.

RESEN [rē'zən] (Heb. *resen*).† An Assyrian city between Nineveh and Calah (Gen. 10:12). The exact location of the city is uncertain, and proposals that have been made thus far have not been likely.

RESHEPH [rĕsh'əf, rē'shĕf] (Heb. *rešep*).†

1. An Ephraimite, son of Rephah and father of Telah (1 Chr. 7:25). The name may represent a clan or town.

2. A Canaanite deity of plague (Ugar. *ršp*; cf. Heb. *rešep* "flame," perhaps related to fever; cf. Akk. Nergal). Such mythological sense may underlie biblical usage of the Hebrew term, often translated "plague" (Deut. 32:24, "burning heat"; cf. Cant. 8:6). The usage at Job 5:7; Pss. 76:3 (MT 4); 78:48 connoting the flash of flying (perhaps flaming) arrows may derive from the Ugaritic epithet of Resheph *b'l ḥṣ* "lord of the arrow" (cf. the identification of the Canaanite deity with Apollo, whose arrows bring sickness). At Hab. 3:5 "pestilence" and "plague" (Heb. *deber*) escort Yahweh as he marches in theophany, reminiscent of Ugaritic paired deities. *See* PESTILENCE.

RESURRECTION (Gk. *anástasis, égersis, exanástasis*).† The raising from death to new life, in biblical usage specifically a raising of the righteous of all ages at the end of earthly history. Implicit in the very idea of resurrection is a positive valuation of life in the physical body, which sets Christianity against worldnegating mysticisms that see the body as an impediment that must be sloughed off. The expectation of the resurrection is thought by most Christians to include also the unrighteous, whose resurrection will be followed by their consignment to eternal punishment. The Christian hope of the resurrection of mankind is based on the resurrection of Christ, which has already occurred in history rather than waiting for the end of history and which is understood as a proleptic preview of the final destination of history.

I. Old Testament and Early Judaism

The idea of resurrection is not attested in early parts of the Old Testament and appears only in postexilic apocalyptic literature. The general conception was of a shadowy existence for the dead in Sheol, and some Old Testament texts seem to deny any possibility of life after death (e.g., Job 14:12-21). In Ezekiel's vision of the valley of dry bones (Ezek. 37:1-14) the striking image of return from death simply foreshadows the return of the exiles from Babylon, but an over-literal interpretation of this prophecy may, however, have contributed later to a genuine resurrection belief. Other texts that speak of a return from death also employ such a thought as a metaphor for national revival (Isa. 25:8; 26:19; Hos. 6:2; 13:14 [but cf. RSV]). Ps. 16:10; 49:15 (MT 16) refer not to a return from death but to God's protection of the psalmist in circumstances that might otherwise lead to death. Job 19:25-27 speaks of a vindication after death, but places it in a momentary vision of the vindicator, not in a lasting resurrection. Dan. 12:2, however, predicts that "many" will rise from death, the righteous (the Maccabean martyrs) to reward, the wicked to "everlasting contempt." According to some scholars, the idea of the resurrection may have been borrowed by the Jews from Zoroastrianism, encountered in the Persian Empire during the Exile.

In post-Old Testament Judaism the resurrection doctrine became widely held, but with a number of variations concerning who will rise—only some or all of the righteous, or both the righteous and the wicked—and concerning whether this rising is to be spiritual, or physical with the return of the very body that died, or experienced as a transformation into a glorious angelic form. Belief in the coming resurrection was not universal among Jews; the Sadducees specifically denied such a belief (cf. Acts 23:8).

II. New Testament

The entire New Testament was written in the shadow of the resurrection of Jesus. This event has, of course, affected what is said about the coming general resurrection, though what is said still falls within the general range of possibilities presented by Jewish belief in the resurrection. What was believed about the coming general resurrection was understood to be in accord with Jewish belief and in conflict with the beliefs of most Gentiles regarding the condition of mankind after death (Acts 24:15, 21).

Jesus himself believed that both the righteous and the wicked would be present at the final judgment (Matt. 10:15; 12:41-42). He also believed in physical resurrection in its most literal sense, such that wounds inflicted in this life would be carried over into eternal life (18:8-9). Jesus' words about the resurrected righteous becoming like angels (Mark 12:25) mean only that marriage will not be part of existence after the resurrection. He also apparently believed in an intermediate state between death and the final judgment, wherein the righteous poor would enjoy bliss in the presence of Abraham, while the wicked rich would suffer in flames in Hades (Luke 16:22-24).

Paul viewed the coming resurrection as the deliverance of creation from bondage, the preparation of the individual for eternal glorious life, and the triumph of Christ on God the Father's behalf (Rom. 8:19-23; 1 Cor. 15:23-28, 35-49). He does not refer in his letters to the wicked as being involved in the resurrection (cf. Acts 24:15). In response to questions that arose because of the death of some Christians, Paul described them as "those who are asleep" (1 Thess. 4:13; cf. 1 Cor. 15:18), but this use of a common euphemism for death need not imply any particular view of the intermediate state (cf. John 11:11-14). The possibility of his own death before the return of Christ did cause Paul to think more definitely about the time between death and resurrection, which he viewed negatively (2 Cor. 5:1-4), though he continued to believe that death would bring him immediately into the presence of Christ (v. 8; Phil. 1:23).

John of Patmos writes of the resurrection of Christian martyrs who will reign with Christ during the millennium, after which all the rest of the dead, good and evil, will rise to be judged by their recorded works, the roll of the saved already having been set down in the book of life (Rev. 20:4-6, 11-15). He also mentions an uncomfortable intermediate state of the martyrs (6:9-11).

The New Testament writers link the future general resurrection closely with the past event of Jesus' resurrection, which is regarded as the first stage of the general resurrection (1 Cor. 15:23; Col. 1:18), as the model of the future resurrection of believers (Phil. 3:21), as that which guarantees believers' resurrection (1 Cor. 15:17-20; 1 Thess. 4:14-16), and as instrumental to believers' resurrection (Rom. 8:11; 1 Cor. 15:21-22). Along with his death on the cross, Jesus' resurrection is considered essential to the present salvation of believers (Rom. 4:25; 1 Pet. 3:21).

While the resurrection of Jesus is thus a central event for the faith of the New Testament writers, the nature of the risen Jesus is portrayed in differing ways. Sometimes an effort is made to distinguish the nature of the resurrected Jesus from the nature of Jesus as he had lived before the cross, so that place can be made for his spiritual presence and his transcendent lordship (1 Cor. 15:44-45, 50; 1 Pet. 3:18; cf. Rom. 1:4). Thus Jesus is able to appear in closed rooms (John 20:19), to disappear suddenly (Luke 24:31), and to appear in forms other than a simple human being on earth (Acts 7:55-56; 9:3-5; 22:6-8; 26:13-15; cf. 1 Cor. 15:8). At other times, however, the physical humanness of Jesus after the resurrection is emphasized (Luke 24:36-43).

Mark, probably the earliest of the Gospels, announces the resurrection of Jesus and depicts his tomb as being empty (Mark 16:1-8). Appearances of the risen Jesus came to be described in the later Gospels (and in late additions to Mark; e.g., vv. 9-20), although 1 Cor. 15:5-7 shows that from earliest times preaching of the gospel included accounts of appearances of the risen Jesus. The account of the discovery of the empty tomb itself developed into a resurrection appearance story (compare Mark 16:1-8 with the parallels in the other Gospels), which then underwent development in different directions.

All of the resurrection appearance stories, however, have the same emphasis on the surprise the event produced in the followers of Jesus and on the risen Jesus' relation to the community of his followers, an emphasis that becomes especially important in references to Jesus' inauguration of the mission of the Church after his resurrection (Matt. 28:18-20; Luke 24:44-49; John 20:21-22; 21:15-17; Acts 1:6-8). It was to believers alone (and those who would become believers) that Jesus appeared, and it was as witnesses of the risen Jesus that the early preachers of the gospel spoke (v. 22; 2:32; 3:15; 4:33).

At some points, aspects of Jesus' burial, his resurrection, and his appearances after his resurrection are mentioned to help attest that his resurrection did, indeed, occur (John 20:20-27; 1 Cor. 15:5-7). His resurrection itself then is regarded as proof of what God is doing in salvation history (e.g., Acts 17:31).

The resurrection of Jesus and the coming general resurrection are used together as a metaphor for the spiritual experience of believers (Rom. 6:4; Eph. 2:5-6; Phil. 3:10; Col. 2:12-13; 3:1-3). This metaphor does not mean that the final physical resurrection was no longer expected (cf. Phil. 3:11; Col. 3:4), though its use did provide the basis for an overrealized eschatology that did deny the future resurrection (2 Tim. 2:18). Such a redefinition of "resurrection" was probably the basis for the problems addressed at 1 Cor. 15.

Bibliography. R. H. Fuller, *The Formation of the Resurrection Narratives* (Philadelphia: 1980); M. J. Harris, *Raised Immortal* (Grand Rapids: 1985); W. Künneth, *The Theology of the Resurrection* (St. Louis: 1965); G. E. Ladd, *I Believe in the Resurrection of Jesus* (Grand Rapids: 1975); P. Perkins, *Resurrection* (Garden City: 1984).

RETURN. * The immediate postexilic period, during which the exiled Israelites left Mesopotamia and resettled in their Palestinian homeland.

For biblical use of the verb "to return" (Heb. *šûḇ*; Gk. *metanoéō*) *see* REPENTANCE.

RETURN OF CHRIST. See SECOND COMING.

REU [rōō, rē′ū] (Heb. *rᵉʿû* "friend" or a short form of Reuel; Gk. *Rhagau*). A son of Peleg, descendant of Shem, and ancestor of Abraham and Jesus (Gen. 11:18-21; 1 Chr. 1:25; Luke 3:35; KJV "Ragau").

REUBEN [rōō′bən] (Heb. *rᵉʾûḇēn* "See, a son"). The firstborn of the twelve sons of Jacob and four sons of Leah (Gen. 29:31-32; 49:3), and the Israelite tribe descended from Reuben.

Reuben saved his brother Joseph's life by convincing the other brothers not to kill him, suggesting instead that they put him in a deep well, intending secretly to return and save Joseph. But Reuben's plan was foiled when the other brothers sold Joseph into slavery (37:21-30; cf. 42:22). Reuben also offered his own two sons as surety for the return of Benjamin, Joseph's full brother, from Egypt (v. 37). Yet Reuben lost favor by having sexual relations with his father's concubine, Bilhah (35:22; 49:4; 1 Chr. 5:1); the act may have represented or been interpreted as an attempt to usurp his father's authority (cf. 2 Sam. 3:7; 16:21-22).

Reuben was the father of Hanoch, Pallu, Hezron, and Carmi (Gen. 46:9). The tribe descended from these four sons, after helping the other tribes of Israel conquer the Canaanites (Num. 32:16-19), was given an allotment in the Transjordanian plateau north of the Arnon river and south of the region of Gad/Gilead (Josh. 13:15-23). The tribe was basically pastoral in economy and society. From the start the Jordan river seems to have isolated Reuben from the other tribes. The Song of Deborah chastises the Reubenites for staying with their flocks rather than joining in battle with the other tribes (Judg. 5:15-16; cf. Deut. 32:6). After the initial stages of their settlement Reuben, Gad, and Manasseh established their own Transjordanian center of worship, probably at Gilgal, an act that angered the other tribes; the center was then identified as a mere memorial, and war was averted (Josh. 22).

Some scholars believe, on the basis of 1 Chr. 5:1-10, 26, that the tribe of Reuben retained a distinct identity in Transjordan until all Transjordanian Israelites were taken into exile by Tiglath-pileser III (*ca.* 732 B.C.). Others contend that by the time of Saul (*ca.* 1020)

Reuben had already been absorbed into Gad and Moab.

The tribe may never have been large, as Deut. 33:6 clearly hints, and is always associated with the tribe of Gad (e.g., Num. 32:6, 33; 1 Chr. 26:32). The town lists of Num. 32:34-38 indicate that Gad had cities both north and south of Reuben. The Reubenite cities, on the other hand, take up a small area around Mt. Nebo, much smaller than Reuben's tribal allotment, which was occupied by Moab much of the time. The tribe of Reuben plays no part in the history of Israel after King Saul, although some individuals were identified as Reubenites in David's time (1 Chr. 11:42). The Moabite Stone (the Mesha stele, ninth century; *ANET*, p. 320) says that Gad "had always dwelt in the land of Ataroth," but it makes no mention of Reuben. Neither is Reuben mentioned in the census of David, though both Gad and Gilead are (2 Sam. 24:5-6).

Reuben is, however, assigned a place in the eschatological restoration of Israel (Ezek. 48:6, 31; Rev. 7:5).

REUEL [rōō′əl] (Heb. *rᵉʿûʾēl* "friend of God").
1. A son of Esau whose four sons were Edomite chiefs (Gen. 36:4, 10, 13, 17; 1 Chr. 1:35, 37).
2. A name used for the father-in-law of Moses, "the priest of Midian" (Exod. 2:18) who is usually called JETHRO. Reuel may be a clan name (cf. Num. 10:29; KJV "Raguel"; *see* HOBAB).
3. The father of Eliasaph, chief of the tribe of Gad (Num 2:14). He is also called Deuel (1:14; 7:42, 47; 10:20), which suggests that one of these forms has resulted from scribal error.
4. An ancestor of Meshullam of the tribe of Benjamin (1 Chr. 9:8).

REUMAH [rōō′mə] (Heb. *rᵉʾûmâ*). The concubine of Abraham's brother Nahor, and the mother of Tebah, Gaham, Tahash, and Maacah (Gen. 22:24).

REVELATION (Heb. verb *gālâ*; Gk. verbs *apokalýptō, dēlóō, phaneróō*, nouns *apokálypsis, phanérōsis, epipháneia*).† God's deliberate disclosure to mankind of true knowledge of himself and his purposes and actions on behalf of mankind.

I. Old Testament

The concept of a self-revealing God was fundamental to the experience of the people of Israel. This idea was anchored in the fundamental spiritual paradox that God cannot be known by mankind, because of both God's infinitude (Isa. 40:13-14; Job 11:7) and humanity's sinful condition (Hos. 4:1-6), but that happiness and productivity, even life itself, depend upon knowing God (Ps. 34:8-9 [MT 9-10]; 36:9 [MT 10]). Therefore God "gave himself" to be known. Revelation occurs when God's *word* tells of his *actions* (Isa. 41:26; 42:9; 48:6-7; Amos 3:7).

The knowledge of God with which the Old Testament is concerned is an experiential knowledge, the knowledge that one person has for another, rather than a merely factual knowledge. God reveals himself by involving himself personally in the history of his people. The Exodus was the primary event of revelation (Exod. 10:1-2; Deut. 4:37-39), but other events that convey knowledge of God are expected in both the present and the future (Ps. 100:3; Prov. 2:1-5; Ezek. 28:25-26; 37:6). See KNOW, KNOWLEDGE.

God reveals his true nature to Israel through the offer of his covenant (Gen. 12:1-3; cf. Ps. 89). By its terms he shows himself to be loving, saving, faithful, and holy (Lev. 11:44-45; 2 Kgs. 13:23; Isa. 43:1-7; Hos. 2:19-23). When it becomes apparent that Israel has failed to fulfill its own side of the covenant, Jeremiah prophesies a new covenant that God will reveal to the heart, with the purpose that "they shall all know me" (Jer. 31:31-34).

II. New Testament

The New Testament is built on the belief that with Christ a new step has been taken in God's self-revelation (Matt. 1:23; Luke 2:29-32; John 1:17-18; Heb. 1:12; 1 Pet. 1:10-12). Since Jesus is himself the incarnate God (John 1:1, 14), not only what he accomplished but who he is in every respect is a revelation of God. By knowing him, mankind knows God (Matt. 11:27; John 14:9; 2 Cor. 4:6).

In the opening chapters of Romans Paul summarizes the history of revelation: God gave himself to be known through his creation, but mankind "by their wickedness suppress the truth" and choose idolatry instead of worship of God (Rom. 1:18-28); God initiated a special effort of self-disclosure through the Law and prophets that the Jews possess (3:1-2), but they too failed in their particular responsibility so that all humanity was shown to be guilty of turning from the knowledge of God (vv. 9-20); finally, "apart from law" God gave himself to be known in Christ (vv. 21-22), especially in his death (v. 25), which reveals God's "righteousness," i.e., his saving action on behalf of mankind (1:17).

The Holy Spirit is the agent who brings revelation home to the human heart (John 14:26; 16:13-15; Rom. 8:15-16; 1 Cor. 2:10-12; Gal. 4:6). Paul's gospel was received by the revelation of Christ (1:11-12) and is consequently the word of God rather than a human word (Col. 1:25; 1 Thess. 2:13; cf. Rom. 1:16-17). The claim of the New Testament books to be the revelatory word of God is made on the basis of this understanding of the apostolic proclamation.

The word "revelation" is also used in the New Testament to describe a spoken prophecy given in the congregation to inspire obedience (Gal. 2:2) or understanding (1 Cor. 14:6, 26), or a more personal illumination (2 Cor. 12:1, 7). This is revelation in a subordinate and derived sense, subject to the authority of the unchanging gospel (1 Cor. 15:1-3; cf. 14:29). The second coming of Christ on the Day of the Lord is also sometimes called "the revealing of our Lord Jesus Christ" (1:7; 2 Thess. 1:7).

III. Theological Issues

The biblical idea of revelation is an indispensable element of the gospel of the self-giving God, and has always been a center of theological discussion. A particular focus of discussion of revelation since the second century A.D. has been the relative roles of reason and revelation in a person's understanding of God. Reason is, in this regard, that which receives both God's "special" revelation to his people and his "gen-

eral" revelation, i.e., what can be learned about God from the existence and order of the created world. Continuing debate about general revelation concerns the role of the created order as Paul discusses it at Rom. 1–2. Some interpreters see nature as a sure guide to certain kinds of knowledge about God, while others understand Paul to be denying that fallen humanity can read the message any longer. The important point for Paul is that God's "eternal power and deity" (1:20) are sufficiently evident in creation to condemn humankind for their determined evasion of the truth of God's lordship.

Another related question is whether it is truer to say that God reveals himself through propositions (i.e., statements about himself) or whether he reveals himself as a person. But this is a false dilemma, since any person becomes known by the gradual accumulation of relevant facts or impressions. The book of Proverbs is in large part a collection of propositions about wise living, and yet the key to its instruction and the goal of its pursuit of wisdom is knowledge of God (Prov. 1:7; 2:1-5).

Bibliography. G. C. Berkouwer, *General Revelation* (Grand Rapids: 1955); L. Morris, *I Believe in Revelation* (Grand Rapids: 1976).

REVELATION, BOOK OF.† The last book in the New Testament. Also called the Apocalypse, it is the only book of the New Testament completely written in apocalyptic style and language.

I. Authorship

The author of the book of Revelation introduces himself as John, a servant of Christ and a "brother" of the Christians in Asia (Rev. 1:1, 9). The early Church held that this was John the apostle, the author also of the fourth gospel and 1–3 John. But differences in language and theological emphasis led some as early as the third century to conclude that Revelation was written by someone besides the author of the other Johannine books. Papias (died 130) mentions two Johns in Asia who reminisced about the Lord: the apostle and "John the elder." It has been suggested that one of these was responsible for the Apocalypse and the other for the rest of the Johannine literature, or that different disciples of the apostle wrote the books. The question is further complicated by the thorny issue of the authorship of the fourth gospel, and each of these theories, including apostolic authorship of all of the books, finds advocates today. An increasing number of scholars, however, prefers to leave the matter open, simply affirming the witness of the text that the author was a Jewish-Christian prophet named John. SEE JOHN 8.

II. Origin and Date

John composed the Apocalypse either on the island of Patmos, on which he had been imprisoned for his Christian faith (1:9), or later at nearby Ephesus after his release. The persecution that had resulted in his imprisonment and the atmosphere of persecution that pervades Revelation (2:10, 13; 3:10; 6:9; 17:6; 18:24; 19:2) suggest a date of composition close to the Neronian persecution (A.D. 64-67) or that of Domitian (A.D. 95). While some have argued for the earlier

The island of Patmos, where the book of
Revelation was written (A. D. Baly)

date, most scholars accept the tradition of the early
Fathers that it was under Domitian that John was imprisoned. Emperor worship, referred to at 13:4, became a general custom only after Nero. The deterioration of some of the churches described in chs. 2–3 is
also considered evidence of the later date.

III. Language

The syntax and literary style of Revelation is inelegant
and sometimes crude. Its awkward grammar is perhaps the result of John's thinking in Aramaic and writing in Greek. The strangeness of the language is further
explainable by John's deep dependence on the Old
Testament and its imagery, as well as by the startling
subject matter he is expounding. The book combines
three biblical literary forms in a unique blend: as an
epistle (1:4), it is addressed to specific Christians at
a certain time and place; as an apocalypse (v. 1), it
embodies Christian truth in complex imagery and
speaks of events that have been determined before
their time and of a catastrophic end to history; and as
a prophecy (v. 3), it expresses urgent warning and encouragement to the Church.

IV. Canonicity

Revelation was more readily accepted by the Church
in the West than in the East. In the second century the
rationalistic "Alogi" of Asia Minor rejected its millennial promise; later, Dionysius of Alexandria and
Eusebius of Caesarea questioned its apostolic authorship. But in the fourth century Athanasius threw his
great influence toward its support. The book of Revelation was recognized as canonical by the Third Council of Carthage in the West (397) and by the Third
Council of Constantinople in the East (680).

V. Contents

Seven letters and a series of visions are bracketed by
a prologue (ch. 1) and an epilogue (22:6-21). The
prologue introduces the Apocalypse and sets it within
the perspective of the lordship of Christ over his Church
and over history. John's messages to each of the seven
churches in Asia Minor (chs. 2–3) probe their strengths
and weaknesses, and provide direction and encouragement as necessary. This is done in the urgency of
the impending calamities about to be revealed.
  Chs. 4–20 portray God's sovereign loosing of his

divine wrath upon the wickedness of the world, together with his love for and vindication of the faithful
Church. Chs. 4–5 show that Jesus, the redeemer, is
alone worthy to dispense the judgment of God to those
who had refused redemption. The judgment begins
with the breaking of seven seals of a scroll (ch. 6),
bringing destruction and death on the earth and its
inhabitants—but the people of God are "sealed" to
safety (ch. 7). The sounding of seven trumpets (chs.
8–11) unleashes ever more severe disaster, and the
murder and resurrection of two prophetic witnesses
produce widespread fear of God. Then a great heavenly drama is unveiled (chs. 12–15), depicting the
rise of the Church and its persecution by the powers
of darkness, as well as the rise of a demonic world
power. Seven bowls of wrath (ch. 16) bring climactic
ruin to the earth, the sun, and the stars, and a special
description is given of the final fall of "Babylon," the
cruel and blasphemous world government (chs. 17–
19). The process is completed with the victory of God
over Satan and the final judgment at the white throne
(ch. 20).
  Chs. 21–22 describe the majesty of the new heaven
and new earth, the eternal home of the Church. The
epilogue (22:6-21) reiterates the urgency of the message, and with it the offer of life.

VI. Interpretation

Because its apocalyptic language can be cryptic, Revelation has been interpreted in many different ways.
Luther remarked that "Revelation is not revealing,"
but others before and after him have found rich significance in its pages.
  Among the several main lines of approach to the
book's interpretation is the historicist position, which
finds references throughout the book to sequential developments in Church history; for instance, the command to prophesy from the open scroll of 10:8-11 is
sometimes related to the preaching of the Reformation. The futurist position can understand the seven
letters to the churches as depicting seven subsequent
ages of the Church's history, like the historicist approach, or as documents that speak to the situations
of the actual first-century churches addressed. But the
futurist position invariably interprets everything from
4:1 on to refer to the last few years of history, especially to the "great tribulation" of Matt. 24:21.
  Most likely the visions of Rev. 4–20 are to be thought
of not as descriptions of chronologically ordered events,
but as overlapping portrayals of human hubris and the
suffering of the Church as these might be experienced
at any time, and divine sovereignty in judgment as it
is expected in the end times. The most common approach to the book in modern scholarship sees the
Apocalypse as a response to a first-century situation,
valuable not for its prediction of future events but for
the continuing relevance of its understanding of the
conflict between human and divine power and the final
triumph of the divine. While this takes seriously the
historical setting of the book's imagery, it can fail to
do full justice to the book's claim to foretell events
(1:19; 4:1).
  In every age the book of Revelation has been a
source of speculation concerning the meaning of history and current events. Elaborate theories have some-

times been linked to destructive fanaticism. The other side of the picture is the comfort that Revelation has brought to every generation of believers, especially those who face distress or martyrdom. In an especially potent way, the book has served to communicate the truth of God's absolute lordship in the Church and the world, and the assurance of his final triumph.

See APOCALYPTIC; MILLENNIUM; SIX HUNDRED AND SIXTY-SIX.

Bibliography. G. R. Beasley-Murray, *The Book of Revelation,* rev. ed. NCBC (1981); G. B. Caird, *The Revelation of St. John the Divine.* HNTC (1966); R. H. Charles, *A Critical and Exegetical Commentary on the Revelation of St. John,* 2 vols. ICC (1920); A. Y. Collins, *Crisis and Catharsis* (Philadelphia: 1984); E. S. Fiorenza, *The Book of Revelation* (Philadelphia: 1985); R. H. Mounce, *The Book of Revelation.* NICNT (1977).

REWARD (Heb. *śāḵār, pᵉrî, šālam, ʿeqeḇ, gāmal;* Gk. *misthós, apodídōmi, antapódosis, misthapodosía*).† The idea of God's reward being given in response to the faithfulness of his people is explicitly stated as early as the Abrahamic covenant (Gen. 15:1). But already there it is made clear by the context that the reward is not deserved from God, but is rather an expression of God's grace toward the human covenant partner whom God has chosen. The reward is intended, nonetheless, as a motivation to faithfulness. God's reward is spoken of a number of other times in the Old Testament: Ruth was rewarded for choosing to join herself with Israel (Ruth 2:12); Saul hoped that David might be rewarded for being faithful and for sparing his life (1 Sam. 24:19 [MT 20]); and the people of God are rewarded for keeping God's law (Ps. 19:11 [MT 12]; Prov. 13:13) and for righteousness (Ps. 18:20 [MT 21]; 58:11 [MT 12]; Prov. 11:18). Where the nature of the reward is specified, it is most often prosperity and security in the land (e.g., Exod. 20:12; Lev. 25:18-19; 26:3-12).

With the eschatological focus of New Testament faith, God's reward becomes a more significant concept. It is to be withheld from those who are not distinguishable from others by righteousness (Matt. 5:46; 6:1) and from those who already "have their reward" in the human glory they seek and gain by their outwardly pious actions (vv. 2, 5, 16). God's reward is to be expected, however, by those persecuted for Jesus' sake (5:12; cf. Heb. 11:26) and those distinguished by true but hidden piety (Matt. 6:4, 6, 18). Those who respond positively to the preaching of the gospel will receive God's reward (10:41-42; Mark 9:41), as will those who do good when no earthly return can be expected (Luke 6:35), those who preach the gospel faithfully (1 Cor. 3:14), those who faithfully fulfill their role in life (Col. 3:24), and those who cling to the faith in the face of temptation to abandon it (Heb. 10:35; 2 John 8). In these contexts the reward intended is simply God's gift of eternal salvation (e.g., Matt. 25:34; Rev. 11:18). That the reward is given in response to "works" is certain (Matt. 16:27; Rom. 2:6; 1 Pet. 1:17; Rev. 22:12), but this does not mean that differentiation will be made among the rewards of the saved in response to the degree of their accomplish-

ments—an idea that appears, in fact, to be denied by Matt. 20:1-16.

See CROWN.

REZEPH [rē'zĕf] (Heb. *reṣep*). A city conquered by the Assyrians (2 Kgs. 19:12 par. Isa. 37:12). Rezeph (Akk. *Raṣappa*) was a caravan station north of Palmyra and a short distance south of the Euphrates river in Syria; possibly modern Rezzafeh. When the representatives of Assyria spoke of Rezeph to Hezekiah toward the end of the eighth century B.C., the city had already been incorporated into Assyria for about a hundred years.

REZIA (1 Chr. 7:39, KJV). *See* RIZIA.

REZIN [rē'zĭn] (Heb. *rᵉṣîn;* cf. *rāṣôn* "pleasing").
1. The last king of the Aramean kingdom of Damascus. According to the cuneiform reports of Tiglath-pileser III of Assyria (where Rezin's name appears as Akk. *Ra-ḫi-a-nu*), Rezin was forced to pay tribute to Assyria at the same time as Menahem of Israel (738 B.C.). Later, with Pekah of Israel Rezin tried to persuade Judah to join an anti-Assyrian alliance. When Jotham and then Ahaz of Judah rejected this plan, Syria and Israel invaded Judah and sought to install a pretender on its throne; they were unsuccessful, as the prophet Isaiah foretold (2 Kgs. 15:37; 16:5; Isa. 7:1-6). Tiglath-pileser captured Damascus and killed Rezin in 731 (2 Kgs. 16:9).
2. The progenitor of a family of temple sevants who returned from exile in Babylon (Ezra 2:48 par. Neh. 7:50).

REZON [rē'zən] (Heb. *rᵉzôn* "prince"). The son of Eliada who escaped from his master, King Hadadezer of Zobah, headed a "marauding band." Subsequently he founded the Syrian kingdom of Damascus and became, as the ruler of much of Syria, an enemy of Solomon (1 Kgs. 11:23-25). He may be the same as Hezion (15:18).

RHEGIUM [rē'jĭ əm] (Gk. *Rhḗgion*). A port city (modern Reggio di Calabria) on the Strait of Messina on the southern tip of Italy. Toward the end of Paul's journey to Rome his ship docked temporarily at Rhegium (Acts 28:13).

RHESA [rē'sə] (Gk. *Rhēsá*). A descendant of Zerubbabel and ancestor of Jesus (Luke 3:27).

RHODA [rō'də] (Gk. *Rhodē* "rose"). A servant in the house of Mary the mother of John Mark (Acts 12:13). After Peter's miraculous escape from prison, he went to Mary's house and knocked at the door. In her excitement at seeing him there Rhoda forgot to open the gate for him and was unable to convince the members of the household that the apostle was actually standing outside (vv. 14-15).

RHODES [rōdz] (Gk. *Rhodos*).† The largest of the Dodecanese islands of Greece in the southeast Aegean Sea off the southwest coast of Turkey. Rhodes was first settled in the Bronze Age. Dorian colonists who came later (*ca.* 1000 B.C.) founded three city-states, which would become important trade centers from which numerous other colonies were established throughout the Mediterranean region. The city of Rhodes, which came to be the primary city of the island, was founded in the fifth century. The island achieved its greatest prosperity when it became independent following the death of Alexander the Great. The Colossus of Rhodes, a huge statue of the sun-god straddling the entrance to the harbor of the city, added to the fame of the island for the few decades in the third century that it stood before being destroyed by an earthquake.

The Old Testament may refer to the people of Rhodes as a people related to Greece and who engaged in trade. The people called Heb. *dōḏānîm* (Gen. 10:4; some MT manuscripts, LXX, and Syr. at 1 Chr. 1:7) or *rôḏānîm* (1 Chr. 1:7) are named among the descendants of Javan (i.e., Greece). According to Ezek. 27:15 Tyre traded with the *bᵉnê dᵉḏān* (KJV "men of Dedan"), whom the LXX calls *huioí Rhodíōn* (RSV "men of Rhodes"). (The LXX does not show this difference in relation to other occurrences of *dᵉḏān*, which refer to an Arabian people, DEDAN.) The Hebrew letters daleth and resh were often confused, but it remains unclear to what peoples or regions *dᵉḏān* and *dōḏānîm* refer.

In the second century B.C. a weakened Rhodes entered a disadvantageous alliance with Rome. According to 1 Macc. 15:23, Rhodes was one of the places to which Rome sent letters confirming both its treaty with the Jews and the authority of the Jewish high priest Simon. Julius Caesar studied at the famous school of rhetoric on Rhodes. Paul stopped at Rhodes when returning from his third missionary journey (Acts 21:1).

RIB (Heb. *ṣēlāʿ*; Aram. *ʿalaʿ*).† A curved bone, often cartilaginous, attached to the spine and protecting the viscera. It was from one of Adam's ribs that God formed Eve (Gen. 2:21-23; cf. NIV mg.). The second beast in Daniel's vision has three ribs in its mouth (Dan. 7:5; NJV "fangs"). Elsewhere biblical usage is less precise, rendering the Hebrew term as "side," with reference to cultic furnishings (e.g., Exod. 25:12, 14; 26:20), side chambers of the temple (1 Kgs. 6:5-6; Ezek. 41:5), the leaves of a door (1 Kgs. 6:34), and the slope of a hill (2 Sam. 16:13; RSV "hillside"). The KJV also renders Heb. *ḥōmeš* as "rib" (e.g., 2:23; 4:6; RSV "belly"; NIV "stomach").

RIBAI [rī'bī] (Heb. *rîḇay* "Yahweh judges"). The father of Ittai (Ithai), one of David's mighty men (2 Sam. 23:29 par. 1 Chr. 11:31).

RIBLAH [rīb'lə] (Heb. *riḇlâ*). A city on the eastern shore of the Orontes river; modern Ribleh, *ca.* 34 km. (20 mi.) south-southwest of Homs. Riblah is one of the reference points in the definition of the ideal boundaries of the land to be occupied by Israel (Num. 34:11; cf. Ezek. 6:14; KJV "Diblath"). Following victories at Megiddo and Kadesh, Neco II established Egyptian military headquarters at Riblah and in 609 B.C. imprisoned King Jehoahaz of Israel (2 Kgs.

23:33). Here also the sons and leading officials of Zedekiah of Judah were killed by Babylonian conquerors and Zedekiah's eyes put out (25:6-7, 20-21; Jer. 39:5-7; 52:9-11, 26-27).

RIDDLE.† The most common English translation (another being "dark saying") of Heb. *ḥîḏâ* pl. *ḥîḏōṯ*), designating one of the common speech forms employed by the wise (Prov. 1:6). This term is paralleled by the more inclusive *māšāl* (usually "proverb") at Ps. 49:4 (MT 5); 78:2 (RSV "parable"); Prov. 1:6; Ezek. 17:2 (RSV "allegory").

A *ḥîḏâ* need not always be a riddle, but is distinguished by speech that is not immediately clear and requires interpretation. Thus God claims to speak to Moses directly, "not in *ḥîḏōṯ*" (Num. 12:8). At Ezek. 17:2 the *ḥîḏâ* is the allegorical story told at vv. 3-10, for which an interpretation is provided at vv. 11-15. The message requiring interpretation in Ps. 78 is the collection of stories concerning God's deliverance of the nation that has been handed down. The king who "understands riddles" (Dan. 8:23) might be one skilled in using "disinformation" (cf. NIV "master of intrigue"). Uses of *ḥîḏâ* in wisdom contexts (e.g., 1 Kgs. 10:1 [RSV "hard questions"]; Ps. 49:4 [MT 5]; Prov. 1:6) may refer to a particular form of philosophical discussion.

Riddles are known in most cultures and were a common form of entertainment in the ancient world, especially enjoyed as a diversion at feasts and banquets. The clearest biblical use of *ḥîḏâ* in the sense of a riddle occurs in the account of Samson's wedding feast (Judg. 14:12-19). Samson proposes a test involving the solution of a seemingly impossible riddle based on information known only to himself (v. 14). His opponents' answer is a riddle itself (v. 18), the answer to which (love) functions in the situation like a taunt. It is this element of contest that distinguishes the riddle from other forms of "dark speech."

RIGHT HAND (Heb. *[yāḏ] yāmîn*; Gk. *dexiá*).* The right side and right hand are generally associated in figurative language and symbolic use with strength, favor, and good fortune. God's right hand supports in time of battle (Ps. 18:35 [MT 36]; 118:15) and gives guidance (139:10).

A seat on the right side of the royal throne (or of God's throne) was a special position of honor and authority (1 Kgs. 2:19). The king's bride had the honor of standing at his right hand (Ps. 45:9 [MT 10]). In the Old Testament Satan could be an important enough figure in the heavenly court to merit a place at God's right hand (Zech. 3:1). At Ps. 110:1 God instructs the king, who will rule after God has quelled opposition, to sit in the honored place on God's right hand until that time has come. This verse and the notion of the victorious general gaining the seat of honor next to his king lie behind the frequent New Testament depictions of the relationship between Christ and God the Father as Christ's being seated at God's right hand (e.g., Mark 12:36; 14:62; Col. 3:1; Heb. 12:2).

For the "right hand" in terms of geographical orientation, *see* SOUTH; BENJAMIN 1.

RIGHTEOUS, RIGHTEOUSNESS (Heb. *ṣāḏaq, ṣaddîq, ṣeḏeq, ṣᵉḏāqâ;* Gk. *díkaios, dikaiosýnē, dikaíōma*).†

I. Old Testament

"Righteousness" is not simply an abstraction, but possesses a relational aspect set within the context of God's covenant with his people. Biblical usage thus differs from customary modern association of the word with absolute standards, indicating instead that some person, action, or thing meets or fulfills the requirements of a given relationship (e.g., weights, Lev. 19:36; RSV "just"; speech, Prov. 8:8; social and family relationships, Gen. 38:26). Righteousness is also the responsibility of the king and the judges, who are charged with preserving the covenant community (Deut. 16:18-19; 1 Kgs. 10:9; cf. 2 Sam. 8:15). In a dispute within the community judges are to decide in favor of the righteous, i.e., the "innocent" (RSV, Deut. 25:1; Heb. *ṣaddîq*) and uphold the cause of the defenseless (Ps. 72:1-2; Jer. 22:3; cf. Ps. 82:1-4). *See* JUST, JUSTICE.

God is, above all others, the righteous one (Isa. 24:16), the one who preserves the covenant relationship by delivering his people with righteous deeds (Judg. 5:11; RSV "triumphs"; 1 Sam. 12:7; RSV "saving deeds"; Mic. 6:5; RSV "saving acts"). God also upholds the cause of the oppressed (cf. Ps. 9:7-12 [MT 8-13]; 103:6; Prov. 22:22-23), gives justice to the innocent (1 Kgs. 8:32; cf. Isa. 50:8-9), and hears the suit of those in need (Ps. 7:9-11 [MT 10-12]; 35:23-24; Jer. 11:20; 12:1). He presses the case against rebellious Israel (cf. Isa. 3:13-15; Jer. 2:9; Hos. 4:1), and calls creation as his witness (Ps. 50:6; 98:7-9; cf. Mic. 6:1-2). Yet for the repentant God's righteousness takes the form of deliverance (Isa. 45:8; 61:10; cf. 51:4-5). The righteous God calls on his people to make the righteous response of keeping his law (Deut. 6:25; cf. Gen. 6:9) and doing justice (Deut. 24:10-13; Job 29:14-17). To do this is to gain life (Ezek. 18:5-9; Hab. 2:4).

II. New Testament

Part of Jesus' polemic against some of his contemporaries was to point out the distinction between outward righteousness or belief in one's own righteousness on the one hand and true righteousness on the other (Matt. 23:28; Luke 18:9). Within the new eschatological focus "righteousness" in the New Testament can stand for the salvation that God brings in the new age (Matt. 21:32; 2 Pet. 2:21), the ethical possibilities brought by this salvation (Heb. 12:11; Jas. 3:17-18), and the life of God's kingdom, now revealed (Matt. 6:33; 1 Pet. 3:14).

According to Paul, Christ is "our righteousness" (1 Cor. 1:30). God's eschatological revelation of his own righteousness takes place in the gospel of Christ (Rom. 1:16-17) and is received as a gift (5:17). This righteousness of God, which is distinguished from human righteousness (10:3; cf. Phil. 3:6, 9), is God's action for the salvation of mankind. Christ's cross is the "act of righteousness" that saves (Rom. 5:18). Through the sacrifice of Christ believers "become the righteousness of God" (2 Cor. 5:21). *See* JUSTIFICATION.

The Christian's righteousness has both forensic and ethical meanings. In the "legal" sense, it is participation in Christ's righteousness (1 Cor. 1:30; cf. 2 Pet. 1:1), an imputed standing possessed through faith (Rom. 9:30). Righteousness also may be the practical fruit that comes from this justification (Phil. 1:11), i.e., holiness that summons for God's use every element of life (Rom. 6:13, 19; Eph. 4:24). Both forensically and ethically righteousness remains a hope, awaiting its consummation in glory (Gal. 5:5; 2 Pet. 3:13).

Bibliography. J. Reumann, J. A. Fitzmyer, and J. Quinn, *Righteousness in the New Testament* (Philadelphia and New York: 1982); H. Seebass and C. Brown, "Righteousness, Justification," *DNTT* 3 (1978): 352-377.

RIMMON [rĭm′ŏn] (Heb. *rimmôn* "thunder"; Aram. *rammān*; Akk. *ramānu*) (**DEITY**). An epithet of the Syrian deity HADAD (**5**), whom the Syrian commander Naaman worshipped at Damascus (2 Kgs. 5:18; cf. Zech. 12:11, "Hadadrimmon").

RIMMON [rĭm′ŏn] (Heb. *rimmôn* "pomegranate" or "thunder") (**PERSON**). An inhabitant of Beeroth in Benjamin whose two sons, Baanah and Rechab, in an attempt to gain David's favor murdered Ishbosheth, the son of Saul, as he slept (2 Sam. 4:2, 5-12).

RIMMON [rĭm′ŏn] (Heb. *rimmôn* "pomegranate" or "thunder") (**PLACE**).

1. A town in the Negeb region of Judah (Josh. 15:32) settled by Simeonites (1 Chr. 4:32). It is identified with EN-RIMMON (Josh. 19:7; KJV distinguishes between Ain [En-] and Remmon [Rimmon]; cf. 15:32). In its prophecy about the future of the Judean hill country ("from Geba to Rimmon south of Jerusalem") Zech. 14:10 refers to this town. The name is preserved in modern Khirbet Umm er-Ramāmîm, 14 km. (9 mi.) north of Beer-sheba, but recent excavations suggest Tell Khuweilifeh (Tell Halif), slightly to the northwest.

2. A town on the boundary of the tribal territory of Zebulun (Josh. 19:13; KJV "Remmon-methoar" for "Rimmon it bends" [RSV]). The site is modern Rummâneh, *ca.* 10 km. (6 mi.) north-northeast of Nazareth. It was a levitical city of the Merarite branch of the Levites (1 Chr. 6:77 [MT 62]; Heb. *rimmônô;* LXX Gk. *Remmon;* RSV "Rimmono"). Dimnah (*dimnâ*) at Josh. 21:35 should probably be emended to Rimmon.

3. A rock near Gibeah. Near this place six hundred Benjaminites took shelter for four months before being permitted to return home after a group from their tribe had raped a Levite's concubine (Judg. 20:45, 47; 21:13-14). The place is generally associated with a rocky spur *ca.* 6 km. (4 mi.) east of Bethel, near the village of Rammûn.

4.* As part of an attempt to clarify the obscure final part of Isa. 10:27, the RSV (following a suggestion in *BH*) emends the last word, Heb. *šāmēn* "fat(ness)" (cf. KJV "anointing"), to "Rimmon" (*rimmôn*), taking the clause with what follows, the list of names of cities conquered by the Assyrian army as it approaches Jerusalem (vv. 28-32), rather than with what precedes. Some other locality may be referred to; that part of the emendation is least certain. Suggestions have included Samaria, Pene-yeshemon (near Gilgal), Bethel, and "the north."

RIMMONO [rĭ mō'nō] (Heb. *rimmônô*). Alternate form of RIMMON (PLACE) **2** (1 Chr. 6:77 [MT 62]; KJV "Rimmon").

RIMMON-PEREZ [rĭm'ŏn pĕr'ĕz] (Heb. *rimmōn pereṣ* "pomegranate of the breach [or 'pass']").† A place where the Israelites encamped following the Exodus (Num. 33:19-20; KJV "Rimmon-parez"). As with most other locations noted in connection with this journey, the exact location is unknown.

RING (Heb. *ṭabbaʿaṯ, ḥōṯām, nezem, ʿāḡîl*; Gk. *[chryso]daktýlios*). Rings were usually of gold (Gen. 24:22; Jas. 2:2). Finger rings, nose rings, and earrings were worn by women for ornamental purposes (Ezek. 16:12), sometimes in connection with worship of gods (Hos. 2:13 [MT 15]; cf. Gen. 35:4). For men, however, rings generally bore the personal signet of the wearer and so were symbols of authority (Gen. 41:42; Esth. 3:10; 8:8; Luke 15:22; see SEAL, SIGNET). Whether ornamental or as signets, rings represented wealth (Jas. 2:2) and were costly gifts (Gen. 24:22). In figurative language they could represent beauty (Prov. 11:22), or that which is of great value (25:12) or significance to a person (Jer. 22:24; Hag. 2:23).

RINNAH [rĭn'ə] (Heb. *rinnâ* "shout, cry"). A son of Shimon of the tribe of Judah (1 Chr. 4:20).

RIPHATH [rī'făth] (Heb. *rîpaṯ*). A people descended from Gomer (Gen. 10:3; "Diphath" at 1 Chr. 1:6). Josephus identified them with the Paphlagonians, but more recently other peoples in ancient Asia Minor have been suggested.

RISSAH [rĭs'ə] (Heb. *rissâ* "sprinkling [?]"). One of the places where the Israelites camped after their escape from Egypt (Num. 33:21-22). The exact location is unknown.

RITHMAH [rĭth'mə] (Heb. *riṯmâ* "broom plant"). One of the places where the Israelites camped after their escape from Egypt (Num. 33:18-19). Its exact location is unknown.

RIVER, THE.† A designation for the EUPHRATES (Heb. *hannāhār*; e.g., Gen. 31:21; 36:37; Exod. 23:31; 2 Sam. 10:16; the RSV usually "Euphrates") or NILE river (*yeʾōr*; e.g., Gen. 41:1-3, 17-18; Exod. 1:22; RSV "the Nile") or tributaries (e.g., 7:19; cf. 2 Kgs. 19:24; Isa. 7:18; RSV "streams").

RIZIA [rĭ zī'ə] (Heb. *riṣîâʾ*). A son of Ulla of the tribe of Asher (1 Chr. 7:39; KJV "Rezia").

RIZPAH [rĭz'pä] (Heb. *riṣpâ* "glowing coals"). Saul's concubine; the daughter of Aiah. Taken as an overt claim to the throne, Abner's alleged intimate relations with Rizpah after Saul's death led to a conflict between Abner and Saul's son Ishbosheth (2 Sam. 3:6-11). David gave Rizpah's two sons, Armoni and Mephibosheth, along with five of Saul's grandsons, to the Gibeonites, who hanged them in answer to Saul's bloodguilt against

the Gibeonites. When David learned that Rizpah was guarding the corpses against the attacks of wild animals and birds, he gave them a proper burial, as well as the bodies of Saul and Jonathan (21:8-14).

ROBE.† A reading used in English versions to represent a number of words (including Heb. *meʿîl, keṯōneṯ, beḡeḏ, ʾeḏer, ʾadderet, middâ*; Gk. *stolḗ, himátion, esthḗs*), generally for the main garment or an outer garment worn by a man or a woman, rich or poor, as a garment only for ceremonial occasions or one worn every day. Such garments were constructed in a number of ways. Often one might wear a simple rectangular piece of material with a hole in the center for the head. An outer garment might be of a single piece of material wrapped around the body, and perhaps joined with a pin at one shoulder. A robe with sleeves was distinctive enough to merit mention as such, and was indicative of honor, wealth, or position (Gen. 37:3, 23; 2 Sam. 13:18).
See TUNIC.

ROBOAM (Matt. 1:7, KJV). *See* REHOBOAM.

ROCK (Heb. *selaʿ, ṣûr*; Gk. *pétra*).† Because of the rocky lands in which the people of the Bible lived (*see* SELA), it was natural that they used figures of speech referring to stones or rocky places. "Rock" has varied connotations, sometimes involving hardness (Jer. 5:3; 23:29), shade from the desert sun (Isa. 32:2), or the open visibility of a cliff (Ezek. 24:7-8). Most often it represents secure, stable, and immobile support, such as the stability that God gives to life (Ps. 40:2 [MT 3]; Matt. 7:24-27; Luke 6:48). Faithful Israelites are urged to recall the solidity of their heritage in the covenant of God with Abraham and Sarah (Isa. 51:1-2). At Matt. 16:18 the Church is said to be founded upon a rock and therefore able to withstand enemy assaults.

A frequent epithet of God in the Old Testament is "rock" or "the Rock," often in archaic or archaizing poetry, and specifically related to the nation Israel (Deut. 32:4; 1 Sam. 2:2; Ps. 78:35; Isa. 30:29; Hab. 1:12) or an individual (2 Sam. 22:2-3; Ps. 28:1; 42:9 [MT 10]; 71:3; 92:15 [MT 16]; 144:1). This figure also recalls the military advantage of a secure fortress built on or into a cliff, eminently defensible because of its height and solidity (Ps. 61:2 [MT 3]; cf. Obad. 3).

Paul develops the image of the divine rock when he identifies Christ as the "supernatural Rock" that followed the Israelites through the wilderness (1 Cor. 10:4). In doing so he combines the concept of God as a rock with another Old Testament theme—the appearance of water from the rock during the Exodus (Exod. 17:6; Num. 20:8-11)—which is referred to in the Old Testament as an example of God's provision for his people (Neh. 9:15; Ps. 78:15-16, 20; 105:41; Isa. 48:21). Paul uses the tradition in the same way, adding that all Israelites were thus provided for and thus demonstrating the unity of the nation. More significantly, he identifies the rock with Christ himself and views the different occasions when water came from the rock as manifestations of Christ, the single divine rock who not only defends his people but also provides for their needs.

The foundation "rock" of the Church referred to at Matt. 16:18 has been of importance for the Roman Catholic view of the Petrine papacy. The traditional Catholic interpretation of this verse, which developed early in the Church, holds that the "rock" is Peter himself, who was chief among the apostles and the first to preach the gospel to both Jews and Gentiles (Acts 2, 10). Two basic views of Matt. 16:18 have been put forward as alternatives to the Catholic view. According to one, the "rock" is Peter's confession of Jesus as Christ and Son of God (vv. 15-17). This view, also held very early in the Church, takes into account not only the similarity between Gk. *pétra* and *Petros* (the name given to Peter by Jesus, which designates a smaller stone) but also their difference in this context: the confession to which Peter holds is the basis of his strength, yet it is not unique to him but is shared by all the apostles (considered foundational to the Church at Eph. 2:20), of whom he is merely the chief. Another interpretation is that *pétra* refers to Christ himself; this view draws upon the Old Testament predictions of Christ as God's chosen cornerstone and a rock over which mankind will stumble (Ps. 118:22; Isa. 8:14; 28:16; Acts 4:11; Rom. 9:33; 1 Pet. 2:4-8). *See* PETER.

ROCK BADGER (Heb. *šāpān*).† A representative of the order *Hyracoidea,* which are small ungulate mammals. The rock badger (*Procavia syriaca*), also called the Syrian coney, resembles a rabbit except that it has much smaller ears. It prefers rocky areas (Ps. 104:18; Prov. 30:26; RSV "badgers"; KJV "conies") and can be found in the hills around the Jordan valley, the southern deserts of Israel, and the hills surrounding the Sea of Galilee. It was considered unclean, but was mistakenly placed among cud-chewing animals (Lev. 11:5; Deut. 14:7; KJV "coney").

ROD (Heb. *šēḇeṭ, maṭṭeh, maqqēl, ḥōṭer*; Gk. *rhábdos*).† Any kind of substantial branch or stick used as a weapon (Isa. 10:26), as an instrument of miracle-working and magic (so "Aaron's rod," Exod. 4, 7–8; Num. 17, 20), or for corporal punishment (e.g., Exod. 21:20; 2 Sam. 7:14; Ps. 89:32; Prov. 14:3; 2 Cor. 11:25; cf. Deut. 25:2-3). The "rod" (*šēḇeṭ*) and "staff" of the shepherd (Ps. 23:4) are, respectively, a club for driving away predators (Ezek. 20:37) and the shepherd's crook used for guiding the sheep. *See* SCEPTER; STAFF.

RODANIM [rō'də nĭm] (Heb. *rôḏānîm*). A people descended from Javan (i.e., Greece; 1 Chr. 1:7). *See* DODANIM; RHODES.

ROE, ROEBUCK. *See* DEER; GAZELLE.

ROGELIM [rō'gə lĭm] (Heb. *rōḡᵉlîm* "fullers"). The home of Barzillai the Gileadite (2 Sam. 17:27; 19:31 [MT 32]). A location often suggested for Rogelim is Bersînyā, *ca.* 25 km. (15 mi.) north of the Jabbok and 17 km. (10.5 mi.) southeast of the Sea of Galilee in northern Gilead.

ROHGAH [rō'gə] (Heb. Q *rohgâ,* K *rôhᵃgâ*). A son of Shemer of the tribe of Asher (1 Chr. 7:34).

ROMAMTI-EZER [rō măm'tĭ ē'zər] (Heb. *rōmamtî 'ezer* "I have gloried in help").† A Levite and son of Heman; leader of the twenty-fourth division of singers during the days of David (1 Chr. 25:4, 31). Though the names in v. 4 are regarded as personal names later in the same chapter (vv. 13-31), many scholars have concluded that beginning with Hananiah or with Hanani the names actually represent a confused bit of poetic prayer, misinterpreted by the editor of the later part of the chapter as a continuation of the immediately preceding list of names. Redivided and repointed, these names yield: "Be gracious, Lord, be gracious to me; you are my God, whom I magnify and exalt, a helper in the midst of trouble; I spoke and he gave visions abundantly."

ROMANS (Gk. *Rhōmaioi*). A designation of persons in one or more of four categories: representatives of the foreign government to which the Jews were subject (John 11:48; Acts 25:16; 28:17); Jews who had been born in Rome or who lived there (2:10); those who claimed an allegiance to the Roman Empire that (it is implied) others did not possess (16:21); and those who possessed Roman citizenship (vv. 37-38; 22:25-29; 23:27). By law Roman citizens could not be flogged or crucified, and when on trial could appeal to the emperor.

ROMANS, LETTER TO THE.† The sixth book of the New Testament, and the longest of Paul's letters. Romans has become for the Church the Bible's most comprehensive guide to the structure of the Christian faith. As such it has often stood behind renewals of life and thought in the Church, including those associated with the names of Augustine, Luther, Calvin, Wesley, and Barth.

I. The Church at Rome

The New Testament is silent about the beginning of the Roman church. It had been in existence for some time when Paul wrote his letter (cf. Rom. 1:8), and it was only later that Paul had his first face-to-face contact with the Roman Christian community (Acts 28). Peter addressed "visitors from Rome" in his Pentecost message (2:10), so the first Christians in the city may have been Jewish and proselyte pilgrims returning from the Jewish feast day. Furthermore, Christian travelers and traders no doubt carried the gospel with them to Rome. Christian missionary work among Jews, who had settled in Rome as early as the second century B.C., may have caused the disturbances among the Jews (which the Roman historian Suetonius attributes to "the instigation of Chrestus"; *Claud.* xxv.4) that led to their expulsion from the city by Claudius in A.D. 49 (18:2). When many Jews returned to Rome after the death of Claudius in 54, the church there again comprised both Jewish and Gentile Christians (cf. Rom. 1:13; 2:17-25; 7:1; 11:13).

II. Origin

Romans was written from Corinth near the end of Paul's third missionary journey, just before his journey to Jerusalem (Rom. 16:25-27; cf. Acts 20:1–21:15). Phoebe of the church at Cenchreae (Rom. 16:1), a harbor of Corinth, probably traveled with the letter, which was written *ca.* A.D. 56.

III. Major Textual Difficulties

The nature of Romans is complicated by a number of textual problems. (1) In different manuscripts the doxology (16:25-27) is included at the end of ch. 14, at the end of ch. 15, at the end of ch. 16, at the end of both chs. 14 and 16, or not at all. (2) Origen reports that Marcion's text ended at 14:23. (3) According to an ancient list of chapter headings, chs. 15 and 16 (except for the doxology) are excluded from some Latin manuscripts. (4) A small number of sources omit "in Rome" at 1:7, 15. To these textual data can be added the non-Pauline language and ideas of the doxology, the long list of greetings to a church Paul has never visited (16:3-15), and the Asian (rather than Roman) connection of three of those greeted (vv. 3 [cf. 1 Cor. 16:19], 5).

According to one theory Paul intended Romans for a wide audience, and ch. 16 was appended to the copy sent to Ephesus in Asia. Another view sees ch. 16 as what remains of a letter to Ephesus that fortuitously became connected to the letter to Rome.

But the large number of greetings is no problem in a letter written to a church with which Paul has not been in direct contact (cf. Col. 2:1; 4:10-17), especially if it is supposed that Paul meant by the greetings to strengthen his credibility in a situation where some did not know him. The Asian focus of the greetings is not established. Prisca and Aquila had lived in Rome before (Acts 18:2) and may have returned after Claudius' death. The identification of Epaenetus as the first Asian convert (Rom. 16:5) would be less necessary to an Asian address than to a Roman address. Such movement as is thus assumed was not at all uncommon in the empire.

The textual difficulties are best explained as the complicated results of attempts (by the omission of "in Rome" and the greetings) to make a document of universal significance out of a letter that began with a specific address. Different copies thus came to have different endings, and further copyists had to do what they could to reconcile them. The doxology may well be, however, a non-Pauline addition.

IV. Purpose and Contents

The debate concerning the purpose of Romans has been centered on the question of whether the letter is addressed to some situation within the church at Rome or should instead be thought of more as a summary of positions Paul had reached in his Asian and Greek ministry. Both perspectives are necessary for an understanding of the letter.

In his career as apostle to the Gentiles Paul dealt again and again with three dangers: that of the forced submission of Gentile Christians to living like Jews by the requirements of the Torah; that of disunity between Jewish and Gentile Christians, or more specifically, between those who lived by the Torah and those who did not; and that of Gentile Christians falling into their former pagan way of life. When Paul wrote to the Roman Christian community, which actually was not a single congregation but a number of house churches (Rom. 16:5, 14-15), apparently both legalism and antinomianism existed there. Rom. 14:1–15:6, though it should not be read too closely for specific details (based as it is on traditional materials and on Paul's earlier thoughts; cf. 1 Cor. 8–10), provides some idea of these opposite tendencies. This disunity was perhaps exacerbated by the expulsion and return of Jewish Christians and by the immigration of Christians from the east, including some from Pauline churches (Rom. 16:3-11) who would be associated with one who was thought of as an antinomian (3:8; 7:7; 9:1-5; 10:1-2; 11:1-2). A two-sided church calls forth a letter that must fight on several fronts.

Paul writes that he has been wanting to preach the gospel to the Roman Christians (1:15); by this method, an exposition of the gospel, he deals in his letter with the conflicts and problems within their community. His main purposes in this exposition are to encourage the mutual acceptance of each other by Christians who live by Torah and Christians who do not, and to set before them a position on Christian life and ethics that is totally determined neither by law nor by freedom. He also hopes to prepare the Roman Christians for his own arrival, and seeks their support and prayers as he goes on his possibly dangerous mission to Jerusalem (1:10-15; 15:23-32).

At 1:18–4:25 Paul shows how Jews and Gentiles are consistently equal in sin, in justification, and in the blessing of Abraham received by faith: "God shows no partiality" (2:11). All are also equal in Adam's legacy, sin and death, and in Christ's act of righteousness for life (5:12-21). Most of the hortatory section of the letter (12:1–15:13) focuses on love and acceptance in the Church (ch. 12; 13:8–15:13). The defense of mutual acceptance at 14:1–15:13 is summed up in the principle "welcome (i.e., 'accept') one another" (15:7), which finds its application in Jewish-Gentile relations in the Church (vv. 8-12).

But equality is not sameness. The special place in salvation history of Israel and the Jews is recognized even while Paul is showing the equality of Jews and Gentiles (2:9-10, "the Jew first"; 3:1-2, 19). Paul's heavy use of the Old Testament shows the continuity of the gospel with God's earlier work in Israel. Paul underlines his case for mutual acceptance by setting out the different places in salvation history of both Israel and the Gentiles (chs. 9–11). The result of God's work in Israel and in Christ is the praise of a Jewish Christian among the Gentiles (15:9) and the rejoicing of the Gentiles with the Jews (v. 10), a picture of mutual acceptance.

As Paul writes on the Mosaic law (ch. 7; cf. 3:19; 4:9-12) he has a message for each side of the conflict in Rome. To the antinomians he writes that the law is good (7:12). To the legalists he writes that the law cannot justify or free from sin. Not the law, but the experience of God's act in Christ, is the basis of Christian ethical behavior (8:3-4). But this freedom from the law is not license to sin (5:20-6:23; 13:11-14).

Near the end of his letter, Paul becomes more specific as he writes about divisive leaders (16:17-20). Here he probably has in mind both intransigent leaders in Rome and the anti-Pauline preachers he has already encountered.

See JUSTIFICATION; LAW.

Bibliography. C. K. Barrett, *The Epistle to the Romans*. HNTC (1957); C. E. B. Cranfield, *A Critical and Exegetical Commentary on the Epistle to the Romans*, 2 vols. ICC (1975-1979; abridged in 1 vol., Grand Rapids: 1985); K. P. Donfried, ed., *The Romans Debate* (Minneapolis: 1977); E. Käsemann, *Commentary on Romans* (Grand Rapids: 1980); J. Murray, *The Epistle to the Romans*. NICNT (1959-1965; repr. 2 vols. in 1, 1968).

ROME (Gk. *Rhōmē*; Lat. *Roma*).† The empire that had its capital at Rome was of inestimable significance in shaping the world of the New Testament, not only because of its political and economic consolidation of the entire Mediterranean region, but also because of the sharing of cultures across borders that was made possible by the empire and its encouragement of an international culture. The empire united Western Europe, all of the Mediterranean region, and most of the Fertile Crescent under one capital.

I. Early Rome and the Republic

Evidence of occupation on the site of the city of Rome can be traced from the mid-eighth century B.C. These settlements grew through that century and the following into a substantial group of communities throughout the seven hills on which the city was to be built (the Capitoline, Palatine, Quirinal, Viminal, Esquiline, Caelian, and Aventine hills). During the sixth century these settlements coalesced into a city-state with considerable importance in Italian trade, but still under Etruscan domination.

The culture that was becoming dominant in Rome in these early centuries was mainly Eastern, being transmitted by Phoenicians, Etruscans, and, above all, Greeks. Phoenician influence came through trading contacts (though no Phoenician colony was ever established in Italy). The Etruscans settled in Etruria, a region north of Rome, coming perhaps from Asia Minor in the eighth century. It was from the Etruscans that Rome received, among other elements of civilization, an adapted form of the Greek alphabet. Greek colonies were established in Italy from the eighth century.

The last king of Rome, an Etruscan, was expelled from the city, according to tradition, in 509, the Republic being established in place of monarchy. At that time, in the late sixth century, Etruscan power in the Mediterranean and the connections between Phoenician and Greek colonies and their eastern homelands were weakening. Military conflicts among Phoenician, Etruscan, and Greek colonies led to Rome's rise and conquest of these peoples in the western Mediterranean. But Roman power in Italy was not stable until after the fifth century, and Roman culture fell from the achievements it had made under the earlier kings until the third century. Gallic raids in the early to mid-fourth century nearly destroyed Rome.

But by 264 Rome had conquered all of the Italian peninsula. By 201 it had gained control of the western Mediterranean region from Spain to the Dalmatian coast through its first and second wars with the Phoenician city of Carthage in northern Africa (the first in 264-241 and the second in 218-201). The patterns that would be followed by Roman conquest were established in the fourth and third centuries. Native populations were not utterly destroyed, and their political structures often remained in place, but took on a client state relationship to Rome, if they were not replaced by Roman provincial government. Colonies of Roman citizens were established in conquered lands (including Philippi in Macedonia; Acts 16:12, 21). Roman citizenship was more and more broadly granted, until in A.D. 212 it was held by almost all free men in the Mediterranean region.

After 200 B.C. the weakness of the Hellenistic kingdoms of the East, long at war with each other and now threatened by Parthia, drew Rome eastward. Engaged in war with Antiochus III of the Seleucid Empire from 192 to 188 B.C., Rome won control of western Asia Minor (taking Antiochus' son hostage at the time; 1 Macc. 1:10). Roman forces halted Antiochus IV's campaign against Egypt in 167, and he turned against Jerusalem (Dan. 11:30). Roman support of Judea in its struggle against Antiochus IV and his successors was one aspect of Roman efforts to keep the Seleucid monarchy under control. A treaty in which Rome was by far the more powerful partner was made with Judas the Maccabee (161; 1 Macc. 8) and renewed by his brothers Jonathan (*ca.* 144; 12:1-4, 16; cf. 14:16) and Simon (*ca.* 140; v. 24; 15:15-24). Roman support of the Hasmoneans was a decisive factor in the success of the revolt of the latter (14:38-40).

By 133 B.C. Rome controlled almost all of the Mediterranean region as far as western Asia Minor. With this military and political expansion came also Rome's adaptation of much of the culture of the conquered lands, particularly Hellenistic culture.

In the 60s of the first century B.C. Pompey was Rome's great conqueror in the eastern Mediterranean. He brought inland and northern Asia Minor under Roman control by defeating Mithridates VI Eupator of Pontus, as also southern Asia Minor, which had been mainly under the control of pirates. He also brought Syria and Palestine into Rome's growing empire, bringing the Seleucid monarchy to its end. Rival Jewish factions disagreed on what to do when Pompey arrived at Jerusalem, but those who wished to open the city gates to him did so. Those who resisted Pompey held out against the Romans for three months in the temple area. Having conquered the temple, Pompey entered the holy of holies, a great sacrilege in Jewish eyes. The Psalms of Solomon are the response of one Jewish group to the Roman conquest of Jerusalem.

The government of the Roman republic was not sufficient to control the vast empire that was developing under Roman control or even to control Italy with all the changes that had been brought about there by the conquests beyond Italy. Tensions grew through the second and first centuries B.C. One response to the tensions that was to be of great significance later was the attempt to curtail the influence of foreign religions in Rome and Italy. In 139 B.C. Jews and astrologers were expelled from Rome.

II. Rome under the Emperors

A century of conflict, often bloody, in the government of Rome began in 133 B.C. The chaos of the early 40s B.C. issued in Julius Caesar's dictatorship. This ended the Republic, but the relative stability of imperial government came only after Caesar. The designation of Octavian (usually referred to by the title Augustus), Caesar's grand-nephew and adopted son, together with Antony and Lepidus as the second triumvirate in 43 B.C. sealed the end of the Republic. The conflict between Antony and Octavian was decided in the battle of Actium and ended with the suicide of Antony and his ally Cleopatra VII Philopator of Egypt (30 B.C.). Theoretically the Republic continued to exist, but from 27 B.C. Octavian was master of the Roman world.

What actually established control by one man as the new Roman pattern of government was Octavian's bringing peace and efficient government to Italy and the provinces and the fact that he lived long enough (to A.D. 14) to permit such a form of government to begin to be taken for granted. The growth of cultural expression during the reign of Augustus is testimony to the new possibilities brought by relative peace, security, and prosperity. This was the age of the poets Virgil, Horace, and Ovid, of Livy and other historians, and of great building projects and smaller art forms. The models in literature, art, and architecture were Greek, but a distinct Roman spirit emerged. But the blessings of the Augustan age were not unmixed. Before the death of the emperor, literature had declined, to a large extent the result of the concentration on autocratic government as essential to the state's survival.

Because of the combination of Republican ideals and dictatorial realities that came to characterize the government of Rome during Augustus' principate, succession to the throne became a difficult matter. The Julio-Claudian line formed by the marriage of Augustus (adopted into the Julian family) and his wife Livia (a Claudian) supplied the rulers through A.D. 68. But hereditary succession could not be fully accepted where the ruler theoretically received his power from the people and where armies could be the deciding factor. Tiberius (ruled 14-37), Augustus' son, was accepted relatively easily, but Claudius (41-54) was installed by the Praetorian Guard against the opposition of the Senate, and provincial armies rebelled against Nero (54-68). Warring armies placed three men in succession on the throne after the death of Nero and removed them as well. A new dynasty, the Flavians, began with Vespasian (69-79) and continued with his sons Titus (79-81) and Domitian (81-96). During the first century A.D. despotism was emerging as the style of Roman rule, but the following century saw some moderation of this as the Senate gained in power and the ruling families of the first century passed from the throne.

The dominant factor during both centuries was the Pax Romana, the relative peace and security achieved by political unification and a strong military (though these were not often accompanied by efficiency in government as the bureaucracy of the empire grew). It was this that allowed Paul, for instance, to carry his message freely across borders without the threat of war or pirates. A cultural consolidation accompanied the Pax Romana. This cultural consolidation meant, among other things, that the Latin language became dominant in the West, and Greek in the East. Forms

of entertainment (such as gladiatorial shows), social structures, and involvement in Roman-style politics were shared from Rome to the provinces. One can speak of "Greco-Roman culture" most clearly in connection with the first and following centuries A.D.

The Pax Romana was not effective in all parts of the empire. Indeed, it was least effective in Egypt and Judea (for the latter *see* JEWISH REVOLTS). Resistance by some, but by no means all, Jews against Roman political domination was to some extent coupled with resistance to Greco-Roman culture; military and political domination and cultural domination worked together as they had during the Maccabean period. The Pax Romana was also ineffective for the lower classes; social stratification increased, so increasing prosperity did nothing to improve the lives of many.

III. The City

Under Augustus the city gained a number of magnificent buildings, and marble was used far more than it had been before. Particularly important were complexes of new buildings in the Forum, in the Campus Martius outside the city walls to the northwest, and the Pantheon. The sponsorship of magnificent building projects in the capital city came to be a normal part of imperial rule. The most prominent of these buildings, the Colosseum, was built in A.D. 72-80 under the sponsorship of Vespasian and Titus. In the first century A.D. Rome was at the height of its growth. A large number of public buildings, most built by the emperors, were in the heart of the city. Yet while the lavish homes of the wealthy reflected the prosperity of the empire, more than a million poor people lived in blocks of multi-story tenements.

A Jewish community existed in Rome from the second century B.C. and was augmented by Jewish prisoners brought to the city by Pompey and freed in 62 B.C. A Christian community existed in Rome probably before 49 (cf. Acts 18:2).

Except for 28:14-31, which tells of Paul's arrival in Rome and the beginning of his testimony to the Jewish leaders of the city, and possibly some allusions in the book of Revelation, the New Testament records no actual incidents occurring in the city of Rome. But the city does not escape mention, which is to be expected in view of its domination of the world of the time. It was a great desire of Paul to go to Rome (19:21; 23:11; Rom. 1:15; 15:23, 28-29, 32), in line with his ambition to take the gospel to all the Gentile world (1:14; 11:13). "Babylon" came to be used as a figure of speech for Rome in view of its power and its persecution of God's people (1 Pet. 5:13; Rev. 14:8; 16:19; 17:5; ch. 18). Both Paul (cf. 2 Tim. 1:17) and Peter ended their lives in Rome as martyrs for the gospel (*see* MAMERTINE PRISON).

IV. Persecution of Christians

Roman persecution of Christians was based on the Roman experience of the effects of foreign cults on the unruly crowds of the capital (see above in connection with Jews and astrologers), on the secretiveness (both actual and reputed) of Christians, which generated false but believable tales of Christian practices, and, ultimately for official persecution, on consistent Christian refusal to sacrifice to the state gods or the emperor. Christians did not have the advantage of Jews, whose strange religion could at least be identified as the ancient faith of a particular land and people and thus had long been extended official protection.

Persecution as an expression of official policy, at least of a consistent nature, did not begin until after the New Testament period. Persecution is a frequent theme in the New Testament, but what is reflected are localized incidents not founded on Roman policy (like the localized expressions of anti-Semitism that were also generally not countenanced by Rome). The book of Revelation refers to Roman persecution, but the book seems to be predicting a crisis on the basis of the tendency of the pagan imperial power more than speaking of actual experiences; Revelation may well have been written when Domitian was emperor (A.D. 81-96), and there is little evidence of a general persecution of Christians during his reign.

Until A.D. 250 persecution of Christians was mostly local. The correspondence between Pliny and the Emperor Trajan (111-112) shows that although Christianity was against the law, the law was not routinely enforced. After 250 the persecutions were empire-wide and had the objective of ridding the empire of all Christians. The accession of Constantine to a share of the throne in 306 (sole emperor in 323) marked the beginning of a new experience of toleration and even power for Christians in the Roman world.

V. The Legacy of Rome

Rome continues to be very much alive in that it passed on to subsequent Western civilization, which has become dominant in nearly all parts of the world, the social, legal, and cultural structures that it both inherited and modified, on the one hand, and invented, on the other.

Rome mediated Greek styles of art and architecture to the Western world, along with some of its own modification and invention in these areas. Even where it was dominated by what it borrowed, therefore, it has performed a function that Greece, or any other culture influencing Rome, could not have done alone.

The basis of a number of modern languages is Latin, which is testimony itself to the size and power of the Roman Empire. Latin has also been the one language, above others, in which the Western Church's thought has been expressed. The literature of Rome itself, much of which remains and is read today, has been of great influence on the literary forms of the Western world. In particular, Cicero's oratory has been one of the greatest influences on prose styles of the Western world up to the present.

The philosophical styles and movements of Rome have had their legacy in the centuries following the empire. One need only think of the influence of Stoic ethical thought through Christianity (evidenced already with the New Testament) or of the Neoplatonic basis of Augustine's thought.

Under Rome a person might be loyal as a slave or a child (or in some other role) to the household ruled by its paterfamilias, to the ancient city-state (which might carry on its existence as a province or part of a province), to the empire under Caesar, to one's own social class, and to religious observances dictated by any or all of these as well as by personal convictions.

This complexity of social relations was partly the outgrowth of the empire's replacement of the localized polis, as that by which persons defined themselves, with the larger cosmopolitan world. This complexity paved the way for the variety of manners in which persons have chosen to organize and govern themselves and for the conflicts that result. Furthermore, the rise of other-worldly religion with a focus on the individual as an escape from a world over which one has no influence, rather than as a society's means of encountering the world with greater forces from outside the world, can be thought of as partly a product of the removal of government from the locality to the emperor and his bureaucrats and army. Such an understanding of religion is still of great importance today.

The Roman Republic was founded on rule by written law, and on the principle that citizens have not only rights that the state cannot violate but also duties toward that state. Despite all of the Republic's failures to live up to these principles, and even despite the realities of the empire, these principles were transmitted to the Western world from Rome in both state and Church. The structural relation of state and state religion, whether pagan or Christian, was also carried on beyond the life of the empire in the nation states of Christendom.

Bibliography. J. P. V. D. Balsdon, *Rome: The Story of an Empire* (New York: 1968); P. A. Brunt, *Social Conflicts in the Roman Empire* (New York: 1971); F. C. Grant, ed., *Ancient Roman Religion* (Indianapolis: 1957); M. Hadas, *A History of Rome from Its Origins to 529 A.D. as Told by the Roman Historians* (Garden City: 1956); M. I. Rostovtzeff, *Social and Economic History of the Roman Empire*, 2nd ed., 2 vols. (Oxford: 1957); C. G. Starr, *Civilization and the Caesars* (Ithaca: 1954).

ROOF (Heb. *gāg, qôrâ*; Gk. *stégē*). In biblical times the roof of a house was normally part of the house's living space. One might sleep on the roof (1 Sam. 9:25), engage in mourning (Isa. 15:3; Jer. 48:38), offer sacrifices and other forms of worship (19:13; Zeph. 1:5), or build a guest room on the roof (2 Kgs. 4:10). Since so much activity took place there, Deut. 22:8 directs that a parapet be built around the roofs of houses.

ROSE. Heb. *ḥᵃbaṣṣeleṭ* (Cant. 2:1; RSV, KJV "rose [of Sharon]"; Isa. 35:1; RSV "crocus") refers not to the rose (genus *Rosa* of family Rosaceae) but to the asphodel (genus *Asphodelus* of the lily family) or some other flower (*see* CROCUS). Roses were known in Palestine after the Old Testament period and are referred to at Sir. 24:14; 39:13; 50:8 (Gk. *rhódon*).

ROSH [rŏsh] (Heb. *rō'š* "head, chief"). A son of Benjamin (Gen. 46:21). He probably died childless, since his name does not occur in later lists of Benjamin's descendants (Num. 26:38-41; 1 Chr. 7:6-12; ch. 8).

RUBY. KJV translation of Heb. *pᵉnînîm, pᵉnîyîm* (e.g., Prov. 3:15; 8:11; 31:10; RSV "jewels"). As this red variety of corundum is not attested at ancient Palestinian sites, the references are most likely to CORAL (so RSV, Job 28:18; Lam. 4:7).

RUE (Gk. *péganon*). A strong-scented perennial herb (*Ruta graveolens* L.), the green-gray leaves of which produce a bitter etheric oil prized as a purgative and as a condiment. In New Testament times this plant was imported from Greece. According to Luke 11:42, Jesus' referred to a pharisaic practice of tithing rue, but the text may have originally mentioned not rue but dill (Gk. *melánthion*; cf. the variant reading in p⁴⁵ and par. Matt. 23:23); dill was, in fact, tithed, but rue was not (Mishnah *Maʿas.* iv.5; *Šeb.* ix.1).

RUFUS [rōōʹfəs] (Gk. *Rhouphos*; Lat. *rufus* "red-haired").†

1. The son of Simon of Cyrene, and the brother of Alexander (Mark 15:21). Simon's sons are named despite his small role in the narrative, perhaps because they were known in the Church. Therefore, it is commonly thought that Rufus, Simon's son, is the same as **2** below.

2. A prominent Christian in Rome greeted by Paul (Rom. 16:13).

RUHAMAH [rōō hāʹmə]. A new name given to Hosea's daughter (KJV, Hos. 2:1 [MT 3]). *See* NOT PITIED.

RULER OF THE SYNAGOGUE (Gk. *archisynágōgos*, *árchōn tḗs synagōgḗs*). The administrator of a local synagogue whose task it was to supervise the business of the synagogue, to preside over the worship services (cf. Luke 13:14) and to choose from the men present who was to read from the Prophets (cf. 4:16-17), who was to pronounce the prayer, and who was to give the sermon (cf. Acts 13:15). Synagogue rulers were prominent members of their communities and could be quite visible representatives of Jewish groups who lived in Gentile cities (cf. 18:17). Some synagogues had more than one ruler (Mark 5:22; Acts 13:15). Synagogue rulers mentioned by name in the New Testament are Jairus (Mark 5:22; Luke 8:41), Crispus, who became a Christian (Acts 18:8), and Sosthenes (v. 17).

RUMAH [rōōʹmə] (Heb. *rûmâ* "elevation"). The home of Zebidah the mother of Jehoiakim (2 Kgs. 23:36). Rumah has been variously identified with ARUMAH near Shechem and with Khirbet Rûmeh, *ca.* 10 km. (6 mi.) north of Nazareth.

RUSH. *See* REED, RUSH.

RUTH [rōōth] (Heb. *rûṯ* "companion" or "satiation [?]"; Gk. *Rhouth*). A Moabite, the widow of the Judahite Mahlon (Ruth 1:2-5). She is the central figure of the book of Ruth, and an ancestor of David and Jesus (Matt. 1:5; cf. Ruth 4:17-22).

RUTH, BOOK OF.†

I. Place in the Canon

In the Hebrew Bible Ruth is in the third division of the canon, the Writings. Although the Talmud places Ruth first in this division (before Psalms), the MT places it among the five scrolls (Heb. *mᵉgillôṯ*), i.e., with Song of Songs, Ecclesiastes, Lamentations, and

Esther. Each of the five scrolls is assigned to be read at a particular festival, with Ruth prescribed for the Feast of Weeks or Pentecost, a biblical festival originally celebrating the end of the grain harvest.

In the LXX, however, Ruth follows the book of Judges, probably because both books deal with the period of the Confederation, following Israel's taking of the land of Canaan and before the beginning of the Israelite monarchy. Josephus actually takes Ruth to be an appendix to Judges (*Ap.* i.40 [8]). The English versions follow the LXX, placing Ruth immediately after Judges.

II. Contents

The story of Ruth is a story of love and devotion that transcend all limits, bound neither by self-interest nor by national prejudice. It is also specifically a woman's story. With unparalleled artistry, the storyteller presents Naomi and her daughter-in-law, Ruth, as they struggle for survival in a patriarchal culture.

The story opens in Moab where a Judahite family from Bethlehem has sought refuge from famine plaguing their native land. Elimelech, the husband of Naomi, dies in the foreign land. The two sons of Elimelech and Naomi, Mahlon and Chilion, take two Moabite women, Ruth and Orpah, as wives. In the course of time both sons die, leaving their wives as childless widows like their mother (Ruth 1:1-5). Naomi decides to return to Bethlehem, but she tries to persuade her daughters-in-law to remain in Moab. Orpah yields to the urging of Naomi, but Ruth insists on leaving her native Moab and going to Judah with Naomi, declaring her complete devotion to her mother-in-law (vv. 6-18). The decision is radical and, from a cultural perspective, makes no sense.

Arriving in Bethlehem at the beginning of the grain harvest, Ruth takes advantage of the privilege of gleaning that custom accorded the poor (cf. Lev. 19:9-10). As the storyteller puts it, Ruth "happened to come" to the field of Boaz, a kinsman of Elimelech (Ruth 2:3). Boaz treats Ruth with kindness, and at the end of the harvest Naomi sends Ruth to ask Boaz to fulfill the duty of the next of kin, i.e., to produce a male offspring for Elimelech's lineage. After a nearer kinsman waives his right both to purchase the family property and to provide an heir for the deceased, Boaz consents to take Ruth as his wife (2:5–4:12). *See* LEVIRATE LAW.

The son who is born to Ruth is spoken of as Naomi's son, for the continuance of her name and that of her family is now assured (4:13-17). The celebration that follows the child's birth represents more than simply the joy arising from the birth of a male child, for the women of Bethlehem exalt Ruth, a foreign woman who has forsaken all to follow Naomi, as one who means more to Naomi "than seven sons" (v. 15). Naomi, the woman of emptiness, has become a woman of plenty (cf. 1:19-21), and Ruth, the daughter-in-law faithful beyond death, is the one who mediates that transformation. The child, Obed (**1**), through his son Jesse, comes to be the grandfather of David.

III. Literary Features

The book of Ruth has generally been regarded as a perfect example of the Hebrew short story. Complex and elaborate in structure, the story is crafted in a beautiful, highly artistic fashion. The four scenes (corresponding to the four chapters) form a circular pattern in which the third and fourth return to the concerns of the second and first respectively, with variations of this design woven throughout each scene. Meaning is here inseparable from form, and the whole is a work of art. The remarkable literary artistry of the storyteller is evidenced throughout by the use of chiasm, repeated key words and motifs, ring construction or inclusio (such as the balancing of the family history at 1:1-5 against the genealogy at 4:18-22), analogies, allusions, and other literary devices. Among the more obvious analogies are those between Ruth and Abraham (2:11-12; cf. Gen. 12:1-9) and Ruth and Tamar (Ruth 4:12, 18; cf. Gen. 38). It is noteworthy that Ruth and Tamar are two of the four women mentioned in the Matthean genealogy of Jesus (Matt. 1:3, 5).

IV. Author and Date

The text of Ruth contains no clue as to its authorship. According to Talmudic tradition, Samuel was the author of not only the books that bear his name but also Judges and Ruth. This has probably influenced the placement of Ruth after Judges in the LXX.

Various dates have been proposed for the book of Ruth. Talmudic tradition posits an early date (i.e., in the early Monarchy), and a few modern scholars have concurred. Some scholars have sought to differentiate between the story, assigned an early date, and its present form, given a later date. The excellent classical style, use of archaic verbal forms, and affinities with Pentateuchal stories are appropriate for the early period. It has been argued, however, that the present form of the book with its social conventions, "Aramaisms," and spirit of tolerance and universalism should be assigned a late (i.e., postexilic) date. In spite of these arguments, the scholarly consensus has shifted from favoring a date during or after the Exile (as late as 400 B.C.) to favoring one in the period of the Monarchy (tenth-eighth centuries).

V. Purpose

Many suggestions have been made as to the purpose of the book of Ruth, and the question of date has often been linked to this question. The most common suggestions are that the book was written to present the origin of the great King David; to combat the narrow exclusivism of Ezra and Nehemiah, especially the prohibition of mixed marriages; to plead for the extension of the practice of levirate marriage as a humanitarian effort on behalf of childless widows; to present Ruth as the model proselyte; to stress universalism and tolerance that go beyond national barriers; to extol human kindness and friendship that exceed any reasonable requirement of duty; or to simply write a beautiful, well-crafted story. Given the number and variety of suggestions, it is best to be cautious in seeking a single, all-embracing purpose.

Bibliography. E. F. Campbell, *Ruth.* AB 7 (1975); J. Gray, *Joshua, Judges, Ruth,* rev. ed. NCBC (1986); J. M. Sasson, *Ruth: A New Translation with a Philological Commentary and a Formalist-Folklorist Interpretation* (Baltimore: 1979); P. Trible, *God and the Rhetoric of Sexuality.* OBT (1978), pp. 166-199.

S

SABAOTH [săb′ə ōth], **LORD OF** (Gk. *kýrios sabaóth*). New Testament Greek representation of Heb. *YHWH ṣᵉḇāʾôt* "the Lord of hosts" (so RSV, Rom. 9:29; Jas. 5:4; KJV "Lord of Sabaoth"). *See* LORD OF HOSTS.

SABBATH [săb′əth] (Heb. *šabbāṯ*; Gk. *sábbaton*).† The seventh day of the week, observed as a day of rest in Israelite and Jewish religion since earliest times. Inasmuch as every new day was considered to begin with sunset, the Sabbath begins with sunset of Friday evening (Neh. 13:19).

Indications of an origin of the Sabbath outside Israel have often been sought. Canaanite seven-day periods are attested, but they were not a regularly observed measure of time and so have only a distant, if any, relation to the origin of the Israelite Sabbath. In Babylonia the day of the full moon (Akk. *šapattū*) was considered particularly auspicious. The binding of Israel's observance to a mathematical calculation, every seventh day, rather than to observance of lunar phases helped to exclude worship of heavenly bodies as deities. But new moon and Sabbath are mentioned together as days for religious gatherings (Isa. 1:13; Ezek. 46:1), feasting (Hos. 2:11 [MT 13]), and cessation of work (Amos 8:5) and as days especially propitious for seeking divine aid (2 Kgs. 4:23). In Babylonia every seventh day was regarded as an inauspicious day, but Israel's Sabbath was not so regarded; rather, it was a day of rest and religious assembly. A Kenite origin for the Sabbath has been suggested on a number of grounds, but this is far from certain. Indeed, all that can be said with certainty about the origin of Sabbath observance is that it is apparently as old as Israel's religion itself.

The Sabbath regulations of the Old Testament are intended mainly to reinforce the provision of that day as a day of rest (cf. Heb. *šāḇaṯ* "stop"). No work is to be done or allowed on the Sabbath (Exod. 20:10; 23:12; Deut. 25:13-14). The prohibition of work allows no distinction between seasons; even in harvest time the Sabbath is to be observed (Exod. 34:21). No burdens are to be carried or loaded onto animals on that day (Neh. 13:15; Jer. 17:21-22). Food to be eaten on the Sabbath is to be prepared the day before, just as the manna for the Sabbath was gathered on the preceding day (Exod. 16:5, 23-30). No food may be bought from Gentiles (Neh. 10:31; 13:16, 20-21) nor a fire kindled on the Sabbath (Exod. 35:3). The penalty for an individual breaking the Sabbath was death (31:14-15; Num. 15:32-36). For the whole nation, Sabbath-breaking was one of the offenses that led to exile (Neh. 9:13-14; Jer. 17:24-27; Ezek. 20:23-24).

The Sabbath is to be both a sign of and a time for remembering the distinct relationship between Yahweh and the people of Israel (Exod. 31:13; Ezek. 20:20). Because of the command that slaves not be put to work on that day, it is a reminder of Israel's enslavement in Egypt and subsequent deliverance by God (Deut. 5:15). In particular, God's creation of the world in six days and his resting on the seventh is to be called to mind (Gen. 2:2-3; Exod. 20:11; 31:17). The Sabbath is to be a time when the worshippers of God are gathered (Lev. 23:3). The tabernacle's Bread of the Presence was to be set on its table on the Sabbath (24:8; 1 Chr. 9:32), and special sacrifices were made in the temple (Num. 28:9-10; Ezek. 46:4-5). In the synagogues the Sabbath became a time for teaching directed to the whole community (cf. Mark 6:2; Luke 6:6; 13:10; Acts 13:14, 27, 42, 44; 15:21).

All of the annual festivals were to be observed according to the principles of the Sabbath (Lev. 23). The abandonment of the land by those taken into exile under God's judgment is portrayed as "sabbaths" of the land (Lev. 26:34-35; 2 Chr. 36:21; cf. Jer. 25:11-12; 29:10); thus the extension of the sabbath principle present in the Sabbatical Year and the Jubilee (Lev. 25) becomes in retrospect a metaphor for both judgment and hope. An aspect of the eschatological hopes of the last chapters of Isaiah is the restoration of Sabbath-observance and its extension to all peoples in accord with the universalization of the worship of Israel's God (Isa. 56:2, 4-7; 58:13-14; 66:23; cf. Lam. 2:6).

In postbiblical Judaism the Sabbath regulations have been elaborated, again with a view to reinforcing the provision of a day of rest, the violation of which could only have dire consequences. (These regulations may be suspended, however, where the saving of a life is at stake.) The definition of forbidden activities developed largely on the basis of thirty-nine such classes of work listed in Mishnah *Šabb.* vii.2. One controversial restriction was the refusal to fight if an enemy attacked on a Sabbath (1 Macc. 2:32-41; 9:43-49; 2 Macc. 6:11; 15:1-5). A SABBATH DAY'S JOURNEY, the distance one could travel out of town on the Sabbath (cf. Matt. 24:20; Acts 1:12), came to be specified as 2000 cubits (900 m. [1000 yd.]); but journeys twice as long were permitted if prior to the Sabbath enough food was deposited at a point within a "Sabbath day's journey," by which provision this point became a temporary "home" from which the permitted distance was computed. Such regulations are not felt to be restrictions of freedom, but rather that which specifies and allows the beauty of a time of rest, tranquillity, and worship.

The controversies in which Jesus was involved with regard to the Sabbath all hinged on his authority as a teacher over against the Pharisees' interpreters of the Torah (Matt. 12:1-8; John 5:8-18; 7:21-24; ch. 9) or on the appropriateness of redemptive acts normally proscribed as work on the Sabbath (Matt. 12:9-14 par.; Luke 13:10-16; 14:1-6). The early Christian community probably kept the Sabbath as did other Jews (Mark 16:1; Luke 23:56). But with the spread of the Christian faith among Gentiles, the Sabbath commandments were interpreted eschatologically (cf. Heb. 4:1-10) and increasingly removed from Christian practice. Paul appears to have been particularly concerned about Gentile Christian misinterpretation of the Sabbath laws as a form of asceticism (Col. 2:16-23; cf. Gal. 4:9-10). The emerging Christian observance of worship on the first day of the week (cf. John 20:19; Acts 20:7; 1 Cor. 16:2), although based on the Jewish division of time into seven-day periods, was not interpreted as Sabbath observance on a different day; the Old Testament Sabbath regulations were not applied to Sunday until the fourth century A.D.

See also LORD'S DAY.

Bibliography. N.-E. A. Andreasen, *The Old Testament Sabbath.* SBL Dissertation 7 (Missoula: 1972); S. Bacchiocchi, *From Sabbath to Sunday* (Rome: 1977); R. de Vaux, *Ancient Israel* (New York: 1965) 2:475-483.

SABBATH DAY'S JOURNEY (Gk. *sabbátou hodós*). The distance one could travel on the Sabbath without violating the special sanctity of that day. When Israel was receiving the manna in the wilderness the people were not to gather manna on the Sabbath, nor was any person to "go out of his place" on that day (Exod. 16:29). Rabbinic interpretation set the limit of Sabbath travel at 2000 cubits (900 m. [1000 yd.]) beyond the borders of the town in which one is spending the Sabbath. Journeys twice as long are permitted if prior to the Sabbath enough food is deposited at a point within a Sabbath day's journey, by which provision this point becomes a temporary "home" from which the distance is computed. Josephus (*Ant.* xx.8.6 [169]) describes the Mount of Olives as being five stades (the equivalent of 2000 cubits) from Jerusalem, which accords with the distance of Olivet from Jerusalem at Acts 1:12; in both cases the higher parts of the Mount are in mind. Referring to a coming time of trouble, Jesus alludes to the difficulties of those whose flight would be on a Sabbath when travel was limited (Matt. 24:20).

SABBATICAL YEAR. The last of a seven-year cycle, in which according to the law of Moses the land was to be left fallow and the people to eat the stored produce of the previous year as a reminder that the land was, in essence, owned by the Lord and thus "given" by him (Lev. 25:2-4). What grew without being tended was not to be gathered in by landowners (v. 5), but was to be left so that all classes of people, domesticated animals, and even wild animals could have it for food (vv. 6-7; cf. vv. 19-22; Exod. 23:10-11). Debts owed by fellow Israelites were to be cancelled (Deut. 15:1-11). It is possible that slaves were also to be freed with the arrival of the Sabbatical Year, though the seventh year for the freeing of slaves appears to have been measured from the beginning of each slave's period of servitude rather than being dependent on an absolute calendrical reckoning like the Sabbatical Year (Exod. 21:2; Deut. 15:12; cf. Isa. 61:1-2; Jer. 34:8-22). The law was to be read during the Feast of Tabernacles in every Sabbatical Year (Deut. 31:10-11). After seven cycles of seven years came the Year of Jubilee (Lev. 25:8-55), which like the Sabbatical Year represented an extension of the Sabbath principle.

It is not certain whether the Sabbatical Year was ever consistently practiced. The abandonment of the land by those taken into exile under God's judgment is spoken of as the "sabbaths" of the land (26:34-35; 2 Chr. 36:21; Jer. 25:11-12; 29:10). This suggests that the actual observance of the Sabbatical Year had been dropped before the Exile, though the ideal of the institution was held strongly enough to insure its preservation in the Pentateuch. The covenant made under Nehemiah included the restoration of the Sabbatical Year (Neh. 10:31). In the early Hasmonean period the Sabbatical Year was observed at least occasionally (1 Macc. 6:48, 53, referring to 163-162 B.C.). It continued to be observed by Palestinian Jews into the Middle Ages.

SABEANS [sə bē'ənz].†
1 (Heb. *šeḇāʾ, šeḇāʾyîm*). Traders and raiders from Sheba in southern Arabia (Job 1:15; Joel 3:8 [MT 4:8]). *See* SHEBA (PLACE) **2**.
2 (Heb. *seḇāʾîm*). Wealthy traders from Seba (Isa. 45:14; *seḇāʾ*; JB "men of Seba") or possibly from Sheba (KJV, RSV "Sabeans"; cf. **1** above). *See* SEBA.
3. At Ezek. 23:42 the KJV and NIV read "Sabeans" for **Q** *sāḇāʾîm* (cf. **2**). RSV "drunkards" could represent either **Q** or **K** *sôḇeʾîm*. The word is dropped as a dittograph by JB and some commentators.

SABTA [săb'tə] (Heb. *saḇtāʾ*), **SABTAH** (*saḇtâ*). A son of Cush (Gen. 10:7; 1 Chr. 1:9). The name may be preserved in either modern Sabota, a city in Hadramaut in southern Arabia, or Saphtha, a city near the Persian Gulf mentioned by Ptolemy.

SABTECA [săb'tə kə] (Heb. *saḇteḵāʾ*). A son of Cush, probably the name of a location in Arabia not otherwise known (Gen. 10:7; 1 Chr. 1:9; KJV "Sabtecha").

SACHAR [sā'kär] (Heb. *śāḵār*).
1. A Hararite; the father of Ahiam, one of David's "mighty men" (1 Chr. 11:35; KJV "Sacar"). At 2 Sam. 23:33 Ahiam's father is called Sharar.

2. A son of Obed-edom, who was leader of one of the divisions of temple gatekeepers (1 Chr. 26:4; KJV "Sacar").

SACHIA [sə kī′ə] (Heb. *śāḵᵉyâ*). A Benjaminite, son of Shaharaim and Hodesh (1 Chr. 8:10; KJV "Shachia").

SACKCLOTH (Heb. *śaq*; Gk. *sákkos*). A rough, dark (cf. Isa. 50:3; Rev. 6:12) material of spun and woven goat's hair used for sacking. Garments made of sackcloth were worn during mourning (Gen. 37:34; 2 Sam. 3:31), as a sign of repentance (1 Kgs. 21:27; Neh. 9:1; Isa. 22:12; Matt. 11:21), in times of great national distress (2 Kgs. 6:30; 19:1-2; 1 Chr. 21:16; Esth. 4:1-4; Isa. 15:3; Ezek. 7:18), and by captives (1 Kgs. 20:31-32; Isa. 3:24). The two prophets of Rev. 11:3 prophesy in sackcloth as a sign to their hearers of coming trouble. The symbolic value of sackcloth derived probably not from any discomfort in wearing it, but from its association with poverty; sackcloth was sometimes the normal garb of the poor. Rizpah the daughter of Aiah laid sackcloth on a rock to provide a place to sit during her vigil by the bodies of her sons and the sons of Merab (2 Sam. 21:10).

SACRED STONE (Gk. *diopetḗs*).* An object preserved in the temple of Artemis in Ephesus (Acts 19:35; RSV "the sacred stone that fell from the sky"; KJV "the image that fell down from Jupiter"). The Greek adjective, which here occurs substantively, often was used to designate meteorites regarded as statues of deities, in this passage presumably an image of Artemis. The meteorites' lack of resemblance to the human form or to anything else caused little difficulty because of the wonder with which such stones were regarded.

SACRIFICES AND OFFERINGS (Heb. *qorbān*; Gk. *thysía, prosphorá*).† The presentation of animals and plant foods to deities, generally by destruction, as a part of worship. Sacrifice was practiced in almost all ancient religions, including that of Israel and the Jews down into the first century A.D., and is regarded in the Bible as an aspect of human worship of God almost from the beginning (Gen. 4:3-4).

I. Old Testament

The offering of sacrifices on the altar, as it developed among the Israelites, was performed by the priests on behalf of the entire community or of individuals who brought animals or other items for sacrifice. The importance of sacrifice gave the priests a central role in religion and made of the altar a focal point for the people. The fire on the altar was never extinguished under normal circumstances (Lev. 6:12-13 [MT 5-6]).

A. Procedures for Sacrifice. The primary sacrifices required by the Old Testament were animal sacrifices. Grain ("cereal") and wine offerings accompanied almost all offerings of animals.

Animals for sacrifice were brought alive to the tabernacle or temple, slaughtered either by the worshippers who brought them or by the priests, and divided and placed on the altar by a priest. Four different types of animal sacrifices may be distinguished, according to the manner in which the animal was offered. The animal of a burnt offering (ch. 1; 6:8-13 [MT 1-6]) was burned entirely, its blood was poured out around the altar, and none of the meat was eaten. With a peace offering (ch. 3; 7:11-36; 22:18-30) the fat and specified parts of the internal organs were burned on the altar and the blood poured out around the altar, but the worshippers who brought the animal ate the meat in a joyous worship meal (cf. Deut. 12:17-18; 1 Sam. 9:12-13; Zeph. 1:7), the breast and right thigh being allotted to the officiating priest. The flesh of a sin offering (Lev. 4:1-5:13; 6:24-30 [MT 17-23]) was either burned outside the tabernacle or temple area if the sin of the people as a whole or of the high priest occasioned the sacrifice, or eaten by the priests. The blood went to the curtain of the holy of holies, the altar of incense, and the altar of sacrifice, or just to the altar of sacrifice, depending again on whose sin occasioned the sacrifice. The fat was burned on the altar. Guilt offerings (5:14-6:7 [MT 5:26]; 7:1-6) were performed as were sin offerings for individuals other than the high priest: the fat of the animals was burned on the altar, the blood went to the altar of sacrifice, and the priest ate the meat.

Grain offerings (ch. 2) were brought in the form of flour, thin cakes or wafers, or toasted grains. A portion of the grain offerings went to the altar to be burned, with incense if they were in the form of flour, the rest going to the priests to be eaten. Grain offerings which accompanied the peace offerings of thanksgiving were eaten by the worshipper, but part went to the officiating priest (7:13-14). Oil and salt were usually included with the grain offerings. Wine offerings were poured out at the foot of the altar.

Some offerings and portions of offerings were presented as "wave offerings." This ritual probably consisted of elevating (rather than waving or shaking) the offerings toward the most holy place to give to them a special sanctity, before they were burned on the altar (Exod. 29:24-25; Lev. 7:30-31; 8:25-28; 14:12-13), eaten (Exod. 29:26-28; Lev. 7:30-31, 34; 10:14-15; Num. 6:20; 18:11), or put to some other ritual use (Lev. 14:12, 15-18).

B. Occasions for Sacrifice. Sacrifices can be divided by that which occasioned them into regular obligatory sacrifices offered on behalf of the whole community (i.e., the regular daily, Sabbath, New Moon, and annual feast day sacrifices); special obligatory sacrifices, which might be offered on behalf of the whole community or on behalf of individuals; and optional sacrifices (votive and freewill offerings) offered on behalf of individuals. Sacrifices offered by the priests on behalf of the entire community were financed by the half-shekel temple tax paid by all Jews once that had been instituted.

The regular daily sacrifices were burnt offerings of one lamb in the morning and one lamb in the evening (Exod. 29:38-42; Num. 28:3-8). An incense offering was also part of the morning and evening sacrificial routine (Exod. 30:7-8). On the Sabbath the daily sacrifices were doubled (Num. 28:9-10). The Bread of the Presence, twelve loaves set out and then eaten by the priests and replaced every Sabbath, was not treated like the usual grain offerings, but was nonetheless considered a part of the offerings (Lev. 24:5-9).

Akhenaten and Nefertiti presenting offerings to the sun-god Aton. From a relief at Tell el-Amarna (The Metropolitan Museum of Art)

During feast times the feast day sacrifices were observed in addition to the regular daily, Sabbath, and New Moon sacrifices. Num. 28:11–29:38 specifies in detail the burnt offerings to be made on every New Moon and at the annual feast times that involved sacrifices (i.e., the seven days of Passover and the Feast of Unleavened Bread, the Feast of Firstfruits or Weeks, the New Year, the Day of Atonement, and the eight days of the Feast of Tabernacles); on every New Moon and each day of these feasts a sin offering of one goat was also made. The lamb of Passover was an unusual sacrifice. What began as a commemorative meal in which the ritual significance of blood was linked to the history of the people (Exod. 12:3-13) came to be, with the centralization of sacrifice, more like other sacrificial meals (cf. Deut. 16:5-7). During the Feast of Firstfruits a special grain offering was made (Lev. 23:15-17; Num. 28:26). A special offering of incense was presented when the high priest entered the holy of holies on the Day of Atonement (Lev. 16:2, 12-13).

Peace offerings were offered on behalf of individuals as freewill offerings given from devotion rather than in response to an obligation (7:16; 22:21) and as votive offerings in fulfillment of vows made in time of trouble (7:16; 22:21; cf. 2 Sam. 15:7-8). "Thank offering" was at times a term for both freewill and votive offerings (Ps. 56:12-13 [MT 13-14]; cf. 50:14; 54:6-7 [MT 8-9]; 116:14, 17-18) and at other times a term for a different category of peace offerings (Lev. 7:12). Burnt offerings as well as peace offerings could also be given as freewill and votive offerings (22:18; Num. 15:3).

Sin and guilt offerings were considered obligatory in a broad range of situations among which those listed at Lev. 5:1-4, 14; 6:1-5 (MT 5:20-24) are just a sample (cf. 4:2, 13; 5:17). Sin offerings were required in connection with ordination of priests (Exod. 29:14), New Moons and annual feast days (as mentioned above), purification after childbirth (Lev. 12:6), and purification of Nazirites (Num. 6:9-11). Guilt offerings were made to effect atonement in some cases of sexual sin (Lev. 19:20-22). The purification ritual for lepers included a guilt offering and a sin offering (14:10-20). A burnt offering accompanied most sin offerings.

The firstborn sons of human families and the first offspring of female animals were regarded as the property of God (Exod. 22:29b-30 [MT 28b-29]). Sons and unclean animals could be redeemed with sacrifice (13:13; 34:19; Num. 18:15-16; cf. Gen. 22:13), but the firstborn of animals which were accepted as sacrificial animals could not be redeemed; it was necessary to sacrifice them. The meat was to be eaten by the priests (Num. 18:17-18) or by the worshippers (Deut. 15:19-20). The "firstfruits," the first of every year's production from crops, were to be treated in a similar manner (Exod. 23:19; Num. 18:12-13; Deut. 18:4). Wave offerings of firstfruits were made on the feasts of Unleavened Bread (Lev. 23:9-14) and Firstfruits (v. 20). The tithe of agricultural produce (Num. 18:24-28; Deut. 14:22-29) was similar to the offering of firstfruits, perhaps sometimes equated with it.

Little investigation is needed to discover inconsistencies and other difficulties in the sacrificial codes of the Pentateuch and other Old Testament references to matters of sacrifice. This is to be expected in the records of an institution with as long a history as that of sacrifice in the religion of the Israelite people. The sacrificial codes (esp. Lev. 1-7; Num. 28-29), in their present final form, probably represent ideal codes drawn up for the temple after its postexilic rebuilding. Ezekiel presents an ideal set of sacrifices with some differences (Ezek. 43:18-27; 45:18-25; 46:11-15).

C. The Origin of Sacrifice. Similarities may be noted between the sacrificial system described in Old Testament and ancient Mesopotamian and, to a greater extent, ancient southern Arabian sacrificial systems. However, the greatest similarities are to Canaanite sacrificial systems, as would be expected because of geographical proximity and cultural similarities. Many sacrificial terms are common to the two groups, and the most important forms of sacrifice, the total burnt sacrifice and the peace offering, are also shared. The conflict between Hebrew Yahweh worship and Canaanite Baal worship depicted in the Old Testament generally concerned not how worship was to be performed but, rather, the object of worship (cf. 1 Kgs. 18:23-24; 2 Kgs. 5:17). The ritual significance of blood in Israel's worship was not, however, shared by the Canaanites, and may actually represent an older part of Israelite ritual than even sacrifice burned on an altar.

Israel's sacrificial system as presented in the Old Testament is sometimes thought to have been a modification of an earlier system in which the sacrificial victims were human. The law of the redemption of the firstborn (Exod. 13:11-15; 34:19-20) has been taken as evidence of this, along with Gen. 22; Ezek. 20:25-26, which are claimed as evidence of awareness that a change had been made. But it is more likely that Deut. 12:31; 2 Kgs. 16:3; Ps. 106:34-38 are correct in representing sacrifice of children as a Canaanite practice sometimes adopted by Israelites (Judg. 11:30-40; 2 Kgs. 17:17; 21:6; Jer. 7:31; 32:35; Ezek. 16:20-21; 23:37, 39). *See* MOLECH.

D. The Meaning of Sacrifice. Old Testament sacrifice has been interpreted variously as meaning that the sacrificial animal was a gift appeasing an angry God (cf. 1 Sam. 26:19; 2 Sam. 24:25; Job 42:7-8); that it was a substitute for the worshipper, who symbolically died in presenting the animal; and that it was presented as a meal for God's consumption. The substitutionary idea has been related to the requirement that the worshipper lay his hands on the animal before killing it (e.g., Lev. 1:4; 3:2), but it is nowhere stated that this action is intended to represent a transference of sins or identity such as with the goat sent into the wilderness on the Day of Atonement (16:21-22). The idea of sacrifice as a meal for God appears to be clearly stated by some Old Testament sacrificial language (e.g., 3:11; 21:6; Num. 28:2) and has the advantage of Mesopotamian parallels. Ultimately, however, such an idea was rejected from Israelite religion (Deut. 32:37-38); God is not dependent on human provision (Ps. 50:12-13), and the language of food used in reference to sacrifice becomes entirely metaphorical. All of these views may have been related to popular thoughts about sacrificial worship, but none was dominant, official, or determinative.

The Old Testament represents sacrifice most of all as giving to God, even though it is he who has given to his people all that they have—land, identity, and sustenance (cf. 1 Chr. 29:14-17). The instructions for sacrifice emphasize the acts of giving: "waving," burning, pouring out, and eating. In acts of burning and pouring out, the tribute given to God is made unreturnable; something of the worshipper's or the community's life sustenance has been given away to God. Even though God ultimately owns and controls all, tribute—costly tribute—is paid to him by those who worship him through sacrifice. When sacrifices are eaten, the act of eating—of sustaining life—is united in a special way with the worship of the God who has received as tribute a portion of that which is eaten. When the prophets attack the way in which sacrifice is practiced, it appears that the emphasis in the sacrificial cult has shifted from the acts of giving to the quantity of what is given (Isa. 1:11; Mic. 6:7; cf. Ps. 50:8-11; Isa. 40:16-17).

Another emphasis in the sacrificial codes is the ac-

ceptability before God of the worshipper that is brought about by sacrifice properly executed. God is pleased by sacrifice (e.g., Lev. 1:9), and atonement is accomplished by it (v. 4; cf. Gen. 8:21). The ritual significance of blood is connected with atonement (Lev. 17:11). Expiation of sins could normally be expected by means of sacrifice (cf. 1 Sam. 3:14), and the sense of estrangement from God that might result from deliberate or accidental wrongdoing is the concern of the sin offerings and guilt offerings. Sin is removed and the relationship with God is reestablished by sacrifice, but little or no thought is devoted to the means by which sacrifice accomplishes these objectives. One characteristic of sacrificial worship that came under attack by the prophets was the separation of sacrificial religion from the ethical considerations of justice within the community (Isa. 1:11-17; Amos 5:21-24; Mic. 6:6-8). The mere act of sacrifice did not itself magically or independently bring about atonement; it could not be separated from the manner in which the participant lived (Ps. 40:6-8 [MT 7-9]; 51:16-19 [MT 18-21]; Jer. 6:20; 14:12; Hos. 6:6; cf. Prov. 21:3; Isa. 29:13).

See also the entries on particular types of sacrifices.

II. New Testament

The continual daily offerings were interrupted by the destruction of the first temple (587 B.C.), restored with the postexilic building of the second temple (520-516), interrupted again under the persecution by Antiochus Epiphanes (167 B.C.; cf. Dan. 8:11-13; 11:31; 12:11; 1 Macc. 1:44-45), restored three years later (4:52-53), and ended with the destruction of the second temple (A.D. 70; some sacrifices may have been offered at the temple site between the second temple's destruction and the defeat of the Bar Kokhba rebellion in A.D. 135). The Roman city of Aelia Capitolina, from which Jews were barred, was built on the site of Jerusalem after A.D. 135, insuring that the practice of sacrifice was ended within Judaism. But the development of the synagogues with their nonsacrificial worship allowed Judaism to continue without temple, altar, or sacrifices. (Sacrifices had been made at a Jewish temple at Leontopolis in Egypt since 160 B.C., but few Jews held any allegiance to this shrine, and it was destroyed not long after the temple in Jerusalem.)

Jesus continued the prophetic critique of sacrificial religion (Matt. 9:13; cf. Mark 12:32-33), although he did accept the practice of sacrifice (Matt. 5:23-24), his predictions of the temple's destruction notwithstanding (Luke 21:5-6, 20-24). Jesus' "cleansing of the temple" (Matt. 21:10-17 par.) was not a rejection of sacrificial worship, but rather a protest against the encroachment upon the Gentiles' worship space in the temple by the merchandising that facilitated sacrificial worship. The earliest Christian community gathered in the temple and participated in the public functions there (Acts 2:46; 3:1). Paul apparently did not disapprove of participation in the sacrificial ritual by Christian Jews, inasmuch as he took part in it himself (21:23-26; 24:17-18). Stephen's speech shows a negative stance toward sacrificial worship (7:41-43, 48-50) that was probably characteristic of a viewpoint emerging in the Church, represented also in Hebrews.

Along with the nonsacrificial worship of the synagogues, which prepared the way for Christian worship just as it made possible the survival of Judaism, the interpretation of Jesus' death as an atoning sacrifice (Mark 10:45; Eph. 5:2) was decisive for Christians (cf. 1 Cor. 5:7, "Christ, our paschal lamb"; 1 Pet. 1:19). Just as the covenant of Sinai was initiated with sacrifice, so the new covenant is initiated with the sacrifice of Jesus (Luke 22:20; cf. Exod. 24:8; Ps. 50:5). Heb. 4:14–10:31 presents Christ as simultaneously priest and sacrifice, the perfect sacrifice prefigured by the Old Testament sacrifices who makes all further sacrifices unnecessary.

Other figurative uses of sacrificial language in the New Testament refer to the Gentile converts to Christian faith as Paul's offering (Rom. 15:16; Phil. 2:17), to Christian dedication (Rom. 12:1; 1 Pet. 2:5), to praise of God (Heb. 13:5), and to sharing of material things (v. 6). Two issues related to pagan sacrifice are addressed in 1 Corinthians: whether Christians should eat meat that had been dedicated to a pagan deity by a sacrifice of a portion of it—which was the case of almost all meat available in the meat markets (1 Cor. 8; 10:25–11:1; cf. Acts 15:29; Rev. 2:14, 20), and the question facing Christians invited to a ritual meal in a pagan temple (1 Cor. 8:10; 10:14-22).

Bibliography. W. Eichrodt, *Theology of the Old Testament.* OTL (1961) 1:141-172; R. de Vaux, *Ancient Israel* (New York: 1965) 2:415-456; *Studies in Old Testament Sacrifice* (Cardiff: 1964).

SADDUCEES [săd'ōō sēz] (Gk. *Saddoukaioi*; from Heb. *ṣᵉdûqîm*). A party existing within Judaism from some time in the second century B.C. to the war of A.D. 66-70. The name came most likely from that of Zadok, the high priest of David's day from whom the high priests were descended. (The alternate derivation of "Sadducees" from a later Zadok, a disciple of Antigonus of Soko, is late and not trustworthy.) The Sadducees did, indeed, favor the priests and accord them an elevated role in their interpretation of the law. By the time of Jesus they included the families who supplied the high priests, as well as other wealthy aristocrats of Jerusalem. Most members of the Sanhedrin, the central judicial authority of Jewish people, were Sadducees. Thus the Sadducees were the party of those with political power, those allied with the Herodian and Roman rulers, but they were not a group with influence among the people themselves. The views of the Pharisees prevailed among the common people, so that even though the two groups differed with regard to items in the laws of purity and details of temple procedure during the feasts, the Sadducean priests were compelled to operate according to the Pharisees' views.

The differences between the two parties were not merely concentrated on a few details, but extended to their social standing (few Pharisees being aristocrats) and to the very principles by which they answered religious questions. The Sadducees accepted only the written Torah and rejected all "oral Torah," i.e., the traditional interpretation of the Torah accepted by the Pharisees that became of central importance in rabbinic Judaism. Scholars once held that the Sadducees accepted only the Pentateuch and not the prophets.

Such was apparently not the case, although the Sadducees may have weighted their use of the canon toward the Pentateuch. They rejected the doctrine of the future resurrection, belief in angels and spirits as it generally developed in postbiblical Judaism, and the predestinarian views held by the Pharisees. The Sadducees represented in these ways a conservatism that limited both the acceptance of religious ideas not represented in the old sources and the interpretation of every aspect of life by reference to religion, which is precisely what the Pharisees most sought.

The Sadducees and the Pharisees are sometimes mentioned together in the New Testament (Matt. 3:7; 16:1-12). Despite their differences, many members in the two groups apparently were united in opposing the mission of Jesus and the early Church. But their Christian opponents could not always be united (22:15-46; Acts 23:6-9). Christian Pharisees are noted (15:5; Phil. 3:5), but not Christian Sadducees. Jesus and the Christians shared with the Pharisees belief in the coming resurrection; but the emphasis on this belief apparent in the proclamation of Jesus' resurrection, together with the danger of revolution present in the Christian movement (which proved to be more apparent than real), subjected the Christians to stronger Sadducean opposition than the Pharisees experienced (Acts 4:1-3; 5:17-18).

The Sadducees may have been totally annihilated during the early stages of the A.D. 66-70 war. At any rate, their religious outlook was irrelevant for Judaism without the temple.

SAFFRON (Heb. *karkōm*). A pungent bright orange spice made from dried stigmas of *Crocus sativus* L. This purple-flowered plant does not grow in Palestine today, though it may have in biblical times. The saffron of Cant. 4:14, which is among spices and plants in a description of a young woman as an ideal garden, may have been from *Curcuma longa* or *Carthamus tinctorius*.

SAINTS.* Heb. *ḥᵃsîdîm* "faithful and devout ones" and *qᵉdôšîm* "holy ones, those set apart to God" are sometimes translated "saints" in English versions of the Old Testament, although variations of translation are common. These words are often simply terms for the people of God. The KJV also renders *qᵉdôšîm* as "saints" with regard to angels or heavenly beings (Job 5:1; 15:15; Ps. 89:5, 7 [MT 6, 8]; Dan. 8:13 [sing. *qāḏôš*]; Zech. 14:5; RSV "holy ones"). "The saints of the Most High" (Dan. 7:18-27; Aram. *qaddîšê ʿelyônîn*) may be either the Jews or heavenly beings.

Paul's most usual designation for Christians in general is Gk. *hágioi* "saints," literally "holy ones." He uses it of his addressees in the salutations of six letters (Rom. 1:7; 1 Cor. 1:2; 2 Cor. 1:1; Eph. 1:1; Phil. 1:1; Col. 1:2), when referring to the Christians of Judea (Acts 26:10; Rom. 15:25-26, 31; 1 Cor. 16:1; 2 Cor. 8:4; 9:1, 12), greetings (Rom. 16:15; 2 Cor. 13:13; Phil. 4:21 [sing.]-22), and other contexts (e.g., Rom. 8:27; 12:13; 16:2; 1 Cor. 6:1-2; 14:33; 16:15; Eph. 1:15, 18; 3:8; 1 Thess. 3:13). The term is also used in the same general way by other writers (e.g., Acts 9:13, 32, 41; Heb. 13:24; Jude 3; Rev. 5:8; 13:7, 10; 19:8; 20:9). It is also applied to those who were raised from the dead on the occasion of Jesus' death (Matt. 27:52; cf. Acts 3:14).

See HOLINESS, HOLY.

SAKKUTH [săk'əth] (Heb. *sikkûṯ*). The Hebrew phrase *sikkûṯ malkᵉḵem* at Amos 5:26 has been translated variously. At issue in the interpretation of these two words and the phrase that follows (*see* KAIWAN) is whether the verse refers to non-Israelite deities whose worship was adopted by Israelites, or to cultic objects (possibly used in worship of Yahweh).

The RSV and JB follow the most likely interpretation of the first word, taking it as the name of an Akkadian deity associated with Saturn, rendered in the typical Masoretic fashion of adding to the consonants of the non-Israelite deity's name the vowels of *šiqqûṣ* "abomination" (*see* DESOLATING SACRILEGE). KJV "tabernacle" and NIV "shrine" are based on LXX Gk. *skēnḗ* "tent," in turn apparently derived from a Hebrew text reading *sukkaṯ* "tabernacle." Another suggestion has been to regard this first word as *massēḵôṯ* "images."

The second word, *malkᵉḵem*, may be translated literally as "your king" (RSV, JB, NIV). The LXX reads *Moloch* (hence KJV), one of its renderings of Heb. *mōleḵ* (cf. the quotation of Amos 5:26 at Acts 7:43, "the tent of Moloch"; *see* MOLECH).

SALA.
1. In Luke's genealogy of Jesus, the father of Boaz (Luke 3:32; KJV "Salmon"). See SALMON 1.
2. (Luke 3:35, KJV). See SHELAH 1.

SALAH (KJV). *See* SHELAH 1.

SALAMIS [săl'ə mĭs] (Gk. *Salamis*; cf. Sem. *šlm* "peace").† A port city, now a ruin, on the Famagusta Bay of eastern Cyprus, 5 km. (3 mi.) north of Famagusta near modern Seryios. According to ancient tradition founded following the Trojan War, Salamis is named in a seventh-century B.C. tribute list of the Assyrian Assurbanipal. Until supplanted by Paphos in Roman times, it became the principal commercial city on Cyprus. The Jewish colony of Salamis visited by Paul and Barnabas at the beginning of their missionary work beyond Antioch (Acts 13:5) had long been there. The city was destroyed in the Jewish revolt of A.D. 116-117, after which the Roman Trajan expelled the Jews from Cyprus (Dio Cassius *Hist.* lxviii.32.2), and rebuilt in the fourth century as Constantia.

SALATHIEL. See SHEALTIEL.

SALECAH [săl'ə kə] (Heb. *salᵉḵâ*). A city originally in the kingdom of Og of Bashan that marked the extreme northeastern reach of the Transjordanian Israelite tribes after the Conquest (Deut. 3:10; KJV "Salchah"; Josh. 12:5; 13:11; KJV "Salcah"; 1 Chr. 5:11). Salecah was probably located at the site of the modern town Salkhad, built on the core of a long-extinct volcano *ca.* 115 km. (72 mi.) south-southeast of Damascus, near the southern corner of modern Syria.

SALEM [sā'ləm] (Heb. *šālēm* "safe, whole, peace-

ful"). The domain of King Melchizedek (Gen. 14:18), later identified with Jerusalem (Ps. 76:2 [MT 3] par. "Zion"). The Valley of Shaveh, the King's Valley (Gen. 14:17-18), where Melchizedek met Abraham after the Hebrew had defeated Chedorlaomer and the allied kings, may have been near Jerusalem and was possibly identical to the Kidron valley (cf. 2 Sam. 18:18). Ps. 110:4 depicts the Judahite king in Jerusalem ("Zion," v. 2) as the successor of Melchizedek. Philo and Heb. 7:2 interpret the name as meaning "peace" (Heb. *šālôm*).

SALIM [sā'lĭm] (Gk. *Salim*). A place near AENON, where during the early part of Jesus' ministry John the Baptist was baptizing (John 3:23). Although various sites have been proposed, the location is not certain.

SALLAI [săl'ī] (Heb. *sallay*).
1. A postexilic Benjaminite living in Jerusalem (Neh. 11:8).
2. A priestly family of the time of Joiakim the high priest (Neh. 12:20), probably the same as SALLU 2.

SALLU [săl'oo].
1. A postexilic Benjaminite living in Jerusalem (1 Chr. 9:7; Heb. *sallû*'; Neh. 11:7; *sallu*').
2. A postexilic priestly family (Neh. 12:7; Heb. *sallû*), probably the same as SALLAI (2) at v. 20.

SALMA [săl'mə] (Heb. *śalmā*').
1. According to 1 Chr. 2:11, the father of Boaz. *See* SALMON 1.
2. A Calebite, the son of Hur, founder ("father") of Bethlehem (1 Chr. 2:51) and Atroth-beth-joab (KJV "Ataroth, the house of Joab"), and ancestor of the Netophathites, the Zorite half of the Manahathites (KJV "Manahethites"; v. 54), and possibly also the "families of scribes" named at v. 55.

SALMON [săl'mən] (Heb. *śalmôn*; Gk. *Salmōn*).
1. A Judahite, the father of Boaz and an ancestor of David and Jesus (Ruth 4:20-21; Matt. 1:4-5). At Ruth 4:20 the name occurs as Heb. *śalmâ*, at 1 Chr. 2:11 as Salma (1) (*śalmā*'), and at Luke 3:32 as Sala (so RSV; KJV "Salmon").
2. (Ps. 68:14, KJV). See ZALMON (PLACE) 2.

SALMONE [săl mō'nē] (Gk. *Salmōnē*). A promontory pointing toward the north from the eastern end of the island of Crete, modern Cape Sideros. It was apparently a wind out of the northwest that prevented the ship bearing Paul from staying close to the Asian mainland and reaching Cnidus, leading to the decision to sail toward Crete. The ship sailed "under the lee of Crete" (i.e., along the island's southern coast), having come in past Salmone (Acts 27:7).

SALOME [sə lō'mē] (Gk. *Salōmē*; from Heb. *šālôm* "peace").
1. One of the women who witnessed the crucifixion of Jesus and who took spices to the tomb on the morning he was raised from the dead (Mark 15:40; 16:1). Salome was possibly the wife of Zebedee and the mother of the apostles James and John (Matt. 27:56;

cf. 20:20). She is also sometimes identified with the sister of Mary the mother of Jesus (John 19:25).

2. The daughter of Herodias and granddaughter, through her father Herod II, of Herod the Great. Herodias left her first husband Herod II (called Philip at Matt. 14:3; Mark 6:17) to marry Herod Antipas, tetrarch of Perea and Galilee and another son of Herod the Great. After John the Baptist had been put in prison by Antipas, Herodias instigated Salome's request from Antipas for John's execution (Matt. 14:3-11 par.). Salome later married Philip, tetrarch of Iturea, Trachonitis, and other regions (cf. Luke 3:1), who was another son of Herod the Great and half-brother of Salome's father Herod and of Antipas. Salome is not mentioned by name in the New Testament, but is known from Josephus *Ant.* xviii.5.4 (136-37).

SALT (Heb. *melaḥ*; Aram. *mᵉlaḥ*; Gk. *hálas, hála, háls*).† An important preservative in the ancient world, considered essential for life (cf. Ep.Jer. 6:28; Sir. 39:26). Moreover, tasteless food could be made more palatable with salt (cf. Job 6:6). Accordingly, the Seleucid Empire normally imposed a tax on this important substance, gathered from the Dead Sea and the adjoining salt marshes (1 Macc. 10:29; 11:35). In figurative usage, to "eat the salt of the palace" (Ezra 4:14) was to be supported by a royal stipend.

The regular use of salt with food led to its use in ritual as well, such as in sealing a covenant. In the Old Testament a "covenant of salt" is a perpetual covenant (Num. 18:19; 2 Chr. 13:5); thus, "the salt of the covenant with your God" was added to all sacrifices (Lev. 2:13; cf. Ezek. 43:24; Ezra 6:9-10) and to the incense of the tabernacle (Exod. 30:35). Salt flats are characterized as the extreme of unproductive land (Deut. 29:23 [MT 24]; Ps. 107:34 [KJV "barrenness"]; Jer. 17:6; Zeph. 2:9), and salt was sometimes spread on conquered land to prevent agriculture and thus resettlement (Judg. 9:45); but this practice may also have led to a ritual use of salt denoting separation from the past so the area formerly occupied by a city could be put to a new purpose, even resettlement. Such a connotation may underlie 2 Kgs. 2:20-21 as well as the custom of rubbing newborn infants with salt (Ezek. 16:4), still practiced in some places.

Natural salt was abundant enough in some places and trade in salt common enough in Palestine to be reflected in place names such as the valley of Salt, the City of Salt, and, most importantly, the Salt Sea, the most frequent name for the Dead Sea in the Pentateuch and Joshua. The lack of any outlet except evaporation makes the Dead Sea the most saline natural body of water in the world, with a variety of salts (e.g., magnesium chloride, calcium chloride, potassium chloride, sodium chloride). Salt marshes are found at es-Sebkha at the southern end of the Dead Sea (cf. Ezek. 47:11), and the western side of the area south of the sea (as far south as 13 km. [8 mi.] south of the southern shore) is now dominated by salt pans. Jebel Usdum ("Hill of Salt") on the southwestern shore has much rock salt in its slopes, which are eroded into strange formations, many identified as "Lot's Wife" while they have lasted (cf. Gen. 19:26; Wisd. 10:7).

Several New Testament figures of speech drawing upon the uses of salt may have been popular maxims set to the particular uses in which they are now found. In the Gospels, sayings of Jesus mentioning salt have clustered together because of the attraction of the catchword. The "fire" of Mark 9:49 is the fire of sacrifice, and the "salt" is that added to some sacrifices. Similarly, disciples of Jesus are to become sacrifices (cf. Rom. 12:1) in being tested and purified (cf. Mark 9:43-47; 1 Pet. 1:7; 4:12).

Other "salt" sayings of Jesus as well as Col. 4:6 point not to the sacrificial use of salt but to its uses in food and as a preservative (Luke 14:35 may refer to the use of salt in fertilizer, but this is not certain). Salt from the Dead Sea could "lose its saltness," acquiring the alkaline taste of other compounds present as the salt was dissolved out, and so could represent the distinctiveness of the disciples of Jesus over against the world that, if lost, made them of no value (Matt. 5:13; Mark 9:50), like a project begun but not finished, which may as well not have been at all (Luke 14:34; cf. vv. 28-32). This "salt," this distinctiveness, should guard the unity of the disciples (Mark 9:50; cf. vv. 33-35). Tasteless salt might be thrown in the street (Matt. 5:13), the usual place for rubbish; "the salt of the earth" refers to the use of salt as a preservative, keeping things wholesome and worthwhile. Col. 4:6 reflects the use of salt either as a flavoring or to preserve food from corruption (cf. Eph. 5:4).

SALT, CITY OF. *See* CITY OF SALT.

SALT, VALLEY OF (Heb. *gê'-[ham]melaḥ*). A place where Edomite armies were defeated by Judah in the time of David (2 Sam. 8:13; 1 Chr. 18:12; Ps. 60 superscription [MT 2]) and again in the time of Amaziah (2 Kgs. 14:7; 2 Chr. 25:11). Because of its name, the Wâdī el-Milḥ southeast of Beersheba has been identified with the Valley of Salt, but a location closer to Edom, perhaps the area south of the Dead Sea, is more likely.

SALT SEA (Heb. *yām hammelaḥ*). The name used for the DEAD SEA in the Pentateuch and Joshua.

SALU [sā'lōō] (Heb. *sālû'*). A family chief of the tribe of Simeon whose son Zimri, together with a Midianite woman, was killed by Phinehas (Num. 25:14).

SALVATION (Heb. *yēša', yᵉšû'â, tᵉšû'â*; Gk. *sōtēría*, **SAVE** (Heb. *yāša'*, hiphil; Gk. *sōzō, rhýomai*), **SAVIOR** (Heb. *môšía'*; Gk. *sōtḗr*).†

I. Salvation in History

"Salvation" in the Old Testament can refer to an event of rescue from any intolerable situation or great danger from which the person is unable to save himself or herself. The one who rescues can be either human (1 Sam. 11:3; Job 26:2) or divine (Judg. 10:12-15; RSV "deliver"). Most prayers in the Old Testament consist of praise for past events of salvation by God (e.g., 2 Sam. 22:2-20; Ps. 116; cf. 107) and supplication for future acts of salvation (e.g., 2 Chr. 20:9;

Ps. 54:1-3 [MT 3-5]; Hab. 1:2-4; cf. Pss. 59, 79). Because of the moral demands that accompany belief in God, salvation is not available to the fool or the proud sinner (e.g., Ps. 24:3-5; 116:6; cf. 34:18 [MT 19]; 50:23; Jer. 4:14).

The people of Israel were established as the people of God by the Lord's rescuing them from slavery in Egypt and giving them the promised land (Exod. 15:1-21; Hos. 13:4; cf. Neh. 9:9-25; Ps. 105:23-45; Isa. 63:11-14). On the basis of this series of events Israel's God was to be known thenceforth as a saving God. But new events of salvation were necessary as new dangers and disasters arose. Salvation from God was thus experienced again and again, so that it became the framework in which the people of God thought of the Lord. In this way they became aware that no earthly or human deliverance can compare with the deliverance that God himself gives (Ps. 44:3, 6-7 [MT 4, 7-8]; Isa. 26:1; cf. Ps. 108:12 [MT 13]; Hos. 1:7), just as no mere idol could be a savior (Isa. 45:20-22; 46:7; Jer. 2:26-28). God was to be thanked even when human saviors came to deliver the people (Judg. 2:16; Neh. 9:27; cf. Judg. 3:9; 1 Macc. 5:62; Acts 7:25).

Acts of salvation created a bond between God and his people in the same way that human saviors become heroes and leaders of the people. From this history of repeated events of salvation, the people of God learned that their forgetfulness of this bond with their God brought disaster upon them (Judg. 10:6-13; Neh. 9:26-30; Pss. 78, 106; Hos. 13:5-9).

II. Eschatological Salvation

Beyond reference to particular events such as the deliverance of Israel from Egypt, the meaning of "salvation" also encompasses the continuing state of blessing, well-being, and protection from harm that follows an event of rescue (e.g., Isa. 60:18). For the Israelites, events of salvation were repeatedly necessary as new situations of danger and decline came about, and the continuing state of blessedness that followed such events of deliverance proved not to be permanent. For this reason the people who had experienced salvation in the past began to think in terms of an eschatological salvation, a salvation from which there can be no decline, in which the normal state of the world out of which threats to well-being arise is done away with in a total transformation of the social, political, and even physical universe.

First expressed in later parts of the Old Testament, this hope for an eschatological salvation was developed greatly in the apocalyptic writings of postbiblical Judaism. This salvation was to be the vindication and glorification of Israel. Not all persons of Jewish ancestry were to have a part in the eschatological salvation, for not all Jews were faithful to the Judaism of the Torah; but salvation was, nonetheless, to be the possession of Israel as a whole.

Since the primary problems for Jewish faith during the period when the apocalypses were written were the geographical disunity of the Jews and Gentile rule over them and their promised land, so eschatological salvation was to consist of the reuniting of Israel (including the Jews of the Diaspora) in their own land

and the liberation of the land from Gentile rule. The fate of the Gentiles could be envisioned as their conversion to the true God (cf. Isa. 2:2-4), but the dominant theme, especially as apocalyptic eschatology developed through time, was of the subjugation of the oppressive and idolatrous Gentiles to Israel or of their destruction. The eschatological hope of Judaism, even though often conceived in territorial and national terms, became the basis for the understanding of the eschatological salvation proclaimed in the New Testament. *See* APOCALYPTIC.

"Salvation" was a concept known by Gentiles as well as Jews at the time of the New Testament. It was addressed in Gentile cults of the time, and some Gentile rulers were called "savior" (*sōtḗr*). This had some effect on verbal formulations in the New Testament, but was not decisive in the understanding of the Christ event as "salvation." For this, Jewish expressions of hope for release from the troubles of earthly life are the essential background.

A primary focus of salvation in the New Testament is deliverance from sin and from God's eschatological punishment of sinners (Matt. 1:21; Luke 1:77; Acts 2:40; Rom. 5:9; cf. 1 Thess. 1:10). This salvation is not just a release from anxiety concerning God's final retribution, but also involves participation in the life of the age to come. Therefore, in the Synoptic Gospels "salvation" can represent participation in the eschatological kingdom of God proclaimed by Jesus (Matt. 19:25; Luke 8:12; 19:9-10). Because it is directed toward both the eschatological future and the presence of the kingdom brought by Christ, salvation is at the same time a single experience that is already in the past for Christians (1 Cor. 15:2; Eph. 2:5), a process Christians are undergoing in the present (Acts 2:47; 1 Cor. 1:18; Phil. 2:12), and a future experience (Rom. 5:9-10; 13:11; 1 Cor. 5:5; cf. Phil. 3:20); the single term stands for all phases of what God has brought in Christ. The preaching of the gospel is the means by which this salvation is brought to the world (Acts 13:26, 47; 16:17; Rom. 1:16; 10:13-15; Eph. 1:13).

The essential condition for participation in the salvation proclaimed in the New Testament is faith in Christ (Acts 16:31; 1 Cor. 1:21; Eph. 2:8). God is called the "Savior" (Luke 1:47; 1 Tim. 1:1), but the role of Christ is essential; he too is called "Savior" (e.g., Luke 2:11; John 4:42; Acts 5:31). The meaning of Jesus' name, "the Lord is salvation" (Heb. y^e-$hôšûaʿ$), is linked at Matt. 1:21 with his centrality in salvation. His death and resurrection are understood to be the basis of salvation (Rom. 5:10; 10:9; cf. 1 Cor. 15:3).

The focus on the Jewish people in Jewish eschatological hope is somewhat displaced in the New Testament proclamation of salvation by the availability of that salvation to every person, Jew or Gentile, on the basis of faith in Christ. But the focus on the Jewish people is not entirely set aside, with the result that Jewish nonacceptance of Jesus as Messiah is perceived as a difficulty of some proportion (cf. Matt. 23:37-39; esp. Rom. 9–11). In the gospel of John Jesus is presented as the one sent to save "the world" (John 3:17; 4:42; 12:47). This universal focus is the counterpart to a focus on the individual, "whoever believes" (3:16; cf. 10:9). But the New Testament, including John, acknowledges the relationship of the salvation in Christ to the salvation history in the Jewish people (Luke 19:9; John 4:22; cf. Rom. 9:4-5).

In the New Testament "salvation" (Gk. *sōtēría*) and related words appear in uses other than for the eschatological salvation from sin brought in Christ, such as with reference to healing (e.g., Matt. 9:21-22; Mark 5:23; John 11:12; Acts 4:9) and to the saving of lives of those in some danger (27:20), including the destruction of Jerusalem (Matt. 24:22) and the experience of crucifixion (27:40, 49). But even these quite normal uses of the Greek terminology usually encompass some relation to the coming of eschatological salvation in Christ.

SALVE (Gk. *kolloúrion*).* A medicinal powder applied as a paste to the eyes (Rev. 3:18; KJV "eyesalve"). Laodicea was known for its medical school and was, indeed, where some eye salve was manufactured. There is, therefore, some irony in the counsel to the Laodicean Christians that they purchase salve to remedy their spiritual blindness (cf. v. 17).

SAMARIA [sə mârˊĭ ə] (Heb. *šōmrôn*; Aram. *šāmᵉrāyin*; Gk. *Samareia*). The capital city of Israel, the northern kingdom.

Samaria was established as Israel's capital on a hill purchased by King Omri from Shemer (1 Kgs. 16:24). The ruins of the city are at modern Sebastiyeh, *ca.* 9 km. (5.6 mi.) northwest of Nablus. Omri's palace complex and fortifications were expanded under succeeding kings of Israel (e.g., Ahab; 1 Kgs. 22:39). The city and the kingdom fell to the Assyrian Empire in 722-721 B.C. (2 Kgs. 17:6). During a time of Assyrian weakness King Josiah of Judah was able to gain brief control of Samaria and the surrounding region (23:19-20). The city experienced the changes of rule to which the entire Near East was subject, passing from Assyrian to Babylonian to Persian rule. With Alexander's defeat of the Persian Empire, Samaria came under Macedonian control (332) and became a Greek city. The non-Greek people called "Samaritans" inhabited the smaller towns of the region. Samaria was destroyed by John Hyrcanus in 108 as part of his expansion of the Hasmonean realm. The city was rebuilt under Roman rule in 57 B.C. In 30 B.C. it became part of Herod the Great's kingdom, remaining a Gentile city. Herod named it Sebastē (from *Sebastos*, the Greek representation of Lat. *Augustus*), and undertook considerable building operations there. It was again destroyed in the war of A.D. 66-70. It was established as a Roman colony in 200, but by the fifth century was hardly settled.

The considerable archaeological work conducted at Samaria has uncovered remains from each period of settlement. Among the finds are the palace of the Israelite kings, part of the wall built by Omri around the palace complex, and a number of later walls and structures, including extensive remains of the Roman city wall. A pool found inside the palace complex may be the pool mentioned at 1 Kgs. 22:38. A number of inscribed potsherds recording shipments of oil and

An Israelite wall at Samaria (by courtesy of the Israel Department of Antiquities and Museums)

wine during the ninth or eighth century B.C. have been found. Several objects of carved ivory have been found, mainly plaques made for inlaying (cf. 1 Kgs. 22:39; Amos 3:15), which have been very important in showing the range and geographical diffusion of artistic styles in the Iron Age.

The name "Samaria" came to be applied to the territory formerly occupied by the kingdom of Israel after the defeat of that kingdom by Assyria (e.g., 2 Kgs. 23:19; cf. 1 Kgs. 13:32, perhaps an alteration of an earlier text). "Samaria" is used in the New Testament (e.g., John 4:4; Acts 1:8) for the central hill country, the region extending generally to the Jordan river in the east, the valley of Aijalon and Joppa in the south, the Mediterranean Sea in the west, and Caesarea Maritima and the valley of Jezreel in the north.

SAMARITAN PENTATEUCH.† A Hebrew text of the Pentateuch preserved by the Samaritan community (*see* SAMARITANS), characterized by several differences in spelling and wording from the MT. Most of the differences are unimportant, and others are modifications reflecting the particular beliefs of the Samaritans, most often their belief that Mt. Gerizim is the place intended by God for worship (cf. Deut. 11:29-30; 12:5-14). However, the Samaritan Pentateuch also contains agreements with the LXX and, to a lesser degree, with Qumran biblical manuscripts and quotations of the Old Testament in the New Testament, over against the MT. These indicate that the Hebrew text modified to produce the Samaritan Pentateuch is independent of the consonantal text that became the basis of the MT. The overall picture that emerges is of a period of diversity in the Hebrew text that only later in the mainstream of Judaism was gradually supplanted by the dominance of the consonantal text underlying the MT.

The date of the Samaritan Pentateuch is contingent on the date assigned to the final break between the Jews and the Samaritans, since both groups possess essentially the same Pentateuch. This division was formerly thought to have occurred gradually in the fourth century B.C., but is now more often associated with

The Samaritan Pentateuch

the attack of John Hyrcanus on Gerizim in 129-128 B.C. Most manuscripts of the Samaritan Pentateuch are from the thirteenth century A.D. or later, though a small number are earlier.

SAMARITANS [sə măr'ə tənz] (Heb. *haššōmᵉrōnî*; Gk. *Samareitēs*).† Inhabitants of the region of Samaria and adherents of the Samaritan religious tradition.

The Jewish view of the origin and nature of the Samaritans occurs already in the Old Testament, beginning with the judgment (summarized at 2 Kgs. 17:7-23) that the northern kingdom of Israel consistently deviated from the course of true religion. Those living in the territory of the northern kingdom after its destruction by Assyria are regarded as non-Israelites settled there by Assyria who adopted Israel's religion, combining it with their own polytheism (vv. 24-41). Samaritans came to be regarded by Jews as neither fully Gentile nor fully Jewish. "Samaritan" could itself be a term of contempt among Jews (John 8:48). The Mishnah calls the Samaritans "Cuthites" (cf. 2 Kgs. 17:24), thus labeling them as non-Israelite in origin.

The Samaritans' canon contains only the Pentateuch. They regard Moses as the final prophet of God and a superhuman being. Mt. Gerizim they identify as the place where Abraham was prepared to sacrifice Isaac (Gen. 22) and where God intended that Israel's one place of sacrificial worship be established (cf. Deut. 11:29-30; 12:5-14). The Samaritans' alternative to the Jewish history of the relation between the two groups teaches that the Jewish departure from the truth began when Eli set up a shrine at Shiloh (cf. 1 Sam. 1–3), not Gerizim; Ezra compounded the falsehood by altering the Pentateuch and by rebuilding the temple at Jerusalem. Though they acknowledge that non-Israelites entered the region of Samaria under Assyrian auspices, the Samaritans regard themselves as descendants of exiled Israelites who returned to the land.

Only a portion of Israel's population was exiled after defeat by Assyria (cf. 2 Chr. 34:9), and it is possible that some of these did return. Those who remained were assimilated with the new inhabitants the Assyrians had resettled from elsewhere. Furthermore, it would appear that the Jewish view of the Samaritan religion as indebted to non-Israelite religions is exaggerated.

The division between the Jews and the Samaritans developed gradually over a long period of time. King Josiah of Judah (640-609 B.C.) destroyed Samaritan worship places at a time of Assyrian weakness (2 Kgs. 23:19-20). Some of the Samaritans did, nonetheless, continue for some time regular pilgrimages to the Jerusalem temple (Jer. 41:5). Postexilic Judah was reconstituted under the strict reformation of religion under Ezra and Nehemiah, in which the Samaritans could not participate because of their supposed non-Israelite ancestry and syncretism (Ezra 4:2-3; Neh. 2:20). Having been rebuffed by the Judahites, the Samaritans opposed the rebuilding of Jerusalem, and were successful for a time (Ezra 4:9-24; cf. Neh. 2:19; 4:2 [MT 3:34]). The schism was made complete by the building of a Samaritan temple on Mt. Gerizim, probably early in the fourth century B.C. (according to Josephus *Ant.* xi.8.4 [321-324], at the beginning of Alexander's rule over the region), and that temple's destruction by John Hyrcanus in 129-128 B.C.

The Jewish report that the Samaritans willingly paganized their temple under pressure from Antiochus Epiphanes (2 Macc. 6:2) is at least exaggerated. Samaritan worship continues on Mt. Gerizim in modern times, though no temple survives. The Passover lamb is sacrificed every year, and other Pentateuchal feast days are occasions for pilgrimage.

Jesus' ministry was not normally directed to Samaritans, and he directed his disciples as they embarked on speaking and healing missions during his ministry not to go to Samaria (Matt. 10:5-6). In Jesus' encounter with a Samaritan woman (John 4:1-42), the decisive issue of the proper place for worship was faced (v. 20). Isa. 66:1-2 anticipates what Jesus told the woman: the answer is neither this place nor that place, because the religion of spirit and truth will supplant the religion of place (John 4:21-24). Thus, despite his loyalty to Jerusalem (cf. Matt. 23:37-38; Luke 9:52-53) and the Jews (John 4:22), Jesus laid the foundation for a transcendence of the division between the two peoples. Samaritans appear in positive roles in Jesus' teaching and the record of his ministry, mainly because faith and mercy on the part of Samaritans would not be expected by Jesus' Jewish audience and were, therefore, worthy of note (Luke 10:30-37; 17:11-19).

After his resurrection Jesus specifically instructed his apostles to take the gospel to Samaria (Acts 1:8). It was because of persecution directed against the Hellenistic branch of the church at Jerusalem that missionary work in Samaria was begun (8:1, 5-25). The work was successful at least for a time in establishing a lasting Christian fellowship in the region

(9:31; 15:3). What effect this Samaritan Christianity had on the New Testament is disputed. It has been suggested that Stephen's origin was Samaritan and that the gospel of John, particularly its christology, reflects Samaritan influences.

SAMGAR-NEBO [săm′gär nē′bō] (Heb. *samgar-nᵉḇô*). An official in Nebuchadrezzar's government who had a role in the 587 B.C. Babylonian siege of Jerusalem (Jer. 39:3). The string of Hebrew syllables in this verse that is generally interpreted as a list of names, titles, and possibly territories of a group of officials is similar to the less complex list at v. 13. "Samgar-nebo" is usually taken as the combination of "Simmagar," a title, or "Samgar," a territory (so NIV), with the beginning of "Nebo-sarsechim," a personal name, probably a confused form of the "Nebushazban" of v. 13.

SAMLAH [săm′lə] (Heb. *śamlâ* "garment"). A resident of Masrekah and an early king of Edom (Gen. 36:36-37; 1 Chr. 1:47-48).

SAMOS [sā′mŏs] (Gk. *Samos*). A mountainous island in the Aegean Sea, 2 km. (1.4 mi.) from Trogyllium in Asia Minor and southwest of Ephesus. Founded by Ionian colonists in the eleventh century B.C., Samos was an important naval force in ancient times and the birthplace of the philosopher Pythagoras. It was among the free territories to which Rome addressed a document of support for the Hasmonean government of Judea *ca.* 140 B.C. (1 Macc. 15:23). Samos became part of the Roman province of Asia in 84 but became independent under Roman rule in 17 B.C. The ship carrying Paul's party came near to or briefly anchored at (the term used is ambiguous) Samos (perhaps the port city of the same name) en route from Assos to Miletus (Acts 20:15).

SAMOTHRACE [săm′ə thrās] (Gk. *Samothrakē*).† A mountainous island in the northeastern Aegean Sea, *ca.* 40 km. (25 mi.) from the Thracian coast. Although the island has no natural harbor, the ship carrying Paul's party stopped there en route from Troas in northwestern Asia Minor to Neapolis in Macedonia (Acts 16:11).

SAMSON [săm′sən] (Heb. *šimšôn*; from *šemeš* "sun, solar deity"; Gk. *Sampsōn*).† An Israelite hero, regarded as one of the judges. Samson's birth was announced to his mother, the childless wife of the Danite Manoah, by an angel who said that the boy would be a Nazirite and that he would begin to deliver Israel from the Philistines (Judg. 13:2-7). The instructions given to safeguard Samson's status as a Nazirite from birth were repeated to Manoah and his wife (vv. 8-14). When Samson had become a man, "the Spirit of the Lord began to stir him in Mahaneh-dan, between Zorah and Eshtaol" (v. 25), i.e., in the original area of Danite settlement adjacent to Philistine territory.

Samson married an unnamed Philistine woman (14:1-4). At their wedding feast the woman responded to a threat by obtaining from him and then divulging the solution to a riddle Samson had posed. In angry response Samson killed some of her fellow Philistines

and left her; as a result, he lost her to his best man (vv. 10-20). The riddle was itself a reminder of Samson's first heroic deed, his bare-handed killing of a lion (vv. 5-9). Angry because he had thus lost his wife, Samson burned the grain fields and olive orchards of the Philistines in the area (15:1-5). They responded by killing the woman and her father (or her family, following LXX A and Syr.; cf. 14:15) in revenge (15:6). Samson killed more Philistines in response and then went to live in a cave (v. 8). He was given over to his Philistine pursuers by some Judahites, but he broke the ropes with which he was bound and killed another thousand Philistines (vv. 9-17).

After an incident in which God preserved Samson from weakening by thirst that would have made him capturable by the Philistines (vv. 18-19), an ambush was set for him at Philistine Gaza. But by his superhuman strength, Samson was again freed (16:1-3). The Philistine rulers sought the means to put an end to his strength, working through Delilah, another Philistine woman whom Samson loved (vv. 4-5). Samson led Delilah along for a time, telling her first one false means of subduing his strength and then another (vv. 6-14), but then submitted to her entreaties. The secret of his strength was in the maintenance of his Nazirite vow, which would be broken if his hair was cut (vv. 15-17). This was done, Samson was captured, and his eyes were put out so he could be humiliated before the Philistines in the temple of Dagon (vv. 18-27). But God restored his strength (his hair had grown back, v. 22) so that he was able to pull down two supporting pillars of the temple, killing both himself and thousands of Philistines (vv. 28-30). (This narrative may have been preserved partly to combat campaigns against Nazirite vows [cf. Amos 2:11-12].)

The material concerning Samson appears last in the series of narratives concerning the "judges" of Israel (Judg. 3:7–16:31), and Samson himself is called a judge (15:20; 16:31). But he was not, like the other judges, a ruler and organizer of people for battle, but rather an individualistic hero who fought alone. Furthermore, he was not consciously fighting for the liberation of his particular tribe or his nation Israel.

God worked through Samson to destroy many of the Philistines who were threatening Israel's integrity. But through all the incidents presented, Samson's aims were personal and not national. He remained ignorant of the divine working behind his first marriage (14:1-4); he violated Israelite endogamy, thereby threatening the security of his people (cf. v. 3); he destroyed one group of Philistines out of anger at the betrayal of his riddle (vv. 19-20); and he prayed to God only for the preservation of his own honor (15:18) and for personal revenge (16:28), not with any sense of the importance of Israel nor from any sense of obligation to God. Nevertheless, God's Spirit worked through Samson (13:25), making possible his superhuman strength (14:6; 15:14) and giving him success in battle (14:19). Samson's anger and vengefulness were more useful to God in controlling Philistine dominance of Israel than was the cautious compliance of others (15:11-12). But the results were only partial: Dan had to move to a new territory (ch. 18), and the Philistines continued to be a problem for Israel.

SAMUEL [săm'yŏŏ əl] (Heb. *š^emû'ēl* "name of God").† An eleventh-century B.C. prophet, regarded as the last of the judges to rule Israel (Acts 13:20); a Levite (1 Chr. 6:28 [MT 13]; cf. v. 33; KJV "Shemuel"), son of Elkanah and Hannah (1 Sam. 1:20).

Samuel's birth was an answer to prayer (v. 10, "asked of the Lord"; cf. Heb. *šā'al*). Hannah had promised to dedicate her son as a Nazirite, so after weaning him she brought the boy to Eli, priest at Shiloh, to fulfil her vow (vv. 11, 24-28). Under Eli's supervision Samuel served God at the Shiloh sanctuary and grew "in the presence of the Lord" (2:21). In a dark time when prophetic utterance was rare (cf. 3:1) Yahweh spoke frequently to the young boy, and his reputation spread through Israel (vv. 20-21). In particular, God called Samuel to prophesy judgment against the house of Eli for the wickedness of the priest's sons (vv. 12-14).

Twenty years after the great Israelite defeat at Aphek and the loss of the ark of the covenant to the Philistines, Samuel acted as judge, mustering the tribes, renewing the covenant, and delivering Israel from the Philistines at Mizpah. He judged Israel "all the days of his life" from his home in Ramah, each year administering justice within the circuit encompassing Bethel, Gilgal, and Mizpah (ch. 7).

Samuel's greatest contribution was his role in establishing the Israelite monarchy. In his old age he appointed his sons Joel and Abijah as judges, but like Eli's sons they became corrupt, taking bribes and perverting justice (8:1-3). This failure and the desire for a king to lead them into battle prompted the elders of Israel to petition the prophet for a king "like all the nations" (vv. 4-5, 20). Although Samuel disapproved, he heeded the command of Yahweh and granted their request, anointing Saul as king (9:1-10:16; cf. vv. 17-27; 11:15). Continuing to chasten the people regarding the dangers of monarchy (8:11-18), Samuel recorded the rights and duties of the king and placed them before the Lord (10:25). When the new ruler usurped Samuel's role as prophet (13:8-14) and disobeyed the word of the Lord (15:22-23), Yahweh instructed Samuel to reject Saul's kingship (vv. 26-29) and to anoint David as king instead (ch. 16).

Having presented Saul to the people as ruler, Samuel surrendered his judgeship. In a farewell address he recalled his steadfast example and admonished the people to serve Yahweh with respect and faithfulness, cautioning them of disaster should they pursue evil ways (ch. 12). Samuel retired to his home at Ramah, where he died and was buried during Saul's persecution of David (25:1; cf. ch. 28, where Saul summons the advice of Samuel's ghost). Later generations held him in highest esteem as an intercessor second only to Moses, and God's beloved (Ps. 99:6; Jer. 15:1; Sir. 46:13-20; cf. 45:1).

SAMUEL, BOOKS OF.† In English versions, the eighth and ninth books of the Old Testament.

I. Place in Canon

In the Hebrew manuscript tradition, 1-2 Samuel were originally one book, the third book of the Former Prophets. The division into two books originated with the LXX, where they are called 1-2 Kingdoms (Gk.

Basileiōn A, B); this division was followed in the Vulgate (Lat. *1-2 Regnorum*) and later adopted in printed versions of the Hebrew scriptures.

In general, critical scholars place the books of Samuel in the larger context of the Deuteronomic History comprised of Deuteronomy and the Former Prophets, a history of Judah and Israel wherein the people and their kings are evaluated on the basis of their obedience (and disobedience) to the Deuteronomic law.

II. Origin and Transmission

Since the death of Samuel is recorded at 1 Sam. 25:1, the prophet can hardly have been the author of all the material that bears his name. Yet the original unity of 1-2 Samuel and Samuel's major role in the transition from confederacy to monarchy underscore the association of his name with these books. Indeed, Jewish tradition regards him as their author (Talmud *B. Bat.* 14b), and he may well be responsible for some accounts of David's early career (cf. 1 Chr. 29:29).

Scholars in general agree that the materials of 1-2 Samuel were compiled gradually over a period of time. Some accounts have the character of folklore (e.g., the account of Saul and the lost asses, 1 Sam. 9–10) and can be assumed to be very old, while others (e.g., the discussion of the evils of monarchy, ch. 8) seem to reflect the theological perspectives of the prophets and the Monarchy or even the Exile. Earlier collections employed by those who produced 1-2 Samuel seem to have included an Ark Narrative (cf. 1 Sam. 4–6; 2 Sam. 6), cycles of stories about Saul (e.g., his birth and name, 1 Sam. 1:27-28a; lost asses, chs. 9–10; military exploits, chs. 11, 13–15), an account of David's rise to power (1 Sam. 16–2 Sam. 5), and a Succession Narrative or Court History of David (2 Sam. 9–20; 1 Kgs. 1–2; 2 Sam. 21–24 has the character of an appendix).

After the text of 1-2 Samuel was completed (during or shortly after the Exile, according to those who ascribe it to the Deuteronomic History), it was preserved in the manuscripts and memories of early Jewish communities. Scholars have long wrestled with the problems presented by discrepancies between the MT and LXX; the MT is shorter, and in many instances the Hebrew is difficult to understand (texts found at Qumran represent a "middle ground" between the MT and LXX). Scholars have often used the LXX to "correct" the MT, but as texts actually used by believing communities both should be regarded—and respected—as distinctive traditions.

III. Structure and Contents

Scholarly consensus regards 1-2 Samuel to be structured around the accounts of three figures—Samuel, Saul, and David; the precise division of these accounts is subject to interpretation. The account of Samuel begins at 1 Sam. 1:1, and Samuel continues to be the main character of the narrative through 8:22. With 9:1 Saul becomes the focus, though Samuel still figures in the narrative. From 1 Sam. 16:1 through 2 Sam. 24:25 both Samuel and Saul recede into the background as David becomes the key figure. David, in turn, becomes a minor figure when the narrative turns to Solomon at 1 Kgs. 1.

A. Samuel (1 Sam. 1–8). The story of Samuel begins with the account of his conception and birth as an answer to the prayer of his mother Hannah (the play on words at 1:27-28a, which uses four forms of the Hebrew root *šā'al* "ask," would be more appropriate for the name Saul). Samuel becomes a leading figure in Israel, acting as a judge and a prophet leading Israel in the transition from tribal confederacy to the monarchy under Saul. Included here are narratives about Samuel's parents (1:1–2:21), Eli and his family (a priestly family rejected by Yahweh in favor of a priest who would act faithfully; vv. 35-36), and the capture and return of the ark of the covenant (chs. 4–6).

B. Saul (chs. 9–15). In the narrative of 1 Samuel Saul is introduced as a handsome young Benjaminite who approaches Samuel to inquire about his father's lost asses and who is secretly anointed as Israel's king (9:1–10:16). While Israel is gathered at Mizpah, Saul is selected by lot as Yahweh's chosen king (vv. 17-27), but only after his rescue of Jabesh-gilead does his kingship become a significant force in Israel (ch. 11). Saul's victories over Israel's enemies are described (chs. 13–14), as well as the occasions of his disobedience that brought about his rejection and Yahweh's choice of a king who would act faithfully (13:7-15; ch. 15). Within the narratives where Saul is the principal figure Samuel appears in a minor role, warning Israel that they and their king must follow Yahweh (chs. 8, 12, 15), and Jonathan appears as a valiant warrior (ch. 14).

C. David (1 Sam. 16–2 Sam. 24). David was anointed by Samuel and came into the service of King Saul (1 Sam. 16). His military successes in Saul's service—beginning with the defeat of Goliath (ch. 17)—gained for him the admiration of the people of Israel and the mistrust and hatred of Saul. The narrative makes clear that David was not a traitor to his king and people; Jonathan (19:1-7) and even Saul (chs. 24, 26) confess David's loyalty. After the death of Saul and Jonathan (ch. 31) Abner, a commander of Saul's army, makes Saul's son Ishbosheth king over the northern Israelite tribes, and David becomes king over Judah (2 Sam. 2:1-11). After two years of conflict between supporters of David and supporters of Ishbosheth, David becomes king over all Israel (2:12–5:5). 2 Samuel records both the successes and scandals of David's reign, but on the whole the evaluation of his kingship is positive. Yahweh's promise of a perpetual house for David—successors to his throne from among his own descendants—is recorded at ch. 7 (the "Divine charter"). Several characters have minor roles in the narrative of David's rise to power and his reign over Israel, including Jonathan (1 Sam. 19:1-7; ch. 20), Saul (22:6-19; chs. 24, 26; 28:3-25; ch. 31), Abigail (25:14-38), Joab (2 Sam. 11:1, 14-25), Abner (chs. 2–3), and Absalom (chs. 13–18). The last act of David recorded in 2 Samuel is his purchase of the threshing floor of Araunah and his erection of an altar and presentation of offerings there (24:15-25); this anticipates the narrative of Solomon in 1 Kings and the building of the temple.

IV. Theology

The theological similarities between the books of Samuel and Deuteronomic theology are evident in the poetic framework provided by the Song of Hannah (1 Sam. 2:1-10) and the Last Words of David (2 Sam. 23:1-7). These passages reflect the authors' and compilers' understanding of Israel's history and relationship with God, an understanding stemming from their reflection upon Israel's historical and religious traditions—especially the messages of the prophets—in light of the national (and religious) catastrophe represented in the fall of Jerusalem, the destruction of the temple, and the exile from the promised land. The Deuteronomic History demonstrates that when the people were faithful to Yahweh they enjoyed God's blessings upon their land, but when they were unfaithful they suffered many hardships. Within this context 1-2 Samuel introduce the monarchy as an institution with the potential either to enhance Israel's relationship with Yahweh through promoting obedience to the law, or to damage the relationship with God by failing to promote such obedience or even by introducing idolatry. Thus the monarchy, with its potential for either good or evil, is shown to be an institution accepted by the Lord when he promises a sure house for David (2 Sam. 7). Jerusalem (and later the temple), the only appropriate locus for sacrifices to the Lord, is an important concern of the Deuteronomic History (e.g., Deut. 26:2; 1 Kgs. 12:25–13:34; 22:43-44; 2 Kgs. 12:3; 21:1-9; 22:1–23:25), a theme evident in the accounts of David's capture of Jerusalem and the establishment of his capital there (2 Sam. 5:6-12) and of his purchase of the temple site and offering of sacrifices (24:15-25).

1-2 Samuel recount the actions of faithless people who are rejected (Eli and his sons; Saul) and of the great faithful king of Israel, David—his successes and the promise made to him. In recounting the origin of the monarchy, the choice of Jerusalem as Israel's capital, and the purchase of the site upon which the temple would be built they show how Israel came to understand this important period in their history and its consequences for their relationship with Yahweh.

The theology of 1-2 Samuel—and the whole of the Deuteronomic History—can be summarized in equations such as faithfulness to God = success and prosperity in temporal human existence, and disobedience = divine retribution in temporal human existence. The biblical writers knew that sometimes the wicked prosper and the righteous suffer (cf. Eccl. 7:15; 9:11-12), a realization that remains difficult even today. The biblical account demonstrates, however, that God cares deeply for those who suffer and is present with them, sharing their pain. It demonstrates also that God acts in and through the lives of humans as they work to relieve suffering and establish justice (cf. Hab. 2:3-4). 1-2 Samuel affirms that the way in which humans respond to God is vitally important, not because one can always see the consequences of human actions becoming a reality in the world but, rather, because of faith in God.

Bibliography. A. F. Campbell, *1-2 Samuel,* FOTL (forthcoming); H. W. Hertzberg, *I and II Samuel.* OTL (1964); P. K. McCarter, Jr., *I Samuel.* AB 8 (1980); *II Samuel.* AB 9 (1984).

SANBALLAT [săn băl'ət] (Heb. *sanballaṭ*; Akk. *Sin-*

uballiṭ "Sin [a lunar deity] gives life"). A leader of the opposition to Nehemiah's rebuilding of the walls of Jerusalem. Sanballat was a "Horonite," probably a native of Beth-horon in Ephraim or, less likely, of Horonaim in Moab. He probably feared that rebuilt Jerusalem would diminish the loyalty of residents of the province of Samaria, of which (according to the Elephantine papyri) he was governor, and that it might draw a reaction of force from the Persian rulers, with repercussions in Samaria as well. His opposition to Jerusalem's rebuilding took the form of ridicule (Neh. 2:19; 4:1-3 [MT 3:33-35]), threats of violence (vv. 7-8, 11-23 [MT 1-2, 5-17]), attempted treachery (6:1-4, 10-13), and attempts to charge the Judeans with conspiring to rebel against Persia (vv. 5-7).

The names of Sanballat's sons, Delaiah and Shelemiah, are attested in the Elephantine papyri. That both are compounds of a short form of "Yahweh" suggests that Sanballat was a worshipper of Israel's God, and, therefore, a member of the emerging Samaritan religious community (*see* SAMARITANS). Sanballat's daughter married the descendant of a Jerusalem high priest (13:28; this suggests that Sanballat's dislike of Nehemiah's rebuilding program did not initially cut him off from relations with the Judean community as a whole); this priestly son-in-law of Sanballat was expelled from Jerusalem by Nehemiah (vv. 28-29).

According to Josephus, the Samaritan temple was built under a Sanballat, governor of Samaria, and his son-in-law, Manasses, son and brother of Jerusalem high priests (*Ant.* xi.7.2; 8.2, 4 [302-303, 306-312, 322-325]). This Sanballat is connected with Alexander the Great's conquest of Palestine and is, therefore, too late to be the contemporary of Nehemiah. It is likely, nonetheless, that Josephus' account, which is based on both Jewish polemical tales concerning the Samaritan community and Samaritan accounts concerning the origin of their community, confuses the Sanballat of Nehemiah's day with a later person of that name.

SANCTIFY, CONSECRATE (Heb. *mālē᾽ yāḏ*, piel *qāḏaš*, niphal and hiphil *nāzar*; Gk. *hagiázō*).† While holiness is fundamentally a quality of God (Job 6:10; Isa. 6:1-5; Hos. 11:9), by God's action persons, places, or objects can be consecrated or sanctified, i.e., separated from common life or use and dedicated in some way to the service or worship of God.

In the Old Testament God does not simply declare objects or places of worship holy; although he is the sanctifier (Exod. 30:43; cf. 31:13), ceremonial rites are involved in sanctification. The altar was consecrated with sacrifice and anointing (29:36b-37), the tabernacle and its furnishings were anointed when they were first put to use (40:9-11; cf. 30:22-29), and firstling males of flock and herd were to be eaten in a ceremonial meal (Deut. 15:19-20).

Through the ceremonial rites of consecration, it is shown that places and objects are not holy because of their own existence, but because of their involvement in the holiness of God's people and their worship. The holiness even of objects used in worship is, therefore, not an impersonal or neutral quality, but is built upon the relationship between God and his people. While specific persons—e.g., priests (Exod. 30:30;

40:12-15), Levites (Num. 8:5-21; 2 Chr. 29:5), firstborn sons (Exod. 13:2), and Nazirites (Num. 6:1-21)—were consecrated for specific roles, the underlying assumption was that the whole of the people of God were consecrated to Yahweh (cf. Lev. 21:8). This consecration of the whole people was accomplished by rites on some occasions (Exod. 19:10, 14) but was also viewed as the ongoing nature of the people: "You shall be holy; for I the Lord your God am holy" (Lev. 19:2; cf. 1 Pet. 1:15). The sanctification of the people was to be evidenced by obedience to the specific commandments of God (Exod. 31:13; Lev. 20:8), by their adherence to proper ritual (e.g., 19:5-8), by more general ethical behavior (e.g., vv. 17-18), and by their distinctness from other peoples (Exod. 33:16).

The ground upon which the New Testament speaks of believers in Christ as "sanctified" is God's own act, his declaration of their sanctification (John 17:17). This sanctification occurs "in Christ Jesus" (1 Cor. 1:2; cf. v. 30); those who are sanctified are those who believe in him. He is the sanctifier by means of his death (John 17:19; Eph. 5:25-26; Heb. 2:11; 10:10, 14; 13:12). The Holy Spirit and God the Father are also active in the sanctification of Christians (Rom. 15:16; 1 Pet. 1:2; Jude 1). Because sanctification is accomplished by God, Paul's most common term for Christians is "saints" (Gk. *hágioi* "holy ones"; e.g., Rom. 12:13; 1 Cor. 1:2; Gal. 1:1), apart from the measure of their faithfulness to a high standard of life. God's act of sanctifying those who believe in Christ is linked with the ritual of baptism (1 Cor. 6:11; Eph. 5:26) and is evidenced by a changed manner of life most obvious in those whose prior lives were far from God's standards (1 Cor. 6:9-11).

Alongside this view of sanctification as a single event is an understanding of it as a process of ethical growth involving human effort (Rom. 6:19; 1 Thess. 4:1-7; 2 Tim. 2:21; Heb. 12:14). But even this process is dependent on God's prior act and continuing work in believers (1 Thess. 5:23).

See HOLINESS, HOLY.

SANDALS, SHOES (Heb. *na᾿ălayim*; Gk. *sándalia, hypodēmata*). While shoes that completely covered the foot and sometimes part of the leg were worn in biblical times, especially by soldiers (e.g., Heb. *s⁰᾽ôn* "boot"; Isa. 9:5), sandals were much more common. Sandals consisted of a sole attached to the foot by a strap or a number of straps extending over and around the foot. The pattern of sandal-straps varied widely. A typical Egyptian sandal had a single strap attached at both ends between the first two toes and going around the heel. In another common form of sandal, a heavy strap that crossed the ankle was attached to a lighter strap fastened between the first two toes. A common form of sandal, especially for soldiers and among Mesopotamian dignitaries, covered the heel completely and was held in place by straps across the top of the foot. Sandals and shoes were often made with toes curving upward. The quality and style of footwear were a reflection of social standing (cf. Ezek. 16:10), as was its mere presence or absence (cf. Luke 15:22).

Theophanies were occasion for removal of footwear because of respect for the sanctity of the place (Exod.

3:5; Josh. 5:15). Having the feet unshod was also a feature of mourning rituals (2 Sam. 15:30; cf. Ezek. 24:17, 23). The bare feet of captives were also worthy of note (2 Chr. 28:15; Isa. 20:2-4). Footwear was usually taken off by guests when entering a house (cf. Luke 7:38, 44), but not by the owner of the house (cf. 15:22). The wearing of shoes or sandals meant that one was ready for a journey (Exod. 12:11; Mark 6:9; Acts 12:8), but for the poor or the ascetic, even long distances would be traveled with the feet unshod (Matt. 10:10; cf. Luke 9:1-5).

Removal of a sandal was part of a ritual of renunciation of ownership of land performed when a levirate marriage might cloud the claim of inheritance of children already born (Deut. 25:9-10; Ruth 4:6-10). Throwing a shoe or sandal on the ground (or a portion of land) was apparently a way of signifying a claim of possession (cf. Ps. 60:8 [MT 10]). Among the more humble attendants on royalty and aristocracy were sandalbearers; in comparing himself with Jesus, John the Baptist considered himself not worthy of even this humble role (Matt. 3:11; Mark 1:7; Acts 13:25). At Eph. 6:15 the Roman soldier's footwear is a figure for the protection given by "the gospel of peace."

SANHEDRIN [săn hē'drən] (Gk. *synédrion* "seated together," *presbytérion, gerousía, boulé*).† A council in Jerusalem that functioned as the central judicial authority for Jews. The Sanhedrin is mentioned in the New Testament as the body that sought Jesus' arrest (Matt. 26:47; RSV "elders"; John 11:47-53; RSV "council") and before which Jesus (Matt. 26:57–27:2) and some leaders of the early Church (Acts 4:5-21; 5:21-40; RSV "council," "Senate"; 6:12-15; 22:30–23:10) were tried.

Ideally at least, the Sanhedrin had seventy members, actually seventy-one when the president was counted among the members. The high priest was the Sanhedrin's president in the New Testament period (cf. Matt. 26:57). The council's members were drawn mainly from the leading priestly families and the religious instructors known as "scribes" or "teachers of the law." By including both of these groups, the Sanhedrin was composed of both (priestly) Sadducees and (scribal) Pharisees. Also included were "elders" not connected with either party among the members of the council. Some New Testament terms for the Sanhedrin reflect its diverse composition (Matt. 2:4; "chief priests and scribes"; 27:41; "chief priest," "scribes and elders"; Mark 14:55; "chief priests and the whole council"; Luke 22:66; 23:13; "chief priests and the rulers and the people"; Acts 4:5, 23; "rulers and elders and scribes").

Rabbinic tradition links the origin of the central Sanhedrin with the seventy elders who assisted Moses in the wilderness (Num. 11:16-17, 24-25). Actually, a central council or representative body of elders existed only sporadically in preexilic Israel and Judah (1 Kgs. 8:1; 20:7; 2 Kgs. 23:1; 2 Chr. 19:8; Ezek. 14:1; 20:1). Under Ezra and Nehemiah not only assemblies of elders (Ezra 5:5; 6:7; 10:8; Neh. 4:14) but also assemblies of the whole nation were convened (Ezra 10:9; Neh. 7:5). The principle involved in these assemblies of the whole nation continued to be of significance even though such assemblies were no longer

possible. For this reason, terms for the assembly of the nation were applied to the central council, which was thought of as a representative body.

The central Sanhedrin's authority in the affairs of the nation varied according to the fortunes of the nation and the changing nature of its government. Sometimes, particularly under some of the Hasmonean rulers (1 Macc. 12:6, 35-36; 2 Macc. 13:13), it shared in the responsibility of governing the nation. At other times, even its judicial powers were restricted and its authority was nearly limited to the conduct of worship in the temple.

Generally, the Sanhedrin served as the central authority for the civic administration of Jerusalem, for religious instruction, for establishment of policy for the conduct of the temple services, and for justice in cases neither handled locally nor reserved to the Roman authorities, particularly those involving the temple and violations of the Torah. Under Roman rule the authority of the Sanhedrin to impose the death penalty varied with the policy of the governor (cf. John 18:31; Acts 23:27). The Roman governor's authority to halt or investigate any proceedings on his own initiative (e.g., 22:30; 23:28) was the greatest restriction on the Sanhedrin's authority. The authority of the Sanhedrin over Jewish communities outside Judea was exercised through the local synagogues (e.g., 9:1-2) and was not part of the Sanhedrin's direct jurisdiction recognized by the Roman government.

In addition to the central Sanhedrin, the New Testament also refers to local Jewish councils, which could exist in any town with 120 or more Jewish men (Matt. 5:22; 10:17). Such local councils administered justice for the synagogues in their area and had powers of excommunication (John 16:2) and corporal punishment (cf. Matt. 10:17; Acts 22:19; 2 Cor. 11:24). Joseph of Arimathea was apparently a member of such a local council (Mark 15:43).

Bibliography. H. Mantel, *Studies in the History of the Sanhedrin*. HSS 17 (1961).

SANSANNAH [săn săn'ə] (Heb. *sansannâ*). A city in the southern part of the tribal territory of Judah (Josh. 15:31). It is usually identified with modern Khirbet esh-Shamsanīyât, *ca.* 15.5 km. (9.6 mi.) northwest of modern Beersheba.

SAPH [săf] (Heb. *sap*). A giant (KJV mg. "of the sons of Rapha") who fought for the Philistines. He was defeated by Sibbecai the Hushathite at Gob (2 Sam. 21:18). At 1 Chr. 20:4 Saph is called Sippai.

SAPHIR (Mic. 1:11, KJV). *See* SHAPHIR.

SAPPHIRA [sə fī'rə] (Gk. *Sappheirē*; from Aram. *šappîrā'* "beautiful"). The wife of ANANIAS 1. Together they agreed to withhold from the church part of a sum of money gained from sale of property, while claiming to bring it all. Since this amounted to a lie against the Holy Spirit, both were struck dead when the sin was exposed (Acts 5:1-10).

SAPPHIRE (Heb. *sappîr*; Gk. *sáppheiros*).† The precise identity of the stone represented by the Hebrew and Greek terms cannot now be determined with certainty. Although commonly translated "sapphire" in English versions (e.g., KJV, RSV, NIV), they are also rendered "lapis lazuli" (JB, NIV mg., RSV mg.). Sapphire, a transparent or translucent variety of conondrum generally blue in color, was known in the ancient world but was not commonly used because of its great hardness.

One of the three colors of the riders' breastplates at Rev. 9:17 is a blue identified by reference to a stone of uncertain identity (Gk. *hyakínthinos*, *hyákinthos*; RSV "sapphire"; KJV "jacinth"; NIV "dark blue"; JB "hyacinth blue").

See LAPIS LAZULI.

SARAH [sâr'ə].†

1. (Heb. *śārâ* "princess, noble woman"; Gk. *Sarra*). The wife of Abraham and mother of Isaac. Initially called Sarai (Heb. *śāray*, with an archaic feminine ending) the wife of Abram, she is characterized as barren, a condition of humiliation (Gen. 11:29-32; cf. 16:1-4). Having married Abram in Ur, Sarai accompanied her husband and his family to Haran, where the clan settled until the death of Terah their leader (11:31-32). She then migrated with them to southwestern Canaan (12:5).

Famine soon forced the childless couple to seek sustenance in Egypt (v. 10). Despite her apparently advanced age, Sarai was exceedingly beautiful, and Abram feared that the Egyptians would kill him and seize her for themselves; accordingly, he convinced Sarai to pass as his sister (cf. 20:12). The ploy was successful insofar as Abram's life was spared, but Pharaoh—believing Sarai to be unmarried—took her for his wife, compensating Abram appropriately (12:15-16). Only after the Lord afflicted the royal household with plagues did the Egyptian discover Sarai's actual status, whereupon he returned her to her husband and sent them away (vv. 17-20). A similar account is recorded at ch. 20; while sojourning in Gerar, Abraham tells the local king, Abimelech, that Sarah is his sister.

Subsequently God promised Abram a son (15:4ff.), but Sarai was unable to produce this heir. Resigned to her condition, she gave Abram her maid Hagar as surrogate to beget their child; when she conceived, Hagar scorned her mistress (16:1-3). After Sarai's bitter reproach, Abram assured her that she could treat the maid as she wished, whereupon Hagar fled to the wilderness. Only after divine intervention did Hagar return and bear Abram's son Ishmael (vv. 5-15).

Sometime later the Lord appeared to Abram and again proclaimed that Sarai would bear a son. As partial token of this promise he changed their names to Abraham and Sarah (17:1-8, 15ff.). Afterwards, when the Lord visited the couple at Mamre, Sarah laughed in disbelief at the prospect of a ninety-year-old woman bearing a child (18:9-12; cf. 17:17). The Lord reprimanded her, for the promise was certain (18:14-15). Indeed, the aged Sarah did conceive and bear a male child, who was named Isaac ("he laughs"; cf. 17:19); Sarah's laughter was now that of joyful amazement (21:1-7). When Hagar's son Ishmael mocked the lad, Sarah demanded that Abraham expel the Egyptian maid and her son without Ishmael's share of the inheritance as firstborn (vv. 9-14).

Sarah died at Hebron at age 127. The grieving Abraham purchased from Ephron the Hittite the cave in the field of Machpelah to bury her remains (ch. 23).

At Isa. 51:2 Sarah is depicted as the mother of Israel, an example of God's faithfulness to his promise (cf. Rom. 9:8-9; Gal. 4:21-31). Heb. 11:11 cites her among the heroes of the faith. At 1 Pet. 3:6 her obedience to her husband (RSV "lord") is presented as a model for the Christian woman.

2. The daughter of Raguel, who after many obstacles became the bride of Tobias (Tob. 3:7ff.).

3. (Num. 26:46, KJV). *See* SERAH.

SARAPH [sâr'əf] (Heb. *śārāp* "burning"). A descendant of Shelah of the tribe of Judah who ruled Moab for a time (1 Chr. 4:22).

SARDINE STONE (Rev. 4:3, KJV). *See* CARNELIAN; SARDIUS.

SARDIS [sär'dĭs] (Gk. *Sardeis*). A city in western Asia Minor located in the valley of the Hermus river (modern Gediz). Sardis ("Sepharad" at Obad. 20) was the capital of the kingdom of Lydia, which existed from *ca.* 700 to 546 B.C., and then of the Persian satrapy of Lydia. It passed under Macedonian and then Roman control, becoming part of the Roman province of Asia. Although Sardis had been a city of considerable wealth and importance earlier, under Rome it was not, partly because of an earthquake in A.D. 17. Emperor Tiberius provided considerable financial support for the city's reconstruction, and he was worshipped there. Sardis remained a source of woolen cloth and garments; this trade and the city's past importance in military events are reflected in John's letter to the church at Sardis (Rev. 3:1-6).

SARDITES (Num. 26:26, KJV). *See* SERED.

SARDIUS [sär'dĭ əs] (Heb. *'ōḏem*; Gk. *sárdion*). A variety of orange-red stone, usually identified as sardius (RSV, Exod. 28:17; 39:10; KJV also Ezek. 28:13; JB "sard"; NEB "sardin") or carnelian (RSV, Ezek. 28:13). Both sardius (or sard) and carnelian are red varieties of chalcedony, sardius being darker than carnelian but sometimes considered a type of carnelian. "Ruby" (NIV) is less likely because that precious stone was little known in the ancient world. The stone mentioned at Rev. 4:3; 21:20 is probably sardius (so KJV; "sardine stone" at 4:3 is based on a variant reading Gk. *sárdinos*) or carnelian (so RSV, NIV; NEB "cornelian"). *See* CARNELIAN.

SARDONYX (Rev. 21:20, KJV). *See* ONYX.

SAREPTA (Luke 4:26, KJV). *See* ZAREPHATH.

SARGON [sär'gŏn] (Heb. *sargôn*; Akk. *Šarru-kēn* "the king is legitimate").*

1. Sargon of Akkad, Sumerian king of Akkad 2371-2230 B.C.). Formerly vizier to King Ur-zababa of Kish, Sargon overthrew Lugalzagesi of Umma, who had subjugated and unified the Sumerian city-states. Sargon's inscriptions claim dominion over territory from "the lower Sea and its islands to the Upper Sea and its islands," i.e., from Telmun to Cyprus. He maintained control by weakening local autonomy, destroying city walls and resettling ruling families at Akkad.

2. Sargon I, king of Assyria *ca.* 1850 B.C.

3. Sargon II, king of Assyria and Babylonia 721-705 B.C. The son of Tiglath-pileser III, he succeeded his elder brother Shalmaneser V, perhaps by means of palace intrigue. Sargon's first two years of rule were occupied with quelling rebellion, first at Assur and later against a Syropalestinian coalition sponsored by Egypt and led by Hamath and Gaza (cf. 2 Kgs. 17:4); as a result of the latter conflict Samaria was captured and the northern kingdom of Israel dissolved (cf. Isa. 9–10). Previously Sargon had battled Merodach-baladan II of Babylonia to a standstill at Der, thus yielding control of Babylonia for the next decade. He waged successful campaigns against the Mušku (Phrygia) in Asia Minor (716), the Syrians at Carchemish (717-716; 10:9), and the Philistines at Ashdod, a city supported by Assyria's rival Egypt (this victory is used to date the oracle at Isa. 20). By 711 he had driven back the Urartu, and a year later defeated Merodach-baladan and regained control of Babylon. In 706 he completed a new capital at Dur-šarrukin (Khorsabad) near Nineveh. A year later Sargon perished in a minor skirmish against the Cimmerians. He was succeeded by his son Sennacherib.

See ASSYRIA *I.*

SARID [sârʹīd] (Heb. *śārîḍ* "survivor"). A place that defined the southern limit of the tribal territory of Zebulun (Josh. 19:10, 12). Sarid is probably to be identified with Tell Shadûd, in the Jezreel valley *ca.* 8 km. (5 mi.) southwest of Nazareth (cf. R. G. Boling and G. E. Wright, *Joshua.* AB 6 [1982], pp. 442-43).

SARON (Acts 9:35, KJV). *See* SHARON.

SARSECHIM [särʹsə kīm] (Heb. *śarsᵉḵîm*). An official in Nebuchadrezzar's government who had a role in the Babylonian siege of Jerusalem in 587 B.C. (Jer. 39:3). The string of Hebrew syllables in this verse that is generally interpreted as a list of names, titles, and possibly territories of a group of officials is similar to the less confused list at v. 13. The NIV reads the personal name "Nebo-sarsechim," probably a confused form of the "Nebushazban" (KJV "Nebushasban") of v. 13.

SARUCH (Luke 3:35, KJV). *See* SERUG.

SATAN [sāʹtən] (Heb. *śāṭān*). In Hebrew usage, any kind of human or supernatural "adversary" (so RSV), including one who attempted to block the way in a determined fashion (Num. 22:22; cf. v. 32), an enemy one faced in battle (1 Sam. 29:4), an opponent to royal policy (2 Sam. 19:22 [MT 23]), a rival for the throne (1 Kgs. 5:4 [MT 18]), an adversary in international relations (11:14, 23, 25), or an "accuser" in a court of law (RSV, Ps. 109:6; cf. vv. 4, 20; 71:13, where the denominative verb *śāṭan* is used). In time "the *śāṭān*" came to designate a particular nonhuman being,

the archfiend or rival of God. At Job 1:6-12; 2:1-7 (RSV mg. "the adversary") this being is a member of the heavenly court of God who wanders about the earth observing mankind and then stands as mankind's accuser before God, thus functioning as a servant of God; a similar function was performed in the Persian Empire by officials known as "the king's eyes and ears" (cf. Zech. 4:10), and similar officials may have existed also in early Israel (cf. 1 Sam. 22:6-10). At Zech. 3:1-2 the *śāṭān* stands next to Joshua, the high priest at the time of the rebuilding of the temple, to accuse him.

At 1 Chr. 21:1 *śāṭān* appears without the article and has, therefore, become a proper name. Satan, replacing "the anger of the Lord" in the earlier parallel 2 Sam. 24:1, is the adversary of Israel in inciting David to take a military census of Israel.

The LXX generally represents Heb. *śāṭān* with Gk. *diábolos* "accuser, opponent," the source of Eng. "devil," or *satán,* a simple transliteration. These two terms (with *satán* lengthened to *satanás*) are the most common terms in the New Testament for the being who tempts to evil and opposes God's people. The development toward dualism and the greater interest in heavenly beings including angels and demons in post-Old Testament Judaism are the background of the New Testament conception of Satan. Dualism is not dominant in the New Testament, however, because of the distinctive New Testament emphasis on the fall of Satan from his heavenly position (Luke 10:18; Rev. 12:7-12) and more fundamentally because of the belief in Jesus as the victor over Satan. Even while Satan continues his work as the accuser of God's people (Luke 22:31-32), his activity is limited—already during the ministry of Jesus (Matt. 12:28-29; John 12:31), and particularly by Jesus' death and resurrection (Col. 2:14-15). This victory continues to be won in the ongoing life of the Church (Eph. 6:11; Rev. 12:11).

SATRAP [sāʹtrăp] (Heb., Aram. *ʾᵃḥašdarpān*; O.Pers. *xšaśapāvana*). Title of provincial governors in the Persian Empire (Ezra 8:36; Esth. 3:12; 8:9; 9:3; KJV "lieutenants"; Dan. 3:2-3; 6:1-7; KJV "princes"). Herodotus lists 20 satrapies in the empire (*Hist.* iii.89-94), while Esth. 1:1; 8:9 refers to 127 provinces and Dan. 6:1-2 of 120 satraps under three presidents. Herodotus' list is, however, related only to the organization of the empire under Darius Hystapes.

SATYR [sātʹər] (Heb. *śāʿîr* "hairy one, goat, satyr"). The rule that the Israelites in the wilderness were not to slaughter any animals suitable for sacrifice outside the tabernacle—i.e., outside the context of sacrifice to God—was instituted because of the practice that had developed of sacrificing in the open country to "satyrs" (Lev. 17:3-7; KJV "devils"), wilderness demons related to or conceived in the form of goats (NIV "goat idols" may not be correct in its interpretation of the situation; cf. mg. "goat demons"). Such illicit worship may have continued in Israel; idols in the form of goats were made in the northern kingdom under Jeroboam I (2 Chr. 11:15). Isaiah refers to satyrs inhabiting the abandoned capital cities of the defeated kingdoms of Babylon (Isa. 13:21) and Edom (34:14);

in these passages, with their lists of strange creatures (cf. Jer. 50:39), the line between the natural and the demonic is particularly indistinct.

SAUL [sôl] (Heb. *šā'ûl* "asked"; Gk. *Saoul, Saulos*). **1** (Gen. 36:37-38, KJV). *See* SHAUL **1**.

2.† The first king of Israel. The length of Saul's reign, which began in the mid- to late-eleventh century B.C., cannot now be determined precisely because of omissions from the text of 1 Sam. 13:1; "forty years" (Acts 13:21) was a traditional round figure.

Before Saul's reign Israel was not united. The tribes were basically autonomous, holding only a few things in common, such as the shrine at Shiloh (1 Sam. 1–3). No continuous common leadership existed other than that of the elders of the respective tribes; only in times of significant threat to the survival of the nation were the tribes united under a single leader (e.g., ch. 7). Israel had no standing army, although the tribes had numerous longtime common enemies, and the tribes could not be counted on for united military action (cf. Judg. 5:16-17). Other nations with strong centralized leadership often became dominant (e.g., 3:12-14). The most significant military threat came to be that of the expansionist Philistines, based in cities of southwestern Palestine. In this situation the need for greater cohesiveness was clear.

Three narratives record how Saul came to be king. The first, recounting his private anointing by Samuel (1 Sam. 10:1ff.), emphasizes the prophet's initiative. The second (vv. 17-24), narrating the choice of Saul by lot from among the elders of Israel and his recognition by the Israelites as a worthy person (vv. 20-24), emphasizes the initiative of the people (vv. 17-19; cf. ch. 8; 12:1). The narrative of Saul's unexpected, divinely-inspired, and successful response to a military crisis at Jabesh-gilead (ch. 11; cf. 12:12) emphasizes Saul's initiative following God's bidding. The second and perhaps the third narrative imply a negative view of monarchy also reflected in Samuel's warnings concerning what the people's insistence on having a king would mean (8:9, 11-18) and the interpretation of their desire for monarchy as rebellion against God's rule (vv. 7-8; 10:19; 12:12, 17-19).

The separate narratives concerning the beginning of Saul's role as king have been viewed as the products of different lines of tradition combined in the existing account. It is possible, however, that Saul became king through a complicated course of events that itself reflected a fundamental disagreement concerning the appropriateness of monarchy for Israel. Although a central monarchy seemed the reasonable solution to the dangers confronting Israel, objections to the institution in Israel were long-standing; indeed, under the Confederation Yahweh was considered Israel's only king (Exod. 15:18; Num. 23:21; Deut. 33:5; Judg. 8:23).

This ambivalence concerning the new monarchy was resolved as Saul began his reign with God's spirit working through him (1 Sam. 11:6; cf. 10:6, 10). But his initial successes (ch. 11; 13:2-4) were followed by an incident that caused Samuel to predict the premature end of Saul's reign. The king, knowing that sacrifice was needed for God's blessing in battle and impatient of waiting for Samuel, usurped the functions of priest by officiating at the sacrifice (vv. 5-15), an act that threatened the distinction between military and religious leadership implied in his being anointed while Samuel still served.

During the ensuing battle with the Philistines, Saul's forces were seriously outnumbered (vv. 15-23). His son Jonathan became the hero by initiating the attack on the Philistine forces in such a way that the dispirited and even traitorous troops of Israel were rallied around Saul (14:1-23, 31). Saul continued to be successful in organizing the forces of Israel against its enemies, thus preparing the way for David's reign, in which Israel became the dominant power in Syria-Palestine (vv. 47-48). But God's and Samuel's final rejection of Saul came in the midst of his success, because of his failure to carry out the commanded total obliteration of Amalek (ch. 15; cf. Deut. 25:17-19).

While Saul still ruled, Samuel heeded God's instructions and anointed David king (1 Sam. 16:1-13). A court musician (vv. 16-17, 23) and the king's armorbearer (v. 21), David became a hero of Israel by killing Goliath (ch. 17) and through other successes in battle (18:5-7, 13-16, 30). Angry and fearful of the young man's popularity, Saul attempted to kill David (vv. 8-11, 20-27). His desire to do away with David then became so unrelenting that David was forced to flee permanently from the royal court (with Jonathan's protection and assistance), even though he continued to regard himself only as a servant of Saul (chs. 19–20).

From that time Saul's life was dominated by his conflict with David and by war with the Philistines. For his part, David protected the king's life and refused to take advantage of opportunities to kill him (24:3-12; 26:6-25). Nevertheless, David did gather around himself a crowd of disillusioned men (22:2) whom he formed into a fighting unit (23:5; 25:13), later to become the core of his army as king (1 Chr. 12). That such a group could be formed shows the deterioration of Saul's rule and the growing discontent. With this core of troops David continued to be a hero of Israel in opposition to the Philistines (1 Sam. 23:1-5). After a time, however, David sought to protect himself by fleeing into Philistia (27:1-4); there he was able to remain by a pretended alliance with the Philistine city of Gath (vv. 5-7), but he continued to fight other enemies of Israel while the Philistines thought he was fighting to gain Saul's throne (vv. 8-12).

When the Philistines prepared a full-scale attack on Saul's army, the king sought a word from the Lord (1 Sam. 28:1-6); when this failed, he visited a medium to consult the spirit of the now dead Samuel (28:7-15). The king was still desperate for Samuel's support, but the ghost told Saul only that his army would be defeated, that he and his sons would be killed, and that David was now the rightful king (vv. 16-19). Saul's three sons were, in fact, killed in the battle (31:2), and rather than be killed by the Philistines, Saul committed suicide (vv. 3-4). An Amalekite who reported Saul's death to David claimed to have killed Saul at the king's request (2 Sam. 1:1-10), probably thinking of David as an enemy of Saul who would be pleased by the king's death.

A number of significant points in Saul's life were

marked by direct influence by the spirit of God. An experience of ecstatic prophecy inspired by God's spirit that made Saul into "another man" with "another heart" were among the signs to Saul that he had been anointed at God's initiative (1 Sam. 10:5-7, 9-12). Saul's response to the crisis at Jabesh-gilead began when "the spirit of God came mightily" upon him (11:6). But God's rejection of Saul in favor of David is described as the departure of God's spirit from Saul, its coming onto David, and its replacement by an evil spirit sent upon Saul (16:13-23; cf. 18:12). After this Saul again experienced ecstatic prophecy, but not as a sign that God was with him (19:20-24).

Saul was not to be the founder of a dynasty, partly because no clear precedent for hereditary rule existed in Israel but even more so because of the success of David and Solomon. Three of Saul's sons by Ahinoam, his first wife, died in his final battle against the Philistines (31:2). A fourth, Ishbosheth (also called Eshbaal and possibly Ishvi [14:49]), remained, however, and was installed as Saul's successor (2 Sam. 2:8–4:12). After Ishbosheth's death, David became king of all Israel. He kept his covenant with Jonathan (1 Sam. 18:1-4; 20:14-17; cf. 24:21-22) by caring for Jonathan's one remaining son, Mephibosheth (2 Sam. 9; 21:7), but probably partly with the idea of guarding against the son's becoming the center of a Saulide revolt. David permitted seven other descendants of Saul, two of them sons, to be killed by the Gibeonites in revenge for Saul's killing of some Gibeonites (vv. 1-14).

3. According to the book of Acts, an alternate (Semitic and apparently preconversion) name of the apostle PAUL.

SAVE, SAVIOR. *See* SALVATION, SAVE, SAVIOR.

SAW (Heb. nouns *mᵉgērâ, maśśôr*; Gk. verb *prízō*).* Early bronze saws were essentially large knives with irregularly notched cutting edges. As iron came into common use (*ca.* 1200-1000 B.C.), better carpenters' saws with keener edges and regular raked teeth, sometimes set, could be made. Bronze saws for cutting stone were fixed with stone teeth (2 Sam. 12:31; 1 Kgs. 7:9). The relationship of artisan and tool is a metaphor

Carpenters using a saw and a mallet and chisel. From a relief in a Fifth-Dynasty Egyptian tomb (2500-2350 B.C.) (MARBURG/Art Resource, N.Y.)

for the relationship of God to Assyria's king and army at Isa. 10:15. Using saws on human bodies could be a means of torturous execution (Heb. 11:37, probably referring to the legend of Isaiah's execution by sawing).

SCALE ARMOR (Heb. *dᵉbāqîm*). The Hebrew term represents some part of the armor worn by King Ahab when he was killed in battle (1 Kgs. 22:34 par. 2 Chr. 18:33; RSV "scale armor"). He received his mortal wound between this part of his armor and another part of it called Heb. *širyān* (RSV "breastplate''; KJV reads "between the joints of the harness" for the entire phrase). The *dᵉbāqîm* may have been the scale armor protecting Ahab's lower abdomen (the older suggestion "armpits" is unlikely). *See* COAT OF MAIL.

SCAPEGOAT (Lev. 16:8, 10, 26, KJV). *See* AZAZEL.

SCARECROW (Heb. *tōmēr*).* A pillar, perhaps shaped to suggest the human form, set up in a field to frighten away birds or thieves. Jeremiah likens idols to speechless and immobile scarecrows (Jer. 10:5; KJV "upright").

SCARFS (Heb. *rᵉ'ālôt*).* Articles of clothing or adornment named in a list of things to be taken away from the aristocrats of Jerusalem (Isa. 3:19). What is actually signified by the term is not clear. Among suggestions other than "scarfs" (RSV; cf. KJV "mufflers") are "veils" (JB, NIV), "beads," and "coronets" (NEB).

SCARLET, CRIMSON (Heb. *karmîl, tôlā', šānî, tôlā'at šānî, šᵉnî tôlā'at, mᵉtullā'îm*; Gk. *kókkinos*). A red pigment made from the dried bodies of female scale insects (genus *Kermes*) found on oak trees; fabrics dyed with this pigment (Gen. 38:28; Josh. 2:18; 2 Chr. 2:7 [MT 6]; Cant. 4:3; Nah. 2:3 [MT 4]). Gk. *kókkinos* represents both "scarlet" and "crimson."

Garments of scarlet were considered a contribution toward beauty (2 Sam. 1:24; Jer. 4:30) and were particularly worn by aristocracy (Prov. 31:21; Lam. 4:5 [RSV "purple"]; Rev. 18:16) and royalty (Cant. 7:5 [MT 6] [RSV "purple"; KJV "Carmel"]; Matt. 27:28; Rev. 17:4). Scarlet was among the fabrics used extensively in the tabernacle and its furnishings (e.g., Exod. 25:4; 26:1) and in the veil of Solomon's temple (2 Chr. 3:14). A scarlet cord was used in the ritual purification of lepers (Lev. 14:4) and persons made ritually unclean by contact with corpses (Num. 19:6).

A transformation from the red color of scarlet to the white of snow or wool is figurative of the forgiveness of sins (Isa. 1:18).

Aram. *'argᵉwān* (the equivalent of Heb. *'argāmān*), translated "scarlet" in the KJV of Dan. 5:7, 16, 29, refers to purple cloth.

SCENTED WOOD (Gk. *xýlon thýinon*). Fragrant wood from trees of genus *Callitris* (cypress pines), most often sandarac, imported from Africa to ancient Rome and used in making furniture (Rev. 18:12; KJV "thyine wood").

SCEPTER (Heb. *matteh, šēbet, maqqēl, šarbît*; Gk. *rhábdos*). The Old Testament terminology does not distinguish between clubs and sticks as weapons of warfare (e.g., 2 Sam. 23:21; Ps. 2:9; Isa. 14:29) and scepters as symbols of power held by rulers on ceremonial occasions; the symbol of power is a representation of the means of power, which is the threat of violence. Representations of scepters show that they had a variety of forms, generally reminiscent of clubs, spears, pikes, and, in Egypt, shepherds' crooks. A loss of power could be spoken of as the "departure" (Gen. 49:10; Zech. 10:11; cf. Ps. 89:44 [MT 45]) or "breaking" (Isa. 14:5; Jer. 48:17) of a scepter. "Scepter," like "throne," could be a figure of speech for the ruler himself (Num. 24:17) or for the nature of a monarch's rule (Ps. 45:6 [MT 7] [quoted at Heb. 1:8]; 125:3).

SCEVA [sē′və] (Gk. *Skeuas*; Lat. *Scaeva*).† A Jewish "high priest" whose seven sons were among exorcists in Ephesus who attempted to use the name of "Jesus whom Paul preaches" in exorcism (Acts 19:13-14). The demonized person for whom they attempted this attacked them after the demon had challenged their authority to use Jesus' name, and the seven men fled naked and wounded (vv. 15-16). This outcome demonstrated that the Jesus by whom Paul healed (vv. 11-12) was not reducible to a magical formula which could be imitated by any exorcist. It is probable that "Jewish high priest" was a title assumed by—but not properly held by—Sceva, and even possible that the seven men advertised themselves as "sons" of a fictional "Sceva, a Jewish high priest." In Gentile Ephesus, where occult arts were widely practiced, Judaism was regarded as an exotic cult and source of many mysteries. Many Jews did, indeed, practice exorcism among Gentiles.

SCHOOLMASTER (Gal. 3:24-25, KJV). *See* CUSTODIAN.

SCORPION (Heb. ʿaqrāḇ; Gk. *skorpíos*). Any member of the order *Scorpiones* in the class Arachnida (which includes spiders). The different species of scorpions differ mainly in size, ranging from 13 mm. (.5 in.) to 175 mm. (7 in.), but are otherwise very much alike in appearance and characteristics. Every scorpion has a segmented body with eight legs, two claws at the front resembling those of a lobster, and a segmented tail that can be arched up over the body and head. At the end of the tail is a stinger, the venom of which may be nearly harmless or fatal depending on the species (cf. Luke 11:12; Rev. 9:3, 5, 10; at Ezek. 2:6 the sting of scorpions is a figure for the painful situation of rejection of the prophet's word).

Scorpions are generally found in hot climates, and a number of species are found in Palestine. Deut. 8:15 associates scorpions with the desert through which the Israelites crossed after their departure from Egypt. Jesus referred to snakes and scorpions as symbols of the demonic realm (Luke 10:19).

"Scorpion" was a term for a type of lash used only on slaves, but Rehoboam threatened to use such a lash on free conscripted laborers (1 Kgs. 12:11, 14 par.).

SCOURGING. *See* LASH; ROD.

SCREECH OWL (Isa. 34:14, KJV). *See* NIGHT HAG.

SCRIBES (Heb. *sōp̄ēr*; Gk. *grammateús*).† Interpreters and teachers of the Mosaic law. Because of the centrality that the Torah came to have in Judaism from the time of the restoration (Neh. 8–9), teachers of the law who interpreted its application came to play an important part. At first this role was filled by priests and Levites (8:7, 9; cf. 2 Chr. 17:7-9), but in time they were supplanted by lay teachers. By 180 B.C. the office of teacher of the law, the "scribe" who also was involved in judicial matters, was well established (Sir. 38:24–39:11). The work of the scribes became the basis of rabbinic Judaism.

The model for the teachers of the law was Ezra. His designation as Heb. *sōp̄ēr* "secretary, scribe, learned person" (Ezra 7:6) became the standard Hebrew designation for the teachers of the Torah. In the New Testament these teachers are called primarily Gk. *grammateús* "scribe, one learned in the Scriptures," but also *nomodidáskalos* "teacher of the law" and *nomikós* "lawyer." The scribes came to be addressed with respectful titles, particularly "Rabbi" (Heb. *rabbî* "my master, my teacher"; Gk. *rhabbí, kýrie, didáskale*).

The scribes' interpretation of the Torah was directed to establishing for their own age the proper means of living by the various precepts of the Torah, both for judicial purposes and for the instruction of the people, especially disciples who would attach themselves to particular renowned teachers. They also taught on scriptural matters other than religious observance, such as eschatology (cf. Matt. 2:4; 17:10; Mark 12:35). The scribes usually were not paid for performing their educational and judicial duties, but might possess inherited wealth, support themselves by a trade, or be financed by a wealthy patron. Teachers of the law were as a matter of course accorded the greatest respect (cf. Matt. 23:6-7; Mark 12:38-39; Luke 11:43; 20:46).

Most of the scribes were adherents of the Pharisees' interpretation of the Torah. It was the Pharisees, as opposed to the Sadducees, whose concept of "oral Torah" gave the greatest respect to the development of legal traditions in the teachings of the scribes. At the heart of the frequently mentioned scribal opposition to Jesus was his unwillingness to adhere to "the tradition of the elders" (i.e., the oral Torah) in the teaching and example he gave to his disciples (Matt. 15:1ff. par.). Thus it can be assumed that the scribes who opposed Jesus were mainly Pharisees. Indeed, "scribes and Pharisees" (meaning scribes who were Pharisees along with other Pharisees) is a common term for the opposition to Jesus (e.g., 5:20; 12:38; Luke 5:21).

The conflict between Jesus and the scribes, constant and increasingly intense, was focused on a number of issues. When Jesus pronounced forgiveness, he appeared to some of the scribes to be blaspheming (Matt. 9:3 par.). Sometimes the opposition took the form of a request for an attesting sign (12:38; cf. 16:21). As the properly constituted authorities, the scribes were often concerned about the authority for Jesus' healing and teaching ministry (Mark 3:22; 9:14; 11:27). The opposition to Jesus eventually constituted concerted action by the Sanhedrin in Jerusalem, which included a number of scribes (cf. Matt. 16:21; 21:15; 26:57).

Jesus held that the righteousness of the "scribes and Pharisees" was not enough (5:20 par.), apparently contrasting their concentration on specific possible cases with his own focus on total obedience. Jesus did respect the scribal tradition sufficiently to say that a scribe who became a disciple of his benefited from both the old and the new (13:52; cf. 23:34), and he held that his disciples should, indeed, live by the teachings of the scribes, but not by their example (vv. 2-3). He castigated the scribes for their desire for recognition and respectful titles (vv. 5-10), for their use of fine distinctions to construe as unnecessary observance that he considered essential (vv. 16-22), for imposing greater restrictions than he thought right (15:1-11; cf. 23:24)—especially where interaction with nonobservant people and healing were restricted (Mark 2:16-17; Luke 6:6-10), and for neglecting broad issues of social justice and response to the call of God (Matt. 23:23, 26, 29-36). Indeed, Jesus favored the prophets' broadly ethical emphasis over the concerns of the scribes (Mark 12:28-34).

Some scribes were attracted to the teaching of Jesus (vv. 28, 32-33). The early Church included Pharisees (Acts 15:5), and the leading scribes in Jerusalem were not uniformly opposed to the Church (5:34-39; 23:6-9). But one scribe who took the initiative in seeking to become a disciple of Jesus was not encouraged by Jesus, but was told obliquely of the difficulties involved (Matt. 8:19-20).

Jesus' teaching was contrasted directly with that of the usual religious teachers—"he taught them as one who had authority, and not as their scribes" (7:29), i.e., not as one who followed their emphasis on the authority of past interpretations of the Torah. Developing a wide individual reputation, as Jesus did with his teaching, could not be a common goal among the scribes. At the root of the conflict, therefore, lay the question of the authority of his independent interpretation of the Torah. For the scribes, "the tradition of the elders," i.e., the tradition of oral Torah, ruled.

For "scribe" in the Old Testament, see WRITING.

SCROLL (Heb., Aram. $m^e gill\hat{a}$; Gk. *biblíon*). A book in the form of papyrus or leather sections attached end to end and rolled up (Jer. 36; KJV "roll"; Rev. 5:1; KJV "book"). See BOOK; WRITING.

SCURVY (Heb. $g\bar{a}r\bar{a}b$). In biblical usage, a fungal disease, possibly ringworm (RSV, Deut. 28:27; KJV, Lev. 21:20; 22:22; RSV "itch[ing disease]").

SCYTHIANS [sĭth'ĭ ənz] (Akk. *Ašguzai*; Heb. *'aš-k^enaz*; Gk. *Skythai*). A nomadic Indoiranian people from southern Russia who began moving by horseback into the Near East in the eighth century B.C. with other peoples, including the Cimmerians ("Gomer"), with whom they are associated at Gen. 10:3; 1 Chr. 1:6 (RSV "Ashkenaz"). They reached as far as Egypt in the seventh century B.C. At one time scholars identified the enemy approaching Jerusalem from the north spoken of by Jeremiah and Zephaniah (Jer. 1:13-15; 4:5-31; 5:15-17; 6:1-5; Zeph. 1:10) as Scythian raiders. The Scythians were initially allies of the Assyrian Empire at the time of Esarhaddon (681-670), but they revolted along with the Mannai.

Rebuffed by Egyptian pharoah Psammetichus I some time thereafter, they raided Ashkelon and Ashdod on the Palestinian coast. They were later defeated and driven back northward by the Medes and the Persians. Scythian soldiers had a part in the Persian defeat of Babylon in 538 (Jer. 51:27; RSV "Ashkenaz"; KJV "Ashchenaz"). In later literature (e.g., 2 Macc. 4:47; Col. 3:11) the Scythians were regarded as a proverbially backward and barbarian people.

SCYTHOPOLIS [sĭth ŏp'ə lĭs] (Gk. *Skythōn pólis, Skythopolis*). The name of BETH-SHAN from the Hellenistic through the Byzantine periods; the chief city of the Decapolis, 120 km. (75 mi.) northeast of Jerusalem (2 Macc. 12:29-30).

SEA GULL (Heb. *šahap*). An unclean bird (Lev. 11:16; Deut. 14:15) of uncertain identity. Other than "(sea) gull" (so RSV, JB, NIV, following LXX, Vulg.) are "long-eared owl" (NEB) and "bat" (which the Old Testament does list among unclean birds); KJV "cuckoo" is unlikely in a list probably made of of carrioneaters. Gulls (family *Laridae*) are aquatic birds with webbed feet and wings long in proportion to their bodies. They feed on fish, insects, and other small animals. Several varieties of gulls are found on the Palestinian coast and the Sea of Galilee.

SEA, MOLTEN (Heb. *hayyām mûşāq* "sea of cast metal," *yām hann^eḥōšeṭ* "bronze sea").† A large bronze basin on the southwest side of the court of the Solomonic temple near the burnt offering altar (1 Kgs. 7:23-26, 39; 2 Chr. 4:2-5, 10).

The bronze sea was round, its rim flared or otherwise shaped like a flower. Its dimensions are given as 10 cubits (*ca.* 4.5 m. [14.5 ft.]) in diameter, 1 handbreadth (*ca.* 7.5 cm. [3 in.]) in thickness, 30 cubits (*ca.* 13.5 m. [43.5 ft.]) in circumference at the top, 5 cubits (*ca.* 2.2 m. [7.3 ft.]) in height. It was decorated with relief-work in the form of gourds (or oxen according to the MT of 2 Chr. 4:3) and set on a stand in the form of twelve oxen. Its volume was 2,000 baths (*ca.* 44,000 l. [11,000 gal.]) according to 1 Kgs. 7:26 or "over 3,000 baths" (*ca.* 66,000 l. [16,500 gal.]) according to 2 Chr. 4:5. It is possible that the two figures are the rounded results of calculations rather than actual measurements, with 1 Kings assuming that the "sea" was hemispherical and 2 Chronicles

A representation of the molten sea

assuming that it was cylindrical; in any case, the "bath" noted is apparently smaller than the normal Old Testament measurement of *ca.* 22 l. (5.5 gal.).

Like all the bronze objects for Solomon's temple, the sea was made by Hiram, a bronze-caster from Phoenician Tyre (1 Kgs. 7:13-14; 2 Chr. 2:13, "Huramabi"; 4:11, "Huram"). According to Chronicles, it was made from bronze that David had taken as spoil (1 Chr. 18:8) and was made "for the priests to wash in" (2 Chr. 4:6). The use of bronze oxen as a stand and the designation of the basin as a "sea" have suggested to some a mythological basis for its presence in the temple (cf. the conquered sea at, e.g., Ps. 74:13; 93:3-4). King Ahaz appropriated the twelve bronze oxen to make part of a tribute payment to Assyria and replaced them with a stone pediment (2 Kgs. 16:17). The "sea" itself was broken up and carried to Babylon when Jerusalem was conquered in 587-586 B.C. (25:13).

SEA MONSTER (Heb. *tannîn*, pl. *tannînîm*). In Hebrew usage, large sea creatures, whether real or mythological (Job 7:12; pl. Gen. 1:21; Ps. 148:7). Yahweh's taming of the sea (generally regarded by the Israelites as a strange and dangerous place) and its great creatures became a theme in Israel's faith (e.g., Ps. 74:13-14; 89:9-10 [MT 10-11]; 93:3-4; 104:6-9). *See* DEEP; DRAGON; LEVIATHAN; RAHAB 2.

The KJV reads "sea monsters" at Lam. 4:3, taking *tannîm* (Q in two manuscripts) as the plural of *tannîn*; the term should usually, however, be taken as the plural of *tan* "jackal" (so RSV).

SEA OF REEDS. *See* RED SEA.

SEA OF THE PLAIN (KJV). *See* DEAD SEA.

SEAL, SIGNET (Heb. nouns *hôtām, hôtemet, tabba'at*; verb *hātam*; Aram. verb *hatam*; Gk. noun *sphragís*; verb *[kata]sphragízō*).† A device of stone or metal engraved with a reverse design for making an impression in clay, lead, or wax. Such impressions were used to identify documents and other objects and, for security purposes, to place marks on closures so that they could be opened only by breaking the seal. Numerous cylinder seals, which were rolled across wet clay to make an impression (usually pictorial), have been recovered by archaeologists, as have signet rings and other forms of stamp seals.

Each personal seal was different to preclude any doubt concerning identity where seals were used or possessed (cf. Gen. 38:25). The use of personal seals on documents was equivalent to the modern use of signatures (cf. Neh. 9:38 [MT 10:1]). Kings' seals were used on letters to give them the status of royal directives (1 Kgs. 21:8; Esth. 3:12; 8:8, 10); a person who possessed the king's signet had much authority (Gen. 41:42; Esth. 3:10; 8:2; cf. Jer. 22:24). Legal documents were sometimes folded over, sealed with the personal seals of the signers, and then attached to another copy of the document that was kept open (cf. 32:10-11, 14). Seals were set upon the closings of both the lions' den into which Daniel was thrown (Dan. 6:17) and Jesus' tomb (Matt. 27:66) to ensure that no one opened them (cf. also Rev. 20:3).

Seals and the setting of seals are used in a wide

A signet ring from Samaria

variety of figures of speech. A seal can represent ownership (Cant. 8:6; Rev. 7:2-3; 9:4). Because they indicate God's ownership, baptism and the giving of the Holy Spirit are described as "sealing" (2 Cor. 1:22; Eph. 1:13; 4:30). A seal can also give authorization, verification, or affirmation to what already exists (Dan. 9:24; John 3:33; 6:27; Rom. 4:11; 1 Cor. 9:2). Persons are referred to as signets because of their authority (Ezek. 28:12; Hag. 2:23). A seal can represent finality, because a sealed container is ready for storage or delivery (Deut. 32:34; RSV mg., Rom. 15:28) or because a sealed document is completed and ready for delivery (Isa. 8:16).

That which is sealed can be hidden or secret, because what is behind a gate or door upon which a seal has been set is hidden from view—in modern usage, "put under lock and key" (Job 9:7; Cant. 4:12), as are the contents of a container on which a seal has been set (Job 14:17; 37:7; Rev. 10:4). Similarly, sealing can be a figure for incomprehensibility (Isa. 29:11). That which is certain to happen but is reserved for a later time is said to be "sealed" (i.e., settled and sure), effective only after a passage of time (Dan. 12:4, 9); a reversal of this metaphor appears at Rev. 22:10— little time is left. The book "sealed with seven seals" opened by Christ in John's vision (5:1–6:12; 8:1) was a folded or rolled document that was accessible only after all seven seals had been removed, therefore representing the train of events that must occur before the long-awaited response to the prayers of the saints (cf. 6:10; 8:3-5).

God, speaking to Job, describes the change that comes over earth at dawn as "like clay under the seal" (Job 38:14). The scales of Leviathan, who is pictured as a Nile crocodile, are said to be as tightly bound to the body as if they were pressed down with a seal (41:15 [MT 7]). Gk. *sphragís* apparently means "inscription" rather than "seal" at 2 Tim. 2:19 (so JB, NIV).

SEAT (Heb. *môšāb, šebet, kissē'*; Gk. *kathédra, prōtokathedría, prōtoklisía*).* References to seating in the Bible are almost all to such as a representation of honor and authority. Exceptions are the seductress's "seat on the high places of the town" (Prov. 9:14) and the meetings in which "scoffers" sit together to ridicule the way of righteousness (Ps. 1:1).

The greatest seats of honor and authority were royal thrones, such as Solomon's elaborate gold and ivory throne (1 Kgs. 10:18-20; Heb. *kissē'*). To be seated on the royal throne was to be recognized as possessing royal authority (16:11; 2 Kgs. 11:19; Acts 12:21-22). Gk. *thrónos* "throne" is used metonymically for strength and authority (Luke 1:52; KJV "seats"). The image of a king seated and looking down on his sub-

The impression made by a third-millenium Mesopotamian cylinder seal. An agriculture deity holding a plow and receiving offerings (Staatliche Museen zu Berlin, DDR)

jects is used to describe God's sovereignty over creation (Ps. 113:5-6; cf. Ezek. 1:26).

The authority to sit among rulers was a considerable privilege and was controlled with a view to the careful dispensation of relative honor and dishonor (1 Sam. 2:8; 1 Kgs. 10:5; Ps. 113:8). The seating at the monthly three-day banquet at Saul's court was assigned (1 Sam. 20:18), with Saul seated by the wall (in the safest seat), Jonathan opposite him (KJV "Jonathan arose," following MT), and Abner by the king's side (v. 25). A seat on the right side of the royal throne, as might be set up for the mother of the king (1 Kgs. 2:19; Jer. 13:18), was a special position of honor and power (Mark 14:62 par.; Col. 3:1; Heb. 8:1; 12:2). Haman was given a seat "above all the princes who were with him" in the court of Ahasuerus (Esth. 3:1). The kings of conquered lands were accorded seats in the court of the king of Babylon, but these were hardly seats of honor (2 Kgs. 25:28; Jer. 13:18; 52:32).

Rulers and judges heard cases and gave judgments seated in a public place (2 Chr. 19:8; Job 23:3; Ps. 122:5; Amos 6:3; Matt. 27:19; John 19:13; Acts 25:6), often a gate (2 Sam. 19:8; Jer. 26:10). The seated judge is a common image for universal eschatological judgment (e.g., Dan. 7:9; Rom. 14:10; Rev. 20:4, 11). According to Jesus, the scribes and Pharisees occupy "Moses' seat" (Matt. 23:2), having the authority and ability to interpret the law of Moses correctly; here "seat" is both a metaphor for judicial authority and also a reference to a literal stone seat in the front of many synagogues that would be occupied by an authoritative teacher of the law. Respected persons in local communities would be honored with particular seats of honor in synagogues (v. 6; Mark 12:39; Luke 11:43; 20:46; Jas. 2:3) and town squares (Job 29:7), and (usually reclining rather than sitting) at formal dinners (Mark 12:39; Luke 20:46).

See JUDGMENT SEAT; THRONE. For the mercy seat, *see* ARK OF THE COVENANT.

SEBA [sē′bə] (Heb. *s*ᵉ*bā'*). A son of Cush (i.e., Ethiopia), perhaps eponymous ancestor of a land in Africa or western Arabia near Ethiopia (Gen. 10:7; 1 Chr. 1:9; Ps. 72:10; Isa. 43:3). Seba may have been the home of the SABEANS 2 (Isa. 45:14; cf. JB) or perhaps a colony of Arabian SHEBA (PLACE) 2.

SEBAM [sē′băm] (Heb. *s*ᵉ*bām*). Alternate form of

SIBMAH, a city in Moab claimed by Reuben after the defeat of Sihon (Num. 32:3; KJV "Shebam").

SEBAT (Zech. 1:7, KJV). *See* SHEBAT.

SECACAH [sə kā′kə] (Heb. *s*ᵉ*kākâ* "thicket, enclosure").† A town in the Judean wilderness assigned to the tribe of Judah. It is perhaps to be identified with Khirbet es-Samrah, southwest of Khirbet Qumran in the valley of Achor near the northwestern shore of the Dead Sea (Josh. 15:61).

SECHU (1 Sam. 19:22, KJV). *See* SECU.

SECOND COMING.† The expected return of Christ to earth at the end of the present age.

I. Terminology

Although it does not occur in the New Testament, "second coming" has become the most common popular term for Christ's expected return. Common New Testament terms for the second coming are Gk. *parousía* "presence, coming" (e.g., Matt. 24:3; 1 Thess. 2:19; 5:23; Jas. 5:7-8; 1 John 2:28), *apokálypsis* "revelation" (1 Cor. 1:7; 2 Thess. 1:7; 1 Pet. 1:7, 13; 4:13), and *epipháneia* "appearing" (2 Thess. 2:8; 1 Tim. 6:14; 2 Tim. 4:1, 8; Titus 2:13). "Second coming" is an appropriate term because *parousía* and *epipháneia* are also used of Christ's (first) appearance in the first century A.D. (2 Tim. 1:10; 2 Pet. 1:16). Gk. *deúteros* "second" is used with reference to the return of Christ at Heb. 9:28.

In the Synoptic Gospels Jesus often calls himself "the Son of man" when speaking of his second coming (e.g., Matt. 10:23; 16:27-28; 24:27; 25:31; 26:64; Luke 17:30; *see* SON OF MAN). The frequency of the word "day" where the New Testament refers to Christ's second coming arises from the interpretation of the day of the Lord" heralded by the Old Testament prophets as meaning the day of Christ's return (cf. Acts 2:20; *see* DAY OF THE LORD).

II. New Testament

In his teachings Jesus contrasted his first coming and the second coming. In the first, less conspicuous coming of Jesus, the kingdom of God was present but hidden (Matt. 13:31-33); in the second, Christ's presence and the triumph of God's kingdom will be obvious to all and will be "with power and great glory" (24:27-30; cf. Rev. 1:7). In the interim between the first coming and the second Christ is understood to be present with God in heaven (Acts 7:55-56; Eph. 1:20). The second coming is described as Christ's descent from heaven, sometimes "on" or "with" the clouds (Matt. 24:30; 26:64; Acts 1:9, 11; 1 Thess. 1:10; 4:16-17).

The return of Christ is one of the eschatological events that will bring the present age to a close and that include also the resurrection of the righteous (1 Cor. 15:23) and all mankind (John 5:28-29; Acts 24:14-15), the gathering and vindication of God's people (Matt. 24:31; Luke 18:7-8; 1 Thess. 3:13; 4:16-17; 2 Thess. 2:1), the defeat of evil (1 Cor. 15:24; 2 Thess. 2:8), the judgment of all, and the establishment of God's eternal rule (1 Cor. 15:24-28; 2 Tim. 4:1). With these other events, the second coming is thought of both as a hope in the midst of earthly suffering, especially persecution (2 Thess. 1:7; 1 Pet. 1:13), and, because judgment and the rewarding of God's faithful people are linked with it, as the motivation for right living (Matt. 16:26-27; 25:31-46; 2 Cor. 5:10; 2 Tim. 4:1, 8; 1 John 2:28).

The question of when Christ's return would occur arose in the early Church, just as it has in later generations. When his disciples posed the question (Matt. 24:3), Jesus spoke of signs, primarily related to the persecution of the witnesses for Christ, the destruction of Jerusalem, and false claims that would arise, rather than to the second coming (vv. 4-35). The main focus of Jesus' answer concerning the time of his second coming was that it cannot be known (vv. 36-44), hence the disciples must be prepared (vv. 45-51).

Certain recorded sayings of Jesus may have led some to expect his return during the first Christian generation (16:28; 24:33-34). The fact that he did not return in the first or second generation did apparently pose a problem for some Christians (2 Pet. 3:3-7). Paul's view of whether he would be alive when Christ returned may have changed during his career (cf. 1 Thess. 4:17; 1 Cor. 15:51-52; 2 Cor. 5:1-4; Phil. 1:20-26; 2 Tim. 4:6-8); in an early letter he explains that certain events were yet to happen before Christ's return (2 Thess. 2:3-4), and in a later letter he depicts Christ's return as "at hand" (Phil. 4:5; cf. Rom. 13:11-12; Jas. 5:8). Prayers for Christ's return appear in the New Testament (1 Cor. 16:22; Rev. 22:20; *see* MARANATHA).

See ESCHATOLOGY.

Bibliography. G. C. Berkouwer, *The Return of Christ* (Grand Rapids: 1972); A. A. Hoekema, *The Bible and the Future* (Grand Rapids: 1979).

SECOND MAN, THE (Gk. *ho deúteros ánthrōpos*).* A term Paul applies to Christ in view of his being the first to be resurrected and, therefore, a second beginning (after Adam, "the first man") of the human race (1 Cor. 15:47). *See* ADAM *III*.

SECOND QUARTER, THE (Heb. *hammišneh* "the second").* A section of Jerusalem that developed during the monarchic period west of the City of David across the Tyropoeon valley in the southern part of what is now called the Upper City (2 Kgs. 22:14; par. 2 Chr. 34:22; KJV "the college"; NIV "the Second District"; Zeph. 1:10; KJV "the second"; NIV "the New Quarter").

SECRET. *See* MYSTERY.

SECRETARY (Heb. *sōpēr*; Gk. *grammateús*). In the preexilic period a government official who performed various military (2 Kgs. 25:19), financial (12:10-11), and scribal (1 Chr. 24:6; Jer. 36:32; RSV "scribe") functions. Secretaries are often included in lists of high ranking officials (2 Sam. 8:17; 20:25; 1 Kgs. 4:3). During the time of Ezra and later the Hebrew term came to designate one who was qualified to teach the law of Moses (RSV "scribe"; Ezra 7:6, 11; Neh. 8:1). The equivalent Greek term (Sir. 38:24; RSV "scribe") is used in the New Testament for teachers of the law, except at Acts 19:35, where it is used

of an Ephesian official (RSV "town clerk"; see SCRIBES; TOWN CLERK). Rom. 16:22; 1 Pet. 5:12 attest to the practice of employing secretaries to write letters.

SECT. *See* HERESY.

SECU [sē′kū] (Heb. *śēḵû* "lookout" [?]).† A place, perhaps a town, near Ramah, where Saul inquired after the whereabouts of David and Samuel (1 Sam. 19:22; KJV "Sechu"). Rather than a place name, "Secu" may have been a reference to a well-known hill outside Ramah where there was a large cistern. LXX Gk. *Sephi* may represent Heb. *śᵉpî* "bare height" (cf. JB).

SECUNDUS [sə koŏn′dəs] (Gk. *Sekoundos*; Lat. *Secundus* "second"). One of the two Thessalonian Christians who accompanied Paul from Macedonia as he carried the collection for the poor Christians of Jerusalem, going at least as far as Troas on the coast of Asia Minor (Acts 20:4). Since Secundus was probably one of Paul's agents in the collection of the fund and a member of the official party bearing it (cf. 1 Cor. 16:3-4; 2 Cor. 8:23), he probably made the whole journey to Jerusalem.

SEDRACH, APOCALYPSE OF. A writing in the Pseudepigrapha that came into its present Christianized form *ca.* the eleventh century A.D., but probably based on a Jewish work composed as early as the mid-second century A.D. After a Christian sermon on love, the apocalypse describes the journey of Sedrach (the Shadrach of Dan. 1:7; 2:49; ch. 3) into heaven. In his conversation with God in heaven, Sedrach asks why mankind was created, since they were bound to sin and therefore to be punished by God. God's responses explain the fall of Adam. Christ (in the original version probably the archangel Michael) is summoned to take Sedrach into Paradise, but Sedrach is not ready to die. Sedrach and Michael plead with God to reduce the time required for the repentance of a lifelong sinner. God eventually reduces the term to twenty days, whereupon Sedrach is satisfied to enter Paradise.

SEER. *See* PROPHECY, PROPHET.

SEGUB [sē′gŭb] (Heb. *śᵉgûb* "exalted").
1. A son of Hezron, and descendant of the patriarch Judah (1 Chr. 2:21-22).
2. The youngest son of Hiel of Bethel who (with his older brother Abiram) died, possibly as a human sacrifice, when Hiel refounded Jericho at the time of King Ahab (1 Kgs. 16:34). Segub's death fulfilled Joshua's curse upon the city (Josh. 6:26).

SEIR [sē′ər, sā′îr] (Heb. *śēʿîr* "hairy, forested") (PERSON). The progenitor of the Horites, the original inhabitants of Mt. Seir (Gen. 36:20-21; 1 Chr. 1:38; cf. Gen. 14:6; Deut. 2:12, 22).

SEIR [sē′ər, sā′îr] (Heb. *śēʿîr* "hairy, forested") (PLACE).
1.† Mt. Seir, the central mountain range of Edom (modern Jebel esh-Sheraʾ), inhabited first by the Hor-

ites and later by Esau and his descendants, the Edomites (Gen. 14:6; 32:3 [MT 4]; 36:8-9, 20-21; Deut. 2:4-5, 12, 22, 29), and eventually coming under Israelite domination (Num. 24:18; cf. 2 Sam. 8:14; 1 Kgs. 11:15-16). Seir rises steeply from the eastern side of the Arabah from the Gulf of Aqabah in the south to Wâdī el-Ḥesā (Zered), southeast of the Dead Sea, in the north. The name Seir derives from the heavy forests that once covered the region. Seir is also used as an appellative for the Edomite people (Isa. 21:11; Ezek. 35). Because of the descriptions of Mt. Halak as rising "toward Seir" (Josh. 11:17; 12:7) and of the Simeonite settlement on Seir (1 Chr. 4:42-43; possibly 2 below), some scholars suggest that Seir could also designate an area on the western side of the Arabah across from Seir proper (cf. Num. 20:23; Deut. 1:44).

2. A mountain on the northern border of the tribal territory of Judah (Josh. 15:10; possibly mentioned at Deut. 1:44; 1 Chr. 4:42). It is usually identified with modern Sārîs, ca. 4 km. (2.5 mi.) southwest of Kiriath-jearim and 14.5 km. (9 mi.) west of Jerusalem.

SEIRA [sē'ə rə] (Heb. *śeʿîrâ* "forested").† The place to which Ehud escaped after killing King Eglon of Moab (Judg. 3:26; KJV "Seirath"). Seirah was probably in Ephraim (cf. v. 27), though little else can be said about its location.

SELA [sē'lə] (Heb. *[has]selaʿ* "[the] rock").† The name of several Edomite strongholds, often identified with the later Nabatean capital, Petra, ca. 75 km. (46.5 mi.) south of the Dead Sea in modern Jordan.

1. A place marking part of the border of (or "with") the Amorites (some LXX manuscripts read "Edomites") at the time of the early Israelite settlement in Palestine (Judg. 1:36; KJV "the rock"). Although some scholars identify it with Petra (cf. Eusebius *Onom.* cxlii.7), it probably is located in the Arabah closer to the Dead Sea.

2. An Edomite fortification in or near the "Valley of Salt" that was taken by King Amaziah of Judah and renamed Joktheel (2 Kgs. 14:7; KJV "Selah"; JB "the Rock"). This Sela is often identified with Umm el-Bayyârah overlooking Petra (cf. LXX).

3. A place of unknown location, possibly the later Nabatean Petra, named in an oracle against Moab (Isa. 16:1).

4. A place, possibly Petra, named as one of a series of representative distant places (Isa. 42:11; KJV "the rock").

SELAH [sē'lə] (Heb. *selâ*). A term occurring seventy-one times in the Psalms (e.g., Ps. 9:16, 20 [MT 17, 21]; 55:7, 19 [MT 8, 20]; 67:1, 4 [MT 2, 5]; 143:6) and at Hab. 3:3, 9, 13. The word is always suffixed to sentences in these poetic passages, often at significant logical breaks and four times at the end of a psalm. It was apparently some kind of musical direction, but its meaning is not now known. Suggestions have been: "raise in pitch," "sustain," "swell," "pause" (so JB), "lift up" (BDB, pp. 699-700), "instrumental interlude" (cf. LXX *diápsalma* "pause in singing"), and "repeat."

For 2 Kgs. 14:7, KJV, *see* SELA **2.**

SELA-HAMMAHLEKOTH (1 Sam. 23:28, KJV, NIV). *See* ESCAPE, ROCK OF.

SELED [sē'lĕd] (Heb. *seleḏ*). The elder son of Nadab of the tribe of Judah (1 Chr. 2:30). Seled died childless.

SELEUCIA [sə lōō'shə] (Gk. *Seleukia, Seleukeia* "of Seleucus").† The name of several cities in the Seleucid Empire, all founded by Seleucus I Nicator. Most important for biblical studies is Seleucia in Syria (or Seleucia Pieria), the port city of Syrian Antioch (modern Samandağ, Turkey). It was founded by Seleucus in the mid-third century B.C. north of the mouth of the Orontes on a rocky spur of the Pierian plateau; its harbor has long been silted up. The city changed hands several times, falling to Ptolemy III of Egypt during the Third Syrian War (246-241) and to the Seleucid Antiochus III in 219. After 146 Seleucia briefly marked the northern terminus of Ptolemy VI's dominion along the Mediterranean coast (1 Macc. 11:8), but in 138 it reverted to the Seleucids. It became a free city under Pompey (63 B.C.). It was from this port that Paul, Barnabas, and John Mark left for Cyprus on the first missionary journey (Acts 13:4).

SELEUCID [sə lōō'sĭd] **EMPIRE.**† With Ptolemaic Egypt, one of the largest empires formed from the division of territory conquered by Alexander the Great (the "Partition of Babylon," 323 B.C.). With its capital at Antioch in Syria, the Seleucid Empire encompassed Mesopotamia, lands east of Mesopotamia, and southern and eastern Asia Minor.

Palestine, Phoenicia, and southern Syria together were an important bridge between the Ptolemaic and Seleucid empires. They were under Ptolemaic control until 198 B.C., when Antiochus III, the sixth Seleucid ruler (223-187 B.C.), extended his control down to the Egyptian border (cf. Dan. 11:15-16). Because of the failure of other attempted conquests by Antiochus (cf. vv. 18-19), his successor, Seleucus IV (187-175), was forced to lay a heavy burden of taxation on the inhabitants of his empire (cf. v. 20; 2 Macc. 3:4-40).

Under Antiochus IV Epiphanes (175-163) the friction between Jews in Judea who sought to adopt aspects of Greek culture and those who resisted the advance of such Hellenization came to a head (cf. 1 Macc. 1:10-15). Antiochus appointed high priests for the Jerusalem temple according to ability to pay for the office and willingness to promote Hellenization. This intrusion into the affairs of the temple, together with Antiochus' plunder of the temple treasury to finance payment of inherited debts and debts incurred by himself in Egyptian military exploits (cf. Dan. 11:24-30; 1 Macc. 1:16-28; 2 Macc. 5:1-21) and his need eventually to secure Palestine as a buffer against Rome's presence in Egypt, led to a confrontation between the emperor and Jerusalem. As part of the effort to stamp out revolt in Jerusalem and prevent its recurrence, the temple cult was forcibly Hellenized (cf. Dan. 11:31-32; 1 Macc. 1:44-61; 2 Macc. 6:1-6), leading to the Maccabean revolt. For the subsequent events, *see* HASMONEANS.

See ANTIOCHUS; DEMETRIUS.

SELEUCUS [sə loo'kəs] (Gk. *Seleukos*).†

1. Seleucus I Nicator, king of Syria (312-281 B.C.) and founder of the Seleucid dynasty. A cavalry officer under Philip of Macedonia and a general of Alexander the Great, he was granted the satrapy of Babylon following the murder of the regent Perdiccas (321). Ousted in 316 by Antigonus of Phrygia, he regained his territory in 312 when he and Ptolemy I defeated Antigonus at Gaza. By 302 he had conquered Alexander's eastern territories as far as the Indus river, and through the battle of Ipsus (301) gained Syria and parts of Asia Minor. He established Antioch on the Orontes as his capital and founded numerous other cities, according to Jews the rights of full citizens. While seeking to regain the Macedonian territory of Alexander he was assassinated in 281 by Ptolemy Ceraunus.

2. Seleucus II Callinicus, son of Antiochus II and Laodice and successor to Antiochus II as king of Syria (246-226 B.C.). Seeking through the Third Syrian War to retaliate against Ptolemy III's invasion of Syria, he lost the capital Antioch and much of the Seleucid territory. Defeated *ca.* 235 at Ancyra (modern Ankara) by his younger brother Antiochus Hierax, Seleucus fled to Asia Minor. In 226 he died after falling from his horse.

3. Seleucus III Soter (or Ceraunus), son of and successor to Seleucus II. Throughout his entire reign (226-223 B.C.) he sought to regain Asia Minor from Attalus I of Pergamum.

4. Seleucus IV Philopator, son and successor of Antiochus III the Great (187-175 B.C.). Heavily indebted to Rome, he dispatched his chief minister Heliodorus to plunder the Jerusalem temple (2 Macc. 3). He was later assassinated by Heliodorus and, because his son Demetrius was held hostage at Rome, was succeeded by his brother Antiochus IV.

SELF-CONTROL. * At Prov. 25:28 a person without "self-control" (so RSV; Heb. *ma'ṣār lᵉrûḥô*; KJV "rule over his own spirit") is likened to a city open to raiders; the converse at 16:32 shows that control of anger is in mind.

Two word groups represent the idea of "self-control" in the New Testament. Gk. *enkráteia* "self-control" (KJV "temperance") and related words are used in contexts where sexual self-control (1 Cor. 7:9; cf. the related word *akrasía* "lack of self-control" at v.5), the self-deprivation of the competing athlete (9:25), and the capacity to resist sin (Acts 24:25; Gal. 5:23; Titus 1:8; 2 Pet. 1:6) are in view. Gk. *sōphronismós* (2 Tim. 1:7; KJV "a sound mind") and related words emphasize the operation of the mind. A person with this quality is sane (Mark 5:15; Acts 26:25; 2 Cor. 5:13), serious (Titus 2:12; 1 Pet. 4:7), sensible (1 Tim. 2:9, 15; Titus 2:2, 5), and judicious (Rom. 12:3).

SEM (Luke 3:36, KJV). *See* SHEM.

SEMACHIAH [sĕm'ə kī'ə] (Heb. *sᵉmaḵyāhû* "Yahweh has sustained"). One of the Levite gatekeepers who were descendants of Obed-edom (1 Chr. 26:7).

SEMEIN [sĕm'ī ən] (Gk. *Semeïn*; Heb. *šimʿî*). A postexilic ancestor of Jesus (Luke 3:26; KJV "Semei").

SEMITES [sĕm'īts].† A linguistic rather than an ethnic term, first applied in the eighteenth century A.D. to designate various Near Eastern peoples, regarded as the descendants of Shem (Gen. 5:32). The Semitic languages are usually classified as East (or Northeast) Semitic (Akkadian: Babylonian and Assyrian), Northwest Semitic (Aramaic, Canaanite: Eblaite, Ugaritic, Phoenician, Hebrew), and South Semitic (Southeast: Old South Arabic and modern derivatives such as Ethiopic; Southwest: Arabic).

SENAAH [sə nā'ə] (Heb. *sᵉnā'â*). A town some of whose inhabitants returned with Zerubbabel after the Exile (Ezra 2:35; Neh. 7:38). These returnees may be connected with "the sons of Hassenaah" who worked on the rebuilding of the walls of Jerusalem (3:3) and with the Benjaminite family of Hassenuah (1 Chr. 9:7; Neh. 11:9). Senaah may be identified with modern Magdalsenna, *ca.* 13 km. (8 mi.) northeast of Jericho.

SENATE, SENATORS. *See* ELDER; SANHEDRIN.

SENEH [sē'nə] (Heb. *senneh*; cf. *sᵉneh* "thorn bush"). One of two rocky crags flanking a pass along the Wâdī eṣ-Ṣuweinît between Michmash and Geba (1 Sam. 14:4). Seneh is on the south side of the wadi, *ca.* 10 km. (6 mi.) north-northeast of Jerusalem.

SENIR [sē'nər] (Heb. *śᵉnîr*). The Amorites' name for Mt. Hermon (Deut. 3:9; KJV "Shenir"). At 1 Chr. 5:23 Senir and Mt. Hermon are distinguished (unless "and" should be taken as epexegetic "even"); furthermore, "Sanir" is known to have been a name for the entire Anti-lebanon range (as opposed to the single peak of Hermon; cf. Cant. 4:8; KJV "Shenir"; Ezek. 27:5).

See ANTI-LEBANON; HERMON, MOUNT.

SENNACHERIB [sə năk'ər ĭb] (Heb. *sanᵉḥērîb*; Akk. *Sin-aḫḫē-rība* "Sin [the moon-god] multiply brothers").† King of the Assyrian Empire 705-681 B.C. Under Sennacherib's uncle Shalmaneser V and father Sargon II the kingdom of Israel was ended (722-721 B.C.). Following a two-year campaign (704-702) to regain control of Babylon from Merodach-baladan, Sennacherib was confronted with rebellion in Syria-Palestine. He took all the fortified cities of Judah except Jerusalem in 701 (2 Kgs. 18:13 par. 2 Chr. 32:1; Isa. 36:1). Although warned by the prophet Isaiah to resist (2 Kgs. 18:17–19:34 par. Isa. 36:1–37:15), King Hezekiah of Judah, the leader of the coalition, finally capitulated to Assyrian pressure (2 Kgs. 18:14-16) and the seige was lifted. However, according to 19:35, thousands of Assyrian soldiers died in their camp before they had even gone against Jerusalem (v. 35; cf. Herodotus *Hist.* ii.141; Taylor prism, *ANET,* pp. 287-88). Some scholars interpret the biblical account as depicting two campaigns against Jerusalem in 701 or possibly a later attack *ca.* 688. Much of Sennacherib's later reign was consumed with campaigns against Babylon and the Elamites. Having designated a younger son, Esarhaddon, as his successor, he was assassinated by two other sons, Adrammelech and Šarezer (cf. 2 Kgs. 19:36-37).

SENUAH (Neh. 11:9, KJV). *See* HASSENUAH 2.

SEORIM [sē ôr´ĭm] (Heb. *śe'ōrîm*). The leader of the fourth division of priests in the time of David (1 Chr. 24:8).

SEPHAR [sĕ'fər] (Heb. *sᵉpār*). A place named in the description of the limit of the Joktanite settlements (Gen. 10:30). The Joktanites were South Arabian Semites. Sephar is possibly to be identified with Ẓafār in Hadramaut.

SEPHARAD [sĕf'ə răd] (Heb. *sᵉpāraḏ*). A place of Jewish dispersion named at Obad. 20. The Targum and the Peshitta identified Sepharad with Spain, with the result that Iberian Jews are now called "Sephardim." Sepharad is now usually identified with SARDIS (*sprd* in a fifth- or fourth-century B.C. Aramaic inscription; O.Pers. *sparda*; Akk. *saparda*), the capital of Lydia in Asia Minor. Another suggested location is Saparda, a region in Media in which exiled Israelites lived as early as the eighth century B.C.

SEPHARVAIM [sĕf'ər vā'əm] (Heb. *sᵉparwayim*). A place whose inhabitants were resettled by King Sargon II of Assyria in the former territory of the kingdom of Israel sometime after its defeat in 722-721 B.C. (2 Kgs. 17:24). The Sepharvites (*sᵉparwîm*) became one of the components of the Samaritans who imported non-Israelite practices into the Samaritan religion (v. 31). Sepharvaim was formerly identified with the Babylonian city of Sippar, but its being listed with Syrian sites (v. 24; 18:34; 19:13; par. Isa. 36:19; 37:13) makes likely its identification with Šabara'in ("Sibraim" at Ezek. 47:16) in Syria. Another suggested location is Saparda, a region in Media conquered by Sargon in 716-714 B.C. (*see* SEPHARAD).

SEPTUAGINT [sĕp'tŏ ə jĭnt] The third- to second-century B.C. Greek translation of the Old Testament produced in Egypt. Both the name "Septuagint" (Lat. *Septuaginta* "seventy") and the common abbreviation LXX come from the legend of the Greek Pentateuch's translation by seventy-two Jewish scholars at the court of Ptolemy II in seventy-two days (*see* ARISTEAS, LETTER OF). The LXX is of significance because of its inclusion of the APOCRYPHA, which has historically important documents, especially 1 Maccabees; its contribution to understanding the literary history of postbiblical Judaism; its demonstration of the theological and ethical outlook of Alexandrian Judaism; and its contribution to Old Testament textual criticism. The LXX contributed in a large way to the entrance of Judaism into the Hellenistic world and became the basis for much of the literature of Judaism written in Greek and for much of the thought and language of the New Testament writers.

See BIBLE TRANSLATIONS *I.*

SERAH [sĭr'ə] (Heb. *śeraḥ*). The daughter of the patriarch Asher (Gen. 46:17; Num. 26:46; KJV "Sarah"; 1 Chr. 7:30).

SERAIAH [sə rā'yə] (Heb. *śᵉrāyâ, śᵉrāyāhû* "Yahweh is ruler").

1. (Heb. *śᵉrāyâ*). David's secretary (2 Sam. 8:17),

also called Sheva (2 Sam. 20:25), Shavsa (1 Chr. 18:16), and possibly Shisha (1 Kgs. 4:3).

2. The high priest at the time of the Babylonian defeat of Judah, executed in Syria with other leaders of Judah (2 Kgs. 25:18 par. Jer. 52:24). Seraiah was the father of Jehozadak and Ezra and the grandfather of Jeshua (Joshua), the first postexilic high priest (1 Chr. 6:14 [MT 15]; Ezra 7:1; Hag. 1:1).

3. The son of Tanhumeth the Netophathite. He was one of the leaders of Judahite forces who remained in the open country in opposition to the Babylonian takeover until they were persuaded by Gedaliah, the newly-appointed governor, to put down their arms (2 Kgs. 25:23-24 par. Jer. 40:7-9).

4. A Judahite, the son of Kenaz and father of Joab (1 Chr. 4:13-14).

5. A Simeonite prince, the son of Asiel and father of Joshibiah (1 Chr. 4:35).

6. One of those who returned from exile in Babylon with Zerubbabel the governor and Jeshua the high priest (Ezra 2:2). At Neh. 7:7 he is called Azariah **(19)**. This Seraiah may be the same as **9** below (see also **7**).

7. A priest who participated in the sealing of the covenant under Nehemiah (Neh. 10:2 [MT 3]). If, as is probable, the priests' names at Neh. 10 are names of families of priests rather than of individuals, then this Seraiah may be the same as **6** above and **9** below.

8. The supervising priest in the temple in early postexilic Judah (Neh. 11:11), called Azariah **(8)** at 1 Chr. 9:11.

9. A priest who returned from exile in Babylon with Zerubbabel the governor and Jeshua the high priest (Neh. 12:1). Members of his family were among the priests who served under Jeshua's son and successor Joiakim (v. 12). He is possibly the same as **6** above (see also **7**).

10. The son of Neriah and brother of Baruch, Jeremiah's secretary (Jer. 32:12; 51:59). Jeremiah the prophet gave Seraiah, who was quartermaster for King Zedekiah, a scroll of oracles against Babylon and instructed him to read it in Babylon and then throw it into the Euphrates river to emphasize Babylon's coming doom (vv. 60-64).

11. (Heb. *śᵉrāyāhû*). The son of Azriel, and a court official during the reign of King Jehoiakim of Judah (Jer. 36:26). Seraiah was among those who attempted to arrest Jeremiah and Baruch at the king's command.

SERAPHIM [sĕr'ə fĭm] (Heb. *śᵉrāpîm*, from *śārap* "burn").† Beings with six wings each, human voices, hands, and feet that the prophet Isaiah saw in his vision of the Lord in the temple (Isa. 6:1-7; JB, NIV "seraphs").

The significance of the name of these beings is not known for certain. The desert snakes sent by Yahweh to punish the people for murmuring against him (Num. 21:6) are called "fiery" (Heb. *śᵉrāpîm*; cf. Deut. 8:15), i.e., poisonous; the bronze fiery (*śārāp*) snake set up by Moses in response to the ensuing plague (Num. 21:8) became a cult object that was still in use (perhaps in the temple) when Isaiah received his call "in the year that King Uzziah died" (2 Kgs. 18:4; Isa. 6:1). The flying *śārāp* mentioned at 14:29; 30:6 (RSV "flying serpent"; KJV "fiery flying serpent") is among the desert creatures that figure in ancient folklore and mythology as they are reflected in the Old Testament. *See* SERPENT.

The seraphim of Isaiah's vision may be related to ideas connected with such desert animals. Their identity, as established by the vision apart from their name, is that of attendants of God and worshippers of his holiness. For this reason they have often been thought of as a type of angel. Their name may imply a "fiery" or snakelike appearance, and is probably also to be connected with the purification by fire from the altar that one of them performs on Isaiah (6:6-7).

SERED [sĕr′ĕd] (Heb. *sereḏ*). A son of the patriarch Zebulun (Gen. 46:14), and ancestor of the Seredites (Num. 26:26; KJV "Sardites").

SERGIUS PAULUS [sûr′jĭ əs pôl′əs] (Gk. *Sergios Paulos*). A Roman proconsul of the island province of Cyprus who became a Christian through the preaching of Paul and Barnabas (Acts 13:6-12; *ca.* A.D. 45). A man with the Latin name L. Sergius Paullus, a curator of the Tiber at some time during the reign of Claudius (A.D. 41-54), may be the same man.

SERMON ON THE MOUNT.† The collection of Jesus' teachings found at Matt. 5–7, the largest block of teachings uninterrupted by narrative in the Gospels. The designation of these chapters as "the Sermon on the Mount" arises from the description of Jesus sitting on a mountain as he teaches (5:1). The mountain on which Jesus sat to teach has been traditionally identified with the Horns of Hattin, west of Tiberias and south of Magdala.

I. Setting in Matthew

The Sermon on the Mount is the first of five discourse sections into which most of the teachings of Jesus recorded in the gospel of Matthew are organized. Each of these discourse sections has a distinct theme or orientation, that of the Sermon on the Mount being the spiritual and ethical nature of the people of the kingdom. This theme builds on the introduction of Jesus' ministry at 4:17-25; the theme of Jesus' preaching is the coming of the kingdom (vv. 17, 23). Jesus calls individuals to follow him (vv. 18-22), and great crowds come to hear and be healed by him (vv. 22-25; cf. chs. 8–9).

All three of the supposed main sources of the gospel of Matthew are represented in the sermon—the gospel of Mark, the collection of sayings of Jesus (designated "Q") represented in both Matthew and Luke, and the sayings material unique to Matthew (usually called "M"). Because of the highly structured nature of both the Sermon on the Mount and the gospel of Matthew, and because of the combination of different sources in the sermon, it should not be understood as a single proclamation offered on one occasion by Jesus. While a core consisting of a sermon presented on one occasion may have served as a basis for the composition of the passage as it stands, teachings of Jesus spoken on different occasions have been assembled by the writer of Matthew to give a clear focus and organization to certain aspects of Jesus' teaching.

II. Content and Theology

Because of the high (and, according to some, impossible) ethical demands of the Sermon on the Mount, it has been interpreted in a number of ways. (1) It has been viewed as a standard only for the clergy or those living a monastic life and not for ordinary laypeople. (2) Among Protestants the sermon has sometimes been assigned the function given to the law at Gal. 3:23-24, that of posing an impossible standard so as to drive people to reliance on Christ rather than on personal achievement. (3) Extreme dispensationalism has seen the sermon as a standard not for this age but for the "kingdom age," the coming millennial age after the return of Christ. (4) It has been suggested that Jesus foresaw only a short time before the end of the present age and therefore laid out an "interim ethic," not an ethical system intended for a continuing community. (5) The sermon has been accepted at face value as setting the standard for the lives of all Christians in this age. Often, but not always, qualifications are added to this final view, e.g., that some of the sermon's demands (e.g., Matt. 5:42) are not to be applied to all types of human relationships, or that Jesus' intention is not to give specific rules of behavior but general principles.

The broadest context of the Sermon on the Mount is the proclamation of the kingdom to all, which is recorded in the Gospels. This context shows that the sermon's intention is to describe the normative life of all Christians in this age. It is apparent that some hyperbole appears in the sermon (e.g., Matt. 5:29-30). But a continuing search for qualifications of the sermon's demands can cripple the effort to grasp its intent. The sermon does not, at any rate, simply establish an ethical standard. The blessing of the kingdom's presence (v. 3) comes before the imperatives that dominate the sermon and is, therefore, the context in which the imperatives are to be understood. Accordingly, the sermon is focused on the spiritual and ethical nature of the people of the kingdom, i.e., those who have responded to Jesus' message of the coming of the kingdom. Thus it does not suggest an ethical life for any society at large, but only for those who have renounced the world for the kingdom of God.

The first two beatitudes show that the people of the kingdom are those whose place in it is not based on their own accomplishments but paradoxically on their inability and their consequent openness to God's actions among them (vv. 3-4). These people are not proud, easily satisfied, or triumphant by usual standards, but humble, persecuted, and always seeking to accomplish God's justice (vv. 5-12).

Despite the humility described in the beatitudes, the righteousness of the people of the kingdom exceeds that of the scribes and Pharisees, whose lives would normally be admired by the ordinary Jew of Jesus' day as the ideal of living properly by the law of Moses (v. 20). The people of the kingdom have this greater righteousness because they go deeper than the letter of the law to its full intention, not being satisfied with mere external adherence but being concerned with the attitudes implied (vv. 21-48). As such, they give evidence of God's work among them to all who see them (vv. 13-16).

In setting this model before his listeners, Jesus makes

clear that his own relationship to the law of Moses is positive and that he has not come as the law's replacement (vv. 17-19). In that he probably intends a contrast with the rabbinic interpreters of the law. Whereas the rabbinic interpreters seek to understand the exact words of the law as the standard for conduct, Jesus presents himself not as an interpreter, but as the authoritative teacher (cf. 7:29) who can proclaim "but I say to you" (5:22, 28, 32, 34, 39, 44). He seeks to build up not an understanding of the exact requirement of the law's precepts, along with the limitations of their applicability, but a manner of life that takes on the law as a pattern of life even in all of the thoughts and attitudes not touched by the exact words of the law. This appropriation of the law also seeks to move beyond the limitations imposed on it by its being the civil law of a nation with enemies (e.g., the Roman occupation soldier who could force one of Jesus' listeners to carry a burden; v. 41) and in which revenge must be regulated (vv. 38-39). (The second clause of Jesus' citation from the law in v. 43 does not actually occur in the text of the Old Testament, but may have been understood as implied by some Jewish interpreters of the law.)

The people of the kingdom are spiritually sincere and simple (6:1-18). Their concerns are oriented toward the kingdom rather than toward insuring their own material security (vv. 19-34). They are also more mindful of their own judgment before God than of judging other people (7:1-5, 13-14, 21-26).

See BEATITUDES; LORD'S PRAYER.

III. Luke's Sermon on the Plain

Luke 6:20-49 is a sermon of Jesus most of which is paralleled in the Sermon on the Mount in Matthew. The introduction to the sermon in Luke is quite different from that in Matthew, placing Jesus "on a level place" and adding reports of healings and of crowds following Jesus, even from "the seacoast of Tyre and Sidon," i.e., from Gentile territory (vv. 17-19). Both sermons follow the same general outline and include similar groups of beatitudes (Matt. 5:3-12; Luke 6:20-23), teaching on retaliation, love of enemies, and judging (Matt. 5:38-48; 7:1-5; Luke 6:27-38, 41-42), teaching on the evidence of good and evil in "fruits" (Matt. 7:15-20; Luke 6:43-45), the question "Why do you call me 'Lord, Lord'. . . ?" (v.46; expanded at Matt. 7:21-23), and the parable of the two builders (vv. 24-27; Luke 6:47-49). The only parts of Luke's sermon not represented in Matthew's Sermon on the Mount are the woes that answer to the beatitudes (vv. 24-26), and vv. 39-40 (but par. Matt. 15:14; 10:24-25).

While the two sermons are thus similar, a different tone is set by the differences in the beatitudes, where Luke is concerned not so much with the ethical and spiritual nature of the people of the kingdom as with the contrast between their present external conditions—poor, hungry, weeping, and hated—and their future participation in the kingdom. Furthermore, Matthew's specific concern with the relation of the Christian community to the law of Moses is not present in Luke.

Bibliography. D. Bonhoeffer, *The Cost of Discipleship* (New York: 1963); W. D. Davies, *The Setting of the Sermon on the Mount* (Cambridge: 1964); R. A. Guelich, *The Sermon on the Mount* (Waco: 1982); H. K. McArthur, *Understanding the Sermon on the Mount* (1960; repr. Greenwood, Conn.: 1978).

SERPENT. † A wide variety of snakes, both poisonous and nonpoisonous, are common in Palestine and nearby lands. These include the Egyptian asp or cobra (*Naja haje*; Heb. *peṭen*; Gk. *aspís*), the horned viper (*Cerastes cornutus*; Heb. *šᵉpîpōn*), the carpet viper (*Echis colorata*; perhaps Heb. *ṣepaʿ*), the epha (*Echis carinatus*), the black whip snake (*Coluber jugularis*), and numerous others. Heb. *nāḥāš* and Gk. *óphis* are general terms that do not differentiate species; terms for reptiles in general (Heb. *zōḥeleṭ*; Gk. *herpetón*) are sometimes applied to snakes. Gk. *échidna* is a general term for poisonous snakes. Heb. *ṣipʿônî* and *ʾepʿeh* may have been applied to particular kinds of snakes, but which is not now known. Heb. *ʿakšûb* (Ps. 140:3 [MT 4]) should probably be taken as "spider" rather than "viper" (KJV "adder").

Because of the particular place that snakes hold in ancient folk beliefs and mythology, two Hebrew words are used to designate not only snakes but also heavenly and mythological creatures, *tannîn* (*see* DRAGON) and *śārāp* (*see* SEPARPHIM). The association of snakes with mythological creatures, specifically chaos monsters, in relation to the creation of the world in the literatures of other ancient Near Eastern peoples is echoed in the Old Testament (e.g., Job 26:13; *see* LEVIATHAN; RAHAB).

During the Israelites' journeys through the wilderness, God responded to their complaining at one point by sending poisonous ("fiery") snakes among them, which killed many of the people (Num. 21:5-6). The solution given by God was a bronze serpent made by Moses, which the afflicted were to look upon. Just as other ancient Near Eastern peoples associated snakes with deities, especially in Egypt, the bronze serpent later came to be worshipped as an idol and therefore had to be destroyed (2 Kgs. 18:4; cf. NEHUSHTAN).

Poison is commonly referred to as a characteristic of snakes in the Old Testament, even though many Palestinian snakes are harmless. This understanding of snakes as generally poisonous was the basis for the strong and varied association of snakes with evil. A number of figures of speech arose from this association, including figures for the effects of violence on society (Ps. 58:4 [MT 5]; 140:3 [MT 4]), every kind of danger that a person might encounter (91:13), the effects of wine (Prov. 23:32), violent enemies (Deut. 32:33; Jer. 8:17), evil people (Matt. 3:7), and evil and violence in general (Isa. 14:29).

This use of snakes and their venom in figures of speech for evil culminated in the personification of evil in the snake, a recurrent theme in biblical demonology. It is the snake who brings the first temptation to the first humans (Gen. 3; 2 Cor. 11:3). Because of this role, the snake is made to crawl on the ground and is made a perpetual enemy of mankind (Gen. 3:14-15). Later, as the eschatological defeat of evil is spoken of, the snake of mankind's fall into sin is identified with Satan (Rev. 12:9; 20:2; cf. Isa. 65:25). This identification of the snake with Satan, the supreme enemy of God and mankind who is to be destroyed at the end of the age, also draws on the old association of snakes with primordial chaos monsters (cf. 27:1).

SERPENT'S STONE (Heb. *'eben hazzōhelet* "stone of the creeping animal").* A place near the spring of En-rogel south of Jerusalem where Adonijah, David's eldest living son at the time, made ceremonial sacrifices as part of an attempted coup (1 Kgs. 1:9; KJV "stone of Zoheleth").

SERUG [sĕr'ŭg] (Heb. *sᵉrûg*; Gk. *Serouch*). A son of Reu; the father of Nahor, hence an ancestor of Abraham and Jesus (Gen. 11:20-23; 1 Chr. 1:26; Luke 3:35; KJV "Saruch").

SERVANT (Heb. *'ebed*; Gk. *doúlos*).† A male or female person who is under obligation to render obedience to a master.

I. Old Testament

The most common Old Testament word for a slave or servant is Heb. *'ebed*. Other terms include *na'ar* "young man, boy" (e.g., Num. 22:22; 2 Kgs. 4:12); *śākîr,* which refers to free hired servants (Exod. 12:45; Job 7:1; Mal. 3:5), and *mᵉśārēt* (from *šrt*), which represents a person who is the attendant of another (e.g., Exod. 24:13; 1 Kgs. 10:5).

In biblical times servants were usually slaves in the sense that they were the property of another person and totally at that person's disposal. In ancient Israel a number of legal stipulations sought to make treatment of slaves, especially Israelite slaves, more humane. Undergirding these laws was the reminder that all of Israel had been enslaved in Egypt (Deut. 15:15). The Sabbath was for slaves as well as for free persons (Exod. 20:10). A master who assaulted his slave suffered the loss of the slave (21:26). Israelites who became slaves because of poverty (Lev. 25:39) were distinguished from foreign slaves, who were bought (vv. 44-45) or captured in battle (1 Kgs. 9:20-21). Israelite slaves could receive their freedom in six years (Exod. 21:2). However, if an Israelite slave wished to stay with his master because of the threat of poverty or because he had gained a wife and children during his time of servitude, his master would pierce his ear to mark him as one who had made such a choice (Exod. 21:5-6; Deut. 15:16-17). All Israelite slaves were to be set free during the Year of Jubilee (Lev. 25:40-41; see JUBILEE, YEAR OF). But those whose ears had been pierced remained with their masters until death.

Israelites were permitted to sell themselves, their wives, and their children as slaves (especially their daughters as concubines; Exod. 21:7-11). The cost of redeeming oneself from a vow of servitude to God varied from five to fifty shekels of silver, depending on the age and sex of the person (Lev. 27:3-7), and the same range probably applied for slaves (cf. Zech. 11:12). A slave of foreign descent could be circumcised and participate in the great feasts (cf. Exod. 12:44). Children of slaves might have often been circumcised (Gen. 17:12-13). A slave could eventually

hold a position of trust and responsibility, as did Eliezer (15:2; ch. 24) and Joseph (*see* STEWARD).

II. New Testament

The most common Greek word for a slave is *doúlos*. In contrast, *diákonos* refers to free servants. Other terms include *país* "child"; *oikétēs*, a domestic servant who worked within the master's household (*oikía*), and *hypērétēs*, a free servant who worked as a personal attendant, guard, or messenger. Gk. *místhios* and *misthōtós* are New Testament words for free hired servants.

The New Testament presupposes slavery and does not argue for its abolition. Neither does it look at slaves with scorn, and in this way it departs from the general pattern of Greco-Roman attitudes. Slaves are admonished to obey their masters (Eph. 6:5-8; Col. 3:22-25), and Paul returned a runaway slave to his owner (Phlm. 12, 17). The apostle exhorts slaves to be content with their present position, though he adds that should the opportunity to become free arise they should make use of it (1 Cor. 7:21-24). But Paul also expects masters to treat their slaves in a humane fashion (Eph. 6:9; Col. 4:1). Thus while the New Testament does not call for the end of slavery, it does urge improvement of the institution. Furthermore, no distinctions according to social class are to exist within the Christian community itself, for "in Christ" there is neither slave nor free person (Gal. 3:28; cf. 1 Cor. 12:13; Col. 3:11).

III. Religious Language

Devotees of particular gods were often called "servants" of that God. In the Old Testament a "servant" of God was a prominent leader of God's people or an intermediary between God and his people such as Moses or David (e.g., Exod. 14:31; 2 Sam. 3:18; cf. Ps. 19:11 [MT 12]). Jesus is called God's servant (*país*), always in quotations and allusions to the Isaianic servant songs (Matt. 12:18; Acts 3:13, 26; 4:27, 30; cf. RSV mg.; *see* SERVANT OF THE LORD). Gk. *doúlos* is used of Christ only at Phil. 2:7.

Christians are called "servants of God" or "servants of Christ" (Acts 16:17; Titus 1:1; Jas. 1:1; 1 Pet. 2:16; cf. Acts 2:18). Paul uses this terminology to speak of Christ's rescue of the Christian from a life of slavery to sin to become the possession of Christ and of righteousness (Rom. 6:6-7, 17-18; 1 Cor. 6:19b-20; 7:22-23; Gal. 4:3, 8-9). Other texts contrast the "sonship" of Christians with "slavery" (John 8:31-36; Rom. 8:15; Gal. 4:4-7).

Gk. *diákonos* is used as the title of an office ("deacon") in the Church (Phil. 1:1; 1 Tim. 3:8-13) and as a functional description of other ecclesial offices (2 Cor. 6:4; RSV "servants"; Col. 1:7; RSV "minister"), as is *hypērétēs* (Acts 26:16; 1 Cor. 4:1).

Bibliography. J. P. M. van der Ploeg, "Slavery in the Old Testament," *VTS* 22 (1972), 72-87; T. Wiedemann, *Greek and Roman Slavery* (Baltimore: 1981).

SERVANT OF THE LORD (Heb. *'ebed YHWH*).† Devotees of any god were called "servants" of that deity. In the Old Testament individuals such as Moses,

Joshua, and David, various classes of people—especially kings and prophets, and Israel collectively (Ps. 136:22) are called "servants" of Yahweh. In the book of Isaiah the title gains special significance. Four songs at Isa. 40–55 refer to an anonymous servant in whom traits of both a group and an individual are mixed; these Servant Songs are a significant part of the message of consolation in chs. 40–66.

I. Servant Songs

The first of the Servant Songs (Isa. 42:1-4) tells of the call of the servant. His mission is to "bring forth justice to the nations" empowered by God's Spirit. This mission will not fail. In the second song (49:1-6) the servant's mission becomes clearer through the Lord's commission to him. All peoples are called upon to pay attention to the one appointed as a light of salvation (v. 6).

Isa. 50:4-9 does not use the word "servant," but is considered the third servant song on the basis of vocabulary and context (some scholars include also vv. 10-11). Here the servant introduces his method. Although he suffers as an obedient servant, his confidence remains in the Lord. The servant's method is expanded at 52:13–53:12 (the fourth song) by a report on his career. The scene is viewed from Yahweh's perspective (52:13-15; 53:12) and from the perspective of a shocked audience (53:1), probably both Israelites and Gentiles. The servant suffers for the sins of all, and as with the scapegoat, his suffering removes the sins of others (vv. 4-6, 12). His reward hints at resurrection (vv. 10-11). Surprise and dismay accompany the report.

II. Identity of the Servant

Identification of the servant has long been a great problem for interpreters (cf. Acts 8:34). Often in Isaiah the servant may be identified with collective Israel (e.g., Isa. 41:8). Indeed, identification of the servant with Israel fits the context of the book as a whole, and it is assumed in the LXX. However, a collective view of Israel's suffering does not fit all the passages, nor does it explain the atonement achieved for all people by the suffering. A mixing of imagery—especially at 49:4-5, where the servant is identified both as Israel and as an individual who leads Israel back to the Lord—makes the identification more difficult. Suggestions that the servant represents the "corporate personality" of ideal Israel attempt to account for both the collective and individual aspects of the servant. However, the corporate personality does not fit the fourth song with its high level of specificity.

In the late nineteenth century A.D. the Servant Songs were isolated from the oracular material that comprises the balance of Deutero-Isaiah, and different historical individuals were proposed as the servant. Suggestions included prophets such as Isaiah, Jeremiah, or Deutero-Isaiah and kings such as Hezekiah, Uzziah, Jehoiachin, Zerubbabel, or Cyrus. Not many interpreters follow such suggestions today, but both prophetic and royal functions are indeed found in the servant.

The writer of the Servant Songs was looking for an individual who represented both Israel and the Lord, and whose work would bring salvation through suf-

fering. This figure carries a sense of the ideal, but also a sense of theological importance that demands historical enactment. Whether or not the writer viewed this figure as messianic, the historical person who most fulfilled this ideal was Jesus. In the New Testament the servant is, indeed, identified with Christ (Matt. 8:17; 12:17-21; Luke 22:37; Acts 8:32-33; Rom. 15:21). The Servant Songs do not identify the servant with messianic concepts found elsewhere in Isaiah (e.g., Isa. 9, 11), but the identification of the servant with Christ allowed the Church to develop a concept of a suffering Messiah, a concept essentially foreign to Judaism.

Bibliography. H. Blocher, *Songs of the Servant* (Downers Grove: 1975); C. R. North, *The Suffering Servant in Deutero-Isaiah,* 2nd ed. (London: 1956); H. H. Rowley, *The Servant of the Lord and Other Essays on the Old Testament,* 2nd ed. (Oxford: 1965).

SETH [sĕth] (Heb. *šēṯ;* cf. *šāṯ* "appointed"; Gk. *Sēth*). The third son of Adam and Eve, born to replace his older brother Abel who was murdered by Cain (Gen. 4:25; 5:3). Seth was the father of Enosh and the ancestor of Noah (vv. 6-7; 1 Chr. 1:1; KJV "Sheth"; Luke 3:38). Sir. 49:16 refers to Seth and Shem as "honored among men."

SETHUR [sē'thər] (Heb. *sᵉṯûr* "hidden"). An Asherite, the son of Michael who was one of the twelve spies sent into Canaan (Num. 13:13).

SEVEN, THE (Gk. *hoi heptá*).* A designation for the seven men appointed by the Church and ordained by the apostles to "serve tables" and minister to the widows (Acts 6:1-6). The term appears at 21:8. *See* DEACON.

SEVEN WORDS, THE. The sayings of Jesus uttered while he was on the cross. The traditional order of the seven recorded "words" is (1) "Father, forgive them; for they do not know what they do" (Luke 23:34), (2) to one of those being crucified with him, "Truly, I say to you, today you will be with me in Paradise" (v. 43), (3) to Mary his mother and "the disciple whom he loved," "Woman, behold, your son" and "Behold, your mother?" (John 19:26-27), (4) "Eli, Eli, lama sabachthani?" (Matt. 27:46 par. Mark 15:34), (5) "I thirst" (John 19:28), (6) "It is finished" (v. 30), and (7) "Father, into thy hands I commit my spirit" (Luke 23:46).

SEX.* The basis of the biblical view of human sexual activity is a positive view of sex within committed heterosexual marriage, i.e., within a relationship in which procreation is an aim and in which children can be received as a blessing and nurtured. This is evident in the accounts of the creation of mankind as sexual, in the views of marriage and children revealed in narratives, and in the accounts of and regulations concerning sexual sins. The intimacy of sex is acknowledged, however—most immediately by the use of Heb. *yāḏaʿ* "know" for sexual intercourse (e.g., Gen. 4:1; 1 Kgs. 1:4). That human sexuality is ultimately a mystery beyond human understanding is also acknowledged (Prov. 30:18-19).

In the first account of creation the distinction between male and female humans is regarded as part of God's good creation and is focused on procreation (Gen. 1:27-28). The expression of this positive attitude toward human procreational processes is conditioned mainly by the increased social status, especially of women, attached to childbearing. Great desire for children is expressed by those who are childless (e.g., 1 Sam. 1:10-11), they are envious of those who do have children (e.g., Gen. 30:1), and joy surrounds the birth of every child, especially every male child (e.g., 21:6-7; Ps. 127:3-5). The Song of Solomon is conspicuous in that it celebrates the joys and sensual pleasures of romantic love apart from childbearing.

The second creation account and the subsequent account of the fall (Gen. 2:4–3:24) have been thought by some to incorporate a negative view of human sexuality. But the woman is brought to the man by God as the man's only appropriate counterpart (2:20-22; cf. Plato *Symposium* 182); marriage and sex ("one flesh") immediately thereafter become part of the human experience (v. 24), and unashamed nudity is part of this experience before the fall (v. 25). The narrative of the first conception and birth appears after the narrative of the fall (4:1); but it is not said that procreation was made possible by the fall, that it was a result of the fall, or even that it occurred after the fall. It is clear, however, that the fall distorted human sexuality (cf. the view that the forbidden fruit of "knowledge" was sexual intercourse): nudity became a source of shame (3:7, 10), the unity of man and woman was broken (v. 12), and pain of childbirth and male dominance of women began after the fall (v. 16). All these conditions present in the relationships of men and women are thus held to be results of an event that occurred after creation, and not, therefore, any part of the intention of creation itself. Ps. 51:5 (MT 7) has also been thought to evidence a negative view of sex (not nearly so much as that of the Church Father Augustine, who viewed sexual passion as animalistic and therefore sinful), but it is not intended as a comment on the process of procreation but rather as an emphatic declaration of the extent of the psalmist's sinfulness.

Another way in which the Bible recognizes that human sexuality is an area of life in which experience is often a distortion of the Creator's intention is in its condemnation of types of sexual behavior that do not conform to the divine intention. Among such behavior are adultery (Exod. 20:14; Deut. 22:22), premarital sex on the part of women (vv. 13-21), homosexuality (Lev. 18:22; 20:13; Rom. 1:26-27; 1 Cor. 6:9; cf. 1 Tim. 1:10), bestiality (Lev. 18:23; 20:15-16), incest (which included having wives who were of the same family; Lev. 18:6-18; 20:14; cf. 1 Cor. 5:1), and refusal to carry out conjugal obligations, including those of levirate marriage (Gen. 38:9-10 [not concerned with masturbation]; Deut. 25:5-9; 1 Cor. 7:3-5). From the persepctive of ceremonial cleanness, sexual bodily discharges were regarded with awe, perhaps because of their association with the mystery of life's generation; hence menstrual taboos are recorded at Lev. 15:19-24; 18:19 (cf. Ezek. 22:10). Development occurs in relation to some of these norms: the patriarchs appear to be lax in comparison to the Mosaic laws regarding incest (Gen. 20:12; 29:21-30); monogamy was increasingly endorsed over polygamy (Mal. 2:14-15; 1 Tim. 3:2, 12); prostitution was no longer tolerated but indeed disapproved (Gen. 38:15-16; 1 Cor. 6:15-20; but cf. Lev. 19:29), as also divorce (Deut. 24:1; Mal. 2:16; Matt. 5:31-32); and female as well as male homosexuality came to be explicitly condemned (Rom. 1:26-27).

Much of this biblical development toward more precise adherence to the divine intention for sexual activity comes in Jesus' insistence on more radical obedience in all areas of life (e.g., Matt. 5:27-30). However, the effect of the gospel was not always in accord with such teaching, but sometimes favored greater libertinism (e.g., 1 Cor. 5). This was often the result of misinterpretation of Paul's responses to attempts to enforce Gentile Christian adherence to the Mosaic law (cf. Rom. 3:8), though the less stringent standards of the Gentile world were a constant factor (cf. Eph. 4:17; 1 Thess. 4:4-5).

Celibacy was endorsed by Jesus (Matt. 19:12) and Paul (1 Cor. 7:7-8), but was also taught and practiced by others as an overreaction to libertinism (vv. 1-2; 1 Tim. 4:1-3). The basic assumption of the New Testament remains similar to that of the Old: most will be married, and there is no evil in that (cf. vv. 4-5); but because of the eschatological situation brought by Christ, marriage is not to be desired as absolutely as before (1 Cor. 7:25-40; cf. Mark 10:29-30; Luke 18:29-30).

See also MARRIAGE; WOMAN.

SHAALBIM [shā ăl'bĭm] (Heb. *ša'al⁽ᵉ⁾bîm* "foxes"), **SHAALABBIN** [shā'ə lăb'ən] (Heb. *ša'⁽ᵃ⁾labbîn*). An Amorite city in the territory assigned to the tribe of Dan (Josh. 19:42, "Shaalabbin"). Dan was unable to gain control of the city, and the Amorites who continued to live there came to be subject to forced labor for the tribe of Joseph (Judg. 1:35). The city was later the seat of Solomon's second district (1 Kgs. 4:9). It is now usually identified with modern Selbît, on the northern side of the valley of Aijalon 13 km. (8 mi.) north of Beth-shemesh.

SHAALBON [shā ăl'bŏn] (Heb. **ša'al⁽ᵉ⁾bŏn*). The home of Eliahba, one of David's "mighty men" (2 Sam. 23:32; 1 Chr. 11:33). KJV "Shaalbonite" follows the Hebrew gentilic *šaa'al⁽ᵉ⁾bŏnî*, perhaps derived from SHAALBIM, SHAALABBIN.

SHAALIM [shā'ə lĭm] (Heb. *š⁽ᵉ⁾'ālîm*).† A region of unknown location, probably near a border of Benjaminite territory and perhaps named after a city or a prominent natural landmark. Saul and a servant passed through this region while looking for Kish's asses (1 Sam. 9:4; KJV "Shalim"). It is generally associated with SHAALBIM, SHAALABBIN, but a connection with SHUAL north of Bethel is also possible (cf. P. K. McCarter, Jr., *I Samuel*. AB 8 [1980], p. 174).

SHAAPH [shā'ăf] (Heb. *ša'ap*).
1. A son of Jahdai, who was possibly a descendant, wife, or concubine of Caleb (1 Chr. 2:47).
2. A son of Maacah and Caleb, and father of Madmannah (1 Chr. 2:49).

SHAARAIM [shā'ə rā'əm] (Heb. *ša'⁽ᵃ⁾rayim* "two gates").

1. A city in the lowland (Shephelah) region of Judah's tribal territory (Josh. 15:36; KJV "Sharaim"). Shaaraim was at one end of the road along which the Israelites pursued the Philistines after David killed Goliath (1 Sam. 17:52). It was probably located near Azekah, perhaps at Khirbet es-Saʿireh.

2. A Simeonite city (1 Chr. 4:31), also called Sharuhen (Josh. 19:6; cf. R. G. Boling and G. E. Wright, *Joshua.* AB 6 [1982], p. 438). Some scholars identify it with Tell el-Fârʿah on the Nahr Besor, *ca.* 25 km. (15 mi.) from the Mediterranean coast.

SHAASHGAZ [shā āsh′găz] (Heb. *šaʿašgaz*). A eunuch in the court of King Ahasuerus who was in charge of the king's harem (Esth. 2:14).

SHABBETHAI [shăb′ə thī] (Heb. *šabbᵉṭay,* from *šabbāṭ* "Sabbath"; Gk. *Sabbataios*). The name of three postexilic Levites, possibly all the same person.

1. One of those who opposed Ezra's solution to the problem of mixed marriages (Ezra 10:15) or, perhaps, assisted in carrying it out (according to 1 Esdr. 9:14; KJV "Sabbatheus").

2. One of the Levites who interpreted the law for the people while Ezra read it (Neh. 8:7).

3. A chief of the Levites, one of those who supervised the outside work of the temple (Neh. 11:16).

SHACHIA (1 Chr. 8:10, KJV)! See SACHIA.

SHADES. See REPHAIM.

SHADOW (Heb. *ṣēl;* Aram. verb *ṭᵉlal;* Gk. *aposkíasma, skiá*).† In the often sunny and hot climate of generally treeless Palestine, shade and shadows were valued (cf. Isa. 25:5; 32:2; Jonah 4:6; RSV "shade") and were a common literary figure. "Shadow" is thus used for that which protects (Gen. 19:8; RSV "shelter"; Judg. 9:15; Isa. 30:2-3; 32:1-2), including God (Ps. 91:1; 121:5). The expressions "the shadow of thy wings" (17:8; 36:7 [MT 8]) and "the shadow of his/my hand" (Isa. 49:2; 51:16) are sometimes used for God's protection. "Shadow" also conveys the notion of the temporal, transient, or fleeting quality of human existence (1 Chr. 29:15; Job 8:9; 14:2; Ps. 39:6 [MT 7]; 102:11 [MT 12]; 144:4). In a contrasting figure, the lengthening of a shadow as the sun moves across the sky depicts a life prolonged by the behavior of the one who lives it (Eccl. 8:13).

Heb. *ṣalmāweṭ,* translated "shadow of death" in the KJV (e.g., Job 3:5; Ps. 23:4; Isa. 9:2 [MT 1]), is better translated "darkness" (RSV "deep darkness"; cf. JB), i.e., not as a reference to death. This mistaken rendering of *ṣalmāweṭ* occurred early and is represented in the LXX and where the New Testament quotes the LXX of Isa. 9:2 (Matt. 4:16; Luke 1:79).

In three New Testament passages "shadow" is used for that which represents or is a copy of something else that is more real or substantial than the "shadow." The shadow is on earth, while the reality is that which is to be experienced in the eschatological future (Col. 2:17; Heb. 10:1) or is present in heaven (8:5). These passages reflect the distinction common in Hellenistic thought between the universal paradigm or archetype and that which only imitates or represents it in earthly experience.

The reference to a shadow at Jas. 1:17 was difficult already at the time of the copyists, who introduced a number of textual variants. It is clear, however, that the changes which shadows undergo as the sun moves across the sky are here a figure for inconsistency, which is said not to be a quality of God.

SHADRACH [shăd′răk] (Heb. *šaḏraḵ;* cf. Akk. *Šudur-Aku* "command of Aku [a Mesopotamian lunar deity]"). The name given by King Nebuchadnezzar's chief of the eunuchs to Hananiah (Heb. *ḥᵃnanyâ* "Yahweh is gracious"), one of Daniel's companions (Dan. 1:7; 2:49; ch. 3). See ABEDNEGO.

SHAGEE [shā′gī] (Heb. *šāgēh* or *šāgēʾ*). A Hararite and father of Jonathan, one of David's mighty men (1 Chr. 11:34; KJV "Shage"). According to 2 Sam. 23:33 Jonathan's father would appear to be "Shammah the Hararite" (cf. v. 11, "Shammah, the son of Agee the Hararite").

SHAHARAIM [shā′ə rā′əm] (Heb. *šaḥᵃrayim* "two dawns"). A Benjaminite who had numerous offspring (1 Chr. 8:8-11).

SHAHAZUMAH [shā′ə zoo′mə] (Heb. K *šaḥᵃṣûmâ,* Q *šaḥᵃṣîmâ*). A city on the border of Issachar's tribal territory (Josh. 19:22; KJV "Shahazimah"). A suggested site is Tell el-Muqarqash, east-southeast of Mt. Tabor.

SHALEM (Heb. *šālēm*). According to the KJV, a place name (Gen. 33:18; cf. LXX *eis Salēm* "to Salem"). The Hebrew is better translated "safely" (so RSV).

SHALIM (1 Sam. 9:4, KJV). See SHAALIM.

SHALISHAH [shăl′ə shə] (Heb. *šālišâ*). A region through which Saul and a servant passed while looking for his father's lost asses (1 Sam. 9:4; KJV "Shalisha"). While little is certain about the location of this region, Baal-shalishah (2 Kgs. 4:42), usually identified with Kefr Thilth approximately midway between Tel Aviv and Nablus, may have been located there.

SHALLECHETH [shăl′ə kĕth], **GATE OF** (Heb. *šaʿar šalleḵeṭ*). A gate of the Jerusalem temple (1 Chr. 26:16), located on the west side of the temple "on the road that goes up," probably the road from the Tyropoean valley to the temple mount. For JB "Gate of the Felled Tree-trunk," cf. Heb. *šalleḵeṭ* "tree that has been felled" (Isa. 6:13).

SHALLUM [shăl′əm] (Heb. *šallûm, šallum*).

1. The son of Jabesh who conspired against King Zechariah, the son of Jeroboam II. After killing the king, Shallum became king (2 Kgs. 15:10) but reigned only one month (747 B.C.). He was murdered by Menahem, who succeeded him (vv. 13-16).

2. The son of Tikvah and husband of the prophetess

Huldah, who lived during the reign of King Josiah (2 Kgs. 22:14; 2 Chr. 34:22). He was keeper of the wardrobe, though it is not known whether he served in the palace or in the temple.

3. A Judahite, the son of Sismai and father of Jekamiah (1 Chr. 2:40-41).

4. The fourth son and successor of King Josiah of Judah (1 Chr. 3:15; Jer. 22:11). Upon assuming the throne in 609 B.C. Shallum adopted the name of JEHOAHAZ (2) (2 Kgs. 23:30-31; 2 Chr. 36:1-2). After ruling but three months he was removed by the Egyptians in favor of his older brother Jehoiakim (1).

5. A son of Shaul of the tribe of Simeon (1 Chr. 4:24-25).

6. A high priest, the son of Zadok and father of Hilkiah (1 Chr. 6:12-13 [MT 5:38-39]; Ezra 7:2). At 1 Chr. 9:11; Neh. 11:11 he is called Meshullam.

7. A son of the patriarch Naphtali (1 Chr. 7:13). He is called Shillem at Gen. 46:24; Num. 26:49.

8. A chief of the levitical gatekeepers whose descendants returned from exile (1 Chr. 9:17; Ezra 2:42; Neh. 7:45). It is possible that he is the same as Meshelemiah (1 Chr. 9:21), Shelemiah (26:14), Shallum **9**, or Shallum **11** below.

9. A levitical gatekeeper, the son of Kore of the Korahite lineage (1 Chr. 9:19, 31). He may be the same as **8** above.

10. An Ephraimite, the father of Jehizkiah who lived during the reign of King Pekah (2 Chr. 28:12).

11. A levitical gatekeeper among those in the postexilic community who divorced their foreign wives (Ezra 10:24).

12. A layman required to relinquish his non-Israelite wife (Ezra 10:42).

13. The son of Hallohesh, administrator of half of Jerusalem's territory, who with his daughters (possibly meaning forces from subordinate villages under his rule) assisted in the rebuilding of the city walls (Neh. 3:12).

14. The son of Colhozeh and ruler of the district of Mizpah, who rebuilt the Fountain Gate of Jerusalem and the wall of the Pool of Shelah at the King's Garden (Neh. 3:15; KJV "Shallun").

15. An uncle of the prophet Jeremiah and father of Hanamel (Jer. 32:7).

16. The father of Maaseiah, keeper of the temple threshold in the time of Jeremiah (Jer. 35:4). If Shallum is actually Maaseiah's more distant ancestor, he may be the same as **8** above.

SHALMAI [shăl′mī] (Heb. *šalmay* "Yahweh is peace [?]"). The ancestor of a family of temple servants who returned from exile in Babylonia (Neh. 7:48; Ezra 2:46). RSV, JB "Shamlai" at Ezra 2:46 represent a variant reading, Heb. *šamlay.*

SHALMAN [shăl′mən] (Heb. *šalman*). A proper name appearing in an allusion to an apparently well-known battle in which Beth-arbel was destroyed (Hos. 10:14). Probably intended is the invasion of Israel by Shalmaneser III of Assyria in 841, specifically the defeat of the border city at the site of modern Irbid in Jordan.

SHALMANESER [shăl′mə nē′zər] (Heb. *šalman°eser*;

Akk. *Šulmānu-ašarid* "Šulmānu [a deity] is chief ").†

1. Shalmaneser I, king of Assyria 1274-1245 B.C. He conquered Hanigalbat (the remnant of Mitanni), deporting its populace, and subdued the formative confederation of Urartu. Kalhu (biblical Calah) was founded during his reign.

2. Shalmaneser II, king of Assyria 1031-1020 B.C.

3. Shalmaneser III, son of Assurnasirpal II and king of Assyria 858-824 B.C. His subjugation of the Aramean city-state Bit-adini (*see* BETH-EDEN) threatened the commercial activities of Damascus, which under Adad-ʿidri (biblical Ben-hadad) mounted an anti-Assyrian coalition including Irḫuleni of Hamath and Ahab of Israel that turned back the Assyrians at Qarqar in 853 (cf. *ANET*, pp. 279-280). In 849 Shalmaneser overcame Carchemish, thus reestablishing Assyrian control of the upper Euphrates. It was not until 841, when economic pressures and internal disarray had weakened the Syrian coalition, that Shalmaneser was able to defeat Hazael of Damascus and subject the various states, including Israel under Jehu, to tribute (*ANET*, pp. 280-81).

4. Shalmaneser IV, son of Adadnirari III. Most of his reign (782-772 B.C.) was devoted to defense against the encroaching Urartians.

5. Shalmaneser V, son and successor to Tiglathpileser III (727-722 B.C.). King Hoshea of Israel, whom he forced to pay tribute (2 Kgs. 17:3), revolted with Egypt's aid, provoking the Assyrian to imprison Hoshea and initiate a three-year siege of Samaria (vv. 4-5). Although Shalmaneser succeeded in conquering the city, he died before appropriate punishment could be enacted; his brother and successor, Sargon II, apparently reconquered Samaria and exiled its inhabitants in 720 (v. 6; 18:9-12; cf. *ANET*, p. 285).

SHAMA [shā′mə] (Heb. *šāmāʿ* "[God] hears"). A son of Hotham the Aroerite, and one of David's "mighty men" (1 Chr. 11:44).

SHAMARIAH (2 Chr. 11:19, KJV). See SHEMARIAH **2.**

SHAMED (1 Chr. 8:12, KJV). *See* SHEMED.

SHAMER (KJV). *See* SHEMER, **2, 3.**

SHAMGAR [shăm′gär] (Heb. *šamgar*; perhaps Hur. *Shimig-ari* "Shimike [a deity] gave"). The "son of Anath" (perhaps meaning that he was from Beth-anath in Galilee) who delivered Israel by killing six hundred Philistines with an ox goad (Judg. 3:31). At the time of Shamgar, who predated Deborah and Barak, travelers had to keep to secondary routes and caravans were impossible because of raiders (5:6).

SHAMHUTH [shăm′hŭth] (Heb. *šamhûṯ*). An Izrahite, chief of the fifth division of David's army (1 Chr. 27:8). He is sometimes identified with Shammah/Shammoth of Harod (2 Sam. 23:25; 1 Chr. 11:27).

SHAMIR [shā′mər] (Heb. *šāmîr* "thorn bush") **(PERSON).** A Kohathite Levite (1 Chr. 24:24; cf. 23:12, 20).

SHAMIR [shă'mər] (Heb. *šāmîr* "thorn bush") **(PLACE)**.

1. A town in the tribal territory of Judah, one of the towns surrounding Debir north of Beersheba (Josh. 15:48). A suggested location is el-Bîreh, a short distance southeast of Debir.

2. The home and burial place of Tola, a judge of Israel (Judg. 10:1-2). Shamir was in the hill country of Ephraim. It is thought to have been located on the same site as the later city of Samaria.

SHAMLAI. *See* SHALMAI.

SHAMMA [shăm'ə] (Heb. *šammā'*). A son of Zopha of the tribe of Asher (1 Chr. 7:37).

SHAMMAH [shăm'ə] (Heb. *šammâ*).

1. A descendant of Esau, and a chief in Edom (Gen. 36:13, 17; 1 Chr. 1:37).

2. The third son of Jesse, an elder brother of David, and the father of Jonadab (1 Sam. 16:9; 17:13). He is also known as Shimeah (2 Sam. 13:3, 32), Shimea (1 Chr. 2:13; 20:7), and Shimei (2 Sam. 21:21).

3. One of the leading members of David's "mighty men," the son of Agee the Hararite (2 Sam. 23:11-12, 33; cf. 1 Chr. 11:34).

4. Shammah of Harod, one of David's "mighty men" (2 Sam. 23:25); also known as Shammoth (1 Chr. 11:27).

SHAMMAI [shăm'ī] (Heb. *šammay*).

1. A Judahite, a son of Onam and father of Nadab and Abishur (1 Chr. 2:28).

2. A Judahite, son of Rekem and father of Maon (1 Chr. 2:44-45).

3. A son of Mered of the tribe of Judah and of Bithiah the daughter of Pharaoh (1 Chr. 4:17).

SHAMMOTH. Alternate name of SHAMMAH 4 (1 Chr. 11:27).

SHAMMUA [shă mū'ə] (Heb. *šammûa'*).

1. The son of Zaccur; the Reubenite chosen to spy out Canaan (Num. 13:4).

2. One of the sons born to David at Jerusalem (2 Sam. 5:14; KJV "Shammuah"). At 1 Chr. 3:5 he is called Shimea.

3. The father of Abda, a postexilic Levite (Neh. 11:17). In the account at 1 Chr. 9:16 he appears as Shemaiah.

4. The head of the priestly family of Bilgah at the time of the postexilic high priest Joiakim (Neh. 12:18).

SHAMSHERAI [shăm'shə rī] (Heb. *šamš⁽ᵉ⁾ray*). A son of Jehoram, and head of a Benjaminite family dwelling in Jerusalem (1 Chr. 8:26).

SHAPHAM [shă'fəm] (Heb. *šāpām*). A prominent person of the tribe of Gad living in Bashan (1 Chr. 5:12).

SHAPHAN [shă'fən] (Heb. *šāpān* "rock badger"").

1. The son of Azaliah, and secretary to King Josiah of Judah (2 Kgs. 22:3 par. 2 Chr. 34:8). Asked by Josiah to inquire about the compensation provided work-

men restoring the temple at Jerusalem (2 Kgs. 22:3-7), Shaphan was given a favorable report by the high priest Hilkiah, as well as the Book of the Law that had been found in the temple (vv. 8-9). Shaphan's reading of the book in Josiah's presence caused the king to fear God's wrath. The secretary was among those sent to the prophetess Huldah to seek God's guidance for the situation (vv. 11-20). Shaphan had three sons who were also prominent in the court of Judah: Ahikam (v. 12; Jer. 26:24), Elasah (29:3), and Gemariah (36:10). His grandson Gedaliah was governor of Judah after its fall to Babylon (2 Kgs. 25:22).

2. The father of Jaazaniah, who is the only individual actually named among seventy elders of Israel engaging in idolatrous worship in a vision of Ezekiel (Ezek. 8:11). If this Shaphan is the same person as 1 above, Jaazaniah probably is singled out because of the religious decline of his family.

SHAPHAT [shă'făt] (Heb. *šāpāṭ,* from *šāpaṭ* "judge, rule").

1. One of the twelve Israelite spies sent into Canaan, the son of Hori of the tribe of Simeon (Num. 13:5).

2. The father of the prophet Elisha (1 Kgs. 19:16, 19-20; 2 Kgs. 3:11; 6:31).

3. A son of Shemaiah and descendant of Zerubbabel (1 Chr. 3:22).

4. A Gadite who lived in Bashan (1 Chr. 5:12).

5. The son of Adlai; overseer of David's cattle "in the valleys" (1 Chr. 27:29).

SHAPHER, MOUNT (Num. 33:23-24, KJV). *See* SHEPHER, MOUNT.

SHAPHIR [shă'fər] (Heb. *šāpîr* "beautiful, pleasant").† A town mentioned in a prophetic lament over Judah (Mic. 1:11; KJV "Saphir"). The wordplay characteristic of this lament is brought into the couplet on Shaphir if its first line is emended to "Sound the shophar" (cf., e.g., JB), the shophar horn being here an alarm signal. Suggested locations for Shaphir are es-Suwafir, between Ashdod and Ashkelon (following Eusebius)—which would not, however, lie in Judah, and Khirbet el-Kôm, on the Wâdī es-Saffar, *ca.* 13.3 km. (8.3 mi.) west of Hebron.

SHARAI [shâr'ī] (Heb. *šārāy*). One of the sons of Binnui among those required by Ezra to divorce their foreign wives (Ezra 10:40).

SHARAIM (Josh. 15:36, KJV). *See* SHAARAIM 1.

SHARAR [shâr'är] (Heb. *šārār*). A Hararite and the father of Ahiam, one of David's "mighty men" (2 Sam. 23:33). He is called "Sachar" at 1 Chr. 11:35.

SHAREZER [shə rē'zər] (Heb. *śar'eṣer*; from Akk. *šar-uṣur* "may [the deity] protect the king").

1. A son of Sennacherib of Assyria who, with his brother, killed Sennacherib in 681 B.C. and fled to Ararat (2 Kgs. 19:37 par. Isa. 37:38). Sharezer's full name may have been (following Eusebius) Nergal-sharezer "may Nergal protect the king" or, supplying the consonants from "his sons" (*bnyw*; Isa. 37; Q at

2 Kgs. 19), Nabu-sharezer "may Nabu protect the king."

2. One of the leaders of a delegation sent by the people of Bethel to Jerusalem in 518 B.C. to ask if the customary fast of the fifth month (in commemoration of the destruction of the temple; 2 Kgs. 25:8-9) should still be observed (Zech. 7:2; KJV "Sherezer"). Sharezer's full name may have been Bethel-sharezer "may Bethel (a deity) protect the king" (so NEB). The KJV takes Bethel as the geographical goal of the delegation, i.e., "the house of God" in Jerusalem. If either of these readings is correct, the delegation was sent not from Bethel but, probably, from a Jewish community in Mesopotamia.

SHARON [shârʹən] (Heb. *šārôn* "plain"; Gk. *Sarōn, Sarōna*). A fertile, thickly forested plain along the Mediterranean coast from Jaffa to Mt. Carmel, extending *ca.* 16 km. (10 mi.) inland. The "majesty" of Sharon (Isa. 35:2) was its fertility; a prophetic picture of destruction speaks of fertile Sharon becoming "like a desert" (33:9). 1 Chr. 5:16 seems to demand a location east of the Jordan for "Sharon"; it may be, however, that Gadites living east of the Jordan went as far as Sharon for pasture. David had herds grazing on Sharon under the care of Shitrai, called "the Sharonite" (Heb. *šārônî*; 27:29). Part of the restoration of Israel to the land (Isa. 65) is the use again of Sharon for pasture (v. 10). Acts 9:35 reports hyperbolically that all the people of Sharon (KJV "Saron") saw Aeneas after his healing and were converted.

SHARUHEN [shə rōōʹən] (Heb. *šārûhen*). A city in the tribal territory of Simeon (Josh. 19:6; lacking in LXX), usually identified with Shilhim (15:32; assigned to Judah) and Shaaraim (1 Chr. 4:31). Sharuhen is mentioned in an Egyptian document from before the Israelite occupation (see *ANET*, p. 233), where it is the first stronghold of the Asiatic Hyksos after their expulsion from Egypt in the sixteenth century B.C. It can possibly be identified with the southern Tell el-Fârʹah, situated on the Nahr Besor *ca.* 30 km. (19 mi.) west of Beer-sheba, although some scholars propose Tell el-ʹAjjûl.

SHASHAI [shāʹshī] (Heb. *šāšay*). One of those required by Ezra to divorce his foreign wife (Ezra 10:40).

SHASHAK [shāʹshak] (Heb. *šāšāq*). A Benjaminite who had a large number of sons (1 Chr. 8:14, 22-25).

SHAUL [shôl] (Heb. *šāʾûl*, from *šʾl* "ask" [?]).

1. One of the early Edomite kings, a native of Rehoboth on the Euphrates (Gen. 36:37-38; KJV "Saul"; 1 Chr. 1:48-49).

2. A son of the patriarch Simeon and an unnamed Canaanite woman (Gen. 46:10; Exod. 6:15; 1 Chr. 4:24). His descendants are called the Shaulites (Num. 26:13).

3. A Levite of the Kohathite line; son of Uzziah (1 Chr. 6:24 [MT 9]). He may be the same as JOEL 5 (v. 36 [MT 21]).

SHAVEH-KIRIATHAIM [shāʹvə kĭrʹ ĭ ə thāʹəm] (Heb. *šāwēh qiryāṯayim*).† The place in Moab where

Chedorlaomer and the kings allied with him defeated the Emim (Gen. 14:5). Two or more sites have been proposed for Shaveh-kiriathaim with the thought that it was a city. It is likely, however, that the name designates the plain (Heb. *šāwēh*) around the city of Kiriathaim.

SHAVEH [shāʹvə], **VALLEY OF** (Heb. *ʹēmeq šāwēh*). The valley where Abram met the king of Sodom and Melchizedek after his victory over the kings of the east (Gen. 14:17). *See* KINGʹS VALLEY.

SHAVSHA [shăvʹshə] (Heb. *šawšāʾ*). The secretary at the court of David (1 Chr. 18:16). Elsewhere he is called Seraiah (2 Sam. 8:17), Sheva (20:25), and Shisha (1 Kgs. 4:3).

SHEAL [shēʹəl] (Heb. *šeʾāl* "petition"). One of those required by Ezra to divorce their foreign wives (Ezra 10:29).

SHEALTIEL [shē ălʹtĭ əl] (Heb. *šeʾaltîʾēl* "asked of God [?]," *šaltîʾēl*; Gk. *Salathiēl*).† A son of Jeconiah/ Jehoiachin, the last king of Judah; father of the postexilic governor Zerubbabel (1 Chr. 3:17; KJV "Salathiel"; Ezra 3:2; 5:2; Neh. 12:1; Hag. 1:1; 2:2; Matt. 1:12; KJV "Salathiel"). 1 Chr. 3:19 makes Zerubbabel the son of Pedaiah, another son of Jeconiah; it is possible that Shealtiel died childless, whereupon Pedaiah took Shealtiel's widow in levirate marriage and was thus the biological father of Zerubbabel. KJV "Assir" at v. 17 should be read as "the captive" (so RSV), referring to Jeconiah.

The identification of Shealtiel's father as Neri at Luke 3:27 (KJV "Salathiel") does not indicate a levirate marriage (Jer. 22:28-30 does not say that Jeconiah/Coniah was childless, only that the dynastic rule of Judah did not continue after him), but rather reflects Luke's historiographic purposes in presenting Jesus' ancestry.

The identification of Shealthiel (RSV "Salathiel") with Ezra at 2 Esdr. 3:1 is a chronological impossibility; Ezra wrote some one hundred years after Nebuchadrezzar's destruction of Jerusalem. Rather, Ezra's name apparently has been added to a writing ascribed to Salathiel, perhaps to facilitate its combination with materials from an Ezra tradition.

SHEARIAH [shē ʹə rīʹə] (Heb. *šeʾaryâ*). A son of Azel, and descendant of King Saul (1 Chr. 8:38; 9:44).

SHEAR-JASHUB [shē ʹər jāʹshəb] (Heb. *šeʾār yāšûb* "a remnant will return"). A son of the prophet Isaiah (Isa. 7:3), so named to symbolize the promise that only a remnant of the combined Syrian and Israelite armies would return to their homes from their siege of Jerusalem (vv. 4-9; cf. 8:18). Later, the name became a promise applied to Israel in the face of eschatological destruction (10:21-23; cf. 11:11, 16).

SHEBA [shēʹbə] (Heb. *šeḇāʾ, šeḇaʾ*) (**PERSON**).

1. (Heb. *šeḇāʾ*). A descendant of Ham and Cush (Gen. 10:7; 1 Chr. 1:9), probably to be associated with SHEBA (PLACE) 2 and the Sabean traders of southern Arabia (*see* SABEANS 1).

2. A descendant of Shem (Gen. 10:28; 1 Chr. 1:22), possibly to be associated with SHEBA (PLACE) 2 and the SABEANS (2).

3. A grandson of Abraham and Keturah, probably the ancestor of a northern Arabian tribe (Gen. 25:3; 1 Chr. 1:32).

4. (Heb. *šeḇaʿ*). A member of the tribe of Benjamin and the clan of the Bichrites (RSV "the son of Bichri") who lived in the hill country of Ephraim and led an Israelite rebellion against David (2 Sam. 20). The differences between Judah and the other tribes of Israel, which were to issue in permanent political division after the death of Solomon, had existed before David's reign. They led to a serious crisis after the death of Absalom because of separate moves to renew allegiance to David (19:9-15, 41-43). The separation was then taken to the point of rebellion on the part of the northern tribes through the urging of Sheba (20:1-2; cf. 1 Kgs. 12:16). In the face of pursuit by David's men, which was thwarted by their internal rivalries, Sheba was apparently able to retain the loyalty only of those from his own clan, the Bichrites (2 Sam. 20:4-14; KJV, NIV "Berites"). During a siege of Abel of Beth-maacah, where Sheba and his men had taken refuge, the residents cut off Sheba's head and threw it over the wall (vv. 15-22).

5. A Gadite living in Bashan (1 Chr. 5:13).

SHEBA [shē′bə] (PLACE).

1. (Heb. *šeḇaʿ*). A city in the tribal territory of Simeon (Josh. 19:2), probably to be deleted as a dittograph after "Beer-sheba" or identified with Shema in Judah's territory (15:26).

2. (Heb. *šeḇāʾ*). Home of the Sabean traders of southern Arabia and the nearby coast of Ethiopia (*see* SABEANS 1). From these caravanners Israelites and other peoples living north of Arabia obtained gold, frankincense, sweet cane and other spices, gems, and other goods from Africa, India, and the East (Ps. 72:15; Isa. 60:6; Jer. 6:20; Ezek. 27:22; 38:13). "The queen of Sheba" who came to visit King Solomon (1 Kgs. 10 par. 2 Chr. 9) may have ruled some of the Sabeans of southern Arabia or one of their colonies in northwestern Arabia. It is clear that the purpose of her visit was to establish trade relations with the wealthy king; she brought a variety of wares to show (1 Kgs. 10:2), and he responded by showing evidence of his wealth (vv. 4, 7).

SHEBAH (Gen. 26:33, KJV). See SHIBAH.

SHEBAM (Num. 32:3, KJV). See SEBAM, SIBMAH.

SHEBANIAH [shĕb′ə nī′ə] (Heb. *šeḇanyâ, šeḇanyāhû*).

1. (Heb. *šeḇanyāhû*). A priest during the reign of David who was among those who blew trumpets before the ark as it entered Jerusalem (1 Chr. 15:24).

2. (Heb. *šeḇanyâ*). One of the Levites who gave the call to praise during the assembly of fasting and repentance under Ezra (Neh. 9:4-5).

3. A priest who (or whose descendants) participated in the sealing of the covenant under Nehemiah (Neh. 10:4 [MT 5]). He is probably the founder of the priestly family named at 12:14 (cf. Shecaniah 8 at v. 3).

4. A Levite who participated in the sealing of the

covenant under Nehemiah (Neh. 10:10 [MT 11]). He may be the same person as 2 above.

5. Another Levite who sealed Nehemiah's covenant (Neh. 10:12 [MT 13]), perhaps the same as 2.

SHEBARIM [shĕb′ə rĭm] (Heb. *haššeḇārîm* "the quarries"). A place to which the men of Ai chased the Israelites after the Israelites' unsuccessful attempt to capture Ai (Josh. 7:5). "Shebarim" might be intended not as a place name but as a reference to actual quarries (so NEB, NIV).

SHEBAT [shē′băt] (Heb. *šeḇāṭ*; cf. Akk. *šabaṭu*; Gk. *Sabat*). The eleventh month of the Jewish calendar (Jan./Feb.; Zech. 1:7; KJV "Sebat"; 1 Macc. 16:14; KJV "Sabat"). See YEAR.

SHEBER [shē′bər] (Heb. *šeḇer*). A son of Caleb and his concubine Maacah (1 Chr. 2:48).

SHEBNA [shĕb′nə] (Heb. *šeḇnāʾ*), SHEBNAH (*šeḇnâ*).† The palace administrator and, probably at a later time, secretary for King Hezekiah of Judah. As palace administrator, Shebna was cursed by Isaiah the prophet for constructing an ostentatious tomb for himself (Isa. 22:15-25). The prophet threatened Shebna with deportation (vv. 17-18) and loss of his office, which was to be given to Eliakim the son of Hilkiah (vv. 19-24).

It was apparently later, after Eliakim had indeed become palace administrator, that Shebna as secretary, Eliakim, and Joah the recorder heard the Assyrian demand for surrender and pleaded unsuccessfully for it to be given in a language other than Hebrew (1 Kgs. 18:18-37 par. Isa. 36:3-22). The three officials were then sent by Hezekiah to Isaiah the prophet to seek a word from God (2 Kgs. 19:2-7 par. Isa. 37:2-7).

SHEBUEL [shə bū′əl] (Heb. *šeḇûʾēl*), SHUBAEL [shoo′bĭ əl] (Heb. *šûḇaʾēl*).

1. A Levite of the "sons of Gershom," Moses' son; chief treasury officer in David's organization of the Levites for temple service (1 Chr. 23:16; 24:20; 26:24).

2. A son of Heman and leader (or ancestor) of the thirteenth division of temple musicians (1 Chr. 25:4, 20).

SHECANIAH [shĕk′ə nī′ə] (Heb. *šeḵanyâ, šeḵanyāhû* "Yahweh dwells").

1. A descendant of David and Zerubbabel (1 Chr. 3:21-22); head of a father's house that returned from exile (Ezra 8:3).

2. The chief of the tenth division of priests during the time of the Davidic organization (1 Chr. 24:11).

3. A Levite during the reign of Hezekiah who served as a distributor of the temple offerings (2 Chr. 31:15).

4. A son of Jahaziel and descendant of Zattu who returned from exile with three hundred men under the leadership of Ezra (Ezra 8:5).

5. The son of Jehiel of the "sons of Elam." Shecaniah led the Israelites in divorcing their foreign wives (Ezra 10:2-3).

6. The father of Shemaiah, a gatekeeper who participated in the postexilic rebuilding of the walls of Jerusalem (Neh. 3:29).

7. The son of Arah and father-in-law of Tobiah the Ammonite, who had tried to prevent Nehemiah from repairing the walls of Jerusalem (Neh. 6:18). Tobiah's effectiveness among the aristocracy of Judah arose partly from having Shecaniah as his father-in-law.

8. A priest who returned from exile with Zerubbabel (Neh. 12:3). Elsewhere he is called Shebaniah **(3)** (10:4; 12:14).

SHECHEM [shĕk'əm] (Heb. *š*ᵉ*ḵem* "shoulder, neck") **(PERSON).**

1. A son of Hamor, the Hivite chief of the city and environs of Shechem. Shechem became acquainted with Jacob's family when Jacob bought a piece of land from Hamor's descendants (Gen. 33:19). When Dinah, Jacob's daughter, visited among the women of the land, Shechem seized her and raped her (34:2); he then asked his father to secure her for his wife (v. 4). Jacob's sons agreed to Hamor's proposal of a marriage alliance (but not sincerely) on the condition that all the males of the city be circumcised as a partial concession to Israelite ways (vv. 13-17). The men of the city, including Shechem, submitted to the request with hopes for enrichment through intermarriage with the family of the wealthy Jacob (vv. 18-24). While the Shechemites were incapacitated by the operation, two of Jacob's sons, Simeon and Levi, killed all the Shechemite men, plundered the city, and took their sister with them (vv. 25-29).

Jacob's reproof of his sons (v. 30) determines much of the tone of the story in its broader context (but cf. Deut. 7) and is related to the dispersion of the tribes of Simeon and Levi (cf. Gen. 49:5-7).

2. A descendant of Manasseh and progenitor of the Shechemite (Heb. *šiḵmî*) branch of the Manassites (Num. 26:31; Josh. 17:2).

3. A son of Shemida of the tribe of Manasseh (1 Chr. 7:19). This is possibly the same person as **2** above.

SHECHEM [shĕk'əm] (Heb. *š*ᵉ*ḵem* "shoulder, neck") **(PLACE).** A Canaanite and Israelite city in the hill country of Ephraim between Mt. Ebal and Mt. Gerizim; site of the covenant ceremony establishing the Israelite confederation (Josh. 24). The city is mentioned in Twelfth Dynasty Egyptian Execration Texts as the city of the ruler Absh-adad. In the Amarna Letters it is the city of King Labayu, who made it the center of a number of cities he controlled.

Abraham built an altar to the Lord at the oak of Moreh at Shechem after his arrival in Canaan (Gen. 12:6-7; KJV "Sichem"). Jacob pitched his tents here and bought a parcel of ground from the people of Shechem when he returned from Paddan-aram (33:18-19); like Abraham, he also built an altar at Shechem (v. 20). Here also Jacob's daughter Dinah was raped by Shechem **(1)** the son of Hamor, an act avenged by her brothers, Simeon and Levi (ch. 34). Jacob buried the household idols of his wives under an oak near Shechem (35:4), and in the same plot of ground Jacob had purchased from Hamor Joseph's bones were buried (Josh. 24:32; cf. Acts 7:16; KJV "Sychem"). Joshua erected a large stone "under the oak in the sanctuary of the Lord" as part of the covenant-making ceremony at Shechem (Josh. 24:26).

Situated near the border between the tribal territories of Manasseh and Ephraim (Josh. 17:7), Shechem became a city of the Levites and a city of refuge (20:7; 21:21). A temple of Baal-berith (El-berith) stood at Shechem (Judg. 9:4, 46). After Gideon's death the citizens of Shechem made his son Abimelech king, giving him seventy silver pieces from the treasury of this temple (v. 4). When they revolted against his rule, Abimelech destroyed the city (v. 45). The inhabitants of the Tower of Shechem (Heb. *migdal šeḵem*), perhaps a fortified high point outside the city proper (probably the same as BETH-MILLO; vv. 6, 20), fled to the temple, which Abimelech set on fire (vv. 46-49).

After Solomon's death Rehoboam sought to win the northern tribes back to unity with Judah by the conciliatory gesture of coronation in the north at Shechem (1 Kgs. 12 par. 2 Chr. 10). But the northern tribes seceded, making Jeroboam I their king and Shechem their first capital (1 Kgs. 12:20, 25). The city continued as a provincial center even after the northern capital was moved to Tirzah. Shechem was destroyed by Assyria in 722 B.C. Pilgrims from Shechem were among those slain at Mizpah by those who had murdered the Babylonian governor Gedaliah (Jer. 41:5). The city is not mentioned in connection with the postexilic community of Ezra and Nehemiah, but Josephus refers to it as the major city of the Samaritans of the time of Alexander (*Ant.* xi.8.6 [340]) and records that it was destroyed by John Hyrcanus (xiii.9.1 [255]).

The site of Shechem is Tell Balâṭah, 1 km. (1.5 mi.) east of modern Nablus. Occupation of the site began during the Chalcolithic Age with the appearance of several small villages as early as 3600 B.C. During the Middle Bronze II period (1900-1540), particularly the Hyksos era in Egypt, Shechem was an important city-state. The site was violently destroyed in the sixteenth century, but by the fourteenth century Shechem had reemerged as a significant city-state, as attested in the Amarna Letters; this period of occupation ended *ca.* 1125 when the city was destroyed, probably by Abimelech (Judg. 9). The city was rebuilt only after a century or more, and continued until the Assyrian destruction in 722. Shechem was rebuilt by the Samaritans in the Hellenistic period, associated with the Samaritan temple on Mt. Gerizim. After Hyrcanus razed it in 107 B.C. the site was abandoned.

Several temples have been uncovered in the process of excavation. The earliest were courtyard sanctuaries (perhaps built around a tree shrine like those mentioned in Genesis), replaced by a massive fortress temple that during some periods included pillars (perhaps like the standing stone set up by Joshua). It is clear that a sanctuary tradition at Shechem, also reflected in the Old Testament, carried through the site's shifts of political allegiance.

Bibliography. G. E. Wright, *Shechem: The Biography of a Biblical City* (Garden City: 1964).

SHEDEUR [shĕd'ĭ ər] (Heb. *š*ᵉ*dê'ûr* "the Almighty is light"). The father of Elizur, who was the representative to Moses and leader of the tribe of Reuben during Israel's travels through the wilderness (Num. 1:5; 2:10).

SHEEP (Heb. *ṣō'n*; Gk. *próbaton*).† Grazing, cud-chewing animals similar to goats (Genus *Ovis*; family

Bovidae, which includes goats and cattle). Many terms are used in the Bible to specify types of sheep on the basis of age, sex, and breed. The Bible refers to sheep more than five hundred times; in the Old Testament most references are literal, while most in the New Testament are metaphorical.

Wild sheep, in general, can be distinguished from goats only by experts. They have long, straight hair with a wooly undercoat, and are high spirited, daring, and self-reliant, climbing higher than any other animal except the mountain goat. Until recently wild sheep (*Ovis ornata orientalis*) could be found in the mountains south of the Dead Sea; it may be a ram of this species that Abraham found on Mt. Moriah (Gen. 22:13).

The earliest evidence for domestication of sheep comes from Zawi Chemi Shanidar in Iraq, *ca.* 9000 B.C. In this early period sheep were valued for their hides and milk. Sheep were first bred for wool *ca.* 4000. The primary domestic breed of both ancient and modern Palestine is the broad-tailed sheep (*Ovis lauticaudata*); their fat tails can weigh as much as 6.8 kg. (15 lbs.) and are regarded as a delicacy (cf. Exod. 29:22-25).

Unlike goats, domestic sheep prefer flat or rolling grazing grounds. Their teeth allow them to eat down to the roots of plants, and they can live off the stubble left over from barley and wheat harvests, or after other cattle have grazed. The sheep provides most of the necessities of life: milk, meat, hides, and wool. Thus for the pastoral people of the ancient Near East it was a chief source of wealth (cf. Gen. 13). Wool was precious and a good product for trade (Ezek. 27:18, 21). King Mesha of Moab was required to pay to Israel tribute of the wool of a hundred thousand rams (2 Kgs. 3:4). The whiteness of wool was a symbol of purity (Isa. 1:18; Rev. 1:14); it could be woven into a number of useful, warm items (Lev. 13:47-48; Job 31:20). Sheep were favored as sacrificial animals (Lev. 1:10; 4:32; 5:15; 22:21). This preference, in part, underlies the identification of the crucified Jesus as the Lamb of God in Johannine literature (e.g., John 1:29; Rev. 5:6). *See* GOAT; LAMB.

Domestic sheep are gentle and docile, thus largely defenseless and in need of constant supervision. Nathan's parable at 2 Sam. 12 illustrates the bond between sheep and shepherd. The helplessness and utter dependence of the sheep on the shepherd underlie the depiction of the people of God as a flock under the charge of God (e.g., Ps. 78:52; 95:7; Isa. 40:11; Mic. 2:12) or Jesus (Matt. 15:24; John 10; Heb. 13:20; cf. John 21:15-17) or human leaders (e.g., Jer. 23:1ff.; 50:6; Ezek. 34). At night the vulnerable sheep are kept in a sheepfold against the dangers of weather, predators, and robbers (cf. John 10:1-6). *See* SHEPHERD.

SHEEP GATE (Heb. *šaʿar haṣṣōʾn;* Gk. *hē probatikē*). A gate near the northeastern corner of Jerusalem (Neh. 3:1, 32; 12:39) near the pool of Bethesda (John 5:2).

SHEERAH [shēʹə rə] (Heb. *šeʾerâ* "female relative"). The daughter of Ephraim who built Upper and Lower Beth-horon and Uzzen-sheerah (1 Chr. 7:24; KJV "Sherah").

SHEHARIAH [shēʹə rīʹə] (Heb. *šeḥaryâ*). A son of Jehoram; head of a family of the tribe of Benjamin living in Jerusalem (1 Chr. 8:26).

SHEKEL [shĕkʹəl] (Heb. *šeqel*). A unit of both weight and money. Until the beginning of the minting of money in the seventh century B.C., metals used as mediums of exchange were weighed. The numerous Old Testament references to shekels are to a unit of weight generally equivalent to about 11.4 g. (.4 oz.), with the possible exception of Neh. 5:15; 10:32, which may refer to a Median coin of about half that weight. In New Testament times a silver shekel or tetradrachma (Gk. *statér;* Matt. 27:17; KJV "piece of money") was equivalent in value to four drachmas and weighed *ca.* 10-15 g. (.35-.5 oz.).

SHEKINAH [shə kīʹnə] (Heb. *šekînâ* "dwelling," from *šākan* "sit, dwell"). A rabbinic euphemism for God as present among mankind. *See* PRESENCE.

SHELAH [shēʹlə].
1. (Heb. *šelaḥ;* Gk. *Sala*). A son of Arpachshad (Arphaxad), descendant of Shem, and father of Eber (Gen. 10:24; 11:12-15; KJV "Salah"; 1 Chr. 1:18, 24). Luke 3:35-36 (KJV "Sala") follows the LXX in listing Shelah as the son of Cainan and grandson of Arpachshad.
2. (Heb. *šēlâ*). The third son of the patriarch Judah and the daughter of Shua, a Canaanite (Gen. 38:5, 11, 14, 26; 46:12; 1 Chr. 2:3; 4:21). He was the eponymous ancestor of the Shelanites (Heb. *šēlānî;* Num. 26:20; *see* SHILONITE).

SHELAH [shēʹlə], **POOL OF** (Heb. *berēkaṯ haššelaḥ*). A reservoir in the KING'S GARDEN (Neh. 3:15), perhaps the same as the KING'S POOL (2:14) or the "lower pool" (Isa. 22:9). *See* SILOAM, POOL OF.

SHELANITES. *See* SHELAH 2.

SHELEMIAH [shĕlʹə mīʹə] (Heb. *šelemyâ, šelemyāhû* "Yahweh has recompensed").
1. A levitical temple gatekeeper of the Korahite line (1 Chr. 26:14). He is called Meshelemiah at v. 1.
2. One of the postexilic sons of Binnui who divorced their foreign wives (Ezra 10:39).
3. Another of the sons of Binnui required to divorce his foreign wife (Ezra 10:41).
4. The father or ancestor of Hananiah, a man of the time of Nehemiah (Neh. 3:30).
5. A priest appointed by Nehemiah as one of the keepers of the temple storerooms (Neh. 13:13).
6. An ancestor of Jehudi, a contemporary of the prophet Jeremiah (Jer. 36:14).
7. One of the men sent by King Jehoiakim to arrest Jeremiah and Baruch (Jer. 36:26).
8. The father of Jehucal (Jer. 37:3) or Jucal (38:1), a contemporary of Jeremiah.
9. The father of Irijah, a sentry at the time of Jeremiah (Jer. 37:13).

SHELEPH [shēʹlĭf] (Heb. *šelep*). A son of Joktan and descendant of Shem (Gen. 10:26; 1 Chr. 1:20). He was ancestor of an Arabian people.

SHELESH [shē′lĭsh] (Heb. *šeleš*; cf. *šālōš* "three"). A son of Helem; head of a father's house in the tribe of Asher (1 Chr. 7:35).

SHELOMI [shə lō′mī] (Heb. *šelōmî*, from *šālôm* "peace"). The father of Ahihud, who was the representative of the tribe of Asher in the group chosen to superintend the division of the land of Canaan (Num. 34:27).

SHELOMITH [shə lō′mĭth] (Heb. *šelōmîṯ* "peaceful").

1. The daughter of Dibri of the tribe of Dan, and mother of a man who was stoned to death on account of his blasphemy (Lev. 24:10-23).

2. A daughter of Zerubbabel (1 Chr. 3:19).

3 (1 Chr. 23:9, KJV). *See* SHELOMOTH **1**.

4. A Levite of the Kohathite line, the son of Izhar (1 Chr. 23:18). At 24:22 he is called SHELOMOTH (**2**).

5 (1 Chr. 26:25-28, KJV). *See* SHELOMOTH **3**.

6. A child of King Rehoboam and his favored wife Maacah (2 Chr. 11:20).

7. The son of Josiphiah and descendant of Bani who, with one hundred sixty men, returned from exile with Ezra (Ezra 8:10).

SHELOMOTH [shə lō′mŏth] (Heb. *šelōmôṯ*).

1. A Levite, the son of Shimei and a descendant of Gershom (1 Chr. 23:9; KJV "Shelomith").

2. A Levite of the Kohathite line, the son of Izhar (1 Chr. 24:22). He is called *Shelomith* (**4**) at 23:18.

3. A Levite and descendant of Moses' son Eliezer. He and his brothers guarded the treasuries of the dedicated gifts acquired as spoil during the reign of David (1 Chr. 26:25-28; KJV "Shelomith").

SHELUMIEL [shə lōō′mĭ əl] (Heb. *šelumî'ēl* "God is peace"). The son of Zurishaddai, and a representative to Moses and leader of the tribe of Simeon during Israel's travels through the wilderness (Num. 1:6; 2:12; 10:19). He made a number of offerings for the tabernacle worship (7:36-41). Judith's ancestry is traced through Shelumiel (Jdt. 8:1; Gk. *Salamiēl*; RSV "Salamiel"; KJV "Samael").

SHEM [shĕm] (Heb. *šēm* "name, fame"; cf. Akk. *šumu* "name, son"; Gk. *Sēm*). The eldest son of Noah (Gen. 5:32; 6:10; 1 Chr. 1:4), who, with the rest of Noah's family, accompanied Noah into the ark and thus survived the flood (Gen. 7:13; 9:18).

Shem is considered the ancestor of Israel and most of the surrounding peoples speaking Semitic languages (10:21-31; 11:10-26; Luke 3:36; KJV "Sem"; *see* TABLE OF NATIONS; cf. the non-Semitic "Elam" at Gen. 10:22). With Japheth he covered the intoxicated Noah (9:23); in his subsequent blessing of Shem, Noah associated Yahweh, the distinctive Israelite name of God, with Shem, perhaps even referring to Yahweh as "the God of Shem"—in this instance equated with Israel (v. 26; so KJV, RSV mg.).

According to 11:10 two years after the flood, at age one hundred. Shem became the father of Arpachshad. During the remaining five hundred years of his life he fathered several other children (v. 11; 10:22; 1 Chr. 1:17; cf. Gen. 10:23).

SHEMA [shē′mə] (Heb. *šema'* "[God] hears") (**PERSON**).

1. A son of Hebron of the tribe of Judah (1 Chr. 2:43-44).

2. A Reubenite, the son of Joel and father of Azaz (1 Chr. 5:8). He is possibly the same as Shemaiah (**4**) or Shimei (**8**) (v. 4).

3. A Benjaminite, head of a household at Aijalon (1 Chr. 8:13). He is probably the same as Shimei (**11**) at v. 21.

4. One of those who stood on the platform with Ezra as he read from the Book of the Law (Neh. 8:4).

SHEMA [shē′mə] (Heb. *šema'* "[God] hears") (**PLACE**). A city in the southern district of the tribal territory of Judah, associated with Beer-sheba (Josh. 15:26). Sheba (**1**) at 19:2 could be the same city.

SHEMA [shə mä′], THE. A confession of faith, originally Deut. 6:4 but from the second century A.D. including also vv. 5-9; 11:13-21; Num. 15:37-41, recited morning and evening by Jews to the present. The name of the Shema comes from the first word of Deut. 6:4, Heb. *šema'* "hear." The recitation of the Shema came to be thought of as the minimum of study of the Torah. Evidence indicates that Jesus and the early Church considered the confession of God's unity and the commandment to love God that together constitute the first two verses of the Shema (and perhaps the entire content of an early form of the confession) as a fundamental summation of the Torah (Mark 12:28-34 par.; Rom. 3:30; 1 Cor. 8:4; Jas. 2:19; 1 John 4:20).

SHEMAAH [shə mä′ə] (Heb. *šemā'â*). The father of Ahiezer and Joash, two Benjaminites who joined David at Ziklag (1 Chr. 12:3).

SHEMAIAH [shə mā′yə] (Heb. *šema'yâ*, *šema'yāhû* "Yahweh has heard").

1. (Heb. *šema'yâ*). A prophet who prevented King Rehoboam of Judah from waging war with the ten northern tribes when they rebelled under Jeroboam I (1 Kgs. 12:22-24; 2 Chr. 11:2-4, *šema'yāhû*). He prophesied again with words of both judgment and deliverance when Jerusalem was attacked by Pharaoh Shishak of Egypt (2 Chr. 12:5-8). To him and Iddo the seer are ascribed a book of chronicles that included the reign of Rehoboam (v. 15).

2. The son of Shecaniah, and a descendant of David (1 Chr. 3:22).

3. A prince from the tribe of Simeon (1 Chr. 4:37).

4. A son of Joel of the tribe of Reuben (1 Chr. 5:4). He may be the same as Shema (**2**) at v. 8.

5. A Levite of the family of Merari who returned from exile and was one of the supervisors of the outside work of the temple in Nehemiah's time (1 Chr. 9:14; Neh. 11:15).

6. The father of Obadiah, a Levite who returned from exile (1 Chr. 9:16). This Shemaiah is also known as Shammua (**3**) (Neh. 11:17) and is possibly the same as **11** below.

7. A Levite of the time of David who was head of the family of Elizaphan, two hundred members of which were among the Levites who transported the ark into Jerusalem (1 Chr. 15:8, 11-15).

8. A Levite and scribe who recorded the designation by lot of the priests during David's reorganization of the temple worship (1 Chr. 24:6).

9. A Levite; the firstborn son of Obed-edom. He and his sons were temple gatekeepers during David's reign (1 Chr. 26:4, 6-7).

10. (Heb. $\check{s}^e ma^\epsilon y\bar{a}h\hat{u}$). One of a group of Levites whom King Jehoshaphat sent with five princes and two priests to instruct the people of Judah in the law (2 Chr. 17:8).

11. (Heb. $\check{s}^e ma^\epsilon y\hat{a}$). A Levite of the family of Jeduthun who was one of the Levites who cleansed the temple during the reign of King Hezekiah (2 Chr. 29:14). He is possibly the same as **6** above.

12. A Levite at the time of King Hezekiah among those who distributed the offerings to the priests and Levites (2 Chr. 31:15).

13. A Levite at the time of Josiah who contributed to a Passover offering (2 Chr. 35:9).

14. A household head of the family of Adonikam who returned from Babylonia with Ezra (Ezra 8:13).

15. One of those sent by Ezra to Iddo at Casiphia to request that the "leading man" send Levites to join the group going from Babylonia to Jerusalem (Ezra 8:16).

16. A priest of the sons of Harim who divorced his foreign wife after Ezra's ban of mixed marriages (Ezra 10:21).

17. A postexilic Israelite of the sons of Harim (presumably distinct from the line of **16** above) required to divorce his foreign wife (Ezra 10:31).

18. The keeper of the East Gate who repaired part of the wall of Jerusalem when Nehemiah was governor (Neh. 3:29).

19. A prophet hired by Tobiah and Sanballat to intimidate and discredit Nehemiah (Neh. 6:10-13).

20. A priest who set his seal to the covenant made under Nehemiah (Neh. 10:8 [MT 9]).

21. A priest or priestly family who went with Zerubbabel from exile in Babylonia (Neh. 12:6, 18).

22. A prince of Judah who participated in the dedication of the rebuilt walls of Jerusalem (Neh. 12:34).

23. An ancestor of Zechariah (**28**), a levitical musician who played the trumpet in the procession dedicating the rebuilt walls (Neh. 12:35).

24. One of the "priest's sons" who took part in the ceremony rededicating the walls of Jerusalem, a kinsman of Zechariah **28** (Neh. 12:36).

25. A priest in the same company as Nehemiah at the dedication of the rebuilt walls of Jerusalem (Neh. 12:42).

26. (Heb. $\check{s}^e ma^\epsilon y\bar{a}h\hat{u}$). The father of the prophet Uriah of Kiriath-jearim, who was executed under King Jehoiakim (Jer. 26:20).

27. A prophet from Nehelam who wrote a letter from Babylon to the people and priests in Jerusalem to incite them against Jeremiah. Jeremiah in turn announced that God would deny Shemaiah and his descendants the opportunity to see the good things God would do for Judah (Jer. 29:24-32).

28. The father of Delaiah, a high official in the court of King Jehoiakim (Jer. 36:12).

SHEMARIAH [shĕm'ə rī'ə] (Heb. $\check{s}^e mar y\hat{a}$, $\check{s}^e mar$-$y\bar{a}h\hat{u}$ "Yahweh has protected").

1. (Heb. $\check{s}^e mar y\bar{a}h\hat{u}$). A Benjaminite who joined David's rebel force at Ziklag (1 Chr. 12:5 [MT 6]).

2. (Heb. $\check{s}^e mar y\hat{a}$). A son of King Rehoboam of Judah and his wife Mahalath (2 Chr. 11:19; KJV "Shamariah").

3. An Israelite among the sons of Harim required by Ezra to divorce his foreign wife (Ezra 10:32).

4. One of the sons of Binnui who divorced his non-Israelite wife (Ezra 10:41).

SHEMEBER [shĕm ē'bər] (Heb. $\check{s}em$'$\bar{e}ber$). The king of Zeboiim, one of the five kings who rebelled against Chedorlaomer and fought unsuccessfully against his alliance in the valley of Siddim (Gen. 14:2).

SHEMED [shē'mĕd] (Heb. $\check{s}emed$ "destruction"). A Benjaminite, son of Elpaal who, together with his brothers, rebuilt the cities of Ono and Lod after the exile (1 Chr. 8:12; KJV "Shamed"; some manuscripts have Heb. $\check{s}emer$).

SHEMER [shē'mər] (Heb. $\check{s}emer$ "guard").

1. Owner of the hill that Omri purchased for the site of Samaria (1 Kgs. 16:24).

2. A Merarite Levite, son of Mahli (1 Chr. 6:46 [MT 31]; KJV "Shamer").

3. A man of the tribe of Asher (1 Chr. 7:34; KJV "Shamer"). He is called Shomer at v. 32.

SHEMIDA [shə mī'də] (Heb. $\check{s}^e m\hat{i}d\bar{a}^\epsilon$). A son of Gilead of the tribe of Manasseh (Num. 26:32; Josh. 17:2; 1 Chr. 7:19; KJV "Shemidah"), head of the family of Shemidaites (Heb. $\check{s}^e m\hat{i}d\bar{a}^\epsilon\hat{i}$; Num. 26:32).

SHEMINITH [shĕm'ə nĭth] (Heb. $^\epsilon al\,ha\check{s}\check{s}^e m\hat{i}n\hat{i}\underline{t}$ "on the eighth"). A term occurring in the superscriptions of Pss. 6, 12 and at 1 Chr. 15:21. Among suggestions as to its meaning are "octave"—perhaps indicating voices an octave lower, "on an eight-stringed instrument," and "for the eighth stage of the liturgy."

SHEMIRAMOTH [shə mĭr'ə mŏth] (Heb. $\check{s}^e m\hat{i}r\bar{a}m\hat{o}\underline{t}$ "name of the highest").

1. A levitical musician during the days of David (1 Chr. 15:18, 20; 16:5).

2. One of the Levites sent by King Jehoshaphat to instruct the people of Judah in the law (2 Chr. 17:8).

SHEMUEL [shĕm'yŏŏ əl] (Heb. $\check{s}^e m\hat{u}$'$\bar{e}l$).

1. The son of Ammihud, and representative of Simeon who assisted Moses in the division of Canaan (Num. 34:20).

2 (1 Chr. 6:33, KJV). See SAMUEL.

3. A son of Tola; head of a household in the tribe of Issachar (1 Chr. 7:2).

SHEN [shĕn] (Heb. $ha\check{s}\check{s}\bar{e}n$ "the tooth, sharp point"). A place near Mizpah in the territory of Benjamin where Samuel erected a stone to commemorate Israel's victory over the Philistines (KJV, NIV, 1 Sam. 7:12). Shen is generally regarded as identical to JESHANAH (so RSV, JB; cf. LXX $t\hat{e}s\,pala\hat{i}as$ "the old [city]").

SHENAZZAR [shə năz'ər] (Heb. $\check{s}en$'$a\underline{s}\underline{s}ar$; cf. Akk. Sin-ab-$u\underline{s}ur$ "may [the moon-god] Sin protect the father"). A son of Jehoiachin (Jeconiah), the captive king of Judah (1 Chr. 3:18). Shenazzar may be the same as SHESHBAZZAR (Ezra 1:8, 11; 5:14, 16).

SHENIR (KJV). *See* SENIR.

SHEOL [shē'ōl] (Heb. *šeʾôl, šeʾōl*). The abode of the dead (e.g., Ps. 49:14 [MT 15]; Prov. 9:18; KJV usually "grave," "hell"), both the wicked (Ps. 31:17 [MT 18]) and righteous (e.g., Ezek. 32:21, 27). The LXX renders the term Gk. *hádēs*. Often synonymous with death itself (e.g., Gen. 42:38; 1 Kgs. 2:6, 9), Sheol is depicted as located in the depths of the earth (e.g., Gen. 37:35; Prov. 15:24; Ezek. 31:15-18), indeed, the deepest place of all (Deut. 32:22; Job 11:8). It is a place of gloom (Job 10:21-22; cf. Eccl. 9:10) and decay (Isa. 14:11), from which there is no escape (Job 7:9; cf. Isa. 5:14); only God can rescue his people from the clutches of Sheol (Ps. 49:15 [MT 16]).

See HELL *I.*

SHEPHAM [shē'fəm] (Heb. *šepām*). A place named in a description of the ideal eastern boundary of Israel's occupation of Canaan (Num. 34:10-11). Possible locations of Shepham are near Mt. Hermon and the sources of the Jordan river or near Riblah, which was on the Orontes river north of the Anti-lebanon range. Ezekiel's restatement of Israel's boundaries (Ezek. 47:18) omits mention of Shepham.

SHEPHATIAH [shĕf'ə tī'ə] (Heb. *šepaṭyâ, šepaṭyāhû* "Yahweh has judged").
   1. (Heb. *šepaṭyâ*). A son of David and his wife Abital born in Hebron (2 Sam. 3:4; 1 Chr. 3:3).
   2. An ancestor of a group of Benjaminites who dwelled in Jerusalem after the Exile (1 Chr. 9:8).
   3. (Heb. *šepaṭyāhû*). A Haruphite of the tribe of Benjamin who joined David's rebel force in Ziklag (1 Chr. 12:5 [MT 6]).
   4. The son of Maacah; chief of the tribe of Simeon during the reign of David (1 Chr. 27:16).
   5. A son of King Jehoshaphat of Judah (2 Chr. 21:2). He and other of Jehoshaphat's sons were killed by their brother Jehoram after Jehoram's accession to the throne (v. 4).
   6. (Heb. *šepaṭyâ*). The ancestor of two groups of people who returned to Judah after the Exile (Ezra 2:4 par. Neh. 7:9; Ezra 8:8).
   7. One of Solomon's servants whose descendants returned with Zerubbabel from exile in Babylon (Ezra 2:57; Neh. 7:59).
   8. A Judahite whose descendants dwelled in Jerusalem after the Exile (Neh. 11:4).
   9. One of four princes of Judah who demanded that King Zedekiah put Jeremiah to death because of his prophecies (Jer. 38:1-4). This occurred during a lull in the Babylonian siege of Jerusalem (37:11; 588 B.C.). Zedekiah granted their request and gave Jeremiah over to them, and they cast him into a dry cistern to die (38:5-6).

SHEPHELAH [shĕ fā'lə, shĕ fē'lə], **THE** (Heb. *haššepēlâ* "lowland").† In the Old Testament usually a proper name designating the foothills going down westward from the central hill country of Judah to the coastal plains of Philistia (RSV also "lowland"; KJV "vale," "valley[s]," "plain[s]").

   The Shephelah is normally cited in contrast to the hill country of Judah and the Negeb (Deut. 1:7; Josh. 10:40; 11:16; 12:8; Judg. 1:9; 2 Chr. 28:18; Jer. 17:26; 32:44; 33:13; Zech. 7:7); with the "wilderness" to the east adjacent to the Dead Sea, these were the main regions of Judah. Of the districts of Judah named with their cities at Josh. 15:21-62, five districts belong to the Shephelah (vv. 33-47), but two of these districts (vv. 45-47) remained in Philistine hands (according to the LXX of Judg. 1:18-19) and are not part of the Shephelah as it is usually considered (cf. Obad. 19). The Shephelah was known as particularly plentiful in trees (1 Kgs. 10:27; 2 Chr. 1:15; 9:27; cf. 1 Chr. 27:28).

SHEPHER [shē'fər], **MOUNT** (Heb. *har šeper*). A place where the Israelites stopped during their journey through the wilderness after Sinai (Num. 33:23-24; KJV "mount Shapher"). Its location is unknown.

SHEPHERD (Heb. masc. *rōʾeh*, fem. *rōʾâ*; Gk. *poimēn*).† A common occupation in ancient Palestine, commonly referred to in biblical imagery. "Shepherd" could refer to the owner of flocks or herds of sheep or other livestock (e.g., the patriarchs; cf. Gen. 13:2-7), or to a person working for the owner, whether the owner's son (37:2), daughter (29:9), or servant (13:7; 1 Sam. 25:7). A shepherd could reside in a city and leave a servant in charge of the herds at some other location (v. 2).

   Shepherds stayed with their sheep day and night (Luke 2:8). They provided their flocks with food and water, defended them against thieves and wild animals (1 Sam. 17:34-35; Isa. 31:4; Amos 3:12), and searched for any sheep that wandered astray (Ezek. 34:12; Luke 15:4-6). Each shepherd carried a curved staff, used as a walking stick and for guiding and dividing the sheep (Lev. 27:32); a rod or club, used as a weapon; and a sling (1 Sam. 17:40). They might be aided by dogs (Job 30:1).

   Because shepherds were the sole source of provision, protection, and control for sheep, in ancient Near Eastern usage "shepherd" came to be a term descriptive of political leaders. The law codes of Lipit-ishtar and Hammurabi each refer to the ruler as the divinely appointed shepherd of his people. The same image was used by Abdu-heba, Shalmaneser, Tukulti-ninurta, and Tiglath-pileser. This figure is found also in the Bible, particularly in prophetic oracles (e.g., Isa. 44:28, Cyrus). Kings, priests, and prophets of Israel are characterized as faithful (Jer. 3:15; 23:4) or wicked shepherds (Isa. 56:11-12; Jer. 10:21; 23:1-2; 50:6). David in particular is called the shepherd appointed by God (2 Sam. 5:2; Ps. 78:70-72). Israel under inadequate leadership is spoken of as sheep without a shepherd (Num. 27:17; 1 Kgs. 22:17; Matt. 9:36). Shepherd imagery is also applied to God, who guides and cares for his people (e.g., Ps. 23:1-4; 28:9; 80:1 [MT 2]; Isa. 40:11; Jer. 31:10; cf. Gen. 48:15). The eschatological Davidic king is depicted as a shepherd (Ezek. 34:23; Mic. 5:4).

   Jesus is called a shepherd as the leader and guard of his people (Heb. 13:20; 1 Pet. 2:25; Rev. 7:17), as the one who suffers for his people (Matt. 26:31 [quoting Zech. 13:7]; John 10:11-18), as the final judge of the nations (Matt. 25:32-33), and as the leader and example for Church leaders (1 Pet. 5:2-4), who are themselves called shepherds (Acts 20:28ff.; cf. John 21:15; 1 Pet. 5:2-3).

SHEPHERD OF HERMAS. *See* HERMAS, SHEPHERD OF.

SHEPHI [shē'fī] (Heb. *š^epî*), **SHEPHO** [shē'fō] (*š^epô*). The fourth son of the Edomite clan chief Shobal (Gen. 36:23, "Shepho"; 1 Chr. 1:40, "Shephi").

SHEPHUPHAM [shə fū'fəm] (Heb. *š^epûpām*). A son of the patriarch Benjamin, and ancestor of the Shuphamites (Num. 26:39; KJV, NIV "Shupham"). This son is not mentioned elsewhere, and the similarity of his name to names of other descendants of Benjamin—Muppim (Gen. 46:21), Shuppim (1 Chr. 7:21), and Shephuphan (8:5)—suggests that one person, the ancestor of an important Benjaminite line, may be in view.

SHEPHUPHAN [shə fū'fən] (Heb. *š^epûpān*). A son of Bela and grandson of the patriarch Benjamin (1 Chr. 8:5). *See* SHEPHUPHAM.

SHERAH (1 Chr. 7:24, KJV). *See* SHEERAH.

SHEREBIAH [shĕr'ə bī'ə] (Heb. *šērēbyâ* "Yahweh has sent desert heat [?]").† Four postexilic Levites or Levite families, possibly the same family.
  1. A "man of discretion" who came from Casiphia with his sons and kinsmen to join those returning to Judah with Ezra (Ezra 8:18, 24; at v. 24 the NIV does not reckon Sherebiah among the priests).
  2. A Levite (so 1 Esdr. 9:48; the MT distinguishes him from the Levites) among those who interpreted the Book of the Law for the people as Ezra read it (Neh. 8:7) and who gave the call to praise during the subsequent assembly of fasting and repentance (9:4-5).
  3. A Levite who participated in the sealing of the covenant under Nehemiah (Neh. 10:12 [MT 13]).
  4. A chief of the Levites who returned with Zerubbabel from exile (Neh. 12:8, 24).

SHERESH [shĕr'ĕsh] (Heb. *šereš* "root"). A son of Machir and grandson of Manasseh (1 Chr. 7:16).

SHEREZER (Zech. 7:2, KJV). *See* SHAREZER 2.

SHESHACH [shē'shăk]. KJV and NIV rendering of Heb. *šēšak̠*, a cryptogram for Babylon substituting *ššk* for *bbl* (Jer. 25:26; 51:41; RSV "Babylon"). *See* ATHBASH.

SHESHAI [shē'shī] (Heb. *šēšay*). One of the three descendants of Anak who lived at Hebron when the Israelite spies explored the land of Canaan (Num. 13:22). When Caleb took possession of Hebron, he drove the three out (Josh. 15:14; Judg. 1:10, 20). *See* ANAKIM.

SHESHAN [shē'shăn] (Heb. *šēšān*). The son of Ishi of the tribe of Judah (1 Chr. 2:31). Sheshan had no

sons and, to perpetuate his family, gave one of his daughters to Jarha, his Egyptian slave (vv. 34-35).

SHESHBAZZAR [shĕsh băz'ər] (Heb. *šēšbaṣṣar*; cf. Akk. *Sin-ab-uṣur* "may [the moon-god] Sin protect the father").† A prince of Judah whom Cyrus made governor of the Persian province of Judah. Sheshbazzar brought the gold and silver vessels of the temple back to Jerusalem and initiated the reconstruction of the temple (Ezra 1:8-11; 5:14-16). He has been identified by some with Zerubbabel, but he was most likely Zerubbabel's predecessor and possibly the same as SHENAZZAR, son of King Jehoiachin (Jeconiah) of Judah (1 Chr. 3:18).

SHETH [shĕth] (Heb. *šēt*).
  1. "The sons of Sheth" is apparently a designation of Moab in Balaam's prediction of Moab's defeat by Israel (Num. 24:17). Heb. *šēt* should perhaps be emended to *š^e'ēt* "exaltation, defiance" (cf. NIV mg. "noisy boasters") or *šē'ṭ* "desolation" (cf. *šā'ôn* "tumult" at Jer. 48:45, which deliberately echoes Num. 24:17).
  2 (1 Chr. 1:1, KJV). *See* SETH.

SHETHAR [shē'thär] (Heb. *šētār*). One of the seven chief advisers to King Ahasuerus (Esth. 1:14).

SHETHAR-BOZENAI [shē'thär bŏz'ə nī] (Heb. *š^etar bôz^enay*). A Persian official who tried to interfere with the rebuilding of the temple in Jerusalem (Ezra 5:3, 6; 6:6, 13; KJV "Shethar-boznai"), apparently a subordinate of Tattenai the governor.

SHEVA [shē'və] (Heb. *š^ewā'*).
  1. David's secretary (2 Sam. 20:25, **Q**; **K** *šy'*). He is also known as Seraiah (8:17), Shisha (1 Kgs. 4:3), and Shavsha (1 Chr. 18:16).
  2. A son of Caleb and his concubine Maacah (1 Chr. 2:49).

SHIBAH [shī'bə] (Heb. *šib'â*). A well where Isaac's servants found water (Gen. 26:33; KJV "Shebah"; cf. JB). It was from this well, named for the oath (cf. Heb. *šāba'*) made between Isaac and Abimelech, that the city of Beer-sheba received its name (cf. 21:31).

SHIBBOLETH [shĭb'ə lĕth] (Heb. *šibbōlet* "ear of grain" or "torrent"). A word used as a test by Gileadite guards to detect Ephraimites attempting to cross the Jordan (Judg. 12:5-6). Because they spoke a distinct dialect of Hebrew, the Ephraimites would pronounce the word's initial šin (a sibilant) as the consonant sin (a spirant, originally tha [*t*], which merged with šin at an earlier time in Palestinian usage than in Transjordanian), producing *sibbōlet* (written, as in the originally unpointed Hebrew, with a samech to distinguish the sounds).

SHIBMAH (Num. 32:38, KJV). *See* SIBMAH.

SHICRON (Josh. 15:11, KJV). *See* SHIKKERON.

SHIELD. The basic defensive weapon in warfare before the introduction of gunpowder. Shields were used in warfare long before the emergence of Israel. They varied greatly in size, covering as much as the entire body of the soldier (sometimes then carried by a shield-bearer) or as little as the face and upper torso. Where body armor was used, smaller shields that restricted movement less could be used. Shields were generally made of wood covered with hides, though metal might be used as the primary material (rarely) or to strengthen a shield of wood and hide, especially the key part of the shield that protected the face.

Three Hebrew words are used in the Old Testament for shield (KJV sometimes "target"; RSV, KJV sometimes "buckler"). Heb. *māgēn* usually represents a small round shield, usable by archers and swordsmen (1 Chr. 5:18; 2 Chr. 14:8 [MT 7]; 17:17). Heb. *ṣinnâ* usually represents a large rectangular shield, used by those whose offensive weapon was a spear (14:8 [MT 7]). Both terms are also used more loosely, however, probably with variations over time in the forms of shields they represented. Heb. *šeleṭ* was perhaps a more general term.

Both small and large shields made of metal served a decorative purpose in the royal palace (1 Kgs. 10:16-17) and the Jerusalem temple (2 Chr. 23:9; cf. 2 Sam. 8:7). God is often referred to metaphorically as a "shield" (e.g., Gen. 15:1; Ps. 84:11 [MT 12]). At Eph. 6:16 faith is called a "shield" (Gk. *thyreós*).

SHIGGAION [shĭ gā'yŏn] (Heb. *šiggāyôn*), **SHIGIONOTH** [shĭg'ĭ ō'nŏth] (pl. *šigyōnôṭ*). A term appearing in the superscription of Ps. 7 and in a plural form at Hab. 3:1, which is the superscription of a psalm (vv. 2-19). The term may indicate that these are songs to be performed in a lament or dirge style (so JB; cf. Akk. *šegu* "lament") or that their structure and performance are varied from part to part (cf. Heb. *šāgâ* "wander").

SHIHON (Josh. 19:19, KJV). *See* SHION.

SHIHOR [shī'hôr] (Heb. *šiḥôr, šiḥōr, šîḥôr*).† One or more rivers marking the boundary between Egypt and Palestine. The name may derive from Egyp. *P3-š-Ḥr* "Pool of Horus," the ancient name for a body of water of uncertain location, or may be related to Heb. *šāḥōr* "black"; it was no longer understood by the time of the translators of the LXX (cf. Josh. 13:3, Gk. *aoíkētos* "uninhabited"; 1 Chr. 13:5, *hória* "boundaries"; Jer. 2:18, *Geōn* "Gihon"). It is probable that the term designates the Bubastite or Pelusiac branches of the Nile (e.g., Josh. 13:3; KJV "Sihor"; 1 Chr. 13:5; Isa. 23:3). Otherwise, the term may refer to the Nile itself (Jer. 2:18; RSV "Nile").

SHIHOR-LIBNATH [shī'hôr lĭb'năth] (Heb. *šîḥôr libnāṭ*). A landmark identifying the southwestern boundary of the tribal territory of Asher (Josh. 19:26; JB "the streams of the Libnath"; NEB "the swamp of Libnath"). Suggested identifications have included the Kishon river, which flows across the plain of Megiddo northeast of the Carmel ridge; the Nahr ez-Zerqa, a stream that empties into the Mediterranean *ca.* 10 km. (6 mi.) south of Dor; and a city (or, assuming a conflation of terms as in some versions, two cities) otherwise unidentified.

SHIKKERON [shĭk'ə rŏn] (Heb. *šikkerôn*; cf. *šikkārôn* "drunkenness").† A place on the northern border of the tribal territory of Judah (Josh. 15:11; KJV "Shicron"), possibly to be identified with Tell el-Fûl, northwest of Ekron.

SHILHI [shĭl'hī] (Heb. *šilḥî* "warrior"). The father of Azuba, King Jehoshaphat's mother (1 Kgs. 22:42; 2 Chr. 20:31).

SHILHIM [shĭl'hĭm] (Heb. *šilḥîm*). A city in the Negeb district of Judah (Josh. 15:32), usually identified with Sharuhen (19:6) and Shaaraim (2) (1 Chr. 4:31). It may have been located at Tell el-Fârʿah on the Nahr Besor, *ca.* 30 km. (19 mi.) west of Beer-sheba.

SHILLEM [shĭl'əm] (Heb. *šillēm*). A son of Naphtali (Gen. 46:24) ancestor of the Shillemites (Num. 26:49). He is called Shallum (7) at 1 Chr. 7:13.

SHILOAH [shī lō'ə], **WATERS OF** (Heb. *mê haš-šilōaḥ*). A pool and aqueduct in Jerusalem, part of the SILOAM water system (Isa. 8:6).

SHILOH [shī'lō] (Heb. *šilô, šîlô, šilōh*).

1. According to the KJV at Gen. 49:10 (cf. RSV mg., NIV mg.), an appellative of the Messiah (cf. Talmud *Sanh.* 98b). The passage refers to a predicted event that will bring about the transition from the victory and reign of Judah proclaimed at vv. 8-10a to a more glorious period marked by the obedience of many or all peoples to a particular ruler whose time will be marked by great abundance (vv. 10b-12). The nature of the transition event is unclear. It is not likely that the place named "Shiloh" is intended by Heb. *šîlōh* (Q *šîlô*). Among the suggested emendations, the most likely is *šellô*, based on the LXX and most other early versions, thus either "that which belongs to him" or "the one to whom it belongs" (cf. RSV, JB, NIV). In the former case, Judah's earlier form of reign (vv. 8-10a) will give way to a more glorious rule of Judah over "the peoples." If the latter translation is followed, Judah's reign will possibly be ended in favor of the more glorious reign of another, or will reach its climax in the glorious reign of a particular Judahite ruler. In any case, the passage can be regarded as a prediction of either David's brief empire or of the rule of the Messiah.

2. A city that prior to the monarchy was the main center of Israelite worship. Its ruins are at Khirbet Seilûn, *ca.* 30 km. (18.5 mi.) north of Jerusalem, "north of Bethel, on the east of the highway that goes up from Bethel to Shechem, and south of Lebonah" (Judg. 21:19).

Shiloh became an Israelite religious center when the tabernacle was set up there prior to the final division of the land of Canaan among the tribes of Israel (Josh. 18:1–22:9; "at/in Shiloh before [or 'in the presence of'] the Lord," 18:8, 10; 19:51). That war plans were set in motion against the Transjordanian tribes when they built an altar at another location immediately after the division of the land (22:10-12) shows how seriously the single central shrine at Shiloh was taken. The ark of the covenant remained at Shiloh until captured by the Philistines at Ebenezer (1 Sam. 4:3-4), and Shiloh became an important pilgrimage center with a yearly pilgrimage "feast of the Lord" (Judg. 21:19; 1 Sam. 1:3; 2:14). Shiloh's importance as a religious center was almost completely ended when the Philistines captured the ark, which never again returned to Shiloh, and when Eli and his sons, the priests at Shiloh, died (4:12-22; Ps. 78:60-61). Some archaeologists cite evidence of Philistine destruction of Shiloh *ca.* 1050 B.C., probably in the generation after Eli's death.

Later, the prophet Ahijah uttered oracles at Shiloh, but the narrative provides no evidence of the city's former importance (1 Kgs. 11:29-39; 14:2-16). Nevertheless, the site of the shrine at Shiloh may have continued to be a stop for religious pilgrims for some time (cf. Jer. 41:5). Jeremiah's recollection of the destruction of the former religious center was a warning concerning the fate awaiting Jerusalem (7:12, 14; 26:6, 9).

SHILONITE [shī'lə nīt] (Heb. *šîlōnî, šîlônî*).

1. A designation of the prophet Ahijah identifying him as a native of Shiloh (1 Kgs. 11:29; 12:15; 15:29; 2 Chr. 9:29; 10:15).

2. A gentilic designating a family of returnees from exile in Babylon (1 Chr. 9:5; Neh. 11:5). The reference may be to descendants of SHELAH 2 rather than to former residents of Shiloh.

SHILSHAH [shĭl'shə] (Heb. *šilšâ*; cf. *šālōš* "three"). An Asherite, son of Zophah (1 Chr. 7:37).

SHIMEA [shĭm'ĭ ə] (Heb. *šim'ā'* "[God] has heard").

1. The third son of Jesse, and a brother of David (1 Chr. 2:13; KJV "Shimma"), and the father of Jonathan (**4**)/Jonadab (**1**), who killed a Philistine giant (20:7). Shimea is also known as Shammah (**2**) (1 Sam. 16:9; 17:13), Shimeah (**1**) (2 Sam. 13:3, 32), and Shimei (**3**) (21:21; KJV "Shimeah").

2. A son of David born after he had become king of all Israel in Jerusalem (1 Chr. 3:5). He is also called Shammua (**2**) (2 Sam. 5:14; 1 Chr. 14:4).

3. A Levite of the house of Merari (1 Chr. 6:30 [MT 15]).

4. A Levite of the house of Gershom who was the father of Berechiah (1 Chr. 6:39 [MT 24]).

SHIMEAH [shĭm'ĭ ə].

1. (Heb. *šim'â* "[God] has heard"). The third son of Jesse, David's father (2 Sam. 13:3, 32). *See* SHIMEA **1.**

2 (Heb. *šim'â*). The son of Mikloth a Benjaminite (1 Chr. 8:32). He is called Shimeam at 9:38.

SHIMEAM [shĭm'ĭ əm] (Heb. *šim'ām*). A Benjaminite, the son of Mikloth (1 Chr. 9:38). He also occurs as Shimeah (**2**) (8:32).

SHIMEATH [shĭm'ĭ ăth] (Heb. *šim'āt*). An Ammonite woman whose son Jozacar/Zabad was among those who killed King Joash (Jehoash) of Judah (2 Kgs. 12:21; 2 Chr. 24:6).

SHIMEATHITES [shĭm'ĭ ə thīts] (Heb. *šim'ātîm*).

One of "the families of the scribes that dwelt at Jabez" who are listed among the descendants of Caleb and who are also perhaps considered a Kenite or Rechabite group (1 Chr. 2:55).

SHIMEI [shĭm'ĭ ī] (Heb. *šim'î* "Yahweh has heard").

1. A son of Gershon (Gershom) and grandson of Levi (Exod. 6:17; KJV "Shimi"; Num. 3:18; 1 Chr. 6:17; 23:7). His descendants are the Shimeites (Heb. *haššim'î*; Num. 3:21; KJV "Shimites"; Zech. 12:13). Two lists of sons of Shimei are given at 1 Chr. 23:9-10, leading some interpreters to posit a second son of Gershom by that name.

2. A man from Bahurim whose father was Gera and who belonged to the same Benjaminite clan as Saul's house. Shimei, probably motivated by loyalty to Saul's family, publicly cursed and threw stones at King David and his servants as they made their escape from Jerusalem at the time of Absalom's rebellion (2 Sam. 16:5-8). David refused to allow Abishai, one of his men, to kill Shimei (vv. 9-13), and Shimei submitted to David on the king's return (19:16, 18-20 [MT 17, 19-21]). Abishai again counseled David to do away with Shimei, and again David refused (vv. 21-23 [MT 22-24]). Nevertheless, David regarded Shimei as a continued threat to Solomon, his successor to the throne, and suggested that Solomon eventually find some reason to execute Shimei (1 Kgs. 2:8-9). Solomon required Shimei to stay in Jerusalem, which he did until he left to bring back two escaped slaves, after which he was executed (vv. 36-46).

3. The third son of Jesse, David's father (2 Sam. 21:21; KJV "Shimeah"). *See* SHIMEA **1.**

4. A supporter of Solomon during Adonijah's attempted coup (1 Kgs. 1:8).

5. The son of Ela who served as Solomon's governor in Benjamin (1 Kgs. 4:18). He is perhaps the same as **4** above.

6. A brother of Zerubbabel (1 Chr. 3:19).

7. The son of Zaccur of the tribe of Simeon who had sixteen sons and six daughters (1 Chr. 4:26-27).

8. The son of Gog of the tribe of Reuben (1 Chr. 5:4).

9. A Levite of the Merarite line (1 Chr. 6:29 [MT 14]).

10. A Gershomite Levite, the son of Jahath (1 Chr. 6:42-43 [MT 27-28]).

11. A Benjaminite (1 Chr. 8:21; KJV "Shimhi"). He is probably the same as Shema (**3**) (v. 13).

12. Leader of the tenth order of temple musicians in David's time, one of the sons of Jeduthun (1 Chr. 25:3, 17; absent from v. 3 in most manuscripts of the MT, followed by KJV).

13. A man from Ramah who served as overseer of David's royal vineyards (1 Chr. 27:27).

14. A descendant of Heman among the Levites who cleansed the temple during the reign of King Hezekiah (2 Chr. 29:14).

15. A Levite contemporary with King Hezekiah who served under his brother Conaniah in overseeing the contributions to the temple (2 Chr. 31:12-13).

16. A Levite among those required by Ezra to divorce their foreign wives (Ezra 10:23).

17. A layman of the sons of Hashum who divorced his non-Israelite wife (Ezra 10:33).

18. One of the sons of Binnui required to abandon his foreign wife (Ezra 10:38).

19. A Benjaminite who was an ancestor of Mordecai (Esth. 2:5).

SHIMEON [shĭm′ĭ ən] (Heb. *šimʿôn* "[God] has heard"). One of those required by Ezra to divorce his foreign wife (Ezra 10:31).

SHIMHI (1 Chr. 8:21, KJV). *See* SHIMEI **11**.

SHIMI (Exod. 6:17, KJV), **SHIMITES** (Num. 3:21, KJV). *See* SHIMEI **1**.

SHIMMA (1 Chr. 2:13, KJV). *See* SHIMEA **1**.

SHIMON [shī′mən] (Heb. *šîmôn*). A man of the tribe of Judah (1 Chr. 4:20).

SHIMRATH [shĭm′răth] (Heb. *šimrāṯ* "vigilance"). A son of Shimei (**11**) of the tribe of Benjamin (1 Chr. 8:21).

SHIMRI [shĭm′rī] (Heb. *šimrî* "[Yahweh] watches").

1. The son of Shemaiah (**3**) of the tribe of Simeon (1 Chr. 4:37).

2. The father of Jediael and Joha, two of David's mighty men (1 Chr. 11:45).

3. A levitical gatekeeper, the son of Hosah of the house of Merari (1 Chr. 26:10; KJV "Simri").

4. A descendant of Elizaphan who was among the Levites who cleansed the temple during the reign of King Hezekiah (2 Chr. 29:13).

SHIMRITH [shĭm′rĭth] (Heb. *šimrîṯ* "[God] has watched"). A Moabite woman whose son, Jehozabad, was one of the murderers of King Joash (Jehoash) of Judah (2 Chr. 24:26). At 2 Kgs. 12:21 she is called Shomer (**1**).

SHIMRON [shĭm′rŏn] (Heb. *šimrôn*) (**PERSON**). A son of the patriarch Issachar (Gen. 46:13; 1 Chr. 7:1; KJV "Shimrom"), ancestor (or head) of the Shimronites (Heb. *šimrōnî*; Num. 26:24).

SHIMRON (PLACE), SHIMRON-MERON [shĭm′rŏn měr′ŏn] (Heb. *šimrôn [mᵉrʾôn]*). A northern Canaanite city that participated in the ill-fated alliance against the Israelites under Jabin of Hazor (Josh. 11:1). Shimron's unnamed king was defeated by the invading Israelites (12:20), and the city was assigned to the tribe of Zebulun (19:15). Tell Semuniyeh, *ca.* 11 km. (7 mi.) west of Nazareth, has sometimes been identified with Shimron(-Meron), as has Marun, between Tyre and Dan, but there can be no certainty as to the location of the city. The compound form of the name occurs only at Josh. 12:20 and may actually represent two different cities (so LXX). The LXX and Egyptian texts suggest that the name of Shimron was originally *šimʿôn* (cf. JB "Symoon" at 12:20).

SHIMSHAI [shĭm′shī] (Heb. *šimšai*; cf. *šemeš* "sun"). A high official ("scribe") in the western province of "Beyond the River" (which included Palestine) during the reign of King Artaxerxes of Persia (464-424 B.C.). Shimshai and other officials of the province protested the rebuilding of Jerusalem by Jews who had returned from exile under Cyrus, thinking that the Jews intended rebellion (Ezra 4:8-16). The king's initial response was to agree that the rebuilding should cease (vv. 17-23).

SHINAB [shī′năb] (Heb. *šināḇ*; Akk. *Sin-a-bi* "[the moon-god] Sin is my father"). The king of Admah, one of the five cities that rebelled against Chedorlaomer during the time of Abraham (Gen. 14:2).

SHINAR [shī′när] (Heb. *šinʿār*). A designation for Babylonia (Isa. 11:11), or a district of Babylonia that according to the Table of Nations included Babylon (Babel), Uruk (Erech, Warka), and Akkad (Accad, Agade) (Gen. 10:10; KJV also "Calneh"). In later biblical usage the name was equated with Babylon (Dan. 1:2; Zech. 5:11).

SHION [shī′ən] (Heb. *šîʾōn*). A city in the tribal territory of Issachar (Josh. 19:19; KJV "Shihon"). Possible locations include Sirim, 22.5 km. (14 mi.) southeast of Mt. Tabor, and ʿAyun esh-Shaʿin, *ca.* 5 km. (3 mi.) east of Nazareth.

SHIPHI [shī′fī] (Heb. *šipʿî* "abundance"). The son of Allon of the tribe of Simeon (1 Chr. 4:37).

SHIPHMITE [shĭf′mīt] (Heb. *šipmî*). A gentilic ascribed to Zabdi, overseer of the royal vineyards in David's time (1 Chr. 27:27). The term may indicate his origin at Shepham (so JB; cf. Num. 34:10-11) or Siphmoth (cf. 1 Sam. 30:28).

SHIPHRAH [shĭf′rə] (Heb. *šiprâ* "beauty"; Egyp. *Šp-ra*). One of two Hebrew midwives commanded by Pharaoh to kill all male children born to the Israelites (Exod. 1:15-16).

SHIPHTAN [shĭf′tăn] (Heb. *šipṭān* "judgment"). The father of Kemuel, the representative of the tribe of Ephraim among those who assisted Moses in the division of the land (Num. 34:24).

SHIPS AND SAILING.† Biblical terms for ships in general include Heb. *ʾŏnîyâ, ṣî*; Gk. *ploíon* (cf. *naús*, a Classical Greek word found in the New Testament only at Acts 27:41). More specific terms designating a "small boat" are Gk. *ploiárion, skáphē* (also "life boat"). Heb. *ʾŏnî* is a collective term indicating a fleet of ships.

I. Israel and the Near East

The first vessels for water transport in the ancient Near East, as in other parts of the world, were boats and rafts made of logs and reeds. By the third millennium B.C. fairly sophisticated small boats were made in both Egypt and Mesopotamia of bundles of reeds lashed together. Sails were also in use in Egypt by the same time. Crete and Cyprus were other early centers for the development of boats, by the third millennium having regular contact by sea with Anatolia and Syria.

By 2500 seagoing ships were built of boards attached together much like the bundles of reeds in earlier craft or were made of single large hollowed logs with boards attached. Such vessels were equipped with single square sails and ten to twenty oars. Development of more sophisticated construction techniques made possible larger ships. One of the main improvements in overall design was the addition of a keel. The use of square sails and oars continued throughout the ancient period. The number of oarsmen increased not only with the increasing length of ships, but also with additional banks of oars.

The Phoenicians were the first great sea traders on the Mediterranean. Early Israelite involvement in Phoenician seagoing trade is merely suggested (Gen. 49:13; Judg. 5:17). With the greater unification of Israel under kings David and Solomon, Israel came to rely on Phoenician, specifically Tyrian, expertise in shipping and other trades (1 Kgs. 5:9 [MT 23]; 10:11). Solomon built a fleet of trading vessels to bring goods from the south to Ezion-geber on the Gulf of Aqaba (9:26-28) and to sail to "Tarshish" from the Mediterranean coast (10:22), but he depended on the use of Phoenician sailors. By means of this fleet Solomon was able to control some of the trade from Egypt and the south to Syria and Anatolia in the north (cf. v. 29). Later King Jehoshaphat of Judah made an unsuccessful attempt to revive the trade to the south (22:48).

Apart from these brief periods of involvement, Judah and Israel never became sea-going nations. The sea was a terrifying place for Israelites (e.g., Ps. 107:23-30; Isa. 51:15; 57:20; Jer. 31:35). "Tarshish" and other names of places across the seas were used vaguely, sometimes only figuratively to represent distant places known only by traders (e.g., 1 Kgs. 10:22; 22:48; Ps. 72:10; Ezek. 38:13; "ships of Tarshish").

Phoenicia continued to grow through sea trade and the establishment of trading colonies, and the Phoenicians came to be characterized as enjoying great luxury because of trade (Ps. 45:12-13 [MT 13-14]; Zech. 9:3). Ezekiel's lament over Tyre, the chief Phoenician port until its defeat by Nebuchadrezzar, gives a broad view of Phoenician trade, even if from a distance (Ezek. 26:1-28:19; cf. Isa. 23; Joel 3:4-8 [MT 4:4-8]). Phoenicia eventually came into competition with the Greeks and then the Romans, who became in time the only power on the Mediterranean (with the exception of pirates). The lament over "Babylon" (e.g., Rome) at Rev. 18 focuses, as Ezekiel's lament over Tyre, on the city's control of sea trade.

A Phoenician ship

A Roman grain ship

II. New Testament

Paul traveled often as a passenger on cargo ships (cf. 2 Cor. 11:25). The account of his journey from Caesarea to Rome as a prisoner (Acts 27:1-28:14) is an important document for understanding ancient sailing. The "ship of Adramyttium" (27:2) on which his party first embarked on this journey was probably a small vessel that stayed close to the coast of Syria and Asia Minor, especially when, as was the case with this voyage, protection from winds out of the west was needed (v. 4). At Myra in Lycia, from which this small vessel would continue west and then north from port to port toward Adramyttium, the party transferred to one of the ships that carried grain from Egypt to Rome and other cities of the empire, which was also carrying a large number of passengers (vv. 5-6, 37). This larger ship was to have continued for a time on a similar route northward along the western coast of Asia Minor, but at Cnidus progress became impossible because of contrary winds. The ship headed south, found protection south of Crete, and anchored at Fair Havens, the westernmost harbor on the south of Crete, to which it could safely proceed against the wind (vv. 7-8).

Sailing was impossible in winter and difficult during autumn. Paul, an experienced traveler, advised that the ship await spring at Fair Havens, since it was already October (vv. 9-10). But because that was not a suitable harbor in which to winter, the crew set out for Phoenix, a harbor farther west on Crete (vv. 11-12). Good progress was made for a time (v. 13), but a storm out of the northeast made them fear that the ship would be run aground in the Syrtis, the shallow bays on the coast of modern Libya and Tunisia. The wind drove the ship into the lee of an island that could provide only a temporary respite. There the lifeboat, normally pulled behind the ship, was brought up on deck, the hull of the ship was undergirded with cables, and the drift-anchor lowered to slow the ship (vv. 14-17). The violent storm continued, with the ship heading toward the west-northwest. The deck cargo and spare tackle were thrown overboard to lighten the ship (cf. Jonah 1:5; Heb. $s^e p \hat{i} y \hat{a}$). But with the storm obscuring the sky there was no way of knowing the course for sure. It seemed probable that the ship would sink (Acts 27:18-20).

After two weeks the ship came toward the island of Malta at night and was anchored until daybreak.

The main part of the cargo, the grain in the hold of the ship, was thrown overboard (vv. 27-38). At daybreak the crew planned to beach the ship in a nearby bay. The anchors were cut loose, the steering paddles released (rudders were not used on ancient ships), and a small foresail raised. But the ship ran onto an unexpected shoal, the bow became firmly lodged, and the waves began to break apart the stern. Nevertheless, all were able to escape to land (vv. 39-44).

The voyage to Rome the following spring was less eventful, but the account still provides some details regarding sailing. A ship from Alexandria, probably another grain ship, took Paul's party from Malta to Syracuse on Sicily, and, apparently having lost whatever favorable wind it had, was forced to stay there three days, then tack northward to Rhegium, the nearest port on the Italian mainland. Then a favorable wind took them to Puteoli on the Bay of Naples, from which the journey continued overland (28:11-14).

Bibliography. L. Casson, *Ships and Seamanship in the Ancient World* (Princeton: 1971).

SHISHA [shī′shə] (Heb. *šîšāʾ*). The father of Elihoreph and Ahijah, secretaries for King Solomon (1 Kgs. 4:3). Shisha was probably David's secretary, known as Shavsha (1 Chr. 18:16), Seraiah (2 Sam. 8:17), and Sheva (20:25).

SHISHAK [shī′shăk] (Heb. *šîšaq*; Egyp. *ššnq*). Sheshonq I, an Egyptian pharaoh of Libyan origin (*ca.* 945-915 B.C.) and founder of the Twenty-second Dynasty (*ca.* 945-730), which ruled from Tanis in the Nile Delta. Shishak may have been a sponsor of Israel's revolt against the dynasty of David under Jeroboam I after Solomon's death; he was at any rate Jeroboam's protector while Solomon was still alive (1 Kgs. 11:40). Five years after Solomon's death Shishak invaded Judah, seized the treasures of both the temple and the royal palace, and gained possession (perhaps as tribute) of some of Judah's fortified cities (14:25-26; K *šûšaq* or *šôšaq*; 2 Chr. 12:2-9; *ANET*, pp. 242-32, 263-64).

Shishak is sometimes suggested as the pharaoh with whom Solomon entered a marriage alliance, receiving as dowry the city of Gezer (1 Kgs. 3:1; 9:16), but most likely an earlier pharaoh is intended.

See EGYPT *III*.

SHITRAI [shĭt′rī] (Heb. *šiṭray*). A Sharonite, overseer of David's cattle in Sharon (1 Chr. 27:29).

SHITTAH TREE, SHITTIM WOOD (KJV). *See* ACACIA.

SHITTIM [shĭt′ĭm] (Heb. *šiṭṭîm* "acacia trees").
1. A place in Moab where the Israelites stopped during their wilderness journeys (Num. 33:49; "Abel-shittim") and where they were drawn into Moabite worship of Baal of Peor (25:1). Shittim was the last stopping-place east of the Jordan. From there Joshua sent spies to Jericho, the first city to be taken west of the Jordan (Josh. 2:1). The miraculous crossing of the Jordan from Shittim (3:1) to Gilgal (4:19) is recalled at Mic. 6:5. If the widely suggested emendation of

Heb. *šaḥᵃṭâ śēṭîm* at Hos. 5:2 to *šaḥaṭ haššiṭṭîm* "pit of Shittim" is followed (so RSV), this may be a reference to the idolatry in which the Israelites engaged at Shittim (cf. 9:10; but cf. F. I. Andersen and D. N. Freedman, *Hosea*. AB 24 [1980], pp. 286-88). Heb. *śēṭîm* can also be taken as it stands as "rebels" (so NIV; other translations are similar). Shittim has been identified with two sites, Khirbet el-Kefrein and Tell el-Ḥammâm, both not far from the Jordan river opposite Jericho.
2. "The valley of Shittim," a place that receives water from a spring in the temple in a vision of eschatological blessing (Joel 3:18 [MT 4:18]; JB "wadi of Acacias"; cf. NIV). The exact identity of this valley is unknown, but the relationship to the temple at Jerusalem ("the house of the Lord") and the apparent normal dryness of the valley make it probable that it is the Wâdī en-Nâr, the lower part of the Kidron valley as it goes down to the Dead Sea.

SHIZA [shī′zə] (Heb. *šîzāʾ*). A Reubenite; the father of Adina, one of David's mighty men (1 Chr. 11:42).

SHOA [shō′ə] (Heb. *šôaʿ*). A people whose soldiers, probably mercenaries, accompany Babylonian invaders in a vision of an attack against Jerusalem (Ezek. 23:23). This people is commonly identified with the Sutu, a nomadic Aramean tribe known from inscriptions and other sources, but this is far from certain.

SHOBAB [shō′băb] (Heb. *šôḇāḇ* "deserter").
1. A son of Caleb and Azubah (1 Chr. 2:18).
2. A son of David and Bathsheba born in Jerusalem (2 Sam. 5:14; 1 Chr. 3:5; 14:4).

SHOBACH [shō′băk] (Heb. *šôḇaḵ*). The commander of the army of the Aramean king Hadadezer of Zobah in the time of David. When the Arameans (RSV "Syrians") under Shobach fought against David's army at Helam, they were defeated and Shobach died on the field of battle (2 Sam. 10:16-18). He is called Shophach at 1 Chr. 19:16-18.

SHOBAI [shō′bī] (Heb. *šôḇāy* "one who carries away captives" [?]). A levitical gatekeeper whose descendants returned with Zerubbabel from captivity in Babylon (Ezra 2:42; Neh. 7:45).

SHOBAL [shō′bəl] (Heb. *šôḇāl*).
1. A son of Seir and chief of the Horites (Gen. 36:20, 23, 29; 1 Chr. 1:38, 40).
2. A Judahite, son of Hur and ancestor of the inhabitants of Kiriath-jearim (1 Chr. 2:50, 52; 4:1-2).

SHOBEK [shō′běk] (Heb. *šôḇēq*). A participant in the sealing of the covenant under Nehemiah (Neh. 10:24 [MT 25]).

SHOBI [shō′bī] (Heb. *šôḇî*). A son of the Ammonite king Nahash in Rabbah who provided food for David and those with him at Mahanaim as they fled from Absalom (2 Sam. 17:27).

SHOCO, SHOCHO, SHOCHOH (KJV). *See* SOCO.

SHOES. *See* SANDALS, SHOES.

SHOHAM [shō'hăm] (Heb. *šōham*, a variety of precious stone). A son of Jaaziah, and a Levite of the house of Merari (1 Chr. 24:27).

SHOMER [shō'mər] (Heb. *šōmēr* "watcher, protector").

1. The mother of Jehozabad, one of those who killed King Joash (Jehoash) of Judah (2 Kgs. 12:21). She is also known as Shimrith the Moabitess (2 Chr. 24:26).

2. One of the sons of Heber of the tribe of Asher (1 Chr. 7:32). He is also called Shemer (**3**) (v. 34; KJV "Shamer").

SHOPHACH [shō'făk] (Heb. *šôpak*). An alternate name of SHOBACH (1 Chr. 19:16, 18).

SHOPHAN (Num. 32:35, KJV). *See* ATROTH-SHOPHAN.

SHOSHANNIM (KJV). *See* LILY.

SHOWBREAD. *See* BREAD OF THE PRESENCE.

SHRINE (Heb. *bêt ['ᵉlōhîm]* "house [of gods/God]"; Gk. *naós*).* In normal usage a sacred building in which a deity is considered to reside and in which the deity's image might be placed (Judg. 17:5; KJV "house of gods"; 2 Kgs. 17:29, 32; 23:19; KJV "[houses of the] high places"; Acts 17:24; KJV "temples"). But "the silver shrines of Artemis" mentioned at 19:24 were small models of the large temple of ARTEMIS at Ephesus. The "inner shrine" (RSV) referred to at Heb. 6:19 (Gk. *tó esóteron*) is the heavenly sanctuary mentioned at 9:12, 24 (*see* MOST HOLY PLACE).

SHUA [shōō'ə].

1. (Heb. *šûaʿ*). The father of Judah's Canaanite wife (Gen. 38:2, 12; KJV "Shuah"). At 1 Chr. 2:3 the RSV and other English versions transliterate *baṭ-šûaʿ* as the proper name ("Bath-shua") of Judah's wife rather than translating "daughter of Shua" (so KJV, NIV mg.).

2. (Heb. *šûʾāʾ*). An Asherite, the daughter of Heber (1 Chr. 7:32).

SHUAH [shōō'ə].

1. (Heb. *šûaḥ*). One of the sons of Abraham and his concubine Keturah (Gen. 25:2; 1 Chr. 1:32). Shuah is thought to be associated with Šûḫu, a land on the Euphrates river in Syria known from Assyrian inscriptions, and with the Shuhites, to whom Bildad, one of Job's friends, belonged (Job 2:11).

2. (Gen. 38:2, 12, KJV). *See* SHUA **1**.

3. (1 Chr. 4:11, KJV). *See* SHUHAH.

SHUAL [shōō'əl] (Heb. *šûʿāl* "fox") (**PERSON**). A son of Zophah of the tribe of Asher (1 Chr. 7:36).

SHUAL [shōō'əl] (Heb. *šûʿāl* "fox") (**PLACE**). "The land of Shual," a region to which one of three groups of Philistine raiders turned as they came out of their camp at Michmash (1 Sam. 13:17). The direction of this group of raiders is also said to be "toward Ophrah"; from this it is known that they were heading northward from Michmash. Shual cannot be identified more definitely. *See* SHAALIM.

SHUBAEL [shōō'bĭ əl] (Heb. *šûḇāʾēl*). Alternate form of SHEBUEL.

SHUHAH [shōō'hə] (Heb. *šûḥâ* "pit"). The brother of Chelub of the tribe of Judah (1 Chr. 4:11; KJV "Shuah").

SHUHAM [shōō'hăm] (Heb. *šûḥām*). A son of Dan whose descendants were the Shuhamites (Num. 26:42-43). At Gen. 46:23 he is called "Hushim."

SHUHITE [shōō'hīt] (Heb. *šûḥî*). A designation of Bildad, one of Job's friends, probably identifying him as a descendant of SHUAH **1** (Job 2:11; 8:1; 18:1; 25:1; 42:9).

SHULAMMITE [shōō'lə mīt] (Heb. *haššûlammît*).† A gentilic of the young woman in the Song of Solomon (Cant. 6:13 [MT 7:1]). A number of interpretations of this term have been advocated. The term may indicate the woman's origin from an otherwise unknown town of Shulam (so JB), but textual evidence that the original form of the term was *haššûnammît* "the Shunammite" may indicate origin from the town of Shunem; if so, the term may be an allusion to Abishag the Shunammite (1 Kgs. 1:3). "The Shulammite" may, according to another interpretation, be a feminine form of "Solomon" (*šᵉlōmōh*), given as a title to a bride of King Solomon, or a feminine form of the name of a deity (perhaps one named *šālôm* "Šalem" or "peace") given to a consort of the deity, or perhaps an epithet of the Assyrian goddess Ishtar. Yet again, *šûlammît* may be simply a proper name itself (cf. *šᵉlōmît* "Shelomith").

SHUMATHITES [shōō'mə thīts] (Heb. *šumāṭî*). One of the families residing in Kiriath-jearim descended from Shobal the son of Hur (1 Chr. 2:53).

SHUNAMMITE [shōō'nə mīt] (Heb. *šûnammît* "woman of Shunem"), **SHUNEM** [shōō'nəm] (*šûmēm*).† Shunem was a town on the site of modern Sôlem, on the southern slope of the Nebī Daḥī (*see* MOREH **2**), east across the valley of Jezreel from Megiddo and *ca.* 11 km. (7 mi.) south of Nazareth. The town was occupied from the Middle Bronze Age into the Middle Ages. The first mention of Shunem is in a list of cities conquered by Pharaoh Thutmose III (1490-1435 B.C.). According to the Amarna Letters, Shunem ("Shunama") was destroyed in the fourteenth century by Lab'ayu of Shechem and rebuilt by Biridiya of Megiddo. At the time of the Israelite conquest, it was a less significant town than previously. Shunem was assigned to the tribe of Issachar (Josh. 19:18). Before one battle during Saul's reign the Philistine army was encamped here, north of Israel's camp at Mt. Gilboa (1 Sam. 28:4).

Two women and possibly a third are identified as being from Shunem: Abishag the Shunammite (1 Kgs. 1:3, 15; 2:17, 21-22), the unnamed wealthy Shunammite woman who provided food for Elisha whenever the prophet passed by Shunem (2 Kgs. 4:8), and possibly the SHULAMMITE (Cant. 6:13 [MT 7:1]). After a time the second woman and her husband also provided lodging for Elisha (vv. 9-10); in return for her kindness, the prophet pledged that she would have a son (vv. 11-16). When the promised son suddenly became ill and died a few years after his birth, the woman went for Elisha, and he raised the boy from death (vv. 18-37). Later Elisha warned the woman of an approaching famine so that she left her land to stay in Philistia. Upon her return (before which the prophet and her husband had apparently died), her appeal to the king for recovery of her property was assisted by the testimony of Elisha's servant (8:1-6).

SHUNI [shōō'nī] (Heb. *šûnî*). A son of Gad and grandson of Jacob (Gen. 46:16) whose descendants were the Shunites (Heb. *haššûnî*; Num. 26:15).

SHUPHAM (Num. 26:39, KJV), **SHUPHAMITES.**
See SHEPHUPHAM.

SHUPPIM [shŭp'īm] (Heb. *šuppîm, šuppim*).
1.† One of the two sons of Ir of the tribe of Benjamin (1 Chr. 7:12). "Shuppim" and "Huppim" are probably alternate forms of "Shephupham" and "Hupham," which also appear in a Benjaminite genealogy list (Num. 26:39; cf. Gen. 46:21; 1 Chr. 8:5). Their appearance in a quite confused Manassite list (7:15) is probably the result of textual corruption.
2. A levitical gatekeeper at the west gate of the temple at the time of David (1 Chr. 26:16).

SHUR [shōōr] (Heb. *šûr* "wall").† A wilderness region in the northern part of the Sinai peninsula east of Egypt into which the Israelites went after coming out of Egypt and crossing through the Red Sea (Exod. 15:22; cf. Gen. 25:18; 1 Sam. 15:7). The same region is also called the wilderness of Etham (Num. 33:8). Shur was referred to as an indication of direction, generally meaning (for people living in Palestine) "toward Egypt" (Gen. 20:1; 1 Sam. 27:8). The "way to Shur" (Gen. 16:7) was a caravan route going southwest from Hebron and Beer-sheba and crossing the wilderness of Shur beyond the Brook of Egypt.

SHUSHAN (KJV). *See* SUSA.

SHUSHAN EDUTH [shōō'shăn ē'dəth]. *See* LILY.

SHUTHELAH [shōō'thə lə] (Heb. *šûṭelaḥ*).
1. A son of Ephraim whose descendants were the Shuthelahites (Num. 26:35-36; 1 Chr. 7:20; KJV "Shuthalhites").
2. The son of Zabad of the tribe of Ephraim (1 Chr. 7:21). He may be the same as or a descendant of **1**.

SIA [sī'ə] (Heb. *sî'ā'*), **SIAHA** [sī'ə hə] (*sî'ªhā'*). A temple servant whose descendants returned with Zerubbabel from captivity in Babylon (Ezra 2:44, "Siaha"; Neh. 7:47, "Sia").

SIBBECAI [sĭb'ə kī] (Heb. *sibbᵉkay*). A Hushathite, and one of David's "mighty men" who served as com-

mander of the eighth division of David's army and who defeated the giant Saph/Sippai (2 Sam. 21:18; KJV "Sibbechai"; 1 Chr. 11:29; 20:4; 27:11).

SIBBOLETH. *See* SHIBBOLETH.

SIBMAH [sĭb'mə] (Heb. *śibmâ*). A city located in the rural Transjordan (Num. 32:3; here called Sebam; Heb. *śᵉbām*; KJV "Shebam") that was rebuilt and occupied by the Reubenites after its conquest by Israel (v. 38; KJV "Shibmah"; Josh. 13:19). Known for its vineyards, it later came under Moabite control, and thus is mentioned in prophetic laments over Moab (Isa. 16:8-9; Jer. 48:32). Sibmah was probably located near Heshbon (cf. Num. 32:3, 37-38; Isa. 16:8), but its exact location is unknown. The site may be Qurn el-Kibsh, *ca.* 5 km. (3 mi.) southwest of Heshbon.

SIBRAIM [sĭb rā'əm] (Heb. *sibrayim*). An otherwise unknown place in Syria mentioned in Ezekiel's description of Israel's ideal boundaries (Ezek. 47:16). A location at the northern end of the Lebanon and Antilebanon ranges and the source of the Orontes river is indicated by Sibraim's description as "on the border between Damascus and Hamath."

SIBYLLINE [sĭb'ə lēn] **ORACLES.**† A collection of oracles of Jewish and Christian origin that are part of the Pseudepigrapha. "Sibyl" (Gk. *Sibylla*) may have been the name of a specific legendary Greek prophetess, but it became an international term for a type of oracular literature usually focused on predictions of wide-scale disasters, political upheavals, and, sometimes, a golden age under a great world leader. A number of collections of Sibylline oracles from different parts of the Mediterranean world and the Near East existed.

The Jewish Sibylline Oracles and their Christian interpolations and expansions date from the second century B.C. to the seventh century A.D. They exist in fourteen books with a prologue and fragments. Book 9 consists of material also found in books 1–8; book 10 is identical to book 4. About half of the material was written in Egypt. The adoption of the Sibylline literary form by Jewish writers began in the context of attempts to defend Judaism before Gentile readers by linking Judaism with what some considered to be the most ancient of Greek thought. The adoption and expansion of the Jewish books by Christian writers show the same apologetic interest in the attestation of the faith through the prediction of the faith itself by the ancient pagan prophetess. The same interest in politically-oriented eschatological thought as the Gentile non-Christian Sibylline oracles is evidenced in those written by Jews and Christians. History prior to the actual writing of the oracles is fictionally treated as future (from the standpoint of the ancient prophetess) and is divided into definite periods of ten generations or four kingdoms. Eschatology is the basis of ethical exhortation.
See APOCALYPTIC.

SICHEM (Gen. 12:6, KJV). *See* SHECHEM (PLACE).

SICKLE (Heb. *ḥermēš, maggāl*; Gk. *drépanon*). An

implement consisting of a blade attached to a short handle and used to harvest grain (Deut. 16:9; 23:25; Jer. 50:16; Mark 4:29). The earliest sickles were made of small pieces of flint set into a wooden or bone handle. The blades were later made of metal (cf. 1 Sam. 13:19-20). A sickle could symbolize judgment (Joel 3:13 [MT 4:13]; Rev. 14:14-20). *See also* AGRICULTURE.

SIDDIM [sĭd'ĭm], **VALLEY OF** (Heb. *'ēmeq haśśiddîm*). A valley where the forces of Chedorlaomer and his allies defeated the kings of Sodom, Gomorrah, Admah, Zeboiim, and Bela, aided by the bitumen pits in the valley (Gen. 14:3-4, 8-11). Siddim was situated at the southern end of the Dead Sea, probably the shallow portion of the Sea where bitumen still occasionally rises to the surface (v. 3). It may be the same as the valley of Salt (2 Sam. 8:13; 2 Kgs. 14:7) and the valley in which Sodom and Gomorrah stood (Gen. 19:24-25).

SIDON [sī'dən] (Heb. *ṣîḏôn*; Gk. *Sidōn*).† An ancient Phoenician city-state, located at modern Ṣaidā, *ca.* 36 km. (22 mi.) north of Tyre and an equal distance south of Beirut. The site has not been excavated. Located on a small hill that projects into the Mediterranean Sea, the city featured harbors on both the north and the south sides of the site, sheltered by a number of small islands. A fertile plain inland from the city supported agriculture, but, like the other Phoenician cities, the people of Sidon were dependent on sea trade for their livelihood.

Sidon is called the first-born of Canaan at Gen. 10:15 (par. 1 Chr. 1:13; KJV "Zidon"). The city was mentioned already in the Amarna Letters and in the writings of Homer. It was the first Phoenician city to sail ships on the open sea. It came under Egyptian control when the pharaohs of the Eighteenth and Nineteenth dynasties reasserted Egyptian power after ejecting the Hyksos from their land. Until the disruption of Phoenician life by the Sea Peoples from *ca.* 1200 B.C., Sidon was the principal Phoenician city. From that time Tyre became more important, but Sidon was rebuilt and nevertheless remained a significant city. In accord with the common experience of the small states of Syria and Palestine, the balance of Sidon's history was marked by invasions by and payment of tribute to a series of empires, alongside the retention of some vestiges of commercial success. Sidon was destroyed by the Assyrian Esarhaddon in 677, but re-emerged under Egyptian control at the end of the seventh century. Soon conquered by the Babylonian Nebuchadrezzar, the city again reasserted some measure of independence under the Persians. A short-lived revolt against Artaxerxes III in 351 incurred the burning of the city and the loss of thousands of Sidonian lives. Sidon surrendered to Alexander the Great in 332. The city flourished as a commercial center under the Seleucids and Romans.

Mounds of murex shells at Sidon attest to the city's participation in Phoenicia's profitable dye production industry. Evidence of other trades at Sidon points to metalworking, weaving, and, in the Hellenistic period, glassmaking. Other significant discoveries include the sarcophagi and inscriptions of sixth-century kings Tabnit and Ešmunazar II.

In the Old Testament Phoenicians in general are commonly referred to as "Sidonians" (e.g., Deut. 3:9; Judg. 10:12; KJV "Zidonians"; 1 Kgs. 5:6 [MT 20]). Both Jesus and Paul visited Sidon (Mark 7:31; Acts 27:3). Jesus compares Gentile Sidon favorably to Jewish cities of Galilee that had not responded to his preaching (Matt. 11:21-22).

SIEGE. *See* WEAPONS.

SIGN (Heb. *'ôṯ, môpēṯ*; Aram. *'āṯ*; Gk. *sēmeíon*).†

I. Old Testament

"Sign" is often used in the Old Testament to denote a visible reminder or token of the relationship between God and his people, particularly a "sign of the covenant," whether God's covenant with mankind through Noah (Gen. 9:12-13, 17) or with Abraham and his descendants (17:11). Signs of the covenant are like assurances guaranteeing agreements between humans (e.g., Josh. 2:12). Similarly, the blood of the Passover (Exod. 12:13) was a reminder to God that marked his human partners in covenant (cf. Isa. 55:13).

A sign might also be given to attest that some course of events is the outworking of God's actions on behalf of his people. Attesting signs receive the greatest emphasis in references to Israel's salvation from slavery in Egypt (e.g., Exod. 3:12; 4:1-9, 28-30; Num. 14:11; Deut. 4:34; Josh. 24:17; Neh. 9:10; Ps. 78:43; Jer. 32:20-21). Such attesting signs were also given to Gideon (Judg. 6:17-22), Saul (1 Sam. 10:1-9), and Jonathan (14:9-13) as God used these individuals for Israel's deliverance. The fulfillment of a disastrous set of events might, on the other hand, be a sign that God's judgment was being executed on his people (Deut. 28:45-46; 1 Sam. 2:34; 1 Kgs. 13:3, 5; Jer. 44:29-30; Ezek. 14:6-8). Signs as memorials of God's saving acts were sometimes set up by the people themselves (Josh. 4:4-7). In the book of Daniel, Gentile rulers refer to miraclous rescues of Jews as signs performed by God (Dan. 4:2-3 [MT 3:32-33]; 6:27 [MT 28]).

It was expected that prophets would give miraculous signs to attest that their words were from God (Deut. 13:1-2). Indeed, such attesting signs might have little apparent connection with the word from God itself (Isa. 7:14-17; 38:7-8). But more often prophetic "signs" were closely related to the word, especially when the prophet presented himself or his actions as a sign (8:18; 20:3-4; Ezek. 4–5; 12:3-16; 24:24, 27).

Repeated religious observances could also be signs. The use of phylacteries was to be a reminder of God's past saving actions (Exod. 13:9; Deut. 6:8; 11:18). The observance of the Sabbath was to be a sign of God's relationship with his people and with all of creation (Exod. 31:12-17; Ezek. 20:12, 20). A sign might also be given as a reminder of the people's violation of one of the provisions of the covenant, so that the violation would not repeated (Num. 16:36-40 [MT 17:1-5]; 17:10 [MT 25]).

The function of the sun, moon, and stars as "signs" (Gen. 1:14) was apparently fulfilled through their indicating periods of time. The workings of nature were viewed as signs of God's sovereignty just as was the deliverance he has accomplished for his people (Ps. 65:8 [MT 9]).

II. New Testament

"Sign" is a common term for the miracles performed by Jesus and others within the Church. Its use presupposes the idea that miracles can give attestation that a message is from God (Luke 23:8; John 2:18; 6:30; Acts 2:22; 4:16, 21-22; 8:6; 1 Cor. 1:22; 14:22). But Jesus refused to provide such attesting signs when they were demanded (Matt. 12:38-40; 16:1, 4; Mark 8:11-12; but cf. Matt. 11:2-5). In so doing he showed an awareness of the danger of reliance on such attestation; he expected the forces of evil also to perform miracles as false "signs" (Matt. 24:24; cf. 2 Thess. 2:9-10; Rev. 13:13-14; 19:20). Luke's gospel speaks particularly of Jesus himself as a "sign," i.e., like the prophets one whose very person points to God's actions (Luke 2:34; 11:30).

Miraculous "signs" as a source of faith play an important part in the gospel of John (cf. John 20:30). The positive and correct reaction of the people to Jesus' signs is recorded (6:2, 14; 7:31; 10:41-42; 12:18-19). But even in John, Jesus retains a skeptical assessment of faith induced by signs (2:23-25; 4:48) and attempts to point beyond the signs to the demands and promises of his message (3:2-3; 6:26-27, 35-40).

On eschatological signs (Matt. 24:3 par.; Luke 21:11, 25) see ESCHATOLOGY III. A.

SIGNET. See SEAL, SIGNET.

SIHON [sī'hŏn] (Heb. *sîhôn, sîhôn*). King of an Amorite kingdom in Transjordan with its capital at Heshbon who was defeated by the Israelites before their entry into Canaan. Sihon had conquered the territory of the king of Moab as far as the Arnon river (Num. 21:26-30) and was allied with various Midianite princes prior to his defeat (Josh. 13:21). The Israelites requested permission from Sihon to travel through his territory, but he refused permission and marched against them with his army (Num. 21:21-23; Deut. 2:26-32; Judg. 11:19-20). After Sihon's defeat at Jahaz his territory was assigned to the tribes of Reuben and Gad (Num. 32:33). Heshbon was much later referred to as "the house of Sihon" in an oracle against Moab (Jer. 48:45).

SIHOR (KJV). See SHIHOR.

SILAS [sī'ləs] (Gk. *Silas, Silouanos*). A man from the Jerusalem church who became a coworker and traveling companion of Paul. The Greek form of the name used in Acts, *Silas*, derives from Aram. *šeʾîlāʾ*. Gk. *Silouanos*, used in the letters of Peter and Paul, represents Lat. *Silvanus*.

Silas and Judas Barsabbas were "leading men among the brethren" chosen to represent the Jerusalem church in the delivery of a letter from that church's leaders to the Gentile Christians of Antioch (Acts 15:22, 27). These two representatives of Jerusalem were accompanied by Paul and Barnabas, who had come to Je-

rusalem as representatives, in effect, of the Antiochenes and other Gentile Christians. Judas and Silas remained for a short time in Antioch and then returned to Jerusalem (vv. 32-33; v. 34 is a late addition). Shortly after this, Barnabas and Paul had a disagreement that led to their parting company. Silas joined Paul in Barnabas' place, and the two went into Syria and Asia Minor (vv. 36-41). They were the leading members of a group that sometimes included Luke (represented by the first person pronoun at, e.g., 16:10), Timothy, and perhaps a number of others. Silas was, like Paul, a Roman citizen (vv. 37-38).

Silas was part of Paul's company through the second missionary journey at least as far as Corinth, where he is last mentioned in the Acts narrative (18:5). It was probably from Corinth that the two letters from "Paul, Silvanus [Silas], and Timothy" to the church in Thessalonica were written (1 Thess. 1:1; 2 Thess. 1:1); how much of a role Silas and Timothy had in the composition of the two letters has received broadly varying estimates. While at Corinth the three men worked together in the founding of the church there (2 Cor. 1:19).

Paul returned to Antioch by way of Ephesus and Caesarea (Acts 18:18-22), but where Silas went from Corinth is not known for certain. The only possible indication of his later activities is 1 Pet. 5:12: "Through Silvanus . . . I have written briefly to you. . . ." This passage has been interpreted in different ways. Silas had perhaps become a leader among the Christians of Asia Minor to whom the letter was addressed (1:1). On the other hand, he may have been Peter's scribe or the one sent to deliver the letter. If, however, he had a substantial role in the composition of the letter, the Pauline features of the letter may be thereby explained.

SILK. * Silk cultivation, spinning, and weaving began in China and spread to the West only slowly. Raw silk was imported into western Asia by *ca.* the fifth century B.C. (*Coa vestis,* a form of silk derived from cocoons other than those of the true mulberry silkworm, apparently had been produced on the Greek island of Cos for some centuries.) Whether Heb. *mᵉšî* (Ezek. 16:10, 13) is, as it has been traditionally translated, "silk" is disputed; a more general translation, such as "fine material," is better. The KJV reads "silk" at Prov. 31:22 for *šēš,* which is normally translated "fine linen." The only certain biblical reference to silk is at Rev. 18:12 (Gk. *serikón*), where it is listed among the costly goods brought by merchants to "Babylon," i.e., Rome.

SILLA [sīl'ə] (Heb. *sillāʾ*). Perhaps a landmark or section of Jerusalem, mentioned in connection with the house of MILLO 3 (2 Kgs. 12:20).

SILOAM [sī lō'əm] (Gk. *Silōam;* from Heb. *šilōaḥ* [Siloah], "sent out"). A pool or reservoir in Jerusalem, part of a complex of water works that carried water from the Gihon spring, located on the eastern slope of the Ophel ridge above the Kidron valley, into Jerusalem.

Some underground means of obtaining water from

Gihon was already in use before David took the city (2 Sam. 5:8). By the reign of Ahaz (*ca.* 735-715 B.C.) water was being collected from Gihon in a reservoir hewn out of rock. This was the "upper pool" (2 Kgs. 18:17; Isa. 7:3), also possibly the "old pool" (22:11). The gently flowing waters of some part of this water works is a metaphor for Ahaz' policy of loyalty to Assyria at 8:6 ("Shiloah"; cf. 7:1-9).

When Sennacherib's Assyrian army marched into Judah in 701, King Hezekiah ordered all springs outside the city walls stopped up to deny water to the invaders (2 Chr. 32:2-4) and prepared for a siege by diverting the water of Gihon through an underground tunnel to a point west of the Ophel ridge (the city of David) inside the city walls (2 Kgs. 20:20; 2 Chr. 32:30). This tunnel emptied into the pool of Siloam, located on the southwestern slope of Ophel.

Hezekiah's tunnel was 535 m. (585 yd.) long and was S-shaped, because of either inadequate engineering or hard rock that impeded the laborers. An inscription found on the wall at the center of the tunnel recounts how two teams of workers bored toward each other through the stone until they heard each others' voices and broke through to complete the tunnel (*ANET,* p. 321).

At the time of Nehemiah's rebuilding of the city the pool of Siloam or some other reservoir in the same water system was adjacent to a city wall (Neh. 3:15; Heb. *šelaḥ*; RSV "Shelah"; KJV "Siloah"; NIV "Siloam"; JB "conduit"; NJV "irrigation pool").

Jesus said that the unrepentant would perish as surely as had eighteen who died when "the tower in Siloam" fell on them (Luke 13:4). The location of this tower is unknown, but it was probably part of the fortifications of Jerusalem in the area of the pool of Siloam. Jesus healed a blind man by applying a paste of his saliva and mud to the man's eyes and telling him to wash them in the pool of Siloam (John 9:6-11).

SILVANUS. *See* SILAS.

SILVER (Heb. *kesep*; Aram. *kᵉsap*; Gk. *árgyros, argýrion*).* Silver was the metal most commonly used for exchange in Old Testament times (e.g., Gen. 23:16). It was also used for jewelry (Exod. 12:35) and for functional objects where a wealthy appearance was possible and desired, as in palaces and temples (e.g., Gen. 44:2; 2 Kgs. 12:13 [MT 14]). It had been used as a medium of exchange and a luxury substance from before 4000 B.C. Part of Abraham's wealth was in the form of silver (Gen. 13:2). Silver used in the ancient Near East was obtained almost entirely from Asia Minor until the first millennium B.C., during which it became more plentiful and less valuable relative to gold (cf. 1 Kgs. 10:21, 27). *See* MONEY.

SIMEON [sĭm'ĭ ən] (Heb. *šimʿôn* "[God] has heard"; Gk. *Symeōn*).

1. The second son of Jacob and Leah, progenitor of one of Israel's twelve tribes.

Simeon and his brother Levi attacked and killed all the male inhabitants of Shechem to avenge the rape of their sister Dinah (Gen. 34:25-26). Later, when the sons of Jacob sought food in Egypt, Joseph retained

Simeon as security while the others returned to Canaan for their youngest brother (42:24, 36; 43:23). When Jacob arrived in Egypt with his household, Simeon had six sons (46:10; Exod. 6:15); some lists name only five sons of Simeon (Num. 26:12-14; 1 Chr. 4:24). From one census to the next in the wilderness the number of fighting men among the Simeonites was reduced from 59,300 to 22,000 (Num. 1:22-23; 2:12-13; 26:12-14). In Moses' blessing of the tribes (Deut. 33) Simeon is not even mentioned, though the tribe does appear in a list at 27:12-13.

In his blessing on his sons, Jacob predicted that both Simeon's and Levi's descendants would be dispersed among the rest of Israel (Gen. 49:5-7). The Levites retained their tribal identity in the land of Canaan through their role in the worship of God, but the Simeonites ultimately lost their distinctiveness as a tribe. A number of cities in Canaan were assigned to Simeon, but Simeon's territory was contained within the southern part of that assigned to Judah (Josh. 19:1-9; cf. 15:26-32; Judg. 1:3). A Simeonite loyalty to Judah may be reflected in the substantial number of Simeonite troops who joined David at Hebron (1 Chr. 12:25). During David's reign the concept of a territory of Simeon was absent altogether, perhaps because of administrative changes (4:31).

During later generations of the monarchic period, Simeonites did continue to be a recognizable group (2 Chr. 15:9; 34:6). During the reign of Hezekiah, Simeonites took pasture lands by force from non-Israelites both to the west and to the southeast or south of their original territory (1 Chr. 4:34-43).

An eschatological restoration of the existence of the tribe of Simeon is recorded at Ezek. 48:24-25, 33; Rev. 7:7.

2. The grandfather of Mattathias **1** (1 Macc. 2:1).

3. Simon Maccabeus, a son of Mattathias **1** and elder brother of Judas Maccabeus (1 Macc. 2:65). *See* SIMON 2.

4. A devout resident of Jerusalem to whom the Holy Spirit had revealed that he would not die before seeing the Messiah. When Jesus was presented in the temple, Simeon greeted the child as the Savior, blessed Mary and Joseph, and predicted events concerning Jesus and Mary (Luke 2:25-35). *See* NUNC DIMITTIS.

5. An ancestor of Jesus who lived between the time of David and that of the Exile (Luke 3:30).

6. (Acts 13:1, KJV). *See* SYMEON 1.

7. The Hebrew name for Simon Peter (KJV, Acts 15:14). *See* SIMON 5; SYMEON 2.

8. *See* BAR KOCHBA.

SIMHAT TORAH [sĭm'hät tôr'ə] (Heb. *śimḥaṯ tôrâ* "rejoicing in the Torah"). A Jewish celebration of God's giving of the law observed after the close of the feast of Sukkoth on the twenty-third of Tishri. The final passage of the yearly cycle of Torah readings and the first passage that begins the cycle again are read in synagogues. The Torah scrolls are carried in processions through the synagogues, often accompanied by dancing.

SIMON [sī'mən] (Gk. *Simōn*; from Heb. *šimʿôn* "[God] has heard").

1. Simon II, a high priest known for his work in the restoration of the temple and for his elaborate worship services (Sir. 50:1-21). The son of Onias II and father of Onias III and Jason, Simon was high priest when Judea came under Seleucid control (200 B.C.).

2. Simon Maccabeus, a son of Mattathias and brother of Judas Maccabeus (1 Macc. 2:3); called "Simeon" at v. 65. Simon was the second Hasmonean high priest (after his brother Jonathan) and obtained the complete independence of Judea from the Seleucid Empire. *See* MACCABEES.

3. An overseer of the temple who had a disagreement with Onias III the high priest and then informed officials of the Seleucid government of private funds held in the temple treasury in Jerusalem (2 Macc. 3:4-6). Only a "manifestation" from God prevented the removal of these funds by the Seleucid emissary who had been sent to Jerusalem for that purpose (vv. 7-40). Simon then tried to attach to subordinates blame for what he himself had done to Onias (4:1-6).

4. One of Jesus' brothers (Matt. 13:55; Mark 6:3).

5. A form of the Hebrew name for the apostle PETER (e.g., Matt. 16:17).

6. A leper who lived in Bethany at whose home Jesus was anointed by a woman (Matt. 26:6-14 par. Mark 14:3-9). If, as is probable, this incident is the same as the one related at John 12:1-8, then the woman was Mary of Bethany and Simon was a relative of Mary, Martha, and Lazarus, perhaps their father.

7. A man from Cyrene in northern Africa who was forced to carry Jesus' cross to Golgotha (Mark 15:21). It is noted that he was the father of Alexander and Rufus, perhaps men known in the early Church (cf. Rom. 16:13).

8. † One of the twelve disciples/apostles of Jesus. He is called "the Zealot" (Luke 6:15; Acts 1:13; KJV "Zelotes") or "the Cananaean" (Matt. 10:4; Mark 3:18; KJV "Canaanite"), an appellative based on Heb. and Aram. *qannā'* "zealous." "Zeal" was a technical term widely used in Judaism of the Hellenistic period for a desire to preserve the purity of Judaism and the Jewish land, temple, and people—even at the cost of suffering or inflicting death. Simon has often been identified as a member of the "Zealot" party active at the time of Jewish revolt of A.D. 66-70, but it would be more accurate to say that he represented the form of Jewish piety that was later galvanized into revolt and that provided the pattern for those who called themselves "Zealots" at the time of the revolt.

9. A Pharisee in whose home Jesus attended a dinner and was anointed by another visitor (Luke 7:36-50).

10. Simon Iscariot, the father of Judas Iscariot (John 6:71; 13:2).

11. Simon Magus, a magician in Samaria. When Philip preached the gospel and performed miracles in Samaria, Simon was one of those who responded. Later, however, he offered the apostles money so he might be able to bestow the Holy Spirit on others as they had done. For this Peter chastised Simon severely (Acts 8:9-24). It is likely that Simon's interest was simply that of a magician who recognized a power greater than his and sought to master it as he had other magical arts.

In later writings, particularly those of Justin Martyr and Irenaeus, Simon is represented as the father of the Gnostic heresies. The pseudo-Clementine literature and the Acts of Peter describe the legendary conflicts between Peter and Simon.

12. A tanner in Joppa in whose home Peter lodged (Acts 9:43 – 10:32).

13. *See* BAR KOCHBA.

SIMPLICITY. In the Old Testament Heb. *petî* "deceived, naive" and related words are used, mainly in Proverbs, to denote the ignorance of the young and the uneducated. The main points conveyed are the dangers into which such ignorance can lead and from which wisdom can lead away (e.g., Job 5:2; KJV "silly"; Prov. 1:4, 32; 8:5; 9:4, 6; 14:15; 22:3). The "simple" person is not merely disparaged in Proverbs; this Wisdom collection also recognizes that the untaught are able to draw lessons merely by observing the punishment of another (19:25; 21:11). The Psalms refer to the law of God as instruction for the simple (Ps. 19:7 [MT 8]; 119:130) and note God's protection of the simple (116:6).

SIMRI (1 Chr. 26:10, KJV). *See* SHIMRI **3.**

SIN. † In essence, the failure or refusal of human beings to live the life intended for them by God their creator. The biblical terminology for sin as an act (and its commission) as well as a human condition is extensive. Among the Old Testament words are Heb. *ḥāṭā'* (verb) "miss the mark, fail" and related words, *'ābar* "pass beyond, transgress" and related words, *'āwōn* "iniquity, perversion," *pāša'* "revolt, transgress" and related words, *šāgag* and *šāgâ* "err, go astray," *tā'â* "err, wander," *ra'* "evil," and *rāšā'* "wicked, impious." New Testament terminology includes Gk. *hamartía* (noun) and related words, *ponērós* "evil," *adikía* "injustice, unrighteousness" and related words, *parábasis* "transgress" and related words, and *anomía* "lawlessness."

I. Nature of Sin

"Sin" as a characteristic of human beings is manifested in the committing of "sins," individual acts of rebellion against God and against expressions of his intentions for humanity. While the Bible can refer to sin in the abstract, it more often cites concrete acts (sins) in collections of commandments against specific sins (as in the law codes of the Pentateuch), narratives of specific sins (which occupy much of the narrative material of the Old Testament), and lists of sins (e.g., Mark 7:21-22; Gal. 5:19-21).

Sin is not to be identified simply with violation of the moral standards of society, though individual sins, as violations of the divine intention for human interactions, are violations of human moral standards as well. Rather, sin in its basic sense is always ultimately against God himself rather than against mankind or any human person (Ps. 51:4 [MT 6]). This is made clear in the resistance of the pentateuchal laws to any thorough distinction between civil lawbreaking, ritual infractions, and moral wrongs. The society presented with these laws was not pluralistic—the people at worship and the people engaging in business or other relationships were not ultimately distinguishable. More importantly, civil, ritual, and moral commands proceeded equally from the will of the one God. An important basis of the ritual regulations was the understanding of God's holiness as a danger that necessitates appropriate precautions for any who would approach him (cf. Exod. 19:22; 2 Sam. 6:6-7). This view of God's holiness functioned in relation to the understanding of all sins, not just ritual infractions.

II. Extent of Sin

The Bible invariably regards sin as both universal and pervasive. No individual human being is free from sin (except Christ; Heb. 4:15; 1 Pet. 2:22), and no human behavior or action is free from the effects of sin.

The universality of sin is derived as a sober conclusion from examination of human life (Prov. 20:6, 9; Eccl. 7:20), including observation ascribed to God himself (Gen. 6:5; Ps. 14:2-3) and to Christ (Matt. 7:11). This human condition is regarded to begin with the birth of each individual (Ps. 51:5 [MT 7]; cf. Gen. 8:21). Job 15:14 suggests that it is impossible for a person not to sin. Paul and the author of 1 John regard the universality of sin as a fundamental factor in the understanding of God's redemption of mankind in Christ (Rom. 3:23 [cf. vv. 10-20]; 1 John 1:8–2:2).

The pervasive effects of sin on human behavior make it such that even acts intended to be righteous are affected by sin (Isa. 64:6 [MT 5]). Even persons who keep all of God's commandments are no more than "unworthy servants" (Luke 17:10) because of the presence of sin. Underlying this inability of humanity at its best to be free from sin is the possibility of human self-deception (Jer. 17:9).

III. Origin and Effects

Because sin is so great in its effects on humanity, the question naturally arises of the origin of sin. The narrative of the sin of Adam and Eve in the garden (Gen. 3) is an account of the first sin and its effects, but chs. 3–11 can be considered together as an account of the origin, pervasiveness, and effects of sin.

The role of the serpent as a tempter (identified with Satan at Rev. 20:2) is prominent in Gen. 3, but the emphasis in this chapter is on the working and results of human envy and distrust of God. After this envy and distrust are suggested by the serpent (vv. 1-5), the beauty of what is forbidden completes the temptation (v. 6). The sin is very clearly an act of rebellion against a specific injunction of God (2:17) and, because of the content of the temptation, against God himself. How it was possible for the serpent's temptation to be effective—i.e., what human responsiveness to the temptation arises from or is based on—is not a question with which Gen. 3 is concerned. (Paul considers deception to be a factor here; 2 Cor. 11:3; 1 Tim. 2:14.) Nor is the origin of the serpent's behavior as tempter explored.

The primary lessons of the account of the fall are that, though sin is as old as mankind, it arises not from the way in which mankind was created, but from the way in which mankind exercises free will, and that sin is not simply an act, but begins with thought—specifically, thought that denies the truth of what God

says and that seeks some gain for the human creature that has not been provided by God.

The larger part of Gen. 3 (vv. 8-24) is concerned with the effects of the sin. The centrality of this concern continues in the succeeding chapters as they build up a picture of the human situation as it existed prior to the commencement of God's redemption and blessing of humanity with the call of Abraham (ch. 12). The progressive growth of sin is matched by the progressive increase of the effects of sin. These effects come about partly as God's responses to sin by which he controls the extent of the rebellion against him. The first sin leads to pain in childbirth, male dominance, the toilsomeness of work, and death (3:16-19; cf. 6:3). The first murderer (4:1-8) becomes the first fugitive (vv. 12-16) and the progenitor of a vengeful and violent people (vv. 17-24). The growth of human evil leads God to destroy most of life on earth (6:5-7), and the restoration of human life leads only to a new collective act of hubris, which brings about the disintegration of the unified human society (11:1-9).

In accordance with Genesis, Paul understood the first sin committed by "one man" (Adam) as that which led to all further sins, which in turn led to the death of each person (Rom. 5:12 [cf. v. 19]; 6:21, 23). He also describes the growth of sin and of God's judging responses to sin in terms of Gentile practices that Jews found repulsive (1:18-32), and refers to the mastery that sin has over human beings (6:15).

IV. Redemptive Response

The fundamental effect of sin is alienation between God and the person or society that sins (Isa. 59:2). For this reason, reconciliation between God and humanity is the heart of what is accomplished in God's salvation of mankind. Because God is the one against whom sin is directed, he must also be—and is—the one to respond by initiating the process of reconciliation. Indeed, only God can make provision for reconciliation, but a human response to God's actions toward reconciliation is required. This is true with regard to the sacrificial system of the Old Testament as well as to human faith in Christ that answers to the reconciliation God has brought about through Christ.

Part of the process of God's redemptive response and defeat of sin is his taking on the responsibility of guaranteeing that his people will live no longer in sinful patterns but will live, rather, according to his will (Jer. 31:33-34; Ezek. 11:19-20; 36:26-27).

The eschaton will bring the final defeat of sin. Sinners who do not participate in God's redemption will be judged and punished, and their sinfulness will be excluded from the heavenly Jerusalem (Rev. 21:8). God's people will experience a complete release from the sin that has until then remained in their lives (1 John 3:2).

See EVIL; FALL, THE; UNFORGIVABLE SIN.

Bibliography. G. C. Berkouwer, *Sin* (Grand Rapids: 1971); H. E. Brunner, *Man in Revolt* (Philadelphia: 1947); G. Quell, *et al.,* "ἁμαρτάνω," *TDNT* 1 (1964): 267-316.

SIN [sĭn] (Heb. *sîn*) (**PLACE**).
   1. A wilderness region near Mt. Sinai through which

the Israelites traveled after their deliverance from Egypt. As with other locations associated with Israel's journeys toward Canaan from Egypt, the wilderness of Sin cannot be identified with any exactness. Furthermore, the description of its location at Exod. 16:1 as "between Elim and Sinai" is difficult to reconcile with its placement in the itinerary at Num. 33:11-12. It was at the wilderness of Sin that manna was first given, in response to the people's murmuring against Moses and Aaron (Exod. 16). The wilderness of Sin is to be distinguished from the wilderness of Zin, which the Israelites entered later (Num. 33:36).

2. (Ezek. 30:15-16, KJV). *See* PELUSIUM.

SIN OFFERING (Heb. *ḥaṭṭāʾt*). A form of animal sacrifice (Lev. 4:1–5:13; 6:24-30 [MT 17-23]). If the sin of the people as a whole or of the high priest occasioned the sacrifice, the flesh of the animal was to be burned not on the altar but outside the temple or tabernacle area. On other occasions it was to be eaten by the priests. The blood of a sin offering was sprinkled before the veil of the inner sanctuary, placed on the horns of the altar of incense, and poured out before the burnt offering altar or merely poured out before the burnt offering altar, depending again on whose sin occasioned the sacrifice. The fat of the sacrificial animal was burned on the altar. If the person offering the sacrifice was extremely poor, a tenth of an ephah of fine flour could be substituted for the more costly animal.

Sin offerings were made in a variety of situations, some of which are listed at 5:1-4. They were offered when priests were ordained (Exod. 29:14), at the time of the New Moon (Num. 28:15), and on annual feast days (e.g., v. 22; 29:5, 11, 16).

See SACRIFICES AND OFFERINGS.

SINAI [sī'nī] (Heb. *sînay*; Gk. *Seina, Sina*), **MOUNT.**† A mountain of epochal importance in Israelite religion, also called Horeb. At Mt. Sinai Moses received his call from God (Exod. 3:1) and the people of Israel received the law and the covenant (chs. 19–20). Mt. Sinai was again a place of theophany for Elijah (1 Kgs. 19:8) and became a theological anchor for Israelite faith (Judg. 5:5; Neh. 9:13; Ps. 68:8, 17 [MT 9, 18]). At Acts 7:30, 38 Stephen refers to the experiences of Moses and Israel at Sinai. At Gal. 4:24-31 Paul finds in "Sinai" a symbol of the legal righteousness he opposes (cf. Heb. 12:18-29).

The location of Sinai has proven difficult since no corroborating archaeological evidence has been found for Israel's wilderness wanderings. Little record of the Late Bronze Age survives in the Sinai peninsula except for some Egyptian remains along the northern coastal strip. The Old Testament names a number of places near Sinai (e.g., Num. 33:14-17) that suggest that the region was well known in antiquity, but the location of these places cannot be determined with confidence. Such difficulties have led to a number of hypotheses for Sinai's location locating it generally east of the Gulf of Aqaba, in the northern part of the Sinai peninsula, or in the southern part of the peninsula.

Some scholars interpret Exod. 19:16-19 as referring to a volcanic eruption. Since in the general area

in which Sinai must be sought volcanoes are found only in northwest Arabia, Mt. Sinai has also been sought east of Aqaba. But this is unlikely, since the Old Testament often uses such natural imagery to depict the awesomeness of God's presence, particularly in theophanies. The presence of Midianites at Sinai (3:1) proves little since these wandering nomads might well have been anywhere in the general area.

Others have noted Israel's contact with the Amalekites in the vicinity of Kadesh-barnea (Num. 14:43) and have concluded that Moses took a northerly route through the Wilderness of Shur (Exod. 15:22). The presence of quails from the sea (Num. 11:31) and the availability of oasis water along the Mediterranean coast have also been taken as support for a route across the northern part of the Sinai peninsula. However, Sinai is clearly distant from Kadesh (33:16-36; Deut. 1:19), and it took the people three months to reach the mountain from Egypt (Exod. 19:1-2).

Since the fourth century A.D., tradition has located Mt. Sinai in the southern part of the Sinai peninsula. Because of this, numerous monastic centers were located in southern Sinai in the Byzantine era. Mt. Sinai was specifically identified with Jebel Mûsâ (the "mount of Moses"), a prominent mountain surrounded by the terrain required in Exodus (a broad plain for the major Israelite camp, 19:1-2; Num. 33:15). Jebel Mûsâ reaches a height of 2285 m. (7500 ft.) and is in a range of mountains with peaks as high as nearly 2700 m. (8900 ft.). Egyptian copper mines were nearby, which would explain why Jethro is called a "Kenite" (i.e., "smith"; Judg. 1:16): he may have used the ore in his trade.

If the southern location of Sinai is correct, Moses led the Iraelites a considerable distance through the peninsula's most difficult wilderness (cf. Deut. 8:15, where the land is described as "great and terrible"). In A.D. 527 Justinian built the present monastery with its high protective wall that in the eleventh century became known as St. Catherine's Monastery; this monastery continues to preserve extraordinary mosaics, icons, and a manuscript library.

SINEW OF THE HIP. When Jacob wrestled with God, who had appeared to him in human form by the Jabbok river, God defeated Jacob by touching the hollow of Jacob's thigh in such a way that the thigh was put out of joint (Gen. 32:25 [MT 26]). This account is understood to be the origin of a custom in Israel of not eating "the sinew of the hip which is upon the hollow of the thigh" (Heb. *gîd hannāšeh ʾašer ʿal-kap hayyārēk*) of animals (v. 32 [MT 33]). This prohibition was developed in the Mishnah (*Hullin* 7), and is still preserved among observant Jews by the removal of the sciatic nerve during slaughtering.

SINIM (Isa. 49:12, KJV, NIV). *See* SYENE.

SINITES [sīn'īts] (Heb. *sînî*).† One of the Canaanite peoples (Gen. 10:17; 1 Chr. 1:15). Early historians associated the Sinites with the town Sinnu or other sites in Lebanon or with ancient Siyyān (Akk. *Sianu*) in northern Phoenicia, located near the modern village of Siyānū, a short distance inland from Jablah, Syria.

SION.

1. (Deut. 4:48, KJV). *See* SIRION.
2. (Ps. 65:1; NT, KJV). *See* ZION.

SIPHMOTH [sĭf′mŏth] (Heb. *śipmôṯ*). A town in southern Judah to whose inhabitants David sent part of the booty taken from the Amalekites (1 Sam. 30:28). The location of Siphmoth is unknown. Zabdi "the Shiphmite," David's vineyard overseer (1 Chr. 27:27), may have been from Siphmoth.

SIPPAI [sĭp′ī] (Heb. *sippay*). A giant who fought for the Philistines and was defeated by Sibbecai the Hushathite (1 Chr. 20:4). At 2 Sam. 21:18 Sippai is called Saph.

SIRACH [sīr′ăk, sī′rək], **WISDOM OF JESUS THE SON OF.**† The oldest book of the Apocrypha, known in Hebrew as the Wisdom of Jesus (Joshua) ben Sira. Although not included in the Hebrew canon of the Bible, the book remained in use in Judaism until the Middle Ages. By the third century A.D. it was known in the Latin church as Ecclesiasticus ("The Church's Book"), probably because it was regarded as the most important of the deuterocanonical writings. The book is a major source for understanding the Jewish wisdom tradition of the Hellenistic Age. Its identification of the figure of Wisdom, the personification of the divine activity and summons, with the law of Moses (Sir. 24) was an important part of the basis of the development of wisdom christology in the early Church and is significant in understanding the development of Torah as the central symbol of Judaism.

I. Author and Date

Sirach is the only book of the Apocrypha whose author is known (50:27). Joshua ben Sira (Jesus the son of Sirach) was a scribe and sage in Jerusalem who conducted an academy (Heb. *bêṯ miḏrāš,* the first occurrence of the term later used of the rabbinical school; 51:23) where he instructed young men on ethical and religious topics. His career may be mirrored in his description of the office of the scribe (38:24–39:11). On this basis and from other passages the author is seen as a person of independent means (38:24) who traveled widely in search of wisdom (34:11; 39:4; 51:13-22), enduring many life-threatening dangers (34:12). He devoted himself and the training of his students to the study of the law of Moses (39:1) and to the cultivation of those public virtues necessary for eminence in public affairs (38:33; 39:1-4). He clearly sets off the scribal profession from other honorable professions (38:24-31). The description of the scribe concludes by noting the praise and honored memory that will be won by the faithful scribe (39:6-11); this suggests that the author saw his own position as similar to those offices that have been filled by Israel's heroes of piety from antiquity to the present, memorialized in the author's composition in praise of them (chs. 44–50). The author regards himself as the last of a long line of teachers (33:16-18).

The book was probably written *ca.* 180 B.C. Since the author gives no evidence of the crisis that led to Antiochus III Epiphanes' deposition of Onias III, the legitimate high priest of the Zadokite line (2 Macc. 3–4), it is unlikely that the book was composed after 175. In his hymn in praise of the heroes of piety, Ben Sira closes with a eulogy for the high priest Simon (i.e., Simon II, son of Onias II; Sir. 50:1-24), who appears to have died only recently. If this is correct, the book could not have been written prior to 198 (the approximate date of the death of Simon II).

II. Text and Translations

Shortly after 132 B.C. the grandson of Ben Sira translated the book from Hebrew into Greek at Alexandria (Prologue). The complete version of the Wisdom of Jesus Sirach is extant in the Greek translation of the LXX (Gk. *Sophia Sirach* or *Seirach*). In 1896-1900 almost two-thirds of the Hebrew text was recovered in four medieval manuscripts found in the genizah (storeroom) of a synagogue in Cairo. These were supplemented by a fifth manuscript published in 1931 and a few leaves identified at Cambridge in 1958 and 1960. In 1964 excavations at Masada yielded twenty-six leather fragments dating from the early first century B.C. (only about a century after the composition of the book) containing portions of 39:27–44:17. In addition to these fragments, portions of ch. 6 have been found on a fragment from Cave 2 at Qumran, and parts of the acrostic poem with which the book closes (51:13-20, 30) are in a first-century A.D. psalter from Qumran (11QPs*a*). The Masada and Qumran manuscripts make it probable that the Hebrew fragments from Cairo do not represent, as had been commonly thought, a medieval retranslation from Syriac.

III. Style and Contents

The style of Ben Sira's didactic verse is similar to that of the book of Proverbs. Most of the book is composed of couplets of balanced lines in synonymous, antithetic, or synthetic parallelism. Unlike the composer of Prov. 10:1–22:16, Ben Sira does not, however, present his epigrams as independent sayings, but connects them with verses on the same theme to form short poetic essays. A wide variety of subjects are taken up seemingly without regard for their arrangement. Topics include the fear of God, humility, filial piety, care for the poor (Sir. 1:22–4:10), friendship and personal associations (4:11–10:29), riches and dealings with the powerful (10:30–14:19), freedom of choice and God's kindness toward his creatures (14:20–18:26), the way of the wise and the way of sinners (18:27–23:27), advice on wives and daughters (25:16–26:27; cf. 42:9-11), the dishonesty of merchants, forgiveness, lending, the avoidance of violence and strife (26:29–29:28), parental discipline, bodily health, giving and attending banquets (30:1–32:13), and suffering and death (40:1–41:13). The author's concerns are not divorced from the religion of Israel: he discourses on the relationship of ritual and ethical acts and offers a prayer for the deliverance of his people from Gentile oppressors (34:18–36:17).

The book falls into two major divisions, chs. 1–23 and 24–50, each beginning with a poem in praise of Wisdom. Some scholars hold that the two divisions were issued separately, since at 24:30-34 the author refers to a renewal of the prophetic spirit that inspired a further outpouring of teaching. A minor division comes with the end of the didactic essays at 42:14 and the beginning of a series of longer poems—a hymn of praise to God for his works in nature (42:15–43:33), a poem praising past heroes of piety that closes with a eulogy to the high priest Simon (44:1–50:24), a psalm of deliverance from affliction (51:1-12), and a closing acrostic poem recounting Sirach's youthful search for wisdom and his invitation to the untaught to attend his school (vv. 13-30).

IV. Theological and Cultural Concerns

The Wisdom of Jesus the Son of Sirach occupies a central place in recent attempts to trace the continuity and development of Israelite and early Jewish wisdom language and concepts in the Hellenistic period. The book stands in an Old Testament intellectual tradition that transmitted proverbial wisdom and reflected on its own assumptions about a divine ordering of the world and human affairs. Indications of continuity with this tradition are present in the literary forms, in the personification of Wisdom, in the traditional themes of creation and the fear of God, and in the questions of theodicy and the limits of human wisdom to grasp the divine ordering of the world.

The author has made his own contributions to this intellectual tradition (cf. 33:16-18). On issues of theodicy, Ben Sira repeatedly has recourse to the original intent of the Creator, the polarity of things created, and the functions assigned to them from the beginning (15:11-20; 16:6–18:14; 33:7-15; 39:16-35). He acknowledges that all humanity shares the burden of fear of death, but underscores the greater anxiety of the wicked in the face of life's troubles (40:1-17; 41:1-13). While he acknowledges the limits of human understanding (3:21-24), he affirms the availability of wisdom in contrast to Job and Ecclesiastes. Not only has God poured out wisdom on all his works in creation (1:1-10), but Wisdom has also come to dwell preeminently in Israel, in its temple cult and in the "book of the covenant," the law of Moses (24:1-29). Thus Wisdom, the primordial creation and delight of the Creator (Prov. 8:22-31), is no longer inaccessible to the human quest (cf. Job 28), nor is it available only to visionaries who penetrate the heavenly spheres (cf. 1 En. 42). Though not exhausted in Torah and temple, wisdom is supremely manifest in the religious culture and institutions of Second Temple Judaism.

The international tradition of empirical prudential wisdom has come to be linked with the national and religious institutions of early Judaism. The sage who transmits wise counsel on the basis of general human experience, the priest who administers the cult and renders judgment, and the scribe who studies and offers instruction in the revelation of the Mosaic law come together in the Wisdom of Jesus the Son of Sirach. The book's didactic and lyric verse is thus an apologia for the Judean theocracy of the first decades of the second century B.C.

This apologia need not have been motivated by political animus toward the Seleucids or opposition to Hellenistic Jewish syncretism, although some passages in the book have been so interpreted (Sir. 2:12-18; 16:17-23; 41:8; 42:1-2). On the contrary, Ben Sira seems open to Hellenistic influences. His hymn in praise of the heroes of the past is clearly indebted to Hellenistic encomiastic historiography and to the educational and social concerns served in that tradition. While the linking of Torah and Wisdom is evidence of a concern for the sources and authority of wisdom in Israel, it is at the same time an authentic reflection on the extent to which Israel's Torah, sacred history, and heroes of piety may mirror a universal order of righteousness. The author may therefore have been indebted in his reflections to Stoic conceptions of an all-embracing world law.

Bibliography. B. L. Mack, *Wisdom and the Hebrew Epic: Ben Sira's Hymn in Praise of the Fathers* (Chicago: 1985); J. G. Snaith, *Ecclesiasticus.* CBC (1974).

SIRAH [sī′rə], **CISTERN OF** (Heb. *bôr hassirâ* "cistern of the thornbush"). A place from which Joab summoned Abner before killing him (2 Sam. 3:26), according to Josephus (*Ant.* vii.1.5 [34]) 4 km. (2.5 mi.) north of Hebron. More than one location near Hebron has been suggested, including Ṣîret el-Bellaʿ, north of Hebron, and ʿAin Sarah, northwest of Hebron.

SIRION [sîr′ī ən] (Heb. *širyōn*).† The Sidonian name for Mt. Hermon (Deut. 3:9). Heb. *šî′ōn* (KJV "Sion"; NIV "Siyon") is given as an alternative name of Mt. Hermon at Deut. 4:48, corrected by many to "Sirion" (so RSV, JB). At Ps. 29:6b Sirion is the parallel for Lebanon at v. 6a; here it may be a designation for the entire Anti-lebanon range, of which Mt. Hermon is the southern part, or possibly for both the Lebanon and Anti-lebanon ranges. Heb. *śāday* "field" (so KJV, RSV mg.) at Jer. 18:14 is associated with Lebanon and is corrected by some to Sirion (so RSV); other possibilities are to omit *śāday* as an extraneous dittograph (so apparently JB) or to associate it with Akk. *šadu* "mountain." *See* HERMON, MOUNT.

SISERA [sĭs′ə rə] (Heb. *sîserā′*).
1.† The commander of the army of King Jabin of Hazor whose headquarters were at Harosheth-hagoiim ("Harosheth of the nations"; Sisera's name is non-Semitic) (Judg. 4:2). Jabin and Sisera oppressed the Israelites for twenty years (v. 3; cf. 1 Sam. 12:9). Through the prophetess-judge Deborah, God called Barak to gather an army from the northern tribes of Naphtali and Zebulun to fight Sisera in the plain of Esdraelon (Judg. 4:4-7). At Barak's insistence, Deborah joined Barak in the leadership of this Israelite army (vv. 8-10). Sisera's chariot forces, rendered useless by a flash flood of the Kishon (5:21), were routed by the Israelites, and Sisera escaped on foot (4:12-16). He sought refuge with Jael, the wife of Heber, a Kenite, because Jabin and Heber were at peace with each other (v. 17). But after her welcome, Jael proved treacherous toward Sisera and killed him by hammering a tent peg through his skull as he slept (vv. 18-21). The song of victory offered by Deborah and Barak celebrated the rout of Sisera's army and his death (5:19-30; cf. Ps. 83:9-10 [MT 10-11]).
2. The ancestor of a family of temple servants who returned with Zerubbabel from the Babylonian captivity (Ezra 2:53; Neh. 7:55).

SISMAI [sĭs'mī] (Heb. *sismāy*; cf. the Phoenician deity *Ssm*). The son of Eleasah of the tribe of Judah (1 Chr. 2:40; KJV "Sisamai").

SISTER (Heb. *'āḥôṯ*; Gk. *adelphḗ*).* A female sibling, the daughter of the same parents (Num. 26:59; 2 Sam. 13:4) or of one common parent (Gen. 20:12; Lev. 18:9, 11; 2 Sam. 13:2). The term can also represent any female blood relative (Gen. 24:59), a member of the same tribe (Num. 25:18), or a lover (Cant. 4:9-10). At Ruth 1:15 Heb. *yᵉḇemeṯ*, usually translated "sister-in-law," specifies the kinship classification "husband's widow."

In the New Testament, "sister" is a term for a female person in the community of faith (Rom. 16:1; 1 Cor. 7:15; Jas. 2:15). Jesus speaks of his followers as his "brother, sister, and mother" (Matt. 12:50). "Elect sister" at 2 John 13 is a designation of the local Christian community of which the letter's writer is a part. This usage builds on another metaphor, "the elect lady" (v. 1), which represents the church addressed by the letter.

SITHRI [sĭth'rī] (Heb. *siṯrî*). A Levite, the son of Uzziel of the house of Kohath (Exod. 6:22; KJV "Zithri").

SITNAH [sĭt'nə] (Heb. *śiṭnâ* "hostility"). One of two wells in the valley of Gerar over which Isaac's servants and the herdsmen of Gerar fought (Gen. 46:21). It was apparently south of Gerar and north of Rehoboth **2**, somewhere in the area west of Beer-sheba.

SIVAN [sī'văn] (Heb. *sîwān*, from Akk. *simānu*). The third month of the Hebrew year (May/June, Esth. 8:9). The Feast of Weeks (Pentecost) falls on the sixth of Sivan (Lev. 23:15-21). *See* YEAR.

SIX HUNDRED AND SIXTY-SIX (Gk. *hexakósioi hexḗkonta héx*).† The number of "the beast" of Rev. 13 (v. 18). This number should be associated with the primary "beast" of this chapter, not with the secondary "beast" (which is so named only at v. 11). The number is apparently the authorizing mark without which no one can engage in commerce (v. 17).

Before the adoption of Arabic numerals, letters served double duty, representing numbers as well as sounds. In accord with its designation as "a human number" (lit. "the number of a person"; *arithmós anthrṓpou*; v. 18), the number of the beast is usually regarded as an example of a type of cryptogram common in the ancient world in which a person's name is represented by the sum of the numerical values of the letters comprising the name.

The most commonly offered solution to the number's riddle is "Nero Caesar." A possible Hebrew transliteration of Gk. *Neron Kaisar* is *nrwn qsr*, the added numerical value of which is six hundred and sixty-six. The common textual variant "six hundred and sixteen" would result if a Hebrew transliteration of Latin rather than Greek were used (*nrw qsr* for *Nero Caesar*). The book of Revelation is usually thought to have been written during the reign of Domitian, nearly three decades after Nero's death. Its author may, however, be making use of the belief current in the Roman world that Nero would return from death, in this way interpreting the difficulties faced by Christians during the reign of Domitian. Though this may be considered the most likely interpretation, other difficulties face the Nero solution to the riddle of the number. Other solutions have been Gk. *Lateínos* "(the) Latin" or Domitian himself (based on a Greek transliteration of an abbreviation of his full Latin name),

Interpreters sometimes assume that the number of the beast points to someone later than the writing of the book of Revelation, so that the book's original addressees would not know of the person (or institution) indicated. This person is usually understood as the "antichrist" of the end of the age, though that term does not appear in Revelation. Within this assumption, suggested solutions have included a large number of political, religious, and military leaders and institutions throughout history up to the present. It is probable, however, that Rev. 13 describes the military power and religious cults of the Roman Empire and its persecution of Christians at the time the book was written.

The possibility remains that the number is to be thought of as "a human number" or "the number of mankind" rather than "the number of a person" and is not to be associated with a name at all. In this case, it could be interpreted according to the same kind of number symbolism as the rest of the numbers in Revelation. Since six falls one short of seven, the number believed by some to symbolize perfection in Revelation, then 666 is imperfection compounded, carried as a mark by all mankind except the people of God, those who have refused the beast's mark (cf. 20:4).

SKIN (Heb. *ḥēmeṯ*, *nō'ḏ*, *'ôḇ*; Gk. *askós*). Whole animal skins, generally goatskins, were used for protecting and transporting liquids (e.g., Gen. 21:14; Josh. 9:4; Judg. 4:19; 1 Sam. 16:20). Wine was both fermented and stored in skins. Because of the gases released in the process of fermentation, wineskins had to have an opening to prevent their bursting (cf. Job 32:19), and old, weakened skins could not be used for wine still undergoing fermentation (Matt. 9:17 par.). *See* GOATSKINS.

SKULL, THE. *See* GOLGOTHA.

SLAVE. *See* SERVANT.

SLEEP (Heb. nouns *šēnâ*, *šēnā'*, *tardēmâ*, verbs *šāḵaḇ*, *yāšēn*, *rāḏam*, *nûm*; adjective *yāšēn*; Aram. *šᵉnâ*; Gk. noun *hýpnos*, verbs *katheúdō*, *koimáō*, *nystázō*).* Sleep is, on the one hand, the result of a good and properly ordered life (Prov. 3:21-24; Eccl. 5:12) and a sign of trust that God provides life's necessities (Ps. 4:8 [MT 9]; 127:1-2; cf. Isa. 30:15). On the other hand, the desire to sleep can be a dangerous sign of sluggishness (Prov. 6:6-11). Accordingly, sleep can be a figure of speech for spiritual torpor, especially in view of the shortness of time before the end of the age (Mark 13:35-36; Rom. 13:11-13). Sometimes God sends a deep sleep over a person to accomplish his purposes (Gen. 2:21; 15:12; *see* DREAM).

Metaphors of sleep are applied to God. It is said that God does not sleep, meaning that his care for his people is unceasing (Ps. 121:4). Elijah mocks the worshippers of Baal by asking if their god needs to be awakened (1 Kgs. 18:27). But a plea for God to act can be in the form of an attempt to rouse God from sleep (Ps. 44:23 [MT 24]; 59:4-5 [MT 5-6]; cf. 78:65).

Death was commonly referred to as "sleep" (e.g., 1 Cor. 15:20). The ambiguity created by this euphemism was played upon by Jesus in reference to persons he was about to raise from the dead (Luke 8:52; John 11:11-14). A similar figure of speech is represented in the Old Testament view of the ideal death as reunion with sleeping ancestors (e.g., 1 Kgs. 2:10; cf. Gen. 15:15; 35:29). Sleep as a figure for death and sleep as a figure for spiritual sluggishness are combined at Eph. 5:14, where a hymn about the resurrection is used in an exhortation to spiritual watchfulness.

SLIME (KJV). *See* BITUMEN.

SLING (Heb. verb *qālaʿ*, noun *qelaʿ*). A common and very ancient offensive weapon consisting of a small piece of leather or cloth (the "hollow" of the sling, 1 Sam. 25:29) attached to two thongs. A stone was placed in the leather or cloth, the sling whirled, and one of the thongs released, hurling the stone toward its target. A skillful slinger was capable of killing a person from a distance (17:49). Shepherds also used slings as protection against predatory animals. Armies typically had specially trained slingers (Heb. *qallaʿ*; Judg. 20:16; 2 Kgs. 3:25; 1 Chr. 12:2). Slingstones were sometimes made of fired clay, but more often natural stones were used, whether they were gathered when needed (1 Sam. 17:40) or kept ready in armories (2 Chr. 26:14).

SMITH (Heb. *ḥārāš, masgēr, ṣōrēp*).† Workers of refined metals or, in the earliest times, workers of metals found as free elements, thus important craftsmen from the time that metals began to be used. Gold, silver, and copper came into use shortly before 4000 B.C., bronze (a copper-tin alloy) shortly before 3000, and iron *ca.* 2000, becoming dominant from 1200. According to Gen. 4:22, Tubal-cain, a descendant of Cain, was the first smith. The Kenites (e.g., 1 Chr. 2:55) were a tribe or order of traveling smiths associated most with the western slopes of the Arabah, which would place them near large deposits of copper. Their name may connect them with Cain and Tubal-cain.

The Israelites traveling from Egypt to Canaan were

A sling in use

in contact with the Kenites (1 Sam. 15:6) and included in their own number some who had metallurgical skills (Exod. 32:2-4; 35:30-32; Num. 21:9). But once they were settled in the land, they were slower than the neighboring Philistines in learning to work iron, which was quickly becoming the dominant metal for weapons (1 Sam. 13:19-22). When Solomon needed a bronzesmith for his building projects, he used a skilled worker from outside Israel (1 Kgs. 7:13-14). Some suspicion of smiths may have arisen from the fashioning of idols from metals (Deut. 27:15; Isa. 40:19; 41:7; 44:9-12; 46:6; Hos. 13:2). The production of weapons was often the largest part of the smith's work. The smiths were among the significant leaders and skilled craftsmen of Jerusalem whom Nebuchadrezzar took into exile (2 Kgs. 24:14, 16; Jer. 24:1; 29:2).

See also the articles on specific metals.

SMYRNA [smûrʹnə] (Gk. *Smyrna*). An important city, modern Izmir, on a bay immediately south of the Hermus river (the modern Gediz) on the western coast of Asia Minor. Colonized by Aeolian Greeks at the northwest edge of the plain that extends some 14 km. (9 mi.) inland, the city soon came under Ionian control and became part of the Ionian League. The original site was destroyed in the early sixth century by Lydian king Alyattes, and Smyrna remained virtually unoccupied until refounded by Alexander's successors Antigonus I and Lysimachus *ca.* 400 (named for a time Eurydicea after Lysimachus' daughter) at the southwest corner of the plain some 5 km. (3 mi.) to the southwest. Situated at the terminus of a major east-west trade road and featuring an excellent harbor, Smyrna was a wealthy trading center during the Roman period and was honored with the title of "temple warden" in the imperial cult.

The Christian community in Smyrna may have begun from Paul's work in Ephesus (Acts 19:9-10). The letter to the church in Smyrna (Rev. 2:8-11) suggests that this group of Christians was poor, that it came into conflicts with the Jewish community of the city (v. 9), and was likely to experience some form of official persecution (v. 10). Continued Jewish-Christian animosity underlies the account of the A.D. 156 martyrdom of Polycarp, bishop of Smyrna.

SNAIL.† A gastropod mollusk usually enclosed in a spiral shell. The meaning of Heb. *šabbᵉlûl* at Ps. 58:8 (MT 9) is not certain. Its identification as some kind of gastropod, whether a slug (so JB, NIV) or a snail, is found in the Talmud. Current scholarship suggests the meaning "miscarriage," in which case the term parallels "untimely birth" in the second half of the verse. The verse would then be a expression of a wish that the psalmist's enemies had never been born (cf. Job 3:16; 10:18-19).

On Lev. 11:30 (KJV "snail") *see* LIZARD.

SNARES AND TRAPS (Heb. nouns *māṣôḏ, mᵉṣûḏâ, paḥ, ḥeḇel, malkōḏeṯ,* verb *yāqōš*; Gk. *pagís, thḗra*).† A variety of devices were used by hunters for catching birds (esp. Heb. *paḥ*) and mammals. Some used nets (*mᵉṣûḏâ*) that were triggered by the hunter or by the animal when the bait was disturbed. Other devices

made use of nooses, trip ropes (*ḥebel*), or camouflaged pits.

Snares and traps are mentioned in a large number
of metaphorical references to dangers, usually of an
unexpected or sudden nature, such as the unexpected
adversities of life (Eccl. 9:12), violence planned by
evil people (Ps. 140:4-5 [MT 5-6]), the destruction
facing the wicked (Job 18:7-10), military defeat (Ezek.
19:8, following LXX), and eschatological destruction
(Luke 21:34 [v. 35 in some versions]). At Ps. 69:22
(MT 23) (quoted at Rom. 11:9; KJV "stumblingblock") sacrificial meals are likened to the bait that
attracts but then becomes a trap. At Amos 3:5 the
action of a trap illustrates the inevitability of God's
punishment of those who are uniquely his people (cf.
v. 2).

See also NET; PIT.

SNOW (Heb. *šeleg*; Aram. *tᵉlag*; Gk. *chiṓn*). In
Palestine snow falls primarily in the hills, and seldom
heavily. In figures of speech snow represents the
whiteness of skin caused by leprosy (Exod. 4:6; Num.
12:10; 2 Kgs. 5:27), the whiteness of beings seen in
visions or of their clothing (Dan. 7:9; Matt. 28:3; Rev.
1:14), and purity resulting from God's sanctification
of sinners (Ps. 51:7 [MT 9]; Isa. 1:18; cf. Lam. 4:7).
Job 9:30 suggests a belief that snow cleanses more
effectively than water. Snow is named among things
that come from God, and the mystery of its origin
makes it particularly a witness to the power of God
and the ignorance of mankind (37:5-6; 38:22; Ps.
147:16; 148:8).

SNUFFERS.† In translations a word designating a
variety of objects used in the tabernacle and temple.
Heb. *mᵉzammᵉrôṯ* indicates a scissorslike instrument
made of gold or bronze used in the temple of Solomon
for trimming lamp wicks (1 Kgs. 7:50; 2 Kgs. 12:13
[MT 14]; 25:14; 2 Chr. 4:22; Jer. 52:18; NIV "wick
trimmers"; JB "knives"). Heb. *melqāḥayim* apparently represents tongs used to lift coals from the altar,
perhaps to light incense (1 Kgs. 7:49 par. 2 Chr. 4:21;
Isa. 6:6; RSV, KJV "tongs"). A similar word, *malqā-
ḥêyhā*, appears in Exod. 25:38; 37:23; Num. 4:9 (NIV
"wick trimmers"; KJV also "tongs"), always in conjunction with *maḥtâ*, which normally represents different kinds of censers and ash buckets (here RSV
"trays"; KJV "snuff dishes"); both words stand for
certain objects made of gold and used in connection
with the seven-branched lampstand of the tabernacle.
The design and function of these objects is uncertain,
though they may have been used for trimming wicks
and carrying away ashes.

SO [sō] (Heb. *sô'*). A "king of Egypt" with whom
King Hoshea of Israel was in contact, probably with
a view to an alliance, at the time of his rebellion
against Assyria (2 Kgs. 17:4; *ca.* 725 B.C.). For these
actions Hoshea was quickly imprisoned by King Shalmaneser V of Assyria. The identification of So is uncertain. An older view held that Hoshea sought an
alliance not with Egypt (Heb. *miṣrayim*) but with
Muṣri, a north Arabian kingdom, and its king, Silhu.
So is now more commonly sought in Egypt because
of the greater likelihood that an Israelite king would

seek protection from Assyria by an alliance with that
power (cf. Hos. 7:11). Several rulers of districts within
Egypt have been suggested as the ally Hoshea sought
(e.g., the general Sib'e, or a gentilic ["the Saite"] for
a local ruler from Sais in the delta region), as well as
Osorkon IV, who was pharaoh of the whole country
about the time of Hoshea's rebellion. It is also possible
that So represents the place (most likely Sais) where
Hoshea met with Egypt's rulers, the place name having
been distorted in transmission of the text.

SOAP. *See* LYE, SOAP.

SOCO [sō'kō] (Heb. *śôḵô*), **SOCOH** (*śôḵōh*, *śōḵōh*).
1. A city in the lowland (Shephelah) region of Judah (Josh. 15:35). It was at this city that the Philistine
armies gathered before the skirmish between David
and Goliath (1 Sam. 17:1; KJV "Shochoh"). Soco(h)
was also among the cities rebuilt and fortified by King
Rehoboam of Judah, probably in view of the threat of
invasion by Egypt (2 Chr. 11:7; KJV "Shoco"). It was
lost to the Philistines at the time of King Ahaz of
Judah (28:18; KJV "Shocho"). The city has been
identified with Khirbet ʿAbbâd, *ca.* 28 km. (17 mi.)
west-southwest of Jerusalem; the name is preserved
in the name of the nearby village Khirbet Shuweikeh.
2. A city in the southern part of the hill country
region of Judah (Josh. 15:48). It has been identified
with Khirbet Shuweikeh (to be distinguished from the
village named in **1** above), *ca.* 25 km. (15 mi.) northeast of Beer-sheba. "Heber the father of Soco" appears in a Calebite genealogy (1 Chr. 4:18; KJV
"Socho"), probably intended to designate him as the
founder of this city.
3. A city in the second administrative district of
Solomon's kingdom (1 Kgs. 4:10; KJV "Sochoh").
This city, which is mentioned in Egyptian records,
has been identified with Khirbet Shuweiket er-Râs
(Tell er-Râs), (10 mi.) northwest of Samaria and a
short distance north of modern Ṭūlkarm in the plain
of Sharon.

SODI [sō'dī] (Heb. *sôḏî* "my confidant"). The father
of Gaddiel of the tribe of Zebulun, one of the twelve
spies sent into the land of Canaan (Num. 13:10).

SODOM [sŏd'əm] (Heb. *sᵉḏōm*; Gk. *Sodoma*).† The
most prominent of "the cities of the valley" destroyed
by Yahweh at the time of Abraham. "The valley" was
perhaps the Jordan valley north of the Dead Sea (Gen.
13:10), but it is most commonly thought that "the
cities of the valley" were located in the region now
covered by the shallow southern part of the Dead Sea.

Sodom was apparently one of the major cities of
the region. On behalf of his nephew Lot, who had
gone to live in the Jordan valley near Sodom (vv.
10-12), Abraham fought on Sodom's side against the
Mesopotamian rulers against which the city and its
allies had revolted (ch. 14). Later God revealed to
Abraham his intention to destroy Sodom and the
neighboring cities because of their sinfulness (18:16-22;
cf. 13:13). Abraham interceded on behalf of Sodom,
again no doubt because his relative Lot lived there
(18:22-33).

Two angels (or lit. "messengers") went to Sodom

to rescue Lot. All the men of the city came to Lot's door, demanding that he send the angels out so that they could have sexual relations with them; this act was apparently an expression of the citizens' subjugation of the two strangers who had sought shelter under the roof of one who was himself an outsider, even though he had lived in Sodom for a time (19:1-5). Lot, following in radical fashion the customary obligation of the host to protect his guests, sought to divert the men of the city by offering to them his two virgin daughters (vv. 6-8). They refused the offer and attacked Lot, but he was rescued by the two angels (vv. 9-11). The next morning, the angels took Lot and his wife and daughters out of Sodom. The city was destroyed by fire and brimstone (vv. 12-29).

Sodom, often with Gomorrah, became proverbial for conspicuous sinfulness that is ripe for judgment (Deut. 32:32; Isa. 1:10; 3:9; Jer. 23:14; Ezek. 16:49-50; Rev. 11:8) and for thorough destruction sent by God as judgment (Deut. 29:23 [MT 22]; Isa. 1:9; 13:19; Jer. 49:18; 50:40; Lam. 4:6; Amos 4:11; Zeph. 2:9; Luke 17:29). Probably referring to Sodom's attempted violent treatment of messengers from God, Jesus noted that what those two cities would experience on the day of final judgment would be preferable to the fate awaiting some cities in which he and his disciples had taught (Matt. 10:15; 11:23-24).

The idea that the fundamental sin of Sodom was homosexual behavior is not present in the Old Testament and appears only in later documents of the New Testament (Jude 7; cf. 2 Pet. 2:6-10). The Hebrew and Greek words translated "sodomite(s)" at Deut. 23:17 [MT 18]; 1 Kgs. 14:24; 15:12; 22:46; 2 Kgs. 23:7 (KJV; Heb. *qāḏēš*); and 1 Tim. 1:10 (RSV; Gk. *arsenokoítēs*) concern homosexual behavior (male cultic prostitution in the Old Testament passages) but do not include in them any allusion to Sodom as does the translation.

SOJOURNER (Heb. *gēr*). A technical term (from *gûr* "sojourn") designating persons living in a place other than their own home or home country. The *gēr* (RSV, KJV often "stranger"; RSV also "alien") was not a native member of the community in which he resided (in most cases as a permanent resident) but who had certain rights as a resident, hence the alternate translation "resident alien." The sojourner's "community" could be a household of which that person became a dependent (usually a servant) during difficult times (e.g., Gen. 32:4 [MT 5]; Exod. 20:10; 1 Kgs. 17:20; cf. Job 19:15; RSV "guests"; KJV "they that dwell"), or a town, region, or nation in which the sojourner had taken up residence (e.g., Gen. 19:9; Exod. 2:22; Judg. 19:16; Ruth 1:1; 2 Sam. 4:3; 2 Kgs. 8:1-2; 2 Chr. 15:9).

The Old Testament laws sought to protect the sojourner and to define his status in Israelite society. Israel's own experience as a class of mistreated foreigners in Egypt was to be recalled and mercy thus shown the sojourner (Exod. 23:9; Lev. 19:34; Deut. 23:7 [MT 8]). Certain rights were held by sojourners as well as Israelites, including the right to the Sabbath rest (Exod. 23:12), to a fair trial (Deut. 1:16), to participation in sacrificial meals (16:11), and to the gleaning of fields and vineyards alongside other dis-

advantaged people (Lev. 19:9-10). Sojourners were obligated to observe the feasts, sacrifices, and prohibitions associated with Israelite religion (Exod. 12:49; Lev. 16:29; 17:8-9; 18:26; Num. 15:29) once they had identified with the Israelite community by being circumcised (Exod. 12:43-44, 48; cf. v. 45). For an Israelite to become a servant of a prosperous sojourner was considered an unfortunate circumstance (cf. Deut. 28:43) for which special legislative provisions were made (Lev. 25:47-55). Although sojourners were otherwise to be regarded as nearly equivalent to native Israelites, some incidents did occur in which this ideal was not adhered to (1 Chr. 22:2; 2 Chr. 2:17-18 [MT 16-17]).

Other Hebrew terms are applied to foreigners. Heb. *zār* is a general term used in a wide variety of contexts. Heb. *tôšāḇ* is sometimes synonymous with *gēr* (Gen. 23:4), but at other times designates a less assimilated person (Exod. 12:45; KJV "foreigner"). The terms *noḵrî* and *ben-nēḵār* are used for persons who, because of their very foreignness, are distinguished even more from natives of a nation (e.g., Deut. 17:15; 1 Kgs. 8:41-43); the legal status of such a person was quite different from that of the native Israelite or the *gēr* (Exod. 12:43; Lev. 22:25; Deut. 14:21; 15:3). Matters related to eschatological Israel reflect a greater readiness to include foreigners, both *gērîm* (Ezek. 47:22-23) and *bᵉnê nēḵār* (Isa. 56:3, 6-7). The fulfillment of this hope in the Church is recorded at Eph. 2:11-13, 19 (RSV "strangers and sojourners"; KJV "strangers and foreigners"; v. 19, Gk. *xénoi kaí pároikoi*).

The concept of Israel as a sojourner (*gēr*) nation is theologically important in the Old Testament. Even though the land of Canaan, the land of the patriarchs' sojourning, became Israel's possession in accord with God's promises (Gen. 17:8; Exod. 6:4), it continued to belong ultimately to God. Israel inhabited it as sojourners (Lev. 25:23; 1 Chr. 29:15; cf. Heb. 11:8-16). Similarly, the worshipper at the temple sojourns in the place that God owns (Ps. 15:1; cf. 61:4 [MT 5]). The worshipper also knows that he is a sojourner in the sense that his life is temporary and quickly passing (39:12 [MT 13]). The Christian community's relationship to the outside world is expressed in similar terms at 1 Pet. 1:1, 17; 2:11 (cf. Heb. 13:14).

SOLOMON [sŏl'ə mən] (Heb. *šᵉlōmōh* "peace, wellbeing"; Gk. *Solomōn*). The second son of David and Bathsheba (2 Sam. 12:24; cf. 1 Chr. 3:5) and third king of Israel (ca. 970-930 B.C.), following David. In a prophecy by Nathan (2 Sam. 12:25) Solomon is called Jedidiah ("beloved of Yahweh"), perhaps a regnal or throne name.

As David grew old, two factions fought for succession to his throne. With the general Joab and the priest Abiathar, David's eldest living son Adonijah made a bid for the throne at En-rogel (1 Kgs. 1:5-10). The opposing faction supported Solomon and included Bathsheba (apparently the leading personality), Nathan the prophet, Benaiah, the captain of David's bodyguard, and Zadok the priest. This group found favor with David, and even as Adonijah and his group were celebrating Solomon was proclaimed David's coregent and successor (vv. 11-49). In contrast to the accession of Saul and David, neither anointing nor popular acclamation was decisive (though they did occur, v. 39); rather, Solomon gained the throne through the word of the aging prior king.

As king, Solomon consolidated his father's empire. He divided all of the territory except for Judah into twelve districts, ignoring the old tribal boundaries, thus centralizing control in his government at Jerusalem. Each district was responsible for supporting the government and temple for one month of the year (4:7-28 [MT 4:7-20; 5:1-8]). As in other nations of the time, Solomon used foreigners, many of them captives, as forced laborers in his extensive building projects. Eventually the levy included Israelites (5:13-18 [MT 27-32]; cf. 12:4). In the eleventh year of his reign, after seven years of building, he completed the temple for which his father had begun preparation (6:38). His own magnificent palace he completed later (7:1-8). He fortified Jerusalem and other important cities, including Megiddo, Hazor, and Gezer (9:15), which have been among the most significant archaeological sites in Israel.

Solomon's empire was especially important in commerce. He built a great seaport and mining center at Ezion-geber. His ships sailed to the end of the known world, the round trip requiring three years (vv. 26-28; 10:22). He made treaties with neighboring states that were commercial as well as military, such as that with Hiram of Tyre (5:1-12 [MT 15-26]), and some of which were cemented by marriage, as was customary. Solomon even married the daughter of the Egyptian pharaoh, an indication of the importance of his kingdom (3:1). Unfortunately, his foreign wives led Solomon away from the pure worship of the God of Israel (11:1-8), for which is blamed the division of Solomon's kingdom after his death (vv. 9-13).

Both Solomon's great wisdom and his great wealth became proverbial (4:32 [MT 5:12]; 10:23; Matt. 6:29; 12:42). According to 3:5-15, when God appeared to the new king in a dream and granted him one request, Solomon asked for wisdom. Indeed, Solomon's wisdom was so highly celebrated that he became the figure most associated with the wisdom tradition of late Israelite and early Jewish writing. Because of this, two large sections of the book of Proverbs (Prov. 10:1–22:16; 25:1–29:27), the Song of Solomon, Ecclesiastes, Ps. 127, Wisdom of Solomon, Psalms of Solomon, and Odes of Solomon are attributed to him in varying ways.

SOLOMON, BOOK OF THE ACTS OF (Heb. *sēper diḇrê š⁽e⁾lōmōh*).† A book referred to at 1 Kgs. 11:41, thought to be a major source for 3:1–11:40. What was included in this book and what was derived from other sources cannot be determined with certainty, but the reference to both deeds and wisdom (11:41) suggests a wide variety of materials.

SOLOMON, ODES OF. A collection of forty-two hymns included among the Pseudepigrapha. The ascription to Solomon appears only in their title. The Odes are most often considered to have been composed *ca.* A.D. 100, probably in Syriac, by a Christian community in Palestine or Syria. Other suggestions are that they are Jewish compositions with Christian

additions or that they were written by Gnostics. The work survives in Syriac, Greek, and Coptic manuscripts, all discovered in the twentieth century.

Literary and theological affinities exist between the Odes and the gospel of John, the letters of Ignatius, and the Dead Sea Scrolls, but in none of these cases is the nature of the relationship clear. The most significant influence on the form of the Odes is from the canonical book of Psalms. The Odes provide important information on early Christian worship. One outstanding feature is their concentration on the present joy of salvation.

SOLOMON, PSALMS OF.† A collection of eighteen poems in the style of the biblical Psalms, reckoned as part of the Pseudepigrapha (though named in some lists of the Apocrypha). The Psalms of Solomon were written by a group of Jews in Jerusalem as a response to the Roman defeat of Jerusalem in the first century B.C. That event is viewed as the just divine response to Hasmonean rule, but also as evil in itself, since foreign idolatry corrupted many Jews. Deliverance by a Davidic messiah is expected. In addition to these historical and eschatological themes, the prayers and praises of the Psalms of Solomon are interested in the sins of God's people and his mercy toward them.

More specifically, authorship of the psalms has often been attributed to a group of Pharisees, and more recently some scholars have assigned them to the Essenes, but the evidence for either view is slight. The psalms are extant in Greek and Syriac but were probably composed in Hebrew.

SOLOMON, TESTAMENT OF.† A complex pseudepigraphal work that builds on elements of the biblical account of Solomon, but the main interest of which is healing by magical means and by control of the demons that cause disease. Suggested places of origin for the Testament include Egypt, Palestine, Asia Minor, and Babylonia. A probable date is the third century A.D., although earlier materials are probably included. Some Christian elements exist in the present form of the Testament, but it may have begun as a Jewish composition. The Testament reflects the traditional view of Solomon as a master magician and exorcist that existed at least as early as the first century A.D. as an interpretation of 1 Kgs. 4:29-34 (MT 5:9-14).

SOLOMON'S PORTICO (Gk. *hē stoá Solomóntos*). A covered colonnade on the eastern side of the Herodian temple area. The name of this structure came from its supposed antiquity, although none of the Herodian temple dated back to Solomon's day. Solomon's Portico was frequently a place for rabbis to meet with their disciples and to engage in public teaching. It was, therefore, the probable site of a number of events recorded in the Gospels (e.g., Luke 2:46; 20:1; John 7:14). It is named as the specific site of Jesus' teaching on one occasion (10:23). The Beautiful Gate, where Peter healed a lame man (Acts 3:2-10), may have led into the forecourt of the temple (the court of the women) on the side facing Solomon's Portico across the court of the Gentiles; after the healing Peter went into the

portico to address the crowd drawn by the healing (vv. 11-12). The portico came to be a regular meeting place of the church (5:12).

SOLOMON'S SERVANTS (Heb. ʿaḇḏê šᵉlōmōh).* Because of the great size of Solomon's bureaucracy and labor force, 1 Kings mentions on several occasion Solomon's "servants" (cf. esp. 1 Kgs. 3:15; 5:6 [MT 20]). After the Exile one group among those who returned to Judah were known as "the sons of Solomon's servants" (Ezra 2:55-58 par. Neh. 7:57-60); these were probably the descendants of the non-Israelites enslaved by Solomon and who thereby became a distinct class in Israel and Judah (1 Kgs. 9:20-21). They apparently constituted a class of postexilic temple servants (cf. Ezra 7:24), similar in function to the Nethinim.

SON (Heb. bēn; Aram. bar; Gk. huiós).† In the basic sense, a male child of a particular parent. In biblical usage the term could also represent a male descendant beyond the first generation (e.g., Gen. 31:28; Exod. 12:24; Luke 20:41; cf. Exod. 20:5; RSV, KJV "children"). A whole nation might be known as the "sons" of an eponymous ancestor, e.g., "the sons of Israel" (e.g., Gen. 32:32 [MT 33]; RSV "the Israelites") or "the sons of Heth" (23:3; RSV "the Hittites"). A similar expression is "the sons of my people" (v. 11). Geographical terms might also be used in such an expression, e.g., "the son(s) of a foreign land," generally translated "foreigner(s)" (e.g., 17:12; 2 Sam. 22:45), "the sons of the east" (Gen. 29:1; RSV, KJV "the people of the east"), and "the sons of" specified cities and nations (e.g., Ezra 2:25-26, 29-33, 35; cf. Jer. 2:16; RSV "men").

"Son of. . ." was a common Semitic expression indicating "a person displaying the quality of. . ." or the like. Examples (usually paraphrased in translations) include "sons of rebellion" (Num. 17:10 [MT 25]), "sons of Belial" (Deut. 13:13 [MT 14]), "son of strength" (1 Sam. 14:52), "son of virtue" (1 Kgs. 1:52), "sons of exile" (Ezra 4:1), "sons of affliction" (Prov. 31:5), "sons of oil" (Zech. 4:14), "sons of the kingdom" (Matt. 8:12), "sons of disobedience" (Eph. 2:2), and "the son of perdition" (2 Thess. 2:3; cf. Eph. 5:8, "children [Gk. tékna] of light"). Those who practice particular professions are often identified in reference to an eponymous ancestor (e.g., 2 Chr. 35:14-15; superscriptions to Pss. 42, 44) or with an expression denoting membership in a class or guild, e.g., "sons of the perfumers" (Neh. 3:8; cf. 1 Kgs. 20:35; Ezra 2:61).

"The sons of men" (Gen. 11:5; Prov. 8:4, 31; Eccl. 1:13) is a term for mankind as a whole. "Son of man" was originally a term for any man, considered specifically in his humanness or in distinction from a large group of people (Ps. 8:4 [MT 5]; Ezek. 26:2); for the use of this term as a designation specifically for Jesus, see SON OF MAN.

"Sons of God" and "sons of gods" appear as designations for divine or semi-divine beings where reference is made to the heavenly assembly of such beings (Job 1:6; 38:7; Ps. 29:1 [RSV "heavenly beings"]; 82:1, 6; 89:5-7 [MT 6-8]), to myths concerning primordial beings (Gen. 6:2, 4), or to angels (Dan. 3:25).

God calls Israel "my son" (Exod. 4:22-23; Hos. 11:1), the Israelites "my sons (and 'my daughters')" (Isa. 43:6) and "my children" (45:11), and its king "my son" (2 Sam. 7:14; Ps. 2:7; cf. 89:26-27 [MT 27-28]) to indicate his unique covenant relationship with that people. The same understanding of God's people as his children is carried into the New Testament (Rom. 8:15-17, 19; 9:26; Gal. 4:5-7; cf. Matt. 5:45; John 1:12; see ADOPTION). For "Son of God" as a designation for Jesus, see SON OF GOD.

Bibliography. J. Bergman, H. Ringgren, and H. Haag, "bēn," *TDOT* 2, rev. ed. (1977): 145-159; P. Wülfing von Martitz et al., "υἱός," *TDNT* 8 (1972): 334-399.

SON OF GOD (Gk. huiós toú theoú). One who shares a close relationship with God; in the New Testament a designation of Jesus.

"Son of God" was a royal title that made its way from Egypt and the East into the Hellenistic kingdoms and the Roman Empire (e.g., Alexander the Great was called "son of Ammon" and "son of Zeus"). Its use in the Roman Empire was initially more a statement of political ideology than an application of mythological beliefs concerning divine generation (e.g., Octavian, who referred to himself as Lat. divi filius). "God" and "divine" were also applied to outstanding individuals, including poets, philosophers, military leaders, seers, and miracle workers (e.g., Plato, Apollonius of Tyana, Pythagoras); the main idea present in such uses of the term was that of unusual power. In a related sense, members of guilds that formed under the patronage of various gods called themselves "sons" or "children" (Gk. paídes) of that deity. An earlier generation of scholars was quick to make a connection between this Hellenistic use of such terms and the New Testament use of "son of God," but more caution is generally followed now, and the Old Testament and Judaism have come to be seen as the more important background.

In the Old Testament a "son of God" is one who has a divine commission for a specific task. Obedience to the task is sometimes contained within the concept. "Son of God" is so used for the people of Israel (e.g., Exod. 4:22; Isa. 1:2; Jer. 3:22), the king (2 Sam. 7:14; Ps. 2:7), and members of the heavenly court (Job 1:6; Ps. 29:1; Dan. 3:25). In the Apocrypha the same term is used of the righteous Jew (Wis. 2:18; Sir. 4:10). "Son of God" does not appear to have been used in the Old Testament as a messianic title, although its use as a royal title easily lent itself to messianic use in later writings (e.g., 1QSa 2:11-12; 4QFlor 1:10-13; 1 En. 105:2; 2 Esdr. 7:28-29). Nevertheless, "Messiah" and "son of God" clearly were used together in reference to Jesus (Matt. 16:16; Mark 14:61; John 11:27; cf. Luke 1:32).

Except in the gospel of John (John 10:36), Jesus does not call himself "son of God." But his use of "Father" ("Abba") in addressing God (Matt. 11:25-26; Mark 14:36), which was unique in Jewish prayer; his claim of special knowledge of God as Father (Matt. 11:27); and his other allusions to his relationship with the heavenly Father (Mark 12:6; 13:32) clearly indicate that he thought the concept appropriate. Such suggestions, along with supernatural testimonies (Matt.

4:3, 6; Mark 1:11; 3:11; 5:7; 9:7), prepared the way for the Christian identification of Jesus as "son of God." This identification became a simple confession of Christian faith, probably a baptismal form (Acts 8:37; cf. Matt. 28:19; Mark 1:9-11). The interpretation of Christ's resurrection as his being begotten or designated as God's son (Acts 13:33, quoting Ps. 2:7; Rom. 1:4) is probably linked to this baptismal confession.

The use of "son of God" as a title for Christ in the letters of Paul often occurs where the apostle quotes statements of tradition that had already existed for some time in the Church. Most of these statements (or confessions) regarding Jesus as "God's son" are focused on God's giving of Jesus and the atoning significance of Jesus' sufferings (Rom. 8:3, 32; Gal. 4:4-5; Col. 1:13-14; 1 Thess. 1:10; cf. Gal. 2:20). Similar emphases are found in connection with the title in Hebrews (Heb. 4:14; 6:6; 10:29) and in the Johannine literature (John 3:16-17; 1 John 1:7; 4:9-10, 14). In Hebrews "son (of God)" is also a title of Jesus connected with his appointment as priest (Heb. 4:14; 5:5; 7:3), and in the Johannine literature the focus on "the son" as the one who is sent is also the basis for a claim of unique authority given to Jesus by the Father (John 1:18; 3:35; 5:19-27; 6:40; 12:49).

Statements original to Paul that refer to Jesus as "the son (of God)" are linked to a number of themes (e.g., 1 Cor. 1:9; 15:28), but the content of the apostolic preaching is associated with the title often enough (Rom. 1:3, 9; 2 Cor. 1:19; Gal. 1:16) to suggest that the baptismal confession of Jesus as "son of God" was carried through Paul's ministry. Acts 9:20, 22 suggests that in Paul's proclamation of Jesus as "son of God" the title was also intended as a messianic designation. The baptismal confession of Jesus as "son of God" was apparently also quite significant in shaping Johannine theology (John 3:16-18; 11:27; 20:31; 1 John 4:15; 5:5).

In the later history of the Church "son of God" became a term to designate specifically the divine nature of Christ, as distinguished from his human nature ("the son of man"). This was suggested by the balancing of "descended from David according to the flesh" and "designated Son of God . . ." at Rom. 1:3-4. The trinitarian formula "Father, Son, and Holy Spirit" is already found in the New Testament (Matt. 28:19).

Bibliography. M. Hengel, *The Son of God* (Philadelphia: 1976).

SON OF MAN (Gk. *ho huiós toú anthrṓpou*).† Jesus' favorite self-designation in the Synoptic Gospels. The appellative arises from Heb. *ben-ʾāḏām* and Aram. *bar ʾenāš* "son of man," a Semitic idiom for an individual human being or for mankind in general, particularly as distinguished from God (e.g., Num. 23:19; Ps. 8:4 [MT 5]; Ezek. 2:1).

At Dan. 7:13 "son of man" is a title for the people of Israel considered corporately or for their angelic representative in the heavenly court (cf. "the saints of the Most High," v. 18). The Similitudes of Enoch (1 En. 37-71) and 2 Esdr. 13 both draw on Daniel's use of the title, viewing it as an expression for a specific eschatological redeemer figure. Whereas the influence of Dan. 7:13 on New Testament use of the expression is

unquestioned, 2 Esdr. 13 and probably the Similitudes of Enoch are too late to have had any such influence. Jesus' use of the term may have arisen from its use in Aramaic as an oblique substitute for the first person singular pronoun as much as from the use of the term in Daniel.

Indeed, the variety in Jesus' use of the term suggests that no single influence was dominant in the meaning of the term as he used it, that his own creativity played a significant role, and that part of this creativity was to bring ideas from the Servant Songs of Isaiah (esp. Isa. 52:13–53:12) into the "son of man" concept. The uses of the term in the Synoptic Gospels fall into three broad categories. Jesus uses it with respect to himself in describing his activity and the exercise of his authority on earth (Matt. 13:37; Mark 2:10, 28; 10:45; Luke 7:34; 9:58; 12:10; 19:10), in predicting his suffering and death (Mark 8:31; 9:31; 10:33), and when speaking of his eschatological return and rule (e.g., Matt. 10:23; 19:28; 25:31; Mark 8:38; 14:62; Luke 17:22-30; 21:36).

Whether the Synoptic "son of man" sayings actually originated with Jesus has been much debated, as has the relative authenticity of each of the three categories of sayings. Scholars have also suggested that the only authentic sayings are those with an eschatological focus, in which Jesus appears to distinguish between himself and the "son of man," another figure whose eschatological coming Jesus announced (Mark 8:38; 14:62; Luke 12:8). But that all three categories of "son of man" sayings originated with Jesus is plausible within the framework of his own anticipation of his rejection, suffering, and vindication.

The gospel of John uses "the Son of man" for Jesus in relation to John's christology of the descending and ascending redeemer (John 3:13; 6:62; cf. 1:51; 5:27; 6:27) and in relation to the death of Jesus, viewed as his glorification (3:14; 12:23, 34; 13:31).

Bibliography. S. Kim, *The Son of Man as the Son of God* (Grand Rapids: 1985); B. Lindars, *Jesus Son of Man* (Grand Rapids: 1984).

SONG OF SOLOMON.† A book of the Old Testament, placed as the last of the poetic books in English translations and as the second of the five Megilloth in the third division, the Writings, of the Hebrew canon.

I. Title, Authorship, and Date

The Song of Solomon is also known in English as the Song of Songs and as the Canticle of Canticles, both from the Latin title *Canticum Canticorum* "Song of Songs." The Hebrew title, *šîr haššîrîm ʾašer lišlōmōh* "the greatest song [lit. 'the Song of Songs'], which is Solomon's" (Cant. 1:1), has traditionally been understood as a claim to authorship by Solomon. However, the construction employed in this title (and in the superscriptions of some of the Psalms) is ambiguous, and debate continues whether the intent of the preposition *l-* is "to," "for," "by," or even "concerning" Solomon. The references to Solomon in the text of the book (v. 5; 3:7, 9, 11; esp. 8:11-12) suggest that an anonymous author composed the Song, intending by the title to link the book with Solomon as an ideal figure of wisdom and wealth (cf. 1 Kgs. 4:29-34 [MT 5:9-14]; 10:14-23).

Because the author is unknown and because the text itself contains no explicit references to date, scholars have assigned a wide range of dates to the Song of Solomon. An early dating would place the book in the monarchic period on the evidence of the mention of Tirzah (capital of the northern kingdom) in parallel with Jerusalem (Cant. 6:4; cf. 1 Kgs. 16:23). Because of supposed late elements in the language of the book (e.g., the relative particle *ša* and signs of Greek linguistic influence), some have dated its composition to the seventh to fifth centuries B.C. or as late as the third century. Recent studies, especially in Ugaritic, have undermined confidence in the lateness of these linguistic elements and have left the date of the Song an open question.

II. Structure and Composition

The Song of Solomon is made up of a number of poems predominantly in *qînâ* (3:2) meter. The number of these poems and the significance of their arrangement continue to be debated. Some interpreters have attempted to divide the book into seven love songs related to the seven days of the wedding feast. Others have seen only an unordered anthology of twenty-three, twenty-eight, or as many as fifty love poems. Some have also sought to establish the unity of the Song by demonstrating the existence of structural, thematic, and linguistic parallels that bind the whole together as a unity.

Attempts to read the Song as a dramatic composition assume a basic unity of the whole, but lack of any equivalent to dramatic notation in the text has led to divergent treatments (cf., e.g., the headings in NIV and JB). Most such efforts divide the contents between two or three major characters, while others add a chorus and numerous minor actors. These reconstructions occasionally resort to rearrangements of the text.

Cultic interpretation relates the Song to Mesopotamian ritual celebrations of the divine wedding or to Canaanite fertility rituals. Israelite usage has, according to this view, obliterated the pagan origins of the poetry, and considerable reconstruction is necessary to see these origins clearly.

III. Interpretation

While the canonicity of the Song of Solomon has occasionally been questioned, usually in objection to the frankly sexual nature of the words, evidence supports the early acceptance of the book. The growth of allegorical interpretation can be understood as an attempt to deflect attention away from what were regarded as objectionable aspects of a book whose place in Scripture was already assured. This resistance to the literal sexuality of the text and the resultant attempts to uncover a meaning through allegorical interpretation have contributed to perception of the Song as obscure and difficult. It is not entirely clear when allegorical approaches to the Song originated. The LXX exhibits little tendency in this direction, but the practice was firmly established by the second century A.D.

Allegorical interpretation of the Song has been the common practice of both Jews and Christians. In the Talmud (A.D. 100-500) the lovers were understood to be God and his bride, Israel. The later Targum (seventh century) sees in the Song allusions to the history of Israel beginning with the Exodus and continuing until the advent of the Messiah. This interpretation apparently developed in reaction both to mystical tendencies in Jewish Gnosticism and to Christian attempts to read the Song as a description of the relation of Christ and the Church. For the influential eleventh-century interpreter Rashi, the Song expressed the longing of exiled Israel for God, the husband of her youth, who will ultimately return to her.

Early Christian interpretation of the Song also followed allegorical paths. For Hippolytus (*ca.* A.D. 200) the Song describes the love between Christ and the Church. Origen (third century) was aware of the view that the Song was an epithalamium for Solomon and Pharaoh's daughter, but felt that in a higher sense it speaks of Christ and the Church or of the individual soul's relation to the Logos. Literal interpretation was not entirely absent among early Christian exegetes. Near the end of the fourth century, Theodore of Mopsuestia rejected the allegorical interpretation of the Song and insisted that it be taken in its literal sense as an erotic song composed by Solomon. About the same time, the Roman monk Jovinian employed a literal interpretation in his attack on the presumed superiority of celibacy and asceticism. These literal approaches were exceptional, however, and were officially condemned. During the Middle Ages allegorical interpretation was widely developed. Numerous attempts were made to identify parts of the Song with events and elements in the passion of Christ. From the twelfth century there was a growing tendency to identify the bride as the Virgin Mary.

The Reformation changed this course only partially. Luther rejected Jewish and Christian allegorization, but stopped short of acknowledging the frank sexuality of the Song. It was rather Solomon's expression of gratitude to God for the peace and security of his kingdom. Calvin, in reaction to those who viewed the Song as lascivious and unworthy of canonicity, regarded it as indeed a song of human love, but nonetheless inspired. Rationalistic approaches of the eighteenth and nineteenth centuries understood the Song literally as human love poetry. The recognition of the erotic nature of the text raised anew the question of the inspiration of the Song and the appropriateness of its inclusion in the canon. This tended to prolong the allegorical approach among those committed to the book's canonicity.

Recent treatments by both Protestants and Roman Catholics have sought to accept the sexuality of the Song while affirming its divine inspiration. Other interpreters focus on the Song's positive view of sexuality as reflective of the intention of God before the fall (cf. Gen. 2:23-25). The inclusion of the Song in Scripture places human sexuality in its proper context within the whole human experience, physical, mental, and spiritual. The mutual longing and active initiation of contact by both male and female in the Song are taken by some feminists as an affirmation of equality.

Many interpreters, while rejecting the excesses of earlier allegorization, are reluctant to leave it aside altogether. Human love has long provided an important basis for understanding divine love. In the Bible God is portrayed as a father who loves his children and as a husband who woos his unfaithful wife. Drawing on passages from Paul (esp. Eph. 5:21-33), interpreters continue to note parallels between the human love expressed in the Song of Solomon and the love between the Church and its Lord.

Bibliography. G. L. Carr and D. J. Wiseman, *The Song of Solomon.* Tyndale (1984); R. Gordis, *The Song of Songs and Lamentations,* rev. ed. (New York: 1974); M. H. Pope, *Song of Songs.* AB 7C (1977).

SONG OF THE THREE YOUNG MEN. † An apocryphal addition to the book of Daniel (called in the KJV "Song of the Three Holy Children") placed after the Prayer of Azariah, with which it is considered a single composition. It appears in the Greek and Latin versions between Dan. 3:23 and 3:24.

In this song Daniel's three companions praise God supposedly in response to his miraculous protection in the furnace (so the introduction, v. 28; LXX, JB 3:51). But their song makes no reference to their experience in the flames except in one verse, in which they are also referred to by their Hebrew names, Shadrach, Meshach, and Abednego (v. 66; LXX, JB 3:88). Otherwise, the song is a hymn of praise to God who is the creator and the one worshiped in the temple. The song draws on Pss. 103, 136, and 148 at a number of points, and demonstrates liturgical characteristics (e.g., the regular refrain, "sing praises to him and highly exalt him forever").

The original language of the song is uncertain and may have been Hebrew, Aramaic, or Greek.

See also AZARIAH, PRAYER OF.

SONS OF THUNDER. *See* BOANERGES.

SOPATER [sō'pə tər] (Gk. *Sōpatros*). A Christian from Beroea who was a member of the group that accompanied Paul from Greece, Macedonia, and Asia Minor to Jerusalem at the end of Paul's third missionary journey (Acts 20:4). Sopater was probably one of the agents appointed by the churches to take the money gift to the church of Jerusalem (cf. 1 Cor. 16:3-4). He may be the same person as Sosipater (Rom. 16:21).

SOPHERETH [sŏf'ə rĕth] (Heb. *sôpereṭ* "scribe"). One of "Solomon's servants" whose descendants returned with Zerubbabel from exile in Babylon (Neh. 7:57). At Ezra 2:55 he is called Hassophereth.

SORCERY. *See* MAGIC.

SOREK, VALLEY OF [sôr'ĕk] (Heb. *nahal śōreq* "valley of a choice grape vine"). A valley to be identified with Wâdī eṣ-Ṣarâr, which runs in a northwesterly direction from the vicinity of Beth-shemesh (*ca.* 20 km. [13 mi.] west-southwest of Jerusalem) to the Mediterranean, meeting the sea about halfway between Ashdod and Tel Aviv. Delilah's home was in the valley of Sorek, then under Philistine control (Judg. 16:4).

SOSIPATER [sō sĭp'ə tər] (Gk. *Sōsipatros*). A Jewish Christian who was with Paul at the time of the writing of the Epistle to the Romans (probably at Corinth shortly before Paul's final journey to Jerusalem) and whose greetings are conveyed to the church at Rome

(Rom. 16:21). He may be the same person as Sopater (Acts 20:4).

SOSTHENES [sŏs'thə nēz] (Gk. *Sōsthenēs*). A common name in the Roman period. The two individuals mentioned in the New Testament may be the same person.

1. A synagogue ruler at Corinth (Acts 18:17), apparently the successor to Crispus when the latter became a Christian (v. 8). Sosthenes was beaten by the Gentile mob after the proconsul Gallio's hearing of a complaint by the Jews against Paul. Gallio ignored the beating. The incident is related as attestation of the proconsul's rejection of the Jews' complaint against the apostle.

2. A Christian, called "our brother" by Paul, who was with Paul when 1 Corinthians was written and who is mentioned in the salutation of the letter (1 Cor. 1:1).

SOTAI [sō'tī] (Heb. *sôṭay, sôṭay*). One of "Solomon's servants" whose descendants returned with Zerubbabel from exile in Babylon (Ezra 2:55; Neh. 7:57).

SOUL. † The usual translation of Heb. *nepeš* and Gk. *psychḗ* (though most translations retain considerable freedom in their renderings of these terms). As with other terms such as "body," "heart," and "spirit," "soul" does not designate a part of a human being, but rather the whole person considered from one particular aspect of its functioning. As such, it represents primarily the life force of the body (cf. Gen. 2:7) or the inner life of the person, encompassing desires and emotions.

Heb. *nepeš* in some contexts represents the person as that which requires food and water (Ps. 107:5, 9; Prov. 25:25; cf. Isa. 29:8; RSV "thirst"; 32:6; RSV "craving"; Hos. 9:4; RSV "hunger"). This leads immediately to a number of figurative uses of the term (e.g., Ps. 143:6; cf. Isa. 5:14; RSV "appetite"). By a natural extension the soul can also be the person as that which experiences desire (Gen. 34:3; 1 Kgs. 11:37; Ps. 42:1 [MT 2]; Prov. 16:24), and a person's soul can even be that object outside the person which he or she desires (cf. Ps. 35:25; RSV "heart's desire"). To "pour out" one's soul is to express one's desire fervently (1 Sam. 1:15). To engage "all" one's soul in something is to carry all of one's desires into that one object (Deut. 6:5). For a group of people to be of "one soul" (cf. Phil. 1:27; RSV "mind") is for them to be united in their desires. Because it is as a soul that a person experiences hunger and thirst, it is also as a soul that a person experiences need and suffering (Isa. 53:11; cf. Exod. 23:9; RSV, KJV "heart"), and is able to sympathize with the needy (Job 30:25). On this basis "soul" also represents the person as that which experiences all types of emotions (2 Sam. 5:8; Ps. 35:9; Cant. 1:7; Jer. 13:17; Jonah 2:7 [MT 8]; cf. 1 Sam. 1:10 [RSV paraphrases]).

The soul also represents the person as that which must breathe to remain alive—as well as the breath itself. When floodwaters have come up to the soul, a person might drown (cf. Ps. 69:1 [MT 2]; RSV "neck"). A person's soul "departs" when that person dies (Gen. 35:18). By a natural extension of the idea, a person's soul is his or her life, that which is threatened by anything that would bring death (Luke 2:35; cf. 1 Sam. 28:9; RSV "life"; Prov. 8:36; RSV "himself"; Mark 8:36; RSV "life").

Finally, "soul" can simply indicate an individual person, even a dead person (cf. Num. 6:6; RSV, KJV "body"), as distinguished from the mass of humanity (Lev. 22:3; RSV "person"). A group of people also can be called "souls" (Gen. 12:5; RSV "persons"). "Soul" can even, in this sense, function as a simple substitute for a pronoun. Therefore, the RSV often uses a simple pronoun where the Hebrew text has *nepeš* with a pronominal suffix (e.g., 19:19, "me"; 27:19b, "you").

In this sense human beings do not have souls—they are souls (Acts 2:41; cf. Gen. 2:7; *nepeš ḥayyâ*; RSV "living being"). "My soul," "my heart," and "my flesh" are all ways of saying "myself" (e.g., Ps. 84:2 [MT 3]). Such terms are used together (e.g., Deut. 6:5; 1 Thess. 5:23) to emphasize involvement of the whole person. They can also be contrasted, especially in the New Testament: the body can be killed while the soul lives on (Matt. 10:28); the soul can be purified (1 Pet. 1:22; cf. Heb. 12:23), but can also suffer from the assaults of the flesh's passions (1 Pet. 2:11).

Some early Christians believed in the preexistence of souls. Origen (second-third century) held that INCARNATION was the incarceration of the soul in punishment for some sin previously committed in the heavenly realm. Among major modern Christian groups, only Mormons hold to the preexistence of souls, viewing incarnation not as the soul's punishment but as a period of progress and testing. The Bible can be made to teach preexistence only by esoteric exegesis (e.g., when God provides the fallen Adam and Eve with "garments of skin" [Gen. 3:21] he is enclosing their hitherto disembodied souls in bodies of flesh).

Ample evidence points to an intertestamental Jewish belief in immortality of souls, which live on in intermediate places of judgment or blessing awaiting the final judgment and resurrection (e.g., 1 En. 22:1-14; "spirits of the souls of the dead"; 39:3-14). Rev. 6:9 notes the presence in heaven of the souls of martyrs prior to the resurrection.

SOUTH.* Because the Israelites thought of the compass points in relation to a person facing eastward, their words for "south" included Heb. *yāmîn* "on the right, right hand, south" and *têmān*, a related word. Other Hebrew terms for "south" are *negeb*, which is also the name of the southern region of Judah, "the Negeb," and *dārôm*. "The king of the south" is a term for various Ptolemaic rulers of Egypt at Dan. 11. New Testament terms for south are Gk. *nótos* and *mesēmbría* (Acts 8:26), which might also be translated "midday" (cf. RSV mg. "noon"). "The queen of the south" (Matt. 12:42; Luke 11:31) is the queen of Sheba (cf. 1 Kgs. 10:1-10).

SPAIN (Gk. *Spania*).† A state in southwestern Europe, comprising most of the Iberian (or Hispano-Lusitanian) peninsula. At least the southeastern portion of the land was populated by the rugged Iberians from *ca.* 3000 B.C. The Phoenicians established scattered trading outposts, and in the sixth century the Phocaean Greeks colonized the eastern and southern coasts. At the same time the Celts were occupying large portions of the peninsula. During the third century the Carthaginians invaded Spain and established Carthago Nova (modern Cartagena) as their capital. From Spain the general Hannibal mounted the Second Punic War against Rome. Following their victory in 201 the Romans formed two provinces in Spain (Hispania Citerior along the eastern coast and the Ebro river valley, and Hispania Ulterior along the southern coast and the Baetis [Guadalquivir] valley), but native resistance continued until 133. The Roman emperors Trajan, Hadrian, and Theodosius I were of Spanish origin.

Jews in Palestine had heard of Spain and of Roman power there as early as the early- to mid-second century B.C. (1 Macc. 8:3). At Rom. 15:24, 28 Paul tells of his plans to go to Spain, visiting the Christians in Rome on the way. The statement in 1 Clement that Paul "came to the limit of the west" (1 Clem. 5:7) has been taken as indicating that Paul's plans, though interrupted by his arrest in Jerusalem, detention in Caesarea, and trial in Rome, were carried through and that he did go to Spain. It is likely, however, that Clement's words refer to Rome as "the limit of the west," or that they are a conjecture based on Rom. 15 and not on any information that the apostle actually did go as far west as Spain. The latter can also be said about the only other early evidence for a journey by Paul to Spain, the Muratorian canon.

SPAN (Heb. *zeret*). A unit of length based on the distance from the thumb to the fifth finger of a spread hand and equivalent to *ca.* 22.2 cm. (8.75 in.) (Exod. 28:16; 39:9; Ezek. 43:13). In a rhetorical question Isa. 40:12 refers to God's span as that which "marked off the heavens."

SPARROW (Heb. *ṣippôr*; Gk. *strouthíon*).† Several varieties of small birds of family Fringillidae (finches). Heb. *ṣippôr* is a general term for small birds living near human dwellings (RSV, KJV usually "bird"; e.g., Gen. 15:10), but is rendered specifically as "sparrow" at Ps. 84:3 (MT 4); Prov. 26:2 (KJV also Ps. 102:7 [MT 8]). Birds in the category of *ṣippôr* could be considered "clean" for human consumption and sacrifice (Lev. 14). Jesus refers to sparrows as of little value (Matt. 10:29, 31; Luke 12:6-7). The prices he names for the birds are probably those asked when they were bought for food by the poor people of his day.

SPARTA [spär'tə] (Gk. *Spartē*).* A major city of the Peloponnesian peninsula of southern Greece in ancient times, capital of the territory of Laconia. The inhabitants of Sparta were known also as Lacedaemonians. When the Oniad priest Jason fled to Sparta (2 Macc. 5:9, "to the Lacedaemonians"), he was depending not only on the ancient legend of the common origin of the Jews and the Spartans, but probably also on previous diplomatic relations between the two peoples (cf. 1 Macc. 12:7-8, which refers to events occurring at some time in the first half of the third century B.C.), and perhaps on the presence of Jews living in

Sparta. Later, during their struggle against the Seleucid Empire, the Hasmoneans initiated friendly relations with the Spartans (vv. 2, 5-23; 14:16, 20-23).

SPEAR (Heb. *ḥᵃnîṯ, rōmaḥ*; Gk. *lónchē*).† An extremely common offensive weapon consisting of a long shaft with a point made of stone or iron (cf. 1 Sam. 13:22; 17:7) set on one end. In Old Testament usage Heb. *kîḏôn* generally represents a javelin (so usually RSV), a light spear that is thrown as opposed to heavier spears or lances used in close combat. The frequent mention of warriors armed with the *rōmaḥ* and a shield (e.g., 1 Chr. 12:24 [MT 25]) suggests the battle formation in which lances were held protruding from a wall of shields placed side by side. A soldier pierced Jesus' crucified body with a spear to make certain that he was dead (John 19:34).

SPECKLED BIRD OF PREY (Jer. 12:9). *See* BIRDS OF PREY.

SPELT. Heb. *kussemeṯ* represents some form of wheat, probably either spelt (*Triticum spelta* L.) or emmer wheat (*Triticum dicoccum* Schrank). It was grown in Egypt (Exod. 9:32; KJV "rie" or "rye"), Palestine (Isa. 28:25; cf. KJV mg. "spelt"), and Babylonia (Ezek. 4:9; KJV "fitches").

SPICES (Heb. *bōśem, sam*; Gk. *árōma*).† In ancient times spices were used in a number of forms to make the food and living environment of those who could afford them more pleasant. They were added to wines not only for flavoring but also because of the fragrance they emitted (Cant. 8:2), and were used in embalming (2 Chr. 16:14; John 19:39-40) and to offset the odors of a tomb being visited (Mark 16:1; Luke 23:56–24:1). Spices and aromatic oils were considered an essential aspect of physical beauty and played a large part in the imagery of eroticism (Esth. 2:12; Cant. 4:10, 14; 5:1, 13; 6:2; 8:14). Expertise in the use of spices was essential to centralized worship because of their use in anointing oil and incense (Exod. 25:6; 30:22-38; 1 Chr. 9:29-30). Among the spices so used was gum (Heb. *nᵉḵôṯ*), obtained from the resin of such plants as the *Astragalus tragacantha* or *Astragalus gummifer* (Gen. 37:25; KJV "spicery"; 43:11; KJV "spices"; cf. LXX Gk. *thymiáma* "incense"). Accordingly, spices were a significant part of the trade in luxury items (e.g., 1 Kgs. 10:2, 10, 25; Ezek. 27:22; Rev. 18:13). Supplies of spices stored away are mentioned as an indication of wealth (2 Kgs. 20:13).

SPIDER (Heb. *ʿakkāḇîš*). An Arachnid of the order Araneida, of which numerous species exist in Palestine. Distinguished from insects by the division of their bodies into two portions, the cephalothorax and abdomen, spiders are unique among animals because of their spinnerets, appendages to their abdomen which emit through spinning tubes a silky fluid. The manner in which a spider's web is woven is a metaphor for the deliberate sinful actions of the wicked at Isa. 59:5. The web itself typifies the fragile existence of the ungodly at Job 8:14.

The RSV and JB follow the Syriac version in reading "spider" at 27:18a, a metaphor similar to that of

8:14 (KJV, NIV "moth," following MT *ʿāš*; cf. Isa. 50:9). The small animal referred to at Prov. 30:28 (Heb. *śᵉmāmîṯ*) is usually identified as a lizard, though the older identification as a spider (so KJV) remains possible. Heb. *ʿakšûḇ* at Ps. 140:3 (MT 4) (KJV "adder"; RSV "viper") may be a variant of *ʿakkāḇîš* "spider."

SPIKENARD (KJV). *See* NARD.

SPINNING. The action of drawing together and twisting fibers to form yarn or thread (Heb. *ṭāwâ* "spin"; Gk. *néthō*). Spinning was normally considered women's work (Exod. 35:25-26; Prov. 31:19) and was tedious (cf. Matt. 6:8 par. Luke 12:27). A very simple apparatus was used. The unspun fibers of wool, flax, or cotton wound loosely onto the distaff (Heb. *peleḵ*) were twisted by the rotation by hand of the spindle (*kîšôr*). David's curse of Joab's family includes the wish that it may never be without one who "holds a spindle" (2 Sam. 3:29). Some have taken this as a curse of effeminacy, but the context suggests that the LXX is probably correct in interpreting the spindle as a staff or crutch on which a cripple would lean (so KJV, NIV).

SPIRIT (Heb. *rûaḥ*; Gk. *pneúma*).†

I. Old Testament

Heb. *rûaḥ* (as well as LXX Gk. *pneúma*) can mean wind (e.g., Gen. 8:1; Ps. 148:8; Amos 4:13), breath, or spirit. Use of the term in describing aspects of divine or human existence brings into relief the dynamism of God's movement or activity and the inner vitality of individual persons.

The Spirit of God has a role in creation alongside that of the Word of God (Ps. 33:6; cf. Gen. 1:2b, RSV mg.). Adam became a living being only when God breathed into his nostrils the "breath" of life (Heb. *nᵉšāmâ*, 2:7; cf. Job 33:4; Ezek. 37:14; Zech. 12:1). The spirit given by God continues to be the life principle that sustains every living thing (Gen. 6:17; 7:15, 22; Job 10:12; Ps. 104:30; Eccl. 3:19). It returns to God at his command or at death (Job 12:10; 34:14; Ps. 104:29; Eccl. 12:7; cf. Gen. 6:3; Num. 16:22).

A person's "spirit" also includes elements of personality, emotion, and attitude. Thus the spirit of a person can be "broken" or despondent (Exod. 6:9; Job 17:1; Isa. 61:3), obedient (Num. 14:24; Ps. 51:10, 12 [MT 12, 14]; cf. RSV mg.), troubled (Gen. 41:8), jealous (Num. 5:14), patient (Eccl. 7:8), proud (Prov. 16:18; Eccl. 7:8), humble (Prov. 16:19; 29:23), or faithless (Hos. 4:12). Resolve that is the basis of success is linked to the rising or ebbing spirit of the individual (Gen. 45:27; Josh. 5:1; 1 Sam. 30:12; Ps. 143:7). Here, too, as with the continuation of life itself, the spirit is subject to God's rule (Deut. 2:30; 1 Chr. 5:26; Ezra 1:1, 5). God favors the humble spirit (Ps. 34:18 [MT 19]; 51:17 [MT 19]; Isa. 57:15; 66:2).

Ezekiel presents the eschatological promise of "a new spirit" given by God (Ezek. 11:19; 36:26) that bears the closest relationship to God's Spirit (v. 27; 37:7-14). This is an aspect of the promised new age characterized by God's Spirit (Isa. 32:15; 44:3; Ezek. 39:29; Joel 2:28 [MT 3:1]).

II. Intertestamental Judaism

During the centuries that immediately preceded the coming of Christ the concept of "spirit" among Jews was elaborated in various directions. It was during this period that a vast hierarchy of heavenly powers came to be envisioned, referred to as angels or spirits (e.g., 1 En.15:4-10; cf. Acts 23:8). Hellenistic influences led to a greater contrast between spirit and body. Some scholars suggest that exposure to Iranian dualism led to speculation, especially at Qumran, about the perpetual conflict between the two spirits (or angels) of light and darkness, of righteousness and evil (cf. 1QS 3:13–4:26).

III. New Testament

The New Testament continues Old Testament ideas with regard to "spirit." That Gk. *pneúma* means both "wind" and "spirit" is the basis for the wordplay at John 3:8, and *pneúma* as God's "breath" appears at 2 Thess. 2:8 (cf. John 20:22). The *pneúma* given by God is still the principle that creates and sustains life (Rev. 11:11). References to the "spirit" as the arena of personality and emotions similar to those in the Old Testament occur (e.g., Mark 2:8; 8:12; John 11:33; 13:21; 1 Pet. 3:4). That John as a child "became strong in spirit" (Luke 1:80) refers to the developing vitality of his personality. As in the Old Testament death is seen as the release of the spirit to God (Matt. 27:50; Luke 23:46; Acts 7:59; Jas. 2:26). Nonetheless, the dead are sometimes referred to as "spirits," whether simply as disembodied (Luke 24:37, 39), or with an emphasis on a continued conscious existence (1 Pet. 3:18). Elsewhere "spirit" occurs as a generic term for persons (e.g., v. 19; *see* SOUL).

In the New Testament the encounter between God (and his Spirit) and the human spirit is a fundamental aspect of Christian experience (Rom. 8:16; Gal. 6:18). Through Jesus Christ God has now given his Spirit to his people in a new way (John 7:38; Acts 2:1-21, 33, 38; Gal. 3:2, 14; Titus 3:5-6). It is "in spirit" that persons most readily encounter God and experience his life (John 4:24; cf. 1 Cor. 2:13; 14:14-15; Eph. 6:18). In the encounter between the human spirit and God's Spirit positive expectations for control and virtue emerge (Gal. 5:16-26), but the spirit remains an arena of struggle for the Christian (1 Cor. 7:1). This struggle is characterized by Paul as a struggle between spirit and flesh (Rom. 8:3-13; 1 Cor. 3:1; Gal. 3:3; 5:16-17; cf. John 3:6; 6:63). The plurality of spiritual beings and powers that began to be envisioned in post-Old Testament Judaism (e.g., 1 En. 15; 61:10; Jub. 2:2; Tob. 3:8; Acts 23:8; 1 Cor. 12:10) becomes itself the arena in which the Christian (Eph. 6:12) and God himself (cf. vv. 10ff.) are engaged in battle.

It has sometimes been thought on the basis of some New Testament texts that the human being is a composite of two parts, body/flesh and soul/spirit, or three, with soul and spirit reckoned separately. The New Testament does not, however, look at human nature as a collection of components, but as a unity. Different terms, such as "heart," "flesh," "spirit," "soul," and "mind," refer to particular aspects of human existence, life, and consciousness. The New Testament writers occasionally list some of these terms to speak of the totality of human life or set different terms in opposition to each other to emphasize the distinction between differing attitudes (e.g., Rom. 8:10; 1 Cor. 5:5; 2 Cor. 4:16; Eph. 2:3; 1 Thess. 5:23; Heb. 4:12; cf. Mark 12:30). "Spirit" can denote an immediacy of contact with divine realities as opposed to, e.g., a more deliberate and evaluative form of devotion associated with the "mind" (1 Cor. 14:14-15), but all such terms are used to describe ways in which the whole person acts.

See FLESH; HOLY SPIRIT.

Bibliography. H. Kleinknecht, et al., "πνεῦμα," *TDNT* 6(1968): 332-455.

SPIRIT, EVIL (Heb. *rûaḥ rāʿâ*; Gk. *pneúma ponērón*)/**UNCLEAN** (Heb. *rûaḥ ṭumʾâ*; Gk. *pneúma akátharton*).† The Old Testament refers to "evil spirits" in two narratives. In both cases these "spirits" are instruments of God sent to cause an unsettling of political conditions. In the first instance, this was accomplished by introducing enmity between a ruler (Abimelech) and the citizens of Shechem (Judg. 9:23). In the second it resulted in God's causing madness to come on Saul so that an obscure person (David) was brought into prominence in the royal court (1 Sam. 16:14-23) and, later, in increasing Saul's suspicion of David (18:10-11; 19:9). In another incident, a "lying spirit" (Heb. *rûaḥ šeqer*), more personalized than the "evil spirits" but still an instrument of God to accomplish his purposes, works through Ahab's prophet Micaiah to lead the Israelite king to his destruction (1 Kgs. 22:19-23 par. 2 Chr. 18:18-22). Similar corruption of prophecy led a postexilic writer to associate prophecy with an "unclean spirit" (Zech. 13:2).

At the time of the New Testament the existence of malevolent spirits was part of the world view of most Jews (cf. Acts 23:8). A number of terms are used for these beings in the New Testament: "evil spirit(s)" (Luke 7:21; 8:2; Acts 19:12-16), "unclean spirit(s)" (e.g., Mark 1:23-27; Luke 11:24), "unclean demon" (Luke 4:33), "foul spirits" (Rev. 16:13), "demonic spirits" (v. 14), "deceitful spirits" (1 Tim. 4:1), and simply "spirits" (Matt. 8:16). Malevolent spirits are particularly known for controlling individuals and inducing symptoms in them (cf. the "dumb and deaf spirit" at Mark 9:25). Narratives of the activity of such spirits are presented to introduce accounts of healing by Jesus or leaders of the early Church.

See also DEMON; EXORCISM.

SPIRITS IN PRISON (Gk. *tá en phylakḗ pneúmata*).* According to 1 Pet. 3:19-20 Christ "went and preached to the spirits in prison." He went not in flesh but in a spiritual state (the probable meaning of "in which," v. 19), probably after his death and possibly after his resurrection (cf. v. 18). The spirits to which Christ went are identified as those "who formerly did not obey, when God's patience waited in the days of Noah, during the building of the ark." According to an interpretation of Gen. 6 current in Judaism at the time of the New Testament, the "sons of God" who existed during the time of great wickedness before the flood (Gen. 6:2, 4) were angels who as punishment for their corruption of mankind were cast into prison (1 En. 6–10; cf. Jude 6; 2 Pet. 2:4). This understanding of the Genesis account provides the most likely understanding of "the spirits in prison." Christ's preaching to the "spirits" might have been his announcement to these ancient imprisoned beings of his victory over sin (cf. 1 Pet. 3:18) or over death (cf. v. 22). At any rate, the settling of the old matter of the "sons of God" is probably portrayed by Christ's preaching to them, so that his death takes on a uniquely eschatological role. The preaching of the gospel to the dead (4:6) is often taken to refer to the same event, but need not be.

SPIRITUAL GIFTS. Apart from 1 Pet. 4:10, Gk. *chárisma* occurs in the New Testament only in the writings of Paul. It is used primarily in two ways, first as a general reference to God's "free" or "special" gift of his grace, especially in salvation (Rom. 5:15-16; 6:23; 11:29; 1 Cor. 7:7; 2 Cor. 1:9-11), and more frequently by Paul as a designation for specific "spiritual gifts," special endowments to be employed in service to the Christian community. The spiritual gifts are, according to Paul, "the manifestation of the Spirit for the common good" (1 Cor. 12:7), ways in which the one Spirit possessed by all Christians works in diverse forms (vv. 4-6, 11-30; cf. Eph. 4:4-11). While the use of natural or acquired talents for the Church may be involved, the emphasis is on enablement by God.

The effective execution of an ordinary leadership or support task in the body of Christ rests on a spiritual gift (Rom. 12:6-8; cf. 1 Tim. 4:14; 2 Tim. 1:6; 1 Pet. 4:10-11). The spiritual gifts listed at 1 Cor. 12:8-10 are generally of a more extraordinary character and include healing and "the working of miracles." Such manifestations were apparently common in the early Church. Paul emphasizes to the Corinthians that prophecy is the most important of such gifts (14:1-6, 24-25; cf. Acts 2:17). He expects that the exercise of prophecy will lead outsiders to recognize the presence of God in the Christian assembly (1 Cor. 14:24-25).

Paul's greatest concern was that the Corinthians' use of the spiritual gifts in worship be done in an orderly fashion (vv. 31-33, 40), in such a way as to build up the community as a whole rather than just individuals (vv. 4, 12, 26; cf. Eph. 4:12-16), and with the love that is to characterize the people of God (1 Cor. 12:31b–14:1; cf. 8:1b).

See also entries on individual gifts of the Spirit.

SPIT (Heb. verbs *yāraq, rāqaq*, nouns *rōq, rîr* "saliva"; Gk. verb *(em)ptýō*, noun *ptýsma*).† In both the Old and New Testament, spitting is regarded as a sign of contempt (Job 17:6; Heb. *tōpet*; KJV "a tabret"; 30:10; Isa. 50:6; Mark 10:34; 14:65; 15:19). At Deut. 25:9 (and perhaps Num. 12:14) it is part of a legal ritual of humiliation. Ritual uncleanness was conveyed by spitting (Lev. 15:8). "Till I swallow my spittle" (Job 7:19) was an expression meaning "for just a brief moment." Saliva running down from a person's mouth was taken as a sign of insanity (1 Sam. 21:13 [MT 14]). Jesus' use of his saliva in healings (Mark 7:33; 8:23; John 9:6) reflects the understanding of saliva as a curative substance among both Jews and Gentiles.

SPRING, FOUNTAIN (Heb. *῾ayin, ma῾yān, māqôr*; Gk. *pēgē*).† Supplies of water played a decisive role in the lives of the ancient Israelites and their neigh-

bors, and thus could be regarded as the source of life itself (cf. Eccl. 12:6; Heb. *mabbûa῾*). A number of major Israelite cities contained elaborate constructions that enabled the people to obtain water from natural springs, including Jerusalem, Megiddo, Hazor, and Gibeon. Such a water system, secured against attack, was especially important when a city was under siege (as in Hezekiah's Jerusalem, 2 Kgs. 20:20; Sir. 48:17). A number of places were named for the springs that made settlement possible (e.g., En-gannim, En-gedi, En-rogel). God's giving of springs is mentioned in recitations of his blessings (Ps. 84:6 [MT 7]; 104:10). Eschatological visions of an ideal future include life-giving springs (Isa. 35:7; 49:10; Joel 3:18 [MT 4:18]; cf. Ps. 114:8).

"Spring" and "springs" are used in figurative language for God as the source of life (Ps. 36:9 [MT 10]; Jer. 2:13) and guidance (Isa. 35:7; 49:10), and to depict sexual activity (Prov. 5:16), unending vigor (Isa. 58:11; John 4:14; Rev. 7:17), and cleansing from sin (Zech. 13:1). A spring that gives dirty water is figurative for a good man who gives in to evil (Prov. 25:26) and a dry spring for the wicked who have been punished (Ps. 107:33; Hos. 13:15) or who give nothing of value (2 Pet. 2:17).

SQUAD (Gk. *tetrádion*).* A detachment of four soldiers. Probably because Peter had escaped from prison on an earlier occasion (Acts 5:19), Herod Agrippa I placed the apostle under a heavy guard consisting of four squads (12:4; KJV "quaternions").

SQUARE (Heb. *reḥôb*).* The central open public place in towns, usually little more than a widening of one of the streets. For this reason English versions vary considerably in translating terms for such areas (KJV consistently "street"). The square of a town (or one of the squares of a city; 2 Chr. 29:4; 32:6; Ezra 10:9; Neh. 8:1) could be a place of public assembly. When it was desired to make a public display of some kind, a public square immediately came to mind (Deut. 13:16 [MT 17]; 2 Sam. 21:12; Esth. 4:1-7; 6:9-11; Isa. 15:3). The elders of a town might gather at the town square to administer justice and provide instruction for citizens (e.g., Job 29:7; cf. Isa. 59:14). Travelers who lacked lodging might sleep in the open square (Judg. 19:15), but where strangers were disliked this could be dangerous (cf. Gen. 19:2; Judg. 19:20).

STACHYS [stā'kĭs] (Gk. *Stachys*). A Christian in Rome greeted by Paul and called his "beloved" (Rom. 16:9).

STACTE [stăk'tī] (Heb. *nāṭāp*).* One of the "sweet spices" used in making the incense of the tabernacle (Exod. 30:34), probably a resin from the storax tree (*Styrax officinalis* L.).

STADIA [stā'dĭ ə] (Gk. sing. *stádion*). Unit of distance equivalent to 170-190 m. (189-215 yds.). Stadia are always represented by an equal number of "furlongs" in the KJV, but are in the RSV translated to the equivalent in miles (Luke 24:13; John 6:19; 11:18), or brought over simply as "furlongs" (Matt. 14:24) or "stadia" (Rev. 14:20; 21:16). *See* WEIGHTS AND MEASURES.

STAFF (Heb. *maqqēl, maṭṭeh, šēḇeṭ, miš'eneṭ*; Gk. *rhábdos*).† Any kind of substantial stick used as a walking stick (Gen. 32:10 [MT 11]; Matt. 10:10), by shepherds as a defense against predators (Zech. 11:7; cf. Ps. 23:4), as a ceremonial object like a scepter (Gen. 49:10; Isa. 14:5), for punishment (30:32), or as a goad (Num. 22:27), a divining stick (Hos. 4:12), or weapon of war (Isa. 10:24). The use of a staff to support the body is the basis for the expression "the staff of bread" for food sufficient to support a given society (Lev. 26:26; Ps. 105:16; Ezek. 4:16; 5:16; 14:13; cf. Isa. 3:1).

See also ROD; SCEPTER.

STANDARD. *See* BANNER.

STAR (Heb. *kôḵāḇ*; Gk. *astḗr, ástron*). The stars are regarded as among the more majestic of God's creations (Job 22:12; Ps. 8:3-4 [MT 4-5]; 136:7-9). In speaking of their creation, Gen. 1:14-16 follows the customary language of the day in referring to the stars as lights in the heavenly dome (*see* FIRMAMENT).

Worship of stars was part of ancient Mesopotamian religion. Such worship was forbidden to Israel but was nonetheless a frequent threat to Israel's religion (Deut. 4:19; Amos 5:26). At the center of the Old Testament's response to such forms of worship is its teaching concerning the creation of all things by the God of Israel (Ps. 147:4), his continuing sovereignty over all things (Job 9:4-10), and the praise they accord him (Ps. 148:3; cf. 19:1 [MT 2]). Astrology is denigrated as a form of divination (Isa. 47:12-13; Jer. 10:2-3a). The Old Testament does sometimes draw on the language of mythology concerning the stars (Judg. 5:20; Job 38:7).

Stars are mentioned in a number of figures of speech. At Eccl. 12:2 the darkening of the light of sun, moon, and stars behind clouds is a figure for the onset of the disabilities of old age. At Num. 24:17 a future ruler is metaphorically referred to as a rising star (cf. Dan. 8:10; *see* DAY STAR). A ruler who seeks to rule all others is said to be seeking to rise above the stars (Isa. 14:13; cf. Obad. 4). The number of the stars is used to represent an uncountably large number, usually the number of the people of Israel (e.g., Gen. 15:5; Deut. 1:10; Neh. 9:23; Nah. 3:16). The darkening or falling of the stars is an aspect of visions of destruction by God (Isa. 13:10; Ezek. 32:7-8; Joel 2:10; 3:15 [MT 4:15]; Matt. 24:29). The use of "star(s)" to represent rulers and the role of stars in eschatological visions have a recurring place in the language of the book of Revelation, together with the representation of heavenly messengers as stars (Rev. 1:16, 20; 2:1; 6:13; 8:10-12; 9:1; 12:1, 4). "Those who turn many to righteousness" are said to be, after the resurrection, like the stars that shine eternally (Dan. 12:3).

The wise men saw a star "in the East" that they identified as a sign heralding the birth of a king of the Jews, going before them from Jerusalem to stand over the place where they found the infant Jesus (Matt. 2:1-10). The view that this "star" was a unique and miraculous phenomenon remains, but a number of identifications with natural phenomena have been suggested. Among these are Halley's comet, which appeared in 12 B.C., a conjunction of the planets Jupiter and Saturn, that occurred three times in 7 B.C., a

nova that appeared in 5 B.C., and conjunctions of Jupiter and Venus in 3-2 B.C. More than one natural phenomenon may have been involved.

See ASTRONOMY.

STAY AND STAFF (Heb. *maš'ēn ûmaš'ēnâ*). At Isa. 3:1 the prophet announces that God will take away from Jerusalem and Judah "stay and staff," the "stay of bread" (*miš'an-leḥem*) and the "stay of water" (*miš'an-mayim*). Here a staff (probably a walking stick) used for support is a figure for food and water sufficient to support the people.

STEEL. The KJV rendering of Heb. *nᵉḥûšâ* at 2 Sam. 22:35; Job 20:24; Ps. 18:34 (MT 35) and *nᵉḥōšeṭ* at Jer. 15:12, both properly translated "copper" or "bronze." *See* BRONZE.

STEPHANAS [stĕf'ə nəs] (Gk. *Stephanas* "crown"). A Corinthian Christian whose household members were the first Christians in the province of Achaia (1 Cor. 16:15) and who were among the few at Corinth baptized by Paul (1:16). Because they had "devoted themselves to the service of the saints" (16:15), Paul urged the Corinthian Christians to be subject to them (v. 16). Stephanas, along with Fortunatus and Achaicus—perhaps members of his household, came to Paul (probably in Ephesus) shortly before or while he was writing 1 Corinthians (v. 17); they probably brought some of the news about the Corinthian church that formed the basis of 1 Corinthians, perhaps the letter from the church mentioned at 7:1.

STEPHEN [stē'vən] (Gk. *Stephanos* "crown").† One of the seven chosen as representatives of the Hellenists (Greek-speaking Jews) in the early Church in Jerusalem after a dispute concerning the daily distribution to the widows in the Church (Acts 6:1-5).

As with Philip, another of the seven, the description of Stephen's activities is not concerned with the distribution. Instead, it shows that Stephen had a prominent role in miracle-working and in disputations with non-Christian Hellenistic Jews (vv. 8-10). The latter role led to Stephen's trial before the Sanhedrin, where witnesses accused Stephen of speaking against the law of Moses and the temple (vv. 11-14). These accusations show that Stephen (and perhaps the Hellenists in the Church as a whole) had begun to draw far-reaching conclusions from certain statements of Jesus (e.g., Mark 7:14-19; 14:58; John 2:19; 4:21).

In his speech at his trial (Acts 7:2-53) Stephen accuses his hearers of not upholding the law of Moses (v. 53; cf. v. 35). But he shows no positive regard for the temple (vv. 47-50), apparently regarding the movable tabernacle of the wilderness as more in accord with God's will than the fixed temple (vv. 44-45). It is probable, therefore, that the accusations made against him were exaggerated on some but not all points. The main themes of Stephen's speech are God's constant care for the people of Israel in view of their role in salvation-history and the consistent failure of the people to live out that role from the time of Moses on. In response to his speech Stephen was stoned to death in accordance with the law regarding blasphemy (vv. 54-60; Lev. 24:16).

Stephen's trial and death and the persecution that arose subsequently stimulated important changes in the early Church. The persecution was directed mainly against the Hellenists (so that the apostles, not among the Hellenists, were able to stay in Jerusalem; Acts 8:1). These events led to the spread of the gospel beyond Jerusalem, and beyond the Jews to Samaritans (8:4-25), and later to Gentiles (11:19-20). Paul (Saul) had perhaps one of his first contacts with the proclamation of faith in Jesus at Stephen's trial (7:58; 8:1) and became first a persecutor (8:3; 9:1) and then "apostle to the Gentiles" (Rom. 11:13).

Bibliography. F. F. Bruce, *Peter, Stephen, James, and John* (Grand Rapids: 1980); M. H. Scharlemann, *Stephen: A Singular Saint* (Rome: 1968).

STEPHEN, APOCALYPSE OF. An "apocalypse ascribed to Stephen," listed in the sixth-century Gelasian Decree and rejected as apocryphal. This work is not now extant unless it is to be identified with an account, written *ca.* 415 by an elder named Lucian, of a vision that led Lucian to the discovery of the bones of Stephen.

STEWARD. In the basic sense, a person who manages the affairs of a large and wealthy household. The tasks of a steward might in different cases include supervision of the service at the master's table, oversight of other household servants, or management of the master's finances. When Joseph was a leading government official in Egypt, his house was under the management of a steward (Heb. *'al bayit*, lit. one "over the household"; Gen. 43:16 [KJV "ruler"], 19; 44:1, 4).

Among the officials of the kings of Israel were caretakers and supervisors of royal property, whose titles are sometimes translated "steward" (*sōkēn*, Isa. 22:15; KJV "treasurer"; *šar*, 1 Chr. 27:31; KJV "rulers"; 28:1). A lower official or servant who was to care for Daniel and his three companions is designated by the term *melṣar* (Dan. 1:11, 16; RSV "steward"), which is wrongly taken as a proper name ("Melzar") in the LXX and KJV. Heb. *ben-mešeq* at Gen. 15:2 (KJV "steward") should be rendered "heir" with RSV or "the son of Meshek," i.e., as another way of indicating that Eliezer was from Damascus.

Gk. *oikonómos* is used for typical figures that appear in two of Jesus' parables. The first so designated is a servant who supervises the household in his master's absence and who might be rewarded by being made manager of all his master's possessions (Luke 12:42-44). The other is a servant who has oversight of at least some of his master's wealth and thus has the opportunity to waste some of it, thereby risking his position (16:1-2). The latter figure retains his position only by further fraud, illustrating for Jesus' disciples not the benefits of dishonesty but the need to live prudently and wisely (vv. 3-8). An *oikonómos* could also be a civic official (Rom. 16:23; RSV "treasurer"; KJV "chamberlain").

Paul spoke of himself as a "steward" and of his ministry as a "stewardship" (*oikonomía*) of God's mysteries (1 Cor. 4:1-2), of God's grace (Eph. 3:2; KJV "dispensation"), and of the tasks of preaching the gospel (1 Cor. 9:17; RSV "commission"; KJV

"dispensation") and teaching God's word to the Church (Col. 1:25; RSV "office"; KJV "dispensation"). He also applies the term *oikonómos* to bishops as "God's steward," having oversight of the churches (Tit. 1:7). 1 Pet. 4:10 speaks of all Christians as "stewards" of the gifts given by God to the Church.

Gk. *epítropos* is used of persons who fill roles similar to those associated with the name *oikonómos* (Matt. 20:8; Luke 8:3). The two words are used together at Gal. 4:2 for the servants (RSV "guardians and trustees") responsible for the conduct and upbringing of children of wealthy families. The "steward of the feast" (John 2:8-9; Gk. *architríklinos*; KJV "governor/ruler of the feast") supervised the servants who served the tables at a banquet.

STOCKS. † A wooden device used to restrain the feet and sometimes the wrists of prisoners. Heb. *saḏ* at Job 13:27 (cf. 33:11) is thought to represent a block attached to the legs that apparently does not entirely prevent walking (cf. the following clause at 13:27, "and watchest [or 'you mark'] all my paths," and the next, "thou settest a bound to [i.e., 'a boundary around'] the soles of my feet").

The "stocks" into which Pashhur put Jeremiah (Jer. 20:2-3; *mahpeket*; cf. Targum "prison") may have actually been a narrow prison cell. In a letter to the priest Zephaniah (29:26) the temple overseer Shemaiah complained about Zephaniah's failure to restrain Jeremiah by putting him into the *mahpeket* and the *ṣînōq* (KJV "prison and stocks"). RSV is probably correct in taking *ṣînōq* as "collar," i.e., a pillory. In another incident (2 Chr. 16:10) the seer Hanani is placed in a *bêt hammahpeket* (KJV "prison house"; RSV "in the stocks, in prison"), again probably a narrow cell.

The Hebrew of Prov. 7:22c (KJV "as a fool to the correction of the stocks") is obscure; JB "as a stag is caught fast" has the support of the ancient versions.

In the jail at Philippi Paul and Silas' feet were put in stocks (Gk. *xýlon*).

STOICS [stō'ĭks] (Gk. *Stōikoi*). The members of a philosophical school founded by Zeno of Citium (*ca.* 335-263 B.C.) who taught in the *Stoa Poikilē* ("Painted Porch"), a colonnaded building in the Agora at Athens, hence the name. In Stoicism the primary focus is on how life is to be lived, with the attainment of virtue stressed above all. For the Stoics, virtuous living is living in accordance with nature.

Stoicism was attuned to the new international climate created by the conquests of Alexander and Rome, in which rootlessness was a common condition. It came to be the most influential philosophical school in the Hellenistic and Roman worlds, influencing such philosophers as Epictetus and Seneca.

Stoics were in Paul's audience when he spoke at Athens (Acts 17:18), and some scholars contend that the apostle himself was influenced by Stoicism. Indeed, a keynote of Stoicism reflected in Paul's letters is the stress on self-sufficiency, contentment in all circumstances that nature or destiny brings to an individual, and indifference to whether one is poor or wealthy, suffering or not suffering (cf. 1 Cor. 7:17, 20, 24; ch. 9; Phil. 4:11-12; cf. 1 Tim. 6:6-8).

STOMACH. † A number of Hebrew words generally translated "stomach," "belly," or "bowels" are used for the human abdomen considered from different aspects and in relation to different functions, both physical and psychological. Heb. *beṭen* often designates a woman's "womb" (e.g., Gen. 25:23; Ps. 22:9 [MT 10]), but can also be a term for the stomach (Job 20:15; Ezek. 3:3), as well as the abdomen in general (Num. 5:21; Judg. 3:21-22; Cant. 7:2 [MT 3]), male and female reproduction (Deut. 28:11), a rounded architectural structure in Solomon's temple (1 Kgs. 7:20; RSV "rounded projection"), the capacity for faulty or evil reasoning (Job 15:2, 35), desire, sometimes avarice (20:20; RSV "greed"; Prov. 13:25), emotions (Job 32:19; RSV "heart"), the "body" united to the "soul" (Ps. 31:9 [MT 10]; 44:25 [MT 26]), and the deepest parts of the land of the dead (Jonah 2:2 [MT 3]; RSV "belly of Sheol").

Heb. *mē'îm* is another word that represents reproductive capacity (e.g., Ruth 1:11; 2 Sam. 7:12; RSV "body"), the digestive tract (Num. 5:22; 2 Chr. 21:15, 18-19; Job 20:14), emotions (30:27; Cant. 5:4; RSV "heart"; Lam. 1:20; RSV "soul"), and inner thoughts (Ps. 40:8 [MT 9]; RSV "heart").

A general term for the inner organs of the torso is *qereḇ* (e.g., Exod. 12:9; KJV "purtenance"; Prov. 14:33; RSV "heart"; KJV "the midst"). Other Hebrew words that are more specific and used less frequently are *gāḥôn* (Gen. 3:14; Lev. 11:42), *kārēš* (Jer. 51:34), *ḥōmeš* (2 Sam. 2:23; 3:27; 20:10; KJV "fifth [rib]"; cf. 4:6 [RSV mg.]), and *qēḇâ* (Deut. 18:3; KJV "maw").

In the New Testament Gk. *stómachos* "stomach" appears only at 1 Tim. 5:23. More frequent are *koilía* and *splánchna*. Gk. *koilía* is used for inner organs in general (e.g., Matt. 12:40), digestive organs (Matt. 15:17; Mark 7:19), and most often the womb or a person's origin (e.g., Luke 1:15; Acts 3:2 [RSV paraphrases]); it also appears as a figure for avarice at Rom. 16:18; Phil. 3:19. The use of *splánchna* with reference to psychological states, generally mercy or affection (e.g., Luke 1:78; 2 Cor. 6:12; 1 John 3:17), had by the time of the New Testament all but completely supplanted its use for the inner organs—generally intestines (only Acts 1:18 in the New Testament; RSV "bowels")—and had given rise to the verb *splanchnízomai* "have compassion toward."

STOMACHER. The KJV rendering of Heb. *pᵉṯîgîl* (Isa. 3:24). RSV "rich robe" is more likely to be correct and better suits the contrast with "a girding with sackcloth."

STONING. *See* DEATH *II.*

STORK (Heb. *ḥᵃsîḏâ* "kindly"). Any of a group of long-legged, long-necked, and large-billed birds (family *Ciconiidae* of genus Ciconia). These migratory wading birds reach a height of *ca.* 1.2 m. (4 ft.). Two species of storks are known in Palestine, the white stork (*Ciconia ciconia* or *Ciconia alba*) and black stork (*Ciconia nigra*). The stork is related to the heron, and in some passages the Hebrew term may indicate either species.

Storks were among the animals designated unclean by the law of Moses (Lev. 11:19; Deut. 14:18). Jer. 8:7 refers to their migratory patterns, and Ps. 104:17 notes their nesting in treetops. A comparison of the ostrich with the stork may exist at Job 39:13 (so JB, NIV), but the wording of this verse is quite uncertain.

STRAIGHT, STREET CALLED (Gk. *rhýmē kalouménē Eutheia*). A street in Damascus where a Jew named Judas lived, to whose home Paul was directed and where he stayed after his vision of Jesus outside the city (Acts 9:11). The street was the main thoroughfare of the city, running east to west, flanked by colonnades and marked by large gates at either end. The name "Straight" survives (Arab. *Darb al-Mustaqim*), but the location of the street has changed somewhat.

STRANGER. *See* SOJOURNER.

STRANGLING. * Job mentions strangling in connection with Ahithophel's suicide (2 Sam. 17:23; Heb. *ḥānaq*, generally translated "hanged"), remarking that he himself would prefer death by strangling than continuation of his suffering (Job 7:15). Nahum speaks of strangling as a lion's method of killing prey (Nah. 2:12 [MT 13]). The Mosaic prohibition of eating blood (Gen. 9:4; Lev. 3:17; Deut. 12:23-25) led to specific methods of slaughtering in such a way that blood was drained off. Thus strangling was excluded, and what was not slaughtered in the prescribed swift fashion was considered "strangled" (Mishnah *Hullin* 1.2). The prohibition of "blood" and "what is strangled" was passed on to the Gentile Christians of Syria and Asia Minor as an accommodation to the scruples of Jews (Gk. *pniktós*; Acts 15:20-21, 29; 21:25).

STREET. *See* CITY.

STRIPES. *See* LASH.

STRONGHOLD (Heb. *mā'ôz*, *mᵉṣāḏ*, *miḇṣār*). A place of refuge or defense such as a mountain fortress, guard tower, or hideout (Judg. 6:2, 26; 1 Chr. 12:8 [MT 9]; cf. Isa. 33:16; RSV "fortresses"), a strategic point on the walls of a city (25:12; RSV "fortifications"), or simply a well-fortified city as a whole (Ps. 89:40 [MT 41]; Lam. 2:2). "Stronghold" is a frequent metaphor for God as the one who gives judgment on behalf of the oppressed (Ps. 9:9 [MT 10]; Heb. *miśgāḇ*; Jer. 16:19) or the one who guards the lives of those who trust him (Ps. 27:1; Nah. 1:7). At 2 Cor. 10:4 Gk. *ochýrōma* "strongholds" is a metaphor for "arguments and every proud obstacle to the knowledge of God" (v. 5).

STUMBLING BLOCK/STONE (Heb. *mikšōl*; Gk. *próskomma*, *skándalon*). † The Bible's only literal reference to a stumbling block is at Lev. 19:14. The conscious setting of an obstacle in the path of one who is not prepared for it—a blind person in the Leviticus prohibition—is the focus of the subsequent metaphorical references to stumbling blocks. Threatened judgments by God can be referred to as stumbling blocks (Jer. 6:21), as can the sins that lead to judgment (Ezek. 7:19; 14:3-4, 7; 44:12) and occasions for sin set in place by God (3:20). In the New Testament occasions for sin that come from humans are called "stumbling blocks" (Rev. 2:14; cf. Matt. 13:41; RSV "causes of sin"; 1 John 2:10; RSV mg., Matt. 16:23; 18:7; Luke 17:1-2). Paul characterizes any encouragement to violate conscience that arises from differences in practice among Christians as a "stumbling block" (Rom. 14:13; 1 Cor. 8:9).

God is often called Israel's rock, i.e., security (e.g., Deut. 32:4; Ps. 18:46 [MT 47]; 62:2 [MT 3]; Isa. 17:10). But when a word from the prophet Isaiah is not heeded, God becomes a rock for Israel to stumble over (8:14, "a stone of offense [Heb. *'eben negep*], and a rock of stumbling [*ṣûr mikṣôl*]"). Two different effects of the coming of Christ, salvation for some and "stumbling" for others, are portrayed at Rom. 9:33; 1 Pet. 2:6, 8 by the combination of these "rock" metaphors; the double reference to the stone of stumbling at Isa. 8:14 (Gk. *líthos proskómmatos, pétra skandálou*) is combined with the reference to a secure foundation rock at 28:16 (cf. Luke 2:34; 1 Cor. 1:23; Gal. 5:11).

On Ps. 69:22 (MT 23) (quoted at Rom. 11:9, where KJV reads "stumblingblock"), see SNARES AND TRAPS.

SUAH [sŏŏ'ə] (Heb. *sûaḥ*). A son of Zophah of the tribe of Asher (1 Chr. 7:36).

SUCATHITES [sŏŏ'kə thīts] (Heb. *śûkātîm*). One of the families of "the scribes that dwelt at Jabez" listed among the descendants of Caleb and also perhaps considered a Kenite or Rechabite group (1 Chr. 2:55; KJV "Suchathites"). The text of this verse has become confused in the course of transmission.

SUCCOTH [sŭk'əth] (Heb. *sukkôt* "booths").

1. A Transjordanian town, the name of which is traced to Jacob's stay there (Gen. 33:17). Succoth was assigned to the tribal territory of Gad (Josh. 13:27). For their refusal to aid his men during his campaign against the Midianites, Gideon tortured the leading men of Succoth (Judg. 8:4-7, 14-16). King Solomon's bronzeworks were near Succoth (1 Kgs. 7:46 par. 2 Chr. 4:17). "The Vale of Succoth" was the fertile region around Succoth, mentioned at Ps. 60:6 (MT 8); 108:7 as a poetic term for the entire Transjordanian territory of Israel.

The site of Succoth is generally identified as modern Tell Deir ʿallā in the Jordan valley a short distance north of the Jabbok river and *ca.* 5 km. (3 mi.) east of the Jordan, although some scholars favor Tell el-Aḥṣaṣ, *ca.* 2.5 km. (1.5 mi.) closer to the Jordan. The area of these two sites was settled as early as the Chalcolithic period. Tell Deir ʿallā has yielded evidence of occupation by the Sea Peoples.

2. The first place where the Israelites stopped after their departure from Egypt and before crossing the Red Sea (Exod. 12:37; Num. 33:5-6). Israel's consecration of the first-born took place here (Exod. 13:2, 11-15). Succoth is generally identified with Tell el-Maskhûṭah, *ca.* 52 km. (32 mi.) south-southeast of Rameses, where the Israelites' journey began.

SUCCOTH-BENOTH [sŭk'əth bē'nōth] (Heb. *sukkôt bᵉnôt*).† Possibly one (or two) of the non-Israelite deities brought into the religion of the Samaritans by the Babylonians resettled at Samaria by King Sargon II of Assyria (2 Kgs. 17:30). Suggested identifications of the Succoth component of the name include Sakkuth, a Babylonian deity identified with Saturn (cf. Amos 5:26). The Benoth component has been suggested as a reference to Ṣarpanitu (often called "Zir-banitu"), the consort of Marduk, the principal Babylonian deity. The literal meaning of Heb. *sukkôt bᵉnôt* is "booths for girls"; it is possible that no deity is cited but that the name refers to housing built by the Babylonians for cultic prostitutes.

SUKKIIM [sŭk'ĭ ĭm] (Heb. *sukkîîm*).† One of the groups of mercenaries that fought against Judah for Pharaoh Shishak of Egypt (2 Chr. 12:3; KJV "Sukkiims"). "Sukkiim" is probably the equivalent of Egyp. *ṭktn*, a technical term for a class of soldiers from the Libyan oases.

SUKKOTH [sŏŏk'əth] (Heb. *sukkôt*). The Feast of Booths (also called Tabernacles and Ingathering), one of the three great pilgrimage feasts in Judaism. See BOOTHS, FEAST OF.

SUMER, SUMERIANS. See BABYLONIA.

SUN (Heb. *šemeš*; Gk. *hélios*).† Worship of the sun was forbidden to Israel (Deut. 4:19; 17:3), but was sometimes a threat to the purity of Israel's religion (2 Kgs. 23:5, 11). Sun-worship was common in the ancient Near East, particularly in Egypt. The center of worship of the Egyptian sun-god Re was the city of On, where Joseph's father-in-law Potiphera was a priest (Gen. 41:45, 50). On came to be known in Greek as Hēliopolis and in Hebrew as Beth-shemesh, both meaning "city of the sun" (Jer. 43:13). Cities named Beth-shemesh in Palestine (Josh. 15:10; 19:22, 38) might well owe their name to sun-worship practiced in the area.

At the center of the Old Testament's response to sun-worship is its teaching concerning the creation of all things by the God of Israel; his continuing sovereignty over all things, which includes his maintenance of the sun's course (Ps. 104:19; Jer. 31:35; Matt. 5:45) and his ability to alter that course (Josh. 10:12-14; 2 Kgs. 20:9-11; Isa. 38:8) and to withhold the sun's light from the earth (Job 9:7; Heb. *ḥeres*); and the praise of the Creator by all things, including the sun (Ps. 148:3). Ps. 19:4c-6 (MT 5c-7) draws on the ancient mythological personification of the sun to exemplify nature's witness to the creator.

God created the sun to give light to the earth during the day (Gen. 1:16, "the greater light"). In referring to the sun's creation, vv. 14-17 follow the customary language of the day in depicting the sun as a light in the heavenly dome (*see* FIRMAMENT).

The sun occurs in a number of figures of speech. "Before the sun" (2 Sam. 12:12) and "in the sun" (Num. 25:4) mean "publicly," much as the modern idiom "in the light of day." "The sun as he rises in his might" (Judg. 5:31) pictures a victorious warrior. The rising "sun of righteousness" (Mal. 4:2 [MT 3:20]) portrays the coming of a new age in which righteousness will prevail. One picture of God's complete rule in the age to come is the replacement of the sun as Jerusalem's source of light with the light of God himself (Isa. 60:19-20 [cf. vv. 1-3]; Rev. 21:23-25).

SUPERSCRIPTION (KJV). *See* INSCRIPTION.

SUPH [soof] (Heb. *sûp* "reeds").* A place probably in Transjordan, one of the places mentioned at Deut. 1:1 as a means of locating Moses' reading of the law in the plains of Moab. A possible location is Khirbet Sufah, *ca.* 6 km. (4 mi.) southeast of Madeba, but this is far from certain. Suph may be the same place as Suphah (Num. 21:14). The KJV, following the LXX and Vulgate, reads "the Red sea" (i.e., Heb. *[yam]-sûp*) at Deut. 1:1.

SUPHAH [soo'fə] (Heb. *sûpâ*).† A region in Moab, probably near the valley of the Arnon river (Num. 21:14; KJV "the Red sea" [Heb. *(yam)-sûp,* following Vulg.]). Suphah may bear some relation to Khirbet Sufah, *ca.* 6 km. (4 mi.) southeast of Madeba and *ca.* 23 km. (15 mi.) north of the Arnon, and to Suph (Deut. 1:1), but this is not certain.

SUR [soor].†
1. (Heb. *sûr*). An otherwise unknown gate in the city of Jerusalem (2 Kgs. 11:6). The parallel account (2 Chr. 23:5) reads "Gate of the Foundation" (Heb. *y^{e}sôd*). Another suggestion is that *sûr* is a corruption of *sûs* "horse" (cf. v. 16).
2. (Gk. *Sour*). A city, presumably on the Mediterranean coast, who sent envoys to seek peace with the dreaded Holofernes. Dor (Heb. *Dôr*), a port 24 km. (15 mi.) south of Mt. Carmel, has been suggested as the site (cf. *Ṣûr* "Tyre").

SURETY (Heb. verb *'ārab,* noun *'ǎrubâ;* Gk. *éngyos*). A person who voluntarily becomes the legal guarantor of another's debt or responsibility. Advice against becoming surety for others is given in Proverbs (Prov. 11:15; 22:26; cf. 6:1-5; 17:18; RSV "pledge"). The psalmist prays for God to become surety for him, i.e., to protect him from oppression (Ps. 119:122). Jesus is called "the surety of a better covenant" (Heb. 7:22), in that he is not just the mediator of the covenant between God and his people, but also its guarantor.

SUSA [soo'sə] (Heb. *šûšan;* Akk. *šušan*).† The capital city of Elam, located near modern Shush in the Ulai river plain in southwestern Iran; later the winter royal residence for the Persian Empire. Inhabited from the fourth millennium B.C., Susa was situated on the important trade routes and flourished particularly under the Achaemenids and Alexander the Great. It remained occupied until captured by Arab forces in the seventh century A.D. Excavations have uncovered the Persian royal palace, acropolis, and artisans' quarter. Also, an extensive archive has been discovered containing Elamite historical and literary inscriptions as well as Old Akkadian, Ur III, and Old Babylonian texts (including a copy of the Code of Hammurabi).

One of Daniel's visions took him to Susa, which was controlled by Media at the time (Dan. 8:2; KJV "Shushan"); Muslim tradition locates his tomb there.

Susa was the scene of the events described in the book of Esther (Esth. 1:2 and passim). Exiles from Susa were among the residents of Samaria who opposed the rebuilding of Jerusalem (Ezra 4:9-10; KJV "Susanchites"). Nehemiah was cupbearer to the Persian king Artaxerxes at Susa (Neh. 1:1).

SUSANNA [soo zăn'ə] (Gk. *Sousanna;* from Heb. *šôšannâ* "lily").
1. The heroine of the apocryphal work bearing her name. *See* SUSANNA, BOOK OF.
2. One of the women who provided for the financial needs of Jesus and his disciples (Luke 8:3).

SUSANNA, BOOK OF.† An apocryphal addition to the book of Daniel, widely regarded as one of the finest short stories in world literature. In the LXX and the Vulgate, as well as modern Roman Catholic editions, the story is appended to Daniel as ch. 13; in Theodotion's Greek version and in other ancient versions it precedes ch. 1.

Set in Babylon, the story tells of Susanna, the beautiful and faithful wife of a Jewish exile. Two lustful Jewish elders force themselves upon her as she bathes in her garden, threatening false accusations against her if she refuses to yield to their desires. She resists their advances and is accused of adultery with a young man. Despite her protestations of innocence, she is found guilty by the assembly and condemned to death. As she is led away, God inspires Daniel to intervene boldly on her behalf. Permitted to cross-examine the two elders, he leads them to contradict each other and thereby demonstrate their false witness. Susanna is acquitted and the perpetrators are executed in accordance with the law of Moses (Deut. 19:16-19).

The story is a classic illustration of the triumph of good over evil and includes the popular motifs of an innocent person's narrow brush with death and the timely actions of a wise young man. Much as the stories in the canonical book of Daniel, this episode offers hope to those who maintain faith in God and adhere to his will. Of special interest in this regard are the names of the primary figures; Susanna (Heb. *šôšannâ*) means "lily," suggesting innocence and freshness, and Daniel (*dānîyē'l*) means "God has judged" or "God is my judge," suggesting the charismatic judges of early Israel.

Daniel's examination of the two witnesses is thought to reflect the pharisaic practice of the Jewish Sanhedrin in the period following the death of Alexander Jannaeus in 76 B.C. If so, this addition would date to the first century B.C.

SUSI [soo'sī] (Heb. *sûsî* "horse" [?]). The father of Gaddi of the tribe of Manasseh, one of the twelve Israelite spies sent into Canaan (Num. 13:11).

SWADDLING CLOTHS. Strips of cloth (so NIV) in which infants accepted as legitimate (and therefore to be cared for) were wrapped tightly (Gk. *sparganóō* "wrap [an infant] in swaddling cloths"). This was thought to enable the limbs of the child to grow straight (Luke 2:7, 12; cf. Ezek. 16:4). At Job 38:9 the "swaddling band" (Heb. *hǎtullâ*) of a child is a metaphor for the clouds that gather over the sea.

SWALLOW (Heb. $d^e r \hat{o} r$). Any of a number of small birds of family Hirundinidae, characterized by long narrow wings and a forked tail. At Ps. 84:3 (MT 4) the nesting instinct of the swallow is part of a portrayal of the desire of worshippers to "dwell" in God's temple (v. 4 [MT v. 5]). In an argument against the mechanical effectiveness of curses, the swallow that flies about without lighting is a picture of "a causeless curse" (Prov. 26:2).

At Isa. 38:14 the RSV renders Heb. $s\hat{u}s$ as "swallow" (KJV "crane") and at Jer. 8:7 the KJV reads "swallow" for $\check{a}g\hat{u}r$ (RSV "crane"; **Q** $s\hat{i}s$). The lack of a conjunction between the two Hebrew terms at Isa. 38:14 may mean that only one bird is represented (cf. JB, NEB "swallow"); this may also be the case at Jer. 8:7, even though a conjunction is present there. In any case the identification is uncertain. It has been argued that the cry of the $s\hat{u}s$ (Isa. 38:14) and its migratory habits (Jer. 8:7) make the swift (family Apodidae, so NIV) a more likely identification than the swallow. For the $\check{a}g\hat{u}r$, see CRANE.

SWAN (KJV). *See* WATER HEN.

SWEET CANE (Heb. $q\bar{a}neh$ "reed, branch, stick"). In contexts referring to spices, a variety of aromatic cane or grass. The Hebrew term is unqualified at Cant. 4:14 (RSV, KJV "calamus"); Isa. 43:24; Ezek. 27:19. Heb. $q\bar{a}neh\ hat\hat{o}b$ (lit. "good reed") appears at Jer. 6:20 and $q^e n\bar{e}h$-$b\bar{o}\acute{s}em$ (RSV "aromatic cane"; KJV "sweet calamus") at Exod. 30:23. Among the plants thus referred to might be sweet flag (*Acorus calamus*, also called calamus), Indian lemon-grass (*Andropogon citratus*), and other grasses and reeds. These plants were used in perfumes (Cant. 4:14) and in the incense made for the tabernacle and temple worship (Exod. 30:23; Isa. 43:24; Jer. 6:20).

SWINE (Heb. $h^a z\hat{i}r$ "wild boar"; Gk. $h\acute{y}s$ "sow," *choíros* "pig"). The wild hog (*Sus scrofa*) was common in ancient Palestine and is still found there. It generally lived in swamps with dense undergrowth, most notably in the Jordan valley, but also in the forests of Mt. Carmel and the coastal plain, frequently causing damage to crops (cf. Ps. 80:13 [MT 14]).

Swine were classified as unclean animals by the law of Moses, i.e., as unsuitable for both food and sacrifice (Lev. 11:7; Deut. 14:8). Gentiles did sometimes sacrifice swine, as did those Jews who acceded to the Hellenization of their religion under the Seleucid Empire (1 Macc. 1:47). The lowest level of the paganization of God's people is, therefore, portrayed partly by a reference to the eating of swine (Isa. 65:4; 66:17), which faithful Jews refused to do even under the threat of death (2 Macc. 6:18–7:1). The domesticated swine into which Jesus sent demons (Matt. 8:28-33 par.) were kept by Gentiles. The prodigal son's feeding of swine (Luke 15:15-16) indicates the deep degradation to which he had sunk and that the "far country" to which he had gone (v. 13) was Gentile territory.

Swine were proverbial for bad manners (Prov. 11:22), violence (Matt. 7:6), and filth (2 Pet. 2:22).

SWORD (Heb. *hereḇ*; Gk. *máchaira, rhomphaía*).†
Swords were widely used as offensive weapons, and

The sword of an Assyrian officer. From a relief in the palace of Sennacherib (Staatliche Museen zu Berlin, DDR)

are by far the weapon mentioned most often in the Bible. Swords were carried inside a belt or in a sheath suspended from a belt on the side opposite the dominant hand (Exod. 32:27; Judg. 3:21 [cf. v. 15]; 1 Sam. 17:51; 2 Sam. 20:8; 1 Chr. 21:27; Cant. 3:8).

The earliest swords were short and straight, essentially long daggers used for stabbing rather than cutting with a sharpened edge. Curved sickle swords, which represented a development from the battle ax and were used for cutting with the edge rather than stabbing, were of importance from the Sumerian period through the early part of the biblical period. There is probably no biblical reference to a sickle sword, except possibly in the otherwise unknown Hebrew term $m^e \underline{k}\bar{e}r\hat{a}$ (Gen. 49:5b; RSV "swords"; KJV "habitations"; some interpreters suggest "plans, ambitions"; cf. JB).

Longer straight or slightly curved swords, often double-edged (Judg. 3:16; Ps. 149:6) replaced these earlier forms and were used most often for stabbing (e.g., Judg. 3:21-22; 1 Sam. 31:4-5) but also for cutting (1 Sam. 17:51; Ezek. 5:1). Gk. *máchaira* can represent a narrow saber and *rhomphaía* a broadsword, but both terms are used commonly without such precision.

The exercise of God's wrath can be called a "sword" (Ps. 7:12 [MT 13]; Isa. 34:5; Jer. 46:10; 50:35-37; Ezek. 6:3). "The flame of the sword" (the literal meaning of the words at Gen. 3:24; RSV "a flaming sword") placed at the garden of Eden to guard the way to the tree of life is its blade; it represents the unavailability to mankind of God's sustenance of life (cf. vv. 19, 22). A "sword" can also represent military power (Ps. 89:43 [MT 44]), emotional pain (Prov. 12:18; Luke 2:35), conflict among family members (Matt. 10:34), damaging false testimony (Prov. 25:18), governmental authority (Rom. 13:4), divine protection (Ps. 17:13). As the word of God (Eph. 6:17; Heb. 4:12; Rev. 1:16; 2:12) it becomes an instrument of God's wrath (v. 16; 19:15).

SYCAMINE [sĭk'ə mĭn] (Gk. *sykáminos*). The LXX translation of Heb. *šiqmâ* "sycamore." The Greek term probably represents the SYCAMORE also at Luke 17:6, its only New Testament occurrence, rather than the mulberry, with which it is often identified (e.g., JB, NIV).

SYCAMORE (Heb. *šiqmâ*; Gk. *sykamoréa*). A large tree with heart-shaped leaves and edible fruit sometimes called the "fig mulberry" (*Ficus sycomorus* L., not any of the plane trees [*Platanus*] of North America that are called "sycamores"). Sycamores were grown in generally frost-free lowland areas (cf. Ps. 78:47). Sycamore cultivation in the Shephelah, for which David's government had a specific administrator (1 Chr. 27:28), became proverbial in its extent (1 Kgs. 10:27; 2 Chr. 1:15; 9:27). The "dresser" of sycamore trees (Amos 7:14) would pierce the unripe fruit to cause it to sweeten and thus become more palatable. Isa. 9:10 may refer to the use of sycamore wood in building. The "sycamine tree" (JB, NIV "mulberry") of Luke 17:6 is probably the sycamore; its large size increases the impact of the saying (cf. 19:4).

SYCHAR [sī'kär] (Gk. *Sychar*). A city in Samaria said to be the location of Jacob's well and to be "near the field that Jacob gave to his son Joseph" (John 4:5-6). It was by this well that Jesus talked with a Samaritan woman about "living water" (vv. 7-26). The "field" spoken of may be the gift of land mentioned at Gen. 48:22, perhaps Shechem itself (cf. JB, RSV mg.; 33:18-19). Gk. *Sychar* could be a corruption of *Sychem* (Shechem), but the traditional identification of Sychar with a village called ʿAskar immediately north of Shechem (and *ca.* 2 km. [1.2 mi.] north of Nablus) is more likely to be correct. Both locations are near the traditional site of Jacob's well.

SYCHEM (Acts 7:16, KJV). *See* SHECHEM.

SYENE [sī ē'nī] (Heb. *sᵉwēnēh*; Egyp. *Swn*).† A town near the southern border of ancient Egypt (Ezek. 29:10; 30:6), located at modern Aswân. Heb. *sînîm* at Isa. 49:12 (KJV, NIV "Sinim"), which refers to places in the Diaspora from which Jews are to return to Jerusalem, should be corrected to *sᵉwēnîm*, a plural gentilic from this place name (RSV "these from the land of Syene"; cf. 1QIsaᵃ, Heb. *swnyym*). Syene was important as a trading post and because of the granite ("Syenite") quarries in the area. Elephantine was located on an island on the Nile near Syene (*see* ELEPHANTINE PAPYRI).

SYMEON [sĭm'ĭ ən] (Gk. *Symeōn*).
1. A prophet and teacher in the church at Antioch who was surnamed "Niger" and may have been, therefore, black (Lat. *niger*) (Acts 13:1).
2. Another name for Simon Peter (Acts 15:14; 2 Pet. 1:1; KJV "Simon"). *See* PETER.

SYNAGOGUE (Gk. *synagōgḗ*).† Buildings used for Jewish worship and instruction in the Torah. Synagogues came into being in the Persian period and possibly as early as the Exile. In time the synagogues came to be a new focal point of Judaism as Jews lived farther and farther from their ancestral land and the temple that had been the focus of their religion. A parallel development was the transition from leader-

ship by priests and Levites to leadership by scribes. These changes made possible the survival of Judaism as a religion centered around the law of Moses after the destruction of the temple in A.D. 70.

Heb. *môʿēḏ* is commonly used in the Old Testament for any appointed time or place, usually for assembly. At Ps. 74:8 *môʿᵃḏê-ʾēl* "assembly places of God" is apparently a designation of synagogues (so KJV; RSV "meeting places") in Judea. This reference, probably the only mention of synagogues in the Old Testament, may be as late as the Maccabean revolt.

Synagogues were not intended to replace the cultic center in Jerusalem but, rather, to be places of corporate prayer and instruction in the Torah, led not necessarily by priests or Levites but by those members of the community who were qualified by their learning (*see* SCRIBES). Teaching, which consisted mainly of reading of prescribed portions of the Torah, generally with comments, was the focal point of Sabbath meetings in synagogues (e.g., Luke 4:15-19; Acts 13:15; 15:21; 17:2). Study of the Torah on days other than the Sabbath also took place at the synagogues. The synagogues were the focal point of the Jewish community in any town with a Jewish population, Palestinian or Diaspora, and were used for judicial functions (cf. Sus. 41, 60), including punishment of Jewish violators of the Jewish law (cf. Matt. 10:17). Sir. 4:7; Jas. 2:2-4 are concerned with comportment in synagogues.

A number of individual synagogues are mentioned in the New Testament, including synagogues in Nazareth (Matt. 13:54; Mark 6:2; Luke 4:16), Capernaum (Mark 1:21; Luke 7:5; John 6:59), and a number of Diaspora cities in which Paul preached (Acts 13:14; 14:1; 17:1, 10, 17; 18:4; 19:8). One synagogue was established specifically for Greek-speaking Jewish freedmen who had come to Jerusalem (6:9). The "place of prayer" near Philippi (16:13, 16) functioned as a gathering place for a small group of Jews and Gentile worshippers of the God of Israel who did not have a synagogue.

Two synagogues in Asia Minor that had apparently been the source of harassment for Christians in the same cities are called synagogues "of Satan" (Rev. 2:9; 3:9).

Bibliography. S. Safrai, "The Synagogue," pp. 908-944 in S. Safrai and M. Stern, eds., *The Jewish People in the First Century* 2 (Philadelphia: 1976); W. Schrage, "συναγωγή," *TDNT* 7 (1971): 798-852; E. Schürer, *The History of the Jewish People in the Age of Jesus Christ (175 B.C.–A.D. 135)*, rev. ed. 2 (Edinburgh: 1979): 423-454.

SYNOPTIC [sĭn ŏp'tĭk] **GOSPELS.**† A term (from Gk. *synoptikós* "seeing together") referring to the Gospels of Matthew, Mark, and Luke, employed because of their common structure, perspective, and contents as distinguished from the gospel of John.

The similarity of these three Gospels may be seen in their general outline of Jesus' life and activity, details of style and language, and at times exact or nearly exact verbal equivalency. A tabulation of material substantially peculiar to each of the Gospels or shared between two or more is provided by B. F. Westcott (*An Introduction to the Study of the Gospels*, 5th ed. [New York: 1875], p. 191):

	Peculiar	Shared
Mark	7%	93%
Matthew	42	58
Luke	59	41
[John	92	8]

Scholars have concluded that the Synoptics are in some way related to one another. The nature of this relationship, complicated by their sharp divergences in form and content, constitutes what is known as the "Synoptic problem."

I. Solutions

Scholars have wrestled with this problem from as early as Augustine (354-430), who assumed a measure of dependence among the three Gospels (in the order Matthew—Mark—Luke) in order to explain their corresponding portions. But it was not until the eighteenth century that the issue came under close scrutiny. Four general approaches to the Synoptic problem emerged from the discussion.

A. Oral Tradition Hypothesis. According to this view as developed by J. C. L. Gieseler (1818), no literary dependence need be assumed between the Synoptics. Rather, an oral tradition of Jesus' words and deeds was formulated by the Jerusalem church and formed the basis for the three books. The agreements between the Gospels are not based on mutual dependence, for they arose independently of each other.

B. Fragment Hypothesis. As developed by F. Schleiermacher (1817), this theory holds that a large number of depictions of Jesus' words and deeds were circulated and, in turn, collected into categories by various apostles and early Christians. From these collections grew the Gospels, their differences being explained by the variety of ways in which the material had been put to use prior to their compilation.

C. Primitive Gospel Hypothesis. This view, associated with J. G. Eichhorn (1804), posits an original Aramaic gospel that the evangelists had available to them, each in a different form, which in combination with other sources they used for their own purposes.

D. Mutual Usage Hypothesis. Unlike the above three theories, which presuppose no literary connection between the Synoptics themselves, a variety of views concerning the interdependence of the gospel writers grew in acceptance. These are distinguished by their assumptions concerning the priority in time of one gospel over the other two. The prevailing opinion since H. J. Holtzmann (1863) is that Mark was written first and used by Matthew and Luke independently of each other.

This theory commonly posits a second source to account for the material common to Matthew and Luke but not found in Mark. This hypothetical document or common oral tradition is called Q (from Ger. *Quelle* "source"). In this manner scholars arrived at the two-source (Mark and Q) solution to the Synoptic problem, with many variations in details.

In addition to these two major sources used by Matthew and Luke, the material unique to each of these two Gospels needs explanation. It has become common to postulate independent sources for Matthew (M) and Luke (L) from which the Evangelists drew their special material. This variation of the two-

source theory is called the four-source theory. Some measure of freedom has also been attributed to the Evangelists in their use and adaptation of the material from which they constructed their Gospels.

Although this basic theory raises some difficulties, it is the dominant paradigm in contemporary Synoptic studies. The key issue is the priority of Mark. Of Mark's 661 verses, 601 are found in Matthew and Luke, with Matthew using 51 percent of the actual words of Mark, and Luke employing 50 percent of Mark's words. In addition, Mark appears to have provided the general outline for the Synoptics, and where Matthew or Luke diverges from Mark, the other is usually found supporting Mark. For many scholars, the freshness and vividness of Mark's style is an additional witness to its originality. Following these conclusions, the interdependence of the Gospels and their sources can be schematized as follows.

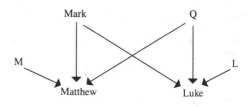

The most significant challenge to this paradigm has been W. R. Farmer's revival (1976) of J. J. Griesbach's (1789) hypothesis that Matthew was written first and used by Luke, with Mark based on both of the longer Gospels. But in terms of content, Matthew's gospel appears to be dependent on Mark and represents a more advanced stage over the more primitive gospel of Mark. Moreover, one tradition holds that Mark was dependent on Peter, interpreting his teaching and creating a written record of what Peter said about Jesus (Eusebius *HE* iii.39.15). As for Luke, he himself claims to have used sources in the composition of his gospel (Luke 1:1-3).

Less evidence exists for the second major source, Q. No such document is attested in the early Church; it is simply posited as a source for material found in both Matthew and Luke, and remains hypothetical. The correspondence between the two Gospels in Q material is sometimes verbatim. The most decisive proof for Q's existence is the occurrence of sayings that appear twice in Matthew or Luke, once on the basis of Mark and once on the basis of another source, presumably Q. The material that has been attributed to Q is comprised almost entirely of teachings of Jesus (*Logia*), with little narrative.

II. Form and Redaction Criticism

Twentieth-century Synoptic scholarship has investigated not only the sources used by the Evangelists in the composition of their Gospels, but also the "form" or structure of independent sections (pericopes) of gospel tradition in their preliterary state. This form criticism (*Formgeschichte*) classifies self-contained pericopes into categories such as controversy stories, miracle stories, parables, and other types of narratives and sayings. It also seeks to identify the life setting (*Sitz im Leben*) in the early Church within which each form would have been used and within which the material classified would have been preserved and transmitted.

This approach to the gospel material has emphasized the relationship between the tradition of Jesus' words and deeds and the ongoing life of the early Church. But the form-critical method had also been accompanied by skeptical presuppositions that have tended to cast doubt on the credibility of much of what has been transmitted in the Gospels. R. Bultmann was the most outstanding example of this approach and these presuppositions, crediting not only the form of the pericopes but also much of their content to the early Church.

A further development in gospel criticism has been redaction criticism (*Redaktionsgeschichte*), which examines the editorial role of the Evangelists as they selected, arranged, and interpreted the received tradition. The gospel writers have come to be viewed as theologians in their own right, who left their distinctive stamp on their Gospels as they addressed through their use of the traditions the issues confronting the Church in their time and place.

The Gospels have thus come to be viewed as the representation of three life settings, the setting of Jesus' own earthly life in which he spoke and acted, the setting of the early Church in which the tradition was used and shaped according to the needs of the different Christian communities, and the setting of the Evangelists themselves in which the tradition was formed into written Gospels directed toward issues and concerns of the Church of their day. Within the setting of the canon of Scripture the three Synoptic Gospels, along with the fourth Gospel, provide kaleidoscopic images of Jesus that appeal to the plurality of settings and perceptions of the Church throughout the ages, as well as correcting individualistic perceptions of his person and work.

Bibliography. K. Aland, ed., *Synopsis of the Four Gospels* [Greek and English], 6th ed. (London: 1972); R. Bultmann, *The History of the Synoptic Tradition*, 2nd ed. (Oxford: 1968); W. R. Farmer, *The Synoptic Problem* (Macon: 1981); P. Feine–J. Behm–W. G. Kümmel, *Introduction to the New Testament,* 17th rev. ed. (Nashville: 1975), pp. 38-80; B. H. Throckmorton, *Gospel Parallels* [English], 4th ed. (Nashville: 1979).

SYNTYCHE [sĭn′tĭ kī] (Gk. *Syntychē* "coincidence, good fortune"). A woman in the church of Philippi whom Paul urged to settle a dispute of an unidentified nature with another woman, Euodia (Phil 4:2-3).

SYRACUSE [sĭr′ə kūs] (Gk. *Syrakousai*). A major city of Sicily, located on the east coast of the island. Colonized by Corinth in 734 B.C., Syracuse enjoyed particular prosperity in the fifth and fourth centuries, connected by a mole with the mainland, where the city established outposts. Attempting to dominate all Sicily, the city was besieged by Athens (415-413), but emerged victorious. Syracuse became subject to Rome after a long siege in 213-211. Under the Roman Empire, Syracuse was a large and prosperous city, re-

nowned for its beauty. Augustus elevated it to the status of a colony in 21 B.C.

The ship carrying Paul from Malta to Puteoli stayed three days at Syracuse (Acts 28:12), probably waiting for the wind that had carried it to the port to rise again.

SYRIA [sĭr′ĭ ə] (Heb. *ʾărām*; Gk. *Syria*). In ancient times, the region bordering the eastern Mediterranean and extending northward from (and sometimes including) Palestine and Phoenicia to the Euphrates in the northeast and the Taurus mountains of southern Turkey in the northwest. In the Old Testament Syria (or "Aram") designates the Aramean kingdom centered at Damascus in southeastern Syria. *See* ARAMEANS.

Syria was a Persian satrapy until conquered by Alexander the Great in 332 B.C. After Alexander's death and the wars of his successors, Syria became the center of the SELEUCID EMPIRE, with its capital at Antioch on the Orontes in northern Syria. Pompey conquered Syria for Rome in 64-63 B.C. and created the Roman province of Syria. This was an important province in the empire because of its position on the border with the Parthians and because of its capital, Antioch, generally considered the third most important city of the empire. Much of Syria remained rural and only superficially touched by Hellenistic culture, however, and much of the population continued to speak Aramaic. Commagene and eastern Cilicia to the north and Ituraea in the south were all incorporated into the province of Syria for at least part of their history under Rome. Judea was a Roman province from A.D. 6 to 41 and again after 44, but its governor was always subordinate to the governor of Syria so that generally Judea was thought of as a part of the province of Syria.

In the New Testament Gk. *Syria* refers to the Roman province of Syria (Luke 2:2), to the Syrian, Phoenician, and Palestinian coastline (Acts 18:18 [cf. v. 22]; 20:3 [cf. 21:2-3]), and to Palestine and the region in which Palestine, Phoenicia, and Syria bordered each other (Matt. 4:24). The province of Syria could also be called "Syria and Cilicia" (Acts 15:23, 41; Gal. 1:21). The commander Naaman, a contemporary of Elisha, is referred to as a "Syrian" (*Syros*; Luke 4:27) in accordance with the LXX at 2 Kgs. 5:20.

SYRIAC [sĭr′ĭ ăk].* A late form of Eastern Aramaic, arising *ca.* the mid-first century A.D. in northern Mesopotamia and generally associated with the city of Edessa (modern Urfa). Its greatest importance as a literary language emerged from the translation of the Old and New Testament into Syriac.

The earliest form of the script derived from cursive Aramaic. Written from right to left, Syriac features an alphabet of twenty-two consonants, ordered as in Hebrew; the written vowel system was introduced in the eighth century.

See ARAMAIC.

SYRIAC VERSIONS.† The standard Syriac version of the Bible is the PESHITTA (lit. the "simple" version). But before the establishment of the Peshitta, earlier Syriac versions of both the Old and New Testament existed.

When the Old Testament was first translated into Syriac is uncertain, as is whether the translation was made by non-Christian Jews or by Jewish Christians. This earliest Syriac Old Testament, the Old Syriac version, was apparently made from some form of Aramaic Targum and became the basis of the later Syriac versions, including the Peshitta.

The first effort toward the rendering of the New Testament into Syriac was apparently the Diatessaron, Tatian's harmony of the four Gospels composed *ca.* A.D. 170. The Diatessaron was probably written in Syriac; less likely is the view that it began in Greek and was translated into Syriac soon after its composition. It served as the Christian canon among Syriac-speaking people until displaced by the Peshitta, and enjoyed considerable popularity in other languages as well. The Syriac Diatessaron is now lost except for fragments. Modern study of the Diatessaron is based mainly on translations and adaptations in other languages.

Old Syriac versions of the four Gospels were made beginning in the third century, influenced by the Diatessaron. Related translations of Acts and the Epistles were made, but are extant now only in citations.

Once thought to be the early fifth-century work of Bishop Rabbula of Edessa, the Peshitta now appears to have been completed by the late fourth century on the basis of earlier Syriac versions. The Peshitta is an uneven work, in terms of both literary quality and its relation to the original languages, which is overliteral at times. For these and other reasons attempts were made to revise or replace the Peshitta. Among the results were the Philoxenian version (early sixth century) and the Harclean version of the New Testament and the Syro-hexaplar version of the Old Testament (seventh century), which are revisions of the Philox-

enian equipped with textual apparatus. The basis of the Philoxenian Old Testament was the LXX, that of the Syro-hexaplar the LXX as found in Origen's Hexapla. The Palestinian Syriac version is really a western Aramaic version of both the Old and New Testament written in a script resembling that used in the Syriac versions. However, none of these other versions was able to displace the popularity of the Peshitta.

The Syriac versions are important in the text criticism of both Old and New Testament. The Syro-hexaplar is one of the more important witnesses to Origen's recension of the LXX. The Peshitta, which has had its own complex texual history, is an important witness for both the Old and New Testament.

SYROPHOENICIA [sī'rō fə nĭsh'ə]. A woman from whose daughter Jesus exorcised a demon is identified as "a Greek, a Syrophoenician (Gk. *Syrophoinissa*) by birth" (Mark 7:26). "Greek" in this identification is not an indication of nationality but means simply "Gentile." "Syrophoenician" identifies the woman as a native of Phoenicia, the region Jesus was in at the time (v. 24, "the region of Tyre and Sidon"), called Syrophoenicia because of its inclusion in the Roman province of Syria. The parallel account calls the woman "a Canaanite" (Matt. 15:22), citing the older name of Phoenicia.

SYRTIS [sûr'təs], **THE** (Gk. *hē Syrtis*). The two shallow bays that form a broad gulf on the coast of modern Libya and Tunisia, Syrtis Major (now called the Gulf of Sidra or Sirte) to the southeast and Syrtis Minor to the northwest, south and southwest of Sicily. The sailors of the ship Paul boarded in Myra of Lycia feared that the wind from the northeast they encountered off Crete would drive the ship "on the Syrtis" (Acts 27:17; KJV "quicksands").

T

TAANACH [tāʹə năk] (Heb. *taʿᵃnāk̲*). A Canaanite and Israelite city located on important trade routes *ca.* 8 km. (5 mi.) south-southeast of Megiddo on the southern edge of the Jezreel (Esdraelon) valley.

Occupied from the mid-third millennium B.C., Taanach is first mentioned in a fifteenth-century inscription of Egyptian pharaoh Thutmose III. It was, with Megiddo, one of the northern Canaanite cities that strongly resisted the Israelite takeover. Its king was defeated by Joshua (Josh. 12:21). The city was assigned to Manasseh, though it lay within the territory of Issachar and Asher (17:11), and was designated a levitical city (21:25; KJV "Tanach"). Nevertheless, it remained under Canaanite rule (Judg. 1:27). Taanach was one focus of the battle of Deborah and Barak against the northern Canaanites (5:19). Perhaps as a result of that battle Taanach's Canaanite residents were put to forced labor by the Israelites (1:28). Taanach was a leading city of Solomon's fifth administrative district, which included Megiddo and Beth-shean (1 Kgs. 4:12). It was destroyed by Pharaoh Shishak *ca.* 918, shortly after Solomon's reign (*ANET,* p. 243).

Tell Taʿannak was excavated from 1902 to 1904 and again in the 1960's. Evidence of the destructions of the city or parts of the city *ca.* 1468 (by Thutmose), 1125 (Joshua), and 918 (Shishak) has been discovered, as well as a variety of buildings and fortifications. Thirteen Akkadian clay tablets dating to *ca.* 1450 contain personal names suggesting that Taanach had a very mixed population. Numerous cultic objects from the period of Israelite occupation were also recovered.

TAANATH-SHILOH [tāʹə năth shīʹlō] (Heb. *taʿᵃnat̲ šilōh*). A border city in the tribal territory of Ephraim (Josh. 16:6). It is perhaps to be identified with Khirbet Taʿnah el-Fôqā, *ca.* 11 km. (7 mi.) southeast of Nablus.

TABBAOTH [tăbʹə ŏth] (Heb. *ṭabbāʿôt̲*; cf. *ṭabbaʿat* "[signet] ring"). The ancestor (or head) of a group of temple servants who returned with Zerubbabel from the Babylonian exile (Ezra 2:43; Neh. 7:46).

TABBATH [tăbʹəth] (Heb. *ṭabbāt̲*). A place near Abel-meholah (Judg. 7:22), possibly the elevation Râs Abū Tābât on the Gilead slopes east of the Jordan river and north of Wâdī Kufrinjeh.

TABEEL [tăbʹĭ əl].

1.† (Heb. *ṭāb̲ʾēl* "God is good"). One of three Persian officials who wrote a letter to King Artaxerxes I (465-424 B.C.; Ezra 4:7). This letter may have opposed the rebuilding of Jerusalem, but it is not the same document preserved at vv. 11-16.

2. (Q *ṭāb̲ᵉʾal* "good-for-nothing"). The father or place of origin of an otherwise unknown man whom Rezin of Syria and Pekah of Israel hoped to place on the throne of Judah in an attempt to coerce Judah into their anti-Assyrian alliance (Isa. 7:6; KJV "Tabeal"). Heb. *bêt̲ ṭāb̲ʾēl,* known from an Assyrian text of the time, was located northeast of Ammon and Gilead. "The son of Tabeel" may be a gentilic designating a Judahite whose mother was a Syrian princess and who lived or was born in this town.

TABERAH [tăbʹə rə] (Heb. *tab̲ʿērâ* "burning"). A place in the southeastern part of the Sinai peninsula where the Israelites camped (Num. 11:3; Deut. 9:22). Because the Israelites complained about their misfortunes, Yahweh punished them by setting fire to the camp's outer edges.

TABERNACLE (Heb. *miškān,* *ʾōhel môʿēd̲*; Gk. *skēnḗ*).† A portable structure that the Israelites made as commanded by God at Sinai and in which he dwelled during the wilderness wanderings. It was called also the "tabernacle of the testimony" (Exod. 38:21), referring to the two tables of the Ten Commandments placed in the ark (31:18; cf. 25:16, 21-22); and, most frequently, the "tent of meeting" (27:21; cf. 40:2, "tabernacle of the tent of meeting"). There God would meet Moses and speak with him; the tabernacle and its court were too small to serve as a meeting place for God and all the people. Some scholars contend that the description of the tabernacle in Exodus is a "retrojection" based on the later Jerusalem temple, and that the actual wilderness shrine was a simpler structure described at 33:7-11.

I. Construction

God showed Moses the pattern for the tabernacle (Exod. 25:9, 40; Acts 7:44; Heb. 8:5). The actual construction was undertaken by Bezalel and Oholiab with their assistants (Exod. 31:1-11; 36:1), with the Israelites providing the materials through voluntary contributions (25:1-7; 35:4-9, 20-29). The work was completed one year after the Exodus (40:2, 17) and nine months after Israel had arrived at Sinai (cf. 19:1).

The tabernacle consisted of an outer structure that defined the public court and a smaller structure, the tabernacle proper, which was divided into the holy place and the holy of holies. The tabernacle proper (ch. 26) consisted of gold-plated boards each 10 cubits (4.45 m. [14.6 ft.]) high and 1.5 cubits (66.7 cm. [26.3 in.]) wide. Twenty boards each were on the south and north sides, with eight (six plus the two corner boards) on the west side. Every board was placed in two silver pedestals, having external golden rings through which cross boards were slid. The east side remained open, closed off by a curtain. Over the wooden frame were placed curtains made from four materials: a double layer of multicolored fine linen curtains embroidered with cherubim, a double layer of goat's-hair curtains, and an outer covering made of rams' skins dyed red and taḥaš skins (RSV "goatskins"; perhaps an Asiatic or East African sea cow).

A multicolored, embroidered veil of fine linen, hanging on four pillars of acacia wood overlaid with gold, divided the tabernacle into the most holy place or holy of holies, which was a cube 10 cubits (4.45 m. [14.6 ft.]) on each side, and the holy place, 20 cubits (8.89 m. [29.2 ft.]) long and 10 cubits wide and high. The ark of the covenant was sheltered in the holy of holies. In the holy place were the table of showbread on the north side, the golden lampstand on the south side, and the golden incense altar in front of the veil of the holy of holies. The holy place was separated from the court outside by a curtain of fine linen hanging on five pillars of acacia wood.

The court (27:9-18) was 100 cubits (44.45 m. [145.8 ft.]) long and 50 cubits (22.23 m. [72.9 ft.]) wide,

fenced off by sixty pillars 5 cubits (2.22 m. [7.3 ft.]) high. In the court were the bronze altar for the burnt-offering (vv. 1-8) and the laver (30:17-21). A curtain of fine linen was hung over the four pillars at the center of the east side of the court (40:33; RSV "screen"); this served as the entrance to the tabernacle grounds. Similar curtains hung over the other pillars of the court.

II. Transport

When the tabernacle and its contents were moved from place to place, the boards and curtains of the tent could be carried on oxcarts, but its furnishings were to be mounted on acacia-wood poles and carried by Levites (25:12-15, 26-28; 27:6-7; 30:4-5; Num. 4:1-15; 7:6-9). The poles used to carry the ark of the covenant were never to be removed from their position in the rings mounted on the sides of the ark. Above all, the Levites who carried the tabernacle furnishings were never to touch them, on pain of death (4:15). When David retrieved the ark from its Philistine captors, it was transported by oxcart. During that journey Uzzah put out his hand to steady the ark on the tottering cart, immediately forfeiting his life (2 Sam. 6:2-7).

III. History

After the wilderness journeys the tabernacle was set up at Shiloh (Josh. 18:1). Subsequently a permanent temple was built there to house the ark (1 Sam. 1:9; 3:3); it was apparently destroyed after the Philistines took the ark in battle (4:1-11; Ps. 78:60-64; Jer. 7:12-15), though a priest continued to serve at Shiloh (1 Sam. 14:3). The tabernacle itself may have been moved to Nob (21:1-9 [MT 2-10]); later it is located at Gibeon (1 Chr. 16:39; 21:29; 2 Chr. 1:3-6). Solomon had remains of the tabernacle transferred to his temple in Jerusalem (1 Kgs. 8:4).

IV. Meaning

The tabernacle was the dwelling of Yahweh, the holy place of his presence among his people (Exod. 25:8). Although God was present among the people, they

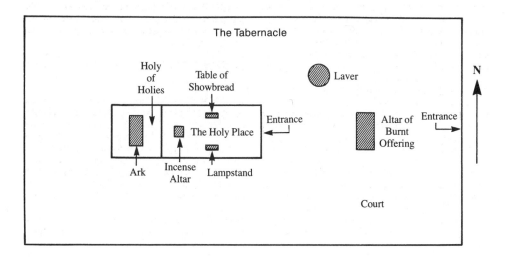

did not have full access to him, for the tabernacle remained enclosed. God's dwelling among his people was preceded by his descending in the cloud of his majesty (40:34-35). This was made possible only by the presence of priests and sacrifices (chs. 28–29; cf. 29:45).

The tabernacle foreshadowed a time when God's dwelling with mankind would be not temporary but permanent. The priesthood and sacrifices are regarded as types of the work of Christ, the great high priest, toward this goal (Heb. 8–9). The tabernacle itself prefigures the earthly ministry of Christ, who "became flesh and dwelt (Gk. *eskḗnōsen* 'tabernacled') among us" (John 1:14). The tabernacle is also an earthly representation of heaven, God's dwelling place (Heb. 8:5; cf. 9:24; Rev. 11:19). As such, it points to a time when heaven and earth will meet, and God will dwell among his people for eternity (21:3).

TABERNACLES, FEAST OF. *See* BOOTHS, FEAST OF.

TABITHA [tăb'ĭ thə] (Gk. *Tabithá*; Aram. *ṭᵉḇîṭāʾ* "gazelle"). Aramaic name of DORCAS, a Christian at Joppa noted for her good works who was raised from the dead by Peter (Acts 9:36).

TABLE OF NATIONS.† A schematic representation, in genealogical form (Gen. 10; cf. 1 Chr. 1:4-24), of the relationship between ancient peoples with whom Israel had dealings, thus providing the historical setting for the call and life of Abraham. As such, the Table of Nations is the bridge between the earlier part of Genesis, which tells of mankind as a whole, and the story of Israel's beginnings. By giving the genealogy of Noah's first son Shem last, Gen. 10 places Israel's ancestry at the end (to be taken up again at 11:10). Japheth (10:2-5) is the ancestor of peoples with whom Israel had only limited contact; with the descendants of Ham—Egypt and the Canaanites (vv. 6-19)—Israel had much more contact.

The names in the Table of Nations are variously attested outside the Bible as names of peoples or places; some are true gentilics in form, others plurals used as gentilics. The division of these nations into three groups corresponding to the three sons of Noah is not a racial or a linguistic division; rather, for the political purposes noted, the names are divided for the most part geographically. Japheth is the ancestor of peoples and places of Asia Minor and the Aegean, as well as the Medes (Madai) (vv. 2-5). Egypt and its sphere of influence, including northern Africa, eastern and southern Arabia, Crete, Lydia, and Canaan, are represented by the descendants of Ham (vv. 6-20). Shem is the ancestor of peoples of southern Arabia, Syria, and Mesopotamia, and, through Arpachshad, of Israel (vv. 21-31). Despite the inclusion of the Mesopotamian powers of Elam and Asshur among the sons of Shem (v. 22), a descendant of Cush (Ethiopia) and Ham, Nimrod, is credited with initiating the process of kingdom- and city-building in Mesopotamia (vv. 8-12; cf. Mic. 5:6). This tension and other aspects of the chapter, most notably the combination of narrative material (Gen. 10:8-12, 18b-19, 25, 30) with more

purely genealogical material, has been explained as arising from the combination of two sources, an earlier Yahwistic source and a later Priestly source (*see* PENTATEUCH).

TABLELAND.* RSV translation of Heb. *mîšôr* as applied to that part of the Transjordanian plateau north of the Arnon and east of the Dead Sea around the cities of Bezer and Medeba (Deut. 3:10; 4:43; Josh. 13:9, 16-17, 21; 20:8; Jer. 48:21; KJV "plain"). In its basic sense the Hebrew term designated any level ground (cf. 1 Kgs. 20:23; "plain").

TABOR [tā'bər] (Heb. *tāḇôr*).
1. A solitary mountain *ca.* 9 km. (6.5 mi.) east of Nazareth in the northeastern corner of the valley of Jezreel. Though it rises only 562 m. (1843 ft.) above sea level, its appearance from the southwest is quite magnificent. The borders of Zebulun, Issachar, and Naphtali met at Mt. Tabor (Josh. 19:12, 22, 34 [Chisloth-tabor and Aznoth-tabor were villages near the mountain; cf. 3 below]), and there Barak gathered the forces of Zebulun and Naphtali to fight Sisera (Judg. 4:6, 12, 14). Tabor was a center of Baal worship (cf. Deut. 33:19; Hos. 5:1).

Tabor is linked with Mt. Hermon as a representative of creation's praise of God (Ps. 89:12 [MT 13]). The unmistakable appearance of Tabor is a figure for the irresistible advance of Nebuchadrezzar against Egypt (Jer. 46:18). According to ancient tradition, Tabor is the mountain of transfiguration, where Christ's face and garments became infused with light.

2. An oak (or terebinth; so NJV; NIV "great tree") where Saul was directed by Samuel to meet three pilgrims (1 Sam. 10:3; KJV "plain of Tabor"). This apparently well-known landmark was probably in the tribal territory of Benjamin near Bethel.

3. A levitical city assigned to the Merarites (1 Chr. 6:77). This city was located in the tribal territory of Zebulun and was probably on or near Mt. Tabor. It may have been the same as Chisloth-tabor (Josh. 19:12).

TABRET (KJV). *See* TIMBREL.

TABRIMMON [tăb rĭm'ən] (Heb. *ṭaḇrimmōn* "[the deity] Rammānū is good"). The son of Hezion and father of King Ben-hadad I of Syria (1 Kgs. 15:18; cf. *ANET*, p. 655).

TACHMONITE (2 Sam. 23:8, KJV). *See* TAHCHEMONITE

TADMOR [tăd'môr] (Heb. *taḏmōr*). A city in the desert fortified (RSV "built") by King Solomon (2 Chr. 8:4). The reference to Hamath in the same verse makes it likely that this city was Tadmor (Palmyra ["city of palms"], modern Tudmur) in Syria, an important caravan city *ca.* 215 km. (135 mi.) northeast of Damascus and *ca.* 120 km. (75 mi.) from the Euphrates. It may, however, be the same as TAMAR (**1**) in Judah, mentioned at 1 Kgs. 9:18 (Q *taḏmōr*).

TAHAN [tā'hăn] (Heb. *taḥan*). A descendant of Ephraim whose descendants were the Tahanites (Num. 26:35; 1 Chr. 7:25; cf. "Tahath" at v. 20).

TAHAPANES (Jer. 2:16, KJV). *See* TAHPANHES.

TAHASH [tā'hăsh] (Heb. *taḥaš* "porpoise, sea-cow" [?]). The third son of Nahor and his concubine Reumah (Gen. 22:24; KJV "Thahash").

TAHATH [tā'hăth] (Heb. *taḥaṯ* "beneath, humble") **(PERSON)**.
1. An ancestor of the prophet Samuel (1 Chr. 6:24, 37 [MT 9, 22]; at v. 33 [MT 18] also Heman the temple musician). Although the genealogies of vv. 22-28, 33-38 (MT 7-13, 18-23) are somewhat confused, they are intended to identify Samuel as a Levite, of the family of Kohath.
2. An Ephraimite, the son of Bered (1 Chr. 7:20).
3. An Ephraimite, son of Eleadah and grandson of Tahath 2 (1 Chr. 7:20).

TAHATH [tā'hăth] (Heb. *taḥaṯ* "beneath, humble") **(PLACE)**. A place where the Israelites camped during the wilderness wanderings (Num. 33:26-27). Its exact location is unknown.

TAHCHEMONITE [tä kē'mə nīt] (Heb. *taḥkᵉmōnî*). A gentilic ascribed to Josheb-basshebeth, one of David's mighty men (2 Sam. 23:8; KJV "Tachmonite"; NIV "Tahkemonite"). The name may be a scribal error for "the Hachmonite" (*haḥakmōnî* or *ben-ḥakᵉmônî*), in which case Josheb-bassebeth may be the same person as "Jashobeam, a Hachmonite" (1 Chr. 11:11).

TAHPANHES [tä'pə nēz] (Heb. *taḥpanḥēs*; Egyp. *T3-ḥ[t]-[n.t]-p3-nḥsy* "fortress of Penhase"). A city on Egypt's eastern border at the Nile Delta, modern Tell Defneh *ca.* 43 km. (27 mi.) south-southwest of Port Said. After the murder of Gedaliah, governor of Judah following the fall of Jerusalem in 587/586 B.C., a group of Jews under the leadership of a certain Johanan fled to Tahpanhes, taking the prophet Jeremiah with them against his will (Jer. 43:5-7). There Jeremiah prophesied that Nebuchadrezzar would be victorious over Egypt (vv. 8-13), possibly referring to Nebuchadrezzar's raid into Egypt in 567, and reprimanded the Jewish colonists for their idolatry (44:1-10). Earlier in his ministry Jeremiah mentioned Tahpanhes when he spoke of what Judah suffered from the Egyptians in 609 (2:16; KJV "Tahapanes"). Later the city is mentioned in Ezekiel's prediction of divine punishment for Egypt (Ezek. 30:18; Heb. *tᵉḥapnᵉḥēs*; RSV, KJV "Tehaphnehes"). Tahpanhes was called Daphnae by the Greeks (cf. Herodotus *Hist.* ii.30).

TAHPENES [tä'pə nēz] (Heb. *taḥpᵉnês*; cf. Egyp. *t.ḥmt.nsw* "wife of the king"). An Egyptian queen whose sister became the wife of the Edomite Hadad, Solomon's adversary (1 Kgs. 11:19). According to v. 20 Tahpenes helped rear her nephew Genubath.

TAHREA [tär'ĭ ə] (Heb. *taḥᵃrēaʿ*). A son of Micah, and descendant of King Saul (1 Chr. 9:41). At 8:35 his name appears as Tarea (Heb. *taʾrēaʿ*).

TAHTIM-HODSHI [tä'tĭm hŏd'shĭ] (Heb. *taḥtîm ḥoḏšî* "lowland of Hodshi [?]"). An otherwise unknown region visited by David's census takers (KJV, 2 Sam. 24:6). The text is commonly emended to *haḥittîm*

qāḏēšâ "to Kadesh (in the land of the) Hittites" (so RSV, JB following one LXX reading). However, while David's kingdom did extend to Kadesh on the Orontes, it seems unlikely that the census takers would have gone from Gilead to the Syrian Kadesh and then to Dan; perhaps Kedesh 3 in Naphtali is intended.

TALENT (Heb. *kikkār*; Gk. *tálanton*). In the Old Testament, a unit of weight equivalent to *ca.* 34.27 kg. (75.6 lb.). In the New Testament, a unit of money (not actually minted) equivalent to *ca.* 6000 drachmas.

TALITHA CUMI [tə lē'thə kōō'mē] (Gk. *talithá koúm*). Mark's Greek transliteration of the Aramaic phrase *ṭalyᵉṭāʾ* [or *tᵉliṭāʾ*] *qûmî* "little girl, arise" spoken by Jesus to Jairus' daughter as he raised her from the dead (Mark 5:41).

TALMAI [tăl'mī] (Heb. *talmay*).
1. One of the Anakim who, along with his brothers, was expelled by Caleb from Hebron (Num. 13:22; Josh. 15:14; Judg. 1:10).
2. The king of Geshur and father of Maacah, one of David's wives (2 Sam. 3:3; 13:37; 1 Chr. 3:2).

TALMON [tăl'mən] (Heb. *ṭalmōn, ṭalmôn*). The ancestor of a group of postexilic Levite gatekeepers (1 Chr. 9:17; Ezra 2:42; Neh. 7:45; 11:19; 12:25).

TALMUD [täl'mōōd] (Heb. *talmûḏ* "teaching, study, learning").† The repository of centuries of Jewish law, legend, and wisdom contained in two large collections, the Palestinian Talmud (also called the Jerusalem Talmud) and the Babylonian Talmud. The latter collection is in many respects the most important document of Jewish religion and culture, surpassing even the Bible in its direct influence on the theory and practice of Jewish life.

According to Jewish faith, the Talmud is founded on the oral law that, along with the written law, was revealed to Moses at Sinai and handed down from generation to generation, and that serves to interpret the written law and adapt it to changing conditions. Several periods are distinguished in the transmission of the oral law. The prophets received it from Moses, Joshua, and the elders and passed it on to Ezra and his successors, the scribes (ending *ca.* 270 B.C.). The period of the scribes was followed by a succession of five "pairs" (Heb. *zûḡôṯ*) of teachers, the last of whom were Hillel and Shammai at the end of the first century B.C. The era of the Tannaim (from Aram. *tᵉnā* "repeat, hand down orally")—those rabbinic sages whose teachings are recorded in the Mishnah—began with the "schools" (disciples) of Hillel and Shammai and closed *ca.* A.D. 200 with the completion of the Mishnah of Rabbi Judah the Prince. The Mishnah quickly was adopted as the authoritative canon of the oral law and became the basis of the work of the Amoraim (from *ᵃmôrā* "interpreter") of the Talmudic era (200-500).

The Talmud is composed of two parts, the Mishnah in Hebrew and the Gemara (from *gᵉmārāʾ* "learning by heart"), which is commentary on the Mishnah, a summary of centuries of discussion and elucidations of the Mishnah by Palestinian sages in the schools of Tiberias, Caesarea, and Sepphoris and by Babylonian sages in the major academies of Sura, Nehardea, Pumbeditha, and Mechuza. The Gemara is recorded mainly in the Aramaic dialects spoken by Jews in the East and the West, but the rabbis' discussions also draw on traditions formulated in Hebrew (especially the Baraitot, tannaitic discussions related to but outside the Mishnah).

A fundamental distinction can be made in the Talmud and in all the rabbinic literature between Halakhah, legal teaching, and Haggadah, nonlegal material that includes ethical teachings, anecdotes about rabbis and others, and long digressions on a wide range of topics. Halakhah is dominant in the Talmud and includes clarification of words and sentences of the Mishnah text, comparison of traditions in order to reconcile teachings stemming from different schools or authorities, discernment of the reasons and underlying logic of a tradition, scriptural exegesis, and attempts to derive the oral law from the written law.

The Gemara of the Palestinian Talmud covers the first four of the six orders of the Mishnah, those on agriculture, feasts, women, and damages. The Gemara of the Babylonian Talmud covers the orders on feasts, women, and damages and the fifth order on holy things, but almost none of the first order on agriculture and the sixth order on purities. The conventional dates for the Palestinian Talmud are A.D. 200-400 and for the Babylonian Talmud A.D. 200-500. However, under the growing influence of Babylonian Jewish leadership that continued into the Islamic Period, the Babylonian Talmud underwent extensive editing for two more centuries, with the result that on the threshold of the Middle Ages its authority was recognized wherever Jews lived.

Since the Talmud combines in a distinctive manner orderly and logical argumentation, acute analysis, and free association of ideas, readers of the Talmud require guidance to enter into its conversation. Therefore, many commentaries on the Talmud have been written. The classical commentary of Rashi (Rabbi Solomon bar Isaac of Troyes, France, 1040-1105), the glosses of the French rabbis of the twelfth and thirteenth centuries known as Tosafot ("Additions"), and numerous other aids to understanding appear on the margins of each page in printed editions of the Babylonian Talmud.

The Talmud is the embodiment of the central religious obligation of rabbinic Judaism to study the Torah. While organized and executed as a commentary on a book of law, it goes beyond the concern for legislation and its practical application. The Talmud receives the elements of the tradition as if they were part of the natural order of things—to be meticulously examined and comprehensively questioned in order to be better understood and perhaps even reshaped.

Bibliography. J. Neusner, *Invitation to the Talmud*, rev. ed. (San Francisco: 1984); A. Steinsaltz, *The Essential Talmud* (New York: 1976); H. L. Strack, *Introduction to the Talmud and Midrash* (1931; repr. New York: 1969).

TAMAH (Neh. 7:55, KJV). *See* TEMAH.

TAMAR [tā′mər] (Heb. *tāmār* "date palm") (**PERSON**).

1. A Canaanite woman who became the wife of Judah's eldest son, Er (Gen. 38:6). After Er's death the patriarch ordered his second son, Onan, to assume levirate responsibility (v. 8); but fearing that his own inheritance would be diminished, Onan withdrew prematurely during intercourse and thus, according to v. 10, was slain by God. Judah then proposed that his daughter-in-law return to her father's house until Shelah, Judah's youngest son, had matured, because he was fearful that failure to comply with the levirate would lead to Shelah's death as well (v. 11).

When Judah apparently failed to fulfill his pledge to dispatch Shelah for the purpose of producing an heir, Tamar posed as a prostitute (vv. 12-15) to trick Judah himself into having sexual relations with her. When she disclosed this three months later, Judah admitted that he was the father of the child she was carrying and that, because of his concern for maintaining the lineage, she was more righteous than he (vv. 16-26). In due time Tamar became the mother of twin boys, Perez and Zerah (vv. 27-30). Perez, Tamar's elder son (Ruth 4:12), was an ancestor of King David (v. 22) and of Jesus (Matt. 1:3; Gk. *Thamar*; KJV "Thamar").

2. The daughter of David and Maacah, and the sister of Absalom (2 Sam. 13:1; cf. 1 Chr. 3:2, 9). Tamar, a beautiful young woman, prepared food for her sick half brother, Amnon, unaware that he was feigning his illness for the opportunity of seducing her (2 Sam. 13:2-11). Though she resisted his seduction and tried to convince him of the folly of such a disgrace, Amnon forced himself upon her (vv. 12-14). Once the rape had been committed, Amnon threw her out of his chamber in spite of her protests that to do so would be a greater wrong than the rape itself (vv. 15-18). Tamar rubbed ashes on her head and tore her robe as signs of mourning (v. 19). She then reported Amnon's abuse to her brother Absalom (vv. 20-22). Two years later Absalom took vengeance, arranging for Amnon's murder (vv. 23-29). The consequent impossibility of Absalom's returning to David's presence was one factor that led to Absalom's revolt.

3. The daughter of Absalom (2 Sam. 14:27). The LXX identifies her as the wife of Rehoboam (in the same verse), therefore as the same person as MAACAH **4**, but it is often assumed that she was actually the mother of Maacah.

TAMAR [tā′mər] (Heb. *tāmār* "date palm") (**PLACE**).

1. A city fortified by King Solomon (1 Kgs. 9:18). Heb. **Q** *taḏmōr* suggests that the city in view may be the same as Tadmor, mentioned at 2 Chr. 8:4. However, if "the land" at 1 Kgs. 9:18 is understood as the territory of Judah (RSV supplies "of Judah"), this would not be the well-known Syrian city of Tadmor (Palmyra).

2. A place in the wilderness of Judah near the southern end of the Dead Sea that marked the southeastern corner of the ideal boundaries of Israel in the vision of Ezekiel (Ezek. 47:19; 48:28). Some scholars emend Heb. *tāmōddû* "you shall measure" at 47:18 to *tāmārâ* "to Tamar," following the Syriac version (so RSV, JB). Proposed identifications of the site have been ʿAin el-ʿArûs (identified by some with Hazazon-tamar), *ca.* 10 km. (6 mi.) southwest of the Dead

Sea, and ʿAin Hoṣob (identified by some with Oboth), *ca.* 32 km. (20 mi.) southwest of the Dead Sea.

TAMARISK [tăm'ə rĭsk] (Heb. *ʾēšel*). A shrub or small tree of the genus *Tamarix*, several species of which are found from the Nile to the Euphrates. Some are desert plants; others can be found along the seashore and rivers. Tamarisks usually have bluish-green scalelike leaves that cover the long, slender branches, thus giving little shade. Near the Dead Sea and the Jordan tamarisk shrubs often dominate the view; these shrubs are beautiful when clusters of the pink blossoms open. Particular tamarisk trees are mentioned in the Old Testament as the focal point of a shrine (Gen. 21:33; KJV "grove") and as prominent landmarks (1 Sam. 22:6; 31:13; KJV "grove"). Some interpreters identify the manna with which God fed Israel during the wilderness wanderings as a resinous exudate of the common tamarisk (*Tamarix gallica*, salt cedar or French tamarisk).

TAMBOURINE. See TIMBREL.

TAMMUZ [tăm'ŭz] (Heb. *tammûz*; Akk. *Tamūzu*; Sum. *Dumu-zi* "faithful son").†

1. A Sumerian and Babylonian god of agriculture, manifest in milk and grain. Tammuz is first encountered as a shepherd god-king (*ANET*, pp. 41-42); according to the Sumerian king list (p. 265), an antediluvian king Dumuzi ruled Uruk (biblical Erech, modern Warka) for thirty-six thousand years. Through time he came to be identified with the natural forces that lead to the creation of new human, animal, and plant life in the spring. In various contexts he is described as Damu ("the child"), that power which produces new life in the watery deep (also manifest in the sap of trees and bushes); Amu-ušumgal-anna ("the single great source of the date clusters" or perhaps "the mother of the dragon is heaven"), the power of the date palm to produce fruit; and the power of barley, particularly in beer. Tammuz was linked with Inanna (Ishtar), the goddess primarily responsible for sexual love, fertility, and procreation. A number of Sumerian myths focus on their sexual relationship or on Tammuz as a dying and rising god of vegetation (e.g., Inanna's Descent to the Nether World, *ANET*, pp. 52-57; cf. pp. 106-9; Adapa, pp. 101-3). In the Sumerian New Year festival the king and a priestess played the part of Tammuz and Inanna in a portrayal of the gods' "sacred marriage" intended to assure the fecundity and prosperity of Sumer for the coming year.

The myth of the dying and rising god of fertility had wide currency in the ancient Near East. The prophet Ezekiel saw a vision of a number of idolatrous practices being carried out in the temple in Jerusalem, among them women engaged in ritual mourning for Tammuz (Ezek. 8:14). In Syria he was worshiped as Adoni.

2. The fourth month of the Babylonian year (June/July), named after 1.

TANACH (Josh. 21:25, KJV). See TAANACH.

TANHUMETH [tăn hū'mĭth] (Heb. *tanḥumet* "com-

fort"). A Netophathite and the father of Seraiah, a general in Judah when Gedaliah was governor (2 Kgs. 25:23; Jer. 40:8).

TANIS (Jdt. 1:10). See ZOAN.

TANNING. The treatment of animal skins with various substances to make leather. Although the Old Testament repeatedly refers to useful objects made of leather, it nowhere mentions the occupation of the tanner who prepared the skins for use. The ram's skins used in the tabernacle were tanned (e.g., Exod. 25:5; 26:14; Heb. *meʾāddām*, from *ʾādam* "be red"). The occupation of tanning was held in low esteem among Jews because it involved working with dead animals and with impure materials such as urine and excrement and because of the odors produced. Entering a tannery necessarily rendered one ritually unclean (Mishnah *Šabb.* i.2). Thus, it was required that tanneries be outside of Jewish towns (*B. Bat.* ii.9). The tannery of Simon (12) the tanner (Gk. *byrseús*) was at Joppa, near the Mediterranean coast (Acts 10:6, 32).

See LEATHER.

TAPHATH [tā'făth] (Heb. *ṭāpaṯ*). The daughter of King Solomon and wife of Ben-abinadab, administrator of the district of Naphath-dor (1 Kgs. 4:11).

TAPPUAH [tăp'yŏŏ ə] (Heb. *tappuaḥ, tappûaḥ* "apple tree" or "quince").

1. (Heb. *tappûaḥ*). One of the northern Canaanite cities defeated by the Israelites under Joshua (Josh. 12:17). Situated on the northern border of the tribal territory of Ephraim (16:8), the town was assigned to Ephraim but the adjoining territory to Manasseh (17:8; cf. LXX, which refers here to the spring En-tappuah at v. 7). It is probably to be identified with modern Sheikh Abū Zarad, *ca.* 13 km. (8 mi.) south-southwest of Shechem, and is thought to be the same as TIPHSAH 2 (2 Kgs. 15:16; RSV "Tappuah," following LXX Gk. *Taphōe*).

2. A town in the Shephelah region of Judah (Josh. 15:34), usually identified with Beit Nettif (Bethletepha), *ca.* 20 km. (12.5 mi.) west of Bethlehem.

3. (Heb. *tappuaḥ*). A "son" of the Calebite city of Hebron (1 Chr. 2:43). The name probably refers to the town of Beth-tappuah (Josh. 15:53), apparently founded by or in a subordinate relationship with Hebron.

TARAH (Num. 33:27-28, KJV). See TERAH (PLACE).

TARALAH [tăr'ə lə] (Heb. *tarʾªlâ*). A town in the tribal territory of Benjamin (Josh. 18:27), in the district northwest of Jerusalem. A suggested site is Khirbet Irha, located near Tell el-Fûl (Gibeah).

TAREA [târ'ĭ ə] (Heb. *taʾªrēaʿ*). A descendant of King Saul (1 Chr. 8:35). At 8:41 he is called Tahrea.

TARES (Matt. 13:25-40, KJV). See WEEDS.

TARGUM [tär'gŭm] (Aram. *targûm* "interpretation, translation").† An Aramaic translation or paraphrase of an Old Testament text. The extant written Targums had their beginnings with the oral rendering into the

Aramaic vernacular of portions of the Hebrew Bible that took place as part of regular worship in synagogues during the centuries when the Jews of Palestine and Babylonia spoke dialects of Aramaic (cf. Ezra 8:7-8). While the origins of this practice in the synagogues are pre-Christian, the growth of the Targum traditions continued for centuries and have been preserved in written compositions that are not only the product of synagogue liturgy, but of the rabbinic academies as well.

Among the factors contributing to the recent upsurge of interest in the Targums are the the publication in 1930 of Targum fragments found in the Cairo Genizah dating from the seventh century A.D. (and thus considerably older than the extant medieval transcriptions), the identification in 1956 of a nearly complete text of the Palestinian Targum to the Pentateuch (Codex Neofiti I of the Vatican Library), and the publication of Aramaic fragments from Qumran, including extensive fragments of a Targum of Job (11QtgJob). With study of the newly discovered and identified materials has come a reevaluation of the significance of the Targums for the understanding of Judaism in the milieu of Jesus and his first followers. Since the Targums originated in the synagogue, they are likely to be the best testimony to popular forms of early Judaism that were the preserve of special groups. While this point and the pre-Christian origin of the practice of oral translation in the synagogue services are generally acknowledged by scholars, the further claim that some of the extant written Targums are as a whole pre-Christian is vigorously debated.

Despite this uncertainty with regard to dating, the Targums have been drawn on extensively in recent New Testament studies to illuminate themes, exegetical traditions, and particular linguistic features. Further progress in this area of comparison will probably depend on advances in other areas to which the study of the Targums also belongs, such as the history of the Aramaic language, the place of the Targums in the history of early biblical interpretation and in the evolution of Jewish liturgy, and the assessment of the relationship between Targum traditions and rabbinic Midrash.

Bibliography. J. W. Bowker, *The Targums and Rabbinic Literature* (Cambridge: 1969); B. D. Chilton, *A Galilean Rabbi and His Bible* (Wilmington: 1984); B. Grossfeld, *A Bibliography of Targum Literature*, 2 vols. (New York: 1972-1977); M. McNamara, *Targum and Testament* (Grand Rapids: 1972).

TARPELITES [tär'pə līts]. The KJV rendering of Aram. *ṭarpᵉlāyēʾ* (Ezra 4:9), which has been variously interpreted as a gentilic term (NIV "men from Tripolis" [on the Phoenician coast]) and as a title for a class of Persian officials (so RSV, JB).

TARSHISH [tär'shĭsh] (Heb. *taršîš* "beryl [?]") (PERSON).
1. One of the "sons of Javan" (Gen. 10:4; 1 Chr. 1:7). *See* TARSHISH (PLACE).
2. A Benjaminite, son of Bilhan (1 Chr. 7:10; KJV "Tharshish").
3. One of the seven nobles of King Ahasuerus who had most direct access to the king (Esth. 1:14).

TARSHISH [tär'shĭsh] (Heb. *taršîš*) (PLACE).† A place presumably associated with the Mediterranean Sea to the west of the Palestinian and Phoenician coast. While "Tarshish" probably arose from the name of some actual place, in the Old Testament it is primarily a term for a vague, faraway place or for such places in general (e.g., Ps. 72:10). Such usage probably stems from the ordinary Israelites' lack of direct contact with the sea and sea commerce.

A number of places have been suggested as the original and actual "Tarshish." Perhaps most likely is Tartessus, a Phoenician colony on the Guadalquivir river of southern Spain. Josephus identifies Tarshish with Cilicia in southern Asia Minor, noting the similarity of the name of Cilicia's principal city, Tarsus (*Ant.* i.6.1 [127]), but this is not likely to be correct. Where "Tarshish" appears in genealogies (Gen. 10:4; 1 Chr. 1:7), it is associated with other names related to Asia Minor (Javan [Ionia], Kittim [Cyprus]). That Heb. *taršîš* is also the name of some precious stone (*see* BERYL) offers little or no clue to the location of Tarshish, because of the uncertain identification of the stone so designated.

Approximately one-third of the Old Testament occurrences of Tarshish are in reference to large seagoing trade ships ("ships of Tarshish") used by Phoenicia (Isa. 23:1, 14; Ezek. 27:25) and Israel (1 Kgs. 10:22; 22:48; KJV "Tharshish"; 2 Chr. 9:21), regardless of their port of origin or destination. The destination of these ships is sometimes said to be Tarshish, but this is so only in late texts written at some remove from the actual practice of sea trading (2 Chr. 20:36-37; Isa. 23:6; Ezek. 27:25; Jonah 1:3; 4:2). This near-legendary place is pictured as a source of great wealth (Jer. 10:9; Ezek. 27:12; 38:13). Tyre was so dependent on sea trade for its wealth that it could be called the "daughter of Tarshish" (Isa. 23:10).

In eschatological settings (Ps. 48:7 [MT 8]; Isa. 2:16) the "ships of Tarshish" are not merchant ships but battleships of the enemies, themselves conceived in the most general terms, of God's people. At 60:9, however, they become the ships that will bring the Diaspora of Israel to Jerusalem. Isa. 66:19-20 looks forward to the return of the Diaspora from Tarshish and other faraway lands.

TARSUS [tär'səs] (Gk. *Tarsos*).† An important city in the Roman province of Cilicia in southeastern Asia Minor; the birthplace of the apostle Paul (Acts 9:11; 21:39; 22:3). Situated *ca.* 18 km. (11 mi.) from the Mediterranean Sea on the Cydnus river, Tarsus prospered (cf. 21:39, "no mean city") because the river branched out into a lake below the city, forming an easily accessible natural harbor, thoroughly safe for shipping. The plain was accessible from the north through the Cilician Gates in the Taurus mountains and from the east through the Syrian Gates in the Amanus mountains, allowing armies and caravans to move along the trade routes on which the city was located.

Excavations at Gozlu Kule, a mound near the city, have revealed occupation as early as the fifth millennium B.C.; fortified settlements existed on the site as early as the third millennium. Mentioned in chronicles of the Hittites, who dominated the area from

One of the "Cilician Gates," narrow passes north of Tarsus which enabled the city to become an important trading center (B. Van Elderen)

1400 to 1200, Tarsus had long been established as a coastal center. Hittite control was interrupted by the Sea Peoples *ca.* 1200. The Black Obelisk of Shalmaneser III (858-824) mentions Tarsus among the cities he conquered. Following a rebellion, the city was sacked by Sennacherib in 698.

Under Persian domination, Tarsus was capital of Cilicia. It was taken by Alexander the Great in 333 and then passed under the control of the Seleucid dynasty. According to 2 Macc. 4:30, when Antiochus IV presented Tarsus and Mallus as a gift to his mistress Antiochis, the citizens revolted. A year later it became a self-governing Greek city (170), renamed "Antiocheia on the Cydnus." The influence of Greek education and civilization made Tarsus a center of intellectual life. Under Roman power, Cilicia became a province with Tarsus as its capital.

The renowned Roman statesman, Cicero, was governor of Tarsus in 50 B.C. After Julius Caesar conferred with Cilician representatives at Tarsus in 47, the city assumed the name Juliopolis in his honor. Following Caesar's assassination, Tarsus opposed Cassius and was treated harshly by him in 43 B.C. Antony

later rewarded the city for this opposition by exempting it from taxes. Under the rule of Augustus (27 B.C.–A.D. 14), Tarsus was restored as a free city, and it soon became one of the foremost centers of intellectual life in the Roman Empire, rivaling Alexandria and Athens. Tarsus was also known particularly for the weaving of linen.

From 170 B.C. a community of Jews lived in Tarsus, encouraged originally by the Seleucids to stimulate economic growth. These Jews were granted rights equal to those of the Greek inhabitants of the city. Following Paul's conversion and initial ministry in Damascus and Jerusalem, he was sent from Caesarea to Tarsus to escape death at the hands of his Jewish opponents (Acts 9:30). Barnabas went later to Tarsus to enlist Paul's help in teaching the Gentile converts at Antioch (11:25-26).

TARTAK [tär′tăk] (Heb. *tartāq*). A deity worshipped by the Avvites (2 Kgs. 17:31). Tartak is probably to be identified with Atargatis, the Syrian fish-goddess and consort of Dagon; she was worshipped in Babylonia as Derketo, mother of the city's legendary founder, Semiramis.

TARTAN [tär′tăn] (Heb. *tartān*; Akk. *turtānu, tartanu*). A high functionary in the Assyrian army, possibly commander in chief (so RSV at Isa. 20:1; cf. NIV "supreme commander"); the JB rendering "cup-bearer in chief" suggests an even more significant rank. The Old Testament alludes to two such officials without giving their names (KJV omits the definite article): one sent by Sargon II to destroy Ashdod (Isa. 20:1; 711 B.C.) and the other dispatched by Sennacherib to King Hezekiah of Judah (2 Kgs. 18:17; 701).

TASSEL. A dangling ornament of white woolen threads and a blue cord attached to the four corners of one's garment as a reminder of God's presence, salvation, and commandments in accordance with the instructions given at Num. 15:38-41 (Heb. *ṣîṣiṯ*; KJV "fringe"); Deut. 22:12 (*gᵉḏilîm*; KJV "fringes"). With the decline in the wearing of four-cornered garments, the tallit or prayer shawl, with tassels attached to the corners in a prescribed elaborate fashion, came to be worn by Jewish men during daytime prayer times. Many modern Orthodox Jewish men also wear the tallit katan, a smaller tallit with tassels, under their shirts.

It may have been the tassels of Jesus' garment that the woman with a hemorrhage touched (Matt. 9:20 par.) and that were the means of healing for others (14:36 par.); Gk. *kráspedon* (RSV "fringe[s]") might represent simply the edge of Jesus' garment (KJV "border, hem") or the distinctive Jewish tassels, referred to at 23:5.

TATIAN [tā′shǝn]. *See* DIATESSARON; SYRIAC VERSIONS.

TATTENAI [tăt′ǝ nī] (Aram. *tattᵉnay*). The Persian governor of the province Beyond the River (Ezra 5:3, 6; 6:6, 13; KJV "Tatnai"). When Tattenai asked King

Darius I Hystaspes for more information concerning the reconstruction of Jerusalem (*ca.* 520 B.C.), the king told him not to prevent this work.

TAX (Heb. nouns *maś'ēṭ, middâ,* verb hiphil *'āraḵ* "assess the value of"; Aram. nouns *mindâ, bᵉlô, hᵃlāḵ;* Gk. nouns *phóros, kḗnsos,* pl. *télē*).†

Payments in kind and forced labor were very much part of life in the ancient Near East. Pharaoh placed a levy on the people of Egypt in order to obtain part of their grain in preparation for anticipated famine (Gen. 41:34-36), and Israel required forced labor of the conquered Canaanites (Deut. 20:11; Josh. 16:10; 17:13; Judg. 1:28-35). That such practices would come upon the Israelites from their own king was predicted by Samuel when they asked for a king (1 Sam. 8:11-17). Although this was to come true, internal taxation of the Israelites apparently did not exist until the reign of Solomon. Solomon's father, David, had been able to support his government with the spoils of war, tribute, and the revenue of his private estates (2 Sam. 8; 1 Chr. 27:25-31). That Solomon was the first Israelite king to impose state taxes on his people is suggested by his appointment of twelve officers over Israel in order to insure that the king and his household would have enough to eat (1 Kgs. 4:7-19). The burden of taxation placed upon the people reached the saturation point when Solomon's son, Rehoboam, chose to increase the demand his father had placed on the people. In response to this short-sighted action (and other long-standing grievances and division), Jeroboam led a rebellion and established rule in the northern part of Solomon's kingdom (ch. 12).

During the last days of the monarchy, kings of both the northern and southern kingdoms were compelled to pay tribute to foreign powers such as Assyria (2 Kgs. 18:13-16), Egypt (23:33, 35), and Babylon (24:13; *see* TRIBUTE). After Judah was conquered, its rulers continued to collect revenue from the people but this revenue was not "tribute" in the strict sense. At first, tribute payments were made directly to the foreign master, but under Persian rule the procedure was changed. The provincial governor, the satrap, paid a direct sum into the Persian royal treasury. To raise this sum, the satrap collected taxes. The terms "tribute, custom, and toll" at Ezra 4:13, 20; 7:24 provide some idea of the diverse means of taxation employed. Artaxerxes I exempted the priests and Levites of Judah from taxation (7:24). In addition to the tax due for the royal revenue, a local tax ("bread for the governor"; RSV "food allowance") was collected to meet the needs of the local governor (Neh. 5:14-15).

Under the Ptolemies and the Seleucids, the foreign king "farmed out" the tax franchise to the highest bidder (Josephus *Ant.* xii.4.1, 4-5 [155, 175-185]). This practice was the cause of much suffering and hardship. Tax collectors made considerable profit because they could pocket anything above the amount of their bid. With the beginning of Roman rule (63 B.C.), heavy taxes remained a part of life, though Julius Caesar did relieve some of the burden (xiv.10.5-6 [202-6]).

Herod the Great taxed nearly every aspect of commerce (cf. xvii.8.4 [204-5]), including agricultural products (xv.9.1 [303]). After Herod, the Roman procurators farmed out the taxes to the highest bidder as the Ptolemies and Seleucids had done. Many of the taxes, including tolls (customs imposed on imports and exports, both at seaports and city gates), were collected by "tax collectors" (Gk. sing. *telónēs*; KJV "publican").

The tax collector was employed by a wealthy entrepreneur who purchased the rights to a tax franchise. One possible example of such a person of wealth is Zacchaeus, a "chief tax collector" (Luke 19:2). The ordinary tax collector, an employee of such a wealthy person, sat in a tax office (*telónion*) and collected taxes, or sat by the roadside and inspected the goods of those who were traveling and charged a toll tax. Because the tax collectors were Jews working for the hated Romans, they were considered traitors by fellow Jews. Moreover, they were well known for their greed because, after having met their financial responsibility to the one for whom they worked, they were free to keep any surplus for themselves. Tax collectors were grouped with sinners (Matt. 9:10; cf. 21:31) and despised by the Pharisees (9:11). But Jesus befriended them and chose one, Matthew, to be an apostle (9:9; 10:3).

Jesus was asked by fellow Jews whether it was right to pay tribute to the Roman government. His answer was affirmative, but it was phrased in such a way as to turn the Jewish awareness of the conflict between God's rule and Caesar's rule into a question concerning personal responsibility to God (22:17-21). Paul also counseled the payment of tribute (Rom. 13:6-7).

The temple tax was an amount paid by every Jewish male in Palestine and the Diaspora for the support of the Jerusalem temple. The basis for this tax was Exod. 30:11-16, according to which every male Jew twenty years or older was to pay one-half shekel (Gk. *dídrachma* at Matt. 17:24). For a period the tax was one-third of a shekel (Neh. 10:32 [MT 33]), but by Jesus' time it was again a half-shekel, collected annually. When Peter was asked whether Jesus paid the temple tax, Jesus' answer was not unequivocal in view of the eschatological nature of his mission and of the community gathered around him, but he felt it should be paid "not to give offense." The temple tax was paid for both Jesus and Peter by a shekel found miraculously in the mouth of a fish (Matt. 17:24-27). After the destruction of the temple in A.D. 70 the Jews were still obligated to pay the tax, but it was then collected by the Romans for the support of the temple of Jupiter Capitolinus (Josephus *BJ* vii.6.6 [218]).

TEACHING (Gk. *didachḗ, didáskō,* and related words).† Teaching is mentioned often in the New Testament because it was a characteristic activity of Jesus and the leaders of the early Church. While an absolute distinction cannot be made between public "preaching" and private "teaching" in the ministry of Jesus, he did give only to his close disciples instruction concerning what he would experience in Jerusalem (Mark 8:31-32), explanations of his parables (4:10-12), and instruction for their missionary work (Matt. 10). His public preaching was centered on the proclamation of the coming of the kingdom and the call to repentance

(4:17). The early Church also distinguished between, on the one hand, the proclamation of Jesus' resurrection and of God's work of salvation in him, and the call to repentance (Acts 2:22-39; 17:30-31; 1 Cor. 2:1-5) and, on the other hand, the teaching of those who had responded to the call and joined the Christian community (Acts 2:42; 1 Cor. 2:6-7). These two tasks overlapped considerably, however, depending on the needs of the community (3:1-3; Col. 1:28; Heb. 6:1-2).

Teaching is listed among the gifts of the Spirit (Rom. 12:7; 1 Cor. 14:6, 26 [Gk. *didachḗ*, RSV "lesson"]) and can be thought of as the primary function involved in other gifts of the Spirit, such as "the utterance of wisdom" and "the utterance of knowledge" (12:8). It is apparent, however, that specific individuals were designated as "teachers" (*didáskalos*) in the early churches; such individuals were distinguished from apostles, prophets, and others (v. 28). Eph. 4:11 appears to suggest that teachers were also "pastors." Congregations were urged to respect teachers and provide for their livelihood (Gal. 6:6; 1 Tim. 5:17). The most apparent positive quality of a teacher would be the effective transmission without distortion of what the teacher had learned from his or her predecessors (1 Cor. 4:17; 2 Tim. 2:2). Teaching was a primary function of the office of bishop as that office developed (1 Tim. 3:2).

TEACHING OF THE TWELVE APOSTLES. *See* DIDACHE.

TEBAH [tē′bə] (Heb. *ṭebaḥ* "slaughtering"). The eldest son of Nahor and his concubine Reumah (Gen. 22:24). His name is associated with the names of the cities Betah (2 Sam. 8:8) and Tibhath (1 Chr. 18:8).

TEBALIAH [tĕb′ə lī′ə] (Heb. *ṭebalyāhû* "Yahweh has purified"). A levitical gatekeeper, the third son of Hosah, and a descendant of Merari (1 Chr. 26:11).

TEBETH [tē′bĕth] (Heb. *ṭēbēṯ*; Akk. *ṭebītu*). The tenth month of the Hebrew year (Dec.–Jan.). In this month Esther was taken to Ahasuerus' palace, where she was made queen (Esth. 2:16). Following the fall of Jerusalem in 587-586 B.C., the Jews initiated a fast on the tenth of Tebeth (cf. Zech. 8:19), the date Nebuchadrezzar's siege of the city had begun (cf. 2 Kgs. 25:1). *See* YEAR.

TEHAPHNEHES [tə hăf′nə hēz] (Heb. *teḥapneḥēs*). Alternate name of the Egyptian city TAHPANHES (Ezek. 30:18).

TEHINNAH [tə hĭn′ə] (Heb. *teḥinnâ* "mercy"). A Judahite, son of Eshton and "father" (i.e., founder) of the city of Irnahash (1 Chr. 4:12).

TEIL TREE (Isa. 6:13, KJV). *See* TEREBINTH.

TEKOA [tə kō′ə] (Heb. *teqôaʿ*; Gk. *Thekōe*). An agricultural town in the highlands of Judah, the founding of which is ascribed to Ashhur, a Calebite (1 Chr. 2:24; 4:5). The name is preserved in that of the modern site, Khirbet Teqûʿ, located *ca.* 8 km. (5 mi.) south

of Bethlehem. East of Tekoa was a wilderness area named for the city (2 Chr. 20:20; 1 Macc. 9:33).

Joab sent to Tekoa for a wise woman who could bring about a reconciliation between David and Absalom (2 Sam. 14:2; KJV "Tekoah"). Tekoa was also the home of Ira the son of Ikkesh, one of David's mighty men (23:26; 1 Chr. 11:28; 27:9), and of the prophet Amos (Amos 1:1). Rehoboam fortified Tekoa (2 Chr. 11:6), and after the Exile some Tekoites (Heb. *teqôʿîm*) were among those who worked on the rebuilding of the walls of Jerusalem (Neh. 3:5, 27).

TEL-ABIB [tĕl′ə bīb′] (Heb. *tēl ʾābîb*; Akk. *Til-abûbi* "mound of the flood"). A mound of ruins in Babylon where a group of Jewish exiles lived (Ezek. 3:15; NIV "Tel Aviv"). It was located by the Chebar river, a canal near Babylon.

TELAH [tē′lə] (Heb. *telaḥ*). An Ephraimite, ancestor of Joshua (1 Chr. 7:25).

TELAIM [tə lā′əm] (Heb. *telāʾîm*). A place where Saul organized his troops to attack Amalekite forces (1 Sam. 15:4), probably the same as the town of Telem (Josh. 15:24). The name may also occur as Telam, possibly mentioned at 1 Sam. 27:8 as marking a boundary of the Amalekites and other peoples (reading *miṭṭēlām* "from Telam," as suggested by some LXX manuscripts [so JB] in place of MT *mēʿôlām* "from of old" [so RSV]). Because the Amalekites dwelled in the northern part of the Sinai peninsula, Telaim/Telem would have been located in the southern part of Judah (cf. Josh. 15:21). Khirbet Umm eṣ-Ṣalafeh, near Ziph (1), has been suggested as the site.

TEL-ASSAR [tĕl ăs′ər] (Heb. *telaʾśśār*, *telaśśār*). A place inhabited by the "people of Eden," named in a message of an Assyrian official to King Hezekiah of Judah as one of the places destroyed by Assyrian forces (2 Kgs. 19:12; KJV "Thelasser"; Isa. 37:12). It is perhaps to be identified with Til-Aššuri, a Babylonian city located in Media near Ecbatana. Some interpreters suggest that the text is corrupt and that the place should be identified as Til Bašir, capital of Bit-adini on the upper Euphrates (so JB "Tel Basar").

TELEM [tē′lĕm] (Heb. *telem* "brightness") (PERSON). A postexilic levitical gatekeeper among those who divorced their foreign wives (Ezra 10:24).

TELEM [tē′lĕm] (Heb. *telem* "brightness") (PLACE). A city in the Negeb region of Judah (Josh. 15:24). *See* TELAIM.

TEL-HARSHA [tĕl här′shə] (Heb. *tēl haršāʾ* "hill of the deaf one"). A city in Babylonia from which Jewish exiles returned to Judah with Zerubbabel (Ezra 2:59; KJV "Telharsa"; Neh. 7:61; KJV "Telharesha"). Its exact location is unknown. The *tēl* element in its name suggests that the Jewish settlement there was established on the site of an old city.

TELL (Arab. *tell* "ruin heap, mound"; Heb. *tēl* "Tel"). The regularly sloping hill that results from the growth of the successive layers of an ancient town, built on the remains of preceding occupations (cf. Turk. *tepe*, *hüyük*). Often readily recognizable to the observer, such sites can be assumed to contain the remains of ancient settlements and thus as suitable for excavation. The term occurs as an element in the modern names of many such sites. In some instances it identifies a natural hill.

TELL EL-AMARNA [těl ĕl ə mär′nə]. The site of Akhetaten, the royal city built by Egyptian pharaoh Amenhotep IV (*ca.* 1375-1362 B.C.) and dedicated to the sun-god Aton. The modern name is derived from the Beni ʿAmran tribe who occupied the region. The site is located *ca.* 320 km. (200 mi.) south of Cairo on the east bank of the Nile.

Early in his reign, for reasons still uncertain, Amenhotep, tenth ruler of the Eighteenth Dynasty, broke with the influential priests of the god Amon at Thebes by devoting himself to the worship of Aton and changing his name to Akhenaten ("It is well with Aton"). He built three cities dedicated to Aton in different areas of the Egyptian empire. Akhetaten ("the horizon of Aton"), the most elaborate of these cities, became the home of the royal family and thus the administrative capital of Egypt. Nobles, wealthy landowners, and bureaucrats lived here, supported by peasants in surrounding villages.

Akhenaten's devotion to Aton sparked what is often called the "Amarna revolution." Scholars have long argued whether the pharaoh was a true monotheist or, rather, practiced a henotheism in which the existence of other gods was also accepted. While the sun disk had been part of Egyptian religion for some time, it apparently had come to be identified as a deity only shortly before Akhenaten came to power. Any influence of Amarna religion on Israelite monotheism (through Moses or by other means) is now generally discredited. Another important characteristic of the Amarna revolution was the abandonment of stylized representations of the pharaoh on monuments: Akhenaten and his wife Nefertiti were portrayed as they actually looked in life.

Despite Egyptian expansion in Palestine and success in international commerce, a weakening of Egyptian power during Akhenaten's reign led him to seek reconciliation with the powerful priests of Amon. He was unsuccessful, and suddenly disappeared from history in about his twelfth regnal year. Tutankhaten, the half-brother of Nefertiti (according to some scholars Akhenaten's immediate successor and, as queen, coregent during the final years of his reign), assumed power, changing his name to Tutankhamen to signal Amon's return to prominence. No evidence survives to indicate that Amarna was occupied before or after this brief period in Akhenaten's reign.

Tell el-Amarna was excavated extensively during the first half of the twentieth century by British and German archaeologists. The AMARNA LETTERS, an important collection of cuneiform diplomatic correspondence from the reigns of Amenhotep III and IV, were recovered at the site.

TEL-MELAH [těl mē′lə] (Heb. *těl melaḥ* "hill of

salt"). A city in Babylonia from which exiled Jews returned with Zerubbabel to Jerusalem (Ezra 2:59; Neh. 7:61). Its site is unknown.

TEMA [tē′mə] (Heb. *têmāʾ*). A son of Ishmael (Gen. 25:15; 1 Chr. 1:30). The name also designates his descendants (who constituted an Arabian tribe) and their home in northwest Arabia (modern Teimā; Isa. 21:14; Jer. 25:23). This oasis, *ca.* 360 km. (220 mi.) east-southeast of modern Aqaba, was an important caravan station (cf. Job 6:19). Nabonidus, Babylon's last king, withdrew to Tema for a number of years, leaving his son Belshazzar to reign at Babylon (*ANET*, pp. 306, 313; cf. 562-63).

TEMAH [tē′mə] (Heb. *temaḥ*). A temple servant whose descendants returned with Zerubbabel from captivity in Babylon (Ezra 2:53; KJV "Thamah"; Neh. 7:55; KJV "Tamah").

TEMAN [tē′mən] (Heb. *têmān* "[place] to the south").† A son of Eliphaz and grandson of Esau who became a chief in Edom (Gen. 36:11, 15, 42). The place in Edom where his descendants dwelled also came to be known as Teman. The site is probably to be identified as modern Tawīlân, located a short distance east of Petra. An important population center and trading station during the Edomite period, Teman is mentioned in prophetic oracles against Edom (Jer. 49:7, 20; Ezek. 25:13; Amos 1:12; Obad. 9). Habakkuk depicts God as coming toward Judah from Teman, i.e., from Sinai by way of Edom (Hab. 3:3; cf. Deut. 33:2).

TEMANITE [tē′mə nīt] (Heb. *têmānî*).†
1. A gentilic designating an inhabitant of Edomite Teman (Gen. 36:34; 1 Chr. 1:45).
2. A gentilic ascribed to Job's would-be comforter, Eliphaz (e.g., Job 2:11), apparently indicating that he was from Tema in Arabia (cf. 6:19).

TEMENI [těm′ə nī] (Heb. *têmᵉnî*). A son of Ashhur and Naarah of the tribe of Judah (1 Chr. 4:6). The name appears to be a gentilic (cf. JB "Timnites"), meaning perhaps "the people of the south."

TEMPLE (Heb. *hêḵāl, bayiṯ*; Gk. *hierón, naós*).† A building, generally thought of as the dwelling-place of a deity, in which the corporate worship of that deity is centered. The basic plan of many ancient Palestinian and Syrian temples consisted of two rooms adjoined end to end, with a single entrance at the end of the larger room. The worshipper would proceed through this entrance and through the larger room to reach the smaller room, the inner sanctuary. The addition of a vestibule outside the entrance (attested in some archaeological examples) and a courtyard in which sacrificial animals were slaughtered and burned characterize the basic plan of Israel's primary places of worship: the tabernacle of the wilderness (which lacked the vestibule), Solomon's temple, the second (Nehemiah's) temple, and Herod's temple.

I. Before Solomon

Israel's first temple was the portable tabernacle of the

A late Bronze Age temple at Lachish (by courtesy of the Israel Department of Antiquities and Museums)

wilderness, which Moses was directed to construct (Exod. 25–31; 33–40) so that God could dwell among his people (25:8; see TABERNACLE). After the people had entered the land of Canaan, they established or adopted shrines and sanctuaries in various locations. Some of these were places where the tabernacle or the ark were located (e.g., Shiloh, Josh. 18:1; Bethel, Judg. 20:26-27; Kiriath-jearim, 1 Sam. 7:1-2; Gibeon, 1 Chr. 16:39; 21:29; 2 Chr. 1:3). Some were sites of significant events (Gilgal, Josh. 4:19-24; 5:13-15; Shiloh, 22:12; Shechem, ch. 24 [cf. v. 26]; Mizpah, Judg. 20; 1 Sam. 7:5-12). Some were sites of existing ancient shrines (Shechem, Gen. 12:6-7; 33:18-20; Bethel, 13:3-4; 31:13; perhaps Gibeon, 2 Sam. 21:6; 1 Kgs. 3:4). At Shiloh (and perhaps elsewhere) a temple was built (Judg. 18:31; 1 Sam. 3:3) and an annual pilgrimage feast was held (Judg. 21:19). After Shiloh had been destroyed, priests of Shiloh maintained a shrine at Nob that possessed some of the furnishings of the tabernacle (1 Sam. 21–22; cf. 14:3).

II. Solomon's Temple

David brought the ark to Jerusalem and placed it in a tent (2 Sam. 6). He made plans to erect a temple in Jerusalem, but was forbidden by God to do so (7:5-16; 1 Chr. 22:8). He did, however, acquire a site (the threshing floor of Araunah/Ornan, perhaps a pre-Israelite sacred site) and made preparations for the temple's construction (1 Chr. 22). Solomon began building the temple in the fourth year of his reign (ca. 958 B.C.) and completed it seven years later. Its construction was supervised by Phoenician craftsmen (1 Kgs. 7:13-14, 40-45), Phoenician materials were used (5:6, 8-10), and the temple no doubt reflected Phoenician styles.

Attempts to construct a model of the temple on the basis of the biblical accounts and analogies from other ancient Near Eastern temples cannot be completely accurate, because the Bible's descriptions are not complete and appear to be in conflict at some points. Nevertheless, some of the larger features of Solomon's temple can be described. The temple was surrounded by a courtyard in which stood the "molten sea" and the altar of sacrifice. The temple proper was rec-

tangular and was divided into three sections from front to back, each 20 cubits (8.9 m. [29 ft.]) wide. Directly in front of the first section, the vestibule, were two free-standing bronze pillars. The vestibule was 10 cubits (4.5 m. [14.5 ft.]) from front to back. The second section was the "holy place," where much of the priestly activity took place. It was 40 cubits (18 m. [58 ft.]) from front to back and contained the altar of incense, ten golden lampstands, and the table for the Bread of the Presence. The inner sanctuary, the "most holy place" or "holy of holies," was 20 cubits (8.9 m. [29 ft.]) wide and deep. Two large cherubim were in the inner sanctuary above the ark. This room was entered only by the high priest and only on the Day of Atonement. Although the temple was constructed of huge blocks of stone, the interior was covered with paneling and elaborate woodwork so that no stonework was visible. Many items in the central room and in the inner sanctuary were inlaid with gold. Three stories of storage rooms were built around the back and sides of the temple proper. These rooms probably housed priests on duty, supplies, the temple treasury, gifts and tribute, and perhaps even weapons (1 Kgs. 7:51; 14:25-26; 15:18; 2 Kgs. 11:10; 12:4).

Solomon's great ceremony of dedication involving "all the assembly of Israel" (1 Kgs. 8:14; cf. v. 1) shows how the new temple served to unite all phases of Israel's religion. The construction of the temple occurred a generation after the establishment of the Davidic monarchy in Israel and of the royal capital in Jerusalem. In the ancient world, the building of a temple served as a visible symbol of the presence of a god, as well as of his approval of the temple's builder, thus justifying the current leadership. It also demonstrated that the king's authority over subservient peoples was legitimate, a crucial factor in an empire as large as Solomon's.

Changes took place in the temple after the time of Solomon as it was plundered by outsiders and raided by Judean kings for tribute payments. Some kings deliberately introduced changes in the furnishings (esp. Ahaz; 2 Kgs. 16:7-18). When Jerusalem fell in 587/ 586 Nebuchadrezzar removed the remaining sacred items from the temple and burned it to the ground. Nevertheless, even after its destruction pilgrimages were still made to the temple site (Jer. 41:5).

III. Ezekiel's Vision

After the destruction of Solomon's temple the prophet Ezekiel had a vision of a restored temple and its ordinances (Ezek. 40–44) as part of a series of visions concerning the restored community in the land of Israel (chs. 33–48). Some have held that Ezekiel was providing architectural guidance for the postexilic building of the second temple, but the information the prophet gave was not sufficient for such a purpose. Instead, these chapters should be understood as a statement of hope for the exiles that looks ahead symbolically to God's dwelling in the midst of a people restored to holiness and reestablished in their own land. This hope balanced the recent events of the fall of Jerusalem, while his vision of the return of God's glory (i.e., his "aura" or "presence") to the temple (ch. 43) counterbalanced his earlier vision of its de-

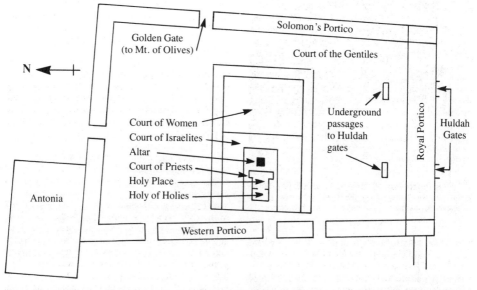

Herod's Temple

parture (chs. 10–11). The basic inspiration for the layout of Ezekiel's temple was Solomon's temple, though there are a number of differences.

IV. Second Temple

After the Babylonian exile efforts to rebuild the temple began *ca.* 537, but lagged until *ca.* 520, when the prophecies of Haggai and Zechariah and the leadership of Zerubbabel provided the incentive to complete the task (Ezra 5:1-2; 6:14). Little is known about this temple. It was built on the same site and according to the same plan and style of workmanship as Solomon's temple, but its furnishings were inferior to those of its predecessor (Ezra 3:12; Hag. 2:3), in spite of the return of some of the treasures carried off by Nebuchadrezzar. The authority represented by the temple was no longer royal, but exclusively priestly. From this period until its eventual destruction, the temple symbolized the religious heart of Israel, not only for Jews in Palestine but for those in the Diaspora as well.

In 167 Antiochus IV Epiphanes set up the "abomination that makes desolate" (Dan. 11:31) on the altar of sacrifice. After three years of warfare, the Maccabees were able to repurify the temple, reinstitute temple worship, and fortify the structure considerably. A century later the Roman conqueror Pompey impiously entered the temple, but out of respect for its sanctity he took no plunder.

V. Herod's Temple

In 20-19 B.C. Herod the Great began dismantling the temple in order to replace it with one of grander design constructed in Hellenistic-Roman style. Although he completed the basic construction in ten years, work on this temple continued until A.D. 64, just a few years before it was destroyed (cf. John 2:20). During the time of this rebuilding, sacrifices continued uninterrupted. Herod was known for his building proj-

ects, and this one had a particularly political motivation. As an Idumean not related to any family with a claim to rule over the Jews, Herod was not accepted by many Jews. His primary reason for building the temple was to ingratiate himself to the people and thereby alleviate political tension.

Herod's temple was built on a large hill, the Temple Mount, which was built up artificially and surrounded by high retaining walls of distinctive Herodian masonry (cf. Mark 13:1). The exact size of this hill remains subject to debate; most scholars hold that it conformed closely to the modern Haram esh-Sharif, but others contend that it was nearly square in shape and corresponded approximately to the southern two-thirds of the Haram. The perimeter of the temple enclosure was marked by colonnades, including Solomon's Portico on the eastern side (Acts 3:11; 5:12), with gates leading in through the colonnades. The Huldah gates, however, gave access to tunnels under the Royal (southern) Portico. The fortress of Antonia adjoined the temple at its northwestern corner.

A large part of the Temple Mount was occupied by the Court of the Gentiles, which Gentiles could enter (cf. Mark 11:15-17). The Court of Women marked the limit of access for Jewish women and the Court of Israelites for Jewish men. The Court of Priests was an area immediately around the temple proper, before which stood the altar of burnt sacrifice. The temple proper was 100 cubits (44.5 m. [146 ft.]) long and high, made of huge white stones and ornately decorated.

Two trends within Judaism of the postexilic to Roman periods lessened the importance of the temple in Jerusalem for some Jews. One was the growth of the Diaspora. Diaspora Jews remained loyal to the temple in Jerusalem. But this did not preclude the building of temples to the God of Israel in Egypt, specifically at Elephantine (sixth-fifth centuries) and at Leontopolis (built by Onias IV *ca.* 164 and maintained until its destruction by the Romans in A.D. 73). (A different situation is represented by the Samaritan temple at Mt. Gerizim.) While these temples did not represent the sentiments of the vast majority of Diaspora Jews, the synagogues in the Diaspora (and in Palestine) provided a new focus for Jewish worship that was able to survive the destruction of the Jerusalem temple and become the basis for a Judaism without a temple.

A second trend was the rise of sectarianism in Judaism of the Hellenistic and early Roman periods. For Qumran, at least, and perhaps in other ways in other Jewish sects, the center of concern became the sect rather than the worship center in Jerusalem. The people of Qumran did not necessarily reject the temple itself, but they did reject as illegitimate the priests who controlled the temple and their ritual as corrupted.

VI. New Testament

The temple elicited strong feelings in Jews, including Jesus. He saw the temple as the place where God dwelled among his people Israel (Matt. 23:21; John 2:16), sanctifying all that was in it (Matt. 23:17-21). Jesus' cleansing of the temple courts was his attempt to restore them to their proper function (Mark 11:15-17). But Jesus claimed to be greater than the temple (Matt. 12:6) and predicted its destruction (Mark 13:2).

The early Church continued for a time to worship at the temple on a regular basis (Acts 2:46; cf. Luke 24:53). It was a focal point for the ministry of the apostles (Acts 3; 5:12, 20, 42). Paul, too, participated in temple rites (21:26; 22:17). Yet in the Hellenist wing of the Church were the seeds of a changing attitude: God does not dwell in houses made by human hands (7:44-50; cf. 17:24).

In Paul's epistles the word "temple" refers no longer to a physical building (even though the temple in Jerusalem was still standing), but to a community of Christian believers (1 Cor. 3:16-17; Eph. 2:19-22). At 2 Cor. 6:16-7:1 this idea is linked to specific Old Testament prophecies, and the emphasis on purity is identical to Ezekiel's in his vision of the new temple (cf. Ezek. 43:7-12; 1 Cor. 6:19).

Revelation speaks of a heavenly temple (Rev. 7:15; 11:19; 14-16; cf. Ps. 11:4) analogous to the heavenly tabernacle of Hebrews (Heb. 8-9). But Revelation envisions no temple building in the new Jerusalem; God himself and the lamb will be the temple for that city (Rev. 21:22), and God will dwell among his people (vv. 2-3).

TEMPLE SERVANTS (Heb. *n^eṭînîm* "those who are given [i.e., to the service of the sanctuary]").† A group of temple personnel known from Ezra-Nehemiah and 1 Chr. 9:2 (KJV "Nethinims") and listed with four other groups in what appears to be a descending order of status: priests, Levites, singers, gatekeepers, and temple servants (Ezra 2:70; 7:7; Neh. 10:28). Most likely this group performed the most menial tasks of temple service.

The origins of the temple servants are unclear, but certain precedents may clarify the historical note that David had established this body to assist the Levites (Ezra 8:20). The Levites themselves were "given" to the priests (Num. 3:9) and "appointed for all the service of the tabernacle" (1 Chr. 6:48). Num. 31:30 records that Moses gave some Midianite prisoners of war to the Levites, and Josh. 9:27 tells of the Gibeonites who were made woodcutters and water carriers for the congregation and the altar. Some scholars have concluded from these passages and from the foreign names in the list of temple servant family heads (Ezra 2:43-54; Neh. 7:46-56) that the temple servants were of foreign extraction, perhaps descendants of prisoners of war from David's time; but others believe them to be of Israelite descent. In any case, by the time of Ezra and Nehemiah the temple servants were full members of the Israelite congregation (Neh. 10:28-29), and thus it is unlikely that Ezekiel's protest (Ezek. 44:6-8) refers to them.

The temple servants, together with the descendants of Solomon's servants (perhaps a technical term for another class of temple personnel), comprised 392 people who accompanied Zerubbabel to Jerusalem after the Exile (Ezra 2:58; Neh. 7:60). When Ezra came to Jerusalem, he brought 220 temple servants with him (Ezra 8:15-20). They were among the first to resettle in their own cities (1 Chr. 9:2). Like the other four temple-related groups, the temple servants were exempt from taxes (Ezra 7:24).

TEMPTATION (Heb. piel *nsh*; Gk. verb *(ek)peir-ázō*).† The testing of human beings, usually enticement to sin or to apostasy from God. The two paradigmatic biblical stories concerning temptation are those concerning Eve and Adam's temptation and sin in the garden of Eden (Gen. 3) and Jesus' successful resistance of Satan's temptations in the wilderness (Matt. 4:1-11; Mark 1:12-13; Luke 4:1-13).

The Genesis account of the events leading to the fall is exemplary of the nature of temptation. Temptation comes from a personal being external to the one who is tempted, in this case "the serpent" (Gen. 3:1), later identified as Satan (e.g., Rev. 12:9). The temptation directly challenges God's instructions regarding what is permitted and forbidden, distorting what God has said and finally denying its truth (Gen. 3:1, 4; cf. John 8:44); not just an impersonal law of God, but the very intention of God for mankind is challenged (Gen. 3:5). Moreover, what is aesthetically

An inscription placed at the periphery of the Court of Women in the temple of Herod warning Gentiles not to proceed further, the penalty being death (by courtesy of the Israel Department of Antiquities and Museums)

pleasing and pleasurable to the senses is made an ally of the temptation and an enemy of God's intention for mankind (v. 6).

The temptation of Jesus also exemplifies certain aspects of temptation. While the devil is the tempter, God's Spirit can set a person in the place in which that person is sure to meet temptation (Matt. 4:1). Temptation can find an ally in immediate personal need (vv. 2-3). The tempter can even quote Scripture (v. 6). A fundamental factor in temptation displayed clearly in the temptation of Jesus is the tempter's endeavor to overthrow the working of God's salvation of mankind. Not merely Jesus' obedience at particular points but also the nature of his messianic ministry is challenged. The three specific temptations recorded do not question Jesus' messiahship, but they do set forth means of making that messiahship effective alternative to the way that God has determined for Jesus, the way of the cross.

Christ's victory over sin does not eliminate temptation. But it does allow for a positive human response, and provides the possibility of not sinning and not abandoning God. A fundamental assumption of the way in which persons are to face temptation is that God is never the tempter; his goodness can never be doubted (Jas. 1:13), even though he does test people by placing them in situations in which an alternative to God's will can be offered (cf. Gen. 22:1). Christ's personal experience as one who was tempted means not only that he has won a victory over sin, but also that his followers are able to see in him one who has led the way through temptation and who understands that way (Heb. 4:15). Paul proclaims that deliverance can occur even during temptation (1 Cor. 10:13); nevertheless, Christians are expected to pray to be delivered from the very experience of temptation (Matt. 6:13) and to respond appropriately, by flight or resistance, when temptation arises (cf. 2 Tim. 2:22; Jas. 4:7).

TEN COMMANDMENTS. A summary statement of the covenant stipulations binding Israel (cf. Exod. 19:5-6) that has come to be a fundamental statement of religious responsibility and social morality. The Ten Commandments are found in two slightly different forms at Exod. 20:2-17; Deut. 5:6-21, and are referred to elsewhere as the "ten words" (Exod. 34:28; Deut. 4:13; 10:4; thus the alternate designation "Decalog," from LXX Gk. *déka lógoi* "ten words"). They were revealed to the people at Sinai directly by God in theophany, rather than through Moses as were other components of Israelite law.

Scholars have noted that the Decalog is structured according to the pattern of ancient Near Eastern treaties between a monarch and a vassal state. These treaties included (1) a personal introduction (cf. "I am the Lord your God"), (2) a historical summary ("who brought you out of Egypt"), (3) basic stipulations (the commandments), and (4) blessings for obedience and curses for breaking the covenant/treaty; these sanctions may be combined with the commandments (Exod. 20:5-6, 7). Because they follow this form, the commandments are based on the prior grace of God in redeeming his people "out of the land of Egypt, out of the house of bondage" (v. 2). The first four commandments concern the relationship between God and his people; the remainder deal with human relationships. The Decalog may have been recited at covenant renewal ceremonies (cf. Deut. 27; Josh. 24); indeed, the stipulations are well suited to preserving the stability of the fragile community of formative Israel. *See* COVENANT.

At what points the Decalog is to be divided into precisely ten commandments has long been a matter of disagreement (e.g., some traditions regard v. 2 as the first commandment, combining vv. 3 and 4-6; others take vv. 3-6 as the first and divide v. 17 into two commandments). Debate also focuses on just where to divide the commandments into "two tables" (cf. 32:15; 34:4, 28; Deut. 4:13); the second table of stone may represent the customary second copy of a treaty. Both tables were placed in the ark of the covenant (Exod. 40:20; Deut. 10:1-5).

Parallels to the Ten Commandments can be found in other parts of the law of Moses, and some scholars argue that these parallels are actually the more ancient forms. While the first four commandments are unique to Israel, some parallels to the other commandments can be found in ancient Near Eastern law collections such as the Code of Hammurabi.

TENT (Heb. *'ōhel*; Gk. *skēnḗ*).† A cloth dwelling used by nomads and transhumants, as well as soldiers and caravaneers. The fabric was woven of goat hair (usually black; cf. Cant. 1:5) and was supported by three or more rows of poles and fastened to ropes tied to wooden stakes (cf. Judg. 4:21).

The importance of Israel's wilderness experience is shown by the use of tent imagery even after the people had settled in permanent dwellings in towns and villages. Such imagery refers to the temporality of human life (Isa. 38:12; 2 Cor. 5:1, 4; cf. RSV mg., 2 Pet. 1:13), the sky (e.g., Ps. 104:2), and the figurative abodes of particular human qualities (Job 11:14; 15:34). The fate of a people's "tent" is the fate of that people (8:22; 29:4; Jer. 4:20; 30:18; Hos. 9:6; Zech. 12:7). Since the growth of a household was accommodated by adding new sections of cloth to the tent, the enlargement of "the place of your tent" represents the people's prosperity (Isa. 54:2).

For the tent of meeting *see* TABERNACLE.

TENTMAKER (Gk. *skēnopoiós*). The occupation of Paul, Priscilla, and Aquila (Acts 18:3). While the Greek term means lit. "maker of tents," it is probable that it actually was used of leatherworkers and, therefore, that Paul was a leatherworker. Older commentaries suggest that Paul was a weaver of goat's hair, a trade particularly associated with Cilicia, the apostle's home, but Paul probably learned his trade in Jerusalem (22:3).

TEPHON [tē'fŏn] (Gk. *Tephōn*). A city in Judah fortified by Bacchides (1 Macc. 9:50; KJV "Taphon"). It has been identified variously with Tappuah and Tekoa.

TERAH [těr'ə] (Heb. *teraḥ*; Gk. *Thara*; cf. Akk. *turaḥu* "ibex"; Aram. *yᵉraḥ* "moon") (**PERSON**). The son of Nahor, and the father of Abraham, Nahor, and Haran (Gen. 11:24-27; 1 Chr. 1:26; Luke 3:34; KJV

"Thara"). Terah took his family from Ur of the Chaldeans to Haran, where they "served other gods" (Gen. 11:31; Josh. 24:2).

TERAH [tĕr'ə] (Heb. *teraḥ*) (**PLACE**). A place where the Israelites encamped during their journey through the wilderness (Num. 33:27-28; KJV "Tarah"). Its location is unknown.

TERAPHIM [tĕr'ə fīm] (Heb. *tᵉrāpîm*). A technical term designating a particular kind of idol. The Hebrew term is a plural form, but is used for one or more idols. Although its etymology remains uncertain (cf. LXX Gk. *therapeúō* "heal"; Targums Aram. *tō-rep* "obscenity"), the term bears linguistic and cultural similarity to Hitt. *tarpiš*, a spirit that can be either protective or malevolent, perhaps associated with the Underworld and the cult of the dead, as well as to Luwian *tarpalli* "substitute," suggesting its use in substitutionary rites.

While no biblical citation describes teraphim in detail, it appears that usually they were relatively small in size (Gen. 31:34; KJV "images"; RSV "household gods"; but cf. 1 Sam. 19:13-16). Teraphim are encountered as part of the paraphernalia of pagan religious practices (2 Kgs. 23:24) and of divination (Ezek. 21:21 [MT 26]; Zech. 10:2). The word functions metonymically as a term for idolatry and divination in general at 1 Sam. 15:23 (RSV "idolatry"). The use of such objects by Israelites violated the prohibition of images (Exod. 20:4-5). Teraphim are mentioned in connection with an ephod (Judg. 17:5; 18:14-20; Hos. 3:4), an ancient symbol of Israelite religion (Exod. 28) that had perhaps been reduced to an object for divination.

A teraphim is put to a more prosaic use at 1 Sam. 19:13-16 (RSV "image"). David's wife Michal aids in his escape from Saul by laying a teraphim in David's bed and clothing it to resemble him. Rachel's theft of her father's teraphim (Gen. 31:19) has often been related to texts from Nuzi indicating that inheritance rights were connected with possession of the household's gods. Although direct Nuzi influence has been challenged, in early Israelite practice also the teraphim may have been tokens of clan or family status, with implications for inheritance and/or succession.

TEREBINTH [tĕr'ə bĭnth] (Heb. *'ēlâ*). A broad, though not very tall, Mediterranean tree (*Pistacia terebinthus* of the sumac family) prized for the shade it gives during summer (Sir. 24:16; KJV "turpentine tree," referring to the product of its resinous sap). The Hebrew term is generally translated "oak."

At Isa. 6:13 the destruction of the southern kingdom is likened to the felling of a terebinth (LXX Gk. *terébinthos;* KJV "teil tree," the lime or linden) because a remnant of the Israelites would remain just as the stump of the felled tree would remain standing. At Hos. 4:13 Israel is castigated for making pagan sacrifices under oaks, poplars, and terebinths (KJV "elms"). *See* OAK.

TERESH [tĕr'ĕsh] (Heb. *tereš*). One of the two eunuchs who guarded the royal threshold of King Ahasuerus and planned to kill the king. Mordecai discovered their plot and had Esther report it to the king (Esth. 2:21-23; cf. 6:2).

TERROR ON EVERY SIDE (Heb. *māgôr missābîb*). An epithet given by Jeremiah to the chief temple official Pashhur (3) to indicate that he would become fearful to his friends and to himself (Jer. 20:3-4; KJV "Magor-missabib"; cf. 6:25; 20:10; 49:29). Pashhur's Egyptian name may have been connected with Heb. *paššāḥ sᵉhôr* "destruction all about," so that "Terror on every side" was a play on words.

TERTIUS [tûr'shĭ əs] (Gk. *Tertios*; Lat. *Tertius* "third"). Paul's secretary who at the apostle's dictation wrote the Letter to the Romans, adding his own greetings (Rom. 16:22).

TERTULLUS [tər tŭl'əs] (Gk. *Tertyllos*; diminutive of Lat. *Tertius*). The hired spokesman of the Jewish accusers of the apostle Paul before Felix, the Roman governor at Caesarea (Acts 24:1). Although he may have been a Jew, his name is Roman in form. Schooled in rhetoric and probably in both Roman and Jewish law, Tertullus began his speech by flattering the court (vv. 2-3) and then stating the case of the accusers: that Paul was a "pestilent fellow" and an agitator among the Jews, "a ringleader of the sect of the Nazarenes" (probably implying that Paul promoted a political messianism), and one who attempted to profane the temple in Jerusalem (vv. 5-6). (The Western text adds that the Jews charged the Roman tribune [RSV mg. "chief captain"], Claudius Lysias, with taking the case out of its proper Jewish jurisdiction; KJV, JB, vv. 6b-8a). Tertullus closed his speech with an invitation to the governor to examine the accused himself (or Lysias, if the Western text is followed) about these matters (v. 8). After Tertullus had presented the case against Paul—recorded by Luke only in outline—the Jewish delegation reiterated the charges (v. 9).

TESTAMENT (KJV). *See* COVENANT; WILL.

TESTAMENTS OF THE TWELVE PATRI-ARCHS. A collection of twelve self-contained works contained in the Pseudepigrapha, presented as the last words of the twelve sons of Jacob and based on the pattern of the Blessing of Jacob (Gen. 49). With some variations, each Testament follows a similar structure: the aged or dying patriarch gathers his sons around him, reviews events of his life, focusing on a particular virtue or vice, and exhorts his progeny to follow or not follow in his footsteps. Often Joseph is held up as a particularly good example of the pursuit of virtue and avoidance of vice. In each case the father makes some predictions about the future of Israel; each Testament then concludes with the death and burial of the patriarch.

In spite of some obvious Christian interpolations that have led a few scholars to consider the Testaments a Christian production, most believe the original document to be the work of a single Jewish author, writing perhaps in the second half of the second century B.C. in Syria or Palestine. Further debate centers on the original language. Some scholars believe the work was composed in Hebrew or Aramaic, but it is more likely that the original language was Greek (although Semitic sources may have been used).

A number of affinities have been discovered between the Testaments and the Essene writings from Qumran, particularly in the ethical dualism expressed (the spirit of truth versus the spirit of error, led by Beliar) and in eschatological motifs. The latter can be illustrated by the priority given in both the Testaments of the Twelve Patriarchs and the Qumran literature to the tribes of Levi and Judah. From these tribes will come two eschatological leaders; from Judah will come the king, but the eschatological priest from Levi will be his superior and God's agent of redemption. It is quite probable that the movements which produced these sets of writings shared some common roots. Their divergence at a number of points is illustrative of the variegated nature of Judaism in this period. One example of this variance is that the ethical emphasis of the Testaments is based more on universal virtues than on any appeal to the Torah. This characteristic sets the Testaments apart from the Qumran community and the nascent pharisaic movement, both of which strove to incorporate the Torah into their daily lives, and demonstrates as well that at least some elements of Judaism were open to the influence of non-Jewish culture.

TESTIMONIA [tĕs tə mō′nĭ ə] (Lat. pl. of *testimonium* "evidence").† A techical term for Old Testament texts cited in the New Testament as testimonies to the messiahship of Jesus. Since different New Testament writers sometimes used similar combinations of Old Testament texts (cf. Rom. 9:32-33; 10:11; 1 Pet. 2:6, 8), it is apparent that certain choices and concatenations of texts were carried by tradition to various parts of the Christian movement. Although various testimony tracts may have circulated in New Testament times, it it not likely that any authoritative written "testimony book" existed before the writing of the New Testament books, as has been suggested. The testimonies were not simply prooftexts. Rather, they often evidence a thought-out christological understanding.

TESTIMONY (Heb. ʿēḏâ, ʿēḏûṯ; Gk. *martyría, martýrion*). In the administration of justice, the oral (or written) declarations of witnesses were the primary means of proof. At least two witnesses were necessary for conviction (Num. 35:30; Deut. 19:15; cf. Matt. 18:19-16). Refusal to testify concerning a crime that one witnessed or heard about was not permitted (Lev. 5:1; cf. Prov. 29:24). The ninth commandment categorically forbade the presentation of false witness (Exod. 20:16). Judges were obligated to investigate the testimony of witnesses. A witness making a false accusation suffered the actual punishment for the crime he claimed to have witnessed (Deut. 19:16-19). In some cases the execution of the convicted criminal was to be begun by the witnesses (17:7).

Heb. ʿēḏâ is used, always in the plural, to refer to the laws of the Torah as divine "testimonies" (e.g., Deut. 4:45; 6:20; Ps. 119 passim). Heb. ʿēḏûṯ is associated with the ten commandments, especially in relation to the tabernacle (e.g., Exod. 38:21; Num. 1:50; 18:2), the ark (e.g., Exod. 25:22; Num. 4:5), and the tables of the law (Exod. 31:18; 32:15). The

ark (16:34; 27:21) and the tables (25:16, 21) are, indeed, sometimes called simply "the testimony." At Isa. 8:16, 20 *tᵉʿûḏâ* represents the prophetic word of Yahweh.

TETRAGRAMMATON [tĕt′rə grăm′ə tän] (Gk. Tetragrammaton "four letters").* The sacred name of Israel's God. The term came into use partly because of the uncertainty concerning which vowel sounds were used in the pronounciation of the four-consonant name (*YHWH*) and partly because in the MT the ineffable name was written with the vowel points for Heb. ʾᵃḏōnāy "my Lord," signaling the reader to pronounce aloud only the Kethib form. *See* YAHWEH.

TETRARCH [tĕt′rärk] (Gk. *tetraárchēs*). Originally the "ruler of a fourth part" of some region; later used more broadly of a number of client rulers in the Roman Empire lower in rank than kings. After the death of Herod the Great, his kingdom was divided among three of his sons, Archelaus receiving the title of ethnarch and Herod Antipas and Philip receiving the lesser title of tetrarch (Matt. 14:1; Luke 3:1, 19; 9:7; Acts 13:1). Antipas is informally called a king in Mark 6:14, 26. Luke 3:1 also refers to Lysanias, the tetrarch of Abilene.

TEXT. *See* BIBLE, TEXT OF THE.

TEXTUS RECEPTUS [tĕks′təs rĭ sĕp′təs] (Lat. "received [or 'accepted'] text"). The form of New Testament text (generally representing the Byzantine text type) that became standard in the sixteenth and seventeenth centuries A.D. and forms the basis for older translations such as the King James Version. The name refers to the 1550 edition of the Greek New Testament by Robert Stephanus (Estienne), an almost verbatim version of the fifth edition compiled in 1535 by Desiderius Erasmus that became the standard edition in the English-speaking world. The use of the term arose from the Latin preface to a 1633 edition of the New Testament by the Dutch printers Elzevir: "You have the text, now, received (or 'recognized') by all, in which we give nothing altered or corrupted." The Elsevir edition, based on Stephanus' third edition, came to be used as the standard text on the Continent. The Textus Receptus remained dominant until the progress of New Testament textual criticism in the nineteenth century caused it to be replaced by newer editions.

THADDAEUS [thăd′ĭ əs] (Gk. *Thaddaios*; from Aram. *taddāʾ* "breast"). One of the twelve apostles, usually identified with Judas (8) the son (or brother) of James (Matt. 10:3; Mark 3:18; cf. Luke 6:16; John 14:22; Acts 1:13).

THADDEUS, ACTS OF. A fifth- or sixth-century Greek writing developed on the basis of the legend of Thaddeus' evangelization of Edessa as the fulfillment of a promise made by Jesus to Agbar, king of Edessa. This legend is also represented in Eusebius *HE* i.13; ii.1.5-7 and in a late third- or early fourth-century Syriac work known as the Doctrine of Addai.

THAHASH (Gen. 22:24, KJV). *See* TAHASH.

THAMAH (Ezra 2:53, KJV). *See* TEMAH.

THAMAR (Matt. 1:3, KJV). *See* TAMAR (PERSON) **1.**

THANK OFFERING (Heb. *[zibeh] tôḏâ).** A term used in the sacrificial language of the Old Testament with some amount of flexibility (RSV often "thanksgiving"). It was at times a term for peace offerings given as freewill or votive offerings (Ps. 56:12-13 [NT 13-14]; cf. 50:14; 54:6-7 [MT 8-9]; 116:14, 17-18) and at other times a term for a separate category of peace offerings (Lev. 7:12-14).

THANKSGIVING (Heb. hiphil *yḏh*; Gk. *eucharistéō*).† In biblical usage the response due to God from his people. Specific grounds for thanksgiving to God are numerous and include God's faithfulness to the covenant (Ps. 57:9-10 [MT 10-11]; 107:8; 138:2), and his protection and deliverance of his people from enemies (35:17-18; 44:7-8 [MT 8-9]; 54:6 [MT 8]), from prison (142:7 [MT 8]), from death (86:12-13); Isa. 38:18-19), and from those who would use the courts against them (Ps. 109:30). God is also thanked for the prospect of final judgment (Ps. 75), for his mercy toward sinners (Isa. 12:1), for miraculous healings (30:4-5 [MT 5-6]; Luke 17:16), and for his acts of salvation (2:38). Reflection on God's past acts of mercy lead to thanksgiving (Ps. 63:5-7 [MT 6-8]). The fundamental sin of the Gentiles is said to be their failure to "honor him as God or give thanks to him" (Rom. 1:21).

Thanksgiving was the focus of Old Testament worship (cf. 1 Chr. 16:4; Ps. 42:4 [MT 5]), especially of pilgrimages to Jerusalem for feasts (100:4; 138:2). In the New Testament also thanksgiving is an activity that takes place in the community and with the focus of attention on the community (2 Cor. 1:11; Eph. 1:16; Phil. 1:3). The thanksgivings of God's people are one means by which knowledge of God is spread (Ps. 57:9 [MT 10]), and increased thanksgiving is the result of that proclamation (2 Cor. 4:15).

True thanksgiving does not consist primarily of deeds, but of the disposition of the heart, and it brings persons nearer to God and enables them to see God's salvation (Ps. 50:23). If a person gives thanks merely for that possessed within himself, then that person expresses self-exaltation and self-deception rather than responding to the grace of God (Luke 18:11-14; cf. 1 Cor. 4:7).

THARA (Luke 3:34, KJV). *See* TERAH (PERSON).

THARSHISH.
1. (1 Kgs. 10:22; 22:48, KJV). *See* TARSHISH (PLACE).
2. (1 Chr. 7:10, KJV). *See* TARSHISH (PERSON) **2.**

THEATER (Gk. *théatron*, from *theáomai* "view, observe"). An outdoor structure for dramatic performances or spectacles among the Greeks and Romans. Remains of several ancient theaters survive at biblical sites, including Gerasa, Caesarea Maritima, Corinth, and Byblos.

Following the uproar of the silversmiths, who were incensed over the negative effect of Paul's preaching on their business, the Ephesian mob went to the city's theater to stage a demonstration, dragging along two of Paul's companions (Acts 19:29). This open-air construction, built in a semicircle and capable of seating some twenty-four thousand spectators, was located at the foot of Mt. Pion (Panayir), between the agora and the stadium.

THEBES [thēbz] (Heb. *nōʾ [ʾāmôn]*; Egyp. *nìwt* [ʾImn] "city [of Amon]").† The major city of Upper Egypt and capital of the united kingdom. The magnificent city straddled both sides of the Nile river at a site *ca.* 500 km. (300 mi.) south of Cairo. On the east bank was the temple complex of the Egyptian god Amon (the Karnak temple), whom the Greeks later identified with Zeus (naming the city *Dios pólis* "city of Zeus"). To the south was the spectacular temple of Luxor. Located on the west bank were numerous tombs and sacred precincts belonging to the nobility of the New Kingdom, as well as the palace of Pharaoh Amenhotep III. Within the desert cliffs can still be seen the great temple of Queen Hatshepsut and the Valley of the Kings (where King Tutankhamen's tomb was opened in 1922). Adjacent hills hid countless tunnel-tombs of leading ancient Egyptian families.

Thebes was perhaps Egypt's most important city for almost 1500 years. The tradition of building gigantic monuments and temples there spans from the Middle Kingdom (*ca.* 2200 B.C.) to the Ptolemaic era. During times of political unity from the Eleventh Dynasty (*ca.* 2040) until the siege of the city by Assurbanipal of Assyria (*ca.* 663) Thebes was the capital of Egypt. When Upper and Lower Egypt were divided Thebes remained the capital of the South and the cult center of Amon. When Egypt flourished, Thebes flourished.

Nahum, the seventh-century prophet, compares the imminent fall of Assyria with the conquest of Thebes that has already happened (Nah. 3:8, 10; KJV "No"; JB "No-amon"). Jeremiah, taken to Egypt following the fall of Jerusalem in 586 (Jer. 43:4-7), predicts a severe devastation of Thebes at the hands of Nebuchadrezzar of Babylon (46:25-26). Ezekiel includes Thebes in his list of Egyptian cities that will be destroyed by the Lord through the conquests of the Babylonians (Ezek. 30:14-16).

THEBEZ [thē'bəz] (Heb. *tēḇēṣ*). A city in Ephraim that Abimelech the son of Gideon besieged and conquered, except for the "strong tower," from which a woman threw a millstone at his head, crushing his skull (Judg. 9:50-54; 2 Sam. 11:21). The city is usually identified with modern Ṭūbâṣ, *ca.* 16 km. (10 mi.) northeast of Nablus.

THEFT (Heb. *gᵉnēḇâ*; Gk. *klémma, klopḗ*). Stealing is forbidden in the eighth commandment of the Decalog (Exod. 20:15; Deut. 5:19; cf. Lev. 19:11). Exod. 22:1-4 (MT 21:37–22:3) contains specific regulations with regard to the punishment of theft. If an ox or a sheep was stolen and then killed or sold, restitution was to be made by paying back five oxen for one ox or four sheep for one sheep (v. 1 [MT 21:37]; cf. 2 Sam. 12:6). If restitution was beyond the means of the thief, he was to be sold into slavery to raise the price of restitution (Exod. 22:3b [MT 2b; RSV 1b]). If the stolen animal was found alive in the thief's possession, only a twofold compensation was required, as with stolen goods or money (vv. 4, 7 [MT 3, 6]). Prov. 6:30-31 mentions sevenfold restitution.

The law of Hammurabi was more severe in this respect, directing that a thirtyfold restitution be made by a citizen who had stolen an ox, sheep, ass, pig, or boat that belonged to a god or to the palace. If the stolen item belonged to a subordinate member of the community, the restitution was to be tenfold, and if the thief had nothing to make payment with, he was killed (§ 8; *ANET*, p. 166). Hittite legislation speaks of a fifteenfold restitution (p. 192), and later Roman law directs that the compensation be fourfold if the thief was caught in the act.

According to Exod. 22:2 (MT 1) if a thief is caught breaking in at night and is struck a lethal blow, no bloodguilt is to be involved because of the presumption that the nighttime burglar might become a murderer if not prevented (cf. Matt. 24:43). If, however, the thief is killed during daylight the killer is guilty of murder (Exod. 22:3 [MT 2]). The situation addressed here is that of a thief who digs through the clay wall of a house (cf. Matt. 6:19-20).

Theft is mentioned in lists of vices in the New Testament (Matt. 15:19; Mark 7:21; 1 Cor. 6:10; 1 Pet. 4:15; Rev. 9:21; cf. Eph. 4:28).

THEODOTION [thē′ə dō′shən].* A second-century A.D. scholar known for his revision of the LXX or some other early Greek translation of the Old Testament. Little is known about Theodotion. Irenaeus identified him as a Jewish proselyte from Ephesus. Jerome called him an Ebionite. He was also identified as a Marcionite.

Theodotion corrected the text he had in hand only where necessary and used Greek prose that would convey the precise meaning of the Hebrew text. Because his translations are often strikingly similar to some New Testament quotations of the Old Testament, some scholars have suggested the existence of an earlier Theodotion-type version used by the New Testament writers. Origen placed Theodotion's text last in the six columns of his Hexapla, while the more literal translation of Aquila was placed second, next to the Hebrew original. Theodotion's version was used to fill in gaps in several manuscripts of the LXX (especially in Job and Jeremiah). His version of Daniel is thought to have supplanted that of the LXX in most manuscripts.

THEODOTUS [thē ŏd′ə təs] (Gk. *Theodotos*).* One of the ambassadors sent by Nicanor to Judas Maccabeus to establish peace (2 Macc. 14:19).

THEOPHANY (Gk. *theopháneia* "appearance of God").† The visual manifestation of a deity to human beings, often accompanied by an auditory revelation. Theophanies recorded in the Bible are largely limited to the Old Testament, particularly the Pentateuch and prophetic books. The literary genre of theophany consists of vivid poetic accounts employing extensive mythological imagery and archaic (or archaizing) style; typically, Yahweh approaches from some distance, with

cataclysmic effect on all creation (e.g., Deut. 33:2; Judg. 5:4-5; 2 Sam. 22:8-16 par. Ps. 18:7-15 [MT 8-16]; Ps. 68:7ff. [MT 8ff.]; Hab. 3:2-19). Other less stylized accounts appear to have no set pattern to their elements or timing, though they are often the vehicles for important teachings to the people of God. Consequently, authorities sometimes differ on whether a particular event is a true theophany.

Some Old Testament theophanies begin when Yahweh "appears to" or "meets" someone without preamble. This is the case at Gen. 17, when the covenant of circumcision is established; ch. 18, when Abraham dickers with God over the fate of Sodom's inhabitants; Exod. 4, when Yahweh meets Moses on his journey back to Egypt; and Judg. 13, when the birth of Samson is predicted.

Many biblical theophanies feature a strong anthropomorphic element. These include Adam and Eve hearing the sound of God walking in Eden (Gen. 3:8), the "three men" who visit Abraham at Mamre (18:1-2), Jacob's wrestling (32:24, 28), and Moses' view of God's back (Exod. 33:18-23). The angel of the Lord, who conveys divine messages (Gen. 16:7-12; 21:17-18; Num. 22:32-35), sometimes turns out to be Yahweh himself (Gen. 18:16-17; Judg. 13). This makes for a curious situation: initially Abraham did not recognize the Lord among his visitors (Gen. 18:2-8), yet when God reveals himself the patriarch registers no surprise (vv. 9-33). Such comfortable relationships between humans and the wholly other are characteristic of the encounters recorded in Genesis.

God also commonly appears in such natural phenomena as clouds, storms, lightning, and fire (Exod. 3:2-6; 13:21; 19:18-19; 24:15-18; Isa. 30:27-28). Such representations of deity were standard among the religions of the ancient Near East. The important difference between biblical and other ancient accounts is that, while Yahweh's presence is signaled by the forces of nature, he is not, for instance, the storm itself but its creator.

On occasion the power or anger of God is depicted as a consuming fire (Num. 11:1-3; 16:35; 1 Kgs. 18:38; Isa. 30:27, 30, 33), which also serves as the context out of which his voice speaks (Exod. 3:2-6; Deut. 4:33; 5:24). The account of the founding of the Abrahamic covenant (Gen. 15) would not be considered a theophany per se by some scholars; while it does feature the voice of God and representations of his power (smoking fire pot and blazing torch; v. 17), the covenant ceremony takes place while Abraham is in deep sleep.

Fantastic representations of God are found in what might be called eschatological theophanies, all of which occur when the human witness is in a state of ecstasy. Included are the vision leading to Isaiah's commission as a prophet (Isa. 6:1-4), Ezekiel's visions of "the appearance of the likeness of the glory of the Lord" (Ezek. 1), and John's description of the risen Christ (Rev. 1:12-16).

THEOPHILUS [thē ŏf′ə ləs] (Gk. *Theophilos* "dear to God" or "friend of God"). A person (rather than, as some suggest, a symbolic "friend of God") to whom Luke dedicated his gospel (Luke 1:3) and its sequel, the Acts of the Apostles (Acts 1:1). Theophilus may have been a member of the equestrian class, though the honorific title "most excellent" (Gk. *krátistos*; Luke 1:3) is used both in addressing Roman officials, notably procurators (e.g., Acts 23:26; 24:2; 26:25) and as a common courteous address (Josephus *Vita* 76 [430]; *Ap.* i.1 [1]). Since a fruitful reading of the third gospel and Acts requires some acquaintance with Judaism and, in the case of the gospel, the topography of Palestine, Theophilus was most likely a Gentile "God-fearer" in need of an "orderly account" of the gospel, about which he may have had some knowledge.

THESSALONIANS [thĕs'ə lō'nĭ ənz], **LETTERS TO THE.**† The thirteenth and fourteenth books of the New Testament, generally considered the two earliest canonical Pauline letters (though some scholars consider Galatians to be earlier).

I. Origin

Pauline authorship of 1 Thessalonians has generally been acknowledged, but many scholars are not as willing to accept that Paul wrote 2 Thessalonians. They have noted the difference in theological outlook between 1 Thessalonians, which stresses that Christ's return will come without warning, and 2 Thessalonians, where a number of events are expected to precede Christ's return. Though A. Harnack's suggestion that Paul addressed Gentile Christians in the first letter and Jewish Christians in the second has found a degree of acceptance, consideration of the circumstances under which the two letters were composed—particularly communications concerning the Thessalonian Christians Paul may have received between the composition of the two letters—may provide a more accurate understanding of the differences between them. There is no lack of external evidence ascribing 2 Thessalonians to the hand of Paul.

During his second missionary journey Paul visited a number of Greek cities, including Thessalonica (*ca.* A.D. 49-50). There he preached the gospel in the local synagogue for two or three weeks (depending on whether Gk. *sábbata* at Acts 17:2 is understood as "sabbath days" [so KJV] or as full weeks [RSV]). Because of strong opposition from Jews who had become jealous of the large number of Gentiles being won to the gospel (v. 5), Paul was forced to depart and go to Beroea (v. 10) where he left his companions, Silas and Timothy (v. 14). He sent for them when he reached Athens (v. 15), but it was not until later when they rejoined him at Corinth with the report of the steadfastness of the Thessalonian believers that the apostle knew he had made progress with his missionary labors there (18:5; 1 Thess. 3:6). It was at that time that the first letter was written. The second letter, which presupposes the first (cf. 2 Thess. 2:15), was most likely written from the same place soon after the first (both *ca.* A.D. 51). Though both letters claim authorship by "Paul, Silvanus (Silas), and Timothy," Paul was no doubt the dominate personality in their composition. This is evident from the use of "I" (1 Thess. 5:27), the emphatic claim at 2 Thess. 3:17, and 1 Thess. 3:1 where the pronoun "we" must refer to Paul alone.

II. 1 Thessalonians

Though his companion Timothy informed Paul that the Thessalonians had remained steadfast in their faith (3:6), Timothy also apparently reported that they remained puzzled about Christ's return. Specifically, they asked whether Christ would return soon and what would happen to Christians who had died before his return, thinking that those not alive at the time of Christ's return would not share in the blessings of that event (4:13-17). They also wondered whether it would be worth their while to continue to work (5:11). In his first letter Paul attempted to answer these questions.

After a salutation (1:1) and a glowing thanksgiving on behalf of the Church (vv. 2-10), Paul recounts his own recent circumstances (2:1–3:10) and expresses his wish to be reunited with the Thessalonians (3:11-13). Ending this personal section with an exhortation to holy living (4:1-12), the apostle then treats the subject of Christ's return (4:13–5:11). He concludes his letter with general admonitions (5:12-22) and personal greetings (vv. 23-28).

Paul notes that Christ's return will come "like a thief in the night" (5:2; cf. v. 4), i.e., suddenly. The apostle does not imply, however, that believers were to spend their lives carousing (vv. 4-7); instead, he urges them to continue in faith and love (v. 8; cf. 3:6), and to admonish idlers among them to find gainful employment (5:14). As for the destiny of those already passed away, they will be included in the general resurrection (4:14) and will meet the Lord "in the air" (v. 17).

A strong factor in the content of the letter is the freshness in Paul's mind, shared with his readers, of their experience of turning from paganism to the gospel (esp. 1:9-10). The apostolic mission to the Thessalonians and their response to it are still recent and can be called on in the apostle's thanksgiving and exhortation (vv. 5-8; 2:1-12; 4:1-2). Paul seeks to communicate to them an understanding of themselves as the suffering people of God who have received the word of God, in contrast to those who resist the word (2:13-16). This contrast is, finally, eschatological, seen in terms of what each group is awaiting (cf. 1:10; 2:16; 5:9). Even now the Thessalonian Christians are people of faith and love (3:6), but what they already are is the basis for exhortation to live out their Christianity even more (4:9-12).

III. 2 Thessalonians

Paul's first letter apparently did not produce the desired effect, for the believers in Thessalonica still had such questions as whether the Day of the Lord had already come and gone. They were also perhaps confounded by a message unjustly attributed to Paul (2 Thess. 2:1-2). 2 Thessalonians is the apostle's attempt to clarify further his views on the return of Christ.

This letter also starts with a salutation (2 Thess. 1:1-2) and thanksgiving on behalf of the Church (vv. 3-12); it ends with a general admonition (3:1-15) and personal greetings (vv. 16-18). At 2:1-12 the apostle further clarifies his position on Christ's return, warning that the Thessalonian believers should not be too easily swayed by any rumor that Christ has already returned.

This event, he explains, will be preceded by a rebellion (v. 3), by the exposure of "the man of lawlessness" who is presently restrained but will proclaim himself divine (vv. 3-7), and finally by Christ's destruction of this person (v. 8).

Paul again confronts certain believers who continued their refusal to work because they felt that the imminent return of Christ rendered labor unnecessary. Citing his own ministry among them as an example to be followed (3:7-9), Paul repeats the command he had given in person that anyone refusing to work not be sustained by the others (v. 10). He then urges the idle believers to earn their living (v. 12).

2 Thessalonians may be less affectionate in tone than its predecessor, but its corrective comments on Christ's return have admirably comforted believers through the centuries.

See also ESCHATOLOGY *II, III. A.*

Bibliography. F. F. Bruce, *1 & 2 Thessalonians.* WBC 45 (1982); I. H. Marshall, *1 and 2 Thessalonians.* NCBC (1983); L. Morris, *The First and Second Epistles to the Thessalonians.* NICNT (1959).

THESSALONICA [thĕs'ə lə nī'kə] (Gk. *Thessalonikē*). A major city of Macedonia, modern Salonika or Thessaloniki.

Originally an Ionian settlement named after the half-sister of Alexander the Great, the wife of King Cassander (*ca.* 315 B.C.), Thessalonica enjoyed prosperity and fame as the capital of the second Macedonian district (from 167) and as the chief city of the Roman province of Macedonia (from 148). Its prosperity was greatly enhanced by its location on the Thermaic Gulf (modern Gulf of Salonika) on the northwest side of the Chalcidice peninsula, and as a trade center along the important Egnatian Way, which connected Rome with its eastern colonies as far as Byzantium.

When Paul visited the city on his second missionary journey (Acts 17:1-10), Thessalonica had a large and mixed population. The Jewish community strongly opposed Paul (vv. 5-13). Paul wrote two letters to the Christian community that had formed because of his work in Thessalonica. He may have visited the city again on his third missionary journey (cf. 20:1-2).

Archaeological excavations have uncovered a first-century Roman forum flanked by stoas on the east and the south sides, a Hellenistic agora, and a hippodrome. Inscriptions confirm the use of the title *politárchai* (17:6; RSV "city authorities") at Thessalonica in New Testament times and the presence of a Samaritan synagogue.

THEUDAS [thoo'dəs] (Gk. *Theudas*). A Jewish insurrectionist, who may have claimed to be the Messiah and who won some four hundred men over to his cause (Acts 5:36). He was slain (according to one manuscript he committed suicide), and his followers were scattered. This incident occurred before the revolt of Judas (**9**) the Galilean (v. 37), which took place in A.D. 6. Theudas' revolt may have been part of the disturbances that took place immediately after the death of Herod the Great (4 B.C.).

Josephus tells of a Theudas who claimed to be a prophet and persuaded a large crowd to take their possessions to the Jordan river, which would be parted (as it had been when Israel crossed into the land of Canaan; Josh. 4). This Theudas was captured and executed. His actions are dated to the time of the procurator Cuspius Fadus (A.D. 44-46; *Ant.* xx.5.1 [97-99]). It has commonly been concluded that Luke anachronistically introduces an account of this Theudas into Gamaliel's speech, which must have occurred about ten years earlier than the governorship of Fadus. However, the reference in Acts may be to an earlier Theudas who is otherwise unknown.

THIGH (Heb. *yārēḵ*; Aram. *yarḵâ*; Gk. *mērós*). The upper part of the leg. The proximity of the thighs to the genitals allows the word to be a euphemism for "genitals." The placing of one's hand under a person's thigh—i.e., touching the genitals, the seat of life—in the course of swearing an oath places one into contact with the life-force (i.e., the procreative powers) of the other person and so underlines the seriousness of the oath (cf. Gen. 32:25, 32 [MT 26, 33]). In two instances this symbolic action is associated with the transfer of familial authority shortly before the death of the family head (24:2, 9; 47:29). For a woman's thigh to "fall away" (Num. 5:21-22, 27) may have been for her to suffer a miscarriage, but this figure of speech remains obscure. A man's "offspring" (so RSV paraphrases) could be spoken of as "those who came from his thigh" (Exod. 1:5).

Warriors are noted as wearing their sword attached to the thigh (Judg. 3:16; Ps. 45:3 [MT 4]; Cant. 3:8). Slapping one's thigh was a gesture indicative of remorse (Jer. 31:19; Ezek. 21:12 [MT 17]). A dietary practice is related to the injury of a patriarch's thigh at Gen. 32:24-32 (MT 25-33) (*see* SINEW OF THE HIP).

It was often specified that the (right) thigh (Heb. *šôq*; KJV "shoulder") of sacrificial animals, one of the preferred portions (cf. Ezek. 24:4), was to be given to the priests (e.g., Lev. 7:32-34; 8:25-27).

THIMNATHAH (Josh. 19:43, KJV). *See* TIMNAH (PLACE) **2**.

THISTLE (Heb. *dardar, ḥôaḥ*; Gk. *tríbolos*). Any of various prickly or spiny plants with composite flowers. A large number of thistles are common in the dry land of Palestine, and it is never clear which kind of thistle is referred to in biblical texts. Some of the most common thistles of the region are *Carthamus glaucus*, the wild safflower, a common thistle having a relatively thin stem and narrow, prickly leaves; *Centaurea pallescens*, not a true thistle but a cornflower with soft leaves and yellow or lilac-colored flower heads surrounded by sharp spines; *Echinops viscosus*, a splendid spherical thistle with violet flowers that grows everywhere in Palestine; *Notabasis syriaca*, which has white-veined leaves and red flowers; *Silybum marianum*, called the Mary thistle, an impressive plant with extremely large, white-veined leaves and relatively small, lilac-colored flower heads surrounded by large spines; and *Cynara syriaca*, a close relative of the artichoke, found mainly in the plains. This plant grows to more than 2 m. (6.5 ft.) in height and has

30-50 cm. (12-20 in.) leaves and purple flower heads. It dies in the autumn, but its structure is so rigid that it remains standing for a long time.

Thistles are mentioned, often in conjunction with other nonbeneficial plants, as evidence of the undesirability of a land (Gen. 3:18; Heb. 6:8) and of the ruination of a formerly prosperous or populated land (Job 31:40; RSV "thorns"; Isa. 34:13; Hos. 10:8). In a figure of speech used by Jesus, thorns and thistles represent that which can be expected by its very appearance to be unfruitful (Matt. 7:16 par.). In King Jehoash of Israel's response to Amaziah (2 Kgs. 14:9) the overture of Judah is likened to that of the small and fragile thistle to a mighty cedar.

THOMAS [tŏm'əs] (Gk. *Thōmas*). One of Jesus' twelve disciples (Matt. 10:3; Mark 3:18; Luke 6:15; Acts 1:13). He is usually called Thomas, though this was probably not his given name; the Greek form of his name is a transliteration of Aram. *tĕ'ômā'* "twin," which John also represents with a Greek translation (Gk. *Dídymos* "[the] Twin"; John 11:16; 20:24; 21:2). An early tradition identifies Thomas' given name as Judas. The Acts of Thomas identifies him as the twin of Jesus, but this is related to the particular standing of Thomas in that document.

When Jesus indicated to his disciples his desire to go to Judea to visit the grave of Lazarus, Thomas was eager to accompany him, even though some there would surely stone them both (John 11:16). A few days later, as Jesus tried to explain to the disciples his approaching return to the Father, Thomas candidly confessed his ignorance of the place and manner of Christ's journey (14:3-5). After Jesus' resurrection Thomas expressed grave doubts about the reality of that event when it was reported to him (20:24-25). He was invited by Christ a week later to inspect the marks of crucifixion on his body and to believe (vv. 26-27). A climactic point in John's gospel is reached with Thomas' reaction: "My Lord and my God" (v. 28).

According to later traditions, Thomas worked as a missionary in Parthia (so Eusebius) or India (so the Acts of Thomas).

THOMAS, ACTS OF.† An extensive apocryphal writing from the third century A.D. deriving from Syrian Christianity and composed, most probably, in Syriac. Complete texts have survived in Syriac and Greek and portions in Ethiopic, Latin, and Armenian. The work follows the ministry of the apostle Thomas from his commission to his martyrdom and, like other apocryphal acts of apostles, emphasizes his miraculous deeds.

At the beginning of the Acts, Thomas and the other apostles gather to determine the locations of their respective ministries, and India falls to the lot of Thomas. Because he is unwilling to go, his master (and twin; *see* THOMAS), Jesus, sells him as a slave to a messenger of the Indian king. During his journey to India and throughout his sojourn there, Thomas preaches the virtue of sexual abstinence, which, together with other forms of asceticism, characterizes his own life. One long section relates the story of a woman who, in response to Thomas' preaching, renounces marital relations with her husband and strives to remain faithful to her new husband, Jesus Christ, while her stricken husband makes every effort to restore their marriage. It is not unlikely that this passage represents fairly what actually happened when such teaching was taken seriously.

Numerous other anecdotes are told, but the work is especially known for the mystical hymns and prayers that the author collected and included, particularly the Hymn of the Pearl. This hymn is full of rich imagery and beauty, and presents an allegory of the descent of the soul into the sensory world, its deliverance, and its ascent to the home from which it came.

The Acts of Thomas is of little historical value, but it may contain kernels of reliable tradition, such as the early belief that Thomas actually went to India and the name of a first-century Indian king. Whether the work is Gnostic or not is debated; most scholars believe that it was originally Gnostic but has been edited by more orthodox hands. This would explain its popularity in both Gnostic and orthodox circles. The Acts of Thomas is valued today because of the evidence it provides regarding early modes of celebrating the sacraments, as well as what it reveals of Syrian Gnostic Christianity in the third century.

THOMAS, COPTIC GOSPEL OF.† A collection of 114 "logia" or sayings purporting to be from Jesus, composed in Greek *ca.* A.D. 140, probably in Syria. This work was mentioned by several ancient writers, but its content remained unknown until the discovery

Oxyrynchus Papyrus 1; logia 26b-28 of the gospel of Thomas in Greek (Bodleian Library, Oxford)

of the Gnostic library at Nag Hammadi in 1946. The recovery there of a virtually intact Coptic translation inaugurated modern study of the Gospel of Thomas and revealed that some sayings of Jesus known previously from the Greek Oxyrhynchus papyri belonged to this work.

The sayings are strung together with no apparent plan and with little narrative framework. Many of the logia closely parallel New Testament sayings of Jesus without being literal reproductions, others vary considerably, and forty are entirely new—the largest extant collection of noncanonical sayings of Jesus. Much of the material that differs from the canonical sayings shows the distinct influence of Gnosticism. A strong esoteric element is present, including a stress on the need to understand secret meanings so as to avoid experiencing death and an emphasis on the importance of recognizing one's true origin and destiny.

Much debate has focused on the relationship between the sayings in the Gospel of Thomas and those in the canonical Gospels. Some of the sayings in Thomas are longer than their canonical parallels, indicating probably that they are later expanded forms, though whether Thomas is literarily dependent on any of the canonical Gospels is debated. Some of the sayings in Thomas are, on the other hand, shorter and more concise than the canonical parallels, possibly indicating that they represent a more primitive form than what is found in the New Testament. Many of the individual logia were clearly in existence well before their compilation near the mid-second century, and some of the forty new sayings may be true agrapha, i.e., genuine sayings of Jesus not recorded by the canonical writers.

THOMAS, INFANCY GOSPEL OF. * A second-century A.D. apocryphal gospel describing many amazing deeds performed by the child Jesus between the ages of five and twelve and ending with an expanded version of the temple incident of Luke 2:41-51. This collection of tales of improbable and grotesque supernatural works performed by a child whose character bears no resemblance to that of the canonical Jesus appears to have been occasioned more by curiosity about the early years of Jesus than by any sectarian motive. Included are a story of Jesus making birds from clay and then causing them to fly, several angry and deadly outbursts against those who displease the boy, and incidents demonstrating the impossibility of teaching a child who is already far more knowledgeable than any mortal person. Docetic tendencies are obvious throughout—this Jesus is no human child. The unbridled nature of these tales shows by contrast the admirable restraint of the canonical gospel writers. In spite of all its excesses, however, and the offense it caused to many, the Infancy Gospel of Thomas enjoyed widespread popularity and was translated into numerous languages from its original Greek.

THORN. A number of Hebrew words are used in the Old Testament for thorns and plants bearing thorns. These words are not likely to have been used with great precision because of the large variety of thorny plants that grow in Palestine. Heb. *qôṣ* is the term

most widely used and was probably of quite broad application. Another broad term is *ḥôaḥ,* translated by the RSV as "hook," "thistle," "thorn," and "bramble." Several other terms occur less frequently; these have represented particular species, but cannot be identified with certainty now.

Thornbushes are mentioned, often in conjunction with other nonbeneficial plants or by means of more than one word for thorny plants, as evidence of the undesirability of a land (Gen. 3:18; Heb. 6:8) and of the ruination of a formerly prosperous or populated place (Isa. 5:6; 7:23-25; 32:13; 34:13; Hos. 10:8). The reversal of such a condition is spoken of at Isa. 55:13. In a figure of speech used by Jesus, thorns (Gk. *ákantha*) and thistles represent that which can be expected by its appearance to be unfruitful (Matt. 7:16 par.). At Mic. 7:4 a brier (Heb. *ḥēḏeq*) and a thorn hedge (*mᵉsûḵâ*) represent that which is fragile and therefore unreliable. The flammability of thornbushes, which were used for fuel (Ps. 58:9 [MT 10]; Eccl. 7:6), is used figuratively with regard to God's wrath (Isa. 9:18 [MT 17]; 10:17; 27:4; Nah. 1:10). This plus the fact that thornbushes provide little protection from the sun underlies the ironic climax of Jotham's fable at Judg. 9:8-15. Thorns can also represent that which is painful and dangerous (e.g., Num. 33:55; Josh. 23:13; Ezek. 2:6; 28:24). Thus Paul speaks (probably) of a chronic disease he suffered as a "thorn" (Gk. *skólops* "pointed stake") in his flesh (2 Cor. 12:7).

It cannot be determined what type of thorns made up the crown placed upon Jesus' head before his crucifixion (Matt. 27:29), but it is unlikely to have been either the Christ thorn (*Zizyphus spina-christi*) or paliuris (*Paliurus spina-christi*). The former occurs naturally only in the lower parts of Palestine and not in the Judean mountains; the latter is not found in central or southern Palestine. A more likely candidate is thorny burnet (*Poterium spinosum*), which is quite common throughout Palestine; it has small red flowers and numerous thorns. Other thorny plants include the box-thorn (*Lycium europaeum*) and camelthorn (*Alhagi camelorum*).

THOUSAND (Heb. *'elep*; Aram. *'ᵃlap*; Gk. *chiliás, chílioi*).* Some of the seemingly inflated numbers of soldiers and other groups of persons in the Old Testament may be accounted for by a technical meaning of Heb. *'elep,* perhaps related to a form *'allûp* "chief, commander" (cf. Num. 1-2; 26; 1 Kgs. 20:29; 2 Chr. 17:14-18). Furthermore, *'elep* was apparently originally a term for a social unit (such as a "clan") of no particular size (Judg. 6:15; RSV "clan"; KJV "family"; cf. 1 Sam. 10:19; 23:23). Clearly a military unit called a "thousand" (Exod. 18:21; Deut. 33:17; 1 Chr. 12:14) did not necessarily consist of as many as a thousand soldiers. In time *'elep* did indeed come to represent the number one thousand; thus interpretation of texts from different periods in the development of the language is often quite confusing.

It remains true that multiples of a thousand were used as round numbers to represent simply large quantities that are not even estimated, and that their use is sometimes hyperbolical (cf. Mark 5:13; Acts 2:41). This is a natural outgrowth of the use of one thousand as a figure of speech for that which is limitless (Exod.

20:6; Deut. 7:9; Ps. 68:17 [MT 18]; 84:10 [MT 11]; 90:4; Dan. 7:10).

For "thousand years" (Rev. 20:2-7), *see* MILLEN-NIUM.

THRACE [thrās] (Gk. *Thrakē*).† The region between the rivers Strymon and Danube in the eastern Balkan peninsula north of the Aegean Sea, less commonly called Thracia. Among the indigenous population were the Thracians, indomitable indoeuropean peoples who remained independent of Greek control. Thracians often served as mercenaries for other powers (e.g., Xerxes [Herodotus *Hist.* vii.185]; Alexander the Great); it may be in such a capacity that a Thracian horseman is recorded as having helped Gorgias, the governor of Idumea, escape in a battle with Judas Maccabeus *ca.* 163 B.C. (2 Macc. 12:35). Situated between western Macedonia and the eastern Greek colonies near the Bosporus, Thrace was made a Roman province *ca.* A.D. 44. A Thracian regiment followed the Royal Guard in the funeral procession of Herod the Great. Although Paul and Silas passed through Amphipolis on the east bank of the Strymon, no missionary activities are recorded in Thrace itself.

THREE TAVERNS (Gk. *Treis Tabernai*). A station about 48 km. (30 mi.) south of Rome on the great Roman highway, the Appian Way. The Christians of the church at Rome met Paul here to encourage him as he came to stand trial in the imperial capital (Acts 28:15).

THRESHING FLOOR (Heb. *gōren*; Aram. *'iddar*; Gk. *hálōn*).† A flat outdoor area used for threshing grain. Threshing floors were set on hilltops so that they were exposed to the wind that blew away chaff (cf. Dan. 2:35) in a threshing process that has survived to modern times in parts of the world.

The harvested grain was laid out on the threshing floor and was threshed by oxen driven over it, pulling a threshing sledge (Heb. *môrag*) equipped with sharp teeth dragged over it, or by beating with sticks (Isa. 28:27-28; 41:15). Wooden forks were then used to throw the grain into the air so that the wind would blow off the chaff while the heavier grain fell back to the floor.

The grain of threshing floors was of course essential for life; threshing floors were, therefore, objects of raids and military conflicts (1 Sam. 23:1). Workers might sleep overnight on the threshing floor to guard the grain (Ruth 3:6-7). Gideon was forced by the frequency of Midianite raids to thresh his grain in a winepress (Judg. 6:11). Threshing floors were often prominent landmarks (cf. 1 Sam. 19:22 [LXX *tóu phréatos tóu hálō* "the cistern of the threshing floor"; RSV following MT "the great well"]), so that Heb. *gōren* came to be regarded almost as a place name (e.g., Gen. 50:10-11; 2 Sam. 6:6; 1 Chr. 13:9).

Grain from the threshing floor was an element in sacrifices of thanksgiving to God (Num. 15:20). The threshing floor and winepress together were the focus of the blessings of the harvest (Deut. 15:14; 16:13; 2 Kgs. 6:27; Hos. 9:2) and are mentioned as signs of God's eschatological blessing of his people (Joel 2:24). In addition to being the setting for harvest celebrations

(cf. Deut. 16:13-15), threshing floors were associated with divination and theophanies, perhaps because of their role in the processing of life-sustaining grain (e.g., 2 Sam. 6:6; 24:16-17; 1 Kgs. 22:10; cf. Judg. 6:37; Hos. 9:1; cf. P. K. McCarter, Jr., *I Samuel*. AB 8 [1980] at 1 Sam. 14:2). It was presumably such a connection that marked the threshing floor of Ornan as a sacred site and prompted David to locate the future temple there (2 Sam. 24:15-25; 1 Chr. 21:15–22:1).

In prophetic imagery threshing is a common representation of divine judgment (Isa. 21:10; 27:12; Jer. 51:33; Hos. 13:3; Mic. 4:12-13; Matt. 3:12). At Amos 1:3 threshing is a figure for torture of humans by humans.

THRESHOLD (Heb. *sap, miptān*). The door sill or lower horizontal stone of a stone doorframe.

Thresholds and doorways had important symbolic meanings in ancient Israel and surrounding countries. A particular home and household was distinguished from others by its doorway (cf. the practice of boring through the ear of an Israelite slave on a doorframe to symbolize his or her voluntary permanent attachment to that household; Exod. 21:5-6; Deut. 15:16-17). The doorways of Israelite homes were marked with the blood of the Passover lamb (Exod. 12:7, 13), and representative passages from the law were affixed to doorposts (Deut. 6:9).

The threshold of a home or temple marked a boundary with the outside world, so that crossing the threshold was, in effect, movement from one realm to another (e.g., Judg. 19:27; 1 Kgs. 14:17). Servants who guarded doorways were of particular importance (e.g., 2 Kgs. 12:9; 22:4; Esth. 2:21; Jer. 35:4). The threshold of a temple was regarded as sacred (cf. Ezek. 46:2). A taboo against stepping on the threshold of the Philistine temple of Dagon is traced to an incident in which the statue of the deity fell and broke, with the head and hands of the statue falling on the threshold (1 Sam. 5:4-5); the practice of leaping over the threshold (whether of temples or houses is unclear), perhaps because of a similar but more broadly applied taboo, is mentioned as a non-Israelite practice followed by some in Judah (Zeph. 1:9). Excessive familiarity with Yahweh was implied by the crowding of the threshold of his temple with human habitations (Ezek. 43:8). In a vision of the prophet Ezekiel the glory of God twice moves from above the cherubim in the inner part of the temple to the threshold of the temple to speak to a symbolic scribe (9:3; 10:4, 18).

THRONE (Heb. *kissē'*; Aram. *kārsē'*; Gk. *thrónos*; *béma*).† A seat that symbolizes the authority and dignity of the one seated on it. The greatest seats of honor and authority were royal thrones, such as Solomon's elaborate gold and ivory throne (1 Kgs. 10:18-20). The act of sitting on a royal throne was itself a symbol of the assumption of royal authority (16:11; 2 Kgs. 11:19; Acts 12:21-22). To arise from the throne, on the other hand, could be a gesture symbolizing recognition of a greater power (Jonah 3:6). Judicial authority was often exercised by an individual, a king, judge, or governor, as he sat on a throne (cf. Luke 1:52). Proximity to a royal throne was a sign of particular honor and power (1 Kgs. 2:19; Mark 14:62; Col. 3:1; Heb. 8:1; 12:2; cf. Esth. 3:1).

God in his sovereignty over creation is portrayed as a king seated on the throne and looking down at his subjects (Ps. 113:5-6). His throne is said to be in heaven, sometimes with the earth serving as his footstool (Ps. 103:19; Isa. 66:1; Ezek. 1:26; Matt. 5:34-35; Rev. 4). In Isaiah's vision the temple in Jerusalem is the location of God's throne (Isa. 6:1; cf. Ezek. 43:4-7); this might reflect an understanding of the ark of the covenant as the throne on which God is seated. In an eschatological oracle Jeremiah calls Jerusalem itself the throne of God (Jer. 3:17; cf. 14:21). The judicial office of the king seated on his throne is often the basis of statements concerning the enthronement of God (Ps. 9:4 [MT 5]; Dan. 7:9-10; Rev. 20:4, 11-12), the Messiah (Isa. 16:5; Luke 22:30), or the leaders of God's people (Matt. 25:31-32).

THUMMIM. *See* URIM AND THUMMIM.

THUNDER (Heb. *qôl, ra‛am*; Gk. *brontē*).† Thunder was believed by peoples of the ancient Near East to be the manifestation of God's voice (Heb. *qôl*), an aspect of divine self-revelation in storms (Exod. 19:16, 19; 20:18; 2 Sam. 22:14 par. Ps. 18:13 [MT 14]). Lightning and thunder might signify God's power and majesty (Job 37:2-5; Ps. 29:3-9) or might be part of the exercise of his anger against his people when they are sinful (1 Sam. 12:17-18; Isa. 29:6) or against the enemies of his people (Exod. 9:23; 1 Sam. 2:10; 7:10). John 12:29 notes that some of the crowd interpreted the voice from heaven responding to Jesus at the end of his public ministry as thunder. In Revelation thunder is associated with the divine majesty (Rev. 4:5, possibly an allusion to Exod. 19:16) and with judgment (e.g., Rev. 10:3-4).

THUNDER, SONS OF. *See* BOANERGES.

THUTMOSE [thŭt′mōs] (Egyp. *dḥwty-ms* "Thoth [the lunar deity] is born"; Gk. *Tuthmosis*).* The regnal name (also rendered Thothmes) of four pharaohs of the Egyptian Eighteenth Dynasty (*ca.* 1550-1306 B.C.), a period in which Egypt was the greatest power in the Near East and during which the Israelites were in Egyptian bondage. The dynasty began with the expulsion (or assimilation) of the Hyksos, who had ruled Egypt for two centuries.

1. Thutmose I (1525-*ca.* 1508), husband of Ahmose the daughter of Amenhotep I. Having expanded Egyptian control south into Nubia, he campaigned against the Hyksos and Mitannians in Syria and Palestine, advancing as far as the Euphrates river.

2. Thutmose II (*ca.* 1508-1504), son of Thutmose I and his second wife Metnofret, perhaps the younger sister of Ahmose; husband of his older half-sister Hatshepsut. His short reign was undistinguished, dominated first by his father's first wife Ahmose and then by his wife and actual successor, Hatshepsut.

3. Thutmose III (*ca.* 1504-1450), son of Thutmose II and a minor wife. His succession was reinforced by his father's appointing him coregent at the end of his reign and arranging his marriage to his half-sister Merytre, daughter of Hatshepsut. Neverthe-

less, the powerful coregent Hatshepsut usurped royal power for twenty-two years. At the age of thirty Thutmose regained the throne in 1482 and proved to be an able and energetic leader both on and off the battlefield, bringing Egypt to the zenith of its power. He conducted seventeen campaigns during the first twenty years of his reign, capturing Megiddo in 1482, and began the practice of holding sons of conquered princes hostage until they succeeded their fathers. By the end of Thutmose's reign the Egyptian Empire stretched northward to a line extending from the Euphrates to the Orontes and southward to the fourth cataract of the Nile.

4. Thutmose IV (*ca.* 1425-1412), son and successor of Amenhotep II. His reign was occupied with preserving the territories conquered by his predecessors. He was the last pharaoh of the Eighteenth Dynasty to campaign in Syria and Palestine.

THYATIRA [thī′ə tī′rə] (Gk. *Thyateira*).† A city in the ancient region of Lydia *ca.* 82 km. (50 mi.) northeast of modern Izmir (Smyrna), 62 km. (38 mi.) eastnortheast of Bergama (Pergamum), and 70 km. (42 mi.) from the Aegean coast. The modern city is called Akhisar.

Thyatira was refounded in the the early third century B.C. by Seleucus I on the site of an earlier settlement and became a city of commerce and industry, famous for its purple dye industry and for metalworking and other trades. It was an important stop on the Roman road connecting Pergamum and Laodicea. In the Roman period the craft guilds were each dedicated to the service of a deity and were prominent in the city's social and political life. Lydia, a prominent Christian convert in Philippi, was a seller of purple from Thyatira (Acts 16:14).

In John's letter to the church of Thyatira (Rev. 2:18-29) the Lord calls himself the one "who has eyes like a flame of fire, and whose feet are like burnished bronze" (v. 18), recalling the metal crafts of the city. He praises the Christians of the city (v. 19), but criticizes them for tolerating the existence of an esoteric and licentious cult in their midst, particularly in the person of a woman who is given the probably symbolical name of "Jezebel" (vv. 20-21, 24; cf. 1 Kgs. 16:31).

THYINE WOOD (Rev. 18:12, KJV). *See* SCENTED WOOD.

TIBERIAS [tī bǐr′ī əs] (Gk. *Tiberias*). A city on the western shore of the Sea of Galilee (John 6:23), built *ca.* A.D. 25 by Herod Antipas as the capital of his tetrarchy of Galilee and Perea and named for Emperor Tiberius. Despite initial Jewish resistance to the establishment of the city because it was built on the site of a cemetery, it came to be dominated by Jews. Tiberias had, nonetheless, a mixed populace and was an important center of Hellenism, governed according to Greek customs with a large council of six hundred members and a small council of ten. Surrounded by a strong wall, the city had a synagogue, a palace, and a stadium. The Sanhedrin relocated at Tiberias *ca.* 150, and from the second and third centuries the city was the major western center of Jewish learning. Here the Palestinian Talmud was compiled and the Tiberian system of Hebrew vowel pointing devised.

The Sea of Galilee also came to be called the Sea of Tiberias (v. 1; 21:1).

TIBERIAS, SEA OF. See GALILEE, SEA OF.

TIBERIUS [tī bĭr'ĭ əs] (Gk. *Tiberios*; Lat. *Tiberius*).† The second emperor of the Roman Empire (A.D. 14-42). Tiberius was born in 42 B.C., the son of the Roman officer Tiberius Claudius Nero, for whom he was named. Augustus adopted him (renaming him Tiberius Julius Caesar) and named him his coregent in A.D. 4, and as such he became successor to the throne upon Augustus' death in A.D. 14.

Tiberius undertook a conservative reign that served to extend and strengthen the policies of Augustus. While some later senatorial historians exaggerate the weaknesses of his administration, contemporary sources speak well of his actions. His strict attention to the economy increased the revenues of the empire without requiring oppressive taxation. He raised the standards of civil service and administration of justice throughout the empire. Though a brave soldier and good emperor, he was suspicious and often cruel (cf. John 19:12-13, where at Jesus' trial the Jews threaten Pilate with the emperor's wrath).

When the Roman general Agrippa, husband of Augustus' only child Julia, died in 12 B.C., Augustus' wife Livia prevailed upon the emperor to coerce Tiberius into divorcing his wife Vipsania (another of Agrippa's daughters) and marrying Julia. When Tiberius' nephew and adopted son Germanicus died in A.D. 19 and Drusus, his son by Vipsania, in 23, Tiberius named two sons of his minister Sejanus as heirs; he subsequently had them assassinated as conspirators. Upon his death in 37 Tiberius was succeeded by Sejanus' third son, Caligula.

Tiberius is mentioned by name at Luke 3:1 to designate the time of John the Baptist's public ministry. He is called "Caesar" in other places, where he is mentioned simply as the supreme governmental authority of the time of Jesus' ministry and trial (Matt. 22:17 par.; John 19:12). In the dispute with the Pharisees concerning the payment of taxes to Caesar (cf. Matt. 22:17-21 par.), the coin that Jesus used for illustration was undoubtedly a silver denarius bearing the image of Tiberius; the denarius of this period was inscribed with the official logia "Tiberius Caesar, son of the divine Augustus, Augustus," though Tiberius himself never lay claim to divinity.

TIBHATH [tĭb'hăth] (Heb. *ṭibḥaṯ*). A place in Syria from which David took much spoil after a victory (1 Chr. 18:8). Called Betah in the parallel passage (2 Sam. 8:8), it is possibly to be associated with Tebah (Gen. 22:24). Thought to be situated in the Beqaʿ region, its precise location is unknown.

TIBNI [tĭb'nī] (Heb. *tibnî*). The son of Ginath. He was favored to be king by half of the northern kingdom of Israel after the death of King Zimri (*ca.* 882 B.C.; 1 Kgs. 16:21). But in the three-year civil war that followed Zimri's suicide, those following his rival

Omri soon gained the upper hand, and Tibni lost his life (v. 22).

TIDAL [tī'dəl] (Heb. *tidʿāl*; cf. Hitt. *Tudḫaliyas*). One of Chedorlaomer's allies who helped subdue the rebellious kings of the plain (Gen. 14:1, 9). Neither the king nor the subjects of his kingdom have been identified. See GOIIM.

TIGLATH-PILESER [tĭg'lăth pĭ lē'zər] (Heb. *tiglaṯ pilʾeser* [*tilgaṯ pilnʾeser* in 1–2 Chronicles]; Akk. *Tukulti-apil-ešarra* "my trust [is] in the son of [the temple] Ešarra").†

1. Tiglath-pileser I, king of Assyria *ca.* 1115-1077 B.C. He was occupied largely with conquest of neighboring peoples, including the Muški in the Upper Euphrates region, Commagene and Cappadocia in Anatolia, and the Arameans in northern Syria. By the end of his reign Assyrian control had been extended as far as the Mediterranean.

2. Tiglath-pileser II, king of Assyria *ca.* 967-935 B.C. The father of Assurdan II and a contemporary of King Solomon, little is known of his reign.

3. Tiglath-pileser III, king of Assyria 745-727 B.C., whose leadership brought Assyria out of a period of weakness into the initial years of its greatest power.

Assyria faced enemies on all its borders when Tiglath-pileser seized the throne. Campaigns against Urartu and its Syrian allies (including a coalition led by Uzziah of Judah) brought a number of Syrian and Palestinian cities under Assyrian power, so that they were forced to pay tribute. Civil war in Babylon following the death of King Nabunasir in 734 allowed Tiglath-pileser to take the throne of Babylon under the name of Pul (cf. 2 Kgs. 15:19; 1 Chr. 5:26; an alternate view is that Pūl[u] was his given name and that he had adopted Tiglath-pileser as a throne name).

Unlike those of his predecessors, the military campaigns of Tiglath-pileser were intended to be permanent conquests and not merely tribute-gathering forays. When faced with rebellion in conquered territories he customarily deported the offenders and made their lands provinces of the empire. The rebellions of the city-states and small kingdoms in Syria and Palestine made it necessary for Tiglath-pileser to campaign repeatedly in that area.

The seizure of the throne of Israel by Pekah (*ca.* 737-732) was probably precipitated by dissatisfaction with the policy of capitulation to Assyria followed by Menahem (2 Kgs. 15:19-25). Pekah led an anti-Assyrian coalition that included Rezin of Damascus, which Judah was pressed to join. The refusal of Jotham of Judah to agree to this led Pekah and Rezin to prepare to attack the southern kingdom (v. 37). Jotham died, and his son and successor Ahaz appealed to Tiglath-pileser for aid against Israel and Damascus (16:1-7; cf. 2 Chr. 28), a course against which the prophet Isaiah counseled (Isa. 7). Ahaz sent considerable tribute to Assyria with his request (2 Kgs. 16:8-9).

Tiglath-pileser reacted to the coalition's rebellion and to Ahaz' request by quickly overrunning Israel and proceeding as far as the River of Egypt. Much of Israel's population was deported (15:29; 1 Chr. 5:6, 26), but the total destruction of the kingdom was postponed by the Assyrian's replacement of Pekah with Hoshea, who offered tribute to Tiglath-pileser (2 Kgs. 15:30; *ANET*, p. 284). However, the kingdom of Damascus was destroyed, and Rezin executed (2 Kgs. 16:9).

TIGRIS [tī'grĭs] (Heb. *ḥiddeqel*; Gk. *Tígris*; Akk. *Idiglat*; O.Pers. *Tigra*).† The easternmost of the two major rivers of Mesopotamia. Formed from two branches that originate on the southern slopes of the Taurus mountains in Turkish Armenia, one south of Lake Geuljik and the other southwest of Lake Van, the river flows southeasterly across the Mesopotamian plain to modern Kurna, where it joins with the Euphrates to form the Shaṭṭ el-ʿArab, which empties into the Persian Gulf. Major tributaries include the Upper and Lower (or Greater and Lesser) Zab and the Diyala rivers. The lower course of the river has shifted since ancient times (presumably it once flowed directly into the Persian Gulf), destroying remains of many ancient sites as well as the system of canals linking the Tigris and Euphrates. Important ancient cities on the Tigris included Nineveh, Calah, and Assur.

The Tigris is mentioned as one of the branches of the river flowing out of the garden of Eden (Gen. 2:14; KJV "Hiddekel"). Daniel saw one of his visions while standing on the bank of the Tigris (Dan. 10:4). Sir. 24:25 implies that the river reaches its highest level after the melting of the snow.

TIKVAH [tĭk'və] (Heb. *tiqwâ* "hope").
1. The father of Shallum (2), the husband of the prophetess Huldah (2 Kgs. 22:14). He is called Tokhath at 2 Chr. 34:22 (KJV "Tikvath").
2. The father of Jahzeiah, who opposed Ezra's plan to dissolve the marriages with foreign women (Ezra 10:15).

TILGATH-PILNESER. *See* TIGLATH-PILESER.

TILON [tī'lən] (Heb. *tîlôn*). A son of Shimon of the tribe of Judah (1 Chr. 4:20).

TIMAEUS [tĭ mē'əs] (Gk. *Timaios* "honorable"). The father of the blind beggar Bartimaeus, whom Jesus cured at Jericho (Mark 10:46).

TIMBREL (Heb. *tōp*). A musical instrument, probably a small hand drum, perhaps with bells or small pieces of metal around its periphery. In addition to "timbrel," its most common rendering, the Hebrew term has been translated variously, including "tabret" (KJV) and "tambourine" (RSV).

TIME.* Some distinction can be made between biblical words for a point in time (e.g., Heb. *zᵉmān, ʿēṭ, paʿam*) and words for a period or duration of time (e.g., *yôm*). It has been particularly common to distinguish between the two most common Greek words for time, associating Gk. *chrónos* with duration and *kairós* with a point in time, particularly "the decisive moment." But although *kairós* bore such a meaning in Classical Greek, its distinction from *chrónos* was to some degree blurred by the time of the New Testament.

A distinction is also sometimes drawn between, on the one hand, a cyclical view of time, supposedly held by the Greeks and even more by the Canaanites, who marked the passage of time with ever-recurring seasonal agricultural festivals dedicated to nature gods, and, on the other hand, a linear view of time and history held by the people of Israel. But Israel's religious observances were also repeated and oriented to the agricultural seasons. Furthermore, deities of other nations, including the Canaanites, also were thought of as acting decisively in history. Ecclesiastes, for its part, thinks of history as a meaningless round of futile repetitions with no goal (Eccl. 1:5-10; 3:1-9). Thus one cannot speak of a uniform view of time and history in either the biblical or the nonbiblical perspectives.

It is true, however, that the importation of a platonic view of time and eternity into Christian theology has made understanding the Bible more difficult. This conception of eternal reality as not involved in or conditioned by time and, therefore, of God as unchanging has been in tension with the Bible's portrayal of a living, acting, loving, and responding God. The Bible portrays God as existing in ever-extending time. Eternity is the continuation of time (cf. Rev. 14:11). At 10:6, which has been interpreted to teach that time will cease to exist when the present age ends, *chrónos* should be translated "delay" (so RSV), not "time" (KJV).

The ordering of events in a chronological framework is very important to some biblical writers, most obviously those responsible for the major histories in the Old Testament. The synchronization of the kings of Judah and Israel in 1–2 Kings is a clear example of this concern. Chronology was also important to the apocalyptic writers, though in a different way. They often sought to periodize history, in this way understanding all of history to be under God's sovereign direction. Thus Daniel divides previous history into a series of "weeks of years" (Dan. 9:24) and into a series of pagan empires that oppress God's people.

The apocalyptic doctrine of two ages, the present evil age to be succeeded by the age to come in which all wrongs will be righted and God will reign over all (cf. 2 Esdr. 7:50 [lacking in KJV]), was held by Jesus, but he regarded the age to come, the "kingdom of God," as already present and working in his own ministry (Mark 1:15). Response to the tension created by the continued presence of evil alongside Jesus' ministry and alongside the Church was one of the aspects of the Church's existence that was most productive in New Testament theology. Paul and other early Christians believed that with the resurrection of Jesus and the outpouring of the Holy Spirit the new age had dawned, but in a secret way, in the midst of the old age, causing an overlapping of the ages (Rom. 8:18, 23; 1 Cor. 15:20; Eph. 1:13-14; 2:4-7). This balance or tension between what has already happened and what is still expected determines the attitude that Christians are to bear toward this world (Col. 3:1-4). The emphasis on present fulfillment or on future expectation varies according to the situation being confronted. Within this framework, another aspect of the apocalyptic view of time that is experienced is the stress on the urgent necessity that ethical and spiritual decisions be made in the present moment (e.g., Matt. 22:2-10; 24:32-34; Rom. 13:11-13; 2 Cor. 6:2; 1 Thess. 5:3-8).

Bibliography. J. Barr, *Biblical Words for Time.* SBT 33 (Naperville: 1962); O. Cullmann, *Christ and Time,* rev. ed. (Philadelphia: 1964); S. J. De Vries, *Yesterday, Today and Tomorrow* (Grand Rapids: 1975).

TIMNA [tĭm′nə] (Heb. *timnaʿ, timnāʿ*).
1. The concubine of Esau's son Eliphaz, the mother of Amalek, and the sister of Lotan (Gen. 36:12, 22; 1 Chr. 1:39).
2. A chief of Edom (Gen. 36:40; 1 Chr. 1:51; KJV "Timnah").
3. A son of Eliphaz and descendant of Esau (1 Chr. 1:36). He may be the same as **2**. If the names are taken as eponymous ancestors of social groups, this Timna may represent a different sociopolitical alignment of the same or related people as **1**.

TIMNAH (PERSON) (Gen. 36:40; 1 Chr. 1:51, KJV). *See* TIMNA **2**.

TIMNAH [tĭm′nə] (Heb. *timnâ* "allotted territory"; Gk. *Tamnatha*) (**PLACE**).
1. A town on the border of the tribal territory of Judah, in the Shephelah region (Josh. 15:10). This town was assigned to the tribe of Dan (19:43; KJV "Thimnathah"), but was apparently dominated by Philistines. It was the hometown of Delilah (Judg. 14:1-2, 5; KJV "Timnath"), whose father was known as "the Timnite" (15:6). Judah and the Philistines continued to fight over Timnah (2 Chr. 28:18). It is probably to be identified with Tell el-Batashi, *ca.* 5 km. (3 mi.) west-northwest of Beth-shemesh.
2. A town in the hill country of southern Judah (Josh. 15:57), generally identified with the place to which the patriarch Judah went to have his sheep sheared (Gen. 38:12-14; KJV "Timnath"). It was probably located somewhere southeast of Hebron.
3.* A town in Judea fortified in 160 B.C. by the Seleucid general Bacchides (1 Macc. 9:50; KJV "Thamnatha"). Situated in the hill country, it is probably to be identified with Khirbet Tibneh, *ca.* 14 km. (9 mi.) northwest of Bethel.

TIMNATH-HERES [tĭm′năth hĕr′ĭz] (Heb. *timnaṯ-ḥeres* "territory dedicated to the sun"), **TIMNATH-SERAH** [tĭm′năth sĕr′ə] (*timmaṯ-seraḥ* "leftover portion"). A city in the hill country of Ephraim, generally identified with Khirbet Tibneh, *ca.* 28.5 km. (18 mi.) north-northwest of Jerusalem. The city was given to Joshua (Timnath-serah, Josh. 19:49-50), who was buried there (24:30; Timnath-heres, Judg. 2:9). The form Timnath-serah may have been substituted for an earlier name based on pre-Israelite sun worship at the site. The LXX adds at Josh. 24:30 that the flint knives Joshua used to circumcise the Israelites at Gilgal were placed in his grave (cf. R. G. Boling and G. E. Wright, *Joshua.* AB 6 [1982], pp. 529ff.). Samaritan tradition locates Joshua's grave and that of Caleb at Kefr Haris, about halfway between Khirbet Tibneh and Shechem; no archaeological evidence yet substantiates this tradition, but clear evidence does support occupation of

Khirbet Tibneh at the time of Joshua. It may be the same as TIMNAH **3**.

TIMNITE [tĭm′nīt] (Heb. *timnî*). A gentilic designating an inhabitant of TIMNAH **1** (Judg. 15:6).

TIMON [tī′mən] (Gk. *Timōn*). One of the seven chosen to aid the disciples in the distribution to the widows of the Church (Acts 6:5).

TIMOTHY [tĭm′ə thē] (Gk. *Timotheos* "honoring God").
1.* An Ammonite officer whose forces were defeated in several encounters with Judas Maccabeus and the Jewish rebels (1 Macc. 5:6-7, 11, 34, 37-39; 2 Macc. 8:30-33; 9:3; 12:2-25). He was killed at Gazara (10:24-37).
2. One of Paul's most significant traveling companions and coworkers. Timothy was already a Christian (probably converted during the apostle's first missionary journey) when Paul and Silas passed through Lystra, Timothy's home, during the second missionary journey (Acts 16:1; cf. 14:6-8, 21). Timothy's mother was Jewish but "a believer," and his father, probably deceased, a Gentile. Timothy had not been circumcised, but had received some training in the Jewish scriptures (2 Tim. 3:15). Wanting Timothy to join him and Silas, Paul circumcised the young disciple so that traveling with the son of a marriage regarded as illegal according to Jewish law would not be such an immediate hindrance to work among Jews (Acts 16:2-3).

Forced to leave Macedonia for Athens, Paul left Timothy and Silas behind in Macedonia (17:1-15). When Timothy joined Paul at Athens, the apostle sent him back northward to Thessalonica (1 Thess. 3:1-2). When they were rejoined at Corinth, Timothy again worked alongside Paul (Acts 18:5; 2 Cor. 1:19). His name occurs with Paul's in the letters to Thessalonica written from Corinth (1 Thess. 1:1; 3:6; 2 Thess. 1:1). Again on his third missionary journey, Paul sometimes had Timothy with him as an assistant and sometimes sent him to some location where help was needed but where the apostle could not himself be present (Acts 19:22; 1 Cor. 4:17; 16:10; 2 Cor. 1:1). When Paul was in Corinth on the eve of his journey to Jerusalem, and at least during part of that journey, Timothy was with Paul (Acts 20:4; Rom. 16:21). Later Timothy worked at Ephesus (1 Tim. 1:3), perhaps going there while Paul went on to Jerusalem. If Philippians, Colossians, and Philemon were written from Rome, then Timothy was there with Paul at least for a short time (Phil. 1:1; 2:19; Col. 1:1; Phlm. 1).

Toward the end of Paul's life, Timothy proved to be an especially significant helper whose faithful service was remembered by the apostle, as 2 Timothy bears witness (cf. 1 Cor. 4:17; Phil. 2:22). Paul indeed wanted Timothy to be with him (2 Tim. 4:9, 21). It appears that alongside his faithfulness was a timidity on Timothy's part, which Paul considered a difficulty, and problems with physical health as well (1 Tim. 4:12; 2 Tim. 1:7; 4:1-5). At some time during his career as a Christian worker Timothy was imprisoned (Heb. 13:23).

TIMOTHY, LETTERS TO. Two letters from the

apostle Paul to his coworker Timothy that are generally considered together with the letter of Paul to Titus because of the similarities in the three letters. *See* PASTORAL EPISTLES.

TIN (Heb. *bᵉdîl*).† A metal used from the late fourth millennium B.C. to form bronze, a copper-tin alloy from which most tools and weapons were made throughout the ancient Near East (except Egypt, where tin was not available) until it was surpassed by iron. At Num. 31:22 tin is listed among metals that, as booty, had to be purified in fire. Tinstone was often found in silver ore; its removal by smelting is mentioned in figures of speech at Isa. 1:25 (RSV "alloy"); Ezek. 22:18-20. Tin was brought to Tyre from "Tarshish" (27:12), but the actual source was probably Cyprus or Spain.

TIPHSAH [tĭf′sə] (Heb. *tipsaḥ*).
1. A city mentioned in a general description of the extent of Solomon's empire (1 Kgs. 4:24 [MT 5:4]), modern Dibseh. Situated at a ford of the Euphrates river east-southeast of later Aleppo, it was called Thapsacus by Roman and Greek writers.
2.† A city sacked by Menahem of Israel when it resisted his takeover of the monarchy (2 Kgs. 15:16; RSV "Tappuah"). While the MT reads Heb. *tipsaḥ*, the Lucianic recension of the LXX has Gk. *Taphōe*, leading to the usual identification of this city with TAPPUAH 1.

TIRAS [tī′rəs] (Heb. *tîrās*). According to the Table of Nations, a son of Japheth (Gen. 10:2; 1 Chr. 1:5). His descendants are assumed to have been a component of the Sea Peoples (called Turusa in Egyptian inscriptions and the Tyrsenoi by the Greeks) who were sea pirates in the Aegean and eastern Mediterranean. They were among the Sea Peoples who invaded Egypt in the thirteenth century B.C.

TIRATHITES [tī′rə thīts] (Heb. *tirʿāṭîm*). One of the "families of scribes" (or "Sopherites"; so NIV mg.; cf. JB) among the Kenites (1 Chr. 2:55).

TIRHAKAH [tûr hā′kə] (Heb. *tirhāqâ*; Egyp. *Thrq*; Akk. *Tarqû*).† The son of Piankhy, the Ethiopian king who conquered northern Egypt and ushered in the Twenty-fifth (or Ethiopian) Dynasty, and Piankhy's third successor, ruling *ca.* 689-664 B.C. Pharaoh Shaba-taka (Shebitku) dispatched the young general Tirhakah (also called Taharqa) to aid King Hezekiah of Judah when the southern kingdom was attacked by Sennacherib of Assyria in 701 (2 Kgs. 19:9 par. Isa. 37:9; cf. *ANET*, p. 287). After Sennacherib's death, Tirhakah as pharaoh again fought against Assyria, suffering defeat when Sennacherib's son Esarhaddon invaded Memphis in 671 to retaliate for Tirhakah's anti-Assyrian collusion with Ba'lu, king of Tyre (pp. 290, 292-97). Having escaped to Thebes, Tirhakah recaptured Memphis. Esarhaddon died in 669 en route to a reengagement over the city, but in 667 the Assyrians, aided by Syrian and Palestinian forces, recaptured Memphis. Tirhakah's further efforts to regain the capital failed.

TIRHANAH [tûr hā′nə] (Heb. *tirhᵃnâ*). A son of Caleb and his concubine Maacah (1 Chr. 2:48).

TIRIA [tĭr′ĭ ə] (Heb. *tîryāʾ*). A son of Jehallelel of the tribe of Judah (1 Chr. 4:16).

TIRSHATHA [tûr shā′thə]. The KJV rendering of Heb. *tiršāṭāʾ*, which represents O.Pers. *taršta*, a title given to the postexilic governors of Judah (Ezra 2:63; Neh. 7:65, 70; 8:9; 10:1 [MT 2]; RSV "governor"). *See* GOVERNOR.

TIRZAH [tĭr′zə] (Heb. *tirṣâ* "pleasure, beauty") **(PERSON).** One of the daughters of the Manassite Zelophehad for whom special provision was made that they might inherit their family's land (Num. 26:33; 27:1; 36:11; Josh. 17:3).

TIRZAH [tĭr′zə] (Heb. *tirṣâ* "pleasure, beauty") **(PLACE).†** A Canaanite royal city defeated by Joshua (Josh. 12:24), perhaps associated with a clan of Manasseh related to the Zelophehad line. Tirzah was later a prominent city of the northern kingdom of Israel (1 Kgs. 14:17), serving for a time as its capital until the establishment of Samaria (15:21, 33; 16:8, 15-18, 23). It was from Tirzah that the rebellion of Menahem, probably the city's governor, began (2 Kgs. 15:14, 16). The reference at Cant. 6:4 to the beauty of the city is, in part, a play on the meaning of the Hebrew name.

Tirzah is generally identified with Tell el-Fârʿah, *ca.* 11 km. (7 mi.) northeast of Shechem. Archaeological investigation has found a number of general correspondences between the history of the site and the biblical record, including evidence of the Israelite conquest and remains of a fortress that may well be the one set afire by Zimri (1 Kgs. 16:18).

TISHBE [tĭsh′bē], **TISHBITE** [tĭsh′bīt] (Heb. *hattišbî*).† The designation of Elijah as "the Tishbite" (1 Kgs. 17:1; 21:17, 28; 2 Kgs. 1:3, 8; 9:36) suggests his origin as some place called Tishbe(h). The traditional site of this place is Listib, *ca.* 14 km. (9 mi.) east of the Jordan a short distance south of Wâdī Yâbis, but this identification is not likely.

At 1 Kgs. 17:1 an additional statement is made about Elijah's origin. The most likely understandings of this difficult phrase are those represented in the RSV and KJV. RSV "of Tishbe in Gilead" follows the LXX (representing Heb. *mittišbê gilʿāḏ*) and is not as redundant as might appear after "the Tishbite," because this common epithet ascribed to the prophet's name was not transparent. KJV "of the inhabitants of Gilead" ("settlers," "colonists," or "sojourners" would be better) represents MT *mittōšāḇê* (revocalized to *mittōšᵉḇê*) *gilʿāḏ*. If KJV is correct, Elijah was possibly of non-Israelite origin.

TISHRI [tĭsh′rē] (Heb. *tišrî*). The postexilic Babylonian name for the seventh month of the Jewish civil or economic calendar and the first month of the religious year (Sept./Oct.). The Hebrew name of the month was ETHANIM. The New Year (Rosh Hashanah), the Day of Atonement, and the Feast of Booths all fall in Tishri. *See* YEAR.

TITHE (Heb. piel ʿāśar; Gk. *[apo]dekatóō*).† The dedication of a tenth of agricultural products, of livestock, of goods gained in trade, or of booty to the worship of a deity or to the persons who served that worship. This was a common custom in the ancient world, one probably well-known before Israel's history began. It was practiced already by the patriarchs, but only on specific occasions and not as a customary practice (Gen. 14:20; 28:22).

From the formative period of Israel arising from their covenant with Yahweh, tithing became a regular religious obligation, but one still subject to numerous variations through time. The primary function of the tithe was the support of those who served in the worship of God, primarily the Levites (Num. 18:21-24; Neh. 10:37 [MT 38]; cf. 1 Macc. 3:49), who were then to pass on to the priests a "tithe of the tithes" that they received (Num. 18:25-29, 32; Neh. 10:38 [MT 39]). Sometimes, however, the tithe was given for the support of various classes of poor people, including Levites, but also including poor people who were not religious functionaries (Deut. 26:12-14).

Tithes were given as sacrifices in fulfillment of vows in early times (Gen. 28:22), and it appears from the context of Lev. 27:30-33 that when sacrificial tithes became customary and obligatory rather than voluntary, they were still associated with vows. It was stipulated that the tenth part of the land, of its seed, and of the fruit of the trees would be set aside for God (v. 30). Should someone wish to redeem his tithe (i.e., buy it back for personal use), he was obligated to pay an additional fifth of its value (v. 31). A tithe of livestock, randomly chosen, was to be devoted to God without substituting bad animals for any good animals that might be included in the tithe; in case such an exchange was made, both animals would be included in the tithe and would be unredeemable (vv. 32-33).

Tithes were also gathered at the temple so those presenting them could participate in a communal ceremonial meal. The participation of the Levites was required, so this too was a way of providing for their sustenance (Deut. 14:22-29). When tithes were given directly to support Levites or for sacrifice, a ceremonial meal could still be part of the procedure (Num. 18:30-31; Deut. 12:6-7). It may be that the ceremonial meal in celebration of a successful harvest or some other successful venture was the earliest foundation of the tithe (cf. Gen. 14:18-20). However, the support of the personnel of the worship center came to be the single function of tithes in Israel (Neh. 13:5, 10-13; Amos 4:4; Mal. 3:8-10).

As part of their effort to live according to the law in a detailed and radical fashion, the Pharisees tithed not only the products of the field, but also what was produced in the spice garden (Matt. 23:23; Luke 11:42; cf. 18:12).

TITIUS JUSTUS (Acts 18:7). *See* JUSTUS 2.

TITTLE. The KJV rendering of Gk. *keraía*, a term for a small stroke or hook that probably served to distinguish otherwise similar Hebrew letters (Matt. 5:18; Luke 16:17). *See* DOT.

TITUS [tī'təs] (Gk. *Titos*).

1. Titus Manius, one of two Roman envoys sent to Judea in 165 B.C. with a letter consenting to the concessions of Lysias to the Jews (2 Macc. 11:34; KJV "Titus Manlius"). Attempts at identifying Titus Manius with some otherwise known person have not led to any clear conclusions.

2. Alternate form of Titius Justus. *See* JUSTUS 2.

3. A coworker of Paul. Titus is mentioned in four of Paul's epistles, but his name is absent from Acts. This omission has been explained with the suggestion that Titus was a relative of Luke (cf. 2 Cor. 8:18-19, 22-23).

At Gal. 2:1, 3 Titus is identified as a Gentile (RSV "Greek") who accompanied Paul and Barnabas to the Apostolic Council in Jerusalem (A.D. 49). A fundamental issue at the Council was whether circumcision should be required of Gentile Christians (Acts 15:2). One of the most significant aspects of the Council in Paul's view was that Titus was not compelled to be circumcised (Gal. 2:3).

Titus played an active role in Paul's care for the Corinthian church. Paul sent Titus (probably with the letter mentioned at 2 Cor. 2:4; 7:8) to handle a difficult situation there. Titus returned to Paul at Macedonia and reported that all was well (vv. 5-7, 13-16). On the strength of this report, Paul sent Titus back to Corinth to supervise the collection of money from the Gentile churches for the Christians of Jerusalem, a work Titus had started earlier (8:6). But if chs. 10-13 are part of a letter written later, as is probable, Paul's relations with the Corinthian Christians had again deteriorated.

Titus 1:5 reports that Paul left Titus on Crete to organize the church there. The entire letter reflects the apostle's high regard for his fellow worker, whom he calls his "true child" by virtue of their common faith (v. 4). The personal note at the end of 2 Timothy reports that Titus went on to yet another field, Dalmatia (2 Tim. 4:10).

4. Titus Flavius Sabinus Vespasianus, Roman emperor (A.D. 79-81). Titus accompanied his father Vespasian to Judea to suppress the Jewish revolt in A.D. 67. When his father returned to Rome to become emperor, Titus was left in charge to see the war through to the end, which essentially came with the destruction of Jerusalem in 70. In honor of his achievement the Arch of Titus was erected at the Forum in Rome, featuring reliefs depicting treasures taken as booty from the Jewish temple.

The short reign of Titus was viewed as a favorable, relatively peaceful interlude. Unlike his father (whose rule he had shared under the title "Caesar"), Titus endeared himself to both the populace and the Senate by spending lavishly on public works (including the Colosseum, which was completed during his reign) and by eliminating trials and executions for treason. He is also remembered for aiding the the victims of Mt. Vesuvius in 79 and the people of Rome when fire and plague struck in 80. The Senate deified Titus upon his death.

5. *See* DYSMAS.

TITUS, EPISTLE OF.* A somewhat tedious apocryphal tract, extant only in one eighth-century A.D.

Latin manuscript, and purporting to be a letter from Titus, the coworker of Paul. The aim of this work is to commend the life of virginity and to oppose "spiritual marriages." For its sources it draws on Scripture and on several of the ascetic, apocryphal acts of apostles. Its origins are unclear, but it may well come from a fifth-century ascetic Spanish community.

TITUS, LETTER TO. A letter from the apostle Paul to his coworker Titus. Because of their similarities, it is generally treated together with the two letters of Paul to Timothy. *See* PASTORAL EPISTLES.

TIZITE [tĭ′zīt] (Heb. *tîṣî*). A gentilic applied to one of David's mighty men (1 Chr. 11:45), probably designating a place of origin otherwise unknown.

TOAH [tō′ə] (Heb. *tôaḥ*). A Levite of the Kohathite clan, the son of Zuph and an ancestor of Samuel (1 Chr. 6:34 [MT 19]). Elsewhere he is called Nahath (**2**) (v. 26 [MT 11]) and Tohu (1 Sam. 1:1).

TOB [tŏb] (Heb. *ṭôb* "good"; Gk. *Toubion*).† A place or region in Transjordan, north of the Yarmuk river. One of the Amarna Letters mentions a region called in Akkadian *Dubu*, which corresponds with Egyp. *tuby* on the list of Thutmose II. Here Jephthah fled when driven out by Jephthah's direct heirs (Judg. 11:3, 5). The Ammonites enlisted mercenaries from Tob for the coalition against David (2 Sam. 10:6, 8; KJV "Ishtob"). Judas Maccabeus rescued Jewish inhabitants of the "land of Tob" from attack by Hellenists (1 Macc. 5:13; cf. 2 Macc. 12:17, "Toubiani"). Tob is often identified with modern eṭ-Ṭaiyibeh in the Hauran region east of Gilead, *ca.* 19 km. (12 mi.) southeast of the Sea of Galilee.

TOBADONIJAH [tŏb′ăd ə nī′jə] (Heb. *ṭôb ʾaḏônîyâ* "my Lord Yahweh is good"). A Levite who instructed the people in the law under King Jehoshaphat (2 Chr. 17:8). The name may be a scribal dittograph after "Adonijah, Tobijah" (so JB, which deletes Tobadonijah).

TOBIAD(S) [tō bī′əd(z)]. *See* TOBIAH **2**.

TOBIAH [tō bī′ə] (Heb. *ṭôbîyâ* "Yahweh is good").
1. The ancestor of a clan who, upon their return from the Babylonion exile, were unable to establish their true Israelite descent (Ezra 2:60; Neh. 7:62).
2. An opponent of Nehemiah's plans for rebuilding the walls of Jerusalem (Neh. 2:10, 19; 4:3, 7-8 [MT 3:35; 4:1-2]; 6:1, 12, 14). He is described by Nehemiah as "the servant [Heb. *ʿeḇeḏ*], the Ammonite," a phrase interpreted variously as a derogatory designation (cf. Deut. 23:3 [MT 4]), possibly implying that Tobiah was of mixed ancestry; as the proper designation of a Persian official acting as governor of the province of Ammon; as the name itself of the Persian governor of Ammon (emending the phrase to read "Tobiah and *ʿbd* the Ammonite," a suggestion based on a fifth-century inscription); and as the title of Tobiah as a Samaritan official in the service of Sanballat, with whom Tobiah is associated in Nehemiah. Even

if Tobiah did reside in Ammon, his name, the name of his son Jehohanan (Neh. 6:18), and his association with high-ranking Jewish officials (vv. 17-19; 13:4-5) testify that he was probably a Jew. After the city had been rebuilt, Tobiah was given the use of a room in the courts of the temple, from which he was ousted by Nehemiah (vv. 4-8).

Tobiah may have been a descendant of Tobiah **1** and/or perhaps a member or ancestor of the Tobiad family, which was to have considerable influence in later generations (cf. Josephus *Ant.* xii.4.2 [160]–5.1 [241]). The Tobiads were based in both Jerusalem and in Transjordan and augmented their already great wealth by collecting taxes for the Ptolemies and the Seleucids. They had definite Hellenistic leanings and were opponents of the Oniad high priests.

TOBIAS [tō bī′əs] (Gk. *Tōbias*; from Heb. *ṭôbîyâ* "Yahweh is good").
1. The son of Tobit who, guided by the angel Raphael, healed his father's blindness and drove out a demon from Sarah, the daughter of Raguel. *See* TOBIT, BOOK OF.
2. A prominent and wealthy Jew of the Maccabean period; the father of Hyrcanus (**1**) (2 Macc. 3:11).

TOBIJAH [tō bī′jə] (Heb. *ṭôbîyāhû* "Yahweh is good").
1. One of the Levites sent out by King Jehoshaphat to teach in the cities of Judah (2 Chr. 17:8).
2. One of a handful of returning Babylonian exiles who, according to the vision of Zechariah (Zech. 6:10, 14), were to contribute silver and gold for the crown of the high priest Joshua. Tobijah was possibly one of the descendants of Tobiah (**1**) who were unable to authenticate their Israelite origin (Ezra 2:60; Neh. 7:62).

TOBIT [tō′bĭt] (Gk. *Tōbit*, *Tōbeith*; from Heb. *ṭôbî* "my goodness").* A man of the tribe of Naphtali, son of Tobiel of the line of Asiel, exiled from his home at Thisbe in Galilee to Nineveh (Tob. 1:1-2; Vulg. Lat. *Tobias*). Characterized as a pious Jew, he becomes blind (ch. 2) and eventually is cured by the angel Raphael working through Tobit's son Tobias (11:1-15).
See TOBIT, BOOK OF.

TOBIT, BOOK OF.† A book of the Apocrypha/Deuterocanonical Books recounting the experiences (Tob. 1:1; cf. RSV mg. "words") of the pious Tobit and his family in the Diaspora. In the Vulgate, where it appears following Ezra-Nehemiah, it is called *Tobias*. In some Greek manuscripts it is placed after the Wisdom books.

I. Contents

Tobit is exiled from his home at Thisbe in Naphtali "in the days of Shalmaneser, king of the Assyrians" (v. 2). Righteous in observance of Jewish law (vv. 3, 5-8, 10-12), he performs "many acts of charity" on behalf of his fellow exiles (vv. 3, 16-18). Indeed, because of his concern to bury the bodies of Jews murdered by the Assyrians, he is forced to flee Nineveh (vv. 19-20); later, upon his return, he resumes this practice and, while thus ritually unclean, becomes blind (2:7-10) and, as a result, impoverished (vv. 11-14). His prayer for divine mercy is recorded at 3:1-6.

At Ecbatana, capital of Media, Sarah, the daughter of Tobit's kinsman Raguel, is bereft over the death of four successive husbands, killed on their wedding night by the demon Asmodeus. Sarah also beseeches God to permit her to die and thus escape her plight (vv. 7-15).

God responds to the prayers of Tobit and Sarah, dispatching the angel Raphael (vv. 16-17). In the meantime, Tobit sends his son Tobias to Rages in Media where he has left funds in trust (3:1-2), instructing the lad in the ideals of the Yahwistic covenant (vv. 3-19). As encouraged by his father, Tobias enlists a traveling companion, Raphael (Heb. *rᵉpā'ēl* "God heals"), who disguised as their kinsman Azarias (from *ᶜazaryāhû* "Yahweh helps") serves as guide (ch. 5). En route the angel instructs Tobias in the magical healing properties of organs from a great fish he has caught (6:1-8) and informs him of his right—and duty—to marry the widowed Sarah, thereby maintaining her family's inheritance within the proper bounds of kinship (vv. 9-17). At Ecbatana the two are married (ch. 7), and on their wedding night Tobias uses the fish organs to rout the demon Asmodeus (ch. 8).

Having recovered Tobit's money (ch. 9), Tobias and Sarah return to the anxious Tobit and Anna at Nineveh (ch. 10). Tobias immediately heals his father (11:1-15), and the family celebrates the marriage (vv. 16-19). Raphael then reveals his true identity (ch. 12). Tobit's hymn of praise follows (ch. 13). Counseling his son and grandsons to flee Nineveh, which he believes will be destroyed as Jonah had prophesied, Tobit dies at an advanced age (ch. 14).

II. Origins

The text survives in two major, frequently divergent, recensions, the longer and presumably earlier represented in Codex Sinaiticus and the Old Latin version, the other in Vaticanus and Alexandrinus. Although some scholars contend that the work was composed in Greek at Alexandria, the Semitic character of its vocabulary and style and the discovery of Hebrew and Aramaic fragments at Qumran favor a Semitic original. Moreover, Jerome's preface indicates that he based his Vulgate rendering on a "Chaldean" text. Although some scholars argue for its composition at Jerusalem, the book most likely originated in the Diaspora, perhaps at Antioch or Babylon.

Tobit has been dated as early as the sixth century B.C. and as late as A.D. 70, but the majority of scholars favor an approximate date in the second century B.C.

III. Evaluation

The book of Tobit is classified generally as didactic fiction, in part because of the numerous folkloristic elements (e.g., the meddling demon-lover Asmodeus and the angel in disguise). Moreover, it makes little pretense of historical accuracy. For example, 1:2 sets Tobit's exile at the time of Shalmaneser III (858-824

B.C.; LXX Gk. *Enemessarus*; cf. v. 15, Sennacherib [705-681]; vv. 21-22, Esarhaddon [681-669]); v. 4 would make him a young man at the beginning of the divided monarchy (*ca.* 930).

Primarily intended to encourage Jews of the Diaspora, the book underscores the hope of divine providence (e.g., 3:16-17; 12:6-15; 14:5-7). Accordingly, it encourages the preservation of the Jewish community (cf. 4:12-13; 6:9-12, 15, 17), to no small extent through faithful adherence to the ethical stipulations of the historic covenant (e.g., 3:5-6; 4:7-11, 14-16; 14:9-11).

TOCHEN [tō'kən] (Heb. *tōken*). A Simeonite village, the site of which is unknown (1 Chr. 4:32).

TOGARMAH [tō gär'mə] (Heb. *tōgarmâ, tôgarmâ*). A son of Gomer and descendant of Japheth (Gen. 10:3 par. 1 Chr. 1:6). His name is related to that of the region of BETH-TOGARMAH.

TOHU [tō'hū] (Heb. *tōhû*). The son of Zuph and an ancestor of Samuel (1 Sam. 1:1). He is also known as Nahath (1 Chr. 6:26 [MT 11]) and Toah (v. 34 [MT 19]).

TOI [tō'ī] (Heb. *tō'î*). A king of Hamath who sent his son Joram with lavish gifts to congratulate David for defeating Hadadezer, the king of neighboring Zobah (2 Sam. 8:9-10; JB, NIV, "Tou"). At 1 Chr. 18:9-10 he is called Tou and his son Hadoram.

TOKHATH [tŏk'hăth] (Heb. K *tôqhaṭ*, Q *toqhaṭ*; LXX Gk. *Thekōe*). The father-in-law of the prophetess Huldah (2 Chr. 34:22; KJV "Tikvath"). He is called Tikvah (**1**) at 2 Kgs. 22:14.

TOLA [tō'lə] (Heb. *tôlāᶜ* "crimson").
1. The eldest son of Issachar (Gen. 46:13; 1 Chr. 7:1), whose descendants—heads of fathers' houses and warriors during the reign of King David (v. 2)— were called Tolaites (Heb. *tôlāᶜî*; Num. 26:23).
2. The son of Puah from the tribe of Issachar. A resident of the Ephraimite town of Shamir, he was a judge of Israel for twenty-three years (Judg. 10:1).

TOLAD [tō'lăd] (Heb. *tôlad*). A Simeonite city (1 Chr. 4:29). See ELTOLAD.

TOMB (Heb. *qeber*, *qᵉbûrâ*; Gk. *mnēmeíon, mnēma, táphos*).† A place of burial for the dead, often a natural cave or a chamber dug out for the purpose. Ancient tombs are well known, both from biblical and extrabiblical writings and from the excavation of thousands of tombs.

The literature accords great importance to the practice of proper burial. Of particular significance was the use of family tombs, attested as early as Abraham's purchase of the cave of Machpelah for his wife Sarah (Gen. 23); subsequently he himself and others in his family were buried there (25:9-10; 49:29-32). To be denied burial with one's family was a sign of great shame (1 Kgs. 13:22; Isa. 14:18-20; 2 Macc. 5:10). It was an honor to have a watch kept at one's grave at the time of burial (Job 21:32). In a culture that demanded that the body be buried on the day of death (Deut. 21:23; cf. Matt. 14:12; Acts 5:5-6, 10), the possession of a tomb already prepared to receive the body was very beneficial. In this light, the contribution of Joseph of Arimathea to the burial of Jesus (Matt. 27:57-60) was particularly significant.

The practice of tomb burial may well have influenced Israelite ideas about the nature of Sheol, the abode of the dead. Words describing tombs (e.g., under the earth, dark, dusty, silent, and stony) are also ascribed to Sheol (Gen. 37:35; Job 10:21-22; 17:13, 16; Ps. 94:17; Isa. 14:19; Ezek. 32:21, 27). Indeed, no absolute distinction between the two can be demonstrated, and Heb. *še'ôl* is often appropriately translated "grave" or "tomb."

By New Testament times some Jews believed that building upon and honoring the supposed graves of the prophets was an act of piety (Luke 11:47-48). Herod the Great thought that erecting an impressive monument at the supposed location of David's tomb would compensate for the valuables he had removed from within. Certain tombs also served as landmarks (cf. Gen. 35:20; 1 Sam. 10:2). Since ancient times a traditional site has been attested for David's tomb (Neh. 3:16; Acts 2:29); however, the tradition placing it on the southwestern hill of Jerusalem dates to after the tenth century A.D. and is probably not authentic. More likely, the tomb was located near the bottom of the southeastern hill of the City of David (1 Kgs. 2:10; cf. 2 Chr. 21:20; 24:25; 32:33).

More than one site has been identified as the tomb of Jesus. No location was noted until the fourth century when Bishop Macarius, searching by order of Emperor Constantine, identified Golgotha and Jesus' burial place with the site now occupied by the Church of the Holy Sepulchre. Excavations have shown that this structure stood outside the city walls of Jesus' day, thus overthrowing what was formerly the most serious objection to the authenticity of the site. Although no conclusive proof survives, this location is probably approximately correct. The primary rival to the Church of the Holy Sepulchre is the "Garden Tomb," a simple, rock-cut tomb in a quiet garden north of Jerusalem that gives a clear idea of what Jesus' tomb must have been like. However, as a great many tombs are located in the area, this one has no particular claim to authenticity.

See BURIAL.

TONGS. *See* SNUFFERS.

TONGUE (Heb. *lāšôn*; Gk. *glōssa*).† In biblical usage not only the physical organ (e.g., Ps. 22:15 [MT 16]; Mark 7:33), but also, by extension, the capacity for speaking (Exod. 4:10; Jas. 1:26; KJV, 1 John 3:18; RSV "speech"), different manners of speaking (Job 5:21; Prov. 6:24), and any language as distinguished from other languages (Rev. 5:9; KJV, Gen. 10:5). The KJV also translates Gk. *diálektos* "language" as "tongue" (Acts 1:19; 2:8; 21:40; 22:2; 26:14).

TONGUES.† The terms "speaking in tongues" and "glossolalia" both arise from Gk. *laleín hetérais*

glōssais "to speak in other tongues [i.e., languages]" (Acts 2:4) and similar forms used in the New Testament of miraculous ecstatic speech. Ecstatic speech and praise are common to many religions ancient and modern, and was present among the early prophets of Israel and surrounding nations (1 Sam. 10:5-6, 9-13; 1 Kgs. 18:29).

When the early Church first experienced glossolalia (Acts 2:4-11), it was heard as actual human languages not known to the speakers, but this may have been a miracle of hearing rather than of speaking (cf. vv. 6-8). Otherwise, glossolalia is not normally regarded in the New Testament as actual human language, but as speech directed to God and not intended to be understood by humans (1 Cor. 14:2). It may be, however, a sign given to human beings (here specifically "unbelievers") by the miraculous nature of the speech itself (vv. 21-22). Paul calls glossolalia "tongues of men and of angels" (13:1), the latter designation relating glossolalia to apocalyptic references to "angelic language," "the dialect of the archons," and the like (e.g., T.Job 48:2-3; 49:2; 50:2; cf. 52:7). Paul may also refer to the phenomenon as "sighs too deep for words" (Rom. 8:26).

Beyond ch. 2, references to glossolalia in Acts all concern new converts to Christianity whose speaking in tongues occurs as evidence that they have received the Holy Spirit (Acts 10:45-46; 19:6; cf. 8:14-19; Mark 16:17). In two of these incidents, glossolalia was necessary to demonstrate to the leaders of the Church that the expansion of the gospel into new areas was legitimate (to Samaritans, ch. 8; to Gentiles, 10:47). At Corinth the converts themselves are shown by the glossolalia that accompanies the coming of the Holy Spirit that what they have received goes beyond what they had previously experienced as followers of John the Baptist (19:1-6). Other conversions to Christian faith are recorded in Acts without any reference to glossolalia (e.g., 2:41-42; 4:4; 8:35-38; 9:3-18; 13:12, 43; 16:14-15, 31-33; 17:4, 12); however, all of these, with the exception of the record of Paul's conversion (9:3-18), are so brief that it is difficult to determine whether the author considered glossolalia as normative in Christian experience.

The church in Corinth placed a high value on glossolalia and regarded it as a spectacular evidence of the Spirit's presence. At their meetings large numbers, it appears, were involved in ecstatic speaking. Paul feared that the resulting scene would be needlessly offensive to outsiders (1 Cor. 14:23) and that it would stand in the way of what would be more upbuilding and instructive for both church members and outsiders (vv. 2-6, 12, 16-19, 23-25). He himself was glad that he was able to speak in tongues (v. 18) and wanted all the Corinthian Christians to do so as well (v. 5), but either in private devotions or with the aid of inspired interpretation (vv. 13-19, 28). Such "interpretation" was probably not translation but something closer to the explication of dreams or signs or an activity similar to prophecy. To regain the proper perspective, Paul set a limit of two or three glossalalic utterances in a meeting (v. 27). He also placed glossolalia within the larger context of the gifts of the Spirit (ch. 12) and sought to subordinate the exercise of all the gifts to the rule of love within the congregation (13:8; cf. 8:1), thus seeking to substitute a concern for the Church for a desire for spectacular display.

Bibliography. F. D. Goodman, *Speaking in Tongues: A Cross-Cultural Study of Glossalalia* (Chicago: 1972); W. E. Mills, *Speaking in Tongues* (Grand Rapids: 1986), esp. bibliography, pp. 493-528.

TOPAZ (Heb. *piṭᵉḏâ*; Gk. *topázion*). A mineral (a silicate of aluminum) that occurs in translucent or transparent prismatic, orthorhombic crystals of various colors, valued as a gemstone. At Exod. 28:17; 39:10 this gem is listed as the second stone in the first row of stones on the high priest's breastpiece (NJV "chrysolite"). Topaz is named at Ezek. 28:13 as one of the gems covering the king of Tyre and at Rev. 21:20 as the ninth foundation stone of the heavenly Jerusalem.

In 1900 Topaz was discovered in great quantities on an island in the Red Sea near the Egyptian coast; perhaps the Israelites took Topaz with them when they departed from Egypt. Job 28:19 mentions topaz from Ethiopia.

TOPHEL [tō'fəl] (Heb. *tōpel*). One of the places named in the description of the Transjordanian location of Moses' discourses (Deut. 1:1). It is sometimes identified with eṭ-Ṭafîleh, *ca.* 25 km. (15 mi.) south-southeast of the Dead Sea.

TOPHETH [tō'fĕth] (Heb. *tōpeṯ*). A place in the valley of Hinnom, probably near where that valley met the Kidron valley south of Jerusalem. Children were burned as sacrifices to Molech at Topheth (2 Kgs. 23:10; 2 Chr. 28:3; 33:6; Jer. 7:31; KJV "Tophet"). Jeremiah prophesied that Topheth would become a place of military defeat for the people of Judah (vv. 32-34; 19:6-7, 11-13). Because of its vile associations, the consonantal form of the place name (from Aram. *tepaṯ* "fire pit") was written with the vowels for *bōšeṯ* "shame" (cf. Molech from Heb. *meleḵ* "king").

Heb. *topteh* at Isa. 30:33 (perhaps "funeral pyre"; RSV "burning place") may be emended to *toptōh* "Tophet . . . for him" (cf. KJV). In any case, this verse clearly refers to Molech worship at Topheth.

TORAH (Heb. *tôrâ* "instruction, guidance, law").* A name ascribed to the first division of the Hebrew canon, the five books of Moses or the Pentateuch. In a more general sense, torah indicates the divine law or instruction to which Israel was to live as stipulated in the covenant. *See* LAW; PENTATEUCH.

TORCH (Heb. *lappîḏ*; Gk. *lampás*). A stick of resinous wood or bundle of tow ignited and carried to provide light. Placing their torches under jars enabled Gideon's three hundred men to make a surprise attack on the Midianite camp (Judg. 7:16-21; KJV "lamps"). The use of torches to destroy grain was a common military action (cf. Zech. 12:6). Samson tied torches to the tails of foxes to destroy the grain of the Philistines (Judg. 15:4-5; KJV "[fire]brands"), a tactic paralleled in other ancient accounts of the military use of animals. The practice was also employed to rid

fields of mildew, and was part of ancient religious rites intended to promote fertility, which the story of Samson may be intended to ridicule. Torches were also used in signalling (cf. Jer. 6:1).

Job 41:19 (MT 11), in describing spray reflecting sunlight, may refer to the use of hurled torches as weapons. Elsewhere, torches are descriptive of a glistening body (Dan. 10:6) or gleaming chariots (Nah. 2:4 [MT 5]). A flaming torch and a smoking fire pot represent God's presence in the performance of the covenant ritual between God and Abraham (Gen. 15:17). Salvation is depicted as a torch, the light of which stands out against the dark background of night (Isa. 62:1). In Ezekiel's throne chariot vision, torches in motion represent the unresting justice of God (Ezek. 1:13; cf. Rev. 4:5).

TOU [tō'ū] (Heb. *tō'û*). Alternate form of TOI (1 Chr. 18:9-10).

TOWER (Heb. *migdāl*; Gk. *pýrgos*).† In biblical references, primarily a part of the defensive wall systems of cities. Towers were constructed as part of the heavy city walls and stood out so that the walls could be defended from an advantageous position. Towers could be round (as are the neolithic tower at Jericho and the Hellenistic tower at Samaria), square (as at Megiddo and Hazor), or semi-circular (as at Arad).

Towers as part of the defensive structures of a city: a reconstruction of the Assyrian siege of Lachish as depicted in reliefs from the palace of Sennacherib (by courtesy of the Trustees of the British Museum)

They were placed at intervals around the city (20-25 m. [65-80 ft.] apart at Arad), at strategic junctures and vulnerable spots, and in front of gates (e.g., 2 Chr. 26:9; 32:5; Neh. 3:25-27).

Siege towers and siege mounds were temporary structures thrown up to aid in offensive warfare against walled cities (e.g., 2 Sam. 20:15; Isa. 23:13; Ezek. 4:2). Freestanding towers in advance positions independent of cities enabled sentries to observe movements of the enemy (2 Kgs. 18:8; 2 Chr. 20:24; 26:10; 27:4). Less prominent watchtowers were built in vineyards and fields to guard crops (Matt. 21:33).

"Tower" is used as a figure of speech for God as a source of strength and protection (Ps. 61:3 [MT 4]; Prov. 18:10). In the Song of Solomon it is a metaphor for striking beauty (Cant. 4:4; 7:4 [MT 5]; 8:10).

The word "tower" frequently appears as a component of names of actual towers (Neh. 3:1, 11; Jer. 31:38), of cities that grew up around watchtowers (Josh. 15:37, Migdal-gad; 19:38, Migdal-el), and of the parts of cities that stood on a higher elevation (Judg. 9:46, Tower of Shechem). Herod the Great fortified Jerusalem's prominent west entrance with three massive towers that he named after his wife Mariamne, brother Phasael, and friend Hippicus.

TOWN (Heb. *ʿîr*; Gk. *pólis*).* A relatively small settlement, presumably larger than the village but smaller than the city. Although occasionally distinguished from the village (Josh. 15:45, 47; Matt. 10:11; Luke 13:22; cf. 8:1; Matt. 9:35), precise classification is made difficult because of the town's designation by the same Hebrew and Greek terms elsewhere used for "village" or "city" (e.g., Heb. *ʿîr*; e.g., Judg. 17:8; KJV "city"; Gk. *pólis*; JB, NIV, Luke 2:4; RSV "city"; *kṓmē*; JB, NIV, John 7:42; RSV "village"). The RSV supplies the designation "town" at Josh. 17:8 (Tappuah). In some cases the term may simply indicate a settlement of any size (cf. Matt. 10:5).

Although little attention has yet been devoted to settlements of this type, archaeological evidence does suggest that the early Israelites were heavily concentrated in towns throughout the central Palestinian hill country. Sometimes fortified (1 Sam. 23:7; Prov. 8:3; cf. Heb. *šaʿar* "gate"; Deut. 14:28-29), the town may represent an intermediary stage in urbanization. Even during the Early Iron Age (twelfth-tenth centuries B.C.) the inhabitants remained primarily transhumants. When dependent on larger fortified cities, towns are referred to by the kinship term Heb. *baṭ* "daughter" (e.g., Josh. 15:45, 47; 1 Chr. 2:49; 7:28).

TOWN CLERK (Gk. *grammateús* "scribe").† At Ephesus the highest official of the city, responsible for executing the decrees of the civic assembly (Acts 19:35). As the highest official, he was also responsible to the Roman administration of the province of Asia, which was resident in the city, for what happened there. Accordingly, the town clerk at the time of Paul's visit sought to bring an end to the riot instigated by Demetrius and his fellow silversmiths in protest of Paul's negative influence on their business. The clerk reminded the crowd of the privileges that the city enjoyed and that could be removed by the Romans (vv. 35-36). Insisting that Paul and his coworkers had not

committed any crime against the local cult, he drew attention to the proper procedure for dealing with grievances and warned the people of the dangers facing the city from the Romans (vv. 37-40).

TRACHONITIS [trăk'ə nī'tĭs] (Gk. *Trachōnitis* "rough, uneven district"). A plateau of black basalt in northern Transjordan *ca.* 40 km. (25 mi.) south of Damascus, always sparsely populated and difficult to rule; modern Hauran. The ministry of John the Baptist is dated in part by a reference to the reign of "Philip tetrarch of the region of Ituraea and Trachonitis" (Luke 3:1). Philip's father, Herod the Great, was given Trachonitis by Augustus *ca.* 23 B.C. Philip governed the region until his death in A.D. 34. Herodian rule over Trachonitis continued with Herod Agrippa I (37-44) and II (53-100). In 106 it became part of the new Roman province of Arabia.

TRADE.† International trade is recorded from the earliest times in the Old Testament. The monetary standard followed by Abraham when he bought the field and cave of Machpelah was that of the traveling merchants (Heb. *sōḥēr*; Gen. 23:16). A caravan of north Arabian traders carrying gum, balm, and myrrh to Egypt were willing to buy Joseph for twenty silver shekels; they then sold the slave to an Egyptian royal official (37:25-36). The pre-Israelite inhabitants of Jericho received goods from Shinar (i.e., Babylon; Josh. 7:21; cf. Deut. 6:11). The right to trade in territory controlled by another was prized (cf. Gen. 34:10, 21; 42:34). Kingdoms could be built on taxes levied from traveling merchants (cf. 1 Kgs. 10:14-15; *rôḵēl*; Ezra 4:13, 20).

Coastal peoples, Philistines and especially Phoenicians, dominated Mediterranean sea trade during much of the period of the Old Testament (cf. "merchant, trader," a secondary meaning of *kᵉnaʿan*, *kᵉnaʿᵃnî* "Canaanite [i.e., 'Phoenician']"; e.g., Prov. 31:24; Ezek. 17:4; Zeph. 1:11; Zech. 11:11; 14:21) For the Phoenician cities in particular this interest in sea commerce stemmed largely from geographical necessity in order to obtain essential food items (cf. 1 Kgs. 5:10-11 [MT 24-25]). The Sabeans (the people of Sheba in southern Arabia) controlled the land trade routes of Arabia and brought wares from as far as India to the eastern Mediterranean. Their trade included spices, gold, gemstones, and incense (10:2, 10; Ps. 72:15; Isa. 60:6; Jer. 6:20; Ezek. 27:22; cf. Cant. 3:6). Cities in northern Arabia, including Tema, Dedan, and Ephah, also based their wealth on trade (Job 6:19; Isa. 21:13; Ezek. 27:20-22), as did Damascus in Syria (v. 18).

Trade was organized typically under royal control in the ancient Near East. King Solomon opened trade routes for Israel based in Ezion-geber at the opposite end of Palestine from Phoenicia, but he did so with Phoenician help (1 Kgs. 9:26-28) and mainly as the provider of a subordinate link between the Phoenicians and Arabia and Africa (10:22). Phoenicia continued to trade directly with Arabia (v. 11). A significant part of Solomon's provision for trade was the building of store-cities (9:19). The growth of trade under Solomon greatly enriched the royal house of Jerusalem (10:4-5, 14-21, 23, 25-29). While a variety of products from other places passed through Israel, its own exports were mainly agricultural (Gen. 43:11; 1 Kgs. 5:11 [MT 25]; Ezek. 27:17).

Except during Solomon's reign, Israel and Judah seldom engaged in sea trade (cf. 2 Chr. 20:36-37), although they continued to engage in land trade (cf. 1 Kgs. 20:34; 2 Kgs. 20:13). Judah later had reason to disdain Phoenician and Philistine trade when it drained off wealth from the southern kingdom and led to the enslavement of Judeans to Greeks (Joel 3:4-6 [MT 4:4-6]; the prophecy threatens that Phoenicians and Philistines will, in return, be sold by Judeans to Sabeans [v. 8]). Phoenician exploitation of Judah during the kingdom's waning days was the basis for Ezekiel's extended oracles against Tyre, a Phoenician city renowned for its wealth and its trading ships (Ezek. 26-28; cf. Isa. 23).

Forced internationalization because of exile led to wealth through trade for some Judeans living far from their homeland. Indeed, the growth of the Diaspora was encouraged by possibilities of such aggrandizement. In the Maccabean period and under Herod Jews were involved in trade from the coast of Palestine. Herod built a significant seaport at Caesarea Maritima. The Roman Empire's control of the Mediterranean Sea encouraged tremendous growth in sea trade. The ships on which ordinary passengers traveled were cargo vessels (cf. Acts 21:2-3; Gk. *gómos*; 27:10; *phortíon*). Grain bound mainly from Egypt for the major cities of the empire, especially Rome, constituted a major part of ships' cargoes (cf. 27:38). Conditions were often such in the empire that a person with money in hand could hope to make more by trade (cf. Matt. 25:16; *ergázomai*), but trade along land routes continued to be risky (cf. Luke 10:30).

Because of the concentration of international trade on luxury items for the rich, traders are often criticized in the Bible. The short-sighted secular outlook of the trader (Jas. 4:13-16) is linked with wealth that values luxuries over the lives of the poor (5:1-5; cf. Zeph. 1:10-13). Trade also involved profiteering in essential goods at the expense of the poor (Amos 8:4-6) and the presence of foreigners with their disregard of local religious customs (Neh. 13:15-22). Solomon, the king who encouraged foreign trade in Israel, was also the king who encouraged foreign cults in Jerusalem (2 Kgs. 23:13; cf. Isa. 2:6-8). Merchants (Gk. *émporoi*) dependent on the wealth of "Babylon" (i.e., Rome) weep over the fallen city in John's vision, while the "saints, apostles, and prophets" are called on to rejoice (Rev. 18:3, 11-20; cf. Isa. 30:6-7).

TRADITION.* The handing on of beliefs and practices from one generation to the next or from one group to a related group primarily by oral rather than written means. Because oral communication was more significant in biblical than in modern societies, oral tradition in the form of standardized forms of stories, sayings, and the like was part of the process toward the composition of nearly every type of biblical literature. Therefore, the understanding of the oral stages of the handing on of biblical material is a goal of much of the work of biblical scholarship. *See* BIBLICAL CRITICISM.

The reduction of multiple traditions to written form has differing effects on communities for whom traditions are significant. Of concern here are two sets of references to tradition that occur in the New Testament. Two Greek verbs are used to speak of tradition, *paradídōmi* (and the cognate noun *parádosis* "tradition") for the handing on of traditions and *paralambánō* for the receiving of traditions.

1. "The Traditions of the Elders"

The Gospels frequently refer to the tradition of the scribes and Pharisees (e.g., Matt. 15:3). While the Sadducees viewed the written text of the Torah as alone authoritative, the Pharisees cultivated an elaborate interpretive tradition as a way of dealing with the ambiguities and inexactness of God's commandments. The resultant "tradition of the elders" (or "oral Torah") was considered equal in authority to the written text elaborated by it. It represented simply the unfolding of what was implied in the written commandments, and was said to have been received by Moses from God on Mt. Sinai along with the written commandments and passed down orally from that time.

The prohibitions of work and of travel away from home on the Sabbath, for instance, required a definition of what activities constituted work and how great a distance took one away from home. The goal was to "build a fence around the Torah" (*Pirke Aboth* i.1), i.e., to erect a barrier of rules more exacting than the written law so as to prevent one from coming close to breaking the written commandments. The oral tradition might also, however, relax the written commandment by taking into account new circumstances such as the need to travel to a synagogue on the Sabbath. Eventually the vast tradition was collected and codified in the Mishnah. Ongoing interpretation and application of this authoritative text resulted in the Palestinian and Babylonian Talmuds.

Incidents recorded in the Gospels show Jesus disregarding the tradition and even attacking it in some specific cases. To some extent he demonstrates a characteristic Galilean indifference to ceremonial details. He spurned the traditional hand-washing rules (Mark 7:1-5), the twice-weekly fasts (2:18), and the traditional definitions of what was outlawed on the Sabbath (2:23-3:6; Luke 13:10-16; John 7:22-23). Jesus did not mean to break the Sabbath; rather, his point was that to meet human need on the Sabbath is not to break it. He assailed the Corban rule that allowed one to donate money to the temple instead of using it to support one's parents. In this case, Jesus charged, the tradition ironically had broken the Torah rather than protecting it from being broken (Mark 7:9-13).

Jesus did not totally reject the oral tradition. He affirmed the traditional rules on the tithing of herbs ("these you ought to have done, without neglecting the others"; Matt. 23:23), though he insisted on the relative triviality of the practice. His own interpretation of the Torah in the Sermon on the Mount employs the scribal principle of "building a fence about the Torah"—not simply by restricting external behavior more than the written law, but by pointing out that sinful interior urgings in themselves violate what the Torah seeks to control (5:21-22, 27-28, 38-39; "you have heard that it was said . . . but I say to you . . . ").

Paul's reflections on his life prior to his call by

Christ include the claim that he was "so extremely zealous ... for the traditions of the fathers" (i.e., the same traditional interpretations of the law of Moses), far more than others of his time (Gal. 1:14).

II. Early Church

Although a guarded attitude toward tradition was thus present in the early Church (cf. Gal. 1:11-12; Col. 2:8), the Church—like any other group of people with a common purpose—had its own traditions. Appeals to authoritative Church tradition are found already in the earliest New Testament writings, the letters of Paul. Occasionally explicit reference is made to some material as traditional, including a particular set of ethical instructions (2 Thess. 3:6), a set eucharistic formula (1 Cor. 11:23-26), and a standardized recital of the death, burial, resurrection, and postresurrection appearances of Christ (15:3-7). Also recorded are more generalized references to Church traditions (11:2; Phil. 4:9; 2 Thess. 2:15; cf. Rom. 6:17; Gal. 1:9). The growth of explicit reliance on tradition has, rightly or wrongly, been used to identify some books of the New Testament as originating after the time of the apostles (cf. Jude 3 and the "sure" sayings of the Pastorals; e.g., 1 Tim. 3:1; Titus 1:9).

Form critical examination of every book of the New Testament has made possible an understanding of the forms employed when the written material was being transmitted orally. This understanding goes far beyond the explicit references to tradition described above. The traditional forms were standardized, not by any authoritative Church body, but by the forms of expression that Jesus himself used in his teaching and by the teaching and worship of the Church as it responded to the Church's needs and experiences. Some of these forms are represented by the parables of Jesus, the miracle stories of the Gospels, creedal and confessional formulas (e.g., Rom. 1:3-4; 1 Tim. 3:16), and fragments of hymns (e.g., Phil. 2:6-11; Col. 1:15-20).

In the second-century Church both orthodox and Gnostic Christians appealed to apostolic traditions to validate their teachings. The Gnostic theologian Basilides claimed to have secret traditions stemming from Paul's interpreter Glaukias and from the apostle Matthias; Valentinus derived his teaching from Paul's disciple Theudas; Ptolemaeus also claimed to stand in unbroken succession from the apostles. What bishops such as Irenaeus regarded as the apostolic tradition eventually crystalized in summaries of Christian doctrine referred to as the rule of faith (e.g., the Apostles' Creed). The apostolic succession of bishops arose as a means to guarantee orthodox transmission and interpretation of the tradition, on the assumption that the first bishops had been appointed and catechized by the apostles themselves and could thus maintain the authentic teachings of the apostles (contrary to the claims of the Gnostics). Similarly, the New Testament writings were first valued not as inspired Scripture but as deposits of apostolic tradition in fixed written form, to be interpreted authoritatively by the bishops and according to the rule of faith.

III. Later Christianity

At the time of the Protestant Reformation Martin Luther determined that the tradition and its ecclesiastical interpretation had become corrupt, and that the only undiluted access to pure apostolic tradition lay in the New Testament canon. In response to this doctrine that Scripture alone was authoritative (*sola Scriptura*), which they (correctly) saw as unleashing unprecedented diversity in interpretation, the Roman Catholic Church at the Council of Trent (1546) defined Scripture and tradition as two distinct "fonts" of revelation having equal authority, with the Church's magisterium the infallible interpreter of both. More recently, Catholic theologians have regarded Scripture and tradition as a single authority (they "flow from the same divine wellspring"), noting with some historical justification that Scripture is itself a part and product of apostolic tradition.

Bibliography. F. F. Bruce, *Tradition Old and New* (Exeter: 1970); R. P. C. Hanson, *Tradition in the Early Church* (Philadelphia: 1962).

TRAJAN [trā′jən].† Marcus Ulpius Traianus, Roman emperor A.D. 98-117; also called Germanicus. Born in Spain, he was the first emperor from the provinces rather than Italy proper. In 97 he was adopted by the emperor Nerva, whom he succeeded.

Prior to becoming emperor Trajan had been a soldier and military tribune with service in Syria, Germany, and Spain. He conducted two campaigns in Dacia from 101-107, establishing a secure Roman province there (modern Romania). From 114-116 he captured most of the Parthian Empire, including Armenia and upper Mespootamia. Recalled from the Persian Gulf because of revolts by the Jews and newly conquered peoples (all ruthlessly suppressed; cf. Sib.Or. 12:147-163), Trajan died at Selinus in Cilicia and was succeeded by Hadrian.

In 111-112 Trajan sent Pliny the Younger to reorganize the province of Bithynia. Pliny's correspondence with Trajan included questions about the persecution of Christians, who were perceived as a disruptive influence in Asia Minor. It is difficult to determine Trajan's atttitude toward Christianity from his responses to Pliny, but he advised against summary execution of alleged Christians, requiring proof of the accusation and a public refusal to recant before permitting execution. He also discouraged active searches for Christians and outlawed anonymous accusations. Thus, Trajan permitted leniency, at least toward the less conspicuous practitioners of the proscribed religion.

TRANCE (Gk. *ékstasis*). In RSV and KJV usage, vision-experiences in which God speaks to a person— Peter at Joppa (Acts 10:10; 11:5) and Paul in the temple at Jerusalem (22:17), both as they are being called to take the gospel to Gentiles. In both acounts, the emphasis is not on the experience itself, but on its nature as revelation. Elsewhere the RSV renders the Greek term as "amazement" (Mark 5:42; Luke 5:26; Acts 3:10) and "astonishment" (Mark 16:8).

TRANSFIGURATION (Gk. verb *metamorphóō* "transform, change in form").† The event in which Jesus was "glorified" on a mountain in the presence of Peter, James, and John. This event is recorded in the Synoptic Gospels (Matt. 17:1-8; Mark 9:2-8; Luke 9:28-36), mentioned at 2 Pet. 1:16-18, and possibly alluded to at John 1:14.

The account begins with the initiative of Jesus as he leads the three disciples "apart by themselves." The appearance of Jesus' face and his garments is changed, becoming intensely white and shining "like the sun." In the midst of this glory, Jesus is seen talking with Moses and Elijah about his "departure, which he was to accomplish at Jerusalem" (Luke 9:31), i.e., his crucifixion, resurrection, and ascension. Peter suggests that tents be built for Jesus, Moses, and Elijah, apparently thinking to prolong the experience. As Peter speaks a cloud overshadows them, and a voice from heaven speaks with words reminiscent of those spoken at Jesus' baptism (Matt. 3:17 par.). After the disappearance of Moses and Elijah, the three disciples are enjoined to silence concerning the event.

The transfiguration was above all a revelation of God to Jesus' disciples of the true nature of Jesus. The dazzling appearance of Jesus points to his future glory. The appearance of Moses and Elijah demonstrates that Jesus and his mission fulfill the law (Moses) and the prophets (Elijah). The parallels between the transfiguration and Moses' receiving of the law on Sinai—the changed appearance (Exod. 34:29-35), the cloud on the mountain (24:15-16), and the use of the word *éxodos* "Exodus, departure" (Luke 24:31)—point to an intentional identification of Jesus as a second Moses. Other christological themes are present in the cloud and the voice. The cloud localizes the presence of God and the voice identifies Jesus as the royal son of God (Ps. 2:7), the servant who bears God's Spirit (Isa. 42:1), and the eschatological prophet sent by God (Deut. 18:15).

The transfiguration has been identified by some interpreters as a postresurrection appearance, inserted by the Evangelists into the time before the crucifixion. But Luke associates the transfiguration with the preceding and following accounts concerning the suffering of Jesus (Luke 9:22, 31), and all three Synoptics regard the event as one of a series that reveal the character of Jesus' messiahship. The transfiguration is recorded shortly after Peter's acknowledgement of Jesus as Messiah and Jesus' first prediction of his sufferings to come (Matt. 16:13-23 par.; cf. 17:1, "after six days"; Luke 9:28, "eight days"). The three events together marked a decisive transition point in Jesus' ministry, occurring soon before the beginning of his final journey to Jerusalem (v. 51).

Although the full meaning of the transfiguration remains difficult to fathom, it clearly declared the identity of Jesus as the Messiah and Son of God, and provided assurance for the disciples that the path Jesus had chosen was indeed that sanctioned by God. The dazzling appearance can be seen to point to his future glory, and the appearance of Moses and Elijah may well have been intended to demonstrate that Jesus and his mission fulfilled the law (Moses) and the prophets (Elijah). The cloud localizes the presence of God, and the voice affirms Jesus as the royal son (Ps. 2:7), the Suffering Servant (Isa. 42:1), and the prophet of God (cf. Deut. 18:15). In addition to christological themes, the account portrays Jesus, the mediator of the new covenant, as a second Moses (cf. Exod. 24:12-16; 34:29-35; 2 Cor. 3:7-18).

Tradition traced to the fourth century A.D. identifies the mountain of the transfiguration with Mt. Tabor; Tabor, however, is more than 70 km. (45 mi.) from Caesarea Philippi, where Jesus and his disciples were just before the transfiguration (Matt. 16:13; Mark 8:27). A more likely site is Mt. Hermon, a large mountain north of Caesarea Philippi, or one of its lower peaks.

TRANSGRESSION. *See* SIN.

TRANSJORDAN [trănz jör′dən]. The region east of the Rift valley (i.e., the Sea of Galilee, the Jordan river, and the Arabah) and west of the Syrian and north Arabian desert. Transjordan extends *ca.* 350 km. (220 mi.) from Mt. Hermon in the north to the area southeast of the Dead Sea. The Old Testament knows this region (from north to south, beginning southeast of the Sea of Galilee) as the lands of Bashan, Gilead, Ammon, Moab, and Edom.

I. Description

From most vantage points in the eastern part of Judea or Samaria, Transjordan appears as a wall of rock that towers over the Rift valley. It is an elevated plateau that has been shaped by the same geological forces and primeval seas that created the heartland of Israel. Ancient volcanic mountains in the north merge with massive folds in the granite platform of which all Arabia is made. Decomposed basalt and sedimentary soils make up the terrain, and these blend with the desert sandstone of the east. The ridge is punctuated with four transverse (east-west) clefts that are the result of geologic faulting in the area; these are, from north to south, the Yarmuk, Jabbok, Arnon, and Zered rivers. These gorges along with other minor ones have over time become conduits enabling rainfall to drain west, and today still contain seasonal rivers (wadis). The Yarmuk, for instance, carries as much water as the Jordan at their confluence. But above all, these clefts have served as natural boundaries within the region.

Precipitation in most of Transjordan is limited and is determined by the degree to which the terrain of Israel allows moisture from the Mediterranean to escape into the east. Thus, in the north the east-west valleys of Galilee permit considerable moisture into the elevated reaches of Bashan and Gilead (100-125 cm. [40-50 in.] per year), but Moab and Ammon, across from the lofty Judean and Samarian arch, obtain little (25-50 cm. [10-20 in.]). As a result, the north has been the land of the farmer while the south is inhabited by pastoralists (cf. Num. 32:1; 2 Kgs. 3:4). Arid Edom has been frequented by nomads, shepherds, and traders. In New Testament times the northern regions were intensely cultivated and grain was shipped from Ptolemais (Acco) throughout the Roman Empire. Gilead was densely forested and famous for its fragrant herbs (Jer. 8:22; 46:11).

II. Significance

Transjordan played a vital role in the history of Israel.

When the influence of the imperial powers in Egypt and Mesopotamia receded, Israel's prosperity had to be won among its neighbors. The eastern deserts could bring prosperity when controlled (as under David) or could be the source of considerable adversaries (such as Hadad and Rezin against Solomon; 1 Kgs. 11:14-25). In any event, the eastern kingdoms could not be ignored, for they looked west for expansion and viewed Israel and Judah as primary foes.

This tension first appears when the tribes of Israel enter Transjordan. Because the promised land could not be entered from the south at Kadesh-barnea, the Israelites traveled east across the Arabah, then north, crossing the Zered and Arnon valleys (Num. 21:10-13). Edom and Moab were crossed freely, but the Amorite king Sihon refused passage, declared war, and was defeated (vv. 21-30). Israel's continued interest in Transjordan is seen in the settlement there of the tribes of Gad and Reuben and half the tribe of Manasseh (ch. 32; Josh. 13:8-33). The land was not kept with ease, though, and enemies from the east—often desert peoples—had to be fought by judges such as Ehud (Judg. 3:12-30), Gideon (chs. 6–8), and Jephthah (10:6–12:7). It is a tribute to David's power that he could control the region and even conduct a census there (2 Sam. 24:5-6).

However, the dissolution of Solomon's unified reign signaled new opportunities for the rival powers of Transjordan. They were even invited into the conflicts between the two components of David and Solomon's kingdom when, e.g., Asa of Judah courted Ben-hadad of Damascus in order to gain leverage over the aggressive Baasha of Israel (1 Kgs. 15:16-21). The seriousness of this threat from the east is further seen at ch. 20 when a league of kings under the leadership of Ben-hadad of Syria launches a joint assault on Israel. The arrival of Assyrian and then Babylonian power in the Near East eliminated these local struggles. The fate of Transjordan's inhabitants was in the hands of foreigners.

In the Hellenistic period new settlements arose in the north where agriculture was possible. A league of Greek cities—the Decapolis—prospered under the privileges bestowed by Rome. Transjordan was controlled for the last time by Jewish leadership when Herod the Great obtained sweeping powers from Rome. At his death, his son Philip inherited Old Testament Bashan, now called Gaulanitis. Herod Antipas, the ruler of Galilee, was given central Transjordan, called "Perea."

TRAVELERS, VALLEY OF THE (Heb. *gê ha'ōḇᵉrîm*). A valley located generally "east of the Sea" (i.e., the Dead Sea) in Transjordan, to be given to Gog as a burial place (Ezek. 39:11). The MT reading could be an otherwise unknown name for some Transjordanian place often traversed by the traders common to the area, the name being used here because of its appropriateness to what the verse says—that the valley will no longer be available for travelers because of the great number of soldiers buried there.

However, Heb. *'ōḇᵉrîm* "travelers" should perhaps be emended to *'ᵃḇārîm*; "the mountain(s) of ABARIM" was a name for the highlands of Moab overlooking

the Dead Sea, and "the valley of Abarim" might have been a designation for the area immediately east and northeast of the Dead Sea.

TRAY. See SNUFFERS.

TREASURER (Heb., Aram. *gizbār*; Aram. *gᵉḏāḇaryā'*), **TREASURY** (Heb. *'ôṣār, gᵉnāzîm*; Gk. *gáza, gazophylakeíon, korbanás* [from Heb. *qorbān* "temple treasury"]).† Both royal and temple treasuries are mentioned in the Bible. A treasury, whether royal or sacred, could house a wide variety of materials, including silver, gold, precious stones, spices, documents, temple vessels and furniture, military equipment, and booty obtained in battle (Josh. 6:24; 2 Chr. 32:27; Isa. 39:2; 1 Macc. 14:49; cf. Ezra 5:17, "royal archives").

Named as individuals in charge of royal treasuries in the time of David are Azmaveth and Jonathan (7) (1 Chr. 27:25). (Shebna the "treasurer" [KJV, Isa. 22:15] was actually the majordomo of the royal household [RSV "steward"]). It is clear that the kings of Judah controlled the temple treasury of Jerusalem as well as their own royal treasuries. King Asa attempted to better his political and military situation by offering the silver and gold from both the royal and temple treasuries to Ben-hadad of Syria in exchange for an alliance (1 Kgs. 15:18-19). Hezekiah accumulated a vast amount of wealth that he stored in his treasuries (2 Chr. 32:27; Isa. 39:2), but was forced to take from both his own treasury and that of the temple to meet the tribute demands of the Assyrian king Sennacherib (2 Kgs. 18:13-15). Both Pharaoh and later Nebuchadrezzar of Babylonia carried off the royal and temple treasuries after having conquered Jerusalem (1 Kgs. 14:26; 2 Kgs. 24:13).

Haman offered to deposit ten thousand talents of silver in King Ahasuerus' treasuries as a bribe to allow the destruction of the Jews (Esth. 3:9; 4:7). Treasurers under Nebuchadrezzar (Dan. 3:2-3) and the Persian emperors (Ezra 1:8; 7:21; cf. 6:4) also are mentioned in the Old Testament. Acts 8:27 identifies the Ethiopian eunuch as the chief royal treasurer of his queen.

Long before the building of the temple, during the time of Joshua, portions of booty won in battle were placed in the "treasury of the Lord" (Josh. 6:19). In planning the temple, David made ample provision for storage of treasures (1 Chr. 28:11-12) and appointed supervisors of "the treasuries of the house of God" and "the treasuries of the dedicated gifts" (26:20, 26; cf. 29:8). After Solomon had built the temple, he brought into it the treasures that David had gathered (1 Kgs. 7:51; cf. 1 Chr. 26:27). A group of Levites supervised the temple treasuries of Jerusalem after the postexilic rebuilding of the temple (9:26-27).

Payments and contributions to the temple treasury of Jesus' day (Matt. 27:6; Mark 12:41-43) were placed in thirteen horn-shaped containers, seven designated for particular kinds of offerings and six for freewill offerings (Mishnah *Šeqal.* vi.5). The "treasury" in which Jesus taught (John 8:20) was probably an area in the Court of the Women near these collection receptacles.

Erastus, the city treasurer (Gk. *oikonómos*) of Corinth whose greetings are passed on to the Roman church (Rom. 16:23; KJV "chamberlain"), was probably the same person as an Erastus, "procurator of public buildings," mentioned in an inscription.

TREE (Heb. *'ēṣ*; Aram. *'îlān*; Gk. *déndron, xýlon*). Palestine enjoys a varied climate, soil, and elevation, all of which provide a suitable location for a large variety of trees. These included in biblical times acacia, almond, apple, cedar, cypress, fir, oak, palm, pine, plane, poplar, sycamore, tamarisk, terebinth, and willow trees. Palestine was then more afforested than now, especially in the hills. Soil erosion and clearing of land for agriculture and building have greatly reduced the number of trees.

Trees were used for food, building material, and shade. Lev. 19:23-25 forbids the eating of fruit from trees during the first four years after planting; wanton deforestation in time of war is also forbidden (Deut. 20:19-20).

Trees were sacred symbols in the ancient world. God appeared to Abraham in theophany at sacred groves (Gen. 12:6-7; 13:18; 18:1), and the patriarch thus planted trees at sacred sites (21:33). The Canaanite fertility goddess Asherah was symbolized by trees or treelike pillars. Worship among the trees was condemned by Israel's prophets because of associations with Canaanite religious practices (Deut. 12:2; Isa. 1:29; 57:5; Jer. 2:20; Ezek. 6:13; Hos. 4:12-13).

Trees are often mentioned in biblical parables, stories, and metaphors to represent people in general (Judg. 9:7-15; 2 Kgs. 14:9; Ezek. 20:47 [MT 21:3]), the people of God in particular (Isa. 10:18-19; Ezek. 17:22-24; Rom. 11:17-24), specific nations (Dan. 4:10-26 [MT 7-23]), might (Ezek. 31:3-14), longevity (Isa. 65:22), hope (Job 14:7-9; 19:10), and the wise person who follows the Lord (Ps. 1:3; Jer. 17:8). John the Baptist and Jesus refer to people's faith in terms of trees and their fruit (Matt. 3:10; 7:17-20; 12:33). Jesus compares the kingdom of God in its full manifestation to a mighty tree (13:32).

The tree of life (Gen. 2:9) was a symbol well known in the ancient Near East, depicted on seals, pottery, and reliefs and in literature. Loss of access to this tree as a result of sin (3:22-24) and the restoration of that privilege at the end of the present age (Rev. 2:7; 22:2, 14, 19; cf. 2 Esdr. 8:52; T.Levi 18:10-11) represent the loss and regaining of eternal life. At Prov. 3:18; 11:30; 13:12; 15:4 the "tree of life" is an expression for health and fulness of life. The "tree of the knowledge of good and evil" (Gen. 2:9, 17), also called "the tree . . . in the midst of the garden" (3:3) and simply "the tree" (vv. 6, 11-12) is, on the other hand, unique to Israel. The nature of the "knowledge" represented by this tree has been the subject of much discussion, with a number of solutions offered. It is certain, however, that this tree is present in the story of the fall first as the concrete object of God's commandment and of mankind's sin, so that the connection between the two is unmistakable (v. 17), and second as the representation of the unfortunate human experience of the potential for both good and evil in the universe (vv. 5, 22).

The instrument of Jesus' death is sometimes called a "tree" (Gk. *xýlon*) rather than a "cross" (*staurós*), explicitly recalling the form of execution indicated at Deut. 21:22-23 and thereby associating his death with a curse (Gal. 3:13; cf. Acts 5:30; 13:29; 1 Pet. 2:24).

See also FOREST and the entries on individual varieties of trees.

TRIBE (Heb. *šēbeṭ, maṭṭeh*).† The primary subdivision of Israelite society in the premonarchic period, regarded as the descendants of a common eponymous ancestor, Jacob/Israel (cf. Gen. 35:10-11), and his sons or grandsons (cf. Josh. 19:47). The Israelite tribes were autonomous (cf. the root meanings of the Hebrew terms, "staff, scepter," as symbols of authority) and self-sufficient. Comprised of "clans" (*mišpāḥâ*, more precisely protective associations of families) and "father's houses" (*bēṯ-'āḇ*), the tribes generally banded together only when confronted with a significant external (military) threat (e.g., Judg. 4–5, 6–8; cf. 12:1-6). The role of Israel's unique Yahwistic ideology generally is regarded as the essential factor binding the tribes together. *See* CONFEDERATION.

The Israelite tribes were territorial units of unequal size, as delineated both by their boundaries and by lists of towns (Josh. 13–21; cf. Judg. 1). They were primarily patrilocal (residence with male head of the lineage or father's house; e.g., Gen. 12:1, 4-5; 24:5-8, 58-61), patrilineal (succession and inheritance from father to son; e.g., Deut. 21:15-17; cf. Gen. 15:2; Num. 27:1-11), and endogamous (marriage restricted to members of the same social unit, intended primarily to preserve claim to that unit's property; e.g., ch. 36; Judg. 12:9; cf. Exod. 34:16).

The number, names, and ranking of tribes frequently differ, suggesting different phases of Israelite history. The standard (or ideal) number was twelve (e.g., Gen. 49; Num. 1, 26), but Judg. 5 (the Song of Deborah) lists only ten (including Machir plus two "offspring" of Joseph, Ephraim and Manasseh, listed separately; Judah, Simeon, and Levi are absent), Deut. 33 (the Blessing of Moses) has eleven (omitting Simeon), and the accounts at Gen. 46, 48 suggest thirteen (reckoning Ephraim and Manasseh separately). Levi is missing from the census lists at Num. 1, 26, and Simeon from Deut. 33 (cf. 27:12-13); here Ephraim and Manasseh are named separately. The order by which the tribes are named may reflect varying political importance or alignments. Indeed, the biblical account records the migration of Dan from their originally allotted territory (Josh. 19:47-48; Judg. 1:34-35; cf. 5:17), the development of two "half-tribes" of Manasseh on either side of the Jordan river (e.g., Deut. 32:33-42; Josh. 17:5-10), and the division of Joseph (17:14-18). Simeon appears to have been absorbed by Judah (19:1-9; Judg. 1:3), and other groups may have increased or decreased in status (e.g., Caleb, Dinah).

With the centralization of government under the monarchy, much of the tribes' autonomy was eroded (cf. David's military organization, 1 Chr. 27). Solomon's system of administrative districts (1 Kgs. 4:7-19) clearly was intended to eradicate tribal identity and function.

Interpreters have long differed regarding the distinction between social units and their ancestors, even to the point of denying the historicity of the patriarchs.

Critical scholars in particular often regard the biblical narrative as depicting in varying degree social and historical realities underlying Israelite society. Some sociological critics discount the role of kinship other than as a fictive means of bonding ethnically diverse social units (cf. Exod. 12:38; Num. 11:4; *see* GENEALOGY).

Bibliography. M. H. Fried, *The Notion of Tribe* (Menlo Park, Calif.: 1975); G. E. Mendenhall, *The Tenth Generation* (Baltimore: 1973), pp. 174-197; M. D. Sahlins, *Tribesmen* (Englewood Cliffs: 1968); E. R. Service, *Primitive Social Organization*, 2nd ed. (New York: 1971).

TRIBULATION (Heb. *ṣar, ṣārâ* "straits, distress"; Gk. *thlípsis*).* In the New Testament, the expected experience of those who believe the gospel and follow Jesus (Matt. 13:21 par.; 24:9; John 16:20-22, 33; Acts 14:22; Rev. 1:9; cf. 1 Thess. 3:3; RSV "afflictions").

Tribulation is also a typical motif in eschatological passages. It is the expected destiny of the unrighteous (Rom. 2:9; Rev. 2:22; cf. 2 Thess. 1:6-7). The background for this notion is the affliction expected in the Old Testament as punishment of the sins of God's people (e.g., Deut. 4:30). The righteous are to be preserved through the eschatological destruction of the earth, which will occur as punishment for sin (Rev. 7:14; cf. Dan. 12:1; RSV "a time of trouble"; 1 Pet. 4:7, 12-18). Jesus also spoke of tribulation as a prelude to the eschatological events rather than as a part thereof; the war of A.D. 66-70 and the destruction of the temple (Matt. 24:15-22 par.) are identified as "tribulation" (v. 21 par.) that will precede the eschatological events (vv. 29-31). Some exegetes thus regard "the Great Tribulation" as a distinct period of unprecedented suffering, catastrophe, and persecution that will occur immediately preceding the eschatological deliverance of God and the final coming of Christ.

TRIBUNAL (Gk. *bḗma*).* A public platform where in cities of the Roman Empire civil cases were heard; often a designation for the court official who pronounced the judgment (cf. "the bench" in English usage). It was in such a setting that Paul was brought before the proconsul Gallio at Corinth (Acts 18:12-17; KJV "judgment seat") and Porcius Festus at Caesarea (25:6-21). *See* JUDGMENT SEAT.

TRIBUTE (Heb. *minḥâ, mekes, ʿōneš, maśśāʾ*; Aram. *middâ*; Gk. *kḗnsos, phóros*).† Large payments in money or in kind demanded by a victorious nation in order to impoverish the citizens of a conquered nation, thereby keeping them subservient, and to raise revenue.

Among the small nations of the Near East, tribute was a recurring problem. The people of Israel paid tribute to Moab soon after their settlement in the land of Canaan (Judg. 3:15-18). Much later, however, during the reigns of David and Solomon, David received tribute from Moab (2 Sam. 8:2) and Syria (v. 6). Solomon received tribute from "all the kingdoms from the Euphrates to the land of the Philistines and to the border of Egypt" (1 Kgs. 4:21 [MT 5:1]; cf. Ps. 72:10). Following the division of Israel and Judah, kings of Judah collected tribute from the Philistines, Arabs, and Ammonites (2 Chr. 17:11; 26:8). Hezekiah was

Tribute-bearers depicted in a relief at Persepolis (L. T. Geraty)

given a "present" by the emissaries of Merodachbaladan of Babylon (2 Kgs. 20:12), probably to win Judah, the smaller of the two nations, over to revolt against Assyria. The kingdom of Israel was often forced to pay tribute. King Hoshea's refusal to pay the annual tribute to Assyria brought the kingdom to an end (17:3-6).

See TAX.

TRIGON [trī'gŏn] (Aram. *śabbᵉḵāʾ, sabbᵉḵāʾ*).* A kind of harp or lyre, perhaps triangular in shape and having four strings, mentioned with other musical instruments at Dan. 3:5, 7, 10, 15 (so RSV, JB; KJV "sackbut"; NIV "lyre"; LXX Gk. *sambýkē*).

TRINITY (from Lat. *trinitas*).† An expression for the revelation of the one God (Deut. 6:4) in three "persons," Father, Son, and Holy Spirit. The doctrine of the trinity is a theoretical model intended to systematize various expressions in the Bible. The basis in Scripture on which it was built can be summarized as follows: there is only one God; each of the three divine persons is recognized to be God; God's self-revelation recognizes distinctions among these three persons in that there are interactions among them; and these distinctions are not just a matter of revelation (as received by humans) but are also eternally immanent in the Godhead.

I. Old Testament Roots

The doctrine of the trinity has been related to various aspects of the Old Testament revelation, the most important being possible indications of plurality within the Godhead and indications of the deity and distinctness of the Spirit of God and of the Messiah. The support of all these aspects of the Old Testament revelation for the Christian doctrine of the trinity have been exaggerated, especially what have been taken as indications of plurality in the Godhead. The "us" in "Let us make man in our image" (Gen. 1:26; cf. 3:22; 11:6-7) refers to the "sons of God" or lesser "gods" mentioned elsewhere (6:1-4; Job 1:6; Ps. 29:1), here viewed as a heavenly council centered around the one God (cf. Ps. 82:1). In later usage these probably would be called "angels."

The Holy Spirit of Christian belief began as the Old

Testament "Spirit of the Lord," but the latter is pictured as essentially equivalent to the power of Yahweh that comes upon, seizes, or falls on certain individuals for special tasks (e.g., Exod. 31:3; Num. 11:17, 25; Judg. 3:10; 6:34; 11:29; 14:6; 1 Sam. 10:10; 16:13). The figure of Wisdom at Prov. 8 is a poetic personification, holding up God's wise craftsmanship in creation as an example for mortals to follow, but it contributed to the later development of the doctrine of the trinity. Many "messianic" texts referred originally to the newborn or newly crowned king of Judah in terms derived from Canaanite royal ideology praising the king as a demigod (e.g., Ps. 2:7; 45:6 [MT 7]; Isa. 9:6 [MT 5]; Jer. 23:5-6). Such borrowing in Judah's case was hyperbole. The appearances of the "angel of the Lord" are sometimes taken as "christophanies" foreshadowing the incarnation. In these incidents (e.g., Gen. 16:7, 13; ch. 18; Judg. 6:11, 22-23; 13:3, 22) God has for a moment taken on a human appearance, but not always an entirely human form (note the implication that the angel does not eat; 6:19-21; 13:16; cf. Gen. 18:8; Tob. 12:19; see also Luke 24:39-43).

II. New Testament Roots

The beginnings of trinitarian thought arose from New Testament speculation about Jesus Christ. Some strands of New Testament tradition associate Jesus' attainment of divine sonship with his resurrection (Acts 13:33; Rom. 1:4; cf. Acts 2:32-36). Others stress his miraculous birth; like Adam, he had no human father (Luke 1:35; 3:38). Jesus' sonship began to imply full divinity when "Son of God" was interpreted in the categories of Jewish wisdom speculation. The personification of Wisdom at Prov. 8 had long been the object of speculation similar to the Logos doctrine of Heraclitus and the Stoics. In such works as the Wisdom of Solomon and the writings of Philo Judaeus, Wisdom (or the Word) had indeed become a distinct, quasi-personal aspect of the Godhead. Philo even called the Word/Wisdom God's "firstborn son" (De conf. ling. 62-63). Jesus is interpreted in these categories at Luke 11:49 (cf. Matt. 23:34; compare also 11:28-30 with Sir. 6:18, 24-30); Col. 1:15-19; Heb. 1:2-3 (cf. Wis. 7:24-26).

The second major New Testament source of trinitarian doctrine is the reinterpretation of the Spirit as the Spirit of Christ. Acts 16:6-7 suggests a close linkage, perhaps verging on an outright identification, of the exalted Christ with the Spirit (cf. v. 10). Paul often says the same things now of Christ, now of the Spirit. The Spirit within seems indistinguishable from Christ within. The Spirit is "the Spirit of his Son" (Gal. 4:6). Paul seems to understand the Spirit as the mode whereby the exalted Lord is present on earth with his people, rather than as a person distinct from Christ. Triadic formulas in the New Testament are often regarded as implying a developed doctrine of the trinity, but this is to read too much into them. 1 Cor. 12:4-6; 2 Cor. 13:14 are implicitly subordinationist since they use the formula "Lord (i.e., Christ)-Spirit-God," differentiating the first two from God. Nonetheless, such formulas may indeed embody what might be called "prototrinitarian" thought patterns. This is especially true of Matt. 28:19, a baptismal formula invoking Father (not simply God), Son, and Holy Spirit.

The strongest attempt in the New Testament to deal with the questions implied in the linking of Jesus Christ with the Word and the Spirit may be found in the Johannine writings. Jesus' farewell discourse (John 14–16) depicts a complex interplay between the Father and the Son, each of whom is "in" the other (14:10), and between the Son and the "Comforter" (Gk. paráklētos; RSV "Counselor"), the latter being both the Spirit (vv. 16-17) and the presence of Jesus himself (vv. 18-19). 1 John 5:7 in the Textus Receptus (represented in the KJV) makes it appear that John had arrived at the doctrine of the trinity in explicit form ("the Father, the Word, and the Holy Ghost"), but this text is clearly an interpolation since no genuine Greek manuscript contains it.

Also of importance in the development of the doctrine of the trinity are indications of interaction (and therefore distinction) among the persons of the trinity, most specifically Jesus and "the Father" to whom he prayed (e.g., Matt. 26:39).

III. Early Church

Creedal developments in the Church reflected growing recognition of the importance of the existence of God in three persons, first by the trinitarian form of early creeds, some as early as the second century, which developed into the Apostles' Creed. A second development is seen in the creeds of the ecumenical councils of Nicea (325) and Constantinople (381), which sought to state christological and trinitarian doctrines in such a way as to achieve as much clarity as possible and to guard against the less than adequate ideas put forward by some. The heart of the trinitarian doctrine of the councils was the statement that the persons of the trinity are of the same essence but distinct in their offices.

Irenaeus of Lyons, at the end of the second century, put forth the doctrine of "economic trinitarianism," whereby the Spirit and the Word were first differentiated from the Father at creation (cf. Ps. 33:6). In the fourth century Marcellus of Ancyra would further develop this view in terms of successive economies or dispensations of activity by the Word (here identified with the Spirit): first in the creation, second in the incarnation, and third in the outpouring of the Spirit at Pentecost. At the second coming of Christ the Word will once again be absorbed into God, "that God may be all in all" (KJV, 1 Cor. 15:28).

In the early third century Tertullian introduced the expression "three persons, one essence," meaning by "persons" (Lat. personae) "faces" or "masks." Later in that century Sabellius developed from Tertullian's rather imprecise terminology the alternative doctrine of modalism (also called Patripassianism [lit. "the Father suffers"] or Theopascism ["God suffers"]). According to Sabellius, Father, Son, and Spirit are three transitory modes in which God manifests himself (cf. the popular analogy of the three persons to water, ice, and steam), not three distinct entities in the Godhead.

In the fourth century the three Cappadocian Fathers Gregory of Nyssa, Gregory of Nazianzus, and Basil of Caesarea experimented with Tertullian's schema, substituting the Greek term *hypóstasis*: "three substances, one essence," implying three individual existences sharing one essence. In the eleventh century the nominalist Roscellinus took a tritheist position, arguing that to speak in this way of a divine essence shared by three distinct individuals was in fact to speak of three (incarnate) Gods, just as Peter, James, and John as three individual existences who share one human nature are three different persons (cf. the popular analogy of Father, Son, and Spirit as three bulbs emitting the same light).

Again in the fourth century Augustine of Hippo sought to explain the trinity in terms of relations within a person or between persons. He pictured the trinity as analogous to memory, intellect, and will within a single mind, and to the triad of the lover, the beloved, and their love.

Bibliography. L. Hodgson, *The Doctrine of the Trinity* (New York: 1944); K. Rahner, *The Trinity* (New York: 1970); A. W. Wainwright, *The Trinity in the New Testament* (London: 1962).

TRIPOLIS [trĭp'ə lĭs] (Gk. *Tripolis* "three cities").† A port city on the Phoenician coast, modern Ṭarâbulus el-Šām ("Tripoli of the North," to distinguish it from the Libyan city) located on the el-Mina peninsula *ca.* 70 km. (43 mi.) northeast of Beirut. Probably founded in the seventh century B.C., Tripolis was colonized as the capital of the Phoenician federation of Sidon, Tyre, and Aradus, each faction occupying a district in the city (hence its name). It continued to flourish under the Seleucids and the Romans. In 161 B.C. Demetrius I Soter (who was to be Seleucid emperor, 162-150) escaped from Rome where he had been an official hostage since 176, entered Syria through Tripolis (2 Macc. 14:1; referred to only as an unnamed "city by the sea" in the parallel 1 Macc. 7:1), and overthrew his young cousin Antiochus V Eupator and the regent Lysias.

TROAS [trō'ăs] (Gk. *Trōas*). A port city on the Aegean Sea in northwest Asia Minor *ca.* 25 km. (15 mi.) south-southwest of ancient Troy (Ilium), from which the name is apparently derived. Founded after the death of Alexander the Great by his successor Antigonus (*ca.* 310 B.C.), who named it Antigonia, the city was renamed Alexandreia Troas (Gk. *Alexandreia hē Trōas*) by Lysimachus in honor of the Macedonian conqueror. It became a Roman colony in the time of Augustus and was an important city throughout the period of the Roman Empire.

It was at Troas that Paul had a vision that prompted him to preach the gospel in Macedonia and to terminate his missionary activities in Asia Minor (Acts 16:8-10); Luke may have joined Paul there—one of the "we" passages of Acts begins at v. 10. When Paul was again in Troas he found an "open door" there for the gospel, but he went back to Macedonia, hoping to get news from Titus about the situation in the church of Corinth (2 Cor. 2:12). When his work in Macedonia had been completed, Paul spent seven days in Troas before continuing his final journey to Jerusalem (Acts 20:5-12). At that time or later he may have left his

cloak, books, and parchments at Troas (2 Tim. 4:13).

TROGYLLIUM [trō jĭl'ĭ əm] (Gk. *Trōgyllion*). A promontory of Mt. Mycale, a peninsula on the coast of Asia Minor extending toward the island of Samos. According to the Western text of Acts 20:15, the ship carrying Paul's party reached the island of Samos, where navigational problems in the narrow strait between the island and the promontory compelled the crew to remain at Trogyllium before leaving for Miletus the next day (so KJV, RSV mg.).

TROPHIMUS [trŏf'ə məs] (Gk. *Trophimos* "nutritious"). An Ephesian, one of two Gentile Christians from the province of Asia who accompanied Paul from Troas to Jerusalem with the relief money collected for the Jerusalem Christians from the Gentile Christians of Greece, Macedonia, and Asia Minor (Acts 20:4-6). Trophimus' presence in Jerusalem led some Jewish pilgrims from Asia to conclude that Paul had taken him into part of the temple complex where Gentiles were not allowed. Their accusation caused a riot that led to Paul's arrest (21:27-33). That Paul later left Trophimus ill at Miletus (2 Tim. 4:20) may be taken as evidence that Paul was released from the Roman imprisonment mentioned at the end of Acts and carried on further missionary activity in the East with Trophimus as one of his coworkers.

TRUMPET.† In English translations, a term encompassing both metal trumpets (Heb. *ḥªṣōṣᵉrâ*) and rams' horns (Heb. *šōpār, yôbēl*). Both trumpets and horns are represented by Gk. *sálpinx*.

Trumpets and horns were used mainly to give signals, such as the call to battle (Judg. 3:27; 7:19; 2 Chr. 13:12; 1 Cor. 14:8; RSV "bugle"), the calls to assemble and to break camp (Num. 10:2), and the alarm given at the approach of danger (Neh. 4:18, 20 [MT 12, 14]; Jer. 6:1; Ezek. 33:3-6). In eschatological texts as well the trumpet is mentioned as a signaling instrument (Matt. 24:31; 1 Cor. 15:52; 1 Thess. 4:16).

In ritual and ceremonies trumpets and horns were used, again mainly to give signals. They were used to announce the beginning of the Year of Jubilee (Lev. 25:9) and the Feast of Trumpets (23:24), at the enthronement of rulers (2 Sam. 15:10), and during special worship occasions (1 Chr. 15:28; 2 Chr. 15:14; Ps. 47:5 [MT 6]; 98:6; 150:3), including the New Moon (81:3 [MT 4]). Priests were appointed to sound the trumpets in worship (1 Chr. 16:6; 2 Chr. 5:12; 7:6; Ezra 3:10; Neh. 12:35, 41). The ritual significance of the ram's horn shofar (e.g., 2 Sam. 6:15; 2 Chr. 15:14) was such that it alone of Old Testament musical instruments has survived in Jewish religious ceremony.

Jesus refers metaphorically to almsgiving that calls attention to itself when he speaks of those who "sound a trumpet" before themselves (Matt. 6:2).

TRUMPETS, FEAST OF. The "day of blowing the trumpets" (Heb. *yôm tᵉrû'â*; Num. 29:1) or "memorial of blowing the trumpets" (*zikrôn tᵉrû'â*; Lev. 23:24), which fell on the first day (the new moon) of the seventh month, Tishri (Sept./-Oct.). Announced by the sound of trumpets, all work ceased on that day and a holy convocation was held. Additional sacrifices were offered (Num. 29:2-6), which shows that the occasion had particular significance, perhaps because it stood at the beginning of the month in which the solemn observances of the Day of Atonement and the Feast of Booths were celebrated.

The celebration of the first of Tishri as the beginning of the new year (*rō'š haššānâ*) is certain only in postbiblical Judaism, in which the sound of the ram's horn (*šôpār*) and the themes of judgment, God's kingship, and creation are linked closely to the approaching Day of Atonement. In the Bible Heb. *rō'š haššānâ* appears only at Ezek. 40:1, where it refers to the time of the year (RSV "beginning of the year") but not to a specific day observed with religious ceremonial.

TRUTH.†

I. Old Testament

Heb. *'ĕmet*, usually translated "truth," is related to the verb *'āman* "support, sustain, establish," to the noun *'ĕmûnâ* "firmness, faithfulness," and to *'āmen* "truly," the source of the exclamation "Amen!" Although truth seems to have been a property of things, it was also used in the Old Testament to characterize God and persons. God is referred to as "the God of truth" (e.g., Isa. 65:16; KJV, Deut. 32:4). The force of the term is not so much that Israel's God is the "true God" in contrast to false gods, but that Yahweh is steadfast and unwavering, a God who can be trusted (hence RSV's translation "faithfulness" in some instances). This is underscored by the fact that God's "truth" is frequently mentioned with his "faithful covenant love" (*ḥesed*), emphasizing God's dependability, trustworthiness, and consistency (e.g., Gen. 32:10; Ps. 25:10; 26:3; 40:11 [MT 12]). God's nature and will remain unchanged by circumstances despite the fact that God chooses to reveal himself through them.

For this reason, God's commandments are not arbitrary, but firm and unwavering; they possess *'ĕmet* (Neh. 9:13; RSV "true laws"). Therefore the Old Testament standard of justice is not found in abstract sociological or ethical concepts, but in the manner in which God deals with the world and persons, which is to be reflected in the world that God has created. Therefore, the ruler as God's representative must demonstrate *'ĕmet* (Ps. 45:4 [MT 5]; cf. Zech. 7:9), which is not so much "truth" (RSV) but consistent and reliable adherence to the standards of the law. Similarly, Israel is to abide "consistently" or "faithfully" by the covenant obligations (1 Sam. 12:24; 1 Kgs. 2:4; 2 Kgs. 20:3). Such faithfulness includes not only the corporate aspect of Israel, the nation, but individual adherence as well. It is a process that encompasses the whole of a person's moral and religious life, both thoughts and desires, cognitive as well as affective. God desires "truth in the inward being" (Ps. 51:6 [MT 8]; cf. 15:2; Isa. 59:14-15).

II. New Testament

In the past interpreters related the New Testament understanding of truth (Gk. *alḗtheia*) to Platonic notions of a supreme idea of truth that can only be reflected in earthly reality. However, neither the Old nor the New Testament contains such an idea of a neutral or inactive truth. The New Testament "way of truth" (2 Pet. 2:2) recalls Ps. 119:30 in speaking primarily of the conduct that should characterize those who have been redeemed. The clause "the truth that you have" (2 Pet. 1:12) refers not to doctrines, but to redeeming actions of God that have been experienced. Similarly, "true grace" (1 Pet. 5:12) refers not to a grace expressed in truthful propositions, but to the reality of God's grace experienced even through the turmoil of persecution and oppression (cf. Jas. 1:18; 3:14; 5:19-20).

Gk. *amḗn*, the transliteration of Heb. *'āmen*, and *alēthṓs*, the Greek translation of the same word (both most often rendered "truly" or "verily"), are frequently used in the New Testament, particularly to introduce words of Jesus (e.g., Luke 21:3; John 3:3). This introduction emphasizes that the statement which follows is beyond doubt. Similar affirmations are made to characterize the Christian witness as "true" (e.g., 5:31-32; 8:13-14; Titus 1:13). The gospel itself is the preaching of truth (Gal. 2:5; Col. 1:5-6; 2 Tim. 2:15; Jas. 1:18), which must therefore be obeyed (Gal. 5:7).

At Rom. 1:25 Paul speaks of the Gentile world as having "exchanged the truth about God for a lie." Here "truth" seems to be that which is hidden behind appearances yet can be apprehended by the mind (cf. v. 20). The "truth about God" is not a propositional truth to be contrasted with the "lie" of "worshiping and serving the creature rather than the Creator," but is the true nature of God, which is wrongly interpreted by idolators. In Paul's understanding, hidden aspects of God's dealings with humankind came to light in Christ (16:25-26; 2 Cor. 4:6; cf. 11:10). Thus, the truth in Jesus is God's redemptive work realized in Christ (Eph. 4:21). Indeed, the truth of the gospel of Christ is not only a message, but also a process whereby Christ and the Church are making manifest God's redemption to humankind (2 Cor. 4:2; 2 Thess. 2:12-13).

The concept of truth is prominent in the Johannine writings. John emphasizes that God is true, i.e., reliable in his witness through Jesus whom he has sent (John 3:33; 7:28; 8:26, 40; 17:3; 18:37; 1 John 5:20). Because God's redeeming plan has become actuality in the coming of Jesus, Jesus is "the true light" (John 1:9), "the true bread" (6:32), and "the true vine" (15:1), i.e., the source of the life that comes through God's redemption of mankind. For John Jesus is more than the proclaimer of truth, though he is that (8:40; 18:37)—he is the truth itself (1:14, 17; 14:6). Jesus promises that his work will be continued by the "Spirit of truth" (vv. 16-17; 15:26; cf. 1 John 4:6; 5:7). True Christian life is lived by people who have the truth in them, in that they admit their wrongdoing (1:6, 8; cf. John 3:21)—people made free by their knowledge of the truth (8:32),who have become "true" (or better "genuine") worshippers of God (4:23). Pilate's question "What is truth?" (18:38), which he probably conceived in abstract terms, thus has an ironic ring because the governor is in the position of judging the one who is truth itself and who calls each person to an existential decision regarding the truth.

Bibliography. G. Quell, G. Kittel, and R. Bultmann, "ἀλήθεια," *TDNT* 1 (1964): 232-251.

TRUTH, GOSPEL OF.* Perhaps the best-written and most sublime of all the writings in the ancient library discovered at Nag Hammadi, and one of the clearest surviving statements of Christian Gnosticism. The work was composed in Greek during the middle to late second century A.D. and is perhaps from the Valentinian sect. It is possible but by no means certain that the Gospel of Truth is the writing of the same title condemned by Irenaeus (*Adv. haer.* iii.11.9).

The Gospel of Truth is not a gospel in the New Testament sense of a narrative of the life, work, and sayings of Jesus, though it does show knowledge of much of the New Testament. Nor does it follow the Gnostic "gospel" form of a revelatory dialogue between Jesus and his disciples. The writing is focused on the person and work of Christ, referring to him with many titles, particularly "Word." However, the ultimate concern of this meditation is not Christ. He is indeed the vehicle of revelation, but salvation does not come through him. He brings knowledge, but it is up to each individual to appropriate it and to awaken from the nightmare of ignorance to full self-knowledge, knowledge of one's own divine origin and destiny.

TRYPHAENA [trī fē′nə] (Gk. *Tryphaina* "dainty"). A Christian woman in Rome to whom, along with TRYPHOSA, Paul sends his greetings (Rom. 16:12).

TRYPHO [trī′fō] (Gk. *Tryphōn*).* A general of the Seleucid king Alexander Balas and rebel against the next king, Demetrius II. Trypho (KJV "Tryphon") claimed the throne of Syria for Balas' son Antiochus VI and later for himself (142-138 B.C.). His actual name was Diodotus; "Trypho" was probably an epithet ("Magnificent," "Luxurious").

Trypho gained custody of the young boy Antiochus and proclaimed him king, having won the support of the troops Demetrius II had dismissed earlier (1 Macc. 11:38-40, 54-56). He also gained the support of the Hasmonean leaders of Judea, confirming Jonathan's hold on the high priesthood and on parts of Samaria, and appointing Jonathan's brother Simon governor over the coastal plain from the Ladder of Tyre to the Egyptian border (vv. 57-59; Josephus *Ant.* xiii.5.4 [145-47]). When Jonathan's military strength proved dangerous (1 Macc. 11:67-74), Trypho plotted to eliminate both Jonathan and the boy king (12:39-40). Seeing that he could not defeat Jonathan's large force at Beth-shan, he lured Jonathan to Ptolemais with promises and had him imprisoned (vv. 40-48). Trypho then set out to invade Judea. Taking his prisoner Jonathan with him (13:12), he was met by Simon who was compelled to agree to Trypho's demands for money and hostages (Jonathan's two sons) in return for the high priest's release. But Trypho had Jonathan put to death, though he was prevented from sending his troops to break the siege of the Akra in Jerusalem because of a heavy snowfall (vv. 13-24).

Trypho had young Antiochus killed (vv. 31-32; *Ant.* xiii.7.1 [218-19]) and assumed the Seleucid throne himself for some three years (*ca.* 142-138 B.C.). The Jews deserted his tyrannical regime and renewed their support of Demetrius II in return for the virtual independence of Judea (1 Macc. 13:34-42). After the

Parthians had captured Demetrius II *ca.* 140-139 (14:2-3), his brother Antiochus VII landed at Seleucia and seized the throne (15:10), pursuing Trypho from Dor through Ptolemais and Orthosia (vv. 11-14, 25, 37-39). Trypho perished in the region of Apameia— by his own hand according to Strabo xiv.5.2.

TRYPHOSA [trī fō′sə] (Gk. *Tryphōsa* "delicate"). A Christian woman in Rome to whom Paul sends his greetings (Rom. 16:12). Some scholars suggest that she and TRYPHAENA were sisters, perhaps twins.

TUBAL [tōō′bəl] (Heb. *ṭûbāl, ṭûḇāl*). One of Japheth's sons (Gen. 10:2; 1 Chr. 1:5). The name also designates a people regarded as his descendants (Ezek. 33:26), very likely the Tibarenoi (Akk. *Tabal*) who dwelled southeast of the Black Sea. Except at Isa. 66:19, Tubal is always mentioned together with Meshech, another people living in the same general region. At Ezek. 27:13 they appear as traders supplying slaves and bronze vessels to Tyre, and at 38:2-3; 39:1 as peoples subordinate to "Gog, of the land of Magog." It may be that these names are chosen to represent the enemies of God and his people in general here because of their connotation as far away and little known (cf. Ps. 120:5).

TUBAL-CAIN [tōō′bəl kān] (Heb. *tûḇal-qayin* "Tubal the smith"). A son of Lamech and his wife Zillah, and a descendant of Cain (Gen. 4:22). Tubal-cain is called the (first) "forger of all instruments of bronze and iron," and apparently lived in a period of cultural expansion (cf. vv. 20-21). See KENITES.

TUMORS (Heb. *ṭᵉḥôrîm*, K *'ᵃpālîm*). A punishment inflicted by God on the inhabitants of Ashdod (1 Sam. 5-6; KJV "emerods") and mentioned among the curses of Deut. 28:27 (RSV "ulcers"), probably to be identified as hemorrhoids (cf. KJV, Ps. 78:66).

TUNIC (Heb. *kuttōneṭ*; Aram. *paṭṭîš*; Gk. *chitōn*). An undergarment, the basic unit of clothing for both men and women. The tunic (also called "garment," "coat," or "robe" in translations) was a long- or half-sleeved shirtlike garment that reached to the ankles (Gen. 37:3), usually worn under a cloak (cf. Matt. 5:40). One would wear a waistcloth around the tunic (2 Kgs. 1:8; Jer. 13:1) and might hide a sword inside it (Judg. 3:16). The garments (so RSV) made by God for Adam and Eve (Gen. 3:21) were *kuttᵃnōt* of skin. The priests' tunics were an important part of their vestments (Exod. 28:4, 39-40; Josephus *Ant.* iii.7.2, 4 [153-56, 159-161]).

Tunics were generally made of wool, but the priests' tunics were of linen. Tunics could be made of two pieces or could be woven on a special loom so as to be seamless, like the tunic of Jesus for which soldiers cast lots at his crucifixion (John 19:23-24).

TURBAN.† A headdress made of cloth and wound around the head. Heb. *pᵉ'ēr* is a term for headgear in general, including ceremonial garlands (Isa. 3:20; 61:3, 10; KJV "ornaments," "beauty"; JB "wreath"); it is used once for the high priest's linen turban (Ezek.

44:18). Removal of one's head covering was a normal part of mourning practices (cf. 24:17, 23; KJV "tire").

Another general word for headgear is *ṣānîp*, which is used for the turban of the ordinary free male (Job 29:14; KJV "diadem"; Isa. 3:23; KJV "hoods"), the high priest's turban (Zech. 3:5), and a royal crown (Isa. 62:3; RSV, KJV "diadem").

A linen turban (Heb. *miṣnepeṭ*; KJV "mitre") was worn by Israel's high priest (Exod. 28:4, 39). Attached to this turban was a gold pendant or diadem inscribed "Holy to the Lord" (vv. 36-38; 29:6; 39:30; Lev. 8:9; Sir. 45:12). The priests other than the high priest wore "caps" of fine linen (Heb. *[pa'ªrê ham]migbaʿōṭ*; Exod. 28:40; 29:9; 39:28; Lev. 8:13; KJV "bonnets"), perhaps similar to fezzes. At a later time all the priests apparently wore turbans (Gk. *kídaris*; Jdt. 4:15; KJV "mitre").

TURTLEDOVE (Heb. *tôr, tōr*; Gk. *trygṓn*). A designation for the various species of the genus *Streptopelia*, small gray- and buff-colored pigeons with various kinds of ring-coloring around their necks. In Palestine the turtledove is one of the earliest harbingers of spring (Cant. 2:12; Jer. 8:7; KJV "turtle"). During the summer they can be heard everywhere in hedges and shrubs (the Hebrew term derives from the sound of their call), and the male and female often remain together even after the breeding season. Because the seeds upon which they feed are so plentiful in Palestine, these birds thrive there in great numbers. Turtledoves were among birds considered clean for sacrifice and consumption (Gen. 15:9; Lev. 1:14; 5:7; Luke 2:24). The defenseless people of God are represented as a turtledove at Ps. 74:19 (RSV "dove").

TWELVE, THE (Gk. *hoi dṓdeka*). The central circle of Jesus' disciples, whom he called to be apostles. The term "the Twelve" appears in all four Gospels (even after the death of Judas at John 20:24; cf. Luke 24:9). Lists of the Twelve in the Synoptic Gospels and Acts agree on the number but not entirely on their names (Matt. 10:2-4; Mark 3:16-19; Luke 6:14-16; Acts 1:13). "The Twelve" also appears as a designation for the apostles at 6:2; 1 Cor. 15:5; Rev. 21:14. The uses of the term suggest that a particular significance was attached to the number itself. Jesus related the number of this group to the twelve tribes of Israel in such a way that the apostles become the core of an eschatological Israel (Matt. 19:28 par. Luke 22:30); a similar idea is expressed at Rev. 21:14 (cf. Eph. 2:20). The choosing of Matthias after the death of Judas was an attempt to restore the number of the Twelve (Acts 1:15-26).

TWIN, THE. *See* DIDYMUS; THOMAS.

TWIN BROTHERS (Gk. *Dioskouroi*). In Greek mythology, the twin sons of Zeus and the moon-god Leda, named Castor and Pollux (Polydeuces). They were regarded as heroes worthy of the honors given to gods. A number of their exploits were told of, and they were sometimes connected with the constellation Gemini. They were revered as saviors in all kinds of distress and particularly as protectors of mariners. Many Roman ships bore images of Castor and Pollux,

as did the grain ship that carried Paul from Malta to Puteoli (Acts 28:11; KJV "Castor and Pollux").

TYCHICUS [tĭk'ə kəs] (Gk. *Tychikos* "child of fortune"). A Christian from the province of Asia who accompanied Paul in delivering to the Jerusalem church the relief money collected from the Gentile Christians of Asia Minor, Macedonia, and Greece (Acts 20:4). Tychicus later worked as an emissary for Paul while the apostle was imprisoned (Eph. 6:21; Col. 4:7; 2 Tim. 4:12; Titus 3:12).

TYPOLOGY (Gk. *týpos* "visible impression [created by pressure or a blow, as a seal on wax or a die on metal], copy, pattern, image, example").† A relationship in which something occurring in the past is a copy or pattern of something in the present or future. The principal purpose of such a correspondence is to instruct by presenting a picture rather than data, just as a teacher might seek to acclimate pupils to a difficult concept by presenting a simple illustration before treating the concept directly. Persons, events, or things in the Old Testament, while possessing true historical validity in themselves, also function as divinely appointed illustrations of what is yet to come.

At Rom. 5:14 Paul identifies Adam as a type of Christ, in that Adam singlehandedly affected the course of vast numbers of human beings. (Paul goes on to explain the differences between Adam's effect on humanity and Christ's, at which point the typological correspondence breaks down; vv. 15-21). Paul also identifies Israel's deliverance, provisions, and judgment in the wilderness as types or models for a Christian understanding of the unity and responsibilities of the Church (1 Cor. 10:6, 11; KJV "examples, ensamples"; RSV "warning[s]"). Peter presents baptism as an antitype (i.e., fulfillment or realization; Gk. *antítypos*; KJV "like figure") of the preservation of Noah and his family through the Flood (1 Pet. 3:21).

What is said about the tabernacle demonstrates the thought structure that served as the background of typological interpretation. The earthly reality (the tabernacle built under Moses' instruction) is regarded as the reflection of an already existing heavenly reality (Acts 7:44), but as this metaphysical duality is transformed by interpretation in terms of eschatological dualism, the old earthly tabernacle comes to represent also the event of Christ's gaining salvation for mankind (Heb. 8:5; 9:24).

In addition to *týpos* and related words, the concept of typology is represented also by Gk. *skiá* (Heb. 10:1; RSV "shadow"), *parabolḗ* (9:9; RSV "symbolic"; KJV "figure"; 11:19; NASB "as a type"; RSV "figuratively speaking"), and *hypódeigma* (9:23; RSV "copies"; KJV "patterns"). Typological relationships are also noted without the use of such words, as in the case of Melchizedek, whom the author of Hebrews sees as a type of Christ because of the way he is presented at Gen. 14:18-20; Ps. 110:4 (Heb. 6:20–7:28).

Typological interpretation has, for better or worse, been extended beyond its beginnings in the New Testament through the use of allegory. On this basis, not only the priestly intercession that occurred in the tabernacle, but also each object in the tabernacle and every priestly act occurring there is taken as in some way prefiguring what happened in Christ. The experiences of Old Testament persons (e.g., Joseph, Samson, and Esther) are also taken as types of the experience of Christ and the salvation accomplished by him. Accordingly, typology is a study requiring care so that the finding of types is not taken to extremes. This approach to interpretation is not properly a source of doctrine, but rather shows ways in which doctrine has been illustrated in inscripturated history.

Bibliography. L. Goppelt, *Typos: The Typological Interpretation of the Old Testament in the New* (Grand Rapids: 1982); A. H. J. Gunneweg, *Understanding the Old Testament.* OTL (1978), pp. 21-31; G. von Rad, "Typological Interpretation of the Old Testament," pp. 17-39 in C. Westermann, ed., *Essays on Old Testament Hermeneutics* (1963; repr. Atlanta: 1979), repr. pp. 28-46 in D. K. McKim, ed. *A Guide to Contemporary Hermeneutics* (Grand Rapids: 1986).

TYRANNUS [tĭ răn'əs] (Gk. *Tyrannos* "ruler"). A teacher at Ephesus in whose lecture hall Paul preached when because of opposition he ceased preaching in the synagogue (Acts 19:9).

TYRE [tīr] (Heb. *ṣōr, ṣôr*; Gk. *Tyros*).† A major Phoenician city, in ancient times located on an island off the Mediterranean coast, ca. 40 km. (25 mi.) south of Sidon and 45 km. (28 mi.) north of Akko; modern Ṣûr, now situated on a peninsula. Tyre's appearance as an independent kingdom in nineteenth-century B.C. Egyptian Execration Texts and the fourteenth-century Amarna Letters attests to its antiquity, but ancient tradition of the city's existence as early as the third millennium has not been substantiated. It appears to have been refounded by the Sidonians ca. 1200. A settlement on the mainland opposite the island, referred to as Ušu in cuneiform records, was known to the Greeks as "ancient Tyre" (Gk. *Palaityros*) but appears to have been an independent entity.

As with the rest of Phoenicia, much of Tyre's history took place in the shadow of the waxing and waning power of Egypt. After the Hyksos had been expelled from Egypt a series of pharaohs exerted control over Phoenicia with varying degrees of success. Within this context the Tyrians plied the Mediterranean trade routes, carrying dyed goods, timber, wheat, oil, wine, metal products, and slaves. They also established a number of important commercial colonies, the most successful of which was Carthage. Hiram I, the tenth-century king of Tyre who had close commercial relations with David and Solomon (2 Sam. 5:11; 1 Kgs. 5), established Tyrian dominance in the eastern Mediterranean and ruled over Tyre's first golden age. He initiated considerable building activity in the city and annexed the nearby Island of Hercules (now submerged) (Josephus *Ap.* i.113 [3]). Ethbaal I (*ca.* 887-*ca.* 856) expanded Tyrian influence in commerce as well as diplomacy, and constructed a new main harbor (the "Egyptian port") on the southern end of the island, sheltered by a breakwater 750 m. (820 yds.) long. Under Ethbaal (called "king of the Sidonians") Tyre emerged as supreme among the Phoenician cities and actively engaged in colonization. Ethbaal's daughter Jezebel married Ahab of Israel,

and her daughter Athaliah married King Joram of Judah, leading to the introduction of foreign religious practices (1 Kgs. 16:29-19:18); for this and other sins the Israelite prophets foretold Tyre's destruction (Isa. 23; Ezek. 26:2-28:19; Amos 1:9-10).

The armies of the Assyrian Empire began making forays into Syria and Phoenicia in the early tenth century, and from the ninth century on Tyre was forced to pay tribute to a number of Assyrian rulers. The fall of Assyria in 612 brought no relief to Tyre. For thirteen years (586-573) King Nebuchadrezzar of Babylon besieged the city, which held out to sign a treaty with the invaders. The advent of the Persian Empire further weakened Tyre, which yielded its place of prominence to Sidon, and Carthage severed its ties with Tyre in 520. The city did, however, continue to be involved in trade (Ezra 3:7; Neh. 13:16).

Alexander the Great's defeat of the Persians at Issus in 333 set the stage for Tyre's encounter with yet another empire. The city declared itself neutral as Alexander advanced down the Mediterranean coast, but he laid siege to Tyre for seven months. The city finally fell after the Greeks used rubble from buildings and monuments of "ancient Tyre" to build a causeway out to the island. Many inhabitants of the city were killed or enslaved. Tyre's economy recovered somewhat under the Seleucids, and Greek culture was adopted. In Roman times the city was administered from Syria.

During his Galilean ministry Jesus withdrew for a time to "the district of Tyre and Sidon" (Matt. 15:21-29 par.). People from that region were among the "great multitude" that came to Galilee to hear him preach (Mark 3:8 par.). In an eschatological pronouncement he contrasted the fate of Palestinian cities that had not responded to his ministry with the judgment due this Gentile city (Matt. 11:21-22 par.). Paul spent a few days with Christians living in Tyre on his last journey to Jerusalem (Acts 21:3-7). At 12:20-23 representatives from Tyre are mentioned in the account of the death of Herod Agrippa I.

Bibliography. H. J. Katzenstein, *The History of Tyre* (Jerusalem: 1973).

TYRE, LADDER OF. *See* LADDER OF TYRE.

TYROPOEON [tī'rō pō ē'ən, tī rō'pī ən] **VALLEY.**† The northwest-southeast valley that bisects Jerusalem into the "upper" and "lower" city. The Tyropoeon valley formed the western limit of the city of David; it converges with the Kidron and Hinnom valleys south of the ancient city to form the Wâdī en-Nâr. In the later monarchy (at the time of Hezekiah) and again in the Greco-Roman period Jerusalem expanded, encompassing also another hill to the west, the "upper city." During these periods Jerusalem's western perimeter was the Hinnom valley while the Tyropoeon was considered the "central" valley skirting the temple's western walls. Herod built bridges spanning the valley and connecting the temple with the upper city on the western hill.

When the Roman general Titus destroyed Jerusalem in A.D. 70, much of the debris from the city—especially the temple—was thrown into the Tyropoeon. As a result, the valley today is difficult to define, but its general contours are visible if one walks from the

Temple Mount into the Jewish or Christian quarters of present-day Old Jerusalem. The Arabic name for the road that follows the valley along the temple enclosure is el-Wad ("the valley").

The name "Tyropoeon" comes from the designation of Josephus (Gk. *hē tōn tyropoiōn pháranx*; *BJ* v.4.1 [140]) meaning "valley of the cheesemakers," perhaps a reference to sheep markets (necessary for cheese) at the valley's northernmost end, in the vicinity of the present Damascus Gate. Some scholars connect the name with Heb. *t^erāpîm* "teraphim," possibly referring to idolatrous practices associated with the southern extreme of the valley. Others relate it to *trp* "to tear, rend," derived from the valley's division of the city into two parts.

U

UCAL [ū′kəl] (Heb. *'ukāl*). If a proper name, one of two people whom Agur addressed in his oracle, perhaps his son or nephew (Prov. 30:1). However, the Hebrew in the verse is obscure and some scholars, as do LXX and Vulg., find not names but an expression such as "I am faint" (NIV mg.). *See* ITHIEL **1**.

UEL [ū′əl] (Heb. *'û'ēl* "will of God" [?]). An Israelite at the time of Ezra who had taken a foreign wife (Ezra 10:34). At 1 Esdr. 9:34 he is called Joel (KJV "Juel").

UGARIT [ōō′gə rĭt].† Ancient Syrian coastal city and kingdom, noted for the find of texts yielding abundant information on Late Bronze Age culture and having important implications for the background of the Old Testament. The site at modern Ras Shamra (Arab. *Râs esh-Shamra* "hill of fennel") is .8 km. (.5 mi.) from the Syrian coast opposite the eastern tip of Cyprus, 11 km. (7 mi.) north of modern Latakia. Closely associated is its harbor town at modern Minet el-Beida, the "White Harbor" (Gk. *Leukos Leumēn*) of the sixth-century B.C. Greeks.

I. Excavations

Archaeological excavations, conducted nearly every season since 1929, indicate that occupation of the site began with three phases of a fortified Neolithic settlement (Ugarit level V C-A, *ca.* 6500-5250 B.C.), followed by another three of a smaller Chalcolithic settlement featuring a strong rampart (V C-III B, *ca.* 5250-3000). In the Early Bronze Age (Ugarit III A, 3000-2100) Ugarit was a prosperous fortified city through its first two phases (III A1-2, *ca.* 3000-2300), with polished red and black Khirbet Kerak ware introduced from Anatolia in level III A2 (2500-2300). The first extant mention of Ugarit occurs in an Eblaite name list *ca.* 2400-2250. A period of seeming decline (III A3, *ca.* 2300-2150), contemporary with the empires of Akkad and Ebla, ends with the city abandoned or destroyed, and apparently unoccupied for a time, in an obscure period somewhat comparable to Early Bronze IV in Palestine.

Occupation resumes with three Middle Bronze Age phases (Ugarit II 1-3, *ca.* 2100-1650) when foreign metalworkers (known as the "torque-wearers") settled on the ruins for a time (II 1, *ca.* 2100-1900). The kingdom of Ugarit, commonly attributed to the arrival of the Amorites (evidenced by the dynastic names and seal), rises in level II 2 (*ca.* 1900-1750), with strong relations to the Twelfth Dynasty of Egypt (attested by various inscriptions) and also to Mari, Crete, and Alalakh. Two great temples to Baal and Dagon (or perhaps El) were erected, and assorted statues and steles, including a large limestone stele of Baal, suggest that the religion attested in later texts was already practiced at this time. By the third phase (II 3, *ca.* 1750-1600), Ugarit was a wealthy second-level power, integrated into the greater Syrian political system that had its center of power first in Yamḫad and then in Mitanni to the east.

In the Late Bronze Age (Ugarit I 1-3, *ca.* 1600-1185) the city enjoyed a cosmopolitan era, often rightly called its golden age. Ugarit avoided harmful alliances by remaining neutral at the rise of Mitanni, submitting to Egypt in the reign of Thutmose IV (1426-1417), and transferring allegiance to the Hittite sphere in 1366. The city was eventually destroyed in 1185 by a great fire, usually attributed to invasion by the Sea Peoples (though an earthquake has also been suggested). A few remains on the acropolis attest Persian-Hellenistic occupation *ca.* 550-200, and some Roman occupation during the second century A.D.

The archaeological and textual evidence indicates a strong agricultural economy in grain, wine, and oil; major marine industries such as shipbuilding, and production of purple dye from the murex shell; large royal and private merchant fleets trading in agricultural products, purple, textiles, copper, and luxury goods to the entire eastern Mediterranean; a strong navy to support this merchant marine; and heavy transfer traffic through Ugarit as a port of entry to the powers of inland Syria and beyond. This highly international economy is reflected by texts and inscriptions in seven languages (Ugaritic, Akkadian, Sumerian, Hurrian, Hittite, Egyptian, and Cyprominoan), using five different scripts (alphabetic and syllabic cuneiform, Egyptian and Hittite hieroglyphic, and a local Cyprominoan script), and even by a sanctuary that yielded Hurrian myths and religious texts, liver models for extispicy, and copper statuettes of Hurrian deities.

The resulting prosperity is evident in strong defenses,

including a glacis, major tower, and monumental gate; a huge palace covering 1 ha. (2.5 a.) with ninety rooms and five courtyards; a palace industry of jewelers, goldsmiths, ivory workers, and scribes; large private homes with fine corbel-vaulted family tombs beneath; extensive residential sectors with their own sanctuaries, and abundant objects of art including the palace ivories, gold and alabaster cups and vases, finely crafted ceremonial weapons, and statuettes of deities with gold or silver decorations.

From the same period, the port of Minet el-Beida has yielded residential quarters, cult sites, and warehouses with as many as eighty Canaanite jars for oil and wine; alabaster vases and beautiful ivories sculpted in high relief; and corbel-vaulted tombs containing large numbers of bowls, vases, and plates of Syrian, Anatolian, Cypriot, and especially Mycenean origin or influence. Also relevant is nearby seaside Râs Ibn Hani, possibly the royal summer residence of Ugarit, with palaces and a royal archive of the same type and period destroyed at the same time.

II. Texts

From the Late Bronze period come the many clay tablets that make Ugarit such an important find. The majority are written either in syllabic cuneiform in Akkadian, or in alphabetic cuneiform in the local Northwest Semitic language now called "Ugaritic," closely related to Biblical Hebrew. Found in royal, priestly, and private archives, the texts contain myths about the major gods; epics about heroes of old, Keret, Danel, and Aqhat; lists of deities, and sacrifices for them; rituals, omen literature, and divination texts; medical knowledge and the care of horses; treaties, administrative texts, and legal records; and official corespondence of all kinds. Texts in the language and alphabetic cuneiform of Ugarit have also been found at Kadesh, Tel Sukas, Ras Ibn Hani, Hala Sultan Tekke, Sarepta, Kamid el-Loz, Mt. Tabor, Taanach, Bethshemesh, and Aphek. Together they provide valuable knowledge about the culture and economy of a developed city-state at the time.

Of special interest is the mythology of the popular storm-god Baal and his consort Anat in the so-called "Baal cycle." In the first story (*ANET*, pp. 129-131), Baal fights and defeats Yamm ("Sea"), who represents the chaotic ocean forces, to win the kingship under the higher god El. This victory gives him the desire for a palace, the acquisition of which through persuasion and intrigue to gain consent from El is narrated in the second account (pp. 131-38). From his new palace, Baal issues a bold challenge to his enemies and especially to the ravenous god Mot ("Death"), who rules the Underworld. This precipitates the conflicts forming the third story (pp. 138-141), which describes a series of struggles between the two gods who represent the forces of life and death as they affect humanity. As a dying and rising god, Baal first succumbs to Mot but eventually returns to regain his position— with substantial help from Anat and other deities—to end the cycle in hopeful if impermanent victory. Modern interpreters often understand it at least in part as a reflex of the seasonal cycle, but the myth also conveys a complex worldview in terms of tensions among conflicting forces to explain the many ambiguities of human existence.

The many links between these texts and the Hebrew Bible make them so important for Old Testament studies that scarcely a textbook or commentary neglects them. Along with Aramaic, Moabite, and Phoenician, the Ugaritic language belongs to the same Northwest Semitic group as Biblical Hebrew (though its exact classification remains in dispute), and is closely related in grammar, lexicon, and poetic style. Strong Old Testament resemblances (viewed variously as parallels or borrowings, demythologized poetry, or simply the result of cultural influence) to the Baal cycle portray the God of Israel riding the storm clouds in majesty (Deut. 33:26; Ps. 18:10 [MT 11] par.; 68:4, 33 [MT 5, 34]; 104:3), showing his power in the thunder in association with the divine temple-palace (Ps. 29; 68:28-35 [MT 29-36]), defeating the sea monster Leviathan (Isa. 27:1, with strikingly similar exotic vocabulary; cf. Ps. 74:13-14; Hab. 3:13-14), mastering the chaotic ocean forces (29:3, 10; 89:9-10 [MT 10-11]; 93:3-4; Hab. 3:8, 15), and dealing with the insatiable power of Death (Isa. 5:14; Hab. 2:5). The legendary wise judge Danel of the Aqhat epic appears at Ezek. 14:14, 20; 28:3. Still other texts relate to Old Testament laws and rituals.

As part of a cultural heritage widely shared in Syria-Palestine, the Ugaritic texts reflect the environment in which Israel was born, but opinions vary on the nature and extent of their influence on the Old Testament. One view is the syncretistic, holding that wayward Israelites simply incorporated desirable elements of Canaanite culture almost unchanged into their religion. Another is the polemic, arguing that such features were appropriated to despoil the rival Canaanite religion by ascribing its more attractive elements to Israel's God and changing their content to accord with distinctively Israelite belief. A third interpretation suggests that the Canaanites who were part of Israel's composite origins adapted native religious elements to the newer Yahwism, much as originally non-Christian features came to be included in the Easter celebration. The several views are not all mutually exclusive, and the actual process was doubtless more complex than any one view would imply.

Bibliography. P. C. Craigie, *Ugarit and the Old Testament* (Grand Rapids: 1983); F. M. Cross, *Canaanite Myth and Hebrew Epic* (Cambridge, Mass.: 1973); J. C. L. Gibson, *Canaanite Myths and Legends,* 2nd ed. (Edinburgh: 1978); J. Gray, *The Legacy of Canaan,* 2nd ed. VTS 5 (1965); A. S. Kapelrud, *The Ras Shamra Discoveries and the Old Testament* (Oxford: 1965); G. D. Young, ed., *Ugarit in Retrospect* (Winona Lake: 1981).

UKNAZ [ŭk'năz] (Heb. *ûqnaz*). According to KJV mg. an alternate name for Kenaz (1 Chr. 4:15). The KJV rendering of the name plus Heb. *u-* "even Kenaz" is better. Another possibility is "and Kenaz"; because his father Elah had "sons," some scholars conjecture that sibling names have dropped from the Hebrew text. *See* KENAZ 2.

ULAI [ū'lī] (Heb. *'ûlay*), A river (NIV "canal") in

the province of Elam, near the Persian capital of Susa, where Daniel saw himself in his vision of the ram and the he-goat (Dan. 8:2, 16). Mentioned in an Assyrian inscription *ca.* 640 B.C. (Akk. *U-la-a*) and called Eulaeus by classical writers, the Ulai connected the rivers Choaspes (modern Kerkha) and Coprates (modern Abdizful).

ULAM [ū'ləm] (Heb. *'ûlām* "first").
1. A descendant of Machir of the tribe of Manasseh (1 Chr. 7:16-17).
2. The oldest son of Eshek, a descendant of Saul, and head of a Benjaminite family of archers (1 Chr. 8:39-40; cf. 2 Chr. 14:8b).

ULLA [ū'lə] (Heb. *'ullā'* "yoke"). Head of a family in the tribe of Asher (1 Chr. 7:39).

UMMAH [ŭm'ə] (Heb. *'ummâ*). A city in the tribal territory of Asher (Josh. 19:30). Ummah may be a scribal error for "Acco" (Heb. *'akkô*; the consonants kaph and mem were written similarly and thus easily confused), a significant Canaanite town missing from Joshua's list (vv. 24-31; cf. Judg. 1:31).

UNCIAL [ŭn'shəl].† A designation for Greek manuscripts of the third through ninth centuries A.D. or the style of writing used in these manuscripts.
Greek manuscripts in the first few centuries of the Christian era used a cursive style of lowercase, or small letters, with some contractions and abbreviations. For literary works, however, scribes developed a style of writing in larger letters similar to modern English capital letters. These letters were called uncials (Lat. *uncia* "a twelfth part") because they were commonly large enough to take up one-twelfth of a column line. After the ninth century, manuscripts began to be written with smaller letters called minuscules.
The uncials were the most beautiful of all manuscripts, written on parchment, or vellum, made from specially treated animal skins and often elaborately decorated. *See* BIBLE, TEXT OF THE *II.A*.

UNCLEAN. *See* CLEAN AND UNCLEAN.

UNCTION [ŭnk'shən]. The KJV translation of Gk. *chrísma* at 1 John 2:20 (RSV "anointed"). *See* ANOINT; HOLY SPIRIT *III.B*.

UNFORGIVABLE SIN. A concept derived initially from Jesus' words at Mark 3:28-30 that blasphemy against the Holy Spirit is an eternal sin—it will never be forgiven. The wider biblical context demonstrates that this theme is not peculiar to a single text; several passages indicate the dire consequences of certain actions, e.g., Num. 15:30-31; Matt. 11:21-24; Mark 14:21; Heb. 6:4-6; 10:26-31; 1 John 5:16.
However, examination of the Markan context reveals that blasphemy against the Holy Spirit was not readily committed. Jesus' reference there is to the scribes, the trained theologians and religious leaders of his day, whose duties included the responsibility to recognize the contemporary work of the Holy Spirit. These were the ones who were in danger of commit-

ting an unforgivable sin (the text does not say they had committed it, and Jesus' warning implies opportunity for repentance) by attributing repeatedly (the implication in Greek of "said" at Mark 3:22) to Satan the Holy Spirit-empowered works of Jesus in casting out demons (cf. 1 John 5:10). Such blasphemy was an expression of defiant hostility toward God and a deliberate refusal to see God's Spirit at work. Jesus' warning was not addressed to the people—they were in no position to commit such a sin.
The context at Heb. 6:4-6; 10:26-31 is somewhat different from Mark's, although 10:29 (". . . outraged the Spirit of grace") appears very similar to blasphemy against the Holy Spirit. In Hebrews the focus is on Christian believers, apparently full members of the body of Christ and "partakers" of the riches of grace (6:4), who nevertheless turn away from that grace and refuse to depart from sin. This is no single act or careless word or deed but deliberate apostasy, a continuing and steadfast rejection of God's grace in Christ in spite of previous participation in it. Even though it was God's deep desire and intent in the sending of his Son to provide forgiveness to all who would come, such persons have made themselves unwilling to come. The impossibility of forgiveness rests not upon God's unwillingness to forgive but upon the sinner's incapacity to repent and receive divine forgiveness.

UNICORN (KJV). *See* OX.

UNKNOWN GOD (Gk. *agnóstos theós*). The text of an inscription on an altar seen by Paul at Athens (Acts 17:23), which he used as the theme of his Areopagus address (vv. 22-31). The Greek geographer Pausanias (second century A.D.) noted the existence of "altars to gods unknown" between the harbor Phalerum and the city of Athens; Diogenes Laertius told of similar altars erected to avert a plague at Athens. The fact that no altar with the exact inscription "to an unknown God" (in the singular) has been discovered has led some commentators to believe that Paul changed the plural into the singular for the sake of the monotheistic message of his speech. Whatever the wording of the original inscription, Paul seized this opportunity to acquaint the religious citizens of Athens with the previously unknown "Lord of heaven and earth."

UNLEAVENED BREAD (Heb. *maṣṣâ*; Gk. *ázymos*). Bread or cakes baked without yeast or other leavening. The Hebrews were instructed by Yahweh to celebrate the Passover with unleavened bread (e.g., Exod. 12:8, 15; *see* PASSOVER) and to present cereal offerings baked without leaven (Lev. 2:4; *see* CEREAL OFFERING *I*). At times, bread was baked without leaven simply out of haste (Gen. 19:3; Judg. 6:19; 1 Sam. 28:24).
In the New Testament, Paul uses leaven in the metaphorical sense of impurity which, even in small quantities, will taint the whole body (1 Cor. 5:6-8; cf. vv. 1-2) and must therefore be removed.
See BREAD; LEAVEN.

UNLEAVENED BREAD, FEAST OF (Heb. *ḥag hammaṣṣôt*). A seven-day agricultural festival of the

Hebrews that early on formed an element of the Passover celebration and constituted one of the three pilgrimage festivals requiring the presence of Israelite males at the sanctuary (Exod. 23:14-15). Cakes or loaves of unleavened bread symbolized the haste with which the Hebrews had to flee Egypt (12:14-20, 33-34, 39; cf. 34:18). Recitations of the Passover regulations at Lev. 23:4-6; Num. 28:16-17; Deut. 16:1-8 show how rapidly the Feast of Unleavened Bread was subsumed into the Passover celebration; this blurring of the original distinction between the two is seen in the New Testament as well (Matt. 26:17; Mark 14:1, 12; Luke 22:1, 7; Acts 12:3; 20:6).

See PASSOVER.

UNNI [ŭn'ī] (Heb. *'unnî* "Yahweh has answered").
1. A levitical musician appointed to accompany the ark of the covenant when David brought it to Jerusalem (1 Chr. 15:18, 20).
2. A Levite who returned with Zerubbabel from the Babylonian captivity (Neh. 12:9; so KJV, NIV, following **Q**). The RSV and JB read "Unno" following **K** *'unnô*. The name is omitted in the LXX.

UPHAZ [ū'făz] (Heb. *'ûpāz*). If a proper name, an otherwise unknown site where gold was obtained (Jer. 10:9; Dan. 10:5). Some interpreters, following certain ancient textual sources, suggest that Uphaz is a scribal error for Ophir (cf. JB, Jer. 10:9), a well-known source of gold (1 Kgs. 9:28; 22:48; Job 22:24); others contend that Uphaz is a misspelling of the Hebrew verbal form *mûpāz* "refine" (cf. Dan. 10:5; NIV "finest gold"; JB "pure gold").

UPPER GATE (Heb. *ša'ar bêṯ-YHWH hā'elyôn* "upper gate of the house of the Lord"). One of the temple gates built (NIV "rebuilt") by King Jotham as part of his program to strengthen Judah's defenses (2 Kgs. 15:35 par. 2 Chr. 27:3; KJV "higher gate"). Facing north (Ezek. 9:2), it may have been the same as the upper Benjamin Gate (Jer. 20:2), located on the north side of the temple between the old and the new courts.

At 2 Chr. 23:20 the name may refer to the GATE OF THE GUARDS.

UPPER ROOM. A room or chamber on the flat roof of a Palestinian house. Sometimes it was no more than a tent (2 Sam. 16:22) or a booth (Neh. 8:16-17), but it might be built as a second story (e.g., Judg. 3:20; Jer. 22:13-14 [Heb. *'ªlîyâ*]; Dan. 6:10). Such rooms were often used for guests (e.g., 1 Kgs. 17:19; 2 Kgs. 4:10). For 2 Sam 18:33 (MT 19:1) *see* GATE.

It was in such an upper guest room in Jerusalem that Jesus celebrated the Last Supper with his twelve disciples (Mark 14:15 par. Luke 22:12; Gk. *anágaion*; cf. Matt. 26:18 "at your house"); it was a chamber large enough for thirteen guests to enjoy the Passover meal, reclining on cushions or carpets (cf. RSV "furnished"). This room and house have been variously identified with the house where Jesus appeared to his disciples after his resurrection (Luke 24:33, 36; John 20:19, 26), the upper room where the twelve apostles and others gathered following Jesus' ascension (Acts

1:13; *hyperóon*), and the home of Mary the mother of John Mark (cf. 12:12). Later tradition has located the room, a vaulted chamber called the Coenaculum or Cenacle, on the second floor of the mosque en-Nebi Daud (until the mid-sixteenth century a church), which also contains on the first floor the reputed tomb of David.

UR [ŏor] (Heb. *'ûr* "light") (**PERSON**). The father of Eliphal, one of David's mighty men (1 Chr. 11:35).

UR [ŏor] (Heb. *'ûr*; Akk. *Uri*; Sum. *Urim*) (**PLACE**). A city in Mesopotamia that flourished during the Early Dynastic period (*ca.* 3000-2350 B.C.) and later, functioning as a city-state controlling Sumer, with its own ruler, temple, and pantheon. The site has been identified as modern Tell el-Muqaiyer, 16 km. (10 mi.) west of the Euphrates river (in ancient times it actually was situated on the right bank of the river), halfway between Baghdad and the Persian Gulf.

The site of Ur is roughly oval in shape, longest along the north-south axis. Harbors on the Euphrates were located at the north end and on the western side of the city. A walled area occupies the middle third of the northern half of the site. This "sacred rectangle" enclosed a temple to the moon-god Nanna (Akk. *Su-en* "Sin") featuring a ziggurat (three-stage temple tower) in the center of the court. Perhaps the model for the biblical tower of Babel (Gen. 11:1-8), the ziggurat consisted of a mud-brick core with an external casing of burnt bricks; monumental staircases led up to the top level, where a temple was located. Other facilities in the walled area included a large storehouse, a temple for Nanna's divine consort Ningal, an elaborate temple kitchen, and quarters for the *entu*-princess, a maiden of royal descent chosen to represent the human bride of the moon-god.

Perhaps the most intriguing find at Ur was the mausoleum of the kings of the Third Dynasty of Ur (2113-2006), located in a royal cemetery that dates to *ca.* 2600. The mausoleum's plan resembles that of a private house, with underground tomb chambers. It is constructed of baked bricks set in bitumen. The tombs revealed that royalty were entombed with gold, jewelry, and furniture as well as a retinue of soldiers, musicians, and courtiers, presumably drugged before entering the tomb during the burial ceremony.

While Ur's history spanned some three thousand years, its high point was undoubtedly the Neo-Sumerian Third Dynastic period (2113-2006), when the city-state was ruled by divinely sanctioned autocratic kings supported by a centralized government and a highly developed bureaucracy. Territory in Ur's sphere of influence was divided into outlying provinces (with military governors) and administrative districts (*ensi*). Large storage depots were employed for grain storage and distribution, and metalworking and textile industries were important. Archaeological excavations of Ur, Lagash, and other cities in the Tigris-Euphrates basin have yielded thousands of cuneiform texts detailing aspects of law, diplomacy, and business in the city-state.

Ur-nammu (2113-2094) laid the foundation for Ur's greatness through territorial conquests, large-scale irrigation projects, land reclamation in the Persian Gulf and monumental building projects such as the ziggurat of Ur. To his son, crown prince Šulgi (2093-2046), is attributed the earliest known law code, "Codex Urnammu." In the law of Ur, the ruler was charged with promoting justice in the land by not levying oppressive taxes, by standardizing weights and measures, and by ensuring that the wealthy did not take advantage of the poor. These regulations are in a form reminiscent of the casuistic form of Old Testament law, characterized by a conditional opening statement (protasis) of the case followed by an apodosis containing the sentence of punishment.

Šulgi spent the first half of his reign consolidating Ur's territories, then undertook military campaigns in his latter years. In 2064 a peace agreement was signed with Elam, but Šulgi still had to fight hostile tribes in Kurdistan and near the Zagros mountains. When Amorites (Sum. MAR.TU) sweeping in from the northwest threatened Ur, Šulgi had a 280 km. (185 mi.)-long defensive line built to prevent their infiltrating Ur's lands; this line ran northeast to southwest and was reinforced at intervals by fortresses along its length. Proclaimed a deity during his own lifetime, Šulgi was a great patron of Sumerian arts, literature, and education.

Following Šulgi, Amar-suen and Shu-suen (each of whom reigned nine years) further enlarged the empire, reaching Ebla near the Mediterranean coast. However, the reign of Ibbi-suen (beginning in 2026) witnessed the start of Ur's decline. External pressure from Elam and the Amorites made it difficult for supplies to reach Ur from the provinces. Ibbi-suen erected massive fortifications around Ur and the religious center of Nippur. Although Išbi-irra, the *ensi* of Isin, asserted his independence with the help of the priests of Nippur, Ur continued to exist until overrun by invading Elamites in 2002, when Ibbi-suen was carried off as their prisoner. Išbi-irra later drove the Elamite garrison out of Ur and became sole ruler of Sumer from Isin.

Ur is mentioned in the Old Testament as the home of Abraham's father Terah (Gen. 11:28) and as Abraham's point of departure for Mesopotamia and Canaan (v. 31; 15:7). Although always called "Ur of the Chaldeans" (KJV "Chaldees") in the Bible, the Chaldeans (Kasdim) did not enter Babylonia until *ca.* 1000.

URBANUS [ûr bā′nəs] (Gk. *Ourbanos*; cf. Lat. *Urbanus* "belonging to a city"). A Christian believer at Rome to whom the apostle Paul sent his greetings (Rom. 16:9; KJV "Urbane"). Because the name was common among Roman slaves listed in inscriptions of the Roman imperial household, Urbanus may be one of the members of Caesar's household (cf. Phil 4:22). He is called a "fellow worker" (Gk. *synergós*) of Paul (cf. Prisca and Aquila, Rom. 16:3; Timothy, v. 21).

URI [ŏŏr′ī] (Heb. *'ûrî* "fiery"; possibly an abbreviation of Uriah).

1. A Judahite, and the father of Bezalel, the supervising craftsman employed in building the tabernacle (Exod. 31:2; 35:30; 38:22; 1 Chr. 2:20; 2 Chr. 1:5).

2. (Heb. *'urāy*). The father of Geber, Solomon's officer in Gilead (1 Kgs. 4:19; LXX Gk. *Adai*).

3. A postexilic gatekeeper who had taken a foreign wife (Ezra 10:24).

URIAH [yŏŏ rī′ə] (Heb. *'ûrîyâ, 'ûrîyāhû* "Yahweh is my light"; Gk. *Ourios*).

1. A Hittite among David's mighty men (2 Sam. 23:39 par. 1 Chr. 11:41) who lived in Jerusalem; his name and conduct suggest he had become a follower of Yahweh. His wife was Bathsheba, the daughter of Eliam (2 Sam. 11:3).

While Uriah was serving David faithfully in the siege of the Ammonite capital Rabbah, David had sexual relations with Bathsheba and she conceived. Attempting to hide the consequences of his sin, David brought Uriah home from the front to see his wife. But the dutiful soldier, out of empathy for his fellows still at the battlefield, refused to visit Bathsheba even after David made him drunk. At last, David sent Uriah back to Rabbah, assigned specifically to "the forefront of the hardest fighting"—in essence, with orders for his own execution. When Uriah was indeed killed in battle, David married his widow (11:1-27).

Matthew's genealogy of Jesus mentions Uriah as the husband of Solomon's mother (Matt. 1:6; KJV "Urias").

2. A priest, probably the high priest, during the reign of King Ahaz of Judah and the ministry of the prophet Isaiah. According to Ahaz' instructions, Uriah built at the front of the temple a replica of an altar (probably Assyrian) Ahaz had seen at Damascus and offered sacrifices on it rather than on Solomon's altar, which the king ordered moved (2 Kgs. 16:10-16; KJV "Urijah"). Uriah's part in this episode was omitted in the parallel account at 2 Chr. 28:22-24. At some point during this period Uriah was chosen by Isaiah to testify to the authenticity of the prophet's oracle against Jerusalem (Isa. 8:2). Whatever role Uriah played in the cultic changes Ahaz implemented at Jerusalem, he apparently still enjoyed the esteem of both Isaiah and the people.

3. A descendant of Hakkoz and father of Meremoth, one of Nehemiah's wall builders (Ezra 8:33; Neh. 3:4, 21).

4. One who stood beside Ezra as he read from the book of the law of Moses (Neh. 8:4; KJV "Urijah"). He may be the same as **3**.

5. The son of Shemaiah of Kiriath-jearim who delivered a divine message against Jerusalem and Judah that was as unpopular as Jeremiah's temple prophecy (Jer. 26:20; cf. vv. 1-19; KJV "Urijah"). He fled to Egypt, but was extradited to Jerusalem, killed without mercy, and thrown into a common graveyard (vv. 21-23). The incident was included to emphasize the constant danger that surrounded Jeremiah as a prophet.

URIEL [yŏŏr′ī əl] (Heb. *'ûrî'ēl*; Gk. *Ouriēl*).

1. The chief of the Kohathite Levites (1 Chr. 15:5) who assisted King David in bringing the ark of the covenant to Jerusalem (vv. 11-12). He is probably the same as Uriel the son of Tahath and father of Uzziah at 1 Chr. 6:24 (MT 9).

2. A resident of Gibeah, a maternal grandparent of King Abijah of Judah (2 Chr. 13:2).

3. One of the holy angels who led Enoch on his visionary journeys through the heavens (e.g., 1 En.

21:5; 80:1). According to some manuscripts, he is also named among the four angels of the Presence (9:1). In 2 Esdras, Uriel was the angel sent to Ezra to respond to his complaint against God and his ways (2 Esdr. 4:1; 5:20; 10:28).*See* ARCHANGEL.

URIM [yoʻorʻim] **AND THUMMIM** [thoōmʻim] (Heb. *ʼûrîm weʻtummîm*). Objects used by the priests for determining the will of God. No description of the Urim and Thummim is provided, although it may be assumed that they were small objects because they fit into a pouch on the breastpiece worn on the ephod of the high priest (Exod. 28:29-30; Lev. 8:8; cf. Exod. 29:5). They may have been pebbles or sticks, or made from a precious metal.

The terms may be of foreign derivation. It has been proposed that Urim may mean "light" and Thummim "dark," and that thus one was light-colored and indicated God's will in one direction while the other was dark-colored and gave the opposite side. Another possibility is that the terms indicate the beginning and ending of the Hebrew alphabet (aleph and tau); thus twenty-two letters would have been cast out and read, on the order of a Ouija board. The technique may have been to shake the pouch on the breastplate and then withdraw one of the objects; however, some scholars think that the objects were cast like lots.

Most biblical examples of usage imply a direct question and answer procedure (1 Sam. 23:9-12; 30:7-8). Answers either confirm or negate the question. Saul views the prospective answer as "right" (1 Sam. 14:41), whatever its outcome. Negative answers seem possible, although biblical passages do not explain the procedure clearly. God does not seem to answer at all when a negative response occurs (1 Sam. 14:36-37; 28:6).

The Talmud (*Soṭah* 48a) observes that the usage of Urim and Thummim was lost during the Second Temple period. Ezra 2:63; Neh. 7:65 suggest that discernment by means of Urim and Thummim may have been still possible though rare.

UTHAI [uʻthī] (Heb. *ʻûṭay*).
1. The son of Ammihud of the tribe of Judah. He was among the first to return from exile in Babylon to resettle on his own property in Jerusalem (1 Chr. 9:4).
2. A family head and descendant of Bigvai who returned with Ezra from the Babylonian captivity (Ezra 8:14).

UZ [ŭz] (Heb. *ʻûṣ*) (PERSON).
1. A son of Aram, and grandson of Shem (Gen. 10:23). At 1 Chr. 1:17 he is called a son of Shem.
2. A son of Milcah and Nahor, Abraham's brother (Gen. 22:21; KJV "Huz").
3. A son (or descendant) of the Horite chief Dishan (Gen. 36:28 par. 1 Chr. 1:42). The name may represent a clan or similar social group.

UZ [ŭz] (Heb. *ʻûṣ*) (PLACE). The homeland of Job (Job 1:1), the precise location of which is unknown. Many modern scholars place it somewhere in the desert south of the Dead Sea, perhaps near Edom (Lam.

4:21; cf. Jer. 25:20, which seems to associate it with Philistine territory) or somewhat to the north, in the same apparent vicinity as the homes of Job's three friends (Job 2:11). Others follow Josephus and subsequent Christian and Muslim tradition in placing Uz at Hauron, south of Damascus (possibly the land settled by Aram's son, Gen. 10:23).

UZAI [uʻzī] (Heb. *ʼûzay*). The father of Palal, one who helped build Nehemiah's wall (Neh. 3:25).

UZAL [uʻzəl] (Heb. *ʼûzāl*).
1. A son of Joktan and descendant of Shem (Gen. 10:27 par. 1 Chr. 1:21). His descendants constituted an Arabian tribe located at ʻAzal (modern Sanʻa, the capital of Yemen).
2. A city in Syria, possibly modern Azalla (Ezek. 27:19). The RSV rendering of the difficult Hebrew text makes Uzal a source of wine.

UZZA [ŭzʻə] (Heb. *ʻuzzāʼ*) (PERSON).
1. A Benjaminite; son of Gera (Heglam) and a descendant of Ehud (1 Chr. 8:7).
2. An ancestor of temple servants who returned with Zerubbabel to Jerusalem from exile in Babylon (Ezra 2:49 par. Neh. 7:51).

UZZA [ŭzʻə] (Heb. *ʻuzzāʼ*) (PLACE). A palace garden where the Judahite kings Manasseh and Amon were buried (2 Kgs. 21:18, 26). Why the garden was so named is disputed. The parallel account (2 Chr. 33:20, 25) omits the name.

UZZAH [ŭzʻə] (Heb. *ʻuzzāʻ, ʻuzzâ*).
1. (Heb. *ʻuzzāʼ*). A son of Abinadab, in whose house the ark of the covenant had remained twenty years. Uzzah guided the ox-cart carrying the ark as it was transported to Jerusalem; when the oxen stumbled, he touched the ark to steady it. For this irreverence he was smitten by God and died (2 Sam. 6:3-7; 1 Chr. 13:7-11).
2. (Heb. *ʻuzzâ*). A Levite of the family of Merari (1 Chr. 6:29 [MT 14]).

UZZEN-SHEERAH [ŭzʻən shēʻə rə] (Heb. *ʼuzzēn šeʻeʻrâ* "ear of Sheerah"). One of three villages built by Sheerah, the daughter (or granddaughter) of Ephraim (1 Chr. 7:24; KJV "Uzzen Sherah"). Some scholars have identified the site as modern Beit Sira, 5 km. (3 mi.) southwest of Lower Beth-horon, but others demur.

UZZI [ŭzʻī] (Heb. *ʻuzzî* "my strength").
1. An Aaronic priest descended from Eleazar, son of Bukki and father of Zerahiah (1 Chr. 6:5-6, 51 [MT 5:31-32; 6:36), and an ancestor of Ezra (Ezra 7:4).
2. A son of Tola of the tribe of Issachar (1 Chr. 7:2-3).
3. A son of Bela of the tribe of Benjamin (1 Chr. 7:7).
4. The father of Elah, one of the first Benjaminites to resettle on their own property in Jerusalem after the Babylonian exile (1 Chr. 9:8).
5. The son of Bani, and a descendant of Asaph;

overseer of the postexilic Levites in Jerusalem (Neh. 11:22).

6. The head of Jedaiah's priestly lineage while Joiakim was high priest (Neh. 12:19).

7. A priest who participated in the dedication ceremony of the repaired walls of Jerusalem (Neh. 12:42).

UZZIA [ə zī'ə] (Heb. *ʿuzzîyā*'). An Ashterathite; one of David's mighty men (1 Chr. 11:44). He is absent from the list in 2 Sam. 23:24-39).

UZZIAH [ə zī'ə] (Heb. *ʿuzzîyâ, ʿuzzîyāhû* "Yahweh is my strength"; Gk. *Ōzias*).

1. The son of King Amaziah and Queen Jecoliah, and the ninth king of Judah. Uzziah, his throne name, is used at 2 Kgs. 15:13, 30, 32, 34 and throughout 2 Chr. 26:1–27:2; his personal name, AZARIAH (**3**) ("Yahweh has helped"), was preferred by the author of Kings (2 Kgs. 14:21; 15:1, 6-8, 17, 23, 27). The Hebrew spelling of the two names differs by only one consonant, and the meanings of their root words came to be virtually interchangeable.

Although the precise dates are disputed, both biblical accounts record the length of Uzziah's reign as fifty-two years (*ca.* 783-742; 2 Kgs. 15:2; 2 Chr. 26:3). This almost certainly includes coregencies both with his father Amaziah (perhaps as long as fifteen years) and his son Jotham (ten years or so). Uzziah began to rule at the age of sixteen, acclaimed king by the very people who had rejected and assassinated his father (2 Kgs. 14:21; 15:2; 2 Chr. 26:1). In Matthew's genealogy of Jesus he is called the son of Joram (Matt. 1:8-9; KJV "Ozias").

The author of 2 Kings provides only the barest outline of Uzziah's long and illustrious reign: he feared God, yet did not remove the high places (a deficiency omitted by the Chronicler) and thus as punishment was made a leper (2 Kgs. 15:1-7). The details are supplied by the Chronicler (2 Chr. 26), who focuses on Uzziah's devotion to Yahweh, which led in turn to success in military endeavors and his enthusiasm for agriculture. Yet at the height of his power the proud Uzziah attempted to usurp the temple prerogatives of the priests and thus was stricken with leprosy (*ca.* 750), thus ending his public exercise of kingship. (Josephus *Ant.* ix.225 and later rabbinic tradition assert that the devastating and long-remembered earthquake during Uzziah's reign [Amos 1:1; Zech. 14:5] occurred at the precise moment of his sin.) Uzziah was confined to a "separate house" (2 Chr. 26:21), possi-

bly a hospital or isolation room; more probably the term means that he was relieved of his official duties. Many scholars believe, however, that his influence and perhaps even his authority continued as long as he lived. A tomb inscription from the first century B.C. appears to confirm the Chronicler's statement that Uzziah was buried outside the royal burial ground (v. 23; cf. 2 Kgs. 15:7).

Despite the manner in which his reign ended, Uzziah had ruled long and well. Judah's prosperity during Uzziah's kingship was greater than in any other period after Solomon.

2. (Heb. *ʿuzzîyâ*). The son of Uriel and father of Shaul; a Levite of the Kohathite branch (1 Chr. 6:24 [MT 9]).

3. (Heb. *ʿuzzîyāhû*). The father of Jonathan, an overseer of royal supplies during King David's reign (1 Chr. 27:25).

4. (Heb. *ʿuzzîyâ*). A priest in the time of Ezra who had taken a foreign wife (Ezra 10:21).

5. The father of Athaiah, a Judahite who came to live in Jerusalem after the Babylonian exile (Neh. 11:4).

6. A Simeonite, the son of Micah, and a magistrate of Bethulia (Jdt. 6:15; KJV "Ozias").

UZZIEL [ŭz'ĭ əl] (Heb. *ʿuzzîʾēl* "God is my strength").

1. A grandson of Levi, and one of the four sons of Kohath (Exod. 6:18, 22 par. 1 Chr. 6:2, 18 [MT 5:28; 6:3]); the uncle of Aaron. Uzziel's sons Mishael and Elzaphan carried the bodies of their cousins Nadab and Abihu outside the camp after they were killed offering unholy fire before Yahweh (Lev. 10:4-5). His descendants were the Uzzielites (Heb. *āzzîʾēlî*), who together with the other three Kohathite clans were responsible for care of the sanctuary (Num. 3:27; 1 Chr. 26:23; cf. 23:12, 20; 24:24). Uzzielites also assisted King David in bringing the ark of the covenant to Jerusalem (15:10; cf. v. 2).

2. One of the five sons of Ishi who during the reign of King Hezekiah led five hundred Simeonites to victory over the Amalekites on Mt. Seir (1 Chr. 4:41-43).

3. One of five sons of Bela, head of a Benjaminite family (1 Chr. 7:7).

4. One of the sons of Heman (1 Chr. 25:4), head of a clan of temple musicians appointed by King David. He is called Azarel at v. 18.

5. A Levite of the lineage of Jeduthun, among the Levites who worked to reestablish the temple service during the reforms of King Hezekiah (2 Chr. 29:14).

6. The son of Harhaiah; a goldsmith who helped Nehemiah rebuild the wall of Jerusalem (Neh. 3:8).

V

VAIZATHA [vī'zə thə] (Heb. *wayzāṯāʾ*). One of the ten sons of Haman killed in Susa by the Jews on their day of reprisal against their enemies (Esth. 9:9; KJV "Vajezatha").

VALLEY. The several Hebrew words so translated represent a variety of topographical formations in Palestine. Heb. *biqʿâ* (from *bāqaʿ* "cleave, break open") and *ʿēmeq* (cf. BDB, p. 770, "deepening, depth") normally represent the area between mountains, whether wide, flat plain or narrow cleft, and are often used in contrast with mountains or hills (e.g., Deut. 8:7; Ps. 104:8; Mic. 1:4). Both of these terms are applied occasionally to specific, named valleys (e.g., Num. 32:9, "Valley of Eshcol"; Deut. 34:3, "valley of Jericho"; Josh. 7:24, 26, "Valley of Achor"; cf. 2 Chr. 35:22; RSV "plain of Megiddo"). The more generic term *gayeʾ* (e.g., Num. 21:20) also occurs in place names (2 Chr. 28:3, "valley of the son of Hinnom"; Ezek. 39:11, 15, "Valley of the Travelers [or Abarim], Valley of Hamon-gog"). Although *naḥal* can refer to a permanent stream (e.g., Lev. 11:9; 1 Kgs. 18:40), it more often indicates a wadi, a dry riverbed that becomes a torrent in the rainy season (e.g., Deut. 21:4; Ps. 104:10; RSV "valley"; cf. the figurative use at 124:4; Isa. 66:12; Jer. 47:2). Heb. *šepēlâ*, translated "lowland" (e.g., Deut. 1:7; KJV "vale") or transliterated "Shephelah" (e.g., Jer. 32:44; KJV "valley"), nearly always refers to a specific range of low hills between Judah and Philistia; *see* SHEPHELAH. The only New Testament occurrence of "valley" is Gk. *pháranx* at Luke 3:5, a quotation from the LXX of Isa. 40:4 (Heb. *gayeʾ*).

Inhabited by the Canaanites before the Hebrews conquered the land (Gen. 19:29; Num. 14:25), the valleys of Palestine became battlegrounds (Gen. 14:8; Judg. 7:12) and invited enemy raids (1 Chr. 14:9, 13). Nevertheless, they were fertile, watered by springs and fountains (Deut. 8:7) and rain (11:11), and thus were chosen by the Hebrews for building cities (Judg. 18:28; Jer. 21:13), planting crops (1 Sam. 6:13; Ps. 65:13 [MT 14]; cf. Num. 13:23), and grazing herds (1 Chr. 27:29).

The prophets made significant reference to valleys, whether in condemning idolatry (Jer. 2:23) or in en-couraging the people of Yahweh (Isa. 40:4; Ezek. 37:1-4; cf. Ps. 23:4).

See further the articles on specific valleys.

VALLEY GATE (Heb. *šaʿar haggayeʾ*). A gate in the southwestern wall of Jerusalem leading into the valley of Hinnom. Fortified with towers by King Uzziah (2 Chr. 26:9), the Valley Gate suffered great damage, along with the rest of the city wall, when Jerusalem was destroyed in 587/6 B.C. Before beginning his rebuilding project, Nehemiah passed through the Valley Gate at night to inspect the damage to the walls (Neh. 2:13-15; KJV "gate of the valley"). Neh. 3:13 details the repairs made by Hanun and the inhabitants of Zanoah on the gate and the 1000 cubits of city wall separating it from the Dung Gate.

VANIAH [və nī'ə] (Heb. *wanyâ*; cf. Pers. "worthy of love"). An Israelite in the time of Ezra who had taken a foreign wife (Ezra 10:36).

VANITY. In biblical usage nothingness, emptiness, or chaos, rather than the attitude of arrogance or pride associated with the word in English. The term is also used in connection with idols or idolatry.

The biblical sense is apparent in the most frequent Hebrew word for vanity, *heḇel*, which means primarily "vapor" (Prov. 21:6) or "breath" (Isa. 57:13). The term connotes the transitory nature of life (esp. Eccl. 1:14; 2:11, 17; 4:16; 6:9, where it occurs in parallel with "striving after wind"; cf. Ps. 39:5 [MT 6]; 144:4) or that which is ultimately unsatisfying (62:9 [MT 10]; cf. Job 15:31, *rîq, šāweʾ*).

Vanity is placing one's own self or pursuits above those of God or others. The results are ultimately worthless and as fleeting as vapor, for if one's purposes are not consonant with the eternal purposes of God, then one's efforts are for naught. Vanity thus encompasses the delusion of the person who lives without regard for divine law or God's guidance and sustaining power (Ps. 2:1; 4:2 [MT 3]; cf. KJV, 94:11; Hab. 2:13). It is applied with this sense specifically to the Gentiles (Isa. 30:28; RSV "destruction"; cf. Eph. 4:17; RSV "futility"). Such is the false reality that one creates by deceit or guile (KJV, Job 31:5; RSV "falsehood"; Ps. 12:2 [MT 3]; RSV "lies"; 24:4; RSV "what is false"; cf. Prov. 30:8; Ezek. 13:6, 8-9).

Idols or idolatry are "vanity," worthless images formed by human hands (Deut. 32:21; RSV "no god"; Ps. 31:6 [MT 7]; RSV "vain idols"; cf. Isa. 57:13; Acts 14:15), perishable works of delusion that lack "breath" (Heb. *rûaḥ* "wind, spirit"; Jer. 51:17-18; cf. Isa. 40:17, 23; *tōhû* "chaos").

Heb. *ʾāwen* "wickedness," translated "vanity" by the KJV, is better rendered "mischief" (Job 15:35; Ps. 10:7) or "calamity" (Prov. 22:8).

Similarly, Gk. *mataiótēs* ranges in meaning from "nothingness" (2 Pet. 2:18; RSV "folly") to "chaos" (Rom. 8:20; RSV "futility").

Bibliography. O. Bauernfeind, "μάταιος," *TDNT* 4 (1967): 519-524; K. Seybold, "hebel [hebhel]," *TDOT* 3 (1978): 313:320.

VASHNI (1 Chr. 6:28, KJV). *See* JOEL **1.**

VASHTI [văsh'tī] (Heb. *waštî*; cf. Pers. *vahišta* "the best," *uas* "one who is beloved"). The wife of King Ahasuerus (Xerxes I, 486-465 B.C.; so NIV). On the last day of a great feast the king commanded Vashti to come before his guests to exhibit her beauty (Esth. 1:10-11). Her refusal so enraged him that she was removed from her royal office (vv. 12-19). Though Ahasuerus may soon have regretted his hasty decision (2:1), he accepted his attendants' suggestion that another woman be found to take Vashti's place as queen (vv. 2-4); that woman was Esther (v. 17).

Attempts to identify Vashti with Xerxes' queen Amestris or Stateira, the consort of Artaxerxes II, are unconvincing. Some scholars identify the name as that of an Elamite goddess.

VEGETABLES. A variety of vegetables are mentioned in the Bible, beginning in Genesis where Esau sold his birthright to Jacob for lentil pottage (Gen. 25:29-34). Lentils and beans were among the foodstuffs provided to David and his entourage when he fled from Absalom (2 Sam. 17:28), and were ingredients in Ezekiel's siege bread (Ezek. 4:9) as well.

In the desert the Israelites cried out for the cucumbers, melons, leeks, onions, and garlic they had enjoyed in Egypt. References in the postbiblical literature show that these vegetables were grown in biblical Palestine (cf. 1 Kgs. 21:2); Isa. 1:8 mentions a cucumber field large enough to require a lodge for a watchman (cf. Jer. 10:5). Deut. 11:10-12 indicates that growing vegetables in the promised land could be accomplished without the irrigation needed in Egypt. Prov. 15:17 (cf. 2 Kgs. 4:38-40) suggests that a meal of vegetables alone was less than the best of fare. Nonetheless, a vegetable diet, probably including grains (Dan. 1:12; Heb. *hazzērōʿîm* "things sown"), suited Daniel and his companions quite well (vv. 8-16).

At Rom. 14:2, Paul considers the person who for religious reasons limits his diet to vegetables (Gk. *láchana*; KJV "herbs") to be weak in faith.

See further the individual entries.

VEIL. A covering primarily for a woman's head and shoulders, sometimes including the face. Heb. *ṣāʿip* designates the shawl worn by Rebekah when she first met Isaac (perhaps indicating her marital status; Gen.

24:65) and the wrapper Tamar used to deceive her father-in-law Judah (38:14, 19). The *ṣammâ* was a veil that enhanced rather than hid the beauty of the wearer (Cant. 4:1, 3; 6:7; cf. Isa. 47:2; KJV "locks"). The Old Testament evidence does not suggest that Hebrew women were always required to veil their faces as some Near Eastern women do. Sarai, Abram's wife, made no attempt to hide her beauty from the Egyptians (Gen. 12:14), nor did young Rebekah cover her face when she went to draw water from the city's well (24:15-16).

Moses wore a veil (*masweh*) or mask to cover his face when it was radiant from contact with Yahweh (Exod. 34:29-35). Paul reinterprets and spiritualizes this veil to represent the Jewish inability to understand the Scriptures correctly (2 Cor. 3:7-18; Gk. *kálymma*; cf. 4:3). The same Greek root (*katakalýptō*) is found at 1 Cor. 11:6, part of a very difficult passage where veil (lit. "covering") seems a probable translation (RSV "veil" for Gk. *exousía* "authority" at v. 10 is clearly interpretive).

The most frequently mentioned veil (Heb. *pārōḵeṯ*; KJV "vail") is the multi-colored curtain, decorated with cherubim and suspended from hooks attached to four wooden pillars, placed in the tabernacle between the holy place and the most holy place (e.g., Exod. 26:31-35; 2 Chr. 3:14). This covering signified the separation of the people from God, but also represented a meeting place for the two parties in the covenant (Exod. 30:6). A second curtain hung at the entrance to the tabernacle (26:37; RSV "screen"). When the tabernacle was moved, the inner veil was taken down and used to cover the ark (Num. 4:5).

The Synoptic Gospels note the rending of the temple veil at the moment of Christ's death (Gk. *katapétasma*; Matt. 27:51; Mark 15:38; cf. Luke 23:45), although it is debated which of the two curtains is indicated. Many scholars favor the inner curtain; if so, the holy of holies was exposed, thus opening the way of access to God (cf. Heb. 6:19; 9:3; 10:20, although no mention is made of a torn veil). However, the rending of the inner veil would not have been a public sign, as only a few priests could go inside. More likely the veil implied was that hung at the entrance to Herod's temple and thus visible to the people. As such, its splitting portended the coming destruction of the temple (cf. Mark 13:2; 14:58; 15:29) and of the formal structures of Judaism.

VERMILION (Heb. *šāšēr*; Gk. *míltos*). A bright red mineral pigment used in painting, routinely applied by the Assyrians and the Babylonians to their bas reliefs. Jeremiah condemned King Jehoiakim of Judah for his attention to the furnishing of his own palace, painted in vermilion (Jer. 22:14), rather than to the cause of the poor and needy (vv. 16-17). Ezekiel, in his allegorical condemnation of the idolatry of Samaria and Jerusalem (Ezek. 23), refers to the latter's lusting after Chaldean soldiers "portrayed in vermilion" (vv. 14-16). According to Wis. 13:14, wooden idols were painted with "red paint."

VERSE.* The primary unit of division, together with chapters, of virtually all modern editions and translations of the Bible, yet not found in the original manuscripts. Verse divisions were introduced into the Hebrew Bible in the early centuries of the Christian era and were fixed substantially in their present form *ca.* A.D. 900. The thirty-nine books were divided into approximately 23,100 verses.

The first Bible to be printed with verses (in the margin) appeared in 1528, but with a system different from the present one introduced soon after by the French printer Robert Estienne (Stephanus) in a Greek New Testament he published in 1551. His Latin Bible of 1555 was the first to show such verse divisions in both testaments, and it was followed in English by the Geneva Bible (1560) and the succeeding editions in many languages down to the present day.

These verse divisions facilitated the finding of particular passages in the Bible. But in the early editions each verse was printed with the first line indented, thus each appeared to be a separate paragraph (e.g., KJV; cf. NASB, NKJV). This suggested that each verse of the Bible could be legitimately interpreted in isolation from its literary context, making it more difficult to grasp the point of any whole paragraph or passage. This is a primary reason why several English translations print the verse numbers in the margins, alongside rather than within the text (e.g., Phillips, NEB, JB). Others, with similar motivation, print the verse numbers within the text but indent only the first line of each paragraph (e.g., RSV, NIV, NJV, TEV, NAB).

VERSIONS. *See* BIBLE TRANSLATIONS.

VESPASIAN [věs pā'shən].† Titus Flavius Sabinus Vespasianus (A.D. 9-79), Roman emperor (69-79), founder of the Flavian dynasty. Born into a poor family, Vespasian became a gifted soldier, serving in Germany and Britain, where under Claudius he conquered the Isle of Wight. He became consul in Britain in A.D. 51 and in 63 proconsul of Africa under Nero. In 66 he was given command of the war against the Jews. After Nero's death, Vespasian recognized Otho and then Vitellius. However, in 69 soldiers in Judea and Alexandria proclaimed him emperor. Winning widespread support, including that of the Senate, he returned to Italy to claim his title, entering Rome in 70. In that year his son Titus completed the defeat of Jerusalem and destroyed the holy temple. In the first two years of his reign the Batavian rebellion was likewise suppressed. In 71 Titus joined his father in Rome for a triumphal celebration. At that time Vespasian closed the gates of the temple of Janus and built the temple of peace. He began constructing the Colosseum and acquired further conquests in Germany and Britain. He and Titus kept a tight grip on the consulate and other positions in the government. Upon his death in 79 he was succeeded by Titus.

The Mishnah (*Soṭah* ix.14) mentions that during "Vespasian's war" Jewish bridegrooms stopped wearing crowns, part of a series of losses in dignity and purity suffered by the Jews. The Sibylline Oracles (Sib. Or. 12:99-116) minimize Vespasian's harm to Jerusalem and emphasize his destruction of Phoenicia and Syria.

VIA DOLOROSA [vē'ə dŭ lə rō'sə] (Lat. "way of suffering").† The traditional route taken by Jesus through Jerusalem as he was led to his crucifixion. The Via Dolorosa begins at the traditional site of Jesus' condemnation by Pilate and ends at the tomb of Christ within the Church of the Holy Sepulchre. Along the way are fourteen devotional stations for pilgrims clearly marked on walls. Two stations begin the Via Dolorosa in the vicinity of the Ecce Homo arch (just inside St Stephen's Gate), seven are found along the city street, and five are within the Church of the Holy Sepulchre. Each Friday at 3 p.m. pilgrims may join the Franciscan Fathers of Jerusalem as they walk the route in memory of Jesus' passion.

The notion of retracing Jesus' steps began with the Byzantine Church. The Spanish nun Egeria, a fourth-century pilgrim, records that on Thursday night of Holy Week Christians would march from Gethsemane (in the Kidron valley) to Constantine's great Church of the Holy Sepulchre without stopping at intermediate stations. In the eighth century the route seems to have gone south to Mt. Zion and then on to the Sepulchre. Medieval Latin Christians observed rival ceremonies: some insisted that Pilate resided at Fortress Antonia north of the temple, while others placed his residence on Mt. Zion. This controversy underscores the difficulty of reconstructing the Via Dolorosa. It should begin at the Praetorium, or the Roman governor's quarters; but did Pilate reside at the Antonia as tradition has it, or did he use Herod the Great's magnificent palace on Mt. Zion? Josephus' mention of a later procurator, Florus, using the palace (*BJ* ii.14 [301]) is reasonable in view of the convenience and fortification offered by the latter location.

The present route was established in the eighteenth century, but it had only ten stations. The current arrangement of fourteen stations was agreed on in the nineteenth century.

VIAL (Heb. *paḵ*). A small container for oil or perfume. Samuel used such a container when he anointed Saul as king of Israel (1 Sam. 10:1). The Hebrew term occurs also in the account of one of the sons of the prophets anointing Jehu king at Elisha's command (2 Kgs. 9:1, 3; RSV "flask"; KJV "box").

The KJV translates Gk. *phiálē* as vial with reference to a broad, shallow cup or bowl (so RSV) filled with incense (Rev. 5:8; cf. Josephus *Ant.* iii.6.6) or, symbolically, a portion of the wrath of God to be poured out upon the earth (Rev. 15:7; 16:1-17; 17:1; 21:9).

VILLAGE (Heb. *ḥāṣer*; Gk. *kṓmē*).† A small, generally unfortified settlement (Deut. 3:5; 1 Sam. 16:18; Esth. 9:19), in biblical usage often difficult to distinguish from the TOWN (cf. Luke 13:22). Archaeological evidence suggests that urban life developed from the agricultural village, generally the home base for ancient Palestinian (and ancient Near Eastern) transhumants (cf. Gen. 13:2, 12; 26:12-14). The village might be no more than a hamlet, scarcely distinguishable from the open field (Ezek. 38:11; cf. Lev. 25:34). Villages might be founded by a city (cf. the Hebrew construction *baṯ* X, lit. "daughter of X," especially common in genealogical material; e.g., 1 Chr. 1:50; 2:3, 21, 35, 49; cf. Ps. 48:11 [MT 12]). A number of villages might be associated with a city, thus references to a city "and its villages" (e.g., Josh. 15:32-62; cf. Jer. 49:2-3), and generally were dependent upon the larger walled settlement for protection and might in turn provide military service (Judg. 5:7, 11; *see* PEASANTRY).

VINE (Heb. *gepen*; Gk. *ámpelos*), **VINEYARD** (Heb. *kerem*; Gk. *ampelốn*).† Since antiquity the agriculture of Israel has relied largely on the unfailing produce of a trinity of products: the olive, the fig, and the grape. Often they are mentioned together (e.g., Jotham's parable, Judg. 9:7-15; cf. Ps. 128:3; Sir. 39:26-27) since in the hill country of Israel it is common for all three to be present in any single vista.

The vine is able to flourish in Israel because of its long, hot summers. It sinks its roots down deeply and therefore can withstand the severest draught. Vineyards are often planted on the hillsides in terraces or in the mountain valleys (so Samaria, Jer. 31:5; Shechem, Judg. 9:26-27; Shiloh, 21:19-20; Hebron, Num. 13:22-23), but in Philistia they can be found on the plains (e.g., Timnah, Judg. 14:5; cf. northern Jezreel, 1 Kgs. 21:1). Even the Judean wilderness near the Dead Sea could grow the vine if a spring was available (En-gedi, Cant. 1:14). The same is true of Transjordan, the destruction of whose vines the Old Testament prophets mourned (Isa. 16:8-9; Jer. 48:32). The vine was so characteristic of prosperity that when Joshua and Caleb were sent to spy out the land of Canaan, they returned carrying an enormous cluster of grapes (Num. 13:26-27). The valley of Eshcol ("valley of the cluster") near Hebron that the spies visited remains famous for its vineyards.

I. Cultivation

In the biblical era a number of steps were required to plant a vineyard and successfully harvest its grapes (cf. Isa. 5:1-5, the Song of the Vineyard). Work could be done by the vineyard owner with his laborers (Matt. 20:1-16), or the field might be let out to tenants (Cant. 8:11; Matt. 21:33-41). First, the soil had to be cleared of stones. Then these rocks were employed to build terraces that limited soil erosion and increased acreage. Often a stone wall was built to keep out animals such as boars (Ps. 80:13 [MT 14]) and foxes (Cant. 2:15), as well as thieves (Jer. 49:9). A watchtower might insure the safety of the crop, especially at harvest time (Isa. 5:2).

The vines were planted in parallel rows far enough apart to allow the plow to pass through. The plant was allowed to trail along the ground, but the fruit-bearing branches were propped up with stones or forked sticks. Sometimes vines were allowed to climb a tree, an arbor, or a trellis (1 Kgs. 4:25 [MT 5:5]; Ezek. 19:10-11). Pruning took place twice during the season. First, in February-March the vines were cut back so severely that they appeared to be mere wooden stalks without life. Then in August, when the vine had filled in with leaves, the farmer cut off the new small shoots so that the main fruit-bearing stems would obtain greater nourishment (Isa. 18:5; John 15:2).

The vineyard was ready for harvest in late summer, generally in September. Before this time the grapes would be too sour for consumption (cf. Jer. 31:29-30).

When the crop had ripened sufficiently, laborers would gather the grapes into baskets. The fruit was eaten fresh, dried into raisins (cf. 2 Sam. 6:19; 1 Chr. 16:3), and sometimes boiled into a honey relish. Most important, the vineyard usually had a winepress so that the bulk of the harvest could be crushed to make wine (*see* WINE). Specific laws applied to the harvest: the vineyard should not be stripped bare, and the gleanings had to be left for the poor (Lev. 19:10; Deut. 24:21). In addition, in observance of the Sabbatical Year the vineyard was to be left unpruned and unharvested (Lev. 25:3-5).

II. Imagery

In the Old Testament the vine is a rich symbol for Israel. Yahweh has planted, cultivated, and protected his people, and in return he expects fruit from them. Ps. 80:8-13 (MT 9-14) typically develops this metaphor, emphasizing how Israel was a transplanted vine rescued from Egypt and relocated in good soil. According to Isa. 27:2-3, the Lord protects and rejoices over his vineyard, Israel. But most often the vineyard metaphor depicts the shortcomings of Israel. Its vineyard walls have been broken and its crop ravaged (Ps. 80:12 [MT 13]). The prophets repeat the theme again and again. Jeremiah asks how the vine has become a "wild vine" (Jer. 2:21; cf. 5:10; 12:10-11). Isaiah speaks with utter dismay about the Lord's disappointing harvest of wild grapes despite God's care and nurture (Isa. 5:1-4; cf. Hos. 9:10). This means that the vineyard must be judged. Its wall will be broken, his protection removed, and its vines no longer weeded or hoed; even the rain upon it shall cease (Isa. 5:5-7). Its wood will be burned like useless timber (Ezek. 15; cf. Rev. 14:19-20).

The vine remained an important symbol in intertestamental Judaism (e.g., 2 Esdr. 5:23). An abounding vineyard was the symbol of the goodness of the eschaton or Day of the Lord (2 Apoc.Bar. 29:5). In Sirach wisdom is described as a vine glorious with abundant fruit (Sir. 24:17-22).

In the Roman period even Herod the Great's rebuilt temple adopted the image. Between the porch and the holy place was a golden gate on which was affixed a gold vine. Clusters of gold grapes hung from it, and wealthy families would give gold tendrils, berries, and leaves as gifts so the vine might always grow larger (Josephus *BJ* v.5.4 [120]; Mishnah *Mid.* iii.8).

It comes as no surprise that Jesus would imply the symbolism of the vine in his ministry. In two parables he uses the well-known context of vineyard labor to illustrate God's grace to all who are sent into the "vineyard" (Matt. 20:1-16) and to explain the nature of true obedience (21:28-32). His most important parable is found at Mark 12:1-11, where he sweeps up the prophetic rebuke and criticizes the Jewish leadership as unrighteous tenants of God's vineyard. Here, however, the tenants (rather than the vineyard) will be destroyed and the vineyard passed on to others.

The vine may have been a messianic symbol for Judaism (2 Apoc.Bar. 39:7), for at John 15:1-11 Jesus develops the metaphor of Jesus as the true vine. This means that attachment to Jesus determines one's connection with the people of God (cf. Rom. 11:17-24), with fruitbearing as the natural result (John 15:4). This is consonant with the theology of John wherein Jesus redefines the "people of Israel" (or "descendants of Abraham") by virtue of his own coming (8:34-49; 10:1-18; cf. Rom. 2:28-29).

Bibliography. D. Baly, *The Geography of the Bible*, rev. ed. (New York: 1974), pp. 77-90; H. F. Lutz, *Viticulture and Brewing in the Ancient Orient* (New York: 1922).

VINEGAR (Heb. *ḥōmēṣ*; Gk. *oxós*). A sour liquid made from fermented wine or other strong drink. Its acid content was well known (Prov. 10:26; 25:20), but, when diluted with water, vinegar was not an uncommon drink among the lower classes (cf. KJV, Ruth 2:14; RSV "wine"). Undiluted, it was fit only for one's enemies (Ps. 69:21 [MT 22]).

Vinegar was the drink offered to Jesus on the cross. Matt. 27:48; Mark 15:36 report this as a gesture of compassion, while Luke 23:36 presents it as an attempt to humiliate Jesus. The incident is presented in John as the fulfillment of Scripture (John 19:29-30; Ps. 69:21 [MT 22]). The mixture of wine (Gk. *oînos* [KJV "vinegar"]) and gall that Jesus had refused earlier (Matt. 27:34) was intended as a sedative.

On dietary restrictions for Nazirites at Num. 6:3, *see* NAZIRITE.

VIPER (Heb. *'epʿeh* "hiss"; Gk. *échidna*), Any of a variety of species of snakes (family Viperidae), usually poisonous. It is difficult to identify the biblical references to viper with any particular species.

Because dread of snakes is a widespread phenomenon, it is not surprising that in biblical usage vipers often symbolize evil or evil people (e.g., Ps. 140:3 [MT 4]; Isa. 30:6; 59:5). Job 20:16 exemplifies the ancient (mis)belief that a snake's tongue was poisonous (JB, NIV "adder"). The description of Dan as "a viper by the path" (Gen. 49:17; Heb. *šᵉpîpōn*) reflects the behavior of certain species of desert vipers (perhaps *Echis colorata* or *Cerastes verastes cornutus*; cf. JB mg.).

In the New Testament the Pharisees and company are described graphically as a brood of vipers. Indeed, young vipers in batches of twelve to fifty emerge live from their mother's body, having hatched inside. Both John the Baptist and Jesus found this an apt image of their opponents (Matt. 3:7; 12:34; 23:33; cf. Luke 3:7, where John applies the image to the multitudes rather than the Pharisees).

The one literal reference in the New Testament is Acts 28:3, where Paul is bitten by a viper but, contrary to the expectations of the people of Malta, does not die (vv. 4-6). The *Vipera aspis* may be intended here, a species found along the Mediterranean coast and still present on Sicily and other islands, although no longer on Malta.

VIRGIN (Heb. *bᵉtûlâ*, *'almâ*; Gk. *parthénos*).† In the basic sense, a woman who has not experienced sexual intercourse. The technical term for virgin in the Old Testament is Heb. *bᵉtûlâ*, from a root meaning "separated," hence "a woman living apart." Strictly speaking, the term designates a young woman who is sexually mature and of marriageable age, but who as yet has not had sexual relations. However, the term does not necessarily always mean a literal virgin. In some cases it is clear from the context that the woman at issue is a virgin (e.g., Gen. 24:16; Judg. 21:12), but elsewhere the emphasis on the virginity of the woman is missing (e.g., Jer. 31:13; Lam. 1:4, 18; 2:10, 21; RSV, NIV "maidens"). Sometimes the expression "who had not known man" or "whom no man had known" is added to remove any doubt. A less common term is *'almâ*, which literally means a "young woman" of marriageable age, and does not necessarily imply chastity. Yet in some instances *'almâ* does explicitly mean virgin (e.g., Gen. 24:43; RSV "young woman"; cf. LXX), with no clear distinction from *bᵉtûlâ*. The Greek equivalent for *bᵉtûlâ* is *parthénos*, usually translated "virgin" in the New Testament. Normally, *neánis* "young woman" is used to translate *'almâ* in the LXX except in a few cases where *parthénos* occurs, most notably Isa. 7:14 (RSV mg. "virgin").

The controversy as to how Isa. 7:14 should be interpreted—whether referring to a virgin (KJV, NIV, RSV mg.) or a young (perhaps married) woman (RSV, NEB, NJV; JB "maiden")—is especially important because Matthew uses this verse in his account of Jesus' birth (Matt. 1:18-25, esp. v. 23; "virgin," following LXX; cf. Luke 1:26-38). These accounts of the Nativity are the foundation for the doctrine of the Virgin Birth, that Mary conceived Jesus not by sexual intercourse but by the Holy Spirit (Matt. 1:18, 20, 25; Luke 1:27, 34-35). Both accounts present the birth as the coming of Jesus as the Messiah, God's anointed son. Some interpreters see the very birth as evidence of Jesus' humanity, while others (even though they may contend that normal biological processes occurred) view the statements concerning conception as symbolic of the divine aspect of Jesus. Roman Catholic tradition, in particular, holds that Mary remained a virgin "perpetually," neither conceiving nor bearing other children.

The Mosaic law features certain regulations pertaining to virgins. When a young man dishonored a virgin, he was required to pay her father a dowry and marry the woman (Exod. 22:16-17 [MT 15-16]; cf. Deut. 22:19, 28-29). When a young married woman was suspected of having surrendered her virginity before marriage, her husband could demand that her father produce "tokens of virginity" (Heb. *bᵉtûlîm*), normally a sheet or garment stained with the blood of the consummation from the wedding night (v. 17; cf. 2 Sam. 13:18, where Tamar [as other royal virgins] wore a "long robe with sleeves" as a symbol of her virginity). If such tokens could not be produced, the woman was stoned to death for harlotry (Deut. 22:21). However, the law did distinguish between premarital sexual relations to which the virgin consented (for which she and her partner were both punished; vv. 23-24) and rape, over which she had no control (vv. 25-27).

The Old Testament exalts virginity as a virtue. Some authors mention by name women whose conduct had been exemplary, namely Rebekah before she married Isaac (Gen. 24:16), the daughter of Jephthah who remained a virgin throughout her short life (Judg. 11:37-38), and Tamar who was violated by her brother Amnon (2 Sam. 13:2, 14-15). Virginity is used figuratively to represent the purity of Israel's relationship with Yahweh (e.g., Isa. 62:5). The prophets criticized Jerusalem, Judah, and the northern tribes for not always remaining "chaste"; for instead of being faithful to their covenant God they committed harlotry by serving idols (Jer. 18:13; cf. Ezek. 23:3, 8).

In one of his parables Jesus likened those ready for the kingdom of God to five wise virgins who carried enough oil to keep their lamps burning as they awaited the arrival of the bridegroom, unlike the five foolish virgins whose lamps went out for lack of oil (Matt. 25:1-13). Paul teaches (1 Cor. 7:25-28) that virgins (so KJV, NIV; RSV, "unmarried"; JB, "celibate") could best serve the Lord if they did not marry; his reasoning is that a married woman will have opened herself to more distractions than if she remained single. In another context, Paul extols the Old Testament example of chastity when he tells the Corinthian Christians that he had intended to present them as a "pure bride" to their bridegroom, Jesus Christ (2 Cor. 11:2). John describes the "spotless" followers of Christ as men who are "chaste" (so RSV), undefiled by women (Rev. 14:4; KJV, RSV mg. "virgins"; cf. JB; NIV "pure").

Bibliography. T. D. Boslooper, *The Virgin Birth* (Philadelphia: 1962); R. E. Brown, *The Birth of the Messiah* (Garden City: 1979), pp. 122-164, 517-542; *The Virginal Conception and Bodily Resurrection of Jesus* (New York: 1973).

VIRGIN, APOCALYPSE OF THE. * Two unrelated but somewhat similar works, probably from *ca.* the ninth century A.D. Both were composed in Greek, but one is now extant only in Ethiopic. The Greek text concerns a visit by the Virgin Mary to see the torments of the wicked. The Ethiopic account, which draws heavily on the Apocalypse of Paul and perhaps other works, presents the Virgin as an intercessor on behalf of those in torment.

VIRTUE Gk. *aretḗ*). A human disposition toward good or moral excellence. Virtue as a moral attribute was a concept unfamiliar to the Hebrews. Not found in the RSV Old Testament, "virtue" in the KJV translates Heb. *ḥayil,* which usually denotes "strength," "valor" (thus an "army"), or "wealth," in each case referring to women (Ruth 3:11; RSV "worth"; Prov. 12:4; 31:10; RSV "good"; v. 29; RSV "excellently"). In the New Testament the KJV similarly translates Gk. *dýnamis* "power" (Mark 5:30; Luke 6:19; 8:46).

In the LXX Gk. *aretḗ* is used for the praise due to Yahweh (Isa. 42:8, 12; 43:21; 63:7; Hab. 3:3; Heb. *tᵉhillâ*). Similarly, at 2 Pet. 1:3 it refers to the goodness or "excellence" of God. At 1 Pet. 2:9 the plural designates the "wonderful deeds" of God, the manifestations of his saving power. At Phil. 4:8 (RSV "excellence"); 2 Pet. 1:5 virtue appears as one item in catalogues of ethical qualities. Although the Greek term also appears in Stoic lists of virtues that in places bear similarity to these, the concepts of virtue are quite different. The New Testament sense is dependent upon the LXX much more than on Greek moral philosophy. Furthermore, Christian virtue refers not to some abstract notion of proper behavior, but to the fruit of the Spirit in the life of the believer, produced not by human activity but by divine.

Bibliography. H. Währisch, H.-G. Link–A. Ringwald, and R. P. Martin, "Virtue, Blameless," *DNTT* 3:923-32.

VISION.† A supernatural visual manifestation, which may also involve the aural, that serves as a divine revelation of something otherwise secret. Visions are closely related to such other revelatory phenomena as dreams and journeys through heaven and hell. Nearly every religious tradition, ancient and modern, contains traditions of visions experienced by holy men and women.

In the biblical tradition visions were a means by which Jews and Christians experienced God's self-revelation and were able to learn about the future. In the patriarchical period even before Moses God revealed himself and Israel's destiny through dreams (Gen. 28) or the appearance of an angel (chs. 16, 18). Subsequently various means of DIVINATION were practiced to ascertain God's will, and prophets and cultic personnel sought the advice of oracles. Ecstatic prophets were seized by God's spirit (Heb. *rûaḥ* "stormy wind," "breath of a living being," or "that which bursts out"), which enabled them to prophecy. The writings of the canonical prophets include accounts of their visions (e.g., Isa. 1:1; Obad. 1). A classic example of a prophetic vision is Ezekiel's vision of the valley of dry bones (Ezek. 37:1-14), which serves as a promise that God would restore to life the exiled Jews and the broken kingdom of Israel.

Visions were also an important and distinctive form of Jewish and Christian apocalyptic literature. By means of a vision that serves as a revelation concerning future events, given through a mediator to a seer—usually a significant individual from Israel's past (or pseudonymously attributed to such a figure)—God revealed himself and his control over history. Knowledge of this vision and its correct interpretation served as a type of esoteric insight providing a means of consolation and hope to the chosen elect who were privileged to have access to it. Thus, the writers of the apocalypses maintain the same close connection between God's word and visions as do the prophets. An example of an apocalyptic vision is found at Dan. 7, a vision of four beasts that serves as a symbolic interpretation of world history. The vision itself recalls themes found in Greek and Canaanite mythology, but reinterpreted within the context of the vision. The vision itself is so esoteric that it requires interpretation (cf. v. 16); those who understand it are given a message of confidence: God will one day establish his kingdom and exalt his people who are now humiliated.

Although visions found in the apocalypses tend to be more exaggerated and extreme than those preserved in the canonical prophets, both are nearly identical in form. They comprise first person descriptions, often quite detailed, of what an individual saw, including the date, time, and place of the vision. This description may include an interpretive dialogue between the seer and an angel of God. The vision may end with a report of how the seer felt during or after the vision and what his or her subsequent actions were.

Visions, as well as dreams and heavenly journeys,

differ in one significant way from other divine manifestations such as the angelophanies of the infancy narratives (Matt. 1:20-25; 2:13-15; Luke 1:8-21, 26-38; 2:8-15) or the epiphanies of the resurrected Jesus (Matt. 28:17-20), in which the emphasis is on the message conveyed by the divine emissary or the presence of the divine being himself. For visions the important element is the combination of the cognitive and imaginative processes. Visions tend to be more symbolic and allegorical. They invite those who hear them described or who read them to enter into the experience being recounted and to participate in it, triggering individual mental images of that which is described. Because they are highly suggestive and conducive to subjective visualization they have an abiding appeal.

Scholars have classified the visions into five major categories: throne visions, whether of God's throne or the heavenly divine council (e.g., Isa. 6; Rev. 4:2-11); visions of a heavenly or earthly reality (e.g., Amos 8:1-3; Ezek. 40–48); visions based on a symbol (Amos 7:7-9; Ezek. 37:1-14); allegorical visions, in which each element of the vision has a corresponding element in reality (e.g., Dan. 8:1-14; Rev. 12); and composite revelations combining two or more of these elements (e.g., Dan. 7; Rev. 17).

VISIT, VISITATION (Heb. *pāqaḏ, pᵉqûddâ*). As represented in English translations, a divine action that produces a great change in the position of a subordinate, either for good (with the sense of "comfort"; e.g., Gen. 50:24-25; Jer. 29:10) or for ill (meaning "afflict, inflict upon"; e.g., Exod. 32:34; Isa. 26:14). Heb. *pāqaḏ* and related forms represent the larger semantic range "attend to, observe," "muster, pass in review," and "appoint."

In the Lucan writings the sense of Gk. *episkopḗ, episképtomai* is positive (Luke 1:68; 7:16; 19:44; Acts 15:14), while at 1 Pet. 2:12 the "day of visitation" (lit. "supervision, oversight") will be positive only for some.

VOPHSI [vŏf′sī] (Heb. *wopsî*). A Naphtalite, the father of Nahbi, one of twelve spies sent by Moses to explore the land of Canaan (Num. 13:14).

VOW (Heb. verb *nāḏar,* noun *neḏer, nēḏer;* Gk. *euchḗ*).† A solemn promise made to a deity, either to perform or to refrain from performing some action. The standard Hebrew word for vow, *neḏer* (Ugar., Phoen. *ndr*), connotes the act of consecrating to God an action (Gen. 28:20-22), an offering (Lev. 27), or an abstention (Ps. 132:2-5). Num. 30 uses a different noun, *ʾissār,* and the verb *ʾāsar,* with reference to a vow of abstention through binding oneself. Vows were to be paid promptly, but they were always voluntary (Deut. 23:21-23; cf. Eccl. 5:4-5 [MT 3-4]).

I. Old Testament

Generally a person would vow to undertake some special action after God had delivered him from danger or otherwise shown favor (e.g., human sacrifice, Judg. 11:30-31; dedication of a son to cultic service, 1 Sam. 1:11; worship, 2 Sam. 15:7-8; cf. Ps. 22:25 [MT 26]; 76:11 [MT 12]; 116:18-19).

Since vows to the Lord had to be promised freely, it was not permissible to make a vow for something that was already due the Lord according to Mosaic legislation, e.g., the firstborn cattle. Nor could a vow by paid with the hire of a prostitute (Deut. 23:18), in contrast with the Phoenician practice of devoting earnings of temple prostitutes to the maintenance of the temple. That which was consecrated to the Lord was later given the Hebrew name *qorbān,* i.e. "given to God," or "offering" (Matt. 15:5; Mark 7:11; Gk. *korbán*); the animals permissible for sacrifice could be vowed only as offerings and were subject to the rules of the peace offering.

Lev. 27 gives the valuations that were to be paid for the redemption of persons who had been vowed to the Lord, differing with age and gender. If a person was too poor to pay these amounts, the priest adjusted the valuation in terms of what could be paid (vv. 1-8).

An exchange or substitution of an animal that had been vowed to the Lord was not permissible if it was an animal fit to be used as an offering. If this was done despite the regulation, both animals were to be given to the Lord and declared holy (vv. 9-10; cf. Mal. 1:14). An unclean animal or a house vowed to the Lord was appraised by the priest, and its redemption price was then set at one-fifth more than this amount (Lev. 27:11-15).

Land was to be valued in terms of the amount of seed that could be sown in it. However, the full appraisal was only paid if the field was vowed immediately after the Year of Jubilee. The amount was decreased in accordance with the length of time between the making of the vow and the next Year of Jubilee. Regulations were given for redemption (vv. 16-19) and for protection of the priests (vv. 20-21) and original owners (25:25; 27:22-24).

A person could also vow to abstain from something that in itself might be permissible, even desirable, until such a time that God granted his wish. Examples of abstention vows may be found in Saul's foolish diet during battle (1 Sam. 14:24), Uriah's wartime vow (2 Sam. 11:9-13), and David's vow not to sleep until a place had been found for the Lord (Ps. 132:2-5). Vows undertaken by Nazirites occupy a special position in this category (Num. 6; Mishnah *Nazir*).

Num. 30 gives rules applicable to abstention vows made by married women and by daughters still living in their father's house. The regulations differed depending on whether the father or the husband heard the vow or pledge and said nothing to her concerning it, or expressed his disapproval on the same day that he heard it, rendering it invalid. Because the responsibility for nullifying a vow rested upon the man rather than upon the woman, any vow or pledge made by a widow or a divorced woman would therefore be required of her (v. 9).

II. New Testament

In the Sermon on the Mount Jesus teaches on the abuse of vows (Matt. 5:33-37). He reminds his audience that they were not required to make vows (v. 35), but if made, there was no need to strengthen the oath by an additional word or phrase (i.e., "heaven" or "earth"), a common Jewish practice of the day. Instead, be truthful, Jesus instructs (cf. Deut. 23:21-23 [MT 22-24]).

Two passages demonstrate early Church practice pertaining to vows. At Cenchreae, on Paul's way to Antioch after his work in Corinth, either Paul or Aquila cut his hair because of a vow (Acts 18:18). This may have been a Nazirite vow, although the occasion for the vow is not mentioned.

A second instance of a Nazirite vow occurs when Paul arrived in Jerusalem after his third missionary journey (21:23-26). Four men under a vow had become defiled and were completing their vow period by paying a purification expense (cf. Num. 6:13-15) and by receiving a haircut. Paul purified himself also and paid the expenses for the others, thus identifying with the Jerusalem community.

VULGATE (Lat. *vulgata* "common"). The Latin version of the Bible prepared by the church father Jerome (*ca.* 347-420). Although a great number of Latin translations of the Bible (*see* OLD LATIN VERSIONS) were available in this period, there was great diversity among them and no one standard edition.

In 382, Jerome, the most capable biblical scholar of his day, was commissioned by Pope Damasus to produce a standard Latin version based on the Old Latin and original language manuscripts. He issued the four gospels in 384; the rest of the New Testament, whether revised by Jerome or one of his disciples, appeared in 405. In 386 Jerome moved to Bethlehem and spent the next twenty years working on the Old Testament. He began by translating from the LXX, considered by many to be the "inspired" word of God, but soon decided to work directly from the Hebrew. He completed his task in 405.

In spite of the Vulgate's generally excellent quality, its initial reception, as Jerome had anticipated, was somewhat cold because of the wide popularity enjoyed by the Old Latin (similar to that of the KJV in the twentieth century), and it was not until the ninth century that it finally won acceptance. Frequent copying and recopying from early on introduced numerous inaccuracies and contaminations from the Old Latin into Jerome's text; hence efforts were made periodically to purify it. In 1592 a revision by Pope Clement VIII, known as the Clementine Vulgate, was published and pronounced authoritative for the Roman Catholic Church. In the twentieth century, new editions have appeared in 1954, 1969, and 1979. The newest edition, the 1979 Neo-Vulgate, has now replaced the Clementine Vulgate as the official Roman Catholic version.

Although few Protestants have paid much attention to this "Catholic" Bible, its influence on the language and thought of the Western world has been quite extensive. For example, the first knowledge of the Bible in the British Isles was from the Vulgate. Moreover, the first translation of the Bible into English was from the Vulgate.

VULTURE. Any of several large, carrion-eating birds of the family Accipitridae. Their vision is excellent even at great distances, but their talons are poorly developed and their beaks are weak. The wingspan of the larger species may approach 2.5 m. (8 ft.).

Heb. *nešer* (equivalent to Gk. *aetós* in the New Testament) is usually translated "eagle" (probably referring to the golden or imperial eagle), but may often refer to the griffon vulture (*Gyps fulvus fulvus*) instead. These vultures were quite numerous in biblical times, and in flight are virtually indistinguishable from eagles. In addition, since the biblical attention is focused on the many features shared by these birds rather than on their differences, either translation may indeed be appropriate in most cases. Both the griffon vulture and eagle were large, strong, and long-lived, had common nesting patterns, and ate carrion and prey.

Heb. *nešer* heads the list of unclean birds at Lev. 11:13; Deut. 14:12 (JB "tawny vulture"; RSV, KJV "eagle"). All the other instances (some twenty-six) are metaphorical or illustrative (e.g., Exod. 19:4; Deut. 28:49; Ps. 103:5; Isa. 40:31; Jer. 49:16; Hab. 1:8; RSV "eagle"). Passages where vulture seems clearly to be a preferable translation include Job 39:27-30; Mic. 1:16 (so JB, NIV; the griffon vulture's head was covered with short, light-colored down, and thus appeared bald from a distance); Matt. 24:28 par. Luke 17:37 (so JB, NIV, RSV mg.; eagles do not gather). The RSV also translates the term as vulture (KJV "eagle[s]") at Prov. 30:17 (also JB, NIV); Lam. 4:19; Hos. 8:1 (JB "watchman").

The second unclean bird on the lists at Lev. 11:13; Deut. 14:12 (RSV "vulture"; KJV "ossifrage"; JB "griffon") is Heb. *peres*, which probably refers to the lammergeier or bearded vulture (*Gypaëtus barbatus aureus*). These birds take bones when the griffon vultures have picked them clean and repeatedly drop them from a great height onto the rocks to break them open (cf. *pāras* "break in two, divide") and get at the marrow; they follow a similar procedure with tortoises and snakes.

The third bird on the lists is the *'oznîyâ*, usually translated "osprey" (KJV "ospray") but more probably the black vulture (*Aegypius* [or *Vultur*] *monachus*; so NIV, NJV). Finally, *rāḥām* (Lev. 11:18) and *rāḥāmâ* (Deut. 14:17; RSV "carrion vulture"; KJV "gier eagle"; NIV "osprey"; JB "white vulture"; NJV "bustard") is the Egyptian vulture or pharaoh's hen (*Neophron percnopterus*), about half the size of the other vultures and distinguished, even from a distance, by its black and white plumage. These birds scavenge their living from town garbage heaps. All four species of vultures nest in Palestine.

At Job 28:7 the KJV and JB translate *'ayyâ* as "vulture" (RSV, NIV "falcon").

W

WAGES (Heb. *śāḵār*; Gk. *misthós*).* The compensation, usually monetary, given to a person in exchange for service or work.

During the early, transhumant phase of Israel's existence and into the period after the conquest of Canaan there was no distinct class of people who earned wages as the exclusive means of their support. Hirelings (Heb. *śāḵîr*) were day laborers or paid workers who in the early part of Israel's history were paid for their work with provisions necessary for their sustenance. To these provisions were added some wages (cf. Gen. 29:15).

As Israel made the transition from a rural, transhumant culture to a more settled, urban one concomitant economic changes took place. Urbanization, as well as increased trade and commerce with other nations, brought about a greater specialization of some skills. People could support themselves by selling the fruits of their own labor. Less time was spent on providing for one's own sustenance because farming techniques improved and freed more people for the work force.

In the midst of these changes a social class of salaried workers developed. In exchange for work these hirelings were paid wages of weighed silver or bronze. Hirelings were employed in a variety of occupations: as shepherds (Gen. 29:15), farmers and vineyard laborers (Matt. 20:1-16), nurses (Exod. 2:9), fishers (Mark 1:20), mercenary soldiers (Luke 3:14), and even harlots (Hos. 9:1). Herod's restoration of the temple employed a large number of workers who were paid very generous wages on the spot. Temple workers had the reputation of being the best paid in Israel, drawing from the rich resources of the temple treasury; they were even provided with most forms of assistance when unemployed.

The actual amount of the wages paid to the worker was determined by bargaining between the employer and the hireling (cf. Gen. 30:32-33; Matt. 20:1-2). Although specific wages are not frequently specified (e.g., 1 Sam. 9:8; 2 Chr. 25:6), the concern of the prophets about the conditions of hirelings and the general economy of Israel suggests that those people who earned wages formed a class of poor people. The Mosaic law provided some protection of workers, dictating that the worker, whether Jew or Gentile, should be paid on the same day that work was completed (Lev. 19:13; Deut. 24:14-15). This practice was followed meticulously in the temple, but was not always the case elsewhere (cf. Gen. 31:6-7). The prophets were frequent in their condemnations of employers who took advantage of their workers (cf. Mal. 3:5). By the time of Jesus workers were paid between twelve and twenty-four hours after completion of their work.

"Wages" is also a term with many metaphorical uses throughout the Bible, describing, e.g., God's favor to his people (Isa. 62:11) and the retribution of God's justice (40:10; Rom. 6:23). In the New Testament most references to wages are taken from agriculture and figure prominently in the parables and teaching of Jesus. Jesus affirms that the laborer deserves his wages (Luke 10:7), and in the parable of the laborers in the vineyard uses wages as indication of God's willingness to break with convention and be generous.

WAHEB [wā'hĕb] (Heb. *wāhēb*).† Possibly a place in the Moabite region of Suphah near the river Arnon (Num. 21:14; KJV mg. "Vaheb in Suphah"; cf. JB). It is mentioned in a quotation from the Book of the Wars of the Lord, but the Hebrew is obscure (cf. LXX Gk. *Zoob*); the KJV renders "what he did in the Red Sea."

WANDER. In the RSV Old Testament most occurrences refer to the physical journeying of a person or persons from place to place (e.g., Gen. 4:12, 14 [Cain as a "fugitive and wanderer"; cf. the Kenites]; 20:13; Num. 32:13 [the Israelites in the wilderness]; cf. Heb. 11:38). Occasionally the term implies aimlessness or the state of being lost (Gen. 37:15; Job 12:24-25; Ps. 107:4, 40).

A further, significant use of the English term concerns a spiritual straying from God and/or his commandments (e.g., Ps. 119:10, 21; Prov. 5:6; 21:16; Jer. 14:10). This sense predominates in the New Testament, where straying from the truth is a particularly grave danger (1 Tim. 1:6; 6:10; 2 Tim. 4:4; Jas. 5:19; Jude 13).

WAR (Heb. *milḥāmâ*; Gk. *pólemos*).†

I. Old Testament

Throughout Old Testament history, warfare was an

inevitable fact of life in Israel. One reason is geographical. Although Palestine was not rich in natural resources, its position as a land bridge connecting Egypt and Mesopotamia made it an important commercial and military route. Moreover, its location between the Mediterranean to the west and the desert to the east tended to focus there any conflicts between the Egyptian or Mesopotamian empires, with Palestine often the prize of war. Consequently, in the struggles involving Egypt, Assyria, and Babylonia (not to mention lesser powers such as Moab, Amalek, and the Philistines), the small land of Palestine played an important strategic role.

Another reason is theological: God's judgment upon sinful human beings is frequently expressed in armed conflict through human agents in this particular area of the world. Indeed, all warfare throughout the ancient Near East had a spiritual, theological dimension, with each side in a conflict acting in the name of its patron deity, who was credited with the victory. In the biblical accounts warfare illustrates the sovereign control of Yahweh over human history, guaranteeing victory to those to whom he granted it. Yahweh is called "a man of war" (Exod. 15:3; cf. Ps. 24:8; Isa. 42:13) and referred to frequently as "LORD OF HOSTS," implying not only natural forces and supernatural beings described as armies (cf. Judg. 5:20; 1 Kgs. 22:19; cf. Rev. 12:7) but human armies as well. In particular Yahweh is "the God of the armies of Israel" (1 Sam. 17:45; cf. v. 47) who won battles irrespective of the number of his warriors (14:6). When necessary, however, Yahweh also employed other nations' forces to accomplish his purpose (Isa. 10:5-6; Jer. 25:9).

As Yahweh's agent, Israel carried out his judgment against those who defied him or would frustrate his purpose. The battles of the Conquest, for example, served a twofold objective: they won for Israel land that had been promised to Abraham (Gen. 13:15), and they executed God's judgment upon the indigenous peoples of Canaan for their iniquity (15:16; Deut. 25:17-19; cf. 1 Sam. 15). Furthermore, the practice of utterly destroying certain defeated foes and their property as "devoted to the Lord" (Josh. 6:17-21) emphasized his sovereign authority as well as protecting Israel from the peoples' idolatrous influence (Deut. 20:16-18).

The Mosaic law provided specific instructions for the conduct of this "holy war." Fundamental was the doctrine that God was with Israel and could assure victory against all opponents (vv. 1-4). Soldiers in the conflict must therefore be steadfast and wholehearted, free from distraction (vv. 5-9; 24:5). Other rules concerned camp sanitation (23:10-14) and treatment of vegetation in times of siege (20:19-20). An opposing city must first be offered terms of surrender; if its citizens accepted they were to serve the Israelites as forced labor, but if not their city was to be besieged and their men killed. The exception was cities within the land; these and their inhabitants were to be totally destroyed (vv. 10-18). Captive women taken as wives were to be treated according to a strict rule of courtesy (21:10-14).

Israel's defeats can usually be traced back to disobedience of these or other, more immediate directives concerning warfare (e.g., Josh. 7). Indeed, it was de-

sertion from the fundamental principle of "holy war"—undivided, unswerving confidence in God as the means of obtaining victory—that the prophets decried during the divided monarchy. God's people had forsaken him in favor of building up their own military strength and making alliances with other nations (e.g., Isa. 30:1-2; 31:1-3; Hos. 7:11), adopting the idolatrous customs of these nations in the process. They had lost their distinctiveness as God's people, and were no longer fighting the orthodox kind of war he had decreed. Therefore Yahweh, who had been Israel's champion of war, caused the Assyrians to deport the northern kingdom. When further prophetic warnings failed, he dispatched the Babylonians to capture Jerusalem and to send the southern kingdom into exile in Babylon.

Despite the continual wars that wracked the history of the Old Testament, the prophets make clear that warfare is not history's goal. Rather, these eras of war culminate in a time when war will be abolished and weapons will be put to peaceful use (Isa. 2:4; Mic. 4:3), a time inaugurated by the Messiah, the Prince of Peace (Isa. 9:6-7 [MT 5-6]; Zech. 9:9-10).

II. New Testament

The New Testament attitude toward war appears at first to be exactly the opposite of the "holy war" promoted in the Old Testament. Jesus tells his disciples not to resist an evildoer (Matt. 5:39-41) and to love their enemies (vv. 43-48), rejects efforts to make him a political leader, and warns Peter against relying on a weapon as a matter of course (26:52). Warfare (although manifested in interpersonal struggles; cf. 10:34-36) has apparently shifted from the physical realm to the spiritual, where the enemies are not human but spiritual agencies (Eph. 6:12).

Yet the New Testament does not directly condemn war as an institution nor renounce its Old Testament portrayal. Indeed, military figures appear in a generally good light. John the Baptist does not tell soldiers to rebel or desert (Luke 3:14). One centurion provides Jesus with a supreme example of faith based on military authority (Matt. 8:5-13), and another is leader of the first Gentiles to join the Church (Acts 10).

The contrast may be explained as a shift in emphasis (rather than doctrine) taking into account the changed political structure of the New Testament world. There is no theocratic nation on earth that fights in God's name; Israel is merely a people under control of a foreign power, and God's kingship is "not of this world" (John 18:36). The focus is now upon the Church, a body that includes not only Israelites but potentially people of all nations.

Thus the concept of physical conflict is dropped because it is irrelevant to the Church. A spiritual warfare remains, however, in which the believer must continually fight, continually armed with God's armor (Eph. 6:11-18). The struggle is between God's kingdom and the secular system that includes all the nations of the world, or between God and Satan (Acts 26:18). Living amid such a struggle requires a disciplined mindset that is well described in military language (1 Tim. 1:18; 2 Tim. 2:3-4; 1 Pet. 2:11). The two kingdoms will meet in final, physical conflict as described at Rev. 16:16; 19:11–20:10.

The question of military service for a believer is of great concern to the Church today. While God's people do not take up armed conflict on behalf of his kingdom (cf. John 18:36), they are still under the authority of divinely appointed governments, which claim among their ordained duties the taking of life in certain cases (cf. Rom. 13:1-4); to do so may require maintaining of some military organization. Scripture does not state explicitly whether or not a Christian may participate in war, and historically various attempts have been made to answer the question by inference. These include full participation in a "just war" (to defend against an invasion or preserve order within a land), noncombatant participation in all wars, and total denunciation of warfare in general ("pacifism").

Bibliography. C. Brown, J. Watts, and M. Langley, "War, Soldier, Weapon," *DNTT* 3:958-982; M. C. Lind, *Yahweh Is a Warrior* (Scottdale: 1980).

WARDROBE, KEEPER OF THE (Heb. *šōmēr hab-bᵉgādîm*).* The person in charge of the vestments worn by the king and priests. One such individual, Harhas, is named at 2 Kgs. 22:14 (called Hasrah at 2 Chr. 34:22). At 2 Kgs. 10:22 the worshippers of Baal were supplied with special garments from the keeper of the wardrobe (cf. Jer. 38:11).

WARS OF THE LORD, BOOK OF (Heb. *sēper milḥᵃmōṯ YHWH*). An otherwise unknown document mentioned only at Num. 21:14, where a brief poetic excerpt concerning the boundaries between Moab and the Amorites is quoted as if its source were familiar to the readers. The work may have been a collection of songs commemorating early Israelite battles, perhaps similar to the Book of Jasher (Josh. 10:13; 2 Sam. 1:18), but the scanty evidence permits no definite conclusions.

WASH (Heb. *rāḥaṣ*; Gk. *níptō*). The act of cleansing was performed with regard to personal cleanness as well as ritual purification. The references to ordinary washing mention specifically only the feet (Gen. 18:4; 19:2; 24:32; 43:24), the hands (Exod. 30:19, 21), and the face (Gen. 43:31). In terms of ritual purification, the priests and Levites were required to wash themselves (Exod. 40:12; Lev. 8:6; 16:4, 24), as well as their clothes (Num. 8:21; 19:7), before performing their assigned tasks; according to Exod. 30:20 they must do so "lest they die." To purify themselves from disease or contact with dead flesh, other members of the community were also required to observe ceremonial washings (Lev. 14:8; 15:5; 17:15). Jesus was aware of the customs of washing the feet (Matt. 6:17), the hands (15:2), and the feet (John 13:3-9).

Excavations at Qumran reveal what appear to be the remains of ceremonial washing pools; ritual washings, required in levitical law of priests, apparently were prescribed for all members of the Qumran community.

Washing also connotes cleansing from sin (Ps. 51:2 [MT 4]; Isa. 1:16) and spiritual regeneration (Titus 3:5; cf. John 3:5).

See BATHING.

WASP.† An insect belonging to the order *Hymenoptera*, particularly the *Vespa orientalis* still found in certain portions of Palestine. Gk. *sphḗx*. which in the LXX translates Heb. *ṣirʿâ*, (RSV, KJV "hornet"), is used figuratively with reference to Yahweh's driving out of the pre-Israelite inhabitants of Canaan (Wisd. 12:8; cf. Exod. 23:28; Deut. 7:20; Josh. 24:12; NEB "panic"; NJV "plague"). Some scholars suggest that the wasp here represents the Egyptian empire and its repeated military campaigns into Late Bronze Age Canaan, weakening the city-state defenses and allowing the Israelites to enter and conquer. Others render the Hebrew term "depression" or "discouragement," the result of Yahweh's holy "terror" during war (cf. Exod. 15:14-16; 23:27; Josh. 2:24).

WATCHMAN (Heb. *ṣōpeh, šōmēr*). One whose duty it is to keep vigil, often on a tower or wall, whether for the king (1 Sam. 14:16; 2 Sam. 18:24-27; 2 Kgs. 9:17-20), over a city (Ps. 127:1 [figurative for the Lord]; Cant. 3:3; 5:7), or over a field (Isa. 56:9-10; cf. Jer. 4:17), and often at night (Ps. 127:1; 130:6; Isa. 21:11-12).

In the book of Ezekiel, the prophet is appointed a watchman for the house of Israel, and it becomes his particular responsibility to warn his people to turn from their wicked ways (Ezek. 3:17; 33:2-7; cf. Hos. 9:8).

The "watcher" (Aram. *ʿîr*; Dan. 4:13, 17, 23 [MT 10, 14, 20]) is an angel, a messenger, or an agent of Yahweh.

WATER (Heb. *mayim*; Gk. *hýdōr*).† A primary requirement for the support and survival of plant and animal life. With bread, water has long been understood as the minimum sustenance necessary for human life (cf. Gen. 21:14; Exod. 23:25); lack of either spells dire need and eventual death (Isa. 3:1; Ezek. 4:17; cf. Isa. 30:20). Water is also used extensively for bathing, washing, and ceremonial cleansing.

I. Physical Aspects

Palestine is largely dependent upon rainfall for moisture. Unlike Mesopotamia and Egypt, with their large rivers fed by mountain watersheds, a slight variation in annual rainfall in Palestine can produce a serious drought. Indeed, famine-producing droughts were a particular problem throughout biblical times (Gen. 26:1; 1 Kgs. 17:1).

In normal years, Palestine has a fall and winter rainy season, separated by a summer dry spell (Ps. 32:4). The amount of rain varies widely throughout Palestine, but the coastal plain averages approximately 56 cm. (22 in.) per annum. Generally, northern and western Palestine get the most rain, as do the slopes of mountains that face the sea. Southern Palestine is a virtual desert, especially in the region around the Dead Sea.

Palestine not only lacks large rivers and watersheds, but also adequate natural storage sites for water reserves. Thus historically its inhabitants had to use a variety of human-made storage facilities. Wells (Gen. 21:30; 29:2-8; John 4:11-12) are deep holes which have been dug in the ground to the depth of the water table in order to provide year-round water. Generally, the well is surrounded by a stone wall above ground for safety and below ground to keep the well from

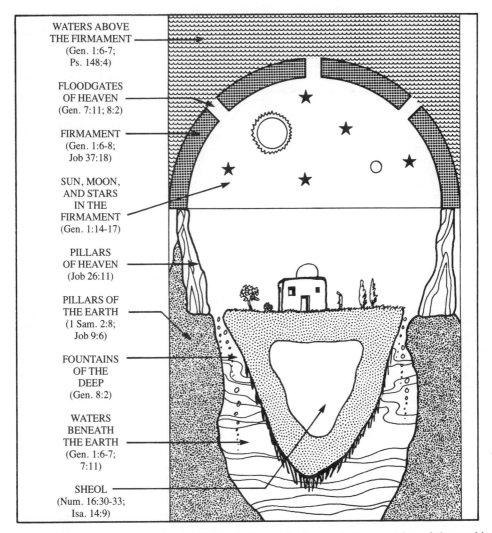

WATERS ABOVE
THE FIRMAMENT
(Gen. 1:6-7;
Ps. 148:4)

FLOODGATES
OF HEAVEN
(Gen. 7:11; 8:2)

FIRMAMENT
(Gen. 1:6-8;
Job 37:18)

SUN, MOON,
AND STARS
IN THE
FIRMAMENT
(Gen. 1:14-17)

PILLARS
OF HEAVEN
(Job 26:11)

PILLARS OF
THE EARTH
(1 Sam. 2:8;
Job 9:6)

FOUNTAINS
OF THE
DEEP
(Gen. 8:2)

WATERS
BENEATH
THE EARTH
(Gen. 1:6-7;
7:11)

SHEOL
(Num. 16:30-33;
Isa. 14:9)

The waters above the firmament and beneath the earth: the ancient conception of the world reflected in the Old Testament

caving in or needing to be redug. Cisterns (2 Chr. 26:10; Jer. 2:13), also dug in the ground, were fed by conduits that directed the rainwater from the roofs or ground surface. Generally both wells and cisterns were covered in order to prevent evaporation or contamination. Pools (2 Sam. 2:13; Isa. 7:3; John 5:2-7), usually left uncovered, were made by damming springs or constructing a shallow pond of masonry. *See* Irrigation.

II. Theological Importance

A. Cosmology. From time immemorial, ancient people must have been aware that water existed above and below the earth. It descended from above in the form of rain and it could be obtained, if one were willing to dig deep enough, from the depths of the earth. In many ancient Near Eastern societies this apparent paradox was explained by the story of the primordial

battle between the hero-god and the dragon of chaos. In the Babylonian version, the victorious Marduk splits the body of the female Tiamat. Then he creates the earth from her body, placing the earth in the womb of chaos below the waters of heaven and above the waters of the deep (cf. Heb. *tᵉhôm* "the deep, sea, ocean"; Akk. *tiâmtu* "Tiamat").

The Old Testament acknowledges this basic understanding of the universe, or cosmogony, but modifies it in the light of Israelite monotheism (the creation account, Gen. 1:1-10; the flood account, 7:11; cf. Exod. 20:4; Deut. 4:18; 2 Sam. 22:14-17; Job 26:5-13; Ps. 104:3-6; 136:6; 148:4-7; Jer. 10:11-13; Amos 9:5-6; Jonah 2:2-6). So the "waters of heaven," or cosmic waters, are the waters above the earth held back by the firmament. Rain falls when God opens the floodgates in the firmament (Gen. 7:11; 8:2; RSV "windows"). The sky is blue (the color of the ocean) because the waters can be seen through the transparent crystal firmament (cf. Ezek. 1:26, which pictures God as seated above the firmament on a throne the color of lapis lazuli [blue or turquoise]—the color of deep water and the sky; so RSV mg., following MT).

B. *Ritual.* The Israelites also reflected a common ancient Near Eastern conception by extending in a metaphysical sense the physical property of water as the primary cleansing agent: water also has the power to make one ceremonially clean. The interpretation of Ezek. 16:4, for example, hinges upon this twofold cleansing property.

The Old Testament ritual for cleansing, in its most basic form, involves bathing, washing one's clothing, and waiting until evening (Lev. 15:5-27; 16:26-28; 17:15; 22:6; Deut. 23:10-11). Thus Aaron and his sons are required to wash with water before they put on the priestly garments (Exod. 29:4-9; cf. 30:17-21; 40:12-15, 30-32). Water is also used for purification in other types of rituals: cleansing the entrails and the legs of a calf or sheep before sacrificing it as a burnt offering (Lev. 1:9, 13), or cleansing a garment or metal vessel from the blood of a sin offering (6:27-28 [MT 20-21]).

Because the water itself could become contaminated (Lev. 11:32-36), later rabbis established the minimum amount of water needed for a ceremonial cleansing bath as forty seahs (264 l. [280 qts.; Mishnah *Miqw.* i.1-8; cf. John 2:6). This amount of water, they felt, guaranteed that the water's natural cleansing power would not become nullified through an inordinate amount of uncleanness.

The most serious cases of uncleanness were cleansed by using "living water" (or running water): water that flowed in such a manner that it was continually renewed and therefore could not be made unclean (Lev. 11:32-36; cf. Mishnah *Miqw.* 1). "Living water" was used for the cleansing of a leper or a house contaminated by leprosy. The priest took two birds, slaying the first over running water. Then he dipped hyssop, cedarwood, scarlet cloth, and the other, living bird into the mixture of blood and water, and sprinkled the fluid seven times on the house or individual. Afterwards, he released the living bird into a nearby field (Lev. 14:1-7, 48-53).

"Living water" is also an element of the "water of bitterness" and the "water for impurity." The "water of bitterness" (Heb. *mê hammārîm ham'ar^arîm*; Num. 5:18-19) was administered by the priest to a woman suspected of adultery (vv. 16-29; cf. Exod. 32:19-20). The priest wrote curses on a slate to which the woman responded, "Amen, Amen" (cf. John 1:51; 3:3, 5). He then washed the slate and mixed the dirty water with dust from the tabernacle and this "holy" water (*mayim q^eḏōšîm*; probably running water; cf. LXX Gk. *hýdōr katharón zōn*). The woman was then forced to drink the water. If she was innocent there would be no damage, but if she were guilty the water would cause her abdomen to swell and her thigh to waste away.

The "water for impurity" (Heb. *mê niddâ*; Num. 19:9; KJV "water of separation") was also water combined with several other ingredients to make its cleansing power more efficacious. A priest offered a red hiefer as a burnt offering outside the camp together with cedarwood, hyssop, and scarlet cloth according to proper ceremony (vv. 1-22). He then mixed the ashes from the fire with running water and sprinkled this "water for impurity" over anyone or anything that had touched a dead body. This was done on the third and the seventh day. After bathing on the seventh day, the offending party was considered ceremonially clean. The Israelites also used the "water of impurity" to purify the Midianite booty they had captured (31:23). The "water of expiation" used to purify the Levites (*mê haṭṭāṯ*; 8:7) is probably identical with the water of impurity.

References to water in the New Testament occur frequently in connection with both Christian baptism (Acts 8:36-39; Heb. 10:22; 1 Pet. 3:20) and John's baptism of repentance (Matt. 3:11; Mark 1:8; Acts 1:5; 11:16). Baptism is a rite of passage that initiates the convert from the world into the community of the regenerate, and hence, in its primary association, an initiatory cleansing ritual. The symbolism of water is particularly appropriate in this ritual. Here the initiate is submerged in the water (reminiscent of the waters of the underworld, and thus symbolic of death). Then he rises to new life (perhaps like the newborn baby emerges from the womb with a burst of water [cf. John 3:5] or reminiscent of the creation of the world "out of water" [Rom. 6:3-4; Col. 2:12]). Baptism is also a cleansing ritual; the initiate emerges with his body "washed with clean water," a symbol of an inner cleansing (Heb. 10:22). *See* BAPTISM.

C. *Holy Spirit.* Several Old Testament passages figuratively use water for the spirit of God (Isa. 44:3-4; cf. Ezek. 36:25-26; Joel 2:23, 28 [MT 3:1]) or for God himself (Jer. 2:13; 17:13). Even more passages refer to the Spirit in terms normally used of a fluid (*šāpak* "pour out," Ezek. 39:29; Joel 2:28-29 [MT 3:1-2]; *yāṣaq*, Isa. 44:3; *nāḇa'*, Prov. 1:23; *'ārâ*, Isa. 32:15; *mālē'* "be filled," Exod. 31:3; 35:31; Deut. 34:9). Also the Spirit is active in creation, where it is found hovering over the face of the waters (Gen. 1:2).

The spirit of God may have come to be associated with the water that gives life or with cleansing (cf. Mishnah *Soṭah* ix.15). Or there may be a deeper, more mythological association between the spirit of God and the cosmic waters (cf. Gen. 1:2; Ezek. 1:26).

The New Testament uses the water for spirit in all of these connections. Luke-Acts, especially, continues the "fluid-oriented" vocabulary of the Spirit ("pour out," Acts 2:17-18; 10:45; "filled," Luke 1:15, 41, 67; Acts 2:4; 4:8; Eph. 5:18).

The most complex water symbolism in the New Testament may be that of the gospel of John, where water occurs as a focal point of several incidents. In addition to the baptism of Jesus (John 1:26-33), seven of these "water" pericopes are unique to John: the transformation of water to wine (2:7-9; 4:46), Jesus' conversation with Nicodemus (3:5) and the Samaritan woman (4:7-15), the healing of the man at the pool of Bethzatha (5:3-7), Jesus' proclamation at Feast of Tabernacles (7:38), the washing of the disciples' feet (13:5), and the blood and water that flowed from the crucified Jesus' side (19:34). John uses water almost exclusively to express his theology of the Spirit, which is closely linked to the activity of the Spirit (1:32-33;

3:5-8; 7:38-39; cf. 19:30) or to the ceremonial cleansings that it displaces (2:6; 13:10-11). The key to this understanding lies in the water libation ritual of the Feast of Booths, which was accompanied by a prayer for the "latter rain" of fall—which the early Church believed to be the outpouring of the Holy Spirit (Acts 2:4, 16-21; cf. Joel 2:28-32 [MT 3:1-5]). Jesus announces that he is the source of such "living water" at this very ceremony (John 7:38-39; cf. in this light the water that flows from the side of the crucified Lord; 19:34; cf. Zech. 12:10; 13:1).

"Water of life" (Rev. 21:6; 22:1, 17; cf. 7:17, "living water") denotes genuine, everlasting life, life eternal, for which those in this earthly life thirst. The image points not only to an ever-flowing source of water but also to its quality, which contains, creates, and communicates life.

Bibliography. L. Goppelt, "ὕδωρ," *TDNT* 8 (1972): 314-333; R. Meyer, "καθαρός C.," *TDNT* 3 (1965): 418-423.

WATER GATE (Heb. *ša'ar hammayim*).† A gate in the eastern wall of Jerusalem on Mt. Zion, apparently opposite the Spring Gihon, restored by Nehemiah (Neh. 12:37). In the square before this gate, Ezra instructed the returning exiles in the law (Neh. 8:1, 3); here also booths were erected for the Feast of Tabernacles in 444 B.C. (v. 16). Some scholars identify the Water Gate with one of the southern gates of the temple area.

WATER HEN (Heb. *tanšemet*).* Apparently one of the nearly two hundred species of Rail birds (order *Rallidae*), which include not only the water hen but rails, gallinules, and coots. Characterized by very short wings, moderately long legs and toes, and a short turned-up tail, Rail birds typically frequent ponds, lakes, and marshes. The only biblical references to *tanšemet* occur in lists of birds that the Israelites were forbidden to eat (Lev. 11:18; JB "horned owl"; Deut. 14:16; KJV "swan"; NIV "white owl"; JB "ibis").

WATER SHAFT (Heb. *ṣinnôr*).† A water spout, tunnel, or shaft by which David was able to conquer the stronghold of Jebus (Jerusalem) (2 Sam. 5:8; JB "conduit"; KJV "gutter"; NIV mg. "scaling hooks"). The context at 2 Sam. 5:8 implies an aspect of security or fortification for time of siege. The other occurrence of the term, Ps. 42:7 (MT 8), associates it with the sound of sea waves (RSV, JB "cataracts"; KJV "waterspouts"; NIV "waterfalls").

Archaeologists have excavated water shafts or tunnels at several sites, including Gezer, Gibeon, and Etham. Indeed, many ancient, fortified cities had elaborate systems for securing access to water in times of siege. Hezekiah's tunnel at Jerusalem was a marvel of engineering whereby water was channeled some 535 m. (1750 ft.) from the Spring Gihon to the pool of Siloam after the other outlets had been sealed; the tunnel was carved through solid rock from the Gihon on the eastern slope of the hill of Zion into the interior of the hill. The water shaft mentioned at 2 Sam. 5:8 may have been a more primitive but similar access to the Spring Gihon or some other water supply. Thus it could be inferred that Jebus was so well fortified that the only possible entry point was the water shaft,

and that it could be easily defended by the blind and lame (but cf. P. K. McCarter, *II Samuel*. AB 9 [1984], pp. 139-140).

WAVE OFFERING (Heb. *tᵉnûpâ*).† The ritual offering of a variety of agricultural products. The Hebrew term is derived from the hiphil form of the verb *nôp* "move back and forth, swing, shake," but the Targums' interpretation of it in terms of the motions "raise, elevate" is more precise. A waving motion seems unlikely since such an action would topple the offering. More likely the offering simply was elevated, thereby dedicating it to the Lord, and then used in sacrifice. Indeed, in the MT the hiphil form of the verb most often occurs in contexts supporting the more logical sense "elevate" (e.g., Isa. 10:15; RSV "lift"; 19:16; RSV "shakes [over]"; cf. 11:15; 13:2). The expression reflects the common ancient Near Eastern practice of elevating those things being offered (cf. Egyptian ritual formulas and reliefs).

The wave offering is a constitutive part of the entire sacrificial system. A number of objects could be the subject of the wave offering, including the breast of the peace offering (Lev. 7:30; 9:21; 10:14-15; Num. 6:20; 18:18); the precious metals used for ornamentation of the tabernacle (Exod. 35:22; 38:24); the thigh, fat, and bread offering of the consecration of priests (29:22-26; Lev. 8:25-29); the loaves and lambs of the peace offering (23:17, 20); the barley sheaf (vv. 11-14); and the oil used to purify the healed leper (14:12, 24). Apparently the ritual could be carried out with a variety of objects simultaneously (Exod. 29:22-24; Lev. 8:25-27). Also waved were the cereal offering of jealousy (Num. 5:25). At 8:11, 15, 21 Aaron symbolically offers the Levites as "a wave offering from the people of Israel."

The wave offering is a ceremony whereby offerings are dedicated to the Lord. Offerings that are the property of their owner when they are brought to the sanctuary must undergo this ritual. Thus, in most cases (except, e.g., the peace offering where the meat offered belongs to and is eaten by the owner [and priest]), the ceremony is unnecessary. Offerings composed of unusual material, used for unusual purposes, or characterized by unusual procedures must undergo the ceremony. Thus the barley sheaf, because it is composed of a substance other than wheat, must be dedicated to the Lord.

The exact nature of the ritual is unclear. One conjecture is that the priest laid the wave offering in the palms of the person bringing the offering, and then put his own hands under the hands of this person and proceeded to move them (cf. Num. 6:19-20). If the priest was bringing his own offering, he took it in his own hands, raised it aloft, and moved it. In both cases, the priest moved the hands holding the pieces of offering forward and backward. He moved them forward to indicate that the offering was presented to the Lord before his altar. He pulled them back to show that the Lord returned the offering, giving it to his priests.

WAY (Heb. *derek*; Gk. *hodós*).† Literally a path, road, or journey. Several such routes are named in the Old Testament. The Way of the Red Sea (Exod. 13:18) refers to the route of the Exodus. The Way of the Land of the Philistines (v. 17) was the Egyptian "Way of Horus," the ancient military highway paralleling the Mediterranean Sea from the frontier fortress of Zilu to Raphia in southwestern Palestine. The main north-south route between Damascus and the Gulf of Syria was the King's Highway (Num. 20:17). The Way of the Sea (Isa. 9:1) led from Dor on the Mediterranean, by the Sea of Chinnereth, to Damascus; it is the probable route of the Assyrian invasion in 732 B.C. (2 Kgs. 15:29). In the New Testament the literal use of "way" is confined to the Synoptic Gospels, usually referring to the route of Jesus' travel.

The metaphorical use is more common in the Bible, and can also be found in other ancient literature. The idea of two contrasting "ways," good and evil (Prov. 14:2; Matt. 7:13-14), is widespread (e.g., 1QS 3:13–4:26; the fable of Hercules at the crossroads, Xenophon *Memorabilia* ii.1.21-34). "Way" often refers to a style of living, either evil or good (e.g., Ps. 1:6; Jude 11). It can also denote a habitual manner or activity, whether of animals (Prov. 30:19) or humans (Lam. 3:40; 1 Cor. 4:17). Death, for example, is "the way of all the earth" (Gen. 19:31; RSV "manner"; Josh. 23:14; 1 Kgs. 2:2). It is in the sense of this dichotomy that divine and human ways differ (Isa. 55:8-9).

By extension, "the way(s) of the Lord" constitutes his will or law (Ps. 119), which is to be followed by believers (Deut. 8:6). In the New Testament and the Dead Sea Scrolls the Way refers to the true faith (1QS 9:17-18; Acts 9:2; 19:9, 23; 22:4). Jesus himself is the new and living "way," the path to God (John 14:4-6; Heb. 9:8; 10:20).

WAYMARK (Heb. *ṣîyûn*).* A heap of stones used to mark a path or road (Jer. 31:21). The same Hebrew word is used to indicate a pile of stones marking the site of a grave (2 Kgs. 23:17; RSV "monument"; KJV "title"; Ezek. 39:15; RSV "sign"; cf. Gen. 35:20).

WEALTH (Heb. *ḥayil, hôn, ʿōšer*; Gk. *ploútos, chréma*).† The more tangible evidence of the power or capability (Heb. *ḥayil, hôn*) to acquire property, such as land, livestock, buildings, or slaves, the basic commodities of the ancient Palestinian agrarian economy.

Fundamental to the Old Testament attitude toward wealth is the concept of Yahweh as Creator and Sovereign over all creation (cf. Ps. 24:1). Indeed, the Israelites were merely stewards over the land of Palestine entrusted to them by Yahweh (Num. 34–36; Josh. 13–19). Israel's failure to acknowledge God as their provider is related to their breaking the covenant and worshipping other gods (cf. Deut. 8:17-20), which eventually resulted in conquest and exile. To the faithful of Israel the promise was voiced that even the wealth of the nations would be brought to Zion (Isa. 45:14; 60:5, 11; Mic. 4:13). Thus wealth and prosperity appeared as a sign of God's blessing, and destruction or loss as a sign of God's wrath (cf. Ps. 1:3-4).

This reward of blessing for obedience or faithfulness, as well as cursing and destruction for disobedience was viewed also on a more individual basis.

Just as God blessed Israel for faithfulness, so also God blessed individuals with wealth and prosperity (e.g., Abraham, Gen. 13:2; 14:23; Solomon, 1 Kgs. 3:13). The book of Job takes issue with at least the more extreme views that faithfulness brings wealth and disobedience results in poverty and tribulation (e.g., Job 21).

Throughout the Old Testament warnings and denouncements are directed against those who pursue wealth through less than honorable means, such as greed or treachery, or against those who take pride and glory in wealth (2 Sam. 12; Isa. 5:8; 10:1-3; Jer. 5:27; 17:3; Ezek. 7:10-11; 28:2-9; Hos. 12:8 [MT 7]; Mic. 2:2; 6:12). In more than a few psalms "rich" is synonymous with "wicked," while "poor" is used for the "faithful" or "righteous" or "godly." Although "poor" here is to be understood in a more religious sense, it points to the socioeconomic milieu of postexilic Judaism in which a growing portion of wealth found its way into the hands of Hellenized Jews, many of whom compromised religious practices that they might ingratiate themselves into commercial favor. Hope is expressed that God might judge those guilty and bring about a reversal of the situation.

The wisdom collected in Proverbs reflects an attitude towards wealth with more equanimity. While "riches" (*ʿōšer*) can be a source of security (Prov. 10:5, 15; 18:11) and ransom for a person's life (13:8), a blessing for righteousness or obedience (3:16; 10:22, 24; 22:4) and a reward for diligence (10:2, 27; cf. Sir. 31:3), ultimately one's reputation and integrity are more important (Prov. 22:1). An imprudent desire for wealth may be the cause of overconfidence and self-importance (28:11; cf. Sir. 11:19), greed (Prov. 28:22), arrogance (18:10-11, 23; cf. 11:28), corruption (28:6; cf. Sir. 31:5, 7-8), and even the eventual loss of wealth (Prov. 13:11; 22:16).

For a proper perspective on the attitude to be taken towards wealth in the Old Testament, one must take into account the attitude towards the poor and all who were weak (widows, orphans, and resident aliens). *See* POOR.

In general the attitude of the New Testament toward wealth is consistent with that of the Old Testament, though with an added stress on the dangers of wealth. Jesus, in particular, warns of the distracting, if not potentially morally deteriorating, quality of wealth. His assessment, "How hard it will be for those who have riches to enter the kingdom of God" (Mark 10:23), is echoed in numerous passages, such as the parable of the rich fool (Luke 12:13-21) and the rich young man who turns away when Jesus instructs him to give up his possessions (Mark 10:17-31). Jesus personifies the evil potential in wealth, exhorting: "You cannot serve God and mammon" (Matt. 6:24). In a more positive vein, he instructs the disciples to provide themselves "a treasure in the heavens that does not fail" (Luke 12:33-34; cf. 10:4; 12:21; 22:36; Matt. 10:10). At the very least, Jesus taught that wealth could be a hindrance to discipleship.

It is important to note that Jesus did not command everyone to give up his/her possessions. The rich young man was a man whose wealth controlled his life, and for this reason Jesus instructed him to give up the possessions that meant so much to him. With respect to the disciples, Jesus was preparing them for the difficult task which lay ahead. Yet neither did Jesus commend poverty; the widow who gave her last coin was commended not for her poverty but her liberality in giving and her devotion to God (Mark 12:41-44).

Although many of Jesus' followers were the poor, such was not exclusively the case, for among them were Zacchaeus (Luke 19:2) and Joseph of Arimathaea (Matt. 27:57). When Jesus said, "Blessed are you poor" (Luke 6:20; cf. Matt. 5:3), he was recalling the spiritual meaning of the term in the Psalms.

The attitude of the early Church seems largely consistent with Jesus' caution toward the dangers of wealth. This finds dramatic embodiment in the sharing of possessions at Acts 4:32-35. Such a communal act of sharing was not a general pattern converts were encouraged to emulate (cf. 5:4), but it does represent a striking instance of the early Christians' willingness to give and share. The apostle Paul urges Christians to work not only for their own needs, but also in order to help others in need (2 Cor. 8:13-15; 2 Thess. 3:12). Yet enslavement to the desire for riches was to be avoided at all costs (1 Cor. 7:30-31).

Although Paul acknowledges problems with wealth in the Church (e.g., 1 Cor. 4:7-8), he seeks primarily to radically redefine wealth or riches as the presence or work of Christ in the Church. Christ was "rich," but became poor in order that his followers might become rich (2 Cor. 8:9; cf. Rom. 2:4; 9:23; 10:12). The word of Christ dwells richly (*plousíōs*) in the community (Col. 3:16; cf. 2 Cor. 8:9), which is enriched in every respect in Christ (1 Cor. 1:5; cf. 2 Cor. 9:11), and in those to whom God has declared "the glory of this mystery" (Col. 1:27; cf. 2:2; Eph. 1:18; 3:16). True riches are to be found in the self-sacrificing love found in Jesus (e.g., 1 Cor. 13:4-13). Even the apostle's task is to proclaim the "unsearchable riches of Christ" (Eph. 3:8).

Later New Testament epistles contain rather striking warnings to the rich concerning the dangers of wealth (Jas. 5:1-6), or concerning deference to the rich (2:1-7). A more temperate attitude is expressed in 1 Timothy, encouraging one to be content with the necessities of life, and admonishing of the dangers of wealth and the desire for riches (1 Tim. 6:8-10, 17-19). Few passages reach the pitch of denouncement that the prosperous church of Laodicea receives for its spiritual lukewarmness (Rev. 3:17; cf. ch. 18).

Bibliography. H. Eising, "ḥayil [chayil]," *TDOT* 4 (1980): 348-355; F. Hauck and W. Kasch, "πλοῦτος," *TDNT* 6 (1968): 318-332.

WEAPONS.† References to a wide variety of weapons of war and instances of their use abound in the Bible, particularly the Old Testament. This is hardly surprising in view of the fact that the Israelites were almost constantly at war throughout their history.

Certainly weapons have been an integral part of all cultures since prehistoric times, whether for hunting or for battle. Skill in using even the most primitive weapons was highly developed, and production of sufficient and suitable arms was a constant focus of tribal existence. Weapons evolved and became increasingly sophisticated over the millennia, and the possession

A Roman soldier with helmet, tunic, lance, sword, and shield

of more advanced weapons often enabled one cultural group to gain the mastery, for a time, over another. In turn, such competition forced the disadvantaged group to achieve or even surpass the technology of their oppressors.

The primary materials of early weapons were wood and stone, with the stone implements used alone or lashed in some way to a piece of wood to form a club or spear. Flint or similar types of stone that could be chipped or flaked to a point or an edge were particularly useful. Bows and arrows and slings also used nonmetallic materials in their construction.

As metallurgy developed in the fifth and fourth millennia B.C., weapon technology advanced tremendously. During this time people began melting, forming, and beating copper into tools and weapons; however, unmixed copper was too soft for such implements, and eventually the technique for making bronze was learned. This alloy of copper and approximately 10 percent tin was far superior to pure copper in hardness and strength.

Bronze served well for some two thousand years, but great upheavals in the ancient world together with a shortage of tin made bronze an increasingly impractical substance. Accordingly, people turned to the much more plentiful iron. Iron may have come into general use earlier for weapons and tools but for one primary fact: its melting point was approximately 330° C. higher than copper, well beyond the capabilities of Bronze Age smiths. As a result, the only kind of iron in use was wrought iron, much inferior to bronze.

At the end of the Bronze Age metalworkers discovered that forging the iron in a fire with charcoal produced a better result, known now as carburized iron (actually a form of steel). Further experimentation with blacksmith procedures such as quenching and tempering produced metal with a very high degree of strength and hardness, far more suitable than wrought iron or bronze for tools and weapons, especially given its ability to take and keep a sharp edge or point. (In biblical usage iron is a symbol of strength;

e.g., Job 40:18; Dan. 2:40.) Thus iron was ideal for swords, daggers, knives, spears, and arrowheads, as well as tools. 1 Sam. 13:19-22 indicates that the Philistines enjoyed an iron monopoly for a time at least, but whether the reason was technological (the Israelites had not yet learned to forge iron; cf. Judg. 1:19; 4:3) or political (the Philistines had successfully outlawed blacksmiths in Israel) is disputed among scholars.

Ancient weapons, biblical and otherwise, are usually classified as offensive or defensive. Defensive weapons consisted primarily of armor and the individual pieces that comprised it. Goliath of Gath had a full set in bronze: helmet, coat of scale armor, greaves, and a shield (1 Sam. 17:5-6; cf. v. 38; 2 Chr. 26:14; Neh. 4:16 [MT 10]; Jer. 46:3-4). The only other defensive weapon mentioned in the Old Testament was Uzziah's "engines," used on the towers at Jerusalem to repel attackers by shooting arrows and hurling large stones (2 Chr. 26:15); whether these engines propelled arrows and stones themselves or served as barricades behind which defenders shot arrows and threw stones is unclear.

Offensive weapons are much more diverse and may be classified according to range of use: short, medium, or long range. Short range weapons include such items as swords or daggers (for cutting or stabbing; Josh. 11:11; Judg. 3:16-22; Matt. 26:47-52), clubs, maces, and battle axes (for breaking in pieces; Jer. 51:20-23; cf. Prov. 25:18; Isa. 10:5, 15), and spears (for thrusting; Num. 25:7-8; 2 Sam. 2:23; John 19:34). Medium range weapons primarily include spears and the similar but lighter javelins (for throwing; 1 Sam. 18:11; 19:10; cf. 17:6-7; Acts 23:23). Long range offensive weapons are represented in the Bible by bows and slings (1 Sam. 17:49; 1 Chr. 12:2; 2 Chr. 26:14; Rev. 6:2). The final offensive weapon, extremely important, is the chariot. Iron chariots in Canaan prevented the Israelites from advancing into a particular area of the promised land (Judg. 1:19) and led to their oppression there (4:3; cf. Rev. 9:9). Solomon's chariot cities and his 1400 chariots were among the components of his great wealth described in 1 Kgs. 10:14-29.

Less plentiful but intriguing are the biblical references to nonliteral, spiritual weapons. At Gen. 15:1; Ps. 3:3 God is referred to as a shield. Ps. 7:11-13 describes the consequences of God's righteous wrath in terms of sword and bow and flaming arrows, while at Isa. 59:17 God the righteous judge dons the breastplate of righteousness and the helmet of salvation. These two items and several others are taken up by Paul at Eph. 6:11-17 as he describes the whole armor of God that the Christian should "put on"; at 2 Cor. 10:4 he refers to the Christians' weapons as "not worldly." Heb. 4:12 compares the word of God to a two-edged sword (cf. Rev. 1:16), similar to Paul's equation of the sword of the Spirit with the word of God (Eph. 6:17).

For specific weapons see the individual entries.

Bibliography. Y. Yadin, *The Art of Warfare in Biblical Lands,* 2 vols. (Jerusalem: 1963).

WEASEL (Heb. *ḥōleḏ*). A small carnivorous mammal of the genus Mustela, some species of which the Israelites considered unclean (Lev. 11:29). The Hebrew term may derive from the common Semitic root *ḥld* "dig, creep." Although the translation "weasel" (*Mustela nivalis*) is supported by the LXX and other versions, more recent translators have preferred the related species "mole" (*Spalax Ehrenbergi*; so JB, NJV) or "mole-rat" (*Spalax typhlus*; so NEB).

WEAVING. A process, common in the ancient world, for making various kinds and patterns of cloth. The basic procedure was to attach a set of threads (warp) to a loom, then interweave cross (woof or weft) threads with the warp and press or beat them successively into the growing fabric.

Three kinds of looms were used in ancient Palestine and Egypt. A vertical loom had warp strings hung from a beam on the top (evidently quite large, for the weaver's beam was the standard to which Goliath's massive spear shaft was compared at 1 Sam. 17:7; cf. 2 Sam. 21:19; 1 Chr. 11:23; 20:5) and weighted at the bottom. The weaver stood in front of the loom and worked down from the top. A second type of vertical loom had beams at both the top and bottom; weavers on each side together worked upwards. The more portable horizontal loom had front and back beams held in place by pegs driven into the ground, while the weaver sat in front. Into which type Delilah wove Samson's hair (Judg. 16:13-14) is a matter of dispute: some scholars envision him sleeping on the ground beside a vertical loom, while others picture him on a cot close to a horizontal loom.

Despite the variety of biblical references to weaving, few specifics are provided. Probably much of the weaving was done by women (Judg. 16:13-14; cf. Exod. 35:25-26; Prov. 31:22), but certain men, whether skilled craftsmen (Exod. 35:35) or members of a guild (linen workers, 1 Chr. 4:21), worked professionally to produce fine work. Biblical examples of woven garments include those worn by Aaron and his sons (Exod. 28:8, 27-28, 39; 39:22, 27) and the seamless tunic of Jesus (John 19:23).

Materials employed in weaving include goats' hair (used in the curtains for the tent over the tabernacle; Exod. 26:7; 36:14) and, most often, linen and wool (Lev. 13:48). Making garments of a mixture of linen and wool was specifically prohibited (Deut. 22:11; cf. the more general Lev. 19:19, "cloth made of two kinds of stuff"). Such prohibitions may well have religious roots, perhaps related to biblical notions of ritual purity and the holiness of God.

Figuratively, the weaver's loom is used to illustrate the passing and ending of life. In one of his laments Job remarks: "My days are swifter than a [weaver's] shuttle and come to an end as the thread runs out" (NEB, Job 7:6). When King Hezekiah learned that his death was imminent, he referred to the ending of his life as being cut off from the loom (Isa. 38:12)— what the weaver does to the cloth when it is finished.

WEEDS. Uncultivated nuisance plants, found in the Old Testament at Job 31:40 (Heb. *bāʾošâ*; RSV "foul weeds"; KJV "cockle"); Hos. 10:4 (*rōš*; RSV "poisonous weeds"; KJV "hemlock"). The reference at Jon. 2:5 (MT 6) probably indicates seaweed (*sûp*). In the New Testament, all instances of Gk. *zizanion* are found in the parable of the weeds of the field and its interpretation (Matt. 13:24-30, 36-43; KJV "tares"). This particular weed was probably darnel (*Lolium tremulentum*), a poisonous weed that closely resembles the young wheat plants as a seedling, thus making early separation of the two almost impossible (cf. v. 29).

In the parable these weeds represent the sons of the evil one who dwell in the world alongside the sons of the kingdom. As with the weeds and the wheat, the separation of good from bad people will not take place until the judgment at the end of the age, represented in the parable by the harvest and the burning of the weeds.

WEEKS, FEAST OF (Heb. *ḥag šāḇuʿôṯ*; Gk. *pentēkostē*).† The second of the three great annual feasts of Israel (Exod. 23:14; 2 Chr. 8:13), to be celebrated seven full weeks (or fifty days) from the beginning of the barley harvest (Lev. 23:15-16; Deut. 16:9). In later Judaism it became an anniversary celebration of the giving of the law at Sinai, and in the New Testament signified God's outpouring of his Holy Spirit upon his people, the birthday of the Christian Church.

I. Old Testament

According to Deut. 16:9 the Israelites were to "begin to count the seven weeks from the time you first put the sickle to the standing grain." This cutting was a part of the waving of the sheaf ceremony recorded at Lev. 23:9-14. The feast itself was originally agricultural in character, as the names Feast of Harvest (Heb. *ḥag haqqāṣîr*; Exod. 23:16) and Day of the First Fruits (*yôm habbikkûrîm*; Num. 28:26) indicate. Other titles, such as Feast of Weeks (Exod. 34:22; Deut. 16:10, 16; 2 Chr. 8:13) and Pentecost (LXX, Lev. 23:16; RSV "fifty weeks") refer to the seven-week or fifty-day period that commenced with the waving of the sheaf and reached its completion on the actual day of celebration itself. Scholars disagree as to the precise significance of this seven-week or fifty-day period. While some have sought to emphasize the importance of the number seven and its multiples (with their obvious connotation of wholeness or completeness), others see the period as possessing no special significance—that it was simply the normal time span required for completion of the harvest. While admitting the crucial role played by the number seven in the structure of Israel's feasts, one must also take into account the fact that nature itself could at times override (as in the case of harvest) adherence to a strict timetable.

Cultic regulations concerning the one-day festival are given in full in the two parallel accounts of Lev. 23:15-21; Num. 28:26-31. Earlier and more brief references to the feast occur at Exod. 23:16; 34:22, with a later treatment (somewhat different in emphasis) at Deut. 16:9-12. On the festal day itself a holy convocation was to be called and no laborious work could be done (Lev. 23:21; Num. 28:26). Pentecost was one of three times during the year when all males were required to appear before the Lord (Exod. 23:17; 34:23). A cereal offering of new grain (two loaves of leavened bread) was offered as first fruits in thanksgiving to the Lord for his bounteous harvest blessings. The two loaves were to be waved before the Lord by

the priest, together with two male lambs a year old (Lev. 23:20). In addition to the cereal offering there was to be a burnt offering—consisting of one bull, two rams and seven male lambs a year old, along with their respective cereal and drink offerings (v. 18; Num. 28:27-29) and a sin offering of one male goat "to make atonement" for their sins (Lev. 23:19; Num. 28:30). Also, each was to make a freewill offering from his own hand, in accordance with the manner in which God had blessed him (Deut. 16:10, 17). Pentecost was a time of rejoicing (v. 11), a time to celebrate and recognize the manifold blessings that Yahweh had bestowed upon his chosen people. This thankfulness was to extend to those outside the fold as well; Israel was to remember that they too had been strangers in a strange land and thus now, in remembrance of their former status, should share their abundance with those less fortunate (Lev. 23:22; Deut. 16:11-12).

In later Judaism Pentecost became an anniversary celebration of the giving of the law on Sinai (cf. Exod. 19:1, which indicates that Israel came into the wilderness of Sinai on the third new moon [the third month] after the exodus from Egypt). The book of Jubilees (second century B.C.) provides a perhaps earlier interpretation of the feast that may have served as a transition to this later equation with the Sinai event. The writer of the book, in an effort to establish the antiquity of "the feast of Shebuot" in Israel's history, sets its origin in the covenant made by God with Noah in the third month when the patriarch had emerged from the ark "in order to renew the covenant in all [respects] year by year" (Jub. 6:17-18); the consonantal form of Heb. "weeks" (*šbʿwt*) here could also connote the meaning "oaths." Other references to the feast (14:20; 15:1-10; 22:1-9) recognize its agricultural (or "weeks") character, yet place the festival within a context more suited to its role as a celebration of covenant renewal ("oaths") (cf. 6:21; 2 Chr. 15:10-15).

The determination of a precise date for the beginning of the festival has remained a matter of long-standing debate in rabbinic writings. The crucial phrase "the morrow after the sabbath" (*mimmāḥᵒraṯ haššabbāṯ*; Lev. 23:15) has been subjected to two major interpretations: that of the Sadducees, who understood the Sabbath as a normal weekly one and began counting the seven weeks the day after (thus the counting could begin anytime during the Passover week, depending upon where the normal Sabbath fell after the first day of Passover), and that of the Pharisees, who interpreted the Sabbath of Lev. 23:15 in a more restrictive sense as the first day of the Passover feast, whereby the counting of the seven weeks always began on the second day of Passover.

Textual evidence for a definite relationship between Pentecost and the giving of the law at Sinai does not emerge until the second century A.D., and many view the events of A.D. 70 (the destruction of Jerusalem) as the major factor in the reinterpretation of the festival. The association of Pentecost with an event of major importance in Israel's history served to elevate the feast from its previously inferior (and original) status as a minor harvest celebration. The transition from God's covenant with Noah (Jub. 6) to the Sinaitic covenant was a natural one that placed Pentecost on

equal footing with Passover and the Feast of Tabernacles.
See PENTECOST.

WEIGHTS AND MEASURES.† A number of difficulties confront the task of transposing biblical measurements into modern systems of measurement. For the most part, what one encounters in the Bible are estimated quantities and measurements based on generally accepted standards rather than on standards enforced by a central authority. Variations within limits are, therefore, a factor for every kind of unit. The accompanying chart provides approximations of equivalents in modern units for units of measurement mentioned in the Bible. Even rough equivalents for some biblical units of measurement cannot be determined. For example, Ehud's sword is said to have been one *gōmer* in length (Judg. 3:16); this unit of length is not otherwise attested, and the reading "cubit" is itself little more than an educated guess. Also, Heb. *šālîš* "third" refers to a unit of capacity not otherwise known (Isa. 40:12; RSV, KJV "measure"; NIV "basket"; JB "bushel").

Various locally or temporarily successful attempts to impose standards for measurements are recorded. Among the duties of the Levites was the maintenance of standards of measurement for the offerings brought to the temple (1 Chr. 23:29). An awareness of changes in the length of a cubit (2 Chr. 3:3) shows that newly imposed standards could differ from old standards. This is reflected in Ezekiel's mention of "long cubits, each being a cubit and a handbreadth in length" (Ezek. 40:5; 43:13); he expects his readers to be familiar with the shorter cubit. The Romans came to use a stable standard for traveling distances, but in the Old Testament distance is measured in terms of time rather than units of distance (e.g., Gen. 30:36; Num. 11:31; Jonah 3:3). The basic unit of weight was the shekel,

A stone one-mina weight from seventh-century Babylonia (by courtesy of the **Trustees** of the **British Museum**)

UNITS OF WEIGHT AND MEASURE With approximate metric and English equivalents		
Biblical[1]	**Metric**	**English**
WEIGHT (*see also* MONEY)		
gerah	————	0.57 gm.	0.02 oz.
beka	10 gerahs	5.7 gm.	0.20 oz.
pim	1.33 bekas	7.6 gm.	0.27 oz.
shekel	2 bekas	11.4 gm.	0.4 oz.
mina	50 shekels	571.2 gm.	1.26 lb.
talent	60 minas	34.27 kg.	75.6 lb.
pound[2]	————	326 gm.	11.5 oz.

LENGTH AND DISTANCE			
Old Testament			
finger	————	1.85 cm.	0.73 in.
handbreadth	4 fingers	7.4 cm.	2.92 in.
span	3 handbreadths	22.2 cm.	8.75 in.
cubit	2 spans	44.4 cm.	17.5 in.
long cubit[3]	7 handbreadths	51.9 cm.	20.4 in.
New Testament:[4]			
cubit	————	42-48 cm.	17-19 in.
fathom	4 cubits	1.8 m.	6 ft.
stade	400 cubits	170-190 m.	189-215 yds.
mile	8 stades	1480 m.	1618 yds.

CAPACITY			
Old Testament:			
log	————	0.3 l.	0.63 pint[5]
kab	4 logs	1.2 l.	1.3 qt.
omer[6]	.10 ephah	2.2 l.	2.3 qt.
hin	12 logs	3.6 l.	1 gal.
"measure"[7]	2 hins	7.3 l.	2 gal.
ephah (dry)	3 "measures"	22 l.	5. 8 gal.
bath (liquid)	3 "measures"	22 l.	5.8 gal.
lethech	5 ephahs	110 l.	29 gal.
cor/homer	10 ephahs	220 l.	58 gal.
New Testament:			
"pot"[8]	————	0.46 l.	1 pt.
"quart"	————	1.1 l.	1.2 qt.
"bushel"[8]	————	7.4 l.	7.8 qt.
metrētés[9]	————	38 l.	10 gal.

[1]RSV terminology except where RSV transposes into modern units.

[2]Gk. *lítra* represents both a unit of weight and a unit of capacity equivalent to about 0.5 l. Either may be in view in the two instances of the term, John 12:3; 19:39.

[3]Ezek. 40:5; 43:13.

[4]New Testament linear measures differ according to whether Roman, Greek, or Palestinian units are used.

[5]English units of capacity are U.S. liquid units.

[6]More commonly referred to as a "tenth," i.e., of an ephah.

[7]Heb. *sᵉ'â* (cf. NIV "seah")

[8]References to both "bushel" (Gk. *módios*, Matt. 5:15 par.) and "pot" (Gk. *xéstēs*, Mark 7:4) are to containers, not to specific units of capacity.

[9]RSV transposes into gallons.

but as with cubits, more than one type of shekel existed. The Bible shows a strong concern for just weights and measurements (Lev. 19:35-36; Deut. 25:13-16; Prov. 20:10, 23; Ezek. 45:10; Amos 8:5; Mic. 6:10-11).

Methods of measuring were developed early. Measuring rods and cords were sometimes used (Ezek. 40:3; Amos 7:17; Zech. 1:16; 2:1 [MT 5]; Rev. 21:15), but more common was the use of arms and hands to measure length. The standard for the cubit was the distance from the tip of the middle finger of the outstretched hand to the elbow; other measurements of length were determined similarly. Weight was measured on beam-balance scales on which stone weights or, less commonly, metals weights were used; the weights were kept in a bag (Deut. 25:13; Prov. 16:11; Mic. 6:11). Jars have been found with names of Old Testament measurements of capacity inscribed on them; these may have been used to standardize measurements. Unfortunately, these jars are not reliable indicators of the capacity indicated by Old Testament terms because of their late date (in some cases) and the differing volumes of similarly inscribed jars.

No units of area appear in the Bible other than the "acre" (so RSV; *ṣemeḏ*), the amount of land that a yoke of oxen could plow in one day (1 Sam. 14:14; RSV mg. "yoke"; Isa. 5:10). Occasionally reference is made to the amount of seed needed to sow a given area (1 Kgs. 18:32; cf. Lev. 27:16). Most often, linear measurements are used in place of measurements of area (e.g., Num. 35:4-5; 1 Kgs. 7:23; Ezek. 40:47-49).

See further the entries on individual units of measurement.

WELL (Heb. *beʾēr, bôr*; Gk. *pēgḗ, phréar*). A source of water, whether a natural surface spring, a shaft sunk to reach a subterranean water supply, or a cistern hewn out and plastered to collect rainwater. In Palestine, where water was scarce, the possession of a water source was extremely important; thus, the finding of water was worth celebrating (Num. 21:16-18), but could also be a bone of contention (Gen. 21:25-30; 26:18-22). Wells served the needs of animals as well as people (24:17-20; 29:1-10; Exod. 2:15-17) and were located in the wilderness (Gen. 16:7, 14), in fields (29:2), in courtyards (2 Sam. 17:18-19; here used also as a hiding place), and near towns. Town wells were usually located outside the city wall (Gen. 24:11; 2 Sam. 23:15; Neh. 2:13; John 4:6-8) and often served as meeting places for the women whose task it was to draw the needed water.

In figurative usage wells represent the lover (Prov. 5:15; Cant. 4:15; but cf. Prov. 23:27) and Jerusalem, a city whose wickedness was always "fresh" (Jer. 6:7). Certainly the best-known example is Jesus' promise to the Samaritan woman at Jacob's well that the water he gives would become "a spring of water welling up to eternal life" (John 4:13-14).

WEST. Although the Hebrews recognized the four points of the compass (Gen. 13:14; 28:14; Deut. 3:27; Luke 13:29; cf. Isa. 11:12; Ezek. 37:9), east held the preeminent place and the other directions were often reckoned and described according to their relationship to that point. Thus west was considered the rear (Joel 2:20) and was opposite to the rising of the sun (Isa. 45:6; 59:19). The usual word for west is Heb. *yām* "sea," referring to the Mediterranean Sea, Palestine's western border (Deut. 11:24; Josh. 15:12).

In Matthew's gospel, west and east are set opposite to one another to represent the ends of the earth from which the righteous will gather (Matt. 8:11; cf. Ps. 107:3; Isa. 43:5-6) and the universal visibility of the coming of the Messiah (Matt. 24:27).

WESTERN SEA (Heb. *hayyām hāʾaḥᵃrôn*). Another name for the Mediterranean Sea (Deut. 11:24; KJV "uttermost sea"; 34:2; KJV "utmost sea"; Joel 2:20; Zech. 14:8; KJV "hinder sea").

WHALE (Gk. *kḗtos*). An aquatic mammal of the order Cetacea, at Matt. 12:40 identified as the "great fish" (so Jonah 1:17) that swallowed and transported the prophet Jonah. The KJV reads "whale" at Job 7:12 (RSV "sea monster"); Ezek. 32:2 (RSV "dragon").

WHEAT (Heb. *ḥiṭṭâ, bar, dāgān*; Gk. *sítos*). A cereal grain and staple food from which flour is ground. Wheat was one of many grains grown in Israel (Deut. 8:8; 2 Sam. 17:28) and the most important for baking bread, including the ceremonial unleavened bread, cakes, and wafers (Exod. 29:2). Wheat harvest time was a seasonal reference point (Gen. 30:14; Judg. 15:1), and it was the firstfruits of the wheat harvest upon which the Feast of Weeks focused (Exod. 34:22; cf. 23:16; Lev. 23:15-20). The processing of wheat is frequently noted in the Bible, including sowing (Jer. 12:13), harvesting (1 Sam. 6:13), threshing (Judg. 6:11; 1 Chr. 21:20), cleaning (2 Sam. 4:6), and winnowing (Matt. 3:12).

In Solomon's time and after, wheat was a valuable commodity; Solomon traded it with Hiram of Tyre for the wood to build his temple (1 Kgs. 5:10-11 [MT 24-25]; cf. 2 Chr. 27:5). In the New Testament wheat represents the righteous in figurative and parabolic language, while chaff and weeds represent the wicked (Matt. 3:12 par. Luke 3:17; Matt. 13:24-30; Luke 22:31). It also symbolizes fruit-bearing and new life, which only appears after the wheat has "died" (John 12:24; 1 Cor. 15:36-37).

WHEEL (Heb. *ʾôpan, galgal*). A circular object or disk capable of turning on an axis at its center. Early wheels were wooden and attached firmly to the axle, but in time lighter, spoked wheels were developed that turned on the axle. In the Bible wheels are mentioned in connection with carts (Isa. 28:27-28) and chariots (Exod. 14:25; Jer. 47:3). Wheels like those of chariots made movable the ten laver stands at Solomon's temple; these were complete with axles, rims, spokes, and hubs (1 Kgs. 7:30-33). At Jer. 47:3; Nah. 3:2 the rumbling of chariot wheels represents God's judgment.

Ezekiel's visions of the glory of the Lord (Ezek. 1:4-28; ch. 10) included wheels with eyes, while in Daniel's vision the fiery throne of the Ancient of Days rested on wheels of burning fire (Dan. 7:9; cf. 1 En. 14:18). Wheels used for threshing grain symbolized a wise king's treatment of the wicked (NIV, Prov. 20:26), and the breaking of a wheel employed to draw water from a cistern represented the end of life (Eccl. 12:6).

WHIP. * Corporal punishment of humans by whipping was probably used in Old Testament Israel; Heb. *yāsar* is a word of broader use ("teach, train, rebuke")

A Roman whip with pieces of metal or bone attached to its cords

that probably indicates whipping in some contexts (e.g., Deut. 21:18; RSV "chastise"; KJV "chasten"; 22:18; RSV "whip"; KJV "chastise"). Punishment by beating with rods was common enough to require careful regulation (25:1-3). Job hyperbolically portrays persons whose social status is lower than his but who are nonetheless mocking him as nomads or vagabonds who are "whipped out of the land," i.e., mistreated by the settled population (Job 30:8; *nikkeʾû*, niphal of *nkʾ*; KJV reads the clause differently). The whip (Gk. *phragéllion*) used by Jesus in his cleansing of the temple (John 2:15; KJV "scourge") was made on the spot from cords. For 1 Kgs. 12:11, 14 par.; Prov. 26:3; Nah. 3:2 (Heb. *šôṭ*) *see* LASH.

WHIRLWIND (Heb. *galgal, sûpâ, saʿar, sᵉʿārâ*).† A violent windstorm of devastating power. Heb. *sûpâ, saʿar,* and *sᵉʿārâ* are used of such storms not necessarily with reference to a whirling motion of the air, and are often translated "storm" or "tempest" (but cf. Jer. 23:19; RSV "whirling tempest"). While tornadoes are rare in Palestine, violent storms are not uncommon during the rainy season. Heb. *galgal* (also translated "wheel"), however, clearly indicates such rotating winds at Ps. 77:18 (MT 19); Isa. 5:28.

Such storms were especially associated with the Negeb (Isa. 21:1; Zech. 9:14; cf. KJV, Job 37:9), and featured winds capable of carrying off persons as well as chaff (27:20; cf. 2 Kgs. 2:1, 11). Their inexorability and thoroughness made them an excellent image for an invading army (Amos 1:14; Hab. 3:14), particularly its chariot wheels (Isa. 5:28; Jer. 4:13; cf. KJV, Isa. 66:15), and for calamity in general (Prov. 1:27; Hos. 8:7). For the same reason God himself is sometimes depicted as employing whirlwinds for judgment, both metaphorically (Isa. 29:6; Jer. 23:19; 30:23; Amos 1:14; Zech. 7:14; cf. KJV, Jer. 25:32) and literally (Ps. 83:15 [MT 16]; RSV "hurricane"; Nah. 1:3; Zech. 9:14). Sometimes a whirlwind was the setting for an actual theophany: God appeared to Job and Ezekiel in a whirlwind (Job 38:1; 40:6; KJV, Ezek. 1:4), and

used one to remove Elijah from the earth (2 Kgs. 2:1, 11).

A lesser whirlwind (Heb. *tîmārâ*) may be implied in the "columns" of smoke at Cant. 3:6; Joel 2:30 (MT 3:3).

The RSV also translates "whirling dust" for *galgal*, identified as the "wheel-shaped dryed calix of the thistle *Gundelia Tournefortii*" (KoB, p. 181), which when blown by a strong wind across plains scatters its ripened seeds. The whirling dust or the tumbleweed (NIV) is a symbol of insignificance at Ps. 83:13 (MT 14) where the psalmist implores God to turn his enemies into tumbleweeds (so RSV mg., JB; KJV "wheel") or chaff, and at Isa. 17:13 where God is said to be chastening the nations before the storm (JB "eddy of dust"; KJV "rolling thing").

WHITE (Heb. *lābān*; Gk. *leukós*).* Heb. *lābān* is normally translated "white," but can also carry the meanings "light," "bright." This broader range of meaning functions when the term is used with reference to skin diseases (eighteen times at Lev. 13). (The comparison of diseased skin to snow [Exod. 4:6; Num. 12:10; 2 Kgs. 5:27; KJV supplies "white" twice, RSV in all three passages] may not indicate white color, but scaling like flakes of snow.) In poetry similes for whiteness refer to snow, wool, and milk (Ps. 51:7 [MT 9]; Isa. 1:18; Lam. 4:7; Rev. 1:14). White garments were worn in times of rejoicing (Eccl. 9:8).

The color white is used frequently in figurative language, almost invariably in a positive sense. The whiteness of milk is part of a picture of agricultural abundance and enjoyment at Gen. 49:12 (cf. Cant. 5:1; Isa. 55:1). Whiteness also represents sinlessness, generally as part of a figure involving washing (Ps. 51:7 [MT 9]; Isa. 1:16, 18; Dan. 11:35; 12:10). In Revelation the figure shifts slightly; the white garments of the sinless are not washed (except at Rev. 7:13-14) but are white already when given to those who persevere (3:4-5, 18; 6:11). Such garments come to be the normal garb of the glorified believers (4:4; 7:9). White garments are also a typical component of theophanic or angelic visions (Dan. 7:9; Aram. *ḥiwwār*; Matt. 17:2; 28:3; Rev. 19:14). Here also, and where white appears in theophanic visions as the color of something other than garments (e.g., 14:14; 20:11), purity is probably again the symbolic value of the color (so also in a different context at Lam. 4:7; Heb. *ṣāḥaḥ* "be white").

White horses were often used in victory processions (and had particular cultic significance in Persia); this may be in mind where white horses are mentioned at Rev. 6:2; 19:11, 14, but the color is less likely to have any symbolic value at Zech. 1:8; 6:3, 6. The "white stone" to be given to persevering Christians in the church of Pergamum (Rev. 2:17) is a metaphor, probably for their reception by God into eternal life; white tesserae were used as tokens for admission to banquets.

WHITEWASH (Heb. *tāpēl*; Gk. *koniáō*). A liquified, plasterlike substance, usually made with lime, used for whitening walls or other objects. In the Bible whitewash is a metaphor for a superficial and ineffectual attempt to deal with a profound difficulty, often representing the external beautification of what cannot in itself be made effective. Job accuses his counselors of whitewashing with lies, i.e., attempting to resolve his dilemma with worthless solutions (Job 13:4). Ezekiel condemns the false prophets because their promises of peace were like a poorly constructed wall, made to appear strong by the application of whitewash (Ezek. 13:10-15; KJV "untempered mortar"; 22:28). Jesus compares the hypocritical scribes and Pharisees to whitewashed tombs—outwardly beautiful but inwardly full of dead persons' bones (Matt. 23:27; cf. Ananias as he stands in judgment of Paul, Acts 23:3; KJV "whited").

WIDOW (Heb. *'almāmâ*; Gk. *chéra*). Together with the fatherless and the sojourners, widows were members of a disadvantaged class in ancient Hebrew society. To help counter their plight, the Mosaic law contained a number of very specific provisions to protect and provide materially for the often needy widow (e.g., Lev. 22:13; Deut. 14:28-29; 16:10-11, 14; 24:17-22). This included the principle of LEVIRATE MARRIAGE, which required a man to marry his deceased brother's widow if there had been no children (25:5-10).

Nevertheless, the widow, in her frequent poverty and dependence upon public charity, was particularly vulnerable and easily exploited. Its repeated mention in the prophets and elsewhere testifies to the prevalence of such treatment (e.g., Isa. 1:17, 23; Ezek. 22:7; 10; cf. Job 22:9; 24:21; Ps. 94:6). In addition, widowhood was held by many to be a disgrace (cf. Ruth 1:19-21; Isa. 4:1; 54:4). Ultimately, however, Yahweh would recompense the oppressors, for widows were among those who enjoyed his special care and favor (Exod. 22:21-24 [MT 20-23]; Deut. 10:18; Ps. 68:5 [MT 6]; 146:9; Mal. 3:5).

The Hebrews' regard for the plight of widows is reaffirmed in the New Testament (e.g., Jas. 1:27). Luke singled out virtuous widows (Luke 2:36-38; Acts 9:39-41). Jesus used them as examples (Mark 12:42-43 par. Luke 21:2-3; 18:3); he exhibited special concern for them (7:12-15) and sharply denounced their oppressors (Mark 12:40 par. Luke 20:47). Acts 6:1-6 records a problem (and its resolution) concerning the charitable distribution of food to needy widows.

Two situations in early churches resulted in discussions about widows. At 1 Cor. 7:8 Paul urges widows to remain single, although he does not forbid remarriage. At 1 Tim. 5:3-16, responding to different circumstances in the Ephesian church, the writer speaks of widows in three categories: those who have children or grandchildren who can (and must) provide for them (vv. 4, 8, 16); younger widows who should remarry (vv. 11-15); and "real" widows. Real widows had no family to support them (v. 5), had lived (and still were living) godly lives (vv. 5, 9b-10; cf. v. 6), and were at least sixty years old (v. 9a). Only these real widows could be put on the list of widows that the Church would support. The text provides no clear indication of an official "order" of widows, who traded the deeds of v. 10 for support by the Church (cf. Polycarp *Phil.* iv.3; Ignatius *Polyc.* iv.1).

In figurative language "widow" can refer to a city that has lost its people (Jerusalem, Lam. 1:1; cf. 5:3;

Isa. 54:4) or its power (Babylon, Isa. 47:9; cf. Rev. 18:7).

WILDGOATS' ROCKS (Heb. *ṣûrê hayyeʿēlîm*). A rocky wilderness region near En-gedi, not far from the western shore of the Dead Sea, where wild goats were (and still are) plentiful (1 Sam. 24:2 [MT 3]). In one of the caves in the area David had an opportunity to kill King Saul, but refused to raise his hand against the Lord's anointed (vv. 3-15 [MT 4-16]).

WILDERNESS (Heb. *miḏbār, ʿarāḇâ, yešîmôn*; Gk. *erēmía, érēmos*). In general, geographical regions beyond the limits of civilization and widely perceived as disorderly and inhospitable. Such areas include desert wastelands (Deut. 32:10; Ps. 106:14), thorny patches (Judg. 8:7, 16), rocky or mountainous regions (1 Sam. 23:14, 25-26), forests (Ezek. 34:25; cf. Isa. 32:15), and pasturelands (Gen. 36:24; Jer. 9:10 [MT 9]).

Most notable in the Bible is that wilderness between Egypt and the promised land of Canaan in which the Israelites wandered for forty years, the period of the "wilderness wanderings" recalled repeatedly in both the Old and New Testament (e.g., Ps. 78:52-54; Amos 2:10; Acts 7:36; 13:18; Heb. 3:17). This was the "great and terrible wilderness" (Deut. 1:19; 8:15; cf. 2 Cor. 11:26) where the Israelites were convinced they would die (Exod. 14:11-12), for there they had neither food (16:2-3) nor water (15:22; 17:1; Num. 21:5). In spite of these dangers, the wilderness was truly a place of God's presence: the Israelites were to sacrifice to God in the wilderness (Exod. 3:18; 5:1), the mountain of God was in the wilderness (4:27; 18:5), and there God remained with them forty years, bearing them as a father bears his son (Deut. 1:31; 2:7; 8:2-5).

Although the names of several specific wilderness areas are noted (Shur, Exod. 15:22; Sin, 16:1; Sinai, 19:2; Paran, Num. 10:12; Zin, 13:21; Etham, 33:8), their precise locations remain unknown (see further the individual entries); thus, the exact route of the wilderness wanderings cannot be reconstructed. *See* EXODUS.

The wilderness played host to a variety of biblical figures. Twice Hagar fled to the wilderness (Gen. 16:7; 21:14), Moses was a shepherd in the wilderness near Horeb (Exod. 3:1), and David received valuable training both in trusting the Lord and in battle skills while he kept sheep in the wilderness (1 Sam. 17:28, 34-37). In New Testament times John the Baptist made his home and, in fulfillment of the prophecy of Isa. 40:3 (cf. Matt. 3:3 par.), prepared the way of the Lord in the wilderness (Luke 1:80; cf. Matt. 3:1 par.; 11:7 par.). Although Jesus' ministry was not based in the wilderness, it was there he endured temptation (4:1 par.), and there he withdrew to pray (Luke 5:16; cf. Rev. 12:6, 14).

Finally, Isaiah speaks of the eschatological renewal of the wilderness, when the Spirit will be poured out from on high, the uninhabitable places will become the seats of righteousness, and the glory and splendor of the Lord will be manifest (Isa. 32:15-16; 35:1-2, 6-10; 41:18-20; 51:3; cf. Ezek. 34:25).

WILL (Gk. *diathḗkē*).† In New Testament usage primarily the (Old Testament) "covenant" (the Greek term was used almost exclusively in the LXX for Heb. *bᵉrît* "covenant"). God is depicted as determining the conditions of the relationship between him and his people, which conditions were finally accomplished through the work of Jesus Christ.

In the Synoptic Gospels Jesus speaks of the blood of the "covenant" (so RSV; Matt. 26:28; Mark 14:24; cf. "new covenant," Luke 22:20; 1 Cor. 11:25; KJV "testament"). By his death Jesus effects the saving will of God. "Will/covenant" was an expression of God's promise and desire for his people (Luke 1:72; Rom. 9:4; 11:27; Eph. 2:12). The old covenant is mentioned in the New Testament (Acts 3:25), often in contrast to the new (Gal. 4:24-31; Heb. 8:6-13; cf. Jer. 31:31-34; 2 Cor. 3:6). The writer of Hebrews is especially fond of the term, using it seventeen times.

In nonbiblical Greek *diathḗkē* means literally "last will and testament," a sense apparent at Gal. 3:15; Heb. 9:16-17 (so RSV). Here the respective writers, in the midst of their discussions, take a side glance at the secular, or popular, understanding of the term. At Gal. 3:15 Paul remarks that God's covenant is inviolable, as is an ordinary will (RSV mg. "covenant"). At Heb. 9:16-17 the author remarks that a "(last) will" does not take effect until the testator dies, a clear reference to the necessity of Christ's death in order to perfect the new covenant.

WILLOW TREE. A plant of the genus *Salix*, generally found growing along streams and rivers. Heb. *ṣapṣāpâ* occurs only in Ezekiel's allegory of the two eagles (Ezek. 17:5), designating a willow, the twigs of which quite readily take root. Heb. *ᶜᵃrābîm* may indicate either the willow or the similar Euphrates poplar. The latter is most likely intended at Ps. 137:2 (so RSV mg., JB, NIV), for it grew commonly by the waters of Babylon where the Israelites hung their lyres while they wept, unable to sing for sorrow. Particular species are uncertain in the other references, such as Lev. 23:40, where booths were constructed (cf. Neh. 8:13-18) and branches waved to celebrate the Feast of Tabernacles (cf. Job 40:22; Isa. 44:4).

WILLOWS, BROOK OF THE (Heb. *naḥal hā'ᵃrābîm*). A wadi on the Moab-Edom border, crossed by Moabite refugees carrying their belongings (Isa. 15:7). This stream, a suitable area for willows, has been identified with the Seil el-Qurahi, the lower course of the Wâdî el-Ḥesā, the biblical "brook Zered"; its crossing by the Israelites marked the end of their wilderness wanderings (Num. 21:12; Deut. 2:13-14). The Brook of the Willows may be the same as the "Brook of the Arabah" (*naḥal hā'ᵃrābâ*), Israel's southern boundary (Amos 6:14).

WIND (Heb. *rûaḥ*; Gk. *pneúma*). The horizontal movement of air. The winds came from the four corners of heaven (the limits of the universe, Jer. 49:32, 36; Mark 13:27), sent by God to do his bidding (Gen. 8:1; Exod. 15:10; Ps. 78:26; 135:7; Ezek. 37:9; Rev. 7:1). Although God was not always "in" the wind (1 Kgs. 19:11), in language reminiscent of archaic Canaanite poetry he was said to ride on its wings (2 Sam. 22:11; Ps. 18:10; 104:3).

Certain winds were well known by reputation, such as the powerful and blighting east wind (Gen. 41:6, 23, 27), which brought the plague of locusts upon Egypt (Exod. 10:13), made the sea into dry land for Israel (14:21), terrorized the wicked (Job 27:21-23), destroyed ships upon the sea (Ps. 48:7 [MT 8]; Ezek. 27:26), and wrought other destruction as well (19:12; Hos. 13:15; Jonah 4:8; cf. Job 1:19; Ps. 55:8 [MT 9]; Matt. 7:27). The west wind, generally the prevailing wind in Palestine, carried the locusts out of Egypt (Exod. 10:19) and brought quails from the sea for the Israelites to eat (Num. 11:31). The north wind brought rain (Prov. 25:23), but the south wind brought great heat (Job 37:17; Luke 12:55 [but cf. Acts 27:13]; cf. Ps. 11:6; Isa. 11:15; 49:10; Jer. 4:11).

Wind was a welcome partner in the threshing process, as it carried away the chaff, although usually wind and chaff are used as a figure for the wicked, scattered by the Lord (Job 21:18; Ps. 1:4; 35:5; Isa. 17:13; 41:16; Jer. 13:24; Dan. 2:35). Wind also represents the emptiness of vain speech (e.g., the arguments at Job 6:26; 8:2; 15:2; 16:3; cf. Jer. 5:13; Mic. 2:11; Eph. 4:14), and of life itself (Eccl. 1:14, 17; 2:11, 17, 26; cf. Prov. 11:29; Isa. 26:18; 41:29). Similarly, wind is used to illustrate the transitory nature of human existence (Ps. 78:39; 103:15-16) and the origin and destiny of those born of the Spirit (John 3:8; cf. Prov. 27:16; Hos. 8:7).

At Acts 2:2 the coming of the Holy Spirit at Pentecost was likened to the rushing of a mighty wind (cf. the use of Heb. *rûaḥ* for both "wind" and "spirit"), and Jesus' disciples learned much from watching him take command of the winds (Matt. 8:23-27 par.; cf. 14:24-33 par.).

WINDOW (Heb. *'ᵃrubbâ, ḥallôn, meḥᵉzâ*; Aram. *kawwîn*; Gk. *thyrís*).† A rectangular opening in the wall of a house. It could be opened as needed (2 Kgs. 13:17), and was often covered with a lattice through which one could look out (Judg. 5:28; 2 Sam. 6:16 par. 1 Chr. 15:29; Prov. 7:6) or in (Cant. 2:9). Windows were usually small and few in number, in order to keep temperatures inside the house warm in winter and cool in summer. Some were still large enough, however, to permit an intruder (Joel 2:9; cf. Jer. 9:21 [MT 20]) or a fugitive (Josh. 2:15; 1 Sam. 19:12; 2 Cor. 11:33; cf. 2 Kgs. 1:2; 9:32) to pass easily through them, and so would usually be placed on upper floors if the building had more than one story (e.g., Dan. 6:10 [MT 11]; the ground floor would be sufficiently illuminated by the doorway). References to the "windows with recessed frames" of Solomon's temple (1 Kgs. 6:4) and Ezekiel's eschatological temple (Ezek. 40:16, 22, 25, 29; 41:16), as well as to the elaborately planned windows in Jehoiakim's house (Jer. 22:14), imply the contrasting simplicity of general window design. It has been suggested also that these latter windows, and Jezebel's window at 2 Kgs. 9:32, included balconies for public appearances, imitating Egyptian royal architecture.

Heb. *'ᵃrubbâ* denotes an opening rather than an architectural feature per se. The image "windows of heaven" thus appears to depict wide openings through which blessing or judgment can cascade to the earth (Gen. 7:11; 8:2; JB "sluices"; 2 Kgs. 7:2, 19; Isa.

24:18; Mal. 3:10; cf. Isa. 60:8; JB "(dove)cote"; Hos. 13:3; KJV "chimney").

The KJV reading "windows" at Isa. 54:12 should probably be rendered "pinnacles" (RSV) or "parapets" (cf. JB, NIV "battlements").

WINE (Heb. *yayin*; Gk. *oínos*).† In the Mediterranean world wine has been favored since antiquity as a preferred and valued beverage (Ps. 104:15). The land and its climate lend themselves favorably to the cultivation of vineyards, and ever since biblical times wine production has been a valued skill. Indeed, the Bible contains more than 140 references to wine. It is no accident that the first tiller of the soil, Noah, planted a vineyard and enjoyed its wine (Gen. 9:20). Wine is found in lists of produce (Deut. 7:13; Jer. 31:12), and because of its color could be called "the blood of the grape" (Gen. 49:11; Deut. 32:14; Isa. 63:3; cf. Rev. 14:20). Sirach (first century B.C.) sums up the Jewish affection for wine: "...What is life to a man who is without wine? It has been created to make men glad..." (Sir. 31:27-28).

In Israel the grape harvest comes in late August or September. In antiquity the fruit was gathered and spread in the sun to ripen further. Even with the later introduction of mechanical wine presses, in both the Old and New Testament eras the grapes were generally crushed by foot in vats, usually circular basins cut out of the bedrock. Grapes were crushed in a first vat, and the juice would run through a channel to a second basin. This was a joyous occasion in Israel, accompanied by merriment and song (Pss. 8, 81, 84 may be vintage songs; "Gittith" in their superscriptions may refer to the wine press; so LXX).

Fermentation began almost immediately. The juice was stored in jars or goatskins, but in the latter case new skins were essential since they needed to expand with the fermenting wine (Job 32:19; Mark 2:22). When the wine was ready it was first strained with cloth to remove foreign matter and any residual pulp (Matt. 23:24) and then poured into metal or pottery cups. Older wine was best, since it had aged longer and was thus sweeter and stronger. Sometimes spices were added to enhance the flavor (Cant. 8:2), and in New Testament times the Romans scented their wine with thyme, cinnamon, roses, and jasmine flowers. Wealthier Jews may have adopted this fashion, but the common person drank his cup either naturally or with some honey. The Romans also mixed their wine with water (2 Macc. 15:39), but this was not the usual Jewish custom (cf. Isa. 1:22).

There is no biblical evidence that wine ever consisted of unfermented grape juice. When such juice is mentioned (cf. Gen. 40:10-11) it is never called wine. Occasionally the Bible refers to "new wine" (Heb. *tîrôš*; Mic. 6:15; KJV, Isa. 65:8; cf. Acts 2:13; Gk. *gleúkos*), but this too was fermented and could intoxicate (Hos. 4:11; the LXX always translates *tîrôš* with Gk. *oínos* "wine"). New wine refers to the first drippings from the vat; it was purer, and because of its higher sugar content fermented into a more substantial drink. Wine could be graded in this manner (cf. the Cana wedding, where the steward is conscious of quality; John 2:10).

In both the Old and New Testament wine is accepted as a commonplace commodity of life. It was a symbol of well-being and of God's blessing (Gen. 27:28), and was often a gift (1 Sam. 25:18; 2 Sam. 16:1) as well as an article of trade (2 Chr. 2:8-10 [MT 7-9]). In the New Testament era, however, wine was not a daily beverage taken with every meal because of the impurity of water; rather, for the common person bread, salt, and water were mainstays that went with all food (cf. Ezek. 4:11; Mishnah *Sukk.* ii.5). On the other hand, wine was drunk at festive occasions when families celebrated circumcision, engagements, or marriage. It was also present at the annual festivals (Passover, Pentecost, Tabernacles), as well as the Sabbath. Finally, wine was considered an excellent medicine (Luke 10:34; 1 Tim. 5:23; cf. Mishnah *Šabb.* xix.2, where wine is used to heal circumcision). When mixed with myrrh it could be a narcotic, and thus was offered to Jesus on the cross (Mark 15:23).

Wine also played a role in Israelite rituals. It was offered as a libation in sacrifice (Exod. 29:40; 1 Sam. 1:24), and in the Hellenistic period it may have been poured at the base of the altar as if it were blood (Sir. 50:15). This connection with sacrifice may explain its eventual use in the Passover Seder (cf. Jub. 49:6) and the rabbinic requirement that Passover wine be red (cf. Mishnah *Pesaḥ.* vii.13, which mentions heated water for mixing with wine). At his final Passover supper with his followers Jesus makes this connection explicit: "This (wine) is my blood of the covenant, which is poured out for many" (Mark 14:24 par.).

Abstinence from wine characterized the piety of priests in service (Lev. 10:9) and those taking a Nazirite vow (Num. 6:3). Rulers were similarly admonished (Prov. 31:4). This voluntary abstinence characterized John the Baptist (Luke 1:15), but did not apply to Jesus. Jesus' willingness to drink wine was well known, and it may have subjected him to criticism (7:33-34; cf. John 2:1-11); abstinence had always been associated with religious zeal or piety, but Jesus refused to be measured by traditional standards.

Although wine is a gift from God and a symbol of abundance, Scripture consistently warns against its abuse (Isa. 5:11; 28:7; Mic. 2:11). Prov. 23:29-35 is virtually a homily against drunkenness (cf. v. 20; 20:1; 21:17). The New Testament lists such abuse as a serious sin (cf. Rom. 13:13; 1 Cor. 5:11; Gal. 5:21; 1 Pet. 4:3) that will not be tolerated among those who wish to inherit the kingdom of God (cf. 1 Cor. 6:10). Thus church leaders must be moderate in their use of wine (1 Tim. 3:8; cf. Titus 2:3). Instead of being drunk with wine, Christians should be "filled with the Spirit" (Eph. 5:18). Paul counsels that even though people possess freedom in Christ, it is correct to abstain from wine in the company of weaker Christians in order to prevent them from stumbling (Rom. 14:21).

WISDOM (Heb. *ḥokmâ*; Gk. *sophía*), **WISDOM LITERATURE.**† Strictly speaking, wisdom literature as a generic category encompasses only the books of Job, Proverbs, and Ecclesiastes in the Old Testament; Sirach and the Wisdom of Solomon in the Apocrypha; and perhaps James in the New Testament. However, Heb. *ḥokmâ* "wisdom" represents a wide semantic field in the Old Testament, and is used in a variety of different contexts. The craftsmen Bezalel and Oholiab are said to be filled "with the Spirit of God, with ability (*ḥokmâ*) and intelligence, with knowledge and all craftsmanship" (Exod. 31:3; 35:31). Wisdom is similarly predicated of skilled persons at Jer. 9:17 (MT 16); 10:9. At Gen. 41:8 Pharaoh calls all the magicians and wise men of Egypt in the hope that they can interpret his dream; although these fail, Joseph succeeds, thereby proving his wisdom (v. 39). The picture of Daniel at Dan. 1–6 is similar. King Solomon is said to have possessed wisdom in legendary proportions, and to have composed 3000 proverbs and 1005 songs; however, the so-called nature wisdom mentioned at 1 Kgs. 4:29-34 (MT 5:9-12) is only rarely found in the book of Proverbs, and it is generally conceded that this picture of Solomon as the wisest man is highly legendary. This use of wisdom is also found in the New Testament, where Gk. *sophós* is used of a "skilled" builder (1 Cor. 3:10) and of the "only wise God" (Rom. 16:27); at Matt. 23:34 the adjective is used as a substantive meaning "wise men."

That wisdom was also institutionalized is suggested by Jer. 18:18 (cf. Ezek. 7:26), which presupposes a professional wisdom institution, generally thought to have been associated with the royal court. It is to this institution that much of the Old Testament's wisdom literature is to be ascribed, though it would be a distortion to assume that no other wisdom institutions existed in ancient Israel. There is good reason to think at least in terms of clan/family wisdom as well as court wisdom, and one plausible theory suggests that the clan is the setting for Israel's "apodictic" legal traditions. Whether or not wisdom schools existed in ancient Israel is open to question, especially for wisdom of the Second Temple (postexilic) period.

Recent scholarship has tended to see as pervasive influence of wisdom on the rest of the Old Testament literature. Deuteronomy is said to be closely related to wisdom, and the prophets Isaiah and Amos have been related to wisdom. Various narratives (e.g., the Joseph narrative, Gen. 37–50; the succession narrative, 2 Sam. 9–20 plus 1 Kgs. 1–2) have been seen as wisdom cast in narrative form. Whether or not these various interpretations are correct remains uncertain, but the Egyptian Tale of the Shipwrecked Sailor suggests that a genre of didactic narrative did exist in the ancient Near East.

I. Genres

Many different genres are associated with Old Testament Wisdom Literature, but five deserve special mention. The "better"-saying (Prov. 16:8) may be formulated with "Better is X than Y" or, contrasting the absolute goodness of A over against the absolute badness of C, "Better is A with B than C with D." The "disputation" (Job) is the genre in which is cast an argument between two or more parties holding differing points of view. The "instruction" (Prov. 1:8–9:18) is a lengthy, self-contained, stylized discourse that aims to prescribe values, rules of conduct, or the like; this genre has been heavily influenced by the Egyptian instruction texts. The "numerical saying" (30:18-19; Aḥiqar 12; cf. Amos 1:3–2:16) is governed by the sequence X . . . X + 1; it is uncertain if this structure reflects a progression in which the final element is emphasized. The sentence-proverb or "aph-

orism" (Prov. 10ff.) is a short utterance, generally containing two clauses written parallelistically, although various items such as motive clauses may also be included within the structure.

II. Ancient Near East

More than any other genre of Old Testament literature, Wisdom Literature reflects its international ancient Near Eastern setting. Wisdom literature has been discovered in Egypt, Syria, Palestine, and Mesopotamia. The concerns of Old Testament wisdom echo throughout the ancient Near Eastern literature. To interpret the Old Testament literature properly, an acquaintance with this material is necessary.

Some twenty wisdom texts survive from Egypt, thirteen *sebayit* ("teaching, instruction") texts and seven examples of speculative wisdom. The texts date from the Old Kingdom (*ca.* 2700-2150 B.C.) to the Hellenistic period (Demotic instructions). It is uncertain whether these texts are pseudonymous. The heart of Egyptian wisdom is encapsulated in Egyp. *maat*, which connotes "truth, justice, order" and refers to the cosmic order established at creation (cf. Ptahotep 5, "Great is justice (*maat*), lasting in effect, Unchallenged since the time of Osiris" (*AEL* 1:69). The instructions are generally introduced with the formula, "The instructions that X made for Y," which is usually expanded significantly. This allows two of the texts to be cast as royal testaments (cf. Deuteronomy): "The Instruction Addressed to King Merikare" and "the Instruction of King Amenemhet I for His Son Sesostris I." Form critically, the pre-Hellenistic instructions closely parallel the structure and genre of Prov. 1–9, while the Demotic instructions are formulated as sentences or aphorisms. Of all the ancient Near Eastern wisdom literature, the Egyptian texts are closest in both form and content to the Old Testament.

Although once thought to be of Mesopotamian origin, the Aramaic text "Words of Aḥiqar" is more likely to be of Syrian origin. This text contains a series of proverbs preceded by a narrative concerning an Assyrian official named Aḥiqar. Unfortunately, the narrative is incomplete. The form of the proverbs themselves is reminiscent of the aphorisms of Prov. 10ff., although the content of the two bodies of literature differs considerably.

A variety of wisdom texts were discovered at Ras Shamra (published in *Ugaritica* V). They are not written in Ugaritic, but in Akkadian, although some proverbs written in Ugaritic are extant. Especially to be noted in RS 22:439, a long collection of proverbs cast in the form of the words of a father to his son as the latter is about to embark on a journey, perhaps a symbol for the course of life. The discovery of collections of proverbs at Ebla has been announced, but the texts themselves have not yet been published.

From Mesopotamia have come a number of Sumerian proverb collections, perhaps numbering more than twenty. Of particular significance are the collected "Instructions of Šuruppak," the written deposit of the instructions of Šuruppak to "his son." It is a matter of dispute how far the designation "wisdom literature" is applicable to Babylonian literature; still, fables, popular sayings, and proverbs are extant from Babylonia. A few such texts might profitably be compared to Job or Ecclesiastes (e.g., the Babylonian "I Will Praise the Lord of Wisdom" and the so-called Sumerian Job [*ANET*, pp. 434-437, 589-591]).

III. Theology

It has recently been argued that Old Testament wisdom was theological from its inception, and that the various wisdom documents reflect the theological critique of these early theological presuppositions. An examination of the earliest aphorisms indicates that three of the theological presuppositions of wisdom were (1) that this is an orderly world, ruled by Yahweh, its Creator; (2) that knowledge of this order is possible to the person who opens himself to wisdom; (3) that the wise person who thus aligns himself with God's order will experience good things, while the fool will suffer for his folly (4). In this context, both Job and Ecclesiastes are seen as critiques of these positions, with Ecclesiastes being the more intense. Whereas for Job the theophanic appearance of Yahweh functions to resolve the questions and problems raised in the preceding chapters, Ecclesiastes subjects these presuppositions to a scathing critique until no hope for wisdom remains. What results from this critique is the Preacher's resolve to make the best of life in all its meaninglessness. Sirach presents a solution that hearkens back to the older theological presuppositions with the innovation that Torah, God's revealed law, is equated with wisdom (Sir. 24, 39). The Wisdom of Solomon adds a different kind of innovation as a solution: the immortality of the soul insures that the demands of justice will eventually be met (Wis. 3:1-4; 5:15-20).

For specific themes see entries on the various books.

IV. New Testament

The New Testament in general presupposes the Jewish wisdom tradition and its genres, in addition to its debt to Hellenistic philosophy and rhetoric. The "natural" wisdom of this age (1 Cor. 2:6) is contrasted with the wisdom of God (Rom. 11:33; Eph. 3:10). As such, God grants wisdom to those Christians who are being tested (Jas. 1:5-8, 16-18). Christ is occasionally identified as the wisdom of God (1 Cor. 1:30) in whom reside "all the treasures of wisdom and knowledge" (Col. 2:3). On the basis of certain sayings in Q and the hymn at Rom. 11:33-36, some scholars have tried to reconstruct an early wisdom christology. Finally, wisdom itself is personified at Matt. 11:19; Luke 7:35, but the interpretation of this passage remains uncertain.

In James, the connection between Christian virtue and wisdom (Jas. 3:13-18) is especially to be noted. An extensive discussion of wisdom may be found at 1 Cor. 1-3.

Bibliography. J. Crenshaw, *Old Testament Wisdom* (Atlanta: 1981); A. W. Jenks, "Theological Presuppositions of Israel's Wisdom Literature," *HBT* 7 (1985): 43-75; D. F. Morgan, *Wisdom in the Old Testament Traditions* (Atlanta: 1982); R. Murphy, *Wisdom Literature.* FOTL 13 (1981); G. von Rad, *Wisdom in Israel* (Nashville: 1972).

WISDOM OF SOLOMON (Gk. *Sophia Salōmōnos*).† One of the more important wisdom compositions in the Apocrypha, in the Vulgate called "the book of Wisdom" (Lat. *Liber sapientia*). The book is the first great attempt to combine the insights of Greek philosophy (especially that of Middle Platonism) with the truths of Jewish faith.

I. Authorship and Date

The book is considered to have been written by an anonymous orthodox Jew who had been strongly influenced by Hellenistic culture and philosophy in Alexandria between 100 B.C. and A.D. 40. While a few scholars still claim the present text is a translation from an original Hebrew document, most are agreed that the author composed the work in Greek. The title refers to the book's traditional connection with Solomon, the great and wise king of Israel (1 Kgs. 4:29-34 [MT 5:9-14]; cf. 3:6-12; 2 Chr. 1:8-12). While Solomon's name never occurs in the book, the author maintains an obvious pretense of Solomonic authorship throughout the first nine chapters (cf. Wisd. 6:12–7:22; 8:2–9:18). By contrast, the latter half (chs. 10-19) features no clear allusions to Solomon.

II. Purpose and Contents

The author's intent is apparently twofold, to convince apostate Jews to return to the ancestral faith, and to convince sympathetic Gentiles of the truth of the claims of the Jewish faith.

Speaking to Jews who have adopted the hedonistic philosophy that if only the soul is immortal, then the gratification of one's physical desires is a matter of moral indifference, the first five chapters are concerned to teach the value of righteousness, which leads to eternal life: "The souls of the righteous are in the hand of God, and no torment will ever touch them" (3:1); "the righteous live forever, and their reward is with the Lord; the Most High takes care of them" (5:15). The wicked, however, will face ultimate punishment: "The ungodly will be punished as their reasoning deserves, who disregarded the rightous man (or 'what is right') and rebelled against the Lord" (3:10); "Do not invite death by the error of your life, nor bring on destruction by the works of your hands" (1:12).

Chs. 6–9 are directed toward the praise of Wisdom, characterized by extensive personification (hypostatization) of Wisdom as the mediator between God and mankind. Wisdom is variously described as "a breath of the power of God," "a pure emanation of the glory of the Almighty" (7:25), "a reflection of eternal light" (v. 26), and "the ordering principle of the universe (8:1). Some interpreters have noted clear connections with the Stoic conception of the LOGOS, a term Philo of Alexandria actually uses to describe this impersonal mediating principle; the connections with the use of Gk. *lógos* "Word" in the prologue to John's gospel are obvious.

Many scholars have noted a decline in skill and inspiration beginning with ch. 10. While some have posited a separate author for these last chapters, most now accept the unity of the book and attribute any diminishment to the vagaries of authorship. Chs. 10–19 are concerned to exhibit the care of Wisdom demonstrated in Israel's history. Beginning with Adam (10:1), Wisdom's protective care is shown for Noah (v. 4), Abraham (v. 5), Lot (v. 6), Jacob (vv. 9-12), and Joseph (vv. 13-14). At v. 15 the discussion shifts to Wisdom's protective guidance of Israel in the events surrounding the Exodus. This discussion is expressed in seven antitheses in which divine punishment of Egypt is paralleled by evidence of Wisdom's care for Israel (e.g., the waters of the Nile were turned to blood, but Israel was provided with water from the rock in the desert; 11:1-14). With the exception of two extensive digressions—considering divine mercy (11:15–12:22) and describing the folly of idolatry (13:1–15:17)—these antitheses occupy the remainder of the book.

III. Theology

As has long been recognized, while the theology of the Wisdom of Solomon is derived from traditional Old Testament sources, it owes much to its reformulation in terms of Greek philosophy. The author was thoroughly familiar with the teaching of Middle Platonism and the Stoics, and employs a host of Greek philosophical and literary forms (e.g., chiasmus, hyperbaton, sorites, antithesis, litotes). Among the religious ideas expressed that result from the influence of Greek philosophy are the preexistence of the soul, the soul's immortality at death in separation from the body, and the association of Wisdom with the concept of the Logos as an intermediating impersonal ordering force. Unlike Ben Sira, the author of Wisdom does not explicitly identify Wisdom and Torah; rather, like the roughly contemporary Philo of Alexandria he views Wisdom as the model of Torah, of which the Mosaic Law is the image. Right understanding of Torah requires further interpretation that only Wisdom can provide.

Bibliography. E. G. Clarke, *The Wisdom of Solomon.* CBC (1973); W. Watson, "Wisdom," *NCCHS.* (1969); D. Winston, *The Wisdom of Solomon.* AB 43 (1979).

WISE MEN (Gk. *mágoi*).† Matthew's account of Jesus' birth in Bethlehem records the visit of "wise men from the East" who came bringing expensive gifts of gold, frankincense, and myrrh (Matt. 2:1-12). They had viewed Christ's "star in the East" (v. 2) and came to Judea in search of the child. Once they consulted with Herod, their search led them to Bethlehem, which according to Matthew would fulfill Micah's prophecy concerning the place for the Messiah's birth (Mic. 5:2 [MT 1]). Soon thereafter they located Jesus and his family, worshiped him, and bestowed upon the child gifts of royalty. Their visit may have occurred sometime after that of Luke's shepherds (Luke 2:8ff.); Herod chooses to kill children who are "two and under" (Matt. 2:16), which implies that Jesus was older than a newborn baby.

Scholars have engaged in considerable debate in attempting to identify these figures. Magi were well known in the ancient East as purveyors of magic, interpreters of dreams and visions, astrologers, and prophets. The book of Daniel (e.g., Dan. 1:20; 2:2), Josephus, and numerous Roman writers record the widespread influence of such magicians. Often the description is pejorative, condemning them as charlatans or practitioners of the occult (cf. Acts 8:9-13; 13:6-12). But in Matthew's story they clearly represent individuals of high nobility.

Reference to the star at Matt. 2:2 suggests that these men were astrologers who employed study of the stars for predictions of future events. This activity flourished in Persia (or Parthia) and may explain their origin. On the other hand, the description of their gifts suggests that they had come from Arabia. Still another suggestion points to Babylon, which had a large community of Jews who could have supplied the *mágoi* with information about the anticipated Messiah.

Matthew's interest in the visit of the *mágoi* is to depict a royal delegation coming from pagan lands to pay homage to Israel's newborn king. This is what both interests and enrages Herod, Israel's current political ruler (vv. 1-2). On a literary level, Herod and Jesus are rivals, and the *mágoi* throw into sharp relief the one who deserves the respect and allegiance of even foreign powers.

Over the centuries the Church has imaginatively embellished the portraits of these figures, even giving them names. Balthasar, Melchior, and Gaspar are names popular in Western traditions. The reckoning of three wise men was speculated from the number of gifts recorded at v. 11. As early as Tertullian in the second century A.D. the eastern Church had begun the tradition that each of the wise men was a king. Further, their remains were valued treasures in the medieval collections of relics, the bulk of which reside today in the cathedral at Cologne.

WITCHCRAFT. *See* MAGIC; MEDIUM, WIZARD.

WITNESS (Heb. *'ēḏ*; Gk. *mártys*).† A person who gives testimony to establish the truth of a charge or a statement of fact. The legal requirement for confirming allegations was that there should be two witnesses (Deut. 19:15). In Old Testament society giving testimony as a witness was a formal confirmation basic to mutual trust in society. Legal documents were signed by witnesses. In the case of capital punishment by means of stoning, witnesses were required to throw the first stone. The importance of witnesses for confirmation is underscored by the Decalog's proscription of perjury (Exod. 20:16).

An altar named "Witness" was erected by the tribes of Reuben and Gad to confirm to future generations that they were a part of the people of God (Josh. 22:26-27). Not to be confused with altars for any type of sacrifice, it was a legal and formal attestation to a fact acknowledged as true by all the people.

When all the people under Joshua promised to serve Yahweh, they became witnesses against themselves if they should ever forsake their Lord (24:22). Joshua set up a large stone at Shechem as a witness confirming this covenant (v. 27).

Jesus claimed that the truth of his Messiahship was witnessed to not by his own testimony alone, but by John the Baptist, by the miracles, by the voice of the Father, and by Moses (John 5:34-47).

The New Testament apostles were commissioned in a unique way to witness to the truth of the resurrection of Jesus Christ (Acts 1:8, 22). This became the basic function of the preaching of the apostles and the basis of the gospel (1 Cor. 15:3-4).

Everyone who is born of the Spirit witnesses to the truth of Jesus Christ, because he has received the witness of the Spirit. This is a strong attestation to the claims of Christ. When a believer declares faith in Christ, "it is the Spirit himself bearing witness with our spirit" (Rom. 8:16).

WIZARD. *See* MEDIUM, WIZARD.

WOLF (Heb. *zeʾēb*; Gk. *lýkos*). A large, generally black member of the dog family (*Canis lupus*). Characteristically fierce predators, Palestinian wolves usually hunt at night (Hab. 1:8), singly or in pairs, and are particularly fond of sheep; voracious eaters, their diet is primarily small animals, although packs have been known to devour deer and other large creatures.

Biblical references to wolves are primarily figurative, often representing wicked leadership (Ezek. 22:27; Zeph. 3:3; Matt. 7:15; Acts 20:29). At Jer. 5:6 wolves are the enemies who attack Judah because of their breach of the covenant. The tribe of Benjamin is a ravenous wolf (Gen. 49:27), while the Babylonians' horses are fiercer than wolves (Hab. 1:8). At Matt. 10:16; Luke 10:3 Jesus warns his disciples as he dispatches them that they will have wolves for opponents.

Because of the long-standing enmity between wolves and sheep (cf. Sir. 13:17), the figure of the two dwelling in harmony is particularly apt for describing the eschatological peace that will characterize the messianic age (Isa. 11:6; 65:25).

WOMAN (Heb. *ʾiššâ*; Gk. *gynḗ*).†

I. Old Testament

Both Genesis accounts of the creation of humanity are careful to mention both sexes, though the treatment of women in the two is very different. In the one judged by critical scholars to be the earlier, Gen. 2:4b–3:24 (attributed to J, the Yahwistic source), the male is created first, then the plants to feed him, and third the animals to keep him company. Because they are not adequate for this task, Yahweh then (fourth) creates the female from the male's rib to be his helper. This does not necessarily imply subordination, as if she were to be his servant. Heb. *ʿēzer* is used of persons thirty times in the Old Testament, twenty-nine times with reference to God himself, and once to King David. But *ṣālāʿ* "rib" (or "side") is a homonym also meaning "stumbling," so the account anticipates that the helper will ironically be the man's downfall. Indeed, both the man (3:12) and God (v. 17) place the blame on her, determinative for later Jewish and Christian views of woman as a temptress to sin. Although man and woman are created as equal companions, God subordinates the woman to the man (v. 16), which accords with the interpretation of the story as an elaborate etiology explaining the origin of sexual relations (2:24), clothing (3:7, 21), mortality (v. 19), and various other matters (v. 14).

The other creation account, Gen. 1:1–2:4a (attributed to P, the Exilic Priestly writer), simply has men and women (probably several of each) created simultaneously on the sixth day (1:27-28). No indication is given of one's subordination to the other; indeed, both are told to rule the rest of creation. In the Priestly Code, attributed to the same source, male and female again appear to be on equal footing; Lev.

15:19-33 contains a series of elaborate rules governing a woman's ritual uncleanness during and after menstruation, but these are exactly paralleled by the juxtaposed laws dealing with male seminal emissions (vv. 1-18).

From other laws it is clear that Hebrew culture was completely patriarchal. The earliest law code, the Book of the Covenant (Exod. 20:22–23:33), guards the rights of a woman sold as a concubine if she displeases her master; she is to be treated well or freed (21:7-11). But another law strongly implies that women were in the category of property. If a man seduces a woman not betrothed, he must pay the brideprice and marry her. But if the seducer is of such bad character that the woman's father will not let her marry him, the seducer must pay the brideprice anyway (22:16-17 [MT 15-16]). The intent of this law is to protect the property rights of the father: he cannot marry off a daughter who is not a virgin, so one way or another he must not lose the due brideprice.

Related laws in the book of Deuteronomy pay little regard to the rights of women. An unbetrothed woman who is raped is to be given to the rapist in marriage, and her father is to be paid the fine as a brideprice (Deut. 22:28-29). The false accusation of a man that his new bride is not really a virgin results in the accuser having to pay a fine to his father-in-law, while she remains married to a husband who hates her (vv. 13-19). Moreover, a man may divorce his wife, but no provision is made for her to divorce him (24:1-4).

Various other indications of the low status of women as the property of men may be found throughout the Old Testament. The tenth commandment forbids its male readers to covet their neighbors' houses, wives, slaves, oxen, or asses, in that order (Exod. 20:17). Boaz sees Ruth and asks not her name but "Whose maiden is this?" (Ruth 2:5). Deeming the virginity of his betrothed daughters less important than the law of hospitality to strangers, the "righteous" Lot tells the Sodomite lynch mob "do to them as you please" (Gen. 19:8).

Of the outstanding women of the Old Testament, some act with decisive ingenuity within the confines of the rigid patriarchal system. Both Tamar (Gen. 38) and Ruth (Ruth 3:1-13) are bold and creative in securing their deprived rights of levirate marriage or kinsman redemption. Jael actually defies her turncoat husband to assassinate Sisera, the enemy of the Kenites and Israelites (Judg. 4:11, 17-22). Esther, the Jewish queen of Persia, saves her people by courageous action within the sphere of womanly propriety: her sexual beauty wins her the throne, and she arranges a feast as an instrument in her strategy to save her people. In this connection one might also call to mind the portrait of the "good wife" at Prov. 31:10-31; her exceptional talents and industry are exercised entirely within the confines of her domestic duties.

The Old Testament heroines who completely escape the female stereotypes are the prophetesses. Miriam, the sister of Moses and Aaron, may have ministered only among the women of Israel (Exod. 15:20-21), but the prophetesses Deborah and Huldah were judges whose oracular decisions governed men as well as women, presumably including their own husbands (Judg. 4:4-5; 2 Kgs. 22:11-20); Deborah's prophecy led to the defeat of the Canaanites, while Huldah's authenticated the book of Deuteronomy. These women could exercise such a role of authority precisely because they acted as the mouthpiece of the deity, a fact to which sexual differences were irrelevant.

II. New Testament

The Gospels preserve no direct teaching of Jesus on the subject of women, although the Talmud records that Jesus instructed that daughters and sons should inherit equally (b. Šabb. 116a-b).

At Mark 7:24-30 Jesus is reluctant to exorcise the daughter of the Syrophoenician woman until she convinces him in argument. Jesus goes against convention in that she is a Gentile, not simply a woman. At Luke 7:36ff. Jesus scandalizes the Pharisee Simon by speaking favorably of the woman who anoints him with her tears, but this is because she is a "sinner" (presumably a prostitute). At John 7:53–8:11 the issue again is that the woman is an adulteress; the mob had brought only the woman for execution, not both partners as the law required, but Jesus does not address that issue. At Mark 5:25-34 Jesus is touched by a woman whose menstrual flow has not ceased for twelve years, rendering her ritually unclean the whole time; her touch would render Jesus, too, unclean, but Jesus did not initiate the contact (nor does Lev. 15 prohibit such touching). At John 4:4-9, 27 Jesus converses with a Samaritan woman. Only here is it noted that he violated social convention by publicly talking, not just with a Samaritan, but with a woman (v. 27). One might see in all these texts an implicit egalitarian thrust, but it is part and parcel with Jesus' general outreach to and approachability by all types of outcasts.

At Luke 10:38-42 Jesus is depicted as teaching Mary of Bethany in a time when women were not usually trained in the Torah. However, the text seems unaware of any flouting of social convention, a fact suggested only by comparison with rabbinic writings. Some scholars suggest that the whole story, unique to Luke, may be intended as an ideal paradigm for the "order of widows" in which Luke has a special interest (cf. Luke 2:26-37; 21:1-4; Acts 6:1).

According to Mark 15:40-41, 47; Luke 8:1-3 Mary Magdalene, Salome, and other wealthy women followed Jesus and paid for his food and expenses. Though a group of women disciples following a teacher is unparalleled in contemporary Judaism, it is very reminiscent of the attraction of wealthy, idle Hellenistic ladies to itinerant mystagogues and teachers attested in the New Testament itself (compare 2 Tim. 3:6-7 with Luke 10:38-42) and elsewhere. Jesus did have women followers—which would have seemed controversial in either cultural setting—yet the fact remains that he did not name any women to his inner circle of the Twelve.

John 20:1-18 depicts the resurrected Christ appearing to Mary alone, apparently waiting till Peter and his companion are gone before showing himself. He then tells her that he is about to ascend and instructs her to tell the male disciples simply that he is ascending now, not that they will see him as in the other Gospels. This pericope, in which Mary is the only one to see the risen Lord, is the earliest example of a wider tradition in the early Church that Mary Magdalene was vouchsafed unique revelations after the resurrection (cf. the gospels of Thomas and Philip, the epistle of the Apostles, and the gospel of Mary).

Women clearly played a widespread role in the early Church as prophetesses. Indeed, Luke regards this fact as a fulfillment of Joel's prediction of the end-time outpouring of the Spirit (Acts 2:17-18; cf. Joel 2:28-29 [MT 3:1-2]). Luke mentions the four unmarried daughters of Philip the Evangelist who prophesied (Acts 21:8-9). Paul discusses the rules of decorum governing women prophesying (1 Cor. 11:5ff.): they must wear a veil that gives them the authority to prophesy. Since Paul says this is the rule in all the churches (v. 16), Christian prophetesses must have been universal.

Paul mentions many women as "fellow workers" in the gospel (a designation also used of Timothy; Rom. 16:21) in his letter of recommendation for Phoebe (ch. 16), a "helper" (meaning religious patron or leader; v. 2). He even mentions Junias (KJV "Junia"), an outstanding apostle (v. 7) and apparently a woman; Junias is a common Roman female name, whereas no evidence supports "Junius" as a male name, which often appears in translations of this verse.

At Gal. 3:28 Paul makes a clear statement of male-female equality in Christ: in Christ "there is neither male nor female." He struggles with this radical innovation at 1 Cor. 11:2-16, first marshaling midrashic arguments to subordinate women to men as merely the glory of men, whereas men are the image and glory of God. Then he reverses himself and returns to his original insight: "Nevertheless, in the Lord woman is not independent of (Gk. chōrís 'different from') man nor man of ('from') woman" (v. 11).

Paul still abides by contemporary decorum enough to warn women not to ask questions at church, but rather to ask their husbands at home, thus echoing Plutarch's advice (14:33b-35). 1 Tim. 2:11-15 also wants women to hold their questions and to learn in silence, but here the author silences them completely. They must neither teach nor usurp the authority properly due, in the writer's eyes, only to men; in his view women are by nature easy marks for the devil and thus liable to fall into heresy more readily than men.

Just as in ancient Hebrew society, the role of women in the early Christian home and family is a function of the surrounding culture. Women are told to submit to their husbands. At Eph. 5:21-33 Paul commands mutual submission of husbands and wives, but his explanation certainly seems to imply that the wife is to submit and obey in a way not asked of the husband. Col. 3:18-19 is a more succinct summary written on the same occasion, making only too clear Paul's intention in both epistles: "Wives, be subject to your husbands." 1 Pet. 3:1-7 (esp. vv. 1, 5-6) describes the husband as the wife's "lord" (Gk. kýrios; v. 6), and calls women "the weaker sex" (v. 7). Nevertheless, husband and wife are "joint heirs of the grace of (eternal) life," and thus equal at least in this respect.

Women's adornment is discussed at 1 Tim. 2:9-10; 1 Pet. 3:2-4, where the use of cosmetics, jewelry, fine clothes, and the braiding of hair are all forbidden. These things denoted unchaste behavior in both Jewish and Hellenistic culture at this time.

According to the writer of the Pastoral Epistles,

woman's place is in the home. Her salvation itself seems to depend on her role as a mother (1 Tim. 2:15), though some interpreters seek rather desperately to make this verse into either a mere promise of safe childbirth ("kept safe through childbirth") or a reference to the virgin birth of Christ ("saved through the birth of the Child"; cf. RSV mg.). Single women ("younger widows"), it is said (5:11-15), are prone to be idle gossips and busybodies; if they want to be godly, they must get married, have children, and run the household. Titus 2:5 summarizes the message: women must be "sensible, chaste, domestic, kind, and submissive to their husbands."

Bibliography. E. S. Fiorenza, ed., *In Memory of Her: A Feminist Theological Reconstruction of Christian Origins* (New York: 1984); P. K. Jewett, *Man as Male and Female* (Grand Rapids: 1975); V. R. Mollenkott, *Women, Men and the Bible* (Nashville: 1977); P. Trible, *God and the Rhetoric of Sexuality.* OBT (1978).

WOOD (Heb. *'ēṣ, ya'ar*; Gk. *xýlon*). Much more plentiful in ancient Israel than in modern Palestine, wood of many varieties was widely used for construction. Noah built his ark of gopher wood (Gen. 6:14), while Moses constructed the tabernacle, including the ark, poles, and altar, of acacia wood (Exod. 25:10, 13, 23, 28; 38:1).

On a larger scale, Solomon imported much timber from Tyre (1 Kgs. 5:10 [MT 24]) and built his temple (in fact, the whole temple-palace complex) of stone and cedar (6:9-10, 15-16, 36; cf. 7:2-3, 7-12), portions of which were carved (6:18; cf. Exod. 31:5; 35:33); the altar was cedar as well (1 Kgs. 6:20). The floors he covered with cypress (v. 15), while the cherubim and two inner doors were carved olivewood and cypress (vv. 23, 31-35). Zerubbabel's temple (Hag. 1:8) and Ezekiel's (Ezek. 41:16-26) were also to be made of wood.

In addition, wood was used for more common dwellings (Lev. 14:45), as well as vessels (Exod. 7:19; Lev. 15:12; 2 Tim. 2:20), weapons (Num. 35:18; Ezek. 39:9-10), threshing sledges, and ox yokes (2 Sam. 24:22). Almug wood for musical instruments (1 Kgs. 10:12) and ebony (Ezek. 27:15) were imported. One all too frequent use of wood was in the making of idols (e.g., Deut. 4:28; Judg. 6:26; 2 Kgs. 19:18; Ezek. 20:32; Dan. 5:23; Rev. 9:20).

A primary and ongoing need of wood was for fuel, both for cooking and heating (cf. Deut. 29:11 [MT 10]; Josh. 9:21-27) and for burnt offerings (Gen. 22:3-9; Lev. 1 passim; 1 Sam. 6:14; 1 Kgs. 18:23, 33, 38), particularly for the fire on the tabernacle altar that must never go out (Lev. 6:12 [MT 5]).

Wood also occurs in a figurative sense, often to represent God's people (Jer. 5:14 [to be "devoured"]; Lam. 4:8 ["dry skin"]; Ezek. 15:2-6 [allegory of the vine]; Luke 23:31 [a proverb]; 1 Cor. 3:12; 2 Tim. 2:20-21).

WORD (Heb. *dābār*; Gk. *lógos*).† The concept of the divine Word, vitally important in conservative and neo-orthodox theology, is no less central in the Bible, dominating every major strand of biblical literature.

It denotes that God is a speaking, revealing, and communicating God.

God is said to have created the world by speaking, thus demonstrating the Semitic equivalence of word/speaking and fact/matter. "God said, 'Let there be light'; and there was light" (Gen. 1:3); each stage of creation is initiated by a similar fiat. The psalmist summarizes: "By the word of the Lord the heavens were made, and all their host by the breath of his mouth" (Ps. 33:6). Thus creation itself is a revelation in which God has spoken for all time of his invisible attributes (19:1-4 [MT 2-5]). Paul takes up this theme in the New Testament, envisioning creation as a primordial preaching of the gospel (cf. Rom. 10:17-18).

The Torah also is the revealed word of God. Thus the "Ten Commandments" are literally "the Ten Words" (Exod. 34:28; so MT; cf. RSV mg.). Most of the rest of the pentateuchal legislation is likewise represented as coming to Moses from the mouth of God (e.g., 20:1; Lev. 4:1).

The prophets of Israel and Judah spoke when "the word of the Lord came" to them (e.g., Isa. 38:4; Jer. 7:1; 16:1; 18:1; 25:1; Ezek. 1:3; Luke 3:2; cf. Jer. 1:14). "Word" here is equivalent to "oracle" (cf. Isa. 2:1; 13:1) or even to "vision" (cf. 1:1). Such a prophetic "word" may mean a sure decree of judgment (9:8-10:4) or of promise (55:10-11).

Related to the "word" motif is the theme of the divine Wisdom that appears in Proverbs, Sirach, and the Wisdom of Solomon. In the Wisdom Literature the stress is on God's wisdom in creation, just as the Genesis account stressed God's creative word. The two are obviously analogous and eventually come to be united as one concept. At Prov. 8 wisdom is the first creation of God (v. 22) and is in turn either the agent of the rest of creation (v. 30) or at least attendant at the scene (v. 27). In the Wisdom of Solomon, wisdom sits beside the divine throne (Wis. 9:4). "A pure emanation of the glory of the Almighty . . . and an image of his goodness" (7:25-26), she assisted in creation (8:6; 9:2, 9).

The Alexandrian Jewish philosopher and exegete Philo (30 B.C.–A.D. 50) transfers all these attributes to the Word; the Logos concept of the Stoics (borrowed by them, in turn, from Heraclitus) already carried many of the same associations. The divine Word was the reason of God and the ordering principle in the world. So close were the Jewish and Stoic concepts that Philo regarded the Stoic *lógos* as a borrowing from the biblical *sophía*. Already in the Wisdom of Solomon the Word is described in terms somewhat analogous to the Wisdom figure (cf. Wis. 18:14-15); although the two are not there identified, it was natural for Philo to make this connection.

The same connection is of course evident in the gospel of John, which declares that without the divine Word nothing was made (John 1:3; Prov. 8). John says that the Word became flesh in Jesus of Nazareth (John 1:14), paralleling Paul's doctrine that the wisdom of God visited earth in the form of Jesus (1 Cor. 1:24; Col. 1:15; cf. Wis. 7:26). Similarly, the writer to the Hebrews directly applies wisdom terminology drawn from Wis. 7:24-26 to Christ (Heb. 1:2-3). So for the New Testament writers, the Word/Wisdom of God is paramountly Jesus Christ.

Occasionally New Testament writers use "word" to refer to the preached gospel (Rom. 10:8; Phil. 2:16; 1 Pet. 1:23-25), to the commandments of the Torah (Mark 7:13), or to God's covenant promise to Israel (Rom. 9:6). The modern use of the expression "word of God" to refer to the canonical scriptures is not exegetically founded, although it is certainly in broad harmony with the various biblical usages of the phrase.

Bibliography. O. Cullmann, *Christology of the New Testament,* rev. ed. NTL (1964); C. H. Dodd, *The Interpretation of the Fourth Gospel* (Cambridge: 1953); C. H. Pinnock, *The Scripture Principle* (San Francisco: 1984); S. Sandmel, *Philo of Alexandria* (New York: 1979).

WORKS.* (Heb. *ma'ăśeh, mᵉlāʾkâ*; Gk. *érgon*).† Deeds or action both of God and humankind. While the Bible always depicts the works of God as good, the works of humankind may be good or bad depending on whether or not one is seeking to conform to the will of God. Generally, good works are those actions performed in response to God's grace and mercy; bad or evil works reflect deeds of one who is either attempting to win God's favor or, more often, has rejected God and is living a life after the flesh.

Literal work, in the sense of toil or occupation, was not a curse placed on humanity by God as punishment for sin. Adam was ordained to work before the fall (Gen. 1:28; 2:15). Even after the fall work is viewed as a normal, natural, and healthy routine of life (Ps. 104:23; cf. 65; 127). Work skills are gifts from God (Exod. 35:30-36:2). Jesus himself was a party to the task of daily manual labor (Mark 6:3; *téktōn* "carpenter," though strictly speaking "artisan" or "craftsman"). Paul likewise was accustomed to honest toil, supporting hmself as a tentmaker (Acts 18:3). *See* LABOR.

The primary understanding of "works" in the Bible is theological. The Bible contains numerous examples of works performed by God and humankind. One of God's works is creation, an act that resulted in such handiwork as heaven and earth (Gen. 1:1), plant and animal life (vv. 11-12, 20-22, 24-25), and people (vv. 26-27; 2:21-24), all of which are called works of God (Ps. 8:3 [MT 4]; 19:1 [MT 2]). In particular, Israel is called the work of the hands of God (Isa. 60:21; 64:8 [MT 7]).

But God's work does not cease with creation, for he maintains (Neh. 9:6; Col. 1:17; Heb. 1:3; cf. Acts 17:28; 1 Cor. 12:6) and controls his creation (Ps. 103:19) by means of natural law (Gen. 8:22; Eccl. 3:1-9), miracle (Exod. 14:21-31; cf. Josh. 24:31; Judg. 2:7, 10), and his word (Deut. 17:18-20). Moreover, God's work encompasses the salvation of his people and the restoration of the universe to its original perfection (Rom. 8:19-22). In the past he rescued his people from danger (Ps. 44:1 [MT 2]; 46:8-9 [MT 9-10]; 64:9 [MT 10]), though not always by ordinary means (Isa. 28:21; cf. 37:36; 45:1). Such is never seen more clearly than in God's redemption of the world to himself through his Son (2 Cor. 5:18-21). Under the heading of "works of God" one can rightfully place the "works of Christ," as is made explicit in John's gospel. The works of Jesus are those of the Father, for the Son's "food is to do the will of him who sent

me, and to accomplish his work" (John 4:34; cf. 5:20, 36; 6:28-29; 9:3-4; 10:25, 37-38; 14:10-14; 15:24). The culmination of God's work will be the accomplishing of his ultimate plan (Rev. 15:3), namely the establishment of the new heaven and new earth (21:1-4).

With regard to humankind, "works" can be divided into the "works of the flesh" and "good works." The idea of flesh (Gk. *sárx*; *see* FLESH) as sinful is a main theme of Paul. To the class of "works of the flesh" he assigns such sins (in contrast to the "fruit of the Spirit," Gal. 5:22-23; cf. v. 16) as "immorality, impurity, licentiousness, idolatry, sorcery, enmity, strife, jealously, anger, selfishness, dissension, party spirit, envy, drunkenness, carousing, and the like" (vv. 19-21). Those who live after the flesh (Rom. 8:12) are characterized by lust (Gal. 5:16; 1 Pet. 4:2; 2 Pet. 2:10; 1 John 2:16) and are dominated by their passions (Eph. 2:3) because their minds are of the flesh (Rom. 8:5, 7). Such people are only capable of wicked (Col. 1:21; 2 John 11; cf. Luke 13:27; John 3:19; 7:7; 1 John 3:12) and ungodly deeds (Jude 15). Their works are of darkness (Rom. 13:12; Eph. 5:11). They have sown to the flesh and will reap destruction (Gal. 6:8).

In contrast to "works of the flesh," the Bible teaches of "good works." Such acts can be described as acts of Christian duty and piety, as evidence of faith in Jesus Christ. Paul is sure to point out that good works are not the basis for salvation (Eph. 2:8-9). To suppose otherwise is to seek God's favor on the basis of the "works of the law" (Gal. 3:10). Such legal "performances," in order to gain God's acceptance, are useless and, in the end, only result in the curse and condemnation of God (2:16, 21; 3:10-14). In essence the "works of the law" can be categorized with the "works of the flesh," in that both are performed without faith in the saving grace of God (Heb. 6:1; 9:14; "dead works").

Instead of viewing good works as the basis for salvation, James teaches that they are proof of, or should result from, salvation. He remarks that, "Faith by itself, if it has no works, is dead" (Jas. 2:17; cf. v. 14). Such a position actually reflects Paul's thinking that a Christian's actions should be worthy of salvation (Acts 26:20). Paul would argue that indeed Christians are saved in order to perform good works (Eph. 2:10; cf. Titus 2:14). The basis of good works is the grace of God (2 Cor. 9:8; cf. Phil. 1:6; 2 Thess. 2:17). The Christian is empowered by the Holy Spirit (Rom. 15:18-19; 1 Thess. 1:5) to execute actions that are both worthy of the Lord (Col. 1:10) and in opposition to the "works of the flesh" (cf. Gal. 5:22-23). For Paul, good works are works of faith (1 Thess. 1:3; 2 Thess. 1:11). Essentially, Christians are saved to perform, not by performing, good works. Jesus exhorted his followers to do good works before other people so that God might be glorified (Matt. 5:16). Among the New Testament examples of people performing good works are Dorcas (Acts 9:36) and Titus (Titus 2:7).

WORLD (Heb. *tēḇēl*; Gk. *kósmos, aiōn*).† To the modern mind the concept of world implies that all individual objects and persons perceived by mankind, despite their wide disparity, finally cohere in a synthetic unity. Whether such unity is the presupposition of human ability to make sense of disparate perceptions, or rather is itself a function of the perceiving process, an artificial "closure" imposed on perception by the mind, is a matter of long-standing philosophical debate. The writers of the Bible were apparently unconcerned with this dimension of the problem, but of the world they do have many things to say—some theological, most ethical.

Old Testament writers refer to the world as the product of God's creation (Ps. 90:2; Jer. 10:12) and the theatre of his manifest glory. They look forward in particular to the day when God will be acknowledged and worshipped by all nations of the world (Isa. 11:9). But these references to the world are better treated under such rubrics as creation.

"World" begins to function as a distinctive and important theological/ethical category in its own right in the New Testament. Here Gk. *kósmos* tends to refer to the created world, the earth, and space; *aión* tends to denote the present age of world history. The two can and do function primarily as synonyms, but sometimes context will clarify whether spatial "world" or temporal "age" is intended.

The range of references to the world in the New Testament, even within works of one writer, has often confused readers. How can John both declare that "God so loved the world that he gave his only Son" to save it (John 3:16) and warn "Love not the world" and "if anyone loves the world, love for the Father is not in him" (1 John 2:15)? Careful scrutiny of context elucidates such apparent contradictions, for "world" is used with several different connotations by the various writers. Once one grasps the range of possible connotations, together with the logical development between them, it is no longer difficult to discern the sense of "world" in most individual texts.

Sometimes "world" means simply the planet, as when Christ's divine origin is stressed. He "came into the world" from without, i.e., he is not a product of it (John 1:9-10; 6:14; 9:39; Heb. 10:5; 1 Tim. 1:15). Or the world as planet earth may be contrasted with heaven, the earth needing the revelation provided from heaven (John 8:23). The world may be the geographic frame of reference for the Church's evangelistic mission, though here lies an interesting ambiguity. Matthew (Matt. 28:19), Mark (Mark 13:10), and Luke (Luke 24:47) refer specifically to "all nations." But Paul's references to "all the world" as his mission field seem to imply only the lands of the Roman Empire or the Mediterranean world, as he seems to regard the gospel as having reached its limits already (Rom. 1:8; Col. 1:6; cf. Rom. 15:24, 28). However, the world in its planetary totality looms in Paul's mind when he thinks of the universality of sin; he even says that if one wanted to avoid all contact with sinners, one would "need to go out of the world" (1 Cor. 5:10).

To speak of the sinfulness of the world implies that one has already begun to move toward the second association of the word: the whole human race. This is the world God loved so much as to send his Son to save it (John 3:16). The sacrificial "Lamb of God, . . . takes away the sin of the world" (1:29), i.e., of all its people. The "woe" due "the world for temptations to sin" is due, strictly speaking, to the one(s)

"by whom the temptation comes" (Matt. 18:7), again meaning the people of the world.

"The world" also means the realm of secular and materialistic concerns. In this sense the world may be considered innocent enough in itself, yet a regrettable if unavoidable distraction from undivided dedication to God (1 Cor. 7:32-35). One must not become overly involved in secular affairs, since this whole order of things will soon disappear (v. 31; cf. Jas. 5:3). For the most part, worldly concerns are viewed as a temptation beckoning one to ignore the gospel. The sown word is choked out by "the cares of the world, and the delight in riches" (Mark 4:19). The backslider Demas is said to have been "in love with this present world" (2 Tim. 4:10). To gain the secular world and its wealth would be to forfeit one's soul (Mark 8:36) since one cannot serve both God and "mammon" (wealth) (Matt. 6:24). Accordingly, it is not the saints who pursue material goods; rather, it is "the nations of the world (who) seek these things" (Luke 12:30). And "the sons of this world" are more shrewd in dealing with their own generation than "the sons of light" (16:8). In light of the dangers of the secular realm, it is no surprise that John warns his readers not to "love the world or the things in the world . . . for all that is in the world (is) the lust of the flesh and the lust of the eyes and the pride of life" (1 John 2:15-16).

The world is also presented as the domain of Satan (lit. "the tempter"), whom John calls "the ruler of this world" (John 12:31; 14:30; 16:11). So great does the worldly power of Satan appear to Paul that the apostle grants him the rather shocking epithet "the god of this world" (2 Cor. 4:4), who is able to blind worldlings to the truth and to energize their sinful works (Eph. 2:2). As such Satan is both in (temporary) control of the world and the object of the (usually unwitting) worship of its inhabitants (1 Cor. 8:5; 10:20-21). Both paganism and Jewish legalism are viewed as slavery to the demonic "elemental spirits (or 'principles') of this world" (Gal. 4:3; cf. Rev. 2:9).

The Temptation Narrative casts Satan's worldly sovereignty in political terms. In accounts common to Luke and Matthew, Satan shows Jesus "all the kingdoms of the world" and offers them to Jesus if he will bow, in turn, to Satan's authority (Matt. 4:8-9 par. Luke 4:5-6).

It is thus natural for New Testament writers, by extension, to view "the world" as the world system of God-rejecters and their cherished worldly values. The world is portrayed as an armed camp, deluded in its imagined self-sufficiency and hostile to the God who gives the lie to its fancy. The opposition between the world on the one hand, and Jesus and his disciples on the other is absolute (John 17:16). The technical language of the covenant underlies the summation "the world knew him not" (1:10); indeed, it hates him (7:7; 15:18), and rejoices at his death (16:20). Jesus has chosen the disciples out of the world (17:9) as "figs from thistles" (Matt. 7:16), so different are the two. Yet he leaves the disciples in the world (John 17:15) like "sheep in the midst of wolves" (Matt. 10:16). For they must bear witness as a light in this world's darkness, even as he has done (compare Matt.

5:14; Phil. 2:15 with John 8:12; 1:4-5). "The reason why the world does not know us is that it did not know him" (1 John 3:1b). James also sees a stark choice to be made: "friendship with the world is enmity with God" (Jas. 4:4). Paul, characteristically, uses the most striking imagery to describe this dichotomy: by "the cross of our Lord Jesus Christ . . . the world has been crucified to me, and I to the world" (Gal. 6:14; Rom. 6:6-11).

If the devil has so turned the world against God, this state of affairs cannot last permanently. Yet while Satan rules, his dominion over the whole world is total (1 John 5:19b). Thus New Testament writers can speak simply of "the world" when they mean this age of world history dominated by Satan, and in this case we may often translate *aiōn* as either "world" or "age" (cf. "age," Matt. 12:32; 13:39-40, 49; Luke 20:34; Gal. 1:4; "world," Luke 16:8; John 12:25; Eph. 2:2). By extension, "world"/"age" may refer to the future age of the kingdom of God (Matt. 12:32; Mark 10:30; Luke 20:35; Heb. 2:5; 6:5).

Bibliography. H. Berkhof, *Christ and the Powers* (Scottdale: 1962); E. R. Dodds, *Pagan and Christian in an Age of Anxiety* (New York: 1965).

WORM. Several Hebrew words designate small, creeping creatures such as larva worms, with the context determining the identification. The most common types represented in the Bible are those larvae or maggots active in the decomposition process (Job 7:5; 17:14; 21:26; Isa. 14:11; cf. Exod. 16:20, 24). The undying worm of Isa. 66:24; Mark 9:48 may well be an extreme portrayal of a type of maggot; the natural destruction of the body will continue eternally in hell.

Deut. 28:39; Jonah 4:7 appear to refer to the larva of some leaf-eating insect, while Isa. 51:8 is a moth worm. At Job 25:6; Ps. 22:6 [MT 7]; Isa. 41:14 the worm is a figure for the state of humiliation of the subject in question, while its use at Acts 12:23 may well be quite literal (cf. 2 Macc. 9:9).

WORMWOOD (Heb. *laʿănâ*; Gk. *ápsinthos*). A small, shrublike plant known for its bitter taste, perhaps a variety of the genus *Artemesia,* and perhaps used as a purgative. All biblical references to wormwood are metaphors for bitterness and sorrow. They describe several unfortunate circumstances, including the results of an illicit affair with a loose woman (Prov. 5:4), the bitterness of judgment for sin (Jer. 9:15 [MT 14]; 23:15) and its resultant affliction (Lam. 3:15, 19), and the bitterness of injustice (Amos 5:7; 6:12). At Rev. 8:10-11 a star named Wormwood falls to earth and turns one-third of the earth's inland waters bitter (cf. Exod. 15:23-25), causing many to die.

WORSHIP (Heb. verb *ʿăḇaḏ,* noun *ʿăḇōḏâ*; Gk. *proskyneō*; Saxon *weorthscipe* "worthship").† To pay homage to or, literally, to ascribe worth to some person or thing. Hence, worship embraces the whole of the reverent life, including piety and liturgy.

I. Old Testament

Although many of the specifics of the patriarchal age remain left to speculation, worship was clearly a central focus of people's lives in the earliest stages of the biblical record. Archaeological evidence together with the Genesis accounts reveal that polytheism and perhaps henotheism were part of the culture. Yet the patriarchal narratives preserve experiences of human encounter with the divine as individuals and within the sphere of history, often in the form of theophanies described in vivid anthropomorphic fashion with appropriate response by the patriarchs. Sacrifice is practiced (Gen. 4:3-4), and basic forms of ritual are observed (v. 26; cf. 8:20-22). Abram's encounter with Melchizedek (Gen. 14) suggests early priestly activity.

Awe or fear of God seems to have been a part of Moses' response to God speaking from the burning bush (Exod. 3:5-6). Pharaoh's response to Moses' request recognizes the legitimacy of pilgrimage for sacrifice (5:1-3). Israel's religious consciousness was heightened by the Exodus experience, and much of their worship tradition appears to derive from (or at least be interpreted in terms of) those events. The Feast of Passover may have had roots in a nomadic feast of firstlings, but it gained new life and meaning associated with the Exodus. Scholars suggest significant influence from surrounding cultures, which may constitute the religious background of many within the "mixed multitude" of early Israel, perhaps implying a process of syncretism or melding of religious rites and practices; the extent would be difficult to gauge Indeed, as Israel gained control over Canaan they also acquired major sanctuaries such as Dan, Gilgal, Beersheba, perhaps Bethel, Shechem, and Shiloh; with that a certain amount of religious practice must have been naturally assimilated (cf. 1 Sam. 1–3, 9–10).

Though David seems responsible for much of the centralization and reform of the cult, it was Solomon who erected the temple. The liturgical calendar consisted primarily in the celebration of three major agricultural feasts: Passover and the Feast of Unleavened Bread, Weeks or Pentecost, and the Feast of Booths or Ingathering. Worship was rich and diverse, and included instrumental and vocal music, solos, anthems, shouting or chanting, dancing, processions with instruments, incense, offerings, tithes, a form of preaching, oracles, recitation of sacred stories, petitions, prayers, vows, vigils, promises, creeds and confessions, sacred meals, washings, and even periods of silence.

The eighth-century prophets' assailing of syncretistic abuses went unheeded or at least abated little the downward spiral of the cult (cf. 2 Kgs. 16:10-16; 18:4). This decline in Yahwistic observances foreshadowed the destruction of the temple and Israel's exile and captivity, cataclysmic events that necessitated a major shift in cultic practice. It seems likely that the synagogue took at least incipient form during this time. In contrast to temple worship with an emphasis on sacrifice, the major feature of synagogue worship was the reading of the Law, followed by a homily around which was organized the offering of blessings and prayers. But with the return from captivity and rebuilding of the temple, the temple regained prominence, but not its prior exclusive role in Israelite worship. In time during the postexilic period a reformed cultus developed. The main feasts were continued, and duties and relationships of the priests and Levites were further refined and delineated. Changes arose in sacrifice as well, with the sin and guilt offerings figuring prominently. In the Second Temple period a morning sacrifice was observed, as well as another between the two evening sacrifices; additional sacrifice took place on Sabbaths and special feasts. The psalms were also widely used, particularly songs of ascents (Pss. 120–134) and the Hallel psalms (113–118; 136).

But these rich traditions of Israelite corporate worship must not eclipse the personal piety that marked many of the people's lives from the patriarchal period on. Many are the intense moments of personal religious experience of the patriarchs and, later, Moses, Aaron, and Joshua. The moving story of Hannah at prayer (1 Sam. 1) affords a vista of personal worship and deep conviction. David, whose hand was likely responsible for many of the psalms (e.g., Pss. 23, 51), lived a life marked by deep conviction and piety (2 Sam. 7:18-19; cf. 6:20-23). Moreover, many of the psalms comprise personal hymns of thanksgiving, repentance, trust, or lamentation. And Jeremiah offers a glimpse of the personal spiritual tribulation and conviction of a rare person whose soul was burdened with a message from Yahweh.

II. New Testament

Scant records and only casual reference to worship practices provide but limited knowledge of early Christian worship until the mid-second century A.D., when Justin Martyr provided a more adequate description. It may be inferred, however, that Christian worship in New Testament times revolved primarily around baptism, preaching, and the Lord's Supper.

Early Christians drew liturgical practices primarily from Jewish sources, though there was some Gentile influence, to form worship as rich and multifaceted as its Old Testament counterpart. Included were public prayer, reading of psalms, Scripture, teaching and preaching, and private devotions. As many of the early Christian followers and leaders were Jewish, early Christian worship draws heavily from its Jewish roots. At first Christians worshipped in the temple, and to that added communal meals (Acts 2:46; 5:42). Soon, however, a rift developed between Jews and Christians, with Christians being denied access to the temple; though it seems certain that such did not occur simultaneously in all places, Christians gradually developed independence from the temple.

Despite heavy borrowing from Jewish worship practices, Christian liturgy underwent a radical transformation. Most importantly, the sacrificial practices of the temple were abandoned, since Christians regarded such as having been fulfilled in the cross (cf. Hebrews). In part an extension and reinterpretation of the Passover meal, the Lord's Supper both recalled and in a sense enacted symbolically Christ's death upon the cross (1 Cor. 11:26). Such elements as Scripture reading, preaching, psalmody, and public prayer were also taken over from Jewish worship.

Gentile influences upon Christian worship remain difficult to trace and gauge. Only the more peripheral elements such as the funeral feast and some marriage customs can be traced directly. The funeral feast was undoubtedly affected profoundly by the belief in the resurrection and the celebration of the Lord's Supper. Speculation remains on the possibility and extent of influence of the mystery religions, with their ritual associated with the dying and rising god and sacred meals. Certainly Christians did not simply adopt, but would have radically transformed appropriate symbol and tradition from the surrounding culture to proclaim the gospel message.

Despite difficulties posed by the nature of the apocalyptic genre, the book of Revelation provides some insight into the nature of Christian worship toward the close of the first century. There appear to be liturgical influences upon the visions (esp. chs. 4–6). Some elements of worship may bear similarity to practices recorded by Justin Martyr in the second century; combined with evidence preserved in a letter from Pliny, governor of Bithynia, to Trajan (ca. A.D. 113), a clearer picture begins to emerge. Christians of Bithynia appear to have observed two separate services, one before dawn that included antiphonal hymnody and a recitation of the Decalog. The early service may have arisen in response to persecution or to accommodate the slaves who made up a large portion of early Christians. Later in the day a communal meal was held (later abandoned when outlawed by the *Lex Julia*); it remains unclear as to whether this meal was the Lord's Supper or simply the communal meal or agape. By the time of Justin the service opened with the reading of Scripture (both the LXX and the Gospels), perhaps involving the use of a lectionary. Following the readings the bishop delivered a sermon seated in his chair (a customary manner of ancient teaching). The congregation then rose for prayers, praying in the Jewish manner with outstretched arms, perhaps using a litany that included the deacons, with individual requests and a concluding collect by the bishop. Such prayers were intoned (spoken prayer developed in medieval times) and concluded with the affirmation of "Amen" by the congregation expressing their assurance in fulfillment (2 Cor. 1:20). The worshippers shared the kiss of peace, followed by the offertory, which consisted in food rather than money (perhaps developed from the practice of the communal meal); the deacons then arranged these elements on the table before the bishop, who offered a prayer of consecration. The service concluded with communion, portions of which were later taken to those absent because of sickness or other reasons. No benediction was offered.

Baptism was an indispensable sign of initiation into full fellowship in the early Christian community (cf. Eph. 4:5). Although the New Testament provides no adequate description of the rite, it apparently was administered by an officiant and involved liturgical confession and a recitation of faith (Acts 8:36-39; cf. 1 Cor. 1:14). Some early confessions in the New Testament may or may not have been associated with baptism (e.g., John 2:22; Rom. 1:3-6; 8:34; 1 Cor. 15:3ff.; 1 Tim. 3:16; 6:13-14; 2 Tim. 2:8; 1 Pet. 3:18-22). In New Testament times baptism was by a single immersion, with triple immersions appearing only later; occasionally, in cases of sickness or lack of water, affusion was practiced. Whether or not infant baptism was observed in New Testament times remains disputed. The origin and role of confirmation are unclear, and it is unclear whether there was a separate laying on of hands in addition to baptism. Converts who after having been baptized were not considered to have received the Holy Spirit are noted at Acts 8:14-17; 19:1-6, but the reference may be related to the display of ecstatic utterances. Several passages do associate the descent of the Spirit with water baptism (e.g., John 3:5; 1 Cor. 6:11; 12:13; Titus 3:5). Quite likely the various rites differed from place to place.

The laying on of hands was also part of the ordination rite that the early Church continued from Judaism, whereby select persons were installed in various offices and duties (Acts 6:1-6; cf. Num. 11:24-25). Early practices also included healings and exorcisms through various means of prayer (e.g., Mark 9:29), anointing (Jas. 5:14), and laying on of hands (Mark 16:18; Acts 9:17). The Church also practiced discipline and, in the case of recalcitrant offenders, excommunication (Matt. 18:17; 1 Cor. 5:3-6).

The development of the Church calendar was a slow process, with surprisingly little borrowing from the Jewish calendar. Other than adaptation of the Passover feast (cf. 1 Cor. 5:6-8), the Church year is primarily the product of the Gentile church. Indeed, the background of many observances such as Christmas, Epiphany, and Ember is pagan. Christians no doubt observed the Jewish calendar until the break with the synagogue was complete. A major innovation was the focus of worship on Sunday in honor of the day of the Lord's resurrection (e.g., John 20:19, 26; Acts 20:7).

Christians adopted the practice of private prayer from Judaism. The Didache (Did. 8) mentions three daily periods of prayer featuring recitation of the Lord's Prayer. The prayer seems to have characterized private rather than corporate worship, until it appeared in the eucharist ca. the fourth century (cf. Cyril of Jerusalem). Gradually, additional hours of prayer were added, until a daily round of six periods of private devotions was established by the time of Hippolytus. Presumably Christians also practiced a more spontaneous form of prayer in their private lives (1 Cor. 7:5; 1 Thess. 5:17; Jas. 5:13). Early Christians also took vows (cf. Acts 18:18; 21:24) and fasted, probably on the Day of Atonement (cf. 27:9), before ordinations (14:23) and other solemn assemblies (13:3), as well as in conjunction with baptism (Did. 7; Justin Martyr *Apol.* i.61). In some localities "station days" or fast days were observed on Wednesday and Friday, in contrast to the pharisaic fast days, Monday and Thursday.

III. Attitude

Both the Old and New Testament share the notion that acceptable worship involves more than simply prescribed rites, namely a correct attitude and concomitant moral rectitude. The prophet Samuel rebukes King Saul with the harsh words: "Behold, to obey is better than sacrifice . . ." (1 Sam. 15:22). Among the wisdom sayings one finds: "The sacrifice of the wicked is an abomination to the Lord, but the prayer of the upright is his delight" (Prov. 15:8; cf. 21:3, 27; Mal. 2:10ff.). Ps. 2 proclaims, "Serve the Lord with fear (reverence)" (v. 11), and throughout Ps. 51 the psalmist offers eloquent voice to the notion of appropriate living and attitude: "The sacrifice acceptable to God is a

broken spirit; a broken and contrite heart, O God, thou wilt not despise" (v. 17; cf. 1 Sam. 15:22). Such an attitude is echoed in the New Testament in the forceful words of Jesus "God is spirit, and those who worship him must worship in spirit and truth" (John 4:24).

Bibliography. O. Cullmann, *Early Christian Worship* (Chicago: 1953); A. S. Herbert, *Worship in Ancient Israel* (Richmond: 1959); R. P. Martin, *Worship in the Early Church* (Grand Rapids: 1975); C. F. D. Moule, *Worship in the New Testament* (Richmond: 1961).

WRATH (Heb. *'ap, ḥēmâ, 'eḇrâ, qeṣep*; Gk. *thymós, orgḗ*).† The response of a holy, just God to that which does not meet his standards of holiness, namely sin. God's wrath is to be distinguished from human wrath chiefly in that human wrath is never pure, even when exercised in defense of God's holiness, but is always tainted by mankind's fallen nature (Rom. 7:18). As a result, human anger is inadequate to achieve God's righteousness (Jas. 1:20).

While God's wrath arises logically from his nature, it is not merely mechanical. The Old Testament especially describes God's wrath in the language of emotion, with words such as *'ap* "nose" (probably referring to snorting and trembling of the nostrils; cf. Ps. 18:8 [MT 9]), *ḥ°rôn 'ap* "burning of anger," and *'eḇrâ* "overflow, fury."

Nor is God's wrath incompatible with his love (contra Marcion and others), since on many occasions God expresses love for the very ones who are to be objects of his wrath. He tells Israel, "I have loved you with an everlasting love" (Jer. 31:3), and at the same time sends Babylon against them in judgment; he declares his love for the world in sending Christ to it (John 3:16; Rom. 5:8; cf. Eph. 2:3), and yet vents his wrath on the unrepentant in everlasting punishment (Matt. 25:41, 46; Jude 13). It is not entirely correct to confine God's love to the sinner and his hatred to the sin, since sinful actions do not exist apart from the agent; rather, the two attitudes should be viewed as existing simultaneously. God is patient and longsuffering toward sinful humanity, but longsuffering has a temporal limit beyond which wrath remains.

God's wrath may be seen in natural catastrophes (Gen. 6:17; 7:11; Joel 1), in personal disasters (Deut. 28:15-68; 2 Sam. 12:15-19), and in the actions of human beings against each other (Hab. 1:5-11). In its final form it appears in the eternal punishment of the unredeemed.

Besides acting directly, God uses angels to carry out his judgments (Exod. 12:23; 2 Sam. 24:16; Matt. 13:39-42; Acts 12:23; Rev. 12:7-12). He also uses individual human beings, who exercise judgment on his behalf against both human and spirit beings (Ps. 149:6-9; Dan. 7:22; Matt. 19:28; 1 Cor. 6:2-3). Entire nations are employed to execute his sentences, even unwittingly (Isa. 10:5-6, 15; Jer. 25:8-10; Rom. 13:1-4).

The preeminent agent of God's wrath, however, is Christ. His title "Son of Man" identifies him with the messianic figure of Dan. 7:13-14 who is given authority over the created order and who exercises judgment by that authority (cf. Matt. 25:31-32; 28:18; Luke 19:12, 14, 27; Rev. 19:11-21). While he does not use this title, John the Baptist announces Messiah's coming as a time of judgment and wrath (Matt. 3:7-12), and identifies Jesus not only as the divine Sacrifice but as Judge (John 1:29-33; compare v. 33 with Matt. 3:11-12). It is his identification with humanity and atoning work on mankind's behalf that qualify him especially to be mankind's judge (John 5:25-29; cf. Rev. 5); consequently the title "Son of Man" is an ever-present reminder of the coming eschatological wrath of God and Christ's part in it (cf. Mark 14:62).

During Old Testament times escape from the wrath of God was found in blood sacrifices, which provided substitutes on which the sentence of physical death, at least, would fall. These sacrifices were not efficacious in themselves, however, but instead foreshadowed the sacrifice of Christ (Heb. 10:1-4). At the crucifixion the wrath of God was vented upon Christ, who as Deity could undergo an infinite experience in finite time. As a result, the one who comes to Christ has a divine Substitute who had endured punishment that for sinful human beings would be everlasting (cf. Isa. 53:4-6). It is to be presumed that those of Old Testament times who committed themselves to Yahweh's care have benefited from this substitution also, even though the event itself had not yet taken place (Rom. 3:25-26). All others experience that wrath directly.

Because God's wrath is a response to sin, it can be viewed as having begun with the entry of sin into the universe. Its exercise toward mankind began with the sin of Adam, as is shown by the presence of death in the human race from that time to the present (5:12-14). By the same token, God's wrath ends concurrently with the end of whatever opposes him or is contrary to his nature. From the viewpoint of redeemed humanity, wrath ends with the great white throne judgment and the dispatch of God's final enemies to the lake of fire (Rev. 20:11-15), whereupon a new heaven and earth appear in which sin—and consequently wrath—are not present. From the viewpoint of the unredeemed, wrath continues throughout eternity in the place of punishment (Matt. 25:41, 46; Rev. 14:11).

Bibliography. H. Schönweiss and H. C. Hahn, "Anger, Wrath," *DNTT* 1 (1975): 105-113; C. R. Schoonhoven, *The Wrath of Heaven* (Grand Rapids: 1966).

WREATH.† A type of decoration, adornment, or art that is made by twisting, wrapping, or intertwining any of various materials. Many different Hebrew and Greek words represent wreaths in English versions. Heb. *gᵉḏilîm* refers to a circle of chain work used to decorate the pillars of Solomon's temple (1 Kgs. 7:17); *ʿaḇōṯ* designates the two braided chains of gold that adorn the ephod of gold (KJV, Exod. 28:14; RSV "cords"); *śᵉḇāḵâ* is used for the network (so RSV) decorating the two bowl-shaped capitals on top of the pillars in Solomon's temple (KJV, 2 Chr. 4:12). Heb. *lōyōṯ* is a technical term for architectural adornment (1 Kgs. 7:29; KJV "additions").

In figurative usage, the verb *śārag* describes the Lord's twisting together of sins into a burdensome yoke (so RSV) to be borne (Lam. 1:14), and *ʿᵃṭārâ* depicts the Lord as a beautiful wreath (RSV "crown of glory") to his people (Isa. 28:5).

Reflecting Hellenistic-Roman society, Gk. *stémma* refers to wreaths used to decorate the gods, presented to Paul and Barnabas, who were thought to be gods at Acts 14:13 (RSV "garlands"). The term *stéphanos* is applied to the wreath given the victor in the Greek games (1 Cor. 9:25).

WRITING.† A conventional symbol system for encoding natural language. The majority of human language, past and present, is speech, which is limited by time and space. The acoustic signal decays rapidly, limiting speech perception to the moment and vicinity of its production. To overcome these restrictions, human communities have devised systems for preserving the information content of speech. All such systems predating electronic technology employ objects, or marks upon objects, as symbols, which constitute writing.

Writing probably developed from systems of counting and record keeping. Distinctively shaped clay objects have been found throughout the Near East from the ninth millennium B.C. onward, in contexts that suggest their use as counters or tokens for verifying and recording transactions. By the fourth millennium are found clay tablets or other objects bearing scratched or impressed signs that resemble the tokens formerly used. Between 3300 and 3000 emerged a system for writing the Sumerian language by means of schematic pictures scratched or pressed into wet clay, or inscribed on stone or metal. When impressed on clay with the edge and corner of a stylus, the lines composing these signs have a characteristic wedge shape, hence the designation "cuneiform," derived from Lat. *cuneus* "wedge."

The several hundred signs that the cuneiform writing system employed could operate at various levels of abstraction. Pictographic signs represent the word that names the object drawn; thus a picture of the sun encodes Sum. *utu* "sun." The same sign might function logographically to write an associated word (e.g., *babbar* "white, bright"); actions and abstractions may be written by a combination of two or more signs. By the rebus principle a sign might represent two homophones similar or identical in sound but unrelated in meaning. By extension of this phonetic principle, a sign may represent any syllable having the same phonetic contours as the sign's pictographic or logographic value; this is its logosyllabic value (e.g., the sign for *ti* "arrow" also can write the syllable *-ti-* in any word). Logosyllabic signs could be used as phonetic complements to indicate which of several possible logographic readings of a sign was intended in a given context. Many signs could also be used as determinatives indicating the class or category of object or action indicated by the preceding sign(s). The cuneiform writing system, as any writing system, was constrained by competing necessities of clarity and economy.

Ca. 2000 B.C. speakers of the Semitic languages known collectively as Akkadian began to employ cuneiform writing. As the Akkadian sound system is entirely different from that of Sumerian, Akkadian cuneiform developed its own set of syllabic and logographic values in addition to those deriving from Sumerian. Cuneiform continued to be used to write

A scribe holding his palette and standing before his king. A relief from Zenjirli, southern Turkey, eighth century B.C. (Staatliche Museen zu Berlin, DDR)

Sumerian long after the language itself ceased to be spoken, and was adopted for the writing of Assyrian, Babylonian, Hittite, Hurrian, and Urartian. A simplified form of cuneiform was used to write Old Persian. Cuneiform texts were copied and composed until *ca.* A.D. 75.

The complexities that cuneiform presented its students made long and rigorous training of scribes a necessity throughout the ancient Near East. For use in schools and chancelleries were developed sign lists, word lists, grammars, bilingual texts, and similar study aids. Archives and libraries were built to house important documents. Cuneiform texts encompass every genre: legal documents (contracts, accounts, receipts), letters, mathematical problems and statistical tables, astronomical and medical observations, omens, prayers, dedications and votive offerings, royal statements, and a variety of literature in prose and poetry.

Writing appears in Egypt *ca.* 3150 B.C. Texts from this early period differ very little from the writing system in widespread use several centuries later. As in cuneiform, signs can be pictographic or logographic; unlike cuneiform they cannot also be acrophonic, representing not complete syllabaries but only the consonants of a word or syllable. Signs can be triconsonantal, biconsonantal, or alphabetic (signifying only the first consonant of the word associated with the object represented). Egyptian hieroglyphics employ thirty signs alphabetically. These frequently are written as pleonastic phonetic complements to bi- or triconsonantal signs (e.g., *nfr* + *f* + *r* = *nefer*).

Whereas cuneiform signs underwent considerable simplification over the course of their use, Egyptian hieroglyphs retained their form virtually unchanged for 3500 years (the last known hieroglyphic inscription is dated August 24, A.D. 394). The number of individual signs increased with time, however. Each sign was a work of art, a stylized naturalistic representation of an object. For quick writing with ink on smooth

surfaces, a cursive hieroglyphic script developed, called hieratic. Later a still more simplified handwriting called demotic was introduced. The hieroglyphic system was never adopted for the writing of languages other than Egyptian (an exception is a single Aramaic text written on papyrus in demotic script), though it did inspire a derivative in which some nine hundred Meroitic inscriptions are written.

The Egyptian scribe, like the Mesopotamian, underwent hard training and could rise to a position of importance in the realm. Taking simple dictation certainly fell to the scribe; but so did scholarship, administration, and literary pursuits.

A number of local writing systems developed in Syria and Palestine. From Byblos in Phoenicia have been found nine documents in linear symbols representing hieroglyphics and dating perhaps from the Middle Bronze Age (*ca.* 2100-1550); recent interpretation of them employing a purely syllabic reading of the script relates them in part to the later South Semitic alphabet.

Two different alphabets are attested from Middle Bronze Age Syria-Palestine, adapted to the most common writing materials then available. For writing with ink on papyrus, potsherds, and stone was a set of twenty-two symbols employing straight lines and curves and representing the Phoenician consonantal inventory. For writing on clay, a wedge alphabet of thirty characters was written dextrograde (left to right) at Ugarit, Sarepta, Tell Sukas, Kamid el-Loz, and Taanach, sinistrograde (right to left) at Tell Nebī Mend, Beth-shemesh, and Wâdī el-Bire.

The Phoenician alphabet was rapidly disseminated throughout the Near East, taking a slightly different form in each of the scribal traditions in which it was employed. In Israel and Judah, a distinctively cursive version served for public inscriptions as well as private documents. The alphabet's simplicity may have facilitated a more widespread literacy than was previously possible, though actual evidence for this notion is limited. The incident narrated at Judg. 8:14 has been cited as evidence that a randomly nabbed youth could write even in premonarchic Israel; more recently Heb. *na'ar* has been recognized as a technical term for a public functionary. Some scholars have argued that many ostraca with Hebrew writing of the preexilic period are school texts, and thus attest to a system of public scribal education in Israel; however, this view has been severely criticized.

Inscriptions intended to endure might be scratched or carved in stone. In Egypt, where stone is abundant and the stoneworker's art reached a high level of sophistication, every sort of text might find its way to permanence on a stone surface. Mesopotamia lacked native stone; imported stone provided kings and dynasts with surfaces on which to immortalize their activities. In Syria and Palestine a variety of stone inscriptions were cut; besides hieroglyphic Egyptian and the rare cuneiform left by neighboring potentates, local powers produced inscriptions in hieroglyphic Luwian, Phoenician, Aramaic, Moabite, and Hebrew. According to Exod. 31:18, Moses received the Decalog inscribed on stone tablets.

A stone or mud brick surface would sometimes be coated with plaster and smoothed to receive a text

A scribe's palette from Eighteenth-Dynasty Egypt. Ink in the hollow at the left end was applied with the sharpened rushes. (by courtesy of the Trustees of the British Museum)

written in ink. An astounding example is a Canaanite text discovered at Deir ʿAllâ in 1967, which recounts a vision of Balaam son of Beor. The recording of the covenant stipulations on such surfaces may be implied at Deut. 27:1-8; Josh. 8:32.

Metal was occasionally used as a writing surface. Gold, silver, copper, and bronze objects are known, inscribed in Sumerian, Akkadian, Hittite, Byblos syllabic, Phoenician and Punic, Hebrew (a silver scroll inscribed with a prayer has been found at Jerusalem), and Ammonite. Lead was used for magical texts. Job 19:23-24 (RSV "iron pen") may refer to a practice of filling the letters of stone inscriptions with lead for greater visibility.

Despite its wide currency, clay is not mentioned as a writing material in the Hebrew Bible. Neither are ostraca (fragments of broken pottery), though their use for writing Hebrew receipts and letters is known from the Samaria Ostraca, the Lachish Letters, and other examples.

Egyptians infrequently wrote on linen, a relatively expensive practice the spread of which was presumably contained by economic factors. From wood, on the other hand, could be made a variety of useful writing boards. The smoothed surface itself could be carved or inked; coated with stucco it could be inked, erased, and reused; waxed, it could receive the impressions of a stylus for quick composition of cuneiform or alphabetic texts with easy erasure. The tablets mentioned at Isa. 8:1; 30:8; Hab. 2:2 may have been coated wooden writing boards. Ivory was an expensive but elegant surface for writing.

Although writing in Egypt appears to have been inspired at least conceptually by the Mesopotamian systems, the Nile valley can be said to have bequeathed writing to the world in two senses. First, in hieroglyphic script was developed the acrophonic principle that, isolated, provided the logic of alphabetic writing. Second, Egypt developed the ideal writing material for such a script: papyrus. Strips of pith from the tall marsh plant were made into supple sheets of great strength; standardized in size and glued into long strips, papyrus made possible documents of every

size and configuration. Papyrus scrolls are known from the third millennium B.C., and by the first millennium had virtually replaced clay and other substances for most kinds of documents. Writing on papyrus was widespread in ancient Israel as elsewhere; it is known from the Hebrew Bible only by implication, however. The scroll of Jeremiah's oracles that was cut up and fed to the flames was certainly papyrus (Jer. 36:23). The Johannine writer expresses his preference for personal encounter over the text written on papyrus (2 John 12; RSV "paper").

Hides were also specially prepared as writing surfaces. Most of the biblical scrolls from Qumran are written on leather. In post-Christian times parchment, which was beautiful, durable, and expensive, was used for the best manuscripts.

The biblical tradition is self-consciously literate. Events themselves are sometimes viewed metaphorically as words in a document that God is writing. Moses could volunteer to be effaced from the record (Heb. *sēper* can hardly mean "book" here) that God had written (Exod. 32:32-33; cf. Ps. 69:28 [MT 29]). In Christianity, the "book of life" was to become a powerful eschatological image (Rev. 13:8).

Bibliography. G. R. Driver, *Semitic Writing: From Pictograph to Alphabet,* 3rd ed. (New York: 1976); I. J. Gelb, *A Study of Writing* (Chicago: 1963); G. Sampson, *Writing Systems: A Linguistic Introduction* (Stanford: 1985).

WRITINGS (Heb. *kᵉṯûḇîm*; Gk. *hagiógrapha* "sacred writings").* The last of the three sections of the Jewish canon (cf. Luke 24:44, "the psalms"). Included are the books of Psalms, Job, Proverbs, Ruth, Song of Solomon, Ecclesiastes, Lamentations, Esther, Daniel, Ezra, Nehemiah, and 1-2 Chronicles. This sequence, found in modern versions of the Hebrew Scriptures, is probably no older than the twelfth century A.D.; in fact, the order varied greatly at different times and was never officially set by the synagogue. The books were probably grouped together between 300 B.C. and A.D. 100. *See* Canon *II;* Bible *II.*

XANTHICUS [zăn'thĭ kəs] (Gk. *Xanthikos*). A month of the Seleucid calendar corresponding to the Jewish month Nisan (Mar./Apr.). This Macedonian name occurs in two letters written to the Jews in 164 B.C. by Antiochus V and the Romans (2 Macc. 11:30, 33, 38).

XERXES [zûrk'sēz] (Aram., Heb. *'ăḥašwērôš*; Gk. *Xerxēs*; O.Pers. *xšayāršan*).†

1. Xerxes I, Achaemenid king of Persia 486-465 B.C.; the eldest son and successor of Darius I and Atossa, daughter of Cyrus the Great. He is best known for his unsuccessful invasion of Greece, described from the Greek point of view in Herodotus' *Persian Wars*; despite initial promise shown by his crossing of the Hellespont in 480, Xerxes' punitive campaign against Greek participation in the Ionian revolt and the battle of Marathon climaxed in the diasastrous sea battle at Salamis later that same year. King Ahasuerus (RSV, KJV) of the book of Esther, who deposed his Persian wife Vashti and married the young Jewish woman Esther (Esth. 1:1–2:1, 16-17), is identified with Xerxes (so NIV; cf. Ezra 4:5-7).

2. Xerxes II, successor to Artaxerxes I (424 B.C.). Assassinated by his brother Sogdianus (Secydianus) after a reign of forty-five days, he was succeeded by Darius II.

Y

YAHWEH [yä′wə, yä′wä].† The covenant name of the God of Israel. According to the biblical account, it is the name by which God identified himself to Moses in the encounter at the burning bush (Exod. 3:14). *See* I AM WHO I AM.

Although the meaning of the name remains subject to debate, Yahweh is most likely a verbal form of Heb. *hāyâ* (perhaps originally *hwy*) "be, become." It is frequently held to be a hiphil form "cause to be," and as such may represent the initial element in a compound such as Yahweh-El ("God, who causes to be"). In historical books from Samuel through Chronicles, Psalms, and especially the prophets the name occurs in the compound *YHWH ṣᵉḇā'ôṯ* "Lord of hosts." It occurs as a divine element in numerous personal names, often in the shortened form Yah or Yahu (e.g., Isaiah, Jeremiah, Nehemiah), and in the liturgical expression *halᵉlû-yāh* "hallelujah."

The name Yahweh occurs on the Moabite Stone and may occur as a divine name or name element in Egyptian, Ugaritic, Nabatean, and Amorite (Mari) texts dating to the second millennium B.C. Moses' burning-bush experience occurred while shepherding the flocks of his father-in-law Jethro, "the priest of Midian," who some scholars thus contend introduced him to a Midianite (or Kenite) god Yahweh (cf. Exod. 18). Early or archaizing poetry depicts Yahweh as approaching from his home in the south, variously identified with the mountains Paran (Deut. 33:2; Hab. 3:3), Seir (Deut. 33:2; Judg. 5:5), Sinai (Deut. 33:2), and Teman (Hab. 3:3), and reminiscences of earlier mythologies are suggested in some accounts (e.g., the attendants Deber and Resheph, Hab. 3:5; the council of the gods, e.g., Ps. 89:7 [MT 8]; cf. Zech. 14:5). Predominant use of the name Yahweh is one of the characteristics associated with the J source of the Pentateuch; *see* YAHWIST.

Because of the utmost sanctity ascribed to the name, Jews from postexilic times on have declined to pronounce it in public reading, and only the consonants were written (*YHWH*; the Dead Sea Scrolls use the archaic, "paleo-Hebrew" script). Although the original pronunciation was thus eventually lost, inscriptional evidence favors *yāhwǣ* or *yāhwē*. The name is represented in the MT by the consonants with the

vowel pointing for *'ᵃḏōnāy* "Lord." From this derived *ca.* the sixteenth century the form "Jehovah" (*yᵉhōwāh*). In modern usage pious Jews often substitute the expression *haš-šēm* "the Name."

See GOD.

Bibliography. D. N. Freedman and M. P. O'Connor, "YHWH," *TDOT* 5 (1986): 500-521.

YAHWIST [yä′wĭst].† The figure or group, according to proponents of the documentary hypothesis, responsible for the J source (from "Jahweh," the German spelling of Yahweh, hence "Jehovah") of the Pentateuch. It is thought to have been compiled in the tenth century, either during or shortly after Solomon's reign, and to represent a reinterpretation of Israel's traditions in view of the crisis posed by the transition from a rural/pastoral confederacy to a wealthy, powerful state.

Critical scholars believe that the formulator(s) of J employed ancient narratives in which the patriarchs faced grave situations to show the Lord's providence and Israel's role as a blessing to the nations (cf. Gen. 12:1-4). Among these narratives are the accounts of barren Sarah, who becomes a mother in her old age (ch. 18), of Israel's brushes with death by famine, from which they are saved by God's power (12:10-20; 26:1-33), and of Joseph's abilities (chs. 41–45). J also includes the premonarchic credo of Deut. 26:5-9 and narrative tradition that focused on the themes of divine promises to Israel and the Exodus.

How far the J materials extend into the Old Testament has been a subject of much debate. Initially it was thought that J could be traced as far as 1-2 Kings. More recent scholars conjecture that J materials are found in Joshua or even Judg. 1.

See BIBLICAL CRITICISM.

YARMUK [yär′mŏok]. The northernmost of a series of rivers east of the Jordan and its major eastern tributary; the Yarmuk, Jabbok, Arnon, and Brook Zered all run through mountain gorges and empty into the Jordan river or the Dead Sea. Although the Yarmuk is not named in the Bible, archaeological evidence attests to extensive settlement along the river throughout the biblical period. The town of Edrei, city of King Og of Bashan (Num. 21:33; Deut. 1:4),

1075

was located on the Yarmuk, which flowed through the northern part of the area known in New Testament times as the Decapolis (Matt. 4:25; Mark 5:20; 7:31).

YEAR (Heb. *šānâ*).† Like all ancient peoples, the ancient Hebrews employed a system to calculate the passage of time, even if they were not capable of modern scientific precision. Although a full statement explaining the Israelite calendar is nowhere presented, the information in the Bible and other ancient Near Eastern records provides a reasonable idea of what their calendar was like, although the particular version in use at any given period is difficult to determine. In the study of Hebrew chronology one must proceed with the realization that in the biblical period the calendar was always in flux.

In Israel and throughout the ancient Near East, the calendar was based in large part on the movement of heavenly bodies: the sun, moon, and stars. To a lesser extent it was determined by such factors as agricultural seasons and cultic festivals, as well as the acts of Yahweh in history. In the Israelite theocratic state, political considerations were of lesser importance. The most fundamental calendrical unit was the year; what varied was the way it was measured.

The two primary approaches to measuring the year in terms of celestial movement were solar and lunar. In solar reckoning, the fixed point for determining the beginning of the year was the equinox, whether in spring or autumn. The solar year normally had 364 or 365 days: twelve months of thirty days, with an additional day each quarter and perhaps at the New Year. Examples of a strict solar reckoning may be found in the book of Jubilees (Jub. 6:23-32), paralleled in 1 Enoch and the Qumran literature.

In lunar reckoning the focal unit was the month, which began when the crescent of the new moon was first visible at sunset. This was referred to as the "new moon day" and was considered holy (Num. 10:10; 28:11; Ps. 81:3 [MT 4]; Isa. 66:23; Hos. 2:11 [MT 13]; Amos 8:5; cf. Col. 2:16). Festivals were celebrated in midmonth, at the full moon (Ps. 81:3 [MT 4]). The lunar year consisted of twelve months, alternating twenty-nine and thirty days (actually 29.5 each), for a total of 354 days. Because this lunar year was approximately eleven days shorter than the actual solar year, it was necessary at intervals to intercalate a thirteenth month in order to keep the New Year in the correct month. This intercalation was done differently in different periods; for example, in later Judaism seven out of every nineteen years included a "second Adar."

Both solar and lunar factors were present in Israelite calendrical reckoning. Passages such as Exod. 23:14-17; 34:18-26 exhibit both: the references to the festivals represent solar reckoning (they took place at the equinoxes), while the months indicate lunar. In another example, the new year began with the new moon closest to the spring equinox. Hence the Hebrew calendar is best described as "lunisolar." Such a calendar, though changing and evolving over the years, was operative throughout the history of Israel.

The months, as has been seen, were calculated on the basis of the moon. Both of the Hebrew words translated "month" (Heb. *yeraḥ*, *ḥōḏeš*) have lunar referents. Early month names in the Old Testament appear to have been borrowed from the Canaanites (only four are mentioned; Exod. 13:4; 1 Kgs. 6:1, 38; 8:2), while Babylonian names appeared in the post-exilic period (e.g., Neh. 1:1; 6:15; Esth. 2:16; 3:7; 8:9; Zech. 1:7). Predominating, however, throughout the whole biblical period and increasingly as time went on, was the use of numerical designations for the months, both along with (e.g., 1 Kgs. 6:1; Esth. 3:7; cf. Exod. 12:2, together with 13:4) and apart from (e.g., Gen. 7:11; Exod. 19:1; Deut. 1:3; Ezra 10:9) the month names. Each of the three nomenclatures represented a year which began in the spring, and a twelve-month system was always in view.

NAMES OF THE MONTHS THAT APPEAR IN THE BIBLE			
Numerical	Canaanite	Babylonian	Modern Equivalent
First	Abib	Nisan	March-April
Second	Ziv	Iyyar	April-May
Third		Sivan	May-June
Fourth		Tammuz	June-July
Fifth		Ab	July-August
Sixth		Elul	August-September
Seventh	Ethanim	Tishri	September-October
Eighth	Bul	Marchesvan	October-November
Ninth		Chislev	November-December
Tenth		Tebeth	December-January
Eleventh		Shebat	January-February
Twelfth		Adar	February-March

Other common units for measuring time included weeks (Exod. 34:22; Lev. 12:5), sabbaths (which often served as points of demarcation; e.g., 23:3, 15; Num. 28:9), and days (vv. 3, 16-18). Agricultural seasons (Exod. 34:21; Num. 13:20; Ruth 1:22) and historical events (Exod. 12:40-42; 1 Kgs. 6:1; Ezek. 33:21) also served as referents, as did cultic feasts and festivals. The festivals were often related to the agricultural cycle as well as to the spring and fall equinoxes. The three major festivals—Passover and the Feast of Unleavened Bread (Exod. 23:15; Lev. 23:5-6), Firstfruits or the Feast of Weeks (Exod. 23:16a; Lev. 23:15-22), and Ingathering or the Feast of Booths, or Tabernacles (Exod. 23:16b; Lev. 23:33-36)—took place in spring, early summer, and fall.

Although the predominance of biblical evidence indicates that the year began in the spring, other passages refer to the beginning or end of the year in the autumn (e.g., Exod. 34:22b; Lev. 25:9 [beginning of the Jubilee Year]; Neh. 1:1, together with 2:1). However, these texts reflect almost exclusively agricultural and seasonal calendars that were not perceived as official, much like modern academic or fiscal years. In addition, the Old Testament contains no certain references to any New Year celebration.

In the New Testament dates are occasionally reckoned according to the reign of certain Roman or Jewish officials (Luke 2:1-2; 3:1-2) or, more commonly, with respect to the Jewish cultic calendar (John 2:13; 7:2; Acts 2:1; 1 Cor. 16:8). Before A.D. 70 Jews followed Sadducean reckoning, which regulated the temple services. Afterwards, the pharisaic system became the norm. It is apparent from John 18:28 that the calendar kept by the Jewish leaders and the one used by Jesus and his disciples were not the same, as the Passover was being celebrated on different days. It is possible, then, that Jesus may have been following a "sectarian" solar calendar such as that of Jubilees and the Qumran community.

YELLOW.* One of the indications of "leprosy" mentioned in the legal provisions for diagnosis of skin diseases is hair that is "yellow [and] thin" (Heb. *ṣāhōb dāq*; Lev. 13:30, cf. vv. 32, 36). Favus, a fungal disease, is characterized by yellowing of the hair, and so may be a part of the complex of skin conditions spoken of at Lev. 13.

YIRON [yĭr'ən] (Heb. *yir'ôn*). A fortified city in the tribal territory of Naphtali (Josh. 19:38; KJV, NIV "Iron"), probably modern Yārûn.

YOKE (Heb. *'ōl, môṭâ, ṣemeḏ*; Gk. *zygós*). A shaped piece of wood placed across the necks of draft animals such as oxen or donkeys (Isa. 30:24) to enable a pair (Deut. 22:10, "unmixed") to pull a plow, cart, or heavy load together (1 Sam. 6:7). As a yoke enabled two to pull as one, the term also denoted a team, a "yoke of oxen" (1 Kgs. 19:19, 21; Job 1:3; 42:12). As a measure of land, "yoke" referred to the area one yoke of oxen could plow in a day, about an acre (cf. 1 Sam. 14:14).

Figurative uses of "yoke" are drawn from its literal characteristics—that it bound one to another and that it teamed one with another. In its binding function, the yoke often represents slavery or servitude (Gen. 27:40; 1 Kgs. 12:4-14; Isa. 47:6; Jer. 27:2-12; 28:10-14; 1 Tim. 6:1), which may be put on (Hos. 10:11) or taken off (Jer. 30:8; Nah. 1:13) by Yahweh. The loosening or breaking of a yoke symbolizes deliverance (Lev. 26:13; Isa. 58:6; Ezek. 34:27), but the reference to an iron yoke at Jer. 28:13-14 indicates a servitude that cannot be broken (cf. Deut. 28:48).

The yoke's teaming function is a pattern for some of Israel's more foolish alliances. Lam. 1:14 refers to transgressions bound into a yoke, while Num. 25:3, 5 depicts Israel's worship of Baal in similar terms. In fact, Israel so often preferred an idol's yoke to Yahweh's (Jer. 2:20; 5:5; cf. KJV, NIV, 2 Cor. 6:14) that the Lord appointed them to a yoke of bondage instead (Hos. 11:1-7).

At Matt. 11:29-30 Jesus issues a call to take on his yoke and learn from him. This is similar in tone to wisdom's call (Sir. 6:23-31; 51:25-26; cf. Prov. 8:1) and to invitations in rabbinic literature to take on the yoke of the law (cf. Lam. 3:27), which was not a burden but a joy. However, Peter and other early Jewish Christians considered the yoke of law, in contrast with the grace of the Lord Jesus, to be a great burden (Acts 15:10-11, 28-29), and Paul argued that Christ had set his followers free from such a yoke of slavery (Gal. 5:1).

YOKEFELLOW. The literal translation of Gk. *sýzygos* "comrade" or "companion," applied to a member (or possibly members) of the church at Philippi charged by Paul to help Euodia and Syntyche resolve their quarrel (Phil. 4:2-3). Scholars have speculated about the identity of this "true yokefellow" and have suggested various persons known from Paul's ministry, such as Epaphroditus, Silas, Luke, Lydia, Timothy, or Titus. More cautious commentators have proposed several less specific options: a well-known associate of Paul's, a leader at Philippi whose name is not mentioned; an otherwise unknown church member whose name is not given; an otherwise unknown church member named Syzygus (unlikely because the word is unattested elsewhere as a name); and the whole congregation addressed as one person.

YOM KIPPUR [yŏm kĭp'ər, yōm kĭ pŏŏr']. The holiest of Jewish holy days from the biblical period on. *See* ATONEMENT, DAY OF.

Z

ZAANAN [zā'ə năn] (Heb. *ṣaʿᵃnān*). An unidentified site in the Shephelah of Judah (Mic. 1:11). It may be the same as Zenan at Josh. 15:37, which also appears in context with Lachish.

ZAANANNIM [zā'ə năn'ĭm] (Heb. *ṣaʿᵃnannîm*). A place on the border of the tribal territory of Naphtali, near Kedesh between Mt. Tabor and the Jordan river (Josh. 19:33). At this site Heber the Kenite pitched his tent (Judg. 4:11; KJV "Zaanaim"); here his wife, Jael, slew Sisera (v. 21) as he fled from Barak.

ZAAVAN [zā'ə văn] (Heb. *zaʿᵃwān*). The second son of Ezer the Horite, leader of an Edomite clan (Gen. 36:27; 1 Chr. 1:42; KJV "Zavan").

ZABAD [zā'băd] (Heb. *zābāḏ* "gift").
1. A descendant of Jerahmeel of the tribe of Judah, son of Nathan and father of Ephlal (1 Chr. 2:36-37).
2. The son of Tahath, and a descendant of Ephraim (1 Chr. 7:21).
3. One of David's mighty men, the son of Ahlai (1 Chr. 11:41).
4. The son of Shimeath the Ammonitess who conspired with Jehozabad to murder King Joash of Judah (2 Chr. 24:26). At 2 Kgs. 12:21 (MT 22) he is called Jozacar (KJV "Jozachar").
5. An Israelite of the sons of Zattu who had taken a foreign wife (Ezra 10:27).
6. One of the sons of Hattum required to divorce his foreign wife (Ezra 10:33).
3. A man among the sons of Nebo who had married a non-Israelite wife (Ezra 10:43).

ZABADEANS [zăb'ə dē'ənz] (Gk. *Zabadaioi*).* An Arab people, apparently named for their village of Zabad, attacked and crushed by Jonathan Maccabeus when the Seleucid opponents he had been pursuing eluded him across the Eleutherus river (probably the Nahr el-Kebir in central Lebanon) (1 Macc. 12:31). Since Jonathan promptly returned to the region of Damascus (v. 32), the village was apparently northwest of that city, probably at modern Zebdani, about 28 km. (17 mi.) from Damascus (cf. Kepherzabad "town of Zabad," northwest of Hamath).

ZABBAI [zăb'ī] (Heb. *zabbay*).
1. An Israelite who had taken a foreign wife (Ezra 10:28).
2. The father of Baruch, who helped repair a section of the wall (Neh. 3:20, **K**; **Q** "Zaccai"). He may be the same as **1**.

ZABBUD (Ezra 8:14, KJV). *See* ZACCUR.

ZABDI [zăb'dī] (Heb. *zabdî* "my gift").
1. An ancestor of Achan of the tribe of Judah (Josh. 7:1, 17-18). He is called Zimri (**3**) at 1 Chr. 2:6.
2. A son of Shimei of the tribe of Benjamin (1 Chr. 8:19).
3. A Shiphmite; steward of David's wine cellar (1 Chr. 27:27).
4. A Levite and son of Asaph (Neh. 11:17). He is probably the same as Zichri (**5**) at 1 Chr. 9:15.

ZABDIEL [zăb'dī əl] (Heb. *zabdîʾēl* "gift of God" or "my gift is God"; Gk. *Sabdiēl*).
1. A Judahite; the father of Jashobeam, commander of David's first army division (1 Chr. 27:2).
2. The son of Haggedolim, and overseer of Jerusalem priests after the Exile (Neh. 11:14).
3. An Arab who decapitated Alexander Balas when he sought refuge in Arabia from the Egyptian king Ptolemy VI Philometor. Zabdiel then sent the head to Ptolemy (1 Macc. 11:17).

ZABUD [zā'bŭd] (Heb. *zābûḏ* "given"). A son of Nathan. He was a priest at the time of Solomon who held the office or position of "king's friend" (1 Kgs. 4:5, **K**; **Q** "Zaccur").

ZABULON (KJV). *See* ZEBULUN.

ZACCAI [zăk'ī] (Heb. *zakkay* "pure"). An Israelite whose descendants returned with Zerubbabel from captivity in Babylon (Ezra 2:9; Neh. 7:14; cf. 3:20, **Q**).

ZACCHAEUS [ză kē'əs] (Gk. *Zakchaios*; from Heb. *zakkay* "pure").†
1. An officer in the Maccabean army (2 Macc. 10:19).

1079

2. A chief tax collector in Jericho whose encounter with Jesus led to his salvation (Luke 19:1-10). Jewish tax collectors were a despised group, hated both for their collaboration with the Romans and for their frequent extortion by overtaxing. Zacchaeus as chief tax collector in prosperous Jericho would have been particularly rich and greatly scorned.

Nonetheless, when he heard Jesus was to pass through his town, Zacchaeus went to some effort to see him, even so far as to climb a tree because he was too short to see above the crowds. When Jesus saw him and invited himself to stay at Zacchaeus' house, Zacchaeus quieted the grumbling and skeptical crowd by promising to give half of his goods to the poor and to repay fourfold anyone whom he had defrauded (cf. Exod. 22:1 [MT 21:37]; Lev. 6:1-5 [MT 5:20-24]; 2 Sam. 12:6). Jesus recognized this deed as a sign of Zacchaeus' salvation; thus, his encounter with Zacchaeus exemplified his mission "to seek and to save the lost" (v. 10).

ZACCUR [zăk´ər] (Heb. *zakkûr* "mindful").
1. The father of the spy Shammua of the tribe of Reuben (Num. 13:4).
2. A Simeonite; the son of Hammuel, and a descendant of Mishma (1 Chr. 4:26; KJV "Zacchur").
3. A Levite of the Merarite line (1 Chr. 24:27).
4. A Levite and son of Asaph who was leader of the third division of temple musicians during the reign of David (1 Chr. 25:2, 10; Neh. 12:35).
5. A descendant of Bigvai who returned from exile with Ezra (Ezra 8:14; KJV "Zabbud," following **K** *zābbûḏ*).
6. A son of Imri who was among those who rebuilt the walls of Jerusalem (Neh. 3:2).
7. A Levite who set his seal to the new covenant under Nehemiah (Neh. 10:12 [MT 13]).
8. The father of Hanan, a Levite who lived during the governorship of Nehemiah (Neh. 13:13).

ZACHARIAH, ZACHARIAS (KJV). *See* ZECHARIAH.

ZACHER (1 Chr. 8:31, KJV). *See* ZECHER.

ZADOK [zā´dŏk] (Heb. *ṣāḏôq, ṣāḏōq* "righteous"; Gk. *Sadōk*).†
1. A young warrior who joined David at Hebron (1 Chr. 12:28 [MT 29]), thought by some to be the same as **2** (cf. Josephus *Ant.* vii.2.2).
2. One of the two leading priests in Jerusalem during the reign of David, and the ancestor of the high priests until 171 B.C. Zadok was the son of Ahitub, a descendant of Aaron's son Eleazar, and the father of Ahimaaz (2 Sam. 8:17; 18:19; 1 Chr. 6:8 [MT 5:34]; 24:3).

Zadok served as the priest of the tabernacle at Gibeon in the early days of David's reign (1 Chr. 16:39-40). Zadok and Abiathar were the leading priests after David became king (2 Sam. 20:25), and Zadok was leader of the Aaronites for the purposes of the military census (1 Chr. 27:17). When David fled from his son Absalom, Zadok and Abiathar carried the ark of the covenant back into Jerusalem and functioned as David's informants concerning developments in the city (2 Sam. 15:24-29; 17:15-16). After Absalom's

death the two priests took a significant part in the restoration of David to his throne (19:11-12 [MT 12-13]).

Abiathar joined Adonijah, David's eldest surviving son, in his attempt to seize the throne from Solomon (1 Kgs. 1:7), but Zadok did not join this conspiracy (vv. 8, 26). Zadok and the prophet Nathan anointed Solomon king (vv. 32-40). Solomon expelled Abiathar and gave Abiathar's priesthood to Zadok (2:26-27, 35; cf. 4:2, 4). Zadok's descendants thus supplanted those of Abiathar (descended from Eli), as foretold at 1 Sam. 2:35, which also predicts that the line of Zadok would continue perpetually. The high priest of Hezekiah's time was a descendant of Zadok (2 Chr. 31:10). By the time of the Exile, the Zadokite high priesthood was firmly established (Ezek. 40:46; 43:19; 44:15; 48:11).
3. The father of Jerusha, the mother of King Jotham of Judah (2 Kgs. 15:33; 2 Chr. 27:1).
4. A descendant of Zadok 2, and ancestor of Jehozadak and Ezra (1 Chr. 6:12 [MT 5:38]; 9:11; Ezra 7:2; Neh. 11:11). The genealogy at Ezra 7:1-5 is telescoped at the name Zadok, so that the ancestors of Zadok 2 appear before the name Zadok and the descendants of this Zadok appear immediately following the name.
5. One who took part in the postexilic rebuilding of the walls of Jerusalem; the son of Baana (Neh. 3:4).
6. The son of Immer who repaired the Jerusalem wall "opposite his house" (Neh. 3:29).
7. One of the "chiefs of the people" who set their seals to the covenant in the time of Nehemiah (Neh. 10:21 [MT 22]).
8. A scribe appointed as one of the keepers of the Levites' storehouses by Nehemiah (Neh. 13:13).
8. An ancestor of Joseph, the legal father of Jesus (Matt. 1:14; KJV "Sadoc").

ZADOKITE [zā´də kīt] **FRAGMENTS.** * A title given to an ancient Hebrew sectarian manual first known through two medieval copies discovered in the Cairo Genizah in 1897. The document was edited and published in 1910 by S. Schechter, who linked the document to the Dositheans, a group related to the Sadducees, since the sect claimed to be the sons of Zadok, the high priest under King Solomon (CD 3:21–4:5; cf. Ezek. 44:15; CD 5:1-5; cf. 2 Kgs. 22). However, the discovery of fragments of this writing among the Dead Sea Scrolls makes it likely that it comes from a group closely associated with Qumran, perhaps a branch of the Essenes. Since the document refers to the "new covenant in the land of Damascus" (CD 6:19; 8:21), it has come to be commonly designated as the Damascus Document or Damascus Rule, usually cited by the abbreviation "CD" for "Cairo, Damascus." The document is divided into two major parts, the Admonitions (A 1:1–8:23; B 1:1–2:34) and the Statutes (A 9:1–16:19). The Qumran fragments reveal that the beginning and end of both sections of the document are missing.

Bibliography. P. R. Davies, *The Damascus Covenant.* JSOTS 25 (1983); C. Rabin, ed., *The Zadokite Documents,* 2nd ed. (Oxford: 1958); S. Schechter, *Documents of Jewish Sectaries,* 2 vols. (1910; repr. New York: 1970).

ZAHAM [zā'hăm] (Heb. *zāham* "disgust"). A son of King Rehoboam of Judah (2 Chr. 11:19).

ZAIR [zā'ər] (Heb. *ṣā'îr* "small"). The site of King Joram's unsuccessful battle to maintain Judaean sovereignty over the Edomites (2 Kgs. 8:21). Zair was probably in or near Edom; however, some LXX manuscripts suggest the name is ZIOR, a town in the Judean hill country (Josh. 15:54).

ZALAPH [zā'lăf] (Heb. *ṣālāp* "caper bush"). The father of Hanun, one of many who worked with Nehemiah to repair the Jerusalem walls (Neh. 3:30).

ZALMON [zăl'mən] (Heb. *ṣalmôn*) (PERSON). An Ahohite, and one of David's mighty men (2 Sam. 23:28). At 1 Chr. 11:29 he is called Ilai.

ZALMON [zăl'mən] (Heb. *ṣalmôn*) (PLACE).
1. A mountain near Shechem from which Abimelech gathered a large amount of brushwood to burn the Tower of Shechem and its people (Judg. 9:48-49).
2. The mountainous site (probably Jebel Ḥauran) of a great but otherwise unknown victory (Ps. 68:14 [MT 15]; KJV "Salmon"). The reference to snow may be literal (RSV) or may figuratively refer to the shining spoil or bleached bones of the vanquished (cf. NIV "like snow").

ZALMONAH [zăl mō'nə] (Heb. *ṣalmōnâ* "dark"). An Israelite campsite during the wilderness wanderings, located between Mt. Hor and Punon (Num. 33:41-42).

ZALMUNNA [zăl mŭn'ə] (Heb. *ṣalmunnāʿ* "without shadow [or "protection")] [?]"). One of a pair of Midianite kings whom Gideon captured and slew because they had murdered his brothers (Judg. 8:4-21; Ps. 83:11 [MT 12]).

ZAMZUMMIM [zăm zŭm'ĭm] (Heb. *zamzumîm*). The name given by the Ammonites to a group of Rephaim who· had dwelt in Canaan. With the Lord's help the Ammonites displaced them, in spite of their great number, strength, and size (Deut. 2:20-21; cf. Gen. 14:5; Deut. 3:11).

ZANOAH [zə nō'ə] (Heb. *zānôaḥ*) (PERSON). The son of Jekuthiel, and a descendant of Mered and his Jewish wife (1 Chr. 4:18).

ZANOAH [zə nō'ə] (Heb. *zānôaḥ*) (PLACE).
1. A city in the northern Shephelah mentioned with Zorah and Jarmuth (Josh. 15:33-35; Neh. 11:29-30), whose residents helped repair the Valley Gate (3:13). The site is commonly identified with Khirbet Zānûʿ (Zānûaḥ), located 5 km. (3 mi.) south of Bethshemesh and situated on a hill that is easily accessible only from the south. Remains of a wall and pottery dating to the Israelite monarchy have been uncovered here.
2. A city in the hill country of Judah (Josh. 15:56; cf. 1 Chr. 4:18, which may refer to the city's founder). Its probable location is near modern Yaṭṭā (biblical Juttah; Josh. 15:55) on the Wâdī Abū Zenah, perhaps

Khirbet Beit Amra, a large hill of ruins and a natural stronghold.

ZAPHENATH-PANEAH [zăf'ə năth pə nē'ə] (Heb. *ṣāp'nat paʿnēaḥ*). The Egyptian name given to Joseph when Pharaoh set him "over all the land of Egypt" (Gen. 41:45; KJV "Zaphnath-paaneah"). The meaning of the name is not certain; its derivation from Egyp. *ḏd-p3-ntr-w.f-ʿnḥ* "the deity speaks and (the bearer of the name) lives" is commonly accepted, but would have to be dated later than Joseph.

ZAPHON [zā'fŏn] (Heb. *ṣāpôn* "north").†
1. A city in the tribal territory of Gad, formerly part of Sihon's kingdom (Josh. 13:27). Here the Ephraimites came to inquire why Jephthah had failed to enlist their aid in his war with the Ammonites (Judg. 12:1). The usual identification of Zaphon is modern Tell eṣ-Ṣaʿîdîyeh, but Tell el-Mazâr has also been proposed. An earlier suggestion, Tell el-Qôs, no longer enjoys much support because of lack of Late Bronze Age remains.
2. In Canaanite mythology the mountain dwelling of the god Baal. At one time the name designated Jebel el-Aqraʿ, a mountain on the Mediterranean coast some 48 km. (30 mi.) north of Ras Shamra (ancient Ugarit), hence the semantic shift of Heb. *ṣāpôn* "north" (cf. *yam* "sea," which came to designate "west"). With regard to ancient mythology, the site shifted among different peoples at different times (e.g., Exod. 14:2 "Baal-zephon"). Zaphon 1 may be another example; at least, it was probably named after the mountain. Hebrew interpretations of this mythology may underlie such texts as Ps. 48:2 (MT 3) (so NJV, NIV); Isa. 14:13 (cf. NIV mg.).

ZARA, ZARAH (KJV). *See* ZERAH (3).

ZARATHUSTRA [zăr'ə thōōs'trə] (Gk. *Zōroastrēs*; O.Pers. *zrdrwšt, zrhwšt,*).† The founder of ZOROASTRIANISM, the major pre-Islamic religion of Iran (628-551 B.C.). He is traditionally said to have converted his patron, King Vistăspa, 258 years before Alexander the Great conquered Persepolis in 330 B.C.
Zarathustra is said to have been born at Rhages in western Iran (modern Rai, south of Tehran), although the Avesta, the earliest group of Zoroastrian texts, indicates an eastern Iranian origin. Both Persian and Greek sources suggest that the spread of Zarathustra's doctrines from eastern to western Iran took a long time. Darius I and his successors worshipped Ahura Mazda as the supreme deity, but their inscriptions do not mention Zarathustra or his doctrine of the entities surrounding Ahura Mazda later known as the Bounteous Immortals. Similarly, Herodotus, who describes the customs of the Magi, the priestly class of the Achaemenids, does not mention Zarathustra. Aristotle, however, refers to the ethical dualism of Zoroastrian doctrine.
The Gāthās, probably the oldest part of the Avesta, are traditionally attributed to Zarathustra. They included the elevation of Ahura Mazda to the position of supreme deity, the names of the Bounteous Immortals, the prohibition of sacrifices to the daivas and the Destructive Spirit, and exhortations to choose truth

rather than falsehood and to live a settled (rather than a nomadic) life as a farmer or cattle breeder. Zarathustra retained the Indoiranian cult of fire. However, the degree to which later Zoroastrianism reflects his teaching is unclear.

ZAREAH (Neh. 11:29, KJV). *See* ZORAH.

ZARED (Neh. 21:12, KJV). *See* ZERED, BROOK.

ZAREPHATH [zăr'ə făth] (Heb. *ṣārᵉpaṭ*; Gk. *Sarepta*). A Phoenician coastal city (modern Ṣarafand) located between Sidon and Tyre (cf. Obad. 20; KJV "Sarepta"). After sending Elijah to Zarephath, God miraculously provided for him from a widow's meager goods and, through Elijah, raised her son from the dead (1 Kgs. 17:9-24; Luke 4:26).

ZARETHAN [zăr'ə thăn] (Heb. *ṣārᵉṭān*). A village in the Jordan valley, probably east of the river, called Zeredah at 2 Chr. 4:17 (NIV "Zarethan") and Zererah at Judg. 7:22. Near Zarethan the waters of the Jordan river "stood up" so the Israelites could cross (Josh. 3:16; KJV "Zaretan"); centuries later Hiram cast there the bronze vessels of Solomon's temple (1 Kgs. 7:45-46; KJV "Zarthan"; cf. 4:12; KJV "Zartanah"). Of the numerous sites proposed, Tell es-Saʿîdîyeh is a prime candidate, fitting many of the accounts; some scholars favor a location on the west bank.

ZARETH-SHAHAR (Josh. 13:19, KJV). *See* ZERETH-SHAHAR.

ZARHITES (KJV). *See* ZERAH **3, 4.**

ZARIUS [zâr'ĭ əs] (Gk. *Zarios*).* The name given in 1 Esdr. 1:38 for a brother of King Jehoiakim of Judea. When Josiah died, the people made his son Jehoahaz king, but after less than a year of failed rule Pharaoh Neco removed Jehoahaz and installed his older brother Jehoiakim. 1 Esdras records that Jehoiakim promptly brought his brother Zarius "up out of" Egypt. Unfortunately this account may be at odds with that provided at 2 Chr. 36 (which 1 Esdr. 1:34-58 summarizes). According to 2 Chr. 36:4 Neco installs Jehoiakim and escorts Jehoiakim's brother Jehoahaz "to" Egypt, where the former king Jehoahaz died (2 Kgs. 23:34; Jer. 22:11-12).

ZATTU [zăt' oo] (Heb. *zattû'*). An Israelite whose descendants returned with Zerubbabel from the Babylonian exile (Ezra 2:8; 8:5 [so RSV, following LXX, 1 Esdr. 8:32; KJV "Zathoe"; lacking in MT]; Neh. 7:13). Six of them are named as having taken foreign wives (Ezra 10:27), and the current head of Zattu's family set his seal to the renewed covenant under Nehemiah (Neh. 10:14 [MT 15]; KJV "Zatthu").

ZAVAN (1 Chr. 1:42, KJV). *See* ZAAVAN.

ZAZA [zā'zə] (Heb. *zāzā'* "fullness [?]"). A Judahite, son of Jonathan (**6**) and descendant of Jerahmeel (1 Chr. 2:33).

ZEAL (Heb. *qin'â*; Gk. *zḗlos*), **ZEALOT** (Gk. *zēlōtḗs*).† In post-Old Testament Judaism a widely used term for the desire to maintain the observance of the law of Moses and the purity of the land, temple, and people of Israel—even when such a desire might require suffering, dying, or killing others, whether apostate Jews or Gentiles who might be threatening the pillars of Jewish life. Jews who considered themselves "zealous" understood themselves as agents of God's judgment. As such they represented the Jewish national self-understanding of the apocalyptic literature and of the violent struggles against Hellenistic kingdoms and Rome. Jewish zeal is encountered in the New Testament as opposition to forms of Christianity that appeared to be a compromise of Jewish principles (Acts 5:17-18; 13:45; 21:20-21; Phil. 3:6; cf. Rom. 10:2). Models of zeal included the Maccabean revolutionaries (1 Macc. 2:15-28, 50), Simeon and Levi (Jdt. 9:2-4; Jub. 30), Elijah (Sir. 48:1-2; 1 Macc. 2:58), and, above all, Phinehas. The Old Testament account of Phinehas provided the terminology of "zeal" (Num. 25:6-13; cf. Sir. 45:23-24; 1 Macc. 2:26). That "zeal" was also ascribed to God (Exod. 20:5; 2 Kgs. 19:31) gave further support to these ideas; KJV "jealous(y)" underscores his uncompromising commitment to Israel (cf. Ezek. 16:35-43). *See* JEALOUSY.

In the New Testament "zeal" is ascribed to Jesus (John 2:17; cf. Matt. 23) as well as his disciple Simon "the Zealot" (Luke 6:15; Acts 1:13), also called "the Cananaean" (cf. Heb., Aram. *qn'*; Mark 3:18 par.), and Paul (Acts 22:3; Gal. 1:14). That these figures were so designated does not mean that they were members of a revolutionary "Zealot" sect or party. Such a group did play a prominent part in the war against Rome of A.D. 66-70, but it was only during and perhaps shortly before the war that "Zealot" became a party designation. It is true, however, that concern for the preservation of Judaism began to be combined with justification for revolution before the war. This hardening of "zeal" into the uncompromising rejection of foreign rule that characterized the revolutionary groups during the war was a position associated with the name of Judas the Galilean, who led an earlier revolt in A.D. 6 (Acts 5:37).

The terminology of "zeal" is also used in reference to attitudes other than the specifically Jewish zeal, both negative (e.g., 1 Cor. 13:4) and positive (e.g., 12:31; 14:1, 39; 2 Cor. 11:2).

ZEBADIAH [zĕb'ə dī'ə] (Heb. *zᵉḇaḏyâ, zᵉḇaḏyāhû* "gift of Yahweh").

1. (Heb. *zᵉḇaḏyâ*). A descendant of Beriah of the tribe of Benjamin (1 Chr. 8:15).

2. A Benjaminite, one of the descendants of Elpaal (1 Chr. 8:17).

3. A Benjaminite, one of two sons of Jeroham of Gedor who joined David at Ziklag (1 Chr. 12:7 [MT 8]).

4. (*zᵉḇaḏyāhû*). A Korahite who served as a gatekeeper in Solomon's temple (1 Chr. 26:2).

5. (*zᵉḇaḏyâ*). The son of Joab's brother Asahel. He succeeded his father as commander of the fourth division of David's army (1 Chr. 27:7).

6. (*zᵉḇaḏyāhû*). One of nine Levites in a commission sent by King Jehoshaphat to teach the law through all the cities of Judah (2 Chr. 17:8).

7. The son of Ishmael, and leader of the house of Judah. He served as supreme justice over civil matters in Jerusalem under King Jehoshaphat (2 Chr. 19:11).

8. ($z^eḇaḏyâ$). The son of Michael of the family of Shephatiah who returned to Jerusalem with Ezra after the Exile (Ezra 8:8).

9. A priest and descendant of Immer who had taken a foreign wife (Ezra 10:20).

ZEBAH [zē′bə] (Heb. *zeḇaḥ* "sacrifice"). A Midianite king whom Gideon captured and slew in retaliation for the murder of his brothers (Judg. 8:4-21; Ps. 83:11 [MT 12]).

ZEBAIM (Ezra 2:57; Neh. 7:59, KJV). *See* POCH-ERETH-HAZZEBAIM.

ZEBEDEE [zĕb′ə dē] (Gk. *Zebedaios*; from Heb. $z^eḇaḏyāhû$ "gift of Yahweh"). The father of James and John, two of Jesus' chosen disciples (Matt. 4:21 par. Mark 1:19; Matt. 10:2 par. Mark 3:17; cf. John 21:2). A fisherman by trade, Zebedee employed his two sons, who were also partners with Simon (Luke 5:10). The facts that he had "hired" servants (Mark 1:20) and that his wife Salome contributed to Jesus' support (Matt. 27:55-56; Mark 15:40-41; cf. Luke 8:2-3) indicate that he was a man of some means. No evidence indicates that Zebedee himself followed Jesus or that he hindered his wife and sons from doing so.

ZEBIDAH [zə bī′də] (Heb. **K** $z^eḇîḏâ$). The daughter of Pedaiah of Rumah, and the mother of King Jehoiakim of Judah (2 Kgs. 23:36; KJV "Zebudah," following **Q** $z^eḇûḏâ$).

ZEBINA [zə bī′nə] (Heb. $z^eḇînā'$ "bought"). One of the postexilic descendants of Nebo who divorced their foreign wives (Ezra 10:43).

ZEBOIIM [zə boi′əm] (Heb. $ṣ^eḇōyim$). One of the five cities in the valley of Siddim near Admah whose king Shemeber tried unsuccessfully to throw off Chedorlaomer's yoke (Gen. 14:2-12; cf. 10:19). The city was destroyed by the Lord along with Sodom and Gomorrah (19:24-29, "all the land of the valley"; cf. Deut. 29:23 [MT 22]) because of their wickedness. For Hosea, the fate of Admah and Zeboiim exemplified God's judgment (Hos. 11:8). Many scholars would locate Zeboiim in an area now beneath the southern part of the Dead Sea.

ZEBOIM [zə bō′əm] (Heb. $ṣ^eḇō'îm$ "hyenas").

1. A valley in Benjamin southeast of Michmash toward the wilderness (1 Sam. 13:18). Its modern designation, Wâdzī Abū Dabā' ("Hyena Valley," which flows into the Wâdī el-Qelt), may preserve the ancient name of the valley.

2. A town in Benjamin to which some of the exiles returned (Neh. 11:34). Mentioned alongside of Hadid and Neballat, Zeboim was probably located north of Lydda.

ZEBUDAH (2 Kgs. 23:36, KJV). *See* ZEBIDA.

ZEBUL [zē′bŏol] (Heb. $z^eḇul$ "height"). The commander of the city of Shechem who informed the judge Abimelech of Gaal's plans to lead the Shechemites in revolt against Israel. After Gaal was defeated, Zebul drove him and his kinsmen from Shechem (Judg. 9:30-41).

ZEBULUN [zĕb′yə lən] (Heb. $z^eḇûlûn$).† The tenth son of Jacob and sixth son of Leah (Gen. 30:19-20; the name is related by folk etymology at v. 20 to Heb. *zbl* "honor, exalt"). The Israelite tribe of Zebulun is regarded as descended from Zebulun through his sons, Sered, Elon, and Jahleel (46:14). By the time the Israelites arrived in the Sinai desert, the tribe of Zebulun had grown large enough to field fifty-seven thousand four hundred soldiers (Num. 1:30-31); this figure increased to sixty thousand five hundred in a later census (26:26-27; $z^eḇûlōnî$ "Zebulunites").

The tribal territory of Zebulun was located in the region of Galilee and shared borders with Asher to the west, Naphtali to the east, Manasseh to the southwest, and Issachar to the southeast. Although this territory may have included part of the plain of Jezreel or the plain of Acco, it was mainly confined to the mountain rim north of Jezreel. Thus Zebulun was situated in a richly forested region, landlocked and removed from the main centers of Canaanite settlement. References to Zebulun living by the sea (Gen. 49:13) and feasting on the abundance of the seas (Deut. 33:19) indicate that the tribe did extend at some time to the Mediterranean (cf. Josephus *Ant.* v.1.22). Zebulun is associated sometimes with Issachar (Gen. 30:17-20; Deut. 33:18-19; Judg. 5:14-15; Ezek. 48:26, 33) and sometimes with Naphtali (Judg. 4:6; 5:18; 6:35; Ps. 68:27 [MT 28]; Isa. 9:1 [MT 8:23]).

Zebulunites fought with Deborah and Barak against the Canaanites (Judg. 4:6, 10; 5:14, 18) and with Gideon against the Midianites (6:35). The judge Elon was a Zebulunite (12:11-12), and the prophet Jonah came from Gath-hepher, a city of Zebulun (2 Kgs. 14:25; cf. Josh. 19:13). Isaiah prophesied that although the territories of Zebulun and Naphtali had been conquered by Assyria, they would have a glorious future (Isa. 9:1-2 [MT 8:23–9:1]); Matt. 4:12-17 applies this prophecy to the beginning of Jesus' ministry in Galilee (KJV "Zabulon").

ZECHARIAH [zĕk′ə rī′ə] (Heb. $z^eḵaryâ$, $z^eḵaryāhû$ "Yahweh has remembered"; Gk. *Zacharias*).†

1. The son of Jeroboam II who reigned over Israel only six months (746 B.C., 2 Kgs. 14:29; KJV "Zachariah"). Shallum killed Zechariah in order to secure the throne for himself (15:8-12). This fulfilled God's word to Jehu that four generations of his sons would be kings (10:30).

2. The father of Abijah (Abi), the mother of King Hezekiah of Judah (2 Kgs. 18:2; KJV "Zachariah"; 2 Chr. 29:1).

3. A chief of the tribe of Reuben (1 Chr. 5:7).

4. A Levite of the Korahite line who was a tabernacle gatekeeper and a "shrewd counselor" during the time of David (1 Chr. 9:21; 26:2, 14).

5. A Benjaminite, possibly a brother of Kish, Saul's father (1 Chr. 9:37). At 1 Chr. 8:31 he is called Zecher (KJV "Zacher"), a shorter form of the name.

6. A Levite and member of David's second division of temple musicians (1 Chr. 15:18, 20; 16:5).

7. A priest of the time of David who blew a trumpet before the ark (1 Chr. 15:24).

8. A Levite among the sons of Uzziel, contemporary with David (1 Chr. 24:25).

9. A levitical gatekeeper of the Merarite line during the time of David (1 Chr. 26:10-11).

10. The father of Iddo, chief of the Manassites in Gilead during David's reign (1 Chr. 27:21).

11. A lay official in Judah during the reign of Jehoshaphat who was one of a group appointed by the king to teach the law in the towns of Judah (2 Chr. 17:7-9).

12. The father of Jahaziel, a Levite of the family of Asaph who prophesied that King Jehoshaphat of Judah would prevail in battle against his Transjordanian enemies (2 Chr. 20:14).

13. A son of King Jehoshaphat of Judah whom his elder brother Jehoram killed upon succeeding their father to the throne (2 Chr. 21:2-4).

14. A son of the high priest Jehoiada who spoke out against the people of the time of King Joash of Judah for turning away from the Lord. At the command of the king the people stoned Zechariah to death in the court of the temple (2 Chr. 24:20-22). Jesus referred to this murder (Matt. 23:35; Luke 11:51; KJV "Zacharias"); Matthew's account calls Zechariah's father Barachiah, apparently confusing this Zechariah with Zechariah the prophet, the son of Berechiah (Zech. 1:1; cf. **29** below).

15. One who instructed King Uzziah of Judah "in the fear of the Lord" (2 Chr. 26:5).

16. A Levite of the family of Asaph who participated in the cleansing of the temple at the time of King Hezekiah (2 Chr. 29:13).

17. A Kohathite Levite who was one of the supervisors of the temple repair during the reign of King Josiah of Judah (2 Chr. 34:12).

18. A "chief officer" of the temple who contributed to the passover offering at the time of King Josiah (2 Chr. 35:8).

19. The head of the family of Parosh that returned from exile with Ezra (Ezra 8:3).

20. The head of the family of Bebai that returned from exile with Ezra (Ezra 8:11).

21. One of the "leading men" whom Ezra sent to Casiphia to seek Levites to come to Jerusalem (Ezra 8:16).

22. One of the men in postexilic Judah who divorced their foreign wives (Ezra 10:26).

23. One of the men who stood with Ezra while he instructed the people in the law (Neh. 8:14).

24. A Judahite of the family of Perez whose descendants settled in Jerusalem after the Exile (Neh. 11:4).

25. A Judahite, called "son of the Shilonite," whose descendants settled in Jerusalem after the Exile (Neh. 11:5).

26. A priest whose postexilic descendants settled in Jerusalem (Neh. 11:12).

27. The postexilic head of the priestly house of Iddo (Neh. 12:16), possibly the same as **31** below.

28. A Levite of the family of Asaph who participated in the dedication of the walls of Jerusalem when Nehemiah was governor (Neh. 12:35).

29. A priest who participated in the dedication of the rebuilt walls of Jerusalem (Neh. 12:41).

30. The son of Jeberechiah who was one of the two "reliable" men summoned by Isaiah as a witness when Isaiah was told by God to write "belonging to Maher-shalal-hash-baz" on a large tablet (Isa. 8:1-2).

31. The son of Berechiah and grandson (or descendant) of Iddo (Zech. 1:1, 7) whose prophetic ministry forms the basis of the book of Zechariah. With Haggai Zechariah encouraged the postexilic community to rebuild the temple in Jerusalem (Ezra 5:1; 6:14). *See* ZECHARIAH, BOOK OF.

32. One of the representatives of the king when the Passover was celebrated in the reign of Josiah (1 Esdr. 1:15; KJV "Zacharias"; cf. 2 Chr. 35:15).

33. The father of Joseph, one of the military commanders under the Maccabees (1 Macc. 5:18; KJV "Zacharias").

34. The father of John the Baptist and husband of Elizabeth, a relative of Jesus' mother Mary; a priest of the division of Abijah. Zechariah and Elizabeth were pious but had remained childless into old age. While Zechariah was burning incense in the temple, a duty that normally fell to a given priest only once in his lifetime, the angel Gabriel appeared beside the incense altar and predicted the birth of a son would prepare God's people for the Messiah. Zechariah did not believe the angel's words and was struck dumb by the angel until the birth of the predicted child. When the child was born, Zechariah gave him the name John in accordance with Gabriel's instructions. His speech returned and he prophesied with the song known as the "Benedictus" (Luke 1:5-25, 57-80; KJV "Zacharias").

ZECHARIAH, BOOK OF.† The eleventh book of the Minor Prophets.

I. Author and Date

The book preserves the visions and utterances of the prophet Zechariah (**31**), son of Berechiah and grandson (or "descendant") of Iddo, and perhaps related to a priestly house. A postexilic contemporary of Haggai (520-518 B.C.), Zechariah's ministry focuses largely on the plight of the recently returned exiles and the necessity of rebuilding the temple at Jerusalem.

II. Literary Aspects

On the basis of style and contents the book clearly divides into two parts, Zech. 1-8 and 9-14. The first section includes a series of eight night visions (1:8-6:8) and oracles concerning the restoration of Jerusalem and Judah (6:9-8:23). The second is largely apocalyptic in nature, concerning the Day of the Lord and the end of the current age. A majority of critical scholars view the latter portion as a later addition, in the fifth or fourth century or even as late as the third; perhaps stemming from persons discontent with the existing leadership of the restoration community, it could also, according to the conservative view, represent the tempered view of a mature Zechariah. The two oracles (cf. superscriptions to 9:1; 12:1; Heb. *maśśā'*) are often associated with the book of Malachi (cf. Mal. 1:1).

III. Contents

An opening prophetic call to repentance is dated to Marcheshvan (Oct./Nov.) 520 (Zech. 1:1-6). The first of eight night visions, dated to Shebat (Jan./Feb.) 519, depicts divine horsemen who patrol the earth, a promise of restoration (vv. 8-17). In the second (vv. 18-21 [MT 2:1-4]) four horns (the mighty nations that dispersed Judah and Israel) will be "terrified" by four smiths, the agents of the Lord. Zech. 2:1-5 (MT 5-9) concerns the restoration (measuring) of Jerusalem, to be protected by the glory of Yahweh; accordingly, in vv. 6-13 (MT 10-17) the prophet appeals to the exiles to flee Babylon and escape to Zion. Judged to be worthy ("clean"), the high priest Joshua is given responsibility in the fourth vision (ch. 3) for both religious and civil aspects of the restoration community. In the fifth vision (ch. 4) both Joshua and Zerubbabel ("the two anointed") share responsibility for the newly unified community (a golden lampstand). At 5:1-4 a flying scroll represents God's curse upon all who steal or swear falsely; vv. 5-11 proclaims the purification of Judah, to be accomplished by dispatching their sin (personified as Wickedness, a woman in an ephah) to Babylon. The final vision (6:1-8) is reminiscent of the first; four chariots and their horses patrol the earth in preparation for the advent of the messianic age.

Zech. 6:9–8:23 contains a series of oracles concerning the messianic age. The first (6:9-15) foretells the crowning of the messianic king. Ch. 7, dated to Chislev (Nov./Dec.) 518, stresses implementation of the prophetic ethical ideal (vv. 9-10) as more appropriate for the restoration community than the prior concern for ritual (cf. 8:19b). Ch. 8 comprises ten utterances proclaiming the restoration of Jerusalem and Judah, with peace and prosperity for all mankind.

The concluding chapters represent two collections of undated poetic and prose utterances. Those contained in the first oracle (chs. 9–11) focus on the restoration of Israel: the humiliation of those hostile to Israel (9:1-8; 11:1-3), the ingathering of God's dispersed people (9:11-17), and the sovereignty of the Lord over nature and history (ch. 10). Zech. 11:4-17 is an allegory of two shepherds (kings), one rejected by his sheep and the other unsympathetic to their needs. The second oracle (chs. 12–14) concerns the coming Day of the Lord when the nations will be destroyed in their final assault upon Jerusalem (ch. 12) and the city purged of idolatry (13:1-6). In ch. 14 only a remnant of Jerusalem escape, and the surviving Gentiles present themselves before the Lord.

IV. Theology

Underlying the prophecy of the book of Zechariah is a clear understanding of Yahweh as sovereign in creation (10:1-2) and history (e.g., 4:6-10; 10:3-12), particularly vivid in depictions of the apocalyptic Day of the Lord (e.g., 2:11-12 [MT 15-16]; chs. 12–14). In harmony with Israel's historic covenant he blesses his people for adherence to its stipulations and curses their

disobedience (e.g., 1:2-6; 2:8-12 [MT 12-16]; 10:6). Despite the prophet's concern for the rebuilding of the temple (e.g., 1:16; 6:12; 8:10), in terms of the covenant he seeks the greater ideals of unity (cf. 3:10; 4:2) and moral behavior (7:9-10).

Of particular significance is Zechariah's interest in the messianic king, a righteous "Branch" (3:8, "my servant"), a scion of the house of David (12:7-8) who shall "(re)build the temple of the Lord" (6:12-13). Presented as a prince of "peace" (9:9-10), he is depicted as a shepherd "doomed to be slain" (11:7ff.; 13:7-9). This imagery underscores the New Testament portrayal of Jesus as Messiah (e.g., Matt. 21:1-11 par., drawing upon Zech. 9:9-10; cf. Matt. 26:14-16 and Zech. 11:12).

Bibliography. J. G. Baldwin, *Haggai, Zechariah, Malachi.* Tyndale (1972); R. A. Mason, *The Books of Haggai, Zechariah and Malachi.* CBC (1977), pp. 27-134; D. L. Petersen, *Haggai and Zechariah 1-8.* OTL (1984).

ZECHER [zē'kər] (Heb. *zeķēr*). A Benjaminite of the line of Gibeon (1 Chr. 8:31; KJV "Zacher"). See ZECHARIAH 5.

ZEDAD [zē'dăd] (Heb. *ṣᵉḏāḏâ* "side"). A place on the northern border of the promised land (Num. 34:8; Ezek. 47:15), usually identified with modern Ṣadâd, *ca.* 105 km. (65 mi.) northeast of Damascus.

ZEDEKIAH [zĕd'ə kī'ə] (Heb. *ṣiḏqîyâ, ṣiḏqîyāhû* "Yahweh is righteousness").

1. The son of Chenaanah, and a prophet during the reign of Ahab of Israel (1 Kgs. 22:11-12, 24; par. 2 Chr. 18:10-11, 23). In contrast to Micaiah the son of Imlah, Zedekiah announced dramatically (and incorrectly) that Ahab would win in battle against Syria at Ramoth-gilead.

2. The last king of Judah (597-586 B.C.); a son of King Josiah (1 Chr. 3:15; cf. v. 16) and brother of Jehoahaz. Originally called Mattaniah (1), Nebuchadrezzar of Babylon changed his name to Zedekiah when he installed him as king of Judah in place of his nephew Jehoiachin (2 Kgs. 24:17-18; cf. 2 Chr. 36:10, "brother").

In spite of the prophet Jeremiah's warnings (Jer. 21:1-7; 24; 27:1-15; 32:3-5; 34:1-5; 38:17-23), Zedekiah renounced his fealty to Nebuchadrezzar, thereby hastening the fall of Judah. In 594-593 he received envoys from Edom, Moab, Ammon, Tyre, and Sidon, who were planning an insurrection against Babylonian rule (27:1-11). During the same period he was summoned to Babylon (51:59), perhaps because Nebuchadrezzar had learned of the conspiracy. Although his response to the envoys is unknown, it is probable that Zedekiah concluded a treaty with Egypt that in turn led to his rebellion against Babylon.

Nebuchadrezzar marched into Judah to suppress the rebellion, and soon only the fortified cities of Lachish, Azekah, and Jerusalem remained (34:7). While the siege of Jerusalem was temporarily lifted because the Babylonians were forced to deal with the threat of an Egyptian army on the borders of Judah (v. 21; 37:5-11; cf. Ezek. 29:1-2; 30:20-26), Zedekiah imprisoned Jeremiah (Jer. 32:2-3; 37:16-21); the king was ultimately unwilling, however, to allow Jeremiah's enemies to kill the prophet (ch. 38). The Egyptian threat was quickly dispelled, and the siege resumed until Jerusalem fell and was destroyed in 586. Although Zedekiah escaped from the city during the night, the Babylonian army overtook him near Jericho. He was brought to Riblah, where he was forced to watch the execution of his sons and then was blinded. He was then sent to Babylon in chains (2 Kgs. 25:1-7), where he remained imprisoned until his death (Jer. 52:11).

3. A son of King Jehoiakim of Judah and brother of Jehoiachin (Jeconiah) (1 Chr. 3:16; cf. 2 Chr. 36:9-10).

4. A priest among those who set their seals to the covenant made under Nehemiah (Neh. 10:1 [MT 9:38]; KJV "Zidkijah").

5. The son of Maaseiah; a prophet among the Babylonian exiles, probably one of those who predicted wrongly that Judah would be freed of Babylonian domination. In a letter to the exiles, Jeremiah announced that this prophet would be executed by Nebuchadrezzar (Jer. 29:21-23).

6. The son of Hananiah; a court official (RSV "prince") under King Jehoiakim of Judah among those who heard Baruch read a scroll of prophecies from Jeremiah and who reported to the king concerning the scroll (Jer. 36:12).

ZEEB [zē′əb] (Heb. *z*ᵉ*ʾēḇ* "wolf "). A Midianite prince who, together with Oreb, was captured by the Ephraimites, who beheaded him at his wine press (or a place so named because of this incident) (Judg. 7:25; 8:3). The defeat of Midian and particularly of Oreb and Zeeb was long remembered in Israel (Ps. 83:11 [MT 12]; cf. Isa. 9:4 [MT 3]; 10:26).

ZELA [zē′lə] (Heb. *ṣēlaʿ* "rib"). A town in the tribal territory of Benjamin (Josh. 18:28; cf. R. G. Boling and G. E. Wright, *Joshua*. AB 6 [1982], p. 428, "Zelaeleph," following LXX A). The site of the family tomb of King Saul (2 Sam. 21:14), Zela was probably Saul's home. Its location is uncertain.

ZELEK [zē′lĕk] (Heb. *ṣeleq*). An Ammonite among David's mighty men (2 Sam. 23:37; 1 Chr. 11:39).

ZELOPHEHAD [zə lō′fə hăd] (Heb. *ṣ*ᵉ*lopᵉḥāḏ* "shadow [thus "protection"] from fear [?]"). A Manassite, the son of Hepher of the lineage of Gilead who "had no sons, but [five] daughters" (Num. 26:33; 1 Chr. 7:15). After Zelophehad died in the wilderness, his daughters asked for the right to receive their father's inheritance in the promised land. Yahweh granted their request, and the decision became a legal precedent in Israel (Num. 27:1-11). Later the stipulation was added that any such daughters must marry within their own tribe to keep their inheritance, lest a tribe lose some of its portion (Num. 36:1-12). When the land was divided, the daughters of Zelophehad received their allotment in the region of Manasseh (Josh. 17:3-6, "daughters of Manasseh").

ZELOTES (Luke 6:15; Acts 1:13, KJV). *See* Simon **8**.

ZELZAH [zĕl′zə] (Heb. *ṣelṣaḥ*). A site on the border (NIV) of the tribal territory of Benjamin, near Rachel's tomb. To confirm his anointing of Saul as king, Samuel gave the young man three signs, the first being that by Rachel's tomb at Zelzah Saul would meet two men bearing a message from his father (1 Sam. 10:2). The exact location of Zelzah (and Rachel's tomb; cf. Gen. 35:19) remains subject to debate (cf. P. K. McCarter, Jr., *I Samuel*. AB 8 [1980], p. 171).

ZEMARAIM [zĕm′ə rā′əm] (Heb. *ṣ*ᵉ*mārayim* "double peak").

1. A town in the tribal territory of Benjamin (Josh. 18:22). It is often identified with modern Râs ez-Zeimara, *ca.* 8 km. (5 mi.) northeast of Bethel.

2. A mountain in the hill country of Ephraim (2 Chr. 13:4), from which King Abijah of Judah addressed Jeroboam and the armies of Israel before defeating them in battle (vv. 4-18).

ZEMARITES [zĕm′ə rīts] (Heb. *ṣ*ᵉ*mārî*). A people associated with the Canaanites (Gen. 10:18; 1 Chr. 1:16). The probable site of their city is modern Sumra, a town on the Phoenician coast between Tripolis and Arvad. This city is named in Assyrian texts (Akk. *Ṣimirra*) and in the Amarna Letters (*Ṣumur*).

ZEMER [zē′mər] (Heb. *ṣemer*). The city of the Zemarites, who served as skilled pilots on the Tyrian ships (Ezek. 27:8; KJV "O Tyrus"; NIV "O Tyre").

ZEMIRAH [zə mī′rə] (Heb. *z*ᵉ*mîrâ* "song" [?]). A son of Becher of the tribe of Benjamin (1 Chr. 7:8).

ZENAN [zē′nən] (Heb. *ṣ*ᵉ*nān* "place of flocks"). A village of the Shephelah of Judah (Josh. 15:37). The site is often identified as modern ʿArâq el-Kharba near Lachish. It is probably the same as Zaanan (Mic. 1:11).

ZENAS [zē′nəs] (Gk. *Zēnas*; abbreviation of *Zēnodōros* "gift of Zeus"). The apparent bearer, together with Apollos, of Paul's epistle to Titus, who is instructed to help them (materially) on their further travels (Titus 3:13). The designation of Zenas as a "lawyer" (Gk. *nomikós*), which in the Synoptic Gospels signifies a scribe versed in the Torah, probably indicates here an expert in Roman law.

ZEPHANIAH [zĕf′ə nī′ə] (Heb. *ṣ*ᵉ*panyâ*, *ṣ*ᵉ*panyāhû* "Yahweh has hidden").

1. A priest in Jerusalem, the son of Maaseiah (2 Kgs. 25:18; Jer. 21:1; 29:25-26). On two occasions King Zedekiah sent Zephaniah to request the intercession of the prophet Jeremiah on behalf of Judah (21:1; 37:3). At another time Zephaniah took the part of Jeremiah in the prophet's dispute with Shemaiah, a false prophet exiled in Babylon (29:24-32). Zephaniah was killed in Riblah after the fall of Jerusalem (2 Kgs. 25:18-21 par. Jer. 52:24-27).

2. A Kohathite Levite (1 Chr. 6:36 [MT 21]).

3. A seventh-century prophet of Judah, the son of Cushi and descendant of Hezekiah (whether Hezekiah the king or another is disputed). Zephaniah was a contemporary of King Josiah (Zeph. 1:1) and appears to have prophesied in the earlier part of Josiah's reign, perhaps beginning *ca.* 630-625 B.C. The duration of his ministry is unknown. His utterances are recorded in the book bearing his name. *See* ZEPHANIAH, BOOK OF.

4. The father of Josiah, who had returned from exile and was living in Jerusalem during the ministry of the prophet Zechariah (Zech. 6:10, 14).

ZEPHANIAH, APOCALYPSE OF. A Jewish pseud-epigraphon ascribed to the prophet Zephaniah, but written between 100 B.C. and A.D. 175—probably before A.D. 70—in Egypt. Its original language was Greek, but it is now extant only in two Coptic manuscripts (which vary in length, contents, and dialect) and in a quotation by Clement of Alexandria. Although much of the work is lost, what remains is sufficient to demonstrate that this apocalypse resembles similar Jewish works from the same period, namely a cosmic journey by the seer in the course of which he sees both the glories of heaven and the terrors of hell. Basic themes focus on aspects of divine judgment: descriptions of punishments of sinners, the need for intercession by the righteous, appeal for repentance while there is still time, and the certainty of God's wrath upon the ungodly.

ZEPHANIAH, BOOK OF.† A book of the Minor Prophets, ninth in the Book of the Twelve.

I. Origins

The prophecies are those of ZEPHANIAH **3**, a descendant of one Hezekiah, perhaps the great reforming king of Judah (Zeph. 1:1); the lengthy genealogy as well as his attention to the offenses of the Jerusalem establishment (vv. 7-9; 3:3-5) supports his royal lineage. His proclamations are dated to the reign of King Josiah (640-609 B.C.), and generally are thought to represent conditions prior to the reforms of 621; some scholars see ch. 3 in the latter part of Josiah's reign as evidence of the reforms' failure (others the entire book, contending that the measures were less than thorough). The first recorded prophetic voice since Isaiah and Micah (beginning of the seventh century) and a contemporary of Jeremiah, Zephaniah himself may have taken part in the reform movement. Attempts to associate the prophet with the Jerusalem temple are inconclusive (cf. 1:4-6; 3:4).

During the early years of Josiah's reign Assyria dominated the ancient Near East (cf. 2:13-15), declining in power rapidly after 626 when Babylonian resurgence precipitated rebellion throughout the empire. Judah had also come under Assyrian influence, largely through syncretistic religious practices fostered during the long reign of the idolatrous Manasseh and continued by his son Amon (cf. 1:4-5). Attempts to identify the coming day of wrath (vv. 14-16) with a Scythian invasion *ca.* 630 (cf. Herodotus *Hist.* i.103-6) are now generally discredited.

II. Contents

Following a detailed superscription (1:1), the prophet proclaims the imminent destruction of all mankind (vv. 2-3; cf. v. 18; 3:8), focusing first on Judah and Jerusalem (1:3-13). He announces the horrible Day of the Lord when God's wrath shall be unleashed (vv. 7-18); only through repentance can the people be spared (2:1-3). Divine judgment is directed also against Judah's neighbors: the Philistine cities to the west (vv. 4-7), Moab and Ammon to the east (vv. 8-11), Ethiopia to the south (v. 12), and Assyria to the north (vv. 13-15). Zech. 3:1-7 returns the focus to Jerusalem, whose inhabitants have defied the religious and ethical demands of the covenant and have rejected the appeal for repentance: "all the more they were eager to make all their deeds corrupt." The book concludes with a message of hope, the conversion of the chastened nations and preservation of a faithful remnant in Judah (vv. 8-20).

III. Theology

Two themes dominate Zephaniah's ministry, judgment (doom, 1:2–3:7) and hope (vv. 8-20). The Day of the Lord is inevitable (e.g., v. 18; 3:8), not only for the heathen nations but also for God's chosen people; immediate repentance could stay the destruction, but Judah refuses to listen (2:1-3; 3:1-7). Yet though God's actions will be drastic, they will have positive effect; through the fire of divine wrath Judah and the nations will be cleansed (vv. 8-9; cf. 2:7; 3:12-13, 17). (Such words of hope were once held to be a later addition to Zephaniah's work; cf. such "postexilic" emphases as universal worship of Yahweh [vv. 9-13] and restoration of the exiles [vv. 19-20]).

Bibliography. A. S. Kapelrud, *The Message of the Prophet Zephaniah* (Oslo: 1975); J. D. W. Watts, *The Books of Joel, Obadiah, Jonah, Nahum, Habakkuk and Zephaniah.* CBC (1975).

ZEPHATH [zē'făth] (Heb. *ṣepaṭ* "watchtower"). A Canaanite city in Judah, not far from Arad, which the Judahites and Simeonites destroyed and renamed HORMAH (Judg. 1:17).

ZEPHATHAH [zĕf'ə thə] (Heb. *ṣepaṭâ* "watchtower"). A valley in Judah near Mareshah (Tell Sandaḥannah) where King Asa met and defeated the Ethiopian Zerah and his forces (2 Chr. 14:9-12 [MT 8-11]).

ZEPHI [zē'fī] (Heb. *ṣepî*), **ZEPHO** [zē'fō] (*ṣepô*). The third son of Eliphaz and grandson of Esau (Zepho, Gen. 36:11; Zephi, 1 Chr. 1:36; NIV "Zepho"). Named among "the chiefs of the sons of Esau" (Gen. 36:15), he was apparently the eponymous ancestor of an Edomite subgroup.

ZEPHON]zē'fŏn] (Heb. *ṣepôn* "expectation"). The eldest son of Gad, ancestor of the Zephonites (Num. 26:15). At Gen. 46:16 his name is given as Ziphion.

ZER [zûr] (Heb. *ṣēr*). A fortified city in the tribal territory of Naphtali (Josh. 19:35), thought by some scholars to be the same as Madon (11:1; 12:19). The Hebrew of the MT is somewhat corrupt, thus the otherwise unattested name may reflect a repetition of the preceding Heb. *weʿārê mibṣār* "fortified cities" (cf. LXX Gk. *Tyros* "Tyre").

ZERAH [zĕr′ə] (Heb. *zeraḥ* "beam of light, dawn").
1. An Edomite chief, descended from Esau and Ish-mael (Gen. 36:13, 17; 1 Chr. 1:37; cf. Gen. 36:2-3).
2. The father of Jobab, the second Edomite king (Gen. 36:33; 1 Chr. 1:44).
3. One of the twin sons of Judah and Tamar (Gen. 38:30; 46:12; KJV "Zarah"; Josh. 7:1, 18, 24; 22:20; 1 Chr. 2:4, 6; 9:6; Neh. 11:24). He is mentioned in Matthew's genealogy of Jesus (Matt. 1:3; KJV "Zara"). His descendants were the Judahite Zerahites (Num. 26:20; KJV "Zarhites").
4. A son of Simeon (1 Chr. 4:24), whose descendants were the Zerahites (Num. 26:13; KJV "Zarhites"). At Gen. 46:10; Exod. 6:15 he is called Zohar.
5. A Levite (or perhaps two individuals) of the family of Gershom (1 Chr. 6:21, 41 [MT 6, 26]).
6. An Ethiopian (so RSV, KJV) or a Cushite (JB, NIV, following MT) who invaded Judah with a great army. King Asa, having sought Yahweh's support, met and vanquished the invader and his forces at Mareshah (2 Chr. 14:9-13 [MT 8-12]).

ZERAHIAH [zĕr′ə hī′ə] (Heb. *zᵉraḥyâ* "Yahweh has arisen" or "has shone").
1. The son of Uzzi and father of Meraioth, a descendant of Aaron (1 Chr. 6:6, 51 [MT 5:32; 6:36]) and ancestor of Ezra (Ezra 7:4).
2. A man of the lineage of Pahath-moab, whose son Eliehoenai returned with Ezra from the Exile (Ezra 8:4).

ZERAHITES [zĕr′ə hīts] (Heb. *zarḥî*). Two Israelite family groups, descendants of ZERAH 4, a Simeonite (Num. 26:13; KJV "Zarhites"), and ZERAH 3, a Judahite (v. 20). To the latter clan belonged Achan, who took booty from the fallen city of Jericho (Josh. 7:17-18), and Sibbecai and Maharai, two of David's officers (1 Chr. 27:11, 13). It is uncertain how long the two groups remained separate, as the tribe of Simeon was eventually absorbed into Judah (cf. Gen. 49:7; Josh. 19:1; cf. also the list of cities of Judah at 15:21-63 with that of Simeon at 19:1-9).

ZERED, BROOK [zĕr′ĕd] (Heb. *naḥal zered*). A brook along the border of Moab and Edom, the crossing of which marked the end of Israel's wilderness wanderings (Num. 21:12, "Valley of Zered"; KJV "Valley of Zared"; Deut. 2:13-14). It has been identified with the Seil el-Qurahi, the lower course of the Wâdī el-Ḥesā, which flows into the southeast end of the Dead Sea. Isaiah refers to this stream as the "Brook of the Willows" (Isa. 15:7); it may be the same as the "Brook of the Arabah" (Amos 6:14).

ZEREDAH [zĕr′ə də].
1. (Heb. *ṣᵉrēḏâ*). The hometown of Jeroboam, probably in the territory of Ephraim (1 Kgs. 11:26; KJV "Zereda"). A location is generally sought near the spring ʿAin Ṣeridah in western Samaria, perhaps Deir Ghassâneh, *ca.* 25 km. (15 mi.) southwest of Shechem and 34 km. (21 mi.) north-northwest of Jerusalem.
2. (Heb. *ṣᵉrēḏāṯâ*). A city in the Jordan valley (2 Chr. 4:17; KJV "Zeredathah"). The reading should probably be "Zarethan" as in the parallel 1 Kgs. 7:46.
3. (Judg. 7:22). See ZERERAH.

ZERERAH [zĕr′ə rə] (Heb. *ṣᵉrērâ*). A place through which the Midianites fled following their ambush by Gideon (RSV, NIV, Judg. 7:22; KJV "Zererath"). The name may be a variant of Zeredah (RSV mg.) or Zarethan (JB).

ZERESH [zĕr′ĕsh] (Heb. *zereš*). The wife of Haman, Mordecai's antagonist (Esth. 5:10). At first she counseled Haman to build a gallows for Mordecai (v. 14), but soon predicted her husband's fall before his Jewish enemy (6:13).

ZERETH [zĕr′ĕth] (Heb. *ṣereṯ* "splendor"). A Judahite and the first son of Ashhur and Helah (1 Chr. 4:7).

ZERETH-SHAHAR [zĕr′ĕth shā′här] (Heb. *ṣereṯ haššaḥar* "splendor of the dawn"). A city in the tribal territory of Reuben situated "on the hill of the valley" (Josh. 13:19; KJV "Zareth-shahar"). The site is probably modern Zârât on Mt. ʿAṭṭarus overlooking the eastern shore of the Dead Sea.

ZERI [zĕr′ī] (Heb. *ṣᵉrî* "balsam"). One of the sons of the levitical family of Jeduthun, set apart by David for musical service in the temple (1 Chr. 25:3). At v. 11 his name is given as Izri (Heb. *yiṣrî*).

ZEROR [zĕr′ôr] (Heb. *ṣᵉrôr* "sharp stone" or "flint"). A Benjaminite and ancestor of Saul (1 Sam. 9:1).

ZERUAH [zə rōō′ə] (Heb. *ṣᵉrûʿâ* "leprous"). The wife of Nebat and mother of King Jeroboam (1 Kgs. 11:26).

ZERUBBABEL [zə rŭb′ə bəl] (Heb. *zᵉrubbāḇel*; Akk. *zēr-bābili* "offspring of Babylon"; Gk. *Zorobabel*). The grandson of King Jehoiachin (Jeconiah) of Judah, governor of Judah after the return from exile, and an ancestor of Jesus through the Davidic line (Matt. 1:12-13; Luke 3:27; KJV "Zorobabel").

Zerubbabel is most often identified as the son of Shealtiel, a son of Jehoiachin (Ezra 3:2; 5:2; Neh. 12:1; Hag. 1:1; 2:2; Matt. 1:12). But 1 Chr. 3:17-19 identifies him as the son of Pedaiah, another son of Jehoiachin. It is possible that Shealtiel died childless and that Pedaiah took Shealtiel's widow in levirate marriage, thus being the actual father of Zerubbabel. An alternate suggestion is that both Shealtiel and Pedaiah had sons named Zerubbabel.

Haggai calls Zerubbabel governor of Judah (Hag. 1:1; 2:2, 21), but it is also said that Cyrus appointed Sheshbazzar as governor over the returning exiles (Ezra 5:14; cf. 1:8). Both Zerubbabel and Sheshbazzar have Babylonian names, and both are mentioned in connection with the laying of the foundation of the temple (Ezra 3:2, 8, 10; 5:16). Because of this Sheshbazzar has been identified by some with Zerubbabel, but he was most likely Zerubbabel's predecessor and possibly the same person as Shenazzar, a son of Jehoiachin and uncle of Zerubbabel (1 Chr. 3:18). The chronology in Ezra is not clear, but most reconstructions of the period represented by Ezra 2-5 propose two waves of Jews returning to Judah, the first led by Sheshbazzar and the second by Zerubbabel (cf. Neh. 7, 12).

The actual date of his arrival in Jerusalem is not known.

By the time work on the temple resumed in 520, Zerubbabel was governor. Haggai and Zechariah invest him with messianic glory: he is the Lord's servant ("the Branch"; Zech. 3:8; 6:12-13) and is to become like a monarch's "signet ring" after God has overthrown the kingdoms of the world (Hag. 2:21-23). How Zerubbabel's governorship ended is unknown, as is his personal fate. Some have suggested that Persian reaction to messianic fervor centered around Zerubbabel led to the governor's death, but there is no clear evidence.

ZERUIAH [zə rōō′yə] (Heb. *ṣᵉrûyâ, ṣᵉruyâ* "perfumed with mastix"). The sister or half sister of David and Abigail, named both as the daughter of Nahash (2 Sam. 17:25) and of Jesse (1 Chr. 2:16); perhaps her mother was married twice. She was the mother of Abishai, Joab, and Asahel, David's nephews and commanders in his army (2 Sam. 8:16; 18:2). She is never mentioned apart from one or more of her sons, who often are named in relation to her but never to their father (e.g., 1 Sam. 26:6; 2 Sam. 2:13, 18; 8:16). This may be because her husband died young or was a foreigner, because she was David's sister, because she was an exceptional woman, or because of a custom that traced descendants along the matriarchal line.

David found Zeruiah's sons difficult to control (3:39; 16:10; 19:22 [MT 23]), for although they were fiercely loyal to him, they were also rash, treacherous, and vindictive in their various dealings (e.g., 1 Sam. 26:8; 2 Sam. 3:27, 30; 16:9; 18:5, 14; 19:21 [MT 22]).

ZETHAM [zē′thəm] (Heb. *zētām* "olive tree"). A Gershomite Levite descended from Ladan (1 Chr. 23:8; 26:22).

ZETHAN [zē′thən] (Heb. *zêṭān* "olive tree" or "one who tends olive trees"). A Benjaminite, son of Bilhan and descendant of Jediael (1 Chr. 7:10).

ZETHAR [zē′thär] (Heb. *zēṭar* "killer"). One of the seven eunuchs who served the Persian king Ahasuerus as chamberlains (Esth. 1:10).

ZEUS [zōōs] (Gk. *Zeus*).† The supreme Greek deity, god of heaven and thunder and commander of the universe. Both Zeus and Jupiter—the supreme Roman deity, with whom Zeus was identified— are forms of the Indoeuropean sky-god (Sanskrit *Dyaus*, from *diu* "heaven, sky, brightness"). Though supreme, Zeus was not held to be eternal; according to Hesiod he was the son of the titan Cronus, who was the son of Heaven and Earth. Hesiod regarded Zeus as the principle of justice, and Aeschylus regarded him as similar to Providence; nevertheless, he was also held to be subject to fate. Zeus was worshiped as the protector of the home and of guests and suppliants. Myths concerning his love affairs with goddesses and human women are now regarded as reflections of the process by which the religion of the Indoeuropean invaders was reconciled with the goddess-worship of the indigenous peoples.

The "god of fortresses" (KJV "forces"; cf. NIV)

whom Antiochus IV Epiphanes wished to honor above all other gods (Dan. 11:37-38) was probably Zeus Olympios. Antiochus promoted the worship of this deity with great zeal, seeking to make it the principle of religious unity within his kingdom (and to gain for himself divine acclaim by identifying himself with this deity). He built a magnificent temple to him in Antioch, desiring to dedicate the Jewish temple in Jerusalem to Zeus Olympios and the Samaritan temple on Mt. Gerizim to Zeus the Protector of Strangers (2 Macc. 6:2; cf. Dan. 11:31; 1 Macc. 1:44-47). It is reported that this venture had greater success among the Samaritans than in Jerusalem, but it may be that Jewish anti-Samaritan propaganda has colored the reports (2 Macc. 6:2; Josephus *Ant.* xii.5.5 [257-264]).

In response to a miraculous healing at Lystra, Barnabas and Paul were taken to be Zeus and Hermes in human form (Acts 14:8-18; KJV "Jupiter," "Mercury," following Vulg. and the practice of Renaissance classicists), perhaps actually local Lycaonian deities who had come to be identified with the Greek gods. This spontaneous crowd response to the healing was perhaps inspired by tales of visits of gods with their identities concealed; Ovid recounts the visit of Zeus and Hermes to an elderly couple of Phrygia, Baucis and Philemon, whom the gods saved from a flood as a reward for their hospitality (*Metamorphoses* viii.626-724).

ZIA [zī′ə] (Heb. *zia‘* "trembling"). A Gadite who lived in Bashan (1 Chr. 5:13).

ZIBA [zī′bə] (Heb. *ṣíbā’, ṣibā’*). A servant of Saul who informed David that Jonathan's son Mephibosheth still lived and could thus receive the kindness David wished to bestow for Jonathan's sake (2 Sam. 9:1-4; cf. 1 Sam. 20:15-17, 42a). David brought Mephibosheth to live in his palace and gave him Ziba and Ziba's fifteen sons and twenty servants for his own servants; the king directed Ziba to cultivate Saul's fields for Mephibosheth (2 Sam. 9:5-11).

Years later when David fled Jerusalem during Absalom's revolt, Ziba came to him with two donkeys laden with food and pretended that Mephibosheth had remained in Jerusalem to regain the kingdom for the house of Saul (16:1-3). David immediately transferred Mephibosheth's possessions to Ziba (v. 4), and when David returned after Absalom's death, Ziba and his servants accompanied the king (19:17). But when the king encountered Mephibosheth, he learned of Ziba's slander and thus divided Saul's land between the two (vv. 24-30).

ZIBEON [zīb′ī ən] (Heb. *ṣib‘ôn* "hyena"). The father of Anah, and the grandfather of Oholibamah, Esau's wife (Gen. 36:14; called a Hivite at v. 2). He is probably the same as Zibeon the Horite clan chief and third son of Seir (vv. 20, 24, 29; 1 Chr. 1:38, 40); the Horites dwelt in Edom, the land of Esau (Gen. 36:8).

ZIBIA [zīb′ī ə] (Heb. *ṣibyā’* "gazelle"). A Benjaminite, one of the seven sons of Shaharaim and Hodesh (1 Chr. 8:9).

ZIBIAH [zīb′ī ə] (Heb. *ṣibyâ* "gazelle"). The mother

of King Joash (Jehoash) of Judah (2 Kgs. 12:1 [MT 2] par. 2 Chr. 24:1).

ZICHRI [zĭk´rī] (Heb. *zikrî* "my remembrance").
1. A Levite, the son of Izhar of the Kohathite line (Exod. 6:21).
2. A Benjaminite, son of Shimei (1 Chr. 8:19).
3. A son of Shashak of the tribe of Benjamin (1 Chr. 8:23).
4. A son of the Benjaminite Jeroham (1 Chr. 8:27).
5. A Levite, son of Asaph (1 Chr. 9:15). At Neh. 11:17 he is called Zabdi (**4**).
6. A Levite descended from Moses' son Eliezer (1 Chr. 26:25).
7. The father of Eliezer, chief of the tribe of Reuben during the reign of David (1 Chr. 27:16).
8. The father of Amasiah, a commander in King Jehoshaphat's army (2 Chr. 17:16).
9. The father of Elishaphat, a commander in Jehoiada's army of revolt against Queen Athaliah of Judah (2 Chr. 23:1).
10. "A mighty man of Ephraim" who murdered the son of King Ahaz and two important court officials of Judah in the Israelite-Syrian invasion of Judah (2 Chr. 28:7).
11. The father of Joel (**13**), who was overseer of the Benjaminites in postexilic Jerusalem (Neh. 11:9).
12. The head of the priestly order of Abijah at the time of the postexilic high priest Joiakim (Neh. 12:17).

ZIDDIM [zĭd´ĭm] (Heb. *ṣiddîm* "sides"). An otherwise unknown fortified city assigned to the tribe of Naphtali (Josh. 19:35).

ZIDKIJAH (Neh. 10:1, KJV). See ZEDEKIAH **4**.

ZIDON (KJV). See SIDON.

ZIF (1 Kgs. 6:1, 37, KJV). See ZIV.

ZIHA [zī´ə] (Heb. *ṣîḥāʾ, ṣiḥāʾ*).
1. The head of a line of temple servants (Nethinim) who returned from the Babylonian Captivity with Zerubbabel (Ezra 2:43; Neh. 7:46).
2. An overseer of the postexilic temple servants (Neh. 11:21).

ZIKLAG [zĭk´lăg] (Heb. *ṣîqlag, ṣiqlag*).† A city assigned to the tribe of Simeon (Josh. 19:5; 1 Chr. 4:30) but elsewhere considered part of the Negeb district of Judah's territory (Josh. 15:31). Ziklag has been identified with modern Tell el-Khuweilfeh (Tell Halif or Lahav), *ca.* 18 km. (11 mi.) northeast of Beersheba. A more likely site, however, is Tell eš-Šerî´ah, *ca.* 15 km. (9.3 mi.) to the west. Excavation of Tell eš-Šerî´ah has uncovered evidence of continuous settlement from the Middle Bronze Age through the Persian period, with some settlement in the Early Bronze Age and earlier. The Early Iron Age Philistine era settlement shows evidence of destruction that is probably to be identified with the burning of the city by the Amalekites mentioned at 1 Sam. 30:14.

Ziklag was a Philistine town until Achish, the Philistine king of Gath, gave it to David when David fled from Saul (1 Sam. 27:5-6). It became David's base for secret military operations against the Philistines, and disaffected Israelite warriors flocked there to join him (1 Chr. 12:1-22). Amalekite raiders attacked Ziklag as David's forces returned there after being rebuffed from serving in the Philistine army (1 Sam. 30). The city was burned and its population carried off, but David pursued the raiders and recovered the booty. David was living in Ziklag when the news of Saul's death reached him (2 Sam. 1:1; 4:10). After the Exile Ziklag was one of the cities occupied by Jews who had returned from Babylonia (Neh. 11:28).

ZILLAH [zĭl´ə] (Heb. *ṣillâ* "shadow" or "protection"). One of Lamech's two wives, and the mother of Tubal-cain and his sister Naamah (Gen. 4:19, 22-23).

ZILLETHAI [zĭl´ə thī] (Heb. *ṣilleʿtay* "Yahweh is a shadow" or "protection").
1. A son of Shimei of the tribe of Benjamin (1 Chr. 8:20; KJV "Zilthai").
2. A Manassite company chief who deserted to David at Ziklag and became a commander in his army (1 Chr. 12:20 [MT 21]; KJV "Zilthai").

ZILPAH [zĭl´pə] (Heb. *zilpâ* "short-nosed" [?]). The maid of Laban, whom he gave to his daughter Leah when she married Jacob (Gen. 29:24). Subsequently Leah, who had become barren, gave Zilpah to Jacob "as a wife"; she bore him Gad and Asher (30:9-13; cf. 35:26; 37:2; 46:18).

ZIMMAH [zĭm´ə] (Heb. *zimmâ* "counsel, plan").
1. A Levite of the family of Gershom, in charge of liturgical music for the temple (1 Chr. 6:20, 42 [MT 5, 27]).
2. The father of the Gershonite Levite Joah (2 Chr. 29:12). He may be the same as **1**.

ZIMRAN [zĭm´răn] (Heb. *zimrān*). The first son of Abraham and Keturah (Gen. 25:2; 1 Chr. 1:32).

ZIMRI [zĭm´rē] (Heb. *zimrî*; Gk. *Zambri*) (**PERSON**).
1. The son of Salu and head of a Simeonite father's house who defied the ban against marriage between Jews and foreigners by bringing a Midianite woman into his family. For this he was slain by Phinehas (Num. 25:6-15; cf. 1 Macc. 2:26; KJV "Zambri").
2. The commander of half of Israelite king Elah's chariot force, Zimri killed Elah and assumed the throne. Though he destroyed the entire house of Baasha as the prophet Jehu had predicted, his own reign lasted only seven days; Zimri committed suicide when the Israelite general Omri captured the capital, Tirzah (1 Kgs. 16:9-20). As a result of his treachery, Zimri's name became an epithet for one who murders his own master (2 Kgs. 9:31).
3. A Judahite, the eldest of the five sons of Zerah (**6**) (1 Chr. 2:6). He is called Zabdi (**1**) at Josh. 7:1, 17-18.
4. A Benjaminite and descendant of Saul through Jonathan (1 Chr. 8:36; 9:42).

ZIMRI [zim´rē] (Heb. *zimrî*) (**PLACE**). A kingdom named in Jeremiah's prophecy concerning the cup of wrath (Jer. 25:25). The name is lacking in the LXX.

ZIN [zĭn] (Heb. *ṣin*), **WILDERNESS OF.** An area (NIV "desert") at the extreme south of Palestine through which the Israelites passed on their way to Canaan. It included Kadesh-barnea and bordered Edom on the east (Num. 20:1; 33:36; 34:3-4; Josh. 15:1, 3). From Kadesh Moses sent twelve representatives to spy out the land of Canaan (Num. 13:1-3, 26, "wilderness of Paran"); there Miriam died (20:1), and there at the waters of Meribah Moses forfeited his right to enter the promised land (vv. 10-13; 27:14; Deut. 32:51).

Named after Zin, a settlement or other place (Num. 34:4), the Wilderness of Zin should be distinguished from the Wilderness of Sin, even though the LXX and Vulgate usually use the same form for both names.

ZINA [zī′nə] (Heb. *zînāʾ*). A Levite, the son of Shimei of the family of Gershom (1 Chr. 23:10). The name may be a scribal error for ZIZAH (so NIV; cf. v. 11).

ZION [zī′ən] (Heb. *ṣîyôn*; Gk. *Siōn*).† The easternmost of the ridges on which Jerusalem is built, adjacent to the Kidron valley and the Spring Gihon. "The stronghold of Zion" was a name for the Jebusite fortress city that David conquered (2 Sam. 5:7; 1 Chr. 11:5), subsequently known as the "city of David" (1 Kgs. 8:1; 2 Chr. 5:2). The city at that time was built entirely on the southern part of the southeastern hill (i.e., "Ophel"). As Jerusalem grew, the name "Zion" came to be used for the entire city, usually in poetic language (e.g., Ps. 14:7; 48:2 [MT 3]; 50:2). Sometimes it designates only the temple mount, the northern extension of the Ophel ridge (20:2 [MT 3]; 125:1; Isa. 18:7; 24:23; Joel 3:17 [MT 4:17]; Obad. 21). In poetic usage the city is personified as the "daughter of Zion" (e.g., 2 Kgs. 19:21; Ps. 9:14 [MT 15]; Isa. 1:8; 52:2; NJV "Fair [Maiden] Zion") and its inhabitants the "sons of Zion" (e.g., Ps. 149:2; cf. Cant. 3:11).

In the New Testament "Zion" (KJV "Sion") represents the newness of the true worship of God that has come in Christ (Heb. 12:22) and the "new Jerusalem" in which Christ and the redeemed will abide (Rev. 14:1). The name usually occurs in quotations from the Old Testament where it is a designation for the geographical focus—whether literal or symbolic— of eschatological fulfillment (Matt. 21:5 par. John 12:15; Rom. 9:33; 11:26; 1 Pet. 2:6).

At present the southwestern hill of the old city of Jerusalem, where the traditional site of David's tomb and the upper room of the Last Supper are located, is called "Mount Zion." Evidently the name had been transferred to the southwestern hill by the time of Josephus, who locates the original city of David there (*BJ* v.4.1 [137]).

ZIOR [zī′ôr] (Heb. *ṣîʿôr* "smallness"). A town in the hill country of Judah south-southwest of Hebron (Josh. 15:54).

ZIPH [zĭf] (Heb. *zîp*) (**PERSON**).
   1. A Calebite of the tribe of Judah (1 Chr. 2:42).
   2. A Judahite, the eldest son of Jehallelel (1 Chr. 4:16).

ZIPH [zĭf] (Heb. *zîp*) (**PLACE**).
   1. A town in the Negeb of Judah (Josh. 15:24), probably modern Khirbet ez-Zeifeh, 40-50 km. (25-30 mi.) west of the southern end of the Dead Sea.
   2. A town in the hill country of Judah near Maon (Josh. 15:55). It has been identified with modern Tell Zif, about 6.5 km. (4 mi.) southeast of Hebron.

In the surrounding Wilderness of Ziph, David hid from King Saul (1 Sam. 23:14-15), renewed his covenant with Jonathan (vv. 16-18), was exposed by the native Ziphites (vv. 19-24; 26:1; cf. Ps. 54 superscription [MT v. 2]; KJV "Ziphims"), narrowly escaped capture by Saul (1 Sam. 23:25-28), and refused an opportunity to kill the one who sought his life (ch. 26).

After the division of the monarchy, Rehoboam fortified Ziph and other cities for defense in Judah (2 Chr. 11:8).

ZIPHAH [zī′fə] (Heb. *zîpâ*). The second son of Jehallelel of the tribe of Judah (1 Chr. 4:16).

ZIPHION [zĭf′ĭ ən] (Heb. *ṣipyôn*). The firstborn son of Gad (Gen. 46:16; NIV "Zephon"). At Num. 26:15 he is called Zephon.

ZIPHRON [zĭf′rŏn] (Heb. *ziprôn*). A city along Israel's northern border, near Hazar-enan (Num. 34:9). The exact location is unknown.

ZIPPOR [zĭp′ôr] (Heb. *ṣippôr, ṣippōr* "bird"). The father of the Moabite king Balak, who sought to hire Balaam to curse Israel (Num. 22:2, 4, 10, 16; 23:18; Josh. 24:9; Judg. 11:25).

ZIPPORAH [zĭ pôr′ə] (Heb. *ṣippōrâ* "swallow"). One of the seven daughters of Jethro (Reuel), a Midianite priest, who gave her as wife to Moses following the Israelite's escape from Egypt (Exod. 2:15-21). Zipporah became the mother of Gershom (v. 22) and Eliezer (18:3-4).

When Moses returned to Egypt to lead the Israelites out of bondage, Zipporah set off with him (4:20). At an unidentified lodging place they met Yahweh, who intended to kill Moses there (v. 24); rabbinic traditions suggest that the cause for the Lord's anger was that Moses had failed to circumcise his son (probably Gershom) as prescribed or that Moses himself had not been circumcised. Indeed, Zipporah sensed that only the circumcision of their son might save Moses' life. She circumcised the lad, touched Moses' (or the son's; MT "his feet") feet (a euphemism for genitals) with the foreskin and exclaimed, "Surely you are a bridegroom of blood to me" (v. 25), suggesting that the circumcision was substitutionarily efficacious for Moses as well. But however the action and exclamation are interpreted, they were effective in saving Moses' life (v. 26).

Apparently Zipporah did not accompany Moses all the way to Egypt. It is reported that Jethro brought Zipporah, Gershom, and Eliezer to Moses when the Israelites had reached Mt. Sinai (18:1-7).

ZITHRI (Exod. 6:22, KJV). *See* SITHRI.

ZIV [zĭv] (Heb. *ziw* "brightness"). An early Canaanite name for the second month of the Hebrew religious year (April/May). Its postexilic Babylonian name was Iyyar. In the month of Ziv Solomon began construction of and laid the foundation for the temple (1 Kgs. 6:1, 37; KJV "Zif").

ZIZ [zĭz] (Heb. *[haṣ]ṣîṣ* "flower"). An ascent near Tekoa (KJV "cliff"; NIV "pass"; JB "slópe") along which the Moabites, the Ammonites, and the Meunites marched against King Jehoshaphat of Judah en route from En-gedi to a valley by the wilderness of Jeruel (2 Chr. 20:16; cf. v. 2). This ascent has been identified with the Wâdī Ḥaṣâṣah, just north of Engedi; accordingly, the name may originally have been Haziz (Heb. *ḥāṣîṣ*; cf. LXX Gk. *Asas*).

ZIZA [zī′zə] (Heb. *zîzā'*).
1. The son of Shiphi who with other Simeonite family heads led an expansion of their tribe toward Gedor (1 Chr. 4:37-40).
2. A son of King Rehoboam of Judah and his second wife, Maacah (2 Chr. 11:20).

ZIZAH [zī′zə] (Heb. *zîzâ*). A Gershonite Levite, the second son of Shimei (1 Chr. 23:11). In the preceding verse the name occurs as Zina (Heb. *zînā'*), quite possibly a scribal error (cf. NIV, NIV mg.).

ZOAN [zō′ən] (Heb. *ṣō'an*; cf. Egyp. *Djanet*; Gk. *Tanis*). An important city in the northeastern Nile delta. The city has been identified with ancient Avaris, refounded by the Hyksos in the sixteenth century B.C. (cf. Num. 13:22). As Tanis it served as capital for the Pharaohs until the seventh century and retained its influence long after that. Recent studies indicate that the earlier identification of Zoan with the store city of Raamses (Exod. 1:11) is unlikely.
Ps. 78:12, 43 places the miracles of the Exodus in "the fields of Zoan," the surrounding region. The continuing prominence of the city in Egypt accounts for its mention by the Hebrew prophets (Isa. 19:11, 13; 30:4; Ezek. 30:14).

ZOAR [zō′ər] (Heb. *ṣō'ar*, *ṣô'ar* "little"). One of the five "cities of the valley" among which Lot chose to dwell (Gen. 13:10-12). The rebellion of Zoar (apparently earlier known as Bela) and the other cities was crushed by Chedorlaomer and his allies at the valley of Siddim (14:1-12).
When angels told Lot that Yahweh was about to destroy his present home of Sodom, he asked permission to flee to Zoar (19:17-23; cf. v. 20, a "little" city); after the other four cities were destroyed (vv. 24-25) Lot was afraid to dwell even in Zoar, so he moved into the nearby hills (v. 30). In later times Zoar was one of the points Moses saw from Pisgah (Deut. 34:3); it is mentioned by the prophets as well (Isa. 15:5; Jer. 48:4, 34).
The exact location of Zoar is uncertain, but it is often sought in the vicinity of modern eṣ-Ṣâfī, near the mouth of the Seil el-Qurahi (brook Zered) about 8 km. (5 mi.) south of the Dead Sea.

ZOBAH [zō′bə] (Heb. *ṣôḇâ*, *ṣôḇā'*). An Aramean city-state at the time of David, located in the Lebanon valley north of Damascus and controlling eastern Syria from Hauron to the Euphrates. Saul fought successfully against the kings of Zobah (1 Sam. 14:47), as did David against King Hadadezer (2 Sam. 8:3-12; 1 Chr. 18:3, 5, 9). Later the Ammonites hired "Syrians of Zobah" to assist in their war against David; however, David's army under Joab and Abishai routed these forces (2 Sam. 10:6-19; 1 Chr. 19:6; cf. Ps. 60 superscription [MT v. 2], "Aram-zobah").
One of David's mighty men was Igal, the son of Nathan of Zobah (2 Sam. 23:36). According to 1 Kgs. 11:23-25, Rezon, who had fled from Hadadezer, became an adversary of Israel at the time of Solomon.
See HAMATH-ZOBAH.

ZOBEBAH [zō bē′bə] (Heb. *ṣôḇēḇâ*). A son (or subgroup) of Koz of the tribe of Judah (1 Chr. 4:8).

ZOHAR [zō′här] (Heb. *ṣōḥar* "tawny").
1. The father of Ephron the Hittite (Gen. 23:8; 25:9), from whom Abraham purchased the cave of Machpelah.
2. An alternate name for Simeon's son Zerah (**4**) (Gen. 46:10; Exod. 6:15).

ZOHELETH (1 Kgs. 1:9, KJV). *See* SERPENT'S STONE.

ZOHETH [zō′hĕth] (Heb. *zôḥēṯ* "strong, proud"). The elder son of Ishi of the tribe of Judah (1 Chr. 4:20).

ZOPHAH [zō′fə] (Heb. *ṣôpaḥ* "bellied jug"). A mighty warrior and family head of the tribe of Asher (1 Chr. 7:35-36).

ZOPHAI [zō′fī] (Heb. *ṣôpay*). The son of Elkanah, a Levite of the family of Kohath and an ancestor of Samuel (1 Chr. 6:26 [MT 11]). At v. 35 (MT 20) he is called Zuph (cf. 1 Sam. 1:1).

ZOPHAR [zō′fär] (Heb. *ṣōpar*, *ṣōpar* "little bird [?]"). One of Job's three "friends"; a native of Naamah, a town possibly located in northwest Arabia (Job 2:11; 42:9; RSV "the Naamathite"). His words of "comfort," beginning at 11:1; 20:1, are characterized by lack of compassion and a popular, commonsense wisdom that misses Job's hurt completely. He is the only one of the three for whom only two speeches are recorded rather than three, which has prompted scholars to seek a third speech somewhere among the words ascribed to Job (e.g., 27:13-23).

ZOPHIM [zō′fĭm] (Heb. *ṣōpîm* "watchers"). The hill to which Balak took Balaam so he could look out over the Hebrews and curse them (Num. 23:14). The "field of Zophim" (or possibly "field of watchers") was located near or on top of Mt. Pisgah in the northern plains of Moab.

ZORAH [zôr′ə] (Heb. *ṣor'â*). A city of the Shephelah, allotted to Judah (Josh. 15:33; KJV "Zoreah") and also to Dan (19:41). The site is modern Ṣarʿah, 3.2 km. (2 mi.) north of Beth-shemesh on the north side of the Wâdī eṣ-Ṣarâr (the biblical valley of Sorek). Zorah was the birthplace of Samson (Judg. 13:2; cf. v. 25), whose tomb was nearby as well (16:31). Later the Danites sent spies from Zorah and Eshtaol to search the land for an inheritance; their favorable report contributed to the capture of northern Laish, which they renamed Dan (ch. 18). Zorah then reverted to Judah. After the division of the monarchy King Rehoboam fortified Zorah (2 Chr. 11:10), and Judahites repopulated the city after their return from exile (Neh. 11:29; KJV "Zareah").

The Zorathites were descendants of Shobal, Judahites who dwelt at Zorah (1 Chr. 2:53; KJV "Zareathites"; 4:2). The Zorites were descendants of Salma, another Judahite clan at Zorah (2:54).

ZOROASTRIANISM. The pre-Islamic religion of Iran, still practiced in isolated parts of Iran and by the Parsis in India, and noted for its tendency toward monotheism and its ethical dualism.

Pre-Zoroastrian Iranian religion was polytheistic and included the cult of fire, animal sacrifices, and the ritual use of an intoxicating beverage (*haoma*); deities were reckoned in two groups, ahuras and daivas. ZARATHUSTRA, the founder of Zoroastrianism, lived probably in the late seventh and early sixth centuries B.C., although some place him much earlier. He worshipped Ahura Mazda (the "wise ahura") as the creator of the world and the greatest of the ahuras—the supreme but not the only god. He stressed the opposition between truth and falsehood. According to early Zoroastrianism, Ahura Mazda (known later as Ormazd) is the father of two antagonistic spirits, the Bounteous Spirit (Spenta Mainyu) and the Destructive Spirit (Angra Mainyu, later Ahriman), who chose, respectively, truth and falsehood. The daivas also chose falsehood. Every human being must choose irrevocably between these two principles in a cosmic war to be won ultimately by truth. This choice affects each person's status in the afterlife, in which good souls are led to paradise and bad souls to hell. On the social level, the followers of truth correspond to settled herders and farmers and the followers of falsehood to nomads. Ahura Mazda is also the creator of the six entities that surround him. Known as the Bounteous Immortals (Amesha Spenta), these personify the divine qualities Truth, Good Mind, Devotion, Power, Wholeness, and Immortality, which can also become qualities of the human followers of truth.

Later Zoroastrianism, which saw considerable development beyond the teachings of Zarathustra, lost sight of the Bounteous Spirit, with the result that the Destructive Spirit became the antagonist of Ahura Mazda. Moreover, with the reemergence of the old gods ignored by Zarathustra, the entities became mere deities whose ethical qualities are no longer accessible to humans.

The primary sacred book of Zoroastrianism, the Avesta, was recorded from oral tradition and is written in Avestan, one of the oldest forms of the Iranian language. It includes hymns, or Gāthās, attributed to Zarathustra and written in a dialect somewhat differ-

ent from that of the rest of the Avesta. The Gathas are the only certain source of information regarding Zarathustra. Later Zoroastrian texts are written in Pahlavi and Persian.

The Jews were made aware of Persian power by Cyrus' conquest of Babylon in 538 B.C.; they returned from exile under Persian Achaemenid rule. Because of this Jewish exposure to Persian religion, aspects of ethical dualism, angelology, eschatology, and even the Jewish and Christian concept of a God who created light and darkness have long been attributed to Iranian influence. The degree of this influence has recently been questioned, however, since the Jewish view of Zoroastrianism as a monotheistic religion would vary according to the period of Zoroastrianism under consideration and since the Jews' apparent lack of curiosity about Persian religion contrasts sharply with the Greek attitude.

Bibliography. J. Barr, "The Question of Religious Influence: The Case of Zoroastrianism, Judaism, and Christianity," *JAAR* 53 (1985): 201-235; M. Boyce, *Zoroastrians* (London: 1979); J. Duchesne-Guillemin, *Religion of Ancient Iran* (Bombay: 1973); R. C. Zaehner, *The Dawn and Twilight of Zoroastrianism* (New York: 1961).

ZOROBABEL (KJV). See ZERUBBABEL.

ZUAR [zōōʹər] (Heb. ṣûʿār "small"). The father of Nethanel, the leader of the tribe of Issachar during the wilderness wanderings (Num. 1:8; 2:5; 7:18, 23; 10:15).

ZUPH [zûf] (Heb. ṣûp "honeycomb") (**PERSON**). An ancestor of Samuel, designated an Ephraimite at 1 Sam. 1:1 and a Levite at 1 Chr. 6:35. He is called Zophai (a Levite) at v. 26.

ZUPH [zûf] (Heb. ṣûp "honeycomb") (**PLACE**). An otherwise unknown district where Saul searched for his father's lost asses (1 Sam. 9:5). Possibly the "land of Zuph" was in Ephraim and received its name from the Ephraimite family of Zuph (cf. Ramathaim-zophim at 1:1).

ZUR [zûr] (Heb. ṣûr "rock").
1. A Midianite prince whose daughter, Cozbi, and her Israelite husband Zimri were killed by Phinehas (Num. 25:15). Zur was one of the five kings of Midian slain in battle against Israel (31:8) and the Amorites (Josh. 13:21).
2. A Benjaminite, the second son of Jeiel and Maacah; the brother of Kish, Saul's father (1 Chr. 8:30; 9:36).

ZURIEL [zōōʹrĭ əl] (Heb. ṣûrîʾēl "God is my rock"). A Levite; son of Abihail, and head of the Merarites during the wilderness wanderings (Num. 3:35).

ZURISHADDAI [zōōʹrĭ shădʹī] (Heb. ṣûrî šadday "Shaddai is my rock"). The father of Shelumiel, the leader of the tribe of Simeon during the wilderness wanderings (Num. 1:6; 2:12; 7:36, 41; 10:19).

ZUZIM [zōō′zĭm] (Heb. *zûzîm*; Gk. *éthnē ischyrá* "strong people"). A people who lived in Ham, east of the Jordan. They were defeated by Chedorlaomer and his allies (Gen. 14:5; KJV "Zuzims"; NIV "Zuzites"). Some scholars identify the Zuzim with the ZAMZUMMIM of Deut. 2:20; the literal meaning of the name, "strong people," fits the description at v. 21; this interpretation is also suggested by the Dead Sea Genesis Apocryphon (1QapGen 21:29).